THE POWER OF
FINE LITERATURE
THE MASTERY OF
LANGUAGE ARTS

PRENTICE HALL
LITERATURE

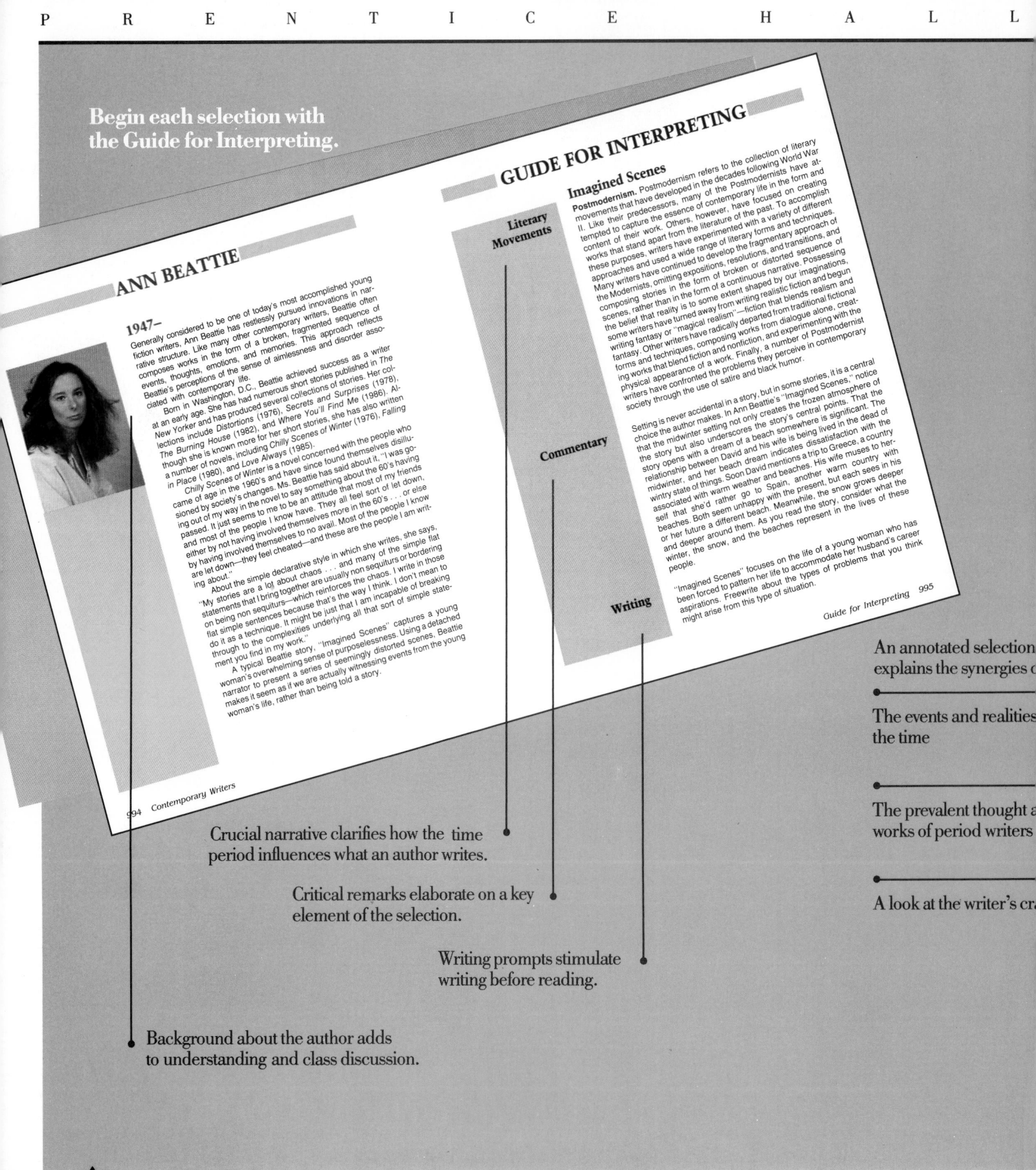

**Begin each selection with
the Guide for Interpreting.**

ANN BEATTIE

1947–

Generally considered to be one of today's most accomplished young fiction writers, Ann Beattie has restlessly pursued innovations in narrative structure. Like many other contemporary writers, Beattie often composes works in the form of a broken, fragmented sequence of events, thoughts, emotions, and memories. This approach reflects Beattie's perceptions of the sense of aimlessness and disorder associated with contemporary life.

Born in Washington, D.C., Beattie achieved success as a writer at an early age. She has had numerous short stories published in *The New Yorker* and has produced several collections of stories. Her collections include *Distortions* (1976), *Secrets and Surprises* (1978), *The Burning House* (1982), and *Where You'll Find Me* (1986). Although she is known more for her short stories, she has also written a number of novels, including *Chilly Scenes of Winter* (1976), *Falling in Place* (1980), and *Love Always* (1985).

Chilly Scenes of Winter is a novel concerned with the people who came of age in the 1960's and have since found themselves disillusioned by society's changes. Ms. Beattie has said about it, "I was going out of my way in the novel to say something about the 60's having passed. It just seems to me to be an attitude that most of my friends and most of the people I know have. They all feel sort of let down, either by not having involved themselves more in the 60's . . . or else by having involved themselves to no avail. Most of the people I am writing about."

About the simple declarative style in which she writes, she says, "My stories are a lot about chaos . . . and many of the simple flat statements that I bring together are usually non sequiturs or bordering on being non sequiturs—which reinforces the chaos. I write in those flat simple sentences because that's the way I think. I don't mean to do it as a technique. It might be just that I am incapable of breaking through to the complexities underlying all that sort of simple statement you find in my work."

A typical Beattie story, "Imagined Scenes," captures a young woman's overwhelming sense of purposelessness. Using a detached narrator to present a series of seemingly distorted scenes, Beattie makes it seem as if we are actually witnessing events from the young woman's life, rather than being told a story.

GUIDE FOR INTERPRETING

Literary Movements

Imagined Scenes

Postmodernism. Postmodernism refers to the collection of literary movements that have developed in the decades following World War II. Like their predecessors, many of the Postmodernists have attempted to capture the essence of contemporary life in the form and content of their work. Others, however, have focused on creating works that stand apart from the literature of the past. To accomplish these purposes, writers have experimented with a variety of different approaches and used a wide range of literary forms and techniques.

Many writers have continued to develop the fragmentary approach of the Modernists, omitting expositions, resolutions, and transitions, and composing stories in the form of broken or distorted sequence of scenes, rather than in the form of a continuous narrative. Possessing the belief that reality is to some extent shaped by our imaginations, some writers have turned away from writing realistic fiction and begun writing fantasy or "magical realism"—fiction that blends realism and fantasy. Other writers have radically departed from traditional fictional forms and techniques, composing works from dialogue alone, creating works that blend fiction and nonfiction, and experimenting with the physical appearance of a work. Finally, a number of Postmodernist writers have confronted the problems they perceive in contemporary society through the use of satire and black humor.

Commentary

Setting is never accidental in a story, but in some stories, it is a central choice the author makes. In Ann Beattie's "Imagined Scenes," notice that the midwinter setting not only creates the frozen atmosphere of the story but also underscores the story's central points. That the story opens with a dream of a beach somewhere is significant. The relationship between David and his wife is being lived in the dead of midwinter, and her beach dream indicates dissatisfaction with the wintry state of things. Soon David mentions a trip to Greece, a country associated with warm weather and beaches. His wife muses to herself that she'd rather go to Spain, another warm country with beaches. Both seem unhappy with the present, but each sees in his or her future a different beach. Meanwhile, the snow grows deeper and deeper around them. As you read the story, consider what the winter, the snow, and the beaches represent in the lives of these people.

Writing

"Imagined Scenes" focuses on the life of a young woman who has been forced to pattern her life to accommodate her husband's career aspirations. Freewrite about the types of problems that you think might arise from this type of situation.

An annotated selection explains the synergies o

The events and realities the time

The prevalent thought a works of period writers

A look at the writer's cr

Crucial narrative clarifies how the time
period influences what an author writes.

Critical remarks elaborate on a key
element of the selection.

Writing prompts stimulate
writing before reading.

Background about the author adds
to understanding and class discussion.

The Power of Fine Literature,
The Mastery of Critical Reading.

Integrate the power of fine literature with in-depth reading to stimulate a critical response.

Begin each unit with Reading Critically.

READING CRITICALLY

The Literature of 1915–1946

World War I had a tremendous impact on the attitudes and outlooks of the American people. This impact is reflected in the literature of the modern age. To fully appreciate modern literature, you must understand how the nation was affected by its involvement in World War I.

Historical Context

Prior to World War I, the mood of American society was confident and optimistic. This mood was shattered by the horrifying realities of American involvement in World War I—a war which caused the death of hundreds of thousands of Americans and Europeans. When the war ended, many people were left with a feeling of distrust toward the ideas and values of the past. People saw the need for change, but they were unsure about the sort of changes that were needed. There was a growing sense of uncertainty, disjointedness, and disillusionment among certain members of American society.

Literary Movements

In the aftermath of World War I, a major literary movement known as Modernism developed. Abandoning many traditional forms and techniques, the Modernists sought to capture the essence of modern life in both the form and content of their work. To reflect the disjointedness of modern life, they constructed their works out of fragments, omitting the expositions, resolutions, interpretations, transitions, and summaries often used in traditional works. The Modernists also frequently expressed their views about modern life in the themes of their works, often focusing on such themes as the uncertainty, bewilderment, and apparent meaninglessness of modern life.

The Writer's Techniques

Because they believed that modern life lacked certainty, the Modernists generally suggested rather than asserted meaning in their works. The theme of a typical Modernist work is implied, not stated, forcing readers to draw their own conclusions. Often, the Modernists used symbols and allusions to suggest themes. They also generally used a limited point of view in their works, because they believed that reality is shaped by people's perceptions. Finally, the Modernists experimented with a number of new literary techniques, including shifting points of view and the stream-of-consciousness technique.

On the following pages is a selection by Sherwood Anderson, an influential modern writer. The notes in the side column show how a reader might read this selection critically.

708   The Modern Age

MODEL

Sophistication
Sherwood Anderson

It was early evening of a day in the late fall and the Winesburg County Fair had brought crowds of country people into town. The day had been clear and the night came on warm and pleasant. On the Trunion Pike, where the road after it left town stretched away between berry fields now covered with dry brown leaves, the dust from passing wagons arose in clouds. Children, curled into little balls, slept on the straw scattered on wagon beds. Their hair was full of dust and their fingers black and sticky. The dust rolled away over the fields and the departing sun set it ablaze with colors.

In the main street of Winesburg crowds filled the stores and the sidewalks. Night came on, horses whinnied. the clerks in the stores ran madly about, children became lost and cried lustily. an American town worked terribly at the task of amusing itself.

Literary Movement: The story begins without an exposition, and background information is revealed as the story progresses. This reflects the Modernist perception of life as ambiguous and fragmented.

Historical Context: The story is set just after the turn of the century.

Writer's Technique: Anderson's description of the town contrasts with the common conception that small-town life is ordered and pastoral.

WEST TISBURY FAIR
Thomas Hart Benton
Collection Mr. Arthur
Levitt, Jr. New York

Sophistication   709

3

Up to 100 Grammar in Action lessons in each ATE . . . the teachable moment for skills mastery.

Enrich your skills teaching with Grammar in Action lessons.

7 Discussion What might postcards represent to the old man?

8 Reading Strategy Have the students invent a story that the man might tell about the postcard. Then have students discuss why the author did not include such a story, but merely alluded to one.

9 Discussion The narrator speaks very little in the scenes with the old man. What does this tell you about her character?

10 Literary Focus Have students look at the way the author establishes each scene. Many of the scenes start abruptly, in the middle of an action. What effect does this have on the reader?

11 Discussion How does this conversation add to your understanding of the relationship between David and the narrator?

7 side there is a box of tissues, a comb and brush, an alarm clock. He sits on the side of the bed, his feet not quite touching the floor, reaching into the drawer without looking. He finds what he wants: an envelope. He removes it and carefully pulls out the flap. He lets her look through the postcards. There is a bird's nest full of cherubs,[1] a picture of a lady elegantly dressed in a high, ruffled collar, curtseying beneath a flowering tree, and one that she looks at longer than the rest: a man in boots and a green jacket, carrying a rifle, is pictured walking down a path through the woods in the moonlight. Stars shine in the sky and illuminate a path in front of him. Tiny silver sparkles still adhere to the postcard. She holds it under the lamp on the night table: the lining of his jacket is silver, the edges of the rocks, a small area of the path. There is a caption: "Joseph Jefferson as Rip Van Winkle."[2] Beneath the caption is a message, ornately written: "Not yet but soon, Pa."

"Did your father write the postcard?"

8 "That's just one I found in a store long ago. I could make up a romantic story to tell you. I love to talk."

She waits, expecting the man's story. He leans back in bed, putting the envelope back in the drawer. His bedroom slippers fall to the floor, and he puts his legs under the covers.

"People get old and they can't improve things," he says, "so they lie all the time."

He waves his hand, dismissing something.

"I trust young people," he says. "I'd even tell you where my money is: in the dresser drawer, in the back of a poetry book."

The snowplow has returned, driving up the other side of the street. The lights cast patterns on the wall. He watches the shadows darken the wallpaper.

1. cherubs (cher' əbz) n.: Representations of heavenly beings as winged children with chubby, rosy faces.
2. Rip Van Winkle: A character who sleeps for twenty years without awakening in a story by Washington Irving.

"I have real stories," he says, pointing to a photograph album on a table by the chair. "Look through and I can tell you some real stories if you want to know."

He is ready to sleep. She arranges the quilt at the bottom of the bed and starts to leave.

9 "The light doesn't bother me," he says, waving her toward the chair. "Look through my album. I'm old and cranky. I'm afraid for my pictures to leave the room."

10 It's early afternoon and no one is in the house. There are dishes on the dining-room table, records and record-album covers. There's a plate, a spoon, two bowls, three coffee cups. How many people have been here? There's no one to ask. There's some food on the counter top—things she doesn't remember buying. An apple pie. She goes into the living room and sits in a chair, looking out the window. More snow is predicted, but now the day is clear and bright, the fields shining in the sun. She goes into the kitchen again to look for the note he hasn't left. On her way to the bedroom to sleep, she looks out the window and sees David coming up the road, only a sweater and scarf on, holding a stick at his side that the dog is jumping for. On the floor by the chair the plant book is open, and several others, books he's studying for his exams. The front door is open. The dog runs into the living room, jumps on her.

"You should be asleep. You can't work at night if you're not going to sleep in the day."

"I thought I'd wait for you to come back."

"You shouldn't have waited. I could have been anywhere."

"Where would you go?"

He's chilled. His knuckles are bright pink, untying the scarf at his throat. He's putting another log on the fire, pushing the screen back into place.

11 "How's the old man?"

"He's no trouble. Last night I fixed his photograph album for him. Some of the pictures had come loose and I glued them in."

"You look like you need sleep."

Grammar in Action

Indirect quotations report the substance of what a person said or thought, rather than the actual words. Unlike a **direct quotation,** an indirect quotation does not require quotation marks; it is punctuated like a simple declarative sentence. Note the following examples:

Direct quotation: "I trust young people," he says.
Indirect quotation: He says that he trusts young people.

Student Activity 1. Select three direct quotations and three indirect quotations from "Imagined Scenes." Explain why a writer would sometimes choose to report a character's words directly and, at other times, use indirect quotations.

Student Activity 2. Rewrite these indirect quotations from "Imagined Scenes" as direct quotations.
1. He told her he wouldn't be working in the fall.
2. Linus Pauling says that a sufficient intake of vitamin C will prevent colds.
3. He wants to show her his postcards.
4. The plant isn't pictured, he tells her, but it may be mentioned in the text.

998

4

The Power of Fine Literature, The Mastery of Grammar and Usage Skills.

Use fine literature as a springboard to teach grammar and usage skills.

"Looks like you've been working," she says, pointing to the books by the chair.

"I've had trouble concentrating. The snow was so beautiful last night. I took the dog out for long walks in the woods."

David is stroking the dog, who lies curled by the fire, panting in his sleep.

"Get some rest," he says, looking at his watch. "I met the people who moved in down the hill and told them I'd help put a sink in. He's very nice. Katherine and Larry Duane."

David kisses her on his way out. The dog wakes and wants to go with him, but at the front door he's told to stay. The dog whines when the door closes, then waits a minute longer before going back to the living room to sleep by the fireplace.

"It's awful. When you get old you expect things to be the same. Sometimes I think the cold air could clear my head. My neighbor is ten years younger than me and he jogs every day, even through snow."

"I'm leaving now," his sister says. She puts on a blue coat and a blue velvet cap that ties under the chin. Her hair is white and copper. She has small, dainty hands. She repeats that she's leaving and pats him on the shoulder, more to make sure he's listening than out of affection. "There are oranges in the bag on your bureau. Linus Pauling says that a sufficient intake of vitamin C will prevent colds."

"How would I get a cold? Every day is the same. I don't go out."

Her coat is buttoned, her hat tied securely. "That's like asking where dust comes from," she says, and disappears down the stairs.

"She's very good to come every day. I forget to thank her. I take it for granted. Fifteen years makes so much difference. She's able to do so much more, but her hands hurt her. She does embroidery so they don't go stiff."

He is looking through a book of Currier and Ives prints.[3] "I suppose I'll have to eat her oranges. There'll be more from Florida when they get back."

She looks at a picture he holds up for her to see, offers to read him science-fiction stories. **13**

"I don't think so. My sister read them this morning. I've had enough make-believe."

3. Currier and Ives prints: Nineteenth-century lithographs depicting the manners, people, and events of the times.

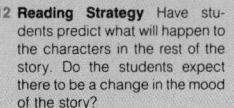

PLEASURES OF WINTER
IN NEW YORK
Francis Peterson

12 Reading Strategy Have students predict what will happen to the characters in the rest of the story. Do the students expect there to be a change in the mood of the story?

13 Critical Thinking and Reading The old man is fond of science fiction. For what might this be a metaphor? Have students discuss the qualities of many science-fiction stories. Then have them relate science fiction to the man's postcard collection.

Humanities Note

Fine art, *Pleasures of Winter in New York*, by Francis Peterson.

Pleasures of Winter in New York is the American painter Francis Peterson's salute to urban childhood. Created in a simplified style, the artist uses bright colors to emphasize the cheer of the scene. The rural appearance of the snow-covered ground and trees is contrasted with the looming buildings visible outside the park. The activities of the children are varied and common to American youth everywhere.

You might use these questions for discussion.
1. What invitation does this scene extend to the viewer?
2. What is the response of the character in this story to a similar scene?

Reinforce learning with blackline masters in the Teaching Portfolio.

5. She asks him if he'll take his cane, but he wants her arm instead.
6. His sister is asking if there is any way she can come back.

Student Activity 3. Rewrite the following direct quotations from "Imagined Scenes" as indirect quotations.
1. "I don't sleep well," he tells her.
2. "I think school was canceled," she says, looking out the window.
3. "My jacket is in the hall closet," he says. "I need the air."
4. "I guess you were walking the dog in the woods," she says.
5. "We'll have to go back for my car," she says.

Guide learning with on-the-spot practice.

999

5

A writing program within a literature program.

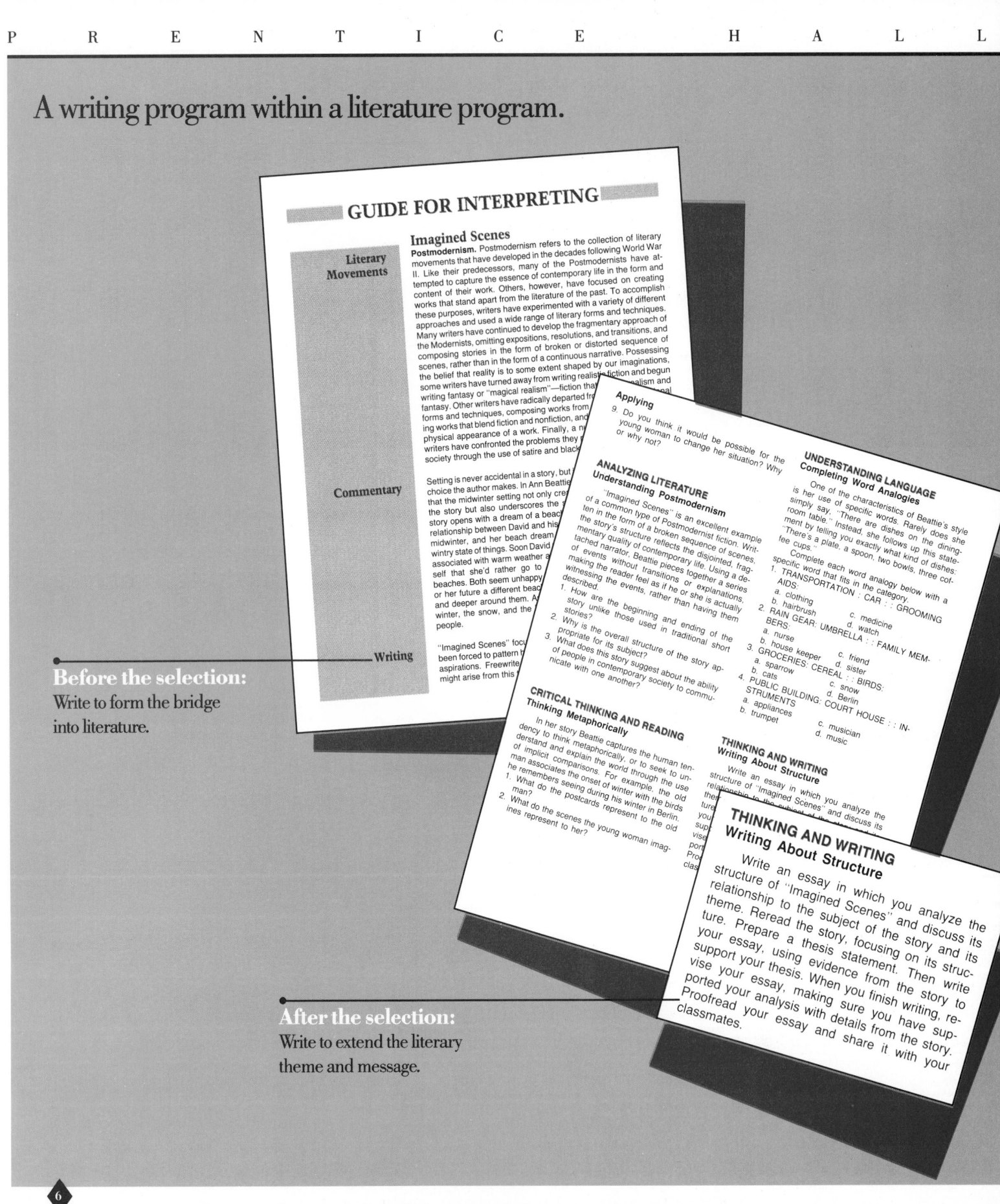

GUIDE FOR INTERPRETING

Literary Movements

Imagined Scenes

Postmodernism. Postmodernism refers to the collection of literary movements that have developed in the decades following World War II. Like their predecessors, many of the Postmodernists have attempted to capture the essence of contemporary life in the form and content of their work. Others, however, have focused on creating works that stand apart from the literature of the past. To accomplish these purposes, writers have experimented with a variety of different approaches and used a wide range of literary forms and techniques. Many writers have continued to develop the fragmentary approach of the Modernists, omitting expositions, resolutions, and transitions, and composing stories in the form of broken or distorted sequence of scenes, rather than in the form of a continuous narrative. Possessing the belief that reality is to some extent shaped by our imaginations, some writers have turned away from writing realistic fiction and begun writing fantasy or "magical realism"—fiction that _____ realism and fantasy. Other writers have radically departed fr_____ forms and techniques, composing works from _____ ing works that blend fiction and nonfiction, and _____ physical appearance of a work. Finally, a n_____ writers have confronted the problems they _____ society through the use of satire and black _____

Commentary

Setting is never accidental in a story, but _____ choice the author makes. In Ann Beattie _____ that the midwinter setting not only cre_____ the story but also underscores the _____ story opens with a dream of a beach _____ relationship between David and his _____ midwinter, and her beach dream _____ wintry state of things. Soon David _____ associated with warm weather _____ self that she'd rather go to _____ beaches. Both seem unhappy _____ or her future a different beac_____ and deeper around them. A _____ winter, the snow, and the _____ people.

"Imagined Scenes" focu_____ been forced to pattern h_____ aspirations. Freewrite _____ might arise from this _____

Writing

Applying
9. Do you think it would be possible for the young woman to change her situation? Why or why not?

ANALYZING LITERATURE
Understanding Postmodernism

"Imagined Scenes" is an excellent example of a common type of Postmodernist fiction. Written in the form of a broken sequence of scenes, the story's structure reflects the disjointed, fragmentary quality of contemporary life. Using a detached narrator, Beattie pieces together a series of events without transitions or explanations, making the reader feel as if he or she is actually witnessing the events, rather than having them described.

1. How are the beginning and ending of the story unlike those used in traditional short stories?
2. Why is the overall structure of the story appropriate for its subject?
3. What does this story suggest about the ability of people in contemporary society to communicate with one another?

CRITICAL THINKING AND READING
Thinking Metaphorically

In her story Beattie captures the human tendency to think metaphorically, or to seek to understand and explain the world through the use of implicit comparisons. For example, the old man associates the onset of winter with the birds he remembers seeing during his winter in Berlin.
1. What do the postcards represent to the old man?
2. What do the scenes the young woman imagines represent to her?

UNDERSTANDING LANGUAGE
Completing Word Analogies

One of the characteristics of Beattie's style is her use of specific words. Rarely does she simply say, "There are dishes on the dining-room table." Instead, she follows up this statement by telling you exactly what kind of dishes: "There's a plate, a spoon, two bowls, three coffee cups".

Complete each word analogy below with a specific word that fits in the category.
1. TRANSPORTATION : CAR :: GROOMING AIDS:
   a. clothing
   b. hairbrush
   c. medicine
   d. watch
2. RAIN GEAR: UMBRELLA :: FAMILY MEMBERS:
   a. nurse
   b. house keeper
   c. friend
   d. sister
3. GROCERIES: CEREAL :: BIRDS:
   a. sparrow
   b. cats
   c. snow
   d. Berlin
4. PUBLIC BUILDING: COURT HOUSE :: INSTRUMENTS
   a. appliances
   b. trumpet
   c. musician
   d. music

THINKING AND WRITING
Writing About Structure

Write an essay in which you analyze the structure of "Imagined Scenes" and discuss its relationship to the subject of th_____ ture. _____ you _____ sup_____ vise _____ por_____ Pro_____ clas_____

THINKING AND WRITING
Writing About Structure

Write an essay in which you analyze the structure of "Imagined Scenes" and discuss its relationship to the subject of the story and its theme. Reread the story, focusing on its structure. Prepare a thesis statement. Then write your essay, using evidence from the story to support your thesis. When you finish writing, revise your essay, making sure you have supported your analysis with details from the story. Proofread your essay and share it with your classmates.

Before the selection:
Write to form the bridge into literature.

After the selection:
Write to extend the literary theme and message.

The Power of Fine Literature, The Mastery of Writing.

Choose from 5 writing activities for each selection.

Extend the power and breadth of your writing program with these additional activities:

- Fine Art Writing activities
- Selection Test essay questions
- Unit Test essay questions
- You the Writer Writing assignment
- You the Critic Writing assignment
- Writing Across the Curriculum activities
- Student writing models

Plus — Writing About Literature Handbook
A writing course right in the student book

Three additional writing activities in the Teaching Portfolio meet the needs of all ability levels:

- Less Challenging
- More Challenging
- The Student as Critic

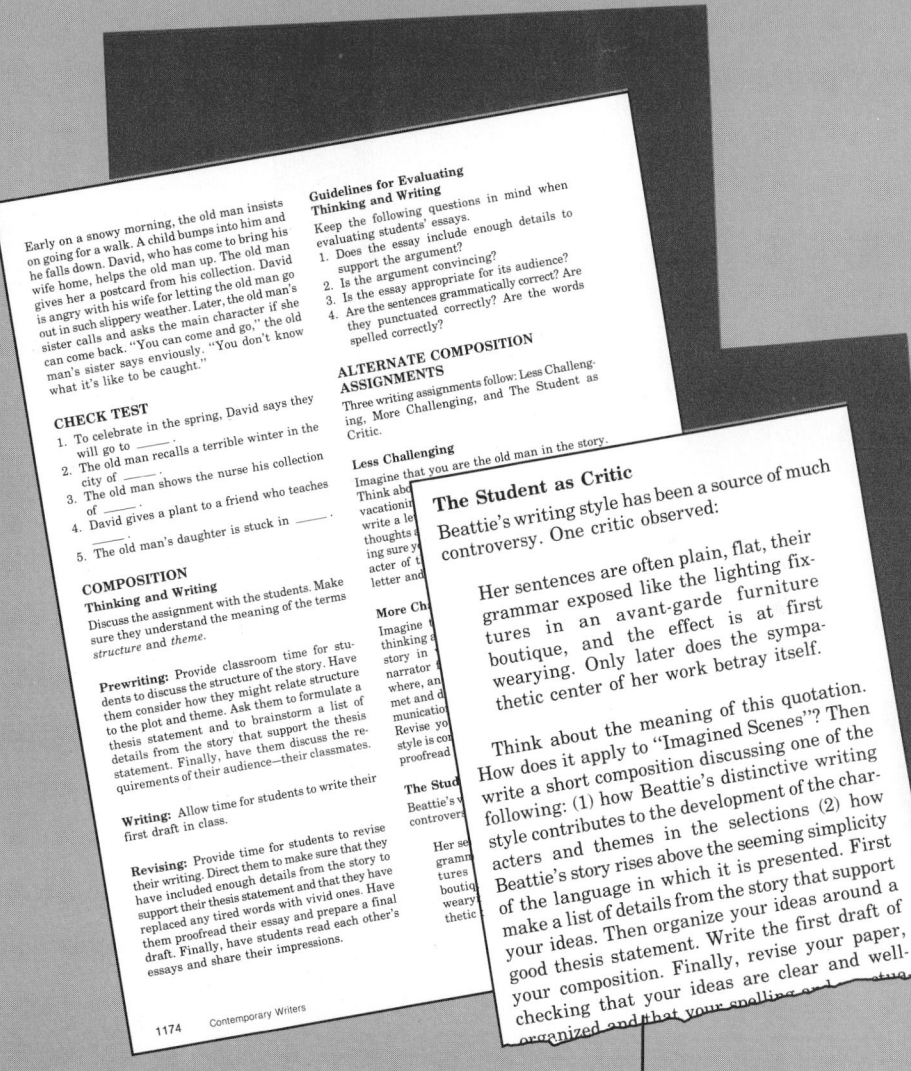

Early on a snowy morning, the old man insists on going for a walk. A child bumps into him and he falls down. David, who has come to bring his wife home, helps the old man up. The old man gives her a postcard from his collection. David is angry with his wife for letting the old man go out in such slippery weather. Later, the old man's sister calls and asks the main character if she can come back. "You can come and go," the old man's sister says enviously. "You don't know what it's like to be caught."

CHECK TEST
1. To celebrate in the spring, David says they will go to _____.
2. The old man recalls a terrible winter in the city of _____.
3. The old man shows the nurse his collection of _____.
4. David gives a plant to a friend who teaches _____.
5. The old man's daughter is stuck in _____.

COMPOSITION
Thinking and Writing
Discuss the assignment with the students. Make sure they understand the meaning of the terms *structure* and *theme*.

Prewriting: Provide classroom time for students to discuss the structure of the story. Have them consider how they might relate structure to the plot and theme. Ask them to formulate a list of thesis statement and to brainstorm a list of details from the story that support the thesis statement. Finally, have them discuss the requirements of their audience—their classmates.

Writing: Allow time for students to write their first draft in class.

Revising: Provide time for students to revise their writing. Direct them to make sure that they have included enough details from the story to support their thesis statement and that they have replaced any tired words with vivid ones. Have them proofread their essay and prepare a final draft. Finally, have students read each other's essays and share their impressions.

1174   Contemporary Writers

Guidelines for Evaluating Thinking and Writing
Keep the following questions in mind when evaluating students' essays.
1. Does the essay include enough details to support the argument?
2. Is the argument convincing?
3. Is the essay appropriate for its audience? Are the sentences grammatically correct? Are
4. Are the sentences grammatically correct? Are they punctuated correctly? Are the words spelled correctly?

ALTERNATE COMPOSITION ASSIGNMENTS
Three writing assignments follow: Less Challenging, More Challenging, and The Student as Critic.

Less Challenging
Imagine that you are the old man in the story.

The Student as Critic
Beattie's writing style has been a source of much controversy. One critic observed:

> Her sentences are often plain, flat, their grammar exposed like the lighting fixtures in an avant-garde furniture boutique, and the effect is at first wearying. Only later does the sympathetic center of her work betray itself.

Think about the meaning of this quotation. How does it apply to "Imagined Scenes"? Then write a short composition discussing one of the following: (1) how Beattie's distinctive writing style contributes to the development of the characters and themes in the selections (2) how Beattie's story rises above the seeming simplicity of the language in which it is presented. First make a list of details from the story that support your ideas. Then organize your ideas around a good thesis statement. Write the first draft of your composition. Finally, revise your paper, checking that your ideas are clear and well-organized and that your spelling and punctua-

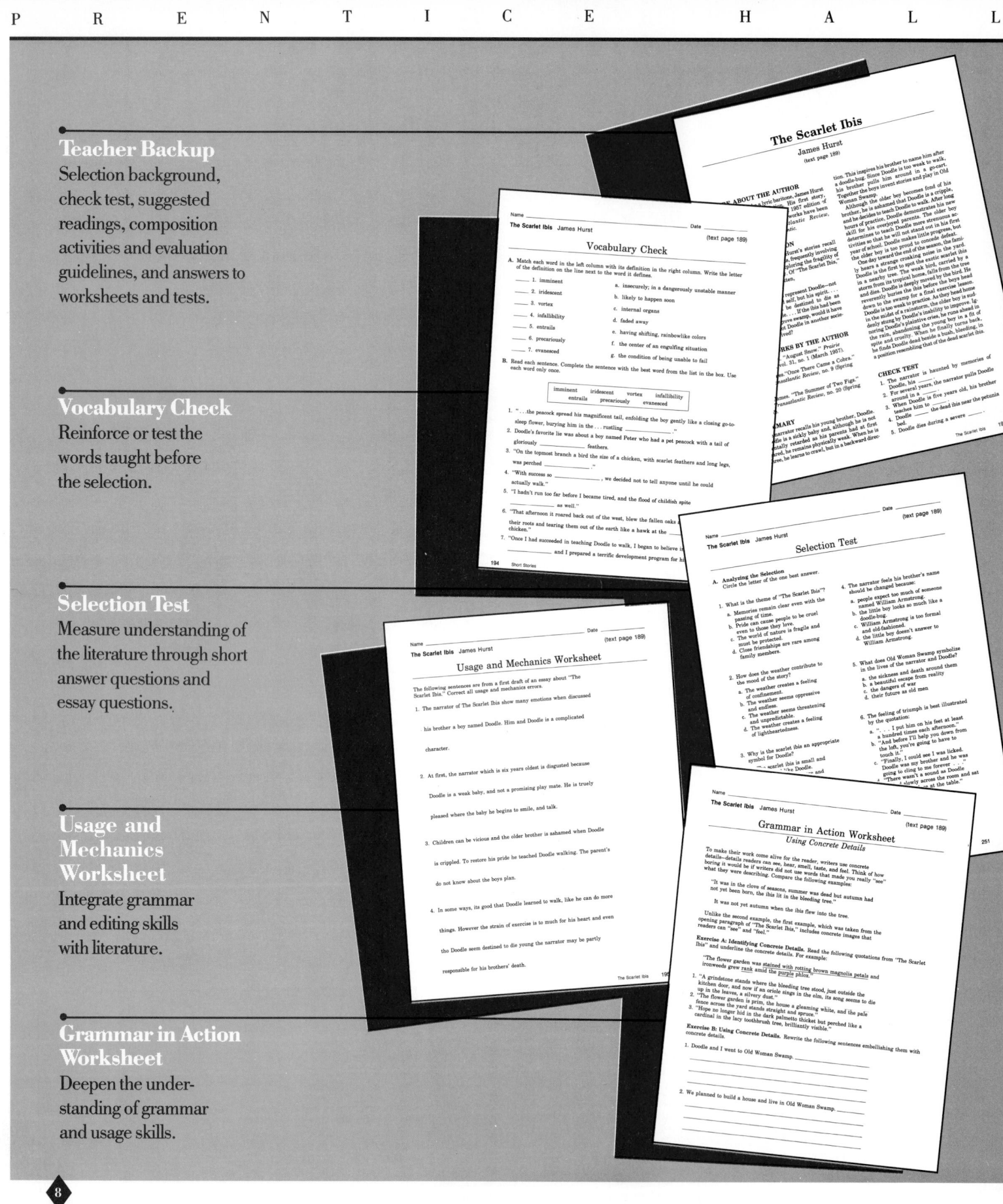

Teacher Backup
Selection background,
check test, suggested
readings, composition
activities and evaluation
guidelines, and answers to
worksheets and tests.

Vocabulary Check
Reinforce or test the
words taught before
the selection.

Selection Test
Measure understanding of
the literature through short
answer questions and
essay questions.

**Usage and
Mechanics
Worksheet**
Integrate grammar
and editing skills
with literature.

**Grammar in Action
Worksheet**
Deepen the under-
standing of grammar
and usage skills.

The Teaching Portfolio – Redefining the Concept of Support for all the Language Arts.

Everything you need to teach a selection is in one place.

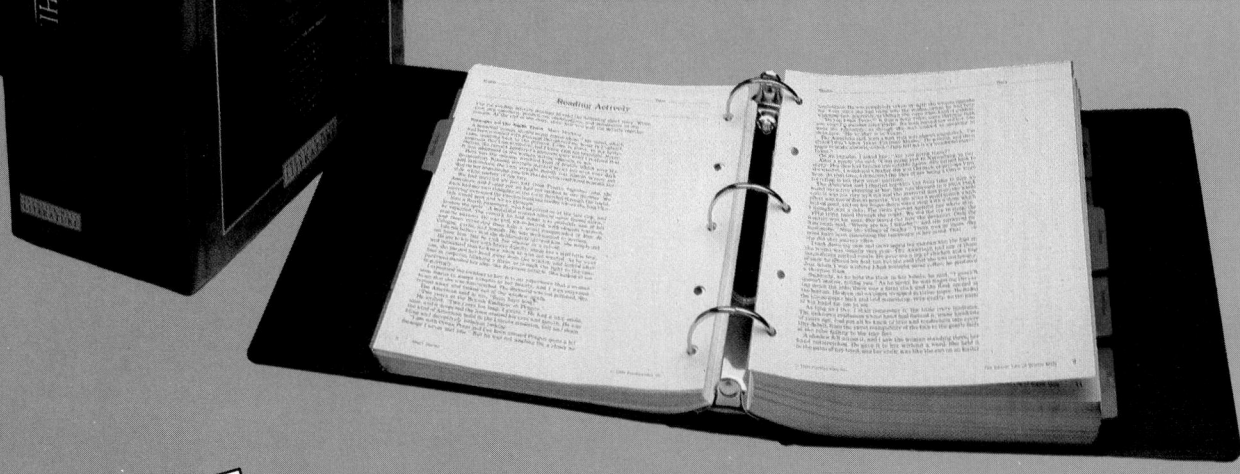

Analyzing Literature Worksheet
Extends understanding of the literary element.

Critical Thinking and Reading Worksheet
Promotes reading and reasoning.

Language Worksheet
Beyond vocabulary to word origins, synonyms, dialects — and more.

Fine Art Transparencies

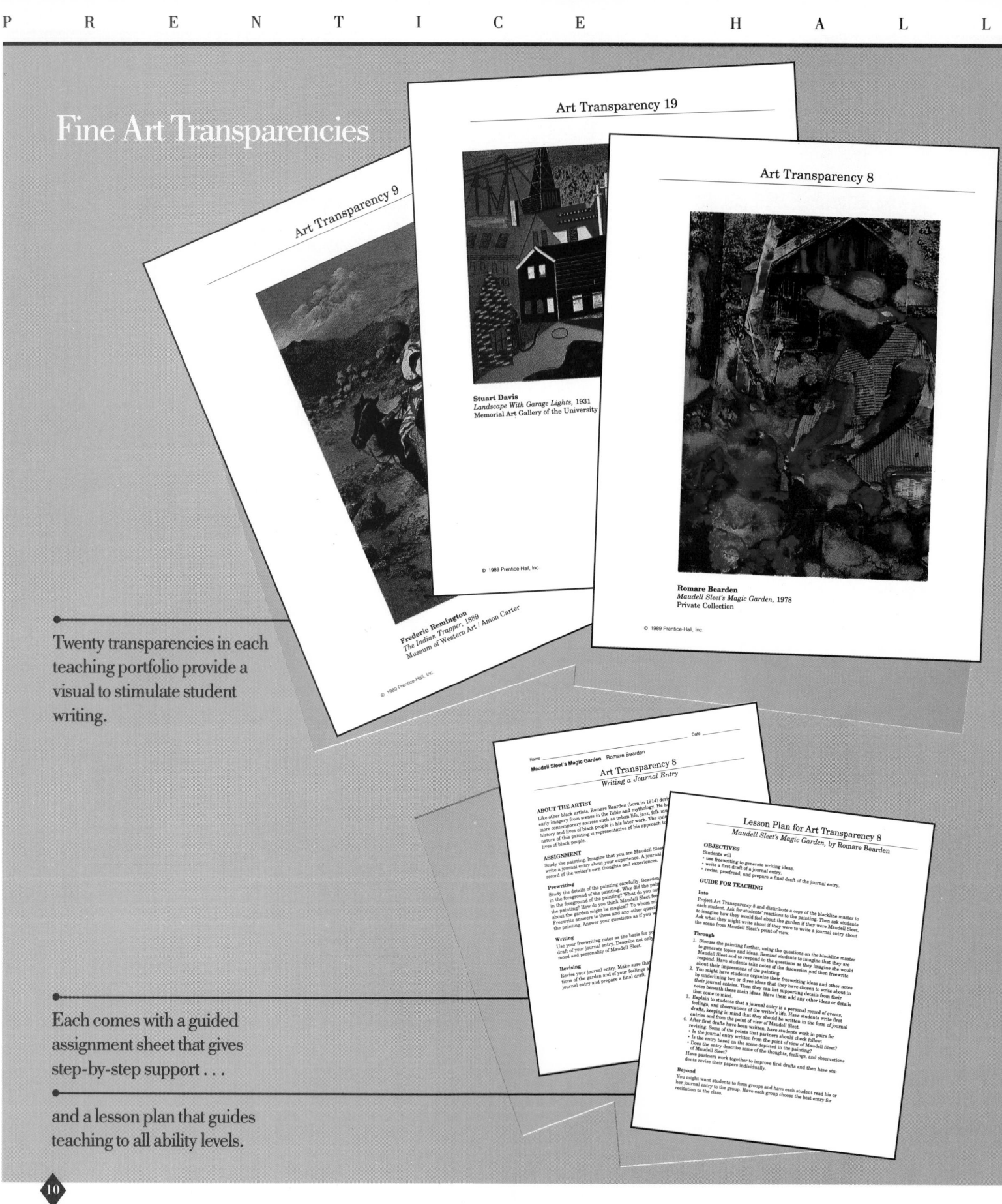

Frederic Remington
The Indian Trapper, 1889
Museum of Western Art / Amon Carter

© 1989 Prentice-Hall, Inc.

Stuart Davis
Landscape With Garage Lights, 1931
Memorial Art Gallery of the University

© 1989 Prentice-Hall, Inc.

Romare Bearden
Maudell Sleet's Magic Garden, 1978
Private Collection

© 1989 Prentice-Hall, Inc.

Twenty transparencies in each teaching portfolio provide a visual to stimulate student writing.

Each comes with a guided assignment sheet that gives step-by-step support . . .

and a lesson plan that guides teaching to all ability levels.

Capture the Power of Integrating
Fine Literature and the Humanities.

A fine arts program and classic cinema connected with literature.

The Library of Video Classics

- Four feature length films per grade level, including the novel and the play.

- Viewing guides link the film with the literature to stimulate new ideas.

Each Viewing Guide provides:

- Previewing and After Viewing Questions — enhance critical thinking skills.

- Speaking and Listening activities — promote oral language skills through the impact of film.

- Writing activities — creative topics enhance students responsiveness.

- Ability level notes — ideas to challenge each student.

Direct students to new discoveries with the dynamic combination of literature and cinema.

Study Guides

What if your favorite novel or play is not in Prentice Hall Literature? We still provide you with teaching support. Complete teaching guides for 40 novels and plays give you fresh insights to make the classic even more interesting and relevant. Each guide contains:

- Author Background
- Synopses of Plot, Setting, Theme and More
- Chapter-by-Chapter Teaching Plans
- Writing Assignments
- Guidelines for Dealing With Provocative Themes
- Blackline Master Handouts and Test

Tailor the Literature Program to Your Own Classes.

Library of Great Works

Now, the time-honored longer works of American, British, and world cultures available with Prentice Hall Literature

- Classic, unabridged editions
- Hardbound versions insure lasting value
- A Novel Study Guide for expert teaching support to bring the work to life

Great Works

Adventures of Huckleberry Finn	Nineteen Eighty Four
Brothers Karamazov	Our Town
Candide	Pride and Prejudice
Death of a Salesman	Red Badge of Courage
Don Quixote	Scarlet Letter
Great Gatsby	Siddartha
Hamlet	Tartuffe
Importance of Being Earnest	Things Fall Apart
Lord of the Flies	Wuthering Heights

Computer Test Bank

Customize your literature testing program with instant tests on each selection

For each selection choose from:
- Selection test
- Essay questions with evaluation guidelines
- Answer key

For each unit, choose from:
- Short answer test
- Essay tests

Powerful word processor for your made to order options.
- Write an unlimited number of new questions
- Delete questions

User friendly format for quick answers.
- Menus
- 800 customer service number

Annotated Teacher's Edition

PRENTICE HALL
LITERATURE

THE AMERICAN EXPERIENCE

SECOND EDITION

PRENTICE HALL
Englewood Cliffs, New Jersey
Needham, Massachusetts

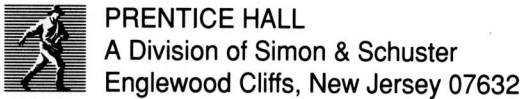

PRENTICE HALL
A Division of Simon & Schuster
Englewood Cliffs, New Jersey 07632

CONTENTS

ACKNOWLEDGMENTS

Grateful acknowledgment is made to the following for permission to reprint copyrighted material.

The Belknap Press of Harvard University Press
Excerpts reprinted by permission of the publishers from *A History of Modern Poetry,* by David Perkins, Cambridge, Mass.: The Belknap Press of Harvard University Press, Copyright © 1976 by the President and Fellows of Harvard College.

Harcourt Brace Jovanovich, Inc.
Excerpts from ''Notes from a Preface'' from *The Complete Poems of Carl Sandburg,* revised and expanded edition by Carl Sandburg. Copyright © 1970, 1969 by Lilian Steichen Sandburg, Trustee. Reprinted by permission of Harcourt Brace Jovanovich, Inc.

Henry Holt and Company, Inc.
Excerpts from ''The Hired Man and Other People'' from *The Pocket Book of Robert Frost's Poems,* With an Introduction and Commentary by Louis Untermeyer. Copyright 1943, © 1971 by Louis Untermeyer. Reprinted by permission of Henry Holt and Company, Inc.

Houghton Mifflin Company
Excerpt from the Introduction, by Mark Helprin, to *The Best American Short Stories 1988,* by Mark Helprin with Shannon Ravenel. Copyright © 1988 by Houghton Mifflin Company and reprinted by permission. Excerpt from the Preface of *The Complete Poetical Works of William Wordsworth* by Alice N. George. Excerpt from *Victorian Poetry and Poetics* by Walter E. Houghton and G. Robert Stange

Liveright Publishing Corporation
Excerpt from Introduction of *Collected Poems* by E. E. Cummings. Copyright © 1923, 1925, 1931, 1935, 1938 by E. E. Cummings. Copyright © 1926 by Boni & Liveright, Inc. Copyright renewed 1954. Reprinted by permission of Liveright Publishing Corporation.

(continued on page 1401)

The Prentice Hall Literature Program
OVERVIEW

THE STUDENT BOOK

The Prentice Hall Literature Program is a complete literature program, offering high-quality, appealing, traditional and contemporary literary selections, with study aids that will guide students into, through, and beyond the literature.

Organization

The selections are organized chronologically to present the literature of the United States in a historical context. The following list shows the units and the sections within each unit into which the selections are organized.

The New Land: Native American Voices, Living in the New Land

The Revolutionary Period

A Growing Nation

New England Renaissance: The Transcendentalists, New England Poets

Division, War, and Reconciliation

Realism and the Frontier: Prose, Poetry

The Modern Age: Fiction, Nonfiction, Poetry, The Harlem Renaissance

Contemporary Writers: Fiction, Nonfiction, Poetry, Drama

The number and variety of selections offer choice and flexibility in meeting curriculum requirements as well as student needs and interests.

Unique Features

Because the Prentice Hall Literature Program puts emphasis on the reading and appreciation of literature, it offers several unique features to help students become active readers.

Reading Critically Each unit begins with a feature called Reading Critically, which includes a summary of the historical context, the literary movements, and the writers' techniques of the period. This feature is followed by a Model for Reading Critically, which is annotated to demonstrate and explain to students how a good reader might apply this information to the analysis of a selection. This technique actively involves the reader in the text before reading and while reading. Such involvement and reaction are necessary if students are to learn. Students are encouraged to use this technique as they read other selections in the unit. This feature provides a method of scaffolding—giving students help and support while they acquire the skills to become successful readers of literature. To give students further practice with this process, there is an additional selection in the Teaching Portfolio, which students can annotate themselves.

Guide for Interpreting All other selections begin with a Guide for Interpreting. These pages contain useful prereading information. The Guide for Interpreting prepares students for successful reading in the following ways:

- A biography of the author provides insight into how the author came to write the selection.
- A literary focus section introduces the literary concept that is taught with the selection.
- A motivational writing activity puts students in an appropriate frame of mind.
- A primary source presents a quotation from the writer or a critic that gives an insight into the writer's work or times.
- Commentaries call out some noteworthy aspect of the work—thematic, stylistic, or meaning-oriented—and offer an insight into it.

This Guide for Interpreting provides the necessary background to encourage comprehension, motivates students to read, and gives them technical support to read successfully.

Each selection is self-contained and complete so that you can use the selections in any order that you like.

After Reading

Features at the end of the selection are designed to foster comprehension and encourage constructive response, either personal or literary. These features encourage the growth of skills needed by students to become independent readers. These features comprise five areas:

Thinking About the Selection: These study questions are built upon three levels of comprehension: the literal, the interpretive, and the applied. The questions are grouped by the levels of increasing complexity: recalling (literal), interpreting (inference, analysis), and applying (generalization, extension, judgment). The different levels may be used as appropriate for different ability levels, or may be used to take all students through different levels of thinking.

Analyzing Literature: This section develops and reinforces the literary concept or skill introduced on the Guide for Interpreting page and applies it to the selection. It helps students to understand literary concepts and appreciate writers' techniques, thereby enabling them to respond appropriately to literature.

Critical Thinking and Reading: This section introduces students to those critical thinking and critical reading skills that are necessary for understanding literature. It gives them an opportunity to apply these skills to the literary selections.

Understanding Language: Knowledge and appreciation of language are developed in this section, which contains activities on language prompted by the selection. The activities may be geared toward helping students appreciate writers' use of language, master skills needed to increase their vocabulary, or prepare for SATs.

Thinking and Writing: This is a composition assignment arising from the selection. This assignment, which may be creative or analytical, is process-oriented, suggesting steps for prewriting, drafting, and revising.

Special Features

Several special features occur throughout this volume: **Cross Currents** present some contemporary or humanities connection to the period or the content of the unit. **Great Works** introduce students to great works of literature, novels and plays that cannot be included in this anthology. This feature places the work in its historical period, indicates the significance of the work, presents a synopsis, and motivates students to read.

End of Unit

You the Writer, You the Critic At the end of each unit, there are six additional writing activities. Three of them, under You the Writer, are creative; three of them, under You the Critic, are analytical. Each activity is developed through the steps of the writing process.

End of Book

Three handbooks are provided at the end of *Prentice Hall Literature:* Handbook of Writing About Literature, Handbook of Critical Thinking and Reading Terms, and Handbook of Literary Terms and Techniques.

Handbook of Writing About Literature The Handbook of Writing About Literature is divided into five sections. The first section introduces the process of writing. The second requires students to analyze and interpret literature and teaches them how to write about the specific elements of literary works. The third requires students to interpret and synthesize while teaching how to write about the work as a whole. The fourth section provides instruction in evaluating literary works and the fifth guides the students in the creation of their own literary works.

This Handbook may be used for direct instruction or as support for the individual writing assignments in *Prentice Hall Literature.*

Handbook of Critical Thinking and Reading Terms The Handbook of Critical Thinking and Reading Terms provides an alphabetical arrangement of the terms taught in the Critical Thinking and Reading activities at the end of selections. Each entry expands upon the original definitions and provides one or more examples. This Handbook can be used to preteach terminology or to review information. It can also be used as an easy reference guide for students as they work on individual Critical Thinking and Reading assignments.

Handbook of Literary Terms and Techniques The Handbook of Literary Terms and Techniques provides an alphabetical guide to the literary terms introduced on the Guide for Interpreting page and taught in the Analyzing Literature activities at the end of selections. Each entry provides a full definition of the term or technique with one or more examples. The Handbook can be used for preteaching, for review, or as a support for students as they work on individual Analyzing Literature activities.

TEACHING SUPPORT

THE ANNOTATED TEACHER'S EDITION

The annotated teacher's edition of *Prentice Hall Literature* is designed to be used both for planning and for actual in-class teaching. It offers planning aids and specific teaching suggestions for all selections. This planning and teaching material appears in the side columns next to the reduced students pages of each selection. These annotations, which correspond to the student material on that page, help you give your students positive and relevant experiences

with literature by asking the right question at the right time and by pointing out what is significant.

Preparing the Lesson: Focus

The annotations on the opening pages of the selection help you plan your presentation of the material. Each selection begins with notes that suggest ways to introduce or enhance the prereading instruction or activities presented in the students' Guide for Interpreting. These notes help you present the material or adapt it for **less advanced** or **more advanced** students. A **vocabulary** list presents, in glossary format, words from the selection that might present difficulty in reading; you may wish to preteach these words. Occasional **spelling tips** give hints for remembering the spelling of a troublesome word. A **critical evaluation** note gives a critic's point of view on the writer of the work. Objectives for each selection are keyed to the end-of-selection material. This page also includes a complete list of support material for this selection in the Teaching Portfolio and other program components. In the column next to the first page of the selection, you will find a **motivation/ prior knowledge** suggestion and a **purpose-setting question** to prepare the students to read. Frequently, **thematic ideas** are given. These suggest other selections in this book that treat themes similar to those under discussion. You may want to use these selections together to integrate and reinforce universal concepts and themes. **ESL strategies** suggest ways to make selections accessible to ESL students. All of these annotations help you effectively prepare your lesson.

Teaching the Lesson: Presentation

You may use the notes throughout the pages of the selection to direct your discussion in class. As you and your students read the selection, you will find additional notes, which enable you to customize the lesson for your class. They let you increase your students' involvement in the work and enrich their reading of it, while enabling them to deal with the particular genres. The following kinds of notes may direct your class discussions:

Master Teacher Notes These tips from master teachers give an approach, a strategy, or a very special bit of information that enlivens the selection or increases appreciation.

Humanities Notes For each piece of fine art in the student book, there is a humanities note giving information on the work of art and the artist. These notes generally point out features of the piece of art that relate it to the work of literature with which it is presented. Additionally, the humanities note concludes with questions that you may use if you wish to discuss the art as part of your discussion of the selection.

Enrichment Enrichment notes provide additional information on points of interest that arise in selection. You may use this information to enrich your students' knowledge of the background of a selection and appreciation of it.

Reading Strategies Strategies to promote student comprehension of the literary text reinforce the emphasis on teaching students to read literature actively.

Clarification Words, phrases, or ideas that might be obstacles to student understanding are clarified to ensure comprehension.

Discussion Throughout the selection, you will find additional questions and points for discussion. These help you proceed through the selection with students, eliciting their understanding and appreciation of significant passages.

Literary Focus To promote understanding of the writer's techniques, literary focus annotations direct attention to those aspects of the selection that reflect the literary concept presented with it.

Critical Thinking and Reading These notes reinforce the critical thinking and reading skills developed throughout the program.

There are probably more notes than you need for presenting any given selection. We emphasize the importance of selecting those annotations that are best suited to your classes and to your course of instruction.

Reader's Response These notes ask a question designed to prompt the students' personal response to the selection.

Grammar in Action Grammar in Action notes integrate language arts skills. These notes demonstrate the writer's use of particular grammatical or style points. They present a direct link between grammar and writing.

Additional **commentary** and **primary source** notes add further background or insight to the selection.

Closure and Extension

Answers are provided for all questions in each feature following the selection. Where questions are open-ended, we present a suggested response or we suggest points that students should note in their answer.

The annotation after the selection also include the following:

Challenge These questions take students beyond those given with the instruction.

Publishing Student Writing For many selections, additional notes suggest ways to publishing the writing students have done in the Thinking and Writing feature.

Writing Across the Curriculum Where appropriate, you will see suggestions for additional assignments or suggestions for relating the Thinking and Writing assignment to students' work in another discipline.

In addition, you will find teaching suggestions for the special features in the student book—Reading Critically, and You the Writer, You the Critic. You will also find annotations in the unit introductions, relating the information there to specific selections.

THE TEACHING PORTFOLIO

The Teaching Portfolio provides support for teaching and testing all of the selections and skills in *Prentice Hall Literature*.

Fine Art Transparencies

Twenty fine-art transparencies with blackline masters are provided in the Teaching Portfolio. These can be used to introduce selections and motivate students to read, or they may be used as additional writing assignments in response to art. Each fine-art transparency has a writing assignment for students and a lesson plan for teaching that assignment. Furthermore, the fine art is keyed into the selections through Master Teacher Notes in the Annotated Teacher's Edition.

Beginning of Unit

Each unit begins with a list of objectives and a skills chart listing literary elements and skills covered in the unit. The skills chart also identifies all the blackline masters in the Teaching Portfolio that correlate to each selection.

The Selections

Full teaching support is provided for each selection. This support material is organized by selection for your convenience. The support for each selection consists of the following: Teaching Backup, Grammar in Action Worksheet, Usage and Mechanics Worksheet, Vocabulary Check, Analyzing Literature Worksheet*, Critical Thinking and Reading Worksheet*, Language Worksheet* (there are always two of the starred three), and a Selection Test.

Teacher Backup Teacher Backup material is provided for each selection. This material consists of more information about the author, a critical quotation about the author, a summary of the selection, and a list of other works by the author. In addition, there is a Check Test that you can use to check if students have read the selection. Help in teaching and evaluating the writing assignment in the student text is provided as well as three alternative composition assignments for the students. One of these is less challenging than the assignment in the student text, one is more challenging, and one requires the student to write in response to literary criticism. Finally, answers to all worksheets and test are provided.

Grammar in Action Worksheets The Grammar in Action worksheet provides further instruction and practice corresponding to Grammar in Action notes in the Annotated Teacher's Edition.

Usage and Mechanics The Usage and Mechanics Worksheet provides sentences dealing with the selection that contain errors in usage and mechanics. These provide practice on such common problems as run-on sentences, sentence fragments, and subject-verb agreement as well as errors in spelling and punctuation; furthermore, the Grammar in Action skills are incorporated into these sentences wherever possible. We suggest you have your students correct these sentences orally so that they can discuss each problem.

Vocabulary Check The Vocabulary Check tests mastery of the vocabulary words listed on the Guide for Interpreting page before each selection. This blackline master can be used as a test or as an in-class or at-home assignment.

Worksheets The Analyzing Literature Worksheet, Critical Thinking and Reading Worksheet, and Language Worksheet support and expand upon the skills taught at the end of the selection in the student book. If no Understanding Language assignment appears in the student book, one is provided in the Teaching Portfolio.

Selection Test A Selection Test is provided for each selection. This test provides a check of comprehension as well as a mastery of the skills taught at the end of the selection.

Annotated Models For each selection that is annotated as a model in the student book, a selection is provided in the Teaching Portfolio for students to annotate themselves.

End of Unit

Each unit ends with two unit tests: a short-answer test and an essay test. Guidelines are provided for evaluating student responses to the essay test questions. In addition, a list of suggested projects, a bibliography, and list of audio-visual aids follow.

End of Portfolio

At the end of the Teaching Portfolio are models of strong and weak student writing and a guide to evaluating student writing.

STUDY GUIDES

Study Guides for major novels and plays are available with *Prentice Hall Literature*. These guides will help you teach many of the novels of your choice as part of your total literature program. Each guide contains an overview of the novel or play, chapter-by-chapter lessons, assignments leading to essays and imaginative writing, guidelines for dealing with provocative themes, a bibliography, and blackline masters of skills and a test.

COMPUTER TEST BANK

The computer test program provides the selection test and unit tests from the Teaching Portfolio on a computer disk. The program allows you to modify the tests by deleting items from the short-answer selection tests supplied, choosing a different essay question, and writing your own questions. You can save your test for future use.

LIBRARY OF VIDEO CLASSICS

The Library of Video Classics provides videotapes of films made of major works in this level. Each tape is accompanied by a Viewing Guide, which gives background on the film or director, a planning overview for the film, and pre-viewing and after-viewing questions and activities.

Composition Strand in Prentice Hall Literature

The following chart shows all composition activities and their location in the program. The activities are organized to take students into, through, and beyond the literature.

Feature	In the Student Materials	In the Teacher Materials	Benefit
Into the Literature			
"Writing" activity *before* each selection	"Guide for Interpreting" page before each selection in student text	"Guide for Interpreting" teaching note in margin of Annotated Teacher's Edition	Writing before reading is an ideal technique for getting students into literature.
Through the Literature			
"Thinking and Writing" composition activity after *each* selection	End of each selection in student text	In Teaching Portfolio: Teaching notes for activity labeled with writing process steps. Evaluation checklist for grading writing In ATE: Suggestions for publishing student writing	The writing activity that follows each selection provides an immediate opportunity to respond to the literary experience. The activity is in writing process format.
Three additional composition activities for *each* selection: Less Challenging, More Challenging, The Student as Critic		Additional activities are in the Teaching Portfolio. These can be used as assignments, or as essay questions for tests	Three additional activities for *each* selection let you meet the needs of lower ability levels, or provide enrichment.
"Unit Test" essay questions that address several selections in a unit		Tests in Teaching Portfolio comes with evaluation checklists	Sharpen critical thinking and writing with thoughtful topics that compare and contrast thematic ideas, literary elements, and unit content.
Beyond the Literature			
"You the Writer" creative writing activity with each unit	End of each unit in student text	Guidelines for evaluating student writing are in Annotated Teacher's Edition	Students try their hand at expressive writing aided by imaginative prompts and step-by-step encouragement.
"You the Critic" literary criticism activity with each unit	End of each unit in student text	Teaching notes and guidelines for evaluating student writing in Annotated Teacher's Edition	Challenge analytical skills as your students respond to literary criticism.
"Writing Across the Curriculum" suggestions		Suggestions in Annotated Teacher's Edition	Broaden writing opportunities to other subjects. Notes suggest assignments and interactions with other departments.
"Fine Art Writing Activity" (from full color art transparency)	Handout sheet	Twenty fine art color transparencies with accompanying blackline masters in Teaching Portfolio	Use the dynamic combination of literature and writing for a humanities-based writing activity.
"Student Writing Models"		In the Teaching Portfolio: Examples of strong and weak student compositions	Use the powerful motivator of peer learning to prompt better writing responses.

Skills Chart for Selections in Each Unit

The following chart shows the literary elements and integrated language arts skills covered with each selection. An asterisk (*) indicates that a worksheet appears in the Teaching Portfolio.

THE NEW LAND

Selection	Analyzing Literature	Critical Thinking and Reading	Understanding Language/ Speaking and Listening	Thinking and Writing	Grammar in Action
Reading Critically					
"Upon the Burning of Our House," Anne Bradstreet, p. 15	Understanding the Puritan plain style*	Appreciating connotations*	Finding word origins	Writing about lyric poetry	Expressing negative ideas*
Native American Voices					
"The Walam Olum," Delaware, p. 22 "The Navaho Origin Legend," Navaho, p. 26	Recognizing myths*	Inferring cultural values*		Comparing and contrasting origin myths	Varying sentence patterns*
"The Iroquois Constitution," Iroquois, p. 29	Recognizing a constitution*	Understanding metaphors*		Comparing and contrasting constitutions	
"From the Houses of Magic," Pima, p. 34 "Spring Song," Chippewa, p. 37 "Song Concerning a Dream of the Thunderbirds," Teton Sioux, p. 38	Understanding the oral tradition*		Using Native American words*	Writing a song	

Selection	Analyzing Literature	Critical Thinking and Reading	Understanding Language/ Speaking and Listening	Thinking and Writing	Grammar in Action
Living in the New Land					
From *The General History of Virginia,* John Smith, p. 44	Understanding history	Recognizing author's purpose/Separating objective from subjective details*	Choosing the meaning that fits the context*	Writing a historical account	Understanding diction*
From *Of Plymouth Plantation,* William Bradford, p. 52	Using modes of discourse*	Making inferences about attitudes	Completing word analogies*	Comparing and contrasting accounts	Understanding the evolution of language* Using participles and participial phrases*
"To My Dear and Loving Husband," Anne Bradstreet, p. 59	Understanding lyric poetry*		Understanding connotation and denotation*		
"Huswifery," Edward Taylor, p. 62 "Upon a Wasp Chilled with Cold," p. 64	Recognizing figurative language		Using context clues*	Writing a conceit	
From *The History of the Dividing Line,* William Byrd, p. 67	Understanding journals*	Recognizing the author's purpose	Exploring tone*	Writing a narrative account	
From *Sinners in the Hands of an Angry God,* Jonathan Edwards, p. 72	Understanding persuasive speeches*	Recognizing persuasive techniques*	Understanding figurative language*	Evaluating persuasive techniques	Appreciating tone*
From *The Wonders of the Invisible World,* Cotton Mather, p. 72	Recognizing a writer's style	Recognizing author's bias*	Appreciating style*	Writing a journal entry	Using active and passive voice*

THE REVOLUTIONARY PERIOD (1750–1800)

Selection	Analyzing Literature	Critical Thinking and Reading	Understanding Language/ Speaking and Listening	Thinking and Writing	Grammar in Action
Reading Critically					
Benjamin Franklin					
"Dialogue Between Franklin and the Gout," Benjamin Franklin, p. 101	Understanding the Age of Reason	Understanding reasoning*	Using suffixes to change parts of speech*	Writing a dialogue	Understanding sentence fragments*
From *The Autobiography,* p. 110	Understanding an autobiography*	Making inferences about the author*		Writing an autobiographical account*	Understanding narrative writing* Using semicolons*
From *Poor Richard's Almanack,* p. 121	Recognizing aphorisms*	Understanding style*		Responding to a statement about style	
"Speech in the Virginia Convention," Patrick Henry, p. 126	Recognizing oratory*	Understanding persuasive techniques*	Delivering a speech	Writing a speech	Understanding parallelism*
From *The Crisis, Number 1,* Thomas Paine, p. 132	Using aphorisms*	Understanding the effect of aphorisms*	Noting synonyms	Writing about revolutionary literature	Understanding persuasive writing*
"To His Excellency, General Washington," Phillis Wheatley, p. 138	Recognizing personification*	Evaluating the effect of personification	Understanding words from Greek myths*	Developing a personification	
"The Declaration of Independence," Thomas Jefferson, p. 144	Recognizing parallelism*	Recognizing charged words*		Comparing and contrasting arguments	Using parallelism*
"Letter to Her Daughter from the New White House," Abigail Adams, p. 150	Recognizing descriptive writing*	Inferring a writer's attitude	Tracing word origins*	Writing a description	
From *Letters from an American Farmer,* Michel-Guillaume Jean de Crèvecoeur, p. 156	Understanding epistles*	Supporting opinions	Appreciating word origins*	Writing an epistle	

A GROWING NATION (1800–1840)

Selection	Analyzing Literature	Critical Thinking and Reading	Understanding Language/ Speaking and Listening	Thinking and Writing	Grammar in Action
Reading Critically					
"To a Waterfowl," William Cullen Bryant, p. 179	Understanding Romanticism*		Understanding archaic words*	Responding to criticism	
"The Devil and Tom Walker," Washington Irving, p. 184	Recognizing folktales*	Inferring cultural attitudes*		Adapting a folktale	Using subordination* Appreciating adjectives*
From *The Prairie*, James Fenimore Cooper, p. 196	Understanding setting*	Predicting later events	Using context clues*	Responding to criticism	Understanding the exclamation mark*
"Thanatopsis," William Cullen Bryant, p. 207	Recognizing blank verse*		Reading with expression Paraphrasing*	Writing a poem using blank verse	
Edgar Allan Poe					
"The Fall of the House of Usher," p. 212	Understanding the single effect*	Supporting statements of theme Providing supporting evidence*		Supporting a statement of theme	Appreciating verb tenses* Understanding parentheses*
"The Raven," p. 227	Using sound devices*		Using sound devices*	Responding to a statement by the author	
"The Oval Portrait," p. 233	Recognizing a frame story	Understanding cause and effect*	Recognizing shares of meaning* Understanding word origins	Comparing and contrasting stories	Understanding adjective clauses*
"To Helen," p. 239	Understanding allusions*		Appreciating poetic language*		

NEW ENGLAND RENAISSANCE (1840–1855)

Selection	Analyzing Literature	Critical Thinking and Reading	Understanding Language/ Speaking and Listening	Thinking and Writing	Grammar in Action
Reading Critically					
"The Skeleton in Armor," Henry Wadsworth Longfellow, p. 265	Understanding the Fireside Poets*		Reading with expression*	Writing a letter	
Ralph Waldo Emerson: From *Nature*, p. 274 from *Self-Reliance*, p. 276	Understanding Transcendentalism*		Completing analogies*	Writing about conformity	
Ralph Waldo Emerson: "The Snowstorm," p. 279 "Concord Hymn," p. 281 "The Rhodora," p. 283 "Brahma," p. 285	Using the apostrophe*	Understanding cause and effect Understanding paradox	Recognizing synonyms* Recognizing antonyms	Writing about history	
From *Walden*, Henry David Thoreau, p. 288	Understanding style*	Evaluating the effect of style*		Comparing and contrasting essays	Using infinitives*
From *Civil Disobedience*, Henry David Thoreau, p. 296	Understanding historical context*		Recognizing synonyms*	Writing a report	
"The Minister's Black Veil," Nathaniel Hawthorne, p. 302	Understanding Anti-Transcendentalism writing*	Recognizing the author's attitudes*		Comparing and contrasting attitudes	Varying sentence structures*
From *Moby-Dick*, Herman Melville, p. 318	Recognizing a symbol*	Analyzing the meaning of a symbol*		Writing about symbolism and theme	Identifying direct and rhetorical questions*

NEW ENGLAND RENAISSANCE (1840–1855) (continued)

Selection	Analyzing Literature	Critical Thinking and Reading	Understanding Language/ Speaking and Listening	Thinking and Writing	Grammar in Action
New England Poets					
Henry Wadsworth Longfellow: "The Tide Rises, The Tide Falls," p. 338 "A Psalm of Life," p. 340 "The Arsenal at Springfield," p. 342	Describing stanza forms*	Evaluating Longfellow's poetry*	Using abstract words		
Oliver Wendell Holmes: "Old Ironsides," p. 348 "The Chambered Nautilus," p. 350	Using meter and scansion*	Understanding personification		Writing a poem in support of a cause	
James Russell Lowell: "Auspex," p. 354 "The First Snowfall," p. 356	Understanding tone*	Understanding similes*		Comparing and contrasting tones	
John Greenleaf Whittier: From *Snowbound*, p. 360 "Hampton Beach," p. 366	Understanding imagery*	Evaluating the effect of imagery*	Using vivid adjectives	Writing a poem using imagery	Analyzing sentences*

Selection	Analyzing Literature	Critical Thinking and Reading	Understanding Language/ Speaking and Listening	Thinking and Writing	Grammar in Action
Emily Dickinson: "'Hope' is the thing with feathers," p. 372 "There's a certain slant of light," p. 373 "I like to see it lap the miles," p. 374 "A Narrow Fellow in the Grass," p. 376 "I never saw a Moor—," p. 378 "Tell all Truth but tell it slant—," p. 379	Understanding style*	Interpreting connotative meaning*			
Emily Dickinson: "Success is counted sweetest," p. 381 "I felt a funeral in my Brain," p. 382 "I heard a Fly buzz—when I died," p. 383 "Because I could not stop for Death—," p. 384 "My life closed twice before its close—," p. 386 "The Bustle in a House," p. 387	Understanding theme*		Finding antonyms*	Responding to criticism	

Selection	Analyzing Literature	Critical Thinking and Reading	Understanding Language/ Speaking and Listening	Thinking and Writing	Grammar in Action
Emily Dickinson: "Much Madness is divinest Sense—," p. 389 "As imperceptibly as grief," p. 390 "The Soul selects her own Society—," p. 391 "How happy is the little Stone," p. 382 "There is a solitude of space," p. 393 "This is my letter to the World," p. 394	Understanding metaphors and similes*		Recognizing synonyms*	Responding to Dickinson's poetry	

DIVISION, WAR, AND RECONCILATION (1855–1865)

Selection	Analyzing Literature	Critical Thinking and Reading	Understanding Language/ Speaking and Listening	Thinking and Writing	Grammar in Action
Reading Critically					
"When Lilacs Last in the Dooryard Bloom'd," Walt Whitman, p. 413	Understanding elegies*	Understanding the multiple meanings of words*	Using synonyms	Writing an elegy	Using appositives*
"Swing Low, Sweet Chariot," p. 426 "Go Down Moses," p. 427	Understanding spirituals* Recognizing a refrain	Understanding the effect of the refrain*		Writing about the role of spirituals	
From *My Bondage and My Freedom*, Frederick Douglass, p. 430	Recognizing an autobiography	Analyzing the effect of style*	Understanding emotive language*	Writing an autobiography	Recognizing gerunds and gerund phrases*
From *Mary Chesnut's Civil War*, Mary Chesnut, p. 437	Understanding a journal*	Recognizing main ideas*		Writing a summary	
Abraham Lincoln: The Gettysburg Address, p. 444 "Letter to Mrs. Bixby," p. 446	Understanding diction*	Analyzing the appropriateness of diction*	Recognizing words with the root *cede*	Comparing and contrasting speeches Writing a letter	
"Letter to His Son," Robert E. Lee, p. 450	Knowing historical context*		Buildings words with the root *cede**	Writing a letter	
"I Will Fight No More Forever," Chief Joseph, p. 454	Understanding tone*	Understanding connotation and denotation*		Writing a speech	

DIVISION, WAR, AND RECONCILATION (1855–1865) (continued)

Selection	Analyzing Literature	Critical Thinking and Reading	Understanding Language/ Speaking and Listening	Thinking and Writing	Grammar in Action
Walt Whitman: From "Preface to the 1855 Edition of *Leaves of Grass*," p. 458 From *Song of Myself*, p. 460 "I Saw in Louisiana a Live-Oak Growing," p. 466 "Beat! Beat! Drums!," p. 468 "When I Heard the Learn'd Astronomer," p. 470 "A Noiseless Patient Spider," p. 472	Recognizing style Recognizing free verse*	Recognizing the author's attitudes*	Recognizing analogies	Writing a personal response Writing a poem in free verse	

REALISM AND THE FRONTIER (1865–1915)

Selection	Analyzing Literature	Critical Thinking and Reading	Understanding Language/ Speaking and Listening	Thinking and Writing	Grammar in Action
Reading Critically					
"Tom Quartz," Mark Twain, p. 495	Understanding point of view*	Understanding exaggeration*	Interpreting dialect	Writing a tall tale	
Prose					
"The Boys' Ambition," Mark Twain, p. 502	Recognizing narration*		Understanding jargon*	Writing a statement of ambition	
"The Notorious Jumping Frog of Calaveras County," Mark Twain, p. 507	Recognizing humor*	Appreciating dialect*		Writing a story using dialect	Understanding the dash*
"The Outcasts of Poker Flat," Bret Harte, p. 518	Understanding regional literature*	Making inferences about attitudes*		Comparing and contrasting characters	Using coordinating conjunctions*

REALISM AND THE FRONTIER (1865–1915) (continued)

Selection	Analyzing Literature	Critical Thinking and Reading	Understanding Language/ Speaking and Listening	Thinking and Writing	Grammar in Action
"An Occurrence at Owl Creek Bridge," Ambrose Bierce, p. 530	Recognizing point of view*	Understanding the sequence of events*		Exploring a different point of view	Eliminating unnecessary words*
"A White Heron," Sarah Orne Jewett, p. 540	Recognizing imagery*	Evaluating the effect of imagery	Appreciating figurative language*	Responding to criticism	Understanding reflexive and intensive pronouns*
"The Story of an Hour," Kate Chopin, p. 550	Recognizing irony*	Recognizing details of irony	Completing word analogies*	Writing about irony	Using adverbs of manner*
"A Wagner Matinée," Willa Cather, p. 556	Understanding characterization*	Making inferences about the effect of setting*	Understanding musical terms	Supporting an opinion	Appreciating concluding sentences*
"To Build a Fire," Jack London, p. 566	Recognizing types of conflict*	Relating conflict to theme*		Writing about conflict and theme	Appreciating sentence structure* Using commas*
"The Open Boat," Stephen Crane, p. 580	Understanding Realism and Naturalism*	Recognizing important passages*		Responding to criticism	Appreciating comparisons* Understanding coordination*
Poetry					
"Song of the Chattahoochee," Sidney Lanier, p. 605	Understanding sound devices*	Analyzing the effect of sound devices	Understanding personification*	Writing an extended personification	
Stephen Crane: "War Is Kind," p. 609 "Think as I Think," p. 611	Understanding irony and tone*		Recognizing assonance and alliteration*	Writing about theme	
Paul Laurence Dunbar: "We Wear the Mask," p. 614 "Douglass," p. 616	Recognizing a sonnet	Comparing sonnet forms*	Completing sentences*	Writing a sonnet	
Edwin Arlington Robinson: "Luke Havergal," p. 620 "Miniver Cheevy," p. 622 "Richard Cory," p. 624	Understanding irony*	Recognizing attitudes Appreciating different points of view*			

REALISM AND THE FRONTIER (1865–1915) (continued)

Selection	Analyzing Literature	Critical Thinking and Reading	Understanding Language/ Speaking and Listening	Thinking and Writing	Grammar in Action
Edgar Lee Masters: "Lucinda Matlock," p. 628 "Fiddler Jones," p. 630	Identifying the speaker in poetry*	Comparing and contrasting speakers*		Writing an epitaph Comparing and contrasting writers	

THE MODERN AGE (1915–1946)

Selection	Analyzing Literature	Critical Thinking and Reading	Understanding Language/ Speaking and Listening	Thinking and Writing	Grammar in Action
Reading Critically					
"Sophistication," Sherwood Anderson, p. 651	Understanding character*	Understanding a character's motivation	Using context clues*	Writing about theme	Identifying noun clauses* Making pronouns agree with antecedents*
Fiction					
"In Another Country," Ernest Hemingway, p. 664	Understanding Modernism*	Analyzing the effect of style*		Responding to a statement by the author	Using direct quotations*
"Winter Dreams," F. Scott Fitzgerald, p. 672	Understanding characterization*	Evaluating a character's behavior*		Writing about historical context	Using dashes* Recognizing adverb clauses* Varying sentence lengths*
"The Jilting of Granny Weatherall," Katherine Anne Porter, p. 694	Understanding stream of consciousness*	Understanding the sequence of events*		Writing about stream of consciousness	Using ellipses* Recognizing formal and informal English*

THE MODERN AGE (1915–1946) (continued)

Selection	Analyzing Literature	Critical Thinking and Reading	Understanding Language/ Speaking and Listening	Thinking and Writing	Grammar in Action
"The Far and the Near," Thomas Wolfe, p. 704	Understanding point of view*	Recognizing period characteristics	Recognizing multiple meanings*	Comparing and contrasting stories	
"A Worn Path," Eudora Welty, p. 710	Interpreting ambiguity*	Making inferences about a character*		Writing a continuation of the story	Understanding coordinate and cumulative adjectives*
"Flight," John Steinbeck, p. 718	Understanding setting*	Analyzing the effect of setting	Using Latin prefixes*	Writing about setting	Recognizing faulty coordination* Using adjectives* Understanding descriptive writing*
"The Bear," William Faulkner, p. 734	Understanding symbols and allusions*		Using suffixes*	Writing about symbols and allusions	Using transitions* Recognizing complex sentences*
"The Signature," Elizabeth Enright, p. 748	Understanding setting	Recognizing important words*	Appreciating adjectives Recognizing synonyms*	Writing about setting	Using concrete details* Recognizing compound adjectives*
Nonfiction					
"Tin Lizzie," John Dos Passos, p. 756	Understanding biography*	Recognizing the writer's attitude	Forming compound words*	Writing an impressionistic biography	
"Walden," E.B. White, p. 762	Understanding personal essays	Recognizing the writer's attitude*	Recognizing antonyms* Fitting the context	Comparing and contrasting essay	Appreciating nominative absolutes*
"The Tooth, the Whole Tooth and Nothing but the Tooth," Robert Benchley, p. 770	Understanding informal essays*	Evaluating the effectiveness of an essay	Recognizing colloquial language	Writing an informal essay	Changing point of view and verb tense*

THE MODERN AGE (1915–1946) (continued)

Selection	Analyzing Literature	Critical Thinking and Reading	Understanding Language/ Speaking and Listening	Thinking and Writing	Grammar in Action
"The Night the Ghost Got In," James Thurber, p. 778	Understanding humor*	Recognizing exaggeration*		Writing a humorous essay	Identifying logical order*
"Lincoln Speaks at Gettysburg," Carl Sandburg, p. 786	Understanding biography*	Evaluating the subject of a biography	Building words using *bene**	Writing a biographical sketch	Recognizing inverted word order* Using elliptical clauses*
Poetry					
Ezra Pound: "In a station of the Metro," p. 800 "The River Merchant's Wife," p. 801 "Canto 13," p. 805	Understanding imagism*		Recognizing connotation*	Writing about imagism	Using specific words*
"The Love Song of J. Alfred Prufrock," T.S. Eliot, p. 810	Understanding stream of consciousness	Interpreting allusions*	Understanding word origins*	Comparing and contrasting works	Using action verbs and linking verbs*
Wallace Stevens: "Disillusionment at Ten O'Clock," p. 818 "Anecdote of the Jar," p. 819	Interpreting symbolism*	Supporting an interpretation*		Responding to a statement by the writer	
"Patterns," Amy Lowell, p. 822	Understanding dramatic monologue*		Understanding word origins*	Comparing and contrasting poems	
H.D. (Hilda Doolittle): "Pear Tree," p. 828 "Heat," p. 830	Understanding imagery*	Analyzing the effect of imagery	Choosing the meaning that fits context*	Writing an imagist poem	
William Carlos Williams: "The Locust Tree," p. 835 "The Red Wheel-barrow," p. 836 "This Is Just To Say," p. 837	Understanding rhythm*		Identifying compounds	Writing an apology	

Selection	Analyzing Literature	Critical Thinking and Reading	Understanding Language/ Speaking and Listening	Thinking and Writing	Grammar in Action
Carl Sandburg: "Grass," p. 840 From *The People, Yes*, p. 842 "Chicago," p. 844	Understanding free verse*		Recognizing slang*	Writing a poem using free verse	
"Renascence," Edna St. Vincent Millay, p. 848	Understanding theme*	Recognizing literary themes*			Identifying prepositional phrases*
"Janet Walking," John Crow Ransom, p. 856 "Ars Poetica," Archibald MacLeish, p. 858 "Poetry," Marianne Moore, p. 860	Understanding pathos Understanding similes*		Identifying antonyms*		
E.E. Cummings: "since feeling is first," p. 864 "anyone lived in a pretty how town," p. 865 "old age sticks," p. 867	Examining style*		Understanding homophones*	Writing about style	
Robert Frost: "Birches," p. 870 "Mending Wall," p. 873 "The Wood-Pile," p. 875 "After Apple-Picking," p. 878	Interpreting symbols*		Recognizing precise language*	Writing about a symbol Writing a poem	Making verbs agree with their subjects*
Robert Frost: "The Death of the Hired Man," p. 881 "Out, Out—," p. 888	Understanding dramatic poetry Understanding narrative poetry*		Choosing the meaning that fits the context*	Writing a dramatic poem	Using apostrophes*

THE MODERN AGE (1915–1946) (continued)

Selection	Analyzing Literature	Critical Thinking and Reading	Understanding Language/ Speaking and Listening	Thinking and Writing	Grammar in Action
Robert Frost: "Fire and Ice," p. 891 "Nothing Gold Can Stay," p. 892 "Stopping By Woods on a Snowy Evening," p. 893 "Acquainted with the Night," p. 894	Understanding rhythm*	Analyzing variations in rhythm	Recognizing degrees of comparison in adjectives*	Supporting a generalization	
W.H. Auden: "Who's Who," p. 898 "The Unknown Citizen," p. 899	Interpreting satire*	Evaluating the effectiveness of satire*			
The Harlem Renaissance					
"Any Human to Another," Countee Cullen, p. 905 "The Tropics in New York," Claude McKay, p. 906	Understanding the Harlem Renaissance*	Comparing and contrasting poems*			
"The Negro Speaks of Rivers," Langston Hughes, p. 911	Identifying the speaker	Comparing and contrasting poems*		Writing a poem about a special place	
"Storm Ending," Jean Toomer, p. 914 "A Black Man Talks of Reaping," Arna Bontemps, p. 916	Understanding metaphor*	Comparing and contrasting poems*			

CONTEMPORARY WRITERS (1946–PRESENT)

Selection	Analyzing Literature	Critical Thinking and Reading	Understanding Language/ Speaking and Listening	Thinking and Writing	Grammar in Action
Reading Critically					
"Night Journey," Theodore Roethke, p. 941	Understanding scansion*		Using concrete words*	Writing a poem about a journey	
Fiction					
"The First Seven Years," Bernard Malamud, p. 946	Understanding epiphany*	Predicting future events	Understanding analogies*	Writing about a character	Using *who* and *whom** Using transitions
"The Life You Save May Be Your Own," Flannery O'Connor, p. 956	Understanding irony*	Seeing irony as a key to theme	Understanding dialect*	Writing a story	Using the subjunctive mood* Using dialect*
"Average Waves in Unprotected Waters," Anne Tyler, p. 968	Understanding foreshadowing*	Identifying rationalization* Ordering events		Responding to criticism	Using varied sentence openers*
"The Slump," John Updike, p. 978	Appreciating diction*		Understanding jargon*	Responding to criticism	
"Journey," Joyce Carol Oates, p. 984	Understanding point of view	Supporting an interpretation*	Using Latin roots*	Writing about symbolic meaning	
"Engineer-Private Paul Klee Misplaces an Aircraft Between Milbertshofen and Cambrai, March 1916," Donald Barthelme, p. 990	Understanding experimental fiction*	Appreciating shades of meaning*	Using words from Latin	Responding to criticism	
"Imagined Scenes," Ann Beattie, p. 996	Understanding Postmodernism*	Thinking metaphorically*	Completing word analogies	Writing about structure	Using direct and indirect quotations* Understanding dialogue*
"Anxiety," Grace Paley, p. 1006	Understanding point of view*	Generalizing about an age	Finding synonyms*	Writing a short story	
"Katherine Comes to Yellow Sky," Mark Helprin, p. 1012	Understanding characters*	Understanding a character's motivation	Understanding similes* Understanding differences in meaning	Responding to criticism	
From *Lonesome Dove,* Larry McMurtry, p. 1020	Understanding setting*	Recognizing sensory language	Understanding word origins	Writing a description	

CONTEMPORARY WRITERS (1946–PRESENT) (continued)

Selection	Analyzing Literature	Critical Thinking and Reading	Understanding Language/ Speaking and Listening	Thinking and Writing	Grammar in Action
Nonfiction					
"Nobel Prize Acceptance Speech," William Faulkner, p. 1028	Understanding oratory*		Using prefixes*	Writing about related themes	
From *The Mortgaged Heart*, Carson McCullers, p. 1032	Understanding argumentation	Understanding paradoxes*	Understanding word roots* Finding word histories	Writing an argumentative essay	
"A Ride Through Spain," Truman Capote, p. 1038	Understanding narration	Appreciating the effect of similes*	Appreciating vivid modifiers*	Writing a personal narrative	
From *Hidden Name and Complex Fate*, Ralph Ellison, p. 1044	Understanding the essay*		Using the meaning that fits context*	Writing a critical response	
"On the Mall," Joan Didion, p. 1052	Understanding exposition	Separating facts from opinions*	Understanding word origins*	Writing about a writer's attitudes	Using quotation marks and italics*
"A Vision Beyond Time and Place," N. Scott Momaday, p. 1060	Understanding classification*	Recognizing cultural attitudes	Understanding shades of meaning*	Comparing and contrasting essays	
"The Edge of the Great Rift," Paul Theroux, p. 1066		Recognizing sensory details*	Completing word analogies*	Writing a description	
From *Arctic Dreams*, Barry Lopez, p. 1070	Using imagery*	Appreciating the effect of imagery	Understanding context clues*	Responding to criticism	Understanding topic sentences and supporting information*
From *Rising from the Plains*, John McPhee, p. 1080	Understanding setting	Understanding the effect of setting*	Understanding word origins*	Comparing and contrasting settings	Identifying predicate nominatives* Using commas to separate items in a series*

Selection	Analyzing Literature	Critical Thinking and Reading	Understanding Language/ Speaking and Listening	Thinking and Writing	Grammar in Action
Poetry					
Theodore Roethke: "The Waking," p. 1094 "Once More the Round," p. 1096	Understanding rhyme*		Using antonyms*	Responding to criticism	
"The Rain Guitar," James Dickey, p. 1100 "Merritt Parkway," Denise Levertov, p. 1102	Understanding visual poetry	Comparing and contrasting writers' styles*	Understanding the meaning of words*	Writing a visual poem	
"The Explorer," Gwendolyn Brooks, p. 1106 "Little Exercise," Elizabeth Bishop, p. 1108 "House Guest," Elizabeth Bishop, p. 1110	Understanding rhythm*		Understanding words from Latin* Understanding word origins	Responding to criticism	
"Hawthorne," Robert Lowell, p. 1114 "The Death of the Ball Turrett Gunner," Randall Jarrell, p. 1119 "Losses," Randall Jarrell, p. 1120	Understanding theme*		Appreciating precise words*	Writing about a writer's attitude	
"Be Beautiful, Nobel, Like the Antique Ant," Jose Garcia Villa, p. 1124 "Expect Nothing," Alice Walker, p. 1126 "Still Life," Reed Whittemore, p. 1128	Understanding lyric poetry*	Analyzing the meaning of allusions	Recognizing abstract words*	Comparing and contrasting poems	

CONTEMPORARY WRITERS (1946–PRESENT) (continued)

Selection	Analyzing Literature	Critical Thinking and Reading	Understanding Language/ Speaking and Listening	Thinking and Writing	Grammar in Action
"The Beautiful Changes," Richard Wilbur, p. 1132 "Gold Glade," Robert Penn Warren, p. 1134 "Evening Hawk," Robert Penn Warren, p. 1136	Understanding imagery*		Appreciating vivid adjectives*	Writing a poem using imagery	
"Mirror," Sylvia Plath, p. 1140 "Those Winter Sundays," Robert Hayden, p. 1143 "Traveling Through the Dark," William Stafford, p. 1144	Understanding confessional poetry*		Understanding word formation* Completing word analogies	Writing a confessional poem	
"Poem," Donald Justice, p. 1148 "Storm Windows," Howard Nemerov, p. 1150 "Lying in a Hammock at William Duffy's Farm in Pine Island, Minnesota," James Wright, p. 1152	Understanding sound devices*	Analyzing the effect of sound devices*		Responding to criticism	

CONTEMPORARY WRITERS (1946-PRESENT) (continued)

Selection	Analyzing Literature	Critical Thinking and Reading	Understanding Language/ Speaking and Listening	Thinking and Writing	Grammar in Action
"The Observer," Adrienne Rich, p. 1156 "Hunger in New York City," Simon Ortiz, p. 1158 "Most Satisfied By Snow," Diana Chang, p. 1160	Understanding parallelism*		Understanding synonyms*	Writing a poem using parallelism Responding to a poem	
"Plucking Out a Rhythm," Lawson Fusao Inada, p. 1164 "Thus Life," Rita Dove, p. 1168	Understanding free verse*		Recognizing antonyms*		
Drama					
The Crucible, Act I, Arthur Miller, p. 1172	Understanding historical context*	Recognizing cultural attitudes*		Writing about setting	Recognizing active and passive voice* Adverbs*
The Crucible, Act II, p. 1201	Understanding characterization*		Appreciating dialect*	Writing a dialogue	Contractions* The four functions of sentences*
The Crucible, Act III, p. 1221	Understanding historical context*		Completing verbal analogies*	Writing about parallels	Specific and concrete words* Terms of direct address*
The Crucible, Act IV, p. 1243	Understanding theme*	Appreciating the importance of casting*		Writing about theme	The dash* Compound and complex sentences*

PRENTICE HALL
LITERATURE
THE AMERICAN EXPERIENCE

PRENTICE HALL
LITERATURE

COPPER

BRONZE

SILVER

GOLD

PLATINUM

THE AMERICAN EXPERIENCE

THE ENGLISH TRADITION

WORLD MASTERPIECES

PRENTICE HALL
LITERATURE

THE AMERICAN EXPERIENCE

SECOND EDITION

 PRENTICE HALL
Englewood Cliffs, New Jersey
Needham, Massachusetts

Humanities Note

Fine art, *Portrait of Captain Joseph Reddeford Walker,* by Alfred Jacob Miller (1810–1874). Miller was a landscape and portrait painter especially noted for his studies of Native Americans and white settlers on the frontier. After studying painting with the American artist Thomas Sully, Miller moved to New Orleans. There he met Captain William Drummond Stewart, whom he accompanied as expedition artist on a trip to the Rocky Mountains. The West was largely unexplored in the late 1830's, and Miller found much to draw and paint. He made more than one hundred sketches of Native Americans and Western scenery. After returning to his home in Baltimore, he spent the rest of his career as a successful portrait painter of distinctive American types, like Captain Joseph Reddeford Walker.

Captian Walker was an American trapper and guide whose trading headquarters were in Independence, Missouri. A member of another expedition to the Rocky Mountains (under Benjamin Bonneville, a French-born explorer of the northwest), Walker also guided an expedition to California.

He was an adventurous and daring personality; Miller's portrait captures the romantic vision of the nineteenth-century American explorer and frontier adventurer. Walker wears the broad-brimmed hat of the westerner and holds the barrel of his rifle in one hand. Wearing the rough clothing of a frontiersman rather than that of a military captain, he is a compelling and romantic figure. This image conveys a set of simple, clear values held in esteem by nineteenth-century Americans.

Art credits begin on page 1393.

COVER AND TITLE PAGE: *Portrait of Captain Joseph Reddeford Walker* (detail), Alfred Jacob Miller, Joslyn Art Museum, Omaha, Nebraska

PRENTICE HALL
A Division of Simon & Schuster
Englewood Cliffs, New Jersey 07632

STAFF CREDITS FOR PRENTICE HALL LITERATURE

Editorial: Eileen Thompson, Ellen Bowler, Philip Fried, Daniel Jackson, Doug McCollum, Jane Standen, Richard Hickox, Carol Schneider, Kelly Ackley

Design: Sue Walrath, Nancy Sharkey, Leslie Osher

Photo Research: Libby Forsyth

Production: Penny Hull, Suse Cioffi, Joan McCulley, Marlys Lehmann, Lisa Meyerhoff, Cleasta Wilburn

Editorial Systems: Andrew Grey Bommarito, Ralph O'Brien

Marketing: Carol Newman, Mollie Ledwith, Tom Maksym

Manufacturing: Laura Sanderson, Denise Herckenrath

Permissions: Doris Robinson

ACKNOWLEDGMENTS

Grateful acknowledgment is made to the following for permission to reprint copyrighted material:

Samuel Allen
"To Satch" by Samuel Allen, reprinted by permission of the author.

The American Scholar
Lines from the poem "Garden of My Childhood" by Kuangchi C. Chang. Reprinted from *The American Scholar*, Volume 26, Number 3, Summer 1957. Copyright © 1957 by the United Chapters of Phi Beta Kappa. Reprinted by permission of the publishers.

Atheneum Publishers, an imprint of Macmillan Publishing Co.
"Poem" from *Selected Poems* by Donald Justice. Copyright © 1969, 1970, 1971, 1972, 1973 by Donald Justice. Reprinted with the permission of Atheneum Publishers, an imprint of Macmillan Publishing Co.

(continued on page 1389)

CONTENTS

vii

A GROWING NATION
1800–1840

NEW ENGLAND RENAISSANCE
1840–1855

New England Poets

DIVISION, WAR, AND RECONCILIATION
1855–1865

REALISM AND THE FRONTIER
1865–1915

THE MODERN AGE
1915–1946

CONTEMPORARY WRITERS
1946–Present

xiii

xiv

PRENTICE HALL
LITERATURE
THE AMERICAN EXPERIENCE

Humanities Note

Fine art, *Landing of Columbus,* 1842, by John Vanderlyn. The early work of John Vanderlyn (1775–1852) so impressed Aaron Burr that Burr arranged for Vanderlyn to study under Gilbert Stuart, the famous portrait painter of George Washington. As the first American artist to study in Paris, Vanderlyn was influenced by the classical style popular in Europe at the time. In this style, historic events and heroic figures are depicted in a grand, elaborate fashion far removed from the experiences of ordinary people.

When Vanderlyn returned to the United States, he found that the American public, with its democratic influences, was less impressed by grandeur than Europeans were. However, Vanderlyn was commissioned to paint the *Landing of Columbus* for one of the panels in the rotunda of the U.S. Capitol. The heroic proportion of the work was suited to the setting. The painting depicts—perhaps glorifies—the arrival of the Italian explorer and his party at San Salvador on October 12, 1492. The focal point of the work, the raised banner, is a patriotic symbol that suggests the assertion of European dominance in the New World.

LANDING OF COLUMBUS
John Vanderlyn
Three Lions

Objectives

1 To understand the history of the New World
2 To appreciate the history of the New World in relation to world events
3 To understand the historical background of the Native Americans
4 To understand the history of the Pilgrims and Puritans
5 To understand the history of the Southern planters
6 To understand and appreciate early American Literature

THE NEW LAND
To 1750

Let England know our willingnesse,
  For that our worke is good;
Wee hope to plant a nation,
  Where none before hath stood.

Thomas Dale
Governor of the Jamestown Colony

Focus

Historical Background In the foreward to *The American Puritans*, Perry Miller wrote this about the importance of understanding the Puritans and their code of ethics: "Because their societies were tightly organized, and above all because they were a highly articulate people, the New Englanders established Puritanism—for better or worse—as one of the continuous factors in American life and thought. It has played so dominant a role because descendants of the Puritans have carried traits of the Puritan mind into a variety of pursuits and all the way across the continent. Many of these qualities have persisted even though the original creed is lost. Without some understanding of Puritanism, and that at its source, there is no understanding of America."

Writing to Learn Write on the chalkboard the following words: *Plymouth*, *Mayflower*, *Puritans*, *settlers*, and *Native Americans*. Ask students to write about what first comes to mind when they see these words. Ask them to write in their journals what they already know about these people, places, and historic names. Have volunteers share their responses with the class. Then have students read the introduction. After they read it, have them add to their journal entries what they learned about this period.

ESL Teaching Strategy The literature in this unit may be difficult for your ESL students. Many of the selections are written in a style and form that is different from those in which we now write. In addition, many of the words are archaic and no longer used regularly. Because of this, you may wish to read these selections aloud, pausing periodically to summarize or clarify certain passages or portions of the work.

Motivation/Prior Knowledge
Ask students if they enjoy discovering new areas of their city or town or visiting new states and countries on vacations. How did they feel during their expeditions? How did they view the "natives"? Were the "natives" friendly to them? Were students friendly with the "natives"? How did it feel not knowing where places were and having to find them alone or seek help? Explore students' feelings about being explorers in what they consider new lands. Then tell them that in this introduction, they will learn about some of the history of those who first settled in America.

Purpose-Setting Question
What are the differences between the New England settlers and the Southern planters? What are the characteristics of early American literature?

1 **Enrichment** Although the Native Americans had not developed any sophisticated writing systems, some Native American literature was recorded in pictographs, or symbols conveying ideas. See the *Walam Olum,* page 22.

2 **Master Teacher Note** To demonstrate the diversity among the Native American peoples, you might compare and contrast the Zuni way of life with that of the Iroquois.

3 **Historical Context** The excerpts from *The General History of Virginia* (page 44) and *Of Plymouth Plantation* (page 52) both reveal a great deal about the relationship between the Native Americans and the earliest settlers.

More than a century after European explorers discovered North America, there were no permanent settlements in the New World north of St. Augustine, Florida. By 1607, however, a small group of English settlers was struggling to survive on a marshy island in the James River in the present state of Virginia. In 1611, Thomas Dale, governor of the colony, wrote a report to the king expressing the colonists' determination to succeed. Despite disease and starvation, Jamestown did survive.

The first settlers were entranced by the presence and, to them, the strangeness of the native inhabitants. They did not at first realize that these earlier Americans, like Europeans, had cultural values and literary traditions of their own. The literature was entirely oral, for the tribes of North America had not yet developed writing systems. This extensive oral literature, along with the first written works of the colonists, forms the beginning of the American literary heritage. | 1

THE HISTORICAL SETTING

When Christopher Columbus reached North America in 1492, the continent was already populated, though sparsely, by several hundred Native American tribes. Europeans did not encounter these tribes all at once. Explorers from different nations came into contact with them at different times. As we now know, these widely dispersed tribes of Native Americans differed greatly from one another in language, government, social organization, customs, housing, and methods of survival. | 2

The Native Americans

No one knows for certain when or how the first Americans arrived in what is now the United States. It may have been as recently as 12,000 years ago or as long ago as 70,000 years. Even if the shorter estimate is correct, Native Americans have been on the continent thirty times longer than the Europeans. Colonists from Europe did not begin arriving on the East Coast of North America until the late 1500's.

What were the earliest Americans doing for those many centuries? To a great extent, the answer is shrouded in mystery. As the historian Samuel Eliot Morison noted, "Even now we cannot write 'The History of America before 1492,' because history presupposes a more or less continuous and dated story." No such story of the Native Americans exists. Archeologists have deduced a great deal from artifacts, however, and folklorists have recorded a rich variety of songs, legends, and myths.

What we do know is that the Native Americans usually, but by no means always, greeted the earliest Europeans as friends. They instructed the newcomers in New World agriculture and woodcraft, | 3 introduced them to maize, beans, squash, maple sugar, snow-shoes, toboggans, and birch bark canoes. Indeed, many more of the European settlers would have succumbed to the bitter Northeastern winters had it not been for the help of these first Americans.

Pilgrims and Puritans

4 A small group of Europeans sailed from England on the *Mayflower* in 1620. The passengers were religious reformers, Puritans who were critical of the Church of England. Having given up hope of "purifying" the church from within, they chose instead to withdraw from the church. This action earned them the name Separatists. We know them as the Pilgrims. They landed in the New World and established a settlement at what is now Plymouth, Massachusetts. With help from friendly tribes of Native Americans, the Plymouth settlement managed to survive the rigors of the New World. The colony never grew very large, however. Eventually, it was engulfed by the Massachusetts Bay Colony, the much larger settlement to the north.

5 Like the Plymouth Colony, the Massachusetts Bay Colony was also founded by religious reformers. These reformers, however, did not withdraw from the Church of England. Unlike the Separatists

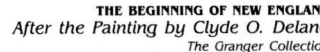
THE BEGINNING OF NEW ENGLAND
After the Painting by Clyde O. Deland
The Granger Collection

Humanities Note

Fine art, *The Beginning of New England,* engraving after the painting by Clyde O. Deland. This engraving is based upon the painting by Clyde O. Deland (1872–1947). The engraving from Deland's work is far removed, both in style and in content, from heroic, classical-style paintings like Vanderlyn's *Landing of Columbus* (pages 4–5). Deland's work shows ordinary people—men and women—working together to build settlements in the new land. The simple depiction of the snowy scene captures both the harshness of nature and the sense of community among the inhabitants.

In the technique of engraving, lines are cut on a metal or wooden plate from which prints are made. The prints may then be colored. Especially before the development of photography, engraving was the primary way in which drawings and painting were reproduced.

Enrichment Galileo Galilei (1564–1642) was an Italian mathematician, astronomer, and physicist. During the period when European explorers were discovering the Americans, Galileo's explorations and experimentations led him to discover that the earth revolved around the sun and was not the center of the universe as had been thought previously. His findings were deemed radical, and he was tried by the Inquisition in Rome in 1633. Rome ordered him to recant his claims and sentenced him to house arrest. Galileo's discoveries were widespread and are the basis for contemporary astronomy. It was Galileo who first used the telescope to study the skies, and he was the first to expand our vision and concept of the universe.

Enrichment The *Bay Psalm Book* was the first book published in the Thirteen Colonies. Written by Richard Mather, John Eliot, and Thomas Weld, it was the common hymnal of the Massachusetts Bay colony. It was originally published in Cambridge, Massachusetts in 1640 as *The Whole Book of Psalms Faithfully Translated into English Metre.*

Enrichment Established May 14, 1607, by the London Company, Jamestown was named after the reigning English monarch, James I. Indian attacks, starvation, and disease diminished the colony, but the London Company continually sent more men and supplies to help rebuild the colony. For much of the first two years, John Smith was the sole leader of the colony until he returned to England in 1609. By the end of 1609 after a severe winter, the settlers were prepared to return to England when a new shipment of men and supplies arrived. Among those who arrived was John Rolfe, who ensured peace with the Indians by marrying Pocahontas.

4

AMERICAN EVENTS

Pre-1492 Native American tribes occupy what is now the United States.

1492 Crew of Christopher Columbus discovers America, sighting land in the Bahamas.

1565 St. Augustine, Florida, first permanent settlement in U.S., founded by Pedro Menéndez.

1570 Iroquois Confederacy established to stop warfare among the Five Nations.

1587 English colony at Roanoke Island disappears; known as the Lost Colony.

1607 First permanent English settlement at Jamestown, Virginia.

1608 **Captain John Smith** writes *A True Relation . . . of Virginia.*

1609 Henry Hudson in the *Half Moon* explores New York harbor and the Hudson River.

1619 House of Burgesses established in Virginia; first legislature in the New World.

1620 Pilgrims land at Plymouth, Massachusetts.

1629 Formation of Massachusetts Bay Company leads to influx of Puritans into New England.

1630 **William Bradford** begins writing *Of Plymouth Plantation*, completes it in 1651.

1636 Harvard University founded in Cambridge, Massachusetts.

1638 First printing press in English-speaking North America arrives in Massachusetts.

1640 *Bay Psalm Book* published; first book printed in the colonies.

Columbus Lands at San Salvador

Captain John Smith

Galileo

The *Mayflower*

Jamestown

The *Mona Lisa*

William Shakespeare

The King James Bible

WORLD EVENTS

1503	Italy: Leonardo da Vinci paints the *Mona Lisa*.
1509	Italy: Michelangelo paints ceiling of Sistine Chapel.
1518	Africa: Algiers and Tunisia founded.
1519–1522	Magellan sails around the world.
1520	Spain: Chocolate introduced to Europe.
1521	Mexico: Cortez conquers Aztecs.
1532	Peru: Pizarro conquers Incas.
1552	Scotland: First golf organization founded.
1558	England: Elizabeth I inherits throne.
1563	England: 20,000 people die in London plague.
1566	Belgium: Bruegel paints *The Wedding Dance*.
1567	South America: 2,000,000 Indians die of typhoid.
1580	France: Montaigne's *Essays* published.
1595	England: Shakespeare completes *A Midsummer Night's Dream*.
1605	England: Shakespeare completes *Macbeth*.
	Spain: Cervantes publishes Part I of *Don Quixote*.
1606	England: Ben Johnson publishes *Volpone*.
1609	Italy: Galileo builds first telescope.
1611	England: King James Bible published.
1633	England: John Donne publishes *Poems*.
1637	Japan: All Europeans expelled.
1639	India: English establish settlement at Madras.

Introduction 5

Enrichment Queen Elizabeth I (1533–1603), daughter of Henry VIII and Anne Boleyn (who was executed in 1536), was one of England's most renowned and influential rulers. Under her reign from 1558 until her death in 1603, England's economy, military, and culture flourished. Her period of reign, also called the Golden Age or the Elizabethan Age, marks the time of great achievement in England and the time when England was united as a nation. Elizabeth's court became a center for poets, musicians, writers, and scholars. Among the most recognizable writers of this time were William Shakespeare, Edmund Spenser, and Walter Raleigh.

Enrichment On Sept. 20, 1519, Portuguese navigator Ferdinand Magellan set sail on the first expedition around the world. On October 18, 1520, Magellan discovered a passage off the southern tip of South America that led from the Atlantic Ocean to another ocean. This passage was later named the Strait of Magellan. Magellan named the new ocean the Pacific, which means "peaceful" because compared to the stormy Atlantic Ocean, the Pacific appeared calm. Magellan's voyage proved that the world is round, not flat as many had previously believed. His voyage also led to future European expeditions to the Pacific.

Enrichment Although he is most well-known as an Italian painter, Leonardo da Vinci was also an accomplished engineer and scientist. Due to his insatiable curiosity about the physical world, da Vinci experimented with numerous studies and inventions in geology, botany, hydraulics, and mechanics. His resulting drawings, which were depicted with scientific precision and artistry, ranged from flying machines to anatomical studies of people, animals, and plants.

AMERICAN EVENTS

Nat Bacon's Rebellion

1647   Massachusetts establishes free public schools.

1650   London publication of **Anne Bradstreet's** *The Tenth Muse. . . .*, a collection of poems.

1662   *The Day of Doom*, by **Michael Wigglesworth**, achieves immediate and widespread fame.

1669   John Eliot, Apostle to the Indians, publishes *The Indian Primer*.

1675   King Philip, chief of the Wampanoags, begins raiding New England frontier towns.

1676   Nat Bacon's ill-fated rebellion launched against Virginia's Governor Berkeley.

1690   By this date, *The New England Primer* is in use in colonial schools.

1692   Salem witchcraft trials result in the execution of 20 "witches."

Woman Accused of Witchcraft in Salem

1693   **Cotton Mather's** *The Wonders of the Invisible World* analyzes evidence against witches.

1704   **Sarah Kemble Knight** begins the journey on horseback on which her *Journal* is based.

1716   First theater in the colonies opens in Williamsburg, Virginia.

1721   Smallpox epidemic breaks out in Boston; **Cotton Mather** argues for inoculation.

1734   **John Peter Zenger** acquitted of libel, furthering freedom of the press.

1735   Great Awakening, a series of religious revivals, begins to sweep the colonies.

1738   **William Byrd** of Virginia makes the trip described in *The History of the Dividing Line*.

1741   **Jonathan Edwards** first delivers his sermon *Sinners in the Hands of an Angry God*.

The Trial of John Peter Zenger   Baron de Montesquieu

The *Night Watch*

Johann Sebastian Bach

Illustration from *Gulliver's Travels*

Illustration from *Robinson Crusoe*

WORLD EVENTS

1642	Holland: Rembrandt paints *Night Watch*.
	England: Civil War begins.
1644	France: Descartes publishes *Principia Philosophicae*.
	China: Ming Dynasty ends.
1660	South Africa: First Dutch settlers arrive.
1667	England: Milton publishes *Paradise Lost*.
1669	France: Molière's *Tartuffe* first performed.
1678	England: John Bunyan publishes *The Pilgrim's Progress*.
1685	China: All ports opened to foreign trade.
1690	India: Calcutta founded by British.
1702	England: First daily newspaper begins publication.
1712	England: Alexander Pope publishes *The Rape of the Lock*.
1719	England: Daniel Defoe publishes *Robinson Crusoe*.
1721	Germany: Bach composes *Brandenburg Concertos*.
1726	England: Jonathan Swift publishes *Gulliver's Travels*.
1727	Brazil: First coffee planted.
1748	France: Montesquieu publishes *The Spirit of the Law*.
1749	Portugal: Sign language invented.

Introduction 7

Enrichment Rembrandt (1606–1669), whose painting *The Night Watch* is shown on this page, is celebrated as the greatest Dutch painter. He began studying painting in 1621, when he was a young boy. During his lifetime, Rembrandt amassed more than 600 paintings, 300 etchings, 1,400 drawings, and 100 self-portraits; a countless number of other works have been lost.

Rembrandt's work represents the height of Dutch portrait painting and illustrates his masterful handling of light and shadow to create atmosphere. Despite his success as a painter, Rembrandt had financial difficulties. He lived in a style beyond his means and collected art on a scale he could not afford. In 1656, he declared bankruptcy; his house and possessions were sold at auction in 1657 and 1658.

Enrichment Johann Sebastian Bach (1685–1750) was a German composer and organist. He was devoted to music from childhood. During his lifetime Bach was better known for his talent as an organist than as a composer. His works were neglected for years after his death. Finally, when the nineteenth-century Romantic composers Mendelssohn and Schumann rediscovered Bach's compositions, his genius, talent, and influence as one of the greatest composers in the world was established.

THE FIRST THANKSGIVING
J. L. G. Ferris
Three Lions

they were Puritans who intended instead to reform the church from within. In America, the Puritans hoped to establish what John Winthrop, governor of the colony, called a "city upon a hill," a community guided in all aspects by the Bible. Their form of government would be a theocracy, a state under the immediate guidance of God.

Religion affected every aspect of Puritan life, although the Puritans were not always as stern and otherworldly as they are sometimes pictured. Their writings occasionally reveal a sense of humor, and the hardships of daily life forced them to be practical. In one sense, the Puritans were radical, since they demanded fundamental changes in the Church of England. In another sense, however, they were conservative. They preached a plain, unadorned Christianity that contrasted sharply with the cathedrals, vestments, ceremony, and hierarchy of the Church of England.

What exactly did the Puritans believe? Their beliefs were far from simple, but they agreed that human beings exist for the glory of God and that the Bible is the sole expression of God's will. They believed in predestination—John Calvin's doctrine that God has already decided who will achieve salvation and who will not. The elect, or saints, who are to be saved cannot take election for granted, however. Because of that, all devout Puritans searched their souls with great rigor and frequency for signs of grace. The Puritans believed in original sin and felt that they could accomplish good only through continual hard work and self-discipline. When people today speak of the "Puritan ethic," that is what they mean.

Puritanism was in decline throughout New England by the early 1700's, as more liberal Protestant congregations attracted followers. A reaction against this new freedom, however, set in around 1735. The Great Awakening, a series of religious revivals led by such eloquent ministers as Jonathan Edwards and George Whitefield, swept the colonies. The Great Awakening attracted thousands of converts to many Protestant groups, but it did little to revive old-fashioned Puritanism. What had been the dominant religion of New England had all but vanished by the time of the American Revolution. Nevertheless, Puritanism made a lasting impression on American attitudes. Its ideals of hard work, frugality, self-improvement, and self-reliance are still regarded as basic American virtues.

The Southern Planters

The Southern colonies differed from New England in climate, crops, social organization, and religion. Prosperous coastal cities grew up in the South, just as in the North, but beyond the Southern cities lay large plantations, not small farms. Despite its romantic image, the plantation was in fact a large-scale agricultural enterprise and a center of commerce. Up to a thousand people, many of them slaves, might live and work on a single plantation. The first black

1621 by the governor of Plymouth Colony, William Bradford. According to a writer of the time, and as indicated by Ferris's work, the settlers "entertained and feasted" the Indians, who, the writer goes on to say, reciprocated by presenting the governor with five deer they had killed for the occasion. The custom of eating turkey for Thanksgiving dinner stems from the fact that

the Pilgrims killed "as much fowl as . . . served the company almost a week." The first national observance of the holiday was proclaimed by President Washington on November 26, 1789.

A particularly American feature of Ferris's work is the humbleness both of the human figures and of the background structures. A sense of good will between the Pilgrims and the Na-

tive Americans pervades the work, and yet there is no forced sentimentality. The scene captures, with quiet sensitivity, a memorable event in the development of the American people.

LANDING AT JAMESTOWN, 1608-09 (ALSO CALLED HOPE OF JAMESTOWN)
John Gadsby Chapman
Mr. and Mrs. Paul Mellon, Upperville, VA

slaves were brought to Virginia in 1619, a year before the Pilgrims landed at Plymouth. The plantation system and the institution of slavery were closely connected from the very beginning, although slavery existed in every colony, including Massachusetts.

Most of the plantation owners were Church of England members who regarded themselves as aristocrats. The first generation of owners, the men who established the great plantations, were ambitious, energetic, self-disciplined, and resourceful, just as the Puritans were. But the way of life on most plantations was more sociable and elegant than that of any Puritan. By 1750, Puritanism was in decline everywhere, despite the Great Awakening, while the plantation system in the South was just reaching its peak.

THE EARLIEST AMERICAN LITERATURE

It was an oddly assorted group that established the foundations of American literature: the Native Americans with their oral traditions, the Puritans with their preoccupation with sin and salvation,

Humanities Note

Fine art, *Landing at Jamestown, 1608–09* by John Gadsby Chapman. John Gadsby Chapman (1808–1889) illustrated a number of books, including Harper's Great Bible (1846). This work, *Landing at Jamestown, 1608–09* (also called *Hope of Jamestown*), is a depiction, intended to inspire a sense of patriotism, of an important episode in American history. The first settlers of Jamestown, who had arrived in 1607, found it difficult to survive the harsh conditions of the new land. Chapman's work shows settlers greeting a newly arrived ship from England. Although the English settlers welcoming the newcomers are more finely dressed and in more "noble" pose than the Indians, the presence of Native Americans suggests a spirit of harmony between the two peoples.

Cooperative Learning In small groups, have students imagine that they have discovered a new world and wish to settle there. Have them write journal entries for the first week of their stay in the new land. Students should take into account and write about all the possible problems they would encounter trying to establish themselves and attempt to solve them. Some of the problems they might consider are dissention and desertion, leadership and government, the climate and terrain of the new world, and so on. Afterward, have students show the location of their new world and share their "experiences" with classmates by reading aloud their journal entries.

11 Enrichment Native American literature reveals a great deal about the attitudes, values, beliefs, and traditions of the Native American people.

12 Master Teacher Note To demonstrate the effect of the Native American languages on American English, you might see how many states with Native American names students can come up with.

Humanities Note

Fine art, *Pilgrims on the Way to Church,* by Charles Yardley Turner. The Englishman Charles Yardley Turner (1773–1857) made some 900 engravings, many of them copies of well-known British paintings. In his painting *Pilgrims on the Way to Church,* Turner depicts the ordinariness of religion in the lives of the European settlers in the New World. The dependence of the people upon their land and upon their livestock is emphasized by the wedding group, as the bride sits upon the back of a bull. The style is slightly impressionistic rather than totally naturalistic.

and the Southern planters with their busy social lives. Indeed, much of the literature that the colonists read was not produced in the colonies. It came from England. Yet by 1750 there were the clear beginnings of a native literature that would one day be honored throughout the English-speaking world.

Their Name Is on Your Waters

For a long time, Native American literature was viewed mainly as folklore. The consequence was that song lyrics, hero tales, migration legends, and accounts of the creation were studied more for their content than for their literary qualities. In an oral tradition, the telling of the tale may change with each speaker, and the words are almost sure to change over time. Thus, no fixed versions of such literary works exist. Still, in cases where the words of Native American lyrics or narratives have been captured in writing, the language is often poetic and moving. As might be expected in an oral setting, oratory was much prized among Native Americans. The names of certain orators, such as Logan and, later, Red Jacket, were widely known.

11

The introductory literature in this unit suggests the depth and power of those original American voices. Interestingly, you can find familiar, one-word examples of the various tribal languages, simply by looking at a map or at road signs. A remarkable number of American place names, including the names of more than half of our fifty states, come from Native American words. In the nineteenth century, Lydia Sigourney wrote a popular poem called "Indian Names."

12

> Ye say they all have pass'd away
> That noble race and brave;
> That their light canoes have vanish'd,
> From off the crested wave;

PILGRIMS ON THE WAY TO CHURCH
Charles Yardley Turner
Three Lions

10   *The New Land*

That mid the forests where they roam'd,
    There rings no hunter's shout;
But their name is on your waters,
    Ye may not wash it out. . . .

"In Adam's Fall/We Sinned All"

13   Just as religion dominated the lives of the Puritans, it also dominated their writings, most of which would not be considered literary works by modern standards. Typically, the Puritans wrote theological studies, hymns, histories, biographies, and autobiographies. The purpose of such writing was to provide spiritual insight and instruction. When Puritans wrote for themselves, in journals or diaries, their aim was the serious kind of self-examination they practiced in other apsects of their lives. The Puritans produced neither fiction nor drama, since they regarded both as sinful.

14   The Puritans did write poetry, however, as a vehicle of spiritual enlightenment. Although they were less concerned with a poem's literary form than with its message, some writers were naturally more gifted than others. A few excellent Puritan poets emerged in the 1600's, among them Anne Bradstreet and Edward Taylor. Anne Bradstreet's moving, personal voice and Edward Taylor's devotional intensity shine through the conventional Puritanism of their themes.

The Puritans were highly literate, with a strong belief in education for both men and women. In 1636, they founded Harvard University to ensure a well-educated ministry. Two years later, they set up the first printing press in the colonies. In 1647, free public schools were established in Massachusetts to combat the influence of "ye ould deluder, Satan." *The New England Primer,* first published around 1690, combined instruction in spelling and reading with moralistic teachings, such as "In Adam's fall/We sinned all."

One of the first books printed in the colonies was the *Bay Psalm Book,* the standard hymnal of the time. Richard Mather, a prominent preacher, was one of its three authors. Increase Mather, Richard's youngest son, served for many years as pastor of the North Church in Boston. He was the author of some 130 books. *Cases of Conscience Concerning Evil Spirits,* published in 1693, was a discourse on the Salem witchcraft trials of the previous year. The trials, conducted in an atmosphere of hysteria, resulted in the hanging of nineteen people as witches.

15   Increase's eldest son, Cotton Mather, far exceeded his father's literary output, publishing at least 450 works in his lifetime. Cotton Mather, like his father, is remembered in part because of his connection with the Salem witchcraft trials. Although he did not actually take part in the trials, his works on witchcraft had helped to stir up some of the hysteria. Still, Cotton Mather was one of the most learned men of his time, a power in the state, and a notable author.

**HARVARD HALL (COLLEGE)
CAMBRIDGE, MASSACHUSETTS,
BUILT 1672–82**
Colored Engraving
The Granger Collection

13 Literary Movement The sermon was also a common form of Puritan literature. Much Puritan thought is preserved in sermons. "Sinners in the Hands of an Angry God," by Jonathan Edwards, page 72, is an example.

14 Literary Movement See the poems by Anne Bradstreet (pages 15 and 59) and Edward Taylor (pages 62 and 64).

15 Literary Movement See the excerpt from *Wonders of the Invisible World* on page 77.

Humanities Note

Fine art, Harvard Hall (College), Cambridge, Massachusetts. The oldest university in the United States, Harvard received a grant, or charter, from the Massachusetts Bay Colony; the school was named for John Harvard, who gave money and his collection of books to the college. This engraving shows one of the earliest buildings.

During the time of the American Revolution, a century later, the buildings of the college were commandeered for the quartering of soldiers. Since the time of its founding, Harvard has played a significant role in the intellectual, political, and economic life of the nation.

16 **Master Teacher Note** To help the students grasp the Puritan's theory of style, you might compare and contrast William Bradford's style (page 50) with that of William Byrd (page 67).

Although the Puritans advocated a plain style—without unnecessary ornamentation or allusions that might be missed by the unlettered—not all New England authors confined themselves to this style. Some elaborate images and occasional flowery language appear in the writings of some New England authors.

17 **Literary Movement** See the excerpt from *The History of the Dividing Line* on page 67.

Humanities Note

Fine art, *The Trial of Two "Witches" at Salem, Massachusetts, in 1692,* Howard Pyle. Howard Pyle (1853–1911) was an illustrator and teacher. In the books he wrote and illustrated for children, and in his illustrations for magazines, he was influenced by the woodcuts of the fifteenth-century German artist Albrecht Dürer, who combined precise details and a kind of spiritualism. Pyle founded a school of art in Wilmington, Delaware; it was free for talented students. He believed in rigorous training for his students, but he encouraged them through his gentleness and devotion.

The Trial of Two "Witches" at Salem captures the horror of the Salem witch trials with insight and compassion. The pointing fingers of the women on the right, who are dressed like the accused women, convey a sense of self-doubt and fear experienced by all the women in the community, as they sought to cast blame on others in order to save themselves from persecution. The pitchforks held behind the accused women evoke a kind of morbid humor. Pyle's illustration

THE TRIAL OF TWO "WITCHES" AT SALEM, MASSACHUSETTS, IN 1692
Illustration by Howard Pyle
The Granger Collection

His theory of writing was simple (although his writing was not): the more information a work contains, the better its style.

In fact, the Puritans in general had a theory of literary style. They believed in a plain style of writing, one in which clear statement is the highest goal. An ornate or clever style would be a sign of vanity and, as such, would not be in accordance with God's will. Despite the restrictions built into their life and literature, the Puritans succeeded in producing a small body of excellent writing.

16

The Planter from Westover

Considering the number of brilliantly literate statesmen who would later emerge in the South, especially in Virginia, it seems surprising that only a few notable Southern writers appeared prior to 1750. As in Puritan New England, those who were educated produced a substantial amount of writing, but it was mostly of a practical nature. Many planters spent long hours each day writing letters. Unlike the Puritans, Southerners did not oppose fiction or drama, and the first theater in America opened in Williamsburg, Virginia, in 1716.

The important literature of the pre-Revolutionary South can be summed up in one name—William Byrd. Byrd lived at Westover, a magnificent plantation on the James River bequeathed to him by his wealthy father. Commissioned in 1738 to survey the boundary line between Virginia and North Carolina, he kept a journal of his experiences. That journal served as the basis for Byrd's book, *The History of the Dividing Line*, which was circulated in manuscript form among Byrd's friends in England. Published nearly a century after Byrd's death, the book was immediately recognized as a minor humorous masterpiece. More of Byrd's papers were published later, establishing his reputation as the finest writer in the pre-Revolutionary South.

17

The writers whose work appears in this unit are not the great names in American literature. They are the founders, the men and women who laid the groundwork for the towering achievements that followed. The modest awakening of American literature seen in this unit had repercussions that echo down the years.

was presumably intended to teach a lesson about justice and decency.

Check Test
1. The _____ were critical of the Church of England.
2. Most Native American literature was transmitted _____.
3. The Puritans' form of government was a _____, a state under the immediate guidance of God.
4. In addition to being an agricultural enterprise, the Southern plantation was a center of _____.
5. The Puritans were called _____ because, having given up hope of "purifying" the Church from within, they withdrew from the Church altogether.

Answers
1. Puritans
2. orally
3. theocracy
4. commerce
5. Separatists

AMERICAN VOICES
Quotations by Prominent Figures of the Period

The voice that beautifies the land,
The voice above,
The voice of the grasshopper,
Among the plants,
Again and again it sounds,—
The voice that beautifies the land.
　　　　　—Navaho

The sun . . . ever shineth on one part or the other [of the Spanish dominions] we have conquered for our king.
　　Captain John Smith, Advertisements for the Unexperienced

They knew they were pilgrims.
　　William Bradford, Of Plymouth Plantation

Welcome, Englishmen.
　　Squanto

The public must and will be served.
　　William Penn, Some Fruits of Solitude

Resolved, never to do anything which I should be afraid to do if it were the last hour of my life.
　　Jonathan Edwards, Seventy Resolutions

Brother! Our lands were once large, and yours were very small. You have now become a great people, and we have scarcely a place left to spread our blankets. You have got our country, but are not satisfied.
　　Red Jacket, Seneca Council Speech

Additional Voices

Our Fathers were Englishmen which came over this great ocean, and were ready to perish in this wilderness.
　　William Bradford, Of Plymouth Plantation

Youth is the time of getting, middle age of improving, and old age of spending.
　　Anne Bradstreet, Meditations Divine and Moral

My case is bad. Lord, be my advocate.
My sin is red: I'm under God's arrest.
　　Edward Taylor, Sacramental Meditations, 8

Intend to live in continual mortification, and never to expect or desire any worldly ease or pleasure.
　　Jonathan Edwards, Diary

I write the wonders of the Christian religion, flying from the depravations of Europe, to the American strand: and, assisted by the Holy Author of that religion, I do, with all conscience of truth, required therein by Him, who is the Truth itself, report that wonderful displays of His infinite power, wisdom, goodness, and faithfulness, wherewith his Divine providence hath irradiated an Indian wilderness.
　　Cotton Mather, Magnalia Christi Americana

Reading Critically The purpose of this feature is to help students place a work of literature in its historical context, understand the literary movements current during the time, and appreciate the techniques writers used to convey the ideas of the period.

Discuss the information on this page with your students. Explain that the selection that accompanies this page, "Upon the Burning of Our House" by Anne Bradstreet, is a model for reading critically. It contains side column notes that draw attention to elements that demonstrate the historical context, the influence of literary movements, and literary techniques used by the writer. Ask students to pay attention to these notes as they read the poem. Also suggest that they make their own comments as they read the poem actively.

To give students further practice with the process of reading critically, use the selection in the Teaching Portfolio, "The Beauty of the World" by Jonathan Edwards, page 6, following the Teacher Backup, which students can annotate themselves. Encourage students to use these strategies as they read the literature in this unit.

Historical Context You might point out that this unit contains literature from two widely different groups: the Native Americans and the first European settlers. The model on the following pages represents the work of one of the early settlers.

The Literature to 1750

When you read literature written during particular time periods, it is important to know the historical background.

Historical Context

Before settlers came to North America, Native Americans lived lives close to the land. Their interaction with nature shows in their literature. The early settlers came from Europe seeking freedom to live and worship as they pleased. For most, their strong religious convictions sustained them as they endured the hardships of life in the New World.

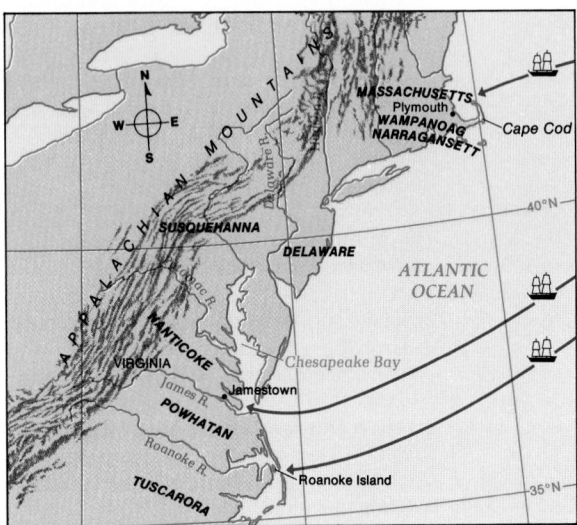

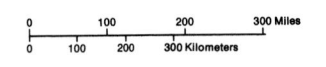

THE FIRST ENGLISH SETTLEMENTS

Literary Movements

The traditional literature of the Native Americans related to their tribal knowledge, customs, and rituals. This literature consists of myths, songs, and chants in the oral tradition.

The early settlers who came from Europe brought with them their knowledge of written communication with its particular style and content. They wrote about their new experiences in forms that were familiar to them—letters, factual records, sermons, and poems.

Writers' Techniques

During this period most writers wrote in a simple, direct, unadorned style, known as the Puritan plain style. Occasionally, writers employed strong images to emphasize their ideas.

On the following pages is a poem by Anne Bradstreet, a devout Puritan woman who lived in the Massachusetts Bay Colony.

14   *The New Land*

Objectives

1 To learn to read critically
2 To recognize the Puritan plain style
3 To appreciate connotations
4 To find word origins
5 To write about lyric poetry

Support Material

Teaching Portfolio
Teacher Backup, p. 3
Reading Critically, "The Beauty of the World" by Jonathan Edwards, p. 6
Grammar in Action Worksheet, *Expressing Negative Ideas*, p. 7
Usage and Mechanics Worksheet, p. 9
Analyzing Literature Worksheet, *Understanding the Puritan Plain Style*, p. 10

Critical Thinking and Reading Worksheet, *Appreciating Connotations*, p. 11
Selection Test, p. 12

Upon the Burning of Our House

July 10th, 1666

Anne Bradstreet

In silent night when rest I took
For sorrow near I did not look
I wakened was with thund'ring noise
And piteous shrieks of dreadful voice.
5　That fearful sound of "Fire!" and "Fire!"
Let no man know is my desire.
I, starting up, the light did spy,
And to my God my heart did cry
To strengthen me in my distress
10　And not to leave me succorless.
Then, coming out, beheld a space
The flame consume my dwelling place.
And when I could no longer look,
I blest His name that gave and took,
15　That laid my goods now in the dust.
Yea, so it was, and so 'twas just.
It was His own, it was not mine,
Far be it that I should repine;
He might of all justly bereft
20　But yet sufficient for us left.
When by the ruins oft I past
My sorrowing eyes aside did cast,
And here and there the places spy
Where oft I sat and long did lie:
25　Here stood that trunk, and there that chest,
There lay that store I counted best.
My pleasant things in ashes lie,
And them behold no more shall I.
Under thy roof no guest shall sit,
30　Nor at thy table eat a bit.
No pleasant tale shall e'er be told,
Nor things recounted done of old.

Literary Movement: Bradstreet writes in a personal voice, sharing her feelings about this incident.

Writer's Technique: Bradstreet uses vivid words to make her purpose clear.

Historical Context: A Puritan's thoughts turn to God on every occasion.

Historical Context: These lines express the Puritan attitude that God's ways are not to be understood so much as simply accepted.

Writer's Technique: Bradstreet's medium is a lyric poem; it expresses her thoughts and feelings.

Upon the Burning of Our House　15

Fine art, *The Parson Barnard House,* nineteenth-century engraving by Henry Marsh. Henry Marsh was a wood engraver who was a partner in the Hitchcock and Marsh firm in Boston from 1848 to 1860. His work appeared in many magazines and books.

The house in this print is not the original Bradstreet house, which burned to the ground in 1666. The Parson Barnard House was built about 1715 on the same lot of land. It appears to be a seventeenth-century house, but structurally the Parson Barnard house is a typical eighteenth-century home.

You may want to ask the following questions:

1. The interior of a seventeenth-century house was different in many ways from that of a modern-day house. What might some of these differences be?
2. What might Anne Bradstreet have treasured in a house like this one?

THE PARSON BARNARD HOUSE
Henry Marsh
North Andover Historical Society

Writer's Technique: Bradstreet writes mostly in the Puritan plain style—clear and precise, making her points directly.

> No candle e'er shall shine in thee,
> Nor bridegroom's voice e'er heard shall be.
> 35 In silence ever shall thou lie,
> Adieu, Adieu,[1] all's vanity.
> Then straight I 'gin my heart to chide,
> And did thy wealth on earth abide?
> Didst fix thy hope on mold'ring dust?
> 40 The arm of flesh didst make thy trust?
> Raise up thy thoughts above the sky
> That dunghill mists away may fly.
> Thou hast an house on high erect,

---

1. adieu (ə dyoo′): "Farewell" (French).

16   *The New Land*

Grammar in Action

Sentences can express **negative ideas** in several ways. Lines 28–30 of Bradstreet's poem illustrate some of these methods:

And them *no more* behold shall I.	(Adverb negated)
Under thy roof *no guest* shall sit.	(Noun negated)
Nor at they table *eat* a bit.	(Verb negated)

However, writers must take care to limit negative words—*no, nor, not, none, never, scarcely, hardly*—so that each clause, each subject-verb unit, contains no more than one negative word.

Student Activity 1. Describe Bradstreet's methods of negation in each of the following lines.

1. For sorrow near I did not look
2. And when I could no longer look,
3. It was His own, it was not mine.

For Further Study A biographical note on Anne Bradstreet appears on page 58, and her poem "To My Dear and Loving Husband" appears on page 59.

Reader's Response How have you felt when you lost something that was precious to you?

> Framed by that mighty Architect,
> 45 With glory richly furnished,
> Stands permanent though this be fled.
> It's purchased and paid for too
> By Him who hath enough to do.
> A price so vast as is unknown
> 50 Yet by His gift is made thine own;
> There's wealth enough, I need no more,
> Farewell, my pelf,² farewell my store.
> The world no longer let me love,
> My hope and treasure lies above.

Writer's Technique: This image presents a Puritan lesson—one's true home is with God, not here on Earth.

Historical Context: The poet ends with her message—not to be attached to earthly things but to live by spiritual ideals.

_____

2. **pelf** *n*.: Money or wealth regarded with contempt.

Upon the Burning of Our House   17

Student Activity 2. Examine Bradstreet's clustering of negative sentences in the section of the poem which details her realization of loss (lines 28–34). Why are there fewer negative sentences before and after this section of the poem?

Student Activity 3. Rewrite these faulty sentences so that each clause contains a single negative word:

1. Bradstreet hadn't hardly expected fire to destroy her home.
2. She couldn't scarcely bear to look at her burned home.
3. She was sorry that she wouldn't be able to offer her usual hospitality to nobody.
4. She realized she didn't need nothing but her faith.
5. She didn't regret the loss of her home no more.

Closure and Extension

ANSWERS TO THINKING ABOUT THE SELECTION

Recalling

1. She blesses God's name.
2. In her mind's eye, she sees the places and possessions that were inside her house before it burned. In reality, she sees the ashes of the things that burned.
3. Her "hope and treasure" lie "above," in heaven with God.

Interpreting

4. She believes that God both gave her the house and took it away, and she believes in following His will. Losing her possessions in the fire has reminded her that her true wealth is not in material things but in her spiritual life.
5. (a) She feels sorrow for the things she lost and nostalgia for the times she spent in the house with friends. (b) She chides herself for her grief over earthly possessions and reminds herself that her real wealth is in heaven with God.
6. She is referring to heaven.
7. (a) The Puritans placed little value on worldly goods. (b) The theme is that people should thank God for what they have and should not place too much value on worldly goods and that they should focus on their spiritual lives.

Applying

8. Suggested Response: Unlike Bradstreet, most people in today's world place a high value on worldly goods.

ANSWERS TO ANALYZING LITERATURE

1. Some plain words used in the poem are "my goods," "that trunk," "that chest," "that store," "My pleasant things," "roof," "table," "candle."
2. Some vivid, colorful words in the poem include "mold'ring dust," "the arm of flesh," "dunghill mists," "mighty Architect," "With glory richly furnished," "my pelf."
3. Examples include: "I blest His name that gave and took"; "it was His own, it was not mine"; "My hope and treasure lies above."

THINKING ABOUT THE SELECTION

Recalling

1. What does the speaker do when she can no longer look at her burning house?
2. What does the speaker see when she passes by her house?
3. In the end, where do the speaker's "hope and treasure" lie?

Interpreting

4. Why does the speaker bless God as her house is burning down?
5. (a) With what emotions is the speaker filled when she passes by the ruins of her house? (b) How does she react to these emotions?
6. To what is the speaker referring when she speaks of the "house on high" in line 43?
7. (a) On the basis of this poem, what generalization would you make about the Puritan attitude toward worldly goods? (b) What seems to be the theme of the poem?

Applying

8. Do you think the contemporary attitude toward worldly goods is similar to or different from that expressed in this poem? Explain your answer.

ANALYZING LITERATURE

The Puritan Plain Style

The writing style of the Puritans reflected the plain style of their lives—spare, simple, and straightforward, with a focus on the essentials of life, not on frivolities. Short words, direct statements, and references to ordinary everyday objects—these were the characteristics of the style. Anne Bradstreet writes mainly in this plain style; however, she does occasionally allow herself some strong, vivid images to present her ideas.

1. Point out three basic, plain words referring to everyday items.
2. Point out three examples of more vivid, colorful words.
3. Find a line that is an example of a direct statement reflecting her Puritan beliefs.

CRITICAL THINKING AND READING

Appreciating Connotations

The **connotation** of a word refers to the suggestions or associations evoked by it—beyond its literal meaning. For example, the word *sky* literally refers to the upper atmosphere or the appearance of this atmosphere. However, *sky* has the connotation of soaring, extreme height. Therefore, when Bradstreet writes "raise up thy thoughts above the sky," in line 41, she is reminding herself of God's province—the highest attainment.

Explain the connotation of the italicized words in each of the following lines.
1. "And did thy *wealth* on earth abide?"
2. "Didst fix thy hope on *mold'ring* dust?"

UNDERSTANDING LANGUAGE

Finding Word Origins

One characteristic of the plain style is the use of short, simple words rather than longer, more difficult words. Many simple words come from Old English, an earlier form of our language, whereas many more difficult words derive from Latin.

Determine whether the following words from the poem come from Old English or Latin. Tell the meaning of the original word.
1. bride 2. bless 3. vanity 4. earth 5. permanent

THINKING AND WRITING

Writing About Lyric Poetry

In her lyrics Anne Bradstreet conveys important Puritan beliefs and concerns. Reread "Upon the Burning of Our House" carefully, noting concerns expressed in the poem. What seems to be her major concern in this poem? Write an essay in which you show how this one concern seems to dominate the poem. Include passages from the poem to support your thesis. Once you have finished writing a draft, revise your paper where needed, and prepare a final copy.

ANSWERS TO CRITICAL THINKING AND READING

1. *Wealth,* in this context, means "spiritual riches and blessings," not "valuable material goods."
2. Here *mold'ring* has the connotation of decay and transiency.

ANSWERS TO UNDERSTANDING LANGUAGE

1. bride: from the Old English word *bryd,* meaning "betrothed"
2. bless: from the Old English word *blod,* meaning "rite of consecration"
3. vanity: from the Latin word *vanitas,* meaning "emptiness"
4. earth: from the Old English word *eorthe,* meaning "earth"
5. permanent: from the Latin word *permanens,* meaning "to remain"

THINKING AND WRITING

After students have finished a draft, have them work in groups reading and suggesting improvements in each other's drafts. Students may then incorporate suggestions in their final drafts.

Native American Voices

PHILIP (METACOMET), AMERICAN WAMPANOAG INDIAN CHIEF
Colored Engraving, 1772, by Paul Revere
The Granger Collection

Humanities Note

Fine art, *Philip (Metacomet), American Wampanoag Indian Chief*, 1772, by Paul Revere. Paul Revere (1735–1818) is best known, of course, for his "midnight ride," of April 18, 1775, to warn of the approach of the British troops at Lexington, Massachusetts. Yet Revere was also an established silversmith and engraver. He made engravings such as this one, and during the American Revolution he printed the government's first currency. After the war he became a well-to-do merchant.

In 1620, Chief Massasoit of the Wampanoag tribe befriended the Pilgrims. Fifty-five years later, King Philip—as his son Metacomet was known—led the final Native American resistance against the colonists in the Massachusetts area. Philip was killed, and the tribe was soon wiped out. Revere's work, done a century after its subject's death, was a kind of historical tribute to a people whose culture and way of life could not survive alongside that of the European settlers, with their more advanced methods of commerce and warfare.

Master Teacher Note In addition to oral literature, the Native Americans used art as a means of communicating their ideas and beliefs. Place Art Transparency 1, *In Search of American Icons* by Marsden Hartley, on the overhead projector. Have students discuss what the painting reveals about Native-American culture. What do each of the figures depicted in the painting represent? What overall message does the painting convey?

Focus

More About the Cultures To this day, members of the **Delaware** tribe hold *The Walam Olum* in great esteem. They recite the story in select ceremonies to keep their heritage alive. Why do you think that it is important for Native Americans to retain a connection to their cultural heritages?

The **Navaho** tribe has retained a great deal of its culture due to oral tradition. One remnant from its past is called "Night Chant." It is a song that lasts for nine days and is used on religious occasions. What difficulties might be involved with maintaining this type of tradition in today's world?

Delaware

Long before the first Europeans arrived in North America, the people of the Delaware tribe lived in parts of what is now Delaware, Pennsylvania, New York, and New Jersey. The Delaware hunted, fished, and farmed. For the most part, the Delaware lived in peace, except when threatened by their powerful enemies, the Iroquois.

In the seventeenth century, European colonists settled in Delaware territory. In 1682 the Delaware signed a treaty with William Penn, the colonial leader, but colonists took the tribe's land. During the next hundred years, eighteen treaties between the colonists and the Delaware were made and broken as the Delaware were pushed westward—eventually, to a reservation in Oklahoma. Today, there are fewer then three thousand Delaware, living primarily in Oklahoma, Wisconsin, and southern Canada.

Living close to the land as they did, the Delaware sought explanations for natural phenomena. Some of their explanations, like *The Walam Olum,* are recorded in pictographs, symbols painted on wood or stone.

Navaho

The Navaho are believed to have settled in the American Southwest between A.D. 1000 and 1400. Fierce warriors and hunters, they intermarried with members of the peaceful Pueblo tribe, who taught them how to weave and raise fruits and vegetables. The Spanish gave the tribe the name "Navaho," which means "cultivator of fields," but the Navaho usually referred to themselves as Dine, "the people." After the Spanish introduced domestic animals to the Navaho, many became herders of sheep and goats.

In the early 1800's, as American settlers began establishing ranches on Navaho land, the Navaho fought to drive the ranchers away. In 1864 U.S. Army troops defeated the Navaho, and seven thousand captives were marched to New Mexico, a trek of more than three hundred miles through the desert. Four years later, they were allowed to return to a reservation on their old land. The Navaho reservation, covering more than 24,000 square miles in Arizona, Utah, and New Mexico, is the largest in the United States. At more than 110,000 people, the Navaho are also the nation's biggest tribe. Today thousands of tribe members choose to live in the traditional Navaho manner, inhabiting earth and log structures as their ancestors did, and practicing their tribal religion.

GUIDE FOR INTERPRETING

from The Walam Olum;
from The Navaho Origin Legend

Literary Forms

Myths. Myths are traditional stories passed down from generation to generation, characteristically involving immortal beings. Myths attempt to explain natural phenomena, the origin of humans, the customs, institutions or religious rites of a people, or events beyond people's control. Indirectly, myths teach the values and ideals of a culture.

The Walam Olum and *The Navaho Origin Legend* are both myths. *The Walam Olum* is the Delaware origin myth. Originally it consisted of a long series of pictographs explaining the origin of the Delaware people as a result of the actions of a manito, or spirit. At traditional ceremonies, a person who had inherited the right to keep *The Walam Olum* would interpret its meaning for the other members of the tribe. *The Navaho Origin Legend*, an important part of the Navaho tradition, also explains the origin of life.

Commentary

For all Native Americans, each creature in nature contains its own power by which it maintains itself and affects others. Each tribe has a different name for this power. The early white settlers learned the Algonquian term Manitou, or Manito. It includes many meanings: power, mystery, magic, spirit, medicine.

Manitos come in all shapes and sizes, from weak to powerful. How did the Native Americans determine the strength of the manito? Outward appearances were not thought a sure sign of power: a small animal or stone could possess great magic. However, close observation of the effects of the creature on other creatures could reveal the extent of its power. Or it could be revealed in a dream or vision.

Many tribes recognize a chief manito, or Great Spirit—an invisible power that is the source of life and good for humans. The Navaho are unusual in that their great manitos are represented primarily in human rather than animal forms.

In the following selections, notice the forms and roles of the manitos. What is their power used for? What does this tell us of the cultural values of the tribe?

Writing

What events that defy explanation occur in the modern world? Are there natural phenomena, such as black holes, that you find mysterious or difficult to understand? List events that are not fully understandable and freewrite about one of them.

Guide for Interpreting 21

Literary Focus Myth appears in two formats: *etiological* and *euhemeristic.* An etiological myth attempts to explain why, while an euhemeristic myth has some basis in historical fact. Ask students to keep these two definitions in mind while reading *The Walam Olum* and *The Navaho Origin Legend*

Writing/Prior Knowledge For extra credit, have students make up an explanation for a mysterious natural phenomenon.

Vocabulary Preteach the following vocabulary words:
ablutions (ab $\overline{loo}'$ shənz) *n.:* A washing or cleansing of the body as part of a religious rite (p. 26)
protruded (prō $\overline{troo}$d id) *v.:* Jutted out (p. 27)

Motivation/Prior Knowledge
Have students imagine they are Native Americans who are about to receive the sacred literature of their tribe in a most important ceremony. In front of them are the elders who will conduct the ceremony, which will grant the initiated ones the right to take their places as spiritual advisors. Would they feel excitement? Would their excitement be tempered by nervousness? Why? Would they feel proud about receiving this great honor? How would they act during the ceremony?

Master Teacher Note This myth expresses the world view of the Delaware tribe. Place the myth in its cultural context by bringing in pictures of Delaware artifacts.

Thematic Idea Another selection that explains the creation of the world is the excerpt from *The Navaho Origin Legend* on page 26.

Purpose-Setting Question How was the world created?

1 **Critical Thinking and Reading** In *The Walam Olum,* the phrases "at all times" and "above the earth" suggest a higher intelligence and different plane of existence.

2 **Discussion** Focus students' attention on the phrase "lost in space." Is this a reference to the Manito's omnipresence?

Enrichment In Algonquian languages, *manito,* also *manitu* and *manitou,* generally refers to a supernatural power or creator. The Delaware term for creator, or the great power, is *ketanto'wit.*

In the Sauk-Delaware tribes, *manito* also often referred to an evil being now identified with Satan.

from # The Walam Olum
Delaware

1
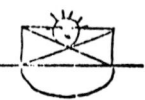

At first, in that place, at all times, above the earth,

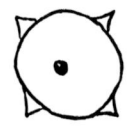

On the earth was an extended fog, and there the great Manito was.

2
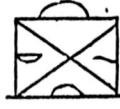

At first, forever, lost in space, everywhere, the great Manito was.

He made the extended land and the sky.

He made the sun, the moon, the stars.

He made them all to move evenly.

Then the wind blew violently, and it cleared, and the water flowed off far and strong.

22   *The New Land*

And groups of islands grew newly, and there remained.

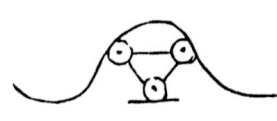

Anew spoke the great Manito, a manito to manitos,

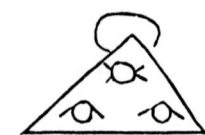

To beings, mortals, souls and all,

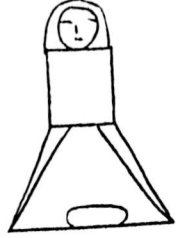

And ever after he was a manito to men, and their grandfather.

He gave the first mother, the mother of beings.

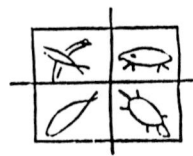

He gave the fish, he gave the turtles, he gave the beasts, he gave the birds.

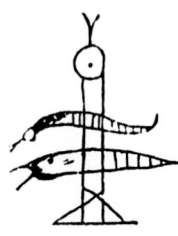

But an evil Manito made evil beings only, monsters.

from *The Walam Olum*   23

3

Humanities Note

Fine art, Delaware Indian symbols. In 1836 Constantine S. Rafinesque, a botanist from Kentucky, published an astounding article in *American Nations* magazine. The article contained copies of pictographs that Rafinesque claimed to have found etched on sticks. His interpretation of this painted record (Walam Olum) was allegedly a history of the Delaware tribe. It included references to the creation of the earth, people crossing the frozen sea (a possible reference to the people leaving Siberia and crossing the Bering Strait), the Manito (Great Creator) and chiefs and spirits, a golden age of peace, and the coming of the white man. A reverence for all life and the natural order of things permeates *The Walam Olum.* No one has been able to prove or disprove Rafinesque's claims. Furthermore, the original sticks were never available for scientific study and their whereabouts are now unknown. Some experts doubt they ever existed.

Have students examine the pictographs and select one. Have them explain, in detail, their interpretation of each line and shape, as it relates to the given interpretation.

3 Discussion How are these two symbols similar to and different from each other?

Grammar in Action

Writers use different types of **sentence patterns** to convey different types of information and to provide variety in their writing. The following line from *The Walam Olum,* in the *complement–linking verb–subject* pattern, provides information about the Great Manito:

. . . there the great Manito was.

In contrast, a *subject–action verb–direct object pattern* is used to describe the Manito's actions in this line:

He made the extended land and the sky.

Student Activity 1. Label the basic parts of each of the remaining lines in *The Walam Olum.* Tell whether each line describes an action or provides information about its subject.

Student Activity 2. Write a paragraph in which you use a variety of basic sentence patterns. Be able to explain why you used each specific pattern.

4 **Discussion** Why is the evil spirit credited with creating flies and gnats?

5 **Discussion** Like the *Walam Olum,* most creation myths include an evil force that disrupts the process of creation. Why do you think that evil plays such an important role in these myths?

Enrichment Located by French scholar Constantine Samuel Rafinesque in 1836, the *Walam Olum* is the Delaware Indian account of their origin and migration. The name, loosely translated as "red score," was chanted. According to tradition, red symbols painted on tally sticks were used as mnemonic devices during the recitation of the legend. In addition to what is considered a usual Native American account of the origin of the universe, the *Walam Olam* also contains lists of the movements and wars of the Delaware Indians and their successive chiefs.

4
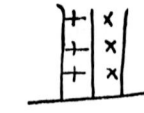
He made the flies, he made the gnats.

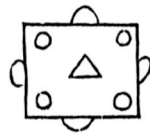
All beings were then friendly.

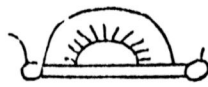
Truly the manitos were active and kindly

To those very first men, and to those first mothers; fetched them wives,

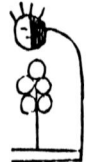
And fetched them food, when first they desired it.

All had cheerful knowledge, all had leisure, all thought in gladness.

5
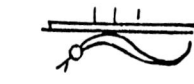
But very secretly an evil being, a mighty magician, came on earth,

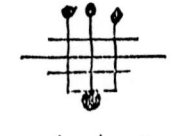 And with him brought badness, quarreling, unhappiness,

 Brought bad weather, brought sickness, brought death.

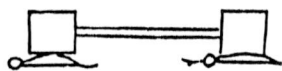 All this took place of old on the earth, beyond the great tidewater, at the first.

THINKING ABOUT THE SELECTION

Recalling

1. List five of the great Manito's creations.
2. What did the evil Manito create?
3. What six troubles did a "mighty magician" bring to the earth?

Interpreting

4. According to *The Walam Olum,* what constitutes a happy life for the Delaware?
5. Examine the pictographs carefully. What evidence is there that the "evil Manito" and the "evil being, a mighty magician" might be the same spirit?

Applying

6. Identify three evils of the twentieth century. Provide an imaginative explanation for the origin of each of these evils.

ANALYZING LITERATURE

Recognizing Myths

Myths, like *The Walam Olum,* are ancient stories, generally involving immortal characters, that explain the mysteries of nature or the customs and religious rites of a people. For example, the excerpt from *The Walam Olum* explains how the universe was created.

1. What supernatural powers does the great Manito have?
2. According to *The Walam Olum,* how did human beings come to inhabit the earth?
3. How does *The Walam Olum* explain bad weather, sickness, and death?

CRITICAL THINKING AND READING

Inferring Cultural Values

Myths like *The Walam Olum* reveal the ideals and values of the people who created them. These ideals and values may not be stated directly, but by reading closely, you can infer them. For example, in *The Walam Olum,* when you read that the first inhabitants of the earth "all had cheerful knowledge, all had leisure, all thought in gladness," you can probably infer that the Delaware value knowledge and leisure, because the statement indicates that knowledge and leisure make people happy.

What can you infer that the Delaware valued from each of the following statements?
1. "He gave the fish, he gave the turtles, he gave the beasts, he gave the birds. . . . All beings were then friendly."
2. ". . . an evil being, a mighty magician, came on earth, And with him brought badness, quarreling, unhappiness. . . ."

from *The Walam Olum* 25

Reader's Response What was your first reaction to this origin tale?

from The Navaho Origin Legend
Navaho

1 On the morning of the twelfth day the people washed themselves well. The women dried themselves with yellow cornmeal; the men with white cornmeal. Soon after the ablutions were completed they heard the distant call of the approaching gods.[1] It was shouted, as before, four times—nearer and

---

1. the approaching gods: The four Navaho gods: White Body, Blue Body, Yellow Body, and Black Body.

THE PLACE OF EMERGENCE AND THE FOUR WORLDS
Navaho
Wheelwright Museum of the American Indian

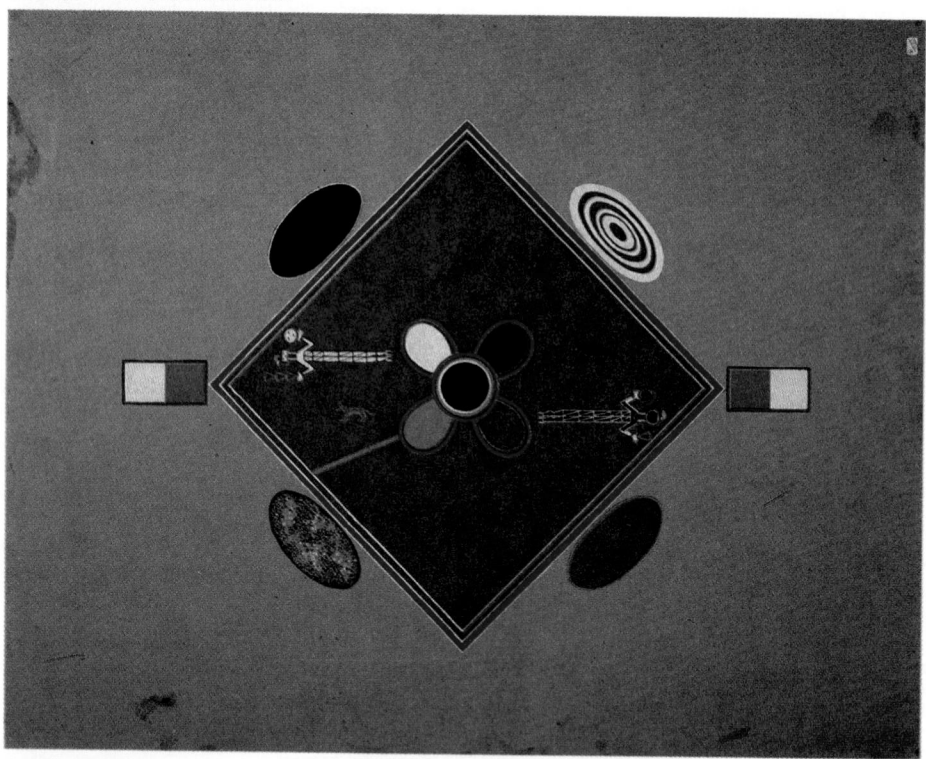

You might ask students what parts of the Navaho legend are represented in the accompanying picture.

louder at each repetition—and, after the fourth call, the gods appeared. Blue Body and Black Body each carried a sacred buckskin. White Body carried two ears of corn, one yellow, one white, each covered at the end completely with grains.

The gods laid one buckskin on the ground with the head to the west; on this they placed the two ears of corn, with their tips to the east, and over the corn they spread the other buckskin with its head to the east; under the white ear they put the feather of a white eagle, under the yellow ear the feather of a yellow eagle. Then they told the people to stand at a distance and allow the wind to enter. The white wind blew from the east, and the yellow wind blew from the west, between the skins. While the wind was blowing, eight of the Mirage People[2] came and walked around the objects on the ground four times, and as they walked the

---

2. **Mirage People:** Mirages personified.

---

eagle feathers, whose tips protruded from between the buckskins, were seen to move. When the Mirage People had finished their walk the upper buckskin was lifted; the ears of corn had disappeared, a man and a woman lay there in their stead.

The white ear of corn had been changed into a man, the yellow ear into a woman. It was the wind that gave them life. It is the wind that comes out of our mouths now that gives us life. When this ceases to blow we die. In the skin at the tips of our fingers we see the trail of the wind; it shows us where the wind blew when our ancestors were created.

The pair thus created were First Man and First Woman (Atsé *Hastín* and Atsé Estsán). The gods directed the people to build an enclosure of brushwood for the pair. When the enclosure was finished, First Man and First Woman entered it, and the gods said to them: "Live together now as husband and wife."

THINKING ABOUT THE SELECTION
Recalling

1. What items do the gods place on the ground?
2. What brings First Man and First Woman to life?
3. What do the gods direct First Man and First Woman to build?

Interpreting

4. Why do the Navaho associate the skin at the tips of the fingers with the trail of the wind?
5. Find evidence in the passage that suggests that the number four is sacred to the Navaho religion.

Applying

6. State two ways in which the wind affects the animals or plants living on the earth.

THINKING AND WRITING
Comparing and Contrasting Myths

Find a myth explaining the origin of life in another culture. Compare and contrast it with the Navaho origin myth. First, prepare a list of similarities and differences between the excerpt from *The Navaho Origin Legend* and the myth you have chosen. Organize your information into an outline, and write a thesis statement about the similarities and differences between the two myths. Then write a short essay in which you support your thesis statement with the information in your lists. When you revise, make sure that you have included corresponding points of comparison and contrast for each myth to support your thesis and that you have used appropriate transitions to show either comparison or contrast.

from *The Navaho Origin Legend* 27

2 **Discussion** This is one of the few myths that deals with life originating from vegetation. Ask students why they feel the Navahos would choose corn to represent the source of their civilization. Is it an appropriate symbol to represent life? Why or why not?

3 **Discussion** Why might the Navahos have viewed the wind as the source of life?

Reader's Response What did you like most about this origin tale? Why?

Interpreting

4. The tips of the fingers have lines. The Navahos believe that these markings were made by the wind when it brought their ancestors to life.
5. Two of the most sacred acts in the passage—the call of the gods and the walk of the Mirage People —occur four times.

Applying

6. Answers will differ. Suggested Response: The wind helps plants reproduce by blowing seeds to where they can germinate. It also moves the clouds that carry rain, supplying plants with water needed for growth.

Challenge What does this selection reveal about the attitudes and values of the Navaho people?

THINKING AND WRITING

For help with this assignment, students can refer to Lesson 16, "Writing a Comparative Evaluation," in the Handbook of Writing About Literature.

After students have completed the assignment, divide them into groups, and have them read their rough drafts to one another and comment on the ways in which their essays could be improved.

Closure and Extension

ANSWERS TO THINKING ABOUT THE SELECTION
Recalling

1. They put down a buckskin and then place two ears of corn on it.
2. The wind gives them life.
3. The gods tell the people to construct an enclosure of brushwood for themselves.

More About the Culture Some historians believe the five tribes of the Iroquois Confederation thought it necessary to unite after white men first appeared in their territories. Intertribal conflicts had weakened the tribes and left them open to outside attack. Note that the constitution provides for a strengthening of the confederation by allowing for the inclusion of other individuals and tribes. What other reasons might the tribes have had for uniting?

Literary Focus The constitution describes the Great Peace as a tree whose spreading roots are strong and whose branches provide shelter for the nations of the confederation. The document's organizational pattern goes from the general to the specific by first describing an envisioned peace and then stating rules to govern this peace.

Writing/Prior Knowledge For extra credit, have students compare and contrast the laws and principles in two different societies.

Vocabulary Preteach the following vocabulary words:
confederate (kən fed′ ər it) *adj.:* United with others for a common purpose (p. 29)
disposition (dis′ pə zish′ ən) *n.:* An inclination or tendency (p. 29)
deliberation (di lib′ ə rā′ shən) *n.:* Careful consideration (p. 30)

Spelling Tip Point out that two words in this group, *disposition* and *deliberation,* have the ending sound spelled *tion.*

Literary Forms

Commentary

Writing

from The Iroquois Constitution

The **Iroquois** were a powerful tribe of Native Americans who lived in what is now the northeast United States. During the fourteenth century, an Iroquoian mystic and prophet named Dekanawidah traveled from village to village urging the Iroquoian-speaking peoples to stop fighting and to band together in peace and brotherhood. Dekanawidah's efforts led to the foundation of the Iroquois Confederation of the Five Nations, a league of five Iroquois tribes: Mohawk, Oneida, Seneca, Cayuga, and Onondaga.

Constitutions. A constitution is a written or unwritten system of fundamental laws and principles governing a society. The Iroquois Constitution, which was unwritten, was first presented to confederate lords of the Five Nations in a speech by Dekanawidah. The confederate lords memorized it and recorded it in symbols on strings of shells.

In most constitutions, laws and principles are listed in a straightforward, factual manner. Because the Iroquois Constitution was spoken rather than written, it had to be presented in a way that would hold the listeners' attention. Therefore, it uses elegant phrasing and metaphors to describe the foundation of the confederation and the system by which the confederation will be governed.

The Iroquois lived in large wooden structures called longhouses. After the confederation was established, the Iroquois called themselves the People of the Longhouse. In this longhouse the most western tribe, the Senecas, were designated the Keepers of the Western Door; and the Mohawks, the most eastern tribe, the Keepers of the Eastern Door. The other three tribes were ranged between them like families in a longhouse, each with their cooking fire. Thus they were the Confederation of the Five Fires. Later, they called the United States "the Thirteen Fires."

The Iroquois were crucial in the struggle between England and France for control of the continent. Expert diplomats and shrewd politicians, the Iroquois played off both sides, finally backing England. As you read the Iroquois Constitution, notice the system of rules it sets up and the language and metaphors it uses to do this. Would you remember the United States Constitution better if it used similar language and metaphors?

Try to imagine a society without laws and principles. What would it be like living there? Freewrite about the function of the laws and principles that govern a society.

Objectives
1 To understand a constitution
2 To interpret metaphors
3 To use Native American words
4 To compare and contrast constitutions

Support Material

Teaching Portfolio
Teacher Backup, p. 27
Usage and Mechanics Worksheet, p. 31
Vocabulary Check, p. 32
Analyzing Literature Worksheet, *Recognizing a Constitution,* p. 33
Critical Thinking and Reading Worksheet, *Understanding Metaphors,* p. 34

Selection Test, p. 35

from The Iroquois Constitution

Iroquois

I am Dekanawidah and with the Five Nations[1] confederate lords I plant the Tree of the Great Peace. I name the tree the Tree of the Great Long Leaves. Under the shade of this Tree of the Great Peace we spread the soft white feathery down of the globe thistle as seats for you, Adodarhoh, and your cousin lords.

We place you upon those seats, spread soft with the feathery down of the globe thistle, there beneath the shade of the spreading branches of the Tree of Peace. There shall you sit and watch the council fire of the confederacy of the Five Nations, and all the affairs of the Five Nations shall be transacted at this place before you.

Roots have spread out from the Tree of the Great Peace, one to the north, one to the east, one to the south and one to the west. The name of these roots is the Great White Roots and their nature is peace and strength.

If any man or any nation outside the Five Nations shall obey the laws of the Great Peace and make known their disposition to the lords of the confederacy, they may trace the roots to the tree and if their minds are clean and they are obedient and promise to obey the wishes of the confederate council, they shall be welcomed to take shelter beneath the Tree of the Long Leaves.

---

1. Five Nations: The Mohawk, Oneida, Onondaga, Cayuga, and Seneca tribes. Together, these tribes formed the Iroquois Confederation.

We place at the top of the Tree of the Long Leaves an eagle who is able to see afar. If he sees in the distance any evil approach-

RED JACKET
George Catlin
The Thomas Gilcrease Institute of American History and Art, Tulsa, Oklahoma

from The Iroquois Constitution   29

Humanities Note

Fine art, *Red Jacket,* by George Catlin. George Catlin (1796–1872) was born in Wilkes-Barre, Pennsylvania. To please his father, he practiced law until 1832, at which time he became intrigued by "the dignity and nobility of the Native Americans." It was then that Catlin decided to devote himself to art and to becoming a historian of Native Americans. He spent eight years among various tribes while on exploratory expeditions along parts of the Mississippi River.

Catlin painted many Native American portraits. This one is of a fiery Seneca orator named Sagoyewatha, who reluctantly followed his people into an alliance with the British. He received from the British a red coat—thus the name "Red Jacket." In Catlin's

Presentation

Motivation/Prior Knowledge Point out that Native Americans often are depicted as ruthless savages in films and on television. Ask students if they believe these to be accurate portrayals. Explain that such depictions are stereotypical. In fact, many tribes wanted peace.

Master Teacher Note Place the Iroquois Constitution in historical perspective by describing some of the forces that led to its adoption. Point out that before the tribes united and established the confederacy, they were plagued by incessant intertribal warfare, which caused great loss of life and ensuing social disruptions. Their conflicts weakened the tribes and left them open to enemy attack.

Thematic Idea Another selection in which a set of principles is established is the Declaration of Independence on page 144.

Purpose-Setting Question What is the purpose of this constitution?

1 **Clarification** A downy growth forms on ripe thistle seeds.

2 **Clarification** Adodarhoh is one of the candidates for the council.

---

painting he is without the coat but is wearing a medal given to him by George Washington after the Revolution.

You might ask students the following questions:
1. What personality traits has the artist tried to capture in this portrait?
2. How are these traits related to the values and ideals set forth in the Iroquois constitution?

29

3 Discussion Compare the council's opening with the way other organizations open their meetings. To what values does the council pay tribute? Are the values very different from those of modern organizations?

4 Enrichment Deer were held in high esteem by Native Americans. They admired the swiftness and cunning of these animals, and felt that antlers symbolized the wisdom that is acquired with age and experience.

5. Discussion The aims of the Iroquois Constitution can be compared with the modern goals of arms control and environmental protection. Have students link these modern movements to the selection. Ask if societies will always be concerned with these types of problems. If so, why?

Reader's Response Do you think the tenets of the constitution are lost in the flowery rhetoric? Why or why not?

ing or any danger threatening he will at once warn the people of the confederacy.

The smoke of the confederate council fire shall ever ascend and pierce the sky so that other nations who may be allies may see the council fire of the Great Peace. . .

Whenever the confederate lords shall assemble for the purpose of holding a council, the Onondaga lords shall open it by expressing their gratitude to their cousin lords and greeting them, and they shall make an address and offer thanks to the earth where men dwell, to the streams of water, the pools, the springs and the lakes, to the maize and the fruits, to the medicinal herbs and trees, to the forest trees for their usefulness, to the animals that serve as food and give their pelts for clothing, to the great winds and the lesser winds, to the thunderers, to the sun, the mighty warrior, to the moon, to the messengers of the Creator who reveal his wishes and to the Great Creator who dwells in the heavens above, who gives all the things useful to men, and who is the source and the ruler of health and life.

Then shall the Onondaga lords declare the council open. . .

All lords of the Five Nations' Confederacy must be honest in all things. . . It shall be a serious wrong for anyone to lead a lord into trivial affairs, for the people must ever hold their lords high in estimation out of respect to their honorable positions.

When a candidate lord is to be installed he shall furnish four strings of shells (or wampum)[2] one span in length bound together at one end. Such will constitute the evidence of his pledge to the confederate

_____
2. wampum (wäm′ pəm) *n.*: Small beads made of shells.

lords that he will live according to the constitution of the Great Peace and exercise justice in all affairs.

When the pledge is furnished the speaker of the council must hold the shell strings in his hand and address the opposite side of the council fire and he shall commence his address saying: "Now behold him. He has now become a confederate lord. See how splendid he looks." An address may then follow. At the end of it he shall send the bunch of shell strings to the opposite side and they shall be received as evidence of the pledge. Then shall the opposite side say:

"We now do crown you with the sacred emblem of the deer's antlers, the emblem of your lordship. You shall now become a mentor of the people of the Five Nations. The thickness of your skin shall be seven spans—which is to say that you shall be proof against anger, offensive actions and criticism. Your heart shall be filled with peace and good will and your mind filled with a yearning for the welfare of the people of the confederacy. With endless patience you shall carry out your duty and your firmness shall be tempered with tenderness for your people. Neither anger nor fury shall find lodgement in your mind and all your words and actions shall be marked with calm deliberation. In all of your deliberations in the confederate council, in your efforts at law making, in all your official acts, self-interest shall be cast into oblivion. Cast not over your shoulder behind you the warnings of the nephews and nieces should they chide you for any error or wrong you may do, but return to the way of the Great Law which is just and right. Look and listen for the welfare of the whole people and have always in view not only the present but also the coming generations, even those whose faces are yet beneath the surface of the ground—the unborn of the future nation."

Closure and Extension

ANSWERS TO THINKING ABOUT THE SELECTION
Recalling

1. They reach out to all corners of the world. They are called the Great White Roots and represent peace and strength.

2. The eagle (known for its keen vision) looks for signs of approaching evil and warns the people of the confederacy about them.
3. They will thank and greet the lords, and will also thank the forces of nature, the messengers of the Creator, and the Creator himself.
4. In this way, he shows the confederate lords the sincerity of this pledge to live by the rules set forth and to exercise justice.

Interpreting

5. The fire symbolizes the peace that exists between the nations and the hope that it will be everlasting.
6. They were conscious of their dependence on the earth, which grew their food and nurtured other forms of life. They respected their environment.

THINKING ABOUT THE SELECTION

Recalling

1. Describe the roots of the Tree of Great Peace.
2. What is the role of the eagle at the top of the Tree of the Long Leaves?
3. How will the Onondaga lords open each council meeting?
4. Why will a candidate lord furnish a string of shells when he is installed?

Interpreting

5. What does the council fire of the Five Nations represent?
6. The constitution tells the lords to "offer thanks to the earth where men dwell." What does this decree suggest about the Iroquois?
7. What conclusions can you draw about Dekanawidah from the constitution he created?

Applying

8. In the constitution, Dekanawidah outlines the qualities he expects the Iroquois lords to possess. What qualities do you think that the leaders of a contemporary society should possess? Explain your answer.

ANALYZING LITERATURE

Recognizing a Constitution

A **constitution** is a written or unwritten system of fundamental principles, laws, and customs that governs a nation or union of nations. The Iroquois Constitution outlines the principles on which the union of the Five Nations is based and presents the manner in which the confederation will be governed.

1. List three principles emphasized in the Iroquois Constitution.
2. (a) What is the function of the confederate council? (b) What sort of behavior is expected of its members?

CRITICAL THINKING AND READING

Interpreting Metaphors

A **metaphor** is an implied comparison between two seemingly dissimilar things. In most constitutions the rules and principles outlined are presented in a direct manner. In contrast, many of the ideas in The Iroquois Constitution are revealed through metaphors. As a result, you must interpret the comparison being made in each metaphor. For example, Dekanawidah uses the thickness of the council lords' skin as a metaphor for their ability to resist anger, offensive actions, and criticism.

1. For what is the planting of the Tree of Great Peace a metaphor?
2. What does Dekanawidah mean when he says that any nation outside the Five Nations that obeys the laws of the Great Peace "shall be welcomed to take shelter beneath the Tree of Long Leaves"?

UNDERSTANDING LANGUAGE

Using Native American Words

The American vocabulary includes many place names and common nouns from Native American languages. For example, the word *Connecticut* was taken from the Algonquian language family, in which it means "place of long river." Using a dictionary, find the Native American language from which each of the following words came, and find the meaning of the word in that language.

1. raccoon
2. Iowa
3. Oklahoma
4. Massachusetts
5. husky
6. Missouri
7. opossum
8. Nebraska
9. totem
10. Kentucky

THINKING AND WRITING

Comparing and Contrasting

Write a short essay contrasting the Iroquois constitution and the United States constitution. Carefully study both documents. In your prewriting, list the similarities and differences between the two documents. Then write a short essay in which you support a thesis statement about the contrasts between the two constitutions. When you revise, make sure that you have organized your writing so that your ideas are clear.

from *The Iroquois Constitution* 31

(Answers begin on p. 30)

ANSWERS TO CRITICAL THINKING AND READING

1. It is a metaphor for the establishment of peace among the five nations.
2. He means that other tribes will be able to join the confederation.

ANSWERS TO UNDERSTANDING LANGUAGE

1. raccoon: Algonquian word meaning "scratcher."
2. Iowa: Dakota word meaning "sleepy one."
3. Oklahoma: Choctaw words meaning "red people"
4. Massachusetts: Algonquian word meaning "at the big hill"
5. husky: Eskimo word meaning "a hardy dog used for pulling sleds"
6. Missouri: Algonquian word meaning "people of the big canoes"
7. opossum: Algonquian word meaning "white beasts"
8. Nebraska: Sioux word meaning "flat water"
9. totem: Algonquian word meaning "his relations"
10. Kentucky: Iroquois word meaning "flat land"

THINKING AND WRITING

For help with this assignment, students can refer to Lesson 16, "Writing a Comparative Evaluation," in the Handbook of Writing About Literature.

Writing Across the Curriculum For extra credit, you might want to have students research and report on the culture of the Iroquois. If you do, perhaps inform the social studies department of this assignment. Social studies teachers might provide guidance for students in conducting their research.

7. He had a great vision. He saw the weaknesses of their society and hoped to overcome them by uniting the Native American people. Because he had great faith in his fellow man, he entrusted his vision to them.

Applying

8. Answers will differ. Suggested Response: They should be responsible, just, honest, unbiased, and farsighted.

Challenge What might the leaders of contemporary societies learn from the *Iroquois Constitution*?

ANSWERS TO ANALYZING LITERATURE

1. Suggested Response: It emphasizes open membership, justice for all, and the integrity of the pledged word.
2. (a) It is responsible for relations with foreign tribes, and it makes laws for the confederacy. (b) They must be honest, unbiased, and just in their actions. However, their justice must be tempered with mercy. In their deliberations, they should be calm rather than emotional. They should respond well to criticism. They must consider the welfare of all people, now and in the future.

Focus

More About the Cultures The **Pima** are primarily known for their craftsmanship. However, their literature, some of which has been preserved through oral tradition, deserves attention as well. What might we learn about the Pima from their literature that we could not learn from their handiworks?

Members of the **Chippewa** tribe still compose verse that celebrates the nuances of nature. Why do you think that it is important for the Chippewa people to keep their oral tradition alive?

The **Sioux** placed a great deal of faith in dreams, which were often used as tools for determining future plans. What do you think people can learn from their dreams?

Pima

The Pima have lived in the Gila and Salt River valleys in southern Arizona for hundreds of years. A peaceful people, the Pima were friendly to both the Spanish explorers and the American settlers who ventured into their region. In the nineteenth century, as American pioneers flooded through Pima land on their way to the new frontier, the Pima fought against only their traditional enemies, the Apaches. Today about 5,500 Pima live on reservations near the Gila and Salt Rivers. Many maintain their oral literature, including songs like "From the Houses of Magic."

Chippewa

When the European settlers arrived in America, the Chippewa were a nomadic people living on the shores of Lake Superior. They sustained themselves by hunting and fishing. After the French gave them guns in exchange for furs, the Chippewa drove the Sioux and Fox tribes out of the Wisconsin area, seizing control of their land. The Chippewa's territory eventually extended from Lake Huron to central North Dakota. Today there are about 30,000 Chippewa living on reservations in North Dakota, Michigan, Wisconsin, and Minnesota, in addition to about 50,000 Chippewa living in Canada. Their early nomadic life made them sensitive to nature. This sensitivity is apparent in "Spring Song."

Teton Sioux

The Teton Sioux are the largest of seven tribes in the Sioux, or Dakota, Confederation. Originally living in the northeastern and north-central part of the country, the Teton Sioux were pushed westward to the midwestern plains by the Chippewa. Like the other tribes of the plains, the Teton Sioux were nomadic hunters who lived in tepees and depended on buffalo for food. In 1874, after gold was discovered on Teton Sioux land, the Teton Sioux became involved in conflicts with the United States Army with increasing frequency. In June of 1876, an army of Sioux defeated General Custer at the Battle of the Little Bighorn. In the months following the battle, the American forces began an intensive campaign that led to the final defeat of the Sioux at Wounded Knee, South Dakota in 1890. Today 40,000 Sioux live on reservations in Minnesota, Nebraska, Montana, North Dakota, and South Dakota.

32   The New Land

Objectives

1 To appreciate the oral tradition
2 To write a song

Support Material

Teaching Portfolio
Teacher Backup, p. 37
Usage and Mechanics Worksheet, p. 41
Vocabulary Check, p. 42
Analyzing Literature Worksheet, *Understanding the Oral Tradition,* p. 43
Language Worksheet, *Using Native American Words,* p. 44
Selection Test, p. 45

Art Transparency 2: *American Totem: Conrnucopia Bear,* by Don Nice

GUIDE FOR INTERPRETING

From the Houses of Magic; Spring Song; Song Concerning a Dream of the Thunderbirds

Literary Forms

The Oral Tradition. The oral tradition refers to the process of passing down sayings, songs, tales, and myths from one generation to the next by word of mouth. Native Americans did not have a written language, though they occasionally recorded myths or historical events in pictographs engraved on wood or hide or in symbols painted on strings of beads. Therefore, members of a tribe memorized the tribal literature and communicated it orally to the next generations. In some tribes, the person who had the best memory became the "keeper" of the tribe's history, songs, and myths.

Native American poetry began as songs chanted to a regular beat. Sometimes complicated melodies accompanied the words. To help the singer remember the poem or song, lines were often repeated, sometimes with a slight variation in the second line. Each line usually contained the same number of accented syllables or beats. Certain images and comparisons were also used so often that the listeners expected to hear them in tribal songs.

Commentary

The prose and poetry of Native Americans differ in purpose, form, and content. Prose stories, rhythmically intoned, tell the adventures of humans, animals, or supernatural beings; they recount ancient times, when the world was new. In this way information, beliefs, and values necessary for the survival of the tribe are passed on.

For Native Americans every thing in the world has its life and purpose, and every event is significant. Poetry attempts to use the magical power of language to connect with this mysterious world. Poems were used only on special occasions and usually dealt with mystical experiences or the symbolic meanings of things or events. They were sung or chanted rhythmically, usually to the accompaniment of drums or other instruments.

To understand the following poems, chant or sing them aloud, noticing the effects of rhythm and repetitions. Do any popular songs use rhythm and repetition in the same way and for the same effects? Explain.

Writing

The lyrics of songs often stand out in our memories. What qualities make lyrics memorable? Freewrite about the feelings you associate with one of your favorite songs and the qualities that make the lyrics easy to remember.

Guide for Interpreting **33**

Literary Focus Point out to students that the oral tradition has been kept alive in many Native American tribes. Discuss how this helps the Native Americans to maintain a connection to their cultural heritages. Why might it be difficult to maintain this connection while living in today's world?

Writing/Prior Knowledge You might want to discuss song lyrics with the class before students complete the freewriting assignment.

Vocabulary

Preteach the following vocabulary words:
gourd (gôrd) *n.:* The dried, hollowed-out shell of a fruit, used as a drinking vessel (p. 35, l. 27)
behold (bi hōld') *v.:* Look (p. 38, l. 1)

Motivation/Prior Knowledge
Ask students to imagine that they are Native Americans living before the arrival of the European settlers. What aspects of nature would seem magical to them?

Master Teacher Note A totem is an animal or natural object considered to be related by blood to a given tribe. To illustrate this concept, place Art Transparency 2, *American Totem: Cornucopia Bear* by Don Nice, on the overhead projector. Have students discuss the reasons why the Native Americans might have chosen the bear as a totem. Point out that "From the Houses of Magic" involves deer, another animal that served as a totem for many Native American tribes. Why would the Native Americans choose the deer as a totem? What does the Native Americans' belief in totems reveal about their relationship with nature?

Thematic Idea The spirituals "Swing Low, Sweet Chariot" (p. 426), and "Go Down, Moses" (p. 427) are also examples of songs that are part of our oral tradition.

Purpose-Setting Question
What is the speaker seeking?

1 **Discussion** What is the significance of the reference to antlers?

From the Houses of Magic

Pima

1

Down from the houses of magic,
Down from the houses of magic;
Blow the winds, and from my antlers
And my ears, they stronger gather.

5 Over there I ran trembling,
Over there I ran trembling,
For bows and arrows pursued me,
Many bows were on my trail.

2

I ran into the swamp confused,
10 There I heard the tadpoles singing.
I ran into the swamp confused,
Where the bark-clothed tadpoles sang.

In the west the dragonfly wanders,
Skimming the surfaces of the pools,
15 Touching only with his tail. He skims
With flapping and rustling wings.

Thence I ran as the darkness gathers,
Wearing cactus flowers in my hair.
Thence I ran as the darkness gathers,
20 In fluttering darkness to the singing-place.

3

At the time of the white dawning,
At the time of the white dawning,
I arose and went away,
At Blue Nightfall I went away.

INDIAN VILLAGE, RIVER GILA
Seth Eastman
Rhode Island School of Design Museum of Art

34   *The New Land*

Primary Source: The Pima

According to Richard Erdoes and Alfonso Ortiz in *American Indian Myths and Legends:*

The Pima, and their closely related neighbors and cousins, the Papago, are thought to be descendants of the ancient Hohokam—Those Who Have Gone Before—prehistoric makers of a vast system of irrigation canals. Members of the Uto-Aztecan language group, the Pima live in southern Arizona near the Gila and Salt rivers. Their earliest contacts with Spaniards occurred in 1589, when they lived in scattered *rancherías* tending their fields of corn, beans, squash, cotton, and tobacco. Like their Hohokam ancestors, they had an advanced system of irrigation. They were consistently peaceful and hospitable to whites.

The typical old-style Pima house was a windowless daub-and-wattle dwelling shaped like an inverted kettle. . . . ; The Pima are possibly the best Indian basket makers. Their women weave beautiful baskets of all shapes, designs, and sizes, from huge, man-high storage baskets to miniature horsehair baskets.

4

25 The evening glow yet lingers,
The evening glow yet lingers:
And I sit with my gourd rattle
Engaged in the sacred chant.
As I wave the eagle feathers
30 We hear the magic sounding.

The strong night is shaking me,
Just as once before he did
When in spirit I was taken
To the great magician's house.

5

35 Pitiable harlot though I am,
My heart glows with the singing
While the evening yet is young.
My heart glows with the singing.

6

Now the swallow begins his singing;
40 Now the swallow begins his singing;
And the women who are with me,
The poor women commence to sing.

The swallows met in the standing cliff;
The swallows met in the standing cliff;
45 And the rainbows arched above me,
There the blue rainbow-arches met.

7

In the reddish glow of the nightfall,
In the reddish glow of the nightfall.
I return to my burrow
50 About which the flowers bloom.

With the four eagle feathers,
With the four eagle feathers,
I stir the air. When I turn
My magic power is crossed.

From the Houses of Magic 35

Most Pima, together with members of the Maricopa community, now live on the Gila River Reservation in Arizona, with headquarters at Sacaton.

Humanities Note

Fine art, *Indian Village, River Gia* by Seth Eastman. Set Eastman (1808–1875) was an American painter known for his depiction of Native American life. After graduating from West Point, he was stationed at forts in Wisconsin and Minnesota. There he made numerous sketches, which he later transformed into paintings and illustrations of the Chippewas and the Sioux. In 1848 he was sent to Texas in Comanche country, where he created many drawings, watercolors, and oils. His unique combination of factual observation and romantic interpretation constitutes a valuable record of Native American life and of the landscape of the time.

This Eastman watercolor (based on a sketch by John Russell Bartlett, a U.S. border-survey commissioner of the 1850's) gives a glimpse into the daily life of a Pima village. Amidst the busy activity is a house under construction. Pima houses were made of saplings bent into domes and then covered with brush. Eastman also provides a romantic view of the landscape in which these people lived.

You might ask the following questions:
1. What might the log structure in the center of the picture be?
2. Which images from "The Houses of Magic" do you find echoed in this painting?
3. What can you learn about daily life in a Pima village from this picture?

2 Discussion Native Americans often used images to describe their deepest feelings and emotions. What do these lines convey about the inner world of the speaker?

Reader's Response Which image do you think is the most beautiful? Why?

NATIVE AMERICAN
CULTURES

0   500   1000 Miles
0   500   1000 Kilometers

THINKING ABOUT THE SELECTION

Recalling

1. Summarize the narrator's movements. What does the narrator do "at the time of the white dawning"?
2. (a) What does the narrator hear while waving the eagle feathers? (b) Where do the swallows meet? (c) What does the narrator do with four eagle feathers at the end of the song?

Interpreting

3. (a) What time of day is described in the poem? (b) What details indicate that it is that time?
4. List three emotions or feelings that the song conveys. How are they conveyed?

Applying

5. The Pima, as well as many other Native American tribes, considered the deer to be a sacred animal. (a) What qualities of deer make them appropriate for being considered sacred? (b) How does the way in which most people today regard deer differ from the Pima view? (c) What does this difference suggest about the contrasts between Pima society and today's society?

ANALYZING LITERATURE

Understanding the Oral Tradition

The oral tradition is the process of passing down literature from generation to generation. Poems and songs were an important part of the Native American oral tradition. Because they had to be memorized, various techniques, such as repeated lines and images and the use of lines with same number of accented syllables, or beats, were used to make them easier to remember. For example, many lines in "From the Houses of Magic" are repeated.

1. What one image, or word picture, is repeated several times in the song?
2. Aside from the use of repetition, in what way are many of the lines similar?

36   The New Land

Spring Song
Chippewa

As my eyes
search
the prairie
1 I feel the summer
in the spring.

Presentation
Motivation/Prior Knowledge
Have students imagine that they are standing in a prairie during the springtime. What do they see? What do they feel?

Thematic Idea N. Scott Momaday discusses the meaning of "Spring Song" in "A Vision Beyond Time and Place" on page 1060.

Purpose-Setting Question
What does the speaker see?

1 **Discussion** What does the speaker mean when he says that he feels "the summer in the spring"?

THINKING ABOUT THE SELECTION

Recalling

1. What two seasons are mentioned in the poem?

Interpreting

2. What type of weather does the speaker of the poem seem to be experiencing?

3. What is meant by the statement "I feel the summer in the spring"?

Applying

4. What seasonal change do you consider to to the most dramatic? Why?

Spring Song 37

Closure and Extension

ANSWERS TO THINKING ABOUT THE SELECTION
Recalling

1. The poem refers to summer and spring.

Interpreting

2. He seems to be experiencing warm weather.
3. The speaker senses the coming of summer.

Applying

4. Answers will differ. Suggested Response: The passage from winter into spring is the most dramatic seasonal change because of the rebirth that occurs in nature during the spring.

Motivation/Prior Knowledge
Have students imagine that they
are standing outside in the midst
of a thunderstorm and are unaware of the scientific explanation for this event. How would
they respond?

Master Teacher Note To set an
appropriate mood, bring in a recording of Native American
chants. Highlight the repetition of
sound and the rhythmic quality of
these chants.

Purpose-Setting Question
What has happened to the
speaker?

1 **Discussion** How does the title
relate to the content of the song?

Humanities Note

Fine Art: *The Mystic,* William R.
Leigh. William R. Leigh (1866–
1955) an American Western artist, was born in West Virginia. In
1906 he made the first of many
trips to the West. It became his
greatest source of inspiration.
Leigh spent time among Native
Americans, cowboys, and "bad
men". He always sketched what
he saw and wrote stories about
them. Leigh considered himself
to be a realist and strict docu-
mentarian. However, his pictures
portray some of the more romantic aspects of life in the West. He
is often referred to as the "Sage-
brush Rembrandt."

This picture shows Leigh's
impression of the mystic. It reveals the sensitivity and respect
he had for the Native Americans.
If this is a romanticized view,
Leigh has used it in a positive
way, to enhance the viewers perception of a truly noble scene.

You might ask students
these questions:
1. What do you think is happening in this picture?
2. How does this art relate to the
song?

Song Concerning a Dream of the Thunderbirds

Teton Sioux

1

Friends, behold!
Sacred I have been made.
Friends, behold!
In a sacred manner
5　I have been influenced
At the gathering of the clouds.
Sacred I have been made,
Friends, behold!
Sacred I have been made.

THE MYSTIC
William R. Leigh
*The Thomas Gilcrease Institute of American History and Art,
Tulsa, Oklahoma*

THINKING ABOUT THE SELECTION
Recalling

1. What two lines appear three times in the song?

Interpreting

2. (a) To what does the "gathering of the clouds" refer? (b) How does it relate to the title of the poem?
3. How does the pattern of the song add emphasis to lines 4–6?

Applying

4. In many ancient cultures, thunderstorms inspired fear and awe. (a) Why did the people of these cultures react this way? (b) What other natural occurrences might have inspired such emotions in these cultures?

THINKING AND WRITING
Writing a Song

Today's songwriters often use some of the same techniques when writing lyrics that the Native American tribes did. Try some of these techniques as you compose a song. First decide on a topic you might like to write a song about and an audience for the song. Brainstorm for ideas about your topic and select some that might work for your audience. Then review your notes about song lyrics and look over the Native American songs once again, taking note of the qualities that make them easy to remember. Once you have a topic and an audience, write a song using the techniques you observed in the songs of the Native American tribes and other song-writers. Then, revise your song, making sure that it is appropriate for your audience, and prepare a final draft.

Closure and Extension

ANSWERS TO THINKING ABOUT THE SELECTION
Recalling
1. The line "Friends, behold!" and "Sacred I have been made" each appear three times.

Interpreting
2. (a) It refers to the time immediately preceding a storm and may be symbolic of the power of Nature. (b) In Native American myth, the thunderbird causes the lightning and thunder that come before the storm.
3. These lines appear between a re-peated series of three lines.

Applying
5. (a) Answers will differ. Suggested Response: Thunderstorms are loud and violent. (b) Suggested Response: Earthquakes and tor-nadoes might have inspired simi-lar responses.

Thinking and Writing

For help with this assignment, students can refer to Lesson 18, "Writing a Poem," in the Hand-book of Writing About Literature.

Publishing Student Writing Ask student volunteers to share their songs with the class.

CROSS CURRENTS

Native American Voices Today

The coming of white settlers to North America in the seventeenth century resulted in almost complete destruction of the Native American societies there. Whole tribes were nearly wiped out in battles or by diseases brought by the Europeans. Survivors were forced off their lands and herded indiscriminately into designated reservations, where many more died. Those left were soon surrounded and controlled by a society they had little knowledge of and no place in.

The land on which each tribe lived was central and sacred to their life. It fed and clothed them. Just as important, the land contained the bones of their ancestors and therefore the knowledge and power of the past, of the Old Ones. Separated from this power and obliged to learn the white man's ways to survive, Native Americans were in danger of losing forever their identity, language, and traditions. Fortunately, through dedicated work by determined tribal members and some enlightened whites, the Native Americans and the United States have not completely lost this heritage.

A REBIRTH OF NATIVE AMERICAN LITERATURE

Recently, Native American voices are once again heard in the land. Some are angry, some sorrowful, others wryly comic—all are powerful. Native Americans are again telling stories and composing poems of their past and present, attempting to create connections between them. Many of their books have become best-sellers.

The one book most credited with beginning the current "rebirth" of Native American literature is N. Scott Momaday's Pulitzer Prize-winning novel *House Made of Dawn*, published in 1969. Momaday (page 1058) was quickly followed by such writers as Leslie Marmon Silko (Laguna Pueblo), Simon Ortiz (Acoma Pueblo), and James Welch (Blackfeet/Gros Ventre).

All these writers vividly portray the struggle of Native Americans to keep hold of their past, live in the present, and create a future. None of the authors romanticize either the past or the present, as many nineteenth-century writers did. The characters in their novels, like themselves, are often only part Native American and must relearn what their grandparents grew up knowing. At the same time, they are living in a modern society where traditional ways of living do not seem possible.

Louise Erdrich

The tragic—and comic—elements of these characters' lives are vividly portrayed by author Louise Erdrich. Erdrich is a member of the Turtle Mountain Chippewa Reservation in North Dakota, where her grandparents lived. She now lives in New Hampshire with her husband, Michael Dorris, a professor of Native American literature at Dartmouth College.

Erdrich has published three novels, two volumes of poetry, and numerous short stories. Her novels are set in the vicinity of the Chippewa territory and are peopled with sev-

eral generations of various Native American families. *Love Medicine*, published in 1984, and *The Beet Queen*, published in 1986, cover roughly the same time period—from 1934 to 1984. *Tracks*, however, published in 1988, precedes the other two chronologically; its events occur between 1912 and 1924. In all three novels, many of the same characters occur but at different points in their lives. The result is a fascinating intertwining of lives and events.

Tracks describes the early twentieth-century struggles of the Native Americans with epidemics, famine, and the dwindling of their lands. In this novel the mysterious, mythic forces of the Chippewa gods are felt strongly through a central character with supernatural powers. This situation is the background for *Love Medicine* and *The Beet Queen*. In these two novels, we meet the families—parents who fight to stay on the grandparents' land and the children who are dislocated between the ways of the reservation and the modern world. Most of the youngest generation have disappeared to Chicago or Minneapolis, but some still recognize their needs for the bonds of family and tradition.

At the end of *Love Medicine*, one of the young men sums up their common situation: "I'd heard that this river was the last of an ancient ocean, miles deep, that once had covered the Dakotas and solved all our problems. It was easy to still imagine us beneath them vast unreasonable waves, but the truth is we live on dry land." His is the voice of the contemporary Native American, struggling to reconcile his place in the modern world with his heritage.

40   The New Land

Living in the New Land

THE ARRIVAL OF THE ENGLISHMEN IN VIRGINIA
Colored Line Engraving, 1590, by Theodor de Bry
The Granger Collection

Humanities Note

Fine art, *The Arrival of the Englishmen in Virginia,* 1590, by Theodor de Bry. Born in Belgium, Theodor de Bry (1528–1598) traveled to England in the 1580's. Although he apparently never left Europe, de Bry illustrated beautiful books on travel and geography, including the *Briefe and True Report of the New Found Land of Virginia* (published in 1595 in Franfurt).

In an age of overseas exploration, maps and illustrations of North America and other faroff regions were of particular interest in Europe, especially among the victims of religious persecution and among mercantile companies seeking to expand their trade routes. The maps by de Bry, presumably based on accounts by travelers, portray the landing of a sailing ship onto a peaceful settlement. The sunken ships and the sea monster symbolize such hazards as violent storms and pirates.

Master Teacher Note To help students envision Puritan New England, place Art Transparency 3, *The Salem Wolf* by Howard Pyle, on the overhead projector. What does the painting reveal about the manner in which the Puritans dressed? What does it suggest about the Puritans' relationship with nature? What does it reveal about the hardships with which the Puritans were faced?

JOHN SMITH

1580–1631

John Smith was a leader in the settlement of Jamestown, Virginia, the first successful English colony in America, and was one of England's most famous New World explorers. The stories of his adventures, often embellished by his own pen, fascinated European readers of his day and continue to provide a wealth of details about the early exploration and colonization of America.

The son of a farmer, Smith was born in Lincolnshire, England. He left home at the age of sixteen to become a soldier. During the next ten years, Smith traveled throughout Europe and the Near East, fought in numerous battles, and was promoted to captain. Then, in 1606, a year after his return to England, Smith led a group of colonists across the Atlantic to establish a settlement in the New World. The group landed in Virginia in 1607 and founded Jamestown.

As president of the colony from 1608 to 1609, Smith helped assure the colony's success, obtaining food, enforcing discipline, and dealing with the native tribes who inhabited the region. In 1608 Smith published *A True Relation of Virginia,* the first English book describing life in America. In 1609, after being burned in a gunpowder accident and involved in disputes with other colonists, Smith traveled back to England.

Smith made two more voyages to America in 1614 and 1615, exploring and mapping the coast of the region he named New England. Then Smith returned to England, settling in London, where he lived for the remainder of his life. During his later years, he published his two most famous works, *A Description of New England* (1616) and *The General History of Virginia, New England, and the Summer Isles* (1624).

Smith was at heart a traveler. He made several determined attempts to reach North America again before reluctantly settling in London. Bad weather, lack of money, and (once) pirates stopped him. Although he was not sympathetic with Puritans, he offered to lead the group sailing on the *Mayflower* in 1620. They did not accept his offer but were happy to use his maps.

In *The General History of Virginia,* which describes the founding of Jamestown, Smith attempts to dispel English misconceptions about America and encourages others to settle in the New World. The book also includes an account of what has become Smith's most famous adventure. According to his story, Smith was captured by the Native Americans and faced execution until the chief's daughter Pocahontas saved him from death. This episode, along with the other experiences Smith describes, provides an understanding and appreciation of what the early colonists' lives were like.

GUIDE FOR INTERPRETING

from The General History of Virginia

Literary Forms

History. A history is a factual account of events in the life or development of a people, nation, institution, or culture. Histories, which usually recount events chronologically, often include analysis and explanation. Some histories are firsthand accounts by people who lived through the events. Other histories are secondhand, or secondary, accounts by people who have researched the events but did not live through them.

Firsthand accounts are likely to be subjective because of the writer's personal involvement with the events. Also, they sometimes lack accuracy because the writer often wrote to persuade or entertain the audiences of the time. For example, John Smith often exaggerates events in *The General History of Virginia*. At the same time, firsthand accounts often capture the flavor of living through those events.

Commentary

All his adventurous life, Smith was in trouble with authority, sometimes because he was more capable than his superiors. The private trading company in England that financed the expedition knew little about the wilderness conditions of the North American continent and was unrealistic in its expectations of material gain from the colony. Smith's practical survival skills saved the settlement, but even that did not keep him from censure and near imprisonment.

It is not surprising, then, that he tried to give his version of the story in his writings. (Although Pocahontas was a real person, Smith's adventure with her is doubtful, since he did not mention it in two earlier accounts of the same events.)

In the following selection, Smith describes, seventeen years later, the hard times in 1607 when the settlers fought to survive until a supply ship could arrive from England. Notice his vivid and detailed description of life then. Notice also when he interprets or explains events or gives his own opinion and when he perhaps exaggerates. Can we ever depend on a history to be completely accurate and unbiased? Could you and another student agree on an account of what happened in class yesterday and why?

Writing

The early American settlers faced a great number of hardships. List the problems you think the colonists faced. Then freewrite about how you would have dealt with each of these hardships if you had been in their situation.

Literary Focus While firsthand accounts may not necessarily be historically accurate, they give the reader a rare opportunity to get acquainted with a historical figure through that figure's own words. The reader is also exposed to the way in which language was used in a particular period of history and is introduced to alternate ways of thinking and interpreting events.

Writing/Prior Knowledge Before students complete the writing activity, have them consider what it would be like to travel to an uncharted land, not knowing what they would find there in terms of climate, forms of life, dangers, and potentially even treasures.

Vocabulary

Preteach the following vocabulary words:
pilfer (pil′ fər) *v.*: Steal (p. 44)
palisades (pal′e sādz′) *n.*: Large pointed stakes set in the ground to form a fence used for defense (p. 44).
conceits (kən sēts′) *n.*: Strange for fanciful ideas (p. 45).
mollified (mäl′ə fīd) *v.*: Soothed; calmed (p. 47).

Spelling Tip Point out the *ei* combination after *c* in *conceits*.

Guide for Interpreting 43

Objectives

1 To recognize historical accounts
2 To recognize the author's purpose
3 To write a historical account

Support Material

Teaching Portfolio
Teacher Backup, p. 47
Grammar in Action, *Understanding Diction,* p. 51
Usage and Mechanics Worksheet, p. 53
Vocabulary Check, p. 54
Critical Thinking and Reading Worksheet, *Separating Objective from Subjective Details,* p. 55

Language Worksheet, *Choosing the Meaning that Fits the Context,* p. 56
Selection Test, p. 57
Art Transparency 2: *American Totem: Cornucopia Bear,* by Don Nice

Presentation

Motivation/Prior Knowledge
Ask your students to imagine that they were among the first settlers to arrive in the new land. How would they feel? How would they feed and shelter themselves? How would they approach the natives?

Master Teacher Note This selection focuses on events that took place in 1607, when a ship carrying English colonists arrived at Jamestown, Virginia. Provide the historical context for the narrative by reviewing English history of the period with students. Point out that Elizabeth I had died only four years before, leaving the throne in the hands of James I, a much less popular monarch. Also point out that the defeat of the Spanish Armada nineteen years earlier had left the seas almost entirely at the disposal of the English.

Thematic Idea Another selection that deals with the arrival of English Settlers in the new world is the excerpt from *Of Plymouth Plantation* by William Bradford (p. 52).

Purpose-Setting Question
What picture do you get of the conditions at Jamestown? What do you learn about John Smith as an individual?

from # The General History of Virginia

John Smith

What Happened Till the First Supply

Being thus left to our fortunes, it fortuned[1] that within ten days, scarce ten amongst us could either go[2] or well stand, such extreme weakness and sickness oppressed us. And thereat none need marvel if they consider the cause and reason, which was this: While the ships stayed, our allowance was somewhat bettered by a daily proportion of biscuit which the sailors would pilfer to sell, give, or exchange with us for money, sassafras,[3] or furs. But when they departed, there remained neither tavern, beer house, nor place of relief but the common kettle.[4] Had we been as free from all sins as gluttony and drunkenness we might have been canonized for saints, but our President[5] would never have been admitted for engrossing to his private,[6] oatmeal, sack,[7] oil, aqua vitae,[8] beef, eggs, or what not but the kettle; that indeed he allowed equally to be distributed, and that was half a pint of wheat and as much barley boiled with water for a man a day, and this, having fried some twenty-six weeks in the ship's hold, contained as many worms as grains so that we might truly call it rather so much bran than corn; our drink was water, our lodgings castles in the air.

With this lodging and diet, our extreme toil in bearing and planting palisades so strained and bruised us and our continual labor in the extremity of the heat had so weakened us, as were cause sufficient to have made us as miserable in our native country or any other place in the world.

From May to September, those that escaped lived upon sturgeon and sea crabs. Fifty in this time we buried; the rest seeing the President's projects to escape these miseries in our pinnace[9] by flight (who all this time had neither felt want nor sickness) so

---

1. **fortuned:** Happened.
2. **go:** Be active.
3. **sassafras:** A tree, the root of which was valued for its supposed medicinal qualities.
4. **common kettle:** Communal cooking pot.
5. **President:** Wingfield, the leader of the colony.
6. **engrossing to his private:** Taking for his own use.
7. **sack** *n.*: A type of white wine.
8. **aqua vitae** (ak′wə vīt′ē): Brandy.
9. **pinnace** (pin′ is) *n.*: A small sailing ship.

Grammar in Action

Diction refers to the words a writer chooses and the way he or she uses these words. Diction is often the most distinctive stylistic mark of a writer. Skilled writers manipulate their diction to communicate specific ideas, to set the tone of their writing, and to elicit certain responses from the reader. For example, when choosing a specific word, writers must keep in mind the purpose of their writing and the connotation of each word they choose. If they wish to persuade their readers, they will choose certain words over others. Because John Smith wished to convey a particular bias toward the settlers and against the Native Americans in *The General History of Virginia,* he used words that would elicit that same bias in the reader. Look at the following example:

"Six or seven weeks those *barbarians* kept him *prisoner,* many strange triumphs and *conjurations* they made of him, yet he so *demeaned* himself amongst them, as he not only diverted them from surprising the fort, but procured his own *liberty,* and got himself and his company such estimation amongst them, that those *savages* admired him."

What does each of the italicized words connote? What impression of the natives do they leave the reader? of the settlers? The

moved our dead spirits as we deposed him and established Ratcliffe in his place . . .

But now was all our provision spent, the sturgeon gone, all helps abandoned, each hour expecting the fury of the savages; when God, the patron of all good endeavors, in that desperate extremity so changed the hearts of the savages that they brought such plenty of their fruits and provision as no man wanted.

And now where some affirmed it was ill done of the Council[10] to send forth men so badly provided, this incontradictable reason will show them plainly they are too ill advised to nourish such ill conceits: First, the fault of our going was our own; what could be thought fitting or necessary we had, but what we should find, or want, or where we should be, we were all ignorant and supposing to make our passage in two months, with victual to live and the advantage of the spring to work; we were at sea five months where we both spent our victual and lost the opportunity of the time and season to plant, by the unskillful presumption of our ignorant transporters that understood not at all what they undertook.

Such actions have ever since the world's beginning been subject to such accidents, and everything of worth is found full of difficulties, but nothing so difficult as to establish a commonwealth so far remote from men and means and where men's minds are so untoward[11] as neither do well themselves nor suffer others. But to proceed.

The new President and Martin, being little beloved, of weak judgment in dangers, and less industry in peace, committed the managing of all things abroad[12] to Captain Smith, who, by his own example, good words, and fair promises, set some to mow, others to bind thatch, some to build houses, others to thatch them, himself always bearing the greatest task for his own share, so that in short time he provided most of them lodgings, neglecting any for himself . . .

Leading an expedition on the Chickahominy River, Captain Smith and his men are attacked by Indians, and Smith is taken prisoner.

When this news came to Jamestown, much was their sorrow for his loss, few expecting what ensued.

Six or seven weeks those barbarians kept him prisoner, many strange triumphs and conjurations they made of him, yet he so demeaned himself amongst them, as he not only diverted them from surprising the fort, but procured his own liberty, and got himself and his company such estimation amongst them, that those savages admired him.

The manner how they used and delivered him is as followeth:

The savages having drawn from George Cassen whither Captain Smith was gone, prosecuting that opportunity they followed him with three hundred bowmen, conducted by the King of Pamunkee,[13] who in divisions searching the turnings of the river found Robinson and Emry by the fireside; those they shot full of arrows and slew. Then finding the Captain, as is said, that used the savage that was his guide as his shield (three of them being slain and divers[14] others so galled),[15] all the rest would not come near him. Thinking thus to have returned to his boat, regarding them, as he marched, more than his way, slipped up to the middle in an oozy creek and his savage with him; yet dared they not come to him till being near dead with cold he threw away his

10. **Council:** The seven persons in charge of the expedition.
11. **untoward:** Stubborn.
12. **abroad:** Outside the palisades.

13. **Pamunkee:** The Pamunkee River.
14. **divers** (dī' vərz) *adj.*: Several.
15. **galled:** Wounded.

from *The General History of Virginia*   45

1 **Enrichment** The London Trading Company, later known as the Virginia Company, was the financial backer of the expedition to Jamestown. The Company knew little about the wilderness conditions of North America and was unrealistic in its expectations of material gain from the colony.

2 **Literary Focus** What is Smith saying in this paragraph? How does this kind of commentary fit into a history?

3 **Reading Strategy** Point out examples of opinions expressed by Smith thus far.

4 **Discussion** How do Smith's references to the Indians reflect his attitudes about them? How could Smith's bias affect the attitudes of readers in his own day and in the future? What repercussions might this have had for the Indians?

5 **Reading Strategy** Ask the students to predict what is to come. What clues does the preceding paragraph give about the outcome of Smith's ordeal with the Indians?

words *barbarians, savages,* and *conjurations* leave readers with the image of wild, uncultured, and dangerous animals who performed magic. Finally, when referring to the settler who was held *prisoner,* Smith says that he *demeaned,* or lowered, himself to gain his *liberty,* connoting that the settler was the one who was the victim and acted appropriately.

Student Activity 1. What does each of the following italicized words connote in the following passage from *The General History of Virginia*? Why do you think Smith chose these words?

"But now was all our provision spent, the sturgeon gone, all helps *abondoned,* each hour expecting the *fury* of the *savages.*

Student Activity 2. To be an active, responsible reader, you must analyze a writer's diction and determine the reasons behind his or her word choice. Select an article from a newspaper and magazine and analyze the writer's diction. For what purpose is the author writing? Is the article biased? What words persuade a reader toward that bias? Rewrite a portion of the article to lead the reader in another direction. Share your work with classmates.

arms. Then according to their composition[16] they drew him forth and led him to the fire where his men were slain. Diligently they chafed his benumbed limbs.

He demanding for their captain, they showed him Opechancanough, King of Pamunkee, to whom he gave a round ivory double compass dial. Much they marveled at the playing of the fly and needle,[17] which they could see so plainly and yet not touch it because of the glass that covered them. But when he demonstrated by that globe-like jewel the roundness of the earth and skies, the sphere of the sun, moon, and stars, and how the sun did chase the night round about the world continually, the greatness of the land and sea, the diversity of nations, variety of complexions, and how we were to them antipodes[18] and many other such like matters, they all stood as amazed with admiration.

Nothwithstanding, within an hour after, they tied him to a tree, and as many as could stand about him prepared to shoot him, but the King holding up the compass in his hand, they all laid down their bows and arrows and in a triumphant manner led him to Orapaks where he was after their manner kindly feasted and well used. . . .

At last they brought him to Werowocomoco, where was Powhatan, their Emperor. Here more than two hundred of those grim courtiers stood wondering at him, as he had been a monster, till Powhatan and his train had put themselves in their greatest braveries. Before a fire upon a seat like a bedstead, he sat covered with a great robe made of raccoon skins and all the tails hanging by. On either hand did sit a young wench of sixteen or eighteen years and along on each side the house, two rows of men and behind them as many women, with all their heads and

---

16. composition: Ways.
17. fly and needle: Parts of a compass.
18. antipodes (an tip′ ə dēz′): On the opposite side of the globe.

shoulders painted red, many of their heads bedecked with the white down of birds, but every one with something, and a great chain of white beads about their necks.

At his entrance before the King, all the people gave a great shout. The Queen of Appomattoc was appointed to bring him water to wash his hands, and another brought him a bunch of feathers, instead of a towel, to dry them; having feasted him after their best barbarous manner they could, a long consultation was held, but the conclusion was, two great stones were brought before Powhatan; then as many as could, laid hands on him, dragged him to them, and thereon laid his head and being ready with their clubs to beat out his brains, Pocahontas, the King's dearest daughter, when no entreaty could prevail, got his head in her arms and laid her own upon his to save him from death; whereat the Emperor was contented he should live to make him hatchets, and her bells, beads, and copper, for they thought him as well of all occupations as themselves.[19] For the King himself will make his own robes, shoes, bows, arrows, pots; plant, hunt, or do anything so well as the rest.

Two days after, Powhatan, having disguised himself in the most fearfulest manner he could, caused Captain Smith to be brought forth to a great house in the woods and there upon a mat by the fire to be left alone. Not long after, from behind a mat that divided the house, was made the most dolefulest noise he ever heard; then Powhatan more like a devil than a man, with some two hundred more as black as himself, came unto him and told him now they were friends, and presently he should go to Jamestown to send him two great guns and a grindstone for which he would give him the country of Capahowasic and forever esteem him as his son Nantaquond.

---

19. as well . . . themselves: Capable of making them just as wel¹ as they could themselves.

6

FOUNDING OF THE FIRST PERMANENT ENGLISH SETTLEMENT
IN AMERICA
A. C. Warren
New York Public Library

Fine art, *Founding of the First Permanent English Settlement in America,* A. C. Warren. Asa Coolidge Warren (1819–1904) was born in Boston. The son of a portrait and miniature painter, Warren was apprenticed in 1833 to jewelers in Boston. Showing an inclination toward engraving, he was then apprenticed to an engraver. He became a reputable line-engraver, but because of eye problems he abandoned engraving for about five years. During this time he drew on wood for other engravers. In 1863 Warren moved to New York and began engraving again, for book publishers. In 1899 he lost the sight in one eye and was compelled to stop engraving altogether. He occupied his later years with painting.

In the art of engraving, a design is created by making incised lines and crevices into a copper or other metal plate. These crevices are filled with ink and the metal surface is then wiped clean, leaving ink in the incised lines. Damp paper is then pressed onto the plate with great pressure, actually forcing the paper into the inked grooves. Due to the amount of pressure required, the edge of the plate actually makes a ridge or "plate mark" along the edges of the design. The inked lines are visibly in relief above the paper surface, when viewed in the proper light. Because every line in an engraving must be carefully planned and executed, the resulting pictures have a tendency to be stiff and cold.

You might use the following questions for discussion:
1. What scene from the selection does this engraving illustrate?
2. Do you think the engraved scene is realistic, or romanticized? Explain.

So to Jamestown with twelve guides Powhatan sent him. That night they quartered in the woods, he still expecting (as he had done all this long time of his imprisonment) every hour to be put to one death or other, for all their feasting. But almighty God (by His divine providence) had mollified the hearts of those stern barbarians with compassion. The next morning betimes they came to the fort, where Smith having used the savages with what kindness he could, he showed Rawhunt, Powhatan's trusty servant, two demiculverins[20] and a millstone to carry Powhatan; they found them somewhat too heavy, but when they did see him discharge them, being loaded with stones, among the boughs of a great tree loaded with icicles, the ice and branches came so tumbling down that the poor savages ran away

---

20. demiculverins (dem' ē kul' vər inz): Large cannons.

from *The General History of Virginia*   47

7 Discussion How does Smith's depiction of the Indians change toward the end of his captivity? How might he have hoped this change would affect the reader's opinion of his character?

8 Discussion Ask the students to think about what happened in Jamestown during Smith's absence. Had anything changed? How might Smith's experiences affect the state of affairs in the colony?

9 Discussion Ask the class to examine how Smith's attitude concerning the settler's situation has changed since the early part of his account.

10 Enrichment John Smith charted the coast of New England in 1614, and, in 1616, he published his findings in a work entitled *A Description of New England.*

Reader's Response Would you like to have been one of the first settlers in the New World? Why or why not?

half dead with fear. But at last we regained some conference with them and gave them such toys and sent to Powhatan, his women, and children such presents as gave them in general full content.

Now in Jamestown they were all in combustion,[21] the strongest preparing once more to run away with the pinnace; which, with the hazard of his life, with saker falcon[22] and musket shot, Smith forced now the third time to stay or sink.

Some, no better than they should be, had plotted with the President the next day to have him put to death by the Levitical law,[23] for the lives of Robinson and Emry; pretending the fault was his that had led

---

21. combustion: Tumult.
22. saker falcon: Small cannon.
23. Levitical law: "He that killeth man shall surely be put to death" (Leviticus 24:17).

them to their ends; but he quickly took such order with such lawyers that he laid them by their heels till he sent some of them prisoners for England.

Now every once in four or five days, Pocahontas with her attendants brought him so much provision that saved many of their lives, that else for all this had starved with hunger.

His relation of the plenty he had seen, especially at Werowocomoco, and of the state and bounty of Powhatan (which till that time was unknown), so revived their dead spirits (especially the love of Pocahontas) as all men's fear was abandoned.

Thus you may see what difficulties still crossed any good endeavor: and the good success of the business being thus oft brought to the very period of destruction; yet you see by what strange means God hath still delivered it.

THINKING ABOUT THE SELECTION

Recalling

1. (a) What hardships do the colonists face during their first several months in the New World? (b) What assistance do they receive?
2. (a) What criticisms does Smith make of the new president and colonist Martin? (b) What does Smith praise?
3. (a) What happens to Smith during his expedition on the Chickahominy River? (b) How is he saved from death?
4. What does Smith discover when he returns to Jamestown after his release?

Interpreting

5. What impression of Smith do you get from this account?
6. What seems to be Smith's attitude toward the Native Americans?
7. Why does Smith write in the third person, referring to himself as "he" instead of "I"?

Applying

8. What are some situations in the world today in which people are coping with great hardships?

ANALYZING LITERATURE

Understanding a History

A **history** is a nonfiction account of events that occurred to a people, nation, institution, or culture. Histories may be either firsthand accounts, written by someone who was involved with the events, or secondhand accounts, written by someone who was not involved in the events. Firsthand accounts, which sometimes lack factual accuracy, tend to be subjective, but they often capture the flavor of the time. For example, while *The General History of Virginia* conveys a sense of life in the Jamestown settlement, most historians consider Smith's account of his rescue by Pocahontas to be greatly exaggerated.

1. Find two examples in which Smith displays subjectivity in recounting events.
2. List three details that capture the flavor of life in Jamestown.

CRITICAL THINKING AND READING

Recognizing Author's Purpose

While the **purpose** of most secondhand historical accounts is to inform, many firsthand ac-

48 *The New Land*

counts are written to entertain or persuade. For example, Smith's primary purpose in writing *The General History of Virginia* was probably to encourage other English men and women to settle in the New World.

1. In what way is the primary purpose of *The General History of Virginia* made apparent?
2. What other purposes does Smith appear to have had?

THINKING AND WRITING

Writing a Historical Account

During our lifetime we all live through or are in some way a part of important events. Think of an important historical event that occurred during your lifetime or an event in your community. Brainstorm to recall details of the event, and, if necessary, research the event in your library. Then, after listing the details in chronological order, write a brief secondhand account. Try to be as objective as possible. When you revise, make sure you have included enough information to inform thoroughly a reader who has no prior knowledge of the event. Try to remove any subjective details you may have included. At this point, you might decide to include tables or maps to make your information clearer. Tables, like the one below, present facts and figures in rows and columns.

Founding of the Colonies

Colony/Date Founded	Leader	Reasons Founded
New England Colonies		
Massachusetts		
Plymouth/1620	William Bradford	Religious freedom
Massachusetts Bay/1630	John Winthrop	Religious freedom
New Hampshire/1622	Ferdinando Gorges John Mason	Profit from trade and fishing
Connecticut		
Hartford/1636	Thomas Hooker	Expand trade; religious and political freedom
New Haven/1639		
Rhode Island/1636	Roger Williams	Religious freedom
Middle Colonies		
New York/1624	Peter Minuit	Expand trade
Delaware/1638	Swedish settlers	Expand trade
New Jersey/1664	John Berkeley George Carteret	Profit from land sales; religious and political freedom
Pennsylvania/1682	William Penn	Profit from land sales; religious and political freedom
Southern Colonies		
Virginia/1607	John Smith	Trade and farming
Maryland/1632	Lord Baltimore	Profit from land sales; religious and political freedom
The Carolinas/1663	Group of eight proprietors	Trade and farming; religious freedom
North Carolina/1712		
South Carolina/1712		
Georgia/1732	James Oglethorpe	Profit, home for debtors; buffer against Spanish Florida

from *The General History of Virginia*   49

Focus

More about the Author Orphaned in the first year of life, William Bradford was trained to be a farmer by relatives. Receiving little formal education, Bradford was forced to educate himself. While his book was not published until more than two hundred years after its completion, it was known to the world and even quoted by colonial historians before its publication. Today, the book is considered by many to be an American classic. What does Bradford's ability to overcome his lack of education tell about his character?

Critical Evaluation Plymouth, Massachusetts, was a microcosm of what the United States was to become. One reason for this was the political and religious guidance of one of the most influential colonists, William Bradford. In *Bradford of Plymouth,* Bradford Smith wrote this about William Bradford's influence and the importance of Plymouth colony: "As in Bradford, so in his little colony of Plymouth we see America in the making . . . Here originate the civil marriage service, outright ownership of land . . . , a classless society in an age of rigid class distinctions, and government by free associations of the governed. The Pilgrims proved that a community of families could survive in the new world and that it could live at peace with the surrounding Indians. Out of Plymouth came a system of government—the town meeting —which colored and enriched the bloodstream of American democracy and which continues a vital force to this day. . . . And out of Plymouth came that most valuable of a people's possessions—the myth, the credo which guides their best efforts and tells them, through an idealized memory of the past, what they ought to be."

1590–1657

Thirteen years after the first permanent English settlement was established in Jamestown, another group of colonists, known as the Pilgrims, landed on the shore of what is now Massachusetts. William Bradford, one of their leaders, recorded the experiences of these early settlers in a factually accurate account.

Bradford was born in Yorkshire, England. Having developed a strong devotion to religion early in life, Bradford joined a group of Puritan extremists, who felt that the Church of England was corrupt and wished to separate themselves from it entirely. In the face of stiff persecution, Bradford's group eventually fled to Leyden, Holland, where Bradford worked as a weaver. Later Bradford and many other group members left Holland to establish a settlement in the New World.

After a difficult voyage aboard the *Mayflower,* a small ship with a cracked beam, the Pilgrims reached North America in November 1620. They landed not in Virginia as intended but much farther north, on the tip of Cape Cod in Massachusetts. Searching the coast in a small boat, they decided to settle in what is now Plymouth. It was mid-December before they could build shelters and all move ashore. During those dreary weeks on the ship, facing an unknown wilderness, Bradford's wife, Dorothy, fell overboard and was drowned.

Once ashore, the Pilgrims encountered not only the hardships experienced by Jamestown's first settlers but also a harsh New England winter. Added to that were disagreements about the validity of the rules of their charter, since it was for Virginia. To silence the argument, Bradford and the other leaders drew up the "Mayflower Compact." This was the first agreement for self-government made in the New World and served as a model for following settlements.

After the death of their first governor, John Carver, the Pilgrims elected William Bradford as their leader. Bradford was reelected governor thirty times. During his tenure as governor, he organized the repayment of debts to financial backers, encouraged new immigration, and established good relations with the Native Americans, without whose help the colony never would have survived.

In 1630 Bradford began writing *Of Plymouth Plantation,* an account of the Pilgrims' voyage to the New World, the founding of Plymouth Plantation, and the Pilgrims' experiences during the early years of the colony's existence. Bradford's work, which was not published until 1856, provides a firsthand view of the Pilgrims' struggle to endure and the courage and unbending religious faith that helped them survive. Written in the simple language that has come to be known as Puritan plain style, *Of Plymouth Plantation* stands as a tribute to the fortitude of Bradford and the other Pilgrim settlers.

Objectives

1 To identify the modes of discourse
2 To make inferences about attitudes
3 To compare and contrast accounts in writing

Support Material

Teaching Portfolio
Teacher Backup, p. 59
Grammar in Action, *Understanding the Evolution of Language,* p. 63; *Using Participles and Participial Phrases,* p. 65
Usage and Mechanics Worksheet, p. 67
Vocabulary Check, p. 68

Analyzing Literature Worksheet, *Using Modes of Discourse,* p. 69
Language Worksheet, *Completing Word Analogies,* p. 70
Selection Test, p. 71

GUIDE FOR INTERPRETING

from Of Plymouth Plantation

Modes of Discourse. Prose is often classified into four modes, or forms, of discourse: narration, description, exposition, and persuasion. Narration is writing that relates a story. The subject may be fictional, as in novels and short stories, or factual, as in historical accounts and biographies. Description presents the details of something, often through appeal to one or more of the five senses— sight, sound, taste, smell, and touch. Exposition uses logical patterns, such as comparison and contrast or definition, to inform or explain. Grammar textbooks and repair manuals are two examples of books containing expository writing. The fourth mode of discourse is persuasion, writing that attempts to convince readers to adopt an opinion or act in a certain way. Examples of persuasion include television advertisements and newspaper editorials.

Most often, the author's main purpose determines which of these categories a work best fits into. However, an author usually uses more than one form of discourse. For example, when writing a narrative, an author is likely to include descriptions of people and places and information about historical events.

Writing

The belief that we should be thankful for what we have, regardless of how difficult our circumstances may be, is often associated with the Pilgrims. What associations do you normally have when you think of the Pilgrims? Write a journal entry in which you discuss the ideas you associate with the Pilgrims.

Primary Source

In Book I of *Of Plymouth Plantation,* Bradford describes his little group of Puritan Separatists as they left the Dutch city of Leyden, headed for England and from there to North America. It is this passage that gave them the name "Pilgrims": "So they left that goodly and pleasant city which had been their resting place near twelve years; but they knew they were pilgrims, and looked not much on those things, but lift up their eyes to the heavens, their dearest country, and quieted their spirits."

Bradford describes their first wintry view of North America as they searched "an unknown coast" for a landing place: ". . . what could they see but a hideous and desolate wilderness, full of wild beasts and wild men—and what multitudes there might be of them they knew not . . . If they looked behind them, there was the mighty ocean . . . to separate them from all the civil parts of the world."

Guide for Interpreting 51

Literary Focus To reinforce the idea that the modes of discourse are often used in combination with each other, bring in a short newspaper article and an editorial. Read them to the class, identifying the writer's use of the various modes of discourse.

Writing/Prior Knowledge Before students write their journal entries, encourage them to think about ideas associated with the Pilgrims. Have them consider how this information relates to their lives, especially with regard to family celebrations of Thanksgiving.

Vocabulary

Preteach the following vocabulary words:
loath (lōth) *adj.:* Reluctant; unwilling (p. 52)
lusty (lus' tē) *adj.:* Strong; hearty (p. 53)
sundry (sun' drē) *adj.:* Various, different (p. 53)

Spelling Tip Some students may confuse the spelling of the adjective *loath* with that of the verb *loathe.*

Motivation/Prior Knowledge
Have your students discuss their impressions of the Pilgrims. What do they think the Pilgrims were really like? What hardships did they face? How did they overcome these hardships?

Master Teacher Note To help familiarize students with the Puritan mind set, you might wish to summarize the plot of Arthur Miller's play *The Crucible*. In what ways do the situations in Miller's play parallel those occurring in modern life?

Purpose-Setting Question
What impressions of Pilgrim life does Bradford's account create?

from Of Plymouth Plantation

William Bradford

Of Their Voyage and How They Passed the Sea; and of Their Safe Arrival at Cape Cod

After they had enjoyed fair winds and weather for a season, they were encountered many times with cross winds and met with many fierce storms with which the ship was shroudly[1] shaken, and her upper works made very leaky; and one of the main beams in the midships was bowed and cracked, which put them in some fear that the ship could not be able to perform the voyage. So some of the chief of the company, perceiving the mariners to fear the sufficiency of the ship as appeared by their mutterings, they entered into serious consultation with the master and other officers of the ship, to consider in time of the danger, and rather to return than to cast themselves into a desperate and inevitable peril. And truly there was great distraction and difference of opinion amongst the mariners themselves; fain would they do what could be done for their wages' sake (being now near half the seas over) and on the other hand they were loath to hazard their lives too desperately. But in examining of all opinions, the master and others affirmed they knew the ship to be strong and firm under water; and for the buckling of the main beam, there was a great iron screw the passengers brought out of Holland, which would raise the beam into his place; the which being done, the carpenter and master affirmed that with a post put

under it, set firm in the lower deck and otherways bound, he would make it sufficient. And as for the decks and upper works, they would caulk them as well as they could, and though with the working of the ship they would not long keep staunch, yet there

THE COMING OF THE MAYFLOWER
N. C. Wyeth
From the Collection of the Metropolitan Life Insurance Company, New York City

---

1. **shroudly:** Wickedly.

52   *The New Land*

Grammar in Action

Since its beginning, the English language has evolved from Old English (450–1150 A.D.) through Middle English (1150–1500 A.D.) to Modern English (1500–present). One work that set the precident for writing was the King James version of the Bible, which was written at the beginning of what we consider the Modern English period. This version, however, contains words and grammatical forms that are not in use today. Characteristic of Modern English is its expanded vocabulary and lengthy sentences as illustrated in this excerpt from William Bradford's *Of Plymouth Plantation*. Although many of the words and phrases Bradford uses have remained, many have been replaced by more contemporary words and expressions. In addition, contemporary writers are concerned with economy of language—saying the most with the fewest possible words. Look at the following examples:

"*. . . fain would they do* what could be done for their wages' sake . . . and on the other hand they were *loath to hazard* their lives too desperately."

Rewritten in standard English, this passage would say something like the following:

would otherwise be no great danger, if they did not overpress her with sails. So they committed themselves to the will of God and resolved to proceed.

In sundry of these storms the winds were so fierce and the seas so high, as they could not bear a knot of sail, but were forced to hull[2] for divers days together. And in one of them, as they thus lay at hull in a mighty storm, a lusty young man called John Howland, coming upon some occasion above the gratings was, with a seel[3] of the ship, thrown into sea; but it pleased God that he

---
2. hull: Drift with the wind.
3. seel: Rolling.

caught hold of the topsail halyards[4] which hung overboard and ran out at length. Yet he held his hold (though he was sundry fathoms under water) till he was hauled up by the same rope to the brim of the water, and then with a boat hook and other means got into the ship again and his life saved. And though he was something ill with it, yet he lived many years after and became a profitable member both in church and commonwealth. In all this voyage there died but one of the passengers, which was William Butten, a youth, servant to Samuel Fuller, when they drew near the coast.

But to omit other things (that I may be brief) after long beating at sea they fell with that land which is called Cape Cod; the which being made and certainly known to be it, they were not a little joyful. After some deliberation had amongst themselves and with the master of the ship, they tacked about and resolved to stand for the southward (the wind and weather being fair) to find some place about Hudson's River for their habitation. But after they had sailed that course about half the day, they fell amongst dangerous shoals and roaring breakers, and they were so far entangled therewith as they conceived themselves in great danger; and the wind shrinking upon them withal,[5] they resolved to bear up again for the Cape and thought themselves happy to get out of those dangers before night overtook them, as by God's good providence they did. And the next day they got into the Cape Harbor[6] where they rid in safety.

Being thus arrived in a good harbor, and brought safe to land, they fell upon their knees and blessed the God of Heaven who had brought them over the vast and furious ocean, and delivered them from all the perils and miseries thereof, again to set their feet on the firm and stable earth, their proper element.

---
4. halyards *n.*: Ropes for raising or lowering sails.
5. withal: Also.
6. Cape Harbor: Now Provincetown Harbor.

from Of Plymouth Plantation 53

1

1 **Discussion** What point of view does Bradford use?

Humanities Note

Fine art, *The Coming of the Mayflower* by N. C. Wyeth. Newell Convers Wyeth (1882–1945) was a prolific American illustrator of great fame. He illustrated many popular or well-known works, including *Robin Hood,* "Rip Van Winkle," *The Yearling,* and *Treasure Island.* He was one of a few American artists to become involved in the difficult art of mural painting. The last mural commission N. C. Wyeth accepted was one he looked forward to with much happiness and enthusiasm. It was a series of eight huge murals expressing the spirit and heritage of New England. *The Coming of the Mayflower* was one of the murals included in this series. Having grown up near Plymouth, Massachusetts, Wyeth took great pride in his New England heritage. He died in 1945 before the completion of this project. His son, Andrew Wyeth, a famous artist himself, and his son-in-law, John McCoy, completed the work he had begun.

You might discuss the following with your students.
1. The wind plays an important part in the first part of Bradford's account. How did N. C. Wyeth demonstrate the power of the wind in his mural?
2. How does the viewpoint lend drama to the picture?
3. Since the actual mural is very large, how do you think you might feel if you were able to stand before the actual mural?

They would gladly have done what they could to save their wages . . . but, on the other hand, they were reluctant to jeopardize their lives too desperately.

Student Activity 1. Rewrite each of the following sentences in standard English.
a. "So they committed themselves to the will of God and resolved to proceed."
b. "In sundry of these storms the winds were so fierce and the seas so high, as they could not bear a knot of sail, but were forced to hull for divers days together."
c. "Yet he held his hold . . . till he was hauled up by the same rope to the brim of the water, and then with a boat hook and

other means go into the ship again and his life saved."
d. "After some deliberation had amongst themselves and with the master of the ship, they tacked about and resolved to stand for the southward . . . to find some place about Hudson's River for their habitation."

Student Activity 2. Find two paragraphs from this selection or other selections in this unit and rewrite them in standard English.

THE LANDING OF THE PILGRIMS AT PLYMOUTH, MASSACHUSETTS, December 22nd, 1620
Currier & Ives, 1876
Museum of the City of New York

The Starving Time

But that which was most sad and lamentable was, that in two or three months' time half of their company died, especially in January and February, being the depth of winter, and wanting houses and other comforts; being infected with the scurvy[7] and other diseases which this long voyage and their inaccommodate[8] condition had brought upon them. So as there died sometimes two or three of a day in the foresaid time, that of one hundred and odd persons, scarce fifty remained. And of these, in the time of most distress, there was but six or seven sound persons who to their great commendations, be it spoken, spared no pains night or day, but with abundance of toil and hazard of their own health, fetched them wood, made them fires, dressed them meat, made their beds, washed their loathsome clothes, clothed and unclothed them. In a word, did all the homely[9] and necessary offices for them which dainty and queasy stomachs cannot endure to hear named; and all this

———
7. scurvy *n.:* A disease caused by vitamin C deficiency.
8. inaccommodate *adj.:* Unfit.

———
9. homely *adj.:* Domestic.

54   *The New Land*

Grammar in Action

A **present participle** is a form of a verb that ends in *-ing* and acts as an adjective. When participles have complements or modifiers of their own, they become participial phrases.

William Bradford uses a participial phrase modifying *Another* in the following line:

Another lay *cursing his wife.* . . .

Participles provide a means of joining short sentences into a more effective longer one.

willingly and cheerfully, without any grudging in the least, showing herein their true love unto their friends and brethren; a rare example and worthy to be remembered. Two of these seven were Mr. William Brewster, their reverend Elder, and Myles Standish, their Captain and military commander, unto whom myself and many others were much beholden in our low and sick condition. And yet the Lord so upheld these persons as in this general calamity they were not at all infected either with sickness or lameness. And what I have said of these I may say of many others who died in this general visitation,[10] and others yet living; that whilst they had health, yea, or any strength continuing, they were not wanting to any that had need of them. And I doubt not but their recompense is with the Lord.

But I may not here pass by another remarkable passage not to be forgotten. As this calamity fell among the passengers that were to be left here to plant, and were hasted ashore and made to drink water that the seamen might have the more beer, and one[11] in his sickness desiring but a small can of beer, it was answered that if he were their own father he should have none. The disease began to fall amongst them also, so as almost half of their company died before they went away, and many of their officers and lustiest men, as the boatswain, gunner, three quartermasters, the cook and others. At which the Master was something strucken and sent to the sick ashore and told the Governor he should send for beer for them that had need of it, though he drunk water homeward bound.

But now amongst his company there was far another kind of carriage[12] in this misery than amongst the passengers. For they that before had been boon[13] companions in drinking and jollity in the time of their health and welfare, began now to desert one another in this calamity, saying they would not hazard their lives for them, they should be infected by coming to help them in their cabins; and so, after they came to lie by it, would do little or nothing for them but, "if they died, let them die." But such of the passengers as were yet aboard showed them what mercy they could which made some of their hearts relent, as the boatswain (and some others) who was a proud young man and would often curse and scoff at the passengers. But when he grew weak, they had compassion on him and helped him; then he confessed he did not deserve it at their hands, he had abused them in word and deed. "Oh!" (saith he) "you, I now see, show your love like Christians indeed one to another, but we let one another lie and die like dogs." Another lay cursing his wife, saying if it had not been for her he had never come this unlucky voyage, and anon cursing his fellows, saying he had done this and that for some of them; he had spent so much and so much amongst them, and they were now weary of him and did not help him, having need. Another gave his companion all he had, if he died, to help him in his weakness; he went and got a little spice and made him a mess[14] of meat once or twice. And because he died not so soon as he expected, he went amongst his fellows and swore the rogue would cozen[15] him, he would see him choked before he made him any more meat; and yet the poor fellow died before morning.

Indian Relations

All this while the Indians came skulking about them, and would sometimes show themselves aloof off, but when any approached near them, they would run away; and once they stole away their tools where they had been at work and were gone to dinner. But about the sixteenth of March, a certain Indian came boldly amongst them and

---

10. **visitation** *n.*: Affliction.
11. **one:** William Bradford.
12. **carriage** *n.*: Behavior.
13. **boon** *adj.*: Close.

14. **mess** *n.*: Meal.
15. **cozen** (kuz' n) *v.*: Cheat.

from Of Plymouth Plantation 55

3 **Clarification** Of the one hundred people on the Mayflower, only about twenty-eight were Pilgrims. The others were sailors and adventurers who came to the New World seeking fortune.

4 **Discussion** Contrast Bradford's portrayal of the sailors' treatment of their ailing companions with that of the Pilgrims'. How does Bradford present the events to teach a lesson?

5 **Critical Thinking and Reading** Ask the students to describe Bradford's attitude toward Indians. Have them compare Bradford's attitudes to John Smith's.

Two sentences: They were now weary of him and did not help him. He had need.

One sentence with participial phrase: They were now weary of him and did not help him, having need.

Student Activity 1. Find five other present participles or participial phrases in the excerpt from *Of Plymouth Plantation*. Identify the noun or pronoun each modifies.

Student Activity 2. Combine the following pairs of sentences by making the first a participial phrase.
Example: The officers considered all opinions.
The officers judged the ship sound.

Combined: Considering all opinions, the officers judged the ship sound.

1. The mariners knew that the voyage was half over. The mariners agreed to go forward.

2. John Howland came on deck for some reason. John Howland fell into the sea.

3. The passengers and crew found refuge in a safe harbor. The passengers and crew thanked God for their landing.

6 **Enrichment** Massasoit was chief of the Wampanoag Indian tribe. He signed the treaty with the Pilgrims in 1621 and remained friendly with them from then until his death in 1661.

7 **Enrichment** Squanto, the Indian who could speak English, had been kidnapped by an English slaver in 1614. When he was finally able to return to his people, the Patuxets, in 1618, he found that the entire tribe had been wiped out by disease.

8 **Discussion** Ask the students to think about this and earlier references to God. What roles does God play in the everyday lives of the Pilgrims?

Reader's Response What do you think was the most difficult part of the Pilgrims' voyage? Why?

Enrichment Massasoit (c. 1580–1661) was chief of the Wampanoag Indians. Also known as Ousamequin, he was one of the most powerful Native American rulers of New England. In 1621 he went to Plymouth to sign this treaty with the Pilgrims, which he observed faithfully until his death.

spoke to them in broken English, which they could well understand but marveled at it. At length they understood by discourse with him, that he was not of these parts, but belonged to the eastern parts where some English ships came to fish, with whom he was acquainted and could name sundry of them by their names, amongst whom he had got his language. He became profitable to them in acquainting them with many things concerning the state of the country in the east parts where he lived, which was afterwards profitable unto them; as also of the people here, of their names, number and strength, of their situation and distance from this place, and who was chief amongst them. His name was Samoset. He told them also of another Indian whose name was Squanto, a native of this place, who had been in England and could speak better English than himself.

Being, after some time of entertainment and gifts dismissed, a while after he came again, and five more with him, and they brought again all the tools that were stolen away before, and made way for the coming of their great Sachem,[16] called Massasoit. Who, about four or five days after, came with the chief of his friends and other attendance, with the aforesaid Squanto. With whom, after friendly entertainment and some gifts given him, they made a peace with him

---

16. **Sachem** (sā′ chəm): Chief.

(which hath now continued this twenty-four years) in these terms:

1. That neither he nor any of his should injure or do hurt to any of their people.
2. That if any of his did hurt to any of theirs, he should send the offender, that they might punish him.
3. That if anything were taken away from any of theirs, he should cause it to be restored; and they should do the like to his.
4. If any did unjustly war against him, they would aid him; if any did war against them, he should aid them.
5. He should send to his neighbors confederates to certify them of this, that they might not wrong them, but might be likewise comprised in the conditions of peace.
6. That when their men came to them, they should leave their bows and arrows behind them.

After these things he returned to his place called Sowams, some 40 miles from this place, but Squanto continued with them and was their interpreter and was a special instrument sent of God for their good beyond their expectation. He directed them how to set their corn, where to take fish, and to procure other commodities, and was also their pilot to bring them to unknown places for their profit, and never left them till he died.

Closure and Extension

ANSWERS TO THINKING ABOUT THE SELECTION
Recalling

1. They encounter strong winds and fierce storms, and their ship falls into disrepair. They consider turning back, but decide against it. One man falls overboard, but survives the ordeal.
2. They get down on their knees and thank God.

THINKING ABOUT THE SELECTION

Recalling

1. What hardships do the Pilgrims endure during their trip across the Atlantic?
2. What is the Pilgrims' first act when they are "brought safe to land?"
3. Explain the situation between the sick and the healthy crew members during the first winter.
4. What are the terms of the peace agreement between the Pilgrims and Native Americans?

Interpreting

5. How would you characterize the Pilgrims' reactions to the hardships they encountered during their first winter in Plymouth?
6. Find two statements by Bradford that convey the Pilgrims' belief that they were being guided and protected by God.
7. (a) What change occurs in Bradford's attitude toward the Native Americans? (b) How does the Native Americans' attitude toward the Pilgrims change? (c) Based on Bradford's descriptions, what do you think brought about these changes in attitude?

Applying

8. Do you feel that the changing attitudes of the settlers toward the Native Americans and the Native Americans toward the settlers reflect typical experiences with newcomers? Why or why not?

ANALYZING LITERATURE

Using Modes of Discourse

Prose is often classified into four modes of discourse: narration, description, exposition, and persuasion. Most often, the author's main purpose determines into which of these modes a work is best classified. However, a writer rarely uses only one form of discourse in a work. For example, while Of Plymouth Plantation is primarily a narrative, because Bradford's main purpose is to tell about a series of events, the work contains many descriptive passages.

1. Find at least two examples of Bradford's use of description.
2. Find two examples of Bradford's use of a third form of discourse.

CRITICAL THINKING AND READING

Making Inferences About Attitudes

Many narratives, such as Of Plymouth Plantation, reveal the attitudes and values of the people being portrayed. However, in most cases cultural attitudes and values are revealed indirectly. As a result, you must make inferences, or draw conclusions, by carefully examining the characters' actions, thoughts, and comments. For example, from Bradford's statement that the Pilgrims "committed themselves to the will of God" you can conclude that Pilgrims had a strong faith in God.

What inferences can you make about the Pilgrims' attitudes and values from each of the following passages?

1. "... there was but six or seven sound persons who ... did all the homely and necessary offices for them [sick Pilgrims] ... willingly and cheerfully, without any grudging in the least. ..."
2. "The boatswain ... would often curse and scoff at the passengers. But when he grew weak, they had compassion on him and helped him. ..."

THINKING AND WRITING

Comparing and Contrasting Accounts

Write an essay comparing and contrasting The General History of Virginia and Of Plymouth Plantation in such areas as style, purpose, objectivity, accuracy, and content. First prepare a list of similarities and differences, and then organize your information into an outline or map. In the essay, use specific examples and passages from both works to support your thesis. When you revise, make sure your essay is well organized and includes supporting information.

from Of Plymouth Plantation 57

(Answers begin on p. 56)

them. (b) The Indians are apprehensive of the colonists at first, stealing from them and running away. Later, the Native Americans are friendly and congenial. (c) The changes in attitudes probably occur when each group realizes that the other means no harm and that each has something to share with the others.

Applying

8. Suggested Response: Yes, at first strangers are usually apprehensive with one another because they don't know what the other will be like, whether the newcomer will be friendly or hostile, or whether the two will get along. Once the stranger becomes familiar, the fear and nervousness diminish.

ANSWERS TO ANALYZING LITERATURE

1. Answers will differ. The first sentence of both the first and second paragraphs use description.
2. Answers will differ. The first two sentences of the third paragraph are examples of narration. An example of exaggeration is found in the second sentence of the second paragraph of "The Starving Time."

ANSWERS TO CRITICAL THINKING AND READING

1. Suggested Response: The Pilgrims were compassionate and selfless.
2. Suggested Response: The Pilgrims were forgiving.

THINKING AND WRITING

For help with this assignment, students can refer to Lesson 16, "Writing a Comparative Evaluation," in the Handbook of Writing About Literature.

Writing Across the Curriculum
The students' history teachers may be interested in reviewing the writing assignments. They may wish to assign secondhand accounts for the students to read and contrast with the subjectivity of the selections by John Smith and William Bradford.

3. The healthy crew members do not help the ill ones. In fact, they mock them and treat them with disdain.
4. The Pilgrims and the Native Americans agree that they will not injure each other, but, if they do, the offender will be punished. They also agree not to steal from one another, to aid each other in times of battle, as well as in peacetime, and to leave their weapons behind when they visit one another.

Interpreting

5. The Pilgrims react to hardships with strength, determination, and a loving, cooperative spirit. Many die and many become ill, yet those who remain well work hard and willingly to nurse and care for the others.
6. Answers will differ. Suggested Responses: "Being thus arrived in good harbor, and brought safe to land, they fell upon their knees and blessed the God of Heaven who had brought them over the

vast and furious ocean ..." and "... but Squanto continued with them and was their interpreter and was a special instrument sent of God for their good. ..."
7. (a) At first, Bradford seems disapproving of the Indians (because the Pilgrims's tools were stolen) and also curious about them. He seems shocked that the Indian who approached them can speak English. Later, he befriends the Indians and enjoys entertaining

More About the Author During Anne Bradstreet's time, it was unusual for a woman to be able to read and write, much less compose poetry. Bradstreet was not encouraged to write by her society, and she had difficulty finding time for her writing. Her duties as wife and mother took up most of her time, and she attended devotional services twice a week. In addition, her physical condition was poor. At the same time, neighbors pressured Bradstreet to be more "feminine." She wrote, "I am obnoxious to each carping tongue/ Who says my hand a needle better fits." How might Bradstreet's situation have influenced her choice of subjects?

Literary Focus You may wish to discuss all of the meanings of the words *lyric, lyrical, lyricism,* and *lyre* with students, to help them understand lyric poetry. Point out that song lyrics may also be a form of poetry.

Writing/Prior Knowledge For extra credit, you might have your **more advanced** students develop their lists into a brief written discussion of the various ways in which people demonstrate their devotion to others.

Vocabulary

Preteach the following vocabulary words:
recompense (rek′ əm pens′) *n.*: Reward (p. 59, 1.8)
manifold (man′ ə fold) *adv.*: In many ways (p. 59, 1.10)

GUIDE FOR INTERPRETING

To My Dear and Loving Husband

Anne Bradstreet (1612–1672) was born in Northampton, England, and raised as a Puritan. In 1630, she and her husband, Simon Bradstreet, left England and settled in the Massachusetts Bay Colony. Bradstreet endured the hardships of life in the New World and raised eight children. In 1650 a collection of her scholarly poems, *The Tenth Muse Lately Sprung Up in America, By a Gentlewoman of Those Parts,* was published in England. Bradstreet's later poems, like "To My Dear and Loving Husband," are more personal, expressing the feeling arising from the joyful but difficult and sometimes tragic experiences of everyday Puritan life.

Literary Forms

Lyric Poetry. Lyric poems, or lyrics, are brief poems that express the writer's personal feelings and thoughts. These poems, which in ancient Greece were sung to the accompaniment of a stringed instrument called a lyre, tend to be melodic and focus on producing a single, unified effect.

Although Bradstreet's early poetry consisted of scholarly poems on such subjects as physics, history, and philosophy, most of her later poems are lyrics. As she became more deeply immersed in her life in the New World, Bradstreet expressed her personal feelings about her family and the difficulties of colonial life.

Commentary

For the Puritans the sole purpose of literature was moral instruction. They were aware of the emotional power of poetry but approved of it only if, like the Psalms, it "moved hearts to righteousness." There were many writers of verse in Puritan times, but few of them were women. Bradstreet was aware that writing was considered unacceptable behavior for women, but she persevered, somehow finding time to write and revise her poems.

Her poetry reflects the Puritans' knowledge of the stories and language of the Bible and their awareness of the relationship between earthly and heavenly life. At the same time, she read the French and English poets of her day and was influenced by their use of comparisons and paradox. Finally, she was among the first American writers—and the first woman—to speak of and thus try to find a place for individual feelings within the context of Puritanism. Notice these different elements as you read her poem. Does the poem seem to you American? Puritan? modern?

Writing

Like most other Puritans, Bradstreet was very devoted to her family. List ways in which people may demonstrate such devotion to others.

58   *The New Land*

Objective
To recognize lyric poetry

Support Material

Teaching Portfolio
Teacher Backup, p. 73
Usage and Mechanics Worksheet, p. 76
Vocabulary Check, p. 77
Analyzing Literature Worksheet, *Understanding Lyric Poetry,* p. 78

Language Worksheet, *Understanding Connotation and Dennotation,* p. 79
Selection Test, p. 80

To My Dear and Loving Husband

Anne Bradstreet

If ever two were one, then surely we.
If ever man were lov'd by wife, then thee;
If ever wife was happy in a man,
1 ☐ Compare with me ye women if you can.
5 I prize thy love more than whole mines of gold,
Or all the riches that the East doth hold.
My love is such that rivers cannot quench,
Nor ought[1] but love from thee, give recompense.
Thy love is such I can no way repay,
10 The heavens reward thee manifold, I pray.
2 ☐ Then while we live, in love let's so persevere,
3 ☐ That when we live no more, we may live ever.

---

1. ought: Anything whatever.

READING WOMAN
Terborch
Three Lions

THINKING ABOUT THE SELECTION

Recalling

1. (a) What does the speaker prize more than "all the riches that the East doth hold"? (b) What "is such that rivers cannot quench"?

Interpreting

2. What does Bradstreet mean by the apparent paradox in the last two lines: ". . . let's so persevere / That when we live no more, we may live ever"?
3. What ideas about heaven and the afterlife does the poem convey?

Applying

4. Do you think personal devotion is as much esteemed today as it was in Anne Bradstreet's day? Support your answer.

ANALYZING LITERATURE

Understanding Lyric Poetry

A **lyric poem** expresses the personal thoughts and feelings of the poet in lively, musical language. For example, "To My Dear and Loving Husband" is a lyric poem that conveys the poet's happiness.
1. What is the main feeling Bradstreet expresses?
2. What other thoughts or feelings does Bradstreet express?
3. How do Bradstreet's repetition and images help to convey the strength of the emotion being expressed?

To My Dear and Loving Husband 59

Although Edward Taylor was an important and influential man, little is known about him. Historians do know that Taylor enrolled in Harvard College shortly after his arrival in Massachusetts when he was 29 years old. His graduation in three years suggests that he had gone to college in England, although no one knows where.

While in England, Taylor taught school. Because he would not sign an oath of loyalty to the Church of England, Taylor left his family and sailed to New England in 1668. Taylor said that he preferred exile in the "howling wilderness" to pledging his loyalty to the Church.

In Westfield, Taylor served as a public servant, a physician, and a minister. His poetry, which was a lifelong ambition, and his ministry were closely tied. Taylor's belief that only a select few were predestined to escape eternal damnation led him to subject himself to continual self-examination in the hope of determining the state of his soul. Although he believed that no amount of good thoughts or deeds would save a person who was damned, he assumed that the select few who were to be saved would act and think in "proper" ways. How might these beliefs have shaped Taylor's poetry? What purpose might his poetry have served for him personally?

EDWARD TAYLOR

1642–1729

Edward Taylor is now generally regarded as the best of the colonial poets. Yet, because Taylor thought of his poetry as a form of personal religious worship, he permitted only two stanzas from one of his poems to be printed while he was alive, and he instructed his heirs not to have any more of his poetry published. As a result, few people knew about his work until his poems were first published more than two centuries after his death.

Before the English government's lack of tolerance for his Puritan beliefs prompted him to emigrate to America, Taylor worked as a teacher in England. After arriving in Boston in 1668, Taylor entered Harvard College and graduated in 1671. Taylor was then asked to serve as the minister and physician of the small farming community of Westfield, Massachusetts. After accepting the position, Taylor walked more than one hundred miles, partly through knee-deep snow, to get to his new home.

Taylor spent the rest of his life in Westfield. It was a life filled with hardships. Because of the fierce battles between the Native Americans and the colonists, Taylor and the other people of Westfield lived in a state of constant fear. Taylor also experienced many personal tragedies. Five of the eight children he had with his first wife died in infancy, and his first wife died while still a young woman. He married a second time, however, and had five or six more children. (Biographers differ on the exact number.)

In spite of the difficulties of his life and the demands of his position, Taylor wrote a considerable amount of poetry. He appears to have been interested in writing poems most of his life. He tried his hand at a great variety of poetic forms: elegies on the deaths of public figures, lyric poems in the style of Elizabethan songs, and a long "debate" poem. Most popular today, however, are what he called "Preparatory Meditations"—short poems written to "unwind" and express the emotional force of the sermon he was preparing for the next day.

Taylor's grandson, to whom Taylor left his poems, described his grandfather as "A man of small stature but firm: of quick Passions—yet serious and grave." In a time when the power of Puritanism was waning, Taylor held intellectually and emotionally to the original doctrines. Nearly all of his poems are expressions of his extremely conservative religious beliefs. Taylor believed that only a select few people were predestined to escape eternal damnation. His poems convey the intensity of the conservative Puritans' devotion to God and the strength of their desire for salvation perhaps better than any of the other poetry of his day.

GUIDE FOR INTERPRETING

Huswifery; Upon a Wasp Chilled with Cold

Writer's Techniques

Figurative Language. Figurative language is language that is not intended to be interpreted literally. To interpret figurative language, you must examine the suggestions and associations it evokes. Writers use figurative language for strength and freshness of expression, to illustrate similarities between things that are seemingly quite different, or to express abstract ideas with concrete images, or word pictures. For example, the statement that a character's "thoughts were like scattered leaves" is figurative. In suggesting that the character's thoughts lacked focus, the phrase creates a concrete picture of an abstract idea and presents an interesting and unusual comparison.

Conceits. One kind of figurative language is a conceit, an elaborate and unusual comparison between two startlingly different subjects. Conceits are often lengthy and intricate, frequently developing through a series of shorter, less elaborate comparisons into the framework for an entire poem. Like the seventeenth-century English poets such as John Donne and George Herbert, whose work he greatly admired, Edward Taylor often used extended conceits in his writing. Yet, while Donne and Herbert used conceits primarily to surprise or shock readers, Taylor used conceits to emphasize the close relationship between God and the natural world.

Commentary

Preachers and poets have much in common. They both appeal to the minds and emotions of their audience. They both use images and examples from everyday life to express abstract or complex concepts. Also, sermons use the rhythm and repetition common in poetry.

The Puritan habit of seeing God's teachings everywhere in nature provided preachers with a ready store of concrete images. For his frontier congregation, Taylor, the preacher, had to keep his comparisons simple. But Taylor the poet, influenced by the conceits of the metaphysical poets and writing for himself, developed ingenious and elaborate comparisons. In the following poems, notice the comparisons that Taylor develops and his purpose in each. Do you ever use comparisons to explain a difficult idea?

Writing

When figurative language is used to express abstract ideas through concrete images, it often adds to our understanding and appreciation of these ideas. Taylor uses figurative language in the poems you will read. List five abstract words, such as *love* and *sorrow*. Then brainstorm about concrete images that illustrate each of these ideas, and record each image beside the idea that it is intended to express.

Guide for Interpreting 61

Writing/Prior Knowledge If students have trouble thinking of concrete images to go with their abstract words, suggest that they first try to think of adjectives. For example, when they think of love, they may think of such words as *comforting* or *sweet*. These words may help lead them to concrete images.

Vocabulary

Preteach the following vocabulary words:
chafes (chāfz) *v*.: Rubs to make warm (p. 64 1. 5)
precepts (prē′ septz) *n*.: Rules of conduct (p. 64, 1. 16)

Objectives

1 To recognize figurative language and conceits
2 To write a conceit

Support Material

Teaching Portfolio
Teacher Backup, p. 83
Usage and Mechanics worksheet, p. 87
Vocabulary Check, p. 88
Analyzing Literature Worksheet, *Recognizing Figurative Language*, p. 89
Language Worksheet, *Using Context Clues*, p. 90
Selection Test, p. 91

Fine art, *Evening,* 1929, Wanda Gág. Gág (1893–1946) was born in Minnesota of Bohemian-Hungarian parents. Determined to become an artist, she went to New York. There she studied at the Art Students League. A painter and illustrator, she began her work in lithography, wood engraving, and etching around 1918. Her first one-woman show was well received. However, she earned a very meager living after that and had to live frugally in a little shack in rural Connecticut and later in New Jersey. As demonstrated in this picture, she had a very personal style in which she drew everyday objects and interiors of country rooms illuminated by the light of a single lamp. Her prints show a clear understanding of the stark realities of life and yet display a kind of exuberance.

You might ask students the following questions.
1. What is the mood of this picture?
2. What lighting effect has the artist used to create the intense mood of the picture?
3. How does the picture relate to the poem?

Motivation/Prior Knowledge
Discuss Puritan values and attitudes with your students. How might these attitudes and values be expressed in the work of a Puritan poet?

Purpose-setting Question
What comparison does the speaker develop?

1 Clarification *Huswifery* means "housekeeping."

2 Clarification Like Anne Bradstreet, Edward Taylor wrote many didactic poems in the style of the English poetry of the time. Also like Bradstreet, Taylor's poems are short and personal. While Bradstreet addressed her husband, however, Taylor's poem speaks fervently and personally to God.

3 Clarification Point out that for Taylor and his contemporaries the spinning wheel and its many parts were familiar objects, and thus were appropriate subjects for an extended metaphor.

EVENING
Wanda Gág
University of New Mexico

Huswifery

Edward Taylor

Make me, O Lord, Thy spinning wheel complete.
    Thy holy word my distaff[1] make for me.
Make mine affections[2] Thy swift flyers[3] neat
    And make my soul Thy holy spoole to be.
5   My conversation make to be Thy reel
    And reel the yarn thereon spun of Thy wheel.

Make me Thy loom then, knit therein this twine:
    And make Thy holy spirit, Lord, wind quills:[4]

---

1. distaff *n.*: A staff on which flax or wool is wound for use in spinning.
2. affections: Emotions.
3. flyers *n.*: The part of a spinning wheel which twists fibers into yarn.
4. quills *n.*: A weaver's spindles or bobbins.

62   *The New Land*

Then weave the web Thyself. The yarn is fine.
10   Thine ordinances⁵ make my fulling mills.⁶
        Then dye the same in heavenly colors choice,
        All pinked⁷ with varnished flowers of paradise.

        Then clothe therewith mine understanding, will,
        Affections, judgment, conscience, memory
15 My words, and actions, that their shine may fill
        My ways with glory and Thee glorify.
        Then mine apparel shall display before Ye
        That I am clothed in holy robes for glory.

---

5. ordinances: Sacraments.
6. fulling mills *n.*: Mills used for cleaning and thickening cloth.
7. pinked: Decorated.

THINKING ABOUT THE SELECTION
Recalling

1. To whom is the poem addressed?
2. (a) What type of machine does Taylor describe? (b) What process does he describe? (c) In what does the speaker ask to be clothed?

Interpreting

3. What does the poem suggest about the speaker's attitude toward God?
4. (a) What seems to be the poem's overall purpose? (b) How do the final two lines convey Taylor's belief that religious grace comes as a gift from God, rather than as a result of a person's efforts?

Applying

5. What process do you think Taylor might have described in the poem if he had written it while living in today's society?

ANALYZING LITERATURE
Noting Figurative Language and Conceits

Figurative language is language that is not meant to be interpreted literally. To grasp the meaning of figurative language, you must examine the suggestions and associations it evokes. For example, the first line of "Huswifery"—"Make me, O Lord, Thy spinning wheel complete"—suggests that the speaker is asking to be made an instrument or agent of God.

A **conceit** is an elaborate, often lengthy comparison between two startlingly different subjects. For example, in "Huswifery," Taylor creates an intricate, extended comparison between the making of cloth and the granting of God's grace.

1. What do each of the following lines from "Huswifery" suggest?
   a. "And make my soul Thy holy spoole to be."
   b. "That I am clothed in holy robes for glory."
2. Taylor believed that the granting of grace involved the transformation of a person from a flawed and imperfect state of being to a state of purity and perfection. How does Taylor's conceit express this belief?
3. What does Taylor's comparison of a common household task with the granting of grace suggest about his beliefs concerning the relationship between God and the earthly world?

Huswifery 63

Reader's Response What is your immediate response to Taylor's poem? Why?

Upon a Wasp Chilled with Cold

Edward Taylor

The bear[1] that breathes the northern blast
Did numb, torpedo-like,[2] a wasp
Whose stiffened limbs encramped, lay bathing
In Sol's[3] warm breath and shine as saving,
5 Which with her hands she chafes and stands
Rubbing her legs, shanks, thighs, and hands.
Her petty[4] toes, and fingers' ends
Nipped with this breath, she out extends
Unto the sun, in great desire
10 To warm her digits at that fire.
Doth hold her temples in this state
Where pulse doth beat, and head doth ache.
Doth turn, and stretch her body small,
Doth comb her velvet capital.[5]
15 As if her little brain pan were
A volume of choice precepts clear.
As if her satin jacket hot
Contained apothecary's shop[6]
Of Nature's receipts,[7] that prevails
20 To remedy all her sad ails,[8]
As if her velvet helmet high
Did turret[9] rationality.
She fans her wing up to the wind
As if her petticoat were lined,
25 With reason's fleece, and hoists sails
And humming flies in thankful gails
Unto her dun curled[10] palace hall
Her warm thanks offering for all.

---

1. The bear: The constellation of Ursa Major, commonly called the Big Dipper.
2. torpedo-like: Capable of producing a strong electrical charge.
3. Sol: Personification of the sun.
4. petty: Small.
5. capital: Head.
6. apothecary's shop: Shop where medicines are prepared and sold.
7. nature's receipts: Natural remedies.
8. ails: Ailments.
9. turret: Contain.
10. dun curled: Dark curved.

64   *The New Land*

Lord clear my misted sight that I
30 May hence view thy divinity.
    Some sparks whereof thou up dost hasp[11]
    Within this little downy wasp

3   In whose small corporation[12] we
    A school and a schoolmaster see
35 Where we may learn, and easily find
    A nimble spirit bravely mind
    Her work in every limb: and lace
    It up neat with a vital grace,
    Acting each part though ne'er so small
40 Here of this fustian[13] animal.

4   Till I enravished climb into
    The godhead[14] on this lather do.
    Where all my pipes inspired upraise
    An heavenly music furred with praise.

---

11. **hasp:** Fasten.
12. **corporation:** Here, body.
13. **fustian:** Coarsely coated.
14. **godhead:** Paradise.

THINKING ABOUT THE SELECTION

Recalling

1. (a) What human features does Taylor use in describing the wasp? (b) How does the wasp warm itself? (c) What does the wasp do after it has warmed itself?
2. (a) To whom is the second stanza addressed? (b) For what does the speaker ask?

Interpreting

3. In the first stanza, the speaker creates a comparison between the warming of the wasp and the granting of God's grace. (a) What does the manner in which the wasp is warmed suggest about Taylor's beliefs concerning the granting of God's grace? (b) With what can the actions of the wasp at the end of the first stanza be compared?

Applying

4. In this poem, the wasp serves as an example for the speaker. List two other insects or animals you feel could serve as an example for humans, and explain what you think we could learn from them.

THINKING AND WRITING

Writing a Conceit

Think of two seemingly different processes that are in some way similar to each other. Then list the stages of each process and try to think of vivid images, or word pictures, to describe each stage. Write a poem in which you develop an extended conceit by directly comparing each of the corresponding stages of the two processes. Your poem does not need to have rhythm or a definite structure. When you revise, make sure that the comparison you are making is clear and that you have used vivid imagery in your descriptions.

Upon a Wasp Chilled with Cold **65**

More About the Author William Byrd's interest in scholarly pursuits, such as language and science, combined with his business background made him somewhat of a Renaissance man. His aristocratic status allowed him to continue his studies and to acquire a large library, while it also kept him active in the civic affairs of his community. As a result his writing style reflects his enlightened, humanistic outlook and his sense of security in his wealth and status. Is such a style appropriate for an account of the explorations of the rugged frontier? Why or why not?

Literary Focus Like firsthand historical accounts, journals provide important insights into the thoughts of historical figures. However, because they may contain subjective judgements and interpretations, they must be read critically.

Writing/Prior Knowledge If students have difficulty thinking of adventures about which to write, encourage them to think about their initial experiences with certain situations. For example, they might explore the first time they flew in an airplane or the first time they rode a bicycle.

Vocabulary

Preteach the following vocabulary words:
unconscionable (un kän' shən ə b'l) *adj.:* Unreasonable (p. 67)
practicable (prak' ti kə b'l) *adj.:* Capable of being put into practice; feasible (p. 67)
quagmire (kwag' mīr) *n.:* Wet, boggy ground (p. 67)
cumbersome (kum' bər səm) *adj.:* Hard to handle or deal with because of size or weight (p. 67)

66

GUIDE FOR INTERPRETING

Literary Forms

Commentary

Writing

from The History of the Dividing Line

William Byrd (1674–1744) helped to develop and expand the early southern colonies. Throughout the course of his life in America, Byrd, a Virginian who spent much of his early life in England, kept diaries that provide us with a firsthand view of early southern life. After his return to Virginia, when he was about thirty years old, Byrd ran his estate while attending to the mapping and expansion of the colonies. Byrd wrote numerous poems, essays, and travel books, and recorded his personal experiences in a diary, *The History of the Dividing Line* (1729), which recounts his experiences during a surveying expedition undertaken to settle a border dispute between the colonies of Virginia and North Carolina.

Journals. A journal, or diary, is a personal record of events, conversations, thoughts, feelings, and observations. Because journals are written on a day-to-day basis, they allow people to record their immediate reactions to their experiences. Most often, people keep journals for their personal use, never intending to have them published. However, keeping a journal allows writers to record descriptions, ideas, and events that they may eventually use in a story, poem, or essay.

William Byrd was a dedicated journal writer, recording his experiences in a code that only he could interpret. *The History of the Dividing Line* is based on an account from Byrd's journal. Though Byrd refined and toned down the original material in preparing *The History,* the work remains in journal form and still captures Byrd's spontaneous responses to the events of the surveying expedition.

Byrd, like John Smith, was not a Puritan. From a Virginia aristocratic family, he was educated as an English gentleman in London, where he had many friends in literary and tavern circles. An active member of the Virginia legislature, Byrd was also an amateur explorer, scientist, and writer. He loved local folk tales and superstitions. His extensive learning—he knew many languages—and sophisticated tastes made him rare among colonials of his day. His secret diaries, filled with intimate details of his rather tempestuous private life, were not decoded and published until the 1940's.

As you read the *History,* notice how Byrd's personal characteristics are evident in his writing. How might William Bradford or Edward Taylor have described this adventure?

What experiences have you had that you feel were adventures? Write a journal entry describing one of these experiences.

66   *The New Land*

Objectives

1 To understand journals
2 To recognize the author's purpose
3 To write a narrative account

Support Material

Teaching Portfolio
Teacher Backup, p. 93
Usage and Mechanics Worksheet, p. 97
Vocabulary Check, p. 98
Analyzing Literature Worksheet, *Understanding Journals,* p. 99
Language Worksheet, *Exploring Tone,* p. 100
Selection Test, p. 101

from The History of the Dividing Line

William Byrd

Into the Dismal Swamp

1 *March 14* Before nine of the clock this morning the provisions, bedding, and other necessaries were made up into packs for the men to carry on their shoulders into the Dismal. They were victualed for eight days at full allowance, nobody doubting but that would be abundantly sufficient to carry them through that inhospitable place; nor indeed was it possible for the poor fellows to stagger under more. As it was, their loads weighed from sixty to seventy pounds, in just proportion to the strength of those who were to bear them. 'Twould have been unconscionable to have saddled them with burdens heavier than that, when they were to lug them through a filthy bog which was hardly practicable with no burden at all. Besides this luggage at their backs, they were obliged to measure the distance, mark the trees, and clear the way for the surveyors every step they went. It was really a pleasure to see with how much cheerfulness they undertook and with how much spirit they went through all this drudgery. For their greater safety, the commissioners took care to furnish them with Peruvian bark,[1] rhubarb, and ipecacuanha,[2] in case they might happen, in that wet 2 journey, to be taken with fevers or fluxes.

Although there was no need of example to inflame persons already so cheerful, yet to enter the people with the better grace, the author and two more of the commissioners accompanied them half a mile into the Dismal. The skirts of it were thinly planted with dwarf reeds and gall bushes, but when we got into the Dismal itself we found the reeds grew there much taller and closer and, to mend the matter, were so interlaced with bamboo briers that there was no scuffling through them without the help of pioneers. At the same time we found the ground moist and trembling under our feet like a quagmire, insomuch that it was an easy matter to run a ten-foot pole up to the head in it without exerting any uncommon strength to do it. Two of the men whose burdens were the least cumbersome had orders to march before with their tomahawks and clear the way in order to make an opening for the surveyors. By their assistance we made a shift to push the line half a mile in three hours and then reached a small piece of firm land about a hundred yards wide, standing up above the rest like an island. Here the people were glad to lay down their loads and take a little refreshment, while the happy man whose lot it was to carry the jug of rum began already, like Aesop's bread carriers,[3] to find it grow a good deal lighter.

After reposing about an hour, the com-

---

1. Peruvian bark: Quinine, used in medicine for treating malaria and other fevers.

2. ipecacuanha (ip′ i ka′ k o͞o an′ yə) *n*.: A plant with roots used for medicinal purposes.

3. Aesop's bread carriers: From a fable in which the man who wanted to carry the lightest load on a journey chose the bread because, though it was the heaviest load at the start of the journey, he knew once it had been distributed he would have only an empty basket to carry.

from *The History of the Dividing Line*   67

Presentation

Motivation/Prior Knowledge
Ask the students if they have ever used a journal to record events and memories about a vacation they took. What kinds of entries did they make? Did they write with an audience in mind or just for themselves? How would their entries have been different if they had known that other people would read them?

Master Teacher Note Byrd's journal was written between 1728 and 1729. It describes the experiences of a group of surveyors who went through the Dismal Swamp to settle a boundary dispute between the states of North Carolina and Virginia.

Purpose-Setting Question
What, according to this account, made the Dismal Swamp, as it is still known today, worthy of its name?

1 **Enrichment** The Boundary Commission began its survey expedition in March of 1728 at the Atlantic shore and traveled westward for several months, finishing the expedition in the fall of that year. Byrd and his companions traveled on horseback.

2 **Clarification** *Fluxes* is a word for dysentery, a condition often caused by drinking impure or stagnant water.

Humanities Note

Fine art, *Dismal Swamp* by Flavius J. Fisher. Fisher (1832–1905) was an American who painted many portraits in Washington, D.C., after the Civil War. He was also a landscape artist.

This landscape is a depiction of the Dismal Swamp. Fisher has captured on canvas the overwhelming atmosphere that one must experience upon visiting a remote part of the swamp. The eerie glow of colors, the crescent moon, and the dramatic silhouettes all add to the mysterious quality felt here.

Consider asking the following questions:
1. What is the atmosphere in this painting of the Dismal Swamp?
2. How does this painting enhance the effect of Byrd's account?

3 Clarification A huzza is a happy cheer, or hurrah.

4 Discussion Notice the sober, practical tone of Byrd's account of the difficulties faced by his group. How might John Smith have related a similar experience? Which account would be more believable and appear more accurate?

5 Enrichment While Byrd's view of the North American wilderness is remarkably detached and devoid of the religious references commonly included by Puritan writers, it includes a significant amount of references to fictional tales. Byrd is known to have loved folk tales and superstitious beliefs and he recorded them in many of his journals.

DISMAL SWAMP
Flavius J. Fisher
Randolph-Macon Women's College, Maier Museum of Art

3 missioners recommended vigor and constancy to their fellow travelers, by whom they were answered with three cheerful huzzas, in token of obedience. This ceremony was no sooner over but they took up their burdens and attended the motion of the surveyors, who, though they worked with all their might, could reach but one mile farther, the same obstacles still attending them which they had met with in the morning. However small this distance may seem to such as are used to travel at their ease, yet our poor men, who were obliged to work with an unwieldy load at their backs, had reason to think it a long way; especially in a bog where **4** they had no firm footing but every step made a deep impression which was instantly filled with water. At the same time they were laboring with their hands to cut down the reeds, which were ten feet high, their legs were hampered with briers. Besides, the weather happened to be warm, and the tallness of the reeds kept off every friendly breeze from coming to refresh them. And indeed it was a little provoking to hear the wind whistling among the branches of the white cedars, which grew here and there amongst the reeds, and at the same time

not to have the comfort to feel the least breath of it.

In the meantime the three commissioners returned out of the Dismal the same way they went in and, having joined their brethren, proceeded that night as far as Mr. Wilson's. This worthy person lives within sight of the Dismal, in the skirts whereof his stocks range and maintain themselves all the winter, and yet he knew as little of it as he did of *Terra Australis Incognita*.[4] He told us a Canterbury tale[5] of a North Briton **5** whose curiosity spurred him a long way into this great desert,[6] as he called it, near twenty years ago, but he, having no compass nor seeing the sun for several days together, wandered about till he was almost famished; but at last he bethought himself of[7] a secret his countrymen make use of to pilot themselves in a dark day. He took a fat louse out

---

4. ***Terra Australis Incognita*** (tĕr′ ə ô strâl′ əs ĭn käg′ nə tə): An unknown southern land.
5. **Canterbury tale:** Here, a remarkable story. *The Canterbury Tales* is a literary work written by medieval English poet Geoffrey Chaucer.
6. **desert:** Here, referring to the swamp.
7. **bethought himself of:** Remembered.

68   *The New Land*

Reader's Response Taking into account the reason they went, would you have gone on Byrd's expedition to the Dismal Swamp? Why or why not?

of his collar and exposed it to the open day on a piece of white paper, which he brought along with him for his journal. The poor insect, having no eyelids, turned himself about till he found the darkest part of the heavens and so made the best of his way toward the North. By this direction he steered himself safe out and gave such a frightful account of the monsters he saw and the distresses he underwent that no mortal since has been hardy enough to go upon the like dangerous discovery.

THINKING ABOUT THE SELECTION

Recalling

1. Describe the contents of the men's packs. How much do their loads weigh?
2. Name two obstacles that the men encounter in the dismal swamp.
3. (a) What, according to Mr. Wilson, did the North Briton use to find his way out of the swamp after becoming lost in it? (b) How did it help him find his way out?

Interpreting

4. How does Byrd's detailed description of the vegetation and surface of the swamp reflect his knowledge of science?
5. Give one example of Byrd's use of humorous exaggeration in this excerpt.

Applying

6. How might this account be different if it had been written by a New England Puritan?

ANALYZING LITERATURE

Understanding Journals

A **journal** is a personal record of thoughts, feelings, insights, conversations, and events. Writers often use material they have recorded in their journals in writing short stories, novels, poems, essays, or other works. For example, *The History of the Dividing Line,* which is written in journal form, is based on an account from William Byrd's journal.

1. How might this account be different if Byrd had written it twenty years after the experience without having a journal to refer to?
2. In his original journal account, Byrd is critical of a number of the other members of the surveying party. In *The History,* however, Byrd is far less critical of these people. Why do you think Byrd toned down his original material when he prepared *The History*?
3. What other changes would you guess Byrd made when revising his original journal account? Explain your answer.

CRITICAL THINKING AND READING

Recognizing the Author's Purpose

William Byrd's decision to tone down his original material when he prepared *The History* shows that the purpose of his journal was different from the purpose of *The History*. While Byrd's journal account served as his personal record of the surveying expedition, *The History* was intended to inform members of the British aristocracy about life in America.

1. What impression of himself and the other colonists does Byrd seem to be trying to convey?
2. What impression of the American wilderness does he seem to be trying to convey?
3. Aside from informing readers, what other purpose does *The History* serve?

THINKING AND WRITING

Writing a Narrative Account

Refer to the journal entry that you wrote before reading this selection. Turn your journal entry into a narrative designed to achieve a certain effect. First determine the effect you would like to achieve. For instance, do you want to persuade someone to undertake an adventure similar to yours? Then, using the information from your journal entry, write your narrative. Revise your narrative, changing or adding details necessary to achieve your effect.

from *The History of the Dividing Line*   69

Closure and Extension

ANSWERS TO THINKING ABOUT THE SELECTION
Recalling

1. They contained provisions for eight days and were as heavy as they possibly could be for carrying, weighing from sixty to seventy pounds.

2. Suggested Response: The tall reeds and other foliage, as well as the wet ground, were two obstacles they faced.
3. (a) He used a louse, an insect with no protective eyelids, which would cause it to turn toward the North, away from the strongest light. (b) The North Briton could then head North and make his way out.

Interpreting

4. He knows the names of all the types of vegetation.
5. Answers will differ. The first sentence of the third paragraph is one example.

Applying

6. Answers will differ. Suggested Response: It might mention God several times and might have praised the efforts of the men who endured the difficulties.

ANSWERS TO ANALYZING LITERATURE

1. Suggested Response: The account might contain fewer details and be less precise if the author had no journal for reference.
2. Suggested Response: Byrd may have toned down the original material to make it more suitable as a history. His aim may have been to appear less biased and less subjective. He also may have wished to avoid the anger of those he had criticized when his account was made available for public reading.
3. Suggested Response: He probably left out some of his feelings about events. He may have omitted comments about any personal discomfort that he felt.

ANSWERS TO CRITICAL THINKING AND READING

1. Suggested Response: Byrd conveys the impression that the colonists were practical and dedicated to their task.
2. Suggested Response: Byrd conveys the impression that the wilderness is very treacherous.
3. Suggested Response: *The History* serves as a firsthand historical report of a particular time and place in America's past. In addition, it provides an interesting story for readers, as well as a description to educate readers about the landscape of the time.

THINKING AND WRITING

After students have written a draft of their narratives, you might have them work in groups, reading one another's drafts and suggesting improvements. Students can then incorporate useful suggestions in their revisions.

More About the Author All through his youth Jonathan Edwards subjected himself to rigorous religious discipline. While not yet twenty-one, he wrote seventy resolutions to follow in his life. Between the ages of eighteen and twenty-two, he kept a diary in which he examined and regularly scrutinized himself and his faith. During this time Edwards still lacked the conviction that he was sufficiently devoted to God. It was not until he was thirty-six that he felt his conversion to be complete. How might Edwards's inner struggles and convictions have affected his expectations of his congregation?

Critical Evaluation Samuel Hopkins (1721–1803) was a student and friend of Jonathan Edwards. Hopkins wrote extensively about Edwards' life and theological works. In the preface to his book, *The Life and Character of the Late Reverend Mr. Jonathan Edwards,* published in Boston in 1765, Hopkins wrote this about Edwards: "President Edwards, in the esteem of all the judicious, who were well acquainted with him, either personally, or by his writings, was one of the *greatest* —*best*—and *most useful* of men, that have lived in this age. . . .

"And no one perhaps has been in our day, more universally esteemed and acknowledged to be a *bright Christian,* an eminently *good man.* His love to God and man; his zeal for God and his cause; his uprightness, humility, self-denial, and weanedness from the world; his close walk with God; his conscientious, constant and universal obedience, in all exact and holy ways of living: In one word, the goodness, the holiness of his heart, has been as evident and conspicuous, as the uncommon greatness and strength of his understanding."

JONATHAN EDWARDS

1703–1758

Though he also wrote extensively, Jonathan Edwards is remembered mainly as one of the most powerful and persuasive Puritan preachers of colonial New England.

Born in East Windsor, Connecticut, Edwards grew up in an atmosphere of devout Puritan discipline. As a young boy, he is said to have demonstrated his religious devotion by preaching sermons to his playmates from a makeshift pulpit he built behind his home. Edwards also displayed academic brilliance at an early age. By the time he was twelve, he had learned to speak Latin, Greek, and Hebrew and had written numerous philosophical and scientific essays. Edwards entered Yale at the age of thirteen and graduated four years later as the valedictorian of his class. Edwards went on to earn his master's degree in theology.

In 1727 Edwards became the assistant to his grandfather, Solomon Stoddard, who was the pastor of the church at Northampton, Massachusetts, one of the largest and wealthiest congregations in the Puritan world. Edwards became the church pastor two years later when his grandfather died, and he also began preaching as a visiting minister throughout New England. Strongly desiring a return to the simplicity and orthodoxy of the Puritan past, Edwards became one of the leaders of the Great Awakening, a religious revival that swept the colonies in the 1730's and 1740's.

The Great Awakening did not last long, however, and in 1750 Edwards was dismissed from his position after many members of his congregation had become displeased with his conservative beliefs. Edwards then moved to Stockbridge, Massachusetts, where he preached to the Native Americans and wrote a number of theological works. In 1757 Edwards became the president of the College of New Jersey (now Princeton University), but he died shortly after taking office.

Although in most of his sermons, books, and essays Edwards appeals to reason and logic, his highly emotional "fire and brimstone" sermon *Sinners in the Hands of an Angry God* is by far his most famous work. This sermon, which was delivered to a congregation in Enfield, Connecticut, in 1741, and is said to have caused listeners to rise from their seats in a state of hysteria, demonstrates Edwards's tremendous powers of persuasion and captures the religious fervor of the Great Awakening.

Support Material

Teaching Portfolio
Teacher Backup, p. 103
Grammar in Action, *Understanding Tone,* p. 108
Usage and Mechanics Worksheet, p. 110
Vocabulary Check, p. 111
Critical Thinking and Reading, *Recognizing Persuasive Techniques,* p. 112

Language Worksheet, *Understanding Figurative Language,* p. 113
Selection Test, p. 114

GUIDE FOR INTERPRETING

from Sinners in the Hands of an Angry God

Literary Forms

Persuasive Speeches. A persuasive speech attempts to convince listeners to think or act in a certain way. The effectiveness of a persuasive speech depends to a large extent on the audience's perception of the speaker, the speaker's consideration of the audience and setting, and the choice of persuasive techniques.

The Speaker's Qualifications. A speaker must establish his or her qualifications to speak on the subject. In many cases the speaker's reputation alone convinces an audience of his or her qualifications. In other cases the speaker must gain the audience's trust by displaying knowledge of the subject or presenting his or her credentials.

Audience. It is also important for the speaker to be aware of the audience he or she is addressing. The writer must take into account the backgrounds, ages, interests, and beliefs of the audience.

Occasion. The time and place at which a speech is presented will also affect its content. The speaker may include references to current events or examples that will appeal to current interests.

Technique. Finally, the speaker must decide which persuasive techniques will best serve his or her purpose. A speaker may choose to present a logical argument or may appeal to past traditions or to the audience's emotions or sense of reason, or he or she may use a variety of other techniques.

Writing

Some of the factors that determine the effectiveness of a television commercial are similar to the factors that determine the effectiveness of a persuasive speech. Brainstorm about television commercials that you consider effective. Then list them and jot down the reasons why you think each one is effective.

Primary Source

In *Jonathan Edwards, Pastor,* Patricia Tracy discusses how Edwards achieved the "terrifying effects" of his sermon:

"Although it conveys the reek of brimstone, the sermon does not say that God will hurl man into everlasting fires—on the contrary, doom will come from God's indifference . . . He holds man above the pit as by a spider's thread, and should He become weary of protecting worthless man, that abominable insect will *drop of his own weight.* Man's preservation lay in God's whim of mercy, and the terror of this message derived from the insecurity of being temporarily protected by an all-powerful being who had an infinite anger. (Was the control of such strong feelings something that Edwards's audience found difficult to understand or to trust?)"

Guide for Interpreting   71

from Sinners in the Hands of an Angry God

Jonathan Edwards

This is the case of every one of you that are out of Christ:[1] That world of misery, that lake of burning brimstone, is extended abroad under you. There is the dreadful pit of the glowing flames of the wrath of God; there is Hell's wide gaping mouth open; and you have nothing to stand upon, nor anything to take hold of; there is nothing between you and Hell but the air; it is only the power and mere pleasure of God that holds you up.

You probably are not sensible of this; you find you are kept out of Hell, but do not see the hand of God in it; but look at other things, as the good state of your bodily constitution, your care of your own life, and the means you use for your own preservation. But indeed these things are nothing; if God should withdraw his hand, they would avail no more to keep you from falling than the thin air to hold up a person that is suspended in it.

Your wickedness makes you as it were heavy as lead, and to tend downwards with great weight and pressure towards Hell; and if God should let you go, you would immediately sink and swiftly descend and plunge into the bottomless gulf, and your healthy constitution, and your own care and prudence, and best contrivance, and all your righteousness, would have no more influence to uphold you and keep you out of Hell, than a spider's web would have to stop a fallen rock. Were it not for the sovereign pleasure of God, the earth would not bear you one moment . . . The world would spew you out, were it not for the sovereign hand of Him who hath subjected it in hope. There are black clouds of God's wrath now hanging directly over your heads, full of the dreadful storm, and big with thunder; and were it not for the restraining hand of God, it would immediately burst forth upon you. The sovereign pleasure of God, for the present, stays[2] his rough wind; otherwise it would come with fury, and your destruction would come like a whirlwind, and you would be like the chaff of the summer threshing floor.

The wrath of God is like great waters that are dammed for the present; they increase more and more, and rise higher and higher, till an outlet is given; and the longer the stream is stopped, the more rapid and mighty is its course, when once it is let loose. It is true, that judgment against your evil works has not been executed hitherto; the floods of God's vengeance have been withheld; but your guilt in the meantime is constantly increasing, and you are every day treasuring up more wrath; the waters are constantly rising, and waxing more and more mighty; and there is nothing but the mere pleasure of God, that holds the waters back, that are unwilling to be stopped, and press hard to go forward. If God should only withdraw his hand from the floodgate, it would immediately fly open, and the fiery floods of the fierceness and wrath of God,

---

1. **out of Christ:** Not in God's grace.

2. **stays:** Restrains.

Grammar in Action

The **tone** of a literary piece can often be its most striking feature, which is certainly true for this excerpt from Jonathan Edwards's sermon, "Sinners in the Hands of an Angry God." Tone can either be an author's attitude toward a subject or tone can be used to designate the mood of the work itself. The various devices used to create mood include diction, sentence structure, repetition, imagery, symbolism, and so on, all of which apply to Edwards's sermon. Look at the following passage:

The bow of God's *wrath* is bent, and the arrow made ready on the string, and *justice* bends the arrow at your heart, and strains the bow, and it is nothing but the mere pleasure of God, and that of an *angry* God, without any promise or obligation at all, that keeps the arrow one moment from being made *drunk* with your blood.

In this passage, Edwards elicits a fearful and angry tone through his use of diction, or word choice. He uses words such as those that are italicized to convey certain feelings and establish his tone. He also uses a lengthy sentence that is filled with symbolism and imagery of weapons and blood that should strike fear in his listeners.

would rush forth with inconceivable fury, and would come upon you with omnipotent power; and if your strength were ten thousand times greater than it is, yea, ten thousand times greater than the strength of the stoutest, sturdiest devil in Hell, it would be nothing to withstand or endure it.

The bow of God's wrath is bent, and the arrow made ready on the string, and justice bends the arrow at your heart, and strains the bow, and it is nothing but the mere pleasure of God, and that of an angry God, without any promise or obligation at all, that keeps the arrow one moment from being made drunk with your blood. Thus all you that never passed under a great change of heart, by the mighty power of the spirit of God upon your souls; all you that were never born again, and made new creatures, and raised from being dead in sin, to a state of new, and before altogether unexperienced light and life, are in the hands of an angry God. However you may have reformed your life in many things, and may have had religious affections, and may keep up a form of religion in your families and closets,[3] and in the house of God, it is nothing but His mere pleasure that keeps you from being this moment swallowed up in everlasting destruction. However unconvinced you may now be of the truth of what you hear, by and by you will be fully convinced of it.

Those that are gone from being in the like circumstances with you, see that it was so with them; for destruction came suddenly upon most of them; when they expected nothing of it, and while they were saying, peace and safety: now they see, that those things on which they depended for peace and safety, were nothing but thin air and empty shadows.

The God that holds you over the pit of Hell, much as one holds a spider, or some loathsome insect over the fire, abhors you, and is dreadfully provoked: his wrath towards you burns like fire; he looks upon you as worthy of nothing else, but to be cast

<hr />

3. closets *n.*: Small, private rooms for meditation.

THE PURITAN
Frank E. Schoonover
Collection of the Brandywine River Museum

into the fire; he is of purer eyes than to bear to have you in his sight; you are ten thousand times more abominable in his eyes, than the most hateful venomous serpent is in ours. . . .

O sinner! Consider the fearful danger you are in: it is a great furnace of wrath, a wide and bottomless pit, full of the fire of wrath, that you are held over in the hand of that God, whose wrath is provoked and incensed as much against you, as against many of the damned in Hell. You hang by a slender thread, with the flames of divine wrath flashing about it, and ready every moment to singe it, and burn it asunder; and you have no interest in any mediator, and nothing to lay hold of to save yourself, noth-

from Sinners in the Hands of an Angry God   73

3 Speaking and Listening Have student volunteers deliver excerpts from Edwards's sermon. Ask other members of the class to critique each delivery in terms of its persuasiveness and power.

4 Discussion What condition do you imagine the congregation would be in at this time?

5 Clarification *Natural condition,* in this context, refers to what Edwards believed to be the original, unsaved state of all humans because of Adam's fall from grace.

---

3 ing to keep off the flames of wrath, nothing of your own, nothing that you ever have done, nothing that you can do, to induce God to spare you one moment. . . .

4 When God beholds the ineffable extremity of your case, and sees your torment to be so vastly disproportioned to your strength, and sees how your poor soul is crushed, and sinks down, as it were, into an infinite gloom; he will have no compassion upon you, he will not forbear the executions of his wrath, or in the least lighten his hand; there shall be no moderation or mercy, nor will God then at all stay his rough wind; he will have no regard to your welfare, nor be at all careful lest you should suffer too much in any other sense, than only that you shall *not suffer beyond what strict justice requires.* . . .

God stands ready to pity you; this is a day of mercy; you may cry now with some encouragement of obtaining mercy. But once the day of mercy is past, your most lamentable and dolorous cries and shrieks will be in vain; you will be wholly lost and thrown away of God, as to any regard to your welfare. God will have no other use to put you to, but to suffer misery; you shall be continued in being to no other end; for you will be a vessel of wrath fitted to destruction; and there will be no other use of this vessel, but to be filled full of wrath. . . .

Thus it will be with you that are in an unconverted state, if you continue in it; the infinite might, and majesty, and terribleness of the omnipotent God shall be magnified upon you, in the ineffable strength of your torments. You shall be tormented in the presence of the holy angels, and in the presence of the Lamb,[4] and when you shall be in this state of suffering, the glorious inhabitants of Heaven shall go forth and look on the awful spectacle, that they may see what the wrath and fierceness of the Almighty is; and when they have seen it, they will fall down and adore that great power and majesty. . . .

_____
4. the Lamb: Jesus.

74   *The New Land*

It would be dreadful to suffer this fierceness and wrath of Almighty God one moment; but you must suffer it to all eternity. There will be no end to this exquisite horrible misery. When you look forward, you shall see a long forever, a boundless duration before you, which will swallow up your thoughts and amaze your soul; and you will absolutely despair of ever having any deliverance, any end, any mitigation, any rest at all. . . .

How dreadful is the state of those that are daily and hourly in the danger of this great wrath and infinite misery! But this is the dismal case of every soul in this congregation that has not been born again, however moral and strict, sober and religious, they may otherwise be. Oh that you would consider it, whether you be young or old! . . . 5 Those of you that finally continue in a natural condition, that shall keep you out of Hell longest will be there in a little time! Your damnation does not slumber; it will come swiftly, and, in all probability, very suddenly upon many of you. You have reason to wonder that you are not already in Hell. It is doubtless the case of some whom you have seen and known, that never deserved Hell more than you, and that heretofore appeared as likely to have been now alive as you. Their case is past all hope; they are crying in extreme misery and perfect despair; but here you are in the land of the living and in the house of God, and have an opportunity to obtain salvation. What would not those poor damned hopeless souls give for one day's opportunity such as you now enjoy!

And now you have an extraordinary opportunity, a day wherein Christ has thrown the door of mercy wide open, and stands in calling and crying with a loud voice to poor sinners; a day wherein many are flocking to him, and pressing into the kingdom of God. Many are daily coming from the east, west, north and south; many that were very lately in the same miserable condition that you are in, are now in a happy state, with their hearts filled with love to him who has loved them, and washed them from their sins in

---

Closure and Extension

ANSWERS TO THINKING ABOUT THE SELECTION
Recalling

1. (a) The hand of God keeps sinners from falling into Hell. (b) If the hand of God were withdrawn, nothing would keep sinners out of Hell.
2. The damned will suffer in Hell for eternity.
3. Edwards says that sinners have an opportunity to obtain mercy and salvation.
4. God's wrath hangs over a "great part of the congregation."

his own blood, and rejoicing in hope of the glory of God. How awful is it to be left behind at such a day! To see so many others feasting, while you are pining and perishing! To see so many rejoicing and singing for joy of heart, while you have cause to mourn for sorrow of heart, and howl for vexation of spirit! . . .

Therefore, let everyone that is out of Christ, now awake and fly from the wrath to come. The wrath of Almighty God is now un-

doubtedly hanging over a great part of this congregation: let everyone fly out of Sodom.[5] "Haste and escape for your lives, look not behind you, escape to the mountain, lest you be consumed."[6]

5. **Sodom:** In the Bible, a city destroyed by fire because of the sinfulness of its people.
6. **"Haste . . . consumed":** From Genesis 19:17, the angels' warning to the only virtuous man in Sodom, Lot, to flee the city before they destroy it.

THINKING ABOUT THE SELECTION

Recalling

1. (a) According to the opening paragraph, what keeps sinners from falling into Hell? (b) What power would the sinners have to keep themselves out of Hell if this were withdrawn?
2. For how long will the damned suffer in Hell?
3. Toward the end of the selection, what does Edwards say the sinners can obtain?
4. According to the last paragraph, over what portion of the congregation is God's wrath hanging?

Interpreting

5. Why do you think Edwards begins his sermon with a vivid description of Hell?
6. (a) State two comparisons Edwards uses to describe God's wrath. (b) How do these comparisons add to the speech's impact?
7. (a) At what point is there a change in Edwards's tone and emphasis? (b) How is this change related to the purpose of the sermon?

Applying

8. Do you think the approach Edwards takes in this sermon would be effective in today's society? Explain your answer.

ANALYZING LITERATURE

Understanding Persuasive Speeches

A **persuasive speech** attempts to convince an audience to think or act in a certain way. For example, in this excerpt from *Sinners in the Hands of an Angry God*, Edwards tries to convince members of a church congregation who

"are out of Christ" that they must dedicate their lives to God to escape eternal damnation. The effectiveness of Edwards's sermon depended to a large extent on the listeners' perception of him, his consideration of the audience and setting, and his choice of persuasive techniques.

1. Why would this sermon have been less effective if Edwards had not had a reputation as a brilliant spiritual leader?
2. In what ways does Edwards exhibit his understanding of the people he is addressing?
3. What emotion does Edwards appeal to? Considering Edwards's purpose, why is this an appropriate choice?
4. This sermon was delivered during the midst of the Great Awakening, a religious revival during which thousands of people converted to Puritanism. Toward the end of his sermon, how does Edwards draw on the occasion to support his argument?

THINKING AND WRITING

Evaluating Persuasive Techniques

Write an essay in which you explain why Edwards's choice of persuasive techniques was appropriate for his audience, setting, and purpose. Carefully reread Edwards's sermon, keeping in mind his audience, setting, and purpose and taking note of the persuasive techniques he uses. Then take some time to think about the relationship between his choice of persuasive techniques and the other factors. After developing a thesis statement, write your essay, making sure that you include passages from the sermon to support your thesis. When you revise, make sure you have touched on all important factors.

from *Sinners in the Hands of an Angry God* 75

More About the Author The combination of a number of factors gave Cotton Mather a complex personality. He came from a prominent New England family. He graduated from Harvard at the age of fifteen and had a reputation for being a genius. He wrote and studied ceaselessly, all the while maintaining his duties as a preacher. He is said to have fasted 450 times during his life, kept vigils, and even publicly humiliated himself in retribution for his sins. What kind of writing might be expected from such a man?

Literary Focus Style is often closely related to a writer's purpose. In *The Wonders of the Invisible World,* for example, Mather's journalistic style is closely related to his desire to make his account seem objective and factual.

Writing/Prior Knowledge For extra credit, you may wish to ask **more advanced** students to write a more formal research paper on the trials. Encourage them to draw their own conclusions about the facts they gather.

Vocabulary

Preteach the following vocabulary words:
calamities (kə lam′ ə tēs) *n.:* Disasters (p. 78)
preternatural (prēt′ ər nach′ ər əl) *adj.:* Differing from or beyond what is normally expected from nature (p. 79)
diabolical (dī′ ə bäl′ ək′l) *adj.:* Of the Devil (p. 80)
rampant (ram′ pənt) *adj.:* Spreading unchecked (p. 80)

GUIDE FOR INTERPRETING

from The Wonders of the Invisible World

Cotton Mather (1663–1728), a descendant of a prominent family of Puritan church leaders, was born in Boston. After receiving two degrees from Harvard College, Mather entered the ministry. He devoted his life to preaching and writing and produced more than four hundred books and pamphlets. His books include *Memorable Providences, Relating to Witchcraft and Possessions* (1689) and *The Wonders of the Invisible World* (1693), a report of the testimony at the Salem witchcraft trials.

Writer's Techniques

Style. Style refers to the manner in which a writer puts his or her thoughts into words. It involves the characteristics of a literary selection that concern form of expression—the choice and arrangement of words, the length and structure of sentences, the relationship between sentences and paragraphs, and the use of literary devices—rather than the ideas conveyed.

Cotton Mather's style is usually characterized by his use of ornate, elegant language and his frequent use of allusions—short references to literary works or figures, places, or events from history, religion, or mythology. In *The Wonders of the Invisible World,* however, Mather used a plain, direct, journalistic style. Mather's choice of words clearly indicates his biased point of view. Mather's purpose in writing the report was to justify the outcome of the trials, and he was careful to choose language that served this purpose.

Commentary

Cotton Mather felt that his generation was falling away from the original vision and purpose of the Puritan immigrants to North America. In the introduction to his account of the witchcraft trials, he reminds his readers that "New Englanders are a people of God settled in those, which were once the devil's territories." Now, warns Mather, the Devil is making a last, forceful attempt to drive them out.

Even though long interested in witchcraft as evidence of the Devil's work, Mather did not take part in the trials. Nor, however, did he speak out against them, even though he became skeptical of some of the evidence offered. In the following selection, notice how Mather's style indicates both his belief in witches and his skeptical attitude as a historian. Who do you think *could* have written the most objective account of the witchcraft trials?

Writing

What sort of impressions do you have of the Salem witchcraft trials? Freewrite about the witchcraft trials, describing the causes of the trials and the lessons we can learn from them.

Objectives

1 To recognize a writer's style
2 To recognize an author's bias
3 To write a journal entry

Support Material

Teaching Portfolio
Teacher Backup, p. 117
Grammar in Action, *Using Active and Passive Voice,* p. 122
Usage and Mechanics Worksheet, p. 124
Vocabulary Check, p. 125
Critical Thinking and Reading, *Recognizing Author's Bias,* p. 126

Language Worksheet, *Appreciating Style,* p. 127
Selection Test, p. 128

from The Wonders of the Invisible World

Cotton Mather

The Trial of Martha Carrier at the Court of Oyer and Terminer,[1] Held by Adjournment at Salem, August 2, 1692

I. Martha Carrier was indicted for the bewitching of certain persons, according to

the form usual in such cases, pleading not guilty to her indictment. There were first brought in a considerable number of the bewitched persons who not only made the court sensible[2] of an horrid witchcraft committed upon them, but also deposed that it

---

1. **Court of Oyer and Terminer:** A court authorized to hear (oyer) and determine (terminer) cases.

---

2. **sensible:** Aware.

A WITCH TRIAL IN SALEM, MASSACHUSETTS, in 1692
The Granger Collection

Humanities Note

Fine art, *A Witch Trial at Salem, Massachusetts, in 1692,* nineteenth century lithograph. The process of lithography, invented in 1799, begins with drawing on a specially prepared stone with a greasy crayon. After the stone is soaked in water, a print is made by inking the stone with a greasy ink that sticks to the crayon lines but is repelled by the wet surface. Paper is then pressed to the stone to receive the ink.

You might ask students the following questions.
1. What is happening in this print?
2. How does this parallel Mather's account of the trial of Martha Carrier?

Presentation

Motivation/Prior Knowledge Inform your students that at some point in their lives they may probably be asked to sit on a jury. Discuss the criteria the students would use to judge whether the evidence presented to them was fair. What kind of testimony would it take for them to be convinced of a defendant's guilt or innocence?

Master Teacher Note Point out to your students that in May of 1692, the Governor of Salem, Massachusetts, appointed a special court to try about nineteen individuals who had been accused of witchcraft. Since Mather was a prominent citizen, a preacher, and an eloquent writer, he was asked to write the account of the trial.

Purpose-Setting Question What does Mather's account suggest about the trial of Martha Carrier?

1 Enrichment Mather viewed the outbreak of witchcraft as a last-ditch attempt by the devil to reclaim the souls of individuals who had once dwelled in his territory. In his introduction, he asserted that if the people could weather this attack, they would soon "enjoy halcyon days with all the vultures of hell trodden under our feet."

2 Discussion Ask the students what they think really happened here. If Martha Carrier was innocent, as most people believe to be the case, what happened to Benjamin Abbott? How could such a large group of people all believe something that was untrue? Compare this mystery with more recent historical events in which large groups of people accepted beliefs or practices that most would find abhorrent, such as the Holocaust or the Jonestown Massacre.

Enrichment Cotton Mather was intent on making all aspects of society their moral best. In *The American Puritans*, Perry Miller describes Mather's crusade as the following: "Accepting the fact that the structure of society had become secularized, Mather prescribed rules for Christian conduct to all the specialized callings—magistrates, doctors, schoolmasters, farmers, ladies, lawyers . . . exhorting them all to assume as part of their status the responsibility of making the moral best of their situations. By trying to form the righteous into "societies" instead of into a society, Mather would subject the unrighteous to an ostracism more formidable than any pronounced by the General Court."

was Martha Carrier, or her shape, that grievously tormented them by biting, pricking, pinching and choking of them. It was further deposed that while this Carrier was on her examination before the magistrates, the poor people were so tortured that everyone expected their death upon the very spot, but that upon the binding of Carrier they were eased. Moreover the look of Carrier then laid the afflicted people for dead; and her touch, if her eye at the same time were off them, raised them again; which things were also now seen upon her trial. And it was testified that upon the mention of some having their necks twisted almost round, by the shape of this Carrier, she replied, "It's no matter though their necks had been twisted quite off."

II. Before the trial of this prisoner several of her own children had frankly and fully confessed not only that they were witches themselves, but that this, their mother, had made them so. This confession they made with great shows of repentance and with much demonstration of truth. They related place, time, occasion; they gave an account of journeys, meetings, and mischiefs by them performed, and were very credible in what they said. Nevertheless, this evidence was not produced against the prisoner at the bar,[3] inasmuch as there was other evidence enough to proceed upon.

III. Benjamin Abbot gave his testimony that last March was a twelvemonth this Carrier was very angry with him upon laying out some land near her husband's. Her expressions in this anger were that she would stick as close to Abbot as the bark stuck to the tree, and that he should repent of it afore seven years came to an end, so as Doctor Prescot should never cure him. These words were heard by others besides Abbot himself, who also heard her say she would hold his nose as close to the grindstone as ever it was held since his name was Abbot. Presently af-

---
3. bar: Court.

---

ter this, he was taken with a swelling in his foot, and then with a pain in his side, and exceedingly tormented. It bred into a sore, which was lanced by Doctor Prescot, and several gallons of corruption ran out of it. For six weeks it continued very bad, and then another sore bred in the groin, which was also lanced by Doctor Prescot. Another sore then bred in his groin, which was likewise cut, and put him to very great misery. He was brought unto death's door and so remained until Carrier was taken and carried away by the constable, from which very day he began to mend and so grew better every day and is well ever since.

Sarah Abbot also, his wife, testified that her husband was not only all this while afflicted in his body, but also that strange, extraordinary, and unaccountable calamities befell his cattle, their death being such as they could guess at no natural reason for.

IV. Allin Toothaker testified that Richard, the son of Martha Carrier, having some difference with him, pulled him down by the hair of the head. When he rose again he was going to strike at Richard Carrier but fell down flat on his back to the ground and had not power to stir hand or foot until he told Carrier he yielded, and then he saw the shape of Martha Carrier go off his breast.

This Toothaker had received a wound in the wars, and he now testified that Martha Carrier told him he should never be cured. Just afore the apprehending of Carrier, he could thrust a knitting needle into his wound four inches deep; but presently after her being seized, he was thoroughly healed.

He further testified that when Carrier and he sometimes were at variance she would clap her hands at him and say he should get nothing by it; whereupon he several times lost his cattle by strange deaths, whereof no natural causes could be given.

V. John Rogger also testified that upon the threatening words of this malicious Carrier his cattle would be strangely bewitched, as was more particularly then described.

Grammar in Action

When the subject of a sentence receives, rather than performs, the verb's action, the **passive voice** is being used. The **active voice,** in which the subject does perform the action, can be transformed into the passive voice by rearranging the words in a sentence. Take note of the following example:

Active: Others *heard* these words.
Passive: These words *were heard* by others.

While most authorities advise that we write in the active voice whenever possible, the passive voice is sometimes used to preserve the vitality of action verbs. For example, Cotton Mather uses the passive voice in the following sentence.

Martha Carrier was *indicted* for bewitching certain persons . . . (p. 77)

By using the passive voice in this sentence, Cotton Mather places the emphasis on Martha Carrier rather than on the court. In other instances, Mather uses the passive voice because the performer of the action is not known.

A WITCH TRIAL IN SALEM, MASSACHUSETTS, in 1692
Tha Granger Collection

Humanities Note

Fine art, *A Witch Trial in Salem, Massachusetts, in 1692,* nineteenth century lithograph. This is another nineteenth century lithograph depicting a witch trial.

Ask students the following questions.
1. What is happening in this picture?
2. What details mentioned in Mather's account are included in the lithograph?

3 **Clarification** *Preternatural* is a word meaning "outside of nature, or extraordinary."

4 **Clarification** A fortnight is a period of fourteen days, or two weeks.

VI. Samuel Preston testified that about two years ago, having some difference with Martha Carrier, he lost a cow in a strange, 3 preternatural, unusual manner; and about a month after this, the said Carrier, having again some difference with him, she told him he had lately lost a cow, and it should not be long before he lost another; which accordingly came to pass; for he had a thriving and well-kept cow which without any known cause quickly fell down and died.

VII. Phebe Chandler testified that about 4 a fortnight before the apprehension of Martha Carrier, on a Lord's day while the psalm was singing in the Church, this Carrier then took her by the shoulder and, shaking her, asked her where she lived. She made her no answer, although as Carrier, who lived next door to her father's house, could not in reason but know who she was. Quickly after this, as she was at several times crossing the fields, she heard a voice that she took to be Martha Carrier's, and it seemed as if it was over her head. The voice told her she should within two or three days be poisoned. Accordingly, within such a little time, one half of her right hand became greatly swollen and very painful, as also part of her face, whereof she can give no account how it came. It continued very bad for some days, and several

from *The Wonders of the Invisible World*   79

Student Activity 1. Identify the performer of the action in these passive sentences; then identify the person to whom Mather would like to attribute the actions:
1. His cattle would be strangely bewitched.
2. The poor people . . . were tortured . . .
3. She should within two or three days be poisoned.
4. She was then struck deaf.

Student Activity 2. Rewrite the four sentences in the first activity as active sentences.

Student Activity 3. Rewrite the following active sentences in passive voice.
1. The court did not produce all the evidence against Martha Carrier.
2. She would hold his nose to the grindstone.
3. Dr. Prescot lanced the sore.
4. The sore put him to very great misery.
5. The devil had promised her she should be queen of Hell.

5 **Discussion** What might the judges have been thinking at this point? What would have made the trial more fair?

6 **Clarification** A specter is "a ghost or apparition."

7 **Discussion** Discuss the strong language used here. Keeping in mind Mather's prominence as a citizen and preacher, how do you imagine the citizens of Salem might have reacted to this account?

Enrichment Five years later one of the judges at the Salem witchcraft trials, Samuel Sewall, publicly apologized for the rulings. Sewall posted a statement of his guilt on the church wall as an apology. Although Mather helped to bring an end to the hangings at the time, he never admitted that he and the judges had made a horrible mistake.

Reader's Response How would you feel if you were one of those accused of being a witch? Why?

times since she has had a great pain in her breast and been so seized on her legs that she has hardly been able to go. She added that lately, going well to the house of God, Richard, the son of Martha Carrier, looked very earnestly upon her; and immediately her hand, which had formerly been poisoned, as is abovesaid, began to pain her greatly, and she had a strange burning at her stomach; but was then struck deaf so that she could not hear any of the prayer or singing till the two or three last words of the psalm.

VIII. One Foster, who confessed her own share in the witchcraft for which the prisoner stood indicted, affirmed that she had seen the prisoner at some of their witch meetings, and that it was this Carrier who persuaded her to be a witch. She confessed that the devil carried them on a pole to a witch meeting; but the pole broke, and she hanging about Carrier's neck, they both fell down, and she then received an hurt by the fall, whereof she was not at this very time recovered.

IX. One Lacy, who likewise confessed her share in this witchcraft, now testified that she and the prisoner were once bodily present at a witch meeting in Salem village, and that she knew the prisoner to be a witch and to have been at a diabolical sacrament, and that the prisoner was the undoing of her and her children by enticing them into the snare of the devil.

X. Another Lacy, who also confessed her share in this witchcraft, now testified that the prisoner was at the witch meeting in Salem village, where they had bread and wine administered unto them.

XI. In the time of this prisoner's trial, one Susanna Sheldon in open court had her hands unaccountably tied together with a wheel band[4] so fast that without cutting it it could not be loosed. It was done by a specter, and the sufferer affirmed it was the prisoner's.

Memorandum. This rampant hag, Martha Carrier, was the person of whom the confessions of the witches and of her own children among the rest agreed that the devil had promised her she should be queen of Hell.

---

4. **wheel band:** A band or strap that goes around a wooden wheel.

Commentary

Three hundred years later, the Salem witch hunt still fascinates and horrifies us. Though the trials and hangings in Salem ended in 1692, the urge to hunt "witches" has certainly not ended. However, the term *witch hunt* has taken on a new meaning. Today a witch hunt is a campaign taken on to uncover alleged disloyalty or subversive activity. In 1953 the American playwright Arthur Miller vividly dramatized the Salem trials in his play *The Crucible* (page 1172). Using historical records of the proceedings, Miller imagined the personal suffering of John and Elizabeth Proctor, both accused of witchcraft.

The play was written and produced during a modern witch hunt: the loyalty hearings of the House Un-American Activities Committee, led by Senator Joseph McCarthy. The hearings were to investigate suspected Communist activity in the federal government. Like the Salem judges, McCarthy used his authority to play on public fear and patriotism and caused many innocent people to be blacklisted, lose their jobs, or be sent to jail. Miller himself was called before the committee in 1956 and, like John Proctor, refused to testify against his colleagues.

Commentary:
Witchcraft Trial Procedures

A set of procedures for conducting witchcraft trials was established by the Puritans to ensure that the accused men, women, young boys, and young girls received a "fair" trial. First the victim complained to the Magistrates about a suspected witch, sometimes doing so through another person. A warrant was then issued for the arrest of the accused. The accused was examined by two or more Magistrates. Next, the case of the accused was presented to the grand jury at which time depositions were introduced as evidence by the accusers. If the accused was indicted by the grand jury, he or she was tried before a jury. If the jury found the defendant guilty, the court passed sentence. In each case, the defendant was sentenced to die by hanging at a specified date. Finally, the sheriff and his deputies carried out the sentence on the appointed day.

During the Massachusetts witchcraft hysteria of 1692, more than 400 persons underwent the horror of being accused of

THINKING ABOUT THE SELECTION

Recalling

1. For what was Martha Carrier indicted?
2. Who was brought in to testify against her?
3. To what had Carrier's children confessed prior to the trial?
4. According to Benjamin Abbot's testimony, what happened to Abbot after Martha Carrier became angry with him?
5. (a) According to Phoebe Chandler's testimony, what did Martha Carrier do to Chandler "on a Lord's day"? (b) What happened "quickly after" this incident?
6. What information does Mather present in his "memorandum" at the end of the excerpt?

Interpreting

7. What detail in Abbot's description of his physical ailments is clearly exaggerated?
8. What does Chandler's testimony that she heard a voice above her head "that she took to be Martha Carrier's" imply about Carrier?

Applying

9. Do you think witnesses might have been likely to fabricate their testimony during the Salem witchcraft trials? Explain your answer.

ANALYZING LITERATURE

Recognizing a Writer's Style

Style refers to the way in which a writer expresses his or her thoughts. For example, in *The Wonders of the Invisible World,* Cotton Mather writes in a plain, direct, journalistic style.

1. How does Mather's style make his report of the trial seem like an objective, factual account?
2. Why would the report be less effective if it had been written in the elaborate, elegant style Mather used in his other works?

CRITICAL THINKING AND READING

Recognizing Author's Bias

Bias means "partiality" or an inclination toward a certain position. Although Mather's report is supposedly an objective account of the trial, his choice of words makes it clear that in reality his report is written from a biased point of view. For example, his reference to Martha Carrier as a "rampant hag" clearly indicates his negative attitude toward her.

1. How does Mather's statement that "a number of bewitched persons" were brought in to testify against Carrier reveal his bias?
2. Find two other examples of language that clearly indicates Mather's bias.
3. Do you think it possible for a person to be completely free of bias? Explain your answer.

THINKING AND WRITING

Writing a Journal Entry

Write a journal entry in which you describe the trial of Martha Carrier from Carrier's point of view. Reread the selection, thinking about how Martha Carrier might have viewed the proceedings. Then write your journal entry, using a plain, journalistic style similar to Mather's. When you revise, make sure your entry is simple and clear.

from *The Wonders of the Invisible World* 81

---

practicing witchcraft. Of these, nineteen were hanged, and one old man who refused to enter a plea at his trial was pressed to death as the sheriff and his men piled weights on him to force him to comply.

Closure and Extension

ANSWERS TO THINKING ABOUT THE SELECTION

Recalling

1. She was indicted for the bewitching of several people.
2. Carrier's own children, plus Benjamin and Sarah Abbot, Allin Toothaker, John Rogger, Samuel Preston, Phebe Cnandler, someone named Foster, two women named Lacy, and Susanna Sheldon all testified against her.
3. They confessed to being witches.
4. His foot swelled, he had a pain in his side that "bred into a sore," and he developed other sores in his groin.
5. (a) She shook her and asked her where she lived. (b) Chandler heard the voice of Carrier telling her she would be poisoned.
6. Mather says that all of the people involved in the case agreed that the devil had promised her that she would be queen of Hell.

Interpreting

7. The detail of his sore excreting several gallons of corruption is exaggerated.
8. It implies that Carrier had supernatural powers.

Applying

9. Suggested Response: They may have fabricated their testimony in response to group pressure and to keep themselves free of suspicion.

ANSWERS TO ANALYZING LITERATURE

1. His style makes the account seem objective, because it creates the appearance that he has limited himself to merely stating the facts.
2. Suggested Response: By using an elegant, elaborate style, Mather would create the impression that he was more concerned with entertaining readers than with presenting the facts.

ANSWERS TO CRITICAL THINKING AND READING

1. His statement makes it clear that he already assumes that Carrier is guilty.
2. Answers will differ. Two examples of his bias are the phrases "horrid witchcraft" and "grievously tormented."
3. Suggested Response: No, because every person has his or her own opinions.

Writing Across the Curriculum

You may wish to inform the students' history teachers about this assignment. They may be able to suggest additional historical sources that would be useful to the students.

81

The writing assignments on page 82 have students write creatively, while those on page 83 have them think about the selections and write critically.

YOU THE WRITER
Guidelines for Evaluating Assignment 1

1. Did the student write five journal entries describing the hardships of an early settler and discussing his or her impressions of the new land?
2. Has the student used simple, direct language?
3. Has the student used sensory details in the descriptions?
4. Is the description clear and coherent, and free from grammar, usage, and mechanics errors?

Guidelines for Evaluating Assignment 2

1. Did the student write a dialogue between a Native American and a settler that reveals the relationship between the two?
2. Has the student written a realistic dialogue?
3. Does the dialogue show some of the differences between the two cultures?
4. Is the dialogue free from grammar, usage, and mechanics errors?

Guidelines for Evaluating Assignment 3

1. Has the student written a creation myth that models those of the Native American oral tradition?
2. Does the myth contain supernatural or superhuman beings?
3. Is the myth written in prose or verse, modeling the style used in the myths in the text?
4. Are the events in the myth clearly described and in a logical order?
5. Is the myth free from grammar, usage, and mechanics errors?

YOU THE WRITER

Assignment

1. Imagine that you are an early settler living in either Plymouth or Jamestown. Write a series of five journal entries describing some of the hardships you and the other settlers face and discussing your impressions of the new land.
    Prewriting. Review the unit introduction (p. 2) and the selections by William Bradford (p. 52) and John Smith (p. 44), noting the hardships the early settlers encountered.
    Writing. When you write your journal entries, use simple, direct language, and use sensory details in describing the landscape.
    Revising. When you revise, make sure your descriptions are clear and coherent. After you have finished revising, proofread your entries and prepare a final copy.

Assignment

2. Because the early settlers and the Native Americans came from dramatically different cultures, it was difficult for them to understand one another when the settlers first arrived. Write a dialogue between a Native American and a settler occurring shortly after the settlers' arrival in the new land. (For the purpose of this assignment, imagine that both speak English.)
    Prewriting. Review the selections by William Bradford (p. 52) and John Smith (p. 44), noting what they reveal about the relationship between the settlers and the Native Americans. Brainstorm about the types of things the early settlers and the Native Americans might have discussed with one another. Then select two characters to have this dialogue.
    Writing. Write the first draft of your dialogue. Try to make your dialogue seem realistic, as if you were recording a conversation that actually occurred.
    Revising. When you revise, make sure your dialogue reveals some of the differences between the two cultures.

Assignment

3. Origin myths were an important part of the Native-American oral tradition. Write a myth describing the origin of the world and the human race. Your myth should be modeled after one of the myths you have read and should include superhuman or supernatural beings.
    Prewriting. Reread the origin myths in this unit. Try to put yourself in the place of the Native Americans, and think of other ways in which they might have explained the origin of the world. Then develop the plot of your origin myth, organizing the events in chronological order.
    Writing. Write your myth in either prose or verse, and model your writing style after the style used in the myths you have read.
    Revising. When you revise, make sure the events in your myth are described clearly. After you have finished revising, proofread your myth and prepare a final copy.

YOU THE CRITIC

Assignment

1. Reading the literature of the new land helps provide us with an awareness of the differences between life in the early settlements in the North and those in the South. Write an essay in which you compare and contrast life in the northern and southern settlements, using evidence from the selections you have read to support your argument.

Prewriting. Review the selections in this unit, noting what they reveal about the similarities and differences between life in the northern and southern settlements.

Writing. When you write your essay, organize your argument according to corresponding points of contrast.

Revising. When you revise, make sure you have used transitions and other linking devices to connect your ideas.

Assignment

2. The literature of the new land is important because of what it reveals about the lives of the settlers. Write an essay in which you discuss the historical significance of early American literature.

Prewriting. Review the selections in this unit, noting what they reveal about life in the early American settlements. Prepare a thesis statement, then organize your information into an outline.

Writing. When you write your essay, use evidence from at least two selections to support your thesis.

Revising. When you revise, make sure your argument is clear and coherent and is organized in a logical manner. After you have finished revising, proofread your essay and prepare a final copy.

Assignment

3. Literature often reveals a great deal about the attitudes and beliefs of different cultures. Write an essay in which you discuss what the literature of the Puritans reveals about their attitudes and values.

Prewriting. Review the selections by Puritan writers that you have read, noting what they reveal about Puritan beliefs. Prepare a thesis statement and organize your notes into an outline.

Writing. When you write your essay, use evidence from at least four selections to support your thesis.

Revising. When you revise, make sure you have thoroughly supported your thesis and have not included any unnecessary information. After you have finished revising, proofread your essay and prepare a final copy.

You the Critic 83

YOU THE CRITIC
Guidelines for Evaluating Assignment 1

1. Does the essay compare and contrast life in northern and southern settlements?
2. Is the essay organized according to corresponding points of contrast?
3. Has the student used transitions and other linking devices to connect ideas?
4. Is the essay free from grammar, usage, and mechanics errors?

Guidelines for Evaluating Assignment 2

1. Has the student written an essay about the historical significance of early American literature, which includes a thesis statement in the introductory paragraph?
2. Has the student given evidence from at least two selections to support the thesis?
3. Has the student presented a clear, coherent argument that is organized in a logical manner?
4. Is the essay free from grammar, usage, and mechanics errors?

Guidelines for Evaluating Assignment 3

1. Has the student written an essay that discusses what the literature of the Puritans reveals about their attitudes and values?
2. Has the student included a thesis statement and supported it with evidence from at least four selections?
3. Has the student eliminated all unnecessary information?
4. Is the essay free from grammar, usage, and mechanics errors?

Humanities Note

Fine art, *The Signing of the Constitution, 1787,* 1940, by Howard Chandler Christy. Many of the works of Ohio-born Howard Chandler Christy (1873–1952) are romanticized, sentimental drawings of elegantly dressed, pampered-looking men and women. In addition, Christy painted portraits of a number of famous people, from Thomas Edison to Edward Rickenbacker, a World War I ace pilot. Christy lent his skills to various causes as well, designing a political campaign poster for Warren G. Harding when Harding ran for president and making advertising posters for such organizations as the American Red Cross.

It was on July 4, 1940, that *The Signing of the Constitution of the United States, 1787* was unveiled in the Capitol building, where it remains. The group of statesmen of the new country are proudly signing the document. This rendering romanticizes the event. A few years later, in 1946–1947, Christy painted *The Signing of the United Nations Charter,* to mark the occasion of the formation of the world organization.

THE SIGNING OF THE CONSTITUTION, 1787
Howard Chandler Christy
The Granger Collection

Objectives

1 To understand the historical setting of the Revolutionary Period
2 To appreciate literature written in a time of crisis

THE REVOLUTIONARY PERIOD
1750–1800

Yesterday the greatest question was decided which ever was debated in America; and a greater perhaps never was, nor will be, decided among men. A resolution was passed without one dissenting colony, that these united colonies are, and of right ought to be, free and independent states.

John Adams

85

Students will be familiar with the historical background of this period of American literature from their social studies class. Ask students to discuss what they know about the causes of the American Revolution. Then tell them that they are about to approach the study of the American Revolution from a literary perspective. Encourage students to keep their historical knowledge of the American Revolution in mind as they read the selections in this unit.

Purpose-Setting Question Why is the literature of the American Revolution largely politically oriented?

Cooperative Learning Ask students to form groups and decide on an emotionally charged issue that they consider a crisis. Once they agree on an issue, students can share their opinions on the issue and keep a list of opinions for a short, one-page paper offering a solution to the crisis.

1 Master Teacher Note As examples of the talents of the founders of the country, you might point out the achievements of Benjamin Franklin and Thomas Jefferson.

2 Enrichment As a result of the advances in science, people came to believe that everything in the world could be explained through the use of reason, and people developed a deep sense of optimism about the present and future.

John Adams, who was to become the second President of the United States, wrote these sentences in a letter to his wife Abigail on the eve of the adoption of the Declaration of Independence. The momentous event of July 4, 1776, capped more than a decade of controversy between England and the American colonies. More than a decade of struggle to establish the new nation followed. During those years—indeed, during the entire second half of the eighteenth century—American literature was largely political. So dominant was the question of our relationship to England, and so talented and literate were the statesmen of the emerging nation, that some of the most notable writers of the period were the founders of the republic.

THE HISTORICAL SETTING

It is easy to forget how long the thirteen original states had been colonies. By 1750, there were fourth- and fifth-generation Americans of European descent living in Virginia and New England. These people were English subjects, and, on the whole, they were well satisfied with that status. Royal governors irritated them from time to time, but the colonial assemblies were locally elected and exercised considerable power, particularly over money. Year by year, decade by decade, Americans acquired experience in the art of self-government. As late as the early 1760's, however, few Americans had given much thought to the prospect of independence.

Between the mid-1760's and the mid-1770's, however, attitudes changed dramatically. King George III and Parliament imposed a number of unwise regulations that threatened the liberties of the colonists. With each succeeding measure, the outrage in America grew, finally erupting into war. As one Revolutionary veteran put it, "We always had governed ourselves, and we always meant to."

The Age of Reason

Great upheavals in history occur when circumstances are ripe. The American Revolution was such an upheaval, and the groundwork for it had been laid by European writers and thinkers as well as by the English king and Parliament. The eighteenth century is often characterized as the Age of Reason, or the Enlightenment. Spurred by the work of seventeenth-century scientists such as Galileo and Sir Isaac Newton, the writers and thinkers of the Enlightenment valued reason over faith. Unlike the Puritans, they had little interest in the hereafter, believing instead in the power of reason and science to further human progress. They spoke of a social contract that forms the basis of government. Above all, they believed that people are by nature good, not evil. A perfect society seemed to them to be more than just an idle dream.

Among the most influential figures of the Enlightenment were the French writer Voltaire, the French philosopher Jean Jacques Rousseau, the English political theorist John Locke, and the Scottish historian David Hume. Educated readers in the American colonies were familiar with the writings of these men.

The American statesmen of the Revolutionary period were themselves figures of the Enlightenment. No history of the period would be complete without mention of the thought and writings of Benjamin Franklin, Thomas Paine, and Thomas Jefferson. These Americans not only expressed the ideas of the Age of Reason, but they also helped to put them spectacularly into practice.

Toward a Clash of Arms

The American Revolution was preceded by the French and Indian War, a struggle between England and France for control of North America. The conflict broke out in the colonies in 1754 and continued for nearly a decade. British forces won the decisive battle of the war at the city of Quebec, Canada, in 1759. When the French and Indian War officially ended in 1763, France gave up its claims to North American territory. There was general jubilation in the thirteen English colonies.

The good feelings were short-lived, however. The British government, wanting to raise revenue in the colonies to pay its war debt, passed the Stamp Act in 1765. This was the first tax other than customs duties ever imposed on the colonists by Great Britain. The act required buying and affixing stamps to each of fifty-four kinds of items, including newspapers, playing cards, legal documents, licenses, and almanacs. Colonial reaction to the Stamp Act was swift and bitter. Stamps were burned. Stamp distributors were

EMBOSSED TAX STAMP ISSUED BY THE BRITISH GOVERNMENT IN 1765 FOR USE IN THE AMERICAN COLONIES
The Granger Collection

3 Enrichment Ironically, Rousseau was also partially responsible for many of the dominant ideas of the Romantic Movement, which followed the Age of Reason. Through reason, Rousseau ultimately concluded that humanity should listen to nature, instinct, and intuition.

Humanities Note

Embossed tax stamp issued by the British government in 1765. The enactment of the Stamp Act by the British Parliament aroused immediate opposition in the colonies. One of the most important acts of protest was the founding of the Sons of Liberty in Boston. This secret organization, under the leadership of Samuel Adams, was made up of lawyers, merchants, journalists, and others who were most directly affected by the tax. Besides making it difficult for the British to collect the tax, members of the Sons of Liberty urged the colonists to boycott British goods. The protest was so effective that, the following year, the British repealed the Stamp Act.

Two French inscriptions, symbols of the British monarchy and nobility, are prominent on the stamp: "Honi soit qui mal y pense" ("Shame be [to anyone] who thinks evil of it"), the motto of the chivalric Order of the Garter, which dates from the fourteenth century; and "Dieu et Mon Doit" ("God and My Right"), the motto of the British monarchy and aristocracy—symbols that were becoming increasingly hateful to the Americans. It was, indeed, more than the tax that they were protesting; it was the very presence of British control.

Enrichment In reaction to the Townshend Acts of 1767, the colonists manufactured their own goods.

Clarification John Adams obtained deathbed testimony from one of the colonists mortally wounded in the Boston Massacre. The dying man held the crowd, not the troops, responsible for the massacre. Samuel Adams, who helped form the Sons of Liberty, was convinced that the massacre was a British plot.

Enrichment "Revolutionary Tea" was a popular song of the 1770's. In it, the colonists called out to England, "Your tea you may have when 'tis steeped enough/ But never a tax from me."

Clarification The First Continental Congress adopted a resolution protesting the Intolerable Acts and voted for an immediate end to all trade with Great Britain.

Enrichment The Second Continental Congress convened in Philadelphia at the Pennsylvania statehouse where the famous Liberty Bell bears the inscription: "Proclaim liberty throughout all the land unto all the inhabitants thereof."

▌AMERICAN EVENTS▐

Benjamin Franklin Conducts His Experiment

1752   **Benjamin Franklin** conducts his kite and key experiment with lightning.

1754   French and Indian War begins for control of North American continent.

1758   *Poor Richard's Almanack* sold to new owner after 25 years under **Benjamin Franklin.**

1763   France, after French and Indian War, gives up claims to North American territory.

1765   Stamp Act passed by British Parliament; colonists protest bitterly.

1767   Townshend Acts impose new taxes, angering colonists further.

        Thomas Godfrey's *The Prince of Parthia* produced as first American play.

1770   British troops fire on an unruly mob in Boston, resulting in Boston Massacre.

        William Billings offers new American hymns in *The New England Psalm–Singer.*

1771   **Benjamin Franklin** begins writing his famous, uncompleted *Autobiography.*

1773   Parliament's Tea Act prompts Boston Tea Party, which led to Intolerable Acts.

        Phillis Wheatley's *Poems on Various Subjects* published in England.

1774   First Continental Congress meets in Philadelphia in response to the Intolerable Acts.

1775   **Patrick Henry** gives his "liberty or death" speech at the Virginia Convention.

        Skirmishes at Lexington and Concord open the American Revolution.

1776   **Thomas Paine's** *Common Sense* helps spur the movement for independence.

        Second Continental Congress adopts Declaration of Independence.

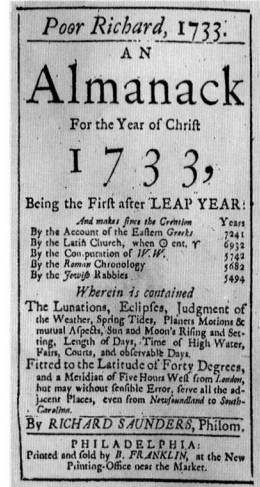

Poor Richard's Almanack

Richard Arkwright's

Phillis Wheatley   Apparatus Used in

88   *The Revolutionary Period*

Voltaire

SPINNING-FRAME.

Spinning Frame

Colonists Protest Stamp Act

Priestley's Experiments

William Hershel

WORLD EVENTS

1751   England: Thomas Gray completes "Elegy Written in a Country Churchyard."

1755   England: Samuel Johnson publishes *Dictionary of the English Language*.

1757   England: Robert Clive defeats native army at Plassey, India.

1759   France: Voltaire publishes *Candide*, satirizing optimism of Rousseau.

1762   France: Jean Jacques Rousseau states his political philosophy in *The Social Contract*.

1763   Seven Years War ends (including French and Indian War in America).

1765   Scotland: James Watt invents an improved steam engine.

1769   England: Richard Arkwright invents a frame for spinning; helped bring about factory system.

1770   Germany: Goethe begins 50 years of work on the dramatic poem *Faust*.

       Germany: Ludwig von Beethoven is born.

1771   England: Tobias Smollett publishes his novel *Humphrey Clinker*.

1772   Poland: First of three major partitions of Poland gives land to Russia, Prussia, and Austria.

1774   England: Joseph Priestley discovers oxygen, named later by Lavoisier.

1778   England: Captain James Cook becomes first European to see Hawaii.

1779   South Africa: First of many Kaffir Wars between blacks and whites breaks out.

1781   Germany: Immanuel Kant publishes his *Critique of Pure Reason*.

       England: William Herschel discovers planet Uranus.

Introduction   89

Enrichment Before Samuel Johnson's dictionary, there had been English dictionaries in the past, the first of which was published by Robert Cawdray in 1604. In *The Story of English*, editors Robert McCrum, William Cran, and Robert MacNeil explain, "Beyond the practical need to make order out of chaos, the rise of dictionaries is associated with the rise of the English middle class, keen to ape their betters and anxious to define and circumscribe the various worlds to conquer—lexical as well as social and commercial. It is highly appropriate that Dr. Samuel Johnson, the very model of an eighteenth-century literary man, as famous in his own time as ours, should have published his *Dictionary* at the very beginning of the heyday of the middle class . . . Rather than have an Academy to settle arguments about language, [Johnson] would write a dictionary; and he would do it single-handed . . . The work was immense. Writing in about eighty large notebooks (and without a library to hand) Johnson wrote the definitions of more than 40,000 words, illustrating their many meanings with some 114,000 quotations drawn from English writing on every subject, from the Elizabethans to his own time. He did not expect to achieve complete originality. Working to a deadline, he had to draw on the best of all previous dictionaries, and to make his a work of heroic synthesis. In fact, it was very much more. Unlike his predecessors, Johnson treated English very practically, as a living language, with many different shades of meaning. He adopted his definitions on the principle of English common law—according to precedent. After its publication, his *Dictionary* was not seriously rivalled for over a century."

AMERICAN EVENTS

1777   American forces defeat British at Battle of Saratoga, a turning point.

1778   France recognizes U.S. independence and signs treaty of alliance.

1781   General Cornwallis surrenders British army to George Washington at Yorktown.

1782   **Michel-Guillaume Jean de Crèvecoeur's** *Letters from an American Farmer* published in London.

1783   Noah Webster's *Spelling Book* first appears; 60 million copies would be sold.

        Peace of Paris ends Revolutionary War and recognizes U.S. independence.

1784   *Pennsylvania Packet and General Advertiser* becomes first long-term daily paper.

1787   Constitutional Convention meets in Philadelphia to draft Constitution.

        Royall Tyler's *The Contrast*, a satiric comedy, is produced in New York City.

1788   *The Federalist*, mainly the work of Alexander Hamilton, appears as a book.

1789   William Hill Brown's *The Power of Sympathy*, first American novel, published anonymously.

        George Washington elected unanimously as first President of United States.

1793   Eli Whitney invents cotton gin.

1795   University of North Carolina opens as America's first state university.

1800   **Thomas Jefferson,** principal author of Declaration of Independence, elected President.

The Constitutional Convention

Eli Whitney's Cotton Gin

Independence Hall, Philadelphia

The Storming of

The British Surrender at Yorktown

The *Death of Socrates*

James Boswell

the Bastille

Napoleon Bonaparte

1785   France: Jean–Pierre Blanchard makes first balloon crossing of English Channel.

1786   Scotland: Robert Burns is widely acclaimed for his first book of poems.

         Austria: Wolfgang Amadeus Mozart creates the comic opera *The Marriage of Figaro*.

1787   France: Jacques–Louis David paints *Death of Socrates*.

1789   France: Storming of Bastille in Paris sets off French Revolution.

1791   England: James Boswell publishes *The Life of Samuel Johnson*.

1793   France: King Louis XVI and Marie Antoinette go to death on guillotine.

1794   England: William Blake publishes *Songs of Experience*, including "Tyger! Tyger!"

1796   England: Edward Jenner develops vaccine against smallpox.

1798   England: Samuel Taylor Coleridge completes "The Rime of the Ancient Mariner."

         England: William Wordsworth publishes *Lyrical Ballads*.

1799   Egypt: Rosetta Stone, key to translating hieroglyphics, found.

         Spain: Goya creates powerfully satiric *Capichos* etchings.

         France: Napoleon Bonaparte becomes First Consul in a coup d'état.

1800   Germany: Ludwig von Beethoven composes *First Symphony*.

Introduction   91

Enrichment Jacques-Louis David was a highly influential French painter for almost a generation. He determined the course of fashion, furniture design, and interior decoration. His work marks a decisive break with tradition, from which point "modern art" is dated.

Clarification The French National Convention voted to abolish the monarchy and make France a republic. Radicals of the Convention wanted to try Louis the XVI for treason, but more moderate revolutionaries suggested that he be imprisoned until the war ended. When the Convention announced that a trunk had been discovered containing letters written by the king, Louis the XVI was doomed. The letters revealed that he was plotting with emigrés to crush the revolution. The convention tried and convicted him of treason, and by a majority of one vote, they sentenced him to death. Louis mounted the steps of the guillotine saying, "People, I die innocent!"

Enrichment The Rosetta stone is a basalt slab inscribed by priests of Ptolemy V in hieroglyphic, demotic, and Greek. Napoleon's troops found the stone near the Arabic city in Northern Egypt, in the Nile River Delta. The British acquired the stone in 1801; now it is in the British Museum.

Fine art, *The Boston Massacre, 5 March 1770,* colored engraving, 1770, by Paul Revere, after the drawing by Henry Pelham. Henry Pelham (1748–1806) made many drawings of Boston, some of them quite beautiful. Because he was a Loyalist, or British sympathizer, however, he fled to London in 1776.

One of the fallen soldiers commemorated at the bottom of Paul Revere's engraving is Crispus Attucks. Probably a runaway black slave (born 1723?), he led a group of about seventy sailors to King Street. There they encountered the hated British soldiers; in the melee that followed, Attucks and several other Americans were killed. Their heroism was celebrated in the oratory of Samuel Adams, who defended the dead Attucks against charges that he had provoked the British soldiers. Crispus Attucks and his companions were thus the first Americans to die in the long series of struggles for independence.

beaten and their shops destroyed. No blood was shed, but the hated stamps were withdrawn within six months, and the Stamp Act was repealed.

Other acts and reactions followed. The Townshend Acts of 1767 taxed paper, paint, glass, lead, and tea. When the colonists organized a boycott, the British dissolved the Massachusetts legislature and sent two regiments of British troops to Boston. In 1770, these Redcoats fired into a taunting mob, causing five fatalities. This so-called Boston Massacre further inflamed passions. Parliament repealed the Townshend duties except for the tax on tea, but a separate Tea Act soon greeted the colonists. The Tea Act gave an English company a virtual monopoly of the American tea trade. Furious, a group of Bostonians dressed as Mohawks dumped a shipment of tea into Boston harbor. As punishment for this Boston Tea Party, the English Parliament passed the Coercive Acts. Colonists immediately dubbed them the Intolerable Acts.

The situation had in fact become intolerable to both the colonists and the British. Colonial leaders, although not speaking

THE BOSTON MASSACRE, 5 MARCH 1770
Colored Engraving, 1770, by Paul Revere After the Drawing by Henry Pelham
The Granger Collection

92   *The Revolutionary Period*

openly of independence, met in Philadelphia for the First Continental Congress. The British, their authority slipping away, appointed General Thomas Gage governor of Massachusetts. The stage was set for war.

"The World Turned Upside Down"

On the night of April 18, 1775, General Gage sent a detail of about 700 British troops from Boston to destroy colonial munitions at Concord. The next morning, these troops met a drawn-up line of some seventy colonial Minutemen on the Lexington green. A musket shot was fired (from which side, no one knows), and the firing became widespread. Before it was over, eight Americans lay dead.

The British continued marching west to Concord, where another skirmish took place. Two more Americans fell, but so did three Redcoats. The British commander ordered a retreat to Boston. American snipers fired on the British troops all the way back, causing a total of 273 casualties.

The encounters at Lexington and Concord, a landmark in American history, have been referred to as "the shot heard round the world." The American revolution had begun, and there would be

THE BATTLE OF LEXINGTON AT THE BEGINNING OF THE COMBAT
Line Engraving, 1832, by Amos Doolittle and John W. Barber
The Granger Collection

Humanities Note

Fine art, *The Battle of Lexington at the Beginning of the Combat,* 1832, by Amos Doolittle and John W. Barber. Engravings of the momentous events of the American Revolution helped keep patriotic sentiment alive. In an age when literacy was not widespread, simple illustrated lessons could appeal to a broad audience.

At the Battle of Lexington, the British defeated a small band of colonial volunteers, or minutemen, alerted by Paul Revere as he rode through the countryside on the night of April 18, 1775. In this engraving, the presence of the Meeting House (5) and the Public Inn (6) made the incident particularly vivid to those familiar with the setting. Finally, legend (4), indicating the march of the British on to Concord, provided continuity with the engraving on page 94.

Fine art, *The Battle of Concord, the Engagement at the North Bridge, 19 April 1775*, 1775, by Amos Doolittle. Like the engraving of the Battle of Lexington (page 93), this work is an easy-to-follow pictorial representation of a historic moment in the American Revolution. At the North Bridge, in Concord, the British were overcome by several hundred colonial volunteers. From Concord the British fled back to Boston, where they were garrisoned. The two battles of April 18–19, 1775, marked the beginning of the Revolutionary War.

4 Enrichment George Washington had commanded British troops during the French and Indian War. Because these troops had suffered several defeats during this war, he recognized the vulnerability of the British army.

5 Enrichment Since the British and French were traditional enemies, it was not surprising that the French aided the Americans.

THE BATTLE OF CONCORD, THE ENGAGEMENT AT THE NORTH BRIDGE, APRIL 19, 1775
Line Engraving, 1775, by Amos Doolittle
The Granger Collection

no turning back. In June, the Americans killed or wounded more than a thousand British soldiers at the Battle of Bunker Hill. Although all the fighting up to this point had taken place in Massachusetts, the revolt involved all the colonies. Two days before Bunker Hill, the Second Continental Congress, meeting in Philadelphia, had named a commander in chief of the official American army. He was George Washington of Virginia.

More than a year would pass before the colonies declared their independence. More than six years would pass before the war ended, although the Battle of Saratoga, in the fall of 1777, marked a turning point. At Saratoga, in upstate New York, the British were surrounded and forced to surrender 5,700 men. When news of this American victory reached Paris, the government of France formally recognized the independence of the United States. Soon afterward, France began to commit troops to aid the American cause.

The war finally came to an end at Yorktown, Virginia, on October 19, 1781. Aided by the French army and the French navy, Gen-

94   *The Revolutionary Period*

eral Washington bottled up the 8,000-man British force under General Cornwallis. Seeing that escape was impossible, Cornwallis surrendered. After the British regiments had stacked their arms, they marched back to camp between rows of American and French soldiers. The British bands played a number of tunes during this ceremony. One of them was an old English song that seemed appropriate to the American troops: "The World Turned Upside Down."

The New Nation

One of the most impressive aspects of the American Revolution is that its original aims were realized. The revolt did not end in a bloodbath, or a military dictatorship, or a regime worse than the one overthrown. Thomas Jefferson recognized the danger of this in 1776 when he warned that "should a bad government be instituted for us in the future, it had been as well to have accepted . . . the bad one offered to us from beyond the water. . . ."

The path to self-government was not always smooth. After the Revolution, the Articles of Confederation established a "league of friendship" among the new states. This arrangement did not work well, however. The federal Constitution that replaced the Articles required many compromises and was ratified only after a long fight. Even then, a Bill of Rights had to be added to placate those who feared the centralized power that the Constitution conferred.

The old revolutionaries, by and large, remained true to their principles and continued their public duties. George Washington became the nation's first President. John Adams, a signer of the Declaration of Independence, succeeded him in that office. Then in 1800, Americans elected as their President the brilliant statesman who had drafted the Declaration, one of the heroes of the Enlightenment, Thomas Jefferson.

LITERATURE IN A TIME OF CRISIS

Like the Puritans in New England, educated Americans in the Age of Reason did a great deal of writing. Unlike the private soul-searching of the Puritans, however, much of what was produced during the Revolutionary period was public writing. By the time of the War for Independence, nearly fifty newspapers had been established in the coastal cities. At the time of Washington's inauguration, there were nearly forty magazines. Almanacs were popular from Massachusetts to Georgia.

During this period, the mind of the nation was on politics. Journalists and printers provided a forum for the expression of ideas. After 1763, those ideas were increasingly focused on relations with Great Britain and, more broadly, on the nature of government. The writing of permanent importance from the Revolutionary era is mostly political writing.

GEORGE WASHINGTON
ADDRESSING THE SECOND
CONTINENTAL CONGRESS AT
PHILADELPHIA
Contemporary Colored
Line Engraving
The Granger Collection

Humanities Note

Fine art, *George Washington Addressing the Second Continental Congress at Philadelphia.* The Second Continental Congress, which met at the Pennsylvania State House, was largely responsible for coordinating the war effort. It was not a sovereign government because the thirteen member states were not legally bound by its actions and decisions.

This contemporary, cartoon-like engraving is a rough-sketch depiction of Washington addressing the assembled group. The work captures a historic scene without sentiment or idealization, in keeping with the revolutionary spirit of democracy of the time.

6 **Master Teacher Note** To help students appreciate the success of the American Revolution, you might contrast it with the results of the French Revolution: the Reign of Terror and the dictatorship of Napoleon.

7 **Literary Movement** Imaginative literature did not flourish in the heat of the Revolution. As diverse as the Puritans and the Enlightenment thinkers were, they shared a suspicion of fiction and a lack of appreciation for imaginative literature in the three major genres: poetry, drama, and fiction.

Fine art, *Patrick Henry Speaking Against the Stamp Act in the Virginia House of Burgesses in 1765.* Patrick Henry (1736–1799) opposed the Stamp Act as a measure not enacted by the colonists' legitimate representatives. The following exchange is reported to have taken place in the House of Burgesses (lower house). Henry: "Ceasar had his Brutus, Charles the First his Cromwell, and George III . . ." Shouts of "Treason! treason!" Henry: ". . . may profit by their example. If *this* be treason, make the most of it."

This colored line engraving imitates the classical style of painting, with formal pillars in the background and the other members of the assembly grouped in a formal pattern. The well-dressed women in the gallery add to the sense of occasion. A dramatic effect is created by the stream of light flooding in through the arched window at the upper right. The beam of sunlight may well be a symbol of the dawning of freedom in the colonies.

8 **Literary Movement** See Patrick Henry's "Speech in the Virginia Convention," page 126.

9 **Literary Movement** See the excerpt from *The Crisis, Number 1* on page 132.

10 **Literary Movement** The Declaration of Independence (page 144) reflects the emphasis on reason and logic that characterized the Age of Reason.

PATRICK HENRY SPEAKING AGAINST THE STAMP ACT IN THE VIRGINIA HOUSE OF BURGESSES IN 1765
Colored Line Engraving, 19th Century
The Granger Collection

Politics as Literature

The public writing and speaking of American statesmen in two tumultuous decades, the 1770's and 1780's, helped to reshape not only the nation but also the world. James Otis of Massachusetts defended colonial rights vigorously in speeches and pamphlets. Otis, an eloquent speaker, is credited with giving Americans their rallying cry: "Taxation without representation is tyranny."

Another spellbinder was Patrick Henry, whose speech against the Stamp Act in the Virginia House of Burgesses brought cries of "Treason!" Ten years later, his electrifying speech to the Virginia Convention expressed the rising sentiment for independence. **8**

One man was more influential than any other in swaying public opinion in favor of independence. He was Thomas Paine, and his pamphlet *Common Sense,* published in January 1776, created an immediate sensation. It swept the colonies, selling 100,000 copies in three months. George Washington praised its "sound doctrine and unanswerable reasoning," as did countless other readers. "Independence rolls in on us like a torrent," said John Adams, who set forth his own ideas in *Thoughts on Government,* published in 1776. **9**

The Declaration of Independence was first drafted by Thomas Jefferson in June 1776. The finished document is largely his work, although a committee of five, including Benjamin Franklin, was involved in its creation. The Declaration, despite some exaggerated charges against King George III, is well reasoned and superbly written. It is one of the most influential political statements ever made. **10**

Another document written by committee that has stood the test of time is the Constitution of the United States, drafted in 1787. The framers, whose new nation contained about four million people, hoped that the Constitution would last a generation. It still survives, amended many times, as the political foundation of a superpower of fifty states and nearly 230 million people. Not everyone in 1787 was pleased with the Constitution. Alexander Hamilton called it a "weak and worthless fabric," and Benjamin Franklin supported it only because "I expect no better."

The doubts of the framers were reflected in the controversy over ratification. Delaware ratified the Constitution within three months, thus becoming the first state in the Union. But the ratification of nine states was necessary before the document could go into effect. The last few states proved difficult. The contest between supporters and opponents was especially hard-fought in New York. Alexander Hamilton, whose opinion of the Constitution was none too high, nevertheless wanted to see it pass in his home state. With James Madison and John Jay, he wrote a series of essays that were first published as letters to three New York newspapers. These essays, collected as *The Federalist,* served their immediate purpose. New York ratified the Constitution by a vote of 30 to 27. Over time, they have also come to be recognized as authoritative statements on the principles of American government.

The Cultural Scene

While politics dominated the literature of the Revolutionary period, not every writer of note was a statesman. Verse appeared in most of the newspapers, and numerous broadside ballads were published. (A broadside is a single sheet of paper, printed on one or both sides, dealing with a current topic.) One of the most popular broadside ballads was called "The Dying Redcoat," supposedly written by a British sergeant mortally wounded in the Revolution. The sergeant in the ballad realizes too late that his sympathy lies with the American cause:

> Fight on, America's noble sons,
> Fear not Britannia's thundering guns:
> Maintain your cause from year to year,
> God's on your side, you need not fear.

One poet of the time whose works were more sophisticated than the broadside ballads was Philip Freneau, a 1771 graduate of Princeton. A journalist and newspaper editor by profession, Freneau wrote poetry throughout his life. A few of his poems, such as "The Wild Honeysuckle" and "The Indian Burying Ground," earned his reputation as America's earliest important lyric poet.

Two other poets of the day were Joel Barlow and Phillis Wheatley. Barlow, a 1778 Yale graduate, is best remembered for "The Hasty Pudding," a mock-heroic tribute to cornmeal mush. Phillis Wheatley, born in Africa and brought to Boston in early childhood as a slave, showed signs of literary genius. A collection of her poems was published in England while she was still a young woman.

COVER OF TOM PAINE'S *COMMON SENSE*, 1776
The Granger Collection

TITLE PAGE OF VOLUME I OF THE *FEDERALIST*, NEW YORK, 1788
The Granger Collection

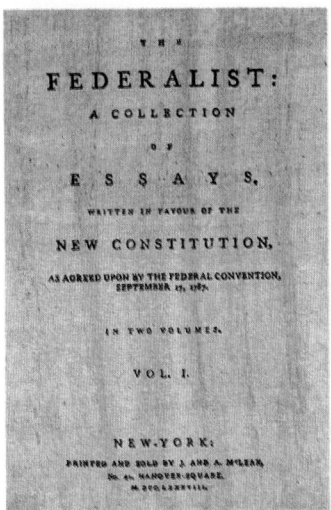

11 **Literary Movement** See "To His Excellency, General Washington" (page 138).

Humanities Note

Cover of Thomas Paine's *Common Sense,* 1776. Thomas Paine (1737–1809) was born in England but came to Philadelphia at the urging of Benjamin Franklin, who met Paine in London. Paine wrote his 50-page pamphlet to urge Americans not simply to protest against the injustices by the British—such as unfair taxation—but to fight for their independence. The pamphlet, which sold half a million copies altogether, was influential in the creation, seven months later, of the Declaration of Independence.

Humanities Note

Title page of Volume I of the *Federalist,* New York, 1788. The authors of the *Federalist* papers sought to calm the fears of opponents of ratification of the Constitution. Anti-federalists, as the opponents were called, were worried, in particular, that the central government under the Constitution would have too much power. Writing anonymously, Alexander Hamilton, James Madison, and John Jay argued that each of the three branches of government would serve as a restraint on the other two, thus preventing any one person or group from gaining too much control. The three advocates of the Constitution asserted, moreover, that the system of checks and balances established in the Constitution—for instance, the President may veto congressional legislation, but the Congress may vote to override the veto—would help protect the rights and interests of less-powerful groups of citizens. The mechanisms set up in the document, they maintained, would make it difficult for well-established, powerful groups to push through measures that would be detrimental to the less privileged in our society.

12 Literary Movement See the excerpt from *Letters from an American Farmer* on page 156.

13 Literary Movement The works of Benjamin Franklin (page 110) are written in the formal, ornate language typical of works from the Age of Reason.

One writer of the Revolutionary period recorded his impressions of everyday American life. He was Michel-Guillaume Jean de Crèvecoeur. Born of an aristocratic French family, Crèvecoeur became a soldier of fortune, a world traveler, and a farmer. For fifteen years he owned a plantation in Orange County, New York, and his impressions of life there were published in London in 1782 as *Letters from an American Farmer*.

12

Perhaps the best-known writing of the period outside the field of politics was done by Benjamin Franklin. His *Poor Richard's Almanack* became familiar to most households in the colonies. A statesman, printer, author, inventor, and scientist, Franklin was a true son of the Enlightenment. His *Autobiography,* covering only his early years, is regarded as one of the finest autobiographies in any language.

13

During this period, America began to establish a cultural identity of its own. Theaters were built from New York to Charleston. A number of new colleges were established after the war, especially in the South. Several outstanding painters were at work in the colonies and the young republic. Among them were John Singleton Copley, Gilbert Stuart, John Trumbull, and Charles Willson Peale. Patience Wright, famous in the colonies as a sculptor of wax portraits, moved to London before the war. While there, she acted as a Revolutionary spy. In music, William Billings produced *The New England Psalm-Singer* and a number of patriotic hymns. This was a turbulent time, a time of action, and its legacy was cultural as well as political.

American Literature at Daybreak

By the early 1800's, America could boast a small body of national literature. The Native Americans had contributed haunting poetry and legends through their oral traditions. The Puritans had written a number of powerful, inward-looking works. The statesmen of the Revolutionary period had produced political documents for the ages. A few poets and essayists had made a permanent mark on the literature of the young republic. There were, however, no American novels or plays of importance. The modern short story had yet to be invented.

The raw materials for a great national literature were at hand, waiting to be used. The nation stood on the threshold of a territorial and population explosion unique in the history of the world. It would take almost exactly a century to close the frontier on the vast and varied continent beyond the Appalachians. During that century, American literature would burst forth with a vitality that might have surprised even the farsighted founders of the nation. The colonial age ended with a narrow volume of memorable literature. The nineteenth century would close with a library of works that form a major part of America's literary heritage.

Check Test

1. _____ imposed taxes and regulations that threatened the liberties of the colonists.
2. The _____ was the first tax ever imposed on the colonists.
3. Important writing of the Revolutionary era is mostly _____ writing.
4. Thomas Paine's _____ was influential in swaying public opinion in favor of independence.
5. The best known writer of the Revolutionary era outside of the political field is _____.

ANSWERS

1. King George III and Parliament
2. Stamp Act
3. political
4. *Common Sense*
5. Benjamin Franklin

AMERICAN VOICES
Quotations by Prominent Figures of the Period

Experience keeps a dear school, but fools will learn in no other.
> **Benjamin Franklin,** *Poor Richard's Almanack*

We must all hang together, or assuredly we shall all hang separately.
> **Benjamin Franklin,** At signing of Declaration of Independence

Caesar had his Brutus; Charles the First his Cromwell; and George the Third ["Treason!" cried the Speaker] *may profit by their example.* If *this* be treason, make the most of it.
> **Patrick Henry,** Speech on the Stamp Act, Virginia House of Burgesses

He that would make his own liberty secure must guard even his enemy from oppression.
> **Thomas Paine,** *Dissertation on First Principles of Government*

For bright Aurora now demands my song.
  Aurora, hail, and all the thousand dyes,
Which deck thy progress through the vaulted skies.
> **Phillis Wheatley,** "An Hymn to the Morning"

The tree of liberty must be refreshed from time to time with the blood of patriots and tyrants.
> **Thomas Jefferson,** Letter to William Stevens Smith

It is not in the still calm of life, or the repose of a pacific station, that great characters are formed. . . . All history will convince you of this. . . . Great necessities call out great virtues.
> **Abigail Adams,** Letter to her son, John Quincy Adams

What then is the American, this new man?
> **Michel-Guillaume Jean de Crèvecoeur,** *Letters from an American Farmer*

Thus briefly sketched the sacred RIGHTS OF MAN,
How inconsistent with the ROYAL PLAN!
> **Philip Freneau,** "On Mr. Paine's *Rights of Man*"

Additional Voices

The next thing most like living one's life over again seems to be a recollection of that life, and to make that recollection as durable as possible by putting it down in writing.
> **Benjamin Franklin,** *Autobiography*

They that can give up essential liberty to obtain a little temporary safety deserve neither liberty nor safety.
> **Benjamin Franklin,** *Historical Review of Pennsylvania* [1759]

When authors and critics talk of the sublime, they see not how nearly it borders on the ridiculous.
> **Thomas Paine,** *The Age of Reason*

Is uniformity [of opinion] attainable? Millions of innocent men, women, and children, since the introduction of Christianity have been burnt, tortured, fined, imprisoned; yet we have not advanced one inch towards uniformity. What has been the effect of coercion? To make one half the world fools, and the other half hypocrites.
> **Thomas Jefferson,** *Notes on the State of Virginia* [1781–1785]

The care of human life and happiness, and not their destruction, is the first and only legitimate object of good government.
> **Thomas Jefferson,** *To the Republican Citizens of Washington County, Maryland* [March 31, 1809]

If we mean to have heroes, statesmen and philosophers, we should have learned women . . . If much depends as is allowed upon the early education of youth and the first principles which are instilled take the deepest root, great benefit must arise from literary accomplishments in women.
> **Abigail Adams,** *Letter to John Adams* [August 14 1776]

Reading Critically The information on this page will help students to read critically the literature of the Revolutionary Period. Discuss the information on this page with your students. Explain that the selection by Benjamin Franklin on the following pages is a model for reading critically. The notes in the side column draw their attention to elements in the writing that reflect the influence of the historical context, the literary movements, and the style of the writer. Have students read the selection through first and then reread it paying attention to the notes. You might have them offer their own comments on the selection as they read it actively.

To give students further practice with the process of reading critically, use the selection in the Teaching Portfolio, from *Travels* by William Bartram, page 146; following the Teacher Backup, which students can annotate themselves. Encourage students to use these strategies as they read the literature in this unit.

READING CRITICALLY

The Literature of 1750–1800

During the years from 1750–1800, almost all writing in America was influenced by the revolutionary spirit or the spirit of the new nation. Recognizing this spirit and the ideas of this period will enable you to understand better the purpose and techniques of the writers of the period.

Historical Context

It was during these years that the American colonists reached the point where they were no longer able to tolerate the British rule. The colonies united and took a stand against Britain. The Revolution was successful, and a proud and practical new nation emerged.

Literary Movements

This was the Age of Reason. The ideas of reason and discipline prevailed in the writing of the time. Because the attention of the nation was on the political events surrounding the Revolution, the literature was mostly political also. There was some personal writing—poetry and letters, for example—but most writing was public—pamphlets, speeches, and other documents—advocating and supporting a break with England.

Writers' Techniques

Logical reasoning is the major technique used by the writers of this period. Public writing offered sound clear arguments in support of the causes. Personal writing too showed the reasoning process.

On the following pages is a selection by Benjamin Franklin. Franklin wrote both political and personal documents. Always interested in self-improvement, he was a thoughtful, forthright, practical representative of the period.

Objectives

1 To read literature critically
2 To recognize the influence of the Age of Reason
3 To understand reasoning
4 To write a dialogue

Support Material

Teaching Portfolio
Teacher Backup, pp. 143–145
Grammar In Action Worksheet, *Understanding Sentence Fragments,* pp. 149–150
Usage and Mechanics Worksheet, p. 151
Critical Thinking and Reading Worksheet, *Understanding Reasoning,* p. 152
Language Worksheet, *Using Suf-*
fixes to Change Parts of Speech, p. 153
Selection Test, pp. 154–155

Dialogue Between Franklin and the Gout

Benjamin Franklin

This dialogue was written during the six-week period in 1780 when Franklin, suffering from gout, was confined to his house.

Midnight, October 22, 1780.

FRANKLIN. Eh! Oh! Eh! What have I done to merit these cruel sufferings?

GOUT. Many things; you have ate and drank too freely, and too much indulged those legs of yours in their indolence.

FRANKLIN. Who is it that accuses me?

GOUT. It is I, even I, the Gout.

FRANKLIN. What! my enemy in person?

GOUT. No, not your enemy.

FRANKLIN. I repeat it: my enemy, for you would not only torment my body to death but ruin my good name, you reproach me as a glutton and a tippler. Now all the world that knows me will allow that I am neither the one nor the other.

GOUT. The world may think as it pleases. It is always very complaisant to itself and sometimes to its friends, but I very well know that the quantity of meat and drink proper for a man who takes a reasonable degree of exercise would be too much for another who never takes any.

FRANKLIN. I take—Eh! Oh!—as much exercise—Eh!—as I can, Madam Gout. You know my sedentary state, and on that account, it would seem, Madam Gout, as if you might spare me a little, seeing it is not altogether my own fault.

GOUT. Not a jot, your rhetoric and your politeness are thrown away, your apology avails nothing. If your situation in life is a sedentary one, your amusements, your recreations, at least, should be active. You ought to walk or ride, or, if the weather prevents that, play at billiards. But let us examine

Literary Movement: Reason prevails during this period. Franklin applies reasoning to determine the cause of his pain.

Writer's Technique: Franklin presents his arguments in the form of a rational but humorous discourse.

Literary Movement: Franklin advocates "reasonable" and responsible behavior on the part of the individual.

Writer's Technique: Franklin has the Gout present reasonable arguments for her case.

Dialogue Between Franklin and the Gout 101

Presentation

Motivation/Prior Knowledge You might have students imagine a conversation with themselves or with some aspect of their personalities. What might be some topics of their conversation? Might an inner conflict be revealed? Point out that the following selection is such a conversation between Benjamin Franklin and a personified physical condition.

Master Teacher Note Because this selection is in the form of a dialogue, consider having students read it aloud, one student reading the part of Franklin and one reading the part of the Gout. Encourage them to read with appropriate expression.

Purpose-Setting Question In this conversation, which speaker presents the more logical arguments?

Clarification Gout is a temporary but painful inflammation of the joints, especially of the feet and hands. In Franklin's time, it was thought to be caused by overindulgence in food and lack of exercise.

Humanities Note

Fine art, *Benjamin Franklin, 1777*, by Augustin de Saint-Aubin. Saint-Aubin was a French engraver who lived in Paris. A prolific and accomplished engraver, he produced more than 1300 prints. Often an engraver will produce prints based on another artist's painting. Saint-Aubin is best known for his portraits modeled after the French painter and engraver Charles Cochin (1715–1790). This engraving of Benjamin Franklin is based on a portrait by Cochin.

You might ask students what personality traits are revealed in this engraving.

BENJAMIN FRANKLIN IN 1777
Augustus de Sainte Aubin
Philadelphia Museum of Art

Historical Context: Note the reference to the great number of documents (newspapers, and so on) available.

Writer's Technique: Franklin presents a clear appeal to a man of sense.

your course of life. While the mornings are long, and you have leisure to go abroad, what do you do? Why, instead of gaining an appetite for breakfast by salutary exercise you amuse yourself with books, pamphlets, or newspapers, which commonly are not worth the reading. Yet you eat an inordinate breakfast: four dishes of tea with cream and one or two buttered toasts with slices of hung beef, which I fancy are not things the most easily digested. Immediately afterward you sit down to write at your desk or converse with persons who apply to you on business. Thus the time passes till one without any kind of bodily exercise. But all this I could pardon in regard, as you say, to your sedentary condition. But what is your practice after dinner? Walking in the beautiful gardens of those friends with whom you have dined would be the choice of men of sense; yours is to be fixed down to chess where you are found engaged for two or three hours! This is your perpetual recreation, which is the least eligible of any for a sedentary man, because, instead of accelerating the motion of the fluids, the rigid attention it requires helps to retard the circulation and obstruct internal secretions. Wrapped in the speculations of this wretched game you destroy your constitution. What can be expected from such a course of living but a body replete with stagnant humors[1] ready to fall a prey to all kinds of dangerous maladies, if I, the Gout, did not occasionally bring you relief by agitating those humors and so purifying or dissipating them? If it was in some nook or alley in Paris, deprived of walks, that you played awhile at chess after dinner, this might

---

1. **humors:** At the time it was believed that the body contained four fluids (humors) which were responsible for a person's health and disposition.

Primary Source

Although few of the writings of the Revolutionary Period fall into the drama genre, Benjamin Franklin's *Dialogue Between Franklin and the Gout* is in its own imaginative way, dramatic. In his collection of essays, *American Literature, 1764–1789: The Revolutionary Years,* Everett Emerson comments on Franklin's potential as a dramatist.

Literary talents, great and small, were put to use during the revolutionary years; no really great ones were used, alas, in the creation of drama. One can imagine the many-talented Benjamin Franklin producing plays with amusing dramatic dialogue, for what he produced in the dialogue between himself and the gout is delightful. The leading writer of the revolutionary years, Franklin as printer, inventor, and statesman accomplished so much that it is easy to disregard his great literary imagination. Combining a brilliant comic sense with an accomplished style, Franklin created probably the most enduring literary works occasioned by the Revolution.

Have students discuss the humorous and dramatic elements of the dialogue before they read it aloud or act it out.

be excusable; but the same taste prevails with you in Passy, Auteuil, Montmartre, or Sanoy, places where there are the finest gardens and walks, a pure air, beautiful women, and most agreeable and instructive conversation, all which you might enjoy by frequenting the walks. But these are rejected for this abominable game of chess. Fie then, Mr. Franklin! But amidst my instructions I had almost forgot to administer my wholesome corrections, so take that twinge, and that.

FRANKLIN. Oh! Eh! Oh! Ohhh! As much instruction as you please, Madam Gout, and as many reproaches; but pray, Madam, a truce with your corrections!

GOUT. No, Sir, no, I will not abate a particle of what is so much for your good—therefore—

FRANKLIN. Oh! Ehhh! It is not fair to say I take no exercise when I do very often, going out to dine and returning in my carriage.

GOUT. That, of all imaginable exercises, is the most slight and insignificant, if you allude to the motion of a carriage suspended on springs. By observing the degree of heat obtained by different kinds of motion we may form an estimate of the quantity of exercise given by each. Thus, for example, if you turn out to walk in winter with cold feet, in an hour's time you will be in a glow all over; ride on horseback, the same effect will scarcely be perceived by four hours' round trotting; but if you loll in a carriage, such as you have mentioned, you may travel all day and gladly enter the last inn to warm your feet by a fire. Flatter yourself then no longer that half an hour's airing in your carriage deserves the name of exercise. Providence has appointed few to roll in carriages, while he has given to all a pair of legs, which are machines infinitely more commodious and serviceable. Be grateful, then, and make a proper use of yours. Would you know how they forward the circulation of your fluids in the very action of transporting you from place to place; observe when you walk that all your weight is alternately thrown from one leg to the other; this occasions a great pressure on the vessels of the foot and repels their contents; when relieved by the weight being thrown on the other foot, the vessels of the first are allowed to replenish, and by a return of this weight this repulsion again succeeds, thus accelerating the circulation of the blood. The heat produced in any given time depends on the degree of this acceleration; the fluids are shaken, the humors attenuated, the secretions facilitated, and all goes well, the cheeks are ruddy and health is established. Behold your fair friend at Auteuil, a lady who received from bounteous nature more really useful science than half a dozen such pretenders to philosophy as you have been able to

Historical Context: The use of battle terminology reflects the ongoing revolutionary events.

Literary Movement: The interest in scientific experiments reflects the attitude of the Age of Reason.

Dialogue Between Franklin and the Gout 103

extract from all your books. When she honors you with a visit, it is on foot. She walks all hours of the day and leaves indolence and its concomitant maladies to be endured by her horses. In this see at once the preservative of her health and personal charms. But when you go to Auteuil, you must have your carriage, though it is no farther from Passy to Auteuil than from Auteuil to Passy.

FRANKLIN. Your reasonings grow very tiresome.

GOUT. I stand corrected. I will be silent and continue my office. Take that, and that.

FRANKLIN. Oh! Ohh! Talk on, I pray you!

GOUT. No, no, I have a good number of twinges for you tonight, and you may be sure of some more tomorrow.

FRANKLIN. What, with such a fever! I shall go distracted. Oh! Eh! Can no one bear it for me?

GOUT. Ask that of your horses, they have served you faithfully.

FRANKLIN. How can you so cruelly sport with my torments?

GOUT. Sport! I am very serious. I have here a list of offenses against your own health distinctly written and can justify every stroke inflicted on you.

FRANKLIN. Read it, then.

GOUT. It is too long a detail, but I will briefly mention some particulars.

FRANKLIN. Proceed. I am all attention.

Historical Context: Franklin served as diplomat to France, where these gardens are located.

GOUT. Do you remember how often you have promised yourself, the following morning, a walk in the grove of Boulogne, in the garden de la Muette, or in your own garden, and have violated your promise, alleging, at one time, it was too cold, at another, too warm, too windy, too moist, or what else you pleased, when in truth it was too nothing but your insuperable love of ease?

FRANKLIN. That I confess may have happened occasionally, probably ten times in a year.

GOUT. Your confession is very far short of the truth. The gross amount is one hundred and ninety-nine times.

FRANKLIN. Is it possible?

GOUT. So possible, that it is fact. You may rely on the accuracy of my statement. You know M. Brillon's gardens and what fine walks they contain, you know the handsome flight of a hundred steps which lead from the terrace above to the lawn below. You have been in the practice of visiting this amiable family twice a week, after dinner, and it is a maxim of your own that "a man may take as much exercise in walking a mile up and down stairs as in ten on level ground." What an oppor-

Grammar in Action

A **sentence fragment** is a group of words expressing an incomplete thought, punctuated as if it were a complete sentence with a subject and a verb. Fragments are usually phrases, subordinate clauses, or words in a series. Nouns and their modifiers need verbs in order to function as complete sentences, just as verbs and their modifiers need nouns in order to stand as complete sentences. Similarly, prepositional and participial phrases cannot stand alone; they can be combined with nearby sentences. Subordinate clauses, clauses that depend on independent clauses, are also considered sentence fragments when they are punctuated like complete sentences. And words that indicate items in a series are also sentence fragments when they are not connected with a subject and a verb.

Although sentence fragments are errors to be avoided in good writing, they are often used in drama or wherever there is dialogue to capture the natural rhythm of the way people speak. Notice Franklin's use of sentence fragments in his dialogue with the Gout.

"What, with such a fever!"

This fragment is Franklin's response to the Gout's promise to pain him with more twinges. It is a prepositional phrase common-

tunity was here for you to have had exercise in both these ways! Did you embrace it, and how often?

FRANKLIN. I cannot immediately answer that question.

GOUT. I will do it for you: not once.

FRANKLIN. Not once?

GOUT. Even so. During the summer you went there at six o'clock. You found the charming lady with her lovely children and friends eager to walk with you and entertain you with their agreeable conversation, and what has been your choice? Why to sit on the terrace, satisfying yourself with the fine prospect and passing your eye over the beauties of the garden below, without taking one step to descend and walk about in them. On the contrary, you call for tea and the chessboard, and lo! you are occupied in your seat till nine o'clock, and that besides two hours' play after dinner; and then, instead of walking home, which would have bestirred you a little, you step into your carriage. How absurd to suppose that all this carelessness can be reconcilable with health without my interposition!

FRANKLIN. I am convinced now of the justness of poor Richard's remark that "Our debts and our sins are always greater than we think for."[2]

Literary Movement: Franklin refers to his own publication, *Poor Richard's Almanack.*

GOUT. So it is. You philosophers are sages in your maxims and fools in your conduct.

FRANKLIN. But do you charge among my crimes that I return in a carriage from Mr. Brillon's?

GOUT. Certainly, for, having been seated all the while, you cannot object the fatigue of the day and cannot want therefore the relief of a carriage.

FRANKLIN. What then would you have me do with my carriage?

GOUT. Burn it if you choose, you would at least get heat out of it once in this way; or, if you dislike that proposal, here's another for you: observe the poor peasants who work in the vineyards and grounds about the villages of Passy, Auteuil, Chaillot, etc., you may find every day among these deserving creatures four or five old men and women bent and perhaps crippled by weight of years and too long and too great labor. After a most fatiguing day these people have to trudge a mile or two to their smoky huts. Order your coachman to set them down. This is an act that will be good for your soul; and, at the same time, after your visit to the Brillons, if you return on foot, that will be good for your body.

Writer's Technique: The Gout presents a logical solution, with a double benefit, in response to Franklin's question.

---

2. **"Our debts . . . for":** From Franklin's *Poor Richard's Almanack.*

Dialogue Between Franklin and the Gout 105

Enrichment Franklin was fond of quoting himself in his writing. Here he quotes himself as Poor Richard from *Poor Richard's Almanack.* For further reading from the *Almanack,* see page 121.

ly used in conversation. Sentence fragments in dialogue quicken the pace of the conversation by eliminating words or phrases that are implied by the writer and understood by the reader. In general, however, sentence fragments caused by incorrect punctuation are errors that detract from the coherence and sophistication of your writing.

Student Activity 1. Locate other sentence fragments in the "Dialogue Between Franklin and the Gout." What purpose do the fragments serve?

Student Activity 2. Write a short dialogue of your own. It can be between you and another person, you and an abstract force (like Franklin's Gout), or two other parties communicating. Use sentence fragments when appropriate to capture the natural flow of conversation. Be careful not to overuse fragments in your dialogue.

Reading Strategy Have students summarize the logical arguments presented by the Gout. Point out that such logical thinking is typical of the Age of Reason.

Reader's Response What situations cause you to reflect in hindsight the way the Gout causes Franklin to reflect on his habits?

FRANKLIN. Ah! how tiresome you are!

GOUT. Well, then, to my office, it should not be forgotten that I am your physician. There.

FRANKLIN. Ohhh! what a devil of a physician!

GOUT. How ungrateful you are to say so! Is it not I who, in the character of your physician, have saved you from the palsy, dropsy, and apoplexy,[3] one or other of which would have done for you long ago but for me?

FRANKLIN. I submit and thank you for the past, but entreat the discontinuance of your visits for the future; for, in my mind, one had better die than be cured so dolefully. Permit me just to hint that I have also not been unfriendly to *you*. I never feed physician or quack of any kind to enter the list against you. If, then, you do not leave me to my repose, it may be said you are ungrateful too.

GOUT. I can scarcely acknowledge that as any objection. As to quacks, I despise them; they may kill you indeed, but cannot injure me. And, as to regular physicians, they are at last convinced that the gout in such a subject as you are is no disease but a remedy, and wherefore cure a remedy?—but to our business—there.

FRANKLIN. Oh! oh!—for Heaven's sake leave me! and I promise faithfully never more to play at chess but to take exercise daily and live temperately.

Historical Context: In line with tenets of the Age of Reason, Franklin promises to work on self-improvement.

GOUT. I know you too well. You promise fair, but, after a few months of good health, you will return to your old habits; your fine promises will be forgotten like the forms of last year's clouds. Let us then finish the account, and I will go. But I leave you with an assurance of visiting you again at a proper time and place, for my object is your good, and you are sensible now that I am your *real friend.*

---

3. apoplexy (ap' ə plek' sē) *n.:* Stroke.

THINKING ABOUT THE SELECTION

Recalling

1. What has Franklin done to merit his suffering?
2. (a) How does Franklin spend his mornings? (b) What is his "practice after dinner"?
3. According to the Gout, how does walking help "forward the circulation of your fluids"?
4. What maxim of Franklin's does the Gout use in her argument?
5. (a) Why does the Gout disregard Franklin's promise "to take exercise daily and live temperately"? (b) With what assurance does the Gout leave Franklin?

Interpreting

6. What do you think might have prompted Franklin to write this dialogue?
7. What does the dialogue reveal about Franklin's personal interests?

Applying

8. Do you think most people today get enough exercise? Why or why not?

ANALYZING LITERATURE

Understanding the Age of Reason

The eighteenth century is often referred to as the Age of Reason because it was characterized by an emphasis on rational thought. At the time, people believed that they could discover all the truths about the world and human existence through scientific observation and the process of reasoning. Because of their faith in reason, people possessed a great deal of optimism about the present and future. People also generally possessed a deep interest in science, a desire to preserve cultural standards and traditions, and a belief in moderation and self-restraint. These attitudes and beliefs are reflected in the literature of the period, which is also characterized by the use of elegant, ornate language.

1. How does Franklin's dialogue reflect a belief in reason?
2. How does the dialogue reflect a belief in moderation and self-restraint?
3. How does the dialogue reflect an interest in science?

CRITICAL THINKING AND READING

Understanding Reasoning

In his dialogue Franklin uses the process of reasoning to analyze his condition. First he assesses the causes of his condition. Then he provides a body of evidence to support his assessment and ends the dialogue by presenting possible solutions to his problem.

1. What are the causes of his condition?
2. Find three examples that he uses to support his assessment of the cause.

THINKING AND WRITING

Writing a Dialogue

Write a dialogue in which you present a logical argument, as Franklin does in "Franklin and the Gout." Think of an ailment or condition that occurs when people do not care for themselves properly. Then write a dialogue between this ailment and a fictional character who suffers from the ailment. Analyze the condition, following the process of reasoning that Franklin uses in his dialogue. When you revise make sure you have included enough evidence to thoroughly support the character's assessment of the causes of his or her condition.

Closure and Extension

ANSWERS TO THINKING ABOUT THE SELECTION
Recalling

1. He has eaten and drunk too much and been lazy about exercise.
2. (a) He eats a large breakfast and reads and writes and talks but gets no exercise. (b) He plays chess.
3. It increases blood circulation by throwing the body's weight from one leg to the other.
4. "A man may take as much exercise in walking a mile up and down stairs as in ten on level ground."
5. (a) She knows too well that after a few months of good health he will go back to his old habits. (b) She promises to visit him again at a proper time and place.

Interpreting

6. He was probably angry with himself for neglecting his physical condition.
7. It shows his interest in social and intellectual pursuits.

Applying

8. Answers will differ. Suggested Response: Yes, we are an exercise-conscious culture.

ANSWERS TO ANALYZING LITERATURE

1. The "gout" is attempting to reason with Franklin.
2. Excess and overindulgence are blamed for bringing on the attack of gout.
3. It gives scientific reasons for the medical condition.

ANSWERS TO CRITICAL THINKING AND READING

1. The causes of his attack of gout are overindulgence and lack of exercise.
2. Suggested Response: He eats an enormous breakfast and takes no morning exercise; he plays chess after dinner, instead of walking; he rides everywhere in his carriage rather than walking.

THINKING AND WRITING

For extra credit, students may try writing a second dialogue from the opposite point of view: a person is giving logical reasons to a malady as to why it should go away.

1706–1790

No other colonial American better embodied the promise of America than Benjamin Franklin. Through hard work, dedication, and ingenuity, Franklin was able to rise out of poverty to become a wealthy, famous, and influential person. Although he never received a formal education, Franklin made important contributions in a variety of fields, including literature, journalism, science, diplomacy, education, and philosophy.

Franklin was born in Boston, one of seventeen children. After leaving school at the age of ten, Franklin spent two years working for his father, before becoming an apprentice to his older brother, who was a printer. When he was seventeen, Franklin left Boston and traveled to Philadelphia, hoping to open his own print shop. Once he established himself as a printer, Franklin began producing a newspaper and an annual publication called *Poor Richard's Almanack*, which contained information, observations, and advice. The *Almanack*, which Franklin published from 1733 through 1758, was very popular and earned Franklin a reputation as a talented writer.

When Franklin was forty-two, he retired from the printing business to devote himself to science. Franklin proved to be as successful a scientist as he had been a printer. Over the course of his lifetime, he was responsible for inventing the lightning rod, bifocals, and a new type of stove; confirming the laws of electricity; and contributing to the scientific understanding of earthquakes and ocean currents.

In spite of his other contributions, Franklin probably is remembered by most as a statesman and diplomat. Franklin played an important role in drafting the Declaration of Independence, enlisting French support during the Revolutionary War, negotiating a peace treaty with Britain, and drafting the United States Constitution.

Franklin, the diplomat and inventor, became an international figure who "played with lightning and the French court." He spent several years in London and nine years in France near Paris. For the French court, the seventy-year-old Franklin played the role of the simple, noble rustic, wearing plain clothes and a frontiersman's fur hat. At the same time, he wrote and published satirical essays, witty "letters," and clever verses. The French idolized him, and he was much sought after as a brilliant storyteller and conversationalist. Franklin's sense of humor, clever wit and knowledge of European and classical literature are evident in all he wrote.

Though it was never completed, Franklin's *Autobiography,* filled with his opinions and suggestions about self-discipline and moral perfection, provides not only a record of his achievements but also an understanding of his character.

108   The Revolutionary Period

More About the Author Like many of his contemporaries, Benjamin Franklin believed an appeal to reason would provide solutions to all human problems. Unlike other philosophers of his time, however, Franklin possessed a keen sense of humor. In what way could Franklin's humor enrich his writing?

Critical Evaluation In his *Literary History of the American Revolution 1763–1783,* M.C. Tyler has the following to say about Benjamin Franklin's literary career: "To treat Franklin as a literary man is like classifying Edison as a letter-writer. One may gather his "works" into a set, but the fact remains that only incidentally was Franklin an author, and seldom even then with anything like creative originality. So far as he wrote at all, he was a journalist: all his life he was connected with newspapers and publishing. His almanacs were journalistic productions. His "Richard Saunders —Philomath" introductions, his amusing arguments concerning the death of his rival almanac-maker, even his proverbs strung down through the weather predictions of his almanac were, as in later years he himself freely confessed, nothing original. From year to year he gave the people what the people wanted, what the people could understand and enjoy."

Objectives

1 To understand an autobiography
2 To make inferences about the author
3 To write an autobiographical account

Support Material

Teaching Portfolio
Teacher Backup, pp. 157-160
Grammar in Action Worksheets, *Understanding Narrative Writing,* pp. 161-162; *Using Semicolons,* pp. 163-164
Usage and Mechanics Worksheet, p. 165
Vocabulary Check, p. 166
Analyzing Literature Worksheet,

Understanding an Autobiography, p. 167
Critical Thinking and Reading Worksheet, *Making Inferences About the Author,* p. 168
Selection Test, pp. 169-170

GUIDE FOR INTERPRETING

from The Autobiography

Literary Forms

Autobiography. An autobiography is a person's account of his or her life. Generally written in the first person, with the author speaking as "I," autobiographies present life events as the writer views them. As a result, the author's portrayals are colored by his or her attitudes, thoughts, and feelings. Thus, they can provide unique insights into the beliefs and perceptions of the author.

People write autobiographies because they feel that their lives are interesting or important or can in some way serve as an example for others. The autobiography has been a popular literary form in America.

Commentary

Franklin wrote the first section of his *Autobiography* in 1771 at the age of sixty-five while vacationing in England. At the urging of friends, he wrote three more sections, the last shortly before his death, but only brought the account of his life to the years 1757–1759, before his diplomatic successes.

The first section is written as a letter to his son, William, then aged forty and Governor of New Jersey. Franklin begins by suggesting that William may be interested in how he rose from poverty to his current state of affluence. This "letter of fatherly advice" is a way for Franklin to tell his remarkable "rags to riches" story without seeming to flaunt his accomplishments.

One of the best known parts of the *Autobiography* is Franklin's description of his earnest attempts to improve himself. This "project for arriving at moral perfection" has sometimes been cited as an example of Franklin's perhaps simplistic faith in the perfectibility of man and the powers of human reason. Franklin, however, writing at the age of seventy-nine, seems to be smiling a little at his youthful vanities and enthusiasm. (In some ways, his methods are not much different from those recommended in popular self-improvement books of today.)

As you read the *Autobiography*, note how you feel about both the young and the older Franklin. Is the idea of "moral perfection" hopelessly old-fashioned, or have you ever thought of trying something similar? What virtues would you list?

Writing

What experiences would you choose to write about if you were preparing your own autobiography? List the experiences that you would be most likely to include.

Presentation

Motivation/Prior Knowledge Many autobiographies, some published only after the author's death, provide an "inside story" about historical or political events that might otherwise be lost. Encourage students to take note of insights in Franklin's *Autobiography* that would not be likely to appear in any other source.

Writing/Prior Knowledge Before having students complete the writing activity, you may want to spend some time discussing the types of experiences and situations that would and would not be appropriate for an autobiography.

Vocabulary

Preteach the following vocabulary words:
approbation (ap′ rə ba′ shən) *n.:* Approval (p. 110)
arduous (är jōō wəs) *adj.:* Difficult (p. 114)
avarice (av′ ər is) *n.:* Greed (p. 115)
vigilance (vij′ ə ləns) *n.:* Watchfulness (p. 116)
disposition (dis′ pə zish′ ən) *n.:* Management (p. 118)
foppery (fäp′ ər ē) *n.:* Foolishness (p. 118)
felicity (fə lis′ ə tē) *n.:* Happiness; bliss (p. 118)

Spelling Tip You might point out that the *s* sound at the end of *avarice* is spelled *ce*.

1 *from* # The Autobiography

Benjamin Franklin

My brother had in 1720 or '21, begun to print a newspaper. It was the second that appeared in America and was called the *New England Courant*. The only one before it was *the Boston News Letter*. I remember his being dissuaded by some of his friends from the undertaking, as not likely to succeed, one newspaper being in their judgment enough for America. At this time (1771) there are not less than five-and-twenty. He went on, however, with the undertaking, and after having worked in composing the types and printing off the sheets, I was employed to carry the papers through the streets to the customers. He had some ingenious men among his friends who amused themselves by writing little pieces for this paper, which gained it credit and made it more in demand, and these gentlemen often visited us. Hearing their conversations and their accounts of the approbation their papers were received with, I was excited to try 2 my hand among them; but, being still a boy, and suspecting that my brother would object to printing anything of mine in his paper if he knew it to be mine, I contrived to disguise my hand, and writing an anonymous paper, I put it in at night under the door of the printing house. It was found in the morning and communicated to his writing friends when they called in as usual. They read it, commented on it in my hearing, and I had the exquisite pleasure of finding it met with their approbation, and that, in their different guesses at the author, none were named but men of some character among us for learning and ingenuity. I suppose now that I 3 was rather lucky in my judges, and that per-

haps they were not really so very good ones as I then esteemed them.

Encouraged however by this, I wrote and conveyed in the same way to the press several more papers, which were equally approved; and I kept my secret till my small fund of sense for such performances was pretty well exhausted, and then I discovered[1] it, when I began to be considered a little more by my brother's acquaintance, and in a manner that did not quite please him, as he thought, probably with reason, that it tended to make me too vain. And perhaps this might be one occasion of the differences that we began to have about this time. Though a brother, he considered himself as my master, and me as his apprentice, and accordingly expected the same services from me as he would from another; while I 4 thought he demeaned me too much in some he required of me, who from a brother expected more indulgence. Our disputes were often brought before our father, and I fancy I was either generally in the right or else a better pleader, because the judgment was generally in my favor. But my brother was passionate and had often beaten me, which I took extremely amiss; and, thinking my apprenticeship very tedious, I was continually wishing for some opportunity of shortening it, which at length offered in a manner unexpected.

One of the pieces in our newspaper, on some political point which I have now forgotten, gave offense to the assembly. He was taken up, censured and imprisoned for a 5

---

1. **discovered:** Revealed.

3 **Discussion** What is Franklin's attitude concerning his first literary success?

4 **Discussion** What does this paragraph reveal about Franklin's relationship with his older brother?

5 **Enrichment** Franklin's brother was jailed for exercising free speech, but Franklin lived long enough to help guarantee free speech in the First Amendment of the Bill of Rights.

month, by the speaker's warrant, I suppose because he would not discover his author. I too was taken up and examined before the council; but though I did not give them any satisfaction, they contented themselves with admonishing me, and dismissed me, considering me perhaps as an apprentice who was bound to keep his master's secrets.

During my brother's confinement, which I resented a good deal, notwithstanding our private differences, I had the management of the paper; and I made bold to give our rulers some rubs in it, which my brother took very kindly, while others began to consider me in an unfavorable light, as a young genius that had a turn for libeling and satire. My brother's discharge was accompanied with an order of the House (a very odd one) "that James Franklin should no longer print the paper called the *New England Courant*."

There was a consultation held in our printing house among his friends what he should do in this case. Some proposed to evade the order by changing the name of the paper; but my brother seeing inconveniences in that, it was finally concluded on as a better way to let it be printed for the future under the name of Benjamin Franklin. And to avoid the censure of the Assembly that might fall on him as still printing it by his apprentice, the contrivance was that my old indenture should be returned to me with a full discharge on the back of it, to be shown on occasion; but to secure to him the benefit of my service, I was to sign new indentures for the remainder of the term, which were to be kept private. A very flimsy scheme it was; however, it was immediately executed, and the paper went on accordingly under my name for several months.

At length a fresh difference arising between my brother and me, I took upon me to assert my freedom, presuming that he would not venture to produce the new indentures. It was not fair in me to take this advantage, and this I therefore reckon one of the first errata[2] of my life; but the unfairness of it

---

2. errata (e rät′ ə): Errors.

BENJAMIN FRANKLIN'S BIRTHPLACE IN BOSTON, MASSACHUSETTS
J. H. Buffords
Metropolitan Museum of Art

weighed little with me when under the impressions of resentment for the blows his passion too often urged him to bestow upon me, though he was otherwise not an ill-natured man: perhaps I was too saucy and provoking.

When he found I would leave him, he took care to prevent my getting employment in any other printing house of the town by going round and speaking to every master, who accordingly refused to give me work. I then thought of going to New York as the nearest place where there was a printer; and I was the rather inclined to leave Boston when I reflected that I had already made myself a little obnoxious to the governing party, and, from the arbitrary proceedings of the Assembly in my brother's case, it was likely I might if I stayed soon bring myself into scrapes. I determined on the point, but my

from *The Autobiography* 111

Humanities Note

Fine art, *Benjamin Franklin's Birthplace in Boston, Massachusetts*, 1883, by J. H. Buffords. John H. Buffords (1835–1871) was a leading American lithographer. He began his career as an apprentice in Boston and then went to New York where he worked for Endicott and Nathaniel Currier. After his return to Boston he founded the firm of J. H. Buffords and Co.

Engravings such as this provide accurate records of places and events from the past. We tend to overlook the value of such images, since contemporary events are recorded through photography and the electronic image.

You might ask students the following:
1. How does this pictorial record of Franklin's house enhance your appreciation of the story?
2. How might a photograph of the house have differed from this engraving?

6 Discussion Here Franklin reveals that he used his brother's legal situation as a means to escape indenture. Do you think Franklin really believed he treated his brother unfairly?

7 Reading Strategy Have students summarize the events that led to Franklin's decision to leave Boston. What impact do they think this decision will have on Franklin's future?

8 **Discussion** What does this passage reveal about the difficulties that faced travelers during Franklin's time? Would today's travelers consider a trip from Boston to New York to be a long journey?

9 **Enrichment** William Bradford (1663–1752) was a well-known printer, who established New York's first newspaper, the *New York Gazette,* in 1725. His grave can be seen at Trinity Church at Wall Street and Broadway in New York City.

10 **Discussion** In what ways could being well-read have been a social asset in Franklin's time? Is a literary education as important today?

father now siding with my brother, I was sensible that if I attempted to go openly, means would be used to prevent me. My friend Collins, therefore, undertook to manage a little for me. He agreed with the captain of a New York sloop for my passage. So I sold some of my books to raise a little money, was taken on board privately, and as we had a fair wind, in three days I found myself in New York near three hundred miles from home, a boy of but seventeen, without the least recommendation to, or knowledge of, any person in the place, and with very little money in my pocket.

My inclinations for the sea were by this time worn out, or I might now have gratified them. But, having a trade, and supposing myself a pretty good workman, I offered my service to the printer in the place, old Mr. William Bradford, who had been the first printer in Pennsylvania, but removed from thence upon the quarrel of George Keith. He could give me no employment, having little to do and help enough already; but, says he, "My son at Philadelphia has lately lost his principal hand, Aquila Rose, by death. If you go thither I believe he may employ you." Philadelphia was one hundred miles farther. I set out, however, in a boat for Amboy,[3] leaving my chest and things to follow me round by sea. In crossing the bay we met with a squall that tore our rotten sails to pieces, prevented our getting into the kill,[4] and drove us upon Long Island. . . .

When we drew near the island, we found it was at a place where there could be no landing, there being a great surf on the stony beach. So we dropped anchor and swung round towards the shore. Some people came down to the water edge and hallowed[5] to us, as we did to them. But the wind was so high and the surf so loud, that we could not hear so as to understand each other. There were canoes on the shore, and we made signs and hallowed that they should fetch us, but they either did not understand us, or thought it impracticable. So they went away, and night coming on, we had no remedy but to wait till the wind should abate; and in the meantime the boatman and I concluded to sleep if we could, and so crowded into the scuttle,[6] and the spray beating over the head of our boat, leaked through to us. In this manner we lay all night with very little rest. But the wind abating the next day, we made a shift to reach Amboy before night, having been thirty hours on the water without victuals or any drink but a bottle of filthy rum, the water we sailed on being salt.

In the evening I found myself very feverish, and went in to bed. But having read somewhere that cold water drank plentifully was good for a fever, I followed the prescription, sweat plentifully most of the Night; my Fever left me, and in the morning crossing the ferry, I proceeded on my journey, on foot, having fifty miles to Burlington, where I was told I should find boats that would carry me the rest of the way to Philadelphia.

It rained very hard all day, I was thoroughly soaked, and by noon a good deal tired; so I stopped at a poor inn where I stayed all night, beginning now to wish I had never left home. I cut so miserable a figure, too, that I found by the questions asked me I was suspected to be some runaway servant, and in danger of being taken up on that suspicion. However I proceeded the next day and got in the evening to an inn within eight to ten miles of Burlington, kept by one Dr. Brown.

He entered into conversation with me while I took some refreshment, and finding I had read a little, became very sociable and friendly. Our acquaintance continued as long as he lived. . . .

At his house I lay that night, and the next morning reached Burlington, but had

---

3. **Amboy:** A town on the New Jersey coast.
4. **kill** *n.:* Channel.
5. **halloed:** Called.

6. **scuttle** *n.:* A small, covered opening or hatchway in the outer hull or deck of a ship.

Grammar in Action

Narrative writing tells a story or relates a series of events. Narration is mainly concerned with capturing action by appealing to the reader's emotions, senses, and imagination. Through the use of concrete details and vivid language, the narrator helps the reader "witness" the events he or she is reading. Notice the vivid language Franklin uses in his narration of his journey to Amboy:

In crossing the bay we met with a squall that tore our rotten sails to pieces, prevented our getting into the kill, and drove us upon Long Island . . . But the wind was so high and the surf so loud, that we could not hear so as to understand each other.

In showing the action of crossing the bay and anchoring at shore, Franklin shows the reader that a "squall" was so severe it damaged their boat and interfered with communication.

Since narration relates a series of events, the events should be arranged in chronological order. Although writers sometimes begin with an event that occurs in the middle or end of the main story, they still maintain a sense of the normal flow of action.

the mortification to find that the regular boats were gone a little before my coming and no other expected to go till Tuesday, this being Saturday. Wherefore I returned to an old woman in the town of whom I had bought gingerbread to eat on the water and asked her advice. She invited me to lodge at her house till a passage by water should offer, and, being tired with my foot traveling, I accepted the invitation. She, understanding I was a printer, would have had me stay at that town and follow my business, being ignorant of the stock necessary to begin with. She was very hospitable, gave me a dinner of oxcheek with great good will, accepting only a pot of ale in return; and I thought myself fixed till Tuesday should come. However, walking in the evening by the side of the river, a boat came by, which I found was going towards Philadelphia with several people in her. They took me in, and as there was no wind, we rowed all the way; and about midnight not having yet seen the city, some of the company were confident we must have passed it, and would row no farther; the others knew not where we were; so we put towards the shore, got into a creek, landed near an old fence, with the rails of which we made a fire, the night being cold in October, and there we remained till daylight. Then one of the company knew the place to be Cooper's Creek, a little above Philadelpia, which we saw as soon as we got out of the creek, and arrived there about eight or nine o'clock on the Sunday morning, and landed at the Market Street Wharf.

I have been the more particular in this description of my journey, and shall be so of

11

DELAWARE RIVER FRONT, PHILADELPHIA
Thomas Birch
Museum of Fine Arts, Boston

11 Discussion Have students review the difficulty Franklin had getting to Philadelphia. Is travel more or less exciting today?

Humanities Note

Fine art, *Delaware River Front, Philadelphia,* 1800, by Thomas Birch. Birch (1779–1851) was born in England and settled in Philadelphia with his father in 1794. He had a fruitful sixty-year career as a printmaker and painter. Birch is considered a leading American marine painter. His work includes paintings of naval engagements from the War of 1812, seascapes (including dramatic paintings of shipwrecks and storms at sea), and ship portraits. Birch also painted landscapes of considerable beauty. His work prefigured the painting of the artists of the Hudson River School.

Birch assisted his father in making watercolor drawings for the portfolio "Views of Philadelphia," published in 1800. This picture is from that group.

You might ask your students these questions:
1. What kinds of activities are seen in this picture?
2. How would a present-day view of the Philadelphia riverfront differ from the view shown here?

Transitions linking events often indicate chronology. Skim the topic sentences of the paragraphs for indicators of chronology. For example, in the following sentences beginning three successive paragraphs, notice the phrases that link events and indicate the timing of events.

"*In the evening* I found myself very feverish, and went in to bed . . .
It rained very hard *all day* . . .
At his house I lay that night, and *the next morning* reached Burlington . . ."

Franklin's topic sentences set the scene and launch the action in the events of his narrative.

Student Activity 1. Analyze pages 112 and 113 for more examples of vivid language and chronological order. Explain how the examples you found help Franklin's narrative achieve its purpose.

Student Activity 2. Write a short, one-page narrative of a series of events in your life.

my first entry into that city, that you may in your mind compare such unlikely beginnings with the figure I have since made there. I was in my working dress, my best clothes being to come round by sea. I was dirty from my journey; my pockets were stuffed out with shirts and stockings; I knew no soul, nor where to look for lodging. I was fatigued with traveling, rowing, and want of rest; I was very hungry; and my whole stock of cash consisted of a Dutch dollar and about a shilling in copper. The latter I gave the people of the boat for my passage, who at first refused it, on account of my rowing; but I insisted on their taking it, a man being sometimes more generous when he has but a little money than when he has plenty, perhaps through fear of being thought to have but little.

Then I walked up the street, gazing about, till near the markethouse I met a boy with bread. I had made many a meal on bread, and inquiring where he got it, I went immediately to the baker's he directed me to in Second Street, and asked for biscuit, intending such as we had in Boston; but they, it seems, were not made in Philadelphia. Then I asked for a threepenny loaf and was told they had none such. So, not considering or knowing the difference of money and the greater cheapness nor the names of his bread, I bade him give me threepenny worth of any sort. He gave me, accordingly, three great puffy rolls. I was surprised at the quantity, but took it, and, having no room in my pockets, walked off with a roll under each arm and eating the other. Thus I went up Market Street as far as Fourth Street, passing by the door of Mr. Read, my future wife's father; when she, standing at the door, saw me and thought I made, as I certainly did, a most awkward, ridiculous appearance. Then I turned and went down Chestnut Street and part of Walnut Street, eating my roll all the way, and, coming round, found myself again at Market Street Wharf, near the boat I came in, to which I went for a draft of the river water; and, being filled with one of my rolls,

gave the other two to a woman and her child that came down the river in the boat with us and were waiting to go farther.

Thus refreshed, I walked again up the street, which by this time had many clean-dressed people in it, who were all walking the same way. I joined them, and thereby was led into the great meetinghouse of the Quakers near the market. I sat down among them, and, after looking round awhile and hearing nothing said, being very drowsy through labor and want of rest the preceding night, I fell fast asleep, and continued so till the meeting broke up, when one was kind enough to rouse me. This was therefore the first house I was in, or slept in, in Philadelphia.

The following excerpt relates events that occurred several years later.

It was about this time I conceived the bold and arduous project of arriving at moral perfection. I wished to live without committing any fault at any time; I would conquer all that either natural inclination, custom, or company might lead me into. As I knew, or thought I knew, what was right and wrong, I did not see why I might not always do the one and avoid the other. But I soon found I had undertaken a task of more difficulty than I had imagined. While my care was employed in guarding against one fault, I was often surprised by another; habit took the advantage of inattention; inclination was sometimes too strong for reason. I concluded, at length, that the mere speculative conviction that it was our interest to be completely virtuous was not sufficient to prevent our slipping; and that the contrary habits must be broken, and good ones acquired and established, before we can have any dependence on a steady, uniform rectitude of conduct. For this purpose I therefore contrived the following method.

In the various enumerations of the moral virtues I had met with in my reading, I found the catalog more or less numerous, as dif-

Grammar in Action

A **semicolon** is used to join independent clauses that express similar or contrasting ideas. In force, a semicolon stands midway between a period, which separates ideas into distinct sentences, and a comma, which joins clauses more closely than does the semicolon.

Notice Franklin's use of semicolons in the following aphorisms:

Eat not to dullness; drink not to elevation.

Resolve to perform what you ought; perform without fail what you resolve.

Student Activity 1. Identify the aphorisms in which Franklin uses semicolons. Then label the sentence elements on each side of the semicolon in each of these aphorisms.

Student Activity 2. The following are some aphorisms from Franklin's *Poor Richard's Almanack*. Punctuate each by placing a semicolon between the independent clauses.

QUAKER MEETING
British, fourth quarter 18th century or first quarter 19th century
Museum of Fine Arts, Boston

Humanities Note

Fine art, *Quaker Meeting,* by an unknown artist, oil on canvas, ca. 1790, Pennsylvania. This painting by an unknown artist is based on a print of a Quaker meeting by Egbert von Heemkirk of London (c. 1670), now in the Quaker collection at Haverford College in Haverford, Pennsylvania. This picture provides a sense of Quaker order and virtue.

You might ask the following questions:
1. The composition of this painting has a certain orderliness to it. How does this relate to Franklin's words?
2. Choose a few of the figures in the painting. What do you suppose each is saying or thinking?

18 **Discussion** Ask students to compile their own list of virtues. How does this list compare with Franklin's?

ferent writers included more or fewer ideas under the same name. Temperance, for example, was by some confined to eating and drinking, while by others it was extended to mean the moderating every other pleasure, appetite, inclination, or passion, bodily or mental, even to our avarice and ambition. I proposed to myself, for the sake of clearness, to use rather more names, with fewer ideas annexed to each, than a few names with more ideas; and I included under thirteen names of virtues all that at that time occurred to me as necessary or desirable, and annexed to each a short precept, which fully expressed the extent I gave to its meaning.

These names of virtues, with their precepts, were:

1. TEMPERANCE Eat not to dullness; drink not to elevation.

18

2. SILENCE Speak not but what may benefit others or yourself; avoid trifling conversation.

from *The Autobiography* 115

1. Wink at small faults remember thou hast great ones.
2. When befriended, remember it when you befriend, forget it.
3. A flatterer never seems absurd the flattered always takes his word.
4. Best is the tongue that feels the rein he that talks much must talk in vain.
5. Anger and folly walk cheek by jowl repentance treads on both their heels.
6. Content makes poor men rich discontent makes rich men poor.

3. ORDER Let all your things have their places; let each part of your business have its time.

4. RESOLUTION Resolve to perform what you ought; perform without fail what you resolve.

5. FRUGALITY Make no expense but to do good to others or yourself; *i.e.*, waste nothing.

6. INDUSTRY Lose no time; be always employed in something useful; cut off all unnecessary actions.

7. SINCERITY Use no hurtful deceit; think innocently and justly, and, if you speak, speak accordingly.

8. JUSTICE Wrong none by doing injuries, or omitting the benefits that are your duty.

9. MODERATION Avoid extremes; forebear resenting injuries so much as you think they deserve.

10. CLEANLINESS Tolerate no uncleanliness in body, clothes, or habitation.

11. TRANQUILLITY Be not disturbed at trifles, or at accidents common or unavoidable.

12. CHASTITY

13. HUMILITY Imitate Jesus and Socrates.[7]

19

My intention being to acquire the *habitude* of all these virtues, I judged it would be well not to distract my attention by attempting the whole at once but to fix it on one of them at a time; and, when I should be master of that, then to proceed to another, and so on, till I should have gone through the thirteen; and, as the previous acquisition of some might facilitate the acquisition of certain others, I arranged them with that view,

as they stand above. *Temperance* first, as it tends to procure that coolness and clearness of head, which is so necessary where constant vigilance was to be kept up, and guard maintained against the unremitting attraction of ancient habits and the force of perpetual temptations. This being acquired and established, *Silence* would be more easy; and my desire being to gain knowledge at the same time that I improved in virtue, and considering that in conversation it was obtained rather by the use of the ears than of the tongue, and therefore wishing to break a habit I was getting into of prattling, punning, and joking, which only made me acceptable to trifling company, I gave *Silence* the second place. This and the next, *Order*, I expected would allow me more time for attending to my project and my studies. *Resolution*, once become habitual, would keep me firm in my endeavors to obtain all the subsequent virtues; *Frugality* and *Industry* freeing me from my remaining debt and producing affluence and independence, would make more easy the practice of *Sincerity* and *Justice*, etc., etc. Conceiving then, that, agreeably to the advice of Pythagoras[8] in his *Golden Verses*, daily examination would be necessary, I contrived the following method for conducting that examination.

I made a little book, in which I allotted a page for each of the virtues. I ruled each page with red ink, so as to have seven columns, one for each day of the week, marking each column with a letter for the day. I crossed these columns with thirteen red lines, marking the beginning of each line with the first letter of one of the virtues, on which line and in its proper column I might mark, by a little black spot, every fault I found upon examination to have been committed respecting that virtue upon that day.

I determined to give a week's strict attention to each of the virtues successively.

7. Socrates (säk' rə tēz'): Ancient Greek philosopher and teacher (470?–399 B.C.).

8. Pythagoras (pi thag' ər əs): An ancient Greek philosopher and mathematician who lived in the sixth century B.C.

Primary Source

In the *Cambridge History of American Literature,* the following commentary makes an important point about Franklin's autobiography:

Franklin attained his eminence, so runs the argument, without academical instruction, with only casual reading, without the benefit of association with men of letters, and "in a society where there was no relish and no encouragement for literature." This statement of Franklin's educational opportunities is manifestly inadequate; but it so pleasantly flatters our longstanding pride in our self-made men that we are loath to challenge it. The hero presented to the schoolboy and preserved in popular tradition is still an "uneducated tradesman of America": a runaway Boston printer walking up Market Street in Philadelphia with his three puffy rolls; directing his fellow shopkeepers the way to wealth; sharply inquiring of extravagant neighbors whether they have not paid too much for their whistle; flying his kite in a thunderstorm; by a happy combination of curiosity and luck making important contributions to science; and, to add the last luster to his name, by a happy combination of industry and frugality, making his fortune.

Thus, in the first week, my great guard was to avoid every[9] the least offense against *Temperance*, leaving the other virtues to their ordinary chance, only marking every evening the faults of the day. Thus, if in the first week I could keep my first line, marked *T*, clear of spots, I supposed the habit of that virtue so much strengthened, and its opposite weakened, that I might venture extending my attention to include the next, and for the following week keep both lines clear of spots. Proceeding thus to the last, I could go through a course complete in thirteen weeks, and four courses in a year. And like him who, having a garden to weed, does not attempt to eradicate all the bad herbs at once, which would exceed his reach and his strength, but works on one of the beds at a time, and, having accomplished the first, proceeds to a second, so I should have, I hoped, the encouraging pleasure of seeing on my pages the progress I made in virtue, by clearing successively my lines of their spots, till in the end, by a number of courses, I should be happy in viewing a clean book, after a thirteen weeks' daily examination . . .

The precept of *Order* requiring that *every part of my business should have its allotted time*, one page in my little book contained the following scheme of employment for the twenty-four hours of a natural day.

THE MORNING. Question. What good shall I do this day?		
	5	Rise, wash, and
	6	address *Powerful Goodness!* Contrive day's business, and take the resolution of the day; prosecute the present study, and breakfast.
	7	
	8	
	9	Work.
	10	
	11	

NOON.	12	Read, or overlook my accounts,
	1	and dine.
	2	
	3	Work.
	4	
	5	
EVENING. Question. What good have I done today?	6	Put things in their places. Supper. Music or diversion, or conversation. Examination of the day.
	7	
	8	
	9	
	10	
	11	
	12	
NIGHT.	1	Sleep.
	2	
	3	
	4	

I entered upon the execution of this plan for self-examination, and continued it with occasional intermissions for some time. I was surprised to find myself so much fuller of faults than I had imagined; but I had the satisfaction of seeing them diminish. To avoid the trouble of renewing now and then my little book, which, by scraping out the marks on the paper of old faults to make room for new ones in a new course, became full of holes, I transferred my tables and precepts to the ivory leaves of a memorandum book, on which the lines were drawn with red ink that made a durable stain, and on those lines I marked my faults with a black-lead pencil, which marks I could easily wipe out with a wet sponge. After a while I went through one course only in a year, and afterward only one in several years, till at length I omitted them entirely, being employed in voyages and business abroad, with a multiplicity of affairs that interfered; but I always carried my little book with me.

My scheme of *Order* gave me the most trouble; and I found that, though it might be

9. **every:** Even.

from *The Autobiography* 117

This picturesque and racy figure is obviously a product of provincial America, the first great Yankee with all the strong lineaments of the type: hardness, shrewdness, ingenuity, practical sense, frugality, industry, self-reliance. The conception of the man here suggested is perhaps sound enough so far as it goes, being derived mainly from facts supplied by Franklin himself in the one book through which he has secured an eternal life in literature. But the popular notion of his personality thus derived in incomplete, because the *Autobiography,* ending at the year 1757, contains no record of the thirty-three years which developed a competent provincial into an able, cultivated, and imposing man of the world.

Literary Focus Here is an example of the use of an anecdote in an autobiography. How does it make the autobiography more entertaining?

22 **Critical Thinking and Reading** Do you think Franklin's description of himself here is an accurate one?

Reader's Response What virtues would be important to you if you were to aim for what Franklin calls "moral perfection"?

practicable where a man's business was such as to leave him the disposition of his time, that of a journeyman printer, for instance, it was not possible to be exactly observed by a master, who must mix with the world and often receive people of business at their own hours. *Order*, too, with regard to places for things, papers, etc., I found extremely difficult to acquire. I had not been early accustomed to it, and, having an exceeding good memory, I was not so sensible of the inconvenience attending want of method. This article, therefore, cost me so much painful attention, and my faults in it vexed me so much, and I made so little progress in amendment, and had such frequent relapses, that I was almost ready to give up the attempt, and content myself with a faulty character in that respect, like the man who, in buying an ax of a smith, my neighbor, desired to have the whole of its surface as bright as the edge. The smith consented to

21 grind it bright for him if he would turn the wheel; he turned, while the smith pressed the broad face of the ax hard and heavily on the stone, which made the turning of it very fatiguing. The man came every now and then from the wheel to see how the work went on, and at length would take his ax as it was, without farther grinding. "No," said the smith, "turn on, turn on; we shall have it bright by and by; as yet, it is only speckled." "Yes," says the man, *"but I think I like a speckled ax best."* And I believe this may have been the case with many, who, having, for want of some such means as I employed, found the difficulty of obtaining good and breaking bad habits in other points of vice and virtue, have given up the struggle, and concluded that *"a speckled ax was best"*; for something, that pretended to be reason, was every now and then suggesting to me that such extreme nicety as I exacted of myself might be a kind of foppery in morals, which, if it were known, would make me ridiculous; that a perfect character might be

attended with the inconvenience of being envied and hated; and that a benevolent man should allow a few faults in himself, to keep his friends in countenance.

In truth, I found myself incorrigible with respect to *Order*; and now I am grown old, and my memory bad, I feel very sensibly the want of it. But, on the whole, though I never arrived at the perfection I had been so ambitious of obtaining, but fell far short of it, yet I was, by the endeavor, a better and a happier man than I otherwise should have been if I had not attempted it; as those who aim at perfect writing by imitating the engraved copies, though they never reached the wished-for excellence of those copies, their hand is mended by the endeavor, and is tolerable while it continues fair and legible.

22

It may be well my posterity should be informed that to this little artifice, with the blessing of God, their ancestor owed the constant felicity of his life, down to his seventy-ninth year in which this is written. What reverses may attend the remainder is in the hand of Providence; but, if they arrive, the reflection on past happiness enjoyed ought to help his bearing them with more resignation. To *Temperance* he ascribes his long-continued health, and what is still left to him of a good constitution; to *Industry* and *Frugality*, the early easiness of his circumstances and acquisition of his fortune, with all that knowledge that enabled him to be a useful citizen, and obtained for him some degree of reputation among the learned; to *Sincerity* and *Justice*, the confidence of his country, and the honorable employs it conferred upon him; and to the joint influence of the whole mass of the virtues, even in the imperfect state he was able to acquire them, all that evenness of temper, and that cheerfulness in conversation, which makes his company still sought for, and agreeable even to his younger acquaintance. I hope, therefore, that some of my descendants may follow the example and reap the benefit.

Closure and Extension

ANSWERS TO THINKING ABOUT THE SELECTION
Recalling

1. Franklin does not think his brother will allow his writing to be published.
2. (a) Franklin's brother is imprisoned for publishing something that offended government officials. (b) Benjamin Franklin runs the paper.

THINKING ABOUT THE SELECTION

Recalling

1. Why does Franklin choose not to sign the first papers he submits for publication?
2. (a) Why is Franklin's brother sent to prison? (b) Who runs the paper while Franklin's brother is confined?
3. (a) What order is given to Franklin's brother when he is released? (b) How does he evade the order?
4. (a) Why does Franklin leave Boston? (b) How old is Franklin when he leaves?
5. What is Franklin's condition when he arrives in Philadelphia?
6. (a) What thirteen virtues does Franklin feel are necessary for moral perfection? (b) Summarize Franklin's plan for arriving at moral perfection. (c) How successful is Franklin in carrying out his plan?

Interpreting

7. (a) What characteristics does Franklin display in his dealings with his brother? (b) What qualities does he display during his trip to Philadelphia?
8. (a) What does Franklin's plan for moral perfection reveal about him? (b) Why is it surprising that the virtue of order gives him the most trouble?
9. (a) Find five examples of self-analysis in the selection. (b) How does Franklin's character change as he grows older?

Applying

10. How can analyzing behavior contribute to personal growth?

ANALYZING LITERATURE

Understanding an Autobiography

An **autobiography** is the story of a person's life written by that person. Because the author's attitudes, thoughts, and feelings color the self-portrayal as well as the portrayal of other people and events, the autobiography is subjective. However, for this same reason, autobiographies often provide insights into the beliefs and perceptions of the author. For example, Franklin's sense of morality is revealed in the excerpt from his *Autobiography.*

1. What impression does Franklin convey of himself as a young man?
2. How might the account of Franklin's early years be different if it had been written by his brother or his father?

CRITICAL THINKING AND READING

Making Inferences About the Author

Because an autobiographical account is colored by the author's viewpoint, you can make **inferences,** or draw conclusions, about the author's personality by examining the manner in which the self, other people, and events are portrayed. For example, one of the inferences that you might make from Franklin's portrayal of himself is that he was a very proud man.

1. What inference can you make about Franklin from his portrayal of his brother? Explain the evidence that supports your inferences.
2. What inference can you make about Franklin from his description of his journey to Philadelphia? Explain the evidence that supports your inference.

THINKING AND WRITING

Writing an Autobiographical Account

Examine the list of experiences you wrote before reading this selection. Decide which one you think others would find most interesting. Outline the events that led up to the experience, and think of what it taught you. Then write an autobiographical account, relating events in chronological order and including descriptive details that help bring the experience to life for your readers. When you finish writing, revise your account; and prepare a final copy.

strengths; however, ordering all of his affairs is more difficult for him.
9. (a) Answers will differ. Students may cite examples of self-analysis in which Franklin admits the following: he was vain about his writings; he might at times have provoked his brother; he was fuller of faults than he had imagined; he was incorrigible with respect to order; and he finds contentment in his "imperfect state." (b) As he grows older, Franklin becomes more even-tempered, and more willing to admit his faults.

Applying

10. Suggested Response: Analyzing behavior can contribute to growth by forcing people to recognize and correct their faults.

Challenge What does this excerpt reveal about Franklin's personality?

ANSWERS TO ANALYZING LITERATURE

1. As a young man Franklin is ambitious and egocentric.
2. Suggested Response: His brother may have depicted Franklin as a pesky younger brother, "saucy and provoking." His father may have depicted him as a rebellious youth.

ANSWERS TO CRITICAL THINKING AND READING

1. Suggested Response: From the way he portrays his brother, we can infer that Franklin is both critical of and resentful toward James.
2. Suggested Response: Franklin's persistence and confidence is evident in the description of his journey to Philadelphia.

THINKING AND WRITING

After your students have completed their accounts divide them into pairs, and have students read and evaluate their partners' rough drafts, suggesting ways in which the accounts could be improved.

3. (a) James Franklin is ordered not to print the paper, the *New England Courant.* (b) He evades the order by having the paper printed under Benjamin Franklin's name.
4. (a) After a falling out with his brother, Franklin is unable to get work and decides to leave Boston. (b) He is seventeen years old.
5. He is dirty, tired, and hungry.
6. (a) Franklin's virtues are temperance, silence, order, resolution, frugality, industry, sincerity, justice, moderation, cleanliness, tranquility, chastity, and humility. (b) Franklin's plan is to devote one week to each of the thirteen virtues and to master the virtue in that time, thus completing his plan for moral perfection in thirteen weeks. (c) Although Franklin admits he never arrived at perfection, he manages to diminish his faults by following the plan.

Interpreting

7. (a) Franklin is "saucy and provoking" in his dealings with his brother. (b) Franklin demonstrates determination, endurance, and a spirit for adventure.
8. (a) Franklin's plan to live a life without faults reveals his moral integrity, his optimism, and his confidence in himself. (b) Order, as Franklin's plan for moral perfection reveals, is one of his

Literary Focus Aphorisms often convey information about the cultures from which they emerged. Many of Franklin's aphorisms, for example, express the values of the merchant class of which Franklin was a member.

Writing/Prior Knowledge For extra credit, you may want to have your **more advanced** students write some of their own aphorisms.

Vocabulary

Preteach the following words:
fasting (fast′ iŋ) *v.:* Eating very little or nothing (p. 121)
squander (skwän dər) *v.:* Spend or use wastefully (p. 122)

GUIDE FOR INTERPRETING

from Poor Richard's Almanack

Literary Forms

Aphorisms. An aphorism is a short, concise statement expressing a wise or clever observation or a general truth. A variety of devices make aphorisms easy to remember. Some aphorisms contain rhymes or repeated words or sounds; others contain two phrases that present contrasting ideas using the same grammatical structure. For example, the contemporary aphorism "when the going gets tough, the tough get going," contains repeated words and contrasting ideas.

Most of Benjamin Franklin's aphorisms are adapted from proverbs, anonymous traditional sayings. Franklin, who believed that clarity and brevity were two of the most important characteristics of good prose, rewrote the traditional sayings, making them short, direct, and witty.

Franklin put an aphorism at the top or bottom of most pages in his almanacs. The aphorisms allowed Franklin to include many moral messages in very little space. Because readers found them entertaining, Franklin's aphorisms contributed to the popularity of *Poor Richard's Almanack.*

Writing

People often use aphorisms or proverbs in everyday speech. What sayings do you use or hear others use? Brainstorm for such sayings, and list as many as you can.

Primary Source

In the almanac of 1758, Richard Saunders, the author/editor created by Franklin and called Poor Richard, claims to overhear a speech made by white-haired Father Abraham to a crowd in front of a store. This speech is made up of most of Poor Richard's aphorisms on prudence and hard work. It was published separately as "The Way to Wealth" and was a tremendous success. By the end of the eighteenth century alone, it was reprinted at least 145 times in seven different languages.

What is Father Abraham's advice? Father Abraham says "plough deep, while Sluggards sleep, and you shall have Corn to sell and to keep . . . If you would have your Business done, go; if not, send . . . And now to conclude, Experience keeps a dear School, but Fools will learn in no other, and scarce in that; for it is true, we may give Advice, but we cannot give Conduct . . . However, remember this, They that won't be counselled, can't be helped, as Poor Richard says: And farther, that if you will not hear Reason, she'll rap your Knuckles."

Poor Richard then comments, "The People heard it, and approved the Doctrine, and immediately practiced the contrary, just as if it had been a common Sermon."

Objectives

1 To recognize aphorisms
2 To respond to a statement about style.

Support Material

Teaching Portfolio
Teacher Backup, pp. 171–173
Usage and Mechanics Worksheet, p. 174
Vocabulary Check, p. 175
Analyzing Literature Worksheet, *Recognizing Aphorisms,* p. 176
Critical Thinking and Reading Worksheet, *Understanding Style,* p. 177
Selection Test, pp. 178–179

from Poor Richard's Almanack

Benjamin Franklin

Hunger is the best pickle.

He that lives upon hope will die fasting.

Fish and visitors smell in three days.

Keep thy shop, and thy shop will keep thee.

If your head is wax, don't walk in the sun.

Necessity never made a good bargain.

Love your neighbor; yet don't pull down your hedge.

A slip of the foot you may soon recover, but a slip of
the tongue you may never get over.

Early to bed, early to rise, makes a man healthy,
wealthy, and wise.

God helps them that help themselves.

Three may keep a secret if two of them are dead.

Fools make feasts, and wise men eat them.

God heals and the doctor takes the fee.

The rotten apple spoils his companions.

If you would know the value of money, try to
borrow some.

A small leak will sink a great ship.

Drive thy business; let it not drive thee.

from *Poor Richard's Almanack*   121

Reader's Response Which of the aphorisms in *Poor Richard's Almanack* could apply to experiences from your life? Explain how at least two aphorisms seem familiar to you from experiences you've had.

Humanities Note

Fine art, *Poor Richard's Almanack*, Benjamin Franklin. *Poor Richard's Almanack* was published annually from 1733 to 1758. Like most almanacs, *Poor Richard's* contained practical information about the calendar, the sun and moon, and the weather. It also contained a wealth of homespun sayings and observations, many of which are still used today. It was these aphorisms, with their characteristic moral overtones, that made the almanac a bestseller. Franklin sold the almanac in 1758 and it continued publication until 1796 under a different name.

You might consider asking the following questions:

1. What letter of the alphabet appeared in a different printed form in 1733 than it does today?
2. After Benjamin Franklin's pseudonym, Richard Saunders, is the title "Philom.," short for philomath. What does "philomath" mean?

Dost thou love life? Then do not squander time; for that's the stuff life is made of.

Genius without education is like silver in the mine.

4 ☐ The cat in gloves catches no mice.

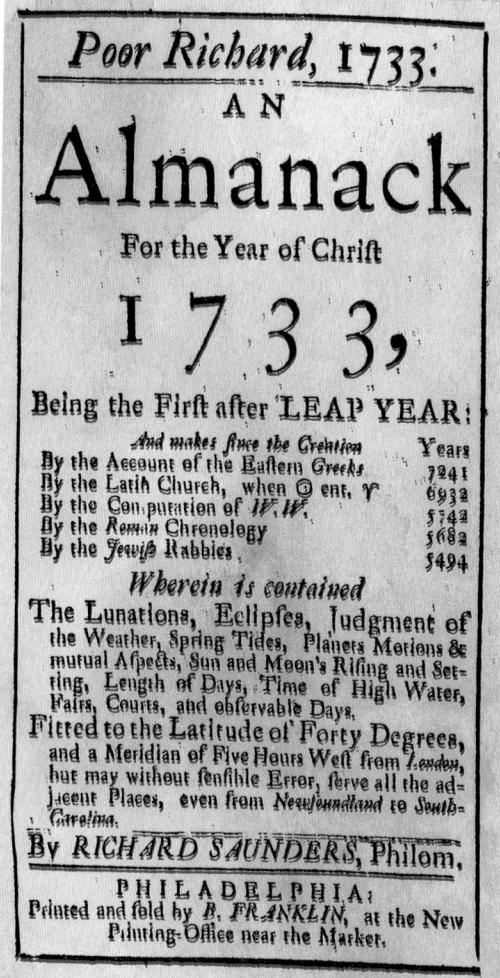

POOR RICHARD'S ALMANACK
The Granger Collection

THINKING ABOUT THE SELECTION

Recalling

1. According to Franklin, what will happen to a person who "lives upon hope"?
2. What makes a person "healthy, wealthy, and wise"?
3. To what does Franklin compare "genius without education"?

Interpreting

4. In what way are the ninth and eighteenth aphorisms related to each other?
5. How are the fourteenth and sixteenth aphorisms related?
6. Which aphorisms express Franklin's belief in the need for self-discipline and self-motivation? Explain why.

Applying

7. Which aphorisms would Franklin apply to business? Which to education? Explain your answers.

ANALYZING LITERATURE

Recognizing Aphorisms

Aphorisms are brief statements expressing wise observations or general truths. A variety of techniques, such as rhymes or repeated words or sounds, are used to make aphorisms easy to remember. For example, in his aphorism "Keep thy shop, and thy shop will keep thee," Franklin uses word repetition to make his saying memorable.

1. Identify Franklin's techniques in each of the following aphorisms, and list them. Then state the meaning of each aphorism, and explain why the aphorisms have more of an impact than the simple statements of their meaning.
   a. "A slip of the foot you may soon recover, but a slip of the tongue you may never get over."
   b. "Early to bed and early to rise, makes a man healthy, wealthy, and wise."
   c. "Fools make feasts, and wise men eat them."
2. Using Franklin's techniques, write three aphorisms for contemporary life.

THINKING AND WRITING

Responding to a Statement About Style

In his essay "On Literary Style," Franklin states that good writing must be "smooth, clear, and short." Examine the excerpt from Franklin's *Autobiography* and the aphorisms from *Poor Richard's Almanack.* Does Franklin's writing meet his own requirements? List passages that support your opinion. Organize your information into an outline. Then write a thesis statement and an essay in which you use transitions to link your ideas, and support your argument with examples of Franklin's writing. When you revise, make sure that your paper meets Franklin's requirements for good writing.

Commentary

In the century following his death, Franklin came to be considered the symbol of success gained by hard work and hard-headed common sense. The twentieth century, however, began to find him lacking in human depth.

This criticism was expressed by the English novelist D.H. Lawrence in his *Studies in Classic American Literature,* published in 1922. Lawrence called Franklin a "virtuous little automaton," and said he could admire Franklin but not like him.

We have many stories and descriptions of Franklin from his contemporaries. From these it seems clear that, while he preferred the useful over the ornamental, Franklin was a very human and humorous man. There is a story that Jefferson was asked to write the Declaration of Independence rather than Franklin because of the fear that Franklin would put a joke in it.

from Poor Richard's Almanack   123

Closure and Extension

ANSWERS TO THINKING ABOUT THE SELECTION
Recalling

1. A person who lives upon hope "will die fasting."

2. "Early to bed, early to rise makes a man healthy, wealthy, and wise."
3. "Genius without education" is compared to unmined silver.

Interpreting

4. Both aphorisms deal with time and with advice on using it wisely.
5. Both point out the greater implications of small problems or mistakes.
6. All but a few of the aphorisms deal, directly or indirectly, with self-discipline and self-motivation. Those that express these ideas most directly are the fourth, eighth, ninth, tenth, sixteenth, seventeenth, and eighteenth aphorisms.

Applying

7. Suggested Response: He would apply the fourth, sixth, eighth, ninth, tenth, fifteenth, seventeenth, and eighteenth to business, because they deal with discipline and management of money and time. He would apply the ninth, tenth, and nineteenth to education, because they deal with self-discipline and self-motivation.

Challenge Are Franklin's aphorisms applicable to life in today's world? Why or why not?

ANSWERS TO ANALYZING LITERATURE

1. (a) He uses rhyme and repeated words. Anyone can recover from a stubbed toe, but a harsh word may inflict greater damage. (b) He uses rhyme and repeated words. Self-discipline increases our health, wealth, and wisdom. (c) He uses repeated sounds. Wise men will feed upon the indiscretions of foolish men.
2. Suggested Response: Never heap too much praise on yourself nor too much criticism on others. A true friend never deserts a friend in need. Money buys cars, but it doesn't buy happiness.

THINKING AND WRITING

Publishing Student Writing Ask student volunteers to share their essays with the rest of the class.

More About the Author Although Patrick Henry was a gifted administrator, his years of public service left him deeply in debt. He enjoyed considerable financial success, however, when he returned to private practice as a criminal lawyer. In what ways could a gift for oration be useful in a court of law?

Critical Evaluation At the time of his fiery speech to the Virginia Convention of Delegates, Patrick Henry had opposed Britain's attempts to impose taxation without representation for nearly ten years. One witness of Henry's speech said that he delivered his final words "with both his arms extended aloft, his brows knit, every feature marked with the resolute purpose of his soul, and his voice swelled to its boldest note of exclamation." Thomas Jefferson listened in astonishment to Patrick Henry's oratory in response to the Stamp Act. Jefferson had been studying law under George Wythe, the most learned lawyer in Virginia and the best classical scholar in the colony. According to Jefferson, Henry "appeared . . . to speak as Homer wrote."

PATRICK HENRY

1736–1799

Remembered most for his fiery battle cry, "Give me liberty or give me death," Patrick Henry is considered the most powerful orator of the American Revolution. Using his talents as a speaker, Henry helped to inspire colonists to unite in an effort to win their independence.

Born on his father's plantation in Hanover County, Virginia, Henry attended school only until the age of ten, though his father continued his schooling at home. After unsuccessfully attempting to run a store with his brother, Henry married at the age of eighteen and took up farming. When his farm was destroyed by a fire several years later, Henry found himself deeply in debt, with several children to support. He then began studying law, and in 1760 he received his license to practice. His talent as a speaker contributed to his reputation as an excellent lawyer.

In 1765 Henry was elected to the Virginia House of Burgesses. Shortly after his election, Henry delivered one of his most powerful speeches, declaring his opposition to the Stamp Act. At the end of his speech, Henry mentioned two kings who had been killed for political reasons and declared that King George III of Britain might "profit by their example." According to legend, this shocked the members of the audience so much that they accused Henry of treason. To this accusation, Henry is reported to have replied, "If this be treason, make the most of it!"

Whatever his actual words may have been, they were effective. Over the protests of some of the most influential members, the Virginia House adopted Henry's resolutions. Virginia thus became the first colony officially to protest the Stamp Act.

Henry rapidly became the leader of Virginia's opposition to British policy. When the royal governor closed the port of Boston in 1774 and dissolved the Virginia legislature, Henry organized a small group of the legislators, who met in a Williamsburg tavern. From there they invited the other colonies to send delegates to what became the First Continental Congress.

In 1775, after he had served as a member of the First Continental Congress, Henry delivered his most famous speech at the Virginia Provincial Convention. While most of the speakers that day argued that the colony should seek a compromise with the British, Henry boldly and dramatically urged armed resistance to England. Henry's speech had a powerful impact on the audience, reinforcing the revolutionary spirit that led to the signing of the Declaration of Independence. In the years that followed, Henry continued to be an important political leader, serving as the governor of Virginia and as a member of the Virginia General Assembly. It was this speech that secured him a place in American history.

Objectives
1 To appreciate oratory
2 To understand persuasive techniques
3 To deliver a persuasive speech
4 To analyze a persuasive speech

Support Material

Teaching Portfolio
Teacher Backup, pp. 181-183
Grammar in Action Worksheet, *Understanding Parallelism,* pp. 184-185
Usage and Mechanics Worksheet, p. 186
Vocabulary Check, p. 187
Analyzing Literature Worksheet, *Recognizing Oratory,* p. 188
Critical Thinking and Reading

Worksheet, *Understanding Persuasive Techniques,* p. 189
Selection Test, pp. 190-191

GUIDE FOR INTERPRETING

Speech in the Virginia Convention

Literary Forms

Oratory. Oratory is the art of skilled, eloquent public speaking. Throughout history talented orators have used their skills to spread messages, gain support, and sway opinions. Oratory has always played an important role in American politics. In fact, to a great extent, America owes its independence to gifted speakers such as Patrick Henry who were responsible for influencing colonists to resist British rule.

An effective orator uses a variety of devices to emphasize important points. Four of these devices are rhetorical questions, restatement, repetition, and parallelism.

Rhetorical questions are questions that the speaker does not expect people to answer verbally. Because people generally will try to answer the questions in their mind, however, the questions force them to think actively about what the speaker is saying.

Restatement, repetition, and parallelism are methods used to highlight important points. A speaker uses restatement to state an idea in a variety of ways. When a speaker uses repetition, he or she restates an idea using the same words. Parallelism involves the use of a repeated grammatical structure.

Commentary

Patrick Henry's ability to rise to his feet and, in a few words and gestures, totally command his audience was extraordinary. This ability, coupled with an intelligent mind, led to his rise to political prominence from rather lowly beginnings.

The Virginia House of Burgesses was largely controlled by men from aristocratic families, wealthy and usually college educated. Henry had little schooling and that mostly informal, but he made good use of it in his speeches. After failing at storekeeping and farming, he studied law on his own and, to everyone's surprise, passed the oral exams.

In 1763 Virginia was again disputing with Britain the right to set prices and taxes in the colony. The case seemed lost for the colonists when Henry rose to speak. Casually, even poorly dressed, rather awkward and unpolished, Henry won the case for Virginia against the king. He was twenty-seven years old. Two years later, he was elected to the House of Burgesses, one of its youngest members.

As you read his "Speech in the Virginia Convention," see and hear him. Notice how he builds logically and emotionally to his famous conclusion.

Writing

What were the main reasons the colonies rebelled against British rule? Spend five minutes brainstorming about the causes of the American Revolution, and list them.

Guide for Interpreting 125

Literary Focus You may wish to have students watch a persuasive speech on television, having them note the use of rhetorical questions, restatement, repetition, and parallelism, as the speaker attempts to persuade the audience.

Writing/Prior Knowledge You may want to have students brainstorm in small groups.

Vocabulary

Preteach the following vocabulary words:
arduous (är′ jōō wəs) *adj.*: Difficult (p. 126)
insidious (in sid′ ē əs) *adj.*: Deceitful; treacherous (p. 126)
subjugation (sub′ jə gā′ shən) *n.*: The act of conquering (p. 126)
vigilant (vij′ ə lənt) *n.*: Alert to danger (p. 128)

Spelling Tip Point out that three words in this list have a *j* sound: *arduous, subjugation, vigilant.* However, only in *subjugation* is that sound spelled with *j* in *arduous* the sound is spelled with *d,* and in *vigilant* with g.

Speech in the Virginia Convention

Patrick Henry

Mr. President: No man thinks more highly than I do of the patriotism, as well as abilities, of the very worthy gentlemen who have just addressed the house. But different men often see the same subject in different lights; and, therefore, I hope it will not be thought disrespectful to those gentlemen, if, entertaining, as I do, opinions of a character very opposite to theirs, I shall speak forth my sentiments freely and without reserve. This is no time for ceremony. The question before the house is one of awful moment[1] to this country. For my own part, I consider it as nothing less than a question of freedom or slavery. And in proportion to the magnitude of the subject ought to be the freedom of the debate. It is only in this way that we can hope to arrive at truth, and fulfill the great responsibility which we hold to God and our country. Should I keep back my opinions at such a time, through fear of giving offense, I should consider myself as guilty of treason toward my country, and of an act of disloyalty toward the Majesty of Heaven, which I revere above all earthly kings.

Mr. President, it is natural to man to indulge in the illusions of hope. We are apt to shut our eyes against a painful truth, and listen to the song of that siren till she transforms us into beasts.[2] Is this the part of wise men, engaged in a great and arduous struggle for liberty? Are we disposed to be of the number of those who having eyes see not, and having ears hear not,[3] the things which so nearly concern their temporal salvation? For my part, whatever anguish of spirit it may cost, I am willing to know the whole truth; to know the worst and to provide for it.

I have but one lamp by which my feet are guided, and that is the lamp of experience. I know of no way of judging of the future but by the past. And judging by the past, I wish to know what there has been in the conduct of the British ministry for the last ten years to justify those hopes with which gentlemen have been pleased to solace themselves and the house? Is it that insidious smile with which our petition has been lately received? Trust it not, sir; it will prove a snare to your feet. Suffer not yourselves to be betrayed with a kiss.[4] Ask yourselves how this gracious reception of our petition comports with those warlike preparations which cover our waters and darken our land. Are fleets and armies necessary to a work of love and reconciliation? Have we shown ourselves so unwilling to be reconciled that force must be called in to win back our love? Let us not deceive ourselves, sir. These are the implements of war and subjugation—the last arguments to which kings resort.

I ask gentlemen, sir, what means this martial array, if its purpose be not to force

---

1. **moment:** Importance.
2. **listen . . . beasts:** In Homer's *Odyssey* the enchantress Circe transforms men into swine after charming them with her singing.
3. **having eyes . . . hear not:** In Ezekiel 12:2 those "who have eyes to see, but see not, who have ears to hear, but hear not" are addressed.
4. **betrayed with a kiss:** In Luke 22:47–48 Jesus is betrayed with a kiss.

126   The Revolutionary Period

PATRICK HENRY BEFORE THE VIRGINIA HOUSE OF BURGESSES
Peter F. Rothermel
Red Hill, The Patrick Henry National Memorial

Speech in the Virginia Convention 127

Fine art, *Patrick Henry Before the Virginia House of Burgesses,* 1852, by Rothermel. Peter F. Rothermel (1817-1895), an American painter who had studied in Munich and Rome, was one of the directors of the Philadelphia Academy. At the time, Philadelphia was the capital of book and magazine publishing and had its own group of painters of historical subjects. The leader of these artists was Rothermel. In his paintings he mixed historical reconstruction with contemporary sentiment. In this painting, Rothermel presents his interpretation of Patrick Henry delivering his famous address to the Virginia House of Burgesses on May 29, 1765.

You might use the following questions for discussion:
1. What is happening in this picture?
2. Which figure is Patrick Henry?
3. How has the artist created a dramatic atmosphere in this painting?

Student Activity 1. In the *Speech in the Virginia Convention,* find an example of each of the following parallel structures.
1. Parallel nouns or noun phrases
2. Parallel verbs or verb phrases
3. Parallel rhetorical questions
4. Parallel statements.

Student Activity 2. Correct the faulty parallelism in the following sentences by rewriting them so that equal ideas are cast in equivalent grammatical structures.
1. In his speech, Henry displayed conviction, skill, and his patriotic feelings.
2. Henry's speech impressed his listeners, and it still sounds good today.

3. Henry had little formal schooling; neither did many leaders of the American Revolution.
4. Did Patrick Henry think he was speaking literally, or were some of his statements deliberate exaggerations?
5. As governor of Virginia, Henry was a supporter of George Washington and sent George Rogers Clark on his northwestern expedition.

7 Discussion In this passage, Henry anticipates an opposing argument (we are not ready to engage Britain) and offers a rebuttal. Why is this so effective?

8 Reading Strategy Have students summarize the passages that led to this final call to action.

Reader's Response Henry argues that the colonists are not likely to acquire strength in submission. In your experience, why is it important to stand up for what you believe when your beliefs are the strongest? On the other hand, how can being patient sometimes work to your advantage?

us to submission? Can gentlemen assign any other possible motive for it? Has Great Britain any enemy in this quarter of the world, to call for all this accumulation of navies and armies? No, sir, she has none. They are meant for us: they can be meant for no other. They are sent over to bind and rivet upon us those chains which the British ministry have been so long forging.

And what have we to oppose to them? Shall we try argument? Sir, we have been trying that for the last ten years. Have we anything new to offer upon the subject? Nothing. We have held the subject up in every light of which it is capable; but it has been all in vain. Shall we resort to entreaty and humble supplication? What terms shall we find which have not been already exhausted? Let us not, I beseech you, sir, deceive ourselves longer.

Sir, we have done everything that could be done to avert the storm which is now coming on. We have petitioned; we have remonstrated; we have supplicated; we have prostrated ourselves before the throne, and have implored its interposition[5] to arrest the tyrannical hands of the ministry and Parliament. Our petitions have been slighted; our remonstrances have produced additional violence and insult; our supplications have been disregarded; and we have been spurned with contempt from the foot of the throne! In vain, after these things, may we indulge the fond[6] hope of peace and reconciliation. There is no longer any room for hope. If we wish to be free, if we mean to preserve inviolate those inestimable privileges for which we have been so long contending, if we mean not basely to abandon the noble struggle in which we have been so long engaged, and which we have pledged ourselves never to abandon until the glorious object of our contest shall be obtained—we must fight! I repeat it, sir, we must fight! An appeal to arms and to the God of Hosts is all that is left us!

7 They tell us, sir, that we are weak—un-

5. **interposition:** Intervention.
6. **fond:** Foolish.

able to cope with so formidable an adversary. But when shall we be stronger? Will it be the next week, or the next year? Will it be when we are totally disarmed, and when a British guard shall be stationed in every house? Shall we gather strength by irresolution and inaction? Shall we acquire the means of effectual resistance by lying supinely on our backs and hugging the delusive phantom of hope until our enemies shall have bound us hand and foot? Sir, we are not weak, if we make a proper use of those means which the God of nature hath placed in our power. Three millions of people, armed in the holy cause of liberty, and in such a country as that which we possess, are invincible by any force which our enemy can send against us. Besides, sir, we shall not fight our battles alone. There is a just God who presides over the destinies of nations and who will raise up friends to fight our battles for us. The battle, sir, is not to the strong alone;[7] it is to the vigilant, the active, the brave. Besides, sir, we have no election.[8] If we were base enough to desire it, it is now too late to retire from the contest. There is no retreat but in submission and slavery! Our chains are forged! Their clanging may be heard on the plains of Boston! The war is inevitable—and let it come! I repeat it, sir, let it come!

It is in vain, sir, to extenuate the matter. Gentlemen may cry, "Peace, peace"—but there is no peace. The war is actually begun! The next gale that sweeps from the north[9] will bring to our ears the clash of resounding arms! Our brethren are already in the field! Why stand we here idle? What is it that gentlemen wish? What would they have? Is life so dear, or peace so sweet, as to be purchased at the price of chains and slavery? Forbid it, Almighty God! I know not what course others may take; but as for me, give me liberty or give me death!

7. **The battle . . . alone:** "The race is not to the swift, nor the battle to the strong." (Ecclesiastes 9:11).
8. **election:** Choice.
9. **The next gale . . . north:** In Massachusetts some colonists had already shown open resistance to the British.

THINKING ABOUT THE SELECTION

Recalling

1. What comment does Henry make about the delegates who have just addressed the House?
2. What does Henry say he would be guilty of if he holds back his opinion?
3. How does Henry say that he judges the future?
4. (a) What does Henry say is the reason for the British military buildup in America? (b) What course of action must the colonists take?
5. What does Henry say "the next gale that sweeps from the north" will bring?
6. To what does Henry compare the colonists' situation?

Interpreting

7. Why do you think Henry begins his speech by stating his opinions of the previous speakers?
8. Why does Henry believe that compromise with the British is not a workable solution?
9. How does Henry answer the objection that the colonists are not ready to fight?

Applying

10. What occasion or situation might prompt a statesman to deliver such a formal, dramatic speech today?

ANALYZING LITERATURE

Recognizing Oratory

Oratory is the art of formal public speaking. A skilled orator uses such devices as rhetorical questions, restatement, repetition, and parallelism to emphasize points. For example, Henry uses restatement in his speech, repeating his declaration, "We must fight!"

1. (a) Find one instance where Henry answers a possible objection to his argument with a series of rhetorical questions. (b) What purpose does this series of questions serve?
2. List two ideas that Henry repeats, using different words.
3. Find one example of parallelism.

CRITICAL THINKING AND READING

Understanding Persuasive Techniques

An effective orator may use a number of persuasive techniques to try to convince an audience to think or act in a certain way. For example, Patrick Henry uses a blend of logical arguments and emotional appeals in his speech.

1. Considering the purpose of Henry's speech, why do you feel these two techniques were appropriate?
2. Why do you think Henry chose to end his speech with an emotional appeal?
3. Rational thought is thinking based on reason. (a) What is the difference between rational thought and rationalization? (b) Which characterizes Henry's speech? Explain.

SPEAKING AND LISTENING

Delivering a Speech

Part of what made Henry's speech successful was his dramatic delivery. Recite Henry's "Speech in the Virginia Convention" to your class, emphasizing the most important points by using gestures and varying the pitch and loudness of your voice. Speak slowly and clearly so that your audience can understand what you are saying.

THINKING AND WRITING

Writing a Speech

Imagine that you are another speaker in the Virginia Provincial Convention and you do not agree with Patrick Henry. Write a speech in which you rebut Henry's points. In your prewriting, list the arguments against Henry's ideas. Then, using some of the same oratorical devices that Henry used, write your speech. As you revise it, strengthen your arguments to make them as persuasive as you can.

Speech in the Virginia Convention 129

Applying

10. Suggested Response: The threat of war might prompt a speaker to deliver a similar speech.

Challenge Do you think that the Revolution would have been successful without the efforts of talented orators such as Henry? Why or why not?

ANSWERS TO ANALYZING LITERATURE

1. (a) Answers will differ. Examples can be found in the openings of the fourth and fifth paragraphs. (b) The series of questions is meant to emphasize the point and stir the listener to action.
2. Answers will differ. One example of the statement of the same idea using different words is in the sixth paragraph: "We have petitioned; we have remonstrated; we have supplicated; we have prostrated ourselves before the throne . . ." Another example is found in the seventh paragraph: "There is no retreat but in submission and slavery! Our chains are forged!"
3. Answers will differ. One example of parallelism occurs at the beginning of the third paragraph.

ANSWERS TO CRITICAL THINKING AND READING

1. Suggested Response: Henry's purpose—to stir the colonists to action—was effectively carried out through emotional appeals to patriotism and threats of loss of freedom and through logical arguments about Britain's goals.
2. Suggested Response: He ends with an emotional appeal to leave a strong impression on his listeners.
3. (a) Rationalization refers to the use of superficially rational, or plausible, explanations or excuses for one's beliefs, while rational thought is thinking based on reasoning. (b) Rational thought characterizes Henry's speeches, because his argument is clearly based on reasoning.

THINKING AND WRITING
Publishing Student Writing
Have student volunteers deliver their speeches. Then have the members of the class evaluate the effectiveness of each speech.

———
129

Closure and Extension

ANSWERS TO THINKING ABOUT THE SELECTION
Recalling

1. He comments that they are patriotic and worthy of respect.
2. He would be a traitor to God and country if he held back his opinion.
3. He judges the future by the past.
4. (a) He believes the purpose of the British military buildup is to force the colonists into submission. (b) The colonists must fight the British.
5. "The next gale that sweeps from the north" will bring the cries of war.
6. Henry compares the colonists' situation to slavery.

Interpreting

7. Suggested Response: By stating his respect for the previous speakers, he creates the impression that he has given consideration to their opinions and makes them more willing to listen to his opinion.
8. Compromise is not a workable solution, because the British have responded to the previous petitions of the colonists with increased repression.
9. Henry answers the objection by saying that if they wait, they will give the British time to build up their forces.

More About the Author Thomas Paine's *The Age of Reason* is considered by many critics to be Paine's greatest literary work. An attack on organized religion, *The Age of Reason* was harshly criticized, as was its author. When Paine died in New York in 1809, he was refused burial in consecrated ground (in a churchyard) and had to be buried on his farm in New Rochelle. In 1819 William Cobbett took the remains to Paine's native England, with the intention of building a monument to Paine. The monument was never erected, and the bones were eventually lost. How is this a loss to the preservation of our historical heritage?

Critical Evaluation According to Evelyn J. Hinz, "Nothing, perhaps, points so forcibly to the importance of a humanistic consideration of the causes and significance of the American Revolution as the role played by Thomas Paine . . . What Paine articulated in his propaganda was his own sense of the injustice he had experienced in the Old World and his dream of a future in the New World, and what makes his propaganda American and accounts at the same time for its impact is that these feelings are the common denominator of one aspect of the American experience. Hence Paine's commitment to the American Revolution is less dramatically messianic than it might appear or has been made to appear; the American Revolution was for him not a new and objective cause but an objective correlative for his own cause, and it was because of the coincidence of his own interests with those patriots that he was able so quickly to grasp and so eloquently to articulate American sentiments."

1737–1809

Though he did not become a journalist until he was in his late thirties, Thomas Paine was the most effective American political writer of the Revolution. Throughout the war, Paine's pamphlets convinced people of the justness of the American cause and helped to inspire faltering American troops.

Born in Thetford, England, Paine left school at thirteen and worked unsuccessfully as a teacher, corset maker, sailor, and grocer. After meeting Benjamin Franklin in London, Paine decided to emigrate to the colonies to start a new life. With a letter of introduction from Franklin, Paine came to America in 1774 and began a career in journalism.

In January 1776, less than two years after his arrival in America, Paine published *Common Sense,* a pamphlet in which he accused the English king of tyranny and argued that Americans had no choice but to fight for their independence. *Common Sense,* which sold more than 120,000 copies in three months, had a powerful effect on the American public. Less than six months after the pamphlet's publication, America declared its independence.

After enlisting in the American army toward the end of 1776, Paine wrote the first of a series of sixteen essays called *The American Crisis.* Paine joined Washington's troops after they had retreated from the British in New York. Suffering from the cold weather and a shortage of provisions, the soldiers were extremely disheartened. As the troops prepared to leave Valley Forge to fight the British at Trenton, General Washington had the first of Paine's inspirational essays read to the men to raise their spirits.

In 1787, several years after the end of the Revolution, Paine traveled to Europe and became involved with the French Revolution. Though Paine supported the revolutionary cause in *The Rights of Man* (1791–1792), the French revolutionaries imprisoned him for pleading against the execution of the overthrown French king. While in prison, he began writing *The Age of Reason* (1784–1785), a sharp attack on organized religion.

When he returned to America in 1802, Paine was treated harshly by the American public for supporting the French Revolution and criticizing religion. Paine died in New York in 1809, an unhappy man, not to be recognized as an American revolutionary hero until years after his death.

Objectives

1 To use aphorisms
2 To understand the effect of aphorisms
3 To note synonyms
4 To write about Revolutionary literature

Support Material

Teaching Portfolio
Teacher Backup, pp. 193-196
Grammar in Action Worksheet, *Understanding Persuasive Writing,* pp. 197-198
Usage and Mechanics Worksheet, p. 199
Vocabulary Check, p. 200
Analyzing Literature Worksheet, *Using Aphorisms,* p. 201
Critical Thinking and Reading

Worksheet, *Understanding the Effect of Aphorisms,* p. 202
Selection Test, pp. 203-204

GUIDE FOR INTERPRETING

from The Crisis, Number I

Writer's Techniques

Aphorisms. An aphorism is a short, pointed statement expressing a wise or clever observation or a general truth. Though aphorisms may appear by themselves, they can also be used as a part of a longer work. Because aphorisms capture our attention and are easy to remember, writers may use them to express or emphasize important points.

Thomas Paine uses aphorisms throughout *The American Crisis* to make his argument strong and memorable. By defending the American cause through a series of statements expressing general truths, Paine creates the impression that the American forces are fighting not only for their own independence but also for the cause of liberty and justice for all humankind.

Commentary

This first of the sixteen *Crisis* papers was often called "The American Crisis." Paine wrote it while retreating with Washington's army across New Jersey during the first, dark winter of the Revolutionary War. The army had just been crushingly defeated at Fort Lee by the British, who had taken the fort and many prisoners. Only about 3,000 men remained with Washington's forces. Washington had the paper read to his troops before they crossed the Delaware River from Philadelphia, where they then defeated the Hessians at Trenton.

Paine's words were inspiring and encouraging, both for the cold, tired, defeated soldiers and for the colonists who read them in December of 1776. The ideas he presents are simple, and they can be clearly and therefore forcefully stated. Sometimes, it is true, he oversimplified an idea or situation to gain force. But he passionately believed in the need to arouse the colonists to immediate rebellion. He knew to whom he was speaking and writing, and made his words easily understood by the average person. He once wrote, "It is my design to make those who can scarcely read understand."

As you read this *Crisis* paper, notice how Paine is speaking personally and directly both to the individual, discouraged soldier standing listening in the cold and to all the colonists. If you were a tired soldier, a resentful colonist, *or* a colonist who supported the British, how would you respond to Paine? How does he logically and emotionally affect you?

Writing

What inspirational sayings or slogans from the American Revolution can you think of? Spend five minutes brainstorming about revolutionary sayings and slogans, and list them.

Literary Focus Students will recall aphorisms from Franklin's *Almanack*. Whereas Franklin's aphorisms are meant to entertain, Paine's aphorisms work on a different level. Have students compare the subject matter and tone of Franklin's aphorisms with those of Paine's.

Writing/Prior Knowledge You may wish to have students brainstorm in small groups.

Vocabulary

Preteach the following vocabulary words:
tyranny (tir′ ə nē) *n.:* Oppressive and unjust government (p. 132)
celestial (sə les′ chəl) *adj.:* Of the heavens (p. 132)
impious (im′ pē əs) *adj.:* Lacking reverence for God (p. 132)
infidel (in′ fə d'l) *n.:* A person who holds no religious belief (p. 132)
ardor (är′ dər) *n.:* Emotional warmth; passion (p. 133)

Motivation/Prior Knowledge
Imagine that you are a soldier in the Colonial army. The year is 1776, and you and the other soldiers are suffering from cold weather and a shortage of provisions. What type of essay might help to raise your spirits?

Thematic Idea Patrick Henry's "Speech in the Virginia Convention" (p. 126) is another important work of Revolutionary literature.

Purpose-Setting Question
What is Paine's message?

1 **Clarification** Paine sometimes referred to this, the first of the sixteen "Crisis" essays that he wrote, as "The American Crisis." He wrote it while retreating across New Jersey with Washington's army after the crushing defeat by the British at Fort Lee. The final essay in the series, "The Crisis, Number 16," written in 1783, announced that the Revolution was "gloriously and happily accomplished."

2 **Discussion** Why is Paine's style suitable for his audience?

3 **Clarification** Here and at the end of the selection, Paine quotes from the Declaratory Act of Parliament (February 1766) that asserted Britain's complete authority over the American colonies.

from The Crisis, Number I

Thomas Paine

These are the times that try men's souls. The summer soldier and the sunshine patriot will in this crisis, shrink from the service of his country; but he that stands it NOW, deserves the love and thanks of man and woman. Tyranny, like hell, is not easily conquered; yet we have this consolation with us, that the harder the conflict, the more glorious the triumph. What we obtain too cheap, we esteem too lightly; 'tis dearness only that gives everything its value. Heaven knows how to put a proper price upon its goods; and it would be strange indeed, if so celestial an article as FREEDOM should not be highly rated. Britain, with an army to enforce her tyranny, has declared that she has a right (not only to TAX) but "to BIND us in ALL CASES WHATSOEVER," and if being bound in that manner, is not slavery, then is there not such a thing as slavery upon earth. Even the expression is impious, for so unlimited a power can belong only to God . . .

I have as little superstition in me as any man living, but my secret opinion has ever been, and still is, that God Almighty will not give up a people to military destruction, or leave them unsupportedly to perish, who have so earnestly and so repeatedly sought to avoid the calamities of war, by every decent method which wisdom could invent. Neither have I so much of the infidel in me, as to suppose that he has relinquished the government of the world, and given us up to the care of devils; and as I do not, I cannot see on what grounds the king of Britain can look up to heaven for help against us: a common murderer, a highwayman, or a housebreaker, has as good a pretense as he . . .

I once felt all that kind of anger, which a man ought to feel, against the mean[1] principles that are held by the Tories:[2] a noted one, who kept a tavern at Amboy, was standing at his door, with as pretty a child in his hand, about eight or nine years old, as I ever saw, and after speaking his mind as freely as he thought was prudent, finished with this unfatherly expression, *"Well! give me peace in my day."* Not a man lives on the continent but fully believes that a separation must some time or other finally take place, and a generous parent should have said, *"If there must be trouble let it be in my day, that my child may have peace"*: and this single reflection, well applied, is sufficient to awaken every man to duty. Not a place upon earth might be so happy as America. Her situation is remote from all the wrangling world, and she has nothing to do but to trade with them. A man can distinguish himself between temper and principle, and I am as confident, as I am that God governs the world, that America will never be happy

---

1. **mean** *adj.*: Here, small-minded.
2. **Tories:** Colonists who remained loyal to Great Britain.

Grammar in Action

Writers use **persuasion** to express their opinions or interpretations, or to defend courses of action. Persuasion tries to appeal to the reader's interest and reason while winning his or her acceptance of the issue being discussed. A persuasive topic must be arguable; therefore, it should be an opinion, not a statement of fact. And the opinion must be supportable with facts and logical arguments. Moreover, persuasive topics should be topics of importance to other people. Thomas Paine's appeal to the disheartened American soldiers in the Revolutionary War is an example of such a topic.

In order to persuade the soldiers to lift their spirits and continue fighting for independence, Paine uses a convincing tone and strong arguments. His ideas and word choice convey his purpose: "to awaken every man to duty." For example, he argues that "not a place on earth might be so happy as America [once] she gets clear of foreign dominion," which will only happen through the persistent, determined effort of the American soldiers.

RECRUITING FOR THE CONTINENTAL ARMY
William T. Ranney
Munson-Williams Proctor Institute

Humanities Note

Fine art, *Recruiting for the Continental Army,* ca. 1857-1859, by William T. Ranney. Ranney (1813-1857) was an American painter born in Connecticut. After his father, a ship's captain, perished at sea, Ranney was apprenticed to a tinsmith. His dissatisfaction with the tin trade led to his love of the frontier. He eventually became an artist and is best known for frontier paintings based on his experiences in Texas. He also executed a variety of other genre scenes, including *Recruiting for the Continental Army.*

Point out to students that this painting was not done to illustrate Thomas Paine's words but rather has been chosen to accompany them here. Ranney has captured what must have been the excitement of the moment through artistic dramatization and exaggeration. The image as a whole rings of patriotism. Since a recruit was paid less than $7 a month, from which the cost of his clothing was deducted, patriotism was obviously the chief recruiting force.

You might use the following questions for discussion:

1. What is happening in this picture?
2. Although this is not an action-packed picture, how does the artist convey the feeling of excitement that must have existed at such a moment?
3. How has the artist expressed feelings of patriotism in this painting?
4. Why is this painting an appropriate choice to illustrate the essay?

till she gets clear of foreign dominion. Wars, without ceasing, will break out till that period arrives, and the continent must in the end be conqueror; for though the flame of liberty may sometimes cease to shine, the coal can never expire . . .

I turn with the warm ardor of a friend to those who have nobly stood, and are yet determined to stand the matter out: I call not upon a few, but upon all; not on *this* state or *that* state, but on *every* state; up and help us; lay your shoulders to the wheel; better

have too much force than too little, when so great an object is at stake. Let it be told to the future world, that in the depth of winter, when nothing but hope and virtue could survive, that the city and the country, alarmed at one common danger, came forth to meet and to repulse it. Say not that thousands are gone, turn out your tens of thousands; throw not the burden of the day upon Providence, but *"show your faith by your works,"* that God may bless you. It matters not where you live, or what rank of life you

from *The Crisis, Number I* 133

Student Activity 1. Study pages 132-133 for more examples of Paine's use of persuasion. How do his ideas and word choice work together to appeal to win the readers' acceptance?

Student Activity 2. Write a short, one-page persuasive article on an issue you consider to be a "crisis." Imitate Paine's persuasive style as you try to win your readers' acceptance of your opinions.

Discussion Near the end of his essay, Paine seems to appeal to both reason and logic. Why is this an effective approach?

Reader's Response Would Thomas Paine's essay have inspired you if you were a disheartened colonist? Explain.

hold, the evil or the blessing will reach you all. The far and the near, the home counties and the back, the rich and the poor, will suffer or rejoice alike. The heart that feels not now, is dead: the blood of his children will curse his cowardice, who shrinks back at a time when a little might have saved the whole, and made *them* happy. (I love the man that can smile at trouble; that can gather strength from distress, and grow brave by reflection.) 'Tis the business of little minds to shrink; but he whose heart is firm, and whose conscience approves his conduct, will pursue his principles unto death. My own line of reasoning is to myself as straight and clear as a ray of light. Not all the trea-

sures of the world, so far as I believe, could have induced me to support an offensive war, for I think it murder; but if a thief breaks into my house, burns and destroys my property, and kills or threatens to kill me, or those that are in it, and to "*bind me in all cases whatsoever,*" to his absolute will, am I to suffer it? What signifies it to me, whether he who does it is a king or a common man; my countryman, or not my countryman; whether it be done by an individual villain or an army of them? If we reason to the root of things we shall find no difference; neither can any just cause be assigned why we should punish in the one case and pardon in the other.

THINKING ABOUT THE SELECTION

Recalling

1. (a) According to the first paragraph, who will "shrink from the service of his country"? (b) What will the people who do not shrink from service deserve?
2. According to the first paragraph, what has Britain declared?
3. Of what is Paine confident in the third paragraph?
4. According to the final paragraph, what will a person "whose heart is firm" pursue "unto death"?
5. What opinion of offensive wars does Paine express in the final paragraph?

Interpreting

6. What does Paine mean when he refers to "the summer soldier" and "the sunshine patriot"?
7. What is the point of Paine's story about the tavernkeeper at Amboy?
8. Name two emotions to which Paine appeals in his essay.
9. (a) What is the main idea of this essay? (b) How does Paine support his main idea?

Applying

10. How might a colonist who had remained loyal to the British react to Paine's argument?

Answers

THINKING ABOUT THE SELECTION
Recalling

1. (a) "The summer soldier and the sunshine patriot" will shrink from the service of their country. (b) Those who do not shrink from service will deserve the love and thanks of all men and women.
2. Britain has declared the absolute

ANALYZING LITERATURE

Using Aphorisms

An **aphorism** is a brief, pointed statement expressing a wise or clever observation or a general truth. Sometimes writers use aphorisms in their works to express or emphasize important points. For example, Paine uses the aphorism, "the harder the conflict, the more glorious the triumph," to express his belief that hardships faced by the American forces during the war will make their eventual victory more meaningful.

1. Find three more aphorisms used in Paine's essay.
2. What point does each of these aphorisms emphasize or express?

CRITICAL THINKING AND READING

Understanding the Effect of Aphorisms

Aphorisms can make a work more forceful and memorable. Because aphorisms express general truths, they can create the impression that the specific argument being presented has a more general application. For example, Paine's use of aphorisms helps to convey his belief that the American Revolution is a part of a greater struggle aimed at attaining liberty and justice for all humankind.

1. Why does the universal application of Paine's argument add to the essay's value as a work of literature?
2. What other historical situations can you think of for which Paine's essay would have been appropriate?

UNDERSTANDING LANGUAGE

Noting Synonyms

Synonyms are words that have the same or almost the same meaning. However, sometimes the slight difference in meaning is very important.

Each group below contains synonyms. Explain the difference in meaning.

1. rational   reasonable   sensible
2. irrational   unreasonable   absurd
3. reason   speculate   deliberate

THINKING AND WRITING

Writing About Revolutionary Literature

Reread the "Speech in the Virginia Convention," "The Declaration of Independence," and the excerpt from *The Crisis, Number 1,* taking notes that will help you to write an essay discussing the common purpose of revolutionary speeches and documents and the various methods used to achieve this purpose. Organize your notes into an outline, and prepare a thesis statement. Then write your essay, being sure to include passages that demonstrate the different methods and arguments used by revolutionary writers to achieve their purpose. When you finish writing, revise your essay, and prepare a final copy.

ANSWERS TO ANALYZING LITERATURE

1. Answers will differ. Some possibilities are: "tyranny, like hell, is not easily conquered"; "what we obtain too cheap, we esteem too lightly"; "'tis the business of little minds to shrink."
2. Answers will differ. The three aphorisms mentioned above have these emphases: The forces of tyranny, like the forces of hell, are difficult to resist. When something is hard to get, we value it more. Those who are small-minded lack conviction and shrink from action.

ANSWERS TO CRITICAL THINKING AND READING

1. It gives it lasting significance.
2. Answers will differ. World War II might be suggested as a time when patriots opposed a dictator who was seeking world domination.

ANSWERS TO UNDERSTANDING LANGUAGE

1. *Rational* means "based on reasoning"; *reasonable* means "showing reason"; and *sensible* means "having or showing good sense."
2. *Irrational* means "contrary to reason"; *unreasonable* means "having or showing little sense or judgement"; *absurd* means "ridiculously unreasonable."
3. *Reason* means "to think logically"; *speculate* means "to ponder"; *deliberate* means "to consider carefully."

THINKING AND WRITING

For help with this assignment, students can refer to Lesson 17, "Evaluating Persuasive Writing," in the Handbook of Writing About Literature.

WRITING ACROSS THE CURRICULUM

You may wish to inform the history department about this assignment. History teachers may be able to provide additional background information that will be useful to students in writing their essays.

---

authority "to bind [the colonies] in all cases whatsoever."

3. Paine is confident that America will never be happy until she is free of foreign domination.
4. A person whose heart is firm "will pursue his principles unto death."
5. Paine likens offensive wars to murder.

Interpreting

6. "The summer soldier and the sunshine patriot" will be available only when things are sunny and bright and will desert in the bleak, harsh, difficult times.
7. The tavernkeeper at Amboy, a Tory, loyal to the British throne, is more interested in keeping the *status quo* than in securing peace for his children.
8. Suggested Response: He appeals to the emotions of fear and anger.
9. (a) The main point of the essay is that the colonists are fighting for a just cause and should endure the difficult times and not lose sight of their purpose. (b) Suggested Response: He uses aphorisms and the story of the tavernkeeper at Amboy.

Applying

10. Suggested Response: He or she might have been angered by Paine's remarks.

Challenge Explain why you do or do not think that Paine's essay is effective.

PHILLIS WHEATLEY

More About the Author Within sixteen months of being purchased by the Wheatleys, Phillis Wheatley learned English well enough to read the most difficult parts of the "Sacred Writings." Mrs. Wheatley's daughter Mary taught Phillis some astronomy, ancient and modern geography, ancient history, the Bible, and the most important Latin classics, including Virgil and Ovid. As Mrs. Wheatley's favorite, Phillis was not allowed to associate with the other servants or do hard work; she was treated as an adopted member of the family.

Many of Phillis Wheatley's eloquent contemporaries, including Patrick Henry, likened the colonists' situation to slavery. In view of this, why is it especially significant that a black slave became a spokeswoman for the American Revolution?

Critical Evaluation In his authoritative edition of Phillis Wheatley's complete works, Julian Mason, Jr., observes: "Her poems are certainly as good [as] or better than those of most of the poets usually included and afforded fair treatment in a discussion of American poetry before 1800, and this same evaluation holds true when she is compared with most of the minor English poets of the eighteenth century who wrote in the neoclassical tradition."

1753[?]–1784

Although she was a black slave whose native language was not English, Phillis Wheatley achieved success as a poet at an early age and went on to become a highly regarded American poet in the Revolutionary period.

Born in West Africa, she was brought to America on a slave ship when she was about eight years old. She was purchased by the Wheatley family of Boston, who gave her their name and converted her to Christianity. Recognizing her extraordinary intelligence, the Wheatleys taught her to read and write. Wheatley learned quickly and was soon reading the Bible, the Latin and Greek classics, and the works of the contemporary English poets. Wheatley also began writing poetry, and when she was thirteen her first poem was published.

In 1770, when she published a poem about the death of George Whitehead, a celebrated English clergyman, Wheatley became famous. Two years later, she accompanied the Wheatley's son on a trip to England, where she was introduced to a number of British aristocrats who were impressed by her poetry and helped to have *Poems on Various Subjects: Religious and Moral* published in London in 1773.

In a foreword to this volume, the publisher claimed that persons who had read the poems felt that "Numbers would be ready to suspect they were not really the Writings of Phillis." Therefore he offered an "attestation" to their authorship, which was signed by eighteen prominent Massachusetts men, among them John Hancock. She was well received by London society, and Benjamin Franklin visited her there. However, *Poems on Various Subjects* was not published in the United States until 1786, two years after her death.

After returning to Boston in the fall of 1773, Wheatley continued to write poetry. During the Revolutionary War, she wrote several poems supporting the American cause, including a poem addressed to George Washington, the commander of the American forces. Washington was so impressed with this poem, "To His Excellency, George Washington," that he invited her to visit him at his headquarters.

Though she was freed in 1778 when John Wheatley died, the last several years of Wheatley's life were filled with hardships. She married John Peters, a free black man, but Peters had trouble maintaining a job and was eventually imprisoned for failing to pay his debts. They had three children, but two of them died in infancy. In addition, Wheatley fell into obscurity as a poet. Though she assembled a second collection of her poetry, the manuscript was lost before it could be published. With her husband in jail and her fame having faded, Phillis Wheatley died alone and impoverished in 1784.

Objectives

1 To recognize personification
2 To evaluate the effect of personification
3 To develop a personification

Support Material

Teaching Portfolio
Teacher Backup, pp. 205-207
Usage and Mechanics Worksheet, p. 208
Vocabulary Check, p. 209
Analyzing Literature Worksheet, *Recognizing Personification*, p. 210
Language Worksheet, *Understanding Words From Greek Myths*, p. 211

Selection Test, pp. 212-213

GUIDE FOR INTERPRETING

To His Excellency, General Washington

Personification. Personification is the attribution of human powers and characteristics to something that is not human, such as an object, an aspect of nature, or an abstract idea. For instance, in the sentence, "The angry wind mercilessly pounded the walls," the wind is personified with two human qualities: anger and lack of mercy.

Throughout history, personification has fulfilled people's need to understand the world in human terms. In ancient religions, gods personified elements of the universe and the natural world. For example, the Greek god Poseidon and the Roman god Neptune were personifications of the ocean. Today, personification is often used as a part of everyday speech. In fact, certain personifications, such as "the screaming of the siren" and "the sighing of the wind," are so common that we do not even think of them as personifications.

In eighteenth-century English literature, poets often drew upon the traditions of the ancient Greek and Roman religions, personifying abstract ideas and elements of the natural world as gods or goddesses. Phillis Wheatley was greatly influenced by the work of the eighteenth-century English poets. This influence is reflected in Wheatley's personification of both America and Great Britain as goddesses in "To His Excellency, General Washington."

Writing

Brainstorm for examples of personification in everyday language, listing your examples.

Primary Source

In October of 1775, when Washington was at his headquarters in Cambridge near Boston, Phillis Wheatley sent him a short letter and the poem addressed to him. Several months later Washington responded.

> I thank you most sincerely for your polite notice of me in the elegant lines you enclosed; and however undeserving I may be of such encomium [high praise] and panegyric [tribute], the style and manner exhibit a striking proof of your poetical talents; in honor of which, and as a tribute justly due you, I would have published the poem, had I not been apprehensive that, while I only meant to give the world this new instance of your genius, I might have incurred the imputation of vanity. This, and nothing else, determined me not to give it a place in the public prints.
>
> If you should ever come to Cambridge, or near headquarters, I shall be happy to see a person so favored by the Muses, and to whom nature has been so beneficent in her dispensations.

Literary Focus Spend some time discussing how personification helps to make it possible for people to understand the world in human terms. Have students try to come up with examples of personification from everyday speech. For example, students might come up with the expression, "the siren screamed."

Writing/Prior Knowledge For extra credit, have students develop one of the examples they come up with into a poem.

Vocabulary

Preteach the following vocabulary words:
celestial (sə les' chəl) *adj.:* Of the heavens (p. 139, l. 1)
refulgent (ri ful' jənt) *adj.:* Radiant; shining (p. 139, l. 4)
propitious (prə pish' əs) *adj.:* Favorably inclined or disposed (p. 139, l. 13)
refluent (ref' loo wənt) *adj.:* Flowing back (p. 139, l. 18)
pensive (pen' siv) *adj.:* Thinking deeply or seriously (p. 140, l. 35)

Humanities Note

Fine art, *George Washington at the Battle of Princeton,* 1783 by Charles Wilson Peale. The son of a poor Maryland school teacher, Peale (1741-1827), studied in London with the famous painter Benjamin West. During his studies, Peale developed a preference for meticulously rendered realism. Back in the United States, he studied natural history and excavated two mastodon skeletons in New York, and he founded Peale's Museum in Philadelphia to house natural curiosities and portraits.

Peale was commissioned to produce a number of versions of this painting. Washington posed for the original painting between December 8th and 13th, 1783, seven years after the battle. The painting demonstrates Peale's realistic style. He combines this style with the abstract feelings of patriotism and glory in a portrait befitting a national hero.

You might ask students the following questions:

1. How do you think the artist felt about George Washington?
2. What symbols has the artist used in this painting? What do you think they represent?
3. Do you imagine Washington was pleased upon viewing this portrait? Why?

GEORGE WASHINGTON AT THE BATTLE OF PRINCETON
Charles Wilson Peale
Yale University Art Gallery

138   *The Revolutionary Period*

To His Excellency, General Washington

Phillis Wheatley

1
   Celestial choir! enthron'd in realms of light,
     Columbia's[1] scenes of glorious toils I write.
   While freedom's cause her anxious breast alarms,
   She flashes dreadful in refulgent arms.
5   See mother earth her offspring's fate bemoan,
   And nations gaze at scenes before unknown!
   See the bright beams of heaven's revolving light
   Involved in sorrows and the veil of night!
     The goddess comes, she moves divinely fair,
2 10   Olive and laurel binds her golden hair:
   Wherever shines this native of the skies,
   Unnumber'd charms and recent graces rise.
     Muse![2] bow propitious while my pen relates
   How pour her armies through a thousand gates,
15   As when Eolus[3] heaven's fair face deforms,
   Enwrapp'd in tempest and a night of storms;
   Astonish'd ocean feels the wild uproar,
3   The refluent surges beat the sounding shore;
   Or thick as leaves in Autumn's golden reign,
20   Such, and so many, moves the warrior's train.
   In bright array they seek the work of war,
   Where high unfurl'd the ensign[4] waves in air.
   Shall I to Washington their praise recite?
   Enough thou know'st them in the fields of fight.
25   Thee, first in peace and honors,—we demand
   The grace and glory of thy martial band.
   Fam'd for thy valor, for thy virtues more,
   Hear every tongue thy guardian aid implore!
     One century scarce perform'd its destined round,
30   When Gallic[5] powers Columbia's fury found;

---

1. Columbia: America personified as a goddess.
2. Muse: The goddess who presides over poetry; one of nine muses presiding over literature, the arts, and the sciences.
3. Eolus (ē′ ə ləs): The Greek god of the winds.
4. ensign (en′ s'n): Flag.
5. Gallic (găl′ ik): French. The colonists, led by Washington, defeated the French in the French and Indian War (1754–1763).

4 **Clarification** "A crown, a mansion, and a throne" are Biblical allusions to the rewards that await those who perform the will of God.

Reader's Response If you were to write a poem to someone you admire the way Wheatley admired General Washington, who would be your subject? Why?

And so may you, whoever dares disgrace
The land of freedom's heaven-defended race!
Fix'd are the eyes of nations on the scales,
For in their hopes Columbia's arm prevails.
35   Anon Britannia[6] droops the pensive head,
While round increase the rising hills of dead.
Ah! cruel blindness to Columbia's state!
Lament thy thirst of boundless power too late.
      Proceed, great chief, with virtue on thy side,
40   Thy ev'ry action let the goddess guide.
A crown, a mansion, and a throne that shine,
With gold unfading, WASHINGTON! be thine.

4

---

6. Britannia: England.

Commentary

From a young age, Phillis Wheatley attracted considerable attention. Her learning and social grace were truly impressive, made more so by the fact that she was a woman, a slave, and a black. In Boston she was "the sooty prodigy"; in London she was all the rage as the "Sable Muse."

Her poetry, although well done, follows the neoclassical conventions of the times. Thomas Jefferson did not think highly of her as a poet: In his *Notes on the State of Virginia* (1781–1782) he writes, "Religion indeed has produced a Phillis Wheatley; but it could not produce a poet." Many equally illustrious persons came to her defense. A college president responded, "I will demand of Mr. Jefferson, or of any other man who is acquainted with American planters, how many of those masters could have written poems equal to those of Phillis Wheatley?"

Although she was largely forgotten by the public in her last years, the abolition movement of the 1830's and 1840's revived her writings, this time as evidence for abolishing slavery. In 1838 in Boston, her poems and those of another slave were published as *Memoir and Poems of Phillis Wheatley, a Native African and a Slave; Also, Poems by a Slave.* Shortly before the end of the Civil War there appeared *The Letters of Phillis Wheatley, the Negro-Slave Poet of Boston.*

Wheatley herself in her poems was not concerned with freedom from slavery but with freedom for all people, an issue of concern in the years before the Revolution.

THINKING ABOUT THE SELECTION

Recalling

1. What cause does Columbia's "anxious breast" alarm?
2. (a) What question does Wheatley ask in line 23? (b) How does she answer this question?
3. According to line 33, whose eyes are fixed "on the scales"?
4. What outcome of the war does Wheatley say that other nations hope for?
5. According to line 39, what does Washington have on his side?

Interpreting

6. (a) Find three instances in which Wheatley indicates a relationship between God and the American cause. (b) What is the nature of this relationship?
7. What does Wheatley suggest about the American forces in comparisons made in lines 13–20?
8. (a) What are the "scales" Wheatley refers to in line 33? (b) Why are eyes fixed on them?
9. What do the last two lines indicate about the influence of the British social and political systems on American thinking?

Applying

10. What does this poem suggest about Wheatley's feelings regarding her country?

ANALYZING LITERATURE

Recognizing Personification

Personification is the attribution of human powers to something that is not human, such as an inanimate object or an abstract idea. For example, in "To His Excellency, General Washington," Phillis Wheatley personifies America as the goddess Columbia.

1. How does Wheatley characterize Columbia?
2. What details does she use in describing Columbia's physical appearance?
3. What is the significance of the physical details Wheatley uses in describing Columbia?
4. What does the god Eolus (line 15) personify?
5. How does Wheatley personify Britain?

CRITICAL THINKING AND READING

Evaluating the Effect of Personification

Personification makes it possible for us to understand a subject in human terms. For example, in "To His Excellency, General Washington" we are able to view American ideals and beliefs as character traits of the goddess Columbia.
1. Explain how Wheatley's use of personification makes us sympathize more readily with the American cause.
2. Compare and contrast Wheatley's personification of America as the goddess Columbia with the common personification of the United States as Uncle Sam.

THINKING AND WRITING

Developing a Personification

What type of person would best personify America today? Prepare to write a poem or several paragraphs in which you personify America. First, develop a list of character traits that express the ideals and beliefs of today's society. Think of how you would describe the physical appearance of a man or woman who personifies America, and think about how this person would behave. Then develop your personification of America as a man or woman through your description of his or her appearance, behavior, and character traits. When you finish writing, revise your poem or paragraphs and prepare a final copy.

7. America's armies are as mighty, valiant, and powerful as the forces of nature.
8. (a) The scales Wheatley refers to are the scales of justice. (b) The eyes of the people of the world await the outcome. They believe that the Americans are fighting for the cause of freedom and justice.
9. The British monarchy has so influenced Americans that Wheatley suggests Washington should be crowned king when he is victorious.

Applying

10. Wheatley was deeply patriotic.

ANSWERS TO ANALYZING LITERATURE

1. Columbia is characterized as a powerful, flashing, resplendent goddess.
2. The goddess moves divinely and her hair is gold and bound by olive and laurel.
3. They imply that America is beautiful and powerful.
4. Eolus personifies the unbeatable American forces.
5. Britain is personified as Britannia, a defeated warrior with a "drooping head."

ANSWERS TO CRITICAL THINKING AND READING

1. Suggested Response: Her use of personification makes us sympathize more readily with the American cause by allowing us to visualize it.
2. Suggested Response: Wheatley's personification is more dignified than the personification of America as Uncle Sam.

THINKING AND WRITING

For help with this assignment, students can refer to Lesson 18, "Writing a Poem," in the Handbook of Writing About Literature.

Publishing Student Writing
Have student volunteers share their personifications with their classmates.

Closure and Extension

ANSWERS TO THINKING ABOUT THE SELECTION
Recalling

1. The cause of freedom.
2. (a) She asks if Washington wishes to hear her praise his troops. (b) She says that she does not have to praise them because he has witnessed their valor in the battlefield.
3. All nations' eyes are fixed "on the scales."
4. Other nations hope that the Americans will prevail over the British forces.
5. Washington has virtue on his side.

Interpreting

6. (a) Suggested Response: In line one Wheatley invokes God's heavenly choir to extol America's cause. In line seven she writes of "heaven's revolving light." In line thirty-two she writes of America as "the land of freedom's heaven-defended race." (b) Because the colonists are fighting for a worthy cause, they have God's power on their side.

THOMAS JEFFERSON

1743–1826

Thomas Jefferson is one of the most widely respected and admired figures in American history. A gifted writer, diplomat, political leader, inventor, architect, philosopher, and educator, with an intense belief in equal rights and individual freedoms, Jefferson played a significant role in the creation and shaping of America.

Born into a wealthy Virginia family, Jefferson received a thorough classical education as a boy. After graduating from the College of William and Mary in 1762, Jefferson spent five years studying law. In 1769, two years after Jefferson received his license to practice law, he was elected to the Virginia House of Burgesses. While serving in the House, Jefferson became an outspoken defender of American rights. After Jefferson displayed his persuasive abilities in his pamphlet *A Summary View of the Rights of British America* (1774), he was chosen to draft the Declaration of Independence at the Second Continental Congress in 1776.

When the Revolutionary War ended, Jefferson served as the American minister to France for several years. He then became America's first Secretary of State in 1789. In 1801, after he served as Vice-President under John Adams, Jefferson became the third American President. While in office, Jefferson nearly doubled the size of the nation by authorizing the purchase of the Louisiana Territory from France.

In 1809 Jefferson retired to Monticello, the Virginia home he had designed, and devoted his time to reading, conducting scientific experiments, collecting paintings, and playing the violin. Jefferson also helped to found the University of Virginia, designing the campus and planning the curriculum.

We owe many further aspects of American life to Jefferson's extremely varied interests and talents. He began collecting an immense library that eventually became the basis of the Library of Congress. He outlined our public school system and proposed the decimal system for American money. He commissioned the Lewis and Clark expedition to find a land route to the Pacific through the then largely unmapped West.

Among his most important legacies to us today are his belief in an aristocracy based on moral character and ability—not on wealth and family name—and his deep faith in the small farmer, the "common man," as the basis of democratic life. "Those who labor in the earth," he wrote, "are the chosen people of God." He wrote eloquently against a belief then current in Europe that in the wilderness life of North America, people would degenerate morally and socially.

On July 4, 1826, the fiftieth anniversary of the Declaration of Independence, Thomas Jefferson died.

GUIDE FOR INTERPRETING

The Declaration of Independence

Parallelism. Parallelism refers to the repeated use of phrases, clauses, or sentences that are similar in structure or meaning. Writers use this technique to emphasize important ideas, create rhythm, and make their writing forceful and direct. In the Declaration of Independence, Thomas Jefferson uses parallelism when listing the reasons that Americans felt compelled to declare their independence. Jefferson's use of parallelism makes his argument grow stronger with each reason he presents.

Commentary

At the Second Continental Congress, Jefferson was elected to join Benjamin Franklin, John Adams, Roger Sherman, and Robert Livingston in drafting a declaration of independence for the colonies. The draft that the committee sent to the Congress was primarily Jefferson's work.

Congress, however, to Jefferson's disappointment, made further changes before approving the final document. They dropped Jefferson's condemnation of the British people for tolerating a corrupt parliament and king, and struck out a strong statement against slavery.

The document finally signed and sent to George III was clearly treasonous. The penalty for treason against the Crown was death—a fact all the delegates were well aware of. Therefore, the two opening paragraphs, preceding the list of grievances, were very important in justifying this act of treason. As you read them and the rest of the Declaration, imagine that you are one of the delegates, and the time has come to sign. What are your chances of *not* being tried and beheaded for treason?

Writing

What does freedom mean to you? Prepare a journal entry in which you discuss your ideas about the concept of freedom. Include specific examples.

Literary Focus Parellelism is an effective rhetorical tool. Point out to students that this technique was also used in the selections by Patrick Henry (p. 126) and Thomas Paine (p. 132).

Writing/Prior Knowledge For extra credit, you may wish to have students develop their journal entry into an essay.

Vocabulary

Preteach the following vocabulary words:

unalienable (un āl' yən ə b'l) *adj.:* Not to be taken away (p. 144)

usurpations (yo͞o' sər pā shənz) *n.:* Unlawful seizures of rights or privileges (p. 144)

candid (kan' did) *adj.:* Impartial (p. 144)

perfidy (pər' fə dē) *n.:* Betrayal of trust (p. 146)

redress (ri dres') *v.:* Compensation for a wrong done (p. 146)

magnanimity (mag'nə nim'ə tē) *n.:* Ability to rise above pettiness or meanness (p. 146)

consanguinity (kän' san gwin' ə tē) *n.:* Kinship (p. 146)

acquiesce (ak' wē es') *v.:* Agree without protest (p. 146)

Spelling Tip Point out that in present-day usage, *unalienable* is spelled *inalienable*.

The Declaration of Independence

Thomas Jefferson

When in the course of human events, it becomes necessary for one people to dissolve the political bands which have connected them with another, and to assume among the powers of the earth, the separate and equal station to which the laws of nature and of nature's God entitle them, a decent respect to the opinions of mankind requires that they should declare the causes which impel them to the separation.

We hold these truths to be self-evident: that all men are created equal; that they are endowed by their Creator with certain unalienable rights; that among these are life, liberty and the pursuit of happiness; that to secure these rights, governments are instituted among men, deriving their just powers from the consent of the governed; that whenever any form of government becomes destructive of these ends, it is the right of the people to alter or to abolish it, and to institute new government, laying its foundation on such principles and organizing its powers in such form, as to them shall seem most likely to effect their safety and happiness. Prudence, indeed, will dictate that governments long established should not be changed for light and transient causes; and accordingly all experience hath shown, that mankind are more disposed to suffer while evils are sufferable than to right themselves by abolishing the forms to which they are accustomed. But when a long train of abuses and usurpations, pursuing invariably the same object, evinces a design to reduce them under absolute despotism,[1] it is their right, it is their duty, to throw off such government, and to provide new guards for their future security. Such has been the patient sufferance of these colonies; and such is now the necessity which constrains[2] them to alter their former systems of government. The history of the present king of Great Britain is a history of repeated injuries and usurpations, all having in direct object the establishment of an absolute tyranny over these states. To prove this, let facts be submitted to a candid world.

He has refused his assent to laws the most wholesome and necessary for the public good.

He has forbidden his governors to pass laws of immediate and pressing importance, unless suspended in their operation till his assent should be obtained; and when so suspended, he has utterly neglected to attend to them.

He has refused to pass other laws for the accommodation of large districts of people, unless those people would relinquish the right of representation in the legislature, a right inestimable to them and formidable to tyrants only.

He has called together legislative bodies at places unusual, uncomfortable, and distant from the depository of their public rec-

---

1. **despotism** (des' pə tiz'm) *n.*: Tyranny.
2. **constrains** *v.*: Forces.

THE DECLARATION OF INDEPENDENCE
John Trumbull
Yale University Art Gallery

ords, for the sole purpose of fatiguing them into compliance with his measures.

He has dissolved representative houses repeatedly, for opposing with manly firmness his invasions on the rights of the people.

He has refused for a long time after such dissolutions to cause others to be elected, whereby the legislative powers, incapable of annihilation, have returned to the people at large for their exercise, the state remaining in the mean time exposed to all the dangers of invasion from without, and convulsions within.

He has endeavored to prevent the population of these states; for that purpose obstructing the laws for naturalization of foreigners, refusing to pass others to encourage their migration hither, and raising the conditions of new appropriations of lands.

He has obstructed the administration of justice, by refusing his assent to laws for establishing judiciary powers.

He has made judges dependent on his will alone, for the tenure of their offices, and the amount and payment of their salaries.

He has erected a multitude of new offices, and sent hither swarms of officers to harass our people and eat out their substance. 〔5〕

He has kept among us in times of peace standing armies without the consent of our legislatures.

He has affected to render the military independent of, and superior to, the civil power.

He has combined with others to subject us to a jurisdiction foreign to our constitution and unacknowledged by our laws, giving his assent to their acts of pretended legislation: for quartering large bodies of 〔6〕

The Declaration of Independence **145**

Humanities Note

Fine art, *The Declaration of Independence,* 1786, by John Trumbull. John Trumbull (1756-1843) was an American who was first drawn to art through his fascination with his older sister's needlework. His father, the governor of Connecticut, found this odd attraction inappropriate for two reasons. First, he believed that gentlemen did not pursue such activities as painting (at the time, the aristocratic view was that picture making was for women and common laborers). Second, John had lost the sight of one eye in an accident. As a result of his father's concerns, Trumbull was sent to Harvard so that he might become a "proper" gentleman. There, he met John Copley, the famous painter, and he soon began to paint, becoming one of the first male aristocrats in the United States to paint seriously. In London he studied with Benjamin West, who urged him to paint small pictures, which his one eye could encompass. Some critics feel that Trumbull's sweeping compositions compressed into a concentrated size are more powerful than West's own large canvases.

This painting is only thirty inches wide, yet it contains forty-eight figures, all grouped naturally and convincingly. Seated at the table is John Hancock, and standing in front of him are Benjamin Franklin, Thomas Jefferson, Robert R. Livingston, Roger Sherman, and John Adams. Trumbull's placement of the heads of his subjects and the sweep of the banners in the background seem to add action and excitement to what might have been a very placid composition.

Ask your students the following questions:
1. How has the artist conveyed the feelings of excitement that must have been in the air at the signing?
2. How might a photograph of this event have differed from this artistic interpretation?

〔5〕 **Reading Strategy** Have students summarize Jefferson's argument up to this point.

〔6〕 **Clarification** The colonists under order of the king had to provide lodging for the British armed forces.

7 **Discussion** Do the charges against King George get more serious as the list of grievances continues?

8 **Discussion** Why does Jefferson use the word *brethren* rather than *brothers*? Why is this choice of words appropriate for the subject and purpose of the Declaration?

Reader's Response Imagine that you are a colonist in the Revolutionary Period. How do you respond to the Declaration of Independence?

armed troops among us; for protecting them by a mock trial from punishment for any murders which they should commit on the inhabitants of these states; for cutting off our trade with all parts of the world; for imposing taxes on us without our consent; for depriving us, in many cases, of the benefits of trial by jury; for transporting us beyond seas to be tried for pretended offenses; for abolishing the free system of English laws in a neighboring province,[3] establishing therein an arbitrary government, and enlarging its boundaries, so as to render it at once an example and fit instrument for introducing the same absolute rule into these colonies; for taking away our charters, abolishing our most valuable laws, and altering fundamentally the forms of our governments; for suspending our own legislatures, and declaring themselves invested with power to legislate for us in all cases whatsoever.

7 He has abdicated government here, by declaring us out of his protection and waging war against us.

He has plundered our seas, ravaged our coasts, burned our towns, and destroyed the lives of our people.

He is at this time transporting large armies of foreign mercenaries to complete the works of death, desolation, and tyranny, already begun with circumstances of cruelty and perfidy scarcely paralleled in the most barbarous ages, and totally unworthy the head of a civilized nation.

He has constrained our fellow citizens taken captive on the high seas to bear arms against their country, to become the executioners of their friends and brethren, or to fall themselves by their hands.

He has excited domestic insurrections amongst us, and has endeavored to bring on the inhabitants of our frontiers, the merciless Indian savages, whose known rule of warfare is an undistinguished destruction of all ages, sexes, and conditions.

In every stage of these oppressions we have petitioned for redress in the most humble terms. Our repeated petitions have been answered only by repeated injury.

A prince whose character is thus marked by every act which may define a tyrant is unfit to be the ruler of a free people.

8 Nor have we been wanting in attentions to our British brethren. We have warned them from time to time of attempts by their legislature to extend an unwarrantable jurisdiction over us. We have reminded them of the circumstances of our emigration and settlement here. We have appealed to their native justice and magnanimity and we have conjured[4] them by the ties of our common kindred to disavow these usurpations which would inevitably interrupt our connections and correspondence. They too have been deaf to the voice of justice and of consanguinity. We must therefore acquiesce in the necessity which denounces[5] our separation and hold them, as we hold the rest of mankind, enemies in war, in peace friends.

We, therefore, the representatives of the United States of America in general congress assembled, appealing to the Supreme Judge of the world for the rectitude of our intentions, do in the name and by authority of the good people of these colonies, solemnly publish and declare that these united colonies are and of right ought to be free and independent states; that they are absolved from all allegiance to the British Crown, and that all political connection between them and the state of Great Britain is and ought to be totally dissolved; and that as free and independent states, they have full power to levy war, conclude peace, contract alliances, establish commerce, and to do all other acts and things which independent states may of right do.

And for the support of this declaration, with a firm reliance on the protection of divine providence, we mutually pledge to each other our lives, our fortunes and our sacred honor.

---

3. neighboring province: Quebec.

4. conjured: Solemnly appealed to.
5. denounces: Here, announces.

Grammar in Action

Parallelism is the use of the same grammatical structure to present equal ideas. When writers use this technique, they must be careful to avoid faulty parallelism. Note Thomas Jefferson's use of parallelism in the following sentence:

He has plundered our seas, ravaged our coasts, burned our towns, and destroyed the lives of our people.

Now note how the sentence might have appeared if Jefferson had used faulty parallelism.

He has plundered our seas, ravaged our coasts, burned our towns, and *will destroy* the lives of our people.

Student Activity 1. Each of the following sentences contains an error in parallel structure. Rewrite each sentence and correct the error.

1. Thomas Jefferson was patriotic, intelligent, imaginative, and he had courage.
2. Jefferson wrote the Declaration of Independence, designed his home at Monticello, and was one of the people who founded the University of Virginia.
3. Patrick Henry was a brilliant speaker; Thomas Jefferson was a gifted writer, and the talented military leader was George Washington.

THINKING ABOUT THE SELECTION

Recalling

1. What are the three "unalienable rights" listed in the second paragraph?
2. (a) According to Jefferson, what is the purpose of a government? (b) When should a government be abolished?
3. List three of the statements Jefferson presents to support his claim that the king's objective is "the establishment of an absolute tyranny over these states"?
4. (a) What does Jefferson claim the colonists have done at "every stage of these oppressions"? (b) How has the king responded to the colonists' actions?
5. What pledge is made in the last paragraph?

Interpreting

6. What effect does Jefferson's long list of specific grievances have on his argument?
7. Why does Jefferson focus his attack on King George III rather than on the British Parliament or people?
8. How is the eighteenth-century faith in reason reflected in the Declaration?

Applying

9. Considering Jefferson's views concerning the purpose of a government, to what governments in today's world might he object?

ANALYZING LITERATURE

Recognizing Parallelism

Parallelism refers to the repeated use of phrases, clauses, or sentences that are similar in structure or meaning. For example, Jefferson lists the colonists' grievances in a series of sentences with the same structure.

1. Find another example of Jefferson's use of parallel structure.
2. In what ways does Jefferson's use of parallelism strengthen his argument?

CRITICAL THINKING AND READING

Recognizing Charged Words

In presenting an argument, a writer may appeal to emotions indirectly through the use of emotionally charged words. **Charged words** are words with strong connotations beyond their literal meanings that are likely to produce an emotional response. For example, the word *tyranny* evokes a feeling of fear. It suggests living in a state of terror, afraid of being jailed or executed for disagreeing with governmental policies.

What associations are evoked by each of the following words from the Declaration of Independence?

1. liberty   2. justice   3. honor

THINKING AND WRITING

Comparing and Contrasting Arguments

The Declaration of Independence and Patrick Henry's "Speech in the Virginia Convention" are both powerful arguments for American independence. In what ways are the two arguments similar? In what ways are they different? Reread both documents carefully and list similarities and differences in format, content, and persuasive techniques. Review your notes to help you develop your thesis statement; then prepare an outline. When you write your essay, make sure that you include passages from both selections to support your argument. After you finish writing, review your essay, making sure you have included enough information to support your thesis.

4. After his retirement, Jefferson conducted scientific experiments, collected paintings, and was a violin player.

Student Activity 2. Write a short paragraph about the Declaration of Independence. In your paragraph include at least five sentences in which you use parallelism correctly.

Closure and Extension

ANSWERS TO THINKING ABOUT THE SELECTION
Recalling

1. Life, liberty, and the pursuit of happiness are the three "inalienable rights."
2. (a) The purpose of government is to secure these inalienable rights. (b) When a government becomes destructive of these rights, it should be altered or abolished.
3. Answers will differ. Among the facts Jefferson presents are the king's refusal to assent to new laws, his dissolution of representative houses, and his refusal to hold elections.
4. (a) At every stage the colonists have petitioned the king for redress. (b) Repeated petitions have been met "only by repeated injury."
5. The lives, fortunes, and sacred honor of the delegates are pledged.

Interpreting

6. The long list of grievances adds both credibility and momentum to his argument.
7. Suggested Response: The focus of Jefferson's argument is on tyranny and, therefore, on the tyrant. He does not wish to pit brethren against brethren.
8. Faith in reason is exhibited in the well-organized, rational argument that Jefferson presents.

Applying

9. Suggested Response: Jefferson would abhor governments that do not uphold "inalienable" human rights.

ANSWERS TO ANALYZING LITERATURE

1. Suggested Response: Jefferson uses parallelism in his list of charges against the king.
2. Suggested Response: His use of parallelism adds momentum to his argument and, in doing so, emphasizes his main points.

ANSWERS TO CRITICAL THINKING AND READING

1. Suggested Response: Liberty suggests an ideal life, characterized by freedom and happiness.
2. Suggested Response: Justice can be associated with freedom and equality.
3. Suggested Response: Honor evokes a sense of morality and dignity.

THINKING AND WRITING
For help with this assignment, students can refer to Lesson 16, "Writing a Comparative Evaluation," in the Handbook of Writing About Literature.

ABIGAIL SMITH ADAMS

1744–1818

Abigail Smith Adams, the wife of John Adams, the second President of the United States, and the mother of John Quincy Adams, the sixth President, was one of the most important and influential American women of her time. A dedicated supporter of women's rights and the American Revolutionary movement, Adams wrote many letters to her husband and other members of her family expressing her opinions. In these letters, Adams included vivid descriptions that capture the essence of life in early America.

Abigail Smith was born in Weymouth, Massachusetts. At the age of twenty, she married John Adams. The couple had four sons and one daughter, and Abigail made sure that her daughter received a thorough education—something few American girls received at the time.

Although her father was a well-to-do minister and her mother from an upper class family, Abigail herself had no formal schooling of any kind. John, of a much more modest social position, was a Harvard graduate. Abigail often excused her lack of schooling by saying that she was frequently ill as a child. However, in later years, she made observations such as this in a letter of 1778: "Every assistance and advantage which can be procured is afforded to the Sons, whilst the daughters are wholly neglected in point of Literature." (By "Literature" she means the liberal arts.)

In 1774, when John left home to serve as a member of the Continental Congress, Abigail assumed the responsibility of managing the family farm in what is now Quincy, Massachusetts. Because of John's political involvement, John and Abigail were separated from each other for most of the next ten years. During this period Abigail became an avid letter writer. In her letters, Abigail provided her husband with information about British troops and ships in the Boston area, stressed the importance of women's rights, and voiced her opposition to slavery.

When John Adams was elected President of the United States, John and Abigail Adams became the first couple to live in the White House. Among the letters Abigail wrote while living there is one to her daughter describing her temporary home. This letter and the others she wrote during this period provide an interesting view of life in the new nation.

Abigail Adams died in 1818, after spending the last seventeen years of her life at the Adams's family home in Massachusetts. In 1840 a volume of her letters was published, and since then three more volumes have been published. Today, Abigail Adams is widely recognized as a writer and a pioneer of the American women's movement.

Objectives
1 To appreciate description
2 To infer a writer's attitude
3 To trace word origins
4 To write a description

Support Material

Teaching Portfolio
Teacher Backup, pp. 227-229
Usage and Mechanics Worksheet, p. 230
Vocabulary Check, p. 231
Analyzing Literature Worksheet, *Recognizing Descriptive Writing*, p. 232

Critical Thinking and Reading Worksheet, *Inferring a Writer's Attitude*, p. 233
Selection Test, pp. 234-235

GUIDE FOR INTERPRETING

Letter to Her Daughter from the New White House

Writer's Techniques

Description. Descriptive writing creates an impression of a person, place, or thing through the use of details appealing to one or more of the five senses—sight, sound, taste, smell, and touch. In a description, a writer includes enough details to enable us to visualize the subject. Because a writer cannot use all the details of the subject in a description, he or she selects those details that create a desired impression.

Abigail Adams lived in the days before cameras were invented. Her descriptions provided the equivalent of snapshots. In passages in her letters, she described for her daughter what the White House looked like and what it was like to live there. When we read Adams's letter, the contrast between her description of the White House and our perceptions of today's White House makes the impression created by Adams even more striking.

Writing

What details would you include in a description of your city hall? List its most significant and striking details.

Primary Source

The letters of Abigail Adams reveal a well-read and politically sensitive writer, well aware of the decisions facing the country. In August 1774, while John was at the Continental Congress in Philadelphia, Massachusetts was in near rebellion. Abigail wrote him, comparing the colonies' position to that of Sparta, a city of ancient Greece, and commenting on the desire for "peace in our time":

> Uncertainty and expectation leave the mind great Scope. Did ever any Kingdom or State regain their Liberty, when once it was invaded without Blood shed? I cannot think of it without horror.
>
> Yet we are told that all the Misfortunes of Sparta were occasioned by their too great Sollicitude for present tranquility, and by an excessive love of peace they neglected the means of making it sure and lasting. They ought to have reflected says Polibius [a Greek historian] that as there is nothing more desirable, or advantageous than peace, when founded in justice and honour, so there is nothing more shameful and at the same time more pernicious when attained by bad measures, and purchased at the price of liberty.

Guide for Interpreting 149

Literary Focus In her essay "Place in Fiction," Eudora Welty encourages every writer to locate within himself or herself a "sense of place"—to find a unique point of view from which to write. You may wish to have your **more advanced** students discuss how two writers can present dramatically different descriptions of the same subject.

Look For You may wish to have your **less advanced** students discuss any trips they have made to Washington, D.C. Did the reality of what they saw live up to their expectations? What were their impressions of the city?

Writing/Prior Knowledge For extra credit, ask your **more advanced** students to write a one-paragraph description of a familiar place, using details that appeal to each of the senses. Then have them rewrite the paragraph, as though they were describing the place through the eyes of one of their ancestors. How has the place changed?

Vocabulary

Preteach the following vocabulary words:
extricate (eks′ trə kāt) *v.* To set free (p. 150)
agues (ā gyo͞oz) *n.:* Fits of shivering (p. 150)

149

Motivation/Prior Knowledge
Have your students imagine that they are the recipients of this letter from Mrs. Adams. What would they want to know about the new White House?

Thematic Idea "Letter to His Son" by Robert E. Lee (p. 450) is another personal letter of historical significance.

Purpose-Setting Question
What overall impression does Adams convey?

1 **Discussion** In 1800 the entire Washington area had a population of only about 8,000 people. How might this city "which is only so in name" have compared to a city like Boston with which Mrs. Adams was familiar?

2 **Enrichment** The White House is a Georgian mansion, designed in the classical Palladian style common in Europe in the 1700's.

3 **Clarification** From 1776 to 1800 the federal government had no permanent capital. Washington, D.C., became the designated capital in 1800. Up to that point, jealousy among the states had blocked every attempt to choose a location. Finally, a compromise was worked out. Northern political leaders agreed to locate the capital in the South in return for some legislation they deemed important.

Letter to Her Daughter from the New White House

Abigail Adams

Washington, 21 November, 1800

My Dear Child:

I arrived here on Sunday last, and without meeting with any accident worth noticing, except losing ourselves when we left Baltimore and going eight or nine miles on the Frederick road, by which means we were obliged to go the other eight through woods, where we wandered two hours without finding a guide or the path. Fortunately, a straggling black came up with us, and we engaged him as a guide to extricate us out of our difficulty; but woods are all you see from Baltimore until you reach *the city*, which is only so in name. Here and there is a small cot, without a glass window, interspersed amongst the forests, through which you travel miles without seeing any human being. In the city there are buildings enough, if they were compact and finished, to accommodate Congress and those attached to it; but as they are, and scattered as they are, I see no great comfort for them. The river, which runs up to Alexandria,[1] is in full view of my window, and I see the vessels as they pass and repass. The house is upon a grand and superb scale, requiring about thirty servants to attend and keep the apartments in proper order, and perform the ordinary business of the house and stables; an establishment very well proportioned to the President's salary. The lighting of the apartments, from the kitchen to parlors and chambers, is a tax indeed; and the fires we are obliged to keep to secure us from daily agues is another very cheering comfort. To assist us in this great castle, and render less attendance necessary, bells are wholly wanting, not one single one being hung through the whole house, and promises are all you can obtain. This is so great an inconvenience, that I know not what to do, or how to do. The ladies from Georgetown[2] and in the city have many of them visited me. Yesterday I returned fifteen visits—but such a place as Georgetown appears—why, our Milton is beautiful. But no comparisons—if they will put me up some bells and let me have wood enough to keep fires, I design to be pleased. I could content myself almost anywhere three months; but, surrounded with forests, can you believe that wood is not to be had because people cannot be found to cut and cart it? Briesler entered into a contract with a man to supply him with wood. A small part, a few cords only, has he been able to get. Most of that was expended to dry the walls of the house before we came in, and yesterday the man told him it was impossible for him to procure it to be cut and carted. He has had recourse to coals; but we cannot get grates made and set. We have, indeed, come into a *new country*.

---

1. **Alexandria:** A city in northeastern Virginia.

2. **Georgetown:** A section of Washington, D.C.

BUILDING THE FIRST WHITE HOUSE

WASHINGTON D.C. 1798

BUILDING THE FIRST WHITE HOUSE
N. C. Wyeth
Copyrighted by the White House Historical Association

Letter to Her Daughter from the New White House 151

Fine art, *Building the First White House,* 1930, by N. C. Wyeth. Newell Convers Wyeth (1882-1945) was a famous and prolific American illustrator. One of his first commercial illustration commissions was for the Pennsylvania Railroad to commemorate the Washington bicentennial year. On May 1, 1930, the railroad advertised that "historical posters in full color, dealing with patriotic subjects have been designed by a well-known painter." In 1971 this painting appeared on the Christmas cards sent by President and Mrs. Nixon.

When viewing this picture, one feels a part of the group in the foreground since the people are facing away from the picture plane. This compositional trick increases the drama of the scene. The pointing figure draws the eye even further into the picture, and the billowing cloud formations add a glorious touch.

You might consider asking these questions:
1. What is unusual about the placement of the figures in this picture?
2. What effect does the placement of the figures have on the viewer?
3. How might Abigail Adams have reacted to this scene?

4 Discussion How are Mrs. Adams's regional prejudices evident in this passage?

Reader's Response At one point or another, everyone finds himself or herself having to adjust to new surroundings. Whether you move into a new house or apartment, or change classrooms or buildings, the differences between your old and new surroundings can be somewhat shocking. Even when your living or studying environment is vastly improved, how can you still feel inconvenienced the way Abigail Smith Adams feels inconvenienced? Why is it difficult to adjust to new surroundings?

You must keep all this to yourself, and, when asked how I like it, say that I write you the situation is beautiful, which is true. The house is made habitable, but there is not a single apartment finished, and all within-side, except the plastering, has been done since Briesler came. We have not the least fence, yard, or other convenience, without, and the great unfinished audience room I make a drying-room of, to hang up the clothes in. The principal stairs are not up, and will not be this winter. Six chambers are made comfortable; two are occupied by the President and Mr. Shaw; two lower rooms, one for a common parlor, and one for a levee room. Upstairs there is the oval room, which is designed for the drawing room, and has the crimson furniture in it. It is a very handsome room now; but, when completed, it will be beautiful. If the twelve years, in which **4** this place has been considered as the future seat of government, had been improved, as they would have been if in New England, very many of the present inconveniences would have been removed. It is a beautiful spot, capable of every improvement, and, the more I view it, the more I am delighted with it.

Since I sat down to write, I have been called down to a servant from Mount Vernon,[3] with a billet[4] from Major Custis, and a haunch of venison, and a kind, congratulatory letter from Mrs. Lewis, upon my arrival in the city, with Mrs. Washington's love, inviting me to Mount Vernon, where, health permitting, I will go before I leave this place.

> Affectionately, your mother,
> Abigail Adams

---

3. Mount Vernon: Home of George Washington, located in northern Virginia.
4. billet (bil' it) *n*.: A brief letter.

THINKING ABOUT THE SELECTION

Recalling

1. By what is Washington, D.C., surrounded?
2. (a) Why are the Adamses "obliged to keep" a fire burning in the fireplace? (b) Why is there very little firewood?
3. Describe the state of the living quarters in the White House.
4. At the end of her letter, what invitation does Adams mention receiving?

Interpreting

5. What do you think is Adams's attitude toward living in the White House? Explain how her selection of details conveys this attitude.

6. Why do you think Adams tells her daughter to keep her complaints about the White House to herself?

Applying

7. Name two contrasts between Adams's description of the White House and Washington, D.C., and the appearance of the building and the city today.

ANALYZING LITERATURE

Recognizing Descriptive Writing

Descriptive writing creates an impression of a person, place, or thing through details appealing to one or more of the five senses. For example, one of the details Abigail Adams includes in her description of the surroundings of the White House is "the river, which runs up to Alexandria."

1. Name four details, including some that appeal to senses other than sight, that Adams includes in her description of the interior of the White House.
2. What impression of the White House does Adams's description create?
3. How does her description of the area surrounding the White House add to this impression?

CRITICAL THINKING AND READING

Inferring a Writer's Attitude

Writers often convey their attitude toward a subject through their description of it. Though in some cases the writer's attitude may be directly stated, most often you have to make inferences, or draw conclusions, about the writer's attitude by examining his or her choice of words or details. For example, from Adams's statement that "woods are all you see from Baltimore until you reach the city, which is so only in name" you can infer that Adams felt that Washington, D.C., was isolated and undeveloped.

What inference can you make from each of the following passages from the "Letter to Her Daughter"?

1. "In the city there are buildings enough, if they were compact and finished, to accommodate Congress and those attached to it; but as they are, and scattered as they are, I see no great comfort for them."

2. "The house is upon a grand and superb scale. . . ."
3. "We have not the least fence, yard, or other convenience, without. . . ."

UNDERSTANDING LANGUAGE

Tracing Word Origins

Many words in English were borrowed or derived from other languages. For example, the word *extricate* comes from the Latin *extricare* meaning "to disentangle."

Using a dictionary that provides etymologies, find the earliest language or origin of each of the following words found in the "Letter to Her Daughter from the New White House."

1. interspersed
2. superb
3. apartment
4. furniture
5. congratulatory

THINKING AND WRITING

Writing a Description

Review your list of details about your city hall. Selecting appropriate details from your list, write a description of some aspect of your city hall, such as the exterior. Write a description, presenting your details in spatial order. When you revise try to think about how someone who has never seen your city hall would respond to your description. Have you included enough details to enable a person to visualize it? Have you included too many for a brief description?

7. Suggested Response: When Adams was writing, Washington was surrounded by forests and was sparsely populated. Today the area is a bustling metropolis.

Challenge What is the historical value of letters such as the one by Adams?

ANSWERS TO ANALYZING LITERATURE

1. Answers will differ. Some details of the interior include: "the great unfinished audience room I make a drying-room of, to hang up the clothes"; the "principal stairs are not up"; "the oval room" has "the crimson furniture"; the need of wood "to keep fires."
2. Suggested Response: Her description conveys a sense of the vastness of the house and its unfinished state.
3. Her description of the surroundings also paints a picture of a vast, unsettled and unfinished area.

ANSWERS TO CRITICAL THINKING AND READING

1. Suggested Response: We can infer that Mrs. Adams thinks Washington is raw and undeveloped and that she is accustomed to comfort and perhaps luxury.
2. Suggested Response: The author is well pleased with the house and sees possibilities for making it to her liking.
3. Suggested Response: Mrs. Adams is accustomed to having all of the necessary conveniences in her house and yard.

ANSWERS TO UNDERSTANDING LANGUAGE

1. interspersed: from Latin
2. superb: from Latin
3. apartment: from Italian
4. furniture: from Old French
5. congratulatory: from Latin

THINKING AND WRITING
Publishing Student Writing

You may wish to encourage students to submit their descriptions to your school's literary magazine.

Closure and Extension

ANSWERS TO THINKING ABOUT THE SELECTION
Recalling

1. Washington, D.C., is surrounded by forests.
2. (a) They are obliged to keep the fires going to stay warm. (b) There are few people who cut and cart wood.

3. (a) Not a single apartment is finished. (b) Six of the chambers are made comfortable.
4. Adams mentions receiving an invitation to Mount Vernon from Mrs. Washington.

Interpreting

5. She is happy to be there but prefers living in New England.
6. It would be unbecoming for the President's wife to make her complaints public.

Critical Evaluation In his collection of essays, *American Literature, 1764-1789: The Revolutionary Years,* Everett Emerson says the following about Michel-Guillaume Jean de Crèvecoeur: "Probably the most striking and penetrating view of America was that provided by an immigrant from France. One who knows other lands is often able to capture the special quality of a place, and so it was with St. John de Crèvecoeur, whose attractive but troubled *Letters from an American Farmer* is a classic worthy to stand beside the *Autobiography* of Benjamin Franklin."

MICHEL-GUILLAUME JEAN DE CRÈVECOEUR

1735–1813

The first writer to compare America to a melting pot, Michel-Guillaume Jean de Crèvecoeur chronicled his experiences and observations as a European immigrant adjusting to life in America. His idealistic descriptions confirmed many people's vision of America as a land of great promise.

Born into a wealthy French aristocratic family, Crèvecoeur emigrated to Canada at the age of nineteen and served for several years as a member of the French army in Quebec. After his military career ended in 1759, Crèvecoeur spent ten years traveling throughout the colonies as a surveyor and Indian trader. In 1769, Crèvecoeur married and settled on a 120-acre farm in Orange County, New York. While living on his farm, which he named Pine Hill, Crèvecoeur began writing about his experiences in America.

Because his position during the Revolutionary War was ambiguous, Crèvecoeur was at one point forced by the revolutionaries to leave his farm; another time he was imprisoned for several months by the British. In 1780 Crèvecoeur sailed to London, where his *Letters from an American Farmer* was published two years later. The book, which was translated into several languages, was successful and made Crèvecoeur famous.

Meanwhile France was moving toward its own revolution. While there, Crèvecoeur prepared an expanded French edition of his *Letters* which was received with wild enthusiasm. He found himself a popular hero who confirmed the evils of the Old World and extolled the promises of the New.

In 1783 he returned to America as the French Consul to New York, New Jersey, and Connecticut. He was so popular that various cities gave him honorary citizenship; St. Johnsbury, Vermont, took its name from the name he used in America, J. Hector St. John.

His good fortune, however, was mixed with bad. On his return, he discovered that his farm had been burned, his wife killed, and his children sent to live with foster parents in Boston. When the French Revolution began in 1789, he was obliged to return to Paris. He never came back to America.

With the outbreak of the Reign of Terror in 1793, Crèvecoeur fled Paris for his family home in Normandy. There he wrote another book about New York and Pennsylvania, which was published in 1801. France and the rest of Europe, however, were by then absorbed in the wars of Napoleon and no longer interested in stories of America.

Crèvecoeur spent the last twelve years of his life largely forgotten amid the political turmoil of Europe.

Objectives

1 To analyze an epistle
2 To support opinions
3 To write an epistle

Support Material

Teaching Portfolio
Teacher Backup, pp. 237-239
Usage and Mechanics Worksheet, p. 240
Vocabulary Check, p. 241
Analyzing Literature Worksheet, *Understanding Epistles,* p. 242
Language Worksheet, *Appreciating Word Origins,* p. 243
Selection Test, pp. 244-245

GUIDE FOR INTERPRETING

from Letters from an American Farmer

Literary Forms

Epistles. An epistle, or literary letter, is a formal composition written in the form of a letter addressed to a distant person or group of people. Unlike common personal letters, which tend to be conversational and private compositions, epistles are carefully-crafted works of literature, intended for a general audience.

The epistle has been a popular literary form throughout history. In ancient Greece and Rome, philosophers recorded their thoughts in epistle form. Centuries later the epistle form was used in the New Testament. During the eighteenth century, European writers frequently composed their works—poems, essays, and novels—using the epistle form.

Influenced by the eighteenth-century European writers, Crèvecoeur chose the epistle form for his essays about life in America. Crèvecoeur's letters are supposedly written by an American farmer named "James" to his friend "Mr. F. B.," but in reality they are intended for a general audience. By presenting his essays in this form, Crèvecoeur is able to maintain a personal tone, while attempting to convince the general public to accept his ideas and opinions.

Commentary

A careful reader of Crèvecoeur's twelve *Letters* will see that life in the New World is not totally idyllic, but that is not what Europe wanted to hear. Although he did not intend to write a piece of immigrant propaganda, luring people to North America, Crèvecoeur does boast in his last letter that he has "caused upwards of a hundred and twenty families to remove thither."

The new country needed hard workers, so it is no wonder that some of its leaders were worried about the popularity of Crèvecoeur's glowing descriptions. Washington called the *Letters* "rather too flattering," but it was up to the wise and witty Ben Franklin to write and publish (first in France) in 1784 *Advice to Such As Would Remove to America*. He begins by warning that even though "there are in that country few people so miserable as the poor of Europe," neither are there many rich. "America is a land of labor," he continues, and what it needs are laborers, farmers, mechanics, and skilled artisans. Gentlemen need not apply.

As you read the selection, note what seems probably true about North America at the time and what seems perhaps wishful exaggeration by Crèvecoeur. Do you *want* to believe him? Why or why not?

Writing

What does being an American mean to you? Freewrite about what you associate with being an American.

Guide for Interpreting 155

Literary Focus You may want to discuss the epistle form used in the Bible. Explain that the New Testament epistles were written to convince their audience to accept the new faith, Christianity. St. Paul speaks of "the new man" in his epistles to the Ephesians (Eph. 4:24) and the Colossians (Col. 3:10). Like St. Paul's epistles, Crèvecoeur's epistle was written to convince his audience of a new faith—a faith in the new American.

Writing/Prior Knowledge Before having students complete the writing activity, spend some time discussing what it means to be an American.

Vocabulary

Preteach the following vocabulary words:
asylum (ə sī′ ləm) *n.:* Place of refuge (p. 156)
penury (pen′ yə rē) *n.:* Lack of money, property, or necessities (p. 156)
metamorphosis (met′ ə môr′ fə sis) *n.:* Transformation (p. 156)
despotic (de spät′ ik) *adj.:* Harsh, cruel, unjust (p. 158)
servile (ser′ v′l) *adj.:* Humbly yielding or submissive (p. 158)
subsistence (səb sis′ təns) *n.:* Means of support (p. 158)

Spelling Tip Point out the *ence* spelling of the suffix in *subsistence*.

from Letters from an American Farmer

Michel-Guillaume Jean de Crèvecoeur

In this great American asylum, the poor of Europe have by some means met together, and in consequence of various causes; to what purpose should they ask one another what countrymen they are? Alas, two thirds of them had no country. Can a wretch who wanders about, who works and starves, whose life is a continual scene of sore affliction or pinching penury, can that man call England or any other kingdom his country? A country that had no bread for him, whose fields procured him no harvest, who met with nothing but the frowns of the rich, the severity of the laws, with jails and punishments; who owned not a single foot of the extensive surface of this planet? No! Urged by a variety of motives, here they came. Everything has tended to regenerate them: new laws, a new mode of living, a new social system; here they are become men: in Europe they were as so many useless plants, wanting vegetative mold[1] and refreshing showers; they withered, and were mowed down by want, hunger, and war; but now by the power of transplantation, like all other plants they have taken root and flourished! Formerly they were not numbered in any civil lists[2] of their country, except in those of the poor; here they rank as citizens. By what invisible power has this surprising metamorphosis been performed? By that of the laws and that of their industry. The laws, the indulgent laws, protect them as they arrive, stamping on them the symbol of adoption; they receive ample rewards for their labors; these accumulated rewards procure them lands; those lands confer on them the title of freemen, and to that title every benefit is affixed which men can possibly require. This is the great operation daily performed by our laws. From whence proceed these laws? From our government. Whence the government? It is derived from the original genius and strong desire of the people ratified and confirmed by the crown. . . .

What attachment can a poor European emigrant have for a country where he had nothing? The knowledge of the language, the love of a few kindred as poor as himself, were the only cords that tied him: his country is now that which gives him land, bread, protection, and consequence: *Ubi panis ibi patria*[3] is the motto of all emigrants. What then is the American, this new man? He is either a European, or the descendant of a European, hence that strange mixture of blood, which you will find in no other country. I could point out to you a family whose grandfather was an Englishman, whose wife was Dutch, whose son married a French woman, and whose present four sons have now four wives of different nations. *He* is an American, who, leaving behind him all his ancient prejudices and manners, receives

---

1. **vegetative mold:** Enriched soil.
2. **civil lists:** Lists of distinguished persons.
3. ***Ubi . . . patria:*** "Where there is bread, there is one's fatherland" (Latin).

new ones from the new mode of life he has embraced, the new government he obeys, and the new rank he holds. He becomes an American by being received in the broad lap of our great *Alma Mater*.[4] Here individuals of all nations are melted into a new race of men, whose labors and posterity will one day cause great changes in the world. Americans are the western pilgrims, who are carrying along with them that great mass of arts, sciences, vigor, and industry which began long since in the east; they will finish the great circle. The Americans were once scattered all over Europe; here they are incorporated into one of the finest systems of population

9

10

---

4. *Alma Mater* (al′ mə mä′ tər): "Fostering mother." Here, referring to America; usually used in reference to a school or college.

INDEPENDENCE (SQUIRE JACK PORTER) 1858
Frank Blackwell Mayer
National Museum of American Art, Smithsonian Institution

from *Letters from an American Farmer*   157

which has ever appeared, and which will hereafter become distinct by the power of the different climates they inhabit. The Ameri-can ought therefore to love this country much better than that wherein either he or his forefathers were born. Here the rewards of his industry follow with equal steps the progress of his labor; his labor is founded on the basis of nature, *self-interest;* can it want a stronger allurement? Wives and children, who before in vain demanded of him a mor-sel of bread, now, fat and frolicsome, gladly help their father to clear those fields whence exuberant crops are to arise to feed and to clothe them all; without any part being claimed, either by a despotic prince, a rich abbot,[5] or a mighty lord. Here religion de-mands but little of him; a small voluntary salary to the minister, and gratitude to God; can he refuse these? The American is a new man, who acts upon new principles; he must therefore entertain new ideas, and form new opinions. From involuntary idleness, servile dependence, penury, and useless labor, he has passed to toils of a very different nature, rewarded by ample subsistence—This is an American.

---

5. abbot *n.*: The head of a monastery.

Commentary

For Europeans and Americans of the eighteenth century, Crèvecoeur expressed age-old dreams of finding a place where they could begin anew—a New World, a Virgin Land, a second Garden of Eden.

To a great extent, Crèvecoeur's vision shaped our history. In one form or an-other, many of his dreams are still with us.

The Old World—Europe—was seen by many more than Crèvecoeur as crowded, corrupt, and repressive. In the New World—North America—the key word was *new*. In this selection alone Crèvecoeur uses it thirteen times, along with words such as *regeneration* and *metamorpho-sis*. *New* carries with it the idea of "bet-ter," an important aspect of American life and thought.

A major source of this "new race of men," according to Crèvecoeur, was the boundless natural resources of the North American continent. For more than a cen-tury, this belief governed our policies on use of land and resources. It is only rela-tively recently that we have found that no resources—trees, water, or land—are limitless.

Crèvecoeur praised highly the bounty and healthy effects of cultivated land and of the life of the small farmer. He was far less enthusiastic about the effects of the wilderness, which at that time made up most of North America, and of the life of the frontiersman. Later in the same *Letter* he writes "[near the woods] men appear to be no better than carnivorous animals of a superior rank." The wildness of the land and the eating of wild meat, he feels, ad-versely affect the frontier dwellers.

Today, the small farmer is an endan-gered species, living a hard and economi-cally marginal life. The woods have been cleared for their lumber and minerals, for subdivisions and golf courses. At the same time, federal and state regulations attempt to preserve what little wilderness remains. And Americans take tents and backpacks in search of the very experience of which Crèvecoeur so highly disap-proved.

THINKING ABOUT THE SELECTION

Recalling

1. What has "tended to regenerate" the European immigrants into America?
2. From what is the colonial system of government "derived"?
3. According to the second paragraph, "what attachment can a poor European have for a country where he had nothing"?
4. What prediction does Crèvecoeur make about the impact the "new race of men" in America will one day have on the rest of the world?

Interpreting

5. (a) What is the logic of Crèvecoeur's arguments? (b) What are his premises? (c) What is his support?
6. (a) How would you summarize Crèvecoeur's definition of an American? (b) Why does he refer to an American as a "new man"?
7. (a) Find two examples of exaggeration in Crèvecoeur's description of life in America. (b) Why does he use exaggeration?

Applying

8. Do you think Crèvecoeur would have written his epistle today? If so, what has stayed essentially the same? If not, what are the important differences?

ANALYZING LITERATURE

Understanding Epistles

An **epistle,** or literary letter, is a formal composition written in the form of a letter addressed to a distant person or group of people. Crèvecoeur's essays in *Letters from an American Farmer* are written in epistle form. The letters are addressed to a fictional character named "Mr. F. B.," though in reality they are intended for a general audience.

One way that Crèvecoeur establishes a personal tone is to use the pronoun *you* in addressing his audience. How does the epistle form allow him to maintain a personal tone, while attempting to convince the general public to accept his ideas and opinions? Support your answer with passages from the selection.

CRITICAL THINKING AND READING

Supporting Opinions

A **fact** can be proved true or false. An **opinion** is a personal belief, attitude, or judgment that cannot be proved. However, an opinion that is supported by facts, we call well-grounded or sound.

Identify the facts Crèvecoeur uses to back up each of the following opinions.

1. ". . . here they are become men: in Europe they were so many useless plants . . ."
2. "The American ought therefore to love this country much better than that wherein either he or his forefathers were born."

THINKING AND WRITING

Writing an Epistle

What does it mean to be an American today? Review your freewriting about being an American. Spend some time brainstorming about the people who live in America, the opportunities they have, and the difficulties they may face. Record your thoughts so that you can write an epistle discussing what it means to be an American today. Address your letter to a fictional person in a foreign country. Then write your letter, using examples to support your opinions. Try to maintain a personal tone. When you revise, make sure that your letter is well-organized and that your opinions are stated clearly.

from Letters from an American Farmer 159

Closure and Extension

ANSWERS TO THINKING ABOUT THE SELECTION

1. "New laws, a new mode of living, a new social system" have regenerated the European immigrants.
2. The government is derived "from the original genius and strong desire of the people ratified and confirmed by the crown."
3. A poor European can have "the

knowledge of the language, the love of a few kindred."
4. "The new race of men" will someday "cause great changes in the world."

Interpreting

5. (a) Crèvecoeur's logic is basically inductive—he is deriving general ideas from particular facts and instances. (b) His basic premise is that America has much to offer, therefore Americans should love their new country. (c) He supports

his premise with descriptions of life in America.
6. (a) Suggested Response: An American is someone who has initiated a new social system through labor, industry, and self-interest. (b) He refers to the American as "new man" because he believes the American has left behind old prejudices and social mores to carve out a wholly new social system and mode of living.
7. (a) Answers will differ. Examples include Crèvecoeur's writing that in America all individuals are "melted into a new race of men" and that Americans are the "western pilgrims" who will finish "the great circle" of civilization. (b) Exaggeration helps him to present an idealized portrait of American life.

Applying

8. Suggested Response: No, because life in today's America is much more complex than it was in Crèvecoeur's day.

Challenge Do you agree with Crèvecoeur's definition of an American? Why or why not?

ANSWERS TO ANALYZING LITERATURE

Suggested Response: It allows him to address his audience in an intimate, personal manner.

ANSWERS TO CRITICAL THINKING AND READING

1. Answers will differ. The facts include Crèvecoeur's comment that "Formerly they were not numbered in any civil lists of their country . . . here they rank as citizens."
2. Answer will differ. Examples include Crèvecoeur's comment that "here they are incorporated into one of the finest systems of population."

THINKING AND WRITING

After students have completed the assignment, divide them into groups, and have them read their rough drafts to one another and suggest ways in which the epistles could be improved.

Motivation/Prior Knowledge
Tell students that they will be reading about how the United States acquired the Statue of Liberty and what the statue has come to represent, not only for Americans, but for people around the world. Ask students what associations they make when they see a picture of the Statue of Liberty. What do they know about the statue, and what does "Lady Liberty" mean to them?

Enrichment You might want to give students specific examples of how France helped America in its war for independence: The French King Louis XVI secretly supplied the American rebels with gunpowder. Nearly all the gunpowder America used during the first two years of the war was from the French. France had been conspiring with Spain to destroy the British Empire. With the decisive American victory at Saratoga, the French openly proclaimed themselves allies and signed a treaty of alliance. Having the support of money, supplies, troops, and the navy of one of the world's great powers secured America's chances of winning the Revolution.

CROSS CURRENTS

The Statue of Liberty

In early July, 1986, the nation's attention was on New York Harbor, where festivities were in progress celebrating the centennial of the Statue of Liberty. The Centennial Year of Liberty, proclaimed by President Reagan, climaxed on October 28 with a rededication of the statue, exactly one hundred years after its unveiling by President Cleveland.

The immense statue was a gift from the people of France to the people of America commemorating the signing of the Declaration of Independence. The gift was an expression of the friendship and the ideal of liberty shared by both nations.

The friendship between the United States and France began in the Revolutionary Period. The help of France had been crucial to the colonists' victory over Great Britain. The French people—and even some of the French aristocracy, such as the Marquis de Lafayette—saw in the American Revolution not only a revolt against a powerful ruler but the successful establishment of a constitutional government with leadership based on ability, not on wealth or family. This ideal motivated France. The victory of the American colonists in 1776 directly influenced the outbreak of revolution in France eight years later. The friendship between the nations remained strong over the next century. When the Statue of Liberty was dedicated in 1886, it was offered as a memorial to the alliance between France and the American colonists who had fought for independence in the Revolutionary War.

THE STATUE'S HISTORY

In Paris in the late 1860's, two men—Édouard-René Lafebvre de Laboulaye, a professor of law, and Frédéric Bartholdi, a young sculptor—conceived the plan of a monument to the ideal of liberty. They greatly admired the United States and felt that such a monument would honor the successful establishment in America of a representative government—something still not achieved and dearly desired in France. France's own revolution had yet to achieve its goals of "Liberty, Equality, Fraternity."

The "Monument to American Independence: Liberty Enlightening the World," as it was officially called, was laboriously built of 350 thin sheets of copper, hammered over wooden molds. By 1885 the completed statue, 150 feet high, towered over the Parisian skyline, waiting to be shipped to the United States.

Meanwhile, in the United States, money was being raised for a suitable pedestal for the statue, which was to be placed in New York harbor. The fund-raising committee asked a young Jewish poet, Emma Lazarus, to write to poem to aid their efforts. Lazarus, who was a tireless crusader for the immigrants who came through New York Harbor, wrote a poem that ends with these lines:

> . . . Give me your tired, your poor,
> Your huddled masses yearning to
>   breathe free,
> The wretched refuse of your teeming
>   shore.
> Send these, the homeless, tempest-
>   tossed to me
> I lift my lamp beside the golden door.

A WORLDWIDE SYMBOL

Since its dedication the statue has come to symbolize far more than the ideal of lib-erty to which it was dedicated. Standing in New York Harbor, it has welcomed multitudes of immigrants, promising hope and opportunity. Emma Lazarus's poem added to Liberty's stern gaze and outstretched arm the voice of a protective mother. In 1903 the poem was engraved on a bronze plaque and affixed to the interior of the pedestal. The large numbers of immigrants linked the statue with the poem's image as "Mother of Exiles."

Over the years, the Lady with the Torch has become a worldwide symbol of human equality and personal liberty. In May, 1989, Chinese students demonstrating for freedom in Beijing's Tiananmen Square carried and raised a Goddess of Democracy as a symbol of their goals. This goddess closely resembled the Statue of Liberty. Her well-known image made a statement that words could not.

Cooperative Learning Ask students to research immigration in the 1880's and apply their findings to Emma Lazarus' poem. Once they have researched, have them form groups of four, and instruct them to pool the results of their research for a group presentation. Their presentation should focus on specific examples of the connections between immigration and the last lines of Lazarus' poem.

Challenge Encourage students to think about how the Statue of Liberty is a worldwide symbol of human equality and personal liberty. Suggest that they read articles on the Chinese students' uprising in Tiananmen Square in Beijing. Ask students to read articles with the following questions in mind: What were the Chinese students' specific goals? How did the Chinese government react? How did the United States react?

The writing assignments on page 162 have students write creatively, while those on page 163 have them think about the selections and write critically.

YOU THE WRITER
Guidelines for Evaluating Assignment 1

1. Has the student written a journal entry that clearly expresses his or her thoughts and feelings about the impending Revolution?
2. Has the student used an informal, conversational style?
3. Does the entry reflect some of the thoughts, hopes, and fears that a colonist might have had?
4. Is the journal entry free from grammar, usage, and mechanics errors?

Guidelines for Evaluating Assignment 2

1. Has the student written a letter to a Revolutionary hero that discusses his or her contributions to the American cause and expresses gratitude?
2. Is the letter written in an informal style?
3. Has the student used transitions and other linking devices to connect ideas?
4. Is the letter organized in a logical manner and free from grammar, usage, and mechanics errors?

Guidelines for Evaluating Assignment 3

1. Has the student written a persuasive essay presenting a series of reasons supported by examples that convince the colonists to revolt?
2. Does the essay reflect ideas of Patrick Henry, Thomas Paine, and Thomas Jefferson?
3. Does the student use persuasive devices?
4. Is the essay logically organized and free from grammar, usage, and mechanics errors?

YOU THE WRITER

Assignment

1. Imagine that you are an American colonist and it has become increasingly apparent to you that a war with the British is inevitable. Write a journal entry in which you express your thoughts and feelings about the impending Revolution.

Prewriting. Spend some time reflecting about how the colonists must have felt as the Revolutionary War approached. List some of the thoughts, hopes, and fears you imagine they must have had.

Writing. When you write your journal entry, use an informal, conversational writing style.

Revising. When you revise, make sure your entry clearly conveys your thoughts and feelings. After you finish revising, proofread your entry and prepare a final copy.

Assignment

2. When the Revolutionary War finally ended and the colonists had won their independence, many of the colonial leaders were viewed as national heroes. Imagine that you are an American who has just lived through the war, and write a letter to a Revolutionary hero, discussing his or her contributions to the American cause and expressing your gratitude.

Prewriting. Choose a Revolutionary hero. Then outline his or her contributions to the American cause.

Writing. When you write your letter, use an informal writing style but make sure the letter is organized in a logical manner.

Revising. When you revise, make sure you have used transitions and other linking devices to connect your ideas. After you finish revising, proofread your letter and prepare a final copy.

Assignment

3. Imagine that it is 1775 and you are a colonial leader who has become increasingly dissatisfied with British rule. Write an essay in which you attempt to persuade other colonists to join together in a unified revolt against British rule.

Prewriting. Start by reviewing the unit introduction (p. 86) and the selections by Patrick Henry (p. 126), Thomas Paine (p. 132), and Thomas Jefferson (p. 144), noting the reasons why the colonists felt compelled to revolt against the British.

Writing. In your essay, present a series of reasons why the colonists must revolt, and use such persuasive devices as restatement and repetition.

Revising. When you revise, make sure your essay is logically organized and that you have used examples to support your argument.

162   *The Revolutionary Period*

YOU THE CRITIC

Assignment

1. During the Colonial Period there was a great deal of emphasis on discipline and restraint. Write an essay in which you discuss how this emphasis is reflected in one of the selections you have read.

Prewriting. Review the selections in this unit, and choose a selection that reflects the colonial emphasis on discipline and restraint. Then reread the selection, noting how the emphasis is reflected in its form and content and in the style in which it is written.

Writing. When you write your essay, use evidence from the selection to support your argument.

Revising. When you revise, make sure your essay is logically organized and that you.have thoroughly supported your argument. After you finish revising, proofread your essay and prepare a final copy.

Assignment

2. The Colonial Period is often called the Age of Reason, because it was characterized by an emphasis on reason and logic. Write an essay in which you analyze how the process of reasoning is used in one of the selections you have read.

Prewriting. Choose a selection in which the reasoning process is used. Then review this selection, noting how the writer uses the reasoning process to develop a logical argument.

Writing. Include your thesis statement in the introduction of your essay. In the body of the essay, present evidence from the selection to support your thesis.

Revising. When you revise, make sure you have included enough evidence to thoroughly support your thesis.

Assignment

3. During the Colonial Period, a revolutionary spirit swept through the land, inspiring the colonists to fight for their independence. Write an essay in which you discuss how this spirit is expressed in the literature of the period.

Prewriting. Choose three selections that express the revolutionary spirit. Reread each of these selections, noting how the spirit is conveyed. Prepare a thesis statement and organize your notes into an outline.

Writing. When you write your essay, use passages from each of the selections to support your thesis.

Revising. When you revise, make sure you have thoroughly supported your thesis and have not included any unnecessary information. After you finish revising, proofread your essay and prepare a final copy.

YOU THE CRITIC
Guidelines for Evaluating Assignment 1

1. Has the student written an essay that discusses how the emphasis on discipline and restraint prevalent during the Colonial Period is reflected in one of the selections?
2. Has the student thoroughly supported his or her thesis with evidence from the selection?
3. Is the essay logically organized?
4. Is the essay free from grammar, usage, and mechanics errors?

Guidelines for Evaluating Assignment 2

1. Has the student analyzed how the process of reasoning is used in one of the selections from the Colonial Period?
2. Does the student include a thesis statement in the introduction of the essay?
3. Does the body of the essay present evidence from the selection that thoroughly supports the thesis?
4. Is the essay free from grammar, usage, and mechanics errors?

Guidelines for Evaluating Assignment 3

1. Does the student make a thesis statement discussing how the revolutionary spirit swept the land, inspiring colonists to fight for independence?
2. Does the student use passages from three selections to support the thesis thoroughly?
3. Has the student eliminated all unnecessary information?
4. Is the essay free from grammar, usage, and mechanics errors?

Humanities Note

Fine art, *Niagara Falls, About 1832–1840,* by Thomas Chambers. Little is known about the life of Thomas Chambers. He was born in England in 1815, lived and painted in the United States, and died after 1866. His works, primarily seascapes, are noted for the dramatic quality of their subject matter.

Niagara Falls is no exception. The painting evokes the forcefulness of nature, as a small figure in the foreground observes the surging falls. The presence of the figure, and of the rustic houses in the background, suggests that human life can exist alongside the powerful elements of nature. The curved shape of the water, spray, and rocks provides visual unity to the work.

NIAGARA FALLS, ABOUT 1832–1840
Thomas Chambers
Wadsworth Atheneum, Hartford

Objectives

1 To understand the historical background of American literature during the period 1800–1840
2 To understand how American literature came of age during this period

A GROWING NATION
1800–1840

America is a land of wonders, in which everything is in constant motion and every change seems an improvement. . . . No natural boundary seems to be set to the efforts of man; and in his eyes what is not yet done is only what he has not yet attempted to do.

Alexis de Tocqueville

165

Humanities Note

Fine art, *Louisiana Purchase Ceremony at New Orleans, 20 December 1803*, by Thor de Thulstrup. Many of the works of Thor de Thulstrup (1848–1930) portray inspiring scenes from American history, like this one and the *Siege of Atlanta*. The purchase of the Louisiana Territory, over three-quarters of a million square miles, not only greatly increased the size of the new nation but averted the occupation of the land by Napoleon's forces.

At the center of the canvas, the raising of the flag is a powerful symbol of America's new possession; the depiction of the ceremonial firing of shots suggest the stirring sounds of the event.

1 Enrichment Another significant writer of this time was Augustus Baldwin Longstreet, a Southern writer whose work influenced both Mark Twain and William Faulkner.

2 Enrichment The land acquired from the French in the Louisiana Purchase extended from the Mississippi River to the Rocky Mountains and from the Gulf of Mexico to Canada.

Humanities Note

Fine art, *Erie Canal near Little Falls,* by W. R. Miller. The Erie Canal, built in 1817–1825, provides a waterway between Lake Erie, at Buffalo, New York, and Albany, north of New York City along the Hudson River. Navigators traveling south on the Hudson could easily reach New York City and the Atlantic Ocean. Overland trade, which had been laborious, expensive, and hazardous, was replaced by economical and efficient canal transport. The waterway thus played a vital role in the development of an industrialized society and in the westward travel of many thousands of immigrants.

LOUISIANA PURCHASE CEREMONY AT NEW ORLEANS, 20 DECEMBER 1803
Thor de Thulstrup
The Granger Collection

ERIE CANAL NEAR LITTLE FALLS
W. R. Miller
Three Lions

In 1831, Alexis de Tocqueville, a young Frenchman, journeyed to the United States to report on the American penitentiary system for his government. He observed far more than prisons during his stay, however. His observations were compiled in a monumental four-volume work, *Democracy in America,* that is considered a classic of political literature. While Tocqueville was impressed by the bustle and optimism that he noted, he was not as impressed by American literature. "America has produced very few writers of distinction," he wrote, adding that the literary output of England "still darts its rays into the forests of the New World."

Tocqueville had perhaps arrived a few years too soon. At the very time he was in the United States, a number of writers of distinction were at work. Among them were Washington Irving, James Fenimore Cooper, William Cullen Bryant, and Edgar Allan Poe, all of whom would achieve fame and acceptance far beyond "the forests of the New World."

THE HISTORICAL SETTING

When Thomas Jefferson was elected President in 1800, three new states, Vermont, Kentucky, and Tennessee, had joined the original thirteen. Then in 1803, at the stroke of a pen, the Louisiana Purchase doubled the nation's territory. By 1837, when Michigan became a state, more than half the present-day fifty states were in the Union.

The rapid growth of the nation brought with it an upsurge of na-

W. R. Miller's painting is a naturalistic view of the canal. As the picture indicates, in the early days mules pulled the barges. The scene is rural, gentle, and apparently untouched by the bustling industrialized communities the canal linked. The woman carrying a pail, the dilapidated house, and the man on a raft lend a rustic quality to the work. The two boys walking down the rocky path seem almost to float. The painter may be suggesting that, as its waters glide by, the canal has not yet changed the tranquil life of places such as Little Falls.

tional pride and identity. Improved transportation helped bind the old and the new states together. Canals, turnpikes, and railroads boomed during this period. Steamboats and sailing packets helped speed people and goods to their destinations. The westward expansion of the United States and its explosive growth in population had profound effects on American life and literature.

Old New York

By 1800, the country's frontier had moved far away from the East Coast. Yet there were other kinds of national frontiers. In the early 1800's, New York, the city that Washington Irving called "Gotham," was becoming a sort of American literary frontier.

New York City had a population of 60,000 in 1800, making it the second largest city in the nation after Philadelphia. A decade later, it passed Philadelphia and was never again challenged for population leadership. By 1840, the population of New York City was 312,000, or about the size of Philadelphia and Boston combined.

The earliest Dutch settlement on Manhattan Island had been at the very southern tip. In 1820, the built-up area extended north to 14th Street and was advancing rapidly up the island. The commercial buildings of the day were low, three or four stories at most.

Despite New York's prosperity, it was not looked upon as a cultural capital. Tocqueville saw it as a center of "all our greatest vices, without any of those interests which counteract their baneful influence." In many people's eyes, Philadelphia remained "the Athens of America," but that was changing. New York, cultivated or not, was attracting America's first professional writers. All four authors represented in this section—Irving, Cooper, Bryant, and Poe—spent important parts of their careers in New York City.

The Growth of Democracy

When Tocqueville looked at American cities such as New York, he foresaw problems. A firm believer in democratic ideals, Tocqueville was concerned about the possible excesses of democracy in urban areas. He thought that cities were too likely to put power "in the hands of a populace carrying out its own impulses."

In fact, the people of the United States had already moved toward giving themselves more direct power over government. The election in 1828 of Andrew Jackson, "the People's President," ushered in the era of the common man. Property requirements for voting began to be eliminated. Presidential electors were increasingly chosen by popular vote, rather than by state legislatures.

Not everyone shared in the triumph of the common man, however. Despite early stirrings of feminism, little political attention was paid to women. The majority of blacks were still slaves, and each slave counted as 3/5 of a person for purposes of congressional rep-

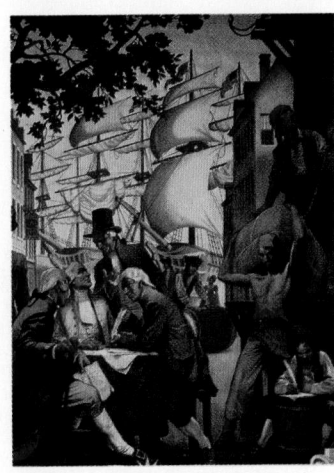

TRADE AND COMMERCE IN MANHATTAN
Karoly and Santo
Three Lions

Humanities Note

Fine art, *Trade and Commerce in Manhattan,* 1790, by Karoly and Santo. *Trade and Commerce in Manhattan,* is a somewhat didactic tribute to both the laboring classes and the merchant classes of a growing nation. Representative endeavors of the period are featured: navigation, textile manufacture, banking or other commercial trading, hotel keeping. The boy sitting behind the barrel writing may symbolize the necessity for education as a means to success in the workaday world. *Trade and Commerce* is, above all, a stylized tribute to the spirit of hard work and of business savvy. These values, the work suggests, are what were to make the new American society thrive and prosper.

3 **Master Teacher Note** To give students a sense of the rate of our nation's growth at this time, you might find and read newspaper accounts of the day: the development of the steamboat, the opening of the Erie Canal, descriptions of turnpike and early railroad travel, and so on.

Enrichment The goals of the Lewis and Clark expedition, which lasted from 1804 to 1806, were to find a land route to the Pacific Ocean, to support American claims to the Oregon territory, and to gather information on the Far West. The importance of the expedition was underscored when Thomas Jefferson made the Louisiana Purchase shortly before Lewis and Clark set out on their journey.

Lewis and Clark were successful in their efforts. They brought back extensive records of their journey and only lost a single man, despite the many hardships they experienced. Their female native American guide, Sacajawea, was an important factor in their success. She acted as an interpreter when they encountered native Americans and was able to obtain horses for them so they could cross the high Rockies.

In this picture the members of the expedition are seen approaching one of the many groups of native Americans they encountered on their journey.

Enrichment The Erie Canal, which opened in 1825, was about 360 miles long. It connected Lake Erie with the Hudson River, providing a waterway from New York City all the way to Buffalo. Canal locks had to be used to compensate for the more than 500-foot difference between the level of the lake and that of the river.

This picture shows some of the bridges built over the canal and, as a small detail, the towpath alongside it. This path was used by the men and animals that towed canalboats.

AMERICAN EVENTS

1803   Louisiana Purchase extends nation's territory to Rocky Mountains.

1804   Lewis and Clark begin expedition exploring and mapping vast region of West.

1807   Robert Fulton's steamboat makes first trip from New York City to Albany.

1809   *A History of New York . . . by Diedrich Knickerbocker* brings recognition to **Washington Irving.**

1812   U.S. declares war on Great Britain; early battles in War of 1812 are at sea.

1814   Bombardment of Fort McHenry inspires Francis Scott Key to write "The Star-Spangled Banner."

1815   Battle of New Orleans occurs after war is officially over.

1817   **William Cullen Bryant** publishes early draft of "Thanatopsis" in a Boston magazine.

1819   **Washington Irving's** *Sketch Book*, including "Rip Van Winkle," begins to appear serially in U.S.

      Spain relinquishes claims to Florida for $5 million.

1820   Missouri Compromise bans slavery in some parts of new territories.

1821   **James Fenimore Cooper** gains widespread fame with *The Spy*, his second novel.

      Emma Willard founds Troy Female Seminary, first women's college in United States.

1823   *The Pioneers* by **James Fenimore Cooper** introduces Natty Bumppo and *Leatherstocking Tales*.

      Monroe Doctrine warns European powers to keep hands off Latin America.

1825   Completion and success of Erie Canal spurs canal building throughout the nation.

168   A Growing Nation

The Lewis and Clark Expedition

The Battle of New Orleans

Rip Van Winkle

The Monroe Doctrine

The Erie Canal

Napoleon in Coronation Robes

Is Established

Jane Austen

John Keats

René Laënnec

WORLD EVENTS

1800 England: Samuel Taylor Coleridge finishes writing "Kubla Khan."

1802 England: J. M. W. Turner, romantic landscape artist, paints *Calais Pier*.

1804 France: Napoleon Bonaparte proclaims himself emperor.

Germany: Friedrich von Schiller gives Swiss their national festival play, *William Tell*.

England: William Wordsworth completes "Ode on Intimations of Immortality."

1805 Germany: Ludwig von Beethoven breaks formal musical conventions with *Third Symphony*.

1812 France: Napoleon Bonaparte suffers disastrous military defeat in Russia.

1813 England: Jane Austen publishes *Pride and Prejudice*, one of the world's great novels.

1815 Belgium: French army under Napoleon routed at Waterloo, Belgium, by British and Prussian forces.

Austria: Congress of Vienna redraws map of Europe following Napoleon's downfall.

1818 England: Mary Wollstonecraft Shelley creates a legend with *Frankenstein*.

1819 England: John Keats writes "Ode to a Nightingale" and "Ode on a Grecian Urn."

France: René Laënnec, a physician, invents the stethoscope.

Scotland: Sir Walter Scott completes *Ivanhoe*, a pioneering historical romance.

1820 England: Percy Bysshe Shelley publishes the four-act drama *Prometheus Unbound*.

1821 Mexico: Mexico gains independence from Spain.

England: George Gordon, Lord Byron completes final work of verse satire, *Don Juan*.

Introduction   169

Enrichment In addition to being one of the greatest English poets, Keats was also one of the most eloquent and passionate letter writers of all time. His personal correspondence is filled with many brilliant insights into the work of Shakespeare, Milton, and Wordsworth. It also contains more general critical formulations that still have validity today. Keats argued, for instance, that poets must demonstrate a quality that he called negative capability —this trait would enable them to tolerate uncertainty and paradox and thereby remain open to experience.

Enrichment Sir Walter Scott (1771–1832) was one of the most popular novelists of his time. Scott is often regarded as the father of both the regional novel, which abounds in local color, and the historical novel, which reconstructs past events. His "Waverley novels," containing romantic tales of Scotland, are examples of the first category. Perhaps his most famous historical novel is *Ivanhoe*, a story set in medieval England.

Enrichment René Laënnec (1781–1826) was a French physician who invented the stethoscope and pioneered its use in detecting diseases of the chest.

Enrichment Byron's *Don Juan*, with its fast-paced wit and antihero, was hailed by modern poets like W.H. Auden as a work ahead of its time.

Enrichment Edgar Allan Poe's story "MS. Found in a Bottle" was published in the Baltimore *Saturday Visiter* [sic], October 19, 1833. Poe also entered this story and other writings in a contest and won the $50 first prize. In addition to the money (a not inconsiderable sum at that time), Poe won the support and friendship of John Pendleton Kennedy, one of the judges of the contest.

Enrichment The Alamo, in San Antonio, Texas, was originally a mission but had been converted into a fortress. In February 1836, it was defended by about 150 Texans against a force of several thousand Mexican soldiers, led by Santa Anna. The battle lasted from February 24 until March 6, when the Mexicans broke into the fortress and there was hand-to-hand fighting. The defenders of the Alamo died (among the dead were James Bowie and Davy Crockett) but their heroism inspired a Texan victory in the battle of San Jacinto six weeks later.

Enrichment Samuel F.B. Morse (1791–1872) was a successful painter as well as an inventor. He studied painting in England and, on his return to the United States, became a well-known portrait painter. In 1832 he learned about the Frenchman Ampere's idea for an electric telegraph. He went on to work for more than a decade on his own version of the telegraph, and in 1844 he successfully demonstrated this invention to Congress. The message he transmitted from Washington to Baltimore was "What hath God wrought."

AMERICAN EVENTS

1826 *Leatherstocking* saga continues with **James Fenimore Cooper's** *The Last of the Mohicans*.

1827 Serial publication of John James Audubon's *The Birds of America* begins in England.

Edgar Allan Poe publishes *Tamerlane*, his first collection of poems.

1828 Noah Webster's *An American Dictionary of the English Language* makes its appearance.

1830 Peter Cooper builds *Tom Thumb*, America's first steam-driven locomotive.

1831 *Poems* by **Edgar A. Poe**, published in New York, includes "To Helen."

1832 **Washington Irving's** *The Alhambra* causes some critics to think he prefers Europe.

1833 "MS. Found in a Bottle" wins contest for **Edgar Allan Poe** and attracts attention to his work.

1834 Cyrus McCormick invents mechanical reaper.

1836 Battles at the Alamo and San Jacinto fought while Texas is a republic.

Ralph Waldo Emerson's essay, *Nature*, signals start of New England's literary renaissance.

1837 *Twice-Told Tales* by **Nathaniel Hawthorne** contains masterpieces that few critics noted.

Samuel F. B. Morse, painter and inventor, patents electromagnetic telegraph.

1838 U.S. army marches Cherokees of Georgia on long "Trail of Tears" to Oklahoma.

1839 "The Fall of the House of Usher," short story by **Edgar Allan Poe**, first appears in print.

1840 After many years, **James Fenimore Cooper's** *Leatherstocking Tales* resume with *The Pathfinder*.

170 A Growing Nation

The Last of the Mohicans

Locomotive "Tom Thumb" Races Horse Car

Samuel Morse

The "Trail of Tears"

Decembrist Uprising in Russia

Stendhal

Alfred, Lord Tennyson

Charles Dickens

WORLD EVENTS

1823 Germany: Jakob and Wilhelm Grimm have *Grimm's Fairy Tales* translated into English.

1824 Hawaii: King Kamehameha III, who favors U.S. interests, ascends the throne.

1825 Denmark: Hans Oersted becomes first scientist to isolate aluminum.

Russia: Decembrist uprising crushed by czarist forces.

1826 Italy: Alessandro Manzoni completes work on his classic novel *The Betrothed.*

1829 England: George Stephenson perfects a steam locomotive for Liverpool-Manchester Railway.

1830 France: Stendhal publishes *The Red and the Black*, first of his great novels.

1831 France: Victor Hugo publishes *Notre Dame de Paris*, popularly called *The Hunchback of Notre Dame.*

1832 England: Alfred, Lord Tennyson completes "The Lady of Shalott," a poem.

1834 France: Eugène Delacroix, a Romantic artist, paints *Women of Algiers.*

1835 Denmark: Hans Christian Andersen publishes his first book of fairy tales.

France: Honoré de Balzac shows his mastery of the novel in *Father Goriot.*

1837 England: Charles Dickens achieves great success with *Oliver Twist.*

England: Thomas Carlyle publishes renowned *The French Revolution, A History.*

1838 England: Elizabeth Barrett Browning adds to her fame with *The Seraphim and Other Poems.*

Introduction 171

Enrichment Today the Grimm brothers are best known to the public for their collection of fairy tales (1812–1815), which were instrumental in reviving an interest in folklore. The Grimm brothers, however, also made important contributions to the study of language. Jakob Grimm wrote a book on German grammar and, with his brother Wilhelm, began work on a comprehensive German dictionary. Jakob also formulated a linguistic law, known as Grimm's law, that is still a subject of investigation: It describes how certain consonants (in the Indo-European language family) have experienced shifts in pronunciation. As the consonant *p* moved from Latin (*pater*-father), for instance, it became *V* in German (*Vater*-father) and *f* in English (father).

Enrichment In the 1930's Victor Hugo's *Notre Dame de Paris* was made into a Hollywood film, starring Charles Laughton as the hunchback Quasimodo. The film itself is mediocre and absurdly imposes a happy ending on the novel. Laughton, however, gave one of the greatest performances of his career in the role of the deformed but soulful hunchback.

Enrichment Alfred, Lord Tennyson (1809–1892) is probably the first great English poet whose voice is preserved for posterity. Tennyson took an interest in science and technology and when the first recording devices were invented, he accepted an invitation to record his voice. The choice of Tennyson for such an honor was natural. From the time he published his book *Poems* (1842), he was regarded as a major English poet. In 1850 he was appointed poet laureate of England. This honor is traditionally conferred by the ruling English monarch on the most respected poet of the time. Today the poet laureate of England is Ted Hughes.

Enrichment Eugène Delacroix (1798–1863) is known as the greatest French painter of the romantic movement. His dramatic compositions are grand in scale and lavish in their use of color. They often portray scenes from mythology, literature, and political or religious history.

Delacroix visited Morocco for four months in 1832. During this time he made many water-color sketches and filled notebooks with his jottings. This material provided the basis for exotic paintings such as *Women of Algiers* (1834).

Fine art, *Andrew Jackson Encouraging His Riflemen at the Battle of New Orleans, 8 January 1815.* The Treaty of Ghent, signed in the Belgian city on December 24, 1814, brought an end to the hostilities of the War of 1812. Nevertheless, word of the truce had not arrived in New Orleans by January 8, 1815, when British troops fired on the Americans. Under Andrew Jackson, commander of the U.S. Army of the Southwest, several thousand soldiers, mostly volunteers, barricaded themselves behind bales of cotton. The unorthodox defense was so effective that the Battle of New Orleans was brief and triumphant.

This nineteenth-century colored engraving is not a finely polished work of art. In a somewhat rough style it shows the soldiers, mostly out of uniform and with their backs to the viewer. The inclusion of smoke and fire creates a sense of immediacy. Except for the depiction of Jackson, the work is not an idealized representation of war. The portrayal of Jackson, on horseback and waving, furthered the image of military hero that, in about a dozen years, would help put him in the White House.

4 Enrichment The United States also strongly objected to British interference with American shipping. Involved in a long conflict with the French, the British blockaded French ports, making it difficult for American merchants to trade with France. Americans also believed that the British had stirred up Indian warfare in the Northwest, obstructing the nation's westward expansion.

5 Enrichment When the war ended, none of the issues that had caused it were resolved.

ANDREW JACKSON ENCOURAGING HIS RIFLEMEN AT THE BATTLE OF NEW ORLEANS, JANUARY 8, 1815
Colored Engraving, 19th Century
The Granger Collection

THE BOMBARDMENT OF FORT MCHENRY, BALTIMORE, ON 13–14 SEPTEMBER 1814
Contemporary American Aquatint Engraving by John Bower
The Granger Collection

resentation. Still, this period saw the beginnings of the feminist and antislavery movements.

One of the tragic aspects of the Jackson era was "Indian removal," the forcible seizure of tribal lands. In the South, many thousands of Native Americans were uprooted and moved to open lands in the West. The most publicized removal was that of the Cherokees from northwestern Georgia to the Indian Territory, now Oklahoma. This 1838 "Trail of Tears" took the lives of about 4,000 of the 15,000 Cherokees who began the long trek.

Despite all this, the first four decades of the 1800's were, on the whole, hopeful ones. The young republic seemed able to weather any storm.

America on the World Stage

One of the storms to be weathered was the War of 1812. This two-and-a-half-year conflict was fought to settle a number of grievances against Great Britain, including the impressment of American seamen by the Royal Navy. Although neither side gained or lost, the war created a number of American military heroes. The British bombardment of Fort McHenry in Baltimore Harbor inspired Francis Scott Key to write "The Star-Spangled Banner." After the war, there was a feeling of solidarity in the United States. Most important, perhaps, the war convinced Europeans that the United States was on the world stage to stay.

That fact was emphasized again in 1823 with the Monroe Doctrine. President James Monroe, fearing European intervention in the newly free nations of Latin America, stated that "the American continents . . . are henceforth not to be considered as subjects for future colonization by any European powers." Monroe's statement attracted little attention at the time. As the United States gained strength and prestige, however, European nations were not eager to challenge it.

Florida and the Southwest raised special problems for the young nation. As late as 1818, Florida was still a Spanish province. Border troubles created tension, and some Americans were killed. The resulting invasion by Andrew Jackson's Tennessee militia convinced Spain to sell Florida rather than have it seized. In 1819 the United States purchased all of Spain's land east of the Mississippi for $5 million.

The situation in Texas was more complicated. Originally a part of Mexico, Texas seceded from Mexico in 1835. The following year, the Mexican army made its famous assault on the Alamo, where every Texan defender was killed. President Jackson recognized the Republic of Texas in 1837. Although Texas wanted to be annexed by the United States, it was not admitted to the Union until 1845. The annexation brought about war between Mexico and the United States. American victory in this war added further territory in the Southwest to the United States.

4

5

172   A Growing Nation

Fine art, *The Bombardment of Fort McHenry, Baltimore, on 13–14 September 1814,* by John Bower. Francis Scott Key was a poet and lawyer from Washington who observed the bombardment of Fort McHenry by the British during the War of 1812. Key's rousing words were later set to the tune of an English song, "To Anacreon in Heaven," as "The Star-Spangled Banner."

This engraving is a crude rendering of the military encounter. Its purpose, presumably, was to make the sequence of events reasonably clear and easy to remember. The land areas are not realistic; the bombs, boats, and other objects are drawn in a cartoonlike style.

AMERICAN LITERATURE COMES OF AGE

In 1783, when the Peace of Paris ended the American Revolution, an eleventh child was born into the family of a wealthy merchant in New York City. The child, Washington Irving, would become the first professional author of the new nation and the first American literary figure to win an international reputation. Other notable writers appeared on the scene in the early nineteenth century. By 1840, Americans could offer convincing answers to British writer Sydney Smith's taunt from 20 years earlier: "In the four quarters of the globe, who reads an American book, or goes to an American play, or looks at an American picture or statue?"

The Professionals

From early colonial times, there were journalists who wrote and edited for a living. Their works were meant for the moment and did not survive as literature. The important literary figures who do survive from those days were outstanding writers, but none made writing his profession. Thomas Jefferson, for example, was a statesman, and Benjamin Franklin was a printer, inventor, and statesman.

America's cultural independence did not come easily. For nearly 200 years American readers had been looking to Europe, mainly Great Britain, for most of their reading material other than the Bible, almanacs, newspapers, magazines, and broadsides. Susanna Rowson, raised in Massachusetts but living in England, wrote America's first best-selling novel, *Charlotte Temple*. It was published in London in 1791 and reprinted in Philadelphia in 1794.

6 In the early nineteenth century, two Scottish writers, Robert Burns and Sir Walter Scott, were popular in the United States. So, too, were three young English poets, Lord Byron, Percy Bysshe Shelley, and John Keats. In addition, classic English works dating back hundreds of years were in print. Tocqueville observed, "There is hardly a pioneer's hut that does not contain a few odd volumes of Shakespeare."

Most American writers of the time could not compete in that company. The names of dozens of writers in the early national period, familiar in their own time, are all but forgotten today. Charles Brockden Brown, James Paulding, Fitz-Greene Halleck, Caroline Kirkland, and N. P. Willis achieved substantial reputations in the early 1800's. All lived in or near New York City, except Kirkland, who was born in New York but moved to frontier Michigan, where she wrote realistic sketches of backwoods life.

A New York Biblical scholar, Clement Clarke Moore, gained more lasting fame with a poem he wrote for his family, with no thought of publication. A relative of Moore's gave a copy of the poem to a newspaper editor in Troy, New York. The poem, popularly known as " 'Twas the Night Before Christmas," thus made its first appearance in 1823.

LAST STAND AT THE ALAMO
N. C. Wyeth
Three Lions

Humanities Note

Fine art, *Last Stand at the Alamo,* by N. C. Wyeth. Newell Convers Wyeth (1882–1945) studied art at the school established in Delaware by Howard Pyle and, in fact, was taught by Pyle. Many of Wyeth's works were drawings or paintings to illustrate magazine articles. Wyeth also painted sympathetic portraits and scenes of Indians of the Southwest.

Last Stand at the Alamo is an unsentimental representation of an American military defeat. There is a gentle expression of sympathy for the soldiers who lost their lives as well as of admiration for their grit. It might be thought of as a work of restrained patriotism.

6 **Enrichment** Byron, Shelley, and Keats were part of the second generation of English Romantic poets. Their work, along with that of the first generation of Romantic poets, influenced the American writers of the time.

7 Enrichment There has been widespread disagreement among writers and critics concerning the quality of Poe's work. Despite these disagreements, Poe is one of the most influential and widely read writers in the history of American literature.

8 Literary Movement Bryant (page 204) was the first American poet to win worldwide critical acclaim. He was also an important journalist and political activist.

9 Literary Movement During his travels Irving learned a great deal about European folklore. Many of Irving's stories, including "The Devil and Tom Walker" (page 184), are adaptations of European folk tales. An interest in folklore was a common Romantic concern.

One writer who had a national reputation was William Gilmore Simms of Charleston, South Carolina. As a young man, Simms lived briefly in New York City and published his first novel, *Martin Faber,* there in 1833. His reputation rests mainly on the romantic novels set in South Carolina that he wrote after returning to Charleston.

The major American authors of the day have already been mentioned. Washington Irving achieved his first great success in 1809 with the satiric *History of New York,* supposedly written by Diedrich Knickerbocker. James Fenimore Cooper introduced his frontier hero Natty Bumppo in *The Pioneers,* published in 1823. William Cullen Bryant, born in Massachusetts, wrote the first draft of his famous poem "Thanatopsis" when he was 17. Edgar Allan Poe, today the most widely read of the four, was a tormented genius. Poe's life, though brief and tragic, produced poems, stories, and criticism that have had a powerful influence on the course of American literature.

Knickerbocker and Leatherstocking

The North American continent offered a vast and exciting vista for American writers, whether in the settled regions or on the advancing edge of settlement. The first who took artistic advantage of this view in any sustained way were New Yorkers, members of two informal literary and artistic groups.

One was the Knickerbocker Group, led by Washington Irving. A notable member of this group was William Cullen Bryant, who moved to New York City in 1825. He remained a dominant literary figure in the city for the rest of his eighty-four years. Other members of stature were James Paulding and Fitz-Greene Halleck. Many Knickerbocker members were of lesser talent. Edgar Allan Poe ridiculed them in a critical review, *The Literati of New York City,* as writers with grand pretensions but limited abilities.

The second New York group, whose leader was James Fenimore Cooper, was called the Bread and Cheese Club. Basically a social club, its members' interests were not restricted to literature. Samuel F. B. Morse, renowned as both a painter and the inventor of the telegraph, was a member. So, too, was William Dunlap, an artist, the founder of the National Academy of Design, and the first professional American playwright and producer.

Not only were these groups located in New York, but the subject matter of their members' work was often local. Irving's *History of New York* and some of the stories in *The Sketch Book* (particularly "Rip Van Winkle" and "The Legend of Sleepy Hollow") make vivid use of local scenes and events. Irving, a world traveler, also used many European settings. The sketches in *The Alhambra,* for example, all involve Spain. Even so, Irving's use of regional materials sparked an interest in American locales, especially the Hudson River valley.

174   *A Growing Nation*

James Fenimore Cooper's fearless, straight-shooting frontier hero enthralled readers here and abroad. Natty Bumppo, a man of complete moral integrity, established the pattern for countless Western heroes to come (although Bumppo himself was not a westerner). Four of the novels about Natty Bumppo, which are collectively known as *The Leatherstocking Tales,* are set on the upstate New York frontier, which was already a dim memory in Cooper's time.

Cooper, like Irving, was a world traveler, and some of his novels have European settings. Yet Cooper, too, found much near at hand to write about, helping to focus attention on the varied literary wellsprings within the new nation.

In 1831, while Irving was in London and Cooper was in Paris, Samuel Francis Smith, a Boston Baptist clergyman, wrote new words for the British song "God Save the King." Smith's words, simple and stirring, expressed the national mood in a timeless hymn: "My country, 'tis of thee,/Sweet land of liberty,/Of thee I sing."

From Reason to Romance

The Puritans were religious fundamentalists who sought salvation. The founders of the republic were political realists who pursued reason. So, then, how can the writers of the early nineteenth century—Irving, Cooper, Bryant, and Poe—be described? Despite unmistakable differences among them, they were all Romantics.

That name can be misleading, because the Romantics do not necessarily write about love. Romanticism can be viewed as an artistic movement, or a state of mind, or both. Romantic writers favor the imagination over reason, intuition over facts. Irving's *History of New York* is not a dry account of actual events; it is a rollicking history that ignores and alters facts at will. Cooper's *The Deerslayer,* the first in the *Leatherstocking* plot sequence, is not a realistic novel of life on the New York frontier. It is a mythical tale of the "natural" man and of lost innocence, of nature versus civilization.

There are other aspects of Romanticism. One is its intense interest in and reverence for nature. The poems of William Cullen Bryant are nearly perfect examples of this characteristic of Romanticism. Most of Bryant's best-known poems exalt the virtues of nature, whatever the poems' individual themes may be. Their titles show this emphasis: "The Yellow Violet," "A Forest Hymn," "Green River," "Summer Wind," and "The Prairies."

Another aspect of Romanticism is its accent on mystery—on the strange and fantastic aspects of human experience. In this realm, Edgar Allan Poe stands supreme. Poe wrote forty-eight brilliantly original lyric poems and a number of short stories whose characters, in the words of a biographer, "are either grotesques or the inhabitants of another world than this."

Not all Romantics were writers. Romanticism pervaded all the

ILLUSTRATION FROM AN 1872
EDITION OF JAMES FENIMORE
COOPER'S *THE LAST OF THE
MOHICANS*
Felix Octavius Carr Darley
The Granger Collection

10 **Literary Movement** Following Natty Bumppo as he moves westward to escape the growth of society, Cooper's *Leather-Stocking Tales* chronicle the westward expansion of American civilization. See the excerpt from *The Prairie* on page 196.

11 **Master Teacher Note** To help students grasp the ideas and attitudes of Romanticism, you might contrast them with the dominant attitudes of the Age of Reason. You might also want to discuss the *Lyrical Ballads* by William Wordsworth and Samuel Taylor Coleridge, the publication of which marked the beginning of the Romantic Age in England. The preface to the *Lyrical Ballads* and Wordsworth's poem "The Tables Turned" both clearly capture the essence of Romanticism.

12 **Literary Movement** Cooper's novels reflect the Romantic emphasis on the natural and the primitive rather than on the elegant and the cultivated.

13 **Literary Movement** Other important aspects of Romanticism were a strong belief in democracy, a concern for common people, an interest in the particular experiences of the individual, and a belief in excess and spontaneity.

14 **Literary Movement** See the selections by Edgar Allan Poe beginning on page 212.

Humanities Note

Illustration from *The Last of the Mohicans,* 1872, by Felix Octavius Carr Darley. Felix Octavius Carr Darley (1822–1888) was a member of the American Art Union, in whose activities the poet William Cullen Bryant was an eager participant. The union distributed inexpensive engravings by many artists, including works by Darley.

Darley's drawings to illustrate James Fenimore Cooper's *The Last of the Mohicans* were made into engravings by a number of artists. According to the publisher of Cooper's novels, the engravers used the more expensive technique for making plates that, until then, had been employed only in printing bank notes.

Darley's illustrations illuminate Cooper's exciting, moralistic narratives. Natty Bumppo is the model hero; the women, Indians, and other minor characters are idealized or stereotyped. Darley's work, nevertheless, has a poignant quality of its own. In an age before photography—and especially, the movies—book illustrations brought fictional characters to life, making reading a vivid, engrossing experience, particularly for young people. Thus a young reader's appreciation of the story was heightened by the skill of the illustrator in capturing the characters' special qualities.

Humanities Note

Fine art, *Kindred Spirits,* by Asher B. Durand. *Kindred Spirits,* by Asher Brown Durand (1796–1886), is a portrait-in-nature of the artist William Cole and the poet William Cullen Bryant. Cole, Durand, and other painters were members of the Hudson River School. The term was originally a derogatory one referring to the painters who preferred to depict scenes from nature rather than to employ the more conventional subject matter (portraits, historical events, and so on). Because of their skill in portraying the wilderness of the American continent, however, the Hudson River artists helped make landscape a respectable subject in American art.

Durand, Cole, and Bryant were close friends, maintaining a correspondence over a number of years, encouraging each other and expressing support. Although a writer, Bryant took an active interest in the busy art world of his day. When Durrand painted *Kindred Spirits,* Cole was already dead, but Bryant, on seeing the picture, expressed his admiration; he felt, in particular, that the painter had successfully captured his likeness. In *Kindred Spirits* Durand has placed the artist and the poet in a beautiful but highly posed setting. The linking of poetry, nature, and art is clear, and there is the suggestion that, indeed, nature should be the principal subject of art and poetry.

KINDRED SPIRITS
Asher B. Durand
New York Public Library

arts in this time of America's youth. Of special note were the landscape painters who came to be known as the Hudson River School. The most influential of this New York group was English-born Thomas Cole. His haunting and dramatic views of the Hudson River and Catskill Mountains have often been compared to Irving's word images. Perhaps the most famous Hudson River School painting is Asher B. Durand's *Kindred Spirits,* in which Thomas Cole and William Cullen Bryant stand on a jutting rock overlooking a picturesque valley.

Seedtime in New England

Although many of the significant literary accomplishments from 1800 to 1840 occurred in New York, cultural activity was by no means limited to that city. Small groups of writers could be found in most major cities on the East Coast, notably Philadelphia, Richmond, and Charleston. After 1840, as New York writing lost its preeminence, an impressive burst of literary activity took place in and around Boston. By that date, the movement that one critic has called, "the flowering of New England," had already begun. In the next fifteen years, it would produce an array of important writers and enduring literary works.

176   A Growing Nation

Check Test
1. The _____ in 1803 doubled the nation's territory.
2. Washington Irving, James Fenimore Cooper, William Cullen Bryant, and Edgar Allan Poe all spent important parts of their careers in _____.
3. The period 1800–1840 witnessed the beginnings of the antislavery and _____ movements.
4. In 1812 America fought a war with _____.
5. Irving, Cooper, Bryant, and Poe can all be described as _____.

Answers
1. Louisiana Purchase
2. New York City
3. feminist
4. Great Britain
5. Romantics

AMERICAN VOICES
Quotations by Prominent Figures of the Period

How convenient it would be to many of our great men and great families of doubtful origin, could they have the privilege of the heroes of yore, who, whenever their origin was involved in obscurity, modestly announced themselves descended from a god.
Washington Irving, *A History of New York*

To see him striding along the profile of a hill on a windy day, with his clothes bagging and fluttering about him, one might have mistaken him for the genius of famine descending upon the earth, or some scarecrow eloped from a cornfield.
Washington Irving, "The Legend of Sleepy Hollow"

I am always at a loss to know how much to believe of my own stories.
Washington Irving, *Tales of a Traveler*

All is contradiction in the settlements, while all is concord in the woods. Forts and churches almost always go together, and yet they're downright contradictions, churches being for peace and forts for war.
James Fenimore Cooper, *The Deerslayer*

Ignorance and superstition ever bear a close, and even a mathematical, relationship to each other.
James Fenimore Cooper, *Jack Tier*

Loveliest of lovely things are they,
On earth, that soonest pass away.
William Cullen Bryant, "A Scene on the Banks of the Hudson"

These are the gardens of the Desert, these
The unshorn fields, boundless and beautiful,
For which the speech of England has no name—
The Prairies.
William Cullen Bryant, "The Prairies"

True!—nervous—very, very dreadfully nervous I had been and am; but why *will* you say that I am mad?
Edgar Allan Poe, "The Tell-Tale Heart"

For the moon never beams without bringing me dreams
Of the beautiful Annabel Lee.
Edgar Allan Poe, "Annabel Lee"

Additional Voices

A sharp tongue is the only edge tool that grows keener with constant use.
Washington Irving, "Rip Van Winkle"

There rise authors now and then, who seem proof against the mutability of language, because they have rooted themselves in the unchanging principles of human nature.
Washington Irving, *The Mutabilities of Literature*

The groves were God's first temples.
William Cullen Bryant, "A Forest Hymn"

Truth, crushed to earth, shall rise again.
William Cullen Bryant, "The Battlefield"

From childhood's hour I have not been
As others were—I have not seen
As others saw.
Edgar Allan Poe, "Alone"

They who dream by day are cognizant of many things which escape those who dream only by night.
Edgar Allan Poe, "Eleonora"

I hold that a long poem does not exist. I maintain that the phrase "a long poem" is simply a flat contradiction in terms.
Edgar Allan Poe, "The Poetic Principle"

READING CRITICALLY

The Literature of 1800–1840

During the years from 1800 to 1840, the new nation grew and expanded at a rapid pace. During this time, the country began developing its own distinctive literary tradition. Because the United States was now an established nation, writers were able to turn from the subject of politics and create literature equal in quality to the work of European writers.

Historical Context

In 1803 President Jefferson completed the Louisiana Purchase, extending the American boundary to the Rocky Mountains. During the years that followed, many Americans traveled westward, seeking new homes and new opportunities. At the same time, the eastern cities grew rapidly, as the United States developed into an industrialized and self-sufficient nation.

Literary Movements

Following the turn of the century, an artistic movement that had originated in Europe swept through the United States. This movement, which came to be known as Romanticism, grew out of a reaction against the dominant attitudes and approaches of the eighteenth century. Unlike the eighteenth-century writers, who emphasized reason, logic, and scientific observation, the Romantics stressed the examination of inner feelings and emotions and the use of the imagination. The Romantic movement was also characterized by an interest in nature and the supernatural, a strong belief in democracy, and a deep awareness of the past.

Writers' Techniques

The attitudes, concerns, and interests of the Romantics are reflected in the themes of the majority of the literary works written between 1800 and 1840. Writers explored the mysteries of nature and the inner self and the relationship between nature and the human imagination. With the establishment of the American identity, writers also began focusing on distinctively American themes and delving into the history of the young nation.

On the following pages is a selection by William Cullen Bryant, the first American poet to win worldwide critical acclaim. The notes in the side column draw your attention to Bryant's literary techniques and to the Romantic concerns that are reflected in the selection.

To a Waterfowl
William Cullen Bryant

Literary Movement: The title indicates this poem will be about nature, which is a characteristic interest of the Romantic movement.

    Whither, midst falling dew,
While glow the heavens with the last steps of day,
Far, through their rosy depths, dost thou pursue
    Thy solitary way?

Literary Movement: Bryant creates vivid images, or word pictures, that capture the beauty of nature.

5   Vainly the fowler's[1] eye
Might mark thy distant flight to do thee wrong,

---

1. fowler's: Referring to a hunter.

To a Waterfowl   179

Presentation

Motivation/Proir Knowledge
Ask students if they have observed migrating birds. What patterns have they observed in the birds? How do the birds seem to know where they are going? Point out that, in this poem, Bryant wonders about a solitary migrating bird.

Thematic Idea Another selection which explores the relationship between humanity and nature is "The Bear" by William Faulkner (p. 734).

Purpose-Setting Question,
What does the speaker learn from his observation of the waterfowl?

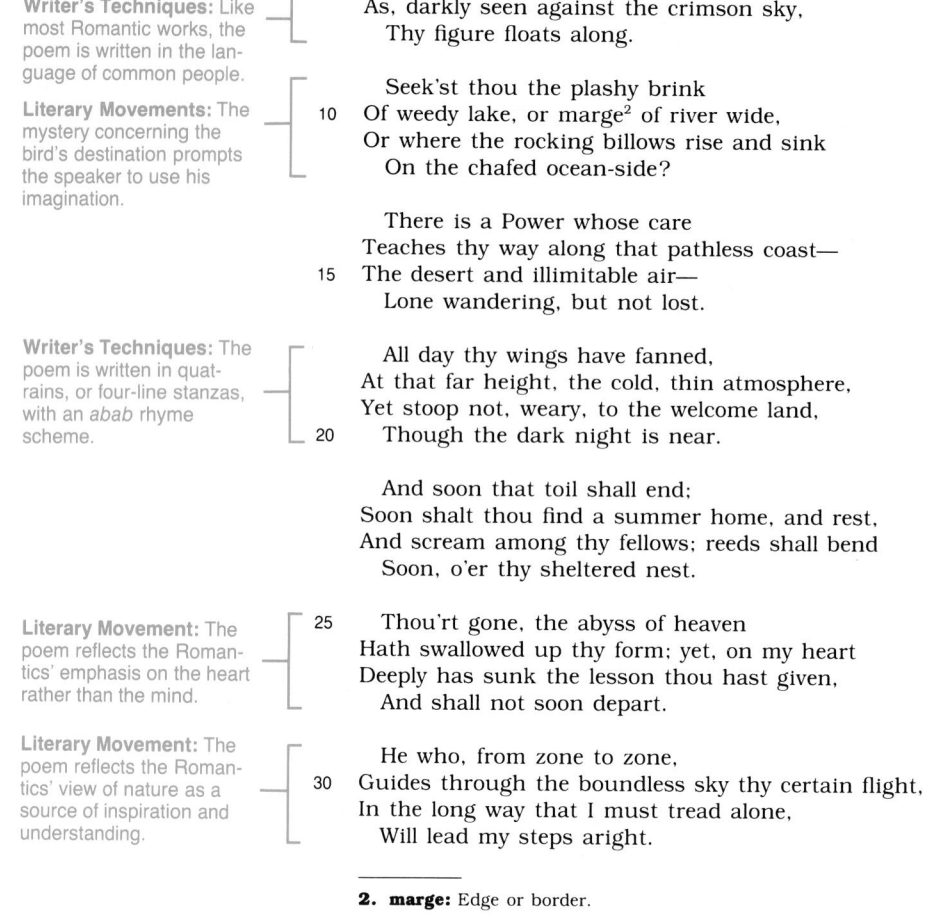

Writer's Techniques: Like most Romantic works, the poem is written in the language of common people.

Literary Movements: The mystery concerning the bird's destination prompts the speaker to use his imagination.

Writer's Techniques: The poem is written in quatrains, or four-line stanzas, with an *abab* rhyme scheme.

Literary Movement: The poem reflects the Romantics' emphasis on the heart rather than the mind.

Literary Movement: The poem reflects the Romantics' view of nature as a source of inspiration and understanding.

As, darkly seen against the crimson sky,
    Thy figure floats along.

    Seek'st thou the plashy brink
10 Of weedy lake, or marge[2] of river wide,
Or where the rocking billows rise and sink
    On the chafed ocean-side?

    There is a Power whose care
Teaches thy way along that pathless coast—
15 The desert and illimitable air—
    Lone wandering, but not lost.

    All day thy wings have fanned,
At that far height, the cold, thin atmosphere,
Yet stoop not, weary, to the welcome land,
20   Though the dark night is near.

    And soon that toil shall end;
Soon shalt thou find a summer home, and rest,
And scream among thy fellows; reeds shall bend
    Soon, o'er thy sheltered nest.

25 Thou'rt gone, the abyss of heaven
Hath swallowed up thy form; yet, on my heart
Deeply has sunk the lesson thou hast given,
    And shall not soon depart.

    He who, from zone to zone,
30 Guides through the boundless sky thy certain flight,
In the long way that I must tread alone,
    Will lead my steps aright.

2. marge: Edge or border.

THINKING ABOUT THE SELECTION

Recalling

1. What questions does the speaker ask the waterfowl in the first three stanzas?
2. What does the "Power" referred to in the fourth stanza teach the waterfowl?
3. What will the waterfowl soon find?
4. What lesson does the speaker learn from the waterfowl?

Interpreting

5. How does the speaker's interest in the waterfowl contrast with the fowler's concern with the bird?
6. What does the speaker learn from his observations of the waterfowl?

Applying

7. What are some other lessons that people might learn from birds or other animals?

ANALYZING LITERATURE

Understanding Romanticism

Romanticism was an artistic movement that grew out of a reaction against the dominant attitudes and approaches of the eighteenth century. The Romantics stressed the examination of inner feelings and emotions and the use of the imagination, rather than the use of reason and logic. They were interested in nature and its mysteries and even in the supernatural. Often, the Romantics sought inspiration and understanding through the observation and contemplation of nature. Possessing a deep awareness of the past, the Romantics turned to legends and folklore as sources of inspiration.

The use of legends and folklore reflected the Romantics' interest in and concern for common people. This concern was also reflected in the Romantics' frequent use of the language of common people in their works.

1. Bryant's poem focuses on the migration of birds, a subject that scientists still cannot fully explain. Why is this an appropriate subject for a Romantic poem?
2. How does the speaker's approach to understanding the waterfowl's flight reflect the concerns of the Romantics?
3. Unlike the writers of the eighteenth century, the Romantics were generally concerned with specific experiences of individuals, rather than with general, universal experiences. How is this concern reflected in Bryant's poem?
4. In writing about the concerns of the Romantic movement, some writers capitalize *Nature.* Explain why this would be appropriate.

THINKING AND WRITING

Responding to Criticism

In discussing "To a Waterfowl," Edgar Allan Poe commented that the poem's main strength is its "completeness," adding that the poem's "rounded and didactic termination has done wonders." Write an essay in which you discuss the poem in relation to this comment. Reread the poem, keeping Poe's comment in mind. Do you think his statement is accurate? Why or why not? When writing your essay, use evidence from the poem to support your argument. When you finish writing, revise your essay, making sure it supports your opinion of the quotation. Proofread your essay and prepare a final draft.

To a Waterfowl 181

ANSWERS TO THINKING ABOUT THE SELECTION

Recalling

1. He asks the bird where it is going. Is it headed for a lake or river, or is it flying to the ocean?
2. It teaches the waterfowl how to find its way "along that pathless coast."
3. It will soon find a summer home.
4. "He who, from zone to zone,/ Guides through the boundless sky thy certain flight,/ In the long way that I must tread alone,/ Will lead my steps aright."

Interpreting

5. The speaker is interested in the bird as a symbol of divine sustenance; the fowler wants to kill it for bodily sustenance.
6. The speaker learns to trust that he too will be guided on his way.

Applying

7. Answers will differ. Suggested Response: We can learn patience, caution, and relaxation from animals.

ANSWERS TO ANALYZING LITERATURE

1. It is appropriate because the Romantics were deeply interested in the mysteries of nature.
2. The speaker takes an intuitive approach.
3. The conclusion that the speaker reaches is internal and personal.
4. Suggested Response: This was appropriate, because they viewed nature as a vital and powerful force.

THINKING AND WRITING

For help with this assignment, students can refer to Lesson 15, "Evaluating a Literary Work," in the Handbook of Writing About Literature.

Writing Across the Curriculum Consider having students investigate and report on migratory habits and patterns of birds. If you do so, you might inform the science teachers who can give guidance and perhaps extra credit to students.

More About the Author Washington Irving became America's first internationally acclaimed man of letters almost in spite of himself. Although he had enjoyed early critical and popular success, he pursued other interests and did not resume writing professionally until financial necessity demanded it. He then published *The Sketch Book* in London with the help of Sir Walter Scott, whom Irving considered the greatest living writer. This work firmly established Irving's literary reputation in England and throughout Europe and gained him prestige at home. You may wish to lead students in a discussion of the various motivations that compel creative writers and other artists to pursue their solitary crafts. Also discuss the significance of early success. What are the benefits of early success? What are the hazards?

Critical Evaluation Edward Wagenknecht made the following evaluation of Irving's work: "It was not his function either to scale the heights or sound the depths of life; neither did he ever pretend to be able to do so. Though he was never so indifferent to either ideas or social evils as his critics would have us believe, he consistently inhabited a middle region which he surveyed and described with a winning, companionable charm. . . . This is the area that Irving inhabits, and whatever other shortcomings it may have, there can be no question that it embraces a good deal of what we generally mean to indicate when we speak of civilization."

WASHINGTON IRVING

1783–1859

Named after the first American President, Washington Irving became the first American writer to achieve an international reputation.

Born into a wealthy New York family, Irving began studying law at the age of sixteen. He had little interest in his studies, however, and spent much time traveling throughout Europe and New York's Hudson Valley and reading European literature. Irving also wrote satirical essays using the pen name Jonathan Oldstyle. When Irving was twenty-four, he and his brother began publishing an anonymous magazine, *Salmagundi* (the name of a spicy appetizer), which carried humorous sketches and essays about New York society.

In 1809 Irving published his first major work, *A History of New York from the Beginning of the World to the End of the Dutch Dynasty,* using the pseudonym Diedrich Knickerbocker. The *History,* a humorous examination of New York during colonial times, was popular and made Irving famous.

From 1815 to 1832, Irving lived in Europe, traveling extensively and learning about European customs, traditions, and folklore. Inspired by the European folk heritage, Irving created two of his most famous stories, "The Legend of Sleepy Hollow" and "Rip Van Winkle," transforming two traditional German tales into distinctly American stories set in the Hudson Valley. When Irving published these two stories in *The Sketch Book* (1820) under the pseudonym Geoffrey Crayon, writers and critics throughout Europe and the United States responded enthusiastically.

Irving produced other books while living in Europe, including *Bracebridge Hall* (1822), *Tales of a Traveller* (1824), and *The Alhambra* (1832). Another of Irving's more famous stories, "The Devil and Tom Walker," an American adaptation of a German legend about a man who sells his soul to the devil, appeared in *Tales of a Traveller*.

Irving's lengthy stay in Europe prompted some to question his loyalty to his native land. Irving responded, "I am endeavoring to serve my country. Whatever I have written has been written with the feelings and published as the writing of an American. Is that renouncing my country? How else am I to serve my country—by coming home and begging an office of it: which I should not have the kind of talent or the business habits requisite to fill?—If I can do any good in this world it is with my pen."

Although Irving continued to write after returning to the United States in 1832, he is remembered mainly for a few of the stories he wrote while in Europe. Like the folktales from which they were adapted, these stories have remained popular for generations, becoming an important part of the American literary heritage.

GUIDE FOR INTERPRETING

The Devil and Tom Walker

Literary Forms

Folk Tales. Folk tales are stories handed down orally among the common people of a particular culture. These stories often relate events that are unrealistic or unlikely to happen in the real world in order to teach a lesson or express a general truth about life. The characters in folk tales tend to be stereotypes or stock characters embodying a single human trait, quality, or emotion. For example, a character in a folk tale may embody hatred or greed.

Washington Irving created "The Devil and Tom Walker" by reshaping a German folk tale about a man who sells his soul to the devil. Irving makes the tale distinctly American by setting it in New England during the late 1720's—a time when Puritanism, especially the belief that a person's life should be devoted to God, was being replaced by commercialism and the desire for personal gain. Like the tale from which it was adapted, Irving's story relates a series of unlikely events, involves stereotyped characters, and teaches an important lesson about life. Because Irving's story is grounded in a specific time and place, it also reveals a great deal about life in New England in the 1720's.

Writing

Do you think that some people today sometimes become so concerned with acquiring money and power that they forget to be sympathetic and compassionate toward other people? Freewrite about your thoughts regarding this question.

Primary Source

In "The Devil and Tom Walker," Irving dramatizes the colonists' attitudes toward Native Americans in a number of passages. Irving commented on the attitudes of colonial Americans in an essay called "Traits of Indian Character." These attitudes were reflected in their treatment of the Indians and in the way early American writers portrayed them in their works. The Indians were "doubly wronged by the white men. They have been dispossessed of their hereditary possessions by mercenary and frequently wanton warfare; and their characters have been traduced by bigoted and interested writers. The colonist has often treated them like beasts of the forest; and the author has endeavored to justify him in his outrages. The former found it easier to exterminate than to civilize; the latter to vilify than to discriminate. The appellations of savage and pagan were deemed sufficient to sanction the hostilities of both; and thus the poor wanderers of the forest were persecuted and defamed, not because they were guilty, but because they were ignorant."

Guide for Interpreting 183

Literary Focus The German folk tale from which Irving adapted "The Devil and Tom Walker" was also the source for many other works of literature. You may wish to make students aware of the fact that folk tales, myths, legends, and even fairy tales have always been a rich source of material for writers. For example, the novels of Mary Renault are drawn largely from Greek mythology, and all vampire tales are based on the folk tales of eastern Europe.

Writing/Prior Knowledge For extra credit, you might have students freewrite about the way in which the subject of greed is dealt with in contemporary literature and films.

Vocabulary

Preteach the following vocabulary words:

termagant (tʉr′ mə gənt) *n.:* A quarrelsome woman (p. 184)

avarice (av′ ər is) *n.:* Greed (p. 187)

usurer (yoo′ zhoo rər) *n.:* A moneylender who charges very high interest (p. 189)

extort (ik stôrt′) *v.:* To obtain by threat or violence (p. 190)

ostentation (äs′tən tā′ shən) *n.:* Boastful display (p. 190)

parsimony (pär′sə mō′ nē) *n.:* Stinginess (p. 190)

Objectives

1 To understand a folk tale
2 To make inferences about cultural attitudes
3 To adapt a folk tale to twentieth-century America

Support Material

Teaching Portfolio
Teacher Backup, p. 269
Grammar in Action Worksheets, *Using Subordination,* p. 272; *Appreciating Adjectives,* p. 274
Usage and Mechanics Worksheet, p. 276
Vocabulary Check, p. 277
Analyzing Literature Worksheet, *Recognizing Folk Tales,* p. 278

Critical Thinking and Reading Worksheet, *Inferring Cultural Attitudes,* p. 279
Selection Test, p. 280

The Devil and Tom Walker

Washington Irving

A few miles from Boston in Massachusetts, there is a deep inlet, winding several miles into the interior of the country from Charles Bay, and terminating in a thickly wooded swamp or morass. On one side of this inlet is a beautiful dark grove; on the opposite side the land rises abruptly from the water's edge into a high ridge, on which grow a few scattered oaks of great age and immense size. Under one of these gigantic trees, according to old stories, there was a great amount of treasure buried by Kidd the pirate.[1] The inlet allowed a facility to bring the money in a boat secretly and at night to the very foot of the hill; the elevation of the place permitted a good look-out to be kept that no one was at hand; while the remarkable trees formed good landmarks by which the place might easily be found again. The old stories add, moreover, that the Devil presided at the hiding of the money, and took it under his guardianship; but this it is well known he always does with buried treasure, particularly when it has been ill-gotten. Be that as it may, Kidd never returned to recover his wealth; being shortly after seized at Boston, sent out to England, and there hanged for a pirate.

About the year 1727, just at the time that earthquakes were prevalent in New England, and shook many tall sinners down upon their knees, there lived near this place a meager, miserly fellow, of the name of Tom Walker. He had a wife as miserly as himself: they were so miserly that they even conspired to cheat each other. Whatever the woman could lay hands on, she hid away; a hen could not cackle but she was on the alert to secure the new-laid egg. Her husband was continually prying about to detect her secret hoards, and many and fierce were the conflicts that took place about what ought to have been common property. They lived in a forlorn-looking house that stood alone, and had an air of starvation. A few straggling savin trees, emblems of sterility, grew near it; no smoke ever curled from its chimney; no traveler stopped at its door. A miserable horse, whose ribs were as articulate as the bars of a gridiron, stalked about a field, where a thin carpet of moss, scarcely covering the ragged beds of puddingstone, tantalized and balked his hunger; and sometimes he would lean his head over the fence, look piteously at the passerby, and seem to petition deliverance from this land of famine.

The house and its inmates had altogether a bad name. Tom's wife was a tall termagant, fierce of temper, loud of tongue, and strong of arm. Her voice was often heard in wordy warfare with her husband; and his face sometimes showed signs that their conflicts were not confined to words. No one ventured, however, to interfere between them. The lonely wayfarer shrunk within himself at the horrid clamor and clapper-clawing;[2] eyed the den of discord askance; and hurried on his way, rejoicing, if a bachelor, in his celibacy.

One day that Tom Walker had been to a

---

1. Kidd the pirate: Captain William Kidd (1645–1701).

2. clapperclawing (klap′ ər klô′ ing): Clawing or scratching.

distant part of the neighborhood, he took what he considered a shortcut homeward, through the swamp. Like most shortcuts, it was an ill-chosen route. The swamp was thickly grown with great gloomy pines and hemlocks, some of them ninety feet high, which made it dark at noonday, and a retreat for all the owls of the neighborhood. It was full of pits and quagmires, partly covered with weeds and mosses, where the green surface often betrayed the traveler into a gulf of black, smothering mud; there were also dark and stagnant pools, the abodes of the tadpole, the bullfrog, and the water-snake; where the trunks of pines and hemlocks lay half-drowned, half-rotting, looking like alligators sleeping in the mire.

Tom had long been picking his way cautiously through this treacherous forest; stepping from tuft to tuft of rushes and roots, which afforded precarious footholds among deep sloughs; or pacing carefully, like a cat, along the prostrate trunks of trees; startled now and then by the sudden screaming of the bittern, or the quacking of a wild duck, rising on the wing from some solitary pool. At length he arrived at a piece of firm ground, which ran out like a peninsula into the deep bosom of the swamp. It had been one of the strongholds of the Indians during their wars with the first colonists. Here they had thrown up a kind of fort, which they had looked upon as almost impregnable, and had used as a place of refuge for their squaws and children. Nothing remained of the old Indian fort but a few embankments, gradually sinking to the level of the surrounding earth, and already overgrown in part by oaks and other forest trees, the foliage of which formed a contrast to the dark pines and hemlocks of the swamp.

It was late in the dusk of evening when Tom Walker reached the old fort, and he paused there awhile to rest himself. Anyone but he would have felt unwilling to linger in this lonely, melancholy place, for the common people had a bad opinion of it, from the stories handed down from the time of the In-dian wars; when it was asserted that the savages held incantations here, and made sacrifices to the evil spirit.

Tom Walker, however, was not a man to be troubled with any fears of the kind. He reposed himself for some time on the trunk of a fallen hemlock, listening to the boding cry of the tree toad, and delving with his walking staff into a mound of black mold at his feet. As he turned up the soil unconsciously, his staff struck against something hard. He raked it out of the vegetable mold, and lo! a cloven skull, with an Indian tomahawk buried deep in it, lay before him. The rust on the weapon showed the time that had elapsed since this deathblow had been given. It was a dreary memento of the fierce struggle that had taken place in this last foothold of the Indian warriors.

"Humph!" said Tom Walker, as he gave it a kick to shake the dirt from it.

"Let that skull alone!" said a gruff voice. Tom lifted up his eyes, and beheld a great black man seated directly opposite him, on the stump of a tree. He was exceedingly surprised, having neither heard nor seen anyone approach; and he was still more perplexed on observing, as well as the gathering gloom would permit, that the stranger was neither Negro nor Indian. It is true he was dressed in a rude half-Indian garb, and had a red belt or sash swathed round his body; but his face was neither black nor copper color, but swarthy and dingy, and begrimed with soot, as if he had been accustomed to toil among fires and forges. He had a shock of coarse black hair, that stood out from his head in all directions, and bore an ax on his shoulder.

He scowled for a moment at Tom with a pair of great red eyes.

"What are you doing on my grounds?" said the black man, with a hoarse growling voice.

"Your grounds!" said Tom with a sneer, "no more your grounds than mine; they belong to Deacon Peabody."

"Deacon Peabody be d——d," said the

The Devil and Tom Walker 185

4 **Reading Strategy** Have students take turns reading aloud the paragraphs that describe Tom's "short cut" through the swamp. Have them emphasize the use of alliteration, assonance, metaphor, and other literary devices to create a feeling of suspense and foreboding.

5 **Enrichment** The tale begins in 1727, before the onset of the French and Indian Wars. The "Indian wars" mentioned here refer to earlier struggles between the Puritan settlers and the Native Americans.

6 **Discussion** What do these passages tell you about the colonists' overall attitude toward the Native American population?

7 **Discussion** What does Tom's reply to the stranger tell you about his character?

8 **Discussion** Do you think Tom's reaction to the stranger is appropriate? How might you react?

9 **Clarification** In the Puritan church, a deacon was a member of the laity elected by the congregation to serve in worship and to help in the administration of church affairs. Some Christian churches still have deacons, but their office does not make them as powerful in the community as the Puritan deacons were.

10 Enrichment The author satirizes hypocritical Puritans who used their prominence to amass wealth. The tale takes place at a time when many Colonial Americans were relinquishing their Puritan ideals for a new set of beliefs related to commercialism. In 1836 Washington Irving was commissioned by John Jacob Astor to write *Astoria,* a novel about the fur trade in the Northwest, from which Astor's immense fortune had grown. At that time Mr. Astor was the personification of a new era of American commercialism called capitalism.

stranger, "as I flatter myself he will be, if he does not look more to his own sins and less to those of his neighbors. Look yonder, and see how Deacon Peabody is faring."

Tom looked in the direction that the stranger pointed, and beheld one of the great trees, fair and flourishing without, but rotten at the core, and saw that it had been nearly hewn through, so that the first high wind was likely to blow it down. On the bark of the tree was scored the name of Deacon Peabody, an eminent man, who had waxed wealthy by driving shrewd bargains with the Indians. He now looked round, and found most of the tall trees marked with the name of some great man of the colony, and all more or less scored by the ax. The one on which he had been seated, and which had evidently just been hewn down, bore the name of Crowninshield; and he recollected a mighty rich man of that name, who made a vulgar display of wealth, which it was whispered he had acquired by buccaneering.

"He's just ready for burning!" said the black man, with a growl of triumph. "You see I am likely to have a good stock of firewood for winter."

"But what right have you," said Tom, "to cut down Deacon Peabody's timber?"

"The right of a prior claim," said the other. "This woodland belonged to me long before one of your white-faced race put foot upon the soil."

"And pray, who are you, if I may be so bold?" said Tom.

"Oh, I go by various names. I am the wild huntsman in some countries; the black miner in others. In this neighborhood I am known by the name of the black woodsman. I am he to whom the red men consecrated this spot, and in honor of whom they now and then roasted a white man, by way of sweet-smelling sacrifice. Since the red men have been exterminated by you white savages, I amuse myself by presiding at the per-

Grammar in Action

Subordination is the joining of an independent clause with one or more subordinate clauses. Look at this example:

It was late in the dusk of evening when Tom Walker reached the old fort, . . . (page 185)

"It was late in the dusk of evening" is the independent clause, the one that could stand alone as a sentence. "When Tom Walker reached the old fort" is the subordinate clause; it could not stand alone as a sentence. Words like *when,* used to introduce a subordinate clause, are called subordinating conjunctions. The independent clause contains the sentence's main idea, while subordinate clauses, which often modify a word in an independent clause, contain less important ideas.

Student Activity 1. Identify the independent and subordinate clauses in the following sentences. Name the subordinating conjunction in each.

secutions of Quakers and Anabaptists;[3] I am the great patron and prompter of slave dealers, and the grandmaster of the Salem witches."

"The upshot of all which is, that, if I mistake not," said Tom, sturdily, "you are he commonly called Old Scratch."

"The same, at your service!" replied the black man, with a half-civil nod.

Such was the opening of this interview, according to the old story; though it has almost too familiar an air to be credited. One would think that to meet with such a singular personage, in this wild, lonely place, would have shaken any man's nerves; but Tom was a hard-minded fellow, not easily daunted, and he had lived so long with a termagant wife, that he did not even fear the Devil.

It is said that after this commencement they had a long and earnest conversation together, as Tom returned homeward. The black man told him of great sums of money buried by Kidd the pirate, under the oak trees on the high ridge, not far from the morass. All these were under his command, and protected by his power, so that none could find them but such as propitiated his favor. These he offered to place within Tom Walker's reach, having conceived an especial kindness for him; but they were to be had only on certain conditions. What these conditions were may easily be surmised, though Tom never disclosed them publicly. They must have been very hard, for he required time to think of them, and he was not a man to stick at trifles where money was in view. When they had reached the edge of the swamp, the stranger paused—"What proof have I that all you have been telling me is true?" said Tom. "There is my signature," said the black man, pressing his finger on Tom's forehead. So saying, he turned off among the thickets of the swamp, and seemed, as Tom said, to go down, down, down, into the earth, until nothing but his head and shoulders could be seen, and so on, until he totally disappeared.

When Tom reached home, he found the black print of a finger, burnt, as it were, into his forehead, which nothing could obliterate.

The first news his wife had to tell him was the sudden death of Absalom Crowninshield, the rich buccaneer. It was announced in the papers with the usual flourish, that "A great man had fallen in Israel."[4]

Tom recollected the tree which his black friend had just hewn down, and which was ready for burning. "Let the freebooter roast," said Tom, "who cares!" He now felt convinced that all he had heard and seen was no illusion.

He was not prone to let his wife into his confidence; but as this was an uneasy secret, he willingly shared it with her. All her avarice was awakened at the mention of hidden gold, and she urged her husband to comply with the black man's terms and secure what would make them wealthy for life. However Tom might have felt disposed to sell himself to the Devil, he was determined not to do so to oblige his wife; so he flatly refused, out of the mere spirit of contradiction. Many and bitter were the quarrels they had on the subject, but the more she talked, the more resolute was Tom not to be damned to please her.

At length she determined to drive the bargain on her own account, and if she succeeded, to keep all the gain to herself. Being of the same fearless temper as her husband, she set off for the old Indian fort towards the close of a summer's day. She was many hours absent. When she came back, she was reserved and sullen in her replies. She spoke something of a black man, whom she had met about twilight, hewing at the root of a tall tree. He was sulky, however, and would not come to terms: she was to go again with a propitiatory offering, but what it was she forbore to say.

---

3. Quakers and Anabaptists: Two religious groups that were persecuted for their beliefs.

4. A . . . Israel: A reference to II Samuel 3:38 in the Bible. The Puritans often called New England "Israel."

The Devil and Tom Walker 187

---

1. As he turned up the soil unconsciously, his staff struck against something hard.
2. This woodland belonged to me long before one of your white-faced race put foot on the soil.
3. When she came back, she was reserved and sullen in her replies.
4. I'll do it tomorrow, if you wish.
5. He prayed loudly and strenuously, as if heaven were to be taken by force of lungs.

Student Activity 2. Combine each pair of sentences, making one into a subordinate clause.

1. A miserable horse stalked about a field.
   A thin carpet of moss tantalized his hunger.
2. They had a long and earnest conversation together.
   Tom returned home.
3. They had reached the edge of the swamp.
   The stranger paused.
4. He seemed to go down . . . into the earth.
   Nothing but his head and shoulders could be seen.

16 **Discussion** What does this sentence and the use of the words *facts* and *historians* tell you about the narrator's point of view?

17 **Reading Strategy** Have several students take turns reading the section that describes Tom's searching for and finding what is left of his wife. Have them supply any sound effects they encounter as they read (the scream of the bittern, the bullfrog's croak, and the hooting owls). Then make students aware of how these effects contribute to the ominous atmosphere.

18 **Discussion** What is ironic about the use of the word *fortitude* in this sentence?

The next evening she set off again for the swamp, with her apron heavily laden. Tom waited and waited for her, but in vain; midnight came, but she did not make her appearance: morning, noon, night returned, but still she did not come. Tom now grew uneasy for her safety, especially as he found she had carried off in her apron the silver teapot and spoons, and every portable article of value. Another night elapsed, another morning came; but no wife. In a word, she was never heard of more.

What was her real fate nobody knows, in consequence of so many pretending to know. It is one of those facts which have become confounded by a variety of historians. Some asserted that she lost her way among the tangled mazes of the swamp, and sank into some pit or slough; others, more uncharitable, hinted that she had eloped with the household booty, and made off to some other province; while others surmised that the tempter had decoyed her into a dismal quagmire, on the top of which her hat was found lying. In confirmation of this, it was said a great black man, with an ax on his shoulder, was seen late that very evening coming out of the swamp, carrying a bundle tied in a checked apron, with an air of surly triumph.

The most current and probable story, however, observes, that Tom Walker grew so anxious about the fate of his wife and his property, that he set out at length to seek them both at the Indian fort. During a long summer's afternoon he searched about the gloomy place, but no wife was to be seen. He called her name repeatedly, but she was nowhere to be heard. The bittern alone responded to his voice, as he flew screaming by; or the bullfrog croaked dolefully from a neighboring pool. At length, it is said, just in the brown hour of twilight, when the owls began to hoot, and the bats to flit about, his attention was attracted by the clamor of carrion crows hovering about a cypress tree. He looked up, and beheld a bundle tied in a checked apron, and hanging in the branches of the tree, with a great vulture perched hard by, as if keeping watch upon it. He leaped with joy; for he recognized his wife's apron, and supposed it to contain the household valuables.

"Let us get hold of the property," said he, consolingly to himself, "and we will endeavor to do without the woman."

As he scrambled up the tree, the vulture spread its wide wings, and sailed off screaming into the deep shadows of the forest. Tom seized the checked apron, but woeful sight! found nothing but a heart and liver tied up in it!

Such, according to the most authentic old story, was all that was to be found of Tom's wife. She had probably attempted to deal with the black man as she had been accustomed to deal with her husband; but though a female scold is generally considered a match for the Devil, yet in this instance she appears to have had the worst of it. She must have died game, however; for it is said Tom noticed many prints of cloven feet deeply stamped about the tree, and found handfuls of hair, that looked as if they had been plucked from the coarse black shock of the woodsman. Tom knew his wife's prowess by experience. He shrugged his shoulders, as he looked at the signs of a fierce clapperclawing. "Egad," said he to himself, "Old Scratch must have had a tough time of it!"

Tom consoled himself for the loss of his property, with the loss of his wife, for he was a man of fortitude. He even felt something like gratitude towards the black woodsman, who, he considered, had done him a kindness. He sought, therefore, to cultivate a further acquaintance with him, but for some time without success; the old blacklegs played shy, for whatever people may think, he is not always to be had for calling for: he knows how to play his cards when pretty sure of his game.

At length, it is said, when delay had whetted Tom's eagerness to the quick, and prepared him to agree to anything rather than not gain the promised treasure, he met the black man one evening in his usual woodsman's dress, with his ax on his shoulder, sauntering along the swamp, and humming a tune. He affected to receive Tom's advances with great indifference, made brief replies, and went on humming his tune.

By degrees, however, Tom brought him to business, and they began to haggle about the terms on which the former was to have the pirate's treasure. There was one condition which need not be mentioned, being generally understood in all cases where the Devil grants favors; but there were others about which, though of less importance, he was inflexibly obstinate. He insisted that the money found through his means should be employed in his service. He proposed, therefore, that Tom should employ it in the black traffic; that is to say, that he should fit out a slave ship. This, however, Tom resolutely refused: he was bad enough in all conscience, but the Devil himself could not tempt him to turn slave-trader.

Finding Tom so squeamish on this point, he did not insist upon it, but proposed, instead, that he should turn usurer; the Devil being extremely anxious for the increase of usurers, looking upon them as his peculiar[5] people.

To this no objections were made, for it was just to Tom's taste.

"You shall open a broker's shop in Boston next month," said the black man.

"I'll do it tomorrow, if you wish," said Tom Walker.

"You shall lend money at two per cent a month."

---

5. **peculiar:** Particular, special.

9

20

19 **Enrichment** This opinion of slave trading does not so much reflect Colonial mores as it does the abolitionist sentiments of the author. By 1824 when Irving wrote *Tales of a Traveller,* which included this selection, the Abolitionist Movement had grown strong in the Northeast, especially in cities like New York. And in England, where Irving was living at the time, antislavery sentiments were widespread.

20 **Critical Thinking and Reading** What does this tell you about Colonial attitudes toward brokers and usurers? Do you think the author shared this view?

Primary Source

Tom's refusal to become a slave-trader reflects Washington Irving's own stand against slavery. Edward Wagenknecht discusses this issue in his biography of Irving:

> In his life of Columbus, Irving condemns both Indian slavery and Negro slavery, which he sees as inviting divine retribution, and in "The Devil and Tom Walker" the one thing Tom will not do to accommodate the Devil is go into the slave trade. Irving was clear on the secession issue as early as 1832, and when Governor James Hamilton of South Carolina, who had entertained him, hoped he would come again, he smiled and replied, "Oh, yes! I'll come with the first troops."

21

Critical Thinking and Reading Take note of the reference to a real person and an actual, historic institution.

22 Discussion What types of people borrow money in today's society? How are these people similar to and different from the ones who borrowed money from Tom Walker?

23 Reading Strategy Have students summarize the story up to this point.

24 Discussion Does Tom's renewed interest in churchgoing seem sincere? Will it eventually cause him to change in other ways? Will it affect the outcome of the story?

"Egad, I'll charge four!" replied Tom Walker.

"You shall extort bonds, foreclose mortgages, drive the merchant to bankruptcy——"

"I'll drive him to the D——l," cried Tom Walker.

"You are the usurer for my money!" said the blacklegs with delight. "When will you want the rhino?"[6]

"This very night."

"Done!" said the Devil.

"Done!" said Tom Walker. So they shook hands and struck a bargain.

A few days' time saw Tom Walker seated behind his desk in a countinghouse in Boston.

His reputation for a ready-moneyed man, who would lend money out for a good consideration, soon spread abroad. Everybody remembers the time of Governor Belcher,[7] when money was particularly scarce. It was a time of paper credit. The country had been deluged with government bills; the famous Land Bank[8] had been established; there had been a rage for speculating; the people had run mad with schemes for new settlements, for building cities in the wilderness; land jobbers[9] went about with maps of grants, and townships, and El Dorados,[10] lying nobody knew where, but which everybody was ready to purchase. In a word, the great speculating fever which breaks out every now and then in the country, had raged to an alarming degree, and everybody was dreaming of making sudden fortunes from nothing. As usual the fever had subsided; the dream had gone off, and the imaginary for-

---

6. **rhino** (rī′ nō): Slang term for money.
7. **Governor Belcher:** Jonathan Belcher, the governor of Massachusetts Bay Colony from 1730 through 1741.
8. **Land Bank:** A bank that financed transactions in real estate.
9. **land jobbers:** People who bought and sold undeveloped land.
10. **El Dorados** (el′ də rä′ dōz): Places that are rich in gold or opportunity. El Dorado was a legendary country in South America sought by early Spanish explorers for its gold and precious stones.

190 A Growing Nation

---

tunes with it; the patients were left in doleful plight, and the whole country resounded with the consequent cry of "hard times."

At this propitious time of public distress did Tom Walker set up as usurer in Boston. His door was soon thronged by customers. The needy and adventurous, the gambling speculator, the dreaming land jobber, the thriftless tradesman, the merchant with cracked credit, in short, everyone driven to raise money by desperate means and desperate sacrifices, hurried to Tom Walker.

Thus Tom was the universal friend of the needy, and acted like a "friend in need"; that is to say, he always exacted good pay and good security. In proportion to the distress of the applicant was the hardness of his terms. He accumulated bonds and mortgages; gradually squeezed his customers closer and closer, and sent them at length, dry as a sponge, from his door.

In this way he made money hand over hand, became a rich and mighty man, and exalted his cocked hat upon 'Change.[11] He built himself, as usual, a vast house, out of ostentation; but left the greater part of it unfinished and unfurnished, out of parsimony. He even set up a carriage in the fullness of his vainglory, though he nearly starved the horses which drew it; and as the ungreased wheels groaned and screeched on the axletrees, you would have thought you heard the souls of the poor debtors he was squeezing.

As Tom waxed old, however, he grew thoughtful. Having secured the good things of this world, he began to feel anxious about those of the next. He thought with regret on the bargain he had made with his black friend, and set his wits to work to cheat him out of the conditions. He became, therefore, all of a sudden, a violent churchgoer. He prayed loudly and strenuously, as if heaven were to be taken by force of lungs. Indeed, one might always tell when he had sinned most during the week, by the clamor of his Sunday devotion. The quiet Christians who

---

11. **'Change:** The exchange, where bankers and merchants did business.

Grammar in Action

An **adjective** is a word used to describe a noun or pronoun or to give it a more specific meaning. Following are examples of adjectives:

She looked to the side and saw the <u>red</u> wingtips of the birds.

The ache in his muscles told him that the load was <u>heavy</u>.

In "The Devil and Tom Walker," Washington Irving makes skillful use of adjectives:

"His reputation for a <u>ready-moneyed</u> man, who would lend money out for a <u>good</u> consideration, soon spread abroad." (p. 190)

"Just then there were <u>three loud</u> knocks at the street door." (p. 191)

The compound adjective <u>ready-moneyed</u> not only provides essential information, but it <u>also</u> helps create a colloquial, even jaunty, tone. In the second example, the information conveyed by the adjectives contributes to the ominous tone.

had been modestly and steadfastly traveling Zionward,[12] were struck with self-reproach at seeing themselves so suddenly outstripped in their career by this new-made convert. Tom was as rigid in religious as in money matters; he was a stern supervisor and censurer of his neighbors, and seemed to think every sin entered up to their account became a credit on his own side of the page. He even talked of the expediency of reviving the persecution of Quakers and Anabaptists. In a word, Tom's zeal became as notorious as his riches.

Still, in spite of all this strenuous attention to forms, Tom had a lurking dread that the Devil, after all, would have his due. That he might not be taken unawares, therefore, it is said he always carried a small Bible in his coat pocket. He had also a great folio Bible on his countinghouse desk, and would frequently be found reading it when people called on business; on such occasions he would lay his green spectacles in the book, to mark the place, while he turned round to drive some usurious bargain.

Some say that Tom grew a little crack-brained in his old days, and that fancying his end approaching, he had his horse newly shod, saddled and bridled, and buried with his feet uppermost; because he supposed that at the last day the world would be turned upside down, in which case he should find his horse standing ready for mounting, and he was determined at the worst to give his old friend a run for it. This, however, is probably a mere old wives' fable. If he really did take such a precaution, it was totally superfluous; at least so says the authentic old legend, which closes his story in the following manner.

One hot summer afternoon in the dog days, just as a terrible black thunder-gust was coming up, Tom sat in his countinghouse in his white linen cap and India silk morning gown. He was on the point of foreclosing a mortgage, by which he would complete the ruin of an unlucky land speculator

12. **Zionward** (zī' ən wôrd): Toward heaven.

for whom he had professed the greatest friendship. The poor land jobber begged him to grant a few months' indulgence. Tom had grown testy and irritated, and refused another day.

"My family will be ruined and brought upon the parish," said the land jobber. "Charity begins at home," replied Tom; "I must take care of myself in these hard times."

"You have made so much money out of me," said the speculator.

Tom lost his patience and his piety—"The Devil take me," said he, "if I have made a farthing!"

Just then there were three loud knocks at the street door. He stepped out to see who was there. A black man was holding a black horse, which neighed and stamped with impatience.

"Tom, you're come for," said the black fellow, gruffly. Tom shrunk back, but too late. He had left his little Bible at the bottom of his coat pocket, and his big Bible on the desk buried under the mortgage he was about to foreclose: never was sinner taken more unawares. The black man whisked him like a child into the saddle, gave the horse the lash, and away he galloped, with Tom on his back, in the midst of the thunderstorm. The clerks stuck their pens behind their ears, and stared after him from the windows. Away went Tom Walker, dashing down the streets, his white cap bobbing up and down, his morning gown fluttering in the wind, and his steed striking fire out of the pavement at every bound. When the clerks turned to look for the black man he had disappeared.

Tom Walker never returned to foreclose the mortgage. A countryman who lived on the border of the swamp, reported that in the height of the thunder-gust he had heard a great clattering of hoofs and a howling along the road, and running to the window caught sight of a figure, such as I have described, on a horse that galloped like mad across the fields, over the hills and down into the black hemlock swamp towards the

The Devil and Tom Walker 191

Student Activity 1. Find three other examples of Irving's skillful use of adjectives, and for each explain how the adjective contributes to the narrative.

Student Activity 2. How would the devil look and behave today? Write a description of a contemporary devil using appropriate adjectives.

31 **Literary Focus** All folks tales have a moral, teach a lesson, or express a universal truth. What is the moral of this tale?

32 **Discussion** To whom in particular is the lesson of the tale addressed?

Reader's Response Which details made the story come to life for you? Explain.

old Indian fort; and that shortly after a thunderbolt falling in that direction seemed to set the whole forest in a blaze.

The good people of Boston shook their heads and shrugged their shoulders, but had been so much accustomed to witches and goblins and tricks of the Devil, in all kind of shapes from the first settlement of the colony, that they were not so much horror struck as might have been expected. Trustees were appointed to take charge of Tom's effects. There was nothing, however, to administer upon. On searching his coffers all his bonds and mortgages were found reduced to cinders. In place of gold and silver his iron chest was filled with chips and shavings; two skeletons lay in his stable

instead of his half-starved horses, and the very next day his great house took fire and was burned to the ground.

Such was the end of Tom Walker and his ill-gotten wealth. Let all griping money brokers lay this story to heart. The truth of it is not to be doubted. The very hole under the oak trees, whence he dug Kidd's money, is to be seen to this day; and the neighboring swamp and old Indian fort are often haunted in stormy nights by a figure on horseback, in morning gown and white cap, which is doubtless the troubled spirit of the usurer. In fact, the story has resolved itself into a proverb, and is the origin of that popular saying, so prevalent throughout New England, of "The Devil and Tom Walker."

THINKING ABOUT THE SELECTION

Recalling

1. Describe Tom Walker and his wife.
2. Describe Tom Walker's first encounter with the stranger in the forest.
3. (a) Why does Walker's wife decide to venture into the forest? (b) What does she bring with her?
4. (a) How does Tom Walker react when his wife does not return? (b) What does he discover when he sets out to find her?
5. (a) What arrangement does Walker finally make with the stranger? (b) What does Walker do when he begins to regret making this arrangement?
6. What happens to Tom Walker and his possessions in the end?

Interpreting

7. What does Irving's description of the Walkers' house and the surrounding land indicate about the kind of people they are?
8. What details indicate that while Tom Walker's condition changes during the story his nature remains the same?
9. (a) What does Irving mean when he says that Walker became "a *violent* churchgoer"? (b) How is the manner in which Walker approaches religion similar to the way he approaches his financial dealings?

Applying

10. Would this story be effective if it were set in contemporary America? Why or why not?

ANALYZING LITERATURE

Recognizing Folk Tales

Folk tales are stories passed down from generation to generation in a particular culture. These stories usually relate unlikely or unrealistic events, involve stereotypes or stock characters, and teach a lesson or express a general truth about life.

1. What trait does Tom Walker embody?
2. What trait does Tom Walker's wife embody?
3. What general truth about life does the story express?

CRITICAL THINKING AND READING

Inferring Cultural Attitudes

"The Devil and Tom Walker" reveals many of the attitudes of the people living in New England in the late 1720's and early 1730's. Because these attitudes are revealed indirectly, you must make inferences, or draw conclusions, about them by examining the evidence presented in the story. For example, when describing the old Indian fort Irving states that, "the stories handed down from the time of the Indian wars . . . asserted that the savages held incantations here, and made sacrifices to the evil spirit." From this passage you can infer that the colonists had a suspicious attitude toward the Native Americans and a firm belief in the devil.

What inferences about the cultural attitudes of the New Englanders of this period can you make from each of the following passages?

1. ". . . the great speculating fever which breaks out every now and then in the country had raged to an alarming degree, and everybody was dreaming of making sudden fortunes from nothing."
2. "The quiet Christians who had been moving modestly and steadfastly traveling Zionward were struck with self-reproach at seeing themselves so suddenly outstripped of their career by this new-made convert."

THINKING AND WRITING

Adapting a Folk Tale

In your library find a folk tale that interests you, perhaps the tale of John Henry, for example. In what ways would this tale be different if it were set in twentieth-century America? Think about how you can reshape the characters and events to make them fit into a contemporary setting. List the qualities that each character in your adaptation will embody, prepare an outline of events, and decide what lesson your tale will teach. When you write your tale, include details of the setting that will ground it in time and place. After you finish writing, revise your tale and prepare a final copy.

The Devil and Tom Walker 193

Interpreting

7. The description shows that the Walkers are too miserly and mean to care for their house and field or feed their horse.
8. Suggested Response: He builds a vast house, but leaves it mostly unfurnished. He almost starves his carriage horses and leaves the carriage wheels ungreased.
9. (a) He means that Tom became loud and strenuous in his observance, particularly in his clamorous repentance. (b) He becomes a stern supervisor of the spiritual accounts of his neighbors and is willing to persecute other sects, just as he harasses his debtors.

Applying

10. Suggested Response: Yes, because greed is still a destructive human character defect.

Challenge Do you think that stories in which the characters and events are exaggerated are as effective as stories that focus on a more realistic portrayal? Why or why not?

ANSWERS TO ANALYZING LITERATURE

1. Tom embodies the trait of greed.
2. Tom's wife embodies the trait of selfishness.
3. Suggested Response: It suggests that it does not pay to be greedy.

ANSWERS TO CRITICAL THINKING AND READING

1. Suggested Response: This suggests a change from the Puritan ethic of hard work and modest living to belief in the values of commercialism, large profits, and consumer expansionism.
2. Suggested Response: This suggests that people placed value on the amount of zeal with which others worshipped.

THINKING AND WRITING

Publishing Student Writing Encourage students to submit their adaptations to your school's literary magazine.

Closure and Extension

ANSWERS TO THINKING ABOUT THE SELECTION
Recalling

1. They are both miserly.
2. Tom learns that the stranger is the Devil. The Devil offers Tom the buried treasure of Captain Kidd in exchange for Walker's soul. Tom responds that he needs time to think about the conditions.
3. (a) Tom's wife decides to drive her own bargain and keep the treasure for herself. (b) She brings "the silver teapot and spoons, and every portable article of value."
4. (a) He grows anxious about her fate and that of his property. (b) He finds her apron tied in a bundle with only a heart and a liver inside.
5. (a) Tom agrees to sell his soul to the Devil and to use the treasure in the Devil's service. (b) He becomes a "violent churchgoer," a religious zealot, and he begins to read the Bible.
6. He is whisked away by the Devil during a thunderstorm, and his possessions are all reduced to cinders and shavings.

More About the Author Although Natty Bumppo, dies at the end of the novel, *The Prairie* was actually the third of the five novels that comprise the *Leatherstocking Tales*. The author began *The Prairie* before departing with his family for an extended stay in Europe. It was completed in Paris in 1826 and published in London the following year. Cooper continued writing prodigiously, but did not resurrect Natty until he responded to the repeated demands of his public more than a dozen years later. He then wrote *The Pathfinder* (1840), which depicts Leatherstocking shortly after the time of *The Last of the Mohicans* (1826); and *The Deerslayer* (1841), in which Natty is a very young man. Ask students whether they think that a writer or any other kind of artist should submit to the public's demands. If so, to what extent?

Critical Evaluation The critic Wayne Fields declared that Cooper was "full of uneasy alliances if not contradictions": "Criticized as incapable of creating believable characters, he created in Leatherstocking one of the most enduring figures in fiction. . . . He honored the genteel and yet, even in the salons of Europe, spun stories of adventure. . . . All these tensions, even the contradictions, should be familiar to us, for they are quint-essentially American. Cooper was, after all, the son of a man who cleared an estate from the New York wilderness and then imported European trees to line his drive. And so, as Americans, are we all."

JAMES FENIMORE COOPER

1789–1851

James Fenimore Cooper was the first successful American novelist. Although his novels were popular when they were published, their literary value was not recognized until decades after Cooper's death.

Cooper grew up on his family's large estate in Cooperstown, New York. When he was thirteen, he entered Yale, but he was expelled during his second year for repeated pranks. He worked for two years as a sailor on a merchant ship; then he joined the navy. Later, when his father died, Cooper left the navy and assumed the life of a gentleman farmer.

According to legend Cooper wrote his first novel after making a bet with his wife that he could write a better book than the British novel he had been reading to her. The novel he wrote, *Precaution* (1820), was actually no better than the one he had been reading, but Cooper developed an interest in writing that led him to write many other successful novels. In fact, his second book, *The Spy* (1821), a historical novel set during the Revolution, was extremely popular and earned critical acclaim.

In 1823 Cooper published *The Pioneers,* the first of five related novels collectively known as *The Leatherstocking Tales.* These novels—*The Deerslayer, The Last of the Mohicans, The Pathfinder, The Pioneers,* and *The Prairie*—portray the life of Natty Bumppo, an American frontiersman who spends his life moving westward as American civilization expands and the wilderness disappears.

During the course of his literary career, Cooper wrote thirty-two novels and a number of nonfiction books. Though readers throughout Europe and the United States responded with enthusiasm to *The Leatherstocking Tales* and many of Cooper's other novels, Cooper's characters and his books were often attacked by the press of his day.

Throughout his life Cooper wrote to develop the unique cultural identity of the United States, apart from European dominance. With his novels he helped create a distinctly American literature, one that used American settings, characters, and themes. "The literature of the United States is a subject of the highest interest to the civilized world," he wrote in 1828; "for when it does begin to be felt, it will be felt with a force, a directness, and a common sense in its application, that has never yet been known. . . . I think the time for the experiment is getting near. . . ."

Following Cooper's death in 1851, his novels came to be thought of as appropriate reading only for schoolchildren. In the 1920's, however, scholars began to reassess Cooper's work and came to regard Cooper as America's first social critic and one of the first writers to explore enduring themes in American literature.

194   A Growing Nation

GUIDE FOR INTERPRETING

from The Prairie

Writer's Techniques

Setting. Setting is the time, environment, and conditions in which the events in a work of literature occur. Though it is rarely the most important element of a literary work, the setting may directly or indirectly affect the characters and events and may be related to the theme, or central idea. Just as real people are often shaped by their environment, characters are often shaped by the setting. As a result, in many literary works, your understanding of the characters' values, attitudes, and behavior depends to some extent on your awareness of the setting. By affecting the characters' behavior, the setting also influences the events in a work. In fact, in some cases, the events are a direct result of the characters' interaction with the setting. The setting may also be closely related to the theme of a work. For example, the theme of a story about a man stranded in the mountains, struggling to survive, might concern the powerlessness of man when confronted with the forces of nature.

Throughout James Fenimore Cooper's *Leatherstocking Tales,* the setting plays a vital role. The novels portray the life of Natty Bumppo, a character molded by the wilderness. During Bumppo's lifetime the American wilderness is being eroded by the westward expansion of civilization. As a result, Bumppo finds himself continually moving westward—from western New York, where he spends his youth, to the midwestern prairies, where he spends his final years—to escape the growth of society. Set on the fringes of the constantly moving frontier, the novels explore the effects of expansion on the American wilderness and people.

Writing

Brainstorm and list the events, characters, and descriptive details that you associate with the expanding American frontier. Before reading, share your list with your classmates.

Primary Source

In his preface to *The Leatherstocking Tales,* Cooper commented on the character of Natty Bumppo. "The author has often been asked if he had any original in his mind, for the character of Leather-Stocking . . . . in a moral sense this man of the forest is purely creation. The idea of delineating a character that possessed little of civilization but its highest principles as they are exhibited in the uneducated, and all of savage life that is not incompatible with these great rules of conduct, is perhaps natural to the situation in which Natty was placed . . . . it appeared to the writer that his hero was a fit subject to represent the better qualities of both conditions, without pushing either to extremes."

Guide for Interpreting   195

Motivation/Prior Knowledge
Ask your students to imagine that they are members of a Native American tribe. How would they feel about the arrival of settlers? Would they make friends with them or try to keep them out? What do they know of the actual effects of westward expansion on the various Indian nations?

Master Teacher Note Display photos and drawings of several extinct or endangered species. For example you might choose the passenger pigeon, the golden condor, and the North American wolf. Lead students into a discussion of the drawbacks of "progress." In doing so, you might discuss such issues as the effects of urbanization, environmental pollution, and the loss of traditional values.

Thematic Idea Another selection that deals with the theme of death is "Thanatopsis" by William Cullen Bryant (p. 207).

Purpose-Setting Question How are the cultures of the Native Americans and the settlers united in the character of Natty Bumppo?

1 **Discussion** What cultural attitude can be inferred from these lines?

2 **Critical Thinking and Reading** Does the reaction of Middleton and his party tell you anything about the overall relations between the Indians and the settlers?

3 **Discussion** What does this passage reveal about the kind of life that the old man has led?

from # The Prairie

James Fenimore Cooper

In the following excerpt, Natty Bumppo is close to death. He is visited by Duncan Uncas Middleton, an army officer whose life Bumppo had saved a year earlier, and Middleton's scouting party. Bumppo has been living with the tribe of Hard-Heart, a young Pawnee chief, whom Bumppo had adopted as a son. As Bumppo's death approaches, both the Indians and the white men are deeply saddened.

When they entered the town, its inhabitants were seen collected in an open space, where they were arranged with the customary deference to age and rank. The whole formed a large circle, in the center of which were perhaps a dozen of the principal chiefs. Hard-Heart waved his hand as he approached, and as the mass of bodies opened he rode through, followed by his companions. Here they dismounted; and as the beasts were led apart, the strangers found themselves environed by a thousand grave, composed, but solicitous faces.

Middleton gazed about him in growing concern, for no cry, no song, no shout welcomed him among a people from whom he had so lately parted with regret. His uneasiness, not to say apprehensions, was shared by all his followers. Determination and stern resolution began to assume the place of anxiety in every eye, as each man silently felt for his arms, and assured himself that his several weapons were in a state for service. But there was no answering symptom of hostility on the part of their hosts. Hard-Heart beckoned for Middleton and Paul[1] to follow, leading the way towards the cluster of forms that occupied the center of the circle. Here the visitors found a solution of all the movements which had given them so much reason for apprehension.

The trapper[2] was placed on a rude seat, which had been made, with studied care, to support his frame in an upright and easy attitude. The first glance of the eye told his former friends that the old man was at length called upon to pay the last tribute of nature. His eye was glazed and apparently as devoid of sight as of expression. His features were a little more sunken and strongly marked than formerly; but there, all change, so far as exterior was concerned, might be said to have ceased. His approaching end was not to be ascribed to any positive disease, but had been a gradual and mild decay of the physical powers. Life, it is true, still lingered in his system; but it was as if at times entirely ready to depart, and then it would appear to reanimate the sinking form, reluctant to give up the possession of a tenement[3] that had never been corrupted by vice or undermined by disease. It would have been no violent fancy to have imagined that the spirit fluttered about the placid lips of the old woodsman, reluctant to depart from a shell that had so long given it an honest and an honorable shelter.

His body was placed so as to let the light of the setting sun fall full upon the solemn features. His head was bare, the long, thin locks of gray fluttering lightly in the evening breeze. His rifle lay upon his knee, and the

---
1. **Paul:** Paul Hover, a young pioneer.

---
2. **The trapper:** Natty Bumppo.
3. **tenement** (ten′ ə mənt) *n.*: Here, body.

other accouterments of the chase were placed at his side, within reach of his hand. Between his feet lay the figure of a hound, with its head crouching to the earth, as if it slumbered; and so perfectly easy and natural was its position, that a second glance was necessary to tell Middleton he saw only the skin of Hector, stuffed, by Indian tenderness and ingenuity, in a manner to represent the living animal. His own dog was playing at a distance with the child of Tachechana and Mahtoree.[4] The mother herself stood at hand, holding in her arms a second offspring, that might boast of a parentage no less honorable than that which belonged to the son of Hard-Heart. Le Balafré[5] was seated nigh the dying trapper, with every mark about his person that the hour of his own departure was not far distant. The rest of those immediately in the center were aged men who had apparently drawn near in order to observe the manner in which a just and fearless warrior would depart on the greatest of his journeys.

The old man was reaping the rewards of a life remarkable for temperance and activity, in a tranquil and placid death. His vigor in a manner endured to the very last. Decay, when it did occur, was rapid, but free from pain. He had hunted with the tribe in the spring, and even throughout most of the summer, when his limbs suddenly refused to perform their customary offices. A sympathizing weakness took possession of all his faculties; and the Pawnees believed that they were going to lose, in this unexpected manner, a sage and counselor whom they had begun both to love and respect. But, as we have already said, the immortal occupant seemed unwilling to desert its tenement. The lamp of life flickered without becoming extinguished. On the morning of the day on which Middleton arrived, there was a general

reviving of the powers of the whole man. His tongue was again heard in wholesome maxims, and his eye from time to time recognized the persons of his friends. It merely proved to be a brief and final intercourse with the world on the part of one who had already been considered, as to mental communion, to have taken his leave of it forever.

When he had placed his guests in front of the dying man, Hard-Heart, after a pause, that proceeded as much from sorrow as decorum, leaned a little forward and demanded:

"Does my father hear the words of his son?"

"Speak," returned the trapper, in tones that issued from his chest, but which were rendered awfully distinct by the stillness that reigned in the place. "I am about to depart from the village of the Loups,[6] and shortly shall be beyond the reach of your voice."

"Let the wise chief have no cares for his journey," continued Hard-Heart with an earnest solicitude that led him to forget, for the moment, that others were waiting to address his adopted parent; "a hundred Loups shall clear his path from briars."

"Pawnee, I die as I have lived, a Christian man," resumed the trapper with a force of voice that had the same startling effect upon his hearers as is produced by the trumpet when its blast rises suddenly and freely on the air after its obstructed sounds have been heard struggling in the distance; "as I came into life so will I leave it. Horses and arms are not needed to stand in the presence of the Great Spirit of my people. He knows my color, and according to my gifts will he judge my deeds."

"My father will tell my young men how many Mingoes[7] he has struck, and what acts of valor and justice he has done, that they may know how to imitate him."

---

4. Tachechana and Mahtoree: Two Sioux Indians. During a battle between the Pawnees and the Sioux, Hard-Heart had killed Mahtoree and taken Mahtoree's widow, Tachechana, as his wife.
5. Le Balafré: An aging Pawnee chief.

---

6. Loups: A Pawnee tribe.
7. Mingoes: Enemy warriors.

4 **Enrichment** Taxidermy, the art of stuffing and preserving animal skins, was widely practiced among Indian tribes. It was one of many crafts the settlers learned from them.

5 **Clarification** *Temperance* refers to moderation or restraint in action, thought, and feeling, especially in the indulgence of appetites and passions.

6 **Discussion** Natty adopted the young chief, Hard-Heart, as his son, and assumed the life style and customs of the Pawnees. Has he also adopted their beliefs about an afterlife? What differences between the Christian and Native American beliefs are suggested in this section?

"A boastful tongue is not heard in the heaven of a white man!" solemnly returned the old man. "What I have done He has seen. His eyes are always open. That which has been well done will he remember; wherein I have been wrong will he not forget to chastise, though he will do the same in mercy. No, my son; a paleface may not sing his own praises and hope to have them acceptable before his God!"

A little disappointed, the young partisan stepped modestly back, making way for the recent comers to approach. Middleton took one of the meager hands of the trapper, and, struggling to command his voice, he succeeded in announcing his presence. The old

THE DEATH OF LEATHERSTOCKING
Felix O. C. Darly
New York Public Library

Primary Source

Critic Donald A. Ringe commented on the importance of the setting in *The Prairie:*

> As in the previous books [of the Leatherstocking series], the relation of man to nature is fundamental to the tale, but the landscape is described as even more vast and sublime so that the characters seem all but completely dwarfed and overpowered by the immensity of grass and sky that stretches in every direction. Cooper had never seen the plains. He relied on books to give him the sense of a scene he did not personally know, and the authenticity of his description has been questioned. But authentic or not, the setting of *The Prairie* serves the perfect aesthetic function in the book. Unlike *The Pioneers, The Prairie* depicts a world that man cannot pretend to master, for it is completely beyond his control; and unlike *The Last of the Mohicans,* it presents a gaunt, bare, hostile nature that leaves man naked to the elements. It is clearly a harsher world than that of the two previous volumes in the series.

man listened like one whose thoughts were dwelling on a very different subject; but when the other had succeeded in making him understand that he was present, an expression of joyful recognition passed over his faded features.

"I hope you have not so soon forgotten those whom you so materially served!" Middleton concluded. "It would pain me to think my hold on your memory was so light."

"Little that I have ever seen is forgotten," returned the trapper; "I am at the close of many weary days, but there is not one among them all that I could wish to overlook. I remember you with the whole of your company; aye, and your gran'ther that went before you. I am glad that you have come back upon these plains, for I had need of one who speaks the English, since little faith can be put in the traders of these regions. Will you do a favor to an old and dying man?"

"Name it," said Middleton; "it shall be done."

"It is a far journey to send such trifles," resumed the old man, who spoke at short intervals, as strength and breath permitted; "a far and weary journey is the same; but kindnesses and friendships are things not to be forgotten. There is a settlement among the Otsego hills—"

"I know the place," interrupted Middleton, observing that he spoke with increasing difficulty; "proceed to tell me what you would have done."

"Take this rifle and pouch and horn, and send them to the person whose name is graven on the plates of the stock—a trader cut the letters with his knife—for it is long that I have intended to send him such a token of my love."

"It shall be so. Is there more that you could wish?"

"Little else have I to bestow. My traps I give to my Indian son; for honestly and kindly has he kept his faith. Let him stand before me."

Middleton explained to the chief what the trapper had said, and relinquished his own place to the other.

"Pawnee," continued the old man, always changing his language to suit the person he addressed, and not unfrequently according to the ideas he expressed, "it is a custom of my people for the father to leave his blessing with the son before he shuts his eyes forever. This blessing I give to you; take it, for the prayers of a Christian man will never make the path of a just warrior to the blessed prai-

from *The Prairie* 199

7 **Reading Strategy** Have students summarize the story up to this point.

8 **Enrichment** In 1790, when the author was a year old, his family moved to a new home in Cooperstown, New York, at the southern tip of Lake Otsego. A year later this area, much of which was owned by Cooper's father, Judge William Cooper, was made Otsego county.

9 **Clarification** Point out to your students that at the time of the story the pouch and horn were necessary equipment for firearms: the pouch kept the gunpowder dry, and the horn was used to funnel it into the flintlock.

10 **Master Teacher Note** Challenge your students to find out whose name is "graven on the plates" of the old man's rifle stock. Tell them to look for the answer in previous chapters of *The Prairie* or in the earlier books of the *Leatherstocking Tales*.

11 **Discussion** Does Bumppo have any regrets about his relationship with the Pawnees? Explain.

12 **Discussion** Is it surprising that Natty asks that his dog be buried with him?

13 **Clarification** Natty has repeatedly been referred to as a trapper in the selection. Here he refers to himself as a hunter. In the previous novels, he *was* a hunter, but in *The Prairie*, he has become a trapper because of his extreme age. By the time of his death he is almost ninety.

14 **Discussion** What images and words suggest that the speaker belongs to two different cultures, the white man's and the Indian's?

ries either longer or more tangled. May the God of a white man look on your deeds with friendly eyes, and may you never commit an act that shall cause him to darken his face. I know not whether we shall ever meet again. There are many traditions concerning the place of Good Spirits. It is not for one like me, old and experienced though I am, to set up my opinions against a nation's. You believe in the blessed prairies, and I have faith in the sayings of my fathers. If both are true, our parting will be final; but if it should prove that the same meaning is hid under different words, we shall yet stand together, Pawnee, before the face of your Wahcondah, who will then be no other than my God. There is much to be said in favor of both religions, for each seems suited to its own people, and no doubt it was so intended. I fear I have not altogether followed the gifts of my color, inasmuch as I find it a little painful to give up forever the use of the rifle and the comforts of the chase. But then the fault has been my own, seeing that it could not have been His. Aye, Hector," he continued, leaning forward a little, and feeling for the ears of the hound, "our parting has come at last, dog, and it will be a long hunt. You have been an honest, and a bold, and a faithful hound. Pawnee, you cannot slay the pup on my grave, for where a Christian dog falls, there he lies forever; but you can be kind to him after I am gone, for the love you bear his master."

"The words of my father are in my ears," returned the young partisan, making a grave and respectful gesture of assent.

"Do you hear, what the chief has promised, dog?" demanded the trapper, making an effort to attract the notice of the insensible effigy of his hound. Receiving no answering look, nor hearing any friendly whine, the old man felt for the mouth and endeavored to force his hand between the cold lips. The truth then flashed upon him, although he was far from perceiving the whole extent of the deception. Falling back in his seat, he hung his head, like one who felt a severe and unexpected shock. Profiting by this momentary forgetfulness, two young Indians removed the skin with the same delicacy of feeling that had induced them to attempt the pious[8] fraud.

"The dog is dead!" muttered the trapper, after a pause of many minutes; "a hound has his time as well as a man; and well has he filled his days! Captain," he added, making an effort to wave his hand for Middleton, "I am glad you have come; for though kind and well-meaning according to the gifts of their color, these Indians are not the men to lay the head of a white man in his grave. I have been thinking, too, of this dog at my feet; it will not do to set forth the opinion that a Christian can expect to meet his hound again; still there can be little harm in placing what is left of so faithful a servant nigh the bones of his master."

"It shall be as you desire."

"I'm glad you think with me in this matter. In order then to save labor, lay the pup at my feet; or for that matter, put him side by side. A hunter need never be ashamed to be found in company with his dog!"

"I charge myself with your wish."

The old man made a long and apparently a musing pause. At times he raised his eyes wistfully, as if he would again address Middleton, but some innate feeling appeared always to suppress his words. The other, who observed his hesitation, enquired in a way most likely to encourage him to proceed whether there was aught else that he could wish to have done.

"I am without kith or kin in the wide world!" the trapper answered; "when I am gone, there will be an end of my race. We have never been chiefs; but honest, and useful in our way. I hope it cannot be denied, we have always proved ourselves. My father lies buried near the sea, and the bones of his son will whiten on the prairies—"

---

8. pious (pī′ əs) *adj.*: Dutiful.

Grammar in Action

The **exclamation mark** should be used to end an exclamatory sentence, a forceful imperative, or an interjection expressing strong emotion. The following examples show the correct use of the exclamation mark for these purposes:

EXCLAMATORY SENTENCE: The sunrise was superb!

IMPERATIVE SENTENCE: Don't try that trick on me!

INTERJECTION: Oh no! I thought the monster was dead!

Cooper makes use of exclamation marks in *The Prairie*:

"'The dog is dead!' muttered the trapper, after a pause of many minutes; 'a hound has his time as well as a man; and well has he filled his days!'" (p. 200)

"'I! no, no, I have no son, . . . No, no, the gun must be sent to him whose name is graven on the lock!'" (p. 201)

The first sentence is an interjection emphasizing Bumppo's surprise that his dog is dead. Once he has thought about the dog's death, however, Bumppo makes his exclamatory judgment of the dog's performance. In the second example, "'I!'" is an interjection while the second sentence is an imperative, or command.

"Name the spot, and your remains shall be placed by the side of your father," interrupted Middleton.

"Not so, not so, Captain. Let me sleep, where I have lived, beyond the din of the settlements! Still I see no need why the grave of an honest man should be hid, like a redskin in his ambushment. I paid a man in the settlements to make and put a graven stone at the head of my father's resting place. It was of the value of twelve beaver skins, and cunningly and curiously was it carved! Then it told to all comers that the body of such a Christian lay beneath; and it spoke of his manner of life, of his years, and of his honesty. When we had done with the Frenchers in the old war[9] I made a journey to the spot, in order to see that all was rightly performed, and glad I am to say, the workman had not forgotten his faith."

"And such a stone you would have at your grave?"

"I! no, no, I have no son, but Hard-Heart, and it is little that an Indian knows of white fashions and usages. Besides I am his debtor, already, seeing it is so little I have done since I have lived in his tribe. The rifle might bring the value of such a thing—but then I know it will give the boy pleasure to hang the piece in his hall, for many is the deer and the bird that he has seen it destroy. No, no, the gun must be sent to him whose name is graven on the lock!"

"But there is one who would gladly prove his affection in the way you wish; he who owes you not only his own deliverance from so many dangers, but who inherits a heavy debt of gratitude from his ancestors. The stone shall be put at the head of your grave."

The old man extended his emaciated hand, and gave the other a squeeze of thanks.

"I thought you might be willing to do it, but I was backward in asking the favor," he

---

9. **the old war:** The French and Indian War (1754–1763).

said, "seeing that you are not of my kin. Put no boastful words on the same, but just the name, the age, and the time of the death, with something from the Holy Book; no more, no more. My name will then not be altogether lost on 'arth; I need no more."

Middleton intimated his assent, and then followed a pause that was only broken by distant and broken sentences from the dying man. He appeared now to have closed his accounts with the world, and to await merely for the final summons to quit it. Middleton and Hard-Heart placed themselves on the opposite sides of his seat, and watched with melancholy solicitude the variations of his countenance. For two hours there was no very sensible alteration. The expression of his faded and timeworn features was that of a calm and dignified repose. From time to time he spoke, uttering some brief sentence in the way of advice, or asking some simple questions concerning those in whose fortunes he still took a friendly interest. During the whole of that solemn and anxious period each individual of the tribe kept his place, in the most self-restrained patience. When the old man spoke, all bent their heads to listen; and when his words were uttered, they seemed to ponder on their wisdom and usefulness.

As the flame drew nigher to the socket, his voice was hushed, and there were moments when his attendants doubted whether he still belonged to the living. Middleton, who watched each wavering expression of his weather-beaten visage with the interest of a keen observer of human nature, softened by the tenderness of personal regard, fancied he could read the workings of the old man's soul in the strong lineaments of his countenance. Perhaps what the enlightened soldier took for the delusion of mistaken opinion did actually occur—for who has returned from that unknown world to explain by what forms, and in what manner, he was introduced into its awful precincts? Without pretending to explain what

from The Prairie 201

15 **Literary Focus** How does the image of the "din of the settlements" contrast with the "peaceful" prairie? How does it express the main purpose of Natty's life?

16 **Clarification** A beaver skin would have been worth about twenty gold dollars in Natty's day, a fairly large sum of money at the time.

17 **Discussions** What indications are there in this passage that Natty has accepted his fate?

18 **Discussion** To what "world" is the narrator referring?

Student Activity 1. Find three other passages in which Cooper uses the exclamation mark. Classify each example as an exclamatory sentence, an imperative sentence, or an interjection.

Student Activity 2. Explain why Cooper uses the exclamation mark so frequently in this particular scene.

Enrichment The critic Donald Ringe declared that Natty Bumppo "dies physically defeated; but intellectually and morally he still maintains his deeply felt philosophy. That the attitude toward the universe which the trapper affirms ought to animate the lives of those who follow him is clearly the meaning of the three books [of the Leatherstocking series]. That human nature being what it is, men will not follow his moral path is equally certain. If they do not, however, men face a serious question of whether or not a free society can survive on a selfishly despoiled and wasted continent."

Ask students how Bumppo would feel about present-day America. Would he lament the end of the frontier? Would he see new and different types of frontiers? Would he work with environmentalists to preserve the remaining wilderness areas?

Reader's Response What would you have said to Bumppo if you had been present as he died?

must ever be a mystery to the quick, we shall simply relate facts as they occurred.

The trapper had remained nearly motionless for an hour. His eyes alone had occasionally opened and shut. When opened, his gaze seemed fastened on the clouds, which hung around the western horizon, reflecting the bright colors, and giving form and loveliness to the glorious tints of an American sunset. The hour—the calm beauty of the season—the occasion, all conspired to fill the spectators with solemn awe. Suddenly, while musing on the remarkable position in which he was placed, Middleton felt the hand which he held, grasp his own with incredible power, and the old man, supported on either side by his friends, rose upright to his feet. For a moment he looked about him, as if to invite all in presence to listen (the lingering remnant of human frailty), and then, with a fine military elevation of the head, and with a voice that might be heard in every part of that numerous assembly, he pronounced the word:

19 "Here!"

A movement so entirely unexpected, and the air of grandeur and humility which were so remarkably united in the mien of the trapper, together with the clear and uncommon force of his utterance, produced a short period of confusion in the faculties of all present. When Middleton and Hard-Heart, each of whom had involuntarily extended a hand to support the form of the old man, turned to him again, they found that the subject of their interest was removed forever beyond the necessity of their care. They mournfully placed the body in its seat, and Le Balafré arose to announce the termination of the scene to the tribe. The voice of the old Indian seemed a sort of echo from that invisible world to which the meek spirit of the trapper had just departed.

"A valiant, a just, and a wise warrior has gone on the path which will lead him to the blessed grounds of his people!" he said. "When the voice of the Wahcondah called him, he was ready to answer. Go, my children; remember the just chief of the pale-faces, and clear your own tracks from briars!"

The grave was made beneath the shade of some noble oaks. It has been carefully watched to the present hour by the Pawnees of the Loup, and is often shown to the traveler and the trader as a spot where a just white man sleeps. In due time the stone was placed at its head, with the simple inscription, which the trapper had himself requested. The only liberty, taken by Middleton, was to add, *"May no wanton hand ever disturb his remains!"* **20**

Commentary

Critics have identified Natty Bumppo as being one in a line of heroic figures who take their place beyond the limits of American literature.

Critic R. W. B. Lewis compared Natty Bumppo to the Biblical Adam—"at home only in the presence of nature and God, who is thrust by circumstances into an actual world and an actual age." He added, "The evolution of the hero as Adam in the fiction of the New World—an evolution which coincides precisely, as I believe, with the evolution of the hero of American fiction generally—begins rightly with Natty Bumppo."

D. H. Lawrence, a British writer and critic, said that the Leatherstocking books formed "a sort of American Odyssey, with Natty Bumppo for Odysseus."

Do you agree with these views of Natty Bumppo? Why or why not?

202 A Growing Nation

THINKING ABOUT THE SELECTION

Recalling

1. Why does Middleton grow concerned when he and his troops enter the Pawnee village?
2. In what condition does Middleton find Natty Bumppo?
3. (a) How does Bumppo respond when Hard-Heart suggests that Bumppo should "tell my young men how many Mingoes he has struck"? (b) How does Hard-Heart react to Bumppo's response?
4. (a) Who is the second person to address Bumppo? (b) What favor does Bumppo ask of this person?
5. (a) According to Bumppo what will happen when he dies? (b) Where does he ask to be buried? (c) What does Middleton promise to put at the head of Bumppo's grave?
6. (a) What is Bumppo's final word? (b) What words does Middleton add to the inscription on Bumppo's gravestone?

Interpreting

7. (a) What do Bumppo's comments about the Christian and Pawnee religions suggest about his character? (b) What differences between the two religions does Bumppo state?
8. How would you describe Bumppo's attitude concerning his death?
9. What is the significance of the fact that both Middleton and Hard-Heart are supporting Bumppo when he dies?

Applying

10. What does Natty Bumppo's life illustrate about relationships between different groups of people?

ANALYZING LITERATURE

Understanding Setting

The **setting** is the time and place in which the events in a work of literature occur. In *The Prairie* the setting is the fringe of the rapidly changing frontier. Setting may directly or indirectly affect the characters and events and may be related to the theme. For example, in Cooper's *Leatherstocking Tales,* there is an obvious relationship between the setting and the theme—that the wilderness provided Americans with an opportunity to free themselves from the restraints of society and live according to the laws of nature.

1. What evidence is there in this selection to indicate that Bumppo's values, attitudes, and behavior have been shaped by the wilderness?
2. What details of the setting are given toward the end of the selection? How are these details related to the events in the selection?

CRITICAL THINKING AND READING

Predicting Later Events

The Prairie is set in the midwestern plains, where Natty Bumppo has settled to escape from the growth of society. Only several years after his death, however, settlers would begin arriving in the area.

1. Considering their relationship with Bumppo, how do you think Hard-Heart and his tribe might react to the arrival of settlers?
2. In what ways might the arrival of settlers have changed the lives of Hard-Heart and the members of his tribe?

THINKING AND WRITING

Responding to Criticism

Commenting on Natty Bumppo's movement westward throughout the *Leatherstocking Tales,* a critic has remarked, "Natty runs from civilization yet opens up the path for civilization to follow." What evidence is there in the excerpt from *The Prairie* to support this statement? Review the excerpt, thinking about what it suggests about the ways in which Bumppo may have opened the path for civilization. Then write a short essay in which you use evidence from the excerpt to support the critic's statement. In your conclusion briefly discuss the irony of the fact that Bumppo dislikes civilization yet opens the way for its expansion. When you finish writing, revise your essay and prepare a final copy.

from *The Prairie* 203

disturb his remains!" are the words on Bumppo's gravestone.

Interpreting

7. (a) His comments suggest that he is tolerant about both religions and believes that each is suited to the needs of its people. (b) Bumppo states the differences in the two religions concerning a person's entry into the afterlife.
8. Bumppo willingly accepts his death.
9. It symbolizes the fact that Bumppo served as a link between the two cultures.

Applying

10. Suggested Response: Natty's life shows the need for understanding and cooperation between different peoples.

Challenge What seems to be Cooper's attitude concerning the destruction of the wilderness?

ANSWERS TO ANALYZING LITERATURE

1. Answers will differ. Students might mention his ability to accept death as a natural part of the cycle of life, his close relationship to both the Indians and the white men, and his request that "no boastful words" be placed on his gravestone.
2. The setting of the sun on the western horizon is described. This echoes both the death of Natty and the decay of the wilderness.

ANSWERS TO CRITICAL THINKING AND READING

1. Suggested Response: Because of Natty's influence, the Pawnees would probably try to keep peace with the settlers and to cooperate whenever possible.
2. Suggested Response: The Native Americans were probably forced from their land.

THINKING AND WRITING

For help with this assignment, students can refer to Lesson 15, "Writing a Critical Evaluation," in the Handbook of Writing About Literature.

Publishing Student Writing Ask the editor of the school newspaper to publish two or three of the best essays.

203

Closure and Extension
ANSWERS TO THINKING ABOUT THE SELECTION
Recalling

1. Middleton becomes concerned because the Indians do not greet him.
2. Natty is dying.
3. (a) He tells Hard-Heart that a boastful tongue will not be heard in "the heaven of a white man." (b) He is disappointed.

4. (a) The second person to address Bumppo is Middleton. (b) He asks Middleton to take his rifle, pouch, and horn to the person whose name is engraved on the rifle stock. He also asks that his dog be buried with him.
5. (a) He says that it will be the end of his race. (b) He asks to be buried on the prairie. (c) He promises to place a tombstone there.
6. (a) His final word is "Here!" (b) "May no wanton hand ever

1794–1878

During William Cullen Bryant's long life, America emerged from its infancy to become a large and powerful nation, and American literature blossomed, earning its place among the world's literature. As a journalist and political activist, Bryant fought to make sure that industrialization and rapid growth did not obscure the democratic values and principles upon which the country was built. As a poet Bryant helped to establish an American literary tradition by producing a number of poems that could be matched against the work of the European poets of his day.

Bryant, a descendant of idealistic Puritans, was born in a rural area in western Massachusetts. His father, a country doctor with a deep interest in nature, encouraged him to explore the surrounding wilderness. Bryant's father also taught his son Greek and Latin and urged him to become an avid reader. As a boy he read the work of eighteenth-century English poets, and during his teens he developed a strong interest in the work of the nineteenth-century English Romantic poets. Bryant began writing poetry at the age of nine, and at nineteen he wrote the first version of "Thanatopsis," his most famous poem. When "Thanatopsis" was published in the *North American Review* in 1817, it was greeted with great enthusiasm. In spite of the poem's success, however, Bryant decided to revise it several years later.

Finding that pursuing a full-time career as a poet was economically impossible, Bryant earned a law degree and practiced law for ten years, continuing to write poetry in his spare time. In 1825 Bryant moved to New York City and began a new career as a journalist. By 1829 he had become editor-in-chief and part owner of the New York *Evening Post,* one of the most highly regarded newspapers in the country. In this position Bryant became an influential and enthusiastic defender of human rights and personal freedoms. He supported such causes as women's rights, freedom of speech and religion, and the abolition of slavery.

Though Bryant did not produce a great quantity of poetry, he was the first American poet to win worldwide critical acclaim. Like the European poets of his day, Bryant explored the connection between nature and humanity in his poetry. His work played a major role in establishing the Romantic movement in American literature and influenced the next generation of American poets.

Objectives

1 To recognize blank verse in poetry
2 To recite a poem with expression
3 To write a poem using blank verse

GUIDE FOR INTERPRETING

Writer's Techniques

Thanatopsis

Blank Verse. Though "Thanatopsis" is not written in rhyme, its lines do have a regular rhythm, that is, a recurring pattern of stressed and unstressed syllables, known as meter. The basic unit of meter is the foot. Usually a *foot* consists of one stressed syllable and one or more unstressed syllables. The most frequently used foot in American and English verse is the *iamb,* which consists of one unstressed syllable followed by a stressed syllable. When the lines in a poem consist of five iambs, as in "Thanatopsis," the poem is written in iambic pentameter. Verse consisting of unrhymed lines of iambic pentameter is called *blank verse*. Below is an example of blank verse from "Thanatopsis." The unstressed syllables are marked with ˘; the stressed syllables with ´.

> Yet not to thine eternal resting place
> Shalt thou retire alone, nor couldst thou wish

Because it effectively re-creates the smooth natural flow of everyday speech in English, blank verse is one of the most common metrical patterns in American and English poetry. However, when poets use blank verse, they often introduce slight variations in the rhythm to avoid monotony.

Writing

What thoughts does nature bring to your mind? Freewrite about nature, considering the relationship between humanity and nature.

Primary Source

Bryant composed the first version of "Thanatopsis" when he was still a teenager. Years later, in 1855, he wrote the following letter in reply to an inquiry about the poem:

> I cannot give you any information of the occasion which suggested to my mind the idea of my poem "Thanatopsis." It was written when I was seventeen or eighteen years old—I have not now at hand the memorandums which would enable me to be precise—and I believe it was composed in my solitary ramblings in the woods. As it was first committed to paper, it began with the half line—"Yet a few days, and thee"—and ended with the beginning of another line with the words—"And make their bed with thee." The rest of the poem—the introduction and the close—was added some years afterward, in 1821, when I published a little collection of my poems at Cambridge.

Literary Focus In order to illustrate the characteristics of blank verse, help students compare the effects of a Shakespearean sonnet with any of the famous dramatic speeches from his plays. Use these selections to demonstrate how Shakespeare employed blank verse to denote "natural" speech, while retaining rhymed iambic pentameter to express heightened emotion.

Writing/Prior Knowledge Before having students complete the writing activity, encourage them to discuss times when they have been alone in a natural setting and have had special thoughts and feelings.

Vocabulary

Preteach the following vocabulary words:
eloquence (el' ə kwəns) *n.:* Persuasive power (l. 5)
sepulcher (sep''l kər) *n.:* Grave; tomb (l. 37)
pensive (pen' siv) *adj.:* Thinking deeply or seriously (l. 39)
venerable (ven' ər ə b'l) *adj.:* Worthy of respect or reverence (l. 40)
melancholy (mal' ən käl' ē) *adj.:* Gloomy (l. 43)

Spelling Tip Point out the ense spelling of the ending sound in eloquence

Humanities Note

Fine art, *Vernal Falls, Yosemite Valley*, by Thomas Moran. Moran (1837–1926) was an English-born American artist, associated with the Hudson River School of painters. He was apprenticed to a wood engraver in Philadelphia, and then, aided by his artist brother, Edward, he turned to painting. In 1862 he traveled to England, where he was captivated by the landscapes of J. M. W. Turner. He copied many of them and remained under their influence for the rest of his life. In 1871 he joined a government expedition to Yellowstone. Inspired by what he saw, Moran created many watercolors and oil paintings, expressing his awe at the riot of colors and grandeur of the sights he beheld.

Dramatic canvases such as *Vernal Falls, Yosemite Valley*, helped Moran achieve success. His recognition was both official and popular, and his work was an important influence in establishing the National Park System in this country. Moran's objective in this painting was not realism, but, rather, idealization. He uses nature as the basis from which to construct a picture of his own sentimental and awestruck feelings. The rich color and drama of this picture clearly demonstrate why his paintings were so popular.

Consider the following questions for discussion:

1. What do you think is the painter's attitude toward nature?
2. In what ways might this painting reflect Bryant's ideas in "Thanatopsis"?

VERNAL FALLS, YOSEMITE VALLEY
Thomas Moran
Three Lions

206   *A Growing Nation*

Primary Source Note

Charles H. Brown, Bryant's biographer, made the following comments on the composition of "Thanatopsis":

"Bryant himself on several occasions when he was asked about the poem said it was written when he was seventeen or eighteen. But he was in his sixties when he replied to the questions, and the circumstantial details had grown dim in his memory, as he once confessed: 'I cannot give you any information of the occasion which suggested to my mind the idea of my poem "Thanatopsis." It was written when I was seventeen or eighteen years old—I have not now at hand the memorandum which would enable me to be precise—and I believe it was composed in my solitary rambles in the woods. . . .' But there is conflicting documentary evidence . . . which lists the date of the poem as 1813. Thus, if one must speculate on the date of the poem, it might be well to trace the development of the young poet's ideas on death in the funerary verse he wrote in 1813 and 1814. This process leads to the conclusion that the poem was composed later than the date usually given and that it was the outgrowth of a real emotional upheaval.

Thanatopsis

William Cullen Bryant

> To him who in the love of Nature holds
> Communion with her visible forms, she speaks
> A various language; for his gayer hours
> She has a voice of gladness, and a smile
> 5 And eloquence of beauty, and she glides
> Into his darker musings, with a mild
> And healing sympathy, that steals away
> Their sharpness, ere[1] he is aware. When thoughts
> Of the last bitter hour come like a blight
> 10 Over thy spirit, and sad images
> Of the stern agony, and shroud, and pall,
> And breathless darkness, and the narrow house,[2]
> Make thee to shudder, and grow sick at heart—
> Go forth, under the open sky, and list
> 15 To Nature's teachings, while from all around—
> Earth and her waters, and the depths of air—
> Comes a still voice—Yet a few days, and thee
> The all-beholding sun shall see no more
> In all his course; nor yet in the cold ground,
> 20 Where thy pale form was laid, with many tears,
> Nor in the embrace of ocean, shall exist
> Thy image. Earth, that nourished thee, shall claim
> Thy growth, to be resolved to earth again,
> And, lost each human trace, surrendering up
> 25 Thine individual being, shalt thou go
> To mix forever with the elements,
> To be a brother to the insensible rock
> And to the sluggish clod, which the rude swain[3]
> Turns with his share,[4] and treads upon. The oak
> 30 Shall send his roots abroad, and pierce thy mold.
>
> Yet not to thine eternal resting place
> Shalt thou retire alone, nor couldst thou wish
> Couch[5] more magnificent. Thou shalt lie down
> With patriarchs of the infant world—with kings,
> 35 The powerful of the earth—the wise, the good,
> Fair forms, and hoary seers of ages past,
> All in one mighty sepulcher. The hills
> Rock-ribbed and ancient as the sun—the vales

---

1. **ere:** Before.
2. **narrow house:** coffin.
3. **swain:** A country youth.
4. **share:** Plowshare.
5. **couch:** Bed.

Presentation

Motivation/Prior Knowledge Have students consider the reasons why death is a common literary subject. Why are people so concerned with death?

Master Teacher Note To help set the mood for the poem, place Transparency 5, *White Mountains, New Hampshire* by Albert Bierstadt, on the overhead projector. What impression of nature does the painting convey?

Thematic Idea Another selection that deals with death is "The First Snowfall" by James Russell Lowell (p. 356).

Purpose-Setting Question What is the theme of Bryant's poem?

1 **Clarification** The title is a composite of the Greek words *thanatos*, which means "death," and *opsis*, which means "a vision."

2 **Literary Focus** Are all of the metric feet in this line iambic? How does the variation emphasize the imagery?

3 **Literary Focus** How is the rhythm varied in this line?

4 **Discussion** Who or what is a "hoary seer"?

"The view that Cullen was led to ponder upon death by his reading of the 'graveyard poets' is plausible, but it is just as likely that he was led to study them to find an answer to the questionings aroused in his own mind by his firsthand experience of death during the summer of 1813 [which saw the deaths of his grandfather and a friend's bride]."

5 Discussion What sound device does Bryant use here?

6 Discussion What is the meaning of lines 71–72?

7 Discussion What sound device is Bryant using here? What is the effect of his use of this device?

Enrichment Bryant wrote at least two versions of "Thanatopsis" between 1817 and 1821. The main problem he faced in revising the poem was writing an introduction and conclusion for the middle portion. In an earlier version of the introduction, he had an inner spirit (a "better genius") speak to the poet: "It was his better genius that was wont/ To steal upon the bard what time his steps/Sought the repose of nature, . . ." Then he revised these lines so that Nature herself speaks to the poet.

Reader's Response Did this poem make you see nature in a different way? Why or why not?

Stretching in pensive quietness between;
40 The venerable woods—rivers that move
In majesty, and the complaining brooks
That make the meadows green; and, poured round all,
Old Ocean's gray and melancholy waste—
Are but the solemn decorations all
45 Of the great tomb of man. The golden sun,
The planets, all the infinite host of heaven,
Are shining on the sad abodes of death,
Through the still lapse of ages. All that tread
The globe are but a handful to the tribes
50 That slumber in its bosom. Take the wings
Of morning,[6] pierce the Barcan[7] wilderness,
Or lose thyself in the continuous woods
Where rolls the Oregon,[8] and hears no sound,
Save his own dashings—yet the dead are there:
55 And millions in those solitudes, since first
The flight of years began, have laid them down
In their last sleep—the dead reign there alone.
So shalt thou rest, and what if thou withdraw
In silence from the living, and no friend
60 Take note of thy departure? All that breathe
Will share thy destiny. The gay will laugh
When thou art gone, the solemn brood of care
Plod on, and each one as before will chase
His favorite phantom; yet all these shall leave
65 Their mirth and their employments, and shall come
And make their bed with thee. As the long train
Of ages glide away, the sons of men,
The youth in life's green spring, and he who goes
In the full strength of years, matron and maid,
70 The speechless babe, and the gray-headed man—
Shall one by one be gathered to thy side,
By those, who in their turn shall follow them.

So live, that when thy summons comes to join
The innumerable caravan, which moves
75 To that mysterious realm, where each shall take
His chamber in the silent halls of death,
Thou go not, like the quarry-slave at night,
Scourged to his dungeon, but, sustained and soothed
By an unfaltering trust, approach thy grave,
80 Like one who wraps the drapery of his couch
About him, and lies down to pleasant dreams.

---

6. Take . . . morning: An allusion to Psalm 139:9.
7. Barcan (bär′ kən): Referring to Barca, a desert region in North Africa.
8. Oregon: A river flowing between Oregon and Washington, now known as the Columbia River.

THINKING ABOUT THE SELECTION

Recalling

1. (a) According to lines 1–3, to whom does nature speak? (b) In what language does nature speak?
2. According to lines 8–15, when should a person "Go forth, under the open sky, and list/To Nature's teachings"?
3. According to lines 22–30, what will eventually happen to you?
4. According to lines 60 and 61, who shares your destiny?
5. According to lines 78 and 79, by what should you be "sustained and soothed"?

Interpreting

6. (a) According to the speaker, how is nature related to human life? (b) How is nature related to death?
7. How is the attitude toward death expressed in the first part of the poem (lines 1–30) different from the attitude expressed in the second half (lines 31–81)?

Applying

8. Bryant's conservative Puritan ancestors believed that only a select few were predestined to go to Heaven. How would the message of this poem be different if it had been written by one of Bryant's ancestors?
9. The contemporary writer Edwin Way Teale has written, "In nature, there is less death and destruction than death and transmutation." First discuss the meaning of this quotation. Then explain how Teale's view of nature compares with Bryant's.

ANALYZING LITERATURE

Recognizing Blank Verse

Blank verse is composed of unrhymed lines of iambic pentameter. In iambic pentameter there are five feet, or beats, per line, and every second syllable is stressed. Below is an example of blank verse from "Thanatopsis."

Shall one by one be gathered to thy side,

By those, who in their turn shall follow them.

1. Find four more lines of blank verse in "Thanatopsis."
2. Find two lines in which the rhythm is varied. Is there any apparent reason why the rhythm is varied besides to break the monotony?

SPEAKING AND LISTENING

Reading with Expression

Recite "Thanatopsis" to your class, being aware of the poem's basic iambic rhythm and its variations. Try to recite the poem at a slow, steady pace, and pronounce each word clearly. Rather than pausing after each line, pause only where a pause is indicated by punctuation.

THINKING AND WRITING

Writing a Poem Using Blank Verse

Think of a natural scene that you could describe in a short poem using iambic pentameter. You might consider one of the following subjects: a waterfall cascading down a mountainside, large snowflakes drifting gently down onto a bed of decaying leaves, large waves crashing on the shore, or a scorching wind screaming across the desert. Once you have decided on your topic, compose a list of details that describe it. Arrange your details in a logical order. Then, using your list of details, compose a brief poem in iambic pentameter. You may vary your rhythm slightly to avoid monotony. When you finish writing, revise your poem and prepare a final copy.

Thanatopsis 209

EDGAR ALLAN POE

1809–1849

Throughout the years following Edgar Allan Poe's death, there have been disagreements among writers and critics concerning the quality of his work. In spite of these disagreements, Poe has remained the most influential and widely read American writer of his time.

Poe was born in Boston in 1809, the son of impoverished traveling actors. Shortly after Poe's birth, his father deserted the family. A year later, Poe's mother died. Young Edgar was taken in, though never formally adopted, by the family of John Allan, a wealthy Virginia merchant. The Allans provided for Poe's education, and in 1826 Poe entered the University of Virginia. However, when he contracted large gambling debts which his stepfather refused to pay, Poe was forced to leave the school.

In 1827, after joining the army under an assumed name, Poe published his first volume of poetry, *Tamerlane and Other Poems,* and in 1829 he published a second volume, *Al Aaraaf.* The following year Poe's stepfather helped him to win an appointment to the United States Military Academy at West Point. Poe was expelled for academic violations within a year, however, and his dismissal resulted in an irreparable break with his stepfather.

During the second half of his life, Poe pursued a literary career in New York, Richmond, Philadelphia, and Baltimore, barely supporting himself by writing and working as an editor for a number of magazines. After his third volume of poetry, *Poems* (1831), failed to bring him either money or acclaim, he turned from poetry to fiction and literary criticism. Five of his short stories were published in newspapers in 1832, and in 1838 he published his only novel, *The Narrative of Arthur Gordon Pym.* Though Poe's short stories gained him some recognition and his poem "The Raven" (1845) was greeted with enthusiasm, he was never able to escape from poverty. In 1849, two years after the death of his beloved wife Virginia, Poe died alone and unhappy.

In the years since his death, Poe's work has received much attention. Some writers and critics have harshly criticized Poe's writing. Others have praised his use of vivid imagery and sound effects and his exploration of altered mental states and the dark side of human nature. Despite Poe's uncertain status among writers and critics, however, his work has remained extremely popular among generations of American readers.

GUIDE FOR INTERPRETING

Writer's Techniques

The Fall of the House of Usher

The Single Effect. More than any other writer, Edgar Allan Poe is responsible for the emergence of the short story as a popular and respected literary form. Poe was the first writer to classify and define the short story as a distinct literary genre and argue that the short story deserved the same status as such other genres as the poem and the novel. In his definition, which first appeared in his review of Nathaniel Hawthorne's *Twice-Told Tales,* Poe asserted that a story should be constructed to achieve "a certain unique or single effect." Poe believed that every character, detail, and incident in a story should contribute to this effect, commenting that "in the whole composition there should be no word written, of which the tendency, direct or indirect, is not to the one preestablished design." Poe even stated that if a writer's "very initial sentence tend not to the outbringing of this effect, then he has failed in his first step."

Writing

What sorts of characters, events, and details make a book or movie terrifying? Brainstorm about terrifying books you have read or movies you have seen. Then compose a list of the characters, events, and details that contributed to the effect of these books or movies.

Primary Source

Poe restated his views about the single effect on more than one occasion. Describing the aims and methods of his writing in *The Philosophy of Composition,* he wrote,

> I prefer commencing with the consideration of an *effect.* Keeping originality *always* in view—for he is false to himself who ventures to dispense with so obvious and so easily attainable a source of interest—I say to myself, in the first place, "Of the innumerable effects, or impressions, of which the heart, the intellect, or (more generally) the soul is susceptible, what one shall I, on the present occasion, select?" Having chosen a novel, first, and secondly a vivid effect, I consider whether it can be best wrought by incident or tone—whether by ordinary incidents and peculiar tone, or the converse, or by peculiarity both of incident and tone—afterward looking about me (or rather within) for such combinations of event, or tone, as shall best aid me in the construction of the effect.

Literary Focus To illustrate the concept of the single effect, you might tell one or two humorous stories or jokes to your class. Point out that all the details, circumstances, and characters lead to the punch line, just as all the elements of Poe's tale lead inevitably to a single climax.

Writing/Prior Knowledge Have your **less advanced** students brainstorm in small groups.

Vocabulary

Preteach the following vocabulary words:
importunate (im pôr′ chə nit) *adj.:* Insistent (p. 212–214)
munificent (myoo nif′ ə s'nt) *adj.:* Generous (p. 214)
equivocal (i kwiv′ ə k'l) *adj.:* Having more than one possible interpretation (p. 214)
appellation (ap′ ə lā shən) *n.:* Name or title (p. 214)
paradoxical (par′ ə däks′ i k'l) *adj.:* Expressing an apparent contradiction (p. 214)
specious (spē′ shəs) *adj.:* Seeming to be good or sound without actually being so (p. 215)
anomalous (ə näm′ ə ləs) *adj.:* Abnormal (p. 216)
sentience (sen′ shəns) *n.:* Capacity of feeling (p. 219)

Spelling Tip Two words in this list, *specious* and *sentience,* have a sh sound in the middle. Point out that in *specious* the sound is spelled *ci,* and in *sentience* the sound is spelled *ti.*

Motivation/Prior Knowledge
Ask your students to imagine
they have been informed by a
close friend that he or she is ill or
in trouble. Would they try to help
their friend? Would they be willing to travel far to see the friend,
even if the circumstances were
unpleasant?

Master Teacher Note Few authors have had their works
adapted for the screen as frequently as Poe. Provide your
class with a list of some Poe
films, and ask students which
ones they have seen. If possible,
screen a portion of the 1966
American International film " The
Fall of the House of Usher." Ask
students why the Poe stories
translate so well to the screen.

Thematic Idea Another selection
that deals with supernatural destruction is "The Devil and Tom
Walker" by Washington Irving
(p. 184).

Purpose-Setting Question
What is the nature of Roderick
Usher's malady?

1 **Discussion** Why has Poe chosen to preface the story with this
French quotation? Do you think
he admired Béranger, a French
writer, who was still alive at the
time? Who in this story do you
think the quotation describes?
The narrator? Roderick Usher?
Both? Does it also refer to Poe's
own ideas about writing? If so,
how?

2 **Discussion** Why did Poe decide
to tell the story from a first-person
point of view?

3 **Clarification** The word *tarn* refers to a deep, steeply-banked
pool or lake.

4 **Enrichment** The use of *boon*
here is archaic. Its meaning is
derived from the French word
bon, which means "good."

The Fall of the House of Usher

Edgar Allan Poe

1

Son cœur est un luth suspendu;
Sitôt qu'on le touche il résonne.[1]

During the whole of a dull, dark, and
soundless day in the autumn of the year,
when the clouds hung oppressively low in
the heavens, I had been passing alone, on
horseback, through a singularly dreary tract
of country, and at length found myself, as
the shades of evening drew on, within view
of the melancholy House of Usher. I know
not how it was—but, with the first glimpse
of the building, a sense of insufferable gloom
pervaded my spirit. I say insufferable; for the

2 feeling was unrelieved by any of that half-
pleasurable, because poetic, sentiment, with
which the mind usually receives even the
sternest natural images of the desolate or
terrible. I looked upon the scene before me—
upon the mere house, and the simple landscape features of the domain—upon the

3 bleak walls—upon the vacant eyelike windows—upon a few rank sedges[2]—and upon a
few white trunks of decayed trees—with an
utter depression of soul, which I can compare to no earthly sensation more properly
than to the afterdream of the reveler upon
opium—the bitter lapse into everyday life—
the hideous dropping off of the veil. There
was an iciness, a sinking, a sickening of the
heart—an unredeemed dreariness of
thought which no goading of the imagina-

tion could torture into aught[3] of the sublime. What was it—I paused to think—what
was it that so unnerved me in the contemplation of the House of Usher? It was a mystery all insoluble; nor could I grapple with
the shadowy fancies that crowded upon me
as I pondered. I was forced to fall back upon
the unsatisfactory conclusion, that while,
beyond doubt, there *are* combinations of
very simple natural objects which have the
power of thus affecting us, still the analysis
of this power lies among considerations beyond our depth. It was possible, I reflected,
that a mere different arrangement of the particulars of the scene, of the details of the
picture, would be sufficient to modify, or
perhaps to annihilate its capacity for sorrowful impression; and, acting upon this idea, I
reined my horse to the precipitous brink of a
black and lurid tarn[4] that lay in unruffled
luster by the dwelling, and gazed down—but
with a shudder even more thrilling than before—upon the remodeled and inverted images of the gray sedge, and the ghastly tree
stems, and the vacant and eyelike windows.

Nevertheless, in this mansion of gloom I
now proposed to myself a sojourn of some
weeks. Its proprietor, Roderick Usher, had
been one of my boon companions in boyhood; but many years had elapsed since our
last meeting. A letter, however, had lately
reached me in a distant part of the country—
a letter from him—which, in its wildly im-

4

---

1. *Son . . . résonne:* "His heart is a suspended lute;
as one touches it, it resounds." From "Le Rufus" by
Pierre Jean de Béranger (1780–1857).
2. sedges (sej′ ez) *n.*: Grasslike plants.

---

3. aught (ôt): Anything.
4. tarn (tärn) *n.*: A small lake.

"I AT LENGTH . . . ," EDGAR ALLAN POE'S TALES OF MYSTERY AND IMAGINATION
Arthur Rackham
New York Public Library, Astor, Lenox and Tilden Foundations

The Fall of the House of Usher   213

Humanities Note

Fine art, *The Fall of the House of Usher* by Arthur Rackham. Arthur Rackham (1867–1936) was born in London. He became one of the best-known book and magazine illustrators. Some of his most famous works were his illustrations for *Grimm's Fairy Tales* (1900). His imaginative and fanciful style was ideally suited to whimsical, grotesque, and gruesome subjects. For example this illustration for *The Fall of the House of Usher* dramatically captures the mood of the story through the artist's use of form and color.

You might ask the following questions:

1. How does Rackham's rendition of this scene compare with the image Poe creates?
2. How has the artist used the elements of form and color to create the mood of the picture?

214

5 Discussion What revelation about the Ushers does the narrator make here? What is the effect of this revelation?

6 Literary Focus How do the narrator's observations in this passage help to create a growing sense of terror?

7 Clarification The word *recked* is here a variant of *reek*, which means "to issue or emanate from."

Master Teacher Note Point out to students the many ways in which the house is separated from the world. First of all, the narrator asserts that it is located in an isolated place. Second, the house gives off "a pestilent and mystic vapor" that further separates it from its surroundings. Finally, the narrator has to cross a causeway to reach the house. Ask students why Poe would want to continually emphasize the way in which the house is cut off from the environment.

portunate nature, had admitted of no other than a personal reply. The MS.[5] gave evidence of nervous agitation. The writer spoke of acute bodily illness—of a mental disorder which oppressed him—and of an earnest desire to see me, as his best and indeed his only personal friend, with a view of attempting, by the cheerfulness of my society, some alleviation of his malady. It was the manner in which all this, and much more, was said—it was the apparent *heart* that went with his request—which allowed me no room for hesitation; and I accordingly obeyed forthwith what I still considered a very singular summons.

Although, as boys, we had been even intimate associates, yet I really knew little of my friend. His reserve had been always excessive and habitual. I was aware, however, that his very ancient family had been noted, time out of mind, for a peculiar sensibility of temperament, displaying itself, through long ages, in many works of exalted art, and manifested, of late, in repeated deeds of munificent yet unobtrusive charity, as well as in a passionate devotion to the intricacies, perhaps even more than to the orthodox and easily recognizable beauties, of musical science. I had learned, too, the very remarkable fact, that the stem of the Usher race, all time-honored as it was, had put forth, at no period, any enduring branch; in other words, that the entire family lay in the direct line of descent, and had always, with very trifling and very temporary variations, so lain. It was this deficiency, I considered, while running over in thought the perfect keeping of the character of the premises with the accredited character of the people, and while speculating upon the possible influence which the one, in the long lapse of centuries, might have exercised upon the other—it was this deficiency, perhaps of collateral issue,[6] and the consequent undeviating transmission, from sire to son, of the

patrimony[7] with the name, which had, at length, so identified the two as to merge the original title of the estate in the quaint and equivocal appellation of the "House of Usher"—an appellation which seemed to include, in the minds of the peasantry who used it, both the family and the family mansion.

I have said that the sole effect of my somewhat childish experiment—that of looking down within the tarn—had been to deepen the first singular impression. There can be no doubt that the consciousness of the rapid increase of my superstition—for why should I not so term it?—served mainly to accelerate the increase itself. Such, I have long known, is the paradoxical law of all sentiments having terror as a basis. And it might have been for this reason only, that, when I again uplifted my eyes to the house itself, from its image in the pool, there grew in my mind a strange fancy—a fancy so ridiculous, indeed, that I but mention it to show the vivid force of the sensations which oppressed me. I had so worked upon my imagination as really to believe that about the whole mansion and domain there hung an atmosphere peculiar to themselves and their immediate vicinity—an atmosphere which had no affinity with the air of heaven, but which had reeked up from the decayed trees, and the gray wall, and the silent tarn—a pestilent and mystic vapor, dull, sluggish, faintly discernible and leaden-hued.

Shaking off from my spirit what *must* have been a dream, I scanned more narrowly the real aspect of the building. Its principal feature seemed to be that of an excessive antiquity. The discoloration of ages had been great. Minute fungi overspread the whole exterior, hanging in a fine tangled web-work from the eaves. Yet all this was apart from any extraordinary dilapidation. No portion of the masonry had fallen; and there appeared to be a wild inconsistency between its still perfect adaptation of parts, and the crum-

---

5. MS.: Manuscript.
6. collateral (kə lat′ ər əl) **issue** *adj.*: Descended from the same ancestors, but in a different line.

---

7. patrimony (pat′ rə mō′ nē) *n.*: Property inherited from one's father.

bling condition of the individual stones. In this there was much that reminded me of the specious totality of old woodwork which has rotted for long years in some neglected vault, with no disturbance from the breath of the external air. Beyond this indication of extensive decay, however, the fabric gave little token of instability. Perhaps the eye of a scrutinizing observer might have discovered a barely perceptible fissure, which, extending from the roof of the building in front, made its way down the wall in a zigzag direction, until it became lost in the sullen waters of the tarn.

Noticing these things, I rode over a short causeway to the house. A servant in waiting took my horse, and I entered the Gothic[8] archway of the hall. A valet, of stealthy step, then conducted me, in silence, through many dark and intricate passages in my progress to the *studio* of his master. Much that I encountered on the way contributed, I know not how, to heighten the vague sentiments of which I have already spoken. While the objects around me—while the carvings of the ceilings, the somber tapestries of the walls, the ebon blackness of the floors, and the phantasmagoric[9] armorial trophies which rattled as I strode, were but matters to which, or to such as which, I had been accustomed from my infancy—while I hesitated not to acknowledge how familiar was all this—I still wondered to find how unfamiliar were the fancies which ordinary images were stirring up. On one of the staircases, I met the physician of the family. His countenance, I thought, wore a mingled expression of low cunning and perplexity. He accosted me with trepidation and passed on. The valet now threw open a door and ushered me into the presence of his master.

The room in which I found myself was very large and lofty. The windows were long, narrow, and pointed, and at so vast a distance from the black oaken floor as to be al-together inaccessible from within. Feeble gleams of encrimsoned light made their way through the trellised panes, and served to render sufficiently distinct the more prominent objects around; the eye, however, struggled in vain to reach the remoter angles of the chamber, or the recesses of the vaulted and fretted[10] ceiling. Dark draperies hung upon the walls. The general furniture was profuse, comfortless, antique, and tattered. Many books and musical instruments lay scattered about, but failed to give any vitality to the scene. I felt that I breathed an atmosphere of sorrow. An air of stern, deep, and irredeemable gloom hung over and pervaded all.

Upon my entrance, Usher arose from a sofa on which he had been lying at full length, and greeted me with a vivacious warmth which had much in it, I at first thought, of an overdone cordiality—of the constrained effort of the *ennuyé*[11] man of the world. A glance, however, at his countenance convinced me of his perfect sincerity. We sat down; and for some moments, while he spoke not, I gazed upon him with a feeling half of pity, half of awe. Surely, man had never before so terribly altered, in so brief a period, as had Roderick Usher! It was with difficulty that I could bring myself to admit the identity of the wan being before me with the companion of my early boyhood. Yet the character of his face had been at all times remarkable. A cadaverousness of complexion; an eye large, liquid, and luminous beyond comparison; lips somewhat thin and very pallid, but of a surpassingly beautiful curve; a nose of a delicate Hebrew model, but with a breadth of nostril unusual in similar formations; a finely molded chin, speaking, in its want of prominence, of a want of moral energy; hair of a more than weblike softness and tenuity—these features, with an inordinate expansion above the regions of the temple, made up altogether a countenance not easily to be forgotten. And now in the mere

---

8. **Gothic:** High and ornate.
9. **phantasmagoric** (fan taz′ mə gôr′ ik) *adj.*: Fantastic or dreamlike.

10. **fretted:** Ornamented.
11. **ennuyé** (än′ wē ā′): Bored (French).

The Fall of the House of Usher 215

exaggeration of the prevailing character of these features, and of the expression they were wont to convey, lay so much of change that I doubted to whom I spoke. The now ghastly pallor of the skin, and the now miraculous luster of the eye, above all things startled and even awed me. The silken hair, too, had been suffered to grow all unheeded, and as, in its wild gossamer texture, it floated rather than fell about the face, I could not, even with effort, connect its Arabesque[12] expression with any idea of simple humanity.

In the manner of my friend I was at once struck with an incoherence—an inconsistency; and I soon found this to arise from a series of feeble and futile struggles to overcome an habitual trepidancy—an excessive nervous agitation. For something of this nature I had indeed been prepared, no less by his letter than by reminiscences of certain boyish traits, and by conclusions deduced from his peculiar physical conformation and temperament. His action was alternately vivacious and sullen. His voice varied rapidly from a tremulous indecision (when the animal spirits seemed utterly in abeyance) to that species of energetic concision—that abrupt, weighty, unhurried, and hollow-sounding enunciation—that leaden, self-balanced, and perfectly modulated guttural utterance, which may be observed in the lost drunkard, or the irreclaimable eater of opium, during the periods of his most intense excitement.

It was thus that he spoke of the object of my visit, of his earnest desire to see me, and of the solace he expected me to afford him. He entered, at some length, into what he conceived to be the nature of his malady. It was, he said, a constitutional and a family evil and one for which he despaired to find a remedy—a mere nervous affection,[13] he immediately added, which would undoubtedly soon pass off. It displayed itself in a host of unnatural sensations. Some of these, as he detailed them, interested and bewildered me; although, perhaps, the terms and the general manner of their narration had their weight. He suffered much from a morbid acuteness of the senses; the most insipid food was alone endurable; he could wear only garments of certain texture; the odors of all flowers were oppressive; his eyes were tortured by even a faint light; and there were but peculiar sounds, and these from stringed instruments, which did not inspire him with horror.

To an anomalous species of terror I found him a bounden slave. "I shall perish," said he, "I *must* perish in this deplorable folly. Thus, thus, and not otherwise, shall I be lost. I dread the events of the future, not in themselves, but in their results. I shudder at the thought of any, even the most trivial, incident, which may operate upon this intolerable agitation of soul. I have, indeed, no abhorrence of danger, except in its absolute effect—in terror. In this unnerved, in this pitiable, condition I feel that the period will sooner or later arrive when I must abandon life and reason together, in some struggle with the grim phantasm, FEAR."

I learned, moreover, at intervals, and through broken and equivocal hints, another singular feature of his mental condition. He was enchained by certain superstitious impressions in regard to the dwelling which he tenanted, and whence, for many years, he had never ventured forth—in regard to an influence whose supposititious[14] force was conveyed in terms too shadowy here to be restated—an influence which some peculiarities in the mere form and substance of his family mansion had, by dint of long sufferance, he said, obtained over his spirit—an effect which the physique of the gray walls and turrets, and of the dim tarn into which they all looked down, had at length, brought about upon the morale of his existence.

---

12. **Arabesque** (ar' ə besk') *n.*: Of complex and elaborate design.
13. **affection:** Affliction.

14. **supposititious** (sə päz' ə tish' əs) *adj.*: Supposed.

Grammar in Action

A good writer never shifts **verb tenses** unnecessarily. If a story or an essay is written in the past tense, for example, and we encounter another tense form, that tense shift is a signal that the writer is moving the account into a different time frame. "The Fall of the House of Usher" is written in past tense, but frequently Poe changes to the past perfect:

Roderick Usher *had been* one of my boon companions . . . (page 212)

A letter, however, *had* lately *reached* me . . . (page 212)

The disease of the lady Madeline *had* long *baffled* the skill of her physicians. (page 217)

By using the past perfect tense, Poe signals his reader that the action of these sentences has been completed (perfected) before the time described in the story.

Student Activity 1. Find ten occurrences of the past perfect tense in the pages of "The Fall of the House of Usher." In each case, identify the previous time to which Poe refers.

He admitted, however, although with hesitation, that much of the peculiar gloom which thus afflicted him could be traced to a more natural and far more palpable origin—to the severe and long-continued illness—indeed to the evidently approaching dissolution—of a tenderly beloved sister, his sole companion for long years, his last and only relative on earth. "Her decease," he said, with a bitterness which I can never forget, "would leave him (him, the hopeless and the frail) the last of the ancient race of the Ushers." While he spoke, the lady Madeline (for so was she called) passed through a remote portion of the apartment, and, without having noticed my presence, disappeared. I regarded her with an utter astonishment not unmingled with dread; and yet I found it impossible to account for such feelings. A sensation of stupor oppressed me as my eyes followed her retreating steps. When a door, at length, closed upon her, my glance sought instinctively and eagerly the countenance of the brother; but he had buried his face in his hands, and I could only perceive that a far more than ordinary wanness had overspread the emaciated fingers through which trickled many passionate tears.

The disease of the lady Madeline had long baffled the skill of her physicians. A settled apathy, a gradual wasting away of the person, and frequent although transient affections of a partially cataleptical[15] character were the unusual diagnosis. Hitherto she had steadily borne up against the pressure of her malady, and had not betaken herself finally to bed; but on the closing in of the evening of my arrival at the house, she succumbed (as her brother told me at night with inexpressible agitation) to the prostrating power of the destroyer; and I learned that the glimpse I had obtained of her person would thus probably be the last I should obtain—that the lady, at least while living, would be seen by me no more.

_____
15. cataleptical (kat' 'l ep' tik 'l) *adj.*: In a state in which consciousness and feeling are suddenly and temporarily lost and the muscles become rigid.

For several days ensuing, her name was unmentioned by either Usher or myself; and during this period I was busied in earnest endeavors to alleviate the melancholy of my friend. We painted and read together, or I listened, as if in a dream, to the wild improvisations of his speaking guitar. And thus, as a closer and still closer intimacy admitted me more unreservedly into the recesses of his spirit, the more bitterly did I perceive the futility of all attempt at cheering a mind from which darkness, as if an inherent positive quality, poured forth upon all objects of the moral and physical universe in one unceasing radiation of gloom.

I shall ever bear about me a memory of the many solemn hours I thus spent alone with the master of the House of Usher. Yet I should fail in any attempt to convey an idea of the exact character of the studies, or of the occupations, in which he involved me, or led me the way. An excited and highly distempered ideality[16] threw a sulfureous[17] luster over all. His long improvised dirges will ring forever in my ears. Among other things, I hold painfully in mind a certain singular perversion and amplification of the wild air of the last waltz of von Weber.[18] From the paintings over which his elaborate fancy brooded, and which grew, touch by touch, into vaguenesses at which I shuddered the more thrillingly, because I shuddered knowing not why—from these paintings (vivid as their images now are before me) I would in vain endeavor to educe more than a small portion which should lie within the compass of merely written words. By the utter simplicity, by the nakedness of his designs, he arrested and overawed attention. If ever mortal painted an idea, that mortal was Roderick Usher. For me at least, in the circumstances then surrounding me, there arose out of the pure abstractions which the hypochondriac contrived to throw upon his

_____
16. ideality (ī' dē al' ə tē) *n.*: Something that is ideal and has no reality.
17. sulfureous (sul fyoor' ē əs) *adj.*: Greenish-yellow.
18. von Weber: Karl Maria von Weber (1786–1826), a German Romantic composer.

The Fall of the House of Usher 217

15 **Literary Focus** Do you think it is merely coincidental that Madeline "succumbs" on the same night that Usher's friend arrives? Or do you think it is a literary contrivance to heighten the single effect?

16 **Discussion** What image used at the beginning of the story does image of "his speaking guitar" echoe?

17 **Master Teacher Note** Play a few recordings of von Weber's works (the very descriptive overtures from the operas *Oberon* and *Der Freischütz* would be good choices) or the works of other Romantic composers, such as Chopin and Liszt. Tell students that von Weber had a great influence on later Romantic composers, as Poe has had on other writers.

Student Activity 2. Combine each pair of sentences, changing the verb in the first to past perfect tense to indicate that the action in the first sentence occurred before that in the second.
1. Usher and the narrator were boyhood friends.
   Still, the narrator knew very little about Usher.
2. Age greatly discolored the mansion.
   Yet, the masonry remained intact.
3. Usher was lying on a sofa when his guest arrived.
   He arose and came to greet his friend.
4. The narrator obtained a glimpse of lady Madeline.
   The glimpse told him that she was very ill.
5. Usher's head fell to his chest.
   When the narrator looked up, he knew Usher was awake.

canvas, an intensity of intolerable awe, no shadow of which felt I ever yet in the contemplation of the certainly glowing yet too concrete reveries of Fuseli.[19]

One of the phantasmagoric conceptions of my friend, partaking not so rigidly of the spirit of abstraction, may be shadowed forth, although feebly, in words. A small picture presented the interior of an immensely long and rectangular vault or tunnel, with low walls, smooth, white and without interruption or device. Certain accessory points of the design served well to convey the idea that this excavation lay at an exceeding depth below the surface of the earth. No outlet was observed in any portion of its vast extent, and no torch or other artificial source of light was discernible; yet a flood of intense rays rolled throughout, and bathed the whole in a ghastly and inappropriate splendor.

I have just spoken of that morbid condition of the auditory nerve which rendered all music intolerable to the sufferer, with the exception of certain effects of stringed instruments. It was, perhaps, the narrow limits to which he thus confined himself upon the guitar which gave birth, in great measure, to the fantastic character of his performances. But the fervid facility of his impromptus could not be so accounted for. They must have been, and were, in the notes, as well as in the words of his wild fantasias (for he not unfrequently accompanied himself with rhymed verbal improvisations), the result of that intense mental collectedness and concentration to which I have previously alluded as observable only in particular moments of the highest artificial excitement. The words of one of these rhapsodies I have easily remembered. I was, perhaps, the more forcibly impressed with it as he gave it because, in the under or mystic current of its meaning, I fancied that I perceived, and for the first time, a full

consciousness on the part of Usher of the tottering of his lofty reason upon her throne. The verses, which were entitled "The Haunted Palace," ran very nearly, if not accurately, thus:

I

In the greenest of our valleys,
By good angels tenanted,
Once a fair and stately palace—
Radiant palace—reared its head.
In the monarch Thought's dominion—
It stood there!
Never seraph[20] spread a pinion
Over fabric half so fair.

II

Banners yellow, glorious, golden,
On its roof did float and flow
(This—all this—was in the olden
Time long ago)
And every gentle air that dallied,
In that sweet day,
Along the ramparts plumed and
pallid,
A winged odor went away.

III

Wanderers in that happy valley
Through two luminous windows saw
Spirits moving musically
To a lute's well-tunèd law;
Round about a throne, where sitting
(Porphyrogene!)[21]
In state his glory well befitting,
The ruler of the realm was seen.

IV

And all with pearl and ruby glowing
Was the fair palace door,
Through which came flowing, flowing,
flowing
And sparkling evermore,

---

19. Fuseli: Johann Heinrich Fuseli (1742–1825), a Swiss-born painter who lived in England and was noted for his work in the supernatural.

20. seraph (ser' əf): Angel.
21. Porphyrogene (pôr fər ō jēn'): Born to royalty or "the purple."

A troop of Echoes whose sweet duty
 Was but to sing,
In voices of surpassing beauty,
 The wit and wisdom of their king.

V

But evil things, in robes of sorrow,
 Assailed the monarch's high estate;
(Ah, let us mourn, for never morrow
 Shall dawn upon him, desolate!)
And, round about his home, the glory
 That blushed and bloomed
Is but a dim-remembered story
 Of the old time entombed.

VI

And travelers now within that valley,
 Through the red-litten[22] windows see
Vast forms that move fantastically
 To a discordant melody;
While, like a rapid ghastly river,
 Through the pale door,
A hideous throng rush out forever,
 And laugh—but smile no more.

20 I well remember that suggestions arising from this ballad led us into a train of thought wherein there became manifest an opinion of Usher's which I mention not so much on account of its novelty (for other men have thought thus), as on account of the pertinacity with which he maintained it. **21** This opinion, in its general form, was that of the sentience of all vegetable things. But, in his disordered fancy the idea had assumed a more daring character, and trespassed, under certain conditions, upon the kingdom of inorganization.[23] I lack words to express the full extent, or the earnest abandon of his persuasion. The belief, however, was connected (as I have previously hinted) with the gray stones of the home of his forefathers. The conditions of the sentience had been here, he imagined, fulfilled in the method of collocation of these stones—in the order of their arrangement, as well as in that of the many fungi which overspread them, and of the decayed trees which stood around—above all, in the long undisturbed endurance of this arrangement, and in its reduplication in the still waters of the tarn. Its evidence—the evidence of the sentience—was to be seen, he said (and I here started as he spoke), in the gradual yet certain condensation of an atmosphere of their own about the waters and the walls. **22** The result was discoverable, he added, in that silent yet importunate and terrible influence which for centuries had molded the destinies of his family, and which made him what I now saw him—what he was. Such opinions need no comment, and I will make none.

Our books—the books which, for years, had formed no small portion of the mental existence of the invalid—were, as might be supposed, in strict keeping with this character of phantasm. We pored together over such works as the *Ververt et Chartreuse*[24] of Gresset; the *Belphegor* of Machiavelli; the *Heaven and Hell* of Swedenborg; the *Subterranean Voyage of Nicholas Klimm* by Holberg; the *Chiromancy* of Robert Flud, of **23** Jean D'Indaginé and of De la Chambre; the *Journey into the Blue Distance* of Tieck; and the *City of the Sun* of Campanella. One favorite volume was a small octavo edition of the *Directorium Inquisitorium*, by the Dominican Eymeric de Gironne; and there were passages in Pomponius Mela, about the old African Stayrs and Œgipans, over which Usher would sit dreaming for hours. His chief delight, however, was found in the perusal of an exceedingly rare and curious book in quarto Gothic—the manual of a forgotten church—the *Vigiliæ Mortuorum secundum Chorum Ecclesiae Maguntinae.* **24**

I could not help thinking of the wild ritual of this work, and of its probable influence upon the hypochondriac, when, one evening, having informed me abruptly that the lady Madeline was no more, he stated his

---

22. litten: Lighted.
23. inorganization: Inanimate objects.

---

24. *Ververt et Chartreuse*, etc.: All of the books listed deal with magic or mysticism.

The Fall of the House of Usher   219

20 Discussion What are the "suggestions" to which the narrator refers?

21 Discussion What is the significance of Usher's belief? What does it reveal about his character?

22 Discussion Why does the narrator "start" as Usher is speaking?

23 Clarification An octavo edition is a book in which the pages are six by nine inches.

24 Clarification A quarto Gothic is a book in which the pages are approximately nine by twelve inches and are printed in Gothic type.

26 **Critical Thinking and Reading** Is the revelation that Madeline and Roderick are twins surprising? What is the significance of this fact? How might it be related to the theme of the story?

27 **Discussion** How has the deterioration of Usher's physical and mental state affected his creativity?

28 **Discussion** What might be Usher's secret?

29 **Critical Thinking and Reading** Note that the narrator has become infected by Usher's condition. How might this be related to a possible theme of the story?

intention of preserving her corpse for a fortnight (previously to its final interment), in one of the numerous vaults within the main walls of the building. The worldly reason, however, assigned for this singular proceeding, was one which I did not feel at liberty to dispute. The brother had been led to his resolution (so he told me) by consideration of the unusual character of the malady of the deceased, of certain obtrusive and eager inquiries on the part of her medical men, and of the remote and exposed situation of the burial ground of the family. I will not deny that when I called to mind the sinister countenance of the person whom I met upon the staircase, on the day of my arrival at the house, I had no desire to oppose what I regarded as at best but a harmless, and by no means an unnatural precaution.

At the request of Usher, I personally aided him in the arrangements for the temporary entombment. The body having been encoffined, we two alone bore it to its rest. The vault in which we placed it (and which had been so long unopened that our torches, half smothered in its oppressive atmosphere, gave us little opportunity for investigation) was small, damp, and entirely without means of admission for light; lying, at great depth, immediately beneath that portion of the building in which was my own sleeping apartment. It had been used, apparently, in remote feudal times, for the worst purposes of a donjon-keep, and, in later days, as a place of deposit for powder, or some other highly combustible substance, as a portion of its floor, and the whole interior of a long archway through which we reached it, were carefully sheathed with copper. The door, of massive iron, had been, also, similarly protected. Its immense weight caused an unusually sharp, grating sound, as it moved upon its hinges.

Having deposited our mournful burden upon trestles within this region of horror, we partially turned aside the yet unscrewed lid of the coffin, and looked upon the face of the tenant. A striking similitude between the brother and sister now first arrested my attention; and Usher, divining, perhaps, my thoughts, murmured out some few words from which I learned that the deceased and himself had been twins, and that sympathies of a scarcely intelligible nature had always existed between them. Our glances, however, rested not long upon the dead—for we could not regard her unawed. The disease which had thus entombed the lady in the maturity of youth, had left, as usual in all maladies of a strictly cataleptical character, the mockery of a faint blush upon the bosom and the face, and that suspiciously lingering smile upon the lip which is so terrible in death. We replaced and screwed down the lid, and, having secured the door of iron, made our way, with toil, into the scarcely less gloomy apartments of the upper portion of the house.

And now, some days of bitter grief having elapsed, an observable change came over the features of the mental disorder of my friend. His ordinary manner had vanished. His ordinary occupations were neglected or forgotten. He roamed from chamber to chamber with hurried, unequal, and objectless step. The pallor of his countenance had assumed, if possible, a more ghastly hue—but the luminousness of his eye had utterly gone out. The once occasional huskiness of his tone was heard no more; and a tremulous quaver, as if of extreme terror, habitually characterized his utterance. There were times, indeed, when I thought his unceasingly agitated mind was laboring with some oppressive secret, to divulge which he struggled for the necessary courage. At times, again, I was obliged to resolve all into the mere inexplicable vagaries[25] of madness, for I beheld him gazing upon vacancy for long hours, in an attitude of the profoundest attention, as if listening to some imaginary sound. It was no wonder that his condition terrified—that it infected me. I felt creeping

---

25. vagaries (və ger′ ēz) *n.*: Odd, unexpected actions or notions.

Grammar in Action

Parentheses are the strongest separators that writers can use. Although material enclosed in parentheses is not essential to the sentence's meaning, a writer indicates that the material is important and calls attention to it by using parentheses. Following are examples of the use of parentheses:

Her duties (or so her boss told her) would be very undemanding.

Pablo Picasso (1881–1973) was one of the greatest artists of the twentieth century.

In "The Fall of the House of Usher," Poe inserts parenthetical material to explain statements, qualify them, and create atmosphere:

"The brother had been led to his resolution (so he told me) by consideration of the unusual character of the malady of the deceased. . . ." (p. 220)

"The vault in which we placed it (and which had been so long unopened that our torches, half smothered in its oppressive atmosphere, gave us little opportunity for investigation) was small, damp, and entirely without means of admission for light. . . ." (p. 220)

upon me, by slow yet uncertain degrees, the wild influences of his own fantastic yet impressive superstitions.

It was, especially, upon retiring to bed late in the night of the seventh or eighth day after the placing of the lady Madeline within the donjon, that I experienced the full power of such feelings. Sleep came not near my couch—while the hours waned and waned away. I struggled to reason off the nervousness which had dominion over me. I endeavored to believe that much, if not all of what I felt, was due to the bewildering influence of the gloomy furniture of the room—of the dark and tattered draperies, which, tortured into motion by the breath of a rising tempest, swayed fitfully to and fro upon the walls, and rustled uneasily about the decorations of the bed. But my efforts were fruitless. An irrepressible tremor gradually pervaded my frame; and, at length, there sat upon my very heart an incubus[26] of utterly causeless alarm. Shaking this off with a gasp and a struggle, I uplifted myself upon the pillows, and, peering earnestly within the intense darkness of the chamber, hearkened—I know not why, except that an instinctive spirit prompted me—to certain low and indefinite sounds which came, through the pauses of the storm, at long intervals, I knew not whence. Overpowered by an intense sentiment of horror, unaccountable yet unendurable, I threw on my clothes with haste (for I felt that I should sleep no more during the night), and endeavored to arouse myself from the pitiable condition into which I had fallen by pacing rapidly to and fro through the apartment.

I had taken but few turns in this manner, when a light step on an adjoining staircase arrested my attention. I presently recognized it as that of Usher. In an instant afterward he rapped, with a gentle touch, at my door, and entered, bearing a lamp. His countenance was, as usual, cadaverously wan—but, moreover, there was a species of mad hilarity in his eyes—an evidently restrained hysteria in his whole demeanor. His air appalled me—but anything was preferable to the solitude which I had so long endured, and I even welcomed his presence as a relief.

"And you have not seen it?" he said abruptly, after having stared about him for some moments in silence—"you have not then seen it?—but, stay! you shall." Thus speaking, and having carefully shaded his lamp, he hurried to one of the casements, and threw it freely open to the storm.

The impetuous fury of the entering gust nearly lifted us from our feet. It was, indeed, a tempestuous yet sternly beautiful night, and one wildly singular in its terror and its beauty. A whirlwind had apparently collected its force in our vicinity; for there were frequent and violent alterations in the direction of the wind; and the exceeding density of the clouds (which hung so low as to press upon the turrets of the house) did not prevent our perceiving the lifelike velocity with which they flew careering from all points against each other, without passing away into the distance. I say that even their exceeding density did not prevent our perceiving this—yet we had no glimpse of the moon or stars, nor was there any flashing forth of the lightning. But the under surfaces of the huge masses of agitated vapor, as well as all terrestrial objects immediately around us, were glowing in the unnatural light of a faintly luminous and distinctly visible gaseous exhalation which hung about and enshrouded the mansion.

"You must not—you shall not behold this!" said I, shuddering, to Usher, as I led him, with a gentle violence, from the window to a seat. "These appearances, which bewilder you, are merely electrical phenomena not uncommon—or it may be that they have their ghastly origin in the rank miasma[27] of

---

26. **incubus** (iŋ′ kyə bəs) n.: Something nightmarishly burdensome.

27. **miasma** (mī az′ mə) n.: An unwholesome atmosphere.

32 Enrichment A prolixity is something that is overly long and drawn out, with an excess of words. Some critics have accused Poe of this fault. Ask your students whether they do or do not agree.

33 Discussion What is the significance of the narrator's choice of reading material?

34 Discussion What is Roderick Usher doing as the narrator reads?

35 Discussion How is this passage from the *Mad Trist* related to the events of the story?

the tarn. Let us close this casement;—the air is chilling and dangerous to your frame. Here is one of your favorite romances. I will read, and you shall listen:—and so we will pass away this terrible night together."

The antique volume which I had taken up was the *Mad Trist* of Sir Launcelot Canning;[28] but I had called it a favorite of Usher's more in sad jest than in earnest; for, in truth, there is little in its uncouth and unimaginative prolixity which could have had interest for the lofty and spiritual ideality of my friend. It was, however, the only book immediately at hand; and I indulged a vague hope that the excitement which now agitated the hypochondriac, might find relief (for the history of mental disorder is full of similar anomalies) even in the extremeness of the folly which I should read. Could I have judged, indeed, by the wild overstrained air of vivacity with which he hearkened, or apparently hearkened, to the words of the tale, I might well have congratulated myself upon the success of my design.

I had arrived at that well-known portion of the story where Ethelred, the hero of the Trist, having sought in vain for peaceable admission into the dwelling of the hermit, proceeds to make good an entrance by force. Here, it will be remembered, the words of the narrative run thus:

"And Ethelred, who was by nature of a doughty heart, and who was now mighty withal, on account of the powerfulness of the wine which he had drunken, waited no longer to hold parley with the hermit, who, in sooth, was of an obstinate and maliceful turn, but feeling the rain upon his shoulders, and fearing the rising of the tempest, uplifted his mace outright, and, with blows, made quickly room in the plankings of the door for his gauntleted hand; and now pulling therewith sturdily, he so cracked, and ripped, and tore all asunder, that the noise of the dry and hollow-sounding wood alar-

---

28. *Mad Trist* of Sir Launcelot Canning: A fictional book and author.

222   *A Growing Nation*

umed and reverberated throughout the forest."

At the termination of this sentence I started and, for a moment, paused; for it appeared to me (although I at once concluded that my excited fancy had deceived me)—it appeared to me that, from some very remote portion of the mansion, there came, indistinctly to my ears, which might have been, in its exact similarity of character, the echo (but a stifled and dull one certainly) of the very cracking and ripping sound which Sir Launcelot had so particularly described. It was, beyond doubt, the coincidence alone which had arrested my attention; for, amid the rattling of the sashes of the casements, and the ordinary commingled noises of the still increasing storm, the sound, itself, had nothing, surely, which should have interested or disturbed me. I continued the story:

"But the good champion Ethelred, now entering within the door, was sore enraged and amazed to perceive no signal of the maliceful hermit; but, in the stead thereof, a dragon of a scaly and prodigious demeanor, and of a fiery tongue, which sate in guard before a palace of gold, with a floor of silver; and upon the wall there hung a shield of shining brass with this legend enwritten—

Who entereth herein, a conqueror hath bin;
Who slayeth the dragon, the shield he shall win.

And Ethelred uplifted his mace, and struck upon the head of the dragon, which fell before him, and gave up his pesty breath, with a shriek so horrid and harsh, and withal so piercing, that Ethelred had fain to close his ears with his hands against the dreadful noise of it, the like whereof was never before heard."

Here again I paused abruptly, and now with a feeling of wild amazement—for there could be no doubt whatever that, in this instance, I did actually hear (although from

---

Primary Source

Richard Wilbur has argued that the character Roderick Usher is a symbol:

"Roderick Usher, then, is a part of the narrator's self, which the narrator reaches by way of reverie. We may think of Usher, if we like, as the narrator's imagination, or as his visionary soul. Or we may think of him as a *state of mind* which the narrator enters at a certain stage of his progress into dreams. Considered as a state of mind, Roderick Usher is an allegorical figure representing the hypnagogic state.

• • •

"Roderick Usher stands for the hypnagogic state, which as Poe said is a teetering condition of mind occurring 'upon the very brink of sleep.' Since Roderick is the embodiment of a state of mind in which *falling*—falling asleep—is imminent, it is appropriate that the building which symbolizes his mind should promise at every moment to fall. The House of Usher stares down broodingly at its reflection in the tarn below, as in the hypnagogic state the conscious mind may stare into the subconscious; the

what direction it proceeded I found it impossible to say) a low and apparently distant, but harsh, protracted, and most unusual screaming or grating sound—the exact counterpart of what my fancy had already conjured up for the dragon's unnatural shriek as described by the romancer.

Oppressed, as I certainly was, upon the extraordinary coincidence, by a thousand conflicting sensations, in which wonder and extreme terror were predominant, I still retained sufficient presence of mind to avoid exciting, by an observation, the sensitive nervousness of my companion. I was by no means certain that he had noticed the sounds in question; although, assuredly, a strange alteration had, during the last few minutes, taken place in his demeanor. From a position fronting my own, he had gradually brought round his chair; so as to sit with his face to the door of the chamber; and thus I could but partially perceive his features, although I saw that his lips trembled as if he were murmuring inaudibly. His head had dropped upon his breast—yet I knew that he was not asleep, from the wide and rigid opening of the eye as I caught a glance of it in profile. The motion of his body, too, was at variance with this idea—for he rocked from side to side with a gentle yet constant and uniform sway. Having rapidly taken notice of all this, I resumed the narrative of Sir Launcelot, which thus proceeded:

"And now, the champion, having escaped from the terrible fury of the dragon, bethinking himself of the brazen shield, and of the breaking up of the enchantment which was upon it, removed the carcass from out of the way before him, and approached valorously over the silver pavement of the castle to where the shield was upon the wall; which in sooth tarried not for his full coming, but fell down at his feet upon the silver floor, with a mighty great and terrible ringing sound."

No sooner had these syllables passed my lips, than—as if a shield of brass had indeed, at the moment, fallen heavily upon a floor of silver—I became aware of a distinct, hollow, metallic, and clangorous, yet apparently muffled, reverberation. Completely unnerved, I leaped to my feet; but the measured rocking movement of Usher was undisturbed. I rushed to the chair in which he sat. His eyes were bent fixedly before him, and throughout his whole countenance there reigned a stony rigidity. But, as I placed my hand upon his shoulder, there came a strong shudder over his whole person; a sickly smile quivered about his lips; and I saw that he spoke in a low, hurried, and gibbering murmur, as if unconscious of my presence. Bending closely over him I at length drank in the hideous import of his words.

"Not hear it?—yes, I hear it, and have heard it. Long—long—long—many minutes, many hours, many days, have I heard it—yet I dared not—oh, pity me, miserable wretch that I am!—I dared not—I *dared* not speak! *We have put her living in the tomb!* Said I not that my senses were acute? I *now* tell you that I heard her first feeble movement in the hollow coffin. I heard them—many, many days ago—yet I dared not—*I dared not speak!* and now—tonight—Ethelred—ha! ha!—the breaking of the hermit's door, and the death cry of the dragon, and the clangor of the shield—say, rather, the rending of her coffin, and the grating of the iron hinges of her prison, and her struggles within the coppered archway of the vault! Oh! wither shall I fly? Will she not be here anon? Is she not hurrying to upbraid me for my haste? Have I not heard her footstep on the stair? Do I not distinguish that heavy and horrible beating of her heart? Madman!"—here he sprang furiously to his feet, and shrieked out his syllables, as if in the effort he were giving up his soul—"*Madman! I tell you that she now stands without the door!*"

As if in the superhuman energy of his utterance there had been found the potency of a spell, the huge antique panels to which the speaker pointed threw slowly back, upon the instant, their ponderous and ebony jaws. It

36 **Discussion** Who is "the romancer"?

37 **Literary Focus** How does the narrator's recital of this passage contribute to the growing sense of terror?

38 **Reading Strategy** Ask students to predict what Roderick is about to reveal.

39 **Discussion** Why was Roderick afraid to voice his fears? Why did he not try to rescue Madeline?

house threatens continually to collapse because it is extremely easy for the mind to slip from the hypnagogic state into the depths of sleep; and when the House of Usher *does* fall, the story ends, as it must, because the mind, at the end of its inward journey, has plunged into the darkness of sleep."

40 **Discussion** Do you agree with the narrator's action? What do you think his fate might have been if he had remained?

41 **Literary Focus** Lead students in a discussion of how the destruction of the House of Usher by means of its expanding fissure represents the culmination of the story's single effect.

Reader's Response What could a contemporary filmmaker learn from Poe about horror and suspense?

was the work of the rushing gust—but then without those doors there *did* stand the lofty and enshrouded figure of the lady Madeline of Usher. There was blood upon her white robes, and the evidence of some bitter struggle upon every portion of her emaciated frame. For a moment she remained trembling and reeling to and fro upon the threshold—then, with a low moaning cry, fell heavily inward upon the person of her brother, and in her violent and now final death agonies, bore him to the floor a corpse, and a victim to the terrors he had anticipated.

From that chamber, and from that mansion, I fled aghast. The storm was still abroad in all its wrath as I found myself crossing the old causeway. Suddenly there shot along the path a wild light, and I turned to see whence a gleam so unusual could have issued; for the vast house and its shadows were alone behind me. The radiance was that of the full, setting, and blood-red moon, which now shone vividly through that once barely discernible fissure, of which I have before spoken as extending from the roof of the building, in a zigzag direction, to the base. While I gazed, this fissure rapidly widened—there came a fierce breath of the whirlwind—the entire orb of the satellite burst at once upon my sight—my brain reeled as I saw the mighty walls rushing asunder—there was a long tumultuous shouting sound like the voice of a thousand waters—and the deep and dank tarn at my feet closed sullenly and silently over the fragments of the *"House of Usher."*

THINKING ABOUT THE SELECTION

Recalling

1. (a) What is the narrator's first impression of the House of Usher? (b) Why has he come to the house?
2. (a) When the narrator meets Usher, what startles him most about Usher's appearance? (b) What strikes him about Usher's behavior?
3. (a) According to Usher, what is "the nature of his malady"? (b) To what is Usher a "bounden slave"?
4. (a) Why is the narrator "forcibly impressed" with Usher's performance of "The Haunted Palace"? (b) What opinion does Usher offer following his performance?
5. (a) What does the narrator assist Usher with following the death of Usher's sister, Madeline? (b) What does the narrator notice when he and Usher turn aside the cover of Madeline's coffin?

6. (a) What noises does the narrator hear in the midst of reading the *Mad Trist*? (b) How does Usher explain these noises? (c) What happens immediately after Usher finishes his explanation?
7. What happens to the House of Usher at the end of the story?

Interpreting

8. (a) How is the physical appearance of the interior of the House of Usher related to the condition of Usher's mind? (b) How is it related to his physical appearance?
9. What details early in the story foreshadow, or hint at, the ending?
10. Critics have argued that Madeline and Roderick are not only twins but are physical and mental components of the same being. What evidence is there in the story to support this claim?
11. What is the significance of the fact that, rather than helping Usher, the narrator finds

---

Closure and Extension

ANSWERS TO THINKING ABOUT THE SELECTION
Recalling

1. (a) The house strikes him as "melancholy" and gives him a

sense of "insufferable gloom." (b) He arrives in response to a compelling letter from his boyhood friend.
2. (a) He is startled by the degree of change in his friend's appearance, especially "the pallor of his skin, and the now miraculous luster of the eye. . . ." (b) He is struck by the incoherence and inconsistency of Usher's behavior.

3. (a) Usher describes his malady as a constitutional, family "evil"; a "nervous affection." (b) Usher is filled with terror and fear.
4. (a) The narrator feels that it shows that Usher is aware of his mental state. (b) Usher expresses his belief in the human quality of matter and his conviction that the house and its surroundings are themselves alive.
5. (a) He helps Usher bring his sister's body to a vault beneath the

house for temporary entombment. (b) He notices the striking resemblance between the brother and sister, who are twins.
6. (a) First he hears the cracking and ripping of wood; next he hears a grating shriek; then he hears loud, metallic clanging. (b) Usher says they are the sounds of Madeline, who has been buried alive, coming for him. (c) The door opens, Madeline collapses into Usher's arms, and they both fall dead.

himself becoming infected by Usher's condition?

12. Explain the two meanings of the story's title.
13. (a) In what way is the ending of the story ambiguous? (b) What do you think has happened?

Applying

14. Poe's story may suggest that the human imagination is capable of producing false perceptions of reality. Do you agree with this suggestion? Why or why not?

ANALYZING LITERATURE

Understanding the Single Effect

In his definition of a short story, Edgar Allan Poe asserted that a story should be constructed to achieve a single effect and that every word, detail, character, and incident in a story should contribute to this effect. Carefully constructed to create a growing sense of terror, "The Fall of the House of Usher" is a perfect illustration of Poe's theory.

How do each of the following events or details contribute to the growing sense of terror in "The Fall of the House of Usher"?

1. The description of the House of Usher
2. The description of Usher's painting
3. The entombment of Madeline
4. Storms and other natural phenomena
5. Madeline's appearance at the end of the story

CRITICAL THINKING AND READING

Supporting Statements of Theme

In his definition of the short story, Poe went on to state that "truth is often, and in very great degree, the aim" of the short story. In other words, in addition to being constructed to achieve a single effect, short stories are often written to make a point, or express a general truth about life. The general truth a story expresses is the story's **theme.** There have been many different interpretations of the theme of "The Fall of the House of Usher." Find evidence from the story to support each of the following statements of possible themes.

1. In the absence of contact with the real world, the human imagination can produce a distorted perception of reality.
2. When isolated from the real world, a person can be infected by another person's fears and false perceptions of reality.
3. If artists (many critics believe that Roderick Usher represents a typical creative artist) completely turn away from the external world and become drawn into the internal world of their imaginations, they ultimately destroy their capacity to create and may eventually destroy themselves.

THINKING AND WRITING

Supporting a Statement of Theme

Develop one of your answers from the Critical Thinking and Reading exercise into an essay. Review the story to see if there is additional evidence you can use to support the statement. Take note of specific passages from the story that you can use in your essay. Organize your support into an outline. Develop the statement of theme into a thesis statement. When you write your essay, use transitions to link your ideas. When you revise make sure that your argument is well organized and clearly presented.

(Answers begin on p. 224.)

altered by many internal and external factors.

Challenge How does the story's theme—reality versus the distortions of the imagination—suit Poe's style of writing?

ANSWERS TO ANALYZING LITERATURE

1. The description of the House of Usher gets the story off to an ominous beginning and sets a mood of gloom and bleakness.
2. Usher's painting suggests he feels isolated and alone inside the house and that the house is his tomb.
3. Madeline's entombment makes real Roderick's frightening fantasies of being finally trapped within the bowels of the house.
4. The storms reinforce the growing terror inside the house.
5. Her appearance embodies the final terror for Roderick and for many of us: the fear of being buried alive.

ANSWERS TO CRITICAL THINKING AND READING

1. Answers will differ. Evidence includes the fact that Usher is isolated from the real world, and as the story progresses, his perceptions of reality grow increasingly distorted.
2. Answers will differ. Evidence includes the fact that the narrator becomes infected by Usher's condition.
3. Answers will differ. Evidence includes the fact that Usher's physical and mental deterioration ultimately strips him of his creative ability.

THINKING AND WRITING

For help with this assignment, students can refer to Lesson 11, "Writing About Theme," in the Handbook of Writing About Literature.

After students have completed the assignment, divide them into groups, and have them read their rough drafts to one another and suggest improvements.

---

7. It is completely destroyed.

Interpreting

8. (a) Like Usher's mind, the house is sorrowful and gloomy. (b) It is gloomy and in a state of decay.
9. Suggested Response: The author's description of the house and its surroundings; the image of the tarn engulfing the house; and the fungi that cover the house and the fissure that divides it all foreshadow the ending.

10. Suggested Response: Roderick seems always to know what Madeline is experiencing, especially when she is entombed; he does not attempt to rescue her because he knows they are both doomed; he mentions the extremely intuitive feelings that have always been between them.
11. It indicates that when a person is isolated from the real world, he or she can become infected by another person's psychological maladies.

12. The "house of Usher" refers to both the house itself and the Usher family as an institution.
13. (a) The reason for the house's collapse is not explained, and we do not know what ultimately happens to the narrator. (b) Answers will differ. Students may suggest that the house was destroyed by an earthquake.

Applying

14. Suggested Response: Yes, because the imagination can be

Literary Focus Read over the definitions with your students to make sure that they can make the distinction between alliteration, assonance, and consonance. Point out that poets also use a variety of other sound devices, including internal rhyme and onomatopoeia.

Writing/Prior Knowledge Before your **less advanced** students complete the writing activity, allow them to brainstorm in groups to recall monsters or other characters from horror and science fiction films that scared them.

Vocabulary

Preteach the following vocabulary words:
obeisance (o′ bā′ s'ns) *n.*: Gesture of respect (l. 39)
beguiling (bi gīl′ in) *v.*: Charming (l. 43)
countenance (koun′ tə nəns) *n.*: Facial expression (l. 44)
craven (krā′ vən) *adj.*: Very cowardly (l. 45)
ominous (äm′ ə nəs) *adj.*: Threatening; sinister (l. 71)

The Raven

Writer's Techniques

Sound Devices. Alliteration, consonance, and assonance are three sound devices that poets use to give their writing a musical quality. Alliteration is the repetition of similar sounds, usually consonants, at the beginnings of words or accented syllables. Notice the repetition of the *n* sound in the following line from "The Raven": "While I nodded, nearly napping, suddenly there came a tapping." Consonance is the repetition of consonant sounds at the ends of words or accented syllables. For example, Poe ends several stanzas of "The Raven" with a line containing a repeated *v* sound: "Quoth the Raven, 'Nevermore.'" Assonance is the repetition of vowel sounds. For example, the *ur* sound is repeated in line 13 of "The Raven": "And the silken, sad, uncertain rustling of each purple curtain."

The repetition of similar sounds in poetry pleases the ear and reinforces meaning by emphasizing important words. Poe's use of alliteration, consonance, and assonance throughout "The Raven" creates a hypnotic effect that draws us into the speaker's irrational world. As a result, we are persuaded temporarily to abandon our conception of reality and accept the speaker's vision as reality. At the same time, the repetition of sounds emphasizes certain words that contribute to the mood and reinforce the meaning of the poem.

Writing

Describe a creature that you find frightening or mysterious. Try to use descriptive details that convey the fear or uncertainty that you associate with this creature.

Primary Source

In *The Philosophy of Composition,* Poe described how he used the repetition of the Raven's response, "Nevermore," according to his

> design of varying, at every turn, the *application* of the word repeated. . . . I saw that I could make the first query propounded by the lover—the first query to which the Raven should reply "Nevermore"—that I could make this first query a commonplace one—the second less so—the third still less, and so on—until at length the lover, startled from his original *nonchalance* by the melancholy character of the word itself—by its frequent repetition—and by a consideration of the ominous reputation of the fowl that uttered it—is at length excited to superstition, and wildly propounds queries of a far different character—. . . because he experiences a frenzied pleasure in so modeling his questions as to receive from the *expected* "Nevermore" the most delicious because the most intolerable of sorrow.

Objectives

1 To appreciate sound devices
2 To respond to an author's statement

Support Material

Teaching Portfolio
Teacher Backup, p. 321
Usage and Mechanics Worksheet, p. 324
Vocabulary Check, p. 325
Analyzing Literature Worksheet, *Using Sound Devices,* p. 326
Language Worksheet, *Using Sound Devices,* p. 327
Selection Test, p. 328

THE RAVEN
Edouard Manet
Courtesy, Museum of Fine Arts, Boston

The Raven

Edgar Allan Poe

1
Once upon a midnight dreary, while I pondered, weak and weary,
Over many a quaint and curious volume of forgotten lore,
While I nodded, nearly napping, suddenly there came a tapping,
As of someone gently rapping, rapping at my chamber door.
5 " 'Tis some visitor," I muttered, "tapping at my chamber door—
                              Only this, and nothing more."

2
Ah, distinctly I remember it was in the bleak December,
And each separate dying ember wrought its ghost upon the floor.
Eagerly I wished the morrow—vainly I had tried to borrow
3 10 From my books surcease[1] of sorrow—sorrow for the lost Lenore—
4 For the rare and radiant maiden whom the angels name Lenore—
                              Nameless here for evermore.

And the silken, sad, uncertain rustling of each purple curtain
Thrilled me—filled me with fantastic terrors never felt before;
15 So that now, to still the beating of my heart, I stood repeating
" 'Tis some visitor entreating entrance at my chamber door—
Some late visitor entreating entrance at my chamber door—
                              This it is and nothing more."

---

1. surcease (sur sēs'): End.

The Raven 227

5 Discussion Whom do you think the speaker is hoping to see?

6 Clarification Pallas was also the patron of Athens, which was the birthplace of modern philosophy and the arts.

7 Discussion What causes the speaker to smile?

Presently my soul grew stronger; hesitating then no longer,
20 "Sir," said I, "or Madam, truly your forgiveness I implore;
But the fact is I was napping, and so gently you came rapping,
And so faintly you came tapping, tapping at my chamber door,
That I scarce was sure I heard you"—here I opened wide the door—
     Darkness there, and nothing more.

25 Deep into that darkness peering, long I stood there wondering, fearing,
Doubting, dreaming dreams no mortal ever dared to dream before;
But the silence was unbroken, and the darkness gave no token,
And the only word there spoken was the whispered word, "Lenore!"
This *I* whispered, and an echo murmured back the word, "Lenore!"
30   Merely this, and nothing more.

Then into the chamber turning, all my soul within me burning,
Soon I heard again a tapping somewhat louder than before.
"Surely," said I, "surely that is something at my window lattice;
Let me see, then, what thereat is, and this mystery explore—
35 Let my heart be still a moment and this mystery explore—
     'Tis the wind, and nothing more!"

Open here I flung the shutter, when, with many a flirt and flutter,
In there stepped a stately raven of the saintly days of yore;
Not the least obeisance made he; not an instant stopped or stayed he;
40 But, with mien of lord or lady, perched above my chamber door—
Perched upon a bust of Pallas[2] just above my chamber door—
     Perched, and sat, and nothing more.

Then this ebony bird beguiling my sad fancy into smiling,
By the grave and stern decorum of the countenance it wore,
45 "Though thy crest be shorn and shaven, thou," I said, "art sure no craven,
Ghastly grim and ancient raven wandering from the Nightly shore—
Tell me what thy lordly name is on the Night's Plutonian[3] shore!"
     Quoth the raven, "Nevermore."

Much I marveled this ungainly fowl to hear discourse so plainly,
50 Though its answer little meaning—little relevancy bore;
For we cannot help agreeing that no sublunary being
Ever yet was blessed with seeing bird above his chamber door—
Bird or beast upon the sculptured bust above his chamber door,
     With such name as "Nevermore."

---

2. Pallas (pal' əs): Pallas Athena, the ancient Greek goddess of wisdom.
3. Plutonian (ploo tō' nē ən) *adj.*: Referring to Pluto, the Greek and Roman god of the underworld.

55 But the raven, sitting lonely on the placid bust, spoke only
That one word, as if his soul in that one word he did outpour.
Nothing farther then he uttered—not a feather then he fluttered—
Till I scarcely more than muttered, "Other friends have flown
   before—
On the morrow *he* will leave me, as my hopes have flown before."
60   Quoth the raven, "Nevermore."

Wondering at the stillness broken by reply so aptly spoken,
"Doubtless," said I, "what it utters is its only stock and store,
Caught from some unhappy master whom unmerciful Disaster
Followed fast and followed faster—so, when Hope he would adjure,
65 Stem Despair returned, instead of the sweet Hope he dared
   adjure—
                              That sad answer, "Nevermore!"

But the raven still beguiling all my sad soul into smiling,
Straight I wheeled a cushioned seat in front of bird, and bust, and
   door;
Then upon the velvet sinking, I betook myself to linking
70 Fancy unto fancy, thinking what this ominous bird of yore—

THE RAVEN
Edouard Manet
Courtesy, Museum of Fine Arts, Boston

The Raven   229

8 **Literary Focus** The mood shifts again to sadness. How does Poe use sound devices to emphasize this change?

9 **Critical Thinking and Reading** Does the speaker's mood change again? How can you tell even before grasping the meaning of the lines?

Humanities Note

Fine art, *The Raven,* 1875, by Édouard Manet. This print is another transfer lithograph that Édouard Manet created for Mallarme's translation of Edgar Allan Poe's "The Raven." Manet's interest in the Japanese technique of brush drawing is evident in this print. He drew this lithograph with black inkwash in the Japanese manner of fluid sweeps and daubs, creating a deceptively casual line with an oriental respect for the white spaces of the page.

You might discuss the following:
1. What part of the poem does this picture illustrate?
2. Using adjectives from the poem, describe the mood of this illustration.

10 Literary Focus Which sound device is used in this description of the raven?

11 Enrichment Poe often uses words that allude to the Arab world. The late eighteenth century began a new era of relations with the Ottoman Empire and a long period of artistic interest in Arab culture, which was considered exotic.

12 Discussion Ask students to recall the three things the speaker has asked the raven. What is the effect of the bird's repeated answer?

What this grim, ungainly, ghastly, gaunt, and ominous bird of yore
      Meant in croaking "Nevermore."

This I sat engaged in guessing, but no syllable expressing
To the fowl whose fiery eyes now burned into my bosom's core;
75 This and more I sat divining, with my head at ease reclining
On the cushion's velvet lining that the lamplight gloated o'er,
But whose velvet violet lining with the lamplight gloating o'er,
      She shall press, ah, nevermore!

Then, methought, the air grew denser, perfumed from an unseen censer
80 Swung by angels whose faint foot-falls tinkled on the tufted floor.
"Wretch," I cried, "thy God hath lent thee—by these angels he hath sent thee
Respite—respite and nepenthe[4] from thy memories of Lenore!
Let me quaff this kind nepenthe and forget this lost Lenore!"
      Quoth the raven, "Nevermore."

85 "Prophet!" said I, "thing of evil!—prophet still, if bird or devil!—
Whether Tempter sent, or whether tempest tossed thee here ashore,
Desolate, yet all undaunted, on this desert land enchanted—
On this home by Horror haunted—tell me truly, I implore—
Is there—*is* there balm in Gilead?[5]—tell me—tell me, I implore!"
90   Quoth the raven, "Nevermore."

"Prophet!" said I, "thing of evil!—prophet still, if bird or devil!
By that Heaven that bends above us—by that God we both adore—
Tell this soul with sorrow laden if, within the distant Aidenn,[6]
It shall clasp a sainted maiden whom the angels name Lenore—
95 Clasp a rare and radiant maiden whom the angels name Lenore."
      Quoth the raven, "Nevermore."

"Be that word our sign of parting, bird or fiend!" I shrieked, upstarting—
"Get thee back into the tempest and the Night's Plutonian shore!
Leave no black plume as a token of that lie thy soul hath spoken!
100 Leave my loneliness unbroken!—quit the bust above my door!
Take thy beak from out my heart, and take thy form from off my door!"
      Quoth the raven, "Nevermore."

---

4. nepenthe (ni pen′ thē) *n*.: A drug that the ancient Greeks believed could relieve sorrow.
5. balm in Gilead (gil′ ē əd): In the Bible, a healing ointment was made in Gilead, a region of ancient Palestine.
6. Aidenn (ā′den): Arabic for *Eden* or *heaven*.

And the raven, never flitting, still is sitting, still is sitting
On the pallid bust of Pallas just above my chamber door;
And his eyes have all the seeming of a demon that is dreaming,
And the lamplight o'er him streaming throws his shadow on the
    floor;
And my soul from out that shadow that lies floating on the floor
                          Shall be lifted—nevermore!

THINKING ABOUT THE SELECTION

Recalling

1. (a) How does the speaker respond to the noise he hears? (b) How does he try to explain this noise?
2. (a) How does the raven get into the chamber? (b) Upon what does it land?
3. According to lines 81-83, what does the speaker want to forget?
4. (a) What does the speaker implore the raven to tell him in lines 88 and 89? (b) What question does the speaker ask the raven in lines 93–95? (c) What does the speaker order in lines 97–101?

Interpreting

5. (a) What is the mood? (b) How is the mood established in the first two stanzas?
6. (a) During the course of the poem, what changes occur in the speaker's attitude toward the raven? (b) What brings about each of these changes? (c) What does the raven finally come to represent?
7. (a) How does the speaker's emotional state change during the poem? (b) How are these changes related to the changes in his attitude toward the raven?
8. How is the word spoken by the raven related to the speaker's emotional state at the end of the poem?

Applying

9. "The Raven" has been popular for well over one hundred years. What do you think accounts for its continuing appeal?

ANALYZING LITERATURE

Using Sound Devices

Alliteration, consonance, and **assonance** are three sound devices used in poetry. Alliteration is the repetition of similar sounds, usually consonants, at the beginnings of words or accented syllables (for example, "surcease of sorrow," line 10). Consonance is the repetition of consonant sounds at the ends of words or accented syllables (for example, "chamber door," line 14). Assonance is the repetition of vowel sounds (for example, "weak and weary," line 1).

Find three more examples of each of these techniques in "The Raven." Explain how each contributes to the poem's hypnotic effect.

THINKING AND WRITING

Responding to a Statement

Poe stated, "A poem, in my opinion, is opposed to a work of science by having, for its *immediate* object, pleasure, not truth. . ." Review the poem, considering how Poe's use of sound devices and his choice of subject relate to the poem's *immediate* purpose. Try to determine the general truth, or theme, the poem expresses. Think about how the theme relates to the poem's *overall* purpose. Then, after deciding how you will respond to Poe's statement, find passages from the poem to support your response. Start your essay with Poe's statement, followed by your response. Then develop an argument supporting your response. When you finish writing, revise your essay, and prepare a final copy.

The Raven   231

---

13 **Discussion** What does the raven perched on top of the bust of Pallas symbolize?

14 **Discussion** Will the speaker now recover from his grief?

6. (a) At first he is amused; then he marvels that the bird can speak; he tries to figure out its meaning; he begins to believe that the bird is an omen from heaven; then he thinks it is evil; he finally becomes angry and orders the bird to leave. (b) The bird's repetition of the word "Nevermore" causes these changes. (c) It represents the speaker's permanent state of madness.
7. (a) The speaker's emotional state fluctuates from sorrow to amusement to hope to despair. (b) They directly correspond to his changes in attitude toward the raven.
8. The speaker has lapsed into an irrational state and may never regain his sanity.

Applying

9. Suggested Response: People respond to the sound effects and rhythm and to the fantasy of the poem.

Challenge Why did Poe choose to use a raven, rather than some other type of bird?

ANSWERS TO ANALYZING LITERATURE

Answers will differ. There are numerous examples of each of these devices in the poem. These devices combine to create a hypnotic effect that draws the reader into the poem.

THINKING AND WRITING

For help with this assignment, students can refer to Lesson 15, "Evaluating a Literary Work," in the Handbook of Writing About Literature.

Publishing Student Writing If there are any regional writing contests for high school students, offer to help prepare the most promising essays for submission.

Closure and Extension

ANSWERS TO THINKING ABOUT THE SELECTION
Recalling

1. (a) He at first thinks it is someone at the door, and he goes to the door and opens it. (b) He decides that it is being caused by the wind.
2. (a) It steps in through the window.

(b) It lands above the door on top of a bust of the Greek goddess, Pallas.
3. He wants to forget his dead Lenore.
4. (a) He implores the raven to tell him whether there is "balm in Gilead," whether he will be healed in the hereafter. (b) He asks if he will be reunited with Lenore in heaven. (c) He orders the raven to leave.

Interpreting

5. (a) The mood is gloomy and sorrowful. (b) The mood is established by the time of night, the bleak weather, and the statement that the speaker is trying to forget his sorrow by studying books.

Literary Focus Point out that the frame technique is also used in flashbacks and dream sequences in films and on television, and is usually signaled by a change in lighting.

Writing/Prior Knowledge Before students complete the writing activity, have them discuss their travels and decide which is the most beautiful place they have visited.

Vocabulary

Preteach the following vocabulary words:

incipient (in sip′ ē ənt) *adj.*: Just beginning (p. 233)

delirium (di lir′ ē əm) *n.*: A temporary state of extreme mental confusion (p. 233)

countenance (koun′ tə nəns) *n.*: Facial expression (p. 234)

austere (ô stir′) *adj.*: Showing strict self-discipline (p. 234)

reveries (rev′ ər ēz) *n.*: Day-dreaming (p. 234)

tremulous (trem′ yoo ləs) *adj.*: Quivering (p. 236)

pallid (pal′ id) *adj.*: Pale (p. 236)

aghast (ə gast′) *adj.*: Horrified (p. 236)

Spelling Tip Point out the *ance* spelling of the ending sound in *countenance*.

The Oval Portrait

Literary Forms

The Frame Story. A frame story is a story told within the framework of another story. For example, in "The Oval Portrait" a story about a painter's attempt to capture the beauty of his young wife on canvas is told within the framework of a story about a wounded man's retreat into an abandoned chateau.

In "The Oval Portrait," Poe uses the frame, or outer story, to provide a setting and create an atmosphere for the frame story. At the same time, the reactions and observations of the wounded man, the narrator, in the frame reinforce the symbolic, or hidden, meaning of the frame story. In a sense the two stories also parallel each other, because both relate the story of a character's temporary retreat from consciousness.

Writing

Think of a person, place, or animal that you find exceptionally beautiful. Write a short description of this person, place, or animal. Then write a few sentences about how you think the passage of time will affect the beauty of your subject, and reflect upon how its beauty might be captured permanently in a work of art.

Commentary

The horror story as we know it today was born in 1764. That year Horace Walpole, an English nobleman, published *The Castle of Otranto*. Its setting, a thirteenth-century Gothic castle, provided the name Gothic Romance to the type of novel that quickly developed in this genre. Novels in the Gothic tradition included dark and dreary settings, much like the castle the narrator enters in "The Oval Portrait." Dark villains and saintly heroines, flickering lights and strange noises, and reliance on the supernatural were among other elements intended to create horror in Gothic romances. The best-known of this genre was Ann Radcliffe's *The Mysteries of Udolpho*.

Out of this tradition emerged Poe's stories. As you read "The Oval Portrait," you will notice that it, like "The Fall of the House of Usher," belongs in the tradition of the Gothic Romance. How does Poe use Gothic elements to create a style that was entirely his own? How is the Gothic tradition continued today?

Objectives

1 To understand a frame story
2 To understand word origins
3 To understand cause and effect
4 To compare and contrast stories

Support Material

Teaching Portfolio
Teacher Backup, p. 331
Grammar in Action Worksheet, *Understanding Adjective Clauses*, p. 334
Usage and Mechanics Worksheet, p. 336
Vocabulary Check, p. 337
Analyzing Literature Worksheet, *Recognizing a Frame Story*, p. 338

Language Worksheet, *Recognizing Shades of Meaning*, p. 339
Selection Test, p. 340

The Oval Portrait

Edgar Allan Poe

The chateau into which my valet had ventured to make forcible entrance, rather than permit me, in my desperately wounded condition, to pass a night in the open air, was one of those piles of commingled gloom and grandeur which have so long frowned among the Apennines,[1] not less in fact than in the fancy of Mrs. Radcliffe.[2] To all appearance it had been temporarily and very lately abandoned. We established ourselves in one of the smallest and least sumptuously furnished apartments. It lay in a remote turret of the building. Its decorations were rich, yet tattered and antique. Its walls were hung with tapestry and bedecked with manifold and multiform armorial trophies, together with an unusually great number of very spirited modern paintings in frames of rich golden arabesque.[3] In these paintings, which depended from the walls not only in their main surfaces, but in very many nooks which the bizarre architecture of the chateau rendered necessary—in these paintings my incipient delirium, perhaps, had caused me to take deep interest; so that I bade Pedro to close the heavy shutters of the room—since it was already night—to light the tongues[4] of a tall candelabrum which stood by the head of my bed—and to throw open far and wide the fringed curtains of black velvet which enveloped the bed itself. I wished all this done that I might resign myself, if not to sleep, at least alternately to the contemplation of these pictures, and the perusal of a small volume which had been found upon the pillow, and which purported to criticize and describe them.

Long—long I read—and devoutly, devotedly I gazed. Rapidly and gloriously the hours flew by and the deep midnight came. The position of the candelabrum displeased me, and outreaching my hand with difficulty, rather than disturb my slumbering valet, I placed it so as to throw its rays more fully upon the book.

But the action produced an effect altogether unanticipated. The rays of the numerous candles (for there were many) now fell within a niche of the room which had hitherto been thrown into deep shade by one of the bedposts. I thus saw in vivid light a picture all unnoticed before. It was the portrait of a young girl just ripening into womanhood. I glanced at the painting hurriedly, and then closed my eyes. Why I did this was not at first apparent even to my own perception. But while my lids remained thus shut, I ran over in my mind my reason for so shutting them. It was an impulsive movement to gain time for thought—to make sure that my vision had not deceived me—to calm and subdue my fancy for a more sober and more certain gaze. In a very few moments I again looked fixedly at the painting.

---

1. **Apennines** (ap′ ə nīnz): A mountain range located in central Italy.
2. **Mrs. Radcliffe:** Ann Radcliffe (1764–1823), an English novelist.
3. **arabesque** (ar′ ə besk′): Complex and elaborate design.
4. **tongues** (tuŋz): Candles.

The Oval Portrait 233

233

That I now saw aright I could not and would not doubt; for the first flashing of the candles upon that canvas had seemed to dissipate the dreamy stupor which was stealing over my senses, and to startle at once into waking life.

The portrait, I have already said, was that of a young girl. It was a mere head and shoulders, done in what is technically termed a *vignette*[5] manner; much in the style of the favorite heads of Sully.[6] The arms, the bosom, and even the ends of the radiant hair melted imperceptibly into the vague yet deep shadow which formed the background of the whole. The frame was oval, richly gilded and filigreed in *Moresque*.[7] As a thing of art nothing could be more admirable than the painting itself. But it could have been neither the execution of the work, nor the immortal beauty of the countenance, which had so suddenly and so vehemently moved me. Least of all, could it have been that my fancy, shaken from its half slumber, had mistaken the head for that of a living person. I saw at once that the peculiarities of the design, of the *vignetting*, and of the frame, must have instantly dispelled such idea—must have prevented even its momentary entertainment. Thinking earnestly upon these points, I remained, for an hour perhaps, half sitting, half reclining, with my vision riveted upon the portrait. At length, satisfied with the true secret of its effect, I fell back within the bed. I had found the spell of the picture in an absolute life-likeliness of expression, which, at first startling, finally confounded, subdued, and appalled me. With deep and reverent awe I replaced the candelabrum in its former position. The cause of my deep agitation being thus shut from view, I sought eagerly the volume which

---

5. *vignette* (vin yet') *n.*: A picture or photograph with no definite border.
6. Sully: Thomas Sully (1783–1872), an American painter born in England.
7. *Moresque* (mô resk'): Decoration characterized by intricate tracery and bright colors.

discussed the paintings and their histories. Turning to the number which designated the oval portrait, I there read the vague and quaint words which follow:

"She was a maiden of rarest beauty, and not more lovely than full of glee. And evil was the hour when she saw, and loved, and wedded the painter. He, passionate, studious, austere, and having already a bride in his art; she a maiden of rarest beauty, and not more lovely than full of glee; all light and smiles, and frolicsome as the young fawn; loving and cherishing all things; hating only the art which was her rival; dreading only the pallet and brushes and other untoward instruments which deprived her of the countenance of her lover. It was thus a terrible thing for this lady to hear the painter speak of his desire to portray even his young bride. But she was humble and obedient, and sat meekly for many weeks in the dark, high turret chamber where the light dripped upon the pale canvas only from overhead. But he, the painter, took glory in his work, which went on from hour to hour, and from day to day. And he was a passionate, and wild, and moody man, who became lost in reveries; so that he *would* not see that the light which fell so ghastly in that lone turret withered the health and the spirits of his bride, who pined visibly to all but him. Yet she smiled on and still on, uncomplainingly, because she saw that the painter (who had high renown) took a fervid and burning pleasure in his task, and wrought day and night to depict her who so loved him, yet who grew daily more dispirited and weak. And in sooth[8] some who beheld the portrait spoke of its resemblance in low words, as of a mighty marvel, and a proof not less of the power of the painter than of his deep love for her whom he depicted so surpassingly well. But at length, as the labor drew nearer to its conclusion, there were admitted none into the

---

8. sooth (sooth): Truth; fact.

Grammar in Action

An **adjective clause** is a subordinate clause that modifies a noun or a pronoun by providing additional information. Adjective clauses are introduced by relative pronouns—*which, that, who, whom, whose*—which, in addition to joining the subordinate clause to the independent clause, serve as sentence elements within the adjective clause. In these examples from "The Oval Portrait," the relative pronouns serve as subjects of the adjective clauses:

The painter . . . took glory in his work, *which* went on from day to day. . . .

Some *who* beheld the portrait spoke of its resemblance in low words, as of a mighty marvel. . . .

Sometimes, the relative pronoun serves as the direct object of the adjective clause, or as the object of a preposition:

The painter stood . . . before the work *which* he had wrought.

The chateau into *which* my valet had ventured to make forcible entrance . . . was one of those commingled piles of gloom and grandeur. . . .

"HE TURNED SUDDENLY . . . ," EDGAR ALLAN POE'S TALES OF MYSTERY AND IMAGINATION
Arthur Rackham
New York Public Library, Astor, Lenox and Tilden Foundations

Humanities Note

Fine art, *The Oval Portrait,* 1935, by Arthur Rackham. Arthur Rackham (1867-1936), was one of the best known British illustrators of his time. He had an imaginative style, which was ideally suited for illustrating work such as Poe's.

This illustration appeared in *Tales of Mystery and Imagination,* 1935. The caption beneath the illustration in the book reads, "He turned suddenly to regard his beloved: She was dead!" The colors in this illustration are pale and fragile. The patterns in the drapery and other forms present a sense of foreboding. The light from the window adds drama. These elements combine effectively to portray the mood of the story.

You might use these questions for discussion:
1. What part of the story does this picture illustrate?
2. What mood has the artist created in this illustration?
3. What has the artist used to create this mood?

The Oval Portrait 235

Student Activity 1. Find five more adjective clauses in "The Oval Portrait," and identify the function of the relative pronoun within each adjective clause.

Student Activity 2. Combine the following pairs of sentences, replacing the italicized expression with a relative pronoun and forming an adjective clause.
1. The narrator stayed in a small apartment.
   The apartment was richly ornamented.
2. He saw the portrait of a young girl.
   The young girl was just reaching maturity.
3. He reached for a book.
   In *the book* were histories of the paintings around him.
4. The portrait's model had loved everything but her husband's work.
   Her husband's work was her only rival.

Sidebar annotations

13 Reading Strategy Have students summarize what they have read so far.

14 Critical Thinking and Reading In "The Fall of the House of Usher," how does Roderick Usher's similar immersion in his creative life destroy his real life?

15 Literary Focus Why does Poe choose not to return to the frame?

Reader's Response What are the qualities that you value most in a portrait?

Main text

turret; for the painter had grown wild with the ardor of his work, and turned his eyes from canvas rarely, even to regard the countenance of his wife. And he *would* not see that the tints which he spread upon the canvas were drawn from the cheeks of her who sat beside him. And when many weeks had passed, and but little remained to do, save one brush upon the mouth and one tint upon the eye, the spirit of the lady again flickered up as the flame within the socket of the lamp. And then the brush was given, and then the tint was placed; and, for one moment, the painter stood entranced before the work which he had wrought; but in the next, while he yet gazed, he grew tremulous and very pallid, and aghast, and crying with a loud voice, 'This is indeed *Life* itself!' turned suddenly to regard his beloved—*She was dead!*"

THINKING ABOUT THE SELECTION
Recalling

1. (a) Why does the narrator's valet break into the chateau? (b) How does the narrator describe the chateau's appearance?
2. (a) What painting does the narrator see when he moves the candelabrum? (b) What is his immediate reaction to the painting? (c) What causes this reaction?
3. (a) What is the relationship between the subject of the painting and the artist? (b) What happens to the subject when the artist finally finishes the painting?

Interpreting

4. (a) What details in the first few paragraphs suggest that the narrator experiences a temporary retreat from consciousness? (b) What details in the frame story indicate that the painter experiences a temporary retreat from consciousness while painting his wife?
5. What makes the artist's remark at the end of the story ironic, or surprising?
6. When this story was first published, it was called "Life in Death." Which title do you find the most effective? Explain your answer.
7. The critic G. R. Thompson has suggested that the entire story can be read as "the dream of a man delirious from pain and lack of sleep." What is your opinion of this interpretation? Support your opinion with details from the story.

Applying

8. In "The Oval Portrait," the narrator has a strong emotional reaction to the painting of the young woman. What do you think causes people to react in this way to certain works of art?
9. Jacques Barzun has written, "Art distills sensation and embodies it with enhanced meaning in memorable form—or else it is not art." (a) How do Barzun's words relate to painting? (b) How do they relate to writing?

ANALYZING LITERATURE
Recognizing a Frame Story

The story of the painter and his wife in "The Oval Portrait" is an example of a **frame story,** a story told within the framework of another story. In the "Oval Portrait," the **frame,** or outer story, provides a setting and creates an atmosphere for the frame story. The narrator's reactions and observations in the frame also reinforce the symbolic, or hidden, meaning of the frame story.

1. What details of the setting in the frame create an appropriate atmosphere for the frame story?
2. In the frame story, the young woman's spirit and beauty are symbolically drawn out of her and into her husband's painting. Through this process her beauty and passion are released from their mortal bonds and permanently cap-

---

Closure and Extension

ANSWERS TO THINKING ABOUT THE SELECTION
Recalling

1. (a) He wants to find shelter for his wounded master. (b) The chateau is grand and gloomy, richly decorated with tattered antiques. Its walls are covered with tapestries and paintings.
2. (a) He sees a painting of a beautiful young woman. (b) He closes his eyes. (c) He is stunned by its "life-likeliness."
3. (a) The woman is the artist's wife. (b) She dies.

Interpreting

4. (a) Suggested Response: He is seriously wounded; he is semi-delirious, yet cannot sleep; he does not trust his initial perception of the painting and shuts his eyes. (b) He is lost in a "reverie" and does not notice his wife's deteriorating health; he is "wild with ardor" and rarely looks away from

tured in her husband's painting. How does the narrator's response to the painting reinforce this interpretation?

CRITICAL THINKING AND READING
Understanding Cause and Effect

A **cause** is the reason why something happens. An **effect** is what happens, or the result.

Answer each of the following questions by finding the result of each cause.

1. The narrator is in a desperately wounded condition. As a result, what does his servant do?
2. The narrator is feeling delirious as he looks at the paintings. What is the result?
3. The narrator wants to study the paintings. As a result, what does he ask his servant to do?
4. The narrator moves the candle. What is the unanticipated effect?
5. The picture has "an absolute life-likeliness of expression." What is its effect?

UNDERSTANDING LANGUAGE
Understanding Word Origins

Many words in English originated in other languages. For example, in the book the narrator reads this description of the painter: "And he was a passionate, and wild, and moody man, who became lost in *reveries* . . ." The word *reverie* means "dreamy thinking or imagining." It comes from a Middle French word that meant "to wander." Do you see the connection? When you engage in reverie, you let your mind wander.

Find the origin of each of the words below. Explain the connection between the original word and the word today.

1. oval
2. arabesque
3. bizarre
4. candelabrum
5. vignette
6. filigree

THINKING AND WRITING
Comparing and Contrasting Stories

Write an essay comparing and contrasting "The Oval Portrait" with "The Fall of the House of Usher." First review both stories and take note of the characters, setting, mood, and theme of each story. List the similarities and differences between the two stories in each of these areas. Organize your information into an outline and write a thesis statement. Then write an essay in which you support your thesis statement with the information from your lists. When you revise make sure that you have used appropriate transitions to indicate either comparison or contrast.

The Oval Portrait 237

(Answers begin on p. 236.)

2. He is so startled by its "life-likeliness" that at first he shuts his eyes to it.

ANSWERS TO CRITICAL THINKING AND READING

1. He breaks into the chateau.
2. He takes a deep interest in the paintings.
3. He asks his servant to close the shutters.
4. He saw a picture that he had not previously noticed.
5. It causes the narrator to close his eyes.

ANSWERS TO UNDERSTANDING LANGUAGE

1. oval: from the Latin word *ovum*, meaning "egg." An oval is shaped like an egg.
2. arabesque: from the Arab word *arab*, refering to Moorish designs in architecture. Arabesque refers to designs similar to the Moorish designs.
3. bizarre: from the Italian word *bizarro*, meaning "angry, fierce, strange." Bizarre still refers to that which is odd or strange.
4. candelabrum: from the Latin word *candela*, meaning "candle." A *candelabrum* is a large, branched candlestick.
5. vignette: from the French word *vigne*, meaning "a vine." A vine does not seem to have a definite end.
6. filigree: from the Latin word *filum*, meaning "a thread. *Filagree* refers to delicate, threadlike ornamental work of intertwined wire.

THINKING AND WRITING

For help with this assignment, students can refer to Lesson 16, "Writing a Comparative Evaluation," in the Handbook of Writing About Literature.

Writing Across the Curriculum You might wish to inform the art department about this assignment. Art teachers might help students to appreciate how life and beauty can be immortalized in art—a theme of both stories.

237

his canvas; he becomes entranced by his finished painting and does not notice at first that his wife has died.
5. His wife dies just as he claims to have captured life on canvas.
6. Suggested Response: "Life in Death" is a better title, because it captures the theme of the story.
7. Suggested Response: This is an incorrect interpretation. One detail that suggests that the interpretation is incorrect is the fact that the narrator closes his eyes when he

first sees the painting and is struck by the same impression when he reopens them.

Applying

8. Suggested Response: Many paintings by great artists have the beauty and emotional power to move us in different ways.
9. (a) and (b) Suggested Responses: Both painters and writers attempt to embody their subjects with enhanced meaning.

Challenge What is the purpose of art? Is it possible for artists to create works that eternally capture beauty and life? Why or why not?

ANSWERS TO ANALYZING LITERATURE

1. The gloomy, abandoned chateau; the richly furnished turret room; the dark tapestries and hanging drapes; and the candlelight, all help to create the atmosphere.

GUIDE FOR INTERPRETING

To Helen

Writer's Techniques

Allusions. An allusion is a reference to another literary work or a figure, place, or event from history, religion, or mythology. For example, in the first stanza of "To Helen," Poe alludes to Helen of Troy, a legendary Greek woman known for her incomparable beauty.

The theme or central idea of "To Helen"—that the purest, most enduring form of beauty is spiritual beauty rather than physical beauty—is revealed through the progression of allusions Poe uses in the poem. By interpreting the meaning of each allusion, we can see through the course of the poem the speaker's ideal conception of beauty transformed from an actual woman to a nymph, and ultimately to the mind and soul.

Writing

What does beauty mean to you? Freewrite about the thoughts and feelings you associate with the concept of beauty.

Primary Source

What accounts for Poe's strange imagination? In "The Cabinet of Edgar Allen Poe," Angela Carter imagines the childhood of the young Poe, whose parents were in the theater.

> Consider the theatrical illusion with special reference to this impressionable child, who was exposed to it at an age when there is no reason for anything to be real.
>
> He must often have toddled onto the stage when the theater was empty and the curtains down . . . .
>
> Here he will find a painted backdrop of, say, an antique castle—a castle! such as they don't build here; a Gothic castle all complete with owls and ivy. The flies are painted with segments of trees, massy oaks or something like that, all in two dimensions. Artificial shadows fall in all the wrong places. Nothing is what is seems. You knock against a gilded throne or horrid rack that looks perfectly solid, thick, immovable, and you kick it sideways, it turns out to be made of papier mâché, it is as light as air—a child, you yourself, could pick it up and carry it off with you and sit in it and be a king or lie in it and be in pain.
>
> A creaking, an ominous rattling scares the little wits out of you; when you jump round to see what is going on behind your back, why, the very castle is in mid-air! Heave-ho and up she rises, amid the inarticulate cries and muttered oaths of the stagehands, and down comes Juliet's tomb or Ophelia's sepulcher, and a super scuttles in, clutching Yorrick's skull.

238   *A Growing Nation*

To Helen

Edgar Allan Poe

1 Helen, thy beauty is to me
      Like those Nicéan barks[1] of yore,
   That gently, o'er a perfumed sea,
      The weary, way-worn wanderer bore
5   To his own native shore.

2 On desperate seas long wont to roam,
      Thy hyacinth[2] hair, thy classic face,
   Thy Naiad airs have brought me home
      To the glory that was Greece,
10   And the grandeur that was Rome.

3 Lo! in yon brilliant window-niche
      How statue-like I see thee stand,
      The agate lamp within thy hand!
   Ah, Psyche, from the regions which
15   Are Holy Land!

---

1. **Nicéan** (nī sē′ ən) **barks:** Boats from the shipbuilding city of Nicea in Asia Minor.
2. **hyacinth** (hī′ ə sinth′) *adj.*: Wavy; lustrous.

PROSERPINE
Dante Gabriel Rossetti
The Tate Gallery, London

THINKING ABOUT THE SELECTION

Recalling

1. To what does the speaker compare Helen's beauty in lines 2–5?
2. To what is the speaker brought home in lines 9 and 10?
3. (a) How is Helen standing in line 12? (b) What does she have in her hand?

Interpreting

4. During the course of the poem, Helen leads the speaker on a journey. What type of journey is the speaker taking?
5. Toward the end of the poem, the speaker looks to art as a possible source of the purest form of beauty. How is this indicated in lines 11–13?

Applying

6. What do you think is the purest form of beauty? Explain your answer.

ANALYZING LITERATURE

Recognizing Allusions

An **allusion** is a reference to another literary work or a figure, place, or event from history, religion, or mythology. For example, in the first stanza, Poe alludes to Helen of Troy, a woman known for her incomparable beauty.

1. Identify the meaning of each of the following allusions. a. Naiad b. Psyche
2. How do these allusions relate to the overall meaning of the poem?

To Helen   239

Presentation

Motivation/Prior Knowledge
Have students envision the most beautiful person, place, or thing that they can think of. Does this image represent pure beauty to them? Why or why not?

Purpose-Setting Question
What insight about beauty does the poem convey?

Humanities Note

Fine art, *Proserpine,* 1877, by Dante Gabriel Rossetti. Rossetti (1828-1882) was born in London of Italian parents. He was a founder of the Pre-Raphaelite Brotherhood, a movement of artists that existed only from 1848 to 1860 but had a lasting influence on British art. The Pre-Raphaelites rebelled against the abuses and excesses of the art of their day. They created a new style of painting, which emulated the simplicity and honesty of the primitive Christian painters before Raphael. They looked back to the romance of chivalry in medieval times, and strove to produce noble and serious paintings, true to nature. Their work blends romantic idealism, scientific rationalism, and morality.

This painting is one of eight versions of *Proserpine,* which were started in the last decade of Rossetti's life.

You might ask students why this painting is an appropriate choice to accompany "To Helen."

1 **Enrichment** The image of the "perfumed sea" (the Aegean) is borrowed from Homer. It occurs, along with other images of the sea, throughout *The Odyssey.*

2 **Discussion** Who has been long roaming on "desperate seas"?

3 **Critical Thinking and Reading** Give a synonym for agate.

Closure and Extension

ANSWERS TO THINKING ABOUT THE SELECTION
Recalling

1. He compares Helen's beauty to Nicean barks that bear wanderers home.
2. He is brought home to "the glory that was Greece and the grandeur that was Rome."
3. (a) She is standing like a statue. (b) She is holding an agate lamp.

Interpreting

4. He takes an imaginative journey in which he tries to envision beauty in its purest form.
5. He envisions Helen as a beautiful statue.

Applying

6. Suggested Response: Spiritual beauty is the purest form of beauty.

ANSWERS TO ANALYZING LITERATURE

1. (a) A Naiad was a water nymph in Greek and Roman mythology. (b) Psyche refers to the soul and the mind.
2. Through the progression of allusions in the poem, we see that the speaker's conception of pure beauty is transformed from an actual woman, to a nymph, to the mind and soul.

Alfred J. Hitchcock (1899–1980)

"At sixteen I discovered the work of Edgar Allan Poe," recalled Alfred Hitchcock, the great director of horror and suspense films. "When I came home from the office where I worked I went straight to my room, took the cheap edition of his *Tales of the Grotesque and Arabesque*, and began to read. I still remember my feelings when I finished 'The Murders in the Rue Morgue.' I was afraid, but this fear made me discover something I've never forgotten since: Fear, you see, is an emotion people like to feel when they know they're safe."

In his more than fifty-year career of film making, Alfred Hitchcock has given viewers plenty of opportunity to experience fear. He began directing films during the silent era, and by the 1930's he had established his reputation as a director of suspense thrillers. By the time he directed *Vertigo* (1958), *Psycho* (1960), and *The Birds* (1963), he had moved beyond suspense into terror.

POE'S INFLUENCE

Hitchcock learned much from Edgar Allan Poe, the master of terror and suspense. Poe's influence is evident in Hitchcock's vision of a morally ambiguous world in which the seemingly ordinary person is susceptible to madness and corruption. Like the characters Poe created, Hitchcock's characters frequently must cope with the hallucinatory effects of guilt, paranoia, and loss of identity. A character in *Psycho* seems to capture Hitchcock's view of the world when he says, "We all go a little mad from time to time."

THEMES AND TECHNIQUES

Hitchcock's psychological thrillers explore many of the themes and ideas that Poe used in his stories and poems. Most striking is the recurring conflict between appearance and reality. Many of Hitchcock's films examine the way the human mind can distort the world, resulting in a life of fantasy bordering on insanity. To illustrate obsession and mental distortion, he often focused his films through a single character's consciousness, as in *Suspicion*. Poe used a narrator to create the same effect. Sometimes, notably in *Rear Window*, Hitchcock allowed the viewer

to observe secretly the private lives of others to emphasize how claustrophobic and perverse the mind in isolation becomes.

Another Hitchcock theme that recalls Poe is the power of the dead over the living. This idea is examined in such films as *Rebecca* and *Vertigo*.

The techniques with which Hitchcock created his effects resemble those Poe used in his tales of horror and suspense. In the typical Hitchcock film, the plot is less important than the development of character and theme, so the viewer is drawn deeply into the moral world of the film. Hitchcock also used the technique of beginning with apparently normal and safe settings that slide almost imperceptibly into depravity and nightmare.

As a result, everyday objects and familiar things—staircases, rooms, birds—become the machinery of terror.

Like Poe, Hitchcock was interested in the black humor of the macabre; he intermixed humor with horror, as if to lure the audience into a false mood of security and nervous relief. For Hitchcock as for Poe, the world was one in which disorder and death lurked beneath the surface of everyday life. And the audience for both loves to experience the fear and terror that exists in this world.

Alfred Hitchcock

Enrichment Both Poe and Hitchcock loved to hide personal details in their work. Poe, for instance, gives the protagonist of his story "William Wilson" his own birthdate: January 19th. Hitchcock was notorious for including a brief cameo shot of himself—walking down a hallway, perhaps, or climbing onto a bus—in his films.

QUESTIONS

1. Explain what Hitchcock meant when he said, "Fear, you see, is an emotion people like to feel when they know they're safe."
2. Do you agree with this observation of Hitchcock's? Why or why not?
3. Explain how Poe and Hitchcock shared a similar view of the world.
4. Why do you think a mixture of humor and horror appeals to some people?
5. Suppose you were a director making a film of Poe's "The Fall of the House of Usher." What would be the most difficult challenge you would face?

ACTIVITIES

1. Have students get together in small groups and devise a brief, suspenseful scene for a movie. Encourage them to include suggested camera angles in addition to dialogue and descriptions of action.
2. Ask students to view a Hitchcock film and report on it to the class. Students' reports should include a description of Hitchcock's strategies for creating suspense.
3. Have students write a brief memorandum suggesting how "The Fall of the House of Usher" could be made into a film.

The writing assignments on page 242 have students write creatively, while those on page 243 have them think about the selections and write critically.

YOU THE WRITER

Guidelines for Evaluating Assignment 1

1. Has the student written a journal entry in an informal style?
2. Is the information in the entry organized in chronological order?
3. Are the descriptions clear and complete?
4. Is the entry free from grammar, usage, and mechanics errors?

Guidelines for Evaluating Assignment 2

1. Has the student written a lyric poem, using a regular rhythm and rhyme?
2. Does the poem express the speaker's thoughts about the subject?
3. Has the student expressed abstract ideas in concrete images?
4. Is the poem free of grammar, usage, and mechanics errors?

Guidelines for Evaluating Assignment 3

1. Has the student written a realistic conversation?
2. Does the dialogue capture the contrast between the Romantic and the eighteenth-century attitudes?
3. Is the dialogue free from grammar, usage, and mechanics errors?

YOU THE WRITER

Assignment

1. Imagine that the year is 1840 and you have lived through the period of rapid growth that occurred in the years between 1800 and 1840. Write a journal entry describing some of the changes that have occurred during your lifetime and present your reactions to these changes.

Prewriting. Review the unit introduction to refresh your memory about the important events that occurred during the period. Prepare a list of these events.

Writing. When you write your journal entry, use an informal writing style and organize your information in chronological order.

Revising. When you revise, make sure your descriptions are clear and complete. After you have finished revising, proofread your entry and prepare a final copy.

Assignment

2. The Romantics had a strong interest in nature and in humanity's relationship with nature. Write a lyric poem in the Romantic tradition, focusing on an aspect of nature or exploring the relationship between humanity and nature.

Prewriting. After deciding on a subject, develop a list of sensory details you can use in your poem. Arrange these details in a logical order.

Writing. When writing your poem, focus on having the speaker express his or her thoughts about the subject. Use a regular rhythm and pattern of rhyme.

Revising. When you revise, make sure any abstract ideas are linked to concrete images, or word pictures. After you have finished revising, proofread your poem and share it with your classmates.

Assignment

3. The attitudes and concerns of the Romantics were dramatically different from those of the writers of the Colonial Period. Write a dialogue in which a Romantic and a writer from the Colonial Period discuss their ideas and interests.

Prewriting. Review the unit introductions for the Colonial Period and for a Growing Nation, noting the differences in the attitudes and concerns of the writers of the two periods.

Writing. Develop a dialogue between an important writer from each period. Try to make the conversation seem realistic, as if it might have actually occurred had the two writers been alive at the same time.

Revising. When you revise, make sure your dialogue captures the contrast between Romantic and eighteenth-century attitudes.

YOU THE CRITIC

Assignment

1. The Romantics had a strong interest in mystery and the supernatural. Write an essay in which you discuss how this interest is reflected in one of the Romantic selections you have read.

    Prewriting. Choose a selection that reflects the Romantic interest in mystery and the supernatural. Carefully reread the selection, noting the elements of mystery and/or the supernatural that it includes.

    Writing. Include a thesis statement in the introduction of your essay. Develop and support your thesis in the body paragraphs.

    Revising. When you revise, make sure you have thoroughly supported your thesis and have not included any unnecessary information. After you finish writing, proofread your essay and prepare a final copy.

Assignment

2. Although all the writers in this unit were Romantics, they each had slightly different concerns and approaches to writing. Write an essay in which you compare and contrast two of the writers whose works you have just read.

    Prewriting. After choosing two writers, review the author biography of each writer and carefully reread the selections by each writer, noting similarities and differences in their concerns and approaches.

    Writing. When you write your essay, organize your argument according to corresponding points of contrast; use evidence from their works for support.

    Revising. When you revise, make sure you have used transitions and other linking devices to connect your ideas and have varied the length and structure of your sentences.

Assignment

3. Romanticism is an extremely broad concept, encompassing a wide variety of different concerns and beliefs. Write an essay in which you discuss the various Romantic attitudes, interests, and approaches reflected in the literature written between 1800 and 1840.

    Prewriting. Review the selections in this unit, noting the Romantic concerns and beliefs that they reflect. Prepare a thesis statement, then organize your notes into an outline.

    Writing. When you write your essay, support your thesis with evidence from at least one selection by each of the writers in this unit.

    Revising. When you revise, make sure your essay is organized in a logical manner. After you have finished revising, proofread your essay and prepare a final copy.

You the Critic   243

YOU THE CRITIC
Guidelines for Evaluating Assignment 1

1. Has the student included a thesis statement that indicates the Romantic interest in the supernatural in one of the selections in this unit?
2. Has the student supported his or her thesis with details from the selection?
3. Has the student included only relevant information?
4. Is the essay free from grammar, usage, and mechanics errors?

Guidelines for Evaluating Assignment 2

1. Has the student compared and contrasted two writers and their works?
2. Has the student used evidence from the works of the writers to support his or her points?
3. Has the student used transitional devices to link ideas and varied the length and structure of the sentences?
4. Is the essay free from grammar, usage, and mechanics errors?

Guidelines for Evaluating Assignment 3

1. Has the student effectively presented in an essay the Romantic concerns and beliefs?
2. Has the student supported his or her thesis statement with evidence from selections by each writer in the unit?
3. Is the essay well-organized?
4. Is the essay free from grammar, usage, and mechanics errors?

Humanities Note

Fine art, *Boston Harbor,* by Fitz Hugh Lane. Fitz Hugh Lane (1804–1865) was born in Gloucester, Massachusetts. Although a youthful illness left him handicapped, he was able, with the aid of the crutches he used throughout his life, to travel a good deal. The gentle, still quality of his landscapes and seascapes has been compared, in their thoughtful depiction of the natural world, with the writings of Thoreau and Emerson.

The work in the text was one of many drawings and paintings Lane did of Boston Harbor. In the 1840's a sculptor noted the beauty of a sailing vessel like the one in Lane's work, remarking on the "majestic form of her hull as she rushes through the water" and "the symmetry of her spars and rigging."

Lane's picture has a luminous quality; it is realistic in its careful attention to details. Lane may have been influenced by the work of J. M. W. Turner, the famous British landscape painter. To Lane, the sea had a gentleness and particular beauty. In this painting, the harbor dominates; the city is barely visible on the horizon, and yet the sea is not portrayed as a threatening element.

BOSTON HARBOR
Fitz Hugh Lane
Museum of Fine Arts, Boston

244

Objectives

1 To learn about the historical developments that occurred in the United States between 1840 and 1855
2 To learn about the literary flowering that took place in New England during this period
3 To learn about the major authors and literary movements of the period

NEW ENGLAND RENAISSANCE

1840–1855

One man's justice is another's injustice; one man's beauty another's ugliness; one man's wisdom another's folly.

Ralph Waldo Emerson

245

Historical Context Tell students that this period was an age of rapid change in the United States. Developments in industry, technology, transportation, and agriculture transformed the United States into one of the most advanced nations in the world. In addition, the country was growing larger as a steady progression of people headed West in search of undeveloped land and new opportunities.

Also point out to students that this period was an age characterized by a tremendous outpouring of literary achievement. Then have students discuss how the fact that the United States had established itself as a secure and well-developed nation might have contributed to the literary flowering that occurred between 1840 and 1855.

Writing to Learn Have students write a journal entry in which they explore their preconceptions of what life was like in America during this period. As students move through the unit, encourage them to look back at their journal entries and think about the ways in which their conceptions may have changed.

ESL Teaching Strategy Pair each ESL student with a native speaker. Have them read through the unit introduction together, taking turns reading aloud. Instruct the native speaker to clarify the meanings of any words with which the ESL student is unfamiliar.

Motivation/Prior Knowledge
Have your students share their prior knowledge of the historical events and developments that took place in the United States between 1840 and 1855. Then explain that this unit introduction will help to enhance their understanding of this period of American history and will help them to appreciate how the historical developments relate to the literary flowering that occurred.

Purpose-Setting Question What were the main historical events and developments of the period? What were the causes of the literary flowering that took place during the period?

1 **Enrichment** As the United States was transformed into an industrialized nation, the differences between the South and the North became more pronounced. One of the most significant differences concerned the attitude toward slavery. While more and more northerners opposed the slavery, the southerners held onto the belief that their economy would collapse if slavery were abolished.

2 **Enrichment** A classic study of this period is *The Flowering of New England* by Van Wyck Brooks (E. P. Dutton, 1936; Houghton Mifflin, paperback, 1981).

3 **Literary Movement** See the excerpt from *Nature* on page 268.

By 1840 it was clear that the American experiment in democracy had succeeded. England, rebuffed in the "Second American War for Independence," was no longer a threat to the survival of the republic. Andrew Jackson, the first "People's President," had served two tempestuous terms in office. New states were entering the Union; Arkansas had come in as the 25th state in 1836, and Michigan was soon to follow. Despite the Panic of 1837, the mood in America was buoyant; the best was yet to come. Alexis de Tocqueville, a French traveler in the 1830's, observed that Americans had "a lively faith in the perfectibility of man," and they "admit that what appears to them today to be good may be superseded by something better tomorrow."

Although the great early presidents of the Virginia and Massachusetts dynasties had passed from the scene, a bright new galaxy of statesmen could be seen in Washington, D.C.: Daniel Webster from Massachusetts, Henry Clay from Kentucky, Thomas Hart Benton from Missouri, and John C. Calhoun from South Carolina. As these men struggled with political issues that would ultimately break the nation apart, American literature blossomed suddenly and brilliantly in the New England states, particularly in Massachusetts, and specifically in Boston, Concord, Salem, Pittsfield, and Amherst. Historians have called this brief, sunlit era in American cultural history a "flowering," a "renaissance," and a "golden day." Its guiding spirit was Ralph Waldo Emerson, a Unitarian minister who in 1832 had left the pulpit of the Second Church of Boston for a broader stage. Wrote one historian, "The year 1836, when Emerson published his essay on *Nature,* may be taken as the focus of a period in American thought corresponding to 1776 in American politics."

Hub of the Solar System

When the New England literary group burst into flower, Boston was a vibrant, expanding city of nearly 100,000 people. Then, as now, it was the metropolis of the region, a cosmopolitan city whose clipper ships were known from Liverpool to Singapore. Oliver Wendell Holmes, a Boston physician and man of letters, said, tongue-in-cheek, "Boston State House is the hub of the solar system."

Certainly, Boston's four-story Tremont House, with 170 guest rooms, was at mid-century one of the finest hotels in America. In 1842 Charles Dickens, twenty-nine years old and already a world-famous author, stayed at the Tremont House. As a climax to his visit, the Young Men of Boston staged a great dinner in his honor, scarcely imagining that some of their close friends would one day have international literary reputations to rival that of Dickens.

Just as the city of Boston, a center of culture and commerce, was growing, so were a great many Massachusetts factory and mill towns. Of the 1,200 cotton factories in the United States in 1840, two-thirds were located in New England. Francis C. Lowell, who developed the first American power loom, devised a plan to attract

246   *New England Renaissance*

conscientious workers. He hired high-principled young women, most of them from nearby farms, to work in the textile mills of Lowell, Waltham, Lawrence, and other towns on the Merrimack River. These so-called "Lowell factory girls" lived in boarding houses under strict supervision, and worked from 5:00 A.M. to 7:30 P.M., with two half-hour breaks for meals. While the Lowell plan was far from typical, the factory system in general was an economic success. Textile companies prospered. The town of Lowell mushroomed from 200 people in 1820 to over 30,000 by 1845.

If New England was growing and changing, so was the rest of the country. The factory system, with its mass production, would eventually change the face of America, but that change was mostly in the future. America was still an agricultural nation. More often than not, the Lowell factory girls returned to their family farms after a few years, more mature, ready to marry, and by no means part of an urban American underclass. City populations were growing throughout the United States, but so was the number of American farms. The nation as a whole experienced a period of spectacular growth during these years of New England's literary prime. Cities, farms, factories—all were booming.

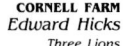

CORNELL FARM
Edward Hicks
Three Lions

Humanities Note

Fine art, *Cornell Farm,* by Edward Hicks. A Quaker background significantly influenced the work of Edward Hicks (1780–1849). Some of his many representations of the signing of Penn's Treaty with the Indians bear the inscription that the pact was the "foundation of religious and civil liberty in the United States." Other works by Hicks show jungle animals side by side with farm animals, as if the artist were proclaiming peace among the creatures of the earth.

Hick's style, as in *Cornell Farm,* combines primitiveness, fantasy, and naturalism. The farm animals, in a striking row-upon-row arrangement, receive greater prominence than the Pennsylvania farmer James Cornell and his two brothers. The painting shows a peaceful, bucolic farm scene representative of the agricultural aspect of the nation at this time.

Enrichment In the years before Texas joined the Union, Texans were involved in a bloody struggle to free themselves from Mexican control. The Texans declared their independence from Mexico on March 2, 1836. At the same time, however, a small army of Texans was involved in a heroic battle in San Antonio. Taking refuge in an old Spanish mission known as the Alamo, a group of 188 soldiers fought bravely to fend off thousands of Mexican troops. After the Mexicans had shelled the Alamo for twelve days, they launched an all-out assault on the mission. Eventually, all of the Texan soldiers were killed. Yet by keeping the Mexican army engaged for close to two weeks, they had provided the Texan leader Sam Houston with enough time to organize a large army. Several weeks later, Houston's army soundly defeated the Mexicans in the Battle of San Jacinto and they forced the Mexican general to sign a treaty granting Texas its independence.

The Texans set up their own government modeled after that of the United States. Yet the new government faced huge problems. Not only had the Mexican government refused to accept the treaty that their general had signed, but also Texas faced serious economic problems that almost forced it into bankruptcy. To solve these problems, most Texans hoped to become part of the United States. This wish was ultimately granted in 1845, when the American Congress passed a joint resolution admitting Texas into the Union.

AMERICAN EVENTS

1840   The Transcendentalist magazine, *The Dial*, begins publication.

1841   **Ralph Waldo Emerson** publishes *Essays*.

Brook Farm, the Transcendental community, established near Boston.

Henry Wadsworth Longfellow publishes "The Skeleton in Armor."

1842   Anesthesia first used for medical purposes.

Webster-Ashburton Treaty eases boundary disputes between the United States and Canada.

1843   **John Greenleaf Whittier** publishes *Lays of My Home and Other Poems*.

1844   First telegraph message sent.

Ralph Waldo Emerson publishes *Essays: Second Series*.

1845   Texas admitted to the Union.

1846   Mexican War begins.

Oliver Wendell Holmes publishes *Poems*.

Herman Melville publishes *Typee*, his first novel.

Abraham Lincoln first elected to Congress.

1847   **Henry Wadsworth Longfellow** publishes *Evangeline*.

First adhesive postage stamps issued.

John Greenleaf Whittier   Henry Wadsworth Longfellow

Mexican War

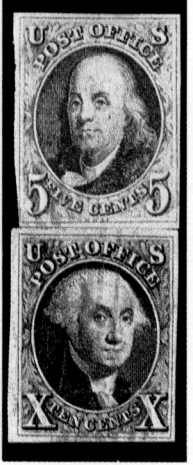
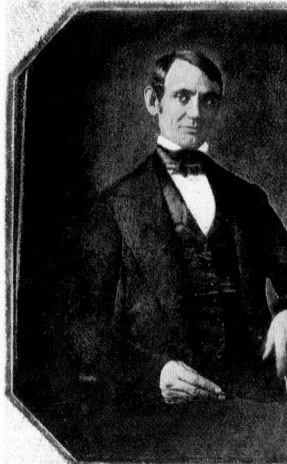

First Postage Stamps   Abraham Lincoln

Alfred, Lord Tennyson

Irish Potato Famine

Emily Brontë   Charlotte Brontë

WORLD EVENTS

1840   Canada: Upper and Lower Canada united.

England: Thomas Hardy is born.

1841   Antarctica: First explored by Englishman James Ross.

South Pacific: New Zealand becomes a British colony.

1842   Asia: Hong Kong becomes a British colony.

England: Alfred, Lord Tennyson publishes *Poems*.

France: Honoré de Balzac publishes *The Human Comedy*.

1843   England: Charles Dickens publishes *A Christmas Carol*.

1844   Germany: Heinrich Heine publishes *Germany: A Winter's Tale*.

France: Alexandre Dumas publishes *The Three Musketeers*.

1845   Ireland: Famine results from failure of potato crop.

1846   Russia: Fyodor Dostoyevsky publishes *Poor Folk*.

1847   Italy: Verdi's opera *Macbeth* first performed.

England: Charlotte Brontë publishes *Jane Eyre*.

England: Emily Brontë publishes *Wuthering Heights*.

Enrichment The great Russian novelist Fyodor Dostoevksy (1821-1881) was born in Moscow, the son of a staff doctor at the Hospital for the Poor. He attended the Military Engineering Academy in St. Petersburg, graduating in 1843. Three years after his graduation, he published his first novel, *Poor People,* which was greeted with enthusiasm by critics. In the same year, he also published his second novel, *The Double.* Yet critics regarded this novel as a failure.

In 1849 Dostoevsky and a group of his friends were arrested because of their advocacy of political reform and social change. After being tried and found guilty of subversion of the government of Czar Nicholas I, they were sentenced to death. Subsequently, they were taken to the place of their execution, blindfolded, and placed in front of a firing squad. Just as the executioners were being ordered to take aim, a horseman suddenly appeared, bearing a reprieve from the czar. This sequence of events had been prearranged to discourage Dostoevsky and his friends from questioning the czar's policies.

Obviously, this experience had a tremendous impact on Dostoevsky, as did his experiences in the Siberian prison camp he was sent to following the aborted execution. Having been sentenced to five years of hard labor, followed by five years of military service in a penal battalion, he spent close to a decade in Siberia. By the time he was finally permitted to leave, he was a changed man. Having rejected the liberal ideas he had previously embraced, he had become a staunch conservative and a devoutly religious man. His experiences had not dampened his enthusiasm for writing, however, and his greatest literary achievements were still to come.

Dostoevsky completed *Notes from Underground,* the first of his great works, in 1864. This work tracks the experiences and expresses the thoughts of a nameless hero who rebels against all outside influences and asserts his personal freedom. Dostoevsky continued to explore the issue of personal freedom in *Crime and Punishment* (1865), a novel about a man who resorts to murder as a means of asserting his independence. Two more successful novels, *The Idiot* (1869) and *The Possessed* (1869), followed. These works set the stage for Dostoevsky's finest work, *The Brothers Karamazov* (1880).

250

Enrichment The Mexican War ended with the signing of the Treaty of Guadalupe Hidalgo. This treaty required Mexico to relinquish control of all of California and the New Mexico Territory to the United States. In return, the United States paid Mexico 15 million dollars and agreed to respect the rights of Spanish-speaking people in the ceded territories. More information about the Mexican War appears on the Guide for Interpreting on page 287.

Enrichment The California gold rush began in 1848 when a builder named James Marshall discovered gold in the American River north of Sacramento. Within just a few days, news of the gold strike had spread to San Francisco. In the ensuing months, hoardes of Californians abandoned their jobs and headed north in search of gold. By 1849, people from all over the world were flocking to California hoping to discover gold. Over 40,000 people traveled to California in 1849. The rise in population and the greed of many of the miners caused a rapid increase in the California crime rate. Hoping to put an end to the lawlessness, the Californians asked to be admitted to the Union. In 1850 their request was granted.

AMERICAN EVENTS

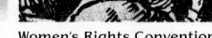

1848   Mexican War ends; United States expands borders.

        James Russell Lowell publishes *A Fable for Critics* and *The Bigelow Papers*.

        California gold rush begins.

        Women's Rights Convention held in Seneca Falls, New York.

1849   **Henry David Thoreau** publishes *A Week on the Concord and Merrimack Rivers*.

        Edgar Allan Poe dies.

1850   *Harper's Magazine* founded.

        Nathaniel Hawthorne publishes *The Scarlet Letter*.

        Ralph Waldo Emerson publishes *Representative Man*.

        California admitted to the Union.

1851   **Herman Melville** publishes *Moby-Dick*.

        Nathaniel Hawthorne publishes *The House of Seven Gables*.

        The New York Times begins publication.

1852   Harriet Beecher Stowe publishes *Uncle Tom's Cabin*.

        Nathaniel Hawthorne publishes *The Blithedale Romance*.

1853   Arizona and New Mexico purchased from Mexico.

        John Greenleaf Whittier publishes *The Chapel of the Hermits*.

1854   **Henry David Thoreau** publishes *Walden*.

        Republican Party organized.

1855   **Henry Wadsworth Longfellow** publishes *The Song of Hiawatha*.

250   *New England Renaissance*

Henry David Thoreau

Women's Rights Convention

Japan Opens Ports to Trade

Louis Napoleon

California Gold Rush

Ralph Waldo Emerson

Taiping Rebellion

Robert Browning

WORLD EVENTS

1848   Belgium: Karl Marx and Friedrich Engels publish *The Communist Manifesto*.

England: Women first admitted to University of London.

1849   England: Matthew Arnold publishes *The Strayed Reveller and Other Poems*.

1850   France: Life insurance introduced.

England: Elizabeth Barrett Browning publishes *Sonnets from the Portuguese*.

England: Charles Dickens publishes *David Copperfield*.

Germany: Wagner's opera *Lohengrin* first performed.

China: Taiping Rebellion begins.

England: Alfred, Lord Tennyson appointed poet laureate.

1851   Australia: Gold discovered in New South Wales.

Norway: Henrik Ibsen writes *Norma*.

1852   Russia: Leo Tolstoy publishes *Childhood*.

Europe: Crimean War begins.

France: Louis Napoleon proclaims himself emperor.

1853   Japan: Ports opened to trade.

1854   England: Charles Dickens publishes *Hard Times*.

1855   England: Robert Browning publishes *Men and Women*.

Introduction   251

Enrichment The Crimean War began in 1854 when France and Britain declared war on Russia to prevent Russia from gaining too much influence over the weak Ottoman Empire. The Italian state of Sardinia entered the war on the side of France and Britain, who achieved victory in 1856. Sardinia's participation in the war ultimately played an important role in bringing about Italian unification. By assisting the French in the Crimean War, the Sardinians were able to gain the support of the French in putting an end to Austrian influence in Italy. Once Austrian influence had been removed, it became possible for Sardinia to seize control of the other Italian states and establish a unified Italian kingdom.

Enrichment Before the Japanese ports were reopened in 1853, Japan had existed in a state of strict seclusion for over two hundred years. This period of self-imposed exile resulted from the desire of the Japanese leaders to put an end to the spread of foreign ideas and beliefs.

Telegraph key used by Samuel F. B. Morse to send the first telegraph message, May 24, 1844. Samuel F. B. Morse (1791–1872) studied art in England, where he was exposed to the classical style. When he returned to the United States, Morse became a portrait painter; his subjects included the poet William Cullen Bryant. In the 1830's he gave up painting and turned his attention to the development of the telegraph. In his device, Morse used the recently discovered electromagnet to create an electric circuit as the key is pressed. At first, the transmitted signal appeared as a system of dots and dashes (the Morse Code) on a paper roll. Later the signal was carried by sound. As the first long-range communication system, the telegraph, along with the telephone (1870's), had an immense impact on all aspects of industrial society.

The Way West

In one sense, the entire course of American history since 1607 can be seen as a pageant of continuous westward movement. The first white settlers sailed west from Europe, establishing their homes on the East Coast of the New World. All thirteen original states were on the eastern seaboard, hemmed in by mountain barriers blocking easy access to the interior. As late as 1845 the most western state in the Union was Texas. The last of the fifty states, Hawaii, lying far away to the west of the North American continent, was at that time an independent kingdom.

During the years in which New England literature flowered, American transportation was steadily changing and improving. The Erie Canal, completed in the state of New York in 1825, set off a wave of frenzied canal building in the Northeast. Throughout the 1840's, American railroads competed not only with canals but also with plank roads. A plank road, usually constructed of hemlock boards, was strong enough to support heavy wagons and stagecoaches. Built by private turnpike companies, plank roads enjoyed a brief flurry of popularity in the 1840's. By 1855, however, it was obvious that railroads had clear-cut advantages over plank roads, and in many places railroads had already rendered canals unprofitable. As the Civil War approached, the golden age of railroading was about to begin.

Advances in agriculture followed advances in technology. John Deere, a native of Vermont, developed the steel plow out in Illinois. Cyrus McCormick, a Virginian, invented the reaper. These two inventions contributed immensely to the settlement of the prairies and later the Great Plains, for they helped make farming practical on the vast, sod-covered grasslands. Another invention of the time, the telegraph, had far-reaching effects, enabling people to communicate almost instantly across great distances. Inventor Samuel F. B. Morse's message from Washington to Baltimore in 1844 could serve as the motto for this era of innovation: "What hath God wrought!"

TELEGRAPH KEY USED BY SAMUEL F. B. MORSE TO SEND THE FIRST TELEGRAPH MESSAGE OF MAY 24, 1844
The Granger Collection

Clouds in a Summer Sky

"In this refulgent summer," wrote Emerson, "it has been a luxury to draw the breath of life. The grass grows, the buds burst, the meadow is spotted with fire and gold in the tint of flowers. The air is full of birds, and sweet with the breath of pine, the balm-of-Gilead, and the new hay. . . . One is constrained to respect the perfection of this world in which our senses converse."

Ever the optimist, Emerson, as one critic said, "counted on things to take care of themselves. He could not be angry, he could not be sad." Yet it was evident to even the most cheerful observer that the United States, in the middle of the nineteenth century, faced growing problems as well as shining promises. The factories and mills that were building prosperity did not always offer the clean boarding houses, matronly chaperons, and pleasant camaraderie of Lowell at its best. More often the factory system brought increasingly fierce competition, which sometimes led to "those dark Satanic mills" of the English poet William Blake's grim vision, in which child labor, low wages, long hours, and unsafe working conditions combined to produce a situation that cried for reform.

4 In the anthracite mines of Pennsylvania, boys as young as seven or eight spent long days working as slate pickers in cavernous coal breakers. These boys, blackened by coal dust, supplemented the income of their fathers, whose own twelve to fourteen hours of labor brought in too little money to support the family. Their plight was worse than most, but in time even the Lowell factory girls lost many of their benefits, saw their wages slashed, and began to think about striking.

5 Nor were most other women at mid-century living in idyllic circumstances. In many states women could not vote, make a will, or file a lawsuit. A woman's property was under the absolute control of her husband, making her, as one woman wrote, "a ward, an appendage." The 1840's and 1850's saw an outburst of energy directed toward increasing the rights of women. One of the pivotal events in the women's movement, the Seneca Falls Convention, organized by Lucretia Mott and Elizabeth Cady Stanton, took place in 1848. Susan B. Anthony, a superb organizer and tireless campaigner, soon joined the movement. Women were active in other reform movements as well. Dorthea Dix crusaded for better treatment of the mentally ill, while Julia Ward Howe and Harriet Beecher Stowe attacked the institution of slavery. Sarah and Angelina Grimké advocated women's rights and freedom for the slaves, as did Lucy Stone and the eloquent Sojourner Truth, who had been born a slave.

135,000 SETS, 270,000 VOLUMES SOLD.

UNCLE TOM'S CABIN

FOR SALE HERE.

AN EDITION FOR THE MILLION, COMPLETE IN 1 Vol., PRICE 37 1-2 CENTS.
" " IN GERMAN, IN 1 Vol., PRICE 50 CENTS.
" " IN 2 Vols., CLOTH, 6 PLATES, PRICE $1.50.
SUPERB ILLUSTRATED EDITION, IN 1 Vol. WITH 153 ENGRAVINGS,
PRICES FROM $2.50 TO $5.00.

The Greatest Book of the Age.

HARRIET BEECHER STOWE, 1853
Alanson Fisher
The Granger Collection

AMERICAN BOOKSELLER'S ANNOUNCEMENT
FOR *UNCLE TOM'S CABIN*, 1852
The Granger Collection

Utopias and Lyceums

"What a fertility of projects for the salvation of the world!" exclaimed Emerson. With reform in the air, it is little wonder that utopias, or "perfect communities," were on many people's minds. One of the most famous of these utopias was Brook Farm, located only nine miles from Boston. Brook Farm was established in 1841 by George Ripley, an ex-Unitarian minister like Emerson, and strongly influenced by Emerson's views. The community attracted a number of prominent writers, including Nathaniel Hawthorne. It soon fell under the influence of Fourierism, a communal system promoted by New York journalist Arthur Brisbane. Since Fourierism held scant appeal for the gentle Bostonians who had established the community, Brook Farm gradually withered away. Meanwhile, three other utopias had been founded in New England: Hopedale, Fruitlands, and Northampton. All failed.

Indeed, very few utopian communities anywhere ever prospered. Among the few that did were seven small Amana colonies, settled in 1855 near the Iowa River in east central Iowa. The woolen goods from Amana, especially blankets, became commercially popular, and today the colonies still survive, their quaint villages attracting many tourists. The 700-member Amana Church Society is virtually all that remains today of the utopian fever that swept America in the 1840's and 1850's.

Another trend of that era, also idealistic in its aims, was the movement for better public and private education. By 1850 most people in the United States seemed to agree that free public elementary and secondary schools should be provided for all children and that higher education should be available for students who were able to pay. Adult education had its advocates, too. The lyceum movement, which originated in Millbury, Massachusetts, gained great momentum during these years. A lyceum (like the chautauqua that eventually replaced it) was a popular society established for literary and scientific study. One of the most famous lyceums was Boston's Lowell Institute, founded in 1839. Lyceums offered lectures, debates, scientific demonstrations, and other entertainments. Many authors of the period, including those of the New England renaissance, appeared frequently as paid lyceum speakers.

LITERATURE IN FULL FLOWER

Elaborate theories have been devised to explain why sudden outbursts of creativity occur at certain places and times. The facts are often more fascinating than the theories—and easier to comprehend. In New England between 1840 and 1855, and mostly around Boston, an array of writers, now world-famous, produced a remarkable body of work that bulks large in the American literary tradition.

THE NOTCH OF THE WHITE MOUNTAINS (CRAWFORD NOTCH), 1839
Thomas Cole
National Gallery of Art, Washington, D. C.

Goodbye, Courtly Muses

Ralph Waldo Emerson published his first essay anonymously in 1836. The next year he delivered his famous oration, *The American Scholar,* before the Phi Beta Kappa Society of Harvard, a speech that attracted widespread attention. Oliver Wendell Holmes called the address "our intellectual Declaration of Independence," which is precisely what Emerson had in mind. Emerson believed that American writers "had listened too long to the courtly muses of Europe" and should begin to interpret their own culture in new, and not borrowed, ways. Emerson named no names, but few readers could deny that Washington Irving and James Fenimore Cooper sometimes sounded like transplanted Englishmen. Edgar Allan Poe never did, but not all American critics, then or later, took Poe seriously—"three-fifths genius," James Russell Lowell, a Bostonian, called him, "and two-fifths sheer fudge."

Critics would be much kinder to the writers who arose in New England in the 1840's and early 1850's. There was the sanguine Emerson himself, whose essays, poems, journals, and letters hold a permanent place in our literature. There was Henry David Thoreau, fourteen years younger than Emerson and something of a

Humanities Note

Fine art, *The Notch of the White Mountains (Crawford Notch),* 1839, by Thomas Cole. William Cullen Bryant, in a funeral oration for Thomas Cole (1801–1848), spoke of the artist's "scenes of wild grandeur." As a young man, Cole was apprenticed to an engraver; however, he preferred to paint scenes from nature, and was devoted to music and poetry as well. Cole's preference for subjects from the natural world led him to become a founding member of the Hudson River School.

Cole himself, in his writings, described the Crawford Notch as desolate; he and his companions felt overwhelmed as they hiked through the region and beheld the dramatic cleft in the soaring White Mountains. According to Cole, the family that had lived in the small house shown in the painting had perished in a landslide. Indeed, Nathaniel Hawthorne wrote a story, "The Ambitious Guest," about just such an incident in the White Mountains. Although a figure on horseback appears in the foreground, the focus of the work is clearly on nature, in its starkness, as suggested by the bare trees and stumps, and in its power, as represented by the centrally placed notch. In an age of exploration of the vast North American continent, artists like Cole sought to portray the majesty and untamed wilderness of the land.

7 Literary Movement Although these writers fit into three small, distinct literary movements, they were also all part of the much broader Romantic Movement that began in the early 1800's.

Learning Across the Curriculum Students might be interested in learning more about the ideas that the Transcendentalists looked to for inspiration. Divide your class into six groups. Then assign each group one of the following topics: the philosophy of Immanuel Kant, the ideas of Plato, the findings of Pascal, the discoveries of Swedenborg, the fundamental beliefs of Buddhism, and the foundations of Hinduism. Have each group research the topic they have been assigned. When they have completed their research, have them share their findings with the rest of the class.

protégé, although a very individualistic one, who lived in the Emerson household for two years. Thoreau's classic work, *Walden,* appeared in 1854. On the darker side there was Nathaniel Hawthorne, whose powerful, sometimes enigmatic style reached its peak in *The Scarlet Letter,* published in 1850. Then there was a volatile New Yorker living in Pittsfield, the ex-sailor of the South Seas, Herman Melville, whose masterpiece, *Moby-Dick,* met with indifference at first and lavish praise later. In Amherst, living quietly and publishing almost nothing in her lifetime, was the young, brilliantly gifted poet, Emily Dickinson.

Those were the giants, or so they seem to us today. In 1850 the reading public in the United States might have pointed more quickly to four other New England writers. Henry Wadsworth Longfellow, a Harvard professor until 1854 and a tremendously popular poet, was a leading figure among New England intellectuals. So was Oliver Wendell Holmes, the unofficial poet laureate of the group. Two other celebrated writers of the day were John Greenleaf Whittier, who came from a hardworking Quaker farm family, and James Russell Lowell, born to wealth and position. Both Whittier and Lowell were antislavery crusaders as well as poets.

Transcendentalism

Most, if not all, of these writers of the period were influenced by the Transcendental movement then flourishing in New England. Emerson and Thoreau were the best-known Transcendentalists, but the ferment of Transcendental ideas affected many other writers, some of whom hovered on the fringes of the movement, some of whom opposed it.

Transcendentalism demands careful definition, yet it is very hard to define. It has many facets, many sources, and encompasses a range of beliefs whose specific principles depend on the individual writer or thinker. The term itself and some of the ideas came from the German philosopher Immanuel Kant. In his *Critique of Practical Reason,* published in 1788, Kant refers to the "transcendental," which to him meant the knowledge or understanding a person gains intuitively, although it lies beyond direct physical experience. New England Transcendentalism drew on other philosophical theories besides Kant's. These included Plato's as well as those of Pascal, the French mathematician and moralist, and Swedenborg, the Swedish scientist and mystic. In addition, it drew on Buddhist thought and German idealism.

The movement was not essentially religious, but there were religious overtones. Even though a hundred years had passed since Jonathan Edwards, a Calvinist minister in Northampton, Massachusetts, had preached that human beings can share directly in the divine light, Edwards's idea continued to exert influence in the mid-nineteenth century. More recently, William Ellery Channing, minister

256   *New England Renaissance*

of the Federal Street Church, Boston, had broken with the Calvinism of his day to become the apostle of Unitarianism. Channing's sermons and essays, promoting more tolerant religious attitudes and various social causes, reflected his own optimism and idealism. The inscription on a statue of him in the Boston Public Garden reads, "He breathed into theology a humane spirit."

Beyond that, Channing helped to lay the groundwork for New England's Transcendentalism. His influence on American literature was substantial; Emerson, Longfellow, Lowell, and Holmes all acknowledged their debt to him. To a remarkable degree, his views became their views. Seven years before Emerson's *American Scholar* address, Channing's *Remarks on American Literature* had called for American writers to cease imitating British models and to find their inspiration closer to home.

Philosophy, religion, literature—all merged in New England Transcendentalism, producing a native blend that was romantic, intuitive, mystical, and considerably easier to recognize than to explain. Emerson, believing in the divinity of human nature, embodied the spirit of it. Thoreau, in *Walden,* provided it with its most sustained expression. Yet Transcendentalism was, and is, hard to pin down. To some in the luminous literary group in Boston and its environs, whose members met from time to time—a group which outsiders came to call the "Transcendental Club,"—the movement meant intense individualism and self-reliance. To others it meant practically the opposite and was considered a single-minded commitment to improving the lot of the poor and oppressed. The Transcendentalists could accept such differences, for theirs was a democracy of intellect. They recognized few absolutes beyond an all-encompassing belief in the unity of God and the world. Even self-contradictions might be necessary, as Emerson stated in a much-quoted sentence: "A foolish consistency is the hobgoblin of little minds."

For Transcendentalists the point was that the real truths, the fundamental truths, lay outside the experience of the senses, residing instead in the "Over-Soul . . . a universal and benign omnipresence . . . a God known to men only in moments of mystic enthusiasm, whose visitations leave them altered, self-reliant, and purified of petty aims."

If that seems a bit obscure, as it did to many people in the United States, and often to the press, so did the essays in *The Dial,* the quarterly magazine of New England Transcendentalism, which grew out of the informal and sporadic meetings of the Transcendentalists. Published from 1840 to 1844, *The Dial*'s first editor was Margaret Fuller, a dominant personality and zealous feminist, whose book, *Woman in the Nineteenth Century,* was the first serious American exploration of feminism. Margaret Fuller, astonishingly erudite, was accepted as the intellectual equal, or even superior, of the most honored members of the circle. Under her editorship, how-

8

9

8 Literary Movement An emphasis on individualism and a concern for the poor and oppressed are both important components of Romanticism.

9 Literary Movement See the discussion of Transcendentalism in the Guide for Reading on page 273.

10 **Literary Movement** The Transcendentalists' beliefs reflected the Romantic interest in nature and its relationship to humanity.

11 **Literary Movement** See the selections by Emerson, pages 274–285.

12 **Literary Movement** See the selections by Thoreau, pages 288–296.

13 **Literary Movement** See the discussion of Anti-Transcendentalism on page 301.

14 **Master Teacher Note** To help students grasp the ideas of the Anti-Transcendentalists, contrast them to those of the Transcendentalists.

ever, *The Dial,* like Transcendentalism, seemed to lack a clear focus and may have bewildered as many people as it enlightened.

Nodding Fields and Walden Pond

If the Transcendentalists, and Emerson himself, lacked a well-defined philosophy, there were certain basic areas of agreement. The Transcendentalists revered nature. Emerson titled his first major work *Nature,* and although the essay deals with many topics—beauty, discipline, idealism, spirit, and others—Nature (with a capital N) provides its unifying theme. "The fields and woods," wrote Emerson, "nod to me, and I to them." This essay is considered the first full-scale expression of American Transcendentalism.

Both of Henry David Thoreau's important works, *Walden* and the earlier *A Week on the Concord and Merrimack Rivers,* emphasize the central importance of nature. *Walden* begins, "When I wrote the following pages, or rather the bulk of them, I lived alone, in the woods, a mile from any neighbor, in a house which I had built myself, on the shore of Walden Pond, in Concord, Massachusetts, and earned my living by the labor of my hands only." The book comprises eighteen essays that deal with matters ranging from the pickerel in Walden Pond to a battle between red and black ants. Nature is the central subject, and from its development emerges Thoreau's philosophy of individualism, simplicity, and passive resistance to injustice.

Brook Farm, as a kind of back-to-nature venture, reflected the Transcendentalists' interest in putting theories into practice. Nathaniel Hawthorne, partly at the urging of Elizabeth Peabody, a Transcendentalist and a friend of Margaret Fuller, bought two shares of stock in Brook Farm and took up residence there in 1841. He hated it. "It is my opinion," he wrote to his fiancée, "that a man's soul may be buried and perish under a dungheap or in a furrow of the field just as well as under a pile of money." Hawthorne, who never shared the optimism of Emerson and Thoreau, found nothing at Brook Farm to alter his view that the world is more complex and less perfectible than the Transcendentalists believed.

The Possibility of Evil

Although the Transcendentalists were widely influential, their view of life seemed far too rosy to many writers. If Emerson and Thoreau can be conveniently paired as Transcendentalists, Nathaniel Hawthorne and Herman Melville can be paired as Anti-Transcendentalists. They were writers who, in Hawthorne's words, "burrowed into the depths of our common nature" and found the area not always shimmering, but often "dusky."

Just as the younger Thoreau had apprenticed, in a sense, in Emerson's household, so Melville, fifteen years younger than Hawthorne, sought the counsel and friendship of the older and more widely acclaimed Hawthorne. It happened almost by accident. Melville, in his early thirties, had moved from New York City to Pittsfield in western Massachusetts, where, on a farm he called "Arrowhead," he wrote his monumental book, *Moby-Dick*. It was published in 1851, a year after Hawthorne's *The Scarlet Letter* appeared. Although *Moby-Dick* would be recognized as a great work only after Melville's death, *The Scarlet Letter* achieved immediate fame in both the United States and England.

Meanwhile, Hawthorne had moved to Lenox, Massachusetts, in the Berkshires, a few miles south of Pittsfield. There he was working on the manuscript of *The House of the Seven Gables*. Melville, pessimistic about *Moby-Dick*—"the product is a final hash," he wrote, "and all my books are botches"—approached Hawthorne, seeking solace. According to a biographer, the young Melville was in "a state of exhaustion and hyper-excitability"; his "impetuous soul rushed out to embrace Hawthorne's . . . in headlong and abso-

15

16

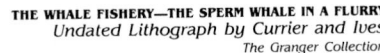

THE WHALE FISHERY—THE SPERM WHALE IN A FLURRY
Undated Lithograph by Currier and Ives
The Granger Collection

15 Literary Movement See the excerpts from *Moby-Dick* beginning on page 318.

16 Literary Movement See the stories by Hawthorne on page 302.

Humanities Note

Fine art, *The Whale Fishery—The Sperm Whale in a Flurry* by Currier and Ives. Nathaniel Currier (1813–1888) and James Merritt Ives (1824–1895) were the largest American publishers of lithographs in the nineteenth century. Lithographs are produced by making a drawing in reverse on stone with a greasy crayon and then inking the stone. Only the crayoned areas accept the ink. The stone is then pressed against paper and a print is made. In the Currier and Ives firm, the coloring of the print was often done by a group of women; the first would apply one color, then pass the print to the next worker, and so on until the coloring process was complete.

The technique of harpooning whales from a small, open boat had been adopted from an Eskimo custom. The print suggests the harshness of the practice. The word *flurry* refers to the violent movement of a dying whale; the print sympathetically portrays the animal's hopeless struggle against the harpoon, while the crew is not glorified. In its time, the scene was highly topical. Before the development of petroleum for industry, sperm whaling was widespread as a means of obtaining necessary lubricants. Herman Melville's novel about Captain Ahab's obsession with his prey is an allegorical study of a driven man. The work, though its whaling-ship setting was familiar enough, did not achieve significant acceptance until the twentieth century.

17 **Literary Movement** Hawthorne's work reflects the Romantic interest in the strange and mysterious.

18 **Enrichment** Hawthorne's importance is examined in contemporary poet Robert Lowell's poem "Hawthorne," page 1114.

19 **Enrichment** Hawthorne also served as a customs officer in Boston and in Salem.

20 **Literary Movement** Emerson's Transcendentalist ideas are reflected in his poetry (pages 279–285).

lute devotion." Hawthorne may have been surprised by this adulation, but he and Melville became and remained friends.

Their visions, however, while equally dark, were very different. Hawthorne's Puritan heritage, which included an ancestor who was a judge at the Salem witchcraft trials, was never far from his consciousness. *The Scarlet Letter* is a historical romance set in Puritan Boston in the middle of the seventeenth century. In it Hawthorne deals with sin and concealed guilt, with hypocrisy and humility, in a dark tale that shows his insight into the Puritan conscience. In *The House of the Seven Gables,* he delves into seventeenth-century witchcraft, insanity, and a legendary curse. These unhappy themes do not reflect the easy optimism of the Transcendentalists, and yet Hawthorne, despite a tendency toward solitude, was stable and self-possessed, absorbed by questions of evil and moral responsibility, yet a shrewd man without illusions.

Melville, by contrast, was a maelstrom of emotions, a man at odds with the world, a tortured and cryptic personality. He was an artist raging against the fates, much like Captain Ahab was in *Moby-Dick,* when he unleashed his fury against the white whale that had torn away his leg. Melville dedicated *Moby-Dick* to Nathaniel Hawthorne "in token for my admiration for his genius." Melville was a genius, too, but an embittered one, a great writer rejected by the public. Only in his later years, with the short novel *Billy Budd,* did he affirm that the cruelties of existence might be overcome by the strength and nobility of the human spirit. Perhaps by then, after long years of obscurity as a customs inspector in New York, he had acquired in his personal life some of the serenity of Hawthorne.

When Poetry Was in Bloom

During the flowering of New England, Americans were avid readers of poetry. Newspapers and magazines published poems, and books of poetry sold briskly. Longfellow was acclaimed as the American bard; Whittier's eightieth birthday was marked by a national celebration; Holmes's comic verse made him a celebrity here and abroad. Today, when poetry is widely written but not so widely read, it may be hard to picture a time in which the names and works of poets were part of the national consciousness. "Poets," said the English poet Shelley in 1821, "are the unacknowledged legislators of the world." In the 1840's and 1850's there were Americans who still believed this.

Among the Transcendentalists, Emerson wrote poetry of an exceptionally high quality. Thoreau declared, "My life has been the poem I would have writ," but in fact he produced some fine poetry on paper as well. Hawthorne concentrated on prose, but Melville in his later years wrote a number of noteworthy poems, especially during the Civil War.

21
22

The popular poets of the day, though, were a group commonly known as the Fireside Poets: Longfellow, Whittier, Holmes, Lowell, and a few lesser-known writers. Working separately—they had no "club" as the Transcendentalists did—the Fireside Poets created verse that the average reader could understand and appreciate. Some of their poems were on inspiring or patriotic themes; others dealt with love, nature, home, family, and children. At their best, the Fireside Poets appealed to well-educated, highly literate readers as well as to the less sophisticated. Longfellow, in particular, had a towering reputation in his own time, and is the only American with a bust in the Poet's Corner of Westminster Abbey in London.

Later critics have tended to rank these poets below Emerson, Thoreau, Hawthorne, and Melville in the literary pantheon. Many of

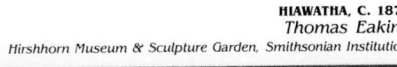

HIAWATHA, C. 1871
Thomas Eakins
Hirshhorn Museum & Sculpture Garden, Smithsonian Institution

21 Literary Movement The Fireside Poets, who were well-known in New England in the 1840's, acquired a national audience after 1850. Their popularity was unrivalled in the quarter century before World War I. The word *fireside* indicates that they had a family audience, and their poetry was read aloud in the family circle. Their themes were home, family, children, nature, idealized love, religion, love of country, history, legend, and anecdote. A very popular work was Longfellow's "Song of Hiawatha."

22 Literary Movement See the selections by Longfellow (pages 338–342), Holmes (pages 348–350), Lowell (pages 354–356), and Whittier (pages 360 and 366).

Humanities Note

Fine art, *Hiawatha*, c. 1871, by Thomas Eakins. Thomas Eakins gained the reputation of being, after Winslow Homer, the finest American painter of the nineteenth century. His work is realistic and penetrating, much of it based on his personal experience and extensive interests, including a series of paintings on boxing.

Hiawatha is not typical of Eakins's work. It is a highly impressionistic, evocative study of the subject of Longfellow's poem *The Song of Hiawatha* (1855). The legendary fifteenth-century chief of the Onondaga tribe, Hiawatha, in a passionate quest for harmony among the Indian nations, helped to found the League of the Iroquois, a confederation of the Mohawk, Cayuga, Oneida, Seneca, and Onondaga tribes. Eakin's fluid, silhouette-like image of Hiawatha, and the vaguely defined shapes of buffalo, deer, and bear, suggest the magical, mystical qualities associated with Longfellow's subject. The work may, in fact, be unfinished.

23 **Enrichment** During her lifetime, not many people saw Emily Dickinson's poems, yet today she holds an important place in American literature. Dickinson had one of the most original minds of her time; she did not look at the world in a conventional way. She wrote about common subjects, such as nature and death. She was not sentimental, but she did not show much optimism. Her poems show a lot of strong emotion and a great deal of wit.

24 **Literary Movement** See the poems by Emily Dickinson on pages 372–394.

their works are still read, however, and the Fireside Poets appear to have earned a permanent place in the hearts of Americans. They lived in New England and were part of its literary blossoming, but they are no longer considered to have been its finest blooms. Even so, their output of memorable poetry helped to build an American myth that still survives and enriches our culture.

At Home in Amherst

At the time Charles Dickens visited Boston and met its emerging literary figures, a young girl was growing up in the valley town of Amherst, Massachusetts. She was not yet writing poetry, at least not seriously, but when she did begin to write, her achievements would catapult her (although not in her lifetime) into the company of the greatest poets in American literature.

Emily Dickinson cannot be easily assigned to any literary category. Her gem-like poetry is unique, just as her life was unique. A recluse for the last twenty-five years of her life, she did not write for publication, or even for her family. Only a few of her poems appeared in print during her lifetime, and those were released without her consent. Why, then, did she write? She may have done so partly to resolve the questions about death, immortality, and the soul that orthodox Calvinism raised but, to her inquiring mind, did not satisfactorily answer.

23

Since her poems were not published until 1890, and since a definitive edition of them did not appear until 1955, it is hard to pigeonhole Emily Dickinson, even historically. She was not a Transcendentalist. She wrote many of her poems during the Civil War, but she was wholly uninfluenced by the conflict. Since she was a New Englander, and since her remarkable poetry with its dazzling brevity and breath-taking images adds a special luster to the New England literary renaissance, her work appears in this unit rather than a later one.

24

Beyond the Flowering

The renaissance did not end abruptly in 1855, of course, but as the storm clouds of war gathered, the great sunburst of creativity in the Northeast did subside. Americans increasingly turned their attention to the coming struggle, and antislavery writers, such as Emerson, Melville, Whittier, and Lowell, strongly supported the northern war effort. Thoreau and Hawthorne died before the last shot was fired. Oliver Wendell Holmes, energetic and cheerful, lived on, outlasting all the rest of that renowned generation of writers, thus becoming "the last leaf upon the tree," to quote his own words. Holmes had written his well-known poem, "The Last Leaf," about Herman Melville's grandfather, "a venerable relic of the Revolution." The poem had been published sixty-three years earlier, in 1831, back when Holmes was a young man and before New England had even begun to bloom.

AMERICAN VOICES
Quotations by Prominent Figures of the Period

Hitch your wagon to a star.
Ralph Waldo Emerson, "Society and Solitude," from
Civilization

Any man more right than his neighbor constitutes a majority
of one.
Henry David Thoreau, *Civil Disobedience*

The mass of men lead lives of quiet desperation.
Henry David Thoreau, *Walden*

If a man does not keep pace with his companions, perhaps it
is because he hears a different drummer. Let him step to the
music which he hears, however measured or far away.
Henry David Thoreau, *Walden*

Life is made up of marble and mud.
Nathaniel Hawthorne, *The House of the Seven Gables*

Call me Ishmael.
Herman Melville, *Moby-Dick*

I 'spect I growed. Don't think nobody never made me.
Harriet Beecher Stowe, *Uncle Tom's Cabin*

If we could read the secret history of our enemies, we should
find in each man's life sorrow and suffering enough to disarm
all hostility.
Henry Wadsworth Longfellow, *Driftwood*

Put not your trust in money, but your money in trust.
Oliver Wendell Holmes, *The Autocrat of the Breakfast Table*

And what is so rare as a day in June?
  Then, if ever, come perfect days.
James Russell Lowell, *The Vision of Sir Launfal*

If I feel physically as if the top of my head were taken off, I
know that is poetry.
Emily Dickinson, *Life and Letters of Emily Dickinson*

Additional Voices

On the threshold she paused,—turned partly round,—for, perchance, the idea of entering, all alone, and all so changed, the home of so intense a former life, was more dreary and desolate than even she could bear. But her hesitation was only for an instant, though long enough to display a scarlet letter on her breast.
Nathaniel Hawthorne, *The Scarlet Letter*

. . . Our day of dependence, our long apprenticeship to the learning of other lands, draws to a close. The millions that around us are rushing into life, cannot always be fed on the sere remains of the foreign harvests. Events, actions arise, that must be sung, that will sing themselves. Who can doubt that poetry will revive and lead in a new age, as the star in the constellation Harp which now flames our zenith, astronomers announce, shall one day be the pole-star for a thousand years.
Ralph Waldo Emerson, "The American Scholar"

This world is a place of business. What an infinite bustle! I am awakened almost every night by the panting of the locomotive. It interrupts my dreams. There is no sabbath. It would be glorious to see mankind at leisure for once. . . . I think that there is nothing, not even crime, more opposed to poetry, to philosophy, ay, to life itself, than this incessant business.
Henry David Thoreau, "Life Without Principle"

Reading Critically The information on this page is intended to
help students read critically the
literature of the New England
Renaissance. This page summarizes the historical context, the
literary movements, and the writers' techniques of the period. On
the following pages, the notes in
the side column point out how a
typical selection of the period,
"The Skeleton in Armor," reflects
these characteristics. It is a model for reading critically the literature of the period. Ask students
to pay attention to these notes as
they read the selection and suggest that they add their own comments. Encourage them to read
the other selections in this unit
with the same attention to the
characteristics of the period.

To give students further
practice with the process of
reading critically, use the selection in the Teaching Portfolio,
"The Hollow of the Three Hills" by
Nathaniel Hawthorne, page 370,
following the Teacher Backup,
which students can annotate
themselves. Encourage students
to use these strategies as they
read the literature in this unit.

Literary Movement New York
and Philadelphia had been the
centers of the American Romantic Movement. Now Boston and
its surrounding area, the stronghold of the "Yankees" who had
been the targets of such writers
as William Cullen Bryant and
Washington Irving, became the
literary capital of the nation.

READING CRITICALLY

The Literature of 1840–1855

During the years from 1840 to 1855, the United States continued to expand rapidly. A steady flow of American pioneers traveled westward, settling in the new frontier. At the same time, a group of writers in New England brought about a literary renaissance that earned the country a place among the world's great literary traditions.

Historical Context

The rapid growth and expansion of the United States helped bring about scientific advances that established the United States as one of the most technologically advanced nations in the world. New agricultural machines were invented, new roads, canals, and railroads were built, and telegraph lines were put into place. These developments brought about an overwhelming sense of optimism about the country's future.

Literary Movements

The sense of optimism that dominated many people's thoughts during this period was reflected in the ideas of the Transcendentalists, the members of one of the main intellectual and artistic movements of the period. Possessing a deep faith in human potential, the Transcendentalists believed that all forms of being are spiritually united through a shared universal soul. In contrast, two major writers who have come to be known as Anti-Transcendentalists espoused a much darker vision of the world, believing that the truths of existence tend to be elusive and disturbing. A third group of writers known as the Fireside Poets also made important contributions during this period. By creating poetry that was inspiring and easy to read, these poets helped to establish poetry as a popular literary form among the American public.

Writers' Techniques

Focusing on popular themes such as love and nature, the Fireside Poets wrote poetry using traditional poetic forms and techniques. Although Ralph Waldo Emerson, the founder of the Transcendentalists, also wrote poetry, the Transcendentalists are remembered mainly for their essays expressing their ideas and beliefs. The Anti-Transcendentalists, on the other hand, expressed their beliefs through the themes of their novels and short stories, often using symbols to convey their themes.

On the following pages is a selection by Henry Wadsworth Longfellow. The notes in the side column should draw your attention to Longfellow's literary techniques and help you to place the selection in its historical context.

264   *New England Renaissance*

Objectives

1 To read literature critically
2 To appreciate the Fireside Poets
3 To read poetry with expression
4 To write a letter

Support Material

Teaching Portfolio
Teacher Backup, p. 376
Reading Critically, "The Hollow of the Three Hills" by Nathaniel Hawthorne, p. 370
Usage and Mechanics Worksheet, p. 374
Analyzing Literature Worksheet, *Understanding the Fireside Poets*, p. 375

Speaking and Listening Worksheet, *Reading with Expression*, p. 376
Selection Test, p. 377

The Skeleton in Armor

Henry Wadsworth Longfellow

Literary Movements: Like much of the poetry of the Fireside Poets, this poem deals with a subject of interest to the common people.

This poem was written after a skeleton clothed in armor was unearthed near Fall River, Massachusetts.

"Speak! speak! thou fearful guest!
Who, with thy hollow breast
Still in rude armor drest,
    Comest to daunt me!
5 Wrapt not in Eastern balms,
But with thy fleshless palms
Stretched, as if asking alms,
    Why dost thou haunt me?"

Historical Context: The discovery of a skeleton in armor made it apparent that the Vikings had explored America long before the arrival of Columbus.

Then, from those cavernous eyes
10 Pale flashes seemed to rise,
As when the Northern skies
    Gleam in December;
And, like the water's flow
Under December's snow,
15 Came a dull voice of woe
    From the heart's chamber.

Writer's Technique: Notice the traditional poetic form. This poem is written in octaves, or eight-line stanzas, with an *aaabcccb* rhyme scheme.

"I was a Viking old!
My deeds, though manifold,
No Skald[1] in song has told,
20   No Saga taught thee!
Take heed, that in thy verse,
Thou dost the tale rehearse,[2]
Else dread a dead man's curse;
    For this I sought thee.

Literary Movement: The poem's subject reflects the Fireside Poets' interest in capturing the American heritage.

25 "Far in the Northern Land,
By the wild Baltic's strand,

---

1. **Skald** (skôld): An ancient Scandinavian poet.
2. **rehearse** (ri hʉrs') *v.:* Narrate.

The Skeleton in Armor   265

Presentation

Motivation/Prior Knowledge
Ask students to imagine that construction workers in their community uncovered a skeleton in a suit of armor. What story could they invent to explain who the skeleton was and how it came to be there? Then explain that Longfellow's poem is such an explanation.

Master Teacher Note You might develop the background of this poem by eliciting from students their knowledge of ancient Viking explorers and warriors—their homelands, their adventures, and their reputation, for example. Tell them that the subject of this poem is a Viking warrior. How does the Viking in this poem compare with their ideas of Vikings?

Purpose-Setting Question What story does the poem tell?

Enrichment Sagas are Icelandic or other Scandinavian medieval stories of the adventures of heroes, especially those of certain important families. The adventures in sagas may be legendary or historical. The term saga has come to be used for a historical legend developed through the oral tradition. Longfellow drew material from *Heimskringla* for his *Sage of King Olaf.*

Critical Thinking and Reading
Ask students to determine who is speaking in the first stanza and who is being addressed. Who is the "I" of the remainder of the poem?

Enrichment The modern word *berserk,* meaning "in a state of violently destructive rage," comes from the behavior of these ancient Scandinavian warriors, like the Berserks in lines 53, who fought with frenzied violence.

Writer's Technique: This poem is an example of a narrative poem—a poem that tells a story. Longfellow's narrative poems played an important role in establishing poetry as a popular literary form.

      I, with my childish hand,
          Tamed the gerfalcon;[3]
      And, with my skates fast-bound,
30   Skimmed the half-frozen Sound,
      That the poor whimpering hound
          Trembled to walk on.

      "Oft to his frozen lair
      Tracked I the grisly bear,
35   While from my path the hare
          Fled like a shadow;
      Oft through the forest dark
      Followed the werewolf's bark,
      Until the soaring lark
40   Sang from the meadow.

Writer's Technique: Longfellow uses sound devices to give his poetry a musical quality.

      "But when I older grew,
      Joining a corsair's[4] crew,
      O'er the dark sea I flew
          With the marauders.
45   Wild was the life we led;
      Many the souls that sped,
      Many the hearts that bled,
          By our stern orders.

      "Many a wassail bout[5]
50   Wore the long Winter out;
      Often our midnight shout
          Set the cocks crowing,
      As we the Berserk's[6] tale
      Measured in cups of ale,
55   Draining the oaken pail,
          Filled to o'erflowing.

      "Once as I told in glee[7]
      Tales of the stormy sea,
      Soft eyes did gaze on me,
60   Burning yet tender;
      And as the white stars shine

---

3. gerfalcon (jʉr′ fal′ k'n) *n.*: A large, fierce falcon of the Arctic.
4. corsair's (kôr′ serz): Referring to a pirate ship.
5. wassail bout (wäs′ l bout): A celebration.
6. Berserk (bər sʉrk′): A legendary Norse warrior who worked himself into a frenzy before battle.
7. glee (glē) *n.*: An unaccompanied song.

THE FIRST CARGO, 1910
N. C. Wyeth
New York Public Library

The Skeleton in Armor 267

Humanities Note

Fine art, *The First Cargo*, 1910, by N. C. Wyeth. N. C. Wyeth, (1882–1945), was a very famous and successful American illustrator. Some of his best known work was done for a series of classic books for Scribner's Sons, *e.g., Kidnapped, Treasure Island, Last of the Mohicans,* and *Mysterious Island.* His work appeared in many other books and magazines and may have totalled almost 3000 illustrations. He also worked on many commissioned mural projects.

This illustration, *The First Cargo,* was created for a story by A. C. Doyle and appeared in *Scribner's Magazine* in December 1910. Wyeth produced a picture that conveys the gloriously heroic and virile qualities of the Vikings. His powerful composition emphasizes the strength of the men.

You might use the following questions for discussion:

1. Illustrations describe without using words. How would you describe Wyeth's picture of the Vikings using words from the poem?
2. Although this illustration was not done for "The Skeleton in Armor," what scene in the poem might it portray?

Longfellow often reverses standard English word order. This technique reflects his training in Classical and Romance languages, which allow more variation in word order. The variation in English word order that Longfellow employed offered him more flexibility in rhyming and gave him the opportunity to place words where they most effectively supported meaning. On this page, for example, lines 64, 72, 75, 95–96, and 97 are examples of lines in which Longfellow has inverted normal word order. You might ask students to find other examples.

On the dark Norway pine,
On that dark heart of mine
        Fell their soft splendor.

Literary Movement: Longfellow's use of simple, straightforward language reflects the desire of the Fireside Poets to appeal to a general audience.

65 "I wooed the blue-eyed maid,
Yielding, yet half afraid,
And in the forest's shade
        Our vows were plighted.
Under its loosened vest
70 Fluttered her little breast,
Like birds within their nest
        By the hawk frighted.

Writer's Technique: Longfellow focuses on the popular theme of love.

"Bright in her father's hall
Shields gleamed upon the wall,
75 Loud sang the minstrels all,
        Chanting his glory;
When of old Hildebrand
I asked his daughter's hand,
Mute did the minstrels stand
80   To hear my story.

"While the brown ale he quaffed,
Loud then the champion laughed,
And as the wind gusts waft
        The sea foam brightly,
85 So the loud laugh of scorn,
Out of those lips unshorn,
From the deep drinking-horn
        Blew the foam lightly.

Literary Movement: Notice the different stations in life of the Viking and his love. Longfellow's sympathetic treatment of the Viking reflects his belief in the American ideals of freedom and equality.

"She was a Prince's child,
90 I but a Viking wild,
And though she blushed and smiled,
        I was discarded!
Should not the dove so white
Follow the sea mew's[8] flight,
95 Why did they leave that night
        Her nest unguarded?

"Scarce had I put to sea,
Bearing the maid with me,
Fairest of all was she
100   Among the Norsemen!

----

8. sea mew: Seagull.

Primary Source

In the introduction to an anthology of poetry of the New England Renaissance, George F. Whicher explores the reason why a literary flowering occurred in New England rather than in another part of the country:

If poetic impulses were made articulate in New England more readily than elsewhere, the explanation may be found in the conditions peculiar to the region. One of these was a long-standing tradition of literacy, resulting from the fact that instruments of culture were more fully developed in New England than in other parts of America. The church, the school, the college, the town meeting, the local newspaper, and the lyceum were well-established vehicles of expression and communication. From earliest colonial times New Englanders had set great store on the leadership of highly educated men and had taken pains to assure a supply of learned ministers and magistrates. The cultivation of poetry was an inevitable by-product of a literary education. Cotton Mather at the close of seventeenth century could advise young scholars to lighten their theological studies with "a little recreation of poetry." A hun-

When on the white sea-strand,[9]
Waving his armèd hand,
Saw we old Hildebrand,
　　With twenty horsemen.

Writer's Technique: Take note of what the Viking's actions reveal about his personality.

105 "Then launched they to the blast,
Bent like a reed each mast,
Yet we were gaining fast,
　　When the wind failed us;
And with a sudden flaw
110 Came round the gusty Skaw,[10]
So that our foe we saw
　　Laugh as he hailed us.

"And as to catch the gale
Round veered the flapping sail,
115 'Death!' was the helmsman's hail,
　　'Death without quarter!'
Mid-ships with iron keel
Struck we her ribs of steel;
Down her black hulk did reel
120 　　Through the black water!

"As with his wings aslant,
Sails the fierce cormorant,[11]
Seeking some rocky haunt,
　　With his prey laden—
125 So toward the open main,
Beating to sea again,
Through the wild hurricane,
　　Bore I the maiden.

"Three weeks we westward bore,
130 And when the storm was o'er,
Cloud-like we saw the shore
　　Stretching to leeward;
There for my lady's bower
Built I the lofty tower,

Historical Context: Longfellow refers to an ancient stone tower in Newport Rhode Island, thought to be evidence of a prehistoric Scandinavian settlement.

---

9. sea-strand: Seashore.
10. Skaw (skô): The cape at the northern tip of the Jutland peninsula, Denmark.
11. cormorant (kôr′ mə rənt) *n.*: A large, diving bird with a hooked beak and webbed toes.

The Skeleton in Armor 269

Speaking and Listening Tell students that the poetry of Longfellow and the other Fireside Poets was often read aloud by members of families gathered together in their living rooms. Have a student or a group of students read aloud "A Skeleton in Armor." Instruct the student or students to recite the poem as expressively as possible and to pronounce each word clearly.

dred years later the desire to produce imaginative literature had become a vocation which John Quincy Adams most unwillingly abandoned for the more profitable study of law, and which young Henry Wadsworth Longfellow insisted on pursuing despite parental admonitions. Every village newssheet had its "poet's corner," and it was as a newspaper poet that John Greenleaf Whittier first attracted notice. Emily Dickinson, when she needed a companionship which her world could not supply, turned to poetry as "my only playmate."

135   Which, to this very hour,
      Stands looking seaward.

"There lived we many years;
Time dried the maiden's tears;
She had forgot her fears,
140   She was a mother;
Death closed her mild blue eyes,
Under that tower she lies;
Ne'er shall the sun arise
    On such another!

145 "Still grew my bosom then,
Still as a stagnant fen!
Hateful to me were men,
    The sunlight hateful!
In the vast forest here,
150 Clad in my warlike gear,
Fell I upon my spear,
    Oh, death was grateful!

Literary Movement: Notice the heroic sentiments expressed by this poem. Such sentiments were characteristic of the Fireside Poets.

"Thus, seamed with many scars,
Bursting these prison bars,
155 Up to its native stars
    My soul ascended!
There from the flowing bowl
Deep drinks the warrior's soul,
Skoal![12] to the Northland! *skoal!*"
160   Thus the tale ended.

---

12. Skoal (skōl) *interj.*: A drinking toast, meaning "to your health."

THINKING AND WRITING

Recalling

1. Why has the spirit of the Viking sought the poet?
2. Describe the Viking's activities when he was young and as he grew older.
3. How does the Viking get the woman he loves?
4. How does the Viking escape his pursuers?
5. What does the Viking do when his wife dies?

Interpreting

6. How would you characterize the Viking?
7. What does the final stanza reveal about the Viking's attitude concerning his own life?
8. Legends are traditional stories that are popularly believed to be based on fact and often serve to explain something. In what respects is Longfellow's poem similar to a legend?

Applying

9. Do you sympathize with the Viking's actions in the poem? Why or why not?

ANALYZING LITERATURE

Understanding the Fireside Poets

The Fireside Poets were a group of poets who helped to establish poetry as a popular literary form by creating poetry that the average reader could understand and appreciate. They wrote poems for a family audience, exploring such popular themes as love, nature, home and family, and patriotism. Because of their use of sound devices and regular rhythms and rhyme, their poetry is especially effective when read aloud. As a result, poetry readings developed into a popular family activity during the New England Renaissance.

1. Why might the subject of this poem be likely to appeal to a general audience?
2. Though the poems of the Fireside Poets often focus on specific subjects or situations, they usually express general, universal themes. In what sense is the theme of "The Skeleton in Armor" universal?

SPEAKING AND LISTENING

Reading with Expression

Recite Longfellow's poem to your classmates, capturing the poem's musical quality in your reading. Hesitate only where a pause is indicated by punctuation, by the meanings of words, or by the natural rhythms of the language. Vary the pitch and loudness of your voice, and be sure to speak slowly and clearly enough so that your classmates can understand you.

THINKING AND WRITING

Writing a Letter

Write a letter to Longfellow discussing the reasons why poetry is less popular today than it was during his time. Also mention the types of subjects that would appeal to a general audience today. Use informal language, but make sure that you follow the rules of grammar, usage, and punctuation. When you finish writing, revise and proofread your letter and prepare a final copy.

The Skeleton in Armor 271

6. Suggested Response: He is determined, strong, and willful.
7. The final stanza reveals that the Viking believed he lived a life worthy of the afterlife reserved for the greatest warriors.
8. Suggested Response: Viking ruins and a skeleton in armor were unearthed. These provided a limited basis in fact. Longfellow wrote this poem to suggest an explanation.

Applying

9. Answers will differ. Students may comment that they do sympathize with the Viking's determination to be with the woman he loves but cannot condone the fact that he sank another ship.

ANSWERS TO ANALYZING LITERATURE

1. Suggested Response: The poem may appeal to a general audience because of the Viking's adventurous life, the setting in the distant past, and the romantic story. The poem, written in the manner of a ballad, is also suitable for reading aloud.
2. The theme of love overcoming obstacles is universal.

SPEAKING AND LISTENING

You might have students practice reading aloud to classmates in groups. Then have a different student read each stanza to the class.

THINKING AND WRITING

Publishing Student Writing
Consider collecting the students' letters in a single folder or booklet entitled "Letters to Longfellow." You can make this publication available for class members to read when time permits.

Closure and Extension

ANSWERS TO THINKING ABOUT THE SELECTION
Recalling

1. The Viking's spirit has sought the poet to tell its story and have the poet record it.
2. When he was young, the Viking trained falcons, skated, and hunted. He joined the crew of a pirate ship when he was old enough and led a wild and dangerous life.
3. The Viking kidnaps the woman he loves when her father refuses to let him marry her.
4. He rams their ship and sinks it. Then he sails to the New World.
5. He kills himself by falling on his spear.

More About the Author Ralph Waldo Emerson was widely sought as a lecturer throughout the nation. Many of his essays began as lectures; Emerson kept working on the ideas until he honed them into the essay form. His talks attracted people of many ages and social classes, but it was the young people of his time who were most receptive to the thoughts of this often controversial philosopher. What modern philosophers have also enjoyed a wide following among young people?

Critical Evaluation James Russell Lowell wrote of Emerson, "There is no man living to whom, as a writer, so many of us feel and thankfully acknowledge so great an indebtedness for ennobling impulses—none whom so many cannot abide. . . . We look upon him as one of the few men of genius whom our age has produced, and there needs no better proof of it than his masculine faculty of fecundating other minds. Search for eloquence in his books and you will perchance miss it, but meanwhile you will find that he has kindled all your thoughts. For choice and pith of language he belongs to a better age than ours. . . . His eye for a fine, telling phrase that will carry true is like that of a backwoodsman for a rifle. . . . A diction that is at once so rich and so homely as his I know not where to match in these days of writings by the page; it is like homespun cloth-of-gold. The many cannot miss his meaning, and only the few can find it. It is the open secret of all true genius."

RALPH WALDO EMERSON

1803–1882

Ralph Waldo Emerson was an essayist, a poet, an orator, and, more than anything else, a philosopher. Throughout the course of his life, Emerson's mind was constantly in motion, bringing forth new ideas and refining and redefining his view of the world. As a result, Emerson's philosophy was reflected in all of his work—his essays, his poems, and his lectures.

Emerson was born in Boston, the son of a Unitarian minister. When Emerson was eight, his father died, leaving the family in a state of poverty. Despite his family's financial difficulties, Emerson received a thorough education. At the age of fourteen, he entered Harvard, where he began recording his ideas in a journal. After his graduation, Emerson taught for several years before deciding to become a minister. In 1825 Emerson entered Harvard Divinity School. Four years later, he became the pastor of the Second Church of Boston.

Saddened by the death of his young wife, Ellen, and dissatisfied with the spiritual restrictions of Unitarianism, Emerson resigned his ministry in 1832. Following his resignation, Emerson traveled to Europe, where he met English poets William Wordsworth and Samuel Taylor Coleridge. When Emerson returned to America, he settled in Concord, Massachusetts, remarried, and began his lifelong career of writing and lecturing.

Emerson's second wife, Lydia Jackson of Plymouth, provided a supportive and secure family life. Emerson was now receiving money from his first wife's legacy. For the first time in his life, he was not living in poverty. The Emerson household, which for a while included Henry David Thoreau, welcomed a slowly widening circle of friends and admirers.

During the 1830's and 1840's, Emerson and a small group of intellectuals gathered regularly to discuss philosophy, religion, and literature. This group, which came to be known as the Transcendental Club, developed a philosophical system that stressed intuition, individuality, and self-reliance. In 1836 Emerson—the group's most influential member—published *Nature,* a lengthy essay that became the Transcendental Club's unofficial statement of belief.

Emerson first achieved national fame in 1841 when he published *Essays,* a collection of essays based on material from his journals and lectures. Emerson went on to publish several more volumes of essays, including *Essays, Second Volume* (1844), *Representative Man* (1849), and *The Conduct of Life* (1860). Though Emerson was known mostly for his essays and lectures, he also published two successful volumes of poetry, *Poems* (1847) and *May-Day and Other Pieces* (1867).

Objectives

1 To understand Transcendentalism
2 To complete word analogies
3 To write about conformity

Support Material

Teaching Portfolio
Teacher Backup, p. 379
Usage and Mechanics Worksheet, p. 382
Vocabulary Check, p. 383
Analyzing Literature Worksheet, *Understanding Transcendentalism,* p. 384
Language Worksheet, *Completing Word Analogies,* p. 385
Selection Test. p. 386

GUIDE FOR INTERPRETING

from Nature; *from* Self-Reliance

Literary Movements

Transcendentalism. Transcendentalism was an intellectual movement that directly or indirectly affected most of the writers of the New England Renaissance. The Transcendentalists, led by Ralph Waldo Emerson, believed that the human senses can know only physical reality. The fundamental truths of being and the universe lie outside the reach of the senses and can be grasped only through intuition. As a result, in their quest for understanding, the Transcendentalists focused their attention on the human spirit. The Transcendentalists were also interested in the natural world and its relationship to humanity. They felt that if they explored nature thoroughly, they would come to know themselves and the universal truths better. Through this exploration, they discovered that the human spirit is reflected in nature. This led them to the conclusion that formed the heart of their beliefs: All forms of being—God, nature, and humanity—are spiritually united through a shared universal soul, or Over-Soul.

Commentary

Emerson was a quiet, soft-spoken, sober man, given neither to physical nor emotional excesses. His ideas, however, were neither cautious nor conventional. They often shocked conservative believers. His speech to the graduating class of the Harvard Divinity School in 1838 aroused a tremendous furor. He was accused of speaking against established tenets of Christianity. As a result, he was not invited to speak again at Harvard for thirty years.

His ideas were deeply and fervently held, and his training as a preacher helped him effectively express them. He saw himself as a seer and poet rather than a coolly objective philosopher with a logically developed argument. Many of his lectures and essays were put together from notes from his extensive journals.

His writings abound in these insights, expressed in vivid statements, which are then developed in a paragraph. Here are some examples: "To go into solitude, a man needs to retire as much from his chamber as from society" and "A man is a god in ruins" (from *Nature*); "The civilized man has built a coach, but has lost the use of his feet" (from "Self-Reliance"); and "Books are the best of things, well used; abused, among the worst" (from "The American Scholar").

Writing

Emerson writes about the effect of nature on him. What do *you* enjoy about nature? What effect does the natural world have on you? Freewrite about your perceptions of the natural world and its effect on you.

Literary Focus Transcendentalism was never a fixed set of beliefs; it was chiefly an attitude toward humans, nature, and the world. Point out that the lack of a systematic set of beliefs was both the chief strength and the chief weakness of the movement.

Writing/Prior Knowledge Before students complete the writing activity, discuss how people's moods can affect their perceptions of nature.

Vocabulary

Preteach the following vocabulary words:

blithe (blith) *adj.:* Carefree (p. 274)

connate (kän′ āt) *adj.:* Having the same origin or nature (p. 274)

chaos (kā′ äs) *n.:* The disorder of formless matter and infinite space, supposed to have existed before the ordered universe (p. 276)

aversion (ə vʉr′ zhən) *n.:* An intense or definite dislike (p. 276)

suffrage (suf′ rij) *n.:* A vote or voting (p. 276)

divines (də vīnz′) *n.:* Clergymen (p. 276)

from # Nature

Ralph Waldo Emerson

Nature is a setting that fits equally well a comic or a mourning piece. In good health, the air is a cordial of incredible virtue. Crossing a bare common,[1] in snow puddles, at twilight, under a clouded sky, without having in my thoughts any occurrence of special good fortune, I have enjoyed a perfect exhilaration. I am glad to the brink of fear. In the woods, too, a man casts off his years, as the snake his slough, and at what period soever of life is always a child. In the woods is perpetual youth. Within these plantations of God, a decorum and sanctity reign, a perennial festival is dressed, and the guest sees not how he should tire of them in a thousand years. In the woods, we return to reason and faith. There I feel that nothing can befall me in life—no disgrace, no calamity (leaving me my eyes), which nature cannot repair. Standing on the bare ground—my head bathed by the blithe air and uplifted into infinite space—all mean egotism vanishes. I become a transparent eyeball: I am nothing: I see all: the currents of the Universal Being circulate through me: I am part or parcel of God. The name of the nearest friend sounds then foreign and accidental: to be brothers, to be acquaintances, master or servant, is then a trifle and a disturbance. I am the lover of uncontained and immortal beauty. In the wilderness, I find something more dear and connate than in the streets or villages. In the tranquil landscape, and especially in the distant line of the horizon, man beholds somewhat as beautiful as his own nature.

The greatest delight which the fields and

---

1. **common:** Piece of open public land.

SUNSET
Frederick E. Church
Munson-Williams-Proctor Institute
Museum of Art, Utica, New York

woods minister is the suggestion of an occult relation between man and the vegetable. I am not alone and unacknowledged. They nod to me, and I to them. The waving of the boughs in the storm is new to me and old. It takes me by surprise, and yet is not unknown. Its effect is like that of a higher thought or a better emotion coming over me, when I deemed I was thinking justly or doing right.

4   Yet it is certain that the power to produce this delight does not reside in nature, but in man, or in a harmony of both. It is necessary to use these pleasures with great temperance. For nature is not always tricked[2] in holiday attire, but the same scene which yesterday breathed perfume and glittered as for the frolic of the nymphs is overspread with melancholy today. Nature always wears the colors of the spirit. To a man laboring under calamity, the heat of his own fire hath sadness in it. Then there is a kind of contempt of the landscape felt by him who has just lost by death a dear friend. The sky is less grand as it shuts down over less worth in the population.

5

_____

2. tricked: Dressed.

THINKING ABOUT THE SELECTION
Recalling

1. According to Emerson, where can we "return to reason and faith"?
2. What happens to Emerson when he stands on the bare ground with his head "uplifted into infinite space"?
3. Where does man behold "somewhat as beautiful as his own nature"?
4. What is "the greatest delight which the fields and woods minister"?
5. What "colors" does nature wear?

Interpreting

6. What does Emerson mean when he comments that in the woods "a man casts off his years"?
7. What does Emerson mean when he describes himself as a "transparent eyeball"?

Applying

8. In what ways is Emerson's attitude toward nature different from a scientist's attitude?

ANALYZING LITERATURE
Understanding Transcendentalism

Transcendentalism was an intellectual movement that held that knowledge of fundamental reality was derived through intuition rather than through sensory experience. This movement focused on the human spirit and the spiritual relationship between humanity and nature. The Transcendentalists ultimately reached the conclusion that all forms of being are spiritually united through a shared universal soul, or Over-Soul.

Emerson's essay *Nature,* published in 1836, was the Transcendentalists' unofficial statement of belief.

1. What does *Nature* reveal about the Transcendentalists' attitude toward nature?
2. What does *Nature* reveal about the Transcendentalists' perceptions of human nature?
3. How does the essay convey the Transcendentalists' belief in the Over-Soul?
4. Do you find any evidence of Transcendentalist beliefs in today's poetry and song lyrics? Explain.

from *Nature*   275

Closure and Extension

_____

275

from Self-Reliance

Ralph Waldo Emerson

There is a time in every man's education when he arrives at the conviction that envy is ignorance; that imitation is suicide; that he must take himself for better, for worse, as his portion; that though the wide universe is full of good, no kernel of nourishing corn can come to him but through his toil bestowed on that plot of ground which is given to him to till. The power which resides in him is new in nature, and none but he knows what that is which he can do, nor does he know until he has tried. Not for nothing one face, one character, one fact makes much impression on him, and another none. This sculpture in the memory is not without preestablished harmony. The eye was placed where one ray should fall, that it might testify of that particular ray. We but half express ourselves, and are ashamed of that divine idea which each of us represents. It may be safely trusted as proportionate and of good issues, so it be faithfully imparted, but God will not have his work made manifest by cowards. A man is relieved and gay when he has put his heart into his work and done his best; but what he has said or done otherwise, shall give him no peace. It is a deliverance which does not deliver. In the attempt his genius deserts him; no muse befriends; no invention, no hope.

Trust thyself: every heart vibrates to that iron string. Accept the place the divine providence has found for you; the society of your contemporaries, the connection of events. Great men have always done so and confided themselves childlike to the genius of their age, betraying their perception that the absolutely trustworthy was stirring at their heart, working through their hands, predominating in all their being. And we are now men, and must accept in the highest mind the same transcendent destiny; and not minors and invalids in a protected corner, but guides, redeemers, and benefactors, obeying the Almighty effort and advancing on Chaos and the Dark. . . .

Society everywhere is in conspiracy against the manhood of every one of its members. Society is a joint-stock company in which the members agree for the better securing of his bread to each shareholder, to surrender the liberty and culture of the eater. The virtue in most request is conformity. Self-reliance is its aversion. It loves not realities and creators, but names and customs.

Whoso would be a man must be a nonconformist. He who would gather immortal palms must not be hindered by the name of goodness, but must explore if it be goodness. Nothing is at last sacred but the integrity of our own mind. Absolve you to yourself, and you shall have the suffrage of the world. . . .

A foolish consistency is the hobgoblin of little minds, adored by little statesmen and philosophers and divines. With consistency a great soul has simply nothing to do. He may as well concern himself with his shadow on the wall. Speak what you think now in hard words and tomorrow speak what tomorrow thinks in hard words again, though it contradict everything you said today. "Ah, so you shall be sure to be misunderstood?"—Is it so bad, then, to be misunderstood? Pythagoras was misunderstood, and Socrates, and Jesus, and Luther, and Copernicus, and Galileo, and Newton,[1] and every pure and wise spirit that ever took flesh. To be great is to be misunderstood. . . .

9

1. **Pythagoras . . . Newton:** Individuals who made major contributions to scientific, philosophical, or religious thinking.

THINKING ABOUT THE SELECTION

Recalling

1. According to the first paragraph, at what conviction does every person arrive?
2. According to the second paragraph, what must every person accept?
3. How does Emerson describe society?
4. What is Emerson's comment about consistency?

Interpreting

5. What does he mean when he comments, "no kernel of nourishing corn can come to him but through his toil bestowed on that plot of ground which is given to him to till"?
6. Why, according to Emerson, should people trust themselves?
7. How does Emerson believe people should be affected by the way others perceive them?
8. How does Emerson support his claim that "to be great is to be misunderstood"?

Applying

9. Toward the end of the essay, Emerson writes, "Speak what you think now in hard words and tomorrow speak what tomorrow thinks in hard words again, though it contradict everything you said today." Explain your reaction to this view.

UNDERSTANDING LANGUAGE

Completing Analogies

A verbal analogy is an expression of a relationship between two words. Analogy questions on standardized tests ask you to choose two words that are related in the same way as a given pair. For example, OLD : NEW : : LONG : SHORT. In this example, the two sets of words are antonyms.

Complete each of the following analogies. Choose the pair of words whose relationship is most similar to that expressed by the capitalized pair.

1. BETTER : WORSE : :
   a. quiet : loud   c. easier : softer
   b. narrow : long   d. pompous : ambitious
2. SOCIETY : CULTURE : :
   a. resolve : ambition c. grasp : hold
   b. ambivalent : angry d. amnesty : emotion
3. SCHOOL : EDUCATION : :
   a. class : writing   c. teacher : student
   b. book : test   d. hospital : operation
4. SCULPTURE : ART : :
   a. poem : literature c. athlete : sport
   b. flower : florist   d. water : flood

THINKING AND WRITING

Writing About Conformity

What are the advantages of conforming to society's expectations? Of not conforming? Make notes about your thoughts on the subject. Then take a stand and present your ideas in an essay. Begin by writing a draft explaining your reasons. Conclude by indicating your agreement or disagreement with Emerson's ideas on conformity. Revise your essay so that your points are clear and supported.

from *Self-Reliance*   277

Reader's Response What is your reaction to Emerson's thoughts concerning self-reliance?

277

Literary Focus Discuss the reasons why Emerson might have been more likely to use apostrophe than a poet who did not share his beliefs. Considering his beliefs, what types of things would Emerson be most likely to address in his poetry?

Writing/Prior Knowledge For extra credit, **more advanced** students may develop their discussion into a poem.

Vocabulary

Preteach the following vocabulary words:

radiant (rā′ dē ənt) adj.: Shining brightly (p. 279, 1.8)

tumultuous (too mult′ choo wəs) adj.: Greatly agitated (p. 279, 1.9)

bastions (bas′ chənz) n.: Fortifications (p. 279, 1.13)

rude (rood) adj.: Crude or rough in form or workmanship (p. 281, 1.1)

sages (sāj′ əz) n.: People widely respected for their wisdom (p. 283, 1.9)

pine (pīn) v.: To have an intense longing or desire (p. 285 1.14)

Writer's Techniques

Writing

Primary Source

The Snowstorm; Concord Hymn; The Rhodora; Brahma

Apostrophe. Apostrophe is a literary device in which a writer directly addresses an inanimate object, an abstract idea, or an absent person. A writer may address a person who is no longer living, an ocean, or a season. For example, the English poet Shelley addresses the wind in these lines: "O Wind,/If Winter comes, can Spring be far behind?"

The Transcendentalists believed that all living things were spiritually united through a shared universal soul, or Over-Soul. In "The Rhodora" Emerson uses apostrophe to express this spiritual unity, directly addressing a flower as if it were a person.

Freewrite, describing a scene that suggests the majesty of nature. Explore your thoughts and reactions to this scene.

Emerson was keeping journals and writing poetry well before the publication of *Nature,* and he continued both activities to the end of his life. Despite his success as a speaker and an essayist, he always regarded himself as a poet.

In February 1835 he wrote to his fiancée, Lydia Jackson, explaining why he could not live in Plymouth, her hometown: He is a poet of nature, not of the city. "Under this morning's severe but beautiful light I thought dear friend that hardly should I get away from Concord. I must win you to love it. I am born a poet, of a low class without doubt yet a poet. That is my nature & vocation. My singing be sure is very "husky," & is for the most part in prose. Still am I a poet in the sense of a perceiver & dear lover of the harmonies that are in the soul & in matter, & specially of the correspondences between these and those. A sunset, a forest, a snowstorm, a certain river-view, are more to me than many friends & do ordinarily divide my day with my books. Wherever I go therefore I guard & study my rambling propensities with a care that is ridiculous to people, but to me is the care of my high calling. Now Concord is only one of a hundred towns in which I could find these necessary objects but Plymouth I fear is not one. Plymouth is streets; I live in the wide [countryside]."

Like the English Romantics and his younger contemporary, the poet Walt Whitman, Emerson saw the poet as a bard or prophet speaking the higher truths to his society. In "The Poet" (1844) he speaks of the poet's "*dream*-power . . . a power transcending all limit and privacy," and proclaims, "The poets are thus liberating gods."

Objectives

1 To understand cause and effect
2 To write about history
3 To understand apostrophe
4 To find antonyms
5 To recognize and explain paradox

Support Material

Teaching Portfolio

Teacher Backup, p. 389

Usage and Mechanics Worksheet, p. 393

Vocabulary Check, p. 394

Analyzing Literature Worksheet, *Understanding Apostrophe,* p. 395

Language Worksheet, *Understanding Synonyms,* p. 396

Selection Test, p. 397

FARM YARD, WINTER
George Henry Durrie
Courtesy of the New York Historical Society

The Snowstorm

Ralph Waldo Emerson

<pre>
   Announced by all the trumpets of the sky,
   Arrives the snow, and, driving o'er the fields,
   Seems nowhere to alight: the whited air
   Hides hills and woods, the river, and the heaven,
5 And veils the farmhouse at the garden's end.
   The sled and traveler stopped, the courier's feet
   Delayed, all friends shut out, the housemates sit
   Around the radiant fireplace, enclosed
   In a tumultuous privacy of storm.
</pre>

The Snowstorm 279

Motivation/Prior Knowledge
Ask students to imagine that it is snowing heavily outside. How would they react to the snow? How would other people be affected by it?

Thematic Idea Another poem that describes a snowstorm is *Snowbound* by John Greenleaf Whittier (p. 360).

Purpose-Setting Question How does Emerson view the snowstorm and its effects?

1 **Discussion** How does the inversion of word order in the first lines help begin the poem on a triumphant note?

Humanities Note

Fine art, *Farmyard Winter,* 1862, by George Henry Durrie. George Henry Durrie (1820–1863) was an American artist who made his reputation working for Currier and Ives. Besides creating pictures for this company, Durrie also painted in oils and was well-known for his appealing landscapes, such as *Farmyard Winter.* Durrie's grasp on the popular tastes in America is evident in this picture. It has an anecdotal quality, which enables the viewer to relate to the scene in a personal way.

Have students look at this painting and keep it in mind as they read the poem. After they have read the poem, you might ask these questions:
1. What details in this painting reflect details from the poem?
2. What words and phrases from Emerson's poem could be used to describe the painting?

2 Critical Thinking and Reading
Note the extended image of the north wind acting as a craftsman or artist carving forms of the snow.

3 Discussion What specific images has the north wind carved?

4 Discussion Who is the "he" of the last stanza?

5 Discussion What is the effect of this metaphor?

Reader's Response What emotions do the images in Emerson's poem evoke in you? Why?

Closure and Extension

ANSWERS TO THINKING ABOUT THE SELECTION
Recalling

1. "The trumpets of the sky" announce the storm.
2. It hides hills, woods, river, and the heavens.
3. The speaker describes the works the snow has constructed.
4. The storm has left behind "astonished art" and "frolic architecture."

Interpreting

5. He establishes a mood of excitement outside and of enforced quiet inside.
6. The outer turmoil is forcing privacy within each home.
7. (a) The storm is described as an artificer who has carved, formed, and hung shapes. (b) The storm has left overnight work that mimics human art that has taken ages to create. (c) Humans find a parallel of their own creative force in nature, and both humanity and natural creativity are part of the Over-Soul.

Applying

8. Suggested Response: Many people might see the destructive and limiting forces caused by a snowstorm.

---

10   Come see the north wind's masonry.
       Out of an unseen quarry evermore
2 Furnished with tile, the fierce artificer
       Curves his white bastions with projected roof
       Round every windward stake, or tree, or door.
15   Speeding, the myriad-handed, his wild work
       So fanciful, so savage, nought cares he
       For number or proportion. Mockingly,
3 On coop or kennel he hangs Parian[1] wreaths;
       A swan-like form invests the hidden thorn;
20   Fills up the farmer's lane from wall to wall,

       Maugre[2] the farmer's sighs; and at the gate
       A tapering turret overtops the work.
       And when his hours are numbered, and the world
4 Is all his own, retiring, as he were not,
25   Leaves, when the sun appears, astonished Art
       To mimic in slow structures, stone by stone,
       Built in an age, the mad wind's nightwork,
5 The frolic architecture of the snow.

---

1. Parian (per'ē ən) *adj.*: Referring to a fine, white marble of the Greek city Paros.
2. Maugre (mô' gər) *prep.*: In spite of.

THINKING ABOUT THE SELECTION
Recalling

1. What announces the storm's arrival?
2. What does "the whited air" hide?
3. What does the speaker describe in the second stanza?
4. According to lines 25–28, what has the storm left behind "when the sun appears"?

Interpreting

5. What mood does Emerson establish in the first stanza?
6. Explain what Emerson means when he refers to the "tumultuous privacy of the storm" in line 9.

7. In this poem Emerson compares the storm and an artist at work. (a) How does he develop this comparison in the second stanza? (b) How does he extend the comparison in the final stanza? (c) How does this comparison express Emerson's belief in a spiritual unity between humanity and nature?

Applying

8. Emerson expresses a favorable attitude toward the snowstorm. Why might some people living in northern climates not share Emerson's attitude?

Concord Hymn

Sung at the Completion of the Battle Monument, April 19, 1836

Ralph Waldo Emerson

1 *This poem was written for the unveiling of a monument commemorating the Minute Men, who fought the British in the first two battles of the Revolutionary War at Lexington and Concord, Massachusetts, in April of 1775.*

2 By the rude bridge that arched the flood,
    Their flag to April's breeze unfurled,
Here once the embattled farmers stood,
    And fired the shot heard round the world.

5 The foe long since in silence slept;
    Alike the conqueror silent sleeps;
And Time the ruined bridge has swept
    Down the dark stream which seaward creeps.

On this green bank, by this soft stream,
10   We set today a votive[1] stone;
3 That memory may their deed redeem,
    When, like our sires, our sons are gone.

4 Spirit, that made those heroes dare
    To die, and leave their children free,
15 Bid Time and Nature gently spare
    The shaft we raise to them and thee.

---

1. **votive** (vōt′ iv) *adj.*: Dedicated in fulfillment of a vow or pledge.

Concord Hymn 281

Closure and Extension

ANSWERS TO THINKING ABOUT THE SELECTION
Recalling

1. "Embattled farmers stood and fired the shot heard round the world."
2. The bridge has been swept away.
3. Memory may redeem their deeds.
4. Spirit "made those heroes dare to die."

Interpreting

5. (a) It refers to the opening shots of the American Revolution. (b) It was heard around the world, because the Revolution had an important impact on the rest of the world, most notably in the French Revolution which began a decade later.
6. He implies that the same spirit which inspired the revolutionaries to fight also controls Time and Nature.

Applying

7. Suggested Response: Many wars are not fought for such high ideals, and many wars leave a nation in worse condition than before; this poem commemorates a war that enabled Americans to begin the great experiment with democracy.

ANSWERS TO CRITICAL THINKING AND READING

Answers will differ. Suggested Response: Many of the causes are reflected in the Declaration of Independence (p. 144).

THINKING AND WRITING

For help with this assignment, students can refer to Lesson 12, "Writing a Poem," in the Handbook of Writing About Literature.

Primary Source

In addition to writing poetry, Emerson spoke and wrote about the source of poetry, the characteristics of good poetry, and the role of the poet in society. The following passage is from the essay "The Poet," his most complete exploration of the subject of poetry:

> The Poet is the sayer, the namer, and represents beauty. He is a sovereign, and stands on the center. For the world is not painted, or adorned, but is from the beginning

THINKING ABOUT THE SELECTION
Recalling

1. What memorable event took place "by the rude bridge"?
2. What has since happened to the bridge?
3. According to the third stanza, what may redeem the deeds of the embattled farmers?
4. According to the final stanza, what "made those heroes dare / To die"?

Interpreting

5. (a) What is meant by "the shot heard round the world"? (b) In what way was this shot heard round the world?
6. How does Emerson express his belief in the existence of a shared universal soul, or Over-Soul, in the final stanza?

Applying

7. What aspects of a poem like this would be appropriate for the dedication of other war monuments? Why?

CRITICAL THINKING AND READING
Understanding Cause and Effect

"Concord Hymn" commemorates a historical event. To understand history, you must understand causes and effects, or the reasons behind actions and the results of these actions.

Do some library research on the Revolutionary War. What causes led up to the battles at Lexington and Concord? What were the results of these battles? Prepare an oral report and present your findings to your classmates.

THINKING AND WRITING
Writing About History

History is all around us. Wherever you live, your town or county or state may have been the site for some important historical event. Interview people in your town to find out about a local historical event. Use this information to write a short poem commemorating this event.

Relate events in chronological order. When you revise, make sure you have made clear what makes the event significant. Proofread your poem and share it with your classmates.

Commentary

In 1837 the Women's Anti-Slavery Society was founded in Concord. Among the charter members were Mrs. Thoreau and her two daughters. Henry David Thoreau, encouraged by them and other friends, became a fiery and popular speaker against slavery. Emotions ran high throughout the nation.

In the summer of 1844, the Society invited Emerson to speak on the occasion of the tenth anniversary of the British emancipation of slaves in the West Indies. In his speech Emerson narrated the history of the seventy-year struggle to abolish slavery in the British West Indies, then drew parallels with the United States. Speaking

calmly and deliberately, he described the moral issue of slavery, denouncing it as a supreme violation of human rights. He proclaimed his faith in Americans and their government to correct this obvious injustice.

For Emerson and the abolitionists, therefore, the passage of the Fugitive Slave Act in 1850 was a moral outrage as well as a bitter disappointment. They swore not to obey it. Their faith in the government was not restored until Lincoln's Emancipation Proclamation in 1862 and the ratification in 1865 of the 13th Amendment to the Constitution, which abolished slavery at last.

---

beautiful; and God has not made some beautiful things, but Beauty is the creator of the universe. Therefore the poet is not any permissive potentate, but is the emperor in his own right. . . . The poet does not wait for the hero or the sage, but, as they act and think primarily, so he writes primarily what will and must be spoken, reckoning others through primaries also, yet, in respect to him, secondaries and servants; as sitters or models in the studio of a painter, or as assistants who bring building materials to an architect.

For poetry was all written before time was, and whenever we are so finely organized that we can penetrate into

The Rhodora

On Being Asked, Whence is the Flower?

Ralph Waldo Emerson

In May, when sea winds pierced our solitudes,
I found the fresh Rhodora in the woods,
Spreading its leafless blooms in a damp nook,
To please the desert and the sluggish brook.
5 The purple petals, fallen in the pool,
Made the black water with their beauty gay;
Here might the red-bird come his plumes to cool,
And court the flower that cheapens his array.
Rhodora! if the sages ask thee why
10 This charm is wasted on the earth and sky,

The Rhodora 283

Presentation

Purpose-Setting   Question
What does the rhodora represent?

Reading   Strategy Students should read the poem through. Ask them to identify the lines where the speaker stops talking about the rhodora and begins to address the flower.

1 **Clarification** *Whence* means "from what source or origin."

2 **Literary Focus** The speaker addresses the rhodora.

3 **Discussion** What purpose does the rhodora serve?

that region where the air is music, we hear those primal warblings, and attempt to write them down, but we lose ever and anon a word, or a verse, and substitute something of our own, and thus miswrite the poem. The men of more delicate ear write down these cadences more faithfully, and these transcripts, though imperfect, become the songs of the nations. For nature is as truly beautiful as it is good, or as it is reasonable, and must as much appear, as it must be done, or known. Words and deeds are quite indifferent modes of divine energy. Words are also actions, and actions are a kind of words.

The sign and credentials of the poet are, that he announces that which no man foretold. He is the true and only doctor; he knows and tells; he is the only teller of news, for he was present and privy to the appearance which he describes. He is the beholder of ideas, and an utterer of the necessary and casual. For we do not speak now of the men of poetical talents, or of industry and skill in meter, but of the true poet. . . . Our poets are men of talents who sing, and not the children of music. The argument is secondary, the finish of the verses is primary.

283

4
Tell them, dear, that if eyes were made for seeing,
Then Beauty is its own excuse for being:
5
Why thou wert there, O rival of the rose!
I never thought to ask, I never knew:
6 15 But, in my simple ignorance, suppose
The self-same Power that brought me there brought you.

THINKING ABOUT THE SELECTION

Recalling

1. (a) When does the speaker find "the fresh Rhodora in the woods"? (b) Where does he find it?
2. (a) According to the speaker, what question might the sages ask the rhodora? (b) How does he suggest the rhodora should respond?
3. In the final line, how does the speaker explain the rhodora's existence?

Interpreting

4. What larger concept does the rhodora represent?
5. (a) How is the sages' attitude toward nature different from the speaker's attitude? (b) Which attitude seems to produce a more meaningful understanding of nature? Explain your answer.
6. What is unexpected about the speaker's reference to his "simple ignorance" in line 15?
7. How does the final line express Emerson's belief in a spiritual unity among all living things?

Applying

8. At another time, Ralph Waldo Emerson wrote, "Though we travel the world over to find the beautiful, we must carry it with us or we find it not." Explain the view of beauty Emerson expresses here. How is it similar to or different from the view of beauty expressed in "The Rhodora"?

ANALYZING LITERATURE

Understanding Apostrophe

Apostrophe is a literary device in which a writer directly addresses an inanimate object, an abstract idea, or an absent person. Emerson directly addresses a flower in "The Rhodora."
1. What is the effect of the use of apostrophe?
2. How does Emerson's use of apostrophe reinforce the meaning of the poem?

UNDERSTANDING LANGUAGE

Finding Antonyms

Antonyms are words that have the opposite, or nearly the opposite, meaning. For example, the words *sluggish* and *active* are antonyms.
Choose an antonym for each of the following words.
1. ARRAY:
   a. rags b. gown c. display d. splendor
2. COURT:
   a. desire b. propose c. shun d. madden
3. SAGE:
   a. wisdom b. fool c. herb d. flavor
4. RIVAL:
   a. friend b. competitor c. teacher
   d. playmate

Brahma[1]

Ralph Waldo Emerson

1
If the red slayer think he slays,
   Or if the slain think he is slain,
They know not well the subtle ways
   I keep, and pass, and turn again.

2
5   Far or forgot to me is near;
   Shadow and sunlight are the same;
The vanished gods to me appear;
   And one to me are shame and fame.

They reckon ill who leave me out;
10   When me they fly, I am the wings;
I am the doubter and the doubt,
   And I the hymn the Brahmin[2] sings.

3
The strong gods pine for my abode,
   And pine in vain the sacred Seven;[3]
15 But thou, meek lover of the good!
   Find me, and turn thy back on heaven.

---

1. **Brahma** (brä′ mə): In Hindu religion, the supreme and eternal essence or spirit of the universe.
2. **Brahmin:** A Hindu priest.
3. **sacred Seven:** The most sacred Hindu saints.

THINKING ABOUT THE SELECTION

Recalling

1. According to the first stanza, what do the red slayer and the slain "know not well"?
2. According to the final stanza, who pines for the speaker's abode?

Interpreting

3. Who is the speaker of the poem?
4. What does the speaker mean when he refers to "gods" in lines 7 and 13?
5. In the sacred Hindu writings, Brahma is the supreme essence, or spirit, of the universe. What does this poem reveal about Brahma's powers?
6. How does Emerson use the concept of Brahma to express his belief that the fundamental truths of the universe lie beyond the reach of our senses?

Applying

7. In what way is the Hindu belief in Brahma similar to the Transcendentalist belief in a universal soul, or Over-Soul?

CRITICAL THINKING AND READING

Understanding a Paradox

A **paradox** is a statement that seems contradictory but in reality contains a possible truth. In "Brahma" Emerson explores the subject of death from a Hindu perspective. In doing so he presents a series of paradoxes—apparent contradictions that are resolved in the higher reality, or the universal truth, of Brahma. For example, the paradox, "Far . . . is near," is presented in line 5. That something can be both far and near seems contradictory, but in the speaker's context, there is truth in the statement.

1. What paradox related to death is presented in the opening stanza?
2. Name three paradoxes presented in the second and third stanzas. Explain each of these paradoxes.
3. What two paradoxes are presented in the final stanza? Explain these paradoxes.

Presentation

Master Teacher Note It might be helpful to read about Hinduism in a book about comparative religion or in a substantial encyclopedia article. Hinduism regards the material world as unreal and transitory and the spiritual world as real and permanent. Hindu gods frequently appear as avatars—transitory human incarnations of the eternal gods.

1 Discussion What are some apparent contradictions in what the speaker says?

2 Discussion Would a Westerner be likely to agree or disagree with the speaker?

3 Critical Thinking and Reading The speaker is not advocating a Western idea of turning away from heaven toward hell; instead the speaker advocates turning from the Western concept of heaven.

Critical Thinking and Reading The poem is written in simple quatrains with *abab* rhymes. Have students consider how the simplicity of the form contrasts sharply with ideas that are far from simple.

ANSWERS TO CRITICAL THINKING AND READING

1. The statement that the slain thinks he is slain is a paradox, because it is not possible for a slain person to think.
2. Suggested Responses: Far or forgot is near; shadow and sunlight are the same; vanished gods appear; shame and fame are one; and the speaker is both the doubter and the doubt. These paradoxes are explained by the fact that all contradictions are resolved in Brahma.
3. Those who long to find Brahma cannot, while a meek lover of the good can. In finding Brahma, a person must turn his or her back on heaven. An explanation would suggest that ultimate reality is beyond human comprehension.

285

Closure and Extension

ANSWERS TO THINKING ABOUT THE SELECTION

Recalling

1. They know not well the subtle ways of the speaker.
2. The strong gods and the sacred Seven pine for the abode.

Interpreting

3. Brahma, the supreme spirit, is the speaker.

4. He is actually referring to people.
5. Brahma's powers are all-encompassing, and in Brahma all contradictions are resolved.
6. Through the concept of Brahma, he points out that what our senses perceive as contradictions may actually be fundamental truths.

Applying

7. Both Brahma and the Over-Soul are all-encompassing entities that exist in all forms of being.

More About the Author Although Henry David Thoreau lived alone at Walden Pond for two years, he was not a hermit who avoided people. He went into Concord from time to time to see his friends and to get a few supplies. His stay at Walden Pond brought his ideas about himself and about the world into clearer focus. When he was near death, a friend asked if he had made his peace with God. Thoreau replied, "We have never quarreled." Ask students to think of other writers who are closely identified with a particular place, as Thoreau is with Walden Pond. How might this type of association affect a writer's reputation?

Critical Evaluation In his eulogy for Thoreau, Ralph Waldo Emerson commented that "Thoreau was sincerity itself, and might fortify the convictions of prophets in the ethical laws by his holy living. It was an affirmative experience which refused to be set aside. A truth-speaker he, capable of the most deep and strict conversation; a physician to the wounds of any soul; a friend, knowing not only the secret of friendship, but almost worshipped by those few persons who resorted to him as their confessor and prophet, and knew the deep value of his mind and great heart. . . . His virtues, of course, sometimes ran into extremes. It was easy to trace the inexorable demand on all for exact truth that austerity which made this willing hermit more solitary even than he wished. Himself a perfect probity, he required not less of others. He had a disgust at crime, and no worldly success would cover it. He detected paltering as readily in dignified and prosperous persons as in beggars, and with equal scorn. Such dangerous frankness was in his dealing that his admirers called him 'that terrible Thoreau,' as if he spoke when

HENRY DAVID THOREAU

1817–1862

When Henry David Thoreau died of tuberculosis at the age of forty-four, his work had received little recognition. Yet he had achieved an inner success that few others have experienced. Speaking at Thoreau's funeral, Ralph Waldo Emerson commented, "The country knows not yet, or in the least part, how great a son it has lost. . . . But he, at least, is content. His soul was made for the noblest society; he had in a short life exhausted the capabilities of this world; wherever there is knowledge, wherever there is virtue, wherever there is beauty, he will find a home."

Thoreau was born and raised in Concord, Massachusetts. After graduating from Harvard, Thoreau became a teacher. When his objection to corporal punishment forced him to quit his first job, he and his older brother John opened their own school. The school was quite successful, but they had to close it when John became ill.

In 1842 Thoreau moved into Emerson's house. He lived there for two years, performing odd jobs to pay for his room and board. Thoreau became Emerson's close friend and devoted disciple. Deciding not to go back to teaching and refusing to pursue another career, Thoreau dedicated himself to testing the Transcendentalist philosophy through experience. By simplifying his needs, Thoreau was able to devote the rest of his life to exploring and writing about the spiritual relationship between humanity and nature and supporting his political and social beliefs.

For two years (1845–1847) Thoreau lived alone in a cabin he built himself at Walden Pond. Thoreau's experiences during this period provided him with the material for his masterwork, *Walden* (1854). Condensing his experiences at Walden Pond into one year, Thoreau used the four seasons as a structural framework for the book. A unique blend of natural observation, social criticism, and philosophical insight, *Walden* is now generally regarded as the supreme work of Transcendentalist literature.

Thoreau wrote throughout his life; however, only *A Week on the Concord and Merrimack Rivers* and some poems were published—and at Thoreau's own expense—during his lifetime. *The Maine Woods, Cape Cod,* and *A Yankee in Canada* were published posthumously. Carefully and deliberately crafted, Thoreau's work reflects the economy for which he strove throughout his life and about which he wrote in *Walden.*

Thoreau's reputation has steadily grown since his death. His work has inspired and influenced writers, environmentalists, and social and political leaders. It has made generations of readers aware of the possibilities of the human spirit and the limitations of society.

286   New England Renaissance

silent, and was still present when he had departed. I think the severity of his ideal interfered to deprive him of healthy sufficiency of human society."

Objectives

1 To appreciate style
2 To evaluate the effect of style
3 To compare and contrast essays

Support Material

Teaching Portfolio
Teacher Backup, p. 399
Grammar in Action Worksheet, *Using Infinitives,* p. 403
Usage and Mechanics Worksheet, p. 405
Vocabulary Check, p. 406
Analyzing Literature Worksheet, *Understanding Style,* p. 407
Critical Thinking and Reading Worksheet, *Evaluating the*

GUIDE FOR INTERPRETING

from Walden; *from* Civil Disobedience

Style. Style refers to the manner in which a writer puts his or her thoughts into words. In *Walden* Thoreau's style is closely related to his purpose, which is to encourage us to examine the way we live and think. To achieve his purpose, Thoreau constructs paragraphs so that the sentences build to a climax.

The Mexican War. The Mexican War was a conflict between Mexico and the United States that took place from 1846 to 1848. The war was caused by a dispute over the boundary between Texas and Mexico and Mexico's refusal to discuss selling California and New Mexico to the United States. Believing that President Polk intentionally provoked the conflict before having congressional approval, Thoreau and many other Americans strongly objected to the war. To demonstrate his disapproval, Thoreau refused to pay taxes. His gesture led to his arrest, and he was forced to spend a night in jail.

How do you think you would respond to living alone in the wilderness? Write about how you think you would manage.

In 1954 E. B. White, a well-known author of essays and children's books *(Charlotte's Web),* wrote an article in honor of the one-hundredth anniversary of the publication of *Walden.*

> *Walden* is an oddity in American letters. It may very well be the oddest of our distinguished oddities . . . . Many think it a sermon; many set it down as an attempt to rearrange society; some think it an exercise in nature-loving; some find it a rather irritating collection of inspirational puffballs by an eccentric show-off. I think it none of these. It still seems to me the best youth's companion yet written by an American, for it carries a solemn warning against the loss of one's valuables, it advances a good argument for traveling light and trying new adventures, it rings with the power of positive adoration, it contains religious feeling without religious images, and it steadfastly refuses to record bad news. . . . Thoreau, very likely without knowing quite what he was up to, took man's relation to nature and man's dilemma in society and man's capacity for elevating his spirit and he beat all these matters together, in a wild free interval of self-justification and delight, and produced an original omelette from which people can draw nourishment in a hungry day. *Walden* is one of the first of the vitamin-enriched American dishes.

Literary Focus Throeau's style involves the use of humor and the unexpected turn of thought as well as the building of sentences to create a climax. He can lead a reader along his line of thought even though that reader may, upon reflection, not agree with him.

Writing/Prior Knowledge Students who have spent time in the wilderness may want to express their reactions and discuss the lessons they have learned.

Vocabulary

Preteach the following words:
dilapidated (di lap′ ə dāt id) *adj.:* In disrepair (p. 289)
terrestrial (tə res′ trēəl) *adj.:* Of this world (p. 290–291)
sublime (sə blīm′) *adj.:* Noble; majestic (p. 291)
superfluous (soo pʉr′ floo wəs) *adj.:* Not needed (p. 285)
evitable (ev′ ə tə b′l) *adj.:* Avoidable (p. 291)
magnanimity (mag′ nə nim′ ə tē) *n.:* Generosity (p. 293)
expedient (ik spē′ dēənt) *n.:* Resource (p. 296)
integrity (in teg′ rə tē) *n.:* Adherence to a code of values (p. 296)
posterity (päs ter′ ə tē) *n.:* All succeeding generations (p. 296)
alacrity (ə lak′ rə tē) *n.:* Speed (p. 296)

Spelling Tip Four nouns in this list end in *ity.* The basic pattern in American English is to use *ity* as a noun ending for this sound.

from Walden

Henry David Thoreau

from Where I Lived, and What I Lived For

1 At a certain season of our life we are accustomed to consider every spot as the possible site of a house. I have thus surveyed the country on every side within a dozen miles of where I live. In imagination I have bought all the farms in succession, for all were to be bought, and I knew their price. I walked over each farmer's premises, tasted his wild apples, discoursed on husbandry[1] with him, took his farm at his price, at any price, mortgaging it to him in my mind; even put a higher price on it—took everything but a deed of it—took his word for his deed, for I dearly love to talk—cultivated it, and him too to some extent, I trust, and withdrew when I had enjoyed it long enough, leaving him to carry it on. This experience entitled me to be regarded as a sort of real-estate broker by my friends. Wherever I sat, there I might live, and the landscape radiated from me accordingly. What is a house but a *sedes*, a seat?—better if a country seat.

2 I discovered many a site for a house not likely to be soon improved, which some might have thought too far from the village, but to my eyes the village was too far from it. Well, there I might live, I said; and there I did live, for an hour, a summer and a winter life; saw how I could let the years run off, buffet the winter through, and see the spring come in. The future inhabitants of this region, wherever they may place their houses, may be sure that they have been anticipated. An afternoon sufficed to lay out the land into orchard woodlot and pasture, and to decide what fine oaks or pines should be left to stand before the door, and whence each blasted tree could be seen to the best advantage; and then I let it lie, 3 fallow[2] perchance, for a man is rich in proportion to the number of things which he can afford to let alone.

4 My imagination carried me so far that I even had the refusal of several farms—the refusal was all I wanted—but I never got my fingers burned by actual possession. The nearest that I came to actual possession was when I bought the Hollowell Place, and had begun to sort my seeds, and collected materials with which to make a wheelbarrow to carry it on or off with; but before the owner gave me a deed of it, his wife—every man has such a wife—changed her mind and wished to keep it, and he offered me ten dollars to 5 release him. Now, to speak the truth, I had but ten cents in the world, and it surpassed my arithmetic to tell, if I was that man who had ten cents, or who had a farm, or ten dollars, or all together. However, I let him keep the ten dollars and the farm too, for I had

---

1. **husbandry** (huz' bən drē) *n.*: Farming.

2. **fallow** (fal'ō) *adj.*: Left uncultivated or unplanted.

From J. Lyndon Shanley, ed., *Walden: The Writings of Henry D. Thoreau.* Copyright © 1971 by Princeton University Press. Excerpts, pp. 81–98 and 320–333, reprinted with permission of Princeton University Press.

carried it far enough; or rather, to be generous, I sold him the farm for just what I gave for it, and, as he was not a rich man, made him a present of ten dollars, and still had my ten cents, and seeds, and materials for a wheelbarrow left. I found thus that I had been a rich man without any damage to my poverty. But I retained the landscape, and I have since annually carried off what it yielded without a wheelbarrow. With respect to landscapes:

> "I am monarch of all I *survey*,
> My right there is none to dispute."[3]

I have frequently seen a poet withdraw, having enjoyed the most valuable part of a farm, while the crusty farmer supposed that he had got a few wild apples only. Why, the owner does not know it for many years when a poet has put his farm in rhyme, the most admirable kind of invisible fence, has fairly impounded it, milked it, skimmed it, and got all the cream, and left the farmer only the skimmed milk.

The real attractions of the Hollowell farm, to me, were: its complete retirement, being about two miles from the village, half a mile from the nearest neighbor, and separated from the highway by a broad field; its bounding on the river, which the owner said protected it by its fogs from frosts in the spring, though that was nothing to me; the gray color and ruinous state of the house and barn, and the dilapidated fences, which put such an interval between me and the last occupant; the hollow and lichen-covered apple trees, gnawed by rabbits, showing what kind of neighbors I should have; but above all, the recollection I had of it from my earliest voyages up the river, when the house was concealed behind a dense grove of red maples, through which I heard the house-dog bark. I was in haste to buy it, before the proprietor finished getting out some rocks, cutting down the hollow apple trees, and grubbing up some young birches which had sprung up in the pasture, or, in short, had made any more of his improvements. To enjoy these advantages I was ready to carry it on; like Atlas,[4] to take the world on my shoulders—I never heard what compensation he received for that—and do all those things which had no other motive or excuse but that I might pay for it and be unmolested in my possession of it; for I knew all the while that it would yield the most abundant crop of the kind I wanted if I could only afford to let it alone. But it turned out as I have said.

All that I could say, then, with respect to farming on a large scale (I have always cultivated a garden) was that I had had my seeds ready. Many think that seeds improve with age. I have no doubt that time discriminates between the good and the bad; and when at last I shall plant, I shall be less likely to be disappointed. But I would say to my fellows, once for all, As long as possible live free and uncommitted. It makes but little difference whether you are committed to a farm or the county jail.

Old Cato,[5] whose "De Re Rustica" is my "Cultivator," says, and the only translation I have seen makes sheer nonsense of the passage, "When you think of getting a farm, turn it thus in your mind, not to buy greedily; nor spare your pains to look at it, and do not think it enough to go round it once. The oftener you go there the more it will please you, if it is good." I think I shall not buy greedily, but go round and round it as long as I live, and be buried in it first, that it may please me the more at last. . . .

I do not propose to write an ode to dejection, but to brag as lustily as chanticleer[6] in the morning, standing on his roost, if only to wake my neighbors up.

---

3. "I am . . . dispute.": From William Cowper's *Verses Supposed to Be Written by Alexander Selkirk.*

4. **Atlas** (at' ləs): From Greek mythology, a Titan who supported the heavens on his shoulders.
5. **Old Cato:** Roman statesman (234–149 B.C.). "De Re Rustica" is Latin for "Of Things Rustic."
6. **chanticleer** (chan' tə klir') n.: A rooster.

from *Walden* 289

6 **Discussion** What does Thoreau mean when he says, "I had been a rich man without any damage to my poverty"?

7 **Discussion** What does Thoreau consider the "most valuable part of a farm"?

8 **Literary Focus** Have the students examine the number and variety of details Thoreau includes in describing the farm. How do these contribute to the effectiveness of his writing?

9 **Critical Thinking and Reading** Point out that Thoreau's comments about the seeds can be interpreted both literally and metaphorically.

10 **Discussion** What does Thoreau mean when he comments that it makes little difference whether you are committed to a farm or a county jail?

11 **Enrichment** Thoreau had an excellent classical education. He often translated passages from Greek and Latin. The classical allusions are references he assumed other educated people of his time would recognize.

12 Discussion Do you think that it was really an accident that Thoreau began living in the woods on Independence Day?

13 Discussion What impression does Thoreau convey of his house? What does the wind represent?

Master Teacher Note Have your students compare and contrast Thoreau's description of his house with E. B. White's description of the site of the house (p. 766). Use the following questions for discussion: What changes occurred during the years between Thoreau's stay at Walden Pond and White's visit to the pond? Do you think that these changes reflect larger changes in society as a whole? How do you think Thoreau would have reacted if he had seen Walden Pond in the condition in which White found it? Considering Thoreau's emphasis on simplicity, how do you think he would feel about the nature of life in America today?

12 When first I took up my abode in the woods, that is, began to spend my nights as well as days there, which, by accident, was on Independence Day, or the fourth of July, 1845, my house was not finished for winter, but was merely a defense against the rain, without plastering or chimney, the walls being of rough weatherstained boards, with wide chinks, which made it cool at night. The upright white hewn studs and freshly planed door and window casings gave it a **13** clean and airy look, especially in the morning, when its timbers were saturated with dew, so that I fancied that by noon some sweet gum would exude from them. To my imagination it retained throughout the day more or less of this auroral[7] character, reminding me of a certain house on a mountain which I had visited the year before. This was an airy and unplastered cabin, fit to entertain a traveling god, and where a goddess might trail her garments. The winds which passed over my dwelling were such as sweep over the ridges of mountains, bearing the broken strains, or celestial parts only, of ter-

_____
7. auroral (ô rôr′ əl) *adj.*: Resembling the dawn.

Grammar in Action

An **infinitive** is a sentence element that can function as a noun, an adjective, or an adverb. It consists of the verb without endings and, usually, the word *to*. An infinitive can bring with it complements and modifiers, resulting in an infinitive phrase. Here are some examples from *Walden:*

I dearly love *to talk*. (Infinitive as noun)

For most men . . . have somewhat hastily concluded that it is the chief end of man here to "*glorify God* . . ." (Infinitive phrase as adjective)

This was an airy . . . cabin, fit *to entertain a god*. (Infinitive phrase as adverb)

Infinitives serve to compress short sentences into a longer one, cutting out repetitious elements and focusing important ideas. Thoreau might have written:

At last I shall plant. Then I shall probably not be disappointed.

Through subordination and the use of an infinitive, he produced, instead, this more cohesive sentence:

restrial music. The morning wind forever blows, the poem of creation is uninterrupted; but few are the ears that hear it. Olympus[8] is but the outside of the earth everywhere. . . .

I went to the woods because I wished to live deliberately, to front only the essential facts of life, and see if I could not learn what it had to teach, and not, when I came to die, discover that I had not lived. I did not wish to live what was not life, living is so dear; nor did I wish to practice resignation, unless it was quite necessary. I wanted to live deep and suck out all the marrow of life, to live so sturdily and Spartanlike[9] as to put to rout all that was not life, to cut a broad swath and shave close, to drive life into a corner, and reduce it to its lowest terms, and, if it proved to be mean, why then to get the whole and genuine meanness of it, and publish its meanness to the world; or if it were sublime, to know it by experience, and be able to give a true account of it in my next excursion. For most men, it appears to me, are in a strange uncertainty about it, whether it is of the devil or of God, and have *somewhat hastily* concluded that it is the chief end of man here to "glorify God and enjoy him forever."[10]

Still we live meanly, like ants; though the fable tells us that we were long ago changed into men; like pygmies we fight with cranes;[11] it is error upon error, and clout upon clout, and our best virtue has for its occasion a superfluous and evitable wretchedness. Our life is frittered away by detail. An honest man has hardly need to count more than his ten fingers, or in extreme cases he may add his ten toes, and lump the rest. Simplicity, simplicity, simplicity! I say, let your affairs be as two or three, and not a hundred or a thousand; instead of a million count half a dozen, and keep your accounts on your thumbnail. In the midst of this chopping sea of civilized life, such are the clouds and storms and quicksands and thousand-and-one items to be allowed for, that a man has to live, if he would not founder and go to the bottom and not make his port at all, by dead reckoning,[12] and he must be a great calculator indeed who succeeds. Simplify, simplify. Instead of three meals a day, if it be necessary eat but one; instead of a hundred dishes, five; and reduce other things in proportion. Our life is like a German Confederacy,[13] made up of petty states, with its boundary forever fluctuating, so that even a German cannot tell you how it is bounded at any moment. The nation itself, with all its so-called internal improvements, which, by the way, are all external and superficial, is just such an unwieldy and overgrown establishment, cluttered with furniture and tripped up by its own traps, ruined by luxury and heedless expense, by want of calculation and a worthy aim, as the million households in the land; and the only cure for it as for them is in a rigid economy, a stern and more than Spartan simplicity of life and elevation of purpose. It lives too fast. Men think that it is essential that the *Nation* have commerce, and export ice, and talk through a telegraph, and ride thirty miles an hour, without a doubt, whether *they* do or not; but whether we should live like baboons or like men, is a little uncertain. If we do not get out sleepers,[14] and forge rails, and devote days and nights to the work, but go to tinkering upon our *lives* to improve *them*, who will build railroads? And if railroads are not

---

8. Olympus (ō lim′ pəs): In Greek mythology, the home of the gods.
9. Spartanlike: Like the people of Sparta, an ancient Greek state, whose citizens were known to be hardy, stoical, simple, and highly disciplined.
10. "glorify . . . forever.": The answer to the question "What is the chief end of man?" in the Westminster catechism.
11. like . . . cranes: In the *Iliad*, the Trojans are compared to cranes fighting against pygmies.

---

12. dead reckoning: Navigating without the assistance of stars.
13. German Confederacy: At the time, Germany was a loose union of thirty-eight independent states, with no common government.
14. sleepers (slē′ pərz) *n.*: Ties supporting railroad tracks.

14 **Discussion** Why did Thoreau go to live in the woods?

15 **Discussion** What is meant by "I wanted to live deep and suck out all the marrow of life"?

16 **Discussion** What is Thoreau's remedy for a life that "is frittered away by detail"?

17 **Discussion** What is Thoreau's attitude toward progress? Do you agree with this attitude? Why or why not?

When at last I shall plant, I shall be less likely to be disappointed.

Student Activity 1. Find at least six infinitives or infinitive phrases in the paragraph on page 291 that begins "I went to the woods. . . ." Identify the function of the infinitive in each.

Student Activity 2. Complete these sentences by adding infinitive phrases.
1. When the farmer's wife changed her mind, Thoreau had just begun. . . .
2. Thoreau went to Walden Pond hoping. . . .
3. Thoreau wants us. . . .

4. He makes us question always being in a hurry. . . .
5. Thoreau said that time was merely a stream. . . .

18 Critical Reading and Thinking Examine Thoreau's metaphor comparing life to a stream. How does he extend his original metaphor?

19 Discussion Why did Thoreau leave the woods?

20 Critical Reading and Thinking Thoreau uses several metaphors to explain how, even in the woods, his life fell into a pattern and how he wanted to remain free of habit and open to experience.

21 Discussion What does Thoreau believe he has learned?

22 Discussion What is the meaning of Thoreau's reference to "castles in the air"?

23 Critical Thinking and Reading Students should be encouraged to compare Thoreau's image of a different drummer with Emerson's view of the nonconformist (page 276).

24 Enrichment Thoreau had lost his father and a brother he loved dearly; he was not impoverished, but was certainly not wealthy. His comments are based on his own circumstances and experiences.

built, how shall we get to heaven in season? But if we stay at home and mind our business, who will want railroads? We do not ride on the railroad; it rides upon us. . . .

18 Time is but the stream I go a-fishing in. I drink at it; but while I drink I see the sandy bottom and detect how shallow it is. Its thin current slides away, but eternity remains. I would drink deeper; fish in the sky, whose bottom is pebbly with stars. I cannot count one. I know not the first letter of the alphabet. I have always been regretting that I was not as wise as the day I was born. The intellect is a cleaver; it discerns and rifts its way into the secret of things. I do not wish to be any more busy with my hands than is necessary. My head is hands and feet. I feel all my best faculties concentrated in it. My instinct tells me that my head is an organ for burrowing, as some creatures use their snout and forepaws, and with it I would mine and burrow my way through these hills. I think that the richest vein is somewhere hereabouts; so by the divining rod[15] and thin rising vapors I judge; and here I will begin to mine. . . .

from The Conclusion

19
20 I left the woods for as good a reason as I went there. Perhaps it seemed to me that I had several more lives to live, and could not spare any more time for that one. It is remarkable how easily and insensibly we fall into a particular route, and make a beaten track for ourselves. I had not lived there a week before my feet wore a path from my door to the pondside; and though it is five or six years since I trod it, it is still quite distinct. It is true, I fear that others may have fallen into it, and so helped to keep it open. The surface of the earth is soft and impress-

15. **divining rod:** A forked branch or stick alleged to reveal underground water or minerals.

ible by the feet of men; and so with the paths which the mind travels. How worn and dusty, then, must be the highways of the world, how deep the ruts of tradition and conformity! I did not wish to take a cabin passage, but rather to go before the mast and on the deck of the world, for there I could best see the moonlight amid the mountains. I do not wish to go below now.

21 I learned this, at least, by my experiment; that if one advances confidently in the direction of his dreams, and endeavors to live the life which he has imagined, he will meet with a success unexpected in common hours. He will put some things behind, will pass an invisible boundary; new, universal, and more liberal laws will begin to establish themselves around and within him; or the old laws be expanded, and interpreted in his favor in a more liberal sense, and he will live with the license of a higher order of beings. **22** In proportion as he simplifies his life, the laws of the universe will appear less complex, and solitude will not be solitude, nor poverty poverty, nor weakness weakness. If you have built castles in the air, your work need not be lost; that is where they should be. Now put the foundations under them. . . .

23 Why should we be in such desperate haste to succeed, and in such desperate enterprises? If a man does not keep pace with his companions, perhaps it is because he hears a different drummer. Let him step to the music which he hears, however measured or far away. It is not important that he should mature as soon as an apple tree or an oak. Shall he turn his spring into summer? If the condition of things which we were made for is not yet, what were any reality which we can substitute? We will not be shipwrecked on a vain reality. Shall we with pains erect a heaven of blue glass over ourselves, though when it is done we shall be sure to gaze still at the true ethereal heaven far above, as if the former were not?. . . .

24 However mean your life is, meet it and live it; do not shun it and call it hard names.

Commentary: Thoreau's Style

Although Thoreau's work received little notoriety during his lifetime, he is now widely recognized as a masterful prose stylist. Not surprisingly, Ralph Waldo Emerson was one of the few people of Thoreau's day to appreciate Thoreau's literary gift. In fact, Emerson openly marvelled at the powerful manner in which Thoreau expressed ideas in writing. After reading passages from Thoreau's journal, Emerson wrote, "That oaken strength which I noted whenever [Thoreau] walked, or worked, or surveyed woodlots, the same unhesitating hand with which a field-laborer accosts a piece of work, which I should shun as a waste of strength, Henry shows in his literary task. He has muscle, and ventures on and performs feats which I am forced to decline. In reading him, I find the same thought, the same spirit that is in me, but he takes a step beyond, and illustrates by excellent images that which I should have conveyed in a sleepy generality. It is as if I went into a gymnasium, and saw youths leap, climb, and swing with a force unapproachable—though their feats are only continuations of my initial grapplings and jumps."

Like Emerson, most contemporary readers and critics are struck by the strength and vigor of Thoreau's style. For this reason, his style is often characterized as powerfully extrava-

It is not so bad as you are. It looks poorest when you are richest. The faultfinder will find faults even in paradise. Love your life, poor as it is. You may perhaps have some pleasant, thrilling, glorious hours, even in a poorhouse. The setting sun is reflected from the windows of the almshouse[16] as brightly as from the rich man's abode; the snow melts before its door as early in the spring. I do not see but a quiet mind may live as contentedly there, and have as cheering thoughts, as in a palace. The town's poor seem to me often to live the most independent lives of any. Maybe they are simply great enough to receive without misgiving. Most think that they are above being supported by the town; but it oftener happens that they are not above supporting themselves by dishonest means, which should be more disreputable. Cultivate poverty like a garden herb, like sage. Do not trouble yourself much to get new things, whether clothes or friends. Turn the old; return to them. Things do not change; we change. Sell your clothes and keep your thoughts. God will see that you do not want society. If I were confined to a corner of a garret[17] all my days, like a spider, the world would be just as large to me while I had my thoughts about me. The philosopher said: "From an army of three divisions one can take away its general, and put it in disorder; from the man the most abject and vulgar one cannot take away his thought." Do not seek so anxiously to be developed, to subject yourself to many influences to be played on; it is all dissipation. Humility like darkness reveals the heavenly lights. The shadows of poverty and meanness gather around us, "and lo! creation widens to our view."[18] We are often reminded that if there were bestowed on us the wealth of Croesus,[19] our aims must still be the same, and our means essentially the same. Moreover, if you are restricted in your range by poverty, if you cannot buy books and newspapers, for instance, you are but confined to the most significant and vital experiences; you are compelled to deal with the material which yields the most sugar and the most starch. It is life near the bone where it is sweetest. You are defended from being a trifler. No man loses ever on a lower level by magnanimity on a higher. Superfluous wealth can buy superfluities only. Money is not required to buy one necessary of the soul. . . .

The life in us is like the water in the river. It may rise this year higher than man has ever known it, and flood the parched uplands; even this may be the eventful year, which will drown out all our muskrats. It was not always dry land where we dwell. I see far inland the banks which the stream anciently washed, before science began to record its freshets. Everyone has heard the story which has gone the rounds of New England, of a strong and beautiful bug which came out of the dry leaf of an old table of apple-tree wood, which had stood in a farmer's kitchen for sixty years, first in Connecticut, and afterward in Massachusetts—from an egg deposited in the living tree many years earlier still, as appeared by counting the annual layers beyond it; which was heard gnawing out for several weeks, hatched perchance by the heat of an urn. Who does not feel his faith in a resurrection and immortality strengthened by hearing of this? Who knows what beautiful and winged life, whose egg has been buried for ages under many concentric layers of woodenness in

---

16. almshouse *n.*: A home for people too poor to support themselves.
17. garret (gar′ it) *n.*: Attic.
18. "and . . . view": From the sonnet "To Night" by British poet Joseph Blanco White (1775–1841).

19. Croesus (krē′ səs): The King of Lydia (d. 546 B.C.), believed to be the wealthiest person of his time.

25 Discussion Do you think Thoreau would give the same advice about poverty today? Why or why not?

26 Master Teacher Note Point out that Thoreau had the benefit of a Harvard education and of family and friends who were educated. He had chosen a life of simplicity and relative poverty—although he had the pencil business that his father had begun. His definition of poverty may be very different from a modern definition.

27 Discussion What is Thoreau's purpose in telling the story of the bug in the wood?

---

gant. Within Thoreau's most effective paragraphs, the sentences build upon one another to create a mounting effect that can be compared to a hammer driving a nail into a piece of wood: Each sentence reinforces the ideas in the preceding sentences, and the paragraph is likely to end with a powerful clincher sentence that drives his points home.

The strength of Thoreau's writing also results partly from his aphoristic sentences, his brief allegories, his striking metaphors and similes, and his use of rhetorical devices such as repetition, parallelism, and rhetorical questions. In his paragraph on simplicity (p. 291), for example, Thoreau uses nearly all of these devices.

Enrichment During Thoreau's lifetime most people viewed him as an extremely eccentric man lacking in both direction and ambition. However, Thoreau was undaunted by the scorn of others, and he continued to live his life exactly as he pleased. In the following passage from his essay "Life without Principle," Thoreau examines society's response to his views and conveys his belief in the need to assert one's individuality in the face of the demands of society:

If a man walks in the woods for love of them half of each day, he is in danger of being regarded as a loafer; but if he spends his whole day as a speculator, shearing off these woods and making the earth bald before her time, he is esteemed an industrious and enterprising citizen. As if a town had no interest in its forests but to cut them down! . . .

The community has no bribe that will tempt a wise man. You may raise money enough to tunnel a mountain, but you cannot raise money enough to hire a man who is minding *his own* business. An efficient and valuable man does what he can, whether the community pay him for it or not. The inefficient offer their inefficiency to the highest bidder, and are forever expecting to be put into office. One would suppose that they are rarely disappointed.

Perhaps I am more than usually jealous with respect to my freedom. I feel that my connection with and obligation to society are still very slight and transient. Those slight labors which afford me a livelihood, and by which it is allowed that I am to some extent serviceable to my contemporaries, are yet commonly a pleasure to me, and I am not often reminded that they are a necessity. So far I am successful. But I foresee, that, if my wants should

the dead dry life of society, deposited at first in the alburnum[20] of the green and living tree, which has been gradually converted into the semblance of its well-seasoned tomb—heard perchance gnawing out now for years by the astonished family of man, as they sat round the festive board—may unexpectedly come forth from amidst society's most trivial and handselled furniture, to enjoy its perfect summer life at last!

I do not say that John or Jonathan[21] will realize all this; but such is the character of that morrow which mere lapse of time can never make to dawn. The light which puts out our eyes is darkness to us. Only that day dawns to which we are awake. There is more day to dawn. The sun is but a morning star.

20. **alburnum** (al bur′ nəm) *n.*: Soft wood between the bark and the heartwood where water is conducted.

21. **John or Jonathan:** The average person.

be much increased, the labor required to supply them would become a drudgery. If I should sell both my forenoons and afternoons to society, as most appear to do, I am sure, that, for me, there would be nothing left worth living for. I trust that I shall never thus sell my birthright for a mess of pottage. I wish to suggest that a man may be very industrious, and yet not spend his time well. There is no more fatal blunder than he who consumes the greater part of his life getting his living. All great enterprises are self-supporting. The poet, for instance, must sustain his body by his poetry, as a steam-planing mill feeds its boilers with the shavings it makes. You must get your living by loving. But as it is said of the merchants that ninety-seven in a hundred fail, so the life of men generally, tried by this standard, is a failure, and bankruptcy may surely be prophesied.

Reader's Response What is your reaction to the ideas that Thoreau expresses in this selection?

THINKING ABOUT THE SELECTION

Recalling

1. What does Thoreau imagine doing?
2. (a) On what day does Thoreau begin spending nights in his "abode in the woods"? (b) What condition is the cabin in at the time?
3. For what reasons does Thoreau go to live in the woods?
4. Why does he leave the woods?
5. What does he learn from his "experiment"?
6. What advice does Thoreau offer to those who live in poverty?

Interpreting

7. What does Thoreau mean when he comments, "It makes but little difference whether you are committed to a farm or the county jail"?
8. (a) How does Thoreau's decription of the wind convey the Transcendentalist belief in the existence of a shared universal soul, or Over-Soul? (b) What does he suggest about peoples' awareness of the Over-Soul?
9. Why does Thoreau believe that living in the woods will enable him to "live deep and suck all the marrow out of life"?
10. Considering the attitude toward commitments that Thoreau expresses in his discussion of farms, why is it not surprising that he decides to leave Walden?
11. In your own words, describe Thoreau's attitude toward individuality and conformity.
12. Why, according to Thoreau, are people better off being poor than wealthy?
13. (a) What does the story of the "beautiful bug" reveal about our capacity to experience a spiritual awakening? (b) What does Thoreau believe we can do to help bring about this type of rebirth?

Applying

14. Explain why you either do or do not believe that it would be possible for Thoreau to conduct his "experiment" in today's society.

ANALYZING LITERATURE

Understanding Style

Style refers to the way in which a writer expresses his or her thoughts. For example, Thoreau writes in a powerfully excessive style, constantly reinforcing his main points.

1. How does the paragraph on simplicity (page 285) demonstrate Thoreau's tendency to make sentences build to a climax? Find one other paragraph that is structured in this manner.
2. Thoreau often starts a paragraph by discussing specific incidents or examples. He then applies them to a larger truth. Find one paragraph in which he uses this technique.

CRITICAL THINKING AND READING

Evaluating the Effect of Style

Some critics have argued that Thoreau overstates his main points in *Walden*. Thoreau, however, felt that it was impossible to overstate the truth about human potential. He deliberately repeated his main ideas to reinforce what he was saying.

Examine the paragraph on simplicity. Explain whether the structure of the paragraph contributes to its effectiveness.

THINKING AND WRITING

Comparing and Contrasting Essays

Write an essay in which you compare and contrast the excerpt from *Walden* with the excerpt from Emerson's *Nature* (page 268). Start by carefully rereading the two selections. Take notes on the ideas expressed in each selection. Organize your notes according to corresponding points of contrast. Then draft your essay, supporting your points with passages from each selection. When you revise, make sure that you have varied the length and structure of your sentences and connected your ideas with transitions. Proofread and prepare a final draft.

from Walden 295

10. He clearly does not want to be bound to any place—not even Walden Pond. As a result, it is not surprising that he leaves when he has gained as much from the experience as he feels he can.
11. Conformity restricts a person; one must follow the voice within.
12. Wealth demands attention to the nonessential details of life; it becomes a kind of prison.
13. (a) Unseen forces can lie deep beneath the surface, and the right timing and circumstances can bring them out. (b) We should open up our minds by freeing ourselves from unnecessary burdens.

Applying

14. Answers will differ. Students may comment that life today is too complex to enable a person to conduct such an experiment.

Challenge Would you be interested in conducting an experiment similar to Thoreau's? Why or why not?

ANSWERS TO ANALYZING LITERATURE

1. He begins with a simile about ants and proceeds to a statement about detail. Then he urges simplicity and gives examples about simplifying individual lives. He then makes another comparison and launches an attack on the complexities of progress.
2. The paragraph about the Hollowell farm is one example.

ANSWERS TO CRITICAL THINKING AND READING

The structure does contribute to its effectiveness. Because the sentences build to a climax, Thoreau's main point is constantly being reinforced.

THINKING AND WRITING

For help with this assignment, students can refer to Lesson 16, "Writing a Comparative Evaluation," in the Handbook of Writing About Literature.

After students have completed their essays divide them into groups, and have them read their essays to one another and suggest ways in which the essays could be improved.

Closure and Extension

ANSWERS TO THINKING ABOUT THE SELECTION

Recalling

1. He imagines buying and living on many different farms.
2. (a) He begins spending time in the woods on Independence Day. (b) The cabin keeps out rain but is not yet ready for winter.
3. He wanted to live with only life's essential needs.
4. He left the woods when he found himself falling into a routine.
5. He learned that "if one advances confidently in the direction of his dreams, and endeavors to live the life he has imagined, he will meet with a success unexpected in common hours."
6. They should love their lives and find the best in it.

Interpreting

7. Living in either place places constraints on your liberty.
8. (a) The wind sweeps across the earth, blowing forever, carrying melodies. Thoreau is using the wind to represent the all-encompassing Over-Soul. (b) He suggests that few people are aware of it.
9. By reducing the nonessentials, life in the woods will enable him to experience the essentials more fully.

Motivation/Prior Knowledge
Have students imagine that they
strongly object to a governmental policy. How would they voice
their objections?

Purpose-Setting Question
What is Thoreau's attitude concerning the role of government?

1 Discussion What groups today
might be most likely to agree or
disagree with the opening statement?

2 Discussion Is it possible to have
a government which "governs
not at all"?

3 Critical Thinking and Reading
Students should note the play on
the words "expedient" and "inexpedient." It may be necessary to
clarify their meanings.

4 Critical Thinking and Reading
Students may want to compare
this passage to Emerson's analogy of the joint-stock company
(p. 276).

5 Discussion Can you think of parallel situations from recent history?

6 Discussion What is the meaning of Thoreau's reference to a
wooden gun?

7 Critical Thinking and Reading
Help students recognize that
Thoreau credits the people, not
the government, for the development of the country. Ask students to compare the American
government's role to the roles of
other governments.

8 Discussion What type of government does Thoreau want?

Reader's Response Do you
agree with Thoreau's ideas
about government? Why or why
not?

from Civil Disobedience

Henry David Thoreau

I heartily accept the motto, "That government is best which governs least";[1] and I
should like to see it acted up to more rapidly
and systematically. Carried out, it finally
amounts to this, which also I believe: "That
government is best which governs not at all";
and when men are prepared for it, that will
be the kind of government which they will
have. Government is at best but an expedient; but most governments are usually, and
all governments are sometimes, inexpedient.
The objections which have been brought
against a standing army, and they are many
and weighty, and deserve to prevail, may also
at last be brought against a standing government. The standing army is only an arm of
the standing government. The government
itself, which is only the mode which the people have chosen to execute their will, is
equally liable to be abused and perverted before the people can act through it. Witness
the present Mexican war, the work of comparatively a few individuals using the standing government as their tool; for in the
outset, the people would not have consented
to this measure.

This American government—what is it
but a tradition, though a recent one, endeavoring to transmit itself unimpaired to posterity, but each instant losing some of its integrity? It has not the vitality and force of a
single living man; for a single man can bend
it to his will. It is a sort of wooden gun to the
people themselves; and, if ever they should
use it in earnest as a real one against each
other, it will surely split. But it is not the
less necessary for this; for the people must
have some complicated machinery or other,
and hear its din, to satisfy that idea of government which they have. Governments
show thus how successfully men can be imposed on, even impose on themselves, for
their own advantage. It is excellent, we must
all allow; yet this government never of itself
furthered any enterprise, but by the alacrity
with which it got out of its way. *It* does not
keep the country free. *It* does not settle the
West. *It* does not educate. The character inherent in the American people has done all
that has been accomplished; and it would
have done somewhat more, if the government had not sometimes got in its way. For
government is an expedient by which men
would fain succeed in letting one another
alone; and, as has been said, when it is most
expedient, the governed are most let alone by
it. Trade and commerce, if they were not
made of India rubber,[2] would never manage
to bounce over the obstacles which legislators are continually putting in their way;
and, if one were to judge these men wholly
by the effects of their actions, and not partly
by their intentions, they would deserve to be
classed and punished with those mischievous persons who put obstructions on the
railroads.

But, to speak practically and as a citizen,
unlike those who call themselves no government men, I ask for, not at once no government, but *at once* a better government. Let
every man make known what kind of government would command his respect, and that
will be one step toward obtaining it. . . .

---

1. **"That . . . least":** The motto of the *United States
Magazine and Democratic Review,* a literary-political
journal.

2. **India rubber:** A form of crude rubber.

Objectives
1 To understand historical
   context
2 To write a report

Support Material

Teaching Portfolio
Teacher Backup, p. 411
Usage and Mechanics Work-
   sheet, p. 415
Vocabulary Check, p. 416
Analyzing Literature Worksheet,
   *Understanding More About His-
   torical Context,* p. 417
Language Worksheet, *Recogniz-
   ing Synonyms,* p. 418
Selection Test, p. 419

THINKING ABOUT THE SELECTION

Recalling

1. What motto does Thoreau heartily accept?
2. According to Thoreau, what is the American public's attitude toward the Mexican War?
3. How does Thoreau suggest people can contribute to improving the government?

Interpreting

4. (a) How would you summarize Thoreau's attitude concerning the role of the government? (b) In what ways does he believe the American government has failed to serve this role?

Applying

5. (a) Considering the beliefs expressed in this essay, what government policies do you think Thoreau would object to? (b) What policies would he endorse?

ANALYZING LITERATURE

Understanding Historical Context

Thoreau wrote *Civil Disobedience* after spending a night in jail for refusing to pay his taxes to demonstrate his disapproval of the Mexican War and of slavery. In the essay he urged people to follow his example by resisting governmental policies with which they disagree. The essay has become one of Thoreau's most famous works, influencing a number of important historical figures such as Mahatma Gandhi and Martin Luther King, Jr.

1. In this excerpt, what does Thoreau suggest is responsible for the Mexican War?
2. What does he indicate about his reasons for disapproving of the war?
3. How does he use the war to support his argument concerning the role of the government?

THINKING AND WRITING

Writing a Report

Write a brief report about the Mexican War. Start by researching the war in encyclopedias and history books in your library. List the events leading up to the war, the important battles, and the outcome. Prepare an outline. Then write your report, making sure that you mention each of the important events related to the war. When you revise, make sure that the events in your report are presented in chronological order.

Commentary

It is not surprising that the residents of Concord should wonder why a twenty-eight-year-old Harvard graduate was playing house in the woods. Seven years (and as many complete revisions later), Thoreau answered their questions in *Walden*—in his own fashion.

He begins by slyly criticizing their narrow interest in the business of making money: "My purpose in going to Walden Pond was not to live cheaply nor to live dearly there, but to transact some private business with the fewest obstacles . . ." Village life, he felt, was deadening: "The mass of men lead lives of quiet desperation."

He did not need to go far to find the freedom he needed to become a "wiser savage." His cabin was less than a two-mile walk from the Emersons' home, where he often went for dinner. He had no intention of being a hermit or of conducting an experiment in wilderness living.

The "wildness" sought by Thoreau was primarily of the spirit and could be found in a rural setting. He recommends the experience of being lost in the woods at night and of eating wild meat, both of which he did (he didn't like the taste of the woodchuck).

from *Civil Disobedience* 297

Closure and Extension

ANSWERS TO THINKING ABOUT THE SELECTION
Recalling

1. "That government is best which governs least."
2. The people do not want the war.
3. They should express their opinions concerning the type of government that they want.

Interpreting

4. (a) Government should do as little as possible. (b) It has imposed the will of the few upon the majority.

Applying

5. Suggested Response: Thoreau would probably believe that the government interferes too much in people's lives.

Challenge How do your views of government compare with Thoreau's?

ANSWERS TO ANALYZING LITERATURE

1. He suggests that it is the result of the desire of a few individuals to use the government as their tool.
2. He objects to it because the people would not have consented to it.
3. He uses it as an example of how the government has abused its authority.

Writing Across the Curriculum You might want to inform the history department about this assignment. History teachers might be able to assist students with their research.

CROSS CURRENTS

Contemporary Thoreaus

During Henry David Thoreau's lifetime, his writings were known only by a small group of friends and acquaintances. Soon after his death, however, his reputation began spreading, until today it is worldwide.

Thoreau's account of his "experiment" at Walden Pond has inspired many people to do the same. They have retreated to such places as snowbound cabins, hill farms, and mountain huts. Some have written reflective accounts of their experiences. Among these modern-day Thoreaus are two American writers, Annie Dillard and Edward Abbey.

Both Dillard and Abbey followed Thoreau's recommendation to go to nature to "explore thyself." In their books they accurately record and vividly describe the natural world, seeking its spiritual meanings. Yet each writer's experience and account of living alone is unique.

ANNIE DILLARD

Annie Dillard spent a year in a small cabin next to Tinker Creek in West Virginia, her only company a goldfish named Ellery Channing. She described her life and thoughts there in the award-winning book *Pilgrim at Tinker Creek*, published in 1974.

"I propose," she tells us in the first chapter, "to keep here what Thoreau called 'a meteorological journal of the mind,' telling some tales and describing some of the sights of this rather tamed valley, and exploring, in fear and trembling, some of the unmapped dim reaches and unholy fastnesses to which those tales and sights so dizzyingly lead." Her exploration leads her to horrifying scenes and joyous moments in the natural world around her.

Dillard has a mystical vision of nature, expressed with intense emotional lyricism. She seeks and sees the face of God and of the unknown in the trees, water, and changing seasons of Tinker Creek. A few years later on an island in Puget Sound, she wrote *Holy the Firm* (published in 1978), a theological meditation on the ultimate meaning of life.

EDWARD ABBEY

Edward Abbey's retreat was a small government-issue trailer at Arches National Monument, where he spent several summers as a park ranger. His account of his experiment, *Desert Solitaire: A Season in the Wilderness*, was published in 1968. As Thoreau did in *Walden*, Abbey compresses the events of several seasons into one.

The harsh and delicate beauty of the Utah desert inspires him: "I am twenty miles or more from the nearest fellow human, but instead of loneliness I feel loveliness. Loveliness and a quiet exultation." The desert and its inhabitants, both animal and human, also bring many doubts and questions about his and all humans' purpose on earth.

It is, however, Thoreau as skeptical observer and critic of society that seems most to attract Abbey. Even more than Thoreau, he is outspoken, witty, sometimes sarcastic in his criticisms of dubious "improvements" made in the land by individuals and government agencies. He is often irreverent and outrageous in condemning the ignorance and greed he sees destroying the last vestiges of wildness. His purpose, like Thoreau's, is to wake up his neighbors before it is too late.

Fiercely against mechanization, Abbey is proud to be a "river rat." In the fall of 1980, he floated down the canyons of the Green and Colorado rivers. With him he took "a worn and greasy paperback copy of a book called *Walden, or Life in the Woods*." He described this trip in "Down the River with Henry Thoreau," first published in 1981.

"Thoreau's mind has been haunting mine for most of my life," he admits. Throughout the river trip he quotes from, talks about, and argues with Thoreau.

At the last rapid, before returning to "civilization, such as it is," Abbey concludes, "Henry thou should be with us now. . . . Wherever there are deer and hawks, wherever there is liberty and danger, wherever there is wilderness, wherever there is a living river, Henry Thoreau will find his eternal home."

More About the Author In 1828, before he wrote most of his short stories, Nathaniel Hawthorne published his first novel, *Fanshawe*. It was not well received, and Hawthorne turned to writing short stories, because there was a better market for stories than for novels. He began to draw heavily on the traditions and superstitions of New England for his material, and it was in his native element that his work matured. Ask students to discuss the ways in which a writer might benefit by exploring familiar subjects in his or her work. Why are writers likely to be unsuccessful if they choose to write about subjects about which they are unfamiliar?

Critical Evaluation The literary scholar Edward H. Davidson has written: "That a century after he lived he should be included in a collection of major writers of America would have baffled and amused Hawthorne. During his lifetime the profession of letters was so poorly rewarded, and Hawthorne himself had been so consistently ignored, that to be a subject for literary study and analysis, to be termed a 'classic' among American writers, would have seemed nothing short of grotesque. Yet, aside from the poor pay and the lack of recognition . . . Hawthorne has not suffered the slow or sudden loss of popularity which befell many of his contemporaries, nor has he been made into a fashionable literary mode, a literary cliché of our own time. Indeed, his literary reputation has maintained its high place more steadily than that of any other major American writer . . ."

NATHANIEL HAWTHORNE

1804–1864

Despite his admiration for Ralph Waldo Emerson, Nathaniel Hawthorne found it impossible to accept the optimistic world view of the Transcendentalists. Haunted by the intolerance and cruelty of his Puritan ancestors, Hawthorne viewed evil as one of the dominant forces in the world. As a result, his works express a gloomy vision of the world, which contrasts sharply with the positive view of the Transcendentalists.

Hawthorne was born in Salem, Massachusetts, a descendant of a prominent Puritan family. His ancestors included a judge known for his persecution of the Quakers and a judge who played an important role in the Salem witchcraft trials. Though Hawthorne himself was not a Puritan, he was deeply aware of the actions of his ancestors, and his character was shaped by a sense of inherited guilt.

After graduating from Bowdoin College in Maine in 1825, Hawthorne lived in seclusion in his mother's house in Salem for twelve years, devoting his energy to developing his skills as a writer. Hawthorne's self-imposed isolation lasted until 1837, when he published his first collection of stories, *Twice-Told Tales*. The book sold poorly, but it established him as a respected writer.

After moving out of his mother's house, Hawthorne lived briefly at Brook Farm, the Transcendentalist commune. Then, in 1842, he married Sophia Peabody and moved to the Old Manse at Concord, Massachusetts, where Emerson had lived. While living in Concord, he became a friend of both Emerson and Thoreau and published a second collection of stories, *Mosses from an Old Manse* (1846).

When he received a political appointment at the Salem customhouse, he moved back to Salem. A change of administrations forced him out of office, and Hawthorne once again focused on his writing. In 1850 he published *The Scarlet Letter,* a powerful novel about sin and guilt among early Puritans. *The Scarlet Letter* was extremely successful, earning Hawthorne international fame. During the next two years, Hawthorne published two more novels, *The House of the Seven Gables* (1851) and *The Blithedale Romance* (1852).

When his college friend Franklin Pierce became President, Hawthorne was made the American consul at Liverpool, England. After spending several years in England and Italy, Hawthorne returned to Massachusetts. Hawthorne's experiences in Italy provided him with the material for his final novel, *The Marble Faun* (1860). Four years after the book's publication, Hawthorne died in his sleep while on a walking tour in New Hampshire.

Objectives

1 To understand Anti-Transcendentalism
2 To recognize the author's attitudes
3 To compare and contrast attitudes

Support Material

Teaching Portfolio
Teacher Backup, p. 421
Grammar in Action Worksheet, *Varying Sentence Structures*, p. 424
Usage and Mechanics Worksheet, p. 426
Vocabulary Check, p. 427
Analyzing Literature Worksheet, *Understanding Anti-Transcen-*

dentalism, p. 428
Critical Thinking and Reading Worksheet, *Interpreting Symbols*, p. 429
Selection Test, p. 430

GUIDE FOR INTERPRETING

The Minister's Black Veil

Literary Movements

Anti-Transcendentalism. Anti-Transcendentalism was a literary movement that essentially consisted of only two writers. Yet these two writers, Nathaniel Hawthorne and Herman Melville, were easily the greatest fiction writers of their time. They focused on the limitations and potential destructiveness of the human spirit rather than on its possibilities.

Writer's Techniques

Allegory. An allegory is a work of literature in which events, characters, and details of setting have a symbolic meaning. For example, a character in an allegory may represent a single human trait, such as jealousy, greed, or compassion. Allegories are used to teach or explain moral principles and universal truths.

Commentary

The truths Hawthorne suggests in his allegories were often themselves mysterious and dimly seen. He was seeking them in the innermost workings of the human heart and mind, an area largely unexplored even today. Ordinary humans as well as the natural world around us, he felt, contained dark places that the cold light of reason alone could not penetrate—at least not without risking one's peace of mind. Truths lay in the shadows, in the time between sleeping and waking, in the world transformed by moonlight.

To entice his readers into this almost dreamlike world, Hawthorne used the voice of the storyteller, the humble teller of folk tales, which we know are not strictly "true" but nevertheless fascinate us. He always called his stories "tales" and his novels "romances," and he explained what he meant.

Rather than sticking closely to the ordinary reality of the novel, he said, the romance writer could best "present the truth of the human heart" by using his artistic imagination to create a rich, shadowy atmosphere or mood. He can, Hawthorne continues, then manage this atmosphere so "as to bring out or mellow the lights and deepen and enrich the shadows of the picture." Finally, in a tale or romance, he can "mingle the Marvelous" with the ordinary and the legendary past with the present.

As you read the following story, listen for the voice of the storyteller speaking directly to you. Notice how Hawthorne creates an atmosphere by mingling not only real and unreal and past and present, but also light and dark and good and evil. Can people or events today be both good and bad, ordinary and marvelous, or a mingling of other opposites?

Writing

Freewrite about how a person's physical appearance can isolate him or her from other people.

Guide for Interpreting 301

Literary Focus The Anti-Transcendentalists displayed a deep awareness of human flaws in their works. Point out to students that nearly all the characters in Hawthorne's work have flaws, and these flaws are usually the points on which the story turns.

Writing/Prior Knowledge Students may want to discuss the difference between the elements of physical appearance that are self-imposed, such as grooming and dress, and those elements that a person is born with or acquires through an accident.

Vocabulary

Preteach the following vocabulary words:
venerable (ven′ ər ə b'l) *adj.:* Commanding respect (p. 301)
iniquity (in ik′ wətē) *n.:* Sin (p. 302)
indecorous (in dek′ ər əs) *adj.:* Improper (p. 303)
ostentatious (äs′ tən tā′ shəs) *adj.:* Intended to attract notice (p. 304)
sagacious (sə gā′ shəs) *adj.:* Shrewd (p. 305)
vagary (və ger′ ē) *n.:* An unpredictable occurrence (p. 306)
tremulous (trem′ yo͞o ləs) *adj.:* Characterized by trembling (p. 307)
waggery (wag′ ər ē) *n.:* Mischievous humor (p. 308)
impertinent (im pɜr′ t'n ənt) *adj.:* Not showing proper respect (p. 308)
obstinacy (äb′ stə nə sē) *n.:* Stubbornness (p. 309)

Spelling Tip Point out that *ostentatious* and *sagacious* have the same ending sound, but the ending of *ostentatious* is spelled *tious* while the ending of *sagacious* is spelled *cious*.

Motivation/Prior Knowledge
Have students imagine that some highly respected member of their community suddenly appeared in public with a mask on or with some other unexpected form of dress. How would they react? What would they want to ask?

Master Teacher Note You may wish to set the tone for this story by discussing the use of a mask as a literary device. Such stories as *The Man in the Iron Mask* and *The Phantom of the Opera* employ masks as symbols of despair and punishment. In other kinds of fiction a mask is used as a symbol of mystery and power.

Thematic Idea Another selection in which a symbol is used as a key to theme is the excerpt from *Moby Dick* by Herman Melville (p. 318).

Enrichment Hawthorne often used the theme of "hidden sin" in his stories, particularly in his novel *The Scarlet Letter*.

Purpose-Setting Question Is the minister wearing the veil for himself or for others?

1 **Clarification** A parable is a short allegorical tale that teaches some kind of lesson. Students should try to identify the lesson taught.

2 **Critical Thinking and Reading** Have students take note of how Hawthorne uses dialogue skillfully for dramatic effect. For example, the veil is first mentioned in dialogue, and the minister's identity is first questioned in dialogue.

3 **Critical Thinking and Reading** The narrator begins by minimizing the aura of the veil, but by the middle of the paragraph an increasingly gloomy aura is attributed to it.

The Minister's Black Veil

Nathaniel Hawthorne

A Parable

1

The sexton[1] stood in the porch of Milford meetinghouse, pulling busily at the bell rope. The old people of the village came stooping along the street. Children, with bright faces, tripped merrily beside their parents, or mimicked a graver gait, in the conscious dignity of their Sunday clothes. Spruce bachelors looked sidelong at the pretty maidens, and fancied that the Sabbath sunshine made them prettier than on weekdays. When the throng had mostly streamed into the porch, the sexton began to toll the bell, keeping his eye on the Reverend Mr. Hooper's door. The first glimpse of the clergyman's figure was the signal for the bell to cease its summons.

2
"But what has good Parson Hooper got upon his face?" cried the sexton in astonishment.

All within hearing immediately turned about, and beheld the semblance of Mr. Hooper, pacing slowly his meditative way towards the meetinghouse. With one accord they started, expressing more wonder than if some strange minister were coming to dust the cushions of Mr. Hooper's pulpit.

"Are you sure it is our parson?" inquired Goodman[2] Gray of the sexton.

"Of a certainty it is good Mr. Hooper," replied the sexton. "He was to have exchanged pulpits with Parson Shute, of Westbury; but Parson Shute sent to excuse himself yesterday, being to preach a funeral sermon."

The cause of so much amazement may appear sufficiently slight. Mr. Hooper, a gentlemanly person, of about thirty, though still a bachelor, was dressed with due clerical neatness, as if a careful wife had starched his band, and brushed the weekly dust from his Sunday's garb. There was but one thing remarkable in his appearance. Swathed about his forehead, and hanging down over his face, so low as to be shaken by his breath, Mr. Hooper had on a black veil. On a nearer view it seemed to consist of two folds of crape,[3] which entirely concealed his features, except the mouth and chin, but probably did not intercept his sight, further than to give a darkened aspect to all living and inanimate things. With this gloomy shade before him, good Mr. Hooper walked onward, at a slow and quiet pace, stooping somewhat, and looking on the ground, as is customary with abstracted men, yet nodding kindly to those of his parishioners who still waited on the meetinghouse steps. But so wonderstruck were they that his greeting hardly met with a return.

"I can't really feel as if good Mr. Hooper's face was behind that piece of crape," said the sexton.

"I don't like it," muttered an old woman, as she hobbled into the meetinghouse. "He has changed himself into something awful, only by hiding his face."

"Our parson has gone mad!" cried Goodman Gray, following him across the threshold.

3

4

5

---

1. sexton (seks′ tən) *n.*: A person in charge of the maintenance of a church.
2. Goodman: A title of respect similar to "Mister."

3. crape (krāp) *n.*: A piece of black cloth worn as a sign of mourning.

4 **Discussion** How does the description of Mr. Hooper contrast with the effects of the veil?

5 **Discussion** Why is the reaction to the veil so strong?

WINTER SUNDAY IN NORWAY, MAINE
Unidentified Artist
New York State Historical Association, Cooperstown

Fine art, *Winter Sunday in Norway, Maine,* c. 1870, anonymous folk artist. Folk painting provides a source of unity between past and present. Such painting offers an intimate view of America through the eyes of the common people—unsophisticated, non-intellectual, and emotional. Unschooled yet charming, folk painting is an art form that draws upon native designs, creativity, and craftsmanship, and reflects American social history.

You might use the following for discussion:
1. Describe the picture.
2. What elements or details of the picture correspond to "The Minister's Black Veil"?

6 Literary Focus Whereas the first reactions were verbal, the next are physical. Both forms of reaction reveal the limitations of the people who respond.

7 Reading Strategy At this point the suggestion is first made that the veil is a symbol. Ask the students to suggest what it might symbolize.

8 Discussion Why might the minister find the sight of the congregation frightening?

A rumor of some unaccountable phenomenon had preceded Mr. Hooper into the meetinghouse, and set all the congregation astir. Few could refrain from twisting their heads towards the door; many stood upright, and turned directly about; while several little boys clambered upon the seats, and came down again with a terrible racket. There was a general bustle, a rustling of the women's gowns and shuffling of the men's feet, greatly at variance with that hushed repose which should attend the entrance of the minister. But Mr. Hooper appeared not to notice the perturbation of his people. He entered with an almost noiseless step, bent his head mildly to the pews on each side, and bowed as he passed his oldest parishioner, a white-haired great-grandsire, who occupied an armchair in the center of the aisle. It was strange to observe how slowly this venerable man became conscious of something singular in the apearance of his pastor. He seemed not fully to partake of the prevailing wonder, till Mr. Hooper had ascended the stairs, and showed himself in the pulpit, face to face with his congregation, except for the black veil. That mysterious emblem was never once withdrawn. It shook with his measured breath, as he gave out the psalm; it threw its obscurity between him and the holy page, as he read the Scriptures; and while he prayed, the veil lay heavily on his uplifted countenance. Did he seek to hide it from the dread Being whom he was addressing?

Such was the effect of this simple piece of crape, that more than one woman of delicate nerves was forced to leave the meetinghouse. Yet perhaps the palefaced congregation was almost as fearful a sight to the minister, as his black veil to them.

Mr. Hooper had the reputation of a good

The Minister's Black Veil 303

304

9 Discussion How is the minister's sermon related to the veil?

10 Discussion Does the veil make the minister's sermon more effective? Why or why not?

11 Critical Thinking and Reading This is one of several hints about the reason the minister chose to wear the veil. Students should be encouraged to note the various hints throughout the story and to evaluate the credibility of each.

12 Critical Thinking and Reading Note how the narrator uses irony to expose human nature.

13 Critical Thinking and Reading The lady states the essence of the situation: each person responds to the symbol, not to the piece of cloth.

14 Discussion How does the veil affect Mr. Hooper's personality?

Master Teacher Note Explain to your students that the veil's symbolic meaning is revealed through the comments and actions of Parson Hooper and his parishioners. For example, the parishioners' sense of relief at the close of the services hints at the meaning of the veil. The parishioners are "conscious of lighter spirits the moment they [lose] sight of the veil" because they are subconsciously aware that the veil represents their secret sins.

preacher, but not an energetic one: he strove to win his people heavenward by mild, persuasive influences, rather than to drive them thither by the thunders of the Word. The sermon which he now delivered was marked by the same characteristics of style and manner as the general series of his pulpit oratory. But there was something, either in the sentiment of the discourse itself, or in the imagination of the auditors, which made it greatly the most powerful effort that they had ever heard from their pastor's lips. It was tinged, rather more darkly than usual, with the gentle gloom of Mr. Hooper's temperament. The subject had reference to secret sin, and those sad mysteries which we hide from our nearest and dearest, and would fain conceal from our own consciousness, even forgetting that the Omniscient[4] can detect them. A subtle power was breathed into his words. Each member of the congregation, the most innocent girl, and the man of hardened breast, felt as if the preacher had crept upon them, behind his awful veil, and discovered their hoarded iniquity of deed or thought. Many spread their clasped hands on their bosoms. There was nothing terrible in what Mr. Hooper said, at least, no violence; and yet, with every tremor of his melancholy voice, the hearers quaked. An unsought pathos came hand in hand with awe. So sensible were the audience of some unwonted attribute in their minister, that they longed for a breath of wind to blow aside the veil, almost believing that a stranger's visage would be discovered, though the form, gesture, and voice were those of Mr. Hooper.

At the close of the services, the people hurried out with indecorous confusion, eager to communicate their pent-up amazement, and conscious of lighter spirits the moment they lost sight of the black veil. Some gathered in little circles, huddled closely together, with their mouths all whispering in the center; some went homeward alone, wrapt in silent meditation; some talked loudly, and profaned the Sabbath day

---

4. Omniscient (äm nish′ ent): All-knowing God.

304 *New England Renaissance*

with ostentatious laughter. A few shook their sagacious heads, intimating that they could penetrate the mystery; while one or two affirmed that there was no mystery at all, but only that Mr. Hooper's eyes were so weakened by the midnight lamp, as to require a shade. After a brief interval, forth came good Mr. Hooper also, in the rear of his flock. Turning his veiled face from one group to another, he paid due reverence to the hoary heads, saluted the middle-aged with kind dignity as their friend and spiritual guide, greeted the young with mingled authority and love, and laid his hands on the little children's heads to bless them. Such was always his custom on the Sabbath day. Strange and bewildered looks repaid him for his courtesy. None, as on former occasions, aspired to the honor of walking by their pastor's side. Old Squire Saunders, doubtless by an accidental lapse of memory, neglected to invite Mr. Hooper to his table, where the good clergyman had been wont to bless the food, almost every Sunday since his settlement. He returned, therefore, to the parsonage, and, at the moment of closing the door, was observed to look back upon the people, all of whom had their eyes fixed upon the minister. A sad smile gleamed faintly from beneath the black veil, and flickered about his mouth, glimmering as he disappeared.

"How strange," said a lady, "that a simple black veil, such as any woman might wear on her bonnet, should become such a terrible thing on Mr. Hooper's face!"

"Something must surely be amiss with Mr. Hooper's intellects," observed her husband, the physician of the village. "But the strangest part of the affair is the effect of this vagary, even on a sober-minded man like myself. The black veil, though it covers only our pastor's face, throws its influence over his whole person, and makes him ghostlike from head to foot. Do you not feel it so?"

"Truly do I," replied the lady; "and I would not be alone with him for the world. I wonder he is not afraid to be alone with himself!"

Grammar in Action

The use of **varied sentence structures** makes prose interesting and, therefore, keeps the reader's attention from wandering. Good writing includes a mixture of simple sentence patterns, coordinated clauses, and subordinated structures.

Although modern readers sometimes think Nathaniel Hawthorne's writing is complicated, involving many long, complex sentences, careful analysis will show that Hawthorne uses a variety of sentence patterns to keep his prose lively and to emphasize important ideas or moments.

Student Activity 1. Look at the paragraph on page 304 that begins "At the close of the services. . . ." The first five sentences average thirty-six words, quite lengthy by our standards. But then Hawthorne writes:

Such was always the custom on the Sabbath day.

After this nine-word sentence, the patterns begin to grow long and intricate again. Discuss the effect of this short, simple sentence set in the midst of the long, convoluted ones.

"Men sometimes are so," said her husband.

The afternoon service was attended with similar circumstances. At its conclusion, the bell tolled for the funeral of a young lady. The relatives and friends were assembled in the house, and the more distant acquaintances stood about the door, speaking of the good qualities of the deceased, when their talk was interrupted by the appearance of Mr. Hooper, still covered with his black veil. It was now an appropriate emblem. The clergyman stepped into the room where the corpse was laid, and bent over the coffin, to take a last farewell of his deceased parishioner. As he stooped, the veil hung straight down from his forehead, so that, if her eyelids had not been closed forever, the dead maiden might have seen his face. Could Mr. Hooper be fearful of her glance, that he so hastily caught back the black veil? A person who watched the interview between the dead and living, scrupled not to affirm, that, at the instant when the clergyman's features were disclosed, the corpse had slightly shuddered, rustling the shroud and muslin cap, though the countenance retained the composure of death. A superstitious old woman was the only witness of this prodigy. From the coffin Mr. Hooper passed into the chamber of the mourners, and thence to the head of the staircase; to make the funeral prayer. It was a tender and heart-dissolving prayer, full of sorrow, yet so imbued with celestial hopes, that the music of a heavenly harp, swept by the fingers of the dead, seemed faintly to be heard among the saddest accents of the minister. The people trembled, though they but darkly understood him when he prayed that they, and himself, and all of mortal race, might be ready, as he trusted this young maiden had been, for the dreadful hour that should snatch the veil from their faces. The bearers went heavily forth, and the mourners followed, saddening all the street, with the dead before them, and Mr. Hooper in his black veil behind.

"Why do you look back?" said one in the procession to his partner.

"I had a fancy," replied she, "that the minister and the maiden's spirit were walking hand in hand."

"And so had I, at the same moment," said the other.

That night, the handsomest couple in Milford village were to be joined in wedlock. Though reckoned a melancholy man, Mr. Hooper had a placid cheerfulness for such occasions, which often excited a sympathetic smile where livelier merriment would have been thrown away. There was no quality of his disposition which made him more beloved than this. The company at the wedding awaited his arrival with impatience, trusting that the strange awe, which had gathered over him throughout the day, would now be dispelled. But such was not the result. When Mr. Hooper came, the first thing that their eyes rested on was the same horrible black veil, which had added deeper gloom to the funeral, and could portend nothing but evil to the wedding. Such was its immediate effect on the guests that a cloud seemed to have rolled duskily from beneath the black crape, and dimmed the light of the candles. The bridal pair stood up before the minister. But the bride's cold fingers quivered in the tremulous hand of the bridegroom, and her deathlike paleness caused a whisper that the maiden who had been buried a few hours before was come from her grave to be married. If ever another wedding were so dismal, it was that famous one where they tolled the wedding knell.[5] After performing the ceremony, Mr. Hooper raised a glass of wine to his lips, wishing happiness to the new-married couple in a strain of mild pleasantry that ought to have brightened the features of the guests, like a cheerful gleam from the hearth. At that instant, catching a glimpse of his figure in the looking glass, the black veil involved his own spirit in the horror with which it overwhelmed all others. His frame shuddered, his lips grew white, he

---

5. If . . . knell: A reference to Hawthorne's short story "The Wedding Knell." A *knell* is the slow ringing of a bell, as at a funeral.

The Minister's Black Veil   305

15 **Discussion** What suggestion is implied in this paragraph about the reason the minister began wearing the veil?

16 **Enrichment** Hawthorne spent a great deal of time interviewing country people to become familiar with their superstitions and history.

17 **Critical Thinking and Reading** The dialogue reinforces the suggestion of a connection between the girl's death and the minister's veil.

18 **Critical Thinking and Reading** Notice the contrast between the paragraph describing the funeral and this one.

19 **Master Teacher Note** Refer to "The Wedding Knell," another story in *Twice-Told Tales*. In that story, an elderly, twice-widowed woman hears a death knell as she enters the church to marry her childhood sweetheart. He appears at the wedding in a shroud, and they marry knowing that death is not far off.

20 **Discussion** How does the minister respond to seeing himself wearing the veil? How does his reaction compare to his congregants' reactions?

Student Activity 2. In the paragraph that begins "That night the handsomest couple . . ." (page 305), examine these sentences:

But such was not the result.

The bridal pair stood up before the minister.

Explain how the writer's emphasis and his sentence structures change after the short sentences.

Student Activity 3. Write, or select from your collected writing, two short, consecutive paragraphs. Try to join the paragraphs by inserting a short, direct, pivotal sentence between them. If your new, longer paragraph requires a revised topic sentence, write one.

21 **Critical Thinking and Reading**
The narrator makes it clear that the villagers are concerned with what the veil conceals, not with the cloth itself.

22 **Discussion** Why would the busybodies avoid asking the question? What does their reluctance reveal about human nature?

23 **Discussion** Why does the delegation chosen to discuss the veil avoid doing so?

24 **Critical Thinking and Reading**
The narrator introduced Mr. Hooper as a bachelor; now the reader first learns that he has a fiancée. Ask your students to consider why she does not appear earlier in the story.

25 **Discussion** What is Elizabeth's tone when she first speaks of the veil?

spilt the untasted wine upon the carpet, and rushed forth into the darkness. For the Earth, too, had on her Black Veil.

21   The next day, the whole village of Milford talked of little else than Parson Hooper's black veil. That, and the mystery concealed behind it, supplied a topic for discussion between acquaintances meeting in the street, and good women gossiping at their open windows. It was the first item of news that the tavernkeeper told to his guests. The children babbled of it on their way to school. One imitative little imp covered his face with an old black handkerchief, thereby so affrighting his playmates that the panic seized himself, and he well nigh lost his wits by his own waggery.

22   It was remarkable that of all the busybodies and impertinent people in the parish, not one ventured to put the plain question to Mr. Hooper, wherefore he did this thing. Hitherto, whenever there appeared the slightest call for such interference, he had never lacked advisers, nor shown himself averse to be guided by their judgment. If he erred at all, it was by so painful a degree of self-distrust that even the mildest censure would lead him to consider an indifferent action as a crime. Yet, though so well acquainted with this amiable weakness, no individual among his parishioners chose to make the black veil a subject of friendly remonstrance. There was a feeling of dread, neither plainly confessed nor carefully concealed, which caused each to shift the responsibility upon another, till at length it was found expedient to send a deputation of the church, in order to deal with Mr. Hooper about the mystery, before it should grow into a scandal. Never did an embassy so ill discharge its duties. The minister received them with friendly courtesy, but became silent, after they were seated, leaving to his visitors the whole burden of introducing their important business. The topic, it might be supposed, was obvious enough.

23 There was the black veil swathed round Mr. Hooper's forehead, and concealing every feature above his placid mouth, on which, at times, they could perceive the glimmering of a melancholy smile. But that piece of crape, to their imagination, seemed to hang down before his heart, the symbol of a fearful secret between him and them. Were the veil but cast aside, they might speak freely of it, but not till then. Thus they sat a considerable time, speechless, confused, and shrinking uneasily from Mr. Hooper's eye, which they felt to be fixed upon them with an invisible glance. Finally, the deputies returned abashed to their constituents, pronouncing the matter too weighty to be handled, except by a council of the churches, if, indeed, it might not require a general synod.[6]

  But there was one person in the village unappalled by the awe with which the black veil had impressed all beside herself. When the deputies returned without an explanation, or even venturing to demand one, she, with the calm energy of her character, determined to chase away the strange cloud that appeared to be settling round Mr. Hooper, every moment more darkly than before. As

24 his plighted wife,[7] it should be her privilege to know what the black veil concealed. At the minister's first visit, therefore, she entered upon the subject with a direct simplicity, which made the task easier both for him and her. After he had seated himself, she fixed her eyes steadfastly upon the veil, but could discern nothing of the dreadful gloom that had so overawed the multitude: it was but a double fold of crape, hanging down from his forehead to his mouth, and slightly stirring with his breath.

25   "No," said she aloud, and smiling, "there is nothing terrible in this piece of crape, except that it hides a face which I am always glad to look upon. Come, good sir, let the sun shine from behind the cloud. First lay aside your black veil: then tell me why you put it on."

  Mr. Hooper's smile glimmered faintly.

---

6. **synod** (sin′ əd) *n.*: A high governing body in certain Christian churches.
7. **plighted wife:** Fiancée.

Primary Source

"The Minister's Black Veil" reflects Hawthorne's intense awareness of the distrustfulness and intolerance of his Puritan ancestors. In his introduction to *The Scarlet Letter,* Hawthorne wrote,

> It is nearly two centuries and a quarter since the original Briton, the earliest emigrant of my name, made his appearance in the wild and forest-bordered settlement, which has since become a city. And here his descendants have been born and died, and have mingled their earthly substance with the soil; until no small portion of it must necessarily be akin to the mortal frame wherewith, for a little while, I walk the streets. . . . The figure of that first ancestor, invested by family tradition with a dim and dusky grandeur, was present to my boyish imagination, as far back as I can remember. It still haunts me, and induces a sort of home-feeling with the past. . . . He was a soldier, legislator, judge; he was a ruler in the Church; he had all the Puritanic traits, both good and evil. He was likewise a bitter persecutor; as witness the Quakers, who have remembered him in their histories, and relate an incident of his hard severity towards a woman of their sect, which will last longer, it is to

"There is an hour to come," said he, "when all of us shall cast aside our veils. Take it not amiss, beloved friend, if I wear this piece of crape till then."

"Your words are a mystery, too," returned the young lady. "Take away the veil from them, at least."

"Elizabeth, I will," said he, "so far as my vow may suffer me. Know, then, this veil is a type and a symbol, and I am bound to wear it ever, both in light and darkness, in solitude and before the gaze of multitudes, and as with strangers, so with my familiar friends. No mortal eye will see it withdrawn. This dismal shade must separate me from the world: even you, Elizabeth, can never come behind it!"

"What grievous affliction hath befallen you," she earnestly inquired, "that you should thus darken your eyes forever?"

"If it be a sign of mourning," replied Mr. Hooper, "I, perhaps, like most other mortals, have sorrows dark enough to be typified by a black veil."

"But what if the world will not believe that it is the type of an innocent sorrow?" urged Elizabeth. "Beloved and respected as you are, there may be whispers that you hide your face under the consciousness of secret sin. For the sake of your holy office, do away this scandal!"

The color rose into her cheeks as she intimated the nature of the rumors that were already abroad in the village. But Mr. Hooper's mildness did not forsake him. He even smiled again—that same sad smile, which always appeared like a faint glimmering of light, proceeding from the obscurity beneath the veil.

"If I hide my face for sorrow, there is cause enough," he merely replied; "and if I cover it for secret sin, what mortal might not do the same?"

And with this gentle, but unconquerable obstinacy did he resist all her entreaties. At length Elizabeth sat silent. For a few moments she appeared lost in thought, considering, probably, what new methods might be tried to withdraw her lover from so dark a fantasy, which, if it had no other meaning, was perhaps a symptom of mental disease. Though of a firmer character than his own, the tears rolled down her cheeks. But in an instant, as it were, a new feeling took the place of sorrow: her eyes were fixed insensibly on the black veil, when, like a sudden twilight in the air, its terrors fell around her. She arose, and stood trembling before him.

"And do you feel it then, at last?" said he mournfully.

She made no reply, but covered her eyes with her hand, and turned to leave the room. He rushed forward and caught her arm.

"Have patience with me, Elizabeth!" cried he, passionately. "Do not desert me, though this veil must be between us here on earth. Be mine, and hereafter there shall be no veil over my face, no darkness between our souls! It is but a mortal veil—it is not for eternity! O! you know not how lonely I am, and how frightened, to be alone behind my black veil. Do not leave me in this miserable obscurity forever!"

"Lift the veil but once, and look me in the face," said she.

"Never! It cannot be!" replied Mr. Hooper.

"Then farewell!" said Elizabeth.

She withdrew her arm from his grasp, and slowly departed, pausing at the door, to give one long shuddering gaze, that seemed almost to penetrate the mystery of the black veil. But, even amid his grief, Mr. Hooper smiled to think that only a material emblem had separated him from happiness, though the horrors, which it shadowed forth, must be drawn darkly between the fondest of lovers.

From that time no attempts were made to remove Mr. Hooper's black veil, or, by a direct appeal, to discover the secret which it was supposed to hide. By persons who claimed a superiority to popular prejudice, it was reckoned merely an eccentric whim, such as often mingles with the sober actions of men otherwise rational, and tinges them all with its own semblance of insanity. But

26 **Discussion** Why does Mr. Hooper refuse to remove the veil for his fiancée.

27 **Discussion** On what grounds does she appeal to him to remove the veil?

28 **Critical Thinking and Reading** Point out that he responds on totally different grounds.

29 **Discussion** Why does the veil, which did not trouble her at first, now terrify her?

30 **Discussion** Why does she finally leave him?

31 **Reading Strategy** This is a turning point in the story. Ask the students what they think will become of the minister.

32 **Discussion** Why would the narrator comment at this point that the veil is "only a material emblem"?

be feared, than any record of his better deeds, although these were many. His son, too, inherited the persecuting spirit, and made himself so conspicuous in the martyrdom of the witches, that their blood may fairly be said to have left a stain upon him. . . . I know not whether these ancestors of mine bethought themselves to repent, and ask pardon of Heaven for their cruelties; or whether they are now groaning under the heavy consequences of them, in another state of being. At all events, I, the present writer, as their representative, hearby take shame upon myself for their sakes, and pray that any curse incurred by them—as I have heard, and as the dreary and unprosperous condition of the race, for many a long year back, would argue to exist—may now and henceforth be removed.

Humanities Note

Fine art, *Cemetery*, 1970, by Peter McIntyre. McIntyre was born in New Zealand in 1910. At age twenty he went to London to study art. He became involved in illustration for books and magazines and in stage design. During World War II, while serving in a New Zealand volunteer unit in London, he was appointed the "Official War Artist" and served in this capacity in Greece, Crete, North Africa, and Italy. After the war he returned to New Zealand. He has since traveled around the world, visiting the Antarctic, Hong Kong, the Pacific, and the American West.

This painting was done during McIntyre's trip to the United States and was published in a book entitled *Peter McIntyre's West* in 1970. This picture may at first seem to be an attempt at photographic likeness. However, a sense of the artist's presence and his feelings about this place soon become evident.

You might use the following for discussion:
1. Describe the atmosphere in this picture.
2. What has the artist done to create this atmosphere?

33 Discussion Do you imagine that the people's suspicions are correct? Why or why not? What do the villagers' suspicions reveal about their personalities?

CEMETERY
Peter McIntyre
Courtesy of the artist

with the multitude, good Mr. Hooper was irreparably a bugbear.[8] He could not walk the street with any peace of mind, so conscious was he that the gentle and timid would turn aside to avoid him, and that others would make it a point of hardihood to throw themselves in his way. The impertinence of the latter class compelled him to give up his customary walk at sunset to the burial ground; for when he leaned pensively over the gate, there would always be faces behind the gravestones, peeping at his black veil. A fable went the rounds that the stare of the dead people drove him thence. It grieved him, to the very depth of his kind heart, to observe how the children fled from his approach, breaking up their merriest sports, while his melancholy figure was yet afar off. Their instinctive dread caused him to feel more strongly than aught else, that a preternatu-

ral[9] horror was interwoven with the threads of the black crape. In truth, his own antipathy to the veil was known to be so great that he never willingly passed before a mirror, nor stooped to drink at a still fountain, lest, in its peaceful bosom, he should be affrighted by himself. This was what gave plausibility to the whispers, that Mr. Hooper's conscience tortured him for some great crime too horrible to be entirely concealed, or otherwise than so obscurely intimated. Thus, from beneath the black veil, there rolled a cloud into the sunshine, an ambiguity of sin or sorrow, which enveloped the poor minister, so that love or sympathy could never reach him. It was said that ghost and fiend consorted with him there. With self-shudderings and outward terrors, he walked continually in its shadow, groping

33

---

8. bugbear *n.*: Something causing needless fear.

9. preternatural (prēt′ ər nach′ ər əl) *adj.*: Supernatural.

308   *New England Renaissance*

Commentary: Hawthorne and the Theme of Guilt

Partly due to his belief that he had an inherited responsibility for the sins of his Puritan ancestors, Hawthorne was haunted by feelings of guilt throughout his life. He wrote, "A cloudy veil stretches over the abyss of my nature. I have, however, no love of secrecy and darkness. I am glad to think that God sees through my heart, and, if any angel has power to penetrate into it, he is welcome to know everything that is there."

Not surprisingly, a large number of Hawthorne's works focus on the subject of guilt. Hawthorne felt that all people are haunted by a sense of guilt on either a conscious or an unconscious level. He commented, "When people think I am pouring myself out in a tale or an essay, I am merely telling what is common to human nature, not what is peculiar to myself. I sympathize with them, not they with me."

Two of Hawthorne's best novels, *The Scarlet Letter* and *The House of the Seven Gables,* deal with characters who are haunted by guilt. In *The Scarlet Letter,* the main character, Hester Prynne, is forced to wear a scarlet letter "A" to symbolize that she has committed adultery. Her secret lover, Arthur Dimmesdale, is tormented by guilt as a result of his action and his

darkly within his own soul or gazing through a medium that saddened the whole world. Even the lawless wind, it was believed, respected his dreadful secret, and never blew aside the veil. But still good Mr. Hooper sadly smiled at the pale visages of the worldly throng as he passed by.

Among all its bad influences, the black veil had the one desirable effect, of making its wearer a very efficient clergyman. By the aid of his mysterious emblem—for there was no other apparent cause—he became a man of awful power over souls that were in agony for sin. His converts always regarded him with a dread peculiar to themselves, affirming, though but figuratively, that, before he brought them to celestial light, they had been with him behind the black veil. Its gloom, indeed, enabled him to sympathize with all dark affections. Dying sinners cried aloud for Mr. Hooper, and would not yield their breath till he appeared; though ever, as he stooped to whisper consolation, they shuddered at the veiled face so near their own. Such were the terrors of the black veil, even when Death had bared his visage! Strangers came long distances to attend service at his church, with the mere idle purpose of gazing at his figure, because it was forbidden them to behold his face. But many were made to quake ere they departed! Once, during Governor Belcher's[10] administration, Mr. Hooper was appointed to preach the election sermon. Covered with his black veil, he stood before the chief magistrate, the council, and the representatives, and wrought so deep an impression that the legislative measures of that year were characterized by all the gloom and piety of our earliest ancestral sway.

In this manner Mr. Hooper spent a long life, irreproachable in outward act, yet shrouded in dismal suspicions; kind and loving, though unloved, and dimly feared; a man apart from men, shunned in their health and joy, but ever summoned to their aid in mortal anguish. As years wore on, shedding their snows above his sable veil, he acquired a name throughout the New England churches, and they called him Father Hooper. Nearly all his parishioners, who were of mature age when he was settled, had been borne away by many a funeral: he had one congregation in the church, and a more crowded one in the churchyard; and having wrought so late into the evening, and done his work so well, it was now good Father Hooper's turn to rest.

Several persons were visible by the shaded candlelight, in the death chamber of the old clergyman. Natural connections[11] he had none. But there was the decorously grave, though unmoved physician, seeking only to mitigate the last pangs of the patient whom he could not save. There were the deacons, and other eminently pious members of his church. There, also, was the Reverend Mr. Clark, of Westbury, a young and zealous divine, who had ridden in haste to pray by the bedside of the expiring minister. There was the nurse, no hired handmaiden of death, but one whose calm affection had endured thus long in secrecy, in solitude, amid the chill of age, and would not perish, even at the dying hour. Who, but Elizabeth! And there lay the hoary head of good Father Hooper upon the death pillow, with the black veil still swathed about his brow, and reaching down over his face, so that each more difficult gasp of his faint breath caused it to stir. All through life that piece of crape had hung between him and the world: it had separated him from cheerful brotherhood and woman's love, and kept him in that saddest of all prisons, his own heart; and still it lay upon his face, as if to deepen the gloom of his darksome chamber, and shade him from the sunshine of eternity.

For some time previous, his mind had been confused, wavering doubtfully between the past and the present, and hovering forward, as it were, at intervals, into the indis-

10. **Governor Belcher:** Jonathan Belcher (1682–1757), the royal governor of the Massachusetts Bay Colony from 1730 through 1741.

11. **natural connections:** Relatives.

The Minister's Black Veil 309

309

34 **Discussion** What is the significance of the fact that nature respects his veil?

35 **Discussion** Why does the veil make the minister a "very efficient clergyman"?

36 **Discussion** How has the veil isolated the minister? Would his calling alone have isolated him?

37 **Discussion** Why has Elizabeth remained loyal all this time? What does that tell us about her character?

inability to confess his sin to the public. In *The House of the Seven Gables*, the members of the Pyncheon family suffer from the guilt they have inherited from one of their ancestors, who was responsible for having an innocent man executed as a wizard.

In "The Minister's Black Veil" all of the characters suffer from guilt, though few are conscious of it. Parson Hooper's veil repels his parishioners because it represents the secret sins of which they are guilty. However, with the exception of people approaching their deaths, none of the characters will allow themselves to recognize the true meaning of the veil. Yet their instinctive dread of the veil and their inability to look directly at Parson Hooper's face suggest that they are subconsciously aware of what the veil represents. No living character becomes conscious of its mean-

ing, however, until the end of the story, when Parson Hooper dies. As he approaches his death, Parson Hooper finally reveals what the veil represents, exclaiming, "Why do you tremble at me alone? . . . Tremble also at each other! Have men avoided me, and women shown no pity, and children screamed and fled, only for my black veil? What, but the mystery which it obscurely typifies, has made this piece of crape so awful? When the friend shows his inmost heart to his friend; the lover to his best beloved; when man does not vainly shrink from the eye of his Creator, loathsomely treasuring up the secret of his sin; then deem me a monster, for the symbol beneath which I have lived, and die! I look around me, and, lo! on every visage a Black Veil!"

38

Critical Thinking and Reading Note that Reverend Clark refers to another symbolic veil, the one between this life and eternity.

39 Discussion How does Reverend Clark interpret the veil's symbolic meaning?

40 Discussion According to Mr. Hooper, what is the meaning of the veil? How does this fit in with the beliefs of the Anti-Transcendentalists?

Reader's Response If you had been in Parson Hooper's place, would you have revealed your reason for wearing the veil? Why or why not?

tinctness of the world to come. There had been feverish turns, which tossed him from side to side, and wore away what little strength he had. But in his most convulsive struggles, and in the wildest vagaries of his intellect, when no other thought retained its sober influence, he still showed an awful solicitude lest the black veil should slip aside. Even if his bewildered soul could have forgotten, there was a faithful woman at his pillow, who, with averted eyes, would have covered that aged face, which she had last beheld in the comeliness of manhood. At length the death-stricken old man lay quietly in the torpor of mental and bodily exhaustion, with an imperceptible pulse, and breath that grew fainter and fainter, except when a long, deep, and irregular inspiration seemed to prelude the flight of his spirit.

The minister of Westbury approached the bedside.

"Venerable Father Hooper," said he, "the moment of your release is at hand. Are you ready for the lifting of the veil that shuts in time from eternity?"

Father Hooper at first replied merely by a feeble motion of his head; then, apprehensive, perhaps, that his meaning might be doubtful, he exerted himself to speak.

"Yea," said he, in faint accents, "my soul hath a patient weariness until that veil be **38** lifted."

"And is it fitting," resumed the Reverend Mr. Clark, "that a man so given to prayer, of such a blameless example, holy in deed and thought, so far as mortal judgment may pronounce; is it fitting that a father in the church should leave a shadow on his memory, that may seem to blacken a life so pure? I pray you, my venerable brother, let not this thing be! Suffer us to be gladdened by your triumphant aspect as you go to your reward. Before the veil of eternity be lifted, let me cast aside this black veil from your face!"

And thus speaking, the Reverend Mr. Clark bent forward to reveal the mystery of so many years. But, exerting a sudden energy, that made all the beholders stand aghast, Father Hooper snatched both his hands from beneath the bedclothes, and pressed them strongly on the black veil, resolute to struggle, if the minister of Westbury would contend with a dying man.

"Never!" cried the veiled clergyman. "On earth, never!"

"Dark old man!" exclaimed the affrighted minister, "with what horrible crime upon your soul are you now passing to the judgment?"

39

Father Hooper's breath heaved; it rattled in his throat; but, with a mighty effort, grasping forward with his hands, he caught hold of life, and held it back till he should speak. He even raised himself in bed; and there he sat, shivering with the arms of death around him, while the black veil hung down, awful, at that last moment, in the gathered terrors of a lifetime. And yet the faint, sad smile, so often there, now seemed to glimmer from its obscurity, and linger on Father Hooper's lips.

"Why do you tremble at me alone?" cried he, turning his veiled face round the circle of pale spectators. "Tremble also at each other! Have men avoided me, and women shown no pity, and children screamed and fled, only for my black veil? What, but the mystery which it obscurely typifies, has made this piece of crape so awful? When the friend shows his inmost heart to his friend; the lover to his best beloved; when man does not vainly shrink from the eye of his Creator, loathsomely treasuring up the secret of his sin; then deem me a monster, for the symbol beneath which I have lived, and die! I look around me, and, lo! on every visage a Black Veil!"

40

While his auditors shrank from one another, in mutual affright, Father Hooper fell back upon his pillow, a veiled corpse, with a faint smile lingering on the lips. Still veiled, they laid him in his coffin, and a veiled corpse they bore him to the grave. The grass of many years has sprung up and withered on that grave, the burial stone is moss-grown, and good Mr. Hooper's face is dust; but awful is still the thought that it moldered beneath the Black Veil!

THINKING ABOUT THE SELECTION

Recalling

1. How do the members of the parish react when they first see Parson Hooper wearing his black veil?
2. (a) What is different about Parson Hooper's sermon on the first day he wears the veil? (b) What is the subject of the sermon?
3. How does Elizabeth react when Parson Hooper refuses to remove the veil?
4. What is its "one desirable effect"?
5. (a) What happens when Reverend Mr. Clark tries to remove the veil while Parson Hooper is lying on his deathbed? (b) What does Parson Hooper suggest is the reason that people have been terrified by his veil?

Interpreting

6. (a) How does the black veil affect Parson Hooper's perceptions of the world? (b) In what ways does it isolate him from the rest of the world? (c) Why does it make him a more effective minister?
7. What does Parson Hooper mean when he tells Elizabeth, "There is an hour to come . . . when all of us shall cast aside our veils"?
8. (a) Why does the black veil have such a powerful effect on people? (b) What do you think it represents?
9. Why do you think Hawthorne chooses not to reveal the reason that Parson Hooper begins wearing the veil?

Applying

10. Hawthorne suggests that all people have certain secrets that they choose not to reveal to anyone. Explain why you either do or do not agree with this suggestion.

ANALYZING LITERATURE

Understanding Anti-Transcendentalism

In "The Minister's Black Veil" Hawthorne conveys a dark vision of the world that is characteristic of **Anti-Transcendentalist** writing.

1. In what way does the story reflect the Anti-Transcendentalists' belief that people possess the potential for both good and evil?
2. The Anti-Transcendentalists believed that the truths of existence tend to be elusive and disturbing. What disturbing truth does Hawthorne convey through Parson Hooper and his black veil?
3. How does the parishioners' inability to grasp the meaning of Parson Hooper's veil reflect the Anti-Transcendentalists' belief in the elusiveness of truth?

CRITICAL THINKING AND READING

Recognizing the Author's Attitudes

Hawthorne had a gloomy vision that was possibly shaped by his awareness of the intolerance and cruelty of his Puritan ancestors. Therefore, he was unable to accept the optimistic views of the Transcendentalists.

Like a number of Hawthorne's other works, "The Minister's Black Veil" is set in Puritan New England. Judging from the story, do you think Hawthorne had a negative attitude toward the Puritans? Support your answer.

THINKING AND WRITING

Comparing and Contrasting Attitudes

Write an essay in which you compare and contrast the attitude toward human nature expressed in "The Minister's Black Veil" with the attitude expressed by the Transcendentalists. Start by reviewing the discussions of Transcendentalism and Anti-Transcendentalism on pages 273 and 301. Take note of the beliefs characterizing each movement. Then review "The Minister's Black Veil," noting the attitudes it expresses. Organize your notes by corresponding points of comparison and contrast. When you write your essay, make sure you support your argument with passages from the story. When you revise, make sure that you have clearly expressed the two attitudes being compared and contrasted.

The Minister's Black Veil 311

9. By not revealing the reason, he creates ambiguity and forces the reader to interpret the reason by examining the evidence in the story.

Applying

10. Answers will differ. Students may respond that they do agree with the suggestion, because all people have some thoughts and concerns that they feel they have to keep to themselves.

Challenge Why do people often have difficulty accepting differences in physical appearance?

ANSWERS TO ANALYZING LITERATURE

1. Suggested Response: The way in which the people respond to the minister's veil demonstrates the potential for evil. The human potential for good is demonstrated through the devotion of the minister's one-time fiancee.
2. All people have committed some acts they regret as sinful, and all put some barriers between themselves and others.
3. The people's inability to grasp the truth of the veil is representative of humanity's overall difficulty in grasping the truths of existence.

ANSWERS TO CRITICAL THINKING AND READING

Suggested Response: It does reflect a negative view of Puritan New England, because the characters are hypocritical and lack compassion.

THINKING AND WRITING

For help with this assignment, students can refer to Lesson 16, "Writing a Comparative Evaluation," in the Handbook of Writing About Literature.

After students have completed the assignment, divide them into groups, and have them read their rough drafts to one another and make suggestions about how the essays could be improved.

---

neath the veil.
2. (a) His sermon is more powerful than usual. (b) Its subject is secret sin.
3. She leaves, and in effect their engagement is broken.
4. It makes him a very efficient clergyman.
5. (a) Mr. Hooper refuses to remove it "on earth." (b) They are terrified by it, because it symbolizes their secret sins.

Closure and Extension

ANSWERS TO THINKING ABOUT THE SELECTION
Recalling

1. They are shocked, and they wonder if it is really Mr. Hooper be-

Interpreting

6. (a) It darkens his own view of the world. (b) It creates a barrier in human relations. (c) The veil makes the people fear him, and as a result they are more moved by his sermons.
7. He means that our true natures will be exposed when our judgment day comes.
8. (a) It has a powerful effect on people, because it reminds them of their secret sins. (b) It is a symbol of secret sin.

Presentation

Motivation/Prior Knowledge
Tell students that when they open *The Scarlet Letter* they will be transported back in time to the 1640's. They will become immersed in the lives of a group of fictional Puritans who have recently settled in Boston, and they will be introduced to a character named Hester Prynne, who has committed adultry and has been condemned to wear a scarlet letter "A" as a symbol of her sin.

Before they begin reading, you may want to have them discuss their conceptions of Puritan life. Encourage them to keep this discussion in mind as they read the novel and to consider whether Hawthorne's depiction of Puritan life matches their earlier conception.

Humanities Note

Fine Art, Cover of *The Scarlet Letter* by Hugh Thompson. Thompson (1860–1920) was an English painter and illustrator whose 1915 edition of Hawthorne's novel has come to be regarded as a classic. In this picture Hester is shown leaving prison with her baby in her arms. By including the picture on the cover, Thompson introduces readers to Hester even before they open the book. Through Hester's proud posture and upraised chin, the artist immediately conveys the impression that Hester is a strong character with the ability to endure.

You might want to use the following questions to discuss the art:

1. What impression does the artist convey of Hester? Explain.
2. What impression does he convey of the setting?
3. Why do you think that this illustration was chosen for the cover of Hawthorne's novel?
4. If you were the editor of an illustrated version of *The Scarlet Letter,* what type of picture would you choose for the cover? Why?

GREAT WORKS

THE SCARLET LETTER
by Nathaniel Hawthorne

On the breast of her gown, in red cloth, surrounded with an elaborate embroidery and fantastic flourishes of gold thread, appeared the letter A.
The Scarlet Letter

Cover of THE SCARLET LETTER
Hugh Thomson

Who was the writer who knew so well Puritan politics and the fruits of sin? Nathaniel Hawthorne was the descendant of a Puritan judge who sentenced a Quaker woman to be whipped and dragged through the streets of Salem and of another Puritan judge who condemned his fellow townspeople to death in the Salem witchcraft trials. A stern Puritan morality and temperament were a strong part of Hawthorne's heritage, and they loomed importantly in *The Scarlet Letter,* considered the first great American novel and Hawthorne's best work. Recognized as a classic even by Hawthorne's contemporaries, respect for this uniquely American work of literature has only increased through the years.

The Writing of *The Scarlet Letter*

Shortly before he began writing *The Scarlet Letter* in September 1849, Hawthorne was unjustly accused of "corruption, iniquity, and fraud" as Surveyor of the Boston Custom House and forcibly removed from the job he had held for three years. Almost at the same time, Hawthorne's mother, who had been living with him, became seriously ill and died. Hawthorne, married and with two children, was without a job. With serious family responsibilities and in need of money, Hawthorne turned to writing. The public and private events of the summer had produced an emotional upheaval in him and, with the anger and hurt of recent events fresh in his mind, he worked on his new book feverishly, completing it in six months.

Hawthorne was well prepared for the novel he set out to write. He had been unable to pursue his writing while working as a surveyor, and he had been formulating ideas for new tales and sketches. Furthermore, for many years he had steeped himself in the customs and values of Puritan New England, filling his notebooks and journals with ideas drawn from wide reading. In previous stories he had also experimented with the projection of psychological dilemmas through characters and situations.

Hawthorne had hoped to write something pleasing and popular, but the new book seemed to take on a life of its own. To a friend, Hawthorne described his work as "positively a hell-fired story, into which I found it almost impossible to throw any cheering light."

Illustration from THE SCARLET LETTER
Hugh Thomson

A Tale of Guilt and Shame

The Scarlet Letter is a dark tale of public guilt and private shame set in Boston in the 1640's, shortly after the first settlers arrived from England. On the day of his arrival in Boston, an old man finds his much younger wife, Hester Prynne, standing on the town pillory, a baby in her arms and a scarlet *A* sewn to her dress. The old man, who had remained in Europe, had sent his wife ahead to the New World. Hester is being punished for adultery and has been condemned to wear the scarlet letter, the symbol of her sin. Hester steadfastly refuses to reveal the name of her child's father, and the old man, who soon afterward assumes the name Roger Chillingworth, vows to uncover the name of the child's father and to have his revenge.

Great Works 313

Humanities Note

Fine Art, Illustration from *The Scarlet Letter* by Hugh Thompson. In this picture Arthur Dimmesdale is shown leaning on a window sill in the room of the evil Roger Chillingworth. Dimmesdale is seen in a despairing pose, with his head resting on one hand, while holding a religious book in his other hand behind his back. Chillingworth, on the other hand, is intently examining the leaves of a plant he has picked. Outside the window of Chillingworth's room is a graveyard, a remainder to Dimmesdale of his mortality and a symbol of his fear of damnation.

You might want to use the following questions to discuss the art:

1. How would you describe the style in which this picture is painted? Why?
2. What impression does the picture convey of Dimmesdale? Explain.
3. What impression does it convey of Chillingworth? Explain.
4. What does the painting suggest about the relationship between the two men?
5. What might the graveyard outside the window symbolize, or represent? Explain.

Illustration from THE SCARLET LETTER
Hugh Thomson

The man whose name Hester refuses to reveal is Arthur Dimmesdale, a highly respected young minister. Dimmesdale is tormented by the guilt of his sin but is unable to admit his crime to the world. Chillingworth correctly recognizes Dimmesdale as Hester's lover. Posing as Dimmesdale's friend and physician, Chillingworth uses conversation and discussion cunningly to increase Dimmesdale's mental torment without revealing that Chillingworth is Hester's husband.

No man, for any considerable period, can wear one face to himself, and another to the multitude, without finally getting bewildered as to which may be the true.

After seven years, Hester and Dimmesdale meet and agree to flee together to Europe. Their escape is frustrated, however, when Chillingworth recognizes their plan and Dimmesdale's inability to live with the guilt of his sin. After delivering his finest sermon, Dimmesdale mounts the town scaffold before the gathered townspeople, finally admits his sin, and reveals the scarlet letter that remorse has carved on his breast. With this act of confession, Dimmesdale escapes Chillingworth's grip on his soul and dies in Hester's arms.

Hawthorne's Study of Sin and Guilt

Much of the greatness of Hawthorne's novel lies in its careful and minute consideration of guilt and its impact. Hawthorne was not so concerned with sin itself as with "the wages of sin," and the way the lives of each of his three main characters are changed by sin in vastly different ways.

Hester Prynne emerges as the main character of *The Scarlet Letter*. Like Parson Hooper's veil in "The Minister's Black Veil," Hester's scarlet *A* serves as a public symbol of her private sin. Because Hester is able to declare her guilt openly, she is freed from excessive remorse, and her sin serves to enrich and dignify rather than to destroy her. At first shunned and humiliated by the townspeople, Hester behaves with decorum and grace, helping others who are hungry, sick, or in need. Slowly the disdain of the townspeople turns to admiration, and the scarlet letter comes to stand for *able* rather than *adultery*. Hester is also helped in her spiritual recovery by her belief that her adultery is a sin against human, not divine, laws. She dreams of a new social order with laws more in keeping with human nature and the quest for happiness.

314   New England Renaissance

Arthur Dimmesdale, on the other hand, is tormented by his sin and enjoys no peace. He lacks the courage to risk his important position in society by admitting his sin publicly, but is unable to achieve any inner calm while living with his hypocrisy. Dimmesdale never doubts that he has sinned against God. Publicly he becomes more and more passionate and effective in his moral counsels to his congregation. Privately he is torn with self-hatred, and his body wastes away because of the remorse that gnaws at his soul.

Roger Chillingworth is the tale's arch villain, a man whose all-consuming thirst for vengeance turns him into a monster. Chillingworth's sin is the worst sin of all, for he invades the sanctity of another person's soul. A learned man, a scientist and physician, he uses all his knowledge of the human heart to deepen Dimmesdale's agony. But Dimmesdale is not the only victim of Chillingworth's quest for revenge. Chillingworth's relentless hatred degrades and transforms him into a devil without ultimately destroying Dimmesdale's immortal soul.

A Work of "Inexhaustible Charm and Mystery"

Critics widely recognize that the way in which Hawthorne treated questions of sin and its consequences transcends the immediate seventeenth-century setting of his story and has meaning for the modern reader. The great nineteenth-century novelist Henry James gave *The Scarlet Letter* a great boost when he applauded the book in his 1879 biography of Hawthorne. His evaluation of the way Hawthorne described "the subtleties and mysteries of life, the moral and spiritual maze" remains true today, for James recognized that "*The Scarlet Letter* has the beauty and harmony of all original and complete conceptions . . . One can often return to it; it supports familiarity, and has the inexhaustible charm and mystery of great works of art."

Among many morals which press upon us from the poor minister's miserable experience, we put only this into a sentence: "Be true! Be true! Show freely to the world, if not your worst, yet some trait whereby the worst may be inferred."

Illustration from THE SCARLET LETTER
Hugh Thomson

Fine Art, Illustration from *The Scarlet Letter* by Hugh Thompson. In this illustration Thompson depicts Arthur Dimmesdale walking through the forest while Hester waits to approach him. Dimmesdale is a picture of despair and ill health, leaning sadly on his stick, his head bent forward, his hand on his breast. In contrast, Hester stands upright and certain, sure of the step she will take. The moral dilemma of the two characters is echoed by the thick foliage, gnarled trees, and uneven ground of the surrounding landscape. Yet the small patch of blue sky visible beyond the boundaries of the forest hints at the possibility of happier times in the distant future.

You might want to use the following questions to discuss the art:
1. What does this picture suggest about Arthur Dimmesdale's condition?
2. How does Hester's condition seem to contrast with that of Dimmesdale?
3. How would you describe the landscape surrounding the two characters?
4. How does the composition of the surrounding landscape echo the situation of the two characters?

Closure and Extension

QUESTIONS AND ACTIVITIES

1. Throughout his life, Hawthorne was haunted by the deeds of his Puritan ancestors, such as those of his ancestor who played an important role in the Salem witchcraft trials. How do you think Hawthorne's preoccupation with the acts of his ancestors might have shaped his writing of *The Scarlet Letter*?
2. Write a paper in which you discuss the parallels between *The Scarlet Letter* and Hawthorne's short story "The Minister's Black Veil" (p. 302).

Critical Evaluation The literary scholar Richard Chase has written: "Melville's reputation is not only great; it seems also secure, for it is impossible to imagine an America of the future which will not honor and read this author. There is therefore much irony in the fact that when Melville died in 1891, he had long outlived the popularity and fame that he briefly enjoyed during the late 1840's, when his South-Seas adventure tales—notably *Typee* (1846)—were in vogue . . ."

HERMAN MELVILLE

1819–1891

Herman Melville is one of America's great novelists. Unfortunately, his work was never fully appreciated during his lifetime, and he lived a life that was often filled with frustration and despair.

Melville was born in New York City, the son of a wealthy merchant. His family's financial situation changed drastically in 1830, however, when his father's import business failed. Two years later his father died, leaving the family in debt. Forced to leave school, Melville spent the rest of his childhood working as a clerk, a farmhand, and a teacher to help support his family.

After becoming a sailor at the age of nineteen, Melville spent several years exploring the South Pacific. Working on a number of different whaling ships, he visited many exotic places and even spent several weeks living among natives in the Marquesas Islands. He did not return to the United States until 1844, after a brief period of service in the navy.

Using his adventures in the South Pacific as material for his novels, Melville started a new career as a writer. He quickly established himself as a popular writer with two successful novels, *Typee* (1846) and *Omoo* (1847), both set in the Pacific islands. His readers found his third novel, *Mardi* (1849), confusing, however, and his fame rapidly faded.

Using the profits from his novels, Melville bought a farm near Pittsfield, Massachusetts. He became a close friend of Nathaniel Hawthorne, who lived in a neighboring village. Encouraged by Hawthorne's interest and influenced by his reading of Shakespeare, Melville's work became more sophisticated.

In 1851 he published his masterpiece *Moby-Dick*, under the title *The Whale. Moby-Dick* is a novel with several layers of meaning. On the surface it is the story of the fateful voyage of a whaling ship. On another level, it is the story of a bitter man's quest for vengeance and search for truth. On still another level, it is a philosophical examination of humanity's relationship to the natural world.

Unable to appreciate the novel's depth, readers responded unfavorably to *Moby-Dick.* They also reacted negatively to Melville's next two novels, *Pierre* (1852) and *The Confidence Man* (1859). As a result, Melville fell into debt and was forced to accept a job as an inspector at the New York customshouse.

Disillusioned and bitter, Melville turned away from writing fiction during the latter part of his life. He produced only a handful of short stories and a powerful novella, *Billy Budd.* He died in 1891, unnoticed and unappreciated. In the 1920's, his work was rediscovered by scholars, and he finally received the recognition he deserved.

316   New England Renaissance

GUIDE FOR INTERPRETING

from Moby-Dick

Writer's Techniques

Symbolism. A symbol is a person, place, or thing that has a meaning in itself and also represents something larger than itself. For example a flag symbolizes the character, attitude, and values of a country.

While some symbols are easy to interpret, others are complex, having a number of possible meanings. The white whale in Melville's *Moby-Dick* is an example of an extremely complex symbol. Only by examining all of the meanings suggested by its appearance and behavior do we realize that the whale ultimately represents all that is paradoxical, unexplainable, and uncontrollable in nature. Like nature, Moby-Dick is massive and threatening but beautiful and awe-inspiring. Moby-Dick is nourishing and destructive, powerful and graceful. Moby-Dick is unpredictable and mindless, yet it is controlled by natural laws. Like nature, Moby-Dick seems indestructible and immortal and at the same time indifferent to human mortality.

Another quality that contributes to the whale's symbolism is its color. Like the other aspects of the whale's appearance, its whiteness conveys contradictions. It suggests purity and goodness but at the same time signifies emptiness and death. Because of the whale's blank whiteness, each crew member attaches a different meaning to the whale—just as each person attaches a different meaning to the mysteries of nature.

Writing

Determination is often considered a positive characteristic. Freewrite, exploring how it can also be a negative characteristic.

Primary Source

In *Melville and His World,* the biographer Gay Wilson Allen describes Melville's early sailing adventures on the whaling ship *Acushnet.* Then he continues:

> Throughout this trip, and even long before he had signed on the *Acushnet,* Melville frequently heard tall tales about a fabulous white whale variously known as 'Mocha Dick,' or 'Moby Dick.' In 1834 Emerson had heard of him as 'Old Tom, who rushed upon the boats which attacked him and crushed the boats to small chips in his jaws, the men generally escaping by jumping overboard and being picked up . . .'
>
> The monstrous albino whale with a scar on his head had already become a myth in whaling folklore before Melville began his voyage. But some of the stories of a whale chewing up rowboats, or ramming a whale ship, were based on fact. An English ship had such an experience in July 1840, and a Russian ship a month later.

Literary Focus Each of Melville's characters sees the adventure from his own perspective. Their different views of the journey help establish different layers of the symbolism. For example, Starbuck, the first mate, offers a literal interpretation of the adventure.

Writing/Prior Knowledge Before having students complete the assignments, discuss the distinction between an obsession and a goal.

Vocabulary

Preteach the following vocabulary words:

inscrutable (in skro͞ot′ ə b′l) *adj.:* Not able to be easily understood (p. 324)

maledictions (mal′ ə dik′ shən) *n.:* Curses (p. 326)

prescient (prē′ shē ənt) *adj.:* Having foreknowledge (p. 328)

pertinaciously (pʉr′ tə nā′ shəs lē) *adv.:* Holding firmly to some purpose (p. 330)

Guide for Interpreting 317

Motivation/Prior Knowledge
Ask students whether they have ever been in a strange town and have tried a restaurant on the recommendation of someone they hardly knew. What did they expect to find?

Master Teacher Note You might wish to set the mood for the selection by bringing in illustrations of whaling ships, such as those in *Men, Ships, and the Sea,* published by the National Geographic Society. Explain to students that, at the time, whaling was a major industry throughout the world. You might also bring in pictures and accounts of waterfront life in such cities as New York and Boston.

Thematic Idea Another story that involves a character's obsession is "Winter Dreams" by F. Scott Fitzgerald (p. 672).

Purpose-Setting Question What is the true purpose of the journey?

1 Enrichment The names Ahab and Ishmael are both from the Old Testament. In I Kings, 16:33, it is written that "Ahab did more to provoke the Lord God of Israel to anger than all the kings of Israel that were before him." In Genesis, Ishmael is the son of Abraham by his wife's handmaiden. Ishmael and his mother are banished into the wilderness.

2 Clarification Each of the three harpooners has a different non-Western backgrounds. Queequeg is a native of "an island far away to the West and South," probably in Polynesia; Tashtego is an American Indian from Gay Head, Massachusetts; and Daggoo is a giant black man from Africa.

from **Moby-Dick**

Herman Melville

Moby-Dick is the story of a man's obsession with the dangerous and mysterious white whale that years before had taken off one of his legs. The man, Captain Ahab, guides the Pequod, a whaling ship, and its crew in relentless pursuit of this whale, Moby-Dick. Among the more important members of the crew are Starbuck, the first mate; Stubb, the second mate; Flask, the third mate; Queequeg, Tashtego, and Daggoo, the harpooners; and Ishmael, the young sailor who narrates the book.

In the following excerpt, Ishmael and Queequeg sample some famous chowder before their voyage.

Chowder

It was quite late in the evening when the little Moss came snugly to anchor, and Queequeg and I went ashore; so we could attend to no business that day, at least none but a supper and a bed. The landlord of the Spouter Inn had recommended us to his cousin Hosea Hussey of the Try Pots, whom he asserted to be the proprietor of one of the best kept hotels in all Nantucket,[1] and moreover he had assured us that Cousin Hosea, as he called him, was famous for his chowders. In short, he plainly hinted that we could not possibly do better than try potluck at the Try Pots. But the directions he had given us about keeping a yellow warehouse on our starboard[2] hand till we opened a white church to the larboard, and then keeping that on the larboard hand till we made a corner three points to the starboard, and that done, then ask the first man we met where the place was; these crooked directions of his very much puzzled us at first, especially as, at the outset, Queequeg insisted that the yellow warehouse—our first point of departure—must be left on the larboard hand, whereas I had understood Peter Coffin to say it was on the starboard. However, by dint of beating about a little in the dark, and now and then knocking up a peaceful inhabitant to inquire the way, we at last came to something which there was no mistaking.

Two enormous wooden pots painted black, and suspended by ass's ears, swung from the crosstrees of an old topmast, planted in front of an old doorway. The horns of the crosstrees were sawed off on the other side, so that this old topmast looked not a little like a gallows. Perhaps I was oversensitive to such impressions at the time, but I could not help staring at this gallows with a vague misgiving. A sort of crick was in my neck as I gazed up to the two remaining horns; yes, *two* of them, one for Queequeg, and one for me. It's ominous, thinks I.

---

1. **Nantucket** (nan tuk′ it): An island off the coast of Massachusetts.
2. **Starboard** *adj.*: The right-hand side of a ship. Larboard refers to the left-hand side.

318   *New England Renaissance*

3 Clarification On whaling ships, try pots were huge iron pots used to render whale blubber into oil.

4 Critical Thinking and Reading Notice the play on words, "try potluck at the Try Pots."

5 Literary Focus Call attention to the symbolic nature of the name Peter Coffin. Coffin was the landlord of the Spouter Inn where Ishmael and Queequeg stayed before moving on. In the next paragraph Ishmael himself notes the symbolism. Have students look for other symbolic foreshadowings as they read.

6 Discussion What might the image of the topmast foreshadow?

Enrichment During the late 1700's and the early 1800's, Nantucket was one of the world's major whaling centers. At one time well over one hundred whaling boats used the island as their main port. However, in the middle of the nineteenth century, the whaling industry began to decline, and the island developed into a popular resort and artists' colony.

A coffin my innkeeper upon landing in my first whaling port; tombstones staring at me in the whalemen's chapel; and here a gallows! and a pair of prodigious black pots too! Are these last throwing out oblique hints touching Tophet?[3]

I was called from these reflections by the sight of a freckled woman with yellow hair and a yellow gown, standing in the porch of the inn, under a dull red lamp swinging there, that looked much like an injured eye, and carrying on a brisk scolding with a man in a purple woolen shirt.

---

3. Tophet (tō′ fit): Hell.

"Get along with ye," said she to the man, "or I'll be combing ye!"

"Come on, Queequeg," said I, "all right. There's Mrs. Hussey."

And so it turned out; Mr. Hosea Hussey being from home, but leaving Mrs. Hussey entirely competent to attend to all his affairs. Upon making known our desires for a supper and a bed, Mrs. Hussey, postponing further scolding for the present, ushered us into a little room, and seating us at a table spread with the relics of a recently concluded repast, turned round to us and said "clam or cod?"

"What's that about cods, ma'am?" said I, with much politeness.

from *Moby-Dick* 319

320

7 Discussion What seem to be Ishmael's expectations of the meal?

8 Clarification The word *chowderhead* is sometimes used to refer to a fool. Ishmael wonders if eating so much chowder might turn him into a chowderhead.

9 Discussion What impression of the Try Pots does Melville convey?

10 Enrichment A harpoon is a kind of spear with a barbed tip and a handle that is attached to a rope. Harpoons are used to capture whales or fish, which are then hauled in and killed with spears or lances. Harpooners were highly valued crew members on whaling ships, and they prized their harpoons.

11 Discussion On what note does the chapter end?

"Clam or cod?" she repeated.

"A clam for supper? a cold clam; is *that* what you mean, Mrs. Hussey?" says I! "but that's a rather cold and clammy reception in the winter time, ain't it, Mrs. Hussey?"

But being in a great hurry to resume scolding the man in the purple shirt who was waiting for it in the entry, and seeming to hear nothing but the word "clam," Mrs. Hussey hurried towards an open door leading to the kitchen, and bawling out "clam for two," disappeared.

"Queequeg," said I, "do you think that we can make a supper for us both on one clam?"

However, a warm savory steam from the kitchen served to belie[4] the apparently cheerless prospect before us. But when that smoking chowder came in, the mystery was delightfully explained. Oh! sweet friends, hearken to me. It was made of small juicy clams, scarcely bigger than hazel nuts, mixed with pounded ship biscuits, and salted pork cut up into little flakes! The whole enriched with butter, and plentifully seasoned with pepper and salt. Our appetites being sharpened by the frosty voyage, and in particular, Queequeg seeing his favorite fishing food before him, and the chowder being surpassingly excellent, we dispatched it with great expedition: when leaning back a moment and bethinking me of Mrs. Hussey's clam and cod announcement, I thought I would try a little experiment. Stepping to the kitchen door, I uttered the word "cod" with great emphasis, and resumed my seat. In a few moments the savory steam came forth again, but with a different flavor, and in good time a fine cod chowder was placed before us.

We resumed business; and while plying our spoons in the bowl, thinks I to myself, I wonder now if this here has any effect on the head? What's that stultifying saying about chowder-headed people? "But look, Quee-

---

4. **belie** (bi lī') *v.*: Prove false.

---

queg, ain't that a live eel in your bowl? Where's your harpoon?"

Fishiest of all fishy places was the Try Pots, which well deserved its name; for the pots there were always boiling chowders. Chowder for breakfast, and chowder for dinner, and chowder for supper, till you began to look for fish bones coming through your clothes. The area before the house was paved with clam shells. Mrs. Hussey wore a polished necklace of codfish vertebra; and Hosea Hussey had his account books bound in superior and old shark-skin. There was a fishy flavor to the milk, too, which I could not at all account for, till one morning happening to take a stroll along the beach among some fishermen's boats, I saw Hosea's brindled[5] cow feeding on fish remnants, and marching along the sand with each foot in a cod's decapitated head, looking very slipshod, I assure ye.

Supper concluded, we received a lamp, and directions from Mrs. Hussey concerning the nearest way to bed; but, as Queequeg was about to precede me up the stairs, the lady reached forth her arm, and demanded his harpoon; she allowed no harpoon in her chambers. "Why not?" said I; "every true whaleman sleeps with his harpoon—but why not?" "Because it's dangerous," says she. "Ever since young Stiggs coming from that unfort'nt v'y'ge of his, when he was gone four years and a half, with only three barrels of *ile*,[6] was found dead in my first floor back, with his harpoon in his side; ever since then I allow no boarders to take sich dangerous weepons in their rooms at night. So, Mr. Queequeg" (for she had learned his name), "I will just take this here iron, and keep it for you till morning. But the chowder; clam or cod tomorrow for breakfast, men?"

"Both," says I, "and let's have a couple of smoked herring by way of variety."

---

5. **brindled** (brin' d'ld) *adj.*: Having a gray or tawny coat with streaks of darker color.
6. **ile** (īle): Oil.

Primary Source

In the aftermath of the public's unfavorable reception of his third novel, *Mardi*, Melville struggled to reconcile his desire to write serious fiction with the need to appeal to a general audience. In the following letter to his friend Nathaniel Hawthorne, Melville discusses his internal struggle and its effect on his writing of *Moby-Dick:*

> In a week or so, I go to New York, to bury myself in a third-story room, and work and slave on my "Whale" while it

is driving through the press. *That* is the only way I can finish it now,—I am so pulled hither and thither by circumstances. The calm, the coolness, the silent grass-growing mood in which a man *ought* to compose,—that, I fear, can seldom be mine. Dollars damn me; and the malicious Devil is forever grinning in upon me, holding the door ajar. My dear Sir, a presentiment is on me,—I shall at last be worn out and perish, like an old nutmeg-grater, grated to pieces by constant attrition of wood, that is, the nutmeg. What I feel most moved to write, that is banned,—it will not pay. Yet, altogether, write the *other* way I cannot. So the product is a final hash, and all my books are botches. . . . But I was talking about the "Whale." As the fishermen say, 'he's in his

When the crew signed aboard the Pequod, the voyage was to be nothing more than a business venture. However, early in the voyage, Ahab makes clear to the crew that his purpose is to seek revenge against Moby-Dick.

from The Quarter-Deck

One morning shortly after breakfast, Ahab, as was his wont, ascended the cabin gangway to the deck. There most sea captains usually walk at that hour, as country gentlemen, after the same meal, take a few turns in the garden.

Soon his steady, ivory stride was heard, as to and fro he paced his old rounds, upon planks so familiar to his tread, that they were all over dented, like geological stones, with the peculiar mark of his walk. Did you fixedly gaze, too, upon that ribbed and dented brow; there also, you would see still stranger footprints—the footprints of his one unsleeping, ever-pacing thought.

But on the occasion in question, those dents looked deeper, even as his nervous step that morning left a deeper mark. And, so full of his thought was Ahab, that at every uniform turn that he made, now at the mainmast and now at the binnacle,[7] you could almost see that thought turn in him as he turned, and pace in him as he paced; so completely possessing him, indeed, that it all but seemed the inward mold of every outer movement.

"D'ye mark him, Flask?" whispered Stubb; "the chick that's in him pecks the shell. 'Twill soon be out."

The hours wore on—Ahab now shut up within his cabin; anon, pacing the deck, with the same intense bigotry of purpose[8] in his aspect.

It drew near the close of day. Suddenly he came to a halt by the bulwarks, and inserting his bone leg into the auger hole there, and with one hand grasping a shroud, he ordered Starbuck to send everybody aft.

"Sir!" said the mate, astonished at an order seldom or never given on shipboard except in some extraordinary case.

"Send everybody aft," repeated Ahab. "Mastheads, there! come down!"

When the entire ship's company were assembled, and with curious and not wholly unapprehensive faces, were eyeing him, for he looked not unlike the weather horizon when a storm is coming up, Ahab, after rapidly glancing over the bulwarks, and then darting his eyes among the crew, started from his standpoint; and as though not a soul were nigh him resumed his heavy turns upon the deck. With bent head and half-slouched hat he continued to pace, unmindful of the wondering whispering among the men; till Stubb cautiously whispered to Flask, that Ahab must have summoned them there for the purpose of witnessing a pedestrian feat. But this did not last long. Vehemently pausing, he cried:

"What do ye do when ye see a whale, men?"

"Sing out for him!" was the impulsive rejoinder from a score of clubbed voices.

"Good!" cried Ahab, with a wild approval in his tones; observing the hearty animation into which his unexpected question had so magnetically thrown them.

"And what do ye next, men?"

"Lower away, and after him!"

"And what tune is it ye pull to, men?"

"A dead whale or a stove[9] boat!"

More and more strangely and fiercely glad and approving, grew the countenance of the old man at every shout; while the mariners began to gaze curiously at each other, as if marveling how it was that they them-

---

7. binnacle (bin′ ə k'l) *n.*: The case enclosing the ship's compass.
8. bigotry of purpose: Complete singlemindedness.

9. stove: Broken, smashed.

---

12 Clarification The quarter-deck is part of the upper deck of a sailing ship. It runs back from the midship or mainmast to the stern, or back, of the ship.

13 Enrichment In Melville's time, the captain had unlimited authority on board of the ship. Punishment for failing to follow orders was often harsh and arbitrary, as Melville himself pointed out in several works. Most crew members were careful not to challenge the captain directly.

14 Critical Thinking and Reading Note that the author moves from the literal to the figurative in this paragraph.

15 Critical Thinking and Reading Note the imagery in Stubb's comment.

16 Discussion Why does Ahab's order surprise Starbuck?

17 Critical Thinking and Reading The answers to Ahab's questions would be obvious to anyone who ever served on a whaling ship.

---

flurry' when I left him some three weeks ago. I'm going to take him by his jaw, however, before long, and finish him up in some fashion or other. What's the use of elaborating what, in its very essence, is so short-lived a modern book? . . . All fame is patronage. Let me be infamous: there is no patronage in *that*. What 'reputation' H. M. [Herman Melville] has is horrible. Think of it! To go down to posterity is bad enough, any way; but to go down as a 'man who lived among the cannibals'! When I speak of posterity, in reference to myself, I only mean that babies who will probably be born in the moment immediately ensuing upon my giving up the ghost. I shall go down to some of them, in all likelihood. 'Typee' will be given to them, perhaps, with

their gingerbread. I have come to regard this matter of Fame as the most transparent of all vanities. . . . I did not think of Fame, a year ago, as I do now. My development has been all within a few years past. I am like one of those seeds taken out of the Egyptian Pyramids, which, after being planted in English soil, it developed itself, grew to greenness, and then fell to mould. So I. Until I was twenty-five, I had no development at all. From my twenty-fifth year I date my life. Three weeks have scarcely passed, at any time between then and now, that I have not unfolded within myself. But I feel that I am now come to the inmost leaf of the bulb, and that shortly the flower must fall to the mould.

18 **Discussion** Why does Ahab offer a reward to the sailor who spots the white whale?

Master Teacher Note "The Quarter-Deck" is one of the most important chapters in the novel. During this chapter Ahab becomes the novel's dominant character; the vengeful, obsessive nature of his personality is conveyed; his conflict with Moby-Dick is established; and the true purpose of the voyage is revealed. After students have finished reading "The Quarter-Deck," have them explain why they think this chapter is important. Why might this chapter be viewed as the turning point of the novel?

selves became so excited at such seemingly purposeless questions.

But, they were all eagerness again, as Ahab, now half-revolving in his pivot hole, with one hand reaching high up a shroud,[10] and tightly, almost convulsively grasping it, addressed them thus:

"All ye mastheaders have before now heard me give orders about a white whale. Look ye! d'ye see this Spanish ounce of gold?"—holding up a broad bright coin to the sun—"it is a sixteen-dollar piece, men. D'ye see it? Mr. Starbuck, hand me yon topmaul."

While the mate was getting the hammer, Ahab, without speaking, was slowly rubbing the gold piece against the skirts of his jacket, as if to heighten its luster, and without using any words was meanwhile lowly humming to himself, producing a sound so strangely muffled and inarticulate that it seemed the mechanical humming of the wheels of his vitality in him.

Receiving the topmaul from Starbuck, he advanced towards the mainmast with the hammer uplifted in one hand, exhibiting the gold with the other, and with a high raised voice exclaiming: "Whosoever of ye raises me a white-headed whale with a wrinkled brow and a crooked jaw; whosoever of ye raises me that white-headed whale, with three holes punctured in his starboard fluke[11]—look ye,

---

10. **shroud** *n.*: A set of ropes from a ship's side to the masthead.

11. **starboard fluke** (flo͞ok) *n.*: The right half of a whale's tail.

322 *New England Renaissance*

whosoever of ye raises me that same white whale, he shall have this gold ounce, my boys!"

"Huzza! huzza!" cried the seamen, as with swinging tarpaulins they hailed the act of nailing the gold to the mast.

"It's a white whale, I say," resumed Ahab, as he threw down the topmaul: "a white whale. Skin your eyes for him, men; look sharp for white water; if ye see but a bubble, sing out."

All this while Tashtego, Daggoo, and Queequeg had looked on with even more intense interest and surprise than the rest, and at the mention of the wrinkled brow and crooked jaw they had started as if each was separately touched by some specific recollection.

"Captain Ahab," said Tashtego, "that white whale must be the same that some call Moby-Dick."

"Moby-Dick?" shouted Ahab. "Do ye know the white whale then, Tash?"

"Does he fantail[12] a little curious, sir, before he goes down?" said the Gay-Header deliberately.

"And has he a curious spout, too," said Daggoo, "very bushy, even for a parmacetty,[13] and mighty quick, Captain Ahab?"

"And he have one, two, tree—oh! good many iron in him hide, too, Captain," cried Queequeg disjointedly, "all twiske-tee be-twisk, like him—him—" faltering hard for a word, and screwing his hand round and round as though uncorking a bottle—"like him—him——"

"Corkscrew!" cried Ahab, "aye, Queequeg, the harpoons lie all twisted and wrenched in him; aye, Daggoo, his spout is a big one, like a whole shock of wheat, and white as a pile of our Nantucket wool after the great annual sheepshearing; aye, Tashtego, and he fantails like a split jib in a squall. Death and devils! men, it is Moby-Dick ye have seen—Moby-Dick—Moby-Dick!"

"Captain Ahab," said Starbuck, who, with Stubb and Flask, had thus far been eyeing his superior with increasing surprise, but at last seemed struck with a thought which somewhat explained all the wonder. "Captain Ahab, I have heard of Moby-Dick—but it was not Moby-Dick that took off thy leg?"

"Who told thee that?" cried Ahab; then pausing, "Aye, Starbuck; aye, my hearties all round; it was Moby-Dick that dismasted me; Moby-Dick that brought me to this dead stump I stand on now. Aye, aye," he shouted with a terrific, loud, animal sob, like that of a heart-stricken moose; "Aye, aye! it was that accursed white whale that razeed me; made a poor pegging lubber[14] for me forever and a day!" Then tossing both arms, with measureless imprecations he shouted out: "Aye, aye! and I'll chase him round Good Hope, and round the Horn, and round the Norway Maelstrom, and round perdition's flames before I give him up. And this is what ye have shipped for, men! to chase that white whale on both sides of land, and over all sides of earth, till he spouts black blood and rolls fin out. What say ye, men, will ye splice hands on it, now? I think ye do look brave."

"Aye, aye!" shouted the harpooneers and seamen, running closer to the excited old man: "A sharp eye for the white whale; a sharp lance for Moby-Dick!"

"God bless ye," he seemed to half sob and half shout. "God bless ye, men. Steward! go draw the great measure of grog. But what's this long face about, Mr. Starbuck; wilt thou not chase the white whale? art not game for Moby-Dick?"

"I am game for his crooked jaw, and for the jaws of Death too, Captain Ahab, if it fairly comes in the way of the business we follow; but I came here to hunt whales, not my commander's vengeance. How many bar-

---

12. **fantail:** To spread the tail like a fan.
13. **parmacetty:** Dialect for *spermaceti*, a waxy substance taken from a sperm whale's head and used to make candles.

14. **lubber** (lub′ ər) *n*.: A slow, clumsy person.

19 **Discussion** What are Ahab's orders?

20 **Clarification** Tashtego is called the Gay-Header because he comes from Gay Head, Massachusetts.

21 **Discussion** What are some details that distinguish Moby-Dick from other whales?

22 **Reading Strategy** Have students watch for the different points of view held by Ahab and Starbuck. Students should note that Starbuck usually raises practical considerations.

23 **Enrichment** Sailors on a whaling ship usually signed on for a share of the net profits. While some also hoped for adventure, the purpose of the voyage was to capture whales and bring back whale oil, whalebone, and other valuable products for the ship's owners to sell.

24 **Discussion** What does Starbuck's comment reveal about his character?

rels will thy vengeance yield thee even if thou gettest it, Captain Ahab? it will not fetch thee much in our Nantucket market."

"Nantucket market! Hoot! But come closer, Starbuck; thou requirest a little lower layer. If money's to be the measurer, man, and the accountants have computed their great countinghouse the globe, by girdling it with guineas, one to every three parts of an inch; then, let me tell thee, that my vengeance will fetch a great premium *here*!"

"He smites his chest," whispered Stubb, "what's that for? methinks it rings most vast, but hollow."

"Vengeance on a dumb brute!" cried Starbuck, "that simply smote thee from blindest instinct! Madness! To be enraged with a dumb thing, Captain Ahab, seems blasphemous."

"Hark ye yet again—the little lower layer. All visible objects, man, are but as pasteboard masks. But in each event—in the living act, the undoubted deed—there, some unknown but still reasoning thing puts forth the moldings of its features from behind the unreasoning mask. If man will strike, strike through the mask! How can the prisoner reach outside except by thrusting through the wall? To me, the white whale is that wall, shoved near to me. Sometimes I think there's naught beyond. But 'tis enough. He tasks me; he heaps me; I see in him outrageous strength, with an inscrutable malice sinewing it. That inscrutable thing is chiefly what I hate; and be the white whale agent, or be the white whale principal, I will wreak that hate upon him. Talk not to me of blasphemy, man; I'd strike the sun if it insulted me. For could the sun do that, then could I do the other; since there is ever a sort of fair play herein, jealousy presiding over all creations. But not my master, man, is even that fair play. Who's over me? Truth hath no confines. Take off thine eye! more intolerable than fiends' glarings is a doltish stare! So, so; thou reddenest and palest; my heat has melted thee to anger-glow. But look ye, Starbuck, what is said in heat, that thing unsays

itself. There are men from whom warm words are small indignity. I meant not to incense thee. Let it go. Look! see yonder Turkish cheeks of spotted tawn—living, breathing pictures painted by the sun. The pagan leopards—the unrecking and unworshiping things, that live, and seek, and give no reasons for the torrid life they feel! The crew, man, the crew! Are they not one and all with Ahab, in this matter of the whale? See Stubb! he laughs! See yonder Chilean! he snorts to think of it. Stand up amid the general hurricane, thy one tossed sapling cannot, Starbuck! And what is it? Reckon it. 'Tis but to help strike a fin; no wondrous feat for Starbuck. What is it more? From this one poor hunt, then, the best lance out of all Nantucket, surely he will not hang back, when every foremasthand has clutched a whetstone. Ah! constrainings seize thee; I see! the billow lifts thee! Speak, but speak!— Aye, aye! thy silence, then, *that* voices thee. (*Aside*) Something shot from my dilated nostrils, he has inhaled it in his lungs. Starbuck now is mine; cannot oppose me now, without rebellion."

"God keep me!—keep us all!" murmured Starbuck, lowly.

But in his joy at the enchanted, tacit acquiescence of the mate, Ahab did not hear his foreboding invocation; nor yet the low laugh from the hold; nor yet the presaging vibrations of the winds in the cordage; nor yet the hollow flap of the sails against the masts, as for a moment their hearts sank in. For again Starbuck's downcast eyes lighted up with the stubbornness of life; the subterranean laugh died away; the winds blew on; the sails filled out; the ship heaved and rolled as before. Ah, ye admonitions and warnings! why stay ye not when ye come? But rather are ye predictions than warnings, ye shadows! Yet not so much predictions from without, as verifications of the foregoing things within. For with little external to constrain us, the innermost necessities in our being, these still drive us on.

"The measure! the measure!" cried Ahab.

Grammar in Action

Rhetorical questions are questions that are not intended to be answered orally. Yet, because listeners generally will try to answer these questions in their minds, the questions force them to think actively about what is being said. **Direct questions,** on the other hand, are questions that are expected to be answered. Because people frequently use rhetorical questions and direct questions in everyday speech, both types of questions are often used in realistic prose. Note the following examples from *Moby-Dick*:

Rhetorical questions:

". . . Look ye! d'ye see this Spanish ounce of gold?"

. . . "How can the prisoner reach out except by thrusting through the wall? To me, that white whale is that wall, shoved near me. . . ." (p. 324)

Direct Questions:

. . . "Captain Ahab, I have heard of Moby-Dick—but it was not Moby-Dick that took off thy leg?"

. . . "Do you know the white whale then, Tash?"

Receiving the brimming pewter, and turning to the harpooneers, he ordered them to produce their weapons. Then ranging them before him near the capstan,[15] with their harpoons in their hands, while his three mates stood at his side with their lances, and the rest of the ship's company formed a circle round the group; he stood for an instant searchingly eyeing every man of his crew. But those wild eyes met his, as the bloodshot eyes of the prairie wolves meet the eye of their leader, ere he rushes on at their head in the trail of the bison; but, alas! only to fall into the hidden snare of the Indian.

"Drink and pass!" he cried, handing the heavy charged flagon to the nearest seamen. "The crew alone now drink. Round with it, round! Short drafts—long swallows, men; 'tis hot as Satan's hoof. So, so; it goes round excellently. It spiralizes in ye; forks out at the serpent-snapping eye. Well done; almost drained. That way it went, this way it comes. Hand it me—here's a hollow! Men, ye seem the years; so brimming life is gulped and gone. Steward, refill!

"Attend now, my braves. I have mustered ye all round this capstan; and ye mates, flank me with your lances; and ye harpooneers, stand there with your irons; and ye, stout mariners, ring me in, that I may in some sort revive a noble custom of my fishermen fathers before me. O men, you will yet see that— Ha! boy, come back? bad pennies come not sooner. Hand it me. Why, now, this pewter had run brimming again, wer't not thou St. Vitus' imp[16]—away, thou ague![17]

"Advance, ye mates! cross your lances full before me. Well done! Let me touch the axis." So saying, with extended arm, he grasped the three level, radiating lances at their crossed center; while so doing, sud- denly and nervously twitched them; mean- while glancing intently from Starbuck to Stubb; from Stubb to Flask. It seemed as though, by some nameless, interior volition, he would fain have shocked into them the same fiery emotion accumulated within the Leyden jar[18] of his own magnetic life. The three mates quailed before his strong, sus- tained, and mystic aspect. Stubb and Flask looked sideways from him; the honest eye of Starbuck fell downright.

"In vain!" cried Ahab; "but, maybe, 'tis well. For did ye three but once take the full- forced shock, then mine own electric thing, *that* had perhaps expired from out me. Per- chance, too, it would have dropped ye dead. Perchance ye need it not. Down lances! And now, ye mates, I do appoint ye three cup- bearers to my three pagan kinsmen there— yon three most honorable gentlemen and no- blemen, my valiant harpooneers. Disdain the task? What, when the great Pope washes the feet of beggars, using his tiara for ewer? Oh, my sweet cardinals! your own condescen- sion, *that* shall bend ye to it. I do not order ye; ye will it. Cut your seizings and draw the poles, ye harpooneers!"

Silently obeying the order, the three har- pooneers now stood with the detached iron part of their harpoons, some three feet long, held, barbs up, before him.

"Stab me not with that keen steel! Cant them; cant them over! know ye not the gob- let end? Turn up the socket! So, so; now, ye cup-bearers, advance. The irons! take them; hold them while I fill!" Forthwith, slowly go- ing from one officer to the other, he brimmed the harpoon sockets with the fiery waters from the pewter.

"Now, three to three, ye stand. Commend the murderous chalices! Bestow them, ye who are now made parties to this indissolu- ble league. Ha! Starbuck! but the deed is

---

15. capstan (kap′ stən) *n*.: A large cylinder, turned by hand, around which cables are wound.

16. St. Vitus' imp: Offspring of St. Vitus. Saint Vitus is the patron saint of people stricken with the nervous disorder chorea, characterized by irregular, jerking movements.

17. ague (ā′ gyo͞o) *n*.: A chill or fit of shivering.

---

18. Leyden (līd′'n) **jar** *n*.: A glass jar coated inside and out with tinfoil with a metal rod passing through the lid and connected to the inner lining; used to store condensed static electricity.

from Moby-Dick 325

---

30 Discussion Why does Ahab or- der the harpooners to produce their weapons?

31 Critical Thinking and Reading Point out the ceremonial quality of this action.

32 Discussion For what is the Ley- den jar a metaphor? What is the effect of this metaphor?

33 Clarification The "three pagan kinsmen" are Queequeg, Tashte- go, and Daggoo.

34 Literary Focus Here the symbol- ic acts take on an almost reli- gious aspect.

Student Activity Identify each of the questions in the following passages as either a rhetorical question or a direct question.

1. ". . . But what's this long face about, Mr. Starbuck; wilt thou not chase the white whale? Art not game for Moby-Dick?"

2. "Stab me not with that keen steel? Cant them; cant them over! know ye not the goblet end? Turn up the socket! . . ."

3. "There's the difference between man's old age and matter's. But aye, old mast, we both grow old together; sound in our hulls, though, are we not, my ship? Aye, minus a leg, that's all. . . ."

4. ". . . But the chowder; clam or cod tomorrow for breakfast, men?"

"Both," says I, "and let's have a couple of smoked herring by way of variety."

35 **Clarification** The whale hunting is done from smaller boats that are propelled by oars, while the ship itself stands ready to process the whale and pick up any sailors who have lost their boats. This is the final chapter in the book.

36 **Enrichment** On a ship, the crew members take turns staying on duty, sleeping, and resting.

37 **Discussion** Why is Ahab's description of himself appropriate?

38 **Critical Thinking and Reading** Point out that Ahab clearly expresses a negative view of the world, and in the wind he sees an enemy that is even harder to conquer than Moby-Dick. How do Ahab's views reflect those of the Anti-Transcendentalists?

done! Yon ratifying sun now waits to sit upon it. Drink, ye harpooneers! drink and swear, ye men that man the deathful whale-boat's bow— Death to Moby-Dick! God hunt us all, if we do not hunt Moby-Dick to his death!" The long, barbed steel goblets were lifted; and to cries and maledictions against the white whale, the spirits were simultaneously quaffed down with a hiss. Starbuck paled, and turned, and shivered. Once more, and finally, the replenished pewter went the rounds among the frantic crew; when, waving his free hand to them, they all dispersed; and Ahab retired within his cabin.

After Moby-Dick has been sighted in the Pacific Ocean, the Pequod's boats pursue the whale for two days. One of the boats has been sunk, and Ahab's ivory leg has been broken off. However, as the next day dawns, the chase continues.

35 **The Chase–Third Day**

36 The morning of the third day dawned fair and fresh, and once more the solitary night man at the foremasthead was relieved by crowds of the daylight lookouts, who dotted every mast and almost every spar.

"D'ye see him?" cried Ahab; but the whale was not yet in sight.

"In his infallible wake, though; but follow that wake, that's all. Helm there; steady, as thou goest, and hast been going. What a lovely day again! were it a new-made world, and made for a summerhouse to the angels, and this morning the first of its throwing open to them, a fairer day could not dawn upon that world. Here's food for thought, had Ahab time to think; but Ahab never

37 thinks; he only feels, feels, feels; *that's* tingling enough for mortal man! to think's audacity. God only has that right and privilege. Thinking is, or ought to be, a coolness and a calmness; and our poor hearts throb, and our poor brains beat too much for that. And yet, I've sometimes thought my brain was very calm—frozen calm, this old skull cracks

so, like a glass in which the contents turned to ice, and shiver it. And still this hair is growing now; this moment growing, and heat must breed it; but no, it's like that sort of common grass that will grow anywhere, between the earthy clefts of Greenland ice or in Vesuvius lava. How the wild winds blow it; they whip it about me as the torn shreds of split sails lash the tossed ship they cling to. A vile wind that has no doubt blown ere this through prison corridors and cells, and wards of hospitals, and ventilated them, and now comes blowing hither as innocent as fleeces.[19] Out upon it!—it's tainted. Were I the wind, I'd blow no more on such a wicked, miserable world. I'd crawl somewhere to a cave, and slink there. And yet, 'tis a noble and heroic thing, the wind! who ever conquered it? In every fight it has the last and bitterest blow. Run tilting at it, and you but run through it. Ha! a coward wind that strikes stark-naked men, but will not stand to receive a single blow. Even Ahab is a braver thing—a nobler thing than *that*. Would now the wind but had a body but all the things that most exasperate and outrage mortal man, all these things are bodiless, but only bodiless as objects, not as agents. There's a most special, a most cunning, oh, a most malicious difference! And yet, I say again, and swear it now, that there's something all glorious and gracious in the wind. These warm trade winds, at least, that in the clear heavens blow straight on, in strong and steadfast, vigorous mildness; and veer not from their mark, however the baser currents of the sea may turn and tack, and mightiest Mississippis of the land swift and swerve about, uncertain where to go at last. And by the eternal poles! these same trades that so directly blow my good ship on; these trades, or something like them—something so unchangeable, and full as strong, blow my keeled soul along! To it! Aloft there! What d'ye see?"

"Nothing, sir."

38

_____

19. **fleeces** (flēs′ əz) n.: Sheep.

"Nothing! and noon at hand! The doubloon[20] goes a-begging! See the sun! Aye, aye, it must be so. I've oversailed him. How, got the start? Aye, he's chasing *me* now; not I, *him*—that's bad; I might have known it, too. Fool! the lines—the harpoons he's towing. Aye, aye, I have run him by last night. About! about! Come down, all of ye, but the regular lookouts! Man the braces!"

Steering as she had done, the wind had been somewhat on the *Pequod*'s quarter, so that now being pointed in the reverse direction, the braced ship sailed hard upon the breeze as she rechurned the cream in her own white wake.

"Against the wind he now steers for the open jaw," murmured Starbuck to himself, as he coiled the new-hauled main brace upon the rail. "God keep us, but already my bones feel damp within me, and from the inside wet my flesh. I misdoubt me that I disobey my God in obeying him!"

"Stand by to sway me up!" cried Ahab, advancing to the hempen basket.[21] "We should meet him soon."

"Aye, aye, sir," and straightway Starbuck did Ahab's bidding, and once more Ahab swung on high.

A whole hour now passed; gold-beaten out to ages. Time itself now held long breaths with keen suspense. But at last, some three points off the weather bow, Ahab descried the spout again, and instantly from the three mastheads three shrieks went up as if the tongues of fire had voiced it.

"Forehead to forehead I meet thee, this third time, Moby-Dick! On deck there!—brace sharper up; crowd her into the wind's eye. He's too far off to lower yet, Mr. Starbuck. The sails shake! Stand over that helmsman with a topmaul! So, so; he travels fast, and I must down. But let me have one more good round look aloft here at the sea; there's

time for that. An old, old sight, and yet somehow so young; aye, and not changed a wink since I first saw it, a boy, from the sand hills of Nantucket! The same!—the same!—the same to Noah as to me. There's a soft shower to leeward. Such lovely leewardings! They must lead somewhere—to something else than common land, more palmy than the palms. Leeward! the white whale goes that way; look to windward, then; the better if the bitterer quarter. But good-bye, good-bye, old masthead! What's this?—green? aye, tiny mosses in these warped cracks. No such green weather stains on Ahab's head! There's the difference now between man's old age and matter's. But aye, old mast, we both grow old together; sound in our hulls, though, are we not, my ship? Aye, minus a leg, that's all. By heaven this dead wood has the better of my live flesh every way. I can't compare with it; and I've known some ships made of dead trees outlast the lives of men made of the most vital stuff of vital fathers. What's that he said? he should still go before me, my pilot; and yet to be seen again? But where? Will I have eyes at the bottom of the sea, supposing I descend those endless stairs? and all night I've been sailing from him, wherever he did sink to. Aye, aye, like many more thou told'st direful truth as touching thyself, O Parsee; but, Ahab, there thy shot fell short. Good-bye, masthead—keep a good eye upon the whale, the while I'm gone. We'll talk tomorrow, nay, tonight, when the white whale lies down there, tied by head and tail."

He gave the word; and still gazing round him, was steadily lowered through the cloven blue air to the deck.

In due time the boats were lowered; but as standing in his shallop's stern, Ahab just hovered upon the point of the descent, he waved to the mate—who held one of the tackle ropes on deck—and bade him pause.

"Starbuck!"

"Sir?"

"For the third time my soul's ship starts upon this voyage, Starbuck."

---

20. **doubloon** (du blōōn′) *n.*: The gold coin Ahab offered as reward to the first man to spot the whale.
21. **hempen basket:** A rope basket constructed earlier by Ahab, in which he could be raised, by means of a pulley device, to the top of the mainmast.

from *Moby-Dick*   327

39 **Discussion** Is Moby-Dick really chasing the ship?

40 **Critical Thinking and Reading** Note Starbuck's comment. Discuss how Starbuck serves as a foil.

41 **Literary Focus** The number three is often symbolic. This is the third day, and Ahab is meeting Moby-Dick for the third time.

42 **Literary Focus** Note the symbolic nature of the comparison Ahab makes between himself and the mast.

43 **Clarification** Parsee is a Persian sailor who disappeared in the previous chapter. Earlier in the book, a prediction was made that Parsee would die before Ahab, but that Ahab would see him once more before his own death.

44 **Literary Focus** Once again the number three is mentioned.

"Aye, sir, thou wilt have it so."

"Some ships sail from their ports, and ever afterwards are missing, Starbuck!"

"Truth, sir: saddest truth."

"Some men die at ebb tide; some at low water; some at the full of the flood—and I feel now like a billow that's all one crested comb, Starbuck. I am old—shake hands with me, man."

Their hands met; their eyes fastened; Starbuck's tears the glue.

"Oh, my captain, my captain!—noble heart—go not—go not!—see, it's a brave man that weeps; how great the agony of the persuasion then!"

"Lower away!"—cried Ahab, tossing the mate's arm from him. "Stand by the crew!"

In an instant the boat was pulling round close under the stern.

"The sharks! the sharks!" cried a voice from the low cabin window there; "O master, my master, come back!"

But Ahab heard nothing; for his own voice was high-lifted then; and the boat leaped on.

Yet the voice spake true; for scarce had he pushed from the ship, when numbers of sharks, seemingly rising from out the dark waters beneath the hull, maliciously snapped at the blades of the oars, every time they dipped in the water; and in this way accompanied the boat with their bites. It is a thing not uncommonly happening to the whaleboats in those swarming seas; the sharks at times apparently following them in the same prescient way that vultures hover over the banners of marching regiments in the east. But these were the first sharks that had been observed by the Pequod since the White Whale had been first descried; and whether it was that Ahab's crew were all such tiger-yellow barbarians, and therefore their flesh more musky to the senses of the sharks—a matter sometimes well known to affect them—however it was, they seemed to follow that one boat without molesting the others.

"Heart of wrought steel!" murmured Starbuck gazing over the side, and following with his eyes the receding boat—"canst thou yet ring boldly to that sight?—lowering thy keel among ravening sharks, and followed by them, open-mouthed to the chase; and this the critical third day?—For when three days flow together in one continuous intense pursuit; be sure the first is the morning, the second the noon, and the third the evening and the end of that thing—be that end what it may. Oh! my God! what is this that shoots through me, and leaves me so deadly calm, yet expectant—fixed at the top of a shudder! Future things swim before me, as in empty outlines and skeletons; all the past is somehow grown dim. Mary, girl; thou fadest in pale glories behind me; boy! I seem to see but thy eyes grown wondrous blue.[22] Strangest problems of life seem clearing; but clouds sweep between—Is my journey's end coming? My legs feel faint; like his who has footed it all day. Feel thy heart—beats it yet? Stir thyself, Starbuck!—stave it off—move, move! speak aloud!—Masthead there! See ye my boy's hand on the hill?—Crazed—aloft there!—keep thy keenest eye upon the boats—mark well the whale!—Ho! again!—drive off that hawk! see! he pecks—he tears the vane"—pointing to the red flag flying at the maintruck—"Ha, he soars away with it!—Where's the old man now? see'st thou that sight, oh Ahab!—shudder, shudder!"

The boats had not gone very far, when by a signal from the mastheads—a downward pointed arm, Ahab knew that the whale had sounded; but intending to be near him at the next rising, he held on his way a little sideways from the vessel; the becharmed crew maintaining the profoundest silence, as the head-beat waves hammered and hammered against the opposing bow.

"Drive, drive in your nails, oh ye waves! to their uttermost heads drive them in! ye but strike a thing without a lid; and no coffin and no hearse can be mine:—and hemp only can kill me! Ha! ha!"

Suddenly the waters around them slowly

22. **Mary . . . blue.:** A reference to Starbuck's wife and son.

swelled in broad circles; then quickly up-heaved, as if sideways sliding from a sub-merged berg of ice, swiftly rising to the surface. A low rumbling sound was heard; a subterraneous hum; and then all held their breaths; as bedraggled with trailing ropes, and harpoons, and lances, a vast form shot lengthwise, but obliquely from the sea. Shrouded in a thin drooping veil of mist, it hovered for a moment in the rainbowed air; and then fell swamping back into the deep. Crushed thirty feet upwards, the waters flashed for an instant like heaps of foun-tains, then brokenly sank in a shower of flakes, leaving the circling surface creamed like new milk round the marble trunk of the whale.

"Give way!" cried Ahab to the oarsmen, and the boats darted forward to the attack; but maddened by yesterday's fresh irons that corroded in him, Moby-Dick seemed combinedly possessed by all the angels that fell from heaven. The wide tiers of welded tendons overspreading his broad white fore-head, beneath the transparent skin, looked knitted together; as head on, he came churning his tail among the boats; and once more flailed them apart; spilling out the irons and lances from the two mates' boats, and dashing in one side of the upper part of their bows, but leaving Ahab's almost with-out a scar.

While Daggoo and Queequeg were stop-ping the strained planks; and as the whale swimming out from them, turned, and showed one entire flank as he shot by them again; at that moment a quick cry went up. Lashed round and round to the fish's back; pinioned in the turns upon turns in which, during the past night, the whale had reeled the involutions of the lines around him, the half-torn body of the Parsee was seen; his sa-ble raiment frayed to shreds; his distended eyes turned full upon old Ahab.

The harpoon dropped from his hand.

"Befooled, befooled!"—drawing in a long lean breath—"Aye, Parsee! I see thee again—Aye, and thou goest before; and this, *this* then is the hearse that thou didst promise.

But I hold thee to the last letter of thy word. Where is the second hearse? Away, mates, to the ship! those boats are useless now; repair them if ye can in time, and return to me; if not, Ahab is enough to die—Down, men! the first thing that but offers to jump from this boat I stand in, that thing I harpoon. Ye are not other men, but my arms and my legs; and so obey me—Where's the whale? gone down again?"

But he looked too nigh the boat; for as if bent upon escaping with the corpse he bore, and as if the particular place of the last en-counter had been but a stage in his leeward voyage, Moby-Dick was now again steadily swimming forward; and had almost passed the ship—which thus far had been sailing in the contrary direction to him, though for the present her headway had been stopped. He seemed swimming with his utmost velocity, and now only intent upon pursuing his own straight path in the sea.

"Oh! Ahab," cried Starbuck, "not too late is it, even now, the third day, to desist. See! Moby-Dick seeks thee not. It is thou, thou, that madly seekest him!"

Setting sail to the rising wind, the lonely boat was swiftly impelled to leeward, by both oars and canvas. And at last when Ahab was sliding by the vessel, so near as plainly to distinguish Starbuck's face as he leaned over the rail, he hailed him to turn the vessel about, and follow him, not too swiftly, at a judicious interval. Glancing upwards he saw Tashtego, Queequeg, and Daggoo, eagerly mounting to the three mastheads; while the oarsmen were rocking in the two staved boats which had just been hoisted to the side, and were busily at work in repairing them. One after the other, through the port-holes, as he sped, he also caught flying glimpses of Stubb and Flask, busying them-selves on deck among bundles of new irons and lances. As he saw all this; as he heard the hammers in the broken boats; far other hammers seemed driving a nail into his heart. But he rallied. And now marking that the vane or flag was gone from the main masthead, he shouted to Tashtego, who had

from *Moby-Dick*   329

50 **Critical Thinking and Reading** Note how the omen about the Parsee becomes reality; the body appears lashed to Moby-Dick's back. The hand of destiny is clearly indicated.

51 **Discussion** Why does Ahab go on despite all the omens of dis-aster?

52 **Discussion** Why does Starbuck plead with Ahab to stop? What does this indicate about his feel-ings toward Ahab?

53 Critical Thinking and Reading
Note that the narrator suggests that Moby-Dick may be giving up the fight. How does this adds to the suspense.

54 Discussion Does Ahab expect to survive?

55 Critical Thinking and Reading
Point out that the events are becoming increasingly kaleidoscopic. The reader catches brief bits of action, very much as a sailor at the scene would see action upon action with little apparent connection between them.

just gained that perch, to descend again for another flag, and a hammer and nails, and so nail it to the mast.

Whether fagged by the three days' running chase, and the resistance to his swimming in the knotted hamper he bore; or whether it was some latent deceitfulness and malice in him: whichever was true, the White Whale's way now began to abate, as it seemed, from the boat so rapidly nearing him once more; though indeed the whale's last start had not been so long a one as before. And still as Ahab glided over the waves the unpitying sharks accompanied him; and so pertinaciously stuck to the boat; and so continually bit at the plying oars, that the blades became jagged and crunched, and left small splinters in the sea, at almost every dip.

"Heed them not! those teeth but give new rowlocks to your oars. Pull on! 'tis the better rest, the sharks' jaw than the yielding water."

"But at every bite, sir, the thin blades grow smaller and smaller!"

"They will last long enough! pull on!— But who can tell"—he muttered—"whether these sharks swim to feast on the whale or on Ahab?—But pull on! Aye, all alive, now— we near him. The helm! take the helm! let me pass"—and so saying, two of the oarsmen helped him forward to the bows of the still flying boat.

At length as the craft was cast to one side, and ran ranging along with the White Whale's flank, he seemed strangely oblivious of its advance—as the whale sometimes will—and Ahab was fairly within the smoky mountain mist, which, thrown off from the whale's spout, curled round his great Monadnock[23] hump; he was even thus close to him; when, with body arched back, and both arms lengthwise high-lifted to the poise, he darted his fierce iron, and his far fiercer curse into the hated whale. As both steel and

---

23. **Monadnock** (mə nad' näk): A mountain in New Hampshire.

curse sank to the socket, as if sucked into a morass, Moby-Dick sidewise writhed; spasmodically rolled his nigh flank against the bow, and, without staving a hole in it, so suddenly canted the boat over, that had it not been for the elevated part of the gunwale to which he then clung, Ahab would once more have been tossed into the sea. As it was, three of the oarsmen—who foreknew not the precise instant of the dart, and were therefore unprepared for its effects—these were flung out; but so fell, that, in an instant two of them clutched the gunwale again, and rising to its level on a combing wave, hurled themselves bodily inboard again; the third man helplessly dropping astern, but still afloat and swimming.

Almost simultaneously, with a mighty volition of ungraduated, instantaneous swiftness, the White Whale darted through the weltering sea. But when Ahab cried out to the steersman to take new turns with the line, and hold it so; and commanded the crew to turn round on their seats, and tow the boat up to the mark; the moment the treacherous line felt that double strain and tug, it snapped in the empty air!

"What breaks in me? Some sinew cracks!—'tis whole again; oars! oars! Burst in upon him!"

Hearing the tremendous rush of the sea-crashing boat, the whale wheeled round to present his blank forehead at bay; but in that evolution, catching sight of the nearing black hull of the ship; seemingly seeing in it the source of all his persecutions; bethinking it—it may be—a larger and nobler foe; of a sudden, he bore down upon its advancing prow, smiting his jaws amid fiery showers of foam.

Ahab staggered; his hand smote his forehead. "I grow blind; hands! stretch out before me that I may yet grope my way. Is't night?"

"The whale! The ship!" cried the cringing oarsmen.

"Oars! oars! Slope downwards to thy depths, O sea that ere it be forever too late,

---

Commentary: The Five Parts of *Moby-Dick*

An extremely long and complex novel, *Moby-Dick* can be divided into five major parts: Chapters 1 through 22, which focus on Ishmael and his relationship with Queequeg; Chapters 23 through 45, which develop the conflict between Ahab and Moby-Dick; Chapters 46 through 72, which focus on the business of the *Pequod*; Chapters 73 through 105, which provide information about whales and whaling; and Chapters 106 through 135, which tell the story of the search for and confrontation with Moby-Dick.

In the first segment of the novel, Melville develops Ishmael's character, establishes his friendship with Queequeg, and prepares the reader for the voyage of the *Pequod*. When Ishamael first meets Queequeg at the Spouter-Inn in New Bedford, he greets him with suspicion. The two men quickly become close friends, however, and together they travel to Nantucket. There, despite warnings of impending doom, they sign up for a whaling voyage aboard the *Pequod*. Then, on a bleak Christmas night, they begin their voyage, and Ishmael comments, "we gave three heavy-hearted cheers, and blindly plunged like fate into the lone Atlantic."

56 **Critical Thinking and Reading**
This is the first time that Ahab seems concerned with the welfare of his ship.

57 **Discussion** What is Starbuck's chief concern now?

56 Ahab may slide this last, last time upon his mark! I see: the ship! the ship! Dash on, my men! will ye not save my ship?"

But as the oarsmen violently forced their boat through the sledge-hammering seas, the before whale-smitten bow-ends of two planks burst through, and in an instant almost, the temporarily disabled boat lay nearly level with the waves; its half-wading, splashing crew, trying hard to stop the gap and bale out the pouring water.

Meantime, for that one beholding instant, Tashtego's masthead hammer remained suspended in his hand; and the red flag, half wrapping him as with a plaid, then streamed itself straight out from him, as his own forward-flowing heart; while Starbuck and Stubb, standing upon the bowsprit beneath, caught sight of the down-coming monster just as soon as he.

"The whale, the whale! Up helm, up helm! Oh, all ye sweet powers of air, now hug me close! Let not Starbuck die, if die he must, in a woman's fainting fit. Up helm I say—ye fools, the jaw! the jaw! Is this the end of all my bursting prayers? all my life-long fidelities? Oh, Ahab, Ahab, lo, thy work. Steady! helmsman, steady. Nay, nay! Up helm again! He turns to meet us! Oh, his un-appeasable brow drives on towards one, whose duty tells him he cannot depart. My God, stand by me now!" 57

from *Moby-Dick*   331

During the second segment, Ishmael and Queequeg move into the background, as Captain Ahab assumes the role of the dominant character. After introducing the various members of the crew, including Starbuck, Stub, Flask, Tashtego, and Daggoo, Melville focuses on developing Ahab's character. The conflict between Ahab and Moby-Dick is then introduced during the climactic quarter-deck scene in which Ahab convinces his crew to join him in his obsessive quest to destroy Moby-Dick.

58 **Literary Focus** The whale has become a symbol of retribution.

59 **Literary Focus** The symbols of death, which may have begun with the name Peter Coffin, increase in number.

60 **Critical Thinking and Reading** Have students note the manner of Ahab's death. While the whale was involved in his death, it did not kill him directly.

Enrichment In the epilogue, Ishmael reveals that he is the sole survivor. Ironically, he has been saved by a floating coffin, and he floats on it until a ship picks him up on the second day.

"Stand not by me, but stand under me, whoever you are that will now help Stubb; for Stubb, too, sticks here. I grin at thee, thou grinning whale! Who ever helped Stubb, or kept Stubb awake, but Stubb's own unwinking eye? And now poor Stubb goes to bed upon a mattress that is all too soft; would it were stuffed with brushwood! I grin at thee, thou grinning whale! Look ye, sun, moon, and stars! I call ye assassins of as good a fellow as ever spouted up his ghost. For all that, I would yet ring glasses with thee, would ye but hand the cup! Oh, oh! oh, oh! thou grinning whale, but there'll be plenty of gulping soon! Why fly ye not, O Ahab! For me, off shoes and jacket to it; let Stubb die in his drawers! A most moldy and oversalted death, though—cherries! cherries! cherries! Oh, Flask, for one red cherry ere we die!"

"Cherries? I only wish that we were where they grow. Oh, Stubb, I hope my poor mother's drawn my part-pay ere this; if not, few coppers will now come to her, for the voyage is up."

From the ship's bows, nearly all the seamen now hung inactive; hammers, bits of plank, lances, and harpoons, mechanically retained in their hands, just as they had darted from their various employments; all their enchanted eyes intent upon the whale, which from side to side strangely vibrating his predestinating head, sent a broad band of overspreading semicircular foam before him as he rushed. Retribution, swift vengeance, eternal malice were in his whole aspect, and spite of all that mortal man could do, the solid white buttress of his forehead smote the ship's starboard bow, till men and timbers reeled. Some fell flat upon their faces. Like dislodged trucks, the heads of the harpooneers aloft shook on their bull-like necks. Through the breach, they heard the waters pour, as mountain torrents down a flume.

"The ship! The hearse!—the second hearse!" cried Ahab from the boat; "its wood could only be American!"

Diving beneath the settling ship, the whale ran quivering along its keel; but turning under water, swiftly shot to the surface again, far off the other bow, but within a few yards of Ahab's boat, where, for a time, he lay quiescent.

"I turn my body from the sun. What ho, Tashtego! let me hear thy hammer. Oh! ye three unsurrendered spires of mine; thou uncracked keel; and only god-bullied hull; thou firm deck, and haughty helm, and Pole-pointed prow—death-glorious ship! must ye then perish, and without me? Am I cut off from the last fond pride of meanest shipwrecked captains? Oh, lonely death on lonely life! Oh, now I feel my topmost greatness lies in my topmost grief. Ho, ho! from all your furthest bounds, pour ye now in, ye bold billows of my whole foregone life, and top this one piled comber of my death! Towards thee I roll, thou all-destroying but unconquering whale; to the last I grapple with thee; from hell's heart I stab at thee; for hate's sake I spit my last breath at thee. Sink all coffins and all hearses to one common pool! and since neither can be mine, let me then tow to pieces, while still chasing thee, though tied to thee, thou damned whale! *Thus*, I give up the spear!"

The harpoon was darted; the stricken whale flew forward; with igniting velocity the line ran through the groove;—ran foul. Ahab stooped to clear it; he did clear it; but the flying turn caught him round the neck, and voicelessly as Turkish mutes bowstring their victim, he was shot out of the boat, ere the crew knew he was gone. Next instant, the heavy eye splice in the rope's final end flew out of the stark-empty tub, knocked down an oarsman, and smiting the sea, disappeared in its depths.

For an instant, the tranced boat's crew stood still; then turned. "The ship? Great God, where is the ship?" Soon they through dim, bewildering mediums saw her sidelong fading phantom, as in the gaseous fata morgana,[24] only the uppermost masts out of

24. **fata morgana:** A mirage seen at sea.

water; while fixed by infatuation, or fidelity, or fate, to their once lofty perches, the pagan harpooneers still maintained their sinking lookouts on the sea. And now, concentric circles seized the lone boat itself, and all its crew, and each floating oar, and every lance pole, and spinning, animate and inanimate, all round and round in one vortex, carried the smallest chip of the *Pequod* out of sight.

But as the last whelmings intermixingly poured themselves over the sunken head of the Indian at the mainmast, leaving a few inches of the erect spar yet visible, together with long streaming yards of the flag, which calmly undulated, with ironical coincidings, over the destroying billows they almost touched—at that instant, a red arm and a hammer hovered backwardly uplifted in the open air, in the act of nailing the flag faster and yet faster to the subsiding spar. A sky hawk that tauntingly had followed the main-truck downwards from its natural home among the stars, pecking at the flag, and incommoding Tashtego there; this bird now chanced to intercept its broad fluttering wing between the hammer and the wood; and simultaneously feeling that ethereal thrill, the submerged savage beneath, in his deathgasp, kept his hammer frozen there; and so the bird of heaven, with archangelic shrieks, and his imperial beak thrust upwards, and his whole captive form folded in the flag of Ahab, went down with his ship, which, like Satan, would not sink to hell till she had dragged a living part of heaven along with her, and helmeted herself with it.

Now small fowls flew screaming over the yet yawning gulf; a sullen white surf beat against its steep sides; then all collapsed, and the great shroud of the sea rolled on as it rolled five thousand years ago.

THINKING ABOUT THE SELECTION

Recalling

1. What makes the narrator feel uncomfortable at the entrance to the Try Pots?
2. (a) What does Ahab offer to the man who spots Moby-Dick? (b) How do the men respond to his offer?
3. (a) Why is Ahab obsessed with killing Moby-Dick? (b) How does Starbuck interpret Ahab's obsession?
4. (a) What does Ahab tell Starbuck just before his whaleboat is lowered into the water? (b) What follows Ahab's boat as it pulls away from the ship?
5. (a) What happens to Ahab at the end of the novel? (b) What happens to Moby-Dick? (c) What happens to the *Pequod*?

Interpreting

6. How does the narrator's impression of the entrance to the Try Pots foreshadow the outcome of the novel?
7. (a) What does Ahab's obsession with Moby-Dick reveal about his character? (b) In what ways is Starbuck different from Ahab? (c) Why does Starbuck obey Ahab even though he disagrees with him? (d) Why does the rest of the crew join Ahab without hesitation in his quest?
8. On the morning of the third day of the chase, Ahab comments, "Thinking is, or ought to be, a coolness and a calmness; and our poor hearts throb, and our brains beat too much for that." (a) How does this comment apply to Ahab's behavior? (b) How does it apply to the crew?

from *Moby-Dick* 333

9. (a) They indicate that he sees nature as being uncontrollable, unexplainable, and filled with contradictions. (b) His attitude has been shaped by his obsession with Moby-Dick, because he views Moby-Dick as being uncontrollable, unexplainable, and paradoxical.
10. (a) Sharks appear, and Starbuck sees visions of his family. Parsee's body is seen lashed to Moby-Dick. (b) Ahab says that the last part of the omen has not been seen, and he continues to pursue Moby-Dick.
11. It indicates that Moby-Dick is merely a creature following its instincts and is not the evil, scheming creature that Ahab believes it to be.
12. Nature is indifferent to the sufferings of humans, and nature endures in the face of human mortality.

Applying

13. Answers will differ. Students may comment that they agree with Ahab's view.
14. (a) Suggested Response: Obsession can strengthen the effort to reach the goal, but it can also blind people to reality. (b) Answers will differ. Students might mention such goals as financial prosperity and the attainment of political power.

Challenge Compare and contrast the use of symbolism in *Moby-Dick* with the use of symbolism in "The Minister's Black Veil" (p. 302).

ANSWERS TO ANALYZING LITERATURE

1. It symbolizes humanity's efforts to explain and control nature.
2. Suggested Response: It points out that despite people's desires to do so, humans will never be able to completely understand or control nature and that nature will remain powerful, eternal, and indifferent.

ANSWERS TO CRITICAL THINKING AND READING

Suggested Response: Ahab sees the whale as an embodi-

9. (a) What do Ahab's comments about the wind (page 322) at the beginning of "The Chase—Third Day" indicate about his attitude toward nature? (b) How has his obsession with Moby-Dick shaped his attitude?
10. (a) What omens appear as Ahab's whaleboat pulls away from the ship? When Moby-Dick surfaces? (b) How does Ahab respond to these omens?
11. What is the significance of the fact that Moby-Dick seems "strangely oblivious" to the advance of Ahab's boat?
12. What does the final paragraph indicate about the relationship between humanity and nature?

Applying

13. In his speech at the beginning of "The Chase—Third Day," Ahab expresses his belief that people are guided by instinct and intuition rather than reason. React to Ahab's view.
14. (a) How can obsession with achieving a goal affect a person's ability to reach this goal? (b) What types of goals do you think many people are obsessed with reaching in today's world?

ANALYZING LITERATURE

Recognizing a Symbol

A **symbol** is a person, place, or thing that has a meaning in itself and also represents something larger than itself. For example, the crew of the *Pequod,* which includes representatives from many of the world's races and cultures, symbolizes humanity.

1. Given the fact that the crew of the *Pequod* symbolizes humanity and Moby-Dick symbolizes everything in nature that is paradoxical, unexplainable, and uncontrollable, what do

you think the voyage of the *Pequod* symbolizes?
2. Considering the symbolic meaning and the outcome of the journey, what do you think is the theme, or central idea, of the novel?

CRITICAL THINKING AND READING

Analyzing the Meaning of a Symbol

Analyzing Ahab's comments is one effective way to understand the meaning of Moby-Dick as a symbol.

Explain how the following passage from one of Ahab's speeches supports the interpretation of Moby-Dick as a symbol of the mysteries of existence.

"All visible objects, man, are but pasteboard masks. But in each event—in the living act, the undoubted deed—there, some unknown but still reasoning thing puts forth the moldings of its features from behind the unreasoning mask. If man will strike, strike through the mask! How can the prisoner reach outside except by thrusting through the wall? To me, the white whale is that wall, shoved near me."

THINKING AND WRITING

Writing About Symbolism and Theme

Write an essay in which you discuss how the theme, or central idea, of *Moby-Dick* is revealed through Melville's use of symbolism. Start by rereading the excerpt, noting passages in which the meaning of any of the primary symbols in the novel is suggested. Define the meaning of each symbol in your own words. Prepare a chart showing the relationship between the symbols and the theme. Write a thesis statement. Then write your essay. Include enough passages from the novel to support your thesis. When you revise, make sure that your ideas are well-organized and stated clearly.

ment of the mystery which humans must penetrate.

THINKING AND WRITING

For help with this assignment, students can refer to Lesson 11, "Writing About Theme," in the Handbook of Writing About Literature.

After students have completed the writing assignment, divide them into groups, and have them read their rough drafts to one another and comment on ways in which the essays could be improved.

New England Poets

AFTER THE FIRST SNOW IN WINTER IN VERMONT
Charles Hughes
Three Lions

Humanities Note

Fine art, *After the First Snow in Winter in Vermont,* by Charles Hughes. *After the First Snow in Winter in Vermont* is a quiet, naturalistic painting. There is a clear focus on details, such as the spiral knots of the trees; even the snow on the bark of the trees is in a graceful mottled pattern.

The work evokes a sense of calm, of a community whose concerns are bound primarily by the daily activities of living, the church, and nature. The feeling of contentment in a beneficent natural setting is suggested by the horse pulling the sleigh through the newly fallen snow. The covering of snow is represented not as a hardship but rather as a source of pleasure and communion with the natural world. Such scenes inspired some of the poetry of this period.

HENRY WADSWORTH LONGFELLOW

More About the Author Henry Wadsworth Longfellow often employed complex poetic forms. His most ambitious poem, *Evangeline,* used a classical Greek meter which was not well suited to the rhythms of English. How might the use of complex poetic forms help or hinder a poet? In what instances is a simple form more effective than a complex form?

Critical Evaluation The literary scholar George F. Whicher has written: "Longfellow did much more than embody the fresh images, the moral conventions and the domestic sentiments of the age. He became the myth-maker extraordinary to the American people, creating a throng of figures to fill the popular imagination. Evangeline and her lover, Miles Standish and Priscilla the puritan maiden, Hiawatha, Paul Revere—these are but the best known. . . ."

1807–1882

Henry Wadsworth Longfellow once wrote, "Music is the universal language of mankind—poetry their universal pastime and delight." During the latter half of the eighteenth century, Longfellow's poetry certainly was a "universal pastime and delight." His work, which was translated into two dozen foreign languages, was read and enjoyed by millions of readers throughout Europe and the United States.

Born in Portland, Maine, Longfellow attended Bowdoin College, where Nathaniel Hawthorne was one of his classmates. After graduating in 1825, Longfellow spent four years in Europe before returning to Bowdoin as a professor of modern languages. He taught at Bowdoin for five years. Then, after spending another year in Europe, he accepted a position at Harvard University in Cambridge, Massachusetts, which he held for eighteen years.

Longfellow suffered the tragic deaths of two wives. In 1831 when he was twenty-four and a professor at Bowdoin, he married Mary Potter, the attractive and educated daughter of a Portland judge. While traveling in Europe in 1835, Mary, already in delicate health and exhausted by the hardships of traveling, suffered a miscarriage and died of the resulting infection.

Eight years later, after a long courtship, Longfellow married Frances Appleton of Boston. It was an extremely happy but not a long marriage. In 1861 Frances was fatally burned in a household accident. Longfellow's attempts to put out the flames left him badly burned. He had always been cleanshaven, but now the scars on his face made it difficult, if not impossible, to shave. Thus resulted the portrait with the long flowing beard, once so familiar to generations of Americans.

During his years as a professor at Bowdoin and Harvard, Longfellow had a long and successful career as a poet, publishing his first collection of poems, *Voices of the Night,* in 1839. Writing poems that appealed to a general audience, Longfellow established himself as the most popular American poet of his time.

Recognizing the need to maintain a connection to the past, Longfellow found subjects for his poetry in American history. His narrative poems, such as *Evangeline* (1847), *The Song of Hiawatha* (1855), *The Courtship of Miles Standish* (1858), and "Paul Revere's Ride" (1861), gave readers a romanticized view of America during its infancy and expressed the democratic ideals of the young nation.

Longfellow's poetry has been criticized for being overly optimistic and sentimental; yet it was Longfellow's optimism that made him so popular. By writing poetry that soothed and encouraged readers, Longfellow became the first American poet to reach a wide audience and create a national interest in poetry.

Objectives

1 To use abstract words
2 To recognize stanza forms
3 To evaluate Longfellow's poetry

Support Material

Teaching Portfolio
Teacher Backup, p. 445
Usage and Mechanics Worksheet, p. 449
Vocabulary Check, p. 450
Analyzing Literature Worksheet, *Recognizing Stanza Forms,* p. 451
Critical Thinking and Reading Worksheet, *Evaluating Longfellow's Poetry,* p. 452

Selection Test, p. 453
Art Transparency 7, *Stage Fort Across Gloucester Harbor* by Fitz Hugh Lane

GUIDE FOR INTERPRETING

The Tide Rises, The Tide Falls; A Psalm of Life; The Arsenal at Springfield

Writer's Techniques

Stanza Forms. A stanza is a unit of poetry consisting of two or more lines arranged in a pattern according to rhyme and meter, or rhythm. Like paragraphs in prose, stanzas organize ideas into units. Unlike paragraphs in prose, however, stanzas in a poem are generally of a fixed length and share the same pattern of rhyme and meter.

Stanza forms are described in terms of rhyme scheme and length. Rhyme scheme is indicated by assigning a different letter of the alphabet to each new rhyming sound in a stanza. For example, in a stanza in which every other line rhymes, the rhyme scheme is *abab*. Length is determined by the number of lines in a stanza. The following are common stanza lengths:

the couplet	(2 lines)
the tercet	(3 lines)
the quatrain	(4 lines)
the cinquain	(5 lines)
the sestet	(6 lines)
the octave	(8 lines)

Writing

What do the ocean and the constant motion of the tide suggest to you? List the ideas you associate with the ocean and the rising and falling of the tide.

Primary Source

In his poems Longfellow returned again and again to the wooded shores and restless sea of his Maine childhood. In the following excerpts from "My Lost Youth," written when he was forty-eight, he vividly describes Portland:

> Often I think of the beautiful town
>   That is seated by the sea;
> Often in thought go up and down
> The pleasant streets of that dear old town,
>   And my youth comes back to me.
>   . . .
> I remember the black wharves and the slips,
>   And the sea-tides tossing free;
> And Spanish sailors with bearded lips,
> And the beauty and mystery of the ships,
>   And the magic of the sea.

Literary Focus Poets often use rhyme schemes as an organizing element. In addition, people who memorize poems find that the rhymes are useful mnemonic devices. At the same time, the poet who uses rhyme faces the challenge of establishing a pattern of rhyme without altering the intended meaning of the poem.

Writing/Prior Knowledge For extra credit, your **more advanced** students may write poems using the stanza form of one of Longfellow's poems.

Vocabulary

Preteach the following vocabulary words:
bivouac (biv′ wak) *n.:* A temporary encampment (p. 339), l. 18)
sublime (sə blīm′) *adj.:* Noble; majestic (p. 339, l. 26)
beleaguered (bi lē′ gərd) *adj.:* Encircled by an army (p. 342, l. 24) **discordant** (dis kôr′ d'nt) *adj.:* Not in harmony; clashing (p. 344, l. 29)

THE RETURN ALONE
Eugene Higgins
The Phillips Collection, Washington, D.C.

The Tide Rises, The Tide Falls

Henry Wadsworth Longfellow

The tide rises, the tide falls,   **1**
The twilight darkens, the curlew[1] calls;
Along the sea sands damp and brown   **2**
The traveler hastens toward the town,
5   And the tide rises, the tide falls.

Darkness settles on roofs and walls,   **3**
But the sea, the sea in the darkness calls;
The little waves, with their soft, white hands,   **4**
Efface the footprints in the sands,
10   And the tide rises, the tide falls.

The morning breaks; the steeds in their stalls   **5**
Stamp and neigh, as the hostler[2] calls;
The day returns, but nevermore
Returns the traveler to the shore,
15   And the tide rises, the tide falls.   **6**

---

1. curlew (kʉr' lōō) *n.*: A large, long-legged wading bird whose call is associated with the evening.
2. hostler (häs' lər) *n.*: A person who tends horses at an inn or stable.

338   *New England Renaissance*

Thematic Idea Another poem that explores the relationship between nature and death is "The First Snowfall" by James Russell Lowell (p. 356).

Purpose-Setting Question What happens to the traveler?

1 Discussion What does the rising and falling of the tide represent?

2 Discussion Which details would occur day after day? What detail would not recur?

3 Discussion What does the image of darkness suggest?

4 Discussion What do the details in this passage suggest about the relationship between humanity and nature?

5 Discussion What do lines 11–12 suggest?

6 Discussion How does the refrain contribute to the meaning of the poem?

Reader's Response What associations do you have with the rising and falling of the tide? Explain.

THINKING ABOUT THE SELECTION

Recalling

1. What is the setting of the poem?
2. What do the "little waves" do in lines 8–9?
3. What happens in the third stanza?
4. What line is repeated three times in the poem?

Interpreting

5. (a) What details of the setting in the first stanza suggest that the traveler is nearing death? (b) What details in the second stanza suggest that the traveler has died?
6. What does the poem suggest about the relationship between humanity and nature?
7. (a) What is the effect of the refrain, or repeated line? (b) How does the rhythm of the refrain contribute to its meaning?
8. What do the details in lines 11–13 suggest about Longfellow's attitude toward death?

Applying

9. (a) What is the significance of the fact that Longfellow wrote "The Tide Rises, The Tide Falls" near the end of his life? (b) How might the poem have been different if he had written it earlier in life?

UNDERSTANDING LANGUAGE

Using Abstract Words

Concrete words are words that appeal to one or more of the five senses. In contrast, **abstract** words are words that express qualities or concepts apart from any particular or material object. The word *beauty,* for example, is an abstract word, while the word *flower* is concrete.

Define in your own words each of the following words. Check your definitions in a dictionary. Then think of a concrete image, or word picture, that conveys the qualities or concepts expressed by each abstract word.

1. death
2. birth
3. age

Commentary

Longfellow was very influential, both as a teacher and a poet, in acquainting the American public with European literature. At the same time, he actively worked to establish an American literature equal to that of Europe.

While a student at Bowdoin, he showed great aptitude for languages. He began teaching at Bowdoin in 1829, leaving there in 1836 for a professorship at Harvard.

In the early years, he taught languages, writing and publishing his own textbooks since there were none available. At the same time, he was writing and publishing essays on European literature and prose sketches based on his travels in Europe. Firmly American in his point of view, he hoped to create a national literature by giving Americans their rich European heritage. His anthology, *The Poets and Poetry of Europe*, published in 1845, was very popular and accomplished his goal of bringing non-English poetry to the ordinary American reader. Longfellow himself supplied many of the translations.

Translation of foreign literature, especially poetry, was very important to him. For many years his translations greatly outnumbered his original poems. Although he began translating to provide materials for his college students, it is clear that he also found in the foreign poetry inspiration and models for his own work.

Closure and Extension

ANSWERS TO THINKING ABOUT THE SELECTION
Recalling

1. The time is evening, night, and the next morning. The place is near the shore.
2. It effaces, or wipes out, the footprints on the sand.
3. The next day dawns, but the traveler does not return.
4. "The tide rises, the tide falls."

Interpreting

5. (a) The details describe the darkening of the sky and the ending of the day. (b) Darkness has settled and the waves have erased his footprints.
6. Humans come and go, but the rhythms of nature endure. Man is mortal; nature is eternal.
7. (a) It mirrors the repeated motion of the tide. (b) The refrain rises and falls in rhythm, just as the tide rises and falls.
8. A possible answer is that he accepts the fact that life goes on after an individual dies.

Applying

9. (a) He was probably beginning to contemplate his own death. (b) Suggested Response: He would probably have expressed a different attitude toward death.

ANSWERS TO UNDERSTANDING LANGUAGE
Suggested Responses:

1. Death is the end of life. The image of a coffin being lowered into the ground conveys this concept.
2. Birth is the beginning of life. The image of a baby emerging from its mother's womb conveys this image.
3. Age refers to the amount of time that something has lived. The image of a group of people who vary in age from two to seventy conveys this quality.

A Psalm of Life

Henry Wadsworth Longfellow

Tell me not, in mournful numbers,[1]
    Life is but an empty dream!—
For the soul is dead that slumbers,
    And things are not what they seem.

5 Life is real! Life is earnest!
    And the grave is not its goal;
Dust thou art, to dust returnest,
    Was not spoken of the soul.

Not enjoyment, and not sorrow,
10   Is our destined end or way;
But to act, that each tomorrow
    Find us farther than today.

Art is long, and Time is fleeting,
    And our hearts, though stout and brave,
15 Still, like muffled drums, are beating
    Funeral marches to the grave.

In the world's broad field of battle,
    In the bivouac of Life,
Be not like dumb, driven cattle!
20   Be a hero in the strife!

Trust no Future, howe'er pleasant!
    Let the dead Past bury its dead!
Act—act in the living Present!
    Heart within, and God o'erhead!

25 Lives of great men all remind us
    We can make our lives sublime,
And, departing, leave behind us
    Footprints on the sands of time;

Footprints, that perhaps another,
30   Sailing o'er life's solemn main,[2]
A forlorn and shipwrecked brother,
    Seeing, shall take heart again.

---

1. numbers: Verses.
2. main: The open sea.

340   *New England Renaissance*

Commentary: The Writing of "A Psalm of Life"

Longfellow wrote "A Psalm of Life" in 1838, a few months after the deaths of his first wife, Mary, and his brother-in-law, George W. Pierce. Having learned that it was possible to find solace and courage in his work, Longfellow wrote the poem in an attempt to help himself overcome his tremendous loneliness and grief. The poem was intended to serve as an inspiration to himself and others to strive to overcome the tragedies and misfortunes of the past and to live as energetically and productively as possible in the present.

His wife having died in Rotterdam, Germany, Longfellow drew on the influence of German literature, most notably the German writers Johann Wolfgang von Göethe and George Schiller, in writing "A Psalm of Life." In fact, the poem clearly echoes a German motto that Longfellow found especially moving: "Look not mournfully into the Past. It comes not back again. Wisely improve the Present. It is thine. Go forth to meet the shadowy Future, without fear, and with a manly heart."

Originally, the poem was intended to be the first of series of psalms entitled *The Psalms of Life*. However, Longfellow was unable to come up with an appropriate title for the first poem and

Let us, then, be up and doing,
  With a heart for any fate;
35 Still achieving, still pursuing,
  Learn to labor and to wait.

6

THINKING ABOUT THE SELECTION

Recalling

1. (a) What opinion about appearances does the speaker express in line 4? (b) What opinion about life does the speaker express in line 5?
2. What comment concerning time does the speaker make in line 13?
3. (a) What advice does the speaker offer in the fifth stanza? (b) What advice does he offer in the sixth stanza?
4. According to the speaker, what can we learn from the "lives of great men"?
5. What advice does the speaker offer in the final stanza?

Interpreting

6. In your own words summarize the speaker's view of life.
7. How would you describe the speaker's attitude concerning individuality and self-reliance?
8. How does the speaker think our lives can influence future generations?

Applying

9. Give your opinion of the speaker's view of life. Explain your opinion.

A Psalm of Life   341

---

6 Discussion How would a Transcendentalist view this philosophy?

Closure and Extension

ANSWERS TO THINKING ABOUT THE SELECTION
Recalling

1. (a) Things are not what they seem. (b) "Life is real! Life is earnest!"
2. "Time is fleeting."
3. (a) "Be not like dumb, driven cattle! / Be a hero in the strife!" (b) "Act . . . in the living Present!"
4. "We can make our lives sublime" and we can leave "footprints on the sands of time."
5. We should be up and doing "With a heart for any fate."

Interpreting

6. Suggested Response: Life is real, and our response to it should be to do as much as possible to make our lives a guide for those who follow.
7. He suggests that individual actions and self-reliance are very important.
8. We can live in such a way that future generations take courage from our acts.

Applying

9. Answers will differ. Students may comment that they agree with the speaker's view of life, because it is a positive, optimistic outlook.

---

was forced to use the title he had intended for the series. Although he did write several more psalms, they are not easily identified as parts of a series. The second of his psalms, "The Reaper and the Flowers: A Psalm of Death," conveys the message that early death for some is part of the Divine scheme. Two of Longfellow's other psalms are "Footsteps of Angels," which commemorates the deaths of his wife and brother-in-law, and "Midnight Mass for the Dying Year," a poem in which he introduced a new five-line stanza form.

Although "A Psalm of Life" enjoyed tremendous popularity and critical acclaim during Longfellow's time, it has been attacked by many modern critics and readers as being trite and overly sentimental. However, if one keeps in mind the context in which the poem was written, as well as the powerful effect that it had on thousands of nineteenth-century readers, it is difficult to deny the poem's importance.

Motivation/Prior Knowledge
Have students discuss their attitudes toward war. Do they think that a poem or work of fiction about war could in any way alter their opinion? Why or why not?

Clarification An arsenal is a place where military equipment is stored. The Springfield referred to in the poem is in Massachusetts.

Thematic Idea Another selection that confronts the issue of war is "In Another Country" by Ernest Hemingway (p. 664).

Purpose-Setting Question What is Longfellow's view of war?

1 **Critical Thinking and Reading**
Have students note how the style of the first line contrasts with the rest of the poem.

2 **Critical Thinking and Reading**
Have students examine the extended metaphor in which the inside of the arsenal is compared to a huge organ. What are some of the similarities?

3 **Discussion** What are some of the sounds that the speaker hears echoing through time?

The Arsenal at Springfield

Henry Wadsworth Longfellow

This is the Arsenal. From floor to ceiling,
    Like a huge organ, rise the burnished arms;
But from their silent pipes no anthem pealing
    Startles the villages with strange alarms.

5 Ah! what a sound will rise, how wild and dreary,
    When the death angel touches those swift keys!
What loud lament and dismal Miserere[1]
    Will mingle with their awful symphonies!

I hear even now the infinite fierce chorus,
10   The cries of agony, the endless groan,
Which, through the ages that have gone before us,
    In long reverberations reach our own.

On helm and harness rings the Saxon hammer,
    Through Cimbric[2] forest roars the Norseman's song,
15 And loud, amid the universal clamor,
    O'er distant deserts sounds the Tartar[3] gong.

I hear the Florentine, who from his palace
    Wheels out his battle bell with dreadful din,
And Aztec priests upon their teocallis[4]
20   Beat the wild war drums made of serpent's skin:

The tumult of each sacked and burning village;
    The shout that every prayer for mercy drowns;
The soldiers' revels in the midst of pillage;
    The wail of famine in beleaguered towns;

---

1. Miserere (miz′ ə rer′ ē): The 51st Psalm of the Bible (50th in the Douay Version) beginning, "Have mercy upon me, O God."
2. Cimbric (sim′ brik): Pertaining to Germanic people of central Europe who invaded Italy and were defeated by the Romans in 101 B.C.
3. Tartar: Refers to the Tartars, who ruled a region of Asia and eastern Europe in the thirteenth and fourteenth centuries.
4. teocallis (tē′ ə ka′ lis) *n.*: Ancient temples erected by Aztec Indians of Mexico and Central America.

Commentary: The Writing of "The Arsenal at Springfield"

Longfellow wrote "The Arsenal at Springfield" in response to a request from his second wife, Fanny. During the couple's wedding journey in 1843, they visited the arsenal at Springfield, Massachusetts. A devout pacifist, Fanny was extremely moved by the visit and asked her new husband to write a peace poem. Although Longfellow was not as pacifistic as Fanny, his strong belief in the biblical "faith, hope, and charity" made him very responsive to his wife's request.

Because it was also written during the Longfellows' wedding journey, the poem "The Old Clock on the Stairs" is often paired with "The Arsenal at Springfield." Following their visit to Springfield, the couple traveled to the home of Fanny's maternal grandfather in Pittsfield, Massachusetts. There, Longfellow saw an old clock that captured his imagination and inspired him to write a poem. The poem also reflects the influence of an early French missionary, who wrote that eternity is a balance between *forever* and *never*. In fact, Longfellow used the writings of the missionary as the basis for the refrain of his poem: "Forever—never!/Never—forever!"

THE ARMORY, SPRINGFIELD, MASS., 1852
Historical Pictures Service, Chicago

The Arsenal at Springfield 343

Fine art, Engraving, *The Army, Springfield, Mass.*, 1852. The Springfield Armory was established by the Continental Army in 1794 as the first United States Arsenal. Located in Springfield, Massachusetts, this arsenal provided high quality weapons to the United States Army for two hundred years. Most famous of these weapons were the first American-made muskets of the revolution, the Springfield rifle of World War I, and MI rifle of World War II. In 1968 the armory was demilitarized and its handsome brick buildings became home to the Springfield Technical Community College and the Armory Museum, a weapons collection.

In this engraving, the artist shows the armory during the mid-nineteenth century when it was surrounded by a very fashionable residential neighborhood. The denizens of this area enjoyed using the ornamental gardens of the armory for their afternoon promenades.

You might use the following questions for discussion:

1. What impression of the armory does the engraving convey?
2. How does the impression conveyed by the engraving contrast with impression conveyed in Longfellow's poem?

4 **Discussion** What "instruments" is Longfellow referring to in line 30?

5 **Discussion** What is the speaker's suggestion in stanza 9?

6 **Critical Thinking and Reading** Call attention to the continued use of the organ metaphor in the last two stanzas.

Reader's Response What emotions does this poem evoke in you? Why?

25 The bursting shell, the gateway wrenched asunder,
        The rattling musketry, the clashing blade;
    And ever and anon, in tones of thunder
        The diapason of the cannonade,

    Is it, O man, with such discordant noises,
30   With such accursed instruments as these,
    Thou drownest Nature's sweet and kindly voices,
        And jarrest the celestial harmonies?

    Were half the power that fills the world with terror,
        Were half the wealth bestowed on camps and courts,
35 Given to redeem the human mind from error,
        There were no need of arsenals or forts:

    The warrior's name would be a name abhorrèd!
        And every nation, that should lift again
    Its hand against a brother, on its forehead
40   Would wear forevermore the curse of Cain!

    Down the dark future, through long generations,
        The echoing sounds grow fainter and then cease;
    And like a bell, with solemn, sweet vibrations,
        I hear once more the voice of Christ say, "Peace!"

45 Peace! and no longer from its brazen portals
        The blast of War's great organ shakes the skies!
    But beautiful as songs of the immortals,
        The holy melodies of love arise.

THINKING ABOUT THE SELECTION

Recalling

1. To what does the speaker first compare the arms in the arsenal?
2. (a) In the third stanza, what does the speaker hear? (b) Name three sounds that he hears in stanzas 5–7.
3. According to the speaker, what would be different if half the money and half the power devoted to fighting were "Given to redeem the human mind from error"?

Interpreting

4. What is the effect of the speaker's references to historical figures, cultures, places, and events?
5. Throughout the poem Longfellow develops an extended comparison between music and war. What is the effect of this comparison?
6. How would you summarize the speaker's attitude toward war?

Applying

7. Explain whether you think the speaker's attitude toward war is realistic.
8. In what ways do you think the poem might be different if it had been written today?

ANALYZING LITERATURE

Describing Stanza Forms

A **stanza** is a unit of poetry consisting of two or more lines arranged according to rhyme and meter.

Describe the stanza form of each of the following poems in terms of rhyme scheme and length.
1. "The Arsenal at Springfield"
2. "A Psalm of Life"
3. "The Tide Rises, The Tide Falls"

CRITICAL THINKING AND READING

Evaluating Longfellow's Poetry

Longfellow had very definite beliefs about the purpose of poetry and the characteristics of a good poem. First, he believed that poetry should be sweet, musical, and regular. He also thought that poetry should be agreeable in subject matter, not offensive or controversial, and that the subject matter of poetry should be timeless. Finally, he felt that all poetry should teach something about life.

Using one of Longfellow's poems as an example, explain how it fits his beliefs about poetry.

Commentary

Longfellow occasionally found his subjects in historic places or events. "The Arsenal at Springfield" was inspired by a visit to the arsenal. Another of his well-known poems, *Evangeline,* was inspired by an incident that occurred in Nova Scotia in 1755. The inhabitants of a French colony there, known as Acadia, had lived a simple and idyllic life until the British seized and dispersed the colony. Most of the inhabitants were deported. Longfellow developed a long, narrative poem around Evangeline and her betrothed, Gabriel, who are separated and put on different ships in the dispersal. The poem describes Evangeline's lifelong search for Gabriel, whom she ultimately finds on his deathbed.

Evangeline solidified Longfellow's reputation. When it was published in 1847, it was greeted with great enthusiasm both by the public and by critics. Nathaniel Hawthorne wrote in the Salem *Advertiser:* "The author has done himself justice, and has regard to his well-earned fame. . . ."

The Arsenal at Springfield 345

More About the Author Oliver Wendell Holmes was a popular lecturer as well as the dean of the Harvard Medical School. He was also the father of Oliver Wendell Holmes, Jr. (1841–1935), a distinguished Supreme Court Justice. In what ways might Holmes's many interests have been reflected in his work? How does Holmes typify the idea of a "renaissance" in New England?

Critical Evaluation The literary scholar Francis Murphy has noted: "From the 1860's through the 1880's Holmes published several volumes of poems and essays and . . . his professional writing for medical journals continued to win respect. In his last decades Holmes was an American institution, the most famous after-dinner speaker of his time and the most reliably witty writer of poems for special occasions. . . ."

OLIVER WENDELL HOLMES

1809–1894

An extraordinarily energetic man with a variety of talents and interests, Oliver Wendell Holmes made important contributions to both literature and medicine. In addition to serving as a professor of anatomy at Harvard University for thirty-five years and writing numerous professional articles, Holmes wrote three novels and several volumes of poems and essays.

Holmes, a descendant of seventeenth-century poet Anne Bradstreet (page 58), was born in Cambridge, Massachusetts. He attended Harvard University, where he was named class poet in 1829. Following his graduation Holmes entered Harvard Law School. While there, he wrote the poem "Old Ironsides" to protest the planned demolition of the battleship *Constitution,* nicknamed "Old Ironsides" because of its ability to withstand the attacks of British warships during the War of 1812. The poem, which aroused such protest that the ship was preserved as a national monument, earned Holmes national recognition as a poet.

After abandoning the study of law, Holmes studied medicine in Paris for several years. Then, in 1836, he returned to Harvard to complete his medical degree. In that same year Holmes also published his first collection of poetry, *Poems*.

In 1847 Holmes began his lengthy teaching career at Harvard. During his years there, he established himself as a leading medical researcher. At the same time, he continued his literary pursuits with energy and enthusiasm. Along with James Russell Lowell, Holmes helped to found the *Atlantic Monthly,* a literary magazine that is still published today. Holmes published many of his best-known works in the *Atlantic Monthly,* including his poem "The Chambered Nautilus" and a series of humorous essays eventually collected in *The Autocrat of the Breakfast-Table* (1858), his most popular book.

Holmes was known for his wise and witty conversation, which was preserved in *The Autocrat of the Breakfast-Table*. The Autocrat, the speaker in the essays, presides over the conversation among a variety of characters: a divinity student, the landlady, a Poor Relation, and later a School Teacher and two aspects of Holmes himself, the Poet and the Professor. The dramatic interplay among the various personalities provided a perfect excuse for humorous exaggeration, colorful expressions, and quotable quotes. Further essays were collected in *The Professor at the Breakfast-Table* (1860), *The Poet at the Breakfast-Table* (1872), and *Over the Teacups* (1891).

Retiring from medicine in 1882, Holmes devoted the final years of his life to writing and lecturing. He died in 1894, the last member of America's first generation of highly regarded writers.

Support Material

Teaching Portfolio
Teacher Backup, p. 455
Usage and Mechanics Worksheet, p. 459
Vocabulary Check, p. 460
Analyzing Literature Worksheet, *Using Meter and Scansion,* p. 461
Critical Thinking and Reading Worksheet, *Understanding Personification,* p. 462

Selection Test, p. 463

GUIDE FOR INTERPRETING

Old Ironsides; The Chambered Nautilus

Meter and Scansion. Meter is a systematic arrangement of stressed and unstressed syllables in poetry. The basic unit of meter is the foot. Usually a foot consists of one stressed syllable and one or more unstressed syllables. The most common foot in American and English verse is the iamb, which is made up of one unstressed syllable followed by a stressed syllable. Other common feet include the trochee, a stressed syllable followed by an unstressed syllable; the anapest, two unstressed syllables followed by a stressed syllable; and the dactyl, a stressed syllable followed by two unstressed syllables.

Meter is determined by combining the type of foot with the number of feet per line: monometer (one foot), dimeter (two feet), trimeter (three feet), tetrameter (four feet), pentameter (five feet), hexameter (six feet). For example, the following line from "The Chambered Nautilus" is written in iambic pentameter:

Its webs of living gauze no more unfurl;

Often, writers vary the number of feet per line in a poem. For example, a poet may alternate lines of iambic pentameter with lines of iambic trimeter. A poet may also introduce slight variations in the metrical pattern to avoid monotony or emphasize important words. For example, a poem written in iambic trimeter may contain several lines that end with two stressed syllables.

The analysis of the meter of poetry is called **scansion**. To scan a line of poetry, you divide it into feet and mark the stressed and unstressed syllables. You determine the meter by taking note of the type of foot being used and counting the number of feet in each line.

Commentary

Like the rhythm of music, the rhythm of poetry is caused by light and heavy beats, like the beating of a drum. The pattern, or meter, should be just regular enough to establish it but not become monotonous. When the poet wants to change the speed of a line or emphasize a word or phrase, he or she does it by altering the rhythm. The best way both to hear the rhythm and to understand a poem is to read it aloud— several times—as if you were saying it to someone. Try that with the following poems, using the punctuation to help with both rhythm and meaning. Do you ever use the rhythm of a sentence to persuade or command?

Writing

Holmes's poem "Old Ironsides" aroused strong public opinion about a current issue. Make a list of social and political issues about which you have strong opinions.

Literary Focus "Old Ironsides" is composed largely of iambic feet. The lines alternate between iambic tetrameter—four feet to a line—and iambic trimeter—three feet to a line. As in most poetry, the poet occasionally varies the rhythm. For example, line 13 begins with "No more," which is a spondee—two stressed syllables, and line 21 begins with "Nail to," which is a trochee. "The Chambered Nautilus" is also basically iambic.

Writing/Prior Knowledge For extra credit, students might be encouraged to list some of the most important issues from previous ages in history.

Vocabulary

Preteach the following vocabulary words:
vanquished (van′ kwisht) *adj.:* Defeated (p. 348, l. 10)
venturous (ven′ chər əs) *adj.:* Daring (p. 350, l. 3)
crypt (kript) *n.:* An underground chamber or vault (p. 350, l. 14)
lustrous (lus′ trəs) *adj.:* Shining (p. 351, l. 16)

Spelling Tip Point out that *crypt* is one of the few words in English in which a short *i* is spelled *y*.

Fine art, *U.S. Frigate Constitution,* by Nicholas Cammilliri. Americans have always been justifiably proud of their ship-building. Certain ships stand out in history as praiseworthy examples of this craft. The *U.S. Constitution,* nicknamed "Old Ironsides," is foremost among them. This ship remarkably survived many 1812 sea battles against heavy odds. American artists have glorified this ship in drawings, paintings, and prints. *The U.S. Frigate Constitution* by nineteenth-century artist Nicholas Cammilliri is one example. The *Constitution* has been preserved to this day by the United States Navy.

Consider the following questions for discussion:

1. Does the homage paid "Old Ironsides" by the poet match that of the painter? Explain your answer.
2. How is your reading of the poem enhanced by this painting?

Presentation

Motivation/Prior Knowledge Have students imagine that it is 1830, and they have just heard that the *Constitution* is going to be demolished. How would they respond?

Thematic Idea Another poem that was written to promote an important cause is "Douglass" by Paul Laurence Dunbar (p. 616).

Enrichment The *Constitution,* also known as "Old Ironsides," is now moored in Boston Harbor. It still attracts great numbers of visitors each year.

Purpose-Setting Question How does Holmes make his point?

U.S. FRIGATE CONSTITUTION, 1823
Nicholas Cammilliri
The Mariner's Museum, Newport News, Virginia

Old Ironsides

Oliver Wendell Holmes

Ay, tear her tattered ensign down!
    Long has it waved on high,
And many an eye has danced to see
    That banner in the sky;
5   Beneath it rung the battle shout,
    And burst the cannons roar—
The meteor of the ocean air
    Shall sweep the clouds no more.

Her deck, once red with heroes' blood,
10   Where knelt the vanquished foe,
When winds were hurrying o'er the flood,
    And waves were white below,
No more shall feel the victor's tread,
    Or know the conquered knee—

348   *New England Renaissance*

1 Critical Thinking and Reading
Call attention to the patriotic images the speaker uses. Is it the ship itself or its historic role that is most important?

15   The harpies[1] of the shore shall pluck
        The eagle of the sea!

     Oh, better that her shattered hulk
        Should sink beneath the wave;
     Her thunders shook the mighty deep,
20   And there should be her grave;
     Nail to the mast her holy flag,
        Set every threadbare sail,
     And give her to the god of storms,
        The lightning and the gale!

------

1. harpies (här′ pēz): In Greek mythology, hideous, filthy winged monsters with the head and trunk of a woman and the tail, legs, and talons of a bird. Here, the word refers to relentless, greedy, or grasping people.

2

THINKING ABOUT THE SELECTION

Recalling

1. Point out two images, or word pictures, the speaker uses in the first two stanzas to describe the battles in which "Old Ironsides" had been involved.
2. What does the speaker suggest might be a more fitting end for the ship?

Interpreting

3. What human qualities does "Old Ironsides" seem to represent for the speaker?
4. What does Holmes mean when he refers to "Old Ironsides" as "the eagle of the sea" (line 16)?
5. How does Holmes appeal in the poem to the American sense of patriotism?

Applying

6. When "Old Ironsides" was published, it aroused such protest that the ship was saved. Do you believe that a poem could have such a powerful effect on the American public today? Why or why not?

THINKING AND WRITING

Writing a Poem in Support of a Cause

Review your list of social and political issues. Decide which issue is most important to you. List the reasons why you feel so strongly about this issue. Think of some descriptive details that convey your feelings, and come up with some concrete images, or word pictures, related to the issue. Decide on the audience you would like to persuade to accept your opinion. Then use your list of details and images to write a poem expressing your opinion. Keep your audience in mind as you write. Do not worry about rhyme or rhythm. Focus on the content of your poem. When you revise make sure that you have included enough concrete images to allow your audience to visualize your subject.

Old Ironsides   349

Enrichment This poem was written in 1830, when the War of 1812 was still a living memory. It has been memorized and recited by thousands of people since that time.

Reader's Response How important do you think it is to preserve national monuments such as "Old Ironsides"? Explain.

Closure and Extension

ANSWERS TO THINKING ABOUT THE SELECTION
Recalling

1. The speaker relies on images of the flag, cannons bursting, heroes' blood, and victory.
2. He suggests that it would be better if the ship sank and was destroyed by storms and lightning.

Interpreting

3. The ship seems to represent patriotism and heroism.
4. An eagle is both a national symbol and a bird considered to have heroic qualities.
5. He appeals to their sense of patriotism by reminding them of the important battles in which the ship was involved.

Applying

6. Suggested Response: No, because fewer people read poetry.

THINKING AND WRITING

For help with this assignment, students can refer to Lesson 18, "Writing a Poem," in the Handbook of Writing About Literature.

Publishing Student Writing You may want to suggest to students that they submit their poems to your school's literary magazine.

The Chambered Nautilus

Oliver Wendell Holmes

1

This is the ship of pearl, which, poets feign,
    Sails the unshadowed main—
    The venturous bark that flings
On the sweet summer wind its purpled wings
5 In gulfs enchanted, where the Siren[1] sings,
    And coral reefs lie bare,
Where the cold sea-maids rise to sun their streaming hair.

2

Its webs of living gauze no more unfurl;
    Wrecked is the ship of pearl!
10   And every chambered cell,
Where its dim dreaming life was wont to dwell,
As the frail tenant shaped his growing shell,
    Before thee lies revealed—
Its irised[2] ceiling rent, its sunless crypt unsealed!

---

1. Siren (sī′ rən): In Greek mythology, one of several sea nymphs who lured sailors to their deaths by singing enchanting songs.
2. irised *adj.*: Rainbow colored.

15   Year after year beheld the silent toil
      That spread his lustrous coil;
      Still, as the spiral grew,
  He left the past year's dwelling for the new,
  Stole with soft step its shining archway through,
20   Built up its idle door,
  Stretched in his last-found home, and knew the old no more.

  Thanks for the heavenly message brought by thee,
      Child of the wandering sea,
      Cast from her lap, forlorn!
25   From thy dead lips a clearer note is born
  Than ever Triton³ blew from wreathèd horn!
      While on mine ear it rings,
  Through the deep caves of thought I hear a voice that sings:

  Build thee more stately mansions, O my soul,
30   As the swift seasons roll!
      Leave thy low-vaulted past!
  Let each new temple, nobler than the last,
  Shut thee from heaven with a dome more vast,
      Till thou at length art free,
35   Leaving thine outgrown shell by life's unresting sea!

---

3. Triton (trīt' 'n) *n.*: A Greek sea god with the body of a man and the tail of a fish, who usually carried a conch-shell trumpet.

THINKING ABOUT THE SELECTION

Recalling

1. What has happened to the nautilus the speaker is describing?
2. What did the nautilus do "as the spiral grew" (line 17)?
3. What does the voice that rings "through the deep caves of thought" tell the speaker?

Interpreting

4. Each year throughout the course of its life, the nautilus creates a new chamber of shell to house its growing body. How does Holmes compare this process to the development of the human soul?

Applying

5. What is it about the chambered nautilus that makes it appropriate for Holmes's message?
6. What can you learn from the life of the chambered nautilus?

ANALYZING LITERATURE

Using Meter and Scansion

  Meter is a systematic arrangement of stressed and unstressed syllables in poetry. **Scansion** is the process of analyzing meter.
1. Scan each line in the first stanza of "The Chambered Nautilus."
2. Identify the meter in each line.

The Chambered Nautilus   351

---

3 Discussion What is the speaker's attitude toward the "frail tenant" who kept moving into a new home?

4 Discussion What is the "heavenly message" the shell brings?

5 Critical Thinking and Reading The speaker sees the shell as a metaphor for life. What does he view as one purpose of life?

Reader's Response What associations do you have with seashells such as the chambered nautilus? Explain.

Closure and Extension

ANSWERS TO THINKING ABOUT THE SELECTION
Recalling

1. The animal is no longer within it.
2. It left its last dwelling for a newer one which gave it more room for "stretching."
3. The voice tells the speaker to keep building "more stately mansions."

Interpreting

4. The human soul should outgrow its constraints and expand until it is completely free.

Applying

5. Animals grow in other shells, but there are no clearly defined chambers to mark the progress. The nautilus is always moving out from the center into a wider realm.
6. Answers will differ. Students might comment that they can learn that it is important to keep growing throughout life.

ANSWERS TO ANALYZING LITERATURE

1. and 2. The first line is iambic pentameter with a trochee substitution in the first foot. The next two lines are basically iambic trimeter. (The first foot of line 2 has a trochee variation.) Lines 4 and 5 are basically iambic pentameter (with some variation in line 4). Line 6 is iambic trimeter. And line 7 is basically iambic hexameter.

More About the Author James Russell Lowell had strong political opinions, which came through in his writing. Like Thoreau, he opposed the Mexican War. As a Northerner, his first response to the oncoming Civil War was that the North should be separate from the South, but he eventually supported President Lincoln's position during the war. Do you think that writers have an obligation to use their talents to promote causes about which they feel strongly?

Critical Evaluation The literary scholar William Charvat has written:

"Among the Fireside Poets, Lowell was the most versatile, the most erudite, the least popular, and in the broad terms of literary statesmanship, the most influential. His claim to membership in the group was based on a very few well-known poems, and on the fact that the publishers of the group . . . bracketed him with the others and printed his work in editions uniform with theirs. This is not to say that he was not widely known and respected by people who never read him, or that he did not earn such reputation as he achieved; rather, that there was much in his work that could not attract a popular audience. His learning was too conspicuous, his approach to life was too bookish, and he spread his many talents so thin that he never became really famous for any one of them . . ."

JAMES RUSSELL LOWELL

1819–1891

James Russell Lowell may have been the most talented of the Fireside Poets. His literary career was disrupted by personal tragedies, however, and he was never able to fulfill his early promise as a poet. Still, Lowell did make many important contributions to the world of literature as a poet, editor, and critic.

Lowell was born in Cambridge, Massachusetts, the descendant of a prominent family. He graduated from Harvard Law School but quickly lost interest in practicing law. Instead, Lowell decided to pursue a career in literature, publishing his first book of poetry, *A Year's Life,* in 1841. While continuing to write poetry and essays, Lowell also supported the abolitionist movement. He frequently wrote editorials attacking slavery, thereby establishing himself as one of the country's leading abolitionist journalists.

In 1848 Lowell's literary career reached its peak. During that year he published three of his best works: *A Fable for Critics,* a satire of other American writers of his time; *The Biglow Papers,* a collection of poems and letters; and *The Vision of Sir Launfal,* an epic poem about medieval knighthood. All three works were very successful, earning him international fame.

These works, published when Lowell was only twenty-nine, demonstrate his varied interests. *The Vision of Sir Launfal* is the climax of his poetic romanticism. Inspired by the Arthurian legends, it teaches ethical lessons. For years it was regularly found in school texts. In *A Fable for Critics,* Lowell humorously criticizes his contemporaries, among them such established figures as Emerson and Hawthorne, and himself as well. In *The Biglow Papers* Lowell successfully used Yankee dialect and humor in a satire of American imperialism and Southern greed for slave territory.

Unfortunately, Lowell's literary success was overshadowed by tragic events in his personal life. Three of his four children died in infancy, and he lost his beloved wife, Maria, in 1853. Following Maria's death, Lowell lost his focus as a writer, and he found himself unable to produce poems or essays that matched his earlier work.

During the second half of his life, Lowell gradually turned away from writing toward other interests. In 1855 he succeeded Longfellow as professor of languages at Harvard, and he remained there until 1872. Lowell also helped to found the *Atlantic Monthly,* a respected literary magazine, and served as its first editor. Later Lowell became co-editor of the *North American Review,* another distinguished literary magazine. Then, in 1877, Lowell began a career in diplomacy, serving for a number of years as the American ambassador to Spain and, later, Great Britain.

Objectives
To compare and contrast tones

Support Material

Teaching Portfolio
Teacher Backup, p. 465
Usage and Mechanics Worksheet, p. 469
Vocabulary Check, p. 470
Analyzing Literature Worksheet, *Understanding Tone,* p. 471
Critical Thinking and Reading Worksheet, *Understanding Similes,* p. 472
Selection Test, p. 473

GUIDE FOR INTERPRETING

Auspex; The First Snowfall

Writer's Techniques

Tone. Tone refers to the writer's attitude toward his or her subject, characters, or audience. The tone of a work of literature is revealed through the writer's choice of words and portrayal of characters and events. For example, in a work with a humorous tone a writer might use witty language and include amusing descriptions of characters and events.

Tone can dramatically affect the way you respond to the subject and characters in a literary work. For example, if a writer expresses a sympathetic attitude toward a character, you are also likely to be sympathetic toward that character. In contrast, if the writer expresses contempt for a character, you are likely to have a negative response to that character.

Your awareness of tone can be important to your understanding of a literary work, because tone is often closely related to the theme, or central idea. For example, a work written to convey the cruelty and destructiveness of war is likely to have a solemn or despairing tone.

Writing

These two poems by Lowell deal with emotional reactions to some aspect of a season. People often have strong emotional reactions to the first snowstorm of each winter. Describe your typical response to a change of season—either the end of one or the beginning of another.

Primary Source

Lowell's early poetry ranks among the best America has. Although he did not develop this early promise in his later work, Lowell always felt himself to be more than anything else a poet. In a letter to a fellow journalist before beginning work on some Abolition writing, Lowell wrote: "If I have any vocation, it is the making of verse. When I take my pen for that, the world opens itself ungrudgingly before me, everything seems clear and easy, as it seems sinking to the bottom would be as one leans over the edge of his boat in one of those dear coves at Fresh Pond. But, when I do prose, . . . I feel as if I were wasting time and keeping back my message. My true place is to serve the cause as a poet. Then my heart leaps on before me into the conflict."

His engaging sincerity and earnestness are again evident when, in a critical essay, he later writes: ". . . all great poetry must smack of the soil, for it must be rooted in it, must suck life and substance from it, . . . but it must do so with the aspiring instinct of the pine that climbs forever toward diviner air, and not in the groveling fashion of the potato."

Guide for Interpreting 353

Literary Focus Students often have difficulty making the distinction between mood and tone. Emphasize the fact that tone refers to the attitude that the writer expresses, while mood refers to the atmosphere that he or she creates.

Writing/Prior Knowledge Students who live in areas with snow may also wish to describe the appearance of the storm. What type of flakes usually fall in the year's first snowstorm?

Vocabulary

Preteach the following vocabulary words:
delusion (di lōō′ zhən) *n.:* Deception (p. 355, l.13)
gloaming (glō′ miŋ) *n.:* Evening dusk; twilight (p. 356, l.1)

Humanities Note

Fine art, *Low Branch,* 1968, by Scarlett. This is an acrylic painting by a contemporary American artist. Acrylics are a fairly recent innovation in painting. Many artists prefer this type of paint over oils for a variety of reasons. Acrylics are easily mixed with water, making thinning and cleaning up easy. Once the paint is dry, however, it is completely waterproof and very durable. Acrylics dry rapidly, and the colors range from delicate to very intense.

In this painting the artist was able to achieve remarkable detail and complex textures. This close-up of leaves and seed pods provides an opportunity to see and experience a common sight in a new way. It makes the viewer aware of the infinite complexity in nature.

You might use the following questions for discussion:

1. Why do you think a painting of leaves, rather than of birds, was chosen to accompany the poem "Auspex"?
2. What style would you attribute to this painting?
3. What makes this painting a different kind of visual experience from most pictures concerning Nature?

LOW BRANCH, 1968
Scarlett
Courtesy New York Graphic Society

Auspex[1]

James Russell Lowell

1
My heart, I cannot still it,
Nest that had song birds in it;
And when the last shall go,

2
The dreary days, to fill it,
5 Instead of lark or linnet,
Shall whirl dead leaves and snow.

Had they been swallows only,
Without the passion stronger
That skyward longs and sings—

3 10 Woe's me, I shall be lonely
When I can feel no longer
The impatience of their wings!

A moment, sweet delusion,
Like birds the brown leaves hover;

15 But it will not be long
Before their wild confusion

4
Fall wavering down to cover
The poet and his song.

1. Auspex (ôs′ peks) *n.*: In ancient Rome, someone who watched for omens in the flight of birds.

THINKING ABOUT THE SELECTION

Recalling

1. According to the first stanza, what will "fill" the speaker's heart when the songbirds have gone?
2. According to the second stanza, when will the speaker be lonely?
3. (a) What is the "sweet delusion" the speaker refers to in lines 13–14? (b) What will happen when the delusion ends?

Interpreting

4. In this poem Lowell compares songbirds to the happiness that provides him with poetic inspiration. To what does he compare the emptiness following the disappearance of his happiness?
5. (a) What do the swallows (line 7) represent? (b) How is this different from what the songbirds represent?
6. What does the image of the leaves falling and covering the poet represent?

Applying

7. What type of event in Lowell's life might have prompted him to write this poem?

Commentary

To poke fun at your literary contemporaries, without getting into hot water yourself is quite a feat. Lowell managed to do that in *A Fable for Critics*. The work was immensely popular.

Among the introductory "candid remarks" addressed to the reader, he says of the work: "I began it, intending a Fable, a frail, slender thing, rhyme-winged, with a sting in its tail."

The satirical portraits, of Emerson, Whittier, Hawthorne, and others do contain satirical "sting" but also wit and good humor. At the end Lowell laughs at himself:

"There is Lowell, who's striving
   Parnassus to climb
With a whole bale of *isms* tied
   together with rhyme,
He might get on alone, spite of
   brambles and boulders,
But he can't with that bundle he
   has on his shoulders,
The top of the hill he will ne'er
   come nigh reaching
Till he learns the distinction
   'twixt singing and preaching."

Auspex 355

Reader's Response What emotions do the images in Lowell's poem evoke in you?

The First Snowfall

James Russell Lowell

The snow had begun in the gloaming,
    And busily all the night
Had been heaping field and highway
    With a silence deep and white.

5 Every pine and fir and hemlock
    Wore ermine too dear for an earl,
And the poorest twig on the elm tree
    Was ridged inch deep with pearl.

From sheds new-roofed with Carrara[1]
10   Came Chanticleer's[2] muffled crow,
The stiff rails softened to swan's-down,
    And still fluttered down the snow.

I stood and watched by the window
    The noiseless work of the sky,
15 And the sudden flurries of snowbirds,
    Like brown leaves whirling by.

I thought of a mound in sweet Auburn[3]
    Where a little headstone stood;
How the flakes were folding it gently,
20   As did robins the babes in the wood.

Up spoke our own little Mabel,
    Saying, "Father, who makes it snow?"
And I told of the good All-Father
    Who cares for us here below.

25 Again I looked at the snowfall,
    And thought of the leaden sky
That arched o'er our first great sorrow,
    When that mound was heaped so high.

---

1. **Carrara** (kə rä′ rə) *n.*: Fine, white marble.
2. **Chanticleer's** (chan′ tə klirz′): Referring to a rooster.
3. **Auburn:** Mt. Auburn Cemetery in Cambridge, Massachusetts.

I remembered the gradual patience
30   That fell from that cloud like snow,
Flake by flake, healing and hiding
    The scar that renewed our woe.

And again to the child I whispered,
    "The snow that husheth all,
35 Darling, the merciful Father
    Alone can make it fall!"

Then, with eyes that saw not, I kissed her;
    And she, kissing back, could not know
That *my* kiss was given to her sister,
40   Folded close under deepening snow.

7

8

THINKING ABOUT THE SELECTION

Recalling

1. (a) When had the snowfall begun? (b) How much snow covered the "poorest twig on the elm tree" by morning?
2. Of what does the snowstorm make the speaker think?
3. (a) What question does the speaker's daughter ask him? (b) How does he respond at first? (c) What does he later add to his response?
4. What does the speaker's daughter not know when he kisses her?

Interpreting

5. How does the speaker imply that his sorrow resulted from the death of his daughter without directly stating it?
6. (a) To what does the speaker compare his sorrow (lines 25–28)? (b) To what does the speaker compare the process of recovering from his sorrow (lines 29–32)?

7. What does the speaker's comment to his daughter suggest about his belief in the source of emotional healing?
8. In your own words, describe the tone of "The First Snowfall."

Applying

9. This poem suggests that a natural event, such as a snowstorm, can both remind us of sorrow and help to heal it. Explain why you do or do not agree with this suggestion.

THINKING AND WRITING

Comparing and Contrasting Tones

Write an essay in which you compare and contrast the tones of "Auspex" and "The First Snowfall." Start by rereading the two poems, taking note of the similarities and differences in tone and the way in which the tone is revealed. Look over your notes and sum up the similarities and differences in a topic sentence. Then write your essay, using passages from each poem for support. When you finish writing, revise your essay and prepare a final copy.

The First Snowfall   357

More About the Author John Greenleaf Whittier was active in politics as well as literature; he was elected to the Massachusetts legislature, ran unsuccessfully for Congress, and was a founder of the Republican party. Ask students to discuss the implications of a poet's involvement in politics. Might having another career get in a poet's way? Or might it inspire the poet?

Critical Evaluation In the introduction to *Poetry of the New England Renaissance*, George F. Whicher writes: "As a political poet John Greenleaf Whittier had no equal in his generation. He was a plain farmer from north of Boston, untypical only in his devotion to the Quaker creed of his family. He had little education beyond what he could acquire in newspaper offices and by eager reading. With all his honest heart he believed in the promises of democracy, and in the struggle to realize them for even the lowliest of mankind he made himself the incandescent conscience of the American people . . ."

JOHN GREENLEAF WHITTIER

1807–1892

John Greenleaf Whittier stands apart from the other Fireside Poets in several ways. Unlike Longfellow, Holmes, and Lowell, Whittier was born in poverty and received virtually no formal education. He was also more deeply involved with the social issues of his time than were the other poets. Finally, because of his devotion to the abolitionist movement, Whittier, unlike the other poets, did not gain national prominence as a poet until late in his life.

Whittier was born and raised on a farm near Haverhill, Massachusetts. His parents were Quakers, who taught him to believe in hard work, simplicity, pacifism, religious devotion, and social justice. Because he worked long hours on the debt-ridden family farm, Whittier suffered from poor health throughout much of his childhood. Though he was able to attend school for only one year, he educated himself by reading—primarily the Bible and other religious writings and the poetry of Scottish poet Robert Burns. During his teens he began writing poetry, and when he was eighteen his first poem was published in a local newspaper.

As a young man, Whittier became deeply committed to the abolitionist movement. He worked as a writer and editor for antislavery newspapers, wrote a large number of antislavery poems, spoke at abolitionist rallies, and became active in politics, serving a term in the Massachusetts legislature. Unfortunately, Whittier's dedication to abolitionism prevented him from gaining national recognition as a poet until after the Civil War.

His abolitionist work, however, did bring him recognition as a speaker and journalist—as well as personal danger. On a speaking tour in New Hampshire in 1835, he and a British abolitionist were attacked by a hostile mob. Driving their carriage through a hail of bullets, they somehow escaped with their lives.

When the war ended, Whittier turned away from politics, focused his attention on writing poetry, and established himself as one of the country's leading poets. He earned national fame in 1866, when he published his most highly regarded work, *Snowbound*. In this poem and in many later poems, Whittier vividly depicts the warmth and simplicity of life in rural New England.

As the way of life depicted in his poetry disappeared, the popularity of Whittier's poems grew. By the time of his death, Whittier had enjoyed more than twenty-five years of success as a poet. Yet he never allowed his success to affect his warmth, simplicity, and modesty, and he remained faithful at all times to his social and spiritual convictions.

358   New England Renaissance

Objectives

1 To appreciate imagery
2 To evaluate the effect of imagery
3 To use vivid adjectives
4 To write a poem using imagery

Support Material

Teaching Portfolio
Teacher Backup, p. 475
Grammar in Action Worksheet, *Analyzing Sentences,* p. 480
Usage and Mechanics Worksheet, p. 482
Vocabulary Check, p. 483
Analyzing Literature Worksheet, *Understanding Imagery,* p. 484

Critical Thinking and Reading Worksheet, *Evaluating the Effect of Imagery,* p. 485
Selection Test, p. 486

GUIDE FOR INTERPRETING

from Snowbound; Hampton Beach

Imagery. Imagery refers to words or phrases that create mental pictures, or images, that appeal to one or more of the five senses—sight, hearing, touch, smell, or taste. Most often, images appeal to the reader's sense of sight. For example, when Whittier writes, "The sun . . . rose cheerless over hills of gray," he creates a visual picture. Sometimes, however, images present sensations that cannot be visualized. For example, when Whittier refers to "a hard, dull bitterness of cold," he presents an image that you can feel but cannot see. A single image may also appeal to more than one sense. Whittier creates an image that you can both see and feel when he writes, "Unwarmed by any sunset light the gray day darkened into night."

Writing

What images come to mind when you envision the morning after a snowstorm? What images do you associate with the beach? List the images that come to mind when you think of each of these scenes.

Primary Source

During 1864 and 1865 Whittier worked on *Snowbound*. He wrote a prefatory note for the edition of 1892. From it we can see that he drew on the oral history, stories and folk tales of New England, his memories of family and neighbors, and his Quaker religious mysticism.

> The inmates of the family at the Whittier homestead who are referred to in the poem were my father, mother, my brother and two sisters, and my uncle and aunt both unmarried.
> In my boyhood, in our lonely farmhouse, we had scanty sources of information; . . . Under such circumstances storytelling was a necessary resource in the long winter evenings. My father when a young man had traversed the wilderness of Canada, and could tell us of his adventures with Indians and wild beasts, and of his sojourn in the French villages. . . . My mother, who was born in the Indian-haunted region of Somersworth, New Hampshire, . . . told us of the inroads of the savages, and the narrow escape of her ancestors. She described strange people who lived on the [rivers], among whom was Bantam the sorceror. I have in my possession the wizard's 'conjuring book,' which he solemnly opened when consulted. . . .

A quotation from the "conjuring book" ends ". . . as the celestial Fire drives away dark spirits, so also this our Fire of Wood doth the same." Whittier then finishes his note with the first stanza of Emerson's poem "The Snowstorm."

Guide for Interpreting 359

Literary Focus Point out to students that the many detailed images in each poem help to create an overall image.

Writing/Prior Knowledge Students may try writing unconnected phrases suggesting images that add up to a broader picture.

Vocabulary

Preteach the following vocabulary words:
ominous (äm' ə nəs) *adj.:* Sinister (p. 360, l.6)
prophecy (präf' ə sē) *n.:* Prediction of the future (p. 360, l.6)
querulous (kwer' ə ləs) *adj.:* Complaining (p. 360, l.30)
patriarch (pā' trē ärk) *n.:* The father and ruler of a family or tribe (p. 362, l.89)
luminous (loo' mə nəs) *adj.:* Shining (p. 366, l.4)
tremulous (trem' yoo ləs) *adj.:* Trembling (p. 366, l.6)
asunder (ə sun' dər) *adv.:* Into parts or pieces (p. 368, l.36)

Master Teacher Note The lifestyle recorded in "Snowbound" has largely disappeared. To convey a visual image of the time, bring in copies of paintings of mid-nineteenth century America. The watercolor works of Winslow Homer would be among the most appropriate examples.

Thematic Idea Another selection that explores the effects of a snowstorm is "The Snowstorm" by Ralph Waldo Emerson (p. 379).

Purpose-Setting Question How do the people react to being isolated by the storm?

1 Clarification An idyll is a poem usually describing charming aspects of rural life and events.

2 Discussion What is the mood of the first four lines?

3 Critical Thinking and Reading The speaker uses very precise language in his description. He makes a very careful distinction between a portent and a threat.

4 Literary Focus Call attention to the images in lines 12–13 and 15–18. To what senses do these images appeal?

5 Discussion How does the family respond to the threat of the storm?

6 Literary Focus What effect is created by the images in this passage?

7 Discussion How is the storm described?

from **Snowbound**

John Greenleaf Whittier

A Winter Idyll

The sun that brief December day
Rose cheerless over hills of gray,
And, darkly circled, gave at noon
A sadder light than waning moon.
5 Slow tracing down the thickening sky
Its mute and ominous prophecy,
A portent seeming less than threat,
It sank from sight before it set.
A chill no coat, however stout,
10 Of homespun stuff could quite shut out,
A hard, dull bitterness of cold,
That checked, mid-vein, the circling race
Of lifeblood in the sharpened face,
The coming of the snowstorm told.
15 The wind blew east; we heard the roar
Of Ocean on his wintry shore,
And felt the strong pulse throbbing there
Beat with low rhythm our inland air.

Meanwhile we did our nightly chores—
20 Brought in the wood from out of doors,
Littered the stalls, and from the mows
Raked down the herd's-grass for the cows:
Heard the horse whinnying for his corn;
And, sharply clashing horn on horn,
25 Impatient down the stanchion[1] rows
The cattle shake their walnut bows;
While, peering from his early perch
Upon the scaffold's pole of birch,
The cock his crested helmet bent
30 And down his querulous challenge sent.

Unwarmed by any sunset light
The gray day darkened into night,
A night made hoary with the swarm
And whirl-dance of the blinding storm,

---

1. stanchion (stan′ chən): A restraining device fitted around the neck of a cow to confine it to its stall.

35 As zigzag, wavering to and fro,
    Crossed and recrossed the wingèd snow:
    And ere the early bedtime came
    The white drift piled the window frame,
    And through the glass the clothesline posts
40 Looked in like tall and sheeted ghosts.

    So all night long the storm roared on:
    The morning broke without a sun;
    In tiny spherule² traced with lines
    Of Nature's geometric signs,
45 In starry flake, and pellicle,³
    All day the hoary meteor fell;
    And, when the second morning shone,
    We looked upon a world unknown,
    On nothing we could call our own.
50 Around the glistening wonder bent
    The blue walls of the firmament,
    No cloud above, no earth below—
    A universe of sky and snow!
    The old familiar sights of ours
55 Took marvelous shapes; strange domes and towers
    Rose up where sty or corncrib stood,
    Or garden wall, or belt of wood;
    A smooth white mound the brush pile showed,
    A fenceless drift what once was road;
60 The bridle post an old man sat
    With loose-flung coat and high cocked hat;
    The wellcurb had a Chinese roof;
    And even the long sweep,⁴ high aloof,
    In its slant splendor, seemed to tell
65 Of Pisa's leaning miracle.⁵

    A prompt, decisive man, no breath
    Our father wasted: "Boys, a path!"
    Well pleased (for when did farmer boy
    Count such a summons less than joy?)
70 Our buskins⁶ on our feet we drew;
    With mittened hands, and caps drawn low,
    To guard our necks and ears from snow,
    We cut the solid whiteness through.
    And, where the drift was deepest, made

---

2. spherule (sfer' o͞ol): A small sphere.
3. pellicle (pel' i k'l): A thin film.
4. sweep: A pole with a bucket at one end, used for raising water from a well.
5. Pisa's leaning miracle: The famous leaning tower of Pisa in Italy.
6. buskins: High-cut shoes.

from *Snowbound* 361

---

8 Discussion How much time has elapsed since the beginning of the poem?

9 Discussion How does the snow reshape the landscape?

10 Critical Thinking and Reading Note how the speaker captures his father's character in just two lines.

11 Discussion How does the speaker's reference to Aladdin's cave contribute to the sense of mystery concerning the newfallen snow?

12 **Discussion** According to the speaker, what makes the solitude so intense?

13 **Literary Focus** Point out the auditory imagery that the speaker uses.

14 **Critical Thinking and Reading** The descriptions in lines 110–115 focus on the absence of an accustomed sound.

15 **Critical Thinking and Reading** In this stanza, the speaker begins to contrast the cozy warmth indoors to the cold outside.

```
75   A tunnel walled and overlaid
     With dazzling crystal: we had read
     Of rare Aladdin's⁷ wondrous cave,
     And to our own his name we gave,
     With many a wish the luck were ours
80   To test his lamp's supernal powers.
     We reached the barn with merry din,
     And roused the prisoned brutes within,
     The old horse thrust his long head out,
     And grave with wonder gazed about;
85   The cock his lusty greeting said,
     And forth his speckled harem led;
     The oxen lashed their tails, and hooked,
     And mild reproach of hunger looked;
     The hornèd patriarch of the sheep,
90   Like Egypt's Amun⁸ roused from sleep,
     Shook his sage head with gesture mute,
     And emphasized with stamp of foot.

     All day the gusty north wind bore
     The loosening drift its breath before;
95   Low circling round its southern zone,
     The sun through dazzling snow-mist shone.
     No church bell lent its Christian tone
     To the savage air, no social smoke
     Curled over woods of snow-hung oak.
100  A solitude made more intense
     By dreary-voicèd elements,
     The shrieking of the mindless wind,
     The moaning tree boughs swaying blind,
     And on the glass the unmeaning beat
105  Of ghostly fingertips of sleet.
     Beyond the circle of our hearth
     No welcome sound of toil or mirth
     Unbound the spell, and testified
     Of human life and thought outside.
110  We minded that the sharpest ear
     The buried brooklet could not hear,
     The music of whose liquid lip
     Had been to us companionship,
     And, in our lonely life, had grown
115  To have an almost human tone.

     As night drew on, and, from the crest
     Of wooded knolls that ridged the west,
```

7. **Aladdin's:** Referring to Aladdin, a boy in *The Arabian Nights* who found a magic lamp and through its powers discovered a treasure in a cave.
8. **Amun:** An Egyptian god with a ram's head.

Grammar in Action

Being able to **analyze a sentence** can help you to comprehend and appreciate poetry. The first unit to distinguish is the independent clause, which usually ends with a period, a semicolon, or a comma and a conjunction. For example, Whittier includes this independent clause in lines 93–94:

All day the gusty north wind bore
The loosening drift its breath before;

Having identified the independent clause, you may have to pause to analyze poetic inversions of normal word order.

its breath before   = before its breath.

Next, try to identify common sentence elements.

the gusty north wind   = subject
bore   = verb
the loosening drift   = direct object
All day, its breath before   = adverb phrases

Finally, reread the lines as they were written to restore their rhyme and meter.

OLD HOLLEY HOUSE, COS COB
John Henry Twachtman
Cincinnati Art Museum

Fine art, *Old Holley House, Cos Cob* (c. 1890–1900), by John Henry Twachtman. John Henry Twachtman (1853–1902) was born in Cincinnati, Ohio. He was a student at the School of Design of Cincinnati, and he studied in Munich and Paris at the Academie Julien. He was awarded the Webb Prize at the Society of American Artists in 1888, the Temple gold medal in 1895, and was a member of the American Art Club in Munich. In 1898 he founded an organization called "Ten American Painters." Twachtman is regarded as one of the best American landscape painters and was a leading American practitioner of French Impressionism. His style was innovative, especially in his use of iridescent colors, his brush strokes, his lack of traditional form-molding shadows, and his use of blue to depict shadows on snow.

In this painting Twachtman used soft colors. The picture may seem flat, but on closer examination it reveals remarkable depth and vibrance, such as might be seen on a bright, snowy day.

You might use the following questions for discussion:
1. What colors has the artist used in depicting the snow?
2. Why do you think the artist used more than just white paint to depict the snow?
3. What words from the poem can be used to describe the picture?

The sun, a snow-blown traveler, sank
From sight beneath the smothering bank,
120 We piled, with care, our nightly stack
Of wood against the chimney back—
The oaken log, green, huge, and thick,
And on its top the stout backstick;
The knotty forestick laid apart,

from *Snowbound* 363

Student Activity 1. Identify the subject, the verbs, the direct objects, and the adverb in lines 85–86 of the excerpt from *Snowbound*.

Student Activity 2. Notice that Whittier almost never divides an internal grammatical unit with a line break. Analyze lines 110–115 from *Snowbound* and identify the lines that contain each of the following items.
1. the subject of the main clause
2. the verb of the main clause
3. the direct object of the main clause
4. the subject of the subordinate clause
5. the verb of the subordinate clause
6. the direct object of the subordinate clause
7. the subject of the adjective clause
8. the verbs of the adjective clause
9. the predicate nominative of the adjective clause
10. the infinitive adverb phrase in the adjective clause

125 And filled between with curious art
     The ragged brush; then, hovering near,
     We watched the first red blaze appear,
     Heard the sharp crackle, caught the gleam
     On whitewashed wall and sagging beam,
130 Until the old, rude-furnished room
     Burst, flowerlike, into rosy bloom;
     While radiant with a mimic flame
     Outside the sparkling drift became,
     And through the bare-boughed lilac tree
135 Our own warm hearth seemed blazing free.
     The crane and pendent trammels[9] showed,
     The Turks' heads[10] on the andirons glowed;
     While childish fancy, prompt to tell
     The meaning of the miracle,
140 Whispered the old rhyme: *"Under the tree,*
     When fire outdoors burns merrily,
     There the witches are making tea."

     The moon above the eastern wood
     Shone at its full; the hill range stood
145 Transfigured in the silver flood,
     Its blown snows flashing cold and keen,
     Dead white, save where some sharp ravine
     Took shadow, or the somber green
     Of hemlocks turned to pitchy black
150 Against the whiteness at their back.
     For such a world and such a night
     Most fitting that unwarming light,
     Which only seemed where'er it fell
     To make the coldness visible.

155 Shut in from all the world without,
     We sat the clean-winged hearth[11] about,
     Content to let the north wind roar
     In baffled rage at pane and door,
     While the red logs before us beat
160 The frost line back with tropic heat;
     And ever, when a louder blast
     Shook beam and rafter as it passed,
     The merrier up its roaring draft
     The great throat of the chimney laughed;
165 The house dog on his paws outspread

----

9. trammels: Adjustable pothooks hanging from the movable arm, or crane, attached to the hearth.
10. Turks' heads: Turbanlike knots at the top of the andirons.
11. clean-winged hearth: A turkey wing was used for the hearth broom.

Laid to the fire his drowsy head,
The cat's dark silhouette on the wall
A couchant tiger's seemed to fall;
And, for the winter fireside meet,
170 Between the andirons' straddling feet,
The mug of cider simmered slow,
The apples sputtered in a row,
And, close at hand, the basket stood
With nuts from brown October's wood.

THINKING ABOUT THE SELECTION

Recalling

1. (a) What weather conditions forewarn the speaker of the approaching snowstorm? (b) How does the coming storm affect the family's nightly routine?
2. How long does the storm last?
3. (a) After the storm has ended, what does the speaker's father tell the boys to do? (b) How do the boys respond to the request?

Interpreting

4. What does the family's response to the coming of the storm suggest about their relationship with nature?
5. What descriptive details in lines 47–80 convey the speaker's sense of wonder and amazement upon viewing the snow-covered landscape?
6. What descriptive details in lines 93–115 convey a sense of solitude?
7. (a) What details in the final stanza convey a sense of warmth and security? (b) How do the details in lines 143–154 reinforce this?

Applying

8. Though for the most part snowstorms no longer isolate people as they did in Whittier's time, we sometimes experience a similar sense of isolation during power failures. In what ways do you think the response of today's families to a blackout is similar to and different from the family's response to their forced isolation in *Snowbound*?

ANALYZING LITERATURE

Understanding Imagery

Imagery appeals to one or more of the five senses. For example, when Whittier writes, "The sun . . . sank from sight beneath the smothering bank," he creates an image that appeals to your sense of sight.

Select three images in this excerpt from *Snowbound*. Explain to which sense each image appeals.

CRITICAL THINKING AND READING

Evaluating the Effect of Imagery

Because we all share the same capacity for physical sensations, imagery provides a natural link between the writer's observations, ideas, and experiences and our own imaginations. When used effectively, imagery allows us to picture each place and event the writer describes—even places and events unlike any we have actually seen. In *Snowbound*, for example, Whittier's imagery makes it possible for us to visualize his yard the morning after the snowstorm.

1. Explain what makes the imagery Whittier uses in describing the snowstorm effective.
2. Explain what makes the imagery used in describing the scene inside his house the night after the storm effective.

from *Snowbound* 365

(b) It does not affect their nightly routine.
2. It begins in late afternoon, continues through the night, lasts the whole next day, and has stopped by the second morning.
3. (a) He tells them to make a path. (b) They are pleased by his request.

Interpreting

4. It suggests that they live in harmony with nature and do not fear such natural events as a snowstorm.
5. Answers will differ. Details include, "No clouds above, no earth below," and "Around the glistening wonder bent/The blue walls of firmament."
6. Answers will differ. Details include, "The moaning tree boughs swaying blind" and "The buried brooklet could not hear."
7. (a) Answers will differ. Details include, "We sat the clean-winged hearth about" and "The mug of cider simmered slow." (b) They capture a sense of the cold, threatening weather outside.

Applying

8. Answers will differ. Students may comment that today's families experience the same sense of warmth and security during a blackout.

ANSWERS TO ANALYZING LITERATURE

Suggested Response: "Hills of gray" appeals to the sense of sight; "the roar of the ocean" appeals to the sense of hearing; and "the blue walls of the firmament" appeals to the sense of sight.

CRITICAL THINKING AND READING

1. Suggested Response: Whittier's use of vivid details that appeal to a number of the senses makes his description effective.
2. Suggested Response: Whittier's use of vivid details in describing the scene inside and his presentation of contrasting images of the scene outside make the description effective.

Closure and Extension

ANSWERS TO THINKING ABOUT THE SELECTION
Recalling

1. (a) There is hardly any sun to be seen, and the sky is thickening.

Motivation/Prior Knowledge
Have students imagine that they are looking out over a beach at sunset. What types of emotions would they experience?

Purpose-Setting Question
What overall impression of the landscape does the speaker convey?

1 **Literary Focus** Call attention to the cumulative effect of such adjectives as "glitters," "dazzled," "luminous," and "misty."

2 **Discussion** What is meant by the "tremulous shadow of the sea"?

3 **Critical Thinking and Reading** Have students determine where the "we" of the poem are and where they are going.

4 **Literary Focus** In the fourth stanza the predominant images appeal to the sense of touch.

5 **Critical Thinking and Reading** In what way does the fifth stanza serve as a transition?

6 **Literary Focus** What impression does this image convey?

7 **Discussion** How does the focus of the poem change in the sixth stanza?

Hampton Beach

John Greenleaf Whittier

The sunlight glitters keen and bright,
  Where, miles away,
Lies stretching to my dazzled sight
A luminous belt, a misty light,
5 Beyond the dark pine bluffs and wastes of sandy gray.

The tremulous shadow of the sea!
  Against its ground
Of silvery light, rock, hill, and tree,
Still as a picture, clear and free,
10 With varying outline mark the coast for miles around.

On—on—we tread with loose-flung rein
  Our seaward way,
Through dark-green fields and blossoming grain,
Where the wild brier-rose skirts the lane,
15 And bends above our heads the flowering locust spray.

Ha! like a kind hand on my brow
  Comes this fresh breeze,
Cooling its dull and feverish glow,
While through my being seems to flow
20 The breath of a new life, the healing of the seas!

Now rest we, where this grassy mound
  His feet hath set
In the great waters, which have bound
His granite ankles greenly round
25 With long and tangled moss, and weeds with cool spray wet.

Good-bye to pain and care! I take
  Mine ease today:
Here where these sunny waters break,
And ripples this keen breeze, I shake
30 All burdens from the heart, all weary thoughts away.

I draw a freer breath, I seem
  Like all I see—
Waves in the sun, the white-winged gleam
Of sea birds in the slanting beam
35 And far-off sails which flit before the south wind free.

QUODDY HEAD
John Marin
Art Resource

Hampton Beach 367

Humanities Note

Fine art, *Quoddy Head,* 1933, by John Marin. John Marin (1870–1953) was born in Rutherford, New Jersey. He trained as an architect at Stevens Institute and studied painting at the Pennsylvania Academy of Fine Arts and the Art Students League in New York. His work is represented in many great museums, including the Metropolitan Museum of Art in New York, the San Francisco Museum of Art, and the Phillips Memorial Gallery in Washington, D.C. Although he produced many oil paintings and etchings, Marin is best known for his watercolors. His spontaneous brushwork sparkles with freshness, and his style suggests atmosphere by means of loose washes of paint. His work has a quality of dynamic balance: lines and forces seem to be in conflict, yet the work possesses a compositional core.

In this painting, an abstract beach scene, the fragmented forms, lines, and colors unite visually to form a balanced whole.

You might use the following for discussion:

1. What physical sensations, such as temperature and wind quality, does this painting suggest?
2. Why might an abstract picture like this one be more effective than a realistic rendering?
3. What adjectives from the poem can be used in describing this painting?

8 **Discussion** Why would the experience at the beach lead to "listless quietude of mind"?

9 **Discussion** What will the speaker take back from the beach?

Reader's Response What thoughts and emotions does this poem evoke in you? Why?

So when time's veil shall fall asunder,
   The soul may know
No fearful change, nor sudden wonder,
Nor sink the weight of mystery under,
40   But with the upward rise, and with the vastness grow.

   And all we shrink from now may seem
     No new revealing;
   Familiar as our childhood's stream,
   Or pleasant memory of a dream,
45   The loved and cherished past upon the new life stealing.

   Serene and mild the untried light
     May have its dawning;
   And, as in summer's northern night
   The evening and the dawn unite,
50   The sunset hues of time blend with the soul's new morning.

   I sit alone; in foam and spray
     Wave after wave
   Breaks on the rocks which, stern and gray,
   Shoulder the broken tide away,
55   Or murmurs hoarse and strong through mossy cleft and cave.

   What heed I of the dusty land
     And noisy town?
   I see the mighty deep expand
   From its white line of glimmering sand
60   To where the blue of heaven on bluer waves shuts down!

   In listless quietude of mind,
     I yield to all
   The change of cloud and wave and wind;
   And passive on the flood reclined,
65   I wander with the waves, and with them rise and fall.

   But look, thou dreamer! wave and shore
     In shadow lie;
   The night-wind warns me back once more
   To where, my native hilltops o'er,
70   Bends like an arch of fire the glowing sunset sky.

   So then, beach, bluff, and wave, farewell!
     I bear with me
   No token stone nor glittering shell,
   But long and oft shall memory tell
75   Of this brief thoughtful hour of musing by the sea.

THINKING ABOUT THE SELECTION

Recalling

1. (a) What does the speaker walk through as he heads toward the sea? (b) Where does he stop to rest?
2. (a) As the speaker sits by the sea, what does he vow to "shake" from his heart? (b) What thoughts does he vow to "shake" away?
3. What does the speaker do "In listless quietude of mind"?
4. (a) What "warns" the speaker to start heading home? (b) What does he "bear with" him when he leaves?

Interpreting

5. What details in the first three stanzas convey the beauty of the coast?
6. (a) In the fifth stanza, how does the speaker personify, or attribute human qualities to, the bluff on which he settles? (b) How does this help to convey his sense of oneness with nature?
7. (a) What do you think might be the "burdens" from which the sea helps the speaker to escape? (b) What does the speaker mean when he says that he seems like the waves, sea birds, and far-off sails? (c) Why does escaping from his burdens make him feel this way?
8. (a) What event is the speaker describing when he writes, "when time's veil shall fall asunder"? (b) How does he feel his respite by the sea helps to prepare him for this event?
9. Why does the speaker need "no token stone nor glittering shell" to remind him of his afternoon by the sea?

Applying

10. Whittier suggests that the ocean has the power to heal and soothe. Do you agree? Why or why not?

UNDERSTANDING LANGUAGE

Using Vivid Adjectives

The clarity and effectiveness of Whittier's imagery is to a large extent the result of his use of **vivid adjectives**. For example, Whittier's use of the adjective *misty* in his image "misty light" (line 4) creates an image of diffuse light.

Define each of the following adjectives as it is used in the poem. Then use each adjective in an original sentence, in which you create an image.

1. sandy (line 5)   4. broken (line 54)
2. silvery (line 8)   5. glimmering (line 59)
3. feverish (line 18)

THINKING AND WRITING

Writing a Poem Using Imagery

Using the images you have already listed, write a poem describing either a beach or a landscape the morning after a snowstorm. Start by trying to come up with new images that you can add to your list. Try to include a number of images appealing to senses other than sight. Use vivid adjectives in your images to make them clear and effective. When you finish developing your list, focus your subject and write your poem. Imagine that your readers have never seen a scene similar to the one you are describing. When you finish writing, revise, adding details to make your description thorough and clear.

Closure and Extension

ANSWERS TO THINKING ABOUT THE SELECTION
Recalling

1. (a) He walks through dark-green fields with grain. (b) He stops to rest on a grassy mound.
2. (a) He vows to shake all burdens from his heart. (b) He vows to shake away all weary thoughts.
3. He yields to the rhythms of nature.
4. (a) The shadows and night winds are coming on. (b) He bears his memories with him.

Interpreting

5. Some details are the glittering sunlight, the luminous belt and misty light beyond the pine bluffs, the "tremulous shadow of the sea," the silvery light, the dark-green fields, and blossoming grain.
6. (a) He describes the mound as having its feet in the water and "granite ankles" surrounded by moss and weeds. (b) By personifying the mound, the speaker brings it to his own level.
7. (a) They are probably the burdens of daily life. (b) He feels free. (c) It makes him feel free, because it relieves his mind of worry.
8. (a) He is referring to death. (b) It makes him feel as if he is in harmony with nature.
9. His memory will endure.

Applying

10. Answers will differ. Students may comment that they believe that the sound of the ocean has a healing and soothing effect.

ANSWERS TO UNDERSTANDING LANGUAGE

1. sandy: sand-colored; Suggested sentence: The shadows descended over the sandy cliffs.
2. silvery: appearing silver in color; Suggested sentence: As the moon rose, the entire landscape was layered with silvery light.
3. feverish: greatly excited or agitated; Suggested sentence: We were all startled by his feverish stare.
4. broken: splintered; Suggested sentence: The ground was covered with shards of broken glass.
5. glimmering: shining; Suggested sentence: The glimmering waves rolled gently onto the shore, as the sun slowly descended into the horizon.

THINKING AND WRITING

For help with this assignment, students can refer to Lesson 18, "Writing a Poem," in the Handbook of Writing About Literature.

Publishing Student Writing Students who choose to make their poems available for others may wish to record readings of their poems.

More About the Author Although Emily Dickinson published few poems in her lifetime, she apparently thought about the possibility of fame. In a letter to Higginson, she wrote, "If fame belongs to me, I could not escape her—if she did not, the longest day would pass me on the chase." After she died, her sister Lavinia discovered the poems in Emily's dresser drawers. Dickinson's first books of poetry were published in 1900. The titles of her poems are taken from the first lines. Lead a discussion about what motivates a poet to write, aside from the desire for recognition. How might Emily Dickinson's life and literary output have differed, had she become famous while she lived?

Critical Evaluation The literary scholar George F. Whicher has written: "Emily Dickinson . . . was quintessentially native to the region [New England] and completely innocent of literary sophistication. As a daughter of the leading lawyer of Amherst, she might normally have married a young minister or lawyer from the college he served as treasurer, but this fulfillment was denied to her. To compensate for her disaster of the heart she seems to have turned to poetry, and in single-minded concentration of what most concerned her to have immersed herself behind the hemlock hedges of the Dickinson house. There she secretly recorded day after day her vivid awarenesses of both outer and inner weather. Only after her death was the extent of her achievement known, and only slowly and with many vexatious delays was the evidence of it laid before the public . . ."

EMILY DICKINSON

1830–1886

During her life, Emily Dickinson wrote at least 1,775 poems. Yet only seven of these were published—anonymously—in her lifetime. Dickinson was a private person, extremely reluctant to reveal herself and her work to the public. As a result, few people outside her family and small circle of friends were aware of her poetic genius until after her death. Today, however, she is generally regarded as one of the greatest American poets.

Dickinson was born in Amherst, Massachusetts, the daughter of a prominent lawyer. Though she traveled to Boston, Washington, and Philadelphia to visit friends when she was young, she rarely left her home town as she grew older. In fact, during the last ten years of her life, she refused to leave her house and garden. Her circle of friends grew smaller and smaller, and she communicated with her remaining friends mainly through notes and fragments of poems. She dressed only in white and would not allow her neighbors or any strangers to see her. When her health failed, she permitted her doctor to examine her only by observing her from a distance. In 1886, after fighting illness for two years, Dickinson died in the same house in which she was born.

Though she chose to live most of her life in virtual isolation, Emily Dickinson was a very intense, energetic person. Having a clear sense of purpose, she devoted most of her energy to her poetry. Yet, because she shared her work with few people, she sometimes doubted her abilities. In 1862 she sent four poems to Thomas Wentworth Higginson, an influential literary critic, and asked him to tell her if her verse was "alive." Like the editors who first published her work after her death, Higginson sought to change her unconventional style—her eccentric use of punctuation and her irregular use of meter and rhyme. He did not realize that Dickinson crafted her poetry with great precision and that her unique style was an important element of her poetry. Still, he did recognize her talent and encouraged her to keep writing.

The extent of Dickinson's talent was not widely recognized until 1955, when a complete, unedited edition of her poems was published. Viewing her work in its original form, writers and critics could see that Dickinson was unlike the other poets of her time. For the first time, Dickinson's unique style, her concrete imagery, and her simple but forceful language were appreciated. Dickinson's work was compared with that of the modern poets, and she was acknowledged as a poet who was truly ahead of her time.

Support Material

Teaching Portfolio
Teacher Backup, p. 489
Usage and Mechanics Worksheet, p. 494
Vocabulary Check, p. 495
Analyzing Literature Worksheet, *Understanding Style*, p. 496
Critical Thinking and Reading Worksheet, *Interpreting Connotative Meaning*, p. 497
Selection Test, p. 498

GUIDE FOR INTERPRETING

"Hope" is the thing with feathers; There's a certain Slant of light; I like to see it lap the miles; A narrow Fellow in the Grass; I never saw a Moor; Tell all the Truth but tell it slant

Writer's Techniques

Style. Style refers to the manner in which a writer puts his or her ideas into words. It involves the characteristics that concern form of expression rather than the thoughts conveyed. In poetry, for example, style is determined by such factors as choice and arrangement of words, length and arrangement of lines, stanza length and format, use of punctuation and capitalization, and use of literary devices.

Emily Dickinson's unique style distinguishes her poetry from that of any other American poet. The most striking characteristics of her style are her unconventional use of punctuation and capitalization and the brevity of most of her lines and stanzas. Most of her poetry is written in quatrains, or four-line stanzas. In her quatrains she usually rhymes only the second and fourth lines, and she often uses slant rhymes, or partial rhymes—rhymes in which the final sounds of the words are similar but not identical. For the most part, she uses iambic rhythm—rhythm in which every second syllable is stressed—but she includes frequent variations in rhythm.

Another notable characteristic of Dickinson's style is her tendency to use figurative language—language that is not intended to be interpreted literally—to convey her ideas. Her use of figurative language adds depth to her poetry.

Commentary

Emily Dickinson's poems should not be considered only as coded messages to be deciphered for their meaning. It is true that in many poems she struggles with difficult questions of existence and death. In others, however, she paints, in quick, vivid strokes, moments from our everyday world. Dickinson sees her surroundings with the clear-eyed, sometimes mischievous, wonder of a child and breathlessly tells us about them. Sometimes she just wants us to see; other times she searches for the meaning in what she sees.

As you read her poems, notice when she is speaking only of what she is describing and when she is perhaps also speaking of what it signifies or suggests. Do you experience the world in both ways—when you watch a sunset or see a rainbow, for example?

Writing

Most people associate certain emotions with each of the four seasons. Freewrite about the emotions you associate with winter.

Writing/Prior Knowledge Before having your students complete the writing assignment, you may want to have them discuss their attitudes concerning each of the four seasons.

Note About the Poems The poems presented here are from the definitive edition, *The Poems of Emily Dickinson*, edited by Thomas H. Johnson, Harvard University Press, 1951, 1955, 1979, 1983.

Vocabulary

Preteach the following vocabulary words:
abash (ə bash') *v.:* Make ashamed (p. 372, l.7)
oppresses (ə pres' əz) *v.:* Weighs heavily on the mind (p. 373, l.3)
prodigious (prə dij' əs) *adj.:* Wonderful (p. 374, l. 4)
supercilious (soo' pər sil' ē əs) *adj.:* Disdainful (p. 374, l. 6)
docile (däs' 'l) *adj.:* Obedient (p. 374, l. 15)
omnipotent (äm nip' ə tənt) *adj.:* Having unlimited power or authority (p. 374, l. 15)

Guide for Interpreting 371

Motivation/Prior Knowledge
Have students discuss the concept of hope. What does hope represent to them?

Purpose-Setting Question
What does hope represent to the speaker?

1 **Literary Focus** By calling hope "the thing with feathers," what comparison is the speaker making?

2 **Discussion** What is "the tune without the words"?

3 **Critical Thinking and Reading** Point out that there is no break between stanzas one and two; the thought continues.

4 **Discussion** What is the meaning of the final two lines?

Closure and Extension

ANSWERS TO THINKING ABOUT THE SELECTION
Recalling

1. (a) Hope perches in the soul. (b) It sings a tune without words. (c) It never stops.
2. (a) The speaker has heard the bird "in the chillest land" and "on the strangest Sea." (b) It never asked a crumb of her.

Interpreting

3. It makes it possible to understand the abstract concept of hope in concrete terms.
4. (a) It possesses determination and selflessness. (b) It suggests that hope does not disappear even in the worst circumstances and that it gives but asks for nothing in return.
5. If it wants nothing from us, we can do nothing to influence it.
6. It suggests that with the help of hope, humans are able to endure hardships.

"Hope" is the thing with feathers—

Emily Dickinson

1   "Hope" is the thing with feathers—
That perches in the soul—
2   And sings the tune without the words—
3   And never stops—at all—

5   And sweetest—in the Gale—is heard—
And sore must be the storm—
That could abash the little Bird
That kept so many warm—

I've heard it in the chillest land—
10 And on the strangest Sea—
4   Yet, never, in Extremity,
It asked a crumb—of Me.

THINKING ABOUT THE SELECTION
Recalling

1. (a) According to the speaker, what "perches in the soul"? (b) What type of tune does it sing? (c) When does it stop singing?
2. (a) Name two places where the speaker has heard the "little Bird"? (b) What has the "little Bird" never done?

Interpreting

3. Throughout the poem Dickinson develops a comparison between hope and a "little Bird." What is the effect of this comparison?
4. (a) What qualities does the "little Bird" possess? (b) What does this suggest about the characteristics of hope?
5. In what way do the final two lines suggest that hope is something that we cannot consciously control?
6. What does this poem suggest about the human ability to endure hardships?

Applying

7. (a) What does hope mean to you? (b) In what situations do you think of hope?

372   *New England Renaissance*

Applying

7. (a) Answers will differ. Students might comment that hope represents the ability to maintain a positive outlook during difficult times. (b) Answers will differ. Students might comment that they look to hope when they are experiencing difficulties in their personal lives.

There's a certain Slant of light,

Emily Dickinson

FEBRUARY 1890–1900
John Henry Twachtman
Museum of Fine Arts, Boston

There's a certain Slant of light,
Winter Afternoons—
That oppresses, like the Heft
Of Cathedral Tunes— **1**

5 Heavenly Hurt, it gives us—
We can find no scar,
But internal difference,
Where the Meanings, are— **2**

None may teach it—Any—
10 'Tis the Seal Despair—
An imperial affliction
Sent us of the Air— **3**

When it comes, the Landscape listens—
Shadows—hold their breath—
15 When it goes, 'tis like the Distance
On the look of Death— **4**

THINKING ABOUT THE SELECTION

Recalling

1. (a) When does the "certain Slant of light" come? (b) What does it do? (c) What does it give us?
2. (a) What may none teach? (b) What is "the Seal Despair"?
3. (a) What does the landscape do when the "Slant of light" comes? (b) What do the shadows do?
4. What is the situation when the "Slant of light" goes?

Interpreting

5. (a) What mood does the "Slant of light" create? (b) What does it seem to represent to the speaker?

6. (a) What is paradoxical, or self-contradictory, about Dickinson's reference to "Heavenly Hurt" (line 5)? (b) How does this paradox suggest that suffering is precious as well as painful?
7. What does the third stanza suggest about the source of despair?
8. In the final stanza, Dickinson suggests that despair makes us more aware of our spiritual relationship with the natural world. What do the final two lines suggest about the connection between despair and our awareness of our own mortality?

Applying

9. Why do you think that weather conditions have such a powerful effect on our moods?

There's a certain Slant of light 373

Motivation/Prior Knowledge
Have your students discuss the effects of advances in technology. What are some of the ways in which people respond to these advances?

Purpose-Setting Question
What object is the speaker describing?

1 Discussion What metaphor does Dickinson establish in the first stanza?

2 Critical Thinking and Reading Point out to your students that they may lose the train of thought if they pause at the ends of stanzas.

3 Discussion How does Dickinson develop the metaphor that she established in the first stanza?

4 Discussion What is "its own stable door"?

Reader's Response What associations do you have with trains? Why?

I like to see it lap the miles,

Emily Dickinson

I like to see it lap the miles,
And lick the valleys up,
And stop to feed itself at tanks;
And then, prodigious, step

5　Around a pile of mountains,
And, supercilious, peer
In shanties by the sides of roads;
And then a quarry pare

To fit its sides, and crawl between,
10　Complaining all the while
In horrid, hooting stanza;
Then chase itself down hill

And neigh like Boanerges;[1]
Then, prompter than a star,
15　Stop—docile and omnipotent—
At its own stable door.

---

1. Boanerges (bō′ ə ner′ jēz): A loud, forceful preacher.

Primary Source

In the April, 1862, edition of *Atlantic Monthly,* the noted critic Thomas Higginson published "Letter to a Young Contributor," an article offering practical advice to inexperienced writers. Responding to this article, Emily Dickinson wrote to Higginson and asked him to respond to several of her poems. Dickinson's letter marked the beginning of a lifelong correspondence. Although Higginson was quick to recognize Dickinson's talent, he was critical of her irregular meter and line length and her unusual use of punctuation. Dickinson wrote back:

Your second letter surprised me, and for a moment, swung—I had not supposed it. Your first—gave no dishonor, because the True—are not ashamed—I thanked you for your justice—but could not drop the Bells whose jingling cooled my Tramp—Perhaps the balm, seemed better, because you bled me, first.

I smile when you suggest that I delay 'to publish'—that being foreign to my thought, as Firmament to Fin—

If fame belonged to me, I could not escape her—if she did not, the longest day would pass me on the chase—and the approbation of my Dog, would forsake me—then—My Barefoot-Rank is better—

AMERICAN RAILROAD SCENE
Currier and Ives
Three Lions

Fine art, *American Railroad Scene,* by Currier and Ives. The lithograph firm of Currier and Ives became famous for its scenes of nineteenth-century American life. Railroad travel in all of its aspects was a common subject of Currier and Ives prints, which were very popular with the American public. The train in this scene is snowbound; the workers are clearing snow from the tracks. The beam from the headlight provides a dramatic point of interest.

As students look at this print, you might ask this question: What image might Emily Dickinson have used to describe this scene?

Closure and Extension

ANSWERS TO THINKING ABOUT THE SELECTION
Recalling

1. (a) It licks them up. (b) It feeds itself at tanks. (c) It peers into shanties at the roadsides. (d) It chases itself down hill. (e) It stops at its own stable door.

Interpreting

2. The comparison is revealed through Dickinson's imagery: it stops "to feed itself at tanks"; it neighs "like Boanerges"; it stops "at its own stable door."
3. It is supercilious; it looks into houses; and it complains.
4. Something that is docile has been tamed, but it is also omnipotent—all-powerful—and that suggests a potential to burst loose.
5. (a) She likes to see it and is amused by it, but she recognizes its shortcomings. (b) It may suggest that she accepts it but sees its flaws.

Applying

6. Suggested Response: She would have accepted them with some reservations.

THINKING ABOUT THE SELECTION

Recalling

1. (a) What does "it" do to the valleys? (b) Where does it stop to feed itself? (c) What does it peer into? (d) What does it "chase itself down"? (e) Where does it stop?

Interpreting

2. In this poem Dickinson develops an implied comparison between a railroad train and a horse. With what words and images does Dickinson reveal this comparison?

3. What human qualities are attributed to the train in the second and third stanzas?
4. What does the description of the train as "docile and omnipotent" suggest?
5. (a) What seems to be Dickinson's attitude toward the train? (b) What does this suggest about her attitude toward industrialization?

Applying

6. Considering the attitude she expresses in this poem, how do you think Dickinson would have reacted to the numerous technological advances that have occurred since her death?

I like to see it lap the miles 375

You think my gait 'spasmodic'—I am in danger—Sir—
You think me 'uncontrolled'—I have no Tribunal. . . .
     If I might bring you what I do—not so frequent to trouble you—and ask you if I told it clear—'twould be control, to me . . .
     Will you be my Preceptor, Mr. Higginson?

Fine art, *Hedgerow Wildlife,* by Peter Barret. Peter Barret is a contemporary British illustrator who resides in Devon, England. The watercolor illustration *Hedgerow Wildlife* was done for London's *Sunday Times Magazine,* August 6, 1978. It is a colorful and beautifully detailed watercolor painting of the flora and fauna of a hedgerow—thicket of shrubs and small trees that form a barrier to enclose a meadow or field. Close examination reveals a wealth of birds and tiny creatures, including a rabbit, a snake, a snail, a frog, a hedgehog and a butterfly—to mention only a few. The flowers, berries, and even a spider web are all delineated with astounding realism and detail. Working in this finely controlled realistic style, Peter Barret has executed illustration commissions for many leading publications in Britain.

You might use the following questions for discussion:
1. What do you think this artist's intense study of nature says about his regard for nature?
2. What attitude does the artist seem to convey toward the snake?
3. How is his attitude toward the snake similar to or different from Dickinson's?

Presentation

Purpose-Setting Question
What is the subject of the poem?

1 **Critical Thinking and Reading**
Note the precise details in the description of the grass.

2 **Discussion** How does Dickinson personify the snake in these two lines?

Primary Source

Thomas Higginson not only had the rare opportunity of reading Emily Dickinson's poetry during her lifetime, but he also was one of the few people, aside from family members and personal acquaintances, who had the chance to meet Dickinson. After his visit Higginson wrote to his wife:

WILDLIFE AND VEGETATION OF A HEDGEROW
Drawing by Peter Barrett
The Sunday Times, The Sunday Times
Magazine, 6 August, 1978

A narrow Fellow in the Grass

Emily Dickinson

A narrow Fellow in the Grass
Occasionally rides—
You may have met Him—did you not
His notice sudden is—

5 The Grass divides as with a Comb—
A spotted shaft is seen—
And then it closes at your feet
And opens further on—

He likes a Boggy Acre
10 A Floor too cool for Corn—
Yet when a Boy, and Barefoot—
I more than once at Noon

I shan't sit up tonight to write you all about E.D. dearest but if you had read Mrs. Stoddard's novels you could understand a house where each member runs his or her own selves. Yet I only saw her.

A large country lawyer's house, brown brick, with great trees and a garden—I sent up my card. A parlor dark and cool and stiffish, a few books and engravings and an open piano . . .

A step like a pattering child's in entry and in glided a little plain woman with two smooth bands of reddish hair and a face a little like Belle Dove's; not plainer—with no good feature—in a very plain and exquisitely clean white pique and a blue net worsted shawl. She came to me with

Have passed, I thought, a Whip lash
Unbraiding in the Sun
15 When stooping to secure it
It wrinkled, and was gone—

3 [Several of Nature's People
I know, and they know me—
I feel for them a transport
20 Of cordiality—

4 [But never met this Fellow
Attended, or alone
Without a tighter breathing
And Zero at the Bone—

THINKING ABOUT THE SELECTION

Recalling

1. How does the grass divide when the "narrow Fellow" moves through it?
2. What does the narrow fellow like?
3. What happens when the speaker tries to catch the narrow fellow?
4. What happens each time the speaker meets the narrow fellow?

Interpreting

5. (a) What is the narrow fellow? (b) Why do you think Dickinson does not name her subject?
6. In line 11 Dickinson indicates that the speaker of the poem is a boy. Why do you think she uses a male speaker?
7. What is the speaker's attitude toward the narrow fellow?

Applying

8. (a) What is your own attitude toward the subject of the poem? (b) Explain why you do or do not think most other people share your attitude.

ANALYZING LITERATURE

Understanding Style

Style refers to the way in which a writer expresses his or her thoughts. Though writers often write about similar subjects, each writer has his or her own distinctive style. As a result, we can often distinguish the work of different writers by examining style. For example, we can easily identify Emily Dickinson's poetry once we are familiar with some of the unique characteristics of her style.
1. What is unusual about Dickinson's use of punctuation?
2. What is unusual about her use of capitalization?
3. What are two other characteristics of her style revealed in this poem?

A narrow Fellow in the Grass 377

3 **Discussion** What is the significance of lines 17–20?

4 **Discussion** What emotion is captured in the image in the final two lines?

Closure and Extension

ANSWERS TO THINKING ABOUT THE SELECTION
Recalling

1. It divides as if a comb is dividing it.
2. He likes "a Boggy Acre" and a "floor too cool for Corn."
3. It disappears.
4. The speaker gets a sensation of tight breathing and "Zero at the Bone."

Interpreting

5. (a) It is a snake. (b) Answers will differ. One possible reason is that the snake itself is not seen, just the signs of its passing.
6. Students may suggest a variety of answers. One possibility is that in her time boys were more likely to go barefoot and were not expected to be afraid of snakes.
7. The narrow fellow creates an instinctive bodily reaction—a chill and a tightening of breath.

Applying

8. (a) Answers will differ. Students may comment that they are afraid of snakes. (b) Answers will differ. Students may comment that they feel that most people are afraid of snakes because of the snakes' quick, slithering motion.

ANSWERS TO ANALYZING LITERATURE

1. She relies heavily on dashes and rarely uses periods or commas.
2. She capitalizes many nouns that are not ordinarily capitalized.
3. Suggested Response: Her frequent use of quatrains and partial rhymes is revealed.

two day lilies which she put in a sort of childlike way into my hand and said "These are my introduction" in a sort frightened breathless childlike voice—and added under her breath "Forgive me if I am frightened; I never see strangers and hardly know what to say"—but she talked soon and thenceforward continuously—and deferentially —sometimes stopping to ask me to talk instead of her— but readily recommencing. Manner between Angie Tilton and Mr. Alcott—but thoroughly ingenuous and simple which they are not and saying many things which you would have thought foolish and I wise—and some things you would have liked. . . .

Fine art, *Near Harlech, North Wales*, by Benjamin W. Leader. Benjamin William Leader (1831–1923) was a British painter. Born Benjamin Williams, he added the surname *Leader* to give distinction to his name. Educated at the schools of the Royal Academy, Leader was also influenced by the Pre-Raphaelites. He developed a reputation as an individualistic painter of landscape devoted to truth in nature.

Near Harlech, North Wales, is a beautiful rendering of a heather-strewn moor. The Pre-Raphaelite influence is obvious in the careful details and bright colors of the scene. The landscape paintings of Benjamin William Leader were a great success with the British people.

1. What mood or feeling does the painting convey?
2. What aspects of the scene in this painting reflect details of Dickinson's poem?

Presentation

Purpose-Setting Question
What truths about life do we arrive at through intuition?

1 **Clarification** A moor is open land with heather and other wild plants on it. Moors are not usually found in the United States.

2 **Critical Thinking and Reading** Call attention to the simplicity of the wording and to the way in which this simplicity contrasts with the complexity of the underlying thought.

3 **Discussion** How do the ideas in the second stanza parallel those in the first stanza?

4 **Discussion** What is the speaker's message?

NEAR HARLECH, NORTH WALES
Benjamin William Leader
Bridgeman-Art Resource

I never saw a Moor—

Emily Dickinson

1   I never saw a Moor—
     I never saw the Sea—
2   Yet know I how the Heather looks
     And what a Billow[1] be.

3 5   I never spoke with God
     Nor visited in Heaven—
4   Yet certain am I of the spot
     As if the Checks[2] were given—

---

1. Billow: Large wave.
2. Checks: Colored seat checks indicating the destinations of passengers on a train after their tickets have been collected.

378   *New England Renaissance*

THINKING ABOUT THE SELECTION

Recalling

1. (a) What two things has the speaker never seen? (b) What does she know in spite of never having seen them?
2. (a) With whom has the speaker never spoken? (b) Where has she never visited? (c) Of what is she certain?

Interpreting

3. (a) How might the speaker have acquired the knowledge she claims to possess in the first stanza? (b) In what way is the knowledge presented in the second stanza different from that of the first stanza? (c) How might she have acquired the knowledge presented in the second stanza?
4. How does the information in the first stanza affect your reaction to the second stanza?

Applying

5. What things do you think you know through intuition rather than through experience?

Closure and Extension

ANSWERS TO THINKING ABOUT THE SELECTION
Recalling

1. (a) She has never seen a moor or the sea. (b) She knows how heather looks and "what a Billow be."
2. (a) She has never spoken with God. (b) She has never visited Heaven. (c) She is certain of the spot.

Interpreting

3. (a) She may have read about it or heard about it. (b) The knowledge in the first stanza concerns visible things, while the knowledge in the second stanza concerns things that are not openly visible to people on earth. (c) She might have acquired it through intuition.

4. The information in the first stanza demonstrates that one can know something without firsthand experience and makes us more willing to accept the ideas presented in the second stanza."

Applying

5. Suggested Response: People gain an awareness of their spiritual relationship with nature through intuition.

Tell all the Truth but tell it slant—

Emily Dickinson

1
2
3

Tell all the Truth but tell it slant—
Success in Circuit lies
Too bright for our infirm Delight
The Truth's superb surprise
5   As Lightning to the Children eased
With explanation kind
The Truth must dazzle gradually
Or every man be blind—

THINKING ABOUT THE SELECTION

Recalling

1. According to the speaker, what is "too bright for our infirm Delight"?
2. Why must the Truth "dazzle gradually"?

Interpreting

3. What does Dickinson mean when she tells us to "tell all the Truth but tell it slant"?

4. To what type of "Truth" do you think Dickinson is referring?

Applying

5. To what types of truths do you think people have to be led gradually? Explain your answer.

Presentation

Motivation/Prior Knowledge
Have students discuss the importance of telling the truth. In what instances might it be acceptable to avoid directly stating the truth?

Purpose-Setting Question
What advice does the speaker relate?

1 Discussion What does the first line seem to suggest?

2 Discussion How does the second line explain the idea expressed in the first?

3 Discussion What comparison does the speaker use to support her argument? How effective is this comparison?

Reader's Response How might you apply Dickinson's message to your own life?

Closure and Extension

ANSWERS TO THINKING ABOUT THE SELECTION
Recalling

1. The truth's "superb surprise" is too "bright for our infirm Delight."
2. It will blind us if it does not "dazzle gradually."

Interpreting

3. She means that people have to be gradually led to the truth.
4. She is referring to the major truths of human existence.

Applying

5. Answers will differ. Students may comment that people have to be gradually led to disturbing truths about themselves and the people they care about.

Literary Focus In poetry, themes are often difficult to grasp. Point out to students that they may have to read a poem several times to interpret its theme.

Writing/Prior Knowledge Before the students write their own definitions of success, conduct a brainstorming session in which students try to come up with unusual definitions. Appoint two or three students to record the off-the-cuff suggestions. Then review them with the class.

Vocabulary

Preteach the following vocabulary words:
gossamer (gäs' ə mər) n.: A very thin, soft, filmy cloth (p. 384, l. 15)
cornice (kôr' nis) n.: The projecting decorative molding along the top of a building (p. 384, l. 20)
surmised (sər mīzd') v.: Guessed (p. 384, l. 23)

Success is counted sweetest; I felt a Funeral, in my Brain; I heard a Fly buzz—when I died; Because I could not stop for Death; My life closed twice before its close; The Bustle in a House

Writer's Techniques

Theme. A theme is the central idea or insight into life that a writer conveys in a work of literature. In some literary works, the theme is directly stated. More often, however, the theme is implied, or revealed indirectly. In poetry, theme is often implied through figurative language—language that is not meant to be interpreted literally. It is important to look beyond the literal meaning of the words in a poem and try to determine their underlying, or hidden, meaning.

Writing

One of Dickinson's poems is about success. What does success mean to you? Write your definition of success. Then suggest other views that people might hold about success.

Primary Source

In 1862 Emily Dickinson wrote to the critic and journalist Thomas Wentworth Higginson:

> Are you too deeply occupied to say if my Verse is alive?
> The Mind is so near itself—it cannot see, distinctly—and I have none to ask—
> Should you think it breathes—and had you the leisure to tell me, I should feel quick gratitude—
> If I make the mistake—that you dared to tell me—would give me sincere honor—toward you—
> I enclose my name—asking you, if you please—Sir—to tell me what is true?
> That you will not betray me—it is needless to ask—since Honor is its own pawn—

Ten days later she replies to his encouraging letter:

> . . . Thank you for the surgery—it was not so painful as I supposed . . .
> While my thought is undressed—I can make the distinction, but when I put them in the Gown—they look alike, and numb . . .

Objective
To respond to criticism

Support Material

Teaching Portfolio
Teacher Backup, p. 501
Usage and Mechanics Worksheet, p. 505
Vocabulary Check, p. 506
Analyzing Literature Worksheet, *Understanding Theme*, p. 507
Language Worksheet, *Finding Antonyms*, p. 508
Selection Test, p. 509

Success
is counted
sweetest

Emily Dickinson

1
    Success is counted sweetest
    By those who ne'er succeed.
2
    To comprehend a nectar
    Requires sorest need.

3
5   Not one of all the purple Host
    Who took the Flag today
    Can tell the definition
    So clear of Victory

    As he defeated—dying—
10 On whose forbidden ear
    The distant strains of triumph
    Burst agonized and clear!

THINKING ABOUT THE SELECTION

Recalling

1. (a) By whom is success "counted sweetest"? (b) What is required "to comprehend a nectar"?
2. For whom do the "distant strains of triumph burst agonized and clear"?

Interpreting

3. What does the "nectar" in line 3 represent?
4. In what way is the ear of the defeated man "forbidden" in line 10?
5. How do the descriptions of victorious and defeated soldiers in the second and third stanzas support the generalization made in the first two lines?
6. (a) What point does the poem make about failure? (b) What point does it make about our ability to comprehend success?

Applying

7. Explain why you do or do not agree with the points that the poem makes about success and failure.

What is the speaker actually describing?

1 **Discussion** How does the opening line grasp the reader's attention?

2 **Discussion** What does this passage reveal about the speaker's psychological state?

3 **Discussion** What is suggested by the speaker's reference to boots of lead?

4 **Discussion** What is the speaker describing in the fourth stanza?

5 **Discussion** What does the speaker mean when she comments that "a Plank in Reason, broke"?

6 **Discussion** What do the last three lines suggest?

Closure and Extension

ANSWERS TO THINKING ABOUT THE SELECTION
Recalling

1. The speaker feels a funeral in her brain.
2. The funeral service, which is like a drum, keeps beating.
3. Space begins to toll.
4. (a) A "Plank in Reason" breaks. (b) The speaker drops downward and finishes knowing.

Interpreting

5. (a) The mourners might represent those who care about her and who may consider her to be outside their reach. (b) The stanzas are filled with auditory images that convey the increasing strain being placed upon her soul. (c) She speaks of silence and of herself being wrecked and solitary.

Applying

6. Answers will differ. Students might suggest a traumatic event, such as the loss of a close friend.

I felt a Funeral, in my Brain,

Emily Dickinson

1

    I felt a Funeral, in my Brain,
    And Mourners to and fro
    Kept treading—treading—till it seemed
    That Sense was breaking through—

2

5 And when they all were seated,
    A Service, like a Drum—
    Kept beating—beating—till I thought
    My Mind was going numb—

3

    And then I heard them lift a Box
10 And creak across my Soul
    With those same Boots of Lead, again,
    Then Space—began to toll,

4

    As all the Heavens were a Bell,
    And Being, but an Ear,
15 And I, and Silence, some strange Race
    Wrecked, solitary, here—

5

    And then a Plank in Reason, broke,

6

    And I dropped down, and down—
    And hit a World, at every plunge,
20 And Finished knowing—then—

THINKING ABOUT THE SELECTION

Recalling

1. What does the speaker feel in her brain?
2. What keeps "beating" until she thinks her mind is going numb?
3. What begins "to toll" in the third stanza?
4. (a) What breaks in the final stanza? (b) What does the speaker do when it breaks?

Interpreting

5. (a) What do you think the mourners might represent? (b) How do the images in the second and third stanzas convey the speaker's growing sense of despair? (c) How do the images in the fourth stanza convey the speaker's sense of isolation?

Applying

6. Many of Emily Dickinson's poems grew out of reactions to events in her personal life. What type of event do you think might have led her to write this poem?

I heard a Fly buzz—when I died—

Emily Dickinson

1
I heard a Fly buzz—when I died—
The Stillness in the Room
Was like the Stillness in the Air—
Between the Heaves of Storm—

2
5   The Eyes around—had wrung them dry—
And Breaths were gathering firm
For that last Onset—when the King
Be witnessed—in the Room—

3
I willed my Keepsakes—Signed away
10 What portion of me be
Assignable—and then it was
There interposed a Fly—

With Blue—uncertain stumbling Buzz—
Between the light—and me—
15 And then the Windows failed—and then
I could not see to see—

ROOM WITH A BALCONY
Adolph von Menzel
Staatliche Museen Preußischer Kulturbesitz, Nationgalerie, Berlin (West)

THINKING ABOUT THE SELECTION

Recalling

1. (a) What does the speaker hear? (b) When does she hear it?
2. To what does the speaker compare the stillness in the room?
3. For what were breaths gathering firm in the second stanza?
4. What does the speaker sign away in the third stanza?
5. According to the final stanza, what happens when the windows fail?

Interpreting

6. Why does the buzzing of the fly heighten the speaker's awareness of the stillness and tension in the room?
7. (a) What does the speaker's attitude toward death seem to be? (b) How is this attitude reflected in her awareness of the fly?

Applying

8. Explain how Dickinson's attitude toward death is similar to and different from the attitude of another writer whose work you have read.

I heard a Fly buzz—when I died   383

1 Critical Thinking and Reading Note that the first two lines suggest that Death is courteous.

2 Discussion What belief is implied in line 4?

3 Critical Thinking and Reading The second stanza reinforces the notion of courtesy that was established in the first lines of the poem.

4 Discussion What do lines 10–13 add to the poem?

5 Discussion What might the setting sun represent?

6 Discussion What does the house represent?

7 Discussion What does the final stanza reveal about the speaker's conception of time?

Reader's Response What emotions does this poem evoke in you? Why?

Because I could not stop for Death—

Emily Dickinson

Because I could not stop for Death—
He kindly stopped for me—
The Carriage held but just Ourselves—
And Immortality.

5 We slowly drove—He knew no haste
And I had put away
My labor and my leisure too,
For His Civility—

We passed the School, where Children strove
10 At Recess—in the Ring—
We passed the Fields of Gazing Grain—
We passed the Setting Sun—

Or rather—He passed Us—
The Dews drew quivering and chill—
15 For only Gossamer, my Gown—
My Tippet[1]—only Tulle[2]—

We paused before a House that seemed
A Swelling of the Ground—
The Roof was scarcely visible—
20 The Cornice—in the Ground—

Since then—'tis Centuries—and yet
Feels shorter than the Day
I first surmised the Horses Heads
Were toward Eternity—

---

1. Tippet: A scarflike garment worn over the shoulders and hanging down in front.
2. Tulle (tool) *n.*: A thin, fine netting used for scarves.

WAITING OUTSIDE NO. 12
Anonymous
Crane Kalman Gallery

Humanities Note

Fine art, *Waiting Outside No. 12,* c. 1850, Anonymous British Folk Artist. In this oil painting, the artist has provided a startling image. A first glance seems to show an ordinary street scene of the mid-1800's. However, a closer examination produces an impression of isolation, as though this were the only house on the street.

You might consider using the following questions for discussion.
1. What elements in the picture work to create a sense of isolation?
2. What lines from the poem do you feel are represented in this painting?

THINKING ABOUT THE SELECTION

Recalling

1. (a) Explain why Death stops for the speaker. (b) What does Death's carriage hold?
2. What does the speaker "put away" in the second stanza?
3. (a) In the third stanza, what three things does the carriage pass? (b) Where does the carriage pause in the fifth stanza?
4. How long has it been since Death stopped for the speaker?

Interpreting

5. (a) How is Death portrayed in the first two stanzas? (b) What is ironic about this portrayal?
6. What stages of the speaker's life might be represented by the three things the carriage passes in the third stanza?
7. How does the speaker's attitude toward Death seem to change in the fourth stanza?
8. (a) What does the "House" in the fifth stanza represent? (b) Why do they pause there?
9. How does Death affect the speaker's conception of time?

Applying

10. What does Dickinson's interest in Death indicate about her?

Closure and Extension

ANSWERS TO THINKING ABOUT THE SELECTION
Recalling

1. (a) Death stops because the speaker cannot stop for Death. (b) The carriage holds Death, the speaker, and Immortality.
2. The speaker puts away her labor and her leisure.
3. (a) In the third stanza, the carriage passes a school with children playing, the fields of gazing grain, and the setting sun. (b) It pauses at a house in the ground.
4. It is centuries since Death stopped for the speaker.

Interpreting

5. (a) Death is portrayed as a courteous gentleman driving a carriage. (b) Unlike common conceptions of death, the image is not frightening and is, in fact, rather appealing.
6. The images might represent childhood, maturity, and old age.
7. The speaker seems to become aware of a coldness and her own frailty.
8. (a) The House seems to represent heaven or an afterworld. It could also represent a grave because it is "A Swelling of the Ground." (b) It is her final resting place.
9. It makes centuries seem shorter than a day.

Applying

10. Answers will differ. Students may comment that it reveals that she was not completely happy.

1 **Discussion** What is the "third event" to which the speaker refers?

2 **Discussion** What is the speaker describing in lines 5–6?

3 **Critical Thinking and Reading** The last two lines could stand by themselves. Yet in the context of the poem they take on a more specific meaning. How could parting relate to both heaven and hell?

Closure and Extension

ANSWERS TO THINKING ABOUT THE SELECTION
Recalling

1. (a) Her life closed twice before its close. (b) It remains to be seen if immortality will unveil a third event to the speaker.
2. "Parting is all we know of heaven/ And all we need of hell."

Interpreting

3. (a) The speaker is referring to being separated from loved ones. (b) It is revealed in line 7.
4. (a) The third event is death itself. (b) It too is huge and hopeless to conceive.
5. (a) Parting is related to our knowledge of both heaven and hell. (b) Suggested Response: We know nothing about heaven until we part from the earth; parting from someone we love is like being in hell.

Applying

6. (a) Answers will differ. Students may comment that it makes them very unhappy. (b) Answers will differ. Students may comment that their reaction is not as intense as Dickinson's.

My life closed twice before its close—

Emily Dickinson

1 [
My life closed twice before its close—
It yet remains to see
If Immortality unveil
A third event to me,

2 [
5   So huge, so hopeless to conceive
As these that twice befell.

3 [
Parting is all we know of heaven,
And all we need of hell.

THINKING ABOUT THE SELECTION
Recalling

1. (a) What has happened twice to the speaker? (b) What remains to be seen?
2. How does the speaker describe parting in the second stanza?

Interpreting

3. (a) What type of events caused the speaker's life to close "twice before its close"? (b) In what line is the nature of these events revealed?

4. (a) What is the "third event" to which the speaker refers? (b) How is this related to the first two events?
5. (a) What is paradoxical, or self-contradictory, about Dickinson's description of parting? (b) How do you explain this paradox?

Applying

6. (a) What is your own response to the departure of close friends? (b) In what ways is your own response similar to and different from Dickinson's response?

The Bustle in a House

Emily Dickinson

The Bustle in a House
The Morning after Death
Is solemnest of industries
Enacted upon Earth—

5   The Sweeping up the Heart
And putting Love away
We shall not want to use again
Until Eternity.

Presentation

Motivation/Prior Knowledge
How is the speaker affected by the loss of a loved one?

1 **Critical Thinking and Reading**
Note that the first stanza can be taken literally.

2 **Discussion** What is the effect of the metaphor in lines 5–6?

3 **Discussion** How do the last two lines relate to the rest of the poem?

THINKING ABOUT THE SELECTION

Recalling

1. According to the speaker, what "is solemnest of industries/Enacted upon Earth"?
2. What shall we "not want to use again/Until Eternity"?

Interpreting

3. What does the first stanza indicate about people's attempts to subdue the grief that results from the death of a loved one?
4. (a) What does the speaker compare with house cleaning in the second stanza? (b) What makes this different from cleaning? (c) Is Dickinson's metaphor effective? Why or why not?
5. What do the last two lines suggest about Dickinson's belief in immortality?

Applying

6. It has been claimed that the true beginnings of modern American poetry can be traced to Emily Dickinson and Walt Whitman. Explain how Dickinson's poems are similar to and different from the modern and contemporary poems you have read.

THINKING AND WRITING

Responding to Criticism

A critic has stated that Emily Dickinson's poetry "is exploration on a variety of levels of the ultimate meaning of life itself and equally important of the depths and heights of her own inner nature." Using evidence from the poems you have just read, write an essay supporting this statement. Reread the poems, looking for evidence to support the critic's comment. Organize your notes into an outline, then write your essay. When you finish writing, revise and proofread your essay.

The Bustle in a House   387

Closure and Extension

ANSWERS TO THINKING ABOUT THE SELECTION
Recalling

1. The "solemnest of industries" is the bustle in a house after a death.
2. We shall not want to use the love we put away.

Interpreting

3. They try to keep busy, but the activity is solemn.
4. (a) The speaker compares sweeping up and storing away feelings to cleaning. (b) This is an emotional activity, rather than a physical activity. (c) Suggested Response: Yes, because it is an activity that people commonly perform to keep themselves busy.
5. They suggest that she does believe in immortality.

Applying

6. Suggested Response: Like Dickinson's work, most contemporary poetry contains a great deal of figurative language.

Challenge What does this group of poems reveal about Dickinson's attitudes toward life, misfortune, and death?

THINKING AND WRITING

For help with this assignment, students can refer to Lesson 15, "Evaluating a Literary Work," in the Handbook of Writing About Literature.

After students have completed the assignment, divide them into groups and have them read their rough drafts to one another and comment on ways in which the essays could be improved.

Literary Focus Review the Emily Dickinson poems that you have already covered, pointing out examples of similes and metaphors.

Writing/Prior Knowledge For extra credit have students develop some of their details into similes and metaphors.

Vocabulary

Preteach the following vocabulary words:

assent (ə sent') v.: Agree (p. 389, l. 6)

demur (di mur') v.: Object (p. 389, l. 7)

perfidy (pur' fə dē) n.: Treachery (p. 390, l. 4)

sequestered (si kwes' tərd) v.: Withdrawn; secluded (p. 390, l. 8)

harrowing (har' ō iŋ) v.: Distressing (p. 390, l. 11)

exigencies (ek' sə jən sēz) n.: Pressing needs; demands (p. 392, l. 4)

finite (fī' nīt) adj.: Having measurable or definable limits (p. 393, l. 8)

GUIDE FOR INTERPRETING

Much Madness is divinest Sense; As imperceptibly as grief; The Soul selects her own Society; How happy is the little Stone; There is a solitude of space; This is my letter to the World

Writer's Techniques

Simile and Metaphor. A simile is an explicit comparison between two seemingly dissimilar things. In a simile the comparison is clearly indicated by either *like* or *as*. For example, the word *like* signals the similarity in the sound of rain and a heartbeat in the following simile: The sound of the rain gently falling on the pavement echoed through the air *like* thousands of tiny heartbeats.

A metaphor is also a comparison between two apparently different things. In a metaphor, however, the comparison is implied rather than stated. A metaphor allows us not only to think that two dissimilar things are in some way alike but to pretend that one thing actually *is* something totally different. For example, the metaphor in Emily Dickinson's poem "Hope is the thing with feathers," leads us not only to see the similarities between a bird and hope but to imagine that hope *is* a bird.

Similes and metaphors enable us to visualize connections that our senses may not be able to perceive. By making it possible for us to relate our inner selves to the outer world, they allow us to visualize abstract concepts such as emotions and enable us to understand the external world in human terms.

Writing

Prepare a list of descriptive details and emotions that you associate with the end of summer.

Primary Source

Thomas Wentworth Higginson first visited Emily Dickinson in 1870. In a letter to his wife he reports some of the things she said to him:

"If I read a book [and] it makes my whole body so cold no fire ever can warm me I know *that* is poetry. If I feel physically as if the top of my head were taken off, I know *that* is poetry. These are the only way I know it. Is there any other way?"

"Could you tell me what home is?"

"I never had a mother. I suppose a mother is one to whom you hurry when you are troubled."

Higginson then describes her effect on him: "I never was with any one who drained my nerve power so much. Without touching her, she drew from me. I am glad not to live near her. She often thought me *tired* & seemed very thoughtful of others."

388 *New England Renaissance*

Objectives

1 To understand similes and metaphors
2 To respond in writing to Dickinson's poetry

Support Material

Teaching Portfolio
Teacher Backup, p. 513
Usage and Mechanics Worksheet, p. 517
Vocabulary Check, p. 518
Analyzing Literature Worksheet, *Understanding Metaphors and Similes*, p. 519
Language Worksheet, *Recognizing Synonyms*, p. 520
Selection Test, p. 521

Much Madness is divinest Sense—

Emily Dickinson

1
        Much Madness is divinest Sense—
        To a discerning Eye—
2
        Much Sense—the starkest Madness—
        'Tis the Majority
3
5   In this, as All, prevail—
        Assent—and you are sane—
        Demur—you're straightway dangerous—
        And handled with a Chain—

THINKING ABOUT THE SELECTION

Recalling

1. (a) According to the speaker, what is "divinest Sense"? (b) What is "the starkest Madness"?
2. (a) According to the speaker, how are you judged if you assent? (b) What happens if you demur?

Interpreting

3. (a) What is paradoxical, or self-contradictory, about the first line? (b) How can this paradox be true?
4. (a) According to the speaker, how does society define sanity? (b) How does it define madness?
5. (a) What is the speaker's attitude toward individuality? (b) What is the speaker's attitude toward society?

Applying

6. In this poem Dickinson suggests that our own perceptions can be shaped by the perceptions of others. Explain how this may be so.
7. The contemporary poet Theodore Roethke wrote, "What's madness but Divinest sense at odds with circumstance?" Compare Roethke's words with the theme of Dickinson's poem.

Humanities Note

Fine art, *Progress*, 1853, by Asher B. Durand. Born in New Jersey, Durand (1796–1886) acquired the fundamental skills of an engraver in his father's watchmaking shop. He was then apprenticed to an engraver in Newark, N.J., from 1812–1817. After establishing himself as one of the finest engravers in America, he ceased engraving to devote himself entirely to painting. Influenced by the work of Thomas Cole, Durand is identified with the Hudson River School of painters and is often referred to as the "Father of American landscape painting."

In his painting Durand has depicted a harmony between Nature and human progress. On the left are symbols of the "old nature": a ravaged tree, a storm, and Native Americans. On the right are smoke from steamboats, a locomotive, and buildings—symbols of the new age.

You might consider using the following questions for discussion.

1. What symbols of nature do you find in the picture?
2. What symbols of human progress do you find?
3. How does the message of the painting relate to the message of the poem?

Presentation

Purpose-Setting Question In what sense can grief be imperceptible?

1 **Discussion** How could the passage of summer seem like perfidy?

2 **Discussion** What is the effect of the images in the second and third stanzas?

3 **Discussion** How is the tone of the last stanza is different from that of the first?

390

As imperceptibly as grief

Emily Dickinson

1
   As imperceptibly as grief
   The summer lapsed away,—
   Too imperceptible, at last,
   To seem like perfidy.

2
5 A quietness distilled,
   As twilight long begun,
   Or Nature, spending with herself
   Sequestered afternoon.

   The dusk drew earlier in,
10 The morning foreign shone,—
   A courteous, yet harrowing grace,
   As guest that would be gone.

3
   And thus, without a wing,
   Or service of a keel,
15 Our summer made her light escape
   Into the beautiful.

THINKING ABOUT THE SELECTION

Recalling

1. What lapses away "as imperceptibly as grief"?

Interpreting

2. How would you describe the mood?
3. What do you think is the meaning of the final two lines?

Applying

4. (a) How are you affected by the passing of summer? (b) What changes do you associate with it?

ANALYZING LITERATURE
Understanding Metaphors and Similes

Both **similes** and **metaphors** are comparisons between two seemingly dissimilar things.
1. (a) Find two similes in "As imperceptibly as grief." (b) What two qualities are being compared in each simile?
2. Each of the similes contributes to the development of a metaphor that extends throughout the entire poem. (a) What two things are being compared in this metaphor? (b) What details in the second and third stanzas develop this comparison?
3. How does this metaphor relate the inner self to the outer world?

Closure and Extension

ANSWERS TO THINKING ABOUT THE SELECTION
Recalling
1. The summer lapses away.

Interpreting
2. Suggested Response: The mood is melancholy.
3. Suggested Response: Summer moved on to create beauty in other parts of the world.

Applying
4. (a) Answers will differ. Students may respond that they are saddened by the passing of summer. (b) Answers will differ. Students may respond that they associate all seasonal changes with the maturing process.

Challenge How does the passing of each of the other seasons affect you?

ANSWERS TO ANALYZING LITERATURE

1. (a) Suggested Response: The summer lapses away as imperceptibly as grief. The distilled quietness is like twilight long begun. (b) The first compares the summer's lapsing to the passing of grief. The second compares quietness to twilight.
2. (a) The passing of summer is compared to the grief resulting from the departure of a loved one.

The Soul selects her own society—

Emily Dickinson

The Soul selects her own Society—   1
Then—shuts the Door—
To her divine Majority—   2
Present no more—

5   Unmoved—she notes the Chariots—pausing—
At her low Gate—   3
Unmoved—an Emperor be kneeling
Upon her Mat—

I've known her—from an ample nation—   4
10 Choose One—
Then—close the Valves of her attention—   5
Like Stone—

PROGRESS
Asher B. Durand
The Warner Collection of Gulf States Paper Corp, Tuscaloosa, Alabama

---

THINKING ABOUT THE SELECTION

Recalling

1. According to the first stanza, what does the soul select?
2. What two things leave the soul unmoved in the second stanza?
3. (a) What does the soul choose in the third stanza? (b) What does the soul do after making this choice?

Interpreting

4. (a) What is the soul's "divine Majority"?

(b) Of how many people does the soul's "Society" actually consist?
5. How would you describe the soul's attitude toward the rest of the world?
6. What does line 9 suggest about the speaker's relationship to the soul?

Applying

7. In real life people select a wide variety of different "societies." List as many as you can. What do you think this tendency indicates about human nature?

The Soul selects her own Society   391

(b) All of the details in the second and third stanzas develop this comparison.
3. The inner grief is reflected in the passing of seasons in the outer world.

Presentation

Purpose-Setting Question
What does the soul select?

1 **Discussion** What do the first two lines mean?

2 **Discussion** What is the "divine Majority"?

3 **Critical Thinking and Reading** Note that the society the "Soul selects" is not determined by wealth or power.

4 **Discussion** What "divine Majority" is suggested by line 10?

5 **Discussion** What is the effect of the image presented in the final lines?

Closure and Extension

ANSWERS TO THINKING ABOUT THE SELECTION
Recalling

1. The soul selects her own society.
2. Chariots passing at the gate and a kneeling emperor leave the soul unmoved.
3. (a) The soul may choose just one individual. (b) Then the valves of her attention are closed.

Interpreting

4. (a) Suggested Response: The people to whom she reveals herself. (b) The soul's society may actually consist of one other person.
5. It is indifferent to the rest of the world.
6. It suggests that the speaker is referring to her own soul.

Applying

7. Suggested Response: The fact that people select a wide variety of "societies" indicates that the human race is a very diverse group.

1 **Literary Focus** What metaphor does Dickinson establish in the first several lines?

2 **Discussion** How does Dickinson characterize the stone?

3 **Discussion** What does the "Coat of elemental Brown" suggest?

4 **Discussion** What is the main source of the stone's happiness?

Reader's Response How would you describe Dickinson's poetry to a friend who has never read any Dickinson poems? Explain.

Closure and Extension

ANSWERS TO THINKING ABOUT THE SELECTION
Recalling

1. (a) The stone rambles in the road alone. (b) It does not care about careers. (c) It fulfills its "absolute Decree in casual simplicity."

Interpreting

2. (a) The human qualities she attributes to the stone are solitude, indifference to careers and necessity, simplicity and lack of pretence, and independence. (b) Suggested Response: These qualities allow it to be faithful to its own nature and to be unaffected by others.

Applying

3. Answers will differ. Students might mention lions, because of their strength and determination; and ants, because of their industriousness.

How happy is the little Stone

Emily Dickinson

```
     How happy is the little Stone
     That rambles in the Road alone,
     And doesn't care about Careers
     And Exigencies never fears—
5    Whose Coat of elemental Brown
     A passing Universe put on,
     And independent as the Sun
     Associates or glows alone,
     Fulfilling absolute Decree
10   In casual simplicity—
```

THINKING ABOUT THE SELECTION

Recalling

1. (a) Where does the little stone ramble? (b) What does it not care about? (c) What does it fulfill?

Interpreting

2. In this poem the speaker sees the little stone as a model for humanity's spiritual self-sufficiency. (a) What human qualities does she attribute to the stone? (b) Why do these qualities make it an appropriate model?

Applying

3. What other elements of the natural world do you think could serve as models for human behavior? Explain your choices.

There is a solitude of space

Emily Dickinson

GENESEE SCENERY
Thomas Cole
Museum of Art, Rhode Island School of Design

1 There is a solitude of space
A solitude of sea
2 A solitude of death, but these
Society shall be
3 5 Compared with that profounder site
That polar privacy
4 A soul admitted to itself—
Finite Infinity.

THINKING ABOUT THE SELECTION

Recalling

1. What three forms of solitude does the speaker mention in the first three lines?
2. What "profounder site" does the speaker describe in lines 6–7?

Interpreting

3. (a) What do you think the speaker means by "a soul admitted to itself"? (b) What makes this concept different from the three forms of solitude mentioned in the first three lines? (c) How does it relate to the paradox, or apparent contradiction, presented in the final line?

Applying

4. Explain how it is possible for a person to live in solitude while surrounded by other people.

There is a solitude of space 393

393

1 **Critical Thinking and Reading**
The letter to the world might refer just to this poem or to the whole body of Dickinson's poetry. Ask the students to suggest which they believe to be the "this" of the first line.

2 **Discussion** What do lines 3–4 suggest about Dickinson's source of poetic inspiration?

Humanities Note

Fine art, *Twilight in the Wilderness,* 1860, by Frederick Edwin Church. Church (1826–1900) was an American painter whose large, dramatic landscapes made him one of the most popular artists of his time. Early in his career, Church was a leading member of the Hudson River School of landscape painting. His early works, including *Twilight in the Wilderness,* are panoramic compositions with emphatic visual effects. Although Church had painted other sunsets, *Twilight in the Wilderness* is his crowning statement.

Consider these questions for discussion:

1. What statement does the artist seem to be making in this painting?
2. How does it compare with the statement Emily Dickinson is making in this poem?

Reader's Response If you were to write a "letter to the world," what would you say? Why?

This is my letter to the World

Emily Dickinson

1   This is my letter to the World
    That never wrote to Me—
2   The simple News that Nature told—
    With tender Majesty

5   Her Message is committed
    To Hands I cannot see—
    For love of Her—Sweet—countrymen—
    Judge tenderly—of Me

TWILIGHT IN THE WILDERNESS
Frederick E. Church
The Cleveland Museum of Art

394   *New England Renaissance*

THINKING ABOUT THE SELECTION

Recalling

1. To whom does the speaker address her letter?
2. What request does the speaker make in the final line?

Interpreting

3. In this poem Dickinson addresses the potential audience of her poetry. What evidence in the poem suggests that she does not expect this audience to read her poetry until after her death?
4. How does Dickinson convey her sense of isolation from the rest of the world?
5. To what does Dickinson give credit for providing the material for her poetry?
6. How does Dickinson indicate that she believes her purpose should be taken into consideration when her poetry is judged?

Applying

7. Explain whether this poem would be an appropriate introduction to a collection of Dickinson's poetry.

THINKING AND WRITING

Responding to Dickinson's Poetry

Respond to Dickinson's letter to the world by writing a letter to her in which you express your personal reactions to her poetry. Review her poems and record your response to them. Then think about your reaction to her poetry. How does it affect you emotionally? Do you find it difficult to understand? If so, why? Do you find that it helps you to understand yourself? Start your letter by summing up your reaction. Then support your reactions with specific examples from several of her poems. When you finish writing, revise your letter and prepare a final copy.

Commentary

The last years of Emily Dickinson's life undoubtedly correspond to the popular picture of the pale recluse in the upstairs room, speaking to almost no one. That she did become very eccentric is clear from her letters, and there is more than a touch of "divine madness" in her poems. But Emily Dickinson was also an ordinary person who could love and be hurt.

From her letters we know that Emily Dickinson did fall passionately in love at least twice during her life. During her years from twenty-eight to thirty-two, she wrote three drafts of letters (which were perhaps never sent) to an unknown recipient whom she calls "Master." The letters are full of the pain, sorrow, and insecurity of love: "I want to see you more—Sir—than all I wish for in this world—and the wish—altered a little—will be my only one—for the skies."

In 1878 she fell deeply in love with a family friend, Judge Phil Lord, and he with her. She was forty-eight and he about twenty years older; they had known each other socially for many years. Only rough drafts of fifteen letters to him remain, but these are filled with passionate intensity: "I confess that I love him—I rejoice that I love him—. . . the exultation floods me. I cannot find my channel—the Creek turns Sea—at thought of thee—."

Lord pushed her to marry him and live in Salem. Although drawn strongly to him and even to the idea of marriage, she resisted. In 1884 he died of a stroke. Two years later she was dead.

This is my letter to the World 395

ANSWERS TO THINKING ABOUT THE SELECTION
Recalling

1. The speaker addresses the letter to the world.
2. The speaker asks that the world judge her tenderly.

Interpreting

3. Her request that the world judge her tenderly and her comment that "her message is committed" to hands she cannot see suggest that she does not expect her work to be read while she is alive.
4. She says that the world never wrote to her.
5. Dickinson credits Nature for supplying the material for the poetry.
6. She suggests that she is conveying Nature's message and that people should consider that when judging her poetry.

Applying

7. Suggested Response: It would make an appropriate introduction, because it reveals the purpose of her poetry and provides insights into her personality.

Challenge If you could write a letter to the world, what would you say?

THINKING AND WRITING

Publishing Student Writing Have students volunteer to read their letters to the class, and use these letters as a springboard for a class discussion about Dickinson's poetry.

The writing assignments on page 396 have students write creatively, while those on page 397 have them think about the selections and write critically.

YOU THE WRITER
Guidelines for Evaluating Assignment 1

1. Has the student written five journal entries that describe the experiences a Transcendentalist might have had while living in the wilderness?
2. Does the student use concrete details in describing the experiences?
3. Do the journal entries convey what the Transcendentalist learned from the experiences?
4. Are the journal entries clear and coherent, and free from grammar, usage, and mechanics errors?

Guidelines for Evaluating Assignment 2

1. Has the student written a lyric poem on the theme of love, nature, home and family, or patriotism, which is easy to read and inspiring?
2. Does the speaker in the poem express thoughts and feelings about the subject?
3. Is there a regular rhythm and rhyme scheme?
4. Has the student used concrete imagery in expressing his or her ideas?
5. Is the poem free from grammar, usage, and mechanics errors?

Guidelines for Evaluating Assignment 3

1. Has the student written a dialogue between a Transcendentalist and an Anti-transcendentalist that clearly contrasts their different philosophies?
2. Does the dialogue seem realistic?
3. Does the dialogue express the dominant ideas of both philosophies?
4. Is the dialogue free from grammar, usage, and mechanics errors?

YOU THE WRITER

Assignment

1. Imagine that you are a Transcendentalist living during the New England Renaissance. Like Thoreau, you have decided to test your beliefs by living in the wilderness. Write a series of five journal entries in which you describe the types of experiences you would expect to have in this situation.

Prewriting. Brainstorm about the types of experiences you might have in the wilderness. How would you react to these experiences? What insights might you gain from the experiences?

Writing. When you write your journal entries, use concrete details in describing your experiences. Make sure you convey what you have gained from the experiences.

Revising. When you revise, make sure you have described your experiences and expressed your ideas clearly and coherently.

Assignment

2. In the tradition of the Fireside Poets, write a lyric poem that would have appealed to a family audience during the New England Renaissance. Your lyric should be inspiring and easy to read and should focus on one of the following themes: love, nature, home and family, or patriotism.

Prewriting. Choose a subject for your poem. Then prepare a list of concrete details related to this subject.

Writing. When writing your lyric, have your speaker express his or her thoughts and feelings about the subject. Use a regular rhythm and follow a regular rhyme scheme.

Revising. When you revise, make sure you have used concrete imagery in expressing your ideas. After you have finished revising, share your poem with your classmates.

Assignment

3. As you have learned in this unit, there was a sharp contrast between the ideas of the Transcendentalists and those of the Anti-Transcendentalists. Write a dialogue in which one of the Transcendentalists and one of the Anti-Transcendentalists discuss their different philosophies.

Prewriting. Review the discussion of the philosophies of Transcendentalism and Anti-Transcendentalism in the unit introduction (p. 246) and in the Guides for Interpreting on pages 273 and 301, paying close attention to the differences in the two philosophies.

Writing. Try to make your dialogue seem realistic, as if you were merely recording a conversation that really occurred.

Revising. When you revise, make sure you have clearly expressed the dominant ideas of both philosophies. After you have finished revising, proofread your dialogue and prepare a final copy.

YOU THE CRITIC

Assignment

1. Although the Fireside Poets shared a common purpose, the poems they created were often quite different from one another. Write an essay in which you compare and contrast two poems by two different Fireside Poets.

Prewriting. Review the poetry of the Fireside Poets, and choose two poems that are in some ways similar and in some ways different from each other. Then reread the poems, noting the similarities and differences.

Writing. Organize your essay according to corresponding points of contrast, using passages from each poem to support your argument.

Revising. When you revise, make sure you have used transitions and other linking devices to connect your ideas. After you have finished revising, proofread your essay and prepare a final copy.

Assignment

2. As the world changes, popular philosophies or views of life sometimes become outdated. Which philosophy do you think is more applicable to contemporary life: that of the Transcendentalists or that of the Anti-Transcendentalists?

Prewriting. Review the discussion of the philosophies of Transcendentalism and Anti-Transcendentalism in the unit introduction. Then spend some time thinking about how effectively each philosophy can be applied to contemporary life.

Writing. When writing your essay, make sure you thoroughly support your opinion with facts and examples.

Revising. When you revise, make sure you have expressed your ideas clearly and coherently.

Assignment

3. While the Transcendentalists, the Anti-Transcendentalists, and the Fireside Poets had very different philosophies and concerns, they were all part of the Romantic movement that began in the early 1800's. Write an essay in which you discuss the Romantic attitudes and interests reflected in the works of the writers involved with one of the three movements of the New England Renaissance.

Prewriting. Review the discussion of Romanticism in the introduction to the Growing Nation unit. Then reread one group of selections in this unit, noting the Romantic ideas and interests they reflect.

Writing. When you write your essay, use evidence from several works to support your argument.

Revising. When you revise, make sure you have thoroughly supported your argument. Proofread your essay and prepare a final draft.

You the Critic **397**

1. Has the student compared and contrated poems by two different Fireside Poets to show that although the poets had a common purpose, the poems they wrote were quite different from one another?
2. Is the essay organized according to corresponding points of contrast, using passages from the poems to support the argument?
3. Has the student used transitions and other linking devices to connect ideas?
4. Is the essay free from grammar, usage, and mechanics errors?

Guidelines for Evaluating Assignment 2

1. Has the student written an essay stating which philosophy, Transcendentalism or Anti-transcendentalism, is more applicable to contemporary life?
2. Has the student supported his or her opinion thoroughly with facts and examples?
3. Has the student clearly and coherently expressed his or her ideas?
4. Is the essay free from grammar, usage, and mechanics errors?

Guidelines for Evaluating Assignment 3

1. Does the essay discuss the Romantic attitudes, ideas, and interests reflected in the works of writers involved in one of the three movements of the New England Renaissance?
2. Does the student give enough evidence from several works to support his or her argument thoroughly?
3. Is the essay logically arranged?
4. Is the essay free from grammar, usage, and mechanics errors?

Humanities Note

Fine art, *Let Us Have Peace (Grant and Lee),* by J. L. G. Ferris. The painter Jean Leon Gerome Ferris (1863–1930) is noted for the American themes in his works—works that stress harmony, peace, and a spirit of hope. *Let Us Have Peace (Grant and Lee)* is such a painting. The event depicted is the surrender of the Confederate forces, under General Robert E. Lee, to the Union commander, Ulysses S. Grant. The setting is Appomattox Court House, in Virginia, on April 9, 1865.

Ferris has chosen, in his title, to emphasize the affirmation by the two generals—and, it was hoped, by the nation as a whole —to heal the wounds of war and to rebuild a country wrenched apart by strife and bitterness. The painting, in the simplicity of the central handshake, and in the somber poses of the figures in attendance, focuses the viewer's eye on the physical representation of the pledge by the two generals to "have peace."

LET US HAVE PEACE (GRANT AND LEE)
J. L. G. Ferris
Three Lions

Objectives

1 To understand the events and developments that led up to the Civil War
2 To learn about the events and developments that shaped the outcome of the war
3 To learn about the literature that emerged during the Civil War era

DIVISION, WAR, AND RECONCILIATION

1855–1865

Skimming lightly, wheeling still,
  The swallows fly low
Over the fields in clouded days,
  The forest-field of Shiloh—
                    Herman Melville

399

Historical Context Tell students that the Civil War was the bloodiest and possibly the most tragic war in American history. Approximately 620,000 soldiers died during the course of the conflict —more than in the Revolutionary War, the War of 1812, the Mexican War, World War I, World War II, the Korean War, and the Vietnam War combined. In addition, the war created deep psychological wounds that took decades to heal. Although the conflict had a tremendous impact on the North, the South paid an even greater price. Not only were many Southern cities, towns, and industries completely destroyed but also the Southern way of life was irreversibly changed. Aside from putting an end to slavery, the war had few positive effects. Yet despite the devastation brought about by the conflict, a number of fine works of American literature emerged from the war era.

Writing to Learn Have students write a journal entry in which they discuss what they know about the Civil War. As they move through the unit, encourage them to look back at their journal entries and explore how the literature of the war era may have enhanced their understanding of the war.

ESL Teaching Strategy Pair each of your ESL students with a native-speaking student. Have the pairs read through the unit introduction together, taking turns reading aloud. Instruct the native speaker to clarify the meanings of any words with which the ESL student is unfamiliar.

If your students have studied or are currently studying American history, you might want to have them share their prior knowledge of the Civil War and its impact on the American people. Then have them try to come up with examples of literary works that either focus on the war or were written during the war. You might also want to have them discuss movies they have seen that are set during the war. What impression of the war do these movies convey? Do they think this impression is accurate? Why or why not?

Purpose-Setting Question What were the major causes of the war? What type of impact did the war have on the American people? What important literary works were written during the war years?

1 **Master Teacher Note** The photographs of Matthew Brady, the first of their kind, form a compelling record of the Civil War. They can be found in many books about the Civil War. You might display samples of them as the basis for a discussion of the vast upheaval caused by the war. For additional information about Brady, see the Cross Currents, pages 474–475.

The Civil War moved Herman Melville to write a volume of sensitive poetry that treated incidents of the war in a quiet, mournful tone. His poem about the Battle of Shiloh is called, "A Requiem," since it was written to honor the soldiers who had died there. The battle, fought in western Tennessee in April 1862, was one of the bloodiest contests of the American Civil War. With more than 10,000 casualties on each side, Shiloh was a decisive event. It proved that the war, begun the previous spring with cheering, flag waving, and brave rhetoric, would be a long and bitter struggle.

1

Like the Revolution before it, the Civil War, or the War Between the States, absorbed the creative energies of the nation. Notable speeches, songs, letters, memoirs, and journals appeared, but little in the way of memorable fiction. Many writers became involved with the war, and some of the most important wartime literature was produced by the leaders from both sides. One towering literary figure did emerge during the wartime era, however—the poet Walt Whitman.

THE HISTORICAL SETTING

Opposition to slavery did not begin with the Civil War. Thomas Jefferson's first draft of the Declaration of Independence described the slave trade as a "cruel war against human nature itself, violating its most sacred rights of life and liberty." This language did not find its way into the final document, however. Slavery eventually disappeared in the North, where it had never been very profitable. In the South, however, slavery became the foundation of the plantation system.

The Missouri Compromise in 1820 and the Compromise of 1850 held off confrontations between slave states and free states for many years. But nothing short of secession from the Union (which the South often threatened) or freedom for the slaves (which many in the North demanded) could finally end the controversy. The northern and southern states entered the 1850's on a collision course. Would the new territories in the West enter the Union as free states or as slave states? Walt Whitman later saw this continuing conflict not as a "struggle between two distinct and separate peoples" but rather as one between "the passions and paradoxes" within the United States.

Passions and Paradoxes

The North and South had clearly developed along very different lines. In the North, commerce, not cotton, was king. The Industrial Revolution and cheap transportation had helped turn northern towns and cities into centers of bustling activity. Education, banking, science, and reform movements—all were topics of interest and concern. Immigration, too, was changing the face of the North. A rising tide of Irish and Germans, among others, were seeking a new life

400   *Division, War, and Reconciliation*

in the United States. Most of these newcomers landed at seaports between Boston and Baltimore and settled in the northern states.

The South, by contrast, was a slower-paced region of plantations and small farms. There were cities, to be sure, but the area was most truly defined by its cotton plantations, large and small. Sugar, rice, and tobacco were also important crops. The march of technological progress, with its hotly debated social issues and problems, had little impact on the prewar South.

One issue, however, made an indelible impression. That issue was slavery. The South believed its lifeblood to depend on the "peculiar institution" of slavery. Statesmen might make tactical compromises on such matters as free states or slave states being carved from the new territories, but there could be no compromise on the legality of slavery.

Firebrands on the other side of the issue, mostly northerners, were just as adamant. William Lloyd Garrison published an aboli-

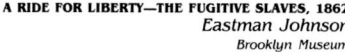

A RIDE FOR LIBERTY—THE FUGITIVE SLAVES, 1862
Eastman Johnson
Brooklyn Museum

Enrichment One of the bloodiest battles of the Civil War, the Battle of Antietam took place on September 17, 1862 in Maryland. Over 24,000 Union and Confederate soldiers were either killed or wounded. Neither side achieved a victory. Yet because the Southern forces left Antietam on the night after the battle, the Northern forces claimed that they had won.

Enrichment The Battle of Shiloh was even more devastating than the Battle of Antietam. More soldiers died in one day at Shiloh than in the American Revolution, the War of 1812, and the Mexican War combined. Although the North suffered severe losses in the battle, it was able to achieve a victory. By doing so it gained control of river traffic on the northern Mississippi.

Enrichment The Battle of Gettysburg, which took place from July 1 through July 3 in 1863, represented a major turning point in the war. After an all-out attack on the strongest Union position ended in failure, the Confederate army was forced to retreat into Virginia, their numbers greatly depleted and their morale severely damaged. In the aftermath of the battle, it seemed less probable that the Confederate forces would be able to overcome the Union's advantages in both resources and manpower.

AMERICAN EVENTS

Bombardment of Fort Sumter

1855   **Walt Whitman** publishes first edition of *Leaves of Grass.*

My Bondage and My Freedon, **Frederick Douglass's** second autobiography, makes its appearance.

1858   **Oliver Wendell Holmes** publishes *The Autocrat of the Breakfast Table.*

Lincoln-Douglas debates help to make **Abraham Lincoln** a national figure.

1859   John Brown, radical abolitionist, raids federal arsenal at Harpers Ferry; he is hanged for treason.

1860   Essays by **Ralph Waldo Emerson** published as *The Conduct of Life.*

Henry Timrod's *Poems* appears; his only collection published during his lifetime.

1861   **Lincoln** inaugurated in March; Civil War begins in April with firing on Fort Sumter.

1862   **Emily Dickinson** writes many superb poems in what, for unknown reasons, is a crucial year for her.

Major battles are fought at Shiloh, Antietam, and Fredericksburg.

Julia Ward Howe writes "The Battle Hymn of the Republic."

After Antietam, **Lincoln** issues the Emancipation Proclamation.

1863   Union forces lose at Chancellorsville, but win at Gettysburg and Vicksburg.

1864   War nears an end with battles of the Wilderness, Atlanta, and Nashville.

1865   **General Robert E. Lee** surrenders to General Ulysses S. Grant at Appomattox Court House.

Within days of Lee's surrender, **President Lincoln** is assassinated.

Charles Darwin

Sepoy Rebellion

Battle of the Wilderness

402   *Division, War, and Reconciliation*

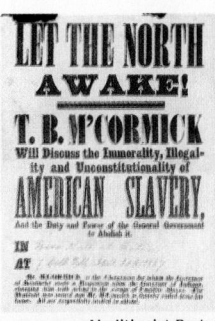

Abolitionist Poster

Frederick Douglass

John Brown

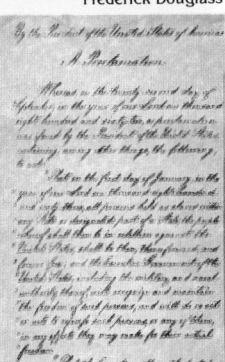

Emancipation Proclamation

The Surrender at Appomattox

1855   England: Alfred, Lord Tennyson publishes his long poem *Maud*.

1856   England: Bessemer steel process makes modern steelmaking possible.

1857   France: Gustave Flaubert completes *Madame Bovary*, classic novel of realism.

India: Start of doomed Sepoy Rebellion; native soliders fight British rule.

1859   England: Charles Darwin introduces theory of evolution in *Origin of Species*.

England: Charles Dickens adds to his fame with *A Tale of Two Cities*.

1860   England: Florence Nightingale founds Nightingale School for training nurses.

1861   England: George Eliot (Mary Ann Evans) publishes her popular novel *Silas Marner*.

Italy: Unification of Italy achieved; Count Camillo Cavour led movement.

1862   France: Louis Pasteur proposes modern germ theory of disease.

Russia: Ivan Turgenev publishes *Fathers and Sons*, his masterpiece.

1863   Mexico: French occupy Mexico City and establish Maximilian as emperor of Mexico.

France: Jean François Millet paints *The Man with the Hoe*.

1864   England: *Dramatis Personae* by Robert Browning appears; it includes the poem "Prospice."

1865   England: Lewis Carroll completes *Alice's Adventures in Wonderland*.

Introduction   403

Enrichment In *Origin of Species,* Charles Darwin introduced his Theory of Evolution. According to this theory, all forms of life evolve, or change, over a long period of time. Simpler forms of life evolve into more complex forms, and new forms evolve out of older ones. Darwin believed that this occurred because all beings struggled with each other for the necessities of life. Only the fittest survived this competition and passed their superior characteristics on to subsequent generations.

Because they felt that Darwin's theories contradicted the Bible, many people attacked his ideas. Others, however, embraced Darwin's ideas and applied them to the social and political issues of the 1800's. The English philosopher Herbert Spencer, for example, used Darwin's theories as an explanation for the inequalities of life.

Enrichment After suppressing the Sepoy Rebellion, an uprising of Indian soldiers who served in European armies, the British government established full colonial rule in India. British rule lasted until 1947, when England passed the India Independence Act, which established two independent nations on the subcontinent: India, which was dominated by Hindus; and Pakistan, which was dominated by Moslems.

2 **Literary Movement** The excerpt from *Mary Chestnut's Civil War,* page 437, gives a first-hand account of the incident at Fort Sumter.

3 **Literary Movement** A letter from Robert E. Lee to his son appears on page 450.

Learning Across the Curriculum
Your students might be interested in learning more about the Civil War. Divide your class into groups of three or four. Then have each group choose an important event in the years leading up to the war or a major battle that occurred during the war. The groups should then research the topic they have chosen. When the groups have completed their research, they should present their findings to the rest of the class. Because social studies teachers may be able to help guide the students' research, you may want to notify the social studies department about this assignment.

tionist weekly, *The Liberator,* that demanded immediate, uncompensated freedom for all slaves. His first issue proclaimed: "I am in earnest—I will not equivocate—I will not excuse—I will not retreat a single inch—*and I will be heard*." Few people in the antislavery movement were as extreme as Garrison. Their basic goal was, nonetheless, unacceptable to most southerners.

The controversy between North and South came to a head in 1860. In that year, Abraham Lincoln was elected President of the United States in a bitter four-way race. Lincoln had once said, "If slavery is not wrong, nothing is wrong." The national paradoxes and passions that Walt Whitman observed could no longer be contained by compromise.

The Union Is Dissolved

Even before Lincoln was inaugurated, the legislature of South Carolina had declared unanimously that "the union now subsisting between South Carolina and other States . . . is hereby dissolved." Other southern states soon followed South Carolina's lead. In February 1861, delegates from seven states met in Montgomery, Alabama, to establish the Confederate States of America.

Some northerners were willing to accept secession, but President Lincoln was not. Once he had made his position clear, war seemed inevitable. The fighting began on April 12, 1861, when Confederate artillery fired on Union troops holding Fort Sumter, in Charleston Harbor. Three days later, Lincoln issued a call for 75,000 Union volunteers to put down the rebellion. Two days after that, Virginia seceded from the Union, and its militia seized the United States Naval yard at Norfolk. The Civil War was on.

Most people in the North expected the Union to win a quick, decisive victory over the Confederacy. It was not to be. Even with the North's formidable economic, industrial, and numerical advantages, four years of war lay ahead. The South's one main advantage over the Union was its superior military leadership. In the end, however, not even the incomparable General Robert E. Lee could prevail against the much larger Union force under General Ulysses S. Grant. Battles raged as far north as Pennsylvania, as far south as Georgia and Florida, and throughout the Mississippi Valley. The names of the major battles are carved on countless Civil War monuments across the United States: Bull Run, Fort Donelson, Shiloh, Antietam, Fredericksburg, Chancellorsville, Gettysburg, Vicksburg, Chattanooga, Atlanta, Petersburg, and, finally, Appomattox Court House.

The Civil War was the first American war in which black troops fought in large numbers. By the end of the war, there were some 180,000 black soldiers in more than a hundred Union regiments. On the Confederate side, both slaves and free blacks accompanied the army as cooks, teamsters, and laborers. A few Native American

TIDINGS FROM THE FRONT
Gilbert Gaul
Three Lions

Humanities Note

Fine art, *Tidings from the Front*, by William Gilbert Gaul. William Gilbert Gaul (1855–1919) was born in New Jersey and studied art in the United States. Gaul is best known for the paintings he did of the Civil War. His works were realistic and believable; they won him a number of important honors. Gaul's subjects include both military scenes and, as in *Tidings from the Front*, images of the impact of the war on ordinary people.

In *Tidings from the Front* intentness is displayed on the faces of the listeners as the central figure reads the letter. The presence of an elderly black man and a young black boy indicates the artist's concern for all Americans. Around the assembled figures the intricate pattern of foliage provides a kind of pictorial frame. What the letter says, of course, is left to the viewer's imagination.

regiments served the Union cause on the frontier. Women's contributions to the war effort, North and South, were monumental. Clara Barton, organizer of the American Red Cross, became known as the "Angel of the Battlefield" for her tireless work as a nurse in army camps and hospitals.

The war finally ended in 1865, when General Lee surrendered to General Grant at Appomattox. Although the nation was reunited, deep wounds had been opened that would take decades to heal. Unfortunately, the nation's unity had to be restored without the leadership of President Lincoln. Lincoln was assassinated on the eve of the final victory.

Introduction 405

Humanities Note

Fine art, *The Confederate Battle Flag—Faithful Troops Cheer General Lee,* by N. C. Wyeth. A prolific painter and illustrator of magazine articles, Newell Convers Wyeth (1882–1945), especially in his later years, was hired by several firms to provide paintings to be used on calendars they produced. *The Confederate Battle Flag—Faithful Troops Cheer General Lee* is from a calendar, entitled "Flags in American History," commissioned by John Morrell and Company for 1944.

The painting, oil on panel, is more than a tribute to the Confederate flag. It is a Civil War scene that combines the heroic and the simple. Lee, prominently depicted in the foreground, waves his hat to the troops. The mostly ragtag soldiers, in turn, greet him with raised arms and raised rifles. The earnestness of their gestures, especially in contrast to the stately-looking Lee, seems to be Wyeth's way of expressing sympathy, perhaps for all soldiers. And, indeed, it is the troops who are carrying the flag, rather than their leader.

FAITHFUL TROOPS CHEER GENERAL LEE, 1865
N. C. Wyeth
U. S. Naval Academy Museum

406 *Division, War, and Reconciliation*

EPIC IN BLUE AND GRAY

Literature deals with conflict, and there was plenty of real-life conflict in the United States between 1855 and 1865. The antislavery and proslavery forces, North and South, argued vehemently in public and in private. Other notable struggles pitted the United States Army against Native Americans, open-range ranchers against settlers, wage-earners against powerful new corporations, reformers against a host of real or imagined evils. All these conflicts would eventually find their way into American literature. For quite some time, however, the attention of writers was riveted on the immediate, cataclysmic event—the Civil War, its causes, clashes, and consequences.

Oh, Freedom!

When white Europeans came to America, they usually arrived with hope and the promise of a better life. Black Africans arrived as slaves, facing a life of bondage. Yet not all of them remained slaves. Some slaves, in the North and the South, were freed even before the Revolution. By the time of the Civil War, there were a great many free blacks in the United States, including a large number in the South.

Of the blacks who remained in slavery in the 1850's, more than half worked on cotton plantations. On these plantations and elsewhere, the slaves developed a unique style of music, the black spiritual. Spirituals fused traditional African music with other familiar materials—the Bible, Protestant hymns, and the popular music of the day. To the slave, spirituals were more than just deeply moving expressions of faith. They were also work songs in the fields and mills, rowing and hauling songs, war songs, laments, lullabies, and funeral dirges.

Among the best-known spirituals are "Roll, Jordan, Roll" and "Poor Rosy." Lucy McKim, a nineteenth-century collector of spirituals, quotes a slave woman who claimed that "Poor Rosy" could be sung only with "a full heart and a troubled spirit." McKim qualifies as an unsung heroine herself. Her *Slave Songs of the United States,* published in 1867, is a valuable source of music that might otherwise have been lost forever.

Not all the black voices of the period surfaced in spirituals. One of the great black abolitionist leaders was Frederick Douglass, born into slavery in Maryland. Douglass escaped as a young man and settled in the North, where he became a persuasive orator against slavery. Later he founded and published the *North Star,* a weekly antislavery newspaper. In his autobiography, *Narrative of the Life of Frederick Douglass,* Douglass agreed with the slave woman who spoke to Lucy McKim. "The songs of the slave," he wrote, "represent the sorrows of his heart; and he is relieved by them only as an aching heart is relieved by its tears."

4

5

4 Master Teacher Note To give students a sense of the melodies and rhythms of spirituals, you might play a recording of some spirituals. One possibility is the recording by Paul Robeson on the Vanguard label (#79193).

5 Literary Movement Two examples of spirituals are presented on pages 426 and 427.

Enrichment In his novel *The Red Badge of Courage,* Stephen Crane offers some graphic descriptions of the fighting during the Civil War. He writes:

The regiment bled extravagantly. Grunting bundles of blue began to drop. The orderly sergeant of the youth's company was shot through the cheeks. Its supports being injured his jaw hung afar down, disclosing in the wide cavern of his mouth a pulsing mass of blood and teeth. And with it all he made attempts to cry out. In his endeavor there was a dreadful earnestness, as if he was convinced that one great shriek would make him well.

The youth saw him presently go rearward. His strength seemed in nowise impaired. He ran swiftly, casting wild glances for succor.

Others fell down about the feet of their companions. Some of the wounded crawled out and away, but many lay still, their bodies twisted into impossible shapes.

6 **Literary Movement** For examples of Lincoln's moving writing, read "The Gettysburg Address," on page 444, and a letter he wrote to Mrs. Bixby, on page 446.

7 **Literary Movement** An excerpt from Mary Chestnut's dairy begins on page 437.

Enrichment Black soldiers made an important contribution to the Union victory in the Civil War. The 54th regiment was a company of free Massachusetts blacks who answered President Lincoln's call to arms. They were led by Colonel Robert Gould Shaw, a member of a prominent Boston family. Shaw and many of his men died in an attack on Fort Wagner, South Carolina. Their experiences are documented in the 1989 film *Glory*.

When the Civil War broke out, the familiar spirituals went into battle. They were joined by new songs born of the conflict, such as "Many Thousand Gone" and "Oh, Freedom!" The words of these songs were still sad, but they often expressed a new-found hope:

> Oh, freedom! Oh, freedom!
> Oh, freedom over me;
> And before I'll be a slave,
> I'll be buried in my grave,
> And go home to my Lord, and be free.

According to one historian, the spiritual "made it possible for human beings to accept their fate when they could do nothing else, and it summoned them to a sustained protest against that same fate whenever the hour struck."

Wartime Voices

In a symbolic sense, the hour struck in September 1862 for all the slaves who lived in the Confederate States of America. It was then, in the midst of war, that Lincoln signed the Emancipation Proclamation. This proclamation declared that as of January 1, 1863, slaves in the Confederacy would be "then, thenceforward, and forever free." In order for the promise to be kept, however, the Union had to win the war.

Abraham Lincoln is generally regarded as one of our greatest presidents. His fame rests largely on his deeds, but his words could be equally impressive. No American statesman is more often quoted. Lincoln's two inaugural addresses, his letters, and his brief, inspiring speech at Gettysburg have earned him a permanent place in American literature. 6

Perhaps surprisingly, Lincoln's two most able commanders—Ulysses S. Grant and William T. Sherman—produced memoirs that are still regarded as models of their kind. In fact, the quality of writing done by high-ranking officers on both sides is remarkable. Also noteworthy were the diaries of ordinary soldiers and civilians. One of the most perceptive diarists was Mary Boykin Chesnut, wife of 7 a Confederate officer. Her vivid, close-up views of wartime life in Charleston, South Carolina, were published as *A Diary from Dixie*.

A great many patriotic songs were written and sung during the war. Among the most popular ones in the North were "The Battle Cry of Freedom" and "Tenting Tonight on the Old Campground." "Taps," composed by General Daniel Butterfield, was first played in July 1862. The most famous Union song of all is probably Julia Ward Howe's stirring "The Battle Hymn of the Republic." Among southerners, "The Bonny Blue Flag" and "The Yellow Rose of Texas" were favorites, as was the well-known "Dixie."

Countless novels have been written about the Civil War, but few of any consequence were written until many decades later. One original novel of the Confederacy, *Macaria, or Altars of Sacrifice*,

UNION SOLDIERS RALLY AROUND THE FLAG
William Winner
Art Resource

Fine art, *Union Soldiers Rally Around the Flag,* by William Winner. Little is known about the life of William E. Winner (c. 1815–1883). It is thought that, in the 1840's, he may have painted a portrait of Edgar Allan Poe; as it happened, the artist and the writer lived not far from each other in Philadelphia at the time. The painting was not discovered until 1936, and was tentatively identified by Winner's grandniece.

Union Soldiers Rally Around the Flag is a dramatic tribute to the northern cause and to the Stars and Stripes. The arrangement of the soldiers around the dominant figure creates a pyramid-like shape, with the flag at its apex. Thus the viewer's eye is drawn to the banner, raised high by the central figure. A sense of drama is created, as well, by the horse standing on its hind legs, and by a kind of tumultuous sky. The effect of the scene is a channeling of the tensions of both war and nature in a patriotic display of the symbol for which the soldiers are fighting.

by Augusta Jane Wilson, was published in Richmond in 1864. Another novel, written from the Union viewpoint, was John W. DeForest's *Miss Ravenel's Conversion from Secession to Loyalty,* published in 1867.

Many of the northern writers who were active before the war continued to write during it. William Cullen Bryant, Ralph Waldo Emerson, Henry Wadsworth Longfellow, John Greenleaf Whittier, Oliver Wendell Holmes, James Russell Lowell, Herman Melville, and Emily Dickinson all produced wartime works. Only Melville, however, wrote memorably of the war itself. In the South, Henry Timrod composed poems that led some to call him "the laureate of the Confederacy." Born in Charleston, he developed a diamond-clear style combined with lyrical power. Illness forced Timrod's discharge from the Confederate Army. He died of tuberculosis two years after the war ended. Poets throughout the nation lamented his death, believing that his promise had been largely unfulfilled.

Introduction 409

Check Test

1. Abraham Lincoln was first elected President of the United States in _____.
2. The Civil War began when Confederate troops fired on the Union soldiers holding _____, in Charleston Harbor.
3. The supreme leader of the Confederate armies was _____.
4. In 1862 Abraham Lincoln signed _____, which officially abolished slavery.
5. Probably the greatest writer to emerge from the Civil War era was _____, the author of *Leaves of Grass*.

ANSWERS

1. 1860
2. Fort Sumter
3. Robert E. Lee
4. the Emancipation Proclamation
5. Walt Whitman

The Good Gray Poet

A northern poet who wrote about the war unforgettably was Walt Whitman, one of the giants of American literature. A New Yorker, Whitman worked as a journalist and editor of various newspapers, including the *Brooklyn Eagle*. In his youth, Whitman was something of a dandy, with a neatly trimmed beard, well-tailored clothes, and a spruce cane. He later acquired the better-known image of "the good gray poet"—shaggy beard, rough workman's clothes, large felt hat, and red shirt open at the collar.

Leaves of Grass, the first collection of Whitman's poems, originally appeared in 1855. Although the book achieved little public success, it was well received critically. In a letter to Whitman, Ralph Waldo Emerson hailed the work. "I greet you at the beginning of a great career," he wrote. Whitman continued to revise and expand *Leaves of Grass* throughout his life, producing several expanded editions.

After the Civil War broke out, Whitman's younger brother George enlisted in the Union army. When George was wounded at the Battle of Fredericksburg, Whitman went to Virginia to care for him. He remained in Washington, D.C., for the rest of the war, working as a volunteer in military hospitals. Out of this experience came such masterful poems as "Cavalry Crossing a Ford," "By the Bivouac's Fitful Flame," and "Beat! Beat! Drums!" Upon the assassination of Lincoln, Whitman wrote the much-quoted "O Captain! My Captain" and the classic elegy "When Lilacs Last in the Dooryard Bloom'd."

Whitman's poetry, unusual in both content and style, exalted democracy and the common man. No one had seen anything quite like it before. It was, said one critic, "impossible to transfix with a phrase or a theory." *Leaves of Grass* has been called the most influential volume of poetry in the history of American literature.

8

My brother sitting on the tree of life,
And he heard when Jordan roll,
  Roll, Jordan, roll, Jordan!
  Roll, Jordan, roll!
    Black Spiritual

"A house divided against itself cannot stand." I believe this government cannot endure permanently half slave and half free.
  Abraham Lincoln, Speech, Republican State Convention, 1858

With malice toward none; with charity for all; with firmness in the right, as God gives us to see the right, let us strive on to finish the work we are in. . . .
  Abraham Lincoln, Second Inaugural Address

I felt so tall within—I felt as if the power of the nation was with me.
  Frederick Douglass, *Life and Times of Frederick Douglass*

Mine eyes have seen the glory
  Of the coming of the Lord,;
He is trampling out the vintage
  Where the grapes of wrath are stored.
    Julia Ward Howe, "The Battle Hymn
    of the Republic"

I hear America singing, the varied carols I hear.
  Walt Whitman, *Leaves of Grass,* "I Hear America Singing"

I say we are no better than our judges in the North, and no worse. We are human beings of the nineteenth century, and slavery has to go, of course.
  Mary Boykin Chesnut, *A Diary from Dixie*

Christmas won't be Christmas without any presents.
  Louisa May Alcott, *Little Women*

Additional Voices

I have always thought that all men should be free; but if any should be slaves, if should be first those who desire it for themselves, and secondly those who desire it for others. Whenever I hear anyone arguing for slavery, I feel a strong impulse to see it tried on him personally.
  Abraham Lincoln, Address to an Indiana Regiment

Important principles may and best be inflexible.
  Abraham Lincoln, Last Public Address

The life of the nation is secure only while the nation is honest, truthful, and virtuous.
  Frederick Douglass, Speech on the twenty-third anniversary of the Emancipation Proclamation

When justice is denied, where poverty is enforced, where ignorance prevails, and where any one class is made to feel that society is in an organized conspiracy to oppress, rob, and degrade them, neither persons nor property will be safe.

  Frederick Douglass, Speech on the twenty-fourth anniversary of the Emancipation Proclamation

O Captain! my Captain! our fearful trip is done,
The ship has weathered every rack, the prize we sought is won,
The port is near, the bells I hear, the people all exulting.
  Walt Whitman, "O Captain! My Captain!"

Reading Critically The purpose
of this page is to help students
read critically the literature of the
period of Division, War, and Reconciliation in American history.
The information here will help
students to place the literary
works of this period in their historical context, understand the
literary movements of the time,
and appreciate the writers' techniques.

As students read "When
Lilacs Last in the Dooryard
Bloom'd" on the following pages,
have them pay attention to the
notes in the side column. These
notes provide a model for reading critically. They point out the
aspects of Whitman's poem that
reflect the historical context, the
literary movements, and Whitman's techniques. Suggest that
students also make their own
comments as they read the
poem.

To give students further
practice with the process of
reading critically, use the selection in the Teaching Portfolio,
from *Behind the Scenes* by Elizabeth Keckley, page 545, following the Teacher Backup, which
students can annotate themselves. Encourage students to
use these strategies as they read
the literature in this unit.

READING CRITICALLY

The Literature of 1855–1865

Nearly all of the literary activity that occurred during the years
from 1855 to 1865 was in some way related to the Civil War. By reading the literature of the period, you can gain a better understanding of
the causes of the war and the ways in which it affected the American
people.

Historical Context

During the early part of the nineteenth century, industrialization
swept through the northern states, while the southern states clung to
their traditional rural lifestyle. The division between the North and
South became more and more pronounced, and a great deal of controversy developed over the issue of slavery. As a movement to abolish slavery gained force in the North, southerners, who believed that
their economy depended on slavery, became increasingly concerned. This concern reached its peak when Abraham Lincoln, an opponent of slavery, was elected president in 1860. Following Lincoln's
election, the southern states began seceding from the Union, and on
April 12, 1861, the Civil War began. The conflict lasted four years, taking thousands of lives and causing a tremendous amount of pain and
suffering among the American people.

Literary Movements

In the literary world, the decade between 1855 and 1865 was a
period of transition during which no new movements developed.
However, the wartime era did produce one of the most important and
influential poets in the history of American literature, Walt Whitman.
While the country was being torn apart by war, Whitman was reaf-
firming the principles upon which the country was founded by expressing American democratic ideals in his poetry.

Writers' Techniques

A number of notable speeches, songs, letters, memoirs, and journals were written by people who were directly or indirectly involved
with the Civil War. At the same time, a new type of poetry was created
by Walt Whitman—a type of poetry in which traditional poetic forms
were abandoned in favor of free verse.

On the following pages is a selection by Walt Whitman. The notes
in the side column should draw your attention to the historical context,
literary movements, and writer's techniques. Understanding these
features will help you to fully appreciate the selection.

Objectives

1 To understand an elegy
2 To recognize synonyms
3 To write an elegy

Support Material

Teaching Portfolio
Teacher Backup, p. 541
Reading Critically, from *Behind
the Scenes, or Thirty Years a
Slave, and Four Years in the
White House* by Elizabeth Keck-
ley, p. 545
Grammar in Action Worksheet,
Using Appositives, p. 549
Usage and Mechanics Work-
sheet, p. 550

Analyzing Literature Worksheet,
Understanding Elegies, p. 551
Critical Thinking and Reading
Worksheet, *Understanding the
Multiple Meanings of Words,* p.
552
Selection Test, p. 553

When Lilacs Last in the Dooryard Bloom'd

Walt Whitman

1

When lilacs last in the dooryard bloom'd,
And the great star early droop'd in the western sky in the
    night,
I mourn'd, and yet shall mourn with ever-returning spring.

Ever-returning spring, trinity sure to me you bring,
5   Lilac blooming perennial and drooping star in the west,
And thought of him I love.

Historical Context: This poem was written in honor of President Lincoln following Lincoln's death.

2

O powerful western fallen star!
O shades of night—O moody, tearful night!
O great star disappear'd—O the black murk that hides the
    star!
10   O cruel hands that hold me powerless—O helpless soul of
    me!
O harsh surrounding cloud that will not free my soul.

Writer's Technique: The "powerful western fallen star" symbolizes President Lincoln.

3

In the dooryard fronting an old farmhouse near the white-
    wash'd palings,
Stands the lilac bush tall-growing with heart-shaped leaves
    of rich green,
With many a pointed blossom rising delicate, with the
    perfume strong I love,
15   With every leaf a miracle—and from this bush in the
    dooryard,
With delicate-color'd blossoms and heart-shaped leaves of
    rich green.
A sprig with its flower I break.

Writer's Technique: The poem is written in free verse—verse that has irregular meter and line length. Whitman was the first American writer to use free verse.

4

In the swamp in secluded recesses,
A shy and hidden bird is warbling a song.

When Lilacs Last in the Dooryard Bloom'd   413

Presentation

Motivation/Prior Knowledge Have students consider the impact on a country when its president is assassinated. How does the loss of a leader affect the citizens?

Master Teacher Note Whitman wrote this poem in 1865 within a year after the death of Lincoln, while Whitman was feeling the stress of his deep sorrow. Even though Whitman had never met Lincoln, he had seen him from a distance quite often in Washington. Lincoln's death moved Whitman to compose this elegy "for the sweetest, wisest, soul of all my days and lands."

Purpose-Setting Question What consolation does the poet find?

20 Solitary the thrush,
    The hermit withdrawn to himself, avoiding the settlements,
    Sings by himself a song.

    Song of the bleeding throat,
    Death's outlet song of life, (for well dear brother I know,
25 If thou wast not granted to sing thou would'st surely die.)

5

    Over the breast of the spring, the land, amid cities,
    Amid lanes and through old woods, where lately the violets
        peep'd from the ground, spotting the gray debris,
    Amid the grass in the fields each side of the lanes, passing
        the endless grass,
    Passing the yellow-spear'd wheat, every grain from its
        shroud in the dark-brown fields uprisen,
30 Passing the apple-tree blows[1] of white and pink in the
        orchards,
    Carrying a corpse to where it shall rest in the grave,
    Night and day journeys a coffin.

---

1. blows: Blossoms.

414   *Division, War, and Reconciliation*

THE FUNERAL OF PRESIDENT LINCOLN, NEW YORK, APRIL 25, 1865
Currier & Ives
Anne S. K. Brown Military Collection, Brown University Library

Literary Focus The poet uses images to show how the whole country, including nature and people, is mourning as the coffin passes. What are some of these images?

Enrichment Whitman had developed a deep sense of admiration and respect for Lincoln long before Lincoln's death. Whitman once wrote to a friend:

(Lincoln) has a face like a hoosier Michael Angelo, so awful ugly it becomes beautiful, with its strange mouth, its deep cut, criss-cross lines, and its doughnut complexion. My notion is, too, that underneath his outside mannerism, and stories from third-class country bar-rooms, (it is his humor,) Mr. Lincoln keeps a fountain of first-class practical telling wisdom. I do not dwell on the supposed failures of his government; he has shown, I sometimes think, an almost supernatural tact in keeping the ship afloat at all, with head steady, not only not going down, and now certain not to, but with proud and resolute spirit, and flag flying in sight of the world, menacing and high as ever. I say never yet captain, never ruler, had such a perplexing, dangerous task as his, the past two years. I more and more rely upon his idomatic western genius, careless of court dress or court decorums.

6

Coffin that passes through lanes and streets,
Through day and night with the great cloud darkening the
    land,
35 With the pomp of the inloop'd flags with the cities draped
    in black,
With the show of the states themselves as of crape-veil'd
    women standing,
With processions long and winding and the flambeaus[2] of
    the night,
With the countless torches lit, with the silent sea of faces
    and the unbared heads,
With the waiting depot, the arriving coffin, and the somber
    faces,
40 With dirges through the night, with the thousand voices
    rising strong and solemn,
With all the mournful voices of the dirges pour'd around
    the coffin,
The dim-lit churches and the shuddering organs—where
    amid these you journey,

Writer's Technique: Whitman uses parallelism, repeating similarly structured phrases, clauses, or sentences to establish a pattern and emphasize important ideas.

---

2. flambeaus (flam′ bōz): Torches.

When Lilacs Last in the Dooryard Bloom'd   **415**

Clarification An orb is a sphere or globe. In line 55, Whitman is using it to refer to the western star.

With the tolling tolling bells' perpetual clang,
Here, coffin that slowly passes,
45   I give you my sprig of lilac.

7

(Nor for you, for one alone,
Blossoms and branches green to coffins all I bring,
For fresh as the morning, thus would I chant a song for
   you O sane and sacred death.

Writer's Technique: Whitman expresses his deep admiration for Lincoln, whom he viewed as a symbol of the American democratic ideal.

All over bouquets of roses,
50   O death, I cover you over with roses and early lilies,
But mostly and now the lilac that blooms the first,
Copious I break, I break the sprigs from the bushes,
With loaded arms I come, pouring for you,
For you and the coffins all of you O death.)

8

55   O western orb sailing the heaven,
Now I know what you must have meant as a month since I
   walk'd,
As I walk'd in silence the transparent shadowy night,
As I saw you had something to tell as you bent to me night
   after night,
As you droop'd from the sky low down as if to my side
   (while the other stars all look'd on,)
60   As we wander'd together the solemn night (for something I
   know not what kept me from sleep,)
As the night advanced, and I saw on the rim of the west
   how full you were of woe,
As I stood on the rising ground in the breeze in the cool
   transparent night,
As I watch'd where you pass'd and was lost in the
   netherward[3] black of the night,
As my soul in its trouble dissatisfied sank, as where you
   sad orb,
65   Concluded, dropt in the night, and was gone.

9

Sing on there in the swamp,
O singer bashful and tender, I hear your notes, I hear your
   call,

---

3. netherward *adj.:* Moving downward.

416   Division, War, and Reconciliation

Primary Source

Just after the end of the Civil War, Whitman wrote a journal entry in which he recorded some of his observations of the conflict and speculated about how the war might be recorded in history books. He wrote:

> And so good-bye to the war. I know not how it may have been, or may be, to others—to me the main interest I found, (and still, on recollection, find) in the rank and file of the armies, both sides, and in those specimens amid the hospitals, and even the dead on the field. To me the points illustrating the latent personal character and eligibilities of these States, in the two or three millions of American young and middle-aged men, North and South, embodied in those armies—and especially the one-third or one-fourth of their number, stricken by wounds or disease at some time in the course of the contest—were of more significance even than the political interests involved. . . . Future years will never know the seething hell and the black infernal battleground of countless minor scenes and interiors, (not the official surface-courteousness of the Gener-

I hear, I come presently, I understand you,
But a moment I linger, for the lustrous star has detain'd
    me,
70   The star my departing comrade holds and detains me.

10

O how shall I warble myself for the dead one there I loved?
And how shall I deck my song for the large sweet soul that
    has gone?
And what shall my perfume be for the grave of him I love?

Sea winds blown from east and west,
75   Blown from the eastern sea and blown from the western
    sea, till there on the prairies meeting,
These and with these and the breath of my chant,
I'll perfume the grave of him I love.

11

O what shall I hang on the chamber walls?
And what shall the pictures be that I hang on the walls,
80   To adorn the burial house of him I love?

Pictures of growing spring and farms and homes,
With the fourth-month[4] eve at sundown, and the gray
    smoke lucid and bright,
With floods of the yellow gold of the gorgeous, indolent,
    sinking sun, burning, expanding the air,
With the fresh sweet herbage[5] under foot, and the pale
    green leaves of the trees prolific,
85   In the distance the flowing glaze, the breast of the river,
    with a wind-dapple here and there,
With ranging hills on the banks, with many a line against
    the sky, and shadows,
And the city at hand with dwellings so dense, and stacks of
    chimneys,
And all the scenes of life and the workshops, and the
    workmen homeward returning.

12

Lo, body and soul—this land,
90   My own Manhattan with spires, and the sparkling and

---

4. **fourth-month:** April.
5. **herbage:** Grass.

als, not the few great battles) of the Secession war; and it is best they should not—the real war will never get in the books. In the mushy influences of current times, too, the fervid atmosphere and typical events of those years are in danger of being totally forgotten. I have at night watch'd by the side of a sick man in the hospital, one who could not live many hours. I have seen his eyes flash and burn as he raised himself and recurr'd to the cruelties on his surrender'd brother, and mutilations of the corpse afterward. . . . Such was the war. It was not a quadrille in the ball-room. Its interior history will never be written—its practicality, minutiae of deeds and passions, will never even be suggested.

The actual soldier of 1862–65, North and South, with all his ways, his incredible dauntlessness, habits, practices, tastes, language, his fierce friendship, his appetite, rankness, his superb strength and animality, lawless gait, and a hundred unnamed lights and shades of camp, I say, will never be written—perhaps must not and should not be.

Reading Strategy Help students to see how Whitman returns to his three major symbols: the lilac, the star, and the thrush. How do they represent impressions of smell, sight, and hearing?

Writer's Technique In lines 104 and 105, Whitman continues his use of invocation. You might have students note earlier examples, particularly in Section 2. This technique adds to the sorrowful, prayerful tone of the elegy.

hurrying tides, and the ships,
The varied and ample land, the South and the North in the light, Ohio's shores and flashing Missouri,
And ever the far-spreading prairies cover'd with grass and corn.

Lo, the most excellent sun so calm and haughty,
The violet and purple morn with just-felt breezes,
95   The gentle soft-born measureless light,
The miracle spreading bathing all, the fulfill'd noon,
The coming eve delicious, the welcome night and the stars,
Over my cities shining all, enveloping man and land.

13

Sing on, sing on you gray-brown bird,
100   Sing from the swamps, the recesses, pour your chant from the bushes,
Limitless out of the dusk, out of the cedars and pines.

Sing on dearest brother, warble your reedy song,
Loud human song, with voice of uttermost woe.

O liquid and free and tender!
105   O wild and loose to my soul!—O wondrous singer!
You only I hear—yet the star holds me, (but will soon depart,)
Yet the lilac with mastering odor holds me.

14

Now while I sat in the day and look'd forth,
In the close of the day with its light and the fields of spring, and the farmers preparing their crops,
110   In the large unconscious scenery of my land with its lakes and forests,
In the heavenly aerial beauty (after the perturb'd winds and the storms,)
Under the arching heavens of the afternoon swift passing, and the voices of children and women,
The many-moving sea tides, and I saw the ships how they sail'd,
And the summer approaching with richness, and the fields all busy with labor,
115   And the infinite separate houses, how they all went on,

ABRAHAM LINCOLN
William Willard
National Portrait Gallery, Smithsonian Institution

Humanities Note

Fine art, *Abraham Lincoln,* by William Willard. This portrait of Lincoln hangs in the National Portrait Gallery in the Smithsonian Institution in Washington, D.C. The artist has used a bright background for a striking effect.

You might want to use the following questions to discuss the art:
1. Which qualities of Lincoln's character are captured in this portrait? Explain.
2. How does this portrait compare with other paintings of Lincoln you have seen?
3. If you were the curator of a museum of historical art, would you include this painting in your collection? Why or why not?

each with its meals and minutia[6] of daily usages,
And the streets how their throbbings throbb'd, and the
  cities pent—lo, then and there,
Falling upon them all and among them all, enveloping me
  with the rest,
Appear'd the cloud, appear'd the long black trail,
And I knew death, its thought, and the sacred knowledge of
  death.

120   Then with the knowledge of death as walking one side of
  me,
And the thought of death close-walking the other side of
  me,
And I in the middle as with companions, and as holding
  the hands of companions,
I fled forth to the hiding receiving night that talks not,

---

6. minutia (mi nü′ s͟hē ə) *n.*: Small and trivial detail.

When Lilacs Last in the Dooryard Bloom'd   419

Down to the shores of the water, the path by the swamp in
    the dimness,
125 To the solemn shadowy cedars and ghostly pines so still.

And the singer so shy to the rest receiv'd me,
The gray-brown bird I know receiv'd us comrades three,
And he sang the carol of death, and a verse for him I love.

From deep secluded recesses,
130 From the fragrant cedars and the ghostly pines so still,
Came the carol of the bird.

And the charm of the carol rapt me,
As I held as if by their hands my comrades in the night,
And the voice of my spirit tallied[7] the song of the bird.

135 *Come lovely and soothing death,*
Undulate[8] round the world, serenely arriving, arriving,
In the day, in the night, to all, to each,
Sooner or later delicate death.

Prais'd be the fathomless universe,
140 *For life and joy, and for objects and knowledge curious,*
And for love, sweet love—but praise! praise! praise!
For the sure-enwinding arms of cool-enfolding death.

Dark mother always gliding near with soft feet,
Have none chanted for thee a chant of fullest welcome?
145 *Then I chant it for thee, I glorify thee above all,*
I bring thee a song that when thou must indeed come,
*   come unfalteringly.*

Approach strong deliveress,
When it is so, when thou hast taken them I joyously sing
*   the dead,*
Lost in the loving floating ocean of thee,
150 *Laved[9] in the flood of thy bliss O death.*

From me to thee glad serenades,
Dances for thee I propose saluting thee, adornments and
*   feastings for thee,*

---

7. tallied: Corresponded with.
8. undulate *v.*: To move in waves.
9. laved *v.*: Washed.

Grammar in Action

An **appositive** is a noun, pronoun, or phrase placed near another noun or pronoun which it renames for clarification or emphasis. Walt Whitman uses appositives and appositive phrases extensively. For example, he writes:

Solitary the thrush,
The hermit withdrawn to himself. . . .

The star *my departing comrade* holds and detains me.
In the distance the flowing glaze, *the breast of the river.*

Appositives are punctuated like adjective clauses. If they contain material essential to the meaning of the sentence, they are not set off by commas. If the material is not essential to understanding the sentence, they are set off by commas.

Walt Whitman, *the good gray poet,* wrote *Leaves of Grass.*

His poem *"When Lilacs Last in the Dooryard Bloom'd"* is a tribute to Abraham Lincoln.

And the sights of the open landscape and the high-spread
    sky are fitting,
And life and the fields, and the huge and thoughtful
    night.

155 *The night in silence under many a star,*
The ocean shore and the husky whispering wave whose
    voice I know,
And the soul turning to thee O vast and well-veil'd death,
And the body gratefully nestling close to thee.
Over the treetops I float thee a song,
160 *Over the rising and sinking waves, over the myriad fields*
    and the prairies wide,
Over the dense-pack'd cities all and the teeming wharves
    and ways,
I float this carol with joy, with joy to thee O death.

15

To the tally of my soul,
Loud and strong kept up the gray-brown bird,
165 With pure deliberate notes spreading filling the night.

Loud in the pines and cedars dim,
Clear in the freshness moist and the swamp perfume,
And I with my comrades there in the night.

While my sight that was bound in my eyes unclosed,
170 As to long panoramas of visions.

And I saw askant[10] the armies,
I saw as in noiseless dreams hundreds of battle flags,
Borne through the smoke of the battles and pierc'd with
    missiles I saw them,
And carried hither and yon through the smoke, and torn
    and bloody,
175 And at last but a few shreds left on the staffs (and all in
    silence,)
And the staffs all splinter'd and broken.

Historical Context: Whitman is referring to the armies that fought in the Civil War. The flags they carry are torn, just as the country was torn apart by the war.

I saw battle corpses, myriads of them,
And the white skeletons of young men, I saw them,

---

10. askant: Askance; with a sideways glance.

Enrichment Although Whitman was from the North, he found the need to show reconciliation with the South. In Section 15, he sees the war for what it does to all victims. His compassion for all who died or were maimed is poignantly expressed.

Student Activity 1. Find three appositive phrases in line 188 and two in lines 199–200 of "When Lilacs Last in the Dooryard Bloom'd."

Student Activity 2. Place an appositive or appositive phrase after the italicized noun or phrase in each of the following sentences. Set off the nonessential appositives with commas.
1. *Abraham Lincoln* _____ was assassinated in 1865.
2. *Walt Whitman* _____ wrote a long poem in honor of Lincoln.
3. In his poem Whitman repeatedly refers to *the flowers he would offer Lincoln* _____.
4. A *thrush and a star* _____ appear throughout the poem.
5. The poet also describes the effects of a *terrible war* _____.

Enrichment The poet repeatedly refers to his poem as a song. Help students to find other instances that suggest that Whitman thought of poetry as music. How did this thought help to free his poetry from the formality of the past?

Reader's Response What is your impression of Abraham Lincoln? How does your impression compare with the impression that Whitman conveys in this poem?

Historical Context: Whitman refers to the thousands of soldiers who lost their lives during the Civil War and to the suffering that the war caused among the American people.

I saw the debris and debris of all the slain soldiers of the war,
180 But I saw they were not as was thought,
They themselves were fully at rest, they suffer'd not,
The living remain'd and suffer'd, the mother suffer'd,
And the wife and the child and the musing comrade suffer'd,
And the armies that remain'd suffer'd.

16

185 Passing the visions, passing the night,
Passing, unloosing the hold of my comrades' hands,
Passing the song of the hermit bird and the tallying song of my soul,
Victorious song, death's outlet song, yet varying ever-altering song,
As low and wailing, yet clear the notes, rising and falling, flooding the night,
190 Sadly sinking and fainting, as warning and warning, and yet again bursting with joy,
Covering the earth and filling the spread of the heaven,
As that powerful psalm in the night I heard from recesses,
Passing, I leave thee lilac with heart-shaped leaves,
I leave thee there in the dooryard, blooming, returning with spring.

195 I cease from my song for thee,
From my gaze on thee in the west, fronting the west, communing with thee,
O comrade lustrous with silver face in the night.

Yet each to keep and all, retrievements out of the night,
The song, the wondrous chant of the gray-brown bird,
200 And the tallying chant, the echo arous'd in my soul,
With the lustrous and drooping star with the countenance full of woe,
With the holders holding my hand nearing the call of the bird,
Comrades mine and I in the midst, and their memory ever to keep, for the dead I loved so well,
For the sweetest, wisest soul of all my days and lands—and this for his dear sake,
205 Lilac and star and bird twined with the chant of my soul,
There in the fragrant pines and the cedars dusk and dim.

THINKING ABOUT THE SELECTION

Recalling

1. According to section 1, when did the speaker mourn?
2. (a) How do the people react to the funeral procession in section 6? (b) What does the speaker place on the coffin?
3. Name three of the "pictures of growing spring" presented in section 11.
4. (a) What walks on each side of the speaker in section 14? (b) To where does the speaker flee? (c) Who receives him there?
5. (a) What two things does the speaker see in section 15? (b) What does he realize about what he sees?
6. (a) Where does the speaker leave the lilac in section 16? (b) What happens to the lilac, the star, and the bird in the poem's final lines?

Interpreting

7. What is the significance of the recurring images of spring in the poem?
8. What do the images in section 6 suggest about the reaction of the American public to Lincoln's death?
9. What is the significance of the speaker's gesture at the end of section 6?
10. (a) What does the speaker learn from his observations at the beginning of section 14? (b) What does he learn from his visions in section 15?

Applying

11. What are some of the reasons why people greatly admire Abraham Lincoln?

ANALYZING LITERATURE

Understanding Elegies

Whitman's poem is an example of an elegy—a mournful poem lamenting the death of

an individual or the passing of life and beauty, or meditating on the nature of death.

1. How would you describe the tone of Whitman's poem?
2. Why is this tone appropriate for an elegy?
3. What conclusion about death does the speaker ultimately reach in the poem?

UNDERSTANDING LANGUAGE

Using Synonyms

Synonyms are words that have the same or nearly the same meaning. For example, *advancement* and *development* are synonyms.

The capitalized words are from "When Lilacs Last in the Dooryard Bloom'd." Choose the word that is nearest in meaning to each of the capitalized words, as it is used in the poem.
1. HELPLESS: (a) forlorn (b) inconsiderate (c) protected (d) isolated
2. SECLUDED: (a) concealed (b) isolated (c) exclusive (d) retired
3. PERPETUAL: (a) perennial (b) constant (c) durable (d) persistent
4. LUSTROUS: (a) robust (b) colorful (c) luminous (d) luxuriant

THINKING AND WRITING

Writing an Elegy

Write an elegy mourning the death of a historical figure whom you greatly admire. Your elegy should be solemn in tone and should be written in formal language. It should capture the importance of the subject's life and should convey the sense of loss that resulted from his or her death. When you revise, make sure that you have expressed your ideas using concrete images. When you have completed your revision, share your elegy with your classmates.

ing; it is the remaining living who suffer.
6. (a) He leaves it in the dooryard to bloom again. (b) They become intertwined with the chant of the speaker's soul among the pines and cedars.

Interpreting

7. Spring signifies life and rebirth, and perhaps an afterlife.
8. The images in section 6 suggest that the public was stunned and saddened by his death.
9. He places a symbol of life on the coffin.
10. (a) The speaker comes to know death. (b) He understands that the dead no longer suffer, but that those who mourn them do.

Applying

11. Answers will differ. Suggested Responses: He guided the nation through the Civil War; he ended slavery.

ANSWERS TO ANALYZING LITERATURE

1. Suggested Response: The tone of the poem is mournful.
2. It is appropriate because an elegy laments death and extolls the virtues of the person who has died.
3. He concludes that death will be replaced by new life.

Challenge

What is the effect of Whitman's repeated references to the poem as a "song"?

ANSWERS TO UNDERSTANDING LANGUAGE

1. (a)   2. (b)   3. (b)   4. (c)

THINKING AND WRITING

For help with this assignment, students can refer to Lesson 19, "Writing a Poem," in the Handbook of Writing About Literature.

Writing Across the Curriculum

For extra credit, you might have students research and write about the aspects of Abraham Lincoln's character and life that made him admired and loved. If you inform the social studies department, perhaps social studies teachers could give students guidance.

Closure and Extension

ANSWERS TO THINKING ABOUT THE SELECTION

Recalling

1. He mourned in the spring, when the lilacs last bloomed.
2. (a) They bare their heads and are silent. They sing dirges. (b) The speaker places a sprig of lilac on the coffin.

3. Suggested Response: The "pictures of growing spring" include a golden April sunset, the fresh sweet grass, and the pale green leaves of trees.
4. (a) Death walks on each side of him. (b) He flees into the night, down to the shores of a forest lake. (c) The gray-brown bird who sings receives him.
5. (a) He sees the armies and the corpses and skeletons of the casualties. (b) He realizes that the dead are at rest and not suffer-

More About the Literature Spirituals are an important part of the American musical heritage. They are often performed by today's gospel singers, and their influence is apparent in a number of forms of contemporary music, including blues and jazz. Ask your students if they have any prior knowledge of spirituals, blues, or jazz. If so, have them share this knowledge with the rest of the class and have them discuss the ways in which blues and jazz reflect the influence of spirituals. Then discuss other forms of music that have influenced the music of today.

You might also want to offer students some information about one of best-known performers, composers, and arrangers of spirituals, Harry Thacker Burleigh (1866–1949). Born in Erie, Pennsylvania, Thacker was one of the first performers to sing spirituals on the concert stage. He arranged dozens of well-known spirituals, including "Deep River" and "Nobody Knows the Troubles I've Seen."

SPIRITUALS

Spirituals are folk songs that originated among black slaves. They served as an important means of communication and a way of expressing the slaves' desire for freedom and religious salvation. At the same time, the songs helped to replace their lost African religious traditions and allowed them to maintain a connection to their musical heritage.

Spirituals were inspired by the religious hymns of the white revivalists of the early nineteenth century and shaped by memories of traditional African music. Because of their religious content, most slave owners openly accepted these songs. Many of the spirituals had a double meaning, however, conveying not only the slaves' religious faith but also their desire to escape from their bondage. In fact, some of the songs were used to transmit secret messages that their masters and overseers would be unable to understand. For example, the spiritual "Follow the Drinking Gourd" advised runaway slaves to follow the Big Dipper, which points to the north.

Many spirituals were work songs that the slaves made up while they harvested cotton or sugar cane or loaded and unloaded ships. Many others were directly based on Methodist hymns, which the slaves turned into entirely new songs by adding a strong rhythm and depth of feeling. Many of these work and church songs followed a call-and-response form in which individuals made up new verses and were answered by the group, which acted like a chorus.

Most spirituals included references to people, places, or events in the Bible. They frequently referred to Moses, who in the Old Testament led the Jews out of slavery in Egypt. The black slaves compared their own enslavement with the plight of the ancient Jews. In spirituals such as "Swing Low, Sweet Chariot" and "Go Down, Moses," the black slaves expressed their hope that they would someday escape to their own "promised land" just as the Israelites had escaped to ancient Israel.

Spirituals were almost unknown outside the South until after the Civil War. In 1867 a collection of black music called *Slave Songs of the United States* was published. A few years later, in 1871, a group of black singers, the Jubilee Singers from Fisk University, traveled throughout the United States and to England and Germany singing spirituals to raise money for their school. Students from other schools followed their example and helped popularize the spiritual.

424   *Division, War, and Reconciliation*

Objectives

1 To recognize refrain
2 To write about the role of spirituals

Support Material

Teaching Portfolio
Teacher Backup, p. 555
Usage and Mechanics Worksheet, p. 558
Vocabulary Check, p. 559
Analyzing Literature Worksheet, *Understanding Spirituals,* p. 560
Critical Thinking and Reading Worksheet, *Understanding the Effect of the Refrain,* p. 561
Selection Test, p. 562

GUIDE FOR INTERPRETING

Swing Low, Sweet Chariot;
Go Down, Moses

The Writer's Techniques

Refrain. A refrain is a word, phrase, line, or group of lines repeated at regular intervals in a poem or song. For example, the line "Coming for to carry me home" is repeated throughout "Swing Low, Sweet Chariot."

Most spirituals include at least one, and sometimes more than one, refrain. The refrain emphasizes the most important ideas and establishes the rhythm. In a spiritual the refrain was usually sung by a chorus, with the other words being sung by a soloist. Because spirituals were passed orally from person to person and group to group, the words apart from the refrain often changed. In fact, soloists often improvised, creating new lyrics while singing. Since the refrains were frequently repeated, however, they were easy to remember and rarely changed. As a result, there is little variation in the refrain among different versions of a spiritual.

Writing

Why does music often produce a strong emotional response in people? Freewrite about the emotional impact of music. Try to include examples.

Primary Source

Frederick Douglass (1817?–1895) escaped from slavery at the age of twenty-one and went on to become one of the nation's foremost orators. In his autobiography he gave his explanation for why the slaves sang spirituals as they worked.

> Slaves are generally expected to sing as well as to work. A silent slave is not liked by masters or overseers. *"Make a noise, make a noise,"* and *"bear a hand,"* are the words usually addressed to the slaves when there is silence amongst them. This may account for the almost constant singing heard in the southern states. There was, generally, more or less singing among the teamsters, as it was one means of letting the overseer know where they were, . . .
>
> The remark is not unfrequently made, that slaves are the most contented and happy laborers in the world. They dance and sing, and make all manner of joyful noises—so they do; but it is a great mistake to suppose them happy because they sing. The songs of the slave represent the sorrows rather than the joys, of his heart; and he is relieved by them, only as an aching heart is relieved by its tears.

Literary Focus To help students grasp the concept of refrain, you might want to review Henry Wadsworth Longfellow's use of the technique in "The Tide Rises, the Tide Falls" (p. 338).

Writing/Prior Knowledge Before having students complete the freewriting activity, spend some time discussing the ways in which music affects people.

Vocabulary

Preteach the following vocabulary words:
oppressed (ə prest') *adj.:* Kept down by cruel or unjust power or authority (p. 427, l. 7)
smite (smît) *v.:* To kill by a powerful blow (p. 427, l. 15)

Motivation/Prior Knowledge
Have students discuss the oppression of various groups of
people. What can these people
do to improve their situations?
How can oppressed people
communicate with one another?

Master Teacher Note Have students discuss the concept of
freedom. What does freedom
mean to most people? Are all
of today's Americans free? Are
there any situations in which a
person should be denied his or
her freedom?

Purpose-Setting Question What
message does the spiritual convey?

1 **Discussion** What do the words
"Jordan" and "angels" imply?

2 **Literary Focus** How are the refrains used in "Swing Low, Sweet
Chariot"? Which refrain seems to
be predominant? How does the
use of this refrain emphasize the
yearning of the speaker? What is
that yearning?

Reader's Response What emotions does this spiritual evoke in
you? Why?

Swing Low, Sweet Chariot

Spiritual

Swing low, sweet chariot,
Coming for to carry me home,
Swing low, sweet chariot,
Coming for to carry me home.

5 I looked over Jordan and what did I see
Coming for to carry me home,
A band of angels coming after me,
Coming for to carry me home.

If you get there before I do,
10 Coming for to carry me home,
Tell all my friends I'm coming too,
Coming for to carry me home.

Swing low, sweet chariot,
Coming for to carry me home,
15 Swing low, sweet chariot,
Coming for to carry me home.

THINKING ABOUT THE SELECTION

Recalling

1. What message does the speaker wish to convey to his friends?

Interpreting

2. (a) If you interpret this spiritual as a religious
song, what does the chariot represent? (b)
What does home represent? (c) What is
the subject of the song?

3. (a) If you interpret this spiritual as an expression of the slaves' desire for freedom, what

does the chariot represent? (b) What does
home represent? (c) What does Jordan,
the river that formed the boundary to the
promised land of the ancient Israelites, represent? (d) What does the band of angels
represent?

Applying

4. (a) For what types of events and situations
do people write protest songs today? (b)
Name two recent protest songs. (c) What
messages do these two songs convey?

426   *Division, War, and Reconciliation*

Closure and Extension

ANSWERS TO THINKING ABOUT THE SELECTION
Recalling

1. He is coming home.

Interpreting

2. (a) It could symbolize death. (b)
Home represents Heaven. (c) It is
about death.

3. (a) It might symbolize the underground railroad. (b) It might refer
to freedom. (c) It might symbolize
the boundary between the slave
states and the free states. (d) It
represents those who will help the
slaves achieve their goal.

Applying

4. Answers will differ. Suggested Responses: (a) They protest against
war, hunger, nuclear power, and
the destruction of the environ-

ment. (b) Two popular ones are
"Where Have All the Flowers
Gone" and "We Are the World."
(c) The first song tells of the futility
of war, and the second protests
world hunger.

Go Down, Moses

Spiritual

Go down, Moses,
Way down in Egypt land
Tell old Pharaoh
To let my people go.

5 When Israel was in Egypt land
Let my people go
Oppressed so hard they could not stand
Let my people go.

Go down, Moses,
10 Way down in Egypt land
Tell old Pharaoh
"Let my people go."

"Thus saith the Lord," bold Moses said,
"Let my people go;
15 If not I'll smite your first-born dead
Let my people go."

Go down, Moses,
Way down in Egypt land,
Tell old Pharaoh,
20 "Let my people go!"

THINKING ABOUT THE SELECTION

Recalling

1. What does the speaker ask Moses to tell the old Pharaoh?
2. What is the condition of the people of Israel in Egypt?
3. What message does Moses deliver to the Pharaoh?

Interpreting

4. In this poem a comparison is developed between the captivity of the ancient Israelites in Egypt and the enslavement of the blacks in America. Egypt represents the South and Moses represents a leader helping blacks escape from slavery. (a) Who does the old Pharaoh represent? (b) Whom do the people of Israel represent?

Applying

5. Harriet Tubman led other black slaves out of bondage to freedom in the North. Known by the code name of Moses, she once said, "We got to go free or die. And freedom's not bought with dust." What other American heroes can you think of who would agree with her words? Explain your choices.

ANALYZING LITERATURE

Recognizing a Refrain

A **refrain** is a word, phrase, line, or group of lines repeated at regular intervals in a poem or song.
1. What refrain is used in the song?
2. Explain how this refrain conveys the main idea.

THINKING AND READING

Writing About the Role of Spirituals

Write an essay in which you discuss what made spirituals such an important part of slave life. Prepare a list of reasons for the spirituals' importance. Then find passages in "Swing Low, Sweet Chariot" and "Go Down, Moses" that support your reasons. Prepare an outline and a thesis statement. Then write your essay. When you revise, eliminate any unnecessary information and make sure that your essay is coherent and well organized.

Go Down, Moses 427

More About the Author As an abolitionist, orator, and journalist, Frederick Douglass favored political methods for emancipating the slaves and bringing them into the mainstream of American life. As a young child, he had recognized that education was the necessary factor for achieving political ends. Does education play an important role in bringing about other kinds of changes?

Critical Evaluation In the preface to Douglass's autobiography, the noted American journalist and social reformer William Lloyd Garrison (1805–1879) comments that the autobiography "contains many affecting incidents, many passages of great eloquence and power; but I think the most thrilling one of them all is the description Douglass gives of his feelings, as he stood soliloquizing respecting his fate, and the chances of his one day being a freeman, on the banks of the Chesapeake Bay—viewing the receding vessels as they flew with their white wings before the breeze, and apostrophizing them as animated by the living spirit of freedom. Who can read that passage, and be insensible to its pathos and sublimity?"

1817[?]–1895

Frederick Douglass rose out of slavery to become one of the most gifted writers and orators of his time. Using these talents, he dedicated his life to fighting for the abolition of slavery and for black civil rights. Douglass's life served as an inspiration and example for both blacks and whites throughout the country.

Douglass was born on a Maryland plantation. When he was eight, he was sent to live with the family of Hugh Auld in Baltimore. There, he learned to read and write, at first with the encouragement of Mrs. Auld and later despite her objections. When his desire for freedom was fueled by his reading, Douglass escaped from slavery at the age of twenty-one.

In 1841, three years after his escape, Douglass was asked to speak at a convention of the Massachusetts Anti-Slavery Society. Though he had never spoken in public before, Douglass delivered a tremendously powerful, moving speech. Impressed by his eloquence, the society immediately hired him as a lecturer.

Although he lived in constant fear of being arrested as a fugitive slave, Douglass spent the next four years lecturing throughout the Northeast. In 1845 he published his autobiography, *Narrative of the Life of Frederick Douglass*. Fearing the book's publication would lead to his re-enslavement, Douglass fled to England, where he spent two years trying to gain British support for the abolitionist cause.

After several of his English friends raised money finally to buy his freedom, Douglass returned to the United States. Upon his return, he established the *North Star*, a newspaper for blacks, and began lecturing again. In 1855 he published *My Bondage and My Freedom*, an updated version of his autobiography.

During the Civil War, Douglass helped to recruit black soldiers for the Union army. After the war ended and slavery was abolished, he fought for black civil rights. He also held several government positions such as the marshal and recorder of deeds of the District of Columbia and the United States minister to Haiti.

In 1883, speaking as a vigorous fighter for civil rights, Douglass commented that the American people "must learn, or neglect to do so at their own peril, . . . that 'Equal Manhood means Equal Rights,' and that further, that the American people must stand each for all and all for each, without respect to color or race. . . . I expect to see the colored people of this country enjoying the same freedom, voting at the same ballot-box, using the same cartridge-box, going to the same schools, attending the same churches, . . . proud of the same country, fighting the same foe, and enjoying the same peace and all its advantages. . . ."

428   *Division, War, and Reconciliation*

GUIDE FOR INTERPRETING

from My Bondage and My Freedom

Literary Forms

Autobiography. An autobiography is a person's account of his or her own life. In an autobiography the writer presents a continuous narrative of what he or she feels are the most significant events in his or her life. Because the writer's life is presented as he or she views it, the portrayal of people and events is colored by the author's feelings and beliefs. In fact, some of the writer's attitudes and beliefs may be directly stated.

Usually, the writers of autobiographies believe that their lives are interesting or important or can in some way serve as examples for others. Frederick Douglass, for instance, wrote his autobiography because he believed that his life proved that blacks were no less perceptive, intelligent, and capable than whites. Written in a plain and direct style that was also fluent and forceful, Douglass's autobiography demonstrated not only that blacks were capable of overcoming great hardships and achieving success but also that they could express themselves eloquently.

Writing

Frederick Douglass's life served as an example for both blacks and whites throughout the country. Prepare a list of other men and women whose lives have served as an example for other people.

Primary Source

In 1879, when Frederick Douglass was in his 60's, the *Rochester Democrat and Chronicle* described him as "among the greatest men, not only of this city, but of the nation as well . . ." It went on to say

> Frederick Douglass can hardly be said to have risen to greatness on account of the opportunities which the republic offers to self-made men, and concerning which we are apt to talk with an abundance of self-gratulation. To him, the republic offered no opportunities. It sought to fetter his mind equally with his body. . . . So far as he was concerned, freedom was a mockery, and law was the instrument of tyranny. . . . There is no sadder commentary upon American slavery than the life of Frederick Douglass. He put it under his feet and stood erect in the majesty of his intellect; but how many intellects as brilliant and as powerful as his it stamped upon and crushed no mortal can tell. . . . Not alone did his voice proclaim emancipation. Eloquent as was that voice, his life, in its pathos and in its grandeur, was more eloquent still . . .

Literary Focus While autobiographies reflect the writer's perspective, they do not tend to be as objective as biographies. How might an autobiographical account differ from a biographical one?

Writing/Prior Knowledge Before having students complete the writing activity, spend some time discussing important historical figures.

Vocabulary

Preteach the following vocabulary words:

congenial (kən jēn′ yəl) *adj.:* Compatible (p. 430)

benevolent (bə nev′ ə lənt) *adj.:* Kindly; charitable (p. 430)

stringency (strin′ jən ŝē) *n.:* Strictness; severity (p. 430)

depravity (di prav′ ə tē) *n.:* Corruption; wickedness (p. 430)

consternation (kän′ stər nā′ shən) *n.:* Great fear or shock that makes one feel helpless or bewildered (p. 431)

unperverted (un′ pər vʉrt′id) *adj.:* Uncorrupted (p. 432)

redolent (red″l ənt) *adj.:* Suggestive (p. 432)

Spelling Tip Point out that two words in this list, *benevolent* and *redolent,* have the same ending sound spelled *ent.* Note that this ending is preceeded by a single *l.*

Motivation/Prior Knowledge
Have students discuss the following question: Is education a right or a privilege?

Master Teacher Note The abolitionist movement in America did not come about through the efforts of politicians or clergymen. It was begun by humble people who lived by their own labor and who took their Christian and democratic convictions seriously.

Purpose-Setting Question How is it possible to be a "good" slave owner?

1 Discussion Why was Mrs. Auld at first inclined to teach Douglass how to read and write? What changed her mind?

from My Bondage and My Freedom

Frederick Douglass

I lived in the family of Master Hugh, at Baltimore, seven years, during which time—as the almanac makers say of the weather—my condition was variable. The most interesting feature of my history here, was my learning to read and write, under somewhat marked disadvantages. In attaining this knowledge, I was compelled to resort to indirections by no means congenial to my nature, and which were really humiliating to me. My mistress—who had begun to teach me—was suddenly checked in her benevolent design, by the strong advice of her husband. In faithful compliance with this advice, the good lady had not only ceased to instruct me, herself, but had set her face as a flint against my learning to read by any means. It is due, however, to my mistress to say, that she did not adopt this course in all its stringency at the first. She either thought it unnecessary, or she lacked the depravity indispensable to shutting me up in mental darkness. It was, at least, necessary for her to have some training, and some hardening, in the exercise of the slaveholder's prerogative, to make her equal to forgetting my human nature and character, and to treating me as a thing destitute of a moral or an intellectual nature. Mrs. Auld—my mistress—was, as I have said, a most kind and tender-hearted woman; and, in the humanity of her heart, and the simplicity of her mind, she set out, when I first went to live with her, to treat me as she supposed one human being ought to treat another.

It is easy to see, that, in entering upon the duties of a slaveholder, some little experience is needed. Nature has done almost nothing to prepare men and women to be either slaves or slaveholders. Nothing but rigid training, long persisted in, can perfect the character of the one or the other. One cannot easily forget to love freedom; and it is as hard to cease to respect that natural love in our fellow creatures. On entering upon the career of a slaveholding mistress, Mrs. Auld was singularly deficient; nature, which fits nobody for such an office, had done less for her than any lady I had known. It was no easy matter to induce her to think and to feel that the curly-headed boy, who stood by her side, and even leaned on her lap; who was loved by little Tommy, and who loved little Tommy in turn; sustained to her only the relation of a chattel. I was *more* than that, and she felt me to be more than that. I could talk and sing; I could laugh and weep; I could reason and remember; I could love and hate. I was human, and she, dear lady, knew and felt me to be so. How could she, then, treat me as a brute, without a mighty struggle with all the noble powers of her own soul. That struggle came, and the will and power of the husband was victorious. Her noble soul was overthrown; but, he that overthrew it did not, himself, escape the consequences.

Primary Source

In the month of August, 1841, I attended an anti-slavery convention in Nantucket, at which it was my happiness to become acquainted with Frederick Douglass . . . I shall never forget his first speech at the convention—the extraordinary emotion it excited in my own mind—the powerful impression it created upon the crowded auditory, completely taken by surprise—the applause which followed from the beginning to the end of his felicitous remarks. I think I have never hated slavery so intensely as at that moment; certainly, my perception of the enormous outrage which is inflicted by it, on the godlike nature of its victims, was rendered far more clear than ever. There stood one, in physical proportion and stature commanding and exact—in intellect richly endowed—in natural eloquence a prodigy—in manifestly "created but a little lower than the angels"—yet a slave, ay, a fugitive slaver, trembling for his safety, hardly daring to believe that on the American soil, a single white person could be found who

He, not less than the other parties, was injured in his domestic peace by the fall.

When I went into their family, it was the abode of happiness and contentment. The mistress of the house was a model of affection and tenderness. Her fervent piety and watchful uprightness made it impossible to see her without thinking and feeling—"that woman is a Christian." There was no sorrow nor suffering for which she had not a tear, and there was no innocent joy for which she did not a smile. She had bread for the hungry, clothes for the naked, and comfort for every mourner that came within her reach. Slavery soon proved its ability to divest her of these excellent qualities, and her home of its early happiness. Conscience cannot stand much violence. Once thoroughly broken down, *who* is he that can repair the damage? It may be broken toward the slave, on Sunday, and toward the master on Monday. It cannot endure such shocks. It must stand entire, or it does not stand at all. If my condition waxed bad, that of the family waxed not better. The first step, in the wrong direction, was the violence done to nature and to conscience, in arresting the benevolence that would have enlightened my young mind. In ceasing to instruct me, she must begin to justify herself *to* herself; and, once consenting to take sides in such a debate, she was riveted to her position. One needs very little knowledge of moral philosophy, to see *where* my mistress now landed. She finally became even more violent in her opposition to my learning to read, than was her husband himself. She was not satisfied with simply doing as *well* as her husband had commanded her, but seemed resolved to better his instruction. Nothing appeared to make my poor mistress—after her turning toward the downward path—more angry, than seeing me, seated in some nook or corner, quietly reading a book or a newspaper. I have had her rush at me, with the utmost fury, and snatch from my hand such newspaper or book, with something of the wrath and consternation which a traitor might be supposed to feel on being discovered in a plot by some dangerous spy.

Mrs. Auld was an apt woman, and the advice of her husband, and her own experience, soon demonstrated, to her entire satisfaction, that education and slavery are incompatible with each other. When this conviction was thoroughly established, I was most narrowly watched in all my movements. If I remained in a separate room from the family for any considerable length of time, I was sure to be suspected of having a book, and was at once called upon to give an account of myself. All this, however, was entirely *too late*. The first, and never to be retraced, step had been taken. In teaching me the alphabet, in the days of her simplicity and kindness, my mistress had given me the "inch," and now, no ordinary precaution could prevent me from taking the "ell."[1]

Seized with a determination to learn to read, at any cost, I hit upon many expedients to accomplish the desired end. The plea which I mainly adopted, and the one by which I was most successful, was that of using my young white playmates, with whom I met in the street, as teachers. I used to carry, almost constantly, a copy of Webster's spelling book in my pocket; and, when sent on errands, or when play time was allowed me, I would step, with my young friends, aside, and take a lesson in spelling. I generally paid my *tuition fee* to the boys, with bread, which I also carried in my pocket. For a single biscuit, any of my hungry little comrades would give me a lesson more valuable to me than bread. Not everyone, however, demanded this consideration, for there were those who took pleasure in teaching me, whenever I had a chance to be taught by them. I am strongly tempted to give the names of two or three of those little boys, as a slight testimonial of the gratitude and af-

1. **ell** *n.*: A former English measure of length, equal to forty-five inches.

would befriend him at all hazards, for the love of God and humanity! Capable of high attainments as an intellectual and moral being—needing nothing but a comparatively small amount of cultivation to make him an ornament to society and a blessing to his race—by the law of the land, by the voice of the people, and by the terms of the slave code, he was only a piece of property, a beast of burden, a chattle personal, nevertheless!

2 **Critical Thinking and Reading** How does slavery affect the slaveholder as well as the slave? What deficiency does Douglass see in Mrs. Auld? In Mr. Auld? Why is slavery a "violence done to nature and to conscience"? Is Douglass correct when he says that "Nature has done almost nothing to prepare men and women to be either slaves or slaveholders"?

3 **Discussion** Why are education and slavery incompatible? How did Douglass continue his education in spite of the obstacles created by the Aulds?

4 **Enrichment** Maryland was not one of the states that joined the Confederacy during the Civil War. The first seven states to join were South Carolina, Georgia, Louisiana, Mississippi, Florida, Alabama, and Texas. They were later joined by Arkansas, North Carolina, Virginia, and Tennessee.

5 **Discussion** How does Douglass come to the inescapable conclusion that slavery is intolerable? What effect does the *Columbian Orator* have on him?

fection I bear them, but prudence forbids; not that it would injure me, but it might, possibly, embarrass them; for it is almost an unpardonable offense to do anything, directly or indirectly, to promote a slave's freedom, in a slave state. It is enough to say, of my warm-hearted little play fellows, that they lived on Philpot Street, very near Durgin & Bailey's shipyard.

Although slavery was a delicate subject, and very cautiously talked about among grownup people in Maryland, I frequently talked about it—and that very freely—with the white boys. I would, sometimes, say to them, while seated on a curbstone or a cellar door, "I wish I could be free, as you will be when you get to be men." "You will be free, you know, as soon as you are twenty-one, and can go where you like, but I am a slave for life. Have I not as good a right to be free as you have?" Words like these, I observed, always troubled them; and I had no small satisfaction in wringing from the boys, occasionally, that fresh and bitter condemnation of slavery, that springs from nature, unseared and unperverted. Of all consciences let me have those to deal with which have not been bewildered by the cares of life. I do not remember ever to have met with a *boy*, while I was in slavery, who defended the slave system; but I have often had boys to console me, with the hope that something would yet occur, by which I might be made free. Over and over again, they have told me, that "they believed *I* had as good a right to be free as *they* had"; and that "they did not believe God ever made anyone to be a slave." The reader will easily see, that such little conversations with my play fellows, had no tendency to weaken my love of liberty, nor to render me contented with my condition as a slave.

When I was about thirteen years old, and had succeeded in learning to read, every increase of knowledge, especially respecting the free states, added something to the almost intolerable burden of the thought—"I am a slave for life." To my bondage I saw no end. It was a terrible reality, and I shall never be able to tell how sadly that thought chafed my young spirit. Fortunately, or unfortunately, about this time in my life, I had made enough money to buy what was then a very popular schoolbook, the *Columbian Orator*. I bought this addition to my library, of Mr. Knight, on Thames street, Fell's Point, Baltimore, and paid him fifty cents for it. I was first led to buy this book, by hearing some little boys say they were going to learn some little pieces out of it for the Exhibition. This volume was, indeed, a rich treasure, and every opportunity afforded me, for a time, was spent in diligently perusing it. . . . The dialogue and the speeches were all redolent of the principles of liberty, and poured floods of light on the nature and character of slavery. As I read, behold! the very discontent so graphically predicted by Master Hugh, had already come upon me. I was no longer the light-hearted, gleesome boy, full of mirth and play, as when I landed first at Baltimore. Knowledge had come. . . . This knowledge opened my eyes to the horrible pit, and revealed the teeth of the frightful dragon that was ready to pounce upon me, but it opened no way for my escape. I have often wished myself a beast, or a bird—anything, rather than a slave. I was wretched and gloomy, beyond my ability to describe. I was too thoughtful to be happy. It was this everlasting thinking which distressed and tormented me; and yet there was no getting rid of the subject of my thoughts. All nature was redolent of it. Once awakened by the silver trump[2] of knowledge, my spirit was roused to eternal wakefulness. Liberty! the inestimable birthright of every man, had, for me, converted every object into an asserter of this great right. It was heard in every sound, and beheld in every object. It was ever present, to torment me with a sense of my

---

2. trump: Trumpet.

432   *Division, War, and Reconciliation*

Grammar in Action

A gerund is a verb form ending in *-ing* that functions as a noun. When complements and modifiers accompany a gerund, we have a **gerund phrase**. Notice Frederick Douglass's use of gerunds and gerund phrases in this excerpt from *My Bondage and My Freedom*. For example, he writes:

The most interesting feature . . . was *my learning to read and write, under somewhat marked disadvantages.*

It was at least necessary for her to have *some training,* and *some hardening,* in . . . the slaveholder's prerogative.

Student Activity 1. In the selection from *My Bondage and My Freedom,* find at least ten more gerunds or gerund phrases.

Student Activity 2. Replace each italicized expression in the following sentences with an appropriate gerund or gerund phrase. Note the gerund's emphasis on action, rather than on static condition. (Do not add *-ing* to the verb form of the noun given; find a fresh action word.)

A HOME ON THE MISSISSIPPI
Currier & Ives
The Museum of the City of N.Y.

from *My Bondage and My Freedom* 433

1. Douglass's *composition* about his boyhood raises many questions about liberty.
2. His sights were set on *the attainment of* his freedom.
3. At first Mrs. Auld's *comprehension of* Douglass's intelligence inspired her to help him.
4. Under the pressure of her husband's *insistence,* she stopped *her assistance* with Douglass's lessons.

6 Discussion Why does Douglass explain that Mrs. Auld, as an individual, was not cruel toward him in any physical way? Why does he say that she was as much a victim as he?

Reader's Response What is your reaction to Mrs. Auld's treatment of Douglass in this selection? Do you agree with Douglass's view that slaveholders as well as slaves were victims of slavery? Why or why not?

wretched condition. The more beautiful and charming were the smiles of nature, the more horrible and desolate was my condition. I saw nothing without seeing it, and I heard nothing without hearing it. I do not exaggerate, when I say, that it looked from every star, smiled in every calm, breathed in every wind, and moved in every storm.

6 I have no doubt that my state of mind had something to do with the change in the treatment adopted, by my once kind mistress toward me. I can easily believe, that my leaden, downcast, and discontented look, was very offensive to her. Poor lady! She did not know my trouble, and I dared not tell her. Could I have freely made her acquainted with the real state of my mind, and given her the reasons therefor, it might have been well for both of us. Her abuse of me fell upon me like the blows of the false prophet upon his ass; she did not know that an *angel* stood in the way;[3] and—such is the relation of master

---

3. blows . . . the way: An allusion to a biblical tale (Numbers 22 : 21–35) about an ass that cannot move, though she is beaten by her master, because her path is blocked by an angel.

and slave—I could not tell her. Nature had made us *friends*; slavery made us *enemies*. My interests were in a direction opposite to hers, and we both had our private thoughts and plans. She aimed to keep me ignorant; and I resolved to know, although knowledge only increased my discontent. My feelings were not the result of any marked cruelty in the treatment I received; they sprung from the consideration of my being a slave at all. It was *slavery*—not its mere *incidents*—that I hated. I had been cheated. I saw through the attempt to keep me in ignorance. . . . The feeding and clothing me well, could not atone for taking my liberty from me. The smiles of my mistress could not remove the deep sorrow that dwelt in my young bosom. Indeed, these, in time, came only to deepen my sorrow. She had changed; and the reader will see that I had changed, too. We were both victims to the same overshadowing evil—*she*, as mistress, *I*, as slave. I will not censure her harshly; she cannot censure me, for she knows I speak but the truth, and have acted in my opposition to slavery, just as she herself would have acted, in a reverse of circumstances.

Commentary

The *Columbian Orator*, which Frederick Douglass mentions, was one of the most popular schoolbooks of its time. Written by Caleb Bingham and published in 1806, the 300-page book quickly displaced the Bible as a textbook for advanced readers.

In the preface to the *Columbian Orator*, Bingham noted that the book was "a new selection of lessons for reading and speaking in American schools," that no works of romantic fiction were included, and that "tales of love have not gained admission." Bingham emphasized that the book did not contain "a word or a sentiment which would raise a blush on the cheek of modesty."

The *Orator* was filled with patriotic speeches, poetry, extracts from literature, and rules for proper speech. But perhaps its best remembered selection was a poem that began this way:

You'd scarce expect one of my age,
To speak in public, on the stage;
And if I chance to fall below
Demosthenes or Cicero,
Don't view me with a critic's eye,
But pass my imperfections by.
Large streams from little fountains flow;
Tall oaks from little acorns grow . . .

434 Division, War, and Reconciliation

434

THINKING ABOUT THE SELECTION

Recalling

1. (a) How long does Douglass live with the Aulds? (b) What is the "most interesting" aspect of his history with the Aulds?
2. Explain the change in Mrs. Auld's attitude toward Douglass.
3. (a) What does Douglass pay the boys who give him lessons in spelling? (b) What is their attitude toward slavery?
4. (a) What popular schoolbook does Douglass buy? (b) How does reading this book affect him?

Interpreting

5. Why does Douglass view slaveholders as well as slaves as victims of slavery?
6. Why is education incompatible with slavery?
7. Why do you think the white children's attitude toward slavery is different from that of their parents?
8. How would you describe Douglass's attitude toward Mrs. Auld?
9. Douglass writes, "My feelings were not the result of any marked cruelty in the treatment I received; they sprung from the consideration of my being a slave at all. It was *slavery*—not its mere *incidents*—that I hated." Explain the difference between *slavery* and the *incidents* of slavery. Why does the first have a so much stronger effect on the emotions?

Applying

10. Mohandas Gandhi wrote, "The moment the slave resolves that he will no longer be a slave, his fetters fall." React to this statement. Then explain whether or not you feel Douglass was free even while in bondage.

ANALYZING LITERATURE

Recognizing an Autobiography

An **autobiography** is a person's account of his or her own life. Most autobiographies convey many of the writer's attitudes and beliefs. For example, Frederick Douglass expresses his attitude toward slavery in *My Bondage and My Freedom*.

1. Find a passage in which Douglass directly states his attitude toward slavery.
2. Find one passage in which Douglass conveys his opposition to slavery through his description of events.
3. How do you think this account would be different if it had been written by Mrs. Auld?

CRITICAL THINKING AND READING

Analyzing the Effect of Style

My Bondage and My Freedom is written in a plain but eloquent style. Douglass describes events in a straightforward, factual manner, offering little interpretation of the significance of the events. He lets the facts speak for themselves and allows readers to draw their own conclusions about the meaning of his experiences.

Considering that Douglass wrote his autobiography because he believed that his life could serve as an example, why do you think that his style is effective?

THINKING AND WRITING

Writing an Autobiography

College applications frequently ask prospective students to write a brief autobiographical sketch describing an important experience. Imagine that you are filling out an application that includes this request. Think about the type of impression you want to make on the admissions committee. Then decide on the experience that you want to describe. Make a list of the important details related to the experience. When you write your sketch, describe the ways in which the experience affected you and what you think it reveals about your personality. When you revise, try to think about how the members of the admissions committee would be likely to respond to your sketch.

from My Bondage and My Freedom 435

Closure and Extension

ANSWERS TO THINKING ABOUT THE SELECTION
Recalling

1. (a) He stays with them seven years. (b) It was his learning to read and write.
2. At first, she was benevolent and kind. Then, as a result of pressure from her husband she becomes an oppressor.
3. (a) He gives them bread. (b) They are opposed to it.
4. (a) He buys the *Columbian Orator*. (b) It increased his longing for freedom.

Interpreting

5. This system keeps the slaveholders from living in harmony with their own souls.
6. Education makes the slaves dissatisfied with their situation.
7. They have not yet learned how to be slaveholders.
8. He does not blame her for becoming an oppressor and sees her as being a victim of the institution of slavery.
9. *Slavery* is the institution which denies men and women their freedom; the *incidents* of slavery are the individual instances in which slaves are mistreated. Because the institution as a whole encompasses the instances of mistreatment of slaves and the denial of the slaves' human rights.

Applying

10. Suggested Response: In one sense he was free, because he realized that the slaveowners were no better than he was.

ANSWERS TO ANALYZING LITERATURE

1. Suggested Response: He expresses his views at the end when he describes both the slave and slaveholder as victims.
2. Suggested Response: The paragraph that begins "When I went into their family" is an example of this approach.
3. Suggested Response: She would have denied any change in her personality and would have seen her actions as proper.

ANSWERS TO CRITICAL THINKING AND READING

His style is effective, because straightforward descriptions of his experiences do not need interpretations; they stand by themselves.

THINKING AND WRITING

Publishing Student Writing Encourage students to save their sketch so that they can refer to it when filling out college applications.

More About the Author Mary Chestnut never wrote novels or poetry for publication. Still, she did express herself in the manner commonly chosen by the women of her time—journal or diary entries. The time in which she lived and wrote was one of stress for the entire country, but she limited her observations to what was going on around her.

Literary Focus Both the journal and the diary have had a great impact in literary history. Some of the more celebrated examples of this literary form were written by Samuel Pepys, James Boswell, Henry David Thoreau, Virginia Woolf, and Anne Frank.

Writing/Prior Knowledge For extra credit, you might have students imagine that they are somehow involved in the Civil War, and have them write a journal entry describing their experiences and presenting their attitudes concerning the war.

Vocabulary

Preteach the following vocabulary words:
capitulate (kə pich′ ə lāt′) *v.*: Surrender conditionally (p. 438)
audaciously (ô dā′ shəs lē) *adj.*: Boldly (p. 438)
foreboding (fôr bōd′ iŋ) *n.*: Prediction (p. 438)
obstinate (äb′ stə nit) *adj.*: Stubborn (p. 438)
imprecations (im′ prə kā′ shənz) *n.*: Curses (p. 438)
serenity (sə ren′ ə tē) *n.*: Calmness (p. 440)

GUIDE FOR INTERPRETING

from Mary Chesnut's Civil War

Mary Boykin Chesnut (1823–1886) was the daughter of a United States senator from South Carolina, and she was brought up in an aristocratic family in Charleston, South Carolina. When she was seventeen, Mary Boykin married James Chesnut, Jr., a wealthy lawyer, who was later elected to the Senate. The cruelty of the war deeply disturbed her. Through her journal we can share firsthand the joy and sorrow of the people of the South in victory and defeat.

Literary Forms

Journals. A journal, or diary, is a personal record of events, conversations, thoughts, feelings, and observations. Written on a day-to-day basis, journals allow writers to record their most immediate responses to their experiences. Usually, writers keep journals for their own personal use, not intending to have them published. As a result, journals tend to be written in an informal, personal style and capture the writer's innermost thoughts and feelings.

Commentary

Many people keep journals, but few journals have as widespread interest as that of Mary Chesnut. What kind of woman was Chesnut? What qualities did she bring to her role as journal writer?

According to one historian, Chesnut had unusual qualifications as a diarist. "[S]he was well informed; she knew most, if not all the leaders of the Confederate Government, and of the Confederate Army; she knew the way of life of the well-born and the wealthy southern planter; she knew a little about the way of life of poorer white people; and she knew the Negro." She was also intelligent and articulate, "expressing herself easily and clearly." Finally, "she was an interesting individual, a devoted wife and a loyal friend without being blind to the faults of her husband, or of her friends—or of herself. She had a bluntness which must have dealt many wounds, and a warmth which must have made it easy to forgive her blunt speech."

What great events might a journal writer describe today? What special qualities would be important for the writer to have in order to make the events interesting to others?

Writing

Freewrite about books you have read and movies you have seen about the Civil War. Discuss what the books and movies reveal about how the war changed people's lives. Also explain what you think the American people learned from the conflict.

436   *Division, War, and Reconciliation*

Objectives

1 To understand a journal
2 To recognize main ideas
3 To write a summary

Support Material

Teaching Portfolio
Teacher Backup, p. 577
Usage and Mechanics Worksheet, p. 580
Vocabulary Check, p. 581
Analyzing Literature Worksheet, *Understanding a Journal,* p. 582
Critical Thinking and Reading Worksheet, *Recognizing Main Ideas,* p. 583
Selection Test, p. 584

from Mary Chesnut's Civil War

Mary Chesnut

April 7, 1861. Today things seem to have settled down a little.

One can but hope still. Lincoln or Seward[1] have made such silly advances and then far sillier drawings back. There may be a chance for peace, after all.

Things are happening so fast.

My husband has been made an aide-de-camp[2] of General Beauregard.

Three hours ago we were quietly packing to go home. The convention has adjourned.

Now he tells me the attack upon Fort Sumter[3] may begin tonight. Depends upon Anderson and the fleet outside. The *Herald* says that this show of war outside of the bar is intended for Texas.

John Manning came in with his sword and red sash. Pleased as a boy to be on Beauregard's staff while the row goes on. He has gone with Wigfall to Captain Hartstene with instructions.

Mr. Chesnut is finishing a report he had to make to the convention.

Mrs. Hayne called. She had, she said, "but one feeling, pity for those who are not here."

Jack Preston, Willie Alston—"the take-life-easys," as they are called—with John Green, "the big brave," have gone down to the island—volunteered as privates.

Seven hundred men were sent over. Ammunition wagons rumbling along the streets all night. Anderson burning blue lights—signs and signals for the fleet outside, I suppose.

Today at dinner there was no allusion to things as they stand in Charleston Harbor. There was an undercurrent of intense excitement. There could not have been a more brilliant circle. In addition to our usual quartet (Judge Withers, Langdon Cheves, and Trescot) our two governors dined with us, Means and Manning.

These men all talked so delightfully. For once in my life I listened.

That over, business began. In earnest, Governor Means rummaged a sword and red sash from somewhere and brought it for Colonel Chesnut, who has gone to demand the surrender of Fort Sumter.

And now, patience—we must wait.

---

1. **Seward:** William Henry Seward (1801–1872), U.S. Secretary of State from 1861 through 1869.
2. **aide-de-camp:** An officer serving as assistant and confidential secretary to a superior.
3. **Fort Sumter:** A fort in Charleston Harbor, South Carolina. At the time, the fort was occupied by Union troops commanded by Major Robert Anderson.

Presentation

Motivation/Prior Knowledge Have students imagine that the Civil War has just begun. What are their reactions? What are their hopes? What are their fears? To whom are they loyal?

Purpose-Setting Question What do Chesnut's journal entries reveal about the war?

Enrichment Fort Sumter was a fortification in South Carolina, at the mouth of the Charleston harbor. South Carolina had seceded from the Union on December 20, 1860, and demanded all the Federal property within the state. Major Anderson resisted the surrender of Sumter, and the Confederate troops opened fire on April 12, 1861, bombarding the fort for thirty-four hours. The Civil War had begun.

Discussion The first entry we read is dated April 7, 1861. Why is this significant? What makes Chesnut listen to the dinner conversation that evening? What does Mrs. Hayne's remark tell us about both her and Chesnut? How does Chesnut characterize Anderson?

2 Discussion What kinds of activities take up most of Chesnut's entries for April 12?

3 Discussion When referring to her husband in her entries, what form does Chesnut use from time to time? Why would she call him Mr. Chesnut? Is there any difference between her attitude toward what is going on and her husband's attitude?

Why did that green goose Anderson go into Fort Sumter? Then everything began to go wrong.

Now they have intercepted a letter from him, urging them to let him surrender. He paints the horrors likely to ensue if they will not.

He ought to have thought of all that before he put his head in the hole.

April 12, 1861. Anderson will not capitulate.

Yesterday was the merriest, maddest dinner we have had yet. Men were more audaciously wise and witty. We had an unspoken foreboding it was to be our last pleasant meeting. Mr. Miles dined with us today. Mrs. Henry King rushed in: "The news, I come for the latest news—all of the men of the King family are on the island"—of which fact she seemed proud.

While she was here, our peace negotiator—or envoy—came in. That is, Mr. Chesnut returned—his interview with Colonel Anderson had been deeply interesting—but was not inclined to be communicative, wanted his dinner. Felt for Anderson. Had telegraphed to President Davis[4] for instructions.

What answer to give Anderson, etc., etc. He has gone back to Fort Sumter with additional instructions.

When they were about to leave the wharf, A. H. Boykin sprang into the boat, in great excitement; thought himself ill-used. A likelihood of fighting—and he to be left behind!

I do not pretend to go to sleep. How can I? If Anderson does not accept terms—at four—the orders are—he shall be fired upon.

I count four—St. Michael chimes. I begin to hope. At half-past four, the heavy booming of a cannon.

I sprang out of bed. And on my knees—prostrate—I prayed as I never prayed before.

There was a sound of stir all over the house—pattering of feet in the corridor—all seemed hurrying one way. I put on my double gown and a shawl and went, too. It was to the housetop.

The shells were bursting. In the dark I heard a man say "waste of ammunition."

I knew my husband was rowing about in a boat somewhere in that dark bay. And that the shells were roofing it over—bursting toward the fort. If Anderson was obstinate—he was to order the forts on our side to open fire. Certainly fire had begun. The regular roar of the cannon—there it was. And who could tell what each volley accomplished of death and destruction.

The women were wild, there on the housetop. Prayers from the women and imprecations from the men, and then a shell would light up the scene. Tonight, they say, the forces are to attempt to land.

The *Harriet Lane*[5] had her wheelhouse[6] smashed and put back to sea.

We watched up there—everybody wondered. Fort Sumter did not fire a shot.

Today Miles and Manning, colonels now—aides to Beauregard—dined with us. The latter hoped I would keep the peace. I give him only good words, for he was to be under fire all day and night, in the bay carrying orders, etc.

Last night—or this morning truly—up on the housetop I was so weak and weary I sat down on something that looked like a black stool.

"Get up, you foolish woman—your dress is on fire," cried a man. And he put me out.

---

4. President Davis: Jefferson Davis (1808–1889), president of the Confederacy (1861–1865).

5. The *Harriet Lane*: A federal steamer that had brought provisions to Fort Sumter.

6. wheelhouse *n.*: An enclosed place on the upper deck of a ship, in which the helmsman stands while steering.

438   *Division, War, and Reconciliation*

THE HOUSETOPS IN CHARLESTON DURING THE BOMBARDMENT OF FORT SUMTER
Harper's Weekly, May 4, 1961
Library of Congress

from *Mary Chesnut's Civil War*　439

Fine art, *The Housetops in Charleston During the Bombardment of Fort Sumner.* This wood engraving was done by an unknown artist for *Harper's Weekly* (May 4, 1861). *Harper's Weekly* was one of the two major northern illustrated newspapers that provided on-the-spot coverage of the Civil War. Correspondents and artists were dispatched by the paper to war zones to provide a steady flow of written and pictorial information for the readers. Although the process of photography was in existence at this time, there was as yet no means of reproducing photographs in a newspaper. On-the-scene drawings were the means by which events of the war were visually recorded for the public. These drawings were sent to the newspaper where a skilled artisan engraved the image into a block of wood which was inked and pressed onto paper to transfer the image. These engravings greatly increased the drama of the written reports that they accompanied.

Have students examine the drawing, and ask these questions:

1. What details correspond to those in Mary Chestnut's account?
2. How does the artist convey the fright of the people and sense of unreality in this scene?
3. Does this print of a major event (for that time) have more or less impact on the view than a photograph of the same scene would? Explain your answer.

4 **Discussion** What makes it impossible to have regular meals in the Chesnut home?

5 **Discussion** Nine days have passed from the first diary entry to the last. How has Chesnut shown her awareness that the foundation of her antebellum civilization has been cracked?

Reader's Response Does Mary Chesnut seem like a person you would have liked to have met? Why or why not?

It was a chimney, and the sparks caught my clothes. Susan Preston and Mr. Venable then came up. But my fire had been extinguished before it broke out into a regular blaze.

Do you know, after all that noise and our tears and prayers, nobody has been hurt. Sound and fury, signifying nothing.[7] A delusion and a snare. . . .

Somebody came in just now and reported Colonel Chesnut asleep on the sofa in General Beauregard's room. After two such nights he must be so tired as to be able to sleep anywhere. . . .

April 13, 1861. Nobody hurt, after all. How gay we were last night.

Reaction after the dread of all the slaughter we thought those dreadful cannons were making such a noise in doing.

Not even a battery[8] the worse for wear.

Fort Sumter has been on fire. He has not yet silenced any of our guns. So the aides—still with swords and red sashes by way of uniform—tell us.

But the sound of those guns makes regular meals impossible. None of us go to table. But tea trays pervade the corridors, going everywhere.

Some of the anxious hearts lie on their beds and moan in solitary misery. Mrs. Wig-

fall and I solace ourselves with tea in my room.

These women have all a satisfying faith.

April 15, 1861. I did not know that one could live such days of excitement.

They called, "Come out—there is a crowd coming."

A mob indeed, but it was headed by Colonels Chesnut and Manning.

The crowd was shouting and showing these two as messengers of good news. They were escorted to Beauregard's headquarters. Fort Sumter had surrendered.

Those up on the housetop shouted to us, "The fort is on fire." That had been the story once or twice before.

When we had calmed down, Colonel Chesnut, who had taken it all quietly enough—if anything, more unruffled than usual in his serenity—told us how the surrender came about.

Wigfall was with them on Morris Island when he saw the fire in the fort, jumped in a little boat and, with his handkerchief as a white flag, rowed over to Fort Sumter. Wigfall went in through a porthole.

When Colonel Chesnut arrived shortly after and was received by the regular entrance, Colonel Anderson told him he had need to pick his way warily, for it was all mined.

As far as I can make out, the fort surrendered to Wigfall.

But it is all confusion. Our flag is flying there. Fire engines have been sent to put out the fire.

Everybody tells you half of something and then rushes off to tell something else or to hear the last news. . . .

7. **Sound . . . nothing:** From Shakespeare's *Macbeth*, Act V, Scene v, lines 27–28. Macbeth is contemplating the significance of life and death, after learning of his wife's death.
8. **battery** *n.*: Artillery unit.

Primary Source

In the introduction to *Mary Chesnut's Civil War*, C. Vann Woodward notes:

Mary Chesnut adheres faithfully to the style, tone, and circumstantial limitations of the diarist and conveys fully the sense of chaotic daily life. To all appearances she respects the Latin meaning of the word *diarum* and its denial of knowledge of the future. Unforeseen events crowd in, unexpected guests arrive, messengers come and go. Each day brings its surprises. Illnesses, accident, violence, crime, death, and tragedy strike randomly and overwhelm. Ambitions, love affairs, conspiracies, and intrigues intimately traced in their day-to-day course, hang fire unfulfilled and await unforeseeable developments. Close friends pictured in the flush of triumph or the gaiety of the social whirl return next day from the front, as corpses. Over all hangs endless speculation, suspense, and anxiety about the fortunes of the war and the outcome of the struggle for Southern independence. The diarist agonizes over these uncertainties. She frets over the

THINKING ABOUT THE SELECTION

Recalling

1. (a) When does the attack on Fort Sumter take place? (b) What happens to Mary Chesnut while she is watching the attack?
2. According to the entry for August 13, what does the sound of the guns make impossible?
3. (a) When do the Union troops at Fort Sumter surrender to the Confederate forces? (b) Who explains how the surrender came about?

Interpreting

4. What does this excerpt reveal about Mary Chesnut's attitude toward the war?
5. What does this excerpt reveal about Mary Chesnut's attitude toward the Confederacy?

Applying

6. In what ways do you think this excerpt would be different if it had been written by someone actively involved in the attack on Fort Sumter?
7. In what ways do you think this excerpt would have been different if Mary Chesnut had been from the North?

ANALYZING LITERATURE

Understanding a Journal

A **journal** is a personal record of events, conversations, thoughts, feelings, and observations. In *Mary Chesnut's Civil War,* Mary Chesnut's journal from the war years, for example, Chesnut records her personal responses to the important events and people of the Civil War.

1. Mary Chesnut's descriptions are often colored by her dislike for the war. What evidence is there in Chesnut's description of the attack on Fort Sumter and the events preceding it that she dreaded the coming of the war?
2. Name two characteristics of Mary Chesnut's personality that are revealed in her journal.

CRITICAL THINKING AND READING

Recognizing Main Ideas

When reading a journal, it is important to recognize the main ideas being expressed and the main events being described. One of the main ideas expressed in Mary Chesnut's journal entry for April 12, for example, is that her husband believes that the attack on Fort Sumter may begin that night.

List three other main ideas and events in the excerpt from *Mary Chesnut's Civil War.*

THINKING AND WRITING

Writing a Summary

Write a summary of the events described in the excerpt from *Mary Chesnut's Civil War.* Reread the selection. Then look at your list of main ideas and events from the Critical Thinking and Reading exercise, making sure that you have not omitted any. Write your summary in chronological order, using transitions to link ideas and indicate the order of events. When you revise, make sure that your summary is clear and concise.

interruption of her diary writing, weeps over the disappointments of her hopes and the tragedies of her friends, and rages over the beastliness of men, the unfairness of life, and the cruelties of fortune.

Closure and Extension

ANSWERS TO THINKING ABOUT THE SELECTION
Recalling

1. (a) It begins on April 12, 1861. (b) Her clothes catch fire.
2. Regular meals are no longer possible.
3. (a) They surrender on April 15. (b) Colonel Chesnut gives details about the surrender.

Interpreting

4. She thinks the South has no choice but to fight, but she is afraid of the consequences of war.
5. She is sympathetic toward it.

Applying

6. Answers will differ. Suggested Response: It would have been less chatty and more concerned with action.
7. Suggested Response: She would have seen the Union soldiers who defended Fort Sumter as heroes.

ANSWERS TO ANALYZING LITERATURE

1. She could not sleep beforehand. She accidentally set herself on fire. Her quotation of Macbeth also expresses her feelings.
2. Suggested Response: She is well-educated. She has a good eye for detail.

ANSWERS TO CRITICAL THINKING AND READING

Suggested Response: Chesnut did not want war but sympathized with the South; people still hoped for peace; the South shelled Fort Sumter; and the North surrendered Fort Sumter.

THINKING AND WRITING

Publishing Student Writing Have student volunteers read their paragraphs to the class, and have the other students point out any important ideas and events that have been omitted.

Abraham Lincoln had not been President of the United States during one of the most trying periods of the country's history, he would almost certainly have been remembered for his words. It has been computed that his printed speeches and writings contain 1,078,365 words. These words, however, are more significant for their quality than for their quantity. How important is it for a political leader to be a talented writer and speaker?

Critical Evaluation Following President Lincoln's death, Walt Whitman wrote the following passage in his journal: "[Abraham Lincoln] leaves for America's history and biography, so far, not only its most dramatic reminiscence—he leaves, in my opinion, the greatest, best, most characteristic, artistic, moral personality. Not but that he had faults, and show'd them in the Presidency; but honesty, goodness, shrewdness, conscience, and (a new virtue, unknown to other lands, and hardly yet really known here, but the foundation and tie of all, as the future will grandly develop,) UNIONISM, in its truest and amplest sense, form'd the hard-pan of his character. These he seal'd with this life. The tragic splendor of his death, purging, illuminating all, throws round his form, his head, his aureole that will remain and will grown brighter through time, while history lives, and love of country lasts. By many has this Union been helped; but if one name, one man, must be pick'd out, he, most of all, is the conservator of it, to the future."

ABRAHAM LINCOLN

1809–1865

Serving as president during one of the most tragic periods in American history, Abraham Lincoln fought to reunite a nation torn apart by war. His courage, strength, and dedication in the face of an overwhelming national crisis have made him one of the most admired and respected American presidents.

Lincoln was born in a log cabin in Kentucky. When he was seven, his family moved to Indiana. Because he had to help his family clear land, split timber, build a home, and plant crops, Lincoln was able to attend school only occasionally. Lincoln managed to educate himself, however, by reading a wide variety of books.

When Lincoln was twenty-one, his family moved to Illinois, and he took a job as a store clerk. He soon developed an interest in politics, and in 1832 he ran for the Illinois state legislature. Though he lost his first election, he won a seat in the legislature—which he held for four terms—two years later.

In 1846 Lincoln was elected to the United States Congress. He earned a reputation as a champion of emancipation by sponsoring a bill that called for the abolition of slavery. The bill was defeated, however, and Lincoln failed to win reelection. Following his defeat Lincoln left politics to practice law. Yet his interest in politics was once again aroused in 1854, when the Missouri Compromise, which protected the balance between slave states and free states, was repealed. In 1858 Lincoln ran for the United States Senate against Stephen Douglas, a strong supporter of the Missouri Compromise. Lincoln lost the election, but his heated debates with Douglas won him national recognition.

Lincoln was elected president of the United States in 1860. Soon after his election, a number of states seceded from the Union and the Civil War began. Throughout the war, Lincoln longed for the day when the states would be reunited and the country's wounds would be healed. Lincoln had little chance to celebrate the end of the war, because he was assassinated just five days after it ended.

In addition to being a strong leader, Abraham Lincoln was a gifted speaker and writer. His most famous speech, "The Gettysburg Address," was delivered at the dedication ceremonies for the national cemetery at Gettysburg. The direct, forceful speech, which captured the determination and despair of the divided nation, is one of the most significant speeches in American history.

442   *Division, War, and Reconciliation*

Objectives

1 To appreciate diction
2 To analyze the appropriateness of diction
3 To compare and contrast speeches
4 To recognize words with the root *cede*
5 To write a letter

Support Material

Teaching Portfolio
Teacher Backup, p. 587
Usage and Mechanics Worksheet, p. 590
Vocabulary Check, p. 591
Analyzing Literature Worksheet, *Understanding Diction,* p. 592
Critical Thinking and Reading Worksheet, *Analyzing the Appropriateness of Diction,* p. 593
Selection Test, p. 594

GUIDE FOR INTERPRETING

The Gettysburg Address;
Letter to Mrs. Bixby

The Writer's Techniques

Diction. Diction refers to a writer's choice of words. An important aspect of style, diction must be appropriate to the subject, audience, occasion, and literary form. For example, if a writer is preparing an essay describing a mountain range for people who have never been there, he or she must use vivid, concrete language that enables the reader to visualize what is being described.

Writing

"The Gettysburg Address" is regarded as one of the most important speeches in American history because it captured the sorrow and determination of the war-torn nation. Freewrite about the Civil War and its effect on the American people.

Primary Source

In October 1863 President Lincoln was invited to make "a few appropriate remarks" at a November dedication of the battlefield at Gettysburg as a sacred resting place. Lincoln's remarks were to follow a two-hour speech by the renowned orator Edward Everett.

In describing Lincoln's speech, the reporter for the *Cincinnati Commercial* wrote, "The President rises slowly, draws from his pocket a paper, and when commotion subsides, in a sharp, unmusical treble voice, reads the brief and pithy remarks." The speech was so unexpectedly short that a photographer, preparing his photographic plates while his black box stood ready on its tripod, did not even have time to take a picture.

Some newspapers that generally opposed Lincoln's policies found fault with his address. The *Chicago Times* referred to it as "silly, flat, and dish-watery utterances." Other newspapers, however, recognized its significance. The *Springfield Republican* called the speech "a perfect gem; deep in feeling, compact in thought and expression, and tasteful and elegant in every word and comma." A writer in *Harper's Weekly* noted that the President's words "were from the heart to the heart. They can not be read, even, without kindling emotion." The *Providence Journal* asked, "Could the most elaborate and splendid oration be more beautiful, more touching, more inspiring, than those thrilling words of the President?" The *Chicago Tribune,* however, was the most prophetic when it commented, "The dedicatory remarks of President Lincoln will live among the annals of man."

Writing/Prior Knowledge For extra credit, have students freewrite about the effect of Vietnam War on the nation.

Master Teacher Note Point out to your students that today's political speeches are very different from the political speeches of Lincoln's time. Unlike the politicians of past eras, most of today's politicians have writers who prepare their speeches for them. Prior to the invention of radio and television, politicians could reach only a limited audience. In contrast, many of today's political speeches are broadcast on television and are heard by millions of Americans. Have your students discuss the ways in which they think television may have changed the nature of political speeches. Do they imagine that forms of nonverbal communication, such as gestures and facial expressions, have gained importance as a result of television? Why or why not?

Vocabulary

Preteach the following vocabulary words:
consecrate (kän′ sə krāt′) *v.:* Cause to be revered or honored (p. 444)
hallow (hal′ o) *v.:* Honor as sacred (p. 444)
beguile (bi gīl′) *v.:* Deceive (p. 446)
assuage (ə swāj) *v.:* Lessen (p. 446)
bereavement (bi rēv′ mənt) *n.:* Sadness resulting from the loss or death of a loved one (p. 446)

The Gettysburg Address
Abraham Lincoln

Four score and seven years ago our fathers brought forth on this continent, a new nation, conceived in Liberty, and dedicated to the proposition that all men are created equal.

Now we are engaged in a great civil war, testing whether that nation, or any nation so conceived and so dedicated, can long endure. We are met on a great battlefield of that war. We have come to dedicate a portion of that field, as a final resting place for those who here gave their lives that that nation might live. It is altogether fitting and proper that we should do this.

But, in a larger sense, we can not dedicate—we cannot consecrate—we cannot hallow—this ground. The brave men, living and dead, who struggled here, have consecrated it, far above our poor power to add or detract. The world will little note, nor long remember what we say here, but it can never forget what they did here. It is for us the living, rather, to be dedicated here to the unfinished work which they who fought here have thus far so nobly advanced. It is rather for us to be here dedicated to the great task remaining before us—that from these honored dead we take increased devotion to that cause for which they gave the last full measure of devotion—that we here highly resolve that these dead shall not have died in vain—that this nation, under God, shall have a new birth of freedom—and that government of the people, by the people, for the people, shall not perish from the earth.

ABRAHAM LINCOLN'S ADDRESS AT THE DEDICATION OF THE GETTYSBURG NATIONAL CEMETERY, 19 NOVEMBER 1863
The Granger Collection

THINKING ABOUT THE SELECTION

Recalling

1. To what "proposition" is the United States dedicated?
2. What is the Civil War "testing"?
3. (a) Where is the audience gathered? (b) Why have they gathered there?
4. What is the "task remaining before us"?

Interpreting

5. (a) Why does Lincoln believe that the war will have an impact on the entire world? (b) How does he convey this belief in his speech? (c) How does it add to the impact of the speech?
6. What is the purpose of Lincoln's speech?
7. Lincoln begins his speech by describing the birth of the nation and ends it by describing his vision of the nation's eventual rebirth. Considering Lincoln's purpose, why is this an effective way of structuring his speech?

Applying

8. (a) In what ways is Lincoln's speech different from the presidential addresses you have heard or seen on television? (b) How do you explain these differences?

ANALYZING LITERATURE

Understanding Diction

Diction refers to the writer's choice of words. Diction may be formal or informal, abstract or concrete. For example, "The Gettysburg Address" is written in formal, dignified language.

1. Find five words or phrases in "The Gettysburg Address" that contribute to its formal, dignified diction.
2. What words or phrases do you think Lincoln might have used in place of the five you chose in question 1 if the speech had been written using informal language?
3. The Shakespearean scholar A. L. Rowse has noted that many of Lincoln's speeches could easily be put into blank verse. In what ways do you find the language of "The Gettysburg Address" similar to the language of a poem?

CRITICAL THINKING AND READING

Analyzing Appropriateness of Diction

A writer must use language that is appropriate to the subject, audience, occasion, and literary form. For example, in writing "The Gettysburg Address," Lincoln used formal language because he felt it best suited the subject and occasion.

1. Why is Lincoln's diction appropriate?
2. Why would the speech have been less effective if it had been written using informal language?

THINKING AND WRITING

Comparing and Contrasting Speeches

Write an essay in which you compare and contrast "The Gettysburg Address" with Patrick Henry's "Speech in the Virginia Convention." Start by rereading both speeches, taking note of similarities and differences in purpose, directness, forcefulness, tone (the writer's attitude toward his or her subject), diction, structure, and methods of persuasion. Arrange your notes according to the points of contrast. Prepare a thesis statement. Then write your essay, focusing each of your body paragraphs on a single point of contrast. When you revise, make sure that you have varied the lengths and structures of your sentences and used transitions to link your ideas. Proofread your essay and prepare a final draft.

The Gettysburg Address 445

6. Lincoln wanted to stress the significance of the conflict and inspire Americans to persevere.
7. It highlights the fact that the soldiers are fighting to preserve the ideals of their forefathers and bring about an expansion of American freedoms in the future.

Applying

8. (a) Suggested Response: It is more brief and more poetic. (b) Suggested Response: Unlike most Presidential addresses, Lincoln's speech was delivered on a momentous occasion.

ANSWERS TO ANALYZING LITERATURE

1. Suggested Responses: Examples include: "Four score and seven years ago"; "far above our poor power to add or detract"; "engaged in a great civil war,"; "nobly advanced"; "—that we here highly resolve."
2. Suggested Responses: He might have said: 87 years ago; more than we can do now; in the middle of a bloody civil war; accomplished; decide or conclude.
3. Suggested Response: The language has a rhythmical, almost musical, quality.

ANSWERS TO CRITICAL THINKING

1. It is appropriate because of the emotional yet solemn nature of the subject and occasion.
2. It would have been less effective, because the language would have lacked the power and dignity needed for such a solemn occasion.

THINKING AND WRITING

For help with this assignment, students can refer to Lesson 16, "Writing a Comparative Evaluation," in the Handbook of Writing About Literature.

Writing Across the Curriculum
You may want to inform the history department about this assignment. History teachers might help students to grasp the historical significance of the two speeches.

Closure and Extension

ANSWERS TO THINKING ABOUT THE SELECTION
Recalling

1. All men are created equal.
2. It is testing whether or not a nation based on this proposition can endure.
3. (a) They are gathered on a "great battlefield" of the Civil War. (b) They have come there to dedicate part of the field as a cemetery for those who died there.
4. The task is to make sure that the soldiers have not died in vain and to make sure that the government does not perish.

Interpreting

5. (a) He believes that it will have an impact on the entire world, because it will demonstrate whether or not a democratic government can survive. (b) He comments that the world will never forget what the dead soldiers have done, and he states that the war is testing whether "any nation" dedicated to democratic ideals can survive. (c) It highlights the significance of the conflict and points out that the soldiers are fighting for an ideal as well as for the survival of their government.

445

Motivation/Prior Knowledge
Have students imagine that they are President Lincoln and have just received a letter from a woman who has lost five sons in battle. How would they respond?

Purpose-Setting Question
What is President Lincoln's attitude concerning Mrs. Bixby's loss?

1 **Discussion** Can grief be eased by letters of condolence? How does Lincoln manage to impart sincerity to his message?

Reader's Response What does this letter add to your conception of Abraham Lincoln? Why?

Humanities Note

Fine art, *Lincoln Proclaiming Thanksgiving,* 1938, by Dean Cornwell. Dean Cornwell (1892–1960), a famous American illustrator, was born in Louisville, Kentucky. Cornwell's method of creating pictures was very thorough; he made dozens of carefully worked-out variations for each project. His finished work was always complex, but seemingly effortless.

This illustration, *Lincoln Proclaiming Thanksgiving,* is a detail from an advertising illustration, commissioned by the Lincoln National Life Foundation of Fort Wayne, Indiana. It is an oil painting, rich, not only in color, but also in the human quality of thoughtfulness. Cornwell makes us truly feel the presence of a living, thinking, beloved man.

Have students describe Lincoln's look and his pose. You might ask these questions:
1. What can you infer about Lincoln from this painting?
2. Within the context of the "Letter," what might Lincoln be thinking about in this picture?
3. What art elements (e.g. color, light, composition), has the artist used to add drama to the picture?

Letter to Mrs. Bixby

Abraham Lincoln

Executive Mansion, Washington,
November 21, 1864

Mrs. Bixby, Boston, Massachusetts:

Dear Madam:

1   I have been shown in the files of the War Department a statement of the Adjutant-General of Massachusetts that you are the mother of five sons who have died gloriously on the field of battle. I feel how weak and fruitless must be any words of mine which should attempt to beguile you from the grief of a loss so overwhelming. But I cannot refrain from tendering to you the consolation that may be found in the thanks of the Republic they died to save. I pray that our Heavenly Father may assuage the anguish of your bereavement, and leave you only the cherished memory of the loved and lost, and the solemn pride that must be yours to have laid so costly a sacrifice upon the altar of freedom.

Yours very sincerely and respectfully,

Abraham Lincoln

**LINCOLN PROCLAIMING
THANKSGIVING**
Dean Cornwell
*Louis A. Warren Lincoln Library and
Museum, Fort Wayne, Indiana*

THINKING ABOUT THE SELECTION
Recalling

1. What has President Lincoln been shown in the files of the War Department?
2. For what does President Lincoln pray?

Interpreting

3. What is the purpose of this letter?
4. How would you describe the tone, or the writer's attitude toward the subject?
5. (a) What does the "altar of freedom" represent? (b) What is the sacrifice which Mrs. Bixby has laid upon it?
6. What does this letter reveal about Lincoln?

Applying

7. (a) What effect do you think this letter would have on Mrs. Bixby? (b) What is it about this letter that would create this effect?
8. In the sixth century B.C., the Chinese philosopher Confucius wrote, "If language be not in accordance with the truth of things, affairs cannot be carried on to success." Explain how Lincoln's letter is in keeping with this advice. Then tell whether or not you think this is good advice for all types of writing.

UNDERSTANDING LANGUAGE
Recognizing Words with the Root *cede*

Many English words are based on the Latin root *cede,* which means "to halt or give way." For example, the word *secede* means "to withdraw or separate formally."

Keeping the definition of *cede* in mind, try to determine the meaning of each of the following words. Then check your answer in a dictionary.

1. accede
2. precede
3. recede
4. concede
5. intercede

THINKING AND WRITING
Writing a Letter

Imagine that you are Mrs. Bixby. Write a letter to Lincoln in response to his letter to you. First freewrite, exploring your reactions to Lincoln's letter. Then prepare your first draft. Choose your language carefully and remember to make the tone appropriate for the audience (the President of the United States) and the purpose. Revise your letter, making sure you have used the appropriate form for a letter.

Commentary

Abraham Lincoln was known as an exquisite stylist. In much of his formal writing, he drew largely on his early reading of Shakespeare and of the Bible, and he stated ideas with elegance and precision. However, Lincoln was equally well known for another language style—a style that was looser and more familiar, one that was as plain and homespun as the man himself.

On one occasion a woman asked President Lincoln to intercede on her behalf at the War Department. Lincoln responded that he could be of no help because "they do things in their own way over there, and I don't amount to pig tracks in the War Department."

Lincoln sometimes coined his own words. He used the word *dupenance,* for example, to describe the quality of being easily duped. Someone who interrupted too often might be called *interruptious.* Lincoln also freely sprinkled his speeches, letters, and daily speech with such words as *bogus*, *skedaddle*, and *deadhead*, newly-coined words that were just then entering the language.

Lincoln was also known for his humorous turns of phrase. When asked whether he had enjoyed a certain lengthy paper, Lincoln is said to have remarked, "Well, for those who like that sort of thing, I should think it is just about the sort of thing they would like."

Letter to Mrs. Bixby 447

ANSWERS TO THINKING ABOUT THE SELECTION
Recalling

1. He has been shown a statement by the Adjutant General of Massachusettes that Mrs. Bixby had five sons who died during the Civil War.
2. He prays that God will comfort Mrs. Bixby in her hour of sorrow so that she can remember the good times and feel proud of her sons.

Interpreting

3. The purpose of the letter is to express sympathy for Mrs. Bixby and to lift her spirits with the knowledge that her sons did not die in vain.
4. The tone may be described as reverent, humane, and comforting.
5. (a) The "altar of freedom" represents the Civil War. (b) Mrs. Bixby had laid the lives of her five sons upon it.
6. Suggested Response: He is a kind, thoughtful, caring man.

Applying

7. (a) Suggested Response: It would soothe her. (b) Suggested Response: The fact that the letter is from the President would create this effect.
8. Suggested Response: The language of Lincoln's letter is sorrowful and compassionate, mirroring the truth of the situation.

ANSWERS TO UNDERSTANDING LANGUAGE

1. accede: to give assent
2. precede: to go before
3. recede: to go or move back
4. concede: to admit as true or valid
5. intercede: to intervene for the purpose of producing an agreement

THINKING AND WRITING

Publishing Student Writing
Have student volunteers share their letters with the class.

More About the Author The Virginia family from which Robert E. Lee was descended was distinguished for its service to our nation. One ancestor was an original colonist, another was a diplomat and agent of the Continental Congress, two others signed the Declaration of Independence and served in Congress. Why is it understandable that Lee was reluctant to see his state secede from the Union?

Critical Evaluation Robert E. Lee may have been the most respected and admired Southerner of his time. Even Ulysses S. Grant, the Union general who forced Lee to surrender, was well aware of the respect that Lee commanded in the South. Following Lee's death, Grant remarked, "There was not a man in the Confederacy whose influence with the whole people was as great as his."

ROBERT E. LEE

1807–1870

A descendant of a number of distinguished patriots and statesmen, Robert E. Lee was born into a respected family in Virginia. He attended the United States Military Academy at West Point, graduating with high honors in 1829. During the Mexican War, he earned a reputation as one of the country's finest military leaders. In fact, he was so highly regarded that when the Civil War began, President Lincoln offered Lee command of the Union forces.

Although he opposed secession, Lee refused Lincoln's offer. Determined not to harm his native state, Lee resigned his commission in the United States Army. In his letter of resignation, Lee vowed never to draw his sword again except in the defense of Virginia.

Shortly after his resignation, Lee agreed to command the army of northern Virginia. During the early stages of the war, he led his troops to several brilliant victories. As a result, Lee was named general-in-chief of all the Confederate armies. The Confederate forces were eventually defeated, however, and Lee was forced to surrender to Ulysses S. Grant at Appomattox on April 9, 1865.

After the war Lee urged fellow southerners to accept defeat gracefully and expressed his hope that the wounds caused by the war would soon be healed. During his final years, he served as president of Washington College, which was renamed Washington and Lee in his honor the year after his death.

Lee was an avid letter writer. During the war he frequently wrote to the members of his family, explaining his actions and expressing his feelings. Lee's letters not only provide insights into many of the most important events of the time, but they also reveal the personality of one of the greatest military leaders in American history.

The Proclamation of Amnesty and Reconciliation of 1865 barred the leaders of the Confederacy from holding public office. However, following the provisions of the proclamation, Lee applied for a complete pardon. His application was not honored during his lifetime, but in 1975 Congress restored him to full citizenship.

Lee once said that the most sublime word in the English language was *duty*. His fame rests on his military accomplishments against overwhelming odds during the Civil War as well as on his personal character in following his principles regardless of personal cost. At the time of Lee's death, the distinguished British soldier Viscount Garnet Wolseley said of Lee: "I have met many of the great men of my time, but Lee alone impressed me with the feeling that I was in the presence of a man who was cast in a grander mold and made of different and finer metal . . ."

GUIDE FOR INTERPRETING

Letter to His Son

The Civil War. When Abraham Lincoln, a vocal opponent of slavery, won the Republican nomination for president in 1860, many southern leaders urged the southern states to withdraw from the Union if Lincoln should win the election. Many southerners believed Lincoln would abolish slavery, and they felt that their economy would collapse if he were to do so. People from the North generally opposed slavery, however, and with their support Lincoln won the election.

In December of 1860, shortly after Lincoln was elected, South Carolina became the first state to secede from the Union. A month later five more states—Mississippi, Florida, Alabama, Georgia, and Louisiana—withdrew. In February of 1860, the six states established the Confederate States of America.

The Civil War began on April 12, 1861, when Confederate forces fired on Fort Sumter, a Union military post in Charleston, South Carolina. Shortly after the attack, five more states—Virginia, Arkansas, North Carolina, Tennessee, and Texas—joined the Confederacy. The war lasted for four years, ending on April 9, 1865. During the course of the conflict, more than 620,000 soldiers were killed.

Robert E. Lee's "Letter to His Son" was written on January 23, 1861. In the letter Lee expresses his opposition to secession and his hope that the dispute between the North and South can be resolved peacefully.

Commentary

Robert E. Lee once told the following anecdote in connection with his son Custis. One winter day, when Custis was little, Lee took him walking in the snow. After a while, the boy dropped behind. When Lee looked over his shoulder, he saw Custis imitating all his movements, holding his head and shoulders erect and placing his feet exactly in his father's footprints. "When I saw this," Lee said, "I said to myself, 'It behooves me to walk very straight, when this fellow is already following in my tracks.' "

Although Lee was frequently away from home, he tried to help his seven children "follow in his tracks" by writing to them frequently. As you read Lee's "Letter to His Son," you will see that Lee confided many of his important thoughts to his children. How did Lee's attitude toward shaping his children's lives contribute to our current knowledge about him?

Writing

How would you write a letter to a friend expressing your feelings about a current event? Think of an event that you feel is important. Then list your ideas and opinions concerning this event.

Guide for Interpreting 449

Historical Context Emphasize the fact that the Civil War was a very traumatic experience for the entire nation. Also point out that it took decades for some of the wounds opened by the war to heal.

Writing/Prior Knowledge Before having your students complete the writing assignment, spend some time discussing the reasons why people choose to write letters to their friends, rather than calling them on the telephone.

Vocabulary

Preteach the following vocabulary words:
perusal (pə r$\overline{oo}'$ z'l) *n.:* The act of reading (p. 450)
anarchy (an' ər kē) *n.:* The absence of government (p. 450)
redress (re' dres) *n.:* Atonement; rectification (p. 451)
calamity (kə lam' ə tē) *n.:* Disaster (p. 451)

Letter to His Son

Robert E. Lee

January 23, 1861

1 I received Everett's[1] *Life of Washington* which you sent me, and enjoyed its perusal. How his spirit would be grieved could he see the wreck of his mighty labors! I will not, however, permit myself to believe, until all ground of hope is gone, that the fruit of his noble deeds will be destroyed, and that his precious advice and virtuous example will so soon be forgotten by his countrymen. As far as I can judge by the papers, we are between a state of anarchy and civil war. May God avert both of these evils from us! I fear that mankind will not for years be sufficiently Christianized to bear the absence of restraint and force. I see that four states[2] have declared themselves out of the Union; four more will apparently follow their example. Then, if the border states are brought into the gulf of revolution, one half of the country will be arrayed against the other. I must try 2

---
1. Everett's: Referring to Edward Everett (1794–1865), an American scholar and orator who made a long speech at Gettysburg before Lincoln delivered his famous address.

2. four states: South Carolina, Mississippi, Florida, and Alabama.

THE BATTLE ABBEY MURALS: THE FOUR SEASONS OF THE CONFEDERACY
The Summer Mural, Charles Hoffbauer
The Virginia State Historical Society

and be patient and await the end, for I can do nothing to hasten or retard it.

The South, in my opinion, has been aggrieved by the acts of the North, as you say. I feel the aggression and am willing to take every proper step for redress. It is the principle I contend for, not individual or private benefit. As an American citizen, I take great pride in my country, her prosperity and institutions, and would defend any state if her rights were invaded. But I can anticipate no greater calamity for the country than a dissolution of the Union. It would be an accumulation of all the evils we complain of, and I am willing to sacrifice everything but honor for its preservation. I hope, therefore, that all constitutional means will be exhausted before there is a resort to force. Secession is nothing but revolution. The framers of our Constitution never exhausted so much labor, wisdom, and forbearance in its formation, and surrounded it with so many

guards and securities, if it was intended to be broken by every member of the Confederacy at will. It was intended for "perpetual union," so expressed in the preamble, and for the establishment of a government, not a compact, which can only be dissolved by revolution or the consent of all the people in convention assembled. It is idle to talk of secession. Anarchy would have been established, and not a government, by Washington, Hamilton, Jefferson, Madison, and the other patriots of the Revolution. . . . Still, a Union that can only be maintained by swords and bayonets, and in which strife and civil war are to take the place of brotherly love and kindness, has no charm for me. I shall mourn for my country and for the welfare and progress of mankind. If the Union is dissolved, and the government disrupted, I shall return to my native state and share the miseries of my people; and, save in defense, will draw my sword on none.

THINKING ABOUT THE SELECTION

Recalling

1. How does Lee describe the current state of the Union?
2. What is Lee willing to do?
3. What does Lee view as the greatest calamity for the country?
4. At the end of his letter, what does Lee vow to do?

Interpreting

5. (a) In your own words, summarize Lee's argument against secession. (b) How does Lee link his acknowledgment of his son's gift to his argument?

Applying

6. In what ways do you think Lee's attitudes might have been different if he had been from the North?

ANALYZING LITERATURE

Knowing Historical Context

Lee wrote "Letter to His Son" as the tension leading to the Civil War was mounting. At the time Lee felt torn between his devotion to his country and his deep attachment to his native state. How does he convey this feeling?

THINKING AND WRITING

Writing a Letter

Write a letter to a friend expressing your feelings concerning a current event. Start by reviewing your list of ideas and opinions. Then begin your letter, writing in a casual, informal style. Mention the important details of the event. When you revise, check to see that your opinions are clearly expressed, and make sure there are no errors in spelling, grammar, or punctuation.

Letter to His Son 451

Closure and Extension

3 **Discussion** Why does Lee feel that the South has some justification for seeking "redress"?

4 **Discussion** Is secession another name for revolution? Does Lee see revolution as a proper course of action?

Reader's Response If you were Lee's son, how would you respond to this letter? Why?

---

union and others are likely to do so in the near future.
2. He feels that the South has been unjustly treated by the North and will take whatever steps are necessary to right this wrong. However, he is also willing to sacrifice "everything but honor" to preserve the Union.
3. Dissolution of the Union is the worst disaster that could happen to the country.
4. If the Union breaks up, he will go home and share the fate of other Virginians. He will fight only in self-defense.

Interpreting

5. (a) He thinks secession would cause more problems than it would solve. Secession is also in direct conflict with the ideas and intentions of the framers of the Constitution. (b) Lee asserts that Washington would be upset if he knew that the Union he worked so hard to create would so soon be destroyed.

Applying

6. Suggested Response: He would not feel that the southern States were justified in seceding from the Union.

ANSWERS TO ANALYZING LITERATURE

Suggested Response: He gives arguments that support both sides.

THINKING AND WRITING

Publishing Student Writing Encourage students to mail their letters to their friends.

ANSWERS TO THINKING ABOUT THE SELECTION
Recalling

1. The union is "between a state of anarchy and civil war." Four states have already seceded from the

451

More About the Author Chief
Joseph of the Nez Percé tribe
was one of the ablest generals
the Native Americans ever produced. After broken treaties by
the government, the Nez Percé,
led by Chief Joseph, put up a
resistance that aroused the respect and admiration even from
their white antagonists. But the
Nez Percé were hopelessly outnumbered and were forced—
with their women and children—
into a fighting retreat. This is considered one of the great retreats
of military history. How can
the injustice that Chief Joseph
fought against be corrected?

You might want to divide
your class into groups of three or
four and have each group research the history of a different
native American tribe. Once the
groups have completed their research, have them share their
findings with the rest of the class.
Then use the reports as a springboard for a class discussion
about the experiences of native
Americans during the eighteenth
century.

CHIEF JOSEPH

1840[?]–1904

Chief Joseph was born in the Wallowa Valley in what is now Oregon.
His father, who was one of the chiefs of the Nez Percé tribe, con-
verted to Christianity around the time of Joseph's birth, and he sent
Joseph to a school run by missionaries.

In 1873 Joseph became a chief, succeeding his father. At that
time the United States Government was trying to force the Nez Percé
to relocate in Idaho. The Nez Percé had signed a treaty in 1863 giving
the government control of the tribe's land, but Chief Joseph felt that
the treaty was illegal and refused to recognize it. Chief Joseph tried
to negotiate with the government, but his attempts failed, and in June
of 1877 the dispute erupted into a war. Hoping to join forces with the
Sioux, Joseph led his people on a long march through Idaho and
Montana toward the Canadian border. During the march the Nez
Percé frequently clashed with federal troops and managed to win several battles. The tribe was heavily outnumbered by the government
troops, however, and the Indians were forced to endure great hardships during the course of their retreat. Chief Joseph was forced to
surrender on October 5, after being defeated in a battle in the Bear
Paw Mountains in Montana.

Several Nez Percé leaders were responsible for the strategies of
the military campaign and its early successes. However, because of
the widespread attention that Chief Joseph's surrender speech received, he became in the public's mind a symbol for the heroic Nez
Percé and their tragic plight. During his lifetime he was sometimes
referred to as the "Indian Napoleon."

After a period of imprisonment, Chief Joseph went to live in the
Indian territory in what is now Oklahoma. Inadequate shelter, fall
rains, and winter cold resulted in the deaths of many of the Nez Percé.
In 1885 Chief Joseph and the remainder of his people moved to the
Colville Reservation in Washington. During his later years, he tirelessly campaigned for American Indian rights, contributing several
essays to magazines and making a memorable series of public appearances in Washington, D.C.

Chief Joseph never gave up his dream that his people might
someday return to the Wallowa Valley. Toward the end of his life, he
visited the valley several times, hoping to convince the settlers to sell
land to the Indian Bureau for his people. All his requests were
refused.

Chief Joseph's speech of surrender is powerful and moving, conveying his sense of utter hopelessness and despair. The following excerpt includes some of the most memorable lines in the speech.

452   *Division, War, and Reconciliation*

Objectives

1 To recognize tone
2 To write a speech

Support Material

Teaching Portfolio
Teacher Backup, p. 607
Usage and Mechanics Work-
  sheet, p. 610
Analyzing Literature Worksheet,
  Understanding Tone, p. 611
Critical Thinking and Reading
  Worksheet, *Understanding Con-
  notation and Denotation*, p. 612
Selection Test, p. 613

GUIDE FOR INTERPRETING

I Will Fight No More Forever

**The Writer's
Techniques**

Tone. Tone refers to the writer's attitude toward his or her subject, characters, or audience. The tone of a nonfiction work may be revealed through the writer's choice of words and the portrayal of people and events. In a speech, tone may also be conveyed through the tone of the speaker's voice and through the speaker's facial expressions and hand gestures.

The tones of some works are obvious and clearly defined. For example, a work may clearly have an angry tone or a humorous tone. The tones of other works, however, are less obvious and more complex. For example, in "Letter to His Son" Robert E. Lee conveys an attitude of devotion and disillusionment toward the Union.

Writing

Native American tribes such as the Nez Percé lived close to the land, adapting their lives to their environments. As the United States grew and developed, many tribes, including the Nez Percé, were forced off their land and relocated in different areas. Freewrite about your thoughts concerning the forced relocation of Native American tribes.

Primary Source

A young soldier, C.E.S. Wood, recorded the scene as Chief Joseph surrendered. At about 2 o'clock in the afternoon, Chief Joseph took his rifle and mounted his horse. Five warriors followed on foot as he rode slowly up a hill to meet the army commanders. Wood, who stood behind the commanders, noticed bullet scars on Joseph's forehead, wrist, and back. He recorded that

> Joseph's hair hung in two braids on either side of his face. He wore a blanket—I do not remember the color—I would say gray with a black stripe. . . . He wore moccasin leggings. His rifle was across the pommel in front of him. When he dismounted he picked up the rifle, pulled his blanket closer about him, and walked to General Howard and offered him the rifle. Howard waved him to Miles. He then walked to Miles and handed him the rifle. Then he stepped back, adjusted his blanket to leave his right arm free, and began his speech.

> Wood recalled that as he surrendered, Chief Joseph "held himself very erect and with a quiet pride, not exactly defiance." When Chief Joseph had finished his speech, the officers present were so touched that they could not speak. Chief Joseph then pulled his blanket over his head, ending the war.

Guide for Interpreting 453

Literary Focus The tone of Chief Joseph's brief speech, surrendering to the overwhelming forces of the United States government, is what marks it as an impressive document. How does his despair evoke our sympathy?

Writing/Prior Knowledge Before your students complete the writing activity, you might discuss how the Native American tribes were affected by westward expansion.

Motivation/Prior Knowledge
Have students imagine that they are members of the Nez Percé tribe who have been retreating toward the Canadian border. They have endured cold weather, supply shortages, and numerous battles with government troops, and they have experienced the loss of many fellow tribe members. Would they want to continue fighting?

Purpose-Setting Question How has Chief Joseph been affected by the struggle?

1 Clarification The tribe was trying to get to Canada from their home in Oregon; they were cold, weary, and near starvation when they were offered honorable terms of surrender. The terms were promptly forgotten. Those who were still alive, along with their chief, were shipped to Oklahoma.

2 Discussion Did Chief Joseph have any recourse other than surrender? Explain.

Reader's Response What emotions does Chief Joseph's speech evoke in you? Why?

Humanities Note

Fine art, *Chief Joseph's Surrender to Colonel Nelson A. Miles*, Olaf C. Seltzer. Seltzer (1877–1957), an important western American painter, was born in Denmark. At the age of fifteen, he emigrated to Montana with his mother. He worked as a cowboy, and then for the Railroad, all while sketching in his spare time. He became friends with the famous painter Charles Russell, who had a great influence on his work. At the age of forty-four, Seltzer became a full-time painter. Following Russell's death, Seltzer traveled to New York City to fulfill some of Russell's last commissions. He was immedi-

I Will Fight No More Forever

Chief Joseph

Tell General Howard I know his heart. What he told me before, I have in my heart. I am tired of fighting. Our chiefs are killed. Looking Glass is dead. Toohoolhoolzote is dead. The old men are all dead. It is the young men who say yes and no. He who led on the young men is dead. It is cold and we have no blankets. The little children are freezing to death. My people, some of them, have run away to the hills and have no blankets, no food; no one knows where they are—perhaps freezing to death. I want to have time to look for my children and see how many I can find. Maybe I shall find them among the dead. Hear me, my chiefs. I am tired; my heart is sick and sad. From where the sun now stands I will fight no more forever.

CHIEF JOSEPH'S SURRENDER TO COLONEL NELSON A. MILES
Olaf C. Seltzer
Thomas Gilcrease Institute of American History and Art, Tulsa, Oklahoma

ately successful and continued to paint.

This painting shows that Seltzer was knowledgeable about the dress and ways of Native Americans, in this case the Nez Percé. He has created an expression of compassion for their sad plight.

You might use these questions for discussion:

1. What is happening in this picture?

2. How do you think the artist felt about the plight of Chief Joseph and his people?

THINKING ABOUT THE SELECTION

Recalling

1. Name three of Chief Joseph's reasons for deciding to "fight no more forever."
2. What does Chief Joseph say he wants to have time to do?

Interpreting

3. Chief Joseph's speech is composed mostly of short sentences with the same type of structure. (a) How does his repeated use of short, simple sentences contribute to the impact of his speech? (b) In what way does the simplicity of the language contribute to the impact?
4. What does this speech convey about Chief Joseph's relationship to his people?
5. Although Chief Joseph delivered his speech to notify the federal troops of his tribe's surrender, the speech had a greater purpose. What do you think this purpose was?

Applying

6. The manner in which a speaker delivers a speech often adds to its impact. In what ways do you think Chief Joseph's delivery of his speech might have added to its impact?

ANALYZING LITERATURE

Understanding Tone

Tone refers to the writer's attitude toward his or her subject. For example, a work of literature may have a sad tone or an indifferent tone.

1. How would you describe the tone of "I Will Fight No More Forever"?
2. How is the tone revealed?
3. Is this tone appropriate for its subject? Explain your answer.

THINKING AND WRITING

Writing a Speech

Write a speech in which you express your thoughts concerning an important current event. Start by listing the details of the event and the reasons that the event affects you as it does. Organize your notes into an outline. Then write your speech. Make sure that your attitude toward your subject is clear. When you revise, add transitions to link your ideas. When you finish revising your speech, deliver it to your classmates. Ask them to comment on both the delivery of the speech and its content.

Commentary

Chief Joseph's surrender speech received widespread attention, but later appeals for justice for his people added even more to his legend. Long after his defeat, Chief Joseph continued to impress people with his quiet eloquence and his dedication to his people. Government officials who visited him met a man who combined the courage and passion of a freedom fighter with the dignity and patience of a statesman.

In one of his most widely read appeals, Chief Joseph soberly noted that "too many misunderstandings have come up between the white men about the Indians. If the white man wants to live in peace with the Indian he can live in peace. There need be no trouble. Treat all men alike. Give them all the same law. Give them all an even chance to live and grow. All men are made by the same Great Spirit Chief. They are all brothers. The earth is the mother of all people, and all people should have equal rights upon it."

Chief Joseph's appeals created an upsurge of public support for his cause. They created an atmosphere that led to the return of other Native Americans to their homelands. However, Chief Joseph himself died in exile, never to live beneath the majestic mountains of his beloved Wallowa Valley again.

Closure and Extension

ANSWERS TO THINKING ABOUT THE SELECTION
Recalling

1. The chiefs have been killed; it is cold and his people have no blankets; and his people are without food.
2. He wants to look for his children.

Interpreting

3. (a) It adds emphasis to his main points. (b) It allows the facts to tell the story without any literary contrivances.
4. He loves his people and is dedicated to looking out for their welfare.
5. The greater purpose was to point out the plight of the Native American people.

Applying

6. Suggested Response: The sadness in his eyes, his subdued tone of voice, and his shoulders sagging in despair would have made this speech even more moving.

ANSWERS TO ANALYZING LITERATURE

1. It is one of sadness and despair.
2. It unfolds through Chief Joseph's direct statements about his feelings and his stark descriptions of the suffering of his people.
3. A sad, despairing tone is appropriate because he is expressing the despair of his people.

THINKING AND WRITING

Remind students that the composition of their speech is as important as their delivery.

Critical Evaluation After receiving a complimentary copy of Whitman's *Leaves of Grass*, Ralph Waldo Emerson wrote the following letter to Whitman: "I am not blind to the worth of the wonderful gift of *Leaves of Grass*. I find it the most extraordinary piece of wit and wisdom that America has yet contributed. I am very happy in reading it, as great power makes us happy. It meets the demand I am always making of what seemed the sterile and stingy nature, as if too much handiwork or too much lymph in the temperament, were making our western wits fat and mean. I give you joy of your free and brave thought. I have great joy in it. I find incomparable things said incomparably well, as they must be. I find the courage of treatment, which so delights me, and which large perception only can inspire. I greet you at the beginning of a great career, which yet must have a long foreground somewhere, for such a start. I rubbed my eyes a little to see if this sunbeam were not illusion; but the solid sense of the book is a sober certainty. It has the best of merits, namely, of fortifying and encouraging.

"I did not know until I, last night, saw the book advertised in a newspaper, that I could trust the name as real and available for a post office. I wish to see my benefactor, and have felt much like striking my tasks, and visiting New York to pay you my respects."

456

WALT WHITMAN

1819–1892

In the preface to his first volume of poetry, the 1855 edition of *Leaves of Grass,* Walt Whitman wrote, "The proof of a poet is that his country absorbs him as affectionately as he absorbed it." Unfortunately, Whitman's poetry did not gain the acceptance he had hoped for during his lifetime. Today, however, Whitman is widely recognized as one of the most gifted poets this country has produced.

Whitman was born on Long Island and raised in Brooklyn, New York. When he was twenty-seven, he became the editor of the Brooklyn *Eagle,* a respected newspaper, but the paper discharged him in 1848 because of his strong opposition to slavery. After accepting a position on a paper in New Orleans, Whitman traveled across the country for the first time, observing the diversity of the American landscapes and people.

In 1850 Whitman withdrew from journalism to devote his energy to writing poetry. When his first edition of *Leaves of Grass* was published five years later, the book provoked both positive and negative reactions. Ralph Waldo Emerson responded to the book with great enthusiasm, remarking that the collection was "the most extraordinary piece of wit and wisdom that America has yet contributed." Others, however, responded negatively, strongly objecting to the absence of rhyme and meter in Whitman's poetry. John Greenleaf Whittier, for example, disliked Whitman's poetry so much that he threw his copy of the book into the fireplace.

Throughout the remainder of his life, Whitman continually revised, reshaped, and expanded *Leaves of Grass*. Whitman viewed the work as one long poem, expressing his evolving vision of the world. His poetry conveyed his belief in democracy, equality, and the spiritual unity of all forms of life and celebrated the potential of the human spirit. Though Whitman's philosophy grew out of the ideas of the Transcendentalists, his poetry was mainly shaped by his unique ability to absorb and comprehend everything he observed. In the 383 poems included in the final edition of *Leaves of Grass* (1891), Whitman captures the diversity of the American people and conveys the energy and intensity of all forms of life.

In the years following Whitman's death, *Leaves of Grass* has become one of the most highly regarded collections of poetry ever written. Millions of readers have enjoyed the book, and it has influenced several generations of poets. There is little doubt that, according to his own definition, Whitman has proven himself as a poet.

1 To recognize style
2 To recognize the author's attitudes
3 To write a personal response
4 To recognize analogies
5 To recognize free verse
6 To write a poem in free verse

Support Material

Teaching Portfolio
Teacher Backup, p. 615
Usage and Mechanics Worksheet, p. 620
Vocabulary Check, p. 621
Analyzing Literature Worksheet, *Recognizing Free Verse* p. 622
Critical Thinking and Reading Worksheet, *Recognizing the Author's Attitudes* p. 623
Selection Test, p. 624

Art Transparency 8, *Abraham's Oak* by H. O. Tanner

GUIDE FOR INTERPRETING

Walt Whitman's Poetry

**The Writer's
Techniques**

Style. Style refers to the manner in which a writer puts his or her thoughts into words. It involves forms of expression rather than the thoughts conveyed.

Two of the most important aspects of Whitman's style are his frequent use of catalogs—the piling up of images or concrete details—and parallelism—the repeated use of phrases, clauses, or sentences that are similar in structure or meaning. For example, Whitman creates a catalog of concrete details in "Song of Myself" when he writes, "My tongue, every atom of my blood, formed from this soil, this air/Born here of parents born here from parents the same, and their parents the same" (lines 6–7). Whitman's catalogs were intended to represent the spiritual unity among all forms of being. Similarly, Whitman's use of parallelism helps to create a sense of unity within his poetry. It also provides a structure, creates a rhythm, and emphasizes important ideas in his poetry.

Free Verse. Another important characteristic of Whitman's style is his use of free verse—verse that has irregular meter and line length. Though free verse lacks regular meter, it does not lack rhythm. Free verse is structured to recreate the rising and falling cadences of natural speech, with the lengths of lines being varied according to intended emphasis.

Although free verse had first been used centuries earlier in the Psalms of the Bible, Whitman was the first American poet to use it. For Whitman, who valued freedom and individuality, free verse proved to be the most appropriate form, because it allowed him to express himself without restraint.

Writing

Prepare a list of concrete details or images that express your associations with a natural element such as grass, the ocean, the sun, or the moon.

Primary Source

In his later years, Walt Whitman developed a close friendship with Canadian doctor Richard Maurice Bucke. In describing Whitman Bucke once wrote, "Perhaps . . . no man who ever lived liked so many things and disliked so few as Walt Whitman. All natural objects seemed to have a charm for him. All sights and sounds seemed to please him. He appeared to like (and I believe he did like) all the men, women, and children he saw . . . I never knew him to argue or dispute, and he never spoke of money. . . . He never spoke deprecatingly of any nationality or class of men . . . He never complained or grumbled, either at the weather, pain, illness, or anything else. . . ."

Literary Focus To help students appreciate the concept of style, compare and contrast an Emily Dickinson poem with one by Edward Taylor. Also point out to students that free verse is a dominant poetic form in modern and contemporary poetry.

Writing/Prior Knowledge You may want to have students work in pairs while completing this assignment.

Vocabulary

Preteach the following vocabulary words:
abeyance (ə bā əns) *n.:* Temporary suspension (p. 460, l. 10)
effuse (e fyo͞oz′) *v.:* Spread out; diffuse (p. 464, l. 8)
expostulation (ik späs′ chə lā′ shən) *n.:* Expression of objection (p. 468, l. 16)
beseeching (bi sēch′ iŋ) *v.:* Ask earnestly; implore (p. 468, l. 18)

from **Preface to the 1855 Edition of *Leaves of Grass***

Walt Whitman

1 America does not repel the past or what it has produced under its forms or amid other politics or the idea of castes or the old religions. . . . accepts the lesson with calmness . . . is not so impatient as has been supposed that the slough still sticks to opinions and manners and literature while the life which served its requirements has passed into the new life of the new forms . . . perceives that the corpse is slowly borne from the eating and sleeping rooms of the house . . . perceives that it waits a little

WALT WHITMAN
Thomas Eakins
Courtesy of The Pennsylvania Academy of the Fine Arts

while in the door . . . that it was fittest for its days . . . that its action has descended to the stalwart and well-shaped heir who approaches . . . and that he shall be fittest for his days.

The Americans of all nations at any time upon the earth have probably the fullest poetical nature. The United States themselves are essentially the greatest poem. In the history of the earth hitherto the largest and most stirring appear tame and orderly to their ampler largeness and stir. Here at last is something in the doings of man that corresponds with the broadcast doings of the day and night. Here is not merely a nation but a teeming nation of nations. Here is action untied from strings necessarily blind to particulars and details magnificently moving in vast masses. Here is the hospitality which forever indicates heroes. . . . Here are the roughs and beards and space and ruggedness and nonchalance that the soul loves. Here the performance disdaining the trivial unapproached in the tremendous audacity of its crowds and groupings and the push of its perspective spreads with crampless and flowing breadth and showers its prolific and splendid extravagance. One sees it must indeed own the riches of the summer and winter, and need never be bankrupt while corn grows from the ground or the orchards drop apples or the bays contain fish or men beget children upon women. . . .

THINKING ABOUT THE SELECTION
Recalling

1. (a) What does America "not repel"? (b) What does it accept "with calmness"?
2. What country does Whitman say has the "fullest poetical nature"?

Interpreting

3. In the second paragraph, Whitman states that "the United States themselves are essentially the greatest poem." (a) What is the meaning of this statement? (b) How does Whitman support it?
4. What does Whitman mean when he comments that the United States "is not merely a nation but a teeming nation of nations"?
5. In your own words, describe Whitman's attitude toward America.

Applying

6. What is your definition of an American? Provide examples to clarify your definition.

from *Preface to the 1855 Edition of* Leaves of Grass   459

Motivation/Prior Knowledge
Have students imagine that they have been asked to write a poem that captures the essence of American life. What details would they want to include? What type of voice would they assume?

Master Teacher Note Point out to students that Whitman was born in a family that expected the equal rights and democracy to prevail as America developed. He was influenced by his family's Quaker background and by the Transcendentalism of Emerson.

Thematic Idea Another selection in which the writer explores what it means to be an American is the excerpt from *Letters from an American Farmer* by Michel-Guillaume Jean de Crèvecoeur (p. 156).

Purpose-Setting Question What is Whitman celebrating?

¹ **Discussion** Is Whitman's youthful optimism justified?

² **Critical Thinking and Reading** The speaker looks at the grass with a child. He sees it as "hopeful green stuff," which is the "flag" of his disposition and "the handkerchief of the Lord." How do these images symbolize his optimism about life?

from Song of Myself

Walt Whitman

1

I celebrate myself, and sing myself,
And what I assume you shall assume,
For every atom belonging to me as good belongs to you.

I loaf and invite my soul,
5 I lean and loaf at my ease observing a spear of summer
    grass.

My tongue, every atom of my blood, formed from this soil,
    this air,
Born here of parents born here from parents the same, and
    their parents the same,
I, now thirty-seven years old in perfect health begin,
Hoping to cease not till death.

10 Creeds and schools in abeyance,
Retiring back a while suffced at what they are, but never
    forgotten,
I harbor for good or bad, I permit to speak at every hazard,
Nature without check with original energy.

6

A child said *What is the grass?* fetching it to me with full
    hands,
How could I answer the child? I do not know what it is any
    more than he.

I guess it must be the flag of my disposition, out of hopeful
    green stuff woven.

Or I guess it is the handkerchief of the Lord,
5 A scented gift and remembrancer¹ designedly dropped,
Bearing the owner's name someway in the corners, that we
    may see and remark, and say *Whose?*

       . . .

What do you think has become of the young and old men?
And what do you think has become of the women and
    children?

---

1. remembrancer: Reminder.

Primary Source

Toward the end of his life, Whitman wrote a number of retrospective essays in which he assessed his career as a writer. In the following passage from "A Backward Glance o'er Travel'd Roads," Whitman expresses regret that *Leaves of Grass* had not gained the acceptance that he had hoped it would, and he conveys his hope that the book will receive more recognition in the future:

I look upon *Leaves of Grass,* now finish'd to the end of its opportunities and powers, as my definitive *carte visite* to the coming generations of the New World, if I may assume to say so. That I have not gain'd the acceptance of my own time, but have fallen back on fond dreams of the future—anticipations—that from a worldly and business point of view *Leaves of Grass* has been worse than a failure—that public criticism on the book and myself as author of it yet shows mark'd anger and contempt more than anything else—'I find a solid line of enemies to you everywhere,'—letter from W.S.K., Boston, May 28, 1884—And that solely for publishing it I have been the object of two or three pretty serious special official buffetings—is all probably no more than I ought to have expected. As fulfill'd, or partially fulfill'd, the

They are alive and well somewhere,
10   The smallest sprout shows there is really no death,
And if ever there was it led forward life, and does not wait
    at the end to arrest it,
And ceas'd the moment life appear'd.
All goes onward and outward, nothing collapses,
And to die is different from what anyone supposed, and
    luckier.

9

The big doors of the country barn stand open and ready,
The dried grass of the harvest-time loads the slow-drawn
    wagon,

3

3 **Reading Strategy** Have students determine the activities that the speaker engages in next. How do they encourage his optimism? What "same old law" is being enacted?

best comfort of the whole business (after a small band of the dearest friends and upholders ever vouchsafed to man or cause—doubtless all the more faithful and uncompromising—this little phalanx!—for being so few) is that, unstopp'd and unwarp'd by any influence outside the soul within me, I have had my say entirely my own way, and put it unerringly on record—the value thereof to be decided by time. . . .

Behind all else that can be said, I consider *Leaves of Grass* and its theory experimental—as, in the deepest sense, I consider our American republic itself to be, with its theory. (I think I have at least enough philosophy not to be too absolutely certain of any thing, or any results.) In the second place, the volume is a *sortie*—whether to prove triumphant, and conquer its field of aim and escape and construction, nothing less than a hundred years from now can fully answer. I consider the point that I have positively gain'd a hearing, to far more than make up for any and all other lacks and withholdings. Essentially, *that* was from the first, and has remain'd throughout, the main object. Now it seems to be achiev'd, I am certainly contented to waive any otherwise momentous drawbacks, as of little account. Candidly and dispassionately reviewing all my intentions, I feel that they were creditable—and I accept the result, whatever it may be.

The clear light plays on the brown gray and green intertinged,
The armfuls are pack'd to the sagging mow.

5 I am there, I help, I came stretch'd atop of the load,
I felt its soft jolts, one leg reclined on the other,
I jump from the crossbeams and seize the clover and timothy,
And roll head over heels and tangle my hair full of wisps.

14

The wild gander leads his flock through the cool night,
Ya-honk he says, and sounds it down to me like an invitation,
The pert may suppose it meaningless, but I listening close,
Find its purpose and place up there toward the wintry sky.

5 The sharp-hoof'd moose of the north, the cat on the house-sill, the chickadee, the prairie dog,
The litter of the grunting sow as they tug at her teats,
The brood of the turkey hen and she with her half-spread wings,
I see in them and myself the same old law.

The press of my foot to the earth springs a hundred affections,
10 They scorn the best I can do to relate them.

I am enamor'd of growing outdoors,
Of men that live among cattle or taste of the ocean or woods,
Of the builders and steerers of ships and the wielders of axes and mauls, and the drivers of horses,
I can eat and sleep with them week in and week out.

15 What is commonest, cheapest, nearest, easiest, is Me,
Me going in for my chances, spending for vast returns,
Adorning myself to bestow myself on the first that will take me,
Not asking the sky to come down to my good will,
Scattering it freely forever.

17

These are really the thoughts of all men in all ages and lands, they are not original with me,

Primary Source

In his retrospective essay "A Backward Glance o'er Travel'd Roads," Whitman explains his purpose in writing *Leaves of Grass:*

Given the nineteenth century, with the United States, and what they furnish as area and points of view, *Leaves of Grass* is, or seeks to be, simply a faithful and doubtless self-will'd record. In the midst of all, it gives one man's—the author's—identity, ardors, observations, faiths, and thoughts, color'd hardly at all with any decided coloring from other faiths or identities. Plenty of songs had been sung—beautiful, matchless songs—adjusted to other lands than these—another spirit and stage of evolution; but I would sing, and leave out or put in, quite solely with reference to America and today. Modern science and democracy see'd to be throwing out their challenge to poetry to put them in its statements in contradistinction to the songs and myths of the past. As I see it now (perhaps too late,) I have unwittingly taken up that challenge and made an attempt at such statements—which I certainly would not assume to do now, knowing more clearly what it means.

For grounds for *Leaves of Grass,* as a poem, I abandon'd the conventional themes, which do not appear in it: none of the stock

If they are not yours as much as mine they are nothing, or
    next to nothing,
If they are not the riddle and the untying of the riddle they
    are nothing,
If they are not just as close as they are distant they are
    nothing.
5 This is the grass that grows wherever the land is and the
    water is,
This is the common air that bathes the globe.

51

The past and present wilt—I have fill'd them, emptied them,
And proceed to fill my next fold of the future.

Listener up there! what have you to confide to me?
Look in my face while I snuff the sidle of evening,[2]
5 (Talk honestly, no one else hears you, and I stay only a
    minute longer.)

Do I contradict myself?
Very well then I contradict myself,
(I am large, I contain multitudes.)

I concentrate toward them that are nigh,[3] I wait on the
    door-slab.

10 Who has done his day's work? who will soonest be through
    with his supper?
Who wishes to walk with me?

Will you speak before I am gone? will you prove already too
    late?

52

The spotted hawk swoops by and accuses me, he complains
    of my gab and my loitering.

I too am not a bit tamed, I too am untranslatable,
I sound my barbaric yawp over the roofs of the world.

---

2. **snuff . . . evening:** Put out the hesitant last light of day, which
is moving sideways across the sky.
3. **nigh:** Near.

from *Song of Myself*   463

5 **Discussion** What does Whitman mean when he comments, "I contain multitudes"?

Enrichment Whitman clearly stated his goals as a poet in a 1856 letter to Ralph Waldo Emerson. He wrote, "Swiftly, on limitless foundations, the United States too are founding a literature. It is all as well done, in my opinion, as could be practicable. Each element here is in condition. Every day I go among the people of Manhattan Island, Brooklyn, and other cities, and among the young men, to discover the spirit of them, and to refresh myself. These are to be attended to; I am myself more drawn here than to those authors, publishers, importations, reprints, and so forth. I pass coolly through those, understanding them perfectly well, and that they do the indispensable service outside of men like me, which nothing else could do. In poems, the young men of The States shall be represented, for they out-rival the best of the rest of the earth."

ornamentation, or choice plots of love or war, or high, exceptional personages of Old-World song; nothing, as I may say, for beauty's sake—no legend, or myth, or romance, nor euphemism, nor rhyme. But the broadest average of humanity and its identities in the now ripening nineteenth century, and especially in each of their countless examples and practical occupations in the United States today.

One main contrast of the ideas behind every page of my verses, compared with establish'd poems, is their different relative attitude toward God, toward the objective universe, and still more (by reflection, confession, assumption, etc.) the quite changed attitude of the ego, the one chanting or talking, towards himself and towards his fellow-humanity. It is certainly time for America, above all, to begin this readjustment in the scope and basic point of view of verse; for everything has changed. . . . A firmer, vastly broader, new area begins to exist—nay, is already form'd—to which the poetic genius must emigrate. Whatever may have been the case in years gone by, the true use for the imaginative faculty of modern times is to give ultimate vivification to facts, to science, and to common lives, endowing them with the glows and glories and final illustriousness which belong to every real thing, and to real things only. Without the ultimate vivification—which the poet or other artist alone can give—reality would seem incomplete, and science, democracy, and life itself, finally in vain.

6 **Critical Thinking and Reading**
The speaker bequeaths himself "to the dirt." How does this take the grass and him full cycle?

Reader's Response What are your reactions to the various ideas that Whitman expresses in these verses? Which ideas do you find most appealing? Which ideas do you find least appealing?

The last scud⁴ of day holds back for me,
5   It flings my likeness after the rest and true as any on the shadow'd wilds,
It coaxes me to the vapor and the dusk.

I depart as air, I shake my white locks at the runaway sun,
I effuse my flesh in eddies, and drift it in lacy jags.

6 [

I bequeath myself to the dirt to grow from the grass I love,
10   If you want me again look for me under your boot soles.

You will hardly know who I am or what I mean,
But I shall be good health to you nevertheless,
And filter and fiber your blood.

Failing to fetch me at first keep encouraged,
15   Missing me one place search another,
I stop somewhere waiting for you.

---

4. scud: Low, dark, wind-driven clouds.

THINKING ABOUT THE SELECTION
Recalling

1. (a) Whom does the speaker celebrate? (b) What does he observe?
2. (a) What question does a child ask the speaker? (b) How does the speaker respond?
3. (a) Name three animals that the speaker observes in section 14. (b) What does he see in both the animals and himself?
4. According to section 17, with whom does the speaker share his thoughts?
5. (a) To what does the speaker "bequeath himself" in section 52? (b) Where does he say that we should look for him? (c) For whom is he waiting?

Interpreting

6. (a) In the first section, how does Whitman suggest that the self he is celebrating is not just his individual self but also a representative and shared universal self? (b) In what ways does Whitman's celebration of individuality and belief in the existence of a shared universal self or soul reflect the beliefs of the Transcendentalists?
7. What do lines 6–14 of section 6 reveal about the speaker's attitude concerning death?
8. How do the images of grass and air in section 17 convey the speaker's belief in the spiritual unity and equality of all forms of being?

464   *Division, War, and Reconciliation*

9. In the final section, what does the speaker suggest will happen to his spirit and message once he is gone?

Applying

10. In what ways is your own attitude toward nature similar to and different from the attitude conveyed in "Song of Myself"?

ANALYZING LITERATURE
Recognizing Style

Style refers to the way in which a writer expresses his or her thoughts. Each writer has his or her own distinctive style. Two important characteristics of Whitman's style are his use of catalogs and parallelism. For example, in the following passage from "Song of Myself" Whitman uses both techniques—creating a catalog of concrete images using parallel structures:

> The big doors of the country barn
>   stand open and ready,
> The dried grass of the harvest-time
>   loads the slow-drawn wagon,
> The clear light plays on the brown
>   gray and green intertinged,
> The armfuls are pack'd to the sagging
>   mow.

1. Find another example of a catalog in "Song of Myself."
2. Find two more examples of parallelism.

CRITICAL THINKING AND READING
Recognizing the Author's Attitudes

Whitman's poetry reveals a great deal about his attitudes and beliefs. For example, he reveals his affection for people who work outdoors in lines 11–14 from "Song of Myself."

1. Find two more passages from "Song of Myself" in which Whitman expresses his attitudes or beliefs.
2. What attitude or belief does each of the passages you identified in question 1 reveal?

THINKING AND WRITING
Writing a Personal Response

Write a short personal essay expressing your reactions to "Song of Myself." You should be prepared to share your essay with your classmates, and it should help to stimulate a class discussion. Start by rereading the poem, noting your responses to the style and content of the poem and to the attitudes and beliefs Whitman expresses. When you write your essay, concentrate on expressing your reactions clearly. When you finish writing, revise your essay. Then read your essay to your class and answer any questions your classmates may have.

Commentary

Ralph Waldo Emerson's enthusiastic response to *Leaves of Grass* was contained in a personal letter to Whitman. Emerson's letter is probably the most famous letter in American literary history, and Whitman's use—or misuse—of it is almost as famous.

When it was first published, *Leaves of Grass* was almost completely ignored by reviewers and readers. Whitman resorted to unconventional means to keep it alive. He allowed Emerson's letter to be published in a newspaper without Emerson's permission. He then inserted copies of the letter in copies of the book that he sent to other figures in the literary world.

Emerson was shocked by Whitman's actions though he continued to recommend *Leaves of Grass.* However, Whitman's use of Emerson's letter had its desired effect. His book began to receive reviews and attract interest. Its value remained controversial for many years, but Whitman's self-promotion had rescued his book from oblivion.

from *Song of Myself* 465

---

6. (a) He says "every atom belonging to me as good belongs to you." (b) Suggested Response: It suggests the Transcendentalists's belief in a shared universal soul, or Over-Soul.
7. He feels there really is no death.
8. Whitman points out that the grass grows everywhere and that the air bathes the entire globe. The images of the air and the grass connected to the "thoughts of all men in all ages and lands."
9. He suggests that he and his message will be somewhere waiting.

Applying

10. Answers will differ. Students might comment that they do not share Whitman's sense of unity with nature.

ANALYZING LITERATURE

1. Answers will differ. One example is, "I am enamour'd of growing outdoors,/Of men that live among cattle or taste the ocean of woods,/Of the builders and steerers of ships and the wielders of axes and mauls, and the drivers of horses . . ."
2. Answers will differ. One example occurs in lines 1–4 of Section 9; another example occurs in lines 2–4 of Section 17.

ANSWERS TO CRITICAL THINKING AND READING

1. Answers will differ. He expresses his attitude concerning death in lines 7–14 of Section 6, and he expresses his attitude toward the outdoors in lines 11–14 of Section 14.
2. Attitudes should correspond to passages selected for question 1. Whitman believed that the spirit does not die, and he was enamoured with the outdoors.

THINKING AND WRITING

Publishing Student Writing Have student volunteers share their responses with the class, and use their readings as a springboard for a class discussion.

Closure and Extension

ANSWERS TO THINKING ABOUT THE SELECTION
Recalling

1. (a) He celebrates himself. (b) He observes a spear of summer grass.
2. (a) A child asks what grass is. (b) He does not know how to respond.
3. (a) Suggested Response: He observes a cat, a chickadee, and a prairie dog. (b) He sees in them and himself "the same old law."
4. He shares his thoughts with the "listener up there."
5. (a) He bequeaths himself to the dirt. (b) We should look under our bootsoles. (c) He is waiting for us.

I Saw in Louisiana a Live-Oak Growing

Walt Whitman

I saw in Louisiana a live-oak growing,
And alone stood it and the moss hung down from the branches,
Without any companion it grew there uttering joyous leaves of dark green,
And its look, rude, unbending, lusty, made me think of myself,
5   But I wonder'd how it could utter joyous leaves standing alone there without its friend near, for I knew I could not,
And I broke off a twig with a certain number of leaves upon it, and twined around it a little moss,
And brought it away, and I have placed it in sight in my room,
It is not needed to remind me as of my own dear friends,
(For I believe lately I think of little else than of them,)

THINKING ABOUT THE SELECTION

Recalling

1. (a) What characteristics of the live-oak make the speaker think of himself? (b) In what way is the live-oak different from the speaker?

Interpreting

2. What human characteristics does the speaker attribute to the live-oak?
3. What is revealed about the speaker's personality through his description of the live-oak?
4. (a) How do the last three lines of the poem echo the beginning? (b) What is the effect of this repetition?

Applying

5. What type of natural scene would make you think of yourself? Explain your answer.

10 Yet it remains to me a curious token, it makes me think of
     manly love;
  For all that, and though the live-oak glistens there in
     Louisiana solitary in a wide flat space,
  Uttering joyous leaves all its life without a friend a lover
     near,
  I know very well I could not.

UNDERSTANDING LANGUAGE
Recognizing Analogies

A verbal **analogy** is an expression of a relationship between two words. Analogy questions on standardized tests ask you to choose two words that are related in the same way as a given pair. For example,

tall : short : : big : small

The words in capital letters in the following analogies appear in Walt Whitman's poetry. Complete each analogy by choosing the pair of words whose relationship is most similar to that expressed by the capitalized pair.

1. FRIEND : COMPANION : :
    (a) mother : kitchen
    (b) carousel : cassock
    (c) car : automobile
    (d) carbon : lead

2. BRANCH : TWIG : :
    (a) automobile : tire
    (b) particle : felony
    (c) athlete : field
    (d) abdomen : synapse
3. CHURCH : CONGREGATION : :
    (a) theater : actors
    (b) stadium : athletes
    (c) farm : farmer
    (d) school : students
4. RUDE : LUSTY : :
    (a) boisterous : angry
    (b) sullen : melancholy
    (c) hopeful : crass
    (d) immature : grown
5. SURROUNDED : DETACHED : :
    (a) agitated : confused
    (b) fickle : constant
    (c) hopeful : dejected
    (d) encircled : distant

I Saw in Louisiana a Live-Oak Growing   467

Motivation/Prior Knowledge
Have students imagine how the majority of Americans might have felt after the Battle of Bull Run. Do you think that some people's attitudes may have changed following the Confederate victory in this battle?

Purpose-Setting Question What is the speaker's attitude toward the war?

1 **Discussion** What progression through the country does the speaker make?

2 **Discussion** How does Whitman's use of alliteration contribute to the impact of the poem?

Reader's Response If you had been alive at the time this poem was written, how do you imagine you would have reacted to it? Explain.

Beat! Beat! Drums!

Walt Whitman

This poem was written in response to the defeat of the Union army by Confederate forces in the battle of Bull Run in 1861. The Confederate victory shocked many people who felt that the Union would easily win the war and made it clear that a long and bloody struggle lay ahead.

Beat! beat! drums!—blow! bugles! blow!
Through the windows—through doors—burst like a ruthless force,
Into the solemn church, and scatter the congregation,
Into the school where the scholar is studying;
5 Leave not the bridegroom quiet—no happiness must he have now with his bride,
Nor the peaceful farmer any peace, ploughing his field or gathering his grain,
So fierce you whirr and pound you drums—so shrill you bugles blow.

Beat! beat! drums!—blow! bugles! blow!
Over the traffic of cities—over the rumble of wheels in the streets;
10 Are beds prepared for sleepers at night in the houses? no sleepers must sleep in those beds,
No bargainers' bargains by day—no brokers or speculators—would they continue?
Would the talkers be talking? would the singer attempt to sing?
Would the lawyer rise in the court to state his case before the judge?
Then rattle quicker, heavier drums—you bugles wilder blow.

15 Beat! beat! drums!—blow! bugles! blow!
Make no parley—stop for no expostulation,
Mind not the timid—mind not the weeper or prayer,
Mind not the old man beseeching the young man,
Let not the child's voice be heard, nor the mother's entreaties,
20 Make even the trestles to shake the dead where they lie awaiting the hearses,
So strong you thump O terrible drums—so loud you bugles blow.

THE WOUNDED DRUMMER BOY
Eastman Johnson
The Union League Club, New York City

THINKING ABOUT THE SELECTION

Recalling

1. (a) What activities do the drums and bugles interrupt?   (b) What do they prevent us from noticing?

Interpreting

2. What do the drums and bugles represent?
3. What does this poem suggest about the effect of war on people's everyday lives?
4. (a) How does the rhythm and repetition of lines 1, 8, and 15 add to the impact of the poem?   (b) How does Whitman's use of parallelism reinforce the meaning of the poem?

Applying

5. Whitman's poem suggests that most Americans dreaded the coming of the Civil War. Why do you think the American people might have dreaded the Civil War more than other wars in which the country had participated? Explain your answer.

Beat! Beat! Drums! 469

Humanities Note

Fine art, *The Wounded Drummer Boy,* 1871, by Eastman Johnson. Eastman Johnson (1824–1906) was the son of a wealthy Maine politician. He studied art in Germany, Holland, and France and returned to America in 1855 with the best training of any American genre painter. During the Civil War he used his artistic skills to report events. Many art historians feel that Johnson receded from reportage to sentimentality, as in this painting, *The Wounded Drummer Boy.* Johnson has portrayed a sweetfaced lad with a discreetly bandaged leg. He is being carried on the shoulders of a heroic, burly soldier, against the background of the battle. The boy is bravely rallying the troops with his little drum. The noticeable lack of blood and the presence of a kind of charming pathos show a lack of concern for the actual hardships of war. Despite the present-day criticism of this painting, it was immensely popular in its day, and Johnson was called on to paint several versions.

You might use the following questions for discussion:
1. What is happening in this painting?
2. What purpose does the beating of the drums serve—both in this painting and in the poem?
3. How would you characterize the emotions in this painting?
4. Although *The Wounded Drummer Boy* is often criticized by today's standards as being overly sentimental and lacking in concern for the actual hardships of war, it was immensely popular during the Civil War. Why do you suppose this was so?

Closure and Extension

ANSWERS TO THINKING ABOUT THE SELECTION
Recalling

1. (a) They interrupt worship, study, family life, farming, city commerce, sleep, and law. (b) They prevent us from noticing the child's voice and the mother's entreaties.

Interpreting

2. They represent the ravages of war.
3. The war brings people's everyday lives to a screeching, grinding halt.
4. (a) The forceful rhythm and use of repetition emphasizes the powerful effect of the war. (b) It adds emphasis to Whitman's references to the disrupting effects of the war.

Applying

5. Suggested Response: Americans might have dreaded the Civil War more because it was fought on our own land, state against state, family against family, brother against brother.

Motivation/Prior Knowledge
Robert Browning, an English poet, observed that "a man's reach should exceed his grasp/ Or what's a heaven for?" What does he mean?

Purpose-Setting Question How does the speaker's view contrast with that of the scientist?

1 Literary Focus Whitman often used parallelism to emphasize his message. How is this technique used in the first four lines?

2 Discussion Why does the speaker become bored by the lecture?

3 Discussion Why is the mystery of the heavens sometimes served better by silence than by "charts and diagrams"?

Humanities Note

Fine art, *The Lawrence Tree*, 1929, by Georgia O'Keeffe. Georgia O'Keeffe (1887–1985) knew by the age of ten that she wanted to be an artist. She had her first one-woman show in New York in 1917, having discovered that she could say things with color and shape that she couldn't say any other way. In 1949 she settled in New Mexico, later traveling in Europe, South America, and the Far East.

About *The Lawrence Tree*, O'Keeffe wrote, "I spent several weeks up at the Lawrence ranch that summer (1929). There was a long weathered carpenter's bench under the tall tree in front of the little old house that Lawrence had lived in there. I often lay on that bench looking up into the three—past the trunk and up into the branches. It was particularly fine at night with the stars above the tree." O'Keeffe reveals her very personal experience with this imagery. It is a vision of strength and clarity, and uniquely hers.

When I Heard the Learn'd Astronomer

Walt Whitman

When I heard the learn'd astronomer,
When the proofs, the figures, were ranged in columns
     before me,
When I was shown the charts and diagrams, to add, divide
     and measure them,
When I sitting heard the astronomer where he lectured with
     much applause in the lecture room,
5 How soon unaccountable I became tired and sick,
Till rising and gliding out I wander'd off by myself,
In the mystical moist night air, and from time to time,
Look'd up in perfect silence at the stars.

THE LAWRENCE TREE, 1929
Georgia O'Keeffe
Wadsworth Atheneum, Hartford

Consider using these questions for discussion:
1. What is unusual about the viewpoint of this painting?
2. What is O'Keeffe saying about Nature in this painting?
3. In what way is O'Keeffe's viewpoint in this painting similar to Whitman's in "When I Heard the Learn'd Astronomer"?

THINKING ABOUT THE SELECTION
Recalling

1. What visual aids does the astronomer use during his lecture?
2. How does the speaker respond to the lecture?
3. (a) Where does the speaker go when he leaves the lecture? (b) What does he look up at from time to time?

Interpreting

4. How is the speaker's attitude toward the stars different from that of the astronomer?
5. The word *mystical* means "spiritually significant." Why do you think Whitman chose this word to describe the moist night air in line 7?
6. Who do you think is more "learn'd" in regard to the stars? Explain your answer.
7. (a) What is the theme, or main point, of the poem? (b) How does Whitman's use of parallel structures in the first four lines reinforce the theme?

Applying

8. (a) How would you describe your own attitude toward the stars? (b) Is your attitude more similar to the astronomer's attitude or the speaker's attitude?

ANALYZING LITERATURE
Recognizing Free Verse

Free verse is verse that has irregular meter and line length. Walt Whitman's use of free verse reflects his belief in freedom, democracy, and individuality.

1. Considering the theme of "When I Heard a Learn'd Astronomer," why do you think free verse is an appropriate form for the poem?
2. How would this poem be different if it were written in verse with regular meter and line length?
3. Even great writers do not always receive good reviews. William Allingham wrote of Walt Whitman's poetry, "Of course, to call it poetry, in any sense, would be mere abuse of the language." Respond to Allingham's statement. Do you think Whitman's writing is poetry? Explain your answer.

THINKING AND WRITING
Writing a Poem in Free Verse

Using free verse, write a poem expressing your associations with a natural element such as grass, the ocean, the sun, or the moon. Start by reviewing the list of concrete details you prepared before you began reading. Try to think of additional details you can add to your list. Then write your poem. Structure your verse to recreate the rising and falling cadences of natural speech and vary the lengths of the lines according to intended emphasis. When you finish writing, revise your poem and share it with your classmates.

Interpreting

4. The speaker is attracted by the beauty and mystery of the heavens, while the scientist views the stars as the subject of his scientific studies.
5. He chose the word, because he sees spiritual significance in the stars.
6. Suggested Response: The speaker is more "learn'd," because he has more of an appreciation for the beauty and mystery of the heavens.
7. (a) The theme is that you don't need a formal knowledge of a thing to enjoy a spiritual connection with it. (b) His uses parallelism in the first four lines to reflect the tedious nature of the scientist's approach.

Applying

8. (a) Suggested Response: The stars are beautiful and mysterious. (b) Suggested Response: It is more similar to the speaker's attitude.

ANSWERS TO ANALYZING LITERATURE

1. Free verse is appropriate, because Whitman is emphasizing the value of a free, unconfined approach to understanding the wonders of nature.
2. Suggested Response: The form of the poem would not reflect its meaning.
3. Suggested Response: Whitman's writing is poetry, because it is rhythmical and musical.

THINKING AND WRITING

For help with this assignment, students can refer to Lesson 12, "Writing a Poem," in the Handbook of Writing About Literature.

Publishing Student Writing You may wish to collect the poems into an anthology. To show similarities and differences in the points of view represented by the poems, you might create a table of contents that groups the poems according to theme.

Closure and Extension

ANSWERS TO THINKING ABOUT THE SELECTION
Recalling

1. He uses charts, numbers, columns, diagrams.
2. He is bored by it.
3. (a) He goes outside. (b) He looks at the stars.

472   *Division, War, and Reconciliation*

A Noiseless Patient Spider

Walt Whitman

1

A noiseless patient spider,
I mark'd where on a little promontory it stood isolated,
Mark'd how to explore the vacant vast surrounding,
It launch'd forth filament, filament, filament, out of itself,
5   Ever unreeling them, ever tirelessly speeding them.

2

And you O my soul where you stand,
Surrounded, detached, in measureless oceans of space,
Ceaselessly musing, venturing, throwing, seeking the
    spheres to connect them,
Till the bridge you will need be form'd, till the ductile
    anchor hold,
10 Till the gossamer thread you fling catch somewhere, O my
    soul.

THINKING ABOUT THE SELECTION

Recalling

1. Where is the spider standing when the speaker first sees it?
2. How does the spider explore its "vacant vast surrounding"?
3. (a) Where is the speaker's soul standing? (b) What is it doing?

Interpreting

4. What similarities does the speaker see between his soul and the spider?

5. With what do you think the speaker's soul is seeking connection (lines 8–10)?
6. Like the Transcendentalists, Whitman believed that the human spirit was mirrored in the world of nature. How does this poem reflect this belief?

Applying

7. Whitman presents a paradox, or apparent self-contradiction, in line 7 when he describes the soul as being both "surrounded" and "detached." Why do you think this paradox might be used to describe the position of the poet in society?

A Noiseless Patient Spider   473

Motivation/Prior Knowledge
Have students discuss why photography was an important invention. Make sure that they note that the invention of photography provided a new way of capturing historical events. Point out that the Civil War was one of the first conflicts to be recorded in photographs. Tell them that they are about to learn about Mathew Brady, the photographer who was most responsible for capturing the war on film.

Enrichment Tell students that several of Brady's photographs appear in the Great Works feature on *The Red Badge of Courage,* pages 599 through 602.

Enrichment The Daguerreotype was a form of photography developed by the French inventor Louis Daguerre during the late 1830's. Daguerre's pictures were made using a sheet of silver-coated copper and developed with mercury vapor, and they required an exposure of 15 to 30 seconds.

CROSS CURRENTS

Mathew Brady (1823–1896)

In 1839 photography in its earliest form—the Daguerreotype—was introduced. Many Americans were quick to see its commercial and artistic possibilities. A few others, among them Mathew Brady, also recognized the role it might play in recording history.

BRADY OF BROADWAY

Mathew Brady was born in upstate New York, the son of poor Irish farmers. By the early 1840's, he had moved to New York City where he studied daguerreotyping with Samuel F. B. Morse. Sometime in 1844 he

opened his first portrait studio on New York's busy lower Broadway. By the late 1850's, with numerous operators and chemists in his employ, he was known as "Brady of Broadway," the most fashionable portraitist of his time.

Brady was a businessman, but early in his career he recognized that photography could be more than a commercial enterprise, that the camera could be the "eye of history." In 1845 he began work on a project of preserving for future generations the portraits of distinguished Americans. He began to seek out the great people of his time, cajoling them into visiting his studios. During his career almost all the great politicians, scientists, writers, thinkers, actors, and actresses of his era posed before his cameras.

THE CIVIL WAR

The outbreak of the Civil War filled Brady with a sense of mission. Here was truly an opportunity to preserve history. Using his friendships with government leaders, he secured authorization to enter combat zones and hurried to the front with his cameramen.

Brady and his assistants worked under difficult conditions. They traveled to the scene of battle over rough country roads in heavy wagons containing darkroom tents, hundreds of fragile glass plates, and sensitive chemicals. Once there they often remained crouched for minutes on end in their fragile darkrooms delicately processing plates while outside the earth shook with battle.

Yet Brady and his cameramen were able to photograph almost every phase of the war—battlefields, ruins, officers, men, artil-

474   *Division, War, and Reconciliation*

lery, ships, railroads. Brady's photographs brought home the grim reality of the war— dead men as they had fallen, dead horses and smashed guns as they lay after a murderous assault, ravaged towns and homesteads, the loneliness of camp life. By the end of the war, Brady and his assistants had created more than 7,000 photographic images.

LATER YEARS

Brady's work was little appreciated in the later years of his life. After the Civil War, people were eager to forget the conflict. To pay the debts he incurred to finance his Civil War crews, Brady was forced to sell his negatives for a fraction of their value. He spent his last years in ill health and poverty.

Brady's photography has given us a lasting record of an era. Today the camera is recognized as an important and relatively convenient tool for the preservation of history. Vast improvements in camera technology have enabled modern photographers to record events in ever greater and often more horrifying detail. But Brady's work remains important for the way it confirmed the camera's early promise as a tool for transforming transitory events into lucid, permanent images.

Cross Currents 475

The writing assignments on page 476 have students write creatively, while those on page 477 have them think about the selections and write critically.

YOU THE WRITER
Guidelines for Evaluating Assignment 1

1. Has the student written a journal entry in which a revolutionary war hero expresses thoughts and feelings about the coming Civil War?
2. Is the journal written in an informal writing style?
3. Has the student varied the length and structure of his or her sentences?
4. Is the essay clearly and coherently organized, and free from grammar, usage, and mechanics errors?

Guidelines for Evaluating Assignment 2

1. Has the student written a letter to the President about the secession issue from the point of view of a northerner or a southerner before the Civil War?
2. Are the relevant issues presented?
3. Are thoughts expressed clearly and concisely?
4. Is the letter logically organized and free from grammar, usage, and mechanics errors?

Guidelines for Evaluating Assignment 3

1. Has the student written a short character sketch about an important historical figure to emerge from the Civil War era?
2. Does the student describe the subject's most important personality traits?
3. Does the character sketch give the reader a clear sense of the subject's personality?
4. Is the sketch free from grammar, usage, and mechanics errors?

YOU THE WRITER

Assignment

1. Imagine you are one of the heroes of the American Revolution and have been transported forward in time to the time of the Civil War. Write a journal entry in which you express your thoughts and feelings concerning the war.
   Prewriting. Choose a Revolutionary hero. Imagine how this person might have reacted to the Civil War.
   Writing. When you write your journal entry, use an informal writing style but make sure the ideas are clearly and coherently organized.
   Revising. When you revise, make sure you have varied the length and structure of your sentences. After you finish revising, proofread your entry and prepare a final copy.

Assignment

2. Imagine you are living in either the North or the South just before the start of the Civil War. Write a letter to the President, expressing your thoughts concerning the possible secession of the southern states.
   Prewriting. Brainstorm about the causes of the Civil War, trying to look at the relevant issues from the points of view of the people from both the North and the South.
   Writing. When writing your letter, express your thoughts as clearly and concisely as possible.
   Revising. When you revise, make sure your thoughts are organized in a logical manner. After you have finished revising, proofread your letter and prepare a final copy.

Assignment

3. Many important historical figures emerged from the Civil War era. Several of these figures are represented in this book. Choose one of these people, or another figure with whom you are familiar, and write a short character sketch of that person.
   Prewriting. Review the author biography of the figure you have chosen in addition to the selection or selections by this person, focusing on what they reveal about his or her personality.
   Writing. When you write your sketch, focus on describing your subject's most important personality traits.
   Revising. When you revise, make sure your sketch gives the reader a clear sense of your subject's personality. After you have finished revising, share your sketch with your classmates.

YOU THE CRITIC

Assignment

1. Civil War literature is important because it helps us to understand how the war and the issues surrounding it affected the American people. Choose one of the selections you have read and discuss what it reveals about the effect of the Civil War and/or the issues surrounding it.

Prewriting. Reread the selection, noting what it reveals about the effect of the war and the issues surrounding it. Then develop a thesis statement and prepare an outline.

Writing. When you write your essay, make sure you use passages from the selection to support your thesis.

Revising. When you revise, make sure you have thoroughly supported your thesis and have not included any unnecessary information.

Assignment

2. Although Frederick Douglass, Abraham Lincoln, Robert E. Lee, and Chief Joseph each had a different perspective of the events of the Civil War era, they all shared a number of noble ideals. Write an essay in which you compare and contrast the ideals, attitudes, and perspectives of two of these figures.

Prewriting. After choosing the figures on which you will focus, reread the author biographies of and selections by each figure, noting similarities and differences in attitudes and points of view.

Writing. When writing your essay, organize your ideas according to corresponding points of contrast.

Revising. When you revise, make sure you have used transitions and other linking devices to connect your ideas.

Assignment

3. Write a critical analysis of one of the works you have read, evaluating the quality of the writing, the use of literary devices, and the selection's historical significance.

Prewriting. Carefully reread the selection you chose. How would you evaluate the quality of the writing? How effectively does the selection achieve its purpose? What literary devices does the writer use? What is the selection's historical significance?

Writing. When you write your essay, support your evaluation with evidence from the selection.

Revising. When you revise, make sure you have expressed your opinions in a clear, coherent, and logically organized manner. After you finish revising, proofread your essay and prepare a final copy.

Focus on Writing 477

YOU THE CRITIC
Guidelines for Evaluating Assignment 1

1. Does the essay discuss what the selection reveals about the effect of the Civil War and/or the issues surrounding it?
2. Does the essay develop a thesis statement and support it with passages from the selection?
3. Has the student eliminated all unnecessary information?
4. Is the essay free from grammar, usage, and mechanics errors?

Guidelines for Evaluating Assignment 2

1. Does the essay note similarities and differences in the attitudes, ideals, and points of view of two important figures from the Civil War period?
2. Is the essay organized according to corresponding points of contrast?
3. Has the student used transitions and other linking devices to connect ideas?
4. Is the thesis supported by evidence, fact, passages, or examples?
5. Is the essay free from grammar, usage, and mechanics errors?

Guidelines for Evaluating Assignment 3

1. Does the criticism evaluate the quality of writing, the use of literary devices, and the selection's historical significance?
2. Is the evaluation supported by evidence from the selection?
3. Has the student expressed himself or herself in a clear, coherent, and logically organized manner?
4. Is the essay free from grammar, usage, and mechanics errors?

Fine art, *The Adirondack Guide,* by Winslow Homer. Homer (1836–1910), considered the greatest American painter of the nineteenth century, is probably best known for his watercolors of rain-soaked sailors struggling to stay afloat as rough seas engulf their small, unprotected craft. Homer, who had no formal artistic training, was deeply committed to his work and to his own sense of the meaning of art. He abandoned a lucrative career as an illustrator to serve as artist for the Army of the Potomac. Far from lifeless depictions of the events of the Civil War, his renderings are works of art in their own right—unsentimental evocations of the fear, homesickness, and despair that haunted the battlefield encampments.

After the war, Homer turned to quiet scenes, often of a solitary figure in a natural setting. In *The Adirondack Guide* the calm water and the soft lighting suggest a mood of serenity and peace with nature. Apparently, however, Homer's restless spirit was dissatisfied with the kind of works he was producing. When he was nearly 50, the status of celebrity he had attained in the bustling New York art world had become repugnant to him; he preferred to live, instead, in a quiet, undisturbed village in Maine, where he painted some of his finest works.

THE ADIRONDACK GUIDE
Winslow Homer
Museum of Fine Arts, Boston

Objectives

1 To understand the historical setting for the literature of realism and the frontier
2 To trace the cultural currents of the expanding American nation
3 To help define the frontier experience
4 To enumerate the unsolved challenges that faced Americans
5 To explain Realism in American Literature
6 To define the Realistic movement
7 To distinguish Naturalism from Realism
8 To recognize the characteristics of regional literature

REALISM AND THE FRONTIER
1865–1915

The Palace Hotel at Fort Romper was painted a light blue, a shade that is on the legs of a kind of heron, causing the bird to declare its position against any background. The Palace Hotel, then, was always screaming and howling in a way that made the dazzling winter landscape of Nebraska seem only a gray swampish hush.

Stephen Crane

479

Focus

Historical Background From 1865 through the turn of the century, American writers involved themselves in a rich complexity that brought international attention to their literature. With the rest of the nation, writers continued to dwell on the horrors of the Civil War that had divided the country so terribly. But with the westward expansion they also began to focus on new problems and future challenges that combined to place history in the background of their concerns. The writings of authors like Mark Twain, Sarah Orne Jewett, Willa Cather, and Jack London created a new readership that gladly allowed writers to turn their collective attention to the characters and situations that were uniquely a part of the American experience west of the Mississippi River during the latter half of the nineteenth century.

Motivation/Prior Knowledge Ask students to list the associations they make with the term "wild West." Have them explain their choices of adjectives that are frequently found in descriptions of the lives of settlers.

Purpose-Setting Question What new topics and kinds of characters are likely to appear in the literature of a time that involved the settlement of so vast an area as the American west?

ESL Teaching Strategy Pair your ESL students with partners who are non-ESL pupils. Ask each team jointly to compose a paragraph describing what the life of a settler was like.

Humanities Note

Fine art, *In Search of the Land of Milk and Honey,* by Harvey Dunn. The title of Harvey Dunn's (1884–1952) painting, *In Search of the Land of Milk and Honey,* is somewhat ironic: A family in a covered wagon drawn by two oxen makes its slow way across the plains, hoping to find a place to settle and to make a living. The painting is quite typical of Dunn's work, in which he chose to depict the simple, hard-working people from South Dakota, where he grew up near a buffalo trail, and other parts of the western frontier. Naturalism marks his subject matter, as indicated by such images in one of his paintings as a woman leading a farm animal. Yet Dunn's paintings have a muted quality that evokes, in their style, the works of French impressionists like Renoir. Dunn's use of line and color in *Land of Milk and Honey* even suggests some of the outdoor scenes of Vincent van Gogh.

One of the characters in Stephen Crane's story "The Blue Hotel," published in 1899, is a half-mad Swede who has arrived by train in the tiny town of Fort Romper, Nebraska. Another character guesses that the Swede "has been reading dime novels, and he thinks he's right out in the middle of it—the shootin' and stabbin' and all." A visiting cowboy wonders how the man could be so mistaken, since, as he says, "this ain't Wyoming ner none of them places. This is Nebrasker."

A few years earlier, Nebraska would have been the Wild West, but no longer. America was changing dramatically in the late nineteenth and early twentieth centuries. The Civil War, although devastating to the South, was more and more becoming a hazy memory. The American frontier, which had once seemed so vast, no longer existed by 1915. (This in no way stemmed the tide of western migration, however.) A number of railroads bridged the continent. The Wright Brothers took their first aircraft aloft at Kitty Hawk, North Carolina, in 1903. Science and industry were making great leaps forward.

1

So was literature. After the relative quiet of the immediate postwar years, an impressive array of writers began to appear. The prewar Romantic writers were still widely read, but most of the emerging writers were not Romantics. These new writers wanted to portray life as it was lived, not sentimentally or in flights of fancy. Their goal was Realism, or Naturalism, or Regionalism.

IN SEARCH OF THE LAND OF
MILK AND HONEY
Harvey Dunn
City Library, De Smet,
South Dakota

480   *Realism and the Frontier*

THE HISTORICAL SETTING

American writers were gaining a large and increasingly diverse audience. Between 1865 and 1915, the population of the United States grew by more than 42 million people. This number was larger than the entire population of the United States at the end of the Civil War. This huge population increase stemmed in part from new immigration. Before the 1880's, most immigrants came from western Europe and the Scandinavian countries. In the 1880's immigrants began arriving from southern and eastern Europe, from Italy, Greece, Poland, and Russia. Many of the new immigrants settled in eastern cities, but some joined the relentless western march.

The populations of older cities like Boston and Baltimore tripled or quadrupled during these decades. The populations of large midwestern cities like Chicago and Detroit also skyrocketed. Major new cities sprang up almost overnight. In 1858 Denver had consisted of sixty crude log cabins. Three years later, as a result of the Pikes Peak gold rush, 3,000 people lived there. By 1890 the population of Denver exceeded 100,000.

A Nation on the Move

In many ways, the American experience has been shaped by advances in transportation. European settlers reached the shores of North America as a result of improvements in oceangoing ships. Once here, the settlers advanced westward by stagecoach, and then by railroad. Long journeys that would have been difficult for early writers of the republic were commonplace for Mark Twain. As a journeyman printer, Twain made his way from Hannibal, Missouri, to St. Louis, then New York, then Philadelphia, and back to Keokuk, Iowa. Later he went to New Orleans as a steamboat pilot, to Virginia City, Nevada, as a newspaperman, and to San Francisco as a writer and foreign correspondent. Eventually, he settled in Hartford, Connecticut. This kind of mobility helped to shape both the subject matter and the attitudes of writers in this period.

Mark Twain's *Roughing It* records his experiences in the Far West, including his days in Virginia City, Nevada. In this period, for the first time, a number of writers represented the Midwest or Far West. Some of these writers, like Bret Harte and Willa Cather, were born in the East or South, but later moved west. Harte moved as a young man from New York to California. Cather moved as a child from Virginia to Nebraska. One of the few native California writers was Jack London, born in San Francisco and raised in Oakland. Interestingly, London's first successful stories were not set in California, but farther north and west—in the Klondike, on the Alaskan-Canadian border. London had gone to this region in 1897 to prospect for gold.

THE MINES DURING THE GOLD RUSH, 1849, IN CALIFORNIA
Frank Tenney Johnson
Three Lions

Introduction 481

2 Historical Context After the Civil War, the United States truly became a land of opportunity for all its inhabitants. Waves of immigrants flooded here to escape deprivations in their native countries. Inventions continued to create new industry, and urban centers sprang up from coast to coast.

3 Enrichment The growth of Chicago presents a vivid example of the rapid growth of the time. In 1833 Chicago was a village of 350 inhabitants; by 1870 the population had increased to more than 300,000; by 1880 to 500,000; and by 1890 to more than a million.

4 Enrichment In addition to his travels around the country, Twain took a number of trips abroad, which he fictionalized in *Innocents Abroad*, *A Tramp Abroad*, and *Following the Equator*.

5 Literary Movement A selection from *Roughing It* is included in this unit: "Tom Quartz," page 495.

6 Literary Movement "The Outcasts of Poker Flat" by Bret Harte begins on page 518 and "A Wagner Matinée" by Willa Cather begins on page 556. Jack London's "To Build a Fire," page 556, set in the Klondike, is one of London's best-known stories.

Humanities Note

Fine art, *The Mines During the Gold Rush, 1849, in California,* by Frank Tenney Johnson. Native Americans, miners, cowboys, pioneers, and other images of the Old West are the primary subjects in the works of Frank Tenney Johnson (1874–1939). As shown by this detail of *The Mines During the Gold Rush, 1849, in California,* Johnson could convey details skillfully and believably. The facial expression on the standing figure has been finely rendered, while the actions of the sitting figure holding the pan are convincing.

Gold was discovered in Sutter's Mill, California, in January 1848. Within a year or so, some 80,000 "forty-niners" had arrived in the San Francisco area, in search of fortune, adventure, or both. How many of these pioneers actually struck it rich is doubtful; what is certain is that the gold rush served as an important stimulus to the settlement of the West, especially northern California.

Enrichment During this period, the Statue of Liberty was erected. Many students will remember their own school-sponsored efforts in 1984 and 1985 to help fund the restoration of the Statue of Liberty on its 100th anniversary. Give them a chance to explain how they felt about such a collective fundraising effort for a national monument. Provide an opportunity for those who have visited the statue to explain what they saw and how they felt about the significance of their visit.

AMERICAN EVENTS

1867   **Mark Twain** wins recognition with ''The Notorious Jumping Frog of Calaveras County.''

     Lucy McKim, with others, publishes *Slave Songs of the United States*.

     United States purchases Alaska from Russia for two cents an acre.

1868   Louisa May Alcott's *Little Women* becomes an immediate children's favorite.

1869   Transcontinental railroad completed with driving of golden spike in Utah.

     Women in Wyoming Territory are first to win right to vote.

1870   **Bret Harte** publishes *The Luck of Roaring Camp and Other Stories*.

1876   Alexander Graham Bell patents a telephone and transmits speech over it.

     Sitting Bull's Sioux wipe out General George A. Custer's cavalry at Battle of the Little Bighorn.

     Mark Twain publishes *The Adventures of Tom Sawyer*.

1879   Thomas A. Edison invents electric light bulb.

1883   **Mark Twain** publishes *Life on the Mississippi*.

     Brooklyn Bridge, an engineering marvel of the day, opens.

1884   **Mark Twain's** *The Adventures of Huckleberry Finn* appears.

1885   William Dean Howells publishes *The Rise of Silas Lapham*.

1886   Statue of Liberty dedicated in New York Harbor.

1887   **Sidney Lanier's** *Poems* appears six years after his death.

1888   Great mid-March blizzard in eastern United States piles 30-foot drifts in New York's Herald Square.

1889   Worst flood in American history strikes Johnstown, Pennsylvania.

482   *Realism and the Frontier*

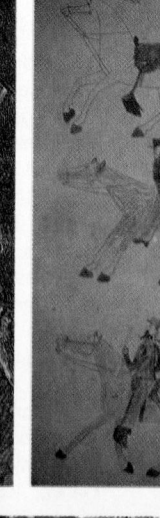

Twenty Thousand Leagues Under the Sea

Proclamation of the German Empire

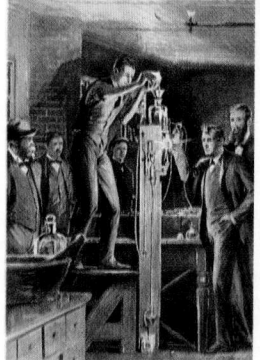

Thomas Edison

Blizzard of 1888

The Battle of Little Bighorn

Mark Twain

Alexander Graham Bell

Inauguration of Statue of Liberty

WORLD EVENTS

1866   Russia: Fyodor Dostoyevsky publishes *Crime and Punishment*.

        Austria: Gregor Mendel reports on basic laws of biological inheritance.

1867   England: Matthew Arnold writes "Dover Beach."

1868   Japan: Emperor gains power when shogunate—Japan's feudal dictatorship—falls.

1869   France: Jules Verne publishes *Twenty Thousand Leagues Under the Sea*.

1871   Germany: End of Franco-Prussian War establishes German empire.

1872   Russia: Leo Tolstoy completes *War and Peace*.

1874   France: Claude Monet gathers Impressionist painters for first exhibition.

1875   France: People in France begin raising money to build U.S. Statue of Liberty.

1878   England: *The Return of the Native* by Thomas Hardy appears in print.

1879   Norway: Henrick Ibsen writes *The Doll's House*.

1880   Russia: Fyodor Dostoyevsky publishes *The Brothers Karamazov*.

        South Africa: Cecil Rhodes founds diamond mining company.

1882   Norway: Henrik Ibsen writes *An Enemy of the People*.

1883   England: Robert Louis Stevenson publishes *Treasure Island*.

1884   Russia: Leo Tolstoy completes "The Death of Ivan Ilyich."

1885   Germany: Karl Benz builds first automobile powered by internal combustion engine.

1886   England: Thomas Hardy publishes *The Mayor of Casterbridge*.

1890 First volume of **Emily Dickinson's** poems is released four years after her death.

Last major battle between U.S. troops and Native Americans fought at Wounded Knee, South Dakota.

1891 Hamlin Garland publishes *Main-Travelled Roads*.

1893 **Ambrose Bierce** publishes *Can Such Things Be?*

1894 **Kate Chopin's** *Bayou Folk* published.

1895 **Stephen Crane** publishes *The Red Badge of Courage*.

1896 **Paul Lawrence Dunbar** publishes *Lyrics of Lowly Life*.

The Country of the Pointed Firs, **Sarah Orne Jewett's** masterpiece, appears.

1897 **Edwin Arlington Robinson** publishes *The Children of the Night*.

1898 Spanish-American War begins.

1901 President William McKinley shot in Buffalo; succeeded by Theodore Roosevelt.

1903 **Jack London** publishes *The Call of the Wild*.

Boston Red Sox and Pittsburgh Pirates play in first World Series.

Wright Brothers stay aloft for 582 feet in their airplane at Kitty Hawk, North Carolina.

1905 **Willa Cather** publishes *The Troll Garden*.

Edith Wharton's *The House of Mirth* appears.

1906 Strong earthquake in San Francisco is followed by devastating fire.

1908 Ford introduces the Model T.

1909 Admiral Robert E. Peary reaches the North Pole.

National Association for the Advancement of Colored People (NAACP) founded.

484 *Realism and the Frontier*

Theodore Roosevelt

San Francisco Earthquake

Albert Einstein

First Flight at

Beginning of

Boxer Rebellion

Ford Model T

Kitty Hawk

Thomas Mann

Spanish-American War

Sigmund Freud

■WORLD EVENTS■

1891 England: Thomas Hardy publishes *Tess of the D'Urbervilles*.

1894 Sino-Japanese War breaks out; Japanese army easily defeats Chinese.

1895 Germany: Wilhelm Roentgen discovers X-rays.

1896 England: A. E. Housman publishes *A Shropshire Lad*.

1897 England: Rudyard Kipling writes *Captains Courageous*.

1898 France: Paul Cézanne begins painting *Bathers*.

France: Pierre Curie and Marie Sklodowska Curie discover radium.

1899 Russia: Anton Chekhov has his play *Uncle Vanya* produced at Moscow Art Theatre.

South Africa: Boer War breaks out between British and Dutch in South Africa.

1900 Austria: Sigmund Freud publishes *The Interpretation of Dreams*.

China: Chinese nationalists begin Boxer Rebellion to expel foreigners.

1901 Germany: Thomas Mann publishes *Buddenbrooks*.

1903 Spain: Pablo Picasso paints *The Old Guitarist*.

Ireland: George Bernard Shaw produces *Man and Superman*.

Ireland: William Butler Yeats publishes *In the Seven Woods*.

1904 Russo-Japanese War begins.

1905 Germany: Albert Einstein proposes his relativity theory.

1910 Mexico: Francisco Madero begins revolution that overthrows dictator Porfirio Díaz.

1914 Europe: World War I begins.

Introduction **485**

Enrichment William Butler Yeats became involved at this time in the growing movement toward Irish independence. He supported the attention that artists and writers directed toward the Gaelic language and the renewed effort to have schools teach basic information about Irish culture and history. These efforts helped to bring about the creation of the Republic of Ireland in 1922.

Cooperative Learning The distinctions that can be made among the tribes of native Americans may interest your students. Divide the class into groups of three or four. Have each choose a different tribe and then research the habits, locations, and lives of the members of that group. Schedule time for presentations to compare and contrast the findings.

The Frontier Experience

In 1827, President John Quincy Adams's secretary of war had predicted that it would take 500 years to fill the American West. By 1890, the superintendent of the census could report that the nation's "unsettled area had been so broken into by isolated bodies of settlement that there can hardly be said to be a frontier line." To many Americans this came as quite a surprise. They had imagined that free, or at least cheap, land would always be available.

The frontier was gone, but its legacy lived on. Frontier dwellers had always been generally mobile, practical, inventive, democratic, and optimistic. Those traits colored the national character and affected American writing. Mark Twain, in his early life and writing, showed all five traits. Yet the frontier itself offered no idyllic existence. It could be lonely and cruel, as in Jack London's "To Build a Fire" or Willa Cather's "A Wagner Matinée." The great majority of Americans never lived on the frontier. American life and literature have nonetheless been enriched by those who did.

Unresolved Challenges

The Civil War and its aftermath spurred the headlong growth of industry in the North. Yet even before the Civil War, writers had observed that industrial growth created hardships as well as benefits. Along with rapid industrial expansion came urban slums, farm problems, and labor unrest. By the 1880's, some of the abuses were bringing insistent demands for reform. Back in 1873, Mark Twain and Charles Dudley Warner had published *The Gilded Age*. This novel dealt with unrestrained greed in a time of financial speculation and uncertain moral values. Around the turn of the century, a group of journalists took up this same theme. Theodore Roosevelt called them "muckrakers," because they uncovered only the muck, or dirt, of American life. Among the leading muckrakers were Ida Tarbell and Lincoln Steffens. Tarbell exposed unethical business practices, while Steffens attacked corruption in city and state governments.

A further challenge facing the nation was its great and increasing diversity. Despite the Depression of 1893, the country as a whole rejoiced in economic good times. Not everyone shared in the prosperity, however. Farmers faced falling agricultural prices, high interest rates for bank loans, and unequal railroad shipping charges. After centuries of conflict, the Native American tribes had been defeated. The slaves had been freed but had not been made full participants in American democracy. Restrictive immigration laws prohibited Chinese workers from entering the United States after 1882; European immigrants often worked long hours in sweatshops and lived in slums; and women were not allowed to vote in national elections.

The literature of the time was as diverse as the nation itself. It

THE BOWERY AT NIGHT, 1895
W. Louis Sonntag, Jr.
Museum of the City of New York

Humanities Note

Fine art, *The Bowery at Night,* 1895, by William Louis Sonntag, Jr. William Louis Sonntag, Jr. (1869–1898), was taught to draw by his father, a well-known painter of landscapes and wilderness scenes. The works of the younger Sonntag, who was born in New York City, have a different quality. They are not the picturesque evocations of natural beauty but, rather, show men and women in simple, everyday settings.

Paintings like *The Bowery at Night,* marked a significant trend in American art—the turn toward realism, the recognition that the lives of ordinary people, often in plain, even ugly surroundings, are a suitable subject for art. *The Bowery at Night* shows well-dressed figures and, also in the foreground, products of America's booming industrialization—streetcars and elevated trains. In works like these, the United States was seeing a new image of itself.

reflected both the promise and the problems of the frontier and of the dynamic expansion of industry.

REALISM IN AMERICAN LITERATURE

The Civil War and its aftermath left Americans less certain about the future than ever before, diminishing their belief in a unity of national purpose. The buoyant spirits of Emerson and the wild imaginings of Poe seemed out of date to many, especially to young writers. In the South, the Jeffersonian dream of a nation of farmers lay shattered like the land itself. The South would have to rebuild on a different foundation, and it would be a long, arduous task.

Under the circumstances, it is small wonder that writers turned away from the Romanticism that had been so popular before the war. The hopes of idealists, these new writers felt, would have to

Humanities Note

Fine art, *Rabbit Stew,* by Gary Niblett. In 1965 a group of artists from the Southwest founded the organization Cowboy Artists of America; their goals were "to perpetuate the memory and culture of the Old West . . . [and] to insure the authentic representation of the life of the West, as it was and as it is." The work of Gary Niblett (b. 1944), one of its members, is marked by sympathetic but unsentimental regard for the subjects he portrays.

Niblett grew up near an Indian reservation in New Mexico. True to the goals of the Cowboy Artists, Niblett has painted scenes of contemporary Native American life, as in his *On the Trail of the Deer. Rabbit Stew,* of course, has a historical setting—travelers in covered wagons stopping to prepare dinner over an open fire. The focus of the painting is on the rugged landscape, including the mesa in the background and the scrub grass in the foreground, on the glow of the fire, and on the sense of camaraderie among the pioneers.

7 **Literary Movement** Realism entailed writing about the environment one knew, including the details of speech, dress, behavior. One viewpoint held that realistic fiction presented a "slice of life," in which the realistic details are important and plot is only incidental.

RABBIT STEW
Gary Niblett
Photograph Courtesy of the Gerald Peters Gallery; Santa Fe, New Mexico, and Dallas, Texas

wait. Even the visions of Hawthorne and the extravagances of Melville did not fit the mood of the times. In place of Romanticism came Realism, a literary movement that sought to portray ordinary life as real people live it and attempted to show characters and events in an objective, almost factual way.

The Realistic Movement

Realistic fiction remains popular today, and it may seem strange that it was once controversial. But it was. Realistic writers saw themselves as being in revolt against Romanticism. Mark Twain wrote an amusing essay whose target was the Romantic writer James Fenimore Cooper. In *The Deerslayer,* Twain claimed, Cooper "has scored 114 offenses against literary art out of a possible 115." One of these offenses, according to Twain, is that "the personages of a tale shall confine themselves to possibilities and let miracles alone; or, if they venture a miracle, the author must plausibly set it forth to make it look possible and reasonable."

Eugene Field, a Chicago journalist, held the opposite view. Field took humorous aim at the new Realistic writers, Hamlin Garland in particular. "Mr. Garland's heroes sweat and do not wear socks," Field wrote. "His heroines eat cold huckleberry pie."

How did Realism originate? There had been Realistic writers in France for some time, notably Honoré de Balzac, Stendhal, and Gustave Flaubert. Although these writers and others had great influence, American Realism had roots in this country, in the experiences of war, on the frontier, and in the cities. Science played a part as well. The objectivity of science struck many writers as a worthy goal for literature. Just as important, perhaps, was a general feeling that Romanticism was wearing thin. Students still recited Romantic poetry and read Romantic novels, but many writers believed these works to be old-fashioned.

One in particular who held that belief was William Dean Howells. Howells held prestigious editorial posts at the *Atlantic Monthly* and *Harper's* and knew virtually every important writer of the day. Although his early works were not Realistic, in the 1880's he began to champion Realism. His best Realistic novel, *The Rise of Silas Lapham,* was published in 1885. Many people considered Howells, a self-educated man, to be the leading literary figure of the time. He often advised his friend Mark Twain and encouraged many younger authors, among them Hamlin Garland and Stephen Crane. In 1891 Howells described his theories about Realism in a book called *Criticism and Fiction*.

Howells and others were aware that Realistic writers ran the risk of becoming boring. A Romantic was limited only by his or her imagination, but a Realist had to find meaning in the commonplace. To do this, the Realist had to be acutely observant and to lay bare to readers the hidden meanings behind familiar words and actions. On the other hand, Realistic writers could deal honestly with characters that a Romantic writer would either avoid or gloss over: factory workers, bosses, politicians, gunfighters. This emphasis did not always please the critics, however. One journalist wrote of Willa Cather's stories: "If the writers of fiction who use western Nebraska as material would look up now and then and not keep their eyes and noses in the cattle yards, they might be more agreeable company." Despite such complaints Realism held sway, and it remains dominant to the present day.

Naturalism

8 | Some writers of the period went one step beyond Realism. Influenced by the French novelist Émile Zola, a literary movement known as Naturalism developed. According to Zola a writer must

8 **Literary Movement** Naturalism frequently seemed to dwell on the unpleasant or ugly themes of life. Naturalist writers dared to write about the poor, the underdogs, the ignored; in doing so, they emphasized the effect of the environment. Speaking of his novel *Maggie: A Girl of the Streets,* Stephen Crane wrote that it "tries to show that environment is a tremendous thing in the world, and frequently shapes lives regardless." In *The Red Badge of Courage* Crane depicts naturalistic forces at work on a young soldier in the Civil War (see page 599).

Fine art, *Queensboro Bridge,* by Glenn Odem Coleman. Glenn Odem Coleman (1887–1932) was born in Ohio but lived most of his adult life in New York City. In a memorial exhibition of his paintings held at the Whitney Musuem of American Art shortly after his death, the artist was praised for the individualism of his style and for his modesty and lack of pretense as a person.

Coleman, attracted by the vitality of city streets and the men and women who throng city neighborhoods, painted mostly the scenes of urban life that were part of his everyday experiences. In *Queensboro Bridge* a group of people lean over a railing as they observe one of the new structures that were bringing New York City into the modern world. The painting, focusing both on human figures and on an intricate engineering feat, suggests that human society has henceforth become linked with technical progress. The bridge is thus more than a span between the boroughs of Manhattan and Queens—it is a link to the future.

QUEENSBORO BRIDGE
Glen Odem Coleman
Hirshhorn Museum and Sculpture Garden
Smithsonian Institution

examine people and society objectively and, like a scientist, draw conclusions from what is observed. In line with this belief, Naturalistic writers viewed reality as the inescapable working out of natural forces. One's destiny, they said, is decided by heredity and environment, physical drives, and economic circumstances. Because they believed people have no control over events, Naturalistic writers tended to be pessimistic.

Only a few major American writers embraced Naturalism. One who did was Stephen Crane. His first novel, *Maggie: A Girl of the Streets,* published in 1893, is the earliest Naturalistic novel by an American writer. Jack London's "To Build a Fire" presents one of the recurring themes of Naturalism, man at the mercy of the brutal forces of nature. Another Naturalistic writer of the time was Frank Norris. *The Octopus,* his best-known novel, concerns the struggle between wheat growers and an all-powerful railroad in the San Joaquin Valley of California.

Regionalism

The third significant literary movement that developed during the latter part of the nineteenth century was Regionalism, or the "local color movement." Through the use of regional dialect and vivid descriptions of the landscape, the Regionalists sought to capture the essence of life in the various different regions of the growing nation.

At its very best, Regional writing transcends the region and becomes part of the national literature. No one today would call Mark Twain a Regionalist or a local colorist. Yet his early short story "The

490   *Realism and the Frontier*

Notorious Jumping Frog of Calaveras County" fits the category. Bret Harte, on the other hand, is generally regarded as the founder of the local color movement. Harte's stories, such as "The Outcasts of Poker Flat," have many of the same elements as Twain's. George Washington Cable, another leader in the local color movement, wrote sketches and novels of Creole life in Louisiana. His writings have charm and style but are seldom read today.

Various reasons have been given to explain the popularity of the local color movement. Perhaps it was the desire of people throughout the reunited nation to learn more about one another after the discord of the Civil War. Whatever its cause, the outpouring of local color was remarkable. Besides Twain, Harte, and Cable, there was Edward Eggleston. Eggleston's novel *The Hoosier Schoolmaster,* portraying the backwoods country of Indiana, became a bestseller in its day. A more critically acclaimed book was Sarah Orne Jewett's *The Country of the Pointed Firs.* Many critics regard this as the finest work of fiction about nineteenth-century rural New England. Mary Wilkins Freeman, too, wrote memorably about rural New England. Kate Chopin, a Louisiana writer, produced outstanding tales of Creole and Cajun life.

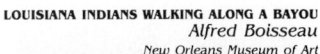

LOUISIANA INDIANS WALKING ALONG A BAYOU
Alfred Boisseau
New Orleans Museum of Art

9 **Literary Movement** According to Mark Twain in his essay "How to Tell a Story," the American humorous story depends on the manner of its telling: "the humorous story is told gravely; the teller does his best to conceal the fact that he even dimly suspects that there is anything funny about it." "The Notorious Jumping Frog of Calaveras Country," page 507, is a good example of Twain's theory of telling stories.

10 **Literary Movement** Realistic regional literature, like Mark Twain's stories, was often published first in local newspapers and, if successful, then serialized in papers throughout the country.

11 **Literary Movement** One of Sarah Orne Jewett's stories, "A White Heron," is included in this unit on page 540. "The Story of an Hour" by Kate Chopin begins on page 550.

Humanities Note

Fine art, *Louisiana Indians Walking Along a Bayou,* by Alfred Boisseau. *Indians Along the Bayou,* by Alfred Boisseau (1823–1901), is an evocative depiction of a simple scene. Wearing their traditional clothing, these Native Americans travel a footpath along the bayou. It is possible that the Indians shown belonged to the Choctaw tribe, an important Native American group in the Louisiana region. The term *bayou,* in fact, comes from the Choctaw for "small stream" and refers to a marsh that was formerly part of a lake, river, or gulf. Perhaps as a result of violent weather conditions, such as a hurricane, the bayou was separated from the larger waterway and became a slow-moving, swamplike stream.

Archeological and other evidence suggests that the Native Americans may have settled, in the region that now encompasses Louisiana, as much as 16,000 years ago. As an indication of their fate after the European settlement of North America began, it is believed that, in 1700—when the Europeans first arrived in the Louisiana area—there were 15,000 Indians; today there may be about 3000.

12 Literary Movement Sidney Lanier's "Song of the Chattahoochee" is on page 605.

13 Literary Movement Two poems by Paul Lawrence Dunbar appear in this unit: "We Wear the Mask," page 614 and "Douglass," page 616.

14 Literary Movement Three of Robinson's poems are in this unit: "Luke Havergal" (page 620), "Miniver Cheevy" (page 622) and "Richard Cory" (page 624).

15 Literary Movement Although Masters had written and published poetry earlier, he found his voice in *Spoon River Anthology*. His inspiration for it came from the Greek Anthology, with its brief epigrams and epitaphs. The poems in *Spoon River Anthology* represent self-spoken epitaphs of citizens buried in an Illinois cemetery. The tone varies from sadness to affirmation of life to disappointment. "Lucinda Matlock" and "Fiddler Jones" are in this unit, on pages 628 and 630 respectively.

Humanities Note

Fine art, *Portrait of Marie Laveau's Daughter,* by François Fleischbein. The portrait attributed to François (or Frantz) Fleischbein (1804–1862), entitled *Portrait of Marie Laveau's Daughter* (also known as *Marie Laveau the Younger*), is highly expressive. The smallness of the face, as well as the intense look of the eyes, suggests a quality of innocence, even vulnerability—traits that are emphasized by the childlike braids. The young girl's hand, holding the trinket hanging from her neck, accentuates the effect still further. The work has, moreover, a sculptural quality.

PORTRAIT OF MARIE LAVEAU'S DAUGHTER
Attributed to Frantz Fleischbein
New Orleans Museum of Art

The poets of this period cannot be easily classified, for each of them speaks in a clear, individual voice. Stephen Crane's poems are short, spare, and untitled. Sometimes they resemble fables and sometimes riddles. Sidney Lanier, whose health was shattered as a Confederate prisoner of war, fused musical and poetical principles. Among the best of his poems are "Song of the Chattahoochee" and "The Marshes of Glynn." Paul Laurence Dunbar, the son of former slaves, used black dialect and folklore in his poetry."

In 1897, one of the finest of all volumes of American poems appeared, Edwin Arlington Robinson's *The Children of the Night*. This volume contains unforgettable psychological portraits of people, including "Luke Havergal" and "Richard Cory." Fifteen years later, the *Spoon River Anthology* by Edgar Lee Masters made that poet's name a household word.

One of the famous short story writers of the time was William Sydney Porter, better known as O. Henry. Sometimes classified as a local colorist, O. Henry portrayed New York City vividly. His stories use the surprise ending to great effect. Like many bestselling authors then and now, O. Henry wrote to formula. In other words he worked within a customary plot structure with certain familiar character types, settings, and situations.

Rarely do formula stories survive as literature, but they can have lasting influence. One type of writing that emerged during this period, the Western, has at times dominated the popular arts. Earlier, James Fenimore Cooper had created an American frontier hero. The settlement of the American West now called for a new breed of hero more closely tied to the Great Plains. Dime-novel westerns introduced this new hero and developed the modern Western formula. Most of the elements of this formula were firmly fixed in Owen Wister's *The Virginian,* published in 1902.

In addition to the poets already named, a number of popular poets were at work during this period. James Whitcomb Riley, using a rustic Hoosier dialect, wrote "Little Orphant Annie," "Knee-Deep in June," and other favorites. Eugene Field, the Denver journalist, wrote "Little Boy Blue" and "Wynken, Blynken, and Nod." Two poets from Oregon also enjoyed a brief popularity: Edwin Markham, whose best-known poem is "The Man with the Hoe," and Joaquin Miller, who wrote "Columbus."

Although, of course, the painting is two-dimensional, the artist has made skillful use of highlighting, especially around the subject's cheekbones, to suggest roundedness, or three-dimensionality.

Check Test

1. Between 1865 and 1915, the _____ of the United States increased dramatically.

2. By 1890, the population of Denver was more than _____.

3. _____ was a literary movement that sought to portray ordinary life as real people live it.

4. The "local color movement" was another name for _____.

5. The _____ believed that people's fates are shaped by forces beyond their control.

ANSWERS

1. population
2. 100,000
3. Realism
4. Regionalism
5. Naturalists

But I reckon I got to light out for the territory ahead of the rest, because Aunt Sally says she's going to adopt me and sivilize me, and I can't stand it. I been there before.
Mark Twain, *Adventures of Huckleberry Finn*

The reports of my death are greatly exaggerated.
Mark Twain, Cable from London to the Associated Press, 1897

Bore: a person who talks when you wish him to listen.
Prejudice: a vagrant opinion without visible means of support.
Ambrose Bierce, *The Devil's Dictionary*

The road was new to me, as roads always are, going back.
Sarah Orne Jewett, *The Country of the Pointed Firs*

The voice of the sea speaks to the soul.
Kate Chopin, *The Awakening*

There are only two or three human stories, and they go on repeating themselves as fiercely as if they had never happened before.
Willa Cather, *O Pioneers!*

Buck did not read the newspapers, or he would have known that trouble was brewing, not alone for himself, but for every tidewater dog, strong of muscle and with warm, long hair, from Puget Sound to San Diego.
Jack London, *The Call of the Wild*

The red sun was pasted in the sky like a wafer.
Stephen Crane, *The Red Badge of Courage*

Silence may be as variously shaded as speech.
Edith Wharton, *The Reef*

We wear the mask that grins and lies,
It hides our cheeks and shades our eyes,—
Paul Laurence Dunbar, *We Wear the Mask*

I shall have more to say when I am dead.
Edwin Arlington Robinson, "John Brown"

Reading Critically This page is designed to give students the background they need to read critically the literature of this period. The information here summarizes the historical context, the literary movements, and the writers' techniques of the period. Students should be able to apply this information to the literary works of the period as done in the model on the following pages, "Tom Quartz." The notes in the side column for "Tom Quartz" provide a model for reading critically. They point out the aspects of the story that reflect the historical context, the literary movements, and techniques that the writer, Mark Twain, used. Suggest that students make their own critical comments as they read the selection.

To give students further practice with the process of reading critically, use the selection in the Teaching Portfolio, "The Bride Comes to Yellow Sky" by Stephen Crane, page 644, following the Teacher Backup, which students can annotate themselves. Encourage students to use these strategies as they read the literature in this unit.

▰READING CRITICALLY▰

The Literature of 1865–1915

When you read literature, it is important to place it in its historical context. Doing so will help you interpret the literary movements that were prevalent during the period and appreciate the techniques the writer used to convey the ideas of the movement.

Historical Context

During 1865–1915 the population of the United States grew dramatically, with many people moving westward and ending up on the frontier. Travel from one part of the country to another became common as a result of new advances in transportation and of the desire of people in various parts of the country to learn more about each other. During his youth, Mark Twain traveled from Hannibal, Missouri, to St. Louis; New York; Philadelphia; New Orleans; Virginia City, Nevada; and San Francisco. As a result of the westward movement and increased travel, more and more of our literature became centered on the Midwest and the Far West.

Literary Movements

During this period writers turned away from Romanticism and strove to portray life as it was actually lived. The major movements of the period were Realism, Naturalism, and Regionalism. **Realism** attempted to present "a slice of life," whereas **Naturalism** went one step further, showing life as the inexorable working out of natural forces beyond our power to control. **Regionalism,** in contrast, was in some ways a blending of Realism and Romanticism. It emphasized locale, or place, and the elements that create local color—customs, dress, speech, and other local differences.

Writer's Techniques

During this period the short story emerged as a popular literary form. In their stories writers used specific details to create a sense of realism and to capture local color. In addition, they tended to draw their characters from the mass of humanity and had them speak in dialect, capturing the flavor and rhythms of common speech.

On the following pages is a selection by Mark Twain, one of the preeminent writers of this period. The notes in the side column should draw your attention to the historical context, literary movements, and writer's techniques. Understanding these features will help you more fully appreciate the selection.

494   *Realism and the Frontier*

Objectives

1 To appreciate point of view
2 To understand exaggeration
3 To interpret dialect
4 To write a tall tale

Support Material

Teaching Portfolio
Teacher Backup, p. 641
Reading Critically, "The Bride Comes To Yellow Sky" by Stephen Crane, p. 644
Usage and Mechanics Worksheet, p. 653
Analyzing Literature Worksheet, *Understanding Point of View* p. 654

Critical Thinking and Reading Worksheet, *Understanding Exaggeration,* p. 655
Selection Test, p. 656

from Roughing It

Mark Twain

Tom Quartz

One of my comrades there[1]—another of those victims of eighteen years of unrequited toil and blighted hopes—was one of the gentlest spirits that ever bore its patient cross in a weary exile: grave and simple Dick Baker, pocket miner of Dead-Horse Gulch. He was forty-six, gray as a rat, earnest, thoughtful, slenderly educated, slouchily dressed, and clay-soiled, but his heart was finer metal than any gold his shovel ever brought to light—than any, indeed, that ever was mined or minted.

Whenever he was out of luck and a little downhearted, he would fall to mourning over the loss of a wonderful cat he used to own (for where women and children are not, men of kindly impulses take up with pets, for they must love something). And he always spoke of the strange sagacity of that cat with the air of a man who believed in his secret heart that there was something human about it—maybe even supernatural.

I heard him talking about this animal once. He said:

"Gentlemen, I used to have a cat here, by the name of Tom Quartz, which you'd 'a' took an interest in, I reckon—most anybody would. I had him here eight year—and he was the remarkablest cat *I* ever see. He was a large gray one of the Tom specie, an' he had more hard, natchral sense than any man in this camp—'n a *power* of dignity—he wouldn't let the Gov'ner of Californy be familiar with him. He never ketched a rat in his life—'peared to be above it. He never cared for nothing but mining. He knowed more about mining, that cat did, than any man *I* ever, ever see. You couldn't tell *him* noth'n' 'bout placer-diggin's—'n as for pocket mining, why he was just born for it. He would dig out after me an' Jim when we went over the hills prospect'n', and he would trot along behind us for as much as five mile, if we went so fur. An' he had the best judgment about mining-ground—why you never see anything like it.

---

1. **there:** California.

Historical Context: Many people rushed to California in 1849 when gold was found there.

Literary Movement: This story is an example of Regionalism. It takes place in a mining camp in California. The main character is a common man, poorly educated and poorly dressed. Note how the narrator presents this character as a jewel of a man.

Writer's Technique: Twain employs a storyteller who speaks in dialect, thus adding local color to the tale.

Literary Movement: The story takes the form of a tall tale, using exaggeration to create humor. Tall tales were a major form of regional writing.

Presentation

Motivation/Prior Knowledge
Have students recall the way that actions in animated cartoons are usually exaggerated. For example, a character's hair may be shown to stand on end when the character is surprised or frightened. Point out that Mark Twain, in the following tall tale, uses exaggeration that calls to mind the same kinds of cartoon-like images.

Purpose-Setting Question
What human characteristics does the narrator give Tom Quartz, the cat?

Enrichment While the Gold Rush brought vast riches to some, it brought only heartbreak to many. Twenty years after gold was discovered, there were still miners in the hills of California, vainly trying to strike it rich. Twain is suggesting that Dick Baker is such a man.

Clarification Placer digging, or placer mining, is a way of obtaining gold or other heavy minerals from gravel and sand deposits. The gold-bearing gravel is shoveled into the upper end of a slanting wooden trough, where it is washed by a water supply. The gold, being heavier than the sand or gravel, settles into the grooves in the bottom of the box while the sand and gravel are washed away. Panning, a form of placer mining, is sometimes used to get gold from streams.

Pocket mining refers to mining small cavities in the earth containing ore.

Writer's Technique: Notice the use of figurative language throughout. This language is not only vivid but also contributes to character development.

When we went to work, he'd scatter a glance around, 'n' if he didn't think much of the indications, he would give a look as much as to say, 'Well, I'll have to get you to excuse *me*,' 'n' without another word he'd hyste his nose into the air 'n' shove for home. But if the ground suited him, he would lay low 'n' keep dark till the first pan was washed, 'n' then he would sidle up 'n' take a look, an' if there was about six or seven grains of gold *he* was satisfied—he didn't want no better prospect'n' that—'n' then he would lay down on our coats and snore like a steamboat till we'd struck the pocket, an' then get up 'n' superintend. He was nearly lightnin' on superintending.

Writer's Technique: Twain has Dick Baker tell this story in the first person. Notice how Twain's storyteller has a gifted imagination and is able to vividly evoke events.

"Well, by an' by, up comes this yer quartz excitement. Everybody was into it—everybody was pick'n' 'n' blast'n' instead of shovelin' dirt on the hillside—everybody was put'n' down a shaft instead of scrapin' the surface. Noth'n' would do Jim, but *we* must tackle the ledges, too, 'n' so we did. We commenced put'n' down a shaft, 'n' Tom Quartz he begin to wonder what in the dickens it was all about. *He* hadn't ever seen any mining like that before, 'n' he was all upset, as you may say—he couldn't come to a right understanding of it no way— it was too many for *him*. He was down on it, too, you bet you— he was down on it powerful—'n' always appeared to consider it the cussedest foolishness out. But that cat, you know, was *always* agin new-fangled arrangements—somehow he never could abide 'em. *You* know how it is with old habits. But by an' by Tom Quartz begin to git sort of reconciled a little, though he never *could* altogether understand that eternal sinkin' of a shaft an' never pannin' out anything. At last he got to comin' down in the shaft, hisself, to try to cipher[2] it out. An' when he'd git the blues, 'n' feel kind o' scruffy, 'n' aggravated 'n' disgusted—knowin' as he did, that the bills was runnin' up all the time an' we warn't makin' a cent—he would curl up on a gunny-sack in the corner an' go to sleep. Well, one day when the shaft was down about eight foot, the rock got so hard that we had to put in a blast—the first blast'n' we'd ever done since Tom Quartz was born. An' then we lit the fuse 'n' clumb out 'n' got off 'bout fifty yards—'n' forgot 'n' left Tom Quartz sound asleep on the gunny-sack. In 'bout a minute we seen a puff of smoke bust up out of the hole, 'n' then everything let go with an awful crash, 'n' about four million ton of rocks 'n' dirt 'n' smoke 'n' splinters shot up 'bout a mile an' a half into the air, an' by George, right in the dead center of it was old Tom Quartz a-goin' end over end, an' a-snortin' an' a-sneez'n', an' a-clawin' an' a-reachin' for things like all pos-

Literary Movement: Twain thought the humorous story should be told in the form of a dramatic monologue. Notice that at no point in this story does Baker suggest that there is anything funny about his tale.

---

2. cipher (sī′ fər) *v.*: Figure.

Commentary

The following quotation, from Kenneth Lynn's *Mark Twain and Southwestern Humor,* provides insight into the voice of the narrator of this selection:

> *Roughing It,* the author's prefatory note announces, is a "personal narrative." The adjective is to be understood in the etymological sense. For the narrator who tells us in the first chapter of the book that he is about to go West as the Secretary of Nevada territory is "young and ignorant," and

"never had been away from home," a description which hardly fits the seasoned steamboat pilot and erstwhile Confederate army officer who, not quite twenty-six years old, made his separate peace in the summer of 1861. The character called "Mark Twain" who is the narrator of *Roughing It* is a persona, as the Mark Twain of *The Innocents [Abroad]* had been. The narrators of the two travel books are, in fact, the same literary character, and *Roughing It* represents a continuation of this innocent's adventures, albeit the continuation has taken us backward in time.

sessed. But it warn't no use, you know, it warn't no use. An' that was the last we see of *him* for about two minutes 'n' a half, an' then all of a sudden it begin to rain rocks and rubbage, an' directly he come down ker-whop about ten foot off f'm where we stood. Well, I reckon he was p'raps the orneriest-lookin' beast you ever see. One ear was sot back on his neck, 'n' his tail was stove up, 'n' his eye-winkers was swinged off, 'n' he was all blacked up with powder an' smoke, an' all sloppy with mud 'n' slush f'm one end to the other. Well, sir, it warn't no use to try to apologize—we couldn't say a word. He took a sort of a disgusted look at hisself, 'n' then he looked at us— an' it was just exactly the same as if he had said—'Gents, maybe *you* think it's smart to take advantage of a cat that ain't had no experience of quartz minin', but *I* think *different'*—an' then he turned on his heel 'n' marched off home without ever saying another word.

"That was jest his style. An' maybe you won't believe it, but after that you never see a cat so prejudiced agin quartz mining as what he was. An' by an' by when he *did* get to goin' down in the shaft ag'in, you'd 'a' been astonished at his sagacity. The minute we'd tetch off a blast 'n' the fuse'd begin to sizzle, he'd give a look as much as to say, 'Well, I'll have to git you to excuse *me*,' an' it was surpris'n' the way he'd shin out of that hole 'n' go f'r a tree. Sagacity? It ain't no name for it. 'Twas *inspiration!*"

I said, "Well, Mr. Baker, his prejudice against quartz mining *was* remarkable, considering how he came by it. Couldn't you ever cure him of it?"

"*Cure him!* No! When Tom Quartz was sot once, he was *always* sot—and you might 'a' blowed him up as much as three million times 'n' you'd never 'a' broken him of his cussed prejudice agin quartz mining."

The affection and the pride that lit up Baker's face when he delivered this tribute to the firmness of his humble friend of other days, will always be a vivid memory with me.

Writer's Technique: Notice how Twain employs a humorless listener who takes the tale seriously. The listener acts like the "straight man" in a modern comedy routine.

from *Roughing It*; Tom Quartz   497

ANSWERS TO THINKING ABOUT THE SELECTION
Recalling

1. Baker tells that the cat had good judgment about mining ground; if he didn't think a prospect looked promising he'd leave; if the ground suited him, he'd wait until he saw six or seven grains of gold, and then go to sleep until the men struck a pocket.
2. Tom Quartz is upset because he doesn't understand the process and he doesn't like "new-fangled arrangements."
3. Tom Quartz comes down into the shaft to figure it out.
4. The miners have to blast the rock. The explosion tosses Tom in the air and makes him mad, and he is forever after prejudiced against quartz mining.

Interpreting

5. Baker admires the cat's good sense and his dignity.
6. Baker considers the cat's sagacity to be inspiration because the cat knows what's going to happen before it happens.
7. Americans have always prided themselves on their common sense and honesty.

Applying

8. Answers will differ. Suggested Response: Life on the frontier was hard; laughter provided relief.

ANSWERS TO ANALYZING LITERATURE

1. He is a quiet man, a man of few words.
2. Dick Baker is good-hearted and kind. He's also talkative.
3. The narrator acts as a "straight man" to Baker's exaggerated story.

ANSWERS TO CRITICAL THINKING AND READING

1. (a) In reality the cat probably would have been seriously injured or killed by such a blast. (b) The cat seems smarter than a person.
2. Each event becomes funnier as it gets more exaggerated.

498

THINKING ABOUT THE SELECTION
Recalling

1. What three things does Baker mention to show that Tom Quartz knew more about mining than any human did?
2. Why is Tom Quartz upset when the men turn to quartz mining?
3. Why does Tom Quartz start going down the shaft himself?
4. How is Tom Quartz's prejudice against quartz mining confirmed?

Interpreting

5. What qualities in Tom Quartz does Dick Baker admire?
6. Why does Baker consider the cat's sagacity really inspiration?
7. Are the qualities the cat displays similar to those we have come to identify as our national character? Explain your answer.

Applying

8. William Thackeray once wrote: "A good laugh is sunshine in the house." Why would the humorous story be so important to people living on the frontier?

ANALYZING LITERATURE
Understanding Point of View

Point of view is the vantage point from which a story is told. Although Twain himself serves as the narrator of this selection, the story of Tom Quartz is recounted by a storyteller, Dick Baker, one of Twain's acquaintances in the mining camp. In some ways Twain fictionalizes both himself and Dick Baker in this tale, creating a persona, or character, for each that contributes to the humor.
1. How would you describe the character Mark Twain creates for himself as the narrator?
2. How would you describe the character he creates for the storyteller, Dick Baker?
3. Compare and contrast the way this story is told with the way a modern comedy team might perform a routine.

498   Realism and the Frontier

CRITICAL THINKING AND READING
Understanding Exaggeration

Exaggeration means magnifying something beyond the limits of truth, often for humorous effect. For example, Mark Twain once joked about the length of sentences in German literature: "Whenever the literary German dives into a sentence, that is the last you are going to see of him till he emerges on the other side of the Atlantic with his verb in his mouth."
1. (a) How is the outcome of the explosion an exaggeration? (b) How is the cat's entire personality an exaggeration?
2. Baker builds his exaggerations, with each getting bigger than the previous one. Explain how this technique contributes to the humor.

UNDERSTANDING LANGUAGE
Interpreting Dialect

Dialect is the colloquial language of people living in a certain region. Writers often use dialect to give their stories local color. For example, Mark Twain has Dick Baker say, "When Tom Quartz was sot once, he was *always* sot, and you might 'a' blowed him up as much as three million times 'n' you'd never 'a' broken him of his cussed prejudice agin quartz-mining."

Find two other examples of dialect in this selection. Does the use of dialect make the tale more or less effective? Explain.

THINKING AND WRITING
Writing a Tall Tale

Write your own tall tale. Imagine someone new has just moved to your neighborhood and to entertain him you want to tell him a tall tale about the exploits of you and your friends. Brainstorm to come up with a list of incredible events. Then start writing your tale. Using a colloquial voice, begin by telling about the event that is most plausible, building to the climax with the event that is most exaggerated. Revise your tale, making sure that your tone is consistent.

ANSWERS TO UNDERSTANDING LANGUAGE

Two examples are: "Gentlemen, I used to have a cat here by the name of Tom Quartz. You would have been interested in him, I think—almost anybody would have been"; and "We began to put down a shaft, and Tom Quartz began to wonder what our activity was all about."

THINKING AND WRITING

Publishing Student Writing You might collect students' tall tales in a class booklet, and make it available for students to read at their leisure.

Prose

TURN HIM LOOSE, BILL
Frederic Remington
Three Lions

Humanities Note

Fine art, *Turn Him Loose, Bill,* by Frederic Remington. Although born in the East, in upstate New York, the young Frederic Remington (1861–1906) showed more enthusiasm for the life of adventure, as symbolized by the West, than he did for the more sedate occupations of the East. After dropping out of Yale University, he headed west, in search of excitement and hoping to make his fortune there. He became an artist-historian of the vanishing frontier.

Remington was not a detached illustrator of the scenes of action he portrayed; he was often a participant, as the inclusion of himself as a subject in some of his works reveals. What interested him most, in any event, was the depiction of vivid, dramatic action, as in *Turn Him Loose, Bill.* In this work, tension is created by the struggle of horse and rider. Quick, violent movement, impulsiveness, readiness to fight— these were the images of the frontier captured by Remington. In the days before western movies, Remington's skill as an illustrator and artist brought the vitality, as well as the brutality, of the frontier to homes throughout the nation and this may have accounted for the immense popularity Remington achieved during his lifetime.

MARK TWAIN

More About the Author Although Mark Twain was reared in rural Missouri, he traveled a great deal in his later life. The following can be included among the American towns where Twain lived at one time or another: St. Louis, New York, Philadelphia, Cincinnati, Elmira, Hartford, and San Francisco. His overseas travels took him throughout Europe with extended visits to England, Germany, Switzerland, and Italy. He also visited Palestine. It is in *A Tramp Abroad,* published in 1880, that he recounts some of his adventures on those trips. Twain's literary style is marked by these influences, and many of his works employ a skillful depiction of country manners and mores balanced by worldly impartiality. In what other ways might a writer benefit from having lived in such different worlds?

Critical Evaluation Maurice LeBreton, a critic, has this to say of Twain's accomplishments: His "work is a panorama of the West in all its variety. He has observed everything: landscapes, environments, ways of life, customs, beliefs, superstitions. Through him we know the little Missouri town . . . He has described for us the Mississippi . . . We follow him into the isolated Arkansas farm . . . The entire West files past us in a succession of precise, faithful images."

1835–1910

Mark Twain earned international fame early in his career by writing humorous tales that captured the local color of the West. He then went on to establish himself as one of the greatest writers in the history of American literature by transforming his childhood observations and experiences into the classic American novels *The Adventures of Tom Sawyer* (1876) and *The Adventures of Huckleberry Finn* (1884). So great was the influence of this later novel, in fact, that Ernest Hemingway wrote, "All modern American literature comes from one book by Mark Twain called *Huckleberry Finn.*"

Twain, who was born Samuel Langhorne Clemens, grew up in the Mississippi River town of Hannibal, Missouri. When he was eleven, his father died, and he left school to become a printer's apprentice. Though he disliked the profession, Twain worked as a printer in a number of different cities before deciding to pursue a career as a riverboat pilot at the age of twenty-one.

When the Civil War closed the Mississippi River, Twain traveled west to Nevada. There he supported himself as a journalist and lecturer, and he developed the entertaining writing style that made him famous. In 1865, when he published "The Notorious Jumping Frog of Calaveras County," his version of a tall tale he had heard in a mining camp, he became an international celebrity.

Following the publication of *The Innocents Abroad* (1869), a successful book of humorous travel letters, Twain moved to Hartford, Connecticut, where he lived for the rest of his life. There, Twain began using his past experiences as the raw material for his books. In *Roughing It* (1872), he drew on his experiences in the western mining regions. He turned to his childhood experiences in writing *The Adventures of Tom Sawyer, Life on the Mississippi* (1883), and *The Adventures of Huckleberry Finn.* In *Huckleberry Finn,* his masterpiece, he delved into the realities of the prewar South, portraying the adventures of a young white orphan and a runaway slave.

During his later years, Twain was unable to reproduce the balance between pessimism and humor that he had captured in *Huckleberry Finn.* In works such as *A Connecticut Yankee in King Arthur's Court* (1889), *Pudd'nhead Wilson* (1894), and *The Man That Corrupted Hadleyburg* (1900), he expressed an increasingly pessimistic vision of society and human nature. However, Twain displayed the same masterful command of language that had already established him as the finest American fiction writer of his time. It was this command of language that compelled the twentieth-century poet T. S. Eliot to write that in Twain he had "discovered a new way of writing . . . a literary language based on American colloquial speech."

Objectives
1 To understand narration
2 To write a statement of ambition

Support Material

Teaching Portfolio
Teacher Backup, p. 659
Usage and Mechanics Worksheet, p. 663
Vocabulary Check, p. 664
Analyzing Literature Worksheet, *Recognizing Narration,* p. 665
Language Worksheet, *Understanding Jargon,* p. 666
Selection Test, p. 667

GUIDE FOR INTERPRETING

The Boys' Ambition

Literary Forms

Narration. Narration is writing that tells a story. The story being related may be fictional, as in novels and short stories, or factual, as in historical accounts, autobiographies, and biographies. However, the distinction between fictional narration and factual narration is not always clear. Fictional narratives are often inspired by or based on real-life events. For example, *The Adventures of Huckleberry Finn,* Mark Twain's finest novel, grew out of Twain's boyhood observations and experiences. Similarly, in some factual narratives certain events and details are fictionalized or exaggerated. For example, in *Life on the Mississippi,* Twain's account of his own experiences as a boy and young man living on the Mississippi River, Twain embellishes certain events and magnifies the traits of certain people.

Commentary

Mark Twain grew up to become a famous and prosperous author. As a grown man, did he still retain his childhood wish to become a riverboat pilot? He claimed that he did—under certain conditions.

In 1880 a twelve-year-old boy named David Watter Bowser wrote Twain a letter. He had chosen Twain as the living man with whom he would most like to change places. In his letter and in a school composition that he enclosed, he explained that Twain had "everything a man could have." Twain was "jolly," "happy," and rich. Would Mr. Twain, Bowser asked, be willing to become a boy again while he, Bowser, settled into Mr. Twain's life?

The boy received an interesting response. Yes, answered Twain, he would be willing to change places, but only if certain conditions were fulfilled. "The main condition should be, that I should emerge from boyhood as a 'cub pilot' on a Mississippi boat, and that I should by and by become a pilot, and remain one." Twain's other conditions included an endless summer filled with blooming oleanders, friends to talk and sing with, and a crew that would never die. The now well-known author also called for fame as a pilot. "And when strangers were informed that I was the celebrated 'Master Pilot of the Mississippi,' . . . and exclaimed, 'O, I know *that* name very well!' I should feel a pleasurable emotion tricking down my spine and know I had not lived in vain."

With what famous writer would you want to change places? How do you think the writer might respond to your request?

Writing

In "The Boy's Ambition," Mark Twain discusses his boyhood ambition to become a steamboatman. Freewrite for five minutes about your ambitions.

Guide for Interpreting 501

Literary Focus Twain often used local vernacular to embellish his narratives. He was particularly adept at capturing regional accents in his writing, providing the reader with a more colorful image of the setting.

Writing/Prior Knowledge If students have reservations about discussing their own ambitions, have them discuss the ambitions of someone they know.

from # Life on the Mississippi
Mark Twain

The Boys' Ambition

When I was a boy, there was but one permanent ambition among my comrades in our village[1] on the west bank of the Mississippi River. That was, to be a steamboatman. We had transient ambitions of other sorts, but they were only transient.

When a circus came and went, it left us all burning to become clowns; the first Negro minstrel show that came to our section left us all suffering to try that kind of life; now and then we had a hope that if we lived and were good, God would permit us to be pirates. These ambitions faded out, each in its turn; but the ambition to be a steamboatman always remained.

Once a day a cheap, gaudy packet[2] arrived upward from St. Louis, and another downward from Keokuk.[3] Before these events, the day was glorious with expectancy; after them, the day was a dead and empty thing. Not only the boys, but the whole village, felt this. After all these years I can picture that old time to myself now, just as it was then: the white town drowsing in the sunshine of a summer's morning; the streets empty, or pretty nearly so; one or two clerks sitting in front of the Water Street stores, with their splint-bottomed chairs tilted back against the wall, chins on breasts, hats slouched over their faces, asleep—with shingle shavings enough around to show what broke them down; a sow and a litter of pigs loafing along the sidewalk, doing a good business in watermelon rinds and seeds; two or three lonely little freight piles scattered about the levee;[4] a pile of skids[5] on the slope of the stone-paved wharf, and the fragrant town drunkard asleep in the shadow of them; two or three wood flats[6] at the head of the wharf, but nobody to listen to the peaceful lapping of the wavelets against them; the great Mississippi, the majestic, the magnificent Mississippi, rolling its mile-wide tide along, shining in the sun; the dense forest away on the other side; the point above the town, and the point below, bounding the river-glimpse and turning it into a sort of sea, and withal a very still and brilliant and lonely one. Presently a film of dark smoke appears above one of those remote points; instantly a Negro drayman,[7] famous for his quick eye and prodigious voice, lifts up the cry, "S-t-e-a-m-boat a-comin'!" and the scene changes! The town drunkard stirs, the clerks wake up, a furious clatter of drays follows, every house and store pours out a human contribution, and all in a twinkling the dead town is alive and moving. Drays, carts, men, boys, all go hurrying from many quarters to a common center, the wharf. Assembled there, the people fasten their eyes upon the coming boat as upon a wonder they are seeing for the first time.

---
1. our village: Hannibal, Missouri.
2. packet *n.*: A boat that travels a regular route, carrying passengers, freight, and mail.
3. Keokuk (kē′ ə kuk′): A town in southeastern Iowa.

4. levee (lev′ ē) *n.*: A landing place along the bank of a river.
5. skids *n.*: Low, movable wooden platforms.
6. flats *n.*: Small flat-bottomed boats.
7. drayman *n.*: The driver of a dray, a low cart with detachable sides.

502   Realism and the Frontier

And the boat *is* rather a handsome sight, too. She is long and sharp and trim and pretty; she has two tall, fancy-topped chimneys, with a gilded device of some kind swung between them; a fanciful pilothouse, all glass and gingerbread, perched on top of the texas deck[8] behind them; the paddle-boxes are gorgeous with a picture or with gilded rays above the boat's name; the boiler deck, the hurricane deck, and the texas deck are fenced and ornamented with clean white railings; there is a flag gallantly flying from the jackstaff;[9] the furnace doors are open and the fires glaring bravely; the upper decks are black with passengers; the captain stands by the big bell, calm, imposing, the envy of all; great volumes of the blackest smoke are rolling and tumbling out of the chimneys—a husbanded grandeur created

with a bit of pitch pine just before arriving at a town; the crew are grouped on the fore-castle:[10] the broad stage is run far out over the port bow, and an envied deckhand stands picturesquely on the end of it with a coil of rope in his hand; the pent steam is screaming through the gauge cocks; the captain lifts his hand, a bell rings, the wheels stop; then they turn back, churning the water to foam, and the steamer is at rest. Then such a scramble as there is to get aboard, and to get ashore, and to take in freight and to discharge freight, all at one and the same time; and such a yelling and cursing as the mates facilitate it all with! Ten minutes later the steamer is under way again, with no flag on the jackstaff and no black smoke issuing from the chimneys. After ten more minutes the town is dead again, and the town drunkard asleep by the skids once more.

---

8. texas deck: The deck adjoining the officers' cabins, the largest cabins on the ship.
9. jackstaff *n*.: A rope that runs up and down a ship's mast.

10. forecastle *n*.: The front part of the upper deck.

PADDLE STEAMBOAT MISSISSIPPI
The Shelburne Museum, Shelburne, Vermont

4
5

4 Clarification "Husbanded grandeur" refers to a deliberately created effect.

5 Clarification Pitch pine is wood from the heart of a pine tree, near the stump. It is heavily saturated with pitch and burns quickly, emitting large amounts of black smoke.

Humanities Note

Fine art, *Paddle Steamboat, Mississippi*. This oil on canvas provides a visual record of a Mississippi steamboat and the banks of the Mississippi River of Mark Twain's era. The three boys waving excitedly at the approaching boat express the excitement Twain describes over the arrival of such a boat.

As students look at the picture, you might ask these questions;
1. What emotion described in the selection is also suggested in this painting?
2. What was it about steamboat travel that excited people like the boys in this picture and young Mark Twain?

503

My father was a justice of the peace, and I supposed he possessed the power of life and death over all men and could hang anybody that offended him. This was distinction enough for me as a general thing; but the desire to be a steamboatman kept intruding, nevertheless. I first wanted to be a cabin boy, so that I could come out with a white apron on and shake a tablecloth over the side, where all my old comrades could see me; later I thought I would rather be the deckhand who stood on the end of the stage plank with the coil of rope in his hand, because he was particularly conspicuous. But these were only daydreams—they were too heavenly to be contemplated as real possibilities. By and by one of our boys went away. He was not heard of for a long time. At last he turned up as apprentice engineer or striker on a steamboat. This thing shook the bottom out of all my Sunday-school teachings. That boy had been notoriously worldly, and I just the reverse; yet he was exalted to this eminence, and I left in obscurity and misery. There was nothing generous about this fellow in his greatness. He would always manage to have a rusty bolt to scrub while his boat tarried at our town, and he would sit on the inside guard and scrub it, where we could all see him and envy him and loathe him. And whenever his boat was laid up he would come home and swell around the town in his blackest and greasiest clothes, so that nobody could help remembering that he was a steamboatman; and he used all sorts of steamboat technicalities in his talk, as if he were so used to them that he forgot common people could not understand them. He would speak of the labboard[11] side of a horse in an easy, natural way that would make one wish he was dead. And he was always talking about "St. Looey" like an old citizen; he would refer casually to occasions when he "was coming down Fourth Street," or when he was "passing by the Planter's House," or when there was a

---

11. **labboard:** Larboard, the left-hand side of a ship.

fire and he took a turn on the brakes of "the old Big Missouri"; and then he would go on and lie about how many towns the size of ours were burned down there that day. Two or three of the boys had long been persons of consideration among us because they had been to St. Louis once and had a vague general knowledge of its wonders, but the day of their glory was over now. They lapsed into a humble silence, and learned to disappear when the ruthless cub engineer approached. This fellow had money, too, and hair oil. Also an ignorant silver watch and a showy brass watch chain. He wore a leather belt and used no suspenders. If ever a youth was cordially admired and hated by his comrades, this one was. No girl could withstand his charms. He cut out every boy in the village. When his boat blew up at last, it diffused a tranquil contentment among us such as we had not known for months. But when he came home the next week, alive, renowned, and appeared in church all battered up and bandaged, a shining hero, stared at and wondered over by everybody, it seemed to us that the partiality of Providence for an undeserving reptile had reached a point where it was open to criticism.

This creature's career could produce but one result, and it speedily followed. Boy after boy managed to get on the river. The minister's son became an engineer. The doctor's and the postmaster's sons became mud clerks; the wholesale liquor dealer's son became a barkeeper on a boat; four sons of the chief merchant, and two sons of the county judge, became pilots. Pilot was the grandest position of all. The pilot, even in those days of trivial wages, had a princely salary—from a hundred and fifty to two hundred and fifty dollars a month, and no board to pay. Two months of his wages would pay a preacher's salary for a year. Now some of us were left disconsolate. We could not get on the river—at least our parents would not let us.

So by and by I ran away. I said I never would come home again till I was a pilot and could come in glory. But somehow I could not manage it. I went meekly aboard a few of the boats that lay packed together like sardines at the long St. Louis wharf, and very humbly inquired for the pilots, but got only a cold shoulder and short words from mates and clerks. I had to make the best of this sort of treatment for the time being, but I had comforting daydreams of a future when I should be a great and honored pilot, with plenty of money, and could kill some of these mates and clerks and pay for them.

12

THINKING ABOUT THE SELECTION
Recalling

1. What is the one permanent ambition of Twain and his boyhood friends?
2. How do the people of Hannibal respond to the daily arrival of the steamboat?
3. (a) How do Twain and the other boys react when one of their friends becomes an apprentice engineer on a steamboat? (b) What does the apprentice do to make sure that the other boys do not forget that he is a steamboatman?
4. (a) What happens to the young apprentice's boat? (b) How do the other boys respond?
5. (a) Why does Twain run away from home? (b) What does he discover after he leaves?

Interpreting

6. What impression of the town of Hannibal, Missouri, is conveyed through Twain's description of the town and its response to the steamboat's arrival?
7. How does Twain's description of the steamboat reflect his boyhood desire to be a steamboatman?
8. (a) How would you describe the attitude of the boys toward the young apprentice engineer? (b) How does their attitude reflect their desire to be steamboatmen?
9. (a) What seems to be Twain's attitude toward himself as a boy? (b) What details in the selection convey his attitude?

Applying

10. Although Twain never earned fame as a steamboat pilot, he did become a famous writer. How do you think Twain's love for the Mississippi River and riverboats contributed to his success as a writer?

ANALYZING LITERATURE
Recognizing Narration

Narration is writing that tells a story. A narrative may be factual or fictional. Yet the distinction between factual narration and fictional narration is not always clear. For example, *Life on the Mississippi* is a factual narrative account of Twain's experiences while growing up on the Mississippi River, but certain details and events in the book are fictionalized or exaggerated.
1. Which details in "The Boys' Ambition" may be exaggerated? Support your answer.
2. What do you think might have been Twain's reasons for fictionalizing some of the details?

THINKING AND WRITING
Writing a Statement of Ambition

College applications often include an essay question in which applicants are asked to discuss their main ambition in life. Prepare to answer this question by reviewing your freewriting concerning your ambitions. Decide what your main ambition is. Then list the reasons for your decision. When you write your essay, make sure you include enough reasons to support your statement of ambition. When you finish writing, revise your essay and prepare a final copy.

from *Life on the Mississippi:* The Boy's Ambition   505

12 **Enrichment** Twain actually did become a riverboat pilot. You may wish to have your students read other excerpts from *Life on the Mississippi* in which he tells of this career.

4. (a) The boat blows up. (b) The other boys are glad.
5. (a) He runs away to become a steamboat pilot. (b) He finds it is difficult to find a position.

Interpreting

6. Suggested Response: Twain gives the impression of a sleepy town with no source of entertainment. The arrival of the steamboat causes the only excitement.
7. He describes the steamboat in glowing terms.
8. (a) They disliked him. (b) They were jealous of his position.
9. (a) Twain seems to recall his attitude as a boy with humor and indulgence. (b) Suggested Response: He describes the packet as cheap and gaudy, and he would someday be a "great and honored pilot . . . and could kill some of these mates and clerks and pay for them."

Applying

10. Suggested Response: Twain used his memories of life along the Mississippi extensively in his writing. His love of the locale is evident in the rich detail of writing which helped give his novels their remarkable clarity and wit.

ANSWERS TO ANALYZING LITERATURE

1. Twain probably exaggerated the details concerning his misery at not being a steamboatman, his loathing of the young man who was, and his relief when the young man's boat blows up.
2. Answers will differ but might include the suggestion that Twain fictionalized some details so that they might better fit the story.

THINKING AND WRITING

Publishing Student Writing Have student volunteers read their compositions to the class.

505

Closure and Extension
ANSWERS TO THINKING ABOUT THE SELECTION
Recalling

1. They all want to be steamboat men.
2. They all stop to greet the boat as it arrives.
3. (a) They are all jealous. (b) He wears his working clothes and peppers his language with nautical terms.

Focus

Literary Focus The humor in Twain's pieces is created by his use of a variety of literary devices, as well as from his own wry observations. The humor created by his use of regional dialect is enhanced by his characters' frequent misuse of words, and his narrative style often neatly underscores the humor in his pieces.

Writing/Prior Knowledge For extra credit, you might have students write a short humorous anecdote, using such techniques as exaggeration and dialect.

Vocabulary

Preteach the following vocabulary words:

garrulous (gar′ ə ləs) *adj.:* Talking too much (p. 507)

conjectured (kən jek′ chərd) *v.:* Guessed (p. 507)

monotonous (mə nät′ nəs) *adj.:* Tiresome because unvarying (p. 507)

interminable (in tʉr′ mi nə b'l) *adj.:* Seeming to last forever (p. 507)

ornery (ôr′ nər ē) *adj.:* Having a mean disposition (p. 508)

The Notorious Jumping Frog of Calaveras County

Writer's Techniques

Humor. In literature, humor refers to writing that is intended to evoke laughter. To accomplish this purpose, writers must have the ability to perceive the ridiculous, comical, or ludicrous aspects of an incident, situation, or personality and to depict them in an amusing manner.

Humorists use a variety of techniques to make their work amusing. For example, the western humorists, including Mark Twain, made extensive uses of exaggeration in their writing. Certain incidents and details were exaggerated to such a great extent that they became comical. Usually, the exaggerated incidents or events were described by a narrator or storyteller in a very serious tone. This tone made the tale more humorous, because it created the impression that the storyteller was unaware of the ridiculousness of what he or she was describing.

Regional dialects—the colloquial languages of people living in certain areas—were another important element of western humor. The use of regional dialects helped to capture local color and made the characters more interesting and amusing. For example, Simon Wheeler's use of regional dialect in "The Notorious Jumping Frog of Calaveras County" helps make him a very entertaining character, and his frequent use of unexpected words adds to the humor of the story.

Commentary

According to one of Mark Twain's biographers, Twain first heard the story that was to become "The Notorious Jumping Frog of Calaveras County" in the barroom of a rundown tavern in Angel's Camp, California, while he himself was prospecting for gold. The storyteller was a former Illinois River pilot named Ben Coon, "a solemn, fat-witted person, who dozed by the stove, or told slow, endless stories, without point or application." Twain found it "soothing and comfortable to listen to his endless narratives, told in that solemn way, with no suspicion of humor."

Like the jumping frog story, many of Twain's stories were based on stories heard in bars, on the trail, or around campfires. To what extent should writers be given credit for stories they merely retell? What do writers need to bring to retold stories to make them their own?

Writing

Think of a humorous story you have heard in which exaggeration was used. Then briefly discuss why you think the use of exaggeration in the story makes it amusing.

Objectives

1 To recognize humor
2 To appreciate dialect
3 To write a story using dialect

Support Material

Teaching Portfolio
Teacher Backup, p. 669
Grammar in Action Worksheet, *Understanding the Dash,* p. 672
Usage and Mechanics Worksheet, p. 674
Vocabulary Check, p. 675
Analyzing Literature Worksheet, *Recognizing Humor,* p. 676
Critical Thinking and Reading

Worksheet, *Appreciating Dialect,* p. 677
Selection Test, p. 678–9

The Notorious Jumping Frog of Calaveras County

Mark Twain

In compliance with the request of a friend of mine, who wrote me from the East, I called on good-natured, garrulous old Simon Wheeler, and inquired after my friend's friend, Leonidas W. Smiley, as requested to do, and I hereunto append the result. I have a lurking suspicion that *Leonidas W.* Smiley is a myth; that my friend never knew such a personage; and that he only conjectured that if I asked old Wheeler about him, it would remind him of his infamous *Jim* Smiley, and he would go to work and bore me to death with some exasperating reminiscence of him as long and as tedious as it should be useless to me. If that was the design, it succeeded.

I found Simon Wheeler dozing comfortably by the barroom stove of the dilapidated tavern in the decayed mining camp of Angel's, and I noticed that he was fat and bald-headed, and had an expression of winning gentleness and simplicity upon his tranquil countenance. He roused up, and gave me good day. I told him a friend of mine had commissioned me to make some inquiries about a cherished companion of his boyhood named *Leonidas W.* Smiley—*Rev. Leonidas W.* Smiley, a young minister of the Gospel, who he had heard was at one time a resident of Angel's Camp. I added that if Mr. Wheeler could tell me anything about this Rev. Leonidas W. Smiley, I would feel under many obligations to him.

Simon Wheeler backed me into a corner and blockaded me there with his chair, and then sat down and reeled off the monotonous narrative which follows this paragraph. He never smiled, he never frowned, he never changed his voice from the gentle-flowing key to which he tuned his initial sentence, he never betrayed the slightest suspicion of enthusiasm; but all through the interminable narrative there ran a vein of impressive earnestness and sincerity, which showed me plainly that, so far from his imagining that there was anything ridiculous or funny about his story, he regarded it as a really important matter, and admired its two heroes as men of transcendent genius in *finesse.* I let him go on in his own way, and never interrupted him once.

"Rev. Leonidas W. H'm, Reverend Le—well, there was a feller here once by the name of *Jim* Smiley, in the winter of '49—or maybe it was the spring of '50—I don't recollect exactly, somehow, though what makes me think it was one or the other is because I remember the big flume[1] warn't finished when he first come to the camp; but anyway, he was the curiousest man about always betting on anything that turned up you ever see, if he could get anybody to bet on the other side; and if he couldn't he'd change sides. Any way that suited the other man would suit *him*—any way just so's he got a bet, *he* was satisfied. But still he was lucky, uncommon lucky; he most always come out winner. He was always ready and laying for a chance; there couldn't be no solit'ry thing

---

1. **flume** (flōōm) *n.*: An artificial channel for carrying water to provide power and transport objects.

The Notorious Jumping Frog of Calaveras County 507

Presentation

Motivation/Prior Knowledge
Students may recall favorite humorous stories that are retold by members of their own families who use exaggeration in order to embellish accounts of funny experiences. Have them explain such accounts and compare their knowledge of what actually happened to the way it is rendered in tales intended to amuse.

Purpose-Setting Question
What expectations do you have for a story that has so promising a title?

Enrichment Twain often continued working on his stories after they were published. For example, on November 18, 1865, his story "The Celebrated Jumping Frog of Calaveras County" was published in the *The Saturday Press*. Twain revised this story later that same year, again in 1867, then in 1872, and published it in its final form in 1875. Twain's final choice of a title was "The Notorious Jumping Frog of Calaveras County."

According to Twain scholar Walter Blair, "Twain's enthusiasm about this story varied; but his characterization of it in 1869 as 'the best humorous sketch America has produced' and his extensive revision before he printed it in its final form in 1875 attest to his belief that it merited painstaking care."

1 **Discussion** How is Twain's formal tone here incongruous with the setting? How does this add to the humor of the piece?

2 **Discussion** How does Twain manage to develop two characters at the same time in this passage?

The accent with which Wheeler speaks lends credibility to the events of the story and to Wheeler's own sense of wonder at them. It also sets up his other observations about the frog, Jim Smiley, and the absurdity of the situation in general.

4 **Literary Focus** Note Twain's use of the classic "punch line."

5 **Discussion** What is so absurd about this situation? How does this absurdity keep the reader from mourning for the dog?

mentioned but that feller'd offer to bet on it, and take ary side you please, as I was just telling you. If there was a horse race, you'd find him flush or you'd find him busted at the end of it; if there was a dogfight, he'd bet on it; if there was a cat fight, he'd bet on it; if there was a chicken fight, he'd bet on it; why, if there was two birds setting on a fence, he would bet you which one would fly first; or if there was a camp meeting,[2] he would be there reg'lar to bet on Parson Walker, which he judged to be the best exhorter about here and so he was too, and a good man. If he even see a straddle bug[3] start to go anywheres, he would bet you how long it would take him to get to—to wherever he was going to, and if you took him up, he would foller that straddle bug to Mexico but what he would find out where he was bound for and how long he was on the road. Lots of the boys here has seen that Smiley, and can tell you about him. Why, it never made no difference to *him*—he'd bet on *any* thing—the dangdest feller. Parson Walker's wife laid very sick once, for a good while, and it seemed as if they warn't going to save her; but one morning he come in, and Smiley up and asked him how she was, and he said she was considerable better—thank the Lord for his inf'nite mercy—and coming on so smart that with the blessing of Prov'dence she'd get well yet; and Smiley, before he thought, says, 'Well, I'll resk two-and-a-half she don't anyway.'

Thish-yer Smiley had a mare—the boys called her the fifteen-minute nag, but that was only in fun, you know, because of course she was faster than that—and he used to win money on that horse, for all she was so slow and always had the asthma, or the distemper, or the consumption, or something of that kind. They used to give her two or three hundred yards start, and then pass her under way; but always at the fag end[4] of the race she'd get excited and desperate like, and come cavorting and straddling up, and scattering her legs around limber, sometimes in the air, and sometimes out to one side among the fences, and kicking up m-o-r-e dust and raising m-o-r-e racket with her coughing and sneezing and blowing her nose—and *always* fetch up at the stand just about a neck ahead, as near as you could cipher it down.

And he had a little small bull-pup, that to look at him you'd think he warn't worth a cent but to set around and look ornery and lay for a chance to steal something. But as soon as money was up on him he was a different dog; his under-jaw'd begin to stick out like the fo'castle[5] of a steamboat, and his teeth would uncover and shine like the furnaces. And a dog might tackle him and bully-rag him, and bite him, and throw him over his shoulder two or three times, and Andrew Jackson—which was the name of the pup—Andrew Jackson would never let on but what *he* was satisfied, and hadn't expected nothing else—and the bets being doubled and doubled on the other side all the time, till the money was all up; and then all of a sudden he would grab that other dog jest by the j'int of his hind leg and freeze to it—not chaw, you understand, but only just grip and hang on till they throwed up the sponge, if it was a year. Smiley always come out winner on that pup, till he harnessed a dog once that didn't have no hind legs, because they'd been sawed off in a circular saw, and when the thing had gone along far enough, and the money was all up, and he come to make a snatch for his pet holt,[6] he see in a minute how he'd been imposed on, and how the other dog had him in the door, so to speak, and he 'peared surprised, and then he looked sorter discouraged-like, and didn't try no more to win the fight, and so he got shucked out bad. He give Smiley a look, as much as to say his heart was broke, and it

---

2. **camp meeting:** A religious gathering at the mining camp.
3. **straddle bug:** An insect with long legs.
4. **fag end:** Last part.

---

5. **fo'castle** (fōk's'l) *n.*: Forecastle; the forward part of the upper deck.
6. **holt:** Hold.

Grammar in Action

The **dash** is a useful punctuation mark, but it should be used with discretion. Mark Twain, in reproducing the speech of Simon Wheeler, uses dashes more than a writer of a formal essay would; yet he uses them consistently. Dashes serve three primary functions: to indicate an interruption or a summary, to set off a dramatic renaming, and to set off a parenthetical expression. Here are examples of each use from Mark Twain's story:

Interruption: Why, it never made no difference to him—he'd bet on anything—the dangest feller.

Renaming: A friend . . . had commissioned me to make some inquiries about a cherished companion of his boyhood named Leonidas W. Smiley—Rev. Leonidas W. Smiley. . . .

Parenthetical expression: He said she was considerable better—thank the Lord for his inf'nite mercy—and coming on . . . smart. . . .

was *his* fault, for putting up a dog that hadn't no hind legs for him to take holt of, which was his main dependence in a fight, and then he limped off a piece and laid down and died. It was a good pup, was that Andrew Jackson, and would have made a name for hisself if he'd lived, for the stuff was in him and he had genius—I know it, because he hadn't no opportunities to speak of, and it don't stand to reason that a dog could make such a fight as he could under them circumstances if he hadn't no talent. It always makes me feel sorry when I think of that last fight of his'n, and the way it turned out.

Well, thish-yer Smiley had rat terriers,[7] and chicken cocks,[8] and tomcats and all them kind of things, till you couldn't rest, and you couldn't fetch nothing for him to bet on but he'd match you. He ketched a frog one day, and took him home, and said he cal'lated to educate him; and so he never done nothing for three months but set in his back yard and learn that frog to jump. And you bet you he *did* learn him, too. He'd give him a little punch behind, and the next minute you'd see that frog whirling in the air like a doughnut—see him turn one summerset, or maybe a couple, if he got a good start, and come down flatfooted and all right, like a cat. He got him up so in the matter of ketching flies, and kep' him in practice so constant, that he'd nail a fly every time as fur as he could see him. Smiley said all a frog wanted was education, and he could do 'most anything—and I believe him. Why, I've seen him set Dan'l Webster down here on this floor—Dan'l Webster was the name of the frog—and sing out, "Flies, Dan'l, flies!" and quicker'n you could wink he'd spring straight up and snake a fly off'n the counter there, and flop down on the floor ag'in as solid as a gob of mud, and fall to scratching the side of his head with his hind foot as indifferent as if he hadn't no idea he'd been doin' any more'n any frog might do. You

never see a frog so modest and straightfor'ard as he was, for all he was so gifted. And when it come to fair and square jumping on a dead level, he could get over more ground at one straddle than any animal of his breed you ever see. Jumping on a dead level was his strong suit, you understand; and when it come to that, Smiley would ante up money on him as long as he had a red.[9] Smiley was monstrous proud of his frog, and well he might be, for fellers that had traveled and been everywheres all said he laid over any frog that ever *they* see.

Well, Smiley kep' the beast in a little lattice box, and he used to fetch him downtown sometimes and lay for a bet. One day a feller—a stranger in the camp, he was—come acrost him with his box, and says:

'What might it be that you've got in the box?'

And Smiley says, sorter indifferent-like, 'It might be a parrot, or it might be a canary, maybe, but it ain't—it's only just a frog.'

And the feller took it, and looked at it careful, and turned it round this way and that, and says, 'H'm—so 'tis. Well, what's *he* good for?'

'Well,' Smiley says, easy and careless, 'he's good enough for *one* thing, I should judge—he can outjump any frog in Calaveras county.'

The feller took the box again, and took another long, particular look, and give it back to Smiley, and says, very deliberate, 'Well,' he says, 'I don't see no p'ints about that frog that's any better'n any other frog.'

'Maybe you don't,' Smiley says. 'Maybe you understand frogs and maybe you don't understand 'em; maybe you've had experience, and maybe you ain't only a amature, as it were. Anyways, I've got *my* opinion, and I'll resk forty dollars that he can outjump any frog in Calaveras county.'

And the feller studied a minute, and then says, kinder sad like, 'Well, I'm only a

---
7. **rat terriers:** Dogs skilled in catching rats.
8. **chicken cocks:** Roosters trained to fight.

---
9. **a red:** A red cent.

The Notorious Jumping Frog of Calaveras County   509

6 **Literary Focus** Note how Wheeler's serious tone contrasts with the subject of the story.

7 **Literary Focus** Another humorous technique is the *aside,* or *throw-away line.* It is used here to make the frog's name even funnier.

8 **Clarification** Daniel Webster was the most famous orator of his day. He was a United States Senator and Secretary of State under William Henry Harrison and John Tyler.

9 **Discussion** Is the stranger as naive as he seems? Explain.

Student Activity 1. Describe the function of the dashes in each of the following sentences.

1. Jest set where you are, stranger, and rest easy—I ain't going to be gone a second.
2. I do wonder what in the nation that frog throwed off for—I wonder if there ain't something the matter with him—he 'pears to look mighty baggy, somehow.
3. When he was going out at the door, he sorter jerked his thumb over his shoulder—so—at Dan'l . . .
4. It warn't no use—he couldn't budge.
5. He . . . filled him pretty near full of quailshot—filled him pretty near up to his chin—and set him on the floor.

Student Activity 2. Insert dashes in the appropriate positions in each of the following sentences.

1. That's all right that's all right if you'll hold my box a minute, I'll go and get you a frog.
2. It might be a parrot, or it might be a canary, maybe, but it ain't it's only just a frog.
3. Smiley said all a frog wanted was education, and he could do 'most anything and I believe him.
4. You'd see that frog whirling in the air like a doughnut see him turn one somersault, or maybe a couple. . . .

Fine art, *Mark Twain Riding the Celebrated Jumping Frog,* Caricature, 1872, by Frederick Waddy. A caricature is a drawing that exaggerates certain traits of a person's appearance so that they become ridiculous, although still recognizable. Caricatures are drawn to satirize or to poke fun. Frederick Waddy was an English caricaturist, whose humorous drawings were reproduced as wood engravings in the *Illustrated London News.* Famous figures, particularly authors, were his favorite subjects. His work is recognizable by the large portrait head and tiny body he liked to use. In this caricature of Mark Twain, he has used the famous "jumping frog" to add humor and further identify Twain.

1. What aspects of Mark Twain —either the man or his work— are being poked fun at in this drawing?

2. What is your opinion of this caricature? Is it fitting? Good-humored? Explain.

10 Reading Strategy Have students predict who will win the bet.

11 Discussion Why is this such an effective ending to the piece? Was the story as boring and tedious as the narrator made it out to be?

Reader's Response What kinds of contests involving animals do you enjoy watching?

MARK TWAIN (SAMUEL L. CLEMENS) RIDING THE CELEBRATED JUMPING FROG
An English Caricature
by Frederic Waddy, 1872
The Granger Collection

10

stranger here, and I ain't got no frog; but if I had a frog, I'd bet you.'

And then Smiley says, 'That's all right— that's all right—if you'll hold my box a minute, I'll go and get you a frog.' And so the feller took the box, and put up his forty dollars along with Smiley's, and set down to wait.

So he set there a good while thinking and thinking to hisself, and then he got the frog out and prized his mouth open and took a teaspoon and filled him full of quail-shot[10]—filled him pretty near up to his chin—and set him on the floor. Smiley he went to the swamp and slopped around in the mud for a long time, and finally he ketched a frog, and fetched him in, and give him to this feller, and says:

'Now, if you're ready, set him alongside of Dan'l, with his forepaws just even with Dan'l's, and I'll give the word.' Then he says, 'One—two—three—*git!*' and him and the feller touched up the frogs from behind, and the new frog hopped off lively, but Dan'l give a heave, and hysted up his shoulders—so—

---

10. quailshot: Small lead pellets used for shooting quail.

like a Frenchman, but it warn't no use—he couldn't budge; he was planted as solid as a church, and he couldn't no more stir than if he was anchored out. Smiley was a good deal surprised, and he was disgusted too, but he didn't have no idea what the matter was, of course.

The feller took the money and started away; and when he was going out at the door, he sorter jerked his thumb over his shoulder—so—at Dan'l, and says again, very deliberate, 'Well,' he says, '*I* don't see no p'ints about that frog that's any better'n any other frog.'

Smiley he stood scratching his head and looking down at Dan'l a long time, and at last he says, 'I do wonder what in the nation that frog throw'd off for—I wonder if there ain't something the matter with him—he 'pears to look mighty baggy, somehow.' And he ketched Dan'l by the nap of the neck, and hefted him, and says, 'Why blame my cats if he don't weigh five pound!' and turned him upside down and he belched out a double handful of shot. And then he see how it was, and he was the maddest man—he set the frog down and took out after that feller, but he never ketched him. And——"

Here Simon Wheeler heard his name called from the front yard, and got up to see what was wanted. And turning to me as he moved away, he said: "Just set where you are, stranger, and rest easy—I ain't going to be gone a second."

But, by your leave, I did not think that a continuation of the history of the enterprising vagabond *Jim* Smiley would be likely to afford me much information concerning the Rev. *Leonidas W.* Smiley, and so I started away.

At the door I met the sociable Wheeler returning, and he buttonholed me and recommenced:

"Well, thish-yer Smiley had a yaller one-eyed cow that didn't have no tail, only just a short stump like a bannanner, and—"

However, lacking both time and inclination, I did not wait to hear about the afflicted cow, but took my leave.

11

Closure and Extension

ANSWERS TO THINKING ABOUT THE SELECTION
Recalling

1. He is bald and looks peaceful in his slumber.
2. Wheeler starts up and barricades the narrator in a corner forcing him to listen to the tall tale.
3. (a) He was infamous, because he would bet on anything and everything. (b) He loved to gamble.

THINKING ABOUT THE SELECTION
Recalling

1. Describe Simon Wheeler as the narrator encounters him.
2. What happens when the narrator asks Simon Wheeler about Leonidas W. Smiley?
3. (a) Why is Jim Smiley described as infamous? (b) What is Jim Smiley's attitude toward gambling?
4. (a) How did Smiley's mare win races? (b) How did Smiley's bull pup win fights? (c) How did the bull pup finally lose?
5. (a) Why was Smiley proud of his frog? (b) What did a stranger do to the frog? (c) What was Smiley's reaction?

Interpreting

6. The story of Jim Smiley is a frame story—a story presented within the framework of another story. How does Twain's use of this technique contribute to the story's effectiveness?
7. The narrator comments that Wheeler did not imagine "that there was anything ridiculous or funny about his story" and that he regarded it "as a really important matter." How does this add to the humor of the story?
8. (a) How would you describe Simon Wheeler's personality? (b) What makes him an interesting and unusual character?

Applying

9. Why do you think people enjoy telling and listening to tall tales such as the one told by Simon Wheeler?

ANALYZING LITERATURE
Recognizing Humor

In literature, **humor** refers to writing intended to evoke laughter. To accomplish this purpose, western humorists made extensive use of exaggeration and regional dialects in their writing. For example, in "The Notorious Jumping Frog of Calaveras County," Simon Wheeler exaggerates when describing the frog's talents. He describes the frog as if it were intelligent and thoughtful, commenting, "You never see a frog so modest and straightforward as he was, for all he was so gifted."

1. (a) Find two more examples of exaggeration in the story. (b) Explain why each of these examples is amusing.
2. (a) How does Simon Wheeler's use of dialect help make him an amusing and entertaining character? (b) Why would the story be less effective if Wheeler spoke in standard English?
3. In "How to Tell a Story" Mark Twain wrote, "The humorous story may be spun out to great length, and may wander around as much as it pleases, and arrive nowhere in particular . . ." Explain how this technique is evident in this tale.
4. Twain continued, "The humorous story is told gravely; the teller does his best to conceal the fact that he even dimly suspects there is anything funny about it." Explain how this technique is evident in this tale.

CRITICAL THINKING AND READING
Appreciating Dialect

Part of what makes Wheeler's use of **dialect** amusing is his frequently unexpected or unusual choice of words. For example, Wheeler's use of the word *monstrous* to describe the extent of Smiley's pride in his frog is unusual.

What is unexpected or unusual about the choice of words in each of the following passages from the story?
1. "And a dog might tackle him and bullyrag him . . ."
2. "Now if you're ready, set him alongside of Dan'l, with his forepaws just even with Dan'l's . . ."

THINKING AND WRITING
Writing a Story Using Dialect

Imagine that your school literary magazine has asked you to write a story in which the characters speak in a regional dialect. Think of a region in which people speak in a distinctive manner. Then develop a story in which you capture the local color of this region through the use of dialect and vivid descriptions of the setting. When you finish writing, revise your story and share it with your classmates.

ANSWERS TO ANALYZING LITERATURE

1. (a) Suggested Response: In describing Smiley, Wheeler says that in order to win a bet Smiley would go so far as to follow a straddle bug to Mexico just to be sure of his destination and how long it took him to get there. Another example is Wheeler describing the bull pup, Andrew Jackson, as having had genius which he unfortunately could not use because the opportunity never presented itself. (b) To think that a man would actually follow, or even be able to follow, a straddle bug all the way to Mexico brings a funny image to mind. In the second example the idea of genius makes one envision a dog that can stand up and compute mathematical equations. It hardly refers to the instinctive and repetitive behavior involved in dog fights.
2. (a) Suggested Response: His use of dialect makes him seem even more unusual. (b) Wheeler's descriptions would be more straightforward and less colorful, and although the exaggerations would still be there, the particular characters would be less well-defined and not as rich or amusing.
3. Suggested Response: Wheeler's tale is not logically organized, following only Wheeler's seemingly disjointed train of thought.
4. Suggested Response: Wheeler tells the story in a straightforward and serious manner.

ANSWERS TO CRITICAL THINKING AND READING

1. Dogs cannot tackle one another.
2. "Forepaws" is unusual in this context because frog legs are not usually referred to as paws.

THINKING AND WRITING

For help with this assignment, students can refer to Lesson 19, "Writing a Short Story," in the Handbook of Writing About Literature.

Publishing Student Writing Encourage students to submit their stories to your school's literary magazine.

4. (a) Because she was sickly, she was always given a head-start, and after everyone had passed her, she would become excited and barrel past all the other horses, kicking and coughing. (b) He would let the fight go on until the wagers had multiplied, and then he would suddenly grab the hind legs of his opponent and hold on until the other dog gave out. (c) One of his opponents had no hind legs for him to grab so he gave up and died.

5. (a) He was proud of it, because he had trained it to jump farther than any other frog. (b) He filled it with quailshot to weigh it down. (c) He was furious and tried to chase down the stranger.

Interpreting

6. This technique adds to the effectiveness, because Wheeler is an amusing character, and his manner of delivery is humorous.
7. It adds to the humor, because his story clearly was ridiculous.

8. (a) Suggested Response: He seems to be an old, gruff miner on the outside but a gentle soul on the inside. (b) Suggested Response: His knack for telling yarns as if he were spouting the absolute truth and his humorous manner of speaking make him an interesting and unusual character.

Applying

9. Answers will differ. Students may respond that people enjoy seeing how far they can stretch the truth.

Presentation

Motivation/Prior Knowledge
Many students will have read, heard, or seen versions of Huckleberry Finn's story. Ask the students what they already know about him. Have them explain what they think of Huck as one of America's great fictional characters.

Humanities Note

Illustration, *Huck Finn,* by E. W. Kemble. This drawing was done for the first edition of Twain's story by Edward Windsor Kemble (1861–1933). It was produced in 1885. Kemble's choice of medium was pen and ink, the traditional nineteenth-century medium. As can be seen here, he preferred to work with lines—straight, curved, and crosshatched.

This series of pictures about Huck by Kemble is the first of many made for the classic Twain story. In fact, this book has been illustrated by many different artists working in various styles. Although Kemble was the artist chosen by Twain, the book has remained in print long after the author's death, and new editors have chosen new artists. As time went on, the paintings were modernized even though each claimed to be faithful to the essence of Huck's character and time.

You might use the following questions to discuss the art:
1. What aspect of this drawing impresses you most?
2. What do you think would be the most difficult part of this kind of sketch for the artist?

GREAT WORKS

THE ADVENTURES OF HUCKLEBERRY FINN
by Mark Twain

HUCK FINN
E. W. Kemble
The Granger Collection

"It's lovely to live on a raft," says Huckleberry Finn. This statement captures a central image of Mark Twain's masterpiece, *The Adventures of Huckleberry Finn*: a makeshift raft, lazily drifting down a river, its passengers free of all responsibility. Huck continues, "We had the sky up there, all speckled with stars, and we used to lay on our backs and look up at them, and discuss whether they was made, or only just happened—Jim he allowed they was made, but I allowed they happened; I judged it would have took too long to *make* so many."

This is the voice of a simple, unsophisticated boy—a runaway, a boy whom the novel shows to be a highly moral character, one who struggles with his conscience to do what he thinks is right, though society tells him it's wrong.

The Source of Modern American Literature

Ernest Hemingway wrote what is perhaps the most famous assessment of Mark Twain's masterpiece, *The Adventures of Huckleberry Finn*: "All modern American literature comes from one book by Mark Twain called *Huckleberry Finn.* . . . There was nothing before. There has been nothing as good since." One of the pivotal novels in the American tradition, *Huckleberry Finn* influenced a number

LEARNING ABOUT MOSES AND THE 'BULRUSHERS'
E. W. Kemble
The Granger Collection

of later writers, such as Sherwood Anderson, William Faulkner, and Hemingway himself, who all admired Twain's realistic use of colloquial language and first-person narrative. But the novel's roots lie in the tradition of American works about the conflicts among the individual, nature, and society written by such early nineteenth-century writers as James Fenimore Cooper, Henry David Thoreau, and Herman Melville.

"Another Boy's Book"

It took Twain eight years to complete the novel that was to become a turning point in American literature. After finishing *The Adventures of Tom Sawyer* in 1876, Twain began to write what he called "another boy's book" about one of the characters who had appeared in *Tom Sawyer*. "It is Huck Finn's autobiography," he wrote to William Dean Howells, the novelist and editor. But Twain did not think much of this new book. "I like it only tolerably well, as far as I have got, and may possibly pigeonhole or burn the [manuscript] when it is done." For some reason Twain had trouble getting past the middle of the novel and put it aside until 1883, when he began to write more intensely. He finished in 1884, and *The Adventures of Huckleberry Finn* was published in 1885.

The Adventures of Huckleberry Finn is narrated by Huck, an uneducated boy, who is about twelve years old and who lives in Missouri along the banks of the Mississippi River before the Civil War, during slavery days. When the novel opens, Huck is living with the Widow Douglas and her sister, Miss Watson, who have taken in the boy in order to "sivilize" him. But Huck has a hard time living in a home where swearing and smoking are not allowed and where he has to wear clothes and shoes all the time. "[I]t was rough living in the house all the time, considering how dismal regular and decent the widow was in all her ways; and so when I couldn't stand it no longer, I lit out." Huck comes back but manages to sneak out at nights to join his friend Tom Sawyer.

Great Works 513

Fine art, *Discovering the Camp Fire,* by E. W. Kemble. Kemble's pictures are historically valuable as well as interesting because Mark Twain chose the artist and presumably approved his work. These views of Huck are a fair representation of Twain's own vision of his hero. It is safe to assume that Twain enjoyed Kemble's ability to use gestures and body poses to express emotion, action, or character.

You might use the following questions to discuss the art:
1. How demanding do you think an author like Twain would be when it came to selecting artwork to accompany stories?
2. How much liberty should an artist have when illustrating characters from fiction?
3. Do you think it is right that new editions of books change the image of characters?

DISCOVERING THE CAMP FIRE
E. W. Kemble
The Granger Collection

One day Huck's father, the town drunkard, shows up demanding the money that Huck had found in the cave with Tom at the end of *Tom Sawyer.* He takes Huck to live with him in a cabin in the woods, where he mistreats the boy, beating and practically starving him. Huck finally decides to run away. So he stages the first of the several charades he will stage in the course of the novel: He kills a pig and, dragging it to the river, leaves a bloody trail that leads the townspeople to think he is dead.

Huck hides on Jackson's Island, known as a refuge for runaway slaves. There he discovers Jim, Miss Watson's slave, who has run away to escape being sold down South for eight hundred dollars. Huck promises Jim he will not turn him in, and soon they decide to travel by raft along the Mississippi River to the Ohio River, on which they can head North, where Jim could be freed.

514   Realism and the Frontier

Runaways from a Corrupt Society

At this point the novel takes on its central form—the journey along the river—and Twain begins to develop one of his major themes—the contrast between what is actually moral and what, according to society, is legal. Huck and Jim are both refugees from a society that Twain condemns for being corrupt and hypocritical. When Huck decides to do what is morally right and help Jim escape slavery, he is also doing what, according to society's laws, is illegal. Judging by what Huck has been taught in school and in church, helping a slave escape is a crime and a sin. When Huck follows his natural inclination to do good and help Jim, even though he believes he will be condemned, Twain ironically exposes the corruption of social laws and customs.

The rest of the novel unfolds episodically, as a string of events that happen as Huck and Jim make their way along the Mississippi. As their relationship develops, Jim becomes a father to the boy, while Huck grows morally as he learns to treat the black man with respect. Their life on the raft is in many ways idyllic. They spend their days "lazying around, listening to the stillness." Nights are spent in watching the twinkling lights on the shore, stargazing, and talking.

Morality and the River

Away from "sivilization," slavery does not violate the natural ties between two human beings. Critics have remarked that the raft floating downriver represents the state of innocence and beauty that Twain felt was still present in nature away from the decadence of society. In these scenes Twain was also drawing upon the nostalgic memories of his own youthful days as a steamboat pilot, depicted in *Life on the Mississippi.*

However, the idyllic portions of their journey are interrupted whenever Huck and

Jim encounter society—whether it is a steamboat that breaks up their raft or involvement with people onshore. Twain uses these encounters with society to expose the moral bankruptcy of human nature when it is driven by greed, ambition, and false sentimentality. Among the more famous episodes are those involving the Shepherdsons and Grangerfords, two families who have been killing each other for years in a feud whose origins are obscure; and the Duke and King, a pair of con men who journey from town to town, duping people out of their money. Each episode reveals how corrupt human nature in society can be. After each disillusioning encounter, Huck retreats to the haven of Jim and the raft.

The Search for Identity

The journey on the river is, therefore, a moral journey for Huck Finn. But it also represents his search for identity, a theme that is common in American literature. With each assault by society upon his moral consciousness, Huck is forced to invent a different story about his parentage, his name, his purpose in being where he is. With these shifts in identity, Twain develops the important theme of the search for the self in society. Only in nature can Huck be his natural self. But in society, the individual is distorted and falsified.

After many complications and dangers, the novel ends with Jim's freedom. Huck, also, seeks freedom for himself. As he writes, ". . . there ain't nothing more to write about, and I am rotten glad of it, because if I'd knowed what a trouble it was to make a book I wouldn't tackle it and ain't agoing to no more. But I reckon I got to light out for the Territory ahead of the rest, because Aunt Sally she's going to adopt me and sivilize me and I can't stand it. I been there before."

Focus

More About the Author Bret Harte's lesser works have been criticized for being too sentimental. Indeed, at eleven years of age when he published his first poem ("Autumn Musings") in the *Sunday Morning Atlas*, members of his family criticized it for being too emotional. Harte later said "I sometimes wonder that I ever wrote another line of verse." Have students discuss the difference between sentiment and sentimentality. How can excessive sentimentality spoil a piece of literature?

Critical Evaluation Richard O'Connor, a biographer of Harte, reports the following: "Kipling said he owed 'many things' to the storyteller's art he learned from reading Harte . . . [and] H.L. Mencken believed he was entitled to a 'sort of immortality' . . . and the even tougher critic Ambrose Bierce granted Harte a place 'very close to the head' of all American writers."

ESL Teaching Strategy Pair each ESL student with a non-ESL partner in class. Have each couple compose a list of words, like *rodeo* or *holster,* associated with the wild west. Then have the non-ESL students teach their partners the correct meaning of each word.

1836–1902

Though relatively few of his stories were successful, Bret Harte played an important role in creating a vivid, lasting portrait of the old West. Harte's stories, filled with intriguing characters and colorful dialogue, provided much of post-Civil-War America with its first glimpse into western life and established the old West as a popular literary setting.

Harte was born and raised in Albany, New York. In 1854, when he was eighteen, he traveled across the country to California. During his first few years in California, a land in a turbulent period of rapid growth brought about by the discovery of gold in 1848, Harte worked as a schoolteacher, tutor, messenger, clerk, and prospector. While Harte's life seemed to have little direction at the time, his observations of the rugged, often violent life in the mining camps and the towns and cities of the new frontier provided him with the inspiration for his most successful short stories.

After working as a typesetter and writer for two California periodicals and publishing two books of verse, *Outcroppings* (1856) and *The Lost Galleon* (1867), Harte became the editor of the *Overland Monthly,* a new literary magazine, in 1868. When Harte published his story "The Luck of Roaring Camp" in the magazine's second issue, he immediately became famous, as the American public, eager to learn about life in the new frontier, responded to the story with enthusiasm. Over the next two years, Harte published "The Outcasts of Poker Flat" and several other similar stories in the *Overland Monthly,* and his popularity grew at a rapid pace.

Following the publication of *The Luck of Roaring Camp and Other Sketches* in 1870, Harte's popularity reached its peak. In 1871 the *Atlantic Monthly,* a distinguished literary magazine, contracted to pay Harte $10,000 for any twelve sketches or stories he contributed over the next year. Harte returned to the East to fulfill his contract, but the stories he wrote were flat and disappointing compared with his earlier work, and his celebrity waned almost as quickly as it had grown.

Harte continued to publish stories, short novels, and plays during the next twenty years, but for the most part, his later work was unsuccessful. From 1878 to 1885, he was a diplomat in Germany and Scotland. He then retired to London, where he lived for the remainder of his life.

516 Realism and the Frontier

Objectives

1 To recognize Regionalism
2 To make inferences about attitudes
3 To compare and contrast characters

Support Material

Teaching Portfolio
Teacher Backup, p. 681
Grammar in Action Worksheet, *Using Coordinating Conjunctions,* p. 685
Usage and Mechanics Worksheet, p. 687
Vocabulary Check, p. 688
Analyzing Literature Worksheet, *Understanding Regional Literature,* p. 690

Critical Thinking and Reading Worksheet, *Making Inferences About Cultural Attitudes,* p. 691
Selection Test, p. 692

GUIDE FOR INTERPRETING

The Outcasts of Poker Flat

Literary Movements

Regionalism. The habits, speech, appearance, customs, and beliefs of people from one geographical region often differ from those of people from other areas. Regional literature captures the essence of life in a particular area, the "local color" of a region, by accurately depicting the distinctive qualities of its people and including vivid, realistic descriptions of the physical appearance of the environment.

During the nineteenth century, the United States grew at a rapid rate. New regions developed as a steady flow of immigrants settled across the land, and as a result the American population became more and more diverse. As the country grew and became more diversified, the American public became curious about the people and the style of life in different parts of the country. Regional literature like "The Outcasts of Poker Flat" satisfied their curiosity.

Commentary

As you read "The Outcasts of Poker Flat," you may wonder how true-to-life Mr. Oakhurst, a gambler and the story's main character, is. Mr. Oakhurst, a generous, genial man who is seemingly nonchalant in the face of danger, is the hero of two of Harte's stories.

Contemporary historian C. W. Haskins supported Harte's description of Mr. Oakhurst. California gamblers, he wrote, "were usually from New Orleans, Louisville, Memphis, Richmond, or St. Louis. Not infrequently they were well-born and well-educated, and among them were as many good, honest, square-dealing men as could be found in any other business; and they were, as a rule, more charitable and more ready to help those in distress."

Harte's biographer Henry Childs Merwin described a gambler named Lucky Bill who demonstrated traits similar to Mr. Oakhurst's. According to Merwin, Lucky Bill "was noted for his generosity, and, though finally hanged by a vigilance committee, he made a 'good end,' for, on the scaffold, he exhorted his son who was among the spectators, to avoid bad company, to keep away from saloons, and to lead an industrious and honest life."

What characteristics do you associate with frontier gamblers? How closely do these characteristics match those described by C. W. Haskins and Henry Childs Merwin?

Writing

Brainstorm for several minutes about films, books, and other sources of your impressions of the old West. Then make a list of typical characters, clothing, speech, situations, and scenic details that you associate with the old West.

Guide for Interpreting 517

Literary Focus To illustrate the idea of Regionalism, suggest to students that they make a list of details that they might use in a story set in their hometown. Can they think of aspects of culture, speech, landscape, and character which are unique to their part of the country? Have students discuss their lists.

Writing/Prior Knowledge Have students share their lists with their classmates.

Vocabulary

Preteach the following vocabulary words:

expatriated (eks pā′ trē āt′ id) *adj.:* Deported; driven from one's native land (p. 518)

anathema (ə nath′ ə mə): *n.:* Curse (p. 518)

bellicose (bel′ ə kōs) *adj.:* Quarrelsome (p. 520)

recumbent (ri kum′ bənt) *adj.:* Resting (p. 520)

equanimity (ek′ wə nim′ ə tē) *n.:* Composure (p. 520)

vociferation (vō sif′ ə rā shən) *n.:* Loud or vehement shouting (p. 522)

vituperative (vī too′ prə tiv) *adj.:* Spoken abusively (p. 523)

querulous (kwer′ ə ləs) *adj.:* Inclined to find fault (p. 523)

The Outcasts of Poker Flat

Bret Harte

As Mr. John Oakhurst, gambler, stepped into the main street of Poker Flat on the morning of the twenty-third of November, 1850, he was conscious of a change in its moral atmosphere since the preceding night. Two or three men, conversing earnestly together, ceased as he approached, and exchanged significant glances. There was a Sabbath lull in the air which, in a settlement unused to Sabbath influences, looked ominous.

Mr. Oakhurst's calm, handsome face betrayed small concern in these indications. Whether he was conscious of any predisposing cause was another question. "I reckon they're after somebody," he reflected; "likely it's me." He returned to his pocket the handkerchief with which he had been whipping away the red dust of Poker Flat from his neat boots, and quietly discharged his mind of any further conjecture.

In point of fact, Poker Flat was "after somebody." It had lately suffered the loss of several thousand dollars, two valuable horses, and a prominent citizen. It was experiencing a spasm of virtuous reaction, quite as lawless and ungovernable as any of the acts that had provoked it. A secret committee had determined to rid the town of all improper persons. This was done permanently in regard of two men who were then hanging from the boughs of a sycamore in the gulch, and temporarily in the banishment of certain other objectionable characters. I regret to say that some of these were ladies. It is but due to the sex, however, to state that their impropriety was professional, and it was only in such easily established standards of evil that Poker Flat ventured to sit in judgment.

Mr. Oakhurst was right in supposing that he was included in this category. A few of the committee had urged hanging him as a possible example, and a sure method of reimbursing themselves from his pockets of the sums he had won from them. "It's agin justice," said Jim Wheeler, "to let this yer young man from Roaring Camp—an entire stranger—carry away our money." But a crude sentiment of equity residing in the breasts of those who had been fortunate enough to win from Mr. Oakhurst overruled this narrower local prejudice.

Mr. Oakhurst received his sentence with philosophic calmness, none the less coolly that he was aware of the hesitation of his judges. He was too much of a gambler not to accept Fate. With him life was at best an uncertain game, and he recognized the usual percentage in favor of the dealer.

A body of armed men accompanied the deported wickedness of Poker Flat to the outskirts of the settlement. Besides Mr. Oakhurst, who was known to be a coolly desperate man, and for whose intimidation the armed escort was intended, the expatriated party consisted of a young woman familiarly known as the "Duchess"; another, who had won the title of "Mother Shipton";[1] and "Uncle Billy," a suspected sluice robber[2] and

---

1. **"Mother Shipton":** An English woman who lived in the sixteenth century and was suspected of being a witch.
2. **sluice robber:** A person who steals gold from sluices, long troughs used for sifting gold.

THE EDGE OF TOWN
Charles Burchfield
Collection of the Kelson-Atkins Museum of Art, Kansas City

5 Reading Strategy Have students discuss the group of outcasts. How do they think the characters will fare together?

Humanities Note

Fine art, *The Edge of Town,* by Charles Burchfield. The unique and individual style of Charles Burchfield (1893–1967) was developed at the Cleveland Institute of Art, where he studied painting. Through his poetic and introspective paintings he describes the invisible forces of nature and the mysterious inner life of buildings.

The watercolor *The Edge of Town* is the last of Burchfield's "main street" paintings. This view of a small-town street on a bleak winter day is filled with the mysterious presence and tension typical of Burchfield. The buildings glow with dull light in eerie contrast to the stormy sky. The figures seem static and so become mere elements of the landscape like stones or bushes. The sky seems the only living force with its roiling clouds changing tones. This painting demonstrates that Charles Burchfield did not relinquish his intense fascination with nature even when painting a human scene.

Consider using the following questions for discussion:
1. What is the mood of the painting?
2. How does the mood of the painting echo the mood of the story?

confirmed drunkard. The cavalcade provoked no comments from the spectators, nor was any word uttered by the escort. Only, when the gulch which marked the uttermost limit of Poker Flat was reached, the leader spoke briefly and to the point. The exiles were forbidden to return at the peril of their lives.

As the escort disappeared, their pent-up feelings found vent in a few hysterical tears from the Duchess, some bad language from Mother Shipton, and a Parthian volley of expletives[3] from Uncle Billy. The philosophic Oakhurst alone remained silent. He listened calmly to Mother Shipton's desire to cut somebody's heart out, to the repeated statements of the Duchess that she would die in the road, and to the alarming oaths that seemed to be bumped out of Uncle Billy as he rode forward. With the easy good humor characteristic of his class, he insisted upon exchanging his own riding horse, "Five Spot," for the sorry mule which the Duchess rode. But even this act did not draw the party into any closer sympathy. The young woman readjusted her somewhat draggled plumes with a feeble, faded coquetry; Mother Shipton eyed the possessor of "Five Spot" with malevolence, and Uncle Billy included the whole party in one sweeping anathema.

The road to Sandy Bar—a camp that, not having as yet experienced the regenerating influences of Poker Flat, consequently seemed to offer some invitation to the emigrants—lay over a steep mountain range. It was distant a day's severe travel. In that advanced season, the party soon passed out of

---

3. Parthian ... expletives: Hostile remarks made while leaving. The Parthians were an ancient society whose cavalrymen usually shot at the enemy while retreating or pretending to retreat.

The Outcasts of Poker Flat 519

6 **Reading Strategy** Have students discuss the character of Mr. Oakhurst. What paradoxes exist in his personality? Why do students think he chose to be a gambler by trade?

7 **Reading Strategy** Have students discuss the character of Tom Simson. How is he different from Mr. Oakhurst? What qualities do they share?

the moist, temperate regions of the foothills into the dry, cold, bracing air of the Sierras.[4] The trail was narrow and difficult. At noon the Duchess, rolling out of her saddle upon the ground, declared her intention of going no farther, and the party halted.

The spot was singularly wild and impressive. A wooded amphitheater, surrounded on three sides by precipitous cliffs of naked granite, sloped gently toward the crest of another precipice that overlooked the valley. It was, undoubtedly, the most suitable spot for a camp, had camping been advisable. But Mr. Oakhurst knew that scarcely half the journey to Sandy Bar was accomplished, and the party were not equipped or provisioned for delay. This fact he pointed out to his companions curtly, with a philosophic commentary on the folly of "throwing up their hand before the game was played out." But they were furnished with liquor, which in this emergency stood them in place of food, fuel, rest, and prescience. In spite of his remonstrances, it was not long before they were more or less under its influence. Uncle Billy passed rapidly from a bellicose state into one of stupor, the Duchess became maudlin, and Mother Shipton snored. Mr. Oakhurst alone remained erect, leaning against a rock calmly surveying them.

6 Mr. Oakhurst did not drink. It interfered with a profession which required coolness, impassiveness, and presence of mind, and, in his own language, he "couldn't afford it." As he gazed at his recumbent fellow exiles, the loneliness begotten of his pariah trade, his habits of life, his very vices, for the first time seriously oppressed him. He bestirred himself in dusting his black clothes, washing his hands and face, and other acts characteristic of his studiously neat habits, and for a moment forgot his annoyance. The thought of deserting his weaker and more pitiable companions never perhaps occurred to him. Yet he could not help feeling the want of that excitement which singularly

---

4. **Sierras** (sē er′ əz): Mountains in eastern California, also called the Sierra Nevadas.

enough, was most conducive to that calm equanimity for which he was notorious. He looked at the gloomy walls that rose a thousand feet sheer above the circling pines around him; at the sky, ominously clouded; at the valley below, already deepening into shadow. And, doing so, suddenly he heard his own name called.

A horseman slowly ascended the trail. In the fresh, open face of the newcomer Mr. Oakhurst recognized Tom Simson, otherwise known as the "Innocent" of Sandy Bar. He had met him some months before over a "little game," and had, with perfect equanimity, won the entire fortune—amounting to some forty dollars—of that guileless youth. After the game was finished, Mr. Oakhurst drew the youthful speculator behind the door and thus addressed him: "Tommy, you're a good little man, but you can't gamble worth a cent. Don't try it over again." He then handed him his money back, pushed him gently from the room, and so made a devoted slave of Tom Simson.

7

There was a remembrance of this in his boyish and enthusiastic greeting of Mr. Oakhurst. He had started, he said, to go to Poker Flat to seek his fortune. "Alone?" No, not exactly alone; in fact (a giggle), he had run away with Piney Woods. Didn't Mr. Oakhurst remember Piney? She that used to wait on the table at the Temperance House? They had been engaged a long time, but old Jake Woods had objected, and so they had run away, and were going to Poker Flat to be married, and here they were. And they were tired out, and how lucky it was they had found a place to camp and company. All this the Innocent delivered rapidly, while Piney, a stout, comely damsel of fifteen, emerged from behind the pine tree, where she had been blushing unseen, and rode to the side of her lover.

Mr. Oakhurst seldom troubled himself with sentiment, still less with propriety; but he had a vague idea that the situation was not fortunate. He retained, however, his presence of mind sufficiently to kick Uncle Billy, who was about to say something, and

---

Primary Source

Richard O'Connor, author of a biography on Bret Harte, relates the following anecdote in an attempt to convey the role of chance in life and death that interested his subject so much.

It is of greater consequence in human affairs that Harte was translated into Russian, among many other languages, and that one of his Russian admirers was, quite unaccountably, Joseph Stalin. Ordinarily the least suggestible and romantic of men, Stalin decided in 1927, after reading Harte's stories of the California gold rush, to set up a gold trust and reopen the Siberian mines. Ten years later the Siberian gold mines were producing $183,000,000 annually, and since then the Soviet Union has been able to survive numerous setbacks . . . by the continuous river of gold flowing from Siberia. Few writers in history have produced an impact to equal that.

Uncle Billy was sober enough to recognize in Mr. Oakhurst's kick a superior power that would not bear trifling. He then endeavored to dissuade Tom Simson from delaying further, but in vain. He even pointed out the fact that there was no provision, nor means of making a camp. But, unluckily, the Innocent met this objection by assuring the party that he was provided with an extra mule loaded with provisions and by the discovery of a rude attempt at a log house near the trail. "Piney can stay with Mrs. Oakhurst," said the Innocent, pointing to the Duchess, "and I can shift for myself."

Nothing but Mr. Oakhurst's admonishing foot saved Uncle Billy from bursting into a roar of laughter. As it was, he felt compelled to retire up the canyon until he could recover his gravity. There he confided the joke to the tall pine trees, with many slaps of his leg, contortions of his face, and the usual profanity. But when he returned to the party, he found them seated by a fire—for the air had grown strangely chill and the sky overcast—in apparently amicable conversation. Piney was actually talking in an impulsive, girlish fashion to the Duchess, who was listening with an interest and animation she had not shown for many days. The Innocent was holding forth, apparently with equal effect, to Mr. Oakhurst and Mother Shipton, who was actually relaxing into amiability. "Is this yer a d—d picnic?" said Uncle Billy with inward scorn as he surveyed the sylvan[5] group, the glancing firelight, and the tethered animals in the foreground. Suddenly an idea mingled with the alcoholic fumes that disturbed his brain. It was apparently of a jocular nature, for he felt impelled to slap his leg again and cram his fist into his mouth.

As the shadows crept slowly up the mountain, a slight breeze rocked the tops of the pine trees, and moaned through their long and gloomy aisles. The ruined cabin, patched and covered with pine boughs, was set apart for the ladies. As the lovers parted, they unaffectedly exchanged a kiss, so honest and sincere that it might have been heard above the swaying pines. The frail Duchess and the malevolent Mother Shipton were probably too stunned to remark upon this last evidence of simplicity, and so turned without a word to the hut. The fire was replenished, the men lay down before the door, and in a few minutes were asleep.

Mr. Oakhurst was a light sleeper. Toward morning he awoke benumbed and cold. As he stirred the dying fire, the wind, which was now blowing strongly, brought to his cheek that which caused the blood to leave it—snow!

He started to his feet with the intention of awakening the sleepers, for there was no time to lose. But turning to where Uncle Billy had been lying, he found him gone. A suspicion leaped to his brain and a curse to his lips. He ran to the spot where the mules had been tethered; they were no longer there. The tracks were already rapidly disappearing in the snow.

The momentary excitement brought Mr. Oakhurst back to the fire with his usual calm. He did not waken the sleepers. The Innocent slumbered peacefully, with a smile on his good-humored, freckled face; the virgin Piney slept beside her frailer sisters as sweetly as though attended by celestial guardians; and Mr. Oakhurst, drawing his blanket over his shoulders, stroked his mustaches and waited for the dawn. It came slowly in a whirling mist of snowflakes that dazzled and confused the eye. What could be seen of the landscape appeared magically changed. He looked over the valley, and summed up the present and future in two words—"snowed in!"

A careful inventory of the provisions, which, fortunately for the party, had been stored within the hut and so escaped the felonious fingers of Uncle Billy, disclosed the fact that with care and prudence they might last ten days longer. "That is," said Mr. Oakhurst, sotto voce[6] to the Innocent, "if you're willing to board us. If you ain't—and

---

5. **sylvan** (sil′vən) *adj*.: Characteristic of the forest.

6. **sotto voce** (sät′ ō vō′ chē): In an undertone.

8 **Critical Thinking and Reading** Ask students how this paragraph hints at what is to come in the story. Make sure they notice the chill in the air which indicates the coming storm, the beginning of changes in the Duchess and Mother Shipton, and Uncle Billy's idea, which later turns out to have been to steal the horses and mules.

9 **Reading Strategy** Have students summarize what has happened in the story so far.

10 **Discussion** Why does Mr. Oakhurst choose not to tell Tom the truth about Uncle Billy's actions?

11 **Discussion** What is ironic about this song? How does it foreshadow the end of the story?

12 **Discussion** Discuss Mr. Oakhurst's views on luck. How do they tie in with his opinion of fate?

perhaps you'd better not—you can wait till Uncle Billy gets back with provisions." For some occult reason, Mr. Oakhurst could not bring himself to disclose Uncle Billy's rascality, and so offered the hypothesis that he had wandered from the camp and had accidentally stampeded the animals. He dropped a warning to the Duchess and Mother Shipton, who of course knew the facts of their associate's defection. "They'll find out the truth about us *all* when they find out anything," he added, significantly, "and there's no good frightening them now."

Tom Simson not only put all his worldly store at the disposal of Mr. Oakhurst, but seemed to enjoy the prospect of their enforced seclusion. "We'll have a good camp for a week, and then the snow'll melt, and we'll all go back together." The cheerful gaiety of the young man, and Mr. Oakhurst's calm, infected the others. The Innocent with the aid of pine boughs extemporized a thatch for the roofless cabin, and the Duchess directed Piney in the rearrangement of the interior with a taste and tact that opened the blue eyes of that provincial maiden to their fullest extent. "I reckon now you're used to fine things at Poker Flat," said Piney. The Duchess turned away sharply to conceal something that reddened her cheeks through its professional tint, and Mother Shipton requested Piney not to "chatter." But when Mr. Oakhurst returned from a weary search for the trail, he heard the sound of happy laughter echoed from the rocks. He stopped in some alarm, and his thoughts first naturally reverted to the whisky, which he had prudently cached.[7] "And yet it don't somehow sound like whisky," said the gambler. It was not until he caught sight of the blazing fire through the still-blinding storm and the group around it that he settled to the conviction that it was "square fun."

Whether Mr. Oakhurst had cached his cards with the whisky as something debarred the free access of the community, I cannot say. It was certain that, in Mother

---

7. **cached** (kasht) *v*.: Hidden.

Shipton's words, he "didn't say cards once" during that evening. Haply the time was beguiled by an accordion, produced somewhat ostentatiously by Tom Simson from his pack. Notwithstanding some difficulties attending the manipulation of this instrument, Piney Woods managed to pluck several reluctant melodies from its keys, to an accompaniment by the Innocent on a pair of bone castanets. But the crowning festivity of the evening was reached in a rude camp-meeting hymn, which the lovers, joining hands, sang with great earnestness and vociferation. I fear that a certain defiant tone and Covenanter's[8] swing to its chorus, rather than any devotional quality, caused it speedily to infect the others, who at last joined in the refrain:

"I'm proud to live in the service
  of the Lord,
And I'm bound to die in
  His army."[9]

The pines rocked, the storm eddied and whirled above the miserable group, and the flames of their altar leaped heavenward as if in token of the vow.

At midnight the storm abated, the rolling clouds parted, and the stars glittered keenly above the sleeping camp. Mr. Oakhurst, whose professional habits had enabled him to live on the smallest possible amount of sleep, in dividing the watch with Tom Simson somehow managed to take upon himself the greater part of that duty. He excused himself to the Innocent by saying that he had "often been a week without sleep." "Doing what?" asked Tom. "Poker!" replied Oakhurst, sententiously; "when a man gets a streak of luck, he don't get tired. The luck gives in first. Luck," continued the gambler, reflectively, "is a mighty queer thing. All you know about it for certain is

---

8. **Covenanter's** (kuv' ə nan' tərz): Seventeenth-century Scottish Presbyterians who resisted the rule of the Church of England.
9. **"I'm . . . army":** Lines from the early American spiritual "Service of the Lord."

Grammar in Action

Coordinating conjunctions are words writers use to join related clauses of equal rank. These conjunctions—*and, but, for, nor, or, so,* and *yet*—join the related clauses more tightly than a semicolon. A comma precedes the coordinating conjunction when it joins two clauses. Here are some examples from "The Outcasts of Poker Flat":

With him life was at best an uncertain game, *and* he

recognized the unusual percentage in favor of the dealer.

The cavalcade provoked no comments from the spectators, *nor* was any word uttered by the escort.

He started to his feet with the intention of awakening the sleepers, *for* there was no time to lose.

Student Activity 1. On pages 522–523, find five more examples of clauses joined by coordinating conjunctions. Identify the subject and verb in each clause to ensure that the examples chosen are coordinated clauses.

that it's bound to change. And it's finding out when it's going to change that makes you. We've had a streak of bad luck since we left Poker Flat—you come along, and slap you get into it, too. If you can hold your cards right along you're all right. For," added the gambler, with cheerful irrelevance,

>" 'I'm proud to live in the service
>   of the Lord,
>And I'm bound to die in
>   His army.' "

The third day came, and the sun, looking through the white-curtained valley, saw the outcasts divide their slowly decreasing store of provisions for the morning meal. It was one of the peculiarities of that mountain climate that its rays diffused a kindly warmth over the wintry landscape, as if in regretful commiseration of the past. But it revealed drift on drift of snow piled high around the hut—a hopeless, uncharted, trackless sea of white lying below the rocky shores to which the castaways still clung. Through the marvelously clear air the smoke of the pastoral village of Poker Flat rose miles away. Mother Shipton saw it, and from a remote pinnacle of her rocky fastness hurled in that direction a final malediction. It was her last vituperative attempt, and perhaps for that reason was invested with a certain degree of sublimity. It did her good, she privately informed the Duchess. "Just you go out there and cuss, and see." She then set herself to the task of amusing "the child," as she and the Duchess were pleased to call Piney. Piney was no chicken, but it was a soothing and original theory of the pair thus to account for the fact that she didn't swear and wasn't improper.

When night crept up again through the gorges, the reedy notes of the accordion rose and fell in fitful spasms and long-drawn gasps by the flickering campfire. But music failed to fill entirely the aching void left by insufficient food, and a new diversion was proposed by Piney—storytelling. Neither Mr. Oakhurst nor his female companions caring to relate their personal experiences, this plan would have failed too but for the Innocent. Some months before he had chanced upon a stray copy of Mr. Pope's[10] ingenious translation of the *Iliad*.[11] He now proposed to narrate the principal incidents of that poem—having thoroughly mastered the argument and fairly forgotten the words—in the current vernacular of Sandy Bar. And so for the rest of that night the Homeric demigods again walked the earth. Trojan bully and wily Greek wrestled in the winds, and the great pines in the canyon seemed to bow to the wrath of the son of Peleus.[12] Mr. Oakhurst listened with quiet satisfaction. Most especially was he interested in the fate of "Ash-heels," as the Innocent persisted in denominating the "swift-footed Achilles."

So with small food and much of Homer and the accordion, a week passed over the heads of the outcasts. The sun again forsook them, and again from leaden skies the snowflakes were sifted over the land. Day by day closer around them drew the snowy circle, until at last they looked from their prison over drifted walls of dazzling white that towered twenty feet above their heads. It became more and more difficult to replenish their fires, even from the fallen trees beside them, now half-hidden in the drifts. And yet no one complained. The lovers turned from the dreary prospect and looked into each other's eyes, and were happy. Mr. Oakhurst settled himself coolly to the losing game before him. The Duchess, more cheerful than she had been, assumed the care of Piney. Only Mother Shipton—once the strongest of the party—seemed to sicken and fade. At midnight on the tenth day she called Oakhurst to her side. "I'm going," she said, in a voice of querulous weakness, "but don't say anything about it. Don't waken the kids. Take the bundle from under my head and open

---

10. Mr. Pope: English poet Alexander Pope (1688–1744).
11. Iliad (il' ē əd): Greek epic poem written by Homer that tells the story of the Trojan War.
12. son of Peleus (pēl' ōōs): Achilles (ə kil' ēz), the Greek warrior hero in the *Iliad*.

The Outcasts of Poker Flat 523

13 **Reading Strategy** Ask students if they see any change in the character of Mother Shipton. Does this passage indicate that she will continue to change?

14 **Discussion** What has Mother Shipton done? Why has she done it? What does this action reveal about her character?

Student Activity 2. Combine each pair of sentences with a coordinating conjunction. Remember to place a comma after the first clause.
1. They had been engaged a long time.
   Old Jake Woods had objected.
2. The accordian and the bones were put aside that day.
   Homer was forgotten.
3. The tears rose to her eyes.
   She hid them from Piney.
4. They slept all that day and the next.
   They did not waken when voices and footsteps broke the silence of the camp.

15 Discussion Contrast the Duchess's character at the beginning of the story with her character at the end. What changed her?

16 Critical Thinking and Reading Point out to students how this passage emphasizes the changes in the personalities of the outcasts.

17 Discussion What is ironic about this statement? What has been the role of the law of Poker Flat in the story?

Reader's Response Can you describe some adverse experience that provided a chance for you to be helpful to others?

it." Mr. Oakhurst did so. It contained Mother Shipton's rations for the last week, untouched. "Give 'em to the child," she said, pointing to the sleeping Piney. "You've starved yourself," said the gambler. "That's what they call it," said the woman, querulously, as she lay down again and, turning her face to the wall, passed quietly away.

The accordion and the bones were put aside that day, and Homer was forgotten. When the body of Mother Shipton had been committed to the snow, Mr. Oakhurst took the Innocent aside, and showed him a pair of snowshoes, which he had fashioned from the old pack saddle. "There's one chance in a hundred to save her yet," he said, pointing to Piney; "but it's there," he added, pointing toward Poker Flat. "If you can reach there in two days she's safe." "And you?" asked Tom Simson. "I'll stay here," was the curt reply.

15 The lovers parted with a long embrace. "You are not going, too?" said the Duchess as she saw Mr. Oakhurst apparently waiting to accompany him. "As far as the canyon," he replied. He turned suddenly, and kissed the Duchess, leaving her pallid face aflame and her trembling limbs rigid with amazement.

Night came, but not Mr. Oakhurst. It brought the storm again and the whirling snow. Then the Duchess, feeding the fire, found that someone had quietly piled beside the hut enough fuel to last a few days longer. The tears rose to her eyes, but she hid them from Piney.

The women slept but little. In the morning, looking into each other's faces, they read their fate. Neither spoke; but Piney, accepting the position of the stronger, drew near and placed her arm around the Duchess's waist. They kept this attitude for the rest of the day. That night the storm reached its greatest fury, and, rending asunder the protecting pines, invaded the very hut.

Toward morning they found themselves unable to feed the fire, which gradually died away. As the embers slowly blackened, the Duchess crept closer to Piney, and broke the silence of many hours: "Piney, can you

524 *Realism and the Frontier*

pray?" "No, dear," said Piney, simply. The Duchess, without knowing exactly why, felt relieved, and, putting her head upon Piney's shoulder, spoke no more. And so reclining, the younger and purer pillowing the head of her soiled sister upon her virgin breast, they fell asleep.

The wind lulled as if it feared to waken them. Feathery drifts of snow, shaken from the long pine boughs, flew like white-winged birds, and settled about them as they slept. The moon through the rifted clouds looked down upon what had been the camp. But all human stain, all trace of earthly travail, was hidden beneath the spotless mantle mercifully flung from above. **16**

They slept all that day and the next, nor did they waken when voices and footsteps broke the silence of the camp. And when pitying fingers brushed the snow from their wan faces, you could scarcely have told from the equal peace that dwelt upon them which was she that had sinned. Even the law of Poker Flat recognized this, and turned away, **17** leaving them still locked in each other's arms.

But at the head of the gulch, on one of the largest pine trees, they found the deuce of clubs pinned to the bark with a bowie knife. It bore the following, written in pencil, in a firm hand:

✝

BENEATH THIS TREE
LIES THE BODY
OF
JOHN OAKHURST,
WHO STRUCK A STREAK OF BAD LUCK
ON THE 23D OF NOVEMBER, 1850,
AND
HANDED IN HIS CHECKS
ON THE 7TH DECEMBER, 1850.

✝

And pulseless and cold, with a Derringer[13] by his side and a bullet in his heart, though still calm as in life, beneath the snow lay he who was at once the strongest and yet the weakest of the outcasts of Poker Flat.

---

13. Derringer: A small pistol.

Closure and Extension

ANSWERS TO THINKING ABOUT THE SELECTION
Recalling

1. (a) The committee had decided to "rid the town of all improper persons." (b) John Oakhurst, a gambler, was escorted to the outskirts of town along with two women and a suspected thief who was also a drunkard.

THINKING ABOUT THE SELECTION

Recalling

1. (a) At the opening of the story, what has the secret committee of Poker Flat decided? (b) Who is in the party escorted to the outskirts of town?
2. (a) Who joins the outcasts at their camp? (b) Why are the new arrivals headed for Poker Flat?
3. What does Mr. Oakhurst discover when he awakens after his first night at the camp?
4. What does Mother Shipton do with her rations?
5. (a) In what condition are Piney and the Duchess when the rescue party arrives? (b) What else does the rescue party discover?

Interpreting

6. (a) What does Harte's statement that Poker Flat "was experiencing a spasm of virtuous reaction, quite as lawless as the acts that provoked it" suggest about his attitude toward the secret committee's decision? (b) What motivates the committee to take action against Mr. Oakhurst?
7. (a) How is Oakhurst's occupation reflected in his attitude toward life? (b) What does Harte mean when he writes that Oakhurst "was at once the strongest and yet the weakest of the outcasts of Poker Flat"?
8. How do Mother Shipton and the Duchess change over the course of the story?

Applying

9. Though the characters in this story have little in common, they band together in support of one another. What kind of situations tend to draw people together in real life?

ANALYZING LITERATURE

Understanding Regional Literature

Regional literature captures the distinctive atmosphere, or "local color," of a particular area by accurately depicting the habits, speech, appearance, customs, and beliefs of its people and vividly describing its appearance.

1. What specific details of the setting does Harte use to create a portrait of the California landscape?
2. Find three examples of a character's use of western dialect.
3. Explain why the story would not be effective if the setting were changed, for example, to New England.

CRITICAL THINKING AND READING

Making Inferences About Attitudes

Cultural attitudes and customs are important aspects of local color. In most cases, however, the distinctive attitudes and customs in regional literature are not explicitly stated by the author. As a result, you must make inferences, or draw conclusions, about the attitudes and customs being depicted by examining the characters' actions, thoughts, and comments.

What inferences about the attitudes and customs of the people of Poker Flat can you make from each of the following passages?

1. "A few of the committee had urged hanging him as a possible example, and a sure method of reimbursing themselves from his pocket of the sums he had won from them."
2. " 'It's a fine justice,' said Jim Wheeler, 'to let this yer young man—an entire stranger—carry away our money.' "

THINKING AND WRITING

Comparing and Contrasting Characters

Think of a character from a western movie, novel, or television series who is in some ways similar to John Oakhurst. In your prewriting, list the similarities and differences between Oakhurst and the character you have chosen. After preparing a thesis statement, write an essay comparing and contrasting the two characters. When you revise, make sure you have included enough information to support your thesis.

The Outcasts of Poker Flat 525

upon them which was she that had sinned."

Applying

9. Answers will differ. Students might comment that people tend to be drawn together by difficult circumstances.

Challenge Would this story be effective if Harte had used a different setting? Why or why not?

ANSWERS TO ANALYZING LITERATURE

1. Some examples are: "the red dust of Poker Flat"; Sandy Bar lay over "a steep mountain range", and Harte's description of the place where the outcasts stop.
2. Some examples are Jim Wheeler's comment that "it's agin justice"; Uncle Billy's question, "is this yer a d—d picnic"; and Piney's comment, "I reckon now you're used to fine things at Poker Flat."
3. Suggested Response: It would not be effective in a different setting, because the characters and events would not be believable and the western flavor that makes the story interesting would be lost.

ANSWERS TO CRITICAL THINKING AND READING

1. Suggested Response: They have a distorted conception of justice and try to use the concept of justice only to serve their own needs.
2. Suggested Response: They could not stand to see a stranger get the best of them.

THINKING AND WRITING

For help with this assignment, students can refer to Lesson 9, "Writing About Character," in the Handbook of Writing About Literature.

After students have completed the assignment, divide them into groups, and have them read their rough drafts to one another and suggest ways in which the drafts could be improved.

2. (a) The outcasts are joined by Tom Simson and his girlfriend, Piney Woods. (b) They are going there to get married.
3. Mr. Oakhurst discovers that it has snowed and that Uncle Billy has stolen the mules and horses.
4. Mother Shipton stores up her rations of food and has Mr. Oakhurst give them to Piney.
5. (a) They are dead. (b) The rescue party discovers that Mr. Oakhurst has killed himself.

Interpreting

6. (a) Harte suggests that the committee's decision was not motivated by a desire for justice or order. (b) Some of the members of the committee had lost money to Mr. Oakhurst.
7. (a) Mr. Oakhurst sees life in terms of a poker game. He was "too much a gambler not to accept Fate . . . and he recognized the usual percentage in favor of the dealer." (b) Harte means that Mr. Oakhurst was strong enough to take care of the others, but he was too weak to put up a fight against the hardships with which the outcasts were faced.
8. Mother Shipton, who began the story as a coarse, hard-hearted woman who had been nicknamed after a suspected witch, ends up starving herself to death so Piney will have more to eat. The Duchess becomes more like the innocent Piney until at the end "you could scarcely have told from the equal peace that dwelt

Motivation/Prior Knowledge
Tell students that they are going to read about an artist whose work depicted an idealized view of a world that was rapidly becoming a thing of the past. Remind them that there is a deeply felt need to retain the memories of better times and that people frequently try to stop themselves and their surroundings from changing too quickly. Ask the students if they can think of writers whose stories sometimes try to capture and hold the special qualities of an earlier time when things seemed to be better, simpler, or more attractive.

Enrichment Have the students study the artwork by Remington on pages 526 and 527 before reading about his life. In a short paragraph have them compare and contrast the two works and prompt them to tell what sort of artist might have done these works. Ask the students to focus their comments on the apparent intent of the artist and have them clarify their estimations by revising their comments after they have read the article on Remington.

Humanities Note

Sculpture, *The Bronco Buster*, by Frederic Remington. Probably the best known artist of cowboys and the Romantic West, Frederic Remington (1861–1901) was primarily an illustrator and most of his subjects were scenes from the old West.

While Remington's paintings capture characters and scenes, his sculpture is concerned with depicting the action and spirit of headlong forward motion. This sculpture, *The Bronco Buster*, is one of his most famous. He copied and recast it many times, working on textures and fine details. All versions of it convey a strong sense of drama and danger.

CROSS CURRENTS

Frederic Remington (1861–1909)

By the time Frederic Remington began his career as an artist in the 1880's, the frontier had almost ceased to exist. Yet, Remington's work provided the images that most strongly represented the old West in late nineteenth and early twentieth-century America.

EARLY YEARS

Remington is considered the best, and was certainly the most popular, painter and sculptor of the old West. Born in New York State, he first traveled west—to Montana in 1881—not as an artist but to seek his for-

THE BRONCO BUSTER
Frederic Remington
Amon Carter Museum, Fort Worth, Texas

tune, possibly in gold mining. In 1883 he traveled west again to try his hand at sheep ranching in Kansas. Later he tried to make his fortune as part owner of a Kansas City saloon. All these ventures met with failure.

During these trips Remington made sketches of landscapes and people. He sold a few of them to popular magazines, and by 1885 he had decided to make art his profession.

Remington's success as an artist came quickly. By 1888 he was one of the nation's most popular magazine illustrators. His sketches of cowboys, soldiers, gunfights, and Indian scenes fed a seemingly unquenchable popular interest in the West. At the same time, Remington began creating paintings. In the 1890's he also turned to sculpture.

REMINGTON'S WEST

Remington's West, the West that gripped the popular imagination through his work, was not the world of the homesteader, of farming and raising families, of small towns and railroading. His West was filled with conflict and action. It was a world of freedom and rugged individualism, of escape from the strictures of society—a world that was quickly passing into history.

Remington's art focused on people, often "wild riders"—cowboys and soldiers on horseback—and his figures usually projected great strength of spirit and physical energy. His work rarely featured generals, chiefs, or ranch owners and instead focused on hardworking, average individuals in a way that made them appear larger-than-life. Remington's frontier had no specific location. For him the landscape functioned mainly as a backdrop for human action. Nature, when it

You might use these questions to discuss the art:
1. Why do you think this image of the wild West was so appealing to the public?
2. How does this sculpture picture the cowboy's personality?

THE OUTLIER
Frederic Remington
The Brooklyn Museum

played any part in his art, was often a remorseless killer.

CHRONICLER OF A ROMANTICIZED PAST

During Remington's lifetime most of the country viewed the "taming" of the West as positive and necessary. For Remington it was a tragic loss. During most of his career, he made annual trips to the West, spending a month or two each year riding with the cavalry or observing cowboys, Mexican *vaqueros,* and Indians. But the West changed rapidly before his eyes, and on one trip he wrote that he would "never come west again. It is all brick buildings—derby hats and blue overalls—it spoils my early illusions."

Remington built his art on his "early illusions," on a romantic view of the West that became more and more distant from reality. As the United States became increasingly industralized, his work fueled the fantasies of many people who longed for a simpler, less complicated time. While time marched on, Remington's art crystallized a way of life that had vanished forever.

Cross Currents 527

More About the Author Ambrose Bierce's early life was marked by extreme poverty. This, combined with his brutal war experiences, led to his obsession with cruelty and death and won him the nickname "Bitter Bierce." There is even a separate book, compiled by Professor Ernest Hopkins and published in 1968, that draws together many of the jottings that would justify that nickname. It is entitled *The Ambrose Bierce Satanic Reader* and contains previously unpublished remarks Bierce made that are challenging, vituperative, or macabre, fitting invective for a person who is hailed as America's greatest nineteenth century iconoclast. What type of stories would you expect a writer with such an obsession to produce?

Critical Evaluation Ernest Hopkins, author of several articles on the subject, claims that Bierce's general philosophy was a "realistic, pessimistic, hard-boiled attitude toward life. This first-handed approach made him rather difficult to work with, no doubt, but it did make his writings refreshingly original and does so today—to read Bierce is to enter a different world."

ESL Teaching Strategy Have your ESL students make a list of five words, other than the vocabulary entries, from this story that can be added to their vocabulary. Be sure to make time to check on the definitions of these words in their notebooks and provide correct pronunciation for each.

AMBROSE BIERCE

1842–1914[?]

Both Ambrose Bierce's literary career and his philosophy of life were shaped by his career as a Union officer in the Civil War. His experiences provided the material for his best short stories and helped determine the unsentimental, cynical, pessimistic view of the world he expressed in his writing.

Bierce was born in Ohio and raised on a farm in Indiana. Having educated himself by reading his father's books, Bierce left the farm during his late teens to attend a military academy in Kentucky. A year later the Civil War broke out, and he enlisted in the Union army. He fought in several important battles and rose from private to major. Toward the end of the conflict, he was seriously wounded, but he returned to battle a few months later.

When the war ended, Bierce settled in San Francisco as a journalist. His column, the "Prattler," which appeared in *The Argonaut* (1877–1879), the *Wasp* (1880–1886), and the *San Francisco Sunday Examiner* (1887–1896), was a mixture of biting political and social satire, literary reviews, and gossip. Bierce also published many of his finest short stories in his column. Bierce's journalistic barbs angered many key political and business figures, yet his reputation as "the wickedest man in San Francisco" only added to his personal popularity. He was a handsome, magnetic figure who charmed those around him despite the malice of his words.

In the early 1890's, Bierce published two collections of his stories: *Tales of Soldiers and Civilians* (1891) and *Can Such Things Be?* (1893). The concise, carefully plotted stories in these collections, set for the most part in the Civil War, capture the cruelty and futility of war and the indifference of death and reflect Bierce's cynical view of human existence. Bierce's pessimistic outlook is also reflected in *The Devil's Dictionary* (1906), a book of humorous and cynical definitions.

Writer George Sterling wrote of Bierce, his longtime friend, that he "never troubled to conceal his justifiable contempt of humanity . . . Bierce was a 'perfectionist,' a quality that in his case led to an intolerance involving merciless cruelty. He demanded in all others, men or women, the same ethical virtues that he found essential to his own manner of life . . . [T]o deviate from his point of view, indeed, to disagree with him even in slight particulars, was the unpardonable sin."

Although Bierce enjoyed a successful career as a writer, his personal life was filled with tragedy and despair. His marriage ended in divorce and his two sons both died at an early age. In 1913 the lonely and disillusioned writer traveled into Mexico, a country in the midst of a bloody civil war, and never returned. The circumstances of his death are still unknown.

Objectives

1 To recognize point of view
2 To understand the sequence of events
3 To explore a different point of view

Support Material

Teaching Portfolio
Teacher Backup, p. 695
Grammar in Action Worksheet, *Eliminating Unnecessary Words,* p. 699
Usage and Mechanics Worksheet, p. 701
Vocabulary Check, p. 702
Analyzing Literature Worksheet, *Recognizing Point of View,* p. 704

Critical Thinking and Reading Worksheet, *Understanding The Sequence of Events* p. 705
Selection Test, p. 706
Library of Video Classics *An Occurrence at Owl Creek Bridge*

GUIDE FOR INTERPRETING

Writer's Techniques

An Occurrence at Owl Creek Bridge

Point of View. Point of view refers to the vantage point or perspective from which a narrative is told. Most stories are told from either a first-person or third-person point of view. In a narrative with a first-person point of view, one of the characters tells the story in his or her own words, using the first-person pronoun *I*. In a narrative with a third-person point of view, the narrator does not participate in the story and refers to characters using the third-person pronouns *he* and *she*. A third-person narrator may be either limited or omniscient. A third-person limited narrator focuses on the thoughts and feelings of only one character. A third-person omniscient narrator conveys the thoughts and feelings of all the characters.

The portrayal of characters and events in a story is often shaped by the point of view. In stories with first-person or limited third-person narrators, the portrayal of characters and events may be colored by the attitudes and feelings of the character from whose point of view the story is being told.

Writing

It has often been suggested that people's lives flash before their eyes as they near death. Freewrite about the thoughts and feelings that you imagine people experience during their final moments.

Primary Source

In "An Occurrence at Owl Creek Bridge," the improbable plays a key role, at least briefly. In his essay "The Short Story," Bierce expressed his view of the value of probability in fiction:

> Probability? Nothing is so improbable as what is true. It is the unexpected that occurs; but that is not saying enough; it also the unlikely—one might almost say the impossible. John, for example, meets and marries Jane. John was born in Bombay of poor but detestable parents; Jane, the daughter of a gorgeous hidalgo, on a ship bound from Vladivostok to Buenos Aires. Will some gentlemen . . . have the goodness to figure out what, at their birth, were the chances that John would meet and marry Jane? Not one in a thousand—not one in a million—not one in a million million! . . .
>
> Fiction has nothing to say to probability; the capable writer gives it not a moment's attention, except to make what is related *seem* probable in the reading—*seem* true. Suppose he relates the impossible; what then? Why, he has but passed over the line into the realm of romance . . . the land of the poets, the home of all that is good and lasting in the literature of the imagination. . . .

Guide for Interpreting 529

Literary Focus Point out that omniscient narrators are rarely used in twentieth-century fiction. This reflects the writers' belief that reality is shaped by peoples' perceptions and, therefore, cannot be viewed objectively.

Writing/Prior Knowledge If students do not feel comfortable exploring the subject of death, have them freewrite about the effects of the Civil War.

Vocabulary

Preteach the following vocabulary words:
acclivity (ə klivʹ ə tē) *n.*: Upward slope (p. 531)
embrasure (im brāʹ zhər) *n.*: Opening (p. 531)
etiquette (etʹ i kət) *n.*: Rules for manners and ceremonies (p. 531)
imperious (im pirʹ ē əs) *adj.*: Overbearing (p. 532)
dictum (dikʹ təm) *n.*: Statement or saying (p. 532)
ramification (ramʹ ə fi kāʹ shən) *n.*: Branchlike division (p. 533)
periodicity (pirʹ ē ə disʹ ə tē) *n.*: Recurrence at regular intervals (p. 533)
oscillation (äsʹ ə lāʹ shən) *n.*: The act of swinging regularly back and forth (p. 533)
preternaturally (prētʹ ər nach ər əl ē) *adv.*: Abnormally (p. 533)
malign (mə līnʹ) *adj.*: Evil (p. 535)

Spelling Tip Point out the sc spelling of the s sound in *oscillation*.

An Occurrence at Owl Creek Bridge

Ambrose Bierce

I

A man stood upon a railroad bridge in northern Alabama, looking down into the swift water twenty feet below. The man's hands were behind his back, the wrists bound with a cord. A rope closely encircled his neck. It was attached to a stout cross timber above his head and the slack fell to the level of his knees. Some loose boards laid upon the sleepers[1] supporting the metals of the railway supplied a footing for him and his executioners—two private soldiers of the Federal army, directed by a sergeant who in civil life may have been a deputy sheriff. At a short remove upon the same temporary platform was an officer in the uniform of his rank, armed. He was a captain. A sentinel at each end of the bridge stood with his rifle in the position known as "support," that is to say, vertical in front of the left shoulder, the hammer resting on the forearm thrown straight across the chest—a formal and unnatural position, enforcing an erect carriage of the body. It did not appear to be the duty of these two men to know what was occur-

---

1. **sleepers** *n.*: Ties supporting a railroad track.

THE RED BRIDGE,
Julian Alden Weir
The Metropolitan Museum of Art

Thematic Idea Another literary work about the American Civil War is explained in a feature dealing with Stephen Crane's *The Red Badge of Courage* (p. 599).

ring at the center of the bridge; they merely blockaded the two ends of the foot planking that traversed it.

Beyond one of the sentinels nobody was in sight; the railroad ran straight away into a forest for a hundred yards, then, curving, was lost to view. Doubtless there was an outpost farther along. The other bank of the stream was open ground—a gentle acclivity topped with a stockade of vertical tree trunks, loopholed for rifles, with a single embrasure through which protruded the muzzle of a brass cannon commanding the bridge. Midway of the slope between bridge and fort were the spectators—a single company of infantry in line, at "parade rest," the butts of the rifles on the ground, the barrels inclining slightly backward against the right shoulder, the hands crossed upon the stock. A lieutenant stood at the right of the line, the point of his sword upon the ground, his left hand resting upon his right. Excepting the group of four at the center of the bridge, not a man moved. The company faced the bridge, staring stonily, motionless. The sentinels, facing the banks of the stream, might have been statues to adorn the bridge. The captain stood with folded arms, silent, observing the work of his subordinates, but making no sign. Death is a dignitary who when he comes announced is to be received with formal manifestations of respect, even by those most familiar with him. In the code of military etiquette silence and fixity are forms of deference.

The man who was engaged in being hanged was apparently about thirty-five years of age. He was a civilian, if one might judge from his habit, which was that of a planter. His features were good—a straight nose, firm mouth, broad forehead, from which his long, dark hair was combed straight back, falling behind his ears to the collar of his well-fitting frock coat. He wore a mustache and pointed beard, but no whiskers; his eyes were large and dark gray, and had a kindly expression which one would hardly have expected in one whose neck was

in the hemp. Evidently this was no vulgar assassin. The liberal military code makes provision for hanging many kinds of persons, and gentlemen are not excluded.

The preparations being complete, the two private soldiers stepped aside and each drew away the plank upon which he had been standing. The sergeant turned to the captain, saluted and placed himself immediately behind that officer, who in turn moved apart one pace. These movements left the condemned man and the sergeant standing on the two ends of the same plank, which spanned three of the crossties of the bridge. The end upon which the civilian stood almost, but not quite, reached a fourth. This plank had been held in place by the weight of the captain; it was now held by that of the sergeant. At a signal from the former the latter would step aside, the plank would tilt and the condemned man go down between two ties. The arrangement commended itself to his judgment as simple and effective. His face had not been covered nor his eyes bandaged. He looked a moment at his "unsteadfast footing," then let his gaze wander to the swirling water of the stream racing madly beneath his feet. A piece of dancing driftwood caught his attention and his eyes followed it down the current. How slowly it appeared to move! What a sluggish stream!

He closed his eyes in order to fix his last thoughts upon his wife and children. The water, touched to gold by the early sun, the brooding mists under the banks at some distance down the stream, the fort, the soldiers, the piece of drift—all had distracted him. And now he became conscious of a new disturbance. Striking through the thought of his dear ones was a sound which he could neither ignore nor understand, a sharp, distinct, metallic percussion like the stroke of a blacksmith's hammer upon the anvil; it had the same ringing quality. He wondered what it was, and whether immeasurably distant or near by—it seemed both. Its recurrence was regular, but as slow as the tolling of a death knell. He awaited each

An Occurrence at Owl Creek Bridge   531

2 **Discussion** Why does Bierce choose to personify death?

3 **Discussion** What is ironic about the "liberal" military code?

4 **Literary Focus** The narrator reveals the condemned man's thoughts. Bierce is using a third-person limited point of view.

2

3

4

5 **Critical Thinking and Reading**
Take note of how this thought sets the stage for the events that follow.

6 **Discussion** Why are these details about the condemned man important to the plot of the story?

7 **Clarification** The uniforms of the Confederate Army were gray.

8 **Discussion** Why does the soldier give Farquhar this information?

stroke with impatience and—he knew not why—apprehension. The intervals of silence grew progressively longer; the delays became maddening. With their greater infrequency the sounds increased in strength and sharpness. They hurt his ear like the thrust of a knife; he feared he would shriek. What he heard was the ticking of his watch.

He unclosed his eyes and saw again the water below him. "If I could free my hands," he thought, "I might throw off the noose and spring into the stream. By diving I could evade the bullets and, swimming vigorously, reach the bank, take to the woods and get away home. My home, thank God, is as yet outside their lines; my wife and little ones are still beyond the invader's farthest advance."

As these thoughts, which have here to be set down in words, were flashed into the doomed man's brain rather than evolved from it the captain nodded to the sergeant. The sergeant stepped aside.

II

Peyton Farquhar was a well-to-do planter, of an old and highly respected Alabama family. Being a slave owner and like other slave owners a politician he was naturally an original secessionist and ardently devoted to the Southern cause. Circumstances of an imperious nature, which it is unnecessary to relate here, had prevented him from taking service with the gallant army that had fought the disastrous campaigns ending with the fall of Corinth, and he chafed under the inglorious restraint, longing for the release of his energies, the larger life of the soldier, the opportunity for distinction. That opportunity, he felt, would come, as it comes to all in war time. Meanwhile he did what he could. No service was too humble for him to perform in aid of the South, no adventure too perilous for him to undertake if consistent with the character of a civilian who was at heart a soldier, and who in good faith and without too much qualification assented to

at least a part of the frankly villainous dictum that all is fair in love and war.

One evening while Farquhar and his wife were sitting on a rustic bench near the entrance to his grounds, a gray-clad soldier rode up to the gate and asked for a drink of water. Mrs. Farquhar was only too happy to serve him with her own white hands. While she was fetching the water her husband approached the dusty horseman and inquired eagerly for news from the front.

"The Yanks are repairing the railroads," said the man, "and are getting ready for another advance. They have reached the Owl Creek bridge, put it in order and built a stockade on the north bank. The commandant has issued an order, which is posted everywhere, declaring that any civilian caught interfering with the railroad, its bridges, tunnels or trains will be summarily hanged. I saw the order."

"How far is it to the Owl Creek bridge?" Farquhar asked.

"About thirty miles."

"Is there no force on this side the creek?"

"Only a picket post[2] half a mile out, on the railroad, and a single sentinel at this end of the bridge."

"Suppose a man—a civilian and student of hanging—should elude the picket post and perhaps get the better of the sentinel," said Farquhar, smiling, "what could he accomplish?"

The soldier reflected. "I was there a month ago," he replied. "I observed that the flood of last winter had lodged a great quantity of driftwood against the wooden pier at this end of the bridge. It is now dry and would burn like tow.[3]

The lady had now brought the water, which the soldier drank. He thanked her ceremoniously, bowed to her husband and rode away. An hour later, after nightfall, he re-

---

2. **picket post:** Troops sent ahead with news of a surprise attack.
3. **tow** *n.:* The coarse and broken fibers of hemp or flax before spinning.

Grammar in Action

In revising a piece of work, a good writer always tries to **eliminate unnecessary words.** Often when a writer combines sentences or clauses, his or her new sentence contains words that can be eliminated without damaging the sentence's force or clarity. For example, Ambrose Bierce writes:

The sentinels, facing the banks of the stream, might have been statues to adorn the bridge.

This sentence may have been derived from a sentence similar to the one that follows:

The sentinels, who were facing the banks of the stream, might have been statues to adorn the bridge.

By editing the words *who were*, Bierce produced a more forceful sentence.

Student Activity 1. Eliminate unnecessary words from these sentences:

passed the plantation, going northward in the direction from which he had come. He was a Federal scout.

III

As Peyton Farquhar fell straight downward through the bridge he lost consciousness and was as one already dead. From this state he was awakened—ages later, it seemed to him—by the pain of a sharp pressure upon his throat, followed by a sense of suffocation. Keen, poignant agonies seemed to shoot from his neck downward through every fiber of his body and limbs. These pains appeared to flash along well-defined lines of ramification and to beat with an inconceivably rapid periodicity. They seemed like streams of pulsating fire heating him to an intolerable temperature. As to his head, he was conscious of nothing but a feeling of fullness—of congestion. These sensations were unaccompanied by thought. The intellectual part of his nature was already effaced; he had power only to feel, and feeling was torment. He was conscious of motion. Encompassed in a luminous cloud, of which he was now merely the fiery heart, without material substance, he swung through unthinkable arcs of oscillation, like a vast pendulum. Then all at once, with terrible suddenness, the light about him shot upward with the noise of a loud plash; a frightful roaring was in his ears, and all was cold and dark. The power of thought was restored; he knew that the rope had broken and he had fallen into the stream. There was no additional strangulation; the noose about his neck was already suffocating him and kept the water from his lungs. To die of hanging at the bottom of a river!—the idea seemed to him ludicrous. He opened his eyes in the darkness and saw above him a gleam of light, but how distant, how inaccessible! He was still sinking, for the light became fainter and fainter until it was a mere glimmer. Then it began to grow and brighten, and he knew that he was rising toward the surface—knew it with reluctance, for he was now very comfortable. "To be hanged and drowned," he thought, "that is not so bad; but I do not wish to be shot. No; I will not be shot; that is not fair."

He was not conscious of an effort, but a sharp pain in his wrist apprised him that he was trying to free his hands. He gave the struggle his attention, as an idler might observe the feat of a juggler, without interest in the outcome. What splendid effort!—what magnificent, what superhuman strength! Ah, that was a fine endeavor! Bravo! The cord fell away; his arms parted and floated upward, the hands dimly seen on each side in the growing light. He watched them with a new interest as first one and then the other pounced upon the noose at his neck. They tore it away and thrust it fiercely aside, its undulations resembling those of a water-snake. "Put it back, put it back!" He thought he shouted these words to his hands, for the undoing of the noose had been succeeded by the direst pang that he had yet experienced. His neck ached horribly; his brain was on fire; his heart, which had been fluttering faintly, gave a great leap, trying to force itself out at his mouth. His whole body was racked and wrenched with an insupportable anguish! But his disobedient hands gave no heed to the command. They beat the water vigorously with quick, downward strokes, forcing him to the surface. He felt his head emerge; his eyes were blinded by the sunlight; his chest expanded convulsively, and with a supreme and crowning agony his lungs engulfed a great draft of air, which instantly he expelled in a shriek!

He was now in full possession of his physical senses. They were, indeed, preternaturally keen and alert. Something in the awful disturbance of his organic system had so exalted and refined them that they made record of things never before perceived. He felt the ripples upon his face and heard their separate sounds as they struck. He looked at the forest on the bank of the stream, saw the individual trees, the leaves and the veining

An Occurrence at Owl Creek Bridge 533

9 Discussion How does this event lend suspense to the story? What is the horrible irony of the hospitality given to the soldier?

1. Boards that were laid upon the sleepers that were supporting the metals of the railway supplied a footing for him.
2. The noose that was about his neck was already suffocating him.
3. He heard the deflected shot that was humming through the air ahead.
4. His wife, who is looking fresh and cool and sweet, steps down from the veranda to meet him.

Student Activity 2. Combine each group of short sentences, eliminating as many unnecessary words as possible. Note the page number given after each group and compare your sentences with those that Bierce wrote.

1. A man stood upon a railroad bridge.
   The bridge was in northern Alabama.
   He was looking down into the swift water.
   The water was about twenty feet below. (page 530)
2. The captain stood with folded arms.
   He was silent.
   He was observing the work of his subordinates.
   He was making no sign. (page 531)

of each leaf—saw the very insects upon them: the locusts, the brilliant-bodied flies, the gray spiders stretching their webs from twig to twig. He noted the prismatic colors in all the dewdrops upon a million blades of grass. The humming of the gnats that danced above the eddies of the stream, the beating of the dragonflies' wings, the strokes of the water spiders' legs, like oars which had lifted their boat—all these made audible music. A fish slid along beneath his eyes and he heard the rush of its body parting the water.

He had come to the surface facing down the stream; in a moment the visible world seemed to wheel slowly round, himself the pivotal point, and he saw the bridge, the fort, the soldiers upon the bridge, the captain, the sergeant, the two privates, his executioners. They were in silhouette against the blue sky. They shouted and gesticulated, pointing at him. The captain had drawn his pistol, but did not fire; the others were unarmed. Their movements were grotesque and horrible, their forms gigantic.

Suddenly he heard a sharp report and something struck the water smartly within a few inches of his head, spattering his face with spray. He heard a second report, and saw one of the sentinels with his rifle at his shoulder, a light cloud of blue smoke rising from the muzzle. The man in the water saw the eye of the man on the bridge gazing into his own through the sights of the rifle. He observed that it was a gray eye and remembered having read that gray eyes were keenest, and that all famous marksmen had them. Nevertheless, this one had missed.

A counterswirl had caught Farquhar and turned him half round; he was again looking into the forest on the bank opposite the fort. The sound of a clear, high voice in a monotonous singsong now rang out behind him and came across the water with a distinctness that pierced and subdued all other sounds, even the beating of the ripples in his ears. Although no soldier, he had frequented camps enough to know the dread signifi-

cance of that deliberate, drawling, aspirated chant; the lieutenant on shore was taking a part in the morning's work. How coldly and pitilessly—with what an even, calm intonation, presaging, and enforcing tranquillity in the men—with what accurately measured intervals fell those cruel words:

"Attention, company! . . . Shoulder arms! . . . Ready! . . . Aim! . . . Fire!"

Farquhar dived—dived as deeply as he could. The water roared in his ears like the voice of Niagara, yet he heard the dulled thunder of the volley and, rising again toward the surface, met shining bits of metal, singularly flattened, oscillating slowly downward. Some of them touched him on the face and hands, then fell away, continuing their descent. One lodged between his collar and neck; it was uncomfortably warm and he snatched it out.

As he rose to the surface, gasping for breath, he saw that he had been a long time under water; he was perceptibly farther down stream—nearer to safety. The soldiers had almost finished reloading; the metal ramrods flashed all at once in the sunshine as they were drawn from the barrels, turned in the air, and thrust into their sockets. The two sentinels fired again, independently and ineffectually.

The hunted man saw all this over his shoulder; he was now swimming vigorously with the current. His brain was as energetic as his arms and legs; he thought with the rapidity of lightning. | 10

"The officer," he reasoned, "will not make that martinet's[4] error a second time. It is as easy to dodge a volley as a single shot. He has probably already given the command to fire at will. God help me, I cannot dodge them all!"

An appalling plash within two yards of him was followed by a loud, rushing sound, *diminuendo*,[5] which seemed to travel back

---

4. **martinet** *n.*: A very strict military disciplinarian.
5. *diminuendo* (də min' yo͞o wen' dō): A musical term used to describe a gradual reduction in volume.

through the air to the fort and died in an explosion which stirred the very river to its deeps! A rising sheet of water curved over him, fell down upon him, blinded him, strangled him! The cannon had taken a hand in the game. As he shook his head free from the commotion of the smitten water he heard the deflected shot humming through the air ahead, and in an instant it was cracking and smashing the branches in the forest beyond.

"They will not do that again," he thought; "the next time they will use a charge of grape.[6] I must keep my eye upon the gun; the smoke will apprise me—the report arrives too late; it lags behind the missile. That is a good gun."

Suddenly he felt himself whirled round and round—spinning like a top. The water, the banks, the forests, the now distant bridge, fort and men—all were commingled and blurred. Objects were represented by their colors only; circular horizontal streaks of color—that was all he saw. He had been caught in a vortex and was being whirled on with a velocity of advance and gyration that made him giddy and sick. In a few moments he was flung upon the gravel at the foot of the left bank of the stream—the southern bank—and behind a projecting point which concealed him from his enemies. The sudden arrest of his motion, the abrasion of one of his hands on the gravel, restored him, and he wept with delight. He dug his fingers into the sand, threw it over himself in handfuls and audibly blessed it. It looked like diamonds, rubies, emeralds; he could think of nothing beautiful which it did not resemble. The trees upon the bank were giant garden plants; he noted a definite order in their arrangement, inhaled the fragrance of their blooms. A strange, roseate light shone through the spaces among their trunks and the wind made in their branches the music of aeolian harps.[7] He had no wish to perfect his escape—was content to remain in that enchanting spot until retaken.

A whiz and rattle of grapeshot among the branches high above his head roused him from his dream. The baffled cannoneer had fired him a random farewell. He sprang to his feet, rushed up the sloping bank, and plunged into the forest.

All that day he traveled, laying his course by the rounding sun. The forest seemed interminable; nowhere did he discover a break in it, not even a woodman's road. He had not known that he lived in so wild a region. There was something uncanny in the revelation.

By night fall he was fatigued, footsore, famishing. The thought of his wife and children urged him on. At last he found a road which led him in what he knew to be the right direction. It was as wide and straight as a city street, yet it seemed untraveled. No fields bordered it, no dwelling anywhere. Not so much as the barking of a dog suggested human habitation. The black bodies of the trees formed a straight wall on both sides, terminating on the horizon in a point, like a diagram in a lesson in perspective. Overhead, as he looked up through this rift in the wood, shone great golden stars looking unfamiliar and grouped in strange constellations. He was sure they were arranged in some order which had a secret and malign significance. The wood on either side was full of singular noises, among which—once, twice, and again, he distinctly heard whispers in an unknown tongue.

His neck was in pain and lifting his hand to it he found it horribly swollen. He knew that it had a circle of black where the rope had bruised it. His eyes felt congested; he could no longer close them. His tongue was swollen with thirst; he relieved its fever by thrusting it forward from between his teeth into the cold air. How softly the turf

---

6. **grape:** A cluster of small iron balls that disperse once fired from a cannon.

7. **aeolian** (ē ō′ lē ən) **harps:** Harps with strings that produce music when air blows over them.

11 **Discussion** How does Bierce's description of the forest foreshadow the end of the story?

12 **Critical Thinking and Reading** Note the powerful effect of Farquhar's inner thoughts here. What is really happening?

11

12

THE SEAT OF JOHN JULIUS PRINGLE, 1800
Charles Fraser
Carolina Art Association, Gibbes Art Gallery

had carpeted the untraveled avenue—he could no longer feel the roadway beneath his feet!

Doubtless, despite his suffering, he had fallen asleep while walking, for now he sees another scene—perhaps he has merely recovered from a delirium. He stands at the gate of his own home. All is as he left it, and all bright and beautiful in the morning sunshine. He must have traveled the entire night. As he pushes open the gate and passes up the wide white walk, he sees a flutter of female garments; his wife, looking fresh and cool and sweet, steps down from the veranda to meet him. At the bottom of the steps she stands waiting, with a smile of ineffable joy, an attitude of matchless grace and dignity. Ah, how beautiful she is! He springs forward with extended arms. As he is about to clasp her he feels a stunning blow upon the back of the neck; a blinding white light blazes all about him with a sound like the shock of a cannon—then all is darkness and silence!

Peyton Farquhar was dead; his body, with a broken neck, swung gently from side to side beneath the timbers of the Owl Creek bridge.

13

THINKING ABOUT THE SELECTION

Recalling

1. (a) As the condemned man is waiting to be hanged, what catches his attention? (b) What sound distracts him?
2. Describe the condemned man's background.
3. (a) What do Farquhar and his wife learn from the visitor? (b) What do you learn about the visitor after he leaves?
4. (a) What sensation does Farquhar experience "with terrible suddenness" after he has been hanged? (b) How does he interpret this sensation?
5. What is Farquhar's fate?

Interpreting

6. In Part I Bierce includes few details about the condemned man and does not reveal the reason why he is being hanged. How does this help to create suspense?
7. (a) In what ways are the condemned man's perceptions of time and motion distorted as he is waiting to be hanged? (b) Why are his distorted perceptions important?
8. (a) What seems to be the narrator's attitude toward Farquhar in Part II? (b) What is the narrator's attitude toward war?
9. (a) Considering the outcome of the story, what is ironic, or surprising, about Farquhar's longing for "the larger life of a soldier"? (b) What is ironic about the fact that Farquhar assents to the "dictum that all is fair in love and war"?
10. (a) What details in Part III suggest that Farquhar's journey occurs in his mind? (b) How is his journey connected with the plan of escape that occurs to him moments before he is hanged?

Applying

11. Explain whether you think the portrayal of Farquhar's final thoughts and sensations is realistic.

ANALYZING LITERATURE

Recognizing Point of View

Point of view refers to the vantage point from which a narrative is told.
1. Why is a limited third-person point of view appropriate for this story?
2. Why would a first-person point of view have been inappropriate?
3. How might the story be different if Bierce had used an omniscient third-person narrator?

CRITICAL THINKING AND READING

Understanding the Sequence of Events

Writers frequently do not present all of the events in a story in chronological order. For example, in "An Occurrence at Owl Creek Bridge," Bierce presents a flashback in which he describes some of the events that led up to Farquhar's hanging.

How does Bierce's use of the flashback technique contribute to the effectiveness of the story?

THINKING AND WRITING

Exploring a Different Point of View

Imagine that your school literary magazine is having a contest in which students are asked to retell "An Occurrence at Owl Creek Bridge" from the point of view of one of the Union soldiers or the Federal scout. Start by thinking about how the character you choose might have felt about the hanging of Peyton Farquhar and what he would have known about the reasons for the hanging. List the events that led up to the hanging and some details you could use in describing these events. Then, after deciding on the order in which you want to present the events, write your story. Remember to focus on the thoughts and feelings of the character you have chosen. When you finish writing, revise your story and prepare a final copy.

Interpreting

6. It makes the reader want to read on to learn more of the details.
7. (a) Things seem to be going in slow motion, even sounds are elongated. (b) His distorted perceptions lead him to believe that he has escaped.
8. (a) Suggested Response: He seems to have feelings of contempt for Farquhar. (b) Suggested Response: He feels that war should not be glorified.
9. (a) His longings ultimately lead to his death. (b) He is deceived by another person who assents to this dictum.
10. (a) The narrator states that Farquhar "was as one already dead" and that he experienced "a sense of suffocation." (b) The journey follows the plan of escape he had envisioned.

Applying

11. Answers will differ. Students may comment that they feel that it is realistic, because they imagine that people have a rush of thoughts immediately before their deaths.

ANSWERS TO ANALYZING LITERATURE

1. It allows Bierce to delve into Farquhar's thoughts, while still depicting his death.
2. Farquhar himself could not have related the story of his death.
3. Suggested Response: The thoughts of the soldiers would have also been presented, and, as a result, the story would have had a different focus.

ANSWERS TO CRITICAL THINKING AND READING

It helps to create suspense.

THINKING AND WRITING

For help with this assignment, students can refer to Lesson 19, "Writing a Short Story," in the Handbook of Writing About Literature.

Publishing Student Writing

Have student volunteers read their stories to the class.

Closure and Extension

ANSWERS TO THINKING ABOUT THE SELECTION

Recalling

1. (a) A piece of driftwood floating downstream catches his attention. (b) The sound of his watch ticking distracts him.
2. He is a well-to-do farmer from Alabama and a Confederate soldier at heart.
3. (a) They learn that the Union army is repairing the railroad at Owl Creek Bridge and preparing to advance. (b) He is a Union soldier.
4. (a) The light about him shoots "upward with the noise of a loud plash," then all became cold and dark. (b) He thinks the rope has broken and he has fallen into the stream.
5. He dies.

More About the Author There are two full-length biographies entitled *Sarah Orne Jewett*. One was published in Boston in 1929 and authored by F. O. Matthiessen. The other, printed in 1960, was written by John T. Frost. Sarah Orne Jewett was strongly influenced by Harriet Beecher Stowe. Jewett, in turn, became an important influence on the writing of Willa Cather, as is described in Cather's book, *Not Under Forty*. What other writers represented in this book were strongly influenced by a writer whom they admired?

Critical Evaluation Josephine Donovan, who has published articles on Jewett, sees parallels in several of her subject's stories. In "A White Heron," as elsewhere, she deals "with the clash between women's loyalty to community versus the male will to destroy and isolate . . . Here, as in *A Country Doctor*, the young woman rejects a potential suitor in the name of loyalty to the sanctuary of the natural community to which she belongs."

ESL Teaching Strategy Pair each ESL student with a non-ESL partner. Allow class time for them to sit separately and quietly read alternate paragraphs of "A White Heron" to each other. Suggest that careful attention be paid to correct pronunciation.

SARAH ORNE JEWETT

1849–1909

Like other Regionalist writers, Sarah Orne Jewett sought to capture the flavor of life in a specific region. Yet while other Regionalists wrote about the new ways of life on the developing frontier, Sarah Orne Jewett portrayed a style of life that was slowly disappearing—the simple, uncomplicated way of life of the people of rural New England. Early settlers in Jewett's native Maine had gravitated toward the long, rugged coast and established successful shipping and shipbuilding businesses. Out of the wealth of the new gentry emerged a graceful, tolerant way of life, filled with tradition. However, the Embargo of 1807 and the Civil War together dealt a fatal blow to the old ways. The Embargo, which prohibited all commerce with foreign nations, seriously hurt all those who made a living from the sea. Later, the Civil War drained the state of many of its young men. As a young woman, Jewett saw industrialization begin to impinge on the area as textile mills and tourists from big cities replaced the graceful clipper ships as sources of livelihood.

Jewett was born in South Berwick, Maine, the daughter of a successful country doctor. During her childhood she often accompanied her father when he visited patients in rural southwestern Maine. Inspired by the people and landscapes she observed during these journeys, Jewett began writing poems and short stories during her early teens. When she was nineteen, she began submitting her work to literary journals, and one of her stories was accepted by the *Atlantic Monthly,* a prestigious magazine.

In 1877 Jewett published *Deephaven,* a collection of tales and sketches about the slow decline of a Maine seaport. Seven years later she published her first novel, *A Country Doctor,* a work that reflected her deep admiration for her father. During the next ten years, Jewett established herself as one of the country's leading Regionalist writers, publishing several more collections of stories and sketches, including *A White Heron and Other Stories* (1886), *A Native of Wimby* (1893), *The Life of Nancy* (1895), and her finest novel, *The Country of the Pointed Firs* (1896).

During Jewett's lifetime the rural lifestyle she had observed as a young girl gradually disappeared. Yet this older way of life lived on in her novels and stories, preserved in her vivid depictions of people and landscapes. In fact, Jewett portrayed life in rural New England so vividly that Willa Cather, a highly regarded American writer, would later comment that Jewett's works "melt into the land and the life of the land until they are not stories at all, but life itself."

538 Realism and the Frontier

Objectives

1 To appreciate imagery
2 To evaluate the effect of imagery
3 To respond to criticism

Support Material

Teaching Portfolio
Teacher Backup, p. 709
Grammar in Action Worksheet, *Understanding Reflexive and Intensive Pronouns,* p. 713
Usage and Mechanics Worksheet, p. 715
Vocabulary Check, p. 716
Analyzing Literature Worksheet, *Recognizing Imagery,* p. 717

Language Worksheet, *Appreciating Figurative Language,* p. 718
Selection Test, p. 719

GUIDE FOR INTERPRETING

A White Heron

Imagery. Imagery refers to words or phrases that create mental pictures, or images, that appeal to one or more of the five senses—sight, hearing, touch, smell, or taste. Most often, images appeal to our sense of sight. For example, Jewett presents a visual image in the first sentence of "A White Heron": "The woods were already filled with shadows . . . though a bright sunset still glimmered through the trees." Yet many visual images also appeal to one or more of the other senses, and some images appeal only to the senses other than sight.

Sarah Orne Jewett and other Regionalist writers used imagery to present vivid, realistic descriptions of the environment. Because people's lives are often shaped by their environments, these descriptions were important in conveying the essence of life in a particular region.

Writing

Think of something, such as an animal, a building, or a tree, that captured your interest when you were a young child. Then freewrite for five minutes about your attachment to this object or animal. Discuss the reasons why it captured your interest and what it represented to you.

Primary Source

In an 1886 review of *A White Heron and Other Stories* in the *Overland Monthly,* one critic noted the following:

> Of Miss Jewett's stories little can ever be said, except to remark afresh on their beauty, their straightforward simplicity, and above all their loving truth to the life of rural New England not merely in its external aspects, but in its very heart and spirit. . . . [The stories] constitute the only record for the future of the real motive and temper of life among the latest (and possibly the last) distinct representatives of the English Puritan colonization of New England; as well as very nearly the only one, in any detail, of its manners and customs. In view of the current misconceptions of the Puritan temper, which threaten to fasten themselves upon history, such authentic records of its rugged kindliness, its intensity of personal affections, its capacity for liberality, are invaluable. Nor can one doubt that these *bona fide* Yankees, yet lingering among the remote farms, are the true descendants in character as well as in blood of the original colonists. . . .

Literary Focus Note how Jewett uses imagery to capture the beauty and wonders of the woods and of the living creatures Sylvia loves.

Writing/Prior Knowledge If students feel uncomfortable about writing about their own experiences, have them write about the experiences of someone whom they know.

Vocabulary

Preteach the following vocabulary words:

dilatory (dil′ ə tôr ē) *adj.:* Slow (p. 540)

squalor (skäl′ ər) *n.:* Filth; wretchedness (p. 542)

hermitage (hʉr′ mit ij) *n.:* A place where a person can live away from other people; a secluded retreat (p. 542)

demure (di myo͞or′) *adj.:* Modest; reserved (p. 543)

ornithologist (ôr′ nə thäl′ ə jist) *n.:* Expert on birds (p. 543)

pinions (pin′ yənz) *n.:* Wings (p. 545)

A White Heron

Sarah Orne Jewett

I

The woods were already filled with shadows one June evening, just before eight o'clock, though a bright sunset still glimmered faintly among the trunks of the trees. A little girl was driving home her cow, a plodding, dilatory, provoking creature in her behavior, but a valued companion for all that. They were going away from the western light, and striking deep into the dark woods, but their feet were familiar with the path, and it was no matter whether their eyes could see it or not.

There was hardly a night the summer through when the old cow could be found waiting at the pasture bars; on the contrary, it was her greatest pleasure to hide herself away among the high huckleberry bushes, and though she wore a loud bell she had made the discovery that if one stood perfectly still it would not ring. So Sylvia had to hunt for her until she found her, and call Co'! Co'! with never an answering Moo, until her childish patience was quite spent. If the creature had not given good milk and plenty of it, the case would have seemed very different to her owners. Besides, Sylvia had all the time there was, and very little use to make of it. Sometimes in pleasant weather it was a consolation to look upon the cow's pranks as an intelligent attempt to play hide and seek, and as the child had no playmates she lent herself to this amusement with a good deal of zest. Though this chase had been so long that the wary animal herself had given an unusual signal of her whereabouts, Sylvia had only laughed when she came upon Mistress Moolly at the swampside, and urged her affectionately homeward with a twig of birch leaves. The old cow was not inclined to wander farther, she even turned in the right direction for once as they left the pasture, and stepped along the road at a good pace. She was quite ready to be milked now, and seldom stopped to browse. Sylvia wondered what her grandmother would say because they were so late. It was a great while since she had left home at half past five o'clock, but everybody knew the difficulty of making this errand a short one. Mrs. Tilley had chased the horned torment too many summer evenings herself to blame anyone else for lingering, and was only thankful as she waited that she had Sylvia, nowadays, to give such valuable assistance. The good woman suspected that Sylvia loitered occasionally on her own account; there never was such a child for straying about out-of-doors since the world was made! Everybody said that it was a good change for a little maid who had tried to grow for eight years in a crowded manufacturing town, but, as for Sylvia herself, it seemed as if she never had been alive at all before she came to live at the farm. She thought often with wistful compassion of a wretched dry geranium that belonged to a town neighbor.

" 'Afraid of folks,' " old Mrs. Tilley said to herself, with a smile, after she had made the unlikely choice of Sylvia from her daughter's houseful of children, and was returning to the farm. " 'Afraid of folks,' they said! I guess she won't be troubled no great with 'em up to the old place!" When they reached the door of the lonely house and stopped to unlock it, and the cat came to purr loudly, and rub against them, a deserted pussy, indeed, but fat with young robins, Sylvia whispered that this was a beautiful place to live in, and she never should wish to go home.

The companions followed the shady wood-road, the cow taking slow steps, and the child very fast ones. The cow stopped long at the brook to drink, as if the pasture were not half a swamp, and Sylvia stood still and waited, letting her bare feet cool themselves in the shoal water, while the great twilight moths struck softly against her. She waded on through the brook as the cow moved away, and listened to the thrushes with a

EVENING IN THE WOODS
Worthington Whittredge
The Metropolitan Museum of Art

Humanities Note

Fine art, *Evening in the Woods,* by Worthington Whittredge. Worthington Whittredge (1820–1910) was an American artist. He began painting portraits about 1840. In 1849 Whittredge traveled to Europe and remained there for ten years, studying painting. Upon returning to America he decided that what he had learned about painting in Europe was unsuited to expressing the grandeur of the American landscape. He endeavored to learn to paint all over again. Whittredge retreated to the Catskill mountain area, where the Hudson River School painters were congregating every summer. His "relearned" painting blossomed in the Hudson River School style. Along with the other painters in this group he was inspired by a sense of mission, combined with patriotism, religion and aesthetics.

This painting by Whittredge indicates that he preferred quiet woodland glens to panoramic vistas. He demonstrates a delicate poetic touch, revealing a sensitivity to atmosphere, the season, even the time of day.

As students look at this painting, you might ask these questions:
1. What season is pictured here? What is the time of day? What sounds might be heard here?
2. What is the mood of this painting?
3. What part of the story does this painting suggest?

5 Discussion Why does the thought of the boy from town frighten her?

6 Discussion What will come of Sylvia's meeting with the young sportsman?

heart that beat fast with pleasure. There was a stirring in the great boughs overhead. They were full of little birds and beasts that seemed to be wide awake, and going about their world, or else saying good night to each other in sleepy twitters. Sylvia herself felt sleepy as she walked along. However, it was not much farther to the house, and the air was soft and sweet. She was not often in the woods so late as this, and it made her feel as if she were a part of the gray shadows and the moving leaves. She was just thinking how long it seemed since she first came to the farm a year ago, and wondering if everything went on in the noisy town just the same as when she was there; the thought of the great red-faced boy who used to chase and frighten her made her hurry along the path to escape from the shadow of the trees.

Suddenly this little woods-girl is horror-stricken to hear a clear whistle not very far away. Not a bird's whistle, which would have a sort of friendliness, but a boy's whistle, determined, and somewhat aggressive. Sylvia left the cow to whatever sad fate might await her, and stepped discreetly aside into the bushes, but she was just too late. The enemy had discovered her, and called out in a very cheerful and persuasive tone, "Halloa, little girl, how far is it to the road?" and trembling Sylvia answered almost inaudibly, "A good ways."

She did not dare to look boldly at the tall young man, who carried a gun over his shoulder, but she came out of her bush and again followed the cow, while he walked alongside.

"I have been hunting for some birds," the stranger said kindly, "and I have lost my way, and need a friend very much. Don't be afraid," he added gallantly. "Speak up and tell me what your name is, and whether you think I can spend the night at your house, and go out gunning early in the morning."

Sylvia was more alarmed than before. Would not her grandmother consider her much to blame? But who could have foreseen such an accident as this? It did not ap-

pear to be her fault, and she hung her head as if the stem of it were broken, but managed to answer "Sylvy," with much effort when her companion again asked her name.

Mrs. Tilley was standing in the doorway when the trio came into view. The cow gave a loud moo by way of explanation.

"Yes, you'd better speak up for yourself, you old trial! Where'd she tucked herself away this time, Sylvy?" Sylvia kept an awed silence; she knew by instinct that her grandmother did not comprehend the gravity of the situation. She must be mistaking the stranger for one of the farmer lads of the region.

The young man stood his gun beside the door, and dropped a heavy game bag beside it; then he bade Mrs. Tilley good evening, and repeated his wayfarer's story, and asked if he could have a night's lodging.

"Put me anywhere you like," he said. "I must be off early in the morning, before day; but I am very hungry, indeed. You can give me some milk at any rate, that's plain."

"Dear sakes, yes," responded the hostess, whose long slumbering hospitality seemed to be easily awakened. "You might fare better if you went out on the main road a mile or so, but you're welcome to what we've got. I'll milk right off, and you make yourself at home. You can sleep on husks or feathers," she proffered graciously. "I raised them all myself. There's good pasturing for geese just below here towards the ma'sh. Now step round and set a plate for the gentleman, Sylvy!" and Sylvia promptly stepped. She was glad to have something to do, and she was hungry herself.

It was a surprise to find so clean and comfortable a little dwelling in this New England wilderness. The young man had known the horrors of its most primitive housekeeping, and the dreary squalor of that level of society which does not rebel at the companionship of hens. This was the best thrift of an old-fashioned farmstead, though on such a small scale that it seemed like a hermitage. He listened eagerly to the old woman's quaint talk, he watched Sylvia's pale face

Grammar in Action

Reflexive and **intensive pronouns,** those which end in *-self* or *-selves,* perform two different functions in sentences, although their forms are the same. Here are some examples of their use in "A White Heron":

"Afraid of folks," old Mrs. Tilley said to *herself* (page 540)

"I'll milk right off, and you make *yourself* at home." (page 542)

As for Sylvia *herself*, it seemed as if she never had been alive at all before she came to live at the farm. (page 540)

In the first two sentences, the pronouns add information by pointing back to a noun or pronoun that appears earlier in the sentence. These are reflexive pronouns. In the second two sentences, the pronouns simply add emphasis to the nouns. These are intensive pronouns.

Student Activity 1. On page 542, find five more reflexive or intensive pronouns and identify the function of each.

Student Activity 2. Add reflexive pronouns to the following sentences.
1. Sylvia thought _____ lucky to live in the country.

and shining gray eyes with ever growing enthusiasm, and insisted that this was the best supper he had eaten for a month; then, afterward, the new-made friends sat down in the doorway together while the moon came up.

Soon it would be berry time, and Sylvia was a great help at picking. The cow was a good milker, though a plaguy¹ thing to keep track of, the hostess gossiped frankly, adding presently that she had buried four children, so that Sylvia's mother, and a son (who might be dead) in California were all the children she had left. "Dan, my boy, was a great hand to go gunning," she explained sadly. "I never wanted for pa'tridges or gray squer'ls while he was to home. He's been a great wand'rer, I expect, and he's no hand to write letters. There, I don't blame him, I'd ha' seen the world myself if it had been so I could.

"Sylvia takes after him," the grandmother continued affectionately, after a minute's pause. "There ain't a foot o' ground she don't know her way over, and the wild creatur's counts her one o' themselves. Squer'ls she'll tame to come an' feed right out o' her hands, and all sorts o' birds. Last winter she got the jay birds to bangeing² here, and I believe she'd 'a' scanted herself of her own meals to throw out amongst 'em, if I hadn't kep' watch. Anything but crows, I tell her, I'm willin' to help support—though Dan he went an' tamed one o' them that did seem to have reason same as folks. It was round here a good spell after he went away. Dan an' his father they didn't hitch³—but he never held up his head ag'in after Dan had dared him an' gone off."

The guest did not notice this hint of family sorrows in his eager interest in something else.

"So Sylvy knows all about birds, does she?" he exclaimed, as he looked round at the little girl who sat, very demure but increasingly sleepy, in the moonlight. "I am making a collection of birds myself. I have been at it ever since I was a boy." (Mrs. Tilley smiled.) "There are two or three very rare ones I have been hunting for these five years. I mean to get them on my own ground if they can be found."

"Do you cage 'em up?" asked Mrs. Tilley doubtfully, in response to this enthusiastic announcement.

"Oh, no, they're stuffed and preserved, dozens and dozens of them," said the ornithologist, "and I have shot or snared every one myself. I caught a glimpse of a white heron three miles from here on Saturday, and I have followed it in this direction. They have never been found in this district at all. The little white heron, it is," and he turned again to look at Sylvia with the hope of discovering that the rare bird was one of her acquaintances.

But Sylvia was watching a hoptoad in the narrow footpath.

"You would know the heron if you saw it," the stranger continued eagerly. "A queer tall white bird with soft feathers and long thin legs. And it would have a nest perhaps in the top of a high tree, made of sticks, something like a hawk's nest."

Sylvia's heart gave a wild beat; she knew that strange white bird, and had once stolen softly near where it stood in some bright green swamp grass, away over at the other side of the woods. There was a open place where the sunshine always seemed strangely yellow and hot, where tall, nodding rushes grew, and her grandmother had warned her that she might sink in the soft black mud underneath and never be heard of more. Not far beyond were the salt marshes and beyond those was the sea, the sea which Sylvia wondered and dreamed about, but never had looked upon, though its great voice could often be heard above the noise of the woods on stormy nights.

"I can't think of anything I should like so much as to find that heron's nest," the handsome stranger was saying. "I would give

---

1. **plaguy** (plā′ gē) *adj.*: Disagreeable.
2. **bangeing** (ban′ jing) *v.*: Lounging around.
3. **hitch:** Relate well to each other.

A White Heron 543

7 **Discussion** What contrasting images does Jewett present?

2. The cow seemed to devise games for Sylvia and _____.
3. Sylvia's grandmother often talked to _____.
4. The hunter thought _____ superior to rural people.
5. Sylvia felt _____ torn between new love and loyalty.

Student Activity 3. Add intensive pronouns to the following sentences.
1. Jewett captures the simplicity of rural life _____.
2. Jewett _____ was brought up in Maine.
3. Many Regionalists had _____ grown up on a frontier.
4. Jewett's stories _____ explore the end of a way of life.

8 **Discussion** In what ways might Sylvia's environment affect her feelings for the young man?

9 **Discussion** What does the idea of climbing the tree represent to Sylvia?

10 **Discussion** What do you think might happen if Sylvia actually climbs the tree? How might climbing the tree change her?

ten dollars to anybody who could show it to me," he added desperately, "and I mean to spend my whole vacation hunting for it if need be. Perhaps it was only migrating, or had been chased out of its own region by some bird of prey."

Mrs. Tilley gave amazed attention to all this, but Sylvia still watched the toad, not divining, as she might have done at some calmer time, that the creature wished to get to its hole under the doorstep, and was much hindered by the unusual spectators at that hour of the evening. No amount of thought, that night, could decide how many wished-for treasures the ten dollars, so lightly spoken of, would buy.

The next day the young sportsman hovered about the woods, and Sylvia kept him company, having lost her first fear of the friendly lad, who proved to be most kind and sympathetic. He told her many things about the birds and what they knew and where they lived and what they did with themselves. And he gave her a jackknife, which she thought as great a treasure as if she were a desert islander. All day long he did not once make her troubled or afraid except when he brought down some unsuspecting singing creature from its bough. Sylvia would have liked him vastly better without his gun; she could not understand why he killed the very birds he seemed to like so much. But as the day waned, Sylvia still watched the young man with loving admiration. She had never seen anybody so charming and delightful; the woman's heart, asleep in the child, was vaguely thrilled by a dream of love. Some premonition of that great power stirred and swayed these young foresters who traversed the solemn woodlands with soft-footed silent care. They stopped to listen to a bird's song; they pressed forward again eagerly, parting the branches, speaking to each other rarely and in whispers; the young man going first and Sylvia following, fascinated, a few steps behind, with her gray eyes dark with excitement.

She grieved because the longed-for white heron was elusive, but she did not lead the guest, she only followed, and there was no such thing as speaking first. The sound of her own unquestioned voice would have terrified her—it was hard enough to answer yes or no when there was need of that. At last evening began to fall, and they drove the cow home together, and Sylvia smiled with pleasure when they came to the place where she heard the whistle and was afraid only the night before.

II

Half a mile from home, at the farther edge of the woods, where the land was highest, a great pine tree stood, the last of its generation. Whether it was left for a boundary mark, or for what reason, no one could say; the woodchoppers who had felled its mates were dead and gone long ago, and a whole forest of sturdy trees, pines and oaks and maples, had grown again. But the stately head of this old pine towered above them all and made a landmark for sea and shore miles and miles away. Sylvia knew it well. She had always believed that whoever climbed to the top of it could see the ocean; and the little girl had often laid her hand on the great rough trunk and looked up wistfully at those dark boughs that the wind always stirred, no matter how hot and still the air might be below. Now she thought of the tree with a new excitement, for why, if one climbed it at break of day, could not one see all the world, and easily discover whence the white heron flew, and mark the place, and find the hidden nest?

What a spirit of adventure, what wild ambition! What fancied triumph and delight and glory for the later morning when she could make known the secret! It was almost too real and too great for the childish heart to bear.

All night the door of the little house stood open, and the whippoorwills came and sang upon the very step. The young sportsman and his old hostess were sound asleep, but Sylvia's great design kept her broad awake and watching. She forgot to think of sleep. The short summer night seemed as long as the winter darkness, and at last when the whippoorwills ceased, and she was afraid the morning would after all come too soon, she stole out of the house and followed the pasture path through the woods, hastening toward the open ground beyond, listening with a sense of comfort and companionship to the drowsy twitter of a half-awakened bird, whose perch she had jarred in passing. Alas, if the great wave of human interest which flooded for the first time this dull little life should sweep away the satisfactions of an existence heart to heart with nature and the dumb[4] life of the forest!

There was the huge tree asleep yet in the paling moonlight, and small and hopeful Sylvia began with utmost bravery to mount to the top of it, with tingling, eager blood coursing the channels of her whole frame, with her bare feet and fingers, that pinched and held like bird's claws to the monstrous ladder reaching up, up, almost to the sky itself. First she must mount the white oak tree that grew alongside, where she was almost lost among the dark branches and the green leaves heavy and wet with dew; a bird fluttered off its nest, and a red squirrel ran to and fro and scolded pettishly at the harmless housebreaker. Sylvia felt her way easily. She had often climbed there, and knew that higher still one of the oak's upper branches chafed against the pine trunk, just where its lower boughs were set close together. There, when she made the dangerous pass from one tree to the other, the great enterprise would really begin.

She crept out along the swaying oak limb at last, and took the daring step across into the old pine tree. The way was harder than she thought; she must reach far and hold fast, the sharp dry twigs caught and held her and scratched her like angry talons, the pitch made her thin little fingers clumsy and stiff as she went round and round the tree's great stem, higher and higher upward. The

---

4. **dumb** *adj.*: Silent.

sparrows and robins in the woods below were beginning to wake and twitter to the dawn, yet it seemed much lighter there aloft in the pine tree, and the child knew that she must hurry if her project were to be of any use.

The tree seemed to lengthen itself out as she went up, and to reach farther and farther upward. It was like a great mainmast to the voyaging earth; it must truly have been amazed that morning through all its ponderous frame as it felt this determined spark of human spirit creeping and climbing from higher branch to branch. Who knows how steadily the least twigs held themselves to advantage this light, weak creature on her way! The old pine must have loved his new dependent. More than all the hawks, and bats, and moths, and even the sweet-voiced thrushes, was the brave, beating heart of the solitary gray-eyed child. And the tree stood still and held away the winds that June morning while the dawn grew bright in the east.

Sylvia's face was like a pale star, if one had seen it from the ground, when the last thorny bough was past, and she stood trembling and tired but wholly triumphant, high in the treetop. Yes, there was the sea with the dawning sun making a golden dazzle over it, and toward that glorious east flew two hawks with slow-moving pinions. How low they looked in the air from that height when before one had only seen them far up, and dark against the blue sky. Their gray feathers were as soft as moths; they seemed only a little way from the tree, and Sylvia felt as if she too could go flying away among the clouds. Westward, the woodlands and farms reached miles and miles into the distance; here and there were church steeples, and white villages; truly it was a vast and awesome world.

The birds sang louder and louder. At last the sun came up bewilderingly bright. Sylvia could see the white sails of ships out at sea, and the clouds that were purple and rose-colored and yellow at first began to fade away. Where was the white heron's nest in

A White Heron 545

11 **Discussion** What is the effect of Jewett's personification of the tree?

11

12 **Discussion** Why does Jewett break her narrative at this point to address Sylvia directly?

13 **Discussion** What is it that suddenly forbids Sylvia to speak? Is it merely a wish to save the bird?

Reader's Response Explain the circumstances that once allowed you to have a special exchange with a pet or wild animal.

the sea of green branches, and was this wonderful sight and pageant of the world the only reward for having climbed to such a giddy height? Now look down again, Sylvia, where the green marsh is set among the shining birches and dark hemlocks; there where you saw the white heron once you will see him again; look, look! a white spot of him like a single floating feather comes up from the dead hemlock and grows larger, and rises, and comes close at last, and goes by the landmark pine with steady sweep of wing and outstretched slender neck and crested head. And wait! wait! do not move a foot or a finger, little girl, do not send an arrow of light and consciousness from your two eager eyes, for the heron has perched on a pine bough not far beyond yours, and cries back to his mate on the nest, and plumes his feathers for the new day!

The child gives a long sigh a minute later when a company of shouting cat-birds comes also to the tree, and vexed by their fluttering and lawlessness the solemn heron goes away. She knows his secret now, the wild, light, slender bird that floats and wavers, and goes back like an arrow presently to his home in the green world beneath. Then Sylvia, well satisfied, makes her perilous way down again, not daring to look far below the branch she stands on, ready to cry sometimes because her fingers ache and her lamed feet slip. Wondering over and over again what the stranger would say to her, and what he would think when she told him how to find his way straight to the heron's nest.

"Sylvy, Sylvy!" called the busy old grandmother again and again, but nobody answered, and the small husk bed was empty, and Sylvia had disappeared.

The guest waked from a dream, and remembering his day's pleasure hurried to dress himself that it might sooner begin. He was sure from the way the shy little girl looked once or twice yesterday that she had at least seen the white heron, and now she must really be persuaded to tell. Here she comes now, paler than ever, and her worn old frock is torn and tattered, and smeared with pine pitch. The grandmother and the sportsman stand in the door together and question her, and the splendid moment has come to speak of the dead hemlock tree by the green marsh.

But Sylvia does not speak after all, though the old grandmother fretfully rebukes her, and the young man's kind appealing eyes are looking straight in her own. He can make them rich with money; he has promised it, and they are poor now. He is so well worth making happy, and he waits to hear the story she can tell.

No, she must keep silence! What is it that suddenly forbids her and makes her dumb? Has she been nine years growing, and now, when the great world for the first time puts out a hand to her, must she thrust it aside for a bird's sake? The murmur of the pine's green branches is in her ears, she remembers how the white heron came flying through the golden air and how they watched the sea and the morning together, and Sylvia cannot speak; she cannot tell the heron's secret and give its life away.

Dear loyalty, that suffered a sharp pang as the guest went away disappointed later in the day, that could have served and followed him and loved him as a dog loves! Many a night Sylvia heard the echo of his whistle haunting the pasture path as she came home with the loitering cow. She forgot even her sorrow at the sharp report of his gun and the piteous sight of thrushes and sparrows dropping silent to the ground, their songs hushed and their pretty feathers stained and wet with blood. Were the birds better friends than their hunter might have been—who can tell? Whatever treasures were lost to her, woodlands and summertime, remember! Bring your gifts and graces and tell your secrets to this lonely country child!

Closure and Extension

ANSWERS TO THINKING ABOUT THE SELECTION
Recalling

1. (a) She is taking her cow back home. (b) She meets a handsome young man. (c) He is an ornithologist, looking for a white heron.
2. (a) He wants to know the location of the white heron's nest. (b) He offers Sylvia ten dollars.
3. (a) Sylvia cannot understand how such a kind man can destroy animals. (b) She is infatuated with him, feeling her femininity for the first time, and wanting a wider view of the world than she has had to date.
4. (a) Sylvia climbs a tall pine tree to locate the heron's nest. (b) She does not tell the young man where to find the heron for fear that the man will kill the bird.

THINKING ABOUT THE SELECTION

Recalling

1. (a) Why is Sylvia walking through the woods at sunset? (b) Whom does she meet during her walk? (c) What is his reason for being in the woods?
2. (a) What does the young man hope Sylvia will show him? (b) How does he promise to reward her?
3. (a) What can Sylvia not understand about the young man? (b) What feelings does he awaken in her?
4. (a) How does Sylvia locate the white heron? (b) Why does Sylvia decide not to tell the young man about her discovery?

Interpreting

5. The name Sylvia is closely related to the word *sylvan,* which means "of the woods." Why is this an appropriate name for the main character?
6. (a) How would you describe Sylvia's attitude toward nature? (b) How is it different from the young man's attitude?
7. (a) What is the young man's attitude toward Sylvia and her family? (b) Find three passages in which this attitude is revealed.
8. (a) What internal conflict does Sylvia experience? (b) How is the conflict resolved?
9. (a) Considering the heron's color and gracefulness and the fact that it is rarely seen, what do you think it symbolizes, or represents? (b) What do you think the great pine tree symbolizes?
10. (a) What does this story reveal about life in the New England wilderness? (b) What details in the story suggest that this life is disappearing?

Applying

11. Explain whether you think or do not think Sylvia makes the right decision at the end of the story.

ANALYZING LITERATURE

Recognizing Imagery

Imagery refers to words or phrases that create images that appeal to one or more of the five senses. For example, in this story Jewett presents a visual image when she writes, "there was the sea with the dawning sun making a golden dazzle over it."
1. Find two other visual images in the story. Explain why these images are effective.
2. Find two images that appeal to other senses. Explain why these images are effective.

CRITICAL THINKING AND READING

Evaluating the Effect of Imagery

When used effectively, imagery allows you to visualize in your mind each place and event the writer describes—even places and events unlike any you have actually seen.
1. Explain whether Jewett's imagery makes it possible for you to visualize the setting.
2. How does Jewett's use of imagery help convey the flavor of life in the New England wilderness?

THINKING AND WRITING

Responding to Criticism

A critic has stated that Sarah Orne Jewett's stories "are always stories of character." Write an essay in which you discuss this comment in relation to "A White Heron." Reread the story keeping the critic's statement in mind. Are character and characterization the most important elements of the story? Why or why not? When you write your essay, use evidence from the story to support your argument. When you revise, make sure your argument is logically organized.

A White Heron 547

(Answers begin on p. 546)

10. (a) The story portrays life in rural New England of the 1800's as being isolated, uncomplicated, unhurried, and somewhat difficult. (b) Details that suggest that the old rural New England lifestyle was disappearing when the story was written are a manufacturing town where Sylvia was born, the woodchoppers who had cut down large numbers of trees, and the sight of villages springing up in the valleys that Sylvia could see from the treetop.

Applying
11. Students may differ in their opinions, but the answer should address Sylvia's moral dilemma.

ANSWERS TO ANALYZING LITERATURE

1. Answers will differ. Visual images include, "the great twilight moths struck softly against her," "as if the pasture were not half a swamp," and "as if she were a part of the gray shadows and moving leaves."
2. Answers will differ. Images that appeal to the sense of feeling or touch include, "with a heart that beat fast with pleasure" and "her bare feet cool themselves in the shoal water."

ANSWERS TO CRITICAL THINKING AND READING

1. Jewett's use of imagery makes the setting of the story easy to visualize because it touches upon the sensory responses one has had in being in a rural woodland.
2. Jewett's use of imagery gives the reader the feeling of isolation and the difficulty of long-term survival that characterized the nineteenth-century New England wilderness.

THINKING AND WRITING

For help with this assignment, students can refer to Lesson 15, "Evaluating a Literary Work," in the Handbook of Writing About Literature.

Divide students into groups, and have them read their rough drafts to one another and suggest ways in which they could be improved.

547

Interpreting
5. Sylvia is a child of the woods, sharing, in some special way, a bond with the creatures and plants that surround her.
6. (a) Sylvia is enchanted with nature and feels comfortable and relaxed within a woodland setting. (b) The young man looks upon the creatures of nature as parts of an interesting study; each bird, for example, is a collector's item.
7. (a) Suggested Response: He has a slightly condescending attitude toward them, viewing them as a convenience and a source of information. (b) Suggested Response: He tells Sylvia to "Speak up" and tell him what her name is; he tells Mrs. Tilley that she can give him "some milk at any rate, that's plain"; and he says that he will give Sylvia ten dollars to help him find a heron.
8. (a) Sylvia must decide whether or not she will cause the heron's death in order to endear herself to the man she has come to adore. (b) The conflict is resolved when Sylvia decides that she cannot reveal the heron's location despite her desire to please the young man.
9. (a) Suggested Response: The heron seems to represent the beauty and dignity of life itself. (b) Suggested Response: The pine tree seems to symbolize the difficulty that people have in ever being able to see the rich gift that we receive simply by being alive.

More About the Author Kate
Chopin was of Creole-Irish descent and it was in the mixed
Natchitoches parish of Louisiana
that she settled with her husband. She acquired an intimate
knowledge of Creole and Cajun
life while living there. It provided
a major influence on her later
work as a writer.

Partly because of the controversy surrounding certain of
her work, there was limited attention paid to her writings for the
half century after her death. But
in 1969 a full-length biography
was published on her by Per Se-
yersted, the same author who
edited her collected works in two
volumes and published them
concurrently with the biography.
Her work is praised now for its
literary accomplishment as well
as for the independence of
thought that is found in her analysis of various characters.

Several weeks after com-
pleting "The Story of an Hour,"
Kate Chopin wrote that if she
could get her husband back, she
would be willing to give up
". . . the past ten years of [her]
growth—[her] real growth." How
might this comment affect the
students' reading of "The Story
of an Hour"?

ESL Teaching Strategy Have
ESL students supplement the
Grammar in Action activities by
composing five brief sentences
that each contain an adverb that
ends with -ly.

KATE CHOPIN

1851–1904

Despite her conservative, aristocratic upbringing, Kate O'Flaherty Chopin became one of the most powerful and controversial writers of her time. In her stories, sketches, and novels, she not only captured the local color of Louisiana but also boldly explored the role of women in society.

Kate O'Flaherty was born in St. Louis, Missouri, the daughter of a wealthy businessman. When she was nineteen, she married Oscar Chopin, a Louisiana cotton trader. The couple settled in New Orleans, where they lived for ten years before moving to a plantation in rural northwestern Louisiana. In 1883 Chopin's husband died, leaving her to raise her six children on her own. Chopin carried on the work of the plantation alone for more than a year, using her knowledge of finance and developing skills as a businesswoman. However, in 1884, she yielded to her mother's urgings, sold most of her holdings, and re-turned to St. Louis with her children. Her mother's sudden death in 1885 left her in deep sorrow. It was at the suggestion of her family doctor, who was concerned about her emotional state, that Chopin began writing fiction. Chopin kept St. Louis as her home for the rest of her life, devoting much of her energy to writing.

Influenced by American Regionalists such as Sarah Orne Jewett and fascinated by the mixture of cultures in Louisiana, Chopin fo-cused on capturing the essence of life in Louisiana in her writing. Like most of her other works, her first novel, *At Fault* (1890), was set in a small Louisiana town inhabited by Creoles, descendants of the origi-nal French and Spanish settlers, and Cajuns, descendants of French Canadian settlers. Through her vivid descriptions and use of dialect, Chopin captured the local color of the region. In her stories, published in *Bayou Folk* (1894) and *Acadie* (1897), she exhibited her deep un-derstanding of the different attitudes and concerns of the Louisiana natives. Yet her charming portraits of Louisiana life often obscured the fact that she explored themes considered radical at the time: the nature of marriage, racial prejudice, and women's desire for social, economic, and political equality.

Her finest novel, *The Awakening* (1899), is a psychological ac-count of a woman's search for independence and fulfillment. Because the novel explored the issue of infidelity, it aroused a storm of protest. The book was severely attacked by critics and eventually banned, and Chopin's reputation was badly damaged. As a result, Chopin's work was virtually ignored for several decades after her death. Today, however, she is widely respected for her intense understanding of fe-male psychology and her ability to capture local color.

Objectives

1 To recognize irony
2 To recognize details that contribute to irony
3 To write about irony

Support Material

Teaching Portfolio
Teacher Backup, p. 721
Grammar in Action Worksheet, *Using Adverbs of Manner,* p. 725
Usage and Mechanics Work-sheet, p. 727
Vocabulary Check, p. 728
Analyzing Literature Worksheet, *Recognizing Irony* p. 729

Language Worksheet, *Recogniz-ing Word Analogies* p. 730
Selection Test, p. 731

GUIDE FOR INTERPRETING

The Story of an Hour

Irony. Irony is a contrast between what is stated and what is meant, or between what is expected to happen and what actually happens. A number of different types of irony are used in literature. Situational irony occurs when the actual result of an action or situation is quite different from the expected result. For example, in "An Occurrence at Owl Creek Bridge," when you are told that Peyton Farquhar assents to the "dictum that all is fair in love and war," you are led to expect that he may become involved in some type of covert or deceptive activity. As it turns out, however, Farquhar himself is the one who is deceived, when he is tricked by a Federal scout who pretends to be a Confederate soldier. Dramatic irony occurs when readers perceive something that a character in a literary work does not know. For example, in Shakespeare's *Romeo and Juliet,* Romeo poisons himself after being told that his beloved Juliet is dead. Yet the audience is aware that in reality Juliet has only been pretending to be dead as part of an elaborate plan to be united with Romeo.

Writing

Imagine an instance in which you or someone you know receives a piece of news that has a powerful effect. Then imagine that the news turns out not to be true. Describe how the news and the discovery that the news was false would affect you.

Primary Source

In "The Story of an Hour," you will meet a married woman who longs for freedom and independence. In this story and others, Kate Chopin recognized that the perfect wife of her time was submissive to her husband in all matters, that "the lack of self-assertion" was a sign of "the perfection of womanliness." Yet Chopin, who never remarried after her husband's death, had another vision of the marriage relationship, which she described in her early story "A Point of Issue":

> [The couple decided] to be governed by no precedential methods. Marriage was to be a form, that while fixing legally their relation to each other, was in no wise to touch the individuality of either; that was to be preserved intact. Each was to remain a free integral of humanity, responsible to no dominating exactions of so-called marriage laws. And the element that was to make possible such a union was trust in each other's love, honor, courtesy, tempered by the reserving clause of readiness to meet the consequences of reciprocal liberty.

Literary Focus Irony is often used to undercut a reader's expectations. Have the students pay attention to how certain expectations are aroused and then frustrated as the story progresses.

Writing/Prior Knowledge For extra credit, you might have students develop their description into a personal narrative.

Vocabulary

Preteach the following vocabulary words:
forestall (fôr stôl') *v.:* Act in advance of (p. 550)
repression (ri presh' ən) *n.:* Restraint (p. 550)
elusive (i lōō' siv) *adj.:* Hard to grasp (p. 550)
tumultuously (tōō mul' chōō wəs lē) *adv.:* Agitatedly (p. 550)
importunities (im' pôr tōōn' ə téz) *n.:* Persistent requests or demands (p. 552)

Motivation/Prior Knowledge
Have the students imagine what life was like for a woman in the late nineteenth century. What freedoms did they enjoy? What freedoms were they denied?

Thematic Idea Another selection in which irony plays a central role is "The love song of J. Alfred Prufrock" by T. S. Eliot (p. 810).

Purpose-Setting   Question
What role does irony play in this story?

1 **Enrichment** Telegrams were the main form of long-distance communication in the nineteenth century.

2 **Discussion** How would you characterize Mrs. Mallard's immediate reaction?

3 **Discussion** Would this be a typical reaction for a woman in the nineteenth century?

The Story of an Hour

Kate Chopin

Knowing that Mrs. Mallard was afflicted with a heart trouble, great care was taken to break to her as gently as possible the news of her husband's death.

It was her sister Josephine who told her, in broken sentences; veiled hints that revealed in half concealing. Her husband's friend Richards was there, too, near her. It was he who had been in the newspaper office when intelligence of the railroad disaster was received, with Brently Mallard's name leading the list of "killed." He had only taken the time to assure himself of its truth by a second telegram, and had hastened to forestall any less careful, less tender friend in bearing the sad message.

She did not hear the story as many women have heard the same, with a paralyzed inability to accept its significance. She wept at once, with sudden, wild abandonment, in her sister's arms. When the storm of grief had spent itself she went away to her room alone. She would have no one follow her.

There stood, facing the open window, a comfortable, roomy armchair. Into this she sank, pressed down by a physical exhaustion that haunted her body and seemed to reach into her soul.

She could see in the open square before her house the tops of trees that were all aquiver with the new spring life. The delicious breath of rain was in the air. In the street below a peddler was crying his wares. The notes of a distant song which someone was singing reached her faintly, and countless sparrows were twittering in the eaves.

There were patches of blue sky showing here and there through the clouds that had met and piled one above the other in the west facing her window.

She sat with her head thrown back upon the cushion of the chair, quite motionless, except when a sob came up into her throat and shook her, as a child who has cried itself to sleep continues to sob in its dreams.

She was young, with a fair, calm face, whose lines bespoke repression and even a certain strength. But now there was a dull stare in her eyes, whose gaze was fixed away off yonder on one of those patches of blue sky. It was not a glance of reflection, but rather indicated a suspension of intelligent thought.

There was something coming to her and she was waiting for it, fearfully. What was it? She did not know; it was too subtle and elusive to name. But she felt it, creeping out of the sky, reaching toward her through the sounds, the scents, the color that filled the air.

Now her bosom rose and fell tumultuously. She was beginning to recognize this thing that was approaching to possess her, and she was striving to beat it back with her will—as powerless as her two white slender hands would have been.

When she abandoned herself, a little whispered word escaped her slightly parted lips. She said it over and over under her breath: "free, free, free!" The vacant stare and the look of terror that had followed it went from her eyes. They stayed keen and bright. Her pulses beat fast, and the cours-

Adverbs of manner modify verbs by answering the question *In what manner?* These adverbs can be single words, phrases, or clauses. Notice the following examples:

Her bosom rose and fell *tumultuously*. (single word)

He decided to tell her *with much hesitation*. (prepositional phrase)

She shook, *as a child who has cried itself to sleep*. (clause)

Most single-word adverbs of manner are derived from adjectives to which the suffix *-ly* or *-ally* is added. Because of their derivation, adverbs of manner can be used to compress sentences. For example, the sentence, "She sat by the window *with a sad expression*," can be written, "She sat *sadly* by the window."

Student Activity 1. On page 550, find three other adverbs of manner that are derived from adjectives. Identify the verbs they modify.

Student Activity 2. Shorten each of the following sentences by changing the italicized adverb phrase to a single-word adverb.
1. The recently widowed lady sobbed *in a tearful way*.

WOMAN WITH A BLACK TIE
Amedeo Modigliani
Private Collection

Fine art, *Woman with a Black Tie,* 1917, by Amadeo Modigliani. The Italian artist Amadeo Modigliani (1884–1920) is an enigma in modern art. He lived in Paris and was a contemporary of the Cubists. He was, however, not affected by their style. His art, paintings of delicate, elongated figures, is considered to be a bridge between the work of Lautrec and the Art Deco style.

Woman with a Black Tie is an example of his portrait style. The subject is elegant and frail; the pale oval of the face is somehow sad and expressive. Color is of little importance in this work. This graphic, decorative style is the result of Modigliani's application of the twentieth-century rules of distortion and linear expression.

Consider these questions for discussion:

1. What might you infer about this woman's character from this portrait?
2. What similarities might you draw between the woman in this painting and Mrs. Mallard?

2. *In private* she began to make plans.
3. The birds sat *with indifferent ease* on the grass.
4. Her brother spoke *with great calm.*
5. The soldier cried *in a loud and bitter voice.*

4 **Reading Strategy** Have students predict the outcome of the story.

5 **Discussion** What is ironic about the doctor's diagnosis?

Reader's Response Can you describe a time when unexpected news made you experience a feeling that you would not have anticipated?

ing blood warmed and relaxed every inch of her body.

She did not stop to ask if it were or were not a monstrous joy that held her. A clear and exalted perception enabled her to dismiss the suggestion as trivial.

She knew that she would weep again when she saw the kind, tender hands folded in death; the face that had never looked save with love upon her, fixed and gray and dead. But she saw beyond that bitter moment a long procession of years to come that would belong to her absolutely. And she opened and spread her arms out to them in welcome.

There would be no one to live for her during those coming years; she would live for herself. There would be no powerful will bending hers in that blind persistence with which men and women believe they have a right to impose a private will upon a fellow creature. A kind intention or a cruel intention made the act seem no less a crime as she looked upon it in that brief moment of illumination.

And yet she had loved him—sometimes. Often she had not. What did it matter! What could love, the unsolved mystery, count for in face of this possession of self-assertion which she suddenly recognized as the strongest impulse of her being!

"Free! Body and soul free!" she kept whispering.

Josephine was kneeling before the closed door with her lips to the keyhole, imploring for admission. "Louise, open the door! I beg; open the door—you will make yourself ill.

What are you doing, Louise? For heaven's sake open the door."

"Go away. I am not making myself ill." No; she was drinking in a very elixir of life[1] through that open window.

Her fancy was running riot along those days ahead of her. Spring days, and summer days, and all sorts of days that would be her own. She breathed a quick prayer that life might be long. It was only yesterday she had thought with a shudder that life might be long.

She arose at length and opened the door to her sister's importunities. There was a feverish triumph in her eyes, and she carried herself unwittingly like a goddess of Victory. She clasped her sister's waist, and together they descended the stairs. Richards stood waiting for them at the bottom.

Someone was opening the front door with a latchkey. It was Brently Mallard who entered, a little travel-stained, composedly carrying his gripsack[2] and umbrella. He had been far from the scene of accident, and did not know there had been one. He stood amazed at Josephine's piercing cry; at Richards's quick motion to screen him from the view of his wife.

But Richards was too late.

When the doctors came they said she had died of heart disease—of joy that kills.

---

1. **elixir of life** (i lik' sər) *n.*: An imaginary substance thought by medieval alchemists to prolong life indefinitely.
2. **gripsack** (grip' sak) *n.*: A small bag for holding clothes.

THINKING ABOUT THE SELECTION

Recalling

1. Why is great care taken to break the news of Brently Mallard's death to Mrs. Mallard "as gently as possible"?
2. (a) How does Mrs. Mallard first react to the news of her husband's death? (b) How does her reaction change?
3. (a) Who opens the front door toward the end of the story? (b) How does Mrs. Mallard react when she sees him?

Interpreting

4. At the beginning of the story, when Chopin states that Mrs. Mallard "was afflicted with a heart trouble," she seems to be referring to a medical problem. Considering Mrs. Mallard's response to her husband's death, what other meaning do you think this statement might have?
5. How do the details of the scene outside Mrs. Mallard's room foreshadow the feelings that gradually sweep over Mrs. Mallard as she sits in her armchair?
6. What has Mrs. Mallard apparently resented about her marriage?
7. Why do you think Chopin chooses to reveal little about Mrs. Mallard's personality aside from her feelings concerning her marriage, her husband, and her independence?
8. What do you think is the actual reason for Mrs. Mallard's death?
9. What do you think is the significance of the story's title?

Applying

10. Mrs. Mallard realizes, "There would be no one to live for her during these coming years; she would live for herself." Do you think that it is important for people to live for themselves? Explain your answer.

ANALYZING LITERATURE

Recognizing Irony

Irony is a contrast between what is stated and what is meant, or between what is expected to happen and what actually happens. Situational irony and dramatic irony are two of the types of irony used in literature. An example of situational irony occurs in "The Story of an Hour," when, after you have been led to expect that Mrs. Mallard will be deeply disturbed by the news of her husband's death, she is actually overcome by a sense of joy.

1. Why is Mrs. Mallard's sudden death also an example of situational irony?
2. Why is the diagnosis of the cause of Mrs. Mallard's death an example of dramatic irony?

CRITICAL THINKING AND READING

Recognizing Details of Irony

A writer creates situational irony by including details that create certain expectations. For example, in "The Story of an Hour," Chopin leads you to expect that Mrs. Mallard will be upset by the news of her husband's death by mentioning that Josephine and Richards take great care to break the news to her as gently as possible.

Find two details that help create the situational irony of Mrs. Mallard's death.

THINKING AND WRITING

Writing About Irony

Write an essay in which you discuss the role of irony in "The Story of an Hour." Reread the story focusing on Chopin's use of irony. Develop a thesis statement. When you write your essay, use evidence from the story to support your thesis. When you revise your essay, make sure you have not included any unnecessary information.

Interpreting

4. It might refer to her lack of love for her husband and her unenthusiastic outlook on life.
5. The details convey a sense of rebirth.
6. Suggested Response: Mrs. Mallard resented the limits placed upon her freedom.
7. Suggested Response: She wants to keep the story focused on the events being described and on Mrs. Mallard's reactions to these events.
8. Her death is caused by the feelings of shock and disappointment that result from the return of her husband.
9. The action of the story takes place within the period of an hour; the title reflects the irony of how quickly events can change within an hour.

Applying

10. Suggested Response: Yes, people must live for themselves in order to have self-esteem.

Challenge Why do you think "The Story of an Hour" provoked a controversial reaction when it was first published?

ANSWERS TO ANALYZING LITERATURE

1. Mrs. Mallard's sudden death is an example of situational irony, because she has just begun to look forward to leading a long life.
2. It is an example of dramatic irony, because readers are aware that the doctor's diagnosis is incorrect.

ANSWERS TO CRITICAL THINKING AND READING

Suggested Response: She had just been "drinking in the very elixir of life" and she had "breathed a quick prayer that life might be long."

THINKING AND WRITING

Publishing Student Writing Have student volunteers read their essays to the class, and use the readings as a springboard for a class discussion about irony.

Closure and Extension

ANSWERS TO THINKING ABOUT THE SELECTION

Recalling

1. Great care is taken in breaking the news to Mrs. Mallard because of her heart condition.
2. (a) Mrs. Mallard reacts by weeping with wild abandonment. (b) Her reaction changes to joy and a sense of freedom.
3. (a) Her husband, Brently Mallard, opens the front door. (b) When she sees him, she dies.

WILLA CATHER

1873–1947

Willa Cather was born in a small town in western Virginia. When she was ten, her family moved to a farm near the frontier town of Red Cloud, Nebraska. Here, many of Cather's new neighbors were immigrants—Swedes, Germans, Slavs, and Russians—struggling to build a life for themselves in their new land and determined to preserve the culture of the land they left behind. Through her interaction with this diverse group of people, Cather developed an awareness of certain qualities shared not only by people of the frontier but by people from all over the world. She also gained a rich cultural background, studying foreign languages, history, and classical music and opera. She wrote of her childhood: "On Sundays we could drive to a Norwegian church and listen to a sermon in that language, or to a Danish or Swedish church. We could go to a French Catholic settlement or into the Bohemian township and hear one in Czech, or we could go to the church with the German Lutherans."

After graduating from the University of Nebraska in 1895, Cather worked as an editor for a Pittsburgh newspaper, while writing poems and short stories in her spare time. Her first collection of stories, *The Troll Garden,* was published in 1905. The following year she moved to New York, where she worked as the managing editor for *McClure's Magazine.* In 1912, the year after she published her first novel, *Alexander's Bridge,* she left the magazine to devote all her energy to writing. During the next several years, she produced three novels: *O Pioneers!* (1913); *The Song of the Lark* (1915); and *My Antonia* (1918), which captured the flavor of life in the midwestern prairies. In 1923 she won the Pulitzer Prize for her novel *One of Ours* (1922).

Cather shifted her attention from the Midwest to the Southwest in *Death Comes for the Archbishop* (1927) and to seventeenth-century Quebec in *Shadows on the Rock* (1931). She also published two collections of short stories: *Youth and the Bright Medusa* (1920) and *Obscure Destinies* (1932); and a collection of critical essays and recollections of earlier writers: *Not Under Forty.*

In her work Cather displayed her admiration for the courage and spirit of the immigrants and other settlers of the frontier while at the same time conveying an intense awareness of the loss felt by some of the pioneers as well as the loneliness and isolation from which they suffered. In "A Wagner Matinée" Cather captures this sense of loneliness and isolation by contrasting the stark realities of frontier life with the possibilities of life in a more cultured world.

554   Realism and the Frontier

GUIDE FOR INTERPRETING

A Wagner Matinée

Characterization. Characterization is the means by which a writer reveals a character's personality. Writers generally develop a character through one of the following methods: direct statements about the character, physical descriptions of the character, the character's actions, the character's thoughts and comments, or other characters' reactions to or comments about the character.

In the late 1800's and early 1900's, writers began turning to the first-person and third-person limited points of view. When a writer limits the point of view to one character, as Cather does in "A Wagner Matinée," most of what is revealed about the characters is shaped by the thoughts of the character from whose point of view the story is being told.

Writing

Ralph Waldo Emerson wrote, "[Music] takes us out of the actual and whispers to us dim secrets that startle us to wonder as to who we are, and for what, whence, and whereth." Discuss the meaning of this quotation. Think about the powerful effect music often has on people's memories and emotions. Recall a piece of music—one that has no lyrics—that can produce a strong effect on your memories and emotions. Then freewrite about it.

Primary Source

As you read "A Wagner Matinée," you will notice Willa Cather's harsh portrayal of the Midwest. Although this portrayal incensed many members of Cather's family, Edith Lewis, a close friend, found herself agreeing with it. Here Lewis recalls how she felt during one trip she took with Cather to Red Cloud, Nebraska.

> A new convention had to be created for [Nebraska]; a convention that had nothing to do with woods and water-falls, streams and valleys and picturesque architecture. . . . There it lay; and it was as new, as unknown to art as it was to the pioneer.
>
> Although I had grown up in Nebraska, I remember how lost in the prairies Red Cloud seemed to me . . . as if the hot wind that so much of the time blew over it went on and left it behind, isolated, forgotten by the rest of the world. It seemed flattened down against the sea of earth as a boat of ship-wrecked men is flattened down, almost imperceptible, among the waves. And I felt again that forlornness, that terrible restlessness that comes over young people born in small towns in the middle of the continent; the sense of being cut off from all the great currents of life and thought.

Guide for Interpreting 555

Literary Focus Ask students to discuss whether one person can ever tell the whole truth about another person. Have them keep their responses in mind as they read the narrator's description of his Aunt Georgiana.

Writing/Prior Knowledge Explain to students that many writers have felt an affinity for music. Ask them to discuss why this might be so. What qualities do music and literature share? You might want to have your **more advanced** students discuss the following comparison by Lawrence Durrell: "As poetry is the harmony of words, so music is that of notes."

Vocabulary

Preteach the following vocabulary words:
callow (kal′ ō) *adj.:* Immature; inexperienced (p. 556)
reverential (rev′ ə ren′ shəl) *adj.:* Showing or caused by a feeling of deep respect, love, and awe (p. 560)
tremulously (trem′ yo͞o ləs lē) *adv.:* Fearfully; timidly (p. 558)
semi-somnambulant (sem′i säm nam′ byo͞o lənt) *adj.:* Half sleepwalking (p. 558)
inert (in urt′) *adj.:* Motionless (p. 559)
trepidation (trep′ə dā′ shən) *n.:* Fearful anxiety; apprehension (p. 559)
jocularity (jäk′ yə lar′ə tē) *n.:* Joking good humor (p. 562)

A Wagner Matinée

Willa Cather

1

I received one morning a letter written in pale ink, on glassy, blue-lined notepaper, and bearing the postmark of a little Nebraska village. This communication, worn and rubbed, looking as though it had been carried for some days in a coat pocket that was none too clean, was from my Uncle Howard. It informed me that his wife had been left a small legacy by a bachelor relative who had recently died, and that it had become necessary for her to come to Boston to attend to the settling of the estate. He requested me to meet her at the station, and render her whatever services might prove necessary. On examining the date indicated as that of her arrival, I found it no later than tomorrow. He had characteristically delayed writing until, had I been away from home for a day, I must have missed the good woman altogether.

2

The name of my Aunt Georgiana called up not alone her own figure, at once pathetic and grotesque, but opened before my feet a gulf of recollections so wide and deep that, as the letter dropped from my hand, I felt suddenly a stranger to all the present conditions of my existence, wholly ill at ease and out of place amid the surroundings of my study. I became, in short, the gangling farmer boy my aunt had known, scourged with chilblains and bashfulness, my hands cracked and raw from the corn husking. I felt the knuckles of my thumb tentatively, as though they were raw again. I sat again before her parlor organ, thumbing the scales with my stiff, red hands, while she beside me made canvas mittens for the huskers.

The next morning, after preparing my landlady somewhat, I set out for the station. When the train arrived I had some difficulty in finding my aunt. She was the last of the passengers to alight, and when I got her into the carriage she looked not unlike one of those charred, smoked bodies that firemen lift from the *débris* of a burned building. She had come all the way in a day coach; her linen duster[1] had become black with soot and her black bonnet gray with dust during the journey. When we arrived at my boardinghouse the landlady put her to bed at once, and I did not see her again until the next morning.

3

Whatever shock Mrs. Springer experienced at my aunt's appearance she considerately concealed. Myself, I saw my aunt's misshapen figure with that feeling of awe and respect with which we behold explorers who have left their ears and fingers north of Franz Josef Land,[2] or their health somewhere along the upper Congo.[3] My Aunt Georgiana had been a music teacher at the Boston Conservatory, somewhere back in the latter sixties. One summer, which she had spent in the little village in the Green Mountains[4] where her ancestors had dwelt for generations, she had kindled the callow fancy of the most idle and shiftless of all the village lads, and had conceived for this Howard Carpenter one of those absurd and extravagant passions which a handsome

---

1. **duster** *n.*: A short, loose smock worn to protect clothing from dust.
2. **Franz Josef Land:** A group of islands in the Arctic Ocean that are now part of the U.S.S.R.
3. **Congo:** River in central Africa.
4. **Green Mountains:** Mountains in Vermont.

FROM ARKANSAS
George Schreiber
Sheldon Swope Art Gallery, Terre Haute, Indiana

A Wagner Matinée 557

Fine art, *From Arkansas,* 1939, by George Schreiber. George Schreiber (1904–1977) was born in Belgium and immigrated to the United States in the 1920's. Like so many American artists during the Depression, Schreiber turned his focus to the great midwestern farmland. In *From Arkansas,* he portrays the subject of an aproned woman with stark realism. The hardships endured and the strength with which they were met are both reflected in the woman's countenance. A mood of loneliness and desolation is evoked by the distant shed and the bare tree branches. Although Schreiber was not a major figure in the Regionalist art movement, this painting demonstrated that he was caught up in recording the spirit of rural America during the Depression.

Ask students the following questions:

1. In what way does the woman in the painting seem like Aunt Georgiana?
2. What feelings can you infer from the way she holds her arms in front of her?

4

Clarification In 1862, Congress passed the Homestead Act as a way of encouraging the settlement of the prairielands of the West. The land offered a quarter-section, 160 acres, of free land to anyone over twenty-one years of age who was a citizen or who had declared intention to become one. Permanent ownership of the land came after five years of residence or after six months and the payment of $1.50 an acre.

5 **Enrichment** When this story was published, it created a hue and cry in Nebraska, where some of Cather's fellow Nebraskans claimed it was unfair to the state in which she had been raised and responded sharply to her portrait of Aunt Georgiana. Cather defended her story, saying that it paid tribute to the brave women who endured the desolation and loneliness of the old days of life on the frontier.

6 **Discussion** What effect is created by the use of the word *martyrdom* here? How does this word relate to Aunt Georgiana's statement at the end of the paragraph?

7 **Master Teacher Note** In *Euryanthe,* an opera by Weber, Euryanthe is falsely accused and led into the desert to die by Adolar, the man she loves.

Notice how Euryanthe's story echoes the theme of martyrdom. Have students discuss why hearing the music aroused such a strong reaction in Aunt Georgiana.

country boy of twenty-one sometimes inspires in a plain, angular, spectacled woman of thirty. When she returned to her duties in Boston, Howard followed her; and the upshot of this inexplicable infatuation was that she eloped with him, eluding the reproaches of her family and the criticism of her friends by going with him to the Nebraska frontier. Carpenter, who of course had no money, took a homestead in Red Willow County,[5] fifty miles from the railroad. There they measured off their eighty acres by driving across the prairie in a wagon, to the wheel of which they had tied a red cotton handkerchief, and counting its revolutions. They built a dugout in the red hillside, one of those cave dwellings whose inmates usually reverted to the conditions of primitive savagery. Their water they got from the lagoons where the buffalo drank, and their slender stock of provisions was always at the mercy of bands of roving Indians. For thirty years my aunt had not been farther than fifty miles from the homestead.

But Mrs. Springer knew nothing of all this, and must have been considerably shocked at what was left of my kinswoman. Beneath the soiled linen duster, which on her arrival was the most conspicuous feature of her costume, she wore a black stuff dress whose ornamentation showed that she had surrendered herself unquestioningly into the hands of a country dressmaker. My poor aunt's figure, however, would have presented astonishing difficulties to any dressmaker. Her skin was yellow from constant exposure to a pitiless wind, and to the alkaline water which transforms the most transparent cuticle into a sort of flexible leather. She wore ill-fitting false teeth. The most striking thing about her physiognomy, however, was an incessant twitching of the mouth and eyebrows, a form of nervous disorder resulting from isolation and monotony, and from frequent physical suffering.

5. **Red Willow County:** County in southwestern Nebraska that borders on Kansas.

In my boyhood this affliction had possessed a sort of horrible fascination for me, of which I was secretly very much ashamed, for in those days I owed to this woman most of the good that ever came my way, and had a reverential affection for her. During the three winters when I was riding herd for my uncle, my aunt, after cooking three meals for half a dozen farmhands, and putting the six children to bed, would often stand until midnight at her ironing board, hearing me at the kitchen table beside her recite Latin declensions and conjugations, and gently shaking me when my drowsy head sank down over a page of irregular verbs. It was to her, at her ironing or mending, that I read my first Shakespeare; and her old textbook of mythology was the first that ever came into my empty hands. She taught me my scales and exercises, too, on the little parlor organ which her husband had bought her after fifteen years, during which she had not so much as seen any instrument except an accordion, that belonged to one of the Norwegian farmhands. She would sit beside me by the hour, darning and counting, while I struggled with the "Harmonious Blacksmith"; but she seldom talked to me about music, and I understood why. She was a pious woman; she had the consolation of religion; and to her at least her martyrdom was not wholly sordid. Once when I had been doggedly beating out some passages from an old score of "Euryanthe" I had found among her music books, she came up to me and, putting her hands over my eyes, gently drew my head back upon her shoulder, saying tremulously, "Don't love it so well, Clark, or it may be taken from you. Oh! dear boy, pray that whatever your sacrifice be it is not that."

When my aunt appeared on the morning after her arrival, she was still in a semi-somnambulent state. She seemed not to realize that she was in the city where she had spent her youth, the place longed for hungrily for half a lifetime. She had been so wretchedly trainsick throughout the journey

6
7

that she had no recollection of anything but her discomfort, and, to all intents and purposes, there were but a few hours of nightmare between the farm in Red Willow County and my study on Newbury Street. I had planned a little pleasure for her that afternoon, to repay her for some of the glorious moments she had given me when we used to milk together in the straw-thatched cowshed, and she, because I was more than usually tired, or because her husband had spoken sharply to me, would tell me of the splendid performance of Meyerbeer's *Les Huguenots*[6] she had seen in Paris in her youth. At two o'clock the Boston Symphony Orchestra was to give a Wagner[7] program, and I intended to take my aunt, though as I conversed with her I grew doubtful about her enjoyment of it. Indeed, for her own sake, I could only wish her taste for such things quite dead, and the long struggle mercifully ended at last. I suggested our visiting the Conservatory and the Common[8] before lunch, but she seemed altogether too timid to wish to venture out. She questioned me absently about various changes in the city, but she was chiefly concerned that she had forgotten to leave instructions about feeding half-skimmed milk to a certain weakling calf, "Old Maggie's calf, you know, Clark," she explained, evidently having forgotten how long I had been away. She was further troubled because she had neglected to tell her daughter about the freshly opened kit of mackerel in the cellar, that would spoil if it were not used directly.

I asked her whether she had ever heard any of the Wagnerian operas, and found that she had not, though she was perfectly familiar with their respective situations and had once possessed the piano score of *The Flying Dutchman.* I began to think it would have been best to get her back to Red Willow County without waking her, and regretted having suggested the concert.

From the time we entered the concert hall, however, she was a trifle less passive and inert, and seemed to begin to perceive her surroundings. I had felt some trepidation lest one might become aware of the absurdities of her attire, or might experience some painful embarrassment at stepping suddenly into the world to which she had been dead for a quarter of a century. But again I found how superficially I had judged her. She sat looking about her with eyes as impersonal, almost as stony, as those with which the granite Ramses[9] in a museum watches the froth and fret that ebbs and flows about his pedestal, separated from it by the lonely stretch of centuries. I have seen this same aloofness in old miners who drift into the Brown Hotel at Denver, their pockets full of bullion, their linen soiled, their haggard faces unshorn, and who stand in the thronged corridors as solitary as though they were still in a frozen camp on the Yukon, or in the yellow blaze of the Arizona desert, conscious that certain experiences have isolated them from their fellows by a gulf no haberdasher could conceal.

The audience was made up chiefly of women. One lost the contour of faces and figures, indeed any effect of line whatever, and there was only the color contrast of bodices past counting, the shimmer and shading of fabrics soft and firm, silky and sheer, resisting and yielding: red, mauve, pink, blue, lilac, purple, ecru, rose, yellow, cream, and white, all the colors that an impressionist finds in a sunlit landscape, with here and there the dead black shadow of a frock coat. My Aunt Georgiana regarded them as though they had been so many daubs of tube paint on a palette.

---

6. **Les Huguenots** (hyoo′ gə nät′): Opera written in 1836 by Giacomo Meyerbeer (1791–1864).
7. **Wagner** (väg′ nər): Richard Wagner (1813–1883), a great German composer who is responsible for the development of the musical drama.
8. **Common:** Boston Common, a small park in Boston.

9. **Ramses** (ram′ sēz): Egyptian kings who ruled from c.1315 to c.1090 B.C.

8 Reading Strategy Have students use a map to trace Aunt Georgiana's probable route from Red Willow county to Boston.

9 Discussion To what long struggle does Clark refer? Why does he use the word *mercifully* here? How does this word echo back to the word *martyr*?

10 Master Teacher Note *The Flying Dutchman* was a milestone in the career of Richard Wagner. In this opera, because of a rashly uttered oath, a Dutch sea captain is doomed to roam the seas forever until the curse is broken by the love of a faithful woman. Have students discuss how Aunt Georgiana's rash decision doomed her to a fate similar to the Dutchman's.

11 Discussion In what way have Clark's judgments of his Aunt up to this point been superficial?

12 Discussion Have students discuss whether they agree with Clark that certain experiences can isolate people from their fellow human beings.

13 **Discussion** Have students compare and contrast the world Clark is showing her with the world Aunt Georgiana left behind in Nebraska.

14 **Master Teacher Note** *Tannhauser* is an opera in three acts by Richard Wagner. The overture musically reveals the powerful struggle within Tannhauser. He has been lured into the Venusburg by the seductive beauty of Holga (Venus), the goddess of love. With difficulty, he tears himself from her, vowing to begin a new life and win the love of the virtuous Elizabeth.

Consider the effects of this warring duality on Georgiana, who is expressing her own internal struggles. After thirty years of neglect, she is awakening to the thrill of music. Shall she allow herself to be fully possessed by it, or must she yield to the grim knowledge of her obligation to return to the farm?

15 **Master Teacher Note** *Tristam and Isolde* is an opera in three acts by Richard Wagner. In this tragic story, Isolde has been promised to the King, and it is Tristam's duty to bring her to him. They declare their love for each other, and are surprised in the King's garden by one of his knights. Tristam is mortally wounded and Isolde breathes her last breath over his body.

Point out to students that here is another example of a tragic ending brought about by love.

When the musicians came out and took their places, she gave a little stir of anticipation, and looked with quickening interest down over the rail at that invariable grouping; perhaps the first wholly familiar thing that had greeted her eye since she had left old Maggie and her weakling calf. I could feel how all those details sank into her soul, for I had not forgotten how they had sunk into mine when I came fresh from plowing forever and forever between green aisles of corn, where, as in a treadmill, one might walk from daybreak to dusk without perceiving a shadow of change in one's environment. I reminded myself of the impression made on me by the clean profiles of the musicians, the gloss of their linen; the dull black of their coats, the beloved shapes of the instruments, the patches of yellow light thrown by the green-shaded stand-lamps on the smooth, varnished bellies of the cellos and the bass viols in the rear, the restless, wind-tossed forest of fiddle necks and bows; I recalled how, in the first orchestra I had ever heard, those long bow strokes seemed to draw the soul out of me, as a conjuror's stick reels out paper ribbon from a hat.

The first number was the Tannhäuser overture. When the violins drew out the first strain of the Pilgrims' chorus, my Aunt Georgiana clutched my coat sleeve. Then it was that I first realized that for her this singing of basses and stinging frenzy of lighter strings broke a silence of thirty years, the inconceivable silence of the plains. With the battle between the two motifs, with the bitter frenzy of the Venusberg[10] theme and its ripping of strings, came to me an overwhelming sense of the waste and wear we are so powerless to combat. I saw again the tall, naked house on the prairie, black and grim as a wooden fortress; the black pond where I had learned to swim, the rain-gullied clay about the naked house; the four dwarf

ash seedlings on which the dishcloths were always hung to dry before the kitchen door. The world there is the flat world of the ancients; to the east, a cornfield that stretched to daybreak; to the west, a corral that stretched to sunset; between, the sordid conquests of peace, more merciless than those of war.

The overture closed. My aunt released my coat sleeve, but she said nothing. She sat staring at the orchestra through a dullness of thirty years, through the films made, little by little, by each of the three hundred and sixty-five days in every one of them. What, I wondered, did she get from it? She had been a good pianist in her day, I knew, and her musical education had been broader than that of most music teachers of a quarter of a century ago. She had often told me of Mozart's operas and Meyerbeer's, and I could remember hearing her sing, years ago, certain melodies of Verdi. When I had fallen ill with a fever she used to sit by my cot in the evening, while the cool night wind blew in through the faded mosquito netting tacked over the window, and I lay watching a bright star that burned red above the cornfield, and sing "Home to our mountains, oh, let us return!" in a way fit to break the heart of a Vermont boy near dead of homesickness already.

I watched her closely through the prelude to *Tristan and Isolde*, trying vainly to conjecture what that warfare of motifs, that seething turmoil of strings and winds, might mean to her. Had this music any message for her? Did or did not a new planet swim into her ken? Wagner had been a sealed book to Americans before the sixties. Had she anything left with which to comprehend this glory that had flashed around the world since she had gone from it? I was in a fever of curiosity, but Aunt Georgiana sat silent upon her peak in Darien.[11] She preserved

---
10. **Venusberg** (vē′ nəs bʉrg′): A legendary mountain in Germany where Venus, the Roman goddess of love, held court.

---
11. **peak in Darien** (der′ ē ən): The mountain on the Isthmus of Panama. From "On First Looking at Chapman's Homer" by English poet John Keats (1795–1821).

560   Realism and the Frontier

Grammar in Action

The **concluding sentence** of a paragraph can summarize the information in the paragraph, reinforce the main point, or mark the completion of a unit of thought. Willa Cather was a master of forceful concluding sentences. For example, the first paragraph on page 558 concludes with the following sentence:

For thirty years, my aunt had not been farther than fifty miles from the homestead.

This sentence forcefully concludes the paragraph by highlighting the impact of moving to Nebraska on Aunt Georgiana's life.

Student Activity 1. Describe the purpose served by each of the concluding sentences on pages 560 and 561. Explain why you do or do not feel that these sentences are effective.

Student Activity 2. Write a forceful concluding sentence for the following paragraph:

Cather's story "A Wagner Matinée" explores the power of art even over people who may not experience it frequently. The narrator, a young man who lives in Boston, watches the reaction of his aunt, who has lived isolated on the prairie for more than thirty years, to a concert of

AT THE OPERA
Mary Stevenson Cassatt
Museum of Fine Arts, Boston

this utter immobility throughout the numbers from the *Flying Dutchman,* though her fingers worked mechanically upon her black dress, as though of themselves they were recalling the piano score they had once played. Poor old hands! They were stretched and pulled and twisted into mere tentacles to hold, and lift, and knead with; the palms unduly swollen, the fingers bent and knotted, on one of them a thin worn band that had once been a wedding ring. As I pressed and gently quieted one of those groping hands, I remembered, with quivering eyelids, their services for me in other days.

Soon after the tenor began the "Prize Song," I heard a quick-drawn breath, and turned to my aunt. Her eyes were closed, but the tears were glistening on her cheeks, and I think in a moment more they were in my eyes as well. It never really dies, then, the

A Wagner Matinée 561

Wagner's music. The narrator assumes that his aunt's arduous life has coarsened her sensibility to music. However, he has a big surprise.

Student Activity 3. Look at a paragraph you have written recently. See if you can make this paragraph more forceful by adding a concluding sentence that reinforces its main point.

16 Discussion Ask students to discuss the inferences they make about Aunt Georgiana based on the information in this passage. Have her sensibilities really been asleep, as Clark has suggested?

17 Discussion *Trovatore* is an opera by Verdi. Perhaps Aunt Georgiana heard it when she was teaching music in Boston. Why does Clark's comment arouse such a strong reaction in Aunt Georgiana?

18 Discussion Have students explain Aunt Georgiana's reaction.

19 Teaching to Ability Levels Point out Clark's condescending tone. Have your **more advanced** students find other examples of this tone. Ask them to discuss how it colors the picture they receive of Aunt Georgiana.

20 Master Teacher Note *The Ring* refers to *Der Ring des Nibelungen (The Ring of the Nibelung)*, which consists of four musical dramas. It was first performed at Bayreuth, Germany, in 1876.

21 Discussion Have students discuss why she doesn't want to go. Do they think she will return home? Have them find evidence in the selection to support their answers.

Reader's Response What is it about music that makes it appeal to so many people?

---

soul? It withers to the outward eye only, like that strange moss which can lie on a dusty shelf half a century and yet, if placed in water, grows green again. My aunt wept gently throughout the development and elaboration of the melody.

During the intermission before the second half of the concert, I questioned my aunt and found that the "Prize Song" was not new to her. Some years before there had drifted to the farm in Red Willow County a young German, a tramp cow puncher who had sung in the chorus at Bayreuth,[12] when he was a boy, along with the other peasant boys and girls. Of a Sunday morning he used to sit on his blue gingham-sheeted bed in the hands' bedroom, which opened off the kitchen, cleaning the leather of his boots and saddle, and singing the "Prize Song," while my aunt went about her work in the kitchen. She had hovered about him until she had prevailed upon him to join the country church, though his sole fitness for this step, so far as I could gather, lay in his boyish face and his possession of this divine melody. Shortly afterward he had gone to town on the Fourth of July, lost his money at a faro[13] table, ridden a saddled Texas steer on a bet, and disappeared with a fractured collarbone.

"Well, we have come to better things than the old *Trovatore* at any rate, Aunt Georgie?" I queried, with well-meant jocularity.

Her lip quivered and she hastily put her handkerchief up to her mouth. From behind it she murmured, "And you've been hearing this ever since you left me, Clark?" Her question was the gentlest and saddest of reproaches.

"But do you get it, Aunt Georgiana, the astonishing structure of it all?" I persisted.

---

12. **Bayreuth** (bī roit´): A city in Germany known for its annual Wagnerian music festivals.
13. **faro** (fer´ ō): A gambling game in which players bet on the cards to be turned up from the top of the dealer's deck.

"Who could?" she said, absently; "why should one?"

The second half of the program consisted of four numbers from the *Ring*. This was followed by the forest music from *Siegfried*[14] and the program closed with Siegfried's funeral march. My aunt wept quietly, but almost continuously. I was perplexed as to what measure of musical comprehension was left to her, to her who had heard nothing for so many years but the singing of gospel hymns in Methodist services at the square frame schoolhouse on Section Thirteen. I was unable to gauge how much of it had been dissolved in soapsuds, or worked into bread, or milked into the bottom of a pail.

The deluge of sound poured on and on; I never knew what she found in the shining current of it; I never knew how far it bore her, or past what happy islands, or under what skies. From the trembling of her face I could well believe that the *Siegfried* march, at least, carried her out where the myriad graves are, out into the gray, burying grounds of the sea; or into some world of death vaster yet, where, from the beginning of the world, hope has lain down with hope, and dream with dream and, renouncing, slept.

The concert was over; the people filed out of the hall chattering and laughing, glad to relax and find the living level again, but my kinswoman made no effort to rise. I spoke gently to her. She burst into tears and sobbed pleadingly, "I don't want to go, Clark, I don't want to go!"

I understood. For her, just outside the door of the concert hall, lay the black pond with the cattle-tracked bluffs, the tall, unpainted house, naked as a tower, with weather-curled boards; the crook-backed ash seedlings where the dishcloths hung to dry, the gaunt, moulting turkeys picking up refuse about the kitchen door.

---

14. **Siegfried** (sēg´ frēd): An opera based on the adventures of Siegfried, a legendary hero in medieval German literature.

Closure and Extension

ANSWERS TO THINKING ABOUT THE SELECTION

Recalling

1. (a) She has received a small legacy from a bachelor relative and is coming to Boston to settle the estate. (b) The news pulls him back to his childhood, making him feel again the "gangling farmer boy" his aunt had known.

2. (a) Because she loved music and had been a music teacher in Boston before her marriage, Clark thinks the concert will be a treat for her. He wants to thank her for her many kindnesses to him when he was a boy. (b) She seems so asleep, with her sensibilities dead, that he doubts she will enjoy it.

3. She played her little piano organ, which her husband had given her after fifteen years. She told stories of glorious performances she had

THINKING ABOUT THE SELECTION

Recalling

1. (a) Why is Clark's Aunt Georgiana coming to visit? (b) Explain his reaction to the news of her visit.
2. (a) Why does Clark take Aunt Georgiana to the Wagner matinée? (b) Why does he grow doubtful that she will enjoy it?
3. Describe three ways in which Aunt Georgiana indulged her love of music while living on the frontier.

Interpreting

4. (a) What impression is conveyed through the physical descriptions of Red Willow County? (b) Contrast the impression of life in Red Willow County with life in Boston.
5. (a) What does Aunt Georgiana mean when she comments, "Don't love it so well, Clark, or it may be taken from you"? (b) How does this reflect the theme, or main point, of the story?
6. (a) Why does the opera have such a powerful effect on Aunt Georgiana? (b) In what way does the effect of the music on Aunt Georgiana in turn awaken Clark?

Applying

7. (a) In what way can environment shape character? (b) In what way can people shape their environment?

ANALYZING LITERATURE

Understanding Characterization

Characterization is the means by which an author reveals a character's personality. Because of Cather's use of a first-person narrator, much of what we learn about Aunt Georgiana comes from Clark's thoughts and feelings regarding her.

1. What is revealed about Aunt Georgiana through descriptions of her physical appearance?

2. What does Aunt Georgiana's reaction to the opera reveal about her personality?
3. What is revealed about Clark's personality through his thoughts and feelings regarding his aunt?
4. How does the fact that much of what we learn about Aunt Georgiana is revealed through Clark's thoughts and feelings shape our impressions of her?

UNDERSTANDING LANGUAGE

Understanding Musical Terms

Musical terms often appear in works of literature and in everyday language. For example, the word *opera*, which refers to a type of drama in which all or most of the text is set to music, appears in "A Wagner Matinée." Use a dictionary to find the meaning of each of the following musical terms.

1. aria
2. solo
3. libretto
4. requiem
5. crescendo
6. raga
7. octave
8. dissonant

THINKING AND WRITING

Supporting an Opinion

Review the freewriting assignment you completed earlier. Do you think music is a valuable component of daily life? Write a short essay for your teacher discussing whether or not music adds to the quality of life. In your prewriting list evidence from daily life. Then, after organizing your evidence into an outline, write your essay using your evidence to support your argument. Use transitions to link your ideas and vary your sentence structure. When you revise, make sure that you have included enough evidence to adequately support your argument.

---

seen of operas in her youth. She sang songs she remembered and she sought the company of a farmboy who had sang in a chorus in Bayreuth. In addition, she attended church services.

Interpreting

4. (a) The impression of bleakness and desolation is created. (b) In contrast, life in Boston seems rich, varied, and fulfilling.

5. (a) Aunt Georgiana loves music intensely. She is probably referring to the pain she feels because music has been taken from her. (b) The theme of the story refers to the dichotomy where one can be asleep in life and alive in art. The isolation of the frontier has dulled Aunt Georgiana's sensibilities; however, in a way, it has been a saving grace. By being asleep, she can live, it is when she wakes up through music that she can no

longer endure her life.

6. (a) The themes of the operas reflect her own life and awaken the passion within her. (b) It is through the music that Clark comes to understand his aunt.

Applying

7. (a) Suggested Response: Environment can affect people for better or worse. Isolation and hardship can take a great toll on hu-

---

(Answers begin on p. 562.)

man beings. On the other hand, an environment that offers little challenge can weaken character. (b) Suggested Response: People have been known to make paradises out of deserts. Even in a harsh environment, Aunt Georgiana manages to draw from the pool of human resources to pursue her love of music.

Challenge Would it have been better for Aunt Georgiana if she had *not* visited Boston? Why or why not?

ANSWERS TO ANALYZING LITERATURE

1. We see that she has been physically broken by life.
2. It reveals that she is very sensitive.
3. Clark seems to be self-centered and condescending.
4. Since Clark does not understand his aunt until the end, her personality is slowly revealed to us, until we too see her take on tragic dimensions.

ANSWERS TO UNDERSTANDING LANGUAGE

1. an air or melody in an opera, especially one for a solo voice
2. a musical piece meant to be played or sung alone
3. the words or text of an opera
4. a musical setting for a Mass for the dead
5. gradual increase in loudness or intensity
6. a traditional form in Hindu music
7. the eighth full note above a given tone
8. a chord that sounds incomplete

THINKING AND WRITING

For help with this assignment, students can refer to Lesson 21 "Writing an Essay," in the Handbook of Writing About Literature.

Publishing Student Writing Have students read one anothers essays and select the essay they consider the best. Offer it to the school's literary magazine for publication.

More About the Author Many of Jack London's stories have a wolf-like dog as an important character. That animal is usually portrayed as having strong survival instincts. London himself had difficulty surviving. Throughout the latter stages of his life, he suffered from depression and poor health. Discuss the ways in which writers might try either to express or to escape from their personal suffering through their work. Do your students think the writers' problems should be discernible in their work?

Critical Evaluations Here are excerpts from the comments of well-known writers about Jack London:

"He was the true king of our story tellers."

Upton Sinclair

"He was a captive of beauty . . . and of the icy vastness of the Arctic world."

Anna Strunsky

"[Jack London] was an instinctive artist of a high order, and if ignorance corrupted his art, it only made the fact of his inborn mastery the more remarkable."

H. L. Mencken

ESL Teaching Strategy Ask ESL students to study the photo on page 566 carefully. Then have them list ten adjectives to describe the bleakness of the setting. Ask them if they find the scene frightening, and discuss their adjectives to see if they can be placed in clusters dealing with the senses.

JACK LONDON

1876–1916

Jack London endured more hardships during the first twenty-one years of his life than most people experience in a lifetime. Yet he was able to learn from his experiences and use them as the inspiration for his successful career as a writer.

Born in San Francisco, London grew up in extreme poverty. At an early age, he left school to support himself through a variety of menial jobs. He worked as a paper boy, in bowling alleys, on ice wagons, and in canneries and mills. These jobs gave him a strong sympathy for the working class and a lasting dislike of drudgery. At the same time, he was constantly reading, borrowing books of adventure and travel from the public library. London also left San Francisco a number of times, sailing to Japan as part of a sealing expedition and participating in a protest march across the country with a group of unemployed men.

After being arrested for vagrancy near Buffalo, New York, London decided to educate himself and reshape his life. He quickly completed high school, then enrolled in the University of California. London remained in college for only one semester, however, before abandoning his studies and traveling to Alaska in search of gold.

Although he experienced no success as a miner, London's experiences in Alaska taught him about the human desire for wealth and power and about humankind's inability to control nature. Shortly after returning to California, London began transforming his Alaskan adventures into short stories and novels. In 1903 he earned national fame when he published the popular novel *The Call of the Wild*. He soon became the highest paid and most industrious writer in the country. During the course of his career, he produced more than fifty books and earned more than a million dollars. Though many of his works are no longer highly regarded by critics, several of his novels, including *The Call of the Wild (1903), The Sea-Wolf* (1904), and *White Fang* (1906), have become American classics.

London's friend Oliver Madox Huefer recalled that London "was the ideal yarnspinner—his spoken stories were even better than his written—and one reason why I think him likely to be numbered as among the writers of real mark was that he was perfectly unconscious of it. Like Peter Pan, he never grew up, and he lived in his own stories with such intensity that he ended by believing them himself."

Many of London's best short stories and novels depict a person's struggle for survival against the powerful forces of nature. For example, "To Build a Fire" tells the story of a man's fight to survive the harsh cold of the Alaskan winter.

564   *Realism and the Frontier*

Objectives

1 To understand conflict
2 To relate conflict to theme
3 To write about conflict and theme

Support Material

Teaching Portfolio
Teacher Backup, p. 745
Grammar in Action Worksheets, *Appreciating Sentence Structure*, p. 751; *Using Commas*, p. 753
Usage and Mechanics Worksheet, p. 755
Vocabulary Check, p. 756
Analyzing Literature Worksheet, *Understanding Conflict*, p. 757

Critical Thinking and Reading Worksheet, *Relating Conflict to Theme*, p. 758
Selection Test, p. 759

GUIDE FOR INTERPRETING

Writer's Techniques

To Build a Fire

Conflict. Conflict, a struggle between two opposing forces or characters, plays a vital role in the plot development of a literary work. The events of a work are all related to the conflict as the plot develops. Frequently the conflict is resolved by the end of the work, though in many modern and contemporary works the conflict is left unresolved.

Conflict may be internal or external. An internal conflict is a struggle between conflicting thoughts and emotions within a character. For example, in "A White Heron" Sylvia struggles between her eagerness to please the young stranger and her desire to protect the white heron. An external conflict is a struggle between a character and an outside force, such as another character, society, nature, or fate. For example, in *Moby-Dick* Ahab struggles against a great white whale, Moby-Dick.

Writing

Think of an incident in which you witnessed or were confronted with the tremendous power of nature. For example, you may have lived through a hurricane or tornado or experienced extremely hot or cold weather. Briefly describe your responses to this incident and how it shaped your impressions of nature.

Primary Source

The discovery in 1896 of a rich lode of gold in the Yukon led to the Klondike stampede of 1897–1898. Thousands of prospectors headed for the arctic cold of the North where they mined for gold in perpetually frozen ground.

Jack London was among the first of the stampeders. What made him join the Klondike gold rush? He once commented, "I had let career go hang and was on the adventure-path again in quest of fortune." Elsewhere he commented, "True, the new territory was mostly barren; but its several hundred thousand square miles of frigidity at least gave breathing space to those who else would have suffocated at home."

London's contemporary, writer Hamlin Garland, who also made the trip to the Klondike, probably reflected London's feelings when he made the following comments:

> I believed that I was about to see and take part in a most picturesque and impressive movement across the wilderness. I believed it to be the last march of the kind which could ever come in America, so rapidly were the wild places being settled up. . . . I wished to return to the wilderness also, to forget books and theories of art and social problems, and come again face to face with the great free spaces of woods and skies and streams.

Guide for Interpreting 565

Literary Focus In most twentieth-century works, the conflict is left unresolved to reflect the sense of uncertainty associated with modern life.

Writing/Prior Knowledge Before having your students complete the writing assignment, you might want to spend some time discussing the forces of nature and their effect on people.

Vocabulary

Preteach the following vocabulary words:
conjectural (kən jek′ chər əl) *adj.:* Based on guesswork (p. 567)
unwonted (un wun′ tid) *adj.:* Unfamiliar (p. 568)
conflagration (kän′ flə grā′ shən) *n.:* A big, destructive fire (p. 568)
peremptorily (pə remp′ tər ə lē) *adj.:* Commandingly (p. 575)

To Build a Fire

Jack London

Day had broken cold and gray, exceedingly cold and gray, when the man turned aside from the main Yukon[1] trail and climbed the high earth-bank, where a dim and little-traveled trail led eastward through the fat spruce timberland. It was a steep bank, and he paused for breath at the top, excusing the act to himself by looking at his watch. It was nine o'clock. There was no sun nor hint of sun, though there was not a cloud in the sky. It was a clear day, and yet there seemed an intangible pall over the face of things, a subtle gloom that made the day dark, and that was due to the absence of sun. This fact did not worry the man. He was used to the lack of sun. It had been days since he had seen the sun, and he knew that

1

---

1. **Yukon** (yōō′ kän): Territory in northwestern Canada, east of Alaska. Also a river.

a few more days must pass before that cheerful orb, due south, would just peep above the skyline and dip immediately from view.

The man flung a look back along the way he had come. The Yukon lay a mile wide and hidden under three feet of ice. On top of this ice were as many feet of snow. It was all pure white, rolling in gentle undulations where the ice jams of the freeze-up had formed. North and south, as far as his eye could see, it was unbroken white, save for a dark hairline that curved and twisted from around the spruce-covered island to the south, and that curved and twisted away into the north, where it disappeared behind another spruce-covered island. This dark hairline was the trail—the main trail—that led south five hundred miles to the Chilcoot Pass, Dyea,[2] and salt water; and that led north seventy miles to Dawson, and still on to the north a thousand miles to Nulato,[3] and finally to St. Michael on Bering Sea, a thousand miles and half a thousand more.

But all this—the mysterious, far-reaching hairline trail, the absence of sun from the sky, the tremendous cold, and the strangeness and weirdness of it all—made no impression on the man. It was not because he was long used to it. He was a newcomer in the land, a *chechaquo*,[4] and this was his first winter. The trouble with him was that he was without imagination. He was quick and alert in the things of life, but only in the things, and not in the significances. Fifty degrees below zero meant eighty-odd degrees of frost. Such fact impressed him as being cold and uncomfortable, and that was all. It did not lead him to meditate upon his frailty as a creature of temperature, and upon man's frailty in general, able only to live within certain narrow limits of heat and cold; and from there on it did not lead him to the conjectural field of

---

2. **Dyea** (dī′ ā): A former town in Alaska at the start of the Yukon trail.
3. **Dawson** and **Nulato:** Former goldmining villages in the Yukon.
4. **chechaquo** (chē chä′ kwō): Slang for newcomer.

immortality and man's place in the universe. Fifty degrees below zero stood for a bite of frost that hurt and that must be guarded against by the use of mittens, earflaps, warm moccasins, and thick socks. Fifty degrees below zero was to him just precisely fifty degrees below zero. That there should be anything more to it than that was a thought that never entered his head.

As he turned to go on, he spat speculatively. There was a sharp, explosive crackle that startled him. He spat again. And again, in the air, before it could fall to the snow, the spittle crackled. He knew that at fifty below spittle crackled on the snow, but this spittle had crackled in the air. Undoubtedly it was colder than fifty below—how much colder he did not know. But the temperature did not matter. He was bound for the old claim on the left fork of Henderson Creek, where the boys were already. They had come over across the divide from the Indian Creek country, while he had come the roundabout way to take a look at the possibilities of getting out logs in the spring from the islands in the Yukon. He would be in to camp by six o'clock; a bit after dark, it was true, but the boys would be there, a fire would be going, and a hot supper would be ready. As for lunch, he pressed his hand against the protruding bundle under his jacket. It was also under his shirt, wrapped up in a handkerchief and lying against the naked skin. It was the only way to keep the biscuits from freezing. He smiled agreeably to himself as he thought of those biscuits, each cut open and sopped in bacon grease, and each enclosing a generous slice of fried bacon.

He plunged in among the big spruce trees. The trail was faint. A foot of snow had fallen since the last sled had passed over, and he was glad he was without a sled, traveling light. In fact, he carried nothing but the lunch wrapped in the handkerchief. He was surprised, however, at the cold. It certainly was cold, he concluded, as he rubbed his numb nose and cheekbones with his mittened hand. He was a warm-whiskered

2 **Reading Strategy** The author regularly gives information that should prompt the reader to evaluate what is said. The reader should become aware of the need to ask questions. For example, the author writes that the tremendous cold "made no impression on the man." The reader should ponder whether the cold ought to have impressed the man.

3 **Discussion** Why is it important for someone in the man's situation to possess an imagination?

4 **Literary Focus** Note that the conflict between the man and nature is established in the first three paragraphs of the story.

5 **Discussion** What does the detail about spitting tell us about London's familiarity with the Arctic?

6 **Critical Thinking and Reading** Note that the man seems certain that he will reach the camp by six. How does this relate to his lack of imagination?

7 **Discussion** Should he still be surprised at the cold? Why or why not?

8 **Critical Thinking and Reading**
Ask students to consider why the obvious detail about the thermometer is included. What does it serve to underscore?

9 **Discussion** Why is it relevant that nobody has passed there in months?

10 **Discussion** What characteristic of the man is reinforced by his thinking about being in camp by six o'clock?

11 **Master Teacher Note** First-aid books list some characteristics of hypothermia, or extremely low body heat. It would be worthwhile to review such information or to assign a student to find out about it. Many of the symptoms the man experiences are clinically accurate.

man, but the hair on his face did not protect the high cheekbones and the eager nose that thrust itself aggressively into the frosty air.

At the man's heels trotted a dog, a big native husky, the proper wolf dog, gray-coated and without any visible or temperamental difference from its brother, the wild wolf. The animal was depressed by the tremendous cold. It knew that it was no time for traveling. Its instinct told it a truer tale than was told to the man by the man's judgment. In reality, it was not merely colder than fifty below zero; it was colder than sixty below, than seventy below. It was seventy-five below zero. Since the freezing point is thirty-two above zero, it meant that one hundred and seven degrees of frost obtained. The dog did not know anything about thermometers. Possibly in its brain there was no sharp consciousness of a condition of very cold such as was in the man's brain. But the brute had its instinct. It experienced a vague but menacing apprehension that subdued it and made it slink along at the man's heels, and that made it question eagerly every unwonted movement of the man as if expecting him to go into camp or to seek shelter somewhere and build a fire. The dog had learned fire, and it wanted fire, or else to burrow under the snow and cuddle its warmth away from the air.

The frozen moisture of its breathing had settled on its fur in a fine powder of frost, and especially were its jowls, muzzle, and eyelashes whitened by its crystalled breath. The man's red beard and mustache were likewise frosted, but more solidly, the deposit taking the form of ice and increasing with every warm, moist breath he exhaled. Also, the man was chewing tobacco, and the muzzle of ice held his lips so rigidly that he was unable to clear his chin when he expelled the juice. The result was that a crystal beard of the color and solidity of amber was increasing its length on his chin. If he fell down it would shatter itself, like glass, into brittle fragments. But he did not mind the appendage. It was the penalty all tobacco-

chewers paid in that country, and he had been out before in two cold snaps. They had not been so cold as this, he knew, but by the spirit thermometer[5] at Sixty Mile he knew they had been registered at fifty below and at fifty-five.

He held on through the level stretch of woods for several miles, crossed a wide flat, and dropped down a bank to the frozen bed of a small stream. This was Henderson Creek, and he knew he was ten miles from the forks. He looked at his watch. It was ten o'clock. He was making four miles an hour, and he calculated that he would arrive at the forks at half past twelve. He decided to celebrate that event by eating his lunch there.

The dog dropped in again at his heels, with a tail drooping discouragement, as the man swung along the creek bed. The furrow of the old sled trail was plainly visible, but a dozen inches of snow covered the marks of the last runners. In a month no man had come up or down that silent creek. The man held steadily on. He was not much given to thinking, and just then particularly he had nothing to think about save that he would eat lunch at the forks and that at six o'clock he would be in camp with the boys. There was nobody to talk to; and, had there been, speech would have been impossible because of the ice-muzzle on his mouth. So he continued monotonously to chew tobacco and to increase the length of his amber beard.

Once in a while the thought reiterated itself that it was very cold and that he had never experienced such cold. As he walked along he rubbed his cheekbones and nose with the back of his mittened hand. He did this automatically, now and again changing hands. But rub as he would, the instant he stopped his cheekbones went numb, and the following instant the end of his nose went numb. He was sure to frost his cheeks; he knew that, and experienced a pang of regret that he had not devised a nose strap of the

5. **spirit thermometer:** A thermometer, containing alcohol, used in extreme cold.

sort Bud wore in cold snaps. Such a strap passed across the cheeks, as well, and saved them. But it didn't matter much, after all. What were frosted cheeks? A bit painful, that was all; they were never serious.

Empty as the man's mind was of thoughts, he was keenly observant, and he noticed the changes in the creek, the curves and bends and timber jams, and always he sharply noted where he placed his feet. Once, coming around a bend, he shied abruptly, like a startled horse, curved away from the place where he had been walking, and retreated several paces back along the trail. The creek he knew was frozen clear to the bottom—no creek could contain water in that arctic winter—but he knew also that there were springs that bubbled out from the hillsides and ran along under the snow and on top the ice of the creek. He knew that the coldest snaps never froze these springs, and he knew likewise their danger. They were traps. They hid pools of water under the snow that might be three inches deep, or three feet. Sometimes a skin of ice half an inch thick covered them, and in turn was covered by the snow. Sometimes there were alternate layers of water and ice skin, so that when one broke through he kept on breaking through for a while, sometimes wetting himself to the waist.

That was why he had shied in such panic. He had felt the give under his feet and heard the crackle of a snow-hidden ice skin. And to get his feet wet in such a temperature meant trouble and danger. At the very least it meant delay, for he would be forced to stop and build a fire, and under its protection to bare his feet while he dried his socks and moccasins. He stood and studied the creek bed and its banks, and decided that the flow of water came from the right. He reflected awhile, rubbing his nose and cheeks, then skirted to the left, stepping gingerly and testing the footing for each step. Once clear of the danger, he took a fresh chew of tobacco and swung along at his four-mile gait.

In the course of the next two hours he came upon several similar traps. Usually the snow above the hidden pools had a sunken, candied apppearance that advertised the danger. Once again, however, he had a close call; and once, suspecting danger, he compelled the dog to go on in front. The dog did not want to go. It hung back until the man shoved it forward, and then it went quickly across the white, unbroken surface. Suddenly it broke through, floundered to one side, and got away to firmer footing. It had wet its forefeet and legs, and almost immediately the water that clung to it turned to ice. It made quick efforts to lick the ice off its legs, then dropped down in the snow and began to bite out the ice that had formed between the toes. This was a matter of instinct. To permit the ice to remain would mean sore feet. It did not know this. It merely obeyed the mysterious prompting that arose from the deep crypts of its being. But the man knew, having achieved a judgment on the subject, and he removed the mitten from his right hand and helped tear out the ice particles. He did not expose his fingers more than a minute, and was astonished at the swift numbness that smote them. It certainly was cold. He pulled on the mitten hastily, and beat the hand savagely across his chest.

At twelve o'clock the day was at its brightest. Yet the sun was too far south on its winter journey to clear the horizon. The bulge of the earth intervened between it and Henderson Creek, where the man walked under a clear sky at noon and cast no shadow. At half-past twelve, to the minute, he arrived at the forks of the creek. He was pleased at the speed he had made. If he kept it up, he would certainly be with the boys by six. He unbuttoned his jacket and shirt and drew forth his lunch. The action consumed no more than a quarter of a minute, yet in that brief moment the numbness laid hold of the exposed fingers. He did not put the mitten on, but, instead, struck the fingers a dozen sharp smashes against his leg. Then he sat down on a snow-covered log to eat. The sting

12 **Discussion** What details suggest that the man's knowledge of the environment is spotty?

13 **Discussion** What is the nature of the danger?

14 **Discussion** What does this suggest about the relationship between the man and the dog? Is the man concerned about the dog?

15 **Critical Thinking and Reading** The phrase the man "cast no shadow" is literally true in the Arctic winter, but it could have a symbolic meaning as well.

16 Discussion How could he have forgotten to build a fire?

17 Literary Focus Note again the use of understatement. The man was "foolish" for not having built a fire, and he "chuckled." Is he taking the cold seriously?

18 Discussion What does the dog's behavior tell the reader?

19 Reading Strategy Discuss with the class what might have happened if the man and dog had stayed by the fire. Would it have been a reasonable thing to do? Why or why not?

20 Critical Thinking and Reading How has the narrator prepared us for this possibility and what it might mean?

that followed upon the striking of his fingers against his leg ceased so quickly that he was startled. He had had no chance to take a bite of biscuit. He struck the fingers repeatedly and returned them to the mitten, baring the other hand for the purpose of eating. He tried to take a mouthful, but the ice muzzle prevented. He had forgotten to build a fire and thaw out. He chuckled at his foolishness, and as he chuckled he noted the numbness creeping into the exposed fingers. Also, he noted that the stinging which had first come to his toes when he sat down was already passing away. He wondered whether the toes were warm or numb. He moved them inside the moccasins and decided that they were numb.

He pulled the mitten on hurriedly and stood up. He was a bit frightened. He stamped up and down until the stinging returned into the feet. It certainly was cold, was his thought. That man from Sulphur Creek had spoken the truth when telling how cold it sometimes got in the country. And he had laughed at him at the time! That showed one must not be too sure of things. There was no mistake about it, it *was* cold. He strode up and down, stamping his feet and threshing his arms, until reassured by the returning warmth. Then he got out matches and proceeded to make a fire. From the undergrowth, where high water of the previous spring had lodged a supply of seasoned twigs, he got his firewood. Working carefully from a small beginning, he soon had a roaring fire, over which he thawed the ice from his face and in the protection of which he ate his biscuits. For the moment the cold of space was outwitted. The dog took satisfaction in the fire, stretching out close enough for warmth and far enough away to escape being singed.

When the man had finished, he filled his pipe and took his comfortable time over a smoke. Then he pulled on his mittens, settled the earflaps of his cap firmly about his ears, and took the creek trail up the left fork. The dog was disappointed and yearned back toward the fire. This man did not know cold. Possibly all the generations of his ancestry had been ignorant of cold, of real cold, of cold one hundred and seven degrees below freezing point. But the dog knew; all its ancestry knew, and it had inherited the knowledge. And it knew that it was not good to walk abroad in such fearful cold. It was the time to lie snug in a hole in the snow and wait for a curtain of cloud to be drawn across the face of outer space whence this cold came. On the other hand, there was no keen intimacy between the dog and the man. The one was the toil slave of the other, and the only caresses it had ever received were the caresses of the whiplash and of harsh and menacing throat sounds that threatened the whiplash. So the dog made no effort to communicate its apprehension to the man. It was not concerned in the welfare of the man; it was for its own sake that it yearned back toward the fire. But the man whistled, and spoke to it with the sound of whiplashes, and the dog swung in at the man's heels and followed after.

The man took a chew of tobacco and proceeded to start a new amber beard. Also, his moist breath quickly powdered with white his mustache, eyebrows, and lashes. There did not seem to be so many springs on the left fork of the Henderson, and for half an hour the man saw no signs of any. And then it happened. At a place where there were no signs, where the soft, unbroken snow seemed to advertise solidity beneath, the man broke through. It was not deep. He wet himself halfway to the knees before he floundered out to the firm crust.

He was angry, and cursed his luck aloud. He had hoped to get into camp with the boys at six o'clock, and this would delay him an hour, for he would have to build a fire and dry out his footgear. This was imperative at that low temperature—he knew that much; and he turned aside to the bank, which he climbed. On top, tangled in the underbrush about the trunks of several small spruce trees, was a high-water deposit of dry fire-

Grammar in Action

Skilled writers sometimes use **sentence structure** to reinforce their themes. In "To Build a Fire," for example, the sentence patterns and combinations mirror the story's conflict, man versus nature. Consider the topics of the following coordinated clauses:

It was a steep bank, and he paused for breath at the top. (page 566)

He was a newcomer in the land, a chechaquo, and this was his first winter. (page 567)

In each case, a statement about a natural feature or condition is coordinated with a statement about the man.

Student Activity 1. On pages 570–571, find four more examples of the use of sentence coordination to draw contrasts between the man and the natural forces against which he is struggling.

Student Activity 2. As the story progresses, the man finds himself in conflict with the dog and with his own body. On pages 574–575, find five examples of sentence coordination used to express these conflicts.

Student Activity 3. Add a coordinate clause to each of the following sentences. Word your clause so that a conflict is revealed by the coordinated sentence.

wood—sticks and twigs, principally, but also larger portions of seasoned branches and fine, dry, last year's grasses. He threw down several large pieces on top of the snow. This served for a foundation and prevented the young flame from drowning itself in the snow it otherwise would melt. The flame he got by touching a match to a small shred of birch bark that he took from his pocket. This burned even more readily than paper. Placing it on the foundation, he fed the young flame with wisps of dry grass and with the tiniest dry twigs.

He worked slowly and carefully, keenly aware of his danger. Gradually, as the flame grew stronger, he increased the size of the twigs with which he fed it. He squatted in the snow, pulling the twigs out from their entanglement in the brush and feeding directly to the flame. He knew there must be no failure. When it is seventy-five below zero, a man must not fail in his first attempt to build a fire—that is, if his feet are wet. If his feet are dry, and he fails, he can run along the trail for half a mile and restore his circulation. But the circulation of wet and freezing feet cannot be restored by running when it is seventy-five below. No matter how fast he runs, the wet feet will freeze the harder.

All this the man knew. The old-timer on Sulphur Creek had told him about it the previous fall, and now he was appreciating the advice. Already all sensation had gone out of his feet. To build the fire he had been forced to remove his mittens, and the fingers had quickly gone numb. His pace of four miles an hour had kept his heart pumping blood to the surface of his body and to all the extremities. But the instant he stopped, the action of the pump eased down. The cold of space smote the unprotected tip of the planet, and he, being on that unprotected tip, received the full force of the blow. The blood of his body recoiled before it. The blood was alive, like the dog, and like the dog it wanted to hide away and cover itself up from the fearful cold. So long as he walked four miles an hour, he pumped that blood,

willy-nilly, to the surface; but now it ebbed away and sank down into the recesses of his body. The extremities were the first to feel its absence. His wet feet froze the faster, and his exposed fingers numbed the faster, though they had not yet begun to freeze. Nose and cheeks were already freezing, while the skin of all his body chilled as it lost its blood.

But he was safe. Toes and nose and cheeks would be only touched by the frost, for the fire was beginning to burn with strength. He was feeding it with twigs the size of his finger. In another minute he would be able to feed it with branches the size of his wrist, and then he could remove his wet foot-gear, and, while it dried, he could keep his naked feet warm by the fire, rubbing them at first, of course, with snow. The fire was a success. He was safe. He remembered the advice of the old-timer on Sulphur Creek, and smiled. The old-timer had been very serious in laying down the law that no man must travel alone in the Klondike after fifty below. Well, here he was; he had had the accident; he was alone; and he had saved himself. Those old-timers were rather womanish, some of them, he thought. All a man had to do was to keep his head, and he was all right. Any man who was a man could travel alone. But it was surprising, the rapidity with which his cheeks and nose were freezing. And he had not thought his fingers could go lifeless in so short a time. Lifeless they were, for he could scarcely make them move together to grip a twig, and they seemed remote from his body and from him. When he touched a twig, he had to look and see whether or not he had hold of it. The wires were pretty well down between him and his finger ends.

All of which counted for little. There was the fire, snapping and crackling and promising life with every dancing flame. He started to untie his moccasins. They were coated with ice; the thick German socks were like sheaths of iron halfway to the knees; and the moccasin strings were like rods of steel all

To Build a Fire 571

---

21 **Discussion** Why is it so important to build a fire?

22 **Discussion** What is beginning to happen?

23 **Discussion** What else had the old-timer in Sulphur Creek told him? What does his advice represent in the story?

1. It was a scorching day in August, and . . .
2. My parents had hoped I would study medicine, but.
3. He carefully counted his change, for . . .
4. I tried to avoid stepping on the branch, but . . .
5. The dragon hadn't spotted him yet, nor . . .

24 **Discussion** Does he still have a chance for survival? Why or why not?

25 **Discussion** How does this passage add to the reader's understanding of the man's relationship with the dog?

26 **Critical Thinking and Reading** The man's actions are becoming less rational and more panic-driven.

twisted and knotted as by some conflagration. For a moment he tugged with his numb fingers, then, realizing the folly of it, he drew his sheath-knife.

But before he could cut the strings, it happened. It was his own fault or, rather, his mistake. He should not have built the fire under the spruce tree. He should have built it in the open. But it had been easier to pull the twigs from the brush and drop them directly on the fire. Now the tree under which he had done this carried a weight of snow on its boughs. No wind had blown for weeks, and each bough was fully freighted. Each time he had pulled a twig he had communicated a slight agitation to the tree—an imperceptible agitation, so far as he was concerned, but an agitation sufficient to bring about the disaster. High up in the tree one bough capsized its load of snow. This fell on the boughs beneath, capsizing them. This process continued, spreading out and involving the whole tree. It grew like an avalanche, and it descended without warning upon the man and the fire, and the fire was blotted out! Where it had burned was a mantle of fresh and disordered snow.

The man was shocked. It was as though he had just heard his own sentence of death. For a moment he sat and stared at the spot where the fire had been. Then he grew very calm. Perhaps the old-timer on Sulphur Creek was right. If he had only had a trail mate he would have been in no danger now. The trail mate could have built the fire. Well, it was up to him to build the fire over again, and this second time there must be no failure. Even if he succeeded, he would most likely lose some toes. His feet must be badly frozen by now, and there would be some time before the second fire was ready.

Such were his thoughts, but he did not sit and think them. He was busy all the time they were passing through his mind. He made a new foundation for a fire, this time in the open, where no treacherous tree could blot it out. Next, he gathered dry grasses and tiny twigs from the high-water flotsam. He could not bring his fingers together to pull them out, but he was able to gather them by the handful. In this way he got many rotten twigs and bits of green moss that were undesirable, but it was the best he could do. He worked methodically, even collecting an armful of the larger branches to be used later when the fire gathered strength. And all the while the dog sat and watched him, a certain yearning wistfulness in its eyes, for it looked upon him as the fire provider, and the fire was slow in coming.

When all was ready, the man reached in his pocket for a second piece of birch bark. He knew the bark was there, and, though he could not feel it with his fingers, he could hear its crisp rustling as he fumbled for it. Try as he would, he could not clutch hold of it. And all the time, in his consciousness, was the knowledge that each instant his feet were freezing. This thought tended to put him in a panic, but he fought against it and kept calm. He pulled on his mittens with his teeth, and threshed his arms back and forth, beating his hands with all his might against his sides. He did this sitting down, and he stood up to do it; and all the while the dog sat in the snow, its wolf brush of a tail curled around warmly over its forefeet, its sharp wolf ears pricked forward intently as it watched the man. And the man, as he beat and threshed with his arms and hands, felt a great surge of envy as he regarded the creature that was warm and secure in its natural covering.

After a time he was aware of the first far-away signals of sensation in his beaten fingers. The faint tingling grew stronger till it evolved into a stinging ache that was excruciating, but which the man hailed with satisfaction. He stripped the mitten from his right hand and fetched forth the birch bark. The exposed fingers were quickly going numb again. Next he brought out his bunch of sulphur matches. But the tremendous cold had already driven the life out of his fingers. In his effort to separate one match from the others, the whole bunch fell in the snow. He tried to pick it out of the snow, but failed. The dead fingers could neither touch nor clutch. He was very careful. He drove the thought of his freezing feet, and nose, and cheeks, out of his mind, devoting his whole soul to the matches. He watched, using the sense of vision in place of that of touch, and when he saw his fingers on each side the bunch, he closed them—that is, he willed to close them, for the wires were down, and the fingers did not obey. He pulled the mitten on the right hand, and beat it fiercely against his knee. Then, with both mittened hands, he scooped the bunch of matches, along with much snow, into his lap. Yet he was no better off.

After some manipulation he managed to get the bunch between the heels of his mittened hands. In this fashion he carried it to his mouth. The ice crackled and snapped when by a violent effort he opened his mouth. He drew the lower jaw in, curled the

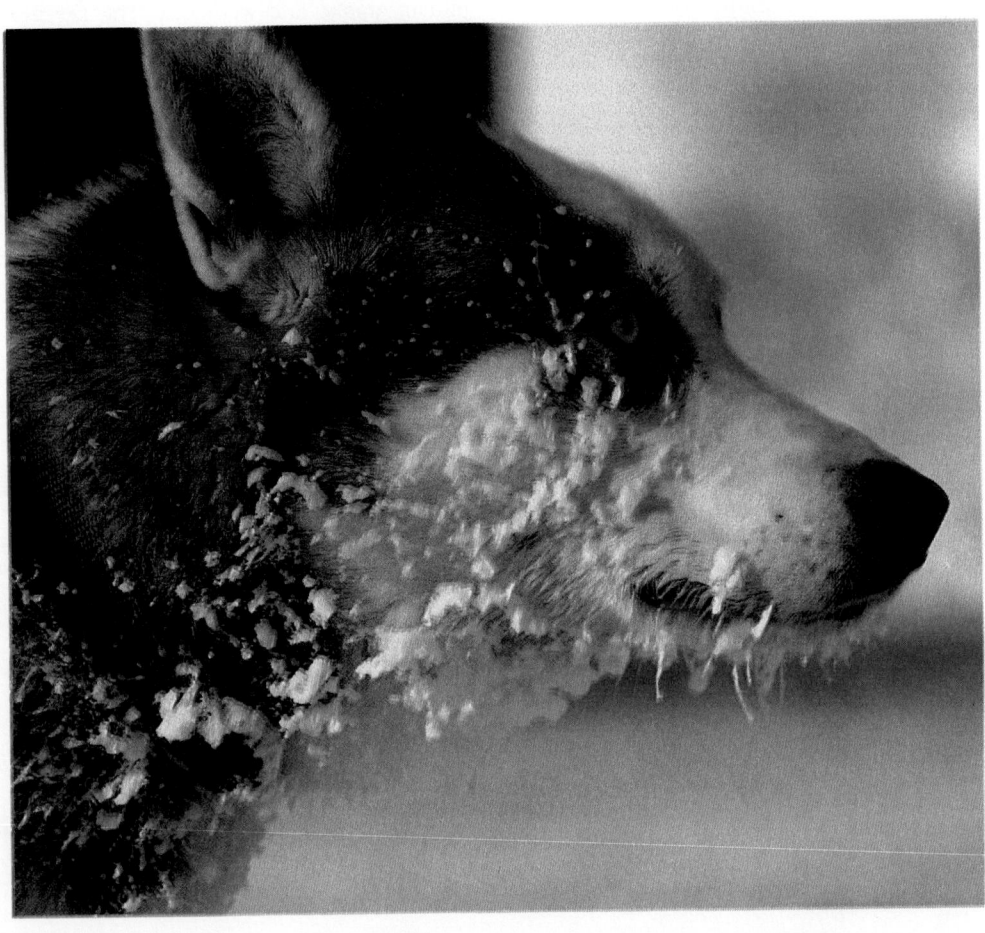

To Build a Fire 573

27 **Discussion** How does the man know his flesh is burning?

28 **Discussion** Do you think people have instincts too? If so, why are they not working well for the man?

upper lip out of the way, and scraped the bunch with his upper teeth in order to separate a match. He succeeded in getting one, which he dropped on his lap. He was no better off. He could not pick it up. Then he devised a way. He picked it up in his teeth and scratched it on his leg. Twenty times he scratched before he succeeded in lighting it. As it flamed he held it with his teeth to the birch bark. But the burning brimstone went up his nostrils and into his lungs, causing him to cough spasmodically. The match fell into the snow and went out.

The old-timer on Sulphur Creek was right, he thought in the moment of controlled despair that ensued: after fifty below, a man should travel with a partner. He beat his hands, but failed in exciting any sensation. Suddenly he bared both hands, removing the mittens with his teeth. He caught the whole bunch between the heels of his hands. His arm muscles not being frozen enabled him to press the hand heels tightly against the matches. Then he scratched the bunch along his leg. It flared into flame, seventy sulphur matches at once! There was no wind to blow them out. He kept his head to one side to escape the strangling fumes, and held the blazing bunch to the birch bark. As

27 he so held it, he became aware of sensation in his hand. His flesh was burning. He could smell it. Deep down below the surface he could feel it. The sensation developed into pain that grew acute. And still he endured it, holding the flame of the matches clumsily to the bark that would not light readily because his own burning hands were in the way, absorbing most of the flame.

At last, when he could endure no more, he jerked his hands apart. The blazing matches fell sizzling into the snow, but the birch bark was alight. He began laying dry grasses and the tiniest twigs on the flame. He could not pick and choose, for he had to lift the fuel between the heels of his hands. Small pieces of rotten wood and green moss clung to the twigs, and he bit them off as well as he could with his teeth. He cherished

the flame carefully and awkwardly. It meant life, and it must not perish. The withdrawal of blood from the surface of his body now made him begin to shiver, and he grew more awkward. A large piece of green moss fell squarely on the little fire. He tried to poke it out with his fingers, but his shivering frame made him poke too far, and he disrupted the nucleus of the little fire, the burning grasses and tiny twigs separating and scattering. He tried to poke them together again, but in spite of the tenseness of the effort, his shivering got away with him, and the twigs were hopelessly scattered. Each twig gushed a puff of smoke and went out. The fire provider had failed. As he looked apathetically about him, his eyes chanced on the dog, sitting across the ruins of the fire from him, in the snow, making restless, hunching movements, slightly lifting one forefoot and then the other, shifting its weight back and forth on them with wistful eagerness.

The sight of the dog put a wild idea into his head. He remembered the tale of the man, caught in a blizzard, who killed a steer and crawled inside the carcass, and so was saved. He would kill the dog and bury his hands in the warm body until the numbness went out of them. Then he could build another fire. He spoke to the dog, calling it to him; but in his voice was a strange note of fear that frightened the animal, who had never known the man to speak in such way before. Something was the matter, and its suspicious nature sensed danger—it knew not what danger, but somewhere, somehow, in its brain arose an apprehension of the man. It flattened its ears down at the sound of the man's voice, and its restless, hunching movements and the liftings and shiftings of its forefeet became more pronounced; but it would not come to the man. He got on his **28** hand and knees and crawled toward the dog. This unusual posture again excited suspicion, and the animal sidled mincingly away.

The man sat up in the snow for a moment and struggled for calmness. Then he pulled on his mittens, by means of his teeth,

Grammar in Action

Writers use **commas** to help make their meaning clear. Commas are visual signals that enable readers to understand the relationships among parts of the sentence. One specific use of the comma is to separate independent clauses in a compound sentence. Notice how the comma is used in these sentences from Jack London's story:

He tried to poke it with his fingers, but his shivering frame made him poke too far.

Something was the matter, and its suspicious nature sensed danger.

Each sentence has two independent clauses joined by a coordinating conjunction. The coordinating conjunctions are *and, but, or, nor, for,* and *yet.*

Student Activity 1. Review the story and point out five other examples of commas being used to separate independent clauses in compound sentences.

Student Activity 2. Check to see if the following sentences are correctly punctuated. Correct errors that you find.

1. He slowed down but she accelerated.
2. They were captured, yet we escaped.

and got upon his feet. He glanced down at first in order to assure himself that he was really standing up, for the absence of sensation in his feet left him unrelated to the earth. His erect position in itself started to drive the webs of suspicion from the dog's mind; and when he spoke peremptorily, with the sound of whiplashes in his voice, the dog rendered its customary allegiance and came to him. As it came within reaching distance, the man lost his control. His arms flashed out to the dog, and he experienced genuine surprise when he discovered that his hands could not clutch, that there was neither bend nor feeling in the fingers. He had forgotten for the moment that they were frozen and that they were freezing more and more. All this happened quickly, and before the animal could get away, he encircled its body with his arms. He sat down in the snow, and in this fashion held the dog, while it snarled and whined and struggled.

But it was all he could do, hold its body encircled in his arms and sit there. He realized that he could not kill the dog. There was no way to do it. With his helpless hands he could neither draw nor hold his sheath-knife nor throttle the animal. He released it, and it plunged wildly away, with tail between its legs, and still snarling. It halted forty feet away and surveyed him curiously, with ears sharply pricked forward. The man looked down at his hands in order to locate them, and found them hanging on the ends of his arms. It struck him as curious that one should have to use his eyes in order to find out where his hands were. He began threshing his arms back and forth, beating the mittened hands against his sides. He did this for five minutes, violently, and his heart pumped enough blood up to the surface to put a stop to his shivering. But no sensation was aroused in the hands. He had an impression that they hung like weights on the ends of his arms, but when he tried to run the impression down, he could not find it.

A certain fear of death, dull and oppressive, came to him. This fear quickly became poignant as he realized that it was no longer a mere matter of freezing his fingers and toes, or of losing his hands and feet, but that it was a matter of life and death with the chances against him. This threw him into a panic, and he turned and ran up the creek-bed along the old, dim trail. The dog joined in behind and kept up with him. He ran blindly, without intention, in fear such as he had never known in his life. Slowly, as he plowed and floundered through the snow, he began to see things again—the banks of the creek, the old timber jams, the leafless aspens, and the sky. The running made him feel better. He did not shiver. Maybe, if he ran on, his feet would thaw out; and, anyway, if he ran far enough, he would reach camp and the boys. Without doubt he would lose some fingers and toes and some of his face; but the boys would take care of him, and save the rest of him when he got there. And at the same time there was another thought in his mind that said he would never get to the camp and the boys; that it was too many miles away, that the freezing had too great a start on him, and that he would soon be stiff and dead. This thought he kept in the background and refused to consider. Sometimes it pushed itself forward and demanded to be heard, but he thrust it back and strove to think of other things.

It struck him as curious that he could run at all on feet so frozen that he could not feel them when they struck the earth and took the weight of his body. He seemed to himself to skim along above the surface, and to have no connection with the earth. Somewhere he had once seen a winged Mercury,[6] and he wondered if Mercury felt as he felt when skimming over the earth.

His theory of running until he reached camp and the boys had one flaw in it: he lacked the endurance. Several times he stumbled, and finally he tottered, crumpled up, and fell. When he tried to rise, he failed.

6. **Mercury:** From Roman mythology, the wing-footed messenger of the gods.

29 **Clarification** The man is becoming disoriented. This is a symptom of severe hypothermia.

30 **Discussion** What do we know about the man's will to live?

3. Bears are intelligent but people are smarter than animals.
4. The husky was injured and the wolves began to circle.
5. The fire went out yet the man stayed warm.

31 Clarification No longer shivering when faced with cold is another symptom of severe hypothermia.

32 Discussion Why does he think of the old-timer from Sulphur Creek at this point?

33 Discussion Why prompts the dog to return to the camp?

Reader's Response Can you explain the details of an experience you once had with nature that frightened you?

He must sit and rest, he decided, and next time he would merely walk and keep on going. As he sat and regained his breath, he noted that he was feeling quite warm and comfortable. He was not shivering, and it even seemed that a warm glow had come to his chest and trunk. And yet, when he touched his nose or cheeks, there was no sensation. Running would not thaw them out. Nor would it thaw out his hands and feet. Then the thought came to him that the frozen portions of his body must be extending. He tried to keep this thought down, to forget it, to think of something else; he was aware of the panicky feeling that it caused, and he was afraid of the panic. But the thought asserted itself, and persisted, until it produced a vision of his body totally frozen. This was too much, and he made another wild run along the trail. Once he slowed down to a walk, but the thought of the freezing extending itself made him run again.

And all the time the dog ran with him, at his heels. When he fell down a second time, it curled its tail over its forefeet and sat in front of him, facing him, curiously eager and intent. The warmth and security of the animal angered him, and he cursed it till it flattened down its ears appeasingly. This time the shivering came more quickly upon the man. He was losing in his battle with the frost. It was creeping into his body from all sides. The thought of it drove him on, but he ran no more than a hundred feet, when he staggered and pitched headlong. It was his last panic. When he had recovered his breath and control, he sat up and entertained in his mind the conception of meeting death with dignity. However, the conception did not come to him in such terms. His idea of it was that he had been making a fool of himself, running around like a chicken with its head cut off—such was the simile that occurred to him. Well, he was bound to freeze anyway, and he might as well take it decently. With this new-found peace of mind came the first glimmerings of drowsiness. A good idea, he thought, to sleep off to death. It was like taking an anaesthetic. Freezing was not so bad as people thought. There were lots worse ways to die.

He pictured the boys finding his body next day. Suddenly he found himself with them, coming along the trail and looking for himself. And, still with them, he came around a turn in the trail and found himself lying in the snow. He did not belong with himself any more, for even then he was out of himself; standing with the boys and looking at himself in the snow. It certainly was cold, was his thought. When he got back to the States he could tell the folks what real cold was. He drifted on from this to a vision of the old-timer on Sulphur Creek. He could see him quite clearly, warm and comfortable, and smoking a pipe.

"You were right, old hoss; you were right," the man mumbled to the old-timer of Sulphur Creek.

Then the man drowsed off into what seemed to him the most comfortable and satisfying sleep he had ever known. The dog sat facing him and waiting. The brief day drew to a close in a long, slow twilight. There were no signs of a fire to be made, and, besides, never in the dog's experience had it known a man to sit like that in the snow and make no fire. As the twilight drew on, its eager yearning for the fire mastered it, and with a great lifting and shifting of forefeet, it whined softly, then flattened its ears down in anticipation of being chidden[7] by the man. But the man remained silent. Later, the dog whined loudly. And still later it crept close to the man and caught the scent of death. This made the animal bristle and back away. A little longer it delayed, howling under the stars that leaped and danced and shone brightly in the cold sky. Then it turned and trotted up the trail in the direction of the camp it knew, where were the other food providers and fire providers.

---

7. chidden: Scolded.

576 Realism and the Frontier

THINKING ABOUT THE SELECTION

Recalling

1. Why does the tremendous cold "make no impression" on the man?
2. (a) How does the man become aware that it is colder than fifty below? (b) What is the actual temperature?
3. How is the dog's awareness of the cold different from the man's awareness?
4. (a) What "traps" is the man careful to avoid? (b) How does the dog assist the man in avoiding one of the traps?
5. (a) What careless mistake does the man make when he tries to build a fire to thaw out his feet? (b) What prevents him from rebuilding the fire?
6. (a) What happens to the man at the end of the story? (b) How does the dog react?

Interpreting

7. (a) How would you characterize the man's relationship with his dog? (b) How is the man's relationship with nature different from the dog's relationship with nature? (c) Which is better equipped to survive in nature? Explain your answer.
8. How do the man's recollections of his conversation with the old man from Sulphur Creek foreshadow the end of the story?
9. At one point in the story, the man gets angry and curses his fate. Do you think the outcome of the story is due to fate or to something within himself? Explain your answer.
10. Why do you think London chose not to give the man in this story a name?
11. What does the story suggest about humanity's place in nature?

Applying

12. Many of the provisions for coping with the cold that exist today did not exist when the story was written. Explain whether the outcome of the story might be different if it were set today.

ANALYZING LITERATURE

Recognizing Types of Conflict

In literature **conflict** refers to a struggle between opposing forces or characters. Conflict may be internal, occurring within a character's mind, or external, occurring between two characters, between a character and society, between a character and nature, or between a character and fate.

1. What type of conflict is central to the plot of "To Build a Fire"?
2. How does the conflict intensify as the plot develops?
3. How is the conflict resolved?

CRITICAL THINKING AND READING

Relating Conflict to Theme

The conflict of a literary work is often closely related to the theme, or general idea. For example, the **theme** of a story in which the **conflict** is between a character and fate might be that people are sometimes unable to control their own destinies.

1. What do you think is the theme of "To Build a Fire"?
2. How is story's conflict related to this theme?

THINKING AND WRITING

Writing About Conflict and Theme

Write an essay in which you discuss the relationship between the conflict and the theme of "To Build a Fire." Review your answers from the Analyzing Literature and Critical Thinking and Reading activities. Then develop a thesis statement and begin writing your essay. Use evidence from the story to support your argument. When you revise, make sure you have varied the length and structure of your sentences. Proofread your essay and prepare a final draft.

8. It foreshadows the ending, because the old-timer had warned him not to travel alone when the weather was this cold.
9. Answers will differ. Suggested Response: The outcome is due to something within himself; an unwarranted belief that he can overcome obstacles of nature.
10. Suggested Response: He did not name him, because the man serves as a symbol for the human desire to control nature.
11. Suggested Response: It suggests that humanity cannot control nature and must respect it. Nature is a much more powerful force than humanity.

Applying
12. Suggested Response: It would be different; because the man would have provisions that would enable him to survive.

ANSWERS TO ANALYZING LITERATURE
1. The conflict is between man and nature.
2. The forces of nature have more and more of an effect on the man as the story progresses.
3. The forces of nature kill the man.

ANSWERS TO CRITICAL THINKING AND READING
1. Suggested Response: The theme is that humans should respect the forces of nature, which have the power to kill.
2. Suggested Response: The conflict is directly related to this theme, because it involves a man's efforts to control nature.

THINKING AND WRITING
For help with this assignment, students can refer to Lesson 11, "Writing About Theme," in the Handbook of Writing About Literature.

After students have completed the assignment, divide them into groups, and have them read their essays to one another and suggest ways in which they could be improved.

Closure and Extension

ANSWERS TO THINKING ABOUT THE SELECTION
Recalling
1. He did not have the imagination to understand the significance of the cold.
2. (a) He spits in the air and sees that his spit crackles before it reaches the ground. (b) It is actually 75° below zero.
3. The dog has an instinctive understanding of the cold. He reacts to what nature tells him.
4. (a) The man carefully avoids the hidden pools under the thin skins of ice that were covered by snow. (b) The man forces the dog to go first.
5. (a) He builds it under a tree that had snow on its boughs, and the snow falls off, putting out the fire. (b) His hands are too numb to rebuild the fire.
6. (a) He freezes to death. (b) The dog goes back to the camp.

Interpreting
7. (a) Suggested Response: The man is the master who rules the dog with the threat of punishment; there is no affection between the two. The two are only interested in what the other can provide for them. (b) The man sees nature as a problem his mind can solve. The dog instinctively understands how to respond to nature. (c) The dog is probably better equipped because he adapts to conditions.

More About the Author In January, 1897, Crane was sent as a reporter to cover the Cuban Revolution. He was aboard the tug *Commodore,* bound for Cuba with guns for the revolutionaries, when the tug sank off the coast of Florida. He and three other men spent almost thirty hours in a small dinghy before landing at Daytona. He wrote a newspaper report of his experience, then later that same year the short story "The Open Boat." Point out to students that in his novel *The Red Badge of Courage,* Crane wrote successfully about experiences that he had not had. Ask students what might be the advantages and the disadvantages of making a story out of their own experiences.

Critical Evaluation The critic Joseph Catz, in *The Portable Stephen Crane,* points out a quotation from Crane "that sounds like Crane trying to explain himself: 'The true artist is the man who leaves pictures of his own time as they appear to him.' Beneath this is a conviction that the world is unpredictable, spontaneous, and discontinuous." Ask your students if what happens in the world seems to them predictable and consistent, or the opposite. Do their individual views differ? Who is "right"?

1871–1900

Stephen Crane died of tuberculosis at the age of twenty-eight. Yet during his short life he established himself as one of the leaders of the Naturalist movement and one of the most highly regarded writers of his time.

The youngest of fourteen children, Crane was born and reared in New Jersey. After briefly attending Syracuse University, where he spent more energy playing baseball than studying, he moved to New York City and found work as a journalist. Inspired by his observations and experiences as a newspaper writer, Crane completed his first novel, *Maggie: A Girl of the Streets* (1893), which he had begun to write while at Syracuse. A grimly realistic depiction of life in the slums of New York City, the novel was so frank and shocking that Crane was unable to find a publisher. He eventually borrowed money and published it at his own expense, but despite praise from a number of writers and critics, the book did not sell.

Crane continued to write, however, and in 1895 he published his second novel, *The Red Badge of Courage: An Episode of the American Civil War*. A psychological exploration of a young soldier's reactions under fire, the novel was a success and earned Crane international acclaim at the age of twenty-four. Readers and critics applauded the book for its convincing descriptions of the young soldier's thoughts and feelings and its realistic depictions of Civil War battles. Yet Crane had neither experienced nor observed military combat. Before writing the novel, however, he had interviewed Civil War veterans and had studied photographs, battle plans, and biographical accounts of military leaders.

Crane soon had the opportunity to view the realities of war first-hand, when he served as a newspaper correspondent during the Greco-Turkish War in 1897 and the Spanish-American War in 1898. His observations convinced him of the accuracy of his depiction of war in *The Red Badge of Courage* and provided material for *War Is Kind* (1899), his second collection of poetry. Crane's experiences as a correspondent also took their toll on his health. During the final months of his life, his physical condition rapidly deteriorated, and he died in Germany shortly after the turn of the century.

Like other Naturalists, Crane depicted characters who were manipulated by forces of society and nature that were beyond their understanding and control. In his story "The Open Boat," for example, the characters are trapped in a tiny lifeboat, floating helplessly in the vast, mysterious, and tremendously powerful Atlantic Ocean. Inspired by a similar real-life experience, the story is one of the most vivid expressions of Crane's Naturalist beliefs.

Objectives

1 To understand realism
2 To understand naturalism
3 To recognize important passages
4 To respond to criticism

Support Material

Teaching Portfolio
Teacher Backup, p. 761
Grammar in Action Worksheets, *Appreciating Comparisons,* p. 765; *Understanding Coordination,* p. 767
Usage and Mechanics Worksheet, p. 769
Vocabulary Check, p. 770
Analyzing Literature Worksheet,

Understanding Realism and Naturalism, p. 771
Critical Thinking and Reading Worksheet, *Recognizing Important Passages,* p. 772
Selection Test, p. 773

GUIDE FOR INTERPRETING

The Open Boat

Realism. Realism was a literary movement that emerged as a reaction against Romanticism. Unlike the Romantic writers, who often portrayed improbable situations and events, the Realists sought to depict real life as faithfully and accurately as possible. Generally, they attempted to present "a slice of life" by delving deeply into the everyday realities of a small group of people or a small portion of the world. The Realists focused on the lives of ordinary people, often writing about lower-class and middle-class characters. In depicting the lives of people faced with poverty and other hardships, the Realists confronted many of the harsh realities of American society, often presenting pessimistic visions of the world dramatically different from the optimistic visions that dominated Romantic literature.

Naturalism. Naturalism, another major literary movement of the late nineteenth and early twentieth centuries, grew out of the Realism movement. Like the Realists, the Naturalists focused on the lives of ordinary people and attempted to depict life truthfully and accurately. Yet, while the Realists searched for the truths of existence by delving beneath the surface of everyday life, the Naturalists already possessed a well-defined, scientific view of the universe that they imposed on their works. The Naturalists believed that a person's fate is determined by environment, heredity, and chance. As a result, Naturalist writers frequently depicted characters whose lives were shaped by forces of nature or society they could not understand or control. However, despite their underlying powerlessness, the characters in Naturalist works generally conduct themselves with strength and dignity in the face of adversity, thereby affirming the significance of their existence. For example, in Crane's novel *The Red Badge of Courage,* a young soldier's experiences in a war he can neither comprehend nor control make him aware of his courage and inner strength and in doing so give his life new meaning.

Writing

Try to imagine what it would be like to be placed in a life-threatening situation, such as being stranded on a lifeboat in the middle of the ocean. Then freewrite about the situation, keeping the following questions in mind: How do you think you might react? What aspects of your personality might the situation bring out? How do you think the situation would affect your interactions with other people? If you survived the situation, how do you think it might alter the way you live your life?

The Open Boat 579

Literary Focus Discuss the definitions in the textbook of Romanticism, Realism, and Naturalism, asking students to explain each term in their own words. Divide them into small groups and ask each group to make up a Romantic short story about boy-meets-girl, then to make a Realistic and then a Naturalistic version of it. Ask each group to tell their stories to the class, asking the class to identify what makes each story Romantic, Realistic, or Naturalistic. If there is time, do the same (in small groups or together) with an adventure or sports story.

Writing/Prior Knowledge Before they freewrite, ask the class to share life-threatening situations they or friends have experienced, they have read about in newspapers or books, or they have seen on television news or in movies. Ask them also what life-threatening situations might realistically happen to them.

Spelling Tip You might point out that *apropos* is a direct borrowing, both in pronunciation and spelling, of the two-word French phrase *à propos,* "to the purpose."

The Open Boat
Stephen Crane

1 **A TALE INTENDED TO BE AFTER THE FACT. BEING THE EXPERIENCE OF FOUR MEN FROM THE SUNK STEAMER *COMMODORE***

I

2 None of them knew the color of the sky. Their eyes glanced level, and were fastened upon the waves that swept toward them. These waves were of the hue of slate, save for the tops, which were of foaming white, and all of the men knew the colors of the sea. The horizon narrowed and widened, and dipped and rose, and at all times its edge was jagged with waves that seemed thrust up in points like rocks.

3 Many a man ought to have a bathtub larger than the boat which here rode upon the sea. These waves were most wrongfully and barbarously abrupt and tall, and each froth top was a problem in small boat navigation.

4 The cook squatted in the bottom and looked with both eyes at the six inches of gunwale which separated him from the ocean. His sleeves were rolled over his fat forearms, and the two flaps of his unbuttoned vest dangled as he bent to bail out the boat. Often he said: "Gawd! That was a narrow clip." As he remarked it he invariably gazed eastward over the broken sea.

The oiler,[1] steering with one of the two oars in the boat, sometimes raised himself suddenly to keep clear of water that swirled in over the stern. It was a thin little oar and it seemed often ready to snap.

5 The correspondent, pulling at the other oar, watched the waves and wondered why he was there.

The injured captain, lying in the bow, was at this time buried in that profound dejection and indifference which comes, temporarily at least, to even the bravest and most enduring when, willy nilly, the firm fails, the army loses, the ship goes down. The mind of the master of a vessel is rooted deep in the timbers of her, though he command for a day or a decade, and this captain had on him the stern impression of a scene in the grays of dawn of seven turned faces, and later a stump of a topmast with a white ball on it that slashed to and fro at the waves, went low and lower, and down. Thereafter there was something strange in his voice. Although steady, it was deep with mourning, and of a quality beyond oration or tears.

"Keep'er a little more south, Billie," said he.

" 'A little more south,' sir," said the oiler in the stern.

A seat in this boat was not unlike a seat upon a bucking bronco, and, by the same token, a bronco is not much smaller. The craft pranced and reared, and plunged like an an-

---

1. **oiler:** The person responsible for oiling machinery in the engine room of a ship.

580 Realism and the Frontier

imal. As each wave came, and she rose for it, she seemed like a horse making at a fence outrageously high. The manner of her scramble over these walls of water is a mystic thing, and, moveover, at the top of them were ordinarily these problems in white water, the foam racing down from the summit of each wave, requiring a new leap, and a leap from the air. Then, after scornfully bumping a crest, she would slide, and race, and splash down a long incline and arrive bobbing and nodding in front of the next menace.

A singular disadvantage of the sea lies in the fact that after successfully surmounting one wave you discover that there is another behind it just as important and just as nervously anxious to do something effective in

6

BENARES
Marshall Johnson
Peabody Museum of Salem

The Open Boat 581

581

6 **Discussion** How does this paragraph carry out a comparison of the boat to a horse?

Humanities Note

Fine art, *Benares,* by Marshall Johnson (1850–1921). This dramatic painting was made by a Boston-born artist who used his own experiences at sea for the subjects of his paintings. Johnson left Boston in 1868 to become a deckhand on a ship called the *Sunbeam,* which sailed from New England to South America. En route the young sailor found himself aboard a burning ship. The *Sunbeam's* fire could not be contained and the ship sank. Only twelve sailors were rescued, Johnson among them. When he returned home, he abandoned life as a seaman for a career as an artist. He went to Europe to study drawing and painting and eventually returned to Boston to set up his own studio.

His experiences at sea obviously influenced his choice of subject and his emphasis on the dramatic. The ship shown here is battling fierce waves and appears to be in imminent danger of sinking. Only a person who had himself experienced the horror of such an ordeal might have focused so graphically on the helplessness of a ship in such seas. The view from above emphasizes the ship's plight and the loneliness of its position in the middle of the raging waves. The choice of color also accents the element of fear and menace. Johnson painted in a nineteenth-century romantic style that exaggerated dramatic moments, but his own experiences in being shipwrecked indicate that the drama of this situation was real.

Consider the following questions for discussion:
1. Why do you think the artist painted some of the sea in tones of white?
2. What does the bird's-eye view emphasize?

7 **Literary Focus** Is this a Romantic or realistic view of the situation?

8 **Clarification** The correspondent is right: houses of refuge have a keeper, boats, and provisions but no crew. Lifesaving stations have crews equipped to rescue boats and people in trouble. The cook is partially right in that there was, in 1897, a house of refuge just north of Mosquito Inlet Lighthouse.

the way of swamping boats. In a ten-foot dinghy one can get an idea of the resources of the sea in the line of waves that is not probable to the average experience, which is never at sea in a dinghy. As each slaty wall of water approached, it shut all else from the view of the men in the boat, and it was not difficult to imagine that this particular wave was the final outburst of the ocean, the last effort of the grim water. There was a terrible grace in the move of the waves, and they came in silence, save for the snarling of the crests.

In the wan light, the faces of the men must have been gray. Their eyes must have glinted in strange ways as they gazed steadily astern. Viewed from a balcony, the whole thing would doubtlessly have been weirdly picturesque. But the men in the boat had no time to see it, and if they had had leisure there were other things to occupy their minds. The sun swung steadily up the sky, and they knew it was broad day because the color of the sea changed from slate to emerald-green, streaked with amber lights, and the foam was like tumbling snow. The process of the breaking day was unknown to them. They were aware only of this effect upon the color of the waves that rolled toward them.

In disjointed sentences the cook and the correspondent argued as to the difference between a lifesaving station and a house of refuge. The cook had said: "There's a house of refuge just north of the Mosquito Inlet Light, and as soon as they see us, they'll come off in their boat and pick us up."

"As soon as who see us?" said the correspondent.

"The crew," said the cook.

"Houses of refuge don't have crews," said the correspondent. "As I understand them, they are only places where clothes and grub are stored for the benefit of shipwrecked people. They don't carry crews."

"Oh, yes, they do," said the cook.

"No, they don't," said the correspondent.

"Well, we're not there yet, anyhow," said the oiler, in the stern.

"Well," said the cook, "perhaps it's not a house of refuge that I'm thinking of as being near Mosquito Inlet Light. Perhaps it's a lifesaving station."

"We're not there yet," said the oiler, in the stern.

II

As the boat bounced from the top of each wave, the wind tore through the hair of the hatless men, and as the craft plopped her stern down again the spray slashed past them. The crest of each of these waves was a hill, from the top of which the men surveyed, for a moment, a broad tumultuous expanse, shining and wind-riven. It was probably splendid. It was probably glorious, this play of the free sea, wild with lights of emerald and white and amber.

"Bully good thing it's an on-shore wind," said the cook. "If not, where would we be? Wouldn't have a show."

"That's right," said the correspondent.

The busy oiler nodded his assent.

Then the captain, in the bow, chuckled in a way that expressed humor, contempt, tragedy, all in one. "Do you think we've got much of a show, now, boys?" said he.

Whereupon the three were silent, save for a trifle of hemming and hawing. To express any particular optimism at this time they felt to be childish and stupid, but they all doubtless possessed this sense of the situation in their mind. A young man thinks doggedly at such times. On the other hand, the ethics of their condition was decidedly against any open suggestion of hopelessness. So they were silent.

"Oh, well," said the captain, soothing his children, "we'll get ashore all right."

But there was that in his tone which

Grammar in Action

Stephen Crane makes many comparisons in his writing. Many of these use *like* followed by a noun or noun phrase. He then further develops the comparisons by using appropriate words, especially verbs and adverbs. Notice how Crane's comparisons effectively describe the situation of the boat in the following examples:

A seat in this boat was *not unlike* [that is, like] *a seat upon a bucking bronco.*

The craft pranced and reared and plunged *like an animal.*

Occasionally, a great spread of water, *like white flames,* swarmed into her.

These comparisons to things that are violent or destructive emphasize the plight of the men in the boat.

Student Activity 1. Find three additional examples of comparisons using *like* in "The Open Boat."

Student Activity 2. Complete the following sentences to make strong and effective comparisons about the art, Benares, on page 581.

1. The boat, like _____, heaved in the turbulent water.
2. The masts snapped like _____.
3. The sailors caught in the storm felt like _____.
4. The power of the ocean seems like _____.

made them think, so the oiler quoth: "Yes! If this wind holds!"

The cook was bailing. "Yes! If we don't catch hell in the surf."

Canton flannel[2] gulls flew near and far. Sometimes they sat down on the sea, near patches of brown seaweed that rolled over the waves with a movement like carpets on a line in a gale. The birds sat comfortably in groups, and they were envied by some in the dinghy, for the wrath of the sea was no more to them than it was to a covey of prairie chickens a thousand miles inland. Often they came very close and stared at the men with black beadlike eyes. At these times they were uncanny and sinister in their unblinking scrutiny, and the men hooted angrily at them, telling them to be gone. One came, and evidently decided to alight on the top of the captain's head. The bird flew parallel to the boat and did not circle, but made short sidelong jumps in the air in chicken-fashion. His black eyes were wistfully fixed upon the captain's head. "Ugly brute," said the oiler to the bird. "You look as if you were made with a jackknife." The cook and the correspondent swore darkly at the creature. The captain naturally wished to knock it away with the end of the heavy painter,[3] but he did not dare do it, because anything resembling an emphatic gesture would have capsized this freighted boat, and so with his open hand, the captain gently and carefully waved the gull away. After it had been discouraged from the pursuit the captain breathed easier on account of his hair, and others breathed easier because the bird struck their minds at this time as being somehow gruesome and ominous.

In the meantime the oiler and the correspondent rowed. And also they rowed.

They sat together in the same seat, and each rowed an oar. Then the oiler took both oars; then the correspondent took both oars; then the oiler; then the correspondent. They rowed and they rowed. The very ticklish part of the business was when the time came for the reclining one in the stern to take his turn at the oars. By the very last star of truth, it is easier to steal eggs from under a hen than it was to change seats in the dinghy. First the man in the stern slid his hand along the thwart and moved with care, as if he were of Sèvres.[4] Then the man in the rowing seat slid his hand along the other thwart. It was all done with the most extraordinary care. As the two sidled past each other, the whole party kept watchful eyes on the coming wave, and the captain cried: "Look out now! Steady there!"

The brown mats of seaweed that appeared from time to time were like islands, bits of earth. They were traveling, apparently, neither one way nor the other. They were, to all intents, stationary. They informed the men in the boat that it was making progress slowly toward the land.

The captain, rearing cautiously in the bow, after the dinghy soared on a great swell, said that he had seen the lighthouse at Mosquito Inlet. Presently the cook remarked that he had seen it. The correspondent was at the oars, then, and for some reason he too wished to look at the lighthouse, but his back was toward the far shore and the waves were important, and for some time he could not seize an opportunity to turn his head. But at last there came a wave more gentle than the others, and when at the crest of it he swiftly scoured the western horizon.

"See it?" said the captain.

"No," said the correspondent, slowly, "I didn't see anything."

"Look again," said the captain. He pointed. "It's exactly in that direction."

At the top of another wave, the correspondent did as he was bid, and this time

---

2. **Canton flannel:** A thick cotton fabric.
3. **painter:** A rope attached to the bow of a boat.

4. **Sèvres** (sev′ rə): A type of fine French porcelain.

The Open Boat 583

9 **Reading Strategy** Crane uses repetition to convey the agonizing monotony and the slow passage of time for the men. Look for repetitions of this "rowing."

10 **Clarification** A thwart is one of a series of ribs running across the boat.

Speaking and Listening In order for the students to hear the objective and ironic tone of the narrator's voice, ask various ones to read aloud passages as you come to them in which the narrator speaks directly to the reader. The repeated passages, e.g., "they rowed and rowed . . ." (pages 583, 589) and "If I drown . . .," (pages 586, 589, 591) could be read as a group.

Student Activity 3. Write a comparison between each of the following pairs in which you use *like* and supporting words.
1. An old woman and a bird
2. Fear and cold water
3. A crowd of people and a river

11 **Critical Thinking and Reading**
Ask students what makes this paragraph important. Then ask them who is speaking.

12 **Clarification** The cook had sailed along the eastern coast within sight of land on a sailing boat with three or more masts ("schooners").

13 **Clarification** In order to steer a boat, it must be moving ("under way"). Therefore, they must keep rowing.

his eyes chanced on a small still thing on the edge of the swaying horizon. It was precisely like the point of a pin. It took an anxious eye to find a lighthouse so tiny.

"Think we'll make it, Captain?"

"If this wind holds and the boat don't swamp, we can't do much else," said the captain.

The little boat, lifted by each towering sea, and splashed viciously by the crests, made progress that in the absence of sea-weed was not apparent to those in her. She seemed just a wee thing wallowing, miraculously, top-up, at the mercy of five oceans. Occasionally, a great spread of water, like white flames, swarmed into her.

"Bail her, cook," said the captain, serenely.

"All right, Captain," said the cheerful cook.

III

It would be difficult to describe the subtle brotherhood of men that was here established on the seas. No one said that it was so. No one mentioned it. But it dwelt in the boat, and each man felt it warm him. They were a captain, an oiler, a cook, and a correspondent, and they were friends, friends in a more curiously iron-bound degree than may be common. The hurt captain, lying against the water jar in the bow, spoke always in a low voice and calmly, but he could never command a more ready and swiftly obedient crew than the motley three of the dinghy. It was more than a mere recognition of what was best for the common safety. There was surely in it a quality that was personal and heartfelt. And after this devotion to the commander of the boat there was this comradeship that the correspondent, for instance, who had been taught to be cynical of men, knew even at the time was the best experience of his life. But no one said that it was so. No one mentioned it.

"I wish we had a sail," remarked the captain. "We might try my overcoat on the end of an oar and give you two boys a chance to rest." So the cook and the correspondent held the mast and spread wide the overcoat. The oiler steered, and the little boat made good way with her new rig. Sometimes the oiler had to scull sharply to keep a sea from breaking into the boat, but otherwise sailing was a success.

Meanwhile the lighthouse had been growing slowly larger. It had now almost assumed color, and appeared like a little gray shadow on the sky. The man at the oars could not be prevented from turning his head rather often to try for a glimpse of this little gray shadow.

At last, from the top of each wave the men in the tossing boat could see land. Even as the lighthouse was an upright shadow on the sky, this land seemed but a long black shadow on the sea. It certainly was thinner than paper. "We must be about opposite New Smyrna,"[5] said the cook, who had coasted this shore often in schooners. "Captain, by the way, I believe they abandoned that life-saving station there about a year ago."

"Did they?" said the captain.

The wind slowly died away. The cook and the correspondent were not now obliged to slave in order to hold high the oar. But the waves continued their old impetuous swooping at the dinghy, and the little craft, no longer under way, struggled woundily over them. The oiler or the correspondent took the oars again.

Shipwrecks are apropos of nothing. If men could only train for them and have them occur when the men had reached pink condition, there would be less drowning at sea. Of the four in the dinghy none had slept any time worth mentioning for two days and two nights previous to embarking in the dinghy, and in the excitement of clambering

---

5. New Smyrna: New Smyrna Beach, a town on the Florida coast, about fifteen miles south of Daytona Beach.

about the deck of a foundering ship they had also forgotten to eat heartily.

For these reasons, and for others, neither the oiler nor the correspondent was fond of rowing at the time. The correspondent wondered ingenuously how in the name of all that was sane could there be people who thought it amusing to row a boat. It was not an amusement; it was a diabolical punishment, and even a genius of mental aberrations could never conclude that it was anything but a horror to the muscles and a crime against the back. He mentioned to the boat in general how the amusement of rowing struck him, and the weary-faced oiler smiled in full sympathy. Previously to the foundering, by the way, the oiler had worked double watch in the engine room of the ship.

"Take her easy, now, boys," said the captain. "Don't spend yourselves. If we have to run a surf you'll need all your strength, because we'll sure have to swim for it. Take your time."

Slowly the land arose from the sea. From a black line it became a line of black and a line of white—trees and sand. Finally, the captain said that he could make out a house on the shore. "That's the house of refuge, sure," said the cook. "They'll see us before long, and come out after us."

The distant lighthouse reared high. "The keeper ought to be able to make us out now, if he's looking through a glass," said the captain. "He'll notify the lifesaving people."

"None of those other boats could have got ashore to give word of the wreck," said the oiler, in a low voice. "Else the lifeboat would be out hunting us."

Slowly and beautifully the land loomed out of the sea. The wind came again. It had veered from the northeast to the southeast. Finally, a new sound struck the ears of the men in the boat. It was the low thunder of the surf on the shore. "We'll never be able to make the lighthouse now," said the captain. "Swing her head a little more north, Billie."

" 'A little more north,' sir," said the oiler.

Whereupon the little boat turned her nose once more down the wind, and all but the oarsman watched the shore grow. Under the influence of this expansion doubt and direful apprehension was leaving the minds of the men. The management of the boat was still most absorbing, but it could not prevent a quiet cheerfulness. In an hour, perhaps, they would be ashore.

Their backbones had become thoroughly used to balancing in the boat and they now rode this wild colt of a dinghy like circus men. The correspondent thought that he had been drenched to the skin, but happening to feel in the top pocket of his coat, he found therein eight cigars. Four of them were soaked with sea water; four were perfectly scatheless. After a search, somebody produced three dry matches, and thereupon the four waifs rode impudently in their little boat, and with an assurance of an impending rescue shining in their eyes, puffed at the big cigars and judged well and ill of all men. Everybody took a drink of water.

IV

"Cook," remarked the captain, "there don't seem to be any signs of life about your house of refuge."

"No," replied the cook. "Funny they don't see us!"

A broad stretch of lowly coast lay before the eyes of the men. It was of dunes topped with dark vegetation. The roar of the surf was plain, and sometimes they could see the white lip of a wave as it spun up the beach. A tiny house was blocked out black upon the sky. Southward, the slim lighthouse lifted its little gray length.

Tide, wind, and waves were swinging the dinghy northward. "Funny they don't see us," said the men.

The surf's roar was here dulled, but its tone was, nevertheless, thunderous and mighty. As the boat swam over the great rollers, the men sat listening to this roar. "We'll swamp sure," said everybody.

14 **Literary Focus** What is the physical condition of the men? Is it described dramatically or in a matter-of-fact, almost detached and ironic tone?

15 **Clarification** If they have to "run a surf," they will try to get the boat through the extremely rough shallow water near the beach.

16 **Enrichment** In Crane's actual experience, the seven other men aboard the *Commodore* when she sank were drowned.

ESL Teaching Strategy At the end of Part III and/or at the end of the story, pair ESL and non-ESL students to write a brief news report of what happened, using short declarative statements. The non-ESL student should act as "coach-editor" for the ESL student who is the "reporter."

17

It is fair to say here that there was not a lifesaving station within twenty miles in either direction, but the men did not know this fact and in consequence they made dark and opprobrious remarks concerning the eyesight of the nation's lifesavers. Four scowling men sat in the dinghy and surpassed records in the invention of epithets.

"Funny they don't see us."

The light-heartedness of a former time had completely faded. To their sharpened minds it was easy to conjure pictures of all kinds of incompetency and blindness and, indeed, cowardice. There was the shore of the populous land, and it was bitter and bitter to them that from it came no sign.

"Well," said the captain, ultimately, "I suppose we'll have to make a try for ourselves. If we stay out here too long, we'll none of us have strength left to swim after the boat swamps."

And so the oiler, who was at the oars, turned the boat straight for the shore. There was a sudden tightening of muscles. There was some thinking.

"If we don't all get shore—" said the captain. "If we don't all get ashore, I suppose you fellows know where to send news of my finish?"

18, 19

They then briefly exchanged some addresses and admonitions. As for the reflections of the men, there was a great deal of rage in them. Perchance they might be formulated thus: "If I am going to be drowned—if I am going to be drowned—if I am going to be drowned, why, in the name of the seven mad gods[6] who rule the sea, was I allowed to come thus far and contemplate sand and trees? Was I brought here merely to have my nose dragged away as I was about to nibble the sacred cheese of life? It is preposterous. If this old ninny-woman, Fate, cannot do better than this, she should be deprived of

---

6. seven mad gods: A reference to the ancient Greek gods.

the management of men's fortunes. She is an old hen who knows not her intention. If she has decided to drown me, why did she not do it in the beginning and save me all this trouble. The whole affair is absurd. . . . But, no, she cannot mean to drown me. She dare not drown me. She cannot drown me. Not after all this work." Afterward the man might have had an impulse to shake his fist at the clouds. "Just you drown me, now, and then hear what I call you!"

The billows that came at this time were more formidable. They seemed always just about to break and roll over the little boat in a turmoil of foam. There was a preparatory and long growl in the speech of them. No mind unused to the sea would have concluded that the dinghy could ascend these sheer heights in time. The shore was still afar. The oiler was a wily surfman. "Boys," he said, swiftly, "she won't live three minutes more and we're too far out to swim. Shall I take her to sea again, Captain?"

"Yes, Go ahead!" said the captain.

This oiler, by a series of quick miracles, and fast and steady oarsmanship, turned the boat in the middle of the surf and took her safely to sea again.

There was a considerable silence as the boat bumped over the furrowed sea to deeper water. Then somebody in gloom spoke. "Well, anyhow, they must have seen us from the shore by now."

The gulls went in slanting flight up the wind toward the gray desolate east. A squall, marked by dingy clouds, and clouds brick-red, like smoke from a burning building, appeared from the southeast.

"What do you think of those lifesaving people? Ain't they peaches?"

"Funny they haven't seen us."

"Maybe they think we're out here for sport! Maybe they think we're fishin'. Maybe they think we're fools."

It was a long afternoon. A changed tide tried to force them southward, but wind and

CALIFORNIA SUITE
Vivian Caldwell

The Open Boat 587

Fine art, *California Suite,* by Vivian Caldwell. Seascapes have been one of America's favorite forms of art since Colonial days. But most paintings of the sea have included boats, shorelines, and a great expanse of ocean.

This painting is an unusual view of the sea, both in its simplicity of subject and in its original angled perspective. Rather than portraying the waves of the ocean as part of a horizontal and limitless expanse, the artist has chosen to focus on the downside of a wave as it breaks toward us. And instead of emphasizing the effect of the powerful wave against ships or rocks, as it often does in seascapes, the painting portrays the inner power of the water as it churns toward us. This is a realist painting; it gives an almost scientific view of light, reflection, and the water's many different patterns. The artist uses a very limited range of color, but within the blues and greens and sky tones there is delicate variation. Each darker area suggests another bit of motion in the sea, just as the lighter spots capture the breaking waves and the sky's reflection. The composition is diagonal, moving the eye from the upper left to the lower right, as though we were riding the crest of the wave.

Use the following questions for discussion.

1. What would your reaction to this wave be if you were a surfer ? a swimmer ? a boater?
2. Where do you imagine the artist would have to be to see the wave from this angle?
3. Is this picture more or less powerful, without a sinking ship in it, than the pictures on pages 581 and 594?
4. How would you describe the artist's attitude toward the sea?

20 Enrichment The *Commodore* had sailed out of Jacksonville, Florida, north of St. Augustine. The dinghy with Crane and the other men aboard came ashore at Daytona Beach, just north of New Smyrna and about fifty miles north of the present Cape Canaveral.

21 Enrichment The rescue boats used by the crews of lifesaving stations were large enough for several people to row at once. They were mounted on large-wheeled carts that were pulled into the water, allowing the crew to launch the boat beyond the dangerous line of surf.

22 Enrichment During the nine-teenth and early twentieth centuries, vacationers usually traveled to seaside hotels by train. Each hotel had its own buses, which brought guests from the train station and took them to the beach or to other places of amusement.

wave said northward. Far ahead, where coastline, sea, and sky formed their mighty angle, there were little dots which seemed to indicate a city on the shore.

"St. Augustine?"[7]

20 The captain shook his head. "Too near Mosquito Inlet."

And the oiler rowed, and then the correspondent rowed. Then the oiler rowed. It was a weary business. The human back can become the seat of more aches and pains than are registered in books for the composite anatomy of a regiment. It is a limited area, but it can become the theater of innumerable muscular conflicts, tangles, wrenches, knots, and other comforts.

"Did you ever like to row, Billie?" asked the correspondent.

"No," said the oiler. "Hang it."

When one exchanged the rowing seat for a place in the bottom of the boat, he suffered a bodily depression that caused him to be careless of everything save an obligation to wiggle one finger. There was cold sea water swashing to and fro in the boat, and he lay in it. His head, pillowed on a thwart, was within an inch of the swirl of a wave crest, and sometimes a particularly obstreperous sea came inboard and drenched him once more. But these matters did not annoy him. It is almost certain that if the boat had capsized he would have tumbled comfortably out upon the ocean as if he felt sure that it was a great soft mattress.

"Look! There's a man on the shore!"

"Where?"

"There! See 'im? See 'im?"

"Yes, sure! He's walking along."

"Now he's stopped. Look! He's facing us!"

"He's waving at us!"

"So he is! By thunder!"

"Ah, now, we're all right! Now we're all right! There'll be a boat out here for us in half an hour."

---

7. St. Augustine: A town on the Florida coast, approximately sixty-five miles north of New Smyrna Beach.

"He's going on. He's running. He's going up to that house there."

The remote beach seemed lower than the sea, and it required a searching glance to discern the little black figure. The captain saw a floating stick and they rowed to it. A bath towel was by some weird chance in the boat, and, tying this on the stick, the captain waved it. The oarsman did not dare turn his head, so he was obliged to ask questions.

"What's he doing now?"

"He's standing still again. He's looking, I think. . . . There he goes again. Toward the house. . . . Now he's stopped again."

"Is he waving at us?"

"No, not now! he was, though."

"Look! There comes another man!"

"He's running."

"Look at him go, would you."

"Why, he's on a bicycle. Now he's met the other man. They're both waving at us. Look!"

"There comes something up the beach."

"What the devil is that thing?"

"Why, it looks like a boat."

"Why, certainly it's a boat."

"No, it's on wheels."

21 "Yes, so it is. Well, that must be the lifeboat. They drag them along shore on a wagon."

"That's the lifeboat, sure."

"No, by——, it's—it's an omnibus."

"I tell you it's a lifeboat."

22 "It is not! It's an omnibus. I can see it plain. See? One of those big hotel omnibuses."

"By thunder, you're right. It's an omnibus, sure as fate. What do you suppose they are doing with an omnibus? Maybe they are going around collecting the life crew, hey?"

"That's it, likely. Look! There's a fellow waving a little black flag. He's standing on the steps of the omnibus. There come those other two fellows. Now they're all talking together. Look at the fellow with the flag. Maybe he ain't waving it!"

"That ain't a flag, is it? That's his coat.

588   *Realism and the Frontier*

Grammar in Action

To communicate effectively writers often combine several ideas into a single sentence, fitting thoughts together according to their relative importance. One way of doing this is to use **coordination** and **coordinating conjunctions** to link or contrast roughly equivalent words, phrases, or clauses. The coordinating conjunctions *and, but, or, nor, for, so,* and *yet* are used to link independent clauses in compound sentences.

Stephen Crane's writing contains many coordinate ideas,

ideas of equal, or coordinate, importance. He expresses these ideas in compound sentences. Notice the following examples:

There was cold sea water swishing to and fro in the boat, *and* he lay in it.

The form of the lighthouse had vanished from the southern horizon, *but* finally a pale star appeared. . . .

Student Activity 1. Point out the coordinating conjunctions in the following sentences. Explain how the ideas joined are coordinate.

1. The birds sat comfortably in groups, and they were envied by some in the dinghy, for the wrath of the sea was not more to them than it was to a covey of prairie chickens. . . .

Why, certainly, that's his coat."

"So it is. It's his coat. He's taken it off and is waving it around his head. But would you look at him swing it!"

"Oh, say, there isn't any lifesaving station there. That's just a winter resort hotel omnibus that has brought over some of the boarders to see us drown."

"What's that idiot with the coat mean? What's he signaling, anyhow?"

"It looks as if he were trying to tell us to go north. There must be a lifesaving station up there."

"No! He thinks we're fishing. Just giving us a merry hand. See? Ah, there, Willie."

"Well, I wish I could make something out of those signals. What do you suppose he means?"

"He don't mean anything. He's just playing."

"Well, if he'd just signal us to try the surf again, or to go to sea and wait, or go north, or go south, or go to hell—there would be some reason in it. But look at him. He just stands there and keeps his coat revolving like a wheel. The ass!"

"There come more people."

"Now there's quite a mob. Look! Isn't that a boat?"

"Where? Oh, I see where you mean. No, that's no boat."

"That fellow is still waving his coat."

"He must think we like to see him do that. Why don't he quit it. It don't mean anything."

"I don't know. I think he is trying to make us go north. It must be that there's a lifesaving station there somewhere."

"Say, he ain't tired yet. Look at 'im wave."

"Wonder how long he can keep that up. He's been revolving his coat ever since he caught sight of us. He's an idiot. Why aren't they getting men to bring a boat out. A fishing boat—one of those big yawls—could come out here all right. Why don't he do something?"

"Oh, it's all right, now."

"They'll have a boat out here for us in less than no time, now that they've seen us."

A faint yellow tone came into the sky over the low land. The shadows on the sea slowly deepened. The wind bore coldness with it, and the men began to shiver.

"Holy smoke!" said one, allowing his voice to express his impious mood, "if we keep on monkeying out here! If we've got to flounder out here all night!"

"Oh, we'll never have to stay here all night! Don't you worry. They've seen us now, and it won't be long before they'll come chasing out after us."

The shore grew dusky. The man waving a coat blended gradually into this gloom, and it swallowed in the same manner the omnibus and the group of people. The spray, when it dashed uproariously over the side, made the voyagers shrink and swear like men who were being branded.

"I'd like to catch the chump who waved the coat. I feel like soaking him one, just for luck."

"Why? What did he do?"

"Oh, nothing, but then he seemed so cheerful."

In the meantime the oiler rowed, and then the correspondent rowed, and then the oiler rowed. Gray-faced and bowed forward, they mechanically, turn by turn, plied the leaden oars. The form of the lighthouse had vanished from the southern horizon, but finally a pale star appeared, just lifting from the sea. The streaked saffron in the west passed before the all-merging darkness, and the sea to the east was black. The land had vanished, and was expressed only by the low and drear thunder of the surf.

"If I am going to be drowned—if I am going to be drowned—if I am going to be drowned, why, in the name of the seven mad gods who rule the sea, was I allowed to come thus far and contemplate sand and trees? Was I brought here merely to have my nose dragged away as I was about to nibble the sacred cheese of life?"

The patient captain, drooped over the

The Open Boat 589

23 **Discussion** In this conversation, there are no indications of speakers. Ask students what would be the effect if Crane had put in "_____ said" after each speech. Why did he choose not to identify the speakers?

24 **Literary Focus** Ask students what impression they have at this point of the relative powers of humanity and of the sea.

25 **Discussion** Ask students what the man with the coat *was* doing. Do we or the men really know?

26 **Reading Strategy** Compare this repetition of "They rowed" with the one that directly precedes the sighting of the men on shore. How is the mood different?

27 **Clarification** The "saffron" refers to the "faint yellow tone" in the western sky mentioned above.

2. The remote beach seemed lower than the sea, and it required a searching glance to discern the little black figure.
3. The cook continued to sleep, but the oiler sat up. . . .

Student Activity 2. Find three more examples of compound sentences. Explain how the ideas combined are coordinate.

590

28 Clarification The term *keep her head up* means to keep the bow of the boat perpendicular to the waves to avoid being swamped.

29 Master Teacher Note This is one of many understatements made by the drily ironic narrator, which undercuts the Romantic possibilities of the story. Discuss "understatement" and read examples like this in a very ironic tone, asking the class to explain why they are understatements and perhaps why they are humorous.

30 Clarification A compass is divided into "points" as a clock is into minutes. The correspondent is to aim the bow of the boat slightly to the right of the light in the north.

water jar, was sometimes obliged to speak to the oarsman.

28 "Keep her head up! Keep her head up!"

" 'Keep her head up,' sir." The voices were weary and low.

29 This was surely a quiet evening. All save the oarsman lay heavily and listlessly in the boat's bottom. As for him, his eyes were just capable of noting the tall black waves that swept forward in a most sinister silence, save for an occasional subdued growl of a crest.

The cook's head was on a thwart, and he looked without interest at the water under his nose. He was deep in other scenes. Finally he spoke. "Billie," he murmured, dreamfully, "what kind of pie do you like best?"

V

"Pie," said the oiler and the correspondent, agitatedly. "Don't talk about those things, blast you!"

"Well," said the cook, "I was just thinking about ham sandwiches, and——"

A night on the sea in an open boat is a long night. As darkness settled finally, the shine of the light, lifting from the sea in the south, changed to full gold. On the northern horizon a new light appeared, a small bluish gleam on the edge of the waters. These two lights were the furniture of the world. Otherwise there was nothing but waves.

Two men huddled in the stern, and distances were so magnificent in the dinghy that the rower was enabled to keep his feet partly warmed by thrusting them under his companions. Their legs indeed extended far under the rowing seat until they touched the feet of the captain forward. Sometimes, despite the efforts of the tired oarsman, a wave came piling into the boat, an icy wave of the night, and the chilling water soaked them anew. They would twist their bodies for a moment and groan, and sleep the dead sleep

once more, while the water in the boat gurgled about them as the craft rocked.

The plan of the oiler and the correspondent was for one to row until he lost the ability, and then arouse the other from his sea-water couch in the bottom of the boat.

The oiler plied the oars until his head drooped forward, and the overpowering sleep blinded him. And he rowed yet afterward. Then he touched a man in the bottom of the boat, and called his name. "Will you spell me for a little while?" he said, meekly.

"Sure, Billie," said the correspondent, awakening and dragging himself to a sitting position. They exchanged places carefully, and the oiler, cuddling down in the sea water at the cook's side, seemed to go to sleep instantly.

The particular violence of the sea had ceased. The waves came without snarling. The obligation of the man at the oars was to keep the boat headed so that the tilt of the rollers would not capsize her, and to preserve her from filling when the crests rushed past. The black waves were silent and hard to be seen in the darkness. Often one was almost upon the boat before the oarsman was aware.

In a low voice the correspondent addressed the captain. He was not sure that the captain was awake, although this iron man seemed to be always awake. "Captain, shall I keep her making for that light north, sir?"

The same steady voice answered him. "Yes. Keep it about two points off the port bow." **30**

The cook had tied a life belt around himself in order to get even the warmth which this clumsy cork contrivance could donate, and he seemed almost stovelike when a rower, whose teeth invariably chattered wildly as soon as he ceased his labor, dropped down to sleep.

The correspondent, as he rowed, looked down at the two men sleeping under foot. The cook's arm was around the oiler's shoulders, and, with their fragmentary clothing and haggard faces, they were the babes of the sea, a grotesque rendering of the old babes in the wood.

Later he must have grown stupid at his work, for suddenly there was a growling of water, and a crest came with a roar and a swash into the boat, and it was a wonder that it did not set the cook afloat in his life belt. The cook continued to sleep, but the oiler sat up, blinking his eyes and shaking with the new cold.

"Oh, I'm awful sorry, Billie," said the correspondent, contritely.

"That's all right, old boy," said the oiler, and lay down again and was asleep.

Presently it seemed that even the captain dozed, and the correspondent thought that he was the one man afloat on all the oceans. The wind had a voice as it came over the waves, and it was sadder than the end.

There was a long, loud swishing astern of the boat, and a gleaming trail of phosphorescence, like blue flame, was furrowed on the black waters. It might have been made by a monstrous knife.

Then there came a stillness, while the correspondent breathed with the open mouth and looked at the sea.

Suddenly there was another swish and another long flash of bluish light, and this time it was alongside the boat, and might almost have been reached with an oar. The correspondent saw an enormous fin speed like a shadow through the water, hurling the crystalline spray and leaving the long glowing trail.

The correspondent looked over his shoulder at the captain. His face was hidden, and he seemed to be asleep. He looked at the babes of the sea. They certainly were asleep. So, being bereft of sympathy, he leaned a little way to one side and swore softly into the sea.

But the thing did not then leave the vicinity of the boat. Ahead or astern, on one side or the other, at intervals long or short, fled the long sparkling streak, and there was to be heard the whiroo of the dark fin. The speed and power of the thing was greatly to be admired. It cut the water like a gigantic and keen projectile.

The presence of this biding thing did not affect the man with the same horror that it would if he had been a picnicker. He simply looked at the sea dully and swore in an undertone.

Nevertheless, it is true that he did not wish to be alone with the thing. He wished one of his companions to awaken by chance and keep him company with it. But the captain hung motionless over the water jar and the oiler and the cook in the bottom of the boat were plunged in slumber.

VI

"If I am going to be drowned—if I am going to be drowned—if I am going to be drowned, why, in the name of the seven mad gods who rule the sea, was I allowed to come thus far and contemplate sand and trees?"

During this dismal night, it may be remarked that a man would conclude that it was really the intention of the seven mad gods to drown him, despite the abominable injustice of it. For it was certainly an abominable injustice to drown a man who had worked so hard, so hard. The man felt it would be a crime most unnatural. Other people had drowned at sea since galleys swarmed with painted sails, but still——

When it occurs to a man that nature does not regard him as important, and that she feels she would not maim the universe by disposing of him, he at first wishes to throw bricks at the temple, and he hates deeply the fact that there are no bricks and no temples. Any visible expression of nature would surely be pelleted with his jeers.

Then, if there be no tangible thing to hoot he feels, perhaps, the desire to confront a personification and indulge in pleas,

31 Critical Thinking and Reading What is the correspondent beginning to hear?

32 Enrichment Anyone swimming in the ocean at night has noticed a trail of blue-green luminescence. This is caused by chemical changes in tiny sea creatures (plankton) when they are disturbed.

33 Literary Focus The correspondent's reaction to the "biding thing" (later identified as a shark) is in keeping with his exhausted physical condition. How might a Hollywood actor play this scene?

34 Critical Thinking and Reading Who is speaking here? How does this connect with the story up to this point?

35 Critical Thinking and Reading Would this be in a newspaper story? Why is it here? What does it add to the story?

bowed to one knee, and with hands supplicant, saying: "Yes, but I love myself."

A high cold star on a winter's night is the word he feels that she says to him. Thereafter he knows the pathos of his situation.

The men in the dinghy had not discussed these matters, but each had, no doubt, reflected upon them in silence and according to his mind. There was seldom any expression upon their faces save the general one of complete weariness. Speech was devoted to the business of the boat.

36 To chime the notes of his emotion, a verse mysteriously entered the correspondent's head. He had even forgotten that he had forgotten this verse, but it suddenly was in his mind.

> A soldier of the Legion[8] lay dying in
>   Algiers,
> There was lack of woman's nursing,
>   there was dearth of woman's tears;
> But a comrade stood beside him, and
>   he took that comrade's hand,
> And he said: "I never more shall see
>   my own, my native land."[9]

In his childhood, the correspondent had been made acquainted with the fact that a soldier of the Legion lay dying in Algiers, but he had never regarded it as important. Myriads of his schoolfellows had informed him of the soldier's plight, but the dinning had naturally ended by making him perfectly indifferent. He had never considered it his affair that a soldier of the Legion lay dying in Algiers, nor had it appeared to him as a matter for sorrow. It was less to him than the breaking of a pencil's point.

Now, however, it quaintly came to him as a human, living thing. It was no longer

---

8. the Legion: The French Foreign Legion.
9. A soldier . . . native land: An incorrectly quoted passage from the poem "Bingen on the Rhine" (1883) by Caroline E. S. Norton.

merely a picture of a few throes in the breast of a poet, meanwhile drinking tea and warming his feet at the grate; it was an actuality—stern, mournful, and fine.

The correspondent plainly saw the soldier. He lay on the sand with his feet out straight and still. While his pale left hand was upon his chest in an attempt to thwart the going of his life, the blood came between his fingers. In the far Algerian distance, a city of low square forms was set against a sky that was faint with the last sunset hues. The correspondent, plying the oars and dreaming of the slow and slower movements of the lips of the soldier, was moved by a profound and perfectly impersonal comprehension. He was sorry for the soldier of the Legion who lay dying in Algiers. 37

The thing which had followed the boat and waited had evidently grown bored at the delay. There was no longer to be heard the slash of the cutwater, and there was no longer the flame of the long trail. The light in the north still glimmered, but it was apparently no nearer to the boat. Sometimes the boom of the surf rang in the correspondent's ears, and he turned the craft seaward then and rowed harder. Southward, someone had evidently built a watch fire on the beach. It was too low and too far to be seen, but it made a shimmering, roseate reflection upon the bluff back of it, and this could be discerned from the boat. The wind came stronger, and sometimes a wave suddenly raged out like a mountain cat and there was to be seen the sheen and sparkle of a broken crest.

The captain, in the bow, moved on his water jar and sat erect. "Pretty long night," he observed to the correspondent. He looked at the shore. "Those lifesaving people take their time."

"Did you see that shark playing around?"

"Yes, I saw him. He was a big fellow, all right."

"Wish I had known you were awake."

Commentary

In *The Red Badge of Courage* Crane proved that he could successfully draw on his imagination to create realistic experiences. However, like so many writers he preferred to draw on his personal history for literary material. His life as a war correspondent provided experiences of hunger, exposure, mortal danger, self doubt. He was able to infer from experiences such as these his reactions to imaginary ordeals.

"The Open Boat" is based on a true experience, which

Crane simplified in some ways. There were five occupants in Crane's boat; in the story, he changes this number to four. Yet he complicated the telling of the story with his ironic and changeable point of view.

Crane's experience with near death by drowning greatly affected him both physically and emotionally. (He was initially reported by the newspapers as drowned.) He spent almost a week in bed to recover from the physical strain. Two months later he hastily wrote a short story "Flanagan and His Short Filibustering Adventure" in an attempt to recreate his experience. It was unsatisfactory and did not face the true horror of the experience. His second attempt later that year resulted in "The Open Boat." After students have completed the story, ask if they feel the story captures the horror of the experience.

Later the correspondent spoke into the bottom of the boat.

"Billie!" There was a slow and gradual disentanglement. "Billie, will you spell me?"

"Sure," said the oiler.

38 As soon as the correspondent touched the cold comfortable sea water in the bottom of the boat, and had huddled close to the cook's life belt he was deep in sleep, despite the fact that his teeth played all the popular airs. This sleep was so good to him that it was but a moment before he heard a voice call his name in a tone that demonstrated the last stages of exhaustion. "Will you spell me?"

"Sure, Billie."

The light in the north had mysteriously vanished, but the correspondent took his course from the wide-awake captain.

Later in the night they took the boat farther out to sea, and the captain directed the cook to take one oar at the stern and keep the boat facing the seas. He was to call out if he should hear the thunder of the surf. This plan enabled the oiler and the correspondent to get respite together. "We'll give those boys a chance to get into shape again," said the captain. They curled down and, after a few preliminary chatterings and trembles, slept once more the dead sleep. Neither knew they had bequeathed to the cook the company of another shark, or perhaps the same shark.

As the boat caroused on the waves, spray occasionally bumped over the side and gave them a fresh soaking, but this had no power to break their repose. The ominous slash of the wind and the water affected them as it would have affected mummies.

"Boys," said the cook, with the notes of every reluctance in his voice, "she's drifted in pretty close. I guess one of you had better take her to sea again." The correspondent, aroused, heard the crash of the toppled crests.

As he was rowing, the captain gave him some whiskey and water, and this steadied the chills out of him. "If I ever get ashore and anybody shows me even a photograph of an oar——"

At last there was a short conversation.

"Billie. . . . Billie, will you spell me?"

"Sure," said the oiler.

VII

39 When the correspondent again opened his eyes, the sea and the sky were each of the gray hue of the dawning. Later, carmine and gold was painted upon the waters. The morning appeared finally, in its splendor, with a sky of pure blue, and the sunlight flamed on the tips of the waves.

On the distant dunes were set many little black cottages, and a tall white windmill reared above them. No man, nor dog, nor bicycle appeared on the beach. The cottages might have formed a deserted village.

The voyagers scanned the shore. A conference was held in the boat. "Well," said the captain, "if no help is coming, we might better try a run through the surf right away. If we stay out here much longer we will be too weak to do anything for ourselves at all." The others silently acquiesced in this reasoning. The boat was headed for the beach. The correspondent wondered if none ever ascended the tall wind tower, and if then they never looked seaward. This tower was a giant, standing with its back to the plight of the ants. It represented in a degree, to the correspondent, the serenity of nature amid the struggles of the individual—nature in the wind, and nature in the vision of men. She did not seem cruel to him then, nor beneficent, nor treacherous, nor wise. But she was indifferent, flatly indifferent. It is, perhaps, plausible that a man in this situation, impressed with the unconcern of the universe, should see the innumerable flaws of his life and have them taste wickedly in his mind and wish for another chance. A distinction between right and wrong seems absurdly

40

38 Discussion Why does the narrator say that the seawater is "cold comfortable"?

39 Discussion What time of day is it? How long have they been in the boat?

40 Literary Focus How does this illustrate the Naturalistic view of nature and life?

WORSENING WEATHER
Anton Otto Fischer
U.S. Coast Guard Museum
New London, Connecticut

clear to him, then, in this new ignorance of the grave-edge, and he understands that if he were given another opportunity he would mend his conduct and his words, and be better and brighter during an introduction, or at a tea.

"Now, boys," said the captain. "she is going to swamp sure. All we can do is to work her in as far as possible, and then when she swamps, pile out and scramble for the beach. Keep cool now, and don't jump until she swamps sure."

The oiler took the oars. Over his shoulders he scanned the surf. "Captain," he said, "I think I'd better bring her about, and keep her head-on to the seas and back her in."

41 "All right, Billie," said the captain. "Back her in." The oiler swung the boat then and, seated in the stern, the cook and the correspondent were obliged to look over their shoulders to contemplate the lonely and indifferent shore.

The monstrous inshore rollers heaved the boat high until the men were again enabled to see the white sheets of water scudding up the slanted beach. "We won't get in very close," said the captain. Each time a man could wrest his attention from the rollers, he turned his glance toward the shore, and in the expression of the eyes during this contemplation there was a singular quality. The correspondent, observing the others, knew that they were not afraid, but the full meaning of their glances was shrouded.

As for himself, he was too tired to grapple fundamentally with the fact. He tried to coerce his mind into thinking of it, but the mind was dominated at this time by the muscles, and the muscles said they did not care. It merely occurrred to him that if he should drown it would be a shame.

There were no hurried words, no pallor, no plain agitation. The men simply looked at the shore. "Now, remember to get well clear

42

594   Realism and the Frontier

41 Literary Focus Is this how the shore looked to the correspondent when he first saw it?

42 Literary Focus Does it seem believable that the correspondent would be so unemotional in the face of almost certain death?

of the boat when you jump," said the captain.

Seaward the crest of a roller suddenly fell with a thunderous crash, and the long white comber came roaring down upon the boat.

"Steady now," said the captain. The men were silent. They turned their eyes from the shore to the comber and waited. The boat slid up the incline, leaped at the furious top, bounced over it, and swung down the long back of the wave. Some water had been shipped and the cook bailed it out.

But the next crest crashed also. The tumbling boiling flood of white water caught the boat and whirled it almost perpendicular. Water swarmed in from all sides. The correspondent had his hands on the gunwale at this time, and when the water entered at that place he swiftly withdrew his fingers, as if he objected to wetting them.

The little boat, drunken with this weight of water, reeled and snuggled deeper into the sea.

"Bail her out, cook! Bail her out," said the captain.

"All right, Captain," said the cook.

"Now, boys, the next one will do for us, sure," said the oiler. "Mind to jump clear of the boat."

The third wave moved forward, huge, furious, implacable. It fairly swallowed the dinghy, and almost simultaneously the men tumbled into the sea. A piece of life belt had lain in the bottom of the boat, and as the correspondent went overboard he held this to his chest with his left hand.

43 The January water was icy, and he reflected immediately that it was colder than he had expected to find it off the coast of Florida. This appeared to his dazed mind as a fact important enough to be noted at the time. The coldness of the water was sad; it was tragic. This fact was somehow so mixed and confused with his opinion of his own situation that it seemed almost a proper reason for tears. The water was cold.

When he came to the surface he was conscious of little but the noisy water. Afterward he saw his companions in the sea. The oiler was ahead in the race. He was swimming strongly and rapidly. Off to the correspondent's left, the cook's great white and corked back bulged out of the water, and in the rear the captain was hanging with his one good hand to the keel of the overturned dinghy.

There is a certain immovable quality to a shore, and the correspondent wondered at it amid the confusion of the sea.

It seemed also very attractive, but the correspondent knew that it was a long journey, and he paddled leisurely. The piece of life preserver lay under him, and sometimes he whirled down the incline of a wave as if he were on a hand sled.

But finally he arrived at a place in the sea where travel was beset with difficulty. He did not pause swimming to inquire what manner of current had caught him, but there his progress ceased. The shore was set before him like a bit of scenery on a stage, and he looked at it and understood with his eyes each detail of it.

As the cook passed, much farther to the left, the captain was calling to him, "Turn over on your back, cook! Turn over on your back and use the oar."

"All right, sir." The cook turned on his back, and, paddling with an oar, went ahead as if he were a canoe.

Presently the boat also passed to the left of the correspondent with the captain clinging with one hand to the keel. He would have appeared like a man raising himself to look over a board fence, if it were not for the extraordinary gymnastics of the boat. The correspondent marveled that the captain could still hold to it.

They passed on, nearer to shore—the oiler, the cook, the captain—and following them went the water jar, bouncing gaily over the seas.

The correspondent remained in the grip

43 Discussion This information (month and place) would come at the beginning of a newspaper report. Why is it here near the end of the story? What would have been the effect if you had known this from the first paragraph?

Primary Source

In late January of 1897, after recovering from his experience at sea, Crane wrote to Cora Taylor, the woman with whom he spent the remainder of his short life. He compares the experience of love to his experience in the dinghy:

"Love comes like the tall swift shadow of a ship at night. There is for a moment the music of water's turmoil, a bell, perhaps, a man's shout, a row of gleaming yellow lights. Then the slow sinking of this mystic shape. Then silence and a bitter silence—the silence of the sea at night."

44 Enrichment The oiler, William Higgins, was hit on the head by a floating timber on the dinghy and actually did drown.

45 Discussion To "interpret" means to "explain the meaning of something difficult to understand or in another language." What might the men tell the people on shore that the sea is saying?

Reader's Response Most adventure stories are exciting struggles of a hero against an enemy of some kind. Is this an exciting story? Are there better adjectives to describe it? Is there a hero and an enemy?

Closure and Extension

ANSWERS TO THINKING ABOUT THE SELECTION
Recalling

1. (a) The oiler decided they couldn't make it and turned the boat back out to sea. (b) The man waves but doesn't seem to understand their desperate situation. (c) The second incident is, finally, more discouraging than the first because they thought the people and bus on shore were from a lifesaving station and would rescue them.
2. They are caught in currents and pulled by waves. The oiler drowns but the rest are saved.

Interpreting

3. (a) The men are enraged because the gulls are comfortable and safe on the waves; one even wants to sit on the captain's head. (b) The gulls represent cold, staring creatures, perhaps vulture-like, who have come to watch them die.
4. (a) The men feel it would be immature and unrealistic to pretend their situation was not life-threatening. (b) Crane means that it would be morally (and psychologically) wrong to say aloud that they had no chance. (Neither simple optimism nor pessimism is a realistic reaction to their situation.)

596

---

of this strange new enemy—a current. The shore, with its white slope of sand and its green bluff, topped with little silent cottages, was spread like a picture before him. It was very near to him then, but he was impressed as one who in a gallery looks at a scene from Brittany[10] or Holland.

He thought: "I am going to drown? Can it be possible? Can it be possible? Can it be possible?" Perhaps an individual must consider his own death to be the final phenomenon of nature.

But later a wave perhaps whirled him out of this small deadly current, for he found suddenly that he could again make progress toward the shore. Later still, he was aware that the captain, clinging with one hand to the keel of the dinghy, had his face turned away from the shore and toward him, and was calling his name. "Come to the boat! Come to the boat!"

In his struggle to reach the captain and the boat, he reflected that when one gets properly wearied, drowning must really be a comfortable arrangement, a cessation of hostilities accompanied by a large degree of relief, and he was glad of it, for the main thing in his mind for some moments had been horror of the temporary agony. He did not wish to be hurt.

Presently he saw a man running along the shore. He was undressing with most remarkable speed. Coat, trousers, shirt, everything flew magically off him.

"Come to the boat," called the captain.

"All right, Captain." As the correspondent paddled, he saw the captain let himself down to bottom and leave the boat. Then the correspondent performed his one little marvel of the voyage. A large wave caught him and flung him with ease and supreme speed completely over the boat and far beyond it. It struck him even then as an event in gymnastics, and a true miracle of the sea. An over-

---

10. **Brittany** (brit′ 'n ē): A former province of northwestern France.

---

596   *Realism and the Frontier*

---

turned boat in the surf is not a plaything to a swimming man.

The correspondent arrived in water that reached only to his waist, but his condition did not enable him to stand for more than a moment. Each wave knocked him into a heap, and the undertow pulled at him.

Then he saw the man who had been running and undressing, and undressing and running, come bounding into the water. He dragged ashore the cook, and then waded toward the captain, but the captain waved him away, and sent him to the correspondent. He was naked, naked as a tree in winter, but a halo was about his head, and he shone like a saint. He gave a strong pull, and a long drag, and a bully heave at the correspondent's hand. The correspondent, schooled in the minor formulae, said: "Thanks, old man." But suddenly the man cried: "What's that?" He pointed a swift finger. The correspondent said: "Go."

In the shallows, face downward, lay the oiler. His forehead touched sand that was periodically, between each wave, clear of the sea.

The correspondent did not know all that transpired afterward. When he achieved safe ground he fell, striking the sand with each particular part of his body. It was as if he had dropped from a roof, but the thud was grateful to him.

It seems that instantly the beach was populated with men with blankets, clothes, and flasks, and women with coffeepots and all the remedies sacred to their minds. The welcome of the land to the men from the sea was warm and generous, but a still and dripping shape was carried slowly up the beach, and the land's welcome for it could only be the different and sinister hospitality of the grave.

When it came night, the white waves paced to and fro in the moonlight, and the wind brought the sound of the great sea's voice to the men on shore, and they felt that they could then be interpreters.

44

45

---

5. (a) The following interactions suggest a "subtle brotherhood": their care in what they say and do not say about their chances of surviving; the oiler's quick defusing of the argument between the cook and the correspondent, the captain's "serene" commands, and the cook's "cheerful" obedience. (b) It probably developed because they are all actually "in the same boat" facing death together, which makes them equal and necessary to each other. (c) The continuing courtesy and the

picture of the "babes at sea" indicate the continuing bond.
6. Despite modern improvements in ships and navigation, the men in the dinghy are as subject to the inscrutable powers of the sea as were ancient seafarers.
7. It is much more frightening to face an unknown menace alone than with someone else.
8. (a) The oiler, a "wily surfman," seems to know more about surviving on the sea than do the rest, including the captain. When the correspondent last sees him,

he is "ahead in the race . . . swimming strongly and rapidly"; therefore, it is ironic that he is the one who drowns. (b) Nature seems to pay no attention to who should, by human reasoning, survive and who should not.
9. (a) The ocean is characterized as angry and threatening. Crane speaks of the waves as animals who "snarl," "growl," or "rage out like a mountain cat." The wave that overturns the boat and throws the men into the surf "moved forward, huge, furious,

THINKING ABOUT THE SELECTION

Recalling

1. (a) What happens when the men first attempt to row to the shore? (b) What happens when they are spotted by a man on the shore? (c) How do these two incidents affect the men's mood?
2. What happens when the men make their final run toward the shore?

Interpreting

3. (a) Why are the men enraged by the presence of the gulls? (b) What do the gulls seem to represent to the men?
4. (a) Why do you think that the men felt that it would be "childish and stupid" to "express any particular optimism"? (b) What does Crane mean when he writes that "the ethics of their condition was decidedly against any open suggestion of hopelessness"?
5. (a) At the beginning of Part III, Crane comments that a "subtle brotherhood" had been established among the four men. How do the men's interactions in the first two parts support this observation? (b) Why did this brotherhood develop among the men? (c) What indications are there that the bond among the men remains strong throughout the story?
6. What parallels between the four men in the dinghy and the seafarers of ancient times are suggested by the allusions to the "seven mad gods who rule the sea"?
7. When the shark first appears, why does the correspondent wish that one of his companions would awaken to "keep him company with it"?
8. (a) Considering each man's physical condition, what is ironic, or surprising, about the fate of the oiler? (b) How does the oiler's fate emphasize the forcefulness and unpredictability of nature?
9. Throughout the story, Crane frequently personifies, or attributes human qualities to, the ocean. (a) How does he generally characterize the ocean in these personifications? (b) How do the personifications add to the impact of the story?

Applying

10. Explain whether you think that the men's behavior in this story represents a typical response to this type of situation.
11. Explain whether you think that the outcome of the story would be different if the setting were changed to the present.

ANALYZING LITERATURE

Understanding Realism and Naturalism

Realism was a literary movement that emphasized the faithful, accurate portrayal of ordinary life. The Realists attempted to present "a slice of life," focusing on the realities of a small portion of the world. For example, in "The Open Boat" Crane focuses on the plight of four men.

Naturalism was a literary movement in which people were generally portrayed as being manipulated by forces of society and nature beyond their understanding or control. For example, in "The Open Boat" the characters are at the mercy of the powerful and unpredictable Atlantic Ocean.

1. Crane's story is filled with detailed descriptions of the ocean, the shore, and the men's movements in the boat. How do these descriptions contribute to the realistic quality of the story?
2. How do you think the fact that the story is based on a similar real-life experience might have contributed to the story's realistic quality?
3. Considering what you have read about the Naturalists' beliefs, why do you think that "The Open Boat" might be viewed as a classic example of a Naturalist story?

CRITICAL THINKING AND READING

Recognizing Important Passages

If you examine the story closely, you will find that at times Crane directly conveys his belief that nature is indifferent to the struggles of humanity. For example, he writes, "When it occurs to a man that nature does not regard him as im-

placable. It fairly swallowed the dinghy." (b) These personifications reinforce the idea of nature being powerful, incomprehensible, and unreasoning.

Applying

10. Suggested Response: These men were perhaps above average in physical and psychological endurance, but their reactions to the idea of dying are probably typical.
11. Suggested Response: Search

helicopters might have been used, but the outcome could have been the same.

ANSWERS TO ANALYZING LITERATURE

1. They make you feel as if you were there and emphasize the agonizingly slow monotony of the passing time.
2. Crane does not have to imagine the details of navigation, of the boat or of the appearance and effects of the waves—he can re-

produce them from his experience.
3. The correspondent, through his experience, comes to see the universe as the Naturalists see it—powerful and indifferent to humanity.

ANSWERS TO CRITICAL THINKING AND READING

Answers may differ. Suggested Response: Following are several passages in which Crane directly conveys his belief in nature's in-

difference to the problems of humanity:

"A high cold star on a winter's night is the word he feels that she [nature] says to him. Thereafter he knows the pathos of his situation." (p. 592)

[The windmill] represented in a degree, to the correspondent, the serenity of nature amid the struggles of the individual—nature in the wind, and nature in the vision of men. She did not seem cruel to him then, nor beneficent, nor treacherous nor wise. But she was indifferent, flatly indifferent." (p. 593)

". . . the cook and the correspondent were obliged to look over their shoulders to contemplate the lonely and indifferent shore." (p. 594)

THINKING AND WRITING

For help with this assignment students can refer to Lesson 15, "Evaluating a Literary Work" in the Handbook of Writing About Literature.

Challenge There are many case studies in psychology that explore what happens to people when their survival is threatened. Find several examples of these and compare them to Crane's story.

Primary Source In several of his works, Crane makes effective use of point of view. What a viewer sees depends not only on the objects seen but on the point of view of the observer. Crane said ". . . I understand that a man is born into the world with his own pair of eyes, and he is not at all responsible for his vision—he is merely responsible for his personal honesty. To keep close to this personal honesty is my supreme ambition." Have students discuss this quotation in relation to the poem on this page, to this short story, and to their own experiences.

portant, and that she feels she would not maim the universe by disposing of him, he at first wishes to throw bricks at the temple, and he hates deeply the fact that there are no bricks and no temples."

Find two other passages in which Crane directly conveys his belief in nature's indifference to the problems of humanity.

THINKING AND WRITING
Responding to Criticism

A literary critic has commented that "The Naturalist often describes his characters as though they are conditioned and controlled by environment, heredity, instinct, or chance. But he also suggests a compensating humanistic value in his characters or their fates which affirms the significance of the individual and of his life."

Write a composition in which you respond to this statement based on your reading of "The Open Boat." Begin by reviewing the story, keeping the critic's comment in mind. Then organize your ideas, and start writing your composition, using passages from the story for support. After you have finished writing, revise your composition, making sure you have presented your ideas in a logical order.

Primary Source

"The Open Boat" provides a good illustration of Crane's use of irony. For example, when Crane describes how picturesque the little boat would have looked to an outsider, he is being ironic. Even before he wrote "The Open Boat," Crane had a strong sense of irony in viewing the sea. Nine months before he himself was shipwrecked and spent time on the open ocean in a small boat, he published a brief poem about the sea, which presents a clear irony of perspective. Consider how this poem is appropriate to the situation in "The Open Boat."

To the maiden
The sea was blue meadow,
Alive with little froth-people
Singing.

To the sailor, wrecked,
The sea was dead gray walls,
Superlative in vacancy,
Upon which nevertheless at fateful time
Was written
The grim hatred of nature.

GREAT WORKS

THE RED BADGE OF COURAGE
by Stephen Crane

A young soldier, Henry Fleming, is about to fight his first battle, not knowing what to expect of the fighting or of himself. Will he stand and fight, or will he become frightened and run?

This is the situation at the opening of *The Red Badge of Courage*, a classic story about a young man's initiation into manhood through an experience that is strange and dangerous.

Stephen Crane's novel *The Red Badge of Courage* was published in 1895. Crane was twenty-four years old, and he had never fought in a war or witnessed battle. The Civil War had ended the decade before his birth. But when *The Red Badge of Courage* appeared, it was embraced as a brutally realistic account of the impact of war on a young recruit. A vivid tale of what Crane called "the red sickness of battle," the novel was also a corrective to the romanticized tales of war that had filled the popular imagination with visions of glory and heroism. Although the young soldier Henry Fleming comes to be regarded by his comrades and superiors as a hero, and he claims to become "a man" in battle, Crane's remark cast doubt over such a conventional reading.

Motivation/Prior Knowledge
Have students discuss the various causes of war. Ask them what types of war, if any, are worth fighting in? Have them determine if a person can profit from fighting in a war. If so, how? Have them also consider the objections that pacifists raise against the concept of war.

Purpose-Setting Question Why would Crane, and many other writers, be so interested in the lives and feelings of soldiers? What is it about those approaching combat that makes them interesting characters?

"War, The Blood-Swollen God"

When the first battle comes, what does Henry Fleming do? He flees in terror and becomes separated from his regiment. As he wanders behind the battle lines, but near enough to hear what is happening, Henry tries to come to terms with his actions and feelings. He seeks to cast blame outside himself—on laws and tradition, on nature, on

fate. "His egotism made him feel safe, for a time, from the iron hands" of these outside forces. Stumbling among the branches and smoke, thirsty and aching, Henry comes face to face with the horrors of war—a dead man propped up against a tree, his face running with ants; wounded and dying men staggering in a march. These encounters strip away the veil of glory and heroism from war, exposing Henry to the realities of human suffering. But these experiences do not seem to bring Henry closer to feeling empathy and compassion for his fellow men. He is preoccupied with his own role and with what the others would think of him if they knew he had fled. He is afraid to return to his own regiment unwounded, bearing no mark of battle that would mark him as a hero. Above all else, he is afraid of his fellow soldiers' scorn.

Still wandering, he soon finds himself in the middle of another battle, in which an entire regiment of men are washed back in defeat. "The column that had butted stoutly at the obstacles in the roadway was barely out of the youth's sight before he saw dark waves of men come sweeping out of the woods and down through the fields. He knew at once that the steel fibers had been washed from their hearts. They were bursting from their coats and their equipment as from entanglements. They charged down upon him like terrified buffaloes." Henry, horror-stricken, watches this scene of terror and chaotic destruction. "The fight was lost. The dragons were coming with invincible strides. The army, helpless in the matted thickets, and blinded by the overhanging night, was going to be swallowed. War, the red animal, war, the blood-swollen god, would have its bloated fill."

As the soldiers rush back upon him, Henry tries to grab one soldier to ask him what is happening. The soldier hits Henry in the head with his rifle, thus "wounding" him. This wound becomes Henry's "red badge of courage," the mark he needs to re-

turn to his regiment without losing face for having fled from the first battlefield.

The Meaning of "Courage" and "Heroism"

The rest of the novel is about Henry's return to his regiment and to battle. Because of his "wound," the men look upon him as a hero. And in the novel's remaining battle scenes, Henry fights ferociously. But Crane wants his readers to question Henry's "courage" and "heroism." In one episode, Henry is fighting so intently that he continues to shoot even after his comrades have stopped and the enemy has retreated. Another time,

insulted by a stray comment made by his general, Henry determines to fight harder. Later, he is portrayed as losing his identity in the "common personality" of the regiment, fighting in a state of "battle-sleep." Crane questions Henry's motives and exposes the unheroic underpinnings of conventional heroism.

Crane's Ironic Tone

One of the important themes of Crane's masterpiece is the conflict between appearance and reality. Writing in the ironic tone that is characteristic of his style, Crane creates a character whose understanding of

Great Works 601

Enrichment Ask students what they think of Crane's comment about not pointing out a particular moral or lesson to his readers. Determine if some members of the class believe writers should be obvious about certain messages contained in the fiction they produce.

Enrichment Have students who volunteer to do so share comments with the class about conversations they have had with relatives who are veterans of wars.

events differs from Crane's and our own interpretations. Recognizing this, Crane's contemporaries saw *The Red Badge of Courage* as a realistic novel. It departed from the popular genteel tradition of the 1890's romantic fiction and pointed toward the psychological realism of modern literature. Many critics today regard the novel as an example of the literature of Naturalism, in which human beings are not seen as individual souls but as a higher order of animal driven by elemental motives and at the mercy of an indifferent world. How one is supposed to interpret this novel, however, Crane left up to the reader. "I try to give the readers a slice out of life," Crane once remarked, "and if there is a moral or lesson in it I do not point it out. I let the reader find it for himself."

602   *Realism and the Frontier*

Poetry

THE GRAND CANYON OF THE YELLOWSTONE, 1893–1901
Thomas Moran
Art Resource

Humanities Note

Fine art, *The Grand Canyon of the Yellowstone,* 1893-1901, by Thomas Moran. By the end of the nineteenth century, explorers and settlers had traveled to most of the vast reaches of the North American continent. Public curiosity, especially about the nation's wilderness, was keen, and Thomas Moran (1837–1926) was one of the artists who painted many of the majestic scenes of natural wonder in the United States.

Yellowstone Park, established in 1872, was the first national park and is the largest. The Grand Canyon of the Yellowstone River is a deep divide, the river winding its way between the massive mountains. Later, of course, such scenes would be commonplace on tourists' postcards. To Moran, however, the depiction of the continent's striking geological formations was more than an attempt at pictorial realism. The impressionistic mood of the scene serves to humanize it, to make the monumental and the spectacular more understandable to the ordinary observer.

More About the Author Sidney Lanier was reared by devoutly religious parents in the traditions of the Old South. He began writing poetry in childhood. During the Civil War he served with the Confederacy and was captured and imprisoned. During that confinement he contracted tuberculosis.

After the war he worked in a law office, taught school, and traveled to the Midwest in the hopes of improving his failing health. For a while he served as first flutist in Baltimore's Peabody Orchestra.

The Song of the Chattahoochee, the volume from which this selection is taken, was published in 1877. After it received favorable attention, Lanier was appointed lecturer in English literature at Johns Hopkins University.

Literary Focus Other sound devices include end rhyme and onomatopoeia.

Writing/Prior Knowledge Some elements of nature, such as the wind, the earth, and the sun, are often personified. Encourage your students to select natural elements that are less frequently personified.

Vocabulary

Preteach the following vocabulary words:
amain (ə mān′) *adv.:* At or with great speed (p. 606, l. 3)
luminous (lōō′ mə nəs) *adj.:* Shining; bright (p. 606, l. 35)

GUIDE FOR INTERPRETING

Song of the Chattahoochee

Sidney Lanier (1842–1881) was a talented musician as well as a gifted poet. He had a strong interest in the relationship between music and poetry. As a result, he abandoned conventional poetic structures and sought to create a musical rhythm in his poetry. Born in Macon, Georgia, Lanier entered Oglethorpe University, where he studied poetry and music. In 1880 he published *The Science of English Verse.* In his book Lanier stated his belief that poetry should have the natural rhythm and fluidity of music and that the sound of a poem should reinforce its meaning.

Writer's Techniques

Sound Devices. Poets use a variety of sound devices to give their writing a musical quality. Four of the most frequently used sound devices are alliteration, consonance, assonance, and internal rhyme.

Alliteration is the repetition of similar sounds, usually consonants, at the beginnings of words or accented syllables. Notice the repetition of the *f* sound in the following line from "Song of the Chattahoochee": "And *f*lee *f*rom *f*olly on every side."

Consonance is the repetition of consonant sounds at the ends of words or accented syllables. For example, the *l* sound is repeated in the following line from "Song of the Chattahoochee": "Vei*l*ing the va*l*leys of Ha*ll.*"

Assonance is the repetition of vowel sounds. For example, the long *a* sound is repeated in the following line: "Av*ai*l: I am f*ai*n for to water the pl*ai*n."

Rhyme refers to the repetition of similar or identical sounds in the accented syllables of two or more words appearing close to each other in a poem. Internal rhyme is rhyme that occurs within a line. An example of internal rhyme appears in the following line from "Song of the Chattahoochee": "With a lover's p*ain* to att*ain* the pl*ain.*"

Writing

In "Song of the Chattahoochee" Lanier personifies, or attributes human characteristics to, a river. Think of another element of nature that a writer might personify. Then prepare a list of human qualities that could be attributed to this element.

Primary Source

Sidney Lanier's ideas about poetry influenced many late nineteenth- and early twentieth-century writers. Among them was American poet and author Hamlin Garland, who wrote, "That he was an immense force in my life . . . I gladly bear witness. He taught me freedom within law. His lines flowed down the printed page like rills of water rippling into whorls of rhyme, pleasantly, unexpectedly, and so easily as to be hardly more confining than prose."

604   Realism and the Frontier

Objectives

1 To recognize sound devices
2 To analyze the effect of sound devices
3 To write an extended personification

Support Material

Teaching Portfolio
Teacher Backup, p. 775
Usage and Mechanics Worksheet, p. 778
Vocabulary Check, p. 779
Analyzing Literature Worksheet, *Understanding Sound Devices,* p. 780
Language Worksheet, *Understanding Personification,* p. 781
Selection Test, p. 782

Song of the Chattahoochee[1]

Sidney Lanier

Out of the hills of Habersham,
  Down the valleys of Hall,[2]
I hurry amain to reach the plain,
Run the rapid and leap the fall,
5 Split at the rock and together again,
Accept my bed, or narrow or wide,
And flee from folly on every side
With a lover's pain to attain the plain
  Far from the hills of Habersham,
10 Far from the valleys of Hall.

———

1. Chattahoochee (chat' ə hoo' chē): A river in western Georgia.
2. Habersham . . . Hall: Two counties through which the Chattahoochee flows.

HARPERS FERRY FROM JEFFERSON ROCK, 1857
Edward Beyer
Virginia State Library

Thematic Idea Another selection in which devices play a vital role is "The Raven" by Edgar Allen Poe (p. 227).

Reader's Response Describe a
special place that has an almost
hypnotic effect on you.

All down the hills of Habersham,
   All through the valleys of Hall,
The rushes cried *Abide, Abide,*
The willful waterweeds held me thrall,
15   The laving laurel turned my tide,
The ferns and the fondling grass said *Stay,*
The dewberry dipped for to work delay,
And the little reeds sighed *Abide, abide,*
      Here in the hills of Habersham,
20   *Here in the valleys of Hall.*

High o'er the hills of Habersham,
   Veiling the valleys of Hall,
The hickory told me manifold
Fair tales of shade, the poplar tall
25 Wrought me her shadowy self to hold,
The chestnut, the oak, the walnut, the pine,
Overleaning, with flickering meaning and sign,
Said, *Pass not, so cold, these manifold*
      Deep shades of the hills of Habersham,
30   *These glades in the valleys of Hall.*

And oft in the hills of Habersham,
   And oft in the valleys of Hall,
The white quartz shone, and the smooth brook-stone
Did bar me of passage with friendly brawl,
35 And many a luminous jewel lone
—Crystals clear or a-cloud with mist,
Ruby, garnet and amethyst—
Made lures with the lights of streaming stone
      In the clefts of the hills of Habersham,
40   In the beds of the valleys of Hall.

But oh, not the hills of Habersham,
   And oh, not the valleys of Hall
Avail: I am fain for to water the plain.
Downward the voices of Duty call—   ⌐ 5
45 Downward, to toil and be mixed with the main,
The dry fields burn, and the mills are to turn,   ⌐ 6
And a myriad flowers mortally yearn,
And the lordly main from beyond the plain
      Calls o'er the hills of Habersham,
50   Calls through the valleys of Hall.

THINKING ABOUT THE SELECTION

Recalling

1. According to the first stanza, toward what is the river racing?
2. (a) What do the little reeds "sigh" in the second stanza? (b) What do the trees "say" in the third stanza?
3. What duties must the river perform before it mixes with the main?

Interpreting

4. Who is the speaker in this poem?
5. In this poem Lanier presents an extended personification of the Chattahoochee River. Name three other elements of nature that Lanier personifies in the poem.
6. (a) Considering Lanier's use of personification and the details he uses in describing the river's flow, what do you think the course of the river symbolizes? (b) What do the obstacles encountered by the river symbolize? (c) What does the "duty" of the plain symbolize? (d) What does the "main" symbolize?

Applying

7. Why is this poem as effective today as it was when it was written?

ANALYZING LITERATURE

Recognizing Sound Devices

Alliteration, consonance, assonance, and internal rhyme are four sound devices used in poetry. **Alliteration** is the repetition of similar sounds, usually consonants, at the beginnings of words or accented syllables (for example, "*R*un the *r*apid," line 4). **Consonance** is the repetition of consonant sounds at the ends of words or accented syllables (for example, "va*ll*eys of Ha*ll*"). **Assonance** is the repetition of vowel sounds (for example, "w*i*th fl*i*ckering," line 27). **Internal rhyme** is rhyme that occurs within a line (for example, "I hurry am*ain* to reach the pl*ain*," line 3).

1. Find two more examples of each of these techniques in "Song of the Chattahoochee."
2. How do these examples convey the natural movement of the river?

CRITICAL THINKING AND READING

Analyzing the Effect of Sound Devices

Sidney Lanier believed that the sound of a poem should help to reinforce its meaning. In "Song of the Chattahoochee" he used sound devices to imitate the natural flowing of a river. For example, his use of alliteration in the line "And flee *f*rom *f*olly on every side" captures the river's dancing, winding movement.

Do you agree with Lanier's contention? Support your answer.

THINKING AND WRITING

Writing an Extended Personification

What would a mountain say if it could speak? What message would the ocean give to humankind? What would a tornado say as it left behind a trail of destruction?

Write a poem or a short narrative essay in which you present an extended personification of an element of nature. Start by reviewing the list of human qualities you have already prepared. Add any other qualities you think of. Then write your personification using the element you are personifying as your speaker or narrator. When you finish writing, revise your personification and share it with your classmates.

abide." (b) The trees say "Pass not, so cold, these manifold/Deep shades of the hills of Haversham."
3. It must water the plain.

Interpreting

4. The river is the speaker of the poem.
5. He also personifies the rushes, waterweeds, hickory, the white quartz, other plants and stones, and duty.
6. (a) Suggested Response: It represents life. (b) Suggested Response: They represent the obstacles that people meet in their lives. (c) Suggested Response: It symbolizes a person's responsibilities and duties in life. (d) Suggested Response: It symbolizes death.

Applying

7. Suggested Response: The elements of sound it relies on still appeal to many people.

ANSWERS TO ANALYZING LITERATURE

1. Some examples of alliteration are "*f*lee *f*rom *f*olly," "*w*illful *w*aterweeds," and "*d*ewberry *d*ipped."
   Examples of consonance include "ra*p*id and lea*p*" and "wi*ll*ful waterweeds held me thra*ll*."
   Examples of assonance include "Av*ai*l: I am f*ai*n" and "flee from folly."
   Some examples of internal rhyme are "I am f*ain* for to water the pl*ain*," "The dry fields b*urn*, and the mills are to t*urn*."
2. Suggested Response: They capture the river's dancing, winding movement.

ANSWERS TO CRITICAL THINKING AND READING

Answers will differ. Students should offer reasons for their agreement or disagreement.

THINKING AND WRITING

After students have completed the assignment, divide them into groups, and have them read their compositions to one another and suggest ways in which they could be improved.

Closure and Extension

ANSWERS TO THINKING ABOUT THE SELECTION

Recalling

1. The river is racing toward the plain.
2. (a) The reeds sigh, "abide,

Many of the poems in *War Is Kind,* Crane's second volume of poetry, dated back to at least 1895. Shortly after its publication the author became seriously ill with tuberculosis and he sought help at a sanitorium in Badenweiler, Germany, where he died on June 5, 1900, at the age of 28.

Literary Focus Students may be encouraged to suggest examples of verbal irony. You may also want to discuss the tones of voice people use for irony.

Writing/Prior Knowledge For extra credit, your students may write short skits involving the use of verbal irony.

Critical Evaluation Crane's lack of recognition during his own time has been replaced by a growing admiration in later generations. John Berryman, a poet, claims that "by a margin, he is probably the greatest American storywriter, he stands as an artist not far below Hawthorne and James, he is one of our few poets, and one of the manifest geniuses the country has produced."

GUIDE FOR INTERPRETING

Writer's Techniques

Writing

Primary Source

War Is Kind; Think as I Think

Stephen Crane (1871–1900), who is primarily remembered for his fiction, was also a gifted poet. He published his harshly realistic and often pessimistic poetry in two volumes, *The Black Riders* (1895) and *War Is Kind* (1899). Generally composed of short, unrhymed lines with an irregular metrical pattern, his poetry was considered highly unconventional in style when it was first published. While Crane's poems were not widely accepted during his lifetime, the blatant honesty of his poems appealed to the following generation.

Irony and **Tone.** Irony is a contrast or a difference between what is stated and what is meant, or between what is expected to happen and what actually happens. Verbal irony is one of a number of forms of irony used in literature. Verbal irony occurs when the literal meaning of a word or statement is quite different from the intended meaning. For example, a character might criticize another character's driving ability by commenting, "He is such a great driver that he's been in ten accidents in the last two years."

Verbal irony can play an important role in revealing tone—the writer's attitude toward his or her subject, characters, or audience. Most often, the use of verbal irony conveys a sarcastic attitude or a sense of anger, bitterness, or disillusionment. For example, the use of verbal irony in a number of Stephen Crane's poems conveys his pessimistic and often bitter attitude.

People often use verbal irony in everyday speech. Prepare a list of examples of verbal irony from conversations you have heard. Then briefly describe what made you aware that each of the statements was not meant to be interpreted literally.

In an 1896 letter, Stephen Crane commented that he personally liked his first book of poems better than his successful novel *The Red Badge of Courage* because in it he had aimed "to give my ideas of life as a whole. . . ." Elsewhere in the same letter he presented some of his fundamental tenets by writing, "it has been a theory of mine ever since I began to write . . . that the most artistic and the most enduring literature was that which reflected life accurately. Therefore I have tried to observe closely, and to set down what I have seen in the simplest and most concise way. . . . Preaching is fatal to art in literature. I try to give to readers a slice out of life; and if there is any moral or lesson in it I do not point it out. I let the reader find it for himself."

Vocabulary

Preteach the following Vocabulary words:
shroud (shroud) *n.:* A cloth sometimes used to wrap a corpse for burial (p. 610, l. 24)
abominably (ə bäm′ ə nə blē) *adv.:* Hatefully (p. 611, l. 2)

Objectives

1 To understand irony and tone
2 To write about theme

Support Material

Selection Test, p. 793

Teaching Portfolio
Teacher Backup, p. 785
Usage and Mechanics Worksheet, p. 788
Vocabulary Check, p. 789
Analyzing Literature Worksheet, *Understanding Irony and Tone,* p. 790
Language Worksheet, *Recognizing Assonance and Alliteration,* p. 792

NEWS FROM THE WAR (DETAIL)
Winslow Homer for Harper's Weekly,
June 14, 1862
Library of Congress

War Is Kind

Stephen Crane

Do not weep, maiden, for war is kind.
Because your lover threw wild hands toward the sky
And the affrighted steed ran on alone,
Do not weep.
5   War is kind.

Hoarse, booming drums of the regiment,
Little souls who thirst for fight,
These men were born to drill and die.
The unexplained glory flies above them,
10 Great is the battle-god, great, and his kingdom—
A field where a thousand corpses lie.

War Is Kind   609

Humanities Note

Fine art, *News from the War*, 1862, by Winslow Homer. Winslow Homer (1836–1910) began his art career as a free-lance illustrator. From 1861–65, he traveled to the war zones and made sketches for *Harper's Weekly*. His drawings were reproduced as woodcuts and appeared frequently during the war. Homer also began painting at the war front.

This Civil War print, *News from the War,* is a detail from a larger montage of sketches showing the various reactions of people as they received news of the war. As a staff artist at the war front for *Harper's Weekly,* Homer was most fascinated by human, everyday scenes such as this, rather than the battles themselves. Many of his early works, such as this one, suffered artistically because they were sent back as sketches and reproduced as woodcuts by other artists; however this print still evokes strong emotion in the viewer. Although the sentimentality of the image might be criticized, it must be remembered that Homer was reporting a cruel reality of the war. The intent of this picture was to illustrate a war-related subject, not to exist as a purely artistic expression.

As students read this poem and look at the picture, you might ask these questions:
1. What is happening in this picture?
2. What emotions does this picture evoke?
3. How does this picture illustrate the irony of the poem?

5 **Discussion** Who are the people addressed in the first, twelfth, and twenty-third lines? Why would the speaker have chosen to address these people?

Reader's Response What are your own thoughts about war?

Closure and Extension

ANSWERS TO THINKING ABOUT THE SELECTION
Recalling

1. (a) The poem is addressed to maiden, babe, and mother. (b) Do not weep because of the horrible things that happened to your lover, father, or son.

Interpreting

2. They are grim images of the fate of men in war.
3. (a) Stanzas 2 and 4 convey glorified images of war. (b) They serve to show the contrast between the image of the glories of war and the realities of war.
4. (a) The theme is that war is cruel, not glorious. (b) Because his repetition is ironic, it reinforces the notion of war's cruelty.

Applying

5. Answers will differ. Students may comment that they have the same attitude toward war.

ANSWERS TO ANALYZING LITERATURE

1. "Great is the battle-god" and "Point for them the virtue of slaughter" are examples of verbal irony.
2. (a) Its tone is bitter. (b) His use of irony conveys a sense of bitterness and disgust.
3. Two details that show the irony of this statement can be found in lines 10–11 and 21–22.

5 | Do not weep, babe, for war is kind.
Because your father tumbled in the yellow trenches,
Raged at his breast, gulped and died,
15 Do not weep.
War is kind.

Swift blazing flag of the regiment,
Eagle with crest of red and gold,
These men were born to drill and die.
20 Point for them the virtue of slaughter,
Make plain to them the excellence of killing
And a field where a thousand corpses lie.

Mother whose heart hung humble as a button
On the bright splendid shroud of your son,
25 Do not weep.
War is kind.

THINKING ABOUT THE SELECTION
Recalling

1. (a) To what three people is the poem addressed? (b) What message does the speaker deliver to them?

Interpreting

2. How are the images presented in stanzas 1, 3, and 5 related to one another?
3. (a) What impressions of war do the images in stanzas 2 and 4 convey? (b) How are these images related to the speaker's message in stanzas 1, 3, and 5?
4. (a) What is the theme of the poem? (b) How does Crane's use of repetition reinforce the theme?

Applying

5. The twentieth century writer George Bernard Shaw wrote, "Peace is not only better than war, but infinitely more arduous." Discuss the meaning and implication of this statement.

610 Realism and the Frontier

ANALYZING LITERATURE
Using Irony and Tone

Verbal irony, one of a number of types of irony used in literature, occurs when the literal meaning of a word or statement is quite different from the intended meaning. For example, when the speaker states that "war is kind," he means that war is cruel.

Because writers often use it to express sarcasm, anger, bitterness, or disillusionment, verbal irony is important in revealing tone.

1. Find two additional examples of verbal irony in the poem.

2. (a) How would you describe the tone of the poem? (b) How does Crane's use of verbal irony help to convey the tone?

3. Find two details from the poem that indicate the statement "war is kind" is being used ironically.

Think as I Think

Stephen Crane

1

"Think as I think," said a man,
"Or you are abominably wicked;
You are a toad."

2

And after I had thought of it,
5   I said, "I will, then, be a toad."

THINKING ABOUT THE SELECTION

Recalling

1. (a) What does the man tell the speaker?
   (b) How does the speaker respond?

Interpreting

2. (a) Explain the last line of the poem. (b) What does the speaker's response reveal about his personality?
3. What does this poem suggest about the choice between conformity and individuality?

Applying

4. In what types of situations do you think people are pressured to conform to the thoughts and desires of others?

THINKING AND WRITING

Writing About Theme

"Think as I Think" focuses on the theme of individuality versus conformity. Write a short personal essay expressing your own thoughts concerning this theme. Start by thinking about how peer pressure and societal pressure can affect people's choices and behavior. Also think about how people's lives are affected by choosing not to conform. List the types of situations in which you think people are most often pressured to conform. Organize your thoughts into an informal outline. Then write your essay expressing your ideas as clearly as possible. When you finish writing, revise your essay and share it with your classmates. Give them an opportunity to respond to it. Then revise your essay again, based on their comments.

Think as I Think   611

Presentation

Motivation/Prior Knowledge
Discuss the concept of conformity with your students. In what ways does society pressure people to conform?

Purpose-Setting Question
What prompts the speaker's response?

1 **Discussion** How does a reader react to the first three lines?

2 **Critical Thinking and Reading**
Note the humor in the tone of the last line. Ask the students what makes that last line humorous.

Reader's Response How would you respond if someone told you to give up thinking independently?

Closure and Extension

ANSWERS TO THINKING ABOUT THE SELECTION
Recalling

1. (a) He tells the speaker, "Think as I think." (b) The speaker replies that he would rather be a toad.

Interpreting

2. The response reveals that the speaker is not easily intimidated.
3. The poem suggests that individuality is preferable to conformity.

Applying

4. Answers will differ. Situations may involve teen-age peer-pressure, political party lines, and many other areas.

THINKING AND WRITING

For help with this assignment, students can refer to Lesson 11, "Writing About Theme," in the Handbook of Writing About Literature.

Publishing Student Writing Have student volunteers read their essays to the class.

Critical Evaluation Not all commentary on Dunbar is favorable. Robert Bone, for instance, writing in *Down Home: A History of Afro-American Short Fiction* has this to say of his merit: "There is a moribund quality in Dunbar's art, attributable at least in part to the limitations of his age. To overcome those limitations, to make the most of his restricted possibilities, to stretch the imaginations of his contemporaries and thereby enlarge their moral horizons, it would have been necessary for Dunbar to adopt a sharply different literary stance. Romanticism would have had to yield to realism; loyalty to satire; pastoral to antipastoral."

ESL Teaching Strategy Ask each of your ESL students to gather five pictures of different masks from magazines or books. Then provide time for them to explain the illustrations while telling classmates what message each mask is supposed to convey to viewers.

PAUL LAURENCE DUNBAR

1872–1906

The first black American to support himself entirely by writing, Paul Laurence Dunbar displayed great versatility as a writer throughout his short career. Dunbar wrote poems, both in a formal, elegant style and in black dialect, and he wrote several novels and numerous short stories.

Dunbar was born in Dayton, Ohio, the son of former slaves. Encouraged by his mother, he began writing poetry at an early age. During high school, Dunbar, who was the only black student in his class, frequently recited his poetry before school assemblies. He also served as the president of the literary society, as class poet, and as editor of the school newspaper.

Following his graduation, he supported himself by working as an elevator operator while continuing to write. He first earned recognition among writers and critics in 1892, when he gave a poetry reading during a meeting of the Western Association of Writers. A year later he published his first collection of poetry, *Oak and Ivy*. In 1895 he published a second collection, *Majors and Minors* (1895), which was received by critics with great enthusiasm. In fact, William Dean Howells, the leading critic of the day, was so impressed with the book that he wrote an introduction for Dunbar's next collection, *Lyrics of a Lowly Life* (1896), which sold over twelve thousand copies and established Dunbar as a widely read and admired American poet.

Dunbar went on to write three more volumes of poetry, four novels, and four volumes of short stories. Dunbar's fiction often focused on daily life in the lost world of the southern plantation. Sometimes, however, it revolved around social problems facing black people in midwestern towns and urban ghettos. His characters included farmers, politicians, preachers, traders, entertainers, and professional people.

Dunbar, however, thought of himself primarily as a poet. He gave readings throughout the United States and Europe. Unfortunately, his life was cut short by tuberculosis in 1906. By the end of his life, his poetry was so popular that he was able to write from Florida that "Down here one finds my poems recited everywhere." One biographer has commented that "young blacks recited his poems and saw in turn what was possible for them."

Despite his success as a poet, Dunbar was disillusioned by the critics' tendency to focus on his poetry written in black dialect, while virtually ignoring his more formal verse. In poems such as "Douglass" and "We Wear the Mask," Dunbar demonstrates a command of the English language that was often overlooked, capturing the despair of black people in a dignified, graceful manner.

612   Realism and the Frontier

Objectives

1 To complete sentences
2 To understand a sonnet
3 To write a sonnet

Support Material

Teaching Portfolio
Teacher Backup, p. 795
Usage and Mechanics Worksheet, p. 798
Vocabulary Check, p. 799
Analyzing Literature Worksheet, *Comparing Sonnet Forms,* p. 800
Language Worksheet, *Completing Sentences,* p. 802
Selection Test, p. 802

GUIDE FOR INTERPRETING

We Wear the Mask; Douglass

Literary Forms

The Sonnet. A sonnet is a fourteen-line lyric poem, usually written in rhymed iambic pentameter—verse with five feet per line, each foot consisting of an unstressed syllable followed by a stressed syllable. A sonnet usually expresses a single complete idea or theme.

The two most common types of sonnets are *English sonnets,* or *Shakespearean sonnets* (named after English playwright William Shakespeare), and *Italian sonnets,* or *Petrarchan sonnets* (named after the fourteenth-century Italian poet Francesco Petrarch). English sonnets are composed of three quatrains (four-line stanzas) followed by a couplet (two rhyming lines), with the rhyme scheme *abab cdcd efef gg.* In most English sonnets, the main idea is presented and developed in the three quatrains, and the couplet offers a conclusion. Italian sonnets consist of an octave (eight lines) followed by a sestet (six lines), usually rhyming *abbaabba cdecde* or *abbaabba cdcdcd.* In some Italian sonnets, a question is raised in the octave and the answer is presented in the sestet. In other Italian sonnets, a single idea is presented in the octave and either developed or contradicted in the sestet.

Writing

In "Douglass" Paul Laurence Dunbar addresses the deceased black leader Frederick Douglass and expresses his people's feelings of despair and their need for Douglass's guidance and comfort. Review the excerpt from Douglass's autobiography (pages 430–434). Then list reasons why Dunbar might have chosen to address his poem to Douglass.

Primary Source

Paul Laurence Dunbar wrote against a backdrop of grave racial injustice. In a July 1903 letter, he used ironic commentary about Independence Day to express his feelings about the situation of black people. Parts of the letter follow.

> [W]e have celebrated the Nation's birthday. Yes, and we black folks have celebrated. . . .
>
> Like a dark cloud, pregnant with terror and destruction, disenfranchisement has spread its wings over our brethren of the South. Like the same dark cloud, industrial prejudice glooms above us in the North. . . . And yet we celebrate. . . .
>
> [W]ith bleeding hands uplifted, still sore and smarting from long beating at the door of opportunity, we raise our voices and sing, "My Country, 'Tis of Thee"; . . . while from the four points of the compass comes our brothers' unavailing cry, and so we celebrate.

Guide for Interpreting 613

Literary Focus Point out that the sonnet is probably the most widely used standard poetic form.

Writing/Prior Knowledge Before writing, students may want to discuss what they might want to say to Douglass today.

We Wear the Mask

Paul Laurence Dunbar

We wear the mask that grins and lies,
It hides our cheeks and shades our eyes—
This debt we pay to human guile;
With torn and bleeding hearts we smile,
5 And mouth with myriad subtleties.

Why should the world be overwise,
In counting all our tears and sighs?
Nay, let them only see us, while
    We wear the mask.

10 We smile, but, O great Christ, our cries
To thee from tortured souls arise.
We sing, but oh the clay is vile
Beneath our feet, and long the mile;
But let the world dream otherwise,
15   We wear the mask!

THINKING ABOUT THE SELECTION

Recalling

1. What purpose does the mask serve?

Interpreting

2. (a) Who is the poem's speaker? (b) How would you describe the speaker's emotional state?
3. What does the mask symbolize?
4. (a) Whom does the mask deceive? (b) Why do you think the speaker chooses not to reveal what is hidden beneath the mask?
5. What is the theme of the poem?

Applying

6. Like the speaker in this poem, most people at times hide their true feelings. Why do you think this is so? Explain your answer.

UNDERSTANDING LANGUAGE

Completing Sentences

Each of the following sentences is incomplete, with one or two words missing. Read each sentence carefully. Choose the lettered word or pair of words that best completes the sentence.

1. When Sue graduated from college, she was confronted with _____ possibilities.
   - a. subtle
   - b. myriad
   - c. tortured
   - d. passionate
2. Plagued by _____, the panel was unable to reach an _____.
   - a. dissension . . . agreement
   - b. defiance . . . solution
   - c. dissent . . . impasse
   - d. confusion . . . arrangement
3. The climber was _____ of the potential dangers that lay ahead.
   - a. suspicious
   - b. careful
   - c. mindful
   - d. observant
4. The boat was trapped _____ a turbulent _____.
   - a. amid . . . storm
   - b. within . . . tempest
   - c. inside . . . squall
   - d. above . . . sea

Commentary

In 1969 Maya Angelou published her autobiography, *I Know Why the Caged Bird Sings*, drawing the title from the Paul Laurence Dunbar poem "Sympathy."

I know why the caged bird sings, ah me,
  When his wing is bruised and his bosom sore,—
When he beats his bars and he would be free;
It is not a carol of joy or glee,
  But a prayer that he sends from his heart's deep core,
But a plea, that upward to Heaven he flings—
I know why the caged bird sings!

Dunbar's "sympathy" for the caged bird grew out of his experience as a black writer forced by circumstances to write for a predominantly white audience. Caged by the expectations of the marketplace, most of Dunbar's poetry and fiction avoided questions of critical importance to him, questions having to do with ending discrimination and racial hatred. Dunbar was the caged bird who sang to keep from shouting out his grief, who laughed to keep from crying.

As a girl Maya Angelou absorbed much of Dunbar's poetry. Like Dunbar, she grew up in a setting that seemed to cage her with discrimination. In her autobiography she detailed how in her rural Arkansas town "whitefolks could[n't] be talked to at all without risking one's life."

Angelou defied discrimination to become a successful writer. She dedicated her autobiography to her son and "all the strong black birds of promise who defy the odds and gods and sing their songs."

We Wear the Mask 615

ANSWERS TO THINKING ABOUT THE SELECTION
Recalling

1. It "grins and lies" and "hides our cheeks and shades our eyes."

Interpreting

2. (a) The speaker is the black people. (b) They are distressed by their condition.
3. It symbolizes their attempt to hide their feelings.
4. (a) It deceives the white people. (b) The decision results from their pride.
5. Suggested Response: The theme is that the black people are suffering but feel compelled to hide their feelings.

Applying

6. Answers will differ. Students may comment that they are motivated by their desire not to let certain people realize that they feel this way.

ANSWERS TO UNDERSTANDING LANGUAGE

1. (b) 2. (a) 3. (c) 4. (a)

Humanities Note

Humanities Note

Humanities Note

Fine art, *Frederick Douglass.* This portrait of the abolitionist/ statesman Frederick Douglass (1817–1895) is a wood engraving, after a photograph by an unidentified artist. It appeared in *Harper's Weekly* in the November 24, 1883 issue.

As students read the poem and look at the portrait, you might ask what characteristics of Douglass are captured in this portrait.

Presentation

Motivation/Prior Knowledge
Have students discuss how important historical figures affect the generations that follow them. How might recalling the actions of these people help the following generations to cope with difficult situations?

Thematic Idea An excerpt from Frederick Douglass's book, *My Bondage and My Freedom,* appears on page 430.

Purpose-Setting Question Why does the speaker address the poem to Douglass?

1 Critical Thinking and Reading
The use of "thou" and "thee" for "you" help establish the formal tone.

2 Discussion How does the speaker use the image of the stormy sea in describing why Douglass is needed?

Reader's Response How would you describe a person who has provided courageous examples for others to follow?

FREDERICK DOUGLASS
Historical Pictures Services, Chicago

Douglass
Paul Laurence Dunbar

1

    Ah, Douglass,[1] we have fall'n on evil days,
        Such days as thou, not even thou didst know,
        When thee, the eyes of that harsh long ago
    Saw, salient, at the cross of devious ways,
5   And all the country heard thee with amaze.
        Not ended then, the passionate ebb and flow,
        The awful tide that battled to and fro;
    We ride amid a tempest of dispraise.

2

    Now, when the waves of swift dissension swarm,
10   And Honor, the strong pilot, lieth stark,
    Oh, for thy voice high-sounding o'er the storm,
        For thy strong arm to guide the shivering bark,[2]
    The blast-defying power of thy form,
        To give us comfort through the lonely dark.

---

1. Douglass: Frederick Douglass, an American abolitionist (1817?–1895).
2. bark: Boat.

616 *Realism and the Frontier*

THINKING ABOUT THE SELECTION

Recalling

1. How does Dunbar's time compare with the days Douglass knew?
2. What does the speaker call for in the second stanza?

Interpreting

3. (a) To what does the speaker compare the struggles of the black people in lines 6–8? (b) How is this comparison developed in the second stanza?
4. What do you think prompted Dunbar to write this poem?
5. How do you think Dunbar might characterize the present times?

Applying

6. (a) What other black leaders do you think the speaker might have called on if the poem had been written today? (b) Explain how the efforts of these leaders compare with Douglass's efforts.

ANALYZING LITERATURE

Recognizing a Sonnet

A **sonnet** is a fourteen-line lyric poem. Sonnets are usually written in rhymed iambic pentameter and express a single, complete thought. The two most common types of sonnets are the English sonnet, or Shakespearean sonnet, and the Italian sonnet, or Petrarchan sonnet. "Douglass" is an example of an Italian sonnet.

1. What is the theme expressed in "Douglass"?
2. At what point in the poem does Dunbar present the main idea?
3. How is the main idea developed in the sestet?
4. How does Dunbar's use of the sonnet form contribute to the poem's effectiveness?

THINKING AND WRITING

Writing a Sonnet

Write a sonnet in which you address an important historical figure, as Dunbar does in "Douglass." Start by thinking of a historical figure who had an important impact on American society. For example, you might select Martin Luther King, Jr., Abraham Lincoln, or Abigail Adams. How would this person respond to contemporary life? Then write a sonnet focusing on issues concerning contemporary society that would be of interest to this person. When you finish writing, revise your sonnet and share it with your classmates.

Commentary

Frederick Douglass was aware of Paul Laurence Dunbar's poetry and once commented to a friend, "He is very young but there is no doubt he is a poet." Dunbar for his part was a youthful admirer of Douglass. The two met in 1893.

At that time Douglass, then almost eighty, was commissioner in charge of the Haitian Pavilion at the World's Columbian Exposition in Chicago—the first world's fair. He hired Dunbar to be a clerk, paying him out of his own pocket. Douglass's interest and encourage-ment helped Dunbar at a key moment in his life. At the Exposition he met other black people active in the arts or in the pursuit of civil rights. His newfound friends included poets and performers.

Dunbar wrote two poems about Douglass, the one you just read and one titled "Frederick Douglass." In this earlier poem, Dunbar celebrated Douglass as a man who was "no soft-tongued apologist." The poem noted, "His heart, his talents, and his hands were free / To all who truly needed aught of him."

Douglass 617

More About the Author Many of Edwin Arlington Robinson's poems explore the difference between the public's perceptions of an individual and that person's view of himself or herself. Robinson himself was a very private person, who saw few people and never married. Do you imagine that most writers are private people? Why or why not?

Critical Evaluation In an essay published shortly after Robinson died, the poet Robert Frost had this to say about his work:

"[Robinson's] theme was unhappiness itself, but his skill was as happy as it was playful. There is that comforting thought for those who suffered to see him suffer. Let it be said at the risk of offending the humorless in poetry's train (for there are a few such): his art was more than playful: it was humorous.

Robinson has gone to his place in American literature and left his human place among us vacant. We mourn, but with the qualification that, after all, his life was a revel in the felicities of language."

ESL Teaching Strategy Ask your ESL students to create names for six characters about whom poems like Robinson's might be written. Have them discuss "what's in a name" and tell what sort of poem would be fitting for each of the names they place on their lists.

EDWIN ARLINGTON ROBINSON

1869–1935

Edwin Arlington Robinson's poetry bridged the gap between two literary eras. Like most nineteenth-century poetry, his work was traditional in form. Yet like the work of modern poets, his poetry was innovative in content, probing beneath the surface of human behavior and exploring the psychological realities of the inner self.

Robinson was raised in Gardiner, Maine, a small town that served as the model for Tilbury Town, the fictional setting of many of his finest poems. When his father, a successful lumber merchant, died, Robinson's family suddenly found itself living in poverty. Robinson attended Harvard for two years before his family's financial problems forced him to leave. He returned to Gardiner and began writing poetry, depending on friends and patrons for financial support. During his four years in Gardiner, Robinson drew back inside himself. He took little interest in the world outside and, instead, read voluminously. He missed the friendships he had made at Harvard and sensed that he was seen as a failure. Despite the despair Robinson experienced during these years, he came through them with a sense of himself as a poet who could speak the truth.

Just before the turn of the century, Robinson published two unsuccessful collections of poetry, *The Torrent and the Night Before* (1897) and *Children of the Night* (1898), at his own expense. Hoping to improve his financial situation, he moved to New York. As it turned out, his situation did improve when President Theodore Roosevelt appointed him to a post at a New York customshouse. Robinson also discovered success as a poet when his fourth volume of poetry, *The Town Down the River* (1910), sold well and received much critical acclaim.

Robinson went on to become a highly regarded poet. His collections *The Man Against the Sky* (1916), *Avon's Harvest* (1922), and *Collected Poems* (1922) were very successful, as was his trilogy of long narrative poems based on the legends of King Arthur: *Merlin, Lancelot,* and *Tristram.* During the 1920's Robinson received more recognition than any other American poet, winning the Pulitzer Prize three times, in 1922, 1925, and 1928.

Growing out of his childhood observations in Gardiner, most of Robinson's best poems focus on people's inner struggles. His poems paint portraits of impoverished characters whose lives are filled with frustration and despair, characters who see their lives as trivial and meaningless, and characters who long to live in another time and place. Yet despite their pessimistic outlook, his poems always possess a certain dignity, resulting from his traditional style, his command of language, and his imagination and wit.

Objectives
1 To appreciate irony
2 To appreciate different points of view

Support Material

Teaching Portfolio
Teacher Backup, p. 805
Usage and Mechanics Worksheet, p. 808
Vocabulary Check, p. 809
Analyzing Literature Worksheet, *Understanding Irony,* p. 810
Critical Thinking and Reading Worksheet, *Appreciating Different Points of View,* p. 811
Selection Test, p. 812

GUIDE FOR INTERPRETING

Luke Havergal; Richard Cory; Miniver Cheevy

Writer's Techniques

Irony. Irony is a contrast between what is stated and what is meant, or between what is expected to happen and what actually happens. Three types of irony used in literature are verbal irony, situational irony, and dramatic irony. Verbal irony occurs when the literal meaning of a word or statement is different from the intended meaning. Situational irony occurs when the actual result of an action or situation is different from the expected result. Dramatic irony occurs when the audience perceives something that a character in a literary work does not know.

Irony is an important element in many of Edwin Arlington Robinson's poems. Robinson possessed an intense awareness of the ironies of everyday life—the contrasts between reality and people's perceptions, between results and expectations, and between the way people view themselves and how they are seen by others—and he sought to capture these ironies in his harshly realistic poetry.

Writing

People are always in search of happiness, but what is happiness? William Saroyan once wrote, "The greatest happiness you can have is knowing that you do not necessarily require happiness." Freewrite, exploring the meaning of this quotation.

Primary Source

In describing Edwin Arlington Robinson's work, poet James Dickey has written:

> It is through people that Robinson found the hints and gleams of the universal condition that he could not help trying to solve. . . . Robinson has been perhaps the only American poet—certainly the only one of major status—interested *exclusively* in human beings as subject matter for poetry—in the psychological, motivational aspects of living, in the inner life as it is projected upon the outer. His work is one vast attempt to tell the stories that no man can really tell, for no man can know their real meaning, their real intention, or even whether such exists. . . . In all Robinson's people the Cosmos seems to be brooding in one way or another. . . .
>
> No poet ever understood loneliness or separateness better than Robinson or knew the self-consuming furnace that the brain can become in isolation. . . . He understood loneliness in all its many forms and depths. . . .

Guide for Interpreting 619

Literary Focus Review the earlier lessons on irony on pages 550 and 609. Discuss some examples of situational irony and dramatic irony. Point out that both situational and dramatic irony are sometimes used for comic effect. Students may be able to cite scenes from movies as examples.

Writing/Prior Knowledge As an alternative assignment, have students free-write about ironic situations that occur in everyday life.

Vocabulary

Preteach the following vocabulary words:
assailed (ə sāld′) *v.:* Attacked violently; assaulted (p. 622, l. 2)
vagrant (vā′ grənt) *n.:* An idle wanderer (p. 622, l. 16)
albeit (ôl bē′ it) *conj.:* Although (p. 622, l. 18)
incessantly (in ses′ ′nt lē) *adv.:* Unceasingly (p. 622, l. 19)
imperially (im pir′ ē əl ē) *adv.:* Majestically (p. 624, l. 4)

Presentation

Purpose-Setting Question
What does the western gate represent?

1 **Discussion** What time of year is it? What is the clue?

2 **Critical Thinking and Reading** The images of the western gate, the autumn, and the twilight all seem to point to the approach to death.

3 **Literary Focus** Note that the last two lines of each stanza repeat its first line.

4 **Discussion** What might be meant by "there is not a dawn in eastern skies"?

5 **Critical Thinking and Reading** Call attention to the paradoxes in lines 12–14. Critics do not agree on the meanings of these lines.

Humanities Note

Fine art, *The Artist's Garden,* by Ralph Albert Blakelock. Ralph Albert Blakelock (1847–1919) was an American landscape painter. Encouraged by his family to pursue a medical career, Blakelock attended the Free Academy of the City of New York (now City College) for a short time. A self-taught painter, Blakelock's eccentric, visionary landscapes and paintings of western scenes were not accepted by the artistic establishment until the pressures of extreme poverty and deprivation drove the artist mad. After his confinement in an institution, Blakelock was recognized as an important and unique artist.

The Artist's Garden is imbued with the mysterious romanticism that characterizes Blakelock's works. His notion that all forces in nature interact is evident in the energetic plant forms of this painting. The paint surface is built up with layers of glaze and dabs of color that create glowing and resonant tones that

seem to pulse with extraordinary energy. The originality of Blakelock's visionary paintings have given him an important place in American art history.

You might use the following questions for discussion:
1. What is the mood of the painting?
2. How does the mood of the painting compare with the mood of "Luke Havergal"?

Luke Havergal

Edwin Arlington Robinson

1
Go to the western gate, Luke Havergal,
There where the vines cling crimson on the wall,
And in the twilight wait for what will come.

2
The leaves will whisper there of her, and some,
5 Like flying words, will strike you as they fall;
But go, and if you listen she will call.

3
Go to the western gate, Luke Havergal—
Luke Havergal.

4
No, there is not a dawn in eastern skies
10 To rift the fiery night that's in your eyes;
But there, where western glooms are gathering,

5
The dark will end the dark, if anything:
God slays Himself with every leaf that flies,
And hell is more than half of paradise.
15 No, there is not a dawn in eastern skies—
In eastern skies.

THE ARTIST'S GARDEN, c. 1880
Ralph Albert Blakelock
National Gallery of Art
Art Resource

620   *Realism and the Frontier*

Out of a grave I come to tell you this,
Out of a grave I come to quench the kiss
That flames upon your forehead with a glow
20 That blinds you to the way that you must go.
6   Yes, there is yet one way to where she is,
    Bitter, but one that faith may never miss.
    Out of a grave I come to tell you this—
    To tell you this.

25 There is the western gate, Luke Havergal,
    There are the crimson leaves upon the wall.
    Go, for the winds are tearing them away,—
    Nor think to riddle the dead words they say,
    Nor any more to feel them as they fall;
30 But go, and if you trust her she will call.
    There is the western gate, Luke Havergal—
    Luke Havergal.

THINKING ABOUT THE SELECTION

Recalling

1. (a) Where does the speaker tell Luke Havergal to go? (b) What will happen when he gets there?
2. (a) From where has the speaker come? (b) What is his reason for coming?

Interpreting

3. What do you think was Luke's relationship to the woman referred to in the poem?
4. (a) Considering that the sun sets in the West and considering the details used in describing the western gate, what do you think the western gate symbolizes? (b) What does the "dawn in eastern skies" symbolize?

5. The speaker may actually be part of Luke Havergal's inner self. If this is so, what does the poem reveal about Luke Havergal's state of mind?
6. Considering Luke's state of mind and the action he is being urged to take, what do you think the speaker means when he comments, "The dark will end the dark"?
7. Robinson's use of repetition in the poem creates a hypnotic effect. How is this effect related to the meaning of the poem?

Applying

8. This poem suggests that a person can never replace a loved one whom he or she has lost. Discuss this view.

Luke Havergal 621

1 **Discussion** What do we learn about Miniver Cheevy from the first stanza?

2 **Discussion** Do you think that Miniver's view of the "days of old" is entirely realistic?

3 **Discussion** What could Miniver Cheevy himself have done to make his time a more glorious one?

4 **Critical Thinking and Reading** Lines 23–24 are clearly ironic in tone. The speaker does not say "knights' armor," which might have some aura of romance, but "iron clothing," which does not sound romantic or graceful.

5 **Discussion** What do lines 25–26 tell us about Miniver Cheevy?

Miniver Cheevy

Edwin Arlington Robinson

Miniver Cheevy, child of scorn,
    Grew lean while he assailed the seasons;
He wept that he was ever born,
    And he had reasons.   **1**

5 Miniver loved the days of old
    When swords were bright and steeds were prancing;
The vision of a warrior bold
    Would set him dancing.   **2**

Miniver sighed for what was not,
10   And dreamed, and rested from his labors;
He dreamed of Thebes[1] and Camelot,[2]
    And Priam's[3] neighbors.

Miniver mourned the ripe renown
    That made so many a name so fragrant;
15 He mourned Romance, now on the town,[4]
    And Art, a vagrant.   **3**

Miniver loved the Medici,[5]
    Albeit he had never seen one;
He would have sinned incessantly
20   Could he have been one.

Miniver cursed the commonplace
    And eyed a khaki suit with loathing;
He missed the medieval grace
    Of iron clothing.   **4**

25 Miniver scorned the gold he sought,
    But sore annoyed was he without it;
Miniver thought, and thought, and thought,
    And thought about it.   **5**

---

1. Thebes (thēbz): A city-state in ancient Greece.
2. Camelot (kam′ ə lät′): The legendary English town where King Arthur's court and Round Table were located.
3. Priam (prī′ əm): King of Troy during the Trojan War.
4. on the town: On public assistance.
5. Medici (med′ ə chē): A rich, powerful family of Florence, Italy, in the fourteenth, fifteenth, and sixteenth centuries.

Miniver Cheevy, born too late,
  Scratched his head and kept on thinking;
Miniver coughed, and called it fate,
  And kept on drinking.

30

6

THINKING ABOUT THE SELECTION

Recalling

1. (a) About what does Miniver Cheevy weep? (b) What does he love? (c) Of what does he dream? (d) What does he mourn? (e) What does he curse? (f) What does he scorn?
2. What does the final line reveal about how Miniver Cheevy copes with his unhappiness?

Interpreting

3. The word *miniver* refers to a white fur used for trimming ceremonial robes during the Middle Ages. Why is this an appropriate name for the character in the poem?
4. Considering Cheevy's condition, what do you think might be the real reason why he eyes "a khaki suit with loathing"?
5. (a) What paradox, or apparent self-contradiction, appears in lines 23–24? (b) What does this paradox reveal about Cheevy's understanding of the past?

Applying

6. Like Miniver Cheevy, people often try to escape from their problems, rather than confronting them and trying to find a solution. Why is this an ineffective way of dealing with problems?

ANALYZING LITERATURE

Understanding Irony

Irony is a contrast between what is stated and what is meant, or between what is expected to happen and what actually happens. Three types of irony used in literature are verbal irony, situational irony, and dramatic irony.

1. In line 2 the speaker comments that Cheevy "assailed the seasons." (a) How is this image related to Cheevy's visions of the past? (b) Why is this image ironic considering Cheevy's life?
2. What is ironic about Miniver's scorning the gold?
3. Explain how the use of irony affects your attitude toward Cheevy.

Miniver Cheevy 623

Richard Cory

Edwin Arlington Robinson

Whenever Richard Cory went down town,
We people on the pavement looked at him:
He was a gentleman from sole to crown,
Clean favored, and imperially slim.

5   And he was always quietly arrayed,
And he was always human when he talked;
But still he fluttered pulses when he said,
"Good-morning," and he glittered when he walked.

THE THINKER
(Portrait of Louis N. Kenton, 1900)
Thomas Eakins
The Metropolitan Museum of Art

624   *Realism and the Frontier*

Consider these questions for discussion:
1. Why do you suppose this picture was chosen to illustrate the poem?
2. About what might the man in the portrait be thinking?
3. How does the artist's use of color affect the message of the painting?

3
10 And he was rich—yes, richer than a king—
And admirably schooled in every grace:
4 In fine, we thought that he was everything
To make us wish that we were in his place.

5 So on we worked, and waited for the light,
And went without the meat, and cursed the bread;
6 **15** And Richard Cory, one calm summer night,
Went home and put a bullet through his head.

THINKING ABOUT THE SELECTION

Recalling

1. What does the speaker notice about Richard Cory each time he comes into town?
2. What does Richard Cory do "one calm summer night"?

Interpreting

3. (a) Who is the poem's speaker? (b) In what ways is the speaker different from Richard Cory?
4. What do the words "crown" (line 3) and "imperially" (line 4) suggest about the speaker's impression of Richard Cory?
5. Why would the poem be less forceful if the speaker had used the pronoun "I" instead of "we"? Explain your answer.
6. What makes the poem's final line surprising?
7. What do you think is the theme of the poem?

Applying

8. (a) Why do you think a person like Richard Cory, who seemingly has every reason to be happy, might in fact be miserable? (b) What do you think are the keys to a person's happiness?

9. The French writer Colette wrote, "What a wonderful life I've had! I only wish I'd realized it sooner." Discuss the meaning of this quotation.

CRITICAL THINKING AND READING

Recognizing Attitudes

This poem points out that each person has a different outlook on life and that it is often difficult for people to perceive or understand the outlooks of others. In the poem we are presented with the speaker's view of Richard Cory, which leads us to expect Cory to be happy. As a result, we are shocked by the ending of the poem and forced to realize that the speaker's impressions were false. The ending also forces us to contemplate Cory's perceptions of himself and the speaker and to think about how they are different from the speaker's perceptions.

1. Considering the outcome of the poem, how do you think Cory's attitude toward himself differs from the speaker's attitude toward him?
2. What do you think might have been Richard Cory's attitude toward the townspeople?

3 Discussion What image do the people in the town have of Richard Cory?

4 Discussion What does line 12 tell us, and how does that help set up the irony of the last stanza?

5 Critical Thinking and Reading Lines 13–14 establish life's reality for the rest of the town. There is an implied contrast between their lives and Richard Cory's life.

6 Discussion Why does the last line have a shock value for those reading the poem for the first time?

Reader's Response Why do people sometimes do totally unexpected things?

Closure and Extension

ANSWERS TO THINKING ABOUT THE SELECTION
Recalling

1. He is a gentleman and people look at him.
2. The speaker clearly admires what he sees of Richard Cory.

Interpreting

3. (a) The townspeople serve as the speaker. (b) The townspeople are ordinary and poor; Richard Cory is wealthy and aristocratic.
4. It suggests that there is a royal air about him.
5. A general public opinion carries more weight than just one person's view.
6. Nothing in the poem leads one to expect it.
7. Suggested Response: Appearances can be deceptive.

Applying

8. (a) Answers will differ. Perhaps his wealth isolates him from people.

(b) Answers will differ. Students may mention love and companionship.
9. People often do not appreciate their lives.

ANSWERS TO CRITICAL THINKING AND READING

1. Richard Cory clearly does not believe that he has everything to live for; the speaker thinks Cory does.
2. Answers will differ. Students may suggest he had difficulty relating to them and felt isolated.

More About the Author In addition to his poetry, Edgar Lee Masters wrote biographies of Abraham Lincoln, Mark Twain, and two poets—Vachel Lindsay and Walt Whitman. Why might a poet also choose to write biographies?

Critical Evaluation In an introduction to *Spoon River Anthology* published in 1962, May Swenson had this to say about Masters:

"It is true that he tried to be a classicist and modernist, reformer and poet, villager and city man, sophisticate and innocent Arcadian. Partly, he failed in all. But the Spoon River compilation impresses one as arising from the most genuine creative springs. On the basis of internal evidence it is neither something purely contrived, nor 'an accident,' but rather a spontaneous synthesis, generating naturally from a deep psychological, as well as inventive, core in Masters."

ESL Teaching Strategy Ask ESL students to pretend that they are going to continue Master's poems by creating characters who would speak about their work. Have them list the occupations of the speakers they would create and then explain why the voices of people with those jobs might be more interesting than others.

EDGAR LEE MASTERS

1868–1950

Edgar Lee Masters is primarily remembered for one volume of his poetry. Yet this volume, *Spoon River Anthology,* is widely regarded as one of the finest collections of poetry ever produced by an American poet.

Masters was born in Kansas but grew up in rural southern Illinois—the area where Abraham Lincoln had spent his early years. After briefly attending Knox College, Masters studied law in his father's law office and eventually passed the bar exam. In 1891 he moved to Chicago, where he became a successful criminal lawyer. During his spare time, he wrote poems, plays, and essays, and he published some of his poems in the highly regarded Chicago magazine *Poetry*.

Masters's early poems, which were traditional in form, received little attention. In 1914, however, Masters's direction as a poet changed dramatically when a friend gave him a copy of *Selected Epitaphs from the Greek Anthology*. This collection included many concise, interconnected epitaphs that each captured the essence of a person's life. Using this structure and abandoning conventional rhyme and meter for free verse, Masters wrote a series of poems about the lives of people in rural southern Illinois. Published under the title *Spoon River Anthology* in 1915, the series provoked strong reactions among critics and became a best seller.

Spoon River Anthology consists of 244 epitaphs for characters buried in the mythical Spoon River cemetery. The dead themselves serve as the speakers of the poems, often revealing secrets they kept hidden throughout their lifetimes. Many types of people are represented, including storekeepers, housewives, and murderers. Some of the characters had lived happy lives, but many more had lived lives filled with frustration and despair. Presented together the epitaphs paint a vivid portrait of the loneliness and isolation with which people living in the Midwest at the time were often confronted.

Poet May Swenson has commented that in *Spoon River Anthology,* Masters gave "outlet to all his grudges, beliefs, indignations, insights, prophesies, discoveries of glaring injustice, revelations of life's mysteries and paradoxes—and his own eccentric philosophy. Miraculously he also created and bequeathed to us a world in microcosm, new in form, timeless in essence."

Several years after *Spoon River Anthology* was published, Masters gave up his law practice to devote all of his energy to writing. Yet, while he was able to produce many other volumes of poetry in addition to novels, biographies, and his autobiography, *Across Spoon River,* he was never able to match the success of *Spoon River Anthology*.

626   Realism and the Frontier

Objectives

1 To write an epitaph
2 To identify the speaker
3 To compare and contrast writers

Support Material

Teaching Portfolio
Teacher Backup, p. 815
Usage and Mechanics Worksheet, p. 819
Vocabulary Check, p. 820
Analyzing Literature Worksheet, *Identifying the Speaker,* p. 821
Critical Thinking and Reading Worksheet, *Comparing and Contrasting Speakers,* p. 822
Selection Test, p. 823

Art Transparency II, *In the Parlor,* by Charles Burchfield

GUIDE FOR INTERPRETING

Lucinda Matlock; Fiddler Jones

The Writer's Techniques

The Speaker. The speaker is the voice of a poem. Although the speaker is often the poet, the speaker may be also be a fictional character or even an inanimate object or another type of nonhuman entity. For example, the speakers in the poems in Edgar Lee Masters's *Spoon River Anthology* are fictional characters buried in the mythical Spoon River cemetery. By using the characters themselves as the speakers, Masters is able to delve deeply into the characters' minds. In each poem a different speaker discusses his or her own life intimately and honestly, candidly expressing his or her most profound thoughts, feelings, and emotions.

Many of the characters are based on people Masters observed or was acquainted with during his childhood. For example, Lucinda Matlock, one of the most forceful speakers, represents Masters's own grandmother.

Writing

In *Spoon River Anthology,* Edgar Lee Masters paints portraits of a variety of characters based on people he observed during his childhood. Think of an interesting or amusing character from books, movies, or even current affairs. Then list details describing this person's appearance, personality, and behavior.

Primary Source

In his essay "The Genesis of Spoon River," Edgar Lee Masters described experiences from his youth in the Illinois towns of Petersburg and Lewiston that contributed to his writing of *Spoon River Anthology.* He then went on to describe his state of mind as he neared completion of the Spoon River poems in December 1914:

> I was nearing exhaustion of body. . . . The flame had now become so intense that it could not be seen, by which I mean that the writing of the pieces did not seem to involve any effort whatever; and yet I should have known that I was being sapped rapidly. I had no auditory or visual experiences which were not the effect of actuality; but I did feel that somehow, by these months of exploring the souls of the dead, by this unlicensed revelation of their secrets, I had convoked about my head swarms of powers and beings who were watching me and protesting and yet inspiring me to go on.
>
> I do not mean by this that I believed that I was so haunted; I only mean I had that sensation, as one in a lonely and eyrie room might suddenly feel that someone was in the next room spying upon him.

Guide for Interpreting 627

Literary Focus A writer needs skill and insight to create different speakers and make their different voices and attitudes credible to a reader.

Writing/Prior Knowledge For extra credit, you might have students develop a character sketch, using their list of details.

Humanities Note

Fine art, *Barn Dance,* 1950, by Grandma Moses. Anna Mary Robertson Moses (1860–1961) born in Greenwich, New York, did not begin to paint seriously until she was in her seventies. She had no formal training. Her pictures are simple scenes of happy rural life, with simple forms, lively colors, and immense detail. Her name is now a household word, and her work blazed the trail for later aspirants to folk art by increasing public awareness and by appealing to almost everyone.

Barn Dance is a typical painting of Grandma Moses—a blend of personal memories and a reflection of her exposure to popular prints such as those of Currier and Ives. A great deal of charming detail is integrated into the landscape. The composition is reminiscent of Currier and Ives prints. *Barn Dance* is one of the last large paintings Grandma Moses created. Almost 90 when she painted it, she admitted that the physical strain was getting to be too much for her. She returned to painting smaller pictures and painted almost until her death at the age of 101.

Consider using these questions for discussion:
1. In what ways does this painting reflect the life of Lucinda Matlock?
2. Discuss what might be termed the "charming appeal" of this painting.
3. What patterns of rhythm and color are represented in this painting?

Master Teacher Note To help students envision the character of Lucinda Matlock, place Art Transparency 11, *In the Parlor* by Charles Burchfield, on the overhead projector. Discuss the woman depicted in the portrait. What impression of the woman's personality does the painting convey?

BARN DANCE, 1950
Grandma Moses
Copyright © 1973, Grandma Moses Properties Co., New York.

Lucinda Matlock

Edgar Lee Masters

1
I went to the dances at Chandlerville,
And played snap-out[1] at Winchester.
One time we changed partners,
Driving home in the moonlight of middle June,
5 And then I found Davis.
2
We were married and lived together for seventy years,
Enjoying, working, raising the twelve children,
Eight of whom we lost
Ere I had reached the age of sixty.

---

1. snap-out: A game often referred to as "crack-the whip," in which a long line of players who are holding hands spin around in a circle, causing the players on the end to be flung off by centrifugal force.

Note about art: Anna Mary Robertson Moses (1860–1961) began painting in old age and became known as "Grandma" Moses. She painted country landscapes and scenes remembered from her childhood.

Purpose-Setting   Question
What is Lucinda Matlock's assessment of her own life?

1 **Discussion** What period of her life is described in lines 1–5?

2 **Literary Focus** Call attention to the speaker's matter-of-fact tone, even when describing the loss of eight children.

3
```
10  I spun, I wove, I kept the house, I nursed the sick,
    I made the garden, and for holiday
    Rambled over the fields where sang the larks,
    And by Spoon River gathering many a shell,
    And many a flower and medicinal weed—
15  Shouting to the wooded hills, singing to the green valleys.
```
4
```
    At ninety-six I had lived enough, that is all,
    And passed to a sweet repose.
```
5
```
    What is this I hear of sorrow and weariness,
    Anger, discontent and drooping hopes?
20  Degenerate sons and daughters,
    Life is too strong for you—
```
6
```
    It takes life to love Life.
```

3 **Discussion** What impression do the details of Lucinda Matlock's life convey?

4 **Discussion** What is her attitude toward her death?

5 **Discussion** To whom are lines 18–20 addressed? What is her attitude toward life's evils?

6 **Discussion** How does the last line help us understand the speaker's personality?

Reader's Response Would you enjoy having Lucinda Matlock as a member of your family? Why?

THINKING ABOUT THE SELECTION

Recalling

1. (a) How does Lucinda Matlock meet her husband? (b) How many years do they spend together? (c) How many children do they have? (d) What happens to eight of the children before Lucinda turns sixty?
2. What does Lucinda Matlock do "for holiday"?
3. When does she decide that she "had lived enough"?
4. What question does Lucinda Matlock ask?
5. What does she say it takes "to love life"?

Interpreting

6. (a) How would you characterize Lucinda Matlock's life? (b) What seems to be Lucinda Matlock's attitude concerning her life?
7. (a) Who are the "sons and daughters" Lucinda addresses in this poem? (b) What is her attitude toward them? (c) How is their attitude toward life different from her own? (d) What is the meaning of her message to them?

Applying

8. Explain whether you agree or disagree with Lucinda Matlock's message.

9. As this poem suggests, the general attitude toward life of one generation is often quite different from that of other generations. What do you think causes these differences?
10. How do you think Lucinda Matlock would respond to people who complain that life today is too complex and confusing?

THINKING AND WRITING

Writing an Epitaph

Imagine that you have entered a contest being held by your school literary magazine in which you are asked to write an epitaph in the style of Edgar Lee Masters. Start by reviewing the list of details you prepared describing an interesting or amusing person. Try to decide which details best capture the essence of the person's life. Then decide what message about life the epitaph should convey. When you write the epitaph, use free verse and try to capture the flavor of the person's life in a limited number of lines. When you finish writing, put your epitaph aside for one day. Then reread it and make any necessary revisions.

Closure and Extension

ANSWERS TO THINKING ABOUT THE SELECTION
Recalling

1. (a) They met driving home from a dance. (b) They spent seventy years together. (c) They had twelve children. (d) They lost eight children by the time she was sixty.
2. For "holiday" she rambled about the fields, gathered shells, shouted, and sang.
3. At ninety-six, she decided she had lived enough.
4. She asks why she hears of sorrow, weariness, anger, discontent, and drooping hopes.
5. She says that it takes life to love life.

Interpreting

6. (a) Suggested Response: It was a busy, difficult life, filled with small pleasures. (b) She seems to think she lived well.
7. (a) They are members of the following generation. (b) She thinks that life is too strong for them, they give in too easily to the woes. (c) She enjoyed the pleasures even though she experienced sorrow; they dwell on the sorrow. (d) They must live and experience the joys and stand up to the sorrows. Living gives one the reason for loving life.

Applying

8. Answers will differ. Students may comment that they agree with her message, because they believe that it is important to think positively.
9. Answers will differ. Some students may note that the experiences of different generations are different.
10. Suggested Response: She would probably say, "Don't worry about the complexity; just go ahead and get on with your lives."

THINKING AND WRITING

Publishing Student Writing Have student volunteers read their compositions to the class.

Fiddler Jones

Edgar Lee Masters

The earth keeps some vibration going
There in your heart, and that is you.
And if the people find you can fiddle,
Why, fiddle you must, for all your life.
5   What do you see, a harvest of clover?
Or a meadow to walk through to the river?
The wind's in the corn; you rub your hands
For beeves hereafter ready for market;
Or else you hear the rustle of skirts
10   Like the girls when dancing at Little Grove.
To Cooney Potter a pillar of dust
Or whirling leaves meant ruinous drouth;[1]
They looked to me like Red-Head Sammy
Stepping it off, to "Toor-a-Loor."
15   How could I till my forty acres
Not to speak of getting more,
With a medley of horns, bassoons and piccolos
Stirred in my brain by crows and robins
And the creak of a windmill—only these?
20   And I never started to plow in my life
That someone did not stop in the road
And take me away to a dance or picnic.
I ended up with forty acres;
I ended up with a broken fiddle—
25   And a broken laugh, and a thousand memories,
And not a single regret.

1 | 2 | 3 | 4 | 5 | 6

---

1. drouth: Drought.

THINKING ABOUT THE SELECTION
Recalling

1. According to Fiddler Jones, what must you do if "the people find you can fiddle"?
2. What are two explanations Fiddler Jones offers for his failures as a farmer?
3. What regrets does Fiddler Jones have about the way he lived his life?

Interpreting

4. What does Fiddler Jones mean when he comments, "The earth keeps some vibration going / There in your heart, and that is you"?
5. What examples does Fiddler Jones use to point out that there are many different ways of viewing the world?
6. How is Fiddler Jones's view of life different from that of other farmers?
7. Explain the last three lines of the poem.

Applying

8. How might you apply the lesson taught by the story of Fiddler Jones to your own life?

ANALYZING LITERATURE
Identifying the Speaker

The **speaker** is the voice of a poem. The speaker may be the poet himself or herself, or it may be a fictional character or even an inanimate object or another type of nonhuman entity.

For example, the speaker in "Fiddler Jones" is Fiddler Jones himself.

1. How would "Fiddler Jones" be different if Masters had used a different speaker?
2. Explain whether the poem would be more or less effective if a different speaker had been used.
3. Fiddler Jones and the other speakers of the poems in *Spoon River Anthology* are dead. Why might this allow them to discuss their lives more openly and honestly than they would have if they were alive?

THINKING AND WRITING
Comparing and Contrasting Writers

Write an essay in which you compare and contrast Edwin Arlington Robinson's poetry with that of Edgar Lee Masters. Start by rereading the poems by Robinson and Masters in this book, noting similarities and differences in style, theme, and choice of subjects. Reread the biographies of Robinson and Masters, again noting similarities and differences between the two writers. Review your notes and prepare a thesis statement. Organize your notes according to corresponding points of contrast. Then begin writing your essay, using passages from the poems to support your argument. When you revise, make sure you have included enough supporting information.

Commentary

Spoon River Anthology shocked many critics and readers at the time of its publication. What accounted for its reception?

One factor, certainly, was its portrayal of small-town life and people. Although the subjects of many of the poems were admirable individuals, a large number were people whose lives were dominated by greed, religious narrow-mindedness, frustration, or inhumanity toward others.

This negative view of small-town life and people ran contrary to popular views.

A second factor was the scandalous portrayal of some of the characters. Numerous readers found these poems distasteful and unwholesome.

Finally, Masters wrote his poems in unadorned free verse. Many critics found the poems overly blunt and graceless.

Fiddler Jones 631

ANSWERS TO THINKING ABOUT THE SELECTION
Recalling

1. You must fiddle.
2. Everything in nature made him think about music; people were always taking him to dances.
3. He says he had no regrets.

Interpreting

4. There are natural impulses to which we respond, and these make us what we are.
5. In a field, one can see a potential clover harvest or a meadow to cross to get to a river. Looking at corn, you can see cattle that will fatten on it or you may be reminded of girls dancing. Dust pillars and whirling leaves may cause you concern about drought or they may remind you of dancing.
6. Fiddler Jones is more interested in music than in farming.
7. Suggested Response: People must pursue their interests.

Applying

8. Answers will differ. Students may comment that they may apply his lesson by not trying to be something that they were clearly not meant to be.

ANSWERS TO ANALYZING LITERATURE

1. Suggested Response: It would have been less personal.
2. Suggested Response: It would have been less effective, because readers would have been offered a less intimate view of Jones's character.
3. Suggested Response: They no longer have anything to prove to the world.

THINKING AND WRITING

For help with this assignment, students can refer to Lesson 16, "Writing a Comparative Evaluation," in the Handbook of Writing About Literature.

After students have completed the assignment, divide them into groups, and have them read their rough drafts to one another and suggest ways in which they could be improved.

The writing assignments on page 632 have students write creatively, while those on page 633 have them think about the selections and write critically.

YOU THE WRITER
Guidelines for Evaluating Assignment 1

1. Has the student written a dialogue between two people?
2. Has the student captured the speakers' dialect?
3. Does the dialogue reveal something of each speaker's personality?
4. Does each character's speech have distinctive characteristics?

Guidelines for Evaluating Assignment 2

1. Has the student written a character sketch?
2. Does the character sketch reveal the most important traits of the character's personality?
3. Is the character sketch free from grammar, usage, and mechanics errors?

Guidelines for Evaluating Assignment 3

1. Has the student written a poem that focuses on a difficulty or problem of life during the nineteenth century?
2. Does the poem use regular rhyme and rhythm?
3. Is the poem free of grammar, usage, and mechanics errors?

YOU THE WRITER

Assignment

1. In their efforts to capture the local color of specific regions, many of the writers of the late nineteenth century used regional dialect in their works. Using regional dialect, write a dialogue between two characters living on the western frontier.

    Prewriting. Review the stories in this unit in which writers use western dialect. Take note of the distinctive characteristics of the characters' speech in these stories.

    Writing. Try to make your dialogue seem realistic, as if you were recording a conversation that really occurred. Also try to reveal something about the characters' personalities through their dialogue.

    Revising. When you revise, make sure the speech of your characters has the same distinctive characteristics as that of the characters in the stories you read.

Assignment

2. As the nation expanded, many Americans left their homes and traveled to the western frontier, hoping to find new opportunities. In pursuing their dreams, these pioneers often had to overcome a great deal of adversity. Write a character sketch of the type of person you imagine would have chosen to make the long and treacherous journey westward.

    Prewriting. Brainstorm about the character traits of a typical American pioneer. Arrange these traits in a logical order.

    Writing. When writing your sketch, focus on describing the most important traits of the character's personality.

    Revising. When you revise, make sure you have conveyed a clear and complete impression of the character's personality. After you finish revising, proofread your sketch and prepare a final copy.

Assignment

3. During the New England Renaissance, the Fireside Poets wrote poetry that was inspiring and optimistic. In the late nineteenth century, however, poets began creating works that expressed a less optimistic outlook, often focusing on the unpleasant realities of human existence. Imagine you are a poet living during the late nineteenth century, and write a poem that focuses on one of the difficulties or problems involved with life at the time.

    Prewriting. Review the unit introduction and the poems in the unit to come up with a topic for your poem.

    Writing. Write your poem, using regular rhyme and rhythm.

    Revising. When you finish writing, revise your poem. Proofread it and share it with your classmates.

YOU THE CRITIC

Assignment

1. As the nation grew and expanded, its population became more and more diverse, and people developed a desire to understand how people lived in other regions of the country. Write an essay in which you discuss how regional literature satisfied this desire.

    Prewriting. Review the selections in this unit, noting what they reveal about life in the various regions of the country. Prepare a thesis statement, then arrange your notes into an outline.

    Writing. When you write your essay, use evidence from several selections to support your thesis.

    Revising. When you revise, make sure you have thoroughly supported your thesis and have not included any unnecessary information.

Assignment

2. The Naturalists were a group of nineteenth-century writers who possessed a well-defined view of the universe. Write an essay in which you discuss how the beliefs of the Naturalists are reflected in their works.

    Prewriting. Review the discussion of Naturalism in the unit introduction. Then review the selections by Jack London and Stephen Crane, noting how they reflect the Naturalists' beliefs.

    Writing. Include a thesis statement in your introduction, and develop and support your thesis in your body paragraphs.

    Revising. When you revise, make sure you have used transitions and other linking devices to connect your ideas. After you have finished revising, proofread your essay and prepare a final copy.

Assignment

3. During the late nineteenth century, writers turned away from Romanticism and began to focus on depicting life as it was actually lived. Write an essay in which you compare and contrast a romantic short story with a realistic story.

    Prewriting. Review the concepts of Romanticism and Realism. Choose a romantic story and a realistic story. For example, you might choose "The Fall of the House of Usher" and "A Wagner Matinée." Carefully reread the stories you choose, focusing on similarities and differences.

    Writing. Organize your essay according to corresponding points of contrast, and use evidence from both stories to support your argument.

    Revising. When you revise, make sure you have varied the length and structure of your sentences.

You the Critic 633

YOU THE CRITIC
Guidelines for Evaluating Assignment 1

1. Does the student's essay contain a thesis statement about regional literature?
2. Has the student used evidence from several selections to support the thesis?
3. Has the student included only relevant information?
4. Is the essay free from grammar, usage, and mechanics errors?

Guidelines for Evaluating Assignment 2

1. Does the student's essay contain a thesis statement about the beliefs of the Naturalists?
2. Has the student supported the thesis statement with examples from the works of Jack London and Stephen Crane?
3. Has the student used transitions and other linking devices to connect ideas?
4. Is the essay free from grammar, usage, and mechanics errors?

Guidelines for Evaluating Assignment 3

1. Has the student written a poem that focuses on a difficulty or problem of life during the nineteenth century?
2. Does the poem use regular rhyme and rhythm?
3. Is the poem free of grammar, usage, and mechanics errors?

Humanities Note

Fine art, *City Roofs*, 1932, by Edward Hopper. Conventional ideas of beauty—handsome men and women, charming interiors, unspoiled natural scenes—had little appeal for Edward Hopper (1882–1967). Hopper found artistic inspiration, instead, in such subjects as the contrasting images of light and shadow against a drab apartment house. The human figures he portrayed are notable for their downcast expressions and their sense of isolation, both physical and spiritual, from the warmth of human companionship.

Hopper studied art under the respected painter Robert Henri, who also rejected traditional assumptions of academism in favor of greater realism. By the 1920's, after the upheaval of world war had destroyed America's sense of innocence and conventionality, Hopper's stark canvases gained acceptance. *City Roofs* is typical of Hopper's work in its depiction of an unlikely setting, with no human figures. The focus is on the triangular and vertical shapes of the rooftop structures. The play of light and dark intensifies the geometric quality. A rooftop, Hopper seems to be saying, can take on a distinct sense of place, a trait that is not dependent on the presence of conventional symbols of beauty or obvious human habitation.

CITY ROOFS, 1932
Edward Hopper
Courtesy of Kennedy Galleries, Inc., New York

Objectives

1 To understand the historical setting of the Modern Age
2 To understand the birth of Modernism

THE MODERN AGE
1915–1946

We asked the cyclone
to go around our barn
but it didn't hear us.
Carl Sandburg
from *The People, Yes*

1

Focus

Historical Background Explain to students that they will be reading about a period in American history in which the United States rose to become a world power both politically and economically. This rise in power had its price, however, as two world wars and a decade of severe economic depression tempered the innocence and optimism that had characterized the mood of the American people at the end of the nineteenth century.

Writing to Learn You might have students write a journal entry or a paragraph exploring their prior knowledge of the people and events of the Modern Age. They might write about social, political, or cultural events from the period. As they read through the unit, students can look back at their writing to see how their initial impressions are shaped or changed by the reading.

ESL Teaching Strategy You might have students who are learning English as a second language share what they know of the social, political, or cultural events that took place in their own culture during the years of the Modern Age (1915–1946).

1 **Literary Movement** These lines by Carl Sandburg are from *The People, Yes*. Sandburg identified himself with the people; he had worked as a common laborer before he started to write.

Motivation/Prior Knowledge
Have students imagine what it might be like to live through a terrible, inhuman war, followed by ten years of unprecedented prosperity, followed by ten years of unprecedented depression, followed by another war that ended with the first atomic bombs being dropped. How might such a series of events have changed the way people viewed themselves and the world in which they lived?

Purpose-Setting Question In what ways did the historical events of the Modern Age influence the writers of that period?

2 **Master Teacher Note** If facilities and time permit, you might show portions of a silent film, such as *All Quiet on the Western Front,* that deals with the impact of World War I. You might also consider using a film that shows the flamboyant optimism of the twenties, such as *The Great Gatsby,* or *The Grapes of Wrath,* which depicts the disillusion of the Depression years. These films would show the wide contrast in the social history of the period.

Carl Sandburg served as a soldier in the Spanish-American War (1898) and wrote his first novel after the Second World War (1948). In the years between, he was a day laborer, a journalist, a salesman, an advertising manager, a world-renowned poet, and a Pulitzer Prize-winning biographer. The focus of Sandburg's writing, like that of Walt Whitman, was America.

The America that Sandburg observed was a nation achieving world dominance, but at the same time losing some of its youthful innocence and brash confidence. Two world wars, a dizzying decade of prosperity, and a devastating worldwide depression marked this era. With these events came a new age in American literature. The upheavals of the early twentieth century ushered in a period of artistic experimentation and lasting literary achievement.

2

THE HISTORICAL SETTING

The years immediately preceding World War I were characterized by an overwhelming sense of optimism. Numerous technological advances occurred, dramatically affecting people's lives, and creating a sense of promise concerning the future. While a number of serious social problems still existed, reforms aimed at solving these problems began to be instituted. When World War I broke out in 1914, however, President Woodrow Wilson was forced to turn his attention away from the troubles at home and focus on the events in Europe.

War in Europe

World War I was one of the bloodiest and most tragic conflicts ever to occur. When the initial advances of the German forces were stalled, the conflict was transformed into a trench war. The introduction of the machine gun made it virtually impossible for one side to launch a successful attack on its opponents' trenches, however, and the war dragged on for several years with little progress being made by either side. Each unsuccessful attack resulted in the deaths of thousands of soldiers, and the war ultimately claimed almost an entire generation of European men.

President Wilson wanted the United States to remain neutral in the war, but that proved impossible. In 1915, a German submarine sank the *Lusitania,* pride of the British merchant fleet. More than 1200 people on board lost their lives, including 128 Americans. After the sinking, American public opinion tended to favor the Allies— England, France, Italy, and Russia. When Germany resumed unrestricted submarine warfare two years later, the United States abandoned neutrality and joined the Allied cause.

At first the reality of war did not sink in. Americans were confident and carefree as the troops set off overseas. That cheerful mood soon passed. A number of famous American writers saw the

636   *The Modern Age*

war firsthand and learned of its horror. E. E. Cummings, Ernest Hemingway, and John Dos Passos served as ambulance drivers. Hemingway later served in the Italian infantry and was seriously wounded. Other, less famous writers fought and died in France. Among them were the poets Joyce Kilmer, who wrote "Trees," and Alan Seeger, who wrote "I Have a Rendezvous with Death."

Prosperity and Depression

The end of the Great War in November 1918 brought little peace to Woodrow Wilson. His dream of the United States joining the League of Nations to prevent future wars failed. The war's end brought little peace to the big cities of America either. In 1919, Prohibition made the sale of liquor illegal, leading to bootlegging, speakeasies, widespread lawbreaking, and sporadic warfare among competing gangs.

Throughout the 1920's, the nation seemed on a binge. After a brief recession in 1920 and 1921, the economy boomed. New buildings rose everywhere, creating new downtown sections in many cities—Omaha, Des Moines, and Minneapolis among them. Radio arrived, and so did jazz. Movies became big business, and spectacular movie palaces sprang up across the country. Fads abounded: raccoon coats, flagpole sitting, the Charleston. The great literary interpreter of the Roaring Twenties was F. Scott Fitzgerald. In *The Beautiful and Damned* and *The Great Gatsby* Fitz-

ARMISTICE DAY, 1918
Gifford Beal
Indiana University Art Museum

Introduction 637

Humanities Note

Fine art, *Armistice Day*, 1918, by Gifford Beal. Gifford Beal (1879–1956) graduated from Princeton University in 1900 and served as president of the highly respected Art Students League from 1914 to 1929. According to his son, writing in the early 1970's, Beal had a joyful, optimistic outlook; he took special pleasure in painting scenes of crowds (as in *Armistice Day*) and circuses. The artist was called an "American Impressionist," and indeed many of his works display the gentle quality of Impressionism.

The news of the end of hostilities frequently draws crowds into the streets in collective celebration, and November 11, 1918, the day World War I ended, was no exception. The curve and sweep of flags and banners forms a festive frame above the assembled throng. The painter recorded the moment when, after more than two years, anxiety, sacrifice, and despair have given way to a kind of ecstatic sense of relief.

AMERICAN EVENTS

1916   *Chicago Poems* by **Carl Sandburg** appears.

1917   United States enters First World War.

1919   Prohibition becomes law, followed by rum-running, speakeasies; law repealed in 1933.

       Sherwood Anderson publishes *Winesburg, Ohio*.

1920   Sinclair Lewis publishes *Main Street*.

       Nineteenth Amendment to Constitution gives U.S. women the right to vote.

1921   Eugene O'Neill's play *Beyond the Horizon* wins the Pulitzer Prize.

1922   **E. E. Cummings** publishes *The Enormous Room*.

       T. S. Eliot publishes *The Waste Land*.

1923   **Wallace Stevens** publishes *Harmonium*.

1925   **F. Scott Fitzgerald** publishes *The Great Gatsby*.

       William Carlos Williams publishes *In the American Grain*.

1926   **Langston Hughes** publishes *The Weary Blues*.

       Ernest Hemingway publishes *The Sun Also Rises*.

James Joyce

Langston Hughes

Signing of Treaty of Versailles

Prohibition Declared

Nineteenth Amendment Adopted

F. Scott Fitzgerald

Carl Sandburg

Mural by José Orozco

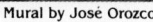
D. H. Lawrence

WORLD EVENTS

1917 Russia: Bolsheviks seize control of Russia in October Revolution.

1918 Worldwide influenza epidemic kills as many as 20 million people.

England: Siegfried Sassoon publishes *Counter-Attack*.

1919 France: Treaty of Versailles ends First World War but sets harsh peace terms.

1921 Mexico: Diego Rivera paints murals that, along with José Orozco's, spark Mexican Renaissance.

England: D. H. Lawrence publishes *Women in Love*.

1922 Ireland: James Joyce publishes *Ulysses*.

1923 Ireland: Nobel Prize for Literature awarded to poet William Butler Yeats.

1924 Germany: Thomas Mann publishes *The Magic Mountain*.

England: E. M. Forster publishes *A Passage to India*.

1925 Czechoslovakia-Germany: *The Trial*, a novel by Franz Kafka, published posthumously.

England: Virginia Woolf publishes *Mrs. Dalloway*.

1926 Russia: Ivan Pavlov reports his experimental findings in *Conditioned Reflexes*.

Introduction 639

Enrichment The Versailles Treaty was signed in the Hall of Mirrors at the palace of Versailles. Only fifty years earlier, German Chancellor Otto Von Bismark had proclaimed a German Empire in the same room following the Franco-Prussian War. The Treaty humiliated Germany, who was not even allowed to participate in the negotiations. Among the conditions set forth in the treaty were that Germany had to surrender territory to France and to the newly created Poland, they had to admit responsibility for the war and pay reparations for the total cost of the war, and they had to dismantle their navy and agree to keep military forces out of the Rhineland.

In the painting on page 638, two German officials are shown on one side of the table. Facing them are Georges Clemençeau of France in the center, David Lloyd George of Great Britain on the right, and President Woodrow Wilson on the left, holding a copy of the treaty.

Enrichment Charles Lindbergh's flight across the Atlantic inspired the nation and transformed Lindbergh into a national hero. The handsome and courageous aviator was hailed by millions on his return from France. Following this feat, Lindbergh toured the country to encourage air mail and air travel.

Enrichment The attack on Pearl Harbor was the greatest military disaster in United States history. The surprise was complete and devastating, as the bulk of our Pacific air force and our most powerful vessels, eight battleships, were destroyed. More than 70 civilians and 2300 servicemen were killed.

AMERICAN EVENTS

1927   Charles Lindbergh flies solo and nonstop from New York to Paris.

1929   **Ernest Hemingway** publishes *A Farewell to Arms*.

      Thomas Wolfe's *Look Homeward, Angel* appears.

      William Faulkner publishes *The Sound and the Fury*.

      Stock market crashes in October, followed by Great Depression of 1930's.

1930   **Katherine Anne Porter** publishes *Flowering Judas*.

      John Dos Passos publishes *The 42nd Parallel*, first novel in *U.S.A.* trilogy.

1931   Pearl S. Buck's *The Good Earth*, wins the Pulitzer Prize.

1933   In the worst year of The Depression, President Franklin D. Roosevelt closes banks; Congress passes New Deal laws.

1938   **Thornton Wilder's** play, *Our Town,* opens.

1939   **John Steinbeck** publishes *The Grapes of Wrath*.

      United States declares neutrality as World War II breaks out in Europe.

1940   Richard Wright publishes *Native Son*.

1941   *A Curtain of Green* by **Eudora Welty** appears.

      Japanese bomb American naval base at Pearl Harbor, bringing U.S. into World War II.

1945   World War II ends after U.S. drops two atomic bombs on Japan.

Charles Lindbergh

Stock Market Crash   Franklin Delano Roosevelt

Woman Working During World War II

Atomic Bombs Dropped on Japan

Adolf Hitler

Nazi Troops

George Orwell

..we here highly resolve that these dead shall not have died in vain...

REMEMBER DEC. 7th!

Japanese Bomb Pearl Harbor

WORLD EVENTS

1927   England: Virginia Woolf publishes *To the Lighthouse*.

1928   China: Chiang Kai-shek becomes head of Nationalist government.

       Germany: Kurt Weill and Bertolt Brecht write and produce *The Threepenny Opera*.

1930   India: Mahatma Gandhi leads famous march to the sea to protest British tax on salt.

1931   Spain: Salvador Dali paints *Persistence of Memory*.

1933   Germany: Adolf Hitler becomes German chancellor and imposes Nazism.

1934   Wales: Dylan Thomas publishes *Eighteen Poems*.

1936   USSR: Stalin starts Great Purge to rid government and armed forces of opposition.

       Spain: Spanish Civil War begins.

1938   England: George Orwell publishes *Homage to Catalonia*.

1939   Poland: German blitzkrieg invasion of Poland sets off Second World War in Europe.

1940   France surrenders to Germany in same railroad car in which Germany had surrendered to France in 1918.

1941   Arthur Koestler publishes *Darkness at Noon*, a novel on totalitarianism.

1942   Albert Camus completes *The Stranger*.

1943   France: Jean-Paul Sartre writes *Being and Nothingness*.

1945   United Nations Charter signed at end of Second World War.

Enrichment The civil war in Spain was the result of a conflict between the republican government in power, which was led by a coalition of liberals, socialists, and communists, and conservative forces led by the clergy, the people who had supported the old Spanish monarchy, and some members of the military. In 1936, after years of unrest and instability, a group of generals, who became known as the Nationalists, led an uprising against the government, known as the Republicans. The Nationalists, led by Francisco Franco, sought to restore the power of the church and eliminate socialism and communism in Spain.

The civil war became an international issue when foreign powers began to take sides. Italian troops were dispatched and the German air force was used to support the Nationalist forces. The U.S.S.R. sent weapons and advisors to support the Republicans.

The civil war ended in 1939 with a victory for the Nationalists. Franco then imposed a fascist dictatorship on Spain.

Humanities Note

Fine art, *The City from Greenwich Village,* 1922, by John Sloan. The influence of John Sloan (1871–1951) on the development of modern art in America was considerable. Raised in Philadelphia, Sloan studied art in Pennsylvania and came to New York in 1904. A few years later Sloan and seven other American artists—known as "The Eight"—formed what is sometimes referred to as the Ashcan School. Although their artistic styles differed, "The Eight" all rejected the prevailing academic standards of painting. They chose, instead, to depict realistic scenes, unhindered by conventional expectations of what constitutes fitting subjects for art. Sloan's cityscapes were at first greeted with scorn; their later acceptance reflected a more general acceptance of modern art in all its forms.

In *The City from Greenwich Village* the visual focal point is the elevated train approaching the viewer. Its curved length contrasts with the prominent verticals of the buildings. From the windows of the buildings, the light seems to glow, suffusing the painting with a warmth that comes, as well, from the greens, yellows, and browns that predominate. The work is thus realistic in subject matter but not harsh in technique.

THE CITY FROM GREENWICH VILLAGE, 1922
John Sloan
National Gallery of Art, Washington, D.C.

gerald showed both the glamorous and the pitiful sides of the American dream.

During the 1920's, artists and writers flocked to Greenwich Village, in New York City. Older buildings in the area, including barns, stables, and houses, were converted to studios, nightclubs, theaters, and shops. In 1923, playwright Eugene O'Neill founded the Greenwich Village Theatre, where experimental dramas were performed. Thomas Wolfe taught English at New York University in the Village while writing his autobiographical novel, *Look Homeward, Angel.*

In late October 1929, the stock market crashed, marking the beginning of the Great Depression. By mid-1932, about 12 million people, or one quarter of the work force, were out of work. Even as bread lines formed and the numbers of unemployed grew, most business leaders remained optimistic. But the situation continued to worsen. In the presidential election of 1932, New York's Governor Franklin D. Roosevelt defeated incumbent President Herbert Hoover. Roosevelt embarked on a far-reaching program, the New Deal, to turn the economic tide. He won reelection in 1936 and again in 1940. While circumstances had improved by then, prosperity did not begin to equal that of the 1920's.

World War II

Only 20 years after the Treaty of Versailles had ended the First World War, the German invasion of Poland touched off the Second World War. As in the earlier war, most Americans wanted to remain neutral. Even after the fall of France in 1940, the dominant mood in the United States was one of isolationism. But when the Japanese attacked Pearl Harbor in Hawaii on December 7, 1941, America could stay neutral no longer. The United States declared war on the Axis powers—Japan, Germany, and Italy.

After years of bitter fighting on two fronts, the Allies—including the United States, Great Britain, the Soviet Union, and France—defeated Nazi Germany. Japan surrendered three months later, after the United States had dropped atomic bombs on two Japanese cities. Peace, and the atomic age, had arrived.

THE BIRTH OF MODERNISM

The devastation of World War I brought about an end to the sense of optimism that had characterized the years immediately preceding the war. Many people were left with a feeling of uncertainty, disjointedness, and disillusionment. No longer trusting the ideas and values of the world out of which the war had developed, people sought to find new ideas that were more applicable to twentieth-century life. The quest for new ideas extended into the world of literature, and a major literary movement known as Modernism was born.

The Modernists experimented with a wide variety of new approaches and techniques, producing a remarkably diverse body of literature. Yet, the Modernists shared a common purpose. They sought to capture the essence of modern life in the form and content of their work. To reflect the fragmentation of the modern world, the Modernists constructed their works out of fragments, omitting the expositions, transitions, resolutions, and explanations used in traditional literature. In poetry, they abandoned traditional forms in favor of free verse. The themes of their works were usually implied, rather than directly stated, creating a sense of uncertainty and forcing readers to draw their own conclusions. In general, Modernist

LIBRARY
Bernard Boruch Zakheim
Coit Tower Mural (WPA)
San Francisco Art Commission

Humanities Note

Fine art, *Library,* Coit Tower Mural (WPA) by Bernard Boruch Zakheim. Artists, like almost all other Americans, suffered during the Depression. Few people had money to buy their works, and artists themselves couldn't afford to purchase needed supplies or rent a studio. In 1935, to give jobs to unemployed Americans in many fields of work, the government set up the WPA—the Works Progress Administration (between 1939 and 1943 it was called the Works Projects Administration). The Federal Arts Project, an offshoot of the WPA, was specifically aimed at helping struggling painters and sculptors by paying them modest wages to create art for public buildings, such as post offices, city halls, and so on.

Many of the WPA works were in the form of murals, and, of these, some were in the social realism style: working-class men and women shown in industrial, urban, or other settings that typified their occupations and their day-to-day surroundings. Paintings done as murals were, often, larger than life, and were composed of a series of related subjects rather than focusing on a specific scene.

The work shown on this page, by Bernard Boruch Zakheim, is from a WPA mural in the Coit Tower in San Francisco. Called *Library,* it is a tribute to the importance of literacy and to the public library system, for the betterment of working people.

4 **Literary Movement** Ezra Pound and other Imagists were profoundly influenced by the poetry of the Orient, in which they saw images distilled to the fewest, most intense words. The Imagists set out to achieve a similar distillation in their poetry. Pound, for example, had written a thirty-line poem about seeing beautiful faces in the Paris subway station; he destroyed this version of his poem and rewrote it in fifteen lines. A year later he reduced this poem to its final two-line form. See the final result, "In a Station of the Metro," page 854.

Humanities Note

Fine art, *Conception Synchromy,* 1914, by Stanton MacDonald-Wright. Born in Virginia, Stanton MacDonald-Wright (1890–1973) moved to California in 1900. At the age of seventeen he went to Paris, where he encountered the works of such major European painters as Cézanne, Matisse, and Picasso. Within a few years MacDonald-Wright and the artist Morgan Russell founded the artistic movement they called *synchromism.* The term, derived from the Greek words for "together" and "color," referred to the "harmony of color" in their paintings. The style, moreover, was one of the first nonrepresentational forms of Western art.

Conception Synchromy is characteristic of the technique. Bright-hued discs and fan-shaped areas are arranged in a flat pattern to form a pleasant display of color. Although the work is nonrepresentational, the colors and pinwheel-like shapes may suggest movement, so that the painting is not static. In some of his later works the artist incorporated still-life images into the synchromatic paintings.

works demanded more from readers than the works of earlier American writers. At the same time, however, the Modernists helped to earn America a place among the world's great literary traditions.

Imagism

The Modernist movement was ushered in by a poetic movement known as Imagism. This movement, which lasted from 1909 to 1917, attracted followers in both the United States and England. The Imagists rebelled against the sentimentality of nineteenth century poetry. They demanded instead hard, clear expression, concrete images, and the language of everyday speech. Their models came from Greek and Roman classics, Chinese and Japanese poetry, and the free verse of the French poets of their day. The early leader of the Imagist movement was Ezra Pound. When Pound abandoned Imagism, other Imagists assumed leadership, among them the poet H. D. (Hilda Doolittle). Amy Lowell, a Massachusetts poet, led the Imagist movement in the United States in its final years.

4

CONCEPTION SYNCHROMY, 1914
Stanton MacDonald-Wright
Joseph H. Hirshhorn Museum

The Expatriates

The postwar disenchantment led a number of American writers to become expatriates, or exiles. Many of these writers settled in Paris, where they were influenced by Gertrude Stein. The writer who coined the phase "lost generation" to describe those who were disillusioned by the First World War, Stein lived in Paris from 1902 until her death in 1946. Stein's home attracted many major authors, including Sherwood Anderson, F. Scott Fitzgerald, and Ernest Hemingway.

Fitzgerald and Hemingway are the best known of the expatriates, but they are by no means the only ones. Ezra Pound spent most of his adult life in England, France, and Italy. T. S. Eliot, born in St. Louis, went to Europe in 1914 and did not return to the United States until 1932. Eliot's long, despairing poem *The Waste Land* appeared in 1922. Some have called it the most important poem of the century.

Most of the lost generation saw very little in their civilization to praise or even accept. Archibald MacLeish, an expatriate from 1923 to 1928, wrote several volumes of verse expressing the chaos and hopelessness of those years. MacLeish eventually broke with the expatriates, however. He returned to the United States in the 1930's and became increasingly concerned about the rise of dictatorships. A supporter of President Roosevelt's New Deal, he served as Librarian of Congress during the Second World War.

New Approaches

5 During the years between the two world wars, writers in both the United States and Europe explored new literary territories. Influenced by developments in modern psychology, writers began using the stream-of-consciousness technique, attempting to re-create the natural flow of a character's thoughts. Named by psychologist William James, the stream-of-consciousness technique involves the presentation of a series of thoughts, memories, and insights, connected only by a character's natural associations. The landmark stream-of-consciousness novel is *Ulysses,* published in 1922 by the Irish writer James Joyce. A number of American novelists soon adopted the technique, most notably William Faulkner in *The Sound and the Fury.*

6 The three novels in John Dos Passos's *U.S.A.* use stream-of-consciousness narration. They include some other unusual devices for a fictional work, such as brief biographies of well-known Americans and quotations from newspapers and magazines. Katherine Anne Porter's short stories also employ stream of consciousness.

7 Poets, no less than novelists and short story writers, sought to stretch the old boundaries. E. E. Cummings's poems attracted special attention because of their wordplay, unique typography, and special punctuation. These devices are more than mere oddities in Cummings's poetry. They are vital to its intent and its meaning.

5 **Writers' Techniques** Very often the Modernists used the device of interior monologue to convey character. This developed into the stream-of-consciousness technique, which was like impressionism in writing. It was a technique used to show a character's state of mind and fragmentation.

6 **Literary Movement** Porter's story "The Jilting of Granny Weatherall" is on page 694.

7 **Literary Movement** Cummings's style expressed his contempt for authority and his reverence for individuality. This mesage of individualism made his poetry fun. See pages 864–867 for examples of his poems.

8 **Literary Movement** This quotation is from Archibald MacLeish's "Ars Poetica," page 858.

9 **Enrichment** Before Eugene O'Neill, American theater showed romantic, sentimental plays, drawing room comedies, melodramas, and the like. O'Neill contributed to a resurgence of serious theater. He tried to revive tragedy in the classic sense in plays like *Mourning Becomes Electra;* he used soliloquies and asides; he also employed symbolic devices such as masks and choruses. O'Neill brought about other changes in the theater by experimenting with scenery and settings and by employing realistic dialogue and character portrayal.

10 **Literary Movement** See page 734 for Faulkner's story "The Bear."

11 **Literary Movement** Hemingway's story "In Another Country" is on page 664. Steinbeck's story "Flight" is on page 718.

Other poets found new devices to express their meaning. William Carlos Williams, a New Jersey physician and poet, called his poetry "objectivist." In his view, a poem is an object that presents its case by the form it assumes. So spare and cryptic are some of Williams's poems that one cannot say for sure what they "mean." This obscurity of meaning did not bother Williams. Nor did it concern other poets who shared Archibald MacLeish's belief that "a poem should not mean but be."

Writers of International Renown

The Modernists dramatically altered the complexion of American literature. At the same time, many of these writers earned international acclaim that equaled that of their European contemporaries.

The Nobel Prize for Literature is an international award. It was established in 1901 from funds left by Alfred Nobel, the Swedish inventor of dynamite. The first American to win the Nobel Prize for Literature was Sinclair Lewis. A native of Sauk Center, Minnesota, Lewis fictionalized his home town as Gopher Prairie in his first important novel, *Main Street*. Lewis, one of the great satirists of his era, wrote two more classics within the next few years. *Babbitt* was about an American businessman, while *Arrowsmith* dealt with the medical profession.

Lewis's Nobel Prize in 1930 was the first of many for American writers. In 1936, the prize went to Eugene O'Neill, ranked by most critics as America's greatest playwright. Among his best-known plays are *Desire under the Elms, The Iceman Cometh,* and *Long Day's Journey into Night*. O'Neill's plays are sometimes autobiographical, generally tragic, and often experimental. His *Strange Interlude,* produced in 1928, uses stream-of-consciousness asides to reveal the inner feelings of characters. These feelings often contrast with their actual spoken words.

In 1938, the Nobel Prize for Literature went to Pearl S. Buck, an American who spent her early years in China. Buck wrote about that country with deep understanding and compassion. *The Good Earth* is considered her finest work.

T. S. Eliot, who had become a British subject in 1927, won the award in 1948. William Faulkner won it the following year. Most of Faulkner's novels and short stories are set in mythical Yoknapatawpha County, Mississippi, which closely resembled the area of Mississippi where Faulkner lived. In addition to *The Sound and the Fury,* Faulkner wrote such enduring works as *Light in August* and *The Hamlet*.

In later years, Ernest Hemingway and John Steinbeck also won Nobel Prizes for Literature. Hemingway's clipped style of writing, evident in such novels as *The Sun Also Rises* and *A Farewell to Arms,* influenced a generation of young writers. His best writing deals with the First World War and its aftermath. Steinbeck's works

646 *The Modern Age*

JUKE BOX
Jacob Lawrence
The Detroit Institute of Arts

Humanities Note

Fine art, *Juke Box,* by Jacob Lawrence. The son of a Pennsylvania coal miner, Jacob Lawrence (b. 1917) was born in Atlantic City and grew up in Harlem, a section of New York City. Many of Lawrence's works reveal a deep commitment to racial justice and to the aspirations of the black people. Lawrence's first series of paintings were based on the life of Toussaint L'Ouverture, a former slave who, around 1800, abolished slavery in Haiti. Other series by Lawrence portray the abolitionist John Brown (1949) and the civil rights struggles of the 1950's and 1960's.

Lawrence's works are highly distinctive in technique. Objects and figures are often stylized. The artist favored flat geometric shapes rather than more naturalistic forms. The prominent pattern of the floor in *Juke Box,* for instance, emphasizes his fascination with spatial arrangements. The effect is not merely decorative, however. The movement of the viewer's eye on the checkerboard foreground echoes, in a way, the jazzy rhythms playing on the juke box. At the same time, the swirls displayed on the instrument provide visual contrast to the assertive foreground. The slightly slouched figure is, again, evocative rather than strictly representational, lending an expressive quality to the painting.

depict the Depression, especially as it affected migrant workers and dust-bowl farmers. Two of Steinbeck's most memorable novels are *Of Mice and Men* and *The Grapes of Wrath.*

The Harlem Renaissance

A new literary age was dawning not only in Greenwich Village and among expatriates in Paris but also in northern Manhattan, in Harlem. Black writers, mostly newcomers from the South, were cre-

Introduction 647

12 **Enrichment** Langston Hughes became one of the more popular and widely anthologized of these writers. He wrote both poetry and short stories. Much of his poetry reflects the changing situation of blacks in the United States—from their discouragement over economic and social conditions to their growing demands for social justice. His poem "The Negro Speaks of Rivers" is on page 911.

13 **Literary Movement** Benchley's essay "The Tooth, the Whole Tooth, and Nothing but the Tooth" is on page 770. Thurber's piece "The Night the Ghost Got In" is on page 778. E. B. White's essay "Walden"—not a humorous essay—is on page 762.

ating their own renaissance there. It began in 1921 with the publication of Countee Cullen's "I Have a Rendezvous with Life (with apologies to Alan Seeger)." Another poem by a black youth—"The Negro Speaks of Rivers," by Langston Hughes—followed six months later.

12

What occurred thereafter was a burst of creative activity by black writers, few of whom, other than Cullen, had been born in New York City. Most of them moved there during the renaissance. Claude McKay, for example, was from Jamaica. His most famous book was *Harlem Shadows,* a collection of poems published in 1922. A year later came Jean Toomer's *Cane,* a collection of stories, verses, and a play.

The Harlem Renaissance was publicly recognized in March 1924, when young black writers met the literary editors of the city. Carl Van Doren, editor of the *Century,* noted that black writers, long "oppressed and handicapped . . . have gathered stores of emotion and are ready to burst forth with a new eloquence."

The Harlem phenomenon continued throughout the 1920's and into the 1930's. Arna Bontemps, born in Louisiana, published his first novel, *God Sends Sunday,* in 1931. The writers of this renaissance belonged to no single school of literature, but they did form a coherent group. They saw themselves as being part of a new and exciting movement. As well as producing their own exceptional works, they opened the door for black writers who would follow them.

Flashes of Wit and Humor

So much of the outstanding writing between the wars echoed disenchantment and despair that the bright, cheery voices of the period tend to be forgotten. The best-known humorist of the time was Will Rogers, the "Cowboy Philosopher" from Oklahoma. He earned that nickname with his homespun humor and wry comments on politics and current events. Rogers died in a 1935 plane crash along with noted American aviator Wiley Post.

The drama critic and popular humorist Robert Benchley wrote clever works with amusing titles. James Thurber was one of a number of humorous writers associated with *The New Yorker* magazine. Thurber, who was also a cartoonist, showed real psychological insight into the odd characters in his works. Another *New Yorker* writer was E. B. White, a subtle humorist and brilliant stylist. White later wrote *Charlotte's Web* and several other stories for children.

13

The Second World War did not end the literary revival that had begun after the First World War. Many of the older writers continued to produce novels, short stories, plays, and poems. Meanwhile, a new generation of writers arose after the war to keep American literature at the leading edge of the world's artistic achievement.

Check Test

1. The world event that most influenced the writers of the Modern Age was _____.
2. Ezra Pound was the early leader of a poetry movement known as _____.
3. Throughout the 1920's and 30's, black writers and artists in New York City were part of a creative movement known as the _____.
4. The stock market collapse in 1929 marked the beginning of the _____.
5. The group of disillusioned writers who left America and settled primarily in Paris were known as the _____.

ANSWERS

1. World War I
2. Imagism
3. Harlem Renaissance
4. Great Depression
5. Expatriates

Quotations by Prominent Figures of the Period

All modern American literature comes from one book by Mark Twain called *Huckleberry Finn*.
Ernest Hemingway, *Green Hills of Africa*

In a real dark night of the soul it is always three o'clock in the morning.
F. Scott Fitzgerald, *The Crack-up*

His name was George F. Babbitt. He was . . . nimble in the calling of selling houses for more than people could afford to pay.
Sinclair Lewis, *Babbitt*

Well, if I called the wrong number, why did you answer the 'phone?
James Thurber, *Cartoon caption*

No more war, no more plague, only the dazed silence that follows the ceasing of the heavy guns. . . .
Katherine Ann Porter, *Pale Horse, Pale Rider*

You Can't Go Home Again
Thomas Wolfe, *Title of novel*

The storm had rolled away to faintness like a wagon crossing a bridge.
Eudora Welty, *"A Piece of News"*

Time is dead as long as it is being clicked off by little wheels; only when the clock stops does time come to life.
William Faulkner, *The Sound and the Fury*

This old anvil laughs at many broken hammers.
There are men who can't be bought.
Carl Sandburg, *The People, Yes*

Literature is news that *stays* news.
Ezra Pound, *ABC of Reading*

April is the cruellest month.
T. S. Eliot, "The Waste Land"

Additional Voices

I am a lover and have not found my thing to love.
Sherwood Anderson, *Winesburg, Ohio*

Most of the change we think we see in life
Is due to truths being in and out of favor.
Robert Frost, *The Black Cottage*

You and me, we've made a separate peace.
Ernest Heminway, *In Our Time*

Good morning, daddy!
Ain't you heard
The boogie-woogie rumble
Of a dream deferred?
Langston Hughes, *Dream Boogie*

I saw a fleet of fishing boats.
. . . I flew down almost touching the craft and yelled at them, asking if I was on the right road to Ireland.
Charles Lindbergh, *Lindbergh's Own Story. In the New York Times (May 23, 1927)*

Okie use'ta mean you was from Oklahoma. Now it means you're scum. Don't mean nothing itself, it's the way they say it.
John Steinbeck, *The Grapes of Wrath*

Reading Critically The information on this page is intended to
give students the background
they need to read critically the
literature of the Modern Age. This
information summarizes the historical context, the literary movements, and the writers' techniques of the period. To read
critically, students should be
able to apply this information to
the literary works of the period as
is done in the model on the following pages, "Sophistication"
by Sherwood Anderson. This story is in many ways typical of the
literature of the period. The notes
in the side column provide a
model for reading critically. They
point out the aspects of the story
that reflect the historical context,
the literary movements, and the
techniques that Anderson used.
Have students pay attention to
these notes and make their own
critical comments as they read.
Also suggest that as they read
other selections in this unit, they
should read them critically, being
aware of the historical context,
the influence of the literary movements, and the writers' techniques.
  To give students further
practice with the process of
reading critically, use the selection in the Teaching Portfolio.
"What Are Years?" by Marianne
Moore, page 849, following the
Teacher Backup, which students
can annotate themselves. Encourage students to use these
strategies as they read the literature in this unit.

READING CRITICALLY

The Literature of 1915–1946

World War I had a tremendous impact on the attitudes and outlooks of the American people. This impact is reflected in the literature
of the modern age. To fully appreciate modern literature, you must
understand how the nation was affected by its involvement in World
War I.

Historical Context

Prior to World War I, the mood of American society was confident
and optimistic. This mood was shattered by the horrifying realities of
American involvement in World War I—a war which caused the death
of hundreds of thousands of Americans and Europeans. When the
war ended, many people were left with a feeling of distrust toward the
ideas and values of the past. People saw the need for change, but
they were unsure about the sort of changes that were needed. There
was a growing sense of uncertainty, disjointedness, and disillusionment among certain members of American society.

**Literary
Movements**

In the aftermath of World War I, a major literary movement known
as Modernism developed. Abandoning many traditional forms and
techniques, the Modernists sought to capture the essence of modern
life in both the form and content of their work. To reflect the disjointedness of modern life, they constructed their works out of fragments,
omitting the expositions, resolutions, interpretations, transitions, and
summaries often used in traditional works. The Modernists also frequently expressed their views about modern life in the themes of their
works, often focusing on such themes as the uncertainty, bewilderment, and apparent meaninglessness of modern life.

**The Writer's
Techniques**

Because they believed that modern life lacked certainty, the Modernists generally suggested rather than asserted meaning in their
works. The theme of a typical Modernist work is implied, not stated,
forcing readers to draw their own conclusions. Often, the Modernists
used symbols and allusions to suggest themes. They also generally
used a limited point of view in their works, because they believed that
reality is shaped by people's perceptions. Finally, the Modernists experimented with a number of new literary techniques, including shifting points of view and the stream-of-consciousness technique.

On the following pages is a selection by Sherwood Anderson, an
influential modern writer. The notes in the side column show how a
reader might read this selection critically.

650   *The Modern Age*

Objectives

1 To understand character
2 To understand a charac-
  ter's motivation
3 To write about theme

Support Material

Teaching Portfolio
Teacher Backup, p. 845
Reading Critically, "What Are
Years?" by Marianne Moore, p.
849
Grammar in Action Worksheets,
Identifying Noun Clauses, p.
850; *Making Pronouns Agree
with Antecedants*, p. 858
Usage and Mechanics Work-
sheet, p. 854

Analyzing Literature Worksheet,
Understanding Character, p.
855
Language Worksheet, *Using
Context Clues*, p. 856
Selection Test, p. 857

Sophistication

Sherwood Anderson

It was early evening of a day in the late fall and the Winesburg County Fair had brought crowds of country people into town. The day had been clear and the night came on warm and pleasant. On the Trunion Pike, where the road after it left town stretched away between berry fields now covered with dry brown leaves, the dust from passing wagons arose in clouds. Children, curled into little balls, slept on the straw scattered on wagon beds. Their hair was full of dust and their fingers black and sticky. The dust rolled away over the fields and the departing sun set it ablaze with colors.

In the main street of Winesburg crowds filled the stores and the sidewalks. Night came on, horses whinnied, the clerks in the stores ran madly about, children became lost and cried lustily, an American town worked terribly at the task of amusing itself.

Pushing his way through the crowds in Main Street, young George Willard concealed himself in the stairway leading to Doctor Reefy's office and looked at the people. With feverish eyes he watched the faces drifting past under the store lights. Thoughts kept coming into his head and he did not want to think. He stamped impatiently on the wooden steps and looked sharply about. "Well, is she going to stay with him all day? Have I done all this waiting for nothing?" he muttered.

George Willard, the Ohio village boy, was fast growing into manhood and new thoughts had been coming into his mind. All that day, amid the jam of people at the Fair, he had gone about feeling lonely. He was about to leave Winesburg to go away to some city where he hoped to get work on a city newspaper and he felt grown up. The mood that had taken possession of him was a thing known to men and unknown to boys. He felt old and a little tired. Memories awoke in him. To his mind his new sense of maturity set him apart, made of him a half-tragic figure. He wanted someone to understand the feeling that had taken possession of him after his mother's death.

There is a time in the life of every boy when he for the first time takes the backward view of life. Perhaps that is the mo-

Literary Movement: The story begins without an exposition, and background information is revealed as the story progresses. This reflects the Modernist perception of life as ambiguous and fragmented.

Historical Context: The story is set just after the turn of the century.

Writer's Technique: Anderson's description of the town contrasts with the common conception that small-town life is ordered and pastoral.

Writer's Technique: George embodies the conflicting emotions associated with the passage from the final stages of childhood to adulthood.

Sophistication 651

Presentation

Motivation/Prior Knowledge
Have students imagine that they are living in a small, pre-industrial town in the Midwest at the turn of the century. What would life be like there? What would people do for a living? for entertainment? Tell students that this is the setting and situation in "Sophistication."

Thematic Idea Another selection in which a character's feelings for another becomes an important step toward maturity is "The White Heron" by Sarah Orne Jewett, on page 540.

Purpose-Setting Question
What changes do the two main characters undergo during the course of this story?

Humanities Note

Fine art, *West Tisbury Fair*, 1963, by Thomas Hart Benton. Thomas Hart Benton (1889–1975) was a famous painter of the American scene. Benton had an early interest in drawing and worked as a cartoonist for a newspaper. After studying at the Art Institute of Chicago and briefly at the academies of Paris, he began painting, searching for a way to combine the new use of pure color (impressionism) with the art of the Renaissance and Baroque. In World War I he served as a draftsman for the Navy, which reinforced his interest in figurative art, and he abandoned abstract art. He traveled throughout America, sketching and painting and deepening his love for his country. He celebrated the American landscape in his paintings, producing spirited images of swinging rhythms and energy. Benton exaggerated the musculature and distorted the poses of his figures to heighten this spirited feeling of energy. Benton loved painting murals and created many to honor America in a career that spanned more than fifty years.

In this painting, Benton presents a view of an event on Martha's Vineyard, an island that he loved and where he maintained a residence. The West Tisbury Agricultural Fair has been held every year for over a century. Originally it occurred when the crops were in, but the date was changed to August to accommodate summer residents. Benton's love of all facets of American life is evident in this celebration of a "small-time" fair. The picture captures the flavor of this particularly American event.

As students look at the painting, have them consider the scene as the setting for "Sophistication."

1. What aspects of the painting are appropriate to "Sophistication"?

WEST TISBURY FAIR
Thomas Hart Benton
Collection Mr. Arthur
Levitt, Jr., New York

Writer's Technique: This is an example of irony. Sophistication is not usually viewed as a source of sadness.

652   The Modern Age

ment when he crosses the line into manhood. The boy is walking through the street of his town. He is thinking of the future and of the figure he will cut in the world. Ambitions and regrets awake within him. Suddenly something happens; he stops under a tree and waits as for a voice calling his name. Ghosts of old things creep into his consciousness; the voices outside of himself whisper a message concerning the limitations of life. From being quite sure of himself and his future he becomes not at all sure. If he be an imaginative boy a door is torn open and for the first time he looks out upon the world, seeing, as though they marched in procession before him, the countless figures of men who before his time have come out of nothingness into the world, lived their lives and again disappeared into nothingness. The sadness of sophistication has come to the boy. With a little gasp he sees himself as merely a leaf blown by the wind through the streets of his village. He knows that in spite of all the stout talk of his fellows he must live and die in uncertainty, a thing blown by the winds, a

2. Benton used distortion to heighten the feeling of spirited energy in his paintings. What is distorted in this painting?

Critical Thinking and Reading
How does the passage on this page tie in with Anderson's view of the Modern Age?

Grammar in Action

A **noun clause** is a subordinate clause that functions as a noun in a sentence. A noun clause may serve as a transition between the sentence in which it appears and other sentences. Here are some examples of transitional noun clauses from "Sophistication":

What George felt, she in her young woman's way felt also.

She knew *that the fact of his presence would create an impression.*

Now that he had found her George wondered *what he had better do and say.*

thing destined like corn to wilt in the sun. He shivers and looks eagerly about. The eighteen years he has lived seem but a moment, a breathing space in the long march of humanity. Already he hears death calling. With all his heart he wants to come close to some other human, touch someone with his hands, be touched by the hand of another. If he prefers that the other be a woman, that is because he believes that a woman will be gentle, that she will understand. He wants, most of all, understanding.

Literary Movement: George's sense of uncertainty reflects the Modernist perception of the ambiguity of life in the modern world.

When the moment of sophistication came to George Willard his mind turned to Helen White, the Winesburg banker's daughter. Always he had been conscious of the girl growing into womanhood as he grew into manhood. Once on a summer night when he was eighteen, he had walked with her on a country road and in her presence had given way to an impulse to boast, to make himself appear big and significant in her eyes. Now he wanted to see her for another purpose. He wanted to tell her of the new impulses that had come to him. He had tried to make her think of him as a man when he knew nothing of manhood and now he wanted to be with her and to try to make her feel the change he believed had taken place in his nature.

As for Helen White, she also had come to a period of change. What George felt, she in her young woman's way felt also. She was no longer a girl and hungered to reach into the grace and beauty of womanhood. She had come home from Cleveland, where she was attending college, to spend a day at the Fair. She also had begun to have memories. During the day she sat in the grandstand with a young man, one of the instructors from the college, who was a guest of her mother's. The young man was of a pedantic turn of mind and she felt at once he would not do for her purpose. At the Fair she was glad to be seen in his company as he was well dressed and a stranger. She knew that the fact of his presence would create an impression. During the day she was happy, but when night came on she began to grow restless. She wanted to drive the instructor away, to get out of his presence. While they sat together in the grandstand and while the eyes of former schoolmates were upon them, she paid so much attention to her escort that he grew interested. "A scholar needs money. I should marry a woman with money," he mused.

Writer's Technique: The story is told from a third-person omniscient point of view. An omniscient narrator was rarely used in Modernist short stories.

Helen White was thinking of George Willard even as he wandered gloomily through the crowds thinking of her. She remembered the summer evening when they had walked together and wanted to walk with him again. She thought that the months she had spent in the city, the going to theaters

By using noun clauses, Anderson is able to refer without repetition to George's feelings, the presence of the instructor, and George's intentions.

Student Activity 1. Identify the noun clauses in the following sentences.

1. He knows that in spite of all the talk of his fellows he must live and die in uncertainty.
2. He believes that a woman will be gentle.
3. You see what I want.
4. I'll say that I want to see her.
5. What he felt was reflected in her.

Student Activity 2. Change the italicized phrases into noun clauses in the following sentences.

1. *George's plans to leave Winesburg* made him moody.
2. He wanted to know *Helen's reaction to his new maturity*.
3. Helen also thought *herself changed by life away from Winesburg*.
4. For a time, the young couple were uncertain of *their feelings for each other*.

and the seeing of great crowds wandering in lighted thoroughfares, had changed her profoundly. She wanted him to feel and be conscious of the change in her nature.

Writer's Technique: Anderson is using the flashback technique, dramatizing events that took place several months earlier.

The summer evening together that had left its mark on the memory of both the young man and woman had, when looked at quite sensibly, been rather stupidly spent. They had walked out of town along a country road. Then they had stopped by a fence near a field of young corn and George had taken off his coat and let it hang on his arm. "Well, I've stayed here in Winesburg—yes—I've not yet gone away but I'm growing up," he had said. "I've been reading books and I've been thinking. I'm going to try to amount to something in life.

"Well," he explained, "that isn't the point. Perhaps I'd better quit talking."

Writer's Technique: George's personality is revealed through his actions and comments.

The confused boy put his hand on the girl's arm. His voice trembled. The two started to walk back along the road toward town. In his desperation George boasted, "I'm going to be a big man, the biggest that ever lived here in Winesburg," he declared. "I want you to do something, I don't know what. Perhaps it is none of my business. I want you to try to be different from other women. You see the point. It's none of my business, I tell you. I want you to be a beautiful woman. You see what I want."

The boy's voice failed and in silence the two came back into town and went along the street to Helen White's house. At the gate he tried to say something impressive. Speeches he had thought out came into his head, but they seemed utterly pointless. "I thought—I used to think—I had it in my mind you would marry Seth Richmond. Now I know you won't," was all he could find to say as she went through the gate and toward the door of her house.

Writer's Technique: Anderson uses the corn as a symbol. The immaturity of the young corn parallels George's lack of maturity.

On the warm fall evening as he stood in the stairway and looked at the crowd drifting through Main Street, George thought of the talk beside the field of young corn and was ashamed of the figure he had made of himself. In the street the people surged up and down like cattle confined in a pen. Buggies and wagons almost filled the narrow thoroughfare. A band played and small boys raced along the sidewalk, diving between the legs of men. Young men with shining red faces walked awkwardly about with girls on their arms. In a room above one of the stores, where a dance was to be held, the fiddlers tuned their instruments. The broken sounds floated down through an open window and out across the murmur of voices and the loud blare of the horns of the band. The medley of sounds got on young Willard's nerves. Everywhere, on all sides, the sense of crowding, moving life closed in about him.

Primary Source

As Mark Schorer states in the following passage, Sherwood Anderson was seeking a new form in which to write. This form eventually took shape in *Winesburg, Ohio,* a collection of stories that are meant to be read and considered as a whole:

> He (Anderson) had observed the pathos, the suffocation of hope and dream in small town characters, the cruelty no less than the comedy. And in form he wanted something loose and impressionistic and without the contrivances of "plot" that would permit him to get under the surface of manners and character, into the secret life, and into what he felt was the soft, warm flow that, taken together, all the secret lives made into life itself. "A man keeps thinking of his own life," he was later to write, in a note probably intended for his *Memoirs,* ". . . life itself is a loose, flowing thing. There are no plot stories in life."

> . . . He would give a certain unification to the separate stories of his twenty-two characters through the background of a single community. As the stories progressed, characters would keep reappearing: someone who had

He wanted to run away by himself and think. "If she wants to stay with that fellow she may. Why should I care? What difference does it make to me?" he growled and went along Main Street and through Hern's Grocery into a side street.

George felt so utterly lonely and dejected that he wanted to weep but pride made him walk rapidly along, swinging his arms. He came to Wesley Moyer's livery barn and stopped in the shadows to listen to a group of men who talked of a race Wesley's stallion, Tony Tip, had won at the Fair during the afternoon. A crowd had gathered in front of the barn and before the crowd walked Wesley, prancing up and down and boasting. He held a whip in his hand and kept tapping the ground. Little puffs of dust arose in the lamplight. "Quit your talking," Wesley exclaimed. "I wasn't afraid, I knew I had 'em beat all the time. I wasn't afraid."

Ordinarily George Willard would have been intensely interested in the boasting of Moyer, the horseman. Now it made him angry. He turned and hurried away along the street. "Old windbag," he sputtered. "Why does he want to be bragging? Why don't he shut up?"

George went into a vacant lot and, as he hurried along, fell over a pile of rubbish. A nail protruding from an empty barrel tore his trousers. He sat down on the ground and swore. With a pin he mended the torn place and then arose and went on. "I'll go to Helen White's house, that's what I'll do. I'll walk right in. I'll say that I want to see her. I'll walk right in and sit down, that's what I'll do," he declared, climbing over a fence and beginning to run.

On the veranda of Banker White's house Helen was restless and distraught. The instructor sat between the mother and daughter. His talk wearied the girl. Although he had also been raised in an Ohio town, the instructor began to put on the airs of the city. He wanted to appear cosmopolitan. "I like the chance you have given me to study the background out of which most of our girls come," he declared. "It was good of you, Mrs. White, to have me down for the day." He turned to Helen and laughed. "Your life is still bound up with the life of this town?" he asked. "There are people here in whom you are interested?" To the girl his voice sounded pompous and heavy.

Helen arose and went into the house. At the door leading to a garden at the back she stopped and stood listening. Her mother began to talk. "There is no one here fit to associate with a girl of Helen's breeding," she said.

Helen ran down a flight of stairs at the back of the house

Literary Movement: Characters in modern fiction are commonly confronted with feelings of loneliness and dejection.

Writer's Technique: Wesley's inability to acknowledge his fears concerning the horse race parallels George's inability to acknowledge his fears regarding his growth into manhood.

Writer's Technique: The vacant lot symbolizes George's feelings of emptiness and isolation.

Sophistication 655

Master Teacher Note Anderson's introduction, which he called "The Book of the Grotesque," to *Winesburg, Ohio,* explains his view of his characters. He calls his characters "grotesques," explaining that their lives are distorted by the frustration and suppression of their desires or by their obsession with a single idea or ambition. The result is that they are isolated from other human beings. You might have students consider and discuss whether George and Helen are examples of Anderson's grotesques.

been a minor figure in one story would presently emerge as the major figure in another, and so on, until a whole sense of the community would emerge. He would supplement . . . unification with another means: in most of the stories George Willard would appear, and while the other characters would come to George in the dumb expectation that he could somehow tell their story, their stories would also be like gifts to him . . .

and into the garden. In the darkness she stopped and stood trembling. It seemed to her that the world was full of meaningless people saying words. Afire with eagerness she ran through a garden gate and, turning a corner by the banker's barn, went into a little side street. "George! Where are you, George?" she cried, filled with nervous excitement. She stopped running, and leaned against a tree to laugh hysterically. Along the dark little street came George Willard, still saying words. "I'm going to walk right into her house. I'll go right in and sit down," he declared as he came up to her. He stopped and stared stupidly. "Come on," he said and took hold of her hand. With hanging heads they walked away along the street under the trees. Dry leaves rustled under foot. Now that he had found her George wondered what he had better do and say.

At the upper end of the Fair Ground, in Winesburg, there is a half decayed old grandstand. It has never been painted and the boards are all warped out of shape. The Fair Ground stands on top of a low hill rising out of the valley of Wine Creek and from the grandstand one can see at night, over a cornfield, the lights of the town reflected against the sky.

Writer's Technique: Like George, Helen embodies the emotions associated with the passage through the final stages between childhood and adulthood.

Writer's Technique: The description of the conflicting forces within people of George's age relates to the theme of the story.

George and Helen climbed the hill to the Fair Ground, coming by the path past Waterworks Pond. The feeling of loneliness and isolation that had come to the young man in the crowded streets of his town was both broken and intensified by the presence of Helen. What he felt was reflected in her.

In youth there are always two forces fighting in people. The warm unthinking little animal struggles against the thing that reflects and remembers, and the older, the more sophisticated thing had possession of George Willard. Sensing his mood, Helen walked beside him filled with respect. When they got to the grandstand they climbed up under the roof and sat down on one of the long bench-like seats.

There is something memorable in the experience to be had by going into a fair ground that stands at the edge of a Middle Western town on a night after the annual fair has been held. The sensation is one never to be forgotten. On all sides are ghosts, not of the dead, but of living people. Here, during the day just passed, have come the people pouring in from the town and the country around. Farmers with their wives and children and all the people from the hundreds of little frame houses have gathered within these board walls. Young girls have laughed and men with beards have talked of the affairs of their lives. The place has been filled to overflowing with life. It has itched and squirmed with life and now it is night and the life has all gone away. The silence is almost terrifying. One

Grammar in Action

Antecedents and **pronouns** must be carefully arranged so that the antecedent of each pronoun is clear and so that the pronoun agrees with its antecedent in number, person, and gender. Notice the way Sherwood Anderson makes his pronouns clear by placing them after their antecedents and making sure they agree with their antecedents:

George and Helen climbed the hill to the Fair Ground, coming by the path past Waterworks Pond. The feeling of loneliness and isolation that had come to the young man in the crowded streets of *his* town was both broken and intensified by the presence of Helen. What *he* felt was reflected in *her*.

Student Activity 1. In the paragraph on page 657 that begins "In the darkness under the roof of the grandstand . . ." identify the antecedent of each pronoun.

Student Activity 2. Supply appropriate pronouns in the following sentences.

1. Young men with shining red faces walked awkwardly about with girls on _____ arms.

AFTER THE SHOW, 1933
Waldo Peirce
Whitney Museum of American Art

conceals oneself standing silently beside the trunk of a tree and what there is of a reflective tendency in his nature is intensified. One shudders at the thought of the meaninglessness of life while at the same instant, and if the people of the town are his people, one loves life so intensely that tears come into the eyes.

In the darkness under the roof of the grandstand, George Willard sat beside Helen White and felt very keenly his own insignificance in the scheme of existence. Now that he had come out of town where the presence of the people stirring about, busy with a multitude of affairs, had been so irritating, the irritation was all gone. The presence of Helen renewed and refreshed him. It was as though her woman's hand was assisting him to make some minute readjustment of the machinery of his life. He began to think of the people in the town where he had always lived with something like reverence. He had reverence for Helen. He wanted to love and to be loved by her, but he did not want at the moment to be confused by her woman-

Writer's Technique: This is an example of irony. The two impulses are directly opposed to each other.

Literary Movement: Characters in modern fiction are commonly confronted with a sense of their own insignificance.

Sophistication   657

Humanities Note

Fine art, *After the Show,* 1933, by Waldo Pierce. Waldo Pierce, (1884–1970), was born in Maine and graduated from Harvard College in 1908. From 1910–1912, he traveled abroad and studied at the Academie Julien in Paris. During World War I he was an ambulance driver for the French army and the American Field Service, and he worked for the American Military Intelligence Department in Spain. He remained in Europe after the war, living in France. He became a friend and traveling companion to Ernest Hemingway. In 1930, he returned to the United States, and resided, at different times, in Maine and Arizona. He was considered to be primarily an Impressionist painter, who worked in oils and watercolors, creating landscapes, seascapes, and still lifes. His work is in the permanent collections of many important museums, including the Metropolitan Museum of Art in New York, the Whitney Museum of American Art, New York, and the Brooklyn Museum. He also illustrated many children's books and won many awards for his art.

There is an energy and excitement that envelopes anyone who attends a typical country fair or tent circus. In this painting, *After the Show,* Pierce has captured the magic of the experience through his use of color, composition, viewpoint. He enables the viewer to feel the lingering air of pleasure and excitement one might feel from the magical world of the carnival.

You might ask this question: George and Helen enter the Fair Ground at the end of the day. How might what they saw and experienced resemble the scene in this painting?

2. George felt so utterly lonely and dejected that _____ wanted to weep but pride made walk rapidly along, swinging _____ arms.
3. As for Helen White, _____ also had come to a period of change: What George felt, _____ in _____ young woman's way felt also.
4. Helen White was thinking of George Willard even as _____ wandered gloomily through the crowds thinking of _____.
5. "Well, _____ ('ve) stayed here in Winesburg—yes— _____ ('ve) not yet gone away but _____ ('m) growing up," he had said.

hood. In the darkness he took hold of her hand and when she crept close put a hand on her shoulder. A wind began to blow and he shivered. With all his strength he tried to hold and to understand the mood that had come upon him. In that high place in the darkness the two oddly sensitive human atoms held each other tightly and waited. In the mind of each was the same thought. "I have come to this lonely place and here is this other," was the substance of the thing felt.

Writer's Technique: The passage of day into night symbolizes George's passage from boyhood into adulthood.

In Winesburg the crowded day had run itself out into the long night of the late fall. Farm horses jogged away along lonely country roads pulling their portion of weary people. Clerks began to bring samples of goods in off the sidewalks and lock the doors of stores. In the Opera House a crowd had gathered to see a show and further down Main Street the fiddlers, their instruments tuned, sweated and worked to keep the feet of youth flying over a dance floor.

In the darkness in the grandstand Helen White and George Willard remained silent. Now and then the spell that held them was broken and they turned and tried in the dim light to see into each other's eyes. They kissed but that impulse did not last. At the upper end of the Fair Ground a half dozen men worked over horses that had raced during the afternoon. The men had built a fire and were heating kettles of water. Only their legs could be seen as they passed back and forth in the light. When the wind blew the little flames of the fire danced crazily about.

Writer's Technique: The corn, now fully grown, symbolizes George's higher level of maturity. The growth of the corn symbolizes the natural movement of life cycles.

George and Helen arose and walked away into the darkness. They went along a path past a field of corn that had not yet been cut. The wind whispered among the dry corn blades. For a moment during the walk back into town the spell that held them was broken. When they had come to the crest of Waterworks Hill they stopped by a tree and George again put his hands on the girl's shoulders. She embraced him eagerly and then again they drew quickly back from that impulse. They stopped kissing and stood a little apart. Mutual respect grew big in them. They were both embarrassed and to relieve their embarrassment dropped into the animalism of youth. They laughed and began to pull and haul at each other. In some way chastened and purified by the mood they had been in, they became, not man and woman, not boy and girl, but excited little animals.

Literary Movement: The story ends without a resolution, leaving the reader with a sense of uncertainty. This reflects the Modernist view of the ambiguous nature of existence.

It was so they went down the hill. In the darkness they played like two splendid young things in a young world. Once, running swiftly forward, Helen tripped George and he fell. He squirmed and shouted. Shaking with laughter, he rolled down the hill. Helen ran after him. For just a moment she stopped in the darkness. There is no way of knowing what woman's thoughts went through her mind but, when the bottom of the hill was reached and she came up to the boy, she took his arm and walked beside him in dignified silence. For some reason they could not have explained they had both got from their silent evening together the thing needed. Man or boy, woman or girl, they had for a moment taken hold of the thing that makes the mature life of men and women in the modern world possible.

Writer's Technique: The final line reflects the theme of the story.

Sherwood Anderson (1876–1941) was one of the most influential writers of the modern age. Born and raised in a small town in Ohio, Anderson used his boyhood observations and experiences as material for his unified collection of short stories, *Winesburg, Ohio* (1919). In this work, from which "Sophistication" is taken, Anderson presents a portrait of small-town life that is strikingly different from those portraits presented in most earlier works of literature. He captures the sense of isolation and despair hidden beneath the surface of the characters' seemingly uneventful lives. He also uses simple, everyday language to capture the true flavor of his characters—a technique that influenced such later twentieth-century writers as Ernest Hemingway. Although Anderson's reputation rests mainly on this single work, he also published several other books, including *Windy McPherson's Sons* (1916), *Triumph of the Egg* (1921), *Horses and Men* (1923), and *Death in the Woods and Other Stories* (1933).

Anderson's preface to *Winesburg, Ohio* explains in a short tale about an old man what Anderson thought of his characters, whom he called "grotesques." This old man believed "that . . . when the world was young there were a great many thoughts but no such thing as truth. Man made the truths himself and. . . . All about in the world were truths and they were beautiful.

"The old man listed hundreds of the truths in his book. I will not try to tell you all of them. . . . Hundreds and hundreds were the truths and they were all beautiful.

"And then the people came along. Each as he appeared snatched up one of the truths. . . . It was the truths that made the people grotesques. . . . It was [the old man's] notion that the moment one of the people took one of the truths to himself, called it his truth, and tried to live his life by it, he became a grotesque and the truth he embraced became a falsehood."

Sophistication   659

More About the Author
Throughout his career, Sherwood Anderson's main concerns were with the sterility of modern life, and with people who did not know how to escape the oppression of the machine age. Anderson himself left his job as manager of a paint factory, abandoned his family, and moved to Chicago to write. Anderson described his departure as follows: "I resorted to slickness, to craftiness. Already I had got a reputation for a kind of queerness among my aquaintances. Men had seen me walking somewhere in the outskirts of the town and suddenly beginning to run. . . . The impression got abroad. I perhaps encouraged it—that I was overworking, was on the point of a nervous breakdown. . . . The thought occurred to me that if men thought me a little insane they would forgive me if I lit out, left the business in which they invested their money on their hands. I did it one day—walked into my office and called my stenographer—It was a bright warm day in summer. I closed the door in my office and spoke to her. A startled look came into her eyes. 'My feet are cold and wet,' I said. 'I have been walking too long on the bed of a river.' Saying these words I walked out of the door leaving her staring after me with frightened eyes. I walked eastward along a railroad track, toward the city of Cleveland. There were five or six dollars in my pocket." Like many of his characters, Anderson's struggle was to escape the confinement of his regulated life. How do other authors you have read reflect their own inner struggles in their work?

Reader's Response What changes have George and Helen undergone through their evening together?

Closure and Extension

1. (a) The Winesburg County Fair is taking place. (b) It brings crowds to town.
2. (a) He wants to be close to her and make her feel that he has matured. (b) She wants to see him for the same reasons.
3. (a) A summer evening that they shared stands out in both of their memories. (b) They walked in the country and George tried to express his feelings about wanting to "amount to something in life."
4. (a) They walk to the Fair Ground. (b) They climb up under the roof of the grandstand and sit on a bench. (c) They leave to get away from the men who are there and to be alone.
5. From their experience George and Helen had taken hold of the "thing" that makes mature life possible.

Interpreting

6. Suggested Response: He conveys the impression of a dull, bleak town that offers no opportunity for growth.
7. (a) Both Helen and George experience the conflict that they are becoming adults, with a new awareness of the world, but still feel bound to the familiar life of Winesburg. (b) Their actions are directly motivated by this conflict.
8. (a) Suggested Response: Anderson generalizes that the passage to adulthood is marked by an ability to take a backward view of life and by the realization of one's need for mature human love. (b) Suggested Response: They act immature but are able to communicate their deeper understanding.
9. Suggested Response: The time of adolescence can be a period of isolation and a time in which love and understanding is needed.
10. (a) Suggested Response: It is the feeling that accompanies an awareness of the true nature of

---

THINKING ABOUT THE SELECTION
Recalling

1. (a) What event is taking place in Winesburg as the story opens? (b) How does this event affect the town?
2. (a) Why does George want to see Helen White? (b) Why does Helen want to see George?
3. (a) What evening stands out in both George's and Helen's memories? (b) How had they spent that evening?
4. (a) Where do George and Helen walk to after they meet outside of Helen's house? (b) What do they do there? (c) Why do they leave?
5. According to the final paragraph, what do George and Helen gain from their experience?

Interpreting

6. What overall impression does Anderson convey through his descriptions of Winesburg and its inhabitants?
7. (a) What internal conflict occurs within both George and Helen? (b) How are their actions in this story related to the conflict?
8. (a) What generalizations does Anderson make about the passage from childhood to adulthood? (b) How do George's and Helen's actions support these generalizations?
9. What is the story's theme, or insight into life?
10. (a) What is the "sadness of sophistication"? (b) Look up the origin of the word *sophistication* in a dictionary. Then explain the meaning of the title.

Applying

11. Do you agree with the generalizations that Anderson makes about the passage from childhood to adulthood? Why or why not?
12. The French biologist and writer Jean Rostand has written, "To be adult is to be alone." How do you think George Willard would react to this comment? Explain your answer.

ANALYZING LITERATURE
Understanding Character

In the introduction to *Winesburg, Ohio,* Anderson suggests that the characters in the book are "grotesques." Anderson explains that grotesques are people who latch onto a single truth, emotion, idea, or ambition and try to live their lives by it.
1. Are George and Helen grotesques? Support your answer.
2. Why is Wesley Moyer a good example of a grotesque?

CRITICAL THINKING AND READING
Understanding a Character's Motivation

In portraying any type of character, a writer must provide a motivation, or a stated or implied reason for the character's actions, to make the character's behavior believable. For example, Anderson directly states that the college instructor's comments on the veranda of Banker White's house are motivated by his desire "to appear cosmopolitan."
1. What motivates George and Helen to find each other?
2. How does Anderson reveal their motivations?

THINKING AND WRITING
Writing About Theme

How would you define the turning point between youth and maturity? Write a brief essay in which you discuss what maturity means to you. Start by listing your thoughts about maturity. Organize your notes into an outline. Prepare a thesis statement. Then write your essay. When you finish writing, revise your essay, making sure you have used vivid examples from life to support your central idea. Finally, proofread your essay and share it with your classmates.

---

life and of the many problems which are a part of life. (b) It refers to wisdom.

Applying

11. Answers will differ. Students may comment that they find the passage into adulthood to be a more gradual comment.
12. Suggested Response: He would agree with the comment, because his passage into adulthood makes him feel lonely.

ANSWERS TO ANALYZING LITERATURE

1. Suggested Response. Yes, because they have both been completely consumed by their feelings concerning their passage into maturity.
2. Wesley Moyer is a "grotesque," because he is obsessed with his desire to boast about his abilities.

ANSWERS TO CRITICAL THINKING AND READING

1. They feel the need to escape from their loneliness and share their feelings for each other.
2. Anderson reveals their motivations by delving into their thoughts.

THINKING AND WRITING
For help with this assignment, students can refer to Lesson 11,

Fiction

8 DECEMBER 1941
Rockwell Kent
The Rockwell Kent Legacies

Humanities Note

Fine art, *8 December 1941,* 1941, by Rockwell Kent. Painter, explorer, architect, wood engraver, lithographer, and writer, Rockwell Kent (1882–1971) was a person of intense energy and passionate interest both in the natural world and in political causes.

Many of Kent's paintings depict rugged scenes of Eskimo life. Others, portraying a less harsh climate, are quiet evocations of rural northeastern United States. The painting *8 December 1941* is in the latter category. The work, in soft autumnal colors, is a kind of understated memorial to one of the most dramatic events in twentieth-century American history. The title, of course, marks the day on which, following the attack on Pearl Harbor, President Franklin D. Roosevelt asked Congress to declare war on the Japanese. The woman in the foreground is waving goodby to the figure receding into the background—presumably going to enlist. Painted in 1941, the work suggests that the tranquility of the scene would soon be shattered by the worldwide catastrophe of war. Thus the figure is bidding farewell to more than a family member—her gesture symbolizes the end of an era.

"Writing About Theme," in the Handbook of Writing About Literature.

After students have completed the assignment, divide them into groups and have them read their first drafts to one another and suggest ways in which they could be improved. The students can then incorporate the suggestions into their revisions.

More About the Author At the beginning of *The Sun Also Rises,* Ernest Hemingway presents Gertrude Stein's famous quotation: "You are all a lost generation." What is the meaning of this quotation? How does it apply to Hemingway?

Critical Evaluation Ray B. West, Jr. made this comment on Hemingway's approach to his work: "Hemingway had said that the old ideals should be reexamined and reappraised. What he meant, as his work will testify, was not that they should be denied and discarded but rather that they should be stripped of the disguise with which an abstract idealism had clothed them, that they should be renewed by an artistic revelation of their relationship to the objects and the events of the immediate present —the violence of war and the disillusionment of apparent corruption and chaos. His subject matter cut through the taboos of genteel society and genteel editorship to discover a world of violence and seeming disorder, but a world struggling to define itself by codes similar in many respects to the old verities—the traditional decorum—of an older society."

ERNEST HEMINGWAY

1899–1961

In his short stories and novels, Ernest Hemingway vividly and forcefully expressed the sentiments of many members of the post-World War I generation. Using a concise, direct style, he wrote about peoples' struggles to maintain a sense of dignity while living in a seemingly hostile and confusing world.

Hemingway was born and raised in Oak Park, Illinois. After graduating from high school, he got a job as a reporter for the Kansas City *Star.* He was eager to serve in World War I, and in 1918 he joined the Red Cross ambulance corps and was sent to the Italian front. Shortly after his arrival, he was severely wounded, and he spent several months recovering in a hospital in Milan. His experiences during the war shaped his views and provided material for his writing.

After the war Hemingway had a difficult time readjusting to life in the United States. Hoping to find personal contentment and establish himself as a writer, he went to Paris where he became friends with Ezra Pound, F. Scott Fitzgerald, Gertrude Stein, and other expatriate writers and artists. His new friends provided him with valuable advice, helped to develop his style, and encouraged his interest in writing.

In 1925 Hemingway published his first major work, *In Our Time,* a series of loosely connected short stories. A year later he published *The Sun Also Rises,* a novel about a group of British and American expatriates searching for sensations that would enable them to forget the pain and disillusionment they associate with life in the modern world. The novel earned him international acclaim, and he remained famous throughout the rest of his life. Yet he was almost as well known for his lifestyle as he was for his writing. Constantly pursuing adventure, he traveled the world, hunting in Africa, deep-sea fishing in the Caribbean, and skiing in Idaho and Europe.

Despite his thirst for adventure, Hemingway remained a productive and successful writer, transforming his observations and experiences into novels and short stories. His novels *A Farewell to Arms* (1926), based on his experiences during World War I, and *For Whom the Bell Tolls* (1940), based on his observations as a war correspondent during the Spanish Civil War, have become American classics. *The Old Man and the Sea* (1952), the story of an old fisherman's struggle to maintain dignity in the face of defeat, won the Pulitzer Prize and helped earn him the Nobel Prize for Literature in 1954.

In 1958 Hemingway defined realism in his art: "From things that have happened and from things as they exist and from all the things that you know and all those that you cannot know, you make something through your invention that is not a representation but a whole new thing truer than any thing true and alive."

662   *The Modern Age*

Objectives
1 To understand Modernism
2 To analyze the effect of style
3 To respond to a statement by the author

Support Material

Teaching Portfolio
Teacher Backup, p. 859
Grammar in Action Worksheet, *Using Direct Quotations,* p. 863
Usage and Mechanics Worksheet. p. 865
Analyzing Literature Worksheet, *Understanding Modernism,* p. 866

Critical Thinking and Reading Worksheet, p. 867
Selection Test, p. 868

GUIDE FOR INTERPRETING

In Another Country

Modernism. Following World War I there was a growing sense of uncertainty, disjointedness, and disillusionment among certain members of American society. Many people came to distrust the ideas and values of the past and sought to find new ideas that seemed more applicable to twentieth-century life. Similarly, writers began turning away from the style, form, and content of nineteenth-century literature and began experimenting with new themes and techniques. A new literary movement, known as Modernism, was born.

The Modernists attempted to capture the essense of modern life in both the form and the content of their work. The uncertainty, bewilderment, and apparent meaninglessness of life were common themes in modern literature. These themes were generally implied, rather than directly stated, to reflect a sense of uncertainty and to enable readers to draw their own conclusions. For similar reasons fiction writers began abandoning the traditional plot structure, omitting the expositions and resolutions that in the past had clarified the work for the reader. Instead, stories and novels were structured to reflect the fragmentation and uncertainty of human experience. A typical modern story or novel seems to begin arbitrarily and to end without a resolution, leaving the reader with possibilities, not solutions.

Writing

Most of Hemingway's stories and novels were based on his observations and experiences. "In Another Country," for example, grew out of his observations during his hospitalization in Milan. Prepare a list of your own observations and experiences that you could use as topics for narratives.

Primary Source

Hemingway's style has been described as simple, objective, and spare. In *Death in the Afternoon* (1932) he wrote,

> If a writer of prose knows enough about what he is writing about he may omit things that he knows and the reader, if the writer is writing truly enough, will have a feeling of those things as strongly as though the writer had stated them. The dignity of movement of an iceberg is due to only one-eighth of it being above water. A writer who omits things because he does not know them only makes hollow places in his writing. A writer who appreciates the seriousness of writing so little that he is anxious to make people see he is formally educated, cultured, or well-bred is merely a popinjay. And this too remember; a serious writer is not to be confounded with a solemn writer. . . .

Guide for Interpreting 663

Literary Focus Hemingway was an important figure in the Modernist movement. His writing style was spare, with no wasted adjectives. Yet it had a lilt to it. Ask the students to analyze how Hemingway's frequent use of "and" gave his prose a special kind of rhythm.

Writing/Prior Knowledge For extra credit, you might ask students to write a narrative account of one of the experiences they have listed.

Vocabulary

Preteach the following vocabulary word:
invalided (in' və lid'd) *v.:* Released because of illness or disability (p. 668)

In Another Country

Ernest Hemingway

In the fall the war[1] was always there, but we did not go to it any more. It was cold in the fall in Milan[2] and the dark came very early. Then the electric lights came on, and it was pleasant along the streets looking in the windows. There was much game hanging outside the shops, and the snow powdered in the fur of the foxes and the wind blew their tails. The deer hung stiff and heavy and empty, and small birds blew in the wind and the wind turned their feathers. It was a cold fall and the wind came down from the mountains.

We were all at the hospital every afternoon, and there were different ways of walking across the town through the dusk to the hospital. Two of the ways were alongside canals, but they were long. Always, though, you crossed a bridge across a canal to enter the hospital. There was a choice of three bridges. On one of them a woman sold roasted chestnuts. It was warm, standing in front of her charcoal fire, and the chestnuts were warm afterward in your pocket. The hospital was very old and very beautiful, and you entered through a gate and walked across a courtyard and out a gate on the other side. There were usually funerals starting from the courtyard. Beyond the old hospital were the new brick pavilions, and there we met every afternoon and were all very polite and interested in what was the matter, and sat in the machines that were to make so much difference.

---

1. **the war:** World War I (1914–1918).
2. **Milan** (mi lan´): A city in northern Italy.

The doctor came up to the machine where I was sitting and said: "What did you like best to do before the war? Did you practice a sport?"

I said: "Yes, football."

"Good," he said. "You will be able to play football again better than ever."

My knee did not bend and the leg dropped straight from the knee to the ankle without a calf, and the machine was to bend the knee and make it move as in riding a tricycle. But it did not bend yet, and instead the machine lurched when it came to the bending part. The doctor said: "That will all pass. You are a fortunate young man. You will play football again like a champion."

In the next machine was a major who had a little hand like a baby's. He winked at me when the doctor examined his hand, which was between two leather straps that bounced up and down and flapped the stiff fingers, and said: "And will I too play football, captain-doctor?" He had been a very great fencer, and before the war the greatest fencer in Italy.

The doctor went to his office in a back room and brought a photograph which showed a hand that had been withered almost as small as the major's, before it had taken a machine course, and after was a little larger. The major held the photograph with his good hand and looked at it very carefully. "A wound?" he asked.

"An industrial accident," the doctor said.

"Very interesting, very interesting," the major said, and handed it back to the doctor.

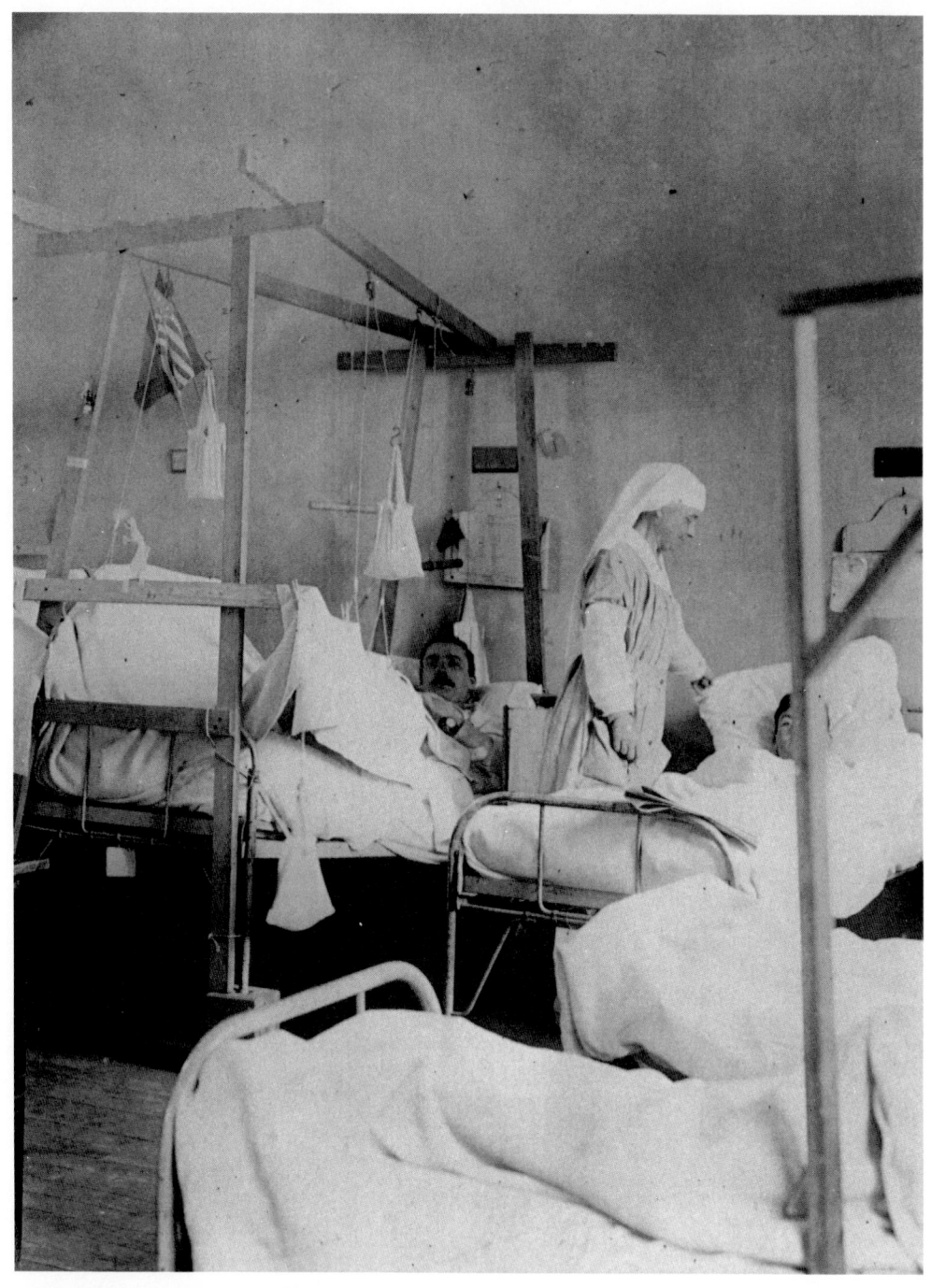

3 **Reading Strategy** Question the students about Hemingway's use of the word *boys*. About how old do they think the narrator is?

4 **Enrichment** La Scala, one of the most celebrated opera houses in the world, was spared during World War I. However, it was bombed during World War II and rebuilt after the war.

5 **Critical Thinking and Reading** Point out to students how the narrator rephrases the opening sentence of the story.

6 **Enrichment** This passage in particular closely parallels Hemingway's own experience in the war. Hemingway never did partake in front-line action. As a Red Cross volunteer, he took food to troops in the trenches. He was hit by a mortar shell and had hundreds of pieces of shrapnel removed from one of his legs. For this, he received medals, accompanied by glowing citations.

"You have confidence?"

"No," said the major.

3 There were three boys who came each day who were about the same age I was. They were all three from Milan, and one of them was to be a lawyer, and one was to be a painter, and one had intended to be a soldier, and after we were finished with the machines, sometimes we walked back together 4 to the Café Cova, which was next door to the Scala.[3] We walked the short way through the communist quarter because we were four together. The people hated us because we were officers, and from a wine-shop someone called out, "A basso gli ufficiali!"[4] as we passed. Another boy who walked with us sometimes and made us five wore a black silk handkerchief across his face because he had no nose then and his face was to be rebuilt. He had gone out to the front from the military academy and had been wounded within an hour after he had gone into the front line for the first time. They rebuilt his face, but he came from a very old family and they could never get the nose exactly right. He went to South America and worked in a bank. But this was a long time ago, and then we did not any of us know how it was going to be afterward. We only knew then that 5 there was always the war, but that we were not going to it any more.

We all had the same medals, except the boy with the black silk bandage across his face, and he had not been at the front long enough to get any medals. The tall boy with a very pale face who was to be a lawyer had been a lieutenant of Arditi[5] and had three medals of the sort we each had only one of. He had lived a very long time with death and was a little detached. We were all a little detached, and there was nothing that held us together except that we met every afternoon at the hospital. Although, as we walked to

the Cova through the tough part of town, walking in the dark, with light and singing coming out of the wine-shops, and sometimes having to walk into the street when the men and women would crowd together on the sidewalk so that we would have had to jostle them to get by, we felt held together by there being something that had happened that they, the people who disliked us, did not understand.

We ourselves all understood the Cova, where it was rich and warm and not too brightly lighted, and noisy and smoky at certain hours, and there were always girls at the tables and the illustrated papers on a rack on the wall. The girls at the Cova were very patriotic, and I found that the most patriotic people in Italy were the café girls—and I believe they are still patriotic.

6 The boys at first were very polite about my medals and asked me what I had done to get them. I showed them the papers, which were written in very beautiful language and full of *fratellanza* and *abnegazione*,[6] but which really said, with the adjectives removed, that I had been given the medals because I was an American. After that their manner changed a little toward me, although I was their friend against outsiders. I was a friend, but I was never really one of them after they had read the citations, because it had been different with them and they had done very different things to get their medals. I had been wounded, it was true; but we all knew that being wounded, after all, was really an accident. I was never ashamed of the ribbons, though, and sometimes, after the cocktail hour, I would imagine myself having done all the things they had done to get their medals; but walking home at night through the empty streets with the cold wind and all the shops closed, trying to keep near the street lights, I knew that I would never have done such things,

---

3. the Scala (ska' la): An opera house in Milan.
4. "A basso gli ufficiali!" (a ba' sō lyē ōō fē cha' lē): "Down with officers!" (Italian).
5. Arditi (ar dē' tē): A select group of soldiers chosen specifically for dangerous campaigns.

---

6. *fratellanza* (fra tāl an' za) **and *abnegazione*** (ab nä ga tzyō' nä): "Brotherhood" and "self-denial" (Italian).

Grammar in Action

The exact reproduction of a person's words is called a **direct quotation.** The person's words are placed inside quotation marks. The introductory or explanatory expression is not enclosed in quotation marks. Take note of the following example:

"An industrial accident," the doctor said.

Most problems with direct quotations arise from the other punctuation marks that accompany the quotation marks. Study-

ing Hemingway's use of direct quotations will help clarify the rules about accompanying punctuation marks.

Student Activity 1. Explain the placement of commas and periods in relation to quotation marks in the following excerpts from "In Another Country."
1. "No," said the major.
2. "He'll lose it," he almost shouted.
3. "I will go to the States."
4. "I am so sorry."

and I was very much afraid to die, and often lay in bed at night by myself, afraid to die and wondering how I would be when I went back to the front again.

The three with the medals were like hunting-hawks; and I was not a hawk, although I might seem a hawk to those who had never hunted; they, the three, knew better and so we drifted apart. But I stayed good friends with the boy who had been wounded his first day at the front, because he would never know now how he would have turned out; so he could never be accepted either, and I liked him because I thought perhaps he would not have turned out to be a hawk either.

The major, who had been the great fencer, did not believe in bravery, and spent much time while we sat in the machines correcting my grammar. He had complimented me on how I spoke Italian, and we talked together very easily. One day I had said that Italian seemed such an easy language to me that I could not take a great interest in it; everything was so easy to say. "Ah yes," the major said. "Why, then, do you not take up the use of grammar?" So we took up the use of grammar, and soon Italian was such a difficult language that I was afraid to talk to him until I had the grammar straight in my mind.

The major came very regularly to the hospital. I do not think he ever missed a day, although I am sure he did not believe in the machines. There was a time when none of us believed in the machines, and one day the major said it was all nonsense. The machines were new then and it was we who were to prove them. It was an idiotic idea, he said, "a theory, like another." I had not learned my grammar, and he said I was a stupid impossible disgrace, and he was a fool to have bothered with me. He was a small man and he sat straight up in his chair with his right hand thrust into the machine and looked straight ahead at the wall while the straps thumped up and down with his fingers in them.

"What will you do when the war is over if it is over?" he asked me. "Speak grammatically!"

"I will go to the States."

"Are you married?"

"No, but I hope to be."

"The more of a fool you are," he said. He seemed very angry. "A man must not marry."

"Why, Signor Maggiore?"[7]

"Don't call me 'Signor Maggiore.' "

"Why must not a man marry?"

"He cannot marry. He cannot marry," he said angrily. "If he is to lose everything, he should not place himself in a position to lose that. He should not place himself in a position to lose. He should find things he cannot lose."

He spoke very angrily and bitterly, and looked straight ahead while he talked.

"But why should he necessarily lose it?"

"He'll lose it," the major said. He was looking at the wall. Then he looked down at the machine and jerked his little hand out from between the straps and slapped it hard against his thigh. "He'll lose it," he almost shouted. "Don't argue with me!" Then he called to the attendant who ran the machines. "Come and turn this damned thing off."

He went back into the other room for the light treatment and the massage. Then I heard him ask the doctor if he might use his telephone and he shut the door. When he came back into the room, I was sitting in another machine. He was wearing his cape and had his cap on, and he came directly toward my machine and put his arm on my shoulder.

"I am so sorry," he said, and patted me on the shoulder with his good hand. "I would not be rude. My wife has just died. You must forgive me."

"Oh—" I said, feeling sick for him. "I am *so* sorry."

---

7. **Signor Maggiore** (sēn yôr′ maj jō′ rā): "Mr. Major" (Italian); a respectful way of addressing an officer.

In Another Country 667

7 **Discussion** This paragraph can serve as the basis for a class discussion. Speaking Italian was easy when the narrator was unaware of the correct grammar. However, as soon as he tried to speak using proper grammar, Italian became difficult. Do your students have the same problem in speaking English? Is there an everyday English that is easy to speak and a separate "classroom grammar" that is difficult and must be learned?

8 **Reading Strategy** At this point have students try to explain why the major has such a negative attitude toward marriage. Then tell them to keep their explanations in mind as they read the rest of the story.

Student Activity 2. Question marks and exclamation marks are placed inside the quotation marks if they are part of the direct quotation; they are placed outside if they are not. Place a question mark or an exclamation mark correctly in these sentences:

1. "Are you to be married"
2. Did he ask if you were "to be married"
3. "Don't argue with me"
4. I was astonished to hear him say "I hope to be"

Student Activity 3. Put quotation marks around the direct quotations in the following items.

1. Someone called, A Basso gli ufficiali! as we passed.
2. Ah yes, the major said. Why, then, do you not take up the use

of grammar?

3. The more of a fool you are, he said.
4. What will you do when the war is over if it is over? he asked me. Speak grammatically!
5. He cannot marry. He cannot marry, he said angrily.

You may check your answers against Hemingway's punctuation on pages 666–667.

Literary Focus The story ends without a resolution, reflecting the Modernist perception of life as being uncertain and confusing.

Reader's Response What emotion was most strongly aroused by their story? Why?

He stood there biting his lower lip. "It is very difficult," he said. "I cannot resign myself."

He looked straight past me and out through the window. Then he began to cry. "I am utterly unable to resign myself," he said and choked. And then crying, his head up looking at nothing, carrying himself straight and soldierly, with tears on both his cheeks and biting his lips, he walked past the machines and out the door.

The doctor told me that the major's wife, who was very young and whom he had not married until he was definitely invalided out of the war, had died of pneumonia. She had been sick only a few days. No one expected her to die. The major did not come to the hospital for three days. Then he came at the usual hour, wearing a black band on the sleeve of his uniform. When he came back, there were large framed photographs around the wall, of all sorts of wounds before and after they had been cured by the machines. In front of the machine the major used were three photographs of hands like his that were completely restored. I do not know where the doctor got them. I always understood we were the first to use the machines. The photographs did not make much difference to the major because he only looked out of the window.

THINKING ABOUT THE SELECTION

Recalling

1. (a) Where does the narrator go every afternoon? (b) Why does he go there?
2. (a) What do the papers reveal about how the narrator acquired his medals? (b) How do the boys' attitude toward the narrator change when they read the papers?
3. (a) What advice does the major give the narrator toward the end of the story? (b) What has happened to the major's wife?
4. (a) What pictures are hanging on the wall when the major returns? (b) Why does the narrator think the pictures are deceptive?

Interpreting

5. What mood do the details of the setting convey?
6. (a) How is the narrator's attitude toward the war different from that of the three boys? (b) How might this difference in attitude be related to their nationalities?
7. What do you think is the significance of the major's interest in grammar?
8. In this story the machines come to symbolize the false hopes and promises of the modern age. What details convey the symbolic meaning of the machines?
9. Considering that the major waited until he was invalided out of the war to marry his wife, what is ironic about her death?

Applying

10. Gertrude Stein wrote, "You are all a lost generation." This epigraph has come to stand for the young people of Hemingway's time. (a) In what way are the young men in this story "lost"? (b) Are there any ways in which they are not lost? Explain your answer.
11. Explain the two meanings suggested by the title of this story.
12. World War I left many people feeling disillusioned because it caused the death of thousands of men, though it seemed to have no purpose. How does this story reflect this sense of disillusionment?

ANALYZING LITERATURE
Understanding Modernism

Modernism was a literary movement in which writers attempted to capture the essence of modern life in both the form and content of their work. One of the themes of "In Another Country," for example, is that in the modern age people are often presented with false hopes and promises.

1. Like most other Modernist stories, "In Another Country" lacks an exposition and a resolution. What Modernist perception does the use of this technique reflect?
2. In this story the narrator makes no direct statements about the war, allowing us to draw our own conclusions. How does this reflect the Modernist belief in the uncertainty of modern life?

CRITICAL THINKING AND READING
Analyzing the Effect of Style

Hemingway's style is easily distinguished from that of most other writers. He wrote in journalistic style, relating events in a straightforward manner with little elaboration and using simple and direct yet rhythmic and precise language.

1. Considering the Modernists' desire to force readers to draw their own conclusions from their works, why is Hemingway's journalistic style appropriate?
2. The nineteenth-century poet Robert Browning wrote, "Less is more." This aphorism was picked up by the twentieth-century architect Ludwig Mies van der Rohe and came to stand for a style in which design was simplified and form was made to serve function. Explain how the aphorism "less is more" can be said to characterize Hemingway's writing style.

THINKING AND WRITING
Responding to a Statement

Hemingway once commented, ". . . I always try to write on the principle of the iceberg. There is seven-eighths of it under water for every part that shows." Write an essay relating this statement to "In Another Country." Start by reviewing the story, taking note of Hemingway's concise style and how he uses such techniques as symbolism and irony to convey meaning. Organize your notes into an outline. Then write your essay, using passages from the story to support Hemingway's statement. When you finish writing, revise your essay, making sure you have backed up your thesis with details from the story. Proofread your essay and share it with your classmates.

Primary Source

Hemingway created realistic characters. In *Death in the Afternoon* (1932), he discussed how to create people in fiction. "When writing a novel a writer should create living people; people not characters. A *character* is a caricature. . . . If the people the writer is making talk of old masters; of music; of modern painting; of letters; or of science then they should talk of those subjects in the novel. If they do not talk of those subjects and the writer makes them talk of them he is a faker, and if he talks about them himself to show how much he knows then he is showing off. No matter how good a phrase or simile he may have if he puts it in where it is not absolutely necessary and irreplaceable he is spoiling his work for egotism. Prose is architecture, not interior decoration. . . ."

In Another Country 669

Closure and Extension

ANSWERS TO THINKING ABOUT THE SELECTION
Recalling

1. (a) He goes to the hospital. (b) He goes for therapy for his leg.
2. (a) The papers reveal that the medals were awarded to him because he was an American. (b) They remain friendly but become more removed.
3. (a) The major advises the narrator not to marry. (b) She has died.
4. (a) There were photographs of wounds, before and after treatment. (b) He thinks they are deceptive, because he always understood that they were the first to use the machines.

Interpreting

5. The details of the setting convey a somber, melancholy mood.
6. (a) The narrator dislikes the war and is afraid to die; the boys were dedicated soldiers, who were proud of their accomplishments in the war. (b) The Italian boys were fighting for their country while the narrator was fighting in a foreign war.

7. Grammar is understandable because it follows set rules, while the war is difficult to understand and seemingly has no rules.
8. Suggested Response: The details include the photographs that supposedly demonstrate the machines' effectiveness, the narrator's comment that the machines "were to make so much difference," and his comment that they were the first to use the machines.
9. The major escaped death in the war but his wife, away from the dangers of war, died after a short illness.

Applying

10. (a) Suggested Response: They are removed from the war, although they have suffered from its effects. (b) Suggested Response: The Italian boys still possess a strong attachment to their country.
11. Suggested Response: The title refers to the fact that the narrator is in a foreign country and to the fact that all of the characters are removed from the war.
12. Suggested Response: The men are disillusioned about the machines, the major is disillusioned about his young wife's sudden death, some townspeople are disillusioned with the officers fighting for them.

ANSWERS TO ANALYZING LITERATURE

1. It reflects their perception of life as uncertain and confusing.
2. It creates a sense of uncertainty concerning the story's meaning that mirrors the Modernist belief that life in general is uncertain and confusing.

ANSWERS TO CRITICAL THINKING AND READING

1. It is appropriate because it omits explanations and interpretations.
2. Hemingway's writing style is spare.

THINKING AND WRITING

For extra credit, have students write a narrative in which they model their own writing after Hemingway's style.

669

More About the Author The times that F. Scott Fitzgerald wrote about, the 1920's, were known as "the Roaring Twenties" or the "Jazz Age." After the stock market collapse in 1929, the Jazz Age ended abruptly and the hard times of the Depression began. Fitzgerald continued to write about the Jazz Age, but readers were no longer receptive to his work. Why do you think that the onset of the Depression might have affected the public's receptiveness to Fitzgerald's writing?

Critical Evaluation In his book, *The Short Story in America: 1900–1950,* Ray B. West, Jr. characterized Fitzgerald's short stories as follows: "Of the non-Southern writers, with the exception of Hemingway, F. Scott Fitzgerald is undoubtedly the most significant writer of short stories. . . . His short stories at their best . . . are studies in manners reflecting a sensitivity to social distinctions —particularly the differences engendered by extreme wealth . . . Unfortunately, Fitzgerald's total production of short stories is marred by hack work, necessitated by his own inordinate need for money. He once wrote a story in a single night, "The Camel's Back." "The Popular Girl," written in a week, brought him fifteen hundred dollars. His best work, however, caught not only the irresponsibility of the years following the first war (World War I) but pointed also to the sources of personal and moral corruption implicit in a society based upon the social and moral prerogatives of wealth."

F. SCOTT FITZGERALD

1896–1940

During the 1920's many Americans lived with reckless abandon, attending wild parties, wearing glamorous clothing, and striving for personal fulfillment through material wealth. Yet this quest for pleasure was often accompanied by a sense of inner despair. In his short stories and novels, F. Scott Fitzgerald captured both the gaiety and the emptiness of the time.

Francis Scott Key Fitzgerald was born in St. Paul, Minnesota, into a family with high social aspirations but little wealth. He entered Princeton University in 1913. Being a romantic young man, he threw himself into the social life at Princeton, living the kind of life for which he became famous in the 1920's. He failed to graduate, and in 1917 he enlisted in the army. He was stationed in Montgomery, Alabama, where he fell in love with Zelda Sayre, a young southern belle. Shortly after being discharged from the army, Fitzgerald published his first novel, *This Side of Paradise* (1920). The novel earned him instant fame and wealth, which enabled him to persuade Zelda to marry him.

The Fitzgeralds soon became a part of the wealthy, extravagant, and hedonistic society that characterized the Roaring Twenties. Spending time in both New York and Europe, the glamorous couple mingled with rich and famous artists and aristocrats, attending countless parties and spending money recklessly. Despite his wild lifestyle, Fitzgerald remained a productive writer. During the twenties he published dozens of short stories and his most successful novel, *The Great Gatsby* (1926), the story of a self-made man whose dreams of love and social acceptance lead to scandal and corruption and ultimately end in tragedy. The novel displayed Fitzgerald's fascination with and growing distrust of the wealthy society he had embraced.

Following the stock market crash in 1929, Fitzgerald's life changed dramatically. His wife suffered a series of nervous breakdowns, his reputation as a writer declined, and financial difficulties forced him to seek work as a Hollywood screenwriter. Despite these setbacks, however, he managed to produce many more short stories and a second fine novel, *Tender Is the Night* (1934). Focusing on the decline of a young American psychiatrist following his marriage to a wealthy patient, the novel reflected Fitzgerald's awareness of the tragedy that can result from an obsession with wealth and social status.

Fitzgerald died of a heart attack in 1940. At the time he was in the midst of writing *The Last Tycoon* (1941), a novel about a Hollywood film mogul.

670   *The Modern Age*

Objectives

1 To understand characterization
2 To evaluate a character's behavior
3 To write about historical context

Support Material

Teaching Portfolio
Teacher Backup, p. 871
Grammar in Action Worksheets, *Using Dashes,* p. 876; *Recognizing Adverb Clauses,* p. 878; *Varying Sentence Length,* p. 880.
Usage and Mechanics Worksheet, p. 882
Vocabulary Check, p. 883

Analyzing Literature Worksheet, *Understanding Characterization,* p. 885

GUIDE FOR INTERPRETING

Winter Dreams

The Writer's Techniques

Characterization. Characterization is the means by which a writer reveals a character's personality. Writers generally develop a character through one or more of the following methods: direct statements about the character, physical descriptions of the character, the character's actions, the character's thoughts and comments, or another character's reactions to or comments about the character. In "Winter Dreams" F. Scott Fitzgerald develops the two main characters using a variety of these methods. For example, he reveals an important aspect of Dexter Green's personality directly, when he comments that Dexter "wanted not association with glittering things and glittering people—he wanted the glittering things themselves."

Commentary

Written in 1922, "Winter Dreams" unfolds against the background of the Jazz Age. The glamour that Dexter Green associates with Judy Jones is connected to her wealth and status. In this story Fitzgerald explores the connections between love and money through Green's obsession with Judy Jones. Focusing on Green's thoughts and feelings, Fitzgerald emphasizes how it feels to be this ambitious young man in the glittering society of the 1920's, who wanted "glittering things": money and Judy Jones. Caught up in the force of his love for Judy, Green idealizes her. In reality she is selfish, arrogant, erratic. But in Green's romanticized vision, she is exhilarating and completely desirable.

But Fitzgerald wants to create sympathy for these two characters, despite their destructive fantasies and values. He explores what critic Lionel Trilling called "the power of love." According to Trilling Fitzgerald was "the last notable writer to affirm the Romantic fantasy"—the nobility of giving your all for a romantic ideal, no matter what. We can criticize Green for being attracted to glamour and for wanting to be rich and to get the richest girl in town, but Fitzgerald also wants us to be a little in awe of Green's devotion, which comes at the cost of his own happiness. This sacrifice to a dream—no matter how illusory—characterizes many of Fitzgerald's heroes. Do people still make sacrifices for romantic ideals?

Writing

In Don Marquis's poem "Unjust," Archy the cockroach writes, "beauty gets the best of it/in this world." Freewrite, exploring your reaction to Archy's comment.

Literary Focus Point out that characterization is usually one of the most important elements of a short story. For most short stories to be effective, the writer must create well-developed characters with whom the readers can sympathize.

Writing/Prior Knowledge Before your students complete the writing activity, you might want to discuss the concept of beauty.

Vocabulary

Preteach the following vocabulary words:
fallowness (fal′ ō nis) *n.:* Inactivity (p. 672)
preposterous (pri päs′ tər əs) *adj.:* Ridiculous (p. 674)
ominous (äm′ə nəs) *adj.:* Threatening; sinister (p. 674)
fortuitous (fôr tōō′ə təs) *adj.:* Fortunate (p. 674)
perturbation (pʉr′ tər bā′ shən) *n.:* Agitation (p. 674)
sinuous (sin′ yōō wəs) *adj.:* Wavy (p. 677)
mundane (mun dān′) *adj.:* Commonplace; ordinary (p. 678)
poignant (poin′ yənt) *adj.:* Sharply painful to the feelings (p. 682)
pugilistic (pyōō′ jə lis′ tik) *adj.:* Like a boxer (p. 683)
somnolent (säm′ nə lənt) *adj.:* Sleepy; drowsy (p. 683)

Guide for Interpreting 671

Winter Dreams

F. Scott Fitzgerald

I

Some of the caddies were poor as sin and lived in one-room houses with a neurasthenic[1] cow in the front yard, but Dexter Green's father owned the second best grocery store in Black Bear—the best one was "The Hub," patronized by the wealthy people from Sherry Island—and Dexter caddied only for pocket money.

In the fall when the days became crisp and gray, and the long Minnesota winter shut down like the white lid of a box, Dexter's skis moved over the snow that hid the fairways of the golf course. At these times the country gave him a feeling of profound melancholy—it offended him that the links should lie in enforced fallowness, haunted by ragged sparrows for the long season. It was dreary, too, that on the tees where the gay colors fluttered in summer there were now only the desolate sandboxes knee deep in crusted ice. When he crossed the hills the wind blew cold as misery, and if the sun was out he tramped with his eyes squinted up against the hard dimensionless glare.

In April the winter ceased abruptly. The snow ran down into Black Bear Lake scarcely tarrying for the early golfers to brave the season with red and black balls. Without elation, without an interval of moist glory, the cold was gone.

Dexter knew that there was something dismal about this Northern spring, just as he knew there was something gorgeous about the fall. Fall made him clinch his hands and tremble and repeat idiotic sentences to himself, and make brisk abrupt gestures of command to imaginary audiences and armies. October filled him with hope which November raised to a sort of ecstatic triumph, and in this mood the fleeting brilliant impressions of the summer at Sherry Island were ready grist to his mill. He became a golf champion and defeated Mr. T. A. Hedrick in a marvelous match played a hundred times over the fairways of his imagination, a match each detail of which he changed about untiringly—sometimes he won with almost laughable ease, sometimes he came up magnificently from behind. Again, stepping from a Pierce-Arrow automobile, like Mr. Mortimer Jones, he strolled frigidly into the lounge of the Sherry Island Golf Club—or perhaps, surrounded by an admiring crowd, he gave an exhibition of fancy diving from the springboard of the club raft. . . . Among those who watched him in open-mouthed wonder was Mr. Mortimer Jones.

And one day it came to pass that Mr. Jones—himself and not his ghost—came up to Dexter with tears in his eyes and said that Dexter was the —— best caddy in the club, and wouldn't he decide not to quit if Mr. Jones made it worth his while, because every other —— caddy in the club lost one ball a hole for him—regularly——

"No, sir," said Dexter decisively, "I don't want to caddy any more." Then, after a pause: "I'm too old."

"You're not more than fourteen. Why the devil did you decide just this morning that

---

1. **neurasthenic** (noor' əs then' ik) *adj.*: Here, weak, tired.

FLOATING ICE, 1910
George Bellows
Collection of the Whitney Museum of American Art

you wanted to quit? You promised that next week you'd go over to the state tournament with me."

"I decided I was too old."

Dexter handed in his "A Class" badge, collected what money was due him from the caddy master, and walked home to Black Bear Village.

"The best —— caddy I ever saw," shouted Mr. Mortimer Jones over a drink that afternoon. "Never lost a ball! Willing! Intelligent! Quiet! Honest! Grateful!"

3 The little girl who had done this was eleven—beautifully ugly as little girls are apt to be who are destined after a few years to be inexpressibly lovely and bring no end of misery to a great number of men. The spark, however, was perceptible. There was a general ungodliness in the way her lips twisted down at the corners when she smiled, and in the—Heaven help us!—in the almost passionate quality of her eyes. Vitality is born early in such women. It was utterly in evidence now, shining through her thin frame in a sort of glow.

She had come eagerly out on to the course at nine o'clock with a white linen nurse and five small new golf clubs in a white canvas bag which the nurse was carrying. When Dexter first saw her she was standing by the caddy house, rather ill at ease and trying to conceal the fact by engaging her nurse in an obviously unnatural conversation graced by startling and irrelevant grimaces from herself.

"Well, it's certainly a nice day, Hilda," Dexter heard her say. She drew down the corners of her mouth, smiled, and glanced furtively around, her eyes in transit falling for an instant on Dexter.

4

Winter Dreams 673

Humanities Note

Fine art, *Floating Ice,* 1910, by George Bellows. Bellows (1882–1925) was born in Columbus, Ohio. He studied at the New York School of Art in 1904 and taught at the Art Students League. The influence of Robert Henri, with whom he had studied at the New York School of Art, was evident in this early work. Henri and Bellows were both associated with the Ashcan School, a group of American realist painters active from about 1908 until World War I.

In *Floating Ice* Bellows reveals a sensitivity to the scenic beauty that can exist in an urban setting. His rich use of color produces an image of cold, raw beauty. The painterly quality of this picture involves the viewer in the infinite textures, movement, and changes in such a scene. What might have been a picture with no focal point, becomes a totally absorbing experience.

You might use these questions for discussion:

1. What art elements has the artist used in this painting to express cold?
2. How has the artist suggested motion?

5 **Discussion** The nurse is a very minor character in this story. Even so, the reader gets to know her. Ask the students what they learn about her in this passage.

6 **Literary Focus** What does this comment reveal about the girl's personality?

7 **Enrichment** Dexter's winter dreams are much like Fitzgerald's own dreams. As Malcolm Cowley, the noted literary critic, said, "[Fitzgerald] acted out his dreams with an extraordinary intensity of emotion."

Then to the nurse:

"Well, I guess there aren't very many people out here this morning, are there?"

The smile again—radiant, blatantly artificial—convincing.

"I don't know what we're supposed to do now," said the nurse looking nowhere in particular.

"Oh, that's all right. I'll fix it up."

Dexter stood perfectly still, his mouth slightly ajar. He knew that if he moved forward a step his stare would be in her line of vision—if he moved backward he would lose his full view of her face. For a moment he had not realized how young she was. Now he remembered having seen her several times the year before—in bloomers.

Suddenly, involuntarily, he laughed, a short abrupt laugh—then, startled by himself, he turned and began to walk quickly away.

"Boy!"

Dexter stopped.

"Boy——"

Beyond question he was addressed. Not only that, but he was treated to that absurd smile, that preposterous smile—the memory of which at least a dozen men were to carry into middle age.

"Boy, do you know where the golf teacher is?"

"He's giving a lesson."

"Well, do you know where the caddy master is?"

"He isn't here yet this morning."

"Oh." For a moment this baffled her. She stood alternately on her right and left foot.

"We'd like to get a caddy," said the nurse. "Mrs. Mortimer Jones sent us out to play golf, and we don't know how without we get a caddy."

Here she was stopped by an ominous glance from Miss Jones, followed immediately by the smile.

"There aren't any caddies here except me," said Dexter to the nurse, "and I got to stay here in charge until the caddy master gets here."

"Oh."

Miss Jones and her retinue now withdrew, and at a proper distance from Dexter became involved in a heated conversation, which was concluded by Miss Jones taking one of the clubs and hitting it on the ground with violence. For further emphasis she raised it again and was about to bring it down smartly upon the nurse's bosom, when the nurse seized the club and twisted it from her hands.

"You little mean old *thing!*" cried Miss Jones wildly.

Another argument ensued. Realizing that the elements of the comedy were implied in the scene, Dexter several times began to laugh, but each time restrained the laugh before it reached audibility. He could not resist the monstrous conviction that the little girl was justified in beating the nurse.

The situation was resolved by the fortuitous appearance of the caddy master, who was appealed to immediately by the nurse.

"Miss Jones is to have a little caddy, and this one says he can't go."

"Mr. McKenna said I was to wait here till you came," said Dexter quickly.

"Well, he's here now." Miss Jones smiled cheerfully at the caddy master. Then she dropped her bag and set off at a haughty mince toward the first tee.

"Well?" The caddy master turned to Dexter. "What you standing there like a dummy for? Go pick up the young lady's clubs."

"I don't think I'll go out today," said Dexter.

"You don't——"

"I think I'll quit."

The enormity of his decision frightened him. He was a favorite caddy, and the thirty dollars a month he earned through the summer were not to be made elsewhere around the lake. But he had received a strong emotional shock, and his perturbation required a violent and immediate outlet.

It is not so simple as that, either. As so frequently would be the case in the future, Dexter was unconsciously dictated to by his winter dreams.

Grammar in Action

The dash is a useful punctuation mark that can serve several different functions. Dashes can be used to set off a nonessential appositive, an interrupting idea, or a long or dramatic parenthetical expression. Here are examples of each use from Fitzgerald's story:

Appositive: When he was twenty-three Mr. Hart—one of the gray-haired men who liked to say "Now there's a boy"—gave him a guest card to the Sherry Island Gold Club for a weekend.

Interrupting Idea: There was a general ungodliness in the way her lips twisted down at the corners when she smiled, and in the—Heaven help us!—in the almost passionate quality of her eyes.

Parenthetical Expression: He remembered the last time he had seen her father, and he was glad the parents were not to be here tonight—they might wonder who he was.

Student Activity 1. Describe the function of dashes in each of the following sentences.

II

Now, of course, the quality and the seasonability of these winter dreams varied, but the stuff of them remained. They persuaded Dexter several years later to pass up a business course at the State university—his father, prospering now, would have paid his way—for the precarious advantage of attending an older and more famous university in the East, where he was bothered by his scanty funds. But do not get the impression, because his winter dreams happened to be concerned at first with musings on the rich, that there was anything merely snobbish in the boy. He wanted not association with glittering things and glittering people—he wanted the glittering things themselves. Often he reached out for the best without knowing why he wanted it—and sometimes he ran up against the mysterious denials and prohibitions in which life indulges. It is with one of those denials and not with his career as a whole that this story deals.

He made money. It was rather amazing. After college he went to the city from which Black Bear Lake draws its wealthy patrons. When he was only twenty-three and had been there not quite two years, there were already people who liked to say: "Now *there's* a boy—" All about him rich men's sons were peddling bonds precariously, or investing patrimonies precariously, or plodding through the two dozen volumes of the "George Washington Commercial Course," but Dexter borrowed a thousand dollars on his college degree and his confident mouth, and bought a partnership in a laundry.

It was a small laundry when he went into it, but Dexter made a specialty of learning how the English washed fine woolen golf stockings without shrinking them, and within a year he was catering to the trade that wore knickerbockers. Men were insisting that their Shetland hose and sweaters go to his laundry, just as they had insisted on a caddy who could find golf balls. A little later he was doing their wives' lingerie as well—and running five branches in different parts of the city. Before he was twenty-seven he owned the largest string of laundries in his section of the country. It was then that he sold out and went to New York. But the part of his story that concerns us goes back to the days when he was making his first big success.

When he was twenty-three Mr. Hart—one of the gray-haired men who like to say "Now there's a boy"—gave him a guest card to the Sherry Island Golf Club for a weekend. So he signed his name one day on the register, and that afternoon played golf in a foursome with Mr. Hart and Mr. Sandwood and Mr. T. A. Hedrick. He did not consider it necessary to remark that he had once carried Mr. Hart's bag over this same links, and that he knew every trap and gully with his eyes shut—but he found himself glancing at the four caddies who trailed them, trying to catch a gleam or gesture that would remind him of himself, that would lessen the gap which lay between his present and his past.

It was a curious day, slashed abruptly with fleeting, familiar impressions. One minute he had the sense of being a trespasser—in the next he was impressed by the tremendous superiority he felt toward Mr. T. A. Hedrick, who was a bore and not even a good golfer any more.

Then, because of a ball Mr. Hart lost near the fifteenth green, an enormous thing happened. While they were searching the stiff grasses of the rough there was a clear call of "Fore!" from behind a hill in their rear. And as they all turned abruptly from their search a bright new ball sliced abruptly over the hill and caught Mr. T. A. Hedrick in the abdomen.

"By Gad!" cried Mr. T. A. Hedrick, "they ought to put some of these crazy women off the course. It's getting to be outrageous."

A head and a voice came up together over the hill:

"Do you mind if we go through?"

"You hit me in the stomach!" declared Mr. Hedrick wildly.

"Did I?" The girl approached the group of men. "I'm sorry. I yelled 'Fore!' "

Winter Dreams 675

8 **Reading Strategy** Ask the students what "enormous thing" they think might happen.

8

1. But he was beginning to be master of his own time now, and he had a rather priggish notion that he—the young and already fabulously successful Dexter Green—should know more about such things.
2. He knew the sort of men they were—the men who when he first went to college had entered from the great prep schools with graceful clothes and the deep tan of healthy summers.
3. When a new man came to town everyone dropped out—dates were automatically cancelled.
4. She had done everything to him except to criticize him—this she had not done—it seemed to him only because it might have sullied the utter indifference she manifested and sincerely felt toward him.
5. It gave him a sense of solidity to go with her—she was so sturdily popular, so intensely "great."

Student Activity 2. Write five sentences of your own in which you use the dash. Two of your sentences should include dashes used to set off an appositive; two should include dashes used to set off parenthetical expressions; and one should include dashes used to set off an interrupting idea.

Her glance fell casually on each of the men—then scanned the fairway for her ball.

"Did I bounce into the rough?"

9 It was impossible to determine whether this question was ingenuous or malicious. In a moment, however, she left no doubt, for as her partner came up over the hill she called cheerfully:

"Here I am! I'd have gone on the green except that I hit something."

As she took her stance for a short mashie shot, Dexter looked at her closely. She wore a blue gingham dress, rimmed at throat and shoulders with a white edging that accentuated her tan. The quality of exaggeration, of thinness, which had made her passionate eyes and down-turning mouth absurd at eleven, was gone now. She was arrestingly beautiful. The color in her cheeks was centered like the color in a picture—it was not a "high" color, but a sort of fluctuating and feverish warmth, so shaded that it seemed at any moment it would recede and disappear. This color and the mobility of her mouth gave a continual impression of flux, of intense life, of passionate vitality—balanced only partially by the sad luxury of her eyes.

She swung her mashie impatiently and without interest, pitching the ball into a sand pit on the other side of the green. With a quick, insincere smile and a careless "Thank you!" she went on after it.

"That Judy Jones!" remarked Mr. Hedrick on the next tee, as they waited—some

10 moments—for her to play on ahead. "All she needs is to be turned up and spanked for six months and then to be married off to an old-fashioned cavalry captain."

"My God, she's good looking!" said Mr. Sandwood, who was just over thirty.

"Good looking!" cried Mr. Hedrick contemptuously, "she always looks as if she wanted to be kissed! Turning those big cow-eyes on every calf in town!"

It was doubtful if Mr. Hedrick intended a reference to the maternal instinct.

"She'd play pretty good golf if she'd try," said Mr. Sandwood.

676   *The Modern Age*

"She has no form," said Mr. Hedrick solemnly.

"She has a nice figure," said Mr. Sandwood.

"Better thank the Lord she doesn't drive a swifter ball," said Mr. Hart, winking at Dexter.

11 Later in the afternoon the sun went down with a riotous swirl of gold and varying blues and scarlets, and left the dry, rustling night of Western summer. Dexter watched from the veranda of the golf club, watched the even overlap of the waters in the little wind, silver molasses under the harvest moon. Then the moon held a finger to her lips and the lake became a clear pool, pale and quiet. Dexter put on his bathing suit and swam out to the farthest raft, where he stretched dripping on the wet canvas of the springboard.

There was a fish jumping and a star shining and the lights around the lake were gleaming. Over on a dark peninsula a piano was playing the songs of last summer and of summers before that—songs from *Chin-Chin* and *The Count of Luxemburg* and *The Chocolate Soldier*[2]—and because the sound of a piano over a stretch of water had always seemed beautiful to Dexter he lay perfectly quiet and listened.

The tune the piano was playing at that moment had been gay and new five years before when Dexter was a sophomore at college. They had played it at a prom once when he could not afford the luxury of proms, and he had stood outside the gymnasium and listened. The sound of the tune precipitated in him a sort of ecstasy and it was with that ecstasy he viewed what happened to him now. It was a mood of intense appreciation, a sense that, for once, he was magnificently attuned to life and that everything about him was radiating a brightness and a glamor he might never know again.

A low, pale oblong detached itself suddenly from the darkness of the Island, spit-

2. Chin-Chin . . . The Chocolate Soldier: Popular operettas of the time.

ting forth the reverberate sound of a racing motorboat. Two white streamers of cleft water rolled themselves out behind it and almost immediately the boat was beside him, drowning out the hot tinkle of the piano in the drone of its spray. Dexter raising himself on his arms was aware of a figure standing at the wheel, of two dark eyes regarding him over the lengthening space of water—then the boat had gone by and was sweeping in an immense and purposeless circle of spray round and round in the middle of the lake. With equal eccentricity one of the circles flattened out and headed back toward the raft.

"Who's that?" she called, shutting off her motor. She was so near now that Dexter could see her bathing suit, which consisted apparently of pink rompers.

The nose of the boat bumped the raft, and as the latter tilted rakishly he was precipitated toward her. With different degrees of interest they recognized each other.

"Aren't you one of those men we played through this afternoon?" she demanded.

He was.

"Well, do you know how to drive a motorboat? Because if you do I wish you'd drive this one so I can ride on the surfboard behind. My name is Judy Jones"—she favored him with an absurd smirk—rather, what tried to be a smirk, for, twist her mouth as she might, it was not grotesque, it was merely beautiful—"and I live in a house over there on the Island, and in that house there is a man waiting for me. When he drove up at the door I drove out of the dock because he says I'm his ideal."

There was a fish jumping and a star shining and the lights around the lake were gleaming. Dexter sat beside Judy Jones and she explained how her boat was driven. Then she was in the water, swimming to the floating surfboard with a sinuous crawl. Watching her was without effort to the eye, watching a branch waving or a sea gull flying. Her arms, burned to butternut, moved sinuously among the dull platinum ripples, elbow appearing first, casting the forearm

back with a cadence of falling water, then reaching out and down, stabbing a path ahead.

They moved out into the lake; turning, Dexter saw that she was kneeling on the low rear of the now uptilted surfboard.

"Go faster," she called, "fast as it'll go."

Obediently he jammed the lever forward and the white spray mounted at the bow. When he looked around again the girl was standing up on the rushing board, her arms spread wide, her eyes lifted toward the moon.

"It's awful cold," she shouted. "What's your name?"

He told her.

"Well, why don't you come to dinner tomorrow night?"

His heart turned over like the flywheel of the boat, and, for the second time, her casual whim gave a new direction to his life.

III

Next evening while he waited for her to come downstairs, Dexter peopled the soft deep summer room and the sun porch that opened from it with the men who had already loved Judy Jones. He knew the sort of men they were—the men who when he first went to college had entered from the great prep schools with graceful clothes and the deep tan of healthy summers. He had seen that, in one sense, he was better than these men. He was newer and stronger. Yet in acknowledging to himself that he wished his children to be like them he was admitting that he was but the rough, strong stuff from which they eternally sprang.

When the time had come for him to wear good clothes, he had known who were the best tailors in America, and the best tailors in America had made him the suit he wore this evening. He had acquired that particular reserve peculiar to his university, that set it off from other universities. He recognized the value to him of such a mannerism and he had adopted it; he knew that to be careless in dress and manner required more con-

12 Reading Strategy Once again, you can ask your students to predict what will happen next. Who is the "figure standing at the wheel"?

13 Literary Focus What does this remark tell the reader about Judy Jones? By now, your students should feel they know the young woman fairly well.

14 Literary Focus What does this conversation reveal about the personalities of Dexter and Judy? Do Judy's comments seem genuine? Why or why not?

fidence than to be careful. But carelessness was for his children. His mother's name had been Krimelich. She was a Bohemian of the peasant class and she had talked broken English to the end of her days. Her son must keep to the set patterns.

At a little after seven Judy Jones came downstairs. She wore a blue silk afternoon dress, and he was disappointed at first that she had not put on something more elaborate. This feeling was accentuated when, after a brief greeting, she went to the door of a butler's pantry and pushing it open called: "You can serve dinner, Martha." He had rather expected that a butler would announce dinner, that there would be a cocktail. Then he put these thoughts behind him as they sat down side by side on a lounge and looked at each other.

"Father and mother won't be here," she said thoughtfully.

He remembered the last time he had seen her father, and he was glad the parents were not to be here tonight—they might wonder who he was. He had been born in Keeble, a Minnesota village fifty miles farther north, and he always gave Keeble as his home instead of Black Bear Village. Country towns were well enough to come from if they weren't inconveniently in sight and used as footstools by fashionable lakes.

They talked of his university, which she had visited frequently during the past two years, and of the nearby city which supplied Sherry Island with its patrons, and whither Dexter would return next day to his prospering laundries.

During dinner she slipped into a moody depression which gave Dexter a feeling of uneasiness. Whatever petulance she uttered in her throaty voice worried him. Whatever she smiled at—at him, at a chicken liver, at nothing—it disturbed him that her smile could have no root in mirth, or even in amusement. When the scarlet corners of her lips curved down, it was less a smile than an invitation to a kiss.

Then, after dinner, she led him out on the dark sun porch and deliberately changed the atmosphere.

"Do you mind if I weep a little?" she said.

"I'm afraid I'm boring you," he responded quickly.

"You're not. I like you. But I've just had a terrible afternoon. There was a man I cared about, and this afternoon he told me out of a clear sky that he was poor as a church mouse. He'd never even hinted it before. Does this sound horribly mundane?"

"Perhaps he was afraid to tell you."

"Suppose he was," she answered. "He didn't start right. You see, if I'd thought of him as poor—well, I've been mad about loads of poor men, and fully intended to marry them all. But in this case, I hadn't thought of him that way, and my interest in him wasn't strong enough to survive the shock. As if a girl calmly informed her fiancé that she was a widow. He might not object to widows, but——"

"Let's start right," she interrupted herself suddenly. "Who are you, anyhow?"

For a moment Dexter hesitated. Then:

"I'm nobody," he announced. "My career is largely a matter of futures."

"Are you poor?"

"No," he said frankly, "I'm probably making more money than any man my age in the Northwest. I know that's an obnoxious remark, but you advised me to start right."

There was a pause. Then she smiled and the corners of her mouth drooped and an almost imperceptible sway brought her closer to him, looking up into his eyes. A lump rose in Dexter's throat, and he waited breathless for the experiment, facing the unpredictable compound that would form mysteriously from the elements of their lips. Then he saw—she communicated her excitement to him, lavishly, deeply, with kisses that were not a promise but a fulfillment. They aroused in him not hunger demanding renewal but surfeit that would demand more surfeit . . . kisses that were like charity, creating want by holding back nothing at all.

It did not take him many hours to decide

Grammar in Action

Adverb clauses are subordinate clauses that modify verbs, adjectives, or adverbs. Adverbs clauses are introduced by subordinating conjunctions, such as *when, because, where,* or *if.* Note how Fitzgerald uses adverb clauses to insert material of secondary importance into the following sentences:

When he crossed the hills, the wind blew cold. . . .

She was so near . . . *that Dexter could see her bathing suit.* . . .

Student Activity 1. Identify the adverb clauses in the following sentences.

1. Then he put these thoughts behind him as they sat down side by side on a lounge and looked at each other.
2. When the corners of her mouth turned down, it was less a smile than an invitation to a kiss.
3. He had wanted Judy Jones ever since he was a proud, desirous little boy.
4. He was, as he found before the summer ended, one of a varying dozen who circulated about her.

that he had wanted Judy Jones ever since he was a proud, desirous little boy.

IV

It began like that—and continued, with varying shades of intensity, on such a note right up to the dénouement. Dexter surrendered a part of himself to the most direct and unprincipled personality with which he had ever come in contact. Whatever Judy wanted, she went after with the full pressure of her charm. There was no divergence of method, no jockeying for position or premeditation of effects—there was a very little mental side to any of her affairs. She simply made men conscious to the highest degree of her physical loveliness. Dexter had no desire to change her. Her deficiencies were knit up with a passionate energy that transcended and justified them.

When, as Judy's head lay against his shoulder that first night, she whispered, "I don't know what's the matter with me. Last night I thought I was in love with a man and tonight I think I'm in love with you——" it seemed to him a beautiful and romantic thing to say. It was the exquisite excitability that for the moment he controlled and owned. But a week later he was compelled to view this same quality in a different light. She took him in her roadster to a picnic supper, and after supper she disappeared, likewise in her roadster, with another man. Dexter became enormously upset and was scarcely able to be decently civil to the other people present. When she assured him that she had not kissed the other man, he knew she was lying—yet he was glad that she had taken the trouble to lie to him.

He was, as he found before the summer ended, one of a varying dozen who circulated about her. Each of them had at one time been favored above all others—about half of them still basked in the solace of occasional sentimental revivals. Whenever one showed signs of dropping out through long neglect, she granted him a brief honeyed hour, which encouraged him to tag along for a year or so longer. Judy made these forays upon the helpless and defeated without malice, indeed half unconscious that there was anything mischievous in what she did.

When a new man came to town everyone dropped out—dates were automatically canceled.

The helpless part of trying to do anything about it was that she did it all herself. She was not a girl who could be "won" in the kinetic sense—she was proof against cleverness, she was proof against charm; if any of these assailed her too strongly she would immediately resolve the affair to a physical basis, and under the magic of her physical splendor the strong as well as the brilliant played her game and not their own. She was entertained only by the gratification of her desires and by the direct exercise of her own charm. Perhaps from so much youthful love, so many youthful lovers, she had come, in self-defense, to nourish herself wholly from within.

Succeeding Dexter's first exhilaration came restlessness and dissatisfaction. The helpless ecstasy of losing himself in her was opiate rather than tonic. It was fortunate for his work during the winter that those moments of ecstasy came infrequently. Early in their acquaintance it had seemed for a while that there was a deep and spontaneous mutual attraction—that first August, for example—three days of long evenings on her dusky veranda, of strange wan kisses through the late afternoon, in shadowy alcoves or behind the protecting trellises of the garden arbors, of mornings when she was fresh as a dream and almost shy at meeting him in the clarity of the rising day. There was all the ecstasy of an engagement about it, sharpened by his realization that there was no engagement. It was during those three days that, for the first time, he had asked her to marry him. She said "maybe some day," she said "kiss me," she said, "I'd like to marry you," she said "I love you"—she said—nothing.

Winter Dreams 679

15 Discussion What is the significance of the fact that Dexter does not mind that Judy lies to him?

16 Clarification Ask your **more advanced** students what they think Fitzgerald means by the "kinetic sense." If they have studied physical science, they may remember that kinetic energy is the energy of motion. Perhaps they will conclude that Fitzgerald means Judy cannot be won actively or dynamically.

5. If any of these assailed her too strongly, she would immediately resolve the affair to a physical basis.

Student Activity 2. Complete the adverb clauses in the following sentences. Be sure you add a complete clause with a subject and a verb.
1. Dexter quit his job caddying because . . .
2. He had made a great deal of money by the time . . .
3. He broke his engagement with Irene although . . .
4. Judy tired of him within a month, just as . . .
5. A man named Devlin brought Dexter news of Judy when. . . .

Student Activity 3. Add independent clauses to the following adverb clauses.
1. When Dexter was a teenager, . . .
2. Later, when he had become a successful businessman, . . .
3. . . . although he knew that she was unfaithful.
4. Because Judy asked him to marry her, . . .
5. . . . as he listened to Devlin describe Judy.

Reading Strategy Although awkwardly constructed, this sentence is important. In fact, it is so important that the narrator tells the reader to remember it. Tell your students to keep it in mind as they finish reading the story.

The three days were interrupted by the arrival of a New York man who visited at her house for half September. To Dexter's agony, rumor engaged them. The man was the son of the president of a great trust company. But at the end of a month it was reported that Judy was yawning. At a dance one night she sat all evening in a motorboat with a local beau, while the New Yorker searched the club for her frantically. She told the local beau that she was bored with her visitor, and two days later he left. She was seen with him at the station, and it was reported that he looked very mournful indeed.

On this note the summer ended. Dexter was twenty-four, and he found himself increasingly in a position to do as he wished. He joined two clubs in the city and lived at one of them. Though he was by no means an integral part of the stag lines at these clubs, he managed to be on hand at dances where Judy Jones was likely to appear. He could have gone out socially as much as he liked—he was an eligible young man, now, and popular with downtown fathers. His confessed devotion to Judy Jones had rather solidified his position. But he had no social aspirations and rather despised the dancing men who were always on tap for the Thursday or Saturday parties and who filled in at dinners with the younger married set. Already he was playing with the idea of going East to New York. He wanted to take Judy Jones with him. No disillusion as to the world in **17** which she had grown up could cure his illusion as to her desirability.

Remember that—for only in the light of it can what he did for her be understood.

Eighteen months after he first met Judy Jones he became engaged to another girl. Her name was Irene Scheerer, and her father was one of the men who had always believed in Dexter. Irene was light-haired and sweet and honorable, and a little stout, and she had two suitors whom she pleasantly relinquished when Dexter formally asked her to marry him.

Summer, fall, winter, spring, another summer, another fall—so much he had given of his active life to the incorrigible lips of Judy Jones. She had treated him with interest, with encouragement, with malice, with indifference, with contempt. She had inflicted on him the innumerable little slights and indignities possible in such a case—as if in revenge for having ever cared for him at all. She had beckoned him and yawned at him and beckoned him again and he had responded often with bitterness and narrowed eyes. She had brought him ecstatic happiness and intolerable agony of spirit. She had caused him untold inconvenience and not a little trouble. She had insulted him, and she had ridden over him, and she had played his interest in her against his interest in his work—for fun. She had done everything to him except to criticize him—this she had not done—it seemed to him only because it might have sullied the utter indifference she manifested and sincerely felt toward him.

When autumn had come and gone again it occurred to him that he could not have Judy Jones. He had to beat this into his mind but he convinced himself at last. He lay awake at night for a while and argued it over. He told himself the trouble and the pain she had caused him, he enumerated her glaring deficiencies as a wife. Then he said to himself that he loved her, and after a while he fell asleep. For a week, lest he imagined her husky voice over the telephone or her eyes opposite him at lunch, he worked hard and late, and at night he went to his office and plotted out his years.

At the end of a week he went to a dance and cut in on her once. For almost the first time since they had met he did not ask her to sit out with him or tell her that she was lovely. It hurt him that she did not miss these things—that was all. He was not jealous when he saw that there was a new man tonight. He had been hardened against jealousy long before.

He stayed late at the dance. He sat for an hour with Irene Scheerer and talked about books and about music. He knew very little about either. But he was beginning to be master of his own time now, and he had a

Grammar in Action

Good writers **vary** their **sentence lengths** to create a rhythm and make their writing more energetic and interesting. For example, note the varying lengths of the sentences in the following passage from "Winter Dreams":

He stayed late at the dance. He sat for an hour with Irene Sheerer and talked about books and about music. He knew very little about either. But he was beginning to be master of his own time now, and he had a rather priggish notion that he—the young and already fabulously successful Dexter Green—should know more about such things.

Student Activity 1. Rewrite the following paragraph from "Winter Dreams," expanding or combining the short sentences and shortening the long sentences, so that all of the sentences are approximately the same length. Then explain why the revised paragraph is less effective than the original.

The dream was gone. Something had been taken from him. In a sort of panic he pushed the palms of his hands into his eyes and tried to bring up a picture of the waters lapping on Sherry Island and the moonlit veranda, and gingham on the golf links and the dry sun and the gold color of her

WINTER HARMONY
John Henry Twachtman
National Gallery of Art, Washington

rather priggish[3] notion that he—the young and already fabulously successful Dexter Green—should know more about such things.

That was in October, when he was twenty-five. In January, Dexter and Irene became engaged. It was to be announced in June, and they were to be married three months later.

The Minnesota winter prolonged itself interminably, and it was almost May when the winds came soft and the snow ran down

---

3. **priggish** (prig′ gish) *adj.*: Excessively precise.

into Black Bear Lake at last. For the first time in over a year Dexter was enjoying a certain tranquillity of spirit. Judy Jones had been in Florida, and afterward in Hot Springs, and somewhere she had been engaged, and somewhere she had broken it off. At first, when Dexter had definitely given her up, it had made him sad that people still linked them together and asked for news of her, but when he began to be placed at dinner next to Irene Scheerer people didn't ask him about her any more—they told him about her. He ceased to be an authority on her.

neck's soft down. And her mouth damp to his kisses and her eyes plaintive with melancholy and her freshness like new fine linen in the morning. Why, these things were no longer in the world! They had existed and they existed no longer.

Student Activity 2. Write two paragraphs describing any activity or event that you enjoy. The paragraphs should each consist of at least eight sentences of varying length.

Humanities Note

Fine art, *Winter Harmony*, by John Henry Twachtman. John Henry Twachtman (1853–1902) was born in Cincinnati, Ohio. He was a student at the School of Design of Cincinnati, and he studied in Munich and Paris at the Academie Julien. In 1898 he founded an organization called "Ten American Painters." Twachtman is considered one of the best American landscape painters and was a leading American practitioner of French Impressionism. His style was innovative, especially in his use of iridescent brush strokes, lack of traditional form-molding shadows, and the use of blue to depict shadows on snow.

Winter Harmony is one of many winter scenes painted by Twachtman. He especially enjoyed painting winter scenes. This painting appears to be similar in composition to many other impressionist paintings. What appears, at first to be random emphasis on a tree trunk here and a water reflection there, or a chance zig-zag repetition of form falls together in a very pleasurable, rhythmic vitality.

Consider using these questions for discussion:
1. What visual repetitions and rhythms are in this painting?
2. The rhythms and repetitions of the painting suggest, among other things, the never ending cycle of the seasons. How does this concept relate to the story?
3. In "Winter Dreams" Dexter has a feeling of "profound melancholy" from the winter landscape. Does this painting suggest such a feeling to you? Explain.

May at last. Dexter walked the streets at night when the darkness was damp as rain, wondering that so soon, with so little done, so much of ecstasy had gone from him. May one year back had been marked by Judy's poignant, unforgivable, yet forgiven turbulence—it had been one of those rare times when he fancied she had grown to care for him. That old penny's worth of happiness he had spent for this bushel of content. He knew that Irene would be no more than a curtain spread behind him, a hand moving among gleaming teacups, a voice calling to children . . . fire and loveliness were gone, the magic of nights and the wonder of the varying hours and seasons . . . slender lips, down-turning, dropping to his lips and bearing him up into a heaven of eyes. . . . The thing was deep in him. He was too strong and alive for it to die lightly.

In the middle of May when the weather balanced for a few days on the thin bridge that led to deep summer he turned in one night at Irene's house. Their engagement was to be announced in a week now—no one would be surprised at it. And tonight they would sit together on the lounge at the University Club and look on for an hour at the dancers. It gave him a sense of solidity to go with her—she was so sturdily popular, so intensely "great."

He mounted the steps of the brownstone house and stepped inside.

"Irene," he called.

Mrs. Scheerer came out of the living room to meet him.

"Dexter," she said, "Irene's gone upstairs with a splitting headache. She wanted to go with you but I made her go to bed."

"Nothing serious, I——"

"Oh, no. She's going to play golf with you in the morning. You can spare her for just one night, can't you, Dexter?"

Her smile was kind. She and Dexter liked each other. In the living room he talked for a moment before he said good night.

Returning to the University Club, where he had rooms, he stood in the doorway for a moment and watched the dancers. He leaned against the doorpost, nodded at a man or two—yawned.

"Hello, darling."

The familiar voice at his elbow startled him. Judy Jones had left a man and crossed the room to him—Judy Jones, a slender enameled doll in cloth of gold: gold in a band at her head, gold in two slipper points at her dress's hem. The fragile glow of her face seemed to blossom as she smiled at him. A breeze of warmth and light blew through the room. His hands in the pockets of his dinner jacket tightened spasmodically. He was filled with a sudden excitement.

"When did you get back?" he asked casually.

"Come here and I'll tell you about it."

She turned and he followed her. She had been away—he could have wept at the wonder of her return. She had passed through enchanted streets, doing things that were like provocative music. All mysterious happenings, all fresh and quickening hopes, had gone away with her, come back with her now.

She turned in the doorway.

"Have you a car here? If you haven't, I have."

"I have a coupé."

In then, with a rustle of golden cloth. He slammed the door. Into so many cars she had stepped—like this—like that—her back against the leather, so—her elbow resting on the door—waiting. She would have been soiled long since had there been anything to soil her—except herself—but this was her own self outpouring.

With an effort he forced himself to start the car and back into the street. This was nothing, he must remember. She had done this before, and he had put her behind him, as he would have crossed a bad account from his books.

He drove slowly downtown and, affecting abstraction, traversed the deserted streets of the business section, peopled here and there where a movie was giving out its crowd or

Primary Source

F. Scott Fitzgerald was an extremely popular and successful writer during his career. According to Arthur Mizener, Fitzgerald struggled with the conflicting demands of a popular and a serious writer:

If the unusual combination of serious and popular writer in Fitzgerald has had a marked effect on the development of his reputation, it had an even more important effect on the character of his work itself. He was, to begin with, only partially successful in living as a writer with the tension between the two sides of his nature. His best work was frequently rejected . . . It constantly exacerbated him that, as he once wrote his agent and friend, Harold Ober, "a cheap story like *The Popular Girl* . . . written in one week while the baby was being born brings $1500.00 & genuinely imaginative thing into which I put three weeks real enthusiasm like *The Diamond in the Sky* . . . brings not a thing."

Part of the time he deliberately wrote what the high-priced magazines wanted, what he called . . . "passably

where consumptive or pugilistic youth lounged in front of pool halls. The clink of glasses and the slap of hands on the bars issued from saloons, cloisters of glazed glass and dirty yellow light.

She was watching him closely and the silence was embarrassing, yet in this crisis he could find no casual word with which to profane the hour. At a convenient turning he began to zigzag back toward the University Club.

"Have you missed me?" she asked suddenly.

"Everybody missed you."

He wondered if she knew of Irene Scheerer. She had been back only a day—her absence had been almost contemporaneous with his engagement.

"What a remark!" Judy laughed sadly—without sadness. She looked at him searchingly. He became absorbed in the dashboard.

"You're handsomer than you used to be," she said thoughtfully. "Dexter, you have the most rememberable eyes."

He could have laughed at this, but he did not laugh. It was the sort of thing that was said to sophomores. Yet it stabbed at him.

"I'm awfully tired of everything, darling." She called everyone darling, endowing the endearment with careless, individual camaraderie.[4] "I wish you'd marry me."

The directness of this confused him. He should have told her now that he was going to marry another girl, but he could not tell her. He could as easily have sworn that he had never loved her.

"I think we'd get along," she continued, on the same note, "unless probably you've forgotten me and fallen in love with another girl."

Her confidence was obviously enormous. She had said, in effect, that she found such a thing impossible to believe, that if it were true he had merely committed a childish indiscretion—and probably to show off. She

---

4. **camaraderie** (käm' ə räd' ər ē) *n.*: Warm, friendly feelings.

---

would forgive him, because it was not a matter of any moment but rather something to be brushed aside lightly.

"Of course you could never love anybody but me," she continued, "I like the way you love me. Oh, Dexter, have you forgotten last year?"

"No, I haven't forgotten."

"Neither have I!"

Was she sincerely moved—or was she carried along by the wave of her own acting?

"I wish we could be like that again," she said, and he forced himself to answer:

"I don't think we can."

"I suppose not. . . . I hear you're giving Irene Scheerer a violent rush."

There was not the faintest emphasis on the name, yet Dexter was suddenly ashamed.

"Oh, take me home," cried Judy suddenly; "I don't want to go back to that idiotic dance—with those children."

Then, as he turned up the street that led to the residence district, Judy began to cry quietly to herself. He had never seen her cry before.

The dark street lightened, the dwellings of the rich loomed up around them, he stopped his coupé in front of the great white bulk of the Mortimer Joneses' house, somnolent, gorgeous, drenched with the splendor of the damp moonlight. Its solidity startled him. The strong walls, the steel of the girders, the breadth and beam and pomp of it were there only to bring out the contrast with the young beauty beside him. It was sturdy to accentuate her slightness—as if to show what a breeze could be generated by a butterfly's wing.

He sat perfectly quiet, his nerves in wild clamor, afraid that if he moved he would find her irresistibly in his arms. Two tears had rolled down her wet face and trembled on her upper lip.

"I'm more beautiful than anybody else," she said brokenly, "why can't I be happy?" Her moist eyes tore at his stability—her mouth turned slowly downward with an exquisite sadness: "I'd like to marry you if

---

sort that would then have whiled away a dreary half hour in a dental office." He was never casual about such stories; he worked on them conscientiously and "there was," as he wrote in his Notebooks, "one little drop of something—not blood, not a tear, not my seed, but me more intimately than these, in every story, it was the extra I had." But again and again, to the very end of his life, he would be carried away by the delight of writing out of his full understanding of life without thinking about the need of the magazines at all.

---

18 Discussion How can anyone be described as having "laughed sadly—without sadness"?

19 Discussion Ask those students who have been antipathetic to Judy if they feel some sympathy for her after her wistful remark about being beautiful but not happy. Has she changed?

20 **Discussion** Explain what has happened to Dexter in this paragraph. Why does he feel such conflicting emotions? What "sediment of wisdom, of convention, of doubt, of honor" has been washed away?

21 **Critical Thinking and Reading** Are you surprised by Dexter's aquiescence? Why or why not? Find evidence from the story to support your argument.

22 **Literary Focus** Summarize what this passage reveals about Dexter.

23 **Discussion** Why might the war have been "greeted . . . with a certain amount of relief" by Dexter and other young men? Would anyone ever be able to view a war in such a way after the experiences of World War I? Why or why not?

you'll have me, Dexter. I suppose you think I'm not worth having, but I'll be so beautfiul for you, Dexter."

20

A million phrases of anger, pride, passion, hatred, tenderness fought on his lips. Then a perfect wave of emotion washed over him, carrying off with it a sediment of wisdom, of convention, of doubt, of honor. This was his girl who was speaking, his own, his beautiful, his pride.

"Won't you come in?" He heard her draw in her breath sharply.

Waiting.

21

"All right," his voice was trembling, "I'll come in."

V

22

It was strange that neither when it was over nor a long time afterward did he regret that night. Looking at it from the perspective of ten years, the fact that Judy's flare for him endured just one month seemed of little importance. Nor did it matter that by his yielding he subjected himself to a deeper agony in the end and gave serious hurt to Irene Scheerer and to Irene's parents, who had befriended him. There was nothing sufficiently pictorial about Irene's grief to stamp itself on his mind.

Dexter was at bottom hard-minded. The attitude of the city on his action was of no importance to him, not because he was going to leave the city, but because any outside attitude on the situation seemed superficial. He was completely indifferent to popular opinion. Nor, when he had seen that it was no use, that he did not possess in himself the power to move fundamentally or to hold Judy Jones, did he bear any malice toward her. He loved her, and he would love her until the day he was too old for loving—but he could not have her. So he tasted the deep pain that is reserved only for the strong, just as he had tasted for a little while the deep happiness.

Even the ultimate falsity of the grounds upon which Judy terminated the engagement that she did not want to "take him away" from Irene—Judy who had wanted nothing else—did not revolt him. He was beyond any revulsion or any amusement.

He went East in February with the intention of selling out his laundries and settling in New York—but the war came to America in March and changed his plans. He returned to the West, handed over the management of the business to his partner, and went into the first officers' training camp in late April. He was one of those young thousands who greeted the war with a certain amount of relief, welcoming the liberation from webs of tangled emotion.

23

VI

This story is not his biography, remember, although things creep into it which have nothing to do with those dreams he had when he was young. We are almost done with them and with him now. There is only one more incident to be related here, and it happens seven years farther on.

It took place in New York, where he had done well—so well that there were no barriers too high for him. He was thirty-two years old, and, except for one flying trip immediately after the war, he had not been West in seven years. A man named Devlin from Detroit came into his office to see him in a business way, and then and there this incident occurred, and closed out, so to speak, this particular side of his life.

"So you're from the Middle West," said the man Devlin with careless curiosity. "That's funny—I thought men like you were probably born and raised on Wall Street. You know—wife of one of my best friends in Detroit came from your city. I was an usher at the wedding."

Dexter waited with no apprehension of what was coming.

"Judy Simms," said Devlin with no particular interest; "Judy Jones she was once."

MANHATTAN TOPS
Herman Rose
Hirschorn Museum and Sculpture Garden, Smithsonian Institution

"Yes, I knew her." A dull impatience spread over him. He had heard, of course, that she was married—perhaps deliberately he had heard no more.

"Awfully nice girl," brooded Devlin meaninglessly, "I'm sort of sorry for her."

"Why?" Something in Dexter was alert, receptive, at once.

"Oh, Lud Simms has gone to pieces in a way. I don't mean he ill-uses her, but he drinks and runs around——"

"Doesn't she run around?"

"No. Stays at home with her kids."

"Oh."

"She's a little too old for him," said Devlin.

"Too old!" cried Dexter. "Why, man, she's only twenty-seven."

He was possessed with a wild notion of rushing out into the streets and taking a train to Detroit. He rose to his feet spasmodically.

"I guess you're busy," Devlin apologized quickly. "I didn't realize——"

"No, I'm not busy," said Dexter, steadying his voice. "I'm not busy at all. Not busy at all. Did you say she was—twenty-seven? No, I said she was twenty-seven."

"Yes, you did," agreed Devlin dryly.

"Go on, then. Go on."

"What do you mean?"

"About Judy Jones."

Devlin looked at him helplessly.

"Well, that's—I told you all there is to it. He treats her like the devil. Oh, they're not going to get divorced or anything. When he's particularly outrageous she forgives him. In fact, I'm inclined to think she loves him. She was a pretty girl when she first came to Detroit."

A pretty girl! The phrase struck Dexter as ludicrous.

"Isn't she—a pretty girl, anymore?"

"Oh, she's all right."

"Look here," said Dexter, sitting down suddenly. "I don't understand. You say she was a 'pretty girl' and now you say she's 'all right.' I don't understand what you mean—Judy Jones wasn't a pretty girl, at all. She was a great beauty. Why, I knew her, I knew her. She was——"

Devlin laughed pleasantly.

"I'm not trying to start a row," he said. "I think Judy's a nice girl and I like her. I can't understand how a man like Lud Simms could fall madly in love with her, but he did." Then he added: "Most of the women like her."

Dexter looked closely at Devlin, thinking wildly that there must be a reason for this, some insensitivity in the man or some private malice.

"Lots of women fade just like *that*," Devlin snapped his fingers. "You must have seen it happen. Perhaps I've forgotten how pretty she was at her wedding. I've seen her so much since then, you see. She has nice eyes."

A sort of dullness settled down upon Dexter. For the first time in his life he felt like getting very drunk. He knew that he was laughing loudly at something Devlin had said, but he did not know what it was or why it was funny. When, in a few minutes, Devlin went he lay down on his lounge and looked out the window at the New York skyline into which the sun was sinking in dull lovely shades of pink and gold.

He had thought that having nothing else to lose he was invulnerable at last—but he knew that he had just lost something more, as surely as if he had married Judy Jones and seen her fade away before his eyes.

The dream was gone. Something had been taken from him. In a sort of panic he pushed the palms of his hands into his eyes and tried to bring up a picture of the waters lapping on Sherry Island and the moonlit veranda, and gingham on the golf links and the dry sun and the gold color of her neck's soft down. And her mouth damp to his kisses and her eyes plaintive with melancholy and her freshness like new fine linen in the morning. Why, these things were no longer in the world! They had existed and they existed no longer.

For the first time in years the tears were streaming down his face. But they were for himself now. He did not care about mouth and eyes and moving hands. He wanted to care, and he could not care. For he had gone away and he could never go back any more. The gates were closed, the sun was gone down, and there was no beauty but the gray beauty of steel that withstands all time. Even the grief he could have borne was left behind in the country of illusion, of youth, of the richness of life, where his winter dreams had flourished.

"Long ago," he said, "long ago, there was something in me, but now that thing is gone. Now that thing is gone, that thing is gone. I cannot cry. I cannot care. That thing will come back no more."

THINKING ABOUT THE SELECTION

Recalling

1. (a) When does Dexter first encounter Judy Jones? (b) What action does her behavior prompt him to take?
2. (a) When does Dexter next encounter Judy? (b) When does she introduce herself to Dexter? (c) When does Dexter realize that he had loved Judy since his childhood?
3. (a) What forces Dexter to view Judy's "exquisite excitability" in a "different light"? (b) What does he learn about Judy before the end of his twenty-fourth summer?
4. Why does Dexter break his engagement to Irene Scheerer?
5. How does Devlin shatter Dexter's image of Judy?

Interpreting

6. (a) How would you describe Judy's personality? (b) According to Devlin's description, how does Judy's personality change following her marriage?
7. (a) What does Judy represent to Dexter? (b) Why does he keep loving her even after he has lost her?
8. (a) What are Dexter's "winter dreams"? (b) What makes them *winter* dreams? (c) How does Judy fit into these dreams?
9. Fitzgerald came to believe that an obsession with wealth and social status ultimately leads to emptiness and dissatisfaction. How does this story reflect this belief?

Applying

10. Explain whether this story would be effective if it were set in contemporary American society.

ANALYZING LITERATURE

Understanding Characterization

Characterization is the means by which an author reveals a character's personality. Writers may use a variety of methods of characterization. For example, we learn a great deal about Judy Jones's personality from her behavior in Part I.

1. What other methods does Fitzgerald use to characterize Judy? Support your answer with examples.
2. What methods does Fitzgerald use to characterize Dexter? Support your answer with examples.
3. (a) In what ways does Fitzgerald show Dexter and Judy to be alike? (b) In what ways does he show them to be different?

CRITICAL THINKING AND READING

Evaluating a Character's Behavior

Literature can often help us better understand ourselves and other people. Evaluating a character's behavior and its effect on the character's life and on other characters can sometimes reveal the implications for our own behavior.

1. Toward the end of Part IV, Judy tells Dexter that she cannot be happy. How do you think her behavior throughout the story might have contributed to her unhappiness?
2. What do you think Dexter's experiences reveal about the potential dangers of an obsession with "glittering things"?

THINKING AND WRITING

Writing About Historical Context

As the biography of Fitzgerald (page 670) states, Fitzgerald's work "captured both the gaiety and the emptiness" of the 1920's. Write an essay in which you discuss how "Winter Dreams" captures the "gaiety and the emptiness" of the 1920's. Use passages from the story to support your argument. When you revise, make sure that you have not included any unnecessary information.

(Answers begin on p. 686)

is obsessed with her and the ideal that she represents to him.
8. (a) His "winter dreams" are his dreams of acquiring "glittering things." (b) They are *winter* dreams, because they will never be fulfilled. (c) Judy is an embodiment of the "glittering things" with which he is obsessed.
9. Dexter gains wealth, but he cannot achieve the social status he desires, and he is ultimately left with a feeling of emptiness and dissatisfaction.

Applying

10. Suggested Response: It would be effective, because many people in today's society have dreams similar to Dexter's.

ANSWERS TO ANALYZING LITERATURE

1. He develops Judy's character through direct statements about her, through physical descriptions, and through other characters' thoughts and comments about her. Examples will differ.
2. He develops Dexter's character through direct statements about him; through his actions, thoughts, and comments; and through the other characters' reactions to and comments about him. Examples will differ.
3. (a) Answers will differ. Students may point out that they are both materialistic. (b) Answers will differ. Students may note that Judy comes from a wealthy background, while Dexter does not.

ANSWERS TO CRITICAL THINKING AND READING

1. Suggested Response: Judy's treatment of suitors might have contributed to her unhappiness.
2. Such obsessions can lead to a sense of emptiness and dissatisfaction.

THINKING AND WRITING

After students have completed the writing assignment, divide them into groups, and have them read their rough drafts to one another and comment on ways in which they could be improved.

herself to Dexter later in the afternoon of the day he met her for the second time. (c) When Dexter began kissing Judy after dinner, he realized he had wanted her since childhood.
3. (a) Dexter viewed Judy's exquisite excitability in a different light after she left Dexter and went off with another man in her car. (b) Dexter learns that Judy, after a one-month-long engagement to another man, broke the engagement.
4. Dexter breaks his engagement to Irene, because he continues to be obsessed with Judy.
5. He reveals that Judy has lost her good looks and is unhappily married.

Interpreting

6. (a) Individual students will describe Judy differently. It is likely though, that most if not all, students will describe her unsympathetically. (b) No longer a dominating person, Judy has become submissive to her husband, forgiving his untoward behavior.
7. (a) She represents the ultimate "glittering thing" to Dexter. (b) He keeps loving her because he

Motivation/Prior Knowledge
You might have students discuss their prior knowledge of the "Roaring Twenties." What do they associate with this term? How did they come to make these associations?

Perhaps some students have already read *The Great Gatsby* on their own, or have seen the film of the same name. If so, have students share their impressions of the work or the film.

GREAT WORKS

THE GREAT GATSBY
by F. Scott Fitzgerald

What images come to mind when you think of the Jazz Age? Music? Flappers? Bathtub gin? No one has described the "Jazz Age," the boom years of the early 1920's, as well as F. Scott Fitzgerald. And nowhere did Fitzgerald better capture the determined gaiety and calculated unconventionality of wealthy society during those years than in his finest novel, *The Great Gatsby.* But perhaps the greatest triumph of *The Great Gatsby* was not in its telling social descriptions but in its portrait of Jay Gatsby as a personification of the American Dream. Over the years the image of Gatsby as the innocent dreamer destroyed by the corruption around him has taken on mythic proportions in American literature.

> . . . his dream must have seemed so close that he could hardly fail to grasp it. He did not know that it was already behind him somewhere back in that vast obscurity beyond the city, where the dark fields of the republic rolled on under the night.
>
> *The Great Gatsby*

Love and Tragedy in the 1920's

The events of *The Great Gatsby* unfold during three months in the summer of 1922. They are recounted as a series of scenes interspersed with recollections and commentary by a narrator, Nick Carroway. Nick is a Midwesterner recently graduated from Yale who lives in a small cottage next door to Gatsby's luxurious mansion on the Long Island shore. During the summer months he slowly becomes more and more involved in the life of the mysterious Gatsby.

Gatsby's house is situated directly across the harbor from that of Daisy Buchanan and her rich but crude husband, Tom. During the summer Gatsby gives lavish parties at which he entertains hundreds of guests in

688   *The Modern Age*

Enrichment The photographs on these pages are stills from the movie, *The Great Gatsby*. If they have not viewed it before, students might be interested in seeing the 1974 film version of the novel. The film starred Robert Redford as Gatsby and Mia Farrow as Daisy. If students both watch the film and read the book, you might have a discussion comparing and contrasting the two works.

the hopes of attracting Daisy's attention. Eventually Gatsby reveals to Nick that he knew Daisy briefly before World War I and that he has acquired his enormous fortune almost entirely in hopes of turning himself into the kind of man he thinks Daisy wants. Nick brings Daisy and Gatsby together and they have a brief romance, but Gatsby is unable to win Daisy away from her husband.

All the elements of the plot come together dramatically and tragically at the end of the novel. Daisy's husband, Tom, has been having a romance with Myrtle Wilson, the vulgar but vital wife of a garage owner. While driving Gatsby's car, Daisy accidentally hits Myrtle, killing her. Tom, now aware of the relationship between Gatsby and his wife, tells Myrtle's husband that Gatsby was driving the car. The husband goes to Gatsby's estate, shoots him, and then shoots himself.

Gatsby's American Dream

Like Dexter Green in "Winter Dreams," Gatsby is obsessed with a young woman and the glittering world she represents. Born in the Midwest, Gatsby has achieved his great wealth through shady means in an effort to acquire Daisy, the golden girl. But Gatsby is unable to see the difference between his world and the world of inherited wealth such as Daisy's. His gaudy mansion, his showy car, his claim to being an Oxford man, the elaborate formality of his speech, all verge on the laughable.

In contrast, Daisy's world is filled with easy grace. Gatsby is astonished when he first meets Daisy at the way she inhabits her beautiful house in Louisville. To Daisy the house "was as casual a thing . . . as his tent out at camp." Daisy's very presence hints at "gay and radiant activities," at shining motorcars, at perpetual grace and beauty.

Gatsby is blind to the carelessness, irresponsibility, and corruption that lie beneath the charmed surface of the lives of people like Tom and Daisy. They are people who "drifted here and there unrestfully wherever people played polo and were rich together."

Great Works 689

Cooperative Learning You might have students work on a class newspaper written from the point of view of people living in the 1920's. One student might report on political news, another on cultural events. Students can write about sports, music, fashion, or other topics related to that time period. Have students assemble their articles into a newspaper format complete with headlines. Perhaps artistically inclined students could contribute illustrations for the articles or create advertisements of products from the period. After the newspaper is assembled, display it where the entire class can enjoy it.

Tom and Daisy are ever on the lookout for something to fill the boredom of their lives. Gatsby is unable to see that beneath their surface glamour they are the kind of people who "smashed up things and creatures and then retreated back into their money or their vast carelessness, or whatever it was that kept them together, and let other people clean up the mess they had made. . . ."

Gatsby is the incurable romantic whose "sensitivity to the promises of life" lead him to seek a dazzling prize whose superficiality and emptiness he is unable to see. He is sure that money can buy him anything, even the dream of love and grace he has carried from his past. He is unable to see the barrenness that lies at the heart of his American Dream.

A Style of Great Suggestibility

Although *The Great Gatsby* is largely judged by the success with which it evokes its grand and doomed hero, it is also praised for the remarkable beauty of its style and the attention to details. Fitzgerald was able to evoke places and characters through descriptions of great suggestibility. The luxurious life style of the Buchanans, for example, is suggested by their lawn, which "started at the beach and ran toward the front door for a quarter of a mile, jumping over sun-dials and brick walks and burning gardens . . ." The reasoning behind Daisy's decision to marry Tom Buchanan is underscored by his gift to her of a pearl necklace valued at

Primary Source

Critic Marius Bewley made the following comments in his essay "Scott Fitzgerald's Criticism of America."

"Critics of Scott Fitzgerald tend to agree that *The Great Gatsby* is somehow a commentary on that elusive phrase, "the American dream." The assumption seems to be that Fitzgerald approved. On the contrary, it can be shown that *The Great Gatsby* offers some of the severest and closest criticism of the American dream that our literature affords.

Read in this way, Fitzgerald's masterpiece ceases to be a pastoral documentary of the Jazz Age and takes its distinguished place among those great national novels whose profound corrective insights into the nature of American experience are not separable from the artistic form of the novel itself. That is to say, Fitzgerald—at least in this one book—is in a line with the greatest masters of American prose. *The Great Gatsby* embodies a criticism of American experience—not of manners, but of a basic historic attitude to life.. . . The theme of *Gatsby* is the withering of the American dream.

". . . We recognize that the great achievement of this novel is that it manages, while poetically evoking a sense of the goodness of that early dream, to offer the most

$350,000. Gatsby's fascination with his newly acquired wealth is demonstrated in a scene in which he throws an enormous pile of expensive shirts, one by one, in front of Daisy, who buries her head in them and cries over their beauty. The character of the bootlegger who has been responsible for Gatsby's wealth is described by his cuff buttons, which are "composed of oddly familiar pieces of ivory" that turn out to be the "finest specimens of human molars."

The Great Gatsby's style is also achieved through the strong sense of mystery that surrounds Gatsby for most of the book. Gatsby's character is revealed slowly through the eyes of Nick, the narrator, as it might be to an acquaintance who is slowly becoming a friend. At the first of Gatsby's fantastic parties that Nick attends, Nick tries to find out who Gatsby is. No one really knows. Rumors abound. He has killed a man, some say. He was a German spy, say others. Facts and details gradually accumulate as Nick's friendship with Gatsby develops. Only at the end of the novel, after Gatsby's death, are the final details revealed.

"Something New, Something Extraordinary"

With *The Great Gatsby*, Fitzgerald had hoped to "write something *new*—something extraordinary and beautiful and simple and intricately patterned." This he achieved, though his novel was not initially a great success. The first printing of 20,000 copies sold slowly, and in 1940, just before his death, Fitzgerald was distressed to discover that many bookstores no longer even carried the novel. Though the highly respected American-born poet and critic T. S. Eliot declared that *The Great Gatsby* was "the first step American fiction has taken since Henry James," at first only a few critics recognized it as a masterpiece.

Over time, however, *The Great Gatsby* has been recognized as the best work of Fitzgerald's generation. Gilbert Seldes noted in his 1925 review, "*The Great Gatsby* is a brilliant work, and it is also a sound one; it is carefully written, and vivid; it has structure, and it has life." Critics have come more and more to agree with this judgment and to recognize that in his tale of Jay Gatsby's grand illusion, Fitzgerald captured the illusion of an age.

damaging criticism of it in American literature. The astonishing thing is that the criticism—if indictment wouldn't be the better word—manages to be part of the tribute. Gatsby, the 'mythic' embodiment of the American dream, is shown to us in all his immature romanticism. His insecure grasp of social and human values, his lack of critical intelligence and self-knowledge, his blindness to the pitfalls that surround him in American society, his compulsive optimism, are realized in the text with rare assurance and understanding. And yet the very grounding of these deficiencies is Gatsby's goodness and faith in life, his compelling desire to realize all the possibilities of existence, his belief that we can have an Earthly Paradise populated by Buchanans. A great part of Fitzgerald's achievement is that he suggests effectively that these terrifying deficiencies are not so much the private deficiencies of Gatsby, but are deficiencies inherent in contemporary manifestations of the American vision itself—a vision no doubt admirable, but stupidly defenseless before the equally American world of Tom and Daisy. Gatsby's deficiencies of intelligence and judgment bring him to his tragic death—a death that is spiritual as well as physical. But the more important question that faces us through our sense of the immediate tragedy is where they have brought America."

KATHERINE ANNE PORTER

More About the Author Glenway Wescott, a friend of Porter, described her in this way: "First, some facts: She was born on May 15, 1890, in Texas, in 'soft backland farming country, full of fruits and flowers and birds,' on the banks of a branch of the Colorado River denominated Indian Creek, small and clear, unimportant but unforgettable. She went to a convent school, perhaps more than one, and was an uneven student: A in history and composition and other subjects having to do with literature, but she admits, 'D in everything else, including deportment, which sometimes went down to E and stopped there.'

She spent an important part of her girlhood in New Orleans, and afterward lived in New York City and in Mexico City and in Paris and in Baton Rouge, Louisiana, and in more recent years, in upper New York State and in southern California and in Connecticut and in Washington, D.C. . . . She is an incomparable letter writer, sparkling, poignant, and abundant, and a famous conversationalist."

Katherine Anne Porter had a deep interest in the effects of social and political change. This interest is apparent in her novel, *Ship of Fools,* which explores the social unrest and political upheaval that took place during the 1930's. Why is an interest in the effects of social and political change an appropriate twentieth-century concern?

1890–1980

Katherine Anne Porter did not produce a great number of literary works during her long life. Yet the works she did produce were skillfully crafted, tightly structured, and written in a clear, elegant style.

Born in Indian Creek, Texas, Porter was raised in poverty. After becoming a journalist, she lived for several years in Mexico. There she developed an interest in writing fiction, and in 1922 she published her first story, "María Conceptión," in *Century,* a highly regarded literary magazine. Eight years later she published her first book, *Flowering Judas* (1930). The book, a collection of six short stories, was praised by critics and earned Porter widespread recognition. *Flowering Judas and Other Stories,* an expanded edition containing ten stories, appeared in 1935 and was followed by several other major works, including *Noon Wine* (1937), *Pale Horse, Pale Rider* (1939), *No Safe Harbor* (1941), *The Leaning Tower and Other Stories* (1944), and *Ship of Fools* (1962)—Porter's only novel. In 1966 she received the Pulitzer Prize and the National Book Award for her *Collected Stories* (1965).

In his review of *The Leaning Tower,* critic Edmund Wilson tried to account for the "elusive" quality that made Porter an "absolutely first-rate artist": "These stories are not illustrations of anything that is reducible to a moral law or a political or social analysis or even a principle of human behavior. What they show us are human relations in their constantly shifting phases and in the moments of which their existence is made. There is no place for general reflections; you are to live through the experience as the characters do."

In her work Porter often explored the sense of uncertainty and disjointedness that results from changes in society. In many of her stories, including "The Jilting of Granny Weatherall," she portrayed families that were drifting apart and losing an awareness of their connection with the past, as the traditional sense of the family as a community disappeared with the coming of the modern age.

In an introduction to the 1940 edition of *Flowering Judas,* Porter offered this view of the meaning of art in an increasingly uncertain world: "All the conscious and recollected years of my life have been lived to this day under the heavy threat of world catastrophe, and most of the energies of my mind and spirit have been spent in the effort to grasp the meaning of those threats, to trace them to their sources, and to understand the logic of this majestic and terrible failure of the life of man in the Western world."

692   The Modern Age

Objectives

1   To appreciate stream of consciousness
2   To understand flashback
3   To understand the sequence of events
4   To write about stream of consciousness

Support Material

Teaching Portfolio
Teacher Backup, p. 889
Grammar in Action Worksheets, *Using Ellipses,* p. 893; *Recognizing Formal and Informal English,* p. 895
Usage and Mechanics Worksheet, p. 897
Vocabulary Check, p. 898
Analyzing Literature Worksheet,

Understanding Stream of Consciousness, p. 899
Critical Thinking and Reading Worksheet, *Sequencing Events,* p. 900
Selection Test, p. 901
Library of Video Classics: The Jilting of Granny Weatherall

GUIDE FOR INTERPRETING

The Jilting of Granny Weatherall

Stream of Consciousness. People's thoughts do not usually flow in a neat, organized manner. Instead, they usually proceed in an unorganized flow of insights, memories, and reflections. When a writer uses the stream-of-consciousness technique, he or she attempts to capture the way the mind works by showing the random movement and natural flow of a character's thoughts. In using this technique, the writer eliminates the transitions used in ordinary prose, instead connecting thoughts through the character's natural associations.

The stream-of-consciousness technique, which reflects the twentieth century interest in psychology, was devised by the Modernists as part of their effort to capture the essence of the fragmented modern world in their work. The Modernists generally believed that there is no external order governing human existence and that, as a result, life is often splintered and disjointed. Their use of the stream-of-consciousness technique reflected this opinion and expressed their belief in the need for people to turn their thoughts inward.

The term "stream of consciousness" was actually coined by the American psychologist William James. He wrote, "Consciousness . . . does not appear to itself chopped up in bits. . . . A 'river' or a 'stream' are the metaphors by which it is most naturally described. In talking of it hereafter, let us call it the stream of thought, of consciousness, or of subjective life."

Flashback. In trying to re-create the natural flow of a character's thoughts, writers often use flashbacks—interruptions in the narrative in which an earlier event is recalled or described. In "The Jilting of Granny Weatherall," for example, flashbacks are used when Granny Weatherall's thoughts drift back to her younger days.

Writing

Try to capture your own "stream of consciousness." Start by thinking about a single person, place, or event. Then write down the various associations that flow through your mind.

Primary Source

Porter learned the use of literary techniques not from any formal instructions but in the works of other writers. Of her schooling Porter said that she received a "fragmentary, but strangely useless and ornamental education. . . ." Instead she was taught "by five writers: Henry James, James Joyce, W. B. Yeats, T. S. Eliot, and Ezra Pound." Porter described what a writer needs to write, as follows: "*first* a *theme,* and then a point of view, a certain knowledge of human nature and strong feeling about it, and style—that is to say, his own special way of telling a thing that makes it precisely his own and no one else's."

Literary Focus The term *stream of consciousness* was first used by American psychologist William James, the brother of Henry James. The stream-of-consciousness technique was first used in literature by Russian novelist Leo Tolstoy in his novel, *Anna Karenina.*

Writing/Prior Knowledge Point out to students that when they freewrite they are essentially recording their stream of consciousness.

Vocabulary

Preteach the following vocabulary words:
piety (pī′ ə tə) *n.:* Devotion to religious duties (p. 699)
frippery (frip′ ər ē) *n.:* Showy display of elegance (p. 700)
dyspepsia (dis pep′ shə)*n.:* Indigestion (p. 700)

The Jilting of Granny Weatherall

Katherine Anne Porter

She flicked her wrist neatly out of Doctor Harry's pudgy careful fingers and pulled the sheet up to her chin. The brat ought to be in knee breeches. Doctoring around the country with spectacles on his nose! "Get along now, take your schoolbooks and go. There's nothing wrong with me."

Doctor Harry spread a warm paw like a cushion on her forehead where the forked green vein danced and made her eyelids twitch. "Now, now, be a good girl, and we'll have you up in no time."

"That's no way to speak to a woman nearly eighty years old just because she's down. I'd have you respect your elders, young man."

"Well, Missy, excuse me," Doctor Harry patted her cheek. "But I've got to warn you, haven't I? You're a marvel, but you must be careful or you're going to be good and sorry."

"Don't tell me what I'm going to be. I'm on my feet now, morally speaking. It's Cornelia. I had to go to bed to get rid of her."

Her bones felt loose, and floated around in her skin, and Doctor Harry floated like a balloon around the foot of the bed. He floated and pulled down his waistcoat and swung his glasses on a cord. "Well, stay where you are, it certainly can't hurt you."

"Get along and doctor your sick," said Granny Weatherall. "Leave a well woman alone. I'll call for you when I want you. . . .

Where were you forty years ago when I pulled through milk leg[1] and double pneumonia? You weren't even born. Don't let Cornelia lead you on," she shouted, because Doctor Harry appeared to float up to the ceiling and out. "I pay my own bills, and I don't throw my money away on nonsense!"

She meant to wave good-bye, but it was too much trouble. Her eyes closed of themselves, it was like a dark curtain drawn around the bed. The pillow rose and floated under her, pleasant as a hammock in a light wind. She listened to the leaves rustling outside the window. No, somebody was swishing newspapers: no, Cornelia and Doctor Harry were whispering together. She leaped broad awake, thinking they whispered in her ear.

"She was never like this, *never* like this!" "Well, what can we expect?" "Yes, eighty years old. . . ."

Well, and what if she was? She still had ears. It was like Cornelia to whisper around doors. She always kept things secret in such a public way. She was always being tactful and kind. Cornelia was dutiful; that was the trouble with her. Dutiful and good: "So good and dutiful," said Granny, "that I'd like to spank her." She saw herself spanking Cornelia and making a fine job of it.

1

----

1. **milk leg:** A painful swelling of the leg.

GARDEN OF MEMORIES, 1917
Charles Burchfield
Collection of The Museum of Modern Art,
New York

"What'd you say, Mother?"

Granny felt her face tying up in hard knots.

"Can't a body think, I'd like to know?"

"I thought you might want something."

"I do. I want a lot of things. First off, go away and don't whisper."

She lay and drowsed, hoping in her sleep that the children would keep out and let her rest a minute. It had been a long day. Not that she was tired. It was always pleasant to snatch a minute now and then. There was always so much to be done, let me see: tomorrow.

Tomorrow was far away and there was nothing to trouble about. Things were finished somehow when the time came; thank God there was always a little margin over for peace: then a person could spread out the plan of life and tuck in the edges orderly. It was good to have everything clean and folded away, with the hair brushes and tonic bottles sitting straight on the white embroidered linen: the day started without fuss and the pantry shelves laid out with rows of jelly glasses and brown jugs and white stone-china jars with blue whirligigs and words painted on them: coffee, tea, sugar, ginger, cinnamon, allspice: and the bronze clock with the lion on top nicely dusted off. The dust that lion could collect in twenty-four hours! The box in the attic with all those let-

The Jilting of Granny Weatherall 695

Humanities Note

Fine art, *Garden of Memories*, 1917, by Charles Burchfield. Charles Burchfield (1893–1967) was an American painter. He attended the Cleveland Institute of Art, where his teacher, Henry Keller, encouraged his individualistic style of painting. Burchfield's early work evoked childhood memories and emotions, and produced a haunting sense of imagination. His later works were more realistic images of the American scene, although there was still evidence of the sinister in his work and his concern for the loneliness that again evoked that highly personal elemental world of his childhood, somewhat surrealistic in character.

This crayon and water color on paper is an example of Burchfield's earlier work, in which he presents his romantic visions of strange phantoms and childhood fears in apparitions of an old woman and a surreal house and garden. His tendency towards melancholy and nostalgia are obvious.

As students look at this art, you might ask these questions:
1. What qualities of this piece of art reflect stream-of-consciousness ideas?
2. How might the figure in the painting represent Granny Weatherall?

2 Literary Focus Take note of the random movement of Granny's thoughts.

3 Discussion What do Granny's thoughts reveal about her character?

4 Discussion Why is Granny concerned about the possibility that her children might discover her letters?

5 Discussion What is Granny's attitude toward death?

6 Discussion What is Cornelia's attitude toward Granny?

7 Discussion How would you describe the relationship between Granny and Cornelia?

8 Discussion Of what accomplishments is Granny most proud? What are the things she fears are still undone?

9 Discussion Why does Granny envision her husband as a young man?

10 Clarification Rural women, living far from hospitals and medical doctors, often depended on the services of neighbors and midwives in delivering their babies.

ters tied up, well, she'd have to go through that tomorrow. All those letters—George's letters and John's letters and her letters to them both—lying around for the children to find afterwards made her uneasy. Yes, that would be tomorrow's business. No use to let them know how silly she had been once.

While she was rummaging around she found death in her mind and it felt clammy and unfamiliar. She had spent so much time preparing for death there was no need for bringing it up again. Let it take care of itself now. When she was sixty she had felt very old, finished, and went around making farewell trips to see her children and grandchildren, with a secret in her mind: This is the very last of your mother, children! Then she made her will and came down with a long fever. That was all just a notion like a lot of other things, but it was lucky too, for she had once for all got over the idea of dying for a long time. Now she couldn't be worried. She hoped she had better sense now. Her father had lived to be one hundred and two years old and had drunk a noggin of strong hot toddy on his last birthday. He told the reporters it was his daily habit, and he owed his long life to that. He had made quite a scandal and was very pleased about it. She believed she'd just plague Cornelia a little.

"Cornelia! Cornelia!" No footsteps, but a sudden hand on her cheek. "Bless you, where have you been?"

"Here, mother."

"Well, Cornelia, I want a noggin of hot toddy."

"Are you cold, darling?"

"I'm chilly, Cornelia. Lying in bed stops the circulation. I must have told you that a thousand times."

Well, she could just hear Cornelia telling her husband that Mother was getting a little childish and they'd have to humor her. The thing that most annoyed her was that Cornelia thought she was deaf, dumb, and blind. Little hasty glances and tiny gestures tossed around her and over her head saying, "Don't cross her, let her have her way, she's

eighty years old," and she sitting there as if she lived in a thin glass cage. Sometimes Granny almost made up her mind to pack up and move back to her own house where nobody could remind her every minute that she was old. Wait, wait, Cornelia, till your own children whisper behind your back!

In her day she had kept a better house and had got more work done. She wasn't too old yet for Lydia to be driving eighty miles for advice when one of the children jumped the track, and Jimmy still dropped in and talked things over: "Now, Mammy, you've a good business head, I want to know what you think of this? . . ." Old. Cornelia couldn't change the furniture around without asking. Little things, little things! They had been so sweet when they were little. Granny wished the old days were back again with the children young and everything to be done over. It had been a hard pull, but not too much for her. When she thought of all the food she had cooked, and all the clothes she had cut and sewed, and all the gardens she had made—well, the children showed it. There they were, made out of her, and they couldn't get away from that. Sometimes she wanted to see John again and point to them and say, Well, I didn't do so badly, did I? But that would have to wait. That was for tomorrow. She used to think of him as a man, but now all the children were older than their father, and he would be a child beside her if she saw him now. It seemed strange and there was something wrong in the idea. Why, he couldn't possibly recognize her. She had fenced in a hundred acres once, digging the post holes herself and clamping the wires with just a negro boy to help. That changed a woman. John would be looking for a young woman with the peaked Spanish comb in her hair and the painted fan. Digging post holes changed a woman. Riding country roads in the winter when women had their babies was another thing: sitting up nights with sick horses and sick children and hardly ever losing one. John, I hardly ever lost one of them! John would see that in

Grammar in Action

Ellipsis marks (. . .) tell the reader that quoted material is incomplete, that the writer has omitted part of the quotation. In Porter's story, Granny often jumps from thought to thought, and some of the characters' comments are interrupted or broken off. Porter uses ellipsis marks to indicate that the sentences that contain these thoughts or comments are incomplete. Note the following examples:

I'll call for you when I want you. . . . (p. 748)

"Yes, eighty years old. . . . "(p. 748)

In these examples, there are four dots, rather than three; the first of the four is the period at the end of the sentence. If it had been appropriate, the first mark would have been a question mark or an exclamation mark. Note the following example:

I want to know what you think of this? . . . (p. 750)

a minute, that would be something he could understand, she wouldn't have to explain anything!

It made her feel like rolling up her sleeves and putting the whole place to rights again. No matter if Cornelia was determined to be everywhere at once, there were a great many things left undone on this place. She would start tomorrow and do them. It was good to be strong enough for everything, even if all you made melted and changed and slipped under your hands, so that by the time you finished you almost forgot what you were working for. What was it I set out to do? she asked herself intently, but she could not remember. A fog rose over the valley, she saw it marching across the creek swallowing the trees and moving up the hill like an army of ghosts. Soon it would be at the near edge of the orchard, and then it was time to go in and light the lamps. Come in, children, don't stay out in the night air.

Lighting the lamps had been beautiful. The children huddled up to her and breathed like little calves waiting at the bars in the twilight. Their eyes followed the match and watched the flame rise and settle in a blue curve, then they moved away from her. The lamp was lit, they didn't have to be scared and hang on to mother any more. Never, never, never more. God, for all my life I thank Thee. Without Thee, my God, I could never have done it. Hail Mary, full of grace.

I want you to pick all the fruit this year and see that nothing is wasted. There's always someone who can use it. Don't let good things rot for want of using. You waste life when you waste good food. Don't let things get lost. It's bitter to lose things. Now, don't let me get to thinking, not when I am tired and taking a little nap before supper. . . .

The pillow rose about her shoulders and pressed against her heart and the memory was being squeezed out of it: oh, push down the pillow, somebody: it would smother her if she tried to hold it. Such a fresh breeze blowing and such a green day with no threats in it. But he had not come, just the same. What does a woman do when she has put on the white veil and set out the white cake for a man and he doesn't come? She tried to remember. No, I swear he never harmed me but in that. He never harmed me but in that . . . and what if he did? There was the day, the day, but a whirl of dark smoke rose and covered it, crept up and over into the bright field where everything was planted so carefully in orderly rows. That was hell, she knew hell when she saw it. For sixty years she had prayed against remembering him and against losing her soul in the deep pit of hell, and now the two things were mingled in one and the thought of him was a smoky cloud from hell that moved and crept in her head when she had just got rid of Doctor Harry and was trying to rest a minute. Wounded vanity, Ellen, said a sharp voice in the top of her mind. Don't let your wounded vanity get the upper hand of you. Plenty of girls get jilted. You were jilted, weren't you? Then stand up to it. Her eyelids wavered and let in streamers of blue-gray light like tissue paper over her eyes. She must get up and pull the shades down or she'd never sleep. She was in bed again and the shades were not down. How could that happen? Better turn over, hide from the light, sleeping in the light gave you nightmares. "Mother, how do you feel now?" and a stinging wetness on her forehead. But I don't like having my face washed in cold water!

Hapsy? George? Lydia? Jimmy? No, Cornelia, and her features were swollen and full of little puddles. "They're coming, darling, they'll all be here soon." Go wash your face, child, you look funny.

Instead of obeying, Cornelia knelt down and put her head on the pillow. She seemed to be talking but there was no sound. "Well, are you tongue-tied? Whose birthday is it? Are you going to give a party?"

Cornelia's mouth moved urgently in strange shapes. "Don't do that, you bother me, daughter."

"Oh, no, Mother. Oh, no. . . ."

The Jilting of Granny Weatherall 697

11 **Clarification** These are the initial lines of a Roman Catholic prayer.

12 **Literary Focus** This flashback helps to clarify the significance of the story's title.

13 **Discussion** Has Granny ever fully recovered from her jilting?

14 **Discussion** Why does Granny want to "hide from the light"?

Student Activity 1. The following sentences are shortened versions of sentences that open paragraphs on pages 750–751. Find the sentences on the page. Then explain what the ellipsis marks replace.

1. . . . She found death in her mind. . . .
2. In her day she . . . had got more work done.
3. It made her feel like rolling up her sleeves. . . .
4. . . . Pick all the fruit . . . and see that nothing is wasted.
5. Instead of obeying, Cornelia knelt down. . . .

Student Activity 2. Rewrite the following sentences, omitting the italicized words and inserting ellipsis marks:

1. Then she made her will and came down with a *long* fever.
2. He had made quite a scandal and was very pleased *about it.*
3. There they were, *made out of her,* and they couldn't get away from that.
4. *That was hell,* she knew hell when she saw it.
5. She must get up and pull the shades down *or she'd never sleep.*

Humanities Note

Fine art, *Lavender and Old Lace,* by Charles Burchfield. The American artist Charles Burchfield (1893–1967) gained fame for his intense and imaginative paintings of nature and his moody, psychological studies of buildings.

Lavender and Old Lace is a watercolor painted between 1939 and 1947. This study of a Victorian house is filled with gloom and mystery. Burchfield has made the building come alive as if its awareness grew on the emotions of those who dwelled there. The melancholy air is nurtured by the overshadowing tree and the gingerbread trim that hangs from the house like a malevolent growth. Burchfield referred to this painting as "an elegy." He used the twilight time of evening and the crowding vegetation to create the sense of mystery that pervades this painting. The unique ability of Charles Burchfield to give life to inanimate objects and plant forms is apparent in this work.

You might ask your students these questions:
1. What mood does this painting evoke?
2. Might this house hold the memories of Granny Weatherall? Explain.

LAVENDER AND OLD LACE
Charles Burchfield, ANA
From the Collection of the New Britain Museum of American Art

Nonsense. It was strange about children. They disputed your every word. "No what, Cornelia?"

"Here's Doctor Harry."

"I won't see that boy again. He just left five minutes ago."

"That was this morning, Mother. It's night now. Here's the nurse."

"This is Doctor Harry, Mrs. Weatherall. I never saw you look so young and happy!"

"Ah, I'll never be young again—but I'd be happy if they'd let me lie in peace and get rested."

She thought she spoke up loudly, but no one answered. A warm weight on her forehead, a warm bracelet on her wrist, and a breeze went on whispering, trying to tell her something. A shuffle of leaves in the everlasting hand of God, He blew on them and they danced and rattled. "Mother, don't mind, we're going to give you a little hypodermic." "Look here, daughter, how do ants get in this bed? I saw sugar ants yesterday." Did you send for Hapsy too?

It was Hapsy she really wanted. She had to go a long way back through a great many rooms to find Hapsy standing with a baby on her arm. She seemed to herself to be Hapsy also, and the baby on Hapsy's arm was Hapsy and himself and herself, all at once, and there was no surprise in the meeting. Then Hapsy melted from within and turned

698   The Modern Age

Grammar in Action

Writers can use either **formal** or **informal English,** depending on their purpose. They use formal English for serious writing. Formal English uses traditional standards of correctness. It is characterized by the use of complex sentence structures and an extensive vocabulary. Writers use informal English to express a casual, everyday tone. It is especially useful for dialogue or for expressing characters' thoughts. Informal English is conversational in tone. It generally uses a smaller vocabulary and shorter sentences than formal English. Notice how Porter uses informal English in the following dialogue:

"Here's Doctor Harry."

"I won't see that boy again. He just left five minutes ago."

"That was this morning, Mother. It's night now. Here's the nurse."

The language in this dialogue is conversational—the way we speak to each other in conversation. It includes contractions, casual expressions, and short sentences. Because "The Jilting of Granny Weatherall" consists primarily of dialogue and the thoughts of the main character, Porter makes extensive use of informal English.

flimsy as gray gauze and the baby was a gauzy shadow, and Hapsy came up close and said, "I thought you'd never come," and looked at her very searchingly and said, "You haven't changed a bit!" They leaned forward to kiss, when Cornelia began whispering from a long way off, "Oh, is there anything you want to tell me? Is there anything I can do for you?"

15 Yes, she had changed her mind after sixty years and she would like to see George. I want you to find George. Find him and be sure to tell him I forgot him. I want him to know I had my husband just the same and my children and my house like any other woman. A good house too and a good husband that I loved and fine children out of him. Better than I hoped for even. Tell him I was given back everything he took away and more. Oh, no, oh, God, no, there was something else besides the house and the man and the children. Oh, surely they were not all? What was it? Something not given back. . . . Her breath crowded down under her ribs and grew into a monstrous frightening shape with cutting edges; it bored up into her head, and the agony was unbelievable: Yes, John, get the Doctor now, no more talk, my time has come.

When this one was born it should be the last. The last. It should have been born first, for it was the one she had truly wanted. Everything came in good time. Nothing left out, left over. She was strong, in three days she would be as well as ever. Better. A woman needed milk in her to have her full health.

16 "Mother, do you hear me?"

"I've been telling you—"

"Mother, Father Connolly's here."

"I went to Holy Communion only last week. Tell him I'm not so sinful as all that."

"Father just wants to speak to you."

He could speak as much as he pleased. It was like him to drop in and inquire about her soul as if it were a teething baby, and then stay on for a cup of tea and a round of cards and gossip. He always had a funny story of some sort, usually about an Irishman who made his little mistakes and confessed them, and the point lay in some absurd thing he would blurt out in the confessional showing his struggles between native piety and original sin. Granny felt easy about her soul. Cornelia, where are your manners? Give Father Connolly a chair. She had her secret comfortable understanding with a few favorite saints who cleared a straight road to God for her. All as surely signed and sealed as the papers for the new Forty Acres. Forever . . . heirs and assigns[2] forever. Since the day the wedding cake was not cut, but thrown out and wasted. The whole bottom dropped out of the world, and there she was blind and sweating with nothing under her feet and the walls falling away. His hand had caught her under the breast, she had not fallen, there was the freshly polished floor with the green rug on it, just as before. He had cursed like a sailor's parrot and said, "I'll kill him for you." Don't lay a hand on him, for my sake leave something to God. "Now, Ellen, you must believe what I tell you. . . ."

So there was nothing, nothing to worry about any more, except sometimes in the night one of the children screamed in a nightmare, and they both hustled out shaking and hunting for the matches and calling, "There, wait a minute, here we are!" John, get the doctor now, Hapsy's time has come. But there was Hapsy standing by the bed in a white cap. "Cornelia, tell Hapsy to take off her cap. I can't see her plain."

Her eyes opened very wide and the room stood out like a picture she had seen somewhere. Dark colors with the shadows rising towards the ceiling in long angles. The tall black dresser gleamed with nothing on it but John's picture, enlarged from a little one, with John's eyes very black when they should have been blue. You never saw him, so how do you know how he looked? But the man insisted the copy was perfect, it was very rich and handsome. For a picture, yes, but it's not my husband. The table by the

---

2. assigns: Persons to whom property is transferred.

The Jilting of Granny Weatherall   699

15 Discussion What is ironic about the fact that Granny wants to find George to tell him that she has forgotten him?

16 Clarification Father Connally has arrived to administer Granny's last rites.

Student Activity. Rewrite the following sentences using formal English.

1. "What'd you say, Mother?"
    Granny felt her face tying up in hard knots.
    "Can't a body think, I'd like to know?"
    "I thought you might want something."
    "I do. I want a lot of things. First off, go away and don't whisper."

2. I want him to know I had my husband just the same and my children and my house like any other woman. A good house too and a good husband that I loved and fine children out of him. Better than I hoped for even.

700

17 Clarification Mass is a Roman Catholic religious service.

18 Critical Thinking and Reading Note that once again Granny's thoughts drift back to her jilting.

19 Discussion Why does Granny tell Cornelia that she has been "taken by surprise"?

20 Discussion Why does Granny feel jilted for a second time, and why is this second jilting so more unforgivable than the first?

Reader's Response Based on her thoughts and statements, do you think that Granny Weatherall was satisfied with the life she led? Why or why not?

---

bed had a linen cover and a candle and a crucifix. The light was blue from Cornelia's silk lampshades. No sort of light at all, just frippery. You had to live forty years with kerosene lamps to appreciate honest electricity. She felt very strong and she saw Doctor Harry with a rosy nimbus around him.

"You look like a saint, Doctor Harry, and I vow that's as near as you'll ever come to it."

"She's saying something."

"I heard you, Cornelia. What's all this carrying on?"

"Father Connolly's saying—"

Cornelia's voice staggered and bumped like a cart in a bad road. It rounded corners and turned back again and arrived nowhere. Granny stepped up in the cart very lightly and reached for the reins, but a man sat beside her and she knew him by his hands, driving the cart. She did not look in his face, for she knew without seeing, but looked instead down the road where the trees leaned over and bowed to each other and a thousand birds were singing a Mass. She felt like singing too, but she put her hand in the bosom of her dress and pulled out a rosary, and Father Connolly murmured Latin in a very solemn voice and tickled her feet.[3] My God, will you stop that nonsense? I'm a married woman. What if he did run away and leave me to face the priest by myself? I found another a whole world better. I wouldn't have exchanged my husband for anybody except St. Michael[4] himself, and you may tell him that for me with a thank you in the bargain.

Light flashed on her closed eyelids, and a deep roaring shook her. Cornelia, is that lightning? I hear thunder. There's going to be a storm. Close all the windows. Call the children in. . . . "Mother, here we are, all of us." "Is that you, Hapsy?" "Oh, no, I'm Lydia. We drove as fast as we could." Their faces drifted above her, drifted away. The rosary fell out of her hands and Lydia put it back. Jimmy tried to help, their hands fumbled together, and Granny closed two fingers

---

3. **murmured . . . feet:** Administered the last rites.
4. **St. Michael:** One of the archangels.

---

around Jimmy's thumb. Beads wouldn't do, it must be something alive. She was so amazed her thoughts ran round and round. So, my dear Lord, this is my death and I wasn't even thinking about it. My children have come to see me die. But I can't, it's not time. Oh, I always hated surprises. I wanted to give Cornelia the amethyst set—Cornelia, you're to have the amethyst set, but Hapsy's to wear it when she wants, and, Doctor Harry, do shut up. Nobody sent for you. Oh, my dear Lord, do wait a minute. I meant to do something about the Forty Acres, Jimmy doesn't need it and Lydia will later on, with that worthless husband of hers. I meant to finish the altar cloth and send six bottles of wine to Sister Borgia for her dyspepsia. I want to send six bottles of wine to Sister Borgia, Father Connolly, now don't let me forget.

Cornelia's voice made short turns and tilted over and crashed. "Oh, Mother, oh, Mother, oh Mother. . . ."

"I'm not going, Cornelia. I'm taken by surprise. I can't go."

You'll see Hapsy again. What about her? "I thought you'd never come." Granny made a long journey outward, looking for Hapsy. What if I don't find her? What then? Her heart sank down and down, there was no bottom to death, she couldn't come to the end of it. The blue light from Cornelia's lampshade drew into a tiny point in the center of her brain, it flickered and winked like an eye, quietly it fluttered and dwindled. Granny lay curled down within herself, amazed and watchful, staring at the point of light that was herself; her body was now only a deeper mass of shadow in an endless darkness and this darkness would curl around the light and swallow it up. God, give a sign!

For the second time there was no sign. Again no bridegroom and the priest in the house. She could not remember any other sorrow because this grief wiped them all away. Oh, no, there's nothing more cruel than this—I'll never forgive it. She stretched herself with a deep breath and blew out the light.

Closure and Extension

THINKING ABOUT THE SELECTION

Recalling

1. (a) How does Granny explain her condition to Doctor Harry? (b) What does she hear Cornelia and Doctor Harry whispering? (c) What does she ask of Cornelia?
2. (a) What had Granny done when she was sixty? (b) How had the experience affected her?
3. (a) What painful memory is "squeezed out" of Granny's heart? (b) With what thought does this memory become mingled?
4. (a) What realization does Granny come to after her children arrive? (b) How does she respond to this realization?
5. (a) What does Granny ask of God just before she blows "out the light"? (b) What happens "for the second time"?

Interpreting

6. Why is "Weatherall" an appropriate surname for Granny?
7. (a) What is ironic about Granny's desire to find George so she can tell him she has forgotten him? (b) What might be the "something not given back" that George took?
8. What detail indicates that Granny's sense of time has become distorted?
9. (a) Why does the jilting dominate Granny's thoughts as she approaches death? (b) How is the jilting related to what she experiences in the final paragraph?
10. What does the light referred to in the last two paragraphs symbolize?

Applying

11. Explain whether you think the thoughts and feelings Granny has in the story are typical for a person in her condition.

ANALYZING LITERATURE

Seeing Stream of Consciousness

When a writer uses the **stream-of-consciousness** technique, he or she re-creates the natural flow of a character's thoughts. The writer accomplishes this by eliminating the transitions used in ordinary prose and by allowing only the character's natural associations to link thoughts.

1. Find two examples from "The Jilting of Granny Weatherall" in which Granny's thoughts drift from one subject to another subject that is seemingly quite different.
2. What natural associations connect the thoughts in each of these examples?

Understanding Flashback

The stream-of-consciousness technique often includes **flashbacks,** or interruptions in the narrative in which an earlier event is recalled or described. For example, early in the story, Granny recalls a series of events that occurred when she was sixty.

1. Find three more examples of flashbacks. What do you learn from each of these flashbacks?
2. How do the flashbacks contribute to Porter's effective use of the stream-of-consciousness technique?

CRITICAL THINKING AND READING

Understanding the Sequence of Events

In a story written using the stream-of-consciousness technique, events are organized according to a character's associations, rather than in chronological order. This means that the narrative jumps around in time. As a result, to understand the sequence you must be able to reorganize the events in the order in which they occurred.

Rearrange the events presented in "The Jilting of Granny Weatherall" in chronological order.

THINKING AND WRITING

Writing About Techniques

Write an essay in which you explain why the stream-of-consciousness technique is particularly appropriate for "The Jilting of Granny Weatherall," considering the subject of the story. Start by thinking about the purpose of the stream-of-consciousness technique and about the subject of the story and noting the reasons why the technique is appropriate for the story. Then prepare a thesis statement, and write your essay. When you finish writing, revise your essay, making sure that you have adequately supported your thesis.

The Jilting of Granny Weatherall 701

the things that have to be done, and her thoughts drift to the way she organized her possessions, to her fears that her children would discover her letters from John and George. Another example is when the priest arrives, and Granny's thoughts drift from the peculiarities of his personality, to the need to provide him a chair, to her "secret comfortable understanding with a few favorite saints."

2. In the first example, her contemplation of the tasks she must complete prompts her to think about the way she organizes her possessions, which leads her to think about her letters and brings out her fears concerning these letters. In the second example, Granny's thoughts about the priest are linked to her thoughts about her "secret understanding with a few favorite saints" by their association with God.

1. Examples include Granny's thoughts about raising her children alone and taking over the role her husband would have played if he had been alive; her memories of her wedding day when George jilted her; and her memories of her work as a midwife.
2. They provide important background information.

ANSWERS TO CRITICAL THINKING AND READING

At age twenty Granny is jilted by George. Granny marries John. Granny has three children. At age forty Granny has milk leg and pneumonia. John dies. Granny continues to raise her children alone. Granny works as a midwife. At age sixty Granny prepares for death and visits her children. At age eighty Granny dies.

THINKING AND WRITING

After students have completed the assignment, divide them into groups, and have them read their rough drafts to one another and suggest ways in which they could be improved.

---

5. (a) She asks God to give her a sign. (b) She is not given a sign.

Interpreting

6. It is appropriate because she has weathered all of the difficult situations that have occurred during the course of her life.
7. (a) It is ironic, because it is clear that she has not forgotten him. (b) The "something not given back" might be her pride or self-esteem.

8. Granny believes that Dr. Harry had just examined her five minutes ago, when it had actually been several hours since he had examined her.
9. (a) It dominates her thoughts, because it was a traumatic event from which she never recovered, and because her memory of this experience has become mingled with her fear of going to hell. (b) She is jilted for a second time.
10. It represents Granny's life.

Applying

11. Suggested Response: Yes, people usually remember the most important events in their lives when they are facing death.

ANSWERS TO ANALYZING LITERATURE

1. Suggested Response: One example is when Granny thinks of all

If Wolfe had not died at such an early age, there is little doubt that his literary output would have been great. In a letter to his mother, Wolfe wrote of his plans for the future. He planned to explore and write about everything: "This is why I think I'm going to be an artist. The things that really mattered sunk in and left their mark. Sometimes only a word—sometimes a peculiar smile—sometimes death—sometimes the smell of dandelions in Spring—once Love. Most people have little more mind than brutes: they live from day to day. I will go everywhere and see everything. I will meet all the people I can. I will think all the thoughts, feel all the emotions I am able, and I will write, write, write."

In his story "Of Time and the River," Thomas Wolfe offers the following definition of an artist: "This is the artist, then—life's hungry man, the glutton of eternity, beauty's miser, glory's slave." What is the meaning of Wolfe's definition? Do you agree with this definition? Why or why not?

THOMAS WOLFE

1900–1938

A man of tremendous energy, appetites, and size, Thomas Wolfe poured out thousands of pages of fiction during his brief career. Unlike such Modernist writers as Hemingway and Fitzgerald, who wrote concise, carefully structured prose, Wolfe wrote elaborate, loosely structured fiction that was often uneven in quality. His novels and short stories tended to be long and somewhat unpolished, yet they were filled with vivid imagery and lyrical language.

Born in Asheville, North Carolina, Wolfe grew up in a large, eccentric family whose members later served as models for characters in his fiction. He attended the University of North Carolina at Chapel Hill, where he developed an interest in playwriting. After a year of postgraduate study at Harvard, he moved to New York. There he taught composition at New York University and wrote plays in his spare time. Unable to find success as a playwright, he turned to fiction. With the assistance of Maxwell Perkins, the leading editor of the time, Wolfe published his first novel, *Look Homeward, Angel,* in 1929. The novel, based on his experiences in Asheville, was a critical and financial success and earned him widespread recognition.

Describing the day that Perkins paid him for the manuscript of *Look Homeward, Angel,* Wolfe wrote: "It was the first time . . . that anyone had concretely suggested to me that anything I had written was worth as much as fifteen cents, and I know that I left the publisher's office that day and entered into the great swarm of men and women who passed constantly along Fifth Avenue at Forty-eighth Street and presently I found myself at 110th Street, and from that day to this I have never known how I got there."

Inspired by the success of his first novel, Wolfe began working on a sequel. Once again Perkins helped him to shorten and shape the novel, which was published as *Of Time and the River* in 1935. The novel sold well, yet Wolfe was criticized for basing his work too closely on his own life and for his reliance on Perkins. Stung by this criticism, Wolfe switched publishers and vowed to abandon his autobiographical mode in his next novel. Unfortunately, he died of a brain infection before he could finish this novel. He did, however, leave several thousand pages of manuscript in the hands of another editor, Edward Aswell, who shaped them into two more books, *The Web and the Rock* (1939) and *You Can't Go Home Again* (1940).

Although he has been criticized for his lack of discipline, Wolfe was clearly a gifted writer. In his novels and short stories, including "The Far and the Near," he displayed a strong sense of time and place, an ability to create vivid, realistic descriptions, and a profound understanding of the human condition.

Objectives

1 To understand point of view
2 To recognize period characteristics
3 To compare and contrast stories

Support Material

Teaching Portfolio
Teacher Backup, p. 903
Usage and Mechanics Worksheet, p. 907
Vocabulary Check, p. 908
Analyzing Literature Worksheet, *Understanding Point of View,* p. 909
Language Worksheet, *Recognizing Multiple Meanings,* p. 910
Selection Test, p. 911

GUIDE FOR INTERPRETING

The Far and the Near

Point of View. Point of view refers to the vantage point or perspective from which a narrative is told. Most stories are told from either a first-person or third-person point of view. In a narrative with a first-person point of view, one of the characters tells the story in his or her own words, using the first-person pronoun *I*. In a narrative with a third-person point of view, the narrator does not participate in the story and refers to characters using the third-person pronouns *he* or *she*. A third-person narrator may be either limited or omniscient. A limited third-person narrator focuses on the thoughts and feelings of only one character. An omniscient third-person narrator conveys the thoughts and feelings of all the characters.

During the Modern Age, fiction writers generally abandoned the use of omniscient narrators in favor of first-person and limited third-person narrators. This practice reflected the Modernist belief that "reality" and "truth" cannot be viewed objectively. Writers also frequently attempted to convey a sense of uncertainty by using a narrator who lacked an understanding or awareness of the nature of human existence.

Commentary

Writing about the way he remembers experiences, Thomas Wolfe once remarked:

> The quality of my memory is characterized, I believe, in a more than ordinary degree by the intensity of its sense impressions, its power to evoke and bring back the odors, sounds, colors, shapes, and feel of things with concrete vividness. . . . the look of an old iron bridge across an American river, the sound the train makes as it goes across it; the spoke-and-hollow rumble of the ties below; the look of the muddy banks; the slow, thick, yellow wash of an American river; an old flat-bottomed boat half-filled with water stogged in the muddy bank. . . .

"The Far and the Near" is filled with the vivid sense impressions that the engineer has piled up in his mind for more than twenty years of traveling the same route on the railroad. As you read, notice Wolfe's descriptions and how they appeal to the engineer's senses and imagination. Wolfe emphasizes the intensity of these impressions by showing how memory, imagination, and longing all spring from the passing impressions of life.

Writing

According to an old Russian proverb, "A toe of the star-gazer is often stubbed." Freewrite, exploring the meaning of this proverb.

Guide for Interpreting 703

Literary Focus In stories that use a limited point of view, the portrayal of characters and events is shaped by the thoughts and feelings of the character from whose point of view that story is being told.

Writing/Prior Knowledge Before having students complete the writing activity, you might want to spend some time discussing how the proverb relates to the discrepancy between reality and people's expectations.

Vocabulary

Preteach the following vocabulary words:
sallow (sal′ ō) *adj.:* Sickly, pale-yellow (p. 706)
sullen (sul′ ən) *adj.:* Sulky; glum (p. 706)
timorous (tim′ ər əs) *adj.:* Full of fear (p. 706)
visage (viz′ ij) *n.:* Appearance (p. 706)

Motivation/Prior Knowledge
Have students imagine that they have been waiting to meet a famous film star whom they have admired for years. Finally, full of expectation, they come face to face with their idol. Does he or she live up to the image? How would students feel if the star simply brushed them aside without a word?

Thematic Idea Another story in which reality does not live up to a character's expectations is "The First Seven Years" by Bernard Malamud (p. 946).

Purpose-Setting Question What is the engineer hoping to find?

1 **Discussion** What single adjective would best describe this house? Are there any details that indicate that the engineer's impressions of the house are not completely accurate?

2 **Critical Thinking and Reading** The narrator uses the phrase "every day" three times in the same paragraph. Why? What is the narrator telling you about the life of the engineer?

3 **Literary Focus** From whose point of view is the story being told?

4 **Critical Thinking and Reading** In two sentences, the narrator sums up the engineer's entire adult life—every bit of "grief, joy, peril, and labor." Four horrible tragedies are listed as an aside in the same sentence that describes his children growing up. What might the narrator really be saying about the "wisdom" this man has gained?

The Far and the Near

Thomas Wolfe

On the outskirts of a little town upon a rise of land that swept back from the railway there was a tidy little cottage of white boards, trimmed vividly with green blinds. To one side of the house there was a garden neatly patterned with plots of growing vegetables, and an arbor for the grapes which ripened late in August. Before the house there were three mighty oaks which sheltered it in their clean and massive shade in summer, and to the other side there was a border of gay flowers. The whole place had an air of tidiness, thrift, and modest comfort.

Every day, a few minutes after two o'clock in the afternoon, the limited express between two cities passed this spot. At that moment the great train, having halted for a breathing space at the town nearby, was beginning to lengthen evenly into its stroke, but it had not yet reached the full drive of its terrific speed. It swung into view deliberately, swept past with a powerful swaying motion of the engine, a low smooth rumble of its heavy cars upon pressed steel, and then it vanished in the cut. For a moment the progress of the engine could be marked by heavy bellowing puffs of smoke that burst at spaced intervals above the edges of the meadow grass, and finally nothing could be heard but the solid clacking tempo of the wheels receding into the drowsy stillness of the afternoon.

Every day for more than twenty years, as the train had approached this house, the engineer had blown on the whistle, and every day, as soon as she heard this signal, a woman had appeared on the back porch of the little house and waved to him. At first she had a small child clinging to her skirts, and now this child had grown to full womanhood, and every day she, too, came with her mother to the porch and waved.

The engineer had grown old and gray in service. He had driven his great train, loaded with its weight of lives, across the land ten thousand times. His own children had grown up and married, and four times he had seen before him on the tracks the ghastly dot of tragedy converging like a cannon ball to its eclipse of horror at the boiler head[1]—a light spring wagon filled with children, with its clustered row of small stunned faces; a cheap automobile stalled upon the tracks, set with the wooden figures of people paralyzed with fear; a battered hobo walking by the rail, too deaf and old to hear the whistle's warning; and a form flung past his window with a scream—all this the man had seen and known. He had known all the grief, the joy, the peril and the labor such a man could know; he had grown seamed and weathered in his loyal service, and now, schooled by the qualities of faith and courage and humbleness that attended his labor, he had grown old, and had the grandeur and the wisdom these men have.

But no matter what peril or tragedy he had known, the vision of the little house and the women waving to him with a brave free motion of the arm had become fixed in the

---

1. **boiler head:** The front section of a steam locomotive.

mind of the engineer as something beautiful and enduring, something beyond all change and ruin, and something that would always be the same, no matter what mishap, grief or error might break the iron schedule of his days.

The sight of the little house and of these two women gave him the most extraordinary happiness he had ever known. He had seen them in a thousand lights, a hundred weathers. He had seen them through the harsh bare light of wintry gray across the brown and frosted stubble of the earth, and he had seen them again in the green luring sorcery of April.

He felt for them and for the little house in which they lived such tenderness as a man might feel for his own children, and at length the picture of their lives was carved so sharply in his heart that he felt that he knew their lives completely, to every hour and moment of the day, and he resolved that one day, when his years of service should be ended, he would go and find these people and speak at last with them whose lives had been so wrought into his own.

That day came. At last the engineer stepped from a train onto the station platform of the town where these two women lived. His years upon the rail had ended. He was a pensioned servant of his company, with no more work to do. The engineer

STONE CITY, IOWA
Grant Wood
Joslyn Art Museum, Omaha, Nebraska

The Far and the Near 705

Humanities Note

Fine art, *Stone City, Iowa*, 1930, by Grant Wood. Grant Wood (1891-1942), an American painter, was a lifelong resident of Iowa. His father's death forced a delay of his artistic training, and as a young man he held many odd jobs, such as farming, silver-smithing, jewelry designing, and making handicrafts. In the 1920's he traveled to Europe. His paint-

ing, especially his landscapes, showed the influence of Impressionism. In 1928, he traveled to Munich, where his style was influenced by the German and Flemish primitives. He now began to paint in a crisp, precisely modelled style. Wood returned to the United States, where he found inspiration for his art in the people and places of Iowa. He became one of the exponents of Regionalism, an artistic move-

ment of the 1930's in America, which strove to break cultural dependence on European art by finding inspiration in everyday local experiences.

Stone City, Iowa is a perfect example of Grant Wood's brand of Regionalism. Although he has painted it in what might be called a realistic style, the picture remains strongly individual in style. Forms take on solid, almost geometric form, casting precise

5 Critical Thinking and Reading The narrator uses the word *sorcery,* meaning "witchcraft," in an unusual context. What does this word suggest about the light in which the engineer sees the two women?

6 Reading Strategy Have students predict what will happen when the engineer carries out his resolution.

shadows. The picture takes on a surrealistic air. Wood's unusual use of perspective and composition add to this unreal quality.

You might use these questions for discussion:

1. "The Far and the Near" is concerned with time and perspective. How does this painting by Grant Wood also indicate time and perspective?

2. What are the notable characteristics of Grant Wood's painting style?

7 Discussion The engineer has seen the town thousands of times before, and yet now it seems as if he had never seen it before. What has given the engineer this new perspective? How has his life changed?

8 Discussion For the first time in his life, the engineer has stepped down from the "high windows of his cab." What might this physical change mean on a symbolic level?

9 Critical Thinking and Reading How does the engineer's state of mind reflect the Modernists' view of the world?

10 Literary Focus You might wish to point out to your **more advanced** students how the function of the narrator changes during the course of the story. At first the narrator simply describes the house, the train, the engineer from a distance. Now the narrator is completely inside the engineer's head, focusing exclusively on his thoughts and feelings.

11 Literary Focus The story is told through the eyes of the engineer, yet in this sentence the reader can make inferences about the woman. If the story were told from her point of view, what might we learn about her thoughts as she meets the engineer?

12 Discussion Would you characterize Wolfe's view of the world as pessimistic, optimistic, or ambivalent? Do you agree?

Reader's Response Have you ever had an experience in which your expectations of something were greater than the actual thing itself? Why are experiences such as these especially disappointing?

walked slowly through the station and out into the streets of the town. Everything was as strange to him as if he had never seen this town before. As he walked on, his sense of bewilderment and confusion grew. Could this be the town he had passed ten thousand times? Were these the same houses he had seen so often from the high windows of his cab? It was all as unfamiliar, as disquieting as a city in a dream, and the perplexity of his spirit increased as he went on.

Presently the houses thinned into the straggling outposts of the town, and the street faded into a country road—the one on which the women lived. And the man plodded on slowly in the heat and dust. At length he stood before the house he sought. He knew at once that he had found the proper place. He saw the lordly oaks before the house, the flower beds, the garden and the arbor, and farther off, the glint of rails.

Yes, this was the house he sought, the place he had passed so many times, the destination he had longed for with such happiness. But now that he had found it, now that he was here, why did his hand falter on the gate; why had the town, the road, the earth, the very entrance to this place he loved turned unfamiliar as the landscape of some ugly dream? Why did he now feel this sense of confusion, doubt and hopelessness?

At length he entered by the gate, walked slowly up the path and in a moment more had mounted three short steps that led up to the porch, and was knocking at the door. Presently he heard steps in the hall, the door was opened, and a woman stood facing him.

And instantly, with a sense of bitter loss and grief, he was sorry he had come. He knew at once that the woman who stood there looking at him with a mistrustful eye

was the same woman who had waved to him so many thousand times. But her face was harsh and pinched and meager; the flesh sagged wearily in sallow folds, and the small eyes peered at him with timid suspicion and uneasy doubt. All the brave freedom, the warmth and the affection that he had read into her gesture, vanished in the moment that he saw her and heard her unfriendly tongue.

And now his own voice sounded unreal and ghastly to him as he tried to explain his presence, to tell her who he was and the reason he had come. But he faltered on, fighting stubbornly against the horror of regret, confusion, disbelief that surged up in his spirit, drowning all his former joy and making his act of hope and tenderness seem shameful to him.

At length the woman invited him almost unwillingly into the house, and called her daughter in a harsh shrill voice. Then, for a brief agony of time, the man sat in an ugly little parlor, and he tried to talk while the two women stared at him with a dull, bewildered hostility, a sullen, timorous restraint.

And finally, stammering a crude farewell, he departed. He walked away down the path and then along the road toward town, and suddenly he knew that he was an old man. His heart, which had been brave and confident when it looked along the familiar vista of the rails, was now sick with doubt and horror as it saw the strange and unsuspected visage of an earth which had always been within a stone's throw of him, and which he had never seen or known. And he knew that all the magic of that bright lost way, the vista of that shining line, the imagined corner of that small good universe of hope's desire, was gone forever, could never be got back again.

THINKING ABOUT THE SELECTION

Recalling

1. Describe the engineer's daily experience for more than twenty years.
2. (a) What four tragedies has the engineer seen during his years with the railroad? (b) What vision remains fixed in his mind despite the tragedies he has known?
3. Explain what happens when the engineer carries out his resolution.
4. What realization does the engineer come to at the end of the story?

Interpreting

5. What does the house come to represent to the engineer?
6. (a) How do the engineer's observations in the final scene contrast with his expectations? (b) When does he first become aware that his experience is unlikely to match his expectations?
7. In what ways does Wolfe use distance and physical movement to symbolize the passage of time in this story?
8. What is the meaning of the story's title?
9. Explain the story's theme.

Applying

10. If you had been in the engineer's place, would you have visited the cottage? Explain your answer.

ANALYZING LITERATURE

Understanding Point of View

Point of view refers to the vantage point or perspective from which a narrative is told. "The Far and the Near" is told from a limited third-person point of view. The narrator does not participate in the story and focuses on the thoughts and feelings of one character, the engineer. The reader seems to step inside the shoes of this

character and see the world through his eyes.

1. How would the story be different if Wolfe had used a first-person point of view?
2. How would it be different if Wolfe had used an omniscient third-person point of view?

CRITICAL THINKING AND READING

Recognizing Period Characteristics

Like "The Far and the Near," most modern short stories are told from a subjective point of view. The author writes in the first person or the third person but limits the perspective to one character.

1. What Modernist belief does the use of the limited third-person point of view reflect?
2. In many modern stories, the character from whose point of view the story is told is naive, lacking understanding of the nature of human existence. In what sense is the engineer naive?
3. How is the engineer's innocence shattered?
4. How does the engineer's loss of innocence reflect the Modernist belief in the uncertainty and confusion of modern life?

THINKING AND WRITING

Comparing and Contrasting Stories

Write an essay in which you compare and contrast Dexter's attachment to Judy Jones in Fitzgerald's "Winter Dreams" with the engineer's attachment to his vision of the little house in "The Far and the Near." Review both stories, noting similarities and differences between the two characters' attachments. Review your notes and prepare a thesis statement. Then write your essay. Organize it according to corresponding points of contrast. Use passages from the two stories to support your points. Then revise, eliminating any unnecessary words or details.

Closure and Extension

ANSWERS TO THINKING ABOUT THE SELECTION

Recalling

1. He passes a cottage on the outskirts of a little town. He blows the train whistle and a woman and her daughter emerge from the cottage and wave.
2. (a) He has seen his train run over a wagon filled with children an automobile filled with people, a hobo, and an unidentified figure. (b) The image of the house and the woman waving stick in his mind.
3. He discovers that the house and the woman are not as he imagined they would be, becomes horrified at their ugliness, and leaves in haste.
4. He realizes that his magical vision is gone forever.

Interpreting

5. The house represents something that is "beautiful and enduring, something beyond all change and ruin."
6. (a) He expected that what he would discover would be beautiful and uplifting, but it turns out to be ugly and upsetting. (b) He realizes it as soon as he steps off the train.
7. The passage of time is symbolized by the movement of the train.

8. The title refers to the contrasts in looking at something from two different vantage points—far and near.
9. Suggested Response: Nothing is as it seems. The world we live in is clouded with doubt and despair with no hope for perfection or a blissful ideal.

Applying

10. Some students might say *no*, because they would rather live life believing that all is well and good. Others might say yes, because they want to see reality for what it is and not live in delusion and ignorance.

Challenge Do you think that the engineer will ever get over his disappointment? Why or why not?

ANSWERS TO ANALYZING LITERATURE

1. Suggested Response: The story would have focused more on the engineer's feelings.
2. Suggested Response: The story would not have been effective, because the reader would know the true character of the woman and her daughter before the engineer's visit.

ANSWERS TO CRITICAL THINKING AND READING

1. It reflects the belief that reality is a product of each individual's thoughts and experiences.
2. He has an unrealistic perception of the cottage and the woman.
3. When he visits the cottage, he discovers that his expectations were unrealistic.
4. When his innocence is shattered, he is left feeling uncertain and confused.

THINKING AND WRITING

For help with this assignment, students can refer to Lesson 16, "Writing a Comparative Evaluation," in the Handbook of Writing About Literature.

After students have completed the assignment, divide them into groups, and have them read their rough drafts to one another and comment on ways in which they could be improved.

More About the Author Regarding the purpose of fiction, Eudora Welty has stated, "I don't think literature—I'm talking about fiction now—I don't think it can exhort. Or it loses every bit of its reality and value. I think it speaks to what is more deeply within, that is, the personal, and conveys its meaning that way. And then one hopes that a person made alert or aroused to be more sensitive to other human beings would go on to look at things on a larger scale by himself. I wouldn't like to read a work of fiction that I thought had an ulterior motive, to persuade me politically. I automatically react the other way . . . I think things should be written to persuade, but openly as a column or an editorial or a speech. But perfectly on the up and up. That's because I understand as a person, not as a motto."

Eudora Welty's characters, like those of her fellow Mississippian William Faulkner, are often exaggerated in their eccentricities. This comes in part from a southern tradition of oral story telling, where details and events become more embellished with each retelling. How else might an oral tradition enrich the work of an author?

EUDORA WELTY

1909–

In her short stories and novels, Eudora Welty captures life in the deep South, creating vivid portraits of the landscape and conveying the shared attitudes and values of the people. She often confronts the hardships and sorrows of life in the poor rural areas. Yet despite her awareness of people's suffering, her outlook remains positive and optimistic.

Welty was born in Jackson, Mississippi, where she has spent most of her life. She attended Mississippi State College for Women, before transferring to the University of Wisconsin, from which she graduated in 1929. Hoping to pursue a career in advertising, she moved to New York and enrolled at Columbia University School of Business. However, because of the worsening Depression, she was unable to find a steady job and returned to Jackson in 1931.

After accepting a job as a publicist for a government agency, she spent several years traveling throughout Mississippi, taking photographs and interviewing people. Her experiences and observations inspired her to write fiction, and in 1936 her first short story, "Death of a Traveling Salesman," was published in a small magazine.

Welty became a leading American writer of this century. Over the years she has published numerous collections of short stories, including *A Curtain of Green* (1941), *The Wide Net and Other Stories* (1943), *The Bride of Innisfallen and Other Stories* (1955), and *Thirteen Stories* (1965). She has also written several novels, including *Delta Wedding* (1946), *The Ponder Heart* (1954), and *Losing Battles* (1970). In 1973 she was awarded the Pulitzer Prize for her novel *The Optimist's Daughter* (1972).

Throughout her work Welty displays an acute sense of detail and a deep sense of compassion toward her characters. In "A Worn Path," for example, she paints a sympathetic portrait of an old woman whose feelings of love and sense of duty motivate her to make a long, painful journey through the woods.

Welty used her fiction to explore private lives like Phoenix Jackson's in "A Worn Path." In "Must the Novelist Crusade," Welty responded to critics who felt that a modern writer had to "better the world or go to his grave reproached for the mess it is in." Welty answered that writers were not crusaders. "Writing fiction is an interior affair. Novels and stories always will be put down little by little out of personal feeling and personal beliefs arrived at alone and at firsthand over a period of time as time is needed. To go outside and beat the drum is only to interrupt, interrupt, and so finally to forget and lose. Fiction has, and must keep, a private address. For life is *lived* in a private place; where it means anything is inside the mind and heart. Fiction has always shown life where it is lived. . . ."

708   *The Modern Age*

GUIDE FOR INTERPRETING

A Worn Path

Writer's Techniques

Ambiguity. Ambiguity refers to uncertainty of intention or meaning. An ambiguous statement is one that can be interpreted in two or more ways. Similarly, when a work of literature is ambiguous or contains ambiguous elements, the work or certain elements of the work can be interpreted in more than one way. Readers may find various possible meanings and look for details that support each interpretation.

During the Modern Age, literary works became increasingly ambiguous. Writers suggested meaning and presented possibilities instead of asserting or directly stating their points. This style reflected the Modernist belief that life in the modern world is confusing and filled with uncertainties rather than definite answers.

Writing

"A Worn Path" is about an old woman, Phoenix Jackson, who repeatedly makes a long, arduous journey into town to get medicine for her grandson. Make a list of journeys that you have made repeatedly during your life. Then jot down your reasons for making each of these journeys.

Primary Source

Welty once wrote an essay called "Is Phoenix Jackson's Grandson Really Dead?" named after the question most often asked her by students.

It's *all right,* I want to say to the students who write me, for things to be what they appear to be, and for words to mean what they say. It's all right, too, for words and appearances to mean more than one thing—ambiguity is a fact of life. A fiction writer's responsibility covers not only what he presents as the facts of a given story but what he chooses to stir up as their implications; in the end, these implications, too, become facts, in the larger fictional sense. But it is not all right, not in good faith, for things *not* to mean what they say.

The grandson's plight was real and it made the truth of the story, which is the story of an errand of love carried out. If the child no longer lived, the truth would persist in the 'worn-ness' of the path. But his being dead can't increase the truth of the story, can't affect it one way or the other. I think I signal this, because the end of the story has been reached before old Phoenix gets home again: she simply starts back. To the question 'Is the grandson really dead?' I could reply that it doesn't make any difference. I could also say that I did not make him up in order to let him play a trick on Phoenix. But my best answer could be: "*Phoenix* is alive."

Literary Focus Give less advanced students examples of ambiguous and nonambiguous statements and ask them to identify them. For example the statement, "The boy is just the same as before" is ambiguous because we do not know how the boy was before.

Writing/Prior Knowledge Before students complete the writing activity, discuss various types of journeys. A pilgrimage is a long journey usually taken for religious reasons. An expedition is a journey of exploration. An odyssey is a wandering journey. A trek connotates a slow and difficult journey. Which types of journeys have students made?

Vocabulary

Preteach the following vocabulary words:
grave (grāv) *adj.:* Serious; solemn (p. 710)
limber (lim′ bər) *adj.:* Flexible (p. 710)
obstinate (äb′stə nit) *adj.:* Stubborn (p. 714)

A Worn Path

Eudora Welty

It was December—a bright frozen day in the early morning. Far out in the country there was an old Negro woman with her head tied in a red rag, coming along a path through the pinewoods. Her name was Phoenix Jackson. She was very old and small and she walked slowly in the dark pine shadows, moving a little from side to side in her steps, with the balanced heaviness and lightness of a pendulum in a grandfather clock. She carried a thin, small cane made from an umbrella, and with this she kept tapping the frozen earth in front of her. This made a grave and persistent noise in the still air, that seemed meditative like the chirping of a solitary little bird.

She wore a dark striped dress reaching down to her shoe tops, and an equally long apron of bleached sugar sacks, with a full pocket: all neat and tidy, but every time she took a step she might have fallen over her shoelaces, which dragged from her unlaced shoes. She looked straight ahead. Her eyes were blue with age. Her skin had a pattern all its own of numberless branching wrinkles and as though a whole little tree stood in the middle of her forehead, but a golden color ran underneath, and the two knobs of her cheeks were illumined by a yellow burning under the dark. Under the red rag her hair came down on her neck in the frailest of ringlets, still black, and with an odor like copper.

Now and then there was a quivering in the thicket. Old Phoenix said, "Out of my way, all you foxes, owls, beetles, jack rabbits, coons and wild animals! . . . Keep out from under these feet, little bobwhites[1]. . . . Keep the big wild hogs out of my path. Don't let none of those come running my direction. I got a long way." Under her small black-freckled hand her cane, limber as a buggy whip, would switch at the brush as if to rouse up any hiding things.

On she went. The woods were deep and still. The sun made the pine needles almost too bright to look at, up where the wind rocked. The cones dropped as light as feathers. Down in the hollow was the mourning dove—it was not too late for him.

The path ran up a hill. "Seem like there is chains about my feet, time I get this far," she said, in the voice of argument old people keep to use with themselves. "Something always take a hold of me on this hill—pleads I should stay."

After she got to the top she turned and gave a full, severe look behind her where she had come. "Up through pines," she said at length. "Now down through oaks."

Her eyes opened their widest, and she started down gently. But before she got to the bottom of the hill a bush caught her dress.

Her fingers were busy and intent, but her skirts were full and long, so that before she could pull them free in one place they were caught in another. It was not possible to allow the dress to tear. "I in the thorny bush," she said. "Thorns, you doing your appointed work. Never want to let folks pass,

---

1. **bobwhites** *n.*: Partridges.

no sir. Old eyes thought you was a pretty little *green* bush."

Finally, trembling all over, she stood free, and after a moment dared to stoop for her cane.

"Sun so high!" she cried, leaning back and looking, while the thick tears went over her eyes. "The time getting all gone here."

At the foot of this hill was a place where a log was laid across the creek.

"Now comes the trial," said Phoenix.

Putting her right foot out, she mounted the log and shut her eyes. Lifting her skirt, leveling her cane fiercely before her, like a festival figure in some parade, she began to march across. Then she opened her eyes and she was safe on the other side.

"I wasn't as old as I thought," she said.

But she sat down to rest. She spread her skirts on the bank around her and folded her hands over her knees. Up above her was a tree in a pearly cloud of mistletoe. She did not dare to close her eyes, and when a little boy brought her a plate with a slice of marble cake on it she spoke to him. "That would be acceptable," she said. But when she went to take it there was just her own hand in the air.

So she left that tree, and had to go through a barbed-wire fence. There she had to creep and crawl, spreading her knees and stretching her fingers like a baby trying to climb the steps. But she talked loudly to herself: she could not let her dress be torn now, so late in the day, and she could not pay for having her arm or her leg sawed off if she got caught fast where she was.

At last she was safe through the fence and risen up out in the clearing. Big dead trees, like black men with one arm, were standing in the purple stalks of the withered cotton field. There sat a buzzard.

"Who you watching?"

In the furrow she made her way along.

"Glad this not the season for bulls," she said, looking sideways, "and the good Lord made his snakes to curl up and sleep in the winter. A pleasure I don't see no two-headed snake coming around that tree, where it come once. It took a while to get by him, back in the summer."

She passed through the old cotton and went into a field of dead corn. It whispered and shook and was taller than her head. "Through the maze now," she said, for there was no path.

Then there was something tall, black, and skinny there, moving before her.

At first she took it for a man. It could have been a man dancing in the field. But she stood still and listened, and it did not make a sound. It was as silent as a ghost.

"Ghost," she said sharply, "who be you the ghost of? For I have heard of nary death close by."

But there was no answer—only the ragged dancing in the wind.

She shut her eyes, reached out her hand, and touched a sleeve. She found a coat and inside that an emptiness, cold as ice.

"You scarecrow," she said. Her face lighted. "I ought to be shut up for good," she said with laughter. "My senses is gone. I too old. I the oldest people I ever know. Dance, old scarecrow," she said, "while I dancing with you."

She kicked her foot over the furrow, and with mouth drawn down, shook her head once or twice in a little strutting way. Some husks blew down and whirled in streamers about her skirts.

Then she went on, parting her way from side to side with the cane, through the whispering field. At last she came to the end, to a wagon track where the silver grass blew between the red ruts. The quail were walking around like pullets, seeming all dainty and unseen.

"Walk pretty," she said. "This the easy place. This the easy going."

She followed the track, swaying through the quiet bare fields, through the little strings of trees silver in their dead leaves, past cabins silver from weather, with the doors and windows boarded shut, all like old women under a spell sitting there. "I walking

The Worn Path 711

6 Critical Thinking and Reading Phoenix says the log is a "trial." What is being tried or tested here? Her age? Her courage? What does her manner of crossing the log tell you about her character?

7 Literary Focus Phoenix often imagines things that are not there. How does this affect the way the reader interprets the story?

8 Reading Strategy Have students sum up what they know about Phoenix so far.

9 Enrichment The bull and the two-headed snake are two of the many Egyptian mythical creatures who guard the underworld.

10 Clarification The word *maze* has a double meaning here—labyrinth and maize (corn).

11 Discussion Ghosts are just one of the many images of death in this story. What other words and images has Welty used so far to create a morbid atmosphere?

12 Critical Thinking and Reading The scarecrow which Phoenix mistakes for a ghost symbolizes death. Why does Phoenix challenge it to dance with her?

13 Discussion To what "end" is Welty referring?

14 Clarification Pullets are young hens.

15 Literary Focus What do you think Phoenix means by this statement? Who or what is sleeping?

16 **Literary Focus** Phoenix's confused mind again creates ambiguity for the reader. For what do you think she is reaching?

17 **Critical Thinking and Reading** What tone of voice does the hunter use with Phoenix? What does this tell you about his attitude toward her?

18 **Clarification** The story was first published in 1949, when the term *colored people* was considered more acceptable than it is today.

19 **Clarification** A cur is a mutt—a dog of mixed breed. It is also a mean-spirited person.

in their sleep," she said, nodding her head vigorously.

In a ravine she went where a spring was silently flowing through a hollow log. Old Phoenix bent and drank. "Sweet gum[2] makes the water sweet," she said, and drank more. "Nobody know who made this well, for it was here when I was born."

The track crossed a swampy part where the moss hung as white as lace from every limb. "Sleep on, alligators, and blow your bubbles." Then the track went into the road.

Deep, deep the road went down between the high green-colored banks. Overhead the live-oaks met, and it was as dark as a cave.

A black dog with a lolling tongue came up out of the weeds by the ditch. She was meditating, and not ready, and when he came at her she only hit him a little with her cane. Over she went in the ditch, like a little puff of milkweed.[3]

16 Down there, her senses drifted away. A dream visited her, and she reached her hand up, but nothing reached down and gave her a pull. So she lay there and presently went to talking. "Old woman," she said to herself, "that black dog come up out of the weeds to stall you off, and now there he sitting on his fine tail, smiling at you."

A white man finally came along and found her—a hunter, a young man, with his dog on a chain.

"Well, Granny!" he laughed. "What are you doing there?"

"Lying on my back like a June bug waiting to be turned over, mister," she said, reaching up her hand.

He lifted her up, gave her a swing in the air, and set her down. "Anything broken, Granny?"

"No sir, them old dead weeds is springy enough," said Phoenix, when she had got her breath. "I thank you for your trouble."

---

2. **sweet gum:** A tree that produces a fragrant juice.
3. **milkweed:** A plant with pods which when ripe release feathery seeds.

"Where do you live, Granny?" he asked, while the two dogs were growling at each other.

"Away back yonder, sir, behind the ridge. You can't even see it from here."

"On your way home?"

"No sir, I going to town."

17 "Why, that's too far! That's as far as I walk when I come out myself, and I get something for my trouble." He patted the stuffed bag he carried, and there hung down a little closed claw. It was one of the bobwhites, with its beak hooked bitterly to show it was dead. "Now you go on home, Granny!"

"I bound to go to town, mister," said Phoenix. "The time come around."

18 He gave another laugh, filling the whole landscape. "I know you old colored people! Wouldn't miss going to town to see Santa Claus!"

But something held old Phoenix very still. The deep lines in her face went into a fierce and different radiation. Without warning, she had seen with her own eyes a flashing nickel fall out of the man's pocket onto the ground.

"How old are you, Granny?" he was saying.

"There is no telling, mister," she said, "no telling."

Then she gave a little cry and clapped her hands and said, "Git on away from here, dog! Look! Look at that dog!" She laughed as if in admiration. "He ain't scared of nobody. He a big black dog." She whispered, "Sic him!"

19 "Watch me get rid of that cur," said the man. "Sic him, Pete! Sic him!"

Phoenix heard the dogs fighting, and heard the man running and throwing sticks. She even heard a gunshot. But she was slowly bending forward by that time, further and further forward, the lids stretched down over her eyes, as if she were doing this in her sleep. Her chin was lowered almost to her knees. The yellow palm of her hand came out from the fold of her apron. Her fingers slid

Grammar in Action

The term **coordinate adjectives** applies to two or more adjectives of equal rank preceding a noun. There are two ways to determine if the adjectives are of equal rank. First, you should be able to reverse their order without changing the meaning of the sentence. Second, you should be able to insert the word **and** between them without changing the meaning of the sentence. Adjectives that pass these tests should be separated by commas. Adjectives that do not pass this test are known as **cumula-** tive adjectives and should not be separated by commas. Note the following examples from "A Worn Path":

  Coordinate: a thin, small cane (p. 710)
  a full, severe look (p. 710)

  Cumulative: a dark striped dress (p. 710)
  a big black dog (p. 710)

Student Activity 1. Apply the two tests to the following noun phrases and decide whether the adjectives are coordinate or cumulative.

1. numberless branching wrinkles
2. a whole little tree
3. big wild hogs
4. a grave persistent noise

down and along the ground under the piece of money with the grace and care they would have in lifting an egg from under a setting hen. Then she slowly straightened up, she stood erect, and the nickel was in her apron pocket. A bird flew by. Her lips moved. "God watching me the whole time. I come to stealing."

The man came back, and his own dog panted about them. "Well, I scared him off that time," he said, and then he laughed and lifted his gun and pointed it at Phoenix.

She stood straight and faced him.

"Doesn't the gun scare you?" he said, still pointing it.

"No, sir, I seen plenty go off closer by, in my day, and for less than what I done," she said, holding utterly still.

He smiled, and shouldered the gun. "Well, Granny," he said, "you must be a hundred years old, and scared of nothing. I'd give you a dime if I had any money with me. But you take my advice and stay home, and nothing will happen to you."

"I bound to go on my way, mister," said Phoenix. She inclined her head in the red rag. Then they went in different directions, but she could hear the gun shooting again and again over the hill.

She walked on. The shadows hung from the oak trees to the road like curtains. Then she smelled woodsmoke, and smelled the river, and she saw a steeple and the cabins on their steep steps. Dozens of little black children whirled around her. There ahead was Natchez[4] shining. Bells were ringing. She walked on.

In the paved city it was Christmas time. There were red and green electric lights strung and criss-crossed everywhere, and all turned on in the daytime. Old Phoenix would have been lost if she had not distrusted her

_____
4. Natchez (nach'iz): A town in southern Mississippi.

eyesight and depended on her feet to know where to take her.

She paused quietly on the sidewalk where people were passing by. A lady came along in the crowd, carrying an armful of red-, green- and silver-wrapped presents; she gave off perfume like the red roses in hot summer, and Phoenix stopped her.

"Please, missy, will you lace up my shoe?" She held up her foot.

"What do you want, Grandma?"

"See my shoe," said Phoenix. "Do all right for out in the country, but wouldn't look right to go in a big building."

"Stand still then, Grandma," said the lady. She put her packages down on the sidewalk beside her and laced and tied both shoes tightly.

"Can't lace 'em with a cane," said Phoenix. "Thank you, missy. I doesn't mind asking a nice lady to tie up my shoe, when I gets out on the street."

Moving slowly and from side to side, she went into the big building, and into a tower of steps, where she walked up and around and around until her feet knew to stop.

She entered a door, and there she saw nailed up on the wall the document that had been stamped with the gold seal and framed in the gold frame, which matched the dream that was hung up in her head.

"Here I be," she said. There was a fixed and ceremonial stiffness over her body.

"A charity case, I suppose," said an attendant who sat at the desk before her.

But Phoenix only looked above her head. There was sweat on her face, the wrinkles in her skin shone like a bright net.

"Speak up, Grandma," the woman said. "What's your name? We must have your history, you know. Have you been here before? What seems to be the trouble with you?"

Old Phoenix only gave a twitch to her face as if a fly were bothering her.

"Are you deaf?" cried the attendant.

But then the nurse came in.

"Oh, that's just old Aunt Phoenix," she

The Worn Path 713

20 Discussion What do you think birds symbolize in this story? Remember that Phoenix herself is described in bird-like terms.

21 Critical Thinking and Reading What does the fact that the hunter points his gun at Phoenix suggest about his character? Why do you think he chased off the black dog with such vigor? Does he enjoy scaring animals and people? If so, why?

22 Discussion Contrast the images of the town with those of the countryside that Phoenix has just walked through.

23 Discussion Why does Welty choose not to identify the big building with the gold seal?

24 Reading Strategy Phoenix has finally arrived at her destination. Have students sum up all the obstacles she has overcome to get there. How would they expect her to react at the end of such a long and hard journey?

5. her small black-freckled hand
6. deep still woods
7. Busy intent fingers
8. long full skirts
9. high green-colored banks
10. a little closed claw

Student Activity 2. Add a coordinate adjective to each of the following sentences and punctuate the adjectives correctly.
1. Old Phoenix had curly _____ hair.
2. She walked through the deep _____ woods.
3. The thorns caught her full _____ skirt.
4. She came upon a playful _____ dog.
5. A pleasant _____ hunter helped her out of a ditch.

said. "She doesn't come for herself—she has a little grandson. She makes these trips just as regular as clockwork. She lives away back off the Old Natchez Trace." She bent down. "Well, Aunt Phoenix, why don't you just take a seat? We won't keep you standing after your long trip." She pointed.

The old woman sat down, bolt upright in the chair.

"Now, how is the boy?" asked the nurse.

Old Phoenix did not speak.

"I said, how is the boy?"

But Phoenix only waited and stared straight ahead, her face very solemn and withdrawn into rigidity.

"Is his throat any better?" asked the nurse. "Aunt Phoenix, don't you hear me? Is your grandson's throat any better since the last time you came for the medicine?"

With her hands on her knees, the old woman waited, silent, erect and motionless, just as if she were in armor.

"You mustn't take up our time this way, Aunt Phoenix," the nurse said. "Tell us quickly about your grandson, and get it over. He isn't dead, is he?"

At last there came a flicker and then a flame of comprehension across her face, and she spoke.

"My grandson. It was my memory had left me. There I sat and forgot why I made my long trip."

"Forgot?" The nurse frowned. "After you came so far?"

Then Phoenix was like an old woman begging a dignified forgiveness for waking up frightened in the night. "I never did go to school, I was too old at the Surrender,[5] she said in a soft voice. "I'm an old woman without an education. It was my memory fail me. My little grandson, he is just the same, and I forgot it in the coming."

---

5. the Surrender: The surrender of the Confederate army. ending the Civil War.

"Throat never heals, does it?" said the nurse, speaking in a loud, sure voice to old Phoenix. By now she had a card with something written on it, a little list. "Yes. Swallowed lye. When was it?—January—two-three years ago—"

Phoenix spoke unasked now. "No, missy, he not dead, he just the same. Every little while his throat begin to close up again, and he not able to swallow. He not get his breath. He not able to help himself. So the time come around, and I go on another trip for the soothing medicine."

"All right. The doctor said as long as you came to get it, you could have it," said the nurse. "But it's an obstinate case."

"My little grandson, he sit up there in the house all wrapped up, waiting by himself," Phoenix went on. "We is the only two left in the world. He suffer and it don't seem to put him back at all. He got a sweet look. He going to last. He wear a little patch quilt and peep out holding his mouth open like a little bird. I remembers so plain now. I not going to forget him again, no, the whole enduring time. I could tell him from all the others in creation."

"All right." The nurse was trying to hush her now. She brought her a bottle of medicine. "Charity," she said, making a check mark in a book.

Old Phoenix held the bottle close to her eyes, and then carefully put it into her pocket.

"I thank you," she said.

"It's Christmas time, Grandma," said the attendant. "Could I give you a few pennies out of my purse?"

"Five pennies is a nickel," said Phoenix stiffly.

"Here's a nickel," said the attendant.

Phoenix rose carefully and held out her hand. She received the nickel and then fished the other nickel out of her pocket and laid it beside the new one. She stared at her palm closely, with her head on one side.

Then she gave a tap with her cane on the floor.

"This is what come to me to do," she said. "I going to the store and buy my child a little windmill they sells, made out of paper. He going to find it hard to believe there such a thing in the world. I'll march myself back where he is waiting, holding it straight up in this hand."

She lifted her free hand, gave a little nod, turned around, and walked out of the doctor's office. Then her slow step began on the stairs, going down.

30

THINKING ABOUT THE SELECTION

Recalling

1. (a) What are the first three obstacles Phoenix Jackson encounters? (b) What does she see after overcoming the third obstacle?
2. (a) What causes Phoenix to fall into a ditch? (b) Who helps her out of the ditch? (c) What does he drop from his pocket? (d) How does Phoenix divert his attention so she can pick it up?
3. (a) What does the nurse ask Phoenix? (b) How does Phoenix explain her inability to answer?

Interpreting

4. What details of the setting help to create a somber, mournful atmosphere?
5. (a) How would you characterize the hunter's attitude toward Phoenix? (b) How would you characterize the nurse's and the attendant's attitudes toward Phoenix?
6. Why do you think Phoenix does not immediately respond to the questions of the nurse and the attendant?
7. What is the significance of the story taking place at Christmas time?
8. What does Phoenix's journey symbolize?

Applying

9. Like Welty's other works, "The Worn Path" is set in the deep South. Do you think the story would be different if the setting were changed? Why or why not?

ANALYZING LITERATURE

Interpreting Ambiguity

When a work of literature is **ambiguous** or contains ambiguous elements, the work or the elements of the work can be interpreted in more than one way. For example, in "A Worn Path" Eudora Welty leaves the question of whether Phoenix Jackson's grandson is still alive open to interpretation.

1. Find two details from the story that support the interpretation that Phoenix's grandson is alive.
2. Find two details that support the interpretation that he is dead.
3. Why do you think Welty chooses not to reveal whether he is alive or dead?

THINKING AND WRITING

Writing a Continuation of the Story

Write a continuation of the story in which Phoenix returns home bearing the medicine. List details you can use to describe the setting. When you write your story, try to use these details to create an appropriate atmosphere and to foreshadow what will be waiting for her when she arrives home. When you finish writing, revise your story, making sure you have maintained a consistent point of view. Then share it with your classmates.

The Worn Path 715

Closure and Extension

ANSWERS TO THINKING ABOUT THE SELECTION
Recalling

1. (a) The first three obstacles are a thorny bush, a brook, and a barbed wire fence. (b) She sees a buzzard.
2. (a) She falls in the ditch after swinging her cane at a black dog. (b) A hunter helps her out of the ditch. (c) He drops a nickel. (d) She gets the man to sic his own dog after the black dog.
3. (a) The nurse asks about Phoenix's sick grandson. (b) She says that she momentarily forgot why she had come.

Interpreting

4. Suggested Response: The pinewoods are dark and full of shadows, dead trees, dead corn, dark

More About the Author In the following excerpt from his Nobel Prize acceptance speech in 1962, Steinbeck said the following about the writer's purpose: "The ancient commission of the writer has not changed. He is charged with exposing our many grievous faults and failures, with dredging up to the light our dark and dangerous dreams for the purpose of improvement.

"Furthermore, the writer is delegated to declare and to celebrate man's proven capacity for greatness of heart and spirit—for gallantry in defeat, for courage, compassion and love. In the endless war against weakness and despair, these are the bright rally flags of hope and emulation. I hold that a writer who does not passionately believe in the perfectability of man has no dedication nor any membership in literature."

John Steinbeck's themes come from the poverty, desperation, and social injustice that he witnessed during the Great Depression of the 1930's, a time when many people suffered under conditions beyond their control. Do you think these themes are relevant today?

JOHN STEINBECK

1902–1968

Reflecting the influence of the Naturalists, John Steinbeck generally portrayed working-class characters who were manipulated by forces beyond their understanding or control. Yet although many of his characters suffered tragic fates, they almost always managed to retain a sense of dignity throughout their struggles.

Steinbeck was born in Salinas, California, the son of a county official and a schoolteacher. The people and the landscape of the area in northern California where he grew up eventually inspired many of the characters and settings of his literary works. After graduating from high school, he enrolled at Stanford University. He left before graduating, however, and spent the next five years drifting across the country, reading, writing, and working at odd jobs.

Steinbeck had little success as a writer until 1935 when he published *Tortilla Flat,* his third novel. Two years later he earned widespread recognition and critical acclaim with the publication of *Of Mice and Men.* This novel, which portrays two drifters whose dream of owning their own farm ends in tragedy, became a best-seller and was made into a Broadway play and a motion picture. Steinbeck then went on to write what is generally regarded as his finest novel, *The Grapes of Wrath* (1939), the accurate and emotional story of the "Okies," Oklahoma farmers dispossessed of their land and forced to become migrant farmers in California. The novel won the National Book Award and the Pulitzer Prize and established Steinbeck as one of the most highly regarded writers of his day.

Steinbeck produced several more successful works during his later years, including *Cannery Row* (1945), *The Pearl* (1947), *East of Eden* (1951), and *The Winter of Our Discontent* (1961). In 1963 he was awarded the Nobel Prize for Literature.

Asked why he writes, Steinbeck answered, "Like everyone, I want to be good and strong and virtuous and wise and loved. I think that writing may be simply a method or technique for communication with other individuals; and its stimulus, the loneliness we are born to. In writing, perhaps we hope to achieve companionship. What some people find in religion, a writer may find in his craft . . . absorption of the small and frightened and lonely into the whole and complete, a kind of breaking through to glory."

In nearly all of his works, including "Flight," Steinbeck creates vivid portraits of the landscape and demonstrates how people are shaped and manipulated by their environments. At the same time, his works reflect his belief in the need for social justice and his hope that people can learn from the suffering of others.

1 To understand setting
2 To analyze the effect of setting
3 To write about setting

Support Material
Teaching Portfolio
Teacher Backup, p. 925
Grammar in Action Worksheets, *Recognizing Faulty Coordination,* p. 929; *Using Adjectives,* p. 931; *Understanding Descriptive Writing,* p. 933
Usage and Mechanics Worksheet, p. 935
Vocabulary Check, p. 936
Analyzing Literature Worksheet,

Understanding Setting, p. 937
Language Worksheet, *Using Latin Prefixes,* p. 938
Selection Test, p. 939

GUIDE FOR INTERPRETING

Flight

Writer's Techniques

Setting. The setting is the time and place in which the events in a work of literature occur. Although it is not usually the most important element in a literary work, the setting can often shape and motivate the characters. In real life people are sometimes viewed as being, to some extent, products of their environments. Similarly, characters in many literary works may be viewed as products of the setting. While a character's attitudes, values, and behavior may be shaped by the long-term effect of the setting, the setting may also have a more immediate impact on a character's actions. For example, in Jack London's story "To Build a Fire," most of the character's actions result directly from his efforts to cope with the extreme cold of the Arctic wilderness.

John Steinbeck believed that people are often manipulated by forces of society and nature beyond their understanding or control. As a result, the setting usually plays an important role in his works, often having both an immediate and long-term effect on the characters. In most of his stories and novels, he describes the setting in exact detail and clearly conveys how it shapes and motivates the characters.

Commentary

As you read "Flight," you will notice the effect of the environment on the action. Critic Edmund Wilson was also struck by Steinbeck's use of nature in his works. "The stories in *The Long Valley* are almost entirely about plants and animals; and Mr. Steinbeck does not give the effect . . . of romantically raising the animals to the stature of human beings, but rather of assimilating the human beings to animals. . . . In 'Flight,' a young Mexican boy, who has killed a man and run away into the mountains, is finally reduced to a state so close to that of the beasts that he is apparently mistaken by a mountain lion for another four-footed animal. . . ." What statement do you think Steinbeck is making about the effect of the environment on characters?

Writing

In "Flight" Steinbeck uses sensory details to paint a vivid portrait of the setting. Prepare a list of sensory details describing your environment. List them in a chart under the headings of *Sight, Smell, Taste, Touch, Hearing.*

Literary Focus Ask your students to name other literary settings that directly affect the characters' actions. Examples include the ocean depths in Jules Verne's *20,000 Leagues Under the Sea* and the wild terrain of William Golding's *Lord of the Flies.*

Writing/Prior Knowledge For extra credit, have students develop their lists into a descriptive paragraph.

Vocabulary

Preteach the following vocabulary words:
insinuating (in sin' yo͞o wāt'iɲ) v.: Hinting or suggesting indirectly; implying (p. 720)
furtive (fʉr'tiv) adj.: Sneaky (p. 722)
monotonous (mə nät''n əs) adj.: Having little or no variation or variety (p. 724)

Motivation/Prior Knowledge
Have students imagine that they are settlers trying to cope with an unfamiliar and harsh environment, such as a windswept desert, a dense forest, or an airless and waterless planet. How might the environment change them? How would they try to overcome its affects?

Master Teacher Note The characters in the story are California farmers of Spanish descent. Bring in magazine and newspaper articles that describe how modern immigrant families—especially migrant farmers—cope with their new environments. Discuss the changes the family members undergo and the hardships they endure.

Thematic Idea Another story that deals with a character's hopes of escaping death is "An Occurrence at Owl Creek Bridge" by Ambrose Bierce (p. 530).

Purpose-Setting Question Will Pepé escape?

1 **Literary Focus** How has the "wild coast" affected the Torres family's farm? Have students point out signs of decay or destruction, such as the farm buildings that huddle and cling against the wind and the rotting barn.

2 **Discussion** The husband was an innocent victim of his environment. What does his manner of death suggest about the fates of the other characters in the story?

3 **Clarification** A truant officer is a school official who deals with students who skip class.

4 **Enrichment** The words *thee* and *thou* are now only used in poetic or religious contexts. Steinbeck is perhaps alluding to Mama Torres's religious background by writing her dialogue in this form.

Flight

John Steinbeck

About fifteen miles below Monterey, on the wild coast, the Torres family had their farm, a few sloping acres above a cliff that dropped to the brown reefs and to the hissing white waters of the ocean. Behind the farm the stone mountains stood up against the sky. The farm buildings huddled like little clinging aphids[1] on the mountain skirts, crouched low to the ground as though the wind might blow them into the sea. The little shack, the rattling, rotting barn were gray-bitten with sea salt, beaten by the damp wind until they had taken on the color of the granite hills. Two horses, a red cow and a red calf, half a dozen pigs and a flock of lean, multicolored chickens stocked the place. A little corn was raised on the sterile slope, and it grew short and thick under the wind, and all the cobs formed on the landward sides of the stalks.

Mama Torres, a lean, dry woman with ancient eyes, had ruled the farm for ten years, ever since her husband tripped over a stone in the field one day and fell full length on a rattlesnake. When one is bitten on the chest there is not much that can be done.

Mama Torres had three children, two undersized black ones of twelve and fourteen, Emilio and Rosy, whom Mama kept fishing on the rocks below the farm when the sea was kind and when the truant officer was in some distant part of Monterey County. And there was Pepé, the tall smiling son of nineteen, a gentle, affectionate boy, but very lazy.

---

1. **aphids** (ā′fidz) *n*.: Small insects that suck the juice from plants.

Pepé had a tall head, pointed at the top, and from its peak, coarse black hair grew down like a thatch all around. Over his smiling little eyes Mama cut a straight bang so he could see. Pepé had sharp Indian cheek bones and an eagle nose, but his mouth was as sweet and shapely as a girl's mouth, and his chin was fragile and chiseled. He was loose and gangling, all legs and feet and wrists, and he was very lazy. Mama thought him fine and brave, but she never told him so. She said, "Some lazy cow must have got into thy father's family, else how could I have a son like thee." And she said, "When I carried thee, a sneaking lazy coyote came out of the brush and looked at me one day. That must have made thee so."

Pepé smiled sheepishly and stabbed at the ground with his knife to keep the blade sharp and free from rust. It was his inheritance, that knife, his father's knife. The long heavy blade folded back into the black handle. There was a button on the handle. When Pepé pressed the button, the blade leaped out ready for use. The knife was with Pepé always, for it had been his father's knife.

One sunny morning when the sea below the cliff was glinting and blue and the white surf creamed on the reef, when even the stone mountains looked kindly, Mama Torres called out the door of the shack, "Pepé, I have a labor for thee."

There was no answer. Mama listened. From behind the barn she heard a burst of laughter. She lifted her full long skirt and walked in the direction of the noise.

Pepé was sitting on the ground with his

5 **Clarification** The "two black ones" refer to Pepé's brother and sister, Emilio and Rosy.

6 **Discussion** Before Pepé flicked the knife, he smiled at the sky. Now he grins self-consciously at it. What is the significance of this action? Who or what makes him self-conscious?

back against a box. His white teeth glistened. On either side of him stood the two black ones, tense and expectant. Fifteen feet away a redwood post was set in the ground. Pepé's right hand lay limply in his lap, and in the palm the big black knife rested. The blade was closed back into the handle. Pepé looked smiling at the sky.

Suddenly Emilio cried, "Ya!"

Pepé's wrist flicked like the head of a snake. The blade seemed to fly open in mid-air, and with a thump the point dug into the redwood post, and the black handle quivered. The three burst into excited laughter.

Rosy ran to the post and pulled out the knife and brought it back to Pepé. He closed the blade and settled the knife carefully in his listless palm again. He grinned self-consciously at the sky.

"Ya!"

The heavy knife lanced out and sunk into the post again. Mama moved forward like a ship and scattered the play.

"All day you do foolish things with the knife, like a toy baby," she stormed. "Get up on thy huge feet that eat up shoes. Get up!" She took him by one loose shoulder and hoisted at him. Pepé grinned sheepishly and

Flight 719

7 Discussion The word *revolution* means "violent change." Why do you think Steinbeck chose such a strong word to describe Pepé at this point? What does it suggest about Pepé's forthcoming trip to Monterey?

8 Discussion Does Pepé's tone of voice sound like that of a man or a boy? Does his mother respond to him as a man, or a boy?

9 Enrichment Reciting *The Lord's Prayer* and *Hail Mary* is a common ritual for practicing Catholics.

10 Discussion Mama keeps calling Pepé foolish and lazy. Pepé insists he is a man. Based on his behavior so far, how would you characterize Pepé?

came halfheartedly to his feet. "Look!" Mama cried. "Big lazy, you must catch the horse and put on him thy father's saddle. You must ride to Monterey. The medicine bottle is empty. There is no salt. Go thou now, Peanut! Catch the horse."

7 A revolution took place in the relaxed figure of Pepé. "To Monterey, me? Alone? *Sí*, Mama."

She scowled at him. "Do not think, big sheep, that you will buy candy. No, I will give you only enough for the medicine and the salt."

8 Pepé smiled. "Mama, you will put the hatband on the hat?"

She relented then. "Yes, Pepé. You may wear the hatband."

His voice grew insinuating, "And the green handkerchief, Mama?"

"Yes, if you go quickly and return with no trouble, the silk green handkerchief will go. If you make sure to take off the handkerchief when you eat so no spot may fall on it. . . ."

"*Sí*, Mama. I will be careful. I am a man."

"Thou? A man? Thou art a peanut."

He went into the rickety barn and brought out a rope, and he walked agilely enough up the hill to catch the horse.

When he was ready and mounted before the door, mounted on his father's saddle that was so old that the oaken frame showed through torn leather in many places, then Mama brought out the round black hat with the tooled leather band, and she reached up and knotted the green silk handkerchief about his neck. Pepé's blue denim coat was much darker than his jeans, for it had been washed much less often.

Mama handed up the big medicine bottle and the silver coins. "That for the medicine," she said, "and that for the salt. That for a candle to burn for the papa. That for *dulces*[2] for the little ones. Our friend Mrs. Rodriguez will give you dinner and maybe a bed for the **9** night. When you go to the church say only

___

2. dulces (do͞ol'säs) *n.:* Candy; sweets.

ten Paternosters[3] and only twenty-five Ave Marias.[4] Oh! I know, big coyote. You would sit there flapping your mouth over Aves all day while you looked at the candles and the holy pictures. That is not good devotion to stare at the pretty things."

The black hat, covering the high pointed head and black thatched hair of Pepé, gave him dignity and age. He sat the rangy horse well. Mama thought how handsome he was, dark and lean and tall. "I would not send thee now alone, thou little one, except for the medicine," she said softly. "It is not good to have no medicine, for who knows when the toothache will come, or the sadness of the stomach. These things are."

10 "Adios, Mama," Pepé cried. "I will come back soon. You may send me often alone. I am a man."

"Thou art a foolish chicken."

He straightened his shoulders, flipped the reins against the horse's shoulder and rode away. He turned once and saw that they still watched him, Emilio and Rosy and Mama. Pepé grinned with pride and gladness and lifted the tough buckskin horse to a trot.

When he had dropped out of sight over a little dip in the road, Mama turned to the black ones, but she spoke to herself. "He is nearly a man now," she said. "It will be a nice thing to have a man in the house again." Her eyes sharpened on the children. "Go to the rocks now. The tide is going out. There will be abalones[5] to be found." She put the iron hooks into their hands and saw them down the steep trail to the reefs. She brought the smooth stone *metate*[6] to the doorway and sat grinding her corn to flour and looking occasionally at the road over which Pepé had gone. The noonday came and then the afternoon, when the little ones beat the abalones on a rock to make them

___

3. Paternosters (pät'ər nôs'tərz): Our Fathers (The Lord's Prayer).
4. Ave Marias (ä' vä mə rē' əz): Hail Marys.
5. abalones (ab'ə lō'nēz) *n.:* Large shellfish.
6. metate (mä tä' tä'): A stone used in the southwestern United States for grinding meal.

tender and Mama patted the tortillas[7] to make them thin. They ate their dinner as the red sun was plunging down toward the ocean. They sat on the doorsteps and watched the big white moon come over the mountain tops.

Mama said, "He is now at the house of our friend Mrs. Rodriguez. She will give him nice things to eat and maybe a present."

Emilio said, "Some day I too will ride to Monterey for medicine. Did Pepé come to be a man today?"

Mama said wisely, "A boy gets to be a man when a man is needed. Remember this thing. I have known boys forty years old because there was no need for a man."

Soon afterwards they retired, Mama in her big oak bed on one side of the room, Emilio and Rosy in their boxes full of straw and sheepskins on the other side of the room.

The moon went over the sky and the surf roared on the rocks. The roosters crowed the first call. The surf subsided to a whispering surge against the reef. The moon dropped toward the sea. The roosters crowed again.

The moon was near down to the water when Pepé rode on a winded horse to his home flat. His dog bounced out and circled the horse yelping with pleasure. Pepé slid off the saddle to the ground. The weathered little shack was silver in the moonlight and the square shadow of it was black to the north and east. Against the east the piling mountains were misty with light; their tops melted into the sky.

Pepé walked wearily up the three steps and into the house. It was dark inside. There was a rustle in the corner.

Mama cried out from her bed. "Who comes? Pepé, is it thou?"

"Sí, Mama."

"Did you get the medicine?"

"Sí, Mama."

"Well, go to sleep, then. I thought you would be sleeping at the house of Mrs. Rodri-

---

7. **tortillas** (tôr tē′əz) n.: Thin, flat cakes of cornmeal.

guez." Pepé stood silently in the dark room. "Why do you stand there, Pepé? Did you drink wine?"

"Sí, Mama."

"Well, go to bed then and sleep out the wine."

His voice was tired and patient, but very firm. "Light the candle, Mama. I must go away into the mountains."

"What is this, Pepé? You are crazy." Mama struck a sulphur match and held the little blue burr until the flame spread up the stick. She set light to the candle on the floor beside her bed. "Now, Pepé, what is this you say?" She looked anxiously into his face.

He was changed. The fragile quality seemed to have gone from his chin. His mouth was less full than it had been, the lines of the lips were straighter, but in his eyes the greatest change had taken place. There was no laughter in them any more, nor any bashfulness. They were sharp and bright and purposeful.

He told her in a tired monotone, told her everything just as it had happened. A few people came into the kitchen of Mrs. Rodriguez. There was wine to drink. Pepé drank wine. The little quarrel—the man started toward Pepé and then the knife—it went almost by itself. It flew, it darted before Pepé knew it. As he talked, Mama's face grew stern, and it seemed to grow more lean. Pepé finished. "I am a man now, Mama. The man said names to me I could not allow."

Mama nodded. "Yes, thou art a man, my poor little Pepé. Thou art a man. I have seen it coming on thee. I have watched you throwing the knife into the post, and I have been afraid." For a moment her face had softened, but now it grew stern again. "Come! We must get you ready. Go. Awaken Emilio and Rosy. Go quickly."

Pepé stepped over to the corner where his brother and sister slept among the sheepskins. He leaned down and shook them gently. "Come, Rosy! Come, Emilio! The mama says you must arise."

The little black ones sat up and rubbed their eyes in the candlelight. Mama was out

Flight 721

---

11 **Discussion** Do you agree with Mama Rodriguez? Why or why not?

12 **Literary Focus** Pepé can see his home—the shack—in the moonlight, but the area beyond it is dark and the mountains unpassable as they "melted into the sky". The contrasting setting reflects Steinbeck's view of nature as mysterious, foreboding, and uncontrollable.

13 **Discussion** How has Pepé's tone of voice changed since he last spoke to his mother?

14 **Discussion** What is the significance of these changes in Pepé?

15 **Reading Strategy** To make sure **less advanced** students understand the subtle details in this paragraph, ask them to describe what happened to Pepé in their own words. Why did he throw the knife at the man? Did he mean to do it? Why must he go to the mountains now?

16 **Enrichment** In the Spanish culture, defending one's honor as Pepé did is considered an act of *machismo* or manliness. Not defending it brings shame and humiliation for the whole family. In this context, Pepé had no choice but to use his knife. The act gives Pepé a reason to flee, yet allows him to retain his dignity and honor.

of bed now, her long black skirt over her nightgown. "Emilio," she cried. "Go up and catch the other horse for Pepé. Quickly, now! Quickly." Emilio put his legs in his overalls and stumbled sleepily out the door.

"You heard no one behind you on the road?" Mama demanded.

"No, Mama. I listened carefully. No one was on the road."

Mama darted like a bird about the room. From a nail on the wall she took a canvas water bag and threw it on the floor. She stripped a blanket from her bed and rolled it into a tight tube and tied the ends with string. From a box beside the stove she lifted a flour sack half full of black stringy jerky. "Your father's black coat, Pepé. Here, put it on."

Pepé stood in the middle of the floor watching her activity. She reached behind the door and brought out the rifle, a long 38-56, worn shiny the whole length of the barrel. Pepé took it from her and held it in the crook of his elbow. Mama brought a little leather bag and counted the cartridges into his hand. "Only ten left," she warned. "You must not waste them."

Emilio put his head in the door. " 'Qui 'st 'l caballo,[8] Mama."

"Put on the saddle from the other horse. Tie on the blanket. Here, tie the jerky to the saddle horn."

Still Pepé stood silently watching his mother's frantic activity. His chin looked hard, and his sweet mouth was drawn and thin. His little eyes followed Mama about the room almost suspiciously.

Rosy asked softly, "Where goes Pepé?"

Mama's eyes were fierce. "Pepé goes on a journey. Pepé is a man now. He has a man's thing to do."

Pepé straightened his shoulders. His mouth changed until he looked very much like Mama.

At last the preparation was finished. The loaded horse stood outside the door. The water bag dripped a line of moisture down the bay shoulder.

The moonlight was being thinned by the dawn and the big white moon was near down to the sea. The family stood by the shack. Mama confronted Pepé. "Look, my son! Do not stop until it is dark again. Do not sleep even though you are tired. Take care of the horse in order that he may not stop of weariness. Remember to be careful with the bullets—there are only ten. Do not fill thy stomach with jerky or it will make thee sick. Eat a little jerky and fill thy stomach with grass. When thou comest to the high mountains, if thou seest any of the dark watching men, go not near to them nor try to speak to them. And forget not thy prayers." She put her lean hands on Pepé's shoulders, stood on her toes and kissed him formally on both cheeks, and Pepé kissed her on both cheeks. Then he went to Emilio and Rosy and kissed both of their cheeks.

Pepé turned back to Mama. He seemed to look for a little softness, a little weakness in her. His eyes were searching, but Mama's face remained fierce. "Go now," she said. "Do not wait to be caught like a chicken."

Pepé pulled himself into the saddle. "I am a man," he said.

It was the first dawn when he rode up the hill toward the little canyon which let a trail into the mountains. Moonlight and daylight fought with each other, and the two warring qualities made it difficult to see. Before Pepé had gone a hundred yards, the outlines of his figure were misty; and long before he entered the canyon, he had become a gray, indefinite shadow.

Mama stood stiffly in front of her doorstep, and on either side of her stood Emilio and Rosy. They cast furtive glances at Mama now and then.

When the gray shape of Pepé melted into the hillside and disappeared, Mama relaxed. She began the high, whining keen[9] of the death wail. "Our beautiful—our brave," she

---

8. 'Qui 'st 'l caballo (kĕst'l kä bä'yō): Here is the horse (colloquial Spanish).

9. keen: A wailing for the dead.

Grammar in Action

Coordination of related clauses is a valuable method of joining short sentences and making writing smoother. However, you must be careful to avoid **faulty coordination.** Faulty coordination is the joining of clauses that are not closely related or that are of unequal importance.

Steinbeck was a master of skillful coordination. Note the following examples:

The knife was with Pepé always, for it had been his father's knife. (p. 718)

Mama's face grew more stern, and it seemed to grow more lean. (p. 721)

Steinbeck was careful not to coordinate unrelated clauses. He left them in separate sentences. For example:

There was no answer. Mama listened. (p. 718)

The roosters crowed the first call. The surf subsided to a whispering surge behind the reef. (p. 718)

cried. "Our protector, our son is gone." Emilio and Rosy moaned beside her. "Our beautiful—our brave, he is gone." It was the formal wail. It rose to a high piercing whine and subsided to a moan. Mama raised it three times and then she turned and went into the house and shut the door.

Emilio and Rosy stood wondering in the dawn. They heard Mama whimpering in the house. They went out to sit on the cliff above the ocean. They touched shoulders. "When did Pepé come to be a man?" Emilio asked.

"Last night," said Rosy. "Last night in Monterey." The ocean clouds turned red with the sun that was behind the mountains.

"We will have no breakfast," said Emilio. "Mama will not want to cook." Rosy did not answer him. "Where is Pepé gone?" he asked.

Rosy looked around at him. She drew her knowledge from the quiet air. "He has gone on a journey. He will never come back."

"Is he dead? Do you think he is dead?"

Rosy looked back at the ocean again. A little steamer, drawing a line of smoke sat on the edge of the horizon. "He is not dead," Rosy explained. "Not yet."

Pepé rested the big rifle across the saddle in front of him. He let the horse walk up the hill and he didn't look back. The stony slope took on a coat of short brush so that Pepé found the entrance to a trail and entered it.

When he came to the canyon opening, he swung once in his saddle and looked back, but the houses were swallowed in the misty light. Pepé jerked forward again. The high shoulder of the canyon closed in on him. His horse stretched out its neck and sighed and settled to the trail.

It was a well-worn path, dark soft leaf-mold earth strewn with broken pieces of sandstone. The trail rounded the shoulder of the canyon and dropped steeply into the bed of the stream. In the shallows the water ran smoothly, glinting in the first morning sun. Small round stones on the bottom were as brown as rust with sun moss. In the sand along the edges of the stream the tall, rich wild mint grew, while in the water itself the cress,[10] old and tough, had gone to heavy seed.

The path went into the stream and emerged on the other side. The horse sloshed into the water and stopped. Pepé dropped his bridle and let the beast drink of the running water.

Soon the canyon sides became steep and the first giant sentinel redwoods guarded the trail, great round red trunks bearing foliage as green and lacy as ferns. Once Pepé was among the trees, the sun was lost. A perfumed and purple light lay in the pale green of the underbrush. Gooseberry bushes and blackberries and tall ferns lined the stream, and overhead the branches of the redwoods met and cut off the sky.

Pepé drank from the water bag, and he reached into the flour sack and brought out a black string of jerky. His white teeth gnawed at the string until the tough meat parted. He chewed slowly and drank occasionally from the water bag. His little eyes were slumberous and tired, but the muscles of his face were hard set. The earth of the trail was black now. It gave up a hollow sound under the walking hoofbeats.

The stream fell more sharply. Little waterfalls splashed on the stones. Five-fingered ferns hung over the water and dripped spray from their fingertips. Pepé rode half over in his saddle, dangling one leg loosely. He picked a bay leaf from a tree beside the way and put it into his mouth for a moment to flavor the dry jerky. He held the gun loosely across the pommel.

Suddenly he squared in his saddle, swung the horse from the trail and kicked it hurriedly up behind a big redwood tree. He pulled up the reins tight against the bit to keep the horse from whinnying. His face was intent and his nostrils quivered a little.

A hollow pounding came down the trail,

---

10. cress: Watercress, an edible white-flowered plant.

Flight 723

723

26 **Discussion** What do the red sun and clouds signify?

27 **Critical Thinking and Reading** How is Pepé like the little steamer on the edge of the horizon? Why does this image indicate to Rosy that Pepé is not dead, but will die soon?

28 **Literary Focus** What details of the setting indicate that it is hostile?

29 **Critical Thinking and Reading** The redwoods are sentinels guarding the trail. Are they working to Pepé's advantage or against him? Note that they block the sun and cut off the sky. How does this affect Pepé's chances of escape?

30 **Discussion** What do the black earth and the hollow sound of the hoofbeats suggest about Pepé's fate?

31 **Clarification** The pommel is the front part of the saddle.

Student Activity 1. Decide whether the following pairs of clauses should be coordinated or left as separate sentences. If a pair should be coordinated, write the coordinated sentence, which will include the correct punctuation and a conjunction.

1. His chin looked hard. His sweet mouth was drawn and thin.
2. The loaded horse stood outside the door. The water bag dripped a line of moisture down the bay shoulder.
3. Moonlight and daylight fought with each other. The two warring qualities made it difficult to see.
4. Emilio and Rosey stood wondering in the dawn. They heard Mama whimpering in the house.

Student Activity 2. Provide a second coordinate clause to follow each of the following initial clauses.

1. Mama told Pepé that he wasn't a man, but . . .
2. Pepé joined the drinking in town, and . . .
3. Pepé's early talk about being a man is ironic, for . . .
4. Pepé was killed in the mountains, and . . .

32 Discussion What do we know about the dark watchers based on Steinbeck's description?

33 Reading Strategy Describe the changes in the setting since Pepé first entered the canyon. How might Pepé feel at this moment?

34 Discussion The hawk is a bird of prey. What is the significance of its appearance at this point in the story?

35 Discussion What do the dead rocks and starving black bushes signify?

and a horseman rode by, a fat man with red cheeks and a white stubble beard. His horse put down its head and blubbered at the trail when it came to the place where Pepé had turned off. "Hold up!" said the man and he pulled up his horse's head.

When the last sound of the hoofs died away, Pepé came back into the trail again. He did not relax in the saddle any more. He lifted the big rifle and swung the lever to throw a shell into the chamber, and then he let down the hammer to half cock.

The trail grew very steep. Now the redwood trees were smaller and their tops were dead, bitten dead where the wind reached them. The horse plodded on; the sun went slowly overhead and started down toward the afternoon.

Where the stream came out of a side canyon, the trail left it. Pepé dismounted and watered his horse and filled up his water bag. As soon as the trail had parted from the stream, the trees were gone and only the thick brittle sage and manzanita[11] and chaparral[12] edged the trail. And the soft black earth was gone, too, leaving only the light tan broken rock for the trail bed. Lizards scampered away into the brush as the horse rattled over the little stones.

Pepé turned in his saddle and looked back. He was in the open now: he could be seen from a distance. As he ascended the trail the country grew more rough and terrible and dry. The way wound about the bases of great square rocks. Little gray rabbits skittered in the brush. A bird made a monotonous high creaking. Eastward the bare rock mountaintops were pale and powder-dry under the dropping sun. The horse plodded up and up the trail toward a little V in the ridge which was the pass.

32 Pepé looked suspiciously back every minute or so, and his eyes sought the tops of the ridges ahead. Once, on a white barren spur,

---

11. **manzanita** (man'zə nēt'ə): Shrubs or small trees.
12. **chaparral** (chap'ə ral') *n.*: A thicket of thorny bushes or shrubs.

724 The Modern Age

he saw a black figure for a moment, but he looked quickly away, for it was one of the dark watchers. No one knew who the watchers were, nor where they lived, but it was better to ignore them and never to show interest in them. They did not bother one who stayed on the trail and minded his own business.

The air was parched and full of light dust blown by the breeze from the eroding mountains. Pepé drank sparingly from his bag and corked it tightly and hung it on the horn again. The trail moved up the dry shale hillside, avoiding rocks, dropping under clefts, climbing in and out of old water scars. When he arrived at the little pass he stopped and looked back for a long time. No dark watchers were to be seen now. The trail behind was empty. Only the high tops of the redwoods indicated where the stream flowed. **33**

Pepé rode on through the pass. His little eyes were nearly closed with weariness, but his face was stern, relentless and manly. The high mountain wind coasted sighing through the pass and whistled on the edges of the big blocks of broken granite. In the air, a red-tailed hawk sailed over close to the ridge and screamed angrily. Pepé went slowly through the broken jagged pass and looked down on the other side. **34**

The trail dropped quickly, staggering among broken rock. At the bottom of the slope there was a dark crease, thick with brush, and on the other side of the crease a little flat, in which a grove of oak trees grew. A scar of green grass cut across the flat. And behind the flat another mountain rose, desolate with dead rocks and starving little black bushes. Pepé drank from the bag again for the air was so dry that it encrusted his nostrils and burned his lips. He put the horse down the trail. The hooves slipped and struggled on the steep way, starting little stones that rolled off into the brush. The sun was gone behind the westward mountain now, but still it glowed brilliantly on the oaks and on the grassy flat. The rocks and the hillsides still sent up waves of the heat they had gathered from the day's sun. **35**

Grammar in Action

The vividness of a descriptive passage usually results to a great extent from the writer's use of **adjectives**. For example, in the following sentences from "Flight" Steinbeck uses adjectives to convey the ruggedness of the mountain landscape:

As he ascended the trail the country grew more *rough* and *terrible* and *dry*.

Eastward the *bare rock* mountaintops were *pale* and *powder-dry* under the dropping sun.

Student Activity 1. Identify the adjectives in each of the following sentences from "Flight" and explain how they contribute to the effectiveness of the description.
1. And there was Pepe, the tall smiling son of nineteen, a gentle, affectionate boy, but very lazy.
2. The weathered little shack was silver in the moonlight and the square shadow of it was black to the north and east.
3. It was a well-worn path, dark soft leaf-mold earth strewn with broken pieces of sandstone.
4. Gradually the sharp snaggled edge of the ridge stood out above them, rotten granite tortured and eaten by the winds of time.
5. Below him lay a deep canyon exactly like the last, waterless, and desolate.

724

Pepé looked up to the top of the next dry withered ridge. He saw a dark form against the sky, a man's figure standing on top of a rock, and he glanced away quickly not to appear curious. When a moment later he looked up again, the figure was gone.

Downward the trail was quickly covered. Sometimes the horse floundered for footing, sometimes set his feet and slid a little way. They came at last to the bottom where the dark chaparral was higher than Pepé's head. He held up his rifle on one side and his arm on the other to shield his face from the sharp brittle fingers of the brush.

Up and out of the crease he rode, and up a little cliff. The grassy flat was before him, and the round comfortable oaks. For a moment he studied the trail down which he had come, but there was no movement and no sound from it. Finally he rode out over the flat, to the green streak, and at the upper end of the damp he found a little spring welling out of the earth and dropping into a dug basin before it seeped out over the flat.

Pepé filled his bag first, and then he let the thirsty horse drink out of the pool. He led the horse to the clump of oaks, and in the middle of the grove, fairly protected from sight on all sides, he took off the saddle and the bridle and laid them on the ground. The horse stretched his jaws sideways and yawned. Pepé knotted the lead rope about the horse's neck and tied him to a sapling among the oaks, where he could graze in a fairly large circle.

When the horse was gnawing hungrily at the dry grass, Pepé went to the saddle and took a black string of jerky from the sack and strolled to an oak tree on the edge of the grove, from under which he could watch the trail. He sat down in the crisp dry oak leaves and automatically felt for his big black knife

36

36 **Discussion** What action indicates that Pepé is losing some of his human dignity?

Flight 725

Student Activity 2. Rewrite each of the following sentences, adding at least two vivid adjectives.

1. The Torres farm was located above a cliff that sloped into the ocean.
2. Mounting his horse, Pepe rode up the trail into the mountains.
3. The moonlight spread across the landscape, illuminating the mountain path.
4. Worn down by the sun, Pepe rested beneath an oak tree.
5. Clinging to the stones with his hands, Pepe struggled to ascend a ridge.

Student Activity 3. Write a paragraph in which you describe a scene from nature, using at least ten adjectives to make your description as vivid as possible.

37 **Discussion** Why does Pepé scare away the quail and the doves, risking a confrontation with the cat?

38 **Clarification** Shod hooves are ones with shoes on them.

39 **Discussion** What is the symbolic significance of Pepé's loss of his hat? Recall that the first time Pepé wears it, when he goes to Monterey, Steinbeck writes that it gave "him dignity and age."

40 **Discussion** What is happening to Pepé at this point? What change has he undergone since losing his horse?

to cut the jerky, but he had no knife. He leaned back on his elbow and gnawed at the tough strong meat. His face was blank, but it was a man's face.

The bright evening light washed the eastern ridge, but the valley was darkening. Doves flew down from the hills to the spring, and the quail came running out of the brush and joined them, calling clearly to one another.

Out of the corner of his eye Pepé saw a shadow grow out of the bushy crease. He turned his head slowly. A big spotted wildcat was creeping toward the spring, belly to the ground, moving like thought.

Pepé cocked his rifle and edged the muzzle slowly around. Then he looked apprehensively up the trail and dropped the hammer again. From the ground beside him he picked an oak twig and threw it toward the spring. The quail flew up with a roar and the doves whistled away. The big cat stood up: for a long moment he looked at Pepé with cold yellow eyes, and then fearlessly walked back into the gulch.

The dusk gathered quickly in the deep valley. Pepé muttered his prayers, put his head down on his arm and went instantly to sleep.

The moon came up and filled the valley with cold blue light, and the wind swept rustling down from the peaks. The owls worked up and down the slopes looking for rabbits. Down in the brush of the gulch a coyote gabbled. The oak trees whispered softly in the night breeze.

Pepé started up, listening. His horse had whinnied. The moon was just slipping behind the western ridge, leaving the valley in darkness behind it. Pepé sat tensely gripping his rifle. From far up the trail he heard an answering whinny and the crash of shod hooves on the broken rock. He jumped to his feet, ran to his horse and led it under the trees. He threw on the saddle and cinched it tight for the steep trail, caught the unwilling head and forced the bit into the mouth. He

felt the saddle to make sure the water bag and the sack of jerky were there. Then he mounted and turned up the hill.

It was velvet dark. The horse found the entrance to the trail where it left the flat, and started up, stumbling and slipping on the rocks. Pepé's hand rose up to his head. His hat was gone. He had left it under the oak tree.

The horse had struggled far up the trail when the first change of dawn came into the air, a steel grayness as light mixed thoroughly with dark. Gradually the sharp snaggled edge of the ridge stood out above them, rotten granite tortured and eaten by the winds of time. Pepé had dropped his reins on the horn, leaving direction to the horse. The brush grabbed at his legs in the dark until one knee of his jeans was ripped.

Gradually the light flowed down over the ridge. The starved brush and rocks stood out in the half light, strange and lonely in high perspective. Then there came warmth into the light. Pepé drew up and looked back, but he could see nothing in the darker valley below. The sky turned blue over the coming sun. In the waste of the mountainside, the poor dry brush grew only three feet high. Here and there, big outcroppings of unrotted granite stood up like moldering houses. Pepé relaxed a little. He drank from his water bag and bit off a piece of jerky. A single eagle flew over, high in the light.

Without warning Pepé's horse screamed and fell on its side. He was almost down before the rifle crash echoed up from the valley. From a hole behind the struggling shoulder, a stream of bright crimson blood pumped and stopped and pumped and stopped. The hooves threshed on the ground. Pepé lay half stunned beside the horse. He looked slowly down the hill. A piece of sage clipped off beside his head and another crash echoed up from side to side of the canyon. Pepé flung himself frantically behind a bush.

He crawled up the hill on his knees and one hand. His right hand held the rifle up off the ground and pushed it ahead of him. He

Primary Source

The following is an abridged analysis by Dan Vogel:

More than a mere allegory, "Flight" reveals characteristics of myth and tragedy. A myth is a story that tries to explain some practice, belief, institution, or natural phenomenon, and is especially associated with religious rites and beliefs. The natural phenomenon, for Steinbeck, is not the facts of nature, with which historical myths deal; rather,

it is . . . the development of innocent childhood into disillusioned manhood. The myth that Steinbeck wrought also contains another quality of myth, the rite. The plot of "Flight" narrates symbolically the ritual: the escape from the Mother, the divestiture of the Father, and the death and burial of Childhood.

At the beginning of the story, Pepe, though 19 years of age, has all the innocence of the "toy-baby" his mother calls him . . .

When his rather domineering mother . . . asks him to go to Monterey, "a revolution took place in the relaxed figure of Pepe."

moved with the instinctive care of an animal. Rapidly he wormed his way toward one of the big outcroppings of granite on the hill above him. Where the brush was high he doubled up and ran, but where the cover was slight he wriggled forward on his stomach, pushing the rifle ahead of him. In the last little distance there was no cover at all. Pepé poised and then he darted across the space and flashed around the corner of the rock.

He leaned panting against the stone. When his breath came easier he moved along behind the big rock until he came to a narrow split that offered a thin section of vision down the hill. Pepé lay on his stomach and pushed the rifle barrel through the slit and waited.

The sun reddened the western ridges now. Already the buzzards were settling down toward the place where the horse lay. A small brown bird scratched in the dead sage leaves directly in front of the rifle muzzle. The coasting eagle flew back toward the rising sun.

Pepé saw a little movement in the brush far below. His grip tightened on the gun. A little brown doe stepped daintily out on the trail and crossed it and disappeared into the brush again. For a long time Pepé waited. Far below he could see the little flat and the oak trees and the slash of green. Suddenly his eyes flashed back at the trail again. A quarter of a mile down there had been a quick movement in the chaparral. The rifle swung over. The front sight nestled in the v of the rear sight. Pepé studied for a moment and then raised the rear sight a notch. The little movement in the brush came again. The sight settled on it. Pepé squeezed the trigger. The explosion crashed down the mountain and up the other side, and came rattling back. The whole side of the slope grew still. No more movement. And then a white streak cut into the granite of the slit and a bullet whined away and a crash sounded up from below. Pepé felt a sharp pain in his right hand. A sliver of granite was sticking out from between his first and second knuckles and the point protruded from his palm. Carefully he pulled out the sliver of stone. The wound bled evenly and gently. No vein nor artery was cut.

Pepé looked into a little dusty cave in the rock and gathered a handful of spider web, and he pressed the mass into the cut, plastering the soft web into the blood. The flow stopped almost at once.

The rifle was on the ground. Pepé picked it up, levered a new shell into the chamber. And then he slid into the brush on his stomach. Far to the right he crawled, and then up the hill, moving slowly and carefully, crawling to cover and resting and then crawling again.

In the mountains the sun is high in its arc before it penetrates the gorges. The hot face looked over the hill and brought instant heat with it. The white light beat on the rocks and reflected from them and rose up quivering from the earth again, and the rocks and bushes seemed to quiver behind the air.

Pepé crawled in the general direction of the ridge peak, zig-zagging for cover. The deep cut between his knuckles began to throb. He crawled close to a rattlesnake before he saw it, and when it raised its dry head and made a soft beginning whirr, he backed up and took another way. The quick gray lizards flashed in front of him, raising a tiny line of dust. He found another mass of spider web and pressed it against his throbbing hand.

Pepé was pushing the rifle with his left hand now. Little drops of sweat ran to the ends of his coarse black hair and rolled down his cheeks. His lips and tongue were growing thick and heavy. His lips writhed to draw saliva into his mouth. His little dark eyes were uneasy and suspicious. Once when a gray lizard paused in front of him on the parched ground and turned its head sideways he crushed it flat with a stone.

When the sun slid past noon he had not gone a mile. He crawled exhaustedly a last hundred yards to a patch of high sharp

41 **Discussion** Steinbeck could have written "Pepé swung over the rifle" instead of "The rifle swung over." What is the significance of this choice of syntax?

42 **Discussion** What do these actions suggest about Pepé's state of mind? Are they the movements of an animal or a human?

43 **Literary Focus** The quivering of the light, the rocks, and the bushes echo Pepé's tense and alert state of mind.

44 **Discussion** Why does Pepé kill the lizard? What does this action reveal about his state of mind?

When Pepe returns, he has killed a man . . . The look of innocence is gone; he has been shocked by a fact of life, an extreme independent act. His mother quickly understands and helps him outfit himself for the flight into the mountains. She gives him especially his father's black coat and rifle. Weighted down by the accoutrements of his father, Pepe separates himself from his mother . . .

The ordeal of transformation from innocence to experience, from purity to defilement begins. There is the physical pain of the ordeal, symbolized by a cut hand that soon becomes gangrenous. There is the psychological pain . . . This realization is symbolized by the . . . presence of the black figures, the "dark watchers" . . .

Only (when) having been separated from his mother and having cleansed himself of all the accoutrements and artifacts of his father, can the youth stand alone. But to Steinbeck this is far from a joyous or victorious occasion. It is sad and painful and tragic. . . . (T)he narrative ends with the man against the sky shot down. . . . Thus innocence is killed and buried in the moment that Man stands alone.

Thus the myth ends, as so many myths do, with violence and melodrama. What the myth described is the natural miracle of entering manhood. When serenity of childhood is lost, there is pain and misery. Yet there is nevertheless a sense of gain and heroism which are more interesting and dramatic.

45 Discussion Why does Pepé leave his father's coat behind? What possessions does he have left?

46 Clarification A draw is a basin through which or into which water drains.

47 Clarification A poultice is a warm and moist mass of material, such as flour and mustard, that healers apply to inflamed wounds.

manzanita, crawled desperately, and when the patch was reached he wriggled in among the tough gnarly trunks and dropped his head on his left arm. There was little shade in the meager brush, but there was cover and safety. Pepé went to sleep as he lay and the sun beat on his back. A few little birds hopped close to him and peered and hopped away. Pepé squirmed in his sleep and he raised and dropped his wounded hand again and again.

The sun went down behind the peaks and the cool evening came, and then the dark. A coyote yelled from the hillside, Pepé started awake and looked about with misty eyes. His hand was swollen and heavy; a little thread of pain ran up the inside of his arm and settled in a pocket in his armpit. He peered about and then stood up, for the mountains were black and the moon had not yet risen. Pepé stood up in the dark. The coat of his father pressed on his arm. His tongue was swollen until it nearly filled his mouth. He wriggled out of the coat and dropped it in the brush, and then he struggled up the hill, falling over rocks and tearing his way through the brush. The rifle knocked against stones as he went. Little dry avalanches of gravel and shattered stone went whispering down the hill behind him.

After a while the old moon came up and showed the jagged ridge top ahead of him. By moonlight Pepé traveled more easily. He bent forward so that his throbbing arm hung away from his body. The journey uphill was made in dashes and rests, a frantic rush up a few yards and then a rest. The wind coasted down the slope rattling the dry stems of the bushes.

The moon was at meridian when Pepé came at last to the sharp backbone of the ridge top. On the last hundred yards of the rise no soil had clung under the wearing winds. The way was on solid rock. He clambered to the top and looked down on the other side. There was a draw like the last below him, misty with moonlight, brushed with dry struggling sage and chaparral. On the other side the hill rose up sharply and at the top the jagged rotten teeth of the mountain showed against the sky. At the bottom of the cut the brush was thick and dark.

Pepé stumbled down the hill. His throat was almost closed with thirst. At first he tried to run, but immediately he fell and rolled. After that he went more carefully. The moon was just disappearing behind the mountains when he came to the bottom. He crawled into the heavy brush feeling with his fingers for water. There was no water in the bed of the stream, only damp earth. Pepé laid his gun down and scooped up a handful of mud and put it in his mouth, and then he spluttered and scraped the earth from his tongue with his finger, for the mud drew at his mouth like a poultice. He dug a hole in

Grammar in Action

Descriptive writing emphasizes what our senses observe—the sensory qualities of a person, an experience, a place, or a thing. It uses language that appeals to the reader's emotions, senses, and imagination. To create these images, writers use sensory details—details appealing to one or more of the five senses. Note Steinbeck's use of sensory details in the following passage from "Flight":

The sun went down behind the peaks and the cool evening came, and then the dark. A coyote yelled from the hillside, Pepé started awake and looked about with misty eyes. His hand was swollen and heavy; a little thread of pain ran up the inside of his arm and settled in a pocket in his armpit.

In looking at this passage, you will notice that the first sentence contains words appealing to the senses of sight and touch, the second sentence appeals to the sense of sound, and the fourth sentence appeals to the sense of touch. These sensory words present a striking, detailed description that evokes a specific image in your imagination.

tle square, soaked it in the water and put it in his mouth. Over and over he filled the cloth and sucked it.

Still the lion sat and watched him. The evening came down but there was no movement on the hills. No birds visited the dry bottom of the cut. Pepé looked occasionally at the lion. The eyes of the yellow beast drooped as though he were about to sleep. He yawned and his long thin red tongue curled out. Suddenly his head jerked around and his nostrils quivered. His big tail lashed. He stood up and slunk like a tawny shadow into the thick brush.

A moment later Pepé heard the sound, the faint far crash of horses' hooves on gravel. And he heard something else, a high whining yelp of a dog.

Pepé took his rifle in his left hand and he glided into the brush almost as quietly as the lion had. In the darkening evening he crouched up the hill toward the next ridge. Only when the dark came did he stand up. His energy was short. Once it was dark he fell over the rocks and slipped to his knees on the steep slope, but he moved on and on up the hill, climbing and scrabbling over the broken hillside.

When he was far up toward the top, he lay down and slept for a little while. The withered moon, shining on his face, awakened him. He stood up and moved up the hill. Fifty yards away he stopped and turned back, for he had forgotten his rifle. He walked heavily down, and poked about in the brush, but he could not find his gun. At last he lay down to rest. The pocket of pain in his armpit had grown more sharp. His arm seemed to swell out and fall with every heartbeat. There was no position lying down where the heavy arm did not press against his armpit.

With the effort of a hurt beast, Pepé got up and moved again toward the top of the ridge. He held his swollen arm away from his body with his left hand. Up the steep hill he dragged himself, a few steps and a rest, and a few more steps. At last he was nearing the

the stream bed with his fingers, dug a little basin to catch water; but before it was very deep his head fell forward on the damp ground and he slept.

The dawn came and the heat of the day fell on the earth, and still Pepé slept. Late in the afternoon his head jerked up. He looked slowly around. His eyes were slits of wariness. Twenty feet away in the the heavy brush a big tawny mountain lion stood looking at him. Its long thick tail waved gracefully, its ears were erect with interest, not laid back dangerously. The lion squatted down on its stomach and watched him.

Pepé looked at the hole he had dug in the earth. A half inch of muddy water had collected in the bottom. He tore the sleeve from his hurt arm, with his teeth ripped out a lit-

48 **Discussion** Compare the movements and actions of the mountain lion with those of Pepé. What similarities are there?

49 **Critical Thinking and Reading** Note that the rifle was Pepé's last possession.

Flight 729

Student Activity 1. Locate five more descriptive passages in "Flight." Then find the sensory details in these passages and identify the sense or senses to which each detail appeals.

Student Activity 2. Write a paragraph describing a place that you know well. It might be a room, a town, or a beautiful scene from nature. Include sensory details in your description.

top. The moon showed the uneven sharp back of it against the sky.

Pepé's brain spun in a big spiral up and away from him. He slumped to the ground and lay still. The rock ridge top was only a hundred feet above him.

50 The moon moved over the sky. Pepé half turned on his back. His tongue tried to make words, but only a thick hissing came from between his lips.

When the dawn came, Pepé pulled himself up. His eyes were sane again. He drew his great puffed arm in front of him and looked at the angry wound. The black line ran up from his wrist to his armpit. Automatically he reached in his pocket for the big black knife, but it was not there. His eyes searched the ground. He picked up a sharp blade of stone and scraped at the wound, sawed at the proud flesh and then squeezed the green juice out in big drops. Instantly he threw back his head and whined like a dog. His whole right side shuddered at the pain, but the pain cleared his head.

In the gray light he struggled up the last slope to the ridge and crawled over and lay down behind a line of rocks. Below him lay a deep canyon exactly like the last, waterless and desolate. There was no flat, no oak trees, not even heavy brush in the bottom of it. And on the other side a sharp ridge stood up, thinly brushed with starving sage, littered with broken granite. Strewn over the hill there were giant outcroppings, and on the top the granite teeth stood out against the sky.

The new day was light now. The flame of the sun came over the ridge and fell on Pepé where he lay on the ground. His coarse black hair was littered with twigs and bits of spider web. His eyes had retreated back into his head. Between his lips the tip of his black tongue showed.

He sat up and dragged his great arm into his lap and nursed it, rocking his body and moaning in his throat. He threw back his head and looked up into the pale sky. A big **51** black bird circled nearly out of sight, and far to the left another was sailing near.

He lifted his head to listen, for a familiar sound had come to him from the valley he had climbed out of; it was the crying yelp of hounds, excited and feverish, on a trail.

Pepé bowed his head quickly. He tried to **52** speak rapid words but only a thick hiss came from his lips. He drew a shaky cross on his breast with his left hand. It was a long struggle to get to his feet. He crawled slowly and mechanically to the top of a big rock on the ridge peak. Once there, he arose slowly, **53** swaying to his feet, and stood erect. Far below he could see the dark brush where he had slept. He braced his feet and stood there, black against the morning sky.

There came a ripping sound at his feet. A piece of stone flew up and a bullet droned off into the next gorge. The hollow crash echoed up from below. Pepé looked down for **54** a moment and then pulled himself straight again.

His body jarred back. His left hand fluttered helplessly toward his breast. The second crash sounded from below. Pepé swung forward and toppled from the rock. His body struck and rolled over and over, starting a little avalanche. And when at last he stopped against a bush, the avalanche slid slowly down and covered up his head.

THINKING ABOUT THE SELECTION

Recalling

1. (a) How had Pepé's father died? (b) What had Pepé inherited from him?
2. (a) Why does Mama Torres send Pepé into town? (b) Why does he return home early?
3. (a) What does Mama Torres give Pepé before he goes away into the mountains? (b) Whom does she tell him to avoid?
4. (a) How does Pepé lose his hat? (b) How does he lose his horse? (c) How is he wounded? (d) How does he lose his rifle?
5. What happens to Pepé at the end of the story?

Interpreting

6. (a) How does Pepé change during the course of the story? (b) What events bring about these changes?
7. How do the descriptions of Pepé's physical appearance during his flight reflect his state of mind?
8. What is the significance of the fact that Pepé never sees his pursuers?
9. During the course of his flight, Pepé is gradually stripped of his possessions, and his behavior becomes more and more animal-like, as he is forced to rely on his instincts. (a) Find three instances in which Steinbeck compares Pepé's actions to those of an animal. (b) What does Pepé do in the end to retain his sense of dignity as a human being?

Applying

10. Do you agree with Mama Torres's statement that "A boy gets to be a man when a man is needed"? Why or why not?

ANALYZING LITERATURE

Understanding Setting

The **setting** is the time and place in which the events in a work of literature occur. Like many of Steinbeck's other works, "Flight" is set in northern California during the later 1800's or early 1900's.

1. What do the details of the setting in the first paragraph suggest about humanity's relationship to nature?
2. How does the landscape change during the course of Pepé's flight?
3. The setting of a literary work sometimes reflects the writer's view of the world. What outlook might the setting of "Flight" reflect?
4. The American writer and social critic Ayn Rand once wrote, "Man's unique reward, however, is that while animals survive by adjusting themselves to their background, man survives by adjusting his background to himself." On the basis of "Flight," do you think John Steinbeck would agree or disagree with this statement? Explain your answer.

CRITICAL THINKING AND READING

Analyzing the Effect of Setting

The **setting** often influences the characters' personalities and behavior. For example, in "Flight" the setting directly affects Pepé's actions as he flees from his pursuers, forcing him to become more and more instinctive and animal-like in his behavior.

1. How have Pepé's and Mama Torres's personalities been shaped by the setting?
2. How do the changes in the landscape during Pepé's flight affect his change of escape?

THINKING AND WRITING

Writing About Setting

Write an essay in which you discuss how the setting has shaped Pepé's personality and how it affects his behavior during the story. Reread the story, thinking about how the setting has shaped Pepé's character and noting the relationship between the details of the setting and Pepé's actions. When you write your essay, use evidence from the story to support your argument. When you revise make sure your essay is logically organized.

Flight 731

beast." He hisses like a snake instead of speaking. (b) He stands up straight to face his attacker.

Applying

10. Answers will differ. Students may respond that they agree with Mama's statement, because people reach maturity by weathering difficult situations.

Challenge Do you think that Pepé had a realistic chance of escaping? Why or why not?

ANSWERS TO ANALYZING LITERATURE

1. The image of aphids huddling and clinging to mountain sides suggests that people are at the mercy of the "wild coast." "Rotting barns, gray-bitten with sea salt" and stunted, wind beaten corn suggest that the terrain has little mercy.
2. The landscape becomes more hostile—harsher, rockier, steeper, and drier.
3. Steinbeck views the world as cruel and unmerciful.
4. Suggested Response: He would disagree, because he believes that people must adapt to their environments.

ANSWERS TO CRITICAL THINKING AND READING

1. Suggested Response: The harsh climate and life have made Mama strong, fierce, and stern when faced with danger and difficulty. As soon as he flees into the mountains, Pepé becomes the same way.
2. The changes in the landscape decrease his chances of escaping.

THINKING AND WRITING

For help with this assignment, students can refer to Lesson 7, in "Writing About Setting", the Handbook of Writing About Literature.

Publishing Student Writing Have student volunteers read their essays to the class, and use the readings as a springboard for a class discussion about setting.

Closure and Extension

ANSWERS TO THINKING ABOUT THE SELECTION

Recalling

1. (a) A rattlesnake had bitten him. (b) Pepé inherits a knife.
2. (a) She needs medicine and salt. (b) He kills a man and must now flee.
3. (a) She gives him a rifle, a water bag, jerky, and his father's coat.

(b) She tells him to avoid the dark watchers.
4. (a) He leaves it under an oak tree. (b) His horse is shot. (c) Pepé is shot in the arm. (d) He forgets his rifle on a hill.
5. He is shot in the breast and, as he falls, he causes an avalanche that buries him.

Interpreting

6. (a) He evolves from being a soft and lazy boy into a wild and desperate man. (b) Violence and

bloodshed—his own and that of the man he kills—bring about the changes.
7. Steinbeck uses animal images to show that Pepé is becoming more helpless, desperate, and wild.
8. Suggested Response: Because he never sees them, he has no chance to fight back. He is totally helpless against the forces around him.
9. (a) Suggested Response: He moves as quietly as a lion. He rises with the effort of a "hurt

731

WILLIAM FAULKNER

1897–1962

William Faulkner is generally regarded as the most innovative American novelist of his time. In his work he experimented with narrative chronology, explored multiple points of view, and delved deeply into the minds of his characters. Yet although he used a variety of forms and techniques in his novels and short stories, most of his works are linked through a common setting, the fictional world of Yoknapatawpha County, Mississippi.

Faulkner grew up in Oxford, Mississippi. Although he never finished high school, he read a great deal and developed an interest in writing at an early age. In 1918 he enlisted in the British Royal Flying Corps and was sent to Canada for training. However, World War I ended before he had a chance to see combat, and he returned to Mississippi. Several years later, longing for a change of scene, he moved to New Orleans. There he became friends with Sherwood Anderson, who offered encouragement and helped get his first novel, *A Soldier's Pay* (1926), published.

In 1926 Faulkner moved back to Oxford and concentrated on his writing. He first earned critical acclaim in 1929 when he published *The Sound and the Fury*, a complex novel exploring the downfall of an old southern family as seen through the eyes of three different characters. A year later he published *As I Lay Dying*, a novel in which the point of view constantly shifts, as Faulkner delves into the varying perceptions of death.

Faulkner went on to write several more inventive novels, including *Light in August* (1932), *Absalom, Absalom* (1936), and *The Wild Palms* (1939). His later works, such as *The Unvanquished* (1938) and *The Hamlet* (1940), were more traditional in form. Yet in these novels, Faulkner continued developing the history of Yoknapatawpha County and its people. Faulkner had invented this imaginative county based on his own in his novel *Sartoris* (1929). It was during the writing of this novel that Faulkner "discovered that my own little postage stamp of native soil was worth writing about and that I would never live long enough to exhaust it, and that by sublimating the actual into the apocryphal I might have complete liberty to use whatever talent I might have to its absolute top. I opened up a gold mine of other people, so I created a cosmos of my own."

Despite the critical success of some of his works, Faulkner did not earn widespread public recognition until 1946, when *The Portable Faulkner*—an anthology in which many of his writings about Yoknapatawpha County were presented in chronological order—was published. Four years later he was awarded the Nobel Prize following the publication of *Intruder in the Dust* (1948), a novel in which he confronted the issue of racism.

GUIDE FOR INTERPRETING

The Bear

Writer's Techniques

Symbols. A symbol is a person, place, or thing that has a meaning in itself and also represents something larger than itself. For example, gold may be used as a symbol of greed, while a rose may symbolize love.

In the aftermath of World War I, many writers came to believe that modern life was filled with uncertainty and lacked any definite meaning. To express this belief, these writers turned away from directly stating their themes and suggested rather than asserted meaning. As a result modern writers frequently used symbols as a means of expressing their themes.

Allusions. An allusion is a reference to another literary work or to a figure, place, or event from history, religion, or mythology.

Allusions serve two important purposes in literature. Like symbols they can contribute to the theme of a literary work. At the same time, they provide writers with a way of maintaining a link to the cultural roots of the past.

Commentary

One of the most striking features of Faulkner's writing style is the way he manipulates time. Rarely do his stories move in a straight line from the past to the present. Instead, he interweaves past, present, and future to show the ways in which they are all intertwined in a person's life. "The Bear" begins when Ike McCaslin is ten, but Faulkner immediately explains that what Ike will do and who he is in the present is part of his inheritance from the past. At the same time, we are given a sense that the events of this hunt are going to be important in the boy's future. In "The Bear" life is presented in flux.

This continuing motion of life is central to Faulkner's ideas about the way people make moral choices. He believed that because life is motion, people do not necessarily have time to make moral judgments while dealing with life. Yet, as Faulkner put it in a famous *Paris Interview* in 1956, people are "compelled to make choices between good and evil sooner or later, because moral consciences demand that. . . ." "The Bear" deals with the boy's developing moral conscience in the context of an exciting hunt. What moral choices must he make?

Writing

"The Bear" is a story about a boy whose experiences during a series of hunting expeditions gradually lead him to an understanding about life. The English novelist Charles Dickens once wrote, "There is a passion for hunting something deeply implanted in the human breast." Freewrite, exploring your reaction to this statement.

Guide for Interpreting 733

Literary Focus Have students think of appropriate symbols for the following concepts: religious beliefs, happiness, hate, and diligence. Ask them to explain precisely why each symbol they have chosen represents the corresponding concept.

Writing/Prior Knowledge Before students begin writing, spend some time discussing the meaning of Dickens's comment.

Enrichment In spite of his lack of formal education, Faulkner's fiction contains many long, difficult words and sentences. Students might benefit from an exercise in which they use the vocabulary words in a series of clauses, linked together in one long sentence.

Vocabulary

Preteach the following vocabulary words:

malevolent (mə lev'ə lənt) *adj.:* Wishing evil or harm to others (p. 734)

anachronism (ə nak'rə niz'm) *n.:* Something that is or seems to be out of its proper time (p. 734)

apotheosis (a päth' ē ō'sis) *n.:* Glorification (p. 734)

abjectness (ab' jekt nəs) *n.:* Wretchedness (p. 735)

effluvium (e floo' vē əm) *n.:* Aura (p. 735)

temerity (tə mer'ə tē) *n.:* Foolhardy or heedless disregard of danger (p. 735)

evanescently (ev'ə nes''nt lē) *adv.:* Fleetingly (p. 739)

immemorial (im'ə môr'ē əl) *adj.:* Extending back beyond memory or record (p. 739)

inviolable (in vī'ə lə b'l) *adj.:* Safe from danger (p. 740)

abrogated (ab'rə gāt'əd) *v.:* Canceled (p. 740)

lucidity (loo sid' i tē) *n.:* Brightness (p. 740)

The Bear

William Faulkner

He was ten. But it had already begun, long before that day when at last he wrote his age in two figures and he saw for the first time the camp where his father and Major de Spain and old General Compson and the others spent two weeks each November and two weeks again each June. He had already inherited then, without ever having seen it, the tremendous bear with one trap-ruined foot which, in an area almost a hundred miles deep, had earned for itself a name, a definite designation like a living man.

He had listened to it for years: the long legend of corncribs rifled, of shotes[1] and grown pigs and even calves carried bodily into the woods and devoured, of traps and deadfalls[2] overthrown and dogs mangled and slain, and shotgun and even rifle charges delivered at point-blank range and with no more effect than so many peas blown through a tube by a boy—a corridor of wreckage and destruction beginning back before he was born, through which sped, not fast but rather with the ruthless and irresistible deliberation of a locomotive, the shaggy tremendous shape.

It ran in his knowledge before he ever saw it. It looked and towered in his dreams before he even saw the unaxed woods where it left its crooked print, shaggy, huge, red-eyed, not malevolent but just big—too big for the dogs which tried to bay[3] it, for the horses which tried to ride it down, for the men and the bullets they fired into it, too big for the very country which was its constricting scope. He seemed to see it entire with a child's complete divination before he ever laid eyes on either—the doomed wilderness whose edges were being constantly and punily gnawed at by men with axes and plows who feared it because it was wilderness, men myriad and nameless even to one another in the land where the old bear had earned a name, through which ran not even a mortal animal but an anachronism, indomitable and invincible, out of an old dead time, a phantom, epitome and apotheosis of the old wild life at which the puny humans swarmed and hacked in a fury of abhorrence and fear, like pygmies[4] about the ankles of a drowsing elephant; the old bear solitary, indomitable and alone, widowered, childless and absolved of mortality—old Priam[5] reft of his old wife and having outlived all his sons.

Until he was ten, each November he would watch the wagon containing the dogs and the bedding and food and guns and his father and Tennie's Jim, the Negro, and Sam Fathers, the Indian, son of a slave woman and a Chickasaw chief, depart on the road to town, to Jefferson, where Major de Spain and the others would join them. To the boy, at seven and eight and nine, they were not going into the Big Bottom to hunt bear and deer, but to keep yearly rendezvous with the bear which they did not even intend

---

1. shotes *n.*: Young hogs.
2. deadfalls *n.*: Traps arranged so that a heavy weight is dropped on prey.
3. bay *v.*: Chase and corner.

4. pygmies (pig′ mēz) *n.*: Members of African and Asiatic races known for their small stature.
5. Priam (prī′ əm): The king of Troy whose wife and children were killed when the Greeks invaded Troy during the Trojan War.

to kill. Two weeks later they would return, with no trophy, no head and skin. He had not expected it. He had not even been afraid it would be in the wagon. He believed that even after he was ten and his father would let him go too, for those two November weeks, he would merely make another one, along with his father and Major de Spain and General Compson and the others, the dogs which feared to bay it and the rifles and shotguns which failed even to bleed it, in the yearly pageant of the old bear's furious immortality.

Then he heard the dogs. It was in the second week of his first time in the camp. He stood with Sam Fathers against a big oak beside the faint crossing where they had stood each dawn for nine days now, hearing the dogs. He had heard them once before, one morning last week—a murmur, sourceless, echoing through the wet woods, swelling presently into separate voices which he could recognize and call by name. He had raised and cocked the gun as Sam told him and stood motionless again while the uproar, the invisible course, swept up and past and faded; it seemed to him that he could actually see the deer, the buck, blond, smoke-colored, elongated with speed, fleeing, vanishing, the woods, the gray solitude, still ringing even when the cries of the dogs had died away.

"Now let the hammers down," Sam said.

"You knew they were not coming here, too," he said.

"Yes," Sam said. "I want you to learn how to do when you didn't shoot. It's after the chance for the bear or the deer has done already come and gone that men and dogs get killed."

"Anyway," he said, "it was just a deer."

Then on the tenth morning he heard the dogs again. And he readied the too-long, too-heavy gun as Sam had taught him, before Sam even spoke. But this time it was no deer, no ringing chorus of dogs running strong on a free scent, but a moiling[6] yap-

***

6. **moiling:** Confused.

***

ping an octave too high, with something more than indecision and even abjectness in it, not even moving very fast, taking a long time to pass completely out of hearing, leaving even then somewhere in the air that echo, thin, slightly hysterical, abject, almost grieving, with no sense of a fleeing, unseen, smoke-colored, grass-eating shape ahead of it, and Sam, who had taught him first of all to cock the gun and take position where he could see everywhere and then never move again, had himself moved up beside him; he could hear Sam breathing at his shoulder and he could see the arched curve of the old man's inhaling nostrils.

"Hah," Sam said. "Not even running. Walking."

"Old Ben!" the boy said. "But up here!" he cried. "Way up here!"

"He do it every year," Sam said. "Once. Maybe to see who in camp this time, if he can shoot or not. Whether we got the dog yet that can bay and hold him. He'll take them to the river, then he'll send them back home. We may as well go back, too; see how they look when they come back to camp."

When they reached the camp the hounds were already there, ten of them crouching back under the kitchen, the boy and Sam squatting to peer back into the obscurity where they huddled, quiet, the eyes luminous, glowing at them and vanishing, and no sound, only that effluvium of something more than dog, stronger than dog and not just animal, just beast, because still there had been nothing in front of that abject and almost painful yapping save the solitude, the wilderness, so that when the eleventh hound came in at noon and with all the others watching—even old Uncle Ash, who called himself first a cook—Sam daubed the tattered ear and the raked shoulder with turpentine and axle grease, to the boy it was still no living creature, but the wilderness which, leaning for the moment down, had patted lightly once the hound's temerity.

"Just like a man," Sam said. "Just like folks. Put off as long as she could having to be brave, knowing all the time that sooner or

The Bear 735

***

6 **Literary Focus** What is the symbolic significance of the hunters' inability to kill the bear?

7 **Reading Strategy** Ask less advanced students to describe in their own words what has just happened.

8 **Reading Strategy** Ask the students to infer what the "grass-eating shape" is. Does the boy actually see it? What senses tell him that it is there?

9 **Discussion** The bear deliberately walks near the hunters' camp. What qualities or characteristics can you infer about the bear based on this action?

10 **Literary Focus** The hounds crouch in fear and obscurity, even though they have not seen the bear. What might the hounds symbolize?

11 **Literary Focus** Faulkner makes a direct connection between the wilderness and the bear. What is the relationship between wilderness and fear, as represented by the bear and the dogs?

12 **Discussion** What do Sam's comments reveal about human nature?

Humanities Note

Fine art, *In the Depths of the Timber,* by W. H. Dunton. W. Herbert (Buck) Dunton (1878–1936) was born in Augusta, Maine. Even at a early age he liked to draw and developed the habit of carrying food, a rifle, and a sketchbook wherever he went. He eventually moved to Wyoming where he worked as a cowboy. He then worked as an illustrator of western stories for several popular magazines but later abandoned the high-pressure magazine work in order to paint the West as it really had been in the early days.

This picture displays Dunton's love of nature. He has successfully created a feeling of depth in the woods through his use of color and detail. His careful rendering of the bear and such details as the playful spots of sunlight against the dark of the trees, all show that Dunton has an intense appreciation of the beauty and complexity of Nature.

You might use the following questions for discussion:

1. The artist used the word *depths* in his title for this painting. How has he created a feeling of depth in this picture?
2. What impression of the bear does Dunton convey? How does it compare with the impression of the boy in this story?

IN THE DEPTHS OF THE TIMBER
W. Herbert Dunton
Courtesy Amon Carter Museum, Fort Worth

736   *The Modern Age*

later she would have to be brave once to keep on living with herself, and knowing all the time beforehand what was going to happen to her when she done it."

That afternoon, himself on the one-eyed wagon mule which did not mind the smell of blood nor, as they told him, of bear, and with Sam on the other one, they rode for more than three hours through the rapid, shortening winter day. They followed no path, no trail even that he could see; almost at once they were in a country which he had never seen before. Then he knew why Sam had made him ride the mule which would not spook. The sound one stopped short and tried to whirl and bolt even as Sam got down, blowing its breath, jerking and wrenching at the rein while Sam held it, coaxing it forward with his voice, since he could not risk tying it, drawing it forward while the boy got down from the marred one.

Then, standing beside Sam in the gloom of the dying afternoon, he looked down at the rotted overturned log, gutted and scored with claw marks and, in the wet earth beside it, the print of the enormous warped two-toed foot. He knew now what he had smelled when he peered under the kitchen where the dogs huddled. He realized for the first time that the bear which had run in his listening and loomed in his dreams since before he could remember to the contrary, and which, therefore, must have existed in the listening and dreams of his father and Major de Spain and even old General Compson, too, before they began to remember in their turn, was a mortal animal, and that if they had departed for the camp each November without any actual hope of bringing its trophy back, it was not because it could not be slain, but because so far they had had no actual hope to.

"Tomorrow," he said.

"We'll try tomorrow," Sam said. "We ain't got the dog yet."

"We've got eleven. They ran him this morning."

"It won't need but one," Sam said. "He ain't here. Maybe he ain't nowhere. The only other way will be for him to run by accident over somebody that has a gun."

"That wouldn't be me," the boy said. "It will be Walter or Major or—"

"It might," Sam said. "You watch close in the morning. Because he's smart. That's how come he has lived this long. If he gets hemmed up and has to pick out somebody to run over, he will pick out you."

"How?" the boy said. "How will he know—" He ceased. "You mean he already knows me, that I ain't never been here before, ain't had time to find out yet whether I—" He ceased again, looking at Sam, the old man whose face revealed nothing until it smiled. He said humbly, not even amazed, "It was me he was watching. I don't reckon he did need to come but once."

The next morning they left the camp three hours before daylight. They rode this time because it was too far to walk, even the dogs in the wagon; again the first gray light found him in a place which he had never seen before, where Sam had placed him and told him to stay and then departed. With the gun which was too big for him, which did not even belong to him, but to Major de Spain, and which he had fired only once—at a stump on the first day, to learn the recoil and how to reload it—he stood against a gum tree beside a little bayou[7] whose black still water crept without movement out of a canebrake[8] and crossed a small clearing and into cane again, where, invisible, a bird—the big woodpecker called Lord-to-God by Negroes—clattered at a dead limb.

It was a stand like any other, dissimilar only in incidentals to the one where he had stood each morning for ten days; a territory new to him, yet no less familiar than that other one which, after almost two weeks, he had come to believe he knew a little—the same solitude, the same loneliness through

---

7. bayou (bī′ oō) n.: A sluggish, marshy inlet or outlet of a lake or river.
8. canebrake n.: An area overgrown with cane plants.

The Bear 737

13 **Discussion** What is the significance of the boy's realization that the bear is mortal? Why do the rotted log and paw print lead him this realization? What lesson has the boy learned about the wilderness?

14 **Critical Thinking and Reading** What quality must the "right" dog have in order to deal with the bear on equal terms?

15 **Discussion** Why would the bear choose the boy?

16 Discussion What is the significance of the fact that the boy
does not see the bear?

17 Literary Focus The eleventh
hound is set apart from the other
ten in this passage and in past
ones. Why? What is the symbolic
significance of her brave, yet futile stance against the bear?

18 Literary Focus Faulkner is alluding to the Civil War which marked
the defeat and decline of the
South. In Faulkner's works, the
Civil War symbolizes the end of
an antebellum ideal in which
family, land, and innocence prevailed. General Compson's de-
scendents, who for the most part
have succumbed to the postwar
corruption of civilization, are the
focus of one of Faulkner's best
novels, *The Sound and the Fury*.

19 Discussion What do the numbers ten and eleven signify in this
story?

which human beings had merely passed
without altering it, leaving no mark, no scar,
which looked exactly as it must have looked
when the first ancestor of Sam Fathers'
Chickasaw predecessors crept into it and
looked about, club or stone ax or bone arrow
drawn and poised; different only because,
squatting at the edge of the kitchen, he
smelled the hounds huddled and cringing
beneath it and saw the raked ear and shoulder of the one who, Sam said, had had to be
brave once in order to live with herself, and
saw yesterday in the earth beside the gutted
log the print of the living foot.

He heard no dogs at all. He never did
hear them. He only heard the drumming of
the woodpecker stop short off and knew that
the bear was looking at him. He never saw it.
He did not know whether it was in front of
him or behind him. He did not move, holding the useless gun, which he had not even
had warning to cock and which even now he
did not cock, tasting in his saliva that taint
as of brass which he knew now because he
had smelled it when he peered under the
kitchen at the huddled dogs.

Then it was gone. As abruptly as it had
ceased, the woodpecker's dry, monotonous
clatter set up again, and after a while he
even believed he could hear the dogs—a murmur, scarce a sound even, which he had
probably been hearing for some time before
he even remarked it, drifting into hearing
and then out again, dying away. They came
nowhere near him. If it was a bear they ran,
it was another bear. It was Sam himself who
came out of the cane and crossed the bayou,
followed by the injured bitch of yesterday.
She was almost at heel, like a bird dog, making no sound. She came and crouched
against his leg, trembling, staring off into
the cane.

"I didn't see him," he said. "I didn't,
Sam!"

"I know it," Sam said. "He done the looking. You didn't hear him neither, did you?"

"No," the boy said. "I—"

"He's smart," Sam said. "Too smart." He
looked down at the hound, trembling faintly
and steadily against the boy's knee. From
the raked shoulder a few drops of fresh blood
oozed and clung. "Too big. We ain't got the
dog yet. But maybe someday. Maybe not next
time. But someday."

So I must see him, he thought. *I must
look at him*. Otherwise, it seemed to him
that it would go on like this forever, as it had
gone on with his father and Major de Spain,
who was older than his father, and even with
old General Compson, who had been old
enough to be a brigade commander in 1865.
Otherwise, it would go on so forever, next
time and next time, after and after and after.
It seemed to him that he could see the two of
them, himself and the bear, shadowy in the
limbo from which time emerged, becoming
time; the old bear absolved of mortality and
himself partaking, sharing a little of it,
enough of it. And he knew now what he had
smelled in the huddled dogs and tasted in
his saliva. He recognized fear. *So I will have
to see him*, he thought, without dread or
even hope. *I will have to look at him*.

It was in June of the next year. He was
eleven. They were in camp again, celebrating
Major de Spain's and General Compson's
birthdays. Although the one had been born
in September and the other in the depth of
winter and in another decade, they had met
for two weeks to fish and shoot squirrels and
turkey and run coons and wildcats with the
dogs at night. That is, he and Boon Hoggenbeck and the Negroes fished and shot squirrels and ran the coons and cats, because the
proved hunters, not only Major de Spain and
old General Compson, who spent those two
weeks sitting in a rocking chair before a tremendous iron pot of Brunswick stew, stirring and tasting, with old Ash to quarrel
with about how he was making it and Tennie's Jim to pour whisky from the demijohn[9]
into the tin dipper from which he drank it,

---

9. **demijohn:** A large bottle with a narrow neck and
a wicker casing and handle.

Grammar in Action

Transitions are words or phrases that clarify the relationships
among ideas in a paragraph. They connect ideas and point out
the directions of ideas. Here are some examples of transitions
from pages 738–739 with the kinds of relationships they express:

Then it was gone . . . (Chronological Order)

Otherwise, it seemed to him like it would go on like this
forever . . . (Contrast)

He went to the little tree *beside* the bayou . . . (Spatial
Order)

It was Sam himself who came out of the cane *and crossed
the bayou,* followed by . . . (Development)

Student Activity 1. Identify the transition in each of the following
sentences and specify the type of relationship it expresses.

1. Otherwise, it would go on so forever, next time and next time,
   after and after and after.
2. He had killed his buck, and Sam Fathers had marked his face
   with the hot blood, and in the next year he killed a bear.
3. By noon he was far beyond the little bayou, farther into the
   new and alien country than he had ever been.

but even the boy's father and Walter Ewell, who were still young enough, scorned such, other than shooting the wild gobblers with pistols for wagers on their marksmanship.

Or, that is, his father and the others believed he was hunting squirrels. Until the third day he thought that Sam Fathers believed that too. Each morning he would leave the camp right after breakfast. He had his own gun now, a Christmas present. He went back to the tree beside the little bayou where he had stood that morning. Using the compass which old General Compson had given him, he ranged from that point; he was teaching himself to be a better-than-fair woodsman without knowing he was doing it. On the second day he even found the gutted log where he had first seen the crooked print. It was almost completely crumbled now, healing with unbelievable speed, a passionate and almost visible relinquishment, back into the earth from which the tree had grown.

He ranged the summer woods now, green with gloom; if anything, actually dimmer than in November's gray dissolution, where, even at noon, the sun fell only in intermittent dappling upon the earth, which never completely dried out and which crawled with snakes—moccasins and water snakes and rattlers, themselves the color of the dappled gloom, so that he would not always see them until they moved, returning later and later, first day, second day, passing in the twilight of the third evening the little log pen enclosing the log stable where Sam was putting up the horses for the night.

"You ain't looked right yet," Sam said.

He stopped. For a moment he didn't answer. Then he said peacefully, in a peaceful rushing burst as when a boy's miniature dam in a little brook gives way, "All right. But how? I went to the bayou. I even found that log again. I—"

"I reckon that was all right. Likely he's been watching you. You never saw his foot?"

"I," the boy said—"I didn't—I never thought—"

"It's the gun," Sam said. He stood beside the fence, motionless—the old man, the Indian, in the battered faded overalls and the frayed five-cent straw hat which in the Negro's race had been the badge of his enslavement and was now the regalia of his freedom. The camp—the clearing, the house, the barn and its tiny lot with which Major de Spain in his turn had scratched punily and evanescently at the wilderness—faded in the dusk, back into the immemorial darkness of the woods. *The gun*, the boy thought. *The gun*.

"Be scared," Sam said. "You can't help that. But don't be afraid. Ain't nothing in the woods going to hurt you unless you corner it, or it smells that you are afraid. A bear or a deer, too, has got to be scared of a coward the same as a brave man has got to be."

The gun, the boy thought.

"You will have to choose," Sam said.

He left the camp before daylight, long before Uncle Ash would wake in his quilts on the kitchen floor and start the fire for breakfast. He had only the compass and a stick for snakes. He could go almost a mile before he would begin to need the compass. He sat on a log, the invisible compass in his invisible hand, while the secret night sounds, fallen still at his movements, scurried again and then ceased for good, and the owls ceased and gave over to the waking of day birds, and he could see the compass. Then he went fast yet still quietly; he was becoming better and better as a woodsman, still without having yet realized it.

He jumped a doe and a fawn at sunrise, walked them out of the bed, close enough to see them—the crash of undergrowth, the white scut,[10] the fawn scudding behind her faster than he had believed it could run. He was hunting right, upwind, as Sam had taught him; not that it mattered now. He had left the gun; of his own will and relinquishment he had accepted not a gambit, not a choice, but a condition in which not

---

10. **scut** *n.*: A short, stumpy tail.

The Bear 739

20 **Clarification** A gobbler is a male turkey.

21 **Discussion** Why might the gun prevent the boy from meeting the bear?

22 **Discussion** What is Faulkner saying about bravery and cowardice? How and why might a coward endanger the wilderness? How and why might the wilderness overcome a coward?

23 **Discussion** What will the boy have to choose between? What does the gun have to do with this choice?

24 **Literary Focus** Why is it significant that the boy has left the gun behind? What might the gun symbolize?

4. As he sat down on the log he say the crooked print . . .
5. . . . it was not because it could not be slain, but because so far they had had no actual hope to.

Student Activity 2. Write a paragraph in which you use at least four transitions. Then identify the kind of relationship that each transition expresses.

25 **Discussion** What is the significance of the boy's decision to abandon his tools?

26 **Discussion** What clues tell us that the boy has arrived at the proper place?

27 **Critical Thinking and Reading** The meeting with the bear is fleeting, leaving the boy with only a brief image, yet it provides him with deep insights into the wilderness that he will carry forever in his memory.

28 **Discussion** Contrast the boy's perceptions of the wilderness at the age of fourteen with his perceptions at the age of ten.

only the bear's heretofore inviolable anonymity but all the old rules and balances of hunter and hunted had been abrogated. He would not even be afraid, not even in the moment when the fear would take him completely—blood, skin, bowels, bones, memory from the long time before it became his memory—all save that thin, clear, quenchless, immortal lucidity which alone differed him from this bear and from all the other bear and deer he would ever kill in the humility and pride of his skill and endurance, to which Sam had spoken when he leaned in the twilight on the lot fence yesterday.

By noon he was far beyond the little bayou, farther into the new and alien country than he had ever been. He was traveling now not only by the compass but by the old, heavy, biscuit-thick silver watch which had belonged to his grandfather. When he stopped at last, it was for the first time since he had risen from the log at dawn when he could see the compass. It was far enough. He had left the camp nine hours ago; nine hours from now, dark would have already been an hour old. But he didn't think that. He thought, *All right. Yes. But what?* and stood for a moment, alien and small in the green and topless solitude, answering his own question before it had formed and ceased. It was the watch, the compass, the stick—the three lifeless mechanicals with which for nine hours he had fended the wilderness off; he hung the watch and compass carefully on a bush and leaned the stick beside them and relinquished completely to it.

He had not been going very fast for the last two or three hours. He went no faster now, since distance would not matter even if he could have gone fast. And he was trying to keep a bearing on the tree where he had left the compass, trying to complete a circle which would bring him back to it or at least intersect itself, since direction would not matter now either. But the tree was not there, and he did as Sam had schooled him—made the next circle in the opposite direction, so that the two patterns would bi-

sect somewhere, but crossing no print of his own feet, finding the tree at last, but in the wrong place—no bush, no compass, no watch—and the tree not even the tree, because there was a down log beside it and he did what Sam Fathers had told him was the next thing and the last.

As he sat down on the log he saw the crooked print—the warped, tremendous, two-toed indentation which, even as he watched it, filled with water. As he looked up, the wilderness coalesced, solidified—the glade, the tree he sought, the bush, the watch and the compass glinting where a ray of sunlight touched them. Then he saw the bear. It did not emerge, appear; it was just there, immobile, solid, fixed in the hot dappling of the green and windless noon, not as big as he had dreamed it, but as big as he had expected it, bigger, dimensionless against the dappled obscurity, looking at him where he sat quietly on the log and looked back at it.

Then it moved. It made no sound. It did not hurry. It crossed the glade, walking for an instant into the full glare of the sun; when it reached the other side it stopped again and looked back at him across one shoulder while his quiet breathing inhaled and exhaled three times.

Then it was gone. It didn't walk into the woods, the undergrowth. It faded, sank back into the wilderness as he had watched a fish, a huge old bass, sink and vanish back into the dark depths of its pool without even any movement of its fins.

He thought, *It will be next fall.* But it was not next fall, nor the next nor the next. He was fourteen then. He had killed his buck, and Sam Fathers had marked his face with the hot blood, and in the next year he killed a bear. But even before that accolade he had become as competent in the woods as many grown men with the same experience; by his fourteenth year he was a better woodsman than most grown men with more. There was no territory within thirty miles of

Grammar in Action

A **complex sentence** consists of a main clause and one or more subordinate clauses. It is the complexity of William Faulkner's sentences, perhaps more than anything else, which makes his prose style unique, and often difficult. Your knowledge of subordinate clauses can help you analyze Faulkner's complex sentences, both to reveal their layers of meaning and to observe the techniques of a writer especially skilled at forming complex sentences.

Study the following analysis of a sentence from the first page of "The Bear." The modifiers are labeled; each line modified the italicized element above it.

It *looked and towered* in his dreams	Main Clause
before he even saw *the unaxed woods*	Adverb clause
where *it* left its crooked print	Adjective clause
shaggy, huge, red-eyed,	
not malevolent	Adjectives
but just *big*—	Adverb and Adjective
too big	Adverb and Adjective
for *the dogs*	Adverb phrase
which tried to bay it,	Adjective clause

the camp that he did not know—bayou, ridge, brake, landmark tree and path. He could have led anyone to any point in it without deviation, and brought them out again. He knew game trails that even Sam Fathers did not know; in his thirteenth year he found a buck's bedding place, and unbeknown to his father he borrowed Walter Ewell's rifle and lay in wait at dawn and killed the buck when it walked back to the bed, as Sam had told him how the old Chickasaw fathers did.

But not the old bear, although by now he knew its footprint better than he did his own, and not only the crooked one. He could see any one of the three sound ones and distinguish it from any other, and not only by its size. There were other bears within those thirty miles which left tracks almost as large, but this was more than that. If Sam Fathers had been his mentor and the backyard rabbits and squirrels at home his kindergarten, then the wilderness the old bear ran was his college, the old male bear itself, so long unwifed and childless as to have become its own ungendered progenitor,[11] was his alma mater. But he never saw it.

He could still find the crooked print now almost whenever he liked, fifteen or ten or five miles, or sometimes nearer the camp than that. Twice while on stand during the three years he heard the dogs strike its trail by accident; on the second time they jumped it seemingly, the voices high, abject, almost human in hysteria, as on that first morning two years ago. But not the bear itself. He would remember that noon three years ago, the glade, himself and the bear fixed during that moment in the windless and dappled blaze, and it would seem to him that it had never happened, that he had dreamed that too. But it had happened. They had looked at each other, they had emerged from the wilderness old as earth, synchronized to that instant by something more than the blood

_____

11. **ungendered progenitor:** Its own parent.

that moved the flesh and bones which bore them, and touched, pledged something, affirmed something more lasting than the frail web of bones and flesh which any accident could obliterate.

Then he saw it again. Because of the very fact that he thought of nothing else, he had forgotten to look for it. He was still-hunting with Walter Ewell's rifle. He saw it cross the end of a long blow-down, a corridor where a tornado had swept, rushing through rather than over the tangle of trunks and branches as a locomotive would have, faster than he had ever believed it could move, almost as fast as a deer even, because a deer would have spent most of that time in the air, faster than he could bring the rifle sights up to it, so that he believed the reason he never let off the shot was that he was still behind it, had never caught up with it. And now he knew what had been wrong during all the three years. He sat on a log, shaking and trembling as if he had never seen the woods before nor anything that ran them, wondering with incredulous amazement how he could have forgotten the very thing which Sam Fathers had told him and which the bear itself had proved the next day and had now returned after three years to reaffirm.

And he now knew what Sam Fathers had meant about the right dog, a dog in which size would mean less than nothing. So when he returned alone in April—school was out then, so that the sons of farmers could help with the land's planting, and at last his father had granted him permission, on his promise to be back in four days—he had the dog. It was his own, a mongrel of the sort called by Negroes a fyce, a ratter, itself not much bigger than a rat and possessing that bravery which had long since stopped being courage and had become foolhardiness.

It did not take four days. Alone again, he found the trail on the first morning. It was not a stalk; it was an ambush. He timed the meeting almost as if it were an appointment with a human being. Himself holding the fyce muffled in a feed sack and Sam Fathers

for *the horses*	Adverb phrase
which tried to ride it down,	Adjective clause
for the men and *the bullets*	Adverb phrase
they fired into it,	Adjective clause
too big	Adverb and Adjective
for *the very country*	Adverb phrase
which was its constricting scope.	Adjective clause

Student Activity 1. Construct a similar analysis for the following sentence from "The Bear":

He sat on a log, shaking and trembling as if he had never seen the woods before nor anything that ran them, wonder-

ing with incredulous amazement how he could have forgotten the very thing which Sam Fathers had told him and which the bear itself had proved the next day and had now returned after three years to reaffirm.

Student Activity 2. Choose another sentence from "The Bear" consisting of one main clause and several subordinate clauses. Analyze the sentence, revealing the structure of the modification.

32 Discussion What images does Faulkner use to portray the bear as larger than life? Why do you think the bear chooses not to attack the boy?

33 Reading Strategy Ask the students to recall the previous three encounters with the bear.

34 Reading Strategy Point out to **less advanced** students that time has passed. The boy has returned home and has described the incident to his father.

35 Enrichment Faulkner is alluding to land treaties drawn up by white men and signed by Indians that transferred land from one group to the other. What is Faulkner's view of such treaties?

36 Discussion What virtues make the hunters part of the wilderness? Does the boy possess these virtues? Did he at the beginning of the story?

---

with two of the hounds on a piece of plowline rope, they lay down wind of the trail at dawn of the second morning. They were so close that the bear turned without even running, as if in surprised amazement at the shrill and frantic uproar of the released fyce, turning at bay against the trunk of a tree, on its hind feet; it seemed to the boy that it would never stop rising, taller and taller, and even the two hounds seemed to take a sort of desperate and despairing courage from the fyce, following it as it went in.

Then he realized that the fyce was actually not going to stop. He flung, threw the gun away, and ran; when he overtook and grasped the frantically pinwheeling little dog, it seemed to him that he was directly under the bear.

32 He could smell it, strong and hot and rank. Sprawling, he looked up to where it loomed and towered over him like a cloudburst and colored like a thunderclap, quite familiar, peacefully and even lucidly familiar, until he remembered: This was the way he had used to dream about it. Then it was gone. He didn't see it go. He knelt, holding the frantic fyce with both hands, hearing the abased wailing of the hounds drawing farther and farther away, until Sam came up. He carried the gun. He laid it down quietly beside the boy and stood looking down at him.

33 "You've done seed him twice now with a gun in your hands," he said. "This time you couldn't have missed him."

The boy rose. He still held the fyce. Even in his arms and clear of the ground, it yapped frantically, straining and surging after the fading uproar of the two hounds like a tangle of wire springs. He was panting a little, but he was neither shaking nor trembling now.

"Neither could you!" he said. "You had the gun! Neither did you!"

34 "And you didn't shoot," his father said. "How close were you?"

"I don't know, sir," he said. "There was a big wood tick inside his right hind leg. I saw that. But I didn't have the gun then."

"But you didn't shoot when you had the gun," his father said. "Why?"

But he didn't answer, and his father didn't wait for him to, rising and crossing the room, across the pelt of the bear which the boy had killed two years ago and the larger one which his father had killed before he was born, to the bookcase beneath the mounted head of the boy's first buck. It was the room which his father called the office, from which all the plantation business was transacted; in it for the fourteen years of his life he had heard the best of all talking. Major de Spain would be there and sometimes old General Compson, and Walter Ewell and Boon Hoggenbeck and Sam Fathers and Tennie's Jim, too, because they, too, were hunters, knew the woods and what ran them.

35 He would hear it, not talking himself but listening—the wilderness, the big woods, bigger and older than any recorded document of white man fatuous enough to believe he had bought any fragment of it or Indian ruthless enough to pretend that any fragment of it had been his to convey. It was of the men, not white nor black nor red, but **36** men, hunters with the will and hardihood to endure and the humility and skill to survive, and the dogs and the bear and deer juxtaposed and reliefed against it, ordered and compelled by and within the wilderness in the ancient and unremitting contest by the ancient and immitigable rules which voided all regrets and brooked no quarter, the voices quiet and weighty and deliberate for retrospection and recollection and exact remembering, while he squatted in the blazing firelight as Tennie's Jim squatted, who stirred only to put more wood on the fire and to pass the bottle from one glass to another. Because the bottle was always present, so that after a while it seemed to him that those fierce instants of heart and brain and cour-

---

Primary Source

Critic Irving Howe wrote the following analysis of "The Bear":

Like many of Faulkner's stories, "The Bear" turns to the past. It turns to a vision of American life not yet soiled by greed or commerce, nor tainted by the anxieties of social existence and the sordidness of urban life. When the men of Yoknapatawpha, taking with them young Isaac McCaslin, go off on their annual visit to the forest . . . their expedition soon takes on the tone of a religious retreat: away from money, away from the town, away from women, away from social distinctions. This yearly hunting trip becomes, as Faulkner said, "a pageant-rite" . . .

In "The Bear" the hunt becomes a ceremony of initiation and maturing, a test of proper conduct through which Isaac McCaslin ceases to be a boy; yet truly to become a man he must retain something of that awe before truth characteristic of boyhood. When he meets the great bear Ben, it is only after having stripped himself of such material objects—and social possessions—as his watch and compass. Seeing the bear, the boy experiences

age and wiliness and speed were concentrated and distilled into that brown liquor which not women, not boys and children, but only hunters drank, drinking not of the blood they had spilled but some condensation of the wild immortal spirit, drinking it moderately, humbly even, not with the pagan's base hope of acquiring thereby the virtues of cunning and strength and speed, but in salute to them.

His father returned with the book and sat down again and opened it. "Listen," he said. He read the five stanzas aloud, his voice quiet and deliberate in the room where there was no fire now because it was already spring. Then he looked up. The boy watched him. "All right," his father said. "Listen." He read again, but only the second stanza this time, to the end of it, the last two lines, and closed the book and put it on the table beside him. " 'She cannot fade, though thou hast not thy bliss, for ever wilt thou love, and she be fair,' "[12] he said.

"He's talking about a girl," the boy said.

"He had to talk about something," his father said. Then he said, "He was talking about truth. Truth doesn't change. Truth is one thing. It covers all things which touch the heart—honor and pride and pity and justice and courage and love. Do you see now?"

He didn't know. Somehow it was simpler than that. There was an old bear, fierce and ruthless, not merely just to stay alive, but with the fierce pride of liberty and freedom, proud enough of that liberty and freedom to see it threatened without fear or even alarm; nay, who at times even seemed deliberately to put that freedom and liberty in jeopardy in order to savor them, to remind his old strong bones and flesh to keep supple and quick to defend and preserve them. There was an old man, son of a Negro slave and an Indian king, inheritor on the one side of the long chronicle of a people who had learned humility through suffering, and pride through the endurance which survived the suffering and injustice, and on the other side, the chronicle of a people even longer in the land than the first, yet who no longer existed in the land at all save in the solitary brotherhood of an old Negro's alien blood and the wild and invincible spirit of an old bear. There was a boy who wished to learn humility and pride in order to become skillful and worthy in the woods, who suddenly found himself becoming so skillful so rapidly that he feared he would never become worthy because he had not learned humility and pride, although he had tried to, until one day and as suddenly he discovered that an old man who could not have defined either had led him, as though by the hand, to that point where an old bear and a little mongrel dog showed him that, by possessing one thing other, he would possess them both.

And a little dog, nameless and mongrel and many-fathered, grown, yet weighing less than six pounds, saying as if to itself, "I can't be dangerous, because there's nothing much smaller than I am; I can't be fierce, because they would call it just noise; I can't be humble, because I'm already too close to the ground to genuflect;[13] I can't be proud, because I wouldn't be near enough to it for anyone to know who was casting that shadow, and I don't even know that I'm not going to heaven, because they have already decided that I don't possess an immortal soul. So all I can be is brave. But it's all right. I can be that, even if they still call it just noise."

That was all. It was simple, much simpler than somebody talking in a book about a youth and a girl he would never need to grieve over, because he could never approach any nearer her and would never have to get any farther away. He had heard about a bear, and finally got big enough to trail it,

---

12. " 'She . . . fair' ": from John Keats's "Ode on a Grecian Urn."

13. **genuflect** (jen' yə flekt') v.: Bend the knee, as in reverence or worship.

an ecstasy of communion which results in his refusal to kill the animal. For to destroy the bear would mean to violate the mute bond with nature that the "pageant-rite" is intended to establish, and thereby to disrupt the fraternity of the men in the hunting camp . . .

Reader's Response Why do you think the boy did not shoot the bear?

and he trailed it four years and at last met it with a gun in his hands and he didn't shoot. Because a little dog— But he could have shot long before the little dog covered the twenty yards to where the bear waited, and Sam Fathers could have shot at any time during that interminable minute while Old Ben stood on his hind feet over them. He stopped. His father was watching him gravely across the spring-rife twilight of the room; when he spoke, his words were as quiet as the twilight, too, not loud, because they did not need to be because they would last, "Courage, and honor, and pride," his father said, "and pity, and love of justice and of liberty. They all touch the heart, and what the heart holds to becomes truth, as far as we know truth. Do you see now?"

Sam, and Old Ben, and Nip, he thought. And himself too. He had been all right too. His father had said so. "Yes, sir," he said.

Commentary

An important theme in American literature is the confrontation between humankind and nature. Many of the works you have already read address this complicated relationship. Many characters in American literature, such as James Fenimore Cooper's Natty Bumppo or Mark Twain's Huck Finn, seek their spiritual identities in nature. In *Walden* Henry David Thoreau explains how he went to the woods to live a truer and simpler life, away from the corruptions and distractions of society.

But as all these works show, the relationship between people and nature is not simple. Whenever people go into the woods, they alter what they find there. They chop down trees and build roads and homes; for food they dig in the earth, fish, and hunt. It is difficult to find a way to live in nature without becoming nature's enemy.

This is one theme to Faulkner's "The Bear" on which critics have commented frequently. One critic, John Lydenberg, had this to say about the conflict between humans and nature in "The Bear": "On one level the story is a symbolic representation of man's relationship to the land, particularly the Southerner's conquest of his native land. In attempting to kill Old Ben, the men are contending with the wilderness itself. In one sense, as men, they have a perfect right to do this, as long as they act with dignity and propriety, maintaining their humility while they demonstrate the ability of human beings to master the brute forces of nature. The hunters from Jefferson are gentlemen and sportsmen, representing the ideals of the old order at its best, the honor, dignity, and courage of the South. In their rapport with nature and their contest with Old Ben, they regain the purity they have lost in their workaday world. . . . But as Southerners they are part of 'that whole edifice intricate and complex and founded upon injustice'; they are part of that South that has bought and sold land and has held men as slaves. Their original sins have alienated them irrevocably from nature. . . . What might in other circumstances have been right, is now a violation of the wilderness and the Southern land."

THINKING ABOUT THE SELECTION

Recalling

1. (a) What had the boy "already inherited" before participating in his first hunting expedition? (b) To what had he listened?
2. According to Sam Fathers, what does the bear do every year?
3. What does the boy realize for the first time when he sees the bear's paw print?
4. (a) Why does the boy finally leave his gun behind when he is tracking the bear? (b) What other objects does he relinquish? (c) When does he first see the bear?
5. (a) What does the boy do when the fyce charges the bear? (b) What comment does Sam make after the bear has gone?
6. How does the boy's father help him to comprehend his inability to shoot the bear?

Interpreting

7. Early in the story, the narrator comments that the wilderness is "being constantly and punily gnawed at by men with axes and plows who feared it because it was wilderness." How are the men who travel to the Big Bottom twice a year different from the "men with axes"?
8. Why does the bear fear a coward more than a brave person?
9. (a) How does the boy's relationship to the wilderness change when he abandons his gun and other "lifeless mechanicals"? (b) How does this set him apart from the "men with axes"?
10. What does the narrator mean by his comment that when the bear and the boy looked at each other they were "synchronized to the instant by something more than blood that moved the flesh and bones which bore them"?
11. What understanding does the boy reach at the end of the story?

Applying

12. (a) Why do you think that people often fear the wilderness? (b) What does this fear suggest about human nature?

ANALYZING LITERATURE

Understanding Symbols

A **symbol** is a person, place, or thing that has a meaning in itself and also represents something larger than itself. The bear, for example, symbolizes the wilderness.

1. Find two descriptions of the bear that help to convey its symbolic meaning.
2. As a symbol of the wilderness, what virtues does the bear embody?
3. Considering the bear's symbolic meaning, what is the significance of its mortality?
4. Who possesses the power to destroy it?

Understanding Allusions

An **allusion** is a short reference to another literary work or to a figure, place, or event from history, religion, or mythology. For example, Faulkner alludes to the poem "Ode on a Grecian Urn" by English Romantic poet John Keats.

1. In Keats's poem the speaker comments on the permanence of a pastoral scene depicted on an urn. In "The Bear" the boy's father repeats two lines describing the urn's portrayal of a young man pursuing a beautiful maiden. How do these lines reinforce the meaning of the story?
2. Keats's poem ends with the following lines: " 'Beauty is truth, truth beauty,'—that is all/Ye know on earth, and all ye need to know." How are these lines related to the meaning of the story?

THINKING AND WRITING

Writing About Symbols and Allusions

Write an essay in which you discuss how Faulkner uses symbols and allusions in conveying the theme of "The Bear." Reread the story, focusing on Faulkner's use of symbols and allusions. Prepare a thesis statement. Then write your essay, using passages from the story to support your thesis.

The Bear 745

Closure and Extension

ANSWERS TO THINKING ABOUT THE SELECTION
Recalling

1. (a) He inherited the legacy of the bear. (b) He had listened to the legends of the bear's exploits.
2. He walks near camp to see who is there.
3. He realizes that the bear is mortal.
4. (a) He understands that the bear does not follow the old rules of hunting and that the gun is useless. (b) He leaves the watch, compass, and stick near a tree. (c) The bear appears as soon as he is standing alone, with no "mechanicals."
5. (a) He drops his gun and rescues the dog. (b) Sam comments that the boy has had two chances to kill the bear but did not shoot.
6. His father reads him a passage from the poem "Ode on a Grecian Urn."

Interpreting

7. The men with axes fear the wilderness and try to destroy it. The men who camp at Big Bottom have a harmonious relationship with the wilderness and go there to admire it.
8. A coward is scared, not afraid, and will try to destroy that which brings on his or her fear.
9. (a) He no longer fears the wilderness and quickly learns to understand it by becoming an experienced woodsman. (b) He no longer seeks to destroy the wilderness with weapons, but rather wishes to become part of it.
10. Suggested Response: He means that they momentarily established an intuitive understanding of each other.
11. He understands that the choice he made, not to shoot the bear, was the right one. He realizes that the bear symbolizes the beauty, freedom, and purity of the wilderness.

Applying

12. (a) Suggested Response: They fear the wilderness because they do not know or understand it. (b) Suggested Response: By nature, humans fear anything that they cannot understand.

ANSWERS TO ANALYZING LITERATURE

1. Suggested Response: "It looked and towered in his dreams before he even saw the unaxed woods where it left its crooked print, shaggy, huge, red-eyed, not malevolent, but just big . . ." and ". . . to the boy it was still no living creature, but the wilderness which . . . had patted lightly once the hound's temerity" are two descriptions that convey its symbolic meaning.
2. The bear embodies the virtues of beauty, courage, honor, pride, pity, and love of justice and of liberty.
3. The wilderness, like the bear, can be destroyed.
4. Humans can destroy it.

---

1. Like the maiden on the urn, the wilderness is eternally beautiful; and though the people can never capture this beauty, they will be able to appreciate it forever.
2. The bear represents the beauty and truth of the wilderness.

THINKING AND WRITING

After students have completed the assignment, divide them into groups, and have them read their rough drafts to one another and comment on ways in which they could be improved.

ELIZABETH ENRIGHT

1909–1968

Elizabeth Enright developed an interest in writing while working as an illustrator of magazines and children's books. At first she wrote stories to accompany her illustrations, but after a time she gave up illustrating to concentrate on writing.

Born in Oak Park, Illinois, Enright spent most of her life in New York City. Inspired by her parents, who were both professional artists, she began drawing and painting at an early age. After studying art in New York and Paris, she began her career as a magazine illustrator. In 1935 she published her first book of illustrations, *Kintu: A Congo Adventure,* for which she also wrote the text.

The author of a number of beloved children's books, Enright won the Newbery Award in 1938 for her book *Thimble Summer,* the story of a young girl on a Wisconsin farm. She also wrote a series of books for children about the Melendy family, which consists of a father, four children, a housekeeper, and a dog. These books, among them *The Saturdays* (1941) and *Spider Web for Two* (1951), confirmed Enright's position as a children's book writer. Critics praised Enright for her realism and her sensitivity to the point of view of children. "The author's brilliant observation of, and probably remembrance of, childhood, makes every page a delight," wrote the *New York Herald Tribune* in 1951. Typical of the reviews her books received was the *Library Journal*'s review in 1938: "There is a swift keen characterization, natural conversation, an almost inspired selection of incident and detail, and rare humor and skill in the telling." The illustrations for her children's books, which Enright drew, also received praise.

After publishing several more children's books, Enright began writing short stories for adults, publishing them in *The New Yorker* and other respected magazines. In 1946 she published her first collection of short stories, *Borrowed Summer and Other Stories*. She went on to publish three more volumes of stories: *The Moment Before the Rain* (1955), *The Riddle of the Fly and Other Stories* (1959), and *Doublefields: Memories and Stories* (1966). Her stories also appeared in such noted anthologies as *Prize Stories: The O. Henry Awards* and *Best American Short Stories*.

Objectives
1 To appreciate setting
2 To appreciate adjectives
3 To write about setting

Support Material
Teaching Portfolio
Teacher Backup, p. 957
Grammar in Action Worksheets, *Using Concrete Details,* p. 961; *Recognizing Compound Adjectives,* p. 963
Usage and Mechanics Worksheet, p. 965
Vocabulary Check, p. 966

Critical Thinking and Reading Worksheet, *Recognizing Important Words,* p. 967
Language Worksheet, *Recognizing Synonyms,* p. 968
Selection Test, p. 969

GUIDE FOR INTERPRETING

The Signature

The Writer's Techniques

Setting. The setting is the time and place in which the events in a work of literature occur. Writers often use the setting to establish a particular atmosphere, or mood, describing it with words that convey the appropriate feeling. For example, a writer might use a secluded, decaying house as the setting of a story to create an atmosphere of loneliness and isolation, using adjectives such as *solitary, empty,* and *vacant* in describing the house.

Writing

"The Signature" tells the story of a woman who finds herself in a world that seems strange and alien. She cannot remember her name or even understand the language she hears. Freewrite, explaining how a person could go about finding out his or her identity in such a situation.

Primary Source

Perhaps because she was the daughter of artists, Enright was especially sensitive to the effect of setting on her characters' moods and thoughts. Setting has an important impact on the woman in "The Signature." In trying to figure out "who and what I was, and why I was in this place," she focuses on the details of her surroundings, searching for clues. At the same time, Enright uses these details and her descriptions to convey to the reader the woman's feelings of alienation and anxiety.

Given the importance of places in Enright's own life, it is not surprising that she focuses her story through a single character's experience of a particular place. In her autobiographical *Doublefields: Memories and Stories,* Enright explains how the apartment she grew up in in New York City became a permanent setting in her imagination for the stories she read about in books. Setting and place are fixtures in her imagination. "As for the apartment itself, it not only refuses to be forgotten, but also has continued all my life to impose itself, in bizarre ways, as a setting. Often I realize this when I am reading. . . . When I read *War and Peace,* where was it that the Rostovs and their guests assembled for the glorious party given to celebrate the name day of the Countess and her young daughter, Natasha? It was in our apartment on the ninth floor of the Woodmere at Broadway and a Hundred and Forty-first Street . . . that place of large light rooms which, for one human being, set a lifetime pattern for all happy backgrounds." As you read, imagine how changing the setting in "The Signature" would affect the story.

Literary Focus Some settings are very specific, while others are quite vague. In "The Signature" Enright purposely uses a vague setting to make it seem as if the story could be occurring in almost any location. This helps to give the story a universal quality and contributes to its impact.

Writing/Prior Knowledge Before students complete the activity, discuss possible solutions to the problem.

Vocabulary

Preteach the following vocabulary words:
unemphatic (un im′ fat′ ik) *adj.*: Not definite; not emphasized (p. 748)
laterally (lat′ər əl lē) *adv.*: In a sideways manner (p. 748)
inimical (in im′i k'l) *adj.*: Hostile; unfriendly (p. 749)
monotony (mə nät′′nē) *n.*: Tiresome sameness of uniformity (p. 749)
periphery (pə rif′ər ē) *n.*: Surrounding space or area (p. 749)
reiterated (rē it′ə rāt′d) *adj.*: Repeated (p. 750)

Enrichment Enright uses vivid words to describe the setting and the narrator's state of mind. Discuss the sensations or images created by these words. Can students visualize an example of a penumbra? Suggest a solar eclipse or a silhouetted figure against a lamp post.

Presentation

Motivation/Prior Knowledge
Ask your students if they have ever had a nightmare in which they found themselves lost in a strange and unfamiliar place. What feelings did the nightmare evoke?

Master Teacher Note The story suggests a town that is old and worn down, perhaps by the ravages of war. To set the scene, show students photographs of war-torn London, Berlin, or other cities. The Time-Life series, *World War II,* is an excellent source for this.

Thematic Idea Another story in which a character searches for direction is "Journey" by Joyce Carol Oates (p. 984).

Purpose-Setting Question
Where is the narrator?

1 **Critical Thinking and Reading**
Why might everything be covered with dust? What are other signs of age and decline? What seems to be missing from the town?

2 **Reading Strategy** Have students predict what might happen to the narrator at the end of the story. Do they think she will find her identity? If so, how?

3 **Discussion** What is the significance of repeated appearance of the symbol?

The Signature
Elizabeth Enright

The street was wide and sloped gently upward ahead of me. It was paved with hard-baked dust almost white in the early-afternoon light, dry as clay and decked with bits of refuse. On either side the wooden houses stood blind to the street, all their shutters closed. The one and two-story buildings—some of them set back a little; there was no sidewalk—had door yards with dusted grass and bushes, but many of them stood flush to the road itself with nothing but a powdered weed or two for grace. All of the houses had an old, foreign look, and all were unpainted, weather-scoured to the same pale color, except for the eaves of some which had been trimmed with wooden zigzags and painted long ago, like the crude, faded shutters, in tones of blue or red.

The sky was blanched with light, fronded with cirrus,[1] unemphatic; just such a sky as one finds near the sea, and this, in addition to the scoured, dry, enduring look of the town, persuaded me that an ocean or harbor must be somewhere near at hand. But when I came up over the rise of the road, I could find no furred line of blue at any horizon. All I could see was the great town—no, it was a city—spread far and wide, low lying, sun bleached, and unknown to me. And this was only one more thing that was unknown to me, for not only was I ignorant of the name of the city, but I was ignorant of my own name, and of my own life, and nothing that I seized on could offer me a clue. I looked at my hands: they were the hands of a middle-aged woman, coarsening at the joints, faintly blotched. On the third finger of the left hand there was a golden wedding ring, but who

had put it there I could not guess. My body in the dark dress, my dust-chalked shoes were also strangers to me, and I was frightened and felt that I had been frightened for a long time, so long that the feeling had become habitual—something that I could live with in a pinch, or, more properly, something that until this moment I had felt that I could live with. But now I was in terror of my puzzle.

I had the conviction that if I could once see my own face, I would remember who and what I was, and why I was in this place. I searched for a pane of glass to give me my reflection, but every window was shuttered fast. It was a season of drought, too, and there was not so much as a puddle to look into; in my pocket there was no mirror and my purse contained only a few bills of a currency unknown to me. I took the bills out and looked at them; they were old and used and the blue numerals and characters engraved on them were also of a sort I had never seen before, or could not remember having seen. In the center of each bill, where ordinarily one finds the pictures of a statesman or a monarch, there was instead an angular, spare symbol: a laterally elongated diamond shape with a heavy vertical line drawn through it at the center, rather like an abstraction of the human eye. As I resumed my walking I was aware of an impression that I had seen this symbol recently and often, in other places, and at the very moment I was thinking this I came upon it again, drawn in chalk on the side of a house. After that, watching for it, I saw it several times: marked in the dirt of the road, marked on the shutters, carved on the railing of a fence.

1. cirrus (sir′əs) *n.*: High, detached wispy clouds.

Grammar in Action

Writers use **concrete details** to describe people, places, objects, or experiences. Concrete details are words that appeal to one or more of the five senses. They create a vivid mental image in the reader's mind. Notice how Elizabeth Enright uses concrete details in the following description from "The Signature":

The street was *wide* and *sloped gently upward* ahead of me. It was paved with *hard-baked* dust *almost white* in the early-afternoon light, *dry as clay and decked with bits of*

refuse. On either side the wooden houses *stood blind to the street,* all their shutters closed. The one and two-story buildings—some of them set back a little; there was no sidewalk—had door yards with *dusted grass and bushes,* but many of them *stood flush to the road* itself with nothing but a *powdered weed or two for grace.*

Enright creates a barren image of the setting through words like "hard-baked," "dry as clay," "bits of refuse," and others. She adds to this a feeling of alienation by describing the houses as "blind to the street." The concrete details appeal to the senses of sight and touch.

It was this figure, this cross-eyed diamond, which reminded me, by its persistence, that the eye of another person can be a little mirror, and now with a feeling of excitement, of possible hope, I began walking faster, in search of a face.

From time to time I had passed other people, men and women, in the street. Their dark, anonymous clothes were like the clothes of Italian peasants, but the language they spoke was not Italian, nor did it resemble any language I had ever heard, and many of their faces had a fair Northern color. I noticed when I met these people that the answering looks they gave me, while attentive, were neither inimical nor friendly. They looked at me with that certain privilege shared by kings and children, as if they possessed the right to judge, while being ignorant of, or exempt from, accepting judgment in return. There is no answer to this look and appeal is difficult, for one is already in a defensive position. Still, I had tried to appeal to them; several times I had addressed the passers-by hoping that one of them might understand me and tell me where I was, but no one could or would. They shook their heads or lifted their empty hands, and while they did not appear hostile, neither did they smile in answer to my pleading smiles. After they had passed I thought it strange that I never heard a whisper or a laugh or any added animation in their talk. It was apparently a matter of complete indifference to them that they had been approached in the street by a stranger speaking a strange language.

Knowing these things I thought that it might be difficult to accomplish my purpose, and indeed this proved to be the case. The next people I met were three women walking together; two were young and one was middle-aged. I approached the taller of the young women, for her eyes were on a level with my own, and looking steadily into them and coming close, I spoke to her.

"Can you tell me where I am?" I said to her. "Can you understand what I am saying?"

The words were a device, I expected no answer and got none of any sort. As I drew close she looked down at the ground; she would not meet my gaze. A little smile moved the corners of her lips, and she stepped aside. When I turned to her companions they also looked away, smiling. This expression on other faces might have been called embarrassment, but not on theirs. The smile they shared seemed noncommittal, secretive, knowledgeable in a way that I could not fathom, and afterward I thought it curious that they had shown no surprise.

For a long time after that I met no one at all. I met no cat, no dog, no cabbage butterfly; not even an ant on the packed, bald dust of the road, and finally rejecting its ugliness and light I turned to the left along another street, narrower and as graceless, and walked by the same monotony of weather-beaten houses. After a few minutes I heard a sound that halted me and I stood listening. Somewhere not far away I heard children's voices. Though their words were foreign they spoke also in the common tongue of children everywhere: voices high, eruptive, excited, sparked with the universal jokes, chants, quarrels of play; and here, listening to them, my memory stirred for the first time— a memory of memory, in fact. For whatever it was that nearly illuminated consciousness was not the memory itself, but a remnant of light which glowed on the periphery of the obstacle before it: a penumbra.[2]

Where are the children, I thought; where are they! With great urgency and longing I set out in the direction of their voices, determined to find them and in doing so to find something of myself. Their voices chattered, skipped, squabbled like the voices of sparrows, never far away, but though I turned and hunted and listened and pursued I could not find them. I never found them, and after a while I could not hear them either. The ghostly light of memory faded and was

---

2. **penumbra** (pi num′ brə) *n.*: The partly lighted area surrounding the complete shadow of a body in full eclipse.

The Signature 749

4 Discussion What contradictions are there in the description of the people? Are they light or dark? Foreign or familiar? Hostile or friendly?

5 Discussion What is the narrator's purpose? Besides speaking to other people, what other ways has she attempted to accomplish this purpose?

6 Reading Strategy Where else have eyes come into play in the story? Have students look for other places where the narrator mentions eyes as they continue reading.

7 Discussion What might these women know that the narrator does not?

8 Clarification The cabbage butterfly is so-named because its larvae destroy cabbage. Why might the author choose to mention this unusual insect, especially in the same sentence with the more ordinary cat and dog?

9 Literary Focus Until now the narrator has described the setting entirely in terms of sight. She now adds a new dimension— sound.

Student Activity 1. Find five more descriptive passages in which Enright uses concrete details. Explain how the details create a mental image in your mind. To what senses do the details appeal?

Student Activity 2. Write a paragraph describing a place that you find especially beautiful or interesting. Use concrete details to create a vivid image of your subject.

Again, the narrator makes a point of mentioning eyes. How do the eyes of the man differ from the eyes of the women that the narrator met before?

11 **Discussion** What is the significance of the narrator's realization?

Humanities Note

Fine art, *Red Suburb*, 1926, by Paul Klee. Klee (1879–1940) was a Swiss painter and etcher. He was involved with the German artist Kandinsky in the Blue Rider Group (an exhibiting society for the avant garde in art) and taught at the prestigious Bauhaus School. The art of Paul Klee is difficult to describe or classify. It was influenced by Freudian dream theories as well as by most of the major movements of modern art. Despite these influences, his art remained uniquely his own, poetic, intellectual and deceptively simple. It was very important to the development and achievement of twentieth-century art.

At first glance, this simplified view of buildings and pine trees in *Red Suburb* has a naive appearance, like a child's drawing. The flattened perspective and geometric shapes of the buildings enhance this impression. Closer examination will, however, bring out the complexity of this painting. The repetition of the unexplained circular shapes lends a sense of mystical importance to the landscape and town. The dark background makes the rosy coloring glow as if lit from behind. A feeling of hidden activity pervades the canvas, springing perhaps from the rhythm of the lines. Paul Klee's fantastic, intuitive art makes it a suitable accompaniment to the "The Signature."

As students look at the painting, you might ask these questions:

RED SUBURB, 1926
Paul Klee
San Francisco Museum of Modern Art

extinguished, and my despair rose up in darkness to take its place.

The next person I met was a man, young and dark-browed, and when I confronted him and asked my questions, it was without hope. I knew he would not meet my look, or let his eyes show me my longed-for, dreaded face. Yet here I was wrong; he stood before me without speaking, but the gaze with which he answered mine was so intense and undeviating that it was I who dropped my eyes and stepped aside. I could not look, and soon I heard him going on his way.

I had been walking a long time, and the light was changing; the sun was low and full in my face. West, I said to myself; at least I know west, and I know that I am a woman, and that that is the sun. When the stars come out I will know those, too, and perhaps they will tell me something else.

After a while I sat down on a wooden step

to rest. I was struck by the silence of the city around me, and I realized this was because it was a city of walkers who walked on dust instead of on pavements. I remembered that I had seen no mark of a wheel on any road, and that nothing had moved in the sky all day except for a few birds in flight.

A breath of dry wind crept along the dust at my feet, and, far away, a noise of knocking started, a sound of stakes being driven into the ground with a wooden mallet. Desolate, reiterated, it sounded as though somewhere in the city they were preparing a gallows or a barricade. Too tired and dispirited to move I sat there listening to the double knock-and-echo of each blow. A few people passed me on their way home, each of them giving me the glance of casual appraisal I had seen so often. Doors opened and doors closed, the sun went down, and soon the street was still again and the knocking

1. What elements or details can you identify in this painting?
2. What is the mood or atmosphere of this painting? What elements of the painting create this mood?
3. What makes this painting a good illustration for "The Signature"?

Grammar in Action

Many of the adjectives that contribute to the atmosphere of "The Signature" are **compound adjectives**—adjectives made up of more than one word. Many compound adjectives, such as *hard-baked* and *early-afternoon,* are hyphenated. Others, such as *hearsay* and *dreamlike,* are written as one word. To be sure whether or not to hyphenate a compound adjective, you must check in a dictionary.

Writers use compound adjectives to compress the meanings of longer phrases. Note the origins of the following compound adjectives:

stopped. Where would I sleep that night, or find a meal? I neither knew nor cared.

One by one the stars came out on the deepening sky, perfect, still, as if they were really what they seemed to be—calm ornaments for hope, promises of stillness and forever.

I looked for Venus, then Polaris,[3] then for Mars. I could not find them, and as the stars grew in number, coming imperceptibly into their light, I saw with slow-growing shock that these were not the stars I knew. The messages of this night sky were written in a language of constellations I had never seen or dreamed. I stared up at the brand-new Catherine wheels,[4] insignias, and fiery thorn crowns on the sky, and I do not think that I was really surprised when I spied at the zenith, small but bright, a constellation shaped like an elongated diamond, like the glittering abstraction of a human eye. . . .

It was just at this moment, before I could marshal or identify my thoughts in the face of such a development, that I heard a sound of trees, wind in the leaves of trees, and I realized, irrelevantly it seemed, that in all my walking in this city—how many hours, how many days?—I had not seen a single tree, and the sound of their presence was as welcome as the sound of rain is after a siege of drought. As I stood up it occurred to me that neither had I seen one child among all the strangers I had met, that though I had heard the children I had not been able to find them, and now to all the other fears was added the fear that the trees, too, would magically elude me.

The street was dark, though light was glimmering through the cracks of the closed shutters. What was left of sunset, green as water, lay on the western horizon. Yet was it really western? In a sky of new stars, was it not possible and in fact probable that what I had believed to be the sun was not really Sun at all? Then what were the compass points, what were the easts and wests of this city? And what would I find when once I found myself?

I heard the beckoning of trees again and as if they were the clue to sanity, I ran along the street in the direction of their sound. I turned a corner, and there, ah yes, there were the trees: a grove of tall, dry, paper-murmuring trees that grew in a little park or public garden where people were walking together or sitting on the dusty grass. At the center of this park or garden there was a great house of stone, the first stone building I had seen all day. It was lighted from top to bottom; the lights of its long windows twittered in gold among the small leaves of the trees, and a door stood open at the head of a flight of steps.

I passed many people on the path, but now I did not look at them or ask them questions. I knew that there was nothing they could do for me. I walked straight to the steps and up them and through the door into the lighted house. It was empty, as I had expected, a great empty ringing house, but there was a splendor about it, even in its emptiness, as if those who had left it—and left it recently—had been creatures of joy, better than people and gayer than gods. But they, who-ever they were, had gone. My footsteps sounded on the barren floor, and the talk of the loiterers outside, the foreign talk, came in the windows clearly on the night air.

The mirror was at the end of the hall. I walked toward it with my fists closed, and my heart walked, too, heavily in my chest. I watched the woman's figure in the dark dress and the knees moving forward. When I was close to it, I saw, low in the right-hand corner of the mirror, the scratched small outline of the eye-diamond, a signature, carved on the surface of the glass by whom, and in what cold spirit of raillery? Lifting my head, I looked at my own face. I leaned forward and looked closely at my face, and I remembered everything. I remembered everything. And I knew the name of the city I would never leave, and, alas, I understood the language of its citizens.

---

3. Polaris (pō lar′ is): North Star.
4. Catherine wheels: A firework like a pinwheel that whirls and throws out colored lights.

The Signature 751

---

12 Critical Thinking and Reading Where else has the narrator seen this symbol?

13 Literary Focus For a second time, the narrator hears a sound, this time the rustling of trees instead of the voices of children. Why does she fear she will not see the trees? Why is it important for her to see the trees?

14 Reading Strategy Again ask the students to predict what will happen at the end of the story. What *will* the woman find?

15 Literary Focus Contrast this setting with the setting at the beginning of the story.

16 Discussion Why does the narrator refer to herself as the "woman's figure in the dark dress"?

17 Clarification The word *raillery* means "teasing or good-natured ridicule."

Reader's Response What do you think the narrator has discovered when she remembers "everything"?

---

weather-scoured from *scoured by the weather*
dust-chalked from *made chalky by dust*
brand-new from *new as a firebrand* (from a furnace)

Student Activity 1. Study the following compound adjectives and indicate the longer phrase from which each is derived.
1. *middle-aged* woman
2. *weather-beaten* houses
3. *dark-browed* man
4. *longed-for* face
5. *slow-growing* shock

Student Activity 2. Form compound adjectives from the following italicized phrases, and place them before the nouns they modify. Hyphenate your new adjectives.
1. the clay *which is as dry as dust*
2. the eaves *which are trimmed with wood*
3. the sky *which is fronded with cirrus*
4. the hands *blotched by age*
5. the windows *shuttered fast*

Closure and Extension

ANSWERS TO THINKING ABOUT THE SELECTION
Recalling

1. (a) The narrator does not know her name, nor the name of the city she is in. (b) She feels terror and fright. (c) She believes that looking at her reflection will reveal her identity.
2. (a) The eye-diamond symbol is in the center of each bill. (b) She also sees it on a house, on a road, on shutters, and on a fence.
3. (a) The people look at the narrator with neither hostility nor friendliness. (b) They respond with indifference, shaking their heads, looking away, not smiling but not being hostile.
4. His gaze is so direct and intense that she cannot look at him.
5. (a) She realizes that she has not seen a single tree. (b) She has not seen any children, either, but has heard them.
6. (a) She remembers who she is. (b) She knows the name of the city and understands the language of its citizens.

Interpreting

7. (a) The city is dry, dusty, barren, sunbleached, rundown, colorless, monotonous. (b) The people act strange and indifferent.
8. (a) It is rundown, filled with dust and refuse, devoid of normal signs of life such as animals, plants, and trees. (b) Suggested Response: She does not see any children, because no children have survived the disaster.
9. Suggested Response: The eye-diamond might be a symbol of the government or society that had existed before the disaster.

Applying

10. Suggested Response: After the war, many people began to fear a nuclear holocaust.

Challenge What is the theme of the story?

752

THINKING ABOUT THE SELECTION
Recalling

1. (a) What two things are unknown to the narrator? (b) What emotion does she feel? (c) What conviction does she have?
2. (a) What symbol is engraved on each bill in her purse? (b) Where else does she see this symbol?
3. (a) How do the people the narrator passes look at her? (b) How do they respond when she addresses them?
4. What happens when the narrator confronts the young, dark-browed man?
5. (a) What does the narrator realize when she hears the wind blowing through the leaves? (b) What occurs to her when she stands up?
6. (a) What happens when the narrator looks in the mirror? (b) What does she realize?

Interpreting

7. (a) How would you characterize the physical appearance of the city in which the narrator finds herself? (b) How would you characterize the people she passes?
8. (a) What evidence in the story suggests that the city has suffered a major disaster, such as a devastating war or a nuclear holocaust? (b) What is the significance of the fact that the narrator never sees any children?
9. What do you think the eye-diamond might symbolize?

Applying

10. Why do you think Enright might have chosen to write a story like this in the aftermath of World War II?

ANALYZING LITERATURE
Understanding Setting

The **setting** is the time and place in which the events in a work of literature occur. In many stories the setting establishes a particular atmosphere, or mood.
1. What atmosphere does the description of the setting in "The Signature" establish?
2. How does the description of the setting reflect the narrator's state of mind?
3. How is the atmosphere especially appropriate to the theme?

UNDERSTANDING ADJECTIVES
Appreciating Adjectives

To establish an atmosphere, a writer will describe the setting with words that convey the appropriate feeling. For example, Enright uses adjectives such as *faded* and *scoured* to help create an atmosphere in "The Signature."
1. Find five other adjectives that help to create the atmosphere in "The Signature."
2. How are these five adjectives related in meaning?

THINKING AND WRITING
Writing About Setting

Write an essay in which you discuss how Enright uses the setting to establish an atmosphere in "The Signature." Prepare a list of details that help to establish the atmosphere. Then write your essay, making sure that you support your thesis. When you finish writing, revise your essay, making sure that you have adequately supported your thesis with details from the short story.

ANSWERS TO ANALYZING LITERATURE

1. The setting establishes an atmosphere of alienation, isolation, terror, confusion, and discomfort.
2. The setting is barren, bleak, and unfamiliar; she is lost and depressed.
3. Suggested Response: The devastated condition of the setting is related to the theme.

ANSWERS TO UNDERSTANDING LANGUAGE

1. Other descriptive adjectives include, hard-baked, dry, blind, dusted, powdered, old, foreign, unpainted, pale, crude, faded, blanched.
2. They are all negative and suggest something old, worn, and washed-out.

THINKING AND WRITING

For help with this assignment, students can refer to Lesson 7, "Writing About Setting," in the Handbook of Writing About Literature.

Writing Across the Curriculum Theater is a discipline where establishing the proper atmosphere is critical to a play's success. For extra credit have

Nonfiction

HANDBALL, 1939
Ben Shahn
The Museum of Modern Art

Humanities Note

Fine art, *Handball,* 1939, by Ben Shahn. As an apprentice to a commercial lithographer when he was a young man, Ben Shahn (1898–1969) developed a life-long interest in hand-lettering and other aspects of the graphic arts. *The Biography of a Painting* (1957, 1966) is a charming book written entirely in Shahn's own handwriting and illustrated with many of his line drawings. Ben Shahn's abiding concern for so-cial, political, and economic jus-tice probably came from his ex-periences, in his native Lithuania, with anti-Semitism (the family emigrated to the United States in 1906). His convictions intensified when he traveled across his adopted country, during the depths of the Depression, as a photographer for the Farm Secu-rity Administration, capturing on camera the unspeakable despair that economic chaos had wrought.

Shahn's works are noted for their emphasis on line; for their clear, bright colors; and for the expressive, often agonized por-trayal of human faces. Some works are, in effect, a cry for justice rendered in assertive black lines and lucid colors. Others, like *Handball,* are less serious in subject matter but still retain the sense of compassion Shahn felt for his subjects. The spatial arrangement of the fig-ures, as well as the variety of their poses, creates a feeling of move-ment that reflects the energy and joyfulness of the handball play-ers.

students write a one-page paper that describes how a set design-er might choose to portray the setting for "The Signature" on stage. Would it be detailed and realistic? Or would the designer create a more ambivalent set? You might inform the drama de-partment of this assignment. Drama teachers may provide guidance for students.

Critical Evaluation George J. Becker wrote in his book on John Dos Passos:

"Throughout his life Dos Passos the novelist also had a parallel vocation as observer, analyst, and philosopher of social institutions. For thirty years this interest was subordinate to and supportive of his fiction. For the last twenty years the relationship was reversed. Fiction mirroring contemporary life yielded place to reflections about it and a search for permanent values by which to judge it, values which he found blazoned in the history of the first decades of the republic. An inductive approach to the contemporary scene gave way to a deductive speculation about what makes a good society. As the writer became more and more disaffected with the present he turned to the past for guidance and comfort.

He was to the end a reporter with an almost obsessive desire to see and to set down what he saw, with a confident reliance on his own senses and his own judgment."

JOHN DOS PASSOS

1896–1970

Although he published numerous novels, essays, and biographical sketches, John Dos Passos is remembered mainly for his experimental trilogy *U.S.A.* In this work Dos Passos blends fiction and nonfiction—interweaving biographies of both fictional characters and real historical figures, newspaper excerpts, passages from popular songs, and quotations from speeches—to paint a biting portrait of early twentieth-century America.

Dos Passos was born in Chicago. He attended private schools and eventually enrolled at Harvard, from which he graduated in 1916. When the United States entered World War I, he joined the United States Army Ambulance Corps. His experiences during the war provided him with the material for his first two novels, *One Man's Initiation—1917* (1920) and *Three Soldiers* (1921).

In 1925 Dos Passos published *Manhattan Transfer,* in which he delved into the complexities of New York City life. In this novel Dos Passos developed the experimental technique which he later perfected in the *U.S.A.* trilogy. He presented scattered fragments of many characters' lives, which combine to form a complete picture of urban life.

Dos Passos published *The 42nd Parallel,* the first novel of the *U.S.A.* trilogy in 1930. The second and third novels, *1919* and *The Big Money,* appeared in 1932 and 1936. In 1937 the trilogy was published in its entirety under the title *U.S.A.*

U.S.A. was admired for its new and dramatic presentation of American culture and history. Dos Passos regarded all writers as "architects of history." "What do you write for then?" he asked. "To convince people of something? That's preaching, and is part of the business of everybody who deals with words; not to admit that is to play with a gun and say you didn't know it was loaded. But outside of preaching I think there is such a thing as writing for writing's sake. A cabinetmaker enjoys whittling a dovetail because he's a cabinetmaker; every type of work has its own delight inherent in it. The mind of a generation is its speech. A writer makes aspects of that speech permanent by putting them in print. He whittles at the words and phrases of today and makes forms for the minds of later generations. That's history. A writer who writes straight is an architect of history."

Dos Passos went on to publish several more novels, including a second trilogy, *District of Columbia* (1952). However, critics generally agree that his later works lack the inventiveness and forcefulness of *U.S.A.*

754   *The Modern Age*

Objectives

1 To analyze an impressionistic biography
2 To recognize the writer's attitude
3 To write an impressionistic biography

Support Material

Teaching Portfolio
Teacher Backup, p. 971
Usage and Mechanics Worksheet, p. 975
Analyzing Literature Worksheet, *Understanding Biography,* p. 976
Language Worksheet, *Forming Compound Words,* p. 977
Selection Test, p. 978

Art Transparency 13, *Landscape Near Chicago* by Aaron Bohrod

GUIDE FOR INTERPRETING

Tin Lizzie

Literary Forms

Biographies. A biography is an account of a person's life written by another person. Most biographies focus on recounting the central events of the subject's life—the events that make that person's life worth reading about. Sometimes, however, a writer will focus on conveying his or her impressions of the subject's character, rather than merely presenting a factual account of the subject's life. The result is what is known as an impressionistic biography. In an impressionistic biography, the writer concentrates on presenting details that help to reveal the subject's personality, often intentionally omitting details that would be included in a factual biography.

In *U.S.A.* Dos Passos presents many short, impressionistic biographical sketches, including ones about Woodrow Wilson and Henry Ford. Together these sketches help to convey Dos Passos's overall impression of America during the first three decades of the twentieth century.

Commentary

In praising Dos Passos's *U.S.A.* trilogy, critic Alfred Kazin compares Dos Passos to the inventors and entrepreneurs of the early twentieth century about whom Dos Passos writes. "What Dos Passos created with [his novel] was in fact another American invention—an American *thing* peculiar to the opportunity and stress of American life, like the Wright Brothers' airplane, Edison's phonograph . . . , Frank Lloyd Wright's first office buildings."

What Kazin was responding to was the new and inventive style of Dos Passos's writing. As you read Dos Passos's impressionistic biography of Henry Ford, pay attention to the way he plays with such things as capitalization, punctuation, and spelling. You may also recognize what Kazin called "the 'poetry' behind the book that makes the 'history' in it live": the different styles of speech that Dos Passos uses to convey his impressions of Henry Ford. Dos Passos varies the rhythms and language in his work to mimic the way people talk in real life. He also imitates the stock phrases and popular writing that appeared in the advertisements and newspapers of his time.

What "poetry" do you hear in the language of your everyday life?

Writing

Imagine that you were writing an impressionistic biography about a public figure or a person you know. Prepare a list of facts about this person's life that contribute to your impressions of his or her character.

Literary Focus An impressionistic biography differs from other biographies in that more biases seep through, both in what the writer says, and in how he or she expresses it. Have your students consider their own speech when expressing strong opinions about a person who is not present. How might the tone change if that person's best friend were present? Are there situations in which telling a simple story might convey more about a person's personality than descriptive details alone? How does this relate to the old adage "a picture is worth a thousand words"?

Writing/Prior Knowledge Have your students jot down five or more adjectives describing the subject of the biography. Students can then work from this list, thinking of facts related to each adjective.

Vocabulary

Preteach the following vocabulary words:
jauntily (jônt′ i lē) *adv.:* In a carefree fashion (p. 756)
practicable (prak′ ti kə b'l) *adj.:* Workable (p. 757)

Spelling Tip Have students be sure to pronounce all syllables in *practicable*. It should not be confused with *practical*.

Motivation/Prior Knowledge
What might life have been like
before most people owned an
automobile? How do students
think mass production changed
life in America? What things in
society could not have existed
without the automobile?

Master Teacher Note To set the
mood for the selection, bring in
books with pictures of Model T
Fords and other early automobiles. You might also place Art
Transparency 13, *Landscape
Near Chicago* by Aaron Bohrod,
on the overhead projector. Direct
the students' attention to how the
Model T is depicted in the painting. How does it differ from today's cars? How do the Model T
and the other cars in the painting
contribute to the overall impression that the painting conveys?

Thematic Idea Another selection
in which the writer conveys a
clear impression of an important
historical figure is "Lincoln
Speaks at Gettysburg" by Carl
Sandburg (p. 786).

Purpose-Setting Question
What is John Dos Passos's attitude toward Henry Ford?

1 **Enrichment** Tin Lizzie was a
nickname for the Model T Ford.
Invented in 1908, the Model T
was the first automobile produced by an assembly line. By
1927, more than fifteen million of
these cars had been sold.

2 **Discussion** What is ironic about
the reference to the Model T as a
"steed"? How is this analogy developed throughout the rest of
the paragraph?

3 **Discussion** What is the effect of
summarizing the first twenty
years of Henry Ford's life in two
long sentences?

Tin Lizzie

John Dos Passos

*"Mr. Ford the automobileer," the feature-
writer wrote in 1900,*

*"Mr. Ford the automobileer began by
giving his steed three or four sharp jerks
with the lever at the righthand side of the
seat; that is, he pulled the lever up and
down sharply in order, as he said, to mix
air with gasoline and drive the charge into
the exploding cylinder. . . . Mr. Ford slipped
a small electric switch handle and there
followed a puff, puff, puff. . . . The puffing
of the machine assumed a higher key. She
was flying along about eight miles an hour.
The ruts in the road were deep, but the machine certainly went with a dreamlike
smoothness. There was none of the bumping common even to a streetcar. . . . By this
time the boulevard had been reached, and
the automobileer, letting a lever fall a little,
let her out. Whiz! She picked up speed with
infinite rapidity. As she ran on there was a
clattering behind, the new noise of the automobile.*

For twenty years or more,

ever since he'd left his father's farm
when he was sixteen to get a job in a Detroit
machineshop, Henry Ford had been nuts
about machinery. First it was watches, then
he designed a steamtractor, then he built a
horseless carriage with an engine adapted
from the Otto gasengine he'd read about in
The World of Science, then a mechanical
buggy with a onecylinder fourcycle motor,
that would run forward but not back;

at last, in ninetyeight, he felt he was far
enough along to risk throwing up his job
with the Detroit Edison Company, where

he'd worked his way up from night fireman
to chief engineer, to put all his time into
working on a new gasoline engine,

(in the late eighties he'd met Edison at a
meeting of electriclight employees in Atlantic
City. He'd gone up to Edison after Edison
had delivered an address and asked him if
he thought gasoline was practical as a motor
fuel. Edison had said yes. If Edison said it,
it was true. Edison was the great admiration
of Henry Ford's life);

and in driving his mechanical buggy, sitting there at the lever jauntily dressed in a
tightbuttoned jacket and a high collar and a
derby hat, back and forth over the level illpaved streets of Detroit,

scaring the big brewery horses and the
skinny trotting horses and the sleekrumped
pacers with the motor's loud explosions,

looking for men scatterbrained enough
to invest money in a factory for building automobiles.

He was the eldest son of an Irish immigrant who during the Civil War had married
the daughter of a prosperous Pennsylvania
Dutch farmer and settled down to farming
near Dearborn in Wayne County, Michigan;

like plenty of other Americans, young
Henry grew up hating the endless sogging
through the mud about the chores, the hauling and pitching manure, the kerosene
lamps to clean, the irk and sweat and solitude of the farm.

He was a slender, active youngster, a
good skater, clever with his hands; what he
liked was to tend the machinery and let the

756   *The Modern Age*

4 **Critical Thinking and Reading**
Have students note that Dos Passos starts many of his paragraphs in the middle of sentences. How does this serve to
emphasize each of the points
that he makes?

5 Literary Focus In leaping from the fact that Ford's father offered him money to Ford's building of a new home, Dos Passos makes it seem inevitable that Ford would accept the money his father offered him. What is Dos Passos implying by not using a smoother transition?

6 Discussion Who actually set the track records? What is the effect of adding the statement about the stuntrider almost as an afterthought?

others do the heavy work. His mother had told him not to drink, smoke, gamble or go into debt, and he never did.

When he was in his early twenties his father tried to get him back from Detroit, where he was working as mechanic and repairman for the Drydock Engine Company that built engines for steamboats, by giving him forty acres of land.

Young Henry built himself an uptodate square white dwellinghouse with a false mansard[1] roof and married and settled down on the farm,

but he let the hired men do the farming;

he bought himself a buzzsaw and rented a stationary engine and cut the timber off the woodlots.

He was a thrifty young man who never drank or smoked or gambled, but he couldn't stand living on the farm.

He moved to Detroit, and in the brick barn behind his house tinkered for years in his spare time with a mechanical buggy that would be light enough to run over the clayey wagonroads of Wayne County, Michigan.

By 1900 he had a practicable car to promote.

He was forty years old before the Ford Motor Company was started and production began to move.

Speed was the first thing the early automobile manufacturers went after. Races advertised the makes of cars.

Henry Ford himself hung up several records at the track at Grosse Pointe and on the ice on Lake St. Clair. In his 999 he

---

1. **mansard** (man' särd): A roof with two slopes on each of the four sides.

Tin Lizzie 757

7 **Literary Focus** Dos Passos ends this sketch about Ford by referring to him as "the great American of his time." Based on these two paragraphs, what were the priorities of this "great American"?

8 **Enrichment** Frederick W. Taylor (1856–1915) pioneered what has become known as time-and-motion study. Its aim was to make workers as machine-like as possible.

9 **Critical Thinking and Reading** Look back at passage number 7. How have the things that Ford "had ideas about" changed? What is the significance of using the same phrasing in both instances? What other phrases can students find that are repeated throughout this selection?

10 **Enrichment** Although he paid relatively high wages, Ford strongly opposed unionization at the Ford Motor Company. Working conditions at the factory were reported to be fairly unpleasant.

11 **Clarification** Have students look closely at the syntax of this sentence. It was the five dollars a day that "made" each of the things on this list.

Reader's Response How is this selection about Henry Ford similar to and different from what you already knew about the man?

did the mile in thirtynine and fourfifths seconds.

But it had always been his custom to hire others to do the heavy work. The speed he was busy with was speed in production, the records records in efficient output. He hired Barney Oldfield, a stunt bicyclerider from Salt Lake City, to do the racing for him.

7 | Henry Ford had ideas about other things than the designing of motors, carburetors, magnetos, jigs and fixtures, punches and dies; he had ideas about sales,

that the big money was in economical quantity production, quick turnover, cheap interchangeable, easilyreplaced standardized parts;

it wasn't until 1909, after years of arguing with his partners, that Ford put out the first Model T.

Henry Ford was right.

That season he sold more than ten thousand tin lizzies, ten years later he was selling almost a million a year.

8 | In these years the Taylor Plan was stirring up plantmanagers and manufacturers all over the country. Efficiency was the word. The same ingenuity that went into improving the performance of a machine could go into improving the performance of the workmen producing the machine.

In 1913 they established the assemblyline at Ford's. That season the profits were something like twentyfive million dollars, but they had trouble in keeping the men on the job, machinists didn't seem to like it at Ford's.

9 | Henry Ford had ideas about other things than production.

He was the largest automobile manufacturer in the world; he paid high wages; maybe if the steady workers thought they were getting a cut (a very small cut) in the profits, it would give trained men an inducement to stick to their jobs,

wellpaid workers might save enough money to buy a tin lizzie; the first day Ford's announced that cleancut properlymarried American workers who wanted jobs had a chance to make five bucks a day (of course it turned out that there were strings to it; always there were strings to it)

10 | such an enormous crowd waited outside the Highland Park plant

all through the zero January night

that there was a riot when the gates were opened; cops broke heads, jobhunters threw bricks; property, Henry Ford's own property, was destroyed. The company dicks[2] had to turn on the firehose to beat back the crowd.

The American Plan; automotive prosperity seeping down from above; it turned out there were strings to it.

11 | But that five dollars a day

paid to good, clean American workmen

who didn't drink or smoke cigarettes or read or think,

and whose wives didn't take in boarders,

made America once more the Yukon of the sweated workers of the world;

made all the tin lizzies and the automotive age, and incidentally,

made Henry Ford the automobileer, the admirer of Edison, the birdlover,

the great American of his time.

---

2. company dicks: Armed guards.

THINKING ABOUT THE SELECTION
Recalling

1. Why did Ford quit his job at the Detroit Edison Company?
2. Whom did Ford look for as he drove his "mechanical buggy" up and down the "illpaved streets of Detroit"?
3. (a) What had Ford grown up hating? (b) What had his mother told him?
4. How did Ford think he could make "the big money"?
5. What happened when the Ford Motor Company announced that it was looking for workers?

Interpreting

6. (a) What details in the excerpt at the beginning of the selection make it clear that the American public knew very little about automobiles in 1900? (b) How is the portrayal of Ford in this excerpt different from the way he is portrayed in the rest of the selection?
7. Find two examples of Dos Passos's use of repetition to emphasize important ideas.
8. (a) What is unconventional about the form of the final sentence? (b) How does the form help to strengthen our final impression of Ford?

Analyzing

9. Dos Passos suggests that a person's accomplishments may reveal little about his or her character. Explain why you do or do not agree with this suggestion.

ANALYZING LITERATURE
Understanding Biography

A **biography** is an account of a person's life written by another person. In an impressionistic biography, the writer focuses on conveying his or her impressions of the subject, rather than merely recounting the central events of that per-

son's life. For example, in "Tin Lizzie" Dos Passos presents his impressions of Henry Ford.

1. What impression does Dos Passos convey of Ford as a young man?
2. How does Dos Passos suggest that Ford thought of his workers as little more than machines?
3. How is Ford's character reflected in his conception of the ideal worker?
4. Considering the impression of Ford the selection conveys, what is ironic, or surprising, about the final line?

CRITICAL THINKING AND READING
Recognizing the Writer's Attitude

Although Dos Passos mentions a number of Ford's achievements in this essay, the way in which they are presented and the way in which Ford's character is portrayed make it clear that Dos Passos actually has a very critical attitude toward Ford and his accomplishments. For example, Dos Passos conveys a negative impression of Ford when he writes that what Ford "liked to do was to tend the machinery and let the others do the heavy work."

Find three other passages that reveal Dos Passos's critical attitude toward Ford.

THINKING AND WRITING
Writing an Impressionistic Biography

Using the list of facts you prepared before reading the selection, write an impressionistic biography. As you are writing, focus on presenting details that convey your impressions of the subject's character. When you finish writing, reread your biography to make sure it conveys the proper impression. After making any necessary revisions, proofread your biography and share it with your classmates.

Tin Lizzie 759

separate lines, almost like poetry. (b) The form of the sentence adds emphasis to each of the individual facts that it contains.

Applying

9. Answers will differ. Students may comment that they do agree with this suggestion, because a person's accomplishments often only relate to a small part of his or her personality.

Challenge Do you imagine that Dos Passos's portrayal of Ford is accurate? Why or why not?

ANSWERS TO ANALYZING LITERATURE

1. Suggested Response: He conveys the impression that Ford was completely absorbed by his own interests and goals and had little concern for others.
2. Dos Passos writes that Ford thought that "The same ingenuity that went into improving the performance of a machine could go into improving the performance of the workmen producing the machine."
3. Ford wanted his workers to follow his example by being clean-cut and not drinking and smoking.
4. Dos Passos conveys a very negative impression of Ford, but in the final line, he refers to Ford as "the great American of his time."

ANSWERS TO CRITICAL THINKING AND READING

Answers will differ. Passages include the ones in which Dos Passos comments that "The same ingenuity that went into improving the performance of a machine could go into improving the performance of the workmen"; that Ford looked "for men scatterbrained enough to invest money in a factory"; and that Ford "made America one more the Yukon of the sweated workers in the world."

THINKING AND WRITING

Publishing Student Writing Encourage students to submit their biographies to your school's literary magazine.

Closure and Extension

ANSWERS TO THINKING ABOUT THE SELECTION
Recalling

1. He wanted to devote his time to developing a new gasoline engine.
2. He was looking for men to invest in his automobile factory.
3. (a) Ford hated chores and he hated the solitude of farm life. (b) His mother had told him not to drink,

smoke, gamble, or go into debt.
4. He felt "the big money" was in economical quantity production of automobiles that he would sell quickly.
5. There was a riot when the gates were opened.

Interpreting

6. (a) The passage is written with a tone of discovery, as though each action Ford performs is being done for the first time. He explains

what he is doing as he does it, and the noise that the machine emits is "the new noise of the automobile." (b) The portrayal of Ford is much more positive than it is in the rest of the selection.
7. The idea of Ford as an admirer of Edison is repeated, as are the facts that he liked to let others do the heavy work; that he never drank, smoked, or gambled; that he did not like farm life; and that he was a man with ideas.
8. (a) The sentence is broken into

E. B. WHITE

More About the Author Another concern that E. B. White had in common with Thoreau was his passion for freedom, as this excerpt from the essay "Freedom," attests: "But a man's free condition is of two parts: the instinctive free-ness he experiences as an animal dweller on a planet, and the practical liberties he enjoys as a privileged member of human society. The latter is, of the two, more generally understood, more widely admired, more violently challenged and discussed. It is the practical and apparent side of freedom. The United States . . . offers the liberties and the privileges and the tools of freedom. In this land the citizens are still invited to write plays and books, to paint their pictures, to meet for discussion, to dissent as well as to agree, to mount soapboxes in the public square, to enjoy education in all subjects without censorship, to hold court and judge one another, to compose music, to talk politics with their neighbors without wondering whether the secret police are listening, to exchange ideas as well as goods, to kid the government when it needs kidding, and to read real news of real events instead of phony news manufactured by a paid agent of the state. This is a fact and should give every person pause."

More proof of E. B. White's admiration for Thoreau can be found in a piece he wrote on the hundredth anniversary of the publication of Thoreau's *Walden*. In the piece, called "A Slight Sound of Evening," White wrote: "I'd like to stroll about the countryside in Thoreau's company for a day, observing the modern scene, inspecting today's snowstorm, pointing out the sights, and offering belated apologies for my sins." If you could spend the day with a writer you admire, who would it be?

1899–1985

Known for his precise, direct style, E(lwyn) B(rooks) White is generally regarded as one of the most important American essayists of the twentieth century. In fact, White's work is still the standard against which the work of many of today's essayists is judged.

After growing up in Mount Vernon, New York, White attended Cornell University. There, he studied literature and served as the editor of the Cornell *Daily Sun*. Several years after his graduation, White joined the staff of *The New Yorker* magazine. His humorous, topical essays helped to establish *The New Yorker* as one of the nation's most successful general-interest magazines.

White produced essays for *The New Yorker* on a weekly basis until 1938. In these essays, many of which are collected in his books *Every Day Is Saturday* (1935) and *Quo Vadimus?* (1939), White used his talents as a humorist to explore numerous social and political themes. Influenced by the teachings of Henry David Thoreau, he strongly believed in individualism and simplicity. In an effort to simplify his own life, he bought a farmhouse in Maine and began spending much of his time there.

While continuing to contribute editorial essays to *The New Yorker,* White wrote for other magazines and published a variety of works: essays, poems, stories, and novels. From 1938 to 1943, he wrote a column for *Harper's* magazine called "One Man's Meat," in which he explored the conflicts of modern life and his decision to move to the country. He published these essays in *One Man's Meat* in 1942. He also reprinted his *New Yorker* editorials on world government in *The Wild Flag* (1946); in *Here Is New York* (1949), he wrote about his impressions of New York City; *The Second Tree from the Corner* (1954) is a collection of essays and poems; and *The Points of My Compass* (1962) contains further essays. He also wrote two much-loved children's books, *Stuart Little* (1945), about a mouse in a human family, and *Charlotte's Web* (1952), about a girl's two pets— a pig and a spider. Always interested in humor, he collaborated with James Thurber and, with his wife Katherine, edited *A Subtreasury of American Humor* (1941). In addition White has been admired and imitated as a brilliant stylist in writing. *The Elements of Style,* a manual of writing by William Strunk, Jr., that White revised in 1959, is widely regarded as one of the most helpful handbooks of writing ever written.

"Walden (June 1939)," an essay from *One Man's Meat,* reflects White's interest in Thoreau and his concern regarding the increasing complexity of modern life. The essay also demonstrates how White's belief in simplicity is reflected in his writing style.

Objectives
1 To understand the personal essay
2 To choose the meaning that fits the context
3 To compare and contrast essays

Support Material
Teaching Portfolio
Teacher Backup, p. 981
Grammar in Action Worksheet, *Appreciating Nominative Absolutes,* p. 985
Usage and Mechanics Worksheet, p. 987
Vocabulary Check, p. 988
Critical Thinking and Reading Worksheet, *Recognizing the Writer's Attitude,* p. 989

Language Worksheet, *Recognizing Antonyms,* p. 990
Selection Test, p. 991

GUIDE FOR INTERPRETING

Walden

Literary Forms

Personal Essays. A personal essay is an informal essay that focuses on a subject that is at least to some extent autobiographical. Personal essays are prose works written in a relaxed, intimate, conversational style. They are generally brief and focus on a limited topic. Despite their narrow focus, personal essays are loosely organized, with the writer at times digressing from the topic to express opinions or discuss related matters. Because of their autobiographical nature, personal essays generally reveal something about the writer's personality. "Walden," for example, reveals White's belief in simplicity.

Writing

"Walden" is written in the form of a letter addressed to Henry David Thoreau, the writer who most influenced White's work. Think of a writer whose work has had a powerful effect on you. Then jot down thoughts you would include in a letter to this writer, discussing the ways in which his or her work affected you.

Primary Source

Style is an important element in essays. White's style is a good guide to his personality and beliefs. An advocate of simple, clear, direct style, White advises inexperienced writers not to try to impress readers with an excess of style. In *Elements of Style,* he writes

> "Young writers often suppose that style is a garnish for the meat of prose, a sauce by which a dull dish is made palatable. Style has no such separate entity; it is nondetachable, unfilterable. The beginner should approach style warily, realizing that it is himself he is approaching, no other; and he should begin by turning resolutely away from all devices that are popularly believed to indicate style—all mannerisms, tricks, adornments. The approach to style is by way of plainness, simplicity, orderliness, sincerity."

Literary Focus To help students appreciate the difference between formal and informal essays, compare and contrast White's essay with the excerpt from Ralph Waldo Emerson's *Nature* (p. 268).

Writing/Prior Knowledge Point out to students that the writer need not be someone still living. The writer can be someone whose works they read as a young child or someone whose most recent book they just put down last week.

Vocabulary

Preteach the following vocabulary words:
impetuous (im pech′ o͞o wəs) *adj.:* Moving with great force or violence (p. 762)
pertinence (pʉr′t'n əns) *n.:* Appropriateness; relevance (p. 762)
stupefaction (sto͞o′ pə fak′ shən) *n.:* Stunned amazement or utter bewilderment (p. 762)
cryptic (krip′tik) *adj.:* Having a hidden or ambiguous meaning (p. 763)
inauspicious (in ôs pish′ əs) *adj.:* Not boding well for the future (p. 764)
petulently (pech′ o͞o lənt lē) *adv.:* Impatiently or irritably (p. 765)

Spelling Tip Point out to students that the short *i* sound is spelled differently in the two syllables in *cryptic.*

Walden

E. B. White

June 1939

Miss Nims, take a letter to Henry David Thoreau. Dear Henry: I thought of you the other afternoon as I was approaching Concord doing fifty on Route 62. That is a high speed at which to hold a philosopher in one's mind, but in this century we are a nimble bunch.

On one of the lawns in the outskirts of the village a woman was cutting the grass with a motorized lawn mower. What made me think of you was that the machine had rather got away from her, although she was game enough, and in the brief glimpse I had of the scene it appeared to me that the lawn was mowing the lady. She kept a tight grip on the handles, which throbbed violently with every explosion of the one-cylinder motor, and as she sheered around bushes and lurched along at a reluctant trot behind her impetuous servant, she looked like a puppy who had grabbed something that was too much for him. Concord hasn't changed much, Henry; the farm implements and the animals still have the upper hand.

I may as well admit that I was journeying to Concord with the deliberate intention of visiting your woods; for although I have never knelt at the grave of a philosopher nor placed wreaths on moldy poets, and have often gone a mile out of my way to avoid some place of historical interest, I have always wanted to see Walden Pond. The account which you left of your sojourn there is, you will be amused to learn, a document of increasing pertinence; each year it seems to gain a little headway, as the world loses ground. We may all be transcendental yet, whether we like it or not. As our common complexities increase, any tale of individual simplicity (and yours is the best written and the cockiest) acquires a new fascination; as our goods accumulate, but not our well-being, your report of an existence without material adornment takes on a certain awkward credibility.

My purpose in going to Walden Pond, like yours, was not to live cheaply or to live dearly there, but to transact some private business with the fewest obstacles. Approaching Concord, doing forty, doing forty-five, doing fifty, the steering wheel held snug in my palms, the highway held grimly in my vision, the crown of the road now serving me (on the righthand curves), now defeating me (on the lefthand curves), I began to rouse myself from the stupefaction which a day's motor journey induces. It was a delicious evening, Henry, when the whole body is one sense, and imbibes delight through every pore, if I may coin a phrase. Fields were richly brown where the harrow, drawn by the stripped Ford, had lately sunk its teeth; pastures were green; and overhead the sky had that same everlasting great look which you will find on Page 144 of the Oxford pocket edition.[1] I could feel the road entering me, through tire, wheel, spring, and cushion; shall I not have intelligence with earth

---

1. Oxford pocket edition: An edition of Thoreau's *Walden* published by the Oxford University Press.

too? Am I not partly leaves and vegetable mold myself?—a man of infinite horsepower, yet partly leaves.

Stay with me on 62 and it will take you into Concord. As I say, it was a delicious evening. The snake had come forth to die in a bloody S on the highway, the wheel upon its head, its bowels flat now and exposed. The turtle had come up too to cross the road and die in the attempt, its hard shell smashed under the rubber blow, its intestinal yearning (for the other side of the road) forever squashed. There was a sign by the wayside which announced that the road had a "cotton surface." You wouldn't know what that is, but neither, for that matter, did I. There is a cryptic ingredient in many of our modern improvements—we are awed and pleased without knowing quite what we are enjoying. It is something to be traveling on a road with a cotton surface.

The civilization round Concord today is an odd distillation of city, village, farm, and manor. The houses, yards, fields look not quite suburban, not quite rural. Under the bronze beech and the blue spruce of the departed baron grazes the milch[2] goat of the heirs. Under the porte-cochère[3] stands the reconditioned station wagon; under the grape arbor sit the puppies for sale. (But why do

---

2. **milch** *adj.*: Milk-giving.
3. **porte-cochère** (pôrt′ kō shâr′): Carport.

5 Discussion How does White use the automobile in comparing and contrasting his age with Thoreau's?

men degenerate ever? What makes families run out?)

It was June and everywhere June was publishing her immemorial stanza; in the lilacs, in the syringa,[4] in the freshly edged paths and the sweetness of moist beloved gardens, and the little wire wickets that preserve the tulips' front. Farmers were already moving the fruits of their toil into their yards, arranging the rhubarb, the asparagus, the strictly fresh eggs on the painted stands under the little shed roofs with the patent shingles. And though it was almost a hundred years since you had taken your ax and started cutting out your home on Walden Pond, I was interested to observe that the philosophical spirit was still alive in Massachusetts: in the center of a vacant lot some boys were assembling the framework of a rude shelter, their whole mind and skill concentrated in the rather inauspicious helter-skelter of studs and rafters. They too were escaping from town, to live naturally, in a rich blend of savagery and philosophy.

That evening, after supper at the inn, I strolled out into the twilight to dream my shapeless transcendental dreams and see that the car was locked up for the night (first open the right front door, then reach over, straining, and pull up the handles of the left rear and the left front till you hear the click, then the handle of the right rear, then shut the right front but open it again, remembering that the key is still in the ignition switch, remove the key, shut the right front again with a bang, push the tiny keyhole cover to one side, insert key, turn, and withdraw). It is what we all do, Henry. It is called locking the car. It is said to confuse thieves and keep them from making off with the laprobe. Four doors to lock behind one robe. The driver himself never uses a laprobe, the free movement of his legs being vital to the operation of the vehicle; so that when he locks the car it is a pure and unselfish act. I have in my life gained very little essential heat from laprobes, yet I have ever been at pains to lock them up.

The evening was full of sounds, some of which would have stirred your memory. The robins still love the elms of New England villages at sundown. There is enough of the thrush in them to make song inevitable at the end of day, and enough of the tramp to make them hang round the dwellings of men. A robin, like many another American, dearly loves a white house with green blinds. Concord is still full of them.

Your fellow townsmen were stirring abroad—not many afoot, most of them in their cars; and the sound which they made in Concord at evening was a rustling and a whispering. The sound lacks steadfastness and is wholly unlike that of a train. A train, as you know who lived so near the Fitchburg line, whistles once or twice sadly and is gone, trailing a memory in smoke, soothing to ear and mind. Automobiles, skirting a village green, are like flies that have gained the inner ear—they buzz, cease, pause, start, shift, stop, halt, brake, and the whole effect is a nervous polytone curiously disturbing.

As I wandered along, the toc toc of ping pong balls drifted from an attic window. In front of the Reuben Brown house a Buick was drawn up. At the wheel, motionless, his hat upon his head, a man sat, listening to Amos and Andy[5] on the radio (it is a drama of many scenes and without an end). The deep voice of Andrew Brown, emerging from the car, although it originated more than two hundred miles away, was unstrained by distance. When you used to sit on the shore of your pond on Sunday morning, listening to the church bells of Acton and Concord, you were aware of the excellent filter of the intervening atmosphere. Science has attended to that, and sound now maintains its intensity without regard for distance. Properly sponsored, it goes on forever.

---

4. **syringa** (sə riŋ′ gə) n.: A plant with large clusters of tiny white flowers.

5. **Amos and Andy:** A popular radio show in the 1930's and 1940's.

Grammar in Action

A **nominative absolute** is a special kind of participial construction. While most participial phrases refer to the subjects of the clauses they modify, nominative absolutes have their own subjects. Note the following examples:

Farmers were already moving the fruits of their toil into their yards, *arranging the rhubarb*. . . . (Participial phrase)

The driver himself never uses a lap-robe, *the free movement of his legs being vital to the operation of a vehicle*. . . . (Nominative Absolute)

In a nominative absolute, words that will be clearly understood without being written can be omitted. For example:

At the wheel, motionless, *his hat [being] upon his head*, a man sat.

Student Activity 1. Indicate the nominative absolutes in the following sentences.
1. We number our highways nowadays, our speed being so great that we can remember little of their quality. . . .
2. The snake had come forth to die . . . on the highway, the wheel upon its head, its bowels flat now and exposed.

A fire engine, out for a trial spin, roared past Emerson's house, hot with readiness for public duty. Over the barn roofs the martins dipped and chittered. A swarthy daughter of an asparagus grower, in culottes, shirt, and bandanna, pedaled past on her bicycle. It was indeed a delicious evening, and I returned to the inn (I believe it was your house once) to rock with the old ladies on the concrete veranda.

Next morning early I started afoot for Walden, out Main Street and down Thoreau, past the depot and the Minuteman Chevrolet Company. The morning was fresh, and in a bean field along the way I flushed an agriculturalist, quietly studying his beans. Thoreau Street soon joined Number 126, an artery of the State. We number our highways nowadays, our speed being so great we can remember little of their quality or character and are lucky to remember their number. (Men have an indistinct notion that if they keep up this activity long enough all will at length ride somewhere, in next to no time.) Your pond is on 126.

I knew I must be nearing your woodland retreat when the Golden Pheasant lunchroom came into view—Sealtest ice cream, toasted sandwiches, hot frankfurters, waffles, tonics, and lunches. Were I the proprietor, I should add rice, Indian meal, and molasses[6]—just for old time's sake. The Pheasant, incidentally, is for sale: a chance for some nature lover who wishes to set himself up beside a pond in the Concord atmosphere and live deliberately, fronting only the essential facts of life on Number 126. Beyond the Pheasant was a place called Walden Breezes, an oasis whose porch pillars were made of old green shutters sawed into lengths. On the porch was a distorting mirror, to give the traveler a comical image of himself, who had miraculously learned to gaze in an ordinary glass without smiling. Behind the Breezes, in a sun-parched clearing, dwelt your philosophical descendants in their trailers, each trailer the size of your hut, but all grouped together for the sake of congeniality. Trailer people leave the city, as you did, to discover solitude and in any weather, at any hour of the day or night, to improve the nick of time; but they soon collect in villages and get bogged deeper in the mud than ever. The camp behind Walden Breezes was just rousing itself to the morning. The ground was packed hard under the heel, and the sun came through the clearing to bake the soil and enlarge the wry smell of cramped housekeeping. Cushman's bakery truck had stopped to deliver an early basket of rolls. A camp dog, seeing me in the road, barked petulantly. A man emerged from one of the trailers and set forth with a bucket to draw water from some forest tap.

Leaving the highway I turned off into the woods toward the pond, which was apparent through the foliage. The floor of the forest was strewn with dried old oak leaves and *Transcript*s.[7] From beneath the flattened popcorn wrapper *(granum explosum)* peeped the frail violet. I followed a footpath and descended to the water's edge. The pond lay clear and blue in the morning light, as you have seen it so many times. In the shallows a man's waterlogged shirt undulated gently. A few flies came out to greet me and convoy me to your cove, past the No Bathing signs on which the fellows and the girls had scrawled their names. I felt strangely excited suddenly to be snooping around your premises, tiptoeing along watchfully, as though not to tread by mistake upon the intervening century. Before I got to the cove I heard something which seemed to me quite wonderful: I heard your frog, a full, clear *troonk*, guiding me, still hoarse and solemn, bridging the years as the robins had bridged them in the sweetness of the village evening. But he soon quit, and I came on a couple of young boys throwing stones at him.

9 **Critical Thinking and Reading** Is White being sarcastic or sincere? Are the vacationers' reasons for going to Walden at all similar to Thoreau's reasons?

---

6. **rice . . . molasses:** The main components of Thoreau's diet at Walden Pond.

7. ***Transcripts:*** *The Evening Transcript,* a Boston newspaper that is no longer published.

---

3. Behind the Breezes . . . dwelt your philosophical descendants in their trailers, each trailer the size of your hut, but all grouped together. . . .
4. The steering wheel held snug in my palms, the highway held grimly in my vision, the crown of the road now serving me . . . now defeating me . . . , I began to rouse myself. . . .

Student Activity 2. Join the following pairs of sentences by changing the second sentence into a nominative absolute.
1. Trailer people leave the city as you did.
   Their motive is to discover solitude.
2. I heard your frog.
   His voice croaked hoarsely and solemnly.

Student Activity 3. Join the following pairs of sentences by changing the first sentence into a nominative absolute:
1. Your account seems each year to gain a little headway.
   The world loses ground.
2. The Golden Pheasant lunchroom came into view.
   I knew I must be nearing your woodland retreat.

10 **Discussion** Does White's tone change as he nears Thoreau's home? If so, in what ways? What might have led to the change in tone?

11 **Discussion** Is White expressing an opinion about this scene? Why does he choose to include the chorus of the song the boys were singing?

12 **Clarification** In *Walden* Thoreau specifies exactly what he spent in building his home, eating meals and otherwise living at Walden. For meals alone he spent $8.74. He estimated that his total expenses were $61.99.

Reader's Response What do you think about the changes at Walden Pond that White has pointed out in this essay? What are the positive aspects of the changes? What are negative aspects?

Your front yard is marked by a bronze tablet set in a stone. Four small granite posts, a few feet away, show where the house was. On top of the tablet was a pair of faded blue bathing trunks with a white stripe. Back of it is a pile of stones, a sort of cairn[8] left by your visitors as a tribute I suppose. It is a rather ugly little heap of stones, Henry. In fact the hillside itself seems faded, browbeaten; a few tall skinny pines, bare of lower limbs, a smattering of young maples in suitable green, some birches and oaks, and a number of trees felled by the last big wind. It was from the bole of one of these fallen pines, torn up by the roots, that I extracted the stone which I added to the cairn—a sentimental act in which I was interrupted by a small terrier from a nearby picnic group, who confronted me and wanted to know about the stone.

I sat down for a while on one of the posts of your house to listen to the bluebottles[9] and the dragonflies. The invaded glade sprawled shabby and mean at my feet, but the flies were tuned to the old vibration. There were the remains of a fire in your ruins, but I doubt that it was yours; also two beer bottles trodden into the soil and become part of earth. A young oak had taken root in your house, and two or three ferns, unrolling like the ticklers at a banquet. The only other furnishings were a DuBarry pattern sheet, a page torn from a picture magazine, and some crusts in wax paper.

Before I quit I walked clear round the pond and found the place where you used to sit on the northeast side to get the sun in the fall, and the beach where you got sand for scrubbing your floor. On the eastern side of the pond, where the highway borders it, the State has built dressing rooms for swimmers, a float with diving towers, drinking fountains of porcelain, and rowboats for hire. The pond is in fact a State Preserve,

---

8. **cairn** (kern) *n.*: A conical heap of stones built as a monument or landmark.
9. **bluebottles** *n.*: Blue-colored blowflies.

and carries a twenty-dollar fine for picking wild flowers, a decree signed in all solemnity by your fellow citizens Walter C. Wardwell, Erson B. Barlow, and Nathaniel I. Bowditch. There was a smell of creosote where they had been building a wide wooden stairway to the road and the parking area. Swimmers and boaters were arriving; bodies plunged vigorously into the water and emerged wet and beautiful in the bright air. As I left, a boatload of town boys were splashing about in mid-pond, kidding and fooling, the young fellows singing at the tops of their lungs in a wild chorus:

> *Amer-ica, Amer-i-ca, God shed his*
>   *grace on thee,*
> *And crown thy good with brother-*
>   *hood*
> *From sea to shi-ning sea!*

I walked back to town along the railroad, following your custom. The rails were expanding noisily in the hot sun, and on the slope of the roadbed the wild grape and the blackberry sent up their creepers to the track.

The expense of my brief sojourn in Concord was:

Canvas shoes $1.95	
Baseball bat .... .25	gifts to
Left-handed fielder's	take back
glove 1.25	to a boy
Hotel and meals 4.25	
In all $7.70	

As you see, this amount was almost what you spent for food for eight months. I cannot defend the shoes or the expenditure for shelter and food: they reveal a meanness and grossness in my nature which you would find contemptible. The baseball equipment, however, is the kind of impediment with which you were never on even terms. You must remember that the house where you practiced the sort of economy which I respect was haunted only by mice and squirrels. You never had to cope with a shortstop.

THINKING ABOUT THE SELECTION

Recalling

1. (a) According to White, what happens as "our common complexities increase"? (b) What happens as "our goods accumulate"?
2. What is White's purpose in going to Walden Pond?
3. How does White describe the civilization around Concord?
4. (a) What marks Thoreau's "front yard"? (b) What shows where his house was located?
5. How does the expense of White's "brief sojourn in Concord" compare with the amount of money Thoreau spent on food while at Walden Pond?

Interpreting

6. (a) What does White's observation of the woman mowing her lawn indicate about humanity's relationship to machines? (b) What do the descriptions of the dead animals on the highway reveal about the effects of modernization on nature?
7. White writes, "Under the bronze beech and the blue spruce of the departed baron grazes the milch goat of the heirs." (a) Who is the departed baron? (b) Who are the heirs?
8. What does this selection reveal about the ways in which Concord and Walden Pond have changed since Thoreau's time?

Applying

9. In what ways would you imagine Concord and Walden Pond have changed since White's visit?

ANALYZING LITERATURE

Understanding Personal Essays

A **personal essay** is a type of informal essay which focuses on a subject that is at least to some extent autobiographical. Because of their autobiographical nature, personal essays generally reveal something about the writer's personality.

1. What does this essay reveal about White's attitude toward Thoreau?
2. What does the essay reveal about White's attitude toward the modern world?
3. List three writers you think White would admire. Explain the reasons for your choices.

UNDERSTANDING LANGUAGE

Fitting the Context

In English, words generally have more than one meaning. When you read, you must choose the meaning that fits the context.

Look up each italicized word below in a dictionary, then select the meaning that fits the context.

"As you see, this amount was almost what you spent for food for eight months. I cannot defend the shoes or the expenditure for *shelter* and food: they reveal a *meanness* and *grossness* in my nature which you would find contemptible. The baseball equipment, however, is the kind of impediment with which you were never on *even* terms. You must remember that the house where you practiced the sort of *economy* which I respect was haunted only by mice and squirrels. You never had to cope with a shortstop."

THINKING AND WRITING

Comparing and Contrasting Essays

Write an essay in which you discuss the ways in which Walden Pond changed from Thoreau's time to White's time. Start by reviewing the excerpt from Thoreau's *Walden* on page 288. Take note of any details describing the pond's appearance. Then review "Walden," taking note of the contrast in the way White describes the pond. When you write your essay, discuss how the contrasts in the pond's appearance reflect the changes that took place in society as a whole. After you finish writing, revise and proofread your essay.

Walden 767

8. The people in the trailer camps ostensibly came to Walden to "discover solitude," just as Thoreau had.

Applying

9. It has become a tourist attraction, and the grounds are covered with litter and graffitti.

Challenge Are surroundings the only consideration in finding a quiet place to contemplate life? Might Thoreau have been able to "live deliberately" and "front only the essential facts of life" in a city, if he had had to? Why or why not?

ANSWERS TO ANALYZING LITERATURE

1. White greatly admired Thoreau.
2. Suggested Response: White finds many aspects of the modern world distasteful.
3. Suggested Response: He would admire Bryant, because of Bryant's interest in nature; Emerson, because of Emerson's Transcendentalist beliefs; and Twain, because of Twain's talents as a humorist.

ANSWERS TO UNDERSTANDING LANGUAGE

shelter: a place that affords protection
meanness: inferiority
grossness: insensitivity
even: equal
economy: restrained or efficient use of one's materials

THINKING AND WRITING

For help with this assignment, students can refer to Lesson 16, "Writing a Comparative Evaluation," in the "Handbook of Writing About Literature."

After students have completed the assignment, divide them into groups, and have them read their rough drafts to one another and suggest ways in which the essays could be improved.

Closure and Extension

ANSWERS TO THINKING ABOUT THE SELECTION
Recalling

1. (a) Tales of simplicity acquire new fascination. (b) Thoreau's report of existence without material adornment takes on a certain awkward credibility.
2. White went to Walden to transact private business with the fewest obstacles.
3. The civilization around Concord is described as an odd distillation of city, village, farm, and manor.
4. (a) Thoreau's "front yard" is marked by a bronze tablet set in a stone. (b) Four small granite posts show where the house was.
5. The amount was almost what Thoreau spent for food for eight months.

Interpreting

6. (a) It indicates that people cannot totally control the machines they have created. (b) Modernization is having a detrimental effect on nature.
7. (a) The departed baron refers to Thoreau. (b) The heirs refer to the current generation.

More About the Author In addition to his work as a writer, editor, and drama critic, Robert Benchley was also known for a series of short, satirical films that he wrote, directed, and acted in himself. He also wrote for and performed on radio. How might the tone of a writer's work be affected by consistent work with the spoken, as well as the written word?

Critical Evaluation Robert Benchley's friend and co-worker at *The New Yorker* magazine, James Thurber, made the following comments about Benchley: "Benchley got off to a fast start ahead of all of us on *The New Yorker,* and our problem was the avoidance of imitation. He had written about practically everything, and his comic devices were easy to fall into. (E.B.) White once showed me something he'd written and asked anxiously, 'Did Benchley say that?' In a 1933 preface I said that we were all afraid that whatever we were engaged in had probably been done better by Robert Benchley in 1924 . . . It got harder and harder for Benchley to write, and he gave it up before he was fifty, but he had done five hundred pieces. Of one of the last he said, 'It was written in blood, I can tell you that.' He left behind a rich legacy of humor, comedy, satire, parody, and criticism—all rolled into one in those thirty-five magnificent movie shorts—but he didn't think he was very good at anything.

"'Being simply a person who writes little articles sporadically, and with no distinction,' he once wrote, 'I am always forced to have something in mind about which to write.' We all heard him say this, in paraphrase, a dozen times.

"In all Benchley, a fresh wind stirs in every page. In all his books, you find him ducking swiftly, looking closely, writing sharply."

ROBERT BENCHLEY

1889–1945

By producing a vast number of humorous essays that generally focused on ordinary situations, Robert Benchley established himself as one of the most popular and most prolific humorists of the modern age.

Benchley was born in Massachusetts and educated at Harvard. Following his graduation, he went into journalism and eventually became the managing editor of the respected magazine *Vanity Fair.* Later in his career, he served as the drama critic for both *Life* and *The New Yorker.*

During the course of his life, Benchley produced a large number of collections of essays, including *Pluck and Luck* (1925), *20,000 Leagues Under the Sea, or David Copperfield* (1928), *From Bed to Worse, or Comforting the Bison* (1934), *My Ten Years in the Quandry, and How They Grew* (1936), and *Benchley Beside Himself* (1943). Following his death, Benchley's work remained popular, and a number of posthumous collections were published. These books include *Chips off the Old Benchley* (1949) and *The Benchley Round-Up* (1954).

The many reviews Benchley wrote as a drama critic for *The New Yorker* reveal his direct and down-to-earth brand of humor. In 1935 he described the drama review department as being

> run solely as a superficial guide to readers—if anything. Certain readers who know its departmental likes and dislikes may be able to gather, from a close study of the page, whether or not they might like the show under discussion. As often as not the decision might be: "If he likes it, I'm not going to waste my money on it." . . .
>
> The only vestige of conscientiousness that goes into these reviews is that if we leave the show early, we make a note of the fact for our readers' information, and if we doze off, we also indicate it as part of the record of our reactions to that particular production. . . .
>
> Aside from these slight points of professional honor, there is nothing which goes into the making of this page which is any different from what any ordinary theatergoer would put into it if talking about the theater at dinner. Any attempt to intimidate us into a more serious attitude will be held as an infringement of the Freedom of the Press.

Objectives

1 To understand an informal essay
2 To evaluate the effectiveness of an essay
3 To write an informal essay

Support Material

Teaching Portfolio
Teacher Backup, p. 993
Grammar in Action Worksheet, *Changing Point of View and Changing Verb Tense,* p. 997
Usage and Mechanics Worksheet, p. 999
Vocabulary Check, p. 1000
Analyzing Literature Worksheet, *Understanding Informal Essays,* p. 1001

Language Worksheet, *Recognizing Colloquial Language,* p. 1002
Selection Test, p. 1003

GUIDE FOR INTERPRETING

The Tooth, the Whole Tooth, and Nothing but the Tooth

Literary Forms

Informal Essays. Like other types of essays, informal essays are short prose works that generally focus on a narrow topic. However, unlike formal essays, which are dignified in style and serious in tone, informal essays are written in a relaxed, intimate, conversational style. Informal essays also tend to be more loosely organized and less serious in purpose than formal essays. While formal essays are written to inform, instruct, or persuade, informal essays are written to amuse and entertain. Often informal essays attempt to evoke laughter, either by exploring an amusing subject or by treating a serious subject in a humorous manner. For example, "The Tooth, the Whole Tooth, and Nothing but the Tooth" extracts humor from the seemingly unpleasant subject of dental problems.

Commentary

If you have ever had to explain a joke to someone, you know why many people believe that humor can only be experienced, and not explained. For example, E. B. White, a witty humorist as well as essayist, wrote, "Humor can be dissected, as a frog can, but the thing dies in the process." Benchley would have agreed with White's reluctance to analyze how humor works. "It is a dangerous thing to attempt to analyze and describe the humor of any writer so that your audience will see that he is humorous," he wrote in *Books and Other Things* (1921). "In fact, it is a dangerous thing to attempt to analyze humor at all. For, by the time you have taken a sentence and pointed out the humorous part and classified it and explained why it is humorous, it dies on you like a fish held too long out of water. And the chances are that the person to whom you have been explaining it won't think it is funny anyway."

However, understanding how a humorist creates his effects can lead to a greater appreciation. One common technique is to put together incongruous elements. Benchley does this right from the start when he takes what for most people is a serious situation—going to the dentist—and writes about it as an event of high comedy. Another technique humorists use is overstatement. Benchley's description of the "appalling moment" when you discover you need a new filling is a good example of overstatement. As you read, notice other passages where Benchley joins incongruous elements or uses overstatement. You might also list other ways he creates humor.

Writing

In "The Tooth, the Whole Tooth, and Nothing but the Tooth," Benchley suggests that most people dread visiting the dentist. Do you agree? Freewrite about dental visits, discussing people's responses to dental visits and exploring the reasons for these responses.

Guide for Interpreting 769

Literary Focus Have students try to come up with appropriate topics for an informal essay. Remind them that the purpose of this type of essay is to amuse or entertain.

Writing/Prior Knowledge Students may wish to start off with a list of words—nouns, verbs, adjectives, and adverbs—that they associate with visits to a dentist. From there students might focus on thoughts they commonly have while sitting in a dentist's waiting room. Do they ever consider the thoughts of the people waiting around them? Have students' attitudes toward dental visits changed since they were younger, or are they basically the same?

Vocabulary

Preteach the following vocabulary words:
obnoxious (əb näk′ shəs) *adj.:* Very unpleasant; objectionable (p. 770)
inscrutable (in skr$\overline{oo}$t′ ə b'l) *adj.:* Not easily understood (p. 770)
dissolutely (dis′ə l$\overline{oo}$t′ lē) *adv.:* Immorally and shamelessly (p. 774)
accost (ə kôst′) *v.:* To approach and speak to in an intrusive way (p. 774)

The Tooth, the Whole Tooth, and Nothing but the Tooth

Robert Benchley

1   Some well-known saying (it doesn't make much difference what) is proved by the fact that everyone likes to talk about his experiences at the dentist's. For years and years little articles like this have been written on the subject, little jokes like some that I shall presently make have been made, and people in general have been telling other people just what emotions they experience when they crawl into the old red plush guillotine.[1]

2   They like to explain to each other how they feel when the dentist puts "that buzzer thing" against their bicuspids,[2] and, if sufficiently pressed, they will describe their sensations on mouthing a rubber dam.

"I'll tell you what I hate," they will say with great relish, "when he takes that little nut-pick and begins to scrape. Ugh!"

"Oh, I'll tell you what's worse than that," says the friend, not to be outdone, "when he is poking around careless-like, and strikes a nerve. Wow!"

3   And if there are more than two people at the experience-meeting, everyone will chip in and tell what he or she considers to be the worst phase of the dentist's work, all present enjoying the narration hugely and none so much as the narrator who has suffered so.

This sort of thing has been going on ever since the first mammoth gold tooth was hung out as a bait to folks in search of a good time. (By the way, when *did* the present obnoxious system of dentistry begin? It can't be so very long ago that the electric auger[3] was invented, and where would a dentist be without an electric auger? Yet you never hear of Amalgam[4] Filling Day, or any other anniversary in the dental year. There must be a conspiracy of silence on the part of the trade to keep hidden the names of the men who are responsible for all this.)

4   However many years it may be that dentists have been plying their trade, in all that time people have never tired of talking about their teeth. This is probably due to the inscrutable workings of Nature who is always supplying new teeth to talk about.

As a matter of fact, the actual time and suffering in the chair is only a fraction of the gross expenditure connected with the affair. The preliminary period, about which nobody talks, is much the worse. This dates from the discovery of the wayward tooth and extends to the moment when the dentist places his foot on the automatic hoist which jacks

---

1. guillotine (gil′ ə tēn′) *n.*: An instrument for beheading by means of a heavy blade dropped between two grooved uprights.
2. bicuspids (bī kus′ pids) *n.*: Eight adult teeth with two-pointed crowns.

3. auger (ô′ gər) *n.*: A tool used for drilling teeth.
4. amalgam (ə mal′ gəm) *n.*: An alloy of mercury used with silver as a dental filling.

you up into range. Giving gas for tooth-extraction is all very humane in its way, but the time for anaesthetics is when the patient first decides that he must go to the dentist. From then on, until the first excavation is started, should be shrouded in oblivion.

There is probably no moment more appalling than that in which the tongue, running idly over the teeth in a moment of carefree play, comes suddenly upon the ragged edge of a space from which the old familiar filling has disappeared. The world stops and you look meditatively up to the corner of the ceiling. Then quickly you draw your tongue away, and try to laugh the affair off, saying to yourself:

"Stuff and nonsense, my good fellow! There is nothing the matter with your tooth. Your nerves are upset after a hard day's work, that's all."

5

The Tooth, the Whole Tooth, and Nothing but the Tooth 771

6 Discussion How long might it take in real life to come to this conclusion? Why does Benchley stretch the moment out, making it seem longer than it actually is?

7 Discussion Is Benchley's humor directed more at people who like to rationalize their actions, at people who procrastinate, or at both? Explain.

8 Reading Strategy How many days will have passed between the first sign of the toothache and the actual appointment with a dentist?

9 Critical Thinking and Reading Do Benchley's exaggerations become bigger, smaller, or stay the same as the day of his dental appointment draws near?

Having decided this to your satisfaction, you slyly, and with a poor attempt at being casual, slide the tongue back along the line of adjacent teeth, hoping against hope that it will reach the end without mishap.

But there it is! There can be no doubt about it this time. The tooth simply has got to be filled by someone, and the only person who can fill it with anything permanent is a dentist. You wonder if you might not be able to patch it up yourself for the time being—a year or so—perhaps with a little spruce gum and a coating of new skin. It is fairly far back, and wouldn't have to be a very sightly job.

But this has an impracticable sound, even to you. You might want to eat some peanut brittle (you never can tell when someone might offer you peanut brittle these days), and the new skin, while serviceable enough in the case of cream soups and custards, couldn't be expected to stand up under heavy crunching.

6 So you admit that, since the thing has got to be filled, it might as well be a dentist who does the job.

This much decided, all that is necessary is to call him up and make an appointment.

Let us say that this resolve is made on Tuesday. That afternoon you start to look up the dentist's number in the telephone book. A great wave of relief sweeps over you when you discover that it isn't there. How can you be expected to make an appointment with a man who hasn't got a telephone? And how can you have a tooth filled without making an appointment? The whole thing is impossible, and that's all there is to it. God knows you did your best.

On Wednesday there is a slightly more insistent twinge, owing to bad management of a sip of ice-water. You decide that you simply must get in touch with that dentist when you get back from lunch. But you know how those things are. First one thing and then another came up, and a man came in from Providence who had to be shown around the office, and by the time you had a minute to yourself it was five o'clock. And,

772   The Modern Age

anyway, the tooth didn't bother you again. You wouldn't be surprised if, by being careful, you could get along with it as it is until the end of the week when you will have more time. A man has to think of his business, after all, and what is a little personal discomfort in the shape of an unfilled tooth to the satisfaction of work well done in the office? **7**

By Saturday morning you are fairly reconciled to going ahead, but it is only a half day and probably he has no appointments left, anyway. Monday is really the time. You can begin the week afresh. After all, Monday is really the logical day to start in going to the dentist.

Bright and early Monday morning you make another try at the telephone book, and find, to your horror, that some time between now and last Tuesday the dentist's name and number have been inserted into the directory. There it is. There is no getting around it: "Burgess, Jas. Kendal, DDS. . . . Courtland—2654." There is really nothing left to do but to call him up. Fortunately the line is busy, which gives you a perfectly good excuse for putting it over until Tuesday. But on Tuesday luck is against you and you get a clear connection with the doctor himself. An appointment is arranged for Thursday afternoon at 3:30. **8**

Thursday afternoon, and here it is only Tuesday morning! Almost anything may happen between now and then. We might declare war on Mexico, and off you'd have to go, dentist appointment or no dentist appointment. Surely a man couldn't let a date to have a tooth filled stand in the way of his doing his duty to his country. Or the social revolution might start on Wednesday, and by Thursday the whole town might be in ashes. You can picture yourself standing, Thursday afternoon at 3:30, on the ruins of the city hall, fighting off marauding bands of reds, and saying to yourself, with a sigh of relief: "Only to think! At this time I was to have been climbing into the dentist's chair!" You never can tell when your luck will turn in a thing like that. **9**

But Wednesday goes by and nothing

Grammar in Action

Robert Benchley's essay is clearly based on his personal experiences with dentistry, yet he has created special effects through the use of special grammatical techniques. Notice that Benchley rarely mentions himself, and when he does, it is only as the chronicler of the essay's events. The first seven paragraphs are written in the third person, their subjects being *everybody* and *people*. Through this technique, Benchley stresses the universal nature of the experiences he will describe. In the eighth paragraph, however, Benchley changes to the second-person narrative form, addressing the reader directly as *you.*

Student Activity 1. Look through the essay and answer the following questions.
1. Where does Benchley speak in his own voice? What is the effect of these "intrusions"?
2. Where does Benchley change back from the second-person to the third-person form? Explain why he does so.

happens. And Thursday morning dawns without even a word from the dentist saying that he has been called suddenly out of town to lecture before the Incisor[5] Club. Apparently, everything is working against you.

By this time, your tongue has taken up a permanent resting place in the vacant tooth, and is causing you to talk indistinctly and incoherently. Somehow you feel that if the dentist opens your mouth and finds the tip of your tongue in the tooth, he will be deceived and go away without doing anything.

The only thing left is for you to call him up and say that you have just killed a man and are being arrested and can't possibly keep your appointment. But any dentist would see through that. He would laugh right into his transmitter at you. There is probably no excuse which it would be possible to invent which a dentist has not already heard eighty or ninety times. No, you might as well see the thing through now.

Luncheon is a ghastly rite. The whole left side of your jaw has suddenly developed an acute sensitiveness and the disaffection has spread to the four teeth on either side of the original one. You doubt if it will be possible for him to touch it at all. Perhaps all he intends to do this time is to look at it anyway. You might even suggest that to him. You could very easily come in again soon and have him do the actual work.

Three-thirty draws near. A horrible time of day at best. Just when a man's vitality is lowest. Before stepping in out of the sunlight into the building in which the dental parlor is, you take one look about you at the happy people scurrying by in the street. Carefree children that they are! What do they know of Life? Probably that man in the silly-looking hat never had trouble with so much as his baby teeth. There they go, pushing and jostling each other, just as if within ten feet of them there was not a man who stands on the brink of the Great Misadventure. Ah well! Life is like that!

---

5. incisor (in sī′zər) *n.*: A front tooth.

Into the elevator. The last hope is gone. The door clangs and you look hopelessly about you at the stupid faces of your fellow passengers. How can people be so clownish? Of course, there is always the chance that the elevator will fall and that you will all be terribly hurt. But that is too much to expect. You dismiss it from your thoughts as too impractical, too visionary. Things don't work out as happily as that in real life.

You feel a certain glow of heroic pride when you tell the operator the right floor number. You might just as easily have told him a floor too high or too low, and that would, at least, have caused delay. But after all, a man must prove himself a man and the least you can do is to meet Fate with an unflinching eye and give the right floor number.

Too often has the scene in the dentist's waiting room been described for me to try to do it again here. They are all alike. The antiseptic smell, the ominous hum from the operating rooms, the ancient *Digest*s, and the silent, sullen group of waiting patients, each trying to look unconcerned and cordially disliking everyone else in the room—all these have been sung by poets of far greater lyric powers than mine. (Not that I really think that they *are* greater than mine, but that's the customary form of excuse for not writing something you haven't got time or space to do. As a matter of fact, I think I could do it much better than it has ever been done before.)

I can only say that, as you sit looking, with unseeing eyes, through a large book entitled *The War in Pictures*, you would gladly change places with the most lowly of God's creatures. It is inconceivable that there should be anyone worse off than you, unless perhaps it is some of the poor wretches who are waiting with you.

That one over in the armchair, nervously tearing to shreds a copy of *The Dental Review and Practical Inlay Worker*. She may have something frightful the trouble with her. She couldn't possibly look more worried. Perhaps it is very, very painful. This

10 Discussion What is Benchley implying about self-pity in this paragraph? How does he get his point across?

11 Discussion Why does Benchley think the people in the waiting room dislike one another?

10

11

Student Activity 2. Benchley also uses an unusual tense form in his essay. Explain why the present tense with second-person narration is more effective for this essay than the past tense with first-person narration would have been.

Student Activity 3. Try Benchley's technique by changing the following first-person, past-tense sentences to the second person and the present tense.
1. As the bus driver glared up at me, I frantically searched my pockets.
2. All too soon, I realized that in my hurry to get to the record store before it closed, I had left all my change in my painting pants.
3. Quickly I scanned the aisle, hoping that I would spot a familiar face.
4. I realized, too, that I was avoiding the accusatory eyes of the driver.
5. Suddenly the bus's engine sputtered and died, and as the driver turned to scrutinize the blinking lights on the panel in front of him, I backed out of the bus.

Student Activity 4. Apply the technique of writing in the second person and the present tense to one of your own descriptions of a personal experience or a dream.

12 **Critical Thinking and Reading**
What is Benchley comparing a visit to the dentist with in this passage?

13 **Discussion** What has led to the patient's change of mood? Is this realistic? In what ways is this paragraph exaggerated?

Reader's Response How do you feel about visiting the dentist? Do you agree or disagree with Benchley's essay? Why?

thought cheers you up considerably. What cowards women are in times like these!

And then there comes the sound of voices from the next room.

"All right, Doctor, and if it gives me any more pain shall I call you up? . . . Do you think that it will bleed much more? . . . Saturday morning, then, at eleven. . . . Goodbye, Doctor."

And a middle-aged woman emerges (all women are middle-aged when emerging from the dentist's office) looking as if she were playing the big emotional scene in *John Ferguson*.[6] A wisp of hair waves dissolutely across her forehead between her eyes. Her face is pale, except for a slight inflammation at the corners of her mouth, and in her eyes is that far-away look of one who has been face to face with Life. But she is through. She should care how she looks.

The nurse appears, and looks inquiringly at each one in the room. Each one in the room evades the nurse's glance in one last, futile attempt to fool someone and get away without seeing the dentist. But she spots you and nods pleasantly. God, how pleasantly she nods! There ought to be a law against people being as pleasant as that.

"The doctor will see you now," she says.

The English language may hold a more disagreeable combination of words than "The doctor will see you now." I am willing to concede something to the phrase "Have you anything to say before the current is turned on." That may be worse for the moment, but it doesn't last so long. For continued, unmitigating depression, I know nothing to equal "The doctor will see you now." But I'm not narrow-minded about it. I'm willing to consider other possibilities.

Smiling feebly, you trip over the extended feet of the man next to you, and stagger into the delivery room, where amid a ghastly array of death-masks of teeth, blue flames waving eerily from Bunsen burners,

---

6. *John Ferguson:* A play by Irish playwright St. John Ervine.

and the drowning sound of perpetually running water which chokes and gurgles at intervals, you sink into the chair and close your eyes.

But now let us consider the spiritual exaltation that comes when you are at last let down and turned loose. It is all over, and what did it amount to? Why, nothing at all. A-ha-ha-ha-ha-ha! Nothing at all.

You suddenly develop a particular friendship for the dentist. A splendid fellow, really. You ask him questions about his instruments. What does he use this thing for, for instance? Well, well, to think of a little thing like that making all that trouble. A-ha-ha-ha-ha-ha! . . . And the dentist's family, how are they? Isn't that fine!

Gaily you shake hands with him and straighten your tie. Forgotten is the fact that you have another appointment with him for Monday. There is no such thing as Monday. You are through for today, and all's right with the world.

As you pass out through the waiting room, you leer at the others unpleasantly. The poor fishes! Why can't they take their medicine like grown people and not sit there moping as if they were going to be shot?

Heigh-ho! Here's the elevator man! A charming fellow! You wonder if he knows that you have just had a tooth filled. You feel tempted to tell him and slap him on the back. You feel tempted to tell everyone out in the bright, cheery street. And what a wonderful street it is too! All full of nice, black snow and water. After all, Life is sweet!

And then you go and find the first person whom you can accost without being arrested and explain to him just what it was that the dentist did to you, and how you felt, and what you have got to have done next time.

Which brings us right back to where we were in the beginning, and perhaps accounts for everyone's liking to divulge their dental secrets to others. It may be a sort of hysterical relief that, for the time being, it is all over with.

Recalling

1. According to Benchley, about what does everyone like to talk?
2. (a) What is a person's immediate reaction to the discovery that a "filling has disappeared"? (b) How does the person manage to put off making an appointment to have the filling replaced? (c) How does the person imagine that he or she might be prevented from keeping the appointment?
3. What observation does Benchley make concerning dentist's waiting rooms?
4. What does Benchley view as the most disagreeable combination of words "for continued, unmitigating depression"?
5. How does a person react when his or her dental work has been completed?

Interpreting

6. (a) Why is the person so reluctant to visit the dentist? (b) Why is the person ultimately so eager to tell others about his or her visit?
7. (a) How does the person's disposition change once the dental work has been completed? (b) What is amusing about this change?

Applying

8. This essay was written before World War II. (a) How do you think people's responses to visiting the dentist have changed since then? (b) What do you think accounts for these changes?

ANALYZING LITERATURE

Understanding Informal Essays

An **informal essay** is a short prose work in which the writer uses a conversational style and a light, personal tone. Informal essays tend to be loosely organized, with the writer at times straying from the topic or interrupting the narrative flow to express related observations or opinions.

1. How does Benchley establish a light, informal tone in the first paragraph?
2. How does he maintain a personal tone throughout the remainder of the essay?
3. Find two instances in which Benchley interrupts the narrative flow to present a related opinion or observation.

CRITICAL THINKING AND READING

Evaluating an Essay

"The Tooth, the Whole Tooth, and Nothing but the Tooth" was clearly written to entertain readers and evoke laughter. For the essay to be successful, the reader must be familiar with the situation it depicts and be able to relate to the reaction it describes and to the attitude it expresses.

1. Explain whether or not you find this essay to be humorous.
2. In what ways is your own attitude toward dental visits similar to and different from the attitude expressed in the essay?
3. How do you think your attitude toward dental visits affected your appreciation of the essay?
4. Do you think this essay is less effective now than when it was written? Why or why not?

THINKING AND WRITING

Writing an Informal Essay

Imagine that your school literary magazine is having a contest to see who can write the best humorous informal essay. Think of an experience which most people dread. Then write an essay in which you describe this experience and people's responses to it in a humorous manner. When you revise, make sure that you have used a conversational style and a humorous tone.

Closure and Extension

ANSWERS TO THINKING ABOUT THE SELECTION
Recalling

1. Everyone likes to talk about their experiences at the dentist.
2. (a) The world stops and you look meditatively up to the corner of the ceiling. Then quickly you draw your tongue away and try to laugh the affair off. (b) The person cannot find the dentist's number in the phone book. (c) Too many "important" things are going on at work.
3. They are all alike, with an antiseptic smell, the ominous hum from the operating rooms, the ancient *Digests,* and the silent, sullen group of waiting patients.
4. "The doctor will see you now."
5. He or she becomes more talkative and friendly toward the dentist.

Interpreting

6. (a) The expectation of what will happen at the dentist's office inspires fear. (b) It probably makes them feel better to share their experiences with others.
7. (a) The person's mood improves dramatically. (b) There seemed to be no reason for the reluctance and fear in the first place.

Applying

8. (a) Suggested Response: People are less reluctant to visit the dentist. (b) Suggested Response: The improvements in dental technology account for this change.

Challenge What are some other topics about which Benchley and his readers might have had similar reactions?

ANSWERS TO ANALYZING LITERATURE

1. Benchley establishes an informal tone by using the first person, inserting a parenthetical statement, and by casually referring to a dentist chair as "the old red plush guillotine."
2. Suggested Response: He uses the second person, seemingly addressing each separate reader.
3. Any parenthetical statements in the essay can serve as correct answers.

ANSWERS TO CRITICAL THINKING AND READING

1. Suggested Response: It is humorous because nearly everyone hates visiting the dentist.
2. Answers will differ. Students might comment that they do not dread visiting the dentist as much as Benchley did.
3. Suggested Response: Someone who does not dislike visiting the dentist will not appreciate the essay.
4. Suggested Response: The essay is less effective, because advances in dental technology have made visits to the dentist less unpleasant.

THINKING AND WRITING

Publishing Student Writing For extra credit, have students reshape their essays into short, comical skits that can be performed in the classroom.

More About the Author James Thurber tended to write humorously about the average man and his harrowing experiences in the modern world. Dominating women and mischievous children continuously frighten and frustrate the oversensitive male characters in Thurber's stories. For example, in Thurber's most famous short story, "The Secret Life of Walter Mitty," Mitty escapes his nagging wife through his daydreams in which he always imagines himself to be a fearless hero. In "The Night the Ghost Got In," how do the ways in which the various characters cope with their environment create a humorous atmosphere?

Critical Evaluation In his introduction to *Thurber: A Collection of Critical Essays,* Charles S. Holmes made the following assessment of Thurber's work: "It is by now a truism to say that James Thurber is the greatest American humorist since Mark Twain. His imagination was tuned to the discords of the twentieth century with preternatural accuracy. In his stories, essays, and drawings we find comic images of our public and private apprehensions: the character of Walter Mitty, as *Time* magazine once said, stands with Leopold Bloom and Hans Castorp as an archetype of modern man. Malcolm Cowley called his prose style one of the best in modern literature, and *The Times Literary Supplement* observed that almost alone among living American writers, he was as 'comprehensible and lovable to the European mind as . . . to the mind of his countrymen.' His first book, *Is Sex Necessary?,* written in collaboration with his friend E.B. White, was a best seller, and throughout his long career he enjoyed a steadily increasing popularity with high and middlebrow readers. . . ."

JAMES THURBER

1894–1961

A noted humorist, James Thurber wrote essays and short stories that generally evolved from his own experiences. In his humorous autobiographical sketches, such as "The Night the Ghost Got In," Thurber embellished the facts and described events in an amusing manner. In his short stories, Thurber created characters who struggled awkwardly against the unpleasant realities of life.

Born in Columbus, Ohio, Thurber attended Ohio State University. Following his graduation, he began a career in journalism, accepting a job as a newspaper reporter in Columbus. In 1927 he joined the staff of the magazine *The New Yorker*. Thurber remained associated with *The New Yorker* for the remainder of his life, contributing stories, essays, and cartoons. At *The New Yorker* he also worked closely with the celebrated writer E. B. White, who influenced his writing. Thurber, White, and other *New Yorker* writers such as Frank Sullivan, Robert Benchley, and S. J. Perelman helped establish a grand tradition of modern American humor. Thurber has written of humor, "Humor is emotional chaos remembered in tranquility." He has also written, "As brevity is the soul of wit, form, it seems to me, is the heart of humor and the salvation of comedy."

During the course of his career, Thurber published a great many books. Some of his books, such as *The Owl in the Attic and Other Perplexities* (1931) and *The Seal in the Bedroom and Other Predicaments* (1932), contain a mixture of short stories, parodies, and cartoons. Other books, including *My Life and Hard Times,* are composed of sketches about his childhood. He also wrote children's stories and collaborated with Elliot Nugent in writing a successful play, *The Male Animal* (1940). Thurber's best-known work is his short story, "The Secret Life of Walter Mitty," which was first published in *The New Yorker* in 1939.

"The Secret Life of Walter Mitty" is characteristic of Thurber's humor. It is the story of a middle-aged man who, unhappy with his everyday life, quietly dreams a life of adventure and heroism for himself. In all of Thurber's most humorous pieces, unhappiness is never far away. Commenting on how humorists get their inspiration, Thurber said, "The little wheels of invention are set in motion by the damp hand of melancholy." The characters in Thurber's essays, stories, and drawings seem to accept the puzzling difficulties of their lives with resignation, even as they explore little escapes.

During the last twenty years of his life, Thurber's vision failed, and he eventually became completely blind. He continued to write and draw as well as he could. Yet his later work is often tinged with a sense of bitterness.

776   *The Modern Age*

Objectives

1 To appreciate humor
2 To recognize exaggeration
3 To write a humorous essay

Support Material

Teaching Portfolio

Teacher Backup, p. 1005
Grammar in Action Worksheet, *Identifying Logical Order,* p. 1009
Usage and Mechanics Worksheet, p. 1011
Vocabulary Check, p. 1012
Analyzing Literature Worksheet, *Understanding Humor,* p. 1013

Critical Thinking and Reading Worksheet, *Recognizing Exaggeration* p. 1014
Selection Test, p. 1015

GUIDE FOR INTERPRETING

The Night the Ghost Got In

Humor. In literature, humor refers to writing that attempts to evoke laughter. To accomplish this purpose, writers must have the ability to perceive the ridiculous, comical, or ludicrous aspects of an incident, situation, or personality and to depict them in an amusing manner. In "The Night the Ghost Got In," for example, Thurber captures the humorous idiosyncrasies of his family members in depicting an amusing, chaotic series of events.

Humorists often exaggerate details and embellish facts in their work. By using exaggeration, a writer can make an amusing event or character seem even more humorous, or a writer can use exaggeration to create humor in an otherwise unamusing situation. For example, in "The Night the Ghost Got In," Thurber uses exaggeration to accentuate the amusing character traits of his family members.

Another technique frequently used by humorists is malapropism—the humorous misuse of words. For example, instead of having a character say that someone "*instigated* a riot," a writer might have the character comment that someone "*insinuated* a riot."

Commentary

In narrating the chaotic events that take place in his house in "The Night the Ghost Got In," Thurber never seems to lose his head. In fact, in reading the story, you may find Thurber's responses to be humorously understated. A houseful of policemen, several mischievous ghosts, a hysterical mother, a grandfather who thinks he is being attacked by "Meade's army" and shoots in defense—these elicit no more emotional a comment than "When I got to the attic, things were pretty confused."

Writing about this typically Thurberesque response to upheaval, critic James D. Hart wrote that Thurber's "fantastic people and animals move with sad persistence through incredible upsets, and are all misshapen and repressed, products of a malignant fate which they stoically survive or combat." Everyone in this story seems a little bizarre, but Thurber suggests that that is because life is very bizarre. The way to arrive at the position of calm and acceptance occupied by Thurber's narrator in this story is to learn to accept that, as the old saying goes, truth is stranger than fiction.

Do you know of true incidents that are "stranger than fiction"?

Writing

Why do we laugh when someone slips on a banana peel? Why do we find it funny when someone is hit in the face by a custard pie? Freewrite, exploring your ideas on what makes someone laugh.

Literary Focus Thurber uses humor in describing most any situation. Simple descriptions are exaggerated or embellished with humorous anecdotes or amusing character traits.

Writing/Prior Knowledge Students may wish to begin by listing some of their humorous experiences. They can then describe some of these experiences in their freewriting.

Vocabulary

Preteach the following vocabulary words:
intuitively (in to͞o′ i tiv lē) *adj.:* Instinctively (p. 779)
blaspheming (blas fēm′ iŋ) *v.:* Cursing (p. 782)

The Night the Ghost Got In

James Thurber

1 The ghost that got into our house on the night of November 17, 1915, raised such a hullabaloo of misunderstandings that I am sorry I didn't just let it keep on walking, and go to bed. Its advent caused my mother to throw a shoe through a window of the house next door and ended up with my grandfather shooting a patrolman. I am sorry, therefore, as I have said, that I ever paid any attention to the footsteps.

They began about a quarter past one o'clock in the morning, a rhythmic, quick-cadenced walking around the dining-room table. My mother was asleep in one room upstairs, my brother Herman in another; grandfather was in the attic, in the old walnut bed which, as you will remember, once fell on my father. I had just stepped out of the bathtub and was busily rubbing myself with a towel when I heard the steps. They were the steps of a man walking rapidly around the dining-room table downstairs. The light from the bathroom shone down the back steps, which dropped directly into the dining-room; I could see the faint shine of plates on the plate-rail; I couldn't see the table. The steps kept going round and round the table; at regular intervals a board creaked, when it was trod upon. I supposed at first that it was my father or my brother Roy, who had gone to Indianapolis but were expected home at any time. I suspected next

THE NIGHT THE GHOST GOT IN
Copyright © 1933, 1961, James Thurber,
From My Life and Hard Times,
published by Harper & Row.

"The ghost got into our house on the night of November 17, 1915 and raised such a hullabaloo of misunderstandings. . . ."

that it was a burglar. It did not enter my mind until later that it was a ghost.

After the walking had gone on for perhaps three minutes, I tiptoed to Herman's room. "Psst!" I hissed, in the dark, shaking him. "Awp," he said, in the low, hopeless tone of a despondent beagle—he always half suspected that something would "get him" in the night. I told him who I was. "There's something downstairs!" I said. He got up and followed me to the head of the back staircase. We listened together. There was no sound. The steps had ceased. Herman looked at me in some alarm: I had only the bath towel around my waist. He wanted to go back to bed, but I gripped his arm. "There's something down there!" I said. Instantly the steps began again, circled the dining-room table like a man running, and started up the stairs toward us, heavily, two at a time. The light still shone palely down the stairs; we saw nothing coming; we only heard the steps. Herman rushed to his room and slammed the door. I slammed shut the door at the stairs top and held my knee against it. After a long minute, I slowly opened it again. There was nothing there. There was no sound. None of us ever heard the ghost again.

The slamming of the doors had aroused mother: she peered out of her room. "What on earth are you boys doing?" she demanded. Herman ventured out of his room. "Nothing," he said, gruffly, but he was, in color, a light green. "What was all that running around downstairs?" said mother. So she had heard the steps, too! We just looked at her. "Burglars!" she shouted intuitively. I tried to quiet her by starting lightly downstairs.

"Come on, Herman," I said.

2 "I'll stay with Mother," he said. "She's all excited."

I stepped back onto the landing.

3 "Don't either of you go a step," said mother. "We'll call the police." Since the phone was downstairs, I didn't see how we were going to call the police—nor did I want the police—but mother made one of her quick, incomparable decisions. She flung up a window of her bedroom which faced the bedroom windows of the house of a neighbor, picked up a shoe, and whammed it through a pane of glass across the narrow space that separated the two houses. Glass tinkled into the bedroom occupied by a retired engraver named Bodwell and his wife. Bodwell had been for some years in rather a bad way and was subject to mild "attacks." Most everybody we knew or lived near had *some* kind of attacks.

It was now about two o'clock of a moonless night; clouds hung black and low. Bodwell was at the window in a minute, shouting, frothing a little, shaking his fist. "We'll sell the house and go back to Peoria," we could hear Mrs. Bodwell saying. It was some time before mother "got through" to Bodwell. "Burglars!" she shouted. "Burglars in the house!" Herman and I hadn't dared to tell her that it was not burglars but ghosts, for she was even more afraid of ghosts than of burglars. Bodwell at first thought that she meant there were burglars in his house, but finally he quieted down and called the police for us over an extension phone by his bed. After he had disappeared from the window, mother suddenly made as if to throw another shoe, not because there was further need of it, but, as she later explained, because the thrill of heaving a shoe through a window glass had enormously taken her fancy. I prevented her.

4

The police were on hand in a commendably short time: a Ford sedan full of them, two on motorcycles, and a patrol wagon with about eight in it and a few reporters. They began banging at our front door. Flashlights shot streaks of gleam up and down the walls, across the yard, down the walk between our house and Bodwell's. "Open up!" cried a hoarse voice. "We're men from Headquarters!" I wanted to go down and let them in, since there they were, but mother wouldn't hear of it. "You haven't a stitch on," she pointed out. "You'd catch your death." I wound the towel around me again. Finally the cops put their shoulders to our big heavy

5

The Night the Ghost Got In 779

2 **Discussion** Why does Herman volunteer to stay with his mother?

3 **Literary Focus** What is amusing about the mother's reaction?

4 **Discussion** What does this reveal about the mother's personality?

5 **Critical Thinking and Reading** Why is this clearly an example of exaggeration?

THE NIGHT THE GHOST GOT IN
Copyright © 1933, 1961, James Thurber,
From My Life and Hard Times, published by
Harper & Row.

front door with its thick beveled glass and broke it in; I could hear a rending of wood and a splash of glass on the floor of the hall. Their lights played all over the living-room and crisscrossed nervously in the dining-room, stabbed into hallways, shot up the front stairs and finally up the back. They caught me standing in my towel at the top. A heavy policeman bounded up the steps. "Who are you?" he demanded. "I live here," I said. "Well, whattsa matta, ya hot?" he asked. I was, as a matter of fact, cold; I went to my room and pulled on some trousers. On my way out, a cop stuck a gun into my ribs. "Whatta you doin' here?" he demanded. "I live here," I said.

The officer in charge reported to mother. "No sign of nobody, lady," he said. "Musta got away—whatt'd he look like?" "There were two or three of them," mother said, "whooping and carrying on and slamming doors." "Funny, said the cop. "All ya windows and doors was locked on the inside tight as a tick."

Downstairs, we could hear the tromping of the other police. Police were all over the place; doors were yanked open, drawers were yanked open, windows were shot up and pulled down, furniture fell with dull thumps. A half-dozen policemen emerged out of the darkness of the front hallway upstairs. They began to ransack the floor: pulled beds away from walls, tore clothes off hooks in the closets, pulled suitcases and boxes off shelves. One of them found an old zither[1] that Roy had won in a pool tournament. "Looky here, Joe," he said, strumming it with a big paw. The cop named Joe took it and turned it over. "What is it?" he asked me. "It's an old zither our guinea pig used to sleep on," I said. It was true that a pet guinea pig we once had would never sleep anywhere except on the zither, but I should never have said so. Joe and the other cop looked at me a long time. They put the zither back on a shelf.

"No sign o' nuthin'," said the cop who

1. **zither** (zith'ər) n.: A musical instrument with thirty to forty strings stretched across a flat sound-board and played with the fingers.

Grammar in Action

A writer must arrange the evidence in a paragraph, or in an entire essay, in a **logical order.** The following are the most frequently used orders:

Chronological order, in which events are described in the sequence in which they happen
Spatial order, in which description moves from near to far, or top to bottom, or side to side

Order of importance, in which the evidence that is most compelling, most important, or most humorous is kept until the end of the paragraph or the essay
Order of comparison and contrast, in which similarities and differences are set against each other

Note that Thurber's paragraph which describes the arrival of the police, on page 779, is ordered by comparing and contrasting the activities of the methodical police with those of the zany family.

had first spoken to mother. "This guy," he explained to the others, jerking a thumb at me, "was nekked. The lady seems historical." They all nodded, but said nothing; just looked at me. In the small silence we all heard a creaking in the attic. Grandfather was turning over in bed. "What's 'at?" snapped Joe. Five or six cops sprang for the attic door before I could intervene or explain. I realized that it would be bad if they burst in on grandfather unannounced, or even announced. He was going through a phase in which he believed that General Meade's men, under steady hammering by Stonewall Jackson, were beginning to retreat and even desert.

When I got to the attic, things were pretty confused. Grandfather had evidently jumped to the conclusion that the police were deserters from Meade's army, trying to hide away in his attic. He bounded out of bed wearing a long flannel nightgown over long woolen underwear, a nightcap, and a leather jacket around his chest. The cops must have realized at once that the indignant white-haired old man belonged in the house, but they had no chance to say so. "Back, ye cowardly dogs!" roared grandfather. "Back t' the lines, ye yellow, lily-livered cattle!" With that, he fetched the officer who found the zither a flat-handed smack alongside his head that sent him sprawling. The others beat a retreat, but not fast enough; grandfather grabbed Zither's gun from its holster and let fly. The report seemed to crack the rafters; smoke filled the attic. A cop cursed and shot his hand to his shoulder. Somehow, we all finally got downstairs again and locked the door against the old gentleman. He fired once or twice more in the darkness and then went back to bed. "That was grandfather," I explained to Joe, out of breath. "He thinks you're deserters." "I'll say he does," said Joe.

THE NIGHT THE GHOST GOT IN
Copyright © 1933, 1961, James Thurber, From My Life and Hard Times, published by Harper & Row.

6 **Literary Focus** This is an example of a malapropism, or humorous misuse of words.

7 **Clarification** During the Civil War, Meade was a general for the Union army, while Jackson was a Confederate general.

8 **Literary Focus** Why is this incident humorous?

Humanities Note

Thurber created this sketch of policemen to illustrate this essay. With a minimum of lines, he has created a humorous picture of frantic activity. You might point out to students that Thurber is able to convey a variety of expressions with his simple line drawings.

You might use these questions for discussion.
1. What expressions are shown on each of the character's faces?
2. What contributes to the humor in this sketch?

Student Activity 1. Identify the type of order Thurber used in the paragraph describing the events in the attic (page 781).

Student Activity 2. Identify the type of order used in the following sequence of events from the essay.
1. The policeman finds the narrator without his pants on.
2. The narrator explains that the guinea pig used to sleep on the zither.
3. The narrator explains to the policemen that the grandfather thinks they are deserters.
4. The narrator tells the reporter there was a ghost.

Student Activity 3. Arrange by order importance the following pieces of evidence supporting the locking of cabinet doors against small children.
1. Children may find and handle poisonous substances.
2. Children don't like shoes and may hide them in cabinets.
3. Children may crawl into large cabinets and fall asleep; then you may think they are lost.
4. Children may take out your belongings and mix them up.
5. Children may take out your belongings and ruin them.

9 Discussion What is the significance of the grandfather's remark?

Reader's Response What did you find to be the most humorous point in this story? Explain.

The cops were reluctant to leave without getting their hands on somebody besides grandfather; the night had been distinctly a defeat for them. Furthermore, they obviously didn't like the "layout"; something looked—and I can see their viewpoint—phony. They began to poke into things again. A reporter, a thin-faced, wispy man, came up to me. I had put on one of mother's blouses, not being able to find anything else. The reporter looked at me with mingled suspicion and interest. "Just what the heck is the real lowdown here, Bud?" he asked. I decided to be frank with him. "We had ghosts," I said. He gazed at me a long time as if I were a slot machine into which he had, without results, dropped a nickel. Then he walked away. The cops followed him, the one grandfather shot holding his now-bandaged arm, cursing and blaspheming. "I'm gonna get my gun back from that old bird," said the zither-cop. "Yeh," said Joe. "You—and who else?" I told them I would bring it to the station house the next day.

"What was the matter with that one policeman?" mother asked, after they had gone. "Grandfather shot him," I said. "What for?" she demanded. I told her he was a deserter. "Of all things!" said mother. "He was such a nice-looking young man."

Grandfather was fresh as a daisy and full of jokes at breakfast next morning. We thought at first he had forgotten all about what had happened, but he hadn't. Over his third cup of coffee, he glared at Herman and me. "What was the idee of all them cops tarry-hootin' round the house last night?" he demanded. He had us there.

Commentary

People who do not write or draw are often curious about how writers and artists come up with ideas for their work. This amused Thurber a great deal, because often he did not come up with ideas for work but actually adjusted his ideas to match the work that appeared on the page. In a humorous essay called "The Lady on the Bookcase," Thurber described the role that accident and even confusion played in his creative process. He labeled this particular type of so-called inspiration the "Concept of the Purely Accidental and the Theory of Haphazard Determination." Under this category he put his famous drawing of a husband and wife in bed with a barking seal on the headboard.

In explaining how he came up with the drawing and caption, Thurber wrote, "The seal on top of the bed, then . . . started out to be a seal on a rock. The rock, in the process of being drawn, began to look like the head of a bed, so I made a bed out of it, put a man and wife in the bed, and stumbled onto the caption as easily and unexpectedly as the seal had stumbled into the bedroom."

"All right, have it your way—you heard a seal bark!"

Recalling

1. (a) What is Thurber doing when he hears the footsteps? (b) What do he and his brother do when they hear the steps coming toward them?
2. Why does Thurber's mother throw a shoe through the neighbors' window?
3. (a) Why will Thurber's mother not allow him to let the police in the house? (b) How do the police finally get in?
4. (a) How does Thurber's grandfather react when the police burst into his room? (b) What prompts this reaction?

Interpreting

5. What role does the lack of communication among the characters play in precipitating the events described?
6. (a) What does the mother's desire to throw a second shoe through the neighbors' window reveal about her character? (b) What does her response to her son's explanation of the grandfather's actions reveal about her character?
7. (a) What is surprising about the question the grandfather asks at breakfast the next morning? (b) What does it reveal about his character?
8. How is Thurber's depiction of himself different from his depiction of the other characters?

Applying

9. Thurber's stories are often filled with eccentrics—people whose idiosyncrasies or peculiarities make them humorously unique. How do people react to eccentrics in real life? Explain your answer.

ANALYZING LITERATURE

Understanding Humor

In literature, **humor** refers to writing which attempts to evoke laughter. Humorists achieve this purpose by depicting comical incidents, situations, or personalities. For example, in "The Night the Ghost Got In," Thurber describes an improbable and humorous series of events involving a number of unusual characters.

1. What makes Thurber's mother an unusual and amusing character?
2. What makes Thurber's grandfather an unusual and amusing character?
3. What is comical about the behavior of the police officers?
4. What malapropism, or humorous misuse of words, does the policeman commit when he describes the mother's behavior?
5. (a) What is the usual reaction to hearing footsteps in the middle of the night? (b) How does the contrast between the usual reaction and the Thurber family's reaction add to the humor of the story?

CRITICAL THINKING AND READING

Recognizing Exaggeration

Humorists often exaggerate details and embellish facts in their work. For example, Thurber clearly exaggerates the number of police officers who showed up at his house.

1. Do you think the actions of the police officers are exaggerated? Why or why not?
2. Do you think the grandfather's personality and behavior are exaggerated? Why or why not?

THINKING AND WRITING

Writing a Humorous Essay

Write an essay describing a humorous incident that you experienced. (If you like, you may make up the incident.) Freewrite, describing an unusual predicament. Then write your essay, using exaggeration to add to the humor of your story. When you finish writing, revise your essay, making sure you have related events in chronological order. Proofread your essay and share it with your classmates.

The Night the Ghost Got In 783

4. (a) He jumps out of bed and attacks them. (b) He jumps to the conclusion that the police are deserters from Meade's army.

Interpreting

5. A lack of communication between Thurber and his mother causes the entire sequence of events to occur.
6. (a) It reveals that she is somewhat irrational. (b) It shows that she is slightly out of touch with reality.
7. (a) It reveals that he was aware of the fact that the men who broke into his room were police officers. (b) It reveals that he is only feigning insanity.
8. He depicts himself as being the only person acting rationally.

Applying

9. Answers will differ. Students may suggest that most people believe that it is rude to laugh at other people's eccentricities.

ANSWERS TO ANALYZING LITERATURE

1. Her irrational behavior makes her an unusual and amusing character.
2. He appears to be completely out of touch with reality.
3. They behave in a highly exaggerated and incompetent manner.
4. He calls her historical instead of hysterical.
5. (a) The usual response is to call the police immediately. (b) The fact that the Thurbers' response is so totally different from the usual response adds to the humor of the story.

ANSWERS TO CRITICAL THINKING AND READING

1. Suggested Response: Yes, the police officers would not have stormed into the house the way that they did.
2. Suggested Response: Yes, the grandfather would not have shot one of the officers.

THINKING AND WRITING

Publishing Student Writing Encourage students to submit their essays to your school's literary magazine.

Closure and Extension

ANSWERS TO THINKING ABOUT THE SELECTION
Recalling

1. (a) He is taking a bath. (b) Herman ran into his room and slammed the door. Thurber slammed the door at the top of the stairs.

2. Because she thinks there are burglars downstairs, she does not want to go down to call the police on her phone. Instead, she wakes her neighbors by throwing a shoe through their window.
3. (a) She will not allow him to go downstairs, because he is only wearing a towel. (b) They break down the door.

More About the Author
Throughout his long career, Carl Sandburg's work reflected his two great desires: to discover the meaning of American history and to voice the concerns of the common people. As a young man, Sandburg traveled throughout the Midwest as a hobo. He later spent almost twenty years of his life as a newspaperman, primarily in Chicago. Why do you think so many literary figures have begun their careers in journalism?

Critical Evaluation The following is an excerpt from a review of Sandburg's biography written by Robert E. Sherwood:

"Twenty years ago Carl Sandburg of Illinois started to write the fullest, richest, most understanding of all the Lincoln biographies. His work is now complete. *The War Years* follows *The Prairie Years* into the treasure house which belongs, like Lincoln himself, to the whole human family. It has been a monumental undertaking; it is grandly realized.

". . . He indulges in one superb lyrical outburst at the conclusion of the chapter in which is described the dedication of the cemetery at Gettysburg; and, in the last volume, after John Wilkes Booth has fired the one bullet in his brass derringer pistol, Mr. Sandburg writes with the poetic passion and the somber eloquence of the great masters of tragedy."

CARL SANDBURG

1878–1967

Born to a family of poor Swedish immigrants in Illinois, where his father worked in the railroad yards, Sandburg left school at the age of thirteen to help support his family. During the next six years he worked as a milkman, a porter in a barber shop, a truck-handler in a brickyard, a dishwasher in Denver and Omaha hotels, and a harvest-hand in Kansas wheatfields. When the Spanish-American War broke out in 1898, Sandburg volunteered and was sent to Puerto Rico, where he enrolled in Lombard College and supported himself by working for the local fire department.

According to poet and critic Louis Untermeyer, "These tasks equipped him, as no amount of learning could have done, to be the laureate of industrial America." Taking as his subjects such unpoetic scenes as Chicago hogyards, a brickyard, or the limited express to Omaha, or writing about America's historical figures, Sandburg sought to be a writer for all the people. Claiming his role as the bard of the common people, he asked, "Who else speaks for the Family of Man? / They are in tune and step / with constellations of universal law." The dignity and strength of the American worker is a dominant theme in his work, as is the search for meaning in American history.

Although he is remembered mostly for his poetry, Carl Sandburg was also a well-known historical biographer. In fact, he wrote what is generally regarded as the definitive biography of Abraham Lincoln, a figure who to Sandburg represented the best of the American character. Sandburg spent thirty years working on this six-volume biography, compiling and organizing information. His collection of resource material grew so large that it outgrew the Lincoln room in his home and the barn had to be set aside for additional storage. The two volumes that comprise *Abraham Lincoln: The Prairie Years* deal with Lincoln's early career. The four volumes that comprise *Abraham Lincoln: The War Years* deal with the Lincoln presidency. Sandburg was rewarded for his efforts in 1940, when his historical biography earned him the Pulitzer Prize for history.

When he was seventy years old, Sandburg, already a famous poet and biographer, published his first book of fiction. Called *Remembrance Rock* (1948), it starts with the Pilgrims in seventeenth-century England, moves to the Revolution, and then westward and through the Civil War. Sandburg hoped the novel would weave "the mystery of the American Dream with the costly toil and bloody struggles that have gone to keep alive and carry farther that Dream."

784   *The Modern Age*

Support Material

Teaching Portfolio
Teacher Backup, p. 1017
Grammar in Action Worksheets, *Recognizing Inverted Word Order,* p. 1021; *Using Elliptical Clauses,* p. 1023
Usage and Mechanics Worksheet, p. 1025
Vocabulary Check, p. 1026
Analyzing Literature Worksheet,

Understanding Biography, p. 1028
Language Worksheet, *Building Words Using bene-,* p. 1029
Selection Test, p. 1030

GUIDE FOR INTERPRETING

Lincoln Speaks at Gettysburg

Literary Forms

Biography. A biography is an account of a person's life written by another person. After carefully researching the subject, a biographer recounts the central events of the subject's life—the events that make that person's life interesting or important. A biographer will also present interpretations of the events, attempting to explain the reasons for the subject's actions and meaning of their lives. For example, in the following chapter from *Abraham Lincoln: The War Years,* Sandburg provides insights into the events leading up to Lincoln's composing his famous Gettysburg Address.

Writing

Freewrite about a person you know or a celebrity you admire, focusing on the reasons why you find this person's life interesting.

Primary Source

In 1936 Sandburg wrote the following in his foreword to *Abraham Lincoln: The War Years*:

> In the story of a great struggle we meet gaps and discrepancies.
>
> How and why did men and women do what they did? And how can we be sure they did what the record may seem to show they did? And of what great war has the final story been written that clears all disputes as to how it moved and what came of it?
>
> If those who are gone who had their parts and roles in it could be summoned back to tell of the gaps and discrepancies, they might give unexpected answers to questions. And many witnesses on being dug up and given speech might again be as noncommittal as ever on this or that circumstance.
>
> This scroll presents events of wild passionate onrush side by side with cruel, grinding monotony—and second and third readings bring out things not seen at first.
>
> The chronicles are abstracted from a record so stupendous, so changing and tumultuous, that anyone dealing with the vast actual evidence cannot use the whole of it, nor tell any of the story.
>
> Supposing all could be told, it would take far longer time to tell it than was taken to act it in life.
>
> Therefore the teller does the best he can and picks what is to him plain, moving, and important—though sometimes gradually taking on interest, even mystery, because of the gaps and discrepancies.

Guide for Interpreting 785

Literary Focus A biography can be more than simply an organized account of the major events of a person's life. Many biographies are interpretive—that is, they use the events of someone's life as a way of focusing on issues that concern the author. Point out to students the ways in which Lincoln was an ideal subject for a writer with Sandburg's interests.

Writing/Prior Knowledge Before having students complete the writing assignment, spend some time discussing the qualities that make a person an appropriate subject for a biography.

Vocabulary

Preteach the following vocabulary words:

eminent (em′ ə nant) *adj.*: Distinguished (p. 786)

auspices (ôs′ pə sēz′) *n.*: Approval and support (p. 788)

demeaned (di mēn′d) *v.*: Behaved; conducted (p. 789)

sallow (sal′ ō) *adj.*: Of a sickly, pale-yellow hue (p. 790)

benevolent (be nev′ ə lənt) *adj.*: Kindly; charitable (p. 791)

sovereignty (säv′ rən tē) *n.*: Supreme and independent political authority (p. 792)

sepulcher (sep′′l kər) *n.*: Tomb (p. 792)

perfunctory (pər fuŋk′ tərē) *adj.*: Done without care or interest or merely as a form or routine (p. 793)

from Abraham Lincoln: The War Years

Carl Sandburg

Lincoln Speaks at Gettysburg

A printed invitation came to Lincoln's hands notifying him that on Thursday, November 19, 1863, exercises would be held for the dedication of a National Soldiers' Cemetery at Gettysburg. The same circular invitation had been mailed to Senators, Congressmen, the governors of northern states, members of the Cabinet, by the commission of Pennsylvanians who had organized a corporation through which Maine, New Hampshire, Vermont, Massachusetts, Rhode Island, Maryland, Connecticut, New York, New Jersey, Pennsylvania, Delaware, West Virginia, Ohio, Indiana, Illinois, Michigan, Wisconsin, and Minnesota were to share the cost of a decent burying ground for the dust and bones of the Union and Confederate dead.

In the helpless onrush of the war, it was known, too many of the fallen had lain as neglected cadavers rotting in the open fields or thrust into so shallow a resting place that a common farm plow caught in their bones. Now by order of Governor Curtin of Pennsylvania seventeen acres had been purchased on Cemetery Hill, where the Union center stood its colors on the second and third of July, and plots of soil had been allotted each State for its graves.

The sacred and delicate duties of orator of the day had fallen on Edward Everett. An eminent cultural figure, perhaps foremost of all distinguished American classical orators, he was born in 1794, had been United States senator, governor of Massachusetts, member of Congress, secretary of state under Fillmore, minister to Great Britain, Phi Beta Kappa poet at Harvard, professor of Greek at Harvard, president of Harvard. . . .

The Union of States was a holy concept to Everett, and the slavery issue secondary, though when president of Harvard from 1846 to 1849 he refused to draw the color line, saying in the case of a Negro applicant, Beverly Williams, that admission to Harvard College depended on examinations. "If this boy passes the examinations, he will be admitted; and if the white students choose to withdraw, all the income of the college will be devoted to his education." Not often was he so provocative. . . .

Serene, suave, handsomely venerable in his sixty-ninth year, a prominent specimen of Northern upper-class distinction, Everett was a natural choice of the Pennsylvania commissioners, who sought an orator for a solemn national occasion. When in September they notified him that the date of the occasion would be October 23, he replied that he would need more time for preparation, and the dedication was postponed till November 19.

Lincoln meanwhile, in reply to the printed circular invitation, sent word to the commissioners that he would be present at the ceremonies. This made it necessary for the commissioners to consider whether the President should be asked to deliver an address when present. Clark E. Carr of Galesburg, Illinois, representing his state on the board of commissioners, noted that the decision of the board to invite Lincoln to speak was an afterthought. "The question was raised as to his ability to speak upon such a grave and solemn occasion . . . . Besides, it was said that, with his important duties and responsibilities, he could not possibly have the leisure to prepare an address. . . . In answer . . . it was urged that he himself, better than anyone else, could determine as to these questions, and that, if he were invited to speak, he was sure to do what, under the circumstances, would be right and proper."

And so on November 2 David Wills of Gettysburg, as the special agent of Governor Curtin and also acting for the several states, by letter informed Lincoln that the several states having soldiers in the army of the Potomac who were killed, or had since died at hospitals in the vicinity, had procured

LINCOLN
Frank E. Schoonover
Wilmington Savings Fund Society

5 **Discussion** What does this indicate about people's attitudes toward Lincoln at the time?

6 **Clarification** Lincoln often wore a tall top hat, or "stovepipe" hat. He occasionally tucked papers into the high band running around the hat.

7 **Enrichment** In 1863 the Civil War was still far from over and Lincoln was not universally popular. It was critical for him to maintain the loyalty of the northern governors if he was to win the war and reunite the nation.

grounds for a cemetery and proper burial of their dead. "These grounds will be consecrated and set apart to this sacred purpose by appropriate ceremonies on Thursday, the 19th instant. I am authorized by the governors of the various states to invite you to be present and participate in these ceremonies, which will doubtless be very imposing and solemnly impressive. It is the desire that after the oration, you, as chief executive of the nation, formally set apart these grounds to their sacred use by a few appropriate remarks."

Mr. Wills proceeded farther as to the solemnity of the occasion, and when Lincoln had finished reading the letter he understood definitely that the event called for no humor and that a long speech was not expected from him. "The invitation," wrote Clark E. Carr, "was not settled upon and sent to Mr. Lincoln until the second of November, more than six weeks after Mr. Everett had been invited to speak, and but little more than two weeks before the exercises were held."

On the second Sunday before the Gettysburg ceremonies were to take place Lincoln went to the studio of the photographer Gardner for a long-delayed sitting. Noah Brooks walked with him, and he carefully explained to Brooks that he could not go to the photographer on any other day without interfering with the public business and the photographer's business, to say nothing of his liability to be hindered en route by curiosity seekers "and other seekers." On the White House stairs Lincoln had paused, turned, walked back to his office, and rejoined Brooks with a long envelope in his hand, an advance copy of Edward Everett's address to be delivered at the Gettysburg dedication. It was thoughtful of Everett to take care they should not cover the same ground in their speeches, he remarked to Brooks, who exclaimed over the length of the Everett address, covering nearly two sides of a one-page supplement of a Boston newspaper. Lincoln quoted a line he said he had read

somewhere from Daniel Webster:[1] "Solid men of Boston, make no long orations." There was no danger that he should get upon the lines of Mr. Everett's oration, he told Brooks, for what he had ready to say was very short, or as Brooks recalled his emphasis, "short, short, short." He had hoped to read the Everett address between sittings, but the photographer worked fast, Lincoln got interested in talk, and did not open the advance sheets while at Gardner's. In the photograph which Lincoln later gave to Brooks an envelope lay next to Lincoln's right arm resting on a table. In one other photograph made by Gardner that Sunday the envelope was still on the table. The chief difference between the two pictures was that in one Lincoln had his knees crossed and in the other the ankles.

Lamon[2] noted that Lincoln wrote part of his intended Gettysburg address at Washington, covered a sheet of foolscap paper[3] with a memorandum of it, and before taking it out of his hat and reading it to Lamon he said that it was not at all satisfactory to him, that he was afraid he would not do himself credit nor come up to public expectation. He had been too busy to give it the time he would like to. . . .

Various definite motives besides vague intuitions may have guided Lincoln in his decision to attend and speak even though half his cabinet had sent formal declinations in response to the printed circular invitations they had all received. Though the Gettysburg dedication was to be under interstate auspices, it had tremendous national significance for Lincoln because on the platform would be the state governors whose cooperation with him was of vast importance.

---

1. **Daniel Webster:** An American statesman and orator (1782–1852).
2. **Lamon:** Ward Hill Lamon (1828–1893), an American lawyer and close associate of Abraham Lincoln.
3. **foolscap paper:** Paper measuring thirteen by sixteen inches in size.

Grammar in Action

Paragraphs consisting of sentences written in the same structure become monotonous and boring. One way writers vary their sentence structure is by using **inverted word order.** The subject follows the verb in sentences written in inverted word order, and often begin with prepositional phrases. Notice how Sandburg's use of inverted word order emphasizes the verb in the following sentence:

Aboard were the three cabinet members, Nicolay and Hay, army and navy representatives . . .

Also, most interrogative sentences are written in inverted word order, as follows:

. . . would the President now give her the next one of her boys?

Student Activity 1. Locate four other examples of inverted sentence patterns in this selection. Write the sentences on a sheet of paper, circling the verbs and underlining the nouns.

Also a slander and a libel had been widely mouthed and printed that on his visit to the battlefield of Antietam nearly a year before he had laughed obscenely at his own funny stories and called on Lamon to sing a cheap comic song. Perhaps he might go to Gettysburg and let it be seen how he demeaned himself on a somber landscape of sacrifice.

His personal touch with Gettysburg, by telegraph, mail, courier, and by a throng of associations, made it a place of great realities to him. Just after the battle there, a woman had come to his office, the doorman saying she had been "crying and taking on" for several days trying to see the President. Her husband and three sons were in the army. On part of her husband's pay she had lived for a time, till money from him stopped coming. She was hard put to scrape a living and needed one of her boys to help.

The President listened to her, standing at a fireplace, hands behind him, head bowed, motionless. The woman finished her plea for one of her three sons in the army. He spoke. Slowly and almost as if talking to himself alone the words came and only those words:

"I have two, and you have none."

He crossed the room, wrote an order for the military discharge of one of her sons. On a special sheet of paper he wrote full and detailed instructions where to go and what to say in order to get her boy back.

In a few days the doorman told the President that the same woman was again on hand crying and taking on. "Let her in," was the word. She had found doors opening to her and officials ready to help on seeing the President's written words she carried. She had located her boy, camp, regiment, company. She had found him, yes, wounded at Gettysburg, dying in a hospital, and had followed him to the grave. And, she begged, would the President now give her the next one of her boys?

As before he stood at the fireplace, hands behind him, head bent low, motionless. Slowly and almost as if talking to himself

alone the words came and as before only those words:

"I have two, and you have none."

He crossed the room to his desk and began writing. As though nothing else was to do she followed, stood by his chair as he wrote, put her hand on the President's head, smoothed his thick and disorderly hair with motherly fingers. He signed an order giving her the next of her boys, stood up, put the priceless paper in her hand as he choked out the one word, "There!" and with long quick steps was gone from the room with her sobs and cries of thanks in his ears.

Thus the Kentuckian, James Speed, gathered the incident and told it. By many strange ways Gettysburg was to Lincoln a fact in crimson mist. . . .

When Lincoln boarded the train for Gettysburg on November 18, his best chum in the world, Tad, lay sick abed and the doctors not sure what ailed him. The mother still remembered Willie[4] and was hysterical about Tad. But the President felt imperative duty called him to Gettysburg.

Provost Marshal General James B. Fry as a War Department escort came to the White House, but the President was late in getting into the carriage for the drive to the station. They had no time to lose, Fry remarked. Lincoln said he felt like an Illinois man who was going to be hanged and as the man passed along the road on the way to the gallows the crowds kept pushing into the way and blocking passage. The condemned man at last called out, "Boys, you needn't be in such a hurry to get ahead, there won't be any fun till I get there."

Flags and red-white-and-blue bunting decorated the four-car special train. Aboard were the three cabinet members, Nicolay and Hay,[5] army and navy representatives, newspapermen, the French and Italian ministers

---

4. **Tad, Willie:** Two of Lincoln's four sons. Willie had died in 1862.
5. **Nicolay and Hay:** John George Nicolay (1832–1901), Lincoln's private secretary, and John Milton Hay (1838–1905), the assistant private secretary.

from *Abraham Lincoln: The War Years—Lincoln Speaks at Gettysburg* 789

8 **Clarification** Antietam Creek, in Maryland, was the site, in 1862, of one of the bloodiest battles of the Civil War. Southern forces were routed and forced to retreat, giving Lincoln a much-needed victory.

9 **Discussion** What do Lincoln's actions reveal about his character?

10 **Critical Thinking and Reading** By referring to Gettysburg as "a fact in crimson mist," Sandburg is using a metaphor to make his point. What is the meaning of this metaphor?

11 **Enrichment** Thomas (Tad) Lincoln recovered from this illness but died eight years later in 1871.

12 **Clarification** Bunting is a thin fabric most often used in the making of flags. In this case, it was in the form of cloths dyed in the nation's colors and loosely draped across the sides of the train.

Student Activity 2. Rewrite the following sentences in inverted word order. If necessary, change the sentence from declarative to interrogative.
1. Beneath the damp leaves the forgotten camp fire smouldered.
2. The frightened bullfighter scrambled over the nearest wall.
3. We are going to the movies tonight.
4. Through the window a young bird flew.
5. You are going to the recital tomorrow night?

13 **Enrichment** William Henry Seward served as Secretary of State under President Lincoln, despite the fact that Lincoln had defeated Seward for the Republican presidential nomination in 1860. Seward was with Lincoln the night the President was slain, and was himself wounded. He is perhaps best remembered for the purchase of Alaska from Russia, an act which was ridiculed at the time.

14 **Discussion** What kind of speech would you expect Lincoln to give based on the information provided up to this point?

15 **Literary Focus** What does Lincoln's response to the serenaders reveal about his character?

and attachés. The rear third of the last coach had a drawing room, where from time to time the President talked with nearly everyone aboard as they came and went. Henry Clay Cochrane, lieutenant of Marines, noted:

"I happened to have a *New York Herald* and offered it to Mr. Lincoln. He took it and thanked me, saying, 'I like to see what they say about us.' The news was about Burnside at Knoxville, Grant and Sherman at Chattanooga and Meade[6] on the Rapidan, all expecting trouble. He read for a little while and then began to laugh at some wild guesses of the paper about pending movements. It was pleasant to see his sad face lighted up. He was looking sallow, sunken-eyed, thin, careworn and very quiet. He returned the paper remarking among other things that when he had first passed over that road on his way to Congress in 1847 he noticed square-rigged vessels up the Patapsco River as far as the Relay House and now there seemed to be only small craft.

13 "At the Calvert Street Station Secretary Seward[7] began to get uneasy as we approached Baltimore. Upon reaching the Calvert Street Station in Baltimore all was quiet, less than two hundred people assembled, among them women with children in arms. They called for the President. He took two or three of the babies up and kissed them which greatly pleased the mothers. General Schenck and staff joined us and soon after the President went forward in the car and seated himself with a party of choice spirits, among whom was Mayor Frederick W. Lincoln of Boston, not a kinsman. They told stories for an hour or so, Mr. Lincoln taking his turn and enjoying it. Approaching Hanover Junction, he arose and said, 'Gentlemen, this is all very pleasant, but the people will expect me to say something to them tomorrow, and I must give the matter some

14

thought.' He then returned to the rear room of the car. . . ."

At sundown the train pulled into Gettysburg and Lincoln was driven to the Wills residence, Seward to the Harper home fronting on the public square. A sleepy little country town of 3,500 was overflowing with human pulses again. Private homes were filled with notables and nondescripts. Hundreds slept on the floors of hotels. Military bands blared till late in the night serenading whomsoever. The weather was mild and the moon up for those who chose to go a-roaming. When serenaders called on the President for a speech, he made again one of those little addresses saying there was nothing to say. "In my position it is sometimes important that I should not say foolish things. [A voice: "If you can help it."] It very often happens that the only way to help it is to say nothing at all. Believing that is my present condition this evening, I must beg of you to excuse me from addressing you further."

15 The crowd didn't feel it was much of a speech. They went next door with the band and blared for Seward. He spoke so low that Hay could not hear him, but he opened the stopgaps of patriotic sentiment, saying in part, "I thank my God for the hope that this is the last fratricidal war which will fall upon the country which is vouchsafed to us by Heaven—the richest, the broadest, the most beautiful, the most magnificent, and capable of a greater destiny than has ever been given to any part of the human race." What more could a holiday crowd ask for on a fair night of moonlit November? Seward gave them more and closed: "Fellow citizens, good night." It was good night for him but not for them. They serenaded five other speakers. . . .

At dinner in the Wills home that evening Lincoln met Edward Everett, a guest under the same roof, and Governor Curtin[8] and others. About ten o'clock he was in his room, with paper and pencil ready to write, when

---

6. **Burnside, Grant, Sherman, Meade:** Union generals.
7. **Seward:** William Henry Seward (1801–1872), U.S. Secretary of State from 1861 to 1869.

8. **Curtin:** Andrew Gregg Curtin (1815–1894), governor of Pennsylvania from 1860 to 1867.

he sent a servant down for Judge Wills to come up. Still later, about eleven o'clock, he sent the servant down again for Judge Wills, who came up and heard Lincoln request to see Mr. Seward. Judge Wills offered to go and bring Seward from next door at the Harpers'. "No, I'll go and see him," said Lincoln, who gathered his sheets of paper and went for a half-hour with his secretary of state.

Whether Seward made slight or material alterations in the text on the sheets was known only to Lincoln and Seward. It was midnight or later that Lincoln went to sleep, probably perfectly clear in his mind as to what his speech would be the next day. The one certainty was that his "few appropriate remarks," good or bad, would go to an immense audience. Also he slept better for having a telegram from Stanton reporting there was no real war news and "On inquiry Mrs. Lincoln informs me that your son is better this evening."

Fifteen thousand, some said thirty thousand or fifty thousand people were on Cemetery Hill for the exercises the next day when the procession from Gettysburg arrived afoot and horseback representing the United States government, the army and navy, governors of states, mayors of cities, a regiment of troops, hospital corps, telegraph-company representatives, Knights Templar, Masonic Fraternity, Odd Fellows, and other benevolent associations, the press, fire departments, citizens of Pennsylvania and other States. They were scheduled to start at ten o'clock and at that hour of the clock Lincoln in a black suit, high silk hat, and white gloves came out of the Wills residence and mounted a horse. A crowd was on hand and he held a reception on horseback. At eleven the parade began to move. The President's horse seemed small for him, as some looked at it. Clark E. Carr, just behind the President, believed he noticed that the President sat erect and looked majestic to begin with and then got to thinking so that his body leaned forward, his arms hung limp, and his head bent far down.

A long telegram sent by Stanton at ten o'clock from Washington had been handed him. Burnside seemed safe though threatened at Knoxville, Grant was starting a big battle at Chattanooga, and "Mrs. Lincoln reports your son's health as a great deal better and he will be out today."

The march of the procession of military and civic bodies began. "Mr. Lincoln was mounted upon a young and beautiful chestnut horse, the largest in the Cumberland Valley," wrote Lieutenant Cochrane. This seemed the first occasion that anyone had looked at the President mounted with a feeling that just the right horse had been picked to match his physical length. "His towering figure surmounted by a high silk hat made the rest of us look small," thought Cochrane. . . . The President rode "easily, bowing occasionally to right or left," noted Cochrane, while Seward lacked dignity, his trousers working up over the shoe tops to show his homemade gray socks. Seward was "entirely unconscious" that the secretary of state looked funny—and nobody really cared. In the town of Gettysburg men with wounds still lingered in hospitals. And many flags along the main street were at half-mast for sorrow not yet over.

Minute guns spoke while the procession moved along Baltimore Street to the Emmitsburg Road, then by way of the Taneytown Road to the cemetery, where troop lines stood in salute to the President.

The march was over in fifteen minutes. But Mr. Everett, the orator of the day, had not arrived. Bands played till noon. Mr. Everett arrived. . . .

The United States House chaplain, the Reverend Thomas H. Stockton, offered a prayer while the thousands stood with uncovered heads. . . .

Benjamin B. French, officer in charge of buildings in Washington, introduced the Honorable Edward Everett, orator of the day, who rose, bowed low to Lincoln, saying, "Mr. President." Lincoln responded, "Mr. Everett." The orator of the day then stood in si-

from Abraham Lincoln: The War Years—Lincoln Speaks at Gettysburg 791

19 Critical Thinking and Reading Point out to students how Sandburg's use of description—the size of the crowd, the vastness and beauty of the land, the deep silence—serves to underscore the importance of the occasion.

20 Discussion What kind of speaker is Everett? What does his speech reveal about his character?

21 Enrichment Pericles was a military leader and statesman of Athens during the fifth century B.C. Everett refers to him, and to Athens, because Athens is regarded as the cradle of democracy and Pericles is thought of as one of democracy's champions.

lence before a crowd that stretched to limits that would test his voice. Beyond and around were the wheat fields, the meadows, the peach orchards, long slopes of land, and five and seven miles farther the contemplative blue ridge of a low mountain range. His eyes could sweep them as he faced the audience. He had taken note of it in his prepared and rehearsed address. "Overlooking these broad fields now reposing from the labors of the waning year, the mighty Alleghenies dimly towering before us, the graves of our brethren beneath our feet, it is with hesitation that I raise my poor voice to break the eloquent silence of God and Nature. But the duty to which you have called me must be performed—grant me, I pray you, your indulgence and your sympathy." Everett proceeded, "It was appointed by law in Athens," and gave an extended sketch of the manner in which the Greeks cared for their dead who fell in battle. He spoke of the citizens assembled to consecrate the day. "As my eye ranges over the fields whose sods were so lately moistened by the blood of gallant and loyal men, I feel, as never before, how truly it was said of old that it is sweet and becoming to die for one's country."

Northern cities would have been trampled in conquest but for "those who sleep beneath our feet," said the orator. He gave an outline of how the war began, traversed decisive features of the three days' battles at Gettysburg, discussed the doctrine of state sovereignty and denounced it, drew parallels from European history, and came to his peroration[9] quoting Pericles[10] on dead patriots: "The whole earth is the sepulcher of illustrious men." The men of nineteen sister states had stood side by side on the perilous ridges. "Seminary Ridge, the Peach-Orchard, Cemetery, Culp, and Wolf Hill, Round Top, Little Round Top, humble names, henceforward dear and famous—no lapse of time, no distance

---

9. peroration (per′ ə rā′ shən) n.: The concluding part of a speech.
10. Pericles (per′ ə klēz′): Ancient Greek statesman and general (495?–429 B.C.).

---

of space, shall cause you to be forgotten." He had spoken for an hour and fifty-seven minutes, some said a trifle over two hours, repeating almost word for word an address that occupied nearly two newspaper pages, as he had written it and as it had gone in advance sheets to many newspapers.

Everett came to his closing sentence without a faltering voice: "Down to the latest period of recorded time, in the glorious annals of our common country there will be no brighter page than that which relates THE BATTLES OF GETTYSBURG." It was the effort of his life and embodied the perfections of the school of oratory in which he had spent his career. His erect form and sturdy shoulders, his white hair and flung-back head at dramatic points, his voice, his poise, and chiefly some quality of inside goodheartedness, held most of his audience to him, though the people in the front rows had taken their seats three hours before his oration closed. . . .

Having read Everett's address, Lincoln knew when the moment drew near for him to speak. He took out his own manuscript from a coat pocket, put on his steel-bowed glasses, stirred in his chair, looked over the manuscript, and put it back in his pocket. The specially chosen Ward Hill Lamon rose and spoke the words "The President of the United States," who rose, and holding in one hand the two sheets of paper at which he occasionally glanced, delivered the address in his high-pitched and clear-carrying voice. The *Cincinnati Commercial* reporter wrote, "The President rises slowly, draws from his pocket a paper, and, when commotion subsides, in a sharp, unmusical treble voice, reads the brief and pithy remarks." Hay wrote in his diary, "The President, in a firm, free way, with more grace than is his wont, said his half dozen words of consecration." Charles Hale of the *Boston Advertiser*, also officially representing Governor Andrew of Massachusetts, had notebook and pencil in hand, took down the slow-spoken words of the President, as follows:

Grammar in Action

An **elliptical clause** is a clause from which certain elements have been deleted to avoid repetition. These deleted (or unstated) elements are clear from the context of the clause. Note the following sentence:

This made it necessary for the commissioners to consider whether the President should be asked to deliver an address when present. (p. 787)

In this sentence *when present* is an elliptical clause, shortened from the clause *when he was present*.

Another example of an elliptical clause appears in the following sentence:

Lincoln was driven to the Wills residence, Seward to the Harper home fronting on the public square.

In this case the verb *was driven* is omitted in the elliptical clause, but because the subjects of the two clauses are different, *Seward* must remain.

Fourscore and seven years ago, our fathers brought forth upon this continent a new nation, conceived in liberty and dedicated to the proposition that all men are created equal.

Now we are engaged in a great civil war, testing whether that nation—or any nation, so conceived and so dedicated—can long endure.

We are met on a great battlefield of that war. We are met to dedicate a portion of it as the final resting place of those who have given their lives that that nation might live.

It is altogether fitting and proper that we should do this.

But, in a larger sense, we cannot dedicate, we cannot consecrate, we cannot hallow, this ground. The brave men, living and dead, who struggled here, have consecrated it, far above our power to add or to detract.

The world will very little note nor long remember what we say here; but it can never forget what they did here.

It is for us, the living, rather, to be dedicated here, to the unfinished work that they have thus far so nobly carried on. It is rather for us to be here dedicated to the great task remaining before us; that from these honored dead we take increased devotion to that cause for which they here gave the last full measure of devotion; that we here highly resolve that these dead shall not have died in vain; that the nation shall, under God, have a new birth of freedom, and that government of the people, by the people, for the people, shall not perish from the earth.

In a speech to serenaders just after the battle of Gettysburg four and a half months before, Lincoln had referred to the founding of the republic as taking place "eighty odd years since." Then he had hunted up the exact date, which was eighty-seven years since, and phrased it "Fourscore and seven years ago" instead of "Eighty-seven years since." Also in the final copy Lincoln wrote "We have come" instead of the second "We are met" that Hale reported.

In the written copy of his speech from which he read Lincoln used the phrase "our poor power." In other copies of the speech which he wrote out later he again used the phrase "our poor power." So it was evident that he meant to use the word "poor" when speaking to his audience, but he omitted it. Also in the copy held in his hands while facing the audience he had not written the words "under God," though he did include those words in later copies which he wrote. Therefore the words "under God" were decided upon after he wrote the text the night before at the Wills residence.

The *New York Tribune* and many other newspapers indicated "[Applause.]" at five places in the address and "[Long continued applause.]" at the end. The applause, however, according to most of the responsible witnesses, was formal and perfunctory, a tribute to the occasion, to the high office, to the array of important men of the nation on the platform, by persons who had sat as an audience for three hours. Ten sentences had been spoken in five minutes, and some were surprised that it should end before the orator had really begun to get his outdoor voice.

A photographer had made ready to record a great historic moment, had bustled about with his dry plates, his black box on a tripod, and before he had his head under the hood for an exposure, the President had said "by the people, for the people" and the nick of time was past for a photograph.

The New York Times reporter gave his summary of the program by writing: "The opening prayer by Reverend Mr. Stockton was touching and beautiful, and produced quite as much effect upon the audience as

from *Abraham Lincoln: The War Years—Lincoln Speaks at Gettysburg*   793

22 **Discussion** What is the central theme of "The Gettysburg Address"?

23 **Reading Strategy** Have students summarize Lincoln's address in their own words.

24 **Enrichment** Most historians agree that Lincoln probably composed five different versions of "The Gettysburg Address," although the differences among them were not great.

25 **Discussion** Have students comment on the differences between the reaction to "The Gettysburg Address" at the time and the verdict of history. Why has this speech come to be highly regarded?

26 **Clarification** Cameras at the time of Abraham Lincoln were much larger than those of today. The camera was covered with a black cloth hood that protected the photographic plates from exposure to light. The photographer ducked under the cloth while taking the shot.

Student Activity 1. Identify the elliptical clauses in the following sentences and explain what has been omitted from each.
1. Burnside seemed safe though threatened at Knoxville.
2. So it was evident that he meant to use the word "poor" when speaking to his audience.
3. The orator must have time to get tuned up, to expatiate and expand while building toward his climaxes. . . .
4. You could not have been excused to make a short address, nor I a long one.
5. I feel, as never before, how truly it was said of old that it is sweet and becoming to die for one's country.

Student Activity 2. Combine each of the following pairs of clauses, omitting unnecessary words from one of the clauses to make it elliptical.
1. Everett was president of Harvard College.
   Everett refused to deny admission to a Negro student.
2. Everett spoke at Gettysburg for nearly two hours.
   Lincoln spoke for only two minutes.
3. Lincoln was at a photographer's studio.
   Lincoln intended to read Everett's speech.

27 **Discussion** Why does Sandburg include this information?

28 **Literary Focus** Sandburg's use of Lincoln's reference to a farming term from his boyhood conveys part of the mythology around Lincoln—the idea that Lincoln represents the common individual and had not lost touch with his humble roots.

the classic sentences of the orator of the day. President Lincoln's address was delivered in a clear loud tone of voice, which could be distinctly heard at the extreme limits of the large assemblage. It was delivered (or rather read from a sheet of paper which the speaker held in his hand) in a very deliberate manner, with strong emphasis, and with a most businesslike air."

The *Philadelphia Press* man, John Russell Young, privately felt that Everett's speech was the performance of a great actor whose art was too evident, that it was "beautiful but cold as ice." The *New York Times* man noted: "Even while Mr. Everett was delivering his splendid oration, there were as many people wandering about the fields, made memorable by the fierce struggles of July, as stood around the stand listening to his eloquent periods. They seem to have considered, with President Lincoln, that it was not what was *said* here, but what was *done* here, that deserved their attention. . . . In wandering about these battlefields, one is astonished and indignant to find at almost every step of his progress the carcasses of dead horses which breed pestilence in the atmosphere. I am told that more than a score of deaths have resulted from this neglect in the village of Gettysburg the past summer; in the house in which I was compelled to seek lodgings, there are now two boys sick with typhoid fever attributed to this cause. Within a stone's throw of the whitewashed hut occupied as the headquarters of General Meade, I counted yesterday no less than ten carcasses of dead horses, lying on the ground where they were struck by the shells of the enemy."

27 | The audience had expected, as the printed program stipulated, "Dedicatory Remarks, by the President of the United States." No eloquence was promised. Where eloquence is in flow the orator must have time to get tuned up, to expatiate and expand while building toward his climaxes, it was supposed. The *New York Tribune* man and other like observers merely reported the

words of the address with the one preceding sentence: "The dedicatory remarks were then delivered by the President." These reporters felt no urge to inform their readers about how Lincoln stood, what he did with his hands, how he moved, vocalized, or whether he emphasized or subdued any parts of the address. Strictly, no address as such was on the program from him. He was down for just a few perfunctory "dedicatory remarks."

According to Lamon, Lincoln himself felt that about all he had given the audience was ordinary garden-variety dedicatory remarks, for Lamon wrote that Lincoln told him just after delivering the speech that he had regret over not having prepared it with greater care. "Lamon, that speech won't *scour*. It is a flat failure and the people are disappointed." On the farms where Lincoln grew up as a boy when wet soil stuck to the mold board of a plow they said it didn't "scour." 28

The nearby *Patriot and Union* of Harrisburg took its fling: "The President succeeded on this occasion because he acted without sense and without constraint in a panorama that was gotten up more for the benefit of his party than for the glory of the nation and the honor of the dead. . . . We pass over the silly remarks of the President; for the credit of the nation we are willing that the veil of oblivion shall be dropped over them and that they shall no more be repeated or thought of. . . ."

Everett's opinion of the speech he heard Lincoln deliver was written in a note to Lincoln the next day and was more than mere courtesy: "I should be glad if I could flatter myself that I came as near to the central idea of the occasion in two hours as you did in two minutes." Lincoln's immediate reply was: "In our respective parts yesterday, you could not have been excused to make a short address, nor I a long one. I am pleased to know that, in your judgment, the little I did say was not entirely a failure. . . ."

The ride to Washington took until midnight. Lincoln was weary, talked little,

Primary Source

Critic Allan Nevins wrote the following about *Abraham Lincoln: The War Years:*

Mr. Sandburg's method is the method of Niagara. He has caught the drainage of the whole vast historical watershed of the Civil War as Niagara catches the Great Lakes, and he pours it forth in a thundering flood.

The most distinctive qualities of Mr. Sandburg's work are two. First, its pictorial vividness, a product of his graphic style, love of concrete detail, and ability to recreate scenes imaginatively in a few sentences; second, the cumulative force of his detail in building up, step by step, an unforgettable impression of the crowded times, with crisis jostling crisis, problems rising in endless welter . . . and an impression of Lincoln patiently finding his talents, learning to endure the storm, and finally mastering it with sad serenity. These two qualities of pictorial vividness and cumulative force are complementary. Neither could have its full effect without the other.. . . [Sandburg] has a graphic, vital fashion of setting his facts on paper, and a

stretched out on one of the side seats in the drawing room and had a wet towel laid across his eyes and forehead.

He had stood that day, the world's foremost spokesman of popular government, saying that democracy was yet worth fighting for. He had spoken as one in mist who might head on deeper yet into mist. He incarnated the assurances and pretenses of popular government, implied that it could and might perish from the earth. What he meant by "a new birth of freedom" for the nation could have a thousand interpretations. The taller riddles of democracy stood up out of the address. It had the dream touch of vast and furious events epitomized for any foreteller to read what was to come. He did not assume that the drafted soldiers, substitutes, and bounty-paid privates had died willingly under Lee's shot and shell, in deliberate consecration of themselves to the Union cause. His cadences sang the ancient song that where there is freedom men have fought and sacrificed for it, and that freedom is worth men's dying for. For the first time since he became President he had on a dramatic occasion declaimed, howsoever it might be read, Jefferson's proposition which had been a slogan of the Revolutionary War—"All men are created equal"—leaving no other inference than that he regarded the Negro slave as a man. His outwardly smooth sentences were inside of them gnarled and tough with the enigmas of the American experiment.

Back at Gettysburg the blue haze of the Cumberland Mountains had dimmed till it was a blur in a nocturne. The moon was up and fell with a bland golden benevolence on the new-made graves of soldiers, on the sepulchers of old settlers, on the horse carcasses of which the onrush of war had not yet permitted removal. The *New York Herald* man walked amid them and ended the story he sent his paper: "The air, the trees, the graves are silent. Even the relic hunters are gone now. And the soldiers here never wake to the sound of reveille."

In many a country cottage over the land, a tall old clock in a quiet corner told time in a ticktock deliberation. Whether the orchard branches hung with pink-spray blossoms or icicles of sleet, whether the outside news was seedtime or harvest, rain or drought, births or deaths, the swing of the pendulum was right and left and right and left in a ticktock deliberation.

The face and dial of the clock had known the eyes of a boy who listened to its ticktock and learned to read its minute and hour hands. And the boy had seen years measured off by the swinging pendulum, and grown to man size, had gone away. And the people in the cottage knew that the clock would stand there and the boy never again come into the room and look at the clock with the query, "What is the time?"

In a row of graves of the unidentified the boy would sleep long in the dedicated final resting place at Gettysburg. Why he had gone away and why he would never come back had roots in some mystery of flags and drums, of national fate in which individuals sink as in a deep sea, of men swallowed and vanished in a man-made storm of smoke and steel.

The mystery deepened and moved with ancient music and inviolable consolation because a solemn man of authority had stood at the graves of the unidentified and spoken the words "We cannot consecrate—we cannot hallow—this ground. The brave men, living and dead, who struggled here, have consecrated it far above our poor power to add or detract. . . . From these honored dead we take increased devotion to that cause for which they gave the last full measure of devotion."

To the backward and forward pendulum swing of a tall old clock in a quiet corner they might read those cadenced words while outside the windows the first flurry of snow blew across the orchard and down over the meadow, the beginnings of winter in a gun-metal gloaming to be later arched with a star-flung sky.

from *Abraham Lincoln: The War Years—Lincoln Speaks at Gettysburg* 795

29 **Critical Thinking and Reading** Point out to students that this final section of narrative differs in form and content from the sections that have preceded it. Ask students why they think Sandburg makes this change and what effect it creates.

30 **Discussion** To what does the metaphor of the clock refer?

Reader's Response Has this selection altered your thoughts about Abraham Lincoln or the Gettysburg Address? If so, how?

cinematographic ease in glancing from point to point, idea to idea, event to event . . .

Doubtless from Sandburg's pages many readers will for the first time gain a clear comprehension of (Lincoln's) greatness. For it is impossible to realize either Lincoln's intellectual or moral stature without understanding the innumerable difficulties which bethorned and quagmired his path, which harried and perplexed him to the melancholy verge of despair.

(It) takes Mr. Sandburg's Niagara of details, drawn from ten thousand sources, condensed, classified, and set down with vehement intensity, to bring out the bewildering confusion of the time, the soul-chilling uncertainty and fear, and the searing human agonies. In these 2500 pages, a distillation from a whole library, we have perhaps the best picture of a nation in racked travail yet written by any pen.

It is not merely a biography; it is a magnificent piece of history, an epic story of the most stirring period of national life, and a narrative which for decades will hearten all believers in the stability of democracy and the potentialities of democratic leadership.

Closure and Extension

ANSWERS TO THINKING ABOUT THE SELECTION
Recalling

1. (a) The occasion was the dedication of a National Soldiers' Cemetery at Gettysburg. (b) The significance for Lincoln was that he would be appearing with the governors of northern states whose cooperation he needed to win the Civil War.
2. (a) Lincoln had granted the request. (b) She had returned, because she discovered that the son Lincoln had released died. The woman sought the release of one of her other sons.
3. Lincoln declines to give a speech to the serenaders by saying, somewhat jokingly, that it is important for a man in his position to "not say foolish things."
4. (a) Everett's speech lasts approximately two hours. (b) Lincoln knows because he has read Everett's prepared remarks and realizes they are drawing to a close.
5. (a) Lincoln thinks the address is a "flat failure." (b) Everett thinks that Lincoln expressed the main idea of the ceremony more succinctly in his short speech than Everett did in his long one.

Interpreting

6. (a) Sandburg seems to have great affection and respect for Lincoln. (b) His attitude is conveyed in his selection of incidents, which reflect characteristics of dignity, humility, humor, and compassion in Lincoln, and in the way he contrasts Lincoln with others such as Everett and Seward.
7. (a) Lincoln's speech is short and straightforward; Everett's is long and flowery, full of rhetoric. (b) The qualities of Lincoln's speech that are highlighted are its simplicity, honesty, and directness.

Applying

8. Suggested Response: It is surprising that more people did not recognize the greatness of the speech at the time, since it has become so famous and highly regarded.

796

THINKING ABOUT THE SELECTION
Recalling

1. (a) What was the occasion of Lincoln's speech? (b) Why did the occasion have "tremendous national significance" for Lincoln?
2. (a) How had Lincoln responded when a woman had asked him to release one of her three sons from the army? (b) Why had she returned several days later?
3. How does Lincoln respond when "serenaders call on" him for a speech just after his arrival in Gettysburg?
4. (a) How long does Edward Everett's speech last? (b) How does Lincoln know when Everett is about to finish speaking?
5. (a) What is Lincoln's assessment of his own address? (b) What is Everett's opinion of Lincoln's address?

Interpreting

6. (a) What is Sandburg's attitude toward Lincoln? (b) How is his attitude conveyed in this selection?
7. (a) How does Lincoln's speech contrast with Everett's speech? (b) What qualities of Lincoln's speech are highlighted by this contrast?

Applying

8. Considering the historical significance of the Gettysburg Address, what is surprising about the immediate responses to the address?

ANALYZING LITERATURE
Understanding Biography

A biography is an account of a person's life written by another person. Biographers recount the central facts of the subject's life and present their interpretations of these events.

1. Why is Lincoln a good subject for a biography?
2. How does Sandburg's frequent use of quotes from eyewitnesses contribute to the reliability and authenticity of his account?

796   The Modern Age

3. What conclusion does Sandburg draw about the addition of the words "under God" to Lincoln's speech?
4. What does Sandburg mean when he comments that Lincoln's "outwardly smooth sentences were inside of them gnarled and tough with the enigmas of the American experience"?
5. Carl Sandburg had great admiration for the American worker—the common man. Why would he have been especially interested in Abraham Lincoln? Explain your answer.

CRITICAL THINKING AND READING
Evaluating the Subject of a Biography

Sandburg's account of the events leading up to and following the Gettysburg Address reveals a good deal about Lincoln's personality. For example, Lincoln's ability to prepare his speech in such a short amount of time reveals the fact that he was a gifted writer and a man of great energy.

1. What does Lincoln's response to the woman's request regarding her three sons reveal about his personality?
2. What does Lincoln's assessment of his own address reveal about his personality?

THINKING AND WRITING
Writing a Biographical Sketch

Imagine that you have been asked to write a biographical sketch for your school newspaper. Review the freewriting you did before reading the selection, and prepare a short list of the central events in the subject's life. When you write your biography, recount the events in chronological order. If possible, use direct quotations. When you revise, make sure that you have included your own insights into your subject's life. Proofread your sketch and prepare a final draft.

ANSWERS TO ANALYZING LITERATURE

1. Lincoln is a good subject for a biography because a great deal of information exists about him, his personality reflected many characteristics valued by Americans, and he was a crucial figure in American history.
2. Sandburg's use of quotes gives the flavor of the times and makes his narrative more objective than if he merely presented his own interpretation of events.
3. The words "under God" were a late addition to Lincoln's speech.
4. Sandburg means that while Lincoln's words were simple and pleasing to the ear, they are suggestive of the difficult struggle for democracy that the United States was undergoing in the Civil War.
5. He would be interested in Lincoln, because Lincoln had humble roots and was known for his concern for common individuals.

ANSWERS TO CRITICAL THINKING AND READING

1. Lincoln's response to the woman suggests that he was a man of great compassion.
2. Lincoln's assessment of his address reveals his modesty.

Poetry

BLACK AND WHITE, 1930
Georgia O'Keeffe
The Whitney Museum of Art

Humanities Note

Fine art, *Black and White*, 1930, by Georgia O'Keeffe. Born in Wisconsin, Georgia O'Keeffe (1887–1986) studied at the Art Institute of Chicago and the Art Students League in New York, two of the most influential art schools in the country. O'Keeffe herself taught art in Texas and became deeply absorbed in the natural surroundings of the Southwest, including the desert. In the late 1940's she settled permanently in Taos, New Mexico.

O'Keeffe's most characteristic works include stark, barren-looking images associated with the desert—the whitish bones of animal skulls against a dark background, for instance. *Black and White* is a more abstract work, although the color scheme is similar. A white triangle emerges from a background of black and gray. The arrangement of color patterns, and the distinct light triangle against a less-defined background, invite the viewer to experience a sense of motion and of the unexpected breakup of space—a kind of minor explosion. The images may suggest, among other things, a night sky showing the movement of celestial bodies.

THINKING AND WRITING

Writing Across the Curriculum
For extra credit, you might want to have students research some aspect of the Civil War. Members of the social studies department may be able to help students conduct this research.

More About the Author Ezra Pound encouraged the early work of many other poets who later became noted. After he had made Fascist propaganda broadcasts from Italy to the United States, most of his literary friends stood by him. They believed that he should be honored for his poetry without regard to his political views. After World War II, he continued to win poetry prizes. Should a poet's views affect the way in which his or her work is judged?

Critical Evaluation David Perkins made the following comments about Ezra Pound: "Pound's achievement in and for poetry was threefold: as a poet, and as a critic, and also as a befriender of genius through personal contact. The least that can be claimed of his poetry is that for over fifty years he was one of the three or four best poets writing in English. During a crucial decade in the history of modern literature, approximately 1912 to 1922, Pound was the most influential and in some ways the best critic of poetry in England or America. He had an almost unerring eye for quality. . . . Finally, he spent much time and energy aiding other writers. W. C. Williams, H.D., Yeats, Frost, Eliot, Joyce, Hemingway, and e.e. cummings were indebted to him for encouragement and criticism when they were still unknown. Some of them were also helped to publication, money (of which he himself had very little), and reputation, not to mention more personal services of miscellaneous kinds. He did this for the sake of literature, for he did not always like the writers he helped. Without his harassed ingenuity, some of the brilliant literature of the early twentieth century would not have been written.

EZRA POUND

1885–1972

More than any other poet, Ezra Pound was responsible for the dramatic changes that occurred in American poetry during the Modern Age. Urging writers to "make it new," Pound influenced many poets of his day to discard the forms, techniques, and ideas of the past and to experiment with new approaches to writing poetry.

Pound was born in Hailey, Idaho, and grew up in Philadelphia. After studying at the University of Pennsylvania and at Hamilton College, he traveled in Europe where he spent most of his life. Settling in London and later moving to Paris, he became a vital part of the growing Modernist movement. He influenced the work of the noted Irish poet William Butler Yeats and that of many American writers, including T. S. Eliot, William Carlos Williams, H. D., Marianne Moore, and Ernest Hemingway. He was also responsible for the development of Imagism, a literary movement that included Williams, H. D., and Moore.

Despite Pound's preoccupation with originality and inventiveness, his poetry reflects a deep interest in the past. In his early work, he often drew upon the poetry of ancient cultures, including Chinese, Japanese, and Provençal French. His dense, complex poems tend to be filled with literary and historical allusions. Often his poems are difficult to understand, because they are void of explanations or generalizations.

After 1920 Pound focused his efforts on writing *The Cantos,* a long poetic sequence in which he expressed his beliefs, reflected upon history and politics, and alluded to a variety of foreign languages and literatures. He eventually produced 116 cantos, which are widely varied in quality.

In 1925 Pound settled in Italy. During World War II, he was an outspoken supporter of the Italian dictator Benito Mussolini, mistakenly believing that a country governed by a powerful dictator was the most conducive environment for the creation of art. In 1943 Pound was indicted by the American government for treason, and a year later he was arrested by American troops and imprisoned. After being flown back to the United States in 1945, he was judged to be psychologically unfit to stand trial and was confined to a hospital for the criminally insane. He remained there until 1958, when he was released largely because of the efforts of his friends in the literary community. After his release he returned to Italy, where he spent the remainder of his life.

798   *The Modern Age*

Objectives
1 To understand Imagism
2 To write about Imagism

Support Material

Teaching Portfolio
Teacher Backup, p. 1033
Grammar in Action Worksheet, *Using Specific Words,* p. 1037
Usage and Mechanics Worksheet, p. 1039
Vocabulary Check, p. 1040
Analyzing Literature Worksheet, *Understanding Imagism,* p. 1041

Language Worksheet, *Recognizing Connotation,* p. 1042
Selection Test, p. 1044

GUIDE FOR INTERPRETING

In a Station of the Metro; The River-Merchant's Wife: A Letter; Canto 13

Imagism. Imagism was a literary movement established in the early part of the twentieth century by Ezra Pound and other poets. As the name suggests, the Imagists concentrated on the direct presentation of images, or word pictures. An Imagist poem expressed the essence of an object, person, or incident, without explanations or generalizations. Through the spare, clean presentation of an image, the Imagists hoped to evoke an emotional response—they hoped to freeze a single moment in time and to capture the emotions of that moment. To accomplish this purpose, the Imagists used the language of everyday speech, carefully choosing each word and avoiding any unnecessary words. Avoiding traditional poetic patterns, they also attempted to create new, musical rhythms in their poetry.

Because they generally focus on a single image, Imagist poems tend to be short. In their length and focus, many Imagist poems reflect the influence of the Japanese verse forms *haiku* and *tanka*. The haiku consists of three lines of five, seven, and five syllables. The tanka is written in five lines of five, seven, five, seven, and five syllables. Like Imagist poems, haikus and tankas generally evoke an emotional response through a single image.

Writing

"In a Station of the Metro" captures an impression of a crowd of people waiting on a dark subway platform. Freewrite about the types of impressions you have when you glance at a large crowd of people.

Primary Source

In the March 1913 issue of *Poetry* magazine, Pound published a set of "rules" for poets. Consider how his rules apply to poetry—not just Imagist poetry, but all poetry, and consider also how these rules apply equally well to any kind of writing. Here are a few of his rules:

> It is better to present one image in a lifetime than to produce voluminous words.
>
> Use no superfluous word, no adjective, which does not reveal something.
>
> Don't use such an expression as 'dim lands of peace.' It dulls the image. It mixes an abstraction with the concrete. It comes from the writer's not realizing that the natural object is always the *adequate* symbol.
>
> Be influenced by as many great artists as you can, but have the decency either to acknowledge the debt outright, or to try to conceal it.

Guide for Interpreting 799

Literary Focus The Imagists wanted their poems to evoke the kinds of emotional responses that paintings evoke. The image itself should stimulate the viewer, or reader, to supply the emotion.

Writing/Prior Knowledge Before having your students complete the writing activity, you might discuss the types of situations in which you are likely to encounter a large crowd.

Vocabulary

Preteach the following vocabulary words:
apparition (ap′ ə rish′ ən) *n.:* The act of appearing or becoming invisible (p. 800, l. 1)
dynastic (dī nas′ tik) *adj.:* Of a period during which a certain family rules (p. 805, l. 2)
savants (sə vänts′) *n.:* Learned persons; scholars (p. 806, l. 43)
deference (def′ ər əns) *n.:* Courteous regard or respect (p. 806, l. 52)

In a Station of the Metro[1]

Ezra Pound

1 The apparition of these faces in the crowd;
Petals on a wet, black bough.

---

1. Metro: The Paris subway.

THINKING ABOUT THE SELECTION
Recalling

1. What is the setting of this poem?

Interpreting

2. Pound compares the faces of people on a subway platform with "petals on a wet, black bough." (a) What does this comparison suggest about the effect of society on individuality? (b) What does the comparison suggest about the fraility of human beings?

Applying

3. How does the image in the poem compare with your own image of the faces of people on a subway platform or at a train station?

ANALYZING LITERATURE
Understanding Imagism

Imagism was a literary movement that focused on evoking emotions through the spare, clean presentations of images, or word pictures. The Imagists also emphasized the creation of new rhythms, the use of common language, and precision in choosing words.

1. In "In a Station of the Metro," Pound juxtaposes, or puts together, two images to capture an impression of faces quickly glimpsed on a dark subway platform. What emotions does the combination of images evoke?
2. Considering the common meaning of apparition as a strange figure appearing suddenly and thought to be a ghost, why do you think Pound chose the word *apparition* rather than *appearance*?
3. How does this word contribute to the emotional impact of the image?

The River-Merchant's Wife: A Letter

Ezra Pound

1
While my hair was still cut straight across my forehead
I played about the front gate, pulling flowers.
You came by on bamboo stilts, playing horse,
You walked about my seat, playing with blue plums.
5 And we went on living in the village of Chokan:[1]
Two small people, without dislike or suspicion.

2
At fourteen I married My Lord you.
I never laughed, being bashful.
Lowering my head, I looked at the wall.
10 Called to, a thousand times, I never looked back.

3
At fifteen I stopped scowling,
I desired my dust to be mingled with yours
Forever and forever and forever.
Why should I climb the lookout?

4 15 At sixteen you departed,
You went into far Ku-to-yen,[2] by the river of swirling eddies,
And you have been gone five months.
The monkeys make sorrowful noise overhead.

5
You dragged your feet when you went out.
20 By the gate now, the moss is grown, the different mosses,
Too deep to clear them away!
The leaves fall early this autumn, in wind.
The paired butterflies are already yellow with August
Over the grass in the West garden;
25 They hurt me. I grow older.
If you are coming down through the narrows of the river
    Kiang,

---

1. **Chokan** (Chō′ kän′): A suburb of Nanking, a city in the People's Republic of China.
2. **Ku-to-yen** (ko͞o′ tō′ yen′): An island in the Yangtze (yäng′ tsē) River.

The River-Merchant's Wife: A Letter   801

Presentation

Motivation/Prior Knowledge
Have the students imagine that they are living in a society in which marriages are arranged by parents. How would they respond to this situation?

Purpose-Setting Question
How does the speaker change as she grows older?

1 **Clarification** The hair cut in bangs is an indication that the speaker was a child at the time.

2 **Clarification** At the time of the poem, marriages in China were arranged by the families.

3 **Discussion** In what ways has the speaker changed between the ages of fourteen and fifteen?

4 **Critical Thinking and Reading** The image of "the river of swirling eddies" reflects both the woman's inner turmoil and the dangers she envisions for her husband.

5 **Discussion** What does line 19 suggest about the husband's feelings about leaving?

Fine art, *Landscape Album in Various Styles,* by Ch'a Shih-piao. Ch'a Shih-piao (1615–1698) was a native of Anhui Province of China. He is counted among the "four Masters of Anhui." Born of a wealthy family that had an extensive art collection, he had the rare opportunity to study closely the work of the old masters. This study partly explains the diversity of styles found in his own work. He was best known for the somber and melancholy landscapes done in the manner of the Yiian painter Ni Tsan.

You might use these questions for discussion:

1. Identify the poetic qualities of this painting.
2. Study the perspective in this painting. How does the use of perspective differ from the traditional western perspective?
3. Does this scene seem to be an appropriate setting for this poem? Explain.

LANDSCAPE ALBUM IN VARIOUS STYLES
Ch'a Shih-piao
The Cleveland Museum of Art

802   *The Modern Age*

Grammar in Action

Writing teachers repeatedly stress the use of **specific words.** One way to make nouns more specific is by adding adjectives or adjective phrases, which will sharpen and clarify them. Note the following examples:

bamboo stilts (p. 801)
the river *of swirling eddies.* (p. 801)

It is important not to overuse adjectives, however. Ezra Pound was sparing in his use of adjectives, choosing his nouns so carefully that they need little modification. Note the following examples:

Lowering my head, I looked at the wall. (p. 801)
The leaves fall early this autumn, in wind. (p. 801)

Student Activity 1. Reread the first stanza of "The River-Merchant's Wife: A Letter." Decide whether more adjectives are used in relation to the girl or the boy. Explain why, in terms of the poem's message, Pound weighted his adjectives as he did.

6 Critical Thinking and Reading
The last four lines of the poem express, in a very understated way, the speaker's eagerness to see her husband again. Why is understatement so effective in this situation?

7 Discussion How has the speaker's attitude toward her husband changed since the time of their marriage?

Reader's Response What feelings and thoughts conveyed in this poem are similar to those you have experienced?

6
7

Please let me know beforehand,
And I will come out to meet you
    As far as Cho-fu-Sa.³

                    By Rihaku

_____

3. Cho-fu-Sa (chō′ f oo′ sä′): A beach along the Yangtze River, several hundred miles from Nanking.

The River-Merchant's Wife: A Letter 803

Student Activity 2. Reread the last stanza of "The River-Merchant's Wife: A Letter." Decide whether more adjectives are used to describe the speaker's feelings or the natural things she views. Explain why Pound chose to apply his adjectives as he did.

Student Activity 3. Rewrite the italicized noun phrases. Try to eliminate modifiers by selecting a more specific noun.

1. We were awakened by a *high-pitched, loud sound*.
2. The director chose an *intentionally humorous drama*.
3. The family lived in a *small, run-down building*.
4. Spiders arouse *a feeling of intense dislike* in her.
5. *His experience of losing* depressed him.
6. I disliked *the sensation that I was losing my balance*.
7. We dug into a *place where water was close to the surface of the ground*.
8. His mother would accept *no explanation of his behavior*.
9. She offered me *a very small piece of food*.
10. Mutt was a *dog descended from several breeds*.

Closure and Extension

ANSWERS TO THINKING ABOUT THE SELECTION
Recalling

1. She married the river-merchant at fourteen. She stopped scowling at fifteen. Her husband left when she was sixteen.
2. The moss has grown too deep to clear away.
3. (a) The paired butterflies in the garden hurt her. (b) She will go to meet him "As far as Cho-fu-Sa."

Interpreting

4. (a) She was bashful and unhappy. (b) She lowered her head, looked at the wall, and would not look back when called. (c) She now loves him.
5. (a) He was unhappy. (b) He dragged his feet.
6. Moss has grown; autumn has come; butterflies are mating.
7. (a) She is unhappy. (b) The unhappiness is reflected in the monkeys' "sorrowful noise" and in her hurt as she watches the butterflies pairing.
8. The tone is respectful and subdued.

Applying

9. Answers will differ. Students may comment that they do not think that arranged marriages have any benefits and that they feel that marriages should be based on love.

THINKING AND WRITING

After students have completed the assignment, divide them into groups, and have them read their rough drafts to one another and suggest ways in which they could be improved.

Primary Source

David Perkins, in his book *A History of Modern Poetry,* made the following comments about Pound's *Cantos:*

> Perhaps the most striking feature of the *Cantos* is the presentation of many different historical cultures: ancient China, eighteenth-century America, the Renaissance, Homeric Greece, twentieth-century Europe and America, the Middle Ages. These times and places are exhibited in concrete samples. There are passages from the letters of John Adams, laws from ancient China . . . , translations or adaptations of poems from diverse times and cultures, extracts from the accounts of medieval Venice . . . , and there are anecdotes of what such figures as Sigismundo Malatesta, Confucius, Yeats, Baldy Bacon, So-Gioku, and Corporal Casey did or said. Such concrete cases embody values, and Pound believed that from so large and varied an accumulation his readers would gradually and tacitly form a sense of what is permanently valuable. Because these values were concretely presented, they would be formative and productive in a way that abstract argument

THINKING ABOUT THE SELECTION
Recalling

1. Summarize the events in the life of the river-merchant's wife at fourteen, at fifteen, and at sixteen.
2. How deep has the moss grown since the river-merchant left?
3. (a) What hurts the river-merchant's wife? (b) What will she do if her husband comes down "through the narrows of the river Kiang"?

Interpreting

4. This poem is adapted from a Chinese poem by Li T'ai Po. When the original poem was written, marriages were arranged by parents according to Chinese custom. (a) How did the river-merchant's wife feel at the time of her marriage? (b) How are these feelings conveyed? (c) How have her feelings for her husband changed since the time of their marriage?
5. (a) How did the river-merchant feel about leaving home? (b) How are his feelings conveyed?
6. How do the details of the setting in the fifth stanza indicate the passage of time?
7. (a) How does the river-merchant's wife feel about her husband's absence? (b) How do the descriptions of the monkeys and butterflies reflect her feelings?

8. Explain how the tone of this poem is appropriate for the society in which the river-merchant's wife lives—a society governed by custom and tradition.

Applying

9. Many societies have believed in arranged marriages. What do you think are the benefits and the drawbacks of arranged marriages both for the individuals involved and for society as a whole?

THINKING AND WRITING
Writing About Imagism

Although "The River-Merchant's Wife" is not a pure Imagist poem, it does possess a number of the characteristics of Imagist poetry. Write an essay in which you discuss these characteristics. Review the poem noting the simplicity and precision of its language, its use of imagery to evoke emotions, and its musical rhythm. Write a thesis statement, and organize your notes into an outline. Then write your essay using passages from the poem to support your argument. When you revise, add transitions to connect your ideas.

Canto 13

Ezra Pound

Kung[1] walked
    by the dynastic temple and into the cedar grove,
      and then out by the lower river,
And with him Khieu, Tchi
5   and Tian the low speaking
And "we are unknown," said Kung,
"You will take up charioteering?
    Then you will become known,
"Or perhaps I should take up charioteering, or archery?
10 "Or the practice of public speaking?"
And Tseu-lou said, "I would put the defenses in order,"
And Khieu said, "If I were lord of a province
I would put it in better order than this is."
And Tchi said, "I would prefer a small mountain temple,
15 "With order in the observances,
    with a suitable performance of the ritual,"
And Tian said, with his hand on the strings of his lute
The low sounds continuing
    after his hand left the strings,
20 And the sound went up like smoke, under the leaves,
And he looked after the sound:
    "The old swimming hole,
"And the boys flopping off the planks,
"Or sitting in the underbrush playing mandolins."
25   And Kung smiled upon all of them equally.
And Thseng-sie desired to know:
    "Which had answered correctly?"
And Kung said, "They have all answered correctly,
"That is to say, each in his nature."
30 And Kung raised his cane against Yuan Jang,
    Yuan Jang being his elder,
For Yuan Jang sat by the roadside pretending to
    be receiving wisdom.
And Kung said
35   "You old fool, come out of it,
Get up and do something useful."

---

1. Kung: Confucius (551?–479? B.C.), Chinese philosopher and
teacher. Confucius emphasized devotion to parents, family and
friends, ancestor worship, and the maintenance of justice and peace.
Khieu, Tchi, Tian, Tseu-lou, Thseng-sie, and Yuan Jang were his disciples.

Presentation

Motivation/Prior Knowledge
Have your students discuss the concept of order. How can people have order within themselves?

Master Teacher Note You might want to have students research Confucius in an encyclopedia before reading the poem.

Thematic Idea Another poem that explores an Eastern religion is "Brahma" by Ralph Waldo Emerson (p. 285).

Purpose-Setting Question
What does this poem reveal about the beliefs of Confucius?

1 **Discussion** Why does Kung suggest that his disciples should take up charioteering?

2 **Discussion** What do Tseu-lou, Khieu, and Tchi each suggest they might do? What do their suggestions reveal about them?

3 **Discussion** How is Tian's response different from those of the others?

can never be. Viewed in this light, the *Cantos* are the most ambitious educative effort that any poet has undertaken in the twentieth century.

The values highlighted in Pound's multiplied and recurrent examples might be generalized as sincerity and productivity. The ideal of sincerity reflects, as he handles it, a Confucian ambience, though the *Cantos* do not associate it only with China. The sincere man has clarified his intellect and will. He is imbued with persisting truths of nature and human nature and judges and acts properly in relation to them. His way of life is sanity, order, and continuity with human tradition.

4 **Discussion** What reason does Kung give for treating Yuan Jang with disrespect?

5 **Clarification** Confucian thinking advises a middle road between excesses.

6 **Discussion** How would Kung's response be viewed in our society?

7 **Critical Thinking and Reading** When the reader reaches lines 62–65, the idea of Kung's wisdom is so firmly established that the reader assumes there is wisdom in Kung's actions.

8 **Discussion** What is the meaning of the final three lines?

Reader's Response Which of the ideas expressed by Kung had the most meaning for you? Why?

And Kung said
4   "Respect a child's faculties
    "From the moment it inhales the clear air,
40   "But a man of fifty who knows nothing
        Is worthy of no respect."
And "When the prince has gathered about him
"All the savants and artists, his riches will be fully
    employed."
And Kung said, and wrote on the bo leaves:
45   If a man have not order within him
He can not spread order about him;
And if a man have not order within him
His family will not act with due order;
    And if the prince have not order within him
50 He can not put order in his dominions.
And Kung gave the words "order"
and "brotherly deference"
And said nothing of the "life after death."
And he said
5 55   "Anyone can run to excesses,
It is easy to shoot past the mark,
It is hard to stand firm in the middle."

6 And they said: If a man commit murder
    Should his father protect him, and hide him?
60 And Kung said:
    He should hide him.

7 And Kung gave his daughter to Kong-Tch'ang
    Although Kong-Tch'ang was in prison.
And he gave his niece to Nan-Young
65   although Nan-Young was out of office.
And Kung said "Wang[2] ruled with moderation,
    In his day the State was well kept,
And even I can remember
A day when the historians left blanks in their writings,
70 I mean for things they didn't know,
But that time seems to be passing."
And Kung said, "Without character you will
    be unable to play on that instrument
Or to execute the music fit for the Odes.
8 The blossoms of the apricot
    blow from the east to the west,
75 And I have tried to keep them from falling."

---

2. Wang: The first emperor of the Chou Dynasty, ruling China from 1122 to 1115 B.C.

806   *The Modern Age*

THINKING ABOUT THE SELECTION

Recalling

1. (a) What would Tseu-lou do to become known? (b) What would Khieu do if he "were the lord of a province"? (c) What would Tchi "prefer"?
2. (a) What does Thseng-sie ask Kung? (b) How does Kung respond?
3. What comment does Kung make about a "man of fifty who knows nothing"?
4. What does Kung write "on the bo leaves"?
5. According to Kung, what should a man do if his son commits murder?

Interpreting

6. This poem presents a dialogue between Confucius, or Kung, and several of his disciples. Confucius first asks his disciples how they will "become known." When they have finished responding, he comments that each has answered correctly "in his nature." (a) What does this comment reveal about his attitude toward his disciples? (b) What does the fact that he "smiled upon them equally" reveal?
7. What attitude concerning youth and old age does Confucius express?
8. (a) What does Confucius mean when he speaks of a person who has "order within him"? (b) Why is it important for a person to have "order within him"?
9. (a) If the "blossoms of the apricot" symbolize the ancient Chinese culture and its traditions, what do you think Confucius means when he says that the blossoms are blowing "from the east to the west"? (b) What does he mean when he says that he has "tried to keep them from falling"?

Applying

10. What ideas does Confucius express that are applicable to life in our society?

Primary Source

Pound's interests in Imagism and Chinese poetry were connected through his theories about metaphor and poetry. As an Imagist who sought to fill his poetry with vivid, concrete images, Pound regarded the written Chinese language as particularly suited to poetry. Because each Chinese character stands for a complete concept or image by itself, unlike English characters which are simply letters, Pound felt that Chinese poetry retains the vividness and concreteness of metaphor—the key element in poetry for the Imagists.

In "The Chinese Written Character as Medium for Poetry," written with Ernest Fenollosa, Pound argued that, because poetry is the representation of nature, written Chinese is the ideal poetic language.

"Metaphor, the revealer of nature, is the very substance of poetry . . . Poetry is finer than prose because it gives us more concrete truth in the same compass of words. Metaphor, its chief device, is at once the substance and nature of language. Poetry only does consciously what the primitive races did unconsciously. The chief work of literary men in dealing with language, and of poets especially, lies in feeling back along the ancient lines of advance.

. . . I have alleged all this because it enables me to show clearly why I believe that the Chinese written language has not only absorbed the poetic substance of nature and built with it a second world of metaphor, but has, through its very pictorial visibility, been able to retain its original creative poetry with far more vigor and vividness than any phonetic tongue. . . ."

Canto 13 807

More About the Author David Perkins wrote the following description of Eliot's outward demeanor in his *A History of Modern Poetry:* "Eliot's demeanor . . . was not the least of his works of art and had much to do with his subsequent authority in the literary world. It changed somewhat as the years went by; in younger days he was relatively more elegant and occasionally waspish . . . , and in later years he was more owlish, clerical, and benevolent. But till the end of his life one encountered on meeting him the sober three-piece suit, the 'necktie rich and modest' like that of Prufrock, the black hair plastered down, the precise conversation in complete sentences, the unbending reserve, propriety, and courtesy. He amused some persons as an eccentric but he overawed more, arousing their insecurities. In short, he was formidable, though he could not have been so through his bearing alone. It was rather the combination of this with intellectual acuteness, force of character, disinterested purpose, moral intensity, and dangerousness—for one could be ambushed by a snub or a sneer—that gave him his personal ascendancy."

Several of T. S. Eliot's plays had successful runs in London and New York. None of them, however, attained the popularity of a musical written after his death. The musical *Cats* is based on the poems in his *Old Possum's Book of Practical Cats.* Would T. S. Eliot have wanted to be remembered for this?

1888–1965

Thomas Stearns Eliot's poetry received more critical acclaim than that of any other American poet of his time. At the same time, his poetry, along with his literary criticism, influenced other writers of the period.

Born into a prominent family in St. Louis, Missouri, Eliot grew up in an environment that promoted his intellectual development. During his years as an undergraduate at Harvard, Eliot published a number of poems in *The Harvard Advocate,* the school's literary magazine. Then, in 1910, the same year in which he earned his master's degree in philosophy, he completed "The Love Song of J. Alfred Prufrock," his first important poem.

When World War I broke out, Eliot settled in England. There he became acquainted with Ezra Pound, another young American poet. Recognizing Eliot's talent, Pound influenced the editor of the American magazine *Poetry* to publish "The Love Song of J. Alfred Prufrock," making Eliot's work available to the public for the first time.

The publication of "Prufrock," along with the other poems in his first book, *Prufrock and Other Observations* (1917), created a stir in the literary world. Eliot had used techniques that had never before been used. Focusing on the frustration and despair of life in modern urban societies, the poems in Eliot's first book also set the tone for the other poems he would produce during the early stage of his career.

In 1922 Eliot published *The Waste Land,* his most famous poem. The poem contrasts the spiritual bankruptcy that Eliot saw as the dominant force in modern Europe with the values and unity that governed the past. The impact of *The Waste Land* on other writers, critics, and the public was enormous, and it is regarded as one of the finest literary works ever written.

In 1928 Eliot became a devout member of the Church of England, after becoming a British citizen the previous year. These changes preceded radical changes in the focus of Eliot's writing, as evidenced by his exploration of religious themes in *Ash Wednesday* (1930) and *Four Quartets* (1943). These poems suggest that Eliot felt that religious belief could be a means for healing the wounds inflicted on a person by the spiritually bankrupt society he depicted in *The Waste Land.*

During his later years, Eliot also produced a sizable body of literary criticism and wrote several plays. His first major play, *Murder in the Cathedral* (1935), is based on the death of Thomas à Becket. His other plays include *The Cocktail Party* (1950), *The Family Reunion* (1939), *The Confidential Clerk* (1954), and *The Elder Statesman* (1958). In 1948 he received the Nobel Prize for Literature.

808   *The Modern Age*

GUIDE FOR INTERPRETING

The Love Song of J. Alfred Prufrock

Writer's Techniques

Stream of Consciousness. Stream of consciousness is a term originated by American psychologist William James to describe the natural flow of a person's thoughts. James noted that people's thoughts do not flow together in a logical, organized manner, but rather take the form of an unorganized and seemingly unconnected series of insights, memories, and reflections. During the early 1900's, writers began incorporating the ideas of James into their work by trying to capture the random movements of a character's thoughts to re-create the natural flow of people's thoughts. In using the stream-of-consciousness technique, the writers abandoned transitions and other linking devices used in ordinary prose, instead connecting thoughts through the character's natural associations.

Writing

William James once wrote, "There is no more miserable human being than one in whom nothing is habitual but indecision." Freewrite, exploring the meaning of this quotation.

Primary Source

Many readers of poetry read to discover the thoughts and feelings of the poet. They consider poetry to be a highly personal expression of one particular poet's views. Eliot disagreed with this concept of poetry. In his classic essay "Tradition and the Individual Talent," he argued that "the emotion of art is impersonal." By this he meant that the poet should not write from personal experience or about his own emotions. Writing poetry is an impersonal act of creation involving material from outside personal experience. Eliot believed that poetry was the interaction of a poet's individual talent and the tradition of poetry. As he explained, "It is not in his personal emotions, the emotions provoked by particular events in his life, that the poet is in any way remarkable or interesting. . . . The business of the poet is not to find new emotions, but to use the ordinary ones and, in working them up into poetry, to express feelings which are not in actual emotions at all. And emotions he has never experienced will serve his turns as well as those familiar to him. Consequently, we must believe that 'emotion recollected in tranquility' is an inexact formula [for poetry]. For it is neither emotion, not recollection, nor, without distortion of meaning, tranquility. It is a concentration, and a new thing resulting from the concentration. . . ."

Literary Focus The stream-of-consciousness technique has been used by writers of both prose and poetry. To use this technique effectively, a writer must imply the subtle connections between the seemingly disjointed thoughts that flow through a character's mind.

Writing/Prior Knowledge Before students complete the writing activity, you might discuss the meaning of the quotation.

Vocabulary

Preteach the following vocabulary words:
insidious (in sid′ ē əs) *adj.*: Secretly treacherous (p. 810, l. 9)
digress (dī gres′) *v.*: Depart temporarily from the main subject (p. 812, l. 65)
malingers (mə liŋ′ gərz) *v.*: Pretends to be ill (p. 813, l. 76)
meticulous (mə tik′ yoo ləs) *adj.*: Extremely careful about details (p. 814, l. 115)
obtuse (äb toos′) *adj.*: Slow to understand or perceive (p. 814, l. 116)

The Love Song of J. Alfred Prufrock

T. S. Eliot

S'io credessi che mia risposta fosse
a persona che mai tornasse al mondo,
questa fiamma staria senza più scosse.
Ma per ciò che giammai di questo fondo
non tornò vivo alcun, s'i'odo il vero,
senza tema d'infamia ti rispondo.[1]

Let us go then, you and I,
When the evening is spread out against the sky
Like a patient etherized[2] upon a table;
Let us go, through certain half-deserted streets,
5   The muttering retreats
Of restless nights in one-night cheap hotels
And sawdust restaurants with oyster-shells:
Streets that follow like a tedious argument
Of insidious intent
10   To lead you to an overwhelming question . . .
Oh, do not ask, "What is it?"
Let us go and make our visit.

In the room the women come and go
Talking of Michelangelo.[3]

The yellow fog that rubs its back upon the window-panes,
15   The yellow smoke that rubs its muzzle on the window-
      panes,
Licked its tongue into the corners of the evening,

---

1. S'io credessi . . . ti rispondo: The epigraph is a passage from Dante's *Inferno* in which one of the damned, upon being requested to tell his story, says: "If I believed my answer were being given to someone who could ever return to this world, this flame (his voice) would shake no more. But since no one has ever returned alive from this depth, if what I hear is true, I will answer you without fear or disgrace."
2. etherized (ē′ thə rīzd) *v*.: Anesthetized with ether.
3. Michelangelo (mī′ kəl an′ jə lō): A famous Italian artist (1475–1564).

Lingered upon the pools that stand in drains,
Let fall upon its back the soot that falls from chimneys,
Slipped by the terrace, made a sudden leap,
20   And seeing that it was a soft October night,
Curled once about the house, and fell asleep.

And indeed there will be time[4]
For the yellow smoke that slides along the street
Rubbing its back upon the window-panes;
25   There will be time, there will be time
To prepare a face to meet the faces that you meet;
There will be time to murder and create,
And time for all the works and days[5] of hands
That lift and drop a question on your plate;
30   Time for you and time for me,
And time yet for a hundred indecisions,
And for a hundred visions and revisions,
Before the taking of a toast and tea.

In the room the women come and go
35   Talking of Michelangelo.

And indeed there will be time
To wonder, "Do I dare?" and, "Do I dare?"
Time to turn back and descend the stair,
With a bald spot in the middle of my hair—
40   (They will say: 'How his hair is growing thin!')
My morning coat, my collar mounting firmly to the chin,
My necktie rich and modest, but asserted by a simple pin—
(They will say: "But how his arms and legs are thin!")
Do I dare
45   Disturb the universe?
In a minute there is time
For decisions and revisions which a minute will reverse.

For I have known them all already, known them all—
Have known the evenings, mornings, afternoons,
50   I have measured out my life with coffee spoons;
I know the voices dying with a dying fall
Beneath the music from a farther room.
    So how should I presume?

---

4. there will be time: Similar to the narrator's plea in English poet
Andrew Marvell's "To His Coy Mistress": "Had we but world enough
and time . . ."
5. works and days: Ancient Greek poet Hesiod wrote a poem about
farming called "Works and Days."

5 Discussion Why does Prufrock
refer to the people at the party as
faces?

6 Literary Focus Point out the play
on the words "visions" and "revisions."

7 Discussion Why does Eliot repeat these two lines?

8 Discussion What is Prufrock's
image of himself?

9 Discussion What does Prufrock
mean when he says that he has
"measured out" his "life with coffee spoons"?

situation is revealed by the different qualities of the sense
images, by references to various historical figures, and by
literary allusions. These form a pattern of contrasts between Prufrock's incapacity to act and the self-fulfillment of
those who have lived by the instinct or principle of creative
activity.

Fine art, *Moonlight, Dovehouse Street, Chelsea,* by Algernon Newton. Newton (1880–1968) was a British artist who worked in watercolors. His painting *Moonlight, Dovehouse Street, Chelsea,* is a watercolor of atmospheric drama. Painted in a realistic style, it is composed of delicate colors that create a mysterious atmosphere. The glowing lamps and subtle glow of twilight in the sky add to the mystery. As our vision is drawn into the picture by the strong perspective line, we are aware of the lack of human presence. No human figures are visible. No lights are in the windows. The quiet of the scene is only slightly disrupted by the recognition of the small figure of a cat silently crossing the street.

Consider using these questions for discussion:
1. How would you describe the atmosphere or mood of this picture?
2. What elements has the artist used to create this mood?
3. In what ways does this painting reflect aspects of the poem?

10 Discussion What is the effect of repeating "how shall I begin" and "how should I presume?"

MOONLIGHT, DOVEHOUSE STREET, CHELSEA
Algernon Newton
Fine Art Society, London Art Resource, NY

And I have known the eyes already, known them all—
55 The eyes that fix you in a formulated phrase,
And when I am formulated, sprawling on a pin,
When I am pinned and wriggling on the wall,
Then how should I begin
10 To spit out all the butt-ends of my days and ways?
60   And how should I presume?
And I have known the arms already, known them all—
Arms that are braceleted and white and bare
(But in the lamplight, downed with light brown hair!)
Is it perfume from a dress
65 That makes me so digress?
Arms that lie along a table, or wrap about a shawl.

812   The Modern Age

Grammar in Action

Verbs are generally categorized as **action verbs** and **linking verbs.** Action verbs express action, while linking verbs express conditions. Note the following examples:

I have seen the eternal Footman *hold* my coat, and *snicker.* (action verbs)

And in short, I *was* afraid. *(linking verb)*

Some action verbs express more vitality or movement than others, and a good writer will choose verbs carefully to express more or less vitality.

Student Activity 1. Compare the verbs in lines 13 and 14 with those in lines 15 to 21. Decide whether Eliot attributes more activity to the women or to the fog outside. Then explain his choice of verbs.

Student Activity 2. Compare the verbs in the passages that describe Prufrock's wish to reveal himself and the verbs in the passages in which he sees the reality of his life. How has Eliot used verbs to intensify the conflict between Prufrock's desires and his actions?

And should I then presume?
And how should I begin?

　　　·　·　·　·　·　·

Shall I say, I have gone at dusk through narrow streets
70　And watched the smoke that rises from the pipes
Of lonely men in shirt-sleeves, leaning out of windows?. . .

11　I should have been a pair of ragged claws
Scuttling across the floors of silent seas.[6]

　　　·　·　·　·　·　·

And the afternoon, the evening, sleeps so peacefully!
75　Smoothed by long fingers,
Asleep . . . tired . . . or it malingers,
Stretched on the floor, here beside you and me.
Should I, after tea and cakes and ices,
Have the strength to force the moment to its crisis?
80　But though I have wept and fasted, wept and prayed,
Though I have seen my head (grown slightly bald) brought
　　in upon a platter,[7]
I am no prophet—and here's no great matter;
I have seen the moment of my greatness flicker,
And I have seen the eternal Footman[8] hold my coat, and
　　snicker,
85　And in short, I was afraid.

12　And would it have been worth it, after all,
After the cups, the marmalade, the tea,
Among the porcelain, among some talk of you and me,
Would it have been worth while,
90　To have bitten off the matter with a smile,
To have squeezed the universe into a ball
To roll it towards some overwhelming question,
13　To say: "I am Lazarus,[9] come from the dead,
Come back to tell you all, I shall tell you all"—
95　If one, settling a pillow by her head,
　　　Should say: "That is not what I meant at all,
　　　That is not it, at all."

---

6. I should . . . seas: In Shakespeare's *Hamlet*, the hero, Hamlet, mocks the aging Lord Chamberlain, Polonius, saying, "You yourself, sir, should be old as I am, if like a crab you could go backward (II.ii. 205–206).
7. head . . . platter: A reference to the prophet John the Baptist, whose head was delivered on a platter to Salome as a reward for her dancing (Matthew 14:1–11).
8. eternal Footman: Death.
9. Lazarus (laz′ ə rəs): Lazarus is resurrected from the dead by Jesus in John 11:1–44.

11 Discussion What does Prufrock mean when he says that he "should have been a pair of ragged claws"? What does this reveal about Prufrock's self-image?

12 Critical Thinking and Reading Note that Prufrock's apprehensive self has won out, and he has decided not to express his feelings to the woman he loves.

13 Discussion Why does Prufrock compare himself to Lazarus?

Student Activity 3. Supply an appropriate verb for each of the following sentences.

1. The wiry detective _____ along the street.
2. The frail invalid _____ along the street.
3. Furiously, I _____ through the door.
4. Timidly, I _____ through the door.
5. The winning team _____ a victory song.
6. The losing team _____ toward their bus.
7. Sir Launcelot _____ into his armor.
8. J. Alfred Prufrock _____ into his morning coat.
9. Prince Hamlet _____ his sword.
10. J. Alfred Prufrock _____ his coffee spoon.

14 **Clarification** In alluding to Shakespeare's *Hamlet,* Prufrock identifies himself with Polonius, an aging and somewhat foolish character, rather than with Prince Hamlet.

15 **Discussion** How does Prufrock envision his remaining years?

16 **Discussion** What might the mermaids represent? Why will they not sing to Prufrock?

17 **Discussion** What is the meaning of the final line?

Reader's Response What did you find to be the strongest feeling or emotion conveyed in the poem? Explain.

And would it have been worth it, after all,
Would it have been worth while,
100 After the sunsets and the dooryards and the sprinkled
    streets,
After the novels, after the teacups, after the skirts that trail
    along the floor—
And this, and so much more?—
It is impossible to say just what I mean!
But as if a magic lantern[10] threw the nerves in patterns on
    a screen:
105 Would it have been worth while
If one, settling a pillow or throwing off a shawl,
And turning toward the window, should say:
        "That is not it at all,
        That is not what I meant, at all."
            . . . . .

No! I am not Prince Hamlet, nor was meant to be;
110 Am an attendant lord, one that will do
To swell a progress,[11] start a scene or two,
Advise the prince; no doubt, an easy tool,
Deferential, glad to be of use,
115 Politic, cautious, and meticulous;
Full of high sentence,[12] but a bit obtuse;
At times, indeed, almost ridiculous—
Almost, at times, the Fool.

I grow old . . . I grow old . . .
120 I shall wear the bottoms of my trousers rolled.

Shall I part my hair behind? Do I dare to eat a peach?
I shall wear white flannel trousers, and walk upon the
    beach.
I have heard the mermaids singing, each to each.

I do not think that they will sing to me.

125 I have seen them riding seaward on the waves
Combing the white hair of the waves blown back
When the wind blows the water white and black.

We have lingered in the chambers of the sea
By sea-girls wreathed with seaweed red and brown
Till human voices wake us, and we drown.

---

10. magic lantern: An early device used to project images on a screen.
11. To swell a progress: To add to the number of people in a parade or scene from a play.
12. Full of high sentence: Speaking in a very ornate manner, often offering advice.

THINKING ABOUT THE SELECTION

Recalling

1. (a) To what does the speaker compare the evening? (b) To what does he compare the streets?
2. For what "will there be time"?
3. (a) In lines 73–74 what does Prufrock say he should have been? (b) In lines 110–120 how does he describe himself? (c) In lines 126–128 whom does he claim to have seen?

Interpreting

4. Prufrock sees himself as being divided into two parts, with one part being eager to take action, while the other part struggles to hold him back. (a) How does the first line suggest that Prufrock sees himself as divided? (b) What do the images in lines 1–12 suggest about his outlook on life?
5. Throughout the poem Prufrock is on his way to an afternoon tea party and is trying to build up enough courage to tell a woman of his love for her. (a) How does Prufrock convey his apprehension and uncertainty in lines 23–48? (b) In what ways does he indicate that he feels that he is growing old? (c) How does the belief that he is growing old affect his decisions?
6. (a) What feelings about the other guests he expects to find at the party does Prufrock convey in lines 49–67? (b) How does he expect to be treated by the other guests? (c) What does he mean when he remarks, "I have measured my life with coffee spoons"?
7. (a) What fears does Prufrock express in lines 80–86? (b) In lines 97–110 how does he convey the fact that he has given in to his apprehension and has decided not to express his love to the woman? (c) How does he attempt to justify his decision?
8. (a) How do the questions Prufrock asks in line 122 contrast with the questions he had found so overwhelming earlier in the poem? (b) How do the images in lines 124–130 contrast with the images in the first stanza? (c) How does the final line sug-

gest that reality has once again intruded upon his thoughts, leaving him in the same condition as when the poem started?

Applying

9. T. S. Eliot felt that the Modern Age was a time of confusion and uncertainty. In what ways does Eliot use Prufrock as an embodiment of the general sentiments of society as a whole?
10. (a) In what ways are many of us similar to Prufrock? (b) In what instances might our behavior be similar to Prufrock's?

ANALYZING LITERATURE

Understanding Techniques

The **stream-of-consciousness technique** allows a writer to re-create the natural flow of a character's thoughts. When using this technique, a writer uses only the character's natural associations to link thoughts. For example, in lines 70–74 Prufrock's thoughts drift from a contemplation of what he will say to the woman to the philosophical observation that he "should have been a pair of ragged claws."

1. Find two other instances in which Prufrock's thoughts drift from his immediate concerns to general philosophical observations.
2. What natural associations connect Prufrock's immediate concerns with his more general concerns?

CRITICAL THINKING AND READING

Interpreting Allusions

Interpreting the meaning of an **allusion**—a reference to another literary work or a figure, place, or event from history, religion, or mythology—may involve research. For example, to interpret the meaning of Eliot's allusion to Shakespeare's *Hamlet* (lines 111–119), you would have to consult the play itself, a critical essay, or a plot summary.

1. (a) Find two other allusions used by Eliot in the poem. (b) Interpret the meaning of each.
2. Do you think the use of allusions enriches the poem? Explain your answer.

The Love Song of J. Alfred Prufrock 815

negative outlook on life.

5. (a) His constant references to time reveal that he is procrastinating. He also questions his personal appearance and repeatedly asks the question, "do I dare?"; he says that he has seen his "greatness flicker"; and he says, "I grow old." (b) He speaks of his thinning hair. (c) He uses the fact that he is growing old as a justification for not expressing his feelings to the woman he loves.
6. (a) He feels they are superficial. (b) He expects them to be painfully aware of his shortcomings. (c) He has spent his days doing trivial things.
7. (a) He expresses his fear of death. (b) He begins speaking about his intentions of declaring his love in the past tense. (c) He attempts to justify his decision by reminding himself that he might have been rejected.
8. (a) They are painfully trivial. (b) These images suggest dreams and imagination of the beautiful; the images in the first stanza capture the bleakness of city life. (c) The references to human voices and drowning suggest an abrupt return to reality.

Applying

9. Prufrock himself is confused and uncertain.
10. (a) Suggested Response: Many of us are afraid of taking risks. (b) We often put off decisions and action.

ANSWERS TO ANALYZING LITERATURE

1. Answers will differ. Examples include lines 42–45 and lines 78–83.
2. Suggested Response: His more general concerns are reflected in his immediate concerns.

CRITICAL THINKING AND READING

1. (a) The poem also includes allusions to Dante, Marvell, Michelangelo, Lazarus, and John the Baptist. (b) Answers will depend on the allusions chosen.
2. Suggested Response: The use of allusions enriches the poem by adding additional layers of meaning.

Closure and Extension

ANSWERS TO THINKING ABOUT THE SELECTION
Recalling

1. (a) He compares it to "a patient etherized upon a table." (b) He compares the streets to a "tedious argument/Of insidious intent."
2. There will be time to prepare a

face, to murder and create, for you and me, and for decisions and revisions.
3. (a) He says he should have been a pair of ragged claws. (b) He describes himself as a bit player of no particular importance and somewhat ridiculous. (c) He claims that he has seen mermaids singing.

Interpreting

4. (a) He refers to himself as both "you" and "I." (b) He has a very

815

ing to David Perkins, "Until the
1950's Wallace Stevens had enjoyed only a gradually spreading
succes d'estime as a 'poet's
poet' or a 'critic's poet.' He now
discovered that graduate students were reading him with enthusiasm, and some wished to
write about him. At this academic
reception he was wryly ironic as
well as incredulous. Honors piled
on him in his sixties and early
seventies, including the offer, in
1954, to serve as Charles Eliot
Norton Professor of Poetry at
Harvard. (He turned it down, for
he was diffident about lecturing
on poetry. He also feared that
acceptance would entail retirement from the insurance company.) Despite his growing reputation, he had been unwilling to
bring out a collected edition,
fearing lest such a climax to his
career might also prove a termination. But in 1954 he admitted
to his publisher . . . that he
would 'have difficulty in putting
together another volume' and authorized publication of the *Collected Poems*."

Wallace Stevens's work was
influenced by movements that
occurred in music and art during
his lifetime. Why might a writer be
influenced by artistic movements
outside of the literary world?

WALLACE STEVENS

1879–1955

Wallace Stevens believed that the goal of poetry is to capture the interaction of the imagination and the real world. As a result he spent
his career writing poems that delved into the ways in which the physical world is perceived through the imagination.

Stevens was born and raised in Reading, Pennsylvania. After
graduating from Harvard, he worked briefly as a journalist before
attending law school. He practiced law for a short time, then took a
job in the legal department of an insurance company in Hartford, Connecticut. Eventually he became the company's vice-president.

Stevens did not publish his first collection of poetry, *Harmonium*
(1923), until he was over forty. Although the book received little recognition from the general public, it earned praise from critics and
other poets. In the poems in this book, Stevens uses dazzling imagery to capture the beauty of the physical world, while expressing the
dependence of this beauty on the perceptions of the observer.

During the second half of his life, Stevens published many more
volumes of poetry, including *Ideas of Order* (1935), *Parts of a World*
(1942), *Transport to Summer* (1947), *The Auroras of Autumn* (1950),
and *Collected Poems* (1955), which earned him the Pulitzer Prize.
Despite his success as a poet, however, Stevens continued his career in insurance. He rarely appeared in public and only began giving
readings toward the end of his life.

While Stevens's early poems explore the ways in which the imagination shapes reality, his later work tended to be more abstract. He
began focusing on such philosophical subjects as death and humanity's relationship with nature. Instead of exploring different ways of
perceiving reality, he delved into different ways of contemplating and
comprehending reality.

In *The Necessary Angel,* a slim book about poetry and reality,
Stevens wrote, "There is, in fact, a world of poetry indistinguishable
from the world in which we live, or, I ought to say, no doubt, from the
world in which we shall come to live, since what makes the poet
the potent figure that he is, or was, or ought to be, is that he creates
the world to which we turn incessantly and without knowing it and that
he gives to life the supreme fictions without which we are unable to
conceive of it."

Throughout his career, however, Stevens's goal as a poet was
"to help people live their lives." Stevens believed that life in the Modern Age was often uncertain and confusing, and that it was the duty
of the poet to provide new ways of understanding the world. By writing
poems that help us to see our role in shaping reality, he was able to
accomplish his goal.

816   *The Modern Age*

Objectives

1 To respond to a state-
   ment by the writer
2 To appreciate symbol-
   ism
3 To support an interpretation

Support Material

Teaching Portfolio
Teacher Backup, p. 1059
Usage and Mechanics Work-
   sheet, p. 1063
Vocabulary Check, p. 1064
Analyzing Literature Worksheet,
   Interpreting Symbolism, p. 1065
Critical Thinking and Reading
   Worksheet, *Supporting Inter-
   pretation,* p. 1066
Selection Test, p. 1067

GUIDE FOR INTERPRETING

Disillusionment of Ten O'Clock; Anecdote of the Jar

Literary Movements

Symbolism. Like many other writers of his time, Stevens was influenced by Symbolism, a literary movement that originated in France in the last half of the nineteenth century. Because people perceive the physical world in different ways, the Symbolist poets believed that the ideas and emotions that people experience are personal and difficult to communciate. As a result these poets avoided directly stating their own ideas and emotions in their poetry. Instead they tried to convey meaning through clusters of symbols—people, places, objects, or actions that have meanings in themselves and also represent something larger than themselves. Because of this reliance on symbols, Symbolist poems can often be interpreted in a number of different ways. Similarly many of Stevens's poems can be interpreted in more than one way.

Commentary

As you read Wallace Stevens's poetry, you will notice that his symbolism encompasses what is real as well as what is not real. Dreams and the imagination are intermixed with concrete objects. Does concrete reality exist outside our imaginations? How does imagination shape our experience of the real world? These are questions Stevens considered. He wanted "not ideas about the thing but the thing itself," as he suggested in another poem. Poetry, he felt, joins imagination and the real world. Consider these ideas as you read "Disillusionment of Ten O'Clock" and "Anecdote of the Jar."

Writing

In "Disillusionment of Ten O'Clock" the subject is people's dreams. Freewrite about dreams and their meanings. How do dreams relate to a person's life? What can dreams reveal about a person? How can people be affected by their dreams?

Literary Focus Point out that writers are often influenced by works that emerged from literary movements of previous eras.

Writing/Prior Knowledge In writing about dreams, students may want to think about some of the symbols that occur in people's dreams.

Vocabulary

Preteach the following vocabulary words:
slovenly (sluv′ ən lē) *adj.*: Untidy (p. 819, l. 3)
dominion (də min′ yən) *n.*: Power to rule (p. 819, l. 9)

Guide for Interpreting 817

Motivation/Prior Knowledge
Discuss the role of the imagination in people's lives. How does an imaginative way of life contrast with a dull, unimaginative way of life?

Thematic Idea Another poem that explores the effects of the imagination is "Still Life" by Reed Wittemore (p. 1128).

Purpose-Setting Question
What is the speaker's attitude toward the imagination?

1 Critical Thinking and Reading
Discuss the difference between white nightgowns and the others mentioned. Is it easy to understand the contrast the poet is setting up?

2 Clarification Ceintures are belts.

3 Discussion What is the speaker's main point?

Reader's Response How important is an active imagination to you?

Closure and Extension

ANSWERS TO THINKING ABOUT THE SELECTION
Recalling

1. They are haunted by "white nightgowns."
2. They will not dream about "baboons and periwinkles."
3. An old, drunk sailor sleeps and dreams of catching "tigers in red weather."

Interpreting

4. (a) The white nightgowns represent the unimaginative; the colorful represent more imaginative ways. (b) The unimaginative do not dream of anything interesting; the more imaginative sailors do.
5. (a) Stevens favors the imaginative. (b) It is characterized by conformity and a lack of imagination.

Disillusionment of Ten O'Clock
Wallace Stevens

The houses are haunted
By white night-gowns.
None are green,
Or purple with green rings,
5 Or green with yellow rings,
Or yellow with blue rings.
None of them are strange,
With socks of lace
And beaded ceintures.
10 People are not going
To dream of baboons and periwinkles.
Only, here and there, an old sailor,
Drunk and asleep in his boots,
Catches tigers
15 In red weather.

THINKING ABOUT THE SELECTION
Recalling
1. By what are the houses haunted?
2. About what are the people "not going to dream"?
3. What happens "only here and there"?

Interpreting
4. In this poem Stevens contrasts an interesting, imaginative way of life with a dull, unimaginative way of life. (a) How does Stevens develop this contrast through his description of nightgowns? (b) How does his description of dreams further develop the contrast?
5. (a) Considering the poem's title and the reference to the houses as "haunted," which way of life do you think Stevens favors? (b) What comment does he seem to be making about modern life?

Applying
6. (a) What are some other things Stevens could have used to symbolize an unimaginative way of life? (b) What are some other things he could have used to symbolize an imaginative way of life?

THINKING AND WRITING
Responding to a Statement
Stevens felt that the goal of a poet was "to help people live their lives." Write an essay in which you discuss Stevens's comment in relation to the poem you have just read. Does it help people to live their lives? If so, how? When you finish writing, revise your essay, making sure that you have included enough evidence to thoroughly support your argument.

Applying

6. (a) Suggested Response: He could have used gray suits, row houses, or briefcases. (b) Suggested Response: He could have used colorful balloons, purple pants, or unusual buildings.

THINKING AND WRITING

For help with this assignment, students can refer to Lesson 15, "Evaluating a Literary Work," in the Handbook of Writing About Literature.

After students have completed the assignment, divide them into groups, and have them read their essays to one another and suggest ways in which they could be improved.

Anecdote of the Jar

Wallace Stevens

1
> I placed a jar in Tennessee,
> And round it was, upon a hill.
> It made the slovenly wilderness
> Surround that hill.

2
> 5 The wilderness rose up to it,
> And sprawled around, no longer wild.
> The jar was round upon the ground
> And tall and of a port in air.

> It took dominion everywhere.
> 10 The jar was gray and bare.
> It did not give of bird or bush,
> Like nothing else in Tennessee.

THINKING ABOUT THE SELECTION
Recalling

1. Where does the speaker place the jar?

Interpreting

2. In your own words, describe the jar's effect on the wilderness.
3. How is the impression of the jar that the speaker conveys in the third stanza different from that conveyed in the first two stanzas?

Applying

4. What types of objects do people create that have a dramatic effect on nature?

ANALYZING LITERATURE
Interpreting Symbolism

Symbolism was a literary movement that originated in France in the late nineteenth century and that influenced many English and American writers of the twentieth century. The Symbolist poets avoided directly stating ideas and emotions in their poetry. Instead they suggested meaning through the use of symbols.

How does this poem reflect the influence of the Symbolist poets?

CRITICAL THINKING AND READING
Supporting an Interpretation

Because of the Symbolists' reliance on symbols, their poetry can often be interpreted in several ways. Similarly, many of Wallace Stevens's poems can be interpreted in more than one way.

Find evidence in the poem to support each of the following interpretations.

1. The jar symbolizes the human imagination, and the poem points out how the appearance of nature is shaped by our perceptions. The poem also points out that our imaginations depend on the physical world for input.
2. The jar symbolizes human interference with nature, and the poem explores the effects of human creations on nature.

Anecdote of the Jar   819

Lowell is also known for her biography of the English poet John Keats and for her works of literary criticism. She also invented "polyphonic prose," a literary form which combines aspects of prose and rhythmic poetry. Do you think that it is important for poets to experiment with other forms of writing?

Critical Evaluation Ludwig Lewisohn felt that Amy Lowell, "trapped by lineage and station in all the popular orthodoxies in politics and culture she projected into literature her fierce revolt against her nature and her personal fate. Thus by her warfare for the liberation of form she seemed allied to the recusants' rebellion and liberation of morals and became something of a banner and a bugler to a generation whose deeper mood she did not share. Nor are her vigor and versatility and talent for the sheer technique of letters to be denied . . .

More and more as the years went on she abandoned the exercises in free verse which nevertheless often had in her hand the hard but permanent glint and cool glow of jade or turquoise or lapis and wrote in the warmer measures closer and more native to the heart . . ."

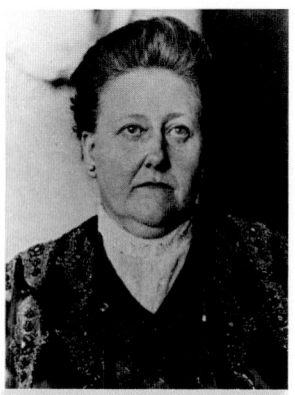

AMY LOWELL

1874–1925

A descendant of New England Renaissance poet James Russell Lowell, Amy Lowell was a strong-minded poet, whose determination helped her to establish herself as the leader of the Imagist movement.

Born in Brookline, Massachusetts, she received an excellent education and traveled extensively as a young girl. In 1913 she published her first volume of poetry, *A Dome of Many Colors,* but the book was not well received. A year later, after reading a poem by the Imagist poet H. D., she traveled to London, hoping to become part of the Imagist movement. She began focusing on creating vivid, precise images in her poetry. At the same time, she energetically promoted the Imagist movement in lectures and essays, and she eventually became the movement's leader. Unfortunately, however, Ezra Pound, the founder of the Imagist movement, found her poetry overly sentimental, and her emergence as the leader of the Imagist circle prompted him to sever his connection with the group.

An outspoken commentator on poets and poetry, Lowell worked hard at defining what were, for her, the ingredients of good poetry: fresh, new rhythms; the language of common speech; clear, concrete, and vivid images. "A demon saleswoman," Eliot called her for her crusade to advertise the new poetry. Reacting against the popular view of the poet as an inspired genius who writes poetry spontaneously—a view inherited from early nineteenth-century Romanticism—Lowell insisted that poetry was a trade like any other. The poet needed to learn and practice writing poetry to do it well. In the preface to her collection *Sword Blades and Poppy Seeds* (1914), she elaborated on this definition of poetry. "No one expects a man to make a chair without first learning how, but there is a popular impression that the poet is born, not made, and that his verses burst from his overflowing heart of themselves. As a matter of fact, the poet must learn his trade in the same manner, and with the same painstaking care, as the cabinetmaker. His heart may overflow with high thoughts and sparkling fancies, but if he cannot convey them to his reader by means of the written word he has no claim to be considered a poet."

Lowell published eleven volumes of poetry between 1913 and 1925, and three others appeared after her death in 1925. Her collection *What's O'Clock* (1925) won her the Pulitzer Prize.

"Patterns," one of her best-known poems, appeared in *Men, Women, and Ghosts,* published in 1916. In this poem she uses colorful images to reflect the emotions of a woman whose fiancé has just been killed in a war.

Objectives

1 To analyze a dramatic monologue
2 To understand word origins
3 To compare and contrast poems

Support Material

Teaching Portfolio
Teacher Backup, p. 1069
Usage and Mechanics Worksheet, p. 1073
Vocabulary Check, p. 1074
Analyzing Literature Worksheet, *Understanding Dramatic Monologue,* p. 1075
Language Worksheet, *Understanding Word Origins,* p. 1076
Selection Test, p. 1077

GUIDE FOR INTERPRETING

Patterns

Literary Forms

Dramatic Monologue. A dramatic monologue is a poem in which one character speaks to one or more silent listeners at a critical point in the speaker's life. The speaker's comments reveal the circumstances surrounding the conversation and offer insights into his or her personality. In T. S. Eliot's poem "The Love Song of J. Alfred Prufrock," for example, the speaker expresses his feelings of uncertainty and disjointedness while debating whether or not to declare his love for a woman.

Commentary

"Patterns" is famous for its rich and brilliant imagery. Writing about Amy Lowell, poet and critic Louis Untermeyer said, "She is, preeminently, the poet of the external world; her visual effects are as 'hard and clear' as the most uncompromising Imagist could desire. The colors with which her words are studded seem like bits of bright enamel; every leaf and flower has a lacquered brilliance. . . . [E]verything flashes, leaps, startles, and burns with dynamic, almost savage speed. . . ."

Through this dynamic imagery, Lowell creates the patterns in this poem. She begins with the concrete pattern of the garden path and moves on to "a pattern called war." This simple story of unfulfilled love begins quietly enough, but it goes on to express a protest against unnatural, artificially imposed patterns that may prevent individuals from fulfilling their lives.

"What are patterns for?" cries the speaker of the poem. What are they for? When do they serve a positive purpose, and when do they restrain? Consider these questions as you read the poem.

Writing

"Patterns" focuses on a woman's reaction to her fiancé's death during a war. Freewrite about the types of emotions that might be evoked by the loss of a loved one during a war.

Guide for Interpreting 821

Humanities Note

Fine art, *In a Shoreham Garden,* c. 1829, by Samuel Palmer. Palmer (1805–1881), an English painter, was considered a child prodigy, exhibiting three drawings at the Royal Academy at the age of fourteen. His painting during his young adulthood was based directly on nature and emanated a mystical spirit, which leaned toward German mysticism rather than the English landscape.

In 1827, Palmer settled in the village of Shoreham in order to commune with nature. It was here that he painted this picture, *In a Shoreham Garden,* a good example of his early work. It is based not on the natural appearance of the garden, but, rather, on an optical and mystical experience of it. The painting resembles the poem "Patterns" through its bright patterns of color, the imaginative qualities of the forms, and its subject—an actual English garden. You might ask student these questions after they have read the poem.

1. What "patterns" can you find in this painting? Consider art elements such as color, shape, and composition.
2. Which words from the poem could be applied to this painting?

Motivation/Prior Knowledge
Have students discuss the ways in which peoples' lives can form a pattern. Does everyone's life form some kind of pattern?

Thematic Idea "The Love Song of J. Alfred Prufrock" is also a dramatic monologue (p. 810).

Purpose-Setting Question
How is the speaker affected by her fiancé's death?

1 Discussion What might the garden-paths symbolize?

Patterns

Amy Lowell

I walk down the garden-paths,
And all the daffodils
Are blowing, and the bright blue squills.
I walk down the patterned garden-paths
5   In my stiff, brocaded gown.
With my powdered hair and jeweled fan,
I too am a rare
Pattern. As I wander down
The garden-paths.
10   My dress is richly figured,
And the train
Makes a pink and silver stain
On the gravel, and the thrift
Of the borders.
15   Just a plate of current fashion,
Tripping by in high-heeled, ribboned shoes.
Not a softness anywhere about me,
Only whalebone and brocade.
And I sink on a seat in the shade
20   Of a lime-tree. For my passion
Wars against the stiff brocade.
The daffodils and squills

822   *The Modern Age*

2 Clarification When a person is a "plate of current fashion" it means that he or she looks like an illustration in a fashion book.

3 Discussion How does the speaker emphasize the contrast between softness and stiffness?

Flutter in the breeze
As they please.
25 And I weep;
For the lime-tree is in blossom
And one small flower had dropped upon my bosom.

And the plashing of waterdrops
In the marble fountain
30 Comes down the garden-paths.
The dripping never stops.
Underneath my stiffened gown
Is the softness of a woman bathing in a marble basin,
A basin in the midst of hedges grown
35 So thick, she cannot see her lover hiding,
But she guesses he is near,
And the sliding of the water
Seems the stroking of a dear
Hand upon her.
40 What is Summer in a fine brocaded gown!
I should like to see it lying in a heap upon the ground.
All the pink and silver crumpled up on the ground.

I would be the pink and silver as I ran along the paths,
And he would stumble after,
45 Bewildered by my laughter.
I should see the sun flashing from his sword hilt and the
    buckles on his shoes.
I would choose
To lead him in a maze along the patterned paths,
A bright and laughing maze for my heavy-booted lover.
50 Till he caught me in the shade,
And the buttons of his waistcoat bruised my body as he
    clasped me
Aching, melting, unafraid.
With the shadows of the leaves and the sundrops,
And the plopping of the waterdrops,
55 All about us in the open afternoon—
I am very like to swoon
With the weight of this brocade,
For the sun sifts through the shade.
Underneath the fallen blossom
60 In my bosom,
Is a letter I have hid.
It was brought to me this morning by a rider from the
    Duke.[1]

---

1. the Duke: Probably John Churchill, Duke of Marlborough (1650–
1722), English general and statesman who commanded the united
English and Dutch armies during the War of the Spanish Succession
(1701–1714).

4 **Critical Thinking and Reading**
The image suggests that the
speaker would burst out of her
culture-imposed cage and follow
her natural desires.

5 **Discussion** What does the brocade symbolize? In what contexts does the speaker mention
it?

6 **Discussion** How is the image of
the fallen blossom related to
what follows?

7 **Discussion** What is the effect of the repetition of lines and images?

8 **Discussion** In what sense is war a "pattern"?

Reader's Response What ideas and emotions expressed in this poem are applicable to people today?

"Madam, we regret to inform you that Lord Hartwell
Died in action Thursday se'nnight."[2]
65   As I read it in the white, morning sunlight,
The letters squirmed like snakes.
"Any answer, Madam," said my footman.
"No," I told him.
"See that the messenger takes some refreshment.
70   No, no answer."
And I walked into the garden,
Up and down the patterned paths,
In my stiff, correct brocade.
The blue and yellow flowers stood up proudly in the sun,
75   Each one.
I stood upright too,
Held rigid to the pattern
By the stiffness of my gown.
Up and down I walked,
80   Up and down.

In a month he would have been my husband.
In a month, here, underneath this lime,
We would have broke the pattern;
He for me, and I for him,
85   He as Colonel, I as Lady,
On this shady seat.
He had a whim
That sunlight carried blessing.
And I answered, "It shall be as you have said."
90   Now he is dead.

In Summer and in Winter I shall walk
Up and down
The patterned garden-paths
In my stiff, brocaded gown.
95   The squills and daffodils
Will give place to pillared roses, and to asters, and to snow.
I shall go
Up and down,
In my gown.
100   Gorgeously arrayed,
Boned and stayed.
And the softness of my body will be guarded from embrace
By each button, hook, and lace.
For the man who should loose me is dead,
105   Fighting with the Duke in Flanders,
In a pattern called a war.
Christ! What are patterns for?

---

2. Thursday se'nnight: A week ago Thursday.

824   The Modern Age

THINKING ABOUT THE SELECTION

Recalling

1. (a) Where does the speaker walk? (b) What is she wearing?
2. (a) About what had a messenger informed the speaker that morning? (b) How had she replied to the message?
3. (a) What does the speaker reveal about Lord Hartwell in the fourth stanza? (b) What does she vow to do in the fifth stanza?

Interpreting

4. The poem's speaker is an upper-class woman living in the early eighteenth century, whose life follows a rigid, formal "pattern." (a) How do her walks in the garden echo the overall pattern of her life? (b) How does the apearance of her dress reflect the pattern of her life? (c) How would getting married have broken the pattern?
5. (a) In what sense is war a "pattern"? (b) What type of "war" seems to be going on in the speaker's mind?
6. How does the final line contrast with the rest of the poem?

Applying

7. Provide your own answer to the woman's final question.

ANALYZING LITERATURE

Understanding Dramatic Monologue

A **dramatic monologue** is a poem in which one character speaks to one or more silent listeners at a critical point in the speaker's life. The speaker's comments reveal the circumstances surrounding the conversation and offer insights into his or her personality. For example, in "Pat-

terns" the speaker's response to her fiancé's death provides insight into her personality.

1. What does the speaker's immediate reaction to the news of her fiancé's death reveal about her personality?
2. What is the speaker's attitude concerning her life?

UNDERSTANDING LANGUAGE

Understanding Word Origins

Many words came into English through French. For example, the English word *fatigue* comes from the French word *fatiguer,* meaning "to weary."

The following words from "Patterns" are of French origin. Use your dictionary to find the meaning of each word. Then give the French word and meaning from which it comes.

1. pattern
2. fashion
3. figure
4. embrace
5. gorgeously

THINKING AND WRITING

Comparing and Contrasting Poems

Write an essay in which you compare and contrast "Patterns" with the Imagist poems of Ezra Pound (pages 800–806). Reread the poems, noting similarities and differences between Lowell's poem and Pound's. Organize your notes according to corresponding points of comparison and contrast. Then write your essay, using evidence from the poems to support your argument. When you finish writing, revise your essay, making sure you have quoted exactly. Proofread your essay and prepare a final draft.

Patterns 825

by others. (b) The dress is stiff and confining, as is her life. (c) She would have been able to break out of restraints and express her love physically.

5. (a) War itself is very regimented, and wars have occurred regularly throughout history. (b) The war in her mind seems to be between her natural impulses and the demands of society.
6. The speaker expresses emotion.

Applying

7. Suggested Response: Patterns can be an important part of life and can help us to accomplish our goals, yet we should not allow ourselves to become caught in patterns that make us unhappy.

ANSWERS TO ANALYZING LITERATURE

1. She is self-disciplined and restrained. She can maintain the outward form of the pattern.
2. Suggested Response: She is displeased with her patterned existence.

UNDERSTANDING LANGUAGE

1. pattern: A form considered worth copying; from *patron,* "something to be imitated."
2. fashion: Accepted custom or style; from *facun,* meaning "company or doing."
3. figure: Form, also a public image; from *figure,* meaning "shape."
4. embrace: To hug, clasp in one's arms; from *embracier,* coming from *brace,* meaning "the two arms."
5. gorgeously: Splendid in appearance or color; from *gorgias,* meaning "fashionable or elegant."

THINKING AND WRITING

For help with this assignment, students can refer to Lesson 16, "Writing a Comparative Evaluation," in the Handbook of Writing About Literature.

After students have completed the assignment, divide them into groups, and have them read their essays to one another and comment on ways in which they could be improved.

Closure and Extension

ANSWERS TO THINKING ABOUT THE SELECTION
Recalling

1. (a) She walks down the garden-paths. (b) She is wearing a stiff, brocaded gown.
2. (a) The messenger had informed the speaker that her fiancé had

died in action. (b) She had said there was no answer.
3. (a) He would have been her husband in a month. (b) She will continue to walk the garden-paths, and she will maintain the pattern of her life.

Interpreting

4. (a) She adheres to the guidelines, the patterns and paths, laid down

More About the Author Along with Ezra Pound, H. D. was responsible for the birth of the Imagist movement. Although the movement was short-lived, it has had a major impact on the poetry of successive generations of writers. Why are emotive images such an important element of poetry?

Critical Evaluation According to Nina Baym, "H.D.'s imagist poetry, for which she was known during her lifetime, represents a perfect expression of the imagist credo with its vivid phrasing, compelling imagery, free verse, short poetic line, and avoidance of abstraction and generalization. . . . Her images come chiefly from nature: austere landscapes of sea, wind, and sand are contrasted with exotic figures of flowers, jewelry, and shells. This contrast can be understood in many ways: it is sterility versus fruitfulness, intellect versus passion, control versus abandon, grief versus joy. . . . Her poetry, though centered on her experience as a woman, was also entirely modernist in its representation of the psyche—anybody's psyche—adrift in a violent, fragmented, alien, and insecure reality."

H. D. (HILDA DOOLITTLE)

1886–1961

In 1913 when Ezra Pound reshaped three of Hilda Doolittle's poems and submitted them to *Poetry* magazine under the name "H. D., Imagiste," the Imagist movement was born. At the same time, it marked the beginning of a successful career for the young poet, who continued to publish her work under the name H. D. throughout the course of her career.

H. D. was born in Bethlehem, Pennsylvania. When she was fifteen she met Pound, who was a student at the University of Pennsylvania. She entered Bryn Mawr College but left because of poor health. In 1911 she moved to London where she renewed her acquaintance with Pound. She married English poet Richard Aldington, a close friend of Pound's, in 1913. Together they studied Greek and developed a deep affection for classical literature. Unfortunately, however, their marriage failed during World War I, when Aldington enlisted in the army and was sent to France.

H. D. remained for a short while in London where she became one of the leaders of the Imagist group. In 1920 she returned to America and settled in California, where she remained for a year before returning to England. After 1921, she lived in Switzerland, where she died in 1961.

Like the Greek lyrics which she greatly admired, H. D.'s early poems were characteristically brief, precise, and direct. Often emphasizing light, color, and physical textures, she created vivid, emotive images. She also abandoned traditional rhythmical patterns, instead creating innovative musical rhythms in her poetry.

In 1925 almost all of H. D.'s early poems were collected in *Collected Poems*. This volume also contains her translations from the *Odyssey* and from the Greek poet Sappho. She also wrote a play, *Hippolytus Temporizes,* which appeared in 1927, and two prose works: *Palimpsest* (1926) and *Hedylus* (1928).

During the later stages of her career, H. D. focused on writing longer works, including *The Walls Do Not Fall* (1944) and *The Flowering of the Rod* (1946). She also wrote an epic poem, *Helen in Egypt.* Comparing her early and late poetry, critic Joseph N. Riddel wrote, "The major distinction . . . is that the [later] poem has become a process or act of discovery. No longer a closed form, a thing itself, it has become a generative act." Despite these later works, however, H. D. is remembered mainly for her early Imagist poetry.

Objectives
1 To write an Imagist poem
2 To understand imagery
3 To analyze the effect of imagery

Support Material

Teaching Portfolio
Teacher Backup, p. 1079
Usage and Mechanics Worksheet, p. 1082
Analyzing Literature Worksheet, *Understanding Imagery,* p. 1083
Language Worksheet, *Choosing the Meaning That Fits the Context,* p. 1084
Selection Test, p. 1085

GUIDE FOR INTERPRETING

Pear Tree; Heat

The Writer's Techniques

Imagery. Imagery refers to words or phrases that create mental pictures, or images, that appeal to one or more of the five senses—sight, hearing, touch, smell, or taste. Most often images appeal to our sense of sight. For example, H. D. creates a visual picture in our minds in "Pear Tree," when she writes "no flower ever opened so staunch a white leaf." Sometimes, however, images do not appeal to our sense of sight, and in some cases a single image appeals to more than one sense.

Imagery was the most vital element of Imagist poems. The Imagists focused on presenting powerful and vivid images, while deleting unnecessary or abstract words and avoiding explanations and generalizations. As a result the Imagists depended on the power of their images to evoke emotions and to capture the readers' attention.

Writing

Think of an image that you find especially striking. For example, you might think of a raging fire, a cherry tree in full bloom, or a snow-covered pine tree swaying in the winter wind. Then prepare a list of sensory details you might use to capture this image.

Primary Source

According to poet and critic Louis Untermeyer, H. D. was the "most important member" of the group of Imagists, including Ezra Pound, with whom she worked.

> She was the only one who steadfastly held to the letter as well as the spirit of its *credo*. She was, in fact, the only true Imagist. Her poems are like a set of Tanagra figurines. Here, at first glance, the effect is chilling—beauty seems held in a frozen gesture. But it is in this very fixation of light, color, and emotion that she achieves intensity. What at first seemed static becomes fluent; the arrested moment glows with quivering tension.
>
> Observe the poem entitled "Heat." Here, in the fewest possible words, is something beyond the description of heat—here is the effect of it. In these lines one feels the weight and solidity of a midsummer afternoon. . . . Her efforts to draw the contemporary world are less happy. H. D. is best in her reflections of clear-cut loveliness in a quietly pagan world; in most of her moods, she seems less a modern writer than an inspired anachronism."

How H. D. uses vivid images to create the "effect" of heat, rather than simply describe it, marks her as one of the Imagists. What effect does she create in "Pear Tree"?

Guide for Interpreting 827

Motivation/Prior Knowledge
Ask students whether they have ever seen a pear tree in bloom. If possible, bring in a picture of a flowering pear tree.

Master Teacher Note You might want to bring in a few twentieth-century paintings of flowers and trees. Discuss the effect of the images in the paintings. Georgia O'Keeffe's flower paintings might be especially effective.

Purpose-Setting Question
What emotions does the image evoke?

1 **Literary Focus** The word *silver* is repeated several times. What is the effect of this repetition?

2 **Discussion** What is the effect of the repetition of the phrase *higher than my arms reach*?

3 **Critical Thinking and Reading**
The final image, like the others in the poem, is primarily visual yet there is an expectation of taste in the phrase *ripe fruits*.

Humanities Note

Fine art, *Orchard in Bloom, Louveçiennes,* 1872, by Camille Pissarro. Pissarro, (1831–1903), born in St. Thomas in the West Indies, traveled to Paris in 1855 in time to see the great exhibit at the World Fair. Soon after he met several prominent Impressionist painters and was deeply influenced by them. In 1863 several of his paintings were exhibited in the Salon des Refusés. From 1866 to 1869, he worked at Pontoise on landscapes painted entirely outside. Although he sold very few paintings, and he and his family lived in poverty, Pissarro was respected and admired by all the Impressionists, for his principles as well as for his art.

In 1895, eye troubles forced him to give up working out-of-doors. He then painted many town views from Paris windows. He died blind. He had been a prolific artist, working not only in oils, but also in etching and lithography as well. His work is in almost every museum of modern art in the world.

This painting, like "Pear Tree," is a poetic expression. Pissarro provides his impression of what he saw in the orchard at Louveçiennes. The colors, forms and spirit of the painting are alive with his true impressions of the moment.

As students look at the painting, you might ask these questions:
1. What is the dominant impression of this painting?
2. What elements of the painting reflect elements of the poem?
3. Pissarro painted this picture out-of-doors, on the spot. How did this add to the "life" of the painting?

Pear Tree

H. D.

1   Silver dust
    lifted from the earth,
    higher than my arms reach,
    you have mounted,
5   O silver,
2   higher than my arms reach
    you front us with great mass;

    no flower ever opened
    so staunch a white leaf,
10 no flower ever parted silver
    from such rare silver;

    O white pear,
    your flower-tufts
    thick on the branch
3 15 bring summer and ripe fruits
    in their purple hearts.

ORCHARD IN BLOOM, LOUVEÇIENNES, 1872
Camille Pissarro
National Gallery of Art, Washington, D.C.

THINKING ABOUT THE SELECTION

Recalling

1. How high has the "silver dust" been "lifted"?
2. What do the flower-tufts of the white pear bring "in their purple hearts"?

Interpreting

3. (a) What is the "silver dust" referred to in the first stanza? (b) In what sense is the silver dust "lifted from the earth"?
4. (a) What time of year is the speaker describing? (b) How is this information conveyed?
5. In the final stanza, H. D. uses apostrophe, directly addressing the pear tree. How does her use of this technique help convey a sense of harmony between humanity and nature?

Applying

6. H. D. uses the color silver several times in her description. What associations do you have with the color silver?

THINKING AND WRITING

Writing an Imagist Poem

Write a poem in which you focus on creating a single vivid and emotive image. Imagine that you are writing your poem for someone who has never seen what you are describing. Start by reviewing the list of sensory details you made before. Add any additional details that come to mind. Write your poem in free verse, trying to capture the natural rhythms of ordinary speech. When you finish writing, revise your poem and share it with your classmates.

Commentary

In "Pear Tree," H. D. writes about a pear tree blossoming in spring. In another poem about a pear tree, entitled "Orchard," H. D. describes the tree at another point in its cycle of nature—late summer. When she addresses the tree in "Pear Tree," she seems to convey a sense of continuity between humanity and nature that is full of beautiful and rich promise. Her address to the pear tree in "Orchard" suggests more tension from beauty too much to bear: "you have flayed us with your blossoms, / spare us the beauty / of fruit-trees!" Comparing "Pear Tree" with "Orchard" may help you understand how imagery works to convey different meanings and moods in H. D.'s poetry.

Orchard

I saw the first pear
as it fell—
the honey-seeking, golden-banded,
the yellow swarm,
was not more fleet than I,
(spare us from loveliness!)

and I fell prostrate,
crying:
you have flayed us with your blossoms,
spare us the beauty
of fruit-trees!

The honey-seeking
paused not;
the air thundered their song,
and I alone was prostrate.

O rough-hewn
god of the orchard,
I bring you an offering—
do you, alone unbeautiful,
son of the god,
spare us from loveliness:
these fallen hazel-nuts,
stripped late of their green sheaths,
grapes, red-purple,
their berries
dripping with wine:
pomegranates already broken,
and shrunken figs,
and quinces untouched,
I bring you as offering.

Pear Tree 829

ANSWERS TO THINKING ABOUT THE SELECTION

Recalling

1. It has been lifted higher than her arms reach.
2. They bring "summer and ripe fruits."

Interpreting

3. (a) It refers to the leaves and flowers of the pear. (b) It has grown upward.
4. (a) It is spring. (b) The tree's blooming anticipates the arrival of summer and its fruits.
5. It makes it seem as if she can communicate with the tree.

Applying

6. Answers will differ. Students may comment that they color silver makes them think of wealth and beauty.

THINKING AND WRITING

For help with this assignment, students can refer to Lesson 19, "Writing a Poem," in the Handbook of Writing About Literature.

Publishing Student Writing
Collect and make copies of the poems, then distribute them in classroom sets.

Humanities Note

Fine art, *Overhanging Cloud,* by Charles Burchfield. Charles Burchfield (1893–1967) grew up in Ohio and attended the Cleveland School of Art. His work shows a haunting sense of imagination, producing a somewhat surrealistic feeling. The strong patterning of the clouds in this picture is especially reminiscent of his early works. The drama of the rays of the sun piercing the picture is made even more intense by Burchfield's viewpoint. The weeds in the foreground bring the viewer into the meadow.

You might use these questions for discussion:
1. What "warm" colors has the artist used in this painting?
2. One of Burchfield's "trademarks" is his use of repetition. How has he used repetition in this painting?
3. Choose words and phrases from the poem and explain how they relate to the painting.

Motivation/Prior Knowledge

Have students imagine that it is a hot, humid day. What types of emotions does the heat evoke?

Purpose-Setting Question To what senses do the images appeal?

1 **Critical Thinking and Reading**
Note that this poem is an apostrophe addressed to the wind. This is indicated by the word *O* in the first line.

OVERHANGING CLOUD IN JULY
Charles Burchfield
The Whitney Museum

Heat

H. D.

1   O wind, rend open the heat,
    cut apart the heat,
    rend it to tatters.

      Fruit cannot drop
5   through this thick air—
      fruit cannot fall into heat
      that presses up and blunts
      the points of pears
      and rounds the grapes.

2

10   Cut the heat—
      plow through it,
      turning it on either side
      of your path.

THINKING ABOUT THE SELECTION
Recalling

1. What does the speaker ask of the wind?
2. According to the speaker, how does the heat affect fruit?

Interpreting

3. (a) What impression of heat does the speaker express? (b) How do the descriptions of the heat's interactions with the wind and fruit convey this impression?
4. What specific type of heat is the speaker describing?

Applying

5. (a) What is your own dominant impression of heat? (b) How does this compare with your dominant impression of cold?

ANALYZING LITERATURE
Understanding Imagery

Imagery refers to language that creates mental pictures, or images, that appeal to one or more of the five senses. For example, when H. D. writes, "Fruit cannot drop through this thick air," she creates an image that appeals to both our sense of touch and our sense of sight.

1. Find another image that appeals to both the sense of touch and the sense of sight.
2. Find an image that appeals only to our sense of touch.

CRITICAL THINKING AND READING
Analyzing the Effect of Imagery

The Imagists relied on imagery to capture the reader's interest and evoke an emotional response. For example, H. D.'s images of a blooming tree in "Pear Tree" are likely to evoke a sense of harmony and beauty and a feeling of hope.

1. What types of feelings do H. D.'s images of heat evoke?
2. Why are H. D.'s images of heat likely to capture the reader's interest?

Heat 831

More About the Author In his long poetic work *Paterson*, William Carlos Williams explored the poet's role in society. Ask students to consider the role that poets play in our lives. How do they help to voice our dreams, shape our thoughts, and give us a new perspective on the world?

Critical Evaluation Critic Kenneth Burke made the following comments about Williams following his death in 1963:

"William Carlos Williams, poet and physician. Trained to crises of sickness and parturition that often came at odd hours. An ebullient man, sorely vexed in his last years, and now at rest. But he had this exceptional good luck: that his appeal as a person survives in is work. To read his books is to find him warmly there, everywhere you turn.

"In some respects, the physician and the poet might be viewed as opposites, as they certainly were at least in the sense that time spent on his patients was necessarily time denied to the writing of poetry. But that's a superficial view. In essence, this man was an imaginative physician and a nosological poet. His great humaneness was equally present in both roles, which contributed essentially to the development of each other."

WILLIAM CARLOS WILLIAMS

1883–1963

A close friend of Ezra Pound, William Carlos Williams was an important member of the Imagist movement. Opposing Pound's belief in using allusions to maintain a link to the past, Williams focused on capturing the common, everyday images of his time in an effort to create poetry with relevance to the lives of ordinary people.

Williams was born in Rutherford, New Jersey, where he spent most of his life. After graduating from the University of Pennsylvania Medical School, he became a pediatrician—a doctor who specializes in the care of children. In 1909 he published his first volume of poetry and began pursuing a double career as a poet and a doctor. Williams felt that his experiences as a doctor helped provide him with inspiration as a poet, crediting medicine for his ability to "gain entrance to . . . the secret gardens of the self."

While Williams's first book was modeled after the work of English Romantic poets, he soon developed his own distinctive voice. This voice emerged with the publication of *Spring and All* (1913), a book of mixed prose and poetry. In this book and in *In the American Grain* (1925), Williams made it clear that his aim was to capture the essence of modern American life by depicting a variety of ordinary people, objects, and experiences using up-to-date, everyday language. He avoided presenting explanations or making generalizations, commenting that a poet should deal in "No ideas but in things." By this he meant that a poet should present concrete images that speak for themselves, evoking emotions and stimulating thoughts and ideas.

In 1948 Williams suffered a heart attack, and three years later he had the first of a series of strokes. He was forced to abandon his medical practice and writing became increasingly difficult. However, he still managed to produce *Paterson* (1946–1958), a five-part epic poem filled with observations about life in the city of Paterson, New Jersey, and two additional collections of poetry, *The Desert Music* (1954) and *Pictures from Breughel and Other Poems* (1962). In 1963 he received the Pulitzer Prize for *Pictures of Breughel*.

Despite his fame and popularity and the prestigious awards he won, Williams always encouraged the young poets who wrote him letters or arrived at his home. He seemed never to forget the loneliness and isolation he himself had felt as a young and struggling poet. "I think the artist, generally speaking, feels lonely," he remarked in 1950. "Perhaps his recourse to art, in any form, comes from his essential loneliness. He is usually in rebellion against the world."

832   *The Modern Age*

Support Material

Teaching Portfolio
Teacher Backup, p. 1087
Usage and Mechanics Worksheet, p. 1090
Analyzing Literature Worksheet, *Understanding Rhythm,* p. 1091
Language Worksheet, *Identifying Compounds,* p. 1092
Selection Test, p. 1093

GUIDE FOR INTERPRETING

The Locust Tree in Flower; The Red Wheelbarrow; This Is Just to Say

Writer's Techniques

Rhythm. William Carlos Williams believed that rhythm—the arrangement of stressed and unstressed syllables in a poem—is the essence of poetry. In writing his poems, he attempted to shape the language of everyday speech into rhythmic units—lines and stanzas—that reflect and reinforce the meaning of the poems. Because each line serves as a separate rhythmic unit, you should read his poetry line by line, pausing briefly at the end of each line and pausing a bit longer at the end of each stanza. These pauses reinforce meaning by adding emphasis to important words, ideas, and images.

Writing

William Carlos Williams's poems focus on ordinary people, objects, and experiences. For example, in this group of poems, he writes about a locust tree, a red wheelbarrow, and the experience of eating plums from the icebox. Prepare a list of other ordinary experiences about which he might have written.

Primary Source

Modernist poets often took modern, industrial America as their subject. Claiming an equal status with English poetry, they asserted that common American subjects and common American language were as appropriate to poetry as the elevated subjects and diction of traditional poetry. In so doing, they also invented a new critical language. Calling a poem a "machine made of words," Williams used a modern, industrial image to refashion conventional ideas about poetry. He wrote in 1944: "A poem is a small (or large) machine made of words. When I say there's nothing sentimental about a poem I mean that there can be no part, as in any other machine, that is redundant.

"Prose may carry a load of ill-defined matter like a ship. But poetry is the machine which drives it, pruned to a perfect economy. As in all machines its movement is intrinsic, undulant, a physical more than a literary character. In a poem this movement is distinguished in each case by the character of the speech from which it arrives. . . .

"There is no poetry of distinction without formal invention, for it is in the intimate form that works of art achieve their exact meaning, in which they most resemble the machine, to give language its highest dignity, its illumination in the environment to which it is native."

Literary Focus Point out how Williams's use of rhythm adds structure to his poems.

Writing/Prior Knowledge For extra credit, have students try to come up with some images related to the experiences they have listed.

Fine art, *Pink Locusts and Windy Moon,* 1959, by Charles Burchfield. Burchfield (1893–1967), an American painter, spent most of his life in Buffalo, New York. His early work, which evoked childhood memories and emotions, produced a haunting sense of imagination. During the 1920's and 1930's, his paintings were more realistic images of the American scene, although there was still evidence of the sinister and imaginative in his work. After 1940, Burchfield's work was once again evoking that highly personal, elemental world of childhood, somewhat surrealistic in character. He even reworked some of his paintings from his more conservative period.

Although *Pink Locusts and Windy Moon* is one of Burchfield's later works, it is reminiscent of his early work, especially in the patterning of the clouds around the moon and the shadows around the house, and the general feeling of the image. It was probably inspired by a walk at night, after which he may have written a "word picture" of the scene to create the appropriate mood before starting to work on the sketch, as was often his routine.

Have students respond to the painting. You might use these questions for discussion:

1. This painting is a strong emotional expression. How would you describe the mood of this picture? How does the painter create this mood?
2. The poem by Williams expresses a great deal with only a few words. Compare and contrast the expressive techniques of Williams and Burchfield.

PINK LOCUSTS AND WINDY MOON, 1959
Charles Burchfield
Collection of the Chase Manhattan Bank

834   *The Modern Age*

Primary Source

Denis Donoghue summed up his opinion of Williams' work as follows:

> Williams' writing, then, has body, substance; he has no interest in finding different ways of saying precious little. There are large issues involved which he understands better than most. Part of what he understands, part of what he teaches, is that life is important, that human beings are important, that the dignity of a human being depends on his power of moral choice. I cannot cite chapter and verse for this, but it seems to me to be deeply involved in his

The Locust Tree in Flower

William Carlos Williams

Among
of
green

1   stiff
5   old
bright

broken
2   branch
come

10   white
sweet
May

again

Recalling

1. This poem describes the locust tree during what season of the year?

Interpreting

2. How does the title help you to understand the poem?
3. (a) Which lines describe the locust tree before it blossoms? (b) Which lines describe the tree after it blossoms?
4. (a) What does this poem reveal about a locust tree's appearance? (b) How does the line arrangement add emphasis to the tree's important characteristics?
5. What is the significance of the final line?

Applying

6. How well does this poem support Williams's claim that poets should deal in "No ideas but in things"?

The Locust Tree in Flower 835

Presentation

Motivation/Prior Knowledge
Have students look at the Burch-field painting on page 834 of a locust tree in flower. Then have them close their eyes and try to envision the tree.

Purpose-Setting Question
What image does Williams create?

1 **Literary Focus** Note that each line in the poem has just one word. Most of those words have one syllable. Yet Williams creates a crisp image.

2 **Discussion** What is the overall effect of the image?

Reader's Response Did you find this poem to be an effective image of spring? Why or why not?

Closure and Extension

ANSWERS TO THINKING ABOUT THE SELECTION
Recalling

1. It describes the tree during spring.

Interpreting

2. Without the title, the reader might not know what the poem is about.
3. (a) Lines 2–8 describe the tree before it blossoms. (b) Lines 9–13 describe the tree after it blossoms.
4. (a) It changes vividly. (b) The line arrangement isolates each important characteristic.
5. It suggests a renewal each year.

Applying

6. Suggested Response: The poem does support Williams's claim because it focuses solely on creating a concrete image.

---

work. It sounds traditional, and perhaps Williams is more traditional than we have assumed. True, by temperament he is more interested in achieving the new than in making obeisance to the old, but he knows the difference between being emancipated and being merely unbuttoned. He wants freedom but not Caliban's freedom; he wants freedom to invent new forms, epiphanies of our time. And surely there can be few things more moving than the labour of such a man toward clarity, self-knowledge, understanding.

Motivation/Prior Knowledge
Ask students to envision a red
wheelbarrow. What does this image bring to mind? What does it
represent to them?

Purpose-Setting   Question
What emotions does the image
evoke?

1 **Discussion** What does the third
stanza add to the description of
the wheelbarrow?

2 **Literary Focus** What images
does the speaker juxtapose?
How do their colors and textures
contrast?

Closure and Extension

***ANSWERS TO THINKING
ABOUT THE SELECTION***
Recalling

1. (a) It is glazed with rain water. (b)
It sits beside white chickens.

Interpreting

2. Answers will differ. Students may
suggest that wheelbarrow is used
for daily chores.
3. They appeal to the sense of sight.

Applying

4. (a) Answers will differ. Students
may respond that they associate
thoughts of childhood with the images. (b) Suggested Response:
The images evoke a feeling of
contentment.

***ANSWERS TO ANALYZING
LITERATURE***

1. Each stanza has a first line of
three words and a second line of
one word.
2. The pattern isolates each image.
3. It emphasizes that rain is made of
water.
4. The chickens are white.

The Red Wheelbarrow

William Carlos Williams

so much depends
upon

a red wheel
barrow

5   glazed with rain
water

beside the white
chickens.

THINKING ABOUT THE SELECTION

Recalling

1. (a) With what is the red wheelbarrow
glazed?   (b) What does it sit beside?

Interpreting

2. What do you think depends on the red wheelbarrow?
3. To what sense do the images in the poem
appeal?

Applying

4. (a) What types of associations do you have
with the images in the poem? (b) What
types of feelings do the images evoke?

ANALYZING LITERATURE

Understanding Rhythm

   In writing his poems, William Carlos Williams
attempted to shape the language of everyday
speech into rhythmic units—lines and stanzas—
that reflect and reinforce the meaning of the
poems. For example, in "The Red Wheelbarrow," Williams calls our attention to the image of
the wheelbarrow by breaking up the word and
presenting it on two separate lines. His presentation of the word also reflects its meaning, since
a wheelbarrow is composed of two separate
parts.

1. What rhythmic and visual pattern does Williams establish in "The Red Wheelbarrow"?
2. How does the pattern help to emphasize
each separate image?
3. How does the line break in the third stanza
call our attention to and reflect the meaning
of the image of rainwater?
4. What characteristic of the chickens is emphasized by the line break in the fourth stanza?

836   *The Modern Age*

Primary Source

In his essay "Williams and the 'New Mode,'" Roy Harvey Pearce
made the following comments about "The Red Wheelbarrow":

   In this notably sentimental piece . . . Williams can only
   dimly specify 'what' depends—himself in his vocation as
   poet. He assures himself that he is what he is by virtue of
   his power to collocate such objects into sharply annotated
   images like these. He must feel himself into the things of his
   world; for he is dependent on them as occasions to be
   himself—as poet. Perhaps—and herein lies the pathos—
   they depend on him as much as he depends on them. 'So
   much depends' too upon a poet's being there to make

This Is Just to Say

William Carlos Williams

I have eaten
the plums
that were in
the icebox
5 and which
you were probably
saving
for breakfast

Forgive me
10 they were delicious
so sweet
and so cold

THINKING ABOUT THE SELECTION

Recalling

1. (a) What has the speaker eaten? (b) For what were the things he has eaten probably being saved?

Interpreting

2. How does the title relate to the poem?
3. To what senses do the images in the poem appeal?
4. (a) Why is the incident described in the poem important to the speaker? (b) How do the last three lines help to reveal the incident's importance?

Applying

5. Why do you think Williams might have chosen to write a poem about such a seemingly insignificant incident?

THINKING AND WRITING

Writing an Apology

"This Is Just to Say" is, after all, a note of apology. However, the speaker doesn't seem to be at all sorry for what he did. Create a similar situation: A character does something he or she knows is incorrect but is actually glad to have done. For example, you might write about a sister borrowing a sweater without asking or a child giving into temptation and sneaking a piece of just-baked pie. Using Williams's poem as a model, write a note of apology. When you revise, make sure you have included details that appeal to the senses.

This Is Just to Say   837

---

them what, at their best, they can be: objects in a poem. At its worst this is togetherness in a chicken-yard. At its best it is an exercise in the creation of the poetic out of the anti-poetic. Not the least significant characteristic of Williams' work is that the best in it cannot but bring out the worst. Like his friend and enemy Pound, he has had the courage to go all the way with his convictions.

Motivation/Prior Knowledge Have students imagine that they are eating plums. How would they describe the experience?

Purpose-Setting Question What does the experience represent to the speaker?

1 **Critical Thinking and Reading** The title is really the first line of the poem. It establishes the poem as a note.

2 **Critical Thinking and Reading** Each stanza adds an additional thought.

Reader's Response Do you think this is an appropriate topic for a poem? Why or why not?

Closure and Extension

ANSWERS TO THINKING ABOUT THE SELECTION
Recalling

1. (a) The speaker has eaten the plums in the icebox. (b) They were probably saved for breakfast.

Interpreting

2. The title leads into the thought of the first line and shows that the poem is a note.
3. They appeal to sight, touch, and taste.
4. (a) It is important because of the sensations the speaker experiences. (b) It reveals the enjoyment the speaker experienced.

Applying

5. Suggested Response: Williams believed there was significance hidden in seemingly insignificant experiences.

THINKING AND WRITING

Publishing Student Writing Have student volunteers share their notes with the class.

More About the Author As the title of Carl Sandburg's book, *The People, Yes,* indicates, the poet had great faith in the spirit of ordinary people. This faith was reflected in his poetry and in his interest in folk songs. You may wish to discuss with students the themes, images, and emotions expressed in folk songs, and play recordings of some in class. Based on this discussion, what do students expect to encounter when they read Sandburg's poems?

Critical Evaluation The following is the conclusion of an address made by poet Archibald MacLeish at the Carl Sandburg Memorial Ceremony in 1967: "What Sandburg knew and said was what America knew from the beginning and said from the beginning and has not yet, no matter what is believed of her, forgotten how to say: that those who are credulous about the destiny of man, who believe more than they can prove of the future of the human race, will *make* that future, *shape* that destiny. This was his great achievement: that he found a new way in an incredulous and disbelieving and often cynical time to say what Americans have always known. And beyond that there was another and even greater achievement: that people listened. They are listening still."

CARL SANDBURG

1878–1967

No poet better captured the spirit of industrial America than did Carl Sandburg. In his poems he paints a vivid portrait of the American working class, capturing its energy and enthususiasm in the lively, accessible manner that made him one of the most popular poets of his day.

The son of Swedish immigrants, Sandburg was born and raised in Galesburg, Illinois. Forced to go to work at an early age, Sandburg attended school on an irregular basis. After spending six years working at a variety of jobs, he enlisted in the army in 1898 to fight in the Spanish-American War. When he returned from the war, he enrolled at Lombard College. He left school shortly before his graduation, however, and spent several years traveling around the country, again working at a variety of jobs.

In 1913 Sandburg settled in Chicago, where he worked as a newspaper reporter. He began publishing poetry in *Poetry* magazine, a highly-regarded literary journal based in Chicago, and in 1916 he published his first book, *Chicago Poems*. The book sold well and was praised for its passion and vigor. Sandburg earned widespread recognition and helped establish Chicago as one of the country's leading literary centers. During the next ten years, Sandburg published three more successful collections of poetry, *Cornhuskers* (1918), *Smoke and Steel* (1920), and *Slabs of the Sunburnt West* (1922).

In 1928 Sandburg offered ten definitions of poetry, among them these two: "Poetry is a search for syllables to shoot at the barriers of the unknown and the unknowable" and "Poetry is the opening and closing of a door, leaving those who look through to guess about what is seen during a moment."

While continuing to write poetry, Sandburg then began touring the country delivering lectures on Walt Whitman and Abraham Lincoln—two men whom he greatly admired—and started a career as a folk singer. He also spent a great deal of time collecting material for a biography of Lincoln, and he prepared an anthology of American folk songs, *The American Songbook* (1927). His multivolume Lincoln biography won the Pulitzer Prize in 1940, and in 1951 he received a second Pulitzer Prize for his *Complete Poems*. Sandburg was also awarded the United States Presidential Medal in 1964, and he was asked to address a joint session of Congress on the 150th anniversary of Lincoln's birth. During his later years, he lived on a farm in North Carolina, where he continued to write poetry and work on his autobiography.

Objectives

1 To write a poem in free verse
2 To understand free verse

Support Material

Teaching Portfolio
Teacher Backup, p. 1095
Usage and Mechanics Worksheet, p. 1098
Vocabulary Check, p. 1099
Analyzing Literature Worksheet, *Understanding Free Verse,* p. 1100
Language Worksheet, *Recognizing Slang,* p. 1101
Selection Test, p. 1102

Art Transparency 15, *Study for Eight Builders* by Jacob Lawrence

GUIDE FOR INTERPRETING

Grass; *from* The People, Yes; Chicago

Free Verse. Heavily influenced by the poetry of Walt Whitman, Carl Sandburg composed his poems using long open lines of free verse—verse that has irregular meter and line length. Written in simple, straightforward language, Sandburg's long free-verse lines capture the activity and energy of industrial America and mirror the natural rhythms of ordinary speech. Sandburg's use of simple language and natural rhythms reflects his interest in common people—who usually served as the subjects of his poems—and his desire to reach a wide audience.

Rather than creating a pattern through regular meter and line length, Sandburg generally establishes a pattern in his poems through the use of parallelism—the repetition of phrases or clauses that are similar in structure or meaning. His use of parallelism also helps to emphasize important ideas and contributes to the natural rhythm of his poetry.

Commentary

Throughout his career Sandburg strove to capture in his poetry the distinctiveness of American life and language. To do this, he wrote from the perspective of ordinary men and women, using the idioms and slang of common speech and treating subjects from ordinary lives. As one critic put it, he "broadened the field" of poetic subjects by writing about industrial scenes, such as packing houses, mills, and factories, as he does in his famous poem "Chicago." He also described and celebrated the lives of the people who worked in these jobs. Sandburg's populist point of view is clearly evident in "The People, Yes," in which he speaks in the voice of the working, struggling people. It is also evident in his poem "Grass," where he reminds us of the common soldier who fought and died in history's many wars.

These characteristics of Sandburg's poetry distinguished his work from that of many of the poets of his day. For example, the poetry of Ezra Pound and T. S. Eliot is filled with sometimes obscure allusions and difficult language. Such poets as Pound and Eliot did not see poetry as primarily a way to portray the thoughts and feelings of common people living their everyday lives. As you read, you may wish to keep in mind Sandburg's different poetic goals.

Writing

In his poem "The People, Yes," Carl Sandburg uses vivid imagery to capture the essence of the American people. Prepare a list of descriptive details you could use in describing the American people.

Literary Focus While Sandburg's free verse attempted to capture the natural rhythms of human speech, his choice of words and images is often an idealized version of the way ordinary people speak.

Writing/Prior Knowledge You may wish to have your **less advanced** students work in groups to complete the writing activity.

Vocabulary

Preteach the following vocabulary words:

cyclonic (sī klän′ ik) *adj.:* Like a cyclone, a windstorm with violent, whirling movement (p. 842, l. 7)

enigmatic (en′ ig mat′ ik) *adj.:* Perplexing; baffling (p. 842, l. 8)

wanton (wän′ t'n) *adj.:* Senseless; unjustified (p. 844, l. 8)

cunning (kun′ iŋ) *adj.:* Skillful in deception; crafty; sly (p. 844, l. 10)

Motivation/Prior Knowledge
Have students discuss what grass represents to them. Does it represent life?

Purpose-Setting Question
What purpose does the grass serve?

1 **Discussion** Who is the speaker of the poem?

2 **Discussion** Why does Sandburg mention several battle sites?

Grass

Carl Sandburg

1

    Pile the bodies high at Austerlitz and Waterloo.[1]
    Shovel them under and let me work—
        I am the grass; I cover all.

2

    And pile them high at Gettysburg
5   And pile them high at Ypres and Verdun.[2]
    Shovel them under and let me work.
    Two years, ten years, and passengers ask the conductor:
        What place is this?
        Where are we now?

10   I am the grass.
        Let me work.

---

1. Austerlitz (ôs′ tər lĭts′) **and Waterloo:** Sites of battles of the Napoleonic Wars.
2. Ypres (ē′ pr) **and Verdun** (vər dŭn′): Sites of battles of World War I.

MARSHES, DUNES AND FIELDS
Jane Freilicher

Fine art, *Marshes, Dunes, and Fields*, by Jane Freilicher. The American painter Jane Freilicher was born in 1924. She studied art at Brooklyn College, Columbia University, and the Hans Hoffman School. Her work is characterized by Long Island landscapes and indoor New York City still lifes.

Jane Freilicher has remained a figurative painter in the face of current trends toward abstract and non-objective painting. Her devotion to realism in landscape results in painterly, romantic scenes of true natural beauty. *Marshes, Dunes, and Fields* was painted at her summer home in Water Mill, Long Island. It is a celebration of the beauty and light of that area.

Consider these questions for discussion:
1. What impression of grass does the artist convey?
2. How does the artist communicate the sense of timelessness with which Sandburg is concerned in this poem?

THINKING ABOUT THE SELECTION

Recalling

1. (a) What "work" does the grass perform at the battle sites mentioned in the poem? (b) What do people ask when they see the sites years after the battles?

Interpreting

2. (a) What is the attitude of the grass toward the events referred to in the poem? (b) What does this attitude suggest about humanity's relationship to nature?

3. How do the questions asked by the passengers reflect the pointlessness of war?
4. (a) Is Sandburg suggesting that it is possible for the death and destruction of war to be covered over and easily forgotten? Support your answer. (b) What is the purpose of the poem?

Applying

5. (a) What types of people do you think might share the attitude of the grass toward war? (b) What types of people do you think might strongly object to this attitude?

Grass   841

Closure and Extension

ANSWERS TO THINKING ABOUT THE SELECTION
Recalling

1. (a) The grass covers the battle sites. (b) They ask, "What place is this?/Where are we now?"

Interpreting

2. (a) The grass is indifferent to the events mentioned. (b) It suggests that nature in general is indifferent to humanity.
3. The fact that nobody remembers the battle sites suggests that most people have forgotten the reasons for the wars.

4. (a) No, he is suggesting that we should not try to cover over or forget the death and destruction of war. This suggestion is conveyed through the tone of the poem. (b) Suggested Response: The purpose of the poem is probably to point out the pointlessness of war.

Applying

5. (a) Answers will differ. Some students may suggest people who want the hurtful memories to pass or people who are indifferent to the suffering of others. (b) Answers will differ. Students may respond that people who have lost loved ones will object strongly to this attitude.

Challenge What can you infer about Sandburg from reading this poem?

Motivation/Prior Knowledge
Discuss the ways in which humanity has changed throughout the course of history. Why has humanity endured? What changes will occur in the future?

Master Teacher Note In "The People, Yes," Carl Sandburg celebrates the American working class. Place Art Transparency 15, *Study for Eight Builders* by Jacob Lawrence on the overhead projector. Have students carefully examine each of the figures depicted in the painting. What dominant impression of these workers does the painting convey?

Purpose-Setting Question
What is the speaker's attitude toward the human experience?

1 **Discussion** What does the speaker admire about people?

2 **Critical Thinking and Reading** Notice how Sandburg re-creates the rhythms of speech in lines 10–20.

3 **Discussion** What does the speaker see as the place of people in the universe?

4 **Discussion** How do the final lines capture humanity's ability to endure hardships?

Reader's Response Do you agree or disagree with the speaker's attitude toward humanity?

from # The People, Yes

Carl Sandburg

1
  The people will live on.
The learning and blundering people will live on.
  They will be tricked and sold and again sold
And go back to the nourishing earth for rootholds,
5   The people so peculiar in renewal and comeback,
  You can't laugh off their capacity to take it.
The mammoth[1] rests between his cyclonic dramas.

The people so often sleepy, weary, enigmatic,
is a vast huddle with many units saying:
10 "I earn my living.
  I make enough to get by
  and it takes all my time.
  If I had more time
  I could do more for myself
2 15 and maybe for others.
  I could read and study
  and talk things over
  and find out about things.
  It takes time.
20 I wish I had the time."

     . . .

  The people know the salt of the sea
  and the strength of the winds
  lashing the corners of the earth.
  The people take the earth
25 as a tomb of rest and a cradle of hope.
  Who else speaks for the Family of Man?
  They are in tune and step
3 with constellations of universal law.

     . . .

In the darkness with a great bundle of grief the people
  march.
30 In the night, and overhead a shovel of stars for keeps, the
4 people march:
    "Where to? what next?"

---

1. **mammoth** (mam′ əth) *n.*: An extinct elephant with hairy skin.

Primary Source

Carl Sandburg described his career as part of "Notes for a Preface" from *The Complete Poems of Carl Sandburg.*

 At the age of six, as my fingers first found how to shape the alphabet, I decided to become a person of letters. At the age of ten I had scrawled letters on slates, on paper, on boxes and walls and I formed an ambition to become a sign-painter. At twenty I was an American soldier in Puerto Rico writing letters printed in the home town paper. At twenty-one I went to West Point, being a classmate of Douglas MacArthur and Ulysses S. Grant III—for two weeks—returning home after passing in spelling, geography, history, failing in arithmetic and grammar. At twenty-three I edited a college paper and wrote many a paragraph that after a lapse of fifty years still seems funny, the same applying to the college yearbook I edited the following year. . . . In a six-year period came four books of poetry having a variety of faults, no other person more keenly aware of their accomplishments and shortcoming than myself. . . . At fifty I had published a two-volume biogra-

THINKING ABOUT THE SELECTION

Recalling

1. What will happen to the "learning and blundering people"?
2. What could the people do if they had more time?
3. (a) What do the people know? (b) As what do they "take the earth"?
4. (a) When do the people march? (b) What do they bring with them?

Interpreting

5. (a) What details suggest that this poem is about working-class people? (b) What is the speaker's attitude toward these people?
6. What does the poem suggest are the reasons why people "live on," while animals such as the mammoth become extinct?

Applying

7. What is the significance of the fact that this poem was written during the Great Depression?

THINKING AND WRITING

Writing a Poem Using Free Verse

Using free verse, write a poem that captures the essence of the American people. Start by reviewing the list of details you prepared before you began reading. Try to think of additional details you can add to your list. When you write your poem, try to structure your verse to recreate the natural rhythms of ordinary speech and try to use parallelism to establish a pattern and to emphasize your important ideas. When you finish writing, revise your poem and share it with your classmates.

Commentary

Many critics of American poetry have noted that Sandburg writes in the tradition of Walt Whitman. Both celebrated the common people in their verse; both used common, everyday language instead of literary language; and both gave great range to free verse.

Another earlier American poet that Sandburg seems aligned with is Edwin Robinson. Both used the idiomatic language of local dialects, with Sandburg staying close to the way Midwesterners talked and Robinson writing the language of his native New England. Both were concerned with the everyday lives of ordinary people. And both wanted to portray the realities of life in America.

For Robinson this meant writing poetry that was completely unsentimental in its vivid portrayal of individual lives. His poetic portraits are psychologically accurate and clearsighted descriptions of the ironies of existence. He wrote about lonely outcasts and misfits without hiding their failures, but with sympathy and without judgment. He records Miniver Cheevy's drinking and Richard Cory's suicide with wry bitterness; but he manages to evoke feelings of tenderness for these characters while he exposes their degradation.

Sandburg's effort to portray the realities of life in America led him to take a different approach. He does not create vivid, psychological portraits of characters. To capture the varieties in everyday life, Sandburg used an impressionistic poetic style, sweeping together individuals into a concept of the "common people." Although his poetry, like Robinson's, is aware of the destructive nature of society, Sandburg's verse is a hymn to the indestructibility of the human spirit. Sandburg seeks to remind us that human virtues will prevail amid the disorder and waste of industrial society. He stresses the bonds between people where Robinson highlights human nature's essential loneliness and isolation.

from *The People, Yes* 843

Closure and Extension

ANSWERS TO THINKING ABOUT THE SELECTION
Recalling

1. They will live on.
2. They could do more for themselves and for others.
3. (a) They know the salt of the sea and the strength of the winds. (b) They take the earth as "a tomb of rest and a cradle of hope."
4. (a) They march in the darkness. (b) They bring with them a "great bundle of grief."

Interpreting

5. (a) The details include the notion that they "go back to the nourishing earth for rootholds," the idea that they are "a vast huddle," and the fact that they know "the salt of the sea/and the strength of the winds." (b) He admires them, despite their shortcomings.
6. The people have the capacity to endure hardships.

Applying

7. The Great Depression sorely tried people's spirits, and the poet saw their capacity to endure despite these hardships.

THINKING AND WRITING

For help with this assignment, students can refer to Lesson 19, "Writing a Poem," in the Handbook of Writing About Literature.

Publishing Student Writing Have students polish their poems. Then encourage them to read them into a tape recorder.

---

phy and *The American Songbag,* and there was puzzlement as to whether I was a poet, a biographer, a wandering troubadour with a guitar, a midwest Hans Christian Anderson, or a historian of current events. . . . I am still studying verbs and the mystery of how they connect nouns. I am more suspicious of adjectives than at any other time in all my born days. I have forgotten the meaning of twenty or thirty of my poems written thirty or forty years ago. I still favor several simple poems published long ago which continue to have an appeal for simple people. I have written by different methods and in a wide miscellany of moods and have seldom been afraid to travel in lands and seas where I met fresh scenes and new songs. All my life I have been trying to learn to read, to see and hear, and to write. . . . I should like to think that as I go on writing there will be sentences truly alive, with verbs quivering, with nouns giving color and echoes. It could be, in the grace of God, I shall live to be eighty-nine, as did Hokusai, and speaking my farewell to earthly scenes, I might paraphrase: "If God had let me live five years longer I should have been a writer."

Presentation

Motivation/Prior Knowledge
Have students look at the photograph of Chicago on page 845. What do they imagine that it was like to live in Chicago at the time the picture was taken?

Purpose-Setting Question
What is the speaker's attitude toward Chicago?

1 **Clarification** At the time this poem was written, Chicago was a center for the nation's meat-packing and grain markets. Many of these industries have now relocated, and Chicago has changed its industrial base.

2 **Discussion** What kind of negative comments about Chicago does the speaker mention? Does he agree or disagree with them?

3 **Discussion** Why does the speaker appreciate Chicago?

4 **Discussion** How does the speaker personify the city?

5 **Critical Thinking and Reading** Note how the last line reflects back on the description at the beginning of the poem?

Reader's Response How does this poem compare with your own impressions of Chicago? Explain.

Chicago

Carl Sandburg

1
Hog Butcher for the World,
Tool Maker, Stacker of Wheat,
Player with Railroads and the Nation's Freight Handler;
Stormy, husky, brawling,
5   City of the Big Shoulders:

2
They tell me you are wicked and I believe them, for I have seen your painted women under the gas lamps luring the farm boys.
And they tell me you are crooked and I answer: Yes, it is true I have seen the gunman kill and go free to kill again.
And they tell me you are brutal and my reply is: On the faces of women and children I have seen the marks of wanton hunger.
And having answered so I turn once more to those who sneer at this my city, and I give them back the sneer and say to them:

3
10   Come and show me another city with lifted head singing so proud to be alive and coarse and strong and cunning.
Flinging magnetic curses amid the toil of piling job on job, here is a tall bold slugger set vivid against the little soft cities;
Fierce as a dog with tongue lapping for action, cunning as a savage pitted against the wilderness,
    Bareheaded,
    Shoveling,
15   Wrecking,
    Planning,
    Building, breaking, rebuilding,

4
Under the smoke, dust all over his mouth, laughing with white teeth,
Under the terrible burden of destiny laughing as a young man laughs,
20   Laughing even as an ignorant fighter laughs who has never lost a battle,
Bragging and laughing that under his wrist is the pulse, and under his ribs the heart of the people,
    Laughing!

5
Laughing the stormy, husky, brawling laughter of Youth, half-naked, sweating, proud to be Hog Butcher, Tool Maker, Stacker of Wheat, Player with Railroads and Freight Handler to the Nation.

844   *The Modern Age*

THINKING ABOUT THE SELECTION

Recalling

1. (a) According to the second stanza, what three things do "they" tell the speaker about Chicago? (b) How does the speaker respond to "those who sneer" at his city?

Interpreting

2. (a) What is the overall impression this poem conveys of the city of Chicago? (b) What human qualities does the speaker attribute to the city?
3. (a) Of what faults concerning his city is the speaker aware? (b) How do these faults seem to affect his attitude toward the city?
4. What details suggest that Chicago was still a young and rapidly developing city when this poem was written?

Applying

5. (a) In what ways is the city described in this poem similar to and different from other cities with which you are familiar? (b) What do the differences among American cities reveal about the nation's character?

ANALYZING LITERATURE

Understanding Free Verse

Carl Sandburg's poems were generally written in long lines of **free verse**—verse that is irregular in meter and line length.

1. How does Sandburg's use of long, open free-verse lines in "Chicago" help to convey the energy, activity, and immensity of the city?
2. How does he emphasize some of the city's important characteristics by varying line length?

Chicago 845

EDNA ST. VINCENT MILLAY

1892–1950

Although she spent only a few years in the New York City community known as Greenwich Village, Edna St. Vincent Millay will always be associated with the unconventional lifestyle and artistic experimentation characteristic of Greenwich Village during the 1920's. An enormously popular poet of her day, Millay embodied the rebellious, questing spirit that emerged in the aftermath of World War I.

Millay was born in Rockford, Maine, and began writing poetry at an early age. "Renascence," the first of her poems to attract public attention, was written when she was still in high school and appeared in a literary anthology when she was only twenty.

After graduating from Vassar College in 1917, Millay moved to Greenwich Village and quickly became part of the New York City artistic scene. While supporting herself by working as an actress and a playwright, she published a number of short stories and several collections of poetry, including *Renascence and Other Poems* (1917), *A Few Figs from Thistles* (1920), and *Second April* (1921). Her collection, *The Harp-Weaver and Other Poems* (1923), was awarded the Pulitzer Prize.

In 1923 Millay married Eugen Boissevain and moved to a farm in upstate New York where she spent the rest of her life. Although she continued to write poetry, she began turning away from writing the intensely personal lyric poems that had made her famous. Instead, deeply disturbed by the rise of fascism in Europe and the resulting war, she started focusing on current events in her poetry.

In her earlier poetry, which is generally regarded as her best, Millay displayed an ability to express the primary concerns of her time in a readily accessible, lyrical style. Like the work of other modern writers, her poetry expressed a rebellious attitude and explored the uncertainty and disillusionment of modern life. Yet her work remained linked to the past through her use of traditional verse forms and poetic devices.

Millay expressed her generation's sense of the intense brevity and beauty of life in *A Few Figs from Thistles:* "My candle burns at both ends; / It will not last the night; / But, ah, my foes, and, oh, my friends— / It gives a lovely light."

846   The Modern Age

GUIDE FOR INTERPRETING

Renascence

The Writer's Techniques

Theme. The theme is the central idea or insight about life that a writer hopes to convey in a literary work. Some themes are universal, occurring again and again in the literature of many eras. For example, the idea that nature is a powerful and wondrous force is a recurring theme in the literature of the Native Americans, the Transcendentalists, and the writers of our own century. Writers also frequently express themes that reflect specific concerns of the eras in which they lived. For example, because of rapid technological changes and the shattering effects of World War I, modern writers often focused on themes related to the uncertain, fragmentary, and confusing nature of life in the modern world.

In "Renascence" Edna St. Vincent Millay explores a universal theme—the idea that a person can be reborn or reawakened to discover a new understanding of the world. However, in describing the need to be reborn, she expresses concerns and attitudes that are characteristic of the modern period.

Commentary

Critics were full of praise for "Renascence" and full of admiration for its young author. Critic and poet Louis Untermeyer described the poem as "[b]eginning like a casual rhyme, it proceeds to a set of climaxes. It is as if a child had, in the midst of ingenuousness, uttered some terrific truth." Harriet Monroe, who founded *Poetry: A Magazine of Verse* in 1912, the year "Renascence" appeared in *The Lyric Year,* praised the poem highly: "The surprise of youth over the universe, the emotion of youth at encountering inexplicable infinities— that is expressed in this poem, and it is a big thing to express. Moreover, it is expressed with a certain triumphant joy, the very mood of exultant youth; and the poet gets a certain freshness into a measure often stilted." Finally, one of Millay's early biographers, Miriam Gurko, wrote: " 'Renascence' would have been a tremendous achievement for a poet of any age. For a young girl it was phenomenal. One reader was to call it 'part birdsong, part essay in philosophy.' It is the overture to all her later work, embodying what were to become her principal themes and techniques. It expresses her feelings about death and her joy at being alive. It is a lyrical rhapsody on nature. At the same time, it reveals her early awareness of suffering and injustice. . . ."

Do you know of any young people who have made achievements that seem to be more appropriate to adults?

Writing

Freewrite, exploring the reasons why a person might feel the need to experience a rebirth.

Literary Focus In some literary works, the theme is directly stated. More often, however, it is implied, or revealed indirectly. In poetry, the theme is often implied through figurative language.

Writing/Prior Knowledge Before having students complete the writing activity, you may want to discuss the concept of a spiritual rebirth.

Vocabulary

Preteach the following vocabulary words:

manifold (man′ ə fōld′) *adj.:* Plentiful and varied (p. 848, l. 38)

omniscience (äm nish′ əns) *n.:* A knowledge of all things (p. 849, l. 55)

gall (gôl) *n.:* Bitterness (p. 849, l. 58)

finite (fī′ nīt) *adj.:* Having measurable limits (p. 850, l. 84)

myriad (mir′ ē əd) *adj.:* Countless (p. 851, l. 139)

sepulchered (sep′′l kərd) *v.:* Entombed; buried (p. 851, l. 140)

herald (her′ əld)*n.:* Messenger (p. 851, l. 149)

Motivation/Prior Knowledge
Discuss the various ways in which people can be "reborn." Why might a person feel the need to experience a rebirth?

Purpose-Setting Question How do the speaker's experiences change her attitude toward the world?

1 Critical Thinking and Reading
The poem begins with very simple lines and ideas. It progresses to complex ideas. The simple lines at the beginning draw the reader into the poem.

2 Critical Thinking and Reading
What is the rhyme scheme of the poem?

3 Discussion Why does the speaker scream?

4 Discussion What is paradoxical about lines 33–34?

Renascence

Edna St. Vincent Millay

All I could see from where I stood
Was three long mountains and a wood;
I turned and looked another way,
And saw three islands in a bay.
5   So with my eyes I traced the line
Of the horizon, thin and fine,
Straight around till I was come
Back to where I'd started from;
And all I saw from where I stood
10   Was three long mountains and a wood.

Over these things I could not see:
These were the things that bounded me.
And I could touch them with my hand,
Almost, I thought, from where I stand!
15   And all at once things seemed so small
My breath came short, and scarce at all.
But, sure, the sky is big, I said:
Miles and miles above my head.
So here upon my back I'll lie
20   And look my fill into the sky.
And so I looked, and after all,
The sky was not so very tall.
The sky, I said, must somewhere stop . . .
And—sure enough!—I see the top!
25   The sky, I thought, is not so grand;
I 'most could touch it with my hand!
And reaching up my hand to try,
I screamed, to feel it touch the sky.

I screamed, and—lo!—Infinity
30   Came down and settled over me;
Forced back my scream into my chest;
Bent back my arm upon my breast;
And, pressing of the Undefined
The definition on my mind.
35   Held up before my eyes a glass
Through which my shrinking sight did pass
Until it seemed I must behold
Immensity made manifold;
Whispered to me a word whose sound
40   Deafened the air for worlds around,

THE SUN
Edvard Munch
Fotograf: O. Vaering

And brought unmuffled to my ears
The gossiping of friendly spheres,
The creaking of the tented sky,
The ticking of Eternity.

45 I saw and heard, and knew at last
The How and Why of all things, past,
And present, and forevermore.
The Universe, cleft to the core,
Lay open to my probing sense,
50 That, sickening, I would fain pluck thence
But could not,—nay! but needs must suck
At the great wound, and could not pluck
My lips away till I had drawn
All venom out,—Ah, fearful pawn:
55 For my omniscience paid I toll
In infinite remorse of soul.

All sin was of my sinning, all
Atoning mine, and mine the gall
Of all regret. Mine was the weight
60 Of every brooded wrong, the hate
That stood behind each envious thrust,
Mine every greed, mine every lust.

Renascence   849

Humanities Note

Fine art, *The Sun,* 1909, oil on canvas, by Edvard Munch. Munch (1863–1944), a Norwegian painter, was one of the forerunners of Expressionism. He spent his early years as an artist in Paris and Berlin. Although the influence of Gaugin is apparent in the bold simplification and shallow spatial effects in his paintings, Munch was more akin to Van Gogh in feeling, which is apparent in the brooding darkness and emotionalism of his work. Although the period between 1889 and 1892 saw many painters falling under the influence of the Impressionist painters, Munch seems to have retained a highly personal and northern individuality in his work. The 1892 exhibition of his work provoked much controversy. Munch became a hero for the younger Expressionists. With his solid powerful forms and distortion of nature for expressive effect, Munch became a leader in the German Expressionist movement.

This painting, considered one of the greatest achievements in modern mural painting, occupies the enormous front place of Oslo University's assembly hall. With its symmetry and power of imagery, it dominates the other murals in the room.

As students look at the painting, you might ask these questions:
1. This painting was created as a large mural. Taking its size into consideration, discuss the visual power of the image it presents.
2. What images from the poem are reflected in this painting?

5 **Discussion** In lines 45–46, of what is the speaker made aware?

6 **Discussion** How does the openness of the Universe affect the speaker?

7 **Discussion** What was the price the speaker paid for knowing everything?

850

And all the while, for every grief,
Each suffering, I craved relief
65 With individual desire;
Craved all in vain! And felt fierce fire
About a thousand people crawl;
Perished with each,—then mourned for all!

A man was starving in Capri;[1]
70 He moved his eyes and looked at me;
I felt his gaze, I heard his moan,
And knew his hunger as my own.
I saw at sea a great fog bank
Between two ships that struck and sank;
75 A thousand screams the heavens smote;
And every scream tore through my throat.

No hurt I did not feel, no death
That was not mine; mine each last breath
That, crying, met an answering cry
80 From the compassion that was I.
All suffering mine, and mine its rod;
Mine, pity like the pity of God.

Ah, awful weight! Infinity
Pressed down upon the finite Me!
85 My anguished spirit, like a bird,
Beating against my lips I heard;
Yet lay the weight so close about
There was no room for it without.
And so beneath the weight lay I
90 And suffered death, but could not die.
Long had I lain thus, craving death,
When quietly the earth beneath
Gave way, and inch by inch, so great
At last had grown the crushing weight,
95 Into the earth I sank till I
Full six feet under ground did lie,
And sank no more,—there is no weight
Can follow here, however great.
From off my breast I felt it roll,
100 And as it went my tortured soul
Burst forth and fled in such a gust
That all about me swirled the dust.

Deep in the earth I rested now.
Cool is its hand upon the brow
105 And soft its breast beneath the head

8

---

1. Capri (ka prē'): An Italian island located near the entrance to the Bay of Naples.

Grammar in Action

A preposition is a word that relates the noun or pronoun that appears with it to another word in the sentence. A preposition is always part of a unit called a **prepositional phrase,** consisting of the preposition and a noun or pronoun called the object of the preposition.

"Renascence" contains many prepositional phrases used to show spatial relationships. Note the following examples:

All I could see *from where I stood*
Was three long mountains and a wood;
I turned and looked another way,
And saw three islands *in a bay.* (p. 848)

The world stands out on *either side*
No wider than the heart is wide;
Above the world is stretched the sky.
No higher than the soul is high. (p. 853)

Student Activity 1. Find prepositional phrases showing spatial relationships in lines 11–28. Then do the same for lines 29–44. In lines 29–44, what do the prepositional phrases indicate about the relation between the speaker and "Infinity"?

Of one who is so gladly dead.
And all at once, and over all
The pitying rain began to fall;
I lay and heard each pattering hoof
110   Upon my lowly, thatchèd roof,
And seemed to love the sound far more
Than ever I had done before.
For rain it hath a friendly sound
To one who's six feet under ground;
115   And scarce the friendly voice or face,
A grave is such a quiet place.

The rain, I said, is kind to come
And speak to me in my new home.
I would I were alive again
120   To kiss the fingers of the rain,
To drink into my eyes the shine
Of every slanting silver line,
To catch the freshened, fragrant breeze
From drenched and dripping apple trees.
125   For soon the shower will be done,
And then the broad face of the sun
Will laugh above the rain-soaked earth
Until the world with answering mirth
Shakes joyously, and each round drop
130   Rolls, twinkling, from its grass-blade top.

How can I bear it, buried here,
While overhead the sky grows clear
And blue again after the storm?
O, multi-colored, multi-form,
135   Belovèd beauty over me,
That I shall never, never see
Again! Spring-silver, autumn-gold,
That I shall never more behold!—
Sleeping your myriad magics through,
140   Close-sepulchred away from you!
O God, I cried, give me new birth,
And put me back upon the earth!
Upset each cloud's gigantic gourd²
And let the heavy rain, down-poured
145   In one big torrent, set me free,
Washing my grave away from me!

I ceased; and through the breathless hush
That answered me, the far-off rush
Of herald wings came whispering

---

2. gourd (gôrd) *n.*: The dried, hollowed-out shell of a piece of fruit from a gourd plant, often used as a dipper or drinking cup.

Renascence   851

9 **Discussion** How does the speaker feel about the rain? What does it represent to her?

10 **Literary Focus** Note the understatement in line 116.

11 **Critical Thinking and Reading** The speaker expresses a desire to relate to the rain; this suggests a desire to come back to life.

12 **Discussion** How is the speaker released from the grave?

Student Activity 2. Identify the prepositional phrases that establish spatial relationships in lines 56–68 and in lines 83–102. How does the poet use prepositional phrases in lines 83–102 to emphasize the speaker's relation to life?

Student Activity 3. Find the prepositional phrases in lines 157–180. Relate the frequency of prepositional phrases to the speaker's experience in this stanza.

Student Activity 4. Identify the prepositional phrases in lines 181–188. How do they express the speaker's new attitude toward life?

13 **Discussion** How is each of her senses brought back to life?

14 **Discussion** What takes place in line 180? How does this complete the rebirth?

150 Like music down the vibrant string
Of my ascending prayer, and—crash!
Before the wild wind's whistling lash
The startled storm-clouds reared on high
And plunged in terror down the sky!
155 And the big rain in one black wave
Fell from the sky and struck my grave.

    I know not how such things can be;
I only know there came to me
A fragrance such as never clings
160 To aught save happy living things;
A sound as of some joyous elf
Singing sweet songs to please himself,
And, through and over everything,
A sense of glad awakening.
165 The grass, a-tiptoe at my ear,
Whispering to me I could hear;
I felt the rain's cool finger-tips
Brushed tenderly across my lips,
Laid gently on my sealèd sight,
170 And all at once the heavy night
Fell from my eyes and I could see!—
A drenched and dripping apple-tree,
A last long line of silver rain,
A sky grown clear and blue again.
175 And as I looked a quickening gust
Of wind blew up to me and thrust
Into my face a miracle
Of orchard-breath, and with the smell,—
I know not how such things can be!—
180 I breathed my soul back into me.

    Ah! Up then from the ground sprang I
And hailed the earth with such a cry
As is not heard save from a man
Who has been dead, and lives again.
185 About the trees my arms I wound;
Like one gone mad I hugged the ground;
I raised my quivering arms on high;
I laughed and laughed into the sky;
Till at my throat a strangling sob
190 Caught fiercely, and a great heart-throb
Sent instant tears into my eyes:
O God, I cried, no dark disguise
Can e'er hereafter hide from me
Thy radiant identity!
195 Thou canst not move across the grass
But my quick eyes will see Thee pass,

Nor speak, however silently,
But my hushed voice will answer Thee.
I know the path that tells Thy way
200 Through the cool eve of every day;
God, I can push the grass apart
And lay my finger on Thy heart!

The world stands out on either side
No wider than the heart is wide;
205 Above the world is stretched the sky,—
No higher than the soul is high.
The heart can push the sea and land
Farther away on either hand;
The soul can split the sky in two,

210 And let the face of God shine through.
But East and West will pinch the heart
That can not keep them pushed apart;
And he whose soul is flat—the sky
Will cave in on him by and by.

THINKING ABOUT THE SELECTION

Recalling

1. (a) In the opening stanza, what does the speaker see "from where she stood"? (b) What does she see when she looks another way? (c) How do the things she sees affect her?
2. In stanza 3, what happens when the speaker screams?
3. (a) In stanza 4, what does the speaker come to know "at last"? (b) What lies open to her "probing sense"? (c) What "toll" does she pay for her "omniscience"?
4. What happens to the speaker when the earth beneath her gives way?
5. (a) What happens when the rain begins to fall? (b) What happens after the sky grows "clear and blue again"?
6. (a) According to the final stanza, how wide is the world? (b) How high is the sky? (c) What will happen to "he whose soul is flat"?

Interpreting

7. In what sense is the speaker "bounded" at the beginning of the poem?
8. (a) What does the action of touching the sky symbolize? (b) Of what does the speaker become aware as a result of this action? (c) How does her awareness affect her?
9. (a) What does the speaker's death symbolize? (b) What realization does she come to that makes her want to be reborn?
10. (a) Restate the ideas presented in the final stanza in your own words. (b) How does the speaker's description of her experiences further develop this theme?

Applying

11. In what ways is the poem's theme reminiscent of Native American and Transcendentalist themes about humanity's spiritual relationship with nature?
12. How does the speaker's need to be reborn reflect the Modernists' sense of disillusionment with the world?

Renascence 853

15 **Discussion** What do lines 203–204 mean?

16 **Discussion** What had the speaker learned?

Reader's Response Have you ever felt "reborn"? That is, have you ever thought or felt about something in a new way that made you feel completely different? Explain.

John Crowe Ransom (1884–1967)

A minister's son, John Crowe Ransom was born in Pulaski, Tennessee, and was educated at Vanderbilt University and at Oxford. He served as a professor of English at Vanderbilt and at Kenyon College. A poet, critic, and editor, he was one of the founders of both *The Fugitive* and *The Kenyon Review,* two important literary magazines. In his seemingly quiet and gentle poems, Ransom subtly expressed his awareness of life's ironies and the frailty of humankind. Much of his work reflected his affection for the rural, agrarian life of the South and his longing for the vanished culture of the pre-Civil War era. Set in a rural environment, "Janet Waking" explores the subject of the death of a child's pet in an aloof, unsentimental manner.

Archibald MacLeish (1892–1982)

A lawyer, teacher, editor, dramatist, and poet, Archibald MacLeish was born in Glencoe, Illinois. He attended Yale, where he distinguished himself in both academics and athletics. He earned a law degree but soon gave up the practice of law to devote himself to literature. His early poems, such as "Ars Poetica," reflect the influence of such Modernist poets as Ezra Pound and T. S. Eliot. However, he eventually changed his style and began using traditional poetic forms in an effort to make his work more accessible. In the 1930's, as fascism rose in Europe and social unrest grew in America, MacLeish became active in politics and began exploring social and political issues in his work. During his career, MacLeish produced more than thirty books and won three Pulitzer Prizes.

Marianne Moore (1887–1972)

Marianne Moore was born in St. Louis, Missouri, and attended Bryn Mawr College. As the editor of the highly-regarded literary journal, *The Dial,* she encouraged many new writers by publishing their work. However, she was hesitant about publishing her own work, despite the fact that it had been read and admired by many noted poets. In fact, her first book, *Poems* (1921), was published without her knowledge.

As part of the Modernist movement, Moore wrote poems that were unconventional in form, precise, inventive, and often witty. However, unlike most other Modernists, she chose not to write about the state of modern civilization. Instead, she wrote poems about such subjects as animals and other elements of nature. "Poetry," one of her most well-known poems, delves into the subject of poetry itself.

GUIDE FOR INTERPRETING

Janet Waking; Ars Poetica; Poetry

The Writer's Techniques

Pathos. Pathos is the quality in a work of literature that evokes a feeling of pity, compassion, or sorrow in the reader. Unlike the pity aroused by a tragedy—a drama in which a character suffers as a result of his or her own mistakes—pathos usually results from situations in which innocent characters suffer through no fault of their own. For example, "Janet Waking" arouses pity for a young girl who awakens to discover that her beloved pet has died.

Similes. A simile is an explicit comparison between two seemingly dissimilar things. This comparison is clearly indicated by a connecting word such as *like* or *as*. For example, the word *like* signals the comparison in the following simile: The sound of the explosion echoed through the air *like* thunder.

Similes force us to use our imaginations to see connections that our senses may not be able to perceive, and they make it possible for us to relate our inner selves to the outer world. Through the use of similes, a poet can enable us to visualize abstract concepts such as emotions and help us to understand the external world in human terms.

Commentary

Marianne Moore was one of the most original poets of her time. Like other Modernists, she sought for ways to break with conventional poetic forms. She experimented with mixing abstract ideas and concrete images and using unusual rhythms, surprising rhymes, and different levels of diction. Her vivid and original images frequently derived from her astonishing range of interests: popular magazines, movies, baseball, boxing, and zoology. Many of her poems, including "Poetry," are striking for the way she arranges long sentences on the page in irregular, unpredictable poetic lines. As you read "Poetry," notice the striking images, and pay attention to the form and meaning of the poem.

Writing

In "Janet Waking" a young girl is devastated by the loss of her pet. Freewrite, exploring why you think children tend to react so strongly to the death of a pet.

Literary Focus Remind students of the differences between similes and metaphors, emphasizing the fact that similes use *like* or *as*.

Writing/Prior Knowledge Before having students complete the writing activity, you might discuss the reasons why pets can mean so much to children.

Vocabulary

Preteach the following vocabulary words:

transmogrifying (trans mäg′ rə fī′ iŋ) *v.:* Transforming in a grotesque manner (p. 857, l. 13)

rigor (rig′ ər) *n.:* Stiffness; rigidity (p. 857, l. 19)

translated (trans lāt′ id) *v.:* Transported (p. 857, l. 23)

palpable (pal′ pə b′l) *adj.:* Able to be touched, felt, or handled (p. 858, l. 1)

derivative (də riv′ ə tiv) *adj.:* Arrived at through complex reasoning (p. 860, l. 8)

literalists (lit′ ər əl ists) *n.:* People who insist on the exact meanings of words (p. 860, l. 20)

Humanities Note

Fine art, *The Sick Chicken,* 1874, by Winslow Homer. Homer (1836–1910) was born in Boston. He was apprenticed to the well-known lithographer J. H. Bufford about 1854. In 1857 he began working as a free-lance illustrator for publications such as *Harper's Weekly.* He moved to New York and studied at the National Academy of Art, where he had his first lessons in oil painting in 1861. He eventually settled on the coast of Maine, where he produced his most famous pictures of the sea and wilderness.

The Sick Chicken shows one of his favorite subjects, a young woman lost in gentle revery. It is delicate in coloring, yet filled with a living light. It has a quiet, contemplative charm, expressing a preoccupation with the suspension of a moment in time.

You might use the following questions for discussion:
1. Look at the quality of light in this painting. What time of day does it appear to be?
2. What details or elements of this painting reflect aspects of "Janet Waking"?
3. What is the emotional effect of this painting?

Presentation

Motivation/Prior Knowledge
Have students imagine that they wake up one morning to discover that a beloved pet has died. How would they react?

Purpose-Setting Question How does the speaker evoke pity for Janet?

1 **Discussion** How is Janet's love for her hen revealed?

THE SICK CHICKEN
Winslow Homer
The Harold T. Pulsifer Memorial Collection
Colby College, Waterville, Maine

Janet Waking

John Crowe Ransom

Beautifully Janet slept
Till it was deeply morning. She woke then
And thought about her dainty-feathered hen,
To see how it had kept.

5 One kiss she gave her mother,
Only a small one gave she to her daddy
Who would have kissed each curl of his shining baby:
No kiss at all for her brother.

"Old Chucky, old Chucky!" she cried,
10 Running across the world upon the grass
To Chucky's house, and listening. But alas,
Her Chucky had died.

It was a transmogrifying bee
Came droning down on Chucky's old bald head
15 And sat and put the poison. It scarcely bled,
But how exceedingly

And purply did the knot
Swell with the venom and communicate
Its rigor! Now the poor comb stood up straight
20 But Chucky did not.

So there was Janet
Kneeling on the wet grass, crying her brown hen
(Translated far beyond the daughters of men)
To rise and walk upon it.

25 And weeping fast as she had breath
Janet implored us, "Wake her from her sleep!"
And would not be instructed in how deep
Was the forgetful kingdom of death.

THINKING ABOUT THE SELECTION
Recalling
1. (a) What does Janet think about when she awakens? (b) What does she do after she kisses her parents?
2. (a) How has Chucky died? (b) How does Janet respond to his death?

Interpreting
3. How do the adjectives used in describing Janet and her hen in the first two stanzas convey a sense of Janet's innocence?
4. How does Janet's behavior toward her family contrast with her behavior toward Chucky?
5. (a) Considering Janet's request in line 26, what is ironic, or surprising, about the title? (b) From what is Janet "waking" as a result of Chucky's death?

Applying
6. Do you think Janet's reaction to Chucky's death is typical for a child in her situation?

ANALYZING LITERATURE
Understanding Pathos

In describing Janet's reaction to Chucky's death, Ransom creates **pathos**—the quality in literature which evokes pity, tenderness, or sorrow in the reader. At the same time, he manages to treat the subject of death without resorting to sentimentalism—an overindulgence in emotion, usually resulting from a conscious effort to induce emotion.
1. How does the fact that the speaker maintains a detached, almost indifferent attitude throughout the poem help prevent the poem from becoming overly sentimental?
2. How does the precision with which the events are described help prevent sentimentalism?
3. Why is Ransom's precise, unsentimental description of the events enough to evoke our pity and sorrow?

Janet Waking 857

Ars Poetica[1]

Archibald MacLeish

A poem should be palpable and mute
As a globed fruit,

Dumb
As old medallions to the thumb,

5   Silent as the sleeve-worn stone
Of casement ledges where the moss has grown—

A poem should be wordless
As the flight of birds.

A poem should be motionless in time
10   As the moon climbs,

1. The title is an allusion to Horace's "Ars Poetica," or "The Art of Poetry," which was composed about 20 B.C.

Leaving, as the moon releases
Twig by twig the night-entangled trees,

Leaving, as the moon behind the winter leaves,
Memory by memory the mind—

15 A poem should be motionless in time
As the moon climbs.

A poem should be equal to:
Not true.

For all the history of grief
20 An empty doorway and a maple leaf.

For love
The leaning grasses and two lights above the sea—

A poem should not mean
But be.

THINKING ABOUT THE SELECTION

Recalling

1. (a) In what sense is a poem like a "globed fruit"? (b) In what sense is a poem like "old medallions of the thumb"? (c) In what sense is a poem like "a sleeve-worn stone"? (d) In what sense is a poem like "the flight of birds"?
2. According to lines 9–16, what should a poem be like?
3. (a) According to lines 17–18, what should a poem be? (b) According to lines 23–24, what should a poem do?

Interpreting

4. (a) What does the speaker mean when he says that a poem should be "wordless"? (b) What does he mean when he says that a poem should be "motionless in time"?
5. (a) How should a poem capture "the history of grief"? (b) How should a poem express love? (c) Why do you think MacLeish chose to focus on the emotions of love and grief?

6. How does the final line sum up the ideas expressed in the poem?

Applying

7. Do you agree with MacLeish's definition of poetry? Why or why not?

ANALYZING LITERATURE

Understanding Similes

A **simile** is an explicit comparison between two seemingly dissimilar things, clearly indicated by a connecting word such as *like* or *as*. For example, MacLeish presents a simile in lines 1 and 2 in which he compares a poem to a globed fruit.
1. What does "globed" suggest about a poem?
2. (a) What comparison is made in the simile in lines 9 and 10? (b) How is this simile developed in the next four lines? (c) How does the simile in lines 9 and 10 help explain the speaker's statement that a "poem should be wordless"?
3. What is the effect of the repetition of this simile in lines 15 and 16?

Ars Poetica 859

---

1. "It is not enough that poems have beauty of form; they must have charm, and draw the hearer's feelings which way they will."
2. "Either follow tradition, or, if you invent, see that your invention be in harmony with itself."
3. "The aim of the poet is either to benefit, or to amuse, or to make his words at once please and give lessons of life."
4. "It is an old question whether a praiseworthy poem be the creation of nature or art. For my part, I do not see what study can do without a rich vein of native gift, nor what the native gift can do without culture: so much does each ask of the other and swear eternal allegiance with it."

---

4 **Discussion** What is the meaning of lines 17–18?

5 **Discussion** How do the last two lines grow out of the preceding stanzas?

Reader's Response What do the final two lines mean to you?

Closure and Extension

ANSWERS TO THINKING ABOUT THE SELECTION
Recalling

1. (a) It is "palpable and mute." (b) It is dumb. (c) It is silent. (d) It is wordless.
2. It should be motionless in time.
3. (a) It should be "equal to:/Not true." (b) It "should not mean/But be."

Interpreting

4. (a) Suggested Response: A poem should be concrete. (b) Suggested Response: A poem should retain its value and significance throughout time.
5. (a) It should capture it through concrete images. (b) It should express love through concrete images. (c) They are two of the strongest emotions.
6. It reinforces the idea that should be concrete.

Applying

7. Answers will differ. Students may respond that they too believe that a poem should be concrete.

Challenge Write your own definition of an effective poem.

ANSWERS TO ANALYZING LITERATURE

1. It should approach some ideal, rounded form.
2. (a) The ideal poem's motionlessness in time is compared to the climbing of the moon. (b) Details of the moon's climbing are described. (c) It reinforces the idea that a poem should be concrete.
3. It reinforces the idea that the simile expresses.

Motivation/Prior Knowledge
Have students discuss the purpose of poetry. Why is poetry such an important literary genre?

Purpose-Setting Question How does the speaker believe a reader should approach a poem?

1 **Discussion** Why is the first line so surprising?

2 **Critical Thinking and Reading** The speaker has lured the reader into the poem with the first line. Then the speaker offers in an understated way some of the reactions poetry can evoke.

3 **Discussion** What statement is illustrated by lines 10–14?

4 **Discussion** About what must one make a distinction?

5 **Discussion** What is the meaning of the final lines?

Reader's Response As a description or definition of poetry, which appeals to you more, "Ars Poetica" or "Poetry"? Explain.

Poetry
Marianne Moore

I, too, dislike it: there are things that are important beyond
    all this fiddle.
        Reading it, however, with a perfect contempt for it, one
            discovers in
    it after all, a place for the genuine.
        Hands that can grasp, eyes
        that can dilate, hair that can rise
5   if it must, these things are important not because a

    high-sounding interpretation can be put upon them but
        because they are
    useful. When they become so derivative as to become
        unintelligible,
    the same thing may be said for all of us, that we do not
        admire what
10   we cannot understand: the bat
            holding on upside down or in quest of something to

    eat, elephants pushing, a wild horse taking a roll, a
        tireless wolf under
    a tree, the immovable critic twitching his skin like a
        horse that feels a flea, the base-
    ball fan, the statistician—
15   nor is it valid
            to discriminate against "business documents and

    schoolbooks"; all these phenomena are important. One
        must make a distinction
        however: when dragged into prominence by half poets,
            the result is not poetry,
    nor till the poets among us can be
20   "literalists of
        the imagination"—above
            insolence and triviality and can present

    for inspection, "imaginary gardens with real toads in
        them," shall we have
        it. In the meantime, if you demand on the one hand,
            the raw material of poetry in
25   all its rawness and
        that which is on the other hand
            genuine, you are interested in poetry.

860   *The Modern Age*

UNTITLED
Alexander Calder
Solomon R. Guggenheim Museum,
New York

THINKING ABOUT THE SELECTION

Recalling

1. What does the speaker say a person discovers when reading poetry "with a perfect contempt for it"?
2. What happens when poems "become so derivative as to become unintelligible"?
3. What happens when poetry is "dragged into prominence by half poets"?
4. What does the speaker say about a person who demands "on the one hand the raw material of poetry in all its rawness and that which is on the other hand genuine"?

Interpreting

5. What type of poetry does the speaker dislike?
6. (a) What does the speaker mean when she says that poets should be "literalists of the imagination"? (b) What does she mean by "imaginary gardens with real toads in them"?
7. What qualities does the speaker believe good poetry should possess?

Applying

8. Do you agree with the speaker's ideas about poetry? Why or why not?
9. Explain the similarities and the differences between Moore's views of poetry and MacLeish's.

Poetry 861

Closure and Extension

ANSWERS TO THINKING ABOUT THE SELECTION
Recalling

1. There is a place for the genuine, a physical contact.
2. They become useless.
3. The result is not real poetry.
4. That person is interested in poetry.

Interpreting

5. The speaker dislikes poetry that needs high-sounding interpretations.
6. (a) They should be able to create imaginary but concrete images. (b) She is referring to imaginary but concrete images grounded in reality.
7. Suggested Response: She believes that poems should be accessible and concrete.

Applying

8. Answers will differ. Students may comment that they agree with Moore's suggestion that poetry should not be inaccessible.
9. The two poets both emphasize the fact that poetry must be concrete. Moore also states her belief that poetry should not be inaccessible.

Cummings' unconventional use of grammar and punctuation helped shape his ideas, as the following excerpt from the introduction to his *Collected Poems* reveals:

"The poems to come are for you and for me and are not for mostpeople

—it's no use trying to pretend that mostpeople and ourselves are alike. Mostpeople have less in common with ourselves than the squarerootofminusone. You and I are human beings; most people are snobs. . . .

you and I are not snobs. We can never be born enough. We are human beings;for whom birth is a supremely welcome mystery, the mystery of growing: the mystery which happens only and whenever we are faithful to ourselves. You and I wear the dangerous looseness of doom and find it becoming.Life, for eternal us, is now; and now is much too busy being a little more than everything to seem anything, catastrophic included."

In addition to his poetry, E.E. Cummings wrote a number of works of prose and a play called *him*. These are as unconventional as his poetry. Why do so many poets choose to explore other genres?

E. E. CUMMINGS

1894–1962

Although E. E. Cummings's poems tend to be very unconventional in form and style, they generally embody traditional thought. In his finest poems, Cummings explores such subjects as love and nature, while innovatively using capitalization, punctuation, and grammar to reinforce meaning.

Following the French poets Guillaume Apollinaire and Stéphane Mallarmé who had experimented with the typography of their poetry, Cummings was a part of the Modernist movement that played with the visual appearance of the poem. His interest in the visual aspects of poetry may have been related to his gifts as a painter. His paintings and drawings are still shown in museums. However, the unpredictability of the printed page in a volume of Cummings's poetry also reflects his lifelong goal of upsetting the conventional expectations of his readers.

Edward Estlin Cummings was born in Cambridge, Massachusetts. He graduated from Harvard and served in the French ambulance corps during World War I. In France he was unjustly imprisoned for three months in a detention camp. His experiences as a prisoner later provided him with the material for a vivid war novel, *The Enormous Room* (1922).

After the war Cummings remained in Paris to study painting but soon returned to the United States and settled in Greenwich Village in New York City. There he began working full-time as an artist, devoting time to both writing and painting. He went on to produce four volumes of poetry. While some critics attacked his unconventional style, all of his collections were well received by the general public. People responded favorably to his playful use of language and his concern with the appearance as well as the content of his poems. He also became known for his concern for the individual, his ability to recognize life's ironies, his interest in human relationships and human emotions, and his humorous approach to many of the confusing aspects of modern life.

Although his most often anthologized poems are his most sentimental ones, Cummings's best and most characteristic works are satirical in their attitude toward the world. He challenged conformity and the comfortable notions of fixed beliefs.

Cummings received a number of awards for his work, including the Boston Fine Arts Poetry Festival Award and the Bollingen Prize in Poetry. In 1968, six years after his death, a complete volume of his poetry, *The Complete Poems, 1913–1962,* was published.

Support Material

Teaching Portfolio
Teacher Backup, p. 1129
Usage and Mechanics Worksheet, p. 1133
Analyzing Literature Worksheet, *Examining Style*, p. 1134
Language Worksheet, *Understanding Homophones*, p. 1135
Selection Test, p. 1136

GUIDE FOR INTERPRETING

since feeling is first; anyone lived in a pretty how town; old age sticks

Writer's Techniques

Style. Style refers to the manner in which a writer puts his or her ideas into words. It involves the characteristics of a literary selection that concern form of expression rather than the thoughts conveyed. In poetry style is determined by such factors as choice and arrangement of words, length and arrangement of lines, stanza length and format, use of punctuation and capitalization, and use of literary devices.

Because he was as concerned with the visual arrangement of his poems as he was with sound and meaning, E. E. Cummings's style is among the most distinctive of any American poet. Cummings strove to mold his poems into unconventional shapes through variations in line length and spaces between letters and lines. Frequently, Cummings used the shape of a poem to convey or reinforce its meaning. For example, his poem about a grasshopper, "r-p-o-p-h-e-s-s-a-g-r," forms the shape of a grasshopper hopping and reforming itself. Cummings also used capitalization and punctuation to reinforce meaning. Many of his poems contain little punctuation. As a result the few marks that are used serve to highlight important ideas. Similarly Cummings rarely used capital letters, except for emphasis. In fact Cummings even used a small *i* when his speakers referred to themselves. This reflected his perception of the self as a small part of a mass society and his belief in the need for modesty.

Writing

"since feeling is first" focuses on the role of emotions in our lives. Freewrite about the ways in which feelings can affect our lives and the reasons why they can have such an impact.

Primary Source

Cummings's typographical games affect what his poetry means and the way it conveys its meaning. The way Cummings breaks the rules of grammar and syntax draws attention to the words on the page and gives them a life of their own. As one critic put it, "the poems are made to misbehave," like individuals fighting against conventional boundaries. Each poem, alive in its own way, affirms individual emotional experience. Cummings's view of what human beings are resembles his ideas about his poetry. Both poems and people should move beyond a machinelike expression of measurable, or restrained, emotions. "I am someone who proudly and humbly affirms that love is the mystery-of-mysteries, and that nothing measurable matters . . . that 'an artist, a man, a failure' is no mere whenfully accreting mechanism, but a givingly eternal complexity . . . whose only happiness is to transcend himself, whose every agony is to grow."

Guide for Interpreting 863

Literary Focus The poet's style enables him to give several possible meanings to his poems. Punctuation in Cummings's work often invites the reader to rearrange possible meanings.

Writing/Prior Knowledge Students may also write about whether they think feeling really is or should be first.

Vocabulary

Preteach the following vocabulary words:
syntax (sin′ taks) *n.:* Orderly or systematic arrangement (p. 864, l. 3)

Motivation/Prior Knowledge
Spend some time discussing syntax. What does syntax represent? Is it compatible with feelings?

Purpose-Setting Question
What is the speaker's outlook on life?

1 **Discussion** How do lines 5–9 support the first line?

2 **Discussion** What is the meaning of the final line?

Reader's Response Can you think of situations in which wisdom is preferable to emotion? Explain.

Humanities Note

Fine art, *Lovers with Flowers,* by Marc Chagall. Chagall (1887–1985) was born in Russia but lived and worked in France. His work is chiefly fantasy, showing his roots in his Russian past and in Russian folklore.

Lovers with Flowers is one of Chagall's many paintings of flowers and lovers. Its soft colors and dreamy atmosphere are appropriate for its subject.
1. Have students identify the details of the painting.
2. How does this painting reflect the sentiments in the poem?

Closure and Extension

ANSWERS TO THINKING ABOUT THE SELECTION
Recalling

1. The person who pays any attention to the syntax of things will never wholly kiss you.
2. Kisses are a better fate than wisdom.
3. Her eyelids flutter.
4. She should laugh because life's not a paragraph.

since feeling is first
E. E. Cummings

since feeling is first
who pays any attention
to the syntax of things
will never wholly kiss you;

5 wholly to be a fool
while Spring is in the world
my blood approves,
and kisses are a better fate
than wisdom
10 lady i swear by all flowers. Don't cry
—the best gesture of my brain is less than
your eyelids' flutter which says

we are for each other: then
laugh, leaning back in my arms
15 for life's not a paragraph

And death i think is no parenthesis

LOVERS WITH FLOWERS
Marc Chagall
The Israel Museum, Jerusalem

THINKING ABOUT THE SELECTION
Recalling

1. Who "will never wholly kiss you"?
2. What does the speaker "swear by all the flowers"?
3. What is more than the "best gesture" of the speaker's brain?
4. For what reasons should the lady laugh?

Interpreting

5. (a) What point does the speaker make about the relationship between reason and emotion? (b) What is his attitude concerning the role of emotions?
6. (a) What does the speaker mean when he says, "life's not a paragraph"? (b) Considering the fact that a parenthesis temporarily interrupts a sentence, what do you think the speaker means when he says, "death i think is no parenthesis"? (c) How is the speaker's perception of death related to his attitude concerning the role of emotions?

Applying

7. Do you agree with the speaker's attitude concerning the role of emotions? Why or why not?

Interpreting

5. (a) Suggested Response: Reason and emotion are not compatible. (b) Emotions should play a more important role than reason.
6. (a) Suggested Responses: Life is not logical. Life does not have a clear beginning and end. Life does not have clear rules. (b) Death is not a mere interruption in something that will continue. (c) If death is a firm ending, then life should be lived to its fullest.

Applying

7. Answers will differ. Students may comment that they feel that reason sometimes needs to be placed ahead of emotion.

anyone lived in a pretty how town

E. E. Cummings

anyone lived in a pretty how town
(with up so floating many bells down)
spring summer autumn winter
he sang his didn't he danced his did.

5   Women and men(both little and small)
cared for anyone not at all
they sowed their isn't they reaped their same
sun moon stars rain

children guessed(but only a few
10   and down they forgot as up they grew
autumn winter spring summer)
that noone loved him more by more

when by now and tree by leaf
she laughed his joy she cried his grief
15   bird by snow and stir by still
anyone's any was all to her

someones married their everyones
laughed their cryings and did their dance
(sleep wake hope and then)they
20   said their nevers they slept their dream

stars rain sun moon
(and only the snow can begin to explain
how children are apt to forget to remember
with up so floating many bells down)

25   one day anyone died i guess
(and noone stooped to kiss his face)
busy folk buried them side by side
little by little and was by was

all by all and deep by deep
30   and more by more they dream their sleep
noone and anyone earth by april
wish by spirit and if by yes.

anyone lived in a pretty how town   865

Presentation

Motivation/Prior Knowledge
Ask students how they would envision a "pretty how town." What would it be like to live in such a town?

Purpose-Setting Question
What impression of life in the "pretty how town" does the speaker convey?

1 **Discussion** To whom does "anyone" refer?

2 **Critical Thinking and Reading** Line 3 is echoed in lines 11 and 34. These lines suggest a natural rhythm of life.

3 **Critical Thinking and Reading** Reading line 7 suggests a negation of the forces of life.

4 **Critical Thinking and Reading** The word "noone" has two possible meanings. One is that nobody loved him; the other is that noone is a person who loves him.

5 **Discussion** How is noone's relation to anyone contrasted with the lives of someones and everyones?

6 **Discussion** How do the people respond to anyone's death?

Women and men(both dong and ding)
summer autumn winter spring
35   reaped their sowing and went their came
sun moon stars rain

Recalling

1. (a) He sang his didn't. (b) He danced his did.
2. (a) They care for him "not at all." (b) "noone" loves him.
3. He is buried.

Interpreting

4. Suggested Response: He wanted to suggest that the characters could be anyone.
5. (a) It suggests an attractive town. (b) They followed a dull routine and cared little for others. (c) He does so through repeated references to the passage of time and through his comment that the people "sowed their isn't and reaped the same."
6. (a) It might mean that they learned to mask their true feelings. (b) Suggested Response: They lived unimaginative lives. (c) Suggested Response: They dreamed of rest from their daily toil.
7. (a) The lines—rearranged each time—"spring summer autumn winter" and "sun moon stars rain" suggest the passage of time. (b) Suggested Response: It reinforces the idea of the passage of time.

Applying

8. Answers will differ. Some students may suggest that the characters would be even more anonymous.

THINKING ABOUT THE SELECTION

Recalling

1. (a) What does "anyone" sing? (b) What does he dance?
2. (a) How do "women and men" feel about "anyone"? (b) Who loves him "more by more"?
3. In the eighth stanza, what happens to "anyone"?

Interpreting

4. This poem tells about the man named "anyone" and his wife named "noone." Why do you think Cummings chose to use these names?
5. (a) What type of town is suggested by the phrase "pretty how"? (b) What type of impression does the speaker convey of the people from this town? (c) How does he convey the impression that their lives are monotonous and dull?
6. (a) What does the speaker mean when he says that the townspeople "laughed their cryings"? (b) What does he mean when he says that they "slept their dream"? (c) What does he mean when he says that they dreamed "their sleep"?
7. (a) What two lines in the poem convey the passage of time? (b) Why does Cummings vary the order of the words in these lines?

Applying

8. How do you think this poem might be different if it were set in a large city rather than a town?

Primary Source

In a series of lectures delivered at Harvard University in 1952 and 1953, Cummings commented on how he felt about the writing of poetry:

". . . so far as I am concerned, poetry and every other art was and is and forever will be strictly and distinctly a question of individuality . . . poetry is being, not doing. If you wish to follow, even at a distance, the poet's calling (and here, as always, I speak from my own totally biased and entirely personal point of view) you've got to come out of the measurable doing universe and into the immeasurable house of being. . . . Nobody else can be alive for you; nor can you be alive for anybody else. Toms can be Dicks and Dicks can be Harrys, but none of them can ever be you. There's the artist's responsibility; and the most awful responsibility on earth. If you can take it, take it—and be. If you can't, cheer up and go about other people's business; and do (or undo) till you drop."

Primary Source

Laurence B. Holland made the following comments on Cummings' poetry:

Cummings was less ambitious in his attempts to reshape poetry than were Eliot, Pound, Stevens, or Williams, partly because he felt a greater continuity with the American past than they did. Standing up for the individual against society was, after all, the main theme of such nineteenth-century writers as Emerson, Thoreau, and Whitman, all three of whom, like Cummings, strove for flexible immediacy of style.

The special signature of Cummings' verse was its use of common speech and elements of popular culture in the diction, and its attention to the visual form of the poem—that is, the poem as it appears on the page rather than as it sounds when read aloud. . . . Some critics took this as mere trickery, but Cummings can be credited with awareness that he lived in a culture where the poem was read rather than spoken. To express his sense that life was always in process, he wrote untitled poems without begin-

old age
sticks

E. E. Cummings

1
old age sticks
up Keep
Off
signs)&

2
5 youth yanks them
down(old
age
cries No

Tres)&(pas)
10 youth laughs
(sing
old age

scolds Forbid
den Stop
15 Must
n't Don't

&)youth goes
right on
gr
20 owing old

Recalling

1. (a) What signs does old age "stick up"?
   (b) What "yanks them down"?
2. (a) What does old age cry? (b) How does youth respond?
3. What is happening to youth?

Interpreting

4. How does youth contrast with old age in this poem?
5. What is ironic about the final stanza?

Applying

6. Why do you think the young and old often have very different attitudes toward life?

ANALYZING LITERATURE

Examining Style

Style refers to the way in which a writer expresses his or her thoughts. We can easily identify E. E. Cummings's poetry once we are familiar with his style.

1. How does Cummings's use of capitalization in "old age sticks" help to emphasize the contrast between youth and old age?
2. How does his use of parentheses in the poem highlight the contrast in the attitudes of the young and the old?
3. How does the shape of the poem reflect its content?

THINKING AND WRITING

Writing About Style

Write an essay in which you discuss how Cummings's style reinforces the meaning of his poems. Review the three poems you have just read, noting how the various elements of Cummings's style, such as his unusual use of punctuation and capitalization, reinforces the meaning of each poem. When you write your essay, use at least one passage from each of the three poems to support your argument. When you revise, make sure that you have clearly defined and thoroughly supported your thesis.

old age sticks 867

nings and endings, consisting of fragmentary lines. There is always much humor in his poetry, along with a willingness, even eagerness, to admit and express such traditional emotions as love and sadness. . . . If his poetry was simpler in thought and technique than the major modernists of his day, it compensated by a gusto and humor that they often lacked.

THINKING AND WRITING

After students have completed the assignment, divide them into groups, and have them read their rough drafts to one another and suggest ways in which they could be improved.

Presentation

Motivation/Prior Knowledge
Discuss the relationship between the young and the elderly. Why should young people respect the elderly?

Purpose-Setting Question
What is youth's attitude toward old age?

1 Discussion What does old age do? Do you think this is an accurate description?

2 Literary Focus What is unusual about Cummings's use of capitalization and punctuation?

Reader's Response Do you agree with the speaker's attitudes concerning young people and old people? Explain.

Closure and Extension

ANSWERS TO THINKING ABOUT THE SELECTION
Recalling

1. (a) It sticks up Keep Off signs.
   (b) Youth yanks them down.
2. (a) It cries "No Trespassing."
   (b) Youth laughs.
3. Youth is growing older.

Interpreting

4. Youth is portrayed as lively and carefree; old age is portrayed as conservative and authoritarian.
5. Youth shows no concern for old age, yet youth is growing old.

Applying

6. Suggested Response: People often change a great deal as they grow older.

ANSWERS TO ANALYZING LITERATURE

1. He capitalizes only the words that focus on the concerns of old age.
2. The lines that concern old age appear inside parentheses, while those that deal with youth do not.

More About the Author Because the sentence structure and wordings in Robert Frost's poetry do not present the difficulties found in the work of many of his contemporaries, some readers have mistakenly assumed that there is not much depth to Frost's poetry. Yet, in reality, Frost's poems tend to have a great deal of depth; and if we read one of his poems several times, we often become aware of underlying meanings. Why do you think that it is important not to judge a work solely upon our first impression?

Critical Evaluation Robert Di-Yanni made the following comments about Frost's poetry:

"Frost was a skilled wordsmith who cared about the sounds of his sentences. He noted more than once how 'the sentence sound says more than the words'; how 'tones of voice' can 'mean more than words.' In such voice tones Frost heard the sounds of sense and captured them in his verse, heightening their expressiveness by combining the inflections of ordinary speech with the measured regularity of meter. Because Frost's achievement in this regard surpasses most other modern American poets, we should be particularly attentive to the way he makes poetry out of the spoken word. His poems often mask the most elegant and subtle of his technical accomplishments. Perhaps the best way to read Frost's poems is to approach them as performances, as poetic acts of skillful daring, of risks taken, of technical dangers overcome. In doing so we may share the pleasure Frost took in poetic performance. In addition, we can see how Frost's poetry often 'begins in delight and ends in wisdom,' offering along the way what he called 'a momentary stay against confusion.'"

ROBERT FROST

1874–1963

In becoming one of America's most loved and respected poets, Robert Frost displayed the same rugged persistence and determination exhibited by the rural New Englanders he depicted in his poems. Although he eventually received four Pulitzer Prizes and read at a presidential inauguration, Frost had a difficult time achieving success as a poet. Only after years of rejection by book and magazine publishers did he finally receive the acceptance for which he worked so hard.

Frost was born in San Francisco, but his father died when he was eleven, and his mother moved the family to Lawrence, Massachusetts. After graduating from high school, he briefly attended Dartmouth College. Disliking college life, he left school and spent time working as a farmer, a mill hand, a newspaper writer, and a schoolteacher. During his spare time, he wrote poetry and dreamed of someday being able to support himself by writing alone.

After marrying and tending a farm in New Hampshire for ten years, Frost moved to England in 1912, hoping to establish himself as a poet. While in England he became friends with a number of well-known poets, including Ezra Pound, and published two collections of poetry, *A Boy's Will* (1913) and *North of Boston* (1914). When he returned home in 1915, he discovered that his success in England had spread to the United States.

Frost went on to publish five more volumes of poetry, for which he received many awards. He also taught at Amherst, the University of Michigan, Harvard, and Dartmouth; lectured and read at dozens of other schools; and farmed in Vermont and New Hampshire. In 1960, at John F. Kennedy's invitation, Frost became the first poet to read his work at a presidential inauguration.

Frost's poetry was popular not only among critics and intellectuals, but also among the general public. In his poems he painted vivid portraits of the New England landscape and captured the flavor of New England life using traditional verse forms and conversational language. Despite their apparent simplicity, however, his poems are filled with hidden meanings, forcing us to delve beneath the surface to fully appreciate his work.

Writing about the effect a poem should have on the reader, Frost once said, "Like a piece of ice on a hot stove the poem must ride on its own melting. A poem may be worked over since it is in being, but may not be worried into being. Its most precious quality will remain its having run itself and carried away the poet with it. Read it a hundred times: it will forever keep its freshness as a petal keeps its fragrance. It can never lose its sense of a meaning that once unfolded by surprise as it went."

Objectives

1 To appreciate symbols
2 To write about a symbol
3 To write a poem

GUIDE FOR INTERPRETING

Birches; Mending Wall;
The Wood-Pile; After Apple-Picking

The Writer's Techniques

Symbols. A symbol is a person, place, or thing that has a meaning in itself and also represents something larger than itself. Frequently, an event or activity in a literary work may have a symbolic meaning. For example, the voyage of the *Pequod* in Herman Melville's *Moby-Dick* symbolizes humanity's quest to conquer everything in nature that seems paradoxical, unexplainable, and uncontrollable.

Symbols create different layers of meaning in a literary work. Because they generally contain symbols, Robert Frost's poems can usually be interpreted in more than one way. On the surface the poems seem straightforward and easy to grasp. Yet by analyzing his use of symbols, we become aware of larger meanings that are hidden beneath the surface.

Commentary

In his poetry Frost combines realism with symbolism. He uses the language of everyday, realistic speech, and the characters and situations he writes about are realistic and believable. But the images he uses and the memorable lines his characters speak suggest their closeness to a symbolic world. For example, in "Mending Wall," the man's repetition of "Good fences make good neighbors" raises the maxim above a mere comment on the immediate need to mend the broken wall. Frost does not simply re-create reality, he illuminates its hidden meanings by shaping it and paring it down. Frost once commented on his view of realism and poetry: "There are two types of realist: the one who offers a good deal of dirt with his potato to show that it is a real one, and the one who is satisfied with the potato brushed clean. I'm inclined to be the second kind. To me, the thing that art does to life is to clean it, to strip it to form." As you read Frost's poetry, notice how he uses images and characters from real life, but how they seem to grow over the course of the poems and become, in a way, much larger than what and who they are. Frost also regarded poetry as discovering meaning in what is already before us: "For me," he wrote in 'The Figure a Poem Makes,' the initial delight is in the surprise of remembering something I didn't know I knew."

Writing

In "Birches" the speaker fondly remembers swinging on the branches of birch trees during his childhood. List some of the activities you enjoyed during the early part of your childhood. Then write down some of your reasons for liking each of these activities.

Guide for Interpreting 869

Literary Focus The reader should keep in mind that Frost is interested in both the literal and symbolic layers of meaning.

Writing/Prior Knowledge After students have completed the assignment, have them discuss the reasons people give up activities they enjoy.

Vocabulary

Preteach the following vocabulary words:
poise (poiz) *n.:* Balance; stability (p. 871, l. 35)
hoary (hôr′ ē) *adj.:* Very old; ancient (p. 878, l. 12)

NEW ENGLAND BIRCHES
Ernest Lawson
The Phillips Collection, Washington, D.C.

Birches

Robert Frost

When I see birches bend to left and right
Across the lines of straighter darker trees,
I like to think some boy's been swinging them.
But swinging doesn't bend them down to stay
5 As ice storms do. Often you must have seen them
Loaded with ice a sunny winter morning
After a rain. They click upon themselves
As the breeze rises, and turn many-colored
As the stir cracks and crazes their enamel.
10 Soon the sun's warmth makes them shed crystal shells
Shattering and avalanching on the snow crust—

Such heaps of broken glass to sweep away
You'd think the inner dome of heaven had fallen.
They are dragged to the withered bracken by the load,
15 And they seem not to break; though once they are bowed
So low for long, they never right themselves:
You may see their trunks arching in the woods
Years afterwards, trailing their leaves on the ground
Like girls on hands and knees that throw their hair
20 Before them over their heads to dry in the sun.
But I was going to say when Truth broke in
With all her matter of fact about the ice storm,
I should prefer to have some boy bend them
As he went out and in to fetch the cows—
25 Some boy too far from town to learn baseball,
Whose only play was what he found himself,
Summer or winter, and could play alone.
One by one he subdued his father's trees
By riding them down over and over again
30 Until he took the stiffness out of them,
And not one but hung limp, not one was left
For him to conquer. He learned all there was
To learn about not launching out too soon
And so not carrying the tree away
35 Clear to the ground. He always kept his poise
To the top branches, climbing carefully
With the same pains you use to fill a cup
Up to the brim, and even above the brim.
Then he flung outward, feet first, with a swish,
40 Kicking his way down through the air to the ground.
So was I once myself a swinger of birches.
And so I dream of going back to be.
It's when I'm weary of considerations,
And life is too much like a pathless wood
45 Where your face burns and tickles with the cobwebs
Broken across it, and one eye is weeping
From a twig's having lashed across it open.
I'd like to get away from earth awhile
And then come back to it and begin over.
50 May no fate willfully misunderstand me
And half grant what I wish and snatch me away
Not to return. Earth's the right place for love:
I don't know where it's likely to go better.
I'd like to go by climbing a birch tree,
55 And climb black branches up a snow-white trunk
Toward heaven, till the tree could bear no more,
But dipped its top and set me down again.
That would be good both going and coming back.
One could do worse than be a swinger of birches.

Birches 871

1 **Discussion** What image does the speaker use to describe the ice fallen from the trees?

2 **Clarification** Bracken is a large, coarse fern.

3 **Discussion** What activity does the speaker prefer? What broader implications might that have?

4 **Literary Focus** In lines 43–47, the wood becomes a metaphor for life and its assaults.

5 **Critical Thinking and Reading** The speaker is quick to make it clear that he wants to return after escaping.

6 **Discussion** What are the possible meanings of the last line?

Reader's Response Do you ever yearn to escape from reality for a little while? Why or why not?

Closure and Extension

ANSWERS TO THINKING ABOUT THE SELECTION

Recalling

1. He likes to think a boy has been swinging on them.
2. Ice storms cause the trees to stay bent.
3. (a) His only play is what he himself invents. (b) He rides them over and over. (c) He learns about not launching out too soon and keeping his poise.
4. He dreams of it when he is "weary of considerations,/And life is too much like a pathless wood."
5. Swinging on birches "would be good both going and coming back."

Interpreting

6. (a) He is very independent and lives in harmony with nature. (b) Suggested Response: He represents the speaker as a young boy. (c) He has a very harmonious relationship with nature.
7. He is describing the vicissitudes of life.
8. He does not want to be taken from earth not to return; in other words he does not want to die.

Applying

9. Suggested Response: A person would be likely to become more inventive, yet he or she might also become lonely.

ANSWERS TO ANALYZING LITERATURE

1. The line suggests that it is desirable to live in harmony with nature and be able to temporarily escape from reality.
2. Suggested Response: This is suggested by the descriptions of the boy's interactions with the birches.
3. Suggested Response: Lines 47–48 and 54–58 suggest the escape from reality.

THINKING AND WRITING

After students have completed the assignment, divide them into groups, and have them read their rough drafts to one another and suggest ways in which they could be improved.

THINKING ABOUT THE SELECTION

Recalling

1. What does the speaker like to think when he sees birches "bend to the left and right"?
2. What causes the birch trees to bend "down to stay"?
3. (a) What is the only play for some boy who lives "too far from town to learn baseball"? (b) How does the boy take the stiffness out of the birch trees? (c) About what does the boy "learn all there was to learn"?
4. When does the speaker dream of "going back to be" a "swinger of birches"?
5. What does the speaker think "would be good both going and coming back"?

Interpreting

6. (a) How would you characterize the boy described in the poem? (b) Whom do you think the boy actually represents? (c) How would you describe the boy's relationship with nature?
7. What type of condition is the speaker describing in lines 44–48?
8. What does the speaker mean when he comments that he hopes that fate will not "half grant" what he wishes?

Applying

9. What are some of the advantages and disadvantages of growing up "too far from town to learn baseball"?

ANALYZING LITERATURE

Interpreting Symbols

A **symbol** is a person, place, object, or action that has a meaning in itself and also represents something larger than itself. For example, in "Birches" the activity of swinging on birch trees symbolizes both a unity between humanity and nature and the notion of a temporary escape from reality.

1. Explain the following line: "One could do worse than be a swinger of birches."
2. What details in the poem suggest that the swinging on birches symbolizes the unity between humanity and nature?
3. What details suggest that the activity symbolizes a temporary escape from reality?

THINKING AND WRITING

Writing About a Symbol

Write an essay in which you discuss the symbolic meaning of the swinging on birches in Frost's poem. Review your answers from the Analyzing Literature activity. Prepare a thesis statement. Then write your essay, using passages from the poem to support your thesis. When you revise, make sure your body paragraphs are arranged in a logical order. Proofread your essay and share it with your classmates.

Mending Wall

Robert Frost

1 Something there is that doesn't love a wall,
That sends the frozen-ground-swell under it
And spills the upper boulders in the sun,
And makes gaps even two can pass abreast.
5 The work of hunters is another thing:
I have come after them and made repair
Where they have left not one stone on a stone,
But they would have the rabbit out of hiding,
To please the yelping dogs. The gaps I mean,
10 No one has seen them made or heard them made,
But at spring mending-time we find them there.

2 I let my neighbor know beyond the hill;
And on a day we meet to walk the line
And set the wall between us once again.
15 We keep the wall between us as we go.
To each the boulders that have fallen to each.
And some are loaves and some so nearly balls
We have to use a spell to make them balance:
"Stay where you are until our backs are turned!"
20 We wear our fingers rough with handling them.

3 Oh, just another kind of outdoor game,
One on a side. It comes to little more:
There where it is we do not need the wall:
He is all pine and I am apple orchard.
25 My apple trees will never get across
And eat the cones under his pines, I tell him.
He only says, "Good fences make good neighbors."

4 Spring is the mischief in me, and I wonder
If I could put a notion in his head:
30 "*Why* do they make good neighbors? Isn't it
Where there are cows? But here there are no cows.
Before I built a wall I'd ask to know
What I was walling in or walling out,
And to whom I was like to give offense.
35 Something there is that doesn't love a wall,
That wants it down." I could say "Elves" to him,
But it's not elves exactly, and I'd rather
He said it for himself. I see him there,
Bringing a stone grasped firmly by the top
40 In each hand, like an old-stone savage armed.

5 He moves in darkness as it seems to me,

Mending Wall 873

Reader's Response Do you agree with the neighbor or with the speaker about the necessity of walls? Can they both be correct? Why or why not?

Closure and Extension

ANSWERS TO THINKING ABOUT THE SELECTION
Recalling

1. The frost-swell causes the gaps.
2. They keep the wall between them.
3. (a) His neighbor has apple trees and he has pine trees; the trees won't cross the wall as cows would. (b) He says, "Good fences make good neighbors."
4. He would want to know what he was walling in or out and if any offense would be given by the wall.

Interpreting

5. (a) Suggested Response: The speaker is practical, considerate, and intelligent. (b) The neighbor is close-minded and stubborn. (c) He finds him difficult to understand and disagrees with his opinions.
6. It suggests that walls are unnatural.
7. (a) It suggests that the barriers between people are often passed from generation to generation. (b) It suggests that he has given little thought to the meaning of his saying.
8. Despite the wall between them, the two men are not good neighbors.

Applying

9. (a) There is nothing to keep out or in. (b) Suggested Response: Walls are necessary if animals or people have to be kept in or out. Walls are also necessary where hostility exists.

THINKING AND WRITING

For help with this assignment, students can refer to Lesson 18, "Writing a Poem," in the Handbook of Writing About Literature.

Not of woods only and the shade of trees.
He will not go behind his father's saying,
And he likes having thought of it so well
45   He says again, "Good fences make good neighbors."

THINKING ABOUT THE SELECTION

Recalling

1. What causes the gaps in the wall?
2. How do the speaker and his neighbor go about repairing the wall?
3. (a) Why does the speaker feel the wall is unnecessary? (b) How does the neighbor respond when the speaker expresses his opinion?
4. What would the speaker ask to know before building a wall?

Interpreting

5. (a) How would you characterize the speaker? (b) How would you characterize the speaker's neighbor? (c) What is the speaker's attitude toward his neighbor?
6. What is the significance of the fact that nature breaks apart the wall each winter?
7. (a) What is suggested by the fact that the neighbor learned his favorite saying from his father? (b) What is the significance of the fact that the saying is a cliché, or an overused expression?

8. How does the speaker's relationship with his neighbor disprove the neighbor's favorite saying?

Applying

9. (a) Why might a wall be unnecessary in the type of environment described in the poem? (b) In what types of environments do you think a wall would be necessary?

THINKING AND WRITING

Writing a Poem

Write a poem that conveys a theme concerning life in contemporary American society. Prepare a list of images, or word pictures, associated with contemporary life. Then use your list of images in developing your poem. When writing your poem, try to avoid using abstract words unless they are linked to concrete images. When you finish writing, revise your poem and share it with your classmates.

874   *The Modern Age*

WOODLOT, MAINE WOODS
Marsden Hartley
The Phillips Collection, Washington, D.C.

The Wood-Pile

Robert Frost

Out walking in the frozen swamp one gray day,
I paused and said, "I will turn back from here.
No, I will go on farther—and we shall see."
The hard snow held me, save where now and then
5 One foot went through. The view was all in lines
Straight up and down of tall slim trees
Too much alike to mark or name a place by
So as to say for certain I was here
Or somewhere else: I was just far from home.

The Wood-Pile 875

Humanities Note

Fine art, *Woodlot, Maine Woods,* 1938, by Marsden Hartley. Hartley (1877–1943) an American painter, was born in Lewiston, Maine but grew up in Cleveland, Ohio. He studied in New York at the Chase School and the National Academy of Design and traveled to Europe where he was exposed to various artistic movements. After returning to America in 1916, he struggled with the concept of integrating the varied styles of twentieth-century painting. After 1928 Hartley finally achieved a personal style characterized by a natural realism.

Woodlot, Maine Woods is one of his later paintings. It demonstrates that Hartley, although evolving an intellectual approach rather than an emotional one, never lost the glowing color that was typical of his earlier abstract period.

You might use these questions for discussion:
1. The subject of the poem and the subject of the painting are the same. What is meant by the term *subject* of a painting?
2. Besides this obvious similarity in subject matter, what else do the poem and painting have in common?

Presentation

Motivation/Prior Knowledge
Have students imagine that they are walking through the wilderness. Would they feel uneasy if they saw no signs of human life?

Purpose-Setting Question
What is the significance of the speaker's discovery?

1 **Discussion** Why does the speaker decide to proceed?

2 Discussion What human characteristics does the speaker attribute to the bird?

3 Critical Thinking and Reading The pile of wood is a sign of human life. Why is the speaker reassured by his discovery?

4 Discussion How does the speaker know that the wood-pile was not made this year or even last year?

5 Clarification Both burning and decay involve oxidation, and decaying wood does produce warmth.

Reader's Response Have you ever felt reassured when you encountered someone or something familiar in an unfamiliar place or situation? Explain.

2

3

4

5

10 A small bird flew before me. He was careful
    To put a tree between us when he lighted,
    And say no word to tell me who he was
    Who was so foolish as to think what *he* thought.
15 He thought that I was after him for a feather—
    The white one in his tail; like one who takes
    Everything said as personal to himself.
    One flight out sideways would have undeceived him.
    And then there was a pile of wood for which
    I forgot him and let his little fear
20 Carry him off the way I might have gone,
    Without so much as wishing him good-night.
    He went behind it to make his last stand.
    It was a cord of maple, cut and split
    And piled—and measured, four by four by eight.
25 And not another like it could I see.
    No runner tracks in this year's snow looped near it.
    And it was older sure than this year's cutting,
    Or even last year's or the year's before.
    The wood was gray and the bark warping off it
30 And the pile somewhat sunken. Clematis[1]
    Had wound strings round and round it like a bundle.
    What held it, though, on one side was a tree
    Still growing, and on one a stake and prop,
    These latter about to fall. I thought that only
35 Someone who lived in turning to fresh tasks
    Could so forget his handiwork on which
    He spent himself, the labor of his ax,
    And leave it there far from a useful fireplace
    To warm the frozen swamp as best it could
40 With the slow smokeless burning of decay.

---

1. clematis (klem′ ə tis) *n*.: A woody vine with bright-colored flowers.

Grammar in Action

In poetry as in other forms of literature, **subject and verb agreement** means that a singular subject must have a singular verb, and a plural subject must have a plural verb. In most sentences, agreement is easily achieved. For example:

He was careful/ To put a tree between us . . .

When the subject and verb are separated by modifiers, agreement requires more care. Note the following example:

No *runner tracks* in this year's snow *looped* near it.

Words like *everything, anyone,* and *nobody* are singular and require singular verbs. *All* is singular or plural depending on its use.

Student Activity. Choose the correct form of the verb in each of the following sentences.
1. The speaker (is, are) walking through a frozen swamp.
2. The speaker (do, does) not know exactly where he is walking.
3. The only objects in sight (appear, appears) to be tall slim trees.
4. Suddenly, away (flutter, flutters) a small bird.

THINKING ABOUT THE SELECTION

Recalling

1. What does the speaker say to himself when he pauses?
2. Why is the speaker unable to "mark or name a place" by the trees?
3. What causes the speaker to forget the bird in which he has developed an interest?
4. How is the speaker able to tell that the woodpile has been there for some time?
5. What type of person does the speaker imagine must have abandoned the woodpile?

Interpreting

6. (a) How does the speaker personify, or attribute human behavior to, the bird? (b) What does his personification of the bird indicate about his response to being isolated in the wilderness?
7. (a) Why is the speaker reassured by his discovery of the woodpile? (b) How does the speaker's discovery fulfill his need to "mark or name a place"?

Applying

8. Why do you think a person isolated in the wilderness might be anxious to find a sign of human life?

5. The speaker, alone and apprehensive, suddenly (find, finds) a cord of firewood in the midst of the woods.
6. The wood (seem, seems) to have been abandoned.

Motivation/Prior Knowledge
Spend some time discussing the effects of ambition. Can a person ever be too ambitious?

Purpose-Setting Question
What does the speaker learn from his experiences?

1 Discussion Why is the speaker done with apple-picking?

2 Clarification The "winter sleep" suggests hibernation.

3 Critical Thinking and Reading The speaker describes that sensation that many of us experience when our sight is blurred from weariness.

4 Discussion Have you ever done something over and over again so that you still see it and feel it when the activity is over?

5 Discussion What is the meaning of the final lines?

After Apple-Picking
Robert Frost

My long two-pointed ladder's sticking through a tree
Toward heaven still,
And there's a barrel that I didn't fill
Beside it, and there may be two or three
5   Apples I didn't pick upon some bough.
But I am done with apple-picking now.
Essence of winter sleep is on the night,
The scent of apples: I am drowsing off.
I cannot rub the strangeness from my sight
10 I got from looking through a pane of glass
I skimmed this morning from the drinking trough
And held against the world of hoary grass.
It melted, and I let it fall and break.
But I was well
15 Upon my way to sleep before it fell,
And I could tell
What form my dreaming was about to take.
Magnified apples appear and disappear,
Stem end and blossom end,
20 And every fleck of russet showing clear.
My instep arch not only keeps the ache,
It keeps the pressure of a ladder-round.
I feel the ladder sway as the boughs bend.
And I keep hearing from the cellar bin
25 The rumbling sound
Of load on load of apples coming in.
For I have had too much
Of apple-picking: I am overtired
Of the great harvest I myself desired.
30 There were ten thousand thousand fruit to touch.
Cherish in hand, lift down, and not let fall.
For all
That struck the earth,
No matter if not bruised or spiked with stubble,
35 Went surely to the cider-apple heap
As of no worth.
One can see what will trouble
This sleep of mine, whatever sleep it is.
Were he not gone,
40 The woodchuck could say whether it's like his
Long sleep, as I describe its coming on,
Or just some human sleep.

THINKING ABOUT THE SELECTION
Recalling

1. What sits beside the ladder?
2. (a) What pictures flash through the speaker's mind as he drifts off to sleep? (b) What sensations does he feel? (c) What does he hear?
3. (a) How had the speaker handled the apples? (b) What happened to the apples that fell to the ground?

Interpreting

4. (a) How would you describe the speaker's condition? (b) What is the cause of his condition?
5. What does the image, or word picture, of "magnified apples" in line 18 suggest about the speaker's desire for a great harvest?
6. How might the speaker's sleep be like the "long sleep" of the woodchuck?
7. What does this poem suggest about the effects of unrestrained ambition?

Applying

8. Why do you think people often become obsessed with reaching a goal?

Primary Source

Frost's early volume of poetry *North of Boston* (1914) contained "Mending Wall," "The Wood-Pile," and "After Apple-Picking"—all poems about the New England countryside. In this volume, according to critic and poet Louis Untermeyer, Frost "found his own full utterance and himself. It is a book full of people, of the folk of New England, of New England itself with its hard hills and harder certainties, its repressions, its cold humor and inverted tenderness. Against this background, Frost has placed some of the most poignant and dramatic poems that the age has produced, perhaps the most authentic and powerful that have ever come out of America. These dramas, sometimes in dialogue, sometimes in monologue, are the antithesis of the 'arranged' and carefully planned pieces of stagecraft. There is a total absence of all the skillful literary mechanics that we have been used to. Discarding the theatrical accessories, Frost has taken the drama out into the air; he lets the sunlight play over his Yankee scenes and allows his actors to talk in a language that is rich and living. No one . . . has put so much of the sharp tang of country life into dramatic poetry; and here . . . every speech is as 'fully flavored as a nut or an apple,' a language that is colloquial and colorful."

After Apple-Picking 879

Closure and Extension

ANSWERS TO THINKING ABOUT THE SELECTION
Recalling

1. An unfilled barrel sits beside the ladder.
2. (a) Images of apples appear. (b) He feels the sensation of the ladder. (c) He hears the sounds of the apples rumbling into the cellar.
3. (a) He had lifted them, cherished them, and not let them fall. (b) They went to the cider heap.

Interpreting

4. (a) He is exhausted. (b) He has been picking apples too long.
5. It suggests that it was unrealistic.
6. The woodchuck hibernates for the winter; the speaker rests from his labors.
7. He suggests that unrestrained ambition can lead to failure and make a person feel depressed.

Applying

8. Suggested Response: People often begin focusing all of their energy on reaching a single goal.

Literary Focus Both narrative poetry and dramatic poetry can tell a story. An example of an earlier narrative poem is "The Skeleton in Armor" on page 265.

Writing/Prior Knowledge Death is a difficult subject for many people to write or talk about. Students may need to distance themselves from the subject by writing in general terms.

Vocabulary

Preteach the following vocabulary words:

musing (my$\overline{oo}$z′ iŋ) v.: Thinking deeply and at length (p. 881, l. 1)

harbor (här′ bər) v.: Shelter or house (p. 881, l. 15)

beholden (bi hōld′ ən) adj.: Owing thanks; indebted (p. 881, l. 21)

piqued (pēkt) v.: Aroused resentment in (p. 883, l. 17)

rueful (r$\overline{oo}$′ fəl) adj.: Feeling or showing sorrow or pity (p. 888, l. 19)

The Death of the Hired Man; "Out, Out—"

Literary Forms

Narrative Poetry. A narrative poem is one that tells a story. Like a short story, a narrative poem has one or more characters, has a setting, a conflict, and describes an event or a series of events. In a narrative poem, the story is told by a single speaker, which may be the voice of the poet or that of a fictional character.

Dramatic Poetry. Unlike narrative poetry, in which events are described in the words of the speaker, dramatic poetry re-creates an event using dialogue or monologue as well as description. In a dramatic poem we see the characters interacting with and talking to one another, and as a result it seems as if we are actually witnessing the event.

Writing

"Out, Out—" tells the story of the death of a young boy and how his family copes with it. Freewrite about the various ways in which people deal with death.

Primary Source

In his poetry Frost uses language that is often simple and matter-of-fact. This is true, for instance, in "The Death of the Hired Man," where the husband and wife speak using ordinary, nonpoetic language. This gives to his poetry a sense of immediacy and reality. One poet and critic, W. H. Auden, wrote at length about the special qualities of Frost's poetic style and its effects. In his essay "Robert Frost," Auden wrote:

> The music [of Frost's poetic style] is always that of the speaking voice, quiet and sensible, and I cannot think of any other modern poet, except [Constantine] Cavafy, who uses language more simply. He rarely employs metaphors, and there is not a word, not a historical or literary reference in the whole of his work which would be strange to an unbookish boy of fifteen. Yet he manages to make this simple kind of speech express a wide variety of emotion and experience. . . .
>
> Frost's poetic speech is the speech of a mature mind, fully awake and in control of itself; it is not the speech of dream or of uncontrollable passion. Except in reported speech, interjections, imperatives, and rhetorical interrogatives are rare. This does not mean, of course, that his poems are lacking in feeling; again and again, one is aware of strong, even violent, emotion behind what is actually said, but the saying is reticent, the poetry has, as it were, an auditory chastity.

880   *The Modern Age*

Objectives

1 To appreciate dramatic poetry
2 To appreciate narrative poetry
3 To write a dramatic poem

Support Material

Teaching Portfolio
Teacher Backup, p. 1153
Grammar in Action Worksheet, *Using Apostrophes,* p. 1156
Usage and Mechanics Worksheet, p. 1158
Vocabulary Check, p. 1159
Analyzing Literature Worksheet, *Understanding Narrative Poetry,* p. 1160

Language Worksheet, *Choosing Meaning That Fits the Context,* p. 1161
Selection Test, p. 1162

The Death of the Hired Man

Robert Frost

Mary sat musing on the lamp-flame at the table,
Waiting for Warren. When she heard his step,
She ran on tiptoe down the darkened passage
To meet him in the doorway with the news
5 And put him on his guard. "Silas is back."
She pushed him outward with her through the door
And shut it after her. "Be kind," she said.
She took the market things from Warren's arms
And set them on the porch, then drew him down
10 To sit beside her on the wooden steps.

"When was I ever anything but kind to him?
But I'll not have the fellow back," he said.
"I told him so last haying, didn't I?
If he left then, I said, that ended it.
15 What good is he? Who else will harbor him
At his age for the little he can do?
What help he is there's no depending on.
Off he goes always when I need him most.
He thinks he ought to earn a little pay,
20 Enough at least to buy tobacco with,
So he won't have to beg and be beholden.
'All right,' I say, 'I can't afford to pay
Any fixed wages, though I wish I could.'
'Someone else can.' 'Then someone else will have to.'
25 I shouldn't mind his bettering himself
If that was what it was. You can be certain,
When he begins like that, there's someone at him
Trying to coax him off with pocket money—
In haying time, when any help is scarce.
30 In winter he comes back to us. I'm done."

"Sh! not so loud: he'll hear you," Mary said.

"I want him to: he'll have to soon or late."

"He's worn out. He's asleep beside the stove.
When I came up from Rowe's I found him here,
35 Huddled against the barn door fast asleep,

Motivation/Prior Knowledge
Discuss the relationship between farm workers and their employers. Why might they develop warm feelings for one another?

Purpose-Setting Question Why does Silas return?

1 **Discussion** What does Mary's behavior reveal about her personality?

2 **Discussion** Why is Warren annoyed with Silas?

3 **Discussion** What do lines 33–39 reveal about the change in Silas?

A miserable sight, and frightening, too—
You needn't smile—I didn't recognize him—
I wasn't looking for him—and he's changed.
Wait till you see."

"Where did you say he'd been?"

40　"He didn't say. I dragged him to the house,
And gave him tea and tried to make him smoke.
I tried to make him talk about his travels.
Nothing would do: he just kept nodding off."

"What did he say? Did he say anything?"

"But little."

45　　　　"Anything? Mary, confess
He said he'd come to ditch the meadow for me."

"Warren!"
　　　　"But did he? I just want to know."

"Of course he did. What would you have him say?
Surely you wouldn't grudge the poor old man
50　Some humble way to save his self-respect.
He added, if you really care to know,
He meant to clear the upper pasture, too.
That sounds like something you have heard before?
Warren, I wish you could have heard the way
55　He jumbled everything. I stopped to look
Two or three times—he made me feel so queer—
To see if he was talking in his sleep.
He ran on Harold Wilson—you remember—
The boy you had in haying four years since.
60　He's finished school, and teaching in his college.
Silas declares you'll have to get him back.
He says they two will make a team for work:
Between them they will lay this farm as smooth!
The way he mixed that in with other things.
65　He thinks young Wilson a likely lad, though daft
On education—you know how they fought
All through July under the blazing sun,
Silas up on the cart to build the load,
Harold along beside to pitch it on."

70　"Yes, I took care to keep well out of earshot."

"Well, those days trouble Silas like a dream.

Grammar in Action

The **apostrophe** has two primary uses. It forms contractions, replacing omitted letters, as in the following examples:

You need*n't* be afraid he*'ll* leave you this time.(p. 883)

You*'ll* be surprised at him—how much he*'s* broken. (p. 886)

The apostrophe, with an *s*, also signals the possessive form of nouns and some pronouns. Note the following examples:

Harold*'s* young college-boy*'s* assurance piqued him. (p. 883)

He takes it out in bunches like big birds*'* nests. (p. 883)

Notice that when the plural noun ends in s—"birds"—the apostrophe follows the *s*.

The possessives of indefinite pronouns—*anybody's, somebody's, nobody's* —are formed by adding *'s*. However, apostrophes are not used in the possessive forms of personal pronouns —*his, its, ours, yours.*

You wouldn't think they would. How such things linger!
Harold's young college-boy's assurance piqued him.
After so many years he still keeps finding
75   Good arguments he sees he might have used.
I sympathize. I know just how it feels
To think of the right thing to say too late.
Harold's associated in his mind with Latin.
He asked me what I thought of Harold's saying
80   He studied Latin, like the violin,
Because he liked it—that an argument!
He said he couldn't make the boy believe
He could find water with a hazel prong—
Which showed how much good school had ever done him.
85   He wanted to go over that. But most of all
He thinks if he could have another chance
To teach him how to build a load of hay—"

"I know, that's Silas' one accomplishment.
He bundles every forkful in its place,
90   And tags and numbers it for future reference,
So he can find and easily dislodge it
In the unloading. Silas does that well.
He takes it out in bunches like big birds' nests.
You never see him standing on the hay
95   He's trying to lift, straining to lift himself."

"He thinks if he could teach him that, he'd be
Some good perhaps to someone in the world.
He hates to see a boy the fool of books.
Poor Silas, so concerned for other folk,
100   And nothing to look backward to with pride,
And nothing to look forward to with hope,
So now and never any different."

Part of a moon was falling down the west,
Dragging the whole sky with it to the hills.
105   Its light poured softly in her lap. She saw it
And spread her apron to it. She put out her hand
Among the harplike morning-glory strings,
Taut with the dew from garden bed to eaves,
As if she played unheard some tenderness
110   That wrought on him beside her in the night.
"Warren," she said, "he has come home to die:
You needn't be afraid he'll leave you this time."

"Home," he mocked gently.

"Yes, what else but home?

The Death of the Hired Man   883

6 **Discussion** What were some of the sources of disagreement between Silas and Harold?

7 **Discussion** How do lines 88–95 contribute to the portrait of Silas?

8 **Discussion** What is the significance of the descriptions of the moonlight?

9 **Discussion** Why does Warren question the use of the word *home?*

Student Activity 1. Indicate whether each apostrophe indicates omission of letters or possession. If it indicates an omission, decide what has been omitted.
1. She took the market things from Warren's arms.
2. What help he is there's no depending on.
3. When I came up from Rowe's I found him here.
4. I shouldn't mind his bettering himself.
5. Where did you say he'd been?
6. I wasn't looking for him—and he's changed.
7. Harold's associated in his mind with Latin.
8. He asked me what I thought of Harold's saying.

Student Activity 2. Choose the appropriate form to complete each of the following sentences.
1. (Frost's, Frosts') poem makes us feel (were, we're) witnessing the action.
2. We overhear the (character's, characters') discussion of (their, they're) hired hand.
3. (Its, It's) clear that (Mary's, Marys') more sympathetic than Warren.
4. The (poems', poem's) ending, with (it's, its) single-word quotation, is sad, but (its, it's) not unexpected.

It all depends on what you mean by home.
115 Of course he's nothing to us, any more
Than was the hound that came a stranger to us
Out of the woods, worn out upon the trail."

"Home is the place where, when you have to go there,
They have to take you in."

             "I should have called it
120 Something you somehow haven't to deserve."

Warren leaned out and took a step or two,
Picked up a little stick, and brought it back
And broke it in his hand and tossed it by.
"Silas has better claim on us you think
125 Than on his brother? Thirteen little miles
As the road winds would bring him to his door.
Silas has walked that far no doubt today.
Why doesn't he go there? His brother's rich,
A somebody—director in the bank."

"He never told us that."

                "We know it, though."
130

"I think his brother ought to help, of course.
I'll see to that if there is need. He ought of right
To take him in, and might be willing to—
He may be better than appearances.
135 But have some pity on Silas. Do you think
If he had any pride in claiming kin
Or anything he looked for from his brother,
He'd keep so still about him all this time?"

"I wonder what's between them."

                 "I can tell you.
140 Silas is what he is—we wouldn't mind him—
But just the kind that kinsfolk can't abide.
He never did a thing so very bad.
He don't know why he isn't quite as good
As anybody. Worthless though he is,
145 He won't be made ashamed to please his brother."

"*I* can't think Si ever hurt anyone."

"No, but he hurt my heart the way he lay
And rolled his old head on that sharp-edged chair-back.

The Death of the Hired Man 885

Primary Source

Poet and critic Louis Untermeyer made the following comments about "The Death of the Hired Man":

"The Death of the Hired Man" is many kinds of poem. It is a narrative, a dialogue, a drama; it has been successfully acted as a one-act play. Three people are portrayed: a farmer, his wife, and an old incompetent hired hand, shiftless and proud—and the character most fully revealed is the one who never appears.

The poem has endeared itself to readers of every kind, and for many reasons. Some readers have praised it for its authentic power, its conversational beauty, its rich sense of ordinary life. Others have been won by its eloquent descriptions. . . .

Perhaps the most famous lines in the poem are those in which husband and wife trade definitions of home. Here the mood changes, and light irony is exchanged for deep pathos. . . .

"The Death of the Hired Man" is one of the most touching human episodes, the more so since it is all so quiet. The story unfolds itself in undertones; a poem heard—or overheard—in whispers.

10 **Discussion** Do you agree or disagree with Warren's definition of home?

11 **Discussion** What is the significance of the fact that Silas never told them he has a brother nearby?

12 Critical Thinking and Reading
The poem returns to the image of the moon begun in lines 103–110.

13 Discussion Why is the ending of the poem so blunt?

Reader's Response With which of the two characters, Mary or Warren, do you most relate? Explain.

He wouldn't let me put him on the lounge.
150 You must go in and see what you can do.
I made the bed up for him there tonight.
You'll be surprised at him—how much he's broken.
His working days are done; I'm sure of it."

"I'd not be in a hurry to say that."

155 "I haven't been. Go, look, see for yourself.
But, Warren, please remember how it is:
He's come to help you ditch the meadow.
He has a plan. You mustn't laugh at him.
He may not speak of it, and then he may.
160 I'll sit and see if that small sailing cloud
Will hit or miss the moon."

                                   It hit the moon.
Then there were three there, making a dim row,
The moon, the little silver cloud, and she.

Warren returned—too soon, it seemed to her—
165 Slipped to her side, caught up her hand and waited.

"Warren?" she questioned.
                                   "Dead," was all he answered.

THINKING ABOUT THE SELECTION

Recalling

1. Why does Warren not want Silas back?
2. (a) In what condition is Silas? (b) What task does he say he has come to perform?
3. According to Warren, what is "Silas's one accomplishment?"
4. What does Silas want to teach Harold Wilson?
5. (a) What does Mary believe is the reason Silas has come? (b) What does she believe is the reason Silas chose not to go to his brother's home?
6. What does Warren tell Mary after he has looked in on Silas?

Interpreting

7. How do the descriptions of the setting help to create a somber mood?
8. (a) How would you characterize Mary? (b) How would you characterize Warren?
9. (a) What do Silas's comments about Harold Wilson reveal about Silas's personality? (b) What do we learn about Silas's personality from his refusal to look to his brother for help?

10. (a) How are Mary's and Warren's definitions of home different? (b) How does this contrast reflect the differences in their personalities?

Applying

11. Do you think Mary and Warren would have been obligated to care for Silas? Why or why not?

ANALYZING LITERATURE

Understanding Dramatic Poetry

A **dramatic poem** is a poem that dramatizes an event using dialogue or monologue as well as description. For example, "The Death of the Hired Man" dramatizes Mary's and Warren's reactions to Silas's arrival.

1. How does Frost's use of dialogue make it seem as if we are actually witnessing the event?
2. Because it depends so much on dialogue, "The Death of the Hired Man" is similar to a scene from a play. What sets it apart from a play?

Primary Source

Through the dialogue between the husband and wife in "The Death of the Hired Man," Frost evokes the character of the hired man and the dignified struggles of life in rural America, a theme he deals with in " 'Out, Out—' " as well. In *The Dyer's Hand and Other Essays*, poet and critic W. H. Auden wrote that "[t]he quality which, after courage, Frost ranks as the highest virtue [is] the self-respect which comes from taking a pride in something. It may be a pride in one's own skill, . . . the pride of the Hired Man who dies from a broken heart since old age has taken from him the one accomplishment, building a load of hay, which had hitherto prevented him from feeling utterly worthless, or it may be a pride which . . . is a folly, the pride of the man who has failed as a farmer, burned his house down for the insurance money, bought a telescope with the proceeds and taken a lowly job as a ticket agent on the railroad. The telescope is not a good one, the man is poor, but he is proud of his telescope and happy."

The Death of the Hired Man 887

ANSWERS TO THINKING ABOUT THE SELECTION
Recalling

1. The year before, Silas had left at haying time.
2. (a) He is worn out. (b) He says he has come to ditch the meadow.
3. Silas knows how to build a load of hay.
4. Silas wants to teach Harold how to build a load of hay.
5. (a) She believes he has come home to die. (b) His brother is ashamed of him, and Silas knows that.
6. Silas is dead.

Interpreting

7. The moon is falling down the west and dragging the sky with it.
8. (a) Mary seems to be sensitive and compassionate. (b) Warren is practical and is less compassionate than his wife.
9. (a) He values hard work more than education. (b) Silas has a certain amount of pride.
10. (a) Warren says that home is the place where they have to take you in. Mary says that home is a place that you do not need to deserve. (b) It reflects the fact that Warren is more cynical than Mary.

Applying

11. Answers will differ. Students may suggest that they would have been obligated to care for him, because he had no one else to do so.

ANSWERS TO ANALYZING LITERATURE

1. It makes it seem as if the event is actually happening, rather than merely being recounted.
2. Suggested Response: Frost's vivid imagery sets it apart from a play.

Motivation/Prior Knowledge
Have students discuss some of
the tragic events that can occur
in rural areas. How does the violent nature of some of these
events contrast with the pastoral
nature of rural life?

Purpose-Setting Question How
does the family respond to the
incident?

1 **Clarification** A buzz saw is a
circular saw rotated by machinery.

2 **Discussion** Lines 10–12 suggest that the boy could have
stopped his work a little sooner.
Why does the speaker mention
this?

3 **Discussion** How does the
speaker personify the saw? What
is the effect of this personification?

4 **Discussion** How does the
speaker dramatize the boy's
death? Why is the boy's death
surprising?

5 **Discussion** What does the final
line suggest about rural life?

Reader's Response What
makes this poem particularly
tragic and horrifying?

"Out, Out—"
Robert Frost

The buzz saw snarled and rattled in the yard
And made dust and dropped stove-length sticks of wood,
Sweet-scented stuff when the breeze drew across it.
And from there those that lifted eyes could count
5   Five mountain ranges one behind the other
Under the sunset far into Vermont.
And the saw snarled and rattled, snarled and rattled,
As it ran light, or had to bear a load.
And nothing happened: day was all but done.
10   Call it a day, I wish they might have said
To please the boy by giving him the half hour
That a boy counts so much when saved from work.
His sister stood beside them in her apron
To tell them "Supper." At the word, the saw,
15   As if to prove saws knew what supper meant,
Leaped out at the boy's hand, or seemed to leap—
He must have given the hand. However it was,
Neither refused the meeting. But the hand!
The boy's first outcry was a rueful laugh,
20   As he swung toward them holding up the hand,
Half in appeal, but half as if to keep
The life from spilling. Then the boy saw all—
Since he was old enough to know, big boy
Doing a man's work, though a child at heart—
25   He saw all spoiled. "Don't let him cut my hand off—
The doctor, when he comes. Don't let him, sister!"
So. But the hand was gone already.
The doctor put him in the dark of ether.[1]
He lay and puffed his lips out with his breath.
30   And then—the watcher at his pulse took fright.
No one believed. They listened at his heart.
Little—less—nothing!—and that ended it.
No more to build on there. And they, since they
Were not the one dead, turned to their affairs.

_____
1. ether (ē thər) *n.*: A chemical compound used as an anesthetic.

THINKING ABOUT THE SELECTION

Recalling

1. (a) When does the accident occur? (b) How does it happen?
2. (a) What is the boy's immediate response to the accident? (b) What does he ask of his sister?
3. (a) What happens to the boy after the doctor comes? (b) How does the family respond?

Applying

4. What does the buzz saw represent? Support your answer.
5. How does the description of the setting contrast with the events in the poem?
6. What does the family's response to the incident suggest about the nature of rural life?
7. The poem's title comes from a scene in Shakespeare's *Macbeth* in which Macbeth laments the premature death of his wife with the following words:

   Out, out, brief candle!
   Life's but a walking shadow, a poor
      player,
   That struts and frets his hour upon the
      stage
   And then is heard no more.

   What does this quote reveal about the poem's theme, or main point?

Applying

8. How do you explain the family's response to the incident?

ANALYZING LITERATURE

Understanding Narrative Poetry

A **narrative poem** is a poem that tells a story. For example, " 'Out, Out—' " tells the story of a tragic accident in Vermont.

1. The events in " 'Out, Out—' " are described by a single speaker. What seems to be the speaker's attitude toward the events?
2. At what point in the poem does the speaker directly state his feelings?

THINKING AND WRITING

Writing a Dramatic Poem

Reshape " 'Out, Out—' " into a dramatic poem. Review "The Death of the Hired Man" paying close attention to Frost's use of dialogue. Then begin writing your poem, using dialogue and description to dramatize the accident and the events surrounding it. When you revise, make sure that your poem will make the reader feel as if he or she is actually witnessing the events.

"Out, Out——" 889

ANSWERS TO THINKING ABOUT THE SELECTION
Recalling

1. (a) The accident occurs just before supper. (b) The saw leaped out of the boy's hand as he was called to supper.
2. (a) He laughs ruefully. (b) He asks her not to let them cut off his hand.
3. (a) The boy is given ether; then he dies. (b) They go on with their affairs.

Interpreting

4. The saw represents the technological invention that humans are unable to completely control. This is indicated by the fact that the boy loses control of the saw.
5. The setting is peaceful and beautiful; the events are violent and tragic.
6. It suggests that rural life is difficult, and people are forced to accept tragedies and continue with their lives.
7. It conveys the fact that life is short and fragile in nature.

Applying

8. Suggested Response: Their lives are difficult, and they have no choice but to accept such tragedies and to keep working to ensure their own survival.

ANSWERS TO ANALYZING LITERATURE

1. Suggested Response: The speaker is disturbed by the events but accepts them as a normal part of rural life.
2. He says, "Call it a day, I wish they might have said."

THINKING AND WRITING

Publishing Student Writing Encourage students to submit their poems to your school's literary magazine.

Literary Focus Many of the preceding Robert Frost poems are written in iambic pentameter. See page 202 to review this term. Some are rhymed. Others are unrhymed iambic pentameter, or blank verse. The poems in this section have a greater variety of rhythm and rhyme than the previous poems.

Writing/Prior Knowledge For extra credit, have students come up with a few details that describe each of the objects on their lists.

Vocabulary

Preteach the following vocabulary words:
suffice (sə fīs′) v.: To be enough (p. 891, l. 9)
luminary (loo′ mə ner′ ē) adj.: Giving off light (p. 894, l. 12)

Fire and Ice; Nothing Gold Can Stay; Stopping by Woods on a Snowy Evening; Acquainted with the Night

Writer's Techniques

Rhythm. Rhythm is the arrangement of stressed and unstressed syllables in a poem. In poems with a regular rhythm, or meter, the arrangement of stressed and unstressed syllables forms a recurring pattern. However, poets usually introduce slight variations in the metrical pattern to avoid monotony or emphasize important words. Poets will also introduce pauses within lines to interrupt the regular rhythm. These pauses, called caesuras, are usually created by punctuation, though they may also be formed by the meanings of words or the natural rhythms of language. For example, the meanings of the words in line 7 of "Fire and Ice" ("To say that for destruction ice") cause a pause to occur between the words *destruction* and *ice*.

Another way poets can vary a regular rhythm is through the use of run-on lines. Unlike end-stopped lines, which end with a pause, run-on lines flow naturally into the next line. For example, in "Fire and Ice," line 7 ("To say that for destruction ice") flows into line 8 ("Is also great").

Writing

In "Nothing Gold Can Stay," Frost writes about the impermanence of beauty. Spend some time thinking about beautiful things that do not last, listing each item that comes to mind.

Primary Source

For Frost the problem of writing poetry had to do with the tensions between freedom and restraint. As he put it in his essay "The Figure a Poem Makes," one mystery of poetry "is how a poem can have a wildness and at the same time a subject that shall be fulfilled." He wondered how the poem could both conform to the poet's intentions and rebel against them to go its own way. He believed that poets begin to write out of a pleasurable impulse to express themselves but find out what they want to say only in the process of saying it. The poem, therefore, leads the poet toward a moment of insight and wisdom. "It should be the pleasure of a poem itself to tell how it can," he continued in his essay. "The figure a poem makes. It begins in delight and ends in wisdom. The figure is the same as for love. No one can really hold that ecstasy should be static and stand still in one place. It begins in delight, it inclines in impulse, it assumes direction with the first line laid down, it runs a course of lucky events, and ends in a clarification of life—not necessarily a great clarification, such as sects and cults are founded on, but in a momentary stay against confusion."

Objectives

1 To appreciate rhythm
2 To analyze variations in rhythm
3 To support a generalization

Support Material

Teaching Portfolio
Teacher Backup, p. 1165
Usage and Mechanics Worksheet, p. 1168
Vocabulary Check, p. 1169
Analyzing Literature Worksheet, *Understanding Rhythm,* p. 1170
Language Worksheet, *Recognizing Degrees of Comparison,* p. 1171

Selection Test, p. 1172
Art Transparency 16, *Calm Morning* by Fairfield Porter

Fire and Ice

Robert Frost

1 {
Some say the world will end in fire,
Some say in ice.

2 {
From what I've tasted of desire
I hold with those who favor fire.
5 But if it had to perish twice,
I think I know enough of hate
To say that for destruction ice
Is also great
And would suffice.

THINKING ABOUT THE SELECTION

Recalling

1. In what two ways do "some say" the world will end?
2. With whom does the speaker hold?
3. What does the speaker feel would also suffice "for destruction"?

Interpreting

4. In this poem the speaker approaches a very serious subject in a seemingly casual manner. What might have been Frost's reasons for taking this type of approach?
5. (a) What emotion does each of the natural elements in the poem represent? (b) What does the speaker suggest that these emotions have in common?

Applying

6. What emotions, aside from the ones referred to in the poem, do you think bring out destructive impulses in people?

Fire and Ice 891

Motivation/Prior Knowledge Have students discuss the title of the poem. What do fire and ice represent to them?

Purpose-Setting Question What is Frost's attitude toward the subject of the poem?

1 Critical Thinking and Reading The first two lines suggest in simple language a thought that terrifies many people. The very simplicity of the language makes the thought even more chilling.

2 Discussion What do fire and ice each represent?

Reader's Response Do you agree with the speaker that desire and hate are equally destructive? Why or why not?

Closure and Extension

ANSWERS TO THINKING ABOUT THE SELECTION
Recalling

1. It will end in fire or ice.
2. The speaker holds with fire.
3. Ice would also suffice.

Interpreting

4. Suggested Response: The casual manner with which he approaches the subject mirrors the many people's attitude about war and destruction and makes the poem even more startling.
5. (a) Fire represents desire and ice represents hate. (b) They both have the power to destroy.

Applying

6. Suggested Response: Jealousy and greed are two other emotions that bring out destructive impulses in people.

Nothing Gold Can Stay

Robert Frost

1 ☐

Nature's first green is gold,
Her hardest hue to hold.
Her early leaf's a flower;
But only so an hour.
5 Then leaf subsides to leaf.
So Eden sank to grief,
So dawn goes down to day.
Nothing gold can stay.

2 ☐

THINKING ABOUT THE SELECTION

Recalling

1. What happens to each of the elements of nature mentioned in the poem?

Interpreting

2. What is the meaning of the first line?
3. (a) What is the poem's theme, or main point? (b) How does the allusion, or reference, to Eden help to convey the theme?

Applying

4. Do you agree with the outlook expressed in this poem? Why or why not?

Stopping by Woods on a Snowy Evening

Robert Frost

1   Whose woods these are I think I know.
His house is in the village though;
He will not see me stopping here
To watch his woods fill up with snow.

2   5   My little horse must think it queer
To stop without a farmhouse near
Between the woods and frozen lake
The darkest evening of the year.

3   He gives his harness bells a shake
10   To ask if there is some mistake.
The only other sound's the sweep
Of easy wind and downy flake.

4   The woods are lovely, dark and deep,
But I have promises to keep,
15   And miles to go before I sleep,
And miles to go before I sleep.

THINKING ABOUT THE SELECTION

Recalling

1. Why does the speaker stop in the woods?
2. (a) What does the speaker imagine that his horse "must think"? (b) Why does the horse give "his harness bells a shake"?
3. What must the speaker do before he sleeps?

Interpreting

4. (a) What do the speaker's actions in this poem reveal about his personality? (b) What internal conflict does the speaker experience? (c) How is the conflict resolved?
5. What difference between humans and animals is revealed through the horse's behavior?

6. (a) How does the repetition of the *d* sound in line 13 reinforce the meaning of the line? (b) What is the effect of Frost's use of repetition in the final two lines?
7. Explain the last three lines of this poem.

Applying

8. Just as swinging from birch trees provides the boy in "Birches" with a temporary escape from reality, pausing to observe nature provides the speaker with a temporary escape from reality in "Stopping by Woods on a Snowy Evening." Why do you think that people at times need to find this type of temporary escape?

Stopping by Woods on a Snowy Evening   893

Presentation

Motivation/Prior Knowledge Have students imagine that they are traveling through the woods on a snowy evening. Would they want to stop just to appreciate the beauty of the scene?

Purpose-Setting Question Why does the speaker interrupt his journey?

1 Critical Thinking and Reading The first stanza sets up the situation. It also establishes the rhythm and rhyme scheme.

2 Critical Thinking and Reading The speaker attributes to his horse an idea he himself may have.

3 Discussion To what senses do the images in the poem appeal?

4 Discussion What is the effect of the repetition in the final two lines?

Reader's Response What thoughts and emotions does this poem evoke?

Closure and Extension

ANSWERS TO THINKING ABOUT THE SELECTION
Recalling

1. He is watching them fill up with snow.
2. (a) It is queer to stop where there are no people. (b) The horse is impatient to move on.
3. He has miles to travel.

Interpreting

4. (a) He has an appreciation of nature and a sense of responsibility. (b) He is torn between his desire to stay and appreciate the woods and his awareness that he has commitments to fulfill. (c) He leaves the woods to fulfill his commitments.
5. Unlike humans, animals are unable to appreciate nature's beauty.
6. (a) The *d* sound echoes the mean-

ing of the line. (b) The repetition of the final two lines creates a hypnotic effect.
7. Suggested Response: The speaker sees the need to fulfill his responsibilities.

Applying

8. Suggested Response: People need to find a temporary escape, because their everyday lives are at times filled with tension and anxiety.

Motivation/Prior Knowledge
Have students discuss what the title suggests to them. What does it mean to be "acquainted with the night"?

Purpose-Setting Question
What is the speaker's view of his own life?

1 **Critical Thinking and Reading**
Note that each image conveys a sense of isolation.

2 **Discussion** What is the effect of line 10?

3 **Discussion** What is the meaning of line 13?

Reader's Response Have you ever felt "acquainted with the night" as the speaker has? Explain.

Acquainted with the Night

Robert Frost

I have been one acquainted with the night.
I have walked out in rain—and back in rain.
I have outwalked the furthest city light.

I have looked down the saddest city lane.
5 I have passed by the watchman on his beat
And dropped my eyes, unwilling to explain.

I have stood still and stopped the sound of feet
When far away an interrupted cry
Came over houses from another street,

10 But not to call me back or say good-by;
And further still at an unearthly height
One luminary clock against the sky

Proclaimed the time was neither wrong nor right.
I have been one acquainted with the night.

THINKING ABOUT THE SELECTION

Recalling

1. (a) Where and in what conditions has the speaker walked? (b) Where has he looked? (c) Whom has he passed?
2. What does the speaker hear that causes him to stand still and stop the sound of feet?
3. What does the "luminary clock" proclaim?

Interpreting

4. What type of mood do the images in lines 1–4 create?
5. (a) The night watchman symbolizes regularity and certainty. Given this fact, what do you think the speaker's response to the watchman suggests? (b) What is the speaker "unwilling to explain"?
6. What does the speaker's comment that "the time was neither wrong nor right" reveal about his life?
7. (a) What does night symbolize in this poem? (b) How does Frost use repetition to help convey the symbolic meaning of the night?

Applying

8. What does this poem suggest about Frost's attitude toward city life?

ANALYZING LITERATURE

Understanding Rhythm

Rhythm is the arrangement of stressed and unstressed syllables in a poem. Poets vary the regular rhythm of a poem in a number of ways. Often poets interrupt the regular rhythm by introducing pauses, or caesuras, within lines. Another way poets vary rhythm is by using run-on lines—lines that flow naturally into the next line.

1. Find two caesuras in "Acquainted with the Night."
2. Find two run-on lines in the poem.

CRITICAL THINKING AND READING

Analyzing Variations in Rhythm

Without some variation, the rhythm of a poem can become monotonous. In fact, an unvaried rhythm may even create a singsong effect that undercuts the meaning of the poem.

Read "Acquainted with the Night" aloud, disregarding run-on lines and caesuras and pausing only at the end of each line. Then reread the poem as Frost meant it to be read. Explain why the run-on lines and caesuras make the poem more effective.

THINKING AND READING

Supporting a Generalization

Write an essay in which you support a generalization about Robert Frost's poetry. Review the Frost poems in this book, noting similarities in form, content, and the attitudes expressed. Look over your notes and prepare a statement making a generalization about Frost's poetry. When you write your essay, use passages from at least four poems to support your statement. When you revise, make sure your essay is well-organized.

Acquainted with the Night 895

Auden collaborated with his long-time friend Chester Kallman to write the libretto for Igor Stravinsky's *The Rake's Progress,* an opera. Auden and Kallman also wrote a modern translation of Mozart's opera, *The Magic Flute.* Why are poets likely to be interested in music?

Critical Evaluation According to David Daiches, following his early poems concerned primarily with political issues, Auden gradually "learned to clarify his imagery and control his desire to shock, and he produced, in the years around 1940, some poems of finely disciplined movement, pellucid clarity, and deep yet unsentimental feeling. At the same time he was developing a more complex view of the world, moving from his earlier diagnosis of modern ills in terms of Freud and Marx to a more religious view of personal responsibility and traditional value without, however, abandoning the ideas and terms he had learned from modern psychology. But he never lost his ear for popular speech or his ability to combine elements from popular art with an extreme technical formality. He was always an experimenter, particularly in ways of bringing together high artifice and a colloquial tone."

W. H. AUDEN

1907–1973

Although he was influenced by the Modernist poets, Wystan Hugh Auden managed to remain his own person. He adopted those aspects of Modernism with which he felt comfortable, while at the same time maintaining many elements of traditional poetry. Throughout his career he wrote with insight into the plight of people struggling to preserve their individuality in an increasingly conformist society.

Auden was born in York, England, and attended Oxford University. In 1930 he published his first collection of poetry, *Poems.* At about the same time, he became very active in politics. He spoke out about the plight of the poor in England and against the emergence of Nazism in Germany, and he actively supported the Republicans who were fighting against the Fascists in the Spanish Civil War. He also used his talents as a poet to express his political beliefs. As a result, many of his early poems focused on political issues.

In 1939 Auden moved to the United States, and in 1946 he became an American citizen. At the time of his move, he rediscovered his Christian beliefs, which grew increasingly stronger during his later years. He expressed his beliefs in *Double Man* (1941) and *For the Times Being* (1944), depicting religion as an effective way of coping with the disjointedness of modern society. In *The Age of Anxiety* (1947), a long narrative poem which earned him a Pulitzer Prize, he explored the confusion and isolation associated with post-World War II life. He went on to publish several more volumes of poetry, including *Nones* (1951), *The Shield of Achilles* (1955), *Homage to Clio* (1960), *About the House* (1967), and *City Without Walls* (1970), and he also produced a large body of literary criticism.

Despite being comforted by his religious beliefs, Auden became increasingly disillusioned with the modern world during his later years. Hoping to find comfort in a university community, he returned to England to teach at Oxford in the late 1950's. Several years later he moved to Austria, where he spent the remainder of his life.

Auden used his poetry and essays to explore the difficulties and responsibilities of being an artist in the modern age. As one who had turned to religious beliefs, he felt that the lack of faith in the modern age made it almost impossible to be an artist—in part, because he saw the absence of religious faith as being similar to an absence of faith in the values of art. If people no longer believed in universal truths, he reasoned, they could not believe in art, which deals with truth. "Poetry is not magic," he wrote in *The Dyer's Hand.* "Insofar as poetry, or any other of the arts, can be said to have an ulterior purpose, it is, by telling the truth, to disenchant and disintoxicate. . . ."

Objective
To understand satire

Support Material

Teaching Portfolio
Teacher Backup, p. 1175
Usage and Mechanics Worksheet, p. 1178
Analyzing Literature Worksheet, *Interpreting Satire,* p. 1179
Critical Thinking and Reading Worksheet, *Evaluating the Effectiveness of Satire,* p. 1180
Selection Test, p. 1182

GUIDE FOR INTERPRETING

Who's Who; The Unknown Citizen

Writer's Techniques

Satire. Satire is a kind of writing in which certain individuals, institutions, types of behavior, or humanity in general are ridiculed or criticized in a humorous manner. The purpose of satire is to promote changes in society or humanity. Satirists write about what they perceive to be the problems and flaws of the world. By poking fun at these problems and flaws or attacking them in a humorous manner, the satirists attempt to use the force of laughter to persuade us to accept their point of view and inspire us to take action to bring about change.

Writing

"Who's Who" explores some of the facts of a famous man's life. Of what types of facts concerning a famous person's life is the public usually aware? Of what types of facts is the public usually unaware? List the sources of the public's knowledge concerning a famous person's life.

Primary Source

Both "Who's Who" and "The Unknown Citizen" portray human beings as a collection of data in order to comment satirically upon the impact of modern society on humanity. "Who's Who" uses somewhat sordid and ordinary biographical facts to undercut our ideas about famous people. In "The Unknown Citizen" Auden shows how the data collected about people in a modern, bureaucratic society undermines our basic notions of what it means to be a human being.

As these poems suggest, Auden considered modern society to be basically hostile to human nature. He also thought that the concerns of this society—especially its focus on power and money—were directly opposed to the poet's interests. He made these comments in his essay "The Poet and the City": "Poets are, by the nature of their interests and the nature of artistic fabrication, singularly ill-equipped to understand politics and economics. Their natural interest is in singular individuals and personal relations, while politics and economics are concerned with large numbers of people, hence with the human average (the poet is bored to death by the idea of the Common Man) and with impersonal, to a great extent, involuntary, relations. The poet cannot understand the function of money in modern society because for him there is no relation between subjective value and market value; he may be paid ten pounds for a poem which he believes is very good and took him months to write, and a hundred pounds for a piece of journalism which costs him but a day's work."

Guide for Interpreting 897

Literary Focus There is a great deal of variation in the tone of satires. For example, some satires are bitter; others are wryly comic.

Writing/Prior Knowledge Before having students complete the writing activity, you might discuss the public's perception of famous people.

Vocabulary

Preteach the following vocabulary word:
psychology (sī köl′ ə jē) *n.:* The science dealing with the mind and with mental and emotional processes (p. 899, l. 12)

Spelling Tip You might point out the difficulties in the spelling of *psychology:* the silent *p* and the *ch* spelling of the k sound.

Motivation/Prior Knowledge
Have students discuss the types of facts that they might not know about a famous person. Would they wish to know these facts?

Purpose-Setting Question
What is revealed about the subject of the poem?

1 Clarification A *shilling life* was a short biography that could be bought for a small amount of money—a shilling.

2 Discussion How do lines 2–6 represent a fairly typical success story?

3 Critical Thinking and Reading The poem is a sonnet. The last two lines of the octave provide a transition to the sextet.

4 Discussion What is ironic about the subject's relationship with his loved one?

Reader's Response What does this poem indicate about the importance of love?

Who's Who

W. H. Auden

1 A shilling life will give you all the facts:
How Father beat him, how he ran away,
What were the struggles of his youth, what acts
2 Made him the greatest figure of his day:
5 Of how he fought, fished, hunted, worked all night,
Though giddy, climbed new mountains; named a sea:
Some of the last researchers even write
3 Love made him weep his pints like you and me.

With all his honors on, he sighed for one
10 Who, say astonished critics, lived at home;
Did little jobs about the house with skill
4 And nothing else; could whistle; would sit still
Or potter round the garden; answered some
Of his long marvelous letters but kept none.

THINKING ABOUT THE SELECTION

Recalling

1. What facts about the subject's youth are mentioned?
2. What acts made the subject "the greatest figure of his day"?
3. What do "some of the last researchers even write"?
4. (a) How did the one he "sighed for" spend her life? (b) What did this person do with his letters?

Interpreting

5. (a) What type of person is this poem about? (b) What do the facts suggest about his personality?

6. (a) What is surprising about the description of the woman whom he loved? (b) How do details in the poem suggest that she did not return his love?
7. (a) What is ironic, or surprising, about the fact that the subject of the poem weeped "pints like you and me"? (b) What does this suggest about the nature of happiness?
8. Explain the title of the poem.

Applying

9. Do you think that famous people are as likely to be unhappy as those who are not famous? Why or why not?

ANSWERS TO THINKING ABOUT THE SELECTION
Recalling

1. His father beat him, and he ran away.
2. He fought, fished, hunted, worked all night, climbed new mountains, and named a sea.
3. Love made him weep.
4. (a) She did little jobs about the house. (b) She answered some and threw them all out.

Interpreting

5. (a) The poem is about a famous man who has achieved a great deal. (b) He was ambitious.
6. (a) On the surface, she seems common and uninteresting, and she does not seem like the type of person with whom a famous man would fall in love. (b) She throws away his letters.
7. (a) It seems surprising that such a noted person would experience the same type of despair experi-enced by common people. (b) It suggests that happiness does not necessarily result from success and fame.
8. The title relates to the title of a book in which famous people are listed.

Applying

9. Suggested Response: Yes, because fame does not ensure happiness.

The Unknown Citizen

W. H. Auden

(To JS/07/M/378
This Marble Monument
Is Erected by the State)

He was found by the Bureau of Statistics to be
One against whom there was no official complaint,
And all the reports on his conduct agree
That, in the modern sense of an old-fashioned word, he was
    a saint,
5 For in everything he did he served the Greater Community.
Except for the War till the day he retired
He worked in a factory and never got fired,
But satisfied his employers, Fudge Motors Inc.
Yet he wasn't a scab[1] or odd in his views,
10 For his Union reports that he paid his dues,
(Our report on his Union shows it was sound)
And our Social Psychology workers found
That he was popular with his mates and liked a drink.
The Press are convinced that he bought a paper every day
15 And that his reactions to advertisements were normal in
    every way.
Policies taken out in his name prove that he was fully
    insured,
And his Health-card shows he was once in hospital but left
    it cured.
Both Producers Research and High-Grade Living declare
He was fully sensible to the advantages of the Installment
    Plan
20 And had everything necessary to the Modern Man,
A phonograph, a radio, a car and a frigidaire.
Our researchers into Public Opinion are content
That he held the proper opinions for the time of year;
When there was peace, he was for peace; when there was
    war, he went.

---

1. **scab** *n.*: A worker who refuses to strike or takes the place of a
striking worker.

The Unknown Citizen   899

Presentation

Motivation/Prior Knowledge
Have students imagine that they are living in a society in which all of their activities are closely monitored by the government. What would their lives be like?

Purpose-Setting Question
What is Auden satirizing?

1 **Clarification** Monuments are often erected for unknown soldiers and sailors.

2 **Discussion** What effect is created by referring to a person in this way?

3 **Discussion** In what ways does the society described resemble the modern world?

4 **Discussion** On what are some of the favorable opinions based?

Discussion What is the effect of the final two lines?

Reader's Response What does this poem indicate to you about modern society?

Closure and Extension

ANSWERS TO THINKING ABOUT THE SELECTION
Recalling

1. He did not do anything to incur an official complaint.
2. (a) He worked at Fudge Motors, Inc. (b) He paid his dues.
3. (a) He was popular with his mates and liked a drink. (b) He bought a paper every day and reacted normally to advertisements. (c) He had the right number of children for a parent of his generation. (d) He never interfered with his children's education.
4. Someone would surely have reported any such problems.

Interpreting

5. (a) It suggests the impersonal, mechanical nature of the society. It also suggests that the citizen has no true identity. (b) The state knows nothing about his feelings or concerns.
6. (a) They work along with the state to account for all of its citizens. (b) The groups want people to conform to the state's desires and to avoid causing any disturbances. (c) It is a society in which people have no freedom and are completely controlled and shaped by the state.
7. (a) Freedom and happiness are not things that they can monitor. (b) They are not concerned with his freedom and happiness.
8. Capitals are used for important state or official institutions.

Applying

9. Answers will differ. Students may respond that the society portrayed in the poem is very different from our society, because freedom is protected in our society.

25 He was married and added five children to the population,
Which our Eugenist[2] says was the right number for a
    parent of his generation,
And our teachers report that he never interfered with their
    education.
Was he free? Was he happy? The question is absurd:
Had anything been wrong, we should certainly have heard.

---

2. Eugenist (ū jen′ ist) *n.*: A specialist in eugenics, the movement devoted to improving the human species through genetic control.

THINKING ABOUT THE SELECTION
Recalling

1. Why is the unknown citizen remembered as a "saint"?
2. (a) Where did the unknown citizen work? (b) What does his union report about him?
3. (a) What do the social psychology workers find? (b) Of what is the press convinced? (c) What does the Eugenist say? (d) What do the teachers report?
4. Why is the question of the citizen's freedom and happiness absurd?

Interpreting

5. (a) What is suggested by the numbers and letters used by the state in referring to the citizen? (b) In what sense is the citizen "unknown" to the state?
6. (a) What is the relationship of the state to the groups mentioned in the poem? (b) What are the primary interests of these groups concerning the citizen? (c) What do the concerns of the groups and their relationship to the state reveal about the society as a whole?
7. (a) Why is it unlikely that the state would have heard anything concerning the citizen's freedom and happiness? (b) What seems to be their attitude toward his freedom and happiness?

900 *The Modern Age*

8. How does Auden use capitalization to reinforce the meaning of the poem?

Applying

9. In what respects is the society portrayed in this poem similar to and different from our society?

ANALYZING LITERATURE
Interpreting Satire

Satire is a kind of writing in which certain individuals, institutions, types of behavior, or humanity in general are ridiculed or criticized in a humorous manner. In "The Unknown Citizen," for example, Auden criticizes the increasingly impersonal and bureaucratic nature of modern society by presenting an exaggerated vision of a state in which people have been almost completely stripped of their individuality.

1. What is Auden's attitude toward the type of society he portrays in the poem?
2. How do the final two lines help to clarify Auden's attitude?
3. Considering Auden's attitude toward the society he portrays, what type of society do you think he supports?

ANSWERS TO ANALYZING LITERATURE

1. He has a tremendous amount of contempt for it.
2. They reveal that he believes that the society is absurd and is angered by its indifference to people's freedom and happiness.
3. He probably supports a society with greater individual freedom.

The Harlem Renaissance

RUBY GREEN SINGING, 1928
James Chapin
Norton Gallery of Art

Humanities Note

Fine art, *Ruby Green Singing,* 1928, by James Chapin. In 1922, disenchanted with the competitive New York art world, James Ormsbee Chapin (1887–1975) moved from Greenwich Village to rural New Jersey. There he painted portraits of the hard-working, simple people he encountered. Chapin made the almost full-length portrait of Ruby Greene (the title of the painting contains a misspelling of her name) after he saw her singing in a choir in New York. The singer's expressive face, slightly raised, her simple pink dress, and her clasped hands suggest both tenderness and power. Although the painting is a portrait of a particular singer, it symbolizes the central role of music in the black experience—the longing for freedom conveyed in Negro spirituals and the feelings of beauty and joy expressed in the melodies sung by Greene and others. Above all, Chapin sought to convey, in the singer's pose, a sense of serenity, dignity, and courage.

Countee Cullen (1903–1946)

Unlike most other poets of his time, Countee Cullen used traditional forms and methods. However, no poet expressed the general sentiments of American blacks during the early 1900's more eloquently than Cullen.

Cullen was born in New York City. He graduated from New York University and later earned a master's degree from Harvard. His first collection of poetry, *Color,* was published in 1925. This was followed by *Copper Sun* (1927), *The Ballad of the Brown Girl* (1927), and *The Black Christ* (1929). In 1932 he published *One Way to Heaven,* a satirical novel about life in Harlem. During his later years he published two children's books, *The Lost Zoo* (1940) and *My Lives and How I Lost Them* (1942).

Cullen was one of leaders of the movement to construct an intellectual and aesthetic culture for blacks in America, especially for those who had come from the South to New York City in the early 1900's. He claimed all of American and English literature as the literary heritage of blacks.

In "Any Human to Another," one of Cullen's best-known poems, he expresses the despair of black people.

Claude McKay (1890–1948)

In much of his work, Claude McKay evokes the rich colors and the rhythms of life on his native island of Jamaica. Yet although McKay considered Jamaica to be "home," he also regarded Harlem as his spiritual and psychic home, even though he frequently lived elsewhere. Writing to fellow Harlem Renaissance poet Langston Hughes from abroad in 1930, McKay said, "I write of America as home [although] I am really a poet without a country."

The son of poor farm workers, McKay moved to Kingston, the capital of the Caribbean island, when he was fourteen. While living in Kingston, he began writing poetry. When his collection *Songs of Jamaica* (1912) won an award from the Institute of Arts and Letters, he was able to emigrate to the United States.

McKay's poem "The Tropics in New York" is marked by a nostalgia for his homeland—a feeling echoed in the title of his autobiography, *A Long Way from Home* (1937).

902   *The Modern Age*

GUIDE FOR INTERPRETING

Any Human to Another; The Tropics in New York

Literary Movements

The Harlem Renaissance. During the late 1800's and early 1900's, many southern blacks moved north, hoping to find opportunities in the northern industrial centers. With this shift in population, the New York City community of Harlem developed into the cultural center for American blacks. There a cultural movement known as the Harlem Renaissance was established during the 1920's. The movement encompassed music, art, and literature, and included such writers as Countee Cullen, Claude McKay, Langston Hughes, Jean Toomer, and Arna Bontemps.

Although the literary forms and techniques used by the Harlem Renaissance writers varied widely, the writers all shared a common purpose: to prove that black writers could produce literature equal in quality to that of white writers. At the same time, the Harlem Renaissance writers focused on capturing the general sentiments of the American blacks of the time. In doing so they expressed their displeasure concerning their overall condition and articulated their cultural heritage.

Writing

In "The Tropics in New York, " Claude McKay presents a series of images, or word pictures, associated with the tropics. Prepare a list of the type of images you would expect to find in this series.

Commentary

One of the issues that the writers of the Harlem Renaissance debated among themselves and explored in their poetry was the relationship between race and poetry. Some viewed their poetry as primarily a vehicle for expressing what it means to be black in America; others regarded their works as dealing with more traditional poetic subjects: love, nature, childhood, home. These subjects were not considered to be exclusive of one another. But many black writers discovered a tension between writing poetry that dealt explicitly with black experiences and poetry that dealt more with universal experiences.

Countee Cullen, whose works have been compared with traditional British and American poetry, sometimes expressed a view that black writers should write within the broader literary tradition and transcend their own racial background. But at other times, he admitted how difficult this was to do. "Somehow or other I find my poetry of itself treating of the Negro, of his joys and his sorrows—mostly of the latter—and of the heights and depths of emotion which I feel as a Negro."

Which view do his poems express?

Guide for Interpreting 903

Literary Focus Emphasize the diversity of the work of the Harlem Renaissance poets.

Writing/Prior Knowledge For extra credit, have students develop a list of images associated with another type of environment.

Vocabulary

Preteach the following vocabulary words:
marrow (mar′ ō) *n.:* The soft tissue that fills the cavities of most bones (p. 905, l. 4)
diverse (dī vʉrs′) *adj.:* Various (p. 905, l. 11)
scorned (skôrnd) *v.:* Refused or rejected as wrong or disgraceful (p. 905, l. 22)
unsheathed (un shēt͟hd′) *adj.:* Removed from its case (p. 905, l. 27)

Humanities Note

Fine art, *Big Meeting,* 1980, by Varnette P. Honeywood. Honeywood is a contemporary Afro-American artist. In *Big Meeting* Honeywood has created a personal interpretation of an "everyday" scene in a black community. The large, solid areas of vibrant color create a life within the picture. As the viewer's eye bounces from form to form, the meeting comes alive. The repetition and intensity of color give a quality of sound to the picture. We can almost hear the people talking and laughing. She has created a unified whole out of a scene involving many different people and conversations. The viewer is at one moment drawn to a particular detail, and then drawn back to view the entire scene with its complexity of motion and interrelationships. Honeywood provides a visual record of an experience in an Afro-American community that shows pride and sensitivity.

Consider these questions for discussion:

1. How does this painting reflect ideas of this poem?
2. What devices has the artist used to keep the viewer's line of vision circulating around the picture?
3. What mood is created by color combinations in this painting?

BIG MEETING, 1980
Varnette P. Honeywood
Black Lifestyles, Los Angeles

Any Human to Another

Countee Cullen

1
The ills I sorrow at
Not me alone
Like an arrow,
Pierce to the marrow,
5 Through the fat
And past the bone.

2
Your grief and mine
Must intertwine
Like sea and river,
10 Be fused and mingle,
Diverse yet single,
Forever and forever.

3
Let no man be so proud
And confident,
15 To think he is allowed
A little tent
Pitched in a meadow
Of sun and shadow
All his little own.

4
20 Joy may be shy, unique,
Friendly to a few,
Sorrow never scorned to speak
To any who
Were false or true.

5
25 Your every grief
Like a blade
Shining and unsheathed
Must strike me down.
Of bitter aloes wreathed,
30 My sorrow must be laid
On your head like a crown.

THINKING ABOUT THE SELECTION

Recalling

1. What pierces the speaker "to the marrow"?
2. What must "intertwine like sea and river"?
3. What should no person think?
4. (a) What must strike the speaker down?
   (b) What must be done with his sorrow?

Interpreting

5. How is the image presented in the first stanza echoed in the final stanza?
6. What is the meaning of the image presented in the third stanza?
7. Why does the speaker feel that joy is more difficult to share than sorrow?

Applying

8. Why do you think sharing feelings of sorrow with others often makes a person feel better?

ANALYZING LITERATURE

Understanding the Harlem Renaissance

The **Harlem Renaissance** was a cultural movement that emerged in Harlem during the 1920's. In their work the writers of the Harlem Renaissance tried to capture the essence of black life and communicate the general sentiments of the black people.

1. What do the emotions discussed in this poem suggest about the overall sentiments of the black people at the time?
2. How does the image presented in the first stanza suggest that the suffering of the black people is deeply rooted in the past?
3. What do you think is the poem's main purpose?

Any Human to Another 905

Presentation

Motivation/Prior Knowledge
Have students imagine they are far from a place they love. How might the memories of this place cause them anguish?

Master Teacher Note You may wish to set the tone for this piece by contrasting Harlem of the 1920's with the countryside of Jamaica, using the encyclopedia and other available sources.

Purpose-Setting Question
What observations remind the speaker of his native land?

1 **Discussion** To what sense do the images in lines 1–3 appeal?

2 **Discussion** Why does the speaker weep?

Reader's Response Have you ever seen, heard, or smelled something that suddenly triggered thoughts and memories of something you hadn't been thinking of? If so, explain.

The Tropics in New York

Claude McKay

1

    Bananas ripe and green, and ginger-root,
        Cocoa in pods and alligator pears,
    And tangerines and mangoes and grape fruit,
        Fit for the highest prize at parish fairs,

5   Set in the window, bringing memories
        Of fruit-trees laden by low-singing rills,
    And dewy dawns, and mystical blue skies
        In benediction over nun-like hills.

2

    My eyes grew dim, and I could no more gaze;
10   A wave of longing through my body swept,
    And, hungry for the old, familiar ways
        I turned aside and bowed my head and wept.

THINKING ABOUT THE SELECTION

Recalling

1. (a) What fruits are "set in the window"? (b) Of what do they bring memories?
2. (a) What emotion sweeps through the speaker's body in the final stanza? (b) How does he respond to this emotion?

Interpreting

3. How does the title contribute to the meaning of the poem?
4. What impression does the speaker convey of his homeland?
5. Which words create especially vivid images? Explain the reason for your choices.
6. How do the speaker's observations in the first stanza lead to the emotions he experiences in the third stanza?

Applying

7. Why do you think people often idealize and long for places from their past?

THINKING AND WRITING

Writing a Poem About a Special Place

Write a poem in which the speaker describes images which lead him or her to recall a place for which he or she has very powerful feelings. Start by listing the images that lead to the speaker's recollections. Then list the speaker's emotions concerning the place he or she recalls. Present the speaker's observations in the first stanza; present his or her associations in the next stanza; and describe his or her emotions in the third stanza. When you finish writing, revise your poem and share it with your classmates.

The Tropics in New York 907

Focus

More About the Author For many people, Langston Hughes is the most important of the writers of the Harlem Renaissance. His works included biographies and children's stories, as well as song lyrics and articles. Yet he is best-known for his poetry, which has been translated into many different languages. Must a writer be especially gifted to experiment with such a variety of genres?

Critical Evaluation David Kalstone wrote that, "Among the many talented black writers connected with the Harlem Renaissance, Langston Hughes was the most popular, the most versatile, and the most durable. Among his important achievements are the incorporation of the rhythms of black music into his poetry, and the creation of an authentic black folk speaker in the persona of Jesse B. Semple. Along with Zora Neale Hurston, and in contrast to Jean Toomer and Countee Cullen (who wanted to work with purely literary patterns, whether traditional or experimental), he wanted to capture the dominant oral and improvisatory traditions of black culture in written form."

1902–1967

Langston Hughes emerged from the Harlem Renaissance as the most prolific and successful black writer in America. Although he is best known for his poetry, he also wrote plays, fiction, autobiographical sketches, and movie screenplays.

Born in Missouri and raised in Illinois and Ohio, Hughes attended high school in Cleveland, where he contributed poetry to the school literary magazine. In 1921 he moved to New York City to attend classes at Columbia University, but a year later he left school to travel to Europe and Africa as a merchant seaman. When he returned to the United States, he met the poet Vachel Lindsay, who helped him publish his first volume of poetry, *The Weary Blues* (1926). The book attracted considerable attention and earned Hughes widespread recognition.

Although Hughes, like many of the Harlem Renaissance writers, was not born in Harlem and lived a large part of his life elsewhere, he identified Harlem as a source of inspiration and life for black artists. Harlem was where he felt at home and nourished, where he felt a sense of community. In his autobiography *Big Sea,* he described his arrival in Harlem in 1921. In his depiction of it, Harlem restores to him his life's breath. "At every subway station I kept watching for the sign: 135TH STREET. When I saw it, I held my breath. . . . I went up the steps and into the bright September sunlight. Harlem! I looked around. Negroes everywhere! . . . I took a deep breath and felt happy again."

Hughes went on to publish several other collections of poetry, including *The Dream Keeper* (1932), *Fields of Wonder* (1947), and *Montage of a Dream Deferred* (1951). In his poetry he experimented with a variety of forms and techniques and often tried to re-create the rhythms of contemporary jazz. Using his talents as a poet, he expressed pride in his heritage and voiced his displeasure with the oppression of blacks.

During the 1950's, Hughes helped to support himself by contributing a number of prose sketches to newspapers. Among the most popular was a series of tales about a fictional character named Jesse B. Semple, whom Hughes often referred to as "Simple." In 1963 Hughes developed these sketches into a musical play, *Simply Heaven*.

Hughes's work not only helped make the general public aware of black life, but it also inspired many other black writers. By eloquently chronicling the heritage of the black people and expressing their pride and determination, Hughes provided his people with a link to their cultural roots and a promise for a better future.

908 *The Modern Age*

Objective

To recognize the speaker

Support Material

Teaching Portfolio
Teacher Backup, p. 1195
Usage and Mechanics Work-
  sheet, p. 1198
Vocabulary Check, p. 1199
Analyzing Literature Worksheet,
  Identifying the Speaker, p. 1200
Critical Thinking and Reading
  Worksheet, *Comparing and
  Contrasting Poems,* p. 1201
Selection Test, p. 1202

GUIDE FOR INTERPRETING

The Negro Speaks of Rivers

The Speaker. The speaker is the voice of a poem. Although the speaker is often the poet himself or herself, the speaker may also be a fictional character, a group of people, or an inanimate object or another type of nonhuman entity. For example, in Carl Sandburg's poem "Grass," the speaker is the grass itself.

In "The Negro Speaks of Rivers," Hughes develops a comparison between rivers and the black people. List some of the characteristics of rivers that you feel reflect certain aspects of the experience of the black people.

Drawing on the populist example of Carl Sandburg's poetry, Hughes described his subject as being the entire community of American blacks: "Workers, roustabouts, and singers, and job hunters on Lenox Avenue in New York, or Seventh Street in Washington or South State in Chicago—people up today and down tomorrow, working this week and fired the next, beaten and baffled, but determined not to be wholly beaten, buying furniture on the installment plan, filling the house with roomers to help pay the rent, hoping to get a new suit for Easter—pawning that suit before the Fourth of July."

In his "documentary, journalistic, and topical" poems, as he called them, Hughes sought to capture the rhythms and resonances of the voices of black America. He also wanted to emphasize black America's connection to its own roots and tradition—in contrast to seeking connection to a European tradition, or to whites in America. In "The Negro Speaks of Rivers," the rivers lead back to black Africa and to slavery in the South. The image of the river was common in the writings of the Harlem Renaissance as an image of the never-ceasing motion of life in Harlem. As critic Sidney H. Bremer writes: "Filled with children as well as adults, women as well as men, Harlem's streets are a neighborhood extension of family life and generation. That does not mean that the Harlem streets are happy—any more than families are always happy. But they are alive, generative. In explicit, repeated contrast to the deadening subway machines and dwarfing skyscraper streets of Anglo New York, Harlem's streets are defined by people walking. They are a 'stream of life.' . . . Even death confirms the generativity of life, as blues spawn the laughter of jazz and street life spills into the cabarets in Langston Hughes's first book of poems, *Weary Blues* (1925)."

Literary Focus Point out that a poem's title sometimes reveals the identity of the speaker.

Writing/Prior Knowledge As an alternate activity, have students identify the river nearest to their homes and discuss the kinds of ties people feel toward that river.

Vocabulary

Preteach the following vocabulary words:
lulled (luld) *v.*: Calmed or soothed by gentle sound or motion (l.5)
dusky (dus′ kē) *adj.*: Dim; shadowy (l.9)

Motivation/Prior Knowledge
Have students discuss the hardships that black people have encountered through the course of history. What other groups of people have experienced similar hardships?

Purpose-Setting Question Who is the speaker of the poem?

The Negro Speaks of Rivers

Langston Hughes

I've known rivers:
I've known rivers ancient as the world and older than the
   flow of human blood in human veins.

My soul has grown deep like the rivers.

I bathed in the Euphrates when dawns were young.
5   I built my hut near the Congo and it lulled me to sleep.
I looked upon the Nile and raised the pyramids above it.
I heard the singing of the Mississippi when Abe Lincoln
   went down to New Orleans, and I've seen its muddy
   bosom turn all golden in the sunset.

I've known rivers:
Ancient, dusky rivers.

10   My soul has grown deep like the rivers.

THINKING ABOUT THE SELECTION

Recalling

1. (a) Who is the speaker of "The Negro Speaks of Rivers"? (b) How does the title help to reveal the speaker's identity?

2. What has happened to the speaker's soul?

3. (a) When and where did the speaker bathe? (b) Where did he build his hut? (c) What did the speaker do after looking upon the Nile? (d) What did the speaker hear when "Abe Lincoln went down to New Orleans"?

Interpreting

4. In this poem Hughes develops a comparison between rivers and the black people. What does the age of rivers imply about the black race?

5. What do the references to specific rivers in lines 4–7 convey about the black experience?

6. (a) What do lines 3 and 10 suggest about how the black race has been affected by its experiences? (b) How do these two lines reflect the poem's theme, or main point?

Applying

7. In what respects can the human race as a whole be compared with rivers?

The Negro Speaks of Rivers 911

Closure and Extension

Focus

More About the Authors Like the preceding authors, **Jean Toomer** was among the leaders of the Harlem Renaissance. Unfortunately, his works remained largely unknown outside the black community until the last quarter of the twentieth century. Why is the work of talented writers sometimes virtually unnoticed?

Arna Bontemps was one of the most versatile writers of the Harlem Renaissance. Yet, until recently, he earned little recognition. Why has the importance of some of the less famous Harlem Renaissance poets only become recognized in recent years?

Critical Evaluation David Perkins, in his *A History of Modern Poetry,* wrote the following about Jean Toomer's most significant work, *Cane:*

"A brilliantly promising book, it was typical of the experimental milieu of the early twenties. It mingled short stories, dramatic sketches, and poems to build up an imaginative impression of the rural South. In the materials it presented it sought the symbolic and the mythical like other works in the high Modernist modes. It also shared their tragic vision of human life. It highlighted the ambiguity and self-conflict of human feelings, the violence and degradation of human nature, and the extent to which actions and emotions are formed by history, in this case by the psychic and social structures grounded in the history of the South."

Jean Toomer (1894–1967)

Like the other Harlem Renaissance writers, Jean Toomer had a deep interest in the cultural roots of the black people. In his work Toomer expressed his belief that maintaining an awareness of and a sense of pride in the black heritage was vital to the happiness and freedom of the black people.

Born in Washington, D.C., Toomer graduated from New York University in 1918. He then taught for several years in Georgia. His observations during his years as a teacher provided him with the material for *Cane* (1923), an unconventional book which consists of prose sketches, stories, poems, and a one-act play, all focusing on the concerns, interests, and experiences of American blacks.

Following the publication of *Cane,* Toomer was for a number of years considered to be the most talented writer of the Harlem Renaissance. During the early 1920's he published in such leading black journals as *The Crisis* and *Opportunity,* as well as in *The Little Review* (the leading journal of the Imagist movement). He was admired not only for his sensitive portrayals of black life, but, as one member of the group put it, for writing "without surrender or compromise of the artist's vision."

Toomer published few other works during the course of his life. After *Cane* fell into obscurity shortly after its publication, Toomer was virtually forgotten as a writer. In recent years, however, *Cane* has come to be recognized as one of the most important works to come out of the Harlem Renaissance and has influenced the work of a number of black writers.

Arna Bontemps (1902–1973)

A talented editor, novelist, dramatist, and poet, Arna Bontemps was one of the most scholarly figures of the Harlem Renaissance.

Bontemps was born in Louisiana and educated at the University of Chicago. He published his first novel, *God Sends Sunday,* in 1931. This book was followed by two novels about slave revolts, *Black Thunder* (1936) and *Drums at Dusk* (1939). Bontemps then went on to produce several volumes of nonfiction, including *The Story of the Negro* (1951) and *One Hundred Years of Negro Freedom* (1961). He also co-edited *The Poetry of the Negro* (1950), an anthology of black poetry, with Langston Hughes, and collaborated with Countee Cullen in writing *St. Louis Women* (1946), a musical play.

Bontemps also wrote poetry throughout his rich, varied literary career. Written in simple, direct language, using traditional forms and techniques, his poems are characterized by what Bontemps himself called "a certain simplicity of expression."

912   The Modern Age

Objectives

1 To understand metaphors
2 To create an extended metaphor

Support Material

Teaching Portfolio
Teacher Backup, p. 1205
Usage and Mechanics Worksheet, p. 1210
Vocabulary Check, p. 1211
Analyzing Literature Worksheet, *Understanding Metaphors,* p. 1212

Critical Thinking and Reading Worksheet, *Comparing and Contrasting Poems,* p. 1213
Selection Test, p. 1214

GUIDE FOR INTERPRETING

Storm Ending; A Black Man
Talks of Reaping

**The Writer's
Techniques**

Metaphor. A metaphor is a comparison between two seemingly dissimilar things. This comparison is implied, rather than stated, and no connecting word is used. While metaphors are often brief, they may also be long, elaborate comparisons. This type of metaphor, in which details developing the comparison are presented throughout the poem, is known as an extended metaphor. For example, Langston Hughes uses an extended metaphor in "The Negro Speaks of Rivers," as he develops a comparison between rivers and the black people throughout the poem.

Commentary

Toomer and Bontemps, like other writers of the Harlem Renaissance, expressed the spirit and complicated rhythms of blues and jazz in their poetry. This was the music that came out of the black culture and became popular during the 1920's among whites, who would travel uptown to Harlem to hear blues and jazz in the Harlem clubs. Seeking to explain the source of the mood and poetic patterns of his poems, Langston Hughes wrote a note to his second volume of poetry in which he described how blues differed from traditional black spiritual music.

> The *Blues,* unlike the *Spirituals,* have a strict poetic pattern: one long line repeated and a third line to rhyme with the first two. Sometimes the second line in repetition is slightly changed and sometimes, but very seldom, it is omitted. The mood of the *Blues* is almost always despondency, but when they are sung people laugh.

The mood of despondency that Hughes speaks of as being typical of the blues is one characteristic mood of the poetry of the Harlem Renaissance. Yet other Harlem Renaissance poets express moods derived from the energy and syncopations of jazz music. Which moods occur in "Storm Ending" and "A Black Man Talks of Reaping"?

Writing

In "Storm Ending" Jean Toomer describes a thunderstorm. Freewrite about the types of images you associate with thunderstorms and discuss the reasons why people have been captivated by thunderstorms.

Guide for Interpreting 913

Vocabulary

914

Humanities Note

Fine Art, *Black Place II,* 1944, by Georgia O'Keeffe. O'Keeffe (1887–1986) is associated with New Mexico, where she settled in 1949, and where she found inspiration for some of her most dramatic paintings.

Black Place II is one of a series of three paintings entitled *Black Place* inspired by a remarkable formation of black earth with a deep vertical cleft down the center. In this version of a fantastic part of desert country, we find a passage from representation to abstraction. The composition is, at one moment, a landscape. Then it flows into an image of flower forms, nature's organic and inorganic forms mimicking each other. O'Keeffe's use of colors and contrasts add drama to this abstraction.

You might ask students these questions:
1. The poem and the accompanying painting by Georgia O'Keeffe both have allegorical qualities. What does this painting represent to you?
2. The poem is dramatic. How does O'Keeffe make her painting dramatic?
3. What words and phrases from the poem can be applied to the poem?

Presentation

Motivation/Prior Knowledge
Have students envision a thunderstorm. What emotions does the image evoke?

Purpose-Setting Question
What two things is the speaker comparing?

1 Discussion Do most people view thunder as being gorgeous? Why or why not?

2 Discussion What does the last line mean?

BLACK PLACE II, 1944
Georgia O'Keeffe
The Metropolitan Museum of Art

Storm Ending

Jean Toomer

1 ☐   Thunder blossoms gorgeously above our heads,
Great, hollow, bell-like flowers,
Rumbling in the wind,
Stretching clappers to strike our ears . . .
5   Full-lipped flowers
Bitten by the sun
Bleeding rain
Dripping rain like golden honey—
2 ☐   And the sweet earth flying from the thunder.

914   *The Modern Age*

Reader's Response What thoughts and emotions do you associate with thunderstorms?

THINKING ABOUT THE SELECTION

Recalling

1. According to line 1, what does thunder do?
2. To what is rain compared in line 8?
3. According to line 9, how does the earth respond to the thunder?

Interpreting

4. (a) What natural event does the poem describe? (b) What is the speaker's attitude toward this event? (c) How is this attitude conveyed?

Applying

5. How would you describe your own attitude toward the type of natural event described in the poem?

ANALYZING LITERATURE

Understanding Metaphors

A **metaphor** is a comparison between two seemingly dissimilar things. An extended metaphor is a comparison which is developed throughout the course of a poem.

1. What two things are compared in the extended metaphor presented in "Storm Ending"?
2. How does Toomer establish this comparison in the first four lines?
3. How does he develop the comparison in the lines that follow?

THINKING AND WRITING

Creating an Extended Metaphor

Write a poem in which you present an extended metaphor. First decide on the two things you are going to compare. Then prepare a list of details developing this comparison. When writing your poem, establish the comparison in the first several lines; then develop it throughout the rest of the poem. After you finish writing, revise your poem, making sure that you have included enough details to adequately develop the comparison. When you finish revising, proofread your poem, and share it with your classmates.

ANSWERS TO THINKING ABOUT THE SELECTION
Recalling

1. Thunder blossoms gorgeously.
2. It is compared to dripping honey.
3. It flies from the thunder.

Interpreting

4. (a) It describes a thunderstorm. (b) The attitude is one of appreciation. (c) The specific images, particularly of flowers and honey, as well as such word choices as *gorgeously* and *sweet,* convey the attitude.

Applying

5. Answers will differ. Students may comment that they are startled by thunderstorms.

ANSWERS TO ANALYZING LITERATURE

1. Thunder is compared to a lush flowering plant.
2. He describes the plant's bell-like flowers.
3. He describes the flowers in more specific detail.

THINKING AND WRITING

For help with this assignment, students can refer to Lesson 19, "Writing a Poem," in the Handbook of Writing About Literature.

Publishing Student Writing Set up an editorial committee of students to select poems from this and other assignment for an anthology of student poetry.

Presentation

Motivation/Prior Knowledge
Have students discuss the title of the poem. How might a black man's view of "reaping" be different from that of a white man?

Thematic Idea Another poem that discusses the black experience is "The Negro Speaks of Rivers" by Langston Hughes (p. 911).

Purpose-Setting Question Who is the speaker of the poem?

1 Discussion What fears did the sower have in his heart?

2 Discussion What is the meaning of the final two lines?

Reader's Response Explain what this poem means to you.

Closure and Extension

ANSWERS TO THINKING ABOUT THE SELECTION
Recalling

1. He plants seeds deep in the fear that wind or birds will take the grain away.
2. (a) He scatters enough seeds to plant the area from Canada to Mexico. (b) He ends up with just a handful.
3. The brother's sons are gathering what he planted.

Interpreting

4. (a) They are not permitted to keep the fruit of their labor. (b) He is speaking of the white people of the country.
5. (a) It refers to other peoples' fields that have already been harvested. (b) "Bitter fruit" refers to the fruit that remains after the field has been harvested.

Applying

6. Answers will differ. Students may note that people of all races cultivate their own food.

916

A Black Man Talks of Reaping
Arna Bontemps

> I have sown beside all waters in my day.
> I planted deep, within my heart the fear
> that wind or fowl would take the grain away.
> I planted safe against this stark, lean year.
>
> 5 I scattered seed enough to plant the land
> in rows from Canada to Mexico
> but for my reaping only what the hand
> can hold at once is all that I can show.
>
> Yet what I sowed and what the orchard yields
> 10 my brother's sons are gathering stalk and root;
> small wonder then my children glean in fields
> they have not sown, and feed on bitter fruit.

THINKING ABOUT THE SELECTION
Recalling

1. Why does the speaker plant "deep"?
2. (a) How much seed does the speaker scatter? (b) With how much grain does he end up?
3. Why are the speaker's brother's sons "gathering stalk and root"?

Interpreting

4. (a) What does this poem suggest about how black people are rewarded for their hard work? (b) Who is the speaker referring to when he mentions his "brother's sons" in line 10?
5. (a) What are the "fields/they have not sown" in lines 11–12? (b) What is the "bitter fruit"?

Applying

6. In what ways do all people of all races and creeds sow and reap?

CROSS CURRENTS

Music in Harlem

Harlem during the 1920's was, for anyone interested in black American culture, the center of the world. "Harlem was like a great magnet for the Negro intellectual," Langston Hughes wrote in his autobiography, *The Big Sea*. Explaining how he felt when he first came to Harlem in 1921, Hughes said, "I really did not want to go to college at all. I didn't want to do anything but live in Harlem, get a job and work there. . . . " Not only did Harlem inspire and nurture such writers as Countee Cullen, Claude McKay, Jean Toomer, Arna Bontemps, Zora Neale Thurston, and Hughes, but it was the home of some of the most important figures in early jazz. Pianists and composers like Duke Ellington and Fats Waller; blues singers like Ethel Waters and Bessie Smith; entertainers like Josephine Baker, Florence Mills, and Bill Robinson were all part of the jazz age of the Harlem Renaissance. Even performers generally associated with other cities—such as Louis Armstrong with New Orleans—came to play in Harlem during the 1920's. "The world's most glamorous atmosphere!" exclaimed a young Duke Ellington upon his arrival in 1923. "Why it is just like the Arabian nights!"

NIGHTLIFE IN HARLEM

It was, according to James Wendell Johnson, "a place where life wakes up at night." A booklet accompanying an early Columbia album called *The Sounds of Harlem* listed almost 125 entertainment spots between 125th and 135th Streets between Lenox and Seventh Avenues. These included

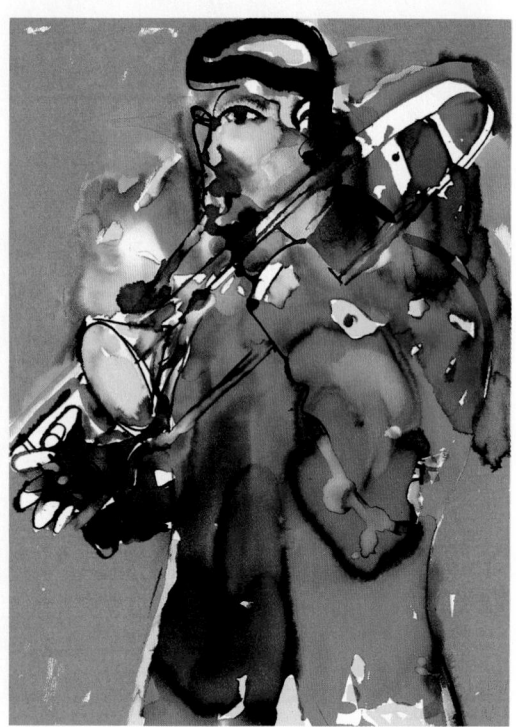

TROMBONE SOLO
Romare Bearden
Courtesy ACA Galleries

at least forty clubs, among them the famous Cotton Club; more than seventeen cafés, speak-easies, cellars, lounges, bar and grills, and other places where blues and jazz were heard nightly; ten theaters and eight ballrooms where the jazz bands played and people danced all night. The most famous of these were the Apollo Theater and the Savoy Ballroom, which took up an entire city block between 140th and 141st Street. The interior of the Savoy reflected the glamour of

Cross Currents   917

Humanities Note

Fine art, *Jazz Village*, by Romare Bearden (1914–1988). Made in 1967, this collage was created by painting, gluing, and tearing away sections of a design to create a varied texture and pattern. Bearden was noted for collages such as *Jazz Village* that combine a variety of images in interesting and striking patterns.

In this collage, a group of four musicians plays together amid a kaleidescope of images. The many different patterns suggest the multi-layered sound of jazz, as does the combination of somber and bright colors. Despite the seemingly haphazard collection of designs and images, the picture has a strong sense of unity, just as the disparate musical lines in jazz make up a coherent musical passage.

You might use the following questions for class discussion:

1. How would you describe the mood of this collage? What forms and colors create this mood?

2. Do you think that this subject is effectively presented through a collage or would another technique convey the subject better? Support your answer.

3. How is this collage characteristic of the work of modernist writers and artists?

JAZZ VILLAGE
Romare Bearden
Courtesy ACA Galleries

the age: there were marble staircases; glass chandeliers; and a polished maple dance floor that had to be replaced every two years because of the wear of several thousand dancers, pounding the floor nightly.

Nightlife in Harlem was like jazz itself: full of energy, spirit, and surprise. People flocked to Harlem from all over the city to hear music and to dance. As the drummer Sammy Greer recalled: "The last show at the Cotton Club went on at two and the Club closed at three-thirty or four. Then everybody would go next door to Happy Roane's or to the breakfast dance at Smalls' Paradise, where the floor show went on at six o'clock in the morning. . . . It was the complete show with twenty-five or thirty people, including the singing waiters and their twirling trays. Show people from all over New York, white and colored, went there Sunday mornings. It's hard to imagine now, musicians coming out from the breakfast dance at eight or nine in the morning with their tuxedos on, and showgirls with evening dresses on. Or Charlie Johnson's band there, at six or seven in the morning, with maybe twenty-five musicians from the bands all over town, white and colored, playing at one time, all the top names in the music business."

918 *The Modern Age*

BLUES AND JAZZ

Black performers of the Harlem Renaissance saw a close connection between their music and black America. "My men and my race are the inspiration of my work," Duke Ellington explained. "I try to catch the character and mood and feeling of my people. The music of my race is something more than the American idiom. It is the result of our transplantation to American soil and it was our reaction in plantation days, to the life we lived. The characteristic, melancholic music of my race has been forged from the very white heat of our sorrow and from our gropings."

The music of the Harlem Renaissance was dominated by two basic forms: blues and jazz. As Ellington suggested, the roots of blues and jazz were in the work songs, spirituals, and shouts of southern slaves, encouraged to sing by masters who thought that singing would keep up the morale of the slaves and make them work better. These slave songs, in turn, had their roots in the music of Africa. The pattern of theme and variation and the rhythmic counterpoint common in blues and jazz are elements in West African music. The blues, specifically, evolved as a folk music after the Civil War, expressing the hardships and struggles of blacks during Reconstruction. As Langston Hughes described the blues: "The music is slow, often mournful, yet syncopated, with a kind of marching bass behind it that seems to say, 'In spite of fate, bad luck, these blues themselves, I'm going on! I'm going to get there.'"

HARLEM AS INSPIRATION

Harlem itself inspired early jazz musicians and composers, much in the way it inspired the writers of the age. In 1927 Fats Waller composed "Lenox Avenue Blues"; in 1928 songs with titles like "Harlem Drag" and "Harlem Twist" were recorded. Harlem seemed to be especially important to Duke Ellington, who recorded "Harlem Flat Blues" (1929), "Harlem Speaks" and "Drop Me Off in Harlem" (1933), and "Harmony in Harlem" (1938). Ellington's famous comment on his "Harlem Air Shaft" (1940) underlines the importance of life in Harlem to his work. It also eloquently describes what everyday life in black Harlem was like: "You get the full essence of Harlem in an air shaft. You hear fights, you smell dinner. . . . You hear intimate gossip floating down. You hear the radio. An air shaft is one great loudspeaker. You see your neighbor's laundry. You hear the janitor's dogs. The man upstairs' aerial falls down and breaks your window. You smell coffee. A wonderful thing, that smell. An air shaft has got every contrast. . . . You hear people praying, fighting, snoring. Jitterbugs are jumping up and down always over you, never below. That's a funny thing about jitterbugs. They're always above you. I tried to put it all down in 'Harlem Air Shaft'. . . . "

The music of blues and jazz that blacks created out of their experiences is considered to be the most important, if not the only, form of music indigenous to America. Begun as a form of expression for blacks amid hardships, blues and jazz were soon copied by prominent white songwriters of the twenties. But in their purest form, blues and jazz are born out of what Duke Ellington called the "dissonant" chord of black America's existence. "Dissonance is our way of life in America. We are something apart, yet an integral part."

Enrichment Duke Ellington (1899–1974) was a jazz composer, bandleader, and pianist. At age 17, Ellington made his first professional performance as a jazz pianist. Two years later, in 1918, he had formed his own band. It was his performances during the late twenties and early thirties at Harlem nightclubs such as The Cotton Club that made Ellington and his band famous. Ellington's orchestra played his own compositions and arrangements, and are responsible for many innovations in jazz. Ellington himself is acknowledged as the first to compose extended jazz works. Many jazz instrumentalists, such as clarinetist Barney Bigard, saxophonists Harry Carney and Johnny Hodges, and trumpeter Cootie Williams, worked closely with Ellington and his band for extended periods of time. As a result of his musical innovations and his popularity, Ellington is one of the most famous and revered figures in the history of jazz music.

GREAT WORKS

OUR TOWN
by Thornton Wilder

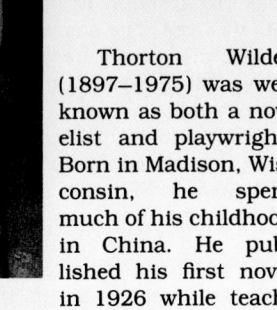

Imagine yourself seated in the audience of a theater awaiting the beginning of a play. The stage has no curtains and no scenery. Soon a stage manager enters and places a few chairs and tables in position. The house-lights dim as he finishes setting the stage. He then turns and watches latecomers arrive. When the auditorium is dark, he speaks directly to the audience, and the play has begun.

This may not seem unusual to you, but in 1938, when *Our Town* opened this way, most theater audiences expected the conventional "box set" in which scenery, sets, and props tied the dramatic action to a particular time and place. The actors performed without any interaction with the audience.

However, in the years between the two world wars, many playwrights had begun moving toward an expression of ideas through fantasy, symbolism, poetry, and other nonliteral techniques. Some began experimenting with more innovative staging technique. Among those who used nonrealistic devices and unusual staging with great success was Thornton Wilder. At its first New York performance, *Our Town* was greeted with wild applause. Its warm portrayal of small-town and family life, its staging, and its timeless themes continue to appeal to wide audiences.

The Author

Thorton Wilder (1897–1975) was well known as both a novelist and playwright. Born in Madison, Wisconsin, he spent much of his childhood in China. He published his first novel in 1926 while teaching French at a private school in New Jersey and a year later published the novel that was to bring him sudden success and a Pulitzer Prize, *The Bridge at San Luis Rey*.

Wilder continued to write novels into the 1930's, but gradually he began to focus his energies on the theater. In 1938 his first major play, *Our Town*, was produced, revealing him as one of the few Americans of the first rank in drama. The play was an immediate hit on Broadway, ran for almost two years, and won a second Pulitzer Prize for Wilder. A leading critic called it "beautifully evocative and "hauntingly beautiful." Wilder went on to write other plays, including *The Skin of Our Teeth* (1942), for which he won a third Pulitzer Prize, and *The Matchmaker* (1954), but *Our Town* remained his masterwork.

920   *The Modern Age*

A Simple Story of Small-Town Life

Our Town portrays the daily routines of Grover's Corners, New Hampshire, on three specific days between 1901 and 1913 along with key events from the lives of George Gibbs and Emily Webb. In Act I, set in 1901 and called "Daily Life," Wilder presents the town and its citizens, particularly the Gibbs and Webb families, engaged in their ordinary pursuits—the milkman delivering milk, the paper carrier delivering the morning newspaper, Mrs. Webb getting the children off to school, Mrs. Webb and Mrs. Gibbs having a casual conversation. He also provides suggestions of a future romantic involvement between young George Gibbs and Emily Webb. In Act II, set in 1904 and called "Love and Marriage," George and Emily fall in love and marry. Again the action is punctuated by casual conversations and scenes of everyday town life. In Act III, set in 1913 and called "Death," Emily is buried in the town cemetery after having died in childbirth. The dead Emily, unwilling to leave life, watches her own funeral and then relives one day from her life, her twelfth birthday, before returning to the peace and tranquillity of the grave.

Unusual Elements

Our Town represented a simplicity in presentation that was unusual for its time. A table, chairs, and a bench, along with ladders to indicate the second stories of houses and a wooden plank to represent a drugstore counter, were among the few props used to support the action. Actors and actresses patted invisible horses, tossed invisible balls, and read invisible newspapers. In this way Wilder forced audience members to participate more actively in the play by using their imaginations to construct the setting and the players' actions.

The play also departed from the conventions of earlier theater by using an omniscient narrator. Ordinarily the feelings and motivations of play characters are revealed through what the characters say and do

Great Works 921

Enrichment During the first run of *Our Town* on Broadway in 1938, Wilder starred in the role of the Stage Manager for two weeks. How might his participation have added to the impact of the play?

and what other characters say about them. Wilder's narrator, the Stage Manager, spoke directly to the audience, commenting on characters' behavior, explaining events, providing background, and even describing future occurrences beyond the scope of the play. At one point the Stage Manager even answered questions asked by characters planted in the audience.

Universal Themes

Wilder used his unusual staging and his narrator to underscore the universality of his themes. His characters were specific people. Yet because of the general way in which they were portrayed, the situations in which they were shown, and the comments made by the Stage Manager, they could also be seen as All People. All elements of the play worked together to show that nothing that happened to these characters might not happen to anyone else. In the same way, because of the lack of scenery and the Stage Manager's remarks, Grover's Corners could also be seen as Anywhere—any spot in the cosmos.

By making his characters and setting emblematic of all people and all places, Wilder was suggesting that his themes applied to life and people everywhere. *Our Town's* portrayal of daily life, love, marriage, and burial underscored the idea that there is a universality in human experience and that people's lives are controlled by nature and are part of a universal and unvarying cycle.

In addition, the play emphasized Wilder's idea that people's lives are essentially tragic. Wilder tried to make people see the priceless value of even the most commonplace events in their lives. The tragedy of human life as Wilder saw it lay in people's inability to appreciate and treasure every moment. People are unhappy, Wilder suggested, not because they fail to achieve great goals, but because they are unable to delight in the beauties of daily existence.

A Popular Classic

Our Town is sometimes seen as a sentimental play, providing an idealized view of small-town American life. At the same time, however, audiences often respond strongly to its ideas about the inevitability of death and the importance of seizing and valuing the moment. An actor who played the Stage Manager in performances of *Our Town* for American troops during World War II recalled that the faces of the soldiers in the audience had "tense, rapt, even desperate looks. Some were wiping tears from their eyes." Willa Cather described Americans living abroad weeping with homesickness after they read the play.

Over the years critics have responded warmly to *Our Town.* One early critic called it "a work of tone and of wisdom" and commented that the play's form enabled Wilder "to build the kind of play he wants to give us—an informal, intimate, and compellingly human drama." Another critic noted, "The life it celebrates is the simplest and least pretentious imaginable . . . yet . . . it has the depth and complexity and richness of a genuine tragic vision."

Our Town has lost none of its emotional power over the years. Audiences continue to leave the theater exhilarated by the play's celebration of affection and family loyalty and its vision of how much more fulfilling and satisfying life can be if we can just stop to appreciate it. Because of the play's timeless themes and its extraordinary success in making the ordinary interesting, *Our Town* remains a popular classic today.

Master Teacher Note If students read and enjoy *Our Town,* you might encourage them to read other early twentieth-century works of literature that focus on small-town life. For example, you might choose *Winesburg, Ohio,* by Sherwood Anderson, or *Main Street* by Sinclair Lewis. The school librarian might be of assistance in choosing other suitable works for students to read. Students could write a paper comparing and contrasting the ideas and themes presented in *Our Town* with the works they read.

The writing assignments on page 924 have students write creatively, while those on page 925 have them think about the selections and write critically.

YOU THE WRITER
Guidelines for Evaluating Assignment 1

1. Does the student use the stream-of-consciousness technique to recreate the natural flow of his or her own thoughts about an important or interesting experience?
2. Does the student only use natural association to link ideas?
3. Has the student eliminated explanations and transitions?
4. Is the stream-of-consciousness piece free from grammar, usage, and mechanics errors?

Guidelines for Evaluating Assignment 2

1. Has the student written a continuation of a modern short story that has no resolution?
2. Does the continuation end with a climax and a resolution?
3. Has the student modeled the writing style of the story's author and kept the characters' actions consistent with their behavior in the original story?
4. Is the continuation free from grammar, usage, and mechanics errors?

Guidelines for Evaluating Assignment 3

1. Has the student written a personal essay that clearly and coherently describes his or her impression of one or two of the most significant events of the Modern Age?
2. Does the student use an informal, conversational writing style?
3. Does the essay reveal something about the student's personality?
4. Is the personal essay free from grammar, usage, and mechanics errors?

Assignment

1. During the Modern Age, writers began using the stream-of-consciousness technique, attempting to recreate the natural flow of their characters' thoughts. Use the stream-of-consciousness technique to re-create the natural flow of your own thoughts.

    Prewriting. Start by thinking of an important or interesting experience you have had at some point in your life. Then let your thoughts flow through the natural associations created by this experience.

    Writing. Record your thoughts as they flow through your mind. Do not add explanations or transitions. Instead, use only your natural associations to link your ideas.

    Revising. After you have finished writing, proofread your paper and prepare a final copy.

Assignment

2. Because writers believed life in the modern world was uncertain and confusing, most modern short stories end without a resolution. Choose a modern story that ends without a resolution, and write a continuation of that story.

    Prewriting. Carefully reread the story you chose, and try to predict the events that might occur after the ending of the story. Then develop a plot for a continuation of the story, ending your continuation with a climax and resolution.

    Writing. When writing your continuation, model your writing style after the style of the story's author.

    Revising. When you revise, make sure your characters' actions are consistent with their behavior in the original story.

Assignment

3. The personal essay became a popular literary form during the Modern Age. Imagine you are living during the Modern Age, and write a personal essay describing your impressions of some of the most significant events of the time.

    Prewriting. Review the unit introduction, trying to imagine how you would have reacted to the events that occurred during the period.

    Writing. When writing your essay, focus on presenting your impressions of one or two important events. Use an informal, conversational writing style. Relate events in chronological order.

    Revising. When you revise, make sure you have conveyed your impressions clearly and coherently. Also make sure your essay reveals something about your personality.

924   *The Modern Age*

YOU THE CRITIC

Assignment

1. During the Modern Age, many poets turned away from conventional poetic forms and techniques, while other poets continued to use traditional forms. Write an essay in which you compare and contrast a poem written in a conventional form with a poem written in an unconventional form.

    Prewriting. Choose a conventional poem and an unconventional poem that have similar themes. Then carefully reread the two poems, noting similarities and differences in form and content.

    Writing. Organize the information in your essay according to corresponding points of contrast, and use passages from both poems to support your argument.

    Revising. When you revise, make sure you have thoroughly supported your argument and have not included any unnecessary information.

Assignment

2. The Modernists associated life in the modern world with a sense of uncertainty, detachment, and disillusionment. Write an essay in which you discuss how this perception of modern life is reflected in the form and content of one of the modern stories you have read.

    Prewriting. Review the unit introduction. Choose a story that reflects the Modernists' perception of life in form and content. Carefully reread the story, focusing on its theme and structure.

    Writing. When you write your essay, use evidence from the story to support your argument.

    Revising. When you revise, make sure your argument is clear and coherent and is organized in a logical manner.

Assignment

3. Literature generally reflects the dominant attitudes and ideas of the period in which it was written. Write an essay in which you discuss the ways in which modern literature reflects the dominant attitudes and ideas of the Modern Age.

    Prewriting. Review the unit introduction. Then review the selections in the unit and find at least five stories or poems that reflect the dominant attitudes of the age.

    Writing. When writing your essay, use evidence from at least five selections to support your argument. State your thesis in your opening paragraph. Support your thesis in the body of your essay. Conclude with a restatement of your main idea.

    Revising. When you revise, make sure your essay is logically organized and that you have used transitions and other linking devices to connect your ideas.

You the Critic   925

YOU THE CRITIC
Guidelines for Evaluating Assignment 1

1. Does the student compare and contrast a poem written in conventional form with a poem written in an unconventional form?
2. Does the student use passages from both poems to support his or her opinion adequately?
3. Has the student organized the essay according to corresponding points of contrast and eliminated any irrelevant information?
4. Is the essay free from grammar, usage, and mechanics errors?

Guidelines for Evaluating Assignment 2

1. Has the student discussed how the Modernists' disillusioned perception of modern life is reflected in the form and content of one of the stories in this section?
2. Has the student presented evidence to adequately support his or her argument?
3. Is the essay organized in a logical manner?
4. Is the essay free from grammar, usage, and mechanics errors?

Guidelines for Evaluating Assignment 3

1. Has the student written an essay in which he or she discusses the ways in which modern literature reflects the dominant attitudes and ideas of the Modern Age?
2. Has the student used evidence from at least five selections to support his or her argument?
3. Has the student used transitions and other linking devices to connect the ideas?
4. Is the essay logically organized and free from grammar, usage, and mechanics errors?

Humanities Note

Fine art, *Golden Gate,* 1955, by Charles Sheeler. When Pennsylvania-born Charles Sheeler (1883–1965) returned to the United States from his European art studies in 1909, he became a photographer. He also set up a painting studio in an old farmhouse in Bucks County, Pennsylvania. His work with the camera influenced his painting; the reverse is true as well. He was influenced, too, by the decorative but utilitarian quality of the Shaker handcrafts produced in the region.

In creating both his paintings and his photographs, Sheeler concentrated on the abstract elements of his subject. Paintings such as *Golden Gate* are based on actual subjects—in this case, the famous San Francisco span—and yet are rendered as geometric shapes juxtaposed in unexpected ways that exaggerate their structural qualities. Rather than provide a literal depiction of the bridge, for instance, Sheeler has broken the subject down into areas of light and dark, so that the viewer's eye moves from one spatial element to another, instead of across the bridge, as in traditional painting. The intensity of the images suggests, first, a three-dimensional quality and, second, a lack of any real connection with the kind of human activity usually associated with such subjects.

GOLDEN GATE, 1955
Charles Sheeler
The Metropolitan Museum of Art

Objectives

1 To gain an understanding of the major events and developments of the contemporary age
2 To gain an understanding of contemporary American literature

926

CONTEMPORARY WRITERS
1946–Present

Maria lay at night in the still of Beverly Hills and saw the great signs soar overhead at seventy miles an hour: *Normandie* 1/4 Vermont 3/4 Hollywood Fwy 1. Again and again she returned to an intricate stretch just south of the interchange where successful passage from the Hollywood to the Harbor required a diagonal move across four lanes of traffic.

Joan Didion

927

Historical Context Point out to students that the world has changed dramatically since the end of World War II. Technological advances, such as the development of the computer, have radically altered the way in which people live their lives. To emphasize the number of developments that have occurred in recent decades, you might want to point out to students that at the end of World War II television was still in its infancy, the first spaceship had yet to be launched, and rock and roll music had yet to be born. Tell students that this introduction will provide them with an overview of the major events and developments of the contemporary period. In addition, it will introduce them to some of the major writers and the important literary trends of the period.

Writing/Prior Knowledge Have students write a journal entry in which they discuss the events of the last several decades that they consider most important. In addition, they should explore their existing perceptions of contemporary American literature. As students move through the unit, encourage them to refer back to their journal entries to see if their understanding of the contemporary period has changed.

ESL Teaching Strategy Pair each of your ESL students with a native speaker. Have the pairs read through the unit introduction together, taking turns reading aloud. Instruct the native speaker to clarify the meanings of any words with which the ESL student is unfamiliar.

Motivation/Prior Knowledge
Have your students share their prior knowledge of the events and developments that have occurred since World War II. Also have them discuss their conceptions of contemporary American literature. Then tell them that they are about to learn more about contemporary American literature as well as about the major events and developments of the contemporary age.

Purpose-Setting Question
What is the most accurate characterization of contemporary American life? How can contemporary American literature be characterized?

¹ **Literary Movement** "On the Mall," an essay by Joan Didion, appears on page 952.

² **Master Teacher Note** To help students appreciate the dramatic changes that have occurred in the last several decades, you might want to compare and contrast life in America today with American life at the turn of the century. Discuss the ways in which people's lives have been affected by the technological advances of the twentieth century. Have students list the ways in which these advances have improved people's lives and the ways in which they have made life more complex.

³ **Enrichment** Relations between the Soviet Union and the West became increasingly strained following the end of World War II. The Soviets helped to establish Socialist governments in the Eastern European countries of Bulgaria, Romania, Hungary, Poland, Czechoslovakia, and eastern Germany. Cutting off nearly all western contact with these nations, the Soviets rapidly expanded their military power. Fearing further Soviet expansion, the western nations established a military alliance known as the North Atlantic Treaty Organization (NATO).

Maria Wyeth, the heroine of Joan Didion's novel *Play It As It Lays,* thinks about freeways, the central metaphor of the story. These freeways, like the Interstate Highway System begun in 1956, speed the movement of traffic. At the same time, however, they pose tricky driving problems. Survival requires skill.

Much of the new technology that has become widespread since 1945—television and computers in particular—can also have consequences beyond their obvious ones. The new technology does make life easier and pleasanter. Paradoxically, it also introduces complexities and problems that were unknown in earlier days.

The years from the end of the Second World War to the present day have been a time of change. Great strides have been made in civil rights and women's rights. Americans have fought in two Asian wars. Popular entertainment has changed dramatically, not just in presentation (from radio to television) but also in style (from big bands to rock music). These changes and others have had an effect on American literature. Their effect seems somehow less dramatic than the changes themselves, however. In general, contemporary writers have absorbed and extended earlier techniques but have introduced few startling innovations.

THE HISTORICAL SETTING

The United States emerged from the Second World War as the most powerful nation on earth. Proud of the part they had played in defeating the Axis, Americans now wanted life to return to normal. Soldiers and sailors came home, the rationing of scarce goods ended, and the nation prospered. But despite postwar jubilation, the dawn of the nuclear age and the ominous actions of the Soviet Union meant that nothing would be the same again.

In 1945, the United Nations was created amid high hopes that it would prevent future wars. Nonetheless, a Cold War between the Soviet Union and the West began as soon as the shooting war ended. In a speech in early 1946, Winston Churchill, Great Britain's wartime Prime Minister, said, "An iron curtain has descended across the continent" of Europe. It was in Asia, however, that the first armed conflict came. In 1950, President Harry S. Truman sent American troops to help anticommunist South Korean forces turn back a North Korean invasion.

From Quiet Pride to Activism

Americans of the 1950's are sometimes referred to as "the Silent Generation." Many of them had lived through both the Great Depression and the Second World War. When peace and prosperity finally arrived, they were only too glad to adopt a quiet, somewhat complacent attitude. They greatly admired President Dwight D. Eisenhower, one of America's wartime heroes.

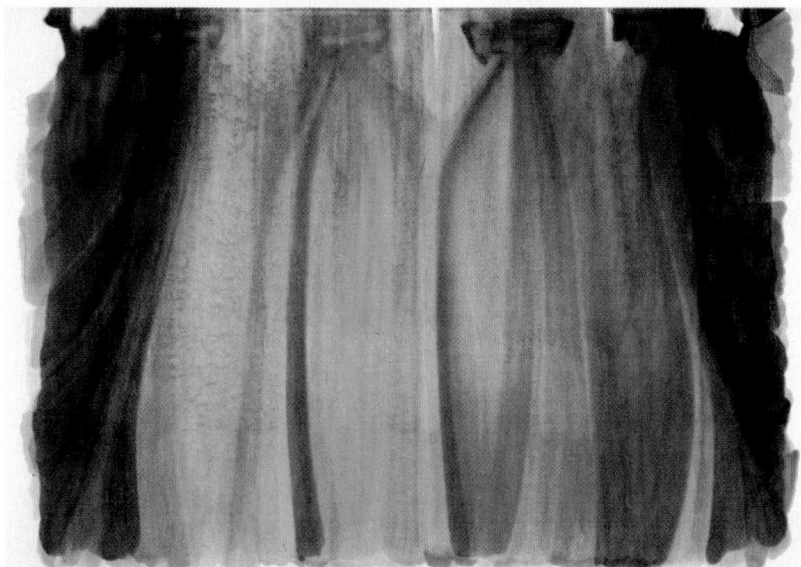

SARABAND, 1959
Morris Louis
Solomon R. Guggenheim
Museum

Near the end of the 1950's, the Soviet Union launched Sputnik, the first artificial satellite to orbit the earth. This Soviet space triumph spurred many people to call for changes in American science and education. President John F. Kennedy, elected in 1960, promised to "get the nation moving again." He had little time to do so, however, before his tragic assassination in 1963.

Kennedy's assassination was followed by an escalating and increasingly unpopular war in Vietnam. A wave of protest followed. Gone were the calm of the Eisenhower years and the high hopes of Kennedy's brief administration. In their place came idealistic but strident demands for rapid change: greater "relevance" in education, more progress on civil rights, an immediate end to the Vietnam War. It was a time of crisis and confrontations.

Real and lasting gains were made in civil rights after the Second World War. Astonishing as it may seem today, blacks could not play baseball in the major leagues until Jackie Robinson broke the color barrier in 1947. Segregation in the public schools was outlawed by the Supreme Court in 1954. Tragedy struck in 1968, when black leader Martin Luther King, Jr. was assassinated in Memphis, Tennessee. Riots broke out in many cities across the nation.

One of the bright moments in a troublesome decade occurred in 1969. In July of that year, American astronaut Neil Armstrong became the first person to set foot on the moon.

Introduction 929

Humanities Note

Fine art, *Saraband,* 1959, by Morris Louis. Unlike many modern painters, Morris Louis (1912–1962), who was born in Baltimore, generally avoided the turbulent art world of New York City; he lived there only in the late 1930's. At his death Louis lived in Washington.

Louis used several different techniques to create his paintings. In one method, for a series called "Veils," he would staple large sheets of canvas onto a scaffold. The thin acrylic paint Louis used would flow down, and the resulting colors would be clear and translucent. In another technique he employed, huge canvases would be left blank in the center, with color applied, in broken diagonal stripes, at the sides. This series he called the "Unfurleds."

The title of the work on this page, *Saraband,* is the name of a slow, stately court dance from the seventeenth and eighteenth centuries. The designation may be intended to reflect a rhythmic quality of the painting.

4 **Enrichment** Martin Luther King, Jr. (1929–1968), a black Baptist minister, was the leader of the American civil rights movement. Advocating a nonviolent approach to fighting racial injustice, he organized demonstrations throughout the South. King's efforts helped to bring about the Civil Rights Act of 1964, which prohibited racial discrimination in public places.

Enrichment North Korea invaded South Korea on June 25, 1950. An emergency meeting of the United Nations Security Council was held later that day. The council passed a resolution condemning the invasion and demanding the immediate withdrawal of the North Korean forces. Two days later, the council recommended that the United Nations provide military aid to South Korea. This recommendation prompted President Truman to send American troops to Korea, where they became part of a joint United Nations fighting force commanded by General Douglas MacArthur.

The Korean War lasted until July 27, 1953, when a cease-fire was signed. By that time, 54,000 Americans and 3,000 soldiers from other United Nations countries had lost their lives in the struggle.

Enrichment The Supreme Court's ruling against public school segregation occurred after the NAACP filed suit against the Board of Education of Topeka, Kansas, on behalf of Linda Brown. The board had denied Brown admission to an all-white school. When the case reached the Supreme Court in 1954, the Court ruled that "separate educational facilities are inherently unequal." "The doctrine of 'separate but equal,'" the Court held, "has no place in public education." A year later the Court ordered school intergration to proceed "with all deliberate speed."

■ AMERICAN EVENTS ■

1945   **Gwendolyn Brooks** publishes *A Street in Bronzeville*.

1946   United States grants independence to the Philippines.

        Robert Penn Warren publishes *All the King's Men*.

        Carson McCullers publishes *The Member of the Wedding*.

1948   Norman Mailer publishes *The Naked and the Dead*.

1949   *Death of a Salesman* by Arthur Miller is first produced; it wins a Pulitzer Prize.

1950   President Harry S. Truman sends troops to South Korea after North Korean invasion.

1951   J. D. Salinger publishes *The Catcher in the Rye*.

1952   **Ralph Ellison** publishes *Invisible Man*.

1953   *The Adventures of Augie March* by Saul Bellow appears.

1954   Supreme Court holds public school segregation to be unconstitutional.

1955   **Flannery O'Connor** publishes *A Good Man Is Hard to Find*.

        Cat on a Hot Tin Roof by Tennessee Williams opens on Broadway.

1959   Alaska and Hawaii admitted to the Union as the 49th and 50th states.

        Robert Lowell's *Life Studies* appears.

1960   **John Updike** publishes *Rabbit Run*.

School Segregation Declared Unconstitutional

Ralph Ellison

Flannery O'Connor

Robert Lowell

State of Israel Established

Jorge Luis Borges

Günter Grass

Fidel Castro

WORLD EVENTS

1945   England: Evelyn Waugh publishes *Brideshead Revisited*.

1947   India-Pakistan: Indian Independence Act grants India and Pakistan independence from Great Britain.

1948   Israel: United Nations establishes state of Israel; war with Arab states begins.

       Germany: Soviet Union blockades Allied sectors of Berlin; leads to Berlin airlift.

       England: The *Heart of the Matter* by Graham Greene published.

1950   England: Doris Lessing publishes *The Grass Is Singing*.

1954   Wales: Poet Dylan Thomas publishes *Under Milk Wood*.

       England: *Lord of the Flies* by William Golding appears.

1955   Argentina: Jorge Luis Borges publishes *Extraordinary Tales*.

1957   Ghana: Ghana becomes first of many new independent African nations to emerge.

       Italy: Alberto Moravia publishes *Two Women*.

       USSR: *Doctor Zhivago* by Boris Pasternak appears.

1959   Cuba: Fidel Castro overthrows regime of Fulgencio Batista and becomes dictator.

       Germany: *The Tin Drum* by Günter Grass appears.

       France: Jean Anouilh produces *Becket*, one of his many plays.

       Canada: Mordecai Richler publishes *The Apprenticeship of Duddy Kravitz*.

Introduction   931

Enrichment Jorge Luis Borges (1899–1986) was born in Buenos Aires, Argentina. He first began enjoying success as a writer during the 1920's and 1930's, when he contributed fiction to Argentine literary magazines. In 1941 he published *The Garden of Forking Paths,* a collection of experimental stories that won him a greater readership among the Argentinian public. His next two books, *Fictions* (1944) and *The Aleph* (1949), were also very successful. In 1962 he established himself as one of the world's most famous and highly regarded writers with the publication of his book *Labyrinths* (1962), which contained translations of some of his best work.

Enrichment Gunter Grass (1927–   ) was born in Danzig, the Baltic seaport that is now the Polish city of Gdansk. During World War II, Grass was imprisoned in the German concentration camp at Dachau. Grass drew on his wartime experiences in writing his novel *The Tin Drum*, a controversial survey of the Nazi era that mixes fairy tale, fantasy, and realism.

Enrichment President John F. Kennedy was assassinated on November 22, 1963, while he was in Dallas on a political tour. The assassination occurred as the Presidential motorcade proceeded from the airport to the center of the city. Hours later, aboard an Air Force jet bound for Washington, Vice President Lyndon Johnson was sworn in as the thirty-sixth President of the United States. Lee Harvey Oswald was arrested and charged with Kennedy's assassination. Before Oswald could be tried, however, he was shot to death by Jack Ruby, while being escorted by the police.

Enrichment In her biography of Sylvia Plath, the literary scholar Linda W. Wagner-Martin offers the following description of "Ariel," the title poem in Sylvia's final collection of poetry: "In 'Ariel' the subject of the poem finds herself through the expansion of her spirit as she rides a beloved horse in early morning. The physical and emotional pleasure allows her to 'unpeel,' to lose what she calls 'dead hands, dead stringencies.' In her new-found freedom from male surveillance, she takes on all the independence, the aggression, that her culture had attempted to deny her."

AMERICAN EVENTS

1961   Joseph Heller publishes *Catch-22*.

1962   Environmental protection movement spurred by Rachel Carson's book *Silent Spring*.

1963   President John F. Kennedy assassinated in Dallas.

1966   *The Fixer*, a novel by **Bernard Malamud**, wins the Pulitzer Prize.

       Ariel, **Sylvia Plath's** last collection of poems, appears.

1968   Martin Luther King, Jr., civil rights leader, murdered in Memphis.

       Joan Didion publishes *Slouching Towards Bethlehem*.

1969   Astronaut Neil Armstrong becomes the first person to set foot on the moon.

       Joyce Carol Oates publishes *Them*.

1972   Last U.S. combat troops leave Vietnam; peace pact signed in 1973.

1973   Toni Morrison publishes *Sula*.

1974   President Richard M. Nixon, faced with impeachment, resigns.

1979   Militant Iranian students take more than 50 Americans hostage in Teheran.

1982   **Alice Walker** publishes *The Color Purple*.

1983   Sally Ride becomes the first American woman to travel in space.

1986   Space shuttle *Challenger* explodes after launch from Cape Canaveral.

1988   George Bush elected President.

1989   Earthquake hits San Francisco.

Mrs. Martin Luther King   Rachel Carson

First Men on the Moon

Violence

Toni Morrison

932   *Contemporary Writers*

John F. Kennedy Assassinated

Breaks Out in Northern Ireland

U.S. Soldier in Vietnam

President Nixon Resigns

The Berlin Wall   Octavio Paz

WORLD EVENTS

1961	Germany: East Germany erects Berlin Wall to keep East Germans from defecting to the West.
	Scotland: Muriel Spark publishes *The Prime of Miss Jean Brodie.*
	Australia: Patrick White publishes *Riders in the Chariot.*
1962	USSR: *One Day in the Life of Ivan Denisovich* by Aleksandr Solzhenitsyn appears.
	USSR: *Selected Poems* published by Yevgeny Yevtushenko.
1965	England: Harold Pinter produces *The Homecoming.*
1967	Israel: Israel gains territory from Arab states in Six-Day War.
	South Africa: Dr. Christiaan Barnard makes medical history with first human heart transplant.
1969	Northern Ireland: Long period of violence begins between Catholics and Protestants.
1972	England: Iris Murdoch publishes *An Accidental Man.*
	Mexico: Octavio Paz publishes *The Other Mexico.*
1973	Middle East: Embargo on Middle East oil produces world shortages.
1979	Vietnam: Repression causes hundreds of thousands of "boat people" to flee Vietnam.
	Trinidad: V. S. Naipaul publishes *A Bend in the River.*
1981	Poland: Polish trade union movement Solidarity suppressed.
1986	USSR: Chernobyl nuclear disaster spreads radioactive cloud across Eastern Europe.
1989	Berlin Wall comes down. Major changes occur in Eastern European governments.

Introduction 933

Enrichment The Russian poet Yevgeny Yevtushenko (1933–) is one of the few contemporary poets known throughout the world. Yevtushenko published his first collection of poetry, *Prospectors of the Future,* in 1953. During the following nine years, he published six more successful books of poetry. In 1962 he wrote a poem that carried his fame around the world. This poem, entitled "Babi Yar," passionately attacked religious prejudice, recalling the brutal murder of 35,000 Jews by German troops at Babi Yar in September of 1941.

Enrichment In discussing the contrasts between Mexican and American culture, the Mexican poet Octavio Paz (1914–) once wrote, "The polar opposites that exist between Americans and Mexicans are epitomized in our attitudes toward change. To us the secret lies not in getting ahead but in managing to stay where we already are. It is the opposition between the wind and a rock . . . we instinctively relate the present to the past, whereas Americans relate it to the future."

5 Enrichment The Watergate scandal resulted from a break-in that occurred at the Democratic Party's national headquarters in 1972. The White House attempted to conceal evidence that linked members of the Nixon Administration to the break-in. The attempt was unsuccessful, however, and an investigation began that ultimately led to the conviction of several White House aides and the initiation of impeachment proceedings against President Nixon. Nixon resigned on August 9, 1974, and he was pardoned by President Gerald Ford on September 8.

6 Master Teacher Note To help students appreciate the effect of television on politics, you might compare and contrast a televised Presidential address with Abraham Lincoln's "Gettysburg Address" (p. 444), or Patrick Henry's "Speech in the Virginia Convention" (p. 126). What are the similarities and differences between the two speeches? How might television account for some of these differences?

Humanities Note

Fine art, *Gotham News,* 1955, by Willem de Kooning. Born in Rotterdam, the Netherlands, Willem de Kooning (b. 1904) came to the United States in his twenties, after studying both fine and applied art for eight years in his native city. His early works were generally representational, but in the 1930's his paintings became increasingly abstract and showed the influence of Picasso and other cubists.

De Kooning's abstract expressionist works, beginning in the 1940's, were, apparently, extensions of the style of the earlier works. Containing no objective imagery, they consist of strong lines, produced by prominent brushstrokes. *Gotham News* is one such work. Oil, enamel, and charcoal sweep in powerful but

GOTHAM NEWS, 1955
Willem de Kooning
Albright-Knox Art Gallery

A Quest for Stability

The upheavals of the 1960's brought a conservative reaction. Many Americans longed for a return to "the good old days." President Richard M. Nixon, elected in 1968, promised to end the Vietnam War and to restore order in the nation. Nixon's first-term achievements, especially in foreign policy, were soon overshadowed by his involvement in the Watergate affair. This scandal forced his resignation from the presidency in 1974. Vice President Gerald Ford took over, proclaiming, "Our long national nightmare is over."

Civil rights activism continued during these years, and another movement attracted growing attention—the women's liberation movement. Although the Nineteenth Amendment to the Constitution, ratified in 1920, had given women the right to vote, discrimination still existed. Women received lower pay than men for the same jobs, and promotion was more difficult. Betty Friedan's *The Feminine Mystique,* published in 1963, called for change. The women's movement grew steadily through the 1970's.

The final months of Jimmy Carter's one-term presidency were marred by high inflation and clouded by Iran's holding of more than fifty American hostages. The nation then sent Ronald Reagan to the White House. A former film star and two-term governor of California, Reagan proved to be a popular and persuasive President. His reelection in 1984 was one of the biggest landslide victories in American history.

The Changing Scene

Commercial television was still in its infancy at the end of the Second World War, but it was on the verge of spectacular growth. TV aerials soon sprouted on rooftops from coast to coast. Over the next few years, television changed the leisure habits of Americans. It even had an impact on presidential politics. John F. Kennedy's youthful but confident demeanor in the televised debates with Richard M. Nixon helped him win the election in 1960.

The postwar period was a time of explosive suburban growth, made possible by the automobile. Despite the recent renewal of certain areas of older cities, the growth of suburbs continues today. At first, most suburban homeowners worked in the nearby city and commuted to their jobs by train, bus, or car. Later, major corporations began establishing suburban headquarters, and workers could live nearby or commute short distances from one suburb to another.

American industry changed rapidly during this period. Automation and foreign competition reduced the number of jobs in heavy industries like steel and automobile manufacturing. At the same time, the electronics industry was experiencing dynamic growth. Along with a sudden increase in the number of high-tech jobs came an increase in the number of service jobs. More leisure time and

5

6

inconclusive lines on the canvas, suggesting curved triangles and other forms. The title of the work may reflect the fact that de Kooning would sometimes place sheets of newspaper over a still-wet painting, and the newspaper copy would be imprinted. If the artist reworked the paint after removing the newspaper, the image would disappear, as in this work; in some paintings, however, he retained the columns of news, ads, and so on that had adhered. (Gotham is a fanciful, satiric name for New York City.)

UNTITLED, 1960–61
Mark Rothko
Art Resource

Humanities Note

Fine art, *Untitled, 1960–1961,* Mark Rothko. Born in Russia, Mark Rothko (1903–1970) emigrated with his family to Oregon when he was ten. Although he studied art in New York City in the 1920's, he considered himself self-taught. During the next two decades his works included expressionistic images of human figures and renderings of delicate lines and playful shapes reminiscent of the style of the Spanish painter Joan Miró.

Untitled, 1960–61 is highly characteristic of the paintings Rothko made in the last twenty years of his life. The light- and dark-colored, softly drawn rectangles, although simple and basically unchanging in form, may elicit different responses: deep red evokes intensity, orange or brown suggests unassertiveness, and so on. Because of the lack of definite background, the rectangles seem to "float," as if not permanently anchored to the canvas. The interplay of color and the suggestion of mobility provide the works with a feeling of poetic tension.

more money to spend brought a need for more employees to serve other people's needs.

The world has changed dramatically since 1945, and it is still changing. These changes have had an impact on the literature of the time, although this impact has not always been obvious.

LITERARY VARIETY AND PROMISE

The turbulence of contemporary times has not fostered a literary revolution of the kind that occurred in the 1920's, yet it has contributed to the development of a wide variety of literary movements that are often collectively referred to as Postmodernism. While many writers have been content to build on the experiments of the Modernists, others have sought to create works that stand apart from the past. Some writers have explored new literary forms and techniques, composing works from dialogue alone, creating works that blend fiction and nonfiction or fantasy and realism, and/or experimenting with the physical appearance of their work. Other writers have focused on capturing the essence of contemporary life in the content of their works, often expressing themes concerning the complex, impersonal, and commercial nature of today's world.

7 Literary Movement See the discussion of Postmodernism in the Guide for Interpreting on page 995.

Introduction 935

8 **Literary Movement** "The First Seven Years" by Bernard Malamud appears on page 946; "The Life You Save May Be Your Own" by Flannery O'Connor appears on page 956; "Average Waves in Unprotected Water" by Anne Tyler appears on page 968; "The Slump" by John Updike appears on page 978; "Journey" by Joyce Carol Oates appears on page 984; and "Imagined Scenes" by Ann Beattie appears on page 996.

9 **Literary Movement** "A Ride Through Spain," an essay by Truman Capote, begins on page 1038.

Authors for a New Era

Although contemporary writers have produced a wide variety of impressive works, it is all but impossible to predict which writers will achieve lasting fame and which will not. Time is needed to certify greatness. Modern readers and modern critics have their favorites, of course. Some of them will undoubtedly become part of America's enduring literary legacy.

Every writer owes a debt to those writers who have gone before. In that sense, literature is cumulative. The earliest American literature, except for that of the Native Americans, was based on European models. Writers in the United States today can look to a rich heritage of their own. Contemporary novelists are well aware of Nathaniel Hawthorne, Mark Twain, Ernest Hemingway, William Faulkner. Short-story writers know Edgar Allan Poe, Willa Cather, Eudora Welty. Poets study Emily Dickinson, Walt Whitman, Langston Hughes. Playwrights are familiar with Eugene O'Neill and Thornton Wilder.

One of the literary giants to whom many modern writers look is not American but Irish: James Joyce. Although Joyce is difficult to read, his technical innovations and major themes have made an indelible mark on American fiction. The stream-of-consciousness technique, although not invented by Joyce, is strongly associated with him. Also influential is Joyce's fusing of the romantic and realistic traditions, achieving a middle ground between myth and reality.

Among the highly acclaimed novelists of our day is Saul Bellow, who won the Nobel Prize for literature in 1976. His novel *Herzog,* about an average man seeking truth in a world that overwhelms him, shows clear parallels with Joyce's *Ulysses.* Ralph Ellison's *Invisible Man,* about a young black man searching for identity, parallels Joyce's *Portrait of the Artist as a Young Man.*

Other contemporary novelists of stature include Carson McCullers, Robert Penn Warren, Norman Mailer, Bernard Malamud, John Updike, Flannery O'Connor, Joyce Carol Oates, Anne Tyler, and Alice Walker. Many of these novelists have written short stories as well. Flannery O'Connor and John Updike are modern masters of the short-story form. Joyce Carol Oates, winner of the National Book Award for her novel *Them,* has also won numerous awards for her short fiction. Other writers, such as Donald Barthelme and Ann Beattie, have written novels but are better known for their short stories. Isaac Bashevis Singer, a Polish-born New Yorker who writes in Yiddish, is renowned for both his novels and his short stories. He won the Nobel Prize for Literature in 1978. John Cheever, a respected novelist, won the Pulitzer Prize for fiction in 1979 for his collected short stories, many of which concern suburban life. 8

Just as realism and romanticism have tended to merge in recent literature, so, curiously, have fiction and nonfiction. Truman Capote's *In Cold Blood,* published in 1966, was billed as a "nonfic- 9 tion novel." Capote, primarily a novelist and short-story writer, used fictional techniques to analyze a real and seemingly senseless crime. Later authors, such as E. L. Doctorow in his novel *Ragtime,* combined historical figures with purely fictional characters. This technique has aroused considerable controversy.

Increasing attention has been paid recently to the place of non-fiction in the literary hierarchy. The essay has always been considered an important literary form, and some outstanding essays are published every year. James Baldwin and John McPhee are accomplished essayists. Among the many notable longer works of nonfiction are Paul Theroux's *The Great Railway Bazaar,* N. Scott Momaday's *The Names,* and Barry Lopez's *Arctic Dreams.*

Poetry Within the Tradition

A number of the famous prewar poets continued to publish extensively after the war. Robert Frost, Marianne Moore, Wallace Stevens, E. E. Cummings, William Carlos Williams, and Ezra Pound all produced major collections of their works. The younger poets, starting out in the shadow of these great names, were mostly content to work within the advances made in the 1920's and 1930's. One critic observed that to a beginning poet "the reassurance of sounding like something already acclaimed" was hard to resist.

The tumultuous 1960's brought great changes in social behavior, which affected the subject matter of all literature. In poetry, as in fiction, the resulting changes were often more personal and thematic than innovative. It seems ironic that out of the turmoil of the 1960's, the finest poetry to emerge follows older patterns.

One of the most respected contemporary poets is Robert Lowell. His *Lord Weary's Castle,* published in 1946, immediately established him as an important poet of his generation. Lowell, a great nephew of the poet James Russell Lowell, is a writer to whom history and historical context are important. His poetry is traditional in form, but its range in theme, method, and tone is breathtaking.

Theodore Roethke, a master of poetic rhythm, was deeply influenced as a man and as a poet by his father, a strong-willed greenhouse owner in Saginaw, Michigan. Some of Roethke's most notable poems are attempts to come to grips with his father's death when Roethke was fourteen. The best of these are often referred to as his "greenhouse poems."

Georgia-born James Dickey is a poet and novelist whose southern heritage is of great importance in his work. Dickey was a decorated fighter pilot in the Second World War and later in Korea. He has also worked as a teacher and as advertising executive. His novel *Deliverance* is perhaps his best-known work.

Two other poets of note are Elizabeth Bishop and Gwendolyn Brooks. Bishop, born in Massachusetts, traveled widely after graduating from Vassar College, finally setting in Brazil. Her poems are

ANSONIA, 1977 (DETAIL)
Richard Estes
Whitney Museum of American Art

10 **Literary Movement** N. Scott Momaday's "A Vision Beyond Time and Place" appears on page 1060; Paul Theroux's "The Edge of the Great Rift" appears on page 1066; an excerpt from Barry Lopez's *Arctic Dreams* appears on page 1070; and an excerpt from John McPhee's *Rising From the Plains* appears on page 1080.

11 **Literary Movement** Robert Lowell's poem "Hawthorne" can be found on page 1114.

12 **Literary Movement** Three of Theodore Roethke's poems are included in this unit: "Night Journey" (page 941), "The Waking" (page 1094), and "Once More, the Round" (page 1096).

13 **Literary Movement** James Dickey's poem "The Rain Guitar" can be found on page 1100.

14 **Literary Movement** This unit includes one poem by Gwendolyn Brooks: "The Explorer" (page 1106). It also includes two poems by Elizabeth Bishop: "Little Exercise" (page 1108) and "House Guest" (page 1110).

Humanities Note

Fine art, *Ansonia,* 1977, Richard Estes. The detail of *Ansonia* reproduced on this page is, in fact, one-half of the painting; the other half is its mirror image. The street scene shown in the work by Richard Estes (b. 1936) is reflected in the window or glass pane in the center of the full picture. The reflection is so lifelike and rendered in such detail that it is difficult to tell which is the actual scene (the one shown on this page) and which is its image-in-glass.

The area around the Ansonia, a hotel on Broadway, in New York City, is one of many cityscapes Estes has made, in the style called Photorealism. The dominant quality is the clarity and precision of the detail—a traffic sign, for instance, is as clearly readable to the viewer as the actual sign would be to a motorist driving up Broadway. The effect is a heightened, almost eerie, sense of reality, more so than in photography itself, simply because the images have been produced by a paint brush and not through a mechanical lens.

Fine art, Untitled (lithograph) 1970, by Richard Diebenkorn. The American painter Richard Diebenkorn was born in 1922. His extensive study of art included work at Stanford University, University of California, California School of Fine Art, and the University of New Mexico. Originally an abstract expressionist, Diebenkorn later turned to gestural figuration in the late 1950's and '60's. In the '70's his style changed once again to the geometric "Ocean Park" phase.

This untitled color lithograph is from Diebenkorn's "Ocean Park" phase. This series is named after an area near his home in Santa Monica, California. These works, both paintings and prints, reflect the meeting of geometry and the colored field or plane. This lithograph is a non-objective study of color relationships within the imposed borders of geometric shapes. In studies such as this, Diebenkorn is attempting to express the concept of "tension beneath calm."

15 **Literary Movement** Postmodern poetry is best characterized by its diversity. While many poets have returned to using the traditional forms and techniques that were abandoned by the Modernists, other poets chose to build on the experiments and developments of the Modernists.

UNTITLED, 1970
Richard Diebenkorn
National Museum of Art,
Smithsonian Institution

beautifully crafted, with precise and memorable descriptions. Brooks, a preeminent black poet, was born in Topeka, Kansas, but spent most of her life in Chicago. Her first collection, *A Street in Bronzeville,* published in 1945, assured her a reputation. This reputation was further enhanced by *Annie Allen,* published in 1949.

Many fine poets are at work today. Nowhere perhaps is America's pluralism displayed more vividly and to better advantage than in its poets. Although it is too early to assess these poets' achievements, it seems likely that some of their works will become the classics of tomorrow.

15

Beyond the Horizon

One of the features of literary history is its unpredictability. No one knows what will happen next. Of this, however, we can be reasonably sure: The novel is not dead, as some were proclaiming in the 1950's and 1960's. Nor is poetry dead, nor the short story. Literature has great resilience. While it may be (and is) profoundly influenced by other media—radio, television, film—it has not yet been replaced by them. Indeed, for sheer technical virtuosity, there has probably never been a more impressive group of American writers at work than at the present time.

Once or twice I have been asked what the peacock is "good for"—a question that gets no answer from me because it deserves none.

Flannery O'Connor, "Peacocks Are a Puzzle"

Ted Williams . . . had met the little death that awaits athletes. He had quit.

John Updike, "Hub Fans Bid Kid Adieu"

You know as well as I that when someone commits an injustice people make mincemeat of the victim, not of the culprit.

Isaac Bashevis Singer, "Advice"

The worst cynicism: a belief in luck.

Joyce Carol Oates, *Do With Me What You Will*

I discovered the difference between good writing and bad, and then made an even more alarming discovery: the difference between very good writing and true art; it is subtle, but savage.

Truman Capote, *Music for Chameleons*

Willy was a salesman. . . . He's a man way out there in the blue, riding on a smile and a shoeshine. . . . Nobody dast blame this man. A salesman is got to dream, boy. It comes with the territory.

Arthur Miller, *Death of a Salesman*

The road curved out and lay into the bank of rain beyond, and Abel was running. Against the winter sky and the long, light landscape of the valley at dawn, he seemed to be standing still, very little and alone.

N. Scott Momaday, *House Made of Dawn*

We will be ourselves and free, or die in the attempt. Harriet Tubman was not our grandmother for nothing.

Alice Walker, *You Can't Keep a Good Woman Down*

Every journey into the past is complicated by delusions, false memories, false namings of real events.

Adrienne Rich, *Of Woman Born*

Additional Voices

There was a disturbance in my heart, a voice that spoke there and said, *I want, I want, I want!* It happened every afternoon, and when I tried to suppress it it got even stronger. . . . It never said a thing except *I want, I want, I want!*

Saul Bellow, *Henderson, the Rain King*

I don't say he's a great man. Willy Loman never made a lot of money. His name was never in the paper. He's not the finest character that ever lived. But he's a human being, and a terrible thing is happening to him. So attention must be paid. He's not to be allowed to fall into his grave like an old dog. Attention, attention must be finally paid to such a person.

Arthur Miller, *Death of a Salesman*

I didn't want to harm the man. I thought he was a very nice gentleman. Soft-spoken. I thought so right up to the moment I cut his throat.

Truman Capote, *In Cold Blood*

We walk through volumes of the unexpressed and like snails leave behind a faint thread of the unexpressed.

John Updike, *The Blessed Man of Boston*

Writers are always selling somebody out.

Joan Didion, *Slouching Towards Bethlehem*

The deep joy we take in the company of people with whom we have just recently fallen in love is undisguisable.

John Cheever, "The Bus to Saint James"

The poem on the following pages, "Night Journey" by Theodore Roethke, is a model for reading critically. The notes in the side column point out the aspects of the poem that reflect the historical context, the literary movements, and Roethke's techniques. Have students pay attention to these notes as they read, and suggest that they make their own critical comments.

To give students further practice with the process of reading critically, use the selection in the Teaching Portfolio, "Story from Big Bear Country" by Leslie Marmon Silko, page 1243, following the Teacher Backup, which students can annotate themselves. Encourage students to use these strategies as they read the literature in this unit.

READING CRITICALLY

The Literature of 1946–Present

In the years since World War II, American life has grown more and more diversified and complex. This diversity is reflected in the wide variety of different types of literary works that have been written in the past several decades.

Historical Context

Soon after the United States dropped the first nuclear bomb on Hiroshima, it became clear that a new era had begun—an era unlike any previous period in the history of humanity. This era has been characterized by rapid change. Air travel has become commonplace, new methods of communication have been developed and old methods have been perfected, computers have become an integral part of American life, and several Americans have walked on the moon. The United States has participated in two wars in Asia and has passed through periods of stability and unrest. As a result of these changes, life in America today is dramatically different from what it was in 1946, and new technological advances make it clear that American life will continue to change.

Literary Movements

A number of small literary movements have developed since World War II. These movements are often referred to as Postmodernism. In fiction, some writers have continued to develop the fragmentary approach of the Modernists. Others have tried blending realism and fantasy in their works, and still others have experimented with radically different fictional forms and techniques. In poetry, many small regional movements have developed, and the poetry that has been written has varied dramatically in form, style, and content.

Writers' Techniques

During the contemporary period, writers have continued to use many of the literary forms and techniques that were popular during the Modern Age. Free verse has remained a dominant poetic form, and many poets have continued to focus on creating vivid, striking images in their poems. In addition to using popular modern devices such as the stream-of-consciousness technique, fiction writers have experimented with a variety of new forms and techniques. For example, writers have composed works from dialogue alone, have created works that blend fiction with nonfiction, and have experimented with the physical appearance of their work.

On the following pages is a selection by Theodore Roethke, a highly regarded contemporary poet. The notes in the side column should help you to place the selection in its historical context.

Objective

To write a poem about a journey

Support Material

Teaching Portfolio
Teacher Backup, p. 1241
Reading Critically, "Story From Big Bear Country" by Leslie Marmon Silko, p. 1243
Usage and Mechanics Worksheet, p. 1245
Vocabulary Check, p. 1246
Analyzing Literature Worksheet *Understanding Scansion*, p. 1247

Language Worksheet, *Using Concrete Words*, p. 1248
Selection Test, p. 1249

Night Journey

Theodore Roethke

Now as the train bears west,
Its rhythm rocks the earth,
And from my Pullman[1] berth
I stare into the night
5 While others take their rest.
Bridges of iron lace,
A suddenness of trees,
A lap of mountain mist
All cross my line of sight,
10 Then a bleak wasted place,
And a lake below my knees.

---

1. **Pullman:** A railroad car with built-in bunks, or berths.

Historical Context:
Roethke describes a train journey. Train travel was much more widely used at the time this poem was written.

Literary Movement:
Roethke is describing a personal experience. Personal experiences are a common subject of contemporary poetry.

Literary Movement: Like many contemporary poets, Roethke conveys a deep awareness of the landscape.

RAILROAD TRAIN
Edward Hopper
Addison Gallery of American Art,
Phillips Academy, Andover, Massachusetts

Night Journey   941

Presentation

Motivation/Prior Knowledge
Have students imagine a journey at night across their region of the country. What features would they see? How would they look at night? Then tell them that this poem records Roethke's images of a similar journey.

Purpose-Setting Question
What is the speaker's feeling about the images he sees?

Humanities Note

Fine art, *Railroad Train,* 1908, by Edward Hopper. Edward Hopper (1882–1967), an American painter of evocative cityscapes and landscapes in a simple realistic style, studied painting in New York City with the dynamic realist painter, Robert Henri. In spite of the powerful personality of his teacher, Hopper developed his own unique form of realism. Hopper exchanged mood for flamboyance and objectivity for humor; above all, he concentrated on capturing the effects of the clean, harsh American light.

    The painting *Railroad Train* is an everyday subject that, prior to Hopper, few artists had ever bothered to paint. It is painted in a simplified style with broad strokes of a large brush. The point of view, that of looking up at the railroad car from below the tracks, adds drama to the painting. Hopper's subjects are always commonplace, but his insight into the psychology of the familiar prevents his paintings from ever being ordinary.

    You might use these questions for discussion:
1. What mood does this painting evoke?
2. How does this painting suggest Roethke's "Night Journey"?
3. Why do you suppose the artist chose to paint only the last car of the train?

ANSWERS TO THINKING ABOUT THE SELECTION
Recalling

1. The speaker observes, among other things, "Bridges of iron lace,/A suddenness of trees,/A lap of mountain mist."
2. He stays up to see the land he loves.

Interpreting

3. While the other passengers are asleep, the speaker is awake and aware of the landscape and the movements of the train.
4. (a) As the train goes around a curve, the speaker feels the strain on his neck. His muscles move with the movements of the train. The train's motion keeps him awake "in every nerve." (b) The train shakes the landscape.
5. (a) Students may mention "Full on my neck I feel/The straining at a curve," and "My muscles move with steel." (b) One example is "We thunder through ravines."
6. The final line ties his observations together and explains why he has chosen not to sleep.

Applying

7. Answers will differ. Students might comment that some people are not in a hurry to get across the country; they may enjoy the leisure of a train ride, or they might want to see the landscape.

THINKING AND WRITING

For help with this assignment, students can refer to Lesson 18, "Writing a Poem," in the Handbook of Writing About Literature.

Publishing Student Writing You might arrange a bulletin board display of students' poems, so that all members of the class can read them.

Writer's Technique: Roethke uses rhyme, a device not often used in contemporary poetry.

Writer's Technique: Roethke creates vivid, striking images.

Writer's Technique: Roethke uses a regular rhythm and line length.

Writer's Technique: Roethke ends the poem by relating the significance of the experience.

Full on my neck I feel
The straining at a curve;
My muscles move with steel,
15 I wake in every nerve.
I watch a beacon swing
From dark to blazing bright;
We thunder through ravines
And gullies washed with light.
20 Beyond the mountain pass
Mist deepens on the pane;
We rush into a rain
That rattles double glass.
Wheels shake the roadbed stone,
25 The pistons jerk and shove,
I stay up half the night
To see the land I love.

THINKING ABOUT THE SELECTION
Recalling

1. What are three of the things the speaker observes from his Pullman berth?
2. Why does the speaker stay up half the night?

Interpreting

3. What sets the speaker apart from the other passengers?
4. (a) How does the train's motion affect the speaker? (b) What effect does the train have on the landscape?
5. (a) Find two images, or word pictures, that appeal to the sense of touch. (b) Find one image that appeals to the sense of hearing.
6. How does the final line help to explain the significance of the experience?

Applying

7. Why do you think some people choose to travel across the country by train rather than by plane?

THINKING AND WRITING
Writing a Poem About a Journey

Write a poem about a journey that you made at some point in your life. List some of the things you observed during your journey. Arrange your observations in chronological order. Then write your poem, using concrete images in describing your observations. End your poem by relating the significance of the experience. When you revise, make sure that you have included enough details to give the reader a complete sense of the experience. Proofread your poem and share it with your classmates.

Fiction

MORNING CALL, 1946
Milton Avery
Hirshhorn Museum

Humanities Note

Fine art, *Morning Call,* 1946, by Milton Avery. The paintings of Milton Avery (1893–1965) show a kinship with the works of Henri Matisse, particularly in the use of decorative shapes of colors. In Avery's *Morning Call,* some of the shapes are clearly derived from objects in the natural world, as are most of the images in the French painter's works. The most prominent image in *Morning Call,* for example, is the head turned on its side and with its mouth open, in some kind of utterance. Other shapes may suggest rather than actually represent objects from the real world.

The early years of Avery's artistic career were periods of fundamental social change, during which many artists were committed to such movements as naturalism or, in the 1930's, social realism. Avery preferred, instead, to depict observed reality in a highly personalized way.

1914–1987

In his novels and short stories, Bernard Malamud depicts the struggles of ordinary people, often focusing on their desire to improve their lives. He uses the Jewish people to represent all of humanity, capturing their attempts to maintain a link to their cultural heritage while trying to cope with the realities of the modern world. While some of Malamud's characters achieve success, others experience failure. By portraying people in both victory and defeat, Malamud captures the essence of the human experience and creates a delicate balance between tragedy and comedy in his work.

Malamud was born in Brooklyn, New York, the son of Russian immigrants. His father was a grocer who worked diligently in an effort to forge a better life for his family. After attending City College of New York and Columbia University, Malamud began publishing short stories in a number of well-known magazines. In 1952 he published his first novel, *The Natural,* which depicted the life of a gifted baseball player. After that he wrote several other novels, including *The Assistant* (1957), *A New Life* (1961), *The Tenants* (1971), and *Dubin's Lives* (1979). His novel about czarist Russia, *The Fixer* (1966), earned him the Pulitzer Prize and the National Book Award. He also received the National Book Award for *The Magic Barrel* (1958), a collection of short stories.

According to his own account, Malamud's boyhood was "comparatively happy." He grew up in a household where both Yiddish and English were spoken. The constant mingling of the two languages contributed to the writer's fine ear for characteristic spoken rhythms. His family's Judaism expressed itself more as culture than as religion, and through his family he gained a taste for Manhattan's Second Avenue Yiddish theater where two of his mother's relatives sometimes performed. Another favored boyhood pastime was listening to his father recount tales of Jewish life in Czarist Russia. Young Bernard began to display his father's gift for telling stories by age nine when, recovering from pneumonia, he spent hours in the back room of the family store writing down the stories he'd made up to tell his friends. Malamud's fondness for his father's stories revealed itself later in the vast number of stories the author drew from Yiddish oral tradition.

Like most of Malamud's work, "The First Seven Years" focuses on the lives of common people. Depicting a Polish immigrant's desire to see his daughter achieve a better life, the story captures the discrepancy that often exists between parents' dreams for their children and their children's actual desires.

GUIDE FOR INTERPRETING

The First Seven Years

The Writer's Techniques

Epiphany. In a traditional short story, the plot moves toward a resolution, a point at which the conflict, or the struggle that the main character undergoes, is resolved and the final outcome of the action becomes clear. During the twentieth century, however, in an effort to capture the uncertainty and confusion of life in the modern world, most fiction writers have turned away from the traditional plot structure by ending their stories without a resolution. Instead, writers often construct plots that move toward an epiphany, a moment when a character has a flash of insight about himself or herself, another character, a situation, or life in general. For example, in "The First Seven Years," the main character, Feld, gains a sudden insight into his own life and his hopes for his daughter.

Writing

Like the main character in "The First Seven Years," many parents are deeply concerned with building better lives for their children. Freewrite about the reasons why parents often hope that their children's lives will be better than their own, discussing the types of actions that result from this desire.

Primary Source

What determines that which is valued by a person or a generation? Some people long for expensive sports cars and fine homes while others value peace of mind or spiritual wealth. Often things most prized in life differ from one generation to the next, and frequently the difference shifts between material and spiritual poles. Bernard Malamud's story, "The First Seven Years," portrays the age-old generational shift as America experienced it in the 1950's. The authors of *American Writers* have written, "The claim that our spiritual lives are being violated by our attachment to material goods and physical comforts is at least as old as the Old Testament. But in America these complaints probably were never so persuasively and variously made as in the late 1950's. . . . Since one of the primary human realities, if not the dominant one, has been material want, our sense of reality is being diminished to the degree that the new prosperity seems to be lessening our sharp responses to want."

In Malamud's story, Miriam has lived a life comfortably provided for by her father. Perhaps her lack of want explains some of the difference between her attitudes toward the relative values of material security and spiritual fulfillment and the attitudes her father holds. Certainly, she and her father live in different worlds.

Guide for Interpreting 945

Literary Focus Your less advanced students may have difficulty understanding the concept of epiphany. It may be helpful to relate it again to a conventional conflict and resolution. Tell your students that in many modern and contemporary stories, the author does not wish to resolve the story thoroughly. Instead, an epiphany is used to focus attention on a particular insight or understanding.

Writing/Prior Knowledge Have students work in small groups to brainstorm about ideas for their freewriting. You may wish to have the students role-play a parent-child situation in which the parent wants a better life for the child.

Vocabulary

Preteach the following vocabulary words:
diligence (dil′ ə jəns) *n.*: Constant, careful effort; perseverance (p. 946)
connivance (kə nī′ vəns) *n.*: Secret cooperation (p. 946)
illiterate (i lit′ ər it) *adj.*: Unable to read or write (p. 946)
unscrupulous (un skroop′ yə ləs) *adj.*: Not restrained by ideas of right and wrong (p. 948)
repugnant (ri pug′ nənt) *adj.*: Offensive; disagreeable (p. 949)
discern (di surn′) *v.*: To perceive or recognize; make out clearly (p. 951)

Spelling Tip Point out that although two words on this list, *diligence* and *connivance,* have the same ending sound, the sound is spelled differently in the two words: *ence* in *diligence* and *ance* in *connivance.*

Motivation/Prior Knowledge
Have students discuss the diffi-culties and rewards of being a parent. What values would they want to pass on to their children? What choices would they want to make for the child? At what age should children begin to make their own choices? Students should carefully express their opinions and listen to the opin-ions of others.

Master Teacher Note This story is about Polish immigrants in America. Some students may be unfamiliar with the life of such immigrants. Have the class dis-cuss what it is like for people to settle in a new country. What types of difficulties do they face? Why might they want to preserve their cultural heritage?

Thematic Idea "The Life You Save May Be Your Own" (p. 956) and "Average Waves in Unpro-tected Waters" (p. 968) also deal with parents who make choices for their children. You might have students compare and contrast Feld with Bet and the old woman.

Purpose-Setting Question How do the events in the story lead to Feld's final realization?

1 Discussion What do you learn about the characters of Feld, So-bel and Miriam from the first par-agraph?

2 Reading Strategy Have stu-dents predict whether Feld will try to arrange a date between Miriam and Max.

The First Seven Years

Bernard Malamud

Feld, the shoemaker, was annoyed that his helper, Sobel, was so insensitive to his reverie that he wouldn't for a minute cease his fanatic pounding at the other bench. He gave him a look, but Sobel's bald head was bent over the last[1] as he worked and he didn't notice. The shoemaker shrugged and continued to peer through the partly frosted window at the nearsighted haze of falling February snow. Neither the shifting white blur outside, nor the sudden deep remem-brance of the snowy Polish village where he had wasted his youth could turn his thoughts from Max the college boy, (a con-stant visitor in the mind since early that morning when Feld saw him trudging through the snowdrifts on his way to school) whom he so much respected because of the sacrifices he had made throughout the years—in winter or direst heat—to further his education. An old wish returned to haunt the shoemaker: that he had had a son instead of a daughter, but this blew away in the snow for Feld, if anything, was a practi-cal man. Yet he could not help but contrast the diligence of the boy, who was a peddler's son, with Miriam's unconcern for an educa-tion. True, she was always with a book in her hand, yet when the opportunity arose for a college education, she had said no she would rather find a job. He had begged her to go, pointing out how many fathers could not afford to send their children to college, but she said she wanted to be independent.

As for education, what was it, she asked, but books, which Sobel, who diligently read the classics, would as usual advise her on. Her answer greatly grieved her father.

A figure emerged from the snow and the door opened. At the counter the man with-drew from a wet paper bag a pair of battered shoes for repair. Who he was the shoemaker for a moment had no idea, then his heart trembled as he realized, before he had thor-oughly discerned the face, that Max himself was standing there, embarrassedly explain-ing what he wanted done to his old shoes. Though Feld listened eagerly, he couldn't hear a word, for the opportunity that had burst upon him was deafening.

He couldn't exactly recall when the thought had occurred to him, because it was clear he had more than once considered sug-gesting to the boy that he go out with Mir-iam. But he had not dared speak, for if Max said no, how would he face him again? Or suppose Miriam, who harped so often on in-dependence, blew up in anger and shouted at him for his meddling? Still, the chance was too good to let by: all it meant was an in-troduction. They might long ago have be-come friends had they happened to meet somewhere, therefore was it not his duty—an obligation—to bring them together, noth-ing more, a harmless connivance to replace an accidental encounter in the subway, let's say, or a mutual friend's introduction in the street? Just let him once see and talk to her and he would for sure be interested. As for Miriam, what possible harm for a working girl in an office, who met only loud-mouthed

---

1. **last** *n*.: A block shaped like a person's foot, on which shoes are made or repaired.

Commentary: The Origin of the Literary Epiphany

The term "epiphany" is derived from Greek mythology where it was used to describe the occasion when a god or goddess, wearing a disguise or concealed in a cloud, would suddenly reveal his or her true identity to a mortal. In many Christian churches, Epiphany (spelled with a capital letter) refers to an annual festival held on January 6 (the twelfth day of Christmas), commemorating the revelation of the baby Jesus to the three wise men (Magi). Influenced by his religious upbringing, the highly regarded Irish novelist James Joyce (1882–1941) was the first writer to use the word as a literary term, defining it as a profound mental or spiritual revelation experienced by a charac-ter in a literary work. Although the term is still most often associated with the works of Joyce, epiphanies also occur in works by many other twentieth-century writers.

In his autobiographical narrative, *Stephen Hero,* which he later reworked into his first novel, *Portrait of the Artist as Young Man,* Joyce offered the following definition of an epiphany: "By an epiphany he [the protagonist, Stephen Daedalus] meant a

3 **Discussion** Why does Feld wait for Sobel to resume his work before talking to Max? What does this reveal about Feld's attitude toward Sobel?

4 **Clarification** Point out to students that Feld's manner of speaking indicates a Yiddish accent. The Yiddish accent is characterized by a musical quality and an uprising tone at the end of each sentence.

salesmen and illiterate shipping clerks, to make the acquaintance of a fine scholarly boy? Maybe he would awaken in her a desire to go to college; if not—the shoemaker's mind at last came to grips with the truth—let her marry an educated man and live a better life.

When Max finished describing what he wanted done to his shoes, Feld marked them, both with enormous holes in the soles which he pretended not to notice, with large white-chalk *x*'s, and the rubber heels, thinned to the nails, he marked with *o*'s, though it troubled him he might have mixed up the letters. Max inquired the price, and the shoemaker cleared his throat and asked the boy, above Sobel's insistent hammering, would he please step through the side door there into the hall. Though surprised, Max did as the shoemaker requested, and Feld went in after him. For a minute they were both silent, because Sobel had stopped banging, and it seemed they understood neither was to say anything until the noise began again. When it did, loudly, the shoemaker quickly told Max why he had asked to talk to him.

"Ever since you went to high school," he said, in the dimly-lit hallway, "I watched you in the morning go to the subway to school,

The First Seven Years   947

sudden spiritual manifestation whether in vulgarity of speech or of gesture or in a memorable phase of the mind itself. He believed it was for the man of letters to record these epiphanies with extreme care, seeing that they themselves are the most delicate and evanescent of moments."

5 **Critical Thinking and Reading**
Have students predict how Max will respond to Feld's proposition. Have them cite information about his character to support their prediction.

6 **Discussion** Why does Feld feel bad about the amount he charges Max for the shoes? Do you think he is justified for feeling this way, or is he over-reacting?

7 **Discussion** What might be the cause of Sobel's outburst?

8 **Reading Strategy** Have students give reasons why they think Malamud introduces this background information here rather than earlier in the story.

9 **Enrichment** Point out to students that many cities have ethnic neighborhoods, such as Little Italy or Little Poland. Have the students discuss the reasons why these neighborhoods exist. How do these neighborhoods make it easier for immigrants to adjust to life in America? What are the possible drawbacks of such communities?

and I said always to myself, this is a fine boy that he wants so much an education."

"Thanks," Max said, nervously alert. He was tall and grotesquely thin, with sharply cut features, particularly a beak-like nose. He was wearing a loose, long slushy overcoat that hung down to his ankles, looking like a rug draped over his bony shoulders, and a soggy, old brown hat, as battered as the shoes he had brought in.

"I am a business man," the shoemaker abruptly said to conceal his embarrassment, "so I will explain you right away why I talk to you. I have a girl, my daughter Miriam—she is nineteen—a very nice girl and also so pretty that everybody looks on her when she passes by in the street. She is smart, always with a book, and I thought to myself that a boy like you, an educated boy—I thought maybe you will be interested sometime to meet a girl like this." He laughed a bit when he had finished and was tempted to say more but had the good sense not to.

Max stared down like a hawk. For an uncomfortable second he was silent, then he asked, "Did you say nineteen?"

"Yes."

"Would it be all right to inquire if you have a picture of her?"

"Just a minute." The shoemaker went into the store and hastily returned with a snapshot that Max held up to the light.

"She's all right," he said.

Feld waited.

"And is she sensible—not the flighty kind?"

"She is very sensible."

After another short pause, Max said it was okay with him if he met her.

"Here is my telephone," said the shoemaker, hurriedly handing him a slip of paper. "Call her up. She comes home from work six o'clock."

Max folded the paper and tucked it away into his worn leather wallet.

"About the shoes," he said. "How much did you say they will cost me?"

"Don't worry about the price."

"I just like to have an idea."

"A dollar—dollar fifty. A dollar fifty," the shoemaker said.

At once he felt bad, for he usually charged two twenty-five for this kind of job. Either he should have asked the regular price or done the work for nothing.

Later, as he entered the store, he was startled by a violent clanging and looked up to see Sobel pounding with all his might upon the naked last. It broke, the iron striking the floor and jumping with a thump against the wall, but before the enraged shoemaker could cry out, the assistant had torn his hat and coat from the hook and rushed out into the snow.

So Feld, who had looked forward to anticipating how it would go with his daughter and Max, instead had a great worry on his mind. Without his temperamental helper he was a lost man, especially since it was years now that he had carried the store alone. The shoemaker had for an age suffered from a heart condition that threatened collapse if he dared exert himself. Five years ago, after an attack, it had appeared as though he would have either to sacrifice his business upon the auction block and live on a pittance thereafter, or put himself at the mercy of some unscrupulous employee who would in the end probably ruin him. But just at the moment of his darkest despair, this Polish refugee, Sobel, appeared one night from the street and begged for work. He was a stocky man, poorly dressed, with a bald head that had once been blond, a severely plain face and soft blue eyes prone to tears over the sad books he read, a young man but old—no one would have guessed thirty. Though he confessed he knew nothing of shoemaking, he said he was apt and would work for a very little if Feld taught him the trade. Thinking that with, after all, a landsman,[2] he would have less to fear than from a complete stranger, Feld took him on and within six

---

2. **landsman** *n.*: A fellow countryman.

Grammar in Action

Many writers find it difficult to use **who** and **whom** correctly. *Who* and *whom* are both interrogative and relative pronouns. As relative pronouns, they are used to form noun clauses and adjective clauses. The function of the pronoun within the clauses determines whether *who* or *whom* is the correct form. *Who* is the nominative case form; *whom* is the objective case form.

Look at the following sentence from Malamud's story:

Yet he could not help but contrast the diligence of the boy, *who* was a peddler's son, with Miriam's unconcern . . . (p. 1042)

Note that *who* is the subject of "who was a peddler's son."

Now look at the following sentence:

[Nothing] could turn his thoughts from Max, the college boy, . . . *whom* he so much respected . . . (p. 1042)

Note that *whom* is the direct object in "whom he so much respected." *Who* and *whom,* then, work like *he* and *him,* or *they* and *them.*

weeks the refugee rebuilt as good a shoe as he, and not long thereafter expertly ran the business for the thoroughly relieved shoemaker.

Feld could trust him with anything and did, frequently going home after an hour or two at the store, leaving all the money in the till, knowing Sobel would guard every cent of it. The amazing thing was that he demanded so little. His wants were few; in money he wasn't interested—in nothing but books, it seemed—which he one by one lent to Miriam, together with his profuse, queer written comments, manufactured during his lonely rooming house evenings, thick pads of commentary which the shoemaker peered at and twitched his shoulders over as his daughter, from her fourteenth year, read page by sanctified page, as if the word of God were inscribed on them. To protect Sobel, Feld himself had to see that he received more than he asked for. Yet his conscience bothered him for not insisting that the assistant accept a better wage than he was getting, though Feld had honestly told him he could earn a handsome salary if he worked elsewhere, or maybe opened a place of his own. But the assistant answered, somewhat ungraciously, that he was not interested in going elsewhere, and though Feld frequently asked himself what keeps him here? why does he stay? he finally answered it that the man, no doubt because of his terrible experiences as a refugee, was afraid of the world.

After the incident with the broken last, angered by Sobel's behavior, the shoemaker decided to let him stew for a week in the rooming house, although his own strength was taxed dangerously and the business suffered. However, after several sharp nagging warnings from both his wife and daughter, he went finally in search of Sobel, as he had once before, quite recently, when over some fancied slight—Feld had merely asked him not to give Miriam so many books to read because her eyes were strained and red—the assistant had left the place in a huff, an incident which, as usual, came to nothing for he

had returned after the shoemaker had talked to him, and taken his seat at the bench. But this time, after Feld had plodded through the snow to Sobel's house—he had thought of sending Miriam but the idea became repugnant to him—the burly landlady at the door informed him in a nasal voice that Sobel was not at home, and though Feld knew this was a nasty lie, for where had the refugee to go? still for some reason he was not completely sure of—it may have been the cold and his fatigue—he decided not to insist on seeing him. Instead he went home and hired a new helper.

Having settled the matter, though not entirely to his satisfaction, for he had much more to do than before, and so, for example, could no longer lie late in bed mornings because he had to get up to open the store for the new assistant, a speechless, dark man with an irritating rasp as he worked, whom he would not trust with the key as he had Sobel. Furthermore, this one, though able to do a fair repair job, knew nothing of grades of leather or prices, so Feld had to make his own purchases: and every night at closing time it was necessary to count the money in the till and lock up. However, he was not dissatisfied, for he lived much in his thoughts of Max and Miriam. The college boy had called her, and they had arranged a meeting for this coming Friday night. The shoemaker would personally have preferred Saturday, which he felt would make it a date of the first magnitude, but he learned Friday was Miriam's choice, so he said nothing. The day of the week did not matter. What mattered was the aftermath. Would they like each other and want to be friends? He sighed at all the time that would have to go by before he knew for sure. Often he was tempted to talk to Miriam about the boy, to ask whether she thought she would like his type—he had told her only that he considered Max a nice boy and had suggested he call her—but the one time he tried she snapped at him—justly—how should she know?

At last Friday came. Feld was not feeling

The First Seven Years   949

10 **Discussion** Why does Sobel require so little? Why does he choose to remain with Feld?

11 **Discussion** Why does the thought of sending Miriam become repugnant to Feld? What might he sense about the relationship between Feld and Miriam?

12 **Reading Strategy** Have students predict how Feld's decision to hire a new helper will affect his life.

13 **Discussion** How does Miriam's attitude about the upcoming date differ from Feld's? Have students cite information from the text that gives them clues about each character's attitudes.

Student Activity 1. Add *who* or *whom* to each of the following sentences.
1. Sobel, _____ read the classics, was Feld's helper.
2. Feld undercharged Max, _____ he wanted to become friends with his daughter.
3. Feld insulted Sobel, _____ he overlooked as a possible husband for Miriam.
4. Sobel, _____ loved Miriam, quit his job.
5. Feld never asked himself _____ Miriam liked.

Student Activity 2. Combine each pair of sentences, using *who* or *whom* to change the second sentence to a clause.
1. Suppose Miriam blew up in anger?
   Miriam harped so often on independence.
2. Feld wanted Miriam to meet the scholarly Max.
   Feld respected Max.
3. Sobel finally came back to work.
   Feld compared Sobel to himself.

949

14 **Reading Strategy** Have students predict whether or not the date will be a success.

15 **Discussion** What seems to be Miriam's attitude about the date?

16 **Discussion** What does Feld's response to the information about Max reveal about his character?

17 **Reading Strategy** Have students predict how Feld will respond to Miriam's statement.

18 **Clarification** The word *materialist* is commonly used with a negative connotation. It is a difficult word, and the Polish-born Feld is unlikely to know its meaning. Discuss what it means for Miriam to know the meaning of a word that Feld does not.

19 **Discussion** Do you think that Feld is a materialist? Discuss similarities and differences between Feld and Max.

particularly well so he stayed in bed, and Mrs. Feld thought it better to remain in the bedroom with him when Max called. Miriam received the boy, and her parents could hear their voices, his throaty one, as they talked. Just before leaving, Miriam brought Max to the bedroom door and he stood there a minute, a tall, slightly hunched figure wearing a thick, droopy suit, and apparently at ease as he greeted the shoemaker and his wife, which was surely a good sign. And Miriam, although she had worked all day, looked fresh and pretty. She was a large-framed girl with a well-shaped body, and she had a fine open face and soft hair. They made, Feld thought, a first-class couple.

Miriam returned after 11:30. Her mother was already asleep, but the shoemaker got out of bed and after locating his bathrobe went into the kitchen, where Miriam, to his surprise, sat at the table, reading.

"So where did you go?" Feld asked pleasantly.

"For a walk," she said, not looking up.

"I advised him," Feld said, clearing his throat, "he shouldn't spend so much money."

"I didn't care."

The shoemaker boiled up some water for tea and sat down at the table with a cupful and a thick slice of lemon.

"So how," he sighed after a sip, "did you enjoy?"

"It was all right."

He was silent. She must have sensed his disappointment, for she added, "You can't really tell much the first time."

"You will see him again?"

Turning a page, she said that Max had asked for another date.

"For when?"

"Saturday."

"So what did you say?"

"What did I say?" she asked, delaying for a moment—"I said yes."

Afterwards she inquired about Sobel, and Feld, without exactly knowing why, said the assistant had got another job. Miriam

said nothing more and began to read. The shoemaker's conscience did not trouble him; he was satisfied with the Saturday date.

During the week, by placing here and there a deft question, he managed to get from Miriam some information about Max. It surprised him to learn that the boy was not studying to be either a doctor or lawyer but was taking a business course leading to a degree in accountancy. Feld was a little disappointed because he thought of accountants as bookkeepers and would have preferred "a higher profession." However, it was not long before he had investigated the subject and discovered that Certified Public Accountants were highly respected people, so he was thoroughly content as Saturday approached. But because Saturday was a busy day, he was much in the store and therefore did not see Max when he came to call for Miriam. From his wife he learned there had been nothing especially revealing about their meeting. Max had rung the bell and Miriam had got her coat and left with him—nothing more. Feld did not probe, for his wife was not particularly observant. Instead, he waited up for Miriam with a newspaper on his lap, which he scarcely looked at so lost was he in thinking of the future. He awoke to find her in the room with him, tiredly removing her hat. Greeting her, he was suddenly inexplicably afraid to ask anything about the evening. But since she volunteered nothing he was at last forced to inquire how she had enjoyed herself. Miriam began something noncommittal but apparently changed her mind, for she said after a minute, "I was bored."

When Feld had sufficiently recovered from his anguished disappointment to ask why, she answered without hesitation, "Because he's nothing more than a materialist."

"What means this word?"

"He has no soul. He's only interested in things."

He considered her statement for a long time but then asked, "Will you see him again?"

"He didn't ask."

Grammer in Action

Transitions are words or phrases that connect thoughts and clarify relationships among ideas. By using transitions, writers can avoid choppiness and make their work smoother and easier to follow. Here are some examples of transitions from Malamud's story with the relationships they express:

During the week, by placing here and there a deft question, he managed . . . (Chronological)

But since she volunteered nothing . . . (Contrast)

Furthermore, this one, though able to do a fair job, knew nothing of grades . . . (Addition)

At the counter the man withdrew from a wet paper bag a pair of battered shoes . . . (Spatial Relationship)

Student Activity 1. Identify the transition used in each of the following sentences and specify the type of relationship it expresses.

1. When it did, loudly, the shoemaker quickly told Max why he had asked to talk to him.

2. Yet in his heart he knew there was no other way, and the first weary day back in the shop thoroughly convinced him, so that

"Suppose he will ask you?"

"I won't see him."

He did not argue; however, as the days went by he hoped increasingly she would change her mind. He wished the boy would telephone, because he was sure there was more to him than Miriam, with her inexperienced eye, could discern. But Max didn't call. As a matter of fact he took a different route to school, no longer passing the shoemaker's store, and Feld was deeply hurt.

Then one afternoon Max came in and asked for his shoes. The shoemaker took them down from the shelf where he had placed them, apart from the other pairs. He had done the work himself and the soles and heels were well built and firm. The shoes had been highly polished and somehow looked better than new. Max's Adam's apple went up once when he saw them, and his eyes had little lights in them.

"How much?" he asked, without directly looking at the shoemaker.

"Like I told you before," Feld answered sadly. "One dollar fifty cents."

Max handed him two crumpled bills and received in return a newly-minted silver half dollar.

He left. Miriam had not been mentioned. That night the shoemaker discovered that his new assistant had been all the while stealing from him, and he suffered a heart attack.

Though the attack was very mild, he lay in bed for three weeks. Miriam spoke of going for Sobel, but sick as he was Feld rose in wrath against the idea. Yet in his heart he knew there was no other way, and the first weary day back in the shop thoroughly convinced him, so that night after supper he dragged himself to Sobel's rooming house.

He toiled up the stairs, though he knew it was bad for him, and at the top knocked at the door. Sobel opened it and the shoemaker entered. The room was a small, poor one, with a single window facing the street. It contained a narrow cot, a low table and sev-eral stacks of books piled haphazardly around on the floor along the wall, which made him think how queer Sobel was, to be uneducated and read so much. He had once asked him, Sobel, why you read so much? and the assistant could not answer him. Did you ever study in a college someplace? he had asked but Sobel shook his head. He read, he said, to know. But to know what, the shoemaker demanded, and to know why? Sobel never explained, which proved he read much because he was queer.

Feld sat down to recover his breath. The assistant was resting on his bed with his heavy back to the wall. His shirt and trousers were clean, and his stubby fingers, away from the shoemaker's bench, were strangely pallid. His face was thin and pale, as if he had been shut in this room since the day he had bolted from the store.

"So when you will come back to work?" Feld asked him.

To his surprise, Sobel burst out, "Never."

Jumping up, he strode over to the window that looked out upon the miserable street. "Why should I come back?" he cried.

"I will raise your wages."

"Who cares for your wages!"

The shoemaker, knowing he didn't care, was at a loss what else to say.

"What do you want from me, Sobel?"

"Nothing."

"I always treated you like you was my son."

Sobel vehemently denied it. "So why you look for strange boys in the street they should go out with Miriam? Why you don't think of me?"

The shoemaker's hands and feet turned freezing cold. His voice became so hoarse he couldn't speak. At last he cleared his throat and croaked, "So what has my daughter got to do with a shoemaker thirty-five years old who works for me?"

"Why do you think I worked so long for you?" Sobel cried out. "For the stingy wages I sacrificed five years of my life so you could have to eat and drink and where to sleep?"

The First Seven Years 951

20 **Literary Focus** The story of Max and Miriam's relationship "ends" here. However, Malamud continues the story past the resolution of the two dates in order to tell of Feld's epiphany.

21 **Discussion** How do the events of the story lead to Feld's heart attack? Which event do you think most influenced Feld's fragile state?

22 **Reading Strategy** Have the students summarize the story up to this point. Then have them suggest events that might hasten Feld's recovery.

23 **Discussion** Why does Feld decide to try to see Sobel again?

24 **Discussion** This is the first line that Sobel has spoken in the story. What reasons might the author have had for having the character remain silent for so long?

25 **Reading Strategy** Have students find indications of Sobel's attachment to Miriam from earlier passages in the story.

26 **Literary Focus** Sobel's revelation of his love for Miriam will trigger the epiphany at the story's end. Discuss the indications that Feld was aware of this situation before he heard it from Sobel.

night after supper he dragged himself to Sobel's rooming house.

3. At once he felt bad, for he usually charged two twenty-five for this kind of job.

4. With his back to Feld, he stood at the window, fists clenched, and his shoulders shook with his choked sobbing.

5. Then he realized that what he had called ugly was not Sobel but Miriam's life if she married him.

Student Activity 2. Write a paragraph in which you use at least four transitions. Then identify the kind of relationship that each transition expresses.

"Then for what?" shouted the shoemaker.

"For Miriam," he blurted—"for her."

The shoemaker, after a time, managed to say, "I pay wages in cash, Sobel," and lapsed into silence. Though he was seething with excitement, his mind was coldly clear, and he had to admit to himself he had sensed all along that Sobel felt this way. He had never so much as thought it consciously, but he had felt it and was afraid.

27 "Miriam knows?" he muttered hoarsely.

"She knows."

"You told her?"

"No."

"Then how does she know?"

"How does she know?" Sobel said, "because she knows. She knows who I am and what is in my heart."

28 Feld had a sudden insight. In some devious way, with his books and commentary, Sobel had given Miriam to understand that he loved her. The shoemaker felt a terrible anger at him for his deceit.

"Sobel, you are crazy," he said bitterly. "She will never marry a man so old and ugly like you."

Sobel turned black with rage. He cursed the shoemaker, but then, though he trembled to hold it in, his eyes filled with tears and he broke into deep sobs. With his back to Feld, he stood at the window, fists clenched, and his shoulders shook with his choked sobbing.

29 Watching him, the shoemaker's anger diminished. His teeth were on edge with pity for the man, and his eyes grew moist. How strange and sad that a refugee, a grown man, bald and old with his miseries, who had by the skin of his teeth escaped Hitler's incinerators,[3] should fall in love, when he had got to America, with a girl less than half his age. Day after day, for five years he had sat at his bench, cutting and hammering away, waiting for the girl to become a woman, unable to ease his heart with speech, knowing no protest but desperation.

"Ugly I didn't mean," he said half aloud.

30
31 Then he realized that what he had called ugly was not Sobel but Miriam's life if she married him. He felt for his daughter a strange and gripping sorrow, as if she were already Sobel's bride, the wife, after all, of a shoemaker, and had in her life no more than her mother had had. And all his dreams for her—why he had slaved and destroyed his heart with anxiety and labor—all these dreams of a better life were dead.

The room was quiet. Sobel was standing by the window reading, and it was curious that when he read he looked young.

32 "She is only nineteen," Feld said brokenly. "This is too young yet to get married. Don't ask her for two years more, till she is twenty-one, then you can talk to her."

Sobel didn't answer. Feld rose and left. He went slowly down the stairs but once outside, though it was an icy night and the crisp falling snow whitened the street, he walked with a stronger stride.

33
34 But the next morning, when the shoemaker arrived, heavy-hearted, to open the store, he saw he needn't have come, for his assistant was already seated at the last, pounding leather for his love.

---

3. Hitler's incinerators: During World War II, millions of Jews were murdered by the Nazis under the direction of German dictator Adolf Hitler (1889–1945).

THINKING ABOUT THE SELECTION
Recalling

1. (a) Why does Feld respect Max? (b) How does Feld arrange to have Max meet Miriam?
2. (a) Why did Feld hire Sobel? (b) Why does he hire a new helper?
3. Why is Miriam uninterested in seeing Max again after their second date?
4. What happens when Feld discovers that his new assistant has been stealing from him?
5. (a) What does Sobel reveal about his feelings for Miriam when Feld visits him? (b) How does Feld respond to this revelation? (c) What does he tell Sobel before he leaves his room?

Interpreting

6. How does Feld's belief that he "wasted his youth" relate to his desires concerning his daughter?
7. (a) What does education represent to Feld? (b) What does it represent to Sobel?
8. What does Feld's inability to accept Miriam's assessment of Max's personality indicate about his own personality?
9. In what ways are Sobel and Feld similar?
10. Explain the title of this story.

Applying

11. "There are only two lasting bequests we can hope to give our children," wrote Hodding Carter. "One of these is roots; the other, wings." First discuss the meaning of this quotation. Then explain how it relates to the theme of this story.

ANALYZING LITERATURE
Understanding Epiphany

In many modern and contemporary stories, the action moves toward an **epiphany**, a moment when a character has a flash of insight about himself or herself, another character, a situation, or life in general.

1. What understanding concerning himself and his hopes for his daughter does Feld reach at the end of the story?
2. Why does he walk "with a stronger stride" when he leaves Sobel's rooming house?

CRITICAL THINKING AND READING
Predicting Future Events

When a writer ends a story without a resolution, it is up to you to predict how the conflict will be resolved or whether it will be resolved at all. To make a valid prediction, you must consider what the story reveals about the characters' personalities and try to determine how they would be likely to act in the future.

1. How do you think Feld's relationship with Sobel will change following the incident at Sobel's rooming house? Support your answer.
2. Do you think Sobel will wait for two years? Explain your answer.
3. Do you think Feld will ever be able to completely accept Sobel as a son-in-law? Why or why not?

THINKING AND WRITING
Writing About a Character

Write an essay in which you analyze Feld's personality. Start by rereading the story, focusing on Feld's feelings, actions, and desires. Then try to determine what his behavior reveals about his character. At some point in your essay, discuss Feld's revelation at the end of the story. Does he change? Do you sympathize with him? When you revise, make sure that you have used passages from the story to support your argument. When you finish revising, proofread your paper and share it with your classmates.

11. Suggested Response: It means that a parent should provide children with an awareness of their cultural heritage and of the experiences of their ancestors, while at the same time giving their children the freedom to shape their own futures. This echoes the theme of the story—that parents cannot shape the destinies of their children, but rather must accept and support the choices that their children make.

Challenge Do you think Feld will tell Miriam about his discussion with Sobel? Why or why not?

ANSWERS TO ANALYZING LITERATURE

1. Feld realizes that despite his desire that his daughter achieve a better life than his own, he cannot shape her life for her.
2. He walks with a stronger stride because of the revelation he has had and the way he has dealt with it.

ANSWERS TO CRITICAL THINKING AND READING

1. Suggested Response: Feld will be more conscious of Sobel's interactions with Miriam. However, his overall attitude toward Sobel probably will not change much.
2. Suggested Response: Yes, because he clearly loves her.
3. Suggested Response: No, because Sobel does not meet the expectations that he had for a son-in-law.

THINKING AND WRITING

For help with this assignment, students can refer to Lesson 9, "Writing About Character," in the Handbook of Writing About Literature.

Writing Across the Curriculum You might have students research and report on the history of a specific group of refugees in America. You may want to inform the history department of this assignment.

Closure and Extension

ANSWERS TO THINKING ABOUT THE SELECTION
Recalling

1. (a) Feld respects Max because he is pursuing further education. (b) When Max comes in to have his shoes repaired, Feld tells him about his daughter.
2. (a) Feld hired Sobel because he needed a helper and Sobel was a fellow Pole. (b) He hires a new helper because Sobel leaves.
3. She decides that he is a materialist and is uninteresting.
4. He has a heart attack.
5. (a) He is in love with her. (b) He is shocked and horrified. (c) He tells Sobel that he can ask Miriam to marry him in two years.

Interpreting

6. He does not want Miriam to waste her youth the way he did.
7. (a) Feld views education as a means of gaining respect and achieving financial success. (b) It represents an opportunity to enrich himself by expanding his knowledge and helping him to better understand the world.
8. Feld cannot accept facts that do not conform to his beliefs; he is stubborn.
9. They both love Miriam and are willing to make sacrifices for her.
10. The title refers to the first seven years of the relationship between Sobel and Miriam.

Flannery O'Connor's stories revolve around deaths and dark
humor. Some critics have objected to the fact that so many of her
stories end with death. O'Connor, however, felt that this structure reflected the lack of possibilities available in many people's
lives. Because of the pain and
difficulty of her disease, she
developed a gallows humor in
the face of death that is entertaining, if somewhat morbid. Ask
students to discuss why her condition might have affected her in
this way. What type of attitude
might she have had about her
own condition?

Critical Evaluation In his article
"The Power of Flannery O'Connor," the well-known literary critic
Frederick Crews observes that
"O'Connor's fiction regularly presents us with a grimmer, more
godforsaken world than we could
have guessed from her collected
remarks about it. At the same
time, however, that world is suffused with a portentousness
whose undeniable source is the
author's religion—her belief in a
looming metaphysical presence
that casts an ironic shadow on
nearly everything her characters
attempt to do. Her best writing is
that in which 'mystery'' as she
called it, drastically intrudes on
the mundane without requiring
us either to embrace a dogma or
to suspend our belief in naturalistic causation."

FLANNERY O'CONNOR

1925–1964

Flannery O'Connor's work reflects her intense commitment to her
personal beliefs. In her exaggerated, tragic, and at times shockingly
violent tales, she forces us to confront such human faults as hypocrisy, insensitivity, self-centeredness, and prejudice.

O'Connor was born in Savannah, Georgia, and was raised in the
small Georgia town of Milledgeville. She was educated at the Georgia
State College for Women and studied at the University of Iowa Writers' Workshop. When she was twenty-seven, she published her first
novel, *Wise Blood,* the story of a violent rivalry among the members
of a fictional religious sect in the South. In 1955 she published her
first collection of short stories, *A Good Man Is Hard to Find*. This was
followed in 1960 by a second novel, *The Violent Bear It Away;* and in
1965 *Everything That Rises Must Converge,* another collection of her
stories, was published.

Unfortunately, throughout most of her adult life, O'Connor suffered from lupus, a rare disease that eventually took her life. Because
her disease set her apart from other people, O'Connor developed a
deep sensitivity to misfits and outsiders. Not surprisingly, many of her
most memorable characters are social outcasts or people who are in
some way mentally or physically disabled. Although she portrays
these characters in an unsentimental manner, there is an underlying
sense of sympathy concerning their pain and suffering.

O'Connor's work reflects her strong Catholic faith, and she had
this to say about the relationship between her faith and her writing:
"When people have told me that because I am a Catholic, I cannot be
an artist, I have had to reply, ruefully, that because I am a Catholic I
cannot afford to be less than an artist." She lived in the true Bible Belt
of the South and acknowledged readily that her people had a strong
sense of the absolute. Whatever she viewed, she viewed from the
standpoint of Christian orthodoxy, which centered on the belief that
sinfulness in humans must be redeemed through Christ. She strongly
believed that man would be defeated unless he acknowledged his obligation to obey God. These beliefs permeate her work. In O'Connor
stories violent or grotesque characters often symbolize moral defor-
mity and are impelled toward damnation from which the only salvation
is divine awareness and redemption.

"The Life You Save May Be Your Own" is a typical O'Connor
story. A grim depiction of a group of outcasts, the story conveys a
powerful moral message, capturing a number of the tragic realities of
life in the modern world.

954 *Contemporary Writers*

GUIDE FOR INTERPRETING

The Life You Save May Be Your Own

Writer's Techniques

Irony. Irony is a contrast or a difference between what is stated and what is meant, or between what is expected to happen and what actually happens. "The Life You Save May Be Your Own" is filled with situational irony—one of a number of different types of irony used in literature. This type of irony occurs when the actual result of an action or situation is quite different from the expected result. Much of the situational irony in O'Connor's story results from the contrast between the main character's comments and actions. This character, Mr. Shiftlet, complains that there is a lack of morality in the world and that people have no concern for others, yet his actions in the story make it clear that he himself lacks morality and has little concern for others.

Flannery O'Connor possessed a deep awareness of the irony and hypocrisy that exist in everyday life. A devoutly religious woman, O'Connor was disturbed by the fact that many people claim to have deep religious convictions yet behave in a manner that totally contradicts this claim. This type of hypocrisy is embodied in the character of Mr. Shiftlet, whose actions clearly contradict the beliefs he professes.

Commentary

Sometimes there is a gulf between what you see and what you hear. As you read this Flannery O'Connor story, you will notice that Mr. Shiftlet says one thing and does another. Ms. O'Connor reflects that situational irony in her story also in the way she first presents the character to you, forcing you to choose between what you are told and what you see. In the first sentence, you meet the old woman at home on her porch, and you are inclined to find her a solid citizen whose impressions you can believe. The narrator tells you she "could tell . . . that this tramp was no one to be afraid of," and you have no reason to mistrust her judgment. However, O'Connor then describes Shiftlet in ways that make you feel uneasy. He has half an arm, and "long black slick hair that hung flat from a part in the middle to beyond the tips of his ears on either side." Although you might intuitively respond to such details with suspicion, you will quickly decide you are wrong since the obviously sound old woman sees nothing to fear in Shiftlet. Thus, O'Connor's subtle writing puts you in the same position as the characters in the story who encounter Mr. Shiftlet.

Writing

The title of the story is a slogan that commonly appeared on American highways a number of years ago. The slogan urged motorists to drive carefully to avoid killing themselves. Discuss the significance of this slogan. Freewrite about this slogan. Whom else might a motorist's reckless driving affect? To what type of motives does the slogan appeal? What does it imply about human nature?

Guide for Interpreting 955

Literary Focus Situational irony is often linked to hypocrisy. Mr. Shiftlet's speeches about morality and the increasing mechanization of the world are hypocritical as well as ironic in view of his actions in the story.

Writing/Prior Knowledge Have the class discuss the meanings of other cautionary signs, such as the surgeon general's warning on cigarettes or the safety belt campaigns. Discuss which slogans they think are most successful, and identify what makes people pay attention to them.

Vocabulary

Preteach the following vocabulary words:

desolate (dəs' ə lit) *adj.:* Forlorn; wretched (p. 956)
listed (list' id) *v.:* Swayed (p. 956)
ominous (äm' ə nəs) *adj.:* Threatening; sinister (p. 957)
ravenous (rav' ə nəs) *adj.:* Extremely eager (p. 960)
morose (mə rōs') *adj.:* Gloomy, sullen (p. 962)
guffawing (gə fo'iŋ) *adj.:* Laughing in a loud, coarse manner (p. 964)

Motivation/Prior Knowledge
Discuss what is necessary for one person to gain another's trust. What attributes make a person trustworthy? What might happen if someone misplaces trust in another person?

Master Teacher Note Like many O'Connor stories, this story deals with characters who are physically disabled. To help students understand the characters' behavior, have them discuss the ways in which a physical handicap can affect a person's behavior and the ways in which it can affect other peoples' behavior toward them.

Thematic Idea Another selection that deals with a handicapped child is "Average Waves in Unprotected Waters" by Anne Tyler, page 968. Have students compare the characters of Lucynell and Arnold.

Purpose-Setting Question
What effect does Mr. Shiftlet have on the family that he visits?

1 **Reading Strategy** Have students pay close attention to the details of the setting. Discuss how the details of the setting reflect the events in the story.

2 **Discussion** What does the old woman's body language tell you about how she plans to deal with the stranger?

The Life You Save May Be Your Own

Flannery O'Connor

The old woman and her daughter were sitting on their porch when Mr. Shiftlet came up their road for the first time. The old woman slid to the edge of her chair and leaned forward, shading her eyes from the piercing sunset with her hand. The daughter could not see far in front of her and continued to play with her fingers. Although the old woman lived in this desolate spot with only her daughter and she had never seen Mr. Shiftlet before, she could tell, even from a distance, that he was a tramp and no one to be afraid of. His left coat sleeve was folded up to show there was only half an arm in it and his gaunt figure listed slightly to the side as if the breeze were pushing him. He had on a black town suit and a brown felt hat that was turned up in the front and down in the back and he carried a tin tool box by a handle. He came on, at an amble, up her road, his face turned toward the sun which appeared to be balancing itself on the peak of a small mountain.

The old woman didn't change her position until he was almost into her yard; then she rose with one hand fisted on her hip. The daughter, a large girl in a short blue organdy dress, saw him all at once and jumped up and began to stamp and point and make excited speechless sounds.

Mr. Shiftlet stopped just inside the yard and set his box on the ground and tipped his hat at her as if she were not in the least afflicted; then he turned toward the old woman and swung the hat all the way off. He had long black slick hair that hung flat from a part in the middle to beyond the tips of his ears on either side. His face descended in forehead for more than half its length and ended suddenly with his features just balanced over a jutting steel-trap jaw. He seemed to be a young man but he had a look of composed dissatisfaction as if he understood life thoroughly.

"Good evening," the old woman said. She was about the size of a cedar fence post and she had a man's gray hat pulled down low over her head.

The tramp stood looking at her and didn't answer. He turned his back and faced the sunset. He swung both his whole and his short arm up slowly so that they indicated an expanse of sky and his figure formed a crooked cross. The old woman watched him with her arms folded across her chest as if she were the owner of the sun, and the daughter watched, her head thrust forward and her fat helpless hands hanging at the wrists. She had long pink-gold hair and eyes as blue as a peacock's neck.

He held the pose for almost fifty seconds and then he picked up his box and came on to the porch and dropped down on the bottom step. "Lady," he said in a firm nasal

Primary Source

In her book *Vulnerable People: A View of American Fiction Since 1945* the literary scholar Josephine Hendin offers the following characterization of O'Connor's work: "Flannery O'Connor is a superb writer whose refusal to feel concerned brought her stories a force and authority that only increased as she fought a losing battle. The writer speaks to the condition of the child, the woman, the sick man whose weakness only marshalls dreams of strength ... O'Connor filled her stories with women who are always in need, or men who are bound to their mothers by infantile need ... The fiction O'Connor lived had its roots in that Southern need to do pretty regardless of what you feel and in her own remarkable ability to divorce behavior from feeling ... O'Connor wrote about what she knew best; what it means to be a living contradiction. For her it meant an eternal cheeriness and suffering; graciousness and fear of human contact, acquiescence and enduring fury. Whether through some great effort of the will or through some more mysterious and unconscious force, she created from that strife a powerful art, and art that was both a release from and a vindication for her life. If she set out to make

voice, "I'd give a fortune to live where I could see me a sun do that every evening."

"Does it every evening," the old woman said and sat back down. The daughter sat down too and watched him with a cautious sly look as if he were a bird that had come up very close. He leaned to one side, rooting in his pants pocket, and in a second he brought out a package of chewing gum and offered her a piece. She took it and unpeeled it and began to chew without taking her eyes off him. He offered the old woman a piece but she only raised her upper lip to indicate she had no teeth.

Mr. Shiftlet's pale sharp glance had already passed over everything in the yard—the pump near the corner of the house and the big fig tree that three or four chickens were preparing to roost in—and had moved to a shed where he saw the square rusted back of an automobile. "You ladies drive?" he asked.

"That car ain't run in fifteen year," the old woman said. "The day my husband died, it quit running."

"Nothing is like it used to be, lady," he said. "The world is almost rotten."

"That's right," the old woman said. "You from around here?"

"Name Tom T. Shiftlet," he murmured, looking at the tires.

"I'm pleased to meet you," the old woman said. "Name Lucynell Crater and daughter Lucynell Crater. What you doing around here, Mr. Shiftlet?"

He judged the car to be about a 1928 or '29 Ford. "Lady," he said, and turned and gave her his full attention, "lemme tell you something. There's one of these doctors in Atlanta that's taken a knife and cut the human heart—the human heart," he repeated, leaning forward, "out of a man's chest and held it in his hand," and he held his hand out, palm up, as if it were slightly weighted with the human heart, "and studied it like it was a day-old chicken, and lady," he said, allowing a long significant pause in which his head slid forward and his clay-colored eyes brightened, "he don't know no more about it than you or me."

"That's right," the old woman said.

"Why, if he was to take that knife and cut into every corner of it, he still wouldn't know no more than you or me. What you want to bet?"

"Nothing," the old woman said wisely. "Where you come from, Mr. Shiftlet?"

He didn't answer. He reached into his pocket and brought out a sack of tobacco and a package of cigarette papers and rolled himself a cigarette, expertly with one hand, and attached it in a hanging position to his upper lip. Then he took a box of wooden matches from his pocket and struck one on his shoe. He held the burning match as if he were studying the mystery of flame while it traveled dangerously toward his skin. The daughter began to make loud noises and to point to his hand and shake her finger at him, but when the flame was just before touching him, he leaned down with his hand cupped over it as if were going to set fire to his nose and lit the cigarette.

He flipped away the dead match and blew a stream of gray into the evening. A sly look came over his face. "Lady," he said, "nowadays, people'll do anything anyways. I can tell you my name is Tom T. Shiftlet and I come from Tarwater, Tennessee. but you never have seen me before: how you know I ain't lying? How you know my name ain't Aaron Sparks, lady, and I come from Singleberry, Georgia, or how you know it's not George Speeds and I come from Lucy, Alabama, or how you know I ain't Thompson Bright from Toolafalls, Mississippi?"

"I don't know nothing about you," the old woman muttered, irked.

"Lady," he said, "people don't care how they lie. Maybe the best I can tell you is, I'm a man; but listen lady," he said and paused and made his tone more ominous still, "what is a man?"

The old woman began to gum a seed.

The Life You Save May Be Your Own   957

3 **Discussion** How are Mr. Shiftlet's and the woman's views of the sunset different?

4 **Discussion** What does Mr. Shiftlet's speech about the doctor suggest about his character?

5 **Discussion** Why do you think Mr. Shiftlet chooses not to answer? Do you think that it is important for the woman to know where he came from? Why or why not?

6 **Literary Focus** Why might Mr. Shiftlet's comments turn out to be ironic?

morals to praise old values, she ended by engulfing all of them in an icy violence. If she began by mocking or damning her murderous heroes she ended by exalting them. Flannery O'Connor became more and more the pure poet of the Misfit, the damaged daughter, the psychic cripple—of all of those who are martyred by silent fury and redeemed through violence."

"What you carry in that tin box, Mr. Shiftlet?" she asked.

"Tools," he said, put back. "I'm a carpenter."

"Well, if you come out here to work, I'll be able to feed you and give you a place to sleep but I can't pay. I'll tell you that before you begin," she said.

There was no answer at once and no particular expression on his face. He leaned back against the two-by-four that helped support the porch roof. "Lady," he said slowly, "there's some men that some things mean more to them than money." The old woman rocked without comment and the daughter watched the trigger that moved up and down in his neck. He told the old woman then that all most people were interested in was money, but he asked what a man was made for. He asked her if a man was made for money, or what. He asked her what she thought she was made for but she didn't answer, she only sat rocking and wondered if a one-armed man could put a new roof on her garden house. He asked a lot of questions that she didn't answer. He told her that he was twenty-eight years old and had lived a varied life. He had been a gospel singer, a foreman on the railroad, an assistant in an undertaking parlor, and he come over the radio for three months with Uncle Roy and his Red Creek Wranglers. He said he had fought and bled in the Arm Service of his country and visited every foreign land and that everywhere he had seen people that didn't care if they did a thing one way or another. He said he hadn't been raised that-away.

A fat yellow moon appeared in the branches of the fig tree as if it were going to roost there with the chickens. He said that a man had to escape to the country to see the world whole and that he wished he lived in a desolate place like this where he could see the sun go down every evening like God made it to do.

"Are you married or are you single?" the old woman asked.

BLACK WALNUTS, 1945
Joseph Pollet
Collection of the Whitney Museum of American Art

Humanities Note

Fine art; *Black Walnuts,* 1945, Joseph Pollet. Joseph Pollet, a Swiss-American painter was born in 1897. He studied painting at the Art Students League in New York City with the innovative American realist painter, John Sloan. The painting *Black Walnuts* shows the influence of Sloan's teachings in the stop-action quality of the scene. This study of a little girl swinging from black walnut trees is presented with a sense of emotion that would not be possible with a photograph. Painters in the Depression era focused on everyday images from the American heartland. Paintings by Americans, for Americans, was the primary motivation for the art of the day.

As students read the story and look at the art, you might ask these questions:

1. What is the mood or feeling evoked by this painting?
2. How does the artist create this mood?
3. In what way is this mood similar to or different from that in the story?
4. What other aspects of this painting reflect aspects of the story?

10 **Reading Strategy** Have students predict what will happen when Mr. Shiftlet comes to live with the family.

11 **Literary Focus** The old woman's assertion that the monks were not as advanced as modern man is ironically juxtaposed with Shiftlet's uncivilized behavior later in the story.

12 **Discussion** The narrator does not mention directly until this point that Lucynell is deaf. Why do you think the narrator omitted this information from the first scene? What clues did the narrator give about Lucynell's condition?

13 **Discussion** Why do you think the woman is "ravenous for a son-in-law?"

14 **Enrichment** The assembly line was introduced by Henry Ford in 1913. Although it greatly increased the efficiency of production, many people feared that the quality of the product might suffer. Discuss the idea of assembly-line production and how the introduction of this system reflects the essence of twentieth-century life.

There was a long silence. "Lady," he asked finally, "where would you find you an innocent woman today? I wouldn't have any of this trash I could just pick up."

The daughter was leaning very far down, hanging her head almost between her knees watching him through a triangular door she had made in her overturned hair; and she suddenly fell in a heap on the floor and began to whimper. Mr. Shiftlet straightened her out and helped her get back in the chair.

"Is she your baby girl?" he asked.

"My only," the old woman said "and she's the sweetest girl in the world. I would give her up for nothing on earth. She's smart too. She can sweep the floor, cook, wash, feed the chickens, and hoe. I wouldn't give her up for a casket of jewels."

"No," he said kindly, "don't ever let any man take her away from you."

"Any man come after her," the old woman said, " 'll have to stay around the place."

Mr. Shiftlet's eye in the darkness was focused on a part of the automobile bumper that glittered in the distance. "Lady," he said, jerking his short arm up as if he could point with it to her house and yard and pump, "there ain't a broken thing on this plantation that I couldn't fix for you, one-arm jackleg or not. I'm a man," he said with a sullen dignity, "even if I ain't a whole one. I got," he said, tapping his knuckles on the floor to emphasize the immensity of what he was going to say, "a moral intelligence!" and his face pierced out of the darkness into a shaft of doorlight and he stared at her as if he were astonished himself at this impossible truth.

10 The old woman was not impressed with the phrase. "I told you you could hang around and work for food," she said, "if you don't mind sleeping in that car yonder."

11 "Why listen, lady," he said with a grin of delight, "the monks of old slept in their coffins!"

"They wasn't as advanced as we are," the old woman said.

The next morning he began on the roof of the garden house while Lucynell, the daughter, sat on a rock and watched him work. He had not been around a week before the change he had made in the place was apparent. He had patched the front and back steps, built a new hog pen, restored a fence, and taught Lucynell, who was completely deaf and had never said a word in her life, to say the word "bird." The big rosy-faced girl followed him everywhere, saying "Burrttddt ddbirrrttdt," and clapping her hands. The old woman watched from a distance, secretly pleased. She was ravenous for a son-in-law.

12

13

Mr. Shiftlet slept on the hard narrow back seat of the car with his feet out the side window. He had his razor and a can of water on a crate that served him as a bedside table and he put up a piece of mirror against the back glass and kept his coat neatly on a hanger that he hung over one of the windows.

In the evenings he sat on the steps and talked while the old woman and Lucynell rocked violently in their chairs on either side of him. The old woman's three mountains were black against the dark blue sky and were visited off and on by various planets and by the moon after it had left the chickens. Mr. Shiftlet pointed out that the reason he had improved this plantation was because he had taken a personal interest in it. He said he was even going to make the automobile run.

14 He had raised the hood and studied the mechanism and he said he could tell that the car had been built in the days when cars were really built. You take now, he said, one man puts in one bolt and another man puts in another bolt and another man puts in another bolt so that it's a man for a bolt. That's why you have to pay so much for a car: you're paying all those men. Now if you didn't have to pay but one man, you could get you a cheaper car and one that had had a personal interest taken in it, and it would be a better car. The old woman agreed with him that this was so.

Grammar in Action

To express a condition that is not factual, use the **subjunctive mood** of the verb. The subjunctive is appropriate in clauses that express two types of conditions: those that express a proposal, a demand, or a request; and those that draw a comparison between something factual and something untrue. Note the following examples:

Mrs. Crater suggested *that Shiftlet marry her daughter.*

Mr. Shiftlet talked *as if he were an ethical person.*

The subjunctive form of a present-tense, third-person singular verb does not have the usual -s or -es ending. Also, the present subjunctive form of *be* is always *be,* and the past form is always *were,* regardless of the subject of the clause.

Student Activity 1. Decide which of the following sentences have a clause in the subjunctive. Then indicate the verb that is in the subjunctive form.

1. She watched him as if she were the owner of the sun.
2. Mr. Shiftlet stopped just inside the yard.

Mr. Shiftlet said that the trouble with the world was that nobody cared, or stopped and took any trouble. He said he never would have been able to teach Lucynell to say a word if he hadn't cared and stopped long enough.

"Teach her to say something else," the old woman said.

"What you want her to say next?" Mr. Shiftlet asked.

The old woman's smile was broad and toothless and suggestive. "Teach her to say 'sugarpie,'" she said.

Mr. Shiftlet already knew what was on her mind.

The next day he began to tinker with the automobile and that evening he told her that if she would buy a fan belt, he would be able to make the car run.

The old woman said she would give him the money. "You see that girl yonder?" she asked, pointing to Lucynell who was sitting on the floor a foot away, watching him, her eyes blue even in the dark. "If it was ever a man wanted to take her away, I would say, 'No man on earth is going to take that sweet girl of mine away from me!' but if he was to say, 'Lady, I don't want to take her away, I want her right here,' I would say, 'Mister, I don't blame you none. I wouldn't pass up a chance to live in a permanent place and get the sweetest girl in the world myself. You ain't no fool,' I would say."

"How old is she?" Mr. Shiftlet asked casually.

"Fifteen, sixteen," the old woman said. The girl was nearly thirty but because of her innocence it was impossible to guess.

"It would be a good idea to paint it too," Mr. Shiftlet remarked. "You don't want it to rust out."

"We'll see about that later," the old woman said.

The next day he walked into town and returned with the parts he needed and a can of gasoline. Late in the afternoon, terrible noises issued from the shed and the old woman rushed out of the house, thinking Lucynell was somewhere having a fit. Lucynell was sitting on a chicken crate, stamping her feet and screaming, "Burrdttt! bddurrd-dttt!" but her fuss was drowned out by the car. With a volley of blasts it emerged from the shed, moving in a fierce and stately way. Mr. Shiftlet was in the driver's seat, sitting very erect. He had an expression of serious modesty on his face as if he had just raised the dead.

That night, rocking on the porch, the old woman began her business, at once. "You want you an innocent woman, don't you?" she asked sympathetically. "You don't want none of this trash."

"No'm, I don't," Mr. Shiftlet said.

"One that can't talk," she continued, "can't sass you back or use foul language. That's the kind for you to have. Right there," and she pointed to Lucynell sitting cross-legged in her chair, holding both feet in her hands.

"That's right," he admitted. "She wouldn't give me any trouble."

"Saturday," the old woman said, "you and her and me can drive into town and get married."

Mr. Shiftlet eased his position on the steps.

"I can't get married right now," he said. "Everything you want to do takes money and I ain't got any."

"What you need with money?" she asked.

"It takes money," he said. "Some people'll do anything anyhow these days, but the way I think, I wouldn't marry no woman that I couldn't take on a trip like she was somebody. I mean take her to a hotel and treat her. I wouldn't marry the Duchesser Windsor," he said firmly, "unless I could take her to a hotel and giver something good to eat.

"I was raised thataway and there ain't a thing I can do about it. My old mother taught me how to do."

"Lucynell don't even know what a hotel is," the old woman muttered. "Listen here,

The Life You Save May Be Your Own 961

961

---

15 **Discussion** Why does Mr. Shiftlet often pass judgment on the world around him? Are his observations usually accurate? Explain.

16 **Reading Strategy** Have students summarize the story up to this point, and predict whether or not Mr. Shiftlet will be interested in marrying Lucynell.

17 **Discussion** What techniques does the woman use to try to convince Mr. Shiftlet that he should marry her daughter? Why does she lie about Lucynell's age?

18 **Clarification** The reference to raising the dead could be interpreted as a reference to Christ's raising of Lazarus from the dead.

19 **Discussion** Do you think that Mr. Shiftlet really wants the money to provide Lucynell with a proper honeymoon?

---

3. He had long black slick hair.
4. Shiftlet proposed that he get the car running.
5. The daughter watched him as if he were a bird.
6. He took a box of wooden matches from his pocket.
7. A fat moon appeared as if it were going to roost there.
8. Mrs. Crater insisted that Shiftlet marry Lucynell.

Student Activity 2. Supply the subjunctive forms of the verbs in each of the following sentences.
1. Shiftlet acted as if he (be) interested in Lucynell.
2. Mrs. Crater demanded that any man who wanted to marry Lucynell (stay) and (live) on the farm.

3. Shiftlet insisted that he (be) able to take Lucynell to a hotel and buy her something to eat.
4. Shiftlet held the match as if he (be) going to set fire to his nose.
5. Shiftlet's peculiar morality required that he (praise) his mother to the hitchhiker.
6. The hitchhiker reached as if he (be) the only person in the story who knew Shiftlet.

Student Activity 3. Explain why O'Connor made extensive use of the subjunctive in this story.

20 Critical Thinking and Reading
Shiftlet's comment foreshadows the outcome of the story.

21 Discussion What does the description of Mr. Shiftlet's smile suggest? Find other examples in which the narrator reveals the characters' personalities through physical descriptions.

22 Discussion Neither the woman nor Mr. Shiftlet consider asking Lucynell about the marriage; they assume that she will agree. Why do they assume this? How do you think Lucynell might feel about the arrangement?

23 Discussion Why didn't the ceremony satisfy Mr. Shiftlet?

Mr. Shiftlet," she said, sliding forward in her chair, "you'd be getting a permanent house and a deep well and the most innocent girl in the world. You don't need no money. Lemme tell you something: there ain't any place in the world for a poor disabled friendless drifting man."

The ugly words settled in Mr. Shiftlet's head like a group of buzzards in the top of a tree. He didn't answer at once. He rolled himself a cigarette and lit it and then he said in an even voice, "Lady, a man is divided into two parts, body and spirit."

The old woman clamped her gums together.

20 "A body and a spirit," he repeated. "The body, lady, is like a house: it don't go anywhere; but the spirit, lady, is like a automobile: always on the move, always . . ."

"Listen, Mr. Shiftlet," she said, "my well never goes dry and my house is always warm in the winter and there's no mortgage on a thing about this place. You can go to the courthouse and see for yourself. And yonder under that shed is a fine automobile." She laid the bait carefully. "You can have it painted by Saturday. I'll pay for the paint."

21 In the darkness, Mr. Shiftlet's smile stretched like a weary snake waking up by a fire. After a second he recalled himself and said, "I'm only saying a man's spirit means more to him than anything else. I would have to take my wife off for the weekend without no regards at all for cost. I got to follow where my spirit says to go."

"I'll give you fifteen dollars for a weekend trip," the old woman said in a crabbed voice. "That's the best I can do."

"That wouldn't hardly pay for more than the gas and the hotel," he said. "It wouldn't feed her."

"Seventeen-fifty," the old woman said. "That's all I got so it isn't any use you trying to milk me. You can take a lunch."

Mr. Shiftlet was deeply hurt by the word "milk." He didn't doubt that she had more money sewed up in her mattress but he had al-

ready told her he was not interested in her money. "I'll make that do," he said and rose and walked off without treating with her further.

22

On Saturday the three of them drove into town in the car that the paint had barely dried on and Mr. Shiftlet and Lucynell were married in the Ordinary's office while the old woman witnessed. As they came out of the courthouse, Mr. Shiftlet began twisting his neck in his collar. He looked morose and bitter as if he had been insulted while someone held him. "That didn't satisfy me none," he said. "That was just something a woman in an office did, nothing but paper work and blood tests. What do they know about my blood? If they was to take my heart and cut it out," he said, "they wouldn't know a thing about me. It didn't satisfy me at all."

23

"It satisfied the law," the old woman said sharply.

"The law," Mr. Shiftlet said and spit. "It's the law that don't satisfy me."

He had painted the car dark green with a yellow band around it just under the windows. The three of them climbed in the front seat and the old woman said, "Don't Lucynell look pretty? Looks like a baby doll." Lucynell was dressed up in a white dress that her mother had uprooted from a trunk and there was a Panama hat on her head with a bunch of red wooden cherries on the brim. Every now and then her placid expression was changed by a sly isolated little thought like a shoot of green in the desert. "You got a prize!" the old woman said.

Mr. Shiftlet didn't even look at her.

They drove back to the house to let the old woman off and pick up the lunch. When they were ready to leave, she stood staring in the window of the car, with her fingers clenched around the glass. Tears began to seep sideways out of her eyes and run along the dirty creases in her face. "I ain't ever been parted with her for two days before," she said.

Mr. Shiftlet started the motor.

"And I wouldn't let no man have her but

Grammar in Action

Dialect is spoken language whose use is restricted to a specific geographical region or to a specific social or ethnic group. When writing dialogue, writers often have their characters speak in dialect to make the conversation seem more realistic and to capture the flavor of the setting. For example, note Flannery O'Connor's use of dialect in the following passage of dialogue from "The Life You Save May Be Your Own":

"That didn't satisfy me none," he said. "That was just something a woman in the office did, nothing but paper work and blood tests. What do they know about my blood? If they was to take my heart and cut it out," he said, "they wouldn't know a thing about me. It didn't satisfy me at all."

"It satisfied the law," the old woman said sharply.

"The law," Mr. Shiftlet said and spit. "It's the law that don't satisfy me."

Student Activity 1. Rewrite all of the following passages of dialogue, replacing the dialect with standard English. Then explain why removing the dialect would make the story less effective.

you because I seen you would do right. Good-bye, Sugarbaby," she said, clutching at the sleeve of the white dress. Lucynell looked straight at her and didn't seem to see her there at all. Mr. Shiftlet eased the car forward so that she had to move her hands.

The early afternoon was clear and open and surrounded by pale blue sky. Although the car would go only thirty miles an hour, Mr. Shiftlet imagined a terrific climb and dip and swerve that went entirely to his head so that he forgot his morning bitterness. He had always wanted an automobile but he had never been able to afford one before. He drove very fast because he wanted to make Mobile by nightfall.

Occasionally he stopped his thoughts long enough to look at Lucynell in the seat beside him. She had eaten the lunch as soon as they were out of the yard and now she was pulling the cherries off the hat one by one and throwing them out the window. He became depressed in spite of the car. He had driven about a hundred miles when he decided that she must be hungry again and at the next small town they came to, he stopped in front of an aluminum-painted eating place called The Hot Spot and took her in and ordered her a plate of ham and grits. The ride had made her sleepy and as soon as she got up on the stool, she rested her head on the counter and shut her eyes. There was no one in The Hot Spot but Mr. Shiftlet and the boy behind the counter, a pale youth with a greasy rag hung over his shoulder. Before he could dish up the food, she was snoring gently.

"Give it to her when she wakes up," Mr. Shiftlet said. "I'll pay for it now."

The boy bent over her and stared at the long pink-gold hair and the half-shut sleeping eyes. Then he looked up and stared at Mr. Shiftlet. "She looks like an angel of Gawd," he murmured.

"Hitchhiker," Mr. Shiftlet explained. "I can't wait. I got to make Tuscaloosa."

The boy bent over again and very carefully touched his finger to a strand of the golden hair and Mr. Shiftlet left.

He was more depressed than ever as he drove on by himself. The late afternoon had grown hot and sultry and the country had flattened out. Deep in the sky a storm was preparing very slowly and without thunder as if it meant to drain every drop of air from the earth before it broke. There were times when Mr. Shiftlet preferred not to be alone. He felt too that a man with a car had a responsibility to others and he kept his eye out for a hitchhiker. Occasionally he saw a sign that warned: "Drive carefully. The life you save may be your own."

The narrow road dropped off on either side into dry fields and here and there a shack or a filling station stood in a clearing. The sun began to set directly in front of the automobile. It was a reddening ball that through his windshield was slightly flat on the bottom and top. He saw a boy in overalls and a gray hat standing on the edge of the road and he slowed the car down and stopped in front of him. The boy didn't have his hand raised to thumb the ride, he was only standing there, but he had a small cardboard suitcase and his hat was set on his head in a way to indicate that he had left somewhere for good. "Son," Mr. Shiftlet said, "I see you want a ride."

The boy didn't say he did or he didn't but he opened the door of the car and got in, and Mr. Shiftlet started driving again. The child held the suitcase on his lap and folded his arms on top of it. He turned his head and looked out the window away from Shiftlet. Mr. Shiftlet felt oppressed. "Son," he said after a minute, "I got the best old mother in the world so I reckon you only got the second best."

The boy gave him a quick dark glance and then turned his face back out the window.

"It's nothing so sweet," Mr. Shiftlet continued, "as a boy's mother. She taught him his first prayers at her knee, she give him

24 **Reading Strategy** Have the students predict how successful the marriage will be. Upon what is the marriage based? Who will be hurt the most if the marriage fails?

25 **Discussion** Lucynell's innocence is referred to throughout the story. What is the reason for her innocence?

26 **Discussion** Why does Mr. Shiftlet leave Lucynell in the diner?

27 **Discussion** Why are Mr. Shiftlet's actions ironic, considering his comments throughout the story?

28 **Critical Thinking and Reading** Have students discuss the significance of the slogan. To what motives does the sign appeal? What does the decision to appeal to these types of motives suggest about human nature?

29 **Discussion** Why does Mr. Shiftlet assume that the boy needs a ride? What are his motives for offering him a ride?

1. "The car ain't run in fifteen year," the old woman said. "the day my husband died, it quit running."

2. "I'm pleased to meet you," the old woman said. "Name Lucynell Crater and daughter Lucynell Crater. What you doing around here, Mr. Shiftlet?"

3. "Lucynell don't even know what a hotel is," the old woman muttered. "Listen here, Mr. Shiftlet," she said, sliding forward in her chair, "you'd be getting a permanent house and a deep well and the most innocent girl in the world. You don't need no money. Lemme tell you something: there ain't any place in the world for a poor disabled friendless drifting man."

4. "It's nothing so sweet," Mr. Shiftlet continued, "as a boy's mother. She taught him his first prayers at her knee, she give him love when no other would, she told him what was right and what wasn't, and she seen that he done the right thin."

5. "My mother was an angel of Gawd," Mr. Shiftlett said in a very strained voice. "he took her from heaven and giver to me and I left her."

Student Activity 2. Write a brief dialogue between two or more characters in which the characters speak in dialect.

30 **Discussion** What is the significance of Mr. Shiftlet's use of the phrase "angel of God" in referring to his mother?

31 **Literary Focus** What is ironic about Mr. Shiftlet's prayer? What is ironic about the way in which it is answered? How does this incident relate to the theme of the story?

Reader's Response What are your feelings about each of the characters in this story?

love when no other would, she told him what was right and what wasn't, and she seen that he done the right thing. Son," he said, "I never rued a day in my life like the one I rued when I left that old mother of mine."

The boy shifted in his seat but he didn't look at Mr. Shiftlet. He unfolded his arms and put one hand on the door handle.

30 "My mother was a angel of Gawd," Mr. Shiftlet said in a very strained voice. "He took her from heaven and giver to me and I left her." His eyes were instantly clouded over with a mist of tears. The car was barely moving.

The boy turned angrily in the seat. "You go to the devil!" he cried. "My old woman is a flea bag and yours is a stinking pole cat!" and with that he flung the door open and jumped out with his suitcase into the ditch.

Mr. Shiftlet was so shocked that for about a hundred feet he drove along slowly with the door still open. A cloud, the exact color of the boy's hat and shaped like a turnip, had descended over the sun, and another, worse looking, crouched behind the car. Mr. Shiftlet felt that the rottenness of the world was about to engulf him. He raised his arm and let it fall again to his breast. "Oh Lord!" he prayed. "Break forth and wash the slime from this earth!"

31 The turnip continued slowly to descend. After a few minutes there was a guffawing peal of thunder from behind and fantastic raindrops, like tin-can tops, crashed over the rear of Mr. Shiftlet's car. Very quickly he stepped on the gas and with his stump sticking out the window he raced the galloping shower into Mobile.

THINKING ABOUT THE SELECTION

Recalling

1. What does the old woman conclude about Mr. Shiftlet as she first sees him?
2. What agreement do Mr. Shiftlet and the old woman reach at the end of the first scene?
3. (a) In what way is Lucynell handicapped? (b) What arguments does the old woman use to persuade Mr. Shiftlet to marry Lucynell? (c) Why does Shiftlet say that he cannot marry her? (d) What causes him to change his mind?
4. Where does Shiftlet abandon Lucynell?
5. What happens when Shiftlet picks up a hitchhiker?

Interpreting

6. (a) What is the significance of Shiftlet's name? (b) What is the significance of the narrator's observation that Shiftlet's figure "formed a crooked cross"?
7. (a) What details in the first scene suggest that the old woman is not really listening to

Shiftlet's comments? (b) With what is she preoccupied?
8. What does the narrator mean when she calls Shiftlet's claim that he has a "moral intelligence" an "impossible truth"?
9. How does Shiftlet's comment that the spirit is "always on the move" foreshadow, or hint at, the outcome of the story?
10. (a) What is the cause of Lucynell's innocence? (b) Considering the cause of her innocence, what does the story imply about a person's ability to remain innocent in the modern world?
11. How does the incident with the hitchhiker relate to the rest of the story?
12. (a) In what ways are the characters in this story realistic? (b) In what ways are they exaggerated?
13. Explain the title of this short story.

Applying

14. Do you think this story could have been written during another period of American history? Explain your answer.

Closure and Extension

ANSWERS TO THINKING ABOUT THE SELECTION
Recalling

1. She decides that he is a harmless tramp.
2. Mr. Shiftlet can stay at the woman's home. She will feed him in exchange for household repairs.
3. (a) Lucynell is deaf. (b) The woman boasts of Lucynell's innocence and youth. (c) Mr. Shiftlet protests because he says that marriage is against his soul; he also says that he needs enough money to treat his wife royally on their honeymoon. (d) The woman offers to give him the car as well as seventy-five dollars for the honeymoon.
4. He leaves her in a roadside diner.
5. The hitchhiker gets angry at Mr. Shiftlet for praising mothers and

yells at him before jumping out of the car.

Interpreting

6. (a) Shiftlet sounds like "shifty" and indicates changeability. (b) He himself is "crooked"; he is a hypocrite because his words are not reflected in his actions.
7. (a) She blankly agrees with many of his pronouncements, then quickly changes the subject. (b) She is analyzing Mr. Shiftlet as a

ANALYZING LITERATURE

Understanding Irony

This story is filled with situational irony—irony that occurs when the actual result of an action or situation is quite different from the expected result. Much of this irony results from the contrast between Mr. Shiftlet's comments and actions.

Explain how situational irony results from each of the following comments.

1. "... people don't care how they lie."
2. "... there's some men that some things mean more to them than money."
3. Mr. Shiftlet said that the trouble with the world was that nobody cared ...
4. "Some people'll do anything anyhow these days, but the way I think, I wouldn't marry no woman that I couldn't take on a trip like she was somebody."

CRITICAL THINKING AND READING

Seeing Irony as a Key to Theme

The irony in this story plays a vital role in conveying its theme. For example, an important aspect of the theme—that people's actions often do not correspond to the beliefs they profess—is expressed through the contradictions between Mr. Shiftlet's comments and behavior.

1. What is ironic about the statement at the end of the story that "Mr. Shiftlet felt that the rottenness of the world was about to engulf him"?
2. This statement, along with Mr. Shiftlet's comment, "The world is almost rotten," suggests that the world is in a state of deterioration. What do the events in the story suggest about the cause of this deterioration?
3. What is ironic about the way in which Shiftlet's prayer at the end of the story is answered?
4. What does this incident suggest will happen to people whose behavior contradicts the beliefs they profess?

THINKING AND WRITING

Writing a Story

Develop a popular slogan into a short story, as Flannery O'Connor did in "The Life You Save May Be Your Own." Start by thinking of a slogan with deeper implications that might not occur to most people. Then develop a plot which expresses these implications. Work the slogan into the story at some point, and use it as the story's title. When you finish writing your story, revise it to make sure that the situational irony is apparent. Proofread your story and share it with your classmates.

Primary Source

Flannery O'Connor was a consummate writer. Her teacher, Paul Engle, recalls his first meeting with Ms. O'Connor in 1946. She had come to his office to speak with him, and he was unable to understand a word of her native Georgian tongue. "Embarrassed, I asked her to write down what she had just said on a pad. She wrote: 'My name is Flannery O'Connor. I am not a journalist. Can I come to the Writer's Workshop?'... I told her to bring examples of her writing and we would consider her, late as it was. Flannery spoke a dialect beyond instant comprehension, but on the page her prose was imaginative, tough, alive: just like Flannery herself. . . . The stories were filled with insights, shrewd about human weakness, hard and compassionate. . . . She was shy about having them read, and when it was her turn to have a story presented in the Workshop, I would read it aloud anonymously. . . . The only communicating gesture she would make was an occasional amused and shy smile at something absurd. The dreary chair she sat in glowed."

The Life You Save May Be Your Own 965

(Answers begin on p. 964)

Applying

14. Suggested Response: No, because the story develops out of the complex and confusing nature of life in the modern world.

Challenge What do you think will happen to each character after the end of the story? Which character will be most affected by the events in the story?

ANSWERS TO ANALYZING LITERATURE

1. Shiftlet himself often lies.
2. Shiftlet is actually swindling the woman out of seventy-five dollars.
3. His actions show that he cares only about himself.
4. He abandons Lucynell in a diner, claiming that she is a hitchhiker. He treats her far worse than anyone has before, not "like she was somebody."

ANSWERS TO CRITICAL THINKING AND READING

1. Shiftlet's actions play an important role in contributing to the rottenness that he senses.
2. The events suggest that the deterioration is caused by people's hypocrisy and self-centeredness.
3. When he asks God to "wash the slime from the earth," a storm breaks out that threatens to wash him from the earth.
4. The incident suggests that people will ultimately pay for their hypocrisy and self-centeredness.

THINKING AND WRITING

For help with this assignment, students can refer to Lesson 19, "Writing a Short Story," in the Handbook of Writing About Literature.

Publishing Student Writing Break students into small groups and have them read their stories to one another. Have the students comment on the work of other students, suggesting how the stories might be improved and indicating the strong points of the stories.

---

possible match for her daughter.
8. He does say morally intelligent things, but his actions clearly contradict his statements.
9. Shiftlet displays the fact that his spirit is always on the move when he abandons Lucynell and continues driving.
10. (a) Her handicap is the cause of her innocence. (b) The story implies that it is impossible to remain innocent in the modern world unless you are in some way handicapped.

11. Shiftlet talks about the separation of a child and its mother after he has caused the separation of Lucynell and her mother. His comments about his behavior toward his mother and his reference to her as an "angel of God" echo his treatment of Lucynell. The hitchhiker then abandons him, just as he abandoned Lucynell.
12. (a) Suggested Response: The characters' situations are realistically depicted, and most of their

reactions are as well. (b) Suggested Response: Their speeches are often exaggerated to give the reader a clear indication of their traits.
13. Suggested Response: The title points out the selfish nature of people in the modern world, because it is taken from a popular slogan that urges people to drive carefully by appealing to selfish motives.

More About the Author Anne Tyler has remained a private person despite her growing acclaim in literary fields. For several years her books were praised, but she remained relatively unknown. Partially as the result of the efforts of authors Gail Godwin and John Updike, she has recently earned more widespread acclaim. Preferring to live in Baltimore rather than in a larger city, she has been called "the nearest thing we have to an urban Southern writer." Ask students to discuss why writers would want to retain their privacy in the face of growing fame. Why might it be easier for writers to retain their privacy than it is for actors?

In discussing the difficulties of balancing her writing with her family obligations, Tyler has commented, "I have spent so long erecting partitions around the part of me that writes, learning how to close the door on it when ordinary life intervenes, how to close the door on ordinary life when it's time to write again—that I'm not sure I could fit the two parts back together again." Have students respond to Tyler's comment. Then have them discuss some of the other difficulties that they imagine might arise from trying to raise a family while pursuing a literary career.

1941–

Inspired by the work of Eudora Welty, Anne Tyler devotes much of her fiction to exposing the latent, unusual characteristics of outwardly ordinary people.

Tyler was born in Minneapolis, Minnesota, spent most of her childhood in Raleigh, North Carolina, and now lives with her family in Baltimore, Maryland. She studied Russian at Duke and at Columbia, while at the same time developing into an enthusiastic and dedicated fiction writer. In 1964, when she was twenty-four, she published her first novel, *If Morning Ever Comes*. Since then, she has published several more novels, including *The Tin Can Tree* (1966), *The Clock Winder* (1973), *Earthly Possessions* (1977), *Dinner at the Homesick Restaurant* (1982), and *The Accidental Tourist* (1985). She has also written a vast number of short stories, many of which she has contributed to *The New Yorker*.

As the wife of a child psychiatrist, mother of two daughters, and committed writer, Ann Tyler orchestrates a balance between family and work in the orderly and highly organized fashion that many of her characters long for. Monday through Thursday she works, seated on a daybed in her starkly plain study. There she writes with a pen in longhand so, as she explains, she can hear her characters speak. She reserves Fridays for errands and weekends for family matters. Her characters are not fictionalizations from her own life but products of a fertile imagination drawn with her gift for fine, realistic detail. During recurrent hours of insomnia, she often records ideas in boxes of index cards.

When Tyler works on a novel, she follows a comfortable pattern that entails writing out a first draft and then reading it to "find out what it means." Then she revises the draft to unify it and to enhance the "subconscious intentions" she has discovered in the work. She keeps the goal of writing "serious" fiction firmly in sight as she revises. "A serious book," she has explained, "is one that removes me to another life as I am reading it. It has to have layers and layers, like life does. It has to be an extremely believable lie." A major satisfaction she derives from her writing comes through the connection she feels in sharing her created worlds with understanding readers. "They in their solitude, and I in mine, have somehow managed to touch without either of us feeling intruded upon. We've spent some time on neutral territory, sharing a life that belongs to neither of us."

"Average Waves in Unprotected Waters" exhibits Tyler's ability to create well-developed, realistic characters and evoke an emotional response through an unsentimental portrayal of the characters' tragic lives.

GUIDE FOR INTERPRETING

Average Waves in Unprotected Waters

The Writer's Techniques

Foreshadowing. Foreshadowing is a technique that writers frequently use in short stories and novels to build **suspense,** or create tension concerning the outcome of the events. When a writer uses foreshadowing, he or she presents details that hint at actions that will occur later in the story or suggest the story's outcome. For example, in her story *The Life You Save May Be Your Own,* Flannery O'Connor hints at the tragic impact that Mr. Shiftlet will have on the lives of the Crater women when she writes that Mr. Shiftlet "paused and made his tone more *ominous* still."

Flashback. A flashback is an interruption in the action of a narrative in which an earlier event is shown or described. Often a flashback takes the form of a reminiscence of one of the characters. For example, in her story "The Jilting of Granny Weatherall," Katherine Anne Porter presents numerous flashbacks as the main character's thoughts drift back to events that occurred in her younger days.

Commentary

Although "Average Waves in Unprotected Waters" concerns two characters, it focuses on Bet, the mother. As you read the story, you will notice that it is a snapshot of one important day in Bet's life, and through the events of that day and her reactions to them, Tyler allows the reader to understand this mother's life. Ms. Tyler has often expressed her "utter lack of faith in change." Notice how she depicts the changeless nature of Bet's character in this story. From childhood when she stood "staunch" in the waves unable to ride them through adulthood when she stayed on in the apartment after Avery had gone, Bet remains steadfastly constant. Bet's resistance to change adds interest to the events of this day, which marks a monumental shift in her life. Perhaps Anne Tyler invites her reader to consider how Bet will manage the transformation. What shape will Bet's life take hereafter? The story's provocative final sentence hints at one possible answer to that question, but the reader must wonder whether or not Tyler means the reader to believe it.

What is your response to change? Do you willingly accept it, or do you resist?

Writing

In "Average Waves in Unprotected Waters," Anne Tyler explores a mother's attempts to cope with a severely handicapped child. Freewrite about some of the difficulties that parents might have in dealing with a handicapped child. What types of emotions might parents experience in this situation? In what ways might a child's handicap affect the parents' lives? What actions might the parents take to make their child's life better?

Guide for Interpreting 967

Average Waves in Unprotected Waters

Anne Tyler

As soon as it got light, Bet woke him and dressed him, and then she walked him over to the table and tried to make him eat a little cereal. He wouldn't, though. He could tell something was up. She pressed the edge of the spoon against his lips till she heard it click on his teeth, but he just looked off at a corner of the ceiling—a knobby child with great glassy eyes and her own fair hair. Like any other nine-year-old, he wore a striped shirt and jeans, but the shirt was too neat and the jeans too blue, unpatched and unfaded, and would stay that way till he outgrew them. And his face was elderly—pinched, strained, tired—though it should have looked as unused as his jeans. He hardly ever changed his expression.

She left him in his chair and went to make the beds. Then she raised the yellowed shade, rinsed a few spoons in the bathroom sink, picked up some bits of magazines he'd torn the night before. This was a rented room in an ancient, crumbling house, and nothing you could do to it would lighten its cluttered look. There was always that feeling of too many lives layered over other lives, like the layers of brownish wallpaper her child had peeled away in the corner by his bed.

She slipped her feet into flat-heeled loafers and absently patted the front of her dress, a worn beige knit she usually saved for Sundays. Maybe she should take it in a little; it hung from her shoulders like a sack.

She felt too slight and frail, too wispy for all she had to do today. But she reached for her coat anyhow, and put it on and tied a blue kerchief under her chin. Then she went over to the table and slowly spun, modeling the coat. "See, Arnold?" she said. "We're going out."

Arnold went on looking at the ceiling, but his gaze turned wild and she knew he'd heard.

She fetched his jacket from the closet—brown corduroy, with a hood. It had set her back half a week's salary. But Arnold didn't like it; he always wanted his old one, a little red duffel coat he'd long ago outgrown. When she came toward him, he started moaning and rocking and shaking his head. She had to struggle to stuff his arms in the sleeves. Small though he was, he was strong, wiry; he was getting to be too much for her. He shook free of her hands and ran over to his bed. The jacket was on, though. It wasn't buttoned, the collar was askew, but never mind; that just made him look more real. She always felt bad at how he stood inside his clothes, separate from them, passive, unaware of all the buttons and snaps she'd fastened as carefully as she would a doll's.

She gave a last look around the room, checked to make sure the hot plate was off, and then picked up her purse and Arnold's suitcase. "Come along, Arnold," she said.

He came, dragging out every step. He

looked at the suitcase suspiciously, but only because it was new. It didn't have any meaning for him. "See?" she said. "It's yours. It's Arnold's. It's going on the train with us."

But her voice was all wrong. He would pick it up, for sure. She paused in the middle of locking the door and glanced over at him fearfully. Anything could set him off nowadays. He hadn't noticed, though. He was too busy staring around the hallway, goggling at a freckled, walnut-framed mirror as if he'd never seen it before. She touched his shoulder. "Come, Arnold," she said.

They went down the stairs slowly, both of them clinging to the sticky mahogany railing. The suitcase banged against her shins. In the entrance hall, old Mrs. Puckett stood waiting outside her door—a huge, soft lady in a black crêpe dress and orthopedic shoes. She was holding a plastic bag of peanut-butter cookies, Arnold's favorites. There were tears in her eyes. "Here, Arnold," she said, quavering. Maybe she felt to blame that he was going. But she'd done the best she could: babysat him all these years and only given up when he'd grown too strong and wild to manage. Bet wished Arnold would give the old lady some sign—hug her, make his little crowing noise, just take the cookies, even. But he was too excited. He raced on out the front door, and it was Bet who had to take them. "Well, thank you, Mrs. Puckett," she said. "I know he'll enjoy them later."

3 "Oh, no . . ." said Mrs. Puckett, and she flapped her large hands and gave up, sobbing.

They were lucky and caught a bus first thing. Arnold sat by the window. He must have thought he was going to work with her; when they passed the red-and-gold Kresge's sign, he jabbered and tried to stand up. "No, honey," she said, and took hold of his arm. He settled down then and let his hand stay curled in hers awhile. He had very small, cool fingers, and nails as smooth as thumbtack heads.

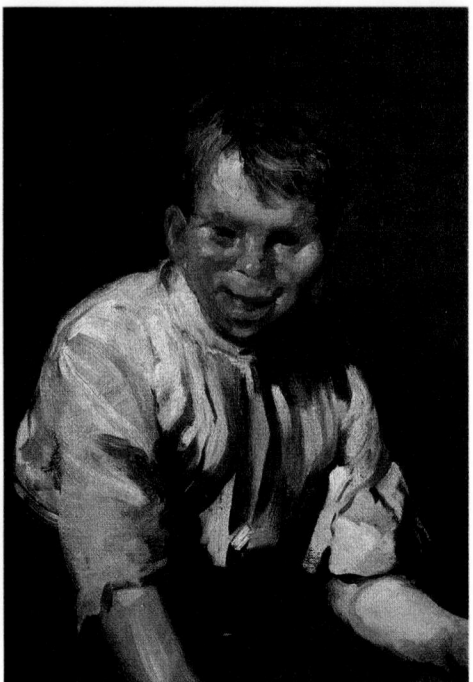

THE LAUGHING BOY
George Bellows
Hirschl & Adler Galleries, Inc.

At the train station, she bought the tickets and then a pack of Wrigley's spearmint gum. Arnold stood gaping at the vaulted ceiling, with his head flopped back and his arms hanging limp at his sides. People stared at him. She would have liked to push their faces in. "Over here, honey," she said, and she nudged him toward the gate, straightening his collar as they walked.

4

He hadn't been on a train before and acted a little nervous, bouncing up and down in his seat and flipping the lid of his ashtray and craning forward to see the man ahead of them. When the train started moving, he crowed and pulled at her sleeve. "That's right, Arnold. Train. We're taking a

Average Waves in Unprotected Waters   969

Humanities Note

Fine art, *The Laughing Boy,* George Bellows. George Wesley Bellows (1882–1925) is an American painter who studied painting with the dynamic realist painter, Robert Henri. Under Henri's tutelage, Bellows learned to take his subjects from his surroundings and to paint them directly and quickly on canvas without preliminary sketches. These lessons from Henri gave his works the emotional impact and fresh immediacy for which they are admired.

The painting *The Laughing Boy* was first exhibited in 1909. It is executed in the somewhat limited palette Bellows preferred in his early works. Through skillful manipulation of color and light, Bellows portrays this child with warmth, sympathy, and humor. He affectionately gives us an honest look at a somewhat homely boy and invites viewers to appreciate his charm and join in his mirth.

You might use the following in your discussion:
1. Describe the character of the boy in the painting.
2. What attitude does the artist seem to have toward this boy?
3. Do you think this boy could represent Arnold in the story? Explain.

3 **Discussion** Why do you think that Mrs. Puckett reacts the way she does?

4 **Reading Strategy** Have students predict where Arnold and Bet are going.

5 Discussion Why did Avery leave Bet and Arnold? Do you think it was wrong for him to leave? Have the students discuss the difficulties of coping with such a situation. Also discuss the issue of assigning blame.

6 Clarification Although it is possible that Arnold's illness was caused by a hereditary link, there is no direct indication that it was. When Bet changes from blaming it on a gene to the marriage in general, the narrator seems to indicate that there is no hereditary link. At the very least, the narrator shows the insignificance of assigning blame in the situation.

trip," Bet said. She unwrapped a stick of chewing gum and gave it to him. He loved gum. If she didn't watch him closely, he sometimes swallowed it—which worried her a little because she'd heard it clogged your kidneys; but at least it would keep him busy. She looked down at the top of his head. Through the blond prickles of his hair, cut short for practical reasons, she could see his skull bones moving as he chewed. He was so thin-skinned, almost transparent; sometimes she imagined she could see the blood traveling in his veins.

When the train reached a steady speed, he grew calmer, and after a while he nodded over against her and let his hands sag on his knees. She watched his eyelashes slowly drooping—two colorless, fringed crescents, heavier and heavier, every now and then flying up as he tried to fight off sleep. He had never slept well, not ever, not even as a baby. Even before they'd noticed anything wrong, they'd wondered at his jittery, jerky catnaps, his tiny hands clutching tight and springing open, his strange single wail sailing out while he went right on sleeping. Avery said it **5** gave him the chills. And after the doctor talked to them Avery wouldn't have anything to do with Arnold anymore—just walked in wide circles around the crib, looking stunned and sick. A few weeks later, he left. She wasn't surprised. She even knew how he felt, more or less. Halfway, he blamed her; halfway, he blamed himself. You can't believe a thing like this will just fall on you out of nowhere.

6 She'd had moments herself of picturing some kind of evil gene in her husband's ordinary, stocky body—a dark little egg like a black jelly bean, she imagined it. All his fault. But other times she was sure the gene was hers. It seemed so natural; she never could do anything as well as most people. And then other times she blamed their marriage. They'd married too young, against her parents' wishes. All she'd wanted was to get away from home. Now she couldn't remember why. What was wrong with home? She

Primary Source

In her essay "Still Just Writing," Anne Tyler shares some of her own perceptions of her career as a writer. She writes,

". . . I do consider that any day now. I will have said all I have to say: I'll have used up all my characters, and then I'll be free to get on with my real life. When I make a note of new ideas on index cards, I imagine I'm clearing out my head, and that soon it will be empty and spacious. I file the cards in a little blue box, and I can picture myself using the final card one day—ah! through at last!—and throwing the blue box away. I'm like a dentist who continually fights tooth decay, working toward a time when he's conquered it altogether and done himself out of a job. But my head keeps loading up again; the little blue box stays crowded and messy. Even when I feel I have no ideas at all, and can't possibly start the next chapter, I have a sense of something still bottled in me, trying to get out. . . .

"I spent my adolescence planning to be an artist, not a writer. After all, books had to be about major events, and none had ever happened to me. All I knew were tobacco workers, stringing the leaves I handed them and talking up a storm. Then I found a book of Eudora Welty's short stories

WAITING ROOM
Raphael Soyer
The Corcoran Gallery of Art

Humanities Note

Fine art, *Waiting Room,* Raphael Soyer. Raphael Soyer (1899–1974) was an American painter who arrived in the United States from Russia in 1912. Educated in art at the Cooper Union, National Academy of Design, and Art Students League, all in New York City, he later taught at these and other prestigious New York art schools. He is remembered today for his socially conscious paintings of the American urban scene during the Great Depression.

Waiting Room was painted in 1938–40. It captures with "stop-action" clarity the sleepy atmosphere, boredom, and depression of a shabby station waiting room. That no effort was made to beautify the people or the surroundings shows the level of realism American artists of this era tried to capture. The artistic device of a mirror reflecting most of the room makes an interesting composition. Although they share a common room, the inhabitants of the waiting room seem isolated from each other. Raphael Soyer is commenting on this isolation and upon the alienation and dehumanization of the American way of life in an industrial age.

Consider the following questions for discussion:
1. What is the dominant feeling in this painting?
2. What contributes to the sense of isolation in it?
3. Did Arnold's mother feel isolated in a similar way?
4. Did the special nature of her dilemma serve to heighten this isolation? Explain.

in the high school library. She was writing about Edna Earle, who was so slow-witted she could sit all day just pondering how the tail of the *C* got through the loop of the *L* on the Coca-Cola sign. Why, I knew Edna Earle. You mean you could *write* about such people? I have always meant to send Eudora Welty a thank-you note, but I imagine she would find it a little strange."

7 Discussion What does her father's behavior reveal about his personality?

8 Clarification Breakers are waves that crest, or break into foam. The term usually applies to waves along a shoreline.

9 Critical Thinking and Reading The flashback is told out of chronological order. Students should notice that this flashback began with a recollection of Arnold as a child, then moved to Bet's childhood, and finally explored her marriage with Avery. Discuss the interior logic that the flashback follows.

10 Discussion Why would Bet never leave Avery? What does her behavior reveal about her character?

11 Discussion Why does Arnold find the situation on the train entertaining?

thought of her parents' humped green trailer, perched on cinder blocks near a forest of masts in Salt Spray, Maryland. At this distance (parents dead, trailer rusted to bits, even Salt Spray changed past recognition), it seemed to her that her old life had been beautifully free and spacious. She closed her eyes and saw wide gray skies. Everything had been ruled by the sea. Her father (who'd run a fishing boat for tourists) couldn't arrange his day till he'd heard the marine forecast—the wind, the tides, the small-craft warnings, the height of average waves in unprotected waters. He loved to fish, offshore and on, and he swam every chance he could get. He'd tried to teach her to bodysurf, but it hadn't worked out. There was something about the breakers: she just gritted her teeth and stood staunch and let them slam into her. As if standing staunch were a virtue, really. She couldn't explain it. Her father thought she was scared, but it wasn't that at all.

She'd married Avery against their wishes and been sorry ever since—sorry to move so far from home, sorrier when her parents died within a year of each other, sorriest of all when the marriage turned grim and cranky. But she never would have thought of leaving him. It was Avery who left; she would have stayed forever. In fact, she did stay on in their apartment for months after he'd gone, though the rent was far too high. It wasn't that she expected him back. She just took some comfort from enduring.

Arnold's head snapped up. He looked around him and made a gurgling sound. His chewing gum fell onto the front of his jacket. "Here, honey," she told him. She put the gum in her ashtray. "Look out the window. See the cows?"

He wouldn't look. He began bouncing in his seat, rubbing his hands together rapidly.

"Arnold? Want a cookie?"

If only she'd brought a picture book. She'd meant to and then forgot. She wondered if the train people sold magazines. If she let him get too bored, he'd go into one of his tantrums, and then she wouldn't be able to handle him. The doctor had given her pills just in case, but she was always afraid that while he was screaming he would choke on them. She looked around the car. "Arnold," she said, "see the . . . see the hat with feathers on? Isn't it pretty? See the red suitcase? See the, um . . ."

The car door opened with a rush of clattering wheels and the conductor burst in, singing "Girl of my dreams, I love you." He lurched down the aisle, plucking pink tickets from the back of each seat. Just across from Bet and Arnold, he stopped. He was looking down at a tiny black lady in a purple coat, with a fox fur piece biting its own tail around her neck. "You!" he said.

The lady stared straight ahead.

"You, I saw you. You're the one in the washroom."

A little muscle twitched in her cheek.

"You got on this train in Beulah, didn't you. Snuck in the washroom. Darted back like you thought you could put something over on me. I saw that bit of purple! Where's your ticket gone to?"

She started fumbling in a blue cloth purse. The fumbling went on and on. The conductor shifted his weight.

"Why!" she said finally. "I must've left it back in my other seat."

"What other seat?"

"Oh, the one back . . ." She waved a spidery hand.

The conductor sighed. "Lady," he said, "you owe me money."

"I do no such thing!" she said. "Viper! Monger! Hitler!"[1] Her voice screeched up all at once; she sounded like a parrot. Bet winced and felt herself flushing, as if *she* were the one. But then at her shoulder she heard a sudden, rusty clang, and she turned and saw that Arnold was laughing. He had his mouth wide open and his tongue curled, the way he did when he watched "Sesame Street." Even after the scene had worn itself out, and the lady had paid and the conductor had moved on, Arnold went on chortling

---

1. **Hitler:** German dictator Adolf Hitler (1889–1945).

Grammar in Action

Good writers use a variety of **sentence openers** to keep their writing from becoming monotonous. Here are some sentence openers from Tyler's story:

Subject: He could tell something was up. (p. 1064)

Adjective: Small though he was, he was strong . . . (p. 1064)

Adverb clause: As soon as it got light, Bet woke him . . . (p. 1064)

Inversion: It was Avery who left . . . (p. 1068)

Transition: In fact, she did stay on . . . (p. 1068)

Quotation: "Easily," said the man.(p. 1070)

In addition, a participle or an infinitive can be used to begin a sentence.

Notice that introductory material is separated from the main clause by a comma. The only exceptions are very short prepositional phrases or one-word modifiers. However, even these must be punctuated if they could lead to confusion. Note the following sentences:

and la-la-ing, and Bet looked gratefully at the little black lady, who was settling her fur piece fussily and muttering under her breath.

From the Parkinsville Railroad Station, which they seemed to be tearing down or else remodeling—she couldn't tell which—they took a taxicab to Parkins State Hospital. "Oh, I been out there many and many a time," said the driver. "Went out there just the other—"

But she couldn't stop herself; she had to tell him before she forgot. "Listen," she said, "I want you to wait for me right in the driveway. I don't want you to go on away."

"Well, fine," he said.

"Can you do that? I want you to be sitting right by the porch or the steps or whatever, right where I come out of, ready to take me back to the station. Don't just go off, and—"

"I *got* you, I got you," he said.

She sank back. She hoped he understood.

Arnold wanted a peanut-butter cookie. He was reaching and whimpering. She didn't know what to do. She wanted to give him anything he asked for, anything; but he'd get it all over his face and arrive not looking his best. She couldn't stand it if they thought he was just ordinary and unattractive. She wanted them to see how small and neat he was, how somebody cherished him. But it would be awful if he went into one of his rages. She broke off a little piece of cookie from the bag. "Here," she told him. "Don't mess, now."

He flung himself back in the corner and ate it, keeping one hand flattened across his mouth while he chewed.

The hospital looked like someone's great, pillared mansion, with square brick buildings all around it. "Here we are," the driver said.

"Thank you," she said. "Now you wait here, please. Just wait till I get—"

"*Lady*," he said. "I'll wait."

She opened the door and nudged Arnold out ahead of her. Lugging the suitcase, she started toward the steps. "Come on, Arnold," she said.

He hung back.

"Arnold?"

Maybe he wouldn't allow it, and they would go on home and never think of this again.

But he came, finally, climbing the steps in his little hobbled way. His face was clean, but there were a few cookie crumbs on his jacket. She set down the suitcase to brush them off. Then she buttoned all his buttons and smoothed his shirt collar over his jacket collar before she pushed open the door.

In the admitting office, a lady behind a wooden counter showed her what papers to sign. Secretaries were clacketing typewriters all around. Bet thought Arnold might like that, but instead he got lost in the lights—chilly, hanging ice-cube-tray lights with a little flicker to them. He gazed upward, looking astonished. Finally a flat-fronted nurse came in and touched his elbow. "Come along, Arnold. Come, Mommy. We'll show you where Arnold is staying," she said.

They walked back across the entrance hall, then up wide marble steps with hollows worn in them. Arnold clung to the bannister. There was a smell Bet hated, pine-oil disinfectant, but Arnold didn't seem to notice. You never knew; sometimes smells could just put him in a state.

The nurse unlocked a double door that had chicken-wired windows. They walked through a corridor, passing several fat, ugly women in shapeless gray dresses and ankle socks. "Ha!" one of the women said, and fell giggling into the arms of a friend. The nurse said, "*Here* we are." She led them into an enormous hallway lined with little white cots. Nobody else was in it; there wasn't a sign that children lived here except for a tiny cardboard clown picture hanging on one vacant wall. "This one is your bed, Arnold," said the nurse. Bet laid the suitcase on it. It was made up so neatly, the sheets might have been painted on. A steely-gray blanket was folded across the foot. She looked over at

Average Waves in Unprotected Waters   973

12 **Discussion** What do Bet's interactions with the cab driver reveal about her state of mind?

13 **Discussion** How does the conflict Bet feels about whether or not to give Arnold a cookie reflect her overall attitude about her son?

14 **Discussion** The nurse calls Bet "Mommy." Do you feel that this is appropriate? Discuss the way that the nurse treats Bet and Arnold.

Before, the house appeared deserted.
Before the house appeared a moving van.

Student Activity 1. Rewrite each sentence so that it begins with the element or technique indicated in brackets. Add commas if they are needed.

1. She blamed their marriage at other times. [adverb]
2. Her father thought she was scared. [inversion]
3. He laughed, curling his tongue. [participle]
4. She walked on, unconscious of the danger. [adjective]
5. She asked if she could buy a magazine. [quotation]

Student Activity 2. Combine the two short sentences so that one becomes an introductory element for the other.

1. Arnold looked around him.
   He made a gurgling sound.
2. She couldn't let him get bored.
   He would throw a tantrum.
3. She had married against her parents' wishes.
   She hadn't known she would be sorry.

15 **Discussion** Why does the hospital prefer to make new patients spend six months without seeing their relatives? Do you agree with this policy? Why or why not?

16 **Discussion** What is the nurse's attitude toward the situation? How is her attitude different from Bet's?

17 **Discussion** Throughout this scene, the narrator has given very little indication of Arnold's response to his new home. How do you think this helps to focus attention on Bet's situation?

18 **Reading Strategy** Have the students summarize the events in the story to this point. Have them predict what will happen at the end of the story.

19 **Discussion** Do you think that Bet overreacts to the fact that the train is delayed? Why or why not?

20 **Discussion** Compare and contrast Bet's new outlook on life as "something to watch" with her father's outlook as captain of a tourist boat.

Reader's Response Do you think that Bet makes the right decision about how to cope with Arnold's condition? Why or why not?

Arnold, but he was pivoting back and forth to hear how his new sneakers squeaked on the linoleum.

15 "Usually," said the nurse, "we like to give new residents six months before the family visits. That way they settle in quicker, don't you see." She turned away and adjusted the clown picture, though as far as Bet could tell it was fine the way it was. Over her shoulder, the nurse said, "You can tell him goodbye now, if you like."

"Oh," Bet said. "All right." She set her hands on Arnold's shoulders. Then she laid her face against his hair, which felt warm and fuzzy. "Honey," she said. But he went on pivoting. She straightened and told the nurse, "I brought his special blanket."

"Oh, fine," said the nurse, turning toward her again. "We'll see that he gets it."

"He always likes to sleep with it; he has ever since he was little."

"All right."

"Don't wash it. He hates if you wash it."

"Yes. Say goodbye to Mommy now, Arnold."

16 "A lot of times he'll surprise you. I mean there's a whole lot to him. He's not just—"

"We'll take very good care of him, Mrs. Blevins, don't worry."

"Well," she said. " 'Bye, Arnold."

She left the ward with the nurse and went down the corridor. As the nurse was unlocking the doors for her, she heard a single, terrible scream, but the nurse only patted her shoulder and pushed her gently on through.

In the taxi, Bet said, "Now, I've just got fifteen minutes to get to the station. I wonder if you could hurry?"

"Sure thing," the driver said.

17
18 She folded her hands and looked straight ahead. Tears seemed to be coming down her face in sheets.

Once she'd reached the station, she went to the ticket window. "Am I in time for the twelve-thirty-two?" she asked.

"Easily," said the man. "It's twenty minutes late."

"What?"

"Got held up in Norton somehow."

"But you can't!" she said. The man looked startled. She must be a sight, all swollen-eyed and wet-cheeked. "Look," she said, in a lower voice. "I figured this on purpose. I chose the one train from Beulah that would let me catch another one back without waiting. I do not want to sit and wait in this station."

"Twenty *minutes*, lady. That's all it is."

"What am I going to do?" she asked him. He turned back to his ledgers.

19 She went over to a bench and sat down. Ladders and scaffolding towered above her, and only ten or twelve passengers were dotted through the rest of the station. The place looked bombed out—nothing but a shell. "Twenty minutes!" she said aloud. "What am I going to do?"

Through the double glass doors at the far end of the station, a procession of gray-suited men arrived with briefcases. More men came behind them, dressed in work clothes, carrying folding chairs, black trunk-like boxes with silver hinges, microphones, a wooden lectern, and an armload of bunting. They set the lectern down in the center of the floor, not six feet from Bet. They draped the bunting across it—an arc of red, white, and blue. Wires were connected, floodlights were lit. A microphone screeched. One of the workmen said, "Try her, Mayor." He held the microphone out to a fat man in a suit, who cleared his throat and said, "Ladies and gentlemen, on the occasion of the expansion of this fine old railway station—"

"Sure do get an echo here," the workman said. "Keep on going."

The Mayor cleared his throat again. "If I may," he said, "I'd like to take about twenty minutes of your time, friends."

20 He straightened his tie. Bet blew her nose, and then she wiped her eyes and smiled. They had come just for her sake, you might think. They were putting on a sort of private play. From now on, all the world was going to be like that—just something on a stage, for her to sit back and watch.

Closure and Extension

ANSWERS TO THINKING ABOUT THE SELECTION
Recalling

1. (a) He will not eat. (b) He moans and rocks and shakes his head, and she has to struggle to get his arms into the sleeves.

2. (a) He becomes nervous and bounces up and down. (b) He grows calmer. (c) There is an argument between one of the

THINKING ABOUT THE SELECTION

Recalling

1. (a) What happens when Bet tries to make Arnold eat? (b) What happens when she tries to put his jacket on him?
2. (a) How does Arnold react when the train first starts moving? (b) What happens when the train reaches a steady speed? (c) What incident occurs on the train that causes Arnold to laugh?
3. (a) What turns out to be the purpose of Bet and Arnold's journey? (b) What does Bet hear just after she leaves Arnold?
4. (a) Why is Bet's train home delayed? (b) What happens while she is waiting for it?

Interpreting

5. When does it first become apparent that Arnold is in some way handicapped?
6. When Bet recalls how her father had tried to teach her to bodysurf, she remembers that she had "just gritted her teeth and stood staunch and let them slam into her." How does this response relate to her reaction to events occurring later in her life?
7. Why does Bet insist that the cab driver wait for her outside the hospital?
8. (a) What impression does Tyler convey in her description of the hospital? (b) What seems to be the nurse's attitude concerning Arnold's situation?
9. Explain the single, terrible scream that Mrs. Blevins hears as the nurse unlocks the doors for her.
10. What is ironic, or surprising, about the mayor's plans to speak in the train station for twenty minutes?
11. (a) What is the meaning of the story's final sentence? (b) How does the story's title relate to its meaning?

Applying

12. Do you think that most people would act as Bet does if they were in her place? Why or why not?

ANALYZING LITERATURE

Understanding Foreshadowing

Foreshadowing refers to the use of hints or clues in a narrative to suggest later events. For example, in the first paragraph of "Average Waves in Unprotected Waters," Tyler hints at a later event when she writes that Arnold "could tell something was up."

1. Find three other examples of foreshadowing in the story.
2. How does Tyler's use of foreshadowing help to build suspense?

CRITICAL THINKING AND READING

Ordering Events

A **flashback** is an interruption in the action of a narrative in which an earlier event is shown or described. For example, a flashback occurs during the train ride when Bet reminisces about her past life. To fully understand a story that contains flashbacks, you must think about the order in which all the events occurred and be able to reorganize them in your own mind.

1. What prompts Bet's flashback?
2. What causes her flashback to end?
3. How does the flashback contribute to your understanding of the story?
4. Rearrange all the events shown or described in "Average Waves in Unprotected Waters" in chronological order.

THINKING AND WRITING

Responding to Criticism

A critic has commented that Anne Tyler "does not trivialize motives with rationalizations. She launches her imagined lives and describes their trajectories with an unpretentious sense of fate." Write an essay in which you discuss "Average Waves in Unprotected Waters" in relation to this statement. When you write your essay, use passages from the story to support your argument. Once you have finished writing, revise and proofread your essay.

Average Waves in Unprotected Waters 975

Applying

12. Suggested Response: Bet seems to have tried to take care of Arnold as well as she was able. Most people would probably agree that Bet's decision was best for both herself and Arnold.

Challenge What do you think the first meeting between Bet and Arnold after six months will be like?

ANSWERS TO ANALYZING LITERATURE

1. Suggested Responses: Arnold eyes the suitcase suspiciously; Mrs. Puckett gives Arnold a going-away present; Arnold has never been on a train before but must take a train trip today; Bet seems nervous and concerned.
2. The foreshadowing helps to increase the reader's interest in discovering the purpose of Bet's trip.

ANSWERS TO CRITICAL THINKING AND READING

1. She watches Arnold as he tries to drift off to sleep and remembers that he had never slept well.
2. Arnold's head snaps up.
3. The flashback provides important information about the events that led up to Bet's current situation.
4. When Bet was a young girl, her father tried to teach her to body-surf. Bet married Avery against her parents' wishes. She and Avery had Arnold, and they soon learned about Arnold's condition. A few weeks after this discovery, Avery left. Several years later, Bet brought Arnold to the hospital. When she returned to the train station, she discovered that the train was delayed. The mayor comes to deliver a speech at the station, and she sits back to watch.

passengers and the conductor.
3. (a) Bet is taking Arnold to a state hospital where he will live. (b) She hears a "single, terrible scream."
4. (a) The train is held up at an earlier station. (b) The mayor of the town delivers a speech at the station.

Interpreting

5. His condition is made apparent in the description of his appearance and behavior at the begin-

ning of the story.
6. Bet does little to change the flow of events; she merely endures them as well as she can.
7. She wants to spend as little time as possible in the hospital, because she feels somewhat guilty about leaving Arnold there.
8. (a) The hospital seems like a cold and unsympathetic place. (b) She seems indifferent to Arnold's situation.
9. The single, terrible scream may be Arnold responding to the fact

that his mother has left him behind.
10. Twenty minutes is the amount of time that Bet's train has been delayed.
11. (a) Bet feels that she will no longer have to participate in the daily agonies that made up her life to this point. (b) The title refers to the events in life that can catch a person off guard, such as Bet's son's condition and her husband's decision to leave her.

THINKING AND WRITING

Arrange students into groups, and have them share their essays with one another. Have students make suggestions about how other students' essays can be improved. Then have students revise their essays, incorporating the suggestion of their peers.

975

JOHN UPDIKE

1932–

In his short stories and novels, John Updike vividly captures the essence of life in contemporary America. Through his depictions of ordinary situations and events, he explores many of the more important issues of our time and offers insights into the underlying significance of everyday life.

Updike was born in Reading, Pennsylvania, and was raised in the nearby town of Shillington. After graduating from Harvard, he spent a year at the Ruskin School of Drawing and Fine Art in England. When he returned to the United States, he joined the staff of *The New Yorker,* a magazine which has published many of his short stories.

Following the publication of his first collection of poetry, *The Carpentered Hen and Other Tame Animals* (1958), Updike published several other collections of poetry, many novels and short stories, numerous essays and book reviews, and a play. His novels include *The Poorhouse Fair* (1959), *Rabbit, Run* (1960), *Of the Farm* (1965), *Couples* (1968), *Rabbit Redux* (1971), *The Coup* (1978), *Rabbit Is Rich* (1981), and *Roger's Version* (1987). He earned the National Book Award for his novel *The Centaur* (1963), and his novel *The Witches of Eastwick* (1984) was made into a major motion picture. His collection of essays and criticism, *Hugging the Shore* (1983), was the winner of the 1983 National Book Critics Circle Award for criticism.

Updike has said, "I'm sure that my capacities to fantasize and to make coherent fantasies, to have patience to sit down day after day and to whittle a fantasy out of paper, all that relates to being an only child." He coped with numerous other personal drawbacks as well. In addition to enduring bouts of hay fever and psoriasis, a painful skin disease, he also stammered. The isolation he suffered from these ills compelled him toward the solitary occupations of drawing and writing. He excelled at both, but in early years focused his hopes on a career as a cartoonist, following in the path of James Thurber. As he matured, his interest shifted toward writing, and by age eighteen, he had decided to follow writing as a career. The aspiration may have been fostered by his mother, who had literary ambitions of her own. She published a novel, *Enchanted,* in 1971.

"The Slump" reflects Updike's awareness of the universal feelings and concerns that develop out of specific situations. By delving into the thoughts of a baseball player in the midst of an extended slump, he captures a sense of uncertainty and insecurity that all people have experienced at some point during their lives.

GUIDE FOR INTERPRETING

Writer's Techniques

The Slump

Diction. Diction refers to a writer's choice of words. When writing a short story or novel, a writer must carefully choose language that is appropriate for the characters and subject. For example, it would not be appropriate for a writer to use ornate, elevated language in a story about uneducated factory workers. However, this type of language would be suitable for a story about a group of scholars

Style. Until the contemporary period, stories were almost always told in the past tense. "He came, she said, they did," authors would write. John Updike was one of the first of the contemporary writers to employ the present tense. In his novel *Rabbit, Run,* Updike used the present tense, a technique he called "a piece of technical daring in 1959," to "emphasize how thoroughly the zigzagging hero lived in the present. . ."

Writing

Updike is one of many writers who have explored the world of sports and the experiences of athletes at work. Freewrite about the reasons why sports are a common subject for literary works. Why do people enjoy reading about sports? What aspects of everyday life are embodied in the world of professional sports? What feelings and experiences do all people share with famous athletes? In what way does the field of sports serve as a metaphor for life?

Primary Source

In "The Slump" the ball player alludes to Soren Kierkegaard, a Danish philosopher who, among other things, expressed a unique view of the concept of repetition as critic Northrop Frye explains. "By [the term] he apparently means, not the simple repeating of an experience, but the recreating of it which redeems or awakens it to life, the end of the process, he says, being the apocalyptic promise: 'Behold, I make all things new.' . . . we face the past: it may be shadowy, but it is all that is there. Plato draws a gloomy picture of man staring at the flickering shapes made on the wall of the objective world by a fire behind us like the sun. But the analogy breaks down when the shadows are those of the past, for the only light we can see them by is the Promethean fire within us. The substance of these shadows can only be in ourselves, and the goal of historical criticism, as our metaphors about it often indicate, is a kind of self-resurrection, the vision of a valley of dry bones that takes on the flesh and blood of our own vision. The culture of the past is not only the memory of mankind, but our own buried life, and study of it leads to a recognition scene, a discovery in which we see, not our past lives, but the total cultural form of our present life. It is not only the poet but his reader who is subject to the obligation to 'make it new.' "

Guide for Interpreting 977

The Slump

John Updike

They say reflexes, the coach says reflexes, even the papers now are saying reflexes, but I don't think it's the reflexes so much—last night, as a gag to cheer me up, the wife walks into the bedroom wearing one of the kids' rubber gorilla masks and I was under the bed in six-tenths of a second, she had the stopwatch on me. It's that I can't see the ball the way I used to. It used to come floating up with all seven continents showing, and the pitcher's thumbprint, and a grass smooch or two, and the Spalding guarantee in ten-point sans-serif,[1] and *whop*! I could feel the sweet wood with the bat still cocked. Now, I don't know, there's like a cloud around it, a sort of spiral vagueness, maybe the Van Allen belt,[2] or maybe I lift my eye in the last second, planning how I'll round second base, or worrying which I do first, tip my cap or slap the third-base coach's hand. You can't see a blind spot, Kierkegaard[3] says, but in there now, between when the ball leaves the bleacher background and I can hear it plop all fat and satisfied in the catcher's mitt, there's somehow just nothing, where there used to be a lot, everything in fact, because they're not keeping me around for my fielding, and al-

ready I see the afternoon tabloid has me down as trade bait.

The flutters don't come when they used to. It used to be, I'd back the convertible out of the garage and watch the electric eye put the door down again and drive in to the stadium, and at about the bridge turnoff I'd ease off grooving with the radio rock, and then on the lot there'd be the kids waiting to get a look and that would start the big butterflies, and when the attendant would take my car I'd want to shout *Stop, thief*, and walking down that long cement corridor I'd fantasize like I was going to the electric chair and the locker room was some dream after death, and I'd wonder why the suit fit, and how these really immortal guys, that I recognized from the bubble-gum cards I used to collect, knew my name. *They* knew *me*. And I'd go out and the stadium mumble would scoop at me and the grass seemed too precious to walk on, like emeralds, and by the time I got into the cage I couldn't remember if I batted left or right.

Now, heck, I move over the bridge singing along with the radio, and brush through the kids at just the right speed, not so fast I knock any of them down, and the attendant knows his Labor Day tip is coming, and we wink, and in the batting cage I own the place, and take my cuts, and pop five or six into the bullpen as easy as dropping dimes down a sewer. But when the scoreboard lights up, and I take those two steps up from the dugout, the biggest two steps in a ball-

---

1. **ten-point sans-serif** (san ser' if): The size and style of the lettering.
2. **Van Allen belt:** A belt of radiation that encircles the earth.
3. **Kierkegaard** (kir' kə gärd'): Søren (sö'rən) Kierkegaard (1813–1855), Danish philosopher and theologian.

4 **Discussion** What does the narrator mean by "hungry?" Discuss
various meanings of the word,
and determine the distinction between "hungry" and "panic hungry."

5 **Discussion** What is the effect of
the narrator's references to Kierkegaard? How does this help to
give the story a universal quality?

Enrichment In an essay about
Updike, Joyce Carol Oates notes
some parallels between Updike
and Flannery O'Connor. She
writes, "Like Flannery O'Connor,
who also studied art before she
concentrated on prose fiction,
Updike pays homage to the visual artist's 'submission' to the
physical stimuli of his world far
more than most writers. He transcribes the world for us, and at
the same time transcribes the
experience of doing so, from the
inside. His world, like O'Connor's, is 'incarnational'—vividly,
lovingly, at times meanly recorded—perhaps because, in Updike, such a synthesis of fidelity
and inventiveness allows an escape of sorts from the tyrannical,
unimaginative cosmology of Calvinism. O'Connor was affirming
her faith through allegorical art;
Updike usually affirms it in words,
but the act of writing itself, the
free lovely spontaneous play of
the imagination, *is* salvation of a
kind . . ."

player's life, and kneel in the circle, giving
the crowd the old hawk profile, where once
the flutters would ease off, now they dig
down and begin.

They say I'm not hungry, but I still feel
hungry, only now it's a kind of panic hungry, and that's not the right kind. Ever
watch one of your little kids try to catch a
ball? He gets so excited with the idea he's going to catch it he shuts his eyes. That's me
now. I walk up to the plate, having come all
this way—a lot of hotels, a lot of shagging—
and my eyes feel shut. And I stand up there
trying to push my eyeballs through my eyelids, and my retinas register maybe a little
green, and the black patch of some nuns in
far left field. That's panic hungry.

Kierkegaard called it dread.[4] It queers
the works. My wife comes at me without the

____

4. dread: Kierkegaard believed that fear, or dread, is
a natural part of the human condition.

The Slump   979

6 Discussion How is the narrator's reference to the empty seats and the lone vendor related to his state of mind?

7 Clarification When a pitcher brushes a batter back, he or she throws the ball inside, forcing the batter to move away from the plate. By brushing a batter back, the pitcher hopes to induce the batter to stand farther away from the plate, making it difficult for the batter to hit an outside pitch.

8 Clarification When a pitcher puts the ball "right down the pike," he or she throws it directly over the center of the plate.

Reader's Response How do you imagine you might feel if you were an athlete nearing the end of your career? Explain.

gorilla mask and when in the old days, *whop!*, now she slides by with a hurt expression and a flicker of gray above her temple. I go out and ride the power mower and I've already done it so often the lawn is brown. The kids get me out of bed for a little fungo and it scares me to see them trying, busting their lungs, all that shagging ahead of them. In Florida—we used to love it in Florida, the smell of citrus and marlin, the flat pink sections where the old people drift around smiling with transistor plugs in their ears—we lie on the beach after a workout and the sun seems a high fly I'm going to lose and the waves keep coming like they've been doing for a billion years, up to the plate, up to the plate. Kierkegaard probably has the clue, somewhere in there, but I picked up *Concluding Unscientific Postscript*[5] the other day and I couldn't see the print, that is, I could see the lines, but there wasn't anything on them, like the rows of deep seats in the shade of the second deck on a Thursday afternoon, just a single ice-cream vendor sitting there, nobody around to sell to, a speck of white in all that shade, old Søren Sock himself, keeping his goods cool.

I think maybe if I got beaned. That's probably what the wife is hinting at with the gorilla mask. A change of pace, like the time DiMaggio[6] broke his slump by Topping's[7] telling him to go to a night club and get plastered. I've stopped ducking, but the trouble is, if you're not hitting, they don't brush you back. On me, they've stopped trying for even the corners; they put it right down the pike. I can see it in his evil eye as he takes the sign and rears back, I can hear the catcher snicker, and for a second of reflex there I can see it like it used to be, continents and cities and every green tree distinct as a stitch, and the hickory sweetens in my hands, and I feel the good old sure hunger. Then something happens. It blurs, skips, fades, I don't know. It's not caring enough, is what it probably is, it's knowing that none of it—the stadium, the averages—is really there, just *you* are there, and it's not enough.

---

5. ***Concluding Unscientific Postscript:*** One of Kierkegaard's major works.

6. **DiMaggio:** Joe DiMaggio (1914–   ), New York Yankee center fielder from 1936 to 1951; now a member of the baseball Hall of Fame.
7. **Topping's:** Refers to Dan Topping, one of the Yankee owners from 1945 to 1964.

THINKING ABOUT THE SELECTION

Recalling

1. (a) How do the coaches and newspapers explain the narrator's slump? (b) How does the narrator himself explain it?
2. (a) How did the narrator feel when he saw "the kids" waiting outside the stadium? (b) How does he now react when he sees them?
3. What now happens when the narrator takes "those two steps up from the dugout" and kneels "in the circle"?
4. (a) What solution does the narrator come up with in the final paragraph? (b) How does he explain his slump in the final sentence?

Interpreting

5. Explain the significance of Kierkegaard's statement, "You can't see a blind spot."

Closure and Extension

ANSWERS TO THINKING ABOUT THE SELECTION
Recalling

1. (a) The coaches and papers say that because the player is older, his reflexes are slower. (b) The narrator feels that it has more to do with the way that he sees the ball.

2. (a) Seeing the kids would cause the "big butterflies" to start. (b) He drives right by them.
3. The flutters "dig down and begin."
4. (a) He decides that getting "beaned" might help him break out of his slump. (b) He attributes the slump to his not caring enough.

Interpreting

5. Answers will differ. Students may respond that the statement means that people cannot be aware of that which they cannot see.

6. (a) He used to be excited and enthusiastic about playing, now he has a matter-of-fact attitude about the game. (b) He conveys this change in attitude by describing how his reaction to arriving at the park has changed.
7. (a) They show that his concerns extend beyond baseball. (b) His

6. (a) How has the narrator's attitude toward baseball changed during the course of his career? (b) How is this change in attitude conveyed?
7. (a) What is the significance of the narrator's observations while lying on the beach in Florida? (b) How do these observations relate to his own situation?
8. Explain the meaning of the conclusion the narrator reaches in the final sentence.
9. (a) What does the story suggest about fame? (b) What does it suggest about aging? (c) What does it suggest about life in general?

Applying

10. The narrator complains, "They say I'm not hungry, but I still feel hungry, only now it's a kind of panic hunger, and that's not the right kind." (a) What does he mean by the word *hungry*? (b) What is the right kind of hunger? (c) Do you think it is necessary to be hungry to succeed? Explain.
11. What other types of situations might produce concerns and feelings similar to the ones experienced by the narrator?

ANALYZING LITERATURE

Appreciating Diction and Style

Diction refers to a writer's choice of words. In fiction a writer must use language that is appropriate for his or her subject and characters.
1. Why is the language in "The Slump" appropriate for the narrator and subject? Support your answer.
2. Would the story still be effective if Updike had used ornate, elevated language? Why or why not?

3. The narrator tells his story in the present tense. (a) How would the effect of this story be different if it were told in the past tense? (b) How effective is this technique? Explain your answer.

UNDERSTANDING LANGUAGE

Understanding Jargon

Jargon refers to the specialized vocabulary of a specific profession. In "The Slump" Updike frequently uses baseball jargon—language which can be understood only by a person with some familiarity with the game. For example, when the narrator comments that he kneels "in the *circle*," he is referring to the on-deck circle, a circle in which the next batter awaits his or her turn at bat.

Use your dictionary to find the meaning of the following baseball terms.
1. batting cage   4. fungo
2. dugout   5. beaned
3. shagging

THINKING AND WRITING

Responding to Criticism

A critic has made the following comment concerning Updike's work: "Knowledgeable about the sports because he played them, Updike understands the difficulties of success and the poignancy of diminished prowess." Write an essay in which you discuss "The Slump" in relation to this comment. Before you start, make sure you understand the critic's comment in its entirety. What does he mean when he refers to "the poignancy of diminished prowess"? Include an explanation of the critic's comment in your essay. When you revise, make sure you have thoroughly supported your argument with passages from the story.

The Slump   981

(Answers begin on p. 980.)

Challenge How would you feel if you were in the narrator's place?

ANSWERS TO ANALYZING LITERATURE

1. The narrator frequently uses baseball terminology, such as *shagging* and *brush-back pitches*. This type of language is appropriate because he is a baseball player and the story is about baseball.
2. No, because ornate, elevated language would not be appropriate for the subject or narrator.
3. (a) The situation and events would seem less immediate. (b) Answers will differ. Students may respond that it is very effective, because it helps to create interest in the outcome of the narrator's situation.

ANSWERS TO UNDERSTANDING LANGUAGE

1. The area in which the next batter waits for his or her turn at the plate
2. A covered shelter near the diamond for the players to sit in when not at bat or in the field
3. Running after and catching
4. A batted ball hit by the batter after he has himself tossed the ball into the air
5. Being hit with a pitch

THINKING AND WRITING

For help with this assignment, students may refer to Lesson 17, Evaluating a Literary Work," in the Handbook of Writing About Literature.

Writing Across the Curriculum
You might wish to have students research and report on one of their favorite athletes. If you do, perhaps inform the physical education department of this assignment. Physical education teachers might provide guidance for students in conducting their research.

observations capture the passage of time, which keeps moving him closer to the end of his career.
8. The narrator observes that his past performance, his status, and the admiration of others are all meaningless, and that he is isolated and must rely on his current abilities to succeed, but he realizes that that isn't enough any more.
9. (a) The story suggests that fame

is both fleeting and unfulfilling. (b) Aging is unavoidable and discouraging. (c) In life it is very difficult to find comfort because you must rely upon yourself and your own perceptions.

Applying

10. (a) He means "eager and determined." (b) The right kind of hunger is eagerness, determination, and desire. (c) Answers will differ. Suggested Response: It is

necessary to be hungry, because hunger provides people with the motivation to succeed.
11. Suggested Response: Any situation that makes him aware of his advancing age could produce similar feelings.

More About the Author After publishing her first collection of stories at the age of 25, Joyce Carol Oates has produced a steady stream of novels and stories as well as nonfiction. She says that one reason for her productivity is that she writes in "flurries" and does not revise her first drafts very much. How do you think a writer could be helped or hindered by not stopping to revise a work in progress?

Critical Evaluation In her book *Vulnerable People: A View of American Fiction Since 1945*, the literary scholar Josephine Hendin writes, "Joyce Carol Oates can be as savage as she is rhapsodic. . . . Oates is no radical. But she is the young American novelist closest to the tradition of social realism. Her subject is not the goodness of the suffering poor but the extent to which being poor creates a divided soul. . . . Oates bares characters who are driven by blind impulse through the pitifully few parts they can play. Oates rhapsodizes the incomprehensibility of their lives. She virtually pleads for their blindness as a way of not seeing how little real mystery there is in lives that seem predestined to be unhappy. . . . Joyce Carol Oates's people hover between the impulse to destroy and a euphoric, tragic acceptance of their own pain at feeling destroyed by others. . . ."

JOYCE CAROL OATES

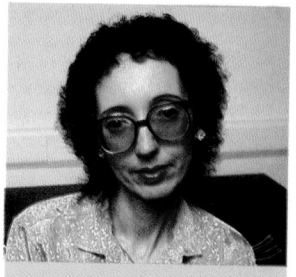

1938–

Joyce Carol Oates is one of the most prolific writers of our time. She has published many novels and collections of stories and has written numerous poems, plays, and critical essays, yet she has never sacrificed quality for productivity. As a result, nearly all of her work possesses a great amount of energy and intensity.

Oates was born in Lockport, New York. Located on the Erie Canal, Lockport was a town so small that Oates attended a one-room schoolhouse. There she had limited exposure to books, but that did not inhibit her from composing her own stories, which she bound with covers of her own design. In order to improve the presentation of her stories, she learned to type by age twelve. She later fictionalized life in Erie County, transforming it into Eden County, the setting for her first volume of stories as well as her first novel. As with Faulkner's Yoknapatawpha County, Oates's fictional Eden County is elaborately conceived and peopled with inhabitants who turn up in various ways from story to story. The practice of using a set cast of characters and familiar landmarks lends credibility to her fiction, continuity to her work, and welcome to readers who move familiarly from volume to volume. But Eden County is not the paradise its name implies. In fact, it is at times insufferable to its inhabitants. It has been suggested that Oates chose the name to remind readers how much we have lost.

Oates began writing at an early age. Her first book, *With Shuddering Fall*, was published in 1964. Since then she has produced novels, collections of short stories, and volumes of poetry at an incredibly rapid pace. Her works of fiction include *Wheel of Love and Other Stories* (1970), *The Assassins* (1975), *Do with Me What You Will* (1978), *The Seduction and Other Stories* (1980), *Bellefleur* (1980), *A Bloodsmore Romance* (1982), and *Mysteries of Winterthurn* (1984). Oates's poetry collections include *Angel Fire* (1973), *The Fabulous Beasts* (1975), and *Love and Its Derangements* and *Other Poems* (1977). She has received numerous awards for her work, including the 1970 National Book Award for her novel *Them* (1968).

In her fiction Oates delves into the varying states of the human mind. Her work often focuses on disturbed characters or characters who are anxiously searching for or struggling to come to terms with their identities. Oates has written, "We are stimulated to emotional response not by works that confirm our sense of the world, but by works that challenge it." "Journey" is the story of a symbolic quest for direction.

Objectives
1 To understand point of view
2 To support an interpretation
3 To use Latin roots
4 To write about symbolic meaning

Support Material

Teaching Portfolio
Teacher Backup, p. 1301
Usage and Mechanics Worksheet, p. 1304
Vocabulary Check, p. 1305
Critical Thinking and Reading Worksheet *Supporting an Interpretation*, p. 1306
Language Worksheet, *Using Latin Roots*, p. 1307
Selection Test, p. 1308

GUIDE FOR INTERPRETING

Journey

Writer's Techniques

Point of View. Point of view refers to the vantage point from which a narrative is told. Most stories are told from either a first-person or a third-person point of view. In contemporary fiction, however, there are rare instances in which a writer uses a second-person point of view. In this type of narrative, the narrator does not participate in the story and refers to the story's protagonist, or main character, as *you*. Generally a second-person narrator is limited, focusing on the thoughts and feelings of only one character.

By using a second-person point of view, a writer can give his or her story a universal quality. Because the narrator refers to the main character as *you*, the reader actually assumes the role of the main character and is forced to view himself or herself performing the actions of the main character in the story. As a result, a second-person narrative may be viewed not as a story about a specific character, but about human behavior in general.

Writing

How might a person's life be described as a journey? Freewrite about the ways in which life can be viewed as a journey.

Primary Source

The reader of Oates's story, "Journey," experiences the journey alone and somewhat fearfully. She has made the reader an "Outsider." The critic Carolyn Walker spoke of the "Outsider" in her work:

> Most interesting of all, perhaps, is Oates's treatment of the fear of being the Outsider. The Outsider is a person who perceives himself as somehow cut off from, shut out of, the human race. He suffers from being uncontrollably different, an aberration. . . .
>
> An important aspect of the Outsider's position is that he is locked out of love, which he sees as the needed path to salvation. . . . Ironically, the Outsider may discover that he is locked out of genuine, meaningful love, even if he has what appears on the surface to be a satisfactory love relationship. He may discover that he is actually locked into a hollow, unfulfilling "love."
>
> Given the horror of his situation, where does the Outsider in Oates's fiction look for comfort and solace? With genuine love unavailable, many of the characters look to art and the act of writing, . . . which results in some kind of spatially ordered pattern. . . . With the aid of the discovered pattern and order the characters hope to find a sense of personal meaning and sanity. . . .

Guide for Interpreting 983

Literary Focus The second-person point of view is fairly rare in fiction. Have your students discuss the limitations inherent in the second-person point of view.

Writing/Prior Knowledge Have small groups of students discuss the assignment before beginning. After completing the assignment, students may wish to share their freewriting with the class.

Vocabulary

Preteach the following vocabulary words:

monotony (mə nät′ 'n ē) *n.*: Lack of variation (p. 984)

hypnotic (hip nät′ ik) *adj.*: Inducing a sleeplike condition (p. 984)

convoluted (kän′ və lo͞ot′ id) *adj.*: Intricate; complicated (p. 984)

Journey

Joyce Carol Oates

You begin your journey on so high an elevation that your destination is already in
sight—a city that you have visited many
times and that, moreover, is indicated on a
traveler's map you have carefully folded up to
take along with you. You are a lover of maps,
and you have already committed this map to
memory, but you bring it with you just the
same.

The highway down from the mountains
is broad and handsome, constructed after
many years of ingenious blasting and leveling and paving. Engineers from all over the
country aided in the construction of this famous highway. Its cost is so excessive that
many rumors have circulated about it—you
take no interest in such things, sensing that
you will never learn the true cost anyway,
and that this will make no difference to your
journey.

After several hours on this excellent
highway, where the sun shines ceaselessly
and where there is a moderate amount of
traffic, cars like your own at a safe distance
from you, as if to assure you that there are
other people in the world, you become sleepy
from the monotony and wonder if perhaps
there is another, less perfect road parallel to
this. You discover on the map a smaller
road, not exactly parallel to the highway and
not as direct, but one that leads to the same
city.

You turn onto this road, which winds
among foothills and forests and goes
through several small villages. You sense by
the attitude of the villagers that traffic on
this road is infrequent but nothing to draw
special attention. At some curves the road
shrinks, but you are fortunate enough to
meet no oncoming traffic.

The road leads deep into a forest, always
descending in small cramped turns. Your
turning from left to right and from right to
left, in a slow hypnotic passage, makes it impossible for you to look out at the forest. You
discover that for some time you have not
been able to see the city you are headed for,
though you know it is still somewhere ahead
of you.

By mid-afternoon you are tired of this
road, though it has served you well, and you
come upon a smaller, unpaved road that evidently leads to your city, though in a convoluted way. After only a moment's pause you
turn onto this road, and immediately your
automobile registers the change—the chas-
sis bounces, something begins to vibrate,
something begins to rattle. This noise is disturbing, but after a while you forget about it
in your interest in the beautiful countryside.
Here the trees are enormous. There are no
villages or houses. For a while the dirt road
runs alongside a small river, dangerously
close to the river's steep bank, and you begin
to feel apprehension. It is necessary for you
to drive very slowly. At times your speedome-
ter registers less than five miles an hour.
You will not get to the city before dark.

The road narrows until it is hardly more
than a lane. Grass has begun to grow in its
center. As the river twists and turns, so does
the road twist and turn, curving around hills
that consist of enormous boulders, bare of
all trees and plants, covered only in patches

MARTHA'S VINEYARD, 1925
Thomas Hart Benton
Collection of Whitney Museum of American Art

by a dull, brown lichen that is unfamiliar to you. Along one stretch rocks of varying sizes have fallen down onto the road, so that you are forced to drive around them with great caution.

 Navigating these blind turns, you tap your horn to give warning in case someone should be approaching. But it is all unnecessary, since you come upon no other travelers.

Late in the afternoon, your foot numb from its constant pressure on the accelerator, your body jolted by the constant bumps and vibrations of the car, you decide to make the rest of your journey on foot, since you must be close to your destination by now.

A faint path leads through a tumble of rocks and bushes and trees, and you follow it enthusiastically. You descend a hill, slipping a little, so that a small rockslide is released; but you are able to keep your balance. At the back of your head is the precise location of your parked car, and behind that the curving dirt road, and behind that the other road, and then the magnificent highway itself: you understand that it would be no difficult feat to make your way back to

Humanities Note

Fine art, *Martha's Vineyard*, 1925, Thomas Hart Benton. Thomas Hart Benton (1889–1975) was one of the foremost American Regionalist painters. The son of a Missouri congressman, Benton had an interesting childhood. He attended the Art Institute of Chicago and the Academie Julien in Paris. After a brief career as a cartoonist, Benton turned to painting in 1912. He rejected the modern trends of the day to paint realistic scenes from American history, folklore, and rural life. His compelling paintings were one of the forces that changed the focus of American painting from Manhattan to the Midwest.

Benton spent many happy summers on Martha's Vineyard with his wife and family. This painting is a view of the Chilmark Town Hall at Beetlebung corner, a place where Benton remembers going to Saturday night square dances in the '20's. This painting was done as a landscape study before Benton focused more intensely on the American scene. The richness of curving shapes and subtle understated colors add to the atmosphere of loneliness suggested by the deserted stretch of road. The title identifies the setting; without the title, this scene could be anywhere.

You might ask the following questions:
1. What might this road symbolize?
2. What is it about this painting that conveys an eerie mood?
3. Given this mood, why is this painting an appropriate illustration for this story?

3 **Discussion** What mood does the story create for the reader? How does the author achieve this mood?

any of these roads, should you decide that going by foot is unwise. But the path, though overgrown, is through a lovely forest, and then through a meadow in which yellow flowers are blooming, and you feel no inclination to turn back.

By evening you are still in the wilderness and you wonder if perhaps you have made a mistake. You are exhausted, your body aches, your eyes are seared by the need to stare so intently at everything around you. Now that the sun has nearly set, it is getting cold; evenings here in the mountains are always chilly.

You find yourself standing at the edge of a forest, staring ahead into the dark. Is that a field ahead, or a forest of small trees? Your path has long since given way to wild grass. Clouds obscure the moon, which should give you some light by which to make your way, and you wonder if you dare continue without this light.

Suddenly you remember the map you left back in the car, but you remember it as a blank sheet of paper.

You resist telling yourself you are lost. In fact, though you are exhausted and it is almost night, you are not lost. You have begun to shiver, but it is only with cold, not with fear. You are really satisfied with yourself. You are not lost. Though you can remember your map only as a blank sheet of paper, which can tell you nothing, you are not really lost.

If you had the day to begin again, on that highway which was so wide and clear, you would not have varied your journey in any way: in this is your triumph.

THINKING ABOUT THE SELECTION

Recalling

1. (a) Where does "your" journey begin? (b) What is "your" destination?
2. (a) Why do "you" turn off the highway? (b) Why do "you" turn onto an unpaved road? (c) Why do "you" decide "to make the rest of the journey on foot"?
3. (a) Where do "you" end up by evening? (b) What do "you" suddenly remember?
4. What conclusion do "you" make at the end of the story?

Interpreting

5. (a) Into what four stages can "your" journey be divided? (b) How does the appearance of the road or path that "you" follow change from stage to stage? (c) How does the appearance of the surrounding landscape change from stage to stage? (d) What other changes occur as "you" pass from stage to stage?
6. What is the significance of the fact that none of the places in the story are named?
7. In the beginning of the story, the narrator comments that "you are a lover of maps." (a) How does this attitude change during the course of the story? (b) What is the signifance of the fact that in the end "you" remember the map "as a blank sheet of paper"?
8. What is the triumph felt at the end of the story?

Applying

9. Explain how this story relates to the following lines from Robert Frost's poem "The Road Not Taken": "Two roads diverged in the wood, and I— / I took the one less traveled by, / and that has made all the difference."

ANALYZING LITERATURE
Understanding Point of View

Point of view refers to the vantage point from which a narrative is told. Unlike most other stories, "Journey" is told from a second-person point of view.

1. How does Oates's use of a second-person point of view help make it clear that the story is meant to be interpreted symbolically?
2. Why would the story be less effective if Oates had used a first-person or third-person point of view?

CRITICAL THINKING AND READING
Supporting an Interpretation

When a story is meant to be interpreted symbolically, you must examine all the details in the story and determine how they fit together and what they represent.

The following is one possible interpretation of the symbolic meaning of "Journey." Support or refute this interpretation using details from the story:

The journey symbolizes a person's life, during which he or she passes from conformity to individuality. At first this person has his or her life carefully mapped out to follow a path that many others have taken. As the person's life pro- gresses, however, he or she begins exploring new directions that fewer and fewer people have followed.

UNDERSTANDING LANGUAGE
Using Latin Roots

The Latin word *navis* means "ship." The root of this word, *nav,* has given us many English words. For example, Oates writes, "Navigating these blind turns, you tap your horn to give warning in case someone should be approach- ing." Originally the word *navigating* meant "di- recting a ship on its course on a body of water." Now the word also means "finding one's way."

Define each of the words below based on the root *nav.*

1. navy
2. navvy
3. navigator
4. navicular

THINKING AND WRITING
Writing About Symbolic Meaning

Develop your answer from the Critical Think- ing and Reading activity into an essay. Review your answer and try to think of additional details that support the interpretation. Organize your essay according to the stages of the journey. When you revise, make sure you have included enough details to thoroughly support your inter- pretation. After revising, proofread your essay.

Journey 987

foot. (b) It indicates you can no longer envision having your jour- ney mapped out.
8. Answers will differ. Students may respond that the triumph refers to the narrator's newly discovered feeling of independence.

Applying

9. Suggested Response: The poet writes of the satisfaction with trav- eling the less-taken route; this sto- ry describes the choice of a wild path over a highway or road as a "triumph."

Challenge Do you agree with the view expressed by the author of this story? Explain how you could apply this view to your own life.

ANSWERS TO ANALYZING LITERATURE

1. By writing the story in the second person, she makes it clear that the situations and events can be ap- plied to anyone's life.
2. If another point of view had been used, it would have appeared that the narrator was merely describ- ing the experiences of a single character.

ANSWERS TO CRITICAL THINKING AND READING

At first "you" are "a lover of maps" and choose a heavily traveled road. You become tired of this road, however, and you spend the rest of your journey seeking out roads that are more and more remote.

ANSWERS TO UNDERSTANDING LANGUAGE

1. the entire sea force of a nation
2. an unskilled laborer
3. one skilled at directing ships or aircraft
4. any of various boat-shaped bones

THINKING AND WRITING

Publishing Student Writing Ask for student volunteers to read their essays aloud. Have stu- dents in the audience record at least one noteworthy feature of each essay.

987

Closure and Extension

ANSWERS TO THINKING ABOUT THE SELECTION
Recalling

1. (a) Your journey begins at a high elevation. (b) Your destination is a city you have visited before.
2. (a) You become sleepy from the monotony of the highway. (b) You have grown tired of the second road. (c) You leave your car be- cause you are numb from driving.
3. (a) By evening you are still in the wilderness. (b) You suddenly re- member that you have left your map in the car.
4. You conclude if you had to begin the day again you would not vary your journey in any way.

Interpreting

5. (a) The journey can be divided into highway, paved road, un- paved road, footpath. (b) The road grows narrower and more wind- ing, and becomes less and less easy to distinguish from the rest of the landscape. (c) The landscape becomes wilder and more over- grown and the signs of human life disappear. (d) The traffic dissi- pates and eventually disappears.
6. The lack of names indicates that the story is meant to be interpret- ed symbolically.
7. (a) You forget completely about your map while you are walking on

More About the Author Donald Barthelme is one of the most experimental and witty of the post-modern authors. His texts are often written in unusual or extreme forms, such as letters, charts, lists, or even drawings. Influenced by the French philosopher Roland Barthes, he is concerned with the actual process of reading words on a page. This concern is often referred to as looking at "text as text" rather than as "experience." Can students see how this concern may have led Barthelme to write about an artist? Discuss the fact that writers convey ideas through the symbols of words while artists are concerned with pictorial images and their placement.

Critical Evaluation In his introduction to a published interview with Donald Barthelme, the literary scholar Jerome Klinkowitz writes, "Barthelme is one of the most prolific short story writers in recent times: of his one-hundred-odd pieces, more than half have not been collected, among them some of his funniest and most inventive fictions. Barthelme's work has become one of the great resources of contemporary American literature: he has according to Philip Stevick become the most imitated fictionist in the United States today."

1931–1989

Donald Barthelme was one of the most innovative fiction writers of our time. Experimenting with a variety of radically different approaches to writing fiction, he frequently abandoned not only traditional forms but also the forms that characterize Modernist fiction.

Barthelme was born in Philadelphia and raised in Houston, Texas. In 1964 he published his first book, *Dr. Caligari*, a collection of satirical and surrealistic stories. Three years later, he produced his first novel, *Snow White*, an elaborately structured work that explores the underlying emptiness of many contemporary ideologies and fads. He went on to publish several novels and numerous collections of short stories and has won a number of awards. He also produced a children's book, *The Slightly Irregular Fire Engine or the Hithering Thithering Djinn* (1971), which earned him the National Book Award for children's literature.

Having worked as a newspaper reporter, a museum director, and a managing editor of an art and literature review, Barthelme's experience has been varied. He also served in the United States Army in Korea and Japan, an epoch in his life to which he devotes some humorous attention in his fiction. He has been called "probably the most perversely gifted writer in the U.S.," a dubious distinction earned in part by his unyielding attempts to broaden both literary forms and the scope of human amusement. Critic Jack Kroll has said, "The world is hysteria but Barthelme doesn't get hysterical about it. He knows it's also funny," In fact, his work is often so humorous that readers may miss his serious intent. The often quirky and absurd nature of Donald Barthelme's work operates as a magnifying agent to trap and focus attention directly on subjects worthy of a second look and reevaluation. Wanting to engage his reader intimately with his writing, he expressed his intention to write in such a manner that readers will identify not just with characters or subjects but with the writer. He hoped to dupe the reader into feeling almost as if the reader is writing the story himself or herself.

As in most Barthelme stories, both the form and content of "Engineer-Private Paul Klee Misplaces an Aircraft Between Milbertshofen and Cambrai, March 1916" are unconventional. Barthelme uses a historical figure, Swiss abstract painter Paul Klee (1879–1940), as the story's main character. Loosely based on an incident that occurred during Klee's period of service with the German air corps during World War I, the story humorously examines the impersonal nature of military life.

Objectives

1 To understand experimental fiction
2 To appreciate shades of meaning
3 To use words from Latin
4 To respond in writing to criticism

Support Material

Teaching Portfolio
Teacher Backup, p. 1311
Usage and Mechanics Worksheet, p. 1314
Vocabulary Check, p. 1315
Analyzing Literature Worksheet *Understanding Experimental Fiction*, p. 1316

Critical Thinking and Reading Worksheet, *Appreciating Shades of Meaning*, p. 1317
Selection Test, p. 1318

GUIDE FOR INTERPRETING

Engineer-Private Paul Klee Misplaces an Aircraft Between Milbertshofen and Cambrai, March 1916

Literary Movements

Experimental Fiction. During the 1960's a number of writers began searching for ways to set their work apart from the literature of the past. This quest led to the development of new and radically different types of fiction in which conventional forms and structures were often completely abandoned. Some writers discarded the use of a narrator in their stories and began composing stories from dialogue alone. Others began experimenting with the physical appearance of their work, at times even using blank pages as a part of a literary work. While basically adhering to conventional structures, other writers began exploring new and unconventional subjects in their works. A number of writers turned their focus inward, writing stories about the process of writing and the forms and techniques of the story itself. Donald Barthelme's story "Sentence," for example, is, as the title suggests, one extremely long sentence about the peculiarities of sentences. Finally, some experimental writers turned to parodying ancient literary works, while others explored the use of historical figures as characters in their works.

Commentary

Repeating words, phrases, and ideas is a tool writers use for various effects. As you read Barthelme's story, notice how he uses repetition for humor. For example, the first time the Secret Police address you, the reader, they repeat "secrets," "omnipresence," and "no one knows," until these become meaningless buzz words, and so the Secret Police who speak the words seem absurd. The Secret Police take on the character of humorous bumblers, a view compounded by the way they take themselves and their task seriously even though it is evident to you, through their ludicrous repetitions of empty words and phrases, that they do not know what they are doing or why they are doing it. Barthelme's use of repetition throughout the story produces humor, but he also uses it to reflect a common view of military life—that it is filled with needless and sometimes mindless repetitions, and that, at least in some aspects, it is also absurd. Do you agree with Barthelme's view of life in the military?

Writing

Barthelme's story focuses on the experiences of Swiss abstract painter Paul Klee during his period of service with the German air corps during World War I. List the reasons why you think it might be difficult for an artist to adjust to life in the military.

Guide for Interpreting 989

Engineer-Private Paul Klee Misplaces an Aircraft Between Milbertshofen and Cambrai[1], March 1916

Donald Barthelme

Paul Klee said:

"Now I have been transferred to the Air Corps. A kindly sergeant effected the transfer. He thought I would have a better future here, more chances for promotion. First I was assigned to aircraft repair, together with several other workers. We presented ourselves as not just painters but artist-painters. This caused some shaking of heads. We varnished wooden fuselages, correcting old numbers and adding new ones with the help of templates. Then I was pulled off the painting detail and assigned to transport. I escort aircraft that are being sent to various bases in Germany and also (I understand) in occupied territory. It is not a bad life. I spend my nights racketing across Bavaria[2] (or some such) and my days in switching yards. There is always bread and wurst and beer in the station restaurants. When I reach a notable town I try to see the notable paintings there, if time allows. There are always unexpected delays, reroutings, backtrackings. Then the return to the base. I see Lily fairly often. We meet in hotel rooms and that is exciting. I have never yet lost an aircraft or failed to deliver one to its proper destination. The war seems interminable. Walden has sold six of my drawings."

The Secret Police said:

"We have secrets. We have many secrets. We desire all secrets. We do not have your secrets and that is what we are after, your secrets. Our first secret is where we are. No one knows. Our second secret is how many of us there are. No one knows. Omnipresence is our goal. We do not even need real omnipresence. The theory of omnipresence is enough. With omnipresence, hand-in-hand as it were, goes omniscience. And with omniscience and omnipresence, hand-in-hand-in-hand as it were, goes omnipotence. We are a three-sided waltz. However our mood is melancholy. There is a secret sigh that we sigh, secretly. We yearn to be known, acknowledged, admired even. What is the good of omnipotence if nobody knows? However that is a secret, that sorrow. Now we are everywhere. One place we are is here watching Engineer-Private Klee, who is escorting three valuable aircraft, B.F.W. 3054/16–17–18, with spare parts, by rail from Milbertshofen to Cambrai. Do you wish to know what Engi-

---

1. Milbertshofen (mil′ berts hof′ ən) **and Cambrai** (käm brā′): Milbertshofen is a town in Bavaria. Cambrai is a town in northern France.
2. Bavaria (bə ver′ ē ə): A state in southwest Germany.

neer-Private Klee is doing at this very moment, in the baggage car? He is reading a book of Chinese short stories. He has removed his boots. His feet rest twenty-six centimeters from the baggage-car stove."

Paul Klee said:

"These Chinese short stories are slight and lovely. I have no way of knowing if the translation is adequate or otherwise. Lily will meet me in our rented room on Sunday, if I return in time. Our destination is Fighter Squadron Five. I have not had anything to eat since morning. The fine chunk of bacon given me along with my expense money when we left the base has been eaten. This morning a Red Cross lady with a squint gave me some very good coffee, however. Now we are entering Hohenbudberg."[3]

The Secret Police said:

"Engineer-Private Klee has taken himself into the station restaurant. He is enjoying a hearty lunch. We shall join him there."

Paul Klee said:

"Now I emerge from the station restaurant and walk along the line of cars to the flatcar on which my aircraft (I think of them as *my* aircraft) are carried. To my surprise and dismay, I notice that one of them is missing. There had been three, tied down on the flatcar and covered with canvas. Now I see with my trained painter's eye that instead of three canvas-covered shapes on the flatcar there are only two. Where the third aircraft had been there is only a puddle of canvas and loose rope. I look around quickly to see if anyone else has marked the disappearance of the third aircraft."

The Secret Police said:

"We had marked it. Our trained policemen's eyes had marked the fact that where three aircraft had been before, tied down on the flatcar and covered with canvas, now there were only two. Unfortunately we had been in the station restaurant, lunching, at the moment of removal, therefore we could not attest as to where it had gone or who

had removed it. There is something we do not know. This is irritating in the extreme. We closely observe Engineer-Private Klee to determine what action he will take in the emergency. We observe that he is withdrawing from his tunic a notebook and pencil. We observe that he begins, very properly in our opinion, to note down in his notebook all the particulars of the affair."

Paul Klee said:

"The shape of the collapsed canvas, under which the aircraft had rested, together with the loose ropes—the canvas forming hills and valleys, seductive folds, the ropes the very essence of looseness, lapsing—it is irresistible. I sketch for ten or fifteen minutes, wondering the while if I might not be in trouble, because of the missing aircraft. When I arrive at Fighter Squadron Five with less than the number of aircraft listed on the manifest,[4] might not some officious person become angry? Shout at me? I have finished sketching. Now I will ask various trainmen and station personnel if they have seen anyone carrying away the aircraft. If they answer in the negative, I will become extremely frustrated. I will begin to kick the flatcar."

The Secret Police said:

"Frustrated, he begins to kick the flatcar."

Paul Klee said:

"I am looking up in the sky, to see if my aircraft is there. There are in the sky aircraft of several types, but none of the type I am searching for."

The Secret Police said:

"Engineer-Private Klee is searching the sky—an eminently sound procedure, in our opinion. We, the Secret Police, also sweep the Hohenbudberg sky, with our eyes. But find nothing. We are debating with ourselves as to whether we ought to enter the station restaurant and begin drafting our preliminary report for forwarding to higher headquarters. The knotty point, in terms of the preliminary report, is that we do not have

---

3. Hohenbudberg (hō ən bud′ berg): A village in northwestern Germany.

4. manifest (man′ ə fest′) *n.*: A cargo list.

991

---

3 Reading Strategy Have students predict how the Secret Police will react when the plane is discovered to be missing.

4 Discussion How does Klee react to the missing plane? What does this tell you about his attitude toward his situation?

5 Discussion How omnipresent are the Secret Police in reality? Discuss the notion of omnipresence, and have students compare the Secret Police in this story with film depictions of spies and double agents.

6 Enrichment Paul Klee has been classified as an Expressionist painter. Expressionism was a movement that one critic describes as "direct visualization of individual emotions." How might Klee's picture differ from another painter's?

7 Discussion How does Klee refer to his act of forgery? Discuss how the use of jargon and formal speech can result in euphemism and ridiculous understatement.

8 Reading Strategy Have students predict how the Secret Police will react to Klee's solution.

9 Discussion Have students compare the Police's reaction with their own predictions. How was the Police's reaction different from what students expected? Have students explain the reasons for the Police's acceptance of the forgery.

10 Discussion What is ironic about Klee's final statement?

Reader's Response Did you enjoy this story? Why or why not?

the answer to the question 'Where is the aircraft?' The damage potential to the theory of omniscience as well as potential to our careers, dictates that this point be omitted from the preliminary report. But if this point is omitted, might not some officious person at the Central Bureau for Secrecy note the omission? Become angry? Shout at us? Omissiveness is not rewarded at the Central Bureau. We decide to observe further the actions of Engineer-Private Klee, for the time being."

Paul Klee said:

"I who have never lost an aircraft have lost an aircraft. The aircraft is signed out to me. The cost of the aircraft, if it is not found, will be deducted from my pay, meager enough already. Even if Walden sells a hundred, a thousand drawings, I will not have enough money to pay for this cursed aircraft. Can I, in the time the train remains in the Hohenbudberg yards, construct a new aircraft or even the simulacrum of an aircraft, with no materials to work with or indeed any special knowledge of aircraft construction? The situation is ludicrous. I will therefore apply Reason. Reason dictates the solution. I will diddle the manifest. With my painter's skill which is after all not so different from a forger's, I will change the manifest to reflect conveyance of *two* aircraft, B.F.W. 3054/16 and 17, to Fighter Squadron Five. The extra canvas and ropes I will conceal in an empty boxcar—this one, which according to its stickers is headed for Essigny-le-Petit.[5] Now I will walk around

---

5. Essigny-le-Petit (es sē nyē′ lə pə tē′): A street or district of St. Quentin in northern France.

town and see if I can find a chocolate shop. I crave chocolate."

The Secret Police said:

"Now we observe Engineer-Private Klee concealing the canvas and ropes which covered the former aircraft into an empty boxcar bound for Essigny-le-Petit. We have previously observed him diddling the manifest with his painter's skill which resembles not a little that of the forger. We applaud these actions of Engineer-Private Klee. The contradiction confronting us in the matter of the preliminary report is thus resolved in highly satisfactory fashion. We are proud of Engineer-Private Klee and of the resolute and manly fashion in which he has dealt with the crisis. We predict he will go far. We would like to embrace him as a comrade and brother but unfortunately we are not embraceable. We are secret, we exist in the shadows, the pleasure of the comradely/brotherly embrace is one of the pleasures we are denied, in our dismal service."

Paul Klee said:

"We arrive at Cambrai. The planes are unloaded, six men for each plane. The work goes quickly. No one questions my altered manifest. The weather is clearing. After lunch I will leave to begin the return journey. My release slip and travel orders are ready, but the lieutenant must come and sign them. I wait contentedly in the warm orderly room. The drawing I did of the collapsed canvas and ropes is really very good. I eat a piece of chocolate. I am sorry about the lost aircraft but not overmuch. The war is temporary. But drawings and chocolate go on forever."

Closure and Extension

ANSWERS TO THINKING ABOUT THE SELECTION
Recalling

1. He works in transport, escorting aircraft to various bases.
2. (a) Their first secret is that no one knows where they are. (b) The second secret is that no one knows how many of them exist.
(c) Their goal is to be everywhere at once.
3. Klee notices that one of the three aircraft is missing.
4. (a) Klee alters the shipping form to indicate that there were only two planes in the shipment. (b) The Secret Police are pleased with his ingenuity.

Interpreting

5. (a) The Secret Police long to be acknowledged for their work, but their duty forbids them from being known. (b) They mechanically accept their role and attempt to perform in a manner that will earn praise from their superiors. (c) Their mechanical attitude is revealed through their mechanical diction. Their desire for praise is indicated by the fact that they are less interested in solving problems than in the appearance of solving problems, as indicated by their appreciation of Klee's solution.

THINKING ABOUT THE SELECTION

Recalling

1. What is Klee's primary duty as a member of the air corps?
2. (a) What is the Secret Police's "first secret"? (b) What is their "second secret"? (c) What is their goal?
3. What does Klee notice when he returns to the flatcar on which his aircraft are carried?
4. (a) How does Klee solve his problem? (b) How do the Secret Police react to Klee's solution?

Interpreting

5. (a) How do the duties of the Secret Police contrast with their desires? (b) What is their attitude toward their service? (c) How is this attitude revealed?
6. (a) What concern do Klee and the Secret Police share? (b) What is the significance of the fact that they share this concern?
7. What is the significance of the mechanical fashion in which both Klee and the Secret Police speak in this story?
8. What is the meaning of Klee's comments about war, drawings, and chocolate?
9. (a) Who, or what, is Barthelme satirizing, or poking fun at, in this story? (b) What is the story's theme, or main point?

Applying

10. Explain why you do or do not think satire is an effective means of protesting war.

ANALYZING LITERATURE

Understanding Experimental Fiction

Barthelme's story is an excellent example of experimental fiction—a radically different type of fiction that developed during the 1960's, as a result of the desire of writers to create work that stood apart from the literature of the past.
1. What is unconventional about the structure of Barthelme's story?
2. How does the structure reflect its meaning?

CRITICAL THINKING AND READING

Appreciating Shades of Meaning

Frequently, words that appear to be identical in meaning actually have slightly different meanings. For example, though the words *monitor* and *observe* are quite similar, they have slightly different meanings. The word *monitor* means "to watch or check on," while *observe* means "to pay special attention to." Use your dictionary to find the slight difference in meaning between the words in each of the following pairs.
1. escort : conduct   3. opinion : belief
2. melancholy : sullen 4. ludicrous : foolish

UNDERSTANDING LANGUAGE

Using Words from Latin

The Latin word *omnis* means "all." It has given us the combining form *omni*, which we use to build new words. For example, in this story the secret police claim to be omnipresent, omnipotent, and omniscient.
1. Define the words *omnipresent, omnipotent,* and *omniscient.*
2. How are these qualities similar to the qualities usually attributed to God?
3. How does this similarity affect the meaning of the story?

THINKING AND WRITING

Responding to Criticism

A critic has commented that despair is one of Barthelme's "favorite subjects for jest." Write an essay in which you discuss this comment in relation to the story you have just read. Reread the story, noting Barthelme's use of satire. Write your essay, using passages from the story to support your argument. When you revise, make sure your essay is logically organized and that you have not included unnecessary information.

ANSWERS TO ANALYZING LITERATURE

1. The story is composed from dialogue alone. No narrator is used.
2. The structure reflects the mechanical and impersonal nature of military life.

ANSWERS TO CRITICAL THINKING AND READING

1. conduct: guide or lead; escort; provide protection for.
2. melancholy: depression of the spirits; sullen; gloomily silent; morose.
3. opinion: a belief stronger than an impression and less strong than positive knowledge; belief: something that one accepts as true.
4. ludicrous: laughable, slightly stronger than foolish; foolish: absurd; ridiculous.

ANSWERS TO UNDERSTANDING LANGUAGE

1. *Omnipresent* means "present at all places at all times"; *omnipotent* means "all-powerful"; *omniscient* means "all-knowing."
2. All three of these qualities are usually attributed to God.
3. The similarities suggest that the Secret Police view themselves as being God-like.

THINKING AND WRITING

For help with this assignment, students can refer to Lesson 15, "Evaluating a Literary Work," in the Handbook of Writing About Literature.

Publishing Student Writing Ask for student volunteers to read their essays aloud. Have students in the audience record at least one noteworthy feature of each essay.

6. (a) They both want to prevent their superiors from becoming angry with them. (b) It indicates that the fear of disapproval from superiors is a common concern among soldiers.
7. It reflects the mechanical nature of military life.
8. Klee points out that he is not very concerned with war, because it will eventually come to an end, unlike culinary creations and art that endure from generation to generation.

9. (a) Barthelme is satirizing the ways in which rigid structures and institutions limit and shape people's behavior. (b) The main point of the story is that rigid structures and institutions are impersonal and ultimately ineffective.

Applying

10. Suggested Response: Satire is an effective tool for protesting war because it captures the reader's attention and makes the reader think. Sometimes it is necessary to exaggerate a view in order to point out the inconsistencies in that view.

Challenge Could this story have been told in a conventional manner? Explain your answer.

More About the Author Ann Beattie is often acknowledged as the foremost champion of the simple prose style favored by many contemporary writers. Some critics link her spare use of language to Hemingway's, others to the flat language of television and modern media. Her work has been praised for accurately reflecting the era in which we live. Ask students to discuss why the critics might think a lean, simple prose style best suited to portraying our times. Why might a style rich in ornate, flowery language be inappropriate for the late twentieth century?

Critical Evaluation In describing Ann Beattie's characters, Clifton Fadiman wrote, "Her people, usually well educated, articulate, sensitive, are often maladjusted . . . ill matched as couples . . . divorced, separated, negative, failed artists, neurotically mod. We conventionally praise fiction writers for their ability to make characters come alive. We should praise Beattie for her ability to make them come half alive, for that is what they are." Tell students to keep Fadiman's comment in mind as they are reading "Imagined Scenes" and to think about how well it applies to the story.

ANN BEATTIE

1947–

Generally considered to be one of today's most accomplished young fiction writers, Ann Beattie has restlessly pursued innovations in narrative structure. Like many other contemporary writers, Beattie often composes works in the form of a broken, fragmented sequence of events, thoughts, emotions, and memories. This approach reflects Beattie's perceptions of the sense of aimlessness and disorder associated with contemporary life.

Born in Washington, D.C., Beattie achieved success as a writer at an early age. She has had numerous short stories published in *The New Yorker* and has produced several collections of stories. Her collections include *Distortions* (1976), *Secrets and Surprises* (1978), *The Burning House* (1982), and *Where You'll Find Me* (1986). Although she is known more for her short stories, she has also written a number of novels, including *Chilly Scenes of Winter* (1976), *Falling in Place* (1980), and *Love Always* (1985).

Chilly Scenes of Winter is a novel concerned with the people who came of age in the 1960's and have since found themselves disillusioned by society's changes. Ms. Beattie has said about it, "I was going out of my way in the novel to say something about the 60's having passed. It just seems to me to be an attitude that most of my friends and most of the people I know have. They all feel sort of let down, either by not having involved themselves more in the 60's . . . or else by having involved themselves to no avail. Most of the people I know are let down—they feel cheated—and these are the people I am writing about."

About the simple declarative style in which she writes, she says, "My stories are a lot about chaos . . . and many of the simple flat statements that I bring together are usually non sequiturs or bordering on being non sequiturs—which reinforces the chaos. I write in those flat simple sentences because that's the way I think. I don't mean to do it as a technique. It might be just that I am incapable of breaking through to the complexities underlying all that sort of simple statement you find in my work."

A typical Beattie story, "Imagined Scenes" captures a young woman's overwhelming sense of purposelessness. Using a detached narrator to present a series of seemingly distorted scenes, Beattie makes it seem as if we are actually witnessing events from the young woman's life, rather than being told a story.

GUIDE FOR INTERPRETING

Imagined Scenes

Literary Movements

Postmodernism. Postmodernism refers to the collection of literary movements that have developed in the decades following World War II. Like their predecessors, many of the Postmodernists have attempted to capture the essence of contemporary life in the form and content of their work. Others, however, have focused on creating works that stand apart from the literature of the past. To accomplish these purposes, writers have experimented with a variety of different approaches and used a wide range of literary forms and techniques. Many writers have continued to develop the fragmentary approach of the Modernists, omitting expositions, resolutions, and transitions, and composing stories in the form of broken or distorted sequence of scenes, rather than in the form of a continuous narrative. Possessing the belief that reality is to some extent shaped by our imaginations, some writers have turned away from writing realistic fiction and begun writing fantasy or "magical realism"—fiction that blends realism and fantasy. Other writers have radically departed from traditional fictional forms and techniques, composing works from dialogue alone, creating works that blend fiction and nonfiction, and experimenting with the physical appearance of a work. Finally, a number of Postmodernist writers have confronted the problems they perceive in contemporary society through the use of satire and black humor.

Look For Your less advanced students may have difficulty following the story as it is told. Have these students make a list of characters as they read, noting their relationships to one another.

Writing Have your more advanced students consider how the situation and problems might be the same or different if a young woman had strong career aspirations and her husband had to pattern his life to accommodate her career. Have them freewrite about the similarities and differences between the two situations.

Commentary

Setting is never accidental in a story, but in some stories, it is a central choice the author makes. In Ann Beattie's "Imagined Scenes," notice that the midwinter setting not only creates the frozen atmosphere of the story but also underscores the story's central points. That the story opens with a dream of a beach somewhere is significant. The relationship between David and his wife is being lived in the dead of midwinter, and her beach dream indicates dissatisfaction with the wintry state of things. Soon David mentions a trip to Greece, a country associated with warm weather and beaches. His wife muses to herself that she'd rather go to Spain, another warm country with beaches. Both seem unhappy with the present, but each sees in his or her future a different beach. Meanwhile, the snow grows deeper and deeper around them. As you read the story, consider what the winter, the snow, and the beaches represent in the lives of these people.

Writing

"Imagined Scenes" focuses on the life of a young woman who has been forced to pattern her life to accommodate her husband's career aspirations. Freewrite about the types of problems that you think might arise from this type of situation.

Vocabulary

Preteach the following vocabulary words:
engrossed (in grōs′t′) v.: Absorbed (p. 997)
impetuous (im pech′ oo wəs) adj.: Acting or done suddenly with little thought; rash; impulsive (p. 997)
adhere (əd hir′) v.: To stick fast; stay attached (p. 998)

Guide for Interpreting 995

Imagined Scenes

Ann Beattie

"I've unlaced my boots and I'm standing barefoot on a beach with very brown sand, ocean in front of me and mountains in the distance, and trees making a pretty green haze around them."

"Pretty," David says.

"Where would that be?"

"Greece?"

1 When she wakes from a dream, David is already awake. Or perhaps he only wakes when she stirs, whispers to him. He doesn't sound sleepy; he's alert, serious, as though he'd been waiting for a question. She remembers last year, the week before Christmas, when she and David had gone out separately to shop. She got back to the house first, her keys lost—or locked in the car. Before she could look for them, headlights lit up the snowy path. David jumped out of his car, excited about his purchases, reaching around her to put the key in the door. Now she expects him to wake up when she does, that they will arrive home simultaneously. But David still surprises her—at the end of summer he told her he wouldn't be working in the fall. He was going back to college to finish the work for his Ph.D.

He sits in a gray chair by the fireplace and reads; she brings coffee to the table by his chair, and he turns off the light and goes up-

PLEASURES OF WINTER IN NEW YORK
Francis Peterson
Three Lions

stairs to bed when she is tired. By unspoken agreement, he has learned to like Roquefort dressing. He pokes the logs in the fireplace because the hot red coals frighten her.

"After I take orals in the spring we'll go to Greece to celebrate."

She wants to go to Spain. Couldn't the beach have been in Spain? No more questions—she should let him sleep. She shakes the thought out of her head.

"No?" he says. "We will. We'll go to Greece when I finish the orals."

The leaves of the plant look like worn velvet. The tops are purple, a shiny, fuzzy purple, and the underside is dark green. Suddenly the plant has begun to grow, sending up a narrow shoot not strong enough to support itself, so that it falls forward precariously, has to be staked. They agree it's strange that a plant should have such a spurt of growth in midwinter. David admires the plant, puts it in a window that gets the morning light and moves it into a side room late in the afternoon. Now when he waters the plant a little plant food is mixed in with the water. David is enthusiastic; he's started to feed the others to see if they'll grow. She comes home and finds him stretched by the fireplace, looking through a book about plants. Their plant isn't pictured, he tells her, but it may be mentioned in the text. She goes into the other room to look at the plant. The shoot appears to be taller. They bought the plant in a food store last winter—not very pretty then. It was in a small cracked pot, wrapped in plastic. They replanted it. In fact, David must have replanted it again.

She puts away the groceries and goes back to the living room. David is still on the rug reading the book. He's engrossed. The coffee would probably get cold if she brought it. She has to work that night. She goes upstairs to take a nap and sets the alarm. She rests, but can't fall asleep, listening to the quiet music downstairs. She pushes in the alarm button and goes back to the living room. David is in his chair, reading the book, drinking coffee.

"I spent the most terrible winter in my life in Berlin. I don't know why, but birds don't leave Berlin in the winter. They're big, strong birds. They nest in the public buildings. I think the winter just comes too suddenly in Berlin, no plans can be made. The birds turn gray, like snowbirds. I think snowbirds are gray."

The old man is looking out the window. He is her patient. His daughter and son-in-law are away for a week, and his sister stays with him in the day. She has been hired to stay with him at night. He is not very ill, but old and unsteady.

She drinks tea with him, tired because she didn't nap.

"I don't sleep well," he tells her. "I want to talk all the time. My daughter doesn't sleep either. In the day we fight, or I worry her, but at night I think she's glad to have someone to talk to."

The snowplow is passing the house, slowly, the lights blinking against the newly plowed snowpiles. The lights illuminate a snowman on the next lawn—crudely made, or perhaps it's just not lit up from the right angle. She remembers her first snowman; her mother broke off the broom handle to give her and helped push the handle through the snowman. Her mother was impetuous, always letting her stay home from school to enjoy the snow, and her father had been surprised when he returned from work to see the broom head on the kitchen table. "Well, we couldn't get out. How could we go out in the snow to get anything?" her mother had asked her father. The snowplow has passed. Except for the wind, it is very quiet outside. In the room, the man is talking to her. He wants to show her his postcards. She's surprised; she hadn't realized she was being spoken to.

"Oh, not that kind of postcard. I'm an old man. Just pretty postcards."

He has opened a night-table drawer. In-

2 **Clarification** In order to get a Ph.D., a student must take "orals," a spoken test administered by professors in the student's major field.

3 **Discussion** What do you learn about the characters from the first scene? Discuss reasons why the author may have chosen to start the story the way she did.

4 **Discussion** What is unusual about the plant's growth? How do you think this image might relate to the relationship between David and the narrator?

5 **Reading Strategy** Have students summarize what they know about the characters so far.

6 **Discussion** The reader learns that the narrator works at night. Why might it be difficult to have a night job? What effect might the job have on her relationship with David?

7 **Discussion** What might post-cards represent to the old man?

8 **Reading Strategy** Have the students invent a story that the man might tell about the postcard. Then have students discuss why the author did not include such a story, but merely alluded to one.

9 **Discussion** The narrator speaks very little in the scenes with the old man. What does this tell you about her character?

10 **Literary Focus** Have students look at the way the author establishes each scene. Many of the scenes start abruptly, in the middle of an action. What effect does this have on the reader?

11 **Discussion** How does this conversation add to your understanding of the relationship between David and the narrator?

7 side there is a box of tissues, a comb and brush, an alarm clock. He sits on the side of the bed, his feet not quite touching the floor, reaching into the drawer without looking. He finds what he wants: an envelope. He removes it and carefully pulls out the flap. He lets her look through the postcards. There is a bird's nest full of cherubs,[1] a picture of a lady elegantly dressed in a high, ruffled collar, curtseying beneath a flowering tree, and one that she looks at longer than the rest: a man in boots and a green jacket, carrying a rifle, is pictured walking down a path through the woods in the moonlight. Stars shine in the sky and illuminate a path in front of him. Tiny silver sparkles still adhere to the postcard. She holds it under the lamp on the night table: the lining of his jacket is silver, the edges of the rocks, a small area of the path. There is a caption: "Joseph Jefferson as Rip Van Winkle."[2] Beneath the caption is a message, ornately written: "Not yet but soon, Pa."

"Did your father write the postcard?"

8 "That's just one I found in a store long ago. I could make up a romantic story to tell you. I love to talk."

She waits, expecting the man's story. He leans back in bed, putting the envelope back in the drawer. His bedroom slippers fall to the floor, and he puts his legs under the covers.

"People get old and they can't improve things," he says, "so they lie all the time."

He waves his hand, dismissing something.

"I trust young people," he says. "I'd even tell you where my money is: in the dresser drawer, in the back of a poetry book."

The snowplow has returned, driving up the other side of the street. The lights cast patterns on the wall. He watches the shadows darken the wallpaper.

---

1. **cherubs** (cher′ əbz) n.: Representations of heavenly beings as winged children with chubby, rosy faces.
2. **Rip Van Winkle:** A character who sleeps for twenty years without awakening in a story by Washington Irving.

"I have real stories," he says, pointing to a photograph album on a table by the chair. "Look through and I can tell you some real stories if you want to know."

He is ready to sleep. She arranges the quilt at the bottom of the bed and starts to leave.

9 "The light doesn't bother me," he says, waving her toward the chair. "Look through my album. I'm old and cranky. I'm afraid for my pictures to leave the room."

10 It's early afternoon and no one is in the house. There are dishes on the dining-room table, records and record-album covers. There's a plate, a spoon, two bowls, three coffee cups. How many people have been here? There's no one to ask. There's some food on the counter top—things she doesn't remember buying. An apple pie. She goes into the living room and sits in a chair, looking out the window. More snow is predicted, but now the day is clear and bright, the fields shining in the sun. She goes into the kitchen again to look for the note he hasn't left. On her way to the bedroom to sleep, she looks out the window and sees David coming up the road, only a sweater and scarf on, holding a stick at his side that the dog is jumping for. On the floor by the chair the plant book is open, and several others, books he's studying for his exams. The front door is open. The dog runs into the living room, jumps on her.

"You should be asleep. You can't work at night if you're not going to sleep in the day."

"I thought I'd wait for you to come back."

"You shouldn't have waited. I could have been anywhere."

"Where would you go?"

11 He's chilled. His knuckles are bright pink, untying the scarf at his throat. He's putting another log on the fire, pushing the screen back into place.

"How's the old man?"

"He's no trouble. Last night I fixed his photograph album for him. Some of the pictures had come loose and I glued them in."

"You look like you need sleep."

Grammar in Action

Indirect quotations report the substance of what a person said or thought, rather than the actual words. Unlike a **direct quotation,** an indirect quotation does not require quotation marks; it is punctuated like a simple declarative sentence. Note the following examples:

Direct quotation: "I trust young people," he says.
Indirect quotation: He says that he trusts young people.

Student Activity 1. Select three direct quotations and three indirect quotations from "Imagined Scenes." Explain why a writer would sometimes choose to report a character's words directly and, at other times, use indirect quotations.

Student Activity 2. Rewrite these indirect quotations from "Imagined Scenes" as direct quotations.
1. He told her he wouldn't be working in the fall.
2. Linus Pauling says that a sufficient intake of vitamin C will prevent colds.
3. He wants to show her his postcards.
4. The plant isn't pictured, he tells her, but it may be mentioned in the text.

"Looks like you've been working," she says, pointing to the books by the chair.

"I've had trouble concentrating. The snow was so beautiful last night. I took the dog out for long walks in the woods."

David is stroking the dog, who lies curled by the fire, panting in his sleep.

"Get some rest," he says, looking at his watch. "I met the people who moved in down the hill and told them I'd help put a sink in. He's very nice. Katherine and Larry Duane."

David kisses her on his way out. The dog wakes and wants to go with him, but at the front door he's told to stay. The dog whines when the door closes, then waits a minute longer before going back to the living room to sleep by the fireplace.

"It's awful. When you get old you expect things to be the same. Sometimes I think the cold air could clear my head. My neighbor is ten years younger than me and he jogs every day, even through snow."

"I'm leaving now," his sister says. She puts on a blue coat and a blue velvet cap that ties under the chin. Her hair is white and copper. She has small, dainty hands. She repeats that she's leaving and pats him on the shoulder, more to make sure he's listening than out of affection. "There are oranges in the bag on your bureau. Linus Pauling says that a sufficient intake of vitamin C will prevent colds."

"How would I get a cold? Every day is the same. I don't go out."

Her coat is buttoned, her hat tied securely. "That's like asking where dust comes from," she says, and disappears down the stairs.

"She's very good to come every day. I forget to thank her. I take it for granted. Fifteen years makes so much difference. She's able to do so much more, but her hands hurt her. She does embroidery so they don't go stiff."

He is looking through a book of Currier and Ives prints.[3] "I suppose I'll have to eat

---
3. Currier and Ives prints: Nineteenth-century lithographs depicting the manners, people, and events of the times.

her oranges. There'll be more from Florida when they get back."

She looks at a picture he holds up for her to see, offers to read him science-fiction stories.

"I don't think so. My sister read them this morning. I've had enough make-believe. No spaceships are coming to Earth today, only snow."

She looks at her watch to see if it's time for his medicine. Her watch isn't there. Did she forget to wear it? He asks for tea, and while the water is boiling in the kitchen she dials David, to see if the watch is on the night table. She hangs up and dials again, but there's still no answer. She looks out the window and sees that it has already begun to snow. Perhaps she lost the watch on the way in. The clasp was loose—she should have asked David to fix it. She turns off the burner and goes outside, looking quickly up and down the front walk before the snow begins to accumulate. She doesn't see it. The car? She looks, but it isn't there. She looks on the front steps and in the entranceway. No. It must be at home. She reheats the water, making tea, and carries the cup and saucer upstairs.

She puts it down quietly on the bureau. He's fallen asleep. She sits in a chair and watches the snow fall, and in a while she closes her eyes and begins imagining things: mountains, and blue, blue water, all the snow melted into water. This time the name of the country comes to her: Greece. She's been sent to Greece to find something on the beach, but she just stands there staring at the mountains in the distance, the water washing over her feet. Her feet are cold; she takes them out of the water, backing up onto the sandy beach. She's lifted her feet from the floor, waking up. She goes to the bureau and gets the tea, even though it's cold. The snow is falling heavily now. Everything is blanketed in whiteness; it clings to the trees, her car is covered with snow. She must have slept through the night. She hears his sister downstairs, closing the door behind her.

"I take her for granted," the old man

12 Reading Strategy Have students predict what will happen to the characters in the rest of the story. Do the students expect there to be a change in the mood of the story?

13 Critical Thinking and Reading The old man is fond of science fiction. For what might this be a metaphor? Have students discuss the qualities of many science-fiction stories. Then have them relate science fiction to the man's postcard collection.

14 Discussion How does the narrator feel about David not being home when she calls? Have students discuss her suspicions, as well as possible reasons for David's absence.

5. She asks him if he'll take his cane, but he wants her arm instead.

6. His sister is asking if there is any way she can come back.

Student Activity 3. Rewrite the following direct quotations from "Imagined Scenes" as indirect quotations.

1. "I don't sleep well," he tells her.
2. "I think school was canceled," she says, looking out the window.
3. "My jacket is in the hall closet," he says. "I need the air."
4. "I guess you were walking the dog in the woods," she says.
5. "We'll have to go back for my car," she says.

15 Literary Focus Many of the fragments end with a pertinent, often ironic quotation or statement. This statement can be applied to the entire story, as well as looked at in context. How does this statement relate to the rest of the story?

16 Critical Thinking and Reading Have the students identify what the plant might represent. Then have them discuss what it means that David has given away the plant.

17 Discussion Why does the old man want to go for a walk in the snow? What precautions should the narrator take before beginning the walk?

---

15 says. "Like snow. Every day I expect more snow."

The plant is gone. She looks in all the rooms and can't find it. Her watch is on the bathroom sink, where she put it when she showered. She showers again and washes her hair, blows it dry. The bathroom is steamy; she can't see her face in the glass.

"David?"

She thought she heard something, but it was only a branch brushing against the bathroom window. She walks naked up to the bedroom and puts on jeans and one of David's sweaters. She notices that some of the books he's been studying have been replaced in the bookcase. Now she's sure she hears him. The dog runs into the house. The front door bangs shut.

"Hi," she calls.

"Hi." David is climbing the steps. "I'm not used to you working for a whole week. I never see you." His cheeks are so cold they sting when he kisses her. "I was down at the Duanes'. They had puppies born this morning."

"What kind?"

"Collies."

"Take me to see them," she says.

"They were going out when I left."

"We could go later in the afternoon."

"They'll think I live there," he laughs.

"It's good for you to be out. You've been working so hard."

"I haven't done any work for a couple of days."

"Yes you have. I saw pages of notes on the dining-room table."

"Larry left his notes behind. He brought them down to read me an article he's working on. He teaches at the university, Botany."

16 "Botany?" she says. "Is that what happened to the plant?"

"They liked it so much I gave it to them. It was such a freak thing, to grow that way in the winter."

She calls early in the morning: 4 A.M.

The telephone rings, and there is no answer. The old man can tell that she's worried when he awakens.

"I tried to get my husband last night but there was no answer."

"Men are heavy sleepers."

"No," she says. "He'd wake up."

"All men are heavy sleepers. I can sleep when people are talking—I don't even hear the children talking on their way to school any more. I can sleep with the light on."

"I think school was canceled," she says, looking out the window.

It has snowed all night. It's still snowing.

"Call my sister and tell her not to come," he says. "If anything happens I can call."

She picks up the phone in the upstairs hallway and gives his sister the message, but the old lady is coming anyway. She has boots and an umbrella, and she's coming. He shakes his head.

"It's terrible to be old. You have no power."

He gets out of bed and opens a bureau drawer.

"Can I help you?"

17 "I'm putting on my things to go for a walk in the snow."

"You should stay inside. It's too cold today."

"I don't feel the cold any more. I can go out."

"Have breakfast first," she says.

"No. I want to go out before she comes."

She leaves the room while he dresses. He takes a long time. Maybe his sister will come early, before they go out. No. He opens the door and walks out without his cane, wearing a sweater and a silk scarf tucked into the neck.

"My jacket is in the hall closet," he says. "I need the air."

She helps him down the stairs. He doesn't weigh much. She asks if he'll take his cane, but he wants her arm instead. She gets his jacket and holds it for him to put on. She takes her own jacket out of the closet and zips it.

It's bright outside. They both stop, mo-

1000 Contemporary Writers

Grammar in Action

When writing **dialogue,** use quotation marks around each speaker's words and begin a new paragraph with each change of speaker. For example, look at the following passage of dialogue from "Imagined Scenes":

His cheeks are so cold they sting when he kisses her. "I was down at the Duanes'. They had puppies born this morning."

"What kind?"

"Collies."

"Take me to see them," she says.

"They were going out when I left."

"We could go later in the afternoon."

Notice that by changing paragraphs as the speakers changed, Beattie could leave out *he said* and *she said* without confusing the reader. Notice also that periods, commas, and question marks are placed inside the quotation marks, and that the expression *she says* is placed outside them.

Student Activity. Write a real or fictional passage of dialogue. Model your dialogue after the dialogue from Beattie's story. Also try to make it seem as natural and realistic as possible.

mentarily blinded by the glare. The snow is wet and deep.

"Just down the walk," she says.

"Yes. All right."

Children, off from school, are playing in the yards. Someone has already built a snowman. He likes it, wants a closer look. They go down the walk to the sidewalk. The children next door call hello. A little boy comes over to tell the old man about the snowman he's built. On another lawn some children are building a fort. Two little girls in snowsuits are carrying snow to the fort in buckets. She sees a big boy push a small boy into a snowbank. It's just fun. It's not just fun—he's kicking snow on him, kicking the little boy.

"Wait!" she says.

The big boy kicks snow in her face and runs. She pulls the younger boy out of the snow, brushing it out of his hair.

"What happened?" she asks him. He's crying, brushing himself and pointing to the boy who ran away at the same time. Now another boy is screaming. She turns and sees that the old man has slipped in the snow. She runs back. He's red in the face, but he's all right. He bent over to make a snowball and one of the children accidentally ran into him. She reaches down to help him up. He's light, but it's hard to get a good grip. The pavement is slippery, she's afraid she might slip. She sends one of the children home to get his mother. But a man walking down the sidewalk has already bent to help the old man up.

18

"What are you doing here?"

"I came to pick you up," David says. "Your car never would have made it up the hill. I had chains put on."

19

They help the old man into the house. In the hallway he brushes snow off his shoulders, embarrassed and angry. He thinks the child knocked him over on purpose. She hangs up his coat and David helps him upstairs. He goes up the stairs more quickly than he came down, talking about the boy who knocked into him. But he's forgotten about it by the time his sister arrives. He's telling David about Berlin in the winter, about the birds. He complains about his memory—Berlin must have been beautiful in the spring. When his sister arrives she's brought fruit for her, too, saying that she's a nurse, she must know about Dr. Pauling. It's her last day. The daughter and the husband will be coming home from Florida. But the sister comes every day, even when they're home—she has an umbrella and high boots. Wait. The old man has something for her: a postcard. He's giving her the postcard. The stars twinkle brightly in her hand.

The children are still playing when she goes outside with David. The big boy she spoke to earlier hides behind a car and tries to hit them with a snowball, but he misses. David's mad at her, mad that she took the old man out. He won't speak.

"We'll have to go back for my car," she says.

No answer.

"I called you last night and there was no answer."

He looks up. "You called?"

"Yes. You weren't there."

"I didn't know it was you. I was asleep. Why were you calling?"

The snow is very deep. He's driving slowly, concentrating so the car doesn't skid. On the radio, the weather forecast calls for more snow.

"I guess you were walking the dog in the woods," she says.

20
21

"I just told you," he says. "I was asleep."

She closes her eyes, imagines him sleeping, then imagines him with the dog, pulling a broken branch out of the snow, holding it high for the dog to jump up. The dog yelps, runs in circles, but the snow is too deep to jump out of. David is asleep, under the covers. He's walking up the hill, the dog barking, jumping for the stick. She tries to imagine more, but she's afraid that if she doesn't open her eyes she'll fall asleep in the car.

22

Back in the house, she closes her eyes again. He's drawn the curtains, and the room is a little less bright. She's very tired. The dog whines outside the door, wanting

Imagined Scenes 1001

18 Discussion How does the scene with the children fighting compare with the other scenes in the story?

19 Discussion Why is it surprising that David comes to pick up the narrator?

20 Discussion Why does the narrator suggest another reason for David's not answering the phone?

21 Enrichment With the Postmodern literary movement, a new critical movement has also evolved. Deconstruction is a type of literary analysis in which scenes, lines, and symbols are analyzed for what they mean both in and out of the story. Have students discuss all possible meanings of the title. What scenes might the narrator be imagining as she is talking with David?

22 Reading Strategy Have students summarize the story up to this point. Then have them predict how the story will end.

23 Discussion What do we learn about the sister's attitude toward her brother? How does this make the reader feel?

24 Discussion What does the woman mean by her final line? Discuss how the narrator might apply the line to her own life.

Reader's Response Do you sympathize with the characters in this story? Why or why not? Do you identify with them in any way? If so, how?

David. David takes his trumpet off the night table and puts it in the case. He must be practicing again.

David leaves, saying that he's going downstairs to clean up. She hears some noise: cups and saucers? and much later, ringing. She's calling David, but there's no answer. David is calling her at the foot of the stairs.

"What?"

"Someone on the phone for you."

She goes downstairs to answer the phone. She sits at a chair by the table. The table is clear. Everything has been cleared away.

"Hello?"

The voice is soft. She can hardly hear. It's the old man's sister. She's tired of the old man and his sister, tired of work. She had already dismissed the old man from her mind, like last week's dreams, but now the old man's sister has called. His sister is upset. She's talking about the snow. Apparently she's snowed in, the snow is deeper than her boots, she's been trying to reach her husband to tell him. The planes from Florida won't land. No planes are landing. The old lady is thanking her for taking care of her brother. Why is she whispering?

"I come every day. I have my umbrella and my high boots so I can do my duty. I always try to bring him things that will please him so he won't think I only do it because I have to. My niece has to get away. He's so demanding. He wants her attention all day and night."

She's still half asleep, squinting against the glare, straining to hear. His sister is at the phone outside his bedroom in the hallway. The plane is still in Florida; it hasn't left because it can't land. His sister is asking if there's any way she can come back.

As she talks, the runway is buried deeper in snow. They're trying to clear it, but the snow is heavy, the planes can't land. The planes from Greece won't land. Now no one is on the beach in Greece, or at home in the United States; they're up in the air, up above the snow. She's sitting in a chair by the table. The table is clear. What was on the table when she came in? David has cleaned the room.

"You're so lucky," the woman whispers. "You can come and go. You don't know what it's like to be caught."

THINKING ABOUT THE SELECTION

Recalling

1. (a) What is the young woman's occupation? (b) What is David's occupation? (c) How do their occupations prevent them from spending a great deal of time together?
2. Why does the old man think that "every day is the same"?
3. (a) What causes the old man to fall down while he is outside? (b) What is his reaction to the incident?
4. Why does the old man's sister call the young woman at the end of the story?

Interpreting

5. How would you describe the story's mood?
6. (a) What hints does Beattie provide that the relationship between the young woman and David is somewhat strained? (b) What might be the main cause of this tension?
7. (a) How is the old man's attitude toward his sister similar to David's attitude toward the young woman? (b) In what sense is the young woman's situation similar to the sister's situation? (c) What is ironic, or surprising, about the sister's final comment?
8. What do you think the snow symbolizes, or represents, in the story?

Closure and Extension

ANSWERS TO THINKING ABOUT THE SELECTION
Recalling

1. (a) She is the night nurse for an elderly man. (b) He is a graduate student. (c) She works at night and sleeps during the day; he works during the day and sleeps at night.
2. He follows the same routine every day, and he never leaves the house.
3. (a) A boy knocks him over while playing in the snow. (b) The man thinks the boy did it on purpose and is very angry.
4. She calls to tell her that she's snowed in and to thank her for taking care of her brother.

Interpreting

5. Suggested Response: The mood is melancholy, detached, and distant.
6. (a) They have a difficult time communicating with each other, and

Applying

9. Do you think it would be possible for the young woman to change her situation? Why or why not?

ANALYZING LITERATURE

Understanding Postmodernism

"Imagined Scenes" is an excellent example of a common type of Postmodernist fiction. Written in the form of a broken sequence of scenes, the story's structure reflects the disjointed, fragmentary quality of contemporary life. Using a detached narrator, Beattie pieces together a series of events without transitions or explanations, making the reader feel as if he or she is actually witnessing the events, rather than having them described.

1. How are the beginning and ending of the story unlike those used in traditional short stories?
2. Why is the overall structure of the story appropriate for its subject?
3. What does this story suggest about the ability of people in contemporary society to communicate with one another?

CRITICAL THINKING AND READING

Thinking Metaphorically

In her story Beattie captures the human tendency to think metaphorically, or to seek to understand and explain the world through the use of implicit comparisons. For example, the old man associates the onset of winter with the birds he remembers seeing during his winter in Berlin.

1. What do the postcards represent to the old man?
2. What do the scenes the young woman imagines represent to her?

UNDERSTANDING LANGUAGE

Completing Word Analogies

One of the characteristics of Beattie's style is her use of specific words. Rarely does she simply say, "There are dishes on the dining-room table." Instead, she follows up this statement by telling you exactly what kind of dishes: "There's a plate, a spoon, two bowls, three coffee cups..."

Complete each word analogy below with a specific word that fits in the category.

1. TRANSPORTATION : CAR : : GROOMING AIDS:
   a. clothing   c. medicine
   b. hairbrush   d. watch
2. RAIN GEAR: UMBRELLA : : FAMILY MEMBERS:
   a. nurse   c. friend
   b. housekeeper   d. sister
3. GROCERIES: CEREAL : : BIRDS:
   a. sparrow   c. snow
   b. cats   d. Berlin
4. PUBLIC BUILDING: COURT HOUSE : : INSTRUMENTS:
   a. appliances   c. musician
   b. trumpet   d. music

THINKING AND WRITING

Writing About Structure

Write an essay in which you analyze the structure of "Imagined Scenes" and discuss its relationship to the subject of the story and its theme. Reread the story, focusing on its structure. Prepare a thesis statement. Then write your essay, using evidence from the story to support your thesis. When you finish writing, revise your essay, making sure you have supported your analysis with details from the story. Proofread your essay and share it with your classmates.

(Answers begin on p. 1002.)

picts? Do you think it is an exaggerated view? Why or why not?

ANSWERS TO ANALYZING LITERATURE

1. The story begins in the middle of an event and ends without a resolution.
2. The fragmentary structure of the story parallels the difficulty that the characters have in communicating with one another and reflects the uncertain and disjointed nature of the narrator's life.
3. The story suggests that the complexities of contemporary life make it difficult for people to communicate with one another.

ANSWERS TO CRITICAL THINKING AND READING

1. To the old man, the postcards represent a romantic and idealized version of the past, an opportunity for him to live through his imagination and make his present life more interesting.
2. The woman feels trapped in her situation. The scenes she imagines allow her freedom, an escape from her present life.

ANSWERS TO UNDERSTANDING LANGUAGE

1. (b)   2. (d)   3. (a)   4. (b)

THINKING AND WRITING

For help with this assignment, students can refer to Lesson 13, "Writing About a Short Story," in the Handbook of Writing About Literature.

After students have completed the assignment, you might want to divide students into groups, and have them read their rough drafts to one another and offer suggestions about the ways in which they could be improved.

---

the woman doesn't seem to completely trust David. (b) The fact that they have such different schedules and that the woman is sacrificing herself to pay for David's schooling may be causing the tension.

7. (a) The old man takes his sister for granted even though he does appreciate her attentions; David also seems to take his wife for granted, giving her little attention or thanks and not sharing much of his life or thoughts with her. (b)

Both women are trapped in situations in which they are sacrificing themselves for people they love. (c) The sister's comment is ironic, because the narrator also feels trapped.

8. The snow may symbolize the coldness in the two situations described in the story and the obstacles that keep the characters from effectively communicating with one another.

Applying

9. Suggested Response: It would be possible for the woman to change her situation, but she would have to take some direct action which seems contrary to her character. She would have to confront her husband and try to establish a new, more sincere understanding between them.

Challenge How would you describe the world that Beattie de-

More About the Author The daughter of Russian immigrants, Grace Paley was raised in New York City. She acknowledges the benefits of growing up at the intersection of two cultures. Ask students to discuss how an author's formative years may influence his or her writing. How might Grace Paley's immigrant background affect the characters and themes she chooses to write about?

Critical Evaluation Grace Paley has earned praise from many fellow contemporary American writers. Donald Barthelme, for example, remarked, "Grace Paley is a wonderful writer and troublemaker. We are fortunate to have her in our country." Another writer who has applauded her work is Philip Roth, who has noted that she has "an understanding of loneliness, lust, selfishness, and fatigue that is splendidly comic and unladylike. . . . "

GRACE PALEY

1922–

Written in a powerful, energetic style, Grace Paley's short stories capture many of the tragedies and ironies that arise in everyday life. Though few in number, Paley's stories have been praised by critics and have earned her a loyal following.

Paley was born and raised in New York City. While attending Hunter College, she developed a serious interest in writing. After her short stories had appeared in a number of major magazines, she published her first collection, *The Little Disturbances of Man: Stories of Women and Men at Love* (1959). Because she has devoted much of her time to supporting her personal beliefs, Paley has gone on to produce only two additional collections, *Enormous Changes at the Last Minute* (1974) and *Later the Same Day* (1985).

Paley's convictions run deep. During the Vietnam War, she devoted a great portion of her time to peaceful demonstration, and her protests landed her in jail. Going to jail, she has said, does not matter if it furthers consciousness about important issues. She is most concerned about urban community life in New York in part, she says, "because that's where I've lived all my life." When asked for her political affiliation, she has replied, "Anarchist, if that's politics." Donald Barthelme, an ardent admirer not only of Paley's stories but also of her political involvement, called her "a wonderful writer and troublemaker. We are fortunate to have her in this country." Some of her friends have suggested that the relatively small body of her work would be much larger if she spent less time on causes, but Ms. Paley protests, "That's not true. It's just my badness . . . I only write when I feel like it. I do write on the subway."

A writer's writer, her stories are favorites for study in writing workshops. She writes without resorting to gimmicks, yet with a solidness of craft that fellow writers admire and writing students emulate. She follows classic rules of writing: She writes what she knows, she does not attempt too much, and she tells a simple, honest story without cliché.

Paley has been quoted as saying about literature, "There isn't a story written that isn't about blood and money. People and their relationships to each other is the blood, the family. And how they live, the money of it."

Like many of Paley's other stories, "Anxiety" is a lively, energetic story that contains little action. Composed mainly from dialogue, the story creates a striking impression of an old woman who is haunted by her fears.

Objectives
1 To appreciate the point of view
2 To generalize about an age
3 To recognize synonyms
4 To write a story

Support Material

Teaching Portfolio
Teacher Backup, p. 1335
Usage and Mechanics Worksheet, p. 1338
Vocabulary Check, p. 1339
Analyzing Literature Worksheet *Understanding Point of View,* p. 1340
Language Worksheet, *Finding Synonyms,* p. 1341
Selection Test, p. 1342

GUIDE FOR INTERPRETING

Anxiety

The Writer's Techniques

Point of View. Point of view refers to the vantage point from which a narrative is told. Most stories are told from either a first-person or third-person point of view. In a narrative with a first-person point of view, one of the characters tells the story in his or her own words, using the first-person pronoun *I*. In a narrative with a third-person point of view, the narrator does not participate in the story and refers to characters using the third-person pronouns *he* or *she*. A third-person narrator may be either limited or omniscient. A third-person limited narrator focuses on the thoughts and feelings of only one character. A third-person omniscient narrator conveys the thoughts and feelings of all the characters.

A story's point of view often affects the way in which the characters are developed and portrayed. By using a third-person limited or first-person point of view, a writer allows you to see directly into the mind of one of the characters. As a result, much of what you learn about the character's personality is revealed through his or her thoughts and feelings. At the same time, this character's impressions are likely to shape the way in which the other characters are depicted.

Commentary

Grace Paley's crisp style seems deceptively simple. As you read "Anxiety," notice that under the quick declarative sentences lurk rich characterization and moral implications worthy of consideration in our age. Ms. Paley creates her portrait of a woman in the window, two fathers, and two children through the voice of the woman, yet we understand the other characters equally well. Paley's use of fine, small detail crystallized her portraits. Rosie is depicted by her wiggling and her "oink oink" as an energetic and bubbling child. Her father, with his "wonderful head of dark well-cut hair" seems self-involved and divorced from what the world was like for him when he was younger. The woman at the window, whom we assume to be quite old, is uniquely characterized by several details. Her "greenhouse marigolds" are flowers grown shut up indoors as she is herself, and her use of the appellation "Son" when addressing the father who is likely not much younger than herself, lets us know that she views herself as old and wise in comparison to him.

What other small details do you find Paley using to build her characters' portraits in this story?

Writing

In "Anxiety" an old woman expresses her fears about the present condition of the world. Brainstorm about the reasons why an elderly person might have a hard time coping with the state of the world today and the types of things that he or she might be likely to fear.

Guide for Interpreting 1005

Literary Focus Have your **more advanced** students consider the different ways in which a single event could be viewed. Have them select an event and discuss the possible points of view from which the event could be described. Evaluate the advantages and disadvantages of each.

Writing/Prior Knowledge Have students discuss what life was like for a young person growing up in the 1960's, the 1940's, and the 1920's. How is life today both simpler and more complex than it was forty years ago?

Vocabulary

Preteach the following vocabulary words:
anxiety (an zī′ ə tē) *n.*: Uneasiness about the future (p. 1006)
tenements (ten′ ə mənts) *n.*: Buildings divided into apartments (p. 1006).

Spelling Tip Point out that *e* is the only vowel in *tenement*.

Anxiety

Grace Paley

1 The young fathers are waiting outside the school. What curly heads! Such graceful brown mustaches. They're sitting on their haunches eating pizza and exchanging information. They're waiting for the 3 P.M. bell. It's springtime, the season of first looking out the window. I have a window box of greenhouse marigolds. The young fathers can be seen through the ferny leaves.

The bell rings. The children fall out of school, tumbling through the open door. One of the fathers sees his child. A small girl. Is she Chinese? A little. Up u-u-p, he says and hoists her to his shoulders. U-u-p, says the second father, and hoists his little boy. The little boy sits on top of his father's head for a couple of seconds before sliding to his shoulders. Very funny, says the father.

They start off down the street, right under and past my window. The two children are still laughing. They try to whisper a secret. The fathers haven't finished their conversation. The frailer father is uncomfortable; his little girl wiggles too much.

Stop it this minute, he says.

Oink oink, says the little girl.

What'd you say?

Oink oink, she says.

The young father says What! three times. Then he seizes the child, raises her high above his head, and sets her hard on her feet.

2 What'd I do so bad, she says, rubbing her ankle. Just hold my hand, screams the frail and angry father.

I lean far out the window. Stop! Stop! I cry.

The young father turns, shading his eyes, but sees. What? he says. His friend says, Hey? Who's that? He probably thinks I'm a family friend, a teacher maybe.

Who're you? he says.

3 I move the pots of marigold aside. Then I'm able to lean on my elbow way out into unshadowed visibility. Once, not too long ago, the tenements were speckled with women like me in every third window up to the fifth story, calling the children from play to receive orders and instruction. This memory enables me to say strictly, Young man, I am an older person who feels free because of that to ask questions and give advice.

Oh? he says, laughs with a little embarrassment, says to his friend, Shoot if you will that old gray head. But he's joking, I know, because he has established himself, legs apart, hands behind his back, his neck arched to see and hear me out.

How old are you? I call. About thirty or so?

Thirty-three.

4 First I want to say you're about a generation ahead of your father in your attitude and behavior toward your child.

Really? Well? Anything else, ma'am.

5 Son, I said, leaning another two, three dangerous inches toward him. Son, I must tell you that madmen intend to destroy this beautifully made planet. That the murder of our children by these men has got to become

ROOM IN BROOKLYN
Edward Hopper
Museum of Fine Arts, Boston

a terror and a sorrow to you, and starting now, it had better interfere with any daily pleasure.

Speech speech, he called.

I waited a minute, but he continued to look up. So, I said, I can tell by your general appearance and loping walk that you agree with me.

I do, he said, winking at his friend; but turning a serious face to mine, he said again, Yes, yes, I do.

Well then, why did you become so angry at that little girl whose future is like a film which suddenly cuts to white. Why did you nearly slam this little doomed person to the ground in your uncontrollable anger.

Let's not go too far, said the young fa-ther. She *was* jumping around on my poor back and hollering oink oink.

When were you angriest—when she wiggled and jumped or when she said oink?

He scratched his wonderful head of dark well-cut hair. I guess when she said oink.

Have you ever said oink oink? Think carefully. Years ago, perhaps?

No. Well maybe. Maybe.

Whom did you refer to in this way?

He laughed. He called to his friend, Hey Ken, this old person's got something. The cops. In a demonstration. Oink oink, he said, remembering, laughing.

The little girl smiled and said, Oink oink.

Shut up, he said.

What do you deduce from this?

Humanities Note

Fine art, *Room in Brooklyn,* 1932, Edward Hopper. The American painter Edward Hopper (1882–1967) led a simple and unre-markable life totally devoted to his art. At seventeen he traveled from his small hometown on the Hudson River to New York City to attend the art classes of the radical American realist painter Robert Henri. The five years of classes with this power-ful teacher gave him technical guidance and the ability to see subject matter in his everyday surroundings. He was not in-fluenced by the dark and flam-boyant style of Henri; Hopper claimed the main influence on his art to be "myself."

In the painting *Room in Brooklyn,* Edward Hopper cap-tures the mood of a time and place. A bleak city room is bathed in sunlight that does little to brighten it. A lone woman, her back to the viewer, sits before empty windows facing a blank sky and an endless vista of red brick facades. The color combi-nations seem strange and grat-ing. Maroon, chartreuse, and aqua combine to give an acid edge to the air of desolation evoked by this painting. Hopper claimed not to have intended his paintings to project the emotion and mood that they so often do. He saw them, rather, as his hon-est attempt to capture the light, color, and familiar surroundings of the American scene.

You might ask the following questions:
1. What might this woman be thinking about as she sits be-fore the window?
2. Does this artist convey the loneliness and desperation of the woman in the story? Ex-plain.

6 **Discussion** How does the woman get the father to change his mind about his actions? Why does she feel it is important to "start again"?

7 **Discussion** How does the ending of the story change the reader's view of the woman's concerns? What new information do we learn in the last two paragraphs?

Enrichment The title of W. H. Auden's poem "The Age of Anxiety" is frequently used to describe the second half of the twentieth century. Discuss why the phrase might be applicable to the times in which we live. Have students provide other phrases that might also summarize our age.

Reader's Response What are your feelings about the old woman who narrates this story? Does she remind you of anyone you know?

That I was angry at Rosie because she was dealing with me as though I was a figure of authority, and it's not my thing, never has been, never will be.

I could see his happiness, his nice grin, as he remembered this.

So, I continued, since those children are such lovely examples of what may well be the last generation of humankind, why don't you start all over again, right from the school door, as though none of this had ever happened.

Thank you, said the young father. Thank you. It would be nice to be a horse, he said, grabbing little Rosie's hand. Come on Rosie, let's go. I don't have all day.

U-up, says the first father. U-up, says the second.

Giddap, shout the children, and the fathers yell neigh neigh, as horses do. The children kick their fathers' horsechests, screaming giddap giddap, and they gallop wildly westward.

I lean way out to cry once more, Be careful! Stop! But they've gone too far. Oh, anyone would love to be a fierce fast horse carrying a beloved beautiful rider, but they are galloping toward one of the most dangerous street corners in the world. And they may live beyond that trisection across other dangerous avenues.

So I must shut the window after patting the April-cooled marigolds with their rusty smell of summer. Then I sit in the nice light and wonder how to make sure that they gallop safely home through the airy scary dreams of scientists and the bulky dreams of automakers. I wish I could see just how they sit down at their kitchen tables for a healthy snack (orange juice or milk and cookies) before going out into the new spring afternoon to play.

Primary Source

We live in an age when thoughts of our final destruction lurk in dark corners never too distant. Teenagers have had much to say in regard to their feelings about nuclear war. Teen correspondents for "TeenAge Magazine" interviewed classmates about nuclear war and about how they saw their futures in the shadow of the arms race. Here's what the students said:

"The possibility of nuclear war makes me adopt a sort of eat-drink-and-be-merry attitude. I try to live each day to the fullest, because I may not live tomorrow." Marilyn Hughes, 17.

"I have better things to think about. If you think about getting blown away every day, you just get paranoid." Alan Seckler, 16.

"I'm angry that I have to consider nuclear war and weapons in my choice. Who wants to have a child and worry about it being blown away?" William Ryan, 15.

"I'll let the politicians think about it. What I think about may be trivial, but it's important to me." Celina Regan, 16.

"I think the schools should be teaching students the truth about nuclear war. If the children of today were taught about it, maybe the adults of tomorrow would do something about it." Teri Magilligan, 17.

"I'll just live for now and not worry about it. But the threat is always there." Thomas Alfieri, 16.

"Working for peace helps me because I know I'm doing something. I'm not sitting around waiting for the world to blow up." Donald Joughin, 13.

THINKING ABOUT THE SELECTION

Recalling

1. What do the young fathers do while they are waiting outside the school?
2. (a) Why does the "frailer father" become angry with his daughter? (b) How does he respond to his anger?
3. (a) When does the father remember having said "oink oink"? (b) How does this memory help him to understand his behavior toward his daughter?

Interpreting

4. (a) Why might the narrator be so interested in the children and their "young fathers"? (b) What do the concerns she expresses reveal about her personality?
5. How does the story's title relate to the narrator's behavior?
6. What is Paley's attitude toward the narrator?
7. What does the father's response to the narrator's remarks reveal about his character?

Applying

8. How do you think most people would react to the narrator's remarks? Support your answer.

ANALYZING LITERATURE

Understanding Point of View

Point of view refers to the vantage point from which a narrative is told. "Anxiety" is told from a first-person point of view, with the old woman relating the story in her own words.

1. How would the story be different if it were told from the "frailer" father's point of view?
2. Why would a third-person omniscient point of view be less effective for this story?

CRITICAL THINKING AND READING

Generalizing About an Age

A common generalization about the period following World War II is that it is an age of anxiety. Prepare a chart with three columns. Label the first column *World*, the second, *Nation*, and the third, *Personal*. Under each heading list conditions or factors that would lead to the development of a sense of anxiety in a person living in today's world. For example, under *World* you might list nuclear war, under *Nation*, unemployment, and under *Personal*, a sense of rootlessness. Share your chart with your classmates.

UNDERSTANDING LANGUAGE

Finding Synonyms

Synonyms are words that have the same or nearly the same meaning. For example, *attitude* and *belief* are synonyms.

The words in capital letters are from "Anxiety." Choose the lettered word that is closest in meaning to each of the capitalized words, as the word is used in the selection.

1. FRAIL: (a) fragile (b) irresolute (c) resistant (d) unintelligent
2. ENABLES; (a) empowers (b) prepares (c) dictates (d) influences
3. ESTABLISHED: (a) organized (b) confirmed (c) entrenched (d) accustomed
4. DEMONSTRATION: (a) display (b) protest (c) representation (d) manifestation
5. ANXIETY: (a) calmness (b) apprehension (c) madness (d) disruption

THINKING AND WRITING

Writing a Short Story

Imagine that your school literary magazine has asked you to write a short story in which you create a striking impression of a character. Start by thinking of interesting or unusual people you know and noting the personality traits that make them interesting or unusual. Then create a fictional character who possesses some of the traits you have listed. When you write your short story, focus on conveying this character's personality through dialogue and action as well as through his or her thoughts. When you finish writing, revise your story, making sure that the character is well developed.

Anxiety 1009

ed. However, he does have a slightly condescending attitude toward the woman.

Applying

8. Suggested Response: Most people probably would not be willing to listen to the woman's comments. People generally avoid strangers and will rarely listen to unsolicited advice.

Challenge How do you think you would respond to meeting the narrator of the story?

ANSWERS TO ANALYZING LITERATURE

1. The portrayal of the old woman would be shaped by the father's impressions. The story would be likely to focus on the woman's eccentricities, and it would convey her fears less effectively. It also might tell of the father's involvement in demonstrations and express his concerns as a parent.
2. A third-person omniscient point of view would be inappropriate because the story's main focus is the woman's anxiety. Presenting other characters' thoughts in addition to the old woman's would lessen the impact of the story.

ANSWERS TO CRITICAL THINKING AND READING

Charts will differ. Students might mention such conditions as pollution, corporate growth, developments in computer technology, and prejudice.

ANSWERS TO UNDERSTANDING LANGUAGE

1. (a) 2. (a) 3. (c) 4. (b) 5. (b)

THINKING AND WRITING

For help with this assignment, students can refer to Lesson 19, "Writing a Short Story," in the Handbook of Writing About Literature.

Publishing Student Writing You might suggest that students submit their stories to your school's literary magazine.

Closure and Extension

ANSWERS TO THINKING ABOUT THE SELECTION

Recalling

1. The fathers sit on their haunches eating pizza and chatting.
2. (a) She wiggles too much and says "oink oink" which he tells her to stop. (b) He seizes her, raises her high above his head, and sets her down roughly.
3. (a) The father had said "oink" to the police during a demonstration. (b) He realizes that he is upset because his daughter was dealing with him as though he were a figure of authority.

Interpreting

4. (a) She is alone, and she likes children and feels that because of her age and experience she can provide important insights to their fathers. (b) She is an anxious, fearful person, worried about the way children are growing up today and concerned about the possibility of nuclear war.
5. The narrator is anxious about everything she sees, and seems unable to control her anxiety about the future.
6. Paley seems to have a sympathetic attitude toward the woman.
7. His response demonstrates that he is fairly patient and openmind-

More About the Author One critic has written that Mark Helprin strives for "loveliness above all else," but other critics have found the author's elegant language and precise characterizations both appealing and rewarding. Ask students to discuss the various goals a writer of fiction may have. Is beauty of language —or, at least, precision of language—an important goal for a writer of short stories?

Critical Evaluation Mark Helprin's works have drawn praise from many fellow contemporary American writers. These include John Garder who has remarked, "Mark Helprin is a wonderful writer. He moves from character to character and from culture to culture as if he'd been born and raised everywhere." Another writer to applaud Helprin's work is Joyce Carol Oates, who has written, "We are in the presence of a storyteller [Helprin] of seemingly effortless and artless charm . . . That storytelling command, that lovely voice, is never lost."

MARK HELPRIN

1947–

One of the most promising young writers in America today, Mark Helprin has been praised for his ability to blend realism and fantasy. Using his imagination, he transforms realistic settings into strange, mystical worlds, creating a type of fiction often referred to as "magical realism."

Helprin was born in New York City. He graduated from Harvard, where he studied Middle Eastern culture. Possessing a thirst for adventure, he is an enthusiastic mountain climber and parachutist and has served in the British merchant navy, the Israeli infantry, and the Israeli air force. Not surprisingly, Helprin has drawn upon his travel experiences in developing the settings for both his novels and short stories.

Because Helprin is a self-professed seeker after truth, his stories are sometimes suffused with touching tones and moral points. In one story, "A Dove of the East," he recounts the story of an Israeli patrolman who risks a great deal by attending to a dove rather than making war. The critic Dan Wakefield said of Helprin's work, "The quality that pervades these stories is love—love of men and women, love of landscapes and physical beauty, love of interior courage as well as the more easily obtainable outward strength. The author never treats his subjects with sentimentality but always with gentleness of a kind that is all too rare in our fiction and our lives."

Helprin has published two novels, *Refiner's Fire* and *Winter's Tale,* and two collections of short stories, *A Dove of the East* and *Ellis Island*. His stories have also been published in many major magazines, including *The New Yorker*.

"Katherine Comes to Yellow Sky," which appears in *A Dove of the East,* exhibits Helprin's sophisticated and elegant style. Set in the late 1800's, the story depicts the westward journey of a young woman, focusing on her thoughts as she travels toward her new home.

Objectives

1 To understand character
2 To understand character motivation
3 To understand differences in meaning
4 To respond in writing to criticism

Support Material

Teaching Portfolio
Teacher Backup, p. 1345
Usage and Mechanics Worksheet, p. 1348
Vocabulary Check, p. 1349
Analyzing Literature Worksheet, *Understanding Characterization,* p. 1350
Language Worksheet *Understanding Similes,* p. 1351
Selection Test, p. 1352

GUIDE FOR INTERPRETING

Katherine Comes to Yellow Sky

The Writer's Techniques

Character. A variety of types of characters are used in literary works. When a character is well developed and possesses a variety of traits, he or she is referred to as a round character. For example, Bet, the main character of Anne Tyler's "Average Waves in Unprotected Waters," is a round character who exhibits conflicting emotions and desires, possessing a deep love for her handicapped son, but also wanting to be relieved of the burden of caring for him. A character who embodies a single trait or quality is referred to as a flat character. For example, Tom Walker, the main character in Washington Irving's "The Devil and Tom Walker," is a flat character who embodies the vice of greed. Characters may also be classified as static or dynamic. A static character is a character who does not change during the course of a literary work. In contrast, a dynamic character is one whose personality undergoes some sort of permanent change. Regardless of the type of character being portrayed, the writer must provide a motivation, or a stated or implied reason for the character's behavior, to make a character's actions believable.

Writing

"Katherine Comes to Yellow Sky" is about a woman who travels westward in the late 1800's to the frontier town of Yellow Sky. Why do you think so many Americans made similar journeys during the nineteenth century? Freewrite about types of motivations people may have had for leaving their homes and moving to the new frontier.

Primary Source

What did Katherine see when she arrived in Yellow Sky? Perhaps it was similar to what another woman who traveled westward saw. In the late nineteenth century, a woman signing herself "Dame Shirley" wrote letters to her sister in New England depicting her new life in the West. In a collection called *The Shirley Letters, From the California Mines*, we find this account of her journey.

> I wish I could give you some faint idea of the majestic solitudes through which we passed; where the pine trees rise so grandly in their awful height, that they seem looking into Heaven itself. . . . But what a lovely sight greeted our enchanted eyes as we stopped for a few moments on the summit of the hill leaning into Rich Bar. Deep in the shadowy nooks of the far down valleys, like wasted jewels dropped from the radiant sky above, lay half a dozen blue-blossomed lagoons, glittering and gleaming and sparkling in the sunlight. . . . It was worth the whole wearisome journey . . . to behold this beautiful vision.

Guide for Interpreting 1011

Literary Focus Your students may find it helpful to review other stories they have read, and identify the characters as flat or round, and static or dynamic. You may also wish to discuss the ways in which stereotypes can be misleading or derogatory.

Writing/Prior Knowledge Have students work together in small groups to discuss conditions of life in the 1880's. Allow students time to organize their ideas before writing.

Vocabulary

Preteach the following vocabulary words:
contemptible (kən temp′ tə b'l) *adj.*: Worthless; despicable (p. 1013)
inevitable (in ev′ ə tə b'l) *adj.*: Certain to happen; unavoidable (p. 1015)

Katherine Comes to Yellow Sky[1]

Mark Helprin

Like a French balloonist who rides above in the clear silence slowly turning in his wicker basket, Katherine rode rapidly forward on a steady-moving train. It glided down depressions and crested hills, white smoke issuing lariat-like from the funnel, but mostly it was committed to the straightness of the path, the single track, the good open way. And as an engine well loved, the locomotive ran down the rails like a horse with a rider.

Passengers sat mainly in silence, not taking one another for granted but rather deeply respectful, for they were unacquainted and there was not the familiarity of one type crossing another. From each could come the unseen, perhaps a strange resolve or stranger ability. Like athletes before a match, they had high mutual regard so that as the day passed from morning to noon each man or woman kept to windows.

Katherine too stared out the imperfect glass ahead at softly glowing grasslands, yellow seas of wheat, seas of wildflowers, and June lilies, and at the dark mountains which were always visible in one direction or another. Having neglected to get a book out of her luggage she could only look, and attempt thoughts and variations. At first it was taking off her thin gold glasses and closing the good left eye so that she could blur the deep permanent colors. This she did, but

saw an old man staring at her and at the way she tilted her head and set her mouth as if waiting for an answer she would never believe. She looked daft when she did that or as if she had some kind of rare nerve dance. Back went the glasses and for a while she stared straight and dignified directly into the distance, this soon giving her the appearance of a gorgeous lunatic. She wore a white dress with high white shoes, and an enormous wide-brimmed hat, which although it glowed as fiercely as the face of a glacier was modified in its absoluteness by the buttercup haze of a yellow saffron band. Her hair was a long bright auburn tied back, and her eyes a striking green, as hazy as the saffron glow and as cool as a spring in the mountains, and if it were not that way the burn of freckles on her face might have consumed her, for they gave this girl a hot and sun-colored redness even in the stillest of white winters and a youth that carried her well into age. The daughter of an Irish quarry worker and a Dublin Jewess, she was taken when small enough to be nicknamed "Carroty" from the west of England to Boston and then to Quincy,[2] where her father became a foreman on a new opening in the granite quarry and her mother took up work in a textile mill. Katherine herself went to normal school,[3] escaping lovers because she was wedded to a dream landscape, and al-

---

1. Katherine . . . Yellow Sky: The title recalls the Stephen Crane short story "The Bride Comes to Yellow Sky."

2. Quincy: A city in eastern Massachusetts.
3. normal school: A school where teachers were trained.

though many sought her she was faithful to a vision of clouds and yellow sky far off to the West in unsettled territories. And she passed quickly from the society of the normal school to the company of a solitary idea. Convinced of new worlds her existence was animated in such a way that she had no answers, not a one, but believed incessantly in what she imagined.

She had read all her life of the openness of the West, of its red rivers and plains leafed in neutral in-breathing gold, of the miraculous Indians and the Rockies, which were mountains of mist that formed and unformed dreams so fast as to confuse even the youngest of dreamers. And strangely enough these substanceless dreams, these short electric pictures, these confused but royally intense sketches, gradually gave to her a strength, practicality, and understanding which many a substantial man would never have. Her vindication, almost God-promised, was as clear as the excellent sea air, or the deep blue pools which in summer formed at the bottom of the quarries, to her father's chagrin. Her father, whose strength had equaled the beauty of her mother, had seen in her very early what he himself had lost, and unlike many fathers he had no envy. He was too good for that. He loved her too much. He saw himself as a stone arch, unbending, sheltering around his wife and daughter, to keep them safe and await the day when his daughter could soar on her visions and be settled.

Katherine, a dreamer, was not hard but tender, and when her parents died one following the other in a general epidemic she was wild. Just to be in Quincy, as gray as a man's suit, afflicted with ice and dark winds, a shabby collection of boards amidst scrub trees like the coat of a dying mare, made her sad in a way which does no good and leads to dead ends and contemptible unbelieving. One day in winter she thought she saw her father standing by her mother, who was gentle and strong and had been the first to die. Her father held a sledgehammer, of the finest wood and with a shining gold head. He said, "I shall free you all," and went to the base of the quarry where he smashed the cast-iron braces and beams which held the rock. The iron rang like a thousand bells and black pieces shattered over the quarry, ringing the pools and echoing off the high walls. And her father continued until every chain was severed and every brace broken, until all metal and all the past were smashed, buried in the clear pools. Free air circulated away from its bounds and the muscular father said to her, a little out of breath but with as good a red color as he had had on the finest days of summer, he said, "Katherine, Katherine, my Carroty, we too have had it with this place. We are not permanently rooted here, and you must go away. I have smashed these bonds, and this I did for you. Pile your hair, tie it firmly, and find a new place."

This she did, about a year later, and headed West, for there she sensed something which would give her the moments she wanted before her death, moments of full cognizance and dream vision, the red roses of her life and its humor. It was good to abandon Quincy and its quarry.

She set her hat at an angle, trying to frame the light blue mountain ranges. The tracks threw up dust and she eyed steam from the locomotive. These billowing clouds became captions for her thoughts, and they centered on Yellow Sky, on a dream quest which had spread to all the people. Yellow Sky. It was still far off.

That night they stopped in Gibson, a town spread across a large rise in the prairie where cattle roads, a flat unnavigable river, and the railroad crossed at angles. Huge yards of seemingly spider-work boards held cattle for boxcar loading, and during the whole of the late spring night, cattle filed past her window in the darkness. Without awakening her assigned roommate, an elderly woman who looked like a tomb, Katherine stepped out of bed and went to the open

---

2 Discussion What do you learn about Katherine from her visions while at normal school?

3 Discussion How is it possible for dreams to give a person "strength, practicality, and understanding?" Discuss what this tells you about Katherine's character.

4 Reading Strategy How many colors has the author referred to up to this point? What is the predominant color in the story? Note how color parallels and highlights mood and characterization throughout the story.

5 Literary Focus Helprin establishes Katherine's character in Massachusetts as yearning and dreaming, but also as strongly practical. Have students note whether her character changed as she grew older.

6 Discussion What does Katherine's vision of her father symbolize? How does the vision help her to make the decision to travel West?

7 Enrichment The second half of the 1800's is often thought of as the time of the Industrial Revolution. The growth of industry was primarily an eastern phenomenon, while the West remained the less civilized, less industrialized frontier. Discuss with students how the description of Quincy shapes the reader's impressions of industrialization. Why does Katherine prefer to imagine the "wild" West?

8 Reading Strategy Have students summarize what they know about Katherine.

9 Literary Focus Point out to students that the characters other than Katherine are flat characters. Because they have little to do in the story, they remain one dimensional.

Fine art, *Across the Continent, Westward the Course of Empire Takes Its Way,* Currier and Ives. The American lithography firm of Currier and Ives operated continuously in New York City from 1840 to 1901. Currier and Ives issued hand-colored woodcut and lithograph prints on various popular subjects for sale to the American public. The firm was first established by Nathaniel Currier (1813–1880), a clever young man who saw the commercial possibilities of producing low-cost, high-quality pictures through lithography. James Ives (1824–1895) joined Currier as partner in 1857. Distributing their prints through mail order, by traveling salesmen, and in their shop, they become phenomenally successful.

Lithographs are prints produced from a drawing done on a fine grained stone slab with a grease crayon. A special ink, which adheres only to the crayon, is applied and paper is pressed onto the stone. This process produces a sharp black-and-white print of the image on the stone. The lithograph, *Across the Continent,* is a comment on the intense movement west of the American people. A train is leaving a pioneer settlement to travel on tracks that stretch to the horizon. Many details of the drawing are obvious symbols of the westward movement: the wagon train; the felling of trees; the buffalo herd; log cabins and Native Americans.

You might ask your students the following questions:

1. The author's description of the train ride in the beginning of the story is filled with western imagery. How do these images compare to the symbols of the West employed by the artist in this print?

2. How is the pioneer settlement pictured similar to the town of Yellow Sky?

ACROSS THE CONTINENT, WESTWARD THE COURSE OF EMPIRE TAKES ITS WAY
Currier & Ives
Museum of the City of New York

window. A high wind carried occasional raindrops past the town and out into the vastly promising darkness from which an endless procession of moody steers was filing—giant animals intent upon moving to their slaughter—to feed the distant cities. She had seen the land-seas of wheat and flowers and from them came these steers, an abundance which kept her awake the rest of the night wide-eyed, waiting for the hoof-beats and dust and drovers' calls to stop, but when morning found her tears were in her eyes as she stared at the clouds of sparkling dust. From where did they come, constantly, without even the slightest break? The land beyond was empty except for storm and mountains, and yet from there the night had been filled with a power so great it drew a shaking tense silence, a joyous fright. The endless power was born somewhere out near Yellow Sky, and Katherine couldn't sleep because she was headed there, as surely and certainly as the warm steel track, or the confident horsemen who often appeared alongside to race the train.

Leaving Gibson, they skirted the wide river and crossed a road on which thousands of cattle were backed up for miles; in the distance they were as even a brown as the drovers' felt hats. For scores of miles the

10

3. How accurate a historic record do you think this print is?

10 Discussion What is the power that Katherine feels? Is this power the same as the vision in her dreams, or different?

Primary Source

In the introduction to a collection of short stories he edited, Helprin discusses why he decided to devote his life to writing. He writes:

". . . I began to develop a deep love for what is unfortunately called literature, a terrible name that sounds affected and pretentious. If you didn't know the word you might guess that it was a surgical technique or an ancient technical term for part of a thatched roof, not the one word for language that can be as beautiful and hypnotic as song, for a vast summing up, in precious few words, of all that is truly important. It includes snowstorms and sunlit forests preserved in their fullness and depth by a miraculous series of

landscape was the same, a rolling plain which looked like masses of brown whales, dotted flowers, banks of lilies, and grasses. The train's exact and faithful forward motion led her to expect something ahead at all moments, and although there was nothing save the glittering May landscape, the convincing direction became in itself more than enough to hold her, and hold her it did, as had her realization of the night power in and around Gibson. She was held fast, but no more than anyone on the train, no more than farmers, fencemen, or drovers outside who were passed by and left to work amid their own silence and claimed lands, no more than boys in Gibson who prodded cattle with dry white cottonwillow sticks, or distant horsemen on a ridge, galloping only to disappear, although leaving the surety of their gallop impressed upon the passengers. A detachment of pony soldiers, '75 blue,[4] rode two by two on a wagon track, swords and buckles shining. They did not always know what they did, but by God they did it, as it was inevitable. Had she not lived her life in grayness and seen the bright only by fantasy? Did she not as the daughter of a man deserve these rich lands which had been declared ready and were being gathered in the arms of those who had come from such long ways away? Yellow Sky was in the mountains, up high, beyond the timberline which was like a skirt. The air was as thin as shell and pearl bright as the lakes and plummeting black-rock streams. She would stop in Yellow Sky but others would pass right on, and yet others right down to the broken beaches of the Pacific. This young impressionable girl alone on the cool wicker-weave seat of a shady railroad car moving out West could not be stopped. The colors in her were bound for Yellow Sky.

At about six in the morning the tired train halted in a cool saddle of the mountains just above the treeline. Men began to carry wood from enormous stockpiles along the track and load it on the coaler. A wooden trough was lowered from a cable-bound barrel tank and mountain water fell into the blackened holds of the locomotive, dribbling, spraying, and steaming from valves of nickel and steel, hissing like a swarm of locusts in the convoluted boilers. The steam from the locomotive's gaskets mingled with the early morning mist, low clouds which hid white gold-flecked mountains of sunrise. The peaks had begun to shine many hours before, and after sunset they would shine even though the night was black, the price for this advanced and delayed burnishing of the mountains being shade and darkness at the extreme hours. Those who lived in that place stared each day in special communication at the shining crowns all about them. The man who had charge of the railroad depot was tall and wore hobnailed boots[5] which awakened passengers as he walked on top of the cars. His boots also awakened his children, a little bear-faced boy and two fat little girls happy to have only their own thousands of private jokes.

The one hundred or so people in the town were miners, bridge workers, and railroad men who rode small mounted donkey engines up and down the passes securing faulted track and removing obstructions. There were always bridges to build, sometimes of several yards, sometimes of a quarter of a mile, because it was ravine country, rocky, high, indifferent to smooth-trafficking men and natural only to birds such as eagles, hawks, crows, and falcons—mountain birds with eyes of wondrous and staggering capabilities. Sharp as a ten-foot glass, they still could not see veins of silver spread variously throughout the ravines and deep into rock where only men could go, and by great effort. The trackers held the land down by use of iron bands, the bridgemen smoothed

---

4. **pony . . . blue:** United States cavalry.

---

5. **hobnailed boots:** Heavy boots with short nails protruding slightly from the soles.

Katherine Comes to Yellow Sky 1015

11 Discussion What does Katherine feel that she deserves? Do you agree with her? Do you think she will fulfill her desires?

11

codes that are of such great effect that they can often be more intense and consequential than the things they describe. It represents the extraordinary courage of a sole human voice confronting death, preserving life beyond its term, standing alone, speaking for as long as the code is conserved, even to others who have not yet been born. Is it not astounding that one can love so deeply characters who are composites, portraits, or born of the thin air, especially when one has never seen or touched them, and they exist only in an imprint of curiously bent lines?

"To make a more concise argument, one lives for a very short time, and life is incomparably precious. To live has much less to do with the senses or with ambition than with the asking of questions that have never been surely answered. To ask and then to answer these questions as far as one can, one needs above all a priceless and taxing involvement with truth and beauty. These are uncommonly plentiful in music and painting, in nature itself in the sciences, in history, and in one's life as it unfolds—if one labors and dares to see them. But nowhere do they run together with such complexity and power as in the gracefully written word. It is not as so many people mistake it, an element of manners, a cultural obligation, a diversion, or a means of opening a conversation at dinner parties. I have devoted my life to it not because I thought it would be a good way to earn money or because I thought it might be pleasant and interesting, but rather, because I love it—I love it not only because it is so pleasingly beautiful, but because it is so deeply consequential."

12 **Discussion** How does the scene of the stopped train add to your understanding of Katherine's journey?

13 **Critical Thinking and Reading** What about the scene depicted here provides further motivation for Katherine's dreams and aspirations?

14 **Discussion** What is the difference between a revelation and a realization? Why is it important that Katherine's understanding here is a realization? What does this tell you about her character?

15 **Literary Focus** Do you think Katherine has changed since the beginning of the train journey? Why or why not?

16 **Discussion** Discuss Katherine's seemingly confused state at the end of the story. What do you think the author intends to convey about Katherine's reaction? Of what is the journey an end? What begins at the end of the story?

Reader's Response What do you imagine it might have been like to have been among the first Americans to settle in the West?

it, and the miners pierced it—as if they were hunters and it a mammoth, succumbing to their studied attack.

The attack was not studied but passionate, and not of greed alone. At each day's end the bridgemen, the railroadmen, the miners looked at the land in the quiet time when the mountains shone softly like lanterns into the dark valley, and they saw that it was not damaged. Work as they did, the peaks were high, the streams excellently fresh, the pastures rich, their iron and wood, their fences and track all but invisible due to the greatness of the land. This, as much as anything else, made them love it. It was invincible and so beckoned, challenging them to make their mark. Impossible, they said when they looked up, for the sky was as blue as a pure packet of indigo,[6] and it reached into deep unconquerable heaven.

The conductor (who had warned Katherine to be careful of sparks—prompting her to say that it was impossible to be careful of sparks) roused her from a fitful, watery-eyed, straight-backed, sitting-up, night never ends sleep and she with the rest of the passengers stepped into a mountain village where they were served tea and rolls. Katherine stood quietly at yet another window, this in the depot, and she saw in the distance the lantern mountains glowing gold in all directions, catching the future sun. There, and just then did she realize, was the source of the

---

6. indigo (in'di go') *n.*: A blue dye.

power she had sensed days before. This time it was realization which struck her, not revelation, and there were no tears or risings within. She simply realized in the deadest and most sober of moments that in those mountains was the source, glancing off high lighted rock faces where no man could ever go, split into rivers eastward and westward running in little fingers to every part of the land, to the oceans where it blended with the newly turned sea foam and sun.

As the sun became stronger, but still not visible, they re-embarked onto the train. When Katherine approached the three-stepped iron stand, the conductor offered her his hand. She wondered why, thinking that perhaps he was going to help her up, something he did not do. But he shook her hand, and barred her way. Why? she said, and then he pointed to her luggage—leather cases and white canvas duffels—and when she still did not understand, to the mountains with golden light like the warm light from a candle. She was struck dumb. The train began to pull away, conductor and all, with a vast exhalation of white steam, and he said to the stunned girl what she already knew, "This is Yellow Sky." As the train vanished she could think only of her father, her mother, and the gray oceans in between. Oceans in between, their lights had lasted, and she had found her way. It came in a flood, and she shuddered. Oceans in between. It was an end. It was a beginning. Katherine had come to Yellow Sky.

THINKING ABOUT THE SELECTION

Recalling

1. What vision dominated Katherine's thoughts while she was in normal school?
2. What did Katherine imagine seeing "one day in winter" after her mother and father had died?
3. Why does the train halt "in a cool saddle of the mountains just above the treeline"?
4. What realization strikes Katherine while she is gazing out the window of the train depot in the small mountain village?

5. Why does the conductor prevent Katherine from reboarding the train?

Interpreting

6. What type of impression does Helprin convey in his description of Quincy?
7. What overall impression of the American landscape does Helprin convey through his depiction of Katherine's observations?
8. (a) Why is the end of the story surprising? (b) What does the ending reveal about Katherine's state of mind?
9. Explain the paradox in the last three sentences: "It was an end. It was a beginning. Katherine had come to Yellow Sky."

Applying

10. Do you think that life in Yellow Sky will live up to Katherine's expectations? Why or why not?

ANALYZING LITERATURE

Understanding Characters

A variety of different types of characters are used in literature. **Round characters** are characters who possess a variety of traits. **Flat characters** are characters who embody a single trait. **Static characters** are characters whose personality does not change during the course of a literary work. **Dynamic characters** are characters whose personalities do change.

1. Is Katherine a flat character or a round character?
2. What personality traits does she possess?
3. Is she a static character or a dynamic character? Support your answer.

CRITICAL THINKING AND READING

Understanding a Character's Motivation

In portraying any type of character, the writer must provide a **motivation,** or a stated or im-plied reason for the character's behavior, to make a character's actions believable. In "Katherine Comes to Yellow Sky," for example, Katherine's decision to travel westward is motivated to a great extent by her childhood visions of the West.

1. How does Helprin's description of Quincy help explain Katherine's motivation for leaving?
2. How does the vision that Katherine has of her mother and father after they have died help explain her decision to leave?

UNDERSTANDING LANGUAGE

Understanding Differences in Meaning

The author writes of Katherine, "There, and just then did she realize, was the source of the power she had sensed before. This time it was realization which struck her, not revelation, and there were no tears or risings within."

1. Explain the difference between the words *realization* and *revelation.*
2. Why might one bring tears and the other none?

THINKING AND WRITING

Responding to Criticism

A critic has commented that "some of Mark Helprin's stories, long on mood and short on plot, seem like watercolor sketches for more finished works." Write an essay in which you discuss this statement in relation to "Katherine Comes to Yellow Sky." Reread the story. Does it seem "long on mood and short on plot"? Does it in some way seem unfinished? When writing your essay, use passages from the story to support your responses to these questions. When you revise, make sure your essay is organized in a logical manner.

Katherine Comes to Yellow Sky 1017

Applying

10. Suggested Response: Katherine's life in Yellow Sky is likely to be happy and successful, because she is aware of the power of the land, and loves it. The reality of the land is likely to meet or exceed her expectations.

Challenge What do you think Katherine's life in Yellow Sky will be like? Describe several situations that might occur.

ANSWERS TO ANALYZING LITERATURE

1. Katherine is a round character.
2. She possesses humor, determination, a dreamy quality, optimism, and an awe of the American landscape.
3. She is a dynamic character because some of her dreamy attitude dissolves when she is confronted with the actual West. Although dazed by it, she is moved in a deeper way than she was in her thoughts.

ANSWERS TO CRITICAL THINKING AND READING

1. Helprin makes the town seem so unpleasant, drab, and suffocating that it is easy to understand wanting to leave.
2. The vision convinces her that her parents would have wanted her to leave.

ANSWERS TO UNDERSTANDING LANGUAGE

1. A revelation is a striking realization.
2. A revelation is a more powerful experience.

THINKING AND WRITING

For help with this assignment, students can refer to Lesson 15, "Evaluating a Literary Work," in the Handbook of Writing About Literature.

Publishing Student Writing Ask for student volunteers to read their essays aloud. Have students in the audience record at least one noteworthy feature of each essay.

1017

Closure and Extension

ANSWERS TO THINKING ABOUT THE SELECTION
Recalling

1. She often thought of "clouds and yellow sky far off to the West."
2. She imagined that she saw her father destroy the quarry with a sledgehammer.
3. The train stops to be refueled with lumber and water.
4. She realizes that the source of the power she felt earlier was in the mountains.
5. The conductor prevents her from reboarding because she has arrived in Yellow Sky.

Interpreting

6. The town is depicted as gray, drab, dark, icy, and suffocating.

7. Helprin conveys a sense of the vastness, mystery, power, and beauty of the landscape.
8. (a) Katherine did not realize that she had reached the destination she had dreamed of reaching for years. (b) It reveals that Katherine has been absorbed in her dreams and awed by her observations of the landscape.
9. It appears to be a contradiction, because the narrator refers to the same event as both a beginning and an end.

LARRY McMURTRY

1936–

In his work Larry McMurtry captures the changing flavor of life in the American West. His realistic and revealing depictions of the West have established him as one of the prominent western writers of our time.

A descendant of two generations of cattle ranchers, McMurtry was born in Wichita Falls, Texas, and raised in the nearby community of Archer City. After graduating from high school, he enrolled at Rice University but soon transferred to North Texas State University. He developed an interest in writing while in college, and while pursuing a master's degree at Rice University, he started work on his first novel, *Horsemen, Pass By*. The novel, better known by its film title, *Hud,* was published in 1961.

McMurtry's grandfather, a frontiersman and cattleman, cherished the romantic cowboy life, but by the time young Larry was growing up in Archer City, the old West had vanished, and only a wistful shadow of the life his grandfather had loved remained. McMurtry wrote, "A part of my generation may keep something of the frontier spirit even though the frontier is lost. What they may keep is a sense of daring and independence, transferred from the life of action to the life of the mind."

Labeled by some critics as the creator of the "urban western," McMurtry first attracted attention as a new kind of writer of western novels who mixed the traditional elements of the genre with sharp social observation and a strong dose of dark humor. His earlier novels, such as *The Last Picture Show* (1966), *Moving On* (1970), and *Terms of Endearment* (1975), capture the changing, rootless character of the American West. These novels created resentment among some citizens of McMurtry's home town who objected to his implicit condemnation of small-town life.

Since his reputation was at first built on his portrayals of the disintegration of cowboy and western folklore, his novel *Lonesome Dove* (1985) represented a startling departure. In this novel, which won a 1986 Pulitzer Prize, he turned to the frontier heritage of the West. The novel, set in the late 1870's, tells about the fortunes of a variety of colorful characters involved in a 2,000-mile cattle drive from the Rio Grande River to northern Montana.

Although he is primarily known as a novelist, McMurtry has also received critical acclaim as an essayist and critic, writing mainly for newspapers and magazines, *In a Narrow Grave: Essays about Texas*, a collection of his nonfiction was published in 1968. He has also written film criticism and screenplays, and he is now a contributing editor to the periodical *American Film*.

GUIDE FOR INTERPRETING

from Lonesome Dove

Setting. The setting is the time and place in which the events in a work of literature occur. While short stories frequently have only one setting, novels often have one or more general settings and numerous specific settings in which the various episodes take place. An effective description of a specific setting enables us to envision the setting and imagine the characters interacting with it. To accomplish this, a writer includes details of such elements of setting as the climate and the physical composition of the land. In describing these elements, writers use sensory language, or language that appeals to one or more of the five senses. In *Lonesome Dove* McMurtry frequently uses language that appeals to our sense of sight. For example, McMurtry creates a visual image, or word picture, when he writes, "The late sun shone through the dust cloud, making the white dust rosy."

As you read the passage from *Lonesome Dove*, notice the familiar pattern of starting out on a journey. The first phase of any journey is exciting. Planning is complete, anticipation runs high, and nervous energy abounds. As horses are selected and positions assigned, we feel the excited anticipation of the drovers about to begin. They picture the way things will be and assume their positions just as their plans dictate. The next phase sees reality set in, and it never exactly matches visions. Sean had not imagined the dust and says, "I didn't know it would be like this." Initial excitement turns to fearful anxiety soon after starting out. This phase is often accompanied by mental or physical discomfort or both. When discomfort becomes acute, a new phase begins—questioning the wisdom of the journey in the first place. "Though everything seemed peaceful. [Call] had an odd, confused feeling at the thought of what they had undertaken." As the drovers head for "bed-ground" at sunset of the first day, we leave them beginning to settle their questions. Can you anticipate the next phase that will shortly overtake them—the settling in of routine?

In this selection the characters are forced to cope with extremely unpleasant conditions caused by the climate. Freewrite about a time when you had to deal with unpleasant conditions related to the climate. In your freewriting explore the ways in which you coped with the conditions, the effect of the conditions on your state of mind, and what you learned from the experience.

Guide for Interpreting 1019

Literary Focus Because this novel is set in the past, in a specific time and place, an awareness of its setting is very important to the reader's understanding of the events. Emphasize to students that setting is a necessary element of storytelling. Then discuss how the landscape described in this selection looked then and how it might look today.

Writing/Prior Knowledge Have your **more advanced** students write this activity in the form of a letter to a friend. Discuss with students what makes a good or interesting story.

Vocabulary

Preteach the following vocabulary words:

deign (dān) *v.*: Condescend (p. 1020)

aggrieved (ə grēv'd') *v.*: Offended (p. 1020)

dismay (dis mā') *n.*: A loss of confidence at the prospect of trouble (p. 1022)

imperative (im per' ə tiv) *adj.*: Absolutely necessary; urgent (p. 1023)

from Lonesome Dove

Larry McMurtry

Captain Woodrow Call and Augustus McCrae are two former Texas Rangers who helped bring peace to the Texas frontier. Call now feels a yearning for adventure. With his friend Augustus, he gathers together a ragtag bunch of cowboys and embarks on a cattle drive from Lonesome Dove, Texas, on the Rio Grande, to the wilderness of Montana.

In the late afternoon they strung a rope corral around the remuda,[1] so each hand could pick himself a set of mounts, each being allowed four picks. It was slow work, for Jasper Fant and Needle Nelson could not make up their minds. The Irishmen and the boys had to take what was left after the more experienced hands had chosen.

Augustus did not deign to make a choice at all. "I intend to ride old Malaria all the way," he said, "or if not I'll ride Greasy."

Once the horses were assigned, the positions had to be assigned as well.

"Dish, you take the right point," Call said. "Soupy can take the left and Bert and Needle will back you up."

Dish had assumed that, as a top hand, he would have a point, and no one disputed his right, but both Bert and Needle were unhappy that Soupy had the other point. They had been with the outfit longer, and felt aggrieved.

The Spettle boys were told to help Lippy with the horse herd, and Newt, the Raineys and the Irishmen were left with the drags. Call saw that each of them had bandanas, for the dust at the rear of the herd would be bad.

They spent an hour patching on the wagon, a vehicle Augustus regarded with scorn. "That dern wagon won't get us to the Brazos,"[2] he said.

"Well, it's the only wagon we got," Call said.

"You didn't assign me no duties, nor yourself either," Augustus pointed out.

"That simple," Call said. "I'll scare off bandits and you can talk to Indian chiefs."

"You boys let these cattle string out," he said to the men. "We ain't in no big hurry."

Augustus had ridden through the cattle and had come back with a count of slightly over twenty-six hundred.

"Make it twenty-six hundred cattle and two pigs," he said. "I guess we've seen the last of the dern Rio Grande. One of us ought to make a speech, Call. Think of how long we've rode this river."

Call was not willing to indulge him in any dramatics. He mounted the mare and went over to help the boys get the cattle started. It was not a hard task. Most of the

---

1. remuda (rə mōō′ də) *n*.: A group of extra saddle horses kept as a supply of remounts.

2. the Brazos (brä′ zəs): A river in central and southeastern Texas.

cattle were still wild as antelope and instinctively moved away from the horsemen. In a few minutes they were on the trail, strung out for more than a mile. The point riders soon disappeared in the low brush.

Lippy and the Spettle boys were with the wagon. With the dust so bad, they intended to keep the horses a fair distance behind.

Bolivar sat on the wagon seat, his ten-gauge across his lap. In his experience trouble usually came quick, when it came, and he meant to keep the ten-gauge handy to discourage it.

Newt had heard much talk of dust, but had paid little attention to it until they actually started the cattle. Then he couldn't help noticing it, for there was nothing else to notice. The grass was sparse, and every hoof sent up its little spurt of dust. Before they had gone a mile he himself was white with it, and for moments actually felt lost, it was so thick. He had to tie the bandana around his nose to get a good breath. He understood why Dish and the other boys were so anxious to draw assignments near the front of the herd. If the dust was going to be that bad all the way, he might as well be riding to Montana with his eyes shut. He would see

nothing but his own horse and the few cattle that happened to be within ten yards of him. A grizzly bear could walk in and eat him and his horse both, and they wouldn't be missed until breakfast the next day.

But he had no intention of complaining. They were on their way, and he was part of the outfit. After waiting for the moment so long, what was a little dust?

Once in a while, though, he dropped back a little. His bandana got sweaty, and the dust caked on it so that he felt he was inhaling mud. He had to take it off and beat it against his leg once in a while. He was riding Mouse, who looked like he could use a bandana of his own. The dust seemed to make the heat worse, or else the heat made the dust worse.

The second time he stopped to beat his bandana, he happened to notice Sean leaning off his horse as if he were trying to vomit. The horse and Sean were both white, as if they had been rolled in powder, though the horse Sean rode was a dark bay.

"Are you hurt?" he asked anxiously.

"No, I was trying to spit," Sean said. "I've got some mud in my mouth. I didn't know it would be like this."

AGAINST THE SUNSET
Frederic Remington
Peterson Galleries

1021

3 **Literary Focus** Have a student volunteer read this description aloud. Discuss what the passage reveals about what it was like to ride in a cattle drive.

4 **Critical Thinking and Reading** Discuss the sensory language used in this description. Have students identify words and phrases that relate to the various senses.

Humanities Note

Fine art, *Against the Sunset,* Frederic Remington. Frederic Remington (1861–1909) was a very important American painter, sculptor, and illustrator of the West. Remington studied painting at the Yale Art School for only one year; he was largely a self-taught talent. Originally his health induced him to travel to the West. While there he worked as a clerk in a general store, a cowboy, and a ranch hand. These experiences gave him the inspiration for his art. Today the name Frederic Remington is synonymous with western art.

The confident and polished style of Frederic Remington portrayed the people of the West with drama, color, and skill. The painting *Against the Sunset* is an essential western scene. A cowboy is traveling on horseback, at top speed, through western terrain. The viewer wonders whether the rider is going for the sheriff, chasing a stray, or simply hurrying home for dinner.

You might ask students the following questions:
1. What scene from *Lonesome Dove* might this painting illustrate?
2. Why do you think this man is in such a hurry?

DRIVING THE HERD
Frank Reaugh
The University of Texas at Austin

"I didn't either," Newt said.

"Well, we better keep up," he added nervously—he didn't want to neglect his responsibilities. Then, to his dismay, he looked back and saw twenty or thirty cattle standing behind them. He had ridden right past them in the dust. He immediately loped back to get them, hoping the Captain hadn't noticed. When he turned back, two of the wild heifers spooked. Mouse, a good cow horse, twisted and jumped a medium-sized chaparral[3] bush in an effort to gain a step on the cows. Newt had not expected the jump and lost both stirrups, but fortunately diverted the heifers so that they turned back into the main herd. He found his heart was beating fast, partly because he had almost been thrown and partly because he had nearly left thirty cattle behind. With such a start, it seemed to him he would be lucky to get to Montana without disgracing himself.

Call and Augustus rode along together, some distance from the herd. They were moving through fairly open country, flats of chaparral with only here and there a strand of mesquite.[4] That would soon change: the first challenge would be the brush country, an almost impenetrable band of thick mesquite between them and San Antonio. Only a few of the hands were experienced in the brush, and a bad run of some kind might cost them hundreds of cattle.

"What do you think, Gus?" Call asked. "Think we can get through the brush, or had we better go around?"

Augustus looked amused. "Why, these cattle are like deer, only faster," he said. "They'll get through the brush fine. The

---

3. chaparral (chap′ ə ral′) *n.:* A thicket of shrubs or thorny bushes.

4. mesquite (mes kēt′) *n.:* A type of small, thorny tree.

class discuss whether or not they expect the cattle drive to be successful.

problem will be the hands. Half of them will probably get their eyes poked out."

"I still don't know what you think," Call said.

"The problem is, I ain't used to being consulted," Augustus said. "I'm usually sitting on the porch drinking whiskey at this hour. As for the brush, my choice would be to go through. It's that or go down to the coast and get et by the mosquitoes."

"Where do you reckon Jake will end up?" Call asked.

"In a hole in the ground, like you and me," Augustus said.

"I don't know why I ever ask you a question," Call said.

"Well, last time I seen Jake he had a thorn in his hand," Augustus said. "He was wishing he'd stayed in Arkansas and taken his hanging."

They rode up on a little knobby hill and stopped for a moment to watch the cattle. The late sun shone through the dust cloud, making the white dust rosy. The riders to each side of the herd were spread wide, giving the cattle lots of room. Most of them were horned stock, thin and light, their hides a mixture of colors. The riders at the rear were all but hidden in the rosy dust.

"Them boys on the drags won't even be able to get down from their horses unless we take a spade and spade 'em off a little," Augustus said.

"It won't hurt 'em," Call said. "They're young."

In the clear late afternoon light they could see all the way back to Lonesome Dove and the river and Mexico. Augustus regretted not tying a jug to his saddle—he would have liked to sit on the little hill and drink for an hour. Although Lonesome Dove had not been much of a town, he felt sure that a little whiskey would have made him feel sentimental about it. Call merely sat on the hill, studying the cattle. It was clear to Augustus that he was not troubled in any way by leaving the border or the town.

"It's odd I partnered with a man like you, Call," Augustus said. "If we was to meet now instead of when we did, I doubt we'd have two words to say to one another."

"I wish it could happen, then, if it would hold you to two words," Call said. Though everything seemed peaceful, he had an odd, confused feeling at the thought of what they had undertaken. He had quickly convinced himself it was necessary, this drive. Fighting the Indians had been necessary, if Texas was to be settled. Protecting the border was necessary, else the Mexicans would have taken south Texas back.

A cattle drive, for all its difficulty, wasn't so imperative. He didn't feel the old sense of adventure, though perhaps it would come once they got beyond the settled country.

Augustus, who could almost read his mind, almost read it as they were stopped on the little knob of a hill.

"I hope this is hard enough for you, Call," he said. "I hope it makes you happy. If it don't, I give up. Driving all these skinny cattle all that way is a funny way to maintain an interest in life, if you ask me."

"Well, I didn't," Call said.

"No, but then you seldom ask," Augustus said. "You should have died in the line of duty, Woodrow. You'd know how to do that fine. The problem is you don't know how to live."

"Whereas you do?" Call asked.

"Most certainly," Augustus said. "I've lived about a hundred to your one. I'll be a little riled if I end up being the one to die in the line of duty, because this ain't my duty and it ain't yours, either. This is just fortune hunting."

"Well, we wasn't finding one in Lonesome Dove," Call said. He saw Deets returning from the northwest, ready to lead them to the bed-ground. Call was glad to see him—he was tired of Gus and his talk. He spurred the mare on off the hill. It was only when he met Deets that he realized Augustus hadn't followed. He was still sitting on old Malaria, back on the little hill, watching the sunset and the cattle herd.

from Lonesome Dove   1023

6 **Discussion** Have students discuss the two options offered: going through the brush or along the coast. Which path do they think the drive should follow?

7 **Literary Focus** Have students describe in their own words what it would be like to be on a cattle drive. Encourage them to use their imaginations to supply details not provided in the story.

8 **Discussion** Why does Augustus think it is odd that he is paired with Call? In what ways are the two men different? What qualities do they share?

9 **Discussion** What distinction does Call make between the cattle drive and his other adventures? Why is it important for Call to feel that what he does is necessary?

10 **Reading Strategy** Have students predict some events that might happen in the rest of the novel. Also discuss the ways in which the characters might interact later in the story.

11 **Discussion** Why is Call bothered by Augustus's talking? Ask the students why they think that Call prefers to ride in silence.

Enrichment *Lonesome Dove* was made into a critically acclaimed television mini-series starring Robert Duvall.

Reader's Response After reading this excerpt, would you be interested in reading the complete novel? Why or why not?

ANSWERS TO THINKING ABOUT THE SELECTION

Recalling

1. Bert and Needle have been with the outfit longer than Soupy and expected one of them would receive the privileged position.
2. (a) The dust makes it impossible for Newt to see anything more than ten yards away. (b) He takes it off and beats it against his leg.
3. Newt is almost thrown by his horse and almost leaves twenty to thirty cattle behind.
4. The brush is very hard to pass through, and very few of the hands have experience in the brush.
5. (a) Augustus thinks it is odd that they are partners because they are so different. (b) According to Augustus, Call knows how to do his duty and fight for a cause but not how to live his own life.

Interpreting

6. (a) His inexperience is indicated by his reaction to the dust storm, his inability to anticipate the move of his "good cow horse," and his misplacement of cattle. (b) He is anxious and enthusiastic.
7. Call is introspective and silent; he thinks that it is important for a man to fulfill a duty. Augustus is talkative and easygoing; he thinks that a man should live his life to the fullest and not worry about what others think of him.

Applying

8. Suggested Response: No, because other pursuits can also make life interesting.

Challenge Who is a more effective leader, Call or Augustus? Explain your answer.

ANSWERS TO ANALYZING LITERATURE

1. He describes the dense, pervasive dust, sparse grass, and occasional thickets of this "fairly open country," the upcoming, nearly impenetrable bush, and the late afternoon light turning the dust clouds rosy.

THINKING ABOUT THE SELECTION

Recalling

1. Why are Bert and Needle unhappy that Soupy is given the left point?
2. (a) How does the dust affect Newt's field of vision? (b) What does he do when the dust becomes caked onto his bandana?
3. What two events cause Newt to conclude that he will be "lucky to get to Montana without disgracing himself"?
4. For what reasons is Call concerned about taking the cattle through the brush?
5. (a) Why does Augustus think it is odd that he and Call are partners? (b) According to Augustus, what does Call know?

Interpreting

6. (a) What evidence in this selection indicates that this is Newt's first cattle drive? (b) What is his attitude concerning his involvement in the cattle drive?
7. What does the conversation between Call and Augustus reveal about their personalities?

Applying

8. Do you think it is necessary for life to be filled with adventure to be interesting? Explain your answer.

ANALYZING LITERATURE

Appreciating Setting

The **setting** is the time and place in which the events in a literary work take place. To describe a setting, writers try to use specific details that create an appropriate image in the reader's mind.

1. What details does McMurtry use to enable you to visualize the setting of this selection?
2. The setting often directly or indirectly affects the characters' actions in a literary work. How does the setting affect Newt's actions in this selection?
3. Usually we think of dust as a nuisance, not as a life-threatening condition. What aspect of the dust storm did you find the most frightening?

CRITICAL THINKING AND READING

Recognizing Sensory Language

When writing a description, writers use **sensory language,** or language that appeals to one or more of the five senses. For example, McMurtry appeals to our sense of sight when he writes, "The grass was sparse, and every hoof sent up its little spurt of dust." He appeals to our sense of touch and taste when he writes, "His bandana got sweaty, and the dust caked on it so that he felt he was inhaling mud."

1. Find two more examples of language that appeals to the sense of sight.
2. Find an example of language that appeals to one of the other senses.
3. Which of these examples do you find most effective? Explain.

UNDERSTANDING LANGUAGE

Understanding Word Origins

Many words came to the English language through Spanish. For example, the English word *corral* comes from the Spanish word *corro,* meaning "a circle or ring."

The following words are of Spanish origin. Use your dictionary to find the meaning of each word. Then give the Spanish word and meaning from which it comes.

1. alcove   4. mosquito
2. guerrilla   5. junta
3. alligator

THINKING AND WRITING

Writing a Description

Describe the conditions you discussed in your freewriting for someone who has never experienced these conditions. Review your freewriting. Then prepare a list of details that you can use in your description. When you write your description, use sensory language to evoke the same types of feelings that you had when you experienced these conditions. When you revise, make sure you have included details that appeal to more than just the sense of sight.

---

2. The setting acts as an antagonist to Newt, almost making him fall off his horse and lose twenty to thirty cattle.
3. Suggested Response: The total lack of visibility was the most threatening aspect.

ANSWERS TO CRITICAL THINKING AND READING

1. Suggested Responses: "The horse and Sean were both white, as if they had been rolled in powder, though the horse Sean rode was a dark bay." "The late sun shone through the dust cloud, making the white dust rosy."
2. Suggested Response: "His bandana got sweaty, and the dust caked on it so that he felt he was inhaling mud."
3. Suggested Response: The description of the dust-caked bandana is the most effective, because it helps to convey an impression of the extent of the storm.

ANSWERS TO UNDERSTANDING LANGUAGE

1. alcove: Recessed portion of a room; *alcoba,* meaning "vault."
2. guerrilla: One who engages in irregular warfare; *guerra,* meaning "war."
3. alligator: A large reptile related to the crocodile; *el lagarto,* meaning "the lizard."
4. mosquito: An insect; *mosca,* meaning "fly."

Nonfiction

PAINTED WATER GLASSES, 1974
Janet Fish
Whitney Museum of Art

Humanities Note

Fine art, *Painted Water Glasses*, 1974, by Janet Fish. A native of Boston, Janet Fish (b. 1938) received degrees from Smith College and Yale University. In 1964 she moved to New York, where she began exhibiting works in artists' collectives. Her works are now in a number of collections, including those owned by some major corporations.

The precision with which Janet Fish has painted her many pictures of water glasses is striking. However, the soft, bright colors Fish uses serve to soften the images of glass containers that have been faceted into hundreds of distinct areas. The pattern of reflected light, in fact, is a major component of such works as *Painted Water Glasses* (1974). In other, similar pictures, Fish has placed flowers in some of the glasses, placed pieces of fruit nearby, or turned some of the empty containers upside-down, to vary the structural arrangements. In most of these paintings, the glass containers are larger than life and surrounded by no distinct background to anchor them in a recognizable setting. The energetic brushstrokes heighten the feeling of an intense representation of a more or less inexpressive object. Even in a society preoccupied with endlessly available products, the painter seems to be suggesting that men and women must find emotional and spiritual values where they can.

5. junta: A council; from *junta*, meaning "the same."

Writing Across the Curriculum
Students might enjoy further exploration of the old West. With the help of history teachers, students might find additional information about the geography and economics of cattle drives.

More About the Author William Faulkner spent most of his life in Oxford, Mississippi. There he absorbed the regional lore and folk wisdom that went into his books, many of which were set in the fictional Yoknapatawpha County. In his writing, he chronicled the political, social, and economic changes that the South experienced after the Civil War. He experimented with new writing forms such as the stream-of-consciousness technique, shifts in point of view, and shifts in time. These styles often make his writing difficult to read. Ask students why a writer would want to experiment with new techniques and approaches. What can the use of experimental devices add to a work?

Shortly after learning that he had been awarded the Nobel Prize Faulkner wrote a letter to the New York correspondent of Stockholm's biggest daily newspaper. This letter included the following passage: "I hold that the award was made, not to me, but to my works—crown to thirty years of the agony and sweat of a human spirit, to make something which was not here before me, to lift up or maybe comfort or anyway at least entertain, in its turn, man's heart. That took thirty years. I am past fifty now; there is probably not much more in the tank. I feel that what remains after thirty years of work is not worth carrying from Mississippi to Sweden, just as I feel that what remains does not deserve to expend the prize on himself, so that it is my hope to find an aim for the money high enough to be commensurate with the purpose and significance of its origin." Read this passage aloud to students. Then have them compare and contrast the ideas it expresses with those Faulkner expresses in his acceptance speech.

WILLIAM FAULKNER

1897–1962

William Faulkner is now generally regarded as one of the finest writers of his time, yet he received little public recognition until 1946, when *The Portable Faulkner,* an anthology of his writings, was published. Four years later he earned further recognition, when he was awarded the Nobel Prize following the publication of his novel *Intruder in the Dust* (1949). When he received the award, Faulkner delivered a powerful and moving speech concerning the duty of writers in contemporary society.

Faulkner grew up on stories of the past glories of the South. For him southern reality mingled with southern myth and memory. In *Intruder in the Dust* he wrote, "For every Southern boy fourteen years old, not once but whenever he wants it, there is the instance when it's still not two o'clock on that July afternoon in 1863, the brigades are in position behind the rail fence, the guns are laid and ready in the woods, and the furled flags are already loosened to break out. . . ."

The bulk of Faulkner's writing centers on Yoknapatawpha County—a fictional area in northern Mississippi. Here, between the 1890's and the late 1930's, the Compsons, the McCaslins, the Sartorises, and the Snopes work out their fates.

On "his own postage stamp of native soil," as he called his home town of Oxford, Mississippi, Faulkner consorted not with literary intellectuals but with townsfolk who, like himself, loved the outdoors. In fact, he rarely discussed his writing life at all and took pride in deeming himself a farmer. A master of reverse snobbery, "Mr. Bill" disliked the telephone and radio and did not own a television set. For years he drove an ancient convertible, crumbling with rust to the degree that books, fish hooks, and bathing suits regularly fell through the floorboards into the Oxford streets. Townsfolk took to calling Faulkner "Count No Count" due in part to his penchant for lies and odd costumes. He sometimes affected a limp and claimed to have a silver plate in his head—souvenirs of a wartime plane crash. Sporting a British officer's uniform complete with swagger stick, he would recount monumental tales of his exploits as a pilot and warrior in World War I when, in fact, he never finished flight school.

In an interview Faulkner said, "The writer's only responsibility is to his art. He will be completely ruthless if he is a good one. He has a dream. It anguishes him so much he must get rid of it. He has no peace until then."

Objectives

1 To appreciate oratory
2 To write about related themes

Support Material

Teaching Portfolio
Teacher Backup, p. 1365
Usage and Mechanics Worksheet, p. 1368
Vocabulary Check, p. 1369
Analyzing Literature Worksheet, *Understanding Oratory,* p. 1370
Language Worksheet, *Using Prefixes,* p. 1371
Selection Test, p. 1372

GUIDE FOR INTERPRETING

Nobel Prize Acceptance Speech

Literary Forms

Oratory. Oratory is the art of skilled, eloquent public speaking. When planning a speech, a skilled orator carefully considers his or her audience and the purpose and occasion of the speech. The speaker focuses on choosing a topic that is appropriate for the occasion and purpose, then writes the speech using language that he or she feels is suited to the audience.

When writing a speech, an orator must also be sure to emphasize his or her main points. To accomplish this, a speaker will use a variety of oratorical devices. Three of these devices are restatement, repetition, and parallelism. When a speaker uses restatement, he or she restates the same idea a number of times in a variety of different ways. When a speaker uses repetition, he or she restates the same idea using the same words. Parallelism refers to the repeated use of phrases, clauses, or sentences that are similar in structure.

Commentary

When you read Faulkner's work, you will notice that he experiments with time, twining past, present, future, and mythical time around whatever present events occur. Thus all of life, or even history, can be lived in a few turnings of the sun. It may be his belief in such time that leads Faulkner to feel man will prevail.

Readers sometimes become confused by Faulkner's time. It may help to consider how many kinds of time each person "lives" within a day, and how those time experiences reciprocate and change each other. For example, a girl wakes in the morning (present) and begins to ponder plans for that evening (future). When she returns to the present moment, she feels an exhilaration brought to it by the anticipation she felt while visiting the future in her mind. While walking to school (present) she smells the autumn leaves and is conveyed to an earlier autumn (past) when she rolled in thick piles of leaves. Regaining the present, she finds that the memory of that ancient autumn has significantly altered this one, leaving her more joyful than she had been before her reverie. As she continues to walk, she begins to view the present world as eternal and changeless, removing her altogether from the clock realm and connecting her with the universe of people who have experienced the world as she does at that moment. Viewed in this way, time is not the simple, metronomic concept most assume it to be. How do you view your own interaction with time?

Writing

Like William Faulkner, many Nobel Prize winners have used the occasion to deliver an important message to the world. Describe the type of message that you would want to deliver if you were awarded the Nobel Prize for your special field of interest.

Literary Focus A classical oratory has seven parts—the entrance, which captures the attention of the audience; the narration, in which the facts are presented; the exposition, in which terms are defined; the proposition, in which the speaker clarifies what is to be proved; the confirmation, in which arguments are presented; the refutation, in which opposing points are refuted; and the conclusion, in which the main points are summarized. Ask students how Faulkner's speech fits this pattern.

Writing/Prior Knowledge Before having students complete the writing activity, you might want to spend some time discussing some of the important issues in today's world.

Vocabulary

Preteach the following vocabulary words:
commensurate (kə men′ shər it) *adj.*: Corresponding in amount, magnitude, or degree (p. 1028)
pinnacle (pin′ ə k′l) *n.*: A lofty peak (p. 1028)
travail (trə vāl′) *n.*: Painfully difficult or burdensome work (p. 1028)
verities (ver′ ə tēz) *n.*: Truths (p.1028)
ephemeral (i fem′ ər əl) *adj.*: Short-lived (p. 1028)

Nobel Prize Acceptance Speech

William Faulkner

Stockholm, Sweden December 10, 1950

1   I feel that this award was not made to me as a man, but to my work—a life's work in the agony and sweat of the human spirit, not for glory and least of all for profit, but to create out of the materials of the human spirit something which did not exist before. So this award is only mine in trust. It will not be difficult to find a dedication for the money part of it commensurate with the purpose and significance of its origin. But I would like to do the same with the acclaim too, by using this moment as a pinnacle from which I might be listened to by the young men and women already dedicated to the same anguish and travail, among whom is already that one who will some day stand here where I am standing.

2   Our tragedy today is a general and universal physical fear so long sustained by now that we can even bear it. There are no longer problems of the spirit. There is only the question: When will I be blown up? Because of this, the young man or woman writing today has forgotten the problems of the human heart in conflict with itself which alone can make good writing because only that is worth writing about, worth the agony and the sweat.

3   He must learn them again. He must teach himself that the basest of all things is to be afraid; and, teaching himself that, forget it forever, leaving no room in his workshop for anything but the old verities and truths of the heart, the old universal truths lacking which any story is ephemeral and doomed—love and honor and pity and pride and compassion and sacrifice. Until he does 4 so, he labors under a curse. He writes not of love but of lust, of defeats in which nobody loses anything of value, of victories without hope and, worst of all, without pity or compassion. His griefs grieve on no universal bones, leaving no scars. He writes not of the heart but of the glands.

   Until he relearns these things, he will write as though he stood among and watched the end of man. I decline to accept the end of man. It is easy enough to say that man is immortal simply because he will endure: that when the last ding-dong of doom has clanged and faded from the last worthless rock hanging tideless in the last red and dying evening, that even then there will still 5 be one more sound: that of his puny inexhaustible voice, still talking. I refuse to accept this. I believe that man will not merely endure: he will prevail. He is immortal, not because he alone among creatures has an inexhaustible voice, but because he has a soul, a spirit capable of compassion and sacrifice

1028 Contemporary Writers

and endurance. The poet's, the writer's, duty is to write about these things. It is his privilege to help man endure by lifting his heart, by reminding him of the courage and honor and hope and pride and compassion and pity and sacrifice which have been the glory of his past. The poet's voice need not merely be the record of man, it can be one of the props, the pillars to help him endure and prevail.

THINKING ABOUT THE SELECTION

Recalling

1. What does Faulkner try "to create out of the materials of the human spirit"?
2. (a) According to Faulkner, what is "our tragedy today"? (b) What have today's young writers forgotten? (c) Why have they forgotten it?
3. What must young writers teach themselves?
4. (a) What does Faulkner "decline to accept"? (b) Why does he believe that humanity "will prevail"? (c) How can young writers help humanity to prevail?

Interpreting

5. Why is fear "the basest of all things"?
6. Faulkner writes, "I believe that man will not only endure, but will prevail." What do you think Faulkner sees as the difference between prevailing and enduring?
7. (a) In your own words, restate Faulkner's message concerning a writer's duty. (b) Why does Faulkner believe that writers will help humanity to endure and prevail by fulfilling their duty?

Applying

8. Explain why you do or do not agree with Faulkner's opinion concerning a writer's duty.

ANALYZING LITERATURE

Understanding Oratory

Oratory is the art of skilled, eloquent public speaking. When preparing a speech, an effective orator considers his audience and the occasion and purpose of the speech. To emphasize his or her main points, the orator will use such oratorical devices as restatement, repetition, and parallelism.

1. What is the purpose of Faulkner's speech?
2. Why is it appropriate for the occasion?
3. Why is the language appropriate for an intelligent, educated audience?
4. Find one example of Faulkner's use of restatement in the speech.
5. Find one example of his use of repetition.
6. Find one example of his use of parallelism.

THINKING AND WRITING

Writing About Related Themes

Write an essay in which you discuss how Faulkner's speech echoes the theme of his short story, "The Bear." Reread "The Bear," focusing on details that reveal its theme. Then reread Faulkner's speech, noting how it echoes the theme of the story. When writing your essay, use passages from both the speech and the short story to support your argument. When you revise, make sure you have not included any unnecessary information.

(Answers begin on p. 1028.)

Applying

8. Answers will differ. Students may comment that they feel that a writer's only duty is to entertain readers.

Challenge The world has changed a great deal since the time when Faulkner delivered his speech. Would Faulkner be pleased with these changes? Why or why not?

ANSWERS TO ANALYZING LITERATURE

1. Faulkner uses the occasion of his acceptance of the Nobel Prize to urge young writers to overcome the fear of nuclear war, and to write about the "old universal truths."
2. It is appropriate because it is an occasion upon which the attention of many young writers is likely to be focused.
3. The language in the speech is sophisticated and conveys complex ideas about writing.
4. Suggested Response: An example of restatement in the speech is the point that only the problems of the human heart in conflict with itself are worth writing about. He restates the point several times in different ways.
5. Suggested Response: Faulkner repeats the "old universal truths": honor and pride and compassion and pity and sacrifice.
6. Suggested Response: An example of parallelism occurs in the first two sentences of the third paragraph.

THINKING AND WRITING

For help with this assignment, students can refer to Lesson 16, Writing a Comparative Evaluation," in the Handbook of Writing About Literature.

Writing Across the Curriculum For extra credit, have students choose a year, after 1901, and research the Nobel Prize winners in all of the different areas for that year. Have students write about any or all of the winners and their achievements. Science and social studies teachers might be able to assist students in researching this subject. _____

problems because they have become concerned with the question of mankind's actual survival.
3. Young writers must teach themselves that fear is "the basest of all things."
4. (a) Faulkner declines to accept the end of man. (b) He believes that humanity "will prevail" because man has "a soul, a spirit capable of compassion and sacrifice and endurance." (c) Faulkner says that young writers can help humanity to prevail by writing

about the problems of the heart: love, honor, pity, pride, compassion, and sacrifice.

Interpreting

5. Suggested Response: It is the basest of all things because it impedes people's ability to function effectively.
6. By *enduring*, he means "merely surviving"; by *prevailing*, he means "thriving and prospering."
7. (a) Suggested Response: A writer's duty is to realize the source of

fear, then to overcome the fear, and to write about the things that truly matter, such as love, honor, compassion, and sacrifice. These things are the only things worth the labor a writer devotes to his work. (b) Faulkner believes that a writer can help humanity to prevail by reminding people of courage, honor, hope, pride, compassion, pity, and sacrifice.

More About the Author When she was fifteen, Carson McCullers had rheumatic fever, the first of many serious illnesses from which she suffered. She also experienced difficulties in her personal life, including a failed marriage. McCullers's works often focus on intense, difficult relationships between depressed or disillusioned individuals. Have students discuss how knowledge of a writer's personal life affects a reader's response to the writer's work. Is it necessary to know about a writer's life in order to understand his or her work? Why or why not?

Critical Evaluation The literary scholar Andrew Hook notes that Carson McCullers's "fiction is filled with violence, perversion and injustice, and deformed by conflict, frustration, pain and grief. She was born in a small town in Georgia, and such a town provides the unromantic setting for most of her work: long summers of glaring heat, drab houses, cafes and small factories, the smells of poverty and decay, and overpowering impression of bleak ugliness. Most of the inhabitants live locked in physical or spiritual isolation, suffering grotesque physical or psychological disfigurement as freaks, oddities, the dispossessed and outcast. Yet Carson McCullers does not create such a world to gain cheap, sensational effects; her central theme is love, its thwarting and failure, and occasionally its grace . . ."

CARSON McCULLERS

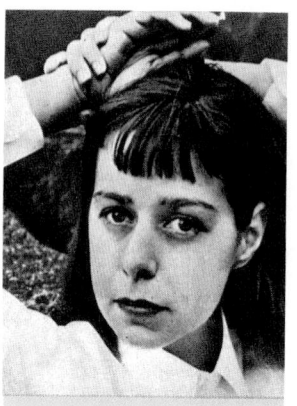

1917–1967

In her writing Carson McCullers captures the feelings of isolation and loneliness sometimes experienced by individuals living in a large, complex, and seemingly indifferent world. Although her works often express a bleak outlook, they also reflect her deep sense of compassion.

Born in Columbus, Georgia, McCullers displayed a great amount of musical talent as a young girl. When she was seventeen, she traveled to New York City to attend the Juilliard School of music, but she lost her tuition money on the subway. Unable to pursue her interest in music, she began taking writing courses at Columbia. She published her first story, "Wunderkind," when she was only nineteen, and her first novel, *The Heart Is a Lonely Hunter* (1940), was published when she was twenty-three.

McCullers went on to publish several more novels, including *The Member of the Wedding* (1945), *The Ballad of the Sad Cafe* (1951), and *Clock with No Hands* (1961). Unfortunately, however, during her late twenties, she suffered a series of strokes that left her partially paralyzed and severely limited her ability to write. She remained steadfast in her efforts despite her physical difficulties. With the left side of her body partially paralyzed, it took her ten years to write *Clock with No Hands*. She completed it by typing with one hand at the rate of one page a day.

Apart from her physical adversities, McCullers endured two difficult marriages—one to Reeves McCullers, from whom she took her name, ended in divorce, and the other, to a deeply troubled man whom her friends regarded as a delayed war casualty, ended in his suicide.

Her life held happy periods as well as troubled ones. Among the best of these were the times spent in a rented brownstone in Brooklyn with a group of writers and artists including Richard Wright, W. H. Auden, Christopher Isherwood, Louis MacNeice, and Gypsy Rose Lee.

The musical talent Ms. McCullers possessed becomes evident in the structure of her fiction. Often themes and character motifs appear early in a novel and disappear for a time to be resumed later. The structure becomes one of introduction, repetition, variation, dissonances, and unresolved harmonies, a form more common to musical composition than to writing.

Four years after McCullers's death, *The Mortgaged Heart* (1971), an edition of her previously uncollected works, was published. In the following selection from this book, McCullers explores the causes of and possible solutions to the problem of loneliness.

Objectives
1 To understand argumentation
2 To understand paradoxes
3 To find word histories
4 To write an argumentative essay

Support Material

Teaching Portfolio
Teacher Backup, p. 1375
Usage and Mechanics Worksheet, p. 1378
Vocabulary Check, p. 1379
Critical Thinking and Reading Worksheet, *Understanding Paradoxes,* p. 1380
Language Worksheet, *Understanding Word Roots,* p. 1381
Selection Test, p. 1382

GUIDE FOR INTERPRETING

The Writer's Techniques

from The Mortgaged Heart

Argumentation. Argumentation is writing that attempts to convince the reader to accept a specific opinion or point of view. An argumentative essay, or an essay which focuses on presenting a convincing argument, can usually be divided into four parts: the introduction of the subject; the analysis of the subject; the presentation of the writer's opinion or point of view; and a brief summary of the writer's main points or ideas. In addition to following this type of logical organization, a writer must use facts and examples to support his or her opinion. The writer must also carefully consider his audience when writing the essay, making sure that his or her choice of facts and examples and use of language are appropriate.

Commentary

Carson McCullers wrote about loneliness. In the years since she wrote, loneliness in America has become an increasing problem, and studies are being conducted to determine its effects. In an article done for *The Washington Post*, David Streitfeld describes health risks associated with loneliness: "The first two-year results from a study of 3,000 Iowans over sixty-five found that the loneliest were five times as likely to be institutionalized. They're also four times as likely to die."

Supporting research at Ohio State University is showing that loneliness may weaken the immune system, the body's defense against infectious and malignant diseases. In studies of medical students and psychiatric inpatients, those who labeled themselves as lonely had lower levels of natural killer cell activity—anti-tumor and anti-viral defense.

There's no long-term data yet, but studies show that people who are widowed, separated, or divorced have a higher mortality rate from certain infectious diseases and cancer.

Loneliness has one good point: It signals that needs aren't being met. "It's like hunger; it tells you to go out and get some nutrients, that there's a demand that isn't being met," says Jeffrey Young, an assistant professor of clinical psychology at Columbia University, "But it can go too far. Just as starvation is not useful, so can extended loneliness be very damaging."

Writing

What do you think are the main causes of loneliness in contemporary society? Prepare a list of reasons for people's loneliness; then list some possible solutions.

Literary Focus Point out to students that, because they will often be asked to write their own argumentative essays, McCullers's essay can serve as an excellent model for their own writing.

Writing/Prior Knowledge Have students discuss the quotation "No man is an island" by the poet John Donne. How does this quotation pertain to the subject of loneliness? For extra credit, have **more advanced** students write an essay using the lists prepared in the writing activity.

Vocabulary

Preteach the following vocabulary words:

pristine (pris′ tēn) *adj.*: Pure, uncorrupted (p. 1032)

corollary (kôr′ ə ler′ ē) *n.*: An easily drawn conclusion (p. 1032)

xenophobic (zen′ ə fō′bik) *adj.*: Afraid of strangers or foreigners (p. 1033)

maverick (mav′ ər ik) *n.*: A nonconformist (p. 1033)

aesthetic (es thet′ ik) *adj.*: Of beauty (p. 1037)

The Mortgaged Heart

Carson McCullers

This city, New York—consider the people in it, the eight million of us. An English friend of mine, when asked why he lived in New York City, said that he liked it here because he could be so alone. While it was my friend's desire to be alone, the aloneness of many Americans who live in cities is an involuntary and fearful thing. It has been said that loneliness is the great American malady. What is the nature of this loneliness? It would seem essentially to be a quest for identity.

To the spectator, the amateur philosopher, no motive among the complex ricochets of our desires and rejections seems stronger or more enduring than the will of the individual to claim his identity and belong. From infancy to death, the human being is obsessed by these dual motives. During our first weeks of life, the question of identity shares urgency with the need for milk. The baby reaches for his toes, then explores the bars of his crib; again and again he compares the difference between his own body and the objects around him, and in the wavering, infant eyes there comes a pristine wonder.

Consciousness of self is the first abstract problem that the human being solves. Indeed, it is this self-consciousness that removes us from lower animals. This primitive grasp of identity develops with constantly shifting emphasis through all our years. Perhaps maturity is simply the history of those mutations that reveal to the individual the relation between himself and the world in which he finds himself.

After the first establishment of identity there comes the imperative need to lose this new-found sense of separateness and to belong to something larger and more powerful than the weak, lonely self. The sense of moral isolation is intolerable to us.

In *The Member of the Wedding*[1] the lovely twelve-year-old girl, Frankie Addams, articulates this universal need: "The trouble with me is that for a long time I have just been an *I* person. All people belong to a *We* except me. Not to belong to a *We* makes you too lonesome."

Love is the bridge that leads from the *I* sense to the *We*, and there is a paradox about personal love. Love of another individual opens a new relation between the personality and the world. The lover responds in a new way to nature and may even write poetry. Love is affirmation; it motivates the *yes* responses and the sense of wider communication. Love casts out fear, and in the security of this togetherness we find contentment, courage. We no longer fear the age-old haunting questions: "Who am I?" "Why am I?" "Where am I going?"—and having cast out fear, we can be honest and charitable.

For fear is a primary source of evil. And when the question "Who am I?" recurs and is unanswered, then fear and frustration project a negative attitude. The bewildered soul can answer only: "Since I do not understand 'Who I am,' I only know what I am *not*." The corollary of this emotional incerti-

---

1. *The Member of the Wedding*: A novel and play by Carson McCullers.

NIGHT CITY
Richard Florsheim
Collection of Jane Golanty

Humanities Note

Fine art, *Night City,* 1956, by Richard Florsheim. The American painter Richard A. Florsheim was born in 1916. His studies at the University of Chicago brought him into contact with the growing American modern art movement. The impetus for this movement was Cubism, the French school of painting that explored the fragmentation of forms into geometric shapes. The pioneer moderns, like Richard Florsheim, applied the principles of this movement to distinctly American images with unique results.

Night City is an interpretation of the essence of a city in a way that was innovative for its time. Florsheim presents an angular geometrical abstraction of a shadow-and-light-filled cityscape. Through the use of color, he turns it into both an image of fiery wickedness and a dazzling paradise of possibility. It is not a static painting but, rather, one that hums, flashes, glows, and dazzles. This arrangement of lines and angles is a fitting way to portray the complexity of a modern city.

You might ask the following questions:
1. How does this painting capture the sense of "I" and the sense of "We" mentioned by Carson McCullers?
2. Does this painting represent the sense of loneliness and isolation discussed by McCullers? If so, how?

tude is snobbism, intolerance and racial hate. The xenophobic individual can only reject and destroy, as the xenophobic nation inevitably makes war.

The loneliness of Americans does not have its source in xenophobia; as a nation we are an outgoing people, reaching always for immediate contacts, further experience. But we tend to seek out things as individuals, alone. The European, secure in his family ties and rigid class loyalties, knows little of the moral loneliness that is native to us Americans. While the European artists tend to form groups or aesthetic schools, the American artist is the eternal maverick—not only from society in the way of all creative minds, but within the orbit of his own art.

Thoreau took to the woods to seek the ul-

7

8

The Mortgaged Heart 1033

7 Discussion McCullers points out the difference between Americans and Europeans. Do you think that the search for belonging extends to all people?

8 Clarification Henry David Thoreau wrote about his experiences living alone in a natural environment in his book *Walden* (p. 288).

9 Clarification Wolfe's first novel, *Look Homeward, Angel,* was set in New York City.

10 Literary Focus McCullers once said that "prose should be like poetry." Does this essay support this statement?

Reader's Response Do you agree with McCullers's observations concerning loneliness? Why or why not?

timate meaning of his life. His creed was simplicity and his *modus vivendi*[2] the deliberate stripping of external life to the Spartan[3] necessities in order that his inward life could freely flourish. His objective, as he put it, was to back the world into a corner. And in that way did he discover "What a man thinks of himself, that it is which determines, or rather indicates, his fate."

On the other hand, Thomas Wolfe turned

---

2. modus vivendi (mō′ dəs vi ven′ dī): Latin for "manner of living."
3. Spartan (spär′ t'n) *adj.*: Characteristic of the people of ancient Sparta: hardy, stoical, severe, frugal.

to the city, and in his wanderings around New York he continued his frenetic and life-long search for the lost brother, the magic door. He too backed the world into a corner, and as he passed among the city's millions, returning their stares, he experienced "That silent meeting [that] is the summary of all the meetings of men's lives."

Whether in the pastoral joys of country life or in the labyrinthine city, we Americans are always seeking. We wander, question. But the answer waits in each separate heart—the answer of our own identity and the way by which we can master loneliness and feel that at last we belong.

THINKING ABOUT THE SELECTION

Recalling

1. According to the first paragraph, what is the nature of loneliness?
2. How does McCullers define maturity in the third paragraph?
3. What need develops after a person establishes his or her identity?

4. What difference between Europeans and Americans does McCullers point out in the eighth paragraph?
5. According to the final paragraph, what "waits in each separate heart"?

Interpreting

6. In the second paragraph, how does McCullers emphasize the urgency of the infant's search for identity?

Closure and Extension

ANSWERS TO THINKING ABOUT THE SELECTION
Recalling

1. According to the first paragraph, the nature of loneliness is "a quest for identity."
2. McCullers defines maturity as "the history of those mutations that reveal to the individual the relation between himself and the world in which he finds himself."
3. After a person establishes his or her identity as a baby, the need is to lose "this new-found sense of separateness and to belong to something larger."
4. McCullers points out that each American's individuality brings a loneliness that is unknown to Europeans, who are more class- and family-conscious.
5. The "answer of our own identity and the way by which we can master loneliness and feel that at last we belong."

7. How is Frankie Addams's age related to the statement she makes?

8. How is McCullers's method of seeking the meaning of life different from Thoreau's?

9. (a) What does McCullers mean by the terms "moral isolation" and "moral loneliness"? (b) What does she mean when she comments that love "motivates the *yes* response"?

Applying

10. Do you think that today's Americans are more likely to be lonely than the early settlers? Why or why not?

ANALYZING LITERATURE

Understanding Argumentation

Argumentation is writing that attempts to convince the reader to accept a specific opinion or point of view. In her essay Carson McCullers attempts to convince readers to accept her conclusions concerning the causes of and possible solutions to the problem of loneliness.

1. Is McCullers's essay organized like a typical argumentative essay? Support your answer.

2. What is McCullers's opinion concerning the cause of loneliness in America?

3. What conclusion does she reach about the solution to the problem?

4. What examples does she use to support her conclusion?

CRITICAL THINKING AND READING

Understanding Paradoxes

A **paradox** is a statement that seems self-contradictory but in reality contains a possible truth. For example, McCullers presents a paradox in the first paragraph of her essay, stating that a friend of hers appreciated living in New York City because it enabled him to be alone.

1. Why does the paradox concerning life in New York City serve as an effective introduction to the essay?

2. What is paradoxical about the "dual motives" of a person to both claim his or her "identity and belong"?

UNDERSTANDING LANGUAGE

Finding Word Histories

McCullers writes, "While the European artists tend to form groups or aesthetic schools, the American artist is the eternal maverick—not only from society in the way of all creative minds, but within the orbit of his own art." The word *maverick* is based on Samuel A. Maverick, a Texas pioneer who did not brand his cattle. Eventually, all unbranded cattle, especially calves separated from their mothers, came to be called mavericks. Finally, the word began to be applied to people who took independent stands. McCullers also writes, "Whether in the pastoral joys of country life or in the labyrinthine city, we Americans are always seeking." Use a dictionary to explain the history of the word *labyrinth*.

THINKING AND WRITING

Writing an Argumentative Essay

What opinions do you have that you would like to convince other people to accept? Think of a subject about which you have a strong opinion. Then write an argumentative essay focusing on this subject. Before you begin writing, decide on the type of audience you wish to address. When you write your essay, keep your intended audience in mind. Present your argument in the logical manner in which typical argumentative essays are organized. When you revise, make sure you have presented your opinions clearly and effectively.

(Answers begin on p. 1034.)

Challenge Do you agree with McCullers's views concerning the causes of loneliness? Why or why not?

ANSWERS TO ANALYZING LITERATURE

1. McCullers's essay is organized like a typical argumentative essay. She introduces the subject in the first paragraph, discusses the subject, presents her opinions throughout, and briefly sums up in the last paragraph. Throughout, she uses examples to support her arguments.

2. McCullers says that loneliness is the search for identity. Because Americans don't have strict guidelines for beliefs and behavior, they are more vulnerable to loneliness.

3. She concludes that we must look into our own hearts for the answers to who we are and how we can master loneliness.

4. She uses the examples of Thoreau and Wolfe, who looked for their identities in two completely different ways.

ANSWERS TO CRITICAL THINKING AND READING

1. It serves as an effective introduction to the essay because it captures the readers' interest and highlights the complexity of the problem of loneliness.

2. To claim one's identity is to separate one's awareness from others; to belong is to join with others.

ANSWERS TO UNDERSTANDING LANGUAGE

The word *labyrinth* comes from the Greek word *labyrinthos* and the Latin word *labyrinthus*, meaning "labor into."

THINKING AND WRITING

Publishing Student Writing Argumentative essays lend themselves very well to being read aloud. Ask for student volunteers to read their essays aloud. Have students in the audience respond to each essay, saying whether they have been convinced by the essay's arguments.

Interpreting

6. McCullers describes the baby's repetitive explorations of its surroundings, and compares the urgency of this quest for identity with the urgency of the infant's need for milk.

7. Frankie is twelve years old. She is just entering the teenage years in which belonging can become so important, and she feels caught between childhood and the beginnings of adulthood.

8. Thoreau went to live by himself in the woods in order to seek the meaning of life; Wolfe went to a big city.

9. (a) McCullers uses "moral" to imply conformity to accepted ideas of right and wrong. A child loses its "moral isolation" by learning the standards of family and society. Americans, who do not have the strict class distinctions of European society, suffer from the "moral loneliness" of deciding correct behavior for themselves. (b) She means that people don't like to deny anything to someone they love.

Applying

10. Suggested Response: While the early settlers had to combat the problem of living in isolation, they usually banded together to help each other out in times of need. Today, families move a great deal, divorce is more prevalent, and people often seem to be out for themselves.

Capote, along with William Faulkner, Carson McCullers, and others, is considered part of the southern Gothic tradition. Strategies of this tradition include exaggeration, parody, irony, and heightened reality. How could an exaggerated or heightened treatment of a subject reveal more than a purely realistic treatment could?

Critical Evaluation The successful American novelist James A. Michener has written "Truman Capote was of tremendous importance to writers like me, for he filled a necessary role in American letters, one from which we profited but which we were ill-equipped to perform ourselves . . . . Because of an unusual combination of circumstances, I was allowed to know Capote tangentially and to assess his performance with some accuracy. I had abiding affection for the man and enormous respect for his talent. I envied the classic manner in which he conducted himself and reveled in his public posturing. His quips were first-class, his best writing of high merit, and his *Cold Blood* exceptional in its mastery."

TRUMAN CAPOTE

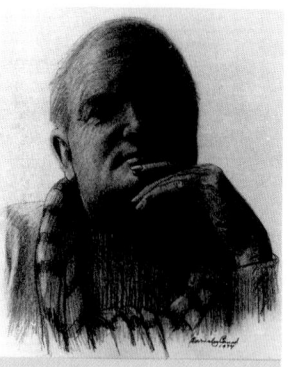

1924–1984

A versatile and talented writer, Truman Capote wrote novels, short stories, plays, movie scripts, and a variety of different types of nonfiction works. Achieving success early in his career, he went on to earn widespread recognition and win numerous awards.

Capote was born and raised in New Orleans. When he was eighteen he moved to New York City, where he spent a number of years working for *The New Yorker* magazine. He published his first novel, *Other Voices, Other Rooms,* in 1948. This book, along with two of his other early works, *A Tree of Night* (1949) and *The Grass Harp* (1951), explores the dark, sinister aspects of human existence. Similarly, his "nonfiction novel," *In Cold Blood* (1966), delves into the underlying motives of a violent crime. Capote also wrote several humorous works, including *The Muses are Heard* (1956) and *Breakfast at Tiffany's* (1958).

Adept at creating fictional characters and illuminating nonfictional ones, he also succeeded in fashioning an image for himself as a colorful eccentric. Capote traveled among the world's social elite. His work is worthy of its praise, but his critical appeal is due at least in part to his unique persona. His comings and goings were widely reported. One episode recounts the time when a friend happened upon Capote in an unlikely neighborhood. To the friend's inquiry about what the author was doing there, Capote rejoined, "Oh, I'm going to have lunch with the Olivers." "Who under earth's heaven are the Olivers?" replied the friend. "You know," answered Capote, "Sir Laurence and Vivian." Capote reserved the right to pronounce his friends' names any way he chose, and it mattered not to him that his friends were those the world has come to term "the beautiful people."

Some photographs of Capote were as strange as his public image. On one book jacket, he is shown "stretched out on a couch, intense eyes peering out from underneath the blond bangs carefully combed over his high forehead and his sensual mouth appearing ready to receive the first plump purple grape popped into it by the first passing Nubian lout." Capote sometimes explained his frivolity in serious tones. ". . . Part of me is always standing in a darkened hallway, mocking tragedy and death. That's why I love champagne and stay at the Ritz."

"A Ride Through Spain" is a personal account of one of Capote's more memorable experiences. The account exhibits Capote's command of language and attention to detail and his ability to bring a scene to life.

1036 *Contemporary Writers*

Objectives

1 To appreciate narration
2 To appreciate the effect of similes
3 To appreciate vivid modifiers
4 To write a personal narrative

Support Material

Teaching Portfolio
Teacher Backup, p. 1385
Usage and Mechanics Worksheet, p. 1388
Vocabulary Check, p. 1389
Critical Thinking and Reading Worksheet, *Appreciating the Effect of Similes,* p. 1390
Language Worksheet, *Appreciating Vivid Modifiers,* p. 1391
Selection Test, p. 1392

GUIDE FOR INTERPRETING

A Ride Through Spain

The Writer's Techniques

Narration. Narration is writing that tells a story. In nonfiction, writers often use narration to recount events and situations from their own lives. When a work focuses on describing a personal experience, it is sometimes referred to as a personal or first-person narrative. Personal narratives are quite similar to anecdotes—brief personal accounts told to make a point or teach a lesson—and autobiographies—full-length accounts of a person's entire life. Like anecdotes and autobiographies, personal narratives generally reveal something about the writer's personality. However, while autobiographies are generally written to inform, personal narratives are often written to amuse or entertain.

Commentary

Truman Capote's masterful use of descriptive details is obvious. Less obvious, perhaps, are his remarkable powers of observation and inference. As you read the beginning of his recounted episode on the Spanish train, notice how keenly he observes many things about the people that surround him. From these observations he concludes things he does not know by adding together the things he sees and what he knows of life. Notice how, in the first page of "A Ride Through Spain," Capote observed and inferred several things. First he observed that the mother in his compartment had "disapproving eyes." When they fell on him, he concluded that the reason she disapproved of him was that he had removed his jacket and that she found that discourteous. Next he observed that the daughter and the soldier had "agreed to flirt," and when the cat appeared, the two played out a routine. Capote inferred that the routine "gave them frequent opportunity to touch each other." Then he noticed that other soldiers enjoyed themselves in the corridors by smoking and laughing. He inferred that this behavior was "wrong of them," since they changed their demeanors when officers passed. Inference from observation is one of the major ways people process experience, but one more thing should be remembered about it—even with the best of information and the most practiced skill, conclusions reached through observation and inference can be wrong. As you read "A Ride Through Spain," do you find any places where Capote's inferences were wrong?

Writing

What incident from your own life do you think might make an interesting subject for a personal narrative? Think of an appropriate incident. Then prepare a list of details that you could use in describing it.

Literary Focus Capote described his book *In Cold Blood* as a nonfiction novel. By that he meant that in telling the story he revealed the actual events and characters in the dramatic way that he would in a novel. "A Ride Through Spain" is also written in this manner.

Writing/Prior Knowledge Autobiographical sketches often contain memorable characters. You may also wish to have students list details about interesting or funny people they have known.

Vocabulary

Preteach the following vocabulary words:
dour (do͞or) *adj.*: Stern; severe (p. 1038)
meandered (mē an′ dər'd) *v.*: Moved lazily (p. 1039)
somber (säm′ bər) *adj.*: Dark and gloomy or dull (p. 1040)
vigor (vig′ ər) *n.*: Active physical or mental force or strength (p. 1040).

A Ride Through Spain

Truman Capote

Certainly the train was old. The seats sagged like the jowls of a bulldog, windows were out and strips of adhesive held together those that were left; in the corridor a prowling cat appeared to be hunting mice, and it was not unreasonable to assume his search would be rewarded.

Slowly, as though the engine were harnessed to elderly coolies,[1] we crept out of Granada.[2] The southern sky was as white and burning as a desert; there was one cloud, and it drifted like a traveling oasis.

We were going to Algeciras, a Spanish seaport facing the coast of Africa. In our compartment there was a middle-aged Australian wearing a soiled linen suit; he had tobacco-colored teeth and his fingernails were unsanitary. Presently he informed us that he was a ship's doctor. It seemed curious, there on the dry, dour plains of Spain, to meet someone connected with the sea. Seated next to him there were two women, a mother and daughter. The mother was an overstuffed, dusty woman with sluggish, disapproving eyes and a faint mustache. The focus for her disapproval fluctuated; first, she eyed me rather strongly because as the sunlight fanned brighter, waves of heat blew through the broken windows and I had removed my jacket—which she considered, perhaps rightly, discourteous. Later on, she took a dislike to the young soldier who also occupied our compartment. The soldier, and the woman's not very discreet daughter, a buxom girl with the scrappy features of a prizefighter, seemed to have agreed to flirt. Whenever the wandering cat appeared at our door, the daughter pretended to be frightened, and the soldier would gallantly shoo the cat into the corridor: this byplay gave them frequent opportunity to touch each other.

The young soldier was one of many on the train. With their tasseled caps set at snappy angles, they hung about in the corridors smoking sweet black cigarettes and laughing confidentially. They seemed to be enjoying themselves, which apparently was wrong of them, for whenever an officer appeared the soldiers would stare fixedly out the windows, as though enraptured by the landslides of red rock, the olive fields and stern stone mountains. Their officers were dressed for a parade, many ribbons, much brass; and some wore gleaming, improbable swords strapped to their sides. They did not mix with the soldiers, but sat together in a first-class compartment, looking bored and rather like unemployed actors. It was a blessing, I suppose, that something finally happened to give them a chance at rattling their swords.

The compartment directly ahead was taken over by one family: a delicate, attenuated, exceptionally elegant man with a mourning ribbon sewn around his sleeve, and traveling with him, six thin, summery girls, presumably his daughters. They were beautiful, the father and his children, all of them, and in the same way: hair that had a dark shine, lips the color of pimientos,[3] eyes

---
1. **coolies:** Unskilled laborers.
2. **Granada** (grə nä′ də): A province in southern Spain.

3. **pimientos** (pi men′ tōz) *n.*: The red, bell-shaped fruit, used for stuffing green olives.

like sherry. The soldiers would glance into their compartment, then look away. It was as if they had seen straight into the sun.

Whenever the train stopped, the man's two youngest daughters would descend from the carriage and stroll under the shade of parasols. They enjoyed many lengthy promenades, for the train spent the greatest part of our journey standing still. No one appeared to be exasperated by this except myself. Several passengers seemed to have friends at every station with whom they could sit around a fountain and gossip long and lazily. One old woman was met by different little groups in a dozen-odd towns—between these encounters she wept with such abandon that the Australian doctor became alarmed: why no, she said, there was nothing he could do, it was just that seeing all her relatives made her so happy.

At each stop cyclones of barefooted women and somewhat naked children ran beside the train sloshing earthern jars of water and furrily squalling *Agua! Agua!*[4] For two pesetas[5] you could buy a whole basket of dark runny figs, and there were trays of curious white-coated candy doughnuts that looked as though they should be eaten by young girls wearing Communion dresses. Toward noon, having collected a bottle of wine, a loaf of bread, a sausage and a cheese, we were prepared for lunch. Our companions in the compartment were hungry, too. Packages were produced, wine uncorked, and for a while there was a pleasant, almost graceful festiveness. The soldier shared a pomegranate with the girl, the Australian told an amusing story, the witch-eyed mother pulled a paper-wrapped fish from between her bosoms and ate it with a glum relish.

Afterward everyone was sleepy; the doctor went so solidly to sleep that a fly meandered undisturbed over his open-mouthed face. Stillness etherized[6] the whole train; in the next compartment the lovely girls leaned loosely, like six exhausted geraniums; even the cat had ceased to prowl, and lay dreaming in the corridor. We had climbed higher, the train moseyed across a plateau of rough yellow wheat, then between the granite walls of deep ravines where wind, moving down from the mountains, quivered in strange, thorny trees. Once, at a parting in the trees, there was something I'd wanted to see, a castle on a hill, and it sat there like a crown.

It was a landscape for bandits. Earlier in the summer, a young Englishman I know (rather, know of) had been motoring through this part of Spain when, on the lonely side of a mountain, his car was surrounded by swarthy scoundrels. They robbed him, then tied him to a tree and tickled his throat with the blade of a knife. I was thinking of this when without preface a spatter of bullet fire strafed the dozy silence.

It was a machine gun. Bullets rained in the trees like the rattle of castanets,[7] and the train, with a wounded creak, slowed to a halt. For a moment there was no sound except the machine gun's cough. Then, "Bandits!" I said in a loud, dreadful voice.

"*Bandidos!*" screamed the daughter.

"*Bandidos!*" echoed her mother, and the terrible word swept through the train like something drummed on a tom-tom. The result was slapstick in a grim key. We collapsed on the floor, one cringing heap of arms and legs. Only the mother seemed to keep her head; standing up, she began systematically to stash away her treasures. She stuck a ring into the buns of her hair and without shame hiked up her skirts and dropped a pearl-studded comb into her bloomers. Like the cryings of birds at twilight, airy twitterings of distress came from the charming girls in the next compartment. In the corridor the officers bumped about yapping orders and knocking into each other.

---

4. agua (ag' wə): Water (Spanish).
5. pesetas (pə sāt' əz): The monetary unit of Spain.
6. etherized (ē' thə rīzd) *v.*: Anesthetized, as with ether.

7. castanets (kas' tə nets') *n.*: Small, hollowed out pieces of wood, held in the hand by a connecting cord and clicked together with the fingers.

A Ride Through Spain 1039

Suddenly, silence. Outside, there was the murmur of wind in leaves, of voices. Just as the weight of the doctor's body was becoming too much for me, the outer door of our compartment swung open, and a young man stood there. He did not look clever enough to be a bandit.

"*Hay un médico en el tren?*"[8] he said, smiling.

The Australian, removing the pressure of his elbow from my stomach, climbed to his feet. "I'm a doctor," he admitted, dusting himself. "Has someone been wounded?"

"*Sí, Señor.* An old man. He is hurt in the head," said the Spaniard, who was not a bandit: alas, merely another passenger. Settling back in our seats, we listened, expressionless with embarrassment, to what had happened. It seemed that for the last several hours an old man had been stealing a ride by clinging to the rear of the train. Just now he'd lost his hold, and a soldier, seeing him fall, had started firing a machine gun as a signal for the engineer to stop the train.

My only hope was that no one remembered who had first mentioned bandits. They did not seem to. After acquiring a clean shirt of mine which he intended to use as a bandage, the doctor went off to his patient, and the mother, turning her back with sour prudery, reclaimed her pearl comb. Her daughter and the soldier followed after us as we got out of the carriage and strolled under the trees, where many passengers had gathered to discuss the incident.

Two soldiers appeared carrying the old man. My shirt was wrapped around his head. They propped him under a tree and all the women clustered about vying with each other to lend him their rosary; someone brought a bottle of wine, which pleased him more. He seemed quite happy, and moaned

a great deal. The children who had been on the train circled around him, giggling.

We were in a small wood that smelled of oranges. There was a path, and it led to a shaded promontory; from here, one looked across a valley where sweeping stretches of scorched golden grass shivered as though the earth were trembling. Admiring the valley, and the shadowy changes of light on the hills beyond, the six sisters, escorted by their elegant father, sat with their parasols raised above them like guests at a *fête champêtre*.[9] The soldiers moved around them in a vague, ambitious manner; they did not quite dare to approach, though one brash, sassy fellow went to the edge of the promontory and called, "*Yo te quiero mucho.*"[10] The words returned with the hollow sub-music of a perfect echo, and the sisters, blushing, looked more deeply into the valley.

A cloud, somber as the rocky hills, had massed in the sky, and the grass below stirred like the sea before a storm. Someone said he thought it would rain. But no one wanted to go: not the injured man, who was well on his way through a second bottle of wine, nor the children who, having discovered the echo, stood happily caroling into the valley. It was like a party, and we all drifted back to the train as though each of us wished to be the last to leave. The old man, with my shirt like a grand turban on his head, was put into a first-class carriage and several eager ladies were left to attend him.

In our compartment, the dark, dusty mother sat just as we had left her. She had not seen fit to join the party. She gave me a long, glittering look. "*Bandidos,*" she said with a surly, unnecessary vigor.

The train moved away so slowly butterflies blew in and out the windows.

---

8. "*Hay . . . el tren?*": "Is there a physician on the train?" (Spanish).

9. *fête champêtre* (fet shän pe′ tr′): An outdoor feast or entertainment.

10. "*Yo . . . mucho*": I like you a lot (Spanish).

THINKING ABOUT THE SELECTION

Recalling

1. (a) With whom does Capote share his compartment on the train? (b) Who occupies the compartment directly ahead of him?
2. What happens each time the train stops?
3. (a) What noise does Capote hear while the other passengers are sleeping? (b) What does he immediately conclude to be the cause of this noise? (c) What turns out to be the true cause?

Interpreting

4. On what do you think Capote bases his conclusions about the attitudes of the "dusty woman" in his compartment?
5. Considering Capote's observations of this woman, why is it not surprising that she alone remembers who precipitated the passengers' reaction to the noise?
6. What seems to be Capote's attitude toward the incident he describes?

Applying

7. Do you think that most people would have reacted as Capote did, considering the circumstances? Why or why not?

ANALYZING LITERATURE

Understanding Narration

Narration is writing that tells a story. A first-person or personal narrative is an account of an event from the writer's life. Personal narratives generally focus on amusing or entertaining readers and usually offer insights into the writer's personality.

1. Why does Capote's experience make a suitable subject for a personal narrative?
2. What does Capote's reaction to the noise reveal about his personality?
3. What do his observations of the passengers reveal about his sense of humor?

CRITICAL THINKING AND READING

Appreciating the Effect of Similes

The vividness of Capote's descriptions in this account results in part from his frequent use of **similes**—comparisons indicated by a connecting word such as *like* or *as*. For example, in his description of the train, he writes that "the seats sagged like the jowls of a bulldog."

1. Find five more similes used by Capote in this selection.
2. Explain how each of these similes helps to create a vivid image, or word picture.

UNDERSTANDING LANGUAGE

Appreciating Vivid Modifiers

The clarity of Capote's descriptions also results partly from his careful choice of modifiers. For example, he uses vivid modifiers to create a clear picture of the woman in his compartment, referring to her as "an *over-stuffed, dusty* woman."

Think of a word that Capote could have used in place of the italicized word in each of the following descriptions from "A Ride Through Spain." Then explain why this word would make the description less effective.

1. *soiled* linen suit (page 1038)
2. *sluggish*, disapproving eyes (page 1038)
3. *stern* stone mountains (page 1038)
4. *gleaming*, improbable swords (page 1038)

THINKING AND WRITING

Writing a Personal Narrative

Using the list of details you prepared before reading the selection, write your own personal narrative. Focus on making your narrative entertaining. When you finish writing, revise your narrative, making sure you have included all the important details related to the incident. Then share your narrative with your classmates.

A Ride Through Spain 1041

Applying

7. Answers may differ. People react differently in times of crisis. However, considering that Capote was in a foreign place under unfamiliar circumstances, Capote did not behave in an illogical way.

ANSWERS TO ANALYZING LITERATURE

1. Capote's experience is interesting and humorous.
2. His reaction reveals that he is somewhat timid and can be affected by his imagination.
3. His observations of the passengers exhibit his wry sense of humor.

ANSWERS TO CRITICAL THINKING AND READING

1. Other similes in the selection include: "the southern sky was as white and burning as a desert"; the cloud "drifted like a traveling oasis"; the officers looked "rather like unemployed actors"; the six girls leaned "like six exhausted geraniums"; a castle on a hill sat "like a crown"; the grass "stirred like the sea before a storm."
2. Each of the similes adds a dimension to the description by providing a different but connected image.

ANSWERS TO UNDERSTANDING LANGUAGE

1. dirty
2. slow
3. angry
4. shining
Student explanations will differ.

THINKING AND WRITING

For extra credit, you may wish to have **more advanced** students write a paper about Capote's use of language in this essay, pointing out his use of similes and metaphors, plot elements, and narrative voice.

Closure and Extension

ANSWERS TO THINKING ABOUT THE SELECTION
Recalling

1. (a) Capote shares his compartment with an Australian doctor, a mother and her grown daughter, and a soldier. (b) The compartment ahead of him contains an elegant man and his six daughters.
2. Whenever the train stops the two youngest daughters "would descend from the carriage and stroll under the shade of parasols."
3. (a) He hears a machine gun fire. (b) He concludes that bandits have stopped the train. (c) An old man had fallen off the back of the train and a soldier, seeing him fall, had fired his gun to signal the engineer to stop.

Interpreting

4. Capote bases his conclusions about the "dusty woman" on her appearance and her behavior.
5. Capote portrays the woman as noticing and disapproving of everything.
6. Capote is both involved in the incident and detached enough to observe his own part in it with wry humor.

More About the Author When Ralph Ellison was first noticed by the literary establishment, he was considered to be not so much a black writer as a writer who was successful despite being black. Ask students to discuss the obstacles that prejudice presents to a writer. Does this prejudice still exist?

Critical Evaluation In his essay "Ralph Ellison and the Uses of the Imagination," the literary critic Robert Bone discusses the significance of Ellison's book *Shadow and Act.* He writes, "with the publication of *Shadow and Act* . . . this remarkable man [Ellison] emerges, at least in silhouette, to the public eye. The book contains most of Ellison's essays, from the beginning of his literary career to the present. There are seven apprentice pieces, written in the forties, which reflect the author's social and political concerns, and seven essays on jazz and blues, which appeared in the late fifties. There are three interviews of the *Paris Review* genre, and three first-rate essays on literary topics. Along the way, we learn a good deal about the author and the forces that have shaped his life."

RALPH ELLISON

1914–

In both his fiction and nonfiction, Ralph Ellison has confronted many of the problems faced by black Americans during the twentieth century. He has portrayed the quests of black men and women to discover and come to terms with their identities and has depicted their struggles against the obstacles of discrimination in American society.

Born in Oklahoma City, Ellison was educated at the Tuskegee Institute in Alabama, where he pursued his strong interest in music. Hoping to become a successful jazz musician, he moved to New York City. There, he met Langston Hughes and Richard Wright, who helped inspire him to become a writer.

In 1952 Ellison published his first novel, *The Invisible Man.* The book, which recounts the often harrowing experiences of a nameless black man, earned Ellison the National Book Award. Ellison's next book, a collection of essays and interviews called *Shadow and Act,* was published in 1964. This book includes "Hidden Name and Complex Fate," an essay in which he explores the relationship between his name and his identity.

Ralph Waldo Ellison is a writer of great magnitude. Since the publication of *The Invisible Man*, his work has enjoyed tremendous acclaim interrupted by some disfavor in the late fifties when portions of black America decried the book as not radical enough in its approach to race difficulties in America. The detractors felt the book advocated blending black America into white America to such a degree that culture would be lost. Ellison has denied the objections as misinterpretations.

Ellison states that being both black and American add greatly to his work. The most valuable resource available to him, he feels, is his "double vision," his simultaneous position of being inside and outside American culture. It is a position, he says, of observation and perspective from which values can be studied in action. "I've always written out of a sense of group experience as filtered through my individual experiences, talent, and vision," comments Ellison of his writing. He goes on to say, "The problem of becoming an artist is related to that of becoming a man, of becoming visible. You need a discipline far more demanding than a loyalty to your racial group." Those who know Ellison describe him as a stylistic perfectionist and "insanely ambitious" about his work. One old friend has said of Ellison's long awaited second novel, it will not be released "until he is sure it is the greatest American novel ever written."

Objectives

1 To appreciate the essay
2 To recognize the meaning that fits the context
3 To write a critical response

Support Material

Teaching Portfolio
Teacher Backup, p. 1395
Usage and Mechanics Worksheet, p. 1398
Vocabulary Check, p. 1399
Analyzing Literature Worksheet, *Understanding the Essay,* p. 1400

Language Worksheet, *Finding the Meaning That Fits the Context,* p. 1401
Selection Test, p. 1402

GUIDE FOR INTERPRETING

from Hidden Name and Complex Fate

Literary Forms

The Essay. An essay is a short prose work that generally focuses on a narrow topic. Essays can generally be divided into two categories: formal essays and informal essays. Formal essays are written using serious, dignified language and are carefully structured to inform, instruct, or persuade. At the beginning of the essay, the topic is clearly defined and an argument is presented. The writer then develops and supports the argument in the body of the essay and concludes with a brief summary or the presentation of an additional insight into the subject. In contrast, informal essays tend to be loosely organized and are generally written in a relaxed, intimate, conversational style. Less serious in purpose than formal essays, informal essays are usually written to amuse or entertain. Often informal essays attempt to evoke laughter, either by exploring an amusing subject or by treating a serious subject in an amusing manner.

Commentary

As you read "Hidden Name and Complex Fate," notice the power of names. At least to some degree, naming is controlling. In language that is obvious, since words are names for things, actions, and the like. The names we assign to represent things are symbols that take the place of things and thus allow people to communicate about them. For example, a young woman may be described repeatedly as a "dumb blonde." She will have no control over the way in which she has been quantified, or named, but it will affect her life greatly. People may pigeonhole her, feeling they know all about her by the derogatory epithet she unwillingly carries. They may not get to know her uniqueness any more than people talking about a tree will be likely to go outside and observe it for themselves. The greatest danger for the young woman, of course, is that she will accept the name applied to her. When that happens, language, one of man's greatest tools, has ceased to function in a positive way and has become a destructive club used for control. What are your feelings about names?

Writing

Freewrite about the relationship between people's names and their identities. How do you think most parents go about choosing names for their children? Why do you think parents often name their children after historical figures? Do you think that a person's name can in some way shape his or her development?

Literary Focus The essay form has existed since the sixteenth century, when the French writer Montaigne published a collection of writings under the name *Essais,* which means "attempts." Today, essays exist all around us, from popular magazine articles on the latest diet and exercise regimens to serious academic and critical studies in scholarly periodicals.

Writing/Prior Knowledge Before having students complete the writing activity, you might want to have them discuss their own names. They might want to ask their parents why they were given their names. In a dictionary of names, students can look up the origin and definitions of their names. How do they feel about the meanings of their names?

Vocabulary

Preteach the following vocabulary words:

furtive (fʉr′ tiv) *adj.*: Secretive (p. 1044)

aggregate (ag′ rə gət) *n.*: Sum total (p. 1044)

facile (fas′ 'l) *adj.*: Fluent (p. 1045)

incongruous (in käŋ′ gro͞o wəs) *adj.*: Incompatible (p. 1045)

juxtaposition (juk′ stə pə zish′ ən) *n.*: Placing side by side (p. 1045)

arduous (är′ jo͞o wəs) *adj.*: Very difficult (p. 1048)

Spelling Tip Point out that the s sound in *facile* is spelled *c*.

Motivation/Prior Knowledge
Ask students if they have ever been teased about their names. Why do they think some people have their names legally changed?

Master Teacher Note Sometimes names have meanings built into them, such as Cruella Deville from the Disney movie *101 Dalmations*. Other times meanings arise around names because of the characters who bear them. One of the most famous of these is Mrs. Malaprop, from Sheridan's play *The Rivals*. Like Archie Bunker in the television show "All in the Family," Mrs. Malaprop frequently and humorously mistook one word for another, entertaining the audience with such comments as "Lead the way, and I'll precede." You may wish to have students research the subject of names in the library, and present their findings to the class.

Purpose-Setting Question
What does the author's name mean to him? How may his name have shaped his identity and his development?

1 Discussion What does Ellison mean here? In what way do our names take on our emotions, hopes, loves, and aspirations?

2 Discussion Why does Ellison say that the names of blacks in particular bear special meaning? What is the irony in the fact that many slaves took the names of their masters? What paradox does Ellison point out?

3 Discussion Ask students what the preacher meant by this. What is the difference between true names and epithets?

4 Enrichment In his poem "The Love Song of J. Alfred Prufrock," T. S. Eliot says, "There will be

from Hidden Name and Complex Fate

Ralph Ellison

Once while listening to the play of a two-year-old girl who did not know she was under observation, I heard her saying over and over again, at first with questioning and then with sounds of growing satisfaction, "I am Mimi Livisay? . . . *I* am Mimi Livisay. I *am* Mimi Livisay . . . I am *Mimi* Li-vi-say! I am Mimi . . ."

And in deed and in fact she was—or became so soon thereafter, by working playfully to establish the unity between herself and her name.

For many of us this is far from easy. We must learn to wear our names within all the noise and confusion of the environment in which we find ourselves; make them the center of all of our associations with the world, with man and with nature. We must charge them with all our emotions, our hopes, hates, loves, aspirations. They must become our masks and our shields and the containers of all those values and traditions which we learn and/or imagine as being the meaning of our familial past.

And when we are reminded so constantly that we bear, as Negroes, names originally possessed by those who owned our enslaved grandparents, we are apt, especially if we are potential writers, to be more than ordinarily concerned with the veiled and mysterious events, the fusions of blood, the furtive couplings, the business transactions, the violations of faith and loyalty, the assaults; yes, and the unrecognized and unrecognizable loves through which our names were handed down unto us. . . .

Perhaps, taken in aggregate, these European names which (sometimes with irony, sometimes with pride, but always with personal investment) represent a certain triumph of the spirit, speaking to us of those who rallied, reassembled and transformed themselves and who under dismembering pressures refused to die. "Brothers and sisters," I once heard a Negro preacher exhort, "let us make up our faces before the world, and our names shall sound throughout the land with honor! For we ourselves are our *true* names, not their epithets! So let us, I say, Make Up Our Faces and Our Minds!"

Perhaps my preacher had read T. S. Eliot, although I doubt it. And in actuality, it was unnecessary that he do so, for a concern with names and naming was very much a part of that special area of American culture from which I come, and it is precisely for this reason that this example should come to mind in a discussion of my own experience as a writer.

Undoubtedly, writers begin their *conditioning* as manipulators of words long before they become aware of literature—certain Freudians[1] would say at the breast.[2] Per-

---

1. Freudians: People who believe in the theories and methods of Sigmund Freud (1856–1939), the founder of psychoanalysis.
2. at the breast: In infancy.

time, there will be time/To prepare a face to meet the faces that you meet."

5 Reading Strategy Have students restate this idea in their own words. How is this idea followed up in the remainder of the paragraph?

haps. But if so, that is far too early to be of use at this moment. Of this, though, I am certain: that despite the misconceptions of those educators who trace the reading difficulties experienced by large numbers of Negro children in Northern schools to their Southern background, these children are, in *their* familiar South, facile manipulators of words. I know, too, that the Negro community is deadly in its ability to create nicknames and to spot all that is ludicrous in an unlikely name or that which is incongruous in conduct. Names are not qualities; nor are words, in this particular sense, actions. To assume that they are could cost one his life many times a day. Language skills depend to a large extent upon a knowledge of the details, the manners, the objects, the folkways, the psychological patterns, of a given environment. Humor and wit depend upon much the same awareness, and so does the suggestive power of names.

"A small brown bowlegged Negro with the name 'Franklin D. Roosevelt Jones' might sound like a clown to someone who looks at him from the outside," said my friend Albert Murray, "but on the other hand he just might turn out to be a fireside operator. He might just lie back in all of that comic juxtaposition of names and manipulate you deaf, dumb and blind—and you not even suspecting it, because you're thrown out of stance by his name! There you are, so dazzled by the F.D.R. image—which you *know* you can't see—and so delighted with your own superior position that you don't realize that it's *Jones* who must be confronted."

Well, as you must suspect, all of this speculation on the matter of names has a purpose, and now, because it is tied up so ironically with my own experience as a writer, I must turn to my own name.

For in the dim beginnings, before I ever thought consciously of writing, there was my own name, and there was, doubtless, a certain magic in it. From the start I was uncomfortable with it, and in my earliest years it

caused me much puzzlement. Neither could I understand what a poet was, nor why, exactly, my father had chosen to name me after one. Perhaps I could have understood it perfectly well had he named me after his own father, but that name had been given to an older brother who died and thus was out of the question. But why hadn't he named me after a hero, such as Jack Johnson,[3] or a soldier like Colonel Charles Young, or a great seaman like Admiral Dewey, or an educator like Booker T. Washington, or a great orator and abolitionist like Frederick Douglass? Or again, why hadn't he named me (as so many Negro parents had done) after President Teddy Roosevelt?

Instead, he named me after someone called Ralph Waldo Emerson, and then, when I was three, he died. It was too early for me to have understood his choice, although I'm sure he must have explained it many times, and it was also too soon for me to have made the connection between my name and my father's love for reading. Much later, after I began to write and work with words, I came to suspect that he was aware of the suggestive powers of names and of the magic involved in naming.

I recall an odd conversation with my mother during my early teens in which she mentioned their interest in, of all things, prenatal culture! But for a long time I actually knew only that my father read a lot, and that he admired this remote Mr. Emerson, who was something called a "poet and philosopher"—so much so that he named his second son after him.

I knew, also, that whatever his motives, the combination of names he'd given me caused me no end of trouble from the moment when I could talk well enough to respond to the ritualized question which grownups put to very young children. Emerson's name was quite familiar to Negroes in Oklahoma during those days when World

---

3. Jack Johnson (1878–1946): The world heavyweight boxing champion from 1908 through 1915.

Humanities Note

Fine art, *Man in a Vest,* by William H. Johnson. William H. Johnson (1901–1970), an African-American painter, was an academically trained artist. He studied at the National Academy of Design in New York City and the Cape Cod School of Art with Charles Hawthorne. He then traveled to France, Scandanavia, and North Africa to broaden his artistic horizons. His constantly evolving style began in the academic tradition, became Impressionistic, then Expressionistic, and finally Primitive. His art is remembered for his regressive primitive style in which he sought to rid himself of academic tradition and adopt the direct emotional expression used by African artists. His paintings of the black experience in this style signaled the beginning of America's acceptance of the black subject in art. William H. Johnson was one of the most dynamic of the Harlem Renaissance artists. His art remains a legacy to all Americans.

The painting *Man in a Vest* was one of the first deliberately primitive paintings done by Johnson. A portrait of a serious man, it is remarkable for its emotional quality, which is enhanced by the simple and direct rendering. Although Johnson used a limited palette of five colors for simplicity, the effect of the colors is not diminished. The vibration of the red chair against the green background and the startling white of the man's shirt emphasize his compelling face.

Consider using these questions for discussion:

1. How does the artist achieve the introspective quality of this portrait?
2. What is conveyed by the posture of the figure in this painting?
3. Basing your answer on Ellison's theory of the importance of names, what kind of a name do you think this man would have?

MAN IN A VEST, 1939–1949
William H. Johnson
National Museum of American Art, Smithsonian Institution

Primary Source

In his essay "Ralph Ellison and the Uses of the Imagination," Robert Bone also discusses how Ellison was influenced by the Transcendentalists. He writes,

Ellison's debt to transcendentalism is manifold, but what is not acknowledged can easily be surmised. He is named, to begin with, for Ralph Waldo Emerson. In this connection he mentions two specific influences: the "Concord Hymn" and "Self-Reliance." The poem presumably inspires him with the willingness to die that one's children may be free; the essay . . . governs his attitude toward Negro culture. He admires Thoreau, plainly enough, for his stand on civil disobedience and his militant defense of John Brown. . . .

In broader terms, it may be said that Ellison's ontology derives from transcendentalism. One senses in his work an unseen reality behind the surface of things. Hence his fascination with guises and disguises, with the con man and the trickster. Hence the felt dichotomy between

War I was brewing, and adults, eager to show off their knowledge of literary figures, and obviously amused by the joke implicit in such a small brown nubbin[4] of a boy carrying around such a heavy moniker,[5] would invariably repeat my first two names and then to my great annoyance, they'd add "Emerson."

And I, in my confusion, would reply, "No, *no, I'm* not Emerson; he's the little boy who lives next door." Which only made them laugh all the louder. "Oh no," they'd say, "*you're* Ralph Waldo Emerson," while I had fantasies of blue murder.

For a while the presence next door of my little friend, Emerson, made it unnecessary for me to puzzle too often over this peculiar adult confusion. And since there were other Negro boys named Ralph in the city, I came to suspect that there was something about the combination of names which produced their laughter. Even today I know of only one other Ralph who had as much comedy made out of his name, a campus politician and deep-voiced orator whom I knew at Tuskegee,[6] who was called in friendly ribbing, *Ralph Waldo Emerson Edgar Allan Poe*, spelled Powe. This must have been quite a trial for him, but I had been initiated much earlier.

During my early school years the name continued to puzzle me, for it constantly evoked in the faces of others some secret. It was as though I possessed some treasure or some defect, which was invisible to my own eyes and ears; something which I had but did not *possess*, like a piece of property in South Carolina, which was mine but which I could not have until some future time. I recall finding, about this time, while seeking adventure in back alleys—which possess for boys a superiority over playgrounds like that

---

4. nubbin *n.*: Anything small and undeveloped.
5. moniker *n.*: Slang for a person's name or nickname.
6. Tuskegee (tus kē′ gē): Tuskegee Institute, the Alabama college which Ellison attended.

which kitchen utensils possess over toys designed for infants—a large photographic lens. I remember nothing of its optical qualities, of its speed or color correction, but it gleamed with crystal mystery and it was beautiful.

Mounted handsomely in a tube of shiny brass, it spoke to me of distant worlds of possibility. I played with it, looking through it with squinted eyes, holding it in shafts of sunlight, and tried to use it for a magic lantern. But most of this was as unrewarding as my attempts to make the music come from a phonograph record by holding the needle in my fingers.

I could burn holes through newspapers with it, or I could pretend that it was a telescope, the barrel of a cannon, or the third eye of a monster—*I* being the monster—but I could do nothing at all about its proper function of making images; nothing to make it yield its secret. But I could not discard it.

Older boys sought to get it away from me by offering knives or tops, agate marbles or whole zoos of grass snakes and horned toads in trade, but I held on to it. No one, not even the white boys I knew, had such a lens, and it was my own good luck to have found it. Thus I would hold on to it until such time as I could acquire the parts needed to make it function. Finally I put it aside and it remained buried in my box of treasures, dusty and dull, to be lost and forgotten as I grew older and became interested in music.

I had reached by now the grades where it was necessary to learn something about Mr. Emerson and what he had written, such as the "Concord Hymn" and the essay "Self-Reliance," and in following his advice, I reduced the "Waldo" to a simple and, I hoped, mysterious "W," and in my own reading I avoided his works like the plague. I could no more deal with my name—I shall never really master it—than I could find a creative use for my lens. . . .

If all this sounds a bit heady, remember that I did not destroy that troublesome mid-

12 Discussion How does Ellison use the photographic lens as a metaphor for his name?

13 Discussion What is ironic about Ellison avoiding the works of Emerson in his own reading?

12

13

the visible and the invisible, public and private, actual and fictive modes of reality. His experience as a Negro no doubt reinforces his ironic awareness of the joke that always lies between appearance and reality, and turns him toward an inner world that lies beyond the reach of insult or oppression. This world may be approached by means of the imagination: it is revealed during the transcendent moment in jazz or the epiphany in literature. *Transcend* is the crucial word in Ellison's aesthetic.

Above all, Ellison admires the transcendentalists for their active democratic faith. They were concerned not only with the slavery question, but with the wider implications of cultural pluralism, with the mystery of the one and the many. . . .

14 **Discussion** What do you think Ellison felt his obligations were to the man who named him?

15 **Discussion** According to Ellison, what is "the cost of change."

16 **Discussion** How does this idea pertain to the condition of black culture in America? What do you think Ellison, as a black writer, was trying to say about the validity of the black person's experience?

17 **Enrichment** In "Self-Reliance," Emerson called on Americans to know themselves, to trust their insights, and to recognize that what was true for them in their own hearts was true for all men.

Reader's Response What are your feelings about your own name?

14 dle name of mine, I only suppressed it. Sometimes it reminds me of my obligations to the man who named me.

It is our fate as human beings always to give up some good things for other good things, to throw off certain bad circumstances only to create others. Thus there is a value for the writer in trying to give as thor-

15 ough a report of social reality as possible. Only by doing so may we grasp and convey the cost of change. Only by considering the broadest accumulation of data may we make choices that are based upon our own hard-earned sense of reality. Speaking from my own special area of American culture, I feel that to embrace uncritically values which are extended to us by others is to reject the validity, even the sacredness, of our own expe-

rience. It is also to forget that the small share of reality which each of our diverse groups is able to snatch from the whirling chaos of history belongs not to the group

16 alone, but to all of us. It is a property and a witness which can be ignored only to the danger of the entire nation.

I could suppress the name of my namesake out of respect for the achievements of its original bearer but I cannot escape the obligation of attempting to achieve some of

17 the things which he asked of the American writer. As Henry James[7] suggested, being an American is an arduous task, and for most of us, I suspect, the difficulty begins with the name.

---

7. Henry James: An American novelist (1843–1916).

Primary Source

Consciously or unconsciously, we all have private pictures of the people who answer to certain names. For their book *The Best Baby Name Book in the Whole Wide World*, Bruce and Vicki Lansky and their researchers have developed a list of names and their stereotypes. Try guessing the stereotypes before you look at them.

Amanda	cultured
Amy	active
Angela	pleasant-looking, somewhat wistful
Ann	ladylike and honest, but not pretty
Elizabeth	seductive
Emily	a sideline-sitter
Jennifer	youthful, yet old-fashioned
Jessica	ambitious and beautiful
Linda	utterly feminine, popular and energetic
Lisa	very frail, well-liked
Margaret	a bit dowdy
Mary	wholesome, womanly, active
Melissa	passive but graceful
Nicole	average on all counts
Patricia	plain

Peggy	spirited, cute
Vicky	very sexy, exceedingly well-liked and frisky
Anthony	tall, wiry, elegant
Benjamin	dishonest
Brian	superstar—macho, dynamic
Charles	masculine, popular, but not overly active
Christopher	diligent, intelligent
David	not quite as terrific as Dave, but still a winner
Eric	a big winner—very strong
Francis	passive, neuter
James	a big winner in all categories
Jason	hugely popular
John	trustworthy, surprisingly passive but manly
Justin	vigorous
Kevin	very popular, virile
Mark	spoiled
Michael	very, very popular
Nicholas	very strong
Richard	very good-looking
Stephen	a winner in all areas
Thomas	large, soft and cuddly
William	kind but not aggressive

Closure and Extension

ANSWERS TO THINKING ABOUT THE SELECTION
Recalling

1. According to the fourth paragraph, blacks are constantly reminded by their names of their former state of slavery.
2. In his "earliest years," Ellison did

THINKING ABOUT THE SELECTION

Recalling

1. According to the fourth paragraph, of what are blacks constantly reminded?
2. Why did Ellison's name puzzle him in his "earliest years"?
3. What was Ellison unable to do with the photographic lens he found as a boy?
4. According to the next-to-last paragraph, what is "our fate as human beings"?
5. According to the final paragraph, from what is Ellison unable to escape?

Interpreting

6. What does Ellison mean when he comments that our names "must become our masks and our shields and the containers of all those values and traditions . . . of our familial past"?
7. What does Ellison mean when he refers to the "suggestive powers of names"?
8. How does Ellison relate his experiences with the photographic lens with his attempts to come to terms with his name?
9. In your own words, state the main point of Ellison's essay.

Applying

10. In *Romeo and Juliet,* Shakespeare wrote, "What's in a name? That which we call a rose/By any other word would smell as sweet." How does the idea about names expressed in these lines compare with the idea Ellison presents?
11. Do you think names play as important a role in people's lives as Ellison suggests? Why or why not?

ANALYZING LITERATURE

Understanding the Essay

Essays are short prose works that focus on a narrow topic. Generally an essay can be classified as either a formal essay or an informal essay. Ellison's essay, however, does not completely fit into either category, because it possesses characteristics of both formal essays and informal essays.

1. How is Ellison's essay organized?
2. What is the purpose of the essay?
3. How would you describe Ellison's use of language?

UNDERSTANDING LANGUAGE

Using Meaning That Fits Context

Many English words have more than one meaning. As a result, you must often examine a word's context, or the words surrounding it, to determine the way in which the word is being used.

Use the context to guess the meaning of the word in italics in each of the following passages from Ellison's essay. If you are unable to do so, consult your dictionary, and choose the definition that fits the context.

1. " . . . all of this *speculation* on the subject of names has a purpose . . ."
2. ". . . he admired this *remote* Mr. Emerson . . . so much so that he named his second son after him . . ."
3. ". . . I feel that to *embrace* uncritically values which are extended to us by others is to reject the validity . . . of our own experience."

THINKING AND WRITING

Writing a Critical Response

Write a formal essay in which you respond to the opinions about names that Ellison expresses in his essay. Reread the essay, carefully noting the opinions Ellison conveys. Decide whether you agree or disagree with each of these opinions. Then begin writing your essay, using examples to support your argument. When you revise, make sure you structured your argument in a logical manner.

from Hidden Name and Complex Fate   1049

(Answers begin on p. 1048.)

It also put him under an obligation to the ideals of Ralph Waldo Emerson, for whom he was named.

Applying

10. The quote contrasts with Ellison's suggestion that people's names help to shape their identities.
11. Answers will differ. Students may say that they do not feel that names play an important role in people's lives.

Challenge Ralph Waldo Emerson is considered one of America's foremost essayists. Discuss why it is suitable for Ellison to be discussing this issue in essay form.

ANSWERS TO ANALYZING LITERATURE
The Essay

1. Ellison's essay is loosely organized, following the progression from introduction, through development, to conclusion.
2. The purpose of the essay is to discuss the topic of names. This topic is one that pertains to all human beings, and which Ellison has personal insight into because of his own experience.
3. Ellison's language varies from elegant and learned to colloquial and informal.

ANSWERS TO UNDERSTANDING LANGUAGE

1. speculation: contemplation
2. remote: distant in time
3. embrace: take hold of

THINKING AND WRITING
Writing Across the Curriculum
For extra credit, you might have students research the opinions of other writers or the views of different cultures on names and the power of naming. Perhaps inform the social studies department of this assignment. Social studies teachers might provide guidance for students researching this topic in the areas of mythology, religion, and sociology.

not know what a poet was nor did he understand why his father had named him after one.

3. Ellison was not able to make it perform its proper function of making images.
4. "It is our fate as human beings always to give up some good things for other good things, to throw off certain bad circumstances only to create others."
5. Ellison is unable to escape the obligation that his name puts him under—"to achieve some of the things which [Emerson] asked of the American Writer."

Interpreting

6. Ellison means that our names are what we show of ourselves to the world. Instead of saying who we are, we say what we are called, and what our fathers have been called before us.
7. Ellison means that names can have an influence on people, as he illustrates with the example of Franklin D. Roosevelt Jones.
8. Ellison could not make the photographic lens work, it was not something he chose, but he could not discard it. Instead, he put it away for a later date.
9. Suggested Response: Ellison says that names are important in many different ways. Using the example of his own name, he shows how he suffered because of it, but also how it told him something about his father, and what his father expected of him.

More About the Author Joan Didion has been criticized by some feminists because, even though she has supported some of the demands of the women's movement, she has publicly rejected its tenets. Ask students to discuss the implications of a writer's political beliefs. What influence can politics have on the reception of a writer's work by the public?

Critical Evaluation In his biography of Joan Didion, Mark Royden Winchell writes, "It is too early to assess Joan Didion's place in American literature and it would be problematical to try to predict the future course of her career. At present, however, she has established herself as being—at the very least—a 'writer's writer.' Her most enthusiastic admirers include other talented literary artists, figures as diverse as Guy Davenport and Joyce Carol Oates, as Brian Moore and Tennessee Williams. Indeed, no less an authority than James Dickey has called her 'the finest woman prose stylist writing in English today.'"

JOAN DIDION

1934–

An innovative writer of both fiction and nonfiction, Joan Didion is known for her precise use of language and her ability to capture the essence of contemporary life using images from her own life.

Born and raised in California, Didion began writing at an early age. She earned a degree from the University of California at Berkeley and worked for a number of years as an editor for *Vogue* magazine. In 1963 she published her first novel, *Run River*. Five years later, she produced a volume of essays, *Slouching Towards Bethlehem*, which captured the flavor of life in San Francisco during the late 1960's. This book, along with a later collection of essays, *The White Album* (1979), earned Didion a reputation as one of the country's premier essayists. Since the publication of *The White Album*, she has published another work of nonfiction, *Salvador* (1983), and *Democracy* (1984), a novel that combines fiction with nonfiction.

Didion has written, "We tell ourselves stories in order to live. . . . We live entirely, especially if we are writers, by the imposition of a narrative line upon disparate images, by the 'ideas' with which we have learned to freeze the shifting phantasmagoria which is our actual experience."

In her essay "On the Mall," Didion displays her direct, precise style and her ability to transform a very ordinary subject into an interesting and entertaining work of literature.

Didion is fond of saying, "Everything you do counts," and she feels each image or gesture tells a story with moral implications. Her images are at times aching blends of elegance and despair, and the near tragic point of view she often strikes shows the vulnerability she feels in her own life and in the lives we all live in our current world. She is particularly adept at depicting the harsh, nonhuman, or even anti-human extremes that surround us in our contemporary world. Her appeal comes from her ability to express a very personal despair in an almost universal way. One striking Didion image shows sunny California as Hell; the image paints the hills of Malibu Beach engulfed in flame while happy surfers ride the waves below. She often portrays such elements as fire or earthquake devastating people's lives while others not personally touched go about their business indifferently.

Ritual, she feels, holds one key to sustaining life through systematizing it and thus subduing its chaos. Often her works explore ritual as a means of survival. Her subjects, or characters, commonly carry on mundane little tasks and routines that give their lives shape and disguise the fact that things around them are, in actuality, falling apart.

1050   *Contemporary Writers*

Support Material

Teaching Portfolio
Teacher Backup, p. 1405
Grammar in Action Worksheet, *Using Quotation Marks and Italics*, p. 1409
Usage and Mechanics Worksheet, p. 1411
Vocabulary Check, p. 1412
Critical Thinking and Reading Worksheet, *Separating Facts From Opinions*, p. 1413

Language Worksheet, *Understanding Word Origins*, p. 1414
Selection Test, p. 1415

GUIDE FOR INTERPRETING

On the Mall

Writer's Techniques

Exposition. Exposition is writing in which factual information is presented. It informs or educates the reader by presenting a series of facts, discussing their significance, and explaining how they relate to one another. In "On the Mall," for example, Didion uses exposition to inform the reader about the theories used in planning shopping malls.

Because it is vital to the reader's understanding of a literary work, exposition plays an important role in both fiction and nonfiction. In fact, many works of nonfiction are classified as expository essays because their primary purpose is to inform or educate the reader.

Commentary

Joan Didion's "On the Mall" looks at aspects of mall design, since it relates to the way in which it affects people. You will notice that the essay does not directly discuss these centers as gathering places, yet that is what they have become for many teens. Teens have traditionally found meeting places for themselves, and the nature of places they meet has reflected the changing times. In the fifties the malt shop was a favorite "hangout" in any town that had one. In the sixties, as American teens became more affluent, suburban car owners took to "cruising," or driving slowly along popular designations in order to see and be seen by their peers. In the seventies parks and beaches had their day, but as shopping malls began to appear all over America, teens discovered that they offered more than places to purchase goods and services. As malls became refined to include inexpensive restaurants and multiplex theaters as well as clothing stores and photo shops, teens began to flock to them as after-school meeting zones. The eighties have seen a vast proliferation of shopping malls in cities and towns alike, and they have remained the number one choice among teens for meeting and conferring with one another. Malls have, in the late eighties, become small towns where young mothers go to do chores and entertain children in one combined trip. Today's shopping malls have become places where one can get most human needs met. In the mall you can cash a check, buy your groceries, have your tires rotated, do your laundry, grab a meal, see a film, get a haircut, catch a bus, order glasses, and ride a merry-go-round. Yet beyond the availability of all these activities, one remains the runaway favorite, at least among the teenage population. Above all, in the late eighties, a mall is a place to meet your friends. What is your experience with malls?

Writing

What sorts of impressions do you have of shopping malls? Freewrite about shopping malls, discussing the reasons for their popularity and your own thoughts concerning them.

Guide for Interpreting 1051

Literary Focus Exposition is one of the modes of discourse. The others are argumentation, persuasion, description, and narration. Often exposition is blended with one or more of the other modes of discourse. Have students think of works that represent each of the different forms of discourse. For instance, Carson McCullers's "The Mortgaged Heart" is an example of argumentation, and Truman Capote's "A Ride Through Spain" is a narrative that also contains description.

Writing/Prior Knowledge Before having students complete the writing activity, you might have them discuss the effect that shopping malls have on small towns. What economic effect do they have? How do they affect the social lives of the people?

Vocabulary

Preteach the following vocabulary words:
egalitarian (i gal' ə ter' ē ən) *adj.*: Asserting, resulting from, or characterized by the belief in the equality of all people (p. 1052)
enigmatic (en' ig mat' ik) *adj.*: Perplexing; mysterious (p. 1052)
indigenous (in dïj' ə nəs) *adj.*: Originating in and characterizing a particular region or country (p. 1052)
eccentric (ik sen' trik) *adj.*: Peculiar (p. 1052)
seminal (sem' ə n'l) *adj.*: Highly original and influencing the development of future events (p. 1054)
recondite (rek' ən dīt') *adj.*: Dealing with very profound, difficult, or abstruse subject matter (p. 1054)

Motivation/Prior Knowledge
Ask the students when they last went to a shopping mall. Do they think that going to a mall is a different experience from going to the supermarket? Why or why not? What are their reasons for going to a mall? How would they describe the atmosphere of a shopping mall?

Master Teacher Note "On the Mall" is from *The White Album,* a collection of essays that were written by Joan Didion during the 1960's on contemporary life. The book takes its title from the name often used to refer to the Beatles album entitled *The Beatles* that was released in 1968. Have students listen to the songs from *The Beatles,* focusing on the lyrics. The themes of these songs illustrate many of the concerns of the times.

Purpose-Setting Question Why do you think shopping malls interest Joan Didion?

1 **Discussion** What is ironic about the names of these shopping malls?

2 **Literary Focus** Didion states ideas about shopping malls that she will support later in the essay. Have students find where she expands on these points.

3 **Discussion** How does the automobile account for suburbia? How does suburbia account for the shopping center?

4 **Discussion** What does Didion mean by this? Was this vision of a new American frontier realized? Compare this kind of frontier to the early American frontier.

5 **Discussion** In what sense was Jere Strizek a frontiersman? What was his frontier?

On the Mall

Joan Didion

They float on the landscape like pyramids to the boom years, all those Plazas and Malls and Esplanades. All those Squares and Fairs. All those Towns and Dales, all those Villages, all those Forests and Parks and Lands. Stonestown. Hillsdale. Valley Fair, Mayfair, Northgate, Southgate, Eastgate, Westgate. Gulfgate. They are toy garden cities in which no one lives but everyone consumes, profound equalizers, the perfect fusion of the profit motive and the egalitarian ideal, and to hear their names is to recall words and phrases no longer quite current. Baby Boom. Consumer Explosion. Leisure Revolution. Do-It-Yourself Revolution. Backyard Revolution. Suburbia. "The Shopping Center," the Urban Land Institute could pronounce in 1957, "is today's extraordinary retail business evolvement. . . . The automobile accounts for suburbia, and suburbia accounts for the shopping center."

It was a peculiar and visionary time, those years after World War II to which all the Malls and Towns and Dales stand as climate-controlled monuments. Even the word "automobile," as in "the automobile accounts for suburbia and suburbia accounts for the shopping center," no longer carries the particular freight it once did: as a child in the late Forties in California I recall reading and believing that the "freedom of movement" afforded by the automobile was "America's fifth freedom." The trend was up. The solution was in sight. The frontier had been reinvented, and its shape was the subdivision, that new free land on which all settlers could recast their lives *tabula rasa.*[1] For one perishable moment there the American idea seemed about to achieve itself, via F.H.A.[2] housing and the acquisition of major appliances, and a certain enigmatic glamour attached to the architects of this newfound land. They made something of nothing. They gambled and sometimes lost. They staked the past to seize the future. I have difficulty now imagining a childhood in which a man named Jere Strizek, the developer of Town and Country Village outside Sacramento (143,000 square feet gross floor area, 68 stores, 1000 parking spaces, the Urban Land Institute's "prototype for centers using heavy timber and tile construction for informality"), could materialize as a role model, but I had such a childhood, just after World War II, in Sacramento. I never met or even saw Jere Strizek, but at the age of 12 I imagined him a kind of frontiersman, a romantic and revolutionary spirit, and in the indigenous grain he was.

I suppose James B. Douglas and David D. Bohannon were too.

I first heard of James B. Douglas and David D. Bohannon not when I was 12 but a dozen years later, when I was living in New York, working for *Vogue,* and taking, by correspondence, a University of California Extension course in shopping-center theory. This did not seem to me eccentric at the

---

1. *tabula rasa* (tab'yə lə rä' sə): Clean slate.
2. **F.H.A.:** Federal Housing Administration.

Primary Source

In her book *Slouching Towards Bethlehem* Joan Didion discusses how her imagination colors her memories. She writes:

Not only have I always had trouble distinguishing between what happened and what merely might have happened, but I remain unconvinced that the distinction, for my purposes, matters. The cracked crab I recall having for lunch the day my father came home from Detroit in 1945 must certainly be embroidery, working into the day's pattern to lend verisimilitude . . . . And yet it is precisely that fictitious crab that makes me see the afternoon all over again, a home movie run all too often, the father bearing gifts, the children weeping, and exercise in family love and guilt. Or that is what it was to me. Similarly, perhaps it never did snow in August in Vermont; perhaps there never were flurries in the night wind, and maybe no one else felt the ground hardening and the summer already dead even as we pretended to bask in it, but that was how

6 time. I remember sitting on the cool floor in Irving Penn's studio and reading, in *The Community Builders Handbook*, advice from James B. Douglas on shopping-center financing. I recall staying late in my pale-blue office on the twentieth floor of the Graybar Building to memorize David D. Bohannon's parking ratios. My "real" life was to sit in this office and describe life as it was lived in Djakarta and Caneel Bay and in the great châteaux of the Loire Valley, but my dream life was to put together a Class-A regional shopping center with three full-line department stores as major tenants.

That I was perhaps the only person I knew in New York, let alone on the Condé Nast[3] floors of the Graybar Building, to have memorized the distinctions among "A," "B," and "C" shopping centers did not occur to me (the defining distinction, as long as I have your attention, is that an "A," or "regional," center has as its major tenant a full-line department store which carries major appliances; a "B," or "community," center has as its major tenant a junior department store which does not carry major appliances; and a "C," or "neighborhood," center has as its major tenant only a supermarket): my interest in shopping centers was in no way casual. I did want to build them. I wanted to build them because I had fallen into the habit of writing fiction, and I had it in my head that a couple of good centers might support this habit less taxingly than a pale-blue office at *Vogue*. I had even devised an original scheme by which I planned to gain enough capital and credibility to enter the

---

3. Condé Nast: Company that publishes a variety of periodicals, including *Vogue* magazine.

it felt to me, and it might as well have snowed, could have snowed, did snow.

9 **Literary Focus** Point out that this paragraph and the one that follows contain facts about shopping malls.

10 **Discussion** What does this sentence indicate about Didion?

11 **Discussion** What sort of person is the woman from Detroit? How does Didion want us to feel about her?

shopping-center game: I would lease warehouses in, say, Queens, and offer Manhattan delicatessens the opportunity to sell competitively by buying cooperatively, from my trucks. I see a few wrinkles in this scheme now (the words "concrete overcoat" come to mind), but I did not then. In fact I planned to run it out of the pale-blue office.

James B. Douglas and David D. Bohannon. In 1950 James B. Douglas had opened Northgate, in Seattle, the first regional center to combine a pedestrian mall with an underground truck tunnel. In 1954 David D. Bohannon had opened Hillsdale, a forty-acre regional center on the peninsula south of San Francisco. That is the only solid bio I have on James B. Douglas and David D. Bohannon to this day, but many of their opinions are engraved on my memory. David D. Bohannon believed in preserving the integrity of the shopping center by not cutting up the site with any dedicated roads. David D. Bohannon believed that architectural setbacks in a center looked "pretty on paper" but caused "customer resistance." James B. Douglas advised that a small-loan office could prosper in a center only if it were placed away from foot traffic, since people who want small loans do not want to be observed getting them. I do not now recall whether it was James B. Douglas or David D. Bohannon or someone else altogether who passed along this hint on how to paint the lines around the parking spaces (actually this is called "striping the lot," and the spaces are "stalls"): make each space a foot wider than it need be—ten feet, say, instead of nine—when the center first opens and business is slow. By this single stroke the developer achieves a couple of important objectives, the appearance of a popular center and the illusion of easy parking, and no one will really notice when business picks up and the spaces shrink.

Nor do I recall who first solved what was once a crucial center dilemma: the placement of the major tenant vis-à-vis the parking lot. The dilemma was that the major tenant—the draw, the raison d'être[4] for the financing, the Sears, the Macy's, the May Company—wanted its customer to walk directly from car to store. The smaller tenants, on the other hand, wanted that same customer to *pass their stores* on the way from the car to, say, Macy's. The solution to this conflict of interests was actually very simple: *two major tenants,* one at each end of a mall. This is called "anchoring the mall," and represents seminal work in shopping-center theory. One thing you will note about shopping-center theory is that you could have thought of it yourself, and a course in it will go a long way toward dispelling the notion that business proceeds from mysteries too recondite for you and me.

A few aspects of shopping-center theory do in fact remain impenetrable to me. I have no idea why the Community Builders' Council ranks "Restaurant" as deserving a Number One (or "Hot Spot") location but exiles "Chinese Restaurant" to a Number Three, out there with "Power and Light Office" and "Christian Science Reading Room." Nor do I know why the Council approves of enlivening a mall with "small animals" but specifically, vehemently, and with no further explanation, excludes "monkeys." If I had a center I would have monkeys, and Chinese restaurants, and Mylar[5] kites and bands of small girls playing tambourine.

A few years ago at a party I met a woman from Detroit who told me that the Joyce Carol Oates novel with which she identified most closely was *Wonderland.*

I asked her why.

"Because," she said, "my husband has a branch there."

I did not understand.

---

4. **raison d'être** (rā′zōn det′rə): Justification for existence.
5. **Mylar** (mī′ lär): Polyester made in extremely thin sheets of great strength.

Grammar in Action

Quotation marks and **italics** (underlining) are used to indicate titles and to mark other special uses of words. Joan Didion's essay includes many of these special uses.

Italics, which in manuscript are shown by underlining, indicate the title of a long written work, a publication issued as a single work, a show, or a work of art. Quotation marks set off the titles of short written works, episodes in a series, songs and parts of long musical compositions. Note the following example of italics from Didion's essay:

I was living in New York, working for *Vogue.* . . . (p. 1052)

Italic type (underlining) is also used to mark foreign words or phrases. For example:

All settlers could recast their lives *tabula rasa.* (p. 1052)

Didion also uses italics for emphasis. Note the following example:

The smaller tenants, on the other hand, wanted that same customer to *pass their stores.* . . . (p. 1054)

"In Wonderland the center," the woman said patiently. "My husband has a branch in Wonderland."

I have never visited Wonderland but imagine it to have bands of small girls playing tambourine.

A few facts about shopping centers.

The "biggest" center in the United States is generally agreed to be Woodfield, outside Chicago, a "super" regional or "leviathan" two-million-square-foot center with four major tenants.

The "first" shopping center in the United States is generally agreed to be Country Club Plaza in Kansas City, built in the twenties. There were some other early centers, notably Edward H. Bouton's 1907 Roland Park in Baltimore, Hugh Prather's 1931 Highland Park Shopping Village in Dallas, and Hugh Potter's 1937 River Oaks in Houston, but the developer of Country Club Plaza, the late J. C. Nichols, is referred to with ritual frequency in the literature of shopping centers, usually as "pioneering J. C. Nichols," "trailblazing J. C. Nichols," or "J. C. Nichols, father of the center as we know it."

Those are some facts I know about shopping centers because I still want to be Jere Strizek or James B. Douglas or David D. Bohannon. Here are some facts I know about shopping centers because I never will be Jere Strizek or James B. Douglas or David D. Bohannon: a good center in which to spend the day if you wake feeling low in Honolulu, Hawaii, is Ala Moana, major tenants Liberty House and Sears. A good center in which to spend the day if you wake feeling low in Ox-

12 Discussion What does being Jere Strizek represent to Didion? What does not being Jere Strizek mean?

12

On the Mall 1055

Quotation marks signal another's words. For example:

  . . . actually this is called "striping the lot,". . . . (p. 1054)

They also indicate words used less than seriously. For example:

  My "real" life was to sit in this office. . . . (p. 1053)

Student Activity 1. Explain the following uses of quotation marks or italics.

1. I went to Ala Moana . . . to buy *The New York Times.*
2. The spaces are "stalls."
3. The solution . . . was actually very simple: *two major tenants,* one at each end of the mall.

Student Activity 2. Provide quotation marks or underlining as needed in the following items.

1. Didion refers to Joyce Carol Oates's novel Wonderland.
2. Didion studied the definitions of A, B, and C centers.
3. Having two major tenants, one at each end of a center is called anchoring the mall.
4. J. C. Nichols is referred to, in the literature Didion read, as trailblazing J. C. Nichols.

1056

13 Discussion How can shopping centers in Hawaii, California, and Mississippi all be "the same place"?

14 Literary Focus Point out that this is one of Didion's main points in the essay.

15 Discussion What does it mean to surrender one's ego to a shopping center? What does this idea suggest about American society?

16 Discussion Has Didion's attitude toward shopping centers changed? What is the emphasis at the end of the essay as opposed to the emphasis at the beginning? Why did Didion buy things she didn't need?

Reader's Response Do you enjoy going to malls? Why or why not?

Closure and Extension

ANSWERS TO THINKING ABOUT THE SELECTION
Recalling

1. (a) As a young girl, Didion believed that "freedom of movement" was "America's fifth freedom." (b) Didion saw Strizek as "a kind of frontiersman, a romantic and revolutionary spirit."
2. (a) Didion hoped to support her fiction writing by building shopping centers which would make money for her. (b) She planned to lease warehouses and offer Manhattan delicatessens the chance to sell competitively by buying cooperatively from her trucks.
3. (a) By making each parking space a foot wider than it has to be, the developer achieves "the appearance of a popular center"

---

nard, California, is The Esplanade, major tenants the May Company and Sears. A good center in which to spend the day if you wake feeling low in Biloxi, Mississippi, is Edgewater Plaza, major tenant Godchaux's. Ala Moana in Honolulu is larger than The Esplanade in Oxnard, and The Esplanade in Oxnard is larger than Edgewater Plaza in Biloxi. Ala Moana has carp pools. The Esplanade and Edgewater Plaza do not.

13
14
These marginal distinctions to one side, Ala Moana, The Esplanade, and Edgewater Plaza are the same place, which is precisely their role not only as equalizers but in the sedation of anxiety. In each of them one moves for a while in an aqueous suspension not only of light but of judgment, not only of judgment but of "personality." One meets no acquaintances at The Esplanade. One gets

no telephone calls at Edgewater Plaza. "It's a hard place to run in to for a pair of stockings," a friend complained to me recently of Ala Moana, and I knew that she was not yet ready to surrender her ego to the idea of the center. **15** The last time I went to Ala Moana it was to buy *The New York Times*. Because *The New York Times* was not in, I sat on the mall for a while and ate caramel corn. In the end I bought not *The New York Times* at all but two straw hats at Liberty House, four bottles of nail enamel at Woolworth's, and a toaster, on sale at Sears. In the literature of shopping centers these would be described **16** as impulse purchases, but the impulse here was obscure. I do not wear hats, nor do I like caramel corn. I do not use nail enamel. Yet flying back across the Pacific I regretted only the toaster.

Primary Source

There are shopping centers and then there is the West Edmonton Mall in Canada. Author Ian Pearson described it like this in an article for *Saturday Night* magazine. "The world's largest collection of stores, restaurants, and fun-fair amusements, West Edmonton Mall is also the latest stage in high-pressure retailing. And it may be the future that awaits consumers everywhere. . . .

"West Edmonton Mall is eight city blocks long and three blocks wide, a two-level, yellow-brick structure that houses a miscellany of modern recreation. There's an indoor amusement park called Fantasyland with carousels, water rides, a miniature train, and a thirteen-story high, triple-loop roller coaster. There are hundreds of video games in two giant arcades which serve as social centers for thousands of teenagers. There's an NHL-sized rink on which the Edmonton Oilers occasionally practice. There's a fountain that shoots fire and water and another that

squirts water in time to the themes from *Chariots of Fire* and *The Pink Panther*.

"Ficus trees and palm trees grow profusely under enormous skylights. Brass railings imbedded with tivoli lights line the edges of the rink, the submarine pond, and the upper level of the mall; . . . on Bourbon Street, a wing of the mall that is a copy of the New Orleans street, there are lifelike statues of jazz musicians. A shopper can traverse an international route from Hollywood West to Rodier of Paris to Casablanca and encounter tigers, bears, moray eels, tropical fish, toucans, flamingos, macaws, and spider monkeys.

" 'Unreal,' the teenagers say, but West Edmonton Mall is having very real and wide-reaching effects. Already malls around the world are following its example, before there's time to answer crucial questions about the financial feasibility and the social effects of this oversized prototype. . . ."

---

and "the illusion of easy parking." (b) By placing two major tenants at either end of a mall, customers may walk directly from their cars to the store and also have the opportunity of passing the smaller stores on their way from one major tenant to the other. (c) This theory is called "anchoring the mall."
4. She doesn't understand why the Community Builder's Council doesn't rank Chinese restaurants along with other restaurants as

deserving a "Hot Spot" location, or why monkeys are excluded from the Council's recommendation of using "small animals" to enliven a mall.
5. She tells of meeting a woman who said that the reason her favorite Joyce Carol Oates' novel was *Wonderland* was that her husband had a branch of his business in a shopping center by that name.
6. (a) The last time she was at the Ala Moana she bought caramel

corn, two straw hats, four bottles of nail enamel, and a toaster. (b) These purchases were unusual because she doesn't like caramel corn, doesn't wear hats, and doesn't use nail enamel.

Interpreting

7. (a) As the Egyptian pharaohs built pyramids to glorify their wealth and power, Americans built shopping malls when times were good. (b) Malls are "profound equalizers" because they

THINKING ABOUT THE SELECTION

Recalling

1. (a) When she was a young girl, what did Didion believe to be "America's fifth freedom"? (b) What impression did she have of Jere Strizek, the developer of Town and Country Village?
2. (a) Why did Didion dream of building shopping centers while she was working at *Vogue*? (b) What scheme did she devise by which she would "gain enough capital and credibility to enter the shopping-center game"?
3. (a) What theory does Didion present concerning the width of parking spaces? (b) What theory does she present concerning the placement of major tenants? (c) What is this theory called?
4. What aspects of shopping-center theory "remain impenetrable" to Didion?
5. What encounter with a woman from Detroit does Didion describe?
6. (a) What did Didion purchase the last time she visited the Ala Moana in Hawaii? (b) What did she find unusual about these purchases?

Interpreting

7. (a) What does Didion mean when she describes shopping malls as "pyramids to the boom years"? (b) In what sense are the malls "profound equalizers"?
8. What does Didion's description of her encounter with the woman from Detroit imply about the priorities of the American public?
9. (a) What seems to be Didion's current attitude concerning her earlier dreams of building shopping centers? (b) What seems to be her current attitude toward shopping malls and shopping-center theory? (c) How are these attitudes conveyed?
10. What point does Didion's essay make concerning the role of shopping centers in American society?

Applying

11. Compare your own attitude toward shopping malls with Didion's current attitude.

ANALYZING LITERATURE

Understanding Exposition

Exposition is writing in which factual information is presented. For example, in the fifth paragraph of "On the Mall," Didion presents a series of facts concerning the "distinctions among 'A,' 'B,' and 'C' shopping centers."

1. What are the distinctions among "A," "B," and "C" shopping centers?
2. Find three more examples of factual information in Didion's essay.
3. Should this essay be classified as an expository essay? Why or why not?

CRITICAL THINKING AND READING

Separating Facts from Opinions

Didion's essay contains both facts and opinions. A **fact** is an objective statement that can be verified, or proved to be true. For example, Didion presents a fact when she writes, "Woodfield Mall, outside Chicago, is a two-million-square-foot center." In contrast, an **opinion** is a subjective statement that cannot be verified. For example, Didion states an opinion when she refers to the years immediately following World War II as a "peculiar and visionary time."

1. Find three more statements of fact presented in Didion's essay.
2. Find three more opinions presented in the essay.

THINKING AND WRITING

Writing About a Writer's Attitudes

Write an essay in which you discuss the attitudes that Didion conveys about shopping malls, shopping-center theory, and the role of shopping malls in American society. Reread the essay, focusing on Didion's attitudes and noting how these attitudes are conveyed. Prepare a thesis statement. Then write your essay, using passages from Didion's essay to support your thesis. When you revise, make sure you have varied the length and structure of your sentences.

On the Mall 1057

---

contemporary life. What other objects or places could be viewed as symbols of contemporary life?

ANSWERS TO ANALYZING LITERATURE

1. An "A" center has as its major tenant a full-line department store; a "B" center has as its major tenant a junior department store; a "C" center has as its major tenant a supermarket.
2. Some examples of exposition are: the facts presented about the achievements of James B. Douglas and David D. Bohannon; the theory concerning the width of parking spaces; and the facts about shopping centers in the seventh through ninth paragraphs.
3. "On the Mall" can be classified as an expository essay. Factual information is presented, the writer discusses its significance, and uses it to make a point.

ANSWERS TO CRITICAL THINKING AND READING

1. Statements of fact include: Jere Strizek was the developer of Town and Country Village outside Sacramento; Didion worked for *Vogue* while taking a correspondence course in shopping-center theory; James B. Douglas opened Northgate in 1950; in 1954 David O. Bohannon opened Hillsdale.
2. Opinions presented in the essay include: shopping centers are "the perfect fusion of the profit motive and the egalitarian ideal;" shopping-center theory is something anyone could think of; all shopping centers are the same place; and others.

---

are the same all over the country, anyone can go into them, they cater to the average person, and no matter what part of the country they are in, they offer the same merchandise and the same experience for the shopper.

8. Didion's experience implies that the average American places a lower value on art than on shopping.

9. (a) Didion seems to be looking back at her dreams with a sense of wonder and amusement. (b) Didion now seems to be interested in shopping malls as a social phenomenon rather than a way that she could make money. (c) She conveys her attitudes toward shopping malls and her own dreams through the description of shopping-mall theory and her experiences in shopping centers.

10. Didion calls malls "profound equalizers, the perfect fusion of the profit motive and the egalitar-ian ideal." She says that malls are used as places where one can escape from reality.

Applying

11. Answers will differ. Students might comment that they enjoy going to shopping malls and, unlike Didion, are not interested in the malls as a social phenomenon.

Challenge Didion clearly sees shopping malls as symbols of

Writing Across the Curriculum

For extra credit, have students research and write about the various movements of the American population: out of the country to the cities; out of the cities to the suburbs. You might wish to inform the social studies department of this assignment. Social studies teachers might guide for students in conducting research.

More About the Author In the mid-1960's, N. Scott Momaday made a pilgrimage from the Rockies in Montana to western Oklahoma. He ended his journey at his grandmother's grave. He wrote about this pilgrimage in *The Way to Rainy Mountain.* Ask students how an experience so personal can pertain to the lives of other people. What can we learn from a writer's personal experiences?

Critical Evaluation In a review of N. Scott Momaday's *The Names,* the noted writer Wallace Stegner observed, *"The Names* is an Indian book, but not a book about wrongs done to Indians. It is a search and a celebration, a book of identities and sources. Momaday is the son of parents who successfully bridged the gulf between Indian and white ways, but remain Indian. In boyhood Momaday made the same choice, and in making it gave himself the task of discovering and in some degree inventing the tradition and history in which he finds his most profound sense of himself . . . Momaday has not invented himself, as many Americans have tried to do. He has let the blood speak, looked for tracks, listened and remembered. Out of ordinary materials . . . he has built a mystical, provocative book. He has pieced together a tradition and created ancestors . . . They empty like feeder streams into the river of his sensibility and awareness. . . ."

N. SCOTT MOMADAY

1934–

Proud of his Native American heritage, N. Scott Momaday has devoted his life to teaching and writing about Native American history, folklore, and mythology.

A Kiowa Indian, Momaday was born in Lawton, Oklahoma. After graduating from the University of New Mexico, he received a doctorate in literature from Stanford University. His first novel, *House Made of Dawn* (1969), an account of a young Indian torn between his ancestral roots and contemporary mainstream society, earned him a Pulitzer Prize. He then published what has become his best-known work, *The Way to Rainy Mountain* (1969), a collection of personal anecdotes and retellings of Kiowa myths and legends. Since then, he has produced several more books, including two volumes of poetry, *Angle of Geese and Other Poems* (1973) and *The Gourd Dancer* (1976), and a collection of anecdotes entitled *The Names* (1976).

Dr. Momaday is devoted to preserving his Kiowa heritage. As a boy he often visited his grandparents, both of whom shared their experiences with their grandson. His grandfather Mammedaty, whose name means "sky walker," was a "peyote man" who "saw things other men do not," according to Momaday. His grandmother had attended the last Kiowa sun dance in the late 1880's. He explains that his grandmother "had a reverence for the sun, a holy regard that now is all but gone out of mankind. There was a warrior in her, and an ancient awe."

His grandparents' home served as a meeting place for aged Kiowas whom Momaday recalls as people "made of lean leather" who "rubbed fat upon their hair and wound their braids with strips of colored cloth. Some," he says, "painted their faces and carried the scars of old and cherished enemies. They were old council warlords come to remind and be reminded of who they were."

N. Scott Momaday acknowledges that the current-day problems of Native American people have become more generally visible, but he also feels the increased awareness is not sufficient. In his writing he strives to preserve the oral tradition of Native American peoples as well as the significance behind their legends.

Like Momaday's other works, "A Vision Beyond Time and Place" helps provide the reader with a better understanding of traditional Native American culture. In the essay Momaday recalls and discusses the significance of an old tribe member's daily prayers to the rising sun.

Objectives
1 To recognize the use of classification
2 To recognize cultural attitudes
3 To compare and contrast essays

Support Material

Teaching Portfolio
Teacher Backup, p. 1917
Usage and Mechanics Worksheet, p. 1920
Vocabulary Check, p. 1921
Analyzing Literature Worksheet, *Understanding Classification,* p. 1922
Language Worksheet, *Understanding Shades of Meaning,* p. 1923

Selection Test, p. 1924
Art Transparency 18, *Sante Fe Landscape* by Stuart Davis

GUIDE FOR INTERPRETING

A Vision Beyond Time and Place

Writer's Techniques

Classification. Classification refers to the process of dividing a subject into categories, or classes. In nonfiction, writers sometimes use classification to clarify the meaning of an idea or concept that may otherwise be difficult to grasp. For example, in "A Vision Beyond Time and Place," N. Scott Momaday uses classification to help define a specific type of "vision" with which most Americans are likely to be unfamiliar.

Writing

Discuss the different ways in which people view the world. Why do you think people from different cultures sometimes view the same thing in completely different ways? Why is it important for different cultures to share their views? How can this contribute to their abilities to understand one another?

Primary Source

The United States government policies toward Native American culture have long been suspect. From the Dawes Act of 1887 until the mid-1930's, government agencies saw no value in preserving Native American heritage. Samuel Eliot Morison wrote in *The Oxford History of the American People*, "The general assumption behind the federal government's policy [on Indians] was an anticipated disappearance of the Indians as a separate and distinct race. Hence it was a good thing to help the process—not, of course, by the earlier crude methods of starvation, disease, and extermination, but by promoting the breakup of reservations into individually owned allotments. Land ownership, it was believed, would make the redskins responsible citizens and assimilate them to the American Way of Life. The interior department speeded up this process through shortening by several years the time that an Indian had to occupy his allotment before [he could] sell it. In one year 60 percent of all Indians receiving titles to their allotments sold out, and most of them squandered the proceeds.

"This does not, however, apply to the Five Civilized Tribes of Oklahoma. They managed to retain much of their own culture, while adapting themselves to that of the Anglo-Saxon American; and many became eminent. Will Rogers, Senator R. L. Owen, and Admiral Joseph J. ("Jocko") Clarke, a great carrier group commander in World War II, were Cherokee; Charles Curtis, Vice President under Hoover, was an Osage, and the list might be extended indefinitely by including artists, professional singers, and ballerinas."

Literary Focus Momaday uses classification to clarify the meaning of abstract ideas. Why would these ideas be more difficult to grasp if he had not used this technique?

Writing/Prior Knowledge Before students complete the writing activity, you may wish to have them research the creation myths of various cultures. Have them discuss similarities and differences among the myths. What is the role of the sun in these myths?

Vocabulary

Preteach the following vocabulary words:
luminous (lōō′ mə nəs) *adj.*: Shining (p. 1060)
impalpable (im pal′ pə b'l) *adj.*: Imperceptible to the sense of touch (p. 1060)
reverence (rev′ ər əns) *n.*: A feeling or attitude of deep respect, love, or awe (p. 1060)
evanescence (ev′ ə nes′ 'ns) *n.*: A fading from sight (p. 1062)
quintessentially (kwin′ tə sen′ shə lē) *adv.*: Purely (p. 1062)

Guide for Interpreting 1059

Motivation/Prior Knowledge
Ask students if they have ever seen the sun rise. What was it like to be up so early in the morning? How would they describe what the sunrise looked like and felt like?

Master Teacher Note There are several excellent books of Native American poetry. Read some of these poems aloud to the class to set the mood for Momaday's essay. Books include *Voices of the Rainbow,* edited by Kenneth Rosen (Viking, 1975), *Contemporary Native American Literature,* edited by Angeline Jacobson (Scarecrow, 1977), and *The Whispering Wind,* edited by Terry Allen and Mae Durham (Exposition Press, 1972). To help students envision the setting of Momaday's essay, place Transparency 18, *Santa Fe Landscape* by Stuart Davis, on the overhead projector. Ask students to imagine what life would be like in this type of environment. How would it be different from life in other settings? How might the people who live there be different from people from other places?

Thematic Idea Another selection that presents a unique vision of nature is "Song Concerning a Dream of the Thunderbirds" (p. 37).

Purpose-Setting Question According to Momaday, what is the purpose of a vision quest?

1 Reading Strategy Have your students discuss this title. What does it indicate about the kind of essay this will be? What do they think the title could mean?

2 Critical Thinking and Reading
Point out how this opening, with its description of the old man going out to pray, contrasts with the more abstract language of the rest of the essay. Ask stu-

A Vision Beyond Time and Place

N. Scott Momaday

When my father was a boy, an old man used to come to [my grandfather] Mammedaty's house and pay his respects. He was a lean old man in braids and was impressive in his age and bearing. His name was Cheney, and he was an arrowmaker. Every morning, my father tells me, Cheney would paint his wrinkled face, go out, and pray aloud to the rising sun. In my mind I can see that man as if he were there now. I like to watch him as he makes his prayer. I know where he stands and where his voice goes on the rolling grasses and where the sun comes up on the land. There, at dawn, you can feel the silence. It is cold and clear and deep like water. It takes hold of you and will not let you go.[1]

I often think of old man Cheney, and of his daily devotion to the sun. He died before I was born, and I never knew where he came from or what of good and bad entered into his life. But I think I know who he was, essentially, and what his view of the world meant to him and to me. He was a man who saw very deeply into the distance, I believe, one whose vision extended far beyond the physical boundaries of his time and place. He perceived the wonder and meaning of Creation itself. In his mind's eye he could integrate all the realities and illusions of the earth and sky; they became for him profoundly intelligible and whole.

Once, in the first light, I stood where Cheney had stood, next to the house which my grandfather Mammedaty had built on a rise of land near Rainy Mountain Creek, and watched the sun come out of the black horizon of the world. It was an irresistible and awesome emergence, as waters gather to the flood, of weather and of light. I could not have been more sensitive to the cold, nor than to the heat which came upon it. And I could not have *foreseen* the break of day. The shadows on the rolling plains became large and luminous in a moment, impalpable, then faceted, dark and distinct again as they were run through with splinters of light. And the sun itself, when it appeared, was pale and immense, original in the deepest sense of the word. It is no wonder, I thought, that an old man should pray to it. It is no wonder . . . and yet, of course, wonder is the principal part of such a vision. Cheney's prayer was an affirmation of his wonder and regard, a testament to the realization of a quest for vision.

This native vision, this gift of seeing truly, with wonder and delight, into the natural world, is informed by a certain attitude of reverence and self-respect. It is a matter of extrasensory as well as sensory perception, I believe. In addition to the eye, it involves the intelligence, the instinct, and the imagination. It is the perception not only of objects

1. **When my father . . . let you go:** From N. Scott Momaday's *The Way to Rainy Mountain.*

dents how this paragraph captures attention and anchors the piece.

3 Discussion In what sense is Cheney a father figure for Momaday? What does Momaday learn from Cheney?

4 Discussion What is Momaday trying to do when he goes to watch the sun rise?

5 Critical Thinking and Reading When Momaday says "original in the deepest sense of the word" he means pertaining to the beginning of things. Ask students how his vision of the sun demonstrates the "native" vision he is discussing.

6 Critical Thinking and Reading Point out the two different ways Momaday uses the word "won-

der" here. Ask students how this emphasizes Momaday's sense of the sunrise as something more than an everyday occurrence.

7 Critical Thinking and Reading This is one of the essay's key paragraphs. In it Momaday defines the "native vision."

THE MEDICINE ROBE
Maynard Dixon
Courtesy of The Buffalo Historical Center, Cody, Wyoming

and forms but also of essences and ideals, as in this Chippewa song:

> *as my eyes*
> *search*
> *the prairie*
> *I feel the summer*
> *in the spring*

8 Even as the singer sees into the immediate landscape, he perceives a now and future dimension that is altogether remote, yet nonetheless real and inherent within it, a quality of evanescence and evolution, a state at once of being and of becoming. He beholds what is there; nothing of the scene is lost upon him. In the integrity of his vision he is wholly in possession of himself and of the world around him; he is quintessentially alive.

Most Indian people are able to see in these terms. Their view of the world is peculiarly native and distinct, and it determines who and what they are to a great extent. It is indeed the basis upon which they identify themselves as individuals and as a race. 9 There is something of genetic significance in such a thing, perhaps, an element of being which resides in the blood and which is, after all, the very nucleus of the self. When old man Cheney looked into the sunrise, he saw as far into himself, I suspect, as he saw into the distance. He knew certainly of his existence and of his place in the scheme of things.

10 In contrast, most of us in this society are afflicted with a kind of cultural nearsightedness. Our eyes, it may be, have been trained too long upon the superficial, and *artificial*, aspects of our environment; we do not see beyond the buildings and billboards that seem at times to be the monuments of our civilization, and consequently we fail to see into the nature and meaning of our own humanity. Now, more than ever, we might do well to enter upon a vision quest of our own, that is, a quest after vision itself. And in this the Indian stands to lead by his example. For 11 with respect to such things as a sense of heritage, of a vital continuity in terms of origin and of destiny, a profound investment of the mind and spirit in the oral traditions of literature, philosophy, and religion—those things, in short, which constitute his vision of the world—the Indian is perhaps the most culturally secure of all Americans.

12 As I see him, that old man, he walks very slowly to the place where he will make his prayer, and it is always the same place, a small mound where the grass is sparse and the hard red earth shows through. He limps a little, with age, but when he plants his feet he is tall and straight and hard. The bones are fine and prominent in his face and hands. And his face is painted. There are red and yellow bars under his eyes, neither bright nor sharply defined on the dark, furrowed skin, but soft and organic, the colors of sandstone and of pollen. His long braids are wrapped with blood-red cloth. His eyes are deep and open to the wide world. At sunrise, precisely, they catch fire and close, having seen. The low light descends upon him. And when he lifts his voice, it enters upon the silence and carries there, like the call of a bird.

Closure and Extension

ANSWERS TO THINKING ABOUT THE SELECTION
Recalling

1. (a) Cheney prayed aloud to the rising sun every morning. (b) Momaday believes that Cheney was able to see beyond the boundaries of time and place.

THINKING ABOUT THE SELECTION

Recalling

1. (a) What did Cheney do every morning? (b) What special abilities does Momaday believe Cheney possessed?
2. According to Momaday, in what terms are most Native Americans "able to see"?
3. How does Momaday believe that the eyes of most people in American society "have been trained"?

Interpreting

4. (a) How does the first paragraph tie together with the final paragraph? (b) What do these two paragraphs add to the rest of the essay?
5. What is the meaning of the Chippewa song Momaday quotes in his essay?
6. Why do some people believe that most people are unable to "see into the nature and meaning" of their "own humanity"?
7. What is Momaday suggesting that other people might learn from Native Americans?

Applying

8. Do you agree with Momaday's statement that most of us "might do well to enter upon a vision quest of our own"? Why or why not?
9. Do you agree with Momaday that "most of us in this society are afflicted with a kind of cultural nearsightedness"? Explain your answer.

ANALYZING LITERATURE

Understanding Classification

Classification refers to the process of dividing a subject into categories. In nonfiction, writers sometimes use classification to help clarify the meaning of difficult-to-grasp ideas or concepts.

1. What are the two types of visions Momaday describes in the essay?

2. How do these two types of visions contrast with each other?
3. How does Momaday use this contrast to help define a traditional Native American vision?

CRITICAL THINKING AND READING

Recognizing Cultural Attitudes

Momaday's attitude reveals a good deal about Native American attitudes and values. For example, toward the end of the essay, Momaday points out that Native Americans deeply value their oral tradition.

1. What do you think this selection reveals about the traditional Native American attitude toward nature?
2. How is this attitude revealed?

THINKING AND WRITING

Comparing and Contrasting Essays

In what ways are Native American beliefs similar to the ideas of the Transcendentalists? Write an essay in which you compare and contrast the Native American beliefs expressed in this essay with the Transcendentalist beliefs Ralph Waldo Emerson expresses in his essay, *Nature*. Start by rereading both essays and reviewing the discussion of the Transcendentalist movement. Note the beliefs each essay conveys about humanity's spiritual relationship with nature. Organize your essay according to corresponding points of contrast and use passages from each essay to support your argument. When you finish writing, revise and proofread your essay.

A Vision Beyond Time and Place 1063

PAUL THEROUX

1941–

An enthusiastic traveler, Paul Theroux has spent much of his life abroad. Possessing a keen eye for detail, he has used many of the exotic places he has visited as settings for his fiction and nonfiction.

Born in Massachusetts, Theroux has worked as a teacher in Singapore, Uganda, Italy, and the African nation of Malawi. He has written numerous essays, several volumes of short stories, and a number of novels. Included among his novels are *Girls at Play* (1969), a satirical account of schoolteachers in Kenya, and *The Mosquito Coast* (1982), the story of an American family that moves to the jungles of Honduras.

Theroux became a traveler and student of distant cultures due at least in part to his service as a Peace Corps volunteer in Africa. Like many volunteers, his life was deeply altered by the experience in a lasting way. He says, "For the past ten years I have lived and worked outside the United States, mainly in equatorial places . . . ; I did not plan to be away so long but that is the way it worked out and, as it happens, expatriation is often my favorite subject. I am not an exile, simply a person who enjoys traveling in temptingly named places (Burma, Java, Singapore, The Congo, Central Africa, the Cotswolds)."

Most of Theroux's work is set outside the United States, and it often contains an almost comic celebration of seediness. His characters are usually dressed in ill-fitting or dirty clothing, or they have entered expensive hotel lobbies in exotic cities having forgotten to put on their socks. The meals his characters eat are often revolting, and they drink their days away in sordid bars then to fall asleep in unmade, dirty beds or on no beds at all.

Theroux has a special love for trains, especially the near-derelict trains that snake through Europe toward Asia hauling decaying sleeping cars. He has remarked that trains are places where conglomerated life occurs. Passengers meet each other who would not otherwise do so. Thus the train allows him to observe unique interaction among people as they view the world traveling by their windows in a transient stream.

Through his travels Theroux has developed a deep awareness of the sharp cultural differences between Third World and industrialized cultures. This awareness is evident in "The Edge of a Great Rift," an essay based on an experience he had while living in the African nation of Nyasaland.

GUIDE FOR INTERPRETING

The Edge of the Great Rift

Writer's Techniques

Description. Description is writing that creates an image of a person, place, or thing in the reader's mind. To create a mental image, a writer uses sensory details—details that appeal to one or more of the five senses. For example, Theroux uses details that appeal to the sense of sight and the sense of touch in the following description of Nyasaland at noon: "there are no clouds and the heat is like a blazing rug thrown over everything."

Commentary

Notice how Paul Theroux attributes life to the landscape he represents in "The Edge of the Great Rift." Landscapes contain life, of course, in the form of forests, plants, and animals, but the life he ascribes to this part of Africa seems almost human, complete with mind and will. When writers describe things as if they were people, they use a technique called personification. Here Theroux personifies Africa largely through his use of vivid action verbs. For example, he says the crack of the Great Rift Valley "seems to be *swallowing* most of East Africa." The picture he evokes in the reader's mind is one of a huge mouth enveloping vast acres of land, and the feeling is that there is a will behind the mouth directing it to do so. Such personification lends a special irony to the seemingly naive questions the writer imagines his schoolchildren asking: "Is fire alive? Is water?" In the context of a personified landscape, the reader is tempted to answer, "Well, yes, perhaps," and so he is drawn into the myth of the living land.

The sun is, of course, a major feature of this African landscape. Theroux attributes several humanlike qualities to it when he describes the sun approaching the hill near his school. "The sun approaches it by *sneaking* behind the clouds until it *emerges to crash* into the hill and *explode* yellow and pink, *to paint* everything in its violent fire." Note the active verb forms and what they do to give the sun a character. It sneaks, emerges, crashes, explodes, and paints. Theroux gives the sun thought and will, showing it stealthily ambushing unsuspecting victims. He endows the rainstorm with similar malevolence when "thunder and close bursts of lightning *charged* all around [him]; the rain *spat* through the palm-leaf walls of the shed."

Does Paul Theroux's use of personification affect the way you feel toward the landscape he examines?

Writing

What types of images come to mind when you think of Africa? Freewrite about your impressions of Africa and discuss the sources of your impressions.

Literary Focus Lopez often makes his writing more intense by using imagery that relates to him personally—that is, he uses images to describe his own feelings about his subject.

Writing/Prior Knowledge As an alternative assignment, have students freewrite about a natural setting or event with which they are familiar.

Vocabulary

Preteach the following vocabulary words:

escarpments (e skärp′ mənts) *n.*: Steep slopes (p. 1066)

vulcanism (vul′ kə niz′m) *n.*: The series of phenomena connected with the origin and movement of molten rock (p. 1066)

stratosphere (strat′ ə sfir′) *n.*: A portion of the upper atmosphere (p. 1066)

luminescent (lo̅o̅′ mə nes′ ′nt) *adj.*: Shining (p. 1066)

Motivation/Prior Knowledge
Have students imagine that they are about to go on a trip to Africa. What would they expect to see? What clothing and equipment might they need? What feelings would they have about meeting people whose language and customs were so different from their own?

Master Teacher Note To set the tone for the essay, you might have students work in small groups, discussing their impressions of Africa. Ask them to find photographs or paintings of Africa and its people to enhance their discussions.

Purpose-Setting Question
What is Theroux saying about the ability of people from dramatically different cultures to understand one another?

1 **Discussion** What kind of environment is Theroux describing? What do you think people's lives might be like here?

2 **Critical Thinking and Reading** Theroux uses imagery that appeals to the senses of sight and touch.

3 **Discussion** How does Theroux personify the sun?

4 **Reading Strategy** Have students explain how the preceding paragraphs help prepare them for the encounter with the boy.

The Edge of the Great Rift

Paul Theroux

September 1, 1964. There is a crack in the earth which extends from the Sea of Galilee[1] to the coast of Mozambique,[2] and I am living on the edge of it, in Nyasaland.[3] This crack is the Great Rift Valley.[4] It seems to be swallowing most of East Africa. In Nyasaland it is replacing the fishing villages, the flowers, and the anthills with a nearly bottomless lake, and it shows itself in rough escarpments and troughs up and down this huge continent. It is thought that this valley was torn amid great volcanic activity. The period of vulcanism has not ended in Africa. It shows itself not only in the Great Rift Valley itself, but in the people, burning, the lava of masses, the turbulence of the humans themselves who live in the Great Rift.

My schoolroom is on the Great Rift, and in this schoolroom there is a line of children, heads shaved like prisoners, muscles showing through their rags. They are waiting to peer through the tiny lens of a cheap microscope so they can see the cells in a flower petal.

Later they will ask, "Is fire alive? Is water?"

The children appear in the morning out of the slowly drifting hoops of fog-wisp. It is chilly, almost cold. There is no visibility at six in the morning; only a fierce white-out where earth is the patch of dirt under their bare feet, a platform, and the sky is everything else. It becomes Africa at noon when there are no clouds and the heat is like a blazing rug thrown over everything to suffocate and scorch.

In the afternoon there are clouds, big ones, like war declared in the stratosphere. It starts to get gray as the children leave the school and begin padding down the dirt road.

There is a hill near the school. The sun approaches it by sneaking behind the clouds until it emerges to crash into the hill and explode yellow and pink, to paint everything in its violent fire.

At night, if there is a moon, the school, the Great Rift, become a seascape of luminescent trees and grass, whispering, silver. If there is no moon you walk from a lighted house to an infinity of space, packed with darkness.

Yesterday I ducked out of a heavy downpour and waited in a small shed for the rain to let up. The rain was far too heavy for my spidery umbrella. I waited in the shed; thunder and close bursts of lightning charged all around me; the rain spat through the palm-leaf walls of the shed.

Down the road I spotted a small African child. I could not tell whether it was a boy or a girl, since it was wearing a long shirt, a yellow one, which drooped sodden to the

---

1. Sea of Galilee (gal'ə lē'): Lake in northeastern Israel, bordering on Syria.
2. Mozambique (mō' zəm bēk'): Country in southeastern Africa.
3. Nyasaland (nyä' sä land'): Former name of Malawi, a country in southeastern Africa, next to Mozambique.
4. Great Rift Valley: A series of valleys extending through eastern Africa and part of southwestern Asia.

ground. The child was carrying nothing, so I assumed it was a boy.

He dashed in and out of the puddles, hopping from side to side of the forest path, his yellow shirt bulging as he twisted under it. When he came closer I could see the look of absolute fear on his face. His only defense against the thunder and the smacking of rain were his fingers stuck firmly into his ears. He held them there as he ran.

He ran into my shed, but when he saw me he shivered into a corner where he stood shuddering under his soaked shirt. We eyed each other. There were raindrops beaded on his face. I leaned on my umbrella and fumbled a Bantu[5] greeting. He moved against a

---

5. **Bantu** (ban' too): A group of African tribes and the languages spoken by those tribes.

palm leaf. After a few moments he reinserted a finger in each ear, carefully, one at a time. Then he darted out into the rain and thunder. And his dancing yellow shirt disappeared.

I stand on the grassy edge of the Great Rift. I feel it under me and I expect soon a mighty heave to send us all sprawling. The Great Rift. And whom does this rift concern? Is it perhaps a rift with the stars? Is it between earth and man, or man and man? Is there something under this African ground seething still?

We like to believe that we are riding it and that it is nothing more than an imperfection in the crust of the earth. We do not want to be captive to this rift, as if we barely belong, as if we were scrawled on the landscape by a piece of chalk.

THINKING ABOUT THE SELECTION
Recalling

1. According to Theroux, what does the Great Rift Valley seem to be doing?
2. (a) Why does Theroux assume that the child he spots during the rainstorm is a boy? (b) How does the child react when he sees Theroux?

Interpreting

3. What overall impression does Theroux's essay convey of the physical appearance of Nyasaland?
4. (a) What do the student's questions suggest about their cultural beliefs? (b) How do their studies contrast with these beliefs?
5. In this essay Theroux uses the Great Rift to symbolize, or represent, the wide cultural gap between people from industrialized and Third World societies. In what sense are Third World cultures being swallowed up?

Applying

6. People from industrialized nations have often tried to change the beliefs of people from Third World countries. Considering the evidence in this essay, do you imagine that Theroux tried to change his students' beliefs when he worked as a teacher in Nyasaland? Why or why not?

THINKING AND WRITING
Writing a Description

Write a description of a place you have been to that you found especially interesting. Prepare a list of sensory details describing this place. Arrange these details in a logical order. Then write your description, trying to convey your overall impression of the place to readers. When you finish writing, revise your description and share it with your classmates.

The Edge of the Great Rift 1067

1945—

Although he also writes fiction, Barry Lopez is known mainly for his nonfiction works about nature and the environment. Written in a vivid, poetic style, his works explore certain aspects of nature from a variety of perspectives, creating a well-rounded view that both informs and entertains readers.

Born in Port Chester, New York, Lopez was educated at the University of Notre Dame and the University of Oregon. In 1976 he published his first book, *Desert Notes: Reflections in the Eye of a Raven,* a collection of fictional narratives. Since then he has produced several additional books and has contributed articles, essays, and short fiction to many major magazines. His most successful work, *Of Wolves and Men* (1978), a nonfiction work examining the relationships between wolves and men and between wolves and other animals, was praised by critics and earned Lopez a number of awards.

From his home in a remote part Oregon, Lopez travels frequently to lecture on the esthetics of the Arctic and the "moral ambiguities" of killing seals for scientific study. He has become a coveted guest on the college lecture circuit and enjoys a tremendous popularity due in part to this country's renewed enthusiasm for nature.

A soft-spoken man with an affable temperament, Lopez spent his early years in California's San Fernando Valley among alfalfa fields, sheep, and horses. His abiding love of nature was apparent early, and he recalls being "mesmerized by the Mojave Desert, summers at Grand Canyon, and at Lake Arrowhead."

But his reverence for nature in all its forms is matched by his expertise with language. Reviewers are nearly unanimous in praise of his prowess as a writer noting his "jewel-like prose," and his "magical, shimmering similes." If his written words dazzle, then his spoken ones do too. When he speaks, he chooses words carefully and feels somewhat embarrassed when his audience's attention becomes, as one observer put it, "almost a physical thing, every heart in the room seeming to beat in time with his own." He says, "I care about language and landscape, both separately and for the connection between them, which is what writing is to me."

Filled with clear, descriptive language, the following excerpt from *Arctic Dreams* paints a vivid portrait of the Arctic wilderness, while examining the reasons why so many people have been drawn to this dangerous, threatening region.

GUIDE FOR INTERPRETING

from Arctic Dreams

Imagery. Lopez's writing has been described as poetic, because it is filled with vivid imagery—words or phrases that create mental pictures, or images, that appeal to one or more of the five senses. While most of Lopez's images appeal to the sense of sight, he also uses some images that cannot be visualized, and some that appeal to more than one sense. For example, he creates an image that appeals to both the sense of sight and the sense of touch when he writes, "the late-night sun, small as a kite in the northern sky, poured forth an energy that burned against my cheekbones."

In *Arctic Dreams* Lopez uses imagery to create a clear, lasting impression of the Arctic wilderness—an impression that helps enlighten readers about the reasons why people are drawn to the Arctic wilderness.

Writing

What are your impressions of the Arctic wilderness? Freewrite about the physical appearance of the Arctic wilderness, the types of animals that inhabit it, and the dangers it poses to people who venture into it.

Primary Source

In March of 1989, the supertanker *Exxon Valdez* ran aground in Alaska's Prince William Sound dumping almost eleven million gallons of petroleum into the pristine seas. It is beyond sad to think what has happened to the Alaska coastline since Barry Lopez wrote the reverent and moving descriptions of *Arctic Dreams*. The following is a record from *Newsweek* magazine of what man has left behind.

Drop by Drop: A Box Score

Oil spilled: **10,836,000 gallons**
Shoreline contaminated by oil: **1,090 miles**
Shoreline treated by Exxon: **1,087 miles**
Shoreline still needing cleaning, according to the state:
  At least 1,000 miles
Number of dead birds: **33,126**
  of dead eagles: **138**
  of dead otters: **980**
Cost of cleanup to Exxon: **$1.28 billion (after-tax cost;**
  insurance companies will reimburse Exxon $400 million)
People involved in cleanup: **12,000**
Vessels and planes used in cleanup: **12,000**
Oil recovered: **2,604,000 gallons (est.)**
Waste from oil cleanup: **24,000 tons**
Lawsuits filed against Exxon: **145**

Guide for Interpreting 1069

Literary Focus "The Edge of the Great Rift" is full of descriptive prose. Description often involves comparisons between a scene and other situations or objects familiar to the reader. This often makes the images more powerful. For example, Theroux calls his umbrella "spidery" and the earth "a platform." Show students how this writing technique can be more effective than a strictly literal description.

Writing/Prior Knowledge Before having students complete the writing activity, you may want to spend some time discussing the African landscape and people.

Vocabulary

Preteach the following vocabulary words:
feigning (fān' iŋ) *v.*: Making a false show of (p. 1070)
fecundity (fi kun' də tē) *n.*: Productivity (p. 1070)
congenial (kən jēn' yəl) *adj.*: Friendly; sympathetic (p. 1072)
implacable (im plak' ə b'l) *adj.*: Relentless (p. 1072)
gracile (gras''l) *adj.*: Slender; slim (p. 1073)
magnanimous (mag nan' ə məs) *adj.*: Noble in mind; rising above pettiness and meanness (p. 1074)
anomalous (ə näm' ə ləs) *adj.*: Deviating from the regular arrangement, general rule, or usual method (p. 1075)
adumbration (ad' um brā' shən) *n.*: Shadowy outline (p. 1076)

Motivation/Prior Knowledge
Have students imagine they are
about to go on a two-week camping trip in Alaska's Brooks
Range. How might reading this
excerpt help them prepare for
the trip?

Master Teacher Note If facilities
permit, you may wish to show
students any one of several nature films about the Arctic region.
One such film is Walt Disney's
Never Cry Wolf.

Thematic Idea Another selection
in which the writer paints a vivid
portrait of the Arctic is "To Build a
Fire" by Jack London (p. 566).

Purpose-Setting Question
What details does Lopez use to
support his view that it is worth
taking certain risks to become
familiar with the Arctic?

1 Discussion What does this passage tell you about the lives of
animals in this region?

2 Discussion What is Lopez bowing to?

3 Literary Focus Lopez uses imagery that appeals to the sense
of touch.

from Arctic Dreams

Barry Lopez

One summer evening I was camped in the western Brooks Range of Alaska with a friend. From the ridge where we had pitched our tent we looked out over tens of square miles of rolling tundra along the southern edge of the calving grounds of the Western Arctic caribou herd. During those days we observed not only caribou and wolves, which we'd come to study, but wolverine and red fox, ground squirrels, delicate-legged whim-brels and aggressive jaegers, all in the un-foldings of their obscure lives. One night we watched in awe as a young grizzly bear tried repeatedly to force its way past a yearling wolf standing guard alone before a den of young pups. The bear eventually gave up and went on its way. We watched snowy owls and rough-legged hawks hunt and caribou drift like smoke through the valley.

On the evening I am thinking about—it was breezy there on Ilingnorak Ridge, and cold; but the late-night sun, small as a kite in the northern sky, poured forth an energy that burned against my cheekbones—it was on that evening that I went on a walk for the first time among the tundra birds. They all build their nests on the ground, so their vul-nerability is extreme. I gazed down at a sin-gle horned lark no bigger than my fist. She stared back resolute as iron. As I ap-proached, golden plovers abandoned their nests in hysterical ploys, artfully feigning a broken wing to distract me from the woven grass cups that couched their pale, darkly speckled eggs. Their eggs glowed with a soft, pure light, like the window light in a Ver-meer[1] painting. I marveled at this intense and concentrated beauty on the vast table of the plain. I walked on to find Lapland long-spurs as still on their nests as stones, their dark eyes gleaming. At the nest of two snowy owls I stopped. These are more formidable animals than plovers. I stood motionless. The wild glare in their eyes receded. One owl settled back slowly over its three eggs, with an aura of primitive alertness. The other watched me, and immediately sought a bond with my eyes if I started to move.

I took to bowing on these evening walks. I would bow slightly with my hands in my pockets, toward the birds and the evidence of life in their nests—because of their fecun-dity, unexpected in this remote region, and because of the serene arctic light that came down over the land like breath, like breathing.

I remember the wild, dedicated lives of the birds that night and also the abandon with which a small herd of caribou crossed the Kokolik River to the northwest, the inci-dent of only a few moments. They pranced through like wild mares, kicking up sheets of water across the evening sun and shaking it off on the far side like huge dogs, a bloom of spray that glittered in the air around them like grains of mica.

I remember the press of light against my face. The explosive skitter of calves among grazing caribou. And the warm intensity of

---

1. **Vermeer** (vər mér'): Dutch painter Jan Vermeer (1632–1675).

4 Reading Strategy Have students summarize the events that lead to the deaths of these men.

the eggs beneath these resolute birds. Until then, perhaps because the sun was shining in the very middle of the night, so out of tune with my own customary perception, I had never known how benign sunlight could be. How forgiving. How run through with compassion in a land that bore so eloquently the evidence of centuries of winter.

During those summer days on Iling-norak Ridge there was no dark night. Darkness never came. The birds were born. They flourished, and then flew south in the wake of the caribou.

The second incident is more fleeting. It occurred one night when I was being driven past a graveyard in Kalamazoo, Michigan. Among the gravestones was one marking the burial place of Edward Israel, a shy young man who sailed north in 1881 with Lieuten-ant Adolphus Greely. Greely and his men es-tablished a base camp on Ellesmere Island, 450 miles from the North Pole, and explored the surrounding territory in the spring of 1882. A planned relief expedition failed to reach them that summer, and also failed again the next year. Desperate, Greely's party of twenty-five retreated south, hopeful of being met by a rescue party in 1884. They wintered at Cape Sabine, Ellesmere Island, where sixteen of them died of starvation and scurvy,[2] another committed suicide, and one man was executed for stealing food. Israel, the expedition's astronomer, died on May 27, 1884, three weeks before the others were

4

---

2. scurvy (skur′ vē) *n*.: A disease caused by vitamin-C deficiency.

from *Arctic Dreams* 1071

one's senses—the high note of the winter wren, the thick perfume of propolis that drifts downwind from spring willows, the brightness of wood chips scattered by beaver —that all this fits together. The indestructibility of these associations conveys a sense of permanence that nurtures the heart, that cripples one of the most insidious of human anxieties, the one that says, you do not belong here, you are unnecessary. . . .

The most moving look I ever saw from a child in the woods was on a mud bar by the footprints of a heron. We were on our knees, making handprints beside the foot-prints. You could feel the creek vibrating in the silt and sand. The sun beat down heavily on our hair. Our shoes were soaking wet. The look said: I did not know until now that I needed someone much older to confirm this, this feeling I have of life here. I can now grow older, knowing it need never be lost.

The quickest door to open in the woods for a child is the one that leads to the smallest room, by knowing the name each thing is called. The door that leads to the cathedral is marked by a hesitancy to speak at all, rather to encourage by example a sharpness of the senses. If one speaks it should only be to say, as well as one can, how wonderfully all this fits together, to indicate what a long, fierce peace can derive from this knowledge.

rescued. The survivors remembered him as the most congenial person among them.

I remember looking out the back window of the car that evening and seeing Israel's grave in the falling light. What had this man hoped to find? What sort of place did he think lay out there before him on that bright June morning in 1881 when the *Proteus* slipped its moorings at Saint John's, Newfoundland?

No one is able to say, of course. He was drawn on by the fixations of his own imagination, as were John Davis and William Baffin before him and as Robert Peary and Vilhjalmur Stefansson[3] would be after him. Perhaps he intended to make his mark as a scientist, to set his teeth in that high arctic landscape and come home like Darwin[4] to a sedate and contemplative life, in the farmlands of southern Michigan. Perhaps he merely hungered after the unusual. We can only imagine that he desired something, the fulfillment of some personal and private dream, to which he pinned his life.

Israel was buried with great public feeling and patriotic rhetoric. His gravestone reads

IN LIFE A TRUE CHILD OF GOD

IN DEATH A HERO

These two incidents came back to me often in the four or five years that I traveled in the Arctic. The one, timeless and full of light, reminded me of sublime innocence, of the innate beauty of undisturbed relationships. The other, a dream gone awry, reminded me of the long human struggle, mental and physical, to come to terms with the Far North. As I traveled, I came to believe that people's desires and aspirations were as much a part of the land as the wind, solitary animals, and the bright fields of stone and

tundra. And, too, that the land itself existed quite apart from these.

The physical landscape is baffling in its ability to transcend whatever we would make of it. It is as subtle in its expression as turns of the mind, and larger than our grasp; and yet it is still knowable. The mind, full of curiosity and analysis, disassembles a landscape and then reassembles the pieces—the nod of a flower, the color of the night sky, the murmur of an animal—trying to fathom its geography. At the same time the mind is trying to find its place within the land, to discover a way to dispel its own sense of estrangement.

The particular section of the Arctic I became concerned with extends from Bering Strait in the west to Davis Strait[5] in the east. It includes great, unrelieved stretches of snow and ice that in summer become plains of open water and an ocean that is the tundra, a tawny island beneath the sky. But there are, too, surprising and riveting sights: Wilberforce Falls on the Hood River suddenly tumbles 160 feet into a wild canyon in the midst of the Canadian tundra, and its roar can be heard for miles. Humboldt Glacier, a towering, 50-mile-long sea margin of the Greenland ice sheet, calves[6] icebergs into Kane Basin with gargantuan and implacable force. The badlands of east-central Melville Island, an eroded country of desert oranges, of muted yellows and reds, reminds a traveler of canyons and arroyos in southern Utah. And there are places more exotic, like the Ruggles River, which flows out of Lake Hazen on Ellesmere Island in winter and runs 2000 feet through the Stygian[7] darkness, wreathed in frost smoke, before it disappears underneath its own ice. South of Cape Bathurst and west of the

---

3. **John Davis . . . Vilhjalmur Stefansson:** Arctic explorers.
4. **Darwin:** Charles Darwin (1809–1882), an English naturalist who formulated the theory of evolution.

5. **Bering Strait . . . Davis Strait:** The Bering Strait separates Siberia and Alaska. The Davis Strait separates Greenland and Baffin Island, Canada.
6. **calves** υ.: Releases.
7. **Stygian** (stij′ ē ən) *adj.*: Characteristic of the river Styx, the river encircling Hades, the land of the dead, in Greek mythology.

Grammar in Action

A **topic sentence** expresses the main idea of a paragraph and defines the scope of the paragraph. The rest of the sentences in a paragraph should support the topic sentence by offering examples, details, facts, reasons, or incidents. The first sentence of the following paragraph is an example of a topic sentence, and the sentences that follow support the topic sentence.

Like other landscapes that initially appear barren, arctic tundra can open suddenly, like the corolla of a flower, when any intimacy is sought. One begins to notice spots of brilliant red, orange, and green, for example, among the monotonic browns of a tundra tussock. A wolf spider lunges at a glistening beetle. A shred of muskox wool lies inert in the lavender blooms of a saxifrage. When Alwin Pederson, a Danish naturalist, first arrived on the northeast coast of Greenland, he wrote, "I must admit to strange feelings at the sight of this godforsaken desert of stone." Before he left, however, he was writing of muskoxen grazing in lush grass higher than the animals' heads in Jameson Land, and of the stark beauty of nunataks, the ice-free spires of rock that pierce the Pleistocene stillness of the Greenland ice cap. I, like Pederson, when stooping

Horton River in the Northwest Territories, bituminous shale fires that have been burning underground for hundreds of years make those coastal hills seem like a vast, smoldering heap of industrial slag. South of the central Kobuk River, one hundred foot dunes rise above hundreds of square miles of shifting sand. In East Greenland lies an arctic oasis called Queen Louisa Land, a valley of wild grasses and summer wildflowers surrounded by the walls of the Greenland ice cap.

The Arctic, overall, has the classic lines of a desert landscape: spare, balanced, extended, and quiet. In the Queen Elizabeth Islands the well-drained tundra plains and low-lying bogs more familiar in the south give way to expanses of weathered rock and gravel, and the illusion of a desert is even more complete. On Baffin and Ellesmere islands and in northern Alaska, sharply pitched arctic mountain ranges, which retain their remoteness even as you stand within them, complete a pervasive suggestion of austerity. The apparent monotony of the land is relieved, however, by weather systems moving through, and by the activities of animals, particularly of birds and caribou. And because so much of the country stands revealed, and because sunlight passing through the dustless air renders its edges with such unusual sharpness, animals linger before the eye. And their presence is vivid.

Like other landscapes that initially appear barren, arctic tundra can open suddenly, like the corolla of a flower, when any intimacy with it is sought. One begins to notice spots of brilliant red, orange, and green, for example, among the monotonic browns of a tundra tussock. A wolf spider lunges at a glistening beetle. A shred of muskox wool lies inert in the lavender blooms of a saxifrage. When Alwin Pederson, a Danish naturalist, first arrived on the northeast coast of Greenland, he wrote, "I must admit to strange feelings at the sight of this godforsaken desert of stone." Before he left, however, he was writing of muskoxen grazing in lush grass that grew higher than the animals' heads in Jameson Land, and of the stark beauty of nunataks, the ice-free spires of rock that pierce the Pleistocene[8] stillness of the Greenland ice cap. I, like Pederson, when stooping to pick up the gracile rib bone of an arctic hare, would catch sudden and unexpected sight of the silken cocoon of an arctic caterpillar.

The wealth of biological detail on the tundra dispels any feeling that the land is empty; and its likeness to a stage suggests impending events. On a summer walk, the wind-washed air proves depthlessly clear. Time and again you come upon the isolated and succinct evidence of life—animal tracks, the undigested remains of a ptarmigan in an owl's casting, a patch of barren-ground willow nibbled nearly leafless by arctic hares. You are afforded the companionship of birds, which follow after you. (They know you are an animal; sooner or later you will turn up something to eat.) Sandpipers scatter before you, screaming *tuituek,* an Eskimo name for them. Coming awkwardly down a scree[9] slope of frost-riven limestone you make a glass-tinkling clatter—and at a distance a tundra grizzly rises on its hind legs to study you; the dish-shaped paws of its front legs deathly still, the stance so human it is unnerving.

Along creek washouts, in the western Arctic especially, you might stumble upon a mammoth tusk. Or in the eastern Arctic find undisturbed the ring of stones used by a hunter 1500 years ago to hold down the edge of his skin tent. These old Dorset camps, located along the coasts where arctic people have been traveling for four millennia, are poignant with their suggestion of the timeless determination of mankind. On rare occasions a traveler might come upon the more

---

8. Pleistocene (plīst′ tə sēn): A geological era characterized by the spreading and recession of continental ice sheets and the appearance of modern man.
9. scree (skrē) *adj.*: A covering of rock fragments on a slope below a rock face.

from *Arctic Dreams* 1073

7 Reading Strategy Have students summarize the details Lopez provides about the quality of light in the Arctic.

8 Literary Focus Lopez uses the phrase "Pleistocene stillness" to evoke an image of an enduring calm that has lasted many millions of years.

9 Enrichment These details support Lopez's earlier image of "Pleistocene stillness." The wooly mammoth became extinct about 11,000 years ago. Incredibly, the remains of mammoths are still being found frozen in the Arctic ground.

to pick up the gracile rib bone of the arctic hare, would catch sudden and unexpected sight of the silken cocoon of an arctic caterpiller.

Student Activity 1. Identify the topic sentences and supporting information in two other paragraphs from the excerpt from *Arctic Dreams.*

Student Activity 2. Write an original paragraph in which you express your opinion about an issue that you feel is important. Make sure that your paragraph has a clear topic sentence and that you thoroughly support your topic sentence with facts, reasons, and details.

10 Discussion How does the modern garbage in the Arctic compare with the ancient remains?

11 Discussion What kinds of changes are taking place in the Arctic?

imposing stone foundations of a large house abandoned by Thule-culture[10] people in the twelfth century. (The cold, dry arctic air might have preserved, even down to its odor, the remains of a ringed seal killed and eaten by them 800 years ago.) More often, one comes upon the remains of a twentieth-century camp, artifacts far less engaging than a scrap of worked caribou bone, or carved wood, or skewered hide at a Dorset or Thule site. But these artifacts disintegrate just as slowly—red tins of Prince Albert brand crimp-cut tobacco, cans of Pet evaporated milk and Log Cabin maple syrup. In the most recent camps one finds used flashlight batteries in clusters like animal droppings, and a bewildering variety of spent rifle and shotgun ammunition.

You raise your eyes from these remains, from whatever century, to look away. The land as far as you can see is rung with a harmonious authority, the enduring force of its natural history, of which these camps are so much a part. But the most recent evidence is vaguely disturbing. It does not derive in any clear way from the land. Its claim to being part of the natural history of the region seems, somehow, false.

It is hard to travel in the Arctic today and not be struck by the evidence of recent change. What is found at modern campsites along the coast points to the sudden arrival of a foreign technology—new tools and a new way of life for the local people. The initial adjustments to this were fairly simple; the rate of change, however, has continued to accelerate. Now the adjustments required are bewildering. And the new tools bring with them ever more complicated sets of beliefs. The native culture, from Saint Lawrence Island to Greenland, is today in a state of rapid economic reorganization and of internally disruptive social readjustment. In a recent article about the residents of Nunivak

---

10. Thule (thōō′ lē) **culture:** An ancient culture that inhabited the northernmost regions of the world.

Island, for example, a scientist wrote that the dietary shift from wild to store-bought foods (with the many nutritional and social complications involved) is proceeding so quickly it is impossible to pin down. "By the time this paper appears in print," he wrote, "much of the information in it will be of historical value only."

Industrial changes have also come to the Arctic, following the discovery of oil at Prudhoe Bay, Alaska, in 1968; the 800-mile-long trans-Alaska pipeline itself, with its recent Kuparuk extension; base camps for oil exploration on Canada's Melville Island and Tuktoyaktuk Peninsula; huge lead-zinc mining operations on northern Baffin and Little Cornwallis islands; hundreds of miles of new roads; and increased ship, air, and truck traffic. The region's normally violent and unpredictable weather, its extreme cold and long periods of darkness, the great distance to supply depots, and the problem of stabilizing permanent structures over permafrost (which melts and shifts in erratic ways) have made the cost of these operations astronomical—indeed, in Canada they could not even be contemplated without massive assistance from the federal government.

Seen as widely separated dots and lines on a map, these recent, radical changes do not appear to amount to very much. But their rippling effect in the settlements and villages of the North—their economic, psychological, and social impact—is acute. And their success, though marginal and in some instances artificial, encourages additional schemes for development. Of special concern to local residents is a growing concentration of power in the hands of people with enormous economic resources but a poorly developed geographic sense of the region. A man from Tuktoyaktuk, a village near the mouth of the Mackenzie River, told me a pointed story. In the 1950's he traveled regularly up and down the coast by dogsled. When a distant early warning (DEW) line radar station went up along his accustomed route, he decided to stop to see what it was. The military

12 **Discussion** What does Lopez mean by a "heedless imposition on the land?" Consider the people who are imposing on the land. Of what exactly are they heedless?

13 **Discussion** How does the desire to comprehend shape knowledge?

Cooperative Learning The massive oil spill that took place off the Alaska coast in 1989 had a devastating impact on the Alaskan environment. Yet it helped to draw national attention to the Alaskan landscape and the importance of preserving it. Divide your class into groups of four or five. Have each group research a topic concerning the Alaskan landscape, such as the effects of the Alaskan pipeline on the Alaskan environment. When the groups have completed their research, have them share their findings with the rest of the class.

men welcomed him not as a resident of the region but as a figure of arctic fable. They enthusiastically fed his dogs a stack of raw steaks. Each time the man came, they pounded him on the back and fed his dogs piles of steak. Their largess seemed so odd and his rapport with them so unrealistic he stopped coming. For months afterward, however, he had tremendous difficulty controlling the dogs anytime they passed near the place.

Passing through the villages, even traveling across the uninhabited land, one cannot miss the evidence of upheaval, nor avoid being wrenched by it. The depression it engenders, because so much of it seems a heedless imposition on the land and on the people, a rude invasion, can lead one to despair. I brooded, like any traveler, over these things; but the presence of the land, the sheer weight of it before the senses, more often drew me away from the contemporary is-

sues. What, I wondered, had compelled me to bow to a horned lark? How do people imagine the landscapes they find themselves in? How does the land shape the imaginations of the people who dwell in it? How does desire itself, the desire to comprehend, shape knowledge? These questions seemed to me to go deeper than the topical issues, to underlie any consideration of them.

In pursuit of answers I traveled with people of differing dispositions. With Eskimos hunting narwhals off northern Baffin Island and walruses in the Bering Sea. With marine ecologists on hundreds of miles of coastal and near-shore surveys. With landscape painters in the Canadian Archipelago. In the company of roughnecks, drilling for oil on the winter ice in high winds at −30°F; and with the cosmopolitan crew of a freighter, sailing up the west coast of Greenland and into the Northwest Passage. They each assessed the land differently—the apparent

from *Arctic Dreams* 1075

14 Literary Focus Lopez uses imagery that appeals to the senses of sight, hearing, and touch.

15 Discussion How might behaving respectfully toward the land cause our "stifling ignorance" to fall away from us?

16 Discussion What kinds of images do these names evoke? What do they tell us of the history of the region?

Reader's Response Would you be interested in visiting Alaska? Why or why not?

emptiness of the tundra, which ran out like a shimmering mirage in the Northern Ocean; the blue-black vault of the winter sky, a cold beauty alive with scintillating stars; a herd of muskoxen, pivoting together on a hilltop to make a defensive stand, their long guard hairs swirling around them like a single, huge wave of dark water; a vein of lead-zinc ore glinting like tiny mirrors in a damp, Mesozoic[11] wall beneath the surface of Little Cornwallis Island; the moaning and wailing in the winter sea ice as the ocean's crust warped and shattered in the crystalline air. All of it, all that the land is and evokes, its actual meaning as well as its metaphorical reverberation, was and is understood differently.

These different views make a human future in that northern landscape a matter of conjecture, and it is here that one encounters dreams, projections of hope. The individual's dream, whether it be so private a wish as that the joyful determination of nesting arctic birds might infuse a distant friend weary of life, or a magnanimous wish, that a piece of scientific information wrested from the landscape might serve one's community—in individual dreams is the hope that one's own life will not have been lived for nothing. The very much larger dream, that of a people, is a story we have been carrying with us for millennia. It is a narrative of determination and hope that follows a

---

11. **Mesozoic** (mes′ ə zō′ik) *adj.*: A geological era characterized by the development and extinction of dinosaurs.

question: What will we do as the wisdom of our past bears down on our future? It is a story of ageless conversation, not only conversation among ourselves about what we mean and wish to do, but a conversation held with the land—our contemplation and wonder at a prairie thunderstorm, or before the jagged line of a young mountain, or at the sudden rise of ducks from an isolated lake. We have been telling ourselves the story of what *we* represent in the land for 40,000 years. At the heart of this story, I think, is a simple, abiding belief: it is possible to live wisely on the land, and to live well. And in behaving respectfully toward all that the land contains, it is possible to imagine a stifling ignorance falling away from us.

Crossing the tree line to the Far North, one leaves behind the boreal owl clutching its frozen prey to its chest feathers to thaw it. Ahead lies an open, wild landscape, pointed off on the maps with arresting and anomalous names: Brother John Glacier and Cape White Handkerchief. Navy Board Inlet, Teddy Bear Island, and the Zebra Cliffs. Dexterity Fiord, Saint Patrick Canyon, Starvation Cove. Eskimos hunt the ringed seal, still, in the broad bays of the Sons of the Clergy and Royal Astronomical Society islands.

This is a land where airplanes track icebergs the size of Cleveland and polar bears fly down out of the stars. It is a region, like the desert, rich with metaphor, with adumbration. In a simple bow from the waist before the nest of the horned lark, you are able to stake your life, again, in what you dream.

THINKING ABOUT THE SELECTION

Recalling

1. (a) What two incidents does Lopez recount in the first several paragraphs? (b) Of what do these two incidents remind Lopez?
2. What is the particular section of the Arctic with which Lopez became concerned?
3. (a) By what is the monotony of the Arctic land "relieved"? (b) What "dispels any feeling that" the Arctic land is "empty"?
4. (a) What "industrial changes" have come to the Arctic since the discovery of oil in 1968? (b) What has become a "special concern" for local residents?
5. What makes "a human future" in the Arctic "a matter of conjecture"?

Interpreting

6. What do the two incidents Lopez recounts in the first several paragraphs reveal about the relationship between man and nature in the Arctic?
7. Although the people who come to the Arctic perceive the landscape in a variety of ways, Lopez argues that they all share a common vision. What is this vision?
8. (a) What is the main point of this essay? (b) How is the title related to the main point?

Applying

9. What other types of dangerous, threatening environments have explorers ventured into during the course of history?

ANALYZING LITERATURE

Using Imagery

Imagery refers to words or phrases that create mental pictures, or images, that appeal to one or more of the five senses. Although most of the imagery in *Arctic Dreams* appeals to the sense of sight, Lopez also uses some images that cannot be visualized and others that appeal to more than one sense.
1. Find five images that appeal to the sense of sight.
2. Find two images that appeal to one of the other senses.
3. Find two images that appeal to more than one sense.

CRITICAL THINKING AND READING

Appreciating the Effect of Imagery

Through the use of imagery, Lopez creates a vivid impression of the Arctic wilderness in his essay. This impression helps provide readers with an understanding of peoples' desires to venture into this dangerous and unforgiving region.
1. What is the dominant impression of the Arctic wilderness that Lopez conveys?
2. How does this impression relate to the main point of the essay?

THINKING AND WRITING

Responding to Criticism

A critic has commented that "A poet slips quietly out of Mr. Lopez's matter-of-fact prose, like an eye on a long nerve-string, to dance and feel." Write a brief essay in which you discuss this comment in relation to the excerpt from *Arctic Dreams*. Reread the essay, focusing on Lopez's use of language. Prepare a thesis statement. Then write your essay, using passages from *Arctic Dreams* to support your thesis. When you revise, make sure you have not included any unnecessary information.

from Arctic Dreams 1077

7. They all share the hope that their lives will not have been lived for nothing.
8. (a) The main point of the essay is that people are attracted to the Arctic by a variety of individual dreams. Once they are there, they become involved in a struggle to understand and somehow control the harsh environment. (b) "Arctic Dreams" refers to the dreams that attract people to the Arctic.

Applying
9. Answers will differ. Students might mention deserts, volcanic regions, and jungles.

ANSWERS TO ANALYZING LITERATURE
1. Visual images include: "the wild glare in their eyes receded". "The serene Arctic light . . . came down over the land like breath"; "a bloom of spray that glittered in the air"; "their eggs glowed with a soft, pure light"; and "sharply, pitched Arctic mountain ranges."
2. Images that appeal to other senses include: "the press of light against my face"; and "the cold, dry Arctic air."
3. Images that appeal to more than one sense include: "the late-night sun, small as a kite in the northern sky, poured forth an energy that burned against my cheekbones"; and "the warm intensity of eggs beneath these resolute birds."

ANSWERS TO CRITICAL THINKING AND READING
1. Suggested Response: He conveys the impression that the wilderness is beautiful yet unforgiving.
2. Suggested Response: The beautiful yet unforgiving quality of the landscape is part of what attracts people to the region.

THINKING AND WRITING
For help with this assignment, students can refer to Lesson 15, "Evaluating a Literary Work," in the Handbook of Writing About Literature.

After students have completed the assignment, divide them into groups, and have them read their rough drafts to one another and comment on ways in which the essays could be improved.

Closure and Extension

ANSWERS TO THINKING ABOUT THE SELECTION
Recalling

1. (a) He remembers watching a golden plover feign a broken wing and seeing Edward Israel's grave. (b) One reminds him of "sublime innocence," the other reminds him of human struggle to come to terms with the Arctic.
2. He is concerned with the section that extends from Bering Strait to Davis Strait.
3. (a) The monotony is relieved by weather systems moving through and by the activities of the animals. (b) The wealth of biological detail dispels any feeling that the land is empty.
4. (a) The industrial changes include base camps for oil exploration, huge lead-zinc mining operations, hundreds of miles of new roads, and increased ship, air, and truck traffic. (b) "Of special concern to local residents is a growing concentration of power in the hands of people with enormous economic resources but a poorly developed geographic sense of the region."
5. The different views of the people who are concerned with the northern landscape make its future a matter of conjecture.

Interpreting
6. The two incidents reveal that humanity and nature are at odds with each other.

More About the Author John McPhee's essays and books are characterized by their depth and thoroughness. How can small details contribute to our overall understanding of a subject?

Critical Evaluation The literary critic Sandra Schmidt Oddo has written, "John McPhee has an eye and an ear and a typewriter that operate like a camera and full crew of a documentary film studio. Give him a theme and he comes up with a picture: edited, cross-cut, spliced and orchestrated, specific and full of the facts and the atmosphere of that theme. The picture, like a good documentary, carries its own emotional impact as well as . . . an urgent imperative.

"McPhee's style is Journalism 101 elevated to the ranks of Art. He uses short sentences, no passive verbs, paragraphs that pursue their subjects with flat-statement, single-minded intensity. He uses them—the art of it—with easy grace, fluidity; and he has the courage to drop raw observations into seemingly unrelated contexts and leave them there reverberating as signals for the reader to interpret. He is also very, very good at breaking down specialized jargon into plain English, at interpreting the ways of scientists for the layman, at understanding and enjoying the processes of thought invention, and human behavior."

1931–

John McPhee is known for his detailed journalistic essays on a wide variety of subjects. In these essays he displays an ability to present a vast amount of information in an organized, unhurried, and interesting manner.

Born and raised in New Jersey, McPhee graduated from Princeton University and studied for a year at Cambridge University in England. After working for *Time* magazine for several years, McPhee became a staff writer for *The New Yorker* in 1964. Given the freedom to explore subjects of his own choice, without the pressure of deadlines, McPhee has remained with the magazine for more than two decades. In addition to publishing his essays in *The New Yorker,* McPhee has written many books, including *Oranges* (1967), *The Pine Barrens* (1968), *Confrontations with the Archdruid* (1971), *The Deltoid Pumpkin Seed* (1973), *Coming into the Country* (1977), *Basin and Range* (1981), *In Suspect Terrain* (1983), and *Rising from the Plains* (1965).

He speaks of his choice of subjects in the following manner: "A great stream of ideas goes by. The problem is how to pick one out that you want to spend a year or more working on. . . . Just about everything I've written touches on subjects that interested me as a kid." He has written about the autocratic headmaster of his prep school and the greats of tennis and basketball, both of which he has enjoyed since childhood.

From his sports figure profiles to his piece on crafting bark canoes in the New Hampshire woods, McPhee's work bears the stamp of expert organization. His respect for organization he credits to Olive McKee, a high school English teacher of the old school who required her students weekly to submit three compositions complete with detailed outlines. To organizational skill McPhee added facility with facts. While an undergraduate at Princeton, he appeared regularly as the teenage panelist on the radio and television quiz show "Twenty Questions" where he was to identify mystery items by asking questions that could be answered only "yes" or "no." The practice taught him how to assemble facts and infer their meanings. Since then he has taught those skills in a course at Princeton titled "The Literature of Fact," a weekly seminar that stresses the "artistic possibilities" in factual writing.

In the following excerpt from *Rising from the Plains,* McPhee recounts the experiences of geologist David Love, who grew up on his family's ranch in Wyoming, using the polished, engaging writing style that has helped to earn him a reputation as one of the finest essayists in America today.

1078   Contemporary Writers

GUIDE FOR INTERPRETING

from Rising from the Plains

Writer's Techniques

Setting. The setting is the time and place in which the events in a literary work occur. In nonfiction, writers sometimes focus on capturing the flavor of life in a specific setting and exploring the effects of the setting on people's personalities and behavior. In the following excerpt from *Rising from the Plains,* for example, McPhee gives the reader a clear impression of what life was like on the Love Ranch in Wyoming during David Love's childhood. At the same time, he reveals a number of ways in which the members of the Love family were shaped by their environment.

Commentary

The roots of the man are in the boy. It is always so. As you read *Rising from the Plains,* notice that from the account of David Love's youth on his family's Wyoming ranch there emerges a rich picture of the times, things, and places that formed the man. Youthful environment affects people directly, creating the life to come one way or another. A person may embrace his youthful life and, in his later life, find ways of perpetuating it. In this way his adulthood can become a comfortable repetition of what he knew when young. A person may also react against the way he lived as a child, choosing a life path as widely divergent from his youth as he can imagine it. If he had been raised on a farm without neighbors, he might choose to live in a high-rise apartment in the heart of a major city, forever leaving the farm behind him. Yet another way of building a life out of one's youthful experience is to blend the old, familiar things with new, strange things. Often people seek the security of childhood amid the turmoil of adult responsibility through incorporating some familiar aspects of their youth with the sometimes exciting and often disturbing new bright wonders of the adult world. David Love's life combined aspects of his youth with the challenges of a career widely different from those he witnessed at the ranch. Of the renowned geologist, McPhee recounts, "Even now, six decades later, David will pass up a cool spring, saying, "If I drink now, I'll be thirsty all day." He retains the trail wisdom of the ranch far away from it in time and place.

Whatever people choose to do with their lives, they never leave their youthful years entirely behind. Whether copied, ignored, or incorporated, those years form the foundation upon which lives are built. What foundations are you developing?

Writing

How do you envision life on a ranch? Freewrite about your impressions of ranch life, discussing the sources of your impressions and the reasons why you think that you would or would not enjoy this type of life.

Guide for Interpreting 1079

Literary Focus The setting is an integral part of this essay. Have students note how McPhee chooses details that bring the setting to life.

Writing/Prior Knowledge Before having students complete the writing activity, you may want to spend some time discussing ranch life.

Vocabulary

Preteach the following vocabulary words:

vernacular (vər nak′ yə lər) *n.*: The native speech, language, or dialect of a country or place (p. 1080)

pragmatic (prag mat′ ik) *adj.*: Practical (p. 1080)

indigenous (in dij′ ə nəs) *adj.*: Existing, growing, or produced naturally in a region or country (p. 1080)

voracity (vô ras′ ə tē) *n.*: Eagerness (p. 1083)

moribund (môr′ ə bund′) *adj.*: Dying; coming to an end (p. 1083)

adroit (ə droit′) *adj.*: Skillful in a physical or mental way (p. 1085)

taciturn (tas′ ə tʉrn′) *adj.*: Almost always silent (p. 1086)

rudimentary (roo də men′ tər ē) *adj.*: Elementary (p. 1086)

truncated (truŋ′ kāt id) *v.*: Cut short (p. 1086)

magisterial (maj′ is tir′ ē əl) *adj.*: Authoritative (p. 1086)

capacious (kə pā′ shəs) *adj.*: Roomy; spacious (p. 1087)

from Rising from the Plains

John McPhee

In the United States Geological Survey's seven-and-a-half-minute series of topographic maps is a quadrangle named Love Ranch. The landscape it depicts lies just under the forty-third parallel and west of the hundred-and-seventh meridian—coordinates that place it twelve miles from the geographic center of Wyoming. The names of its natural features are names that more or less materialized around the kitchen table when David Love was young: Corral Draw, Castle Gardens, Buffalo Wallows, Jumping-Off Draw. To the fact that he grew up there his vernacular, his outlook, his pragmatic skills, and his professional absorptions about equally attest. The term "store-bought" once brightened his eyes. When one or another of the cowpunchers used a revolver, the man did not so much fire a shot as "slam a bullet." If a ranch hand was tough enough, he would "ride anything with hair on it." Coffee had been brewed properly if it would "float a horseshoe." Blankets were "sougans." A tarpaulin was a "henskin." To be off in the distant ranges was to be "gouging around the mountains." In Love's stories of the ranch, horses come and go by the "cavvy." If they are unowned and untamed, they are a "wild bunch"—led to capture by a rider "riding point." In the flavor of his speech the word "ornery" endures.

He describes his father as a "rough, kindly, strong-willed man" who would put a small son on each knee and—reciting "Ride a cockhorse to Banbury Cross to see a fine lady upon a white horse"—give the children bronco rides after dinner, explaining that his purpose was "to settle their stomachs." Their mother's complaints went straight up the stovepipe and away with the wind. When their father was not reciting such Sassenach[1] doggerel, he could draw Scottish poems out of the air like bolts of silk. He had the right voice, the Midlothian[2] timbre. He knew every syllable of *The Lady of the Lake*.[3] Putting his arms around the shoulders of his wee lads, he would roll it to them by the canto, and when they tired of Scott there were in his memory more than enough ballads to sketch the whole of Scotland, from the Caithness headlands to the Lammermuir Hills.

David was fifteen months younger than his brother, Allan. Their sister, Phoebe, was born so many years later that she does not figure in most of these scenes. They were the only children in a thousand square miles, where children outnumbered the indigenous trees. From the ranch buildings, by Muskrat Creek, the Wind River Basin reached out in buffalo grass, grama grass, and edible salt sage across the cambered erosional swells of

---

1. **Sassenach** (sas′ ə nak′): Saxon; English; a term used, often disparagingly, by Irish and Scots.
2. **Midlothian** (mid lō′ thē ən): Referring to a former county in southeastern Scotland.
3. *The Lady of the Lake:* A long poem by Scottish writer Sir Walter Scott (1771–1832).

5 **Reading Strategy** Have students summarize the details of the setting so far.

6 **Discussion** Why does McPhee include this small detail about John Love?

7 **Critical Thinking and Reading** Note the poetic language McPhee uses to describe the wild horses.

the vast dry range. When the wind dropped, this whole wide world was silent, and they could hear from a great distance the squeak of a horned lark. The nearest neighbor was thirteen miles away. On the clearest night, they saw no light but their own.

Old buffalo trails followed the creek and branched from the creek: old but not ancient—there were buffalo skulls beside them, and some were attached to hide. The boys used the buffalo trails when they rode off on ranch chores for their father. They rode young and rode long, and often went without water. Even now, six decades later, David will pass up a cool spring, saying, "If I drink now, I'll be thirsty all day." To cut cedar fence posts, they went with a wagon to Green Mountain, near Crooks Gap—a round trip of two weeks. In early fall, each year, they spent ten days going back and forth to the Rattlesnake Hills for stove wood. They took two wagons—four horses pulling each wagon—and they filled them with limber pine. They used axes, a two-handled saw. Near home, they mined coal with their father—from the erosional wonderland they called Castle Gardens, where a horse-drawn scraper stripped the overburden and exposed the seams of coal. Their father was adept at corralling wild horses, a skill that called for a horse and rider who could outrun these closest rivals to the wind. He caught more than he kept, put his Flatiron brand on the best ones and sold the others. Some of them escaped. David remembers seeing one clear a seven-foot bar in the wild-horse corral and not so much as touch it. When he and Allan were in their early teens,

8 Discussion What does McPhee mean by implying a difference between "choice" and "custom" here?

9 Enrichment John Love's uncle, John Muir, was a famous explorer, naturalist, and writer, whose campaigns for forest conservation in the United States influenced Congress to pass the Yosemite National Park Bill in 1890. Muir persuaded President Theodore Roosevelt to set aside 148 million acres of forest reserves. A redwood forest near San Francisco bears his name.

10 Discussion Why would John Love think of newcomers to the area as "pilgrims"?

11 Clarification *Hypothermia* is "a physiological condition caused by loss of body temperature that often results in the victim freezing to death."

12 Critical Thinking and Reading Note how the small details about frost on the nailheads brings home the reality of the cold.

---

his father sent them repping—representing Love Ranch in the general roundup—and they stayed in cow camp with other cowboys, and often enough their sougans included snow. When they were out on the range, they slept out on the range, never a night in a tent. This was not a choice. It was a family custom.

In the earlier stretch of his life when John Love had slept out for seven years, he would wrap himself in his sougans and finish the package with the spring hooks and D-rings that closed his henskin. During big gales and exceptional blizzards, he looked around for a dry wash and the crease of an overhanging cutbank. He gathered sage and built a long fire—a campfire with the dimensions of a cot. He cooked his beans and bacon, his mutton, his sourdough,[4] his whatever. After dinner, he kicked the fire aside and spread out his bedroll. He opened his waterproof packet of books and read by kerosene lamp. Then he blew out the light and went to sleep on warm sand. His annual expenditures were seventy-five dollars. This was a man who wore a long bearskin coat fastened with bone pegs in loops of rope. This was a man who, oddly enough, carried with him on the range a huge black umbrella—his summer parasol. This was a man whose Uncle John Muir had invented a device that started a fire in the morning while the great outdoorsman stayed in bed. And now this wee bairn[5] with the light-gold hair was, in effect, questioning Love Ranch policy by asking his father what he had against tents. "Laddie, you don't always have one available," his father said patiently. "You want to get used to living without it." Tents, he made clear, were for a class of people he referred to as "pilgrims."

When David was nine, he set up a trap line between the Hay Meadow and the Pinna-

---

cles (small sandstone buttes in Castle Gardens). He trapped coyotes, bobcats, badgers. He shot rabbits. He ran the line on foot, through late-autumn and early-winter snow. His father was with him one cold and blizzarding January day when David's rifle and the rabbits he was carrying slipped from his hands and fell to the snow. David picked up the gun and soon dropped it again. "It was a cardinal sin to drop a rifle," he says, "Snow and ice in the gun barrel could cause the gun to blow up when it was fired." Like holding on to a saddle horn, it was something you just did not do. It would not have crossed his father's mind that David was being careless. In sharp tones, his father said, "Laddie, leave the rabbits and rifle and run for home. Run!" He knew hypothermia when he saw it, no matter that it lacked a name.

Even in October, a blizzard could cover the house and make a tunnel of the front veranda. As winter progressed, rime[6] grew on the nailheads of interior walls until white spikes projected some inches into the rooms. There were eleven rooms. His mother could tell the outside temperature by the movement of the frost. It climbed the nails about an inch for each degree below zero. Sometimes there was frost on nailheads fifty-five inches up the walls. The house was chinked with slaked lime, wood shavings, and cow manure. In the wild wind, snow came through the slightest crack, and the nickel disks on the dampers of the heat stove were constantly jingling. There came a sound of hooves in cold dry snow, of heavy bodies slamming against the walls, seeking heat. John Love insulated his boots with newspapers—as like as not the New York *Times*. To warm the boys in their beds on cold nights, their mother wrapped heated flatirons in copies of the New York *Times*. The family were subscribers. Sundays only. The *Times*,

---

4. sourdough *n.*: Fermented dough saved from one baking so it can be used in the next.
5. bairn (bern) *n.*: Child.

6. rime *n.*: Frost.

Grammar in Action

A **predicate nominative** is a noun or a pronoun that works with a linking verb to rename or identify the subject of the sentence. If used too often, sentences with predicate nominatives can become boring, creating a list of names. Still, these structures are vital for describing uncommon things, people, or ideas. When used by a skilled writer like John McPhee, they can be lively and evocative. Note the following examples:

The Wyoming sheep wagon was the ancestral *Winnebago*. (p. 1085)
"A coyote is the whole *world* to a flea." (p. 1085)

Student Activity 1. Identify the predicate nominatives in the following sentences.
1. He was one of the most celebrated murderers in central Wyoming.
2. The consensus was that the victim had "needed killing."
3. She was a graduate of Wellesley College, and was now a Wyoming bride.

David Love recalls, was "precious." They used it to insulate the house: pasted it against the walls beside the Des Moines *Register*, the Tacoma *News Tribune*—any paper from anywhere, without fine distinction. With the same indiscriminate voracity, any paper from anywhere was first read and re-read by every literate eye in every cow camp and sheep camp within tens of miles, read to shreds and passed along, in tattered circulation on the range. There was, as Love expresses it, "a starvation of print." Almost anybody's first question on encountering a neighbor was "Have you got any newspapers?"

The ranch steadings were more than a dozen buildings facing south, and most of them were secondhand. When a stage route that ran through the ranch was abandoned, in 1905, John Love went down the line shopping for moribund towns. He bought Old Muskrat—including the hotel, the post office, Joe Lacey's Muskrat Saloon—and moved the whole of it eighteen miles. He bought Golden Lake and moved it thirty-three. He arranged the buildings in a rough semicircle that embraced a corral so large and solidly constructed that other ranchers traveled long distances to use it. Joe Lacey's place became the hay house, the hotel became in part a saddlery and cookhouse, and the other buildings, many of them connected, became all or parts of the blacksmith shop, the chicken hatchery, the ice shed, the buggy shed, the sod cellar, and the bunkhouse—social center for all the workingmen from a great many miles around. There was a granary made of gigantic cottonwood logs from the banks of the Wind River, thirty miles away. There were woolsack towers, and a wooden windmill over a hand-dug well. The big house itself was a widespread log collage of old town parts and original construction. It had wings attached to wings. In the windows were air bubbles in distorted glass. For its twenty tiers of logs, John had journeyed a hundred miles to the lodgepole-pine groves of the Wind River Range, returning with ten logs at a time, each round trip requiring two weeks. He collected a hundred and fifty logs. There were no toilets, of course, and the family had to walk a hundred feet on a sometimes gumbo-slick path to a four-hole structure built by a ranch hand, with decorative paneling that matched the bookcases in the house. The cabinetmaker was Peggy Doherty, the stagecoach driver who had first brought Miss Waxham through Crooks Gap and into the Wind River country.

The family grew weary of carrying water into the house from the well under the windmill. And so, as she would write in later years:

> After experiments using an earth auger and sand point, John triumphantly installed a pitcher pump in the kitchen, a sink, and drain pipe to a barrel, buried in the ground at some distance from the house. This was the best, the first, and at that time the only water system in an area the size of Rhode Island.

In the evenings, kerosene lamps threw subdued yellow light. Framed needlework on a wall said "WASH & BE CLEAN." Everyone bathed in the portable galvanized tub, children last. The more expensive galvanized tubs of that era had built-in seats, but the Loves could not afford the top of the line. On the plank floor were horsehide rugs—a gray, a pinto—and the pelt of a large wolf, and two soft bobcat rugs. Chairs were woven with rawhide or cane. John recorded the boys' heights on a board nailed to the inside of the kitchen doorframe. A brass knocker on the front door was a replica of a gargoyle at Notre Dame de Paris.[7]

The family's main sitting and dining room was a restaurant from Old Muskrat.

_____

7. **Notre Dame** (nō′ trə däm′) **de Paris:** A famous cathedral in Paris, built 1163–1257.

from Rising from the Plains 1083

13 **Discussion** What do these details tell you about the Loves and the other people of the region?

14 **Critical Thinking and Reading** Note how the names here add flavor to the narrative.

15 **Critical Thinking and Reading** This small detail about the windows makes all the buildings of the ranch seem more real.

16 **Enrichment** Lodgepole-pines were so called because Native American tribes used the trunks of these tall, straight trees to support the lodges they built for shelter.

17 **Discussion** What does this detail tell you about the values of the Love family?

4. "Throat-cutting, however, became a symbol of immediate death in our young minds, the ultimate horror. . . ."
5. She had a lesser sense of fitting in than she would have had had she been a mare, a cow, or a ewe.

Student Activity 2. Complete the following sentences by adding predicate nominatives. Try to overcome the limitations of the linking verbs by making your predicate nominatives as precise and unusual as you can.

1. My childhood was . . .
2. Her mother remained . . .
3. Reading Walt Whitman is . . .
4. I think eating rattlesnake would be . . .

18 Critical Thinking and Reading
Note how these details provide glimpses into the era that preceded Love Ranch.

19 Discussion What do the titles of these books tell you about Mrs. Love, David, and Allan?

20 Discussion Why might McPhee consider this detail an important part of the description of David?

21 Enrichment In the days before electricity, sewing machines were operated by a foot treadle, much like the foot pump of an organ.

22 Critical Thinking and Reading
Note the irony of Mrs. Love having to leave her sewing to sew a cowboy.

On the walls were polished buffalo horns mounted on shields. The central piece of furniture was a gambling table from Joe Lacey's Muskrat Saloon. It was a poker-and-roulette table—round, covered with felt. Still intact were the subtle flanges that had caused the roulette wheel to stop just where the operator wished it to. And if you reached in under the table in the right place you could feel the brass slots where the dealer kept wild cards that he could call upon when the fiscal integrity of the house was threatened. If you put your nose down on the felt, you could almost smell the gunsmoke. At this table David Love received his basic education—his schoolroom a restaurant, his desk a gaming table from a saloon. His mother may have been trying to academize the table when she covered it with a red-and-white India print.

From time to time, other schoolmarms were provided by the district. They came for three months in summer. One came for the better part of a year. By and large, though, the boys were taught by their mother. She had a rolltop desk, and Peggy Doherty's glassed-in bookcases. She had the 1911 Encyclopædia Britannica, the Redpath Library, a hundred volumes of Greek and Roman literature, Shakespeare, Dickens, Emerson, Thoreau, Longfellow, Kipling, Twain. She taught her sons French, Latin, and a bit of Greek. She read to them from books in German, translating as she went along. They read the *Iliad* and the *Odyssey*.[8] The room was at the west end of the ranch house and was brightly illuminated by the setting sun. When David as a child saw sunbeams leaping off the books, he thought the contents were escaping.

In some ways, there was more chaos in this remote academic setting than there could ever be in a grade school in the heart of a city.

---

8. ***Iliad . . . Odyssey:*** Famous epics by the ancient Greek poet Homer.

The house might be full of men, waiting out a storm, or riding on a round-up. I was baking, canning, washing clothes, making soap. Allan and David stood by the gasoline washing machine reading history or geography while I put sheets through the wringer. I ironed. They did spelling beside the ironing board, or while I kneaded bread; they gave the tables up to fifteen times fifteen to the treadle of the sewing machine. Mental problems, printed in figures on large cards, they solved while they raced across the . . . room to write the answers . . . and learned to think on their feet. Nine written problems done correctly, without help, meant no tenth problem. . . . It was surprising in how little time they finished their work—to watch the butchering, to help drive the bawling calves into the weaning pen, or to get to the corral, when they heard the hoofbeats of running horses and the cries of cowboys crossing the creek.

No amount of intellectual curiosity or academic discipline was ever going to hold a boy's attention if someone came in saying that the milk cow was mired in a bog hole or that old George was out by the wild-horse corral with the biggest coyote ever killed in the region, or if the door opened and, as David recalls an all too typical event, "they were carrying in a cowboy with guts ripped out by a saddle horn." The lessons stopped, the treadle stopped, and she sewed up the cowboy.

Across a short span of time, she had come a long way with these bunkhouse buckaroos. In her early years on the ranch, she had a lesser sense of fitting in than she would have had had she been a mare, a cow, or a ewe. She did not see another woman for as much as six months at a stretch, and if she happened to approach a group of working ranch hands they would loudly call out, "Church time!" She found "the sudden silence . . . appalling." Women were so rare in the country that when she lost a glove on the open range, at least twenty miles from home, a stranger who found it learned easily whose it must be and rode to the ranch to return it. Men did the housekeeping and the cooking, and went off to buy provisions at distant markets. Meals prepared in the bunkhouse were carried to a sheep wagon, where she and John lived while the big house was being built and otherwise assembled. The Wyoming sheep wagon was the ancestral Winnebago. It had a spring bed and a kitchenette.

After her two sons were born and became old enough to coin phrases, they called her Dainty Dish and sometimes Hooty the Owl. They renamed their food, calling it, for example, dog. They called other entrées caterpillar and coyote. The kitchen stool was Sam. They named a Christmas-tree ornament Hopping John. It had a talent for remaining unbroken. They assured each other that the cotton on the branches would not melt. David decided that he was a camel, but later changed his mind and insisted that he was "Mr. and Mrs. Booth." His mother described him as "a light-footed little elf." She noted his developing sense of scale when he said to her, "A coyote is the whole world to a flea."

One day, he asked her, "How long does a germ live?"

She answered, "A germ may become a grandfather in twenty minutes."

He said, "That's a long time to a germ, isn't it?"

She also made note that while David was the youngest person on the ranch he was nonetheless the most adroit at spotting arrowheads and chippings.

When David was five or six we began hunting arrowheads and chippings. While the rest of us labored along scanning gulches and anthills, David rushed by chattering and picking up arrowheads right and left. He told me once, "There's a god of chippings that sends us anthills. He lives in the sky and tinkers with the clouds."

The cowboys competed with Homer in the entertainment of Allan and David. There was one who—as David remembers him— "could do magic tricks with a lariat rope,[9] making it come alive all around his horse, over our heads, under our feet, zipping it back and forth around us as we jumped up and down and squealed with delight." Sombre tableaux,[10] such as butcherings, were played out before them as well. Years later, David would write in a letter:

We always watched the killing with horror and curiosity, although we were never permitted to participate at that age. It seemed so sad and so irrevocable to see the gushing blood when throats were cut, the desperate gasps for breath through severed windpipes, the struggle for and the rapid ebbing of life, the dimming and glazing of wide terrified eyes. We realized and accepted the fact that this was one of the procedures that were a part of our life on the range and that other lives had to be sacrificed to feed us. Throat-cutting, however, became a symbol of immediate death in our young minds, the ultimate horror, so dreadful that we tried not to use the word "throat."

He has written a recollection of the cowboys, no less frank in its bequested fact, and quite evidently the work of the son of his mother.

9. **lariat** (lar′ē it) **rope:** A rope used for tethering grazing horses or cattle.
10. **sombre tableaux** (säm′ bər tab′ lōz): Gloomy dramatic scenes.

from *Rising from the Plains* 1085

23 **Discussion** Why are these details so important in describing the setting and the character of Mrs. Love? What other circumstances might make it especially difficult for a woman on an isolated ranch?

24 **Clarification** A *Winnebago* is a motor home, commonly used for camping and recreation.

25 **Reading Strategy** Have students summarize the details provided about David Love so far.

26 **Enrichment** The land around the Love Ranch was literally littered with the remains of the original Native American inhabitants. Some of the arrowheads might be many hundreds of years old.

27 Discussion What does this description of occupational hazards tell us about the lives of these men?

The cowboys and horse runners who drifted in to the ranch in ever-increasing numbers as the spring advanced were lean, very strong, hard-muscled, taciturn bachelors, nearly all in their twenties and early thirties. They had been born poor, had only rudimentary education, and accepted their lot without resentment. They worked days that knew no hour limitations but only daylight and dark, and weeks that had no holidays. . . . Most were homely, with prematurely lined faces but with lively eyes that missed little. None wore glasses; people with glasses went into other kinds of work. Many were already stooped from chronic saddle-weariness, bowlegged, hip-sprung, with unrepaired hernias[11] that required trusses,[12] and spinal injuries that required a "hanging pole" in the bunkhouse. This was a horizontal bar from which the cowboys would hang by their hands for five to ten minutes to relieve pressure on ruptured spinal disks that came from too much bronc-fighting. Some wore eight-inch-wide heavy leather belts to keep their kidneys in place during prolonged hard rides.

When in a sense it was truly church time—when cowboys were badly injured and in need of help—they had long since learned where to go. David vividly remembers a moment in his education which was truncated when a cowboy rode up holding a bleeding hand. He had been roping a wild horse, and one of his fingers had become caught between the lariat and the saddle horn. The finger was still a part of his hand but was hanging by two tendons. His mother boiled water, sterilized a pair of surgical scissors, and scrubbed her hands and arms. With magisterial nonchalance, she "snipped the tendons, dropped the finger into the hot coals of the fire box, sewed a flap of skin over the stump, smiled sweetly, and said: 'Joe, in a month you'll never know the difference.'"

There was a pack of ferocious wolf-hounds in the country, kept by another flockmaster for the purpose of killing coyotes. The dogs seemed to relish killing rattlesnakes as well, shaking the life out of them until the festive serpents hung from the hounds' jaws like fettuccine.[13] The ranch hand in charge of them said, "They ain't happy in the spring till they've been bit. They're used to it now, and their heads don't swell up no more." Human beings (on foot) who happened to encounter these dogs might have preferred to encounter the rattlesnakes instead. One summer afternoon, John Love was working on a woodpile when he saw two of the wolfhounds streaking down to the creek in the direction of his sons, whose ages were maybe three and four. "Laddies! Run! Run to the house!" he shouted. "Here come the hounds!" The boys ran, reached the door just ahead of the dogs, and slammed it in their faces. Their mother was in the kitchen:

The hounds, not to be thwarted so easily, leaped together furiously at the kitchen windows, high above the ground. They shattered the glass of the small panes, and tried to struggle through, their front feet catching over the inside ledge of the window frame, and their heads, with slavering mouths, reaching through the broken glass. I had only time to snatch a heavy iron frying pan from

---

11. hernias (hŭr' nē əz) *n.*: The protrusion of part of the intestine through the abdominal muscles.
12. trusses *n.*: Appliances for giving support in hernia cases.

13. fettuccine (fet' oo chē' nē) *n.*: Broad, flat noodles.

Grammar in Action

One of the main uses of the **comma** is to **separate the items in a series** of three or more words, phrases, or subordinate clauses. Note the following examples from *Rising from the Plains:*

The milieu of Love Ranch was not all wind, snow, freezing cattle, and killer dogs.

The names of its natural features are names that more or less materialized around the kitchen table when David Love was young: Corral Draw, Castle Gardens, Buffalow Wallows, Jumping-Off Draw.

Student Activity. Insert commas in the appropriate places in each of the following sentences.

1. From the ranch buildings, by Muskrat Creek, the Wind River Basin reached out in buffalo grass grama grass and edible salt sage across the cambered erosional swells of vast dry range.
2. He cooked his beans and bacon his mutton, his sourdough, his whatever.
3. The house was chinked with slaked lime wood shavings and cow manure.

the stove and face them, beating at those clutching feet and snarling heads. The terrified boys cowered behind me. The window sashes held against the onslaught of the hounds, and my blows must have daunted them. They dropped back to the ground and raced away.

In the boys' vocabulary, the word "hound" joined the word "throat" in the deep shadows, and to this day when David sees a wolfhound there is a drop in the temperature of the center of his spine.

The milieu[14] of Love Ranch was not all wind, snow, freezing cattle, and killer dogs. There were quiet, lyrical days on end under blue, unthreatening skies. There were the redwing blackbirds on the corral fence, and the scent of moss flowers in spring. In a light breeze, the windmill turned slowly beside the wide log house, which was edged with flowers in bloom. Sometimes there were teal on the creek—and goldeneyes, pintails, mallards.[15] When the wild hay was ready for cutting, the harvest lasted a week.

> John liked to have me ride with them for the last load. Sometimes I held the reins and called "Whoa, Dan!" while the men pitched up the hay. Then while the wagon swayed slowly back over the uneven road, I lay nestled deeply beside Allan and David in the fragrant hay. The billowy white clouds moving across the wide blue sky were close, so close, it seemed there was nothing else in the universe but clouds and hay.

When the hay house was not absolutely full, the boys cleared off the dance floor of Joe's Lacey's Muskrat Saloon and strapped on their roller skates. Bizarre as it may seem, there was also a Love Ranch croquet ground. And in winter the boys clamped ice skates to their shoes and flew with the wind up the creek. Alternatively, they lay down on their sleds and propelled themselves swiftly over wind-cleared, wind-polished black ice, with an anchor pin from a coyote trap in each hand. Almost every evening, with their parents, they played mah-jongg.[16]

One fall, their mother went to Riverton, sixty-five miles away, to await the birth of Phoebe. For her sons, eleven and twelve, she left behind a carefully prepared program of study. In the weeks that followed, they were in effect enrolled in a correspondence school run by their mother. They did their French, their spelling, their arithmetic lessons, put them in envelopes, rode fifteen miles to the post office and mailed them to her. She graded the lessons and sent them back—before and after the birth of the baby.

> Her hair was the color of my wedding ring. On her cheek the fingers of one hand were outspread like a small, pink starfish.

From time to time, dust would appear on the horizon, behind a figure coming toward the ranch. The boys, in their curiosity, would climb a rooftop to watch and wait as the rider covered the intervening miles. Almost everyone who went through the region stopped at Love Ranch. It had not only the sizable bunkhouse and the most capacious horse corrals in a thousand square miles but also a spring of good water. Moreover, it had Scottish hospitality—not to mention the forbidding distance to the nearest alternative cup of coffee. Soon after Mr. Love and Miss Waxham were married, Nathaniel Thomas, the Episcopal Bishop of Wyoming, came through in his Gospel Wagon, accompanied

---

14. **milieu** (mēl yōō′) *n.*: Environment.
15. **teal ... goldeneyes, pintails, mallards:** Types of ducks.

16. **mah-jongg** (mä′ jôŋ′) *n.*: A game of Chinese origin, played with pieces resembling dominoes.

28

4. He trapped coyotes bobcats badgers.

5. Joe Lacey's place became the hay house, the hotel became a saddlery and cookhouse, and the other buildings, many of them connected, became all or parts of the blacksmith shop the chicken hatchery the ice shed the buggy shed the sod cellar and the bunkhouse—the social center for all the workingmen from a great many miles around.

29 **Enrichment** Wellesley is a well-known college in a Massachusetts town of the same name.

30 **Clarification** A *posse* is a group of lawmen on the trail of a wanted criminal.

by his colleague the Reverend Theodore Sedgwick. Sedgwick later reported (in a publication called *The Spirit of Missions*):

29

> We saw a distant building. It meant water. At this lonely ranch, in the midst of a sandy desert, we found a young woman. Her husband had gone for the day over the range. Around her neck hung a gold chain with a Phi Beta Kappa[17] key. She was a graduate of Wellesley College, and was now a Wyoming bride. She knew her Greek and Latin, and loved her house on the care-free prairie.

The bishop said he was searching for "heathen," and he did not linger.

---

17. Phi Beta Kappa (fī băt′ə kap′ə): An honorary society of U.S. college students of high scholastic rank.

Fugitive criminals stopped at the ranch fairly often. They had to—in much the way that fugitive criminals in lonely country today will sooner or later have to stop at a filling station. A lone rider arrived at the ranch one day with a big cloud of dust on the horizon behind him. The dust might as well have formed in the air the letters of the word "posse." John Love knew the rider, knew that he was wanted for murder, and knew that throughout the country the consensus was that the victim had "needed killing." The murderer asked John Love to give him five dollars, and said he would leave his pocket watch as collateral. If his offer was refused, the man said, he would find a way to take the money. The watch was as honest as the day is long. When David does his field geology, he has it in his pocket.

30

People like that came along with such frequency that David's mother eventually assembled a chronicle called "Murderers I Have Known." She did not publish the manuscript, or even give it much private circulation, in her regard for the sensitivities of some of the first families of Wyoming. As David would one day comment, "they were nice men, family friends, who had put away people who needed killing, and she did not wish to offend them—so many of them were such decent people."

One of these was Bill Grace. Homesteader and cowboy, he was one of the most celebrated murderers in central Wyoming, and he had served time, but people generally disagreed with the judiciary and felt that Bill, in the acts for which he was convicted, had only been "doing his civic duty." At the height of his fame, he stopped at the ranch one afternoon and stayed for dinner. Although David and Allan were young boys, they knew exactly who he was, and in his presence were struck dumb with awe. As it happened, they had come upon and dispatched a rattlesnake that day—a big one,

over five feet long. Their mother decided to serve it creamed on toast for dinner. She and their father sternly instructed David and Allan not to use the word "rattlesnake" at the table. They were to refer to it as chicken, since a possibility existed that Bill Grace might not be an eater of adequate sophistication to enjoy the truth. The excitement was too much for the boys. Despite the parental injunction, gradually their conversation at the table fished its way toward the snake. Casually—while the meal was going down—the boys raised the subject of poisonous vipers, gave their estimates of the contents of local dens, told stories of snake encounters, and so forth. Finally, one of them remarked on how very good rattlers were to eat.

Bill Grace said, "By God, if anybody ever gave me rattlesnake meat I'd kill them."

The boys went into a state of catatonic paralysis. In the pure silence, their mother said, "More chicken, Bill?"

"Don't mind if I do," said Bill Grace.

31 **Discussion** What purpose does this anecdote serve in the narrative?

Reader's Response Would you be interested in living on a ranch? Why or why not?

Commentary

Some critics have noted that the structure of a McPhee article can be its dominant feature, accentuating the subject it holds. His working method shows how such elegant structures are formed.

McPhee builds his carefully constructed articles from hundreds of pages of typewritten notes, the result of months of reading, researching, and interviewing. When interviewing, he shuns tape recorders, finding such devices intrusive. Rather, he relies on keen listening and remarkable powers of observation. Asking few formal questions, he prefers instead to "just hang around" with his subjects until he begins to hear the same stories for the third time. At that point he goes home to write. He has called the writing "a wretched process" that begins with reading and rereading his notes until a pattern of ideas and incidents suggesting possible topics emerges. Then he codes his notes by topic, puts topic headings on individual index cards, and shuffles them until he happens upon a logical outline. Next he codes a duplicate set of notes and cuts them up, filing the hundreds of scraps of information in appropriately labeled folders, one for each index card. With the structural form set, he begins the slow process of writing. As his work continues, he marks his progress with a steel dart on an outline he keeps tacked to a bulletin board.

from *Rising from the Plains*   1089

Closure and Extension

ANSWERS TO THINKING ABOUT THE SELECTION
Recalling

1. He is a "rough, kindly, strong-willed man."
2. They did not use them.
3. He went shopping for abandoned towns.
4. They are "lean, very strong, hard-muscled, taciturn bachelors."
5. He describes the time Bill Grace dines on rattlesnake thinking it is chicken.

Interpreting

6. Because they are so out of touch with civilization, they are "starved for print."
7. They are first-hand accounts and include details McPhee could not have been aware of.
8. He seems to admire their ingenuity and independence.

Applying

9. Suggested Response: People on ranches today have the benefit of labor-saving machines, highways, and communication with the outside world.

Challenge How do the changes in ranch life reflect the changes that have occurred in society as a whole?

ANSWERS TO ANALYZING LITERATURE

1. It discusses the wide extremes of temperature during the seasons, in particular the freezing winters.
2. It gives the impression of a difficult, demanding life with abundant rewards for those willing to endure its hardships.

ANSWERS TO CRITICAL THINKING AND READING

1. It tells you she has learned to keep a cool head in a crisis and to cope with many different situations.
2. He is tough, pragmatic, and watchful for danger.

THINKING ABOUT THE SELECTION
Recalling

1. How does David Love describe his father?
2. What was the Love Ranch policy regarding the use of tents?
3. What did John Love do when the stage route that ran through the ranch was abandoned?
4. How does David Love describe the cowboys and horse runners "who drifted in to the ranch . . . as the spring advanced"?
5. What incident involving the "celebrated" murderer, Bill Grace, does McPhee describe at the end of the selection?

Interpreting

6. How does the way in which the people in the area around Love Ranch treated newspapers reflect their sense of isolation?
7. How do the passages written by David Love and his mother contribute to the authenticity of McPhee's account?
8. What seems to be McPhee's attitude toward David Love and his family?

Applying

9. In what ways do you imagine that life on today's American ranches differs from the type of life described in this essay?

ANALYZING LITERATURE
Understanding Setting

The **setting** is the time and place in which the events in a literary work occur. In *Rising from the Plains,* McPhee focuses on capturing the flavor of life in a specific setting—the Love Ranch in Wyoming.

1. What does this selection reveal about the climate of the area in which Love Ranch is located?
2. What overall impression of life on Love Ranch does the selection convey?

CRITICAL THINKING AND READING
Understanding the Effect of Setting

McPhee's essay also reveals many of the ways in which the members of the Love family were shaped by the setting. For example, in the first paragraph McPhee points out that David Love's experiences growing up on Love Ranch shaped his use of language, his outlook on life, and "his pragmatic skills."

1. What does the way in which David Love's mother deals with the cowboy's injured finger suggest about the effect of the setting on her character?
2. In what ways has David Love's father clearly been shaped by the setting?

THINKING AND WRITING
Comparing and Contrasting Settings

Write an essay in which you compare and contrast the setting of McPhee's essay with the setting Larry McMurtry describes in the excerpt from *Lonesome Dove.* Reread each selection, noting the details of the setting. Organize your notes according to corresponding points of comparison and contrast. Then write your essay, using details from both selections to support your argument. When you revise, make sure you have used transitions to link your ideas and varied the length and structure of your sentences.

THINKING AND WRITING

For help with this assignment, students can refer to Lesson 16, "Writing a Comparative Evaluation," in the Handbook of Writing About Literature.

After students have completed the assignment, you may want to divide them into groups, and have them read their rough drafts to one another and suggest ways in which the essays could be improved.

Poetry

NUMBER 3, 1949
Jackson Pollack
Joseph Hirshhorn Museum

Fine art, *Number 3*, 1949, by Jackson Pollock. Although *Number 3* and the many other scatter-paint works of Jackson Pollock (1912-1956) may look like the haphazard application of oil to canvas, they are actually the result of a more controlled technique. As Pollock dripped or spattered paint from a stick or a can onto large, unstretched sheets of canvas laid out on the floor, he would regulate the direction and thickness of the lines and their three-dimensional quality; he would determine, too, how the colors would interact. The physical energy expended as he moved from one side of the canvas to another created, Pollock felt, a feeling of closeness with the work. Sometimes he would add household objects, like tacks and keys, to achieve surface interest and a sense of the unexpected. What also appealed to Pollock was the fact that viewers could interpret the interplay of lines, colors, and suggested shapes according to their own responses to the canvases. Some of the shapes evoked forms from nature—intricate twigs, for instance.

Pollock, born in Wyoming, was influenced, among others, by Picasso and the surrealist painters. It was in the 1940's that he began producing his famous "drip" paintings (the technique is sometimes referred to as Action Painting). He was both criticized and imitated for his innovations —and eventually gained recognition as one of the foremost abstract expressionist painters of the mid-twentieth century.

More About the Author Theodore Roethke used the extensive notes he took throughout his life as the source for much of his poetry. It has been said that his pockets were always full of notes about his conversations, reflections, and observations. Ask students to discuss what amusing, insightful, or telling observations they have made in the last week. What is the difference between merely reporting these insights and observations and using them as the subject of a poem?

Critical Evaluation The literary scholar Eric Mottram has observed that "Roethke developed a unique poetry out of his sense of links between the unconscious and nature . . . with Yeats as his formal model. His floppy whimsical poems, often in a sort of baby talk, were exceptional in a poetic career of almost desperate stabilities. His strength lay in creating an interior landscape out of a crowded greenhouse or a river estuary which locates, with lyrical precision and a degree of splendor, a sense of alienation, madness and reconciliation which he strives to unify."

THEODORE ROETHKE

1908–1963

Throughout the course of his career, Theodore Roethke focused his poetry on the various aspects of his own life. Although his style changed during the period between the publication of his first book, *Open House* (1941), and the appearance of his posthumous collection, *The Far Field* (1964), Roethke continued to seek a sense of self by exploring his personal experiences in his poetry.

Roethke grew up in Saginaw, Michigan, where his family owned several large commercial greenhouses. In his family's greenhouses, he observed nature putting forth roots and blossoms, as well as falling into dormancy and death. These observations later provided him with ideas and inspiration for many of his poems.

His work was especially influenced by the Transcendentalist movement, and he expressed an abiding affinity for Emerson and Thoreau. His adolescence had been a "hell of bright awareness" as one critic put it. He felt odd in high school where possessing keen intelligence was equated with being a "sissy." Often frustrated because he didn't know what to do with his perceptions, Roethke viewed himself as "odious" and found relating to people a problem well into his university years. Following the Transcendentalist precepts, he took refuge in nature. "When I get alone out under the sky where man isn't too evident—then I'm tremendously exalted and a thousand vivid ideas and sweet visions flood my consciousness."

During much of his life, he lived dangerously close to madness. His mental struggles threatened to destroy both his teaching and poetic careers, and in 1943 he was hospitalized for manic-depressive psychosis, one of two events which formed the foundation for most of his later poetry. The second event shaping his later work was the death of his father, who had been both a stern authoritarian and a sensitive, vulnerable soul. Although it had happened when Roethke was fourteen, the poet waited until his later years to sort out his ambiguous feelings toward Otto Roethke.

After receiving his education at the University of Michigan and Harvard, Roethke taught writing at Bennington College, the Pennsylvania State University, and the University of Washington. A slow, diligent writer, Roethke spent many years assembling poems for his first book. He went on to publish several more volumes, including *The Lost Son* (1948), *The Waking* (1953), and *Words for the Wind* (1958). In 1954 he received a Pulitzer Prize for *The Waking,* and two years after his death he was awarded the National Book Award for *The Far Field.*

1092   *Contemporary Writers*

Support Material

Teaching Portfolio
Teacher Backup, p. 1467
Usage and Mechanics Worksheet, p. 1471
Vocabulary Check, p. 1472
Analyzing Literature Worksheet, *Understanding Rhyme,* p. 1473
Language Worksheet, *Using Antonyms,* p. 1474
Selection Test, p. 1475

GUIDE FOR INTERPRETING

Literary Focus Rhyme is often an important element of song lyrics. Encourage students to find examples of the use of internal, end, exact, and approximate rhyme in popular song lyrics.

Writing/Prior Knowledge Have the students discuss the difference between learning from books and learning through experience. Why are both of these types of learning important?

Vocabulary

Preteach the following vocabulary words:
abiding (ə bīd′ iŋ) *adj.*: Enduring; lasting (p. 1096, 1.6)
questing (kwest′ iŋ) *adj.*: Searching (p. 1096, 1.7)

The Waking; Once More, the Round

Writer's Techniques

Rhyme. Rhyme refers to the repetition of sounds in the accented syllables of two or more words that appear close to each other. Rhyme that occurs at the ends of lines is called end rhyme, while rhyme that occurs within a line is called internal rhyme. When rhyme involves the repetition of identical sounds, it is called exact rhyme. For example, *snow-crow* is an exact rhyme. When the rhyme is not exact, it is called approximate rhyme or slant rhyme. For example, *dream-home* is an approximate rhyme.

Commentary

All poetry has form, but some poems are framed according to very structured "rules," or conventions. You are no doubt familiar with some formal poetry. Haiku, for instance, consists of seventeen syllables arranged in three lines of five, seven, and five syllables respectively. Sonnets each have fourteen lines and follow prescribed rhyme schemes and metrical arrangements. One of the most demanding forms of poetry is the villanelle. So difficult is it to write a good villanelle that poets seldom use this form. Theodore Roethke's "The Waking" is a villanelle. As you read it, notice how it fits the pattern.

A villanelle consists of six stanzas, the first five of which contain three lines each and end rhyme in the first and third lines. The middle lines of all five stanzas rhyme with one another. The first and last lines of the first stanza form a unifying refrain throughout the poem. These lines are split after the first stanza and alternately repeated as the final line of each successive stanza until the sixth and final four-line stanza. In the sixth stanza, the two refrain lines are combined to form the two final lines of the poem. Further conventions govern the villanelle, but these serve to illustrate the constraints under which the poet labors when he creates a villanelle. Roethke follows the conventional formula in this poem except in the fifteenth line where he breaks the convention, or "rule," by slightly altering the line. When a poet breaks a convention, he does so for important reasons, typically to call attention to the place where convention is breached. Why do you think Roethke wanted to call attention to line fifteen in "The Waking"?

Writing

In Roethke's poem "The Waking," the speaker comments, "I learn by going where I have to go." Do you think this is the way most people learn? Freewrite about the ways in which people acquire knowledge during the courses of their lives.

Guide for Interpreting 1093

Motivation/Prior Knowledge
Have the students imagine that they are alone on a camping trip or an outing in the mountains or at the ocean. They have just awakened. It is early morning. What kinds of sounds would they hear? What kinds of colors would they see? How would they feel?

Master Teacher Note Have two of your students read the poem aloud while the rest of the class listens. After the readings, encourage the students to discuss the way in which each student interpreted the poem. How did the two readings differ from one another?

Thematic Idea Another literary work which points out the value of learning through observation and experience is "When I Heard the Learn'd Astronomer" by Walt Whitman (p. 470).

Purpose-Setting Question What is paradoxical about Roethke's statement "I wake to sleep"?

1 **Discussion** What does the speaker mean when he says that he wakes to sleep?

2 **Discussion** What does the speaker mean when he says that we "think by feeling"?

3 **Enrichment** Theodore Roethke suffered through bouts of manic-depression, yet he was recognized as an energetic teacher and writer. His illnesses were sometimes debilitating, but from them he emerged to continue his teaching and writing.

Reader's Response Do you ever learn things "by going where [you] have to go"? Explain.

The Waking

Theodore Roethke

I wake to sleep, and take my waking slow.
I feel my fate in what I cannot fear.
I learn by going where I have to go.

We think by feeling. What is there to know?
5 I hear my being dance from ear to ear.
I wake to sleep, and take my waking slow.

Of those so close beside me, which are you?
God bless the Ground! I shall walk softly there,
And learn by going where I have to go.

10 Light takes the Tree; but who can tell us how?
The lowly worm climbs up a winding stair;
I wake to sleep, and take my waking slow.

Great Nature has another thing to do
To you and me; so take the lively air,
15 And, lovely, learn by going where to go.

This shaking keeps me steady. I should know.
What falls away is always. And is near.
I wake to sleep, and take my waking slow.
I learn by going where I have to go.

1

2

3

THINKING ABOUT THE SELECTION

Recalling

1. (a) In what does the speaker feel his fate? (b) How does he learn? (c) What does he hear? (d) What keeps him steady?

Interpreting

2. (a) What is paradoxical, or seemingly self-contradictory, about the statement, "I wake to sleep"? (b) What is the meaning of this paradox? (c) Find two other paradoxes in the poem. (d) Explain the meaning of each of these paradoxes.
3. What does the speaker mean when he says that he takes his "waking slow"?
4. What is the meaning of lines 3, 9, and 19?
5. (a) What is the other "thing" that Nature has "to do/To you and me"? (b) How does the speaker's reference to this "thing" help clarify the meaning of the poem?
6. Why is the form of this poem appropriate to its subject?
7. Read this poem aloud. (a) What effect is created by the rhythm? (b) How is this effect appropriate for the subject matter?
8. What does this poem suggest about Roethke's attitude toward life?
9. Why is "The Waking" an appropriate title for this poem?

Applying

10. The American novelist Richard Wright has written, "Men can starve from lack of self-realization as much as they can from a lack of bread." Discuss the meaning of this quotation and its relation to "The Waking."

ANALYZING LITERATURE

Understanding Rhyme

Rhyme refers to the repetition of sounds in the accented syllables of two or more words that appear close to each other. Exact rhyme refers to the repetition of identical sounds. The use of the words *fear* and *ear* at the ends of lines 2 and 5 is an example of exact rhyme. When the rhyme is not exact, it is called approximate rhyme or slant rhyme. For example, Roethke uses slant rhyme in lines 5 and 8, when he rhymes the words *ear* and *there*.

1. Find two more examples of exact rhyme.
2. Find another example of slant rhyme.
3. What is the rhyme scheme, or the pattern of end rhymes in the poem?

THINKING AND WRITING

Responding to Criticism

Critic Robert Boyers has commented that Roethke's "best poems permit us to embrace the principle of change as the root of stability." Write an essay in which you discuss this comment in relation to "The Waking." Reread the poem, noting what it suggests about the concepts of change and stability. Develop a thesis statement. Then write your essay, using passages from the poem to support your argument. When you finish writing, revise your essay, making sure that you have included enough supporting information.

The Waking 1095

---

that the "sleep" that the speaker ultimately wakes to is death.

6. The regular pattern and use of repetition reflect the poem's depiction of life as a cycle.
7. (a) The rhythm creates a sense of steadiness and regularity. (b) This steadiness and regularity reflects the poem's depiction of life as a cycle.
8. Suggested Response: The poem suggests that Roethke views life as a slow process in which a person strives to develop an understanding of his or her destiny and purpose.
9. Suggested Response: "The Waking" is an appropriate title because the poem focuses on a type of awakening, the acquisition of knowledge through experience.

Applying

10. The quotation mirrors the poem's emphasis on the acquisition of self-knowledge.

Challenge How does Roethke's attitude compare with your own attitude toward life?

ANSWERS TO ANALYZING LITERATURE

1. Suggested Response: *Stair* and *air* in lines 11 and 14 is an exact rhyme. *Know* and *slow* in lines 16 and 18 is also an exact rhyme.
2. Suggested Response: *Do* and *go* in lines 13 and 15 is a slant rhyme.
3. It has an *aba* rhyme scheme.

THINKING AND WRITING

For help with this assignment, students can refer to Lesson 12, "Writing About a Poem," in the Handbook of Writing About Literature.

After students have completed the assignment, divide them into groups and have them read their rough drafts to one another and suggest ways in which they could be improved.

Closure and Extension

ANSWERS TO THINKING ABOUT THE SELECTION
Recalling

1. (a) He feels his fate in what he cannot fear. (b) He learns by going where he has to go. (c) He hears his being dancing from ear to ear. (d) "This shaking" keeps him steady.

Interpreting

2. (a) It is paradoxical to "wake to sleep," because waking brings sleep to an end. (b) The speaker uses "waking" to refer to the process of acquiring knowledge; sleep is his fate, or final destination. (c) "The shaking keeps me steady" and "What falls away is always" are two other paradoxes. (d) "Shaking keeps me steady" refers to the fact that the uncertainties in life force a person to

follow fate's path. "What falls away is always" refers to the fact that the world is constantly changing.
3. He means that acquiring learning and understanding, and truly assimilating them, is a slow, demanding process.
4. These lines mean that the speaker learns through experience.
5. (a) Nature sees to it that we all eventually die. (b) The speaker's reference helps to make it clear

Once More, the Round

Theodore Roethke

What's greater, Pebble or Pond?
What can be known? The Unknown.
My true self runs toward a Hill
More! O More! visible.

5　Now I adore my life
With the Bird, the abiding Leaf,
With the Fish, the questing Snail,
And the Eye altering all;
And I dance with William Blake[1]
10　For love, for Love's sake;

And everything comes to One,
As we dance on, dance on, dance on.

---

1. **William Blake:** English poet (1757–1827).

WILD FLOWERS, 1978
Samuel Reindorf
Collection: George Williams

THINKING ABOUT THE SELECTION

Recalling

1. What questions does the speaker ask in the first stanza?
2. What elements of nature does the speaker mention in the second stanza?

Interpreting

3. What do the "pebble" and "pond" referred to in the first stanza represent?

4. Why does the speaker's "true self" run "toward a Hill"?
5. What does the speaker mean when he says that "the Eye" alters "all"?

Applying

6. In this poem Roethke compares life to a round dance, a type of dance in which groups of dancers move in a circle. To what other types of dances do you think life might be compared?

Once More, the Round 1097

Closure and Extension

ANSWERS TO THINKING ABOUT THE SELECTION
Recalling

1. The speaker asks "What's greater, Pebble or Pond?" and "What can be known?"
2. The speaker mentions the bird, leaf, fish, and snail.

Interpreting

3. The pebble and pond refer to the big and the small.
4. The true self wants to rise up and find a broader view of life.
5. The speaker means that reality is shaped by people's impressions.

Applying

6. Suggested Response: One example is modern dancing in which there are no set steps. This dance reflects the unpredictability of life.

Challenge Would William Blake share the sentiments Roethke expresses in this poem?

Humanities Note

Fine art, *Wild Flowers,* 1978, by Samuel Reindorf. Samuel Reindorf, born in 1914, is an American painter who immigrated from Poland. He studied art at the Toronto School of Art in Canada and the American Artists School in New York City. He now resides in Mexico.

Wild Flowers is a pleasant, modern rendering of flowers. The subtle blend of colors and simplified shapes combine to produce a harmonious interpretation of a favorite painterly theme.

You might ask students the following questions.
1. What are the artist's feelings about nature as reflected by this painting?
2. How do they compare with the poet's regard for nature?

Focus

Focus

More About the Authors In his poetry **James Dickey** juxtaposes the world of nature and the civilized world. These two worlds are also juxtaposed in his novel, *Deliverance,* which was adapted into a major film. Ask students to discuss the similarities and differences between nature and civilization. Can the same sort of struggles and the same kinds of resolutions be found in both nature and civilization?

Denise Levertov has commented that the work of William Carlos Williams has had a powerful impact on her own poetry. She has stated that Williams "showed us the rhythms of speech as *poetry.*" Have students discuss why so many poets have followed Williams's example by trying to capture the natural rhythms of speech in their work. Is this type of poetry more or less effective than poetry with a more rigid structure?

Critical Evaluation The literary critic David Perkins has written that "Because of his [Dickey's] direct methods, narrative skills, and use of Southern regional materials, James Dickey has affinities with Robert Penn Warren, who has championed Dickey's poetry. Like Warren, Dickey is also a novelist and critic. . . . During the 1970's Dickey put his strength into prose. His novel *Deliverance* was made into a well-known film, but his reputation as a poet declined, partly because his later poems in longer lines and looser forms are less successful than his tighter, earlier ones in strong rhythms. Also, his affirmation of life began to seem too easy and uncritical, and his macho pose in many poems gave offense."

James Dickey (1923–   )

A lover of nature and a devoted outdoorsman, James Dickey is a man of great size (he is six foot three) and energy. Dickey's energy and affection for the outdoors are exhibited in his poetry. In his work he often shows people testing their survival instincts against the primitive elements of the natural world. This reflects his belief that maintaining contact with the world of nature can help people escape from the monotony of everyday existence.

Dickey was born in Atlanta, Georgia. He was a star football player in high school and served as a bomber pilot in World War II. After returning from the war, Dickey began writing poetry while studying at Vanderbilt University. During his senior year, one of his poems was published in *Sewanee Review.*

Dickey went on to publish several volumes of poetry, including *Into the Stone* (1960), *Buckdancer's Choice* (1965), *Poems 1957–1967* (1967) and *Puella* (1982). In 1966 he received the National Book Award for *Buckdancer's Choice.* In addition to poetry, he has written literary criticism and a best-selling novel, *Deliverance* (1970).

Denise Levertov (1923–   )

Denise Levertov has commented that she believes that the poem is the poet's means for discovering the divine in the real world. Acting upon this belief, Levertov writes original, inventive poetry that often explores the hidden meaning in ordinary events. Most of her poems stem from personal experience, but they are not merely personal treatments. She firmly believes a poet's aim should be greater than the narration of pictures, and through her work she strives to impart love of nature, faith in people, and the conviction that life must be fully experienced. Levertov feels the essence of life is paradox and that both communication and silence should be respected. Her poems often bring together the seeming polarities of activity and passivity, sound and silence.

Levertov was born in Essex, England. She began writing poetry at an early age, and in 1946 she published her first collection, *The Double Image.* A year later she married American writer Mitchell Goodman and moved to the United States. She became an American citizen in 1955, and her second book of poetry was published in 1957. Since then, she has written over a dozen more books of poetry, including *With Eyes at the Back of Our Heads* (1960) and *Relearning the Alphabet* (1970). She has also published two books of translations and a book of essays about writing poetry.

1098   Contemporary Writers

Support Material

Teaching Portfolio
Teacher Backup, p. 1477
Usage and Mechanics Worksheet, p. 1482
Vocabulary Check, p. 1483
Critical Thinking and Reading Worksheet, *Comparing and Contrasting Writers' Styles,* p. 1484

Language Worksheet, *Understanding the Meanings of Words,* p. 1485
Selection Test, p. 1486
Art Transparency 19, *Harmonizing,* by Robert Gwatharey
Art Transparency 20, *Urban Freeways,* by Wayne Thiebaud

GUIDE FOR INTERPRETING

The Rain Guitar; Merritt Parkway

Literary Forms

Visual Poetry. Visual poetry refers to poems in which the letters, words, lines, and spaces are arranged to form a shape or create a visual effect. Often the shape of a visual poem in some way reflects or reinforces the poem's meaning. For example, seventeenth-century English poet George Herbert shaped his poem "The Altar" to look like a church altar and shaped his poem "Easter Wings" to resemble a pair of wings.

Commentary

As you read these two poems by Dickey and Levertov, notice that although they differ in many ways, they have more in common than their use of visual effects. Each confronts human isolation and connection and the way that connection between people enriches lives. "The Rain Guitar" brings two apparent strangers into the same place at the same time, though each has come for his own purpose. The speaker declaims, "It mattered to me not at all," about the other upon the bridge. And when we see that the second man has come to fish, the speaker again dissociates himself from the fisherman. "I had no line and no feeling. I had nothing to do with fish. . . ." But the poet suggests a link between the two that neither man yet acknowledges. The speaker's "threads were opening" and the second man "cast a fish thread" into the water. Poets use words precisely, and the repetition of *thread* implies a similarity between these men.

Denise Levertov offers a modern scene that, at first thought, would imply man's complete isolation. Indeed, she recounts the isolation of individuals within their separate cars. But she goes "above" that seclusion in several places and implies a connection between the drivers who share experiences so strikingly similar. She recognizes in "the dreamlike continuum . . ." that people are alike. With this line, "And the people—ourselves!" she expresses not only the link between people but their identity with one another. People, she implies, are not isolated, although they may appear to be except at "gasoline stops." She implies that the viewing of lives as unique and isolated from one another is an illusion we take as real, perhaps because of the speed with which we move "relentlessly" in our quickening world.

What feelings about connection and isolation do these poems evoke in you?

Writing

In "Merritt Parkway," Levertov writes about the experience of traveling along a crowded highway. Freewrite about the thoughts and feelings that you associate with highway travel.

Literary Focus Visual poetry is sometimes referred to as "pattern poems." The typographical arrangement of the poem on the page visually illustrates the poem's subject and thus provides an added dimension of relevance. Why is poetry more vigorously patterned than prose?

Writing/Prior Knowledge Have students categorize their feelings about travel. What is it like to be on a freeway during rush hour? What is it like to travel down a country road? How does highway travel differ from air travel?

Vocabulary

Preteach the following vocabulary words:
wan (wän) *adj.*: Sickly pale (p. 1102, l.4)
continuum (ken tin′ yo͞o wəm) *n.*: A continuous whole with parts that cannot be separated (p. 1102, l.10)

Motivation/Prior Knowledge
Have students imagine that they are fishing in a stream. What types of thoughts might they have? How would they respond if it began to rain?

Master Teacher Note The dueling banjo sequence from the film adaptation of James Dickey's novel, *Deliverance,* is a classic performance scene. It is a gripping scene that fully conveys the sound-picture relationship so unique to the cinematic medium. You may wish to show a videotaped excerpt of this sequence. Discuss the meeting of the two strangers in the film, pointing out the way in which this part of the film parallels the poem.

You may also wish to place Art Transparency 19, *Harmonizing* by Robert Gwatharey, on the overhead projector. Have students discuss the ways in which music can affect people. What types of emotions can music evoke? Why does music often cause people to remember situations and experiences from earlier in their lives?

Thematic Idea Another poem that explores the effects of music is "Plucking Out a Rhythm" by Lawson Fusao Inada (p. 1164)

Purpose-Setting Question How would you describe the shape of this poem?

1 **Discussion** The guitar is used as a motif in a number of James Dickey's poems. What is the relationship between music and poetry?

2 **Clarification** A *weir* is "a fence or enclosure set in a waterway for taking fish, or a dam in a stream that raises the water level or diverts the flow of the stream."

3 **Enrichment** Winchester is a town in South England. Even

The Rain Guitar

James Dickey

England, 1962

The water-grass under had never waved
But one way. It showed me that flow is forever
Sealed from rain in a weir. For some reason having
To do with Winchester, I was sitting on my guitar case
5 Watching nothing but eelgrass trying to go downstream with all the right motions
But one. I had on a sweater, and my threads were opening
Like mouths with rain. It mattered to me not at all
That a bridge was stumping
With a man, or that he came near and cast a fish
10 thread into the weir. I had no line and no feeling.
I had nothing to do with fish
But my eyes on the grass they hid in, waving with the one move of trying
To be somewhere else. With what I had, what could I do?
I got out my guitar, that somebody told me was supposed to improve
15 With moisture—or was it when it dried out?—and hit the lowest
And loudest chord. The drops that were falling just then
Hammered like Georgia railroad track
With E. The man went into a kind of fishing
Turn. Play it, he said through his pipe. There
20 I went, fast as I could with cold fingers. The strings shook
With drops. A buck dance settled on the weir. Where was the city
Cathedral in all this? Out of sight, but somewhere around.
Play a little more
Of that, he said, and cast. Music-wood shone,
25 Getting worse or better faster than it liked:
Improvement or disintegration
Supposed to take years, fell on it
By the gallon. It darkened and rang
Like chimes. My sweater collapsed, and the rain reached
30 My underwear. I picked, the guitar showered, and he cast to the mountain
Music. His wood leg tapped
On the cobbles. Memories of many men
Hung, rain-faced, improving, sealed-off
In the weir. I found myself playing Australian
35 Versions of British marching songs. Mouths opened all over me; I sang,
His legs beat and marched
Like companions. I was Air Force,
I said. So was I; I picked
This up in Burma, he said, tapping his gone leg

when London was ascending to become the central city of England, Winchester remained the center of learning and attracted many religious scholars. This reflects the prominence of its famous cathedral, a magnificent Gothic structure that still stands today. You may wish to refer students to pictures of this cathedral, which they may find in the encyclopedia. What is the contrast between the cathedral background and the marshlike setting?

4 **Discussion** What is the effect of *alliteration* in the opening of this poem?

5 **Discussion** How do these lines parallel the final two lines?

6 **Clarification** Burma is a country in Southeast Asia. The Burma Road played an important part in the defeat of Japan by United States forces during World War II.

With his fly rod, as Burma and the South
west Pacific and North Georgia reeled,
Rapped, cast, chimed, darkened and drew down
Cathedral water, and improved.

7

THINKING ABOUT THE SELECTION
Recalling

1. (a) Whom does the poet meet in the stream? (b) How does this person respond when the speaker begins playing the guitar? (c) What do the two people find they have in common?
2. (a) What are the weather conditions in the poem? (b) How does the speaker think the weather conditions will affect his guitar?

Interpreting

3. To what two senses do most of the images, or word pictures, in the poem appeal? Find examples to support your answer.
4. (a) What do the speaker's actions in the poem suggest about his state of mind? (b) What details in the poem indicate that his war experiences have had a powerful effect on him?
5. This poem is set in Winchester, England, the location of a famous cathedral, which the speaker refers to in the poem. (a) What is the relationship between the cathedral and the speaker's experiences in the poem? (b) What is the significance of the other places mentioned in the poem?

Applying

6. Why do you think music often reminds us of past experiences?

ANALYZING LITERATURE
Understanding Visual Poetry

Visual poetry refers to poems in which the letters, words, lines, and spaces are arranged to form a shape or create a visual effect. Often the shape of a visual poem reflects or reinforces the poem's meaning.
1. What is the visual effect of "The Rain Guitar"?
2. How is the visual effect related to the poem's meaning?

THINKING AND WRITING
Writing a Visual Poem

Imagine that you have been asked to write a visual poem for your school literary magazine. Start by choosing a subject for your poem. Then think about how you can shape the poem to reflect its meaning. Prepare a list of images, or word pictures, related to your subject. Then begin writing your poem, arranging the letters, words, and lines to form the appropriate shape. When you finish writing, revise and proofread your poem.

The Rain Guitar 1101

Closure and Extension

ANSWERS TO THINKING ABOUT THE SELECTION
Recalling

1. (a) The speaker meets a fisherman. (b) The person encourages the speaker to play the guitar. (c) The two men were both in the Air Force.

2. (a) It is raining rather heavily throughout the poem. (b) The speaker once heard that moisture will improve the guitar, but realizes this may be incorrect.

Interpreting

3. The images appeal mostly to the senses of hearing and touch. Examples include, "Hammered like Georgia railroad track" and "My sweater collapsed, and the rain reached / My underwear."

Motivation/Prior Knowledge
Have the students imagine that they are the personification of such vehicles as a truck, a BMW, an Alfa Romeo, a station wagon, or a Volkswagon van. How would each view the other? What kind of world view might each have?

Master Teacher Note To set the mood for the poem, place Transparency 20, *Urban Freeways* by Wayne Thiebaud, on the overhead projector. What impression of contemporary society does the painting convey? What does the painting suggest about the role of highways in contemporary life?

Literary Focus What other visual form could the poet have used for this poem? Take any word or line, and see how, if it were placed elsewhere, the poem would change. What is the relationship of form to content?

1 **Enrichment** The Merritt Parkway runs from New Haven, Connecticut, to Connecticut's border with New York State, where the road becomes the Hutchinson River Parkway. It is a landscaped thoroughfare that was originally conceived by Frederick Law Olmstead to harmoniously combine a roadway with the beauty of a park.

Reader's Response What associations does this poem call to mind? Explain.

Merritt Parkway

Denise Levertov

As if it were
forever that they move, that we
keep moving—

> Under a wan sky where
> 5   as the lights went on a star
>   pierced the haze & now
> follows steadily
>   a constant
> above our six lanes
> 10   the dreamlike continuum . . .

And the people—ourselves!
  the humans from inside the
cars apparent
only at gasoline stops
15   unsure,
  eyeing each other

      drink coffee hastily at the
    slot machines & hurry
back to the cars
20   vanish
  into them forever, to
  keep moving—

Houses now & then beyond the
sealed road, the trees / trees, bushes
25 passing by, passing
    the cars that
      keep moving ahead of
us, past us, pressing behind us
        and
30   over left, those that come
    toward us shining too brightly
moving relentlessly

    in six lanes, gliding
north & south, speeding with
35 a slurred sound—

1. The poem describes moving in a car, down a parkway, stopping only at gas stations.

Interpreting

2. Moving traffic may seem like a "dreamlike continuum" because it is never ending; the driver or riders may view the continuously moving cars in almost a hypnotic or trancelike fashion.
3. Lines 11-22 portray people as isolated and suspicious, more in touch with machines than with each other, rushing into their cars to get away from others.
4. The parkway is sealed from the houses and trees perhaps by a retaining wall, a fence, or a sound barrier, much like the subconscious is sealed in a dream from reality.
5. People are seen here as alienated from their neighbors and isolated in their pursuit of living.
6. The poem is shaped to resemble the flow of traffic moving along the highway.

Applying

7. Suggested Response: Students may say they have a more positive impression of highway travel, because they often pass through beautiful landscapes while traveling on a highway.

Challenge How might the speaker respond if there were an accident on the highway?

THINKING ABOUT THE SELECTION

Recalling

1. What experience does this poem describe?

Interpreting

2. Why might moving traffic seem like a "dreamlike continuum"?
3. How do the details in lines 11–22 suggest that the people feel more comfortable in their cars than with other people?
4. In what sense is the road "sealed"?

5. In this poem Levertov uses highway travel as a metaphor for how people travel through life. Considering this fact, what does the poem suggest about the nature of people's lives in modern society?
6. How does the shape of "Merritt Parkway" reinforce its meaning?

Applying

7. How do the impressions of highway travel presented in the poem compare with your own impressions?

Merritt Parkway 1103

More About the Authors
Gwendolyn Brooks's career can be divided into two distinct periods. Her earlier works provide portraits of unheroic blacks who fled the rural South to become the northern urban poor. They are depictions of people whose lives were filled with grief and pain. Her later works are characterized by her emerging awareness of the problems of color and justice. Ask students to discuss how poetry can express the aspirations and frustrations of disenfranchised people. Is "The Explorer" necessarily a black poem or does it have universal application?

Elizabeth Bishop's poetry is tightly constructed, stark verse that is sometimes witty. Her poetry has been influenced by her experiences growing up in New England and her love of the tropics. She spent much of her adult life traveling and living in Brazil. What would be the similarities and differences in outlook that would come from living in Boston, Massachusetts, and in Rio de Janeiro, Brazil?

Critical Evaluation In his book *A History of Modern Poetry: Modernism and After,* the literary scholar David Perkins comments that Elizabeth Bishop's "work is brilliantly varied, and particular poems unify opposite qualities. She is plain, witty, realistic, imaginative, objective, dreamlike, idyllic, pessimistic, associative, intellectual, and extremely averse to making generalizations. Her assessment of life and its possibilities is clear-eyed to the utmost degree, both in general and on every particular occasion. Her mind is troubled, open, and exploratory."

BIOGRAPHIES

Gwendolyn Brooks (1917–   )

In 1950 Gwendolyn Brooks became the first black writer to win a Pulitzer Prize, receiving the award for her second collection of poetry, *Annie Allen* (1949). Since that time, Brooks's reputation as a writer has steadily grown, and she has become one of the most highly regarded poets of our time.

Brooks was born in Topeka, Kansas, and was raised in a section of Chicago known as "Bronzeville." This area provided her with the setting for her first book of poems, *A Street in Bronzeville* (1945). In this collection and in her other early works, Brooks focused on the suffering of city blacks, whom she saw as uprooted, often abused, untrained, and unable to compete for a living. In her later works, after having, as she put it, "rediscovered her blackness," she became more outspoken, openly expressing her support for the black movement.

Ms. Brooks's own early life differed from the lives of the poor speakers in her poems. Her home was warm and her parents loving and supportive. Of her childhood she recalls, "I loved poetry very early and began to put rhymes together at about seven, at which time my parents expressed most earnest confidence that I would one day be a writer."

Elizabeth Bishop (1911–1980)

Elizabeth Bishop's poetry reflects the influence of the work of Marianne Moore. Like Moore, Bishop is known mainly for her meticulously detailed descriptions of nature and her interest in discovering meaning in ordinary observations.

Bishop was born in Worcester, Massachusetts, and was educated at Vassar College. Following her graduation, she traveled extensively outside the United States, residing in Brazil for a number of years. Bishop's travels provided her with inspiration for many of her poems.

Bishop never confused the natural with the primitive or the elegant with the mannered; she showed the world through a truthful eye, without offering easy philosophical explanations. The critic Ann Stevenson said of her, "The best thing that can be said of her philosophy is that it is not philosophy at all but instinctive awareness." In her work she never told half-truths.

Although she published relatively few collections of poetry during her lifetime, Bishop received many honors and awards. Her awards include the 1956 Pulitzer Prize for *Poems: North and South—A Cold Spring* and the 1969 National Book Award for *Complete Poems.*

Objectives
1 To appreciate word origins
2 To understand rhythm
3 To respond to criticism

Support Material

Teaching Portfolio
Teacher Backup, p. 1489
Usage and Mechanics Worksheet, p. 1493
Vocabulary Check, p. 1494
Analyzing Literature Worksheet, *Understanding Rhythm,* p. 1495
Language Worksheet, *Understanding Word Origins,* p. 1496
Selection Test, p. 1497

GUIDE FOR INTERPRETING

Writer's Techniques

The Explorer;
Little Exercise; House Guest

Rhythm. Rhythm is the arrangement of stressed and unstressed syllables in a poem. In poems with a regular rhythm, or meter, the arrangement of stressed and unstressed syllables forms a recurring pattern. However, poets usually introduce slight variations in the metrical pattern to avoid monotony or emphasize important words. Poets will also introduce pauses within lines to interrupt the regular rhythm. These pauses, called caesuras, are usually created by punctuation, though they may also be created by the meanings of words or the natural rhythms of language.

Another way poets can vary a regular rhythm is through the use of run-on lines. Unlike end-stopped lines, which end with a pause, run-on lines flow naturally into the next line. For example, in House Guest," line 1 ("The sad seamstress") flows into line 2 ("who stays with us this month").

Commentary

As you read the following poems by Gwendolyn Brooks and Elizabeth Bishop, notice that people approach life in different ways. In "The Explorer," the speaker notes "choices," and the reader harbors the hope that his or her life will change for the better if he or she finds and makes the right ones. In "Little Exercise," the speaker challenges the reader to "think" or, more accurately, to imagine. Various pictures come alive through visions beyond the things themselves. In both poems the speaker and the reader entertain human possibilities that are realizable through active minds.

In "House Guest" the reader's attention is focused on the helpless, hopeless seamstress. "No hope," she says when asked, "Can you adjust the TV?" Unlike the speakers in the other poems, she does not feel it will be possible to "adjust" life through choice or thought. She sees only one thwarted opportunity. By using the distasteful seamstress, the poet awakens opposition to her viewpoint in the reader. The reader will not choose to be like the seamstress and may feel she is wrong to give up. In the last third of the poem, the speaker becomes an active character with whom the reader can identify. She poses questions about "our lives," but she does not answer them, allowing the reader full possibilities of thinking and choosing for himself or herself. How do you answer the questions she poses?

Writing

In "Little Exercise" Elizabeth Bishop describes the arrival and passage of a thunderstorm as a sequence of scenes. Think of a similar natural event, such as a snowstorm or a landslide. Then describe the stages of this event in a sequence of scenes.

Guide for Interpreting 1105

Literary Focus Rhythm is difficult to define. It is evident in the flow of the seasons; it is as natural as breathing. One can only give examples of it and categorize the varieties of rhythm, yet it is what is the unique and resplendent make-up of each poem. The word *rhythm* comes from the Greek word meaning "flow." In poetry, both the meter and the pauses contribute to how the poem reads or flows.

Writing/Prior Knowledge Your **less advanced** students, as well as those who are strong visual learners, may benefit from storyboarding this activity. Have the students draw the sequence of events as if it were to be filmed. Then have them outline each step in the sequence from the calm before the storm to the storm, and then the aftermath.

Vocabulary

Preteach the following vocabulary words:
din (din) *n.*: Loud, continuous noise or clamor (p. 1106, l.3)
wily (wī′ lē) *adj.*: Sly; cunning (p. 1106, l.5)

Have students share their likes and dislikes about living in the city or the country. What are the advantages and benefits of living in either the city or the country? What are the forces of nature that one must contend with in the country? What stresses result from the urban condition?

Master Teacher Note Display photographs and paintings that capture both the urban and rural landscape. Particularly appropriate are the photographs of Ansel Adams's Southwest and the portraits of Margaret Bourke-White, Gordon Parks, and Diane Arbus.

1 Literary Focus If these were end-stopped lines, how would it affect the impact of the poem?

2 Discussion What could be the setting of this poem?

3 Clarification A *bourn* is "a stream or rivulet."

Closure and Extension

ANSWERS TO THINKING ABOUT THE SELECTION
Recalling

1. "He kept hunting through the din" for a "still spot in the noise."
2. Behind "throbbing knobs" he finds "only spiraling, high human voices, the scream of nervous affairs, wee griefs, grand griefs. And choices."

Interpreting

3. Most of the images appeal to the sense of hearing. Examples include: "room of wily hush," "spiraling, high human voices," and "the scream of nervous affairs."
4. (a) The person lives in a crowded and chaotic place. (b) The home represents the person's life, and the rooms represent his choices in life. (c) The experiences symbolize the person's inability to find solace, the limitations of the

1106

The Explorer
Gwendolyn Brooks

Somehow to find a still spot in the noise
Was the frayed inner want, the winding, the frayed hope
Whose tatters he kept hunting through the din.
A satin peace somewhere.
5   A room of wily hush somewhere within.

 ⎤
 ⎦ 1

So tipping down the scrambled halls he set
Vague hands on throbbing knobs. There were behind
Only spiraling, high human voices,
The scream of nervous affairs,
10   Wee griefs,
Grand griefs. And choices.

 ⎤
 ⎦ 2

He feared most of all the choices, that cried to be taken.

There were no bourns.
There were no quiet rooms.

 ⎤
 ⎦ 3

THINKING ABOUT THE SELECTION
Recalling

1. What does "he" keep "hunting through the din"?
2. In the second stanza, what does "he" find behind the "throbbing knobs"?

Interpreting

3. To which sense do most of the images in this poem appeal? Find three examples to support your answer.
4. (a) What do the details indicate about the place in which the poem's subject lives? (b) What does this person's home symbolize, or represent? (c) What do his experiences in the poem symbolize?
5. (a) Why does the subject fear choices "most of all"? (b) What conclusions does he reach in the final two lines?

Applying

6. Why do you think people often fear having to make choices?

UNDERSTANDING LANGUAGE
Understanding Word Origins

Many words came into the English Language through Latin. For example, in "The Explorer" Brooks uses the word *vague,* which comes from the Latin word *vagus,* meaning "wandering."

The following words are of Latin origin. Use your dictionary to find the meaning of each word. Then give the Latin word and meaning from which it comes.

1. salute
2. incubate
3. opinion
4. communion
5. transmit

1106   Contemporary Writers

choices with which he is presented, and his difficulty in making these choices.
5. (a) The subject fears choices because his choices seem limited and he is unsure of the direction that he should follow. (b) In the final two lines, he realizes that he will never be able to find the solace for which he has been searching.

Applying

6. Suggested Response: People are

afraid they will not be happy with the results of their decision.

Challenge Does this poem have an urban or rural sensitivity to it? Support your answer.

ANSWERS TO UNDERSTANDING LANGUAGE

1. salute: To greet; from *salus,* meaning "health, safety, greeting."

2. incubate: To maintain under conditions favorable to hatching or development; from *incubatus,* meaning "to lie on."
3. opinion: A view, judgment, or appraisal; from *opinio,* meaning "belief."
4. communion: An act or instance of sharing; from *communio,* meaning "fellowship; mutual participation."
5. transmit: To send; from *transmittere,* meaning "to send across."

THE UNEXPECTED ANSWER
René Magritte
Patrimoine des Musees Royaux des Beaux-Arts

The Explorer 1107

Fine art, *The Unexpected Answer,* 1933, by René Magritte. René Magritte (1898-1967), a Belgian Surrealist painter, studied art at the Academie des Beaux Arts in Brussels and subsequently in Paris where he met avant garde intellectuals and artists. It was through their influence that he was attracted to Surrealism, a style of painting in which ordinary objects are made to appear fantastic or bizarre through unnatural juxtapositions or strange contexts.

The Unexpected Answer shows an ordinary door that is rendered bizarre by the neat free-form cutout that shows the darkness beyond. Magritte's aim in this painting was to emphasize the function of the door as an opening. That opening allows the night into the picture plane. This odd use of reality creates a mood of mystery and tends to disorient the viewer in a deliberate and intellectual way.

You might use the following questions for discussion.
1. What is your response to this painting?
2. How does this painting relate to lines 5 and 15 in "The Explorer"?

GREAT FLORIDA SUNSET, 1887
Martin Johnson Heade
Private Collection USA

Little Exercise

Elizabeth Bishop

Think of the storm roaming the sky uneasily
like a dog looking for a place to sleep in,
listen to it growling.

Think how they must look now, the mangrove[1] keys
5   lying out there unresponsive to the lightning
in dark, coarse-fibred families,

where occasionally a heron[2] may undo his head,
shake up his feathers, make an uncertain comment
when the surrounding water shines.

1

---

1. mangrove: A tropical tree with branches that spread and send down roots, forming new trunks and causing a thick growth over a large area.
2. heron (her′ ən) *n.*: A wading bird with a long neck, long legs, and a long, tapered bill.

10 Think of the boulevard and the little palm trees
all stuck in rows, suddenly revealed
as fistfuls of limp fish-skeletons.

It is raining there. The boulevard
and its broken sidewalks with weeds in every crack
15 are relieved to be wet, the sea to be freshened.

Now the storm goes away again in a series
of small, badly lit battle-scenes,
each in "Another part of the field."[3]

2

Think of someone sleeping in the bottom of a rowboat
20 tied to a mangrove root or the pile of a bridge;
think of him as uninjured, barely disturbed.

3

_____
3. "Another . . . field": A stage direction used to designate different
parts of a battlefield in several of William Shakespeare's plays.

THINKING ABOUT THE SELECTION

Recalling

1. To what does the speaker compare the storm
in the first stanza?
2. What happens occasionally in the mangrove
keys?
3. How does the "boulevard and its broken
sidewalks" respond to the rain?
4. What does the speaker describe in the final
stanza?

Interpreting

5. What details indicate that the poem is set in
a tropical environment?

6. In what way is the speaker's description of
the storm similar to a play?
7. Considering the way in which the storm is described in the first six stanzas, what is ironic,
or surprising, about the scene described in
the final stanza?
8. How does the title relate to the poem?

Applying

9. How does the speaker's vision of a thunderstorm compare with your own image of a
thunderstorm?

Little Exercise   1109

Closure and Extension

ANSWERS TO THINKING ABOUT THE SELECTION
Recalling

1. The storm is compared to a growling dog as it looks for a place to
sleep.
2. Occasionally, a heron may respond to the lightning by moving
its head and shaking its feathers.
3. The "boulevard and its broken
sidewalks" are "relieved to be
wet."
4. The last stanza describes a man
sleeping in a boat, unharmed and
undisturbed.

Interpreting

5. The tropical environment is indicated by the setting in the mangrove keys, and by the references
to herons, palm trees, and the
sea.
6. The storm is described in a sequence of separate scenes.
7. The storm is described as being
loud and violent, yet the main
stanza has barely been disturbed
by it.
8. The poem is an exercise of the
imagination, with the speaker asking us to imagine the various
stages of a storm.

Applying

9. Suggested Response: Students
might comment that the speaker's
reference to the storm as a series
of battle scenes corresponds with
their own impressions of thunderstorms.

_1109_

Motivation/Prior Knowledge
Have the students imagine that they are host to a house guest whom they hardly know. They feel they are responsible for entertaining the guest; however, the guest is unresponsive. Each time they suggest an activity—going to a sporting event, going dancing, going out to eat, going to a movie—the guest responds with only mild interest. How would they begin to feel toward that guest? What would be their attitude about having that person around?

1 Discussion What kind of household would have a seamstress staying with them?

2 Discussion What does the speaker reveal about her attitude towards the seamstress?

3 Discussion From lines 1-3 and lines 36-38 we get a portrait of the seamstress. What does she look like?

4 Clarification A *nun* is "a woman who belongs to a religious order that requires her to take solemn vows of poverty, chastity, and obedience." What might be the motivation for a woman, who has been thwarted in her attempt to enter a convent, to be as despondent as the seamstress?

5 Enrichment The Fates were three stern and gloomy goddesses who ruled people's lives. Clotho was the spinner of the thread, Lachesis decided how long it was to be, and Atropos cut the thread. What kind of metaphor for life is meant by depicting fate as these three goddesses? How does Elizabeth Bishop use this metaphor to serve her poetic purpose?

House Guest

Elizabeth Bishop

The sad seamstress
who stays with us this month
is small and thin and bitter.
No one can cheer her up.
5 Give her a dress, a drink,
roast chicken, or fried fish—
it's all the same to her.

She sits and watches TV.
No, she watches zigzags.
10 "Can you adjust the TV?"
"No," she says. No hope.
She watches on and on,
without hope, without air.

Her own clothes give us pause,
15 but she's not a poor orphan.
She has a father, a mother,
and all that, and she's earning
quite well, and we're stuffing
her with fattening foods.

20 We invite her to use the binoculars.
We say, "Come see the jets!"
We say, "Come see the baby!"
Or the knife grinder who cleverly
plays the National Anthem
25 on his wheel so shrilly.
Nothing helps.

She speaks: "I need a little
money to buy buttons."
She seems to think it's useless
30 to ask. Heavens, buy buttons,

if they'll do any good,
the biggest in the world—
by the dozen, by the gross!
Buy yourself an ice cream,
35 a comic book, a car!

Her face is closed as a nut;
closed as a careful snail
or a thousand-year-old seed.
Does she dream of marriage?
40 Of getting rich? Her sewing
is decidedly mediocre.

Please! Take our money! Smile!
What on earth have we done?
What has everyone done
45 and when did it all begin?
Then one day she confides
that she wanted to be a nun
and her family opposed her.

Perhaps we should let her go,
50 or deliver her straight off
to the nearest convent—and wasn't
her month up last week, anyway?

Can it be that we nourish
one of the Fates in our bosoms?
55 Clotho, sewing our lives
with a bony little foot
on a borrowed sewing machine,
and our fates will be like hers,
and our hems crooked forever?

Reader's Response What is your attitude toward the seamstress? Do you find her to be a sympathetic character? Why or why not?

THINKING ABOUT THE SELECTION

Recalling

1. (a) How does the speaker describe the seamstress's appearance? (b) How do the speaker and her family respond to the seamstress's clothes?
2. (a) For what does the seamstress ask? (b) How does the family respond?
3. (a) What does the seamstress reveal to the family in the seventh stanza? (b) What responses does the speaker contemplate in the eighth stanza?

Interpreting

4. (a) What do the seamstress's actions reveal about her personality? (b) What do the descriptions of her appearance reveal about her personality?
5. (a) What is the speaker's attitude toward the seamstress? (b) How is this attitude conveyed? (c) How does the speaker's attitude change after the seamstress confides in her and her family?

Applying

6. In this poem the seamstress has a strong negative reaction to her inability to fulfill her goal in life. Do you think that most people would respond as negatively as the seamstress does if they were unable to achieve their goals in life? Why or why not?

ANALYZING LITERATURE

Understanding Rhythm

Rhythm is the arrangement of stressed and unstressed syllables in a poem. Poets vary the regular rhythm of a poem in a number of ways. Often poets interrupt the regular rhythm by introducing pauses, or caesuras, within the lines. Another way poets vary rhythm is by using run-on lines—lines that flow naturally into the next line.

1. Find two caesuras in "House Guest."
2. Find two run-on lines in the poem.

THINKING AND WRITING

Responding to Criticism

Critic Candace Stalter has commented that Elizabeth Bishop's "poetry reveals more diffuse sympathy for the oppressed than definite anger at the oppressor." Write an essay in which you discuss this comment in relation to "House Guest." Reread the poem, focusing on the attitude it expresses concerning the seamstress and her unhappiness. When you write your essay, use passages from the poem to support your argument. When you finish writing, revise and proofread your essay.

House Guest   1111

3. (a) She reveals that she wanted to become a nun but her family opposed her. (b) The speaker considers delivering the seamstress to a convent, since the seamstress's month of work has been completed.

Interpreting

4. (a) The seamstress is very unhappy with her life. She has no hope for the future. She has no goals, no desires, no cares. She is simply bearing her unfulfilling life. (b) The descriptions of her appearance reveal that she is a bitter person who is unwilling to share her feelings with others.
5. (a) The speaker is extremely bothered by the seamstress's sad disposition, and she becomes impatient and almost angry with her. (b) Her attitude is conveyed through her descriptions of the seamstress's appearance and behavior, and in the way she describes her family's responses to the seamstress. (c) At the end of the poem, the speaker begins to pity all of humankind, for we are all, in ways, like the seamstress.

Applying

6. Suggested Response: No, most people would seek other means of achieving happiness.

Challenge How do you think the seamstress feels about the speaker?

ANSWERS TO ANALYZING LITERATURE

1. Suggested Response: Caesuras occur in line 40 after "getting rich?" and in line 51 after "nearest convent."
2. Run-on lines occur in lines 1-3 and in lines 23-25.

THINKING AND WRITING

For help with this assignment, students can refer to Lesson 15, "Evaluating a Literary Work," in the Handbook of Writing About Literature.

After students have completed the assignment, divide them into groups and have them read their rough drafts to each other and suggest ways in which they could be improved.

ANSWERS TO THINKING ABOUT THE SELECTION

Recalling

1. (a) She describes her as small, thin, and bitter. (b) Her clothes "give them pause."
2. (a) She asks for money to buy buttons. (b) They respond that they will do anything that might change her disposition.

More About the Authors Robert Lowell is considered one of the most influential American poets of this century. His poetry is disarmingly open and filled with a deep emotional energy. What kind of life might we expect from someone so compelled to write such profound confessional poetry?

Robert Lowell has said that Randall Jarrell is "monstrously knowing and monstrously innocent—one does not know just where to find him . . . a Wordsworth with the obsessions of Lewis Carroll." Discuss with the students the works of Wordsworth and Lewis Carroll. What does Robert Lowell mean by his characterization of Jarrell?

Critical Evaluation In his book *A History of Modern Poetry: Modernism and After,* the literary scholar David Perkins briefly discusses Randall Jarrell's war experiences and the poetry they shaped. He writes: "At the air base [Jarrell] listened to the stories of pilots and read newspaper war reports, and out of these materials he composed, in *Little Friend, Little Friend* (1945) and *Losses* (1948), what remain for many readers the finest 'war' poems of our time. They are vivid and moving incidents of combat, told with an exceptionally sensitive psychological insight and moral perplexity. And the emotions of Jarrell's pilots were in some ways unfamiliar in the literature of modern war . . . in his pilots Jarrell expressed the feelings of alienation, helplessness, regression, irresponsibility, and vulnerability that our vastly unmanageable, bureaucratic, technological civilization seems to create."

Robert Lowell (1917–1977)

Robert Lowell was a member of one of the country's oldest and most prominent families. His ancestors included two noted American poets, James Russell Lowell and Amy Lowell. Considering his background, it is not surprising that he was one of the most history-conscious and influential poets of his time.

Born in Boston, Lowell attended Harvard University for two years, then transferred to Kenyon College in Ohio, where he studied poetry under John Crowe Ransom. Lowell earned widespread recognition early in his career as a poet, winning a Pulitzer Prize for his collection *Lord Weary's Castle.* In the poems in this book and in those in his other early collections, Lowell relied on traditional poetic forms and techniques. During the late 1950's, however, Lowell abandoned his early style and began writing freer, more direct poems. This change first became evident when he published *Life Studies* (1959), a collection of confessional poems—poems in which Lowell openly and frankly explored his own personal life. The book had a tremendous impact on the literary world, giving rise to a school of confessional poets that included Sylvia Plath, John Berryman, and Anne Sexton.

Randall Jarrell (1914–1965)

Randall Jarrell was a talented poet, literary critic, and teacher. His poetry was praised by both writers and critics, including Robert Lowell, who called Jarrell "the most heartbreaking English poet of his day"; and his literary essays, many of which appear in his book *Poetry and the Age* (1953), have been credited with altering the dominant critical trends and tastes of his time.

Jarrell was born and raised in New Orleans, Louisiana. After graduating from Vanderbilt University, he became a teacher, a profession to which he remained dedicated for the rest of his life. During World War II, he served in the United States Air Force. His war experiences provided him with the material for the poems in his book, *Losses* (1948). Many of his other poems, including those in *The Seven League Crutches* (1951) and *The Lost World* (1965), focus on childhood and the sense of innocence with which it is associated. In contrast, the poems in *The Woman at the Washington Zoo* (1960) reflect Jarrell's concern with aging and loneliness.

1112 Contemporary Writers

Objectives

1 To appreciate precise words
2 To understand theme
3 To write about a writer's attitudes

Support Material

Teaching Portfolio
Teacher Backup, p. 1501
Usage and Mechanics Worksheet, p. 1506
Vocabulary Check, p. 1507
Analyzing Literature Worksheet, *Understanding Theme,* p. 1508
Language Worksheet, *Appreciating Precise Words,* p. 1509
Selection Test, p. 1510

GUIDE FOR INTERPRETING

Hawthorne; The Death of the Ball Turret Gunner; Losses

Writer's Techniques

Theme. The theme is the central idea or insight about life that a writer hopes to convey in a work of literature. In some literary works, the theme is stated directly. More often, however, the theme is implied, or revealed indirectly. When interpreting an implied theme, it is important to pay close attention to the writer's choice of details, portrayal of characters and events, and use of literary devices.

Commentary

War and poetry have gone hand in hand as long as men have fought and written. As you read Randall Jarrell's affecting poems, "The Death of the Ball Turret Gunner" and "Losses," notice that they follow the tradition. Jarrell's poems echo the themes of sensitive men who have fought before him. British poets Wilfred Owen and Siegfried Sassoon met and fought in The War to End All Wars, World War I, and saw their generation transformed by trench warfare and nerve-damaging mustard gas. Owen said, "My subject is War, and the pity of War. The Poetry is in the pity." His poetry became a monument to war's futility and waste. Passionately dedicated to humanity and to life, both Sassoon and Owen felt they must understand battle in order to subdue it. They met briefly in a hospital for nervous disorders, fellow casualties of war. Sassoon, the established poet, encouraged young Owen to hone his sensitive poetic gifts and continue to illuminate the horror of young lives wasted to "the Cause," which grew more indistinct as the death tolls steadily climbed. Owen returned to the front to prove his courage under fire so that his protesting poetry would not seem mere cowardice, feeling he must win medals to throw them away. He wrote to Sassoon but did not meet him again. Wilfred Owen was killed just before the war ended.

The cause of Owen and Sassoon and so many other poets who deplored the wasting of young life in war was taken up by Jarrell in World War II, the war that Owen and Sassoon's war was to prevent. Do you feel war poetry serves a purpose?

Writing

"The Death of the Ball Turret Gunner" and "Losses" were inspired by Randall Jarrell's experiences in the United States Air Force. Why do you think writers often use war as a subject for their writing? Freewrite about the reasons why war is such a common literary subject.

Motivation/Prior Knowledge
Have students imagine that they are going to visit the former home of a historical figure whom they greatly admire. What would they expect to find? For what would they look? How would their feelings about the person affect their impressions of his or her former home?

Master Teacher Note This poem alludes to the Salem of Nathaniel Hawthorne (1804-64), the renowned American novelist and short story writer. His novels *The Scarlet Letter* and *The House of the Seven Gables* were written while he lived in Salem, Massachusetts, which was a world-famous port city from its earliest colonial days. Its infamous history includes the witchcraft of the seventeenth century. Hawthorne's fiction provides lively descriptions of Salem. Have your **more advanced** students prepare a literary history of Salem, basing their research on these novels. Supplement these oral reports with maps and pictures of historical Salem, which are available from the Salem Tourism Association, Salem, Massachusetts 01965.

Thematic Idea Another poem in which the writer expresses admiration for an earlier writer is "Douglass" by Paul Lawrence Dunbar (p. 430).

Purpose-Setting Question
What is the reason for Lowell's admiration of Hawthorne?

Hawthorne

Robert Lowell

Follow its lazy main street lounging
from the alms house to Gallows Hill[1]
along a flat, unvaried surface
covered with wooden houses
5   aged by yellow drain
like the unhealthy hair of an old dog.
You'll walk to no purpose
in Hawthorne's Salem.

I cannot resilver the smudged plate.[2]

---

1. Gallows Hill: A hill in Salem, Massachusetts, where nineteen people who were accused of practicing witchcraft were hanged.
2. resilver . . . plate: Early photographs were taken on a metal plate coated with silver.

CROWNINSHIELD'S WHARF. AROUND THE
WHARF ARE THE VESSELS AMERICA, FAME,
PRUDENT, AND BELISAURIUS
George Ropes
Peabody Museum of Salem

10

I drop to Hawthorne, the customs officer,[3]
measuring coal and mostly trying to keep warm—
to the stunted black schooner,
the dismal South-end dock,
the wharf-piles with their fungus of ice.

15 On State Street[4]
a steeple with a glowing dial-clock
measures the weary hours,
the merciless march of professional feet.

Even this shy distrustful ego
20 sometimes walked on top of the blazing roof,
and felt those flashes
that char the discharged cells of the brain.

Look at the faces—
Longfellow, Lowell, Holmes and Whittier!

---

3. customs officer: Hawthorne worked as a customs officer in Salem.
4. State Street: A street in the business district of Boston.

1
2

1 Discussion Is the poet speaking about Hawthorne or might he also be speaking about himself?

2 Clarification Henry Wadsworth Longfellow (1807-82), James Russell Lowell (1819-91), Oliver Wendell Holmes (1809-94), and John Greenleaf Whittier (1807-92), all writers and contemporaries of Hawthorne, wrote popular verse that many now consider overly sentimental. These writers stand in contrast to Hawthorne, whose work is thought of as psychologically dark. Robert Lowell's confessional poetry has also been characterized as being dark and brooding.

Humanities Note

Fine art, *Crowninshield's Wharf*, 1805, by George Ropes. The American painter George Ropes (1788-1819) was the son of a Salem, Massachusetts, sea captain. He was taught to paint by an expatriate French marine artist, Michel Corne. Painting locally, George Ropes captured the port life of Salem during that town's most active years.

The seamen of Salem were proud of their port and the prosperity of the American shipping trade. They hired artists, such as George Ropes, to paint their town, ships, and harbor for proud display in their homes. *Crowninshield's Wharf* was commissioned by George Crowninshield, Sr. This panoramic view of the prosperous wharf lined with world trade ships includes the historic pepper trader *America* at the outer end. American flags proudly fly from warehouses and shipmasts. Dockside, men and horses bustle about their business. Ropes chose an unusual format—long and thin—for this painting. The treatment is formalized but pleasantly rendered in earthtones and blues.

This scene slightly predates the time when Hawthorne was the customs officer in Salem. Nevertheless, the bustling atmosphere of the wharf would have been similar in Hawthorne's time.

Consider using these questions for discussion:
1. What does this scene suggest about Salem?
2. What does Lowell suggest about Hawthorne's relationship with this Salem?

3 **Discussion** What might be one of the many things that Hawthorne and/or Robert Lowell learned from their meditation on the true and insignificant?

Reader's Response Based on the way in which Lowell depicts him, does Hawthorne seem like someone you would have liked to have met? Why or why not?

25 Study the grizzled silver of their beards.
Hawthorne's picture,
however, has a blond mustache
and golden General Custer[5] scalp.
He looks like a Civil War officer.
30 He shines in the firelight. His hard
survivor's smile is touched with fire.

Leave him alone for a moment or two,
and you'll see him with his head
bent down, brooding, brooding,
35 eyes fixed on some chip,
some stone, some common plant,
the commonest thing,
as if it were the clue.
The disturbed eyes rise,
40 furtive, foiled, dissatisfied
from meditation on the true
and insignificant.

3

---

5. General Custer: George Armstrong Custer (1839–1876), a general who served in the Civil War and was killed along with his troops by the Sioux at the Battle of Little Big Horn, had long blond hair.

Primary Source

Robert Lowell writes of Nathaniel Hawthorne's home. Critic Hyatt H. Waggoner, in his pamphlet *Nathaniel Hawthorne*, has the following to say about Hawthorne, his family, and his Salem:

"When Hawthorne was born in Salem, Massachusetts, in 1804 the town was already very old by American standards. The Hathornes had been there from the beginning. (Hawthorne added the *w* to the family name when he began to sign his stories.) By the 1690's one of them was prominent enough to be a judge in the witchcraft trials. His descendants' remarks on him in "The Custom House" introduction to *The Scarlet Letter* mix pride in his prominence and a sense of inherited guilt for his deeds as judge.

"Hawthorne is being a little whimsical in 'The Custom House,' protectively light in his tone, when he takes the judge's guilt on himself and offers to do penance that the family curse may be removed. But there is an undercurrent of seriousness. Salem is a part of him, for good and for ill. The 'mere sensuous sympathy of dust for dust' is perhaps all that is needed to bind town and man together. . . . Hawthorne admits to being haunted by the figure of the prominent but guilty ancestor who 'was present to my boyish imagination, as far back as I can remember.' . . .

"As he grew up, Hawthorne watched Salem decline. The Embargo of 1807 struck the town a heavy blow, and when the end of the War of 1812 made shipping possible again, Salem did not recover its importance as a seaport. The town was repeating the family history, it seemed. . . ."

THINKING ABOUT THE SELECTION

Recalling

1. With what is the "unvaried surface" of the "lazy main street" in Salem covered?
2. (a) What is Hawthorne doing in lines 10–11? (b) According to lines 19–22, what does the "shy distrustful ego" sometimes do?
3. (a) What does the speaker reveal about the physical appearance of Longfellow, Lowell, Holmes, and Whittier? (b) How does he describe Hawthorne's appearance?
4. According to the final stanza, what will you see if you leave Hawthorne "alone for a moment or two"?

Interpreting

5. (a) What type of impression is conveyed by the description of Salem in the first stanza? (b) How does line 9 relate to the description of Salem?
6. What is the significance of the allusion, or reference, to Gallows Hill?
7. (a) What impression of time is conveyed by the image, or word picture, in lines 15–17? (b) What impression of professional people does the image in line 18 convey?
8. (a) What do lines 19–22 reveal about Hawthorne? (b) What do the descriptions in lines 23–31 imply about the contrasts between Hawthorne's personality and the personalities of some of his literary contemporaries?

9. In the final stanza, what is Hawthorne seeking through his observations of common things?

Applying

10. (a) Why do you think Lowell might have chosen to write this poem? (b) What does the poem reveal about Lowell?
11. Proverb 22:28 reads, "Remove not the ancient landmark, which the fathers have set." (a) In what way has Hawthorne served as a literary landmark for Lowell? (b) Think of your own field of interest. Who would serve as a "landmark" for you? Explain the reasons for your choice.

UNDERSTANDING LANGUAGE

Appreciating Precise Words

The effectiveness of Lowell's poetry results in part from his precise choice of words. Find a synonym for each of the italicized words below. Then explain why the synonyms are less effective than are the words Lowell chose.
1. ". . . along the flat, *unvaried* surface . . ."
2. ". . . the *merciless* march of professional feet."
3. "The *disturbed* eyes rise, furtive, foiled, dissatisfied . . ."
4. ". . . from the meditation on the true and *insignificant*."

charged cells of the brain."
3. (a) They all have grizzled silver beards. (b) Hawthorne has a blond mustache and golden hair, and has a hard survivor's smile.
4. You will see Hawthorne brooding, meditating "on the true and insignificant."

Interpreting

5. (a) Salem seems to be an old, quiet community. (b) Despite its outward peacefulness, Salem's infamous history cannot be erased.
6. It stands as a reminder of Salem's violent history.
7. (a) The image creates the impression that time moves slowly and drearily onward. (b) The image creates the impression that professional people are blindly absorbed in their daily routine and have completely lost their concern for anything else.
8. (a) It reveals that he was shy and distrustful and had sudden flashes of insight. (b) The descriptions imply that the four poets are bland and lack originality, while Hawthorne is strong, energetic, and unique.
9. Hawthorne seeks to find truth in the seemingly insignificant objects of everyday life.

Applying

10. Suggested Responses: (a) Lowell may want to show the differences among the early American poets, and his identification with Hawthorne. (b) Lowell obviously respects, admires, and relates to Hawthorne.
11. (a) Suggested Response: Lowell has learned from Hawthorne's ability to find significance in common objects and events. (b) Answers will differ. Students should choose figures who excelled in their specific fields of interest.

Closure and Extension

ANSWERS TO THINKING ABOUT THE SELECTION
Recalling

1. It is covered with wooden houses.
2. (a) Hawthorne is putting coal in his stove and warming himself near it. (b) The ego walked on top of the blazing roof feeling the "flashes that char the dis-

ANSWERS TO UNDERSTANDING LANGUAGE

Suggested Responses:
1. uniform 2. unyielding
3. puzzled 4. trivial

Enrichment Jarrell described a ball turret as "a plexiglass sphere set into the belly of a B-17 or B-24, and inhabited by two .50 caliber machine guns and one man, a short small man. When this gunner tracked with his machine guns a fighter attacking his bomber from below, he revolved with the turret; hunched upside-down in his little sphere, he looked like a fetus in the womb. The fighters which attacked him were armed with cannons firing explosive shells. The hose was a steam hose."

1118   *Contemporary Writers*

The Death of the Ball Turret Gunner

Randall Jarrell

A ball turret was a small space, enclosed in plexiglass, on the underside of the fuselage of certain World War II bombers, which held a small man and two machine guns. When the bomber was attacked by a plane below, the gunner would fire his guns from an upside-down, hunched-up position.

From my mother's sleep I fell into the State,
And I hunched in its belly till my wet fur froze.
Six miles from earth, loosed from its dream of life,
I woke to black flak¹ and the nightmare fighters.
5   When I died they washed me out of the turret with a hose.

---

1. flak *n.*: Anti-aircraft fire.

THINKING ABOUT THE SELECTION

Recalling

1. (a) From what does the ball turret gunner fall?   (b) To what does he wake?
2. What happens when he dies?

Interpreting

3. (a) To what does the word *State* (line 1) refer?   (b) What does Jarrell mean when he writes that the gunner "fell into the State"?
4. (a) To what does Jarrell compare the ball turret gunner in the first two lines?   (b) How does this comparison add to the impact of the poem?
5. Why might the gunner view life on earth as a "dream" (line 3)?
6. What does the final line reveal about the realities of war?
7. How does the brevity of this poem add to its impact?

Applying

8. Why do you think Jarrell chose to write about a ball turret gunner rather than a pilot or another type of soldier?

The Death of the Ball Turret Gunner   1119

Losses

Randall Jarrell

It was not dying: everybody died.
It was not dying: we had died before
In the routine crashes—and our fields
Called up the papers, wrote home to our folks,
5 And the rates rose, all because of us.
We died on the wrong page of the almanac,
Scattered on mountains fifty miles away;
Diving on haystacks, fighting with a friend,
We blazed up on the lines we never saw.
10 We died like aunts or pets or foreigners.
(When we left high school nothing else had died
For us to figure we had died like.)

In our new planes, with our new crews, we bombed
The ranges by the desert or the shore,
15 Fired at towed targets, waited for our scores—
And turned into replacements and woke up
One morning, over England, operational.
It wasn't different: but if we died
It was not an accident but a mistake
20 (But an easy one for anyone to make).
We read our mail and counted up our missions—
In bombers named for girls, we burned
The cities we had learned about in school—
Till our lives wore out; our bodies lay among
25 The people we had killed and never seen.
When we lasted long enough they gave us medals;
When we died they said, "Our casualties were low."

THINKING ABOUT THE SELECTION

Recalling

1. According to lines 6–9, where do the pilots die?
2. (a) What do the pilots bomb (line 14)? (b) At what do they fire (line 15)? (c) What do they burn (line 23)?
3. (a) What happens when the pilots last "long enough" (line 26)? (b) What happens when they die (line 27)?

Interpreting

4. (a) Do the pilots really think that their missions are not difficult? Support your answer. (b) Do they really think that if they died "it was not an accident but a mistake"? Support your answer. (c) Who might be more likely to express these opinions?
5. What is ironic, or surprising, about the fact that the bombers are named for girls?
6. What is the significance of the fact the pilots never see the people they kill?
7. (a) Who is the *they* referred to in the final line? (b) What does their comment reveal about their attitude toward the pilots?

Applying

8. How is this poem similar to and different from some of the other literary works about war you have read?

ANALYZING LITERATURE

Understanding Theme

The **theme** is the central idea or insight about life that a writer hopes to convey in a work of literature. Most often, a theme is revealed indirectly through the writer's choice of details, portrayal of characters and events, and use of literary devices.

1. What is the theme of "Losses"?
2. What details play an important role in conveying the theme?
3. How does the use of irony also help convey the theme?

THINKING AND WRITING

Writing About a Writer's Attitude

Write an essay in which you discuss what "The Death of the Ball Turret Gunner" and "Losses" reveal about Jarrell's attitude toward war. Reread both poems, focusing on their themes. Create a chart, listing details from both poems that help convey the poet's attitude. Prepare a thesis statement. Then write your essay, using passages from the two poems to support your thesis. When you revise, make sure you have included enough supporting information. Check that you have quoted precisely and have punctuated your quotations accurately. Proofread your essay and share it with your classmates.

takes. (c) A superior officer who does not do the actual fighting might express this opinion.
5. It is ironic because the bombers are instruments of destruction, while the girls are likely to be sensitive and compassionate.
6. It demonstrates the impersonal nature of war.
7. (a) "They" refers to the military establishment. (b) It reveals that they place little value on individual lives and are more concerned with kill ratios.

Applying

8. Suggested Response: The attitude it expresses about war is similar to the attitude conveyed in the poem "An Irish Airman Foresees His Death" by William Butler Yeats.

ANSWERS TO ANALYZING LITERATURE

1. The theme is that war is violent, cruel, and impersonal.
2. Suggested Response: The relevant details include the speaker's comment that they never saw the people they killed and the officers' comment that the casualties were low.
3. Suggested Response: Ironic statements, such as "When we died they said, 'Our casualties were low,'" help to highlight the cruel, impersonal nature of war.

THINKING AND WRITING

For help with this assignment, students can refer to Lesson 11, "Writing About Theme," in the Handbook of Writing About Literature.

Writing Across the Curriculum
For extra credit you might want to have your **more advanced** students research and report on the reaction of Vietnam veterans to their war experience. Inform the history department of this assignment. History teachers might provide guidance for students in conducting their research.

Closure and Extension

ANSWERS TO THINKING ABOUT THE SELECTION

Recalling

1. The pilots die "on the wrong pages of the almanac."
2. (a) They bomb "the ranges by the desert or the shore." (b) They fire at towed targets. (c) They burn the foreign cities they had learned about in school.
3. (a) They receive medals. (b) When they die their superiors say, "Our casualties were low."

Interpreting

4. (a) The pilots think their missions are difficult and dangerous. They fight until their lives wear out. (b) No, because they can be shot down without making any mis-

1122

More About the Authors
José García Villa (Vil'-ah) has stated: "I am not at all interested in description or outward appearance, nor in the contemporary scene, but in essence." What might be the primary poetic concerns of a poet who explores the inner life?

Alice Walker has been a voter registration worker in Georgia, a worker at a Head Start program in Mississippi, and a staff member of the welfare department of New York City. Discuss how this kind of work, as well as Walker's commitment to a black identity, may have shaped the poet's observations. How can a poet's personal life shape his or her poetic vision?

Reed Whittemore is a popular poet whom critics have found skillful and amusing. James Dickey has said that Whittemore is one of his favorites, but that there are "dangerous favorites and inconsequential favorites, and favorites like pleasant disease." Discuss James Dickey's remark with your students. How would they categorize their own favorite poets?

Critical Evaluation Reed Whittemore has enjoyed success as both a poet and a literary critic. In discussing Whittemore's achievements in these two realms, the literary scholar Malcolm Bradbury writes: "A witty and critical commentator both in prose and verse (Whittemore's) criticism has stressed the need for poetry to emphasize its rational elements, and his own work varied as it is in theme, is concerned with the quality and accuracy of the mind."

BIOGRAPHIES

José García Villa (1914–   )

José García Villa's poetry reflects his concern for the individual. In fact, Villa himself has commented that his purpose as a poet is to find "man's selfhood and identity in the mystery of Creation."

Born in the Philippines, Villa came to the United States at the age of sixteen. While an undergraduate at the University of New Mexico, he established a reputation as a short-story writer. He began studying poetry while in college but did not have a collection published in the United States until 1942. This book, *Have Come, Am Here,* was followed by a second collection, *Volume Two,* in 1949. Since then Villa has published several more volumes of poetry and a collection of short stories.

Alice Walker (1944–   )

Although she is known mainly for her fiction, Alice Walker has also written a good deal of poetry. Like her other works, her poems reflect her interest in and respect for the black women of America.

Walker was born into a family of sharecroppers in Georgia. Her first book of poetry, *Once* (1968), was inspired by a trip to Africa in the summer of 1964. After publishing another book of poetry, *Revolutionary Petunias and Other Poems,* Walker focused on writing fiction. Her first novel, *Meridian* (1976), has been praised as one of the finest novels to come out of the civil rights movement; and her third novel, *The Color Purple* (1982), earned her a Pulitzer Prize.

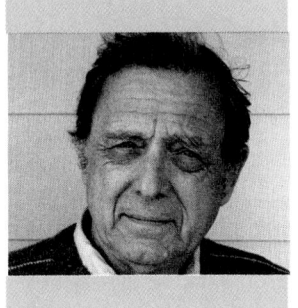

Reed Whittemore (1919–   )

Although Reed Whittemore's poetry is often witty and fanciful, his best poems contain profound observations about contemporary American life.

Born in New Haven, Connecticut, Whittemore attended Yale University. After serving in the United States Army Air Force during World War II, he did graduate work in history at Princeton. While at Princeton, Whittemore published his first book of poetry, *Heroes and Heroines* (1946). Since then he has published many additional poetry collections, several books of essays, and a biography of the poet William Carlos Williams. He has also won numerous awards, including a grant from the National Institute of Arts and a Guggenheim Fellowship.

1 To appreciate lyric poetry
2 To recognize abstract words
3 To compare and contrast poems
4 To analyze the meaning of allusions

Support Material

Teaching Portfolio
Teacher Backup, p. 1513
Usage and Mechanics Worksheet, p. 1518
Vocabulary Check, p. 1519
Analyzing Literature Worksheet, *Understanding Lyric Poetry,* p. 1520
Language Worksheet, *Recognizing Abstract Words,* p. 1521
Selection Test, p. 1522

GUIDE FOR INTERPRETING

Be Beautiful, Noble, Like the Antique Ant; Expect Nothing; Still Life

Literary Forms

Lyric Poetry. A lyric poem expresses the personal thoughts and feelings of the speaker. One of the oldest and most popular forms of poetry, lyrics were originally sung to the accompaniment of a stringed instrument called a lyre. Although lyrics are no longer meant to be sung, they retain a musical quality. Lyrics also tend to be brief and generally focus on producing a single, unified effect.

Writing

In "Be Beautiful, Noble, Like the Antique Ant," José García Villa illustrates the importance of modesty. Freewrite about the value of modesty, exploring the reasons why it is an important virtue.

Primary Source

An unfortunate happenstance of Alice Walker's youth may bear on her poem "Expect Nothing." Here is the incident recounted in *Current Biography Yearbook.*

> In 1952 Alice Walker was accidentally wounded in the eye by a shot from a BB gun fired by one of her brothers. Because they had no access to a car, the Walkers were unable to take their daughter to a hospital for immediate treatment, and when they finally brought her to a doctor a week later, she was permanently blind in that eye. A disfiguring layer of scar tissue formed over it, rendering the previously outgoing child self-conscious and painfully shy. Stared at and sometimes taunted, she felt like an outcast and turned for solace to reading and to poetry writing. Although when she was fourteen the scar tissue was removed—and she subsequently became valedictorian and was voted most popular girl and queen of her senior class—she came to realize that her traumatic injury had had some value: It allowed her to begin 'really to see people and things, really to notice relationships and to learn to be patient enough to care about how they turned out.' Because of the accident, she became eligible for and won a scholarship for handicapped students to attend Spelman College, a black women's college in Atlanta, beginning in 1961. Her neighbors raised the $75 for her bus fare to the state capital.

Motivation/Prior Knowledge
Have the students list virtues such as modesty, charity, and humility. What insects or animals embody these virtues?

Thematic Idea Another poem in which an element of nature is personified is "The Rhodora" by Ralph Waldo Emerson (p. 283).

Purpose-Setting Question
What virtue does Villa have in mind?

Master Teacher Note Discuss with students the fact that contemporary poetry is sometimes difficult or obscure. "Be Beautiful, Noble, Like the Antique Ant" is one such poem. To help students appreciate such poems, you may wish to have students refer to Randall Jarrell's essay "The Obscurity of the Poet" in *Poetry and the Age* (Noonday Press, 1953). In the essay Jarrell says: ". . . when you begin to read a poem, you are entering a foreign country whose laws and language and life are a kind of translation of your own. . . ." Discuss the meaning of this statement. Why is reading contemporary poetry like traveling to a foreign country? Encourage students to talk about the difficulties and rewards of reading poetry.

1 **Clarification** This poem is written in the imperative voice, the grammatical voice that expresses the will to influence. What does the poet achieve by using this voice?

2 **Discussion** Why does the poet use the word "antique" instead of "ancient" or "surviving"?

3 **Discussion** How do the archbishop and soldier dress?

4 **Discussion** Lines 15-20 display internal and end rhyme. How does this contribute to the lyrical quality of the poem?

Be Beautiful, Noble, Like the Antique Ant

José García Villa

Be beautiful, noble, like the antique ant,
Who bore the storms as he bore the sun,
Wearing neither gown nor helmet,
Though he was archbishop and soldier:
5 Wore only his own flesh.

Salute characters with gracious dignity:
Though what these are is left to
Your own terms. Exact: the universe is
Not so small but these will be found
10 Somewhere. Exact: they will be found.

Speak with great moderation: but think
With great fierceness, burning passion:
Though what the ant thought
No annals reveal, nor his descendants
15 Break the seal.

Trace the tracelessness of the ant,
Every ant has reached this perfection.
As he comes, so he goes,
Flowing as water flows,
20 Essential but secret like a rose.

Reader's Response Which animal or insect do you most admire? Why?

THINKING ABOUT THE SELECTION

Recalling

1. What advice does the speaker give at the beginning of each stanza?
2. According to the final stanza, what "perfection" has the ant reached?

Interpreting

3. (a) In what sense can an ant be thought of as "antique"? (b) In what sense is an ant like an "archbishop"? (c) In what sense is an ant like a "soldier"?

4. What does the speaker mean when he refers to the "tracelessness of the ant"?
5. In what sense is a rose "essential but secret"?
6. (a) What human virtue does the speaker attribute to the ant? (b) What does he feel that people can learn from ants?

Applying

7. What other human virtues might be attributed to ants?
8. From what other insects or animals do you think people might learn? Explain your answer.

Be Beautiful, Noble, Like the Antique Ant 1125

Presentation

Master Teacher Note "Expect Nothing" has the lyrical quality of a folk song. We recommend that you play any number of different types of songs so that the lyrical quality of music can be compared and contrasted to that of the poem.

Purpose-Setting Question Who is the speaker of the poem?

1 Discussion What do these lines say about self-esteem? Have the students speculate about the reasons why the poet wrote about disappointment in such a way.

Speaking and Listening A musically inclined student may wish to team up with another student in the class to present a musical reading of this poem. The other poems in this section may also be performed in this way.

Humanities Note

Fine art, *Somewhere in America,* c. 1933-4, by Robert Brackman. Robert Brackman (1898–1980), an American painter, studied at the Ferrer School in San Francisco and at the National Academy of Design in New York with the two important Realist painters Robert Henri and George Bellows. Their influence on Brackman's work was profound. Brackman became an award-winning American Realist painter and a fine teacher.

During the Depression, Brackman worked on New Deal projects. Through these projects he and more than 5000 other artists were subsidized by the federal government to create thousands of works of art. This art was often ordinary in subject, but always expressed authentic American images and ideas, many of which were new to painting. *Somewhere in America* is typical of this period in American art. It is painted in a realistic style that uses soft, clear colors and interesting pattern relationships. In this touching portrait, Robert Brackman may be voicing his dismay at what this little girl can expect.

You might ask students these questions.
1. How does the artist feel about his subject?
2. Does the poet express similar feelings? Explain.

Expect Nothing

Alice Walker

Expect nothing. Live frugally
On surprise.
Become a stranger
To need of pity
5 Or, if compassion be freely
Given out
Take only enough
Stop short of urge to plead
Then purge away the need.

10 Wish for nothing larger
Than your own small heart

Or greater than a star;
Tame wild disappointment
With caress unmoved and cold
15 Make of it a parka
For your soul.

Discover the reason why
So tiny human midget
Exists at all
20 So scared unwise
But expect nothing. Live frugally
On surprise.

SOMEWHERE IN AMERICA
Robert Brackman
National Museum of American Art
Smithsonian Institution

THINKING ABOUT THE SELECTION

Recalling

1. (a) According to the speaker, to what should we "become a stranger"? (b) For what should we wish? (c) How should we deal with "wild disappointment"? (d) What should we "discover"?

Interpreting

2. (a) What is the meaning of lines 3–4? (b) What is the meaning of lines 10–12?
3. How can disappointment be made into "a parka for your soul"?
4. What do lines 18–20 reveal about the speaker's attitude concerning humanity's place in the universe?
5. Explain the title of this poem.

Applying

6. Do you agree with the advice given by the speaker of the poem? Why or why not?

ANALYZING LITERATURE

Understanding Lyric Poetry

"Expect Nothing" is an example of a lyric—a brief poem that expresses the thoughts and feelings of the speaker in lively, musical language.

1. What are the main thoughts and feelings that the speaker expresses in the poem?

2. What does the poem reveal about the speaker's attitude toward life?

UNDERSTANDING LANGUAGE

Recognizing Abstract Words

Concrete words are those which appeal to one or more of the five senses. In contrast, abstract words are ones that express qualities or concepts that exist apart from any material object. For example, the word *love* is abstract, while the word *rose* is concrete.

Define in your own words each of the following words from "Expect Nothing." Check your definitions in the dictionary. Then think of a concrete image, or word picture, that conveys the qualities or concepts expressed by the abstract word.

1. surprise
2. pity
3. compassion
4. disappointment

THINKING AND WRITING

Comparing and Contrasting Poems

Imagine you work for a literary magazine and have been asked to write an article comparing and contrasting "Expect Nothing" with "Be Beautiful, Noble, like the Antique Ant." Reread both poems, noting similarities and differences in purpose and theme. Organize your notes according to corresponding points of contrast. Then write your essay, using passages from the two poems to support your argument. When you revise, make sure you have connected your ideas using transitions and other linking devices.

4. The speaker believes that humanity is only a small, insignificant part of the vast universe.
5. Suggested Response: The title conveys the poem's main point—that we should limit our expectations.

Applying

6. Suggested Response: Yes, because if we expect too much, we leave ourselves open to disappointment.

ANSWERS TO ANALYZING LITERATURE

1. The speaker expresses her sense of humility and her belief in limiting our expectations.
2. The speaker's attitude is that life is full of many disappointments and dashed expectations. However, she believes that by living simply and expecting nothing of others, a person can more easily cope with these disappointments.

ANSWERS TO UNDERSTANDING LANGUAGE

1. *surprise:* Something that happens suddenly or unexpectedly. Suggested image: The facial expression of a woman who has just arrived at a surprise party.
2. *pity:* Sorrow felt for another's suffering or misfortune; sympathy. Suggested image: The facial expression of a person paying a visit to an accident victim.
3. *compassion:* Sorrow for the sufferings or trouble of another, accompanied by the urge to help. Suggested image: A man taking off his coat and offering it to a homeless man on a cold winter day.
4. *disappointment:* The feeling of dissatisfaction; failed hope. Suggested image: The facial expressions of the players on a basketball team that has just lost the championship game.

THINKING AND WRITING

For help with this assignment, students should refer to Lesson 16, "Writing a Comparative Evaluation," in the Handbook of Writing About Literature.

Closure and Extension

ANSWERS TO THINKING ABOUT THE SELECTION
Recalling

1. (a) One should become a "stranger to the need of pity." (b) We should wish for nothing larger than our own hearts or "greater than a star." (c) We should "tame wild disappointment." (d) We should discover the "reason why so tiny midget exists at all."

Interpreting

2. (a) We should not look for and expect pity. (b) Our wishes should be kept simple and personal.
3. One can make disappointment into "a parka for your soul" by learning from it and protecting himself or herself from similar disappointments in the future.

1128

Still Life

Reed Whittemore

1

I must explain why it is that at night, in my own house,
Even when no one's asleep, I feel I must whisper.

2 Thoreau and Wordsworth[1] would call it an act of devotion,
I think; others would call it fright; it is probably
5 Something of both. In my living-room there are matters I'd
    rather not meddle with
Late at night.

I prefer to sit very still on the couch, watching
All the inanimate things of my daytime life—
The furniture and the curtains, the pictures and books—
10 Come alive,
Not as in some childish fantasy, the chairs dancing
And Disney[2] prancing backstage, but with dignity,
The big old rocker presiding over a silent
And solemn assembly of all my craftsmen,
15 From Picasso[3] and other dignities gracing my walls
To the local carpenter benched at my slippered feet.

I find these proceedings
Remarkable for their clarity and intelligence, and I wish I
    might somehow
Bring into daylight the eloquence, say, of a doorknob.
3 20 But always the gathering breaks up; everyone there
Shrinks from the tossing turbulence
Of living,
A cough, a creaking stair.

---

1. Thoreau and Wordsworth: American author Henry David Thoreau (1817–1862) and British poet William Wordsworth (1770–1850).
2. Disney: Famous American film producer, Walt Disney (1901–1966).
3. Picasso: Painter Pablo Picasso (1881–1973).

INTERIOR
Preston Dickinson
The Metropolitan Museum of Art

THINKING ABOUT THE SELECTION

Recalling

1. (a) What does the speaker watch while sitting on his couch late at night? (b) What is his attitude toward what he sees?

Interpreting

2. (a) What effect does nighttime have on the speaker? (b) How does the speaker's nighttime life contrast with his daytime life? (c) How is this contrast conveyed?
3. What does the speaker mean when he comments that he wishes he could "Bring into daylight the eloquence . . . of a doorknob"?
4. What is the significance of the poem's title?

Applying

5. Do you agree with the suggestion the poem makes concerning the effect of nighttime on the imagination? Why or why not?

CRITICAL THINKING AND READING

Analyzing the Meaning of Allusions

An allusion is a short reference to another literary work or a figure, place, or event from history, religion, or mythology. To understand the meaning of an allusion, you must have some knowledge of the work or figure to which the writer is alluding.

In "Still Life" Whittemore alludes to four men known for imagination and creativity. Look up each of these men in an encyclopedia. Then explain the meaning of each allusion and how each contributes to the poem's overall meaning.

Humanities Note

Fine art, *Interior,* by Preston Dickinson. Preston Dickinson (1891–1930), an American painter, studied at the Art Students League under the dynamic teacher and painter, Robert Henri. He then went to Paris to engage in independent study of the old masters. There he became acquainted with the work of Cezanne and the Cubists, both of which had a profound influence on his work. Preston Dickinson returned to the United States and became a key figure in the Precisionist movement, a form of American Cubism.

Interior was done during a period when Dickinson focused on still life. The subtle colors of his palette reflect the influence of Cezanne. The style is abstract with simplified, recognizable shapes and distorted perspectives. The objects in the room are varied and interesting. The painting conveys a sense of waiting, as if someone has just left or will just return. Here the artist has interpreted an ordinary American scene as a decorative and evocative abstract design.

As students look at the art and read the poem, you might use these ideas for discussion.
1. Compare and contrast the way the poet and the artist feel about the "life" of inanimate objects.
2. How does the emotional quality of the empty room in the painting compare with the room described in the poem?

imaginative abilities into the "tossing turbulence" of the daytime.
4. A still life depicts the types of inanimate objects that come to life in the poem.

Applying

5. Answers will differ. Suggested Response: Yes, because darkness has a powerful effect on people.

ANSWERS TO CRITICAL THINKING AND READING

Answers will differ. Suggested Response: The allusion to Thoreau and Wordsworth refers to the two writers' emphasis on tranquility. The allusion to Disney refers to his interest in fantasy.

The speaker alludes to Picasso because of the painter's emphasis on the imagination and the unconscious mind. Each of these allusions relates to the poem's focus on the effect of isolation and the powers of the imagination.

Richard Wilbur (1921–   )

Like many other contemporary poets, Richard Wilbur is known for his elegant and imaginative use of language. Yet, unlike most of the other poets of our time, Wilbur uses traditional poetic forms and techniques in expressing an optimistic outlook toward life and an awareness of the world's beauty.

Wilbur was born in New York City but spent most of his childhood on a farm in rural northern New Jersey. After graduating from Amherst College, he served in the army infantry in Europe during World War II. He began writing poetry during the war and published his first book, *The Beautiful Changes and Other Poems* (1947), while he was a graduate student at Harvard.

Wilbur has gone on to publish many other volumes of poetry. His third book, *Things of This World* (1956), won both the Pulitzer Prize and the National Book Award. He has also published translations of a number of French dramas, a collection of essays, lyrics for an operetta based on Voltaire's novel *Candide,* and two books for children.

Robert Penn Warren (1905–1989)

Robert Penn Warren was one of the most versatile, prolific, and distinguished writers of our time. He wrote poetry, stories, novels, plays, criticism, essays, textbooks, and a biography, and received three Pulitzer Prizes.

Warren was born in Guthrie, Kentucky. When he was sixteen, he entered Vanderbilt University, where he began to write poetry. After graduating from Vanderbilt in 1925, he studied at the University of California, Yale, and Oxford. In 1935 he became one of the founding editors of the literary magazine *The Southern Review.* Just over a decade later, he was awarded his first Pulitzer Prize for his novel, *All the King's Men* (1947), which explores the subject of southern politics. He received his second Pulitzer Prize in 1959 for *Promises,* a volume of poetry; and in 1980 he won a third Pulitzer Prize for *Now and Then* (1979), another collection of poetry.

Warren consistently used southern settings and characters in both his poetry and fiction, but at the same time he focused on universal themes. In his work, he emphasized love of the land, continuity between generations, and the need for self-knowledge and fulfillment in an often violent world.

The Beautiful Changes; Gold Glade; Evening Hawk

Writer's Techniques

Imagery. Imagery refers to words or phrases that create mental pictures, or images, that appeal to one or more of the five senses—sight, hearing, touch, smell, or taste. Most often, images appeal to our sense of sight. For example, Warren creates a visual image in "Evening Hawk," when he writes, "From plane of light to plane, wings dipping through/Geometries and orchids that the sunset builds." Although visual imagery is the most common type of imagery, many images present sensations that we cannot visualize, and some images appeal to more than one sense. For example, in "Gold Glade" when Warren writes that there was "No breathing of air," he creates an image that appeals to both our senses of hearing and touch but not to our sense of sight.

Commentary

Robert Penn Warren, one of America's most respected men of letters, died in September 1989. His friend, poet and novelist James Dickey remembers him as " . . . a remarkable man, a wonderful writer. The main thing about Warren is that he had a powerful, primitive imagination that dealt with the basics of human existence, either personal, political, or religious. . . . And he did it to hell and gone. He was an all-out kind of a writer." Master of all traditional verse forms from lullabies to sonnets, Warren used them to express characteristically twentieth-century themes. Although his subjects came from his southern roots, he endowed them with universal appeal, offering anecdotes to illuminate concerns common to all men. Critic Charles Bohner finds in Warren's work " . . . a gusto . . . reminiscent of the writer who, Warren said, has had the greatest influence on his life—Shakespeare."

In 1986 the United States Congress selected Robert Penn Warren America's first poet laureate. The beauty of his images, language, and truth has enriched American literature and will be his lasting monument.

Writing

To what do you think the title of Richard Wilbur's poem, "The Beautiful Changes," might refer? Explore the possible subjects of the poem by preparing a list of "beautiful changes" that occur in nature, in people's lives, and in people's behavior.

Literary Focus Poetry is the special domain of imagery. Have students come up with examples of images that appeal to each of the five senses.

Writing/Prior Knowledge Discuss the concept of change with your students. How can it be both frightening and beautiful? Why do we sometimes look forward to change and, at other times, find it foreboding?

Vocabulary

Preteach the following vocabulary words:

declivity (di kliv′ ə tē) *n.:* A downward slope (p. 1134, l. 12)

tumultuous (too mul′ choo wəs) *adj.:* Wild and noisy (p. 1136, l. 4)

guttural (gut′ ər əl) *adj.:* Of the throat (p. 1136, l. 5)

QUEEN ANNE'S LACE, 1957
Charles Burchfield
The Detroit Institute of Arts

The Beautiful Changes

Richard Wilbur

One wading a Fall meadow finds on all sides
The Queen Anne's Lace[1] lying like lilies
On water; it glides
So from the walker, it turns
5 Dry grass to a lake, as the slightest shade of you
Valleys my mind in fabulous blue Lucernes.[2]

    1

    2

---

1. Queen Anne's Lace A weed with finely divided foliage and white flowers.
2. Lucernes (lōō sʉrnz′): The Lake of Lucerne, located in central Switzerland.

dissimilar from those of the Postimpressionist painters, such as Cézanne, Seurat, Gauguin, and Van Gogh. Their attempts to render nature, color, and light are intensely patterned. Any of the landscape paintings of these artists reveal this dramatic use of shape, color, and space. Cézanne's *The Arc Valley* and Van Gogh's *Cypresses in the Moonlight* are two examples of such paintings.

1 **Discussion** What does the speaker accomplish by comparing wading in a meadow to wading in water?

2 **Discussion** Is the speaker alone or is he walking with someone?

The beautiful changes as a forest is changed
By a chameleon's tuning his skin to it;
As a mantis, arranged
10   On a green leaf, grows
Into it, makes the leaf leafier, and proves
Any greenness is deeper than anyone knows.

Your hands hold roses always in a way that says
They are not only yours; the beautiful changes
15   In such kind ways,
Wishing ever to sunder
Things and things' selves for a second finding, to lose
For a moment all that it touches back to wonder.

THINKING ABOUT THE SELECTION

Recalling

1. What scene does the speaker describe in the first stanza?
2. (a) How does the chameleon change? (b) How does the mantis change?

Interpreting

3. (a) What comparison does the speaker develop in the first stanza? (b) What type of "change" does this comparison represent?
4. (a) In what sense does the change of the mantis make the "leaf leafier"? (b) Why does the change prove that "any greenness is deeper than anyone knows"?
5. What is unusual about the speaker's use of the word *beautiful*?
6. (a) What does the speaker mean when he comments that change offers a "second finding"? (b) Why does he believe that change can produce a sense of "wonder"?

Applying

7. Do you think that most people perceive changes in nature in the same way as the speaker does? Why or why not?

3

Discussion How do lines 7-11 deal with the cliché "You can't tell the trees from the forest"? Do these lines add anything to this saying?

Reader's Response Which of the changes that occur in nature do you find most interesting? Why?

Closure and Extension

ANSWERS TO THINKING ABOUT THE SELECTION
Recalling

1. The speaker describes an autumn scene of Queen Anne's Lace in a meadow.
2. (a) The chameleon changes by turning its skin to the color of the forest. (b) The mantis changes by arranging itself on a leaf.

Interpreting

3. (a) The speaker compares the meadow filled with Queen Anne's Lace to a lake covered with lilies. (b) It represents the transformations that occur in the imagination.
4. (a) It makes the leaf thicker and more full of life. (b) People do not look at it closely enough to perceive the depth of its color.
5. *Beautiful* is used as a noun rather than as an adjective.
6. (a) Change provides an opportunity to gain new perspective and perceive an object in a different way. (b) Change produces a sense of strangeness and wonder, and with it life becomes new and exciting.

Applying

7. Answers will differ. Suggested Response: No, most people do not give much thought to seasonal changes.

Challenge What types of beauty never change?

Presentation

Thematic Idea Another poem in which the speaker recalls childhood interactions with nature is "Birches" by Robert Frost on page 870.

Reading Strategy Have your students map out the speaker's route from stanza to stanza. Where is the speaker in each stanza? What does he see? What time of day is it? Encourage students to add their own description to each scene.

1 **Discussion** What might be the speaker's disposition as he walks through the golden glade?

2 **Discussion** To what does "it" refer? Does the speaker clarify this in the last stanza?

3 **Literary Focus** This stanza is filled with visual, auditory, and tactile imagery.

4 **Clarification** Montgomery County is in both Kentucky and Tennessee. Todd and Christian are counties in Kentucky. Warren is referring to counties he knew so well from his boyhood in Kentucky.

Gold Glade

Robert Penn Warren

Wandering, in autumn, the woods of boyhood,
Where cedar, black, thick, rode the ridge,
Heart aimless as rifle, boy-blankness of mood,
I came where ridge broke, and the great ledge,
5   Limestone, set the toe high as treetop by dark edge

Of a gorge, and water hid, grudging and grumbling,
And I saw, in mind's eye, foam white on
Wet stone, stone wet-black, white water tumbling,
And so went down, and with some fright on
10   Slick boulders, crossed over. The gorge-depth drew
    night on,

But high over high rock and leaf-lacing, sky
Showed yet bright, and declivity wooed
My foot by the quietening stream, and so I
Went on, in quiet, through the beech wood:
15   There, in gold light, where the glade gave, it stood.

The glade was geometric, circular, gold,
No brush or weed breaking that bright gold of leaf-fall.
In the center it stood, absolute and bold
Beyond any heart-hurt, or eye's grief-fall.
20   Gold-massy in air, it stood in gold light-fall,

No breathing of air, no leaf now gold-falling,
No tooth-stitch of squirrel, or any far fox bark,
No woodpecker coding, or late jay calling.
Silence: gray-shagged, the great shagbark[1]
25   Gave forth gold light. There could be no dark.

But of course dark came, and I can't recall
What county it was, for the life of me.
Montgomery, Todd, Christian—I know them all.
Was it even Kentucky or Tennessee?
30   Perhaps just an image that keeps haunting me.

---

1. shagbark: A hickory tree.

No, no! in no mansion under earth,
Nor imagination's domain of bright air,
But solid in soil that gave it its birth,
It stands, wherever it is, but somewhere.
35 I shall set my foot, and go there.

THINKING ABOUT THE SELECTION

Recalling

1. (a) What does the speaker hear while standing at "the great ledge"? (b) What does he see in his "mind's eye"?
2. How does the speaker describe the glade?
3. What is the speaker now unable to recall about the glade?
4. What does the speaker vow to do at the end of the poem?

Interpreting

5. At what point does the action of the poem shift from the past to the present?
6. (a) What does the speaker mean when he comments that the glade is "beyond any heart-hurt, or eye's grief-fall"? (b) What does he mean when he comments, "There could be no dark"?
7. (a) How many times is the word *gold* used in this poem? (b) What is the significance of this word?

Applying

8. (a) What does the gold glade represent to the speaker? (b) Why is he so anxious to return to the glade?

ANALYZING LITERATURE

Understanding Imagery

Imagery refers to words or phrases that create mental pictures, or images, that appeal to one or more of the five senses—sight, hearing, touch, smell, or taste. Although most of the imagery in "Gold Glade" appeals to our sense of sight, Warren also uses images that appeal to both our sense of hearing and our sense of touch.

1. Find one image that appeals to the sense of hearing and one image that appeals to the sense of touch.
2. How do the visual images used in describing the woods on the ridge (lines 1–5) contrast with the images used in describing the glade (lines 15–25)?

THINKING AND WRITING

Writing a Poem Using Imagery

Write a poem in which you use vivid imagery to re-create an important childhood experience. Start by thinking of an important experience you had as a child. Then prepare a list of concrete details describing the incident. When you write your poem, focus on creating vivid imagery and do not worry about rhythm or rhyme. After you finish writing, revise and proofread your poem, and share it with your classmates.

Gold Glade   1135

SUMMER LANDSCAPE WITH HAWK,
1901–06
Louis M. Eilshemius
The Phillips Collection,
Washington, D.C.

Evening Hawk
Robert Penn Warren

From plane of light to plane, wings dipping through
Geometries and orchids that the sunset builds,
Out of the peak's black angularity of shadow, riding
The last tumultuous avalanche of
5 Light above pines and the guttural gorge,
The hawk comes.

       His wing
Scythes[1] down another day, his motion

————

1. Scythes (sīthz) *v.*: Cuts as with a tool with a long single-edged blade set at an angle on a long, curved handle.

Is that of the honed steel-edge, we hear
10 The crashless fall of stalks of Time.

The head of each stalk is heavy with the gold of our error.

Look! look! he is climbing the last light
Who knows neither Time nor error, and under
Whose eye, unforgiving, the world, unforgiven, swings
15 Into shadow.

        Long now,
The last thrush is still, the last bat
Now cruises in his sharp hieroglyphics.[2] His wisdom
Is ancient, too, and immense. The star
20 Is steady, like Plato,[3] over the mountain.

If there were no wind we might, we think, hear
The earth grind on its axis, or history
Drip in darkness like a leaking pipe in the cellar.

---

2. hieroglyphics (hī′ ər ə glif′ iks) *n.*: Pictures or symbols,
representing words, syllables, or sounds.
3. Plato (427?–347? B.C.): A Greek philosopher.

THINKING ABOUT THE SELECTION

Recalling

1. How is the sunset described in lines 4–5?
2. What comment does the speaker make about the "last light" in lines 13–15?
3. According to the final stanza, what might we hear "If there were no wind"?

Interpreting

4. (a) What contrasting images, or word pictures, does Warren present in the first stanza? (b) How is this contrast developed throughout the rest of the poem?
5. (a) How does the speaker relate the hawk to darkness? (b) How does he relate its movement to time? (c) What does he mean when he comments that the "stalks of Time" are "heavy with the gold of our error"?
6. (a) Why might the speaker consider a bat to be wise? (b) Why might he compare a star to Plato?
7. What does the speaker mean when he describes history as dripping "in darkness like a leaking pipe in the cellar"?

Applying

8. What animals and other elements of nature, aside from the ones mentioned in the poem, do you associate with darkness?

Evening Hawk 1137

More About the Authors Robert Lowell remembers **Sylvia Plath** as "a distinguished, delicate, complicated person." Her poetry reveals a great capacity to experience emotion—to suffer and to love. What risks does a person, take in creating poetry from personal experience?

Although **Robert Hayden** devoted a large portion of his work to exploring black concerns and celebrating black history and culture, he maintained that black poets should be judged by the same criteria as other writers. He warned against "ghettoizing" black writers, or separating them from the rest of the literary world. Do you agree with Hayden's belief that all poetry should be judged by the same criteria?

William Stafford was born and raised in Kansas, a locale which figures prominently in his work. His poetry, critics point out, is serene and unadorned. There is a simplicity and directness to it that stems from his use of natural language. Discuss the differences among the various regions of the United States. How might these differences be reflected in poetry?

Critical Evaluation In her biography of Sylvia Plath the literary scholar Linda W. Wagner-Martin writes: "[Plath] believed in her poetry, and she knew her craft thoroughly. In her poems, she wrote about the crucial issues of her life, but she made expert art aside from those issues. She voiced anger as well as hope; she spoke of sorrow as well as joy. She wrote scathingly about people of whom she disapproved and about her husband who angered her. She wrote peacefully with a calm lyricism, about her children and their daily activities. She wrote politically: Plath cared intensely about the arms race, nuclear power, and people's injustice to others."

Sylvia Plath (1932–1963)

Despite her success as a poet, Sylvia Plath lived a very short, unhappy life. In many of her poems, she expresses her intense feelings of despair and her deep inner pain.

Born in Boston, Plath wrote poetry and received scholastic and literary awards as a child. Although she suffered a nervous breakdown during her junior year, she graduated with highest honors from Smith College. She went on to attend Cambridge University in England. In 1956 she married English poet Ted Hughes, and, after a year in the United States, the couple settled in England. Plath's first volume of poetry, *The Colossus* (1960), was the only collection of her work to appear during her lifetime. Two more books of her poetry and her novel, *The Bell Jar* (1963), were published posthumously.

Robert Hayden (1913–1980)

An extremely versatile poet, Robert Hayden used a variety of poetic forms and techniques and focused on a wide range of subjects. In addition to writing about his personal experiences, Hayden wrote about current and historical events, mythology, and folklore.

Born in Detroit, Hayden attended Wayne State University. He received a master's degree from the University of Michigan and taught there and at Fisk University in Tennessee. He published several collections of poetry, including *Heart-Shape in the Dust* (1940), *The Lion and the Archer* (1948), and *The Night-Blooming Dereus* (1972). His collection *A Ballad of Remembrance* received the Grand Prize for Poetry at the First World Festival for Negro Arts in 1966.

William Stafford (1914–   )

The poetry of William Stafford reflects his love for the natural world and his fear that modern technology will someday destroy the wilderness. Focusing on such subjects as the threat of nuclear war and the beauty of untamed nature, Stafford writes simply and directly about the causes in which he believes.

Born in Hutchinson, Kansas, Stafford attended the University of Kansas. Although he began submitting poems to poetry journals during the 1940's, he did not publish his first book, *West of Your City*, until he was forty-six. Since then he has published several more collections of poetry, including *Traveling Through the Dark*, which earned him the National Book Award in 1962.

1138　*Contemporary Writers*

GUIDE FOR INTERPRETING

Mirror; Those Winter Sundays; Traveling Through the Dark

Literary Forms

Confessional Poetry. Confessional poetry is a type of poetry in which the poet speaks frankly and openly about his or her own life. This type of poetry was introduced by Robert Lowell, when he published his collection *Life Studies* in 1959. Lowell felt that the writing of poetry had become too intellectual and impersonal and needed a "breakthrough back into life." Traditionally, when writers used the first-person pronoun "I" in a poem, readers were taught to think of the "I" as the speaker of the poem, not the poet himself or herself. Even when the "I" clearly did refer to the poet, the poet tended to reveal little about his or her doubts, frustrations, and painful experiences. In *Life Studies*, however, Lowell openly expressed his thoughts and feelings concerning his family, his experiences, and his personal problems. Many other poets followed Lowell's example and confessional poetry became a popular literary form. Other poets known for their confessional poetry include John Berryman, Sylvia Plath, and Anne Sexton.

Commentary

What makes a poem move a reader? The answer is not simple, but recognizable human truths and emotions are common to poetry that affects its readers profoundly. As you read these three poems, you will notice that they contain those elements. Sylvia Plath's mirror shows the inevitable human truth of aging and the devastation we all face with passing years. Plath observes the woman with a close sensitivity that makes the reader care for her and recognize himself or herself in her pain. Robert Hayden frames a tribute to his father by narrating a simple story of habitual Sunday mornings. The truth is evident in his words, but his father's caring eclipses all else. His quiet sacrifices are recognizable as a noble human quality—love. William Stafford's poem recounts a deer, dead on the road, and the dilemma faced by a man stopping to clear it away. The scene, once again, is recognizable even to one who has never experienced it, but even more affecting is the dilemma faced by the man. He must choose to do something, but nothing he does will seem completely satisfactory. He encounters human feelings faced by all people. We recognize the sadness and the paradox, and we respond.

What emotions do you feel as you read these poems?

Writing

In "Those Winter Sundays," Hayden writes about the sacrifices his father made for his family. Freewrite about a person who has in some way tried to make your life easier and more pleasant.

Guide for Interpreting 1139

Literary Focus The most common subjects of confessional poetry include childhood, love and love lost, and death. It is sometimes a brutal and violent poetry that dares to explore the poet's psyche. Point out that confessional poetry may take any number of forms, such as John Berryman's sonnets or the triadic stanzas of William Carlos Williams.

Writing/Prior Knowledge Before students complete the writing activity, have them discuss the reasons why people make sacrifices for the ones they love.

Vocabulary

Preteach the following vocabulary words:

preconceptions (prē′ kən sep′ shənz) *n.:* Ideas formed beforehand (p. 1140, l. 1)

meditate (med′ ə tāt′) *v.:* Think deeply (p. 1140, l. 6)

chronic (krän′ ik) *adj.:* Continuing indefinitely (p. 1143, l. 9)

austere (ô stir′) *adj.:* Showing strict self-discipline and self-denial (p. 1143, l. 14)

Motivation/Prior Knowledge
Have students recall looking in a mirror right after getting ready for some event. How did they respond to the image of themselves in the mirror?

Thematic Idea Another poem in which an inanimate object serves as the speaker is "Song of the Chattahoochee" by Sidney Lanier (p. 605).

Purpose-Setting Question Who is the speaker of the poem?

1 **Discussion** How does the wittiness of line 6 dissolve into the sadness of line 8?

2 **Clarification** This line alludes to Narcissus, the beautiful youth who fell in love with his own image in a pool, whereupon he turned into a flower. What is meant when we say someone is narcissistic? In what way is Narcissus parallel to the woman in the poem?

3 **Discussion** What is the speaker's attitude about growing old?

Reader's Response What is your reaction to the changes that have occurred in your own physical appearance over the last few years?

Mirror

Sylvia Plath

I am silver and exact. I have no preconceptions.
Whatever I see I swallow immediately
Just as it is, unmisted by love or dislike.
I am not cruel, only truthful—
5 The eye of a little god, four-cornered.
Most of the time I meditate on the opposite wall.
It is pink, with speckles. I have looked at it so long
I think it is a part of my heart. But it flickers.
Faces and darkness separate us over and over.
10 Now I am a lake. A woman bends over me,
Searching my reaches for what she really is.
Then she turns to those liars, the candles or the moon.
I see her back, and reflect it faithfully.
She rewards me with tears and an agitation of hands.
15 I am important to her. She comes and goes.
Each morning it is her face that replaces the darkness.
In me she has drowned a young girl, and in me an old woman
Rises toward her day after day, like a terrible fish.

THINKING ABOUT THE SELECTION

Recalling

1. (a) How does the mirror describe its appearance? (b) What does it do with whatever it sees?
2. (a) For what is the woman searching when she "bends over" the mirror? (b) With what does the woman reward the mirror? (c) What "rises toward" the woman in the mirror "day after day"?

Interpreting

3. In what way are the candle and the moon "liars"?

4. (a) Who is the "young girl" who has drowned? (b) Who is the "old woman"? (c) Why is the old woman "like a terrible fish"?
5. (a) How does the woman feel about aging? (b) How is her attitude revealed?

Applying

6. Do you think that most people share the woman's attitude toward aging? Why or why not?

Closure and Extension

ANSWERS TO THINKING ABOUT THE SELECTION
Recalling

1. (a) The mirror is silver and exact. (b) It immediately swallows whatever it sees.
2. (a) The woman is searching for what she really is. (b) The woman rewards the mirror with "tears and an agitation of hands." (c) An old woman rises toward her.

Interpreting

3. The light of the candle and the moon produce dim light in which the woman appears younger and more attractive than she really is.
4. (a) The "young girl" who has drowned is the woman looking in the mirror. (b) The "old woman" is what the woman is becoming. (c) She is "like a terrible fish," because the old woman's face is withered and scaley.
5. (a) She is unhappy about it and has a difficult time accepting it. (b) Her attitude is revealed through her actions: she cries and wrings her hands; she turns her back on the mirror; and she searches desperately in the mirror trying to recapture signs of youth.

Applying

6. Answers will differ. Suggested Response: No, most people have an easier time accepting the fact that they are growing older.

GIRL IN WHITE DRESS
Sir William Orpen
Private Collection
Bridgeman Art Resource

Fine art, *Girl in a White Dress,* by Sir William Orpen. Sir William Neveham Montague Orpen (1878–1931) was a British painter, born in Ireland. He studied art at the Dublin Metropolitan School of Art and the Slade School in London. Orpen became well known for his vivid portraits. During World War II he was appointed an official War Artist.

Girl in a White Dress is a penetrating portrait of a young girl. Painted in subdued, harmonious, grayed colors, this painting shows his indebtedness to the art of Whistler. It not only reveals the appearance of the girl but also informs the viewer of the nature of her personality. This revelation of character is a hallmark of Sir William Orpen's skill as a portraitist.

Consider these questions for discussion:
1. What character traits of this girl can you determine from this portrait?
2. What might she think when she looks in a mirror?

1142   Contemporary Writers

Those Winter Sundays

Robert Hayden

> Sundays too my father got up early
> and put his clothes on in the blueblack cold,
> then with cracked hands that ached
> from labor in the weekday weather made
> 5 banked fires blaze. No one ever thanked him.
>
> I'd wake and hear the cold splintering, breaking.
> When the rooms were warm, he'd call,
> and slowly I would rise and dress,
> fearing the chronic angers of that house,
>
> 10 Speaking indifferently to him,
> who had driven out the cold
> and polished my good shoes as well.
> What did I know, what did I know
> of love's austere and lonely offices?

THINKING ABOUT THE SELECTION

Recalling

1. (a) Why did Hayden's father get up early on Sunday mornings? (b) Why did his father's hands ache?

Interpreting

2. What does the first stanza reveal about Hayden's father's dedication to his family?
3. What does Hayden mean when he says that he could "hear the cold splintering, breaking"?
4. What does Hayden mean when he refers to the chronic angers of his house?
5. How do you think Hayden eventually learned about "love's austere and lonely offices"?

Applying

6. Why do you think that some young people are unable to appreciate the sacrifices their parents make for them? (b) Why do you think young people sometimes have a difficult time communicating with their parents?

ANALYZING LITERATURE

Understanding Confessional Poetry

Confessional poetry is poetry that deals openly and frankly with a poet's personal life. Although confessional poems are autobiographical, the situations and problems on which they focus are often universal. For example, in "Those Winter Sundays," Hayden writes about his indifference toward the sacrifices his father made for his family—an attitude shared by many young people in contemporary society.

1. How has Hayden's attitude toward his father changed since his childhood?
2. How does he make it clear that he now regrets the way he reacted to his father?
3. What is his message to readers?

Those Winter Sundays 1143

Motivation/Prior Knowledge
Have students discuss how nature has been affected by the expansion of civilization. What animals are endangered by highway traffic? Are there any solutions to this problem?

1 **Discussion** Why is the sighting of a dead deer the fitting subject for a poem?

2 **Discussion** Describe the parallel images of the deer's belly and the engine purring under the hood.

3 **Discussion** Why does the speaker push the deer into the river and not into the canyon? What does this reveal about the speaker?

Reader's Response How would you react if you were in the place of the poem's speaker? Why?

Traveling Through the Dark

William Stafford

Traveling through the dark I found a deer
dead on the edge of the Wilson River road.
It is usually best to roll them into the canyon:
that road is narrow; to swerve might make more dead.

5 By glow of the tail-light I stumbled back of the car
and stood by the heap, a doe, a recent killing;
she had stiffened already, almost cold.
I dragged her off; she was large in the belly.

My fingers touching her side brought me the reason—
10 her side was warm; her fawn lay there waiting,
alive, still, never to be born.
Beside that mountain road I hesitated.

The car aimed ahead its lowered parking lights;
under the hood purred the steady engine.
15 I stood in the glare of the warm exhaust turning red;
around our group I could hear the wilderness listen.

I thought hard for us all—my only swerving—,
then pushed her over the edge into the river.

THINKING ABOUT THE SELECTION

Recalling

1. (a) Where does the speaker find the deer? (b) What does he observe about the deer "by glow of the tail-light"? (c) What does he discover when he touches the deer? (d) What does the speaker do with the deer at the end of the poem?

Interpreting

2. (a) How does the speaker personify, or attribute human qualities to, his car in the fourth stanza? (b) How does this image of the car relate to the speaker's discovery of the deer?
3. What does this poem reveal about the relationship between humanity and nature in the modern world?
4. In literature, a journey is often used to symbolize, or represent, life. Assuming that this is the case in Stafford's poem, how might you interpret the poem's title?

Applying

5. Do you think the speaker makes the proper decision about what to do with the deer? Why or why not?

UNDERSTANDING LANGUAGE

Completing Word Analogies

Word analogies often appear on standardized tests. To complete them, you must first identify the relationship in the first pair of words and then add a word to the second pair that has the same relationship. For example,

    DOE: FAWN : : COW:

The relationship between the first pair of words is mother to child. Therefore, to complete the second pair, you must find the word that names the child of a cow. This word is *calf*.

Read each word analogy below: First identify whether the relationship is mother to child or child to mother. Then complete the second pair with the appropriate word.

1. CAT : KITTEN : : BEAR:
2. SOW : PIGLET : : DOG:
3. LAMB : EWE : : DUCK:
4. CHICK : HEN : : GOSLING:

THINKING AND WRITING

Writing a Confessional Poem

Write a poem expressing your feelings of affection and appreciation for a person who has in some way tried to make your life easier or more pleasant. Start by reviewing the freewriting you did before you began reading this group of poems. When you write your poems, use concrete images, or word pictures, in describing your feelings. After revising your poem, share it with the person about whom it is written.

ANSWERS TO THINKING ABOUT THE SELECTION
Recalling

1. (a) The speaker finds the deer on the edge of the Wilson River Road. (b) He observes that she has stiffened and is almost cold. (c) He discovers that the deer is pregnant, and the fawn inside is alive. (d) The speaker pushes the deer over the edge into the river.

Interpreting

2. (a) The car seems to control its own headlights, as if holding a flashlight. Its engine purrs as if it is an animal. It has a warm exhaust, like warm breath. (b) The car is a cold, stiff object on the outside, but inside the engine is warm and 'purring.' Inside the body of the cold, stiff deer is a warm, alive, unborn fawn.
3. Suggested Response: Nature is threatened by the development of human civilization.
4. Suggested Response: The title suggests that there are many dark, depressing aspects of life.

Applying

5. Answers will differ. Suggested Response: Yes, because he has no other option.

ANSWERS TO UNDERSTANDING LANGUAGE

1. cub
2. puppy
3. duckling
4. goose

THINKING AND WRITING

For help with this assignment, students can refer to Lesson 12, "Writing a Poem," in the Handbook Writing of About Literature.

Publishing Student Writing You may want to submit your students' poems to your school's literary magazine.

Focus

More About the Authors Critics generally agree that the central theme of **Donald Justice's** poetry is loss. Does it seem appropriate that a poet who feels loss so keenly would write poetry that is considered conservative?

Howard Nemerov's poetry is sometimes witty and sometimes ludicrous as it focuss on the relationship of history, death, and the universe. This can be quite heavy material, yet Nemerov tempers it with humor. In what way might a poet need to write humorously about the tragic aspects of life?

The Midwest is the turf that **James Wright** poetizes. He writes about an almost brutal Midwest—the Ohio working-class society in which he grew up. Discuss the geography and economics of the Midwest of the last thirty years. Could there be a distinctive voice emerging from this region?

Critical Evaluation In his book *A History of Modern Poetry: Modernism and After,* the literary scholar David Perkins laments James Wright's early death. He writes: "(Wright's) achievement is important as it stands, but he died at a relatively young age, and one regrets both the poems he did not write and the influence he would have had. What was best in him recalls Thomas Hardy—sensitivity to the darker side of experience, direct honesty, seriousness, essentialism, compassion—and we remember that Hardy had published almost none of his poems at the age when Wright died."

Donald Justice (1925–   )

Throughout the course of his career, Donald Justice has experimented with different poetic forms and techniques. In all of his poetry, however, he displays a firm command of language and rhythm.

Born in Miami, Florida, Justice studied at the University of Miami, the University of North Carolina, Stanford University, and the University of Iowa. He began writing poetry in 1952, and in 1960 he published his first book of poems, *The Summer Anniversaries*. Since then he has published four more collections, including *The Local Storm* (1963) and *Selected Poems* (1979), which earned him a Pulitzer Prize.

Howard Nemerov (1920–   )

In his poetry Howard Nemerov has explored various themes. While some of his poems are light and witty, others focus on serious philosophical subjects such as the relationship between humanity and nature.

Born in New York City, Nemerov began writing poetry while attending Harvard. During World War II, he served as a pilot in the Royal Canadian Air Force and the United States Army Air Force. After returning from the war, he published his first collection of poetry, *The Image of the Law* (1947). Since then he has published eleven more volumes of poetry, three novels, two collections of short stories, and six books of literary criticism. In 1978 he won the National Book Award and the Pulitzer Prize for his *Collected Poems*.

James Wright (1927–1980)

In the introduction to his second book, *The Green Wall* (1957), James Wright wrote that his purpose as a poet was to say something that was "humanly important, instead of just showing off language." Throughout his career, Wright achieved this goal, while at the same time writing poetry that is filled with elegant language and rich, vivid imagery.

Wright was born in Martins Ferry, Ohio, and educated at Kenyon College and the University of Washington. During his brief life, he published five books of poetry, including *Saint Judas* (1959), *The Branch Will Not Break* (1963), and *Shall We Gather at the River* (1968). In 1972 he received the Pulitzer Prize for his *Collected Poems* (1971).

1146   Contemporary Writers

Objectives

1 To appreciate sound devices
2 To analyze the effect of sound devices
3 To respond to criticism

Support Material

Teaching Portfolio
Teacher Backup, p. 1549
Usage and Mechanics Worksheet, p. 1554
Vocabulary Check, p. 1555
Analyzing Literature Worksheet *Understanding Sound Devices,* p. 1556
Critical Thinking and Reading Worksheet *Understanding the*

Effect of Sound Devices, p. 1557
Selection Test, p. 1558

GUIDE FOR INTERPRETING

Poem; Storm Windows; Lying in a Hammock at William Duffy's Farm in Pine Island, Minnesota

Writer's Techniques

Sound Devices. Poets use a variety of sound devices to give their writing a musical quality and to emphasize certain words and reinforce meaning. Alliteration, assonance, consonance, and onomatopoeia are four of the most common sound devices.

Alliteration is the repetition of similar sounds, usually consonants, at the beginnings of words or accented syllables. Notice the repetition of the *d* sound in the following line from "Traveling Through the Dark": "Traveling through the *d*ark I found a *d*eer."

Assonance is the repetition of vowel sounds. For example, the *o* sound is repeated in line 3 of "Storm Windows": "Dr*o*ve them indoors. S*o*, coming home at noon."

Consonance is the repetition of consonant sounds at the ends of words or accented syllables. For example, the *k* sound is repeated in line 2 of "Lying in a Hammock at William Duffy's Farm in Pine Island, Minnesota": "Asleep on the blac*k* trun*k*."

Onomatopoeia refers to the use of words whose sounds in some way mimic or suggest their meanings. *Meow, bang,* and *crash* are examples of onomatopoetic words; and in the following line from Robert Penn Warren's "Gold Glade," the word *grumbling* is onomatopoetic: "Of a gorge, and water hid, grudging and *grumbling*."

Commentary

As you read the last line of James Wright's "Lying in a Hammock at William Duffy's Farm in Pine Island, Minnesota," notice that it makes this simple but affecting statement: "I have wasted my life." In contemplative repose the speaker is reflecting on the richness of nature's slow beauty. He is allowed respite from the busy world in which reflection plays no part. People often turn to nature for renewal. A solitary walk on the beach, a hike among the turning leaves of autumn, a rest in a hammock—these allow us to quiet the noise long enough to hear the silent voices of our souls. In our contemporary world it is difficult for us to stop and reflect about the choices we have made and the things that matter most. Does this poem remind us that it is important to do so?

Writing

In "Lying in a Hammock at William Duffy's Farm in Pine Island, Minnesota," the speaker presents his observations of a farm at sunset. What types of details do you think the speaker is likely to have observed? Prepare a list of images, or word pictures, that you associate with farms.

Guide for Interpreting   1147

Literary Focus The world of contemporary poetry asks little of its poets. They may write free of the constraints of rhyme and meter. Subject matter, too, can range from love to storm windows. What is necessary is sound. The sound devices of alliteration, assonance, consonance, and onomatopoeia are what often separates contemporary poetry from prose.

Writing/Prior Knowledge Have the students complete the writing assignment. For extra credit, have students write poems incorporating the images they have listed.

Poem

Donald Justice

This poem is not addressed to you.
You may come into it briefly,
But no one will find you here, no one.
You will have changed before the poem will.

1

PORTRAIT OF DIEGO
Giacometti
Galerie Maeght, Paris

1148   *Contemporary Writers*

5   Even while you sit there, unmovable,
    You have begun to vanish. And it does not matter.
2   The poem will go on without you.
3   It has the spurious glamor of certain voids.

    It is not sad, really, only empty.
10 Once perhaps it was sad, no one knows why.
    It prefers to remember nothing.
    Nostalgias were peeled from it long ago.

    Your type of beauty has no place here.
    Night is the sky over this poem.
15 It is too black for stars.
    And do not look for any illumination.

    You neither can nor should understand what it means.
    Listen, it comes without guitar,
    Neither in rags nor any purple fashion.
20 And there is nothing in it to comfort you.

    Close your eyes, yawn. It will be over soon.
    You will forget the poem, but not before
    It has forgotten you. And it does not matter.
    It has been most beautiful in its erasures.

25 O bleached mirrors! Oceans of the drowned!
    Nor is one silence equal to another.
4   And it does not matter what you think.
    This poem is not addressed to you.

THINKING ABOUT THE SELECTION

Recalling

1. (a) According to the speaker, what will happen to you before the poem changes? (b) What is happening to you "even while you sit there"?
2. According to the sixth stanza, what will happen before you forget the poem?

Interpreting

3. (a) What does the speaker mean when he comments that "Night is the sky over this poem./It is too black for stars"? (b) Why does he believe that "You neither can nor should understand what" the poem means?
4. (a) What does this poem imply about the permanence of art? (b) What does it imply about the relationship between art and humanity?

Applying

5. Do you agree with the speaker's attitude toward poetry? Why or why not?

Poem   1149

Master Teacher Note Poetry, as we have seen in the works of Robert Lowell, Randall Jarrell, Sylvia Plath, and others, tends to be very serious. In contrast, Howard Nemerov writes poetry that contains intrusions of humor. A few of his best poems are built on direct humor, sometimes as a form of irony. Discuss with the students the role of humor in society.

1 **Discussion** While focusing on the subject of storm windows, Nemerov brings in imagery from the sea and the fields of midwestern wheat. How does this affect the poem?

2 **Literary Focus** What sound device is used here?

3 **Discussion** What might the speaker mean by "missed desires"?

Reader's Response What emotions does this poem evoke in you? Why?

Storm Windows

Howard Nemerov

People are putting up storm windows now,
Or were, this morning, until the heavy rain
Drove them indoors. So, coming home at noon,
I saw storm windows lying on the ground,
5 Frame-full of rain; through the water and glass
I saw the crushed grass, how it seemed to stream
Away in lines like seaweed on the tide
Or blades of wheat leaning under the wind.
The ripple and splash of rain on the blurred glass
10 Seemed that it briefly said, as I walked by,
Something I should have liked to say to you,
Something . . . the dry grass bent under the pane
Brimful of bouncing water . . . something of
A swaying clarity which blindly echoes
15 This lonely afternoon of memories
And missed desires, while the wintry rain
(Unspeakable, the distance in the mind!)
Runs on the standing windows and away.

THINKING ABOUT THE SELECTION

Recalling

1. (a) What were people doing this morning? (b) Why did they stop?
2. What does the speaker see when he comes home at noon?
3. (a) To what does the poet compare the crushed grass? (b) What does the "swaying clarity" of the grass blindly echo?

Interpreting

4. How would you describe the mood of this poem?
5. (a) Why does the speaker associate the "dry grass bent under the pane/Brimful of bouncing water" with "missed desires"? (b) How does the "wintry rain" that "runs on the standing windows and away" relate to the speaker's "missed desires"?
6. What do you think is the "Something I should have liked to say to you"?
7. Why is this poem called "Storm Windows"?

Applying

8. What other types of images do you think people might associate with missed chances and desires?
9. According to a Portuguese proverb, "What was hard to bear is sweet to remember." (a) Explain the meaning of this proverb. (b) How does it relate to "Storm Windows"?

ANALYZING LITERATURE

Understanding Sound Devices

Alliteration, assonance, consonance, and onomatopoeia are four sound devices used in literature. Alliteration is the repetition of similar sounds, usually consonants, at the beginnings of words or accented syllables. Assonance is the repetition of vowel sounds. Consonance is the repetition of consonant sounds at the ends of words or accented syllables. Onomatopoeia refers to the use of words whose sounds in some way mimic or suggest their meanings.

1. Find two examples of alliteration in "Storm Windows."
2. Find two examples of assonance.
3. Find one example of consonance.
4. Find one example of onomatopoeia.

CRITICAL THINKING AND READING

Analyzing the Effect of Sound Devices

Poets use sound devices to give their writing a musical quality. Sound devices can also reinforce meaning and contribute to the mood of a poem.

1. Read "Storm Windows" aloud, paying close attention to the use of sound devices. Then explain how the sound devices contribute to the poem's musical quality.
2. (a) How do the sound devices contribute to the mood of the poem? (b) How would you describe the mood of this poem?

3. (a) The crushed grass is compared with seaweed on the tide or blades of wheat leaning under the wind. (b) The "swaying clarity" of grass echoes the "lonely afternoon of memories and missed desires."

Interpreting

4. Suggested Responses: The mood is sad and nostalgic.
5. (a) The missed desires are unreachable, like the grass under the water and glass. (b) The wintry rain runs on the standing windows and disappears like his missed desires.
6. Suggested Response: "I love you."
7. Suggested Response: The poem is called storm windows, because the windows serve as the central symbol of the poem.

Applying

8. Answers will differ. Students might suggest a variety of bleak images, such as rain or snow.
9. (a) It means that people often romanticize the past. (b) The speaker of the poem is romanticizing the past.

ANSWERS TO ANALYZING LITERATURE

1. Examples include "*P*eople are *p*utting" and "*S*omething *s*hould have liked to say.
2. An example is "Dr*o*ve them ind*oo*rs. S*o*, c*o*ming h*o*me."
3. Examples include "mor*n*ing, until the heavy rai*n*" and "Drove the*m* indoors. So, co*m*ing ho*m*e."
4. One example is "The ripple and *splash* of rain."

ANSWERS TO CRITICAL THINKING

1. Suggested Response: The sound devices add to the rhythm.
2. (a) Suggested Response: The sound devices contribute to the mood by slowing the pace. (b) The mood is melancholy.

Closure and Extension

ANSWERS TO THINKING ABOUT THE SELECTION

Recalling

1. (a) People were putting up storm windows. (b) They stopped because it began to rain.
2. The speaker sees storm windows lying on the ground.

Lying in a Hammock at William Duffy's Farm in Pine Island, Minnesota

James Wright

Over my head, I see the bronze butterfly,
Asleep on the black trunk,
Blowing like a leaf in green shadow.
Down the ravine behind the empty house,
5 The cowbells follow one another
Into the distances of the afternoon.

THE POET RECLINING 1915
Marc Chagall
The Tate Gallery, London

To my right,
In a field of sunlight between two pines,
The droppings of last year's horses
10 Blaze into golden stones.
I lean back, as the evening darkens and comes on.
A chicken-hawk floats over, looking for home.
4 I have wasted my life.

THINKING ABOUT THE SELECTION

Recalling

1. (a) What does the speaker see over his head? (b) What does he observe "down the ravine behind the empty house"? (c) What does he observe to his right? (d) What observation does he make about his own life?

Interpreting

2. Metonymy is a literary device in which something very closely associated with a thing is used to suggest or represent the thing itself. Wright uses this technique in line 5, using cowbells to represent cows. How does his use of this technique help him to create an image, or word picture, that appeals to both the sense of hearing and the sense of sight?
3. What overall impression do the images, or word pictures, in the poem convey?
4. (a) Why might the speaker's observations of the farm lead him to the conclusion he reaches at the end of the poem? (b) Do you think the poet means his words to be taken at face value? Explain your answer.

Applying

5. How would you define a well-spent life?

THINKING AND WRITING

Responding to Criticism

A critic has commented that in his poetry Wright focuses "not only on his experience but also on his response to that experience." Write an essay in which you discuss this statement in relation to "Lying in a Hammock at William Duffy's Farm in Pine Island, Minnesota." Use passages from the poem to support your argument. When you revise, make sure that you have adequately supported your opinion with details from the poem.

---

4 **Discussion** What does the final statement reveal about the speaker?

Closure and Extension

ANSWERS TO THINKING ABOUT THE SELECTION
Recalling

1. (a) He sees the bronze butterfly. (b) He observes the cows following one another. (c) He sees the droppings of last year's horses blazed into golden stones in the sunlight. (d) He feels that he has wasted his life.

Interpreting

2. By using cowbells to represent cows, he prompts us to both visualize the cows and hear their bells ringing.
3. The images create an impression of the beauty and tranquility of the landscape.
4. Suggested Response: (a) The speaker might regret the fact that he has not spent his life in a tranquil setting and spent his time appreciating the beauty of nature. (b) Suggested Response: No, because his comment is exaggerated.

Applying

5. Answers will differ. Suggested Response: A life in which a person makes a lasting contribution to the world.

Challenge How would you react if you were in the speaker's place?

THINKING AND WRITING

For help with this assignment, students can refer to Lesson 15, "Evaluating a Literary Work," in the Handbook of Writing About Literature.

After students have completed the assignment, divide them into groups, and have them read their essays to one another and make suggestions about how the essays could be improved.

More About the Authors The poetry of **Adrienne Rich** documents the changing role of women in America. Ask students to discuss how feminist concerns can be expressed in poetry. What are likely to be the subjects and concerns of a female poet writing in the last decade of the twentieth century?

Simon Ortiz's poetry is conversational in tone and contains spiritual and mythic elements. His work frequently explores the connection between the survival of the Native American and the American nation as a whole. Discuss the history of the Native Americans in the West since the American-Indian wars. In what way might the knowledge and wisdom of Native Americans in the Southwest be a part of the sensibility of American Society as a whole?

Diana Chang's ethnic heritage is Chinese. About one-fifth of all the people in the world live in China. The Chinese call their country *Chung-kuo,* which means "middle country," because the ancient Chinese thought of their country as being both the geographical center of the world and the only truly cultured civilization. What might be the cultural paradoxes of having such a heritage and writing for an American audience?

Critical Evaluation In his book *A History of Modern Poetry: Modernism and After,* the literary scholar David Perkins writes that Adrienne Rich's "special gifts as a poet are the honesty and complexity of her emotions and perceptions, together with her power to articulate these in images and metaphors."

BIOGRAPHIES

Adrienne Rich (1929–   )

Adrienne Rich's career as a poet can be divided into two distinct stages. During the early part of her career, she wrote neatly crafted traditional verse. In contrast, her later poems are written in free verse and often explore her deepest personal feelings.

Born and raised in Baltimore, Rich began writing poetry at an early age. Her first volume of poetry, *A Change of World* (1951), was published just after she graduated from Radcliffe College. Since abandoning traditional poetic forms for free verse in the early 1960's, she has produced several collections of poetry. Her later books include *Snapshots of a Daughter-in-Law* (1963), *The Will to Change* (1971), and *Diving into the Wreck* (1973).

Simon Ortiz (1941–   )

An Acoma Pueblo Indian, Simon Ortiz carries on the Native-American tradition of storytelling in his poetry. Not surprisingly, much of his poetry reflects his deep awareness of his cultural heritage.

Ortiz was born in New Mexico. After graduating from the University of New Mexico, he attended the University of Iowa Writers' Workshop. He has worked as a teacher, journalist, and public relations director, and is currently a professor at the University of New Mexico. Possessing a strong belief in the importance of education, Ortiz devotes much of his free time to educating fellow Native Americans.

Diana Chang (1934–   )

Diana Chang, who spent most of her childhood in China, is another contemporary poet whose work reflects her cultural heritage. In fact, many of her poems, including "Most Satisfied by Snow" clearly exhibit the influence of ancient Oriental verse forms.

Born in New York City and raised in China, Chang settled in the United States following World War II. She attended Barnard College, graduating in 1955. In addition to writing poetry, she has written several novels, including *The Frontiers of Love* (1956), *The Only Game in Town,* and *Eye to Eye.* She has also served as the editor of *The American Pen,* a journal published by the international writers' association, P.E.N.

Objectives

1 To understand parallelism
2 To write a poem using parallelism

Support Material

Teaching Portfolio
Teacher Backup, p. 1561
Usage and Mechanics Worksheet, p. 1565
Vocabulary Check, p. 1566
Analyzing Literature Worksheet, *Understanding Parallelism,* p. 1567
Language Worksheet, *Understanding Synonyms,* p. 1568
Selection Test, p. 1569

GUIDE FOR INTERPRETING

The Observer; Hunger in New York City; Most Satisfied by Snow

Writer's Techniques

Parallelism. Parallelism refers to the repeated use of phrases, clauses, or sentences that are similar in structure. Poets often use parallelism to create a sense of unity and establish a pattern in their poems, especially in poems written in free verse—verse that has irregular meter and line length. The use of parallelism also adds emphasis to certain words and phrases and helps to create a rhythm.

Commentary

As you read the three poems on the next few pages, notice that they all concern ways of nurturing the soul. Often in our fast-paced world, we remember to feed our bodies but forget to feed our souls. "The Observer" compares the lives of two people. The speaker envies the simplified, natural existence she envisions Dian Fossey living and implies that Fossey's life in the "pale gorilla-scented dawn" is richer than her own "in the old cell block." The richness she longs for is not material; it is the fullness of the soul.

"Hunger in New York City" addresses soul nourishment more directly. Ortiz expressly sees hunger "asking for food, words, wisdom, young memories. . . ." As you read the poem, notice what things the poem's speaker searches out and finds to feed himself in "the concrete of this city" where he finds little to "eat."

"Most Satisfied by Snow" ends with the words "I, too, flowering." How does a person flower? In the poem the speaker observes and is open to both the insubstantial fog and the very substantial snow. Perhaps, in comparing "us" to these things, she reminds us that the spiritual and the physical components of ourselves are both important and that we can grow, or flower, in soul as well as in body.

How do you nourish your hungry soul? What do you feed it to make it grow healthy and strong? Some people feed their souls nature, some tradition or memories, and some even feed it poetry.

Writing

In Adrienne Rich's poem "The Observer," the speaker contrasts her own life with the life of Dian Fossey, a scientist who studied gorillas by living among them in the African jungle. Freewrite about the type of life that you imagine Fossey might have led while living among the gorillas. Why do you think she chose to lead this sort of life? What dangers do you think she might have faced? Why might she have found the experience rewarding?

Guide for Interpreting 1155

Literary Focus Parallelism is an especially significant device in Hebrew, in the Oriental languages, and in the poetry of Native Americans. Point out that parallelism is apparent in any number of the biblical psalms. For example, Psalm 19 reads: "Day unto day uttereth speech, and night unto night showeth knowledge."

Writing/Prior Knowledge Have the students complete the freewriting assignment. For extra credit you might have them prepare a report on Dian Fossey's scientific studies.

Vocabulary

Preteach the following vocabulary words:

subscribe (səb skrīb′) *v.:* To give support, sanction, or approval (p. 1156, l. 17)

automation (ôt′ ə mā′ shən) *n.:* In manufacturing, a system or process in which many or all of the processes of production, movement, and inspection of parts and materials are automatically performed or controlled by self-operated machinery (p. 1158, l. 20)

humble (hum′ b'l) *adj.:* Not proud; modest (p. 1254, l. 27)

pervade (pər vād′) *v.:* To pass through; to spread throughout (p. 1160, l. 4)

The Observer

Adrienne Rich

Completely protected on all sides
by volcanoes
a woman, darkhaired, in stained jeans
sleeps in central Africa.
5 In her dreams, her notebooks, still
private as maiden diaries,
the mountain gorillas move through their life term:
their gentleness survives
observation. Six bands of them
10 inhabit, with her, the wooded highland.
When I lay me down to sleep
unsheltered by any natural guardians
from the panicky life-cycle of my tribe
I wake in the old cellblock
15 observing the daily executions,
rehearsing the laws
I cannot subscribe to,
envying the pale gorilla-scented dawn
she wakes into, the stream where she washes her hair,
20 the camera-flash of her quiet
eye.

THINKING ABOUT THE SELECTION

Recalling

1. What inhabits the wooded highland with the darkhaired woman?
2. (a) Where is the speaker when she wakes? (b) What does she observe? (c) What does she rehearse?

Interpreting

3. (a) What do the details in the poem suggest about the world in which the speaker lives? (b) How does her world contrast with the world in which the scientist lives? (c) What is the speaker's attitude toward her world? (d) How is this attitude revealed?
4. Why does the speaker envy the scientist?

Applying

5. Do you think that most people in contemporary American society would envy the scientist? Why or why not?

Primary Source

Dian Fossey lived among the gorillas while Jane Goodall, another scientist of great renown, chose a similar life among the chimpanzees of Africa. Here Goodall describes a day three months after her arrival. " . . . I set off alone one morning for the mountain I had climbed on my first afternoon—the mountain that rose directly above our camp. I left at my ususal time, when it was still cool, in the first glimmerings of dawn. After ten minutes or so my heart began to hammer wildly, I could feel the blood pounding in my head, and I had to stop to catch my breath. Eventually I reached an open peak about one thousand feet above the lake. It offered a superb view over the home valley, so I decided to sit there for a while and search for signs of chimpanzees through my binoculars.

"I had been there some fifteen minutes when a slight movement caught my eye. I looked around and saw three chimps standing there staring at me. I expected them to flee, for they were no farther than eighty yards away, but after a moment they moved on again, quite calmly, and were soon lost to sight in some thicker vegetation. . . .

"I remained on my peak, and later on in the morning a group of chimps . . . careered down the opposite mountain slope and began feeding in some fig trees that grew thickly along the streambanks in the valley below me. . . . Although they all stopped and stared and then hastened their steps slightly as they moved on again, the chimpanzees did not run in panic. . . .

"That day, in fact, marked the turning point in my study. The fig trees grow all along the lower reaches of the stream and that year the crop in our valley was plentiful, lasting for eight weeks. Every day I returned to my peak, and every day chimpanzees fed on the figs below. They came in large groups and small groups, singly and in pairs. Regularly they passed me. . . . And because I always looked the same, wearing similar dull-colored clothes, and never tried to follow them or harass them in any way, the shy chimpanzees began to realize, at long last, that after all I was not so horrific and terrifying."

The Observer 1157

ANSWERS TO THINKING ABOUT THE SELECTION
Recalling

1. Six bands of mountain gorillas inhabit the wooded highland.
2. (a) The speaker is in an old cell-block. (b) She observes daily executions. (c) She rehearses laws she cannot subscribe to.

Interpreting

3. (a) The speaker's world is restrictive, unnatural, and dangerous. (b) The scientist's world is natural and unconfined. (c) She has a negative attitude toward her world. (d) It is revealed in her description of her daily activities.
4. The scientist's life is unfettered and subject to the laws of nature, unlike the poet's. She envies the natural, unconfined nature of the scientist.

Applying

5. Answers will differ. Suggested Response: No, because most people would not enjoy living in such conditions.

Motivation/Prior Knowledge
Discuss hunger with your students. Whom have they known who was truly hungry? What is natural hunger like? What is the difference between needing food and wanting food?

Master Teacher Note You may wish to have your **more advanced** students prepare a report on the homeless in the big cities of the United States. Who are they? Why are they there? What has the government done to abet the problem?

1 Enrichment Although Oritz writes about New York City, he is an Acoma Pueblo of the Southwest. His background is almost exactly opposite of the area about which he writes. The Acomas live some seventy miles west of Albuquerque. A small mesa rises three hundred feet or so in a vast landscape of low brown mountains, cliffs and a shallow valley rests green with centuries of nurture and carefully guarded fertility. On top of this mesa sit the irregular adobe houses of Acoma Pueblo, the Sky City, of the same color as the cliffs below and invisible from a distance. This is the matrix of the Acoma people, first built they say, sometime before history when Masaweh, one to the Divine Twins, created by the earth herself, led the people up the cliffs. What might be the perspective of a Native American from this southwestern environment who is suffering from hunger in the urban Northeast?

2 Discussion Why does hunger ask these questions?

3 Discussion In what way might this be a typical Native American response? Why does he express respect for the earth, even though it is not providing him food?

Hunger in New York City

Simon Ortiz

Hunger crawls into you
from somewhere out of your muscles
or the concrete or the land
or the wind pushing you.

5 It comes to you, asking
for food, words, wisdom, young memories
of places you ate at, drank cold spring water,
or held somebody's hand,
or home of the gentle, slow dances,
10 the songs, the strong gods, the world
you know.

That is, hunger searches you out.
It always asks you,
How are you, son? Where are you?
15 Have you eaten well?
Have you done what you as a person
of our people is supposed to do?

And the concrete of this city,
the oily wind, the blazing windows,
20 the shrieks of automation cannot,
truly cannot, answer for that hunger
although I have hungered,
truthfully and honestly, for them
to feed myself with.

25 So I sang to myself quietly:
I am feeding myself
with the humble presence
of all around me;
I am feeding myself
30 with your soul, my mother earth;
make me cool and humble.
Bless me.

Closure and Extension

ANSWERS TO THINKING ABOUT THE SELECTION
Recalling

1. (a) The hunger crawls into you from "out of your muscles/or the concrete or the land/or the wind pushing you." (b) It asks for food, words, wisdom, memories, home

THE LONE TENEMENT
George W. Bellows

Humanities Note

Fine art, *The Lone Tenement*, 1909, by George W. Bellows. George Wesley Bellows (1882–1925), an American painter and lithographer, studied with the realist painter Robert Henri. At the age of 27, Bellows was accepted as a member of the National Academy of design, the youngest man ever to be so honored. His enthusiasm for life was reflected in his dynamic paintings of the ordinary things he saw around him. Lauded as an American artist of remarkable promise, his untimely death at the age of forty-two deprived the art world of a great artistic talent.

The painting *The Lone Tenement* is a view of a single derelict building left standing on a demolition site, an urban scene familiar to all city dwellers. Its loneliness and decrepitude evoke the same feelings of sadness in today's viewer as it did in 1909. The soft blurred technique of the painting tends to increase the depression of the scene. This painting is an example of the realism with which Bellows explored the noise, beauty, color, and ugliness of city life.

Questions for class discussion:
1. What comment is this artist making about city life?
2. What words might you use to describe both the painting and the poem?

THINKING ABOUT THE SELECTION

Recalling

1. (a) From where does hunger crawl into you? (b) For what does it ask? (c) What cannot "answer for" the hunger?
2. What does the speaker sing to himself?

Interpreting

3. How does Ortiz personify hunger?
4. (a) What details indicate that the speaker has moved to the city from another place? (b) How is this place different from the city? (c) What details indicate that the speaker hungers for his original home?

Applying

5. This poem clearly reflects Ortiz's Native-American heritage. What does it reveal about the traditional attitudes of his tribe?

THINKING AND WRITING

Writing a Poem Using Parallelism

Write a free-verse poem in which you use parallelism to establish a pattern. Start by thinking of a subject for your poem. You might want to write about a personal experience, an important event, or an element of nature. Prepare a list of details describing your subject. Arrange your details in logical order. Then write your poem. When you finish writing, revise and proofread your poem.

Hunger in New York City   1159

---

of the gentle, slow dances, songs, gods, and the world you know.
2. The speaker sang, "I am feeding myself/with the humble presence of all around me . . . /with your soul, my mother earth;/make me cool and humble."

Interpreting

3. Hunger crawls, speaks by asking questions, and searches. These are human qualities.
4. (a) The speaker mentions the land, cold spring water, and mother earth—visions that are not of the city. (b) This other place seems quite rural and pastoral. (c) The speaker's hunger centers on the memories of his past in another place, where his human needs were taken care of.

Applying

5. Suggested Response: It reveals the belief in humility and their respect for the earth.

THINKING AND WRITING

For help with this assignment, students can refer to Lesson 18, "Writing a Poem," in the Handbook of Writing About Literature.

Publishing Student Writing You might suggest that students submit their poems to your school's literary magazine.

Motivation/Prior Knowledge
Ask students to discuss how weather affects their mood. How are they likely to feel on a rainy day? What is their reaction to the first snowfall?

1 Discussion This is a short, strong poem, not unlike a haiku. Remind students that a haiku is a Japanese poem consisting of three lines of five, seven, and then five syllables. How is this poem reminiscent of a haiku?

2 Discussion Is this a complete thought? Why is this play on words so powerful?

3 Discussion What does this reveal about the speaker's mood?

Reader's Response What emotions does snow evoke in you? Why?

1

Most Satisfied by Snow

Diana Chang

Against my windows,
fog knows
what to do, too

Spaces pervade
5   us, as well

But occupied by snow,
I see

2

Matter
matters

3

10   I, too,
flowering

CHRISTMAS MORNING, ADIRONDACKS, 1946
Rockwell Kent
Sunne Savage Gallery, Boston

THINKING ABOUT THE SELECTION

Recalling

1. What does the fog against the speaker's windows know?
2. What does the speaker see when she is "occupied by snow"?

Interpreting

3. What does the speaker mean when she comments that "spaces pervade us"?

4. (a) What difference between fog and snow does this poem highlight? (b) How is this contrast embodied in human beings?
5. (a) What is the meaning of the final two lines? (b) What is the poem's overall message?

Applying

6. This poem suggests that we can learn about ourselves by observing nature. Do you agree with this suggestion? Why or why not?

Most Satisfied by Snow 1161

Humanities Note

Fine art, *Christmas Morning, Adirondacks, 1946,* by Rockwell Kent. Rockwell Kent (1882–1971), an American painter and graphic artist, originally studied architecture at Columbia University in New York City. At the same time, he attended evening art classes taught by the realist painter, Robert Henri. He began his career in architecture as a draftsman but soon decided that fine art was more important to him. He then embarked on a unique and rugged lifestyle that combined painting, writing, and travel with various menial jobs. A true nonconformist, Rockwell Kent practiced his belief that each person should strive to live life exactly as he or she pleased.

Christmas Morning, Adirondacks, 1946 is one of Kent's salutes to nature. He loved the rugged country of the Northeast and portrayed it many times. The snow is rendered in a clean, crisp way that emphasizes its cool beauty. A fierce champion of independent art, Kent never succumbed to the popular trends of abstraction and nonobjectivity in his work. His realistic views of the harsh American landscape of the North are his trademark.

Consider using the following questions for discussion:
1. What do both the poet and the painter feel about snow?
2. How can contemplation of this painting allow your imagination to expand?

Focus

More About the Authors Lawson Fusao Inada's poetry seeks to respect differences and recognize similarities. As he puts it, "I am a man trying to do right by my word." The poet Dave Smith calls the writing of poetry "a moral right." Is there a consciousness to poetry? Should there be one? What is the moral right of poetry?

Rita Dove has said that travel helps her gain different perspectives and helps her avoid becoming complacent. Discuss with the students how their own travel experiences have helped them gain a different perspective. In what other ways might travel experiences provide subjects for poetry?

Lawson Fusao Inada (1938–   )

The first Asian-American poet to have a book published by a major American publishing company, Lawson Fusao Inada has established himself as a widely respected member of the American literary community. He is active in cross-cultural concerns and says, "My main interest now is the discovery of Asian-American culture. I have always been involved with Third World culture." A member of the Japanese-American Citizens League, he directs Project S.O.C., Students of Other Cultures, at Southern Oregon State College where he is a revered member of the English department.

Born in Fresno, California, Inada graduated from Fresno State College and later received a master's degree from the University of Oregon. He has taught at several universities, served as a consultant for many literary organizations, and published a number of books, including *Before the War: Poems As They Happen* (1971). He was also responsible for editing *Aiiieeeee!: An Anthology of Asian-American Writers* (1974).

Rita Dove (1952–   )

Rita Dove has commented that "the events of the poem should never be more important than how that event is recreated." Considering this belief, it is not surprising that her poetry can be characterized by her vivid imagery and skillful use of language. She has also said that stock questions such as "What is poetry about?" are fruitless. Poetry, she believes, leads to personal experience and should awaken readers' feelings. She brings together wide varieties of images to help awareness happen. In her poetry Dove tries to combine real events with insights those events might trigger.

Dove is an advocate of travel, finding it an excellent avenue for personal growth and the best way to ward off complacency. Through travel, she feels, people gain different perspectives on history, events, and humanity.

Dove was born in Akron, Ohio. She graduated with highest honors from Miami University in Oxford, Ohio, and later earned a master's degree from the University of Iowa. She has published several collections of poetry, including *The Yellow House on the Corner* (1980) and *Museum* (1983). In 1987 she received the Pulitzer Prize for her book, *Thomas and Beulah*.

Objectives

1 To appreciate free verse
2 To respond to a poem

Support Material

Teaching Portfolio
Teacher Backup, p. 1571
Usage and Mechanics Worksheet, p. 1575
Vocabulary Check, p. 1576
Analyzing Literature Worksheet, *Understanding Free Verse,* p. 1577
Language Worksheet, *Recognizing Antonyms,* p. 1578
Selection Test, p. 1579

GUIDE FOR INTERPRETING

Plucking Out a Rhythm; This Life

Literary Focus Point out to students that Walt Whitman was the first American poet to use free verse and that free verse did not become popular until the early part of the twentieth century. What changes in society might be reflected in the establishment of free verse as a dominant poetic form?

The Writer's Techniques

Free Verse. The majority of contemporary poetry is written in free verse—verse that has irregular meter and line length. Though free verse lacks regular meter, it does not lack rhythm. Yet it does allow poets to experiment with new types of rhythms in their work. For example, Lawson Fusao Inada's use of free verse enables him to capture the natural rhythms of jazz in "Plucking Out a Rhythm."

Commentary

Art communicates imagination and human experience through many forms. Painting, music, poetry, dance, and sculpture can all express similar things. The mediums change, not necessarily the messages. In "Plucking Out a Rhythm" and "This Life," the poets allude to art forms other than poetry to heighten the subjects expressed in the poems—they mix the arts. Lawson Inada builds an imaginative impression of a bass player creating jazz music piece by piece in a room, or in one's imagination, until the daylight and snow scatter it away. The sound and rhythm of the words play on the reader's imagination to build the impression of music. Finally, the reader hears music where there is none. The poetry and music have combined to create an imaginative experience.

Rita Dove uses a visual art form, a Japanese woodcut, in her poem to evoke a human experience for the reader. The scene conveyed in the woodcut is the scene shaped in the speaker's life and in the poem's words. The woodcut scene is static—a girl waiting—and there is no movement in the speaker's life either. By paralleling the experience of the girl in the woodcut to that of the poem's speaker, Ms. Dove doubles the impact of the experience on the reader.

Each of these poets has used hybrid art, that is poem-and-music and poem-and-woodcut, to work upon the reader in more than one way. Inada, a Japanese American, and Dove, a black American, both embrace hybrid cultures within their own experiences. Do they suggest that adding one art to another, like adding one culture to another, enriches experience by allowing a multiple view of it?

Writing/Prior Knowledge Georgia O'Keeffe said about her painting: "I had to create an equivalent for what I felt about what I was looking at—not copy it." You may wish to show students reproductions of a few of O'Keeffe's paintings of the American Southwest. Discuss how the artist used her imagination to capture the reality of the desert landscape. Then have the students complete the free-writing assignment.

Vocabulary

Preteach the following vocabulary words:
posturing (päs′ chər iŋ) v.: Posing (p. 1164, l. 15)
exuding (ig zo͞od′ iŋ) v.: Oozing, discharging (p. 1164, l. 25)

Writing

In "Plucking Out a Rhythm," Lawson Fusao Inada explores how reality affects our imaginations. Freewrite about your own thoughts concerning the effect of reality on people's imaginations.

Presentation

Motivation/Prior Knowledge Have students imagine that they are sitting alone listening to jazz on the radio. What kind of images does the music evoke?

Purpose-Setting Question How is the imagination limited by reality?

Master Teacher Note Jazz is an American art form. It is a major contribution by black Americans to contemporary culture. Primarily a player's art, which involves extemporizing. Jazz has been played by solo pianists, by pianists with the accompaniment of string bass and drums, by brass bands of five to eight pieces, and by the big bands. Inada's poem presents the image of a jazz bassist. Its free verse hints at rhythms and syncopation. There is probably no more talented jazz bassist than Charles Mingus. We recommend listening to any of his albums, which include *Hora Decubitus* (ABC-Impulse Records), *Let My Children Hear Music* (Columbia G-30628), or *Mingus at Monterey* (Fantasy J81002).

1 **Discussion** Develop the description of the room. Is this an urban or rural setting?

2 **Discussion** What are Japanese features? Is the writer using stereotypes?

Plucking Out a Rhythm

Lawson Fusao Inada

Start with a simple room—
a dullish color—
and draw the one shade down. 1
Hot plate. Bed.
Little phonograph in a corner.

Put in a single figure—
medium weight and height—
but oversize, as a child might.

The features must be Japanese. 2

Then stack a black pompadour[1] on,
and let the eyes
slide behind a night of glass.

The figure is in disguise:

slim green suit
for posturing on a bandstand,
the turned-up shoes of Harlem[2] . . .

Then start the music playing—
thick jazz, strong jazz—

and notice that the figure
comes to life:
sweating, growling
over an imaginary bass—
plucking out a rhythm—
as the music rises and the room is full,
exuding with that rhythm . . .

---

1. **pompadour** (päm′pə dôr′) *n.*: A hairdo in which the hair is swept up high from the forehead.
2. **Harlem:** A section of New York City, located in northern Manhattan.

VAUDEVILLE, 1951
Jacob Lawrence
Hirshhorn Museum and Sculpture Garden, Smithsonian Institution

Humanities Note

Fine art, *Vaudeville,* 1951, by Jacob Lawrence. The Afro-American artist Jacob Lawrence was born in 1917 in the Harlem section of New York City. An underpriviledged childhood did not prevent him from finding an outlet for his talent in settlement house art classes. Later, the WPA artist subsidy project gave Lawrence the financial freedom that he needed to devote his time to painting. Working in a deliberate, primitive style characterized by bright colors and exaggeration and distortion of form, Jacob Lawrence's vigorous, narrative paintings of the black experience won him the reputation of America's leading black painter.

The painting *Vaudeville* is a bright decorative salute to the artist's memories of the Apollo Theater in Harlem. The influence of printed cartoons on Lawrence's art is obvious here. The caricatures of the performers and the intense, arbitrary color combinations are reminiscent of the Sunday comics. Lawrence was not recalling any particular show that he saw; rather, he was trying to capture the essence of all of the shows he saw at that theater.

You might use these questions for discussion:

1. What elements of this painting reflect aspects of Inada's poem?
2. If there were music to accompany this painting, what kind of music would it be?

3 Discussion Who or what is really playing in the room?

Reader's Response What is your favorite type of music? What emotions does it evoke in you? Why?

Then have the shade flap up
and daylight catch him
frozen in that pose

as it starts to snow—
30   thick snow, strong snow—

blowing in the window
while the music quiets,
the room is slowly covered,

and the figure is completely
35   out of sight.

Primary Source

Jazz music is an influential American art form. It flowered in the 1920's, the age that took its name. Among the greats of "The Jazz Age," the names Joe "King" Oliver and Louis Armstrong stand out. They played "the real stuff." The writers of Time-Life's *This Fabulous Century* series say this about these greats:

The King's Men

Who played the real stuff? The Negroes of Chicago's South Side agreed that the best group of all in 1923 was King Oliver's Creole Jazz Band. The name "Creole" indicated its origin—the band was almost a Who's Who of the best musicians to come north from New Orleans. Johnny Dodds played the clarinet and his younger brother, called "Baby," was on drums. Joe Oliver, the cornet-playing leader, had long been acknowledged the Crescent City's top brass man and he had with him a new cornet-playing sensation from down home, a cheerful lad named Louis Armstrong. Joe and Louis could read each other's mind and when they did duet breaks, playing in perfect harmony with no rehearsal, the crowd at Chicago's Lincoln Gardens went wild, standing on tables and shouting. The band had, everyone agreed, "that great blue New Orleans sound," and Joe Oliver deserved his title of King.

Oliver was a powerfully built man of formidable girth. When he was about to blow something really hot he would say to the admirers grouped around the bandstand, "Now you'll get a chance to see Papa Joe's red underwear." And as he blew chorus after chorus his stiff shirtfront would pop and the red undershirt— he always wore one—would show through. "I never blew my horn over Joe Oliver at no time," Armstrong recalled, "unless he said, 'Take it!' Never. Papa Joe was a creator—always some little idea—and he exercised them beautifully. I'll never run out of ideas. All I have to do is think about Joe."

THINKING ABOUT THE SELECTION
Recalling

1. (a) What details does the speaker use in describing the "simple room"? (b) How does he describe the appearance of the "single figure"? (c) What is this person wearing? (d) What type of music does he play?
2. What causes the figure to disappear from sight?

Interpreting

3. To what two senses do most of the images, or word pictures, in the poem appeal?
4. How does the image in line 30 echo the image in line 17?
5. What does the impact of the snow on the imaginary musician suggest about the effect of reality on the imagination?

Applying

6. In what way do people's imaginations set them apart from one another?

ANALYZING LITERATURE
Understanding Free Verse

Free verse is verse that has irregular meter and line length. Through the use of free verse, poets are able to experiment with new types of rhythms in their poetry.
1. Why is free verse an appropriate form for "Plucking Out a Rhythm"?
2. How would the poem be different if it were written in verse with regular meter and line length?

THINKING AND WRITING
Responding to a Poem

Imagine that Lawson Fusao Inada has asked you to respond to "Plucking Out a Rhythm." Reread the poem. What do you like about the poem? What do you dislike about it? Organize your thoughts. Then write your response, using passages from the poem to support your opinions. When you finish writing, revise and proofread your response.

Plucking Out a Rhythm 1167

Motivation/Prior Knowledge
Ask students to discuss the possessions that were most important to them when they were younger. What did these possessions mean to them?

Master Teacher Note This poem alludes to a Japanese woodcut. Woodcutting is an art form in which the artist uses a thin block of wood to create a picture. The most famous designers of woodblock prints are Hokusai (1760–1849) and Hiroshige (1797–1858). *The Art of Japan* (Kodansha, 1981) is an excellent source of representations of these paintings.

1 **Discussion** What is most like golden dresses in a nutshell?

Discussion Would you like to know the two people spoken about in this poem? Why or why not?

This Life

Rita Dove

The green lamp flares on the table.
You tell me the same thing
as that one,
asleep, upstairs.
5   Now I see: the possibilities
are like golden dresses in a nutshell.

As a child, I fell in love
with a Japanese woodcut
of a girl gazing at the moon.
10   I waited with her for her lover.
He came in white breeches[1] and sandals.
He had a goatee[2]—he had

your face, though I didn't know it.
Our lives will be the same—
15   your lips, swollen from whistling
at danger,
and I a stranger
in this desert,
nursing the tough skin of figs.

---

1. breeches *n*.: Pants reaching to or just below the knees.
2. goatee (gō tē′) *n*.: A small, pointed beard.

THINKING ABOUT THE SELECTION

Recalling

1. What does the speaker "see" in the first stanza?
2. What childhood memory does the speaker describe in the second stanza?
3. How does the speaker describe her life in the final three lines?

Interpreting

4. Who might the "one" mentioned in line 3 be?

5. What is the meaning of the simile, or comparison, in lines 5 and 6?
6. (a) What is the significance of the speaker's childhood memory? (b) How does it seem to relate to her present life?
7. What attitude does "whistling at danger" suggest?
8. What impression does the image of the "tough skin of figs" convey?

Applying

9. Why do childhood memories seem so vivid?

Closure and Extension

ANSWERS TO THINKING ABOUT THE SELECTION
Recalling

1. The speaker sees that possibilities are like golden dresses in a nutshell.

1168

2. The speaker remembers a Japanese woodcut of a girl gazing at the moon, waiting for her lover.
3. Her life is like that of a stranger in the desert nursing the tough skin of figs.

Interpreting

4. The "one" might be her child.
5. Suggested Response: The possibilities are beautiful but limited.
6. (a) Suggested Response: The speaker associates herself with

the girl in the woodcut. (b) Suggested Response: The speaker feels that her life will be like that of the girl in the woodcut.
7. It suggests an indifferent attitude toward danger.
8. It conveys the impression that her life is filled with hardships.

Applying

9. Answers will differ. Suggest Response: They seem vivid, because they played an important

role in shaping people's current lives.

Challenge How important of a role do our early childhood experiences play in shaping our characters?

Drama

THE FABULOUS INVALID, 1938
Set Design by Donald Oenslayer
The Museum of the City of New York

Humanities Note

Fine art, *The Fabulous Invalid, 1938,* set design by Donald Oenslager. Donald Oenslager (1902–1975), a prominent twentieth-century set designer, originally studied acting; he produced his first stage set at the age of twenty-two. Along with a half-dozen or so other well-known set designers, Oenslager helped modernize the profession.

The Fabulous Invalid, which ran for only sixty-five performances after it opened in 1938, was—fittingly enough—a play about the American theater itself. Each act of the musical work presented a different era in the history of the theater as an art form in the United States. Two other giants of the American theater wrote the libretto and the music for *The Fabulous Invalid:* Moss Hart and George S. Kaufman.

More About the Author During the two years following the production and publication of *The Crucible,* Miller was investigated for possible communist associations and was refused a passport to visit Belgium. In 1956 he was called to testify before the House Committee on UnAmerican Activities. Refusing to offer the information the Committee wanted, Miller was found in contempt of Congress. However, this conviction was reversed the following year by the federal Court of Appeals. Ask students to discuss the role that *The Crucible* might have played in arousing suspicion about Miller's political involvement. Do they think an artistic creation, such as a play, should be judged politically? Why or why not?

Critical Evaluation In his essay "Salem Witchcraft in Recent Fiction and Drama," the American literary scholar David Levin discusses Miller's purpose in depicting the Salem witchcraft trials in *The Crucible* Levin writes, "In the twentieth century as well as the seventeenth, Mr. Miller insists in his preface, . . . [absolute morality and] human pride make devils out of the opponents of orthodoxy and destroy individual freedom. Using the Salem episode to show that it also blinds people to the truth, he has his characters turn the truth upside down."

1915–

Considered among the finest American playwrights of the contemporary era, Miller chronicled the dilemma of common people pitted against powerful and unyielding social forces. His plays have earned acclaim from both critics and the general public.

Miller was born in New York City in 1915. During the Depression, his father suffered severe financial losses that forced the family to move from Manhattan to more modest quarters in Brooklyn. In the aftermath of his family's financial downfall, Miller dropped out of high school and worked as a shipping clerk in an automobile parts warehouse—an experience that he later dramatized in *A Memory of Two Mondays* (1955). Despite his inability to complete high school, in 1934 he persuaded the University of Michigan to accept him as a student and used his savings from his warehouse job to finance the first year of his studies.

It was in college that Miller first began to write plays. After graduation, he continued to write while holding a variety of jobs, including one at the Brooklyn Naval Yard. In 1947 his play *All My Sons* opened on Broadway. The play, which focuses on a businessman whose actions during World War II bring about the disintegration of his family, earned immediate critical acclaim and established Miller as one of the country's most promising playwrights.

Miller fulfilled this promise as a writer two years later, when he completed *Death of a Salesman*. He created, in the character of Willy Loman, a deluded and tragic protagonist whose obsessive and futile quest for material success evoked an ambivalent reaction from the audience. *Death of a Salesman* won a Pulitzer Prize and catapulted Miller to international fame.

Departing from a contemporary milieu, Miller wrote *The Crucible* in 1953. Although it depicts the Salem witchcraft trials of 1692, the play was inspired by Miller's belief that the hysteria surrounding the witchcraft trials paralleled the contemporary political climate of McCarthyism—Senator Joseph McCarthy's obsessive quest to uncover communist infiltration of American institutions.

In 1956 the public spotlight become focused on Miller's personal life, when he married film star Marilyn Monroe. During his five-year marriage to Monroe, Miller did little writing, though he did write the screenplay for *The Misfits* (1961), a film that starred Monroe. After the marriage ended in divorce, Miller once again became a prolific writer. His later plays include *Vichy* (1964), *The Price* (1968), *The Creation of the World and Other Business* (1972), *The Archbishop's Ceiling* (1977), and *The American Clock* (1980).

1170   Contemporary Writers

GUIDE FOR INTERPRETING

The Crucible, Act I

Historical Context

The Salem Witchcraft Trials. In 1692 the colony of Massachusetts was plagued by a witchcraft hysteria that resulted in the death of at least twenty people and the jailing of at least 150 others. Although this event is considered by many to be one of the most tragic incidents in American history, it was actually only a small part of a much larger witchcraft hysteria that swept through the western world during the sixteenth and seventeenth centuries. In fact, historians estimate that between one and nine million alleged witches were either hanged or burned to death in Europe during this two-hundred-year period.

Despite the rampant hysteria in Europe at the time, there had been no mass accusations of witchcraft in Massachusetts prior to 1692. However, the extremely stressful nature of the lives of the Puritans who inhabited the colony made an outbreak such as the one that occurred in 1692 almost inevitable. The colonists endured harsh, cold winters; suffered through outbreaks of fatal diseases; struggled to save their crops in the face of such calamities as drought and insect infestation; experienced devastating fires; and lived through attacks by pirates and Indians, as well as French and Dutch warships. Finding themselves at the mercy of forces beyond their control, many of the colonists attributed their hardships to the Devil and were eager to strike back at the evil forces responsible for their suffering.

The witchcraft hysteria of 1692 originated in the small parish of Salem Village, now Danvers, Massachusetts. Most of the people of Salem Village were poor, uneducated, and superstitious; and they were quick to blame witchcraft when the minister's daughter and niece and several other girls became afflicted by a strange malady involving seizures and lapses into an unconscious state. After the minister, Reverend Samuel Parris, had questioned his daughter and niece for some time, the two girls accused the minister's slave, Tituba, and two other women of being responsible for their suffering. The three accused women were immediately taken into custody, and Tituba was coerced into confirming the girls' accusations. Eventually, other girls began naming people who were supposedly persecuting them, and dozens of people were jailed. Learning of the furor in Salem Village, the Governor of the Massachusetts Bay Colony appointed several of the colony's leading citizens to a court responsible for trying all those accused of witchcraft. It was at this point that the Salem witchcraft trials began.

Writing

Write a journal entry in which you explore your own perceptions of life in the Massachusetts Bay Colony and discuss how you think you would have fared if you had lived there.

Guide for Interpreting 1171

Literary Focus Have a student read aloud the information about the Salem witchcraft trials. Then have students discuss the hardships that the Puritan settlers faced and the reasons why these hardships might have made them especially vulnerable to an outbreak of witchcraft hysteria.

Writing/Prior Knowledge Before students begin their journal entries, you might want to have them read or review one or more of the following selections from The New Land unit: from *Of Plymouth Plantation* by William Bradford (p. 52), from *Sinners in the Hands of an Angry God* by Jonathan Edwards (p. 72), from *The Wonders of the Invisible World* by Cotton Mather (p. 77).

Vocabulary

Preteach the following vocabulary words:

predilection (pred′ 'l ek′ shən) *n.:* An already existing liking

parochial (pə rō′ kē əl) *adj.:* Narrow; limited

ingratiating (in grā′ shē āt iŋ) *adj.:* Having a quality that brings (oneself) into favor

dissembling (di sem′ bliŋ) *n.:* Pretense

subservient (səb sʉr′ vē ənt) *adj.:* Submissive

calumny (kal′ əm nē) *n.:* False accusation; slander

inferentially (in fə ren′ shəl lē) *adv.:* Determined by reasoning from something known or assumed

inculcation (in kul′ kā shən) *n.:* Teaching by repetition and insistent urging

propitiation (prə pish′ ē ā′ shən) *n.:* Appeasement or conciliation

licentious (lī sen′ shəs) *adj.:* Disregarding accepted rules

Spelling Tip Call students' attention to the fact that the words *predilection, inculcation,* and *propitiation* all end with the letters *tion.*

The Crucible

Arthur Miller

CHARACTERS

Reverend Parris	Giles Corey
Betty Parris	Reverend John Hale
Tituba	Elizabeth Proctor
Abigail Williams	Francis Nurse
Susanna Walcott	Ezekiel Cheever
Mrs. Ann Putnam	Marshal Herrick
Thomas Putnam	Judge Hathorne
Mercy Lewis	Deputy Governor Danforth
Mary Warren	Sarah Good
John Proctor	Hopkins
Rebecca Nurse	

ACT I
(An Overture)

1
2
A small upper bedroom in the home of REVEREND SAMUEL PARRIS, *Salem, Massachusetts, in the spring of the year 1692.*

There is a narrow window at the left. Through its leaded panes the morning sunlight streams. A candle still burns near the bed, which is at the right. A chest, a chair, and a small table are the other furnishings. At the back a door opens on the landing of the stairway to the ground floor. The room gives off an air of clean spareness. The roof rafters are exposed, and the wood colors are raw and unmellowed.

As the curtain rises, REVEREND PARRIS *is discovered kneeling beside the bed, evidently in prayer. His daughter,* BETTY PARRIS, *aged ten, is lying on the bed, inert.*

At the time of these events Parris was in his middle forties. In history he cut a villainous path, and there is very little good to be said for him. He believed he was being persecuted wherever he went, despite his best efforts to win people and God to his side. In meeting, he felt insulted if someone rose to shut the door without first asking his permission. He was a widower with no interest in children, or talent with them. He regarded them as young adults, and until this strange crisis he, like the rest of Salem, never conceived that the children were anything but thankful for being permitted to walk straight, eyes slightly lowered, arms at the sides, and mouths shut until bidden to speak.

His house stood in the "town"—but we today would hardly call it a village. The meeting house was nearby, and from this point outward—toward the bay or inland—there

1172   Contemporary Writers

Grammar in Action

When the subject of a sentence receives, rather than performs, the verb's action, the **passive voice** is being used. In contrast, when the subject performs the action, the **active voice** is being used. Note the following examples from *The Crucible:*

Active Voice: He *believed* he was being persecuted wherever he went.

Passive Voice: The parochial snobbery of these people *was* partly *responsible* for their failure to convert the Indians.

While the active voice is preferred whenever possible, the

were a few small-windowed, dark houses snuggling against the raw Massachusetts winter. Salem had been established hardly forty years before. To the European world the whole province was a barbaric frontier inhabited by a sect of fanatics who, nevertheless, were shipping out products of slowly increasing quantity and value.

No one can really know what their lives were like. They had no novelists—and would not have permitted anyone to read a novel if one were handy. Their creed forbade anything resembling a theater or "vain enjoyment." They did not celebrate Christmas, and a holiday from work meant only that they must concentrate even more upon prayer.

Which is not to say that nothing broke into this strict and somber way of life. When a new farmhouse was built, friends assembled to "raise the roof," and there would be special foods cooked and probably some potent cider passed around. There was a good supply of ne'er-do-wells in Salem, who dallied at the shovelboard[1] in Bridget Bishop's tavern. Probably more than the creed, hard work kept the morals of the place from spoiling, for the people were forced to fight the land like heroes for every grain of corn, and no man had very much time for fooling around.

That there were some jokers, however, is indicated by the practice of appointing a two-man patrol whose duty was to "walk forth in the time of God's worship to take notice of such as either lie about the meeting house, without attending to the word and ordinances, or that lie at home or in the fields without giving good account thereof, and to take the names of such persons, whereby they may be accordingly proceeded against." This predilection for minding other people's business was time-honored among the

people of Salem, and it undoubtedly created many of the suspicions which were to feed the coming madness. It was also, in my opinion, one of the things that a John Proctor would rebel against, for the time of the armed camp had almost passed, and since the country was reasonably—although not wholly—safe, the old disciplines were beginning to rankle. But, as in all such matters, the issue was not clear-cut, for danger was still a possibility, and in unity still lay the best promise of safety.

The edge of the wilderness was close by. The American continent stretched endlessly west, and it was full of mystery for them. It stood, dark and threatening, over their shoulders night and day, for out of it Indian tribes marauded from time to time, and Reverend Parris had parishioners who had lost relatives to these heathens.

The parochial snobbery of these people was partly responsible for their failure to convert the Indians. Probably they also preferred to take land from heathens rather than from fellow Christians. At any rate, very few Indians were converted, and the Salem folk believed that the virgin forest was the Devil's last preserve, his home base and the citadel[2] of his final stand. To the best of their knowledge the American forest was the last place on earth that was not paying homage to God.

For these reasons, among others, they carried about an air of innate resistance, even of persecution. Their fathers had, of course, been persecuted in England. So now they and their church found it necessary to deny any other sect its freedom, lest their New Jerusalem[3] be defiled and corrupted by wrong ways and deceitful ideas.

They believed, in short, that they held in their steady hands the candle that would light the world. We have inherited this belief, and it has helped and hurt us. It helped

---

1. shovelboard: A game in which a coin or other disk is driven with the hand along a highly polished board, floor, or table marked with transverse lines.

2. citadel (sit′ ə d'l) n.: A fortified place; stronghold.
3. New Jerusalem: In the Bible, the holy city of heaven.

The Crucible 1173

---

passive voice is sometimes used to preserve the vitality of action verbs or to place emphasis on the subject.

Student Activity 1. Identify the type of voice used in each of the following passages from *The Crucible:*
1. This predilection for minding other people's business was time-honored among the people of Salem, . . .
2. When a new farmhouse was built, friends assembled to "raise the roof," . . .
3. They believed, in short, that they held in their steady hands the candle that would light the world.
4. The Englishmen who landed there were motivated mainly by a hunt for profit.

Student Activity 2. Transform each of the following active sentences into a passive sentence:
1. We have inherited this belief.
2. And I heard a screeching and gibberish coming from her mouth.
3. I'll lead them in a psalm, but let you say nothing of witchcraft yet.
4. However, that experience never raised a doubt in his mind as to the reality of the underworld or the existence of Lucifer's many-faced lieutenants.
5. We discovered he this morning on the high road.

8 Discussion Have students discuss the tone of this passage. What seems to be Miller's attitude toward the people who founded the settlement at Jamestown? Does he really believe that they were "a much more ingratiating group than the Massachusetts men"? On what do you base your answer?

9 Discussion Ask students what seems to be Miller's attitude toward the earliest Puritan settlers. How is his attitude conveyed?

10 Enrichment Tell students that in 1689 the people of Boston rose in revolt, imprisoned the Royal Governor, and established their own government.

11 Discussion Point out to students that Miller draws a comparison between the contemporary age and time in which the Puritans lived. Why might he have viewed the contemporary age as "insoluble and complicated"?

12 Clarification Explain to students that the phrase *laying on* means "attacking."

13 Clarification If students are not familiar with the term *paradox*, call their attention to the information about this term on page 279.

14 Discussion Have students respond to Miller's comment that "It is still impossible for man to organize his social life without repressions." Do they agree with Miller's observation? Why or why not?

them with the discipline it gave them. They were a dedicated folk, by and large, and they had to be to survive the life they had chosen or been born into in this country.

The proof of their belief's value to them may be taken from the opposite character of the first Jamestown settlement, farther south, in Virginia. The Englishmen who landed there were motivated mainly by a hunt for profit. They had thought to pick off the wealth of the new country and then return rich to England. They were a band of individuals, and a much more ingratiating group than the Massachusetts men. But Virginia destroyed them. Massachusetts tried to kill off the Puritans, but they combined; they set up a communal society which, in the beginning, was little more than an armed camp with an autocratic and very devoted leadership. It was, however, an autocracy by consent, for they were united from top to bottom by a commonly held ideology whose perpetuation was the reason and justification for all their sufferings. So their self-denial, their purposefulness, their suspicion of all vain pursuits, their hard-handed justice, were altogether perfect instruments for the conquest of this space so antagonistic to man.

But the people of Salem in 1692 were not quite the dedicated folk that arrived on the *Mayflower*. A vast differentiation had taken place, and in their own time a revolution had unseated the royal government and substituted a junta[4] which was at this moment in power. The times, to their eyes, must have been out of joint, and to the common folk must have seemed as insoluble and complicated as do ours today. It is not hard to see how easily many could have been led to believe that the time of confusion had been brought upon them by deep and darkling forces. No hint of such speculation appears on the court record, but social disorder in any age breeds such mystical suspicions, and when, as in Salem, wonders are brought

---

4. junta (hoon'tə) *n.*: An assembly or council.

forth from below the social surface, it is too much to expect people to hold back very long from laying on the victims with all the force of their frustrations.

The Salem tragedy, which is about to begin in these pages, developed from a paradox. It is a paradox in whose grip we still live, and there is no prospect yet that we will discover its resolution. Simply, it was this: for good purposes, even high purposes, the people of Salem developed a theocracy, a combine of state and religious power whose function was to keep the community together, and to prevent any kind of disunity that might open it to destruction by material or ideological enemies. It was forged for a necessary purpose and accomplished that purpose. But all organization is and must be grounded on the idea of exclusion and prohibition, just as two objects cannot occupy the same space. Evidently the time came in New England when the repressions of order were heavier than seemed warranted by the dangers against which the order was organized. The witch-hunt was a perverse manifestation of the panic which set in among all classes when the balance began to turn toward greater individual freedom.

When one rises above the individual villainy displayed, one can only pity them all, just as we shall be pitied someday. It is still impossible for man to organize his social life without repressions, and the balance has yet to be struck between order and freedom.

The witch-hunt was not, however, a mere repression. It was also, and as importantly, a long overdue opportunity for everyone so inclined to express publicly his guilt and sins, under the cover of accusations against the victims. It suddenly became possible—and patriotic and holy—for a man to say that Martha Corey had come into his bedroom at night, and that, while his wife was sleeping at his side, Martha laid herself down on his chest and "nearly suffocated him." Of course it was her spirit only, but his satisfaction at confessing himself was no lighter than if it had been Martha herself.

Grammar in Action

An adverb is a word that modifies a verb, an adjective, or another adverb. Because the **placement of an adverb** in a sentence indicates the word it is modifying, it is important to place adverbs as close as possible to the words they modify. Note the position of the adverb in the following sentence from *The Crucible*:

No one can *really* know what their lives were like. (p. 1173)

In this sentence, it is clear that the adverb modifies the verb *to know*. If the position of the adverb is changed, the meaning of the entire sentence is altered. Note the difference in meaning between the following sentence and the preceding example:

No one can know what their lives *really* were like.

Student Activity 1. Rewrite the following sentences, moving each adverb closer to the word it is intended to modify:
1. The Puritans went to church during the week frequently.
2. Mrs. Putnam said she wanted to see only if Betty could fly.
3. Two hours had gone by hardly before the whole town was talking.
4. Reverend Parris was in tears almost.

THE TRIAL OF TWO 'WITCHES' AT SALEM, MASSACHUSETTS, IN 1662
Howard Pyle
The Granger Collection

The Crucible 1175

Humanities Note

Fine art, *The Trial of Two "Witches" at Salem, Massachusetts, in 1862* by Howard Pyle. Pyle (1853–1911) was a well-known and influential illustrator of books and magazines. He began his career as an illustrator for *Harper's Weekly* and other periodicals. Later, he became an illustrator of historical books, including President Woodrow Wilson's *History of the American People*. Having developed a love for history as a young boy, Pyle illustrated a wide range of historical topics. In many of his illustrations, including the one seen here, he depicted events that occurred before America gained its independence. Here he shows a woman pointing an accusatory finger at two suspected witches. Notice how he has captured the varying emotions of the people involved in the trial.

You might want to use the following questions to discuss the art:

1. Describe what is happening in this illustration?
2. What emotions are expressed by the various people depicted in the illustration?
3. Why do you think the artist might have chosen to use a dark gray background in this picture?
4. What thoughts and emotions does this illustration arouse in you? Why?

Student Activity 2. Write five original sentences that each contain at least one adverb. Make sure that you place each adverb as close as possible to the word it modifies.

15 Enrichment In the Bible Lucifer was the highest ranking angel in Heaven until he challenged the authority of God. After a tremendous battle, he and his followers were defeated and cast downward into the pit of Hell.

16 Clarification Make sure students realize that Barbados is a Caribbean island in the British West Indies. Also explain to students that slaves such as Tituba were usually given at least rudimentary instruction in the English language and the Christian religion.

17 Discussion Have students discuss what this exchange suggests about Parris's attitude toward Tituba.

18 Enrichment Tell students that the real Abigail Williams was twelve or thirteen when the witchcraft hysteria broke out. Then have them speculate about why Miller might have altered her age.

19 Discussion Have students speculate about why Parris is so quick to dismiss the possibility that Betty's ailment is the result of "unnatural causes." Why does he instruct her to "Go directly home and speak nothing of unnatural causes"?

One could not ordinarily speak such things in public.

Long-held hatreds of neighbors could now be openly expressed, and vengeance taken, despite the Bible's charitable injunctions. Land-lust which had been expressed before by constant bickering over boundaries and deeds, could now be elevated to the arena of morality; one could cry witch against one's neighbor and feel perfectly justified in the bargain. Old scores could be settled on a plane of heavenly combat between Lucifer[5] and the Lord; suspicions and the envy of the miserable toward the happy could and did burst out in the general revenge.

REVEREND PARRIS *is praying now, and, though we cannot hear his words, a sense of his confusion hangs about him. He mumbles, then seems about to weep; then he weeps, then prays again; but his daughter does not stir on the bed.*

The door opens, and his Negro slave enters. TITUBA *is in her forties.* PARRIS *brought her with him from Barbados, where he spent some years as a merchant before entering the ministry. She enters as one does who can no longer bear to be barred from the sight of her beloved, but she is also very frightened because her slave sense has warned her that, as always, trouble in this house eventually lands on her back.*

TITUBA, *already taking a step backward:* My Betty be hearty soon?

PARRIS: Out of here!

TITUBA, *backing to the door:* My Betty not goin' die . . .

PARRIS, *scrambling to his feet in a fury:* Out of my sight! She is gone. Out of my— *He is overcome with sobs. He clamps his teeth against them and closes the door and leans against it, exhausted.* Oh, my God! God help me! *Quaking with fear, mumbling to*

---

5. Lucifer: The Devil.

himself through his sobs, he goes to the bed and gently takes BETTY's *hand.* Betty. Child. Dear child. Will you wake, will you open up your eyes! Betty, little one . . .

He is bending to kneel again when his niece, ABIGAIL WILLIAMS, *seventeen, enters—a strikingly beautiful girl, an orphan, with an endless capacity for dissembling. Now she is all worry and apprehension and propriety.*

ABIGAIL: Uncle? *He looks to her.* Susanna Walcott's here from Doctor Griggs.

PARRIS: Oh? Let her come, let her come.

ABIGAIL, *leaning out the door to call to* SUSANNA, *who is down the hall a few steps:* Come in, Susanna.

SUSANNA WALCOTT, *a little younger than* ABIGAIL, *a hurried girl, enters.*

PARRIS, *eagerly:* What does the doctor say, child?

SUSANNA, *craning around* PARRIS *to get a look at* BETTY: He bid me come and tell you, reverend sir, that he cannot discover no medicine for it in his books.

PARRIS: Then he must search on.

SUSANNA: Aye, sir, he have been searchin' his books since he left you, sir. But he bid me tell you, that you might look to unnatural things for the cause of it.

PARRIS, *his eyes going wide:* No—no. There be no unnatural cause here. Tell him I have sent for Reverend Hale of Beverly, and Mr. Hale will surely confirm that. Let him look to medicine and put out all thought of unnatural causes here. There be none.

SUSANNA: Aye, sir. He bid me tell you. *She turns to go.*

ABIGAIL: Speak nothin' of it in the village, Susanna.

PARRIS: Go directly home and speak nothing of unnatural causes.

Primary Source

In an introductory essay to a volume of his collected plays, Miller discusses the inspiration of *The Crucible*. He writes, "I had known of the Salem witch hunt for many years before 'McCarthyism' had arrived, and it had always remained an inexplicable darkness to me. When I looked into it now, however, it was with the contemporary situation at my back, particularly the mystery of the handing over of conscience which seemed to me the central and informing fact of the time. One finds, I suppose, what one seeks. I doubt I should ever have tempted agony by actually writing a play on the subject had I not come upon a single fact. It was that Abigail Williams, the prime mover of the Salem hysteria,

SUSANNA: Aye, sir. I pray for her. *She goes out.*

ABIGAIL: Uncle, the rumor of witchcraft is all about; I think you'd best go down and deny it yourself. The parlor's packed with people, sir. I'll sit with her.

20

PARRIS, *pressed, turns on her:* And what shall I say to them? That my daughter and my niece I discovered dancing like heathen in the forest?

ABIGAIL: Uncle, we did dance; let you tell them I confessed it—and I'll be whipped if I must be. But they're speakin' of witchcraft. Betty's not witched.

PARRIS: Abigail, I cannot go before the congregation when I know you have not opened with me. What did you do with her in the forest?

ABIGAIL: We did dance, uncle, and when you leaped out of the bush so suddenly, Betty was frightened and then she fainted. And there's the whole of it.

PARRIS: Child. Sit you down.

ABIGAIL, *quavering, as she sits:* I would never hurt Betty. I love her dearly.

21

PARRIS: Now look you, child, your punishment will come in its time. But if you trafficked with spirits in the forest I must know it now, for surely my enemies will, and they will ruin me with it.

ABIGAIL: But we never conjured spirits.

PARRIS: Then why can she not move herself since midnight? This child is desperate! *Abigail lowers her eyes.* It must come out—my enemies will bring it out. Let me know what you done there. Abigail, do you understand that I have many enemies?

ABIGAIL: I have heard of it, uncle.

22

PARRIS: There is a faction that is sworn to drive me from my pulpit. Do you understand that?

ABIGAIL: I think so, sir.

PARRIS: Now then, in the midst of such disruption, my own household is discovered to be the very center of some obscene practice. Abominations are done in the forest—

ABIGAIL: It were sport, uncle!

PARRIS, *pointing at* BETTY: You call this sport? *She lowers her eyes. He pleads:* Abigail, if you know something that may help the doctor, for God's sake tell it to me. *She is silent.* I saw Tituba waving her arms over the fire when I came on you. Why was she doing that? And I heard a screeching and gibberish coming from her mouth. She were swaying like a dumb beast over that fire!

ABIGAIL: She always sings her Barbados songs, and we dance.

PARRIS: I cannot blink what I saw, Abigail, for my enemies will not blink it. I saw a dress lying on the grass.

ABIGAIL, *innocently:* A dress?

PARRIS—*it is very hard to say:* Aye, a dress. And I thought I saw—someone naked running through the trees!

ABIGAIL, *in terror:* No one was naked! You mistake yourself, uncle!

23

PARRIS, *with anger:* I saw it! *He moves from her. Then, resolved:* Now tell me true, Abigail. And I pray you feel the weight of truth upon you, for now my ministry's at stake, my ministry and perhaps your cousin's life. Whatever abomination you have done, give me all of it now, for I dare not be taken unaware when I go before them down there.

ABIGAIL: There is nothin' more. I swear it, uncle.

PARRIS, *studies her, then nods, half convinced:* Abigail, I have fought here three long years to bend these stiff-necked people to me, and now, just now when some good respect is rising for me in the parish, you compromise my very character. I have given you a home, child, I have put clothes upon your back—now give me upright answer. Your

24

The Crucible 1177

so far as the hysterical children are concerned, had a short time earlier been the house servant of the Proctors and now was crying out Elizabeth Proctor as a witch; but more—it was clear from the record that with entirely uncharacteristic fastidiousness she was refusing to include John Proctor, Elizabeth's husband, in her accusation despite the urgings of the prosecutors. Why?"

---

20 Critical Thinking and Reading Ask students what they can infer about Puritan beliefs from Parris's remark.

21 Discussion Have students discuss what this passage reveals about Parris's personality. What indication is there that he is more concerned about himself than about the well-being of his daughter?

22 Literary Focus Tell students that a Puritan minister could be dismissed if a large enough percentage of his parishioners became displeased with him.

23 Discussion Do students think that Abigail is telling the truth? Why or why not?

24 Discussion Have students discuss what this passage reveals about Parris's attitude toward his parishioners. What does he mean when he refers to them as "stiff-necked people"?

25 Enrichment Tell students that in the Puritan villages it was common for families to hire young, unmarried girls as servants. In return for the services of these girls, the families usually provided them with room and board.

26 Discussion Do students imagine that Abigail's characterization of Goody Proctor is accurate? Why or why not?

27 Discussion Remind students that theatergoers would not have access to the information in this stage direction. Considering this fact, why do they think that Miller included it? Why might it be helpful to an actress playing the role of Goody Putnam?

28 Discussion Have students speculate about why one of the villagers might claim to have seen Betty flying "over Ingersoll's barn." What is revealed by the fact that Goody Putnam apparently believes the villager's story?

name in the town—it is entirely white, is it not?

ABIGAIL, *with an edge of resentment:* Why, I am sure it is, sir. There be no blush about my name.

PARRIS, *to the point:* Abigail, is there any other cause than you have told me, for your being discharged from Goody[6] Proctor's service? I have heard it said, and I tell you as I heard it, that she comes so rarely to the church this year for she will not sit so close to something soiled. What signified that remark?

ABIGAIL: She hates me, uncle, she must, for I would not be her slave. It's a bitter woman, a lying, cold, sniveling woman, and I will not work for such a woman!

PARRIS: She may be. And yet it has troubled me that you are now seven month out of their house, and in all this time no other family has ever called for your service.

ABIGAIL: They want slaves, not such as I. Let them send to Barbados for that. I will not black my face for any of them! *With ill-concealed resentment at him:* Do you begrudge my bed, uncle?

PARRIS: No—no.

ABIGAIL, *in a temper:* My name is good in the village! I will not have it said my name is soiled! Goody Proctor is a gossiping liar!

Enter MRS. ANN PUTNAM. *She is a twisted soul of forty-five, a death-ridden woman, haunted by dreams.*

PARRIS, *as soon as the door begins to open:* No—no, I cannot have anyone. *He sees her, and a certain deference springs into him, although his worry remains.* Why, Goody Putnam, come in.

MRS. PUTNAM, *full of breath, shiny-eyed:* It is a marvel. It is surely a stroke of hell upon you.

---

6. Goody: A title used to refer to a married woman; short for Goodwife.

1178 Contemporary Writers

PARRIS: No, Goody Putnam, it is—

MRS. PUTNAM, *glancing at* BETTY: How high did she fly, how high?

PARRIS: No, no, she never flew—

MRS. PUTNAM, *very pleased with it:* Why, it's sure she did. Mr. Collins saw her goin' over Ingersoll's barn, and come down light as bird, he says!

PARRIS: Now, look you, Goody Putnam, she never—*Enter* THOMAS PUTNAM, *a well-to-do, hard-handed landowner, near fifty.* Oh, good morning, Mr. Putnam.

PUTNAM: It is a providence the thing is out now! It is a providence. *He goes directly to the bed.*

PARRIS: What's out, sir, what's—?

MRS. PUTNAM *goes to the bed.*

PUTNAM, *looking down at* BETTY: Why, *her* eyes is closed! Look you, Ann.

MRS. PUTNAM: Why, that's strange. *To* PARRIS: Ours is open.

PARRIS, *shocked:* Your Ruth is sick?

MRS. PUTNAM, *with vicious certainty:* I'd not call it sick; the Devil's touch is heavier than sick. It's death, y'know, it's death drivin' into them, forked and hoofed.

PARRIS: Oh, pray not! Why, how does Ruth ail?

MRS. PUTNAM: She ails as she must—she never waked this morning, but her eyes open and she walks, and hears naught, sees naught, and cannot eat. Her soul is taken, surely.

PARRIS *is struck.*

PUTNAM, *as though for further details:* They say you've sent for Reverend Hale of Beverly?

PARRIS, *with dwindling conviction now:* A precaution only. He has much experience in all demonic arts, and I—

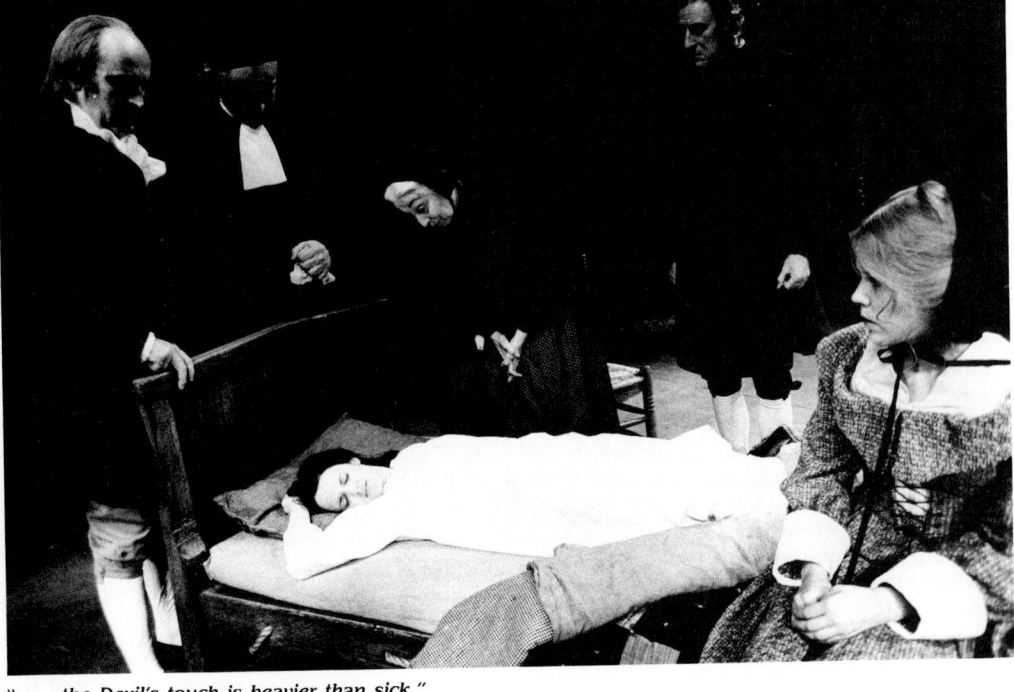

"... the Devil's touch is heavier than sick."

29

MRS. PUTNAM: He has indeed; and found a witch in Beverly last year, and let you remember that.

PARRIS: Now. Goody Ann, they only thought that were a witch, and I am certain there be no element of witchcraft here.

PUTNAM: No witchcraft! Now look you, Mr. Parris—

PARRIS: Thomas, Thomas, I pray you, leap not to witchcraft. I know that you—you least of all, Thomas, would ever wish so disastrous a charge laid upon me. We cannot leap to witchcraft. They will howl me out of Salem for such corruption in my house.

A word about Thomas Putnam. He was a man with many grievances, at least one of which appears justified. Some time before, his wife's brother-in-law, James Bayley, had been turned down as minister at Salem. Bayley had all the qualifications, and a two-thirds vote into the bargain, but a faction stopped his acceptance, for reasons that are not clear.

Thomas Putnam was the eldest son of the richest man in the village. He had fought the Indians at Narragansett, and was deeply interested in parish affairs. He undoubtedly felt it poor payment that the village should so blatantly disregard his candidate for one of its more important offices, especially since he regarded himself as the intellectual superior of most of the people around him.

His vindictive nature was demonstrated long before the witchcraft began. Another former Salem minister, George Burroughs, had had to borrow money to pay for his wife's funeral, and, since the parish was remiss in his salary, he was soon bankrupt.

The Crucible 1179

29 **Discussion** Have students speculate about how Reverend Hale might go about determining whether a person is a witch.

30 **Enrichment** In 1676 and 1677, a group of native American tribes led by Chief Philip, the leader of the Wampanoags, launched an assault against the settlers, prompted by the settlers' encroachments of tribal hunting lands. The settlers retaliated by attacking the stronghold of the Narragansetts near what is now Kingston, Rhode Island. The settlers inflicted heavy losses on the native Americans, and in a later skirmish they killed Chief Philip. This series of battles came to be known as King Philip's War.

31 **Discussion** Given the Puritans' deep commitment to their religious beliefs, do students find it surprising that a group of parishioners would be "remiss" in a minister's salary? Why or why not?

32 Thomas and his brother John had Burroughs jailed for debts the man did not owe. The incident is important only in that Burroughs succeeded in becoming minister where Bayley, Thomas Putnam's brother-in-law, had been rejected; the motif of resentment is clear here. Thomas Putnam felt that his own name and the honor of his family had been smirched by the village, and he meant to right matters however he could.

33 Another reason to believe him a deeply embittered man was his attempt to break his father's will, which left a disproportionate amount to a stepbrother. As with every other public cause in which he tried to force his way, he failed in this.

So it is not surprising to find that so many accusations against people are in the handwriting of Thomas Putnam, or that his name is so often found as a witness corroborating the supernatural testimony, or that **34** his daughter led the crying-out at the most opportune junctures of the trials, especially when—But we'll speak of that when we come to it.

PUTNAM—*at the moment he is intent upon getting* PARRIS, *for whom he has only contempt, to move toward the abyss:*[7] Mr. Parris, I have taken your part in all contention here, and I would continue; but I cannot if you hold back in this. There are hurtful, vengeful spirits layin' hands on these children.

PARRIS: But, Thomas, you cannot—

PUTNAM: Ann! Tell Mr. Parris what you have done.

35 MRS. PUTNAM: Reverend Parris, I have laid seven babies unbaptized in the earth. Believe me, sir, you never saw more hearty babies born. And yet, each would wither in my arms the very night of their birth. I have spoke nothin', but my heart has clamored intimations. And now, this year, my Ruth,

---

7. abyss (ə bis') *n.*: A deep crack in the earth.

my only—I see her turning strange. A secret child she has become this year, and shrivels like a sucking mouth were pullin' on her life too. And so I thought to send her to your Tituba—

PARRIS: To Tituba! What may Tituba—?

MRS. PUTNAM: Tituba knows how to speak to the dead, Mr. Parris.

PARRIS: Goody, Ann, it is a formidable sin to conjure up the dead!

MRS. PUTNAM: I take it on my soul, but who else may surely tell us what person murdered my babies?

PARRIS, *horrified:* Woman!

36 MRS. PUTNAM: They were murdered, Mr. Parris! And mark this proof! Mark it! Last night my Ruth were ever so close to their little spirits; I know it, sir. For how else is she struck dumb now except some power of darkness would stop her mouth? It is a marvelous sign, Mr. Parris!

PUTNAM: Don't you understand it, sir? There is a murdering witch among us, bound to keep herself in the dark. PARRIS *turns to* BETTY, *a frantic terror rising in him.* Let your names make of it what they will, you cannot blink it more.

PARRIS, *to* ABIGAIL: Then you were conjuring spirits last night.

ABIGAIL, *whispering:* Not I, sir—Tituba and Ruth.

37 PARRIS *turns now, with new fear, and goes to* BETTY, *looks down at her, and then, gazing off:* Oh, Abigail, what proper payment for my charity! Now I am undone.

PUTNAM: You are not undone! Let you take hold here. Wait for no one to charge you—declare it yourself. You have discovered witchcraft—

PARRIS: In my house? In my house, Thomas? They will topple me with this! They will make of it a—

Enter MERCY LEWIS, *the Putnams' servant, a fat, sly, merciless girl of eighteen.*

MERCY: Your pardons. I only thought to see how Betty is.

PUTNAM: Why aren't you home? Who's with Ruth?

MERCY: Her grandma come. She's improved a little, I think—she give a powerful sneeze before.

MRS. PUTNAM: Ah, there's a sign of life!

MERCY: I'd fear no more, Goody Putnam. It were a grand sneeze; another like it will shake her wits together, I'm sure. *She goes to the bed to look.*

PARRIS: Will you leave me now, Thomas? I would pray a while alone.

ABIGAIL: Uncle, you've prayed since midnight. Why do you not go down and—

PARRIS: No—no. *To* PUTNAM: I have no answer for that crowd. I'll wait till Mr. Hale arrives. *To get* MRS. PUTNAM *to leave:* If you will, Goody Ann . . .

PUTNAM: Now look you, sir. Let you strike out against the Devil, and the village will bless you for it! Come down, speak to them—pray with them. They're thirsting for your word, Mister! Surely you'll pray with them.

PARRIS, *swayed:* I'll lead them in a psalm, but let you say nothing of witchcraft yet. I will not discuss it. The cause is yet unknown. I have had enough contention since I came; I want no more.

MRS. PUTNAM: Mercy, you go home to Ruth, d'y'hear?

MERCY: Aye, mum.

MRS. PUTNAM *goes out.*

PARRIS, *to* ABIGAIL: If she starts for the window, cry for me at once.

ABIGAIL: I will, uncle.

PARRIS, *to* PUTNAM: There is a terrible power in her arms today. *He goes out with* PUTNAM.

ABIGAIL, *with hushed trepidation:* How is Ruth sick?

MERCY: It's weirdish, I know not—she seems to walk like a dead one since last night.

ABIGAIL, *turns at once and goes to* BETTY, *and now, with fear in her voice:* Betty? BETTY *doesn't move. She shakes her.* Now stop this! Betty! Sit up now!

BETTY *doesn't stir.* MERCY *comes over.*

MERCY: Have you tried beatin' her? I gave Ruth a good one and it waked her for a minute. Here, let me have her.

ABIGAIL, *holding* MERCY *back:* No, he'll be comin' up. Listen, now; if they be questioning us, tell them we danced—I told him as much already.

MERCY: Aye. And what more?

ABIGAIL: He knows Tituba conjured Ruth's sisters to come out of the grave.

MERCY: And what more?

ABIGAIL: He saw you naked.

MERCY, *clapping her hand together with a frightened laugh:* Oh, Jesus!

Enter MARY WARREN, *breathless. She is seventeen, a subservient, naive, lonely girl.*

MARY WARREN: What'll we do? The village is out! I just come from the farm; the whole country's talkin' witchcraft! They'll be callin' us witches, Abby!

MERCY, *pointing and looking at* MARY WARREN: She means to tell, I know it.

MARY WARREN: Abby, we've got to tell. Witchery's a hangin' error, a hangin' like they done in Boston two year ago! We must tell the truth, Abby! You'll only be whipped for dancin', and the other things!

ABIGAIL: Oh, *we'll* be whipped!

The Crucible 1181

38 Critical Thinking and Reading Ask students why Mercy Lewis and Goody Putnam would interpret a sneeze as a sign of life. What, if anything, does this reaction reveal about Puritan beliefs?

39 Discussion Have students discuss why Parris is "swayed" to come down and speak to the crowd.

40 Discussion Have students discuss what is revealed about the three girls and their relationship with one another through their interactions in this scene. What evidence is there that Abigail is the leader of their group of friends? What does Mary Warren's behavior reveal about her character?

41 Clarification Make sure students understand that when Mary refers to witchcraft as a "hangin'" error, she means it is a crime that is punishable by death. Explain that in 1542 the British Parliament had passed a bill making witchcraft a capital crime.

42 Reading Strategy Have students pause and summarize what has happened up to this point. Then have them predict what will happen during the rest of Act I.

43 Discussion Have students imagine that they are early Puritan settlers. Then ask them how they would respond to Betty's behavior.

44 Discussion Have students speculate about why Abigail would drink a "charm to kill John Proctor's wife." What does this reveal about Abigail's character?

45 Discussion Do students think that Abigail's threats should be taken seriously? Why or why not? What does Abigail mean when she says that she "will bring a pointy reckoning that will shudder" the other girls?

46 Discussion Ask students what Miller's attitude toward John Proctor seems to be. How is his attitude conveyed?

47 Discussion Ask students what Miller means when he writes that the Puritans "had no ritual for the washing away of sins." Why does Miller comment that this is a "trait that we inherited from them"?

MARY WARREN: I never done none of it, Abby. I only looked!

MERCY, *moving menacingly toward* MARY: Oh, you're a great one for lookin', aren't you, Mary Warren? What a grand peeping courage you have!

BETTY, *on the bed, whimpers.* ABIGAIL *turns to her at once.*

ABIGAIL: Betty? *She goes to* BETTY. Now, Betty, dear, wake up now. It's Abigail. *She sits* BETTY *up and furiously shakes her.* I'll beat you, Betty! BETTY *whimpers.* My, you seem improving. I talked to your papa and I told him everything. So there's nothing to—

BETTY, *darts off the bed, frightened of* ABIGAIL, *and flattens herself against the wall:* I want my mama!

ABIGAIL, *with alarm, as she cautiously approaches* BETTY: What ails you, Betty? Your mama's dead and buried.

BETTY: I'll fly to Mama. Let me fly! *She raises her arms as though to fly, and streaks for the window, gets one leg out.*

ABIGAIL, *pulling her away from the window:* I told him everything; he knows now, he knows everything we—

BETTY: You drank blood, Abby! You didn't tell him that!

ABIGAIL: Betty, you never say that again! You will never—

BETTY: You did, you did! You drank a charm to kill John Proctor's wife! You drank a charm to kill Goody Proctor!

ABIGAIL, *smashes her across the face:* Shut it! Now shut it!

BETTY, *collapsing on the bed:* Mama, Mama! *She dissolves into sobs.*

ABIGAIL: Now look you. All of you. We danced. And Tituba conjured Ruth Putnam's dead sisters. And that is all. And mark this. Let either of you breathe a word, or the edge of a word, about the other things, and I will come to you in the black of some terrible night and I will bring a pointy reckoning that will shudder you. And you know I can do it; I saw Indians smash my dear parents' heads on the pillow next to mine, and I have seen some reddish work done at night, and I can make you wish you had never seen the sun go down! *She goes to* BETTY *and roughly sits her up.* Now, you—sit up and stop this!

But BETTY *collapses in her hands and lies inert on the bed.*

MARY WARREN, *with hysterical fright:* What's got her? ABIGAIL *stares in fright at* BETTY. Abby, she's going to die! It's a sin to conjure, and we—

ABIGAIL, *starting for* MARY: I say shut it, Mary Warren!

Enter JOHN PROCTOR. *On seeing him,* MARY WARREN *leaps in fright.*

Proctor was a farmer in his middle thirties. He need not have been a partisan of any faction in the town, but there is evidence to suggest that he had a sharp and biting way with hypocrites. He was the kind of man—powerful of body, even-tempered, and not easily led—who cannot refuse support to partisans without drawing their deepest resentment. In Proctor's presence a fool felt his foolishness instantly—and a Proctor is always marked for calumny therefore.

But as we shall see, the steady manner he displays does not spring from an untroubled soul. He is a sinner, a sinner not only against the moral fashion of the time, but against his own vision of decent conduct. These people had no ritual for the washing away of sins. It is another trait we inherited from them, and it has helped to discipline us as well as to breed hypocrisy among us. Proctor, respected and even feared in Salem, has come to regard himself as a kind of fraud. But no hint of this has yet appeared on the surface, and as he enters from the crowded parlor below it is a man in his prime we see, with a quiet confidence and an unexpressed, hidden force. Mary Warren, his servant, can barely speak for embarrassment and fear.

MARY WARREN: Oh! I'm just going home, Mr. Proctor.

PROCTOR: Be you foolish, Mary Warren? Be you deaf? I forbid you leave the house, did I not? Why shall I pay you? I am looking for you more often than my cows!

MARY WARREN: I only come to see the great doings in the world.

PROCTOR: I'll show you a great doin' on your arse one of these days. Now get you home; my wife is waitin' with your work! *Trying to retain a shred of dignity, she goes slowly out.*

MERCY LEWIS, *both afraid of him and strangely titillated:* I'd best be off. I have my Ruth to watch. Good morning, Mr. Proctor.

MERCY *sidles out. Since* PROCTOR'S *entrance,* ABIGAIL *has stood as though on tiptoe, absorbing his presence, wide-eyed. He glances at her then goes to* BETTY *on the bed.*

ABIGAIL: Gad. I'd almost forgot how strong you are, John Proctor!

PROCTOR, *looking at* ABIGAIL *now, the faintest suggestion of a knowing smile on his face:* What's this mischief here?

ABIGAIL, *with a nervous laugh:* Oh, she's only gone silly somehow.

PROCTOR: The road past my house is a pilgrimage to Salem all morning. The town's mumbling witchcraft.

ABIGAIL: Oh, posh! *Winningly she comes a little closer, with a confidential, wicked air.* We were dancin' in the woods last night, and my uncle leaped in on us. She took fright, is all.

PROCTOR, *his smile widening:* Ah, you're wicked yet, aren't y'! *A trill of expectant*

laughter escapes her, and she dares come closer, feverishly looking into his eyes. You'll be clapped in the stocks before you're twenty.

He takes a step to go, and she springs into his path.

ABIGAIL: Give me a word, John. A soft word. *Her concentrated desire destroys his smile.*

PROCTOR: No, no, Abby. That's done with.

ABIGAIL, *tauntingly:* You come five mile to see a silly girl fly? I know you better.

PROCTOR, *setting her firmly out of his path:* I come to see what mischief your uncle's brewin' now. *With final emphasis:* Put it out of mind, Abby.

ABIGAIL, *grasping his hand before he can release her:* John—I am waitin' for you every night.

PROCTOR: Abby, I never give you hope to wait for me.

ABIGAIL, *now beginning to anger—she can't believe it:* I have something better than hope, I think!

PROCTOR: Abby, you'll put it out of mind. I'll not be comin' for you more.

ABIGAIL: You're surely sportin' with me.

PROCTOR: You know me better.

ABIGAIL: I know how you clutched my back behind your house and sweated like a stallion whenever I come near! Or did I dream that? It's she put me out, you cannot pretend it were you. I saw your face when she put me out, and you loved me then and you do now!

PROCTOR: Abby, that's a wild thing to say—

ABIGAIL: A wild thing may say wild things. But not so wild, I think. I have seen you since she put me out; I have seen you nights.

PROCTOR: I have hardly stepped off my farm this seven-month.

The Crucible 1183

53 Clarification Remind students of Betty's earlier observation that Abigail "drank a charm to kill Goody Proctor." How does this exchange between Abigail and John Proctor explain Abigail's earlier actions?

54 Discussion Ask students why Abigail is so angered by the fact that John Proctor calls her a child.

55 Discussion Do students believe John Proctor's vow that he will "cut off [his] hand before [he'll] ever reach for [Abigail] again"? Why or why not?

56 Discussion Do students believe Abigail's assertion that Goody Proctor has been "telling lies" about Abigail? Why or why not?

57 Discussion Have students discuss why Miller introduces the sound of the psalm at this point in the scene. What is the effect of the juxtaposition of the psalm with the exchange between Abigail and Proctor?

"John—I am waitin' for you every night."

ABIGAIL: I have a sense for heat, John, and yours has drawn me to my window, and I have seen you looking up, burning in your loneliness. Do you tell me you've never looked up at my window?

PROCTOR: I may have looked up.

ABIGAIL, *now softening:* And you must. You are no wintry man. I know you, John. I *know* you. *She is weeping.* I cannot sleep for dreamin'; I cannot dream but I wake and walk about the house as though I'd find you comin' through some door. *She clutches him desperately.*

PROCTOR, *gently pressing her from him, with great sympathy but firmly:* Child—

ABIGAIL, *with a flash of anger:* How do you call me child!

PROCTOR: Abby, I may think of you softly from time to time. But I will cut off my hand before I'll ever reach for you again. Wipe it out of mind. We never touched, Abby.

ABIGAIL: Aye, but we did.

PROCTOR: Aye, but we did not.

ABIGAIL, *with a bitter anger:* Oh, I marvel how such a strong man may let such a sickly wife be—

PROCTOR, *angered—at himself as well:* You'll speak nothin' of Elizabeth!

ABIGAIL: She is blackening my name in the village! She is telling lies about me! She is a cold, sniveling woman, and you bend to her! Let her turn you like a—

PROCTOR, *shaking her:* Do you look for whippin'?

A psalm is heard being sung below.

ABIGAIL, *in tears:* I look for John Proctor that took me from my sleep and put knowledge in my heart! I never knew what pretense Salem was, I never knew the lying lessons I was taught by all these Christian women and their covenanted men! And now you bid me tear the light out of my eyes? I will not, I cannot! You loved me, John Proctor, and whatever sin it is, you love me yet! *He turns abruptly to go out. She rushes to him.* John, pity me, pity me!

The words "going up to Jesus" are heard in the psalm, and BETTY *claps her ears suddenly and whines loudly.*

ABIGAIL: Betty? *She hurries to* BETTY, *who is now sitting up and screaming.* PROCTOR *goes to* BETTY *as* ABIGAIL *is trying to pull her hands down, calling "Betty!"*

PROCTOR, *growing unnerved:* What's she doing? Girl, what ails you? Stop that wailing!

The singing has stopped in the midst of this, and now PARRIS *rushes in.*

PARRIS: What happened? What are you doing to her? Betty! *He rushes to the bed, crying,* "Betty, Betty!" MRS. PUTNAM *enters, feverish with curiosity, and with her* THOMAS PUTNAM *and* MERCY LEWIS. PARRIS, *at the bed, keeps lightly slapping* BETTY's *face, while she moans and tries to get up.*

ABIGAIL: She heard you singin' and suddenly she's up and screamin'.

MRS. PUTNAM: The psalm! The psalm! She cannot bear to hear the Lord's name!

PARRIS: No, God forbid. Mercy, run to the doctor! Tell him what's happened here! MERCY LEWIS *rushes out.*

MRS. PUTNAM: Mark it for a sign, mark it!

REBECCA NURSE, *seventy-two, enters. She is white-haired, leaning upon her walking-stick.*

PUTNAM, *pointing at the whimpering* BETTY: That is a notorious sign of witchcraft afoot, Goody Nurse, a prodigious sign!

MRS. PUTNAM: My mother told me that! When they cannot bear to hear the name of—

PARRIS, *trembling:* Rebecca, Rebecca, go to her, we're lost. She suddenly cannot bear to hear the Lord's—

GILES COREY, *eighty-three, enters. He is knotted with muscle, canny, inquisitive, and still powerful.*

REBECCA: There is hard sickness here, Giles Corey, so please to keep the quiet.

GILES: I've not said a word. No one here can testify I've said a word. Is she going to fly again? I hear she flies.

PUTNAM: Man, be quiet now!

Everything is quiet. REBECCA *walks across the room to the bed. Gentleness exudes from her.* BETTY *is quietly whimpering, eyes shut.* REBECCA *simply stands over the child, who gradually quiets.*

And while they are so absorbed, we may put a word in for Rebecca. Rebecca was the wife of Francis Nurse, who, from all accounts, was one of those men for whom both sides of the argument had to have respect. He was called upon to arbitrate disputes as though he were an unofficial judge, and Rebecca also enjoyed the high opinion most people had for him. By the time of the delusion, they had three hundred acres, and their children were settled in separate homesteads within the same estate. However, Francis had originally rented the land, and one theory has it that, as he gradually paid for it and raised his social status, there were those who resented his rise.

Another suggestion to explain the systematic campaign against Rebecca, and inferentially against Francis, is the land war he fought with his neighbors, one of whom was a Putnam. This squabble grew to the proportions of a battle in the woods between partisans of both sides, and it is said to have lasted for two days. As for Rebecca herself, the general opinion of her character was so high that to explain how anyone dared cry her out for a witch—and more, how adults could bring themselves to lay hands on her—we must look to the fields and boundaries of that time.

As we have seen, Thomas Putnam's man for the Salem ministry was Bayley. The Nurse clan had been in the faction that prevented Bayley's taking office. In addition, certain families allied to the Nurses by blood or friendship, and whose farms were contiguous with the Nurse farm or close to it, combined to break away from the Salem town authority and set up Topsfield, a new and independent entity whose existence was resented by old Salemites.

That the guiding hand behind the outcry was Putnam's is indicated by the fact that, as soon as it began, this Topsfield-Nurse faction absented themselves from church in protest and disbelief. It was Edward and Jonathan Putnam who signed

The Crucible   1185

58 **Discussion** Have students explain why Goody Putnam interprets Betty's reaction to the psalm as a sign of witchcraft. Given the Puritans' beliefs, do students find it understandable that Goody Putnam would respond to Betty's behavior in this way? Why or why not?

59 **Discussion** Have students discuss the impact of Betty's behavior on Reverend Parris. Do students think that Parris himself is now convinced that Betty's condition is the result of witchcraft? On what do they base their answer?

60 **Discussion** Ask students if Giles Corey seems eager to see Betty fly. If so, why?

61 **Discussion** Ask students what this passage reveals about what will happen to Rebecca later in the play.

62 **Discussion** Have students discuss what Miller means when he writes that Goody Putnam's charge that Rebecca's spirit tempted "her to iniquity" had "more truth in it than Mrs. Putnam could know."

63 **Discussion** Have students discuss what this passage reveals about Rebecca's character.

64 **Discussion** Explain to students that Goody Putnam is using the word *bewilder* in its original sense, meaning that Ruth has "gone wild."

65 **Discussion** Have students explain the meaning of John Proctor's remark.

66 **Discussion** Ask students what Goody Putnam means when she says that there "are wheels within wheels in this village, and fires within fires."

62 the first complaint against Rebecca; and Thomas Putnam's little daughter was the one who fell into a fit at the hearing and pointed to Rebecca as her attacker. To top it all, Mrs. Putnam—who is now staring at the bewitched child on the bed—soon accused Rebecca's spirit of "tempting her to iniquity," a charge that had more truth in it than Mrs. Putnam could know.

MRS. PUTNAM, *astonished:* What have you done?

REBECCA, *in thought, now leaves the bedside and sits.*

PARRIS, *wondrous and relieved:* What do you make of it, Rebecca?

PUTNAM, *eagerly:* Goody Nurse, will you go to my Ruth and see if you can wake her?

63 **REBECCA,** *sitting:* I think she'll wake in time. Pray calm yourselves. I have eleven children, and I am twenty-six times a grandma, and I have seen them all through their silly seasons, and when it come on them they will run the Devil bowlegged keeping up with their mischief. I think she'll wake when she tires of it. A child's spirit is like a child, you can never catch it by running after it; you must stand still, and, for love, it will soon itself come back.

PROCTOR: Aye, that's the truth of it, Rebecca.

64 **MRS. PUTNAM:** This is no silly season, Rebecca. My Ruth is bewildered, Rebecca; she cannot eat.

REBECCA: Perhaps she is not hungered yet. *To* PARRIS: I hope you are not decided to go in search of loose spirits, Mr. Parris. I've heard promise of that outside.

PARRIS: A wide opinion's running in the parish that the Devil may be among us, and I would satisfy them that they are wrong.

PROCTOR: Then let you come out and call them wrong. Did you consult the wardens before you called this minister to look for devils?

PARRIS: He is not coming to look for devils!

PROCTOR: Then what's he coming for?

PUTNAM: There be children dyin' in the village, Mister!

PROCTOR: I seen none dyin'. This society will not be a bag to swing around your head, Mr. Putnam. *To* PARRIS: Did you call a meeting before you—?

PUTNAM: I am sick of meetings; cannot the man turn his head without he have a meeting?

65 **PROCTOR:** He may turn his head, but not to Hell!

REBECCA: Pray, John, be calm. *Pause. He defers to her.* Mr. Parris, I think you'd best send Reverend Hale back as soon as he come. This will set us all to arguin' again in the society, and we thought to have peace this year. I think we ought rely on the doctor now, and good prayer.

MRS. PUTNAM: Rebecca, the doctor's baffled!

REBECCA: If so he is, then let us go to God for the cause of it. There is no prodigious danger in the seeking of loose spirits. I fear it, I fear it. Let us rather blame ourselves and—

PUTNAM: How may we blame ourselves? I am one of nine sons; the Putnam seed have peopled this province. And yet I have but one child left of eight—and now she shrivels!

REBECCA: I cannot fathom that.

66 **MRS. PUTNAM,** *with a growing edge of sarcasm:* But I must! You think it God's work you should never lose a child, nor grandchild either, and I bury all but one? There are wheels within wheels in this village, and fires within fires!

PUTNAM, *to* PARRIS: When Reverend Hale comes, you will proceed to look for signs of witchcraft here.

PROCTOR, *to* PUTNAM: You cannot command, Mr. Parris. We vote by name in this society, not by acreage.

PUTNAM: I never heard you worried so on this society, Mr. Proctor. I do not think I saw you at Sabbath meeting since snow flew.

PROCTOR: I have trouble enough without I come five mile to hear him preach only hell-fire and bloody damnation. Take it to heart, Mr. Parris. There are many others who stay away from church these days because you hardly ever mention God any more.

PARRIS, *now aroused:* Why, that's a drastic charge!

REBECCA: It's somewhat true; there are many that quail to bring their children—

PARRIS: I do not preach for children, Rebecca. It is not the children who are unmindful of their obligations toward this ministry.

REBECCA: Are there really those unmindful?

PARRIS: I should say the better half of Salem village—

PUTNAM: And more than that!

PARRIS: Where is my wood? My contract provides I be supplied with all my firewood. I am waiting since November for a stick, and even in November I had to show my frostbitten hands like some London beggar!

GILES: You are allowed six pound a year to buy your wood, Mr. Parris.

PARRIS: I regard that six pound as part of my salary. I am paid little enough without I spend six pound on firewood.

PROCTOR: Sixty, plus six for firewood—

PARRIS: The salary is sixty-six pound, Mr. Proctor! I am not some preaching farmer with a book under my arm; I am a graduate of Harvard College.

GILES: Aye, and well instructed in arithmetic!

PARRIS: Mr. Corey, you will look far for a man of my kind at sixty pound a year! I am not used to this poverty; I left a thrifty business in the Barbados to serve the Lord. I do not fathom it, why am I persecuted here? I cannot offer one proposition but there be a howling riot of argument. I have often wondered if the Devil be in it somewhere; I cannot understand you people otherwise.

PROCTOR: Mr. Parris, you are the first minister ever did demand the deed to this house—

PARRIS: Man! Don't a minister deserve a house to live in?

PROCTOR: To live in, yes. But to ask ownership is like you shall own the meeting house itself; the last meeting I were at you spoke so long on deeds and mortgages I thought it were an auction.

PARRIS: I want a mark of confidence, is all! I am your third preacher in seven years. I do not wish to be put out like the cat whenever some majority feels the whim. You people seem not to comprehend that a minister is the Lord's man in the parish; a minister is not to be so lightly crossed and contradicted—

PUTNAM: Aye!

PARRIS: There is either obedience or the church will burn like Hell is burning!

PROCTOR: Can you speak one minute without we land in Hell again? I am sick of Hell!

PARRIS: It is not for you to say what is good for you to hear!

PROCTOR: I may speak my heart, I think!

PARRIS, *in a fury:* What, are we Quakers?[8] We are not Quakers here yet, Mr. Proctor. And you may tell that to your followers!

---

8. Quakers: The Quakers are members of a Christian religious sect that has no formal creed, rites, or priesthood. Parris is asserting his authority as a minister. Unlike the Quakers, the Puritans had a rigid code of conduct and were expected to heed the words of their ministers.

The Crucible 1187

72 Discussion Have students speculate about whether John Proctor's attitude might cause problems for him later in the play.

73 Discussion Ask students to explain what has caused Giles Corey to change his opinion of Reverend Parris.

74 Discussion Have students discuss what this exchange suggests about the relationship among the inhabitants of Salem. Given the Puritan's professed beliefs, do students find it surprising that the inhabitants of the village would be constantly suing one another? Why or why not?

75 Discussion Ask students who they side with in the dispute between Proctor and Putnam. Why?

PROCTOR: My followers!

PARRIS—*now he's out with it:* There is a party in this church. I am not blind; there is a faction and a party.

PROCTOR: Against you?

PUTNAM: Against him and all authority!

PROCTOR: Why, then I must find it and join it.

There is shock among the others.

REBECCA: He does not mean that.

PUTNAM: He confessed it now!

PROCTOR: I mean it solemnly, Rebecca; I like not the smell of this "authority."

REBECCA: No, you cannot break charity with your minister. You are another kind, John. Clasp his hand, make your peace.

PROCTOR: I have a crop to sow and lumber to drag home. *He goes angrily to the door and turns to* COREY *with a smile.* What say you, Giles, let's find the party. He says there's a party.

GILES: I've changed my opinion of this man, John. Mr. Parris, I beg your pardon. I never thought you had so much iron in you.

PARRIS, *surprised:* Why, thank you, Giles!

GILES: It suggests to the mind what the trouble be among us all these years. *To all:* Think on it. Wherefore is everybody suing everybody else? Think on it now, it's a deep thing, and dark as a pit. I have been six time in court this year—

PROCTOR, *familiarly, with warmth, although he knows he is approaching the edge of Giles' tolerance with this:* Is it the Devil's fault that a man cannot say you good morning without you clap him for defamation? You're old, Giles, and you're not hearin' so well as you did.

GILES—*he cannot be crossed:* John Proctor, I have only last month collected four pound damages for you publicly sayin' I burned the roof off your house, and I—

PROCTOR, *laughing:* I never said no such think, but I've paid you for it, so I hope I can call you deaf without charge. Now come along, Giles, and help me drag my lumber home.

PUTNAM: A moment, Mr. Proctor. What lumber is that you're draggin', if I may ask you?

PROCTOR: My lumber. From out my forest by the riverside.

PUTNAM: Why, we are surely gone wild this year. What anarchy is this? That tract is in my bounds, it's in my bounds, Mr. Proctor.

PROCTOR: In your bounds! *Indicating* REBECCA: I bought that tract from Goody Nurse's husband five months ago.

PUTNAM: He had no right to sell it. It stands clear in my grandfather's will that all the land between the river and—

PROCTOR: Your grandfather had a habit of willing land that never belonged to him, if I may say it plain.

GILES: That's God's truth; he nearly willed away my north pasture but he knew I'd break his fingers before he'd set his name to it. Let's get your lumber home, John. I feel a sudden will to work coming on.

PUTNAM: You load one oak of mine and you'll fight to drag it home!

GILES: Aye, and we'll win too, Putnam—this fool and I. Come on! *He turns to* PROCTOR *and starts out.*

PUTNAM: I'll have my men on you, Corey! I'll clap a writ on you!

Enter REVEREND JOHN HALE *of Beverly.*

Mr. Hale is nearing forty, a tight-skinned, eager-eyed intellectual. This is a beloved errand for him; on being called here to ascertain witchcraft he felt the pride of the specialist whose unique knowledge has at last been publicly called for. Like almost all men of learning, he spent a good deal of time pondering the invisible world, especially since he had himself encountered a witch in his parish not long before. That woman, however, turned into a mere pest under his searching scrutiny, and the child she had allegedly been afflicting recovered her normal behavior after Hale had given her his kindness and a few days of rest in his own house. However, that experience never raised a doubt in his mind as to the reality of the underworld or the existence of Lucifer's many-faced lieutenants. And his belief is not to his discredit. Better minds than Hale's were—and still are—convinced that there is a society of spirits beyond our ken. One cannot help noting that one of his lines has never yet raised a laugh in any audience that has seen this play; it is his assurance that "We cannot look to superstition in this. The Devil is precise." Evidently we are not quite certain even now whether diabolism is holy and not to be scoffed at. And it is no accident that we should be so bemused.

Like Reverend Hale and the others on this stage, we conceive the Devil as a necessary part of a respectable view of cosmology. Ours is a divided empire in which certain ideas and emotions and actions are of God, and their opposites are of Lucifer. It is as impossible for most men to conceive of a morality without sin as of an earth without "sky." Since 1692 a great but superficial change has wiped out God's beard and the Devil's horns, but the world is still gripped between two diametrically opposed absolutes. The concept of unity, in which positive and negative are attributes of the same force, in which good and evil are relative, ever-changing, and always joined to the same phenomenon—such a concept is still reserved to the physical sciences and to the few who have grasped the history of ideas. When it is recalled that until the Christian era the underworld was never regarded as a hostile area, that all gods were useful and essentially friendly to man despite occasional lapses; when we see the steady and methodical inculcation into humanity of the idea of man's worthlessness—until redeemed—the necessity of the Devil may become evident as a weapon, a weapon designed and used time and time again in every age to whip men into a surrender to a particular church or church-state.

Our difficulty in believing the—for want of a better word—political inspiration of the Devil is due in great part to the fact that he is called up and damned not only by our social antagonists but by our own side, whatever it may be. The Catholic Church, through its Inquisition,[9] is famous for cultivating Lucifer as the arch-fiend, but the Church's enemies relied no less upon the Old Boy to keep the human mind enthralled. Luther[10] was himself accused of alliance with Hell, and he in turn accused his enemies. To complicate matters further, he believed that he had had contact with the Devil and had argued theology with him. I am not surprised at this, for at my own university a professor of history—a Lutheran,[11] by the way—used to assemble his graduate students, draw the shades, and commune in the classroom with Erasmus.[12] He was never, to my knowledge, officially scoffed at for this, the reason being that the university officials, like most of us, are the children of a history which still sucks at the Devil's teats. At this writing, only England has held back before the temptations of contemporary diabolism. In the countries of the Communist ideology, all resistance of any import is

---

9. Inquisition: The general tribunal established in the thirteenth century for the discovery and suppression of beliefs and opinions opposed to the orthodox doctrines of the Church.
10. Luther: Martin Luther (1483–1546), the German theologian who led the Protestant Reformation.
11. Lutheran: A member of the Protestant denomination founded by Martin Luther.
12. Erasmus: Desiderius Erasmus (1466?–1536), a Dutch humanist, scholar, and theologian.

The Crucible   1189

Discussion Have students describe the tone of this passage. Is Miller being serious when he writes that Tituba's confession was "certain evidence" that people were "communing with, and even worshipping, the Devil in Salem"? On what do students base their answer?

linked to the totally malign capitalist succubi,[13] and in America any man who is not reactionary in his views is open to the charge of alliance with the Red hell. Political opposition, thereby, is given an inhumane overlay which then justifies the abrogation[14] of all normally applied customs of civilized intercourse. A political policy is equated with moral right, and opposition to it with diabolical malevolence. Once such an equation is effectively made, society becomes a congerie[15] of plots and counterplots, and the main role of government changes from that of the arbiter to that of the scourge of God.

The results of this process are no different now from what they ever were, except sometimes in the degree of cruelty inflicted, and not always even in that department. Normally, the actions and deeds of a man were all that society felt comfortable in judging. The secret intent of an action was left to the ministers, priests, and rabbis to deal with. When diabolism rises, however, actions are the least important manifests of the true nature of a man. The Devil, as Reverend Hale said, is a wily one, and until an hour before he fell, even God thought him beautiful in Heaven.

81

The analogy, however, seems to falter when one considers that, while there were no witches then, there are Communists and capitalists now, and in each camp there is certain proof that spies of each side are at work undermining the other. But this is a snobbish objection and not at all warranted by the facts. I have no doubt that people *were* communing with, and even worshiping, the Devil in Salem, and if the whole truth could be known in this case, as it is in others, we should discover a regular and conventionalized propitiation of the dark spirit. One certain evidence of this is the confession of Tituba, the slave of Reverend

Parris, and another is the behavior of the children who were known to have indulged in sorceries with her.

There are accounts of similar *klatches*[16] in Europe, where the daughters of the towns would assemble at night and, sometimes with fetishes,[17] sometimes with a selected young man, give themselves to love, with some bastardly results. The Church, sharp-eyed as it must be when gods long dead are brought to life, condemned these orgies as witchcraft and interpreted them, rightly, as a resurgence of the Dionysiac[18] forces it had crushed long before. Sex, sin, and the Devil were early linked, and so they continued to be in Salem, and are today. From all accounts there are no more puritanical mores in the world than those enforced by the Communists in Russia, where women's fashions, for instance, are as prudent and all-covering as any American Baptist would desire. The divorce laws lay a tremendous responsibility on the father for the care of his children. Even the laxity of divorce regulations in the early years of the revolution was undoubtedly a revulsion from the nineteenth-century Victorian[19] immobility of marriage and the consequent hypocrisy that developed from it. If for no other reasons, a state so powerful, so jealous of the uniformity of its citizens, cannot long tolerate the atomization of the family. And yet, in American eyes at least, there remains the conviction that the Russian attitude toward women is lascivious. It is the Devil working again, just as he is working within the Slav who is shocked at the very idea of a woman's disrobing herself in a burlesque show. Our

---

13. succubi (suk′ yoo bī): Female demons thought to lie on sleeping men.
14. abrogation (ab′ rə gā′ shən): Abolishment.
15. congerie (kän′ jə rē) *n.*: Heap; pile.

16. klatches (kläċh′ əz) *n.*: Informal gatherings.
17. fetishes (fet′ ish əz) *n.*: Objects believed to have magical power.
18. Dionysiac (dī′ ə nis′ ē ak′) *adj.*: Wild, frenzied, and sensuous. Characteristic of Dionysus, the Greek god of wine and revelry.
19. Victorian: Of or characteristic of the time when Victoria was queen of England (1837–1901). The characteristics attributed to this period include respectability, prudery, and bigotry.

Commentary: The Rise of Witchcraft Accusations in Europe

In 1484, Pope Innocent VIII issued an official proclamation requiring that all persons suspected of witchcraft be arrested and punished. This did not mark the first time that the subject of witchcraft was given official attention. Yet following the Pope's pronouncement, prosecutions of witchcraft increased dramatically in almost every European country. In Geneva, Switzerland

alone, five hundred people were burned to death as accused witches in a three-month period during 1515. It is clear from historical records that the accusation of witchcraft was sometimes used by ecclesiastical authorities to silence vocal critics of either the church or the government.

The majority of the people prosecuted for witchcraft were women. It was believed that women were easy prey for the Devil because they were likely to have inherited Eve's vulnerability to evil. Consequently, behavior that was likely to be tolerated in men was considered unacceptable for women and was often used as the grounds for witchcraft accusations.

opposites are always robed in sexual sin, and it is from this unconscious conviction that demonology gains both its attractive sensuality and its capacity to infuriate and frighten.

Coming into Salem now, Reverend Hale conceives of himself much as a young doctor on his first call. His painfully acquired armory of symptoms, catchwords, and diagnostic procedures are now to be put to use at last. The road from Beverly is unusually busy this morning, and he has passed a hundred rumors that make him smile at the ignorance of the yeomanry in this most precise science. He feels himself allied with the best minds of Europe—kings, philosophers, scientists, and ecclesiasts of all churches. His goal is light, goodness and its preservation, and he knows the exaltation of the blessed whose intelligence, sharpened by minute examinations of enormous tracts, is finally called upon to face what may be a bloody fight with the Fiend himself.

He appears loaded down with half a dozen heavy books.

HALE: Pray you, someone take these!

PARRIS, *delighted:* Mr. Hale! Oh! it's good to see you again! *Taking some books:* My, they're heavy!

HALE, *setting down his books:* They must be; they are weighted with authority.

PARRIS, *a little scared:* Well, you do come prepared!

HALE: We shall need hard study if it comes to tracking down the Old Boy. *Noticing* RE-BECCA: You cannot be Rebecca Nurse?

REBECCA: I am, sir. Do you know me?

HALE: It's strange how I knew you, but I sup-

82 **Enrichment** Explain to students that following the invention of the printing press in 1485 many "witch manuals" had been published, offering instruction about how to recognize people who were possessed by the Devil. It is from manuals such as these that Reverend Hale has gained his knowledge of "symptoms, catchwords, and diagnostic procedures."

"We shall need hard study if it comes to tracking down the Old Boy."

83 **Discussion** Ask students to explain why Reverend Hale is embarrassed.

84 **Discussion** Have students respond to Reverend Hale's remark about superstition. On what does Reverend Hale base his pronouncement that the "marks of [the Devil's] presence are as definite as stone"?

85 **Discussion** Have students discuss why Rebecca is "horrified" by Goody Putnam's actions.

86 **Enrichment** Tell students that although the infant mortality rate was high in the early colonial settlements, it was very unusual for a single person to lose this many babies.

87 **Discussion** Ask students why Rebecca turns her face away "with great pain."

pose you look as such a good soul should. We have all heard of your great charities in Beverly.

PARRIS: Do you know this gentleman? Mr. Thomas Putnam. And his good wife Ann.

HALE: Putnam! I had not expected such distinguished company, sir.

PUTNAM, *pleased:* It does seem to help us today, Mr. Hale. We look to you to come to our house and save our child.

HALE: Your child ails too?

MRS. PUTNAM: Her soul, her soul seems flown away. She sleeps and yet she walks . . .

PUTNAM: She cannot eat.

HALE: Cannot eat! *Thinks on it. Then, to* PROCTOR *and* GILES COREY: Do you men have afflicted children?

PARRIS: No, no, these are farmers. John Proctor—

GILES COREY: He don't believe in witches.

PROCTOR, *to* HALE: I never spoke on witches one way or the other. Will you come, Giles?

GILES: No—no, John, I think not. I have some few queer questions of my own to ask this fellow.

PROCTOR: I've heard you to be a sensible man, Mr. Hale. I hope you'll leave some of it in Salem.

83 PROCTOR *goes.* HALE *stands embarrassed for an instant.*

PARRIS, *quickly:* Will you look at my daughter, sir? *Leads* HALE *to the bed.* She has tried to leap out the window; we discovered her this morning on the highroad, waving her arms as though she'd fly.

HALE, *narrowing his eyes:* Tries to fly.

PUTNAM: She cannot bear to hear the Lord's name, Mr. Hale; that's a sure sign of witchcraft afloat.

HALE, *holding up his hands:* No, no. Now let me instruct you. We cannot look to superstition in this. The Devil is precise; the marks of his presence are definite as stone, and I must tell you all that I shall not proceed unless you are prepared to believe me if I should find no bruise of hell upon her.

84

PARRIS: It is agreed, sir—it is agreed—we will abide by your judgment.

HALE: Good then. *He goes to the bed, looks down at* BETTY. *To* PARRIS: Now, sir, what were your first warning of this strangeness?

PARRIS: Why, sir—I discovered her—*indicating* ABIGAIL—and my niece and ten or twelve of the other girls, dancing in the forest last night.

HALE, *surprised:* You permit dancing?

PARRIS: No, no, it were secret—

MRS. PUTNAM, *unable to wait:* Mr. Parris's slave has knowledge of conjurin', sir.

PARRIS, *to Mrs. Putnam:* We cannot be sure of that, Goody Ann—

MRS. PUTNAM, *frightened, very softly:* I know it, sir. I sent my child—she should learn from Tituba who murdered her sisters.

REBECCA, *horrified:* Goody Ann! You sent a child to conjure up the dead? **85**

MRS. PUTNAM: Let God blame me, not you, not you, Rebecca! I'll not have you judging me any more! *To* HALE: Is it a natural work to lose seven children before they live a day? **86**

PARRIS: Sssh!

REBECCA, *with great pain, turns her face away. There is a pause.* **87**

HALE: Seven dead in childbirth.

MRS. PUTNAM, *softly:* Aye. *Her voice breaks; she looks up at him. Silence.* HALE *is impressed.* PARRIS *looks to him. He goes to his books, opens one, turns pages, then reads. All wait, avidly.*

PARRIS, *hushed:* What book is that?

MRS. PUTNAM: What's there, sir?

HALE, *with a tasty love of intellectual pursuit:* Here is all the invisible world, caught, defined, and calculated. In these books the Devil stands stripped of all his brute disguises. Here are all your familiar spirits—your incubi and succubi;[20] your witches that go by land, by air, and by sea; your wizards of the night and of the day. Have no fear now—we shall find him out if he has come among us, and I mean to crush him utterly if he has shown his face! *He starts for the bed.*

REBECCA: Will it hurt the child, sir?

HALE: I cannot tell, If she is truly in the Devil's grip we may have to rip and tear to get her free.

REBECCA: I think I'll go, then. I am too old for this. *She rises.*

88

PARRIS, *striving for conviction:* Why, Rebecca, we may open up the boil of all our troubles today!

REBECCA: Let us hope for that. I go to God for you, sir.

89

PARRIS, *with trepidation—and resentment:* I hope you do not mean to go to Satan here! *Slight pause.*

REBECCA: I wish I knew. *She goes out; they feel resentful of her note of moral superiority.*

PUTNAM, *abruptly:* Come, Mr. Hale, let's get on. Sit you here.

GILES: Mr. Hale, I have always wanted to ask a learned man—what signifies the readin' of strange books?

90

HALE: What books?

GILES: I cannot tell; she hides them.

HALE: Who does this?

---

20. incubi (iŋ′ kyə bī): Spirits or demons thought to lie on sleeping women.

GILES: Martha, my wife. I have waked at night many a time and found her in a corner, readin' of a book. Now what do you make of that?

HALE: Why, that's not necessarily—

GILES: It discomfits me! Last night—mark this—I tried and tried and could not say my prayers. And then she close her book and walks out of the house, and suddenly—mark this—I could pray again!

Old Giles must be spoken for, if only because his fate was to be so remarkable and so different from that of all the others. He was in his early eighties at this time, and was the most comical hero in the history. No man has ever been blamed for so much. If a cow was missed, the first thought was to look for her around Corey's house; a fire blazing up at night brought suspicion of arson to his door. He didn't give a hoot for public opinion, and only in his last years—after he had married Martha—did he bother much with the church. That she stopped his prayer is very probable, but he forgot to say that he'd only recently learned any prayers and it didn't take much to make him stumble over them. He was a crank and a nuisance, but withal a deeply innocent and brave man. In court, once, he was asked if it were true that he had been frightened by the strange behavior of a hog and had then said he knew it to be the Devil in an animal's shape. "What frighted you?" he was asked. He forgot everything but the word "frighted," and instantly replied, "I do not know that I ever spoke that word in my life."

HALE: Ah! The stoppage of prayer—that is strange. I'll speak further on that with you.

GILES: I'm not sayin' she's touched the Devil, now, but I'd admire to know what books she reads and why she hides them. She'll not answer me, y' see.

91

HALE: Aye, we'll discuss it. *To all:* Now mark me, if the Devil is in her you will witness

88 Clarification Explain to students that Reverend Parris is comparing evil to a sore, or boil, that must be lanced before the infected body can be cured.

89 Discussion Have students discuss the meaning of Rebecca's and Parris's remarks to each other. What seems to be Rebecca's attitude toward Parris?

90 Discussion Have students speculate about whether Giles Corey might later regret calling his wife's reading habits to the attention of Reverend Hale.

91 Discussion Have students discuss how Miller captures Giles Corey's lack of education through Corey's lines of dialogue.

92 Discussion Ask students to explain why Reverend Parris is so frightened by the proceedings.

93 Discussion Given what students have learned about Reverend Parris up to this point, do they think it is accurate to describe him as one of the best souls? Why or why not?

94 Enrichment Explain to students that Latin was believed to be the most effective language to use in driving away the Devil.

"I don't know, sir, but the Devil got him numerous witches."

some frightful wonders in this room, so please to keep your wits about you. Mr. Putnam, stand close in case she flies. Now, Betty, dear, will you sit up? PUTNAM *comes in closer, ready-handed.* HALE *sits* BETTY *up, but she hangs limp in his hands.* Hmmm. *He observes her carefully. The others, watch breathlessly.* Can you hear me? I am John Hale, minister of Beverly. I have come to help you, dear. Do you remember my two little girls in Beverly? *She does not stir in his hands.*

92 **PARRIS,** *in fright:* How can it be the Devil? Why would he choose my house to strike? We have all manner of licentious people in the village!

93 **HALE:** What victory would the Devil have to win a soul already bad? It is the best the Devil wants, and who is better than the minister?

GILES: That's deep, Mr. Parris, deep, deep!

PARRIS, *with resolution now:* Betty! Answer Mr. Hale! Betty!

HALE: Does someone afflict you, child? It need not be a woman, mind you, or a man. Perhaps some bird invisible to others comes to you—perhaps a pig, a mouse, or any beast at all. Is there some figure bids you fly? *The child remains limp in his hands. In silence he lays her back on the pillow. Now, holding out his hands toward her, he intones:* In nomine Domini Sabaoth sui filiique ite ad infernos.[21] *She does not stir. He turns to* AB-IGAIL, *his eyes narrowing.* Abigail, what sort of dancing were you doing with her in the forest? **94**

---

21. In nomine Domini Sabaoth sui filiique ite ad infernos (in nō′ mĕ nä dō′ mĕ nē Sab′ á ôt sōō′ ē fē′ lē ē kwä ē′ tä äd in fär′ nōs): "In the name of the lord of hosts and his son get thee to the lower world."

ABIGAIL: Why—common dancing is all.

PARRIS: I think I ought to say that I—I saw a kettle in the grass where they were dancing.

ABIGAIL: That were only soup.

HALE: What sort of soup were in this kettle, Abigail?

ABIGAIL: Why, it were beans—and lentils, I think, and—

HALE: Mr. Parris, you did not notice, did you, any living thing in the kettle? A mouse, perhaps, a spider, a frog—?

PARRIS, *fearfully:* I—do believe there were some movement—in the soup.

ABIGAIL: That jumped in, we never put it in!

HALE, *quickly:* What jumped in?

ABIGAIL: Why, a very little frog jumped—

PARRIS: A frog, Abby!

HALE, *grasping* ABIGAIL: Abigail, it may be your cousin is dying. Did you call the Devil last night?

ABIGAIL: I never called him! Tituba, Tituba . . .

PARRIS, *blanched:* She called the Devil?

HALE: I should like to speak with Tituba.

PARRIS: Goody Ann, will you bring her up? MRS. PUTNAM *exits.*

HALE: How did she call him?

ABIGAIL: I know not—she spoke Barbados.

HALE: Did you feel any strangeness when she called him? A sudden cold wind, perhaps? A trembling below the ground?

ABIGAIL: I didn't see no Devil! *Shaking* BETTY: Betty, wake up. Betty! Betty!

HALE: You cannot evade me, Abigail. Did your cousin drink any of the brew in that kettle?

ABIGAIL: She never drank it!

HALE: Did you drink it?

ABIGAIL: No, sir!

HALE: Did Tituba ask you to drink it?

ABIGAIL: She tried, but I refused.

HALE: Why are you concealing? Have you sold yourself to Lucifer?

ABIGAIL: I never sold myself! I'm a good girl! I'm a proper girl!

MRS. PUTNAM *enters with* TITUBA, *and instantly* ABIGAIL *points at* TITUBA.

ABIGAIL: She made me do it! She made Betty do it!

TITUBA, *shocked and angry:* Abby!

ABIGAIL: She makes me drink blood!

PARRIS: Blood!!

MRS. PUTNAM: My baby's blood?

TITUBA: No, no, chicken blood. I give she chicken blood!

HALE: Woman, have you enlisted these children for the Devil?

TITUBA: No, no, sir, I don't truck with no Devil!

HALE: Why can she not wake? Are you silencing this child?

TITUBA: I love me Betty!

HALE: You have sent your spirit out upon this child, have you not? Are you gathering souls for the Devil?

ABIGAIL: She sends her spirit on me in church; she makes me laugh at prayer!

PARRIS: She have often laughed at prayer!

ABIGAIL: She comes to me every night to go and drink blood!

TITUBA: You beg *me* to conjure! She beg *me* make charm—

The Crucible   1195

95 Discussion Ask students whether they believe Abigail's responses to Reverend Hale's questions. Why or why not?

96 Discussion Ask your students if they are surprised that Abigail places the blame on Tituba. Why or why not? How do they imagine that Tituba will respond to the accusations that she called the Devil and that she forced Abigail to drink blood?

97 Discussion Ask students if they think there is any chance that Tituba will be able to convince Reverend Hale that she has not contacted the Devil. Why or why not? Do they think Reverend Hale has already concluded that Tituba is guilty? Why or why not?

98 Enrichment Explain to students that witches were thought to cast their spirits out in various shapes to harm or seize control of their victims.

99 Discussion What do students think is the real reason why Abigail has "often laughed at prayer"? On what do they base their answer?

100 Discussion Do students think that Abigail is telling the truth? If not, why might the apparent ease with which Abigail concocts lies prove dangerous later in the play?

101 Discussion Ask students what causes this sudden shift in Tituba's story concerning her involvement with the Devil.

102 Enrichment Explain to students that it was believed that witches had transferred their allegiance from God to the Devil and had signed their names in the Devil's book.

103 Enrichment Tell students that although the term *witch* was used to refer to both men and women, 90 percent of the people accused of witchcraft over the centuries were women. Also point out that the terms *wizard* and *warlock* were sometimes used to refer to male witches.

ABIGAIL: Don't lie! *To* HALE: She comes to me while I sleep; she's always making me dream corruptions!

TITUBA: Why you say that, Abby?

ABIGAIL: Sometimes I wake and find myself standing in the open doorway and not a stitch on my body! I always hear her laughing in my sleep. I hear her singing her Barbados songs and tempting me with—

TITUBA: Mister Reverend, I never—

HALE, *resolved now:* Tituba, I want you to wake this child.

TITUBA: I have no power on this child, sir.

HALE: You most certainly do, and you will free her from it now! When did you compact with the Devil?

TITUBA: I don't compact with no Devil!

PARRIS: You will confess yourself or I will take you out and whip you to your death, Tituba!

PUTNAM: This woman must be hanged! She must be taken and hanged!

TITUBA, *terrified, falls to her knees:* No, no, don't hang Tituba! I tell him I don't desire to work for him, sir.

PARRIS: The Devil?

HALE: Then you saw him! TITUBA *weeps.* Now Tituba, I know that when we bind ourselves to Hell it is very hard to break with it. We are going to help you tear yourself free—

TITUBA, *frightened by the coming process:* Mister Reverend, I do believe somebody else be witchin' these children.

HALE: Who?

TITUBA: I don't know, sir, but the Devil got him numerous witches.

HALE: Does he! *It is a clue.* Tituba, look into my eyes. Come, look into me. *She raises her eyes to his fearfully.* You would be a good Christian woman, would you not, Tituba?

TITUBA: Aye, sir, a good Christian woman.

HALE: And you love these little children?

TITUBA: Oh, yes, sir, I don't desire to hurt these children.

HALE: And you love God, Tituba?

TITUBA: I love God with all my bein'.

HALE: Now, in God's holy name—

TITUBA: Bless Him. Bless Him. *She is rocking on her knees, sobbing in terror.*

HALE: And to His glory—

TITUBA: Eternal glory. Bless Him—bless God . . .

HALE: Open yourself, Tituba—open yourself and let God's holy light shine on you.

TITUBA: Oh, bless the Lord.

HALE: When the Devil come to you does he ever come—with another person? *She stares up into his face.* Perhaps another person in the village? Someone you know.

PARRIS: Who came with him?

PUTNAM: Sarah Good? Did you ever see Sarah Good with him? Or Osburn?

PARRIS: Was it man or woman came with him?

TITUBA: Man or woman. Was—was woman.

PARRIS: What woman? A woman, you said. What woman?

TITUBA: It was black dark, and I—

PARRIS: You could see him, why could you not see her?

TITUBA: Well, they was always talking; they was always runnin' round and carryin' on—

PARRIS: You mean out of Salem? Salem witches?

TITUBA: I believe so, yes, sir.

Now HALE *takes her hand. She is surprised.*

HALE: Tituba. You must have no fear to tell

"*I want to open myself!*"

104 **Discussion** Point out to students that Tituba escapes being hanged by confessing to witchcraft. Ask students if they think most people would be likely to falsely confess to witchcraft in order to escape being executed. What is wrong with a type of proceeding in which an admission of guilt is a way in which the accused can escape severe punishment? What is likely to be the outcome of such a proceeding?

105 **Discussion** Ask students to explain who is actually responsible for choosing Tituba to help "cleanse [the] village."

us who they are, do you understand? We will protect you. The Devil can never overcome a minister. You know that, do you not?

TITUBA, *kisses* HALE's *hand:* Aye, sir, oh, I do.

HALE: You have confessed yourself to witchcraft, and that speaks a wish to come to Heaven's side. And we will bless you, Tituba.

TITUBA, *deeply relieved:* Oh, God bless you, Mr. Hale!

HALE, *with rising exaltation:* You are God's instrument put in our hands to discover the Devil's agent among us. You are selected, Tituba, you are chosen to help us cleanse our village. So speak utterly, Tituba, turn your back on him and face God—face God, Tituba, and God will protect you.

The Crucible   1197

106 Clarification Make sure that students understand that a *midwife* is a woman who assists other women during childbirth.

107 Discussion Have students discuss why Abigail speaks out at this point and begins naming people she has supposedly seen with the Devil. Why does Betty join her?

Reader's Response What emotions do the events in this act arouse in you? Why? Which characters do you find the most sympathetic? Why? Which characters do you find the least sympathetic? Why?

Collaborative Learning Your students might be interested in learning more about the Salem witchcraft hysteria as well as about the witchcraft hysteria that swept through Europe in the sixteenth and seventeenth centuries. Divide your class into groups of five. Assign each group one of the following topics: the Salem witchcraft hysteria, other incidents in the American colonies involving witchcraft, the witchcraft hysteria in Europe during the sixteenth century, and the witchcraft hysteria in Europe during the seventeenth century. Have each group research the topic they have been assigned. Then have them present their findings to the rest of the class.

TITUBA, *joining with him:* Oh, God, protect Tituba!

HALE, *kindly:* Who came to you with the Devil? Two? Three? Four? How many?

Tituba pants, and begins rocking back and forth again, staring ahead.

TITUBA: There was four. There was four.

PARRIS, *pressing in on her:* Who? Who? Their names, their names!

TITUBA, *suddenly bursting out:* Oh, how many times he bid me kill you, Mr. Parris!

PARRIS: Kill me!

TITUBA, *in a fury:* He say Mr. Parris must be kill! Mr. Parris no goodly man, Mr. Parris mean man and no gentle man, and he bid me rise out of my bed and cut your throat! *They gasp.* But I tell him "No! I don't hate that man. I don't want kill that man." But he say, "You work for me, Tituba, and I make you free! I give you pretty dress to wear, and put you way high up in the air, and you gone fly back to Barbados!" And I say, "You lie, Devil, you lie!" And then he come one stormy night to me, and he say, "Look! I have *white* people belong to me." And I look—and there was Goody Good.

PARRIS: Sarah Good!

TITUBA, *rocking and weeping:* Aye, sir, and Goody Osburn.

MRS. PUTNAM: I knew it! Goody Osburn were midwife to me three times. I begged you, Thomas, did I not? I begged him not to call Osburn because I feared her. My babies always shriveled in her hands!

HALE: Take courage, you must give us all their names. How can you bear to see this child suffering? Look at her, Tituba. *He is indicating* BETTY *on the bed.* Look at her God-given innocence; her soul is so tender; we must protect her, Tituba; the Devil is out and preying on her like a beast upon the flesh of the pure lamb. God will bless you for your help.

ABIGAIL *rises, staring as though inspired, and cries out.*

ABIGAIL: I want to open myself! *They turn to her, startled. She is enraptured, as though in a pearly light.* I want the light of God, I want the sweet love of Jesus! I danced for the Devil; I saw him; I wrote in his book; I go back to Jesus; I kiss His hand. I saw Sarah Good with the Devil! I saw Goody Osburn with the Devil! I saw Bridget Bishop with the Devil!

As she is speaking, BETTY *is rising from the bed, a fever in her eyes, and picks up the chant.*

BETTY, *staring too:* I saw George Jacobs with the Devil! I saw Goody Howe with the Devil!

PARRIS: She speaks! *He rushes to embrace* BETTY. She speaks!

HALE: Glory to God! It is broken, they are free!

BETTY, *calling out hysterically and with great relief:* I saw Martha Bellows with the Devil!

ABIGAIL: I saw Goody Sibber with the Devil! *It is rising to a great glee.*

PUTNAM: The marshal, I'll call the marshal!

PARRIS *is shouting a prayer of thanksgiving.*

BETTY: I saw Alice Barrow with the Devil!

The curtain begins to fall.

HALE, *as* PUTNAM *goes out:* Let the marshal bring irons!

ABIGAIL: I saw Goody Hawkins with the Devil!

BETTY: I saw Goody Bibber with the Devil!

ABIGAIL: I saw Goody Booth with the Devil!

On their ecstatic cries—

Closure and Extension

ANSWERS TO THINKING ABOUT THE SELECTION
Recalling

1. He summons Reverend Hale, who is known to be an expert in the area of witchcraft, to determine whether witchcraft is responsible for Betty's condition.
2. He questions Tituba because

THINKING ABOUT THE SELECTION

Recalling

1. Why does Reverend Parris summon Reverend Hale?
2. Why does Reverend Hale question Tituba?

Interpreting

3. (a) What do Reverend Parris's comments and actions in the first act reveal about his character? (b) What do Abigail Williams's comments and actions reveal about her character?
4. (a) What is revealed about Ann Putnam's personality? (b) What is revealed about Mary Warren's personality?
5. What seems to be the main motivation for Reverend Parris's concern about Abigail and Betty's behavior in the forest?
6. (a) When Reverend Parris leaves the room, Abigail, Mercy, Mary, and Betty briefly talk in private. What does this discussion reveal about their concerns? (b) How does this scene foreshadow, or hint at, events that will occur later in the play?
7. (a) How does Betty's reaction to the psalm support the assertion that there is "witchcraft afoot"? (b) What other incidents or situations do the various characters use to support this assertion?
8. What evidence is there that sharp divisions exist among the people of Salem Village?
9. (a) What role does Rebecca Nurse serve when she appears in the first act? (b) How would you describe the other characters' attitudes toward her?
10. (a) How would you characterize the manner in which Hale questions Tituba? (b) What causes Tituba to begin naming people whom she had supposedly seen with the Devil?

Applying

11. What types of situations might cause a contemporary American town to become afflicted by a general hysteria?

ANALYZING LITERATURE

Understanding the Historical Context

The Crucible is based on the Salem witchcraft trials of 1692. Considered one of the most tragic incidents in American history, the trials resulted in the death of at least twenty people and the jailing of at least 150 others.

1. Although the play is based on historical fact, some of the events and characters have been fictionalized. Why do you think Arthur Miller might have chosen not to strive for complete historical accuracy?
2. What evidence is there in the first act that Salem Village might be especially susceptible to an outbreak of witchcraft hysteria?

CRITICAL THINKING AND READING

Recognizing Cultural Attitudes

In *The Crucible* Arthur Miller conveys many of the dominant Puritan attitudes and beliefs. For example, during the initial discussion between Parris and Abigail, it is revealed that dancing was viewed as sinful and was strictly forbidden.

1. What evidence is there in the first act that the Puritans believed in severe punishments for those who had sinned?
2. What do the references to the frequent lawsuits and the squabbling over Reverend Parris's salary suggest about the Puritans' attitudes toward money and possessions?

THINKING AND WRITING

Writing About the Setting

Write a paper in which you discuss how the Puritans' attitudes, along with the stresses of their daily lives, may have increased the likelihood of an outbreak of witchcraft hysteria. Along with two other students, review the first act of *The Crucible,* noting what it reveals about the Puritans' ideals and concerns. Also note what it reveals about the stresses of Puritan life. Working on your own, organize your ideas. Then begin writing your paper. After you have finished writing, read your paper to two other students whose job is to suggest how the paper could be improved.

The Crucible 1199

8. Suggested Response: The people are involved in frequent lawsuits. There is talk about "factions" within the village. Several of the characters become involved in arguments during the course of the act.
9. (a) Suggested Response: She serves as a voice of reason. (b) Suggested Response: They deeply respect and admire her.
10. (a) Suggested Response: He questions her in an accusatory manner, making it clear that he has already concluded that she is guilty. (b) She begins naming people because she fears for her own life.

Applying

11. Answers will differ. Students might note that an outbreak of an infectious disease might have a similar effect.

ANSWERS TO ANALYZING LITERATURE

1. Answers will differ. Students may note that Miller is concerned with the implications of the events rather than with the specific details.
2. Suggested Response: There are deep divisions among the people of the village, the people are suspicious of one another, and many of them are not satisfied with their leadership.

ANSWERS TO CRITICAL THINKING AND READING

1. Suggested Response: The characters indicate that singing and dancing are punishable by whipping and that the penalty for witchcraft is death.
2. Suggested Response: It suggests that the Puritans had come to place a great deal of importance on wealth and personal possessions and that many of them were greedy and stingy.

THINKING AND WRITING

Writing Across the Curriculum

You may want to notify the history department about this assignment. History teachers might be able to help students develop a fuller understanding of Puritan life.

Abigail accuses Tituba of contacting the Devil.

Interpreting

3. (a) Answers will differ. Students should note that Parris seems self-important and self-centered and seems more concerned about his own reputation than about Betty's well-being. (b) Answers will differ. Students should note that she is clever, manipulative, and deceitful.
4. (a) Answers will differ. Students should note that she is very suspicious of others. (b) Answers will differ. Students should note that Mary Warren seems timid and weak-willed.
5. Suggested Response: He seems most concerned about how it will affect his own status in the village.
6. (a) Suggested Response: It reveals that they have not divulged the truth about their behavior and that they are afraid they will be accused of being witches. (b) Suggested Response: It shows the girls plotting to save themselves and hints at the fact that they will ultimately do almost anything to avoid punishment.
7. (a) It suggests that she cannot bear to hear God's name. (b) Answers will differ. Students should note Mrs. Putnam's frequent references to the deaths of her babies and her descriptions of her daughter's strange behavior.

GUIDE FOR INTERPRETING

Writer's Techniques

The Crucible, Act II

Characterization. Characterization is the means by which a writer reveals a character's personality. Unlike a short story writer or novelist, a playwright usually cannot make direct statements about a character or reveal a character's thoughts. Instead, a dramatist must develop a character through the character's comments and actions and through other characters' comments about him or her. In fact, everything that the audience learns about the characters, including their names and occupations, must be revealed through the characters' comments and actions. Yet a playwright cannot write a dialogue with the sole intention of conveying details about the characters. The dialogue must seem natural and realistic, as if it were taken from real-life conversations.

In the published version of *The Crucible,* Arthur Miller has included information about historical background and commentary on the events and the actions of the characters. In this text Miller provides biographical information about many of the characters and offers valuable insights into their personalities. However, Miller's comments are meant only for readers of the play and would not be part of a dramatic presentation.

As you read or view a play, you begin to develop certain expectations about a character's behavior based upon what you have learned about his or her personality. Before you begin reading the second act, think about what you have already learned about each of the characters. For example, think about what Reverend Parris's comments and actions in the first act reveal about his personality. Considering what is revealed about Parris's personality in the first act, how do you expect him to conduct himself throughout the remainder of the play? How do you expect other characters, such as Abigail Williams, Mary Warren, John Proctor, Thomas Putnam, and Giles Corey, to conduct themselves?

Writing

Write a journal entry in which you predict what will occur in the second act. In your predictions explore each of the following questions: How rapidly will the witchcraft hysteria progress? Which characters will be accused of witchcraft? What will happen to the characters who are accused? What role will Reverend Hale play in the proceedings? What other types of characters might be introduced?

ACT II

The common room of Proctor's house, eight days later.

At the right is a door opening on the fields outside. A fireplace is at the left, and behind it a stairway leading upstairs. It is the low, dark, and rather long living room of the time. As the curtain rises, the room is empty. From above, ELIZABETH *is heard softly singing to the children. Presently the door opens and* JOHN PROCTOR *enters, carrying his gun. He glances about the room as he comes toward the fireplace, then halts for an instant as he hears her singing. He continues on to the fireplace, leaves the gun against the wall as he swings a pot out of the fire and smells it. Then he lifts out the ladle and tastes. He is not quite pleased. He reaches to a cupboard, takes a pinch of salt, and drops it into the pot. As he is tasting again, her footsteps are heard on the stair. He swings the pot into the fireplace and goes to a basin and washes his hands and face.* ELIZABETH *enters.*

ELIZABETH: What keeps you so late? It's almost dark.

PROCTOR: I were planting far out to the forest edge.

ELIZABETH: Oh, you're done then.

PROCTOR: Aye, the farm is seeded. The boys asleep?

ELIZABETH: They will be soon. *And she goes to the fireplace, proceeds to ladle up stew in a dish.*

PROCTOR: Pray now for a fair summer.

ELIZABETH: Aye.

PROCTOR: Are you well today?

ELIZABETH: I am. *She brings the plate to the table, and, indicating the food:* It is a rabbit.

PROCTOR, *going to the table:* Oh, is it! In Jonathan's trap?

ELIZABETH: No, she walked into the house this afternoon; I found her sittin' in the corner like she come to visit.

PROCTOR: Oh, that's a good sign walkin' in.

ELIZABETH: Pray God. It hurt my heart to strip her, poor rabbit. *She sits and watches him taste it.*

PROCTOR: It's well seasoned.

ELIZABETH, *blushing with pleasure:* I took great care. She's tender?

PROCTOR: Aye. *He eats. She watches him.* I think we'll see green fields soon. It's warm as blood beneath the clods.

ELIZABETH: That's well.

PROCTOR *eats, then looks up.*

PROCTOR: If the crop is good I'll buy George Jacob's heifer. How would that please you?

ELIZABETH: Aye, it would.

PROCTOR, *with a grin:* I mean to please you, Elizabeth.

ELIZABETH—*it is hard to say:* I know it, John.

He gets up, goes to her, kisses her. She receives it. With a certain disappointment, he returns to the table.

PROCTOR, *as gently as he can:* Cider?

ELIZABETH, *with a sense of reprimanding herself for having forgot:* Aye! *She gets up and goes and pours a glass for him. He now arches his back.*

PROCTOR: This farm's a continent when you go foot by foot droppin' seeds in it.

ELIZABETH, *coming with the cider:* It must be.

PROCTOR, *drinks a long draught, then, putting the glass down:* You ought to bring some flowers in the house.

The Crucible   1201

1 **Discussion** Ask students how John Proctor's observation that "It's winter in here yet" might be interpreted figuratively. Does Elizabeth seem to be behaving coldly toward John? On what do students base their answer?

2 **Discussion** Have students discuss why the Puritans might have been especially appreciative of the coming of spring.

3 **Literary Focus** Have students discuss what the interactions between John and Elizabeth Proctor in this scene reveal about the personalities of the two characters. What do the interactions reveal about the status of Proctors' marriage?

4 **Enrichment** The Massachusetts charter gave the royal governor the power to establish a general court and appoint the judges who sit on it. When Proctor says, "They've sent four judges out of Boston," he is referring to the actions of the provincial government.

5 **Clarification** Draw students attention to what this passage indicates about the amount of time that has elapsed since the first act.

ELIZABETH: Oh! I forgot! I will tomorrow.

1 **PROCTOR:** It's winter in here yet. On Sunday let you come with me, and we'll walk the farm together; I never see such a load of flowers on the earth. *With good feeling he goes and looks up at the sky through the open doorway.* Lilacs have a purple smell.
2 Lilac is the smell of nightfall, I think. Massachusetts is a beauty in the spring!

ELIZABETH: Aye, it is.

There is a pause. She is watching him from the table as he stands there absorbing the night. It is as though now she would speak but cannot. Instead, now, she takes up his plate and glass and fork and goes with them to the basin. Her back is turned to him. He turns to her and watches her. A sense of their separation rises.

PROCTOR: I think you're sad again. Are you?

ELIZABETH—*she doesn't want friction, and yet she must:* You come so late I thought you'd gone to Salem this afternoon.

PROCTOR: Why? I have no business in Salem.

ELIZABETH: You did speak of going, earlier this week.

PROCTOR—*he knows what she means:* I thought better of it since.

ELIZABETH: Mary Warren's there today.

3 **PROCTOR:** Why'd you let her? You heard me forbid her go to Salem any more!

ELIZABETH: I couldn't stop her.

PROCTOR, *holding back a full condemnation of her:* It is a fault, it is a fault, Elizabeth—you're the mistress here, not Mary Warren.

ELIZABETH: She frightened all my strength away.

PROCTOR: How may that mouse frighten you, Elizabeth? You—

ELIZABETH: It is a mouse no more. I forbid her go, and she raises up her chin like the daughter of a prince and says to me, "I must go to Salem, Goody Proctor; I am an official of the court!"

PROCTOR: Court! What court?

ELIZABETH: Aye, it is a proper court they have now. They've sent four judges out of Boston, she says, weighty magistrates of the General Court, and at the head sits the Deputy Governor of the Province.   4

PROCTOR, *astonished:* Why, she's mad.

ELIZABETH: I would to God she were. There be fourteen people in the jail now, she says. PROCTOR *simply looks at her, unable to grasp it.* And they'll be tried, and the court have power to hang them too, she says.

PROCTOR, *scoffing, but without conviction:* Ah, they'd never hang—

ELIZABETH: The Deputy Governor promise hangin' if they'll not confess, John. The town's gone wild, I think. She speak of Abigail, and I thought she were a saint, to hear her. Abigail brings the other girls into the court, and where she walks the crowd will part like the sea for Israel.[1] And folks are brought before them, and if they scream and howl and fall to the floor—the person's clapped in the jail for bewitchin' them.

PROCTOR, *wide-eyed:* Oh, it is a black mischief.

ELIZABETH: I think you must go to Salem, John. *He turns to her.* I think so. You must tell them it is a fraud.

PROCTOR, *thinking beyond this:* Aye, it is, it is surely.

ELIZABETH: Let you go to Ezekiel Cheever—he knows you well. And tell him what she said to you last week in her uncle's house.   5

---

1. **part like . . . Israel:** In the Bible God commanded Moses, the leader of the Jews, to part the Red Sea to enable the Jews to escape from the Egyptians into Canaan.

Grammar in Action

Contractions are formed by removing a letter or group of letters from an expression and replacing the missing letters with an apostrophe. Although contractions are often used in informal writing and in dialogue, they are generally not considered acceptable in formal writing. This results partly from the fact that the exact meaning of a contraction is often not immediately clear and must be determined from the context in which it is used. Note the following example from *The Crucible:*

Why'd you let her? You heard me forbid her go to Salem any more!

In this sentence, the contraction could stand for either *why did* or *why would.* By examining the context in which the sentence is used, however, it becomes clear that the contraction stands for *why did.*

Student Activity. Rewrite the following sentences, replacing each of the contractions with the words it represents.
1. She's told you!
2. And I'd as lief you'd not be sending me to Hell.
3. You've ripped the Deputy Governor's warrant, man!

She said it had naught to do with witchcraft, did she not?

PROCTOR, *in thought:* Aye, she did, she did. *Now, a pause.*

ELIZABETH, *quietly, fearing to anger him by prodding:* God forbid you keep that from the court, John. I think they must be told.

PROCTOR, *quietly, struggling with his thought:* Aye, they must, they must. It is a wonder they do believe her.

ELIZABETH: I would go to Salem now, John— let you go tonight.

PROCTOR: I'll think on it.

ELIZABETH, *with her courage now:* You cannot keep it, John.

PROCTOR, *angering:* I know I cannot keep it. I say I will think on it!

ELIZABETH, *hurt, and very coldly:* Good, then, let you think on it. *She stands and starts to walk out of the room.*

PROCTOR: I am only wondering how I may prove what she told me, Elizabeth. If the girl's a saint now, I think it is not easy to prove she's fraud, and the town gone so silly. She told it to me in a room alone—I have no proof for it.

ELIZABETH: You were alone with her?

PROCTOR, *stubbornly:* For a moment alone, aye.

ELIZABETH: Why, then, it is not as you told me.

PROCTOR, *his anger rising:* For a moment, I say. The others come in soon after.

ELIZABETH, *quietly—she has suddenly lost all faith in him:* Do as you wish, then. *She starts to turn.*

PROCTOR: Woman. *She turns to him.* I'll not have your suspicion any more.

ELIZABETH, *a little loftily:* I have no—

PROCTOR: I'll not have it!

ELIZABETH: Then let you not earn it.

PROCTOR, *with a violent undertone:* You doubt me yet?

ELIZABETH, *with a smile, to keep her dignity:* John, if is were not Abigail that you must go to hurt, would you falter now? I think not.

PROCTOR: Now look you—

ELIZABETH: I see what I see, John.

PROCTOR, *with solemn warning:* You will not judge me more, Elizabeth. I have good reason to think before I charge fraud on Abigail, and I will think on it. Let you look to your own improvement before you go to judge your husband any more. I have forgot Abigail, and—

ELIZABETH: And I.

PROCTOR: Spare me! You forget nothin' and forgive nothin'. Learn charity, woman. I have gone tiptoe in this house all seven month since she is gone. I have not moved from there to there without I think to please you, and still an everlasting funeral marches round your heart. I cannot speak but I am doubted, every moment judged for lies, as though I come into a court when I come into this house!

ELIZABETH: John, you are not open with me. You saw her with a crowd, you said. Now you—

PROCTOR: I'll plead my honesty no more, Elizabeth.

ELIZABETH—*now she would justify herself:* John, I am only—

PROCTOR: No more! I should have roared you down when first you told me your suspicion. But I wilted, and, like a Christian, I confessed. Confessed! Some dream I had must have mistaken you for God that day. But you're not, you're not, and let you remember

The Crucible   1203

6 **Discussion** Have students speculate about how the court might respond if John Proctor went into town and revealed what Abigail told him. Would the court be likely to believe him? Why or why not?

7 **Discussion** Ask students to explain why Elizabeth is hurt by her husband's response to her urgings.

8 **Discussion** Have students explain why Elizabeth suddenly loses all faith in John.

9 **Discussion** Given what students have learned about the Proctors' relationship, do they think that Elizabeth has a right to be suspicious of John? Why or why not?

10 **Literary Focus** Have students discuss what John Proctor's reaction to Elizabeth's suspicion reveals about his character.

11 **Discussion** Have students discuss the possible irony of Proctor's statement that he confessed "like a Christian" in light of the various characters' forced confessions to witchcraft later in the play.

4. We've now only come from the jail, and they'll not even let us in to see them.
5. The town's gone wild.
6. Ah, they'd never hang—
7. But she's safe, thank God, for they'll not hurt the innocent child.

12 Literary Focus Point out to students that Miller does not offer the types of in-depth description of Elizabeth that he offers of many of the other characters. Have them explore possible reasons why Miller might have chosen to omit such a description of Elizabeth. Then have them discuss what Miller might have said if he had included a description of Elizabeth.

13 Discussion Have students discuss the ways in which the situation might be different if all of the characters did in fact "love each other."

14 Enrichment Tell students that Sarah Good was one of the first two to be executed during the real Salem witchcraft trials. Then have them discuss why Miller might have altered such details.

15 Enrichment Tell students that Mary's descriptions are similar to much of the testimony of supposed victims of witchcraft during the Salem witchcraft trials.

16 Discussion Have students discuss what might bring Mary Warren to the sudden conclusion that on many occasions Sarah Good had tried to kill her.

it! Let you look sometimes for the goodness in me, and judge me not.

ELIZABETH: I do not judge you. The magistrate sits in your heart that judges you. I never thought you but a good man, John—*with a smile*—only somewhat bewildered.

PROCTOR, *laughing bitterly:* Oh, Elizabeth, your justice would freeze beer! *He turns suddenly toward a sound outside. He starts for the door as* MARY WARREN *enters. As soon as he sees her, he goes directly to her and grabs her by the cloak, furious.* How do you go to Salem when I forbid it? Do you mock me? *Shaking her.* I'll whip you if you dare leave this house again!

Strangely, she doesn't resist him, but hangs limply by his grip.

MARY WARREN: I am sick, I am sick, Mr. Proctor. Pray, pray, hurt me not. *Her strangeness throws him off, and her evident pallor and weakness. He frees her.* My insides are all shuddery; I am in the proceedings all day, sir.

PROCTOR, *with draining anger—his curiosity is draining it:* And what of these proceedings here? When will you proceed to keep this house, as you are paid nine pound a year to do—and my wife not wholly well?

As though to compensate, MARY WARREN *goes to* ELIZABETH *with a small rag doll.*

MARY WARREN: I made a gift for you today, Goody Proctor. I had to sit long hours in a chair, and passed the time with sewing.

ELIZABETH, *perplexed, looking at the doll:* Why, thank you, it's a fair poppet.

MARY WARREN, *with a trembling, decayed voice:* We must all love each other now, Goody Proctor.

ELIZABETH, *amazed at her strangeness:* Aye, indeed we must.

MARY WARREN, *glancing at the room:* I'll get up early in the morning and clean the house. I must sleep now. *She turns and starts off.*

PROCTOR: Mary. *She halts.* Is it true? There be fourteen women arrested?

MARY WARREN: No, sir. There be thirty-nine now—*She suddenly breaks off and sobs and sits down, exhausted.*

ELIZABETH: Why, she's weepin'! What ails you, child?

MARY WARREN: Goody Osburn—will hang!

There is a shocked pause, while she sobs.

PROCTOR: Hang! *He calls into her face.* Hang, y'say?

MARY WARREN, *through her weeping:* Aye.

PROCTOR: The Deputy Governor will permit it?

MARY WARREN: He sentenced her. He must. *To ameliorate it:* But not Sarah Good. For Sarah Good confessed, y'see.

PROCTOR: Confessed! To what?

MARY WARREN: That she—*in horror at the memory*—she sometimes made a compact with Lucifer, and wrote her name in his black book—with her blood—and bound herself to torment Christians till God's thrown down—and we all must worship Hell forevermore.

Pause.

PROCTOR: But—surely you know what a jabberer she is. Did you tell them that?

MARY WARREN: Mr. Proctor, in open court she near to choked us all to death.

PROCTOR: How, choked you?

MARY WARREN: She sent her spirit out.

ELIZABETH: Oh, Mary, Mary, surely you—

MARY WARREN, *with an indignant edge:* She tried to kill me many times, Goody Proctor!

ELIZABETH: Why, I never heard you mention that before.

MARY WARREN: I never knew it before. I never knew anything before. When she come into

THE EXECUTION OF THE REVEREND STEPHEN BURROUGHS
FOR WITCHCRAFT AT SALEM, MASSACHUSETTS, IN 1692
19th Century Engraving
The Granger Collection

The Crucible 1205

Fine art, *The Execution of the Reverend Stephen Burroughs at Salem, Massachusetts, in 1692.* This nineteenth-century engraving captures the execution of one of the people accused of witchcraft during the hysteria in Salem. Like many nineteenth-century engravers who focused on historical subjects, the artist has attempted to be historically accurate. Yet, probably because the artist had access to little factual material about the witchcraft trials, a number of the details in the picture seem out of place. Although the executioner, the minister on horseback, and the accused, are all dressed in Puritan attire, the guards are dressed in costumes that seem to be taken from medieval Europe rather than colonial America. The weapons the guards are holding also seem to be taken from the distant past.

You might want to use the following questions to discuss the art:

1. What does this engraving suggest about Stephen Burroughs's state of mind in the moments preceding his execution?
2. What role does the minister on horseback seem to be playing in the proceedings?
3. What seems unusual about the costumes worn by the guards?
4. What emotions does this engraving evoke in you? Why?

17 **Discussion** Have students discuss their attitudes toward Mary Warren at this point in the play. Which of her comments and actions have contributed most to shaping their attitudes?

18 **Enrichment** The nineteenth-century American writer Nathaniel Hawthorne (p. 300) was a direct descendent of Judge Hathorne. Hawthorne's decision to add a *w* to his family name may have resulted from his shame concerning his ancestor's role in the trial at Salem.

19 **Discussion** Have students discuss Mary Warren's comment that Goody Osburn "condemned herself" by falsely claiming that she was reciting her commandments. What is suggested about Puritan attitudes by the fact that the court regarded Goody Osburn's lie as "hard proof" that she was a witch?

20 **Discussion** Have students discuss the irony of the fact that the court "will not hang [the accused] if they confess."

21 **Discussion** Ask students what change Mary's participation in the court proceedings seems to have brought about in her attitude toward the Proctors and her obligations to them.

17 the court I say to myself, I must not accuse this woman, for she sleep in ditches, and so very old and poor. But then—then she sit there, denying and denying, and I feel a misty coldness climbin' up my back, and the skin on my skull begin to creep, and I feel a clamp around my neck and I cannot breathe air; and then—*entranced*—I hear a voice, a screamin' voice, and it were my voice—and all at once I remembered everything she done to me!

PROCTOR: Why? What did she do to you?

MARY WARREN, *like one awakened to a marvelous secret insight:* So many time, Mr. Proctor, she come to this very door, beggin' bread and a cup of cider—and mark this: whenever I turned her away empty, she *mumbled.*

ELIZABETH: Mumbled! She may mumble if she's hungry.

MARY WARREN: But *what* does she mumble? You must remember, Goody Proctor. Last month—a Monday, I think—she walked away, and I thought my guts would burst for two days after. Do you remember it?

ELIZABETH: Why—I do, I think, but—

MARY WARREN: And so I told that to Judge Hathorne, and he asks her so. "Goody Osburn," says he, "what curse do you mumble that this girl must fall sick after turning you away?" And then she replies—*mimicking an old crone*—"Why, your excellence, no curse at all. I only say my commandments; I hope I may say my commandments," says she!

ELIZABETH: And that's an upright answer.

18 MARY WARREN: Aye, but then Judge Hathorne say, "Recite for us your commandments!"—*leaning avidly toward them*—and **19** of all the ten she could not say a single one. She never knew no commandments, and they had her in a flat lie!

PROCTOR: And so condemned her?

MARY WARREN, *now a little strained, seeing his stubborn doubt:* Why, they must when she condemned herself.

PROCTOR: But the proof, the proof!

MARY WARREN, *with greater impatience with him:* I told you the proof. It's hard proof, hard as rock, the judges said.

PROCTOR, *pauses an instant, then:* You will not go to court again, Mary Warren.

MARY WARREN: I must tell you, sir, I will be gone every day now. I am amazed you do not see what weighty work we do.

PROCTOR: What work you do! It's strange work for a Christian girl to hang old women!

20 MARY WARREN: But, Mr. Proctor, they will not hang them if they confess. Sarah Good will only sit in jail some time —*recalling*—and here's a wonder for you; think on this. Goody Good is pregnant!

ELIZABETH: Pregnant! Are they mad? The woman's near to sixty!

21 MARY WARREN: They had Doctor Griggs examine her, and she's full to the brim. And smokin' a pipe all these years, and no husband either! But she's safe, thank God, for they'll not hurt the innocent child. But be that not a marvel? You must see it, sir, it's God's work we do. So I'll be gone every day for some time. I'm—I am an official of the court, they say, and I—*She has been edging toward offstage.*

PROCTOR: I'll official you! *He strides to the mantel, takes down the whip hanging there.*

MARY WARREN, *terrified, but coming erect, striving for her authority:* I'll not stand whipping any more!

ELIZABETH, *hurriedly, as* PROCTOR *approaches:* Mary, promise you'll stay at home—

MARY WARREN, *backing from him, but keep-*

Primary Source

In the introduction to his *Collected Plays* (1957), Miller reflected on the "social compliance" he observed during the McCarthy hearings. He wrote: "I wondered, at first, whether it must be that self-preservation and the need to hold on to opportunity . . . was what the fear was feeding on . . . It seemed to me after a time that this . . . social compliance is the result of the sense of guilt which individuals strive to conceal by complying . . . Above all, above all horrors, I saw accepted the notion that conscience was no longer a private matter but one of state administration. I saw men handing conscience to other men and thanking other men for the opportunity of doing so." Ask students if the situation Miller describes seems to be happening in the play.

ing her erect posture, striving, striving for her way: The Devil's loose in Salem, Mr. Proctor; we must discover where he's hiding!

PROCTOR: I'll whip the Devil out of you! *With whip raised he reaches out for her, and she streaks away and yells.*

MARY WARREN, *pointing at* ELIZABETH: I saved her life today!

Silence. His whip comes down.

ELIZABETH, *softly:* I am accused?

MARY WARREN, *quaking:* Somewhat mentioned. But I said I never see no sign you ever sent your spirit out to hurt no one, and seeing I do live so closely with you, they dismissed it.

ELIZABETH: Who accused me?

MARY WARREN: I am bound by law, I cannot tell it. *To* PROCTOR: I only hope you'll not be so sarcastical no more. Four judges and the King's deputy sat to dinner with us but an hour ago. I—I would have you speak civilly to me, from this out.

PROCTOR, *in horror, muttering in disgust at her:* Go to bed.

MARY WARREN, *with a stamp of her foot:* I'll not be ordered to bed no more, Mr. Proctor! I am eighteen and a woman, however single!

PROCTOR: Do you wish to sit up? Then sit up.

MARY WARREN: I wish to go to bed!

PROCTOR, *in anger:* Good night, then!

MARY WARREN: Good night. *Dissatisfied, uncertain of herself, she goes out. Wide-eyed, both, Proctor and Elizabeth stand staring.*

ELIZABETH, *quietly:* Oh, the noose, the noose is up!

PROCTOR: There'll be no noose.

ELIZABETH: She wants me dead. I knew all week it would come to this!

PROCTOR, *without conviction:* They dismissed it. You heard her say—

ELIZABETH: And what of tomorrow? She will cry me out until they take me!

PROCTOR: Sit you down.

ELIZABETH: She wants me dead, John, you know it!

PROCTOR: I say sit down! *She sits, trembling. He speaks quickly, trying to keep his wits.* Now we must be wise, Elizabeth.

ELIZABETH, *with sarcasm, and a sense of being lost:* Oh, indeed, indeed!

PROCTOR: Fear nothing. I'll find Ezekiel Cheever. I'll tell him she said it were all sport.

ELIZABETH: John, with so many in the jail, more than Cheever's help is needed now, I think. Would you favor me with this? Go to Abigail.

PROCTOR, *his soul hardening as he senses . . . :* What have I to say to Abigail?

ELIZABETH, *delicately:* John—grant me this. You have a faulty understanding of young girls. There is a promise made in any bed—

PROCTOR, *striving against his anger:* What promise!

ELIZABETH: Spoke or silent, a promise is surely made. And she may dote on it now— I am sure she does—and thinks to kill me, then to take my place.

PROCTOR'S *anger is rising; he cannot speak.*

ELIZABETH: It is her dearest hope, John, I know it. There be a thousand names; why does she call mine? There be a certain danger in calling such a name—I am no Goody Good that sleeps in ditches, nor Osburn, drunk and half-witted. She'd dare not call out such a farmer's wife but there be monstrous profit in it. She thinks to take my place, John.

22 Discussion Have students guess who might have accused Elizabeth in court that day. On what do they base their guesses?

23 Literary Focus Have students discuss what this exchange reveals about Mary Warren's personality. Does her behavior seem almost comical? Why or why not?

24 Discussion Ask students if they think that Elizabeth's conclusions about Abigail are accurate. Why or why not? Given the earlier interactions of the two characters, what do students think would happen if John Proctor went to Abigail? Do they think that he might be able to convince her to refrain from accusing Elizabeth? Why or why not?

25 Discussion Ask students how the information in this passage helps to explain why Goody Good and Goody Osburn were the first two people accused of witchcraft.

Humanities Note

Fine art, *The Hanging of a "Witch" at Salem, Massachusetts, in 1692.* Like the nineteenth-century engravings appearing earlier in the text, this picture depicts an actual historical event. Although the engraving vividly captures the horror of the situation, several of the details seem unrealistic or out of place. For instance, the accused man is shown grasping his neck in pain though the noose has yet to be placed around it. In addition, the hangman is dressed in clothing that seems more appropriate for a frontiersman than for a colonist from Salem.

You might want to use the following questions to discuss the art:

1. How does the artist focus attention on the condemned man?
2. How does he convey the brutality of the event that is about to occur?
3. What impression does he convey of the crowd that has gathered to witness the execution?
4. This is one of many nineteenth-century engravings depicting the Salem witchcraft trials. Why do you think that the witchcraft trials might have been a popular subject among nineteenth-century artists?

THE HANGING OF A 'WITCH' AT SALEM, MASSACHUSETTS, IN 1692
19th Century Engraving
The Granger Collection

1208   *Contemporary Writers*

PROCTOR: She cannot think it! *He knows it is true.*

ELIZABETH, *"reasonably":* John, have you ever shown her somewhat of contempt? She cannot pass you in the church but you will blush—

PROCTOR: I may blush for my sin.

ELIZABETH: I think she sees another meaning in that blush.

PROCTOR: And what see you? What see you, Elizabeth?

ELIZABETH, *"conceding":* I think you be somewhat ashamed, for I am there, and she so close.

PROCTOR: When will you know me, woman? Were I stone I would have cracked for shame this seven month!

ELIZABETH: Then go and tell her she's a whore. Whatever promise she may sense—break it, John, break it.

PROCTOR, *between his teeth:* Good, then. I'll go. *He starts for his rifle.*

ELIZABETH, *trembling, fearfully:* Oh, how unwillingly!

PROCTOR, *turning on her, rifle in hand:* I will curse her hotter than the oldest cinder in hell. But pray, begrudge me not my anger!

ELIZABETH: Your anger! I only ask you—

PROCTOR: Woman, am I so base? Do you truly think me base?

ELIZABETH: I never called you base.

PROCTOR: Then how do you charge me with such a promise? The promise that a stallion gives a mare I gave that girl!

ELIZABETH: Then why do you anger with me when I bid you break it?

PROCTOR: Because it speaks deceit, and I am honest! But I'll plead no more! I see now your spirit twists around the single error of my life, and I will never tear it free!

ELIZABETH, *crying out:* You'll tear it free—when you come to know that I will be your only wife, or no wife at all! She has an arrow in you yet, John Proctor, and you know it well!

Quite suddenly, as though from the air, a figure appears in the doorway. They start slightly. It is MR. HALE. *He is different now—drawn a little, and there is a quality of deference, even of guilt, about his manner now.*

HALE: Good evening.

PROCTOR, *still in his shock:* Why, Mr. Hale! Good evening to you, sir. Come in, come in.

HALE, *to Elizabeth:* I hope I do not startle you.

ELIZABETH: No, no, it's only that I heard no horse—

HALE: You are Goodwife Proctor.

PROCTOR: Aye; Elizabeth.

HALE, *nods, then:* I hope you're not off to bed yet.

PROCTOR, *setting down his gun:* No, no. HALE *comes further into the room. And* PROCTOR, *to explain his nervousness:* We are not used to visitors after dark, but you're welcome here. Will you sit you down, sir?

HALE: I will. *He sits.* Let you sit, Goodwife Proctor.

She does, never letting him out of her sight. There is a pause as HALE *looks about the room.*

PROCTOR, *to break the silence:* Will you drink cider, Mr. Hale?

HALE: No, it rebels my stomach; I have some further traveling yet tonight. Sit you down, sir. PROCTOR *sits.* I will not keep you long, but I have some business with you.

The Crucible 1209

---

26 Discussion What do students see as the reason why John Proctor blushes when Abigail passes by him in church? On what do they base their answer?

27 Literary Focus Have students pause at this point and discuss what they have learned about the characters of John and Elizabeth Proctor during this scene. Then have them predict what will happen to the two characters during the remainder of the play.

28 Discussion Have students discuss why there might be a "quality of deference, even of guilt, about [Hale's] manner" at this point. What does the change in Reverend Hale's demeanor suggest about his response to the events that have taken place since the first act?

29 Discussion Have students speculate about why Reverend Hale has come to visit the Proctors.

30 Enrichment Although the settlers had driven the native Americans back into the wilderness by the time of the play, the settlers still associated many natural and supernatural dangers with darkness. Consequently, they usually avoided traveling at night.

31
32

33

31 Literary Focus Have students discuss whether Reverend Hale's remarks suggest that he is somewhat skeptical about the court's judgment. If so, what does his skepticism reveal about his character?

32 Discussion Have students explain why Elizabeth is so shocked that Rebecca has been charged.

33 Reading Strategy Have students offer predictions about what will happen to Rebecca.

34 Clarification Make sure that students understand that Reverend Hale is using the word *theology* to refer to Proctor's knowledge and doctrines of Christianity as the Puritans interpreted them.

35 Literary Focus Have students respond to Reverend Parris's insistence on having golden candlesticks. What does this action reveal about Parris's character?

PROCTOR: Business of the court?

HALE: No—no, I come of my own, without the court's authority. Hear me. *He wets his lips.* I know not if you are aware, but your wife's name is—mentioned in the court.

PROCTOR: We know it, sir. Our Mary Warren told us. We are entirely amazed.

HALE: I am a stranger here, as you know. And in my ignorance I find it hard to draw a clear opinion of them that come accused before the court. And so this afternoon, and now tonight, I go from house to house—I come now from Rebecca Nurse's house and—

ELIZABETH, *shocked:* Rebecca's charged!

HALE: God forbid such a one be charged. She is, however—mentioned somewhat.

ELIZABETH, *with an attempt at a laugh:* You will never believe, I hope, that Rebecca trafficked with the Devil.

HALE: Woman, it is possible.

PROCTOR, *taken aback:* Surely you cannot think so.

HALE: This is a strange time, Mister. No man may longer doubt the powers of the dark are gathered in monstrous attack upon this village. There is too much evidence now to deny it. You will agree, sir?

PROCTOR, *evading:* I—have no knowledge in that line. But it's hard to think so pious a woman be secretly a Devil's bitch after seventy year of such good prayer.

HALE: Aye. But the Devil is a wily one, you cannot deny it. However, she is far from accused, and I know she will not be. *Pause.* I thought, sir, to put some questions as to the Christian character of this house, if you'll permit me.

PROCTOR, *coldly, resentful:* Why, we—have no fear of questions, sir.

HALE: Good, then. *He makes himself more* comfortable. In the book of record that Mr. Parris keeps, I note that you are rarely in the church on Sabbath Day.

PROCTOR: No, sir, you are mistaken.

HALE: Twenty-six time in seventeen month, sir. I must call that rare. Will you tell my why you are so absent?

PROCTOR: Mr. Hale, I never knew I must account to that man for I come to church or stay at home. My wife were sick this winter.

HALE: So I am told. But you, Mister, why could you not come alone?

PROCTOR: I surely did come when I could, and when I could not I prayed in this house.

HALE: Mr. Proctor, your house is not a church; your theology must tell you that.

PROCTOR: It does, sir, it does; and it tells me that a minister may pray to God without he have golden candlesticks upon the altar.

HALE: What golden candlesticks?

PROCTOR: Since we built the church there were pewter candlesticks upon the altar; Francis Nurse made them y'know, and a sweeter hand never touched the metal. But Parris came, and for twenty week he preach nothin' but golden candlesticks until he had them. I labor the earth from dawn of day to blink of night, and I tell you true when I look to heaven and see my money glaring at his elbows—it hurt my prayer, sir, it hurt my prayer. I think, sometimes, the man dreams cathedrals, not clapboard meetin' houses.

HALE, *thinks, then:* And yet, Mister, a Christian on Sabbath Day must be in church. *Pause.* Tell me—you have three children?

PROCTOR: Aye. Boys.

HALE: How comes it that only two are baptized?

PROCTOR, *starts to speak, then stops, then, as though unable to restrain this:* I like it not that Mr. Parris should lay his hand upon

34

35

36 my baby. I see no light of God in that man. I'll not conceal it.

HALE: I must say it, Mr. Proctor; that is not for you to decide. The man's ordained, therefore the light of God is in him.

PROCTOR, *flushed with resentment but trying to smile:* What's your suspicion, Mr. Hale?

HALE: No, no, I have no—

37 **PROCTOR:** I nailed the roof upon the church, I hung the door—

HALE: Oh, did you! That's a good sign, then.

PROCTOR: It may be I have been too quick to bring the man to book, but you cannot think we ever desired the destruction of religion. I think that's in your mind, is it not?

HALE, *not altogether giving way:* I—have—there is a softness in your record, sir, a softness.

ELIZABETH: I think, maybe, we have been too hard with Mr. Parris. I think so. But sure we never loved the Devil here.

HALE, *nods, deliberating this. Then, with the voice of one administering a secret test:* Do you know your Commandments, Elizabeth?

ELIZABETH, *without hesitation, even eagerly:* I surely do. There be no mark of blame upon my life, Mr. Hale. I am a covenanted Christian woman.

HALE: And you, Mister?

38 **PROCTOR,** *a trifle unsteadily:* I—am sure I do, sir.

HALE, *glances at her open face, then at* JOHN, *then:* Let you repeat them, if you will.

PROCTOR: The Commandments.

HALE: Aye.

PROCTOR, *looking off, beginning to sweat:* Thou shalt not kill.

HALE: Aye.

PROCTOR, *counting on his fingers:* Thou shalt not steal. Thou shalt not covet thy neighbor's goods, nor make unto thee any graven image. Thou shalt not take the name of the Lord in vain; thou shalt have no other gods before me. *With some hesitation:* Thou shalt remember the Sabbath Day and keep it holy. *Pause. Then:* Thou shalt honor thy father and mother. Thou shalt not bear false witness. *He is stuck. He counts back on his fingers, knowing one is missing.* Thou shalt not make unto thee any graven image.

HALE: You have said that twice, sir.

39 **PROCTOR,** *lost:* Aye. *He is flailing for it.*

ELIZABETH, *delicately:* Adultery, John.

40 **PROCTOR,** *as though a secret arrow had pained his heart:* Aye. *Trying to grin it away—to* HALE: You see, sir, between the two of us we do know them all. HALE *only looks at* PROCTOR, *deep in his attempt to define this man.* PROCTOR *grows more uneasy.* I think it be a small fault.

HALE: Theology, sir, is a fortress; no crack in a fortress may be accounted small. *He rises; he seems worried now. He paces a little, in deep thought.*

PROCTOR: There be no love for Satan in this house, Mister.

HALE: I pray it, I pray it dearly. *He looks to both of them, an attempt at a smile on his face, but his misgivings are clear.* Well, then—I'll bid you good night.

ELIZABETH, *unable to restrain herself:* Mr. Hale. *He turns.* I do think you are suspecting me somewhat? Are you not?

41 **HALE,** *obviously disturbed—and evasive:* Goody Proctor, I do not judge you. My duty is to add what I may to the godly wisdom of the court. I pray you both good health and good fortune. *To* JOHN: Good night, sir. *He starts out.*

36 Discussion Do students think that John Proctor's dislike for Reverend Parris is a valid reason for questioning Proctor's religious devotion? Why or why not?

37 Discussion Have students discuss what Proctor's role in constructing the church indicates about the place of religion in his life.

38 Reading Strategy Have students predict whether Proctor will be able to recite his commandments. On what do they base their prediction?

39 Discussion Have students discuss the irony of the fact that Proctor forgets the commandment concerning adultery.

40 Discussion Ask students what Reverend Hale's inability to overlook the omission of a single commandment suggests about Puritan attitudes.

41 Discussion Have students discuss why John Proctor's inability to recite all of the commandments would contribute to Reverend Hale's suspicions about Elizabeth Proctor.

42 Discussion Do students think that Reverend Hale believes Proctor? Why or why not?

43 Discussion Ask students if they think that Proctor is justified in having reservations about appearing before the court. Given what students have already learned about the court proceedings, how do they think the court would be likely to respond to Proctor's testimony?

44 Clarification Explain to students that the Puritans viewed people who did not believe in witchcraft as heretics.

"I do think you are suspecting me somewhat?"

ELIZABETH, *with a note of desperation:* I think you must tell him, John.

HALE: What's that?

ELIZABETH, *restraining a call:* Will you tell him?

Slight pause. HALE *looks questioningly at* JOHN.

PROCTOR, *with difficulty:* I—I have no witness and cannot prove it, except my word be taken. But I know the children's sickness had naught to do with witchcraft.

HALE, *stopped, struck:* Naught to do—?

PROCTOR: Mr. Parris discovered them sportin' in the woods. They were startled and took sick.

Pause.

HALE: Who told you this?

PROCTOR, *hesitates, then:* Abigail Williams.

HALE: Abigail.

PROCTOR: Aye.

HALE, *his eyes wide:* Abigail Williams told you it had naught to do with witchcraft!

PROCTOR: She told me the day you came, sir.

HALL, *suspiciously:* Why—why did you keep this?

PROCTOR: I never knew until tonight that the world is gone daft with this nonsense.

HALE: Nonsense! Mister, I have myself examined Tituba, Sarah Good, and numerous others that have confessed to dealing with the Devil. They have *confessed* it.

PROCTOR: And why not, if they must hang for denyin' it? There are them that will swear to anything before they'll hang; have you never thought of that?

HALE: I have. I—I have indeed. *It is his own suspicion, but he resists it. He glances at* ELIZABETH, *then at* JOHN. And you—would you testify to this in court? — **42**

PROCTOR: I—had not reckoned with goin' into court. But if I must I will.

HALE: Do you falter here?

PROCTOR: I falter nothing, but I may wonder if my story will be credited in such a court. I do wonder on it, when such a steady-minded minister as you will suspicion such a woman that never lied, and cannot, and the world knows she cannot! I may falter somewhat, Mister; I am no fool. — **43**

HALE, *quietly—it has impressed him:* Proctor, let you open with me now, for I have a rumor that troubles me. It's said you hold no belief that there may even be witches in the world. Is that true, sir? — **44**

PROCTOR—*he knows this is critical, and is*

Grammar in Action

All **sentences** can be classified according to one of **four functions:** declarative, interrogative, imperative, and exclamatory. A declarative sentence states an idea and ends with a period. An interrogative sentence asks a question and ends with a question mark. An imperative sentence gives and order or a direction and ends with a period or an exclamation mark. An exclamatory sentence expresses strong emotions and ends with an exclamation mark. Note the following examples from *The Crucible:*

Mr. Parris discovered them sportin' in the woods. (declarative)
Will you tell him? (interrogative)
Go to bed. (imperative) (page 1207)
Abigail Williams told you it had naught to do with witchcraft! (exclamatory)

Student Activity 1. Identify each of the following sentences as declarative, interrogative, imperative, or exclamatory.
1. It's said that you hold no belief that there may even be witches in the world.
2. Question Abigail Williams about the Gospel, not myself!
3. How is Rebecca charged, Mr. Nurse?

striving against his disgust with HALE *and with himself for even answering:* I know not what I have said, I may have said it. I have wondered if there be witches in the world—although I cannot believe they come among us now.

HALE: Then you do not believe—

PROCTOR: I have no knowledge of it; the Bible speaks of witches, and I will not deny them.

HALE: And you, woman?

ELIZABETH: I—I cannot believe it.

HALE, *shocked:* You cannot!

PROCTOR: Elizabeth, you bewilder him!

ELIZABETH, *to* HALE: I cannot think the Devil may own a woman's soul, Mr. Hale, when she keeps an upright way, as I have. I am a good woman, I know it; and if you believe I may do only good work in the world, and yet be secretly bound to Satan, then I must tell you, sir, I do not believe it.

HALE: But, woman, you do believe there are witches in—

ELIZABETH: If you think that I am one, then I say there are none.

HALE: You surely do not fly against the Gospel, the Gospel—

PROCTOR: She believe in the Gospel, every word!

ELIZABETH: Question Abigail Williams about the Gospel, not myself!

HALE *stares at her.*

PROCTOR: She do not mean to doubt the Gospel, sir, you cannot think it. This be a Christian house, sir, a Christian house.

HALE: God keep you both; let the third child be quickly baptized, and go you without fail each Sunday to Sabbath prayer; and keep a solemn, quiet way among you. I think—

GILES COREY *appears in doorway.*

GILES: John!

PROCTOR: Giles! What's the matter?

GILES: They take my wife.

FRANCIS NURSE *enters.*

GILES: And his Rebecca!

PROCTOR, *to* FRANCIS: Rebecca's in the *jail!*

FRANCIS: Aye, Cheever come and take her in his wagon. We've only now come from the jail, and they'll not even let us in to see them.

ELIZABETH: They've surely gone wild now, Mr. Hale!

FRANCIS, *going to* HALE: Reverend Hale! Can you not speak to the Deputy Governor? I'm sure he mistakes these people—

HALE: Pray calm yourself, Mr. Nurse.

FRANCIS: My wife is the very brick and mortar of the church, Mr. Hale—*indicating* GILES—and Martha Corey, there cannot be a woman closer yet to God than Martha.

HALE: How is Rebecca charged, Mr. Nurse?

FRANCIS, *with a mocking, half-hearted laugh:* For murder, she's charged! *Mockingly quoting the warrant:* "For the marvelous and supernatural murder of Goody Putnam's babies." What am I to do, Mr. Hale?

HALE, *turns from* FRANCIS, *deeply troubled, then:* Believe me, Mr. Nurse, if Rebecca Nurse be tainted, then nothing's left to stop the whole green world from burning. Let you rest upon the justice of the court; the court will send her home, I know it.

FRANCIS: You cannot mean she will be tried in court!

HALE, *pleading:* Nurse, though our hearts break, we cannot flinch; these are new times, sir. There is a misty plot afoot so subtle we should be criminal to cling to old respects and ancient friendships. I have seen too many frightful proofs in court—the Devil

The Crucible 1213

45 Literary Focus Have students discuss what Elizabeth Proctor's pronouncements reveal about her character.

46 Discussion Ask students to explain what causes Elizabeth's outburst.

47 Discussion Have students discuss what Reverend Hale's instruction to the Proctors to "keep a solemn, quiet way among [them]" suggests about the Puritan approach to life.

48 Clarification Explain to students that as it is used in this sentence the word *marvelous* means "supernatural."

49 Discussion Ask students if they think that Reverend Hale's assessment of Rebecca Nurse's situation is accurate. Why or why not?

50 Reading Strategy Have students predict whether Reverend Hale will remain supportive of the court throughout the entire play. On what do they base their prediction?

4. Pray calm yourself, Mr. Nurse.
5. They've surely gone wild now, Mr. Hale!

Student Activity 2. Write a brief passage of dialogue in which you use each of the four types of sentences at least once.

51 Enrichment Explain that the Puritans believed that the fact that the Devil was originally a principal angel in Heaven demonstrated it was possible for even the best people to fall under the power of evil.

52 Discussion Ask students what seems to have motivated Walcott to accuse Giles Corey's wife of witchcraft.

53 Discussion Have students discuss the irony of Giles Corey's suggestion that Ezekial Cheever will "burn in Hell" for his role in the witchcraft proceedings.

54 Discussion Have students discuss Ezekial Cheever's apparent attitude toward his role as a clerk of the court. How is his attitude revealed?

55 Discussion Ask students to explain how the court might have gained the knowledge that Elizabeth Proctor had a poppet in her house.

is alive in Salem, and we dare not quail to follow wherever the accusing finger points!

PROCTOR, *angered:* How may such a woman murder children?

HALE, *in great pain:* Man, remember, until an hour before the Devil fell, God thought him beautiful in Heaven.

GILES: I never said my wife were a witch, Mr. Hale; I only said she were reading books!

HALE: Mr. Corey, exactly what complaint were made on your wife?

GILES: That bloody mongrel Walcott charge her. Y'see, he buy a pig of my wife four or five years ago, and the pig died soon after. So he come dancin' in for his money back. So my Martha, she says to him, "Walcott, if you haven't the wit to feed a pig properly, you'll not live to own many," she says. Now he goes to court and claims that from that day to this he cannot keep a pig alive for more than four weeks because my Martha bewitch them with her books!

Enter EZEKIEL CHEEVER. *A shocked silence.*

CHEEVER: Good evening to you, Proctor.

PROCTOR: Why, Mr. Cheever. Good evening.

CHEEVER: Good evening, all, Good evening, Mr. Hale.

PROCTOR: I hope you come not on business of the court.

CHEEVER: I do, Proctor, aye. I am clerk of the court now, y'know.

Enter MARSHAL HERRICK, *a man in his early thirties, who is somewhat shamefaced at the moment.*

GILES: It's a pity, Ezekiel, that an honest tailor might have gone to Heaven must burn in Hell. You'll burn for this, do you know it?

CHEEVER: You know yourself I must do as I'm told. You surely know that, Giles. And I'd as lief you'd not be sending me to Hell. I like not

the sound of it, I tell you; I like not the sound of it. *He fears* PROCTOR, *but starts to reach inside his coat.* Now believe me, Proctor, how heavy be the law, all its tonnage I do carry on my back tonight. *He takes out a warrant.* I have a warrant for your wife.

PROCTOR, *to* HALE: You said she were not charged!

HALE: I know nothin' of it. *To* CHEEVER: When were she charged?

CHEEVER: I am given sixteen warrant tonight, sir, and she is one.

PROCTOR: Who charged her?

CHEEVER: Why, Abigail Williams charge her.

PROCTOR: On what proof, what proof?

CHEEVER, *looking about the room:* Mr. Proctor, I have little time. The court bid me search your house, but I like not to search a house. So will you hand me any poppets that your wife may keep here?

PROCTOR: Poppets?

ELIZABETH: I never kept no poppets, not since I were a girl.

CHEEVER, *embarrassed, glancing toward the mantel where sits* MARY WARREN'S *poppet:* I spy a poppet, Goody Proctor.

ELIZABETH: Oh! *Going for it:* Why, this is Mary's.

CHEEVER, *shyly:* Would you please to give it to me?

ELIZABETH, *handing it to him, asks* HALE: Has the court discovered a text in poppets now?

CHEEVER, *carefully holding the poppet:* Do you keep any others in this house?

PROCTOR: No, nor this one either till tonight. What signifies a poppet?

CHEEVER: Why, a poppet—*he gingerly turns the poppet over*—a poppet may signify—

Now, woman, will you please to come with me?

PROCTOR: She will not! *To* ELIZABETH: Fetch Mary here.

CHEEVER, *ineptly reaching toward* ELIZABETH: No, no, I am forbid to leave her from my sight.

PROCTOR, *pushing his arm away:* You'll leave her out of sight and out of mind, Mister. Fetch Mary, Elizabeth. ELIZABETH *goes upstairs.*

HALE: What signifies a poppet, Mr. Cheever?

CHEEVER, *turning the poppet over in his hands:* Why, they say it may signify that she—*he has lifted the poppet's skirt, and his eyes widen in astonished fear.* Why, this, this—

PROCTOR, *reaching for the poppet:* What's there?

CHEEVER: Why—*He draws out a long needle from the poppet*—it is a needle! Herrick, Herrick, it is a needle!

HERRICK *comes toward him.*

PROCTOR, *angrily, bewildered:* And what signifies a needle!

CHEEVER, *his hands shaking:* Why, this go hard with her, Proctor, this—I had my doubts, Proctor, I had my doubts, but here's calamity. *To* HALE, *showing the needle:* You see it, sir, it is a needle!

HALE: Why? What meanin' has it?

CHEEVER, *wide-eyed, trembling:* The girl, the Williams girl, Abigail Williams, sir. She sat to dinner in Reverend Parris's house tonight, and without word nor warnin' she falls to the floor. Like a struck beast, he says, and screamed a scream that a bull would weep to hear. And he goes to save her, and, stuck two inches in the flesh of her belly, he draw a needle out. And demandin' of her how she come to be so stabbed, she—*to* PROCTOR *now*—testify it were your wife's familiar spirit pushed it in.

PROCTOR: Why, she done it herself! *To* HALE: I hope you're not takin' this for proof, Mister!

HALE, *struck by the proof, is silent.*

CHEEVER: 'Tis hard proof! *To* HALE: I find here a poppet Goody Proctor keeps. I have found it, sir. And in the belly of the poppet a needle's stuck. I tell you true, Proctor, I never warranted to see such proof of Hell, and I bid you obstruct me not, for I—

Enter ELIZABETH *with* MARY WARREN. PROCTOR, *seeing* MARY WARREN, *draws her by the arm to* HALE.

PROCTOR: Here now! Mary, how did this poppet come into my house?

MARY WARREN, *frightened for herself, her voice very small:* What poppet's that, sir?

PROCTOR, *impatiently, points at the doll in* CHEEVER'S *hand:* This poppet, this poppet.

MARY WARREN, *evasively, looking at it:* Why, I—I think it is mine.

PROCTOR: It is your poppet, is it not?

MARY WARREN, *not understanding the direction of this:* It—is, sir.

PROCTOR: And how did it come into this house?

MARY WARREN, *glancing about at the avid faces:* Why—I made it in the court, sir, and—give it to Goody Proctor tonight.

PROCTOR, *to* HALE: Now, sir—do you have it?

HALE: Mary Warren, a needle have been found inside this poppet.

MARY WARREN, *bewildered:* Why, I meant no harm by it, sir.

PROCTOR, *quickly:* You stuck that needle in yourself?

MARY WARREN: I—I believe I did, sir, I—

56

59

57

58

56 Literary Focus Have students discuss what this sequence of events reveals about Abigail's character. If Abigail's accusation were to result in the hanging of Elizabeth Proctor, do students think that Abigail would be guilty of murder? Why or why not?

57 Enrichment Witches were believed to have servants known as *familiars.* Most often, the familiars appeared in the form of animals, such as black cats.

58 Clarification Explain that the Puritans believed it was possible for a witch to inflict harm on someone from a distance by injuring a doll or poppet representing the victim.

59 Reading Strategy Have students pause at this point and predict whether the charges against Elizabeth will be dropped as a result of Mary Warren's admission that she was the one who stuck the needle in the poppet. On what do students base their prediction?

60 **Discussion** Have students explain why Reverend Hale does not continue his questioning of Mary Warren.

61 **Discussion** Have students speculate about whether Proctor's outburst and his ripping of the warrant might later be used against him by the court.

62 **Discussion** Have students speculate about what our society might be like if our courts conducted themselves in the manner that the court in Salem was run. Is it possible to achieve justice in a society in which this type of court system is used? Why or why not?

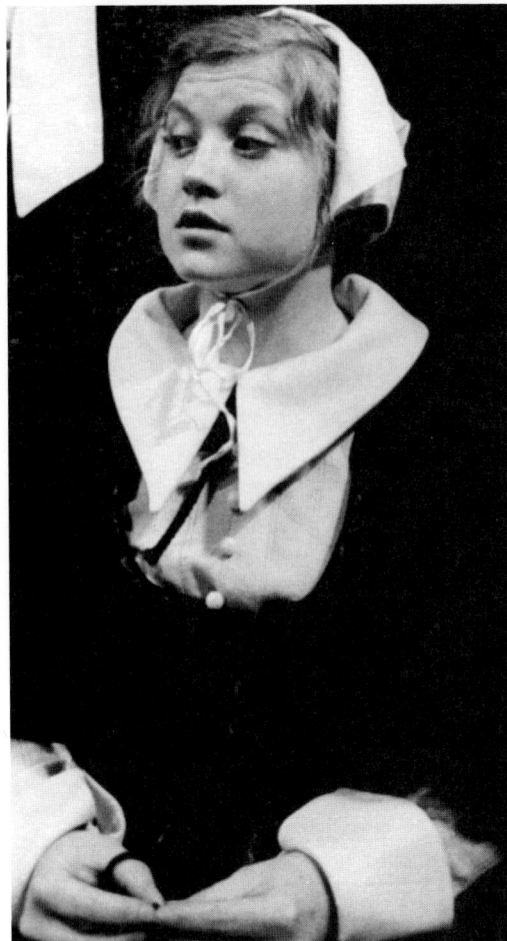

"What poppet's that, sir?"

PROCTOR, *to* HALE: What say you now?

HALE, *watching* MARY WARREN *closely:* Child, you are certain this be your natural memory? May it be, perhaps that someone conjures you even now to say this?

MARY WARREN: Conjures me? Why, no, sir, I am entirely myself, I think. Let you ask Susanna Walcott—she saw me sewin' it in court. *Or better still:* Ask Abby, Abby sat beside me when I made it.

PROCTOR, *to* HALE, *of* CHEEVER: Bid him begone. Your mind is surely settled now. Bid him out, Mr. Hale.

ELIZABETH: What signifies a needle?

HALE: Mary—you charge a cold and cruel murder on Abigail.

MARY WARREN: Murder! I charge no—

HALE: Abigail were stabbed tonight; a needle were found stuck into her belly—

ELIZABETH: And she charges me?

HALE: Aye.

ELIZABETH, *her breath knocked out:* Why—! The girl is murder! She must be ripped out of the world!

CHEEVER, *pointing at* ELIZABETH: You've heard that, sir! Ripped out of the world! Herrick, you heard it!

PROCTOR, *suddenly snatching the warrant out of* CHEEVER's *hands:* Out with you.

CHEEVER: Proctor, you dare not touch the warrant.

PROCTOR, *ripping the warrant:* Out with you!

CHEEVER: You've ripped the Deputy Governor's warrant, man!

PROCTOR: Damn the Deputy Governor! Out of my house!

HALE: Now, Proctor, Proctor!

PROCTOR: Get y'gone with them! You are a broken minister.

HALE: Proctor, if she is innocent, the court—

PROCTOR: If *she* is innocent! Why do you never wonder if Parris be innocent, or Abigail? Is the accuser always holy now? Were

Primary Source

In his analysis of *The Crucible,* the literary scholar Jeffrey Helterman writes:

> Since [Miller's] concern is with the sources of the madness which were plaguing his own times as well as that of the Puritan, Miller explores the multifaceted causes of the growth of the witchhunt. The first sources, social or economic, are rational. Reverend Parris, the village minister, finds it useful to explain his daughter's indecent behavior by attributing it to witchcraft rather than to his own inability to raise her properly, and Mr. Putnam, the town's richest man, finds great advantage in having his rival landowners charged with witchcraft. Because of her testimony, Abigail Williams, a serving girl . . . raises herself to a position of power in the town. As the fever grows, however, its sources lie more and more in the irrationality of the human psyche as both individual and mass hysteria take over the town. Paranoia surfaces: Mrs. Putnam's unfocused despair over the loss of her infants in childbirth turns to a more comforting hatred of Rebecca Nurse. Both Mrs. Putnam and Reverend Parris see a kind of inverse election in being tormented by the devil. Miller very convincingly describes

they born this morning as clean as God's fingers? I'll tell you what's walking Salem—vengeance is walking Salem. We are what we always were in Salem, but now the little crazy children are jangling the keys of the kingdom, and common vengeance writes the law! This warrant's vengeance! I'll not give my wife to vengeance!

ELIZABETH: I'll go, John—

PROCTOR: You will not go!

HERRICK: I have nine men outside. You cannot keep her. The law binds me, John, I cannot budge.

PROCTOR, *to* HALE, *ready to break him:* Will you see her taken?

HALE: Proctor, the court is just—

PROCTOR: Pontius Pilate![2] God will not let you wash your hands of this!

ELIZABETH: John—I think I must go with them. *He cannot bear to look at her.* Mary, there is bread enough for the morning; you will bake, in the afternoon. Help Mr. Proctor as you were his daughter—you owe me that, and much more. *She is fighting her weeping. To* PROCTOR: When the children wake, speak nothing of witchcraft—it will frighten them. *She cannot go on.*

PROCTOR: I will bring you home. I will bring you soon.

ELIZABETH: Oh, John, bring me soon!

PROCTOR: I will fall like an ocean on that court! Fear nothing, Elizabeth.

ELIZABETH, *with great fear:* I will fear nothing. *She looks about the room, as though to fix it in her mind.* Tell the children I have gone to visit someone sick.

She walks out the door, HERRICK *and* CHEE-

---

2. **Pontius** (pän′ shəs) **Pilate** (pī′ lət): The Roman leader who condemned Jesus to be crucified.

VER *behind her. For a moment,* PROCTOR *watches from the doorway. The clank of chain is heard.*

PROCTOR: Herrick! Herrick, don't chain her! *He rushes out the door. From outside:* Damn you, man, you will not chain her! Off with them! I'll not have it! I will not have her chained!

There are other men's voices against his. HALE, *in a fever of guilt and uncertainty, turns from the door to avoid the sight:* MARY WARREN *bursts into tears and sits weeping.* GILES COREY *calls to* HALE.

GILES: And yet silent, minister? It is fraud, you know it is fraud! What keeps you, man?

PROCTOR *is half braced, half pushed into the room by two deputies and* HERRICK.

PROCTOR: I'll pay you, Herrick, I will surely pay you!

HERRICK, *panting:* In God's name, John, I cannot help myself. I must chain them all. Now let you keep inside this house till I am gone! *He goes out with his deputies.*

PROCTOR *stands there, gulping air. Horses and a wagon creaking are heard.*

HALE, *in great uncertainty:* Mr. Proctor—

PROCTOR: Out of my sight!

HALE: Charity, Proctor, charity. What I have heard in her favor, I will not fear to testify in court. God help me, I cannot judge her guilty or innocent—I know not. Only this consider: the world goes mad, and it profit nothing you should lay the cause to the vengeance of a little girl.

PROCTOR: You are a coward! Though you be ordained in God's own tears, you are a coward now!

HALE: Proctor, I cannot think God be provoked so grandly by such a petty cause. The jails are packed—our greatest judges sit in

The Crucible   1217

63 **Discussion** Ask students what Proctor means when he declares that "God will not let [Reverend Hale] wash [his] hands of this."

64 **Literary Focus** Have students discuss what the manner in which Elizabeth handles her arrest reveals about her character.

65 **Discussion** Have students explain what Proctor means when he declares that he will "pay" Herrick.

66 **Literary Focus** Have students discuss their impressions of both Herrick and Cheever. How should the two men be judged?

67 **Discussion** Do students agree with Proctor's opinion that Reverend Hale is "a coward"? Why or why not?

the "positive" effects of paranoia. The "victims" of the witches begin to value themselves more highly than those who have been left alone, since it comforts them that someone, even Satan, is constantly watching out for them. The culmination of the mass hysteria occurs when the girls of Salem, egged on by the calculating deceptions of Abigail, truly believe that they see the devil in the form of a giant bird.

Reading Strategy Have students predict whether John will eventually succeed in convincing Mary to tell the truth about the poppet. On what do they base their prediction?

Cooperative Learning Divide your class into groups of four or five. Then have each group act out a scene from the first two acts. Urge students to pay close attention to Miller's stage directions. Also make sure that they keep in mind the personality of the character whose role they are playing.

Enrichment After the first performance of the play, Miller reacted to critics' reviews by writing an additional scene that took place between Act II and Act III. In this scene, which is set in the woods, Abigail voices her determination to get rid of Elizabeth and to reestablish her relationship with John. However, John vows to thwart her plan. The scene was felt by many to be unnecessary and to disturb the rhythm of the play. Miller came to agree with this assessment and decided not to include the scene in the version of the play that he published in his *Collected Plays*.

Reader's Response What is your opinion of John Proctor at this point in the play? What is your opinion of Elizabeth Proctor? Of Reverend Hale? Of Abigail Williams?

Salem now—and hangin's promised. Man, we must look to cause proportionate. Were there murder done, perhaps, and never brought to light? Abomination? Some secret blasphemy that stinks to Heaven? Think on cause, man, and let you help me to discover it. For there's your way, believe it, there is your only way, when such confusion strikes upon the world. *He goes to* GILES *and* FRANCIS. Let you counsel among yourselves; think on your village and what may have drawn from heaven such thundering wrath upon you all. I shall pray God open up our eyes.

HALE *goes out.*

FRANCIS, *struck by* HALE'S *mood:* I never heard no murder done in Salem.

PROCTOR—*he has been reached by* HALE'S *words:* Leave me, Francis, leave me.

GILES, *shaken:* John—tell me, are we lost?

PROCTOR: Go home now, Giles. We'll speak on it tomorrow.

GILES: Let you think on it. We'll come early, eh?

PROCTOR: Aye. Go now, Giles.

GILES: Good night, then.

GILES COREY *goes out. After a moment:*

MARY WARREN, *in a fearful squeak of a voice:* Mr. Proctor, very likely they'll let her come home once they're given proper evidence.

PROCTOR: You're coming to the court with me, Mary. You will tell it in the court.

MARY WARREN: I cannot charge murder on Abigail.

PROCTOR, *moving menacingly toward her:*

You will tell the court how that poppet come here and who stuck the needle in.

MARY WARREN: She'll kill me for sayin' that! PROCTOR *continues toward her.* Abby'll charge lechery on you, Mr. Proctor!

PROCTOR, *halting:* She's told you!

MARY WARREN: I have known it, sir. She'll ruin you with it, I know she will.

PROCTOR, *hesitating, and with deep hatred of himself:* Good. Then her saintliness is done with. MARY *backs from him.* We will slide together into our pit; you will tell the court what you know.

MARY WARREN, *in terror:* I cannot, they'll turn on me—

PROCTOR *strides and catches her, and she is repeating, "I cannot, I cannot!"*

PROCTOR: My wife will never die for me! I will bring your guts into your mouth but that goodness will not die for me!

MARY WARREN, *struggling to escape him:* I cannot do it, I cannot!

PROCTOR, *grasping her by the throat as though he would strangle her:* Make your peace with it! Now Hell and Heaven grapple on our backs, and all our pretense is ripped away—make your peace! *He throws her to the floor, where she sobs, "I cannot, I cannot . . ." And now, half to himself, staring, and turning to the open door:* Peace. It is a providence, and no great change; we are only what we always were, but naked now. *He walks as though toward a great horror, facing the open sky.* Aye, naked! And the wind, God's icy wind, will blow!

And she is over and over again sobbing, "I cannot, I cannot, I cannot."

Closure and Extension

ANSWERS TO THINKING ABOUT THE SELECTION
Recalling

1. (a) She has been appointed an "official" of the court during the witchcraft proceedings. (b) She gives her a poppet.
2. (a) Elizabeth's name has been mentioned in court, and he wishes to investigate her situation personally. (b) They have come to tell Proctor that their wives have been arrested.
3. They find a poppet in the Proctor house with a needle in its stomach. They had been led to believe that Elizabeth had used a poppet

THINKING ABOUT THE SELECTION

Recalling

1. (a) Why does Mary Warren spend the day in Salem? (b) What does she give to Elizabeth Proctor when she returns?
2. (a) Why does Reverend Hale visit the Proctors? (b) Why do Giles Corey and Francis Nurse appear at the Proctor house?
3. What evidence is used to support Abigail Williams's assertion that Elizabeth Proctor is guilty of witchcraft?

Interpreting

4. At one point, John Proctor identifies revenge as the true evil that is afflicting Salem village. What evidence is there to support Proctor's assertion?
5. What does John Proctor mean when he alludes to Reverend Hale as Pontius Pilate?
6. (a) What is ironic, or surprising, about John Proctor's comment that the witchcraft trials are "a black mischief"? (b) Why is it ironic that Rebecca Nurse is charged with witchcraft? (c) What is ironic about the fact that Ezekiel Cheever is the one who arrests Elizabeth Proctor?

Applying

7. The American court system is based on the principle that a person is assumed to be innocent until proven guilty. Explain whether you think this principle applies to the proceedings in Salem.
8. If you were in Reverend Hale's position, how do you think you would react to the information you had gathered during your visit to the Proctors?

ANALYZING LITERATURE

Understanding Characterization

Characterization is the means by which a writer reveals a character's personality. Generally, playwrights must develop characters solely through dialogue and action.

1. What do Elizabeth Proctor's comments and actions reveal about her personality?
2. What do John Proctor's comments and actions reveal about his personality?
3. What is revealed about Hale's character during his questioning of the Proctors?
4. Review Miller's commentary in the first act and find at least three instances in which he offers insights into a character's personality. Then explain how each of the these characters' comments and actions support the insights that Miller has provided

UNDERSTANDING LANGUAGE

Appreciating Dialect

Dialect is the distinctive manner of speech of people living in a particular region. Writers often use dialect to capture the flavor of a specific region. In *The Crucible* Arthur Miller has the characters speak in the dialect of the early New England settlers. For example, note John Proctor's use of dialect in the following comment: "And why not, if they must hang for denyin' it? There are them that will swear to anything . . ."

1. Two of the characteristics of the dialect in this play are the lack of agreement between subjects and verbs and the use of double negatives. Find two examples of each of these characteristics in the second act.
2. Explain why the play would be less effective if Miller had not used dialect.

THINKING AND WRITING

Writing a Dialogue

Write a dialogue between two residents of Salem Village who are not portrayed in the play. The dialogue should focus on the growing witchcraft hysteria in the village, and it should be written in the appropriate dialect. Start by listing the incidents that you wish to have the characters discuss. Then list the character traits that you want each character to possess. When you write your dialogue, make sure the traits you have listed are revealed through their comments. After you have finished writing, revise your dialogue, making sure it seems natural and realistic.

The Crucible 1219

Literary Focus In February, 1950, Joseph McCarthy delivered a speech in Wheeling, West Virginia, that was to mark the beginning of the McCarthy era. He is reported to have said: "I have here, in my hand [waving a piece of paper] a list of 205 that are known to the secretary of state as being members of the Communist Party and who, nevertheless, are still working and shaping the policy of the State Department." Although McCarthy never revealed the names on his list, his speech touched off a hysteria that plagued the nation throughout the early 1950s.

Have students discuss what it might have been like to live in the United States during the McCarthy era. Then have them explore any parallels that they see between McCarthyism and the Salem witchcraft hysteria of 1692.

Writing/Prior Knowledge Before students begin writing their journal entries, have a class discussion about the atmosphere in Salem during the witchcraft trials. What options were available to those who were accused of witchcraft? What options were available to those whose spouses were accused?

Spelling Tip Call students' attention to the fact that both *contentious* and *prodigious* end in the letters *ious*.

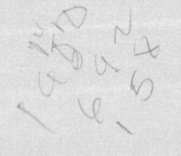

The Crucible, Act III

Historical Context

The McCarthy Era. In a number of ways, the Salem witchhunt parallels another disturbing period of American history, the McCarthy era. Growing out of the existing fears concerning the spread of communism, the McCarthy era began in 1950, when Joseph McCarthy, a Republican senator from Wisconsin, charged that the State Department had been infiltrated by more than two hundred communists. McCarthy's accusation shook the entire nation, resulting in a pervasive atmosphere of fear and suspicion. Although a Senate committee determined McCarthy's claims to be unfounded, he refused to retract his charges, even though he had provided no evidence to support them. Instead, McCarthy appeared on a series of radio and television programs, reasserting his earlier charges and accusing other government officials of subversive activities.

When the Republicans gained control of the Senate in 1952, McCarthy was appointed chairman of the Senate permanent investigations committee. McCarthy exploited his new position by holding widely publicized hearings during which sweeping accusations were made and people were questioned in a hostile, inquisitorial manner. During the hearings, people's private lives were mercilessly scrutinized, with both their personal relationships and their affiliations with various organizations being brought into question. In addition, the members of the committee demanded that witnesses provide names of people who were involved in communist activities or who advocated principles that were remotely connected to communism. Although little concrete evidence was ever uncovered at the hearings, the careers of many government officials were ruined, and the nation lapsed into a state of near hysteria. In 1954, however, McCarthy himself came under investigation for improper conduct and alleged financial improprieties. As a result, McCarthy's influence in the Senate quickly dwindled and the furor he had created eventually died out.

As you read the third act of *The Crucible,* look for the ways that the witchhunt of 1692 parallels the McCarthy era. For example, you might note that the hysteria that swept through Salem in 1692 parallels the atmosphere of fear and suspicion that dominated the McCarthy era.

Writing

How do you think you would respond if you were one of the characters accused of witchcraft? How would you respond if you were a character whose husband or wife had been accused of witchcraft? Freewrite, exploring your answers to these questions and discussing your reactions to the events in the first two acts.

Objectives

1 To understand how the events of the McCarthy era relate to the events in the play
2 To complete verbal analogies
3 To write about the parallels between the Salem witchhunt and the events of the McCarthy era

Support Material

Teaching Portfolio
Teacher Backup, p. 1609
Grammar in Action Worksheets, *Recognizing Specific and Concrete Words,* p. 1613; *Using Terms of Direct Address,* p. 1615
Usage and Mechanics Worksheet, p. 1617
Vocabulary Check, p. 1618
Analyzing Literature Worksheet,

Understanding Historical Context, p. 1619
Language Worksheet, *Completing Verbal Analogies,* p. 1620
Selection Test, p. 1621

ACT III

The vestry room of the Salem meeting house, now serving as the anteroom of the General Court.

As the curtain rises, the room is empty, but for sunlight pouring through two high windows in the back wall. The room is solemn, even forbidding. Heavy beams just out, boards of random widths make up the walls. At the right are two doors leading into the meeting house proper, where the court is being held. At the left another door leads outside.

There is a plain bench at the left, and another at the right. In the center a rather long meeting table, with stools and a considerable armchair snugged up to it.

Through the partitioning wall at the right we hear a prosecutor's voice, JUDGE HATHORNE'S, *asking a question; then a woman's voice,* MARTHA COREY'S, *replying.*

HATHORNE'S VOICE: Now, Martha Corey, there is abundant evidence in our hands to show that you have given yourself to the reading of fortunes. Do you deny it?

MARTHA COREY'S VOICE: I am innocent to a witch. I know not what a witch is.

HATHORNE'S VOICE: How do you know, then, that you are not a witch?

MARTHA COREY'S VOICE: If I were, I would know it.

HATHORNE'S VOICE: Why do you hurt these children?

MARTHA COREY'S VOICE: I do not hurt them. I scorn it!

GILES' VOICE, *roaring:* I have evidence for the court!

Voices of townspeople rise in excitement.

DANFORTH'S VOICE: You will keep your seat!

GILES' VOICE: Thomas Putnam is reaching out for land!

DANFORTH'S VOICE: Remove that man, Marshal!

GILES' VOICE: You're hearing lies, lies!

A roaring goes up from the people.

HATHORNE'S VOICE: Arrest him, excellency!

GILES' VOICE: I have evidence. Why will you not hear my evidence?

The door opens and GILES *is half carried into the vestry room by* HERRICK.

GILES: Hands off, damn you, let me go!

HERRICK: Giles, Giles!

GILES: Out of my way, Herrick! I bring evidence—

HERRICK: You cannot go in there, Giles; it's a court!

Enter HALE *from the court.*

HALE: Pray be calm a moment.

GILES: You, Mr. Hale, go in there and demand I speak.

HALE: A moment, sir, a moment.

GILES: They'll be hangin' my wife!

JUDGE HATHORNE enters. He is in his sixties, a bitter, remorseless Salem judge.

HATHORNE: How do you dare come roarin' into this court! Are you gone daft, Corey?

GILES: You're not a Boston judge, Hathorne. You'll not call me daft!

Enter DEPUTY GOVERNOR DANFORTH *and, behind him,* EZEKIEL CHEEVER *and* PARRIS. *On his appearance, silence falls.* DANFORTH *is a grave man in his sixties, of some humor and sophistication that does not, however, interfere with an exact loyalty to his position and his cause. He comes down to* GILES, *who awaits his wrath.*

DANFORTH, *looking directly at* GILES: Who is this man?

The Crucible   1221

Presentation

Motivation/Prior Knowledge
Have students discuss their prior knowledge of crowd reactions at social or political rallies, sporting events, and concerts. Do they think that people often act differently when they are in the midst of a crowd than they do when they are by themselves? If so, why? How can students apply their observations about crowd psychology to the behavior of the characters in Miller's play?

Master Teacher Note Tell your students that this act starts quietly, then builds to the emotional climax of the play. Many of the major conflicts in the play reach their height as the act draws to a close. Before students begin reading the act, have them jot down each of the conflicts that has been developed up to this point. As students read the act, they should chart the development of each of the conflicts they have noted. In addition, they should look for the appearance of new conflicts and keep track of their development.

Vocabulary

Preteach the following vocabulary words:
contentious (kän ten′ shəs) *adj.:* Argumentative
imperceptible (im′ pər sep′ tə b'l) *adj.:* Barely noticeable
anonymity (an′ ə nim′ ə tē) *n.:* The condition of being unknown or unacknowledged
prodigious (prə dij′ əs) *adj.:* Of great size, power, or extent
effrontery (e frun′ tər ē) *n.:* Shameless boldness
confounded (kən found′ id) *v.:* Confused; dismayed
incredulously (in krej′ oo ləs lē) *adv.:* Skeptically

Purpose-Setting Question Will John Proctor succeed in exposing Abigail as a fraud and securing Elizabeth's release?

1222

PARRIS: Giles Corey, sir, and a more contentious—

GILES, *to* PARRIS: I am asked the question, and I am old enough to answer it! *To* DANFORTH, *who impresses him and to whom he smiles through his strain:* My name is Corey, sir, Giles Corey. I have six hundred acres, and timber in addition. It is my wife you be condemning now. *He indicates the courtroom.*

DANFORTH: And how do you imagine to help her cause with such contemptuous riot? Now be gone. Your old age alone keeps you out of jail for this.

GILES, *beginning to plead:* They be tellin' lies about my wife, sir, I—

DANFORTH: Do you take it upon yourself to determine what this court shall believe and what it shall set aside?

GILES: Your Excellency, we mean no disrespect for—

DANFORTH: Disrespect indeed! It is disruption, Mister. This is the highest court of the supreme government of this province, do you know it?

GILES, *beginning to weep:* Your Excellency, I only said she were readin' books, sir, and they come and take her out of my house for—

DANFORTH, *mystified:* Books! What books?

GILES, *through helpless sobs:* It is my third wife, sir; I never had no wife that be so taken with books, and I thought to find the cause of it, d'y'see, but it were no witch I blamed her for. *He is openly weeping.* I have broke charity with the woman, I have broke charity with her. *He covers his face, ashamed.* DANFORTH *is respectfully silent.*

HALE: Excellency, he claims hard evidence for his wife's defense. I think that in all justice you must—

DANFORTH: Then let him submit his evidence in proper affidavit.[1] You are certainly aware of our procedure here, Mr. Hale. *To* HERRICK: Clear this room.

HERRICK: Come now, Giles. *He gently pushes* COREY *out.*

FRANCIS: We are desperate, sir; we come here three days now and cannot be heard.

DANFORTH: Who is this man?

FRANCIS: Francis Nurse, Your Excellency.

HALE: His wife's Rebecca that were condemned this morning.

DANFORTH: Indeed! I am amazed to find you in such uproar. I have only good report of your character, Mr. Nurse.

HATHORNE: I think they must both be arrested in contempt, sir.

DANFORTH, *to* FRANCIS: Let you write your plea, and in due time I will—

FRANCIS: Excellency, we have proof for your eyes; God forbid you shut them to it. The girls, sir, the girls are frauds.

DANFORTH: What's that?

FRANCIS: We have proof of it, sir. They are all deceiving you.

DANFORTH *is shocked, but studying* FRANCIS.

HATHORNE: This is contempt, sir, contempt!

DANFORTH: Peace, Judge Hathorne. Do you know who I am, Mr. Nurse?

FRANCIS: I surely do, sir, and I think you must be a wise judge to be what you are.

DANFORTH: And do you know that near to four hundred are in the jails from Marblehead to Lynn, and upon my signatures?

FRANCIS: I—

DANFORTH: And seventy-two condemned to hang by that signature?

---

1. **affidavit** (af′ ə dā′ vit) *n.:* A written statement made on oath.

FRANCIS: Excellency, I never thought to say it to such a weighty judge, but you are deceived.

Enter GILES COREY *from left. All turn to see as he beckons in* MARY WARREN *with* PROCTOR. MARY *is keeping her eyes to the ground;* PROCTOR *has her elbow as though she were near collapse.*

PARRIS, *on seeing her, in shock:* Mary Warren! *He goes directly to bend close to her face.* What are you about here?

PROCTOR, *pressing* PARRIS *away from her with a gentle but firm motion of protectiveness:* She would speak with the Deputy Governor.

DANFORTH, *shocked by this, turns to* HERRICK: Did you not tell me Mary Warren were sick in bed?

HERRICK: She were, Your Honor. When I go to fetch her to the court last week, she said she were sick.

GILES: She has been strivin' with her soul all week, Your Honor; she comes now to tell the truth of this to you.

DANFORTH: Who is this?

PROCTOR: John Proctor, sir. Elizabeth Proctor is my wife.

PARRIS: Beware this man, Your Excellency, this man is mischief.

HALE, *excitedly:* I think you must hear the girl, sir, she—

DANFORTH, *who has become very interested in* MARY WARREN *and only raises a hand toward* HALE: Peace. What would you tell us, Mary Warren?

PROCTOR *looks at her, but she cannot speak.*

PROCTOR: She never saw no spirits, sir.

DANFORTH, *with great alarm and surprise, to* MARY: Never saw no spirits!

GILES, *eagerly:* Never.

PROCTOR, *reaching into his jacket:* She has signed a deposition,[2] sir—

DANFORTH, *instantly:* No, no, I accept no depositions. *He is rapidly calculating this: he turns from her to* PROCTOR. Tell me, Mr. Proctor, have you given out this story in the village?

PROCTOR: We have not.

PARRIS: They've come to overthrow the court, sir! This man is—

DANFORTH: I pray you, Mr. Parris. Do you know, Mr. Proctor, that the entire contention of the state in these trials is that the voice of Heaven is speaking through the children?

PROCTOR: I know that, sir.

DANFORTH, *thinks, staring at* PROCTOR, *then turns to* MARY WARREN: And you, Mary Warren, how come you to cry out people for sending their spirits, against you?

MARY WARREN: It were pretense, sir.

DANFORTH: I cannot hear you.

PROCTOR: It were pretense, she says.

DANFORTH: Ah? And the other girls? Susanna Walcott, and—the others? They are also pretending?

MARY WARREN: Aye, sir.

DANFORTH: *wide-eyed:* Indeed. *Pause. He is baffled by this. He turns to study* PROCTOR's *face.*

PARRIS, *in a sweat:* Excellency, you surely cannot think to let so vile a lie be spread in open court.

DANFORTH: Indeed not, but it strike hard upon me that she will dare come here with such a tale. Now, Mr. Proctor, before I decide

---

2. deposition (dep′ ə zish′ ən) *n.:* The testimony of a witness, made under oath but not in open court, and written down to be used during a trial.

The Crucible 1223

6 Discussion Do students think that this is a courageous statement for Francis Nurse to make? Why or why not?

7 Discussion Ask students to describe the internal conflict that Mary Warren seems to have been experiencing. How do they imagine that this conflict will be resolved?

8 Discussion Ask students why Danforth is so alarmed and surprised by this assertion.

9 Discussion How do students explain Parris's outburst. Does he want to prevent Danforth from hearing what John Proctor and Mary Warren have to say? If so, why?

10 Discussion Ask students why Parris begins to sweat. Is he disturbed by the possibility that the accused witches might have been falsely convicted? Or is he afraid of the effect that Mary Warren's revelations might have on him?

11 Discussion Ask students if it seems as if Danforth believes Mary Warren's assertion. On what do they base their answer?

12 Literary Focus Have students explain what Danforth means when he says, "We burn a hot fire here." Given what students learned in the Commentary, does it seem to them that this description could be applied to the McCarthy hearings? Why or why not?

13 Discussion Do students think that the answer to this question seems obvious? If so, why does Danforth ask it?

whether I shall hear you or not, it is my duty to tell you this. We burn a hot fire here; it melts down all concealment.

PROCTOR: I know that, sir.

DANFORTH: Let me continue. I understand well, a husband's tenderness may drive him to extravagance in defense of a wife. Are you certain in your conscience, Mister, that your evidence is the truth?

PROCTOR: It is. And you will surely know it.

DANFORTH: And you thought to declare this revelation in the open court before the public?

PROCTOR: I thought I would, aye—with your permission.

DANFORTH, *his eyes narrowing:* Now, sir, what is your purpose in so doing?

"She never saw no spirits, sir."

Primary Source

In the introduction to his *Collected Plays* (1957), Miller described his perceptions of the atmosphere during the McCarthy era and then discussed the role that these perceptions played in his writing of *The Crucible.* He wrote: "It was as though the whole country had been born anew, without a memory even of certain elemental decencies which a year or two earlier no one would have imagined could be altered, let alone forgotten. Astounded, I watched men pass me by without a nod whom I had known rather well for years; and again, the astonishment was produced by my knowledge, which I could not give up, that the terror in these people was being knowingly planned and consciously engineered, and yet that all they knew was terror. That so interior and subjective an emotion could have been so manifestly created from without was a marvel to me. It underlies every word in *The Crucible.*"

PROCTOR: Why, I—I would free my wife, sir.

DANFORTH: There lurks nowhere in your heart, nor hidden in your spirit, any desire to undermine this court?

PROCTOR, *with the faintest faltering:* Why, no, sir.

CHEEVER, *clears his throat, awakening:* I— Your Excellency.

DANFORTH: Mr. Cheever.

CHEEVER: I think it be my duty, sir— *Kindly, to* PROCTOR: You'll not deny it, John. *To* DAN-FORTH: When we come to take his wife, he damned the court and ripped your warrant.

PARRIS: Now you have it!

DANFORTH: He did that, Mr. Hale?

HALE, *takes a breath:* Aye, he did.

PROCTOR: It were a temper, sir. I knew not what I did.

DANFORTH, *studying him:* Mr. Proctor.

PROCTOR: Aye, sir.

DANFORTH, *straight into his eyes:* Have you ever seen the Devil?

PROCTOR: No, sir.

DANFORTH: You are in all respects a Gospel Christian?

PROCTOR: I am, sir.

PARRIS: Such a Christian that will not come to church but once in a month!

DANFORTH, *restrained—he is curious:* Not come to church?

PROCTOR: I—I have no love for Mr. Parris. It is no secret. But God I surely love.

CHEEVER: He plow on Sunday, sir.

DANFORTH: Plow on Sunday!

CHEEVER, *apologetically:* I think it be evidence, John. I am an official of the court, I cannot keep it.

PROCTOR: I—I have once or twice plowed on Sunday. I have three children, sir, and until last year my land give little.

GILES: You'll find other Christians that do plow on Sunday if the truth be known.

HALE: Your Honor, I cannot think you may judge the man on such evidence.

DANFORTH: I judge nothing. *Pause. He keeps watching* PROCTOR, *who tries to meet his gaze.* I tell you straight, Mister—I have seen marvels in this court. I have seen people choked before my eyes by spirits; I have seen them stuck by pins and slashed by daggers. I have until this moment not the slightest reason to suspect that the children may be deceiving me. Do you understand my meaning?

PROCTOR: Excellency, does it not strike upon you that so many of these women have lived so long with such upright reputation, and—

PARRIS: Do you read the Gospel, Mr. Proctor?

PROCTOR: I read the Gospel.

PARRIS: I think not, or you should surely know that Cain were an upright man, and yet he did kill Abel.[3]

PROCTOR: Aye, God tells us that. *To* DAN-FORTH: But who tells us Rebecca Nurse murdered seven babies by sending out her spirit on them? It is the children only, and this one will swear she lied to you.

DANFORTH *considers, then beckons* HATHORNE *to him.* HATHORNE *leans in, and he speaks in his ear.* HATHORNE *nods.*

HATHORNE: Aye, she's the one.

DANFORTH: Mr. Proctor, this morning, your wife send me a claim in which she states that she is pregnant now.

PROCTOR: My wife pregnant!

---

3. **Cain . . . Abel:** In the Bible Cain, the oldest son of Adam and Eve, killed his brother, Abel.

The Crucible 1225

14 **Discussion** Have students contrast Proctor's behavior during this scene with his behavior at the end of the second act. Do students imagine that Proctor will be able to remain calm and restrained throughout the remainder of the act? Why or why not?

15 **Discussion** Ask students if they agree with Cheever's assertion that he has a duty to reveal this information. Why or why not?

16 **Discussion** Do students believe Danforth's declaration that he judges nothing? Why or why not? What is ironic about this statement?

17 **Discussion** Do students think that this is an effective response to Parris's observation about Cain and Abel? Why or why not?

18 Discussion Ask students if they think Danforth actually believes that this information will motivate Proctor to drop his claim. If not, what do they see as Danforth's purpose in telling John Proctor about his wife's pregnancy and the resulting delay in her execution?

19 Discussion Does it seem to students as if Danforth pays any attention to Parris's remarks? If not, what does this suggest about his opinion of Parris?

20 Enrichment Of the seven magistrates involved in the trials, Samuel Sewall was the only one to publicly apologize for his role. He did so in 1697, when he had a written apology read aloud to his church congregation. Shortly thereafter, he wrote the first antislavery paper to be published in the colonies.

21 Discussion Have students respond to this statement. Does Danforth's opinion fit into the basic principles of our current legal system? Why or why not?

22 Literary Focus Explain to students that during the McCarthy era, people who questioned the authority of McCarthy's Senate committee quickly found themselves under suspicion of guilt. Do students think that this aspect of the McCarthy hearings seems to parallel the proceedings at Salem? Why or why not?

DANFORTH: There be no sign of it—we have examined her body.

PROCTOR: But if she say she is pregnant, then she must be! That woman will never lie, Mr. Danforth.

DANFORTH: She will not?

PROCTOR: Never, sir, never.

DANFORTH: We have thought it too convenient to be credited. However, if I should tell you now that I will let her be kept another month; and if she begin to show her natural signs, you shall have her living yet another year until she is delivered—what say you to that? JOHN PROCTOR *is struck silent.* Come now. You say your only purpose is to save your wife. Good, then, she is saved at least this year, and a year is long. What say you, sir? It is done now. *In conflict,* PROCTOR *glances at* FRANCIS *and* GILES. Will you drop this charge?

PROCTOR: I—I think I cannot.

DANFORTH, *now an almost imperceptible hardness in his voice:* Then your purpose is somewhat larger.

PARRIS: He's come to overthrow this court, Your Honor!

PROCTOR: These are my friends. Their wives are also accused—

DANFORTH, *with a sudden briskness of manner:* I judge you not, sir. I am ready to hear your evidence.

PROCTOR: I come not to hurt the court; I only—

DANFORTH, *cutting him off:* Marshal, go into the court and bid Judge Stoughton and Judge Sewall declare recess for one hour. And let them go to the tavern, if they will. All witnesses and prisoners are to be kept in the building.

HERRICK: Aye, sir. *Very deferentially:* If I may say it, sir. I know this man all my life. It is a good man, sir.

DANFORTH—*it is the reflection on himself he resents:* I am sure of it, Marshal. HERRICK *nods, then goes out.* Now, what deposition do you have for us, Mr. Proctor? And I beg you be clear, open as the sky, and honest.

PROCTOR, *as he takes out several papers:* I am no lawyer, so I'll—

DANFORTH: The pure in heart need no lawyers. Proceed as you will.

PROCTOR, *handing* DANFORTH *a paper:* Will you read this first, sir? It's a sort of testament. The people signing it declare their good opinion of Rebecca, and my wife, and Martha Corey. DANFORTH *looks down at the paper.*

PARRIS, *to enlist* DANFORTH'S *sarcasm:* Their good opinion! *But* DANFORTH *goes on reading, and* PROCTOR *is heartened.*

PROCTOR: These are all landholding farmers, members of the church. *Delicately, trying to point out a paragraph:* If you'll notice, sir— they've known the woman many years and never saw no sign they had dealings with the Devil.

PARRIS *nervously moves over and reads over* DANFORTH'S *shoulder.*

DANFORTH, *glancing down a long list:* How many names are here?

FRANCIS: Ninety-one, Your Excellency.

PARRIS, *sweating:* These people should be summoned. DANFORTH *looks up at him questioningly.* For questioning.

FRANCIS, *trembling with anger:* Mr. Danforth, I gave them all my word no harm would come to them for signing this.

PARRIS: This is a clear attack upon the court!

HALE, *to* PARRIS, *trying to contain himself:* Is every defense an attack upon the court? Can no one—?

PARRIS: All innocent and Christian people

23 are happy for the courts in Salem! These people are gloomy for it. *To* DANFORTH *directly:* And I think you will want to know, from each and every one of them, what discontents them with you!

HATHORNE: I think they ought to be examined, sir.

DANFORTH: It is not necessarily an attack, I think. Yet—

FRANCIS: These are all covenanted Christians, sir.

DANFORTH: Then I am sure they may have nothing to fear. *Hands* CHEEVER *the paper.* Mr. Cheever, have warrants drawn for all of these—arrest for examination. *To* PROCTOR: Now, Mister, what other information do you have for us? FRANCIS *is still standing, horrified.* You may sit, Mr. Nurse.

FRANCIS: I have brought trouble on these people; I have—

24 **DANFORTH:** No, old man, you have not hurt these people if they are of good conscience. But you must understand, sir, that a person is either with this court or he must be counted against it, there be no road between. This is a sharp time, now, a precise time—we live no longer in the dusky afternoon when evil mixed itself with good and befuddled the world. Now, by God's grace, the shining sun is up, and them that fear not light will surely praise it. I hope you will be one of those. MARY WARREN *suddenly sobs.* She's not hearty, I see.

PROCTOR: No, she's not, sir. *To* MARY, *bending to her, holding her hand, quietly:* Now remember what the angel Raphael said to the boy Tobias.[4] Remember it.

---

4. Raphael . . . Tobias: In the Bible Tobias is guided by the archangel Raphael to save two people who have prayed for their deaths. One of the two is Tobias's father, Tobit, who has prayed for his death because he has lost his sight; the other is Sara, a woman who is afflicted by a demon and has killed her seven husbands on their wedding day. With Raphael's assistance, Tobias exorcises the devil from Sara and cures his father of his blindness.

MARY WARREN, *hardly audible:* Aye.

PROCTOR: "Do that which is good, and no harm shall come to thee."

MARY WARREN: Aye.

DANFORTH: Come, man, we wait you.

MARSHAL HERRICK *returns, and takes his post at the door.*

GILES: John, my deposition, give him mine.

PROCTOR: Aye. *He hands* DANFORTH *another paper.* This is Mr. Corey's deposition.

25 **DANFORTH:** Oh? *He looks down at it. Now* HATHORNE *comes behind him and reads with him.*

HATHORNE, *suspiciously:* What lawyer drew this, Corey?

GILES: You know I never hired a lawyer in my life, Hathorne.

26 **DANFORTH,** *finishing the reading:* It is very well phrased. My compliments. Mr. Parris, if Mr. Putnam is in the court, will you bring him in? HATHORNE *takes the deposition, and walks to the window with it.* PARRIS *goes into the court.* You have no legal training, Mr. Corey?

GILES, *very pleased:* I have the best, sir—I am thirty-three time in court in my life. And always plaintiff, too.

DANFORTH: Oh, then you're much put-upon.

GILES: I am never put-upon: I know my rights, sir, and I will have them. You know, your father tried a case of mine—might be thirty-five year ago, I think.

DANFORTH: Indeed.

GILES: He never spoke to you of it?

DANFORTH: No, I cannot recall it.

27 **GILES:** That's strange, he gave me nine pound damages. He were a fair judge, your father. Y'see, I had a white mare that time, and this fellow come to borrow the mare— *Enter* PARRIS *with* THOMAS PUTNAM. *When*

23 Discussion Have students cite evidence from the play that shows that Parris's statement "all innocent and Christian people are happy for the courts in Salem" is inaccurate.

24 Discussion Have students discuss how Danforth's statement echoes the common slogan "America—love it or leave it."

25 Discussion Have students compare and contrast Danforth and Hathorne based on the two men's comments and actions up to this point.

26 Discussion Ask students what Danforth's decision to summon Putnam suggests about the contents of Giles Corey's deposition.

27 Discussion Have students speculate about Giles Corey's motivation for telling Danforth about the case that Danforth tried.

28 **Discussion** Ask students whether the "proof" that Giles Corey is
offering is any different from the
type of proof being used to con-
vict the accused witches.

29 **Discussion** Do students think
that Giles Corey's fears are well-
founded? Why or why not?

30 **Clarification** Explain that in legal
terminology the statement "I
stand mute" is used to indicate a
refusal to reveal information or
answer question.

31 **Enrichment** The real Reverend
Hale was at first deeply involved
in the prosecutions at Salem and
changed his mind only after his
own wife was accused of witchcraft in October 1692. Hale's
change of heart came a month
after the last group of "witches"
was hanged. In 1698 he wrote a
book in which he was critical of
the Salem proceedings but upheld the belief in witchcraft. Yet
he died in 1700, before the book
was published.

he sees PUTNAM, GILES' *ease goes; he is
hard.* Aye, there he is.

DANFORTH: Mr. Putnam, I have here an accusation by Mr. Corey against you. He states
that you coldly prompted your daughter to
cry witchery upon George Jacobs that is now
in jail.

PUTNAM: It is a lie.

DANFORTH, *turning to* GILES: Mr. Putnam
states your charge is a lie. What say you to
that?

GILES, *furious, his fists clenched:* A fart on
Thomas Putnam, that is what I say to that!

DANFORTH: What proof do you submit for
your charge, sir?

GILES: My proof is there! *Pointing to the paper.* If Jacobs hangs for a witch he forfeit up
his property—that's law! And there is none
but Putnam with the coin to buy so great a
piece. This man is killing his neighbors for
their land!

DANFORTH: But proof, sir, proof.

GILES, *pointing at his deposition:* The proof
is there! I have it from an honest man who
heard Putnam say it! The day his daughter
cried out on Jacobs, he said she'd given him
a fair gift of land.

HATHORNE: And the name of this man?

GILES, *taken aback:* What name?

HATHORNE: The man that give you this information.

GILES, *hesitates, then:* Why, I—I cannot give
you his name.

HATHORNE: And why not?

GILES, *hesitates, then bursts out:* You know
well why not! He'll lay in jail if I give his
name!

HATHORNE: This is contempt of the court,
Mr. Danforth!

DANFORTH, *to avoid that:* You will surely tell
us the name.

GILES: I will not give you no name. I mentioned my wife's name once and I'll burn in
hell long enough for that. I stand mute.

DANFORTH: In that case, I have no choice but
to arrest you for contempt of this court, do
you know that?

GILES: This is a hearing; you cannot clap me
for contempt of a hearing.

DANFORTH: Oh, it is a proper lawyer! Do you
wish me to declare the court in full session
here? Or will you give me good reply?

GILES, *faltering:* I cannot give you no name,
sir, I cannot.

DANFORTH: You are a foolish old man. Mr.
Cheever, begin the record. The court is now
in session. I ask you, Mr. Corey—

PROCTOR, *breaking in:* Your Honor—he has
the story in confidence, sir, and he—

PARRIS: The Devil lives on such confidences!
To DANFORTH: Without confidences there
could be no conspiracy, Your Honor!

HATHORNE: I think it must be broken, sir.

DANFORTH, *to* GILES: Old man, if your informant tells the truth let him come here
openly like a decent man. But if he hide in
anonymity I must know why. Now sir, the
government and central church demand of
you the name of him who reported Mr.
Thomas Putnam a common murderer.

HALE: Excellency—

DANFORTH: Mr. Hale.

HALE: We cannot blink it more. There is a
prodigious fear of this court in the country—

DANFORTH: Then there is a prodigious guilt
in the country. Are *you* afraid to be questioned here?

HALE: I may only fear the Lord, sir, but there
is fear in the country nevertheless.

Grammar in Action

To create vivid pictures in their readers' minds, writers must use
concrete and specific words. Concrete words refer to words
that appeal to one or more of the five senses. For example, Giles
Corey uses words that appeal to both the sense of sight and the
sense of touch when he comments that he will "burn in hell."
Specific words are those that have very precise meanings. For
example, Miller uses specific words in the following passage
from his description of the setting on page 1221:

In the center a rather long *meeting table,* with stools and a
considerable *armchair* snugged up to it.

Student Activity 1. Find five more examples of concrete words
from *The Crucible.* Then identify the sense or senses to which
each word appeals.

Student Activity 2. Find five more examples of specific words in
Miller's play. Then suggest a general word that Miller could have
used in place of each of these words.

Student Activity 3. Write a paragraph describing a place that
you find especially beautiful or interesting. Use specific and
concrete words to create a vivid image of your subject.

THE WITCHCRAFT TRIAL OF GILES COREY
AT SALEM, MASSACHUSETTS, IN 1692
19th Century Engraving
The Granger Collection

32 Discussion Have students explain why Danforth seems unwilling to listen to Hale's argument.

33 Discussion Do students agree with Giles Corey's interpretation of Danforth's intentions? Why or why not?

Humanities Note

Fine art, *The Witchcraft Trial of Giles Corey at Salem, Massachusetts, in 1692.* Although the Salem witchcraft proceedings were recorded in writing by a number of the people of the time, the people of seventeenth-century Salem left few visual records of the events. During the nineteenth century, however, many artists produced engravings in which they attempted to re-create the horror and hysteria of the witchcraft trials. This engraving, for example, shows Giles Corey being accused by one of the young girls who played a central role in the witchcraft furor.

You might want to use the following questions to discuss the art:
1. What impression does the artist convey of Giles Corey?
2. Does the artist's depiction of Corey match the way in which you envision him? Why or why not?
3. What impression does the artist convey of the girl who is accusing Corey?

DANFORTH, *angered now:* Reproach me not with the fear in the country; there is fear in the country because there is a moving plot to topple Christ in the country!

HALE: But it does not follow that everyone accused is part of it.

DANFORTH: No uncorrupted man may fear this court, Mr. Hale! None! *To* GILES: You are under arrest in contempt of this court. Now sit you down and take counsel with yourself, or you will be set in the jail until you decide to answer all questions.

GILES COREY *makes a rush for* PUTNAM. PROCTOR *lunges and holds him.*

PROCTOR: No, Giles!

GILES, *over* PROCTOR's *shoulder at* PUTNAM: I'll cut your throat, Putnam, I'll kill you yet!

PROCTOR, *forcing him into a chair:* Peace, Giles, peace. *Releasing him.* We'll prove ourselves. Now we will. *He starts to turn to* DANFORTH.

GILES: Say nothin' more, John. *Pointing at* DANFORTH: He's only playin' you! He means to hang us all!

MARY WARREN *bursts into sobs.*

DANFORTH: This is a court of law, Mister. I'll have no effrontery here!

PROCTOR: Forgive him, sir, for his old age. Peace, Giles, we'll prove it all now. *He lifts up* MARY's *chin.* You cannot weep, Mary. Remember the angel, what he say to the boy. Hold to it, now; there is your rock. MARY *quiets. He takes out a paper, and turns to* DANFORTH. This is Mary Warren's deposition. I—I would ask you remember, sir, while you read it, that until two week ago she were no different than the other children are today. *He is speaking reasonably, restraining all his fears, his anger, his anxiety.* You saw her scream, she howled, she swore familiar spirits choked her; she even testified that Satan, in the form of women now in jail, tried to win her soul away, and then when she refused—

The Crucible 1229

34 Discussion Do students think Danforth should follow Reverend Hale's suggestion? Why or why not?

35 Clarification Remind students that the word *immaculate* appears in the phrase immaculate conception, which describes how the Virgin Mary conceived Jesus. Considering this fact, why is Reverend Hale's use of this word especially appropriate?

36 Enrichment Explain to students that in the British court system the accused are considered guilty until they are proven innocent.

DANFORTH: We know all this.

PROCTOR: Aye, sir. She swears now that she never saw Satan; nor any spirit, vague or clear, that Satan may have sent to hurt her. And she declares her friends are lying now.

PROCTOR *starts to hand* DANFORTH *the deposition, and* HALE *comes up to* DANFORTH *in a trembling state.*

HALE: Excellency, a moment. I think this goes to the heart of the matter.

DANFORTH, *with deep misgivings:* It surely does.

34

HALE: I cannot say he is an honest man; I know him little. But in all justice, sir, a claim so weighty cannot be argued by a farmer. In God's name, sir, stop here; send him home and let him come again with a lawyer—

DANFORTH, *patiently:* Now look you, Mr. Hale—

HALE: Excellency, I have signed seventy-two death warrants; I am a minister of the Lord, and I dare not take a life without there be a proof so immaculate no slightest qualm of conscience may doubt it.

35

DANFORTH: Mr. Hale, you surely do not doubt my justice.

HALE: I have this morning signed away the soul of Rebecca Nurse, Your Honor. I'll not conceal it, my hand shakes yet as with a wound! I pray you, sir, *this* argument let lawyers present to you.

DANFORTH: Mr. Hale, believe me; for a man of such terrible learning you are most bewildered—I hope you will forgive me. I have been thirty-two year at the bar, sir, and I should be confounded were I called upon to defend these people. Let you consider, now— *To* PROCTOR *and the others:* And I bid you all do likewise. In an ordinary crime, how does one defend the accused? One calls up witnesses to prove his innocence. But witch-

36

craft is *ipso facto,*[5] on its face and by its nature, an invisible crime, is it not? Therefore, who may possibly be witness to it? The witch and the victim. None other. Now we cannot hope the witch will accuse herself; granted? Therefore, we must rely upon her victims—and they do testify, the children certainly do testify. As for the witches, none will deny that we are most eager for all their confessions. Therefore, what is left for a lawyer to bring out? I think I have made my point. Have I not?

HALE: But this child claims the girls are not truthful, and if they are not—

DANFORTH: That is precisely what I am about to consider, sir. What more may you ask of me? Unless you doubt my probity?[6]

HALE, *defeated:* I surely do not, sir. Let you consider it, then.

DANFORTH: And let you put your heart to rest. Her deposition, Mr. Proctor.

PROCTOR *hands it to him.* HATHORNE *rises, goes beside* DANFORTH, *and starts reading.* PARRIS *comes to his other side.* DANFORTH *looks at* JOHN PROCTOR, *then proceeds to read.* HALE *gets up, finds position near the judge, reads too.* PROCTOR *glances at* GILES. FRANCIS *prays silently, hands pressed together.* CHEEVER *waits placidly, the sublime official, dutiful.* MARY WARREN *sobs once.* JOHN PROCTOR *touches her hand reassuringly. Presently* DANFORTH *lifts his eyes, stands up, takes out a kerchief and blows his nose. The others stand aside as he moves in thought toward the window.*

PARRIS, *hardly able to contain his anger and fear:* I should like to question—

DANFORTH—*his first real outburst, in which his contempt for* PARRIS *is clear:* Mr. Parris, I bid you be silent! *He stands in silence,*

---

5. ipso facto (ip′ sō fak′ tō): By that very fact.
6. probity (prō′ bə tē): *n.*: Complete honesty; integrity.

looking out the window. Now, having established that he will set the gait: Mr. Cheever, will you go into the court and bring the children here? CHEEVER *gets up and goes out upstage.* DANFORTH *now turns to* MARY. Mary Warren, how came you to this turnabout? Has Mr. Proctor threatened you for this deposition?

MARY WARREN: No, sir.

DANFORTH: Has he ever threatened you?

MARY WARREN, *weaker:* No, sir.

DANFORTH, *sensing a weakening:* Has he threatened you?

MARY WARREN: No, sir.

DANFORTH: Then you tell me that you sat in my court, callously lying, when you knew that people would hang by your evidence? *She does not answer.* Answer me!

MARY WARREN, *almost inaudibly:* I did, sir.

DANFORTH: How were you instructed in your life? Do you not know that God damns all liars? *She cannot speak.* Or is it now that you lie?

MARY WARREN: No, sir—I am with God now.

DANFORTH: You are with God now.

MARY WARREN: Aye, sir.

DANFORTH, *containing himself:* I will tell you this—you are either lying now, or you were lying in the court, and in either case you have committed perjury and you will go to jail for it. You cannot lightly say you lied, Mary. Do you know that?

MARY WARREN: I cannot lie no more. I am with God, I am with God.

But she breaks into sobs at the thought of it, and the right door opens, and enter SUSANNA WALCOTT, MERCY LEWIS, BETTY PARRIS, *and finally* ABIGAIL. CHEEVER *comes to* DANFORTH.

CHEEVER: Ruth Putnam's not in the court, sir, nor the other children.

DANFORTH: These will be sufficient. Sit you down, children. *Silently they sit.* Your friend, Mary Warren, has given us a deposition. In which she swears that she never saw familiar spirits, apparitions, nor any manifest of the Devil. She claims as well that none of you have seen these things either. *Slight pause.* Now, children, this is a court of law. The law, based upon the Bible, and the Bible, writ by Almighty God, forbid the practice of witchcraft, and describe death as the penalty thereof. But likewise, children, the law and Bible damn all bearers of false witness. *Slight pause.* Now then. It does not escape me that this deposition may be devised to blind us; it may well be that Mary Warren has been conquered by Satan, who sends her here to distract our sacred purpose. If so, her neck will break for it. But if she speak true, I bid you now drop your guile and confess your pretense, for a quick confession will go easier with you. *Pause.* Abigail Williams, rise. ABIGAIL *slowly rises.* Is there any truth in this?

ABIGAIL: No, sir.

DANFORTH, *thinks, glances at* MARY, *then back to* ABIGAIL: Children, a very augur bit will now be turned into your souls until your honesty is proved. Will either of you change your positions now, or do you force me to hard questioning?

ABIGAIL: I have naught to change, sir. She lies.

DANFORTH, *to* MARY: You would still go on with this?

MARY WARREN, *faintly:* Aye, sir.

DANFORTH, *turning to* ABIGAIL: A poppet were discovered in Mr. Proctor's house, stabbed by a needle. Mary Warren claims that you sat beside her in the court when she made it, and that you saw her make it

37 Discussion Do students think that Mary Warren is being truthful? On what do they base their answer?

38 Discussion Ask students to characterize the manner in which Danforth questions Mary Warren. Do they imagine that questioning her in this manner is likely to cause her to reconsider her decision to come forward with the truth? Why or why not?

39 Reading Strategy Have students pause and summarize the events that have taken place up to this point in the play. Then have them predict the play's outcome.

40 Discussion Have students discuss what the manner in which Abigail responds to Mary's deposition reveals about Abigail's character.

and witnessed how she herself stuck the needle into it for safe-keeping. What say you to that?

ABIGAIL, *with a slight note of indignation:* It is a lie, sir.

DANFORTH, *after a slight pause:* While you worked for Mr. Proctor, did you see poppets in that house?

ABIGAIL: Goody Proctor always kept poppets.

PROCTOR: Your Honor, my wife never kept no poppets. Mary Warren confesses it was her poppet.

CHEEVER: Your Excellency.

DANFORTH: Mr. Cheever.

CHEEVER: When I spoke with Goody Proctor in that house, she said she never kept no poppets. But she said she did keep poppets when she were a girl.

PROCTOR: She has not been a girl these fifteen years, Your Honor.

HATHORNE: But a poppet will keep fifteen years, will it not?

PROCTOR: It will keep if it is kept, but Mary Warren swears she never saw no poppets in my house, nor anyone else.

PARRIS: Why could there not have been poppets hid where no one ever saw them?

PROCTOR, *furious:* There might also be a dragon with five legs in my house, but no one has ever seen it.

PARRIS: We are here, Your Honor, precisely to discover what no one has ever seen.

PROCTOR: Mr. Danforth, what profit this girl to turn herself about? What may Mary Warren gain but hard questioning and worse?

DANFORTH: You are charging Abigail Williams with a marvelous cool plot to murder, do you understand that?

PROCTOR: I do, sir. I believe she means to murder.

DANFORTH, *pointing at* ABIGAIL, *incredulously:* This child would murder your wife?

PROCTOR: It is not a child. Now hear me, sir. In the sight of the congregation she were twice this year put out of this meetin' house for laughter during prayer.

DANFORTH, *shocked, turning to* ABIGAIL: What's this? Laughter during—!

PARRIS: Excellency, she were under Tituba's power at that time, but she is solemn now.

GILES: Aye, now she is solemn and goes to hang people!

DANFORTH: Quiet, man.

HATHORNE: Surely it have no bearing on the question, sir. He charges contemplation of murder.

DANFORTH: Aye. *He studies* ABIGAIL *for a moment, then:* Continue, Mr. Proctor.

PROCTOR: Mary. Now tell the Governor how you danced in the woods.

PARRIS, *instantly:* Excellency, since I come to Salem this man is blackening my name. He—

DANFORTH: In a moment, sir. *To* MARY WARREN, *sternly, and surprised.* What is this dancing?

MARY WARREN: I—*She glances at* ABIGAIL, *who is staring down at her remorselessly. Then, appealing to* PROCTOR: Mr. Proctor—

PROCTOR, *taking it right up:* Abigail leads the girls to the woods, Your Honor, and they have danced there naked—

PARRIS: Your Honor, this—

PROCTOR, *at once:* Mr. Parris discovered them himself in the dead of night! There's the "child" she is!

DANFORTH—*it is growing into a nightmare, and he turns, astonished, to* PARRIS: Mr. Parris—

---

41 Master Teacher Note Urge students to try to envision how a performance of this scene would appear. How do they picture Abigail? Why? In what tone of voice do they imagine she would deliver her lines in this scene? How do they picture the other characters in the scene? Why?

42 Discussion Have students speculate about whether Proctor will reveal Abigail's motives for wanting to murder his wife. How do students imagine that Danforth and Hathorne would respond to his revelation of this information?

43 Discussion Ask students why Parris keeps interrupting. Is he confident that Abigail and the other girls have been telling the truth? On what do students base their answer?

44 Discussion Ask students if they are surprised that Danforth had not been aware of the girls' dancing. What does his ignorance of this fact reveal about the court proceedings?

PARRIS: I can only say, sir, that I never found any of them naked, and this man is—

DANFORTH: But you discovered them dancing in the woods? *Eyes on* PARRIS, *he points at* ABIGAIL. Abigail?

HALE: Excellency, when I first arrived from Beverly, Mr. Parris told me that.

DANFORTH: Do you deny it, Mr. Parris?

PARRIS: I do not, sir, but I never saw any of them naked.

DANFORTH: But she have *danced*?

PARRIS, *unwillingly:* Aye, sir.

DANFORTH, *as though with new eyes, looks at* ABIGAIL.

HATHORNE: Excellency, will you permit me? *He points at* MARY WARREN.

DANFORTH, *with great worry:* Pray, proceed.

HATHORNE: You say you never saw no spirits, Mary, were never threatened or afflicted by any manifest of the Devil or the Devil's agents.

MARY WARREN, *very faintly:* No, sir.

HATHORNE, *with a gleam of victory:* And yet, when people accused of witchery confronted you in court, you would faint, saying their spirits came out of their bodies and choked you—

MARY WARREN: That were pretense, sir.

DANFORTH: I cannot hear you.

MARY WARREN: Pretense, sir.

PARRIS: But you did turn cold, did you not? I myself picked you up many times, and your skin were icy. Mr. Danforth, you—

DANFORTH: I saw that many times.

PROCTOR: She only pretended to faint, Your Excellency. They're all marvelous pretenders.

HATHORNE: Then can she pretend to faint now?

PROCTOR: Now?

PARRIS: Why not? Now there are no spirits attacking her, for none in this room is accused of witchcraft. So let her turn herself cold now, let her pretend she is attacked now, let her faint. *He turns to* MARY WARREN. Faint!

MARY WARREN: Faint?

PARRIS: Aye, faint. Prove to us how you pretended in the court so many times.

MARY WARREN, *looking to Proctor:* I—cannot faint now, sir.

PROCTOR, *alarmed, quietly:* Can you not pretend it?

MARY WARREN: I—*She looks about as though searching for the passion to faint.* I—have no *sense* of it now, I—

DANFORTH: Why? What is lacking now?

MARY WARREN: I—cannot tell, sir, I—

DANFORTH: Might it be that here we have no afflicting spirit loose, but in the court there were some?

MARY WARREN: I never saw no spirits.

PARRIS: Then see no spirits now, and prove to us that you can faint by your own will, as you claim.

MARY WARREN, *stares, searching for the emotion of it, and then shakes her head.* I—cannot do it.

PARRIS: Then you will confess, will you not? It were attacking spirits made you faint!

MARY WARREN: No, sir, I—

PARRIS: Your Excellency, this is a trick to blind the court!

MARY WARREN: It's not a trick! *She stands.* I—I used to faint because I—I thought I saw spirits.

DANFORTH: *Thought* you saw them!

The Crucible 1233

1233

---

45 Discussion Ask students to explain why Hathorne intervenes at this point. What might he be hoping to accomplish?

46 Discussion How do students explain the coldness of Mary Warren's skin during the earlier court proceedings.

47 Discussion Ask students why Mary Warren is unable to demonstrate how she pretended to faint.

48 Literary Focus Ask students whether Danforth, Hathorne, and Parris are being objective in their questioning of Mary Warren. Then have them discuss whether they imagine that people were questioned objectively during the McCarthy hearings. On what do they base their response? Why is it important for the people who pass judgment during legal proceedings to be as objective as possible?

49 Discussion Ask students if Mary Warren's explanation is believable. Why or why not?

50 Discussion Have students discuss how Abigail's manner of responding to Danforth differs from the way in which other characters respond to him. What do they see as the reason for this difference?

51 Discussion Have students share their reactions to Abigail's performance. What emotions does it arouse in them? Why?

MARY WARREN: But I did not, Your Honor.

HATHORNE: How could you think you saw them unless you saw them?

MARY WARREN: I—I cannot tell how, but I did. I—I heard the other girls screaming, and you, Your Honor, you seemed to believe them, and I—It were only sport in the beginning, sir, but then the whole world cried spirits, spirits, and I—I promise you, Mr. Danforth, I only thought I saw them but I did not.

DANFORTH *peers at her.*

PARRIS, *smiling, but nervous because* DANFORTH *seems to be struck by* MARY WARREN'S *story:* Surely Your Excellency is not taken by this simple lie.

DANFORTH, *turning worriedly to* ABIGAIL: Abigail. I bid you now search your heart and tell me this—and beware of it, child, to God every soul is precious and His vengeance is terrible on them that take life without cause. Is it possible, child, that the spirits you have seen are illusion only, some deception that may cross your mind when—

ABIGAIL: Why, this—this—is a base question, sir.

DANFORTH: Child, I would have you consider it—

ABIGAIL: I have been hurt, Mr. Danforth: I have seen my blood runnin' out! I have been near to murdered every day because I done my duty pointing out the Devil's people—and this is my reward? To be mistrusted, denied, questioned like a—

DANFORTH, *weakening:* Child, I do not mistrust you—

ABIGAIL, *in an open threat:* Let *you* beware, Mr. Danforth. Think you to be so mighty that the power of Hell may not turn *your* wits? Beware of it! There is—*Suddenly, from an accusatory attitude, her face turns, looking into the air above—it is truly frightened.*

DANFORTH, *apprehensively:* What is it, child?

ABIGAIL, *looking about in the air, clasping her arms about her as though cold:* I—I know not. A wind, a cold wind, has come. *Her eyes fall on* MARY WARREN.

MARY WARREN, *terrified, pleading:* Abby!

MERCY LEWIS, *shivering:* Your Honor, I freeze!

PROCTOR: They're pretending!

HATHORNE, *touching* ABIGAIL'S *hand:* She is cold, Your Honor, touch her!

MERCY LEWIS, *through chattering teeth:* Mary, do you send this shadow on me?

MARY WARREN: Lord, save me!

SUSANNA WALCOTT: I freeze, I freeze!

ABIGAIL, *shivering, visibly:* It is a wind, a wind!

MARY WARREN: Abby, don't do that!

DANFORTH, *himself engaged and entered by* ABIGAIL: Mary Warren, do you witch her? I say to you, do you send your spirit out?

With a hysterical cry MARY WARREN *starts to run. Proctor catches her.*

MARY WARREN, *almost collapsing:* Let me go, Mr. Proctor, I cannot, I cannot—

ABIGAIL, *crying to Heaven:* Oh, Heavenly Father, take away this shadow!

Without warning or hesitation, PROCTOR *leaps at* ABIGAIL *and, grabbing her by the hair, pulls her to her feet. She screams in pain.* DANFORTH, *astonished, cries, "What are you about?" and* HATHORNE *and* PARRIS *call, "Take your hands off her!" and out of it all comes* PROCTOR'S *roaring voice.*

PROCTOR: How do you call Heaven! Whore! Whore!

HERRICK *breaks* PROCTOR *from her.*

HERRICK: John!

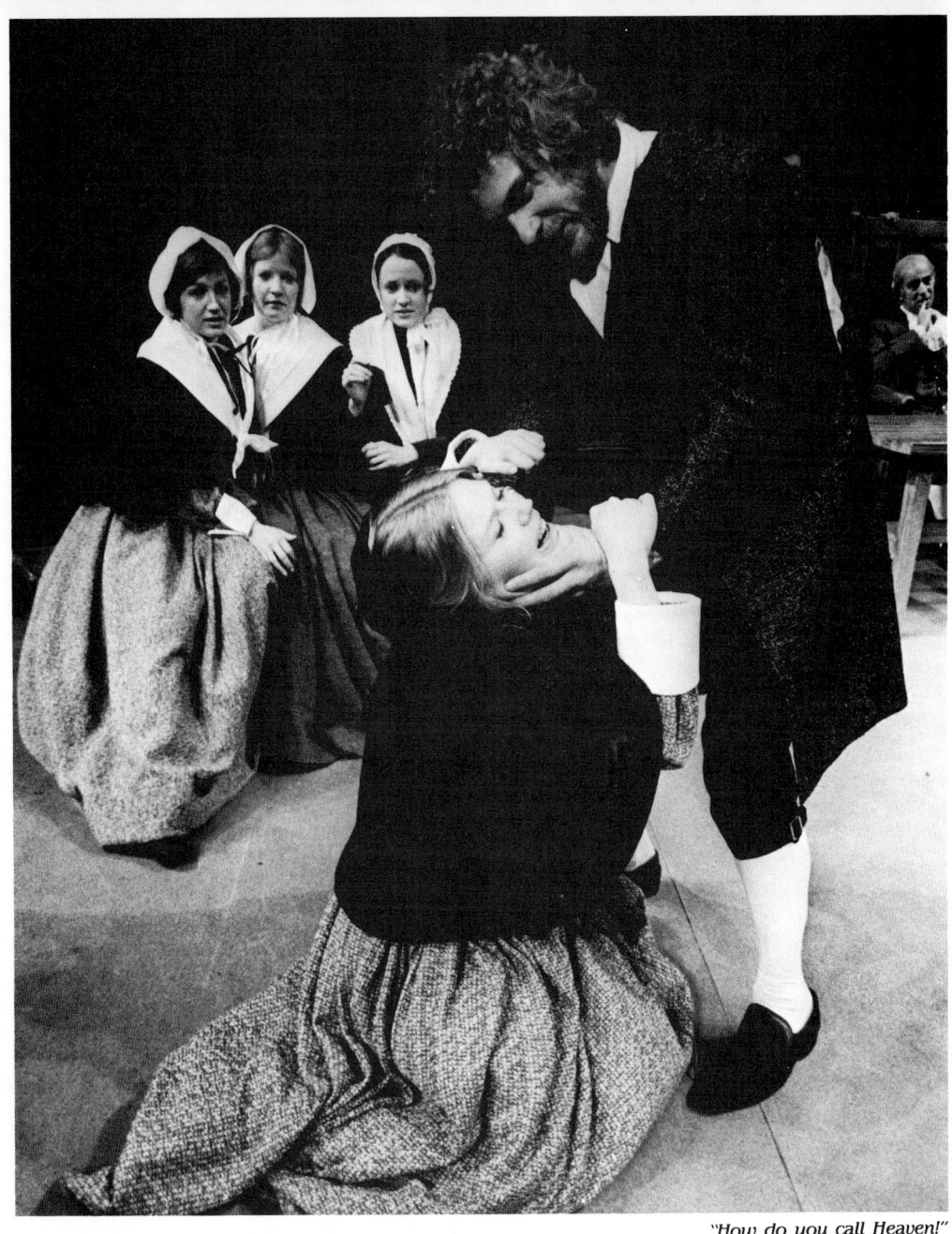

"How do you call Heaven!"

The Crucible   1235

Enrichment In discussing the "dilemma" he faced in trying to identify the similarities between the Salem witchcraft trials and the McCarthy hearings, Miller has noted: "The truth is that the more I worked at this dilemma the less it had to do with Communists and McCarthy and the more it concerned something very fundamental in the human animal: the fear of the unknown, and particularly the dread of social isolation." Have students discuss Miller's comment in relation to the events that have occurred in *The Crucible* up to this point.

52 **Discussion** Have students discuss what Proctor's decision to reveal his involvement with Abigail indicates about his character. What are some of the possible implications of his revelation?

53 **Discussion** Ask students if it seems as though Danforth believes what Proctor has just told him. On what do they base their answer?

54 **Reading Strategy** Have students predict whether Elizabeth will tell the truth about John's involvement with Abigail. On what do students base their predictions?

DANFORTH: Man! Man, what do you—

PROCTOR, *breathless and in agony:* It is a whore!

DANFORTH, *dumfounded:* You charge—?

ABIGAIL: Mr. Danforth, he is lying!

PROCTOR: Mark her! Now she'll suck a scream to stab me with, but—

DANFORTH: You will prove this! This will not pass!

PROCTOR, *trembling, his life collapsing about him:* I have known her, sir. I have known her.

DANFORTH: You—you are a lecher?

FRANCIS, *horrified:* John, you cannot say such a—

PROCTOR: Oh, Francis, I wish you had some evil in you that you might know me! *To* DANFORTH: A man will not cast away his good name. You surely know that.

DANFORTH, *dumfounded:* In—in what time? In what place?

PROCTOR, *his voice about to break, and his shame great:* In the proper place—where my beasts are bedded. On the last night of my joy, some eight months past. She used to serve me in my house, sir. *He has to clamp his jaw to keep from weeping.* A man may think God sleeps, but God sees everything. I know it now. I beg you, sir, I beg you—see her what she is. My wife, my dear good wife, took this girl soon after, sir, and put her out on the highroad. And being what she is, a lump of vanity, sir—*He is being overcome.* Excellency, forgive me, forgive me. *Angrily against himself, he turns away from the* GOVERNOR *for a moment. Then, as though to cry out is his only means of speech left:* She thinks to dance with me on my wife's grave! And well she might, for I thought of her softly. God help me, I lusted, and there *is* a promise in such sweat. But it is a whore's vengeance, and you must see it; I set myself

entirely in your hands. I know you must see it now.

DANFORTH, *blanched, in horror, turning to* ABIGAIL: You deny every scrap and tittle of this?

ABIGAIL: If I must answer that, I will leave and I will not come back again!

DANFORTH *seems unsteady.*

PROCTOR: I have made a bell of my honor! I have rung the doom of my good name—you will believe me, Mr. Danforth! My wife is innocent, except she knew a whore when she saw one!

ABIGAIL, *stepping up to* DANFORTH: What look do you give me? DANFORTH *cannot speak.* I'll not have such looks! *She turns and starts for the door.*

DANFORTH: You will remain where you are! HERRICK *steps into her path. She comes up short, fire in her eyes.* Mr. Parris, go into the court and bring Goodwife Proctor out.

PARRIS, *objecting:* Your Honor, this is all a—

DANFORTH, *sharply to* PARRIS: Bring her out! And tell her not one word of what's been spoken here. And let you knock before you enter. PARRIS *goes out.* Now we shall touch the bottom of this swamp. *To* PROCTOR: Your wife, you say, is an honest woman.

PROCTOR: In her life, sir, she have never lied. There are them that cannot sing, and them that cannot weep—my wife cannot lie. I have paid much to learn it, sir.

DANFORTH: And when she put this girl out of your house, she put her out for a harlot?

PROCTOR: Aye, sir.

DANFORTH: And knew her for a harlot?

PROCTOR: Aye, sir, she knew her for a harlot.

DANFORTH: Good then. *To* ABIGAIL: And if she tell me, child, it were for harlotry, may God spread His mercy on you! *There is a knock. He calls to the door.* Hold! *To* ABI-

Grammar in Action

Terms of direct address are nouns or pronouns that identify the person to whom a remark is addressed. A single comma is used to set off a term of direct address that appears at the beginning or end of a sentence. Two commas are used to set off a term of direct address that appears in the middle of a sentence. Note the following examples from *The Crucible:*

Mr. Danforth, he is lying!

I have known her, sir.
In her life, sir, she have never lied.

Student Activity. Insert the proper punctuation in each of the following sentences from *The Crucible:*

1. Come here woman.
2. Your wife you say is an honest woman.
3. I have paid much to learn it sir.
4. Mary Warren do you witch her?

GAIL: Turn your back. Turn your back. *To* PROCTOR: Do likewise. *Both turn their backs*—ABIGAIL *with indignant slowness.* Now let neither of you turn to face Goody Proctor. No one in this room is to speak one word, or raise a gesture aye or nay. *He turns toward the door, calls:* Enter! *The door opens.* ELIZABETH *enters with* PARRIS. PARRIS *leaves her. She stands alone, her eyes looking for* PROCTOR. Mr. Cheever, report this testimony in all exactness. Are you ready?

CHEEVER: Ready, sir.

DANFORTH: Come here, woman. ELIZABETH *comes to him, glancing at* PROCTOR'S *back.* Look at me only, not at your husband. In my eyes only.

ELIZABETH, *faintly:* Good, sir.

DANFORTH: We are given to understand that at one time you dismissed your servant, Abigail Williams.

ELIZABETH: That is true, sir.

DANFORTH: For what cause did you dismiss her? *Slight pause. Then* ELIZABETH *tries to glance at* PROCTOR. You will look in my eyes only and not at your husband. The answer is in your memory and you need no help to give it to me. Why did you dismiss Abigail Williams?

ELIZABETH, *not knowing what to say, sensing a situation, wetting her lips to stall for time:* She—dissatisfied me. *Pause.* And my husband.

DANFORTH: In what way dissatisfied you?

ELIZABETH: She were—*She glances at* PROCTOR *for a cue.*

DANFORTH: Woman, look at me? ELIZABETH *does.* Were she slovenly? Lazy? What disturbance did she cause?

ELIZABETH: Your Honor, I—in that time I were sick. And I—My husband is a good and righteous man. He is never drunk as some

are, nor wastin' his time at the shovelboard, but always at his work. But in my sickness—you see, sir, I were a long time sick after my last baby, and I thought I saw my husband somewhat turning from me. And this girl—*She turns to* ABIGAIL.

DANFORTH: Look at me.

ELIZABETH: Aye, sir. Abigail Williams—*She breaks off.*

DANFORTH: What of Abigail Williams?

ELIZABETH: I came to think he fancied her. And so one night I lost my wits, I think, and put her out on the highroad.

DANFORTH: Your husband—did he indeed turn from you?

ELIZABETH, *in agony:* My husband—is a goodly man, sir.

DANFORTH: Then he did not turn from you.

ELIZABETH, *starting to glance at* PROCTOR: He—

DANFORTH, *reaches out and holds her face, then:* Look at me! To your own knowledge, has John Proctor ever commited the crime of lechery? *In a crisis of indecision she cannot speak.* Answer my question! Is your husband a lecher!

ELIZABETH, *faintly:* No, sir.

DANFORTH: Remove her, Marshal.

PROCTOR: Elizabeth, tell the truth!

DANFORTH: She has spoken. Remove her!

PROCTOR, *crying out:* Elizabeth, I have confessed it!

ELIZABETH: Oh, God! *The door closes behind her.*

PROCTOR: She only thought to save my name!

HALE: Excellency, it is a natural lie to tell; I beg you, stop now before another is condemned! I may shut my conscience to it no

The Crucible 1237

55 **Discussion** Ask your students to explain why Danforth asks John Proctor and Abigail Williams to turn their backs to Elizabeth.

56 **Discussion** Have students discuss whether they think Elizabeth's characterization of her husband as a "good and righteous man" is accurate.

57 **Discussion** Ask your students why Elizabeth lies about her husband's actions. What does this reveal about her character?

5. Child I do not mistrust you—

6. Lord save me!

7. Your Honor I freeze!

8. What is it child?

9. Your excellency this is a trick to blind the court!

10. You say you never saw no spirits Mary were never threatened or afflicted by any manifest of the Devil or the Devil's agents.

Discussion Do students think that Hale is being truthful when he says that Abigail has "always struck [him] as false"? Why or why not?

59 **Discussion** Ask students if they think that Abigail and the other girls have rehearsed this behavior. If not, why do the other girls so quickly follow Abigail's lead?

60 **Reading Strategy** Have students pause at this point and predict how the third act will end. What will happen to Mary Warren? What will happen to John Proctor? On what do students base their predictions?

---

more—private vengeance is working through this testimony! From the beginning this man has struck me true. By my oath to Heaven, I believe him now, and I pray you call back his wife before we—

DANFORTH: She spoke nothing of lechery, and this man has lied!

HALE: I believe him! *Pointing at* ABIGAIL: This girl has always struck me false! She has—

ABIGAIL, *with a weird, wild, chilling cry, screams up to the ceiling.*

ABIGAIL: You will not! Begone! Begone, I say!

DANFORTH: What is it, child? *But* ABIGAIL, *pointing with fear, is now raising up her frightened eyes, her awed face, toward the ceiling—the girls are doing the same—and now* HATHORNE, HALE, PUTNAM, CHEEVER, HERRICK, *and* DANFORTH *do the same. What's there? He lowers his eyes from the ceiling, and now he is frightened; there is real tension in his voice.* Child! *She is transfixed—with all the girls, she is whimpering, open-mouthed, agape at the ceiling.* Girls! Why do you—?

MERCY LEWIS, *pointing:* It's on the beam! Behind the rafter!

DANFORTH, *looking up:* Where!

ABIGAIL: Why—? *She gulps.* Why do you come, yellow bird?

PROCTOR: Where's a bird? I see no bird!

ABIGAIL, *to the ceiling:* My face? My face?

PROCTOR: Mr. Hale—

DANFORTH: Be quiet!

PROCTOR, *to* HALE: Do you see a bird?

DANFORTH: Be quiet!!

ABIGAIL, *to the ceiling, in a genuine conversation with the "bird," as though trying to talk it out of attacking her:* But God made my face; you cannot want to tear my face. Envy is a deadly sin, Mary.

MARY WARREN, *on her feet with a spring, and horrified, pleading:* Abby!

ABIGAIL, *unperturbed, continuing to the "bird":* Oh, Mary, this is a black art to change your shape. No, I cannot, I cannot stop my mouth; it's God's work I do.

MARY WARREN: Abby, I'm *here!*

PROCTOR, *frantically:* They're pretending, Mr. Danforth!

ABIGAIL—*now she takes a backward step, as though in fear the bird will swoop down momentarily:* Oh, please, Mary! Don't come down.

SUSANNA WALCOTT: Her claws, she stretching her claws!

PROCTOR: Lies, lies.

ABIGAIL, *backing further, eyes still fixed above:* Mary, please don't hurt me!

MARY WARREN, *to* DANFORTH: I'm not hurting her!

DANFORTH, *to* MARY WARREN: Why does she see this vision?

MARY WARREN: She sees nothin!

ABIGAIL, *now staring full front as though hypnotized, and mimicking the exact tone of* MARY WARREN's *cry:* She sees nothin'!

MARY WARREN, *pleading:* Abby, you mustn't!

ABIGAIL AND ALL THE GIRLS, *all transfixed:* Abby, you mustn't!

MARY WARREN, *to all the girls:* I'm here, I'm here!

GIRLS: I'm here, I'm here!

DANFORTH, *horrified:* Mary Warren! Draw back your spirit out of them!

MARY WARREN: Mr. Danforth!

GIRLS, *cutting her off:* Mr. Danforth!

DANFORTH: Have you compacted with the Devil? Have you?

MARY WARREN: Never, never!

GIRLS: Never, never!

DANFORTH, *growing hysterical:* Why can they only repeat you?

PROCTOR: Give me a whip—I'll stop it!

MARY WARREN: They're sporting. They—!

GIRLS: They're sporting!

MARY WARREN, *turning on them all hysterically and stamping her feet:* Abby, stop it!

GIRLS, *stamping their feet:* Abby, stop it!

MARY WARREN: Stop it!

GIRLS: Stop it!

MARY WARREN, *screaming it out at the top of her lungs, and raising her fists:* Stop it!!

GIRLS, *raising their fists:* Stop it!!

MARY WARREN, *utterly confounded, and becoming overwhelmed by* ABIGAIL's—*and the girls'—utter conviction, starts to whimper, hands half raised, powerless, and all the girls begin whimpering exactly as she does.*

DANFORTH: A little while ago you were afflicted. Now it seems you afflict others; where did you find this power?

MARY WARREN, *staring at* ABIGAIL: I—have no power.

GIRLS: I have no power.

PROCTOR: They're gulling you, Mister!

DANFORTH: Why did you turn about this past two weeks? You have seen the Devil, have you not?

HALE, *indicating* ABIGAIL *and the girls:* You cannot believe them!

MARY WARREN: I—

PROCTOR, *sensing her weakening:* Mary, God damns all liars!

DANFORTH, *pounding it into her:* You have seen the Devil, you have made compact with Lucifer, have you not?

PROCTOR: God damns liars, Mary!

MARY *utters something unintelligible, staring at* ABIGAIL, *who keeps watching the "bird" above.*

DANFORTH: I cannot hear you. What do you say? MARY *utters again unintelligibly.* You will confess yourself or you will hang! *He turns her roughly to face him.* Do you know who I am? I say you will hang if you do not open with me!

PROCTOR: Mary, remember the angel Raphael—do that which is good and—

ABIGAIL, *pointing upward:* The wings! Her wings are spreading! Mary, please, don't, don't—!

HALE: I see nothing, Your Honor!

DANFORTH: Do you confess this power! *He is an inch from her face.* Speak!

ABIGAIL: She's going to come down! She's walking the beam!

DANFORTH: Will you speak!

MARY WARREN, *staring in horror:* I cannot!

GIRLS: I cannot!

PARRIS: Cast the Devil out! Look him in the face! Trample him! We'll save you, Mary, only stand fast against him and—

ABIGAIL, *looking up:* Look out! She's coming down!

She and all the girls run to one wall, shielding their eyes. And now, as though cornered, they let out a gigantic scream, and MARY, *as though infected, opens her mouth and screams with them. Gradually* ABIGAIL *and the girls leave off, until only* MARY *is left there, staring up at the "bird," screaming madly. All watch her, horrified by this evident fit.* PROCTOR *strides to her.*

The Crucible 1239

61 Discussion Have students discuss whether they think that this scene is the play's climax. On what do they base their answer?

62 Discussion Ask students if they think that Mary is about to turn away from John Proctor and rejoin Abby and the other girls. How does Miller make it clear that Mary is weakening?

63 Discussion Ask students if they think that it is fair to say that Abigail and Danforth have been involved in a power struggle throughout this scene. If so, who has won?

Enrichment When Miller's play was first performed, a number of critics claimed that the characters were simply "mouthpieces" for Miller's ideas. Among these critics was Walter Kerr, who wrote: "there are many times at the [performance] when one's intellectual sympathies go out to Mr. Miller and to his apt symbols of anguish on stage. But it is the intellect which goes out, not the heart.

"For Salem, and the people who live, love, fear, and die in it, are really only conveniences to Mr. Miller, props to his theme. He does not make them interesting in and for themselves, and you wind up analyzing them, checking their dilemmas against the latest headlines, rather than losing yourself in any rounded, deeply rewarding personalities."

Have students respond to Kerr's statement, explaining why they do or do not agree with it.

64 Discussion Have students explain why Abigail and the other girls stop repeating Mary's words.

65 Discussion Given what has been revealed about Mary Warren's character up to this point, do students find her change of heart surprising? Why or why not?

66 Reading Strategy Have students summarize the events that took place in Act III. Then have them predict what will happen in the final act.

67 Literary Focus Have students discuss how Proctor's comments might be applied to the proceedings during the McCarthy era.

Reader's Response What is your reaction to the events that took place in this act? What emotions did the girls' behavior in the final scene evoke in you? Why?

PROCTOR: Mary, tell the Governor what they—*He has hardly got a word out, when, seeing him coming for her, she rushes out of his reach, screaming in horror.*

MARY WARREN: Don't touch me—don't touch me! *At which the girls halt at the door.*

PROCTOR, *astonished:* Mary!

MARY WARREN, *pointing at* PROCTOR: You're the Devil's man!

He is stopped in his tracks.

PARRIS: Praise God!

GIRLS: Praise God!

PROCTOR, *numbed:* Mary, how—?

MARY WARREN: I'll not hang with you! I love God, I love God.

DANFORTH, *to Mary:* He bid you do the Devil's work?

MARY WARREN, *hysterically, indicating* PROCTOR: He come at me by night and every day to sign, to sign, to—

DANFORTH: Sign what?

PARRIS: The Devil's book? He come with a book?

MARY WARREN, *hysterically, pointing at* PROCTOR, *fearful of him:* My name, he want my name. "I'll murder you," he says, "if my wife hangs! We must go and overthrow the court," he says!

DANFORTH'S *head jerks toward* PROCTOR, *shock and horror in his face.*

PROCTOR, *turning, appealing to* HALE: Mr. Hale!

MARY WARREN, *her sobs beginning:* He wake me every night, his eyes were like coals and his fingers claw my neck, and I sign, I sign . . .

HALE: Excellency, this child's gone wild!

PROCTOR, *as* DANFORTH'S *wide eyes pour on him:* Mary, Mary!

MARY WARREN, *screaming at him:* No, I love God; I go your way no more. I love God, I bless God. *Sobbing, she rushes to* ABIGAIL. Abby, Abby, I'll never hurt you more! *They all watch, as* ABIGAIL, *out of her infinite charity, reaches out and draws the sobbing* MARY *to her, and then looks up to* DANFORTH.

DANFORTH, *to* PROCTOR: What are you? *Proctor is beyond speech in his anger.* You are combined with antichrist,[7] are you not? I have seen your power; you will not deny it! What say you, Mister?

HALE: Excellency—

DANFORTH: I will have nothing from you, Mr. Hale! *To* PROCTOR: Will you confess yourself befouled with Hell, or do you keep that black allegiance yet? What say you?

PROCTOR, *his mind wild, breathless:* I say— I say—God is dead!

PARRIS: Hear it, hear it!

PROCTOR, *laughs insanely, then:* A fire, a fire is burning! I hear the boot of Lucifer, I see his filthy face! And it is my face, and yours, Danforth! For them that quail to bring men out of ignorance, as I have quailed, and as you quail now when you know in all your black hearts that this be fraud—God damns our kind especially, and we will burn, we will burn together.

DANFORTH: Marshal! Take him and Corey with him to the jail!

HALE, *staring across to the door:* I denounce these proceedings!

PROCTOR: You are pulling Heaven down and raising up a whore!

HALE: I denounce these proceedings, I quit this court! *He slams the door to the outside behind him.*

DANFORTH, *calling to him in a fury:* Mr. Hale! Mr. Hale!

7. **antichrist:** In the Bible, the great antagonist of Christ expected to spread universal evil.

1240 Contemporary Writers

1240

Closure and Extension

ANSWERS TO THINKING ABOUT THE SELECTION
Recalling

1. He has evidence that he wants to present.
2. The three depositions are a testimonial to the good characters of Mrs. Proctor, Mrs. Corey, and Mrs. Nurse: a written statement that Putnam was overheard saying he would get Jacob's land after his [Putnam's] daughter accused Jacob of being a witch; and a statement by Mary Warren saying that she never saw any spirits.
3. Mary Warren accuses him of being in league with the Devil and forcing her to try to "overthrow the court."

Interpreting

4. (a) Answers will differ. Students should note that he is very stern

THINKING ABOUT THE SELECTION

Recalling

1. Why does Giles Corey interrupt the court proceedings?
2. What three depositions are presented to Deputy Governor Danforth?
3. Why is John Proctor arrested?

Interpreting

4. (a) How would you characterize Judge Hathorne? (b) How would you characterize Deputy Governor Danforth?
5. Why are Giles Corey's informant and the people who signed the first deposition afraid of being called to testify in court?
6. (a) How has Reverend Hale's character changed since the end of the second act? (b) Which of his comments and actions reveal this change? (c) What is the cause of the change in Hale's character?
7. (a) What is the significance of Reverend Hale's observation that "every defense is considered an attack upon the court"? (b) What is the significance of Danforth's assertion that "a person is either with this court or he must be counted against it"?
8. (a) Why does Elizabeth Proctor lie when she is questioned by Danforth? (b) How might the outcome of the witchcraft hysteria have been different if Elizabeth Proctor had told the truth?
9. Why does Mary Warren recant her admission and turn on John Proctor?

Applying

10. (a) What qualities do you think a judge should possess? (b) Which of these qualities do you think that Hathorne and Danforth are lacking?

ANALYZING LITERATURE

Understanding Historical Context

There are several parallels between the witchcraft hysteria of 1692 and the events that occurred during the McCarthy era in the twentieth century. For example, during both the witchcraft trials and the McCarthy hearings people were questioned in a hostile, inquisitorial manner.

1. During the McCarthy era, people who questioned the authority of McCarthy's Senate committee soon found themselves under suspicion of guilt. What evidence is there in the third act of Miller's play that this also occurred during the Salem witchcraft trials?
2. McCarthy's committee displayed a disregard for legal rights, such as the right to counsel and the right not to be branded guilty by reason of association. What evidence is there in the third act that these rights were also ignored during the Salem witchcraft trials?

UNDERSTANDING LANGUAGE

Completing Verbal Analogies

Word analogy items on standardized tests ask you to see the relationship between two words. Often, the words are either synonyms or antonyms.

Identify the relationship in the first pair of words in each of the following items. Then complete the second pair by choosing a word that expresses the same relationship.

1. flutter : quiver : : commencement :
   - a. beginning   c. ending
   - b. decision   d. festival
2. intermission : break : : contriving :
   - a. developing   c. scheming
   - b. pleasing   d. continuing
3. hurling : catching : : gangling :
   - a. stocky   c. athletic
   - b. lanky   d. healthy

THINKING AND WRITING

Writing About Parallels

Write a paper in which you discuss the parallels between the Salem witchhunt and the events of the McCarthy era. Begin by reviewing the first three acts of the play and rereading the Guides for Interpreting on the Salem witchcraft trials and the McCarthy era. You may also want to consult outside sources to find additional information about these two events.

and all of the convicted "witches" would have been freed.
9. Suggested Response: She is protecting herself against the accusations of Abigail and the other girls, who have united against her.

Applying

10. (a) Answers will differ. Students may respond that judges should be honest, fair, and objective. (b) Answers will differ. Students may note that Danforth and Hathorne are not fair and objective.

ANSWERS TO ANALYZING LITERATURE

1. Suggested Response: Giles refuses to reveal the name of his witness because he feels convinced that the witness will end up in jail. In addition, both Corey and Proctor are treated in a suspicious and hostile manner when they try to present their evidence and they both end up being arrested.
2. Suggested Response: Danforth refuses Hale's plea that Proctor should have a lawyer to present Mary Warren's statement. He also comments that none of the accused witches have a need for a lawyer. Giles's fears about his witness demonstrate the court has a tendency to brand people guilty by reason of association.

Challenge What are some of the differences between the Salem witchcraft trials and the events of the McCarthy era?

ANSWERS TO UNDERSTANDING LANGUAGE

1. a
2. c
3. a

THINKING AND WRITING

Writing Across the Curriculum You may want to inform the history department about this assignment. History teachers may be able to assist students in exploring the parallels between the Salem witchcraft trials and the events of the McCarthy era.

---

and closed-minded. (b) Answers will differ. Students should note that he is arrogant, imposing, and intelligent.
5. Suggested Response: Because they realize that if they are called to testify, it is likely that they will be accused of witchcraft.
6. (a) Suggested Response: He has lost confidence in the court proceedings, has ceased believing the testimony of Abigail and the other girls, and has taken the side of the accused. (b) Suggested Response: Almost everything he says during the course of the act is aimed at making Danforth and Hathorne consider the possibility that the accused are innocent. (c) Answers will differ. Students may respond that the change occurs because he is one of the few characters to consider the implications of the convictions.
7. (a) Suggested Response: It calls attention to the fact that the accused are considered guilty before their trials begin and that they are offered no chance to defend themselves. (b) Suggested Response: It makes it impossible for anyone to critically examine the court and to consider the possibility that its findings may have been wrong.
8. (a) Suggested Response: She does not want to humiliate her husband publicly. (b) Suggested Response: If she had told the truth, Abigail's testimony would probably have been thrown out

Literary Focus Have students discuss Miller's development of each of the themes mentioned in the Writer's Techniques section. Then have them try to come up with other possible themes. Record each of these additional themes on the chalkboard. Before students begin reading, have them jot down all of the themes in their notebook. As they read the final act, they should record passages that relate to each of the themes that have been mentioned.

Writing/Prior Knowledge Before students begin freewriting, have a class discussion in which students share what they know about Reverend Hale's character.

ESL Teaching Strategy Pair each of your ESL students with a native speaker. Have them read through the final act together, taking turns reading aloud. Instruct the native speaker to clarify the meanings of any words with which the ESL student is unfamiliar.

The Crucible, Act IV

Writer's Techniques

Theme. The theme is the central idea or insight into life that a writer hopes to convey in a work of literature. In some literary works, the theme is directly stated. More often, however, the theme is implied, or revealed indirectly, through the portrayal of characters and events or through the use of literary devices such as irony or symbols.

While shorter literary works often have only one theme, longer works are likely to have several themes. *The Crucible,* for example, has many themes. One of these themes is that fear and suspicion are infectious and can produce a state of general hysteria that results in the destruction of public order and rationality. Another theme is that it is possible for people's conceptions of good and evil to become so corrupted that they commit irreversible misdeeds in the name of virtue. Still another theme of the play is that people who claim to be pious and virtuous may in fact be guilty of hypocrisy. This theme is evident in the actions of Reverend Parris, who pretends to be motivated by concerns about the moral health of the village, though in reality he is concerned only about himself.

As you read the fourth act, pay close attention to how each of these themes is conveyed through the comments and actions of the characters. Also look for other possible themes, and note how each of these themes is revealed.

Writing

Although Reverend Hale has realized that the witchcraft proceedings are a tragic mistake, he does not have the power to stop them. Imagine that you were in Reverend Hale's place. How would you feel about the situation in Salem? What would be your attitude toward Danforth and Hathorne? What actions might you take? Freewrite, exploring your responses to these questions and offering predictions about Reverend Hale's behavior in the final act.

Primary Source

When *The Crucible* was first published, Arthur Miller added a note about the play's historical accuracy: "This play is not history in the sense in which the word is used by the academic historian. Dramatic purposes have sometimes required many characters to be fused into one; the number of girls involved in the 'crying-out' has been reduced; Abigail's age has been raised; while there were several judges of almost equal authority, I have symbolized them in Hathorne and Danforth. However, I believe that the reader will discover here the essential nature of one of the strangest and most awful chapters in human history. The fate of each character is exactly that of his historical model, and there is no one in the drama who did not play a similar—and in some cases exactly the same—role in history."

1242   *Contemporary Writers*

Objectives

1 To recognize the themes of the play
2 To appreciate the importance of casting
3 To write about theme

Support Material

Teaching Portfolio
Teacher Backup, p. 1623
Grammar in Action Worksheets, *Using the Dash,* p. 1627; *Understanding Compound and Complex Sentences,* p. 1629
Usage and Mechanics Worksheet, p. 1630
Vocabulary Check, p. 1631
Analyzing Literature Worksheet, *Understanding Theme,* p. 1632

Critical Thinking and Reading Worksheet, *Appreciating the Importance of Casting,* p. 1633
Selection Test, p. 1634

ACT IV

A cell in Salem jail, that fall.

At the back is a high barred window; near it, a great, heavy door. Along the walls are two benches.

The place is in darkness but for the moonlight seeping through the bars. It appears empty. Presently footsteps are heard coming down a corridor beyond the wall, keys rattle, and the door swings open. MARSHAL HERRICK *enters with a lantern.*

He is nearly drunk, and heavy-footed. He goes to a bench and nudges a bundle of rags lying on it.

HERRICK: Sarah, wake up! Sarah Good! *He then crosses to the other bench.*

SARAH GOOD, *rising in her rags:* Oh, Majesty!

Comin', comin'! Tituba, he's here, His Majesty's come!

HERRICK: Go to the north cell; this place is wanted now. *He hangs his lantern on the wall.* TITUBA *sits up.*

TITUBA: That don't look to me like His Majesty; look to me like the marshal.

HERRICK, *taking out a flask:* Get along with you now, clear this place. *He drinks, and* SARAH GOOD *comes and peers up into his face.*

SARAH GOOD: Oh, is it you, Marshal! I thought sure you be the devil comin' for us. Could I have a sip of cider for me goin'-away?

HERRICK, *handing her the flask:* And where are you off to, Sarah?

TITUBA, *as* SARAH *drinks:* We goin' to Barba-

"Oh, it is you, Marshal! I thought sure you be the devil comin' for us."

The Crucible 1243

Motivation/Prior Knowledge Have students share their reactions to the events that occurred in the first three acts. Then have them speculate about how the play will end. What will become of John Proctor? What will become of Elizabeth? What will become of the other accused "witches"? What will become of Abigail and the other girls who have participated in the proceedings?

Purpose-Setting Question Will John Proctor confess to witchcraft in order to save his own life?

Thematic Idea If your students have read Nathaniel Hawthorne's story "The Minister's Black Veil" (page 302), you might want to have them discuss the ways in which it parallels Miller's play.

Vocabulary

Preteach the following vocabulary words:
agape (a gāp′) *adj.:* Wide open
conciliatory (kən sil′ ē ə tôr′ ē) *adj.:* Tending to sooth the anger of
retaliation (ri tal′ ē ā′ s ˌhən) *n.:* The act of returning an injury or wrong
adamant (ad′ ə mənt) *adj.:* Firm; unyielding
cleave (clēv) *v.:* Adhere; cling
sibilance (sib′ 'l əns) *n.:* Hissing sound
tantalized (tan′ tə līzt) *v.:* Tormented; frustrated
purged (pʉrjt) *v.:* Cleansed; purified

Spelling Tip Point out to students that the letter *a* is the only vowel that appears in the word *adamant*.

1244

1 Discussion Have students discuss Tituba's and Sarah Good's behavior in this scene. Do the two women seem to have lost touch with reality? If so, why?

2 Discussion Have students discuss what this comment suggests about Herrick's attitude about the events that are taking place in Salem.

3 Discussion Have students discuss the irony of the fact that Tituba claims to see the Devil just as Danforth is arriving.

4 Discussion Have students discuss how Danforth's attitude toward Reverend Hale has changed. What has brought about this change?

5 Enrichment Since the Puritan government was a theocracy, members of the clergy had as much power as civil authorities.

6 Discussion Ask students if they think that the cold weather is the true cause of Herrick's drinking. Why or why not?

dos, soon the Devil gits here with the feathers and the wings.

HERRICK: Oh? A happy voyage to you.

SARAH GOOD: A pair of bluebirds wingin' southerly, the two of us! Oh, it be a grand transformation, Marshal! *She raises the flask to drink again.*

HERRICK, *taking the flask from her lips:* You'd best give me that or you'll never rise off the ground. Come along now.

TITUBA: I'll speak to him for you, if you desires to come along, Marshal.

HERRICK: I'd not refuse it, Tituba; it's the proper morning to fly into Hell.

TITUBA: Oh, it be no Hell in Barbados. Devil, him be pleasureman in Barbados, him be singin' and dancin' in Barbados. It's you folks—you riles him up 'round here; it be too cold 'round here for that Old Boy. He freeze his soul in Massachusetts, but in Barbados he just as sweet and—*A bellowing cow is heard, and* TITUBA *leaps up and calls to the window:* Aye, sir! That's him, Sarah!

SARAH GOOD: I'm here, Majesty! *They hurriedly pick up their rags as* HOPKINS, *a guard, enters.*

HOPKINS: The Deputy Governor's arrived.

HERRICK, *grabbing* TITUBA: Come along, come along.

TITUBA, *resisting him:* No, he comin' for me. I goin' home!

HERRICK, *pulling her to the door:* That's not Satan, just a poor old cow with a hatful of milk. Come along now, out with you!

TITUBA, *calling to the window:* Take me home, Devil! Take me home!

SARAH GOOD, *following the shouting* TITUBA *out:* Tell him I'm goin', Tituba! Now you tell him Sarah Good is goin' too!

In the corridor outside TITUBA *calls on—"Take me home, Devil: Devil take me*

home!" *and* HOPKINS' *voice orders her to move on.* HERRICK *returns and begins to push old rags and straw into a corner. Hearing footsteps, he turns, and enter* DANFORTH *and* JUDGE HATHORNE. *They are in greatcoats and wear hats against the bitter cold. They are followed in by* CHEEVER, *who carries a dispatch case and a flat wooden box containing his writing materials.*

HERRICK: Good morning, Excellency.

DANFORTH: Where is Mr. Parris?

HERRICK: I'll fetch him. *He starts for the door.*

DANFORTH: Marshal. HERRICK *stops.* When did Reverend Hale arrive?

HERRICK: It were toward midnight, I think.

DANFORTH, *suspiciously:* What is he about here?

HERRICK: He goes among them that will hang, sir. And he prays with them. He sits with Goody Nurse now. And Mr. Parris with him.

DANFORTH: Indeed. That man have no authority to enter here, Marshal. Why have you let him in?

HERRICK: Why, Mr. Parris command me, sir. I cannot deny him.

DANFORTH: Are you drunk, Marshal?

HERRICK: No, sir; it is a bitter night, and I have no fire here.

DANFORTH, *containing his anger:* Fetch Mr. Parris.

HERRICK: Aye, sir.

DANFORTH: There is a prodigious stench in this place.

HERRICK: I have only now cleared the people out for you.

DANFORTH: Beware hard drink, Marshal.

HERRICK: Aye, sir. *He waits an instant for further orders. But* DANFORTH, *in dissatisfac-*

Grammar in Action

In dialogue the dash is often used to indicate a speaker's hesitation or uncertainty. In addition, it is sometimes used at the end of a speech to indicate that the speaker did not finish expressing his or her ideas. Note the following examples from *The Crucible:*

DANFORTH: Why—this is indeed a providence.
PARRIS: There is news, sir, that the court—the court must

reckon with. My niece, sir, my niece—I believe she has vanished.
PARRIS: I had thought to advise you of it earlier in the week, but—
DANFORTH: Reverend Hale have no right to enter this—

Student Activity 1. Insert dashes in the appropriate places in each of the following sentences:
1. But the rumor here speaks of rebellion in Andover, and it
2. That speak of discontent, I think, and
3. My daughter tells me how she heard them speaking of ships last week, and tonight I discover my strongbox is broke into.
4. If retaliation is your fear, know this I should hang ten thousand

tion, turns his back on him, and HERRICK *goes out. There is a pause.* DANFORTH *stands in thought.*

HATHORNE: Let you question Hale, Excellency; I should not be surprised he have been preaching in Andover lately.

DANFORTH: We'll come to that; speak nothing of Andover. Parris prays with him. That's strange. *He blows on his hands, moves toward the window, and looks out.*

HATHORNE: Excellency, I wonder if it be wise to let Mr. Parris so continuously with the prisoners. DANFORTH *turns to him, interested.* I think, sometimes, the man has a mad look these days.

DANFORTH: Mad?

HATHORNE: I met him yesterday coming out of his house, and I bid him good morning—and he wept and went his way. I think it is not well the village sees him so unsteady.

DANFORTH: Perhaps he have some sorrow.

CHEEVER, *stamping his feet against the cold:* I think it be the cows, sir.

DANFORTH: Cows?

CHEEVER: There be so many cows wanderin' the highroads, now their masters are in the jails, and much disagreement who they will belong to now. I know Mr. Parris be arguin' with farmers all yesterday—there is great contention, sir, about the cows. Contention make him weep, sir; it were always a man that weep for contention. *He turns, as do* HATHORNE *and* DANFORTH, *hearing someone coming up the corridor.* DANFORTH *raises his head as* PARRIS *enters. He is gaunt, frightened, and sweating in his greatcoat.*

PARRIS, *to Danforth, instantly:* Oh, good morning, sir, thank you for coming. I beg your pardon wakin' you so early. Good morning, Judge Hathorne.

DANFORTH: Reverend Hale have no right to enter this—

PARRIS: Excellency, a moment. *He hurries back and shuts the door.*

HATHORNE: Do you leave him alone with the prisoners?

DANFORTH: What's his business here?

PARRIS, *prayerfully holding up his hands:* Excellency, hear me. It is a providence. Reverend Hale has returned to bring Rebecca Nurse to God.

DANFORTH, *surprised:* He bids her confess?

PARRIS, *sitting:* Hear me. Rebecca have not given me a word this three month since she came. Now she sits with him, and her sister and Martha Corey and two or three others, and he pleads with them, confess their crimes and save their lives.

DANFORTH: Why—this is indeed a providence. And they soften, they soften?

PARRIS: Not yet, not yet. But I thought to summon you, sir, that we might think on whether it be not wise, to—*He dares not say it.* I had thought to put a question, sir, and I hope you will not—

DANFORTH: Mr. Parris, be plain, what troubles you?

PARRIS: There is news, sir, that the court—the court must reckon with. My niece, sir, my niece—I believe she has vanished.

DANFORTH: Vanished!

PARRIS: I had thought to advise you of it earlier in the week, but—

DANFORTH: Why? How long is she gone?

PARRIS: This be the third night. You see, sir, she told me she would stay a night with Mercy Lewis. And next day, when she does not return, I send to Mr. Lewis to inquire. Mercy told him she would sleep in *my* house for a night.

DANFORTH: They are both gone?!

PARRIS, *in fear of him:* They are, sir.

The Crucible 1245

7 Discussion Have students speculate about what is happening in Andover.

8 Discussion Have students offer their reactions to Cheever's remark. Does Miller seem to be introducing an element of humor into the play? If so, why?

9 Discussion Do students imagine that Cheever's interpretation of Parris's behavior is essentially accurate? Why or why not?

10 Discussion Have students discuss Reverend Hale's possible motives for trying to convince Rebecca Nurse and the others to confess.

11 Discussion Ask students to explain Abigail's disappearance. Then have them speculate about how Danforth will respond to this news.

that dared to rise against the law, and an ocean of salt tears could not melt the resolution of the statues.

5. It is not for me to give, John, I am

Student Activity 2. Write a brief passage of dialogue in which you use the dash to indicate both hesitation and the expression of incomplete thoughts.

12 **Clarification** Make sure students are aware that the *pound* is a British monetary unit. Since Massachusetts was a British colony at the time of the play, the people who lived there used British currency.

13 **Discussion** Have students discuss whether Parris's reaction to Abigail's disappearance is consistent with his behavior throughout the first three acts. What upsets him most about Abigail's disappearance?

14 **Discussion** Have students discuss whether Parris seems to have considered the fact that Abigail's disappearance might imply that she has been lying throughout the witchcraft proceedings

15 **Enrichment** At the time, executions were public events that were intended to strike fear in the spectators and reinforce their awareness of the power of the authorities who governed their society.

16 **Discussion** Have students offer explanations for Danforth's unwillingness to postpone the executions.

DANFORTH, *alarmed:* I will send a party for them. Where may they be?

PARRIS: Excellency, I think they be aboard a ship. DANFORTH *stands agape.* My daughter tells me how she heard them speaking of ships last week, and tonight I discover my—my strongbox is broke into. *He presses his fingers against his eyes to keep back tears.*

HATHORNE, *astonished:* She have robbed you?

PARRIS: Thirty-one pound is gone. I am penniless. *He covers his face and sobs.*

DANFORTH: Mr. Parris, you are a brainless man! *He walks in thought, deeply worried.*

PARRIS: Excellency, it profit nothing you should blame me. I cannot think they would run off except they fear to keep in Salem any more. *He is pleading.* Mark it, sir, Abigail had close knowledge of the town, and since the news of Andover[1] has broken here—

DANFORTH: Andover is remedied. The court returns there on Friday, and will resume examinations.

PARRIS: I am sure of it, sir. But the rumor here speaks rebellion in Andover, and it—

DANFORTH: There is no rebellion in Andover!

PARRIS: I tell you what is said here, sir. Andover have thrown out the court, they say, and will have no part of witchcraft. There be a faction here, feeding on that news, and I tell you true, sir, I fear there will be riot here.

HATHORNE: Riot! Why at every execution I have seen naught but high satisfaction in the town.

PARRIS: Judge Hathorne—it were another sort that hanged till now. Rebecca Nurse is

---

1. **news of Andover:** During the height of the terror in Salem village, witchcraft hysteria broke out in the nearby town of Andover. There, many respected people were accused of and confessed to practicing witchcraft. However, people soon began questioning the reality of the situation, and the terror quicky subsided.

no Bridget that lived three year with Bishop before she married him. John Proctor is not Isaac Ward that drank his family to ruin. *To* DANFORTH: I would to God it were not so, Excellency, but these people have great weight yet in the town. Let Rebecca stand upon the gibbet[2] and send up some righteous prayer, and I fear she'll wake a vengeance on you.

HATHORNE: Excellency, she is condemned a witch. The court have—

DANFORTH, *in deep concern, raising a hand to* HATHORNE: Pray you. *To* PARRIS: How do you propose, then?

PARRIS: Excellency, I would postpone these hangin's for a time.

DANFORTH: There will be no postponement.

PARRIS: Now Mr. Hale's returned, there is hope, I think—for if he bring even one of these to God, that confession surely damns the others in the public eye, and none may doubt more that they are all linked to Hell. This way, unconfessed and claiming innocence, doubts are multiplied, many honest people will weep for them, and our good purpose is lost in their tears.

DANFORTH, *after thinking a moment, then going to* CHEEVER: Give me the list.

CHEEVER *opens the dispatch case, searches.*

PARRIS: It cannot be forgot, sir, that when I summoned the congregation for John Proctor's excommunication there were hardly thirty people come to hear it. That speak a discontent, I think, and—

DANFORTH, *studying the list:* There will be no postponement.

PARRIS: Excellency—

DANFORTH: Now, sir—which of these in your opinion may be brought to God? I will myself strive with him till dawn. *He hands the list to* PARRIS, *who merely glances at it.*

---

2. **gibbet** (jib′ it) *n.:* A gallows.

PARRIS: There is not sufficient time till dawn.

DANFORTH: I shall do my utmost. Which of them do you have hope for?

PARRIS, *not even glancing at the list now, and in a quavering voice, quietly:* Excellency—a dagger— *He chokes up.*

DANFORTH: What do you say?

PARRIS: Tonight, when I open my door to leave my house—a dagger clattered to the ground. *Silence.* DANFORTH *absorbs this.* Now PARRIS *cries out:* You cannot hang this sort. There is danger for me. I dare not step outside at night!

REVEREND HALE *enters. They look at him for an instant in silence. He is steeped in sorrow, exhausted, and more direct than he ever was.*

DANFORTH: Accept my congratulatons, Reverend Hale; we are gladdened to see you returned to your good work.

HALE, *coming to* DANFORTH *now:* You must pardon them. They will not budge.

HERRICK *enters, waits.*

DANFORTH, *conciliatory:* You misunderstand, sir; I cannot pardon these when twelve are already hanged for the same crime. It is not just.

PARRIS, *with failing heart:* Rebecca will not confess?

HALE: The sun will rise in a few minutes. Excellency, I must have more time.

DANFORTH: Now hear me, and beguile yourselves no more. I will not receive a single plea for pardon or postponement. Them that will not confess will hang. Twelve are already executed; the names of these seven are given out, and the village expects to see them die this morning. Postponement now speaks a floundering on my part; reprieve or pardon must cast doubt upon the guilt of them that died till now. While I speak God's law, I will not crack its voice with whimpering. If retaliation is your fear, know this—I should hang ten thousand that dared to rise against the law, and an ocean of salt tears could not melt the resolution of the statutes. Now draw yourselves up like men and help me, as you are bound by Heaven to do. Have you spoken with them all, Mr. Hale?

HALE: All but Proctor. He is in the dungeon.

DANFORTH, *to* HERRICK: What's Proctor's way now?

HERRICK: He sits like some great bird; you'd not know he lived except he will take food from time to time.

DANFORTH, *after thinking a moment:* His wife—his wife must be well on with child now.

HERRICK: She is, sir.

DANFORTH: What think you, Mr. Parris? You have closer knowledge of this man; might her presence soften him?

PARRIS: It is possible, sir. He have not laid eyes on her these three months. I should summon her.

DANFORTH, *to* HERRICK: Is he yet adamant? Has he struck at you again?

HERRICK: He cannot, sir, he is chained to the wall now.

DANFORTH, *after thinking on it:* Fetch Goody Proctor to me. Then let you bring him up.

HERRICK: Aye, sir. HERRICK *goes. There is silence.*

HALE: Excellency, if you postpone a week and publish to the town that you are striving for their confessions, that speak mercy on your part, not faltering.

DANFORTH: Mr. Hale, as God have not empowered me like Joshua to stop this sun

The Crucible **1247**

17 Discussion Have students express their reactions to Reverend Parris's behavior in this scene. Then have them share their overall attitudes toward Parris. Which of Parris's comments and actions played an especially important role in shaping their attitudes? Why?

18 Discussion Have students discuss the irony of Danforth's remarks.

19 Discussion Do your students think that Danforth himself has any doubts about the guilt of the convicted "witches"? On what do they base their answer?

20 Literary Focus Ask your students which of the major themes of the play is reflected in Danforth's speech.

21 Reading Strategy Have students predict whether Danforth will be able to convince John Proctor to confess. On what do they base their predictions?

22 **Discussion** Ask students if Danforth seems to have any concern about the disasterous effects of the witchcraft proceedings. If not, what does this reveal about his character?

23 **Discussion** Have students discuss the irony of Hale's remark that he has "come to do the Devil's work."

24 **Discussion** Have students discuss what Hale's remarks reveal about his character.

25 **Discussion** Have students discuss whether they agree with Hale's pronouncement that "no principle, however glorious, may justify the taking of [life]."

from rising,[3] so I cannot withhold from them the perfection of their punishment.

HALE, *harder now:* If you think God wills you to raise rebellion, Mr. Danforth, you are mistaken!

DANFORTH, *instantly:* You have heard rebellion spoken in the town?

22

HALE: Excellency, there are orphans wandering from house to house; abandoned cattle bellow on the highroads, the stink of rotting crops hangs everywhere, and no man knows when the harlots' cry will end his life—and you wonder yet if rebellion's spoke? Better you should marvel how they do not burn your province!

DANFORTH: Mr. Hale, have you preached in Andover this month?

HALE: Thank God they have no need of me in Andover.

DANFORTH: You baffle me, sir. Why have you returned here?

23

HALE: Why, it is all simple. I come to do the Devil's work. I come to counsel Christians they should belie themselves. *His sarcasm collapses.* There is blood on my head! Can you not see the blood on my head!!

PARRIS: Hush! *For he has heard footsteps. They all face the door.* HERRICK *enters with* ELIZABETH. *Her wrists are linked by heavy chain, which* HERRICK *now removes. Her clothes are dirty; her face is pale and gaunt.* HERRICK *goes out.*

DANFORTH, *very politely:* Goody Proctor. *She is silent.* I hope you are hearty?

ELIZABETH, *as a warning reminder:* I am yet six months before my time.

DANFORTH: Pray be at your ease, we come not for your life. We—*uncertain how to*

---

3. **Joshua . . . rising:** In the Bible Joshua, the leader of the Jews after the death of Moses, asks God to make the sun and the moon stand still during a battle, and his request is granted.

plead, for he is not accustomed to it. Mr. Hale, will you speak with the woman?

HALE: Goody Proctor, your husband is marked to hang this morning.

Pause.

ELIZABETH, *quietly:* I have heard it.

HALE: You know, do you not, that I have no connection with the court? *She seems to doubt it.* I come of my own, Goody Proctor. I would save your husband's life, for if he is taken I count myself his murderer. Do you understand me?

24

ELIZABETH: What do you want of me?

HALE: Goody Proctor, I have gone this three month like our Lord into the wilderness. I have sought a Christian way, for damnation's doubled on a minister who counsels men to lie.

HATHORNE: It is no lie, you cannot speak of lies.

HALE: It is a lie! They are innocent!

DANFORTH: I'll hear no more of that!

HALE, *continuing to* ELIZABETH: Let you not mistake your duty as I mistook my own. I came into this village like a bridegroom to his beloved, bearing gifts of high religion; the very crowns of holy law I brought, and what I touched with my bright confidence, it died; and where I turned the eye of my great faith, blood flowed up. Beware, Goody Proctor—cleave to no faith when faith brings blood. It is mistaken law that leads you to sacrifice. Life, woman, life is God's most precious gift; no principle, however glorious, may justify the taking of it. I beg you, woman, prevail upon your husband to confess. Let him give his lie. Quail not before God's judgment in this, for it may well be God damns a liar less than he that throws his life away for pride. Will you plead with him? I cannot think he will listen to another.

25

Grammar in Action

A **compound sentence** consists of two or more independent clauses joined by a comma and a coordinating conjunction or by a semicolon. A **complex sentence** consists of one main clause and at least one subordinate clause. Note the following examples from *The Crucible:*

COMPOUND SENTENCE: It is a bitter night, and I have no fire here. (p. 1244)
COMPLEX SENTENCE: And next day, when she does not return, I send to Mr. Lewis to inquire. (p. 1245)

1248

Student Activity 1. Identify each of the following sentences as either a compound sentence or a complex sentence:
1. I have sought a Christian way, for damnation's doubled on a minister who counsels men to lie.
2. My honesty is broke, Elizabeth; I am no good man.
3. Suspicion kissed you when I did; I never knew how I should say my love.
4. John, I counted myself so plain, so poorly made, no honest man could come to me!

Student Activity 2. Combine each of the following pairs of sentences into either a compound sentence or a complex sentence.

ELIZABETH, *quietly:* I think that be the Devil's argument.

HALE, *with a climactic desperation:* Woman, before the laws of God we are as swine! We cannot read His will!

ELIZABETH: I cannot dispute with you, sir; I lack learning for it.

DANFORTH, *going to her:* Goody Proctor, you are not summoned here for disputation. Be there no wifely tenderness within you? He will die with the sunrise. Your husband. Do you understand it? *She only looks at him.* What say you? Will you contend with him? *She is silent.* Are you stone? I tell you true, woman, had I no other proof of your unnatural life, your dry eyes now would be sufficient evidence that you delivered up your soul to Hell! A very ape would weep at such calamity! Have the devil dried up any tear of pity in you? *She is silent.* Take her out. It profit nothing she should speak to him!

ELIZABETH, *quietly:* Let me speak with him, Excellency.

PARRIS, *with hope:* You'll strive with him? *She hesitates.*

DANFORTH: Will you plead for his confession or will you not?

ELIZABETH: I promise nothing. Let me speak with him.

A sound—the sibilance of dragging feet on stone. They turn. A pause. HERRICK *enters with* JOHN PROCTOR. *His wrists are chained. He is another man, bearded, filthy, his eyes misty as though webs had overgrown them. He halts inside the doorway, his eyes caught by the sight of* ELIZABETH. *The emotion flowing between them prevents anyone from speaking for an instant. Now* HALE, *visibly affected, goes to* DANFORTH *and speaks quietly.*

HALE: Pray, leave them, Excellency.

DANFORTH, *pressing* HALE *impatiently aside:*

Mr. Proctor, you have been notified, have you not? PROCTOR *is silent, staring at* ELIZABETH. I see light in the sky, Mister; let you counsel with your wife, and may God help you turn your back on Hell. PROCTOR *is silent, staring at* ELIZABETH.

HALE, *quietly:* Excellency, let—

DANFORTH *brushes past* HALE *and walks out.* HALE *follows.* CHEEVER *stands and follows,* HATHORNE *behind.* HERRICK *goes.* PARRIS, *from a safe distance, offers:*

PARRIS: If you desire a cup of cider, Mr. Proctor, I am sure I—PROCTOR *turns an icy stare at him, and he breaks off.* PARRIS *raises his palms toward* PROCTOR. God lead you now. PARRIS *goes out.*

Alone. PROCTOR *walks to her, halts. It is as though they stood in a spinning world. It is beyond sorrow, above it. He reaches out his hand as though toward an embodiment not quite real, and as he touches her, a strange soft sound, half laughter, half amazement, comes from his throat. He pats her hand. She covers his hand with hers. And then, weak, he sits. Then she sits, facing him.*

PROCTOR: The child?

ELIZABETH: It grows.

PROCTOR: There is no word of the boys?

ELIZABETH: They're well. Rebecca's Samuel keeps them.

PROCTOR: You have not seen them?

ELIZABETH: I have not. *She catches a weakening in herself and downs it.*

PROCTOR: You are a—marvel, Elizabeth.

ELIZABETH: You—have been tortured?

PROCTOR: Aye. *Pause. She will not let herself be drowned in the sea that threatens her.* They come for my life now.

ELIZABETH: I know it.

Pause.

26 Discussion Have students explain what Reverend Hale means when he comments that "before the laws of God we are swine."

27 Discussion Do students think that Danforth and Hathorne would agree with Reverend Hale's observation that it is not possible to read God's will? Why or why not?

28 Master Teacher Note Urge students to try to envision the characters performing these actions and engaging in the conversation that follows.

29 Discussion What emotions do students imagine that the two characters are experiencing at this point?

30 Discussion Have students respond to the revelation that John Proctor has been tortured. What does this reveal about the Puritans?

1. That document is a lie. I will not accept it.
2. You will prove your soul's whiteness. You cannot live in a Christian community.
3. It is a weighty name. It will strike the village that Proctor confesses.
4. I speak God's law. I will not crack its voice with whimpering.

"You are a—marvel, Elizabeth."

PROCTOR: None—have yet confessed?

ELIZABETH: There be many confessed.

PROCTOR: Who are they?

ELIZABETH: There be a hundred or more, they say. Goody Ballard is one; Isaiah Goodkind is one. There be many.

PROCTOR: Rebecca?

ELIZABETH: Not Rebecca. She is one foot in Heaven now; naught may hurt her more.

PROCTOR: And Giles?

ELIZABETH: You have not heard of it?

PROCTOR: I hear nothin', where I am kept.

ELIZABETH: Giles is dead.

He looks at her incredulously.

PROCTOR: When were he hanged?

ELIZABETH, *quietly, factually:* He were not hanged. He would not answer aye or nay to his indictment; for if he denied the charge they'd hang him surely, and auction out his property. So he stand mute, and died Christian under the law. And so his sons will have his farm. It is the law, for he could not be condemned a wizard without he answer the indictment, aye or nay.

PROCTOR: Then how does he die?

ELIZABETH, *gently:* They press him, John.

PROCTOR: Press?

ELIZABETH: Great stones they lay upon his chest until he plead aye or nay. *With a tender smile for the old man:* They say he give them but two words. "More weight," he says. And died.

PROCTOR, *numbed—a thread to weave into his agony:* "More weight."

ELIZABETH: Aye. It were a fearsome man, Giles Corey.

Pause.

PROCTOR, *with great force of will, but not quite looking at her:* I have been thinking I would confess to them, Elizabeth. *She shows nothing.* What say you? If I give them that?

ELIZABETH: I cannot judge you, John.

Pause.

PROCTOR, *simply—a pure question:* What would you have me do?

ELIZABETH: As you will, I would have it. *Slight pause:* I want you living, John. That's sure.

PROCTOR, *pauses, then with a flailing of hope:* Giles' wife? Have she confessed?

ELIZABETH: She will not.

Pause.

PROCTOR: It is a pretense, Elizabeth.

ELIZABETH: What is?

PROCTOR: I cannot mount the gibbet like a saint. It is a fraud. I am not that man. *She is silent.* My honesty is broke, Elizabeth; I am no good man. Nothing's spoiled by giving them this lie that were not rotten long before.

ELIZABETH: And yet you've not confessed till now. That speak goodness in you.

PROCTOR: Spite only keeps me silent. It is hard to give a lie to dogs. *Pause, for the first time he turns directly to her.* I would have your forgiveness, Elizabeth.

ELIZABETH: It is not for me to give, John, I am—

PROCTOR: I'd have you see some honesty in it. Let them that never lied die now to keep their souls. It is pretense for me, a vanity that will not blind God nor keep my children out of the wind. *Pause.* What say you?

ELIZABETH, *upon a heaving sob that always threatens:* John, it come to naught that I should forgive you, if you'll not forgive

31

32

33

31 **Enrichment** Tell students that this is in fact the way in which the real Giles Corey died during the Salem witchcraft proceedings.

32 **Discussion** Have students discuss what Giles Corey's final actions reveal about his character. Given what they had learned about him in the preceding acts, would students have expected Giles to react to his indictment in this manner? Why or why not? Do students consider Giles Corey's actions heroic? Why or why not?

33 **Discussion** Have students respond to John Proctor's remarks. Do they agree with Proctor's comment that he is "no good man." Why or why not?

34 **Discussion** Ask students to explain why Elizabeth's remarks cause her husband "great pain."

35 **Clarification** Have students restate these remarks in their own words.

36 **Discussion** Ask students to explain the significance of the way in which Proctor responds to Hathorne's question.

37 **Discussion** Have students discuss Elizabeth's feelings about her husband's decision. Why does his decision cause her to feel terror? Why does she weep? Should she not be happy that John's life will be spared?

38 **Discussion** Have students discuss the irony of Danforth's observation that Proctor will be "blessed in Heaven for [his decision to confess]."

yourself. *Now he turns away a little, in great agony. It is not my soul, John, it is yours. He stands, as though in physical pain, slowly rising to his feet with a great immortal longing to find his answer. It is difficult to say, and she is on the verge of tears. Only be sure of this, for I know it now: Whatever you will do, it is a good man does it. He turns his doubting, searching gaze upon her. I have read my heart this three month, John. Pause. I have sins of my own to count. It needs a cold wife to prompt lechery.*

34 **PROCTOR,** *in great pain:* Enough, enough—

ELIZABETH, *now pouring out her heart:* Better you should know me!

PROCTOR: I will not hear it! I know you!

ELIZABETH: You take my sins upon you, John—

PROCTOR, *in agony:* No, I take my own, my own!

35 **ELIZABETH:** John, I counted myself so plain, so poorly made, no honest love could come to me! Suspicion kissed you when I did; I never knew how I should say my love. It were a cold house I kept! *In fright, she swerves, as* HATHORNE *enters.*

HATHORNE: What say you Proctor? The sun is soon up.

PROCTOR, *his chest heaving, stares, turns to* ELIZABETH. *She comes to him as though to plead, her voice quaking.*

ELIZABETH: Do what you will. But let none be your judge. There be no higher judge under Heaven than Proctor is! Forgive me, forgive me, John—I never knew such goodness in the world! *She covers her face, weeping.*

PROCTOR *turns from her to* HATHORNE; *he is off the earth, his voice hollow.*

PROCTOR: I want my life.

36 **HATHORNE,** *electrified, surprised:* You'll confess yourself?

PROCTOR: I will have my life.

HATHORNE, *with a mystical tone:* God be praised! It is a providence! *He rushes out the door, and his voice is heard calling down the corridor:* He will confess! Proctor will confess!

PROCTOR, *with a cry, as he strides to the door:* Why do you cry it? *In great pain he turns back to her.* It is evil, is it not? It is evil.

ELIZABETH, *in terror, weeping:* I cannot judge you, John, I cannot!

PROCTOR: Then who will judge me? *Suddenly clasping his hands:* God in Heaven, what is John Proctor, what is John Proctor? *He moves as an animal, and a fury is riding in him, a tantalized search.* I think it is honest, I think so; I am no saint. *As though she had denied this he calls angrily at her:* Let Rebecca go like a saint; for me it is fraud!

Voices are heard in the hall, speaking together in suppressed excitement.

ELIZABETH: I am not your judge, I cannot be. *As though giving him release:* Do as you will, do as you will!

PROCTOR: Would you give them such a lie? Say it. Would you ever give them this? *She cannot answer.* You would not; if tongs of fire were singeing you you would not! It is evil. Good, then—it is evil, and I do it!

HATHORNE *enters with* DANFORTH, *and, with them,* CHEEVER, PARRIS, *and* HALE. *It is a businesslike, rapid entrance, as though the ice had been broken.*

DANFORTH, *with great relief and gratitude:* Praise to God, man, praise to God; you shall be blessed in Heaven for this. CHEEVER *has hurried to the bench with pen, ink, and paper.* PROCTOR *watches him.* Now then, let us have it. Are you ready, Mr. Cheever?

PROCTOR, *with a cold, cold horror at their efficiency:* Why must it be written?

DANFORTH: Why, for the good instruction of the village, Mister; this we shall post upon the church door! *To* PARRIS, *urgently:* Where is the marshal?

PARRIS, *runs to the door and calls down the corridor:* Marshal! Hurry!

DANFORTH: Now, then, Mister, will you speak slowly, and directly to the point, for Mr. Cheever's sake. *He is on record now, and is really dictating to* CHEEVER, *who writes.* Mr. proctor, have you seen the Devil in your life? PROCTOR'S *jaws lock.* Come, man, there is light in the sky; the town waits at the scaffold; I would give out this news. Did you see the Devil?

PROCTOR: I did.

PARRIS: Praise God!

DANFORTH: And when he come to you, what were his demand? PROCTOR *is silent.* DANFORTH *helps.* Did he bid you to do his work upon the earth?

PROCTOR: He did.

DANFORTH: And you bound yourself to his service? DANFORTH *turns, as* REBECCA NURSE *enters, with* HERRICK *helping to support her. She is barely able to walk.* Come in, come in, woman!

REBECCA, *brightening as she sees* PROCTOR: Ah, John! You are well, then, eh?

PROCTOR *turns his face to the wall.*

DANFORTH: Courage, man, courage—let her witness your good example that she may come to God herself. Now hear it, Goody Nurse! Say on, Mr. Proctor. Did you bind yourself to the Devil's service?

REBECCA, *astonished:* Why, John!

PROCTOR, *through his teeth, his face turned from* REBECCA: I did.

DANFORTH: Now, woman, you surely see it profit nothin' to keep this conspiracy any further. Will you confess yourself with him?

REBECCA: Oh, John—God send his mercy on you!

DANFORTH: I say, will you confess yourself, Goody Nurse?

REBECCA: Why, it is a lie, it is a lie; how may I damn myself? I cannot, I cannot.

DANFORTH: Mr. Proctor. When the Devil came to you did you see Rebecca Nurse in his company? PROCTOR *is silent.* Come, man, take courage—did you ever see her with the Devil?

PROCTOR, *almost inaudibly:* No.

DANFORTH, *now sensing trouble, glances at* JOHN *and goes to the table, and picks up a sheet—the list of condemned.*

DANFORTH: Did you ever see her sister, Mary Easty, with the Devil?

PROCTOR: No, I did not.

DANFORTH, *his eyes narrow on* PROCTOR: Did you ever see Martha Corey with the Devil?

PROCTOR: I did not.

DANFORTH, *realizing, slowly putting the sheet down:* Did you ever see anyone with the Devil?

PROCTOR: I did not.

DANFORTH: Proctor, you mistake me. I am not empowered to trade your life for a lie. You have most certainly seen some person with the Devil. PROCTOR *is silent.* Mr. Proctor, a score of people have already testified they saw this woman with the Devil.

PROCTOR: Then it is proved. Why must I say it?

DANFORTH: Why "must" you say it! Why, you should rejoice to say it if your soul is truly purged of any love for Hell!

PROCTOR: They think to go like saints. I like not to spoil their names.

DANFORTH, *inquiring, incredulous:* Mr. Proctor, do you think they go like saints?

The Crucible 1253

---

39 Enrichment At the time the most common way in which information was conveyed to the general public was by posting notices or documents on the church door.

40 Discussion Ask students to characterize the manner in which Danforth is questioning Proctor. How does he go about eliciting the information he desires?

41 Discussion Ask students to explain why Rebecca Nurse is brought in at this point. Do Danforth and Hathorne hope that witnessing Proctor's confession will prompt Rebecca to confess?

42 Discussion Ask students why Proctor turns his face away from Rebecca.

43 Discussion Have students discuss the irony of Rebecca's response to Danforth's question.

44 Enrichment Explain to students that this type of questioning was frequently used during the McCarthy hearings. In fact, when Miller himself was called to testify before the Committee in 1956, he was pressed to reveal the names of people who had attended meetings sponsored by the Communist Party. To these requests, Miller responded, "my conscience will not permit me to use the name of another person and bring trouble on him."

PROCTOR, *evading:* This woman never thought she done the Devil's work.

DANFORTH: Look you, sir. I think you mis- take your duty here. It matter nothing what she thought—she is convicted of the unnatural murder of children, and you for sending

"Do what you will. But let none be your judge."

your spirit out upon Mary Warren. Your soul alone is the issue here, Mister, and you will prove its whiteness or you cannot live in a Christian country. Will you tell me now what persons conspired with you in the Devil's company? PROCTOR *is silent.* To your knowledge was Rebecca Nurse ever—

PROCTOR: I speak my own sins; I cannot judge another. *Crying out, with hatred:* I have no tongue for it.

HALE, *quickly to Danforth:* Excellency, it is enough he confess himself. Let him sign it, let him sign it.

PARRIS, *feverishly:* It is a great service, sir. It is a weighty name; it will strike the village that Proctor confess. I beg you, let him sign it. The sun is up, Excellency!

DANFORTH, *considers: then with dissatisfaction:* Come, then, sign your testimony. *To* CHEEVER: Give it to him. CHEEVER *goes to* PROCTOR, *the confession and a pen in hand.* PROCTOR *does not look at it.* Come, man, sign it.

PROCTOR, *after glancing at the confession:* You have all witnessed it—it is enough.

DANFORTH: You will not sign it?

PROCTOR: You have all witnessed it; what more is needed?

DANFORTH: Do you sport with me? You will sign your name or it is no confession, Mister! *His breast heaving with agonized breathing,* PROCTOR *now lays the paper down and signs his name.*

PARRIS: Praise be to the Lord!

PROCTOR *has just finished signing when* DANFORTH *reaches for the paper. But* PROCTOR *snatches it up, and now a wild terror is rising in him, and a boundless anger.*

DANFORTH, *perplexed, but politely extending his hand:* If you please, sir.

PROCTOR: No.

DANFORTH, *as though* PROCTOR *did not understand:* Mr. Proctor, I must have—

PROCTOR: No, no. I have signed it. You have seen me. It is done! You have no need for this.

PARRIS: Proctor, the village must have proof that—

PROCTOR: Damn the village! I confess to God, and God has seen my name on this! It is enough!

DANFORTH: No, sir, it is—

PROCTOR: You came to save my soul, did you not? Here! I have confessed myself; it is enough!

DANFORTH: You have not con—

PROCTOR: I have confessed myself! Is there no good penitence but it be public? God does not need my name nailed upon the church! God sees my name; God knows how black my sins are! It is enough!

DANFORTH: Mr. Proctor—

PROCTOR: You will not use me! I am no Sarah Good or Tituba, I am John Proctor! You will not use me! It is no part of salvation that you should use me!

DANFORTH: I do not wish to—

PROCTOR: I have three children—how may I teach them to walk like men in the world, and I sold my friends?

DANFORTH: You have not sold your friends—

PROCTOR: Beguile me not! I blacken all of them when this is nailed to the church the very day they hang for silence!

DANFORTH: Mr. Proctor, I must have good and legal proof that you—

PROCTOR: You are the high court, your word is good enough! Tell them I confessed myself; say Proctor broke his knees and wept like a woman; say what you will, but my name cannot—

49 **Clarification** Make sure students understand that when Proctor speaks of his *name*, he is referring to his reputation.

50 **Discussion** Ask students to explain why Proctor's reputation is so important to him. Do they sympathize with his feelings? Why or why not?

51 **Enrichment** At public executions, drums were often used to capture the crowd's attention.

52 **Discussion** Draw students' attention to the simile in the final two lines of the play. Then ask them what makes this simile especially effective.

Enrichment Soon after the Salem witchcraft hysteria ended, Parris was voted out of office and forced to leave town. According to legend, Abigail Williams eventually ended up working in a Boston brothel. Elizabeth Proctor, on the other hand, managed to rebound from her husband's death, remarrying four years after his body was laid to rest.

Twenty years after the last execution, compensation was awarded to victims who were still living. In 1712 the government ordered the congregation to rescind the excommunications of the accused. Yet only one of the presiding judges, Samuel Sewall, ever publicly admitted that a dreadful mistake had been made.

Reader's Response What is your overall reaction to the play? Did you enjoy it? Why or why not?

DANFORTH, *with suspicion:* It is the same, is it not? If I report it or you sign to it?

PROCTOR—*he knows it is insane:* No, it is not the same! What others say and what I sign to is not the same!

DANFORTH: Why? Do you mean to deny this confession when you are free?

PROCTOR: I mean to deny nothing!

DANFORTH: Then explain to me, Mr. Proctor, why you will not let—

PROCTOR, *with a cry of his whole soul:* Because it is my name! Because I cannot have another in my life! Because I lie and sign myself to lies! Because I am not worth the dust on the feet of them that hang! How may I live without my name? I have given you my soul; leave me my name!

DANFORTH, *pointing at the confession in* PROCTOR's *hand:* Is that document a lie? If it is a lie I will not accept it! What say you? I will not deal in lies, Mister! PROCTOR *is motionless.* You will give me your honest confession in my hand, or I cannot keep you from the rope. PROCTOR *does not reply.* What way do you go, Mister?

His breast heaving, his eyes staring, PROCTOR *tears the paper and crumples it, and he is weeping in fury, but erect.*

DANFORTH: Marshal!

PARRIS, *hysterically, as though the tearing paper were his life:* Proctor, Proctor!

HALE: Man, you will hang! You cannot!

PROCTOR, *his eyes full of tears:* I can. And there's your first marvel, that I can. You have made your magic now, for now I do think I see some shred of goodness in John Proctor. Not enough to weave a banner with, but white enough to keep it from such dogs. ELIZABETH, *in a burst of terror, rushes to him and weeps against his hand.* Give them no tear! Tears pleasure them! Show honor now, show a stony heart and sink them with it! *He has lifted her, and kisses her now with great passion.*

REBECCA: Let you fear nothing! Another judgment waits us all!

DANFORTH: Hang them high over the town! Who weeps for these, weeps for corruption! *He sweeps out past them.* HERRICK *starts to lead* REBECCA, *who almost collapses, but* PROCTOR *catches her, and she glances up at him apologetically.*

REBECCA: I've had no breakfast.

HERRICK: Come, man.

HERRICK *escorts them out,* HATHORNE *and* CHEEVER *behind them.* ELIZABETH *stands staring at the empty doorway.*

PARRIS, *in deadly fear, to* ELIZABETH: Go to him, Goody Proctor! There is yet time!

From outside a drumroll strikes the air. PARRIS *is startled.* ELIZABETH *jerks about toward the window.*

PARRIS: Go to him! *He rushes out the door, as though to hold back his fate.* Proctor! Proctor!

Again, a short burst of drums.

HALE: Woman, plead with him! *He starts to rush out the door, and then goes back to her.* Woman! It is pride, it is vanity. *She avoids his eyes, and moves to the window.* He drops to his knees. Be his helper!—What profit him to bleed? Shall the dust praise him? Shall the worms declare his truth? Go to him, take his shame away!

ELIZABETH, *supporting herself against collapse, grips the bars of the window, and with a cry:* He have his goodness now. God forbid I take it from him!

The final drumroll crashes, then heightens violently. HALE *weeps in frantic prayer, and the new sun is pouring in upon her face, and the drums rattle like bones in the morning air.*

Closure and Extension

ANSWERS TO THINKING ABOUT THE SELECTION
Recalling

1. (a) Abigail has disappeared. In addition, someone left a dagger above his door one night, making him fear for his life. He is also concerned about how the people of Salem will react to the hangings of John Proctor and Rebecca Nurse. (b) He proposes delaying the executions to allow Reverend Hale time to convince one of the condemned "witches" to confess.

2. He feels that any postponement would indicate uncertainty on his part.

3. Refusing to answer to his indictment, he is pressed to death by heavy stones.

THINKING ABOUT THE SELECTION

Recalling

1. (a) Why is Reverend Parris worried when he meets with Hathorne and Danforth at the beginning of the act? (b) What proposal does Parris make to Danforth?
2. Why does Danforth refuse to postpone the executions?
3. How does Giles Corey meet his death?
4. Why does Danforth arrange a meeting between John and Elizabeth Proctor?

Interpreting

5. (a) What might have motivated Abigail Williams to leave Salem? (b) How does Parris exhibit his self-centeredness when he relates the news of Abigail's disappearance to Hathorne and Danforth?
6. (a) What motivates Reverend Hale to seek confessions from the condemned prisoners? (b) What is ironic about Hale's comment that he has "come to do the Devil's work"?
7. What do Giles Corey's actions as he faces his death reveal about his character?
8. (a) Why is Elizabeth Proctor unable to offer her husband advice concerning his possible confession? (b) Why does Proctor decide to confess? (c) Why does Danforth respond so enthusiastically to Proctor's confession?
9. (a) Why does Proctor refuse to implicate others in his confession? (b) What factors lead him to retract his confession?

Applying

10. (a) Do you think that John Proctor makes the right decision? Why or why not? (b) If you were asked to write Proctor's epitaph, what would you say?

ANALYZING LITERATURE

Understanding Theme

The **theme** is the central idea or insight about life that a writer hopes to convey in a literary work. While shorter literary works often have only one theme, longer works are likely to have several themes. *The Crucible,* for example, has many themes.

1. One of the play's themes is that fear and suspicion are infectious and can produce a state of general hysteria that results in the destruction of public order and rationality. How does Miller convey this theme?
2. Another theme is that people who claim to be pious and virtuous may in fact be guilty of hypocrisy. How is this theme evident in the actions of Parris in the fourth act?
3. Another of the play's themes is that it is more noble to die with integrity than it is to compromise one's principles in order to live. How do the actions of John Proctor and Rebecca Nurse support this idea?

CRITICAL THINKING AND READING

Appreciating the Importance of Casting

Plays are generally written to be performed, not read. As a result, a person's response to a play usually depends to a great extent on the actors' portrayal of the various characters. For this reason, the casting of a dramatic production is extremely important.

Putting yourself in the role of casting director for a dramatic production of *The Crucible,* think of the specific actors or types of actors you would choose to play each of the following roles: Reverend Parris, Abigail Williams, Mary Warren, John Proctor, Elizabeth Proctor, Reverend Hale, Judge Hathorne, and Deputy Governor Danforth. Explain each of your choices.

THINKING AND WRITING

Writing About Theme

Choose one theme that you feel is important. Then write a paper in which you explain how this theme is conveyed. Begin by reviewing the play and noting details that relate to the theme you have chosen. Organize your notes. Then write your essay, using passages from the play for support.

The Crucible 1257

DEATH OF A SALESMAN
by Arthur Miller

What is the American dream? What is it that stirs us on to greater and greater success? In the 1940's, characters of psychological complexity became increasingly common in works of fiction. At the same time, writers were expressing a stronger interest in social problems and in the often disturbing impact on human life and values of social and technological change. With his Pulitzer Prize-winning play *Death of a Salesman*, Arthur Miller presented a complex and shattering portrait of a man destroyed by progress and by his own mistaken vision of the American Dream.

I don't say he's a great man. Willy Loman never made a lot of money. His name was never in the paper. He's not the finest character that ever lived. But he's a human being, and a terrible thing is happening to him. So attention must be paid. He's not to be allowed to fall into his grave like an old dog. Attention, attention must be finally paid to such a person.
Death of a Salesman Act I

Drama Drawn from Experience

Arthur Miller grew up in New York City where his father was a prosperous clothing manufacturer. Miller worked briefly in his father's factory when he was in high school. At the factory he was shocked by the cruelty and hardness of the buyers, who treated his father and the company's salesmen without respect or courtesy.

While working for his father, Miller met one particular salesman who impressed him deeply. When he was seventeen, he wrote a brief short story about the man called "In Memoriam." In the story the narrator accompanies the salesman, who is old, tired, and poor, on his rounds. The man sells nothing and is mistreated by his buyers. In the end

Clarification *Death of a Salesman* is set during the last twenty-four hours of Willy Loman's life. Yet the action moves effortlessly from the present into Loman's memories of the past. In discussing the purpose of the play's frequent temporal shifts, Miller commented that "the play's eye was to revolve from within Willy's head, sweeping endlessly in all directions like a light on the sea."

Enrichment The first production of *Death of a Salesman* was directed by Elia Kazan, who had directed the original Broadway production of Tennessee Williams's *A Streetcar Named Desire* just two years earlier.

the salesman commits suicide by throwing himself in front of a subway train. In 1949 this same salesman was to become the basis for the hero of Miller's widely respected play, *Death of a Salesman*.

An American Tragedy

Death of a Salesman tells the story of an aging traveling salesman, Willy Loman, a man on the verge of psychological collapse as he faces his own failures. Willy has based his life on the notion that success comes to those who are "well liked," and he has raised his son Biff with the same idea. At the time of the play, Biff, now thirty-four years old, has just returned to his father's Brooklyn home. A former high school football star, he has turned into a ne'er-do-well. Unable to feel satisfied with the pleasure he takes in manual labor on a western farm, he feels guilt for failing to achieve the kind of success his father wants for him.

The play proceeds as a series of meetings and confrontations between family members and business associates. In one of the most important confrontations, Willy, tired of traveling, asks his boss to give him a position in New York only to be told that after thirty-six years with the company he is of no

more value. In the play's most critical confrontation, Biff tries to make his father recognize that Biff is just an ordinary man, that his father's dreams of material success for him are just "phony dreams," but that Biff has always loved his father. At the end of the play, Willy, distraught by the loss of his job but exhilarated by the knowledge that his son loves him, kills himself in a car crash in order to give his family the material legacy of his $20,000 life insurance policy.

Much of the play takes place in the present as characters are portrayed realistically drinking coffee, mending stockings, washing the car, or eating in a restaurant. Interwoven with these scenes of ordinary life, however, are Willy's memories of past experiences. An incident or phrase in the present suddenly triggers a memory, which is then given representation by the appearance of such characters as Willy's dead brother, Ben, or by Willy and Biff as their younger selves. The memory sequences occur without the other characters noticing them. Only the audience sees what is going on in Willy's mind.

The Common Man as Tragic Hero

With his protagonist Willy Loman, Miller was demonstrating his notion that tragedy was possible in the modern theater and that the proper hero for modern tragedy was the common man. Willy is distinctly unheroic. Nothing about him is exceptional. He is not particularly articulate or kindhearted. He has failed to achieve the material success he craves. His life and death have no impact on the larger world. Yet audiences everywhere were able to respond to the words of his wife, Linda, when she said "He's not the finest character that ever lived. But he's a human being, and a terrible thing is happening to him. So attention must be paid." Miller was portraying Loman as the stuff of modern tragedy, a man whose fall results from the forces of a society that fails to take human nature into account.

Willy's tragedy lies partly in his victimization by the "system." Willy loses his job because he no longer fills the needs of a changed society. As a young salesman, he was able to achieve a degree of success through the force of personality, by making people like him. As an old man, he faces a business world that has become more "cut and dried," colder, more dependent on the product alone. Most of his old friends and associates have died, Willy is worn out, and he is no longer able to make sales. Instead of finding a place for him, his employer fires him. Willy is a victim of a system that "will eat the orange and throw the peel away," a system that abandons people once they have lost their usefulness.

At the same time, Willy's tragedy also results from his own misinterpretation of the

American Dream. Willy has gradually destroyed himself because he has placed his faith in false values. For Willy the American Dream is symbolized by two different figures. The first is Ben, Willy's brother, a self-made man who has achieved material success through personal daring. Ben's motto is "Never fight fair with a stranger." The second is Dave Singleman, a successful salesman who achieved wealth by virtue of his personal loveableness and appeal. Willy fails to see the emptiness of his dream of material success through the force of personality. He fails to recognize the importance of family and love while spending one's life doing jobs that have their own intrinsic value.

> Willy was a salesman. And for a salesman, there is no rock bottom to the life. He don't put a bolt to a nut, he don't tell you the law or give you medicine. He's a man way out there in the blue, riding on a smile and a shoeshine. And when they start not smiling back—that's an earthquake. And then you get yourself a couple of spots on your hat, and you're finished. Nobody dast blame this man. A salesman is got to dream, boy. It comes with the territory.
>
> *Requiem*

An Enduring Masterpiece

Death of a Salesman continues to provide an overpowering emotional experience to audiences not just in the United States but worldwide. People often see in it an accurate reflection of their own dilemmas and inadequacies. They recognize in the play elements from life that are poignantly and tragically true.

Brooks Atkinson, a critic for *The New York Times*, responded this way to the play when it first opened: "By common consent, this is one of the finest dramas in the whole range of the American theater. Humane in its point of view, it has stature and insight, awareness of life, respect for people and knowledge of American manners and of modern folkways." Atkinson also noted that the play "is so simple in style and so inevitable in theme that it scarcely seems like a thing that has been written and acted. For Mr. Miller has looked with compassion into the hearts of some ordinary Americans and quietly transferred their hopes and anguish to the theater."

Critics continue to hail the play as an American masterpiece. America's finest actors are often eager to play the part of its tragic hero, Willy Loman, for Willy, in all his pain and self-destructiveness, is still clearly recognized as part of the modern Everyman.

Great Works 1261

QUESTIONS AND ACTIVITIES

1. Ask students to identify the play's central theme. Have them support their interpretations with passages from the play. Then have them discuss how they can apply the play's theme to their own lives.
2. Have students put themselves in the place of the producer of a new theatrical production of the play. Then have them explain which of today's actors they would cast in the roles of each of the main characters in the play.
3. Ask students to explain whether they think that Miller's play would have been any different if it had been written today rather than in 1949.
4. Have students locate critics' reviews of early performances of the play and have them share the reviews with their classmates.

CROSS CURRENTS

Aaron Copland (1900–   )

Considered America's most versatile, popular, and important composer, Aaron Copland writes music to express what it feels like to be an American living in America. From his first jazz-influenced compositions of the 1920's to his great western folk ballets and his orchestral pieces echoing complex cityscapes, Copland's music is based on traditional melodies, harmonies, and rhythms that evoke the spirit of America's past and present.

AN AMERICAN COMPOSER

Born Aaron Kaplan to Russian immigrant parents in Brooklyn, New York, Cop-

land decided as a teenager that he wanted to be a composer. Like other aspiring American artists of his generation, he went to Paris to study music. It was abroad—away from America—that Copland realized the importance of his American roots to the kind of music he wished to write. As he later recalled, "The idea that my personal expression in music ought somehow to be related to my own back-home environment took hold of me. The conviction grew inside me that the two things that seemed always to have been so separate in America—music and the life about me—must be made to touch. This desire to make the music I wanted to write come out of the life I had lived in America became a preoccupation of mine. . . . "

AMERICA'S HERITAGE

Copland's early pieces reflect America's jazz age of the twenties with its syncopated rhythms and ambiguous blues sounds. Soon, however, Copland began to search for what he later called a "vernacular music, which, as language, would cause no difficulties to my listeners." Out of this desire to write more simply and directly for the common listener, Copland developed a folksy American style that appealed to a wide audience. His most popular works are the ballets *Billy the Kid* (1938), *Rodeo* (1942), and *Appalachian Spring* (1944). Copland himself described these ballets as having a "musical naturalness" in keeping with America's pastoral heritage as opposed to Europe's classical culture. Based on American folk themes, they incorporate traditional cowboy songs, folk songs, and hymns to convey life on the prairie and in rural nineteenth-century

Enrichment A number of Copland's early works reflect the influence of French and Middle Eastern music of the early 1900's.

Enrichment Copland has written several successful books about music, including *What to Listen for in Music* (1964). *The New Music 1900–1960* and his autobiography, *Copeland: 1900 Through 1942* (1984).

Learning Across the Curriculum Your students might be interested in learning more about Aaron Copland or about another twentieth-century American composer. Divide your class into groups of four or five. Have each group research achievements of a different composer. When the groups have finished their research, have them present their findings to the rest of the class.

America. Recalling America's musical heritage, these works celebrate the American pioneer spirit, evoking the courage, struggle, and isolation of America's settlers. The ballets explore themes that are common in American literature. Both *Billy the Kid* and *Rodeo* are about the conflict between society and the outsider, the first a tragic version, the second a comic one. *Appalachian Spring* is about the domestic security and religious faith of a young newlywed pioneer couple.

Copland's music is a veritable course in American history and culture. His *A Lincoln Portrait* for narrator and orchestra, his suite based on John Steinbeck's *The Red Pony*, his musical settings of twelve poems of Emily Dickinson, and his opera *The Tender Land* reflect Copland's deep interest in America's roots. Copland also wrote the scores for several Hollywood films about small-town America, notably *Of Mice and Men* and *Our Town*. In his later works, Copland departed from the simple expressions of pastoral America to write music that catches the complex vigor of city life.

In addition to his contributions to modern music, Copland has devoted himself to the cause of American music and the advancement of American composers. He has also written books to promote wider acceptance of modern music. It is with good reason that Copland has been called the "Dean of American Composers."

YOU THE WRITER
Guidelines for Evaluating Assignment 1

1. Has the student written a poem about the landscape in which he or she lives?
2. Has the student used concrete imagery to create a vivid picture of the landscape?
3. Are the details in spatial order?
4. Is the poem free from grammar, usage, and mechanics errors?

Guidelines for Evaluating Assignment 2

1. Has the student written an informal essay about important issues of the times?
2. Has the student explained why each issue is important?
3. Is the essay arranged in a logical manner?
4. Is the essay free from grammar, usage, and mechanics errors?

Guidelines for Evaluating Assignment 3

1. Has the student depicted some of the rapid changes in the contemporary period and explored ways these changes have affected people's lives?
2. Has the student chosen an appropriate literary form?
3. Is the writing style and word choice appropriate to the form chosen?
4. Is the piece free from grammar, usage, and mechanics errors?

YOU THE WRITER

Assignment

1. Many contemporary poets convey a deep awareness of the American landscape in their poetry. In doing so, they use vivid, striking imagery that brings the landscape to life for the reader. Write a poem in which you use vivid imagery to describe the appearance of the landscape in the region in which you live.

Prewriting. Prepare a list of concrete details you can use in describing the landscape. Arrange the details in spatial order.

Writing. When you write your poem, do not worry about rhythm or rhyme. Instead, focus on using concrete imagery to create a vivid picture of the landscape you are describing.

Revising. When you finish writing, revise and proofread your poem and share it with your classmates.

Assignment

2. Writers often focus on the dominant issues of their time. What do you feel are the most important issues of the contemporary age? Write a brief informal essay in which you discuss your perceptions of the dominant issues of our time.

Prewriting. Brainstorm about the dominant issues of our time, and list them in order of importance. Then eliminate some of the less important issues.

Writing. When you write your essay, use an informal writing style, but make sure the essay is organized in a logical manner.

Revising. When you revise, make sure you have explained why you think each issue you have discussed is important.

Assignment

3. The contemporary period has been a time of rapid change. Write a short story, narrative poem, personal essay, or journal entry in which you depict some of these changes and explore the ways in which they have affected people's lives. For example, you might write a story in which a middle-aged man reflects upon some of the important events and developments that have occurred during his lifetime.

Prewriting. Prepare a list of changes and brainstorm about how they have affected people's lives. Then decide on the type of literary form that you wish to use.

Writing. When writing your work, make sure your writing style and choice of words are appropriate for the literary form you have chosen.

Revising. When you revise, check for errors in grammar, usage, and mechanics.

1264   *Contemporary Writers*

YOU THE CRITIC

Assignment

1. Many contemporary stories reflect the writers' perception that today's world is complex and impersonal, making it difficult for people to communicate with one another. Write an essay in which you discuss how this perception is reflected in one of the contemporary stories you have read.

    Prewriting. After choosing a story, carefully reread it, focusing on theme, characterization, and the characters' interactions with one another. Prepare a thesis statement and organize your notes into an outline.

    Writing. When you write your essay, use passages from the story to support your thesis.

    Revising. When you revise, make sure you have included enough information to thoroughly support your thesis.

Assignment

2. During the contemporary period, many writers have chosen to build on the developments of the Modernists, applying the Modernist ideas and approaches to contemporary life. Write an essay in which you compare and contrast a modern story with a contemporary story.

    Prewriting. Choose a modern story and a contemporary story that are in some ways similar in form and content. For example, you might choose "In Another Country" and "Imagined Scenes." Then carefully reread the stories, noting similarities and differences in structure and theme.

    Writing. When you write your essay, organize your argument according to corresponding points of contrast.

    Revising. When you revise, make sure you have thoroughly supported your argument with examples from the two stories.

Assignment

3. Contemporary literature is extremely varied and diverse, with writers exploring a wide variety of subjects and approaches. Write an essay in which you discuss the diversity of contemporary poetry or contemporary fiction.

    Prewriting. Reread the discussion of contemporary literature in the unit introduction. Then review the selections in the unit, noting similarities and differences in form and content.

    Writing. When writing your essay, use evidence from at least five selections to support your argument.

    Revising. When you revise, make sure your argument is clear and coherent and is organized in a logical manner.

Focus on Writing 1265

YOU THE CRITIC
Guidelines for Evaluating Assignment 1

1. Has the student written a thesis statement that discusses how the idea that the impersonal world makes communication difficult for people is reflected in a short story?
2. Has the student included enough information to support thoroughly the thesis in the essay?
3. Has the student cited passages from the story for support?
4. Is the essay free from grammar, usage, and mechanics errors?

Guidelines for Evaluating Assignment 2

1. Has the student compared and contrasted a story written by a Modernist with one written by a contemporary author?
2. Has the student thoroughly supported his or her argument with examples from the two stories?
3. Has the student organized the arguments according to corresponding points of contrast?
4. Is the essay free from grammar, usage, and mechanics errors?

Guidelines for Evaluating Assignment 3

1. Has the student presented an argument that explores the diversity of contemporary poetry or fiction?
2. Has the student used evidence from at least five selections to support his or her argument?
3. Is the argument clear, coherent, and logically organized?
4. Is the essay free from grammar, usage, and mechanics errors?

Roethke
teaches

WASHINGTON

Chief Joseph's "I Will Fight No More"

NORTH DAKOTA

OREGON

Chief Joseph born

MONTANA

Sioux Territory

IDAHO

SOUTH DAKOTA

WYOMING

Ezra Pound born

CALIFORNIA

NEVADA

NEBRASKA

Twain's *Roughing It*

UTAH

Twain meets Artemus Ward

Cooper's *The Prairie*
(Natty Bumpo dies)

Willa Cather's stories

COLORADO

Twain's Calaveras County

Katherine Ann Porter lives

KANSAS

G. Brooks born ●

Frost born

W. Stafford born

Steinbeck's
"Flight"

ARIZONA

NEW MEXICO

OKLAHOMA

Navaho Legends

Ralph Ellison born

N. Scott Momaday
born

○ Simon Ortiz lives, writes

● Katherine Anne Porter born

TEXAS

Lopez's
Arctic Dreams

London, Melville, Twain write

McMurty's
● *Lonesome Dove*

ALASKA

HAWAII

Literary Map of the United States

HANDBOOK OF WRITING ABOUT LITERATURE

1268   Contents

Contents *1269*

SECTION 1: UNDERSTANDING THE WRITING PROCESS

Lesson 1: Prewriting

Someone once remarked that easy writing makes difficult reading. Good writing always takes both time and effort. Understanding that writing a paper requires not one step but many can help you to have more realistic expectations of yourself as a writer. A writer does not simply sit down and produce a final version off the top of his or her head. Instead, a writer completes a number of stages that together make up the process of writing.

1. *Prewriting:* planning the piece of writing
2. *Drafting:* getting ideas down on paper in rough form
3. *Revising:* changing and improving the rough draft
4. *Proofreading:* correcting any errors in spelling or mechanics
5. *Publishing:* letting others read and share the writing

In this lesson you will learn about the steps that make up the prewriting stage.

STEP 1: ANALYZE THE SITUATION

You may feel that you should begin any paper by just sitting down and writing. However, a better way to begin is to think first about the entire context in which you will be working. To do so, ask yourself the following questions about the writing situation.

1. *Topic* (the subject that you will be writing about): What, exactly, is this subject? Can you state it in a sentence? Is your subject too broad or too narrow?
2. *Purpose* (what you want your writing to accomplish): Is your purpose to tell a story? to describe? to explain? to persuade? to enter-

tain? Will your writing serve some combination of these purposes?

3. *Audience* (the people for whom you are writing): What are the backgrounds of the people in your audience? Do these people already know a great deal about your topic? Will you have to provide basic background information?
4. *Voice* (the way the writing will sound to the reader): What impression do you want to make on your audience? What tone should the piece of writing have? Should your writing be formal or informal, objective or subjective, emotional or dispassionate?
5. *Content* (the subject and all the information provided about it): How much do you already know about your subject? What will you have to find out? Will you have to do some research? If so, what sources can you use? Can you use books, magazines, newspapers, reference works, or interviews with other people? Can you draw on your own memories and experiences?
6. *Form* (the shape the writing will take, including its length and organization): What will the final piece of writing look like? How long will it be? Will it be written in one or more paragraphs? Will it have a distinct introduction, body and conclusion? What method of organization or organizing principle will you use?

STEP 2: MAKE A PLAN

Ask yourself the questions outlined in Step 1 to clarify the writing task. Answer any questions you can. Then make a plan of action for answering the questions that remain. You may find, for example, that you are unsure about your topic and that you need to do more thinking about it, or you may discover that you need to gather information for your paper and therefore will have to do some research.

STEP 3: GATHER INFORMATION

Ideas and information for writing can come either from within you or from outside sources. If you decide to use outside sources, you can try looking at books, magazines, films, television programs, or reference works of various kinds. You also might try using a computer information service or conducting interviews with people who are knowledgeable about your subject. If you decide to gather information from your own memories and experiences, you might try one of the following techniques.

1. *Analyzing:* Divide your topic into parts, think about these parts, and think about the relationships among the parts and between each part and the whole.
2. *Charting:* Make lists of key ideas or concepts related to your topic. List the parts of the topic, make a pros-and-cons chart, draw a tree diagram, or construct a time line. Make any kind of list or chart that is relevant to your topic.
3. *Clustering:* Write your topic in the middle of a sheet of paper. Then think about the topic and jot down any related ideas that occur to you. Circle these related ideas and connect them, with lines, to the topic. Then think about the related ideas, jot down other ideas, and connect these with lines. Continue in this way until you have filled the paper.
4. *Freewriting:* Without stopping to punctuate or to think about spelling or form, write down everything that comes into your mind as you think about the topic.
5. *Questioning:* Prepare a list of questions that deal with various aspects of your topic. Begin the questions with words such as *who, what,* *where, when, why,* and *how.*

These techniques also can be used to narrow a topic or to come up with a topic idea in the first place.

STEP 4: ORGANIZE YOUR NOTES

Your next step is to organize the information that you have gathered. If you have used note cards, you might organize these. If not, you might make a rough outline. In either case, you need to choose an order in which to present your ideas and information. The order to use is one that grows logically from your materials. The following are some common methods of organization.

1. *Chronological order:* events arranged in order of occurrence in time
2. *Spatial order:* features or items arranged in a physical order or pattern, as from right to left
3. *Degree order:* points arranged from least to most or from most to least according to degree of presence or absence of some property such as complexity, familiarity, frequency, effectiveness, value, or importance

CASE STUDY: PREWRITING

Juanita's English class was studying mass communications. The teacher asked each student to choose one medium of mass communication and to write a paragraph on some topic related to that medium. At first Juanita couldn't think of a topic, so she made the tree diagram (on page 1272) in her notebook.

Juanita studied her diagram and decided that she wanted to write about school newspapers. However, she still needed a more narrow topic, so she did some freewriting and came up with this idea: She would write about the editorial policy of her school newspaper. This would be a good topic to write about because (1) Juanita worked on the school paper and knew something about its editorial policy and (2) because

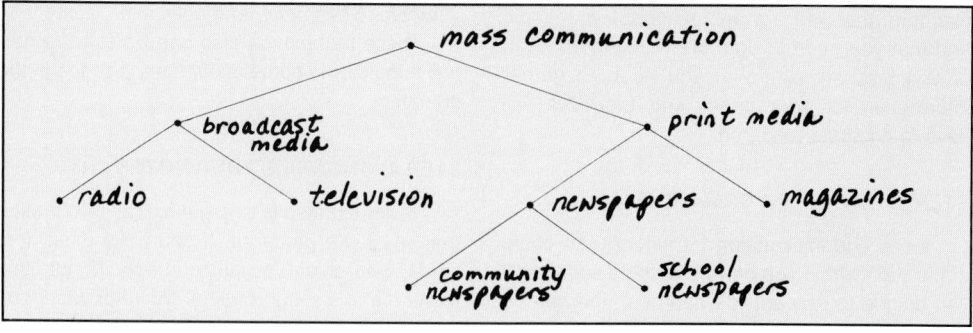

many of the students in Juanita's class probably didn't know what an editorial policy was, much less that the school paper had one.

Juanita then took the following notes.

- Topic: the editorial policy of our school newspaper

- Purpose: to explain the editorial policy to other students

- Audience: other students in my class (all readers of the school paper)

- Voice: relatively formal

- Content: information about the paper's editorial policy (but where am I going to find this information?)

- Form: one paragraph

Looking over her notes, Juanita recognized that she needed to make a plan for gathering information for her paragraph. She decided to interview the editor of the school paper, Colleen Ryan. First Juanita made a list of questions to ask Colleen, and then she arranged an interview. During the interview Juanita took notes, putting quotations around those comments that she got down word for word. Here are some of the notes that Juanita took.

- Does the school paper have an official editorial policy?
  "Yes." Policy is stated in a document

called "The Editorial Policy of the Emerson High School Star Reporter"

- Who determines the editorial policy?
  "The editorial policy is determined by the editorial board, which is made up of the editor (that's me), the assistant editor, and the journalism advisor, Ms. Ortega."

- What, precisely, is the official editorial policy?
  Policy statement deals with lots of issues.
  Mostly, ensures that reporting will be fair, objective, unbiased.
  Also says that policy of paper is to print news of interest to students.
  Spells out what kinds of ads the paper can carry.
  Says who has the final word about what can go into the paper and what can't.

- Who does have the final word?
  Well, I suppose that the final word is Ms. Ortega's. She's the editor-in-chief. But the policy statement also says that the principal has the right to veto publication of any article if she considers doing so to be "in the best interest of the school."

- You mean that the principal can ask you not to print something? Doesn't that violate the freedom of the press?
  "In theory, perhaps it does. However, in

practice, the principal never does stop publication of an article. Besides, every newspaper in the country has an editorial review board that turns thumbs up or thumbs down on particular articles."

- So having the materials in your paper be subject to review doesn't bother you?

No, because the principal is only going to reject an article if it is irresponsible, and "we simply don't allow irresponsible articles to be considered in the first place."

As the interview progressed, Juanita realized that she had found a much more interesting topic to write about than the newspaper's editorial policy. She decided to change her topic to the issue of whether the student press should be completely free or subject to review by the school administration. She knew that this meant changing her statement of purpose as well. Her purpose would be to present both sides of this complicated issue.

ACTIVITIES AND ASSIGNMENTS

A. Answer the following questions about the case study:

1. What method did Juanita use to come up with a topic?
2. When Juanita analyzed the writing situation, what did she realize that she needed to do?
3. How did Juanita change her writing plan during the interview? What other parts of her writing plan will this change affect?

B. Select your own topic, or choose a reading from this book about which you want to comment. Begin work on an informal paragraph by following the prewriting steps discussed in this lesson.

ANSWERS TO ACTIVITIES AND ASSIGNMENTS, SECTION A

1. She made a tree diagram.
2. She realized that she needed a plan for gathering information.
3. She decided to change her topic to the issue of whether the student press should be completely free or subject to review by the school administration. Changing her topic forced her to change her statement of purpose.

Lesson 2: Drafting and Revising

DRAFTING YOUR PAPER

Once your prewriting is finished, you are ready to begin the drafting stage. *Drafting* is the process of getting ideas down on paper in rough form. When you draft, keep the following points in mind:

1. Choose a drafting style that is right for you. Some people like to write a quick and very rough draft and then go back and rework this draft considerably. Other people prefer to write a slow, careful draft, revising as they go. Choose whichever method works best for you. The quick draft has the advantage of allowing you to get all of your ideas down so they can be manipulated easily. The slow draft has the advantage of reducing the amount of revision time required later on.

2. Bear in mind that your first version is a draft and need not be perfect. If you choose to do a slow, careful draft, don't work so slowly and carefully that you interrupt your stream of thought. Make getting your ideas down the main priority. You can go back and work on the details of sentence structure, organization, spelling, and mechanics during the revision and proofreading stages.

3. Keep your audience, purpose, and voice in mind as you write. As you work, try not to stray too far from your original plan. If you find that the original plan isn't workable, go back to the prewriting stage and make a new plan.

4. As you draft, keep yourself open to new ideas. Work from your prewriting notes and your rough outline. However, remember that some of the best ideas occur while people are actually writing. If a new idea occurs to you and it is a good one, then use it. Don't forget that you can revise your prewriting plan at any time if you feel the need to do so.

CHECKLIST FOR REVISION

Topic and Purpose
- ☐ Is my main idea clear?
- ☐ Does the writing achieve its purpose?

Content and Development
- ☐ Have I developed the main idea completely?
- ☐ Have I provided examples or details that support the statements I have made?
- ☐ Are my sources of information unbiased, up-to-date, and authoritative?
- ☐ Have I avoided including unnecessary or unrelated ideas?

Form
- ☐ Have I followed a logical method of organization?
- ☐ Have I used transitions to make the connections between ideas clear?
- ☐ Does the writing have a clear introduction, body, and conclusion?

Audience
- ☐ Will my audience understand what I have said?
- ☐ Will my audience find the writing interesting?
- ☐ Will my audience respond in the way I intend?

Voice and Word Choice
- ☐ Does the writing convey the impression I intended it to convey?
- ☐ Is my language appropriate?
- ☐ Have I avoided vague, undefined terms?
- ☐ Have I used vivid, specific nouns, verbs, and adjectives?
- ☐ Have I avoided jargon?
- ☐ Have I avoided clichés, slang, euphemisms, and gobbledygook except for humorous effect?

---

5. Allow yourself enough time to write. Do not try to do all your writing at the last minute. Give

yourself enough time to write a draft and then to revise and proofread it.

6. Write as many drafts as you need to write. One nice thing about writing is that you can do it over and over until you have a final product you are satisfied with.

REVISING YOUR DRAFT

Revising is the process of reworking a written draft to enhance its content and organization. After you finish your draft, use the checklist on the preceding page to identify ways to improve your paper.

CASE STUDY: DRAFTING AND REVISING

As you will recall from the preceding lesson, Juanita had decided to write a paper presenting two sides of a complicated issue: whether the student press should or should not be subject to review by academic administrators. As Juanita thought about this issue, she decided that she had firm personal opinions about it. She therefore decided to change her topic once again: She would write about why she believed that administrators should have the right to review articles before they appear in the student press.

Juanita wrote a first draft of her paper and then revised it. Here is her draft with the revisions that she made:

~~Two days ago~~ *Recently* I interviewed ~~the editor of our~~ *Colleen Ryan,*

school newspaper, The Emerson High School

During our conversation ~~Star Reporter.~~ ~~She said~~ *Ms. Ryan told me* that the Principal ~~had~~ *has* *according to the paper's editorial policy,*

the right to review any articles before they

could be printed in the paper. Initially I was

inscensed by ~~mad about~~ this ~~. B~~ *B*ecause it seemed to violate

---

the students right to *a* free press. *However,* ~~As~~ I thought

about the issue I realised that their were good

reasons for ~~this~~ *the review policy. First,* High school journalists are not

experienced. They need guidance regarding

such matters as what can be published in a

newspaper and what cannot. No paper can

print just any ~~kind of stuff~~ *sort of material.* The law says that *for example*

papers can be held accountable for ~~anything~~ *material with* *ing* ~~that they print that is libelous.~~ The review policy *malice a forethought©*

ensures that articles that violate the law will not *in the school paper. Second,*

be published. *A*ll newspapers, including

professional ones, have review policies. The

Editor-in-Chief, and sometimes the Publisher,

can veto publication of certain ~~story~~ *ies©*. In the

case of the school paper, the journalism

sponser acts as the editor in chief, and the

Principal acts as the Publisher. They therefore

have the same right to accept or reject certain

articles as would thier counterparts in the world

of proffessional print journalism. Some

students might object to working under the

constraints of the review policy. However, these

students need to realise that they will be

working under the same constraints. When

they ~~enter the world~~ *become* of proffessional journalism. *ists*

ANSWERS TO ACTIVITIES AND ASSIGNMENTS, SECTION A

1. Her original statement was accurate only on the day she wrote the paper.
2. She added the transitions *during our conversation, however, first,* and *second.*
3. She changed *mad about* to *incensed by* and *kind of stuff* to *sort of material.*
4. The fourth and final sentences were fragments. She corrected them by combining them with other sentences.
5. She added references to the school paper and its editorial policy.
6. She did not underline the name of the school newspaper, and she capitalized editor-in-chief. These errors should be corrected during the revising stage.

ACTIVITIES AND ASSIGNMENTS

A. Answer the following questions about the case study:
1. Why did Juanita change the phrase "Two days ago" to the word "Recently"?
2. What transitions did Juanita add to show the logical connections between her ideas?
3. In what places did Juanita replace informal language with language that is more formal?
4. What sentence fragments did Juanita correct? How did she correct these fragments?
5. What information did Juanita add to make her statements clearer?
6. What spelling, punctuation, and capitalization errors did Juanita not correct during revision? During what stage of the writing process should such errors be corrected?

B. Use your notes and outlines from the preceding lesson to draft and revise a paragraph. Follow the procedures described in this lesson.

Lesson 3: Proofreading and Publishing

USING EDITORIAL SYMBOLS

After you have revised your draft, you are ready to begin proofreading. *Proofreading* is the process of checking for errors in spelling, grammar, mechanics, and manuscript form. As you proofread, use the editorial symbols shown on the next page to mark corrections on your draft:

USING A PROOFREADING CHECKLIST

Try to allow time between revising and proofreading. Doing so will make it easier for you to notice minor errors that you might otherwise miss. Proofread carefully, since just a few minor mistakes can distract a reader from many good ideas. Use the checklist at right to guide your proofreading.

When you have a question about some rule of spelling, grammar, mechanics, or manuscript form, check the rule in a dictionary, in a writing text, or in a grammar book. As you proofread, bear in mind the mistakes that you have made on papers in the past and try to avoid repeating these. After you proofread, make a neat final copy of your paper and check this copy as well.

PUBLISHING, OR SHARING, YOUR WORK

The neat final copy of your paper is ready for an audience. Most school papers have a teacher as the main reader, but you or your class can find other ways to share your writing. Here are some suggestions:

1. Share your writing with friends, parents, and other relatives.
2. Mail a copy of a paper you like to grandparents or to other relatives.
3. Read your paper aloud to a discussion group, to the whole class, or to a different class.

CHECKLIST FOR PROOFREADING

Grammar and Usage
☐ Are all my sentences complete? That is, have I avoided sentence fragments?
☐ Do all my sentences express just one complete thought? That is, have I avoided run-on sentences?
☐ Do my verbs agree with their subjects?
☐ Did I use all the words in my paper correctly? Am I sure the meaning and connotation of each word fits the writing?
☐ Does each pronoun clearly refer to something?
☐ Have I used adjectives and adverbs correctly?

Spelling
☐ Is every word correctly spelled?
☐ Have I double-checked the spelling of proper nouns?

Punctuation
☐ Does each sentence end with a punctuation mark?
☐ Have I used commas, semicolons, colons, hyphens, dashes, parentheses, quotation marks, and apostrophes correctly?

Capitalization
☐ Have I eliminated unnecessary capital letters?
☐ Have I capitalized all words that need capital letters?

---

4. Trade papers with other students who sit nearby or who work with you on projects or in groups.
5. Create a publication that contains writing by all the students in your class.
6. Make your own "book" of papers that you have written during the year. Share this book with classmates, with friends, or with relatives.

Proofreading and Publishing 1277

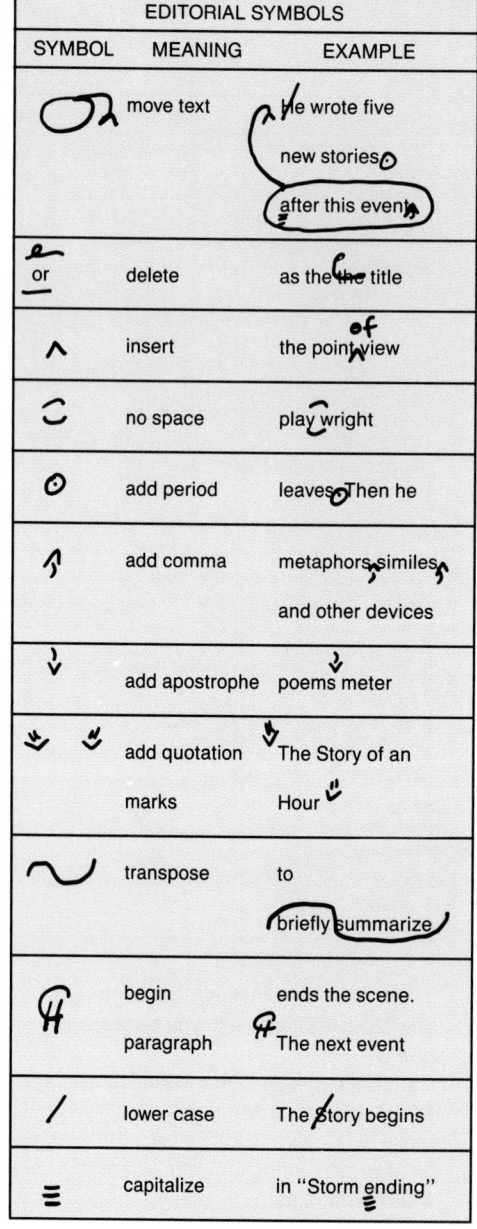

7. Submit some of your writing to the school literary magazine.
8. Start a school literary magazine.
9. Submit your writing to your school newspaper, to the community newspaper, or to another publication that prints works by young writers.
10. Enter your work in an essay or creative writing contest.

CASE STUDY: PROOFREADING AND PUBLISHING

Juanita used the Checklist for Proofreading to find and correct the errors that remained in her rough draft. Here is Juanita's proofread paragraph:

> Recently I interviewed Colleen Ryan, the editor of our school newspaper, The Emerson High School Star Reporter. During our conversation Ms. Ryan told me that according to the paper's editorial policy, the principal has the right to review any articles before they are printed in the paper. Initially I was incensed by this policy because it seemed to violate the students' right to a free press. However, as I thought about the issue, I realized that there were good reasons for the review policy. First high-school journalists are not experienced. They need guidance regarding such matters as what can be published in a newspaper and what cannot. No paper can print just any sort of material.

The law says, for example, that papers can be held accountable for printing libelous materials with malice aforethought. The review policy ensures that articles that violate the law will not be published in the school paper. Second, all newspapers, including professional ones, have review policies. The ~~E~~ditor-in-~~C~~hief, and sometimes the ~~P~~ublisher, can veto publication of certain stories. In the case of the school paper, the journalism sponsͦer acts as the editor-in-chief, and the ~~P~~rincipal acts as the ~~P~~ublisher. They therefore have the same right to accept or reject certain articles as would th~~ie~~r counterparts in the world of prof̂essional print journalism. Some students might object to working under the constraints of the review policy. However, these students need to reali~~z~~se that when they become prof̂essional journalists, they will be working under the same constraints.

After proofreading her paper, Juanita made a clean final copy. Then she checked this copy once again for errors and shared the paper with classmates in a small-group discussion. She and her classmates had a lively debate about the issue.

ACTIVITIES AND ASSIGNMENTS

A. Answer the following questions about the case study:
1. What errors did Juanita correct in spelling, punctuation, capitalization, and manuscript form?
2. Are there any changes that Juanita should have made in her draft that she didn't make?

B. Proofread and share the paragraph that you drafted in the last lesson. Follow these steps:
1. Check your revised draft for errors, using the Checklist for Proofreading, on page 1277. Use standard editorial symbols to make any necessary corrections.
2. Make a neat final copy of your paragraph. Check this copy carefully to make sure you have added all of your final changes and have not made mistakes in copying.
3. Share your draft with your teacher and with your classmates.

ANSWERS TO ACTIVITIES AND ASSIGNMENTS, SECTION A

1. She corrected the spelling of the following words: *incensed, realized, there, professional,* and *sponsor.* She added an apostrophe to the word *students.* She deleted one comma and added another. She added a hyphen to high school. She underlined the name of the school newspaper. She indented the paragraph. She changed the first letter in the following words to lower case: *principal, editor-in-chief,* and *publisher.*
2. Suggested Response: The sentence "They needed guidance regarding such matters as what can be published and what cannot" needs revision.

SECTION 2: UNDERSTANDING THE PARTS OF A LITERARY WORK: ANALYSIS AND INTERPRETATION

Lesson 4: Writing About Images

WHAT IS AN IMAGE?

Sights, sounds, touches, tastes, and smells are physical sensations that people experience. When these sensations are presented in words or phrases, they are called *images.* The following poem uses images, especially those of sight and touch, to create a portrait of a woman:

CHINATOWN 1: *SEATTLE, WASHINGTON*

Laureen Mar

She boards the bus at Chinatown,
holding the brown paper shopping bag
with twine handles that came from
San Francisco or Vancouver.
It is worn thin with creases.
An oil spot darkens one side
where juice dripped from warm
roast duck, another shopping trip.

WHY WRITERS USE IMAGES

Writers use images to convey sensations and emotions. Images are concrete and specific, and they therefore help a writer to describe or express an exact moment, setting, mood, or feeling. For example, notice the imagery used by poet M. Carl Holman in the opening lines of his poem "Three Brown Girls Singing":

In the ribs of an ugly school building
Three rapt faces
Fuse one pure sound in a shaft of April light:
Three girls, choir robes over their arms, in a
    stairwell singing

Holman's imagery accomplishes three purposes. First, it creates a sharp picture, in words, of three girls singing in a stairwell. Second, it suggests a feeling of appreciation for the power and beauty of the "one pure sound" their singing makes. Third, it alerts the reader to the importance of the song and prepares him or her to find out more about its significance.

CASE STUDY: WRITING ABOUT IMAGES

Wendy's English teacher asked the class to write a paragraph analyzing a favorite poem. Wendy decided to write about the use of images in Emily Dickinson's poem, "I felt a Funeral, in my Brain," on page 381.

Prewriting

Wendy began by reading the poem several times. Then she made the following list of images in her prewriting notes:

- Images of sight:
  None

- Images of sound:
  "Kept treading—treading"
  "like a Drum—/Kept beating—beating"
  "creak across my soul"
  "Boots of Lead"
  "all the Heavens were a Bell"

- Images of touch:
  "felt a Funeral, in my Brain"
  "My Mind was going numb"
  "I dropped down, and down—/And hit a
  World, at every plunge"

- Images of taste:
  None

- Images of smell:
  None

Next Wendy asked herself what scene was created by the images and what emotions were associated with that setting. She wrote her answers to these questions in her prewriting notes, as follows:

- Scene created by images:
  A funeral with mourners treading by the casket
  The casket being lifted and carried to the grave site
  The deafening sounds of the bells
  The casket being lowered into the grave

- Mood created by the images:
  Great anguish and pain
  Confusion

Wendy decided to write her paragraph about how Dickinson uses imagery to create a mood of pain and confusion. She made the following rough outline for her paragraph:

- Topic sentence:
  Title and author of poem
  Purpose: to show how Dickinson uses images to create mood of anguish and confusion

- Body of paragraph:
  Describe the images of sound and touch in the poem

- Conclusion of paragraph:
  Indicate how the last five lines summarize the mood of the poem

Drafting and Revising

Using her outline and her prewriting notes, Wendy wrote a draft of her paragraph and then revised it. Wendy's draft, with her revisions marked in standard editorial symbols, is shown at right.

In the poem "I felt a Funeral, in my Brain," Emily Dickenson ~~utilizes~~ *uses* imagery to create a mood of anguish and confusion. The poem describes a funeral from the point of view of the *person inside the casket.* ~~body.~~ The mind protecting itself by numbness ⊙ *An image of touch shows how the person's* ~~is conveyed by an image of touch.~~ The mounting anguish builds with the use of images of sound. For example, the mourners "Kept treading—treading" and the service "Kept beating—beating." The swelling sounds of the bells are contrasted to the *silent world* ~~silence~~ of the dead person. The poem ends with a glimpse at the narrator's loneliness and confusion. The dead person seeks silence to end the pain of hearing the sounds of the funeral. But instead *more terrifying* experiences a plunge into nothingness.

Proofreading and Publishing

Wendy made a fresh copy of her revised paragraph and proofread it carefully. The she shared her final copy with friends in her class and with her teacher.

ACTIVITIES AND ASSIGNMENTS

A. Answer the following questions about the case study:
1. Why did Wendy change "body" to "person inside the casket"?
2. Where did Wendy correct a sentence fragment? How did she correct it?

Writing About Images   1281

1. The word *body* implies a lack of consciousness.
2. The final sentence was a fragment. She corrected it by combining it with the previous sentence.
3. She changed the pattern of the fourth sentence. She did this to make her paper read more smoothly.
4. She changed several words to make the language more precise. She corrected several spelling mistakes. She made two necessary changes in punctuation.
5. Suggested Response: She should have introduced a variation in sentence structure in the sixth through eighth sentences.

3. Where did Wendy change the organization of her paragraph? Why did she make the change?
4. What other changes and corrections did Wendy make? Why did she make them?
5. What other revisions would you make in Wendy's paragraph? Why?

B. Select one of the following poems for a paragraph on images: Emily Dickinson's "There's a certain Slant of light," on page 373; Walt Whitman's "When I Heard the Learn'd Astronomer," on page 470; Edwin Arlington Robinson's "Richard Cory," on page 624; Ezra Pound's "In a Station of the Metro," on page 800; Amy Lowell's "Patterns," on page 822; or H.D.'s "Heat," on page 830. Follow these steps when planning and writing your paragraph:
1. Read the poem several times. Freewrite about the mood the poem creates.
2. Make a list in your notes of the specific images of sight, sound, touch, taste, and smell in the poem. Also note how each image contributes to the mood of the poem as a whole.
3. Use your notes to write a thesis statement that introduces the topic of your paragraph: the mood of the poem and the images that help to create it.
4. Make a rough outline for your paragraph. In the outline, show what information you will present in the introduction, body, and conclusion. Make sure that you include evidence for your thesis statement in the body of your paragraph.
5. Write a draft of your paragraph. Then revise the draft carefully, adding more specific examples from the poem and changing the organization where necessary.
6. Proofread your paper thoroughly and make a final copy of it. Share your paragraph with your classmates and with your teacher.

Lesson 5: Writing About Sound

SOUND AND MEANING

When prose or poetry is read aloud, the way the words sound contributes to the meaning that the listener attaches to the work. In the following poem, sound and meaning are closely related:

THE WORKER

Richard W. Thomas

My father lies black and hushed
Beneath white hospital sheets
He collapsed at work
His iron left him
Slow and quiet he sank
Meeting the wet concrete floor on his way
The wheels were still turning—they couldn't
   stop
And as they carried him out
The whirling and buzzing and humming
   machines
Applauded him
Lapping up his dripping iron
       They couldn't stop

Techniques of Sound

The chart at right describes some common devices of sound that writers use to enhance the meaning of their writing. The examples are from Thomas's poem.

WHY WRITERS USE DEVICES OF SOUND

Devices of sound enrich the meaning of literature in many ways. In "The Worker," for instance, Thomas contrasts the quiet hospital—emphasized by the *sh* sounds in "hu*sh*ed" and "*sh*eets"—with the noisy machinery where the father works—emphasized by the use of cacophony and onomatopoeia. Sound devices can highlight individual words, connect related words, or link words in a pattern that unites a stanza or an entire poem. Repeated sounds can also lead readers to expect and follow a musical pattern.

Alliteration: repetition of initial consonant sounds, as in "Meeting the *w*et concrete floor on his *w*ay / The *w*heels *w*ere still turning."

Assonance: repetition of vowel sounds, as in "B*e*neath ... sh*ee*ts."

Consonance: repetition of consonant sounds at the ends of words or accented syllables, as in "white hospital sheet*s*."

Rhyme: repetition of sounds in the final syllables of words. *Exact rhyme* means words that have identical final syllables, and *slant rhyme* refers to words whose last syllables are similar but not identical, as in "L*apping* up his d*ripping* iron." *End rhyme* occurs when the rhyming words appear at the ends of lines of poetry, and *internal rhyme* is when they appear within the lines.

Cacophony: harsh, unpleasant sounds, as in "Gloved hands twisting knobs."

Euphony: beautiful, pleasant sounds, as in "Slow and quiet he sank."

Onomatopoeia: use of words that sound like what they mean, as in "buzzing and humming."

Parallelism: the use of phrases, clauses, or sentences that have similar grammatical structures, as in "Red and yellow lights flashing/Gloved hands twisting."

Repetition: the repeated use of a sound, word, phrase, or line. The clause "they couldn't stop" is repeated in "The Worker." Alliteration, assonance, consonance, rhyme, and parallelism are examples of repetition.

Meter: the regular rhythmical pattern of words, as in "The whirling and buzzing and humming machines."

Writing About Sound 1283

Motivation/Prior Knowledge
Ask your students why they think that poetry is so frequently read aloud. Point out that the sound of a poem can reinforce and even contribute to a poem's meaning. In "The Raven," for example, Edgar Allan Poe uses sound devices to create a hypnotic effect that draws the reader or listener into the speaker's increasingly irrational world; and in Sidney Lanier's "Song of the Chattahoochee," sound devices are used to echo the movement of the river.

1. The word *suggest* is more precise.
2. His addition explains the effect of the alliteration.
3. He did so because the mood is related to the use of sound devices.
4. The seventh sentence was a run-on sentence. He divided it into two sentences.
5. He removed the reference to himself. He did so because it is improper for the writer to refer to himself or herself in a literary analysis.
6. He made a great number of necessary changes in spelling, punctuation, and word choice.

CASE STUDY: WRITING ABOUT DEVICES OF SOUND

Clyde's English class was studying the use of sound in poetry. For a homework assignment, Clyde decided to write about the following poem:

THE WATCH

Frances Cornford

I wakened on my hot, hard bed,
Upon the pillow lay my head;
Beneath the pillow I could hear
My little watch was ticking clear
I thought the throbbing of it went
Like my continual discontent.
I thought it said in every tick:
I am so sick, so sick, so sick.
O death, come quick, come quick, come quick,
Come quick, come quick, come quick, come
    quick!

Prewriting

First Clyde read the poem aloud several times, listening carefully to its sounds. Then he made a list of the devices of sound in the poem, as follows:

- Alliteration:
  "*h*ot *h*ard bed, / . . . lay my *h*ead"
  "*th*ought the *th*robbing"

- Assonance:
  "B*ea*n*ea*th . . . h*ea*r"
  "l*i*ttle . . . t*i*cking"

- Consonance:
  "har*d* . . . hea*d*"

- Rhyme:
  "bed"/"head"
  "hear"/"clear"
  "went"/"discontent"
  "tick"/"sick"/"quick"

- Cacophony:
  "I wakened on my hot, hard bed"

- Onomatopoeia:
  Last three lines sound like ticking

- Repetition:
  "so sick"
  "come quick"

- Meter:
  Iambic tetrameter—very regular, like the ticking of a watch

Clyde looked over his notes and decided to use a topic organization, discussing each sound device in turn. He then made a rough outline for his paper.

Drafting and Revising

Clyde wrote and revised the draft of his paper shown on the next page.

Proofreading and Publishing

Clyde proofread his paper for errors in grammar, usage, spelling, punctuation, and capitalization. Then he made a final copy of his writing and shared it with his family and with his teacher.

ACTIVITIES AND ASSIGNMENTS

A. Answer the following questions about the case study:
1. Why did Clyde change "show" to "suggest" in the first sentence of his paper?
2. Why did Clyde add the words "emphasizes words to introduce the rhythm of the poem" to the second sentence?
3. Why did Clyde add a reference to the mood of the poem?
4. Where did Clyde correct a run-on sentence? How did he do this?
5. How did Clyde revise his concluding sentence? Why did he revise it?
6. What other changes did Clyde make in his paper? Why did he make them?

B. Choose one of the following poems for a one- to three-paragraph composition on devices of sound: Edgar Allan Poe's "The Raven," on page 227; Ralph Waldo Emerson's "Brahma," on page 285; Henry Wadsworth Longfellow's "The Tide Rises, The Tide Falls," on page 338; Carl Sandburg's "Chicago," on page 844; E. E. Cummings's "anyone lived in a pretty how town," on page 865; or Langston Hughes's "The Negro Speaks of Rivers," on page 911.

Follow these steps when planning and writing your composition:

1. Read the poem aloud several times, listening very carefully to the sounds. Freewrite about the general effect created by these sounds.

2. Make a list in your notes of specific devices of sound used in the poem to create the general effect that you have already noted.

3. Decide in what order you will present the information in your paper. You might discuss the poem line by line, or you might explain each sound device in turn. When you have decided how you intend to organize your writing, make an outline for your composition.

4. Write a draft of your composition, referring often to your outline and to your notes. Then revise your paper, using the Checklist for Revision on page 1274.

5. Proofread your paper, using the Checklist for Proofreading on page 1277. Then make a clean final copy of your composition and share this copy with your classmates and with your teacher.

In her poem entitled "The Watch," Frances Cornford uses many devices of sound to show [*suggest*] a watch ticking. ~~Alliteration is one of them—for~~ [*For example, the*] ~~example,~~ [*in*] "on my *hot*, *hard* bed, / . . . lay my [*emphasizes words to introduce the rythm of the poem*] head." ~~Then she also uses~~ [*The*] assonance as in "Beneath the pillow I could hear" and [*the*] repetition of *t* sounds ~~as~~ in "my *little* watch was [*also shows the rythm*] *ticking* clear" and "continual discontent." [*@*] End rhyme also contributes to the sound of the [*The*] poem. ~~An example of cacophony can be found~~ in the first line—"I wakened on my *hot*, *hard* [*sets up an uncomfortable mood*] bed." Cornford uses words onomatopoetically [*to create the*] in the last three lines, ~~which~~ sound ~~just exactly~~ [*of*] ~~like~~ a watch ticking. Also in the last three lines, the words *so sick* and *come quick* are repeated several times for *affect* [*effect*] and the meter of the entire poem is a very regular iambic tetrameter, [*imitates*] which ~~suggests~~ the ticking of the narrator's watch as well. ~~I liked the way~~ every element in the poem contributed [*contributes*] to a single, ~~real~~ [*very*] striking effect.

Motivation/Prior Knowledge
List the following figures of speech across the top of the chalkboard so that each word has a column beneath it: apostrophe, hyperbole, metaphor, oxymoron, paradox, and simile. Then make sure that all of the students are familiar with each of these devices. Explain any of the figures of speech with which they are unfamiliar. Then have the students try to come up with examples of each of these figures of speech from works of literature they have read. Have one of the students record the responses in the appropriate columns.

Lesson 6: Writing About Figures of Speech

WHAT ARE FIGURES OF SPEECH?

Figures of speech are words or phrases used imaginatively to suggest more than their literal meanings. The following chart defines and illustrates some of the common figures of speech found in literature:

Apostrophe: the direct address of an object, idea, or absent person, as in the following poem:

WHERE HAVE YOU GONE?

Mari Evans

Where have you gone

with your confident
walk with
your crooked smile

why did you leave
me
when you took your
laughter
and departed

Hyperbole: exaggeration or overstatement. The following poem uses hyperbole to describe the energetic feelings of the narrator:

TO SATCH (OR AMERICAN GOTHIC)

Samuel Allen (Paul Vesey)

Sometimes I feel like I will *never*
    stop
Just go on forever
Till one fine mornin
I'm gonna reach up and grab me a
    handfulla stars
Swing out on my long lean leg
And whip three hot strikes burnin
    down the heavens
And look over at God and say
How about that!

Irony: the use of words to suggest the opposite

of what they literally mean. In the following poem, the author uses the word *intelligent* ironically:

EARTH

John Hall Wheelock

"A planet doesn't explode of
    itself," said dryly
The Martian astronomer, gazing off
    into the air—
"That they were able to do it is
    proof that highly
Intelligent beings must have been
    living there."

Metaphor: writing or speaking about one thing as if it were something very different. The following poem speaks metaphorically of the task of writing poetry:

WRITING A POEM

Naomi Long Madgett

Writing a poem is trying to catch
    a fluff of cloud
With open-fingered hands.

Oxymoron: using two contradictory words to describe the same object, as in the last phrase of this poem, "Solitude Late at Night in the Woods," by Robert Bly:

Nothing but bare trunks climbing/
    like cold fire!

Paradox: a statement that seems obviously false but is somehow true. The following poem is based on a paradox:

MUCH MADNESS IS DIVINEST SENSE—

Emily Dickinson

Much Madness is divinest Sense—
To a discerning Eye—
Much Sense—the starkest Madness—
'Tis the Majority

Personification: writing or speaking about a nonhuman subject as if it had human

1286 *Handbook of Writing About Literature*

characteristics, as in these lines from "February Twilight," by Sara Teasdale:

> I stood and watched an evening star
> As long as it watched me.

Simile: a comparison between two dissimilar things using *like* or *as*. Note the examples of simile in the following poem:

UNTITLED

Lucille Clifton

> the thirty eighth year
> of my life,
> plain as bread
> round as a cake
> an ordinary woman.

Figures of speech such as metaphor, personification, and simile have two parts, called the tenor and the vehicle. The *tenor* is the subject that is being described in the figure of speech. The *vehicle* is an object that shares one or more characteristics with the tenor and that is used as a means to describe it. For instance, in the Lucille Clifton poem quoted above, the tenor of both similes is the narrator's life, and the vehicles are bread and a cake.

WHY WRITERS USE FIGURES OF SPEECH

Writers use figurative language, or figures of speech, to make their writing more vivid and concrete. Figurative language can also draw powerful emotional or imaginative responses from a reader. Through interesting comparisons and surprising combinations of words and ideas, figurative language can move the reader and enrich his or her appreciation of the human experience.

CASE STUDY: WRITING ABOUT FIGURES OF SPEECH

Leslie's English teacher asked the class to select a poem and to write a paragraph about the figures of speech used in it. Leslie decided to write about Arna Bontemps's "A Black Man Talks of Reaping," on page 916.

Prewriting

Leslie read the poem several times. She decided that the central figure of speech used in "A Black Man Talks of Reaping" is a metaphor. She made the following observations in her prewriting notes:

- Tenor: racism

- Vehicle: harvest/farming

- Shared characteristics:
    Planting deep
    Kept safe against lean years
    Scattered seeds
    Reap only what hand sows
    Work in fields that others have sown
    Feed on bitter fruit

Leslie decided that the metaphor would be the focus of her paragraph, and she made a rough outline organizing her information.

Drafting and Revising

Leslie used her prewriting notes and her outline to write a draft of her paragraph. Her draft, along with the revisions that she made in it, is shown on the next page.

Proofreading and Publishing

Leslie made a clean final copy of her paragraph for her teacher, who suggested that she read it aloud to the class.

ACTIVITIES AND ASSIGNMENTS

A. Answer the following questions about the draft in the case study:
1. Why did Leslie add "the persistence of" to the first sentence of her paragraph?

¶ In the poem "A Black Man Talks of Reaping",

Arna Bontemps employs a metaphor to illustrate
the persistence of
racial prejudice against the black man.
            is   suggests a
Bontemps metaphor ~~forces the~~ comparison
                              and the
between sowing and reaping the harvest ~~with~~

~~the~~ sowing and reaping of racial prejudice.

Both the farmer and the black man "keep safe"
                              meager
against the lean years when harvests are ~~meek~~
                              farmer
and racial tensions are raw. Like the ~~black~~
        black man
~~man~~, the ~~farmer~~ reaps only what he sows. Yet,

the black man and his children continue to pay

for what others have sown, feeding on the

"bitter fruit" of prejudice.

2. Where did Leslie correct errors in word choice?
3. What spelling and punctuation corrections did Leslie make?
4. Where did Leslie originally confuse the tenor and the vehicle of the metaphor in the poem?

How did she correct her error?

B. Select one of the following poems for a one- to three-paragraph composition on figures of speech: Henry Wadsworth Longfellow's "A Psalm of Life," on page 340; Emily Dickinson's "I heard a Fly buzz—when I died—," on page 383; Walt Whitman's "A Noiseless Patient Spider," on page 473; Paul Laurence Dunbar's "We Wear the Mask," on page 614; Wallace Stevens's "Anecdote of the Jar," on page 819; or Randall Jarrell's "The Death of the Ball Turret Gunner," on page 1119. Follow these steps:
1. Read the poem several times. Make a handwritten copy of the poem to familiarize yourself with the exact language used in it.
2. Find examples of figures of speech in the poem and list them in a chart in your notes.
3. Pick the one or two figures of speech that you think are most important to the poem. Write a thesis statement that tells the title and author of the poem and that introduces the central figure(s) of speech.
4. Write the rest of your composition, based on your prewriting notes. Then revise your paper, making sure that it is logically organized and clear.
5. Proofread your composition and make a clean final copy. Then share it with your classmates and with your teacher.

Lesson 7: Writing About Setting

WHAT IS SETTING?

The writer of a narrative work establishes a *setting*—a time and place in which the action occurs. The description of the setting may present details of the geographical location, the date in history, the season and the weather, the physical buildings and rooms, the social environment, and the characters' dress, manners, and customs.

Ann Petry's story "Doby's Gone" is about a young black girl beginning school. The writer opens the story in this manner:

> When Doby first came into Sue Johnson's life her family were caretakers on a farm way up in New York State. And because Sue had no one else to play with, the Johnsons reluctantly accepted Doby as a member of the family.
>
> The spring that Sue was six they moved to Wessex, Connecticut—a small New England town whose neat colonial houses cling to a group of hills overlooking the Connecticut River.

This description of the setting introduces the location of the story and also the characters' backgrounds.

Often the information provided about the setting includes images of sight, sound, touch, taste, and smell. Notice the imagery used in the opening of Elizabeth Sullivan's "Legend of the Trail of Tears":

> Annakee observed the beauty around her. It was a beautiful day. The fruit tree blossoms were in bloom, corn and tobacco had been planted and the cottonwood leaves were like glass. . . . The south wind sprang up. The clouds became very dark and it began to rain.

In this story the setting is especially important. It represents all that the Creek tribe lost when they had to give up their lands.

HOW WRITERS USE SETTING

The following chart describes some of the functions setting can perform in a literary work:

USES OF SETTING
To make a story seem more believable
To help establish a story's mood
To act as the force against which the protagonist struggles, the source of the central conflict
To symbolize an idea the writer wants to reinforce in the mind of the reader
To reflect or contrast with other elements of the story, such as a character's feelings or a theme

CASE STUDY: WRITING ABOUT SETTING

Alvin read Robert Frost's poem "Stopping by Woods on a Snowy Evening," on page 893. He was intrigued by the setting created by Frost, and he decided to write a paragraph about this setting for his English class.

Prewriting

Alvin reread "Stopping by Woods on a Snowy Evening" and discovered several points about the setting that he had overlooked the first time. Then he made the following notes:

- Important details of the setting:
  - Next to woods
  - Away from village
  - Snowing
  - "without a farmouse near"
  - "frozen lake"
  - "The darkest evening of the year."
  - "the sweep/of easy wind and downy flake"
  - "The woods are lovely, dark and deep"

Writing About Setting 1289

- Mood created by setting:
  Ominous ("frozen lake," "darkest evening")
  Peaceful ("easy wind and downy flake," "lovely, dark and deep")

- Symbolic roles of elements in setting:
  Woods traditional symbols of confusion, of being lost
  Snow and winter traditional symbols of death

Alvin decided that although the setting does indeed provide a backdrop for the poem, there is a more important function that it serves. This function is to symbolize the main idea, or theme, of the poem. Alvin wrote a topic sentence and made a rough outline for his paragraph.

Drafting and Revising

Alvin used his notes and his outline to write the following rough draft of his paragraph:

The Setting of Robert Frosts Stopping by Woods on a Snowey Evening creates more than just a backdrop for the poem. The setting also serves a symbolic purpose that is a key to understanding Frost's meaning. In the poem, the speaker has stopped on a country roadway to watch the "woods filling up with snow." That the speaker is in the countryside is obvious. From the fact that he refers to owner of the woods as being absent and "in the village." in the second stanza of the poem, the reader learns that the speaker beleives that his horse "must think it queer" to be stopping in the woods at this time. After all, the lake is "frozen" and this is "The darkest evening of the year." Stopping at such a time and in such a place can be dangerous, as the ominous words "frozen" and "darkest" suggest. However, the speaker is lulled by "the sweep/Of easy wind and downy flake"—by the fact that "The woods are lovely, dark and deep. In poetry, woods are traditional symbols of confusion—of being lost. Snow and winter are traditional symbols of death. On a symbolic level, therefore, the setting symbolizes the speakers attraction to and longing for the peacefullness that death would bring. In the

final stanza, the speaker reminds himself that he has "promises to keep" and should go on. However, the repetition in the final lines seems to indicate that the speaker is repeating things to himself as one does sometimes before falling off to sleep. The poem might therefor be a warning to poeple not to be attracted to the peacefulness of death or simply a warning against complacency.

Alvin revised his draft to make it more clearly organized and specific. Then he made a fresh copy of the draft for proofreading.

Proofreading and Publishing

Alvin proofread his paragraph for errors in spelling and mechanics. Then he shared the final copy of his paper with his class discussion group and with his English teacher.

ACTIVITIES AND ASSIGNMENTS

A. Revise and proofread Alvin's paragraph. Find and correct a sentence fragment, an error in a quotation, and several errors in spelling and punctuation.

B. Choose one of the following works for a composition on setting: Washington Irving's "The Devil and Tom Walker," on page 184, William Cullan Bryant's "Thanatopsis," on page 207; the selection from John Greenleaf Whittier's "Snowbound," on page 360; Jack London's "To Build a Fire," on page 566; William Faulkner's "The Bear," on page 734; or Wallace Stevens's "Disillusionment of Ten O'Clock," on page 818. Write a one- or two-paragraph analysis of the setting by following these steps:

1. Read the work once. Freewrite about the mood or atmosphere that the setting creates. Then read the story or poem again, noting specific details of the setting used to create the mood. Also write down any other functions that the setting performs and relate these functions to details in the work.

2. Write a topic sentence for your paper that tells the title and author of the work and that introduces the most important function of the setting. Then make an outline for the rest of your paper.
3. Write a draft of your paper, based on your notes and your outline. Make sure that your writing does not stray from your purpose of showing the significance of the setting.
4. Revise your draft, making sure that it has a clear introduction, body, and conclusion. Also check to see that every statement you have made is supported by evidence from the work.
5. Proofread your revised draft for errors in grammar, usage, spelling, punctuation, capitalization, and manuscript form. Make a clean final copy of your paper, and share this copy with classmates who have read the work. Then share your writing with your English teacher.

Lesson 8: Writing About Plot

Motivation/Prior Knowledge

Point out that many twentieth-century writers have chosen to abandon the traditional plot structure. This is why many twentieth-century novels and stories lack an exposition, a resolution, and a denouement. This approach reflects the writers' view of life in the twentieth century as being disillusioning, fragmentary, and confusing.

WHAT IS PLOT?

The series of events or actions in a narrative work is called the *plot.* The basis of the plot is a *conflict,* or struggle. Some plots contain more than one conflict, but most narratives focus on one central conflict involving the protagonist. Conflicts can be internal or external. An *internal conflict* takes place within the mind of a character as he or she struggles with an important decision or with a strong feeling such as fear or hatred. An *external conflict* is a struggle between a character and some outside force. This outside force may be another character or a group of characters; a natural or nonhuman force, such as a flood; or a political or social institution or custom.

THE PARTS OF A PLOT

A plot may be logically divided into six parts, as follows:

1. *Exposition:* Also called the introduction, the exposition is the opening part of a narrative in which the writer gives background information about the setting, the characters, and the basic situation.
2. *Inciting incident:* The inciting incident is the event that sets the story in motion; it introduces the central conflict.
3. *Development:* The development includes all the events that follow from the inciting incident up to the climax. In this part of a narrative, the main character normally struggles to overcome obstacles to achieve some goal.
4. *Climax:* The climax is the high point of interest or suspense in the work.
5. *Resolution:* The resolution is the point in the narrative when the central conflict is ended. In

many stories the resolution and the climax are identical.

6. *Denouement:* The denouement includes all the events that take place after the central conflict has been resolved. In this part of the plot, less important conflicts may be resolved and questions still left in the mind of the reader may be answered.

Not all narratives have this exact plot structure. In some works the inciting incident takes place before the opening of the narrative. Some stories end with the resolution and thus lack a denouement. In addition, writers often employ special techniques that alter the structures of their plots.

SPECIAL TECHNIQUES OF PLOT

The following list describes some techniques writers use to make their plots more interesting and enjoyable for readers:

1. *Foreshadowing:* This technique involves hinting at an event or events that will happen later in the narrative. Foreshadowing is often very subtle, so readers must be constantly on the lookout for clues to how the plot will unfold.
2. *Flashback:* A flashback is a section of a narrative that interrupts the chronological order of events to relate something that happened in the past. Flashbacks may help to explain the motivations behind a character's actions by telling the reader about his or her past experiences.
3. *Suspense:* The tension that builds as the reader wonders how the central conflict will be resolved is known as suspense. Writers create suspense by raising questions in the reader's mind about what will happen next.
4. *Surprise ending:* An unexpected turn of events

at the resolution is called a surprise ending. An effective surprise ending is achieved by leading the reader to expect the conflict to end in a certain way and then abruptly changing the direction of the story.

CASE STUDY: WRITING ABOUT PLOT

Todd's English class learned about plot structure in narrative works. Then his teacher asked the class to select a short story and to write a paragraph analyzing its plot. Todd chose Ambrose Bierce's "An Occurrence at Owl Creek Bridge," on page 530.

Prewriting

Todd read the story several times to familiarize himself with all the techniques the author had used in constructing the plot. Then he made a list of the events in the story. He studied this list and identified the parts of the plot. Finally, he made notes about each part of the plot, as follows:

- Introduction: rich description of a military hanging of a civilian on a railroad bridge in northern Alabama during the Civil War; includes foreshadowing—"If I could free my hands"

- Inciting incident: (occurs before start of story) Peyton Farquhar was caught tampering with a Yankee-held bridge; punishment is hanging

- Development: the rope breaks; Peyton falls into the stream and escapes; detailed description of how Peyton dodges bullets and escapes

- Climax: Peyton eventually reaches the safety of his home

- False resolution: Peyton reaches out to embrace his wife; everything turns silent and dark

- Real resolution/surprise ending: Payton's body swings beneath the timbers of Owl Creek Bridge—he is dead

Drafting and Revising

Todd used his prewriting notes to write a draft of his paragraph. Then he revised his draft to make it clearer and better organized.

Proofreading and Publishing

Todd made a fresh copy of his paragraph and proofread it for errors in spelling and mechanics. Then he made a final copy and shared it with his parents, his classmates, and his teacher.

ACTIVITIES AND ASSIGNMENTS

A. Read the story "An Occurrence at Owl Creek Bridge," on page 530. Then use Todd's prewriting notes from the case study to write a paragraph about the story's plot. Follow these steps:

1. Write a topic sentence that tells the title and author of the story and introduces the main idea of your paragraph. Make an outline for your writing that shows how you will organize the information in your introduction, body, and conclusion.

2. Write a draft of your paragraph, following your outline. Make sure that you support all your main points with specific evidence from the story. Conclude with a sentence or two explaining why the story is an enjoyable one to read.

3. Revise and proofread the paragraph. Share your final copy with a small group of your classmates. Then give your paper to your teacher.

B. Select one of the following short stories for a paragraph on plot: Washington Irving's "The Devil and Tom Walker," on page 184; Edgar Allan Poe's "The Fall of the House of

Usher," on page 212; Bret Harte's "The Outcasts of Poker Flat," on page 518; or Willa Cather's "A Wagner Matinée," on page 556. Follow these steps:

1. Read the story once. Make a list of the events that take place in the story and group them under these headings: Introduction, Inciting incident, Development, Climax, Resolution, and Denouement. Then read the story a second time and look for special techniques of plot that the author has used. Make notes about these techniques and about how they contribute to the story.

2. Write a topic sentence for your paragraph. Then make an outline for the rest of your paragraph from the information in your prewriting notes.

3. Write a draft of your paragraph. Then revise your draft, making sure that it will be clear to your readers.

4. Proofread your revised draft, checking for errors in grammar, usage, spelling, punctuation, capitalization, and manuscript form. Share the final copy of your paragraph wtih your classmates and with your teacher.

Lesson 9: Writing About Character

TYPES OF CHARACTERS

The people and animals who take part in the action of a narrative work are called *characters*. The *protagonist* is the most important character in a work, the character who faces the central conflict. Other characters who play significant roles in the story are called *major characters*, and those who play less important roles are called *minor characters*. A major character who is in direct conflict with the protagonist is called the *antagonist*.

WHAT IS CHARACTERIZATION?

Characterization is the process by which a writer reveals the nature of a particular character. In this passage from "The Snow Keeps Falling," author Janet Campbell characterizes a minor character through a description of her physical appearance:

> She's sitting on the edge of her desk, casual like, one knee drawn up a little. She has greasy, thin hair, blond in places, grey-brown in places, hanging loose and stringy around her face. Little raw-looking red pimples dot her chin and forehead. She has a cold and her nose is red and runny.

By describing what the character looks like, Campbell creates certain expectations in the reader about what the character's personality is like.

James Baldwin, on the other hand, in describing the protagonist in *Go Tell It on the Mountain*, says nothing about the character's physical appearance:

> Everyone had always said that John would be a preacher when he grew up, just like his father. It had been said so often that John, without ever thinking about it, had come to believe it himself. Not until the morning of his fourteenth birthday did he really begin to think about it, and by then it was already too late.

This passage tells the reader something about the character's background and what people expect from him.

HOW WRITERS CREATE CHARACTER

In creating a believable character, a writer may use a number of different techniques of characterization. *Direct characterization* is the simplest method. It involves merely stating what the character is like. A statement such as "Tim had a mischievous streak" is an example of direct characterization.

A more subtle way of revealing a character is through *indirect characterization*. In this case the writer shows what a character is like by describing how the character appears, what the character says and does, and how other characters react to the character. When a writer uses indirect characterization, it is up to the reader to gather clues about the character and to draw conclusions based on those clues.

Elements of Character

A well-developed character in a literary work has many facets, just as a real person does. When you analyze a character, ask yourself the following questions about the portrayal of the character:

1. *Appearance*: How does the character look and dress? What do these aspects of appearance reveal about the character?
2. *Words and actions*: What kinds of things does the character say and do? What kind of language does the character use? What can the reader learn about the character from his or her words and actions?

Writing About Character 1295

Motivation/Prior Knowledge
Have your students discuss how the characters affect their response to a work of fiction. Are they likely to appreciate the work if the characters seem one-dimensional, stereotypical, or unconvincing? Are they likely to appreciate the work if they cannot sympathize with the characters? The students' responses to these types of questions should highlight the importance of characters in literary works.

3. *Background*: Where did the character grow up? What kind of educational background does the character have? What past experiences has the character had? How does the character's background affect his or her thoughts and actions in the present?

4. *Personality*: Does the character tend to be emotional or rational? principled or unscrupulous? obstinate or open-minded? caring or cold?

5. *Motivation*: What makes the character act and speak as he or she does? What does the character value? What are the character's goals? dreams? desires? needs?

6. *Relationships*: How does the character interact with other characters in the work? Who are his or her friends and enemies?

7. *Conflict*: Is the character involved in some conflict? If so, is the conflict *internal*—within the character's mind—or *external*—between the character and an outside force? How is the conflict resolved?

8. *Change*: Does the character change or grow in the course of the story? If so, how? How does the reader know that the character has changed?

CASE STUDY: WRITING ABOUT CHARACTER

Angela's English class was asked to write a paragraph about a character in a narrative work. Angela decided to write about the protagonist of Eudora Welty's short story "A Worn Path," on page 710.

Prewriting

Angela read the story several times, paying close attention to the characterization of Phoenix Jackson, the main character. In her prewriting notes, Angela answered the questions about character listed in this lesson. She also gathered specific details from the story to support her answers. Then she made a rough outline for her paragraph.

Drafting and Revising

Angela wrote the following draft of her paragraph:

> The main character of Eudora Welty's short story: "A Worn Path" is an elderly woman named Phoenix Jackson. Phoenix lives in the country and periodically makes her way along the wooden path to reach Natchez. The author describes Phoenix as small, with her hair tied in a "red rag". Phoenix carries a cane made from an umbrella to steady her step. Phoenix appears to be an independant, courageous character, talking to the animals as she walked. Phoenix meets a hunter along the way but she shows no fear of this stranger. Upon reaching Natchez, Phoenix's motivation for her long walk is revealed—to get medicine for her grandson. With the nickle the hunter dropped and the nickle the nurse gave her she buys a paper windmill for her grandson. We maybe see how a simple windmill signifies for Phoenix the simple but more important joy of love and generosity.

Angela realized that her rough draft needed some major revisions. As she revised, Angela added details, combined sentences, eliminated sentence fragments, and clarified several of her statements.

Proofreading and Publishing

After revising her draft, Angela made a fresh copy and proofread it for errors in spelling, punctuation, and capitalization. Then Angela shared her paragraph with her class discussion group.

ACTIVITIES AND ASSIGNMENTS

A. Revise and proofread the draft in the case study. Follow these steps:

1. Read the draft, noting its overall organization. Does the draft have a topic sentence? Does it contain supporting evidence? Does it have a definite conclusion? Supply whatever parts are missing.

2. Check to see whether any sentences can be improved by combining. Notice that many of Angela's sentences begin in the same way.

Try to vary her sentence openings. Correct any sentence fragments or run-on sentences in the draft.

3. Rewrite any parts that are unclear. Check to make sure that transition words such as *however*, *although*, and *next* have been used to relate the sentences logically to one another.

4. Make sure that Angela's claims about the story are all supported by the text.

5. Make any other changes that you think are necessary. Use the Checklist for Proofreading, on page 1277, to proofread your paragraph. Then share the final copy with your classmates and with your teacher.

B. Select one of the following short stories for a paragraph about character: Edgar Allan Poe's "The Fall of the House of Usher," on page 212; Nathaniel Hawthorne's "The Minister's Black Veil," on page 302; Katherine Anne Porter's "The Jilting of Granny Weatherall," on page 694; or Flannery O'Connor's "The Life You Save May Be Your Own," on page 956.

Follow these steps:

1. Read the story once. Choose one character from the story and freewrite about that character. Then read the story again and gather details the author has used to characterize the person.

2. Use the prewriting notes to write a draft of your paragraph. Revise your draft, making sure that it has a definite introduction, body, and conclusion.

3. Proofread your writing and make a final copy of your paragraph. Share this copy with your classmates and with your teacher.

WHAT ARE NARRATION AND POINT OF VIEW?

Narration is the act of telling a story. A literary work that tells a story is called a *narrative.* Every narrative has a speaker, or voice. This voice is called the *narrator.*

The perspective of the narrator is called the *point of view* of the story. The point of view determines who will tell the story and what details the story will include.

First-person Point of View If the narrator is a character in the story and refers to himself or herself using "I," the story is told from the *first-person point of view.* The opening lines of Willa Cather's "A Wagner Matinée," on page 556, show that the story is told from the first-person point of view:

> I received one morning a letter written in pale ink, on glassy, blue-lined notepaper, and bearing the postmark of a little Nebraska village.

The first-person point of view is almost always *limited.* That is, the narrator does not know the thoughts and feelings of any of the other characters in the story and can offer only his or her own interpretations of their words and actions.

Third-person Point of View When the narrator is not a character in the story but tells it from outside the action, the story is told from the third-person point of view. A third-person narrator never refers to himself or herself as "I" but uses third-person pronouns such as *she*, *they*, *his*, and *them* to talk about the characters. A writer using the third-person point of view may decide that the narrator will know what one of the characters thinks and feels but only what the others say and do. In this case, the narrator speaks from the *limited third-person point of view*. Ann Beattie's short story "Imagined Scenes," on page 996, is told from the limited third-person point of view. Here is a passage from that story:

> When she wakes from a dream, David is already awake. Or perhaps he only wakes when she stirs, whispers to him. He doesn't sound sleepy; he's alert, serious, as though he'd been waiting for a question. She remembers last year, the week before Christmas.

If a third-person narrator is not limited but knows the thoughts and feelings of every character, that narrator is said to be *omniscient,* or "all-knowing." The following passage from Flannery O'Connor's "The Life You Save May Be Your Own," on page 956, shows that the story is told from the *omniscient third-person point of view*:

> The old woman and her daughter were sitting on their porch when Mr. Shiftlet came up their road for the first time. The old woman slid to the edge of her chair and leaned forward, shading her eyes from the piercing sunset with her hand. The daughter could not see far in front of her and continued to play with her fingers.

Reliability and Unreliability

Besides determining what point of view a narrative is told from, a reader must also consider whether the narrator is biased or prejudiced in any way. Deciding if you can trust what a narrator says is making a judgment about the reliability or unreliability of that narrator. Another consideration is whether the narrator gives an objective or a subjective account of the story's events. An objective narrator simply presents the facts and allows the reader to draw his or her own conclusions. A subjective narrator presents his or her own opinions along with the facts, and the reader must be careful to separate the two.

CASE STUDY: WRITING ABOUT NARRATION AND POINT OF VIEW

Darrell's English class was asked to write a paragraph about the narration and point of view of a short story. Darrell decided to write about "The First Seven Years," by Bernard Malamud, on page 946.

Prewriting

After reading the story once, Darrell concluded that it was told from the limited third-person point of view. Then he reread the story and made careful notes about the narration and point of view. The following are Darrell's prewriting notes:

- Point of view: limited third-person—narrator knows Feld's thoughts only

- Function of point of view: reveals the inner life of the main character; causes the reader to identify with Feld

- Narrator: reliable and objective; we see the world through Feld's eyes; narrator withholds his opinions

Darrell made an outline for his paragraph so that he would not stray from his topic when he began writing.

Drafting and Revising

Darrell used his outline and prewriting notes to write a draft of his paragraph. Then he revised his draft, using editorial symbols. Darrell's revised draft is shown at right.

Proofreading and Publishing

Darrell made a fresh copy of his revised draft and proofread it for errors in grammar, usage, spelling, punctuation, capitalization, and manuscript form. Finally, he shared his paragraph with his classmates by reading it aloud before the class.

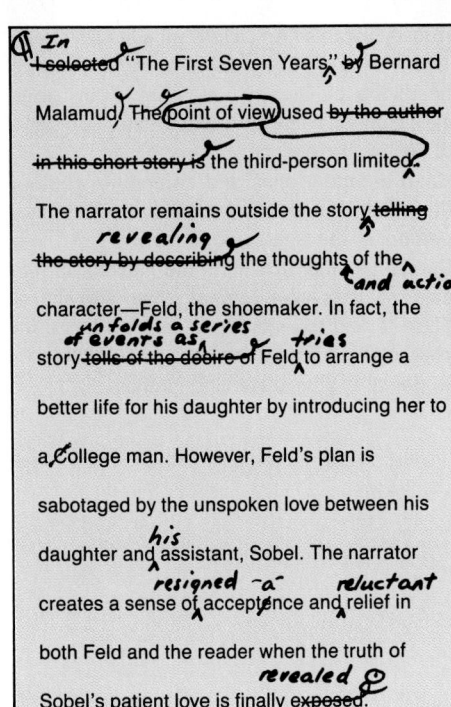

ACTIVITIES AND ASSIGNMENTS

A. Answer the following questions about the case study:
1. What error in manuscript form did Darrell correct in his draft?
2. What sentences did Darrell combine to eliminate unnecessary words?
3. What errors in spelling, punctuation, and capitalization did Darrell correct?
4. To what sentences did Darrell add clarifying details?
5. What informal words and phrases did Darrell replace with language that was more appropriate?

B. Write a two-paragraph composition analyzing the narration and point of view in one of the following short stories: Edgar Allan Poe's "The Fall of the House of Usher," on page 212;

ANSWERS TO ACTIVITIES AND ASSIGNMENTS, SECTION A

1. He indented the paragraph.
2. He combined the first and second sentences.
3. He added a comma to the first sentence. He made the first letter in *college* lower case. He corrected the spelling of *acceptance.*
4. He added clarifying details to the second, third, and fifth sentences.
5. He changed *tells of the desire of* to *unfolds a series of events as.*

Ambrose Bierce's "An Occurrence at Owl Creek Bridge," on page 530; Katherine Anne Porter's "The Jilting of Granny Weatherall," on page 694; or Eudora Welty's "A Worn Path," on page 710. Follow these steps:

1. Read the story once and determine whether the point of view is first-person, limited third-person, or third-person omniscient.

2. Decide whether you think the narrator is reliable or unreliable, objective or subjective. Then reread the story to gather evidence for your opinion about the narrator. Write this evidence in your prewriting notes.

3. Make an outline for your composition. Plan to introduce your topic and to discuss the narrator and point of view of the story in your first paragraph. Then use your second paragraph to discuss the effect the point of view has on a reader or on the presentation of the story.

4. Write a draft of your composition. Then revise your draft, adding details and clarifying ideas where necessary.

5. Proofread your paper and make a clean final copy of it. Share your composition with a small group of your classmates and with your teacher.

Lesson 11: Writing About Theme

WHAT IS THEME?

Although some literary works are intended merely to entertain the reader, most works contain a message that the writer wants to convey. This message is known as the *theme*. A theme usually expresses some insight into the human experience. It may deal with values, ideas, beliefs, or life in general. Complex literary works may express several perceptions about human beings and thus have several different themes.

HOW WRITERS EXPRESS THEMES

In some works the theme may be stated directly, as is the moral in a fable. More often the theme is shown by the impact of the work as a whole. Theme may be revealed through elements of a work such as the title, the characters, the setting, and the resolution of the plot. The writer expects the reader to infer the theme from clues provided by these elements.

CASE STUDY: WRITING ABOUT THEME

Hayley's English class was given an assignment to write about the theme of a poem. Hayley decided to write about the theme of Edwin Arlington Robinson's "Richard Cory," on page 624.

Prewriting

Hayley read the poem several times to make sure that she had not missed any possible clues to its theme. Then she made the following prewriting notes:

- Title: "Richard Cory"
- Author: Edwin Arlington Robinson

- Theme: One should not make generalizations based solely on someone's appearance.

- Ways in which theme is revealed:
  Poem opens with a description of Richard Cory as a gentleman whom everyone admires.
  The townspeople make assumptions about him based on the way he appears to them—handsome, well-spoken, friendly, rich, educated, well-dressed.
  The townspeople continue to work for more money and material things.
  A surprise ending—Richard Cory commits suicide. Where was the "light" in his life? The townspeople did not know him at all.

Drafting and Revising

Hayley wrote a draft of her paragraph, based on her prewriting notes. She began with a topic sentence that stated the title and author of the poem and that introduced the poem's theme. Then, in the body of her paragraph, she used evidence from the poem to show how the theme was revealed. Finally, she wrote a concluding sentence that told how the theme of the poem could be applied to real life. When she had finished her draft, Hayley revised it thoroughly, making sure that all her statements supported her topic sentence.

Proofreading and Publishing

Hayley proofread her revised draft for errors in grammar, usage, spelling, punctuation, capitalization, and manuscript form. Then she made two final copies of her paragraph—one for her English teacher and one for the class literary magazine.

Writing About Theme 1301

Motivation/Prior Knowledge
Explain to your students that interpreting the theme of a literary work will often greatly enhance their appreciation of that work. At the same time, by interpreting the theme of a literary work, they may learn something about themselves, other people, or life in general. However, themes are sometimes difficult to grasp, and students may have to read through a literary work several times to interpret its theme.

ACTIVITIES AND ASSIGNMENTS

A. Using Hayley's prewriting notes from the case study, write a paragraph about the theme of "Richard Cory." Follow these steps:

1. Read the poem once and look at Hayley's prewriting notes. Then read the poem a second time and add to her notes any important details that she omitted. If you think you can state the theme of the poem more accurately than Hayley did in her notes, write a sentence expressing the theme in your own words.
2. Write a topic sentence in which you state the title and author of the poem and its theme. If it will help you to organize your notes, make a rough outline for the rest of your paragraph.
3. Write the body of your paragraph. Make sure that every statement you make is supported by specific evidence from the poem.
4. Write a concluding sentence or two, summarizing the theme and relating it to real life.
5. Revise and proofread the draft carefully. Then make a final copy of your paragraph and share it with a small group of your classmates and with your teacher.

B. Select one of the following works for a paragraph on theme: "Thanatopsis," on page 207; "The Tide Rises, The Tide Falls," on page 338; "Patterns," on page 822; "since feeling is first," on page 864; "Mending Wall," on page 873; "Any Human to Another," on page 873; "Journey," on page 984; or "Mirror," on page 1140. Follow these steps:

1. Read the work once. Try to state the theme in a sentence. Then reread the work, gathering evidence for your statement of theme in your prewriting notes. List all the elements of the work that help to reveal the theme and explain how each accomplishes this task.
2. Revise your statement of theme until it is accurate and clear.
3. Make an outline for your paragraph. In the outline, show how you will present the information in your prewriting notes in the introduction, body, and conclusion of your paragraph.
4. Use your statement of theme to write a topic sentence for your paragraph.
5. Write the body of your paragraph, explaining how each element of the work reveals the theme. Make sure that you include specific details from the work to support your ideas.
6. Write a conclusion of one or two sentences that summarizes the theme of the work and shows how it is relevant to real life.
7. Revise your draft, making sure that all your points are clear. Also check the overall organization of your paragraph and make sure that every statement is related to your purpose.
8. Use the Checklist for Proofreading on page 1277 to proofread your revised draft. Then make a clean final copy of your paragraph, and share this copy with a small group of your classmates before submitting it to your teacher.

Section 3: UNDERSTANDING THE WORK AS A WHOLE: INTERPRETATION AND SYNTHESIS

Lesson 12: Writing About a Short Story

To interpret a short story you must analyze it. First you divide the story into its elements and consider each element separately. Then you think about how each element contributes to the meaning of the work as a whole. The following questions will help you when analyzing a short story:

1. *Author*: Who is the author of the story?
2. *Title*: What is the story's title? Does the title suggest the story's subject or theme?
3. *Setting*: Where and when does the story take place? What details does the writer use to create the setting? Does the setting create a particular mood, or feeling? Is the setting a symbol for an important idea that the writer wants to convey? Does the setting play a role in the central conflict?
4. *Point of view*: Is the story told from the first-person or from the third-person point of view? Is the narrator limited or omniscient? What effect does the point of view have on the way the reader experiences the story?
5. *Central conflict*: What struggle is the main character involved in? Is the central conflict *internal*—within the protagonist's mind—or *external*—between the protagonist and another character, society, or a nonhuman force? How is the conflict resolved?
6. *Plot*: What events take place in the story? Does the story have an introduction? If so, what does the reader learn in the introduction? What is the inciting incident? What happens during the development? When does the climax occur? What event marks the resolution of the central conflict? Does the story have a denouement?

Does the writer make use of special plot devices such as foreshadowing, flashbacks, or a surprise ending? Is the story suspenseful? If so, how does the writer create suspense?

7. *Characterization*: Who is the main character, or protagonist? Who are the other major and minor characters? How does the writer reveal what each of the characters is like? Which characters are in conflict with each other? Do any of the characters change in the course of the work? If so, how and why do they change?
8. *Devices of sound and figures of speech*: Does the writer make use of any devices of sound such as euphony or alliteration? Does the story contain any examples of figurative language such as hyperbole, simile, metaphor, or symbolism? What do these techniques add to the story?
9. *Theme*: What is the theme, or central idea, of the story? How is the theme revealed?

It is often convenient to use a topic organization when writing an analysis of a short story. For example, in the introductory paragraph of your paper, you might state the title, author, and theme of the story. Then you might devote each of your body paragraphs to discussing a particular element of the story and to explaining how this element is related to other elements. For example, one paragraph might explore the setting of the story and show how the setting creates a particular mood. Finally, in your conclud-

1. She combined the first and second sentences.
2. She changed *concealed* to *disguised*, *love* to *kindness*, and *damage* to *ruin*.
3. The second sentence was a run-on sentence.
4. She changed *show* to *shows*. She changed *life* to *lives*.

ing paragraph, you might restate the theme and summarize how each element in the story helps to reveal that theme.

CASE STUDY: WRITING ABOUT A SHORT STORY

Lynn's English teacher asked the class to write a composition presenting an interpretation of a short story. Lynn decided to write about Flannery O'Connor's "The Life You Save May Be Your Own," on page 956.

Prewriting

Lynn read the short story carefully. She then read the list of questions in this lesson and wrote the answers to the questions in her notes. She decided that the main point of her composition would be the theme of the story as suggested by the title. Lynn made the following rough outline for her composition, in which each major heading represents a paragraph:

- Introduction:
  Author
  Title
  Theme

- Plot:
  Of the entire short story
  Of Mr. Shiftlet's story

- Theme as understood by the characters:
  What the old woman and her daughter learned from Mr. Shiftlet
  Idea of story for Mr. Shiftlet

- Conclusion:
  Meaning of the title of the story in light of what has been discussed in preceding paragraphs
  Significance of the theme for readers/real people

Lynn reread the story and added more details to her notes to support her ideas in each paragraph.

Drafting and Revising

Lynn wrote a draft of her four-paragraph composition and then revised it carefully. Here is the first paragraph of Lynn's draft, with her revisions marked in editorial symbols:

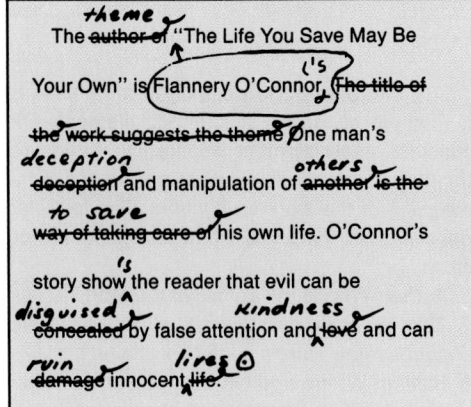

Proofreading and Publishing

Lynn made a fresh copy of her composition and proofread it for errors in spelling and mechanics. Then she shared her composition in a class discussion.

ACTIVITIES AND ASSIGNMENTS

A. Answer the following questions about the revised paragraph in the case study:
1. What sentences did Lynn combine?
2. What words did Lynn replace with ones that were more appropriate?
3. What run-on sentence did Lynn correct?
4. What errors in spelling and punctuation did Lynn correct?

B. Select one of the following short stories for a two- to four-paragraph composition: "The Fall of the House of Usher," on page 212; "The Minister's Black Veil," on page 302; "The Story of an Hour," on page 550; "To Build a Fire," on page 566; "In Another Country," on page 664; "Flight," on page 718; "The Slump," on page 978; or "Anxiety," on page 1006. Follow these steps:

1. Read the story carefully. Answer the questions in this lesson in your prewriting notes.
2. Decide what element of the story will be the focus of your composition. Make a rough outline showing how you will organize your writing.
3. Write a draft of your paragraph. When you revise your draft, make sure that you have provided supporting evidence for each of your statements.
4. Proofread your composition and make a clean final copy of it. Share this copy with your classmates and with your teacher.

Lesson 13: Writing About a Poem

Before you can write an interpretation of a poem as a whole, you must make sure that you understand it thoroughly. To do this, you must analyze the poem and consider each of its parts separately. Then you can assess the meaning of the entire poem. The following steps will guide you in analyzing a poem:

1. Read the poem silently. To make sure that you understand its literal meaning, look up any words or allusions that you do not know in a dictionary or in another reference work. Then paraphrase the poem line by line, restating the literal meaning in your own words.
2. Read the poem aloud several times, listening to the sound of the words as you read them. Ask yourself what effect is created by the sound of the poem.
3. Read the poem silently again. Then make a copy of the poem and mark on the copy any examples of figures of speech and images that you can find.

Answer the following questions in your prewriting notes:

1. *Author:* Who is the author of the poem?
2. *Title:* What is the poem's title? Does the title suggest the poem's subject or theme?
3. *Genre:* What type of poem is it? Is it a lyric poem? a narrative poem? a dramatic poem? If it is a lyric poem, what emotion(s) does it express? Who is the speaker? What is the situation? If it is a narrative poem, what is the plot of the story that it tells? What is the setting? Who are the characters? If it is a dramatic poem, what dramatic techniques—such as monologue or dialogue—does it use? What is the plot? What is the setting? Who are the characters?
4. *Form:* Is the poem divided into stanzas? If so, how many lines are there in each stanza? Does each stanza express a complete thought, like a paragraph in prose writing?

   Is the poem written in any traditional form, such as quatrains, sonnet form, or haiku form? Is the poem written in free verse? What does the poem's form contribute to its meaning?
5. *Imagery:* What images of sight, sound, touch, taste, and smell are used in the poem? What do these images describe? What effect is created by these images?
6. *Figurative language:* Are there any examples of apostrophe in the poem? of hyperbole? of irony? of metaphor? of metonomy? of oxymoron? of paradox? of personification? of simile? of synecdoche? of understatement? What symbols, if any, does the poet use to represent other ideas or things? Does the poet make use of allusion? Is the poem an allegory?
7. *Devices of sound:* What is the rhyme scheme of the poem, if any? What examples of alliteration can you find in the poem? of assonance? of consonance? Does the poet use euphony, cacophony, parallelism, repetition, or a refrain?

   Does the poem have a regular rhythm? If so, what kind of metrical feet does the poem contain? How many feet are there in each line? What effect does the meter of the poem create?
8. *Other elements:* What is the overall mood of the poem? What literary devices create this mood?

   What is the theme of the poem? How is this theme revealed?

CASE STUDY: WRITING ABOUT A POEM

David's English teacher asked the class to select a poem and to write an interpretation of it. David chose Henry Wadsworth Longfellow's "The Tide Rises, The Tide Falls," on page 338.

Prewriting

David began by reading the poem several times, both silently and aloud. Then he made the following notes about the elements of the poem:

- Title: "The Tide Rises, The Tide Falls"

- Author: Henry Wadsworth Longfellow

- Stanza form:
    3 stanzas, 5 lines in each
    First stanza introduces the traveler at dusk.
    Second stanza tells of the traveler's disappearance.
    Third stanza suggests that the traveler is not to be seen again.

- Images of sight:
    "The tide rises, the tide falls"
    "Darkness settles on roofs and walls"
    "The little waves with their soft, white hands"

- Images of sound:
    "The tide rises, the tide falls"
    "the steeds in their stalls stamp and neigh, as the hostler calls"

- Images of touch:
    "sea sands damp and brown"

- Personification:
    "waves with their soft, white hands"

- Rhyme scheme: *aabbc*

- Alliteration:
    "*s*ea *s*ands"
    "*st*eeds in their *st*alls *st*amp and neigh"

- Euphony/repetition:
    "The tide rises, the tide falls"

- Mood:
    Inevitability of tides
    Acceptance of cycle of life

- Theme: The cycle of life and death is as inevitable and as predictable as the rising and falling of the tides.

Drafting and Revising

David used his prewriting notes to write a draft of his composition. In the first paragraph, he discussed the likeness between the life cycle and the ebb and flow of the tide. In the last sentence of the first paragraph, David stated his thesis, or main idea:

> Henry Wadsworth Longfellow, in his poem "The Tide Rises, The Tide Falls," portrays the cycle of life and death as the comforting ebb and flow of the tide.

In his second paragraph, David discussed the three stanzas of the poem. He explained how the poet suggests the cycle of life and death through the use of rhyme, repetition of phrases, and imagery.

In his third and final paragraph, David discussed the theme of the poem and explained the value of the poem to readers.

David wrote several versions of his draft. Then he revised the best of these drafts.

Proofreading and Publishing

After proofreading his draft, David made a final copy and gave it to his English teacher. His teacher suggested that he read the poem and his interpretation aloud to the class.

ACTIVITIES AND ASSIGNMENTS

A. Use David's prewriting notes to write a three-paragraph composition that offers an interpretation of "The Tide Rises, The Tide Falls." Then revise and proofread your composition, and share your final copy with your classmates and with your teacher.

B. Select one of the following poems to analyze in a two- to four-paragraph composition: "A Psalm of Life," on page 340; "Hampton Beach," on page 366; "Because I could not stop for Death—," on page 383; "War Is Kind," on page 609; "Miniver Cheevy," on page 622; "The Love Song of J. Alfred Prufrock," on page 810; "Disillusionment of Ten O'Clock," on page 818; "Poetry," on page 860; "Nothing Gold Can Stay," on page 892; "The Tropics in New York," on page 906; "The Waking," on page 906; "Expect Nothing," on page 1126; or "Most Satisfied by Snow," on page 1160. Follow these steps:

1. Read the poem several times, both silently and aloud. Follow the steps in the lesson for analyzing the poem.
2. Make an outline for your composition. Show what information from your prewriting notes you will include in each of your paragraphs. Make sure that your paper has a definite introduction, thesis statement, body, and conclusion.
3. Write a draft of your composition. Then revise your draft, adding evidence to support your claims where necessary. Also make sure that you have expressed your ideas clearly.
4. Proofread your paper and make a clean final copy of it. Share your composition with your teacher and with classmates who have analyzed the same poem.

Lesson 14: Writing About Drama

DRAMA AS LITERATURE

Dramas, like short stories, novels, and narrative poems, have plots, characters, settings, and themes. Like poetry, a drama may be written in verse and may use imagery, figures of speech, and devices of sound. In these ways, drama has many features in common with other forms of literature.

Drama as Performance

Dramas differ from other literary works in one very important respect. Dramas are written specifically for on-stage performance before an audience. The action is meant to be experienced by seeing and hearing actors move about and speak on stage. When reading a drama, therefore, it is important to try to visualize what the play would be like as a performance.

A *script*, or written form of a drama, has features that reflect the fact that the drama is meant to be performed. The title of the play is followed by a list of characters. The play itself is composed of dialogue and stage directions. *Dialogue* is the words spoken by the characters. The lines of dialogue in a drama follow the names of the characters who speak them. The *stage directions* give instructions for how the play is to be performed. They include details about how the actors should move and speak; how the set should look; what special effects of lighting and sound should be used; and what *properties*, or movable objects, should appear on stage.

When writing about drama, you may approach it as literature or as performance. The following are some suggestions for ways to write about a drama in both fashions:

The drama as literature:

1. Analyze the plot of the drama. Discuss the introduction, the inciting incident, the development, the climax, the resolution, and the denouement. Also address any special techniques of plot used by the playwright, such as suspense, foreshadowing, flashbacks, or a surprise ending.
2. Discuss how the setting of the play creates a certain mood or contributes to the action of the drama.
3. Find the central idea, or theme, of the drama and write about how other elements such as the plot, setting, and characters help to reveal this theme.
4. Select a major character in the play and discuss how the writer reveals the nature of this character. If the character changes in the course of the drama, tell why and how he or she changes.

The drama as performance:

1. Describe how you would create the set for a specific scene in the drama. Include details about the backdrop, the furniture, the properties, and the lighting you would use.
2. Imagine that you are a costume designer for the play. Describe what kinds of costumes you would have the major character wear.
3. If you have the opportunity to attend an actual performance, write a review of the play. Comment on the sets, costumes, lighting, sound, and performances by the actors.

CASE STUDY: WRITING ABOUT DRAMA

Dana's English class was asked to write a paragraph about a drama. Dana decided to write about Thornton Wilder's *Our Town*, which is introduced on page 920.

Writing About a Drama 1309

Prewriting

Dana read *Our Town* carefully and thought about what aspect of the drama he would like to write about. Since he had found the Stage Manager especially intriguing, he decided to make this character the focus of his paper. Dana re-read the drama and made the following notes about the Stage Manager:

- Character: Stage Manager

- Characteristics:
  Knowledgeable
  Speaks directly to audience, but also interacts with characters
  Knows what will happen in the characters' futures

- Role he plays in the drama:
  Establishes the setting by describing it to the audience
  Controls the action of the play
  Introduces the characters
  Explains scene transitions
  Dismisses audience after each act

Drafting and Revising

Dana wanted to make sure that the topic sentence of his paragraph clearly introduced what he intended to write about in the body of the paragraph. He drafted the following sentence:

When I read Thornton Wilder's play *Our Town*, I thought that the Stage Manager was an important role.

Dana read his topic sentence and realized that it needed to be revised. First, he did not want to use the first-person pronoun "I" to refer to himself in the paragraph. Second, he wanted the sentence to emphasize the fact that he thought the Stage Manager was the most important character in the play. Dana rewrote his topic sentence as follows:

The most important character in Thornton Wilder's play *Our Town* is the Stage Manager.

Next Dana wrote the body of his paragraph, in which he gave supporting evidence for his topic sentence. He concluded his paragraph with a sentence that summarized the main idea of his paper. Then Dana revised his paragraph to make sure that his ideas would be clear to his readers.

Proofreading and Publishing

Dana made a fresh copy of his paragraph and proofread it. Then he shared his paragraph with his drama teacher and with other students in the class.

ACTIVITIES AND ASSIGNMENTS

A. Use the notes in the case study to write a paragraph about the Stage Manager in *Our Town*. Follow these steps:

1. Read the play carefully. Then read Dana's notes and add to them any important details about the Stage Manager that you find are missing. Make an outline for your paragraph.
2. If you wish to do so, you may use Dana's revised sentence as the topic sentence for your paragraph, or you may write an original sentence that introduces your own main idea.
3. Write the rest of your paragraph according to your outline.
4. Revise your draft. Make sure that you have provided supporting evidence for all your statements about the Stage Manager and about *Our Town*. Also make sure that all of your ideas are clear.
5. Proofread your paragraph for errors in grammar, usage, spelling, punctuation, capitalization, and manuscript form. Make a clean final copy of your paragraph and share it with your classmates and with your teacher.

B. Select one of the following approaches for a one- to three-paragraph composition about *Our Town*, which is introduced on page 920:

1. Analyze one scene and explain what elements contribute to its overall effect.
2. Describe how you would create the setting for a particular scene in the drama. Explain the mood that would be created by the setting.
3. Analyze the role of a minor character in one scene of the play.
4. Analyze the interaction of the Stage Manager with the audience in one specific scene.
5. Describe how a major character should be portrayed in a certain scene. Tell how you would instruct the actor playing the role to move, act, and speak.
6. Make up your own topic analyzing a specific element of a scene in the play.

C. Follow these steps when planning and writing your composition:

1. Carefully study the scene that you will be analyzing. Read it both silently and aloud. Think about how it would look and sound in a performance.
2. Makes notes about the details in the scene that are relevant to your topic. Then organize your notes and make an outline for your composition.
3. Write a topic sentence that introduces the main idea of your composition. Then write a draft of your paper. Make sure that your writing has a definite introduction, body, and conclusion.
4. Revise and proofread your composition. Share your final copy with your classmates and with your teacher.

SECTION 4: JUDGING A LITERARY WORK: EVALUATION

Lesson 15: Evaluating a Literary Work

WHAT IS EVALUATION?

An *evaluation* is a judgment about the quality or value of something. Every time you decide that you like or do not like something, you are making an evaluation.

To be valid, an evaluation must not be arbitrary but must be based on reasonable *criteria*, or standards. For example, if you were judging the quality of a new brand of potato chips, you might select criteria such as flavor, texture, freshness, and amount of sodium and cholesterol. You would use different criteria to evaluate an automobile, such as ease of handling and effectiveness of brakes. An evaluation must reflect facts about the object being judged. For example, if you said you did not like the flavor of Brand X potato chips because they had too much salt on them, when in fact they had no salt at all, your evaluation would be unsound.

The same principles apply when you evaluate a literary work. Your evaluation must follow a set of reasonable criteria and must reflect facts about the work you are evaluating.

CRITERIA FOR EVALUATING LITERATURE

The following list describes some of the most common criteria, or standards, that are used to evaluate literary works:

1. *Originality:* A work that deals with a subject that has not been dealt with in other literary works shows originality or creativity on the part of the writer. A work that has an unusual subject or sheds an interesting new light on a familiar subject will often be evaluated favorably on grounds of originality. Works that lack originality are trite or contain clichés.

2. *Consistency or completeness of effect:* Most works are intended to leave the reader with a certain feeling by creating an overall effect. If the reader is left feeling confused because the writer has carelessly allowed the effect of the work to be spoiled, the work will not be evaluated favorably. For example, imagine a novel that told the story of a man who had been the victim of cruel fate throughout his entire life. If the novel were to end with the words "Oh, well—that's life," the melancholy mood of the work would be ruined.

3. *Importance:* Some works of literature are judged to be better than others because they deal with matters of greater importance. Works evaluated favorably according to this criterion usually have serious themes or subjects. For example, a poem that offers a profound insight into human nature might be judged to be superior to a poem that simply describes a pretty scene.

4. *Theme:* The theme of a literary work is often an idea about how one should live one's life. If a reader agrees with the theme, he or she is likely to evaluate the work favorably.

5. *Clarity:* Many great works of literature are difficult and require a great deal of study to be understood. However, if a work is incomprehensible simply because the writer has not expressed his or her ideas clearly, the work will be judged to be of poor quality.

CASE STUDY: EVALUATING A LITERARY WORK

Sara's English teacher asked the class to write an evaluation of a literary work. Sara and her classmates had saved all their writing in folders, so Sara decided to write an evaluation of a poem that she had written earlier in the year.

Prewriting

Here is Sara's poem, "Seasonal Changes":

It is springtime.
An infant crawls across
A fragrant lawn
And laughs
As she looks up at
The blossoming cherry tree.

Now it is summer
And a young girl—
Almost a woman—
Leaves a trail of footprints
On the sandy beach.
The tide washes them away.

In the fall
A mature woman
Hurries across the busy street
To her office building.
As a car horn blares
She turns up the collar of her jacket
Against a suddenly chilly wind.

It is winter.
Snow covers the ground
On the lawn outside an old woman's/
    window—
The same lawn
Across which crawled
A laughing infant.

Sara read the poem carefully and decided that it sounded trite and contained clichés. She made the following notes about why she felt the poem was ineffective:

- Criterion for evaluation: originality

- How poem fails to meet criterion:

The theme—likening cycle of life to seasonal changes—is unoriginal. Many other writers have used this analogy. The poem contains clichés such as the "young girl" who is "Almost a woman"; the "trail of footprints/On the sandy beach" that is washed away by the tide; the "suddenly chilly wind"; and the snow outside the window.

Sara made an outline for her evaluation, one that showed how she would organize her ideas in the introduction, body and conclusion of her paper.

Drafting and Revising

Sara used her notes and her outline to write a draft of her composition. Then she revised her paper, adding supporting evidence for her claims and clarifying some of her statements.

Proofreading and Publishing

Sara made a fresh copy of her paper and proofread it carefully. Then she shared the final copy of her evaluation with her class discussion group.

ACTIVITIES AND ASSIGNMENTS

A. Use Sara's prewriting notes to write an evaluation of the poem "Seasonal Changes." Follow these steps:

1. Read the poem carefully. Then look at Sara's notes. If you can think of any other criteria to evaluate the poem, add them to your notes.
2. Make an outline for your evaluation.
3. Write a topic sentence that introduces the purpose of your paper. Then finish writing your draft according to your outline.
4. Revise your draft. Make sure that your purpose is clear and that your topic sentence is

supported with specific evidence from the poem.

5. Proofread your revised draft carefully. Then share your final copy with a small group of your classmates and with your teacher.

B. Select one of the following works for a one- to three-paragraph evaluation: "To a Waterfowl," on page 179; "The Raven," on page 227; "The Chambered Nautilus," on page 350; "A Noiseless Patient Spider," on page 473; "Winter Dreams," on page 672; "Anecdote of the Jar," on page 819; "anyone lived in a pretty how town," on page 865; "The Death of the Hired Man," on page 881; "Storm Ending," on page 914; "Katherine Comes to Yellow Sky," on page 1012; "A Vision Beyond Time and Place," on page 1060; "The Explorer," on page 1106; or "Evening Hawk," on page 1136. Follow these steps:

1. Read the work carefully. Freewrite about why you liked or did not like the work. Then decide which criteria you will use to evaluate the work—originality, completeness of effect, importance, moral or ethical message, or clarity. In your prewriting notes, list specific examples from the work that support your evaluation.

2. Make a rough outline for your composition. Then write a draft of your evaluation, including details to support all your statements.

3. Revise your paper to make sure that it is clear and well organized. Then proofread your revised draft for errors in spelling and mechanics.

4. Share the final copy of your evaluation with your classmates and with your teacher.

Lesson 16: Writing a Comparative Evaluation

WHAT IS A COMPARATIVE EVALUATION?

As you learned in the preceding lesson, an evaluation is a statement about the quality or value of something. A *comparative evaluation* is a statement about the relative quality or value of two or more things. Suppose, for example, that you want to buy a car and there are two models that appeal to you. To decide between these two models, you will have to do a comparative evaluation. First you will choose certain features to compare, such as safety, appearance, cost, and fuel efficiency. Then you will judge the relative value of each model with respect to these features.

COMPARING TWO LITERARY WORKS

When you choose two literary works for a comparative evaluation, the two works should have at least one feature in common—a feature that can be compared. For example, you might choose two works by the same author, two works from the same literary period, two works on the same theme or subject, or two works that make use of the same literary device. The first step in doing a comparative evaluation is to list the works and the feature to be compared in your prewriting notes. The next step is to read each work carefully and to take notes on the feature as it appears in each work. Finally, you need to decide which of the two works is better with respect to the feature you are comparing.

CASE STUDY: WRITING A COMPARATIVE EVALUATION

Marina's English teacher asked the students to choose two works for a comparative evaluation. Marina decided to write about two imagist poems—Ezra Pound's "In a Station of the Metro," on page 800, and William Carlos Williams's "The Red Wheelbarrow," on page 836.

Prewriting

Marina began by listing the works and the feature to be compared in her prewriting notes, as follows:

- Works to be compared: Ezra Pound's "In a Station of the Metro" and William Carlos Williams's "The Red Wheelbarrow"

- Feature to be compared: use of imagery

Next Marina read the two works carefully and made the following notes about the imagery in each:

- Imagery in the poem by Pound:
  faces in train station described as an "apparition," like a ghostly vision
  faces compared to "petals on a wet, black bough"
  imagery is used to report how an ordinary thing can appear to be extraordinary, like a vision or like one of those Oriental watercolors of petals against the limb of a tree, shining black after a rain
  three metaphors, all in a couple of lines (the whole scene = an apparition; the faces = petals; the people's dark clothing = a wet, black bough)

- Imagery in the poem by Williams:
  "a red wheelbarrow"
  "glazed with rain water"
  "beside the white chickens"
  contrast between the red of the wheelbarrow and the white of the chickens
  colors always more vibrant after a rain
  "So much depends" is purposefully

Writing a Comparative Evaluation 1315

Motivation/Prior Knowledge
Point out to students that comparing and contrasting different literary works can enhance their overall understanding of and appreciation for literature. Comparing and contrasting literary works can help your students to comprehend literary trends and movements. This type of evaluation can also help them to make the distinction between sophisticated and unsophisticated works of literature and can help them to appreciate the talents of certain writers.

vague, as though Williams meant to suggest both that the overall appearance of the scene and the state of the speaker of the poem both depend on how the wheelbarrow looks

After making these notes, Marina thought about her reactions to the two poems. She decided that she liked the Pound poem better because it was more sophisticated and because it dealt with a more important subject. Therefore, she added the following comments to her notes:

- Evaluation 1: Ezra Pound's poem is more sophisticated than William Carlos Williams's because of its use of metaphors that bring lots of associations to mind.

- Evaluation 2: Ezra Pound's poem deals with an important subject—how people perceive other people. Williams's poem, on the other hand, deals with a relatively trivial subject—how the beauty of a scene can depend on a single brilliant contrast

Marina decided that she would focus her paper on the relative sophistication of the two poems. She would make the claim that Ezra Pound's poem was better because it showed more artistry in its subtle use of metaphor.

Drafting and Revising

Based on her notes, Marina wrote a four-paragraph paper. In the first paragraph she introduced the two poems, the two authors, and her subject—the imagery in the two poems. In the second paragraph she discussed how Williams used imagery in his poem to create a picture of a wheelbarrow. In the third paragraph she discussed how Pound used imagery in his poem to show that ordinary people can sometimes be strikingly beautiful. Finally, in her fourth paragraph Marina explained why she thought the Pound poem was better than the Williams poem. After finishing the rough draft of her paper, Marina made extensive revisions, using the Checklist for Revision on page 1274.

Proofreading and Publishing

Marina proofread her paper carefully and then shared it with a small group of her classmates. Several people in the group objected to Marina's paper quite strongly. They felt that Williams's poem was more powerful than Pound's precisely because the Williams poem was so simple and direct.

ACTIVITIES AND ASSIGNMENTS

A. If you haven't already done so, read Ezra Pound's "In a Station of the Metro," on page 800, and William Carlos Williams's "The Red Wheelbarrow," on page 836. Then, using the notes from the case study and notes of your own, write a comparative evaluation of the two poems.

B. Choose one of the following pairs of works for a comparative evaluation:
1. Robert Benchley's "The Tooth, the Whole Tooth, and Nothing but the Tooth," on page 770, and James Thurber's "The Night the Ghost Got In," on page 778.
2. Ralph Waldo Emerson's "Concord Hymn," on page 281, and Ralph Waldo Emerson's "Brahma," on page 285.
3. Paul Laurence Dunbar's "We Wear the Mask," on page 614, and Countee Cullen's "Any Human Being to Another," on page 905.
4. Henry Wadsworth Longfellow's "A Psalm of Life," on 340, and the excerpt from Walt Whitman's "Song of Myself," on page 460.

C. Follow these steps when writing your evaluation:
1. Choose some feature you wish to compare.
2. Read both works carefully and take notes on the feature you are comparing.
3. Write a statement of opinion that expresses the relative value of each work with respect to the feature you are comparing.
4. Write an outline for a four-paragraph paper. In the first paragraph you should state what

works and feature you are comparing. In the second paragraph you should discuss one of the works. In the third paragraph you should discuss the other work. In the fourth paragraph you should state your opinion about the relative value of the two works and support this opinion with evidence from the rest of the paper.

5. Write a rough draft based on your outline and your notes. Revise and proofread your draft. Then share it with your classmates and with your teacher.

Lesson 17: Evaluating Persuasive Writing

Persuasion, or *persuasive writing,* is a type of nonfiction in which the writer attempts to convince the audience to accept a certain idea or to act in a certain way. The purpose of persuasive writing, then, is to present the opinion of the writer in such a way as to solicit an active response from the reader. Familiar examples of persuasive writing and speech include advertisements, newspaper editorials, political speeches, and campaign brochures.

SOUND REASONING ABOUT PERSUASION

The opinions presented in persuasive writing and speech are, by definition, statements about which people may disagree. Therefore, to be effective, persuaders must present reasonable arguments to support their opinions. Readers or listeners must then decide whether these opinions are sound. The following are some criteria for evaluating the soundness of opinions:

The Consistency Principle

Is the opinion consistent with known facts? For example, the opinion that it is foolish never to check the oil level in one's car engine is consistent with the fact that to allow the oil to run low is to risk destroying the engine.

The Utility Principle

Does accepting the opinion lead to consequences that are themselves acceptable? For example, the opinion that one should engage in a program of regular exercise is sound because the result of acting on this opinion is a healthier body.

The Principle of Appeal to Authority

Is the opinion consistent with the views of knowledgeable and reliable authorities? For example, the opinion that it will snow this evening is sound if it reflects the views of competent meteorologists. These people study the patterns of the weather and are able to make intelligent predictions about upcoming weather conditions.

Unsound Reasoning About Opinions

Not all persuasive writing and speech contains logically reasoned arguments. Instead, some persuasion makes use of propaganda and logical fallacies. *Propaganda* is language that is emotionally charged and intentionally misleading. A *logical fallacy* is an error in reasoning. The following propaganda devices and logical fallacies are often found in persuasive writing and speech:

Propaganda Devices:

1. *Bandwagon:* urging support for an opinion simply because many other people support the opinion
2. *Loaded language:* using emotionally charged words that have little meaning beyond arousing positive or negative feelings
3. *Argument ad hominem:* (literally, "argument to the person") criticizing or attacking the opponent instead of the opponent's argument
4. *Snob appeal:* urging support for an opinion solely because an admired person or group supports it
5. *Straw man:* exaggerating or misrepresenting the opposing position so that it sounds more ridiculous than it actually is
6. *Stereotyping:* assuming, without sufficient evidence, that everyone in a particular group has certain characteristics

Logical Fallacies:

1. *Begging the question:* stating an opinion without giving evidence to support it; simply assuming the truth of the opinion to be proved

2. *Either/or fallacy:* treating a complicated issue as if there were only two sides or two alternatives when there are actually more
3. *Post hoc, ergo propter hoc:* (literally, "after this, therefore because of this") assuming that one action or event caused another simply because it came earlier in time
4. *False analogy:* falsely treating two subjects as similar in one respect simply because they are similar in some other respect
5. *Non sequitur:* (literally, "It does not follow") stating a conclusion that is not a necessary consequence of the reasons given
6. *Overgeneralization:* making a statement that is too broad in its application

When you evaluate written or spoken persuasion, you must constantly be aware of any devices of propaganda or logical fallacies that appear in the arguments. You should never accept an opinion until you are convinced that it is supported by sound reasoning.

CASE STUDY: EVALUATING PERSUASION

Jodie's English teacher asked the class to find an example of persuasive writing and to evaluate the soundness of its arguments. Jodie found a letter to the editor in a local newspaper that she decided to use for the assignment.

Prewriting

Here is the letter that Jodie found:

Dear Editor:

The outrageous behavior last Friday of five juvenile delinquents at Hampton Mall shows what trouble our country is in! These young hoodlums were playing a game by the public walkways, wildly throwing a saucer-shaped plastic disk. This unruly behavior upset all the hard-working Americans who needed to shop. I'm sure all solid citizens will agree that anyone under eighteen should be banned from malls or parents should be fined when their children run wild in public!

Sincerely,
Maudine Oxley

Jodie read the letter carefully, noting its unsupported assumptions and biased opinions. In her prewriting notes she made a list of the propaganda techniques and logical fallacies in the letter:

- Loaded language: calling the kids "juvenile delinquents" and "hoodlums"; calling shoppers "hard-working Americans"
- Bandwagon or snob appeal: calling on "all solid citizens"
- Either/or fallacy: suggesting banning or fining parents as the only choices
- Non sequitur: assuming that the kids' behavior shows trouble in the entire nation

While Jodie agreed that the behavior discussed in the letter was reprehensible, she nonetheless concluded that the letter was badly flawed because it contained unsupported claims and illogical solutions. She made an outline and drafted a topic sentence based on her prewriting notes and ideas.

Drafting and Revising

Jodie wrote a draft of her essay, including many specific examples from the letter. Then she revised her draft to clarify her points.

Proofreading and Publishing

Jodie proofread her essay and shared it with the class.

ACTIVITIES AND ASSIGNMENTS

A. Use Jodie's prewriting notes to write an essay analyzing the letter to the editor in the case study. Follow these steps:
1. Read the letter carefully. Then look at Jodie's notes and add to them any examples of propaganda devices or logical fallacies that she left out.
2. Make an outline for your essay. Make sure that it is organized logically and that it shows

how you will support each of your claims about the letter.

3. Write a draft of your essay. Then revise the draft, keeping in mind that your ideas must be presented clearly if you want to convince your readers that the letter is actually flawed.

4. Proofread your revised draft and share your final copy with a small group of your classmates before turning it in to your teacher.

B. Write an essay analyzing the propaganda devices or logical fallacies in a piece of persuasive writing. Follow these steps:

1. Find an example of persuasive writing. Look in magazines, in newspapers, and in public relations materials.

2. Analyze your example. What does the writer want the audience to do or to believe? What reasons are given for the audience to accept the opinion expressed in the writing? Look for examples of the propaganda devices and logical fallacies listed in this lesson and record them in your notes.

3. Make an outline for your essay. Then write your first draft, making sure that you include specific details to support your claims.

4. Revise your draft. Make sure that all your ideas are expressed clearly and that you have not wandered from your topic.

5. Proofread your essay, and share your final copy with your classmates.

SECTION 5: WRITING CREATIVELY
Lesson 18: Writing a Short Story

Motivation/Prior Knowledge
Ask your students if they ever tell stories to their friends and family members. Do they enjoy telling stories? Do they enjoy listening to stories? Point out that by writing their stories down, they will have more time to develop them, and they will be able to capture them permanently. Also explain that writing their stories down will allow them to reach a wider audience than they can by relating their stories orally.

Authors have many different purposes for writing short stories. Some want to express serious themes through their narratives. Others want to entertain their audiences with intriguing or amusing tales. Still others want to sketch important or interesting characters.

An idea for a short story can come from any of a number of sources. You can work from your own experience. You can write about historical figures. You can create completely imaginary characters and events. Begin by concentrating on one element of the story—setting, characters, plot, or theme. Then build the rest of your story around this one element.

DEVELOPING YOUR IDEA

The following questions will help you to develop the various parts of your story before you begin writing:

1. *Setting:* Where does the story take place? At what date in history does the action unfold? In what season does the story occur? Are the weather conditions important to the story? What images of sight, sound, touch, taste, and smell will you use to reveal the setting?
2. *Character:* Who will be the main character, or protagonist, of the story? What other major and minor characters will take part in the action? What will each of the characters be like? How will you reveal the nature of each character? Will any of the characters change or grow in the course of the story? What will cause them to change? How will they be different at the end of the story? What will the reader learn from the experiences of the characters?
3. *Conflict:* What central conflict will the protagonist be involved in? Will the conflict be *internal*—within the character's mind—or *external*—between the character and some outside force? How will the conflict be resolved?
4. *Plot:* What events will take place in the story?
   Introduction: What background information about the setting or the characters will you present at the beginning of the story?
   Inciting incident: What event will give rise to the central conflict?
   Development: What events will occur as a result of the inciting incident?
   Climax: What will be the high point of interest or suspense in the story?
   Resolution: How will the central conflict be resolved? Will the resolution and the climax occur at the same time?
   Denouement: What events, if any, will happen after the resolution?
5. Will your story have a message for the reader? What elements in the story will serve to reveal this message, or theme?
6. *Point of view:* Who will be the narrator of the story? Will the narrator be involved in the action of the story or tell the story as an outsider? That is, will the narrator be first person or third person? How much will the narrator know about each of the characters? That is, will the narrator be limited or omniscient?

DRAFTING YOUR STORY

Perhaps the most important point to remember as you write your story is that you must keep

Writing a Short Story 1321

your readers interested and involved. Do not include any pointless or unnecessary passages that will distract the reader or break the tension that you are trying to build as the plot develops. Instead, make sure that every sentence you write has a purpose and contributes to the overall effect of the story.

To make your writing especially interesting, consider where you could add vivid descriptions of people and places using images and figurative language. Also, you might want to employ special plot techniques such as foreshadowing, flashback, or surprise ending.

CASE STUDY: WRITING A SHORT STORY

Andrei's English teacher asked each student in the class to write a short story. All of the stories were to be bound together in a class booklet.

Prewriting

Andrei did not have an idea for his story, so he tried brainstorming about setting, plot, and character. Here are Andrei's brainstorming notes:

- Setting:
  a beach in California
  a stormy night in a dark, abandoned house
  the public library, where I'm studying for a math test
  the United States during the Industrial Revolution
  inside my favorite book
  ten years from now—what will I be doing?

- Plot:
  I meet the girl of my dreams on vacation, but she lives in Greece.
  A kid and his friends are snooping around where they're not supposed to be.

A poor man wants to buy his daughter an expensive doll for her birthday.
I'm reading a book and suddenly I find myself taking part in the action.

- Character:
  myself
  my best friend, Leo
  the characters in my favorite book
  a Siamese cat
  the king of an imaginary land
  a boy who can't decide whether or not to try out for the swim team

Andrei liked the idea of finding himself in the middle of his favorite book. He decided that the purpose of his short story would be to relate the humorous adventures he might have if he could participate in the action of a literary work. He made an outline of the events that would occur in the plot. He also listed the characters that would play roles in his story and described briefly what each would be like. Finally, Andrei made a list of the images he would use to describe the setting of his story.

Drafting and Revising

Andrei used his prewriting notes to write a draft of his short story. When he read the story, he realized that some passages were not essential to the plot and might seem boring to a reader. He deleted these passages.

Proofreading and Publishing

Andrei proofread his story and made a clean final copy. This copy he submitted to his teacher, who added it to the class booklet.

ACTIVITIES AND ASSIGNMENTS

A. Use Andrei's prewriting notes and ideas from the case study to write a story about a student who finds himself or herself in the setting of a literary work. Follow these steps:
1. Select a narrative work that you enjoyed reading. Then decide at what point in the story it

would be interesting for a student to enter. Make notes about what events might occur when the student suddenly appears. Think about what characters the student will meet and how he or she will interact with them.

2. Decide whether you will tell the story from the first-person or the third-person point of view. Then decide whether the narrator will be limited or omniscient.

3. Write a draft of your story. Describe the setting and characters, using images and figures of speech. Tell the events of the story in order. Try to create suspense by making the reader wonder what will happen next.

4. Revise and proofread your draft. Then share your final copy with your classmates and with your teacher.

B. Write an original short story. Follow these steps:

1. If you have trouble thinking of an idea for your story, try brainstorming or freewriting. Once you have decided on a main idea, develop the other elements of the story by answering the questions in this lesson.

2. Write a draft of your story. Then revise the draft, making sure that there are no unnecessary passages that will ruin the effect of your writing. Add new passages where you need to clarify what is happening or where you want to describe something more fully.

3. Proofread your story for errors in spelling and mechanics. Then share your final copy with your classmates and with your teacher.

Lesson 19: Writing a Poem

Poetry is imaginative language that expresses ideas of truth and beauty for the enjoyment of a reader. Poems can tell stories, present dramatic moments, and express human emotions. Because American poetry written during the twentieth century is especially rich, you might want to try writing poems modeled on those appearing in your text. For example, you might try writing an imagist poem such as those written by Ezra Pound, H.D., and William Carlos Williams, or you might try writing a dramatic dialogue such as Robert Frost's "The Death of the Hired Man," on page 881.

WRITING AN IMAGIST POEM

An *imagist poem* presents a single vivid picture in words. See, for example, H.D.'s "Pear Tree," on page 828, and William Carlos Williams's "The Red Wheelbarrow," on page 836. To write an imagist poem, you need first to choose a scene that you want to describe. Then you need to make a list of the elements of the scene. It might be helpful to break up this list into images of sight, sound, touch, taste, and smell. The next step is to decide what characteristic of the scene you want to emphasize. Do you want to create a particular mood? Is there some important aspect of the scene that you want to concentrate on? Decide on a focus for your description. Then make a list of descriptive words you can use in your poem. Toss out any words that are vague or abstract. You want the words in your poem to be as vivid and concrete as possible.

Use your list of words to write a rough draft of your poem. In an imagist poem, the lines do not have to be of any particular length or rhythmical pattern. As you revise, try to make your lines even more vivid and dramatic, and experiment with lines of various lengths and rhythms. Revise the poem as many times as necessary until your final product is a single, vivid picture with a single dominant effect.

WRITING A DRAMATIC POEM

A *dramatic poem* is a poem in which there are two speakers who talk to one another. Often the poem involves some conflict between the speakers and reveals the speakers' personalities. There are many ways to approach writing a dramatic poem. One way is to think, first, of a conflict involving two people. Then write a short scene, in prose, describing a confrontation between these people. In your prose version, use dialogue to reveal the characters' feelings, thoughts, opinions of one another, and the like. Begin with some incident that triggers the central conflict, show how the conflict is developed, and then show how it is resolved.

Once you are satisfied with your prose version of the dialogue, rewrite the lines in verse form. Use unrhymed verse so you will not have to make the lines fit a rhyme scheme, but make sure that each line has the same number of beats, or strong stresses—three, four, or five. Use quotation marks to show when each speaker's lines begin and end. Remember that it is acceptable to include run-on lines (ones that are not end-stopped).

As you revise your poem, check to make sure that the characters' lines sound natural by reading these lines aloud. Also check to make sure that each line has the same number of strong stresses.

CASE STUDY: WRITING A POEM

Arthur's class was studying early twentieth-century poetry. After the class finished studying the movement known as Imagism, the teacher asked each of the students to write an imagist poem.

Prewriting

At first Arthur could not think of a subject to write about. Therefore, he did the following free-writing in his journal:

> What am I going to write about? Imagism. Let's see, images are . . . whatever you can see or touch or taste or hear or smell or—that could be almost anything. I need a really striking, powerful image like—what about a Ferris wheel at night with its lights shining against a dark blue sky?

Arthur then made the following notes:

- Subject: a Ferris wheel at night
- Images: dark sky, Ferris wheel seen from a distance, turning, its colored lights shining
- Mood: maybe the mood could be a little bit scary, as though the Ferris wheel were some kind of creature in the darkness

Arthur also included in his notes a list of words that he could use to describe the scene.

Drafting and Revising

Arthur wrote several drafts of his poem. Here is his final draft, which he titled "The Beast at the Edge of the Wood," with some of the corrections he made:

Across the farms and fields
 darkened
Against ~~a blue~~ sky,
 an indigo

A ferris wheel turns—
A hundred eyes ~~shine~~ in the
 burn

dreamlike distance.

Proofreading and Publishing

Arthur proofread the final copy of his poem. The only error that he found to correct was the capitalization of the word *Ferris*. After correcting this error, Arthur shared his poem with his parents, with his classmates, and with his teacher.

ACTIVITIES AND ASSIGNMENTS

A. Answer the following questions about the case study:

1. Why might Arthur have added the word "darkened" to his first line?
2. Why might Arthur have changed the word "blue" to "indigo"? the word "shine" to "burn"?
3. To what sense does Arthur's poem appeal?
4. What mood does Arthur's poem create?
5. Do you think that Arthur's poem is successful? Why or why not?

B. Write your own imagist poem or dramatic poem. Follow the steps described in this lesson.

ANSWERS TO ACTIVITIES AND ASSIGNMENTS, SECTION A

1. He may have added this word to make the image more precise.
2. These words also make the images more precise.
3. It appeals to the sense of sight.
4. Suggested Response: It creates a dreamlike mood.
5. Answers will differ. Students may respond that Arnold's poem is successful because it creates a vivid image.

Ask students if they sometimes listen to or observe other peoples' conversations. How would they go about recording these observations? How might they be able to alter the conversations so that the peoples' names and identities are revealed through the dialogue? Point out that it is very difficult to reveal character through dialogue, while at the same time making the dialogue seem natural and realistic. This challenge makes playwriting one of the most difficult forms of writing. At the same time, however, the challenge of creating realistic and revealing dialogue makes playwriting an extremely rewarding craft.

A *dramatic sketch* has the same form as a full-length drama except that it has only one brief scene that makes a single point. The elements that make up a drama—dialogue and stage directions—are also found in a dramatic sketch. The *dialogue* is the words spoken by the characters. When a character speaks, his or her name appears, followed by the appropriate lines of dialogue. The *stage directions* are instructions that appear in underlined or italicized text within brackets or parentheses. They give information about how the characters should move and speak; how the stage should appear to the audience; what special effects of lighting and sound should be used; and what *properties*, or movable pieces, should be used by the actors. The setting of a dramatic sketch is often described in stage directions at the very beginning of the work.

The following excerpt from *Our Town*, which is introduced on page 920, shows the form in which a dramatic sketch is written:

MR. WEBB [*suddenly and loudly*]. Well, George, how are you?

GEORGE [*startled, choking over his coffee*]. Oh, fine, I'm fine. (*Pause.*) Mr. Webb, what sense could there be in a superstition like that?

PLANNING A DRAMATIC SKETCH

Planning to write a dramatic sketch is much like planning any other narrative work. You might start by thinking of an interesting main character for the sketch, or you might begin with a creative idea for a plot. No matter how you begin your planning, before you start writing you must have a clear idea of what the setting of your sketch will be; what characters will participate in the action;

how each of the characters will act and speak; and what events will take place in the sketch. If your sketch is to be a serious one with a theme, you must have a plan for revealing that theme. Finally, you must make sure that the setting and action of the sketch can be presented on a stage. For example, a scene with a car chase around mountain curves would be very difficult to reproduce on stage.

WRITING THE SKETCH

Begin your sketch with a title and a list of characters. You may include a brief description of each character, as follows:

DR. TANAKA, a renowned surgeon
ALISA TANAKA, Dr. Tanaka's beautiful daughter

After the list of characters, include a set of stage directions with a detailed description of the setting. The description must be explicit enough so that a director will know exactly what you had in mind when you wrote the sketch. Next write the dialogue and stage directions that describe the action of the sketch. Stop writing from time to time to read the dialogue aloud. You want to make sure that it sounds natural and not stilted or contrived. Add stage directions only where necessary to clarify a particular movement or manner of speaking of one of the characters, or where you want to indicate a special effect of lighting or sound.

When you revise your sketch, make sure that you have not included dialogue or stage directions that are unnecessary to the purpose of the sketch. Remember that the sketch should be brief and should make a single point.

CASE STUDY: WRITING
A DRAMATIC SKETCH

Rosa's English class was asked to write a short dramatic sketch about a historical event in an imaginary town. Rosa decided to write about the establishment of the first trading post in a town called New Pockets, Mississippi.

Prewriting

Rosa thought about the setting, characters, and plot of her dramatic sketch. She made the following notes:

- Title: Local Trade

- Setting: early nineteenth century; pioneer town; wooded area near flooding stream with a cabin under construction

- Characters: Trader Wainwright, Trapper Stockton, Trapper Levar, Abigail Scully, William Scully, Jenny Scully, Nancy Scully

- Plot summary: Despite spring floods, Trader Wainwright manages to open the town's first business, thanks to the help of two trappers and the Scully family.

Drafting and Revising

Rosa used her prewriting notes to write a draft of her sketch. Then she revised the draft. Here is Rosa's revised draft:

Local Trade

[*The scene opens in a wooded area next to a flooding stream. On the left is a cabin, partly constructed. TRADER WAINWRIGHT, the Scully family, and two trappers have formed a line and are passing supplies toward the cabin, trying to save them from the spring floods.*]

TRAPPER STOCKTON. [*Tossing a large parcel toward WAINWRIGHT*] Here you go.

TRADER WAINWRIGHT. Another bolt of fabric. [*Taking the parcel and passing it along*] Can't let the floods take your new summer outfit, can we now, Jenny, my girl?

JENNY SCULLY. No, sir, Mr. Wainwright. [*Continues passing parcel along to others and into the cabin*]

TRAPPER LEVAR. [*At the head of the line, now passing a large sack to STOCKTON*] Corn meal coming next.

TRADER WAINWRIGHT. Ready for a heavy one, Jenny?

NANCY SCULLY. Knowing what that girl eats, she'll be wanting her corn meal johnnycakes lots more than a July dress!

JENNY SCULLY. [*Turning to appeal to her mother, who is in line near the cabin*] Mother! That Nancy is makin' fun of me again! Tell her to leave me be!

ABIGAIL SCULLY. [*Eying both of them*] I do believe we have something better to do today than bicker.

TRAPPER LEVAR. [*Moving out of line*] That does it, Wainwright. Every parcel you brought here for your new trading post is safe from the flood waters now.

WILLIAM SCULLY. [*Coming down from the cabin*] Well, neighbor, we've done it. The west side of the cabin is covered and still dry. And your goods are all up on logs above ground now, too.

TRADER WAINWRIGHT. [*Shaking hands all around*] Thanks to you all. Looks like I'll still open me a trading post this spring.

WILLIAM SCULLY. [*Digging in his pocket*] When I find you a penny, you'll have your first sale, too. I'll take some of that rock candy for my two girls here.

TRADER WAINWRIGHT. Keep your penny, neighbor. The first business done at the Wainwright Trading Post is a fair exchange—neighborly help for a sweet treat. [*Brings a small bag out of the cabin and offers rock candy to the girls*] Looks like we're in business, doesn't it, girls.

Proofreading and Publishing

Rosa proofread her revised draft and made

a clean final copy. Then she and several of her friends performed the sketch for the class.

ACTIVITIES AND ASSIGNMENTS

A. Refer to the sketch in the case study to complete the following exercises:

1. Rosa's sketch lacks a list of characters. Write out a list of characters for the sketch with a brief description of each character.
2. Practice writing dialogue by adding to the sketch another brief conversation or two between characters. Be sure that the dialogue makes sense in the context of the story and that the lines sound natural when read aloud.

B. Write an original dramatic sketch. Follow these steps:

1. Select a suitable topic that can be covered in a short sketch. Decide what the purpose of your sketch will be—to make the audience laugh, to dramatize a historical event, to make a serious point, or whatever—and plan the action around that purpose. Make notes about the setting, characters, plot, and theme of your sketch.
2. Write a draft of your sketch. Then revise your draft, making sure that you have included a title, a list of characters, natural-sounding dialogue, and appropriate stage directions.
3. Proofread your sketch and share it with your classmates and with your teacher.

Lesson 21: Writing a Personal Essay

When you write a *personal essay,* you speak directly to your audience about your own experiences, knowledge, attitudes, and feelings. The way you approach your topic reflects your personal thoughts. The process of writing a personal essay is the same as the process you used to write about literature. It includes prewriting, drafting, revising, proofreading, and publishing.

PLANNING A PERSONAL ESSAY

The topic of a personal essay should be something that really matters to you. The purpose of your essay will determine how you will write about the topic. Suppose, for example, you are planning to write about your experience working at a fast-food restaurant. Depending on the purpose of your writing, you could approach the topic in a number of ways. The following list explains some of the different types of essays you might write:

1. *Narrative essay:* one that tells a story about your experience

   Just getting to work on my first day at the Burger Place turned into an unbelievable adventure.

2. *Descriptive essay:* one that describes the topic vividly so that the reader can almost experience it for himself or herself

   In the peaceful hour before dawn, the kitchen at the Burger Place is already humming with activity.

3. *Expository essay:* one that explains an idea, thing, or process

   The process of preparing a hamburger at the Burger Place involves four simple steps, each performed by a different employee in an assembly line.

4. *Persuasive essay:* one that attempts to convince the audience to accept a particular point of view or to act in a certain way

   The town loitering ordinance should be amended to allow young people to gather peacefully outside popular restaurants such as the Burger Place.

A clear and definite topic sentence, or thesis statement, like the ones listed, is essential to an effective essay. The topic sentence tells the audience what the writer's purpose and topic are, thus creating certain expectations in the mind of the reader. For example, the thesis statement of a persuasive essay leads the reader to expect to find solid arguments for the writer's opinion in the body of the essay. As a writer, you must make sure that these expectations are fulfilled. Regardless of what type of essay you write, you must provide supporting evidence for your topic sentence in the body of your essay.

CASE STUDY: WRITING A PERSONAL ESSAY

John's English teacher asked the class to write a personal essay of three to five paragraphs.

Prewriting

John had no idea what he would write his personal essay about. Since he knew that the prewriting stage would take him longer than usual, he started working on his essay several days before it was due.

John decided to try freewriting to gather ideas for his topic:

Writing a Personal Essay 1329

Motivation/Prior Knowledge
Have students discuss their most interesting or unusual experiences. Point out that these types of experiences would make excellent topics for personal essays. Also explain that personal essays can serve a variety of purposes—they can entertain, they can inform, they can describe, or they can persuade. Ask students to decide what the purpose of their essay would be if they were to write about one of their experiences. Then explain that their purpose will affect how they approach their topic.

1330

1. John used freewriting. He might have used charting, clustering, or brainstorming.
2. All of his points do support his thesis. His outline is well organized. He could improve his outline by numbering his subtopics and lettering his main points.
3. John's thesis statement clearly reveals his viewpoint because it explains his desire to attend restaurant school. The sentence reveals each of John's subtopics in the proper order.

Maybe I could write about my future. Let's see...All I want is to graduate. Then I want to go to hotel school so I can get a good job working for a big chain. Maybe even manage a hotel or motel. Maybe get to pick different places to live. Plus being a trained manager. If I get tired of it I can go work for some other kind of company.

John stopped writing and read what he had written so far. He realized that his freewriting contained a good idea for his essay. He brainstormed to come up with further ideas about why he planned to attend hotel management school, and then he organized his points in an outline, as follows:

- Topic: Going to hotel and restaurant school

- Reasons why I want to go:
  chance for good employment
    can work for one of the major hotel chains
    can rise to a higher-level job with one of these chains or perhaps work for an independent hotel
  chance to have responsibility
    eventually manage a hotel or run a big restaurant
    take care of travelers far from home
    be able to pick where to live, maybe in a resort area or near a beach
    manage a big staff, which is quite a challenge
  chance to have managerial training
    training program combines on-the-job experience with classwork
    managerial training is like business school
    skills could be used in some other kind of business if I don't like the actual hotel work

John decided that his essay would have five paragraphs: an introductory paragraph, a body paragraph for each of the three major reasons listed in his outline, and a concluding paragraph.

Drafting and Revising

John wrote a thesis statement to introduce his topic and his viewpoint. Here is John's thesis statement:

I want to go to hotel and restaurant school because it will give me a chance to get a good job, to take on important responsibilities, and to be trained as a manager.

John began his introductory paragraph with this sentence. Then he wrote the rest of his essay. When he revised his draft, he made sure that all of his points were clear.

Proofreading and Publishing

John proofread his essay and made a clean final copy of it. Then he shared it with his parents and with his English teacher.

ACTIVITIES AND ASSIGNMENTS

A. Answer the following questions about the case study:
1. What method did John use to come up with an idea for his paper? What other methods might he have used?
2. Carefully review John's outline. Do all his points support his thesis? Is the outline well organized? How might his outline be improved?
3. Look at John's thesis statement. Does it reveal his approach, or viewpoint? Explain. What does the sentence make the reader expect to find in the body of John's essay? Does the reader expect to find the points covered in any particular order?

B. Write your own personal essay on any topic that is interesting or important to you. Follow these steps:
1. If you have trouble thinking of a topic, try prewriting techniques such as freewriting or clustering. Once you have settled on a topic, decide whether your essay will be narrative, descriptive, expository, or persuasive.

2. Gather all the ideas and information that you will use in your essay. Then organize your notes into a rough outline for your essay.

3. Write a thesis statement that introduces your topic and purpose. Revise this statement as necessary to make it as clear as possible.

4. Draft your essay, referring to your prewriting notes and to your outline. Make sure that your writing remains focused on your topic and purpose throughout.

5. Revise your draft. Make sure that your points are clear and that you have not made any unsupported statements.

6. Proofread your essay for errors in grammar, usage, spelling, punctuation, capitalization, and manuscript form. Make a clean final copy of your essay, and share this copy with members of your family, with your classmates, and with your teacher.

ACT   See *Drama.*

ALLEGORY   An *allegory* is a story or tale with two or more levels of meaning—a literal level and one or more symbolic levels. The events, setting, and characters in an allegory are symbols for ideas or qualities. Many of Nathaniel Hawthorne's short stories, such as "The Minister's Black Veil," on page 302, are allegories.

ALLITERATION   *Alliteration* is the repetition of consonant sounds at the beginning of words or accented syllables. Sara Teasdale uses alliteration in the second stanza of her poem "Understanding":

> But you I never understood,
>   Your spirit's secret hides like gold
> Sunk in a Spanish galleon
>   Ages ago in waters cold.

Poets and other writers use alliteration to link and to emphasize ideas as well as to create pleasing, musical sounds.

ALLUSION   An *allusion* is a reference to a well-known person, place, event, literary work, or work of art. Writers often make allusions to stories from the Bible, to Greek and Roman myths, to plays by Shakespeare, to political and historical events, and to other materials with which they can expect their readers to be familiar. In the selection from *Hidden Name and Complex Fate,* on page 1044, Ralph Ellison alludes to Freudian psychology, to President Roosevelt's fireside chats, and to many famous Americans. By using allusions, writers can bring to mind complex ideas simply and easily.

ALMANAC   An *almanac* is a magazine or book, published monthly, seasonally, or yearly, that contains weather forecasts, tide tables, important dates, lists of upcoming events, statistics, and other information of use or interest to readers. The selection on page 121 is from *Poor Richard's Almanack* by Benjamin Franklin. Franklin's almanac is famous for its humorous and wise sayings.

ANALOGY   An *analogy* is a comparison between two unlike things. The purpose of an analogy is to describe something unfamiliar by pointing out its similarities to something that is familiar. In "A Noiseless Patient Spider," on page 473, Walt Whitman makes an analogy between a spider weaving its web and the soul seeking connections with things outside itself.
See *Metaphor* and *Simile.*

ANAPEST   See *Meter.*

ANECDOTE   An *anecdote* is a brief story about an interesting, amusing, or strange event. An anecdote is told to entertain or to make a point. In the excerpt from *Life on the Mississippi,* on page 502, Mark Twain tells several anecdotes about his experiences on the Mississippi River.

ANTAGONIST   An *antagonist* is a character or force in conflict with a main character, or protagonist. In Jack London's "To Build a Fire," on page 566, the antagonist is neither a person nor an animal but is rather the extreme cold of the Yukon. Not all stories contain antagonists. However, in many stories the conflict between the antagonist and the protagonist is the basis for the plot.
See *Conflict, Plot,* and *Protagonist.*

APHORISM   An *aphorism* is a general truth or observation about life, usually stated concisely and pointedly. Often witty and wise, aphorisms appear in many kinds of works. An essay writer may have an aphoristic style, making many such statements. Ralph Waldo Emerson was famous for his aphoristic style. His essay entitled "Fate" contains the following aphorisms:

> The book of Nature is the book of Fate.
> Men are what their mothers made them.
> Nature is what you may do.
> So far as a man thinks, he is free.
> A man's fortunes are the fruit of his character.

Used in an essay, an aphorism can be a memorable way to sum up or to reinforce a point or an argument.

APOSTROPHE   An *apostrophe* is a figure of speech in which a speaker directly addresses an absent person or a personified quality, object, or idea. Phillis Wheatley uses apostrophe in this line from "To the University of Cambridge, in New England":

> Students, to you 'tis given to scan the
>   heights

Apostrophe is often used in poetry and in speeches to add emotional intensity.
See *Figurative Language.*

ARGUMENTATION   *Argumentation* is discourse in which the writer presents and logically supports a particular view or opinion. Many critics and scholars distinguish argumentation, or reasoned discourse about opinions, from persuasion, or emotional discourse about opinions. However, some people use the two terms interchangeably.
See *Forms of Discourse* and *Persuasion.*

ASIDE   In a play, an *aside* is a speech delivered by an actor in such a way that other characters on the stage are presumed not to hear it. An aside generally reveals a character's inner thoughts. In Thornton Wilder's *Our Town,* which is introduced on page 920, the Stage Manager uses many asides to communicate to the audi-

ence. In the same play, when the dead speak among themselves during the funeral, they are overheard by the audience but are presumed not to be heard by the living characters.

ASSONANCE   *Assonance* is the repetition of vowel sounds in conjunction with dissimilar consonant sounds. Emily Dickinson uses assonance in the line "The mountain at a g*i*ven d*i*stance." The *i* sound is repeated in the words *given* and *distance,* in the context of the dissimilar consonant sounds *g–v* and *d–s.*

ATMOSPHERE   See *Mood.*

AUTOBIOGRAPHY   An *autobiography* is a form of nonfiction in which a person tells his or her own life story. Notable examples of autobiographies include those by Benjamin Franklin and Frederick Douglass.
See *Biography and Journal.*

BALLAD   A *ballad* is a songlike poem that tells a story, often one dealing with adventure and romance. Most ballads have the following characteristics:
1. Simple language
2. Four- or six-line stanzas
3. Rhyme
4. A regular meter

A *folk ballad* is one that originated in the oral tradition and was passed by word of mouth from generation to generation. Examples of folk ballads include "Yankee Doodle," "Casey Jones," and "John Henry." A *literary ballad* is one written by a specific person in imitation of the folk ballad. Henry Wadsworth Longfellow's "The Wreck of the Hesperus" is an example of a literary ballad. Here is its first stanza:

> 'Twas the schooner Hesperus,
>   That sailed the wintry sea;
> And the skipper had taken his little
>   daughter,
>   To bear him company.

BIOGRAPHY A *biography* is a form of nonfiction in which a writer tells the life story of another person. John Dos Passos's "Tin Lizzie," on page 756, is an example of biographical writing. See *Autobiography*.

BLANK VERSE *Blank verse* is poetry written in unrhymed iambic pentameter. An *iamb* is a poetic foot consisting of one weak stress followed by one strong stress. A *pentameter line* is a line of five poetic feet. Robert Frost's "Birches," on page 870, is written in blank verse.

CAESURA A *caesura* is a pause or break in the middle of a line of poetry. Double slanted lines (*//*) have been used to mark the caesuras in these lines from Jean Toomer's "November Cotton Flower":

Boll weevil's coming,//and the winter's
  cold,
Made cotton stalks look rusty,//seasons
  old

CATALOG A *catalog* is a list of people, places, or things in a literary work. In the following example from "As I Ebb'd with the Ocean of Life," Walt Whitman records what he sees along the shore:

Chaff, straw, splinters of wood,
  weeds, and the sea-gluten.
Scum, scales from shining rocks, leaves
  of salt-lettuce, left by the tide.

Whitman often used catalogs in his verse to suggest the fullness, diversity, and scope of American life or of the human experience.

CHARACTER A *character* is a person or animal who takes part in the action of a literary work. The following are some terms used to describe various types of characters:

The *main character* in a literary work is the one on whom the work focuses. *Major characters* in a literary work include the main character and any other characters who play significant roles. A *minor character* is one who does not play a significant role. A *round character* is one who is complex and multi-faceted, like a real person. A *flat character* is one who is one-dimensional. A *dynamic character* is one who changes in the course of a work. A *static character* is one who does not change in the course of a work.
See *Characterization* and *Motivation*.

CHARACTERIZATION *Characterization* is the act of creating and developing a character. There are two primary methods of characterization: direct and indirect. In *direct characterization*, a writer simply states a character's traits, as when the young girl in "A White Heron," on page 540, is called "a lonely country child." In *indirect characterization*, character is revealed by one of the following means:
1. By the words, thoughts, or actions of the character
2. By descriptions of the character's appearance or background
3. By what other characters say about the character
4. By the ways in which other characters react toward the character
See *Character*.

CINQUAIN See *Stanza*.

CLASSICISM *Classicism* is an approach to literature and the other arts that stresses reason, balance, clarity, ideal beauty, and orderly form in imitation of the arts of ancient Greece and Rome. Classicism is often contrasted with *Romanticism*, which stresses imagination, emotion, and individualism. Classicism also differs from *Realism*, which stresses the actual rather than the ideal.
See *Realism* and *Romanticism*.

CLIMAX The *climax* is the high point of inter

est or suspense in a literary work. For example, William Faulkner's "The Bear," on page 734, reaches its climax when the boy finally meets the bear. The climax generally appears near the end of a story, play, or narrative poem.
See *Plot.*

CONCEIT   A *conceit* is an unusual or surprising comparison between two very different things. In Edward Taylor's "Huswifery," on page 62, the granting of grace is compared to spinning yarn, weaving and dyeing cloth, and making clothes. Such a far-fetched comparison is a conceit.

CONCRETE POEM   A *concrete poem* is one with a shape that suggests its subject.

CONFESSIONAL POETRY   *Confessional poetry* is verse that speaks of personal matters, often with great frankness, or candor. Famous American confessional poets include Maxine Kumin, Robert Lowell, Sylvia Plath, Anne Sexton, and John Berryman.

CONFLICT   A *conflict* is a struggle between opposing forces. Sometimes this struggle is internal, or within a character, as in Bernard Malamud's "The First Seven Years," on page 946. At other times this struggle is external, or between a character and an outside force, as in Jack London's "To Build a Fire," on page 566. Conflict is one of the primary elements of narrative literature because most plots develop from conflicts.
See *Antagonist, Plot,* and *Protagonist.*

CONNOTATION   A *connotation* is an association that a word calls to mind in addition to the dictionary meaning of the word. Many words that are similar in their dictionary meanings, or denotations, are quite different in their connotations. Consider, for example, José Garcia Villa's line, "Be beautiful, noble, like the antique ant." This line would have a very different effect if it were "Be pretty, classy, like the old ant." Poets and other writers choose their words carefully so that the connotations of those words will be appropriate.
See *Denotation.*

CONSONANCE   *Consonance* is the repetition of consonant sounds at the ends of words or accented syllables. Emily Dickinson uses consonance in the following lines:

> But if he ask where you are hi*d*
> Until to-morrow,—happy letter!
> Gesture, coquette, an*d* shake your hea*d*!

COUPLET   See *Stanza.*

CRISIS   In the plot of a narrative, the *crisis* is the turning point for the protagonist—the point at which the protagonist's situation or understanding changes dramatically. In Bernard Malamud's "The First Seven Years," on page 946, the crisis comes when Feld recognizes that Sobel loves Miriam.

DACTYL   See *Meter.*

DENOTATION   The *denotation* of a word is its objective meaning, independent of other associations that the word brings to mind.
See *Connotation.*

DENOUEMENT   See *Plot.*

DESCRIPTION   A *description* is a portrayal, in words, of something that can be perceived by the senses. Writers create descriptions by using images, as N. Scott Momaday does in the following lines from "A Vision Beyond Time and Place," on page 1060:

> His eyes are deep and open to the wide world.
> At sunrise, precisely, they catch fire and close,
> having seen. The low light descends upon him.
> And when he lifts his voice, it enters upon

the silence and carries there, like the call of a bird.

Description is one of the major forms of discourse and appears quite often in literary works of all genres.

See *Image* and *Forms of Discourse*.

DEVELOPMENT   See *Plot*.

DIALECT   A *dialect* is the form of a language spoken by people in a particular region or group. Every dialect differs from every other dialect in the details of its vocabulary, grammar, and pronunciation. Writers often use dialect to make their characters seem realistic and to create local color. See, for example, Mark Twain's "The Notorious Jumping Frog of Calaveras County," on page 507.

See *Local Color* and *Vernacular*.

DIALOGUE   A *dialogue* is a conversation between characters. Writers use dialogue to reveal character, to present events, to add variety to narratives, and to arouse their reader's interest.

See *Drama*.

DICTION   *Diction* is a writer's or speaker's word choice. Diction is part of a writer's style and may be described as formal or informal, plain or ornate, common or technical, abstract or concrete. In the selection from *The Mortgaged Heart,* on page 1032, Carson McCullers uses formal diction suitable to her essay's serious purpose.

See *Style*.

DIMETER   See *Meter*.

DRAMA   A *drama* is a story written to be performed by actors. The playwright supplies dialogue for the characters to speak and stage directions that give information about costumes, lighting, scenery, properties, the setting, and the characters' movements and ways of speaking.

The audience accepts as believable the many dramatic conventions that are used such as soliloquies, asides, poetic language, or the passage of time between acts or scenes. An *act* is a major division in a drama. A *scene* is a minor division.

See *Genre*.

DRAMATIC CONVENTION   See *Drama*.

DRAMATIC DIALOGUE   A *dramatic dialogue* is a poem in which there are two speakers who converse with one another. An example in this text is Robert Frost's "The Death of the Hired Man," on page 881.

See *Dramatic Poem*.

DRAMATIC IRONY   See *Irony*.

DRAMATIC MONOLOGUE   A *dramatic monologue* is a poem or speech in which an imaginary character speaks to a silent listener. T.S. Eliot's "The Love Song of J. Alfred Prufrock," on page 810, is a dramatic monologue.

See *Dramatic Poem* and *Monologue*.

DRAMATIC POEM   A *dramatic poem* is one that makes use of the conventions of drama. Such poems may be monologues or dialogues or may present the speech of many characters. Examples of dramatic poems in this anthology include those from Edgar Lee Masters's *Spoon River Anthology,* on page 628, and Robert Frost's "The Death of the Hired Man," on page 881.

See *Dramatic Dialogue* and *Dramatic Monologue*.

DYNAMIC CHARACTER   See *Character*.

ELEGY   An *elegy* is a solemn and formal lyric poem about death, often one that mourns the passing of some particular person. Walt Whitman's "When Lilacs Last in the Dooryard

Bloom'd," on page 413, is an elegy lamenting the death of President Lincoln.
See *Lyric*.

END-STOPPED LINE   An *end-stopped line* is one in which the end of the line coincides with a pause or with the end of a thought. End-stopped lines are often recognizable because of their end punctuation—a period, a comma, a dash, or some other mark. These lines from "Southern Mansion," by Arna Bontemps, are end-stopped:

> The years go back with an iron clank,
> A hand is on the gate,
> A dry leaf trembles on the wall.
> Ghosts are walking.

See *Run-on Line*.

EPIGRAM   An *epigram* is a brief, pointed statement, in prose or in verse, often characterized by use of some rhetorical device or figure of speech. Benjamin Franklin was famous for his epigrams, which include "Fools make feasts, and wise men eat them," and "A plowman on his legs is higher than a gentleman on his knees."

ESSAY   An *essay* is a short, nonfiction work about a particular subject. The term *essay* comes from the Old French word *essai,* meaning "a trial or attempt." As the history of the word suggests, an essay is meant to be exploratory. It is not meant to be an exhaustive treatment of a subject. Essays can be classified as formal or informal, personal or impersonal. They can also be classified according to purpose, as expository, argumentative, descriptive, persuasive, or narrative.
See *Forms of Discourse*.

EXPOSITION   *Exposition* is writing or speech that explains, informs, or presents information. The main techniques of expository writing include analysis, classification, comparison and contrast, definition, and exemplification, or illus-tration. An essay may be primarily expository, as is Joan Didion's "On the Mall," on page 1052, or it may use exposition to support another purpose such as persuasion or argumentation, as in the selection from Carson McCullers's *The Mortgaged Heart,* on page 1032.

In a story or play, the exposition is that part of the plot that introduces the characters, the setting, and the basic situation.
See *Forms of Discourse* and *Plot*.

EXPRESSIONISM   *Expressionism* was an artistic movement of the early twentieth century. Expressionist painters, sculptors, and writers emphasized the inner experience of the individual rather than the time frame or physical objects of some absolute external reality. The Expressionist movement, exemplified by the works of artists like Van Gogh, influenced such writers as Eugene O'Neill and T.S. Eliot.

EXTENDED METAPHOR   See *Metaphor*.

FABLE   A *fable* is a brief story, usually with animal characters, that teaches a lesson, or moral. James Thurber was a famous American writer of fables.

FALLING ACTION   See *Plot*.

FICTION   *Fiction* is prose writing that tells about imaginary characters and events. Short stories and novels are works of fiction.
See *Genre, Narrative, Nonfiction,* and *Prose*.

FIGURATIVE LANGUAGE   *Figurative language* is writing or speech not meant to be taken literally. Writers use figurative language to express ideas in vivid and imaginative ways. For example, Emily Dickinson begins one poem with the following description of snow:

> It sifts from leaden sieves,
> It powders all the wood

By describing the snow as if it were flour, Dickinson renders a precise and compelling picture of it.
See *Figure of Speech.*

FIGURE OF SPEECH A *figure of speech* is an expression or a word used imaginatively rather than literally. Many types of figures of speech are used by writers in English, including apostrophe, hyperbole, irony, metaphor, metonymy, oxymoron, paradox, personification, simile, synecdoche, and understatement.
See *Figurative Language.* See also the entries for individual figures of speech.

FIRST-PERSON POINT OF VIEW See *Point of View.*

FLASHBACK A *flashback* is a section of a literary work that interrupts the chronological presentation of events to relate an event from an earlier time. A writer may present a flashback as a character's memory or recollection, as part of an account or story told by a character, as a dream or a daydream, or simply by having the narrator switch to a time in the past. A flashback occurs at the beginning of Ann Beattie's "Imagined Scenes," on page 996, when the protagonist remembers a time when she arrived home from shopping, was missing her keys, and was let in by David. Writers often use flashbacks as a dramatic way of providing background information.

FLAT CHARACTER See *Character.*

FOIL A *foil* is a character who provides a contrast to another character. In F. Scott Fitzgerald's "Winter Dreams," on page 672, Irene Scheerer is a foil for the tantalizing Judy Jones.

FOLK BALLAD See *Ballad.*

FOLKLORE *Folklore* is that body of stories, legends, myths, ballads, riddles, sayings, and other works that has arisen out of the oral traditions of peoples around the globe. The folklore traditions of the United States, including those of Native Americans and of the American pioneers, are especially rich.

FOOT See *Meter.*

FORESHADOWING *Foreshadowing* is the use, in a literary work, of clues that suggest events that have yet to occur.

FORMS OF DISCOURSE The *forms of discourse* are the various modes into which writing can be classified. Traditionally, writing has been divided into the following modes:
1. *Exposition,* or expository writing, which presents information
2. *Narration,* or narrative writing, which tells a story
3. *Description,* or descriptive writing, which portrays people, places, or things
4. *Persuasion,* or persuasive writing, which attempts to convince people to think or act in a certain way

Some people distinguish between *persuasion* and *argumentation,* defining the former as an attempt to move an audience by means of an emotional appeal and the latter as an attempt to move an audience by means of a reasoned or rational appeal.

Often, of course, several forms of discourse appear in a single work. A narrative, for example, may contain descriptive or expository passages.
See *Argumentation, Description, Exposition, Narration,* and *Persuasion.*

FREE VERSE *Free verse* is poetry that lacks a regular rhythmical pattern, or meter. A writer of free verse is at liberty to use any rhythms that are appropriate to what he or she is saying. Free verse has been widely used by twentieth-century poets such as Leslie Marmon Silko, who begins

"Where Mountain Lion Lay Down with Deer" with these lines:

> I climb the black rock mountain
> stepping from day to day
>   silently.

See *Meter.*

GENRE A *genre* is a division, or type, of literature. Literature is commonly divided into three major genres: poetry, prose, and drama. Each major genre can in turn be divided into smaller genres. Poetry can be divided into lyric, concrete, dramatic, narrative, and epic poetry. Prose can be divided into fiction (novels and short stories) and nonfiction (biography, autobiography, letters, essays, and reports). Drama can be divided into series drama, tragedy, comic drama, melodrama, and farce.
See *Drama, Poetry,* and *Prose.*

GOTHIC *Gothic* refers to the use of primitive, medieval, wild, or mysterious elements in literature. Gothic elements offended eighteenth-century classical writers but appealed to the Romantic writers who followed them. Gothic novels feature places like mysterious and gloomy castles, where horrifying, supernatural events take place. Their influence on Edgar Allan Poe is evident in "The Fall of the House of Usher," on page 212.

HARLEM RENAISSANCE The *Harlem Renaissance,* which occurred during the 1920s, was a time of black artistic creativity centered in Harlem, in New York City. Writers of the Harlem Renaissance include Countee Cullen, Claude McKay, Jean Toomer, Langston Hughes, and Arna Bontemps.

HEPTAMETER See *Meter.*

HEPTASTICH See *Stanza.*

HERO/HEROINE A *hero* or *heroine* is a character whose actions are inspiring or noble. The most obvious examples of heroes and heroines are the larger-than-life characters of myths and legend. More ordinary characters, however, can also act as heroes and heroines.

HEXAMETER See *Meter.*

HYPERBOLE A *hyperbole* is a deliberate exaggeration or overstatement. In Mark Twain's "The Notorious Jumping Frog of Calaveras County," on page 507, the claim that Jim Smiley would follow a bug as far as Mexico to win a bet is a hyperbole. As this example shows, hyperboles are often used for comic effect.

IAMB See *Meter.*

IAMBIC PENTAMETER *Iambic pentameter* is a line of poetry with five iambic feet, each containing one unstressed syllable followed by one stressed syllable ($\smile\,\prime$). Iambic pentameter may be rhymed or unrhymed. Unrhymed iambic pentameter is called *blank verse.* These concluding lines from Anne Bradstreet's "The Author to Her Book" are in iambic pentameter:

> And for thy, Mother, she alas is poor,
> Which caused her thus to send thee out
> of door.

See *Blank Verse* and *Meter.*

IDYLL An *idyll* is a poem or part of a poem that describes and idealizes country life. John Greenleaf Whittier's "Snowbound," on page 360, is an idyll.

IMAGE An *image* is a word or phrase that appeals to one or more of the five senses—sight, hearing, touch, taste, or smell.
See *Imagery.*

IMAGERY *Imagery* is the descriptive or figurative language used in literature to create word pictures for the reader. These pictures, or images, are created by details of sight, sound, taste, touch, smell, or movement. The following stanza, from Kuangchi C. Chang's "Garden of My Childhood," shows how a poet can use imagery to appeal to several senses:

> I ran past the old maple by the terraced hall
> And the singing crickets under the latticed
>   wall,
> And I kept on running down the walk
> Paved with pebbles of memory big and small
> Without turning to look until I was out of the
>   gate
> Through which there be no return at all.

IMAGISM *Imagism* was a literary movement that flourished between 1912 and 1917. Led by Ezra Pound and Amy Lowell, the Imagist poets rejected nineteenth-century poetic forms and language. Instead, they wrote short poems that used ordinary language and free verse to create sharp, exact, concentrated pictures. "Oread," by H.D., illustrates how the Imagists concentrated on describing a scene or object without making abstract comments:

> Whirl up, sea—
> whirl your pointed pines,
> splash your great pines
> on our rocks,
> hurl your green over us,
> cover us with your pools of fir.

INCITING INCIDENT   See *Plot.*

INCONGRUITY   *Incongruity* is the combination or juxtaposition of incompatible or opposite elements. Many examples of incongruity can be found in T.S. Eliot's "The Love Song of J. Alfred Prufrock," on page 810. The speaker constantly shifts from grand pronouncements like "Do I dare/Disturb the universe?" to pathetic ones like "Do I dare to eat a peach?"

INVERSION   An *inversion* is a reversal or change in the regular word order of a sentence. For instance, Ezra Pound begins one poem with

the line, "Sing we for love and idleness." This line reverses the usual subject-verb order, "We sing."

IRONY   *Irony* is a contrast between what is stated and what is meant, or between what is expected to happen and what actually happens. In *verbal irony* a word or a phrase is used to suggest the opposite of its usual meaning. In *dramatic irony,* there is a contradiction between what a character thinks and what the reader or audience knows to be true. In *irony of situation,* an event occurs that directly contradicts the expectations of the characters, of the reader, or of the audience.

IRONY OF SITUATION   See *Irony.*

JOURNAL   A *journal* is a daily autobiographical account of events and personal reactions. William Byrd's journal, on page 67, records events during an expedition to survey the Virginia-North Carolina boundary, while Mary Chesnut's journal, on page 437, records events during the Civil War.

LEGEND   A *legend* is a traditional story. Usually a legend deals with a particular person—a hero, a saint, or a national leader. Often legends reflect a people's cultural values. American legends include those of the early Native Americans and those about folk heroes such as Davy Crockett and Daniel Boone.
See *Myth.*

LITERARY LETTER   A *literary letter,* or epistle, is a work of literature created for publication and meant to be read by a large general audience but written as though it were a personal letter to an individual. Ezra Pound's "The River Merchant's Wife," on page 801, is a literary letter. See also the selection from de Crèvecoeur's *Letters from an American Farmer,* on page 156.

LOCAL COLOR *Local color* is the use in a literary work of characters and details unique to a particular geographic area. Local color can be created by the use of dialect and by descriptions of customs, clothing, manners, attitudes, scenery, and landscape. Local-color stories were especially popular after the Civil War, bringing readers the West of Bret Harte, the Mississippi River of Mark Twain, and the New England of Sarah Orne Jewett.

See *Realism* and *Regionalism.*

LYRIC POEM A *lyric poem* is a melodic poem that expresses the observations and feelings of a single speaker. Unlike a narrative poem, a lyric focuses on producing a single, unified effect. Types of lyrics include the elegy, the ode, and the sonnet. Among contemporary American poets, the lyric is the most common poetic form.

MAIN CHARACTER See *Character.*

METAPHOR A *metaphor* is a figure of speech in which one thing is spoken of as though it were something else. The identification suggests a comparison between the two things that are identified, as in "death *is* a long sleep" or "the sleeping dead."

A *mixed metaphor* occurs when two metaphors are jumbled together. For example, thorns and rain are illogically mixed in "the thorns of life rained down on him." A *dead metaphor* is one that has been overused and has become a common expression, such as "the arm of the chair" or "nightfall." Metaphors are used to make writing, especially poetry, more vivid, imaginative, and meaningful.

METER The *meter* of a poem is its rhythmical pattern. This pattern is determined by the number and types of stresses, or beats, in each line. To describe the meter of a poem, you must *scan* its lines. *Scanning* involves marking the stressed and unstressed syllables, as follows:

Soon as the sun forsook the eastern main
The pealing thunder shook the heav'nly
plain;

—Phillis Weatley, "An Hymn to the Evening"

As the example shows, each strong stress is marked with a slanted line (´) and each weak stress with a horseshoe symbol (˘). The weak and strong stresses are then divided by vertical lines (|) into groups called *feet.* The following types of feet are common in poetry written in English:

1. *Iamb:* a foot with one unstressed syllable followed by one stressed syllable, as in the word "around"
2. *Trochee:* a foot with one stressed syllable followed by one unstressed syllable, as in the word "broken"
3. *Anapest:* a foot with two unstressed syllables followed by one stressed syllable, as in the phrase "in a flash"
4. *Dactyl:* a foot with one stressed syllable followed by two unstressed syllables, as in the word "argument"
5. *Spondee:* a foot with two stressed syllables, as in the word "airship"
6. *Pyrrhic:* a foot with two unstressed syllables, as in the last foot of the word "imag|ining"
7. *Amphibrach:* a foot with an unstressed syllable, one stressed syllable, and another stressed syllable, as in the word "ungainly"
8. *Amphimacer:* a foot with a stressed syllable, one unstressed syllable, and another stressed syllable, as in "give and take"

Lines of poetry are often described as *iambic, trochaic, anapestic,* or *dactylic.*

Lines are also described in terms of the number of feet that occur in them, as follows:

1. *Monometer:* verse written in one-foot lines

Évĭl

Bĕgéts

Évĭl

   —Anonymous

2. *Dimeter:* verse written in two-foot lines

Thĭs ĭs | thĕ tíme

ŏf thĕ trág|ĭc mán

   —Elizabeth Bishop, "Visits to St. Elizabeth's"

3. *Trimeter:* verse written in three-foot lines:

Óvĕr | thĕ wín|tĕr glácĭĕrs

Ĭ sée | thĕ súm|mĕr glów,

Ănd thróugh | thĕ wíld-|pĭled snówdrĭft

Thĕ wárm |rósĕbŭds | bĕlów.

   —Ralph Waldo Emerson, "Beyond Winter"

4. *Tetrameter:* verse written in four-foot lines:

Thĕ sún | thăt bríef | Dĕcém|bĕr dáy

Rŏse chéer|lĕss óv|ĕr hílls | ŏf gráy

   —John Greenleaf Whittier, *Snowbound*

5. *Pentameter:* verse written in five-foot lines:

Ĭ dóubt | nŏt Gód | ĭs góod, | wĕll-méan|ĭng,

kínd,

Ănd díd | Hĕ stóop | tŏ quíb|blĕ cóuld | tĕll

whý

Thĕ lít|tlĕ búr|ĭed móle | cŏntín|ŭĕs blínd

   —Countee Cullen, "Yet Do I Marvel"

A six-foot line is called a hexameter. A line with seven feet is a *heptameter.*

A complete description of the meter of a line tells both how many feet there are in the line and what kind of foot is most common. Thus the lines from Countee Cullen's poem would be described as *iambic pentameter. Blank verse* is poetry written in unrhymed iambic pentameter.

Poetry that does not have a regular meter is called *free verse.*

MINOR CHARACTER   See *Character.*

MONOLOGUE   A *monologue* is a speech delivered entirely by one person or character. See *Dramatic Monologue* and *Soliloquy.*

MONOMETER   See *Meter.*

MOOD   *Mood,* or atmosphere, is the feeling created in the reader by a literary work or passage. Elements that can influence the mood of a work include its setting, tone, and events. See *Setting* and *Tone.*

MOTIVATION   A *motivation* is a reason that explains a character's thoughts, feelings, actions, or speech. Characters are motivated by their values and by their wants, desires, dreams, wishes, and needs. Sometimes the reasons for a character's actions are stated directly, as in Willa Cather's "A Wagner Matinée," on page 556, when Clark explains his reception of his aunt by saying, "I owed to this woman most of the good that ever came my way in my boyhood." At other times, the writer will just suggest a character's motivation. For example, at the end of Chapter 4 of Stephen Crane's *The Red Badge of Courage,* which is introduced on page 599, the loud soldier leaves a packet for his family with Henry. From the dialogue, the reader can guess that the soldier is motivated by his fear of the upcoming battle. The more effectively and persuasively a writer presents a character's motivations, the more convincing the character will be.

MYTH   A *myth* is a fictional tale that explains the actions of gods or heroes or the causes of natural phenomena. Some myths are a kind of primitive science, explaining how and why natural phenomena came about. Other myths express the central values of the people who created them. The stories of the Navaho and the Delaware peoples included in this text are examples of Native American myths.

NARRATION   *Narration* is writing that tells a story. The act of telling a story is also called *narration.* The *narrative,* or story, is told by a storyteller called the *narrator.* A story is usually told chronologically, in the order that events take place in time, though it may include flashbacks and foreshadowing. Narratives may be true, as are the events recorded in Mary Chesnut's journal, on page 437, or fictional, as are the events in Flannery O'Connor's "The Life You Save May Be Your Own," on page 956. Narration is one of the forms of discourse and is used in novels, short stories, plays, narrative poems, anecdotes, autobiographies, biographies, and reports.
See *Forms of Discourse, Narrative Poem,* and *Narrator.*

NARRATIVE   A *narrative* is a story told in fiction, nonfiction, poetry, or drama.
See *Narration.*

NARRATIVE POEM   A *narrative poem* tells a story in verse. Three traditional types of narrative verse are *ballads,* songlike poems that tell stories; *epics,* long poems about the deeds of gods or heroes; and *metrical romances,* poems that tell tales of love and chivalry. Examples of American narrative poems include Stephen Vincent Benét's *John Brown's Body* and the ballad "John Henry."
See *Ballad.*

NARRATOR   A *narrator* is a speaker or character who tells a story. A story or novel may be narrated by a main character, by a minor character, or by someone uninvolved in the story. The narrator may speak in the first person, as in John Updike's "The Slump," on page 978, or in the third person as in Ann Beattie's "Imagined Scenes," on page 996. In addition, the narrator may have an omniscient or a limited point of view. The *omniscient narrator* is all-knowing, while the *limited narrator* knows only what one character does. Because the writer's choice of narrator helps determine the point of view, this decision affects what version of a story is told and how readers will react to it.
See *Point of View.*

NATURALISM   *Naturalism* was a literary movement among novelists at the end of the nineteenth century and during the early decades of the twentieth century. The Naturalists tended to view people as hapless victims of immutable natural laws. Early exponents of Naturalism included Stephen Crane, Jack London, and Theodore Dreiser.
See *Realism.*

NONFICTION   *Nonfiction* is prose writing that presents and explains ideas or that tells about real people, places, objects, or events. Essays, biographies, autobiographies, journals, and reports are all examples of nonfiction.
See *Fiction* and *Genre.*

NOVEL   A *novel* is a long work of fiction. A novel often has a complicated plot, many major and minor characters, a significant theme, and several varied settings. Novels can be classified in many ways, based on the historical periods in which they are written, on the subjects and themes that they treat, on the techniques that are used in them, and on the literary movements that inspired them. James Fenimore Cooper, author of *The Prairie,* was the earliest well-known American novelist. Classic nineteenth-century novels include *Moby-Dick,* by Herman Melville; *The Scarlet Letter,* by Nathaniel Hawthorne; *The Adventures of Huckleberry Finn,* by Mark Twain; and *Portrait of a Lady,* by Henry James. Well-known twentieth-century novels include *The*

House of Mirth, by Edith Wharton; *O Pioneers!,* by Willa Cather; *An American Tragedy,* by Theodore Dreiser; *The Great Gatsby,* by F. Scott Fitzgerald; *The Sound and the Fury,* by William Faulkner; and *Invisible Man,* by Ralph Ellison. A *novella* is not as long as a novel but is longer than a short story. Ernest Hemingway's *The Old Man and the Sea* is a novella.

NOVELLA See *Novel.*

OCTAVE See *Stanza.*

ODE An *ode* is a long, formal lyric poem with a serious theme that may have a traditional stanza structure. An ode may be written for a private occasion or for a public ceremony. Odes often honor people, commemorate events, respond to natural scenes, or consider serious human problems.
See *Lyric.*

OMNISCIENT POINT OF VIEW See *Point of View.*

ONOMATOPOEIA *Onomatopoeia* is the use of words that imitate sounds. Examples of such words are *buzz, hiss, murmur,* and *rustle.* Isabella Stewart Gardner uses onomatopoeia in "Summer Remembered":

> Sounds sum and summon the remembering of
>   summers.
> The humming of the sun
> The mumbling in the honey-suckle vine
> The whirring in the clovered grass
> The pizzicato plinkle of ice in an auburn
>   uncle's amber glass.

ORAL TRADITION *Oral tradition* is the passing of songs, stories, and poems from generation to generation by word of mouth. The oral tradition in America has preserved Native American myths and legends, spirituals, folk ballads, and other stories or songs originally heard and memorized rather than written down.
See *Ballad, Folklore, Legend, Myth,* and *Spiritual.*

ORATORY *Oratory* is public speaking that is formal, persuasive, and emotionally appealing. Patrick Henry's "Speech in the Virginia Convention," on page 126, is an example of oratory.

ORNATE STYLE *Ornate style* is a way of writing that uses long, complicated sentences with elaborate figures of speech, parallel structures, uncommon allusions, and unfamiliar word choices. This style was used during the seventeenth and eighteenth centuries by writers such as Cotton Mather. Because of its complexity and formality, writing in the ornate style is harder to follow than that in the contrasting plain style.
See *Plain Style* and *Style.*

OVERSTATEMENT See *Hyperbole.*

OXYMORON An *oxymoron* is a figure of speech that combines two opposing or contradictory ideas. An oxymoron, such as "freezing fire" or the often used "conspicuous by his absence," suggests a paradox in just a few words.
See *Figurative Language* and *Paradox.*

PARABLE A *parable* is a brief story, usually with human characters, that teaches a moral lesson. The most famous parables are those told by Christ in the Bible. Some critics would classify Nathaniel Hawthorne's "The Minister's Black Veil," on page 302, as a parable.

PARADOX A *paradox* is a statement that seems to be contradictory but that actually presents a truth. Marianne Moore uses paradox in "Nevertheless" when she says, "Victory won't come/to me unless I go/to it." Because a paradox is surprising or even shocking, it draws

the reader's attention to what is being said.
See *Figurative Language* and *Oxymoron.*

PARALLELISM   *Parallelism* is the repetition of a grammatical structure. Robert Hayden concludes his poem "Astronauts" with these questions in parallel form:

> What do we want of these men?
> What do we want of ourselves?

Parallelism is used in poetry and in other writing to emphasize and to link related ideas.

PARODY   A *parody* is a humorous imitation of a literary work, one that exaggerates or distorts the characteristic features of the original. American author Donald Barthelme was noted for his parodic style, which he used to point out absurd aspects of modern life.

PERSONIFICATION   *Personification* is a figure of speech in which a nonhuman subject is given human characteristics. In "April Rain Song," Langston Hughes personifies the rain:

> Let the rain kiss you.
> Let the rain sing you a lullaby.

Effective personification of things or ideas makes them seem vital and alive, as if they were human.
See *Figurative Language.*

PERSUASION   *Persuasion* is writing or speech that attempts to convince a reader to think or act in a particular way. During the Revolutionary War period, leaders such as Patrick Henry, Thomas Paine, and Thomas Jefferson used persuasion in their political arguments. Persuasion is also used in advertising, in editorials, in sermons, and in political speeches.
See *Argumentation* and *Forms of Discourse.*

PLAIN STYLE   *Plain style* is a way of writing that uses uncomplicated sentences and ordinary words to make simple, direct statements. This style was favored by those Puritans who rejected ornate style because they wanted to express themselves clearly and directly, in accordance with the austerity of their religious beliefs. In the twentieth century, Ernest Hemingway was a master of plain style.
See *Ornate Style* and *Style.*

PLOT   *Plot* is the sequence of events in a literary work. In most novels, dramas, short stories, and narrative poems, the plot involves both characters and a central conflict. The plot usually begins with an *exposition* that introduces the setting, the characters, and the basic situation. This is followed by the *inciting incident,* which introduces the central conflict. The conflict then increases during the *development* until it reaches a high point of interest or suspense, the *climax.* The climax is followed by the end, or *resolution,* of the central conflict. Any events that occur after the resolution make up the *denouement.* The events that lead up to the climax make up the *rising action.* The events that follow the climax make up the *falling action.*
See *Conflict.*

POETRY   *Poetry* is one of the three major types of literature. In poetry, form and content are closely connected, like the two faces of a single coin. Poems are often divided into lines and stanzas and often employ regular rhythmical patterns, or meters. Most poems make use of highly concise, musical, and emotionally charged language. Many also make use of imagery, figurative language, and special devices such as rhyme.
See *Genre.*

POINT OF VIEW   *Point of view* is the perspective, or vantage point, from which a story is told. Three commonly used points of view are first-person, omniscient third-person, and limited third-person.

In the *first-person point of view,* the narrator is a character in the story and refers to himself or herself with the first-person pronoun *I.* "The Fall of the House of Usher," on page 212, is told by a first-person narrator.

The two kinds of third-person point of view, limited and omniscient, are called "third person" because the narrator uses third-person pronouns such as *he* and *she* to refer to the characters. There is no *I* telling the story.

In stories told from the *omniscient third-person point of view,* the narrator knows and tells about what each character feels and thinks. "The Devil and Tom Walker," on page 184, is written from the omniscient third-person point of view.

In stories told from the *limited third-person point of view,* the narrator relates the inner thoughts and feelings of only one character, and everything is viewed from this character's perspective. "An Occurrence at Owl Creek Bridge," on page 530, is written from the limited third-person point of view.
See *Narrator.*

PROSE *Prose* is the ordinary form of written language. Most writing that is not poetry, drama, or song is considered prose. Prose is one of the major genres of literature and occurs in two forms: fiction and nonfiction.
See *Fiction, Genre,* and *Nonfiction.*

PROTAGONIST The *protagonist* is the main character in a literary work. In "The Jilting of Granny Weatherall," on page 694, the protagonist is the dying grandmother.
See *Antagonist.*

PUN A *pun* is a play on words. Robert Frost's "Mending Wall," on page 873, contains a pun in the lines "Before I built a wall I'd ask to know/ What I was walling in or walling out,/And to

whom I was like to give offense." Of course, the word "offense" is meant to suggest, in addition to its normal meaning, the phrase "a fence."

PYRRHIC See *Meter.*

QUATRAIN See *Stanza.*

REALISM *Realism* is the presentation in art of the details of actual life. Realism was also a literary movement that began during the nineteenth century and that stressed the actual as opposed to the imagined or the fanciful. The Realists tried to write truthfully and objectively about ordinary characters in ordinary situations. They reacted against Romanticism, rejecting heroic, adventurous, unusual, or unfamiliar subjects. The Realists, in turn, were followed by the Naturalists, who traced the effects of heredity and environment on people helpless to change their situations. American realism grew from the work of local-color writers such as Bret Harte and Sarah Orne Jewett and is evident in the writings of major figures such as Mark Twain and Henry James.
See *Local Color, Naturalism,* and *Romanticism.*

REFRAIN A *refrain* is a repeated line or group of lines in a poem or song. Most refrains end stanzas, as does "And the tide rises, the tide falls," the refrain in Henry Wadsworth Longfellow's poem on page 338; or "Coming for to carry me home," the refrain in "Swing Low, Sweet Chariot," on page 426. Although some refrains are nonsense lines, many increase suspense or emphasize character and theme.

REGIONALISM *Regionalism* in literature is the tendency among certain authors to write about specific geographical areas. Regional writers, like Willa Cather and William Faulkner, present the distinct culture of an area, including its speech, customs, beliefs, and history. Local-color writing may be considered a type of Re-

gionalism, but Regionalists, like the southern writers of the 1920s, usually go beyond mere presentation of cultural idiosyncracies and attempt, instead, a sophisticated sociological or anthropological treatment of the culture of a region.
See *Local Color* and *Setting.*

REPETITION   *Repetition* is the repeated use of any element of language—a sound, a word, a phrase, a clause, a sentence, a grammatical pattern, or a rhythmical pattern. For example, in "The Mortgaged Heart," on page 1032, Carson McCullers repeats key words—*alone, lonely,* and *loneliness*—to connect and unify her arguments. Careless repetition bores a reader, but successful repetition links ideas and emphasizes main points.

RESOLUTION   See *Plot.*

RHYME   *Rhyme* is the repetition of sounds at the ends of words. Rhyming words have identical vowel sounds in their final accented syllables. The consonants before the vowels may be different, but any consonants, occurring after these vowels are the same, as in *frog* and *bog* or *willow* and *pillow. End rhyme* occurs when rhyming words are repeated at the ends of lines. *Internal rhyme* occurs when rhyming words fall within a line. *Approximate,* or *slant, rhyme* occurs when the rhyming sounds are similar, but not exact, as in *prove* and *glove.*
See *Rhyme Scheme.*

RHYME SCHEME   A *rhyme scheme* is a regular pattern of rhyming words in a poem. To describe a rhyme scheme, one uses a letter of the alphabet to represent each rhyming sound in a poem or stanza. Consider how letters are used to represent the rhymes in the following example:

With innocent wide penguin eyes, three	a
large fledgling mocking-birds below	b
the pussywillow tree,	a
stand in a row.	b
—Marianne Moore, "Bird-Witted"	

The rhyme scheme of this section of Moore's poem is *abab.*
See *Rhyme.*

RHYTHM   *Rhythm* is the pattern of beats, or stresses, in spoken or written language. Prose and free verse are written in the irregular rhythmical patterns of everyday speech.

Consider, for example, the rhythmical pattern in the following free verse lines by Gwendolyn Brooks:

Life for my child is simple, and is good.
He knows his wish. Yes, but that is not all.
Because I know mine too.

Traditional poetry often follows a regular rhythmical pattern, as in the following lines by America's first great female poet, Anne Bradstreet:

In critic's hands beware thou dost not come,
And take thy way where yet thou art not known

—"The Author to Her Book"

See *Meter.*

RISING ACTION   The *rising action* is that part of the plot in a story that leads up to the climax. During the rising action, suspense increases as the complications of the conflict develop. In Mark Helprin's "Katherine Comes to Yellow Sky," on page 1012, the rising action continues until Katherine watches the sunrise and learns that she has reached Yellow Sky.
See *Plot.*

ROMANCE   A *romance* is a story that presents remote or imaginative incidents rather than ordinary, commonplace experiences. Although the events in a romance are improbable or impossible, the characters still reflect what Nathaniel

Hawthorne calls "the truth of the human heart." Hawthorne considered his writings, such as *The House of the Seven Gables,* to be "romances" rather than "novels" because they were imaginative rather than realistic.

See *Novel* and *Romanticism.*

ROMANTICISM *Romanticism* was a literary and artistic movement of the nineteenth century, one that arose in reaction against eighteenth-century Neoclassicism and that placed a premium on fancy, imagination, emotion, nature, individuality, and exotica. Romantic elements can be found in the works of American writers as diverse as Cooper, Poe, Thoreau, Emerson, Dickinson, Hawthorne, and Melville. Romanticism is particularly evident in the works of the New England Transcendentalists.

See *Classicism* and *Transcendentalism.*

ROUND CHARACTER   See *Character.*

RUN-ON LINE   A *run-on line* is one in which the thought continues, without pause, into the next line. Jean Toomer's "Song of the Son" illustrates how a line can run on to the next stanza as well as to the next line:

O Negro slaves, dark purple ripened plums,
Squeezed, and bursting in the pine-wood air,
Passing, before they stripped the old tree
  bare
One plum was saved for me, one seed
  becomes

An everlasting song, a singing tree,

Run-on lines change a poem's rhythm, adding variety and helping avoid monotony.

See *End-Stopped Line.*

SATIRE   *Satire* is writing that ridicules or criticizes individuals, ideas, institutions, social conventions, or other works of art or literature. The writer of a satire, or satirist, may use a tolerant, sympathetic tone or an angry, bitter tone. Some satire is written in prose and some in poetry. Examples of satire in this text include Stephen Crane's "War Is Kind," on page 609, Edwin Arlington Robinson's "Miniver Cheevy," on page 622, and W.H. Auden's "The Unknown Citizen," on page 899.

SCANSION   *Scansion* is the process of analyzing a poem's metrical pattern. When a poem is scanned, its stressed and unstressed syllables are marked to show what poetic feet are used and how many feet appear in each line. The last two lines of Edna St. Vincent Millay's "I Shall Go Back Again to the Bleak Shore" may be scanned as follows:

But I | shall find | the sul|len rocks |
  and skies
Unchanged | from what | they were |
  when I | was young.

See *Meter.*

SCENE   See *Drama.*

SENSORY LANGUAGE   *Sensory language* is writing or speech that appeals to one or more of the five senses.

See *Image.*

SETTING   The *setting* of a literary work is the time and place of the action. A setting may serve any of a number of functions. It may provide a background for the action. It may be a crucial element in the plot or central conflict. It may also create a certain emotional atmosphere, or mood. The setting of Ernest Hemingway's "In Another Country," on page 664, is Milan, Italy, during World War I. The story centers on the hospital where the protagonist receives physical therapy for a war injury. The setting therefore provides a backdrop for the action and is central to the plot. Hemingway also uses his setting to suggest a mood of disillusionment and isolation. See *Mood.*

SHORT STORY   A *short story* is a brief work of fiction. The short story resembles the novel but generally has a simpler plot and setting. In addition, the short story tends to reveal character at a crucial moment rather than to develop it through many incidents. For example, Thomas Wolfe's "The Far and the Near," on page 704, concentrates on what happens to the engineer when he visits the people who waved to him every day. The American writers Washington Irving, Edgar Allan Poe, and Nathaniel Hawthorne were instrumental in creating and developing the short story genre. Other great American writers of short stories include Mark Twain, Bret Harte, Ambrose Bierce, Sarah Orne Jewett, Willa Cather, Jack London, O. Henry, Ernest Hemingway, Katherine Anne Porter, Eudora Welty, Flannery O'Connor, and John Updike.
See *Fiction* and *Genre.*

SIMILE   A *simile* is a figure of speech that makes a direct comparison between two subjects using either *like* or *as.* Here are two examples of similes:

> The trees looked like pitch forks against the sullen sky.

> Her hair was as red as a robin's breast.

See *Figurative Language.*

SOLILOQUY   A *soliloquy* in a play or prose work is a long speech made by a character who is alone and who reveals his or her private thoughts and feelings to the audience. By alternating the speeches of Paul Klee and of the Secret Police in his story on page 990, Donald Barthelme adapts the soliloquy to the short story.
See *Monologue.*

SONNET   A *sonnet* is a fourteen-line lyric poem focused on a single theme. Sonnets have many variations but are usually written in iambic pentameter, following one of two traditional patterns. The *Petrarchan,* or *Italian, sonnet* is divided into two parts, the eight-line octave and the six-line sestet. The octave rhymes *abba abba,* while the sestet generally rhymes *cde cde* or uses some combination of *cd* rhymes. The two parts of the Petrarchan sonnet work together: the octave raises a question, states a problem, or presents a brief narrative, and the sestet answers the question, solves the problem, or comments on the narrative.

The *Shakespearean,* or *English, sonnet* is made up of three quatrains and a concluding couplet and follows the rhyme scheme *abab cdcd efef gg.* Although the three quatrains may state and resolve a problem, as in the Petrarchan octave and sestet, each quatrain usually explores a different aspect of the main theme. The couplet then sums up the rest of the poem. See *Lyric.*

SPEAKER   The *speaker* is the voice of a poem. Although the speaker is often the poet, the speaker may also be a fictional character or even an inanimate object or another type of nonhuman entity. Interpreting a poem often depends upon recognizing who the speaker is, who the speaker is addressing, and what the speaker's attitude, or tone, is. In these lines from Sylvia Plath's "Mushrooms," the speaker is one (or perhaps all) of the mushrooms of the title:

> We shall by morning
> Inherit the earth.
> Our foot's in the door.

See *Point of View.*

SPIRITUAL   A *spiritual* is a type of black American folk song dating from the period of slavery and Reconstruction. A typical spiritual deals both with religious freedom and, on an allegorical level, with political and economic freedom. For example, in some spirituals the Biblical river Jordan was used as a symbol for the Ohio River, which separated slave states from free states, and the Biblical promised land, Canaan, was used as a symbol for the free northern United States. The spirituals were developed on models derived from white American hymns and from African work songs and chants. Most spirituals contained Biblical allusions and made use of repetition, parallelism, and rhyme. Spirituals had a profound influence on the development of both poetry and song in the United States. See "Swing Low, Sweet Chariot," on page 426, and "Go Down, Moses," on page 427.

SPONDEE   See *Meter.*

STAGE DIRECTIONS   See *Drama.*

STANZA   A *stanza* is a group of lines in a poem, considered as a unit. Many poems are divided into stanzas that are separated by spaces. Stanzas often function just like paragraphs in prose. Each stanza states and develops a single main idea.

Stanzas are commonly named according to the number of lines found in them, as follows:
1. *Couplet:* a two-line stanza
2. *Tercet:* a three-line stanza
3. *Quatrain:* a four-line stanza
4. *Cinquain:* a five-line stanza
5. *Sestet:* a six-line stanza
6. *Heptastich:* a seven-line stanza
7. *Octave:* an eight-line stanza

STATIC CHARACTER   See *Character.*

STEREOTYPE   See *Character.*

STREAM OF CONSCIOUSNESS   *Stream of consciousness* is a narrative technique that presents thoughts as if they were coming directly from a character's mind. Instead of being arranged in chronological order, the events of the story are presented from the character's point of view, mixed in with the character's feelings and memories just as they might spontaneously occur in the mind of a real person. Katherine Anne Porter uses this technique in "The Jilting of Granny Weatherall," on page 694, to show Granny's dying thoughts and feelings. Ambrose Bierce also uses the stream-of-consciousness technique in his short story "An Occurrence at Owl Creek Bridge," on page 530. Stream-of-consciousness writing reveals a character's complex psychology and presents it in realistic detail.
See *Point of View.*

STYLE   A writer's *style* is his or her typical way of writing. Style includes word choice, tone, degree of formality, figurative language, rhythm, grammatical structure, sentence length, organization—in short, every feature of a writer's use of language. Ernest Hemingway, for example, is noted for a simple prose style that contrasts with Thomas Paine's aphoristic style and with N. Scott Momaday's reflective style.
See *Diction, Ornate Style,* and *Plain Style.*

SUBPLOT   A *subplot* is a second, less important plot within a story. In Stephen Crane's *The Red Badge of Courage,* which is introduced on page 599, the tall soldier's story is told along with Henry's, thus adding to Crane's picture of the war. A subplot may add to, contrast with, reflect, or vary the main plot.
See *Plot.*

SURPRISE ENDING   A *surprise ending* is a conclusion that violates the expectations of the reader. Often a surprise ending is foreshadowed, or subtly hinted at, throughout the course of a work.

SUSPENSE   *Suspense* is a feeling of growing uncertainty about the outcome of events in a

literary work. Writers create suspense by raising questions in the minds of their readers. Because readers are curious or concerned, they keep reading to find out what will happen next. Suspense builds until the climax of the plot, at which point the suspense reaches its peak. Thereafter, the suspense is generally resolved.
See *Climax* and *Plot.*

SYMBOL A *symbol* is anything that stands for or represents something else. A *conventional symbol* is one that is widely known and accepted, such as a voyage symbolizing life or a skull symbolizing death. A *personal symbol* is one developed for a particular work by a particular author. Examples in this text include Hawthorne's black veil, Melville's white whale, Jewett's white heron, and Faulkner's bear.

SYMBOLISM *Symbolism* was a literary movement during the nineteenth century that influenced many poets, including the Imagists and T.S. Eliot. Symbolists turned away from everyday realistic details, trying instead to express emotions by using a pattern of symbols.
See *Imagism* and *Realism.*

SYNECDOCHE *Synecdoche* is a figure of speech in which a part of something is used to stand for the whole thing. In "Recuerdo," when Edna St. Vincent Millay says, "We hailed, 'Good morrow, mother!' to a shawl-covered head," the shawl-covered head stands for the woman being greeted.
See *Figurative Language.*

TERCET See *Stanza.*

TETRAMETER See *Meter.*

THEME A *theme* is a central message or insight into life revealed by a literary work. An essay's theme is often directly stated in its thesis statement. The theme of a story, poem, or play, however, is usually not directly stated. For example, in "A Worn Path," on page 710, Eudora Welty does not directly say that Phoenix Jackson's difficult journey shows the power of love, but readers learn this indirectly by the end of the story.

THIRD-PERSON POINT OF VIEW See *Point of View.*

TONE The *tone* of a literary work is the writer's attitude toward his or her subject, characters, or audience. A writer's tone may be formal or informal, friendly or distant, personal or pompous. For example, William Faulkner's tone in his "Nobel Prize Acceptance Speech," on page 1028, is earnest and serious, while James Thurber's tone in "The Night the Ghost Got In," on page 778, is humorous and ironic.
See *Mood.*

TRANSCENDENTALISM *Transcendentalism* was an American literary and philosophical movement of the nineteenth century. The Transcendentalists, who were based in New England, believed that intuition and the individual conscience "transcend" experience and thus are better guides to truth than are the senses and logical reason. Influenced by Romanticism, the Transcendentalists respected the individual spirit and the natural world, believing that divinity was present everywhere, in nature and in each person. This last notion, that of an omnipresent divinity, or Over-Soul, shows the influence on Transcendentalism of the Hindu religion and of the Swedish mystic Emanuel Swedenborg. The Transcendentalists included Ralph Waldo Emerson, Henry David Thoreau, Bronson Alcott, W.H. Channing, Margaret Fuller, and Elizabeth Peabody.
See *Romanticism.*

TRIMETER See *Meter.*

TROCHEE See *Meter.*

UNDERSTATEMENT *Understatement* means saying less than is actually meant, generally in an ironic way. An example of understatement is the description of a flooded area as "slightly soggy."
See *Figurative Language, Hyperbole,* and *Irony.*

VERBAL IRONY See *Irony.*

VERNACULAR The *vernacular* is the ordinary language of people in a particular region. Instead of using a more formal literary language, writers may use the vernacular to create realistic characters or to approach readers informally. See *Dialect.*

VILLANELLE A *villanelle* is a nineteen-line poem with only two rhymes that follows a strict pattern popular in traditional French poetry. It has two refrains formed by repeating line 1 in lines 6, 12, and 18 and by repeating line 3 in lines 9, 15, and 19. The three lines in each of the first five 3-line stanzas rhyme *aba;* the final quatrain rhymes *abaa.* An example of a villanelle in this text is Theodore Roethke's "The Waking," on page 1094.

HANDBOOK OF CRITICAL THINKING AND READING TERMS

ABSTRACT *adj.* Anything that is not concrete or definite is *abstract*. The concrete is perceived by one of the senses; the abstract is conceived by the intellect. A portrait is concrete because it contains numerous concrete details—eyes, mouth, nose, hair, clothing, and so on. A stick figure drawing, on the other hand, is abstract because most of these details are left out and the mind must decide what the drawing represents. Words and the ideas that they represent can also be abstract. Some common abstract words are *truth, beauty, love, freedom,* and *courage.* Less obvious examples include *society, realism, nature, sanity,* and *history.* You can point, for instance, to concrete actions and events from history, but you cannot point to history itself.

People can make abstract ideas clear to themselves and to others by using specific examples and illustrations. Suppose, for instance, that a writer wants to convey the abstract idea that a character is wealthy. The writer might do this by showing that the character has many possessions that are normally associated with wealth, such as a sports car, a yacht, and a country estate. Another way to express abstract ideas clearly is to use figures of speech. For example, the simile "time is like a river" uses a concrete image—a river—to describe an abstraction, time.

ANALOGY *n.* An *analogy* is a comparison that explains one subject by pointing out its similarities to another subject. In his famous "Speech in the Virginia Convention," on page 126, Patrick Henry makes an analogy between the crisis facing the American colonies and the Biblical story of Christ's betrayal: "Suffer not yourselves to be betrayed with a kiss." This analogy compares the British to Judas Iscariot, who betrayed Christ by kissing his cheek. A careful writer invents or selects analogies that are likely to fall within the experience of the reader. Patrick Henry, for instance, could reasonably assume that his audience would be familiar with the Biblical story to which he referred. A careful reader evaluates a writer's analogies and rejects those which seem unfair or illogical.

An analogy may be expressed using a variety of literary techniques such as simile, metaphor, and extended metaphor. See the definition of these terms in the Handbook of Literary Terms and Techniques.

ANALYSIS *n.* *Analysis* is the process of studying the parts of a whole. The process of analysis consists of the following steps:

1. Divide the object you are studying into its parts.
2. Observe and describe the characteristics of each part.
3. Look for relationships among the parts and between each part and the whole.

An analysis might also take the form of a series of questions:

1. What are the parts that make up the whole?
2. How are they similar to one another?
3. How are they different?
4. How would the whole be affected if the parts were arranged differently?
5. What function does each part serve?

When you analyze a literary work, break it into parts, observe the characteristics of these parts, and consider how they are related. For example, you might analyze an essay by considering its subject, tone, diction, and structure. A short story or novel could be analyzed into its plot, characters, dialogue, setting, and theme.

ARGUMENT *n.* An *argument* is a set of statements consisting of one or more premises and a conclusion. *Premises* are statements assumed to be true in the context of the argument, and the *conclusion* is a statement that logically follows from the premises. If the premises are true, then the conclusion should also be true. For example, the Declaration of Independence gives a long list of premises—specific examples of King George III's treatment of the Americans—to support the conclusion that the King is a tyrant.

People also present arguments when writing about literature. They use the various parts of a literary work—plot, characters, images, and dialogue, for example—as premises, or evidence, to support their conclusions, or interpretations. For instance, a writer might argue on the basis of details mentioned in T. S. Eliot's "The Love Song of J. Alfred Prufrock", on page 810, that Prufrock is facing some crucial decision in his life.

The term *argument* is also used to describe a brief summary, or synopsis, of a literary work. Thus a paragraph summarizing the plot of Arthur Miller's *The Crucible,* on page 1172, might be described as presenting "the argument of the play."
See *Conclusion, Deduction, Evidence, Induction,* and *Inference.*

BANDWAGON   See *Propaganda Technique.*

BEGGING THE QUESTION   See *Logical Fallacy.*

CATEGORIZATION *n.*   *Categorization* is the process of placing objects or ideas into groups or classes. Objects or ideas possessing similar characteristics may be placed in the same cate-

gory. To categorize something, follow these steps:
1. Observe the characteristics of the object you are studying.
2. Think of other subjects that share these qualities.
3. Select a name or phrase that best characterizes the group.

Literary works may be placed in categories for the purpose of analysis and discussion. Prose and poetry are two very general categories into which all works of literature can be grouped. Each, however, can be further divided into more useful categories. For example, Frederick Douglass's *My Bondage and My Freedom,* on page 430, is a narrative of his own real-life experiences. Therefore, it may be placed into the category of autobiography. Usually, specific categories are more useful than general ones. A standard literary category such as the sonnet, detective story, slave narrative, or biography is called a *genre.*

CAUSE AND EFFECT *n. phrase*   When one event precedes and brings about another event, the first is said to be a *cause* and the second an *effect. Cause and effect* are extremely important in the study of literature. The plot of a short story, for example, is a series of causes and effects. One event causes the next, which causes the next, and so on to the end of the story. In *Moby-Dick,* an excerpt from which appears on page 318, Captain Ahab's loss of his leg causes his obsession with the great white whale. Readers must judge whether the cause-and-effect relationships in a plot are believable or true-to-life.

In addition, writers choose their language carefully in order to cause certain effects in their readers. For example, a writer might describe a battle scene in explicit detail in order to cause the reader to feel the horror and savagery of war.

CIRCULAR REASONING   See *Logical Fallacy.*

COMPARISON *n.*   *Comparison* is the process of observing and pointing out similarities. For example, a comparison of the selections from Walt Whitman and Carl Sandburg might note the following similarities: Each author celebrates common people and democracy, each takes inspiration from the world of nature, and each writes in free verse.
See *Contrast.*

CONCLUSION *n.*   A *conclusion* is anything that follows reasonably from something else. In an argument, the conclusion follows from supporting statements, facts, and reasons. Thus the Declaration of Independence uses a series of reasons to support the conclusion that the colonies are justified in separating from England.

CONTRAST *n.*   *Contrast* is the process of observing and pointing out differences. In any kind of analysis, differences can be as significant as similarities. Contrast, therefore, is an important technique in literary study.
See *Comparison.*

DEDUCTION *n.*   *Deduction* is the form of argument in which the conclusion has to be true if the premises are true. The following is a typical deductive argument:

Major premise: The Civil War was fought from 1861 to 1865.
Minor premise: Stephen Crane was born in 1871.
Conclusion: Stephen Crane did not fight in the Civil War.

If you accept the premises of the argument, then you must also accept the conclusion. Therefore, the argument is a deduction.
See *Generalization* and *Inference.*

DEFINITION *n.*   *Definition* is the process of explaining the meaning of a word or phrase. Definition is essential to the process of communication because it establishes agreed-upon meanings for words. The simplest type of definition, *ostensive definition,* involves pointing to something and saying its name. If you point to an object and say, "book," you are giving an ostensive definition of the word *book.* The most common type of definition is the kind found in dictionaries, *lexical definition.* Lexical definition uses words to explain the meanings of other words and phrases. Definition by synonym, by antonym, by example, and by genus and differentia are all types of lexical definition.

In a *definition by synonym,* you use a word or phrase that has the same meaning: An *attorney* is a "lawyer."

In *definition by antonym,* you use a negation along with a word or a phrase that has an opposite meaning: A *coward* is one who demonstrates a "lack of courage."

In *definition by example,* you list things to which the term being defined applies: The *Transcendentalists* included Henry David Thoreau, Ralph Waldo Emerson, Margaret Fuller, and Bronson Alcott.

In a *genus and differentia definition,* you place the thing to be defined into a general category, group, or *genus.* Then you tell how it differs from other members of the group:

To be defined: *French horn*
Genus, or group: brass musical instruments
Differentia: three valves
    coiled tube
    flaring bell
Definition: A *French horn* is "a brass musical instrument with three valves, a coiled tube, and a flaring bell."

The purpose of definition is to make ideas as clear and exact as possible. Whenever you write about literature, make sure you define your key terms. Use the methods of lexical definition explained here.

EITHER/OR FALLACY   See *Logical Fallacy.*

EVALUATION *n.*   *Evaluation* is the process of making a judgment about the quality or value of something. "'Birches' is one of Robert Frost's best poems" is an evaluation. To evaluate a literary work, you must first analyze it. Only after you understand a work are you in a position to make judgments about it.

Although literary evaluation is not an exact science, there are generally accepted standards, or criteria, for judging literary works. For example, you might ask the following types of questions: Is the language fresh and imaginative? Are the characters convincing? Is the plot original and believable?

When you present an evaluation of a literary work, use elements in the work as evidence to support your evaluation. In addition, try to make your evaluation as specific as possible. Judgments such as "I hated it" are unacceptable because they are too vague.
See *Opinion* and *Judgment.*

EVIDENCE *n.*   *Evidence* is factual information presented to support an argument. Trial lawyers present evidence to support their cases in court. In literary analysis or evaluation, the parts of a work—such as language, plot, characters, and tone—are the evidence that must be used to support an interpretation or judgment. For example, consider the statement, "William Carlos Williams's short poem 'The Red Wheelbarrow' asserts the primary importance of images in literature." You might support this interpretation by pointing out that the poem consists entirely of images, preceded only by the words "so much depends upon."
See *Fact, Reason,* and *Support.*

FACT *n.*   A *fact* is a statement that can be proved true or false by evidence. For example, the following facts are true by definition:

Steam is vaporized water.
Plot is the series of events or actions that make up a work of fiction.

The following facts are true by observation:

Joyce Carol Oates has written many novels, short stories, and poems.
Edward Taylor's "Huswifery" contains three stanzas of six lines each.

Facts are extremely important in literary works. An author uses them to develop characters, settings, and plots. A reader uses them as the evidence or data on which to base predictions, conclusions, and evaluations.
See *Opinion.*

FALSE ANALOGY   See *Logical Fallacy.*

GENERALIZATION *n.*   A *generalization* is a statement that applies to more than one thing. The following are generalizations:

Emily Dickinson's poems are often about death.
Ernest Hemingway's prose style is simple and direct.

The first statement applies to more than one of Dickinson's poems, and the second applies to more than one of Hemingway's prose works.

Deductive arguments usually begin with a generalization. Consider the following deductive argument:

Premise: (a generalization) All of Mark Twain's writings are entertaining.
Conclusion: Twain's "The Notorious Jumping Frog of Calaveras County" is entertaining.

Inductive arguments, on the other hand, often end with generalizations. Consider the following:

Premise: Longfellow's "A Psalm of Life" rhymes.
Premise: Longfellow's "The Arsenal at Springfield" rhymes.
Premise: Longfellow's "The Tide Rises, The Tide Falls" rhymes.

Conclusion: (generalization) Many of Longfellow's poems rhyme.

When making generalizations, be careful not to overgeneralize. For example, the statement "All speeches are boring" is an overgeneralization because many speeches, such as Chief Joseph's "I Will Fight No More Forever," on page 594, are quite interesting. One way to avoid overgeneralization is to use qualifiers, or words that limit statements, such as *some, a few,* or *many*.
See *Conclusion* and *Stereotype*.

INDUCTION *n.* *Induction* is a form of argument in which the conclusion is probably but not necessarily true. For example, if you read several poems by E. E. Cummings and notice that each uses punctuation and syntax in unusual ways, then you might conclude that "All of E. E. Cummings's poems use punctuation and syntax in unconventional ways." This conclusion may be true, but it is not necessarily true because you have not read all of Cummings's poems. To be safe, you would have to limit your conclusion to something like, "Many of E. E. Cummings's poems use punctuation and syntax in unusual ways."
See *Generalization* and *Inference*.

INFERENCE *n.* An *inference* is any logical or reasonable conclusion based on known facts or accepted premises. The conclusions of inductive and deductive arguments are inferences. When reading or thinking about a literary work, one must constantly draw inferences from the details presented by the author. For example, the main character in Eudora Welty's "A Worn Path," on page 710, is described as wearing a dress made from bleached sugar sacks. From this detail the reader might conclude, or infer, that the main character in Welty's story is poor. Additional details in the story confirm this conclusion.
See *Conclusion, Deduction,* and *Induction*.

INTERPRETATION *n.* *Interpretation* is the process of determining the meaning or significance of speech, writing, art, music, or actions. The interpretation of a literary work involves many different processes. These include the following:

1. Reading carefully and actively and responding to each new detail, character, or incident
2. Breaking down the work into its parts, noting the characteristics of each, and looking for relationships among the parts
3. Examining your responses to the work and identifying the details in the work that help to create these responses
4. Pulling separate observations together to make generalizations about the significance of the work

Interpretation usually aims at making clear the theme of a literary work. For example, your reading of Carl Sandburg's poem "Chicago," on page 844, might lead you to this statement of theme: "Sandburg's 'Chicago' recognizes the unsavory aspects of the modern American city but nevertheless affirms and celebrates the vigor of urban life." Sound interpretations will take into account, implicitly or explicitly, all important parts of a work.
See *Analysis*.

JUDGMENT *n.* A *judgment* is a statement about the quality or value of something. Like any conclusion, a judgment must be supported by facts and reasons. A sound judgment of a literary work, therefore, must be based on evidence from the text.
See *Evaluation* and *Opinion*.

LOADED WORDS See *Propaganda Technique*.

LOGICAL FALLACY *n. phrase* A *logical fallacy* is an error in reasoning. Such errors are common in persuasive or argumentative writing and speech. The following are some of the most common types of logical fallacies:

1. *Begging the question:* This fallacy occurs when someone assumes the truth of the statement to be proved without providing any supporting evidence. For example: "Robert Frost was the greatest American poet of the twentieth century." (No evidence is provided to support the claim.)

2. *Circular reasoning:* This fallacy occurs when the evidence given to support a claim is simply a restatement of the claim. For example: "Robert Frost was the greatest American poet because his poems were better than anyone else's." (The second part of the statement simply repeats the assertion made in the first part. No evidence is supplied to support the claim.)

3. *Either/or fallacy:* This fallacy occurs when someone claims that there are only two alternatives when there are actually more. For example: "Either you love Robert Frost's poems or you hate them." (This statement ignores another alternative—that one might not feel strongly about Frost's poems one way or the other.)

4. *False analogy:* This fallacy occurs when someone falsely assumes that two subjects are similar in some respect just because they are similar in some other respect. For example: "Whitman's poems were like leaves of grass: Each was just like the others." (While there may be similarities between Whitman's poems and leaves of grass, it certainly isn't the case that Whitman's poems are all alike.)

5. *Overgeneralization:* This fallacy occurs when someone makes a statement that is too broad or too inclusive. For example: "All of Whitman's poems are about democratic ideals." (While it is true that many of Whitman's poems are about democratic ideals, it is also true that some deal with other subjects.)

6. *Post hoc, ergo propter hoc:* (a Latin phrase meaning "After this, therefore because of this") This fallacy occurs when someone falsely assumes that an event is caused by another event simply because of the order of the events in time. For example: "Robert Frost became a successful poet after he moved to England. Therefore, moving to England made Frost into a great poet." (Of course, Frost's greatness depends on factors totally unrelated to his move to England.)

When you do persuasive writing or speaking, or when you present arguments, try to avoid logical fallacies. Also be on guard against logical fallacies in the speech and writing of others.

MAIN IDEA *n. phrase* The *main idea* is the central point that a speaker or writer wants to communicate. For example, the main idea of "The Gettysburg Address," on page 444, is that the living must dedicate themselves to the "unfinished work" of preserving the Union. In many literary works, especially in poetry and in fiction, the main idea is implied.
See *Purpose.*

OBJECTIVE *adj.* Something is *objective* if it has to do with a reality that is independent of any particular person's mind or personal, internal experiences. Jurors in criminal and civil trials are expected to evaluate cases impartially and objectively. Statements of fact are objective because anyone can, at least in theory, determine whether they are true. Even apparent statements of fact, however, can mask personal or cultural biases. For example, the statement "Columbus discovered America" would seem to be a fact. However, it ignores the external reality that Native Americans and Scandinavian explorers reached this continent long before Columbus. A statement that is not objective, such as "Anne Bradstreet wrote beautiful poetry," is *subjective* because it represents only one indi-

vidual's personal, internal experience.
See *Subjective.*

OPINION *n.*   An *opinion* is a statement that can be supported by facts but is not itself a fact. Opinions may be judgments, predictions, or statements of policy or obligation. The following are opinions:

Judgment: Nathaniel Hawthorne is the most profound American writer of his century.

Prediction: Hispanic writers will play an increasingly prominent role in American literature.

Obligation: We must study the past to understand the present.

Whenever you express an opinion, you should be prepared to support it with facts and with reasoned arguments. A statement that you cannot back up is merely a *prejudice,* which Ambrose Bierce once defined as "a vagrant opinion without visible means of support."
See *Fact, Judgment,* and *Prediction.*

OVERGENERALIZATION   See *Logical Fallacy.*

PARAPHRASE *n.*   A *paraphrase* is a restatement in other words. When you write about a literary work, paraphrasing can be a useful technique for summarizing passages that you do not wish to quote exactly, or *verbatim.* A paraphrase can be used to support an interpretive argument when the exact words of the original are not essential to the argument. When paraphrasing, be careful not to alter the meaning of the original passage. Simply put into your own words what the writer said. You can also test your understanding of a literary work by attempting to paraphrase key passages.

POST HOC, ERGO PROPTER HOC   See *Logical Fallacy.*

PREDICTION *n.*   *Prediction* is the act of making statements about the future. Like inference, prediction is important to active reading. An active reader continually makes and tests predictions on the basis of details presented in a literary work. For example, a reader of Jack London's "To Build a Fire," on page 566, continually predicts, based on each new detail, whether the protagonist is going to survive. Authors often provide clues to future plot developments. These clues make predictions possible. When an author presents clues to future events, he or she is using a technique known as *foreshadowing.* Sometimes an author will intentionally mislead readers into making predictions that will later prove false. This often happens, for example, in mystery stories with surprise endings.
See *Opinion.*

PROBLEM-SOLVING *n. phrase*   *Problem-solving* is the process by which a person comes up with a solution to some difficulty. Advances in medicine and technology represent a common type of problem-solving. For example, polio was once a common and crippling disease among young people in the United States. The creation of a polio vaccine was the solution to that problem. The following steps can be used in any situation that requires problem-solving:

1. State the problem as precisely and as clearly as possible.
2. Identify your goal.
3. Examine the differences between the goal state (the situation that will exist when the problem is solved) and the initial state (the situation at the time when you begin working on the problem).
4. Take steps to reduce the differences between the initial state and the goal state.

The following rules of thumb, or *heuristics,* are useful in solving many problems:

1. Break the problem down into parts and solve the parts separately.

2. Think of similar problems that you have solved before. Use some or all of those solutions to solve the current problem.
3. Restate the problem in various ways or from several points of view.
4. Ask someone to help you with parts of the problem that are especially difficult.
5. Use general thinking strategies such as brainstorming, freewriting, and diagraming to come up with possible solutions.

PROPAGANDA TECHNIQUE *n. phrase* A *propaganda technique* is an improper appeal to emotion, used for the purpose of swaying the opinions of an audience. The following propaganda techniques are often found in persuasive speech and writing:

1. *Bandwagon:* This technique involves encouraging people to think or act in some way simply because other people are doing so. For example: "Everyone's buying these new fashion jeans, so rush on down to Peabody's Department Store. Supplies are limited."
2. *Loaded words:* This technique involves using words with strong positive or negative connotations, or associations. Name-calling is an example of the use of loaded words. So is any use of words that are charged with emotion. For example: "These books should be banned because they are *un-American.*"
3. *Snob appeal:* This technique involves making a claim that one should act or think in a certain way because of the high social status associated with the action or thought. For example: "Diamond jewelry from Katz Jewelers—for those who settle for nothing but the best."
4. *Transfer:* This is the technique of attempting to get readers or listeners to transfer their strong feelings about one thing onto another thing that is unrelated. For example: "To celebrate Abe Lincoln's birthday, we're slashing prices on our bedroom sets. So, come on down to the Lincoln's birthday sale at Fast Freddie's Furniture."
5. *Unreliable testimonial:* This technique involves having an unqualified person endorse a product, an action, or an opinion. For example: "Hello, I'm Anita Stratton, from television's hit series, *Crimefighters.* I'd like to talk to you about a new home security system from Ersatz Industries."
6. *Vague, undefined terms:* This technique involves promoting or challenging an opinion by using words that are so vague or so poorly defined as to be almost meaningless. For example: "This *new* cereal tastes *good* and is *good* for you."

Avoid using propaganda techniques in your own speech and writing, and be on the alert for these techniques in the speech and writing of others.

PURPOSE *n.* The *purpose* is the goal or aim of a literary work. Works are often classified, by purpose, as narrative, descriptive, expository, or persuasive. The purpose of a narrative work is to tell a story. The purpose of a descriptive work is to portray a person, place, or thing. The purpose of an expository work is to explain something or to provide information. The purpose of a persuasive work is to move an audience to take some action or to adopt some opinion. For example, Jonathan Edwards's purpose in "Sinners in the Hands of an Angry God," on page 72, is persuasive. He wants to persuade the members of his audience to change their ways. Complex literary works often involve many purposes. For example, a persuasive work may contain expository passages, or a narrative work may contain passages of description.
See *Main Idea.*

REALISTIC DETAILS/FANTASTIC DETAILS *n. phrases* A *realistic detail* is one that is drawn from actual or possible experience; a *fantastic detail* is one that is not based on actual experience and that is improbable or imaginary. Writers of fiction, poetry, and drama use realistic details to make their plots and characters seem true-to-life. Writers often use fantastic details to heighten interest or to engage the reader's imagination. In "The Raven," on page 227, Edgar Allan Poe introduces a fantastic detail—a raven who flies in and announces "Nevermore!"—into an otherwise realistic setting.

REASON *n.* A *reason* is a statement in support of some conclusion. The term *reason* is also used as a verb to signify the human faculty for thinking logically and rationally.
See *Argument* and *Conclusion*.

SOURCE *n.* A *source* is anything from which ideas and information are taken. Books, magazines, speeches, television programs, conversations, and personal experiences may all serve as sources. Dictionaries, encyclopedias, bibliographies, almanacs, atlases, and other reference works are specifically designed to be used as sources.

There are two basic types of sources, primary sources and secondary sources. *Primary sources* are generally preferable because they are firsthand accounts. Conversations, speeches, documents, and letters are examples of primary sources. *Secondary sources* are accounts or compilations written after the fact. The Iroquois Constitution is a primary source; a history of the Iroquois nation is a secondary source. In literary study, the work itself—the poem, play, novel, or essay—is a primary source, while a work of criticism or a biography of the author would be considered a secondary source.

STEREOTYPE *n.* A *stereotype* is a fixed or conventional notion or characterization. It is a type of overgeneralization. Some examples include the absent-minded professor, the brain-

less beauty queen, the bleeding-heart liberal, and the mad scientist. Although writers occasionally use stereotypes when they do not have sufficient space in which to develop a character fully, good writers generally avoid stereotyping, preferring to create more realistic characters.
See *Generalization*.

SUBJECTIVE *adj.* Something is *subjective* if it is based on personal reactions or emotions rather than on some objective reality. A reader's reaction to a work of literature is subjective because another reader may have a different reaction. All opinions are by definition subjective. However, this does not mean that all opinions are equally valid. A credible opinion is one that is based on facts. For example, if you find Randall Jarrell's poem "Death of a Ball Turret Gunner," on page 1119, strangely disturbing, you might base this opinion on facts about the work. These facts would include all the details in the work that caused your subjective reaction.

When authors invent thoughts, dialogue, and actions for their characters, they are depicting their characters' subjective experiences. Ambrose Bierce's short story, "An Occurrence at Owl Creek Bridge," on page 530, consists almost entirely of the protagonist's subjective experiences while awaiting execution.
See *Objective*.

SUMMARIZE *v.* To *summarize* something is to restate it briefly in other words. Generally, one summarizes long works and paraphrases short passages. A brief summary of Flannery O'Connor's "The Life You Save May Be Your Own," on page 956, might read as follows: "A one-armed tramp named Tom Shiftlet ingratiates himself with Mrs. Crater—the owner of a broken-down farm—and with Mrs. Crater's thirty-year-old deaf-mute daughter, Lucynell. Part miracle worker and part schemer, Shiftlet fixes up the farm, rehabilitates an old, abandoned car on the property, and allows Mrs. Crater to talk him into marrying the wide-eyed Lucy. On their wedding trip, however, Shiftlet abandons Lucy at a roadside eatery and takes off for Florida. On the way he picks up a young runaway boy. The boy quickly flees the car and its one-armed driver."

SUPPORT *v.* To *support* something is to provide evidence for it.
See *Argument* and *Evidence.*

TIME ORDER *n. phrase* *Time order* is organization by order of occurrence, that is, by chronological order. Time order is one of the most common methods of organization and is used in both fiction and nonfiction works.

TRANSFER See *Propaganda Technique.*

UNRELIABLE TESTIMONIAL See *Propaganda Technique.*

GLOSSARY

READING THE GLOSSARY ENTRIES

The words in this glossary are from selections appearing in your textbook. Each entry in the glossary contains the following parts:

1. Entry Word. This word appears at the beginning of the entry, in boldface type.

2. Pronunciation. The symbols in parentheses tell how the entry word is pronounced. If a word has more than one possible pronunciation, the most common of these pronunciations is given first.

3. Part of Speech. Appearing after the pronunciation, in italics, is an abbreviation that tells the part of speech of the entry word. The following abbreviations have been used:

n. noun   **p.** pronoun   **v.** verb
adj. adjective   **adv.** adverb   **conj.** conjunction

4. Definition. This part of the entry follows the part-of-speech abbreviation and gives the meaning of the entry word as used in the selection in which it appears.

KEY TO PRONUNCIATION SYMBOLS
USED IN THE GLOSSARY

The following symbols are used in the pronunciations that follow the entry words:

Symbol	Key Words	Symbol	Key Words
a	asp, fat, parrot	b	bed, fable, dub
ā	ape, date, play	d	dip, beadle, had
ä	ah, car, father	f	fall, after, off
		g	get, haggle, dog
e	elf, ten, berry	h	he, ahead, hotel
ē	even, meet, money	j	joy, agile, badge
		k	kill, tackle, bake
i	is, hit, mirror	l	let, yellow, ball
ī	ice, bite, high	m	met, camel, trim
		n	not, flannel, ton
ō	open, tone, go	p	put, apple, tap
ô	all, horn, law	r	red, port, dear
o͞o	ooze, tool, crew	s	sell, castle, pass
o͝o	look, pull, moor	t	top, cattle, hat
yo͞o	use, cute, few	v	vat, hovel, have
yo͝o	united, cure, globule	w	will, always, swear
oi	oil, point, toy	y	yet, onion, yard
ou	out, crowd, plow	z	zebra, dazzle, haze
u	up, cut, color	ch	chin, catcher, arch
ʉr	urn, fur, deter	sh	she, cushion, dash
		t͟h	thin, nothing, truth
ə	a in ago	t͟h	then, father, lathe
	e in agent	zh	azure, leisure
	i in sanity	ŋ	ring, anger, drink
	o in comply	ʼ	[indicates that a
	u in focus		following l or n is a
ər	perhaps, murder		syllabic consonant, as in
			able (āʼ bʼl)]

This pronunciation key is from *Webster's New World Dictionary*, Second College Edition. Copyright © 1986 by Simon & Schuster. Used by permission.

A

abalone (ab′ ə lō′ nē)   *n.* A large shellfish

abash (ə bash′)   *v.* To make ashamed

aberrations (ab′ ər ā′ s͟hənz)   *n.* Departures from what is right, true, or correct

abeyance (ə bā′ əns)   *n.* A temporary suspension

abiding (ə bīd′ iŋ)   *adj.* Enduring; lasting

abject (ab′ jekt)   *adj.* Wretched

ablution (ab lo͞o′ s͟hən)   *n.* A washing or cleansing of the body as part of a religious rite

abominably (ə bäm′ ə ne b′lē)   *adv.* Hatefully

abrogated (ab′ rə gāt′ əd)   *v.* Canceled

acclivity (ə kliv′ ə tē)   *n.* An upward slope

accost (ə kôst′)   *v.* To approach and speak to in an intrusive way

acquiesce (ak′ wē es′)   *v.* To agree without protest

adamant (ad′ ə mənt)   *adj.* Unyielding

adhere (əd hir′)   *v.* To stick fast; stay attached

adieu (ə dyo͞o′)   *n.* "Farewell" (French)

adroit (ə droit′)   *adj.* Skillful in a physical or mental way

adumbration (ad′ um brā′ s͟hən)   *n.* A shadowy outline

aeolian (ē ō′ lē ən) **harps**   *n.* Harps with strings that produce music when air blows over them

aesthetic (es t͟het′ ik)   *adj.* Of beauty

agape (ə gāp′)   *adj.* Wide open

aggregate (ag′ rə gət)   *n.* The sum total

aggrieve (ə grēv′)   *v.* To offend

aghast (ə gast′)   *adj.* Horrified

ague (ā′ gyo͞o)   *n.* A chill or fit of shivering

alacrity (ə lak′ rə tē)   *n.* Speed

albeit (ô bē′ it)   *conj.* Although

alburnum (al bur′ nəm)   *n.* The soft wood between the bark and the heartwood where water is conducted

amain (ə mān′)   *adv.* At or with great speed

amalgam (ə mal′ gəm)   *n.* An alloy of mercury used with silver as dental filling

ameliorate (ə mēl′ yə rāt′)   *v.* Improve

anachronism (ə nak′ rə niz′m)   *n.* Something that is or seems to be out of its proper time

anarchy (an′ ər kē)   *n.* The absence of government

anathema (ə nat͟h′ ə mə)   *n.* Curse

anomalous (ə näm′ ə ləs)   *adj.* Abnormal; deviating from the regular arrangement, general rule, or usual method

antipodes (an tip′ ə dēz′)   *n.* On the opposite side of the globe

anxiety (aŋ zī′ ə tē)   *n.* An uneasiness about the future

aqua vitae (ä′ kwə vī′ tē)   *n.* Brandy

aphid (ä′ fid)   *n.* Small insect that sucks the juice from plants

apotheosis (a pöt͟h′ ē ō′ sis)   *n.* Glorification

apparition (ap′ ə ris͟h′ ən)   *n.* The act of appearing or becoming invisible

appellation (ap′ ə lā s͟hən)   *n.* A name or title

approbation (ap′ rə bā′ s͟hən)   *n.* Approval

apropros (ap′ rə pō′)   *adv.* At the right time

arabesque (ar′ ə besk′)   *n.* A complex and elaborate design

ardor (är′ dər)   *n.* Emotional warmth; passion

arduous (är′ jōō wəs) *adj.* Very difficult

assail (ə sāl′) *v.* 1. To attack violently; assault; 2. to have a forceful effect on

assent (ə sent′) *v.* To agree

assuage (ə swāj) *v.* To lessen

asunder (ə sun′ dər) *adv.* Into parts or pieces

asylum (ə sī′ ləm) *n.* A place of refuge

attest (ə test′) *v.* To bear witness

audaciously (ô dā′ s/əs lē) *adj.* Boldly

auger (ô′ gər) *n.* A tool used for drilling teeth

auroral (ô rôr′ əl) *adj.* Resembling the dawn

Auspex (ôs′ peks) *n.* In ancient Rome, someone who watched for omens in the flight of birds

auspice (ôs′ pəs) *n.* Approval and support

austere (ô stir′) *adj.* Showing strict self-discipline and self-denial

automation (ôt′ ə mā′ s/ən) *n.* In manufacturing, a system or process in which many or all of the processes of production, movement, and inspection of parts and materials are automatically performed or controlled by self-operated machinery

avarice (av′ ər is) *n.* Greed

aversion (ə vur′ z/ən) *n.* An intense or definite dislike

avidly (av′ id lē) *adv.* Eagerly and enthusiastically

B

banshee (ban′ shē) *n.* In Scottish and Irish folklore, a female spirit believed to wail outside a house as a warning that a death will soon occur in the family

base (bās) *v.* Mean; contemptible

bastion (bas′ chən) *n.* A fortification

bayou (bī′ ōō) *n.* A sluggish, marshy inlet or outlet of a lake or river

beguile (bi gīl′) *v.* To charm; deceive

behold (bi hōld′) *v.* To look

beholden (bi hōld′ ən) *adj.* Owing thanks; indebted

beleaguered (bi lē′ gərd) *adj.* Encircled by an army

belie (bi lī′) *v.* To prove false

bellicose (bel′ ə kōs) *adj.* Quarrelsome

benevolent (bə nev′ ə lənt) *adj.* Kindly; charitable

bereaved (bi rēvd′) *n.* The survivors of recently deceased people

bereavement (bi rēv′ mənt) *n.* The sadness resulting from the loss or death of a loved one

berserk (bər surk′) *adj.* In a frenzy, after a legendary Norse warrior who worked himself into a frenzy before battle

beseech (bi sēch′) *v.* To ask earnestly; implore

bicuspid (bī kus′ pid) *n.* Any of eight adult teeth with two-pointed crowns

billet (bil′ it) *n.* A brief letter

binnacle (bin′ ə k′l) *n.* The case enclosing the ship's compass

bivouac (biv′ wak) *n.* A temporary encampment

blaspheme (blas fēm′) *v.* To curse

blithe (blith) *adj.* Carefree

blunt (blunt) *v.* To make dull

brachycephalic (brak′ i sə fal′ ik) *adj.* Short-headed or broad-headed

brindled (brin′ d′ld) *adj.* Having a gray or tawny coat with streaks of darker color

brocaded (brō kād′ id) *adj.* Having a raised design woven into it

brood (brōōd′) *v.* To pondering in a troubled or mournful way

C

cache (kash) *v.* To hide

cairn (kern) *n.* A conical heap of stones built as a monument or landmark

calamity (kə lam′ ə tē) *n.* A disaster

callow (kal′ ō) *adj.* Immature; inexperienced

calumny (kal′ əm nē) *n.* False accusation; slander

camaraderie (käm′ ə räd′ ər ē) *n.* Warm, friendly feelings

candid (kan′ did) *adj.* Impartial

capacious (kə pā′ s/əs) *adj.* Roomy; spacious

capitulate (kə pich′ ə lāt′) *v.* To surrender conditionally

capstan (kap′ stən) *n.* A large cylinder, turned by hand, around which cables are wound

Carrara (kə rä′ rə) *n.* A fine, white marble

castanets (kas′ tə nets′) *n.* Small, hollowed out pieces of wood, held in the hand by a connecting cord and clicked together with the fingers

cataleptical (kat′ ′l ep′ tik ′l) *adj.* In a state in which consciousness and feeling are suddenly and temporarily lost and the muscles become rigid

celestial (sə les′ chəl) *adj.* Of the heavens

chafe (chāf) *v.* To rub to make warm

chanticleer (chan′ tə klir′) *n.* A rooster

chaos (kā′ äs) *n.* The disorder of formless matter and infinite space, supposed to have existed before the ordered universe

chaparral (chap′ ə ral′) *n.* A thicket of thorny bushes or shrubs

charnel (chär′ n′l) *adj.* Like a graveyard

cherub (cher′ əb) *n.* A representation of a heavenly being as a winged child with a chubby, rosy face

chronic (krän′ ik) *adj.* Continuing indefinitely

cipher (sī′ fər) *v.* To figure

cirrus (sir′ əs) *n.* High, detached wispy clouds

cleave (klēv) *v.* Split

clematis (klem′ ə tis) *n.* A woody vine with bright-colored flowers

collateral (kə lat′ ər əl) *adj.* Descended from the same ancestors, but in a different line

commensurate (kə men′ s/ər it) *adj.* Corresponding in amount, magnitude, or degree

conceit (kən sēt′) *n.* A strange or fanciful idea

conciliatory (kən sil′ ē ə tôr ē) *adj.* Tending to soothe the anger of

confederate (kən fed′ ər it) *adj.* United with others for a common purpose

conflagration (kän′ flə grā s/ən) *n.* A big, destructive fire

congenial (kən jēn′ yəl) *adj.* Compatible; friendly; sympathetic

conjectural (kən jek′ chər əl) *adj.* Based on guesswork

conjecture (kən jek′ chər) *v.* To guess

connate (kän′ āt) *adj.* Having the same origin or nature

connivance (kə nī′ vəns) *n.* Secret cooperation

consanguinity (kän′ saŋ gwin′ ə tē) *n.* Kinship

consecrate (kän′ sə krāt′)   v. To cause to be revered or honored

consternation (kän′ stər nā′ s/hən)   n. A great fear or shock that makes one feel helpless or bewildered

contemptible (kən temp′ tə b′l)   adj. Worthless; despicable

contentious (kän ten′ s/həs)   adj. Quarrelsome

continuum (kən tin′ yōō wəm)   n. A continuous whole with parts that cannot be separated

contrive (kən trīv′)   v. To scheme

convoluted (kän′ və lōōt′ id)   adj. Intricate; complicated

cormorant (kôr′ mə rənt)   n. A large, diving bird with a hooked beak and webbed toes

cornice (kôr′ nis)   n. The projecting decorative molding along the top of a building

corollary (kôr′ ə ler′ ē)   n. An easily drawn conclusion

countenance (koun′ tə nəns)   n. A facial expression

cozen (kuz′ ən)   v. To cheat

crape (krāp)   n. A piece of black cloth worn as a sign of mourning

craven (krā′ vən)   adj. Very cowardly

crescendo (krə s/hen′ dō)   adj. Gradually increasing in loudness or intensity

crypt (kript)   n. An underground chamber or vault

cryptic (krip′ tik)   adj. Having a hidden or ambiguous meaning

cumbersome (kum′ bər səm)   adj. Hard to handle or deal with because of size or weight

cunning (kun′ iŋ)   adj. Skillful in deception; crafty; sly

curlew (kur′ lōō)   n. A large, long-legged wading bird whose call is associated with the evening

cyclonic (sī klän′ ik)   adj. Like a cyclone, a windstorm with violent, whirling movement

cynical (sin′ i k′l)   adj. Denying the sincerity of people's motives and actions

cynicism (sin′ ə siz′m)   n. The denial of the sincerity of people's motives or actions or of the value of living

diabolical (dī′ ə bäl′ ə k′l)   adj. Of the devil

dictum (dik′ təm)   n. A statement or saying

digress (dī gres′)   v. To depart temporarily from the main subject

dilapidated (di lap′ ə dāt id)   adj. In disrepair

dilatory (dil′ ə tôr ē)   adj. Slow

diligence (dil′ ə jəns)   n. A constant, careful effort; perseverance

diligent (dil′ ə jənt)   adj. Hard-working; industrious

din (din)   n. A loud, continuous noise or clamor

discern (di surn′)   v. To perceive or recognize; make out clearly

discordant (dis kôr′ d′nt)   adj. Not in harmony; clashing

dismay (dis mā′)   v. to make afraid; discourage

disposition (dis′ pə zis/h′ ən)   n. An inclination or tendency

dissembling (di sem′ bliŋ)   n. Pretense; hiding under false appearances

dissolutely (dis′ ə lōōt′ lē)   adv. Immorally and shamelessly

diverse (dī vurs′)   adj. Various

divine (də vīn′)   n. A clergyman

docile (däs′ ′l)   adj. Obedient

dolorous (dō′ lər əs)   adj. Sad; mournful

dominion (də min′ yən)   n. The power to rule

doubloon (du blōōn′)   n. The gold coin Ahab offered as reward to the first man to spot the whale

dour (door)   adj. Stern; severe

drayman (drā′ mən)   n. The driver of a dray, a low cart with detachable sides

dubious (dōō′ bē əs)   adj. Questionable

duodecimos (dōō′ ə des′ ə mōz′)   n. Books about five by eight inches

dusky (dus′ kē)   adj. Dim; shadowy

dynastic (dī nas′ tik)   adj. Of a period during which a certain family rules

dyspepsia (dis pep′ s/hə)   n. Indigestion

D

declivity (di kliv′ ə tē)   n. A downward slope

deference (def′ ər əns)   n. A courteous regard or respect

deferential (def′ ə ren′ s/həl)   adj. Very respectful

degenerate (di jen′ ər it)   adj. Deteriorated

deign (dān)   v. To condescend to take or accept

deliberation (di lib′ ə rā′ s/hən)   n. Careful consideration

delirium (di lir′ ē əm)   n. A temporary state of extreme mental confusion

delusion (di lōō′ z/hən)   n. A false belief

demean (di mēn′)   v. To behave; conduct

demiculverin (dem′ ē kul′ vər in)   A large cannon

demur (di mur′)   v. To object

demure (di myoor′)   adj. Modest; reserved

depravity (di prav′ ə tē)   n. Corruption; wickedness

deprecating (dep′ rə kāt′ iŋ)   adj. Expressing disapproval

derivative (də riv′ ə tiv)   adj. Arrived at through complex reasoning

desolate (dəs′ ə lit)   adj. Forlorn; wretched

despotic (de spät′ ik)   adj. Harsh, cruel, unjust

despotism (des′ pə tiz′m)   n. Tyranny

E

eccentric (ik sen′ trik)   adj. Peculiar

efface (i fās′)   v. To wipe out; obliterate

effluvium (e flōō′ vē əm)   n. An aura

effrontery (e frun′ tər ē)   n. Unashamed boldness

effuse (e fyōōz′)   v. To spread out; diffuse

egalitarian (i gal′ ə ter′ ē ən)   adj. Asserting, resulting from, or characterized by the belief in the equality of all people

elixir (i lik′ sər) **of life**   n. An imaginary substance thought by medieval alchemists to prolong life indefinitely

eloquence (el′ ə kwəns)   n. Expressiveness; persuasive power

elusive (i lōō′ siv)   adj. Hard to grasp

emaciated (i mā′ s/hē āt′ id)   adj. Abnormally thin

embrasure (im brā′ z/hər)   n. An opening

eminence (em′ ə nəns)   n. Greatness; celebrity

eminent (em′ ə nant)   adj. Distinguished

engrossed (in grōs′t)   adj. Absorbed

enigmatic (en′ ig mat′ ik)   adj. Perplexing; baffling; mysterious

ephemeral (i fem′ ər əl)   adj. Short-lived

equanimity (ek′ wə nim′ ə tē)   n. Composure

Glossary   1365

equivocal (i kwiv′ ə k′l) *adj.* Having more than one possible interpretation

escarpment (e skärp′ mənt) *n.* A steep slope

eschew (es chōō′) *v.* To abstain from

ether (ē′ t/hər) *n.* A chemical compound used as an anesthetic

etherize (ē′ t/hə rīz) *v.* To anesthetize as with ether

etiquette (et′ i kət) *n.* The rules for manners and ceremonies

evanescence (ev′ ə nes′ ′ns) *n.* A fading from sight

evanescently (ev′ ə nes′ ′nt lē) *adv.* Fleetingly

evitable (ev′ ə tə b′l) *adj.* Avoidable

exigency (ek′ sə jən sē) *n.* A pressing need; demand

expatriated (eks pā′ trē āt′ id) *adj.* Deported; driven from one's native land

expedient (ik spē′ dē ənt) *n.* A resource used in an emergency

expostulation (ik späs′ ơhə lā′ s/hən) *n.* Expression of objection

extort (ik stôrt′) *v.* To obtain by threat or violence

extricate (eks′ trə kāt) *v.* To set free

exude (ig zōōd′) *v.* To ooze, discharge

F

facetious (fə sē′ s/həs) *adj.* Joking at an inappropriate time

facile (fas′ ′l) *adj.* Fluent

fallow (fal′ ō) *adj.* Left uncultivated or unplanted

fallowness (fal′ ō nis) *n.* Inactivity

fast (fast′) *v.* To eat very little or nothing

fecundity (fi kun′ də tē) *n.* Productivity

feign (fān′) *v.* To make a false show of

felicitate (fə lis′ ə tāt) *v.* To congratulate

felicity (fə lis′ ə tē) *n.* Happiness; bliss

festoon (fes tōōn′) *n.* A wreath of flowers or leaves

fettuccine (fet′ ōō chē′ nē) *n.* Broad, flat noodles

finite (fī′ nīt) *adj.* Having measurable or definable limits

flume (flōōm) *n.* An artificial channel for carrying water to provide power and transport objects

folio (fō′ lē ō′) *n.* The largest regular size of books, over eleven inches in height

foppery (fäp′ ər ē) *n.* Foolishness

foreboding (fôr bōd′ iŋ) *n.* A prediction

forestall (fôr stôl′) *v.* To act in advance of

fortuitous (fôr tōō′ ə təs) *adj.* Fortunate

frippery (frip′ ər ē) *n.* A showy display of elegance

frugally (frōō′ g′l ē) *adv.* Thriftily

furtive (fur′ tiv) *adj.* Sneaky; shifty; secretive

G

gall (gôl) *n.* Bitterness

garret (gar′ it) *n.* A attic

garrulous (gar′ ə ləs) *adj.* Talking too much

genuflect (jen′ yə flekt′) *v.* To bend the knee, as in reverence or worship

gerfalcon (jur′ fal′ k′n) *n.* A large, fierce falcon of the Arctic

gesticulate (jes tik′ yə lāt) *v.* To gesture with hands or arms

glean (glēn) *v.* To collect the remaining grain after reaping

gloaming (glō′ miŋ) *n.* The evening dusk; twilight

glee (glē) *n.* An unaccompanied song

goatee (gō tē′) *n.* A small, pointed beard

gossamer (gäs′ ə mər) *n.* A very thin, soft, filmy cloth

gourd (gôrd) *adj.* The dried, hollowed-out shell of a piece of fruit from a gourd plant, often used as a dipper or drinking cup

gracile (gras′ ′l) *adj.* Slender; slim

grandeur (gran′ jər) *adj.* Magnificence

grave (grāv) *adj.* Serious; solemn

gripsack (grip′ sak) *n.* A small bag for holding clothes

guile (gīl) *n.* Craftiness

guillotine (gil′ ə tēn′) *n.* An instrument for beheading by means of a heavy blade dropped between two grooved uprights

guffaw (gə fô′) *adj.* To laugh in a loud, coarse manner

guttural (gut′ ər əl) *adj.* Of the throat

H

hallow (hal′ ō) *v.* To honor as sacred

halyard (hal′ yərd) *n.* A rope for raising or lowering sail

harbor (här′ bər) *v.* A shelter or house

harrow (här′ ō) *v.* To distress

herald (her′ əld) *n.* A messenger

hermitage (hur′ mit ij) *n.* A place where a person can live away from other people; a secluded retreat

hernia (hur′ nē ə) *n.* The protrusion of part of the intestine through the abdominal muscles

heron (her′ ən) *n.* A wading bird with a long neck, long legs, and a long, tapered bill

hieroglyphic (hī′ ər ə glif′ ik) *n.* A picture or symbol representing a word, syllable, or sound

hoary (hôr′ ē) *adj.* Very old; ancient

hostler (häs′ lər) *n.* A person who tends horses at an inn or stable

humble (hum′ b′l) *adj.* Not proud; modest

husbandry (huz′ bən drē) *n.* Farming

hypnotic (hip nät′ ik) *adj.* Inducing a sleeplike condition

I

ideality (ī′ dē al′ ə tē) *n.* Something that is ideal and has no reality

illiterate (i lit′ ər it) *adj.* Unable to read or write

illumination (i lōō′ mə nā′ s/hən) *n.* The supplying of light

imbibe (im bīb′) *v.* To drink in

immemorial (im′ ə môr′ ē əl) *adj.* Extending back beyond memory or record

impalpable (im pal′ pə b′l) *adj.* Imperceptible to the sense of touch

imperative (im per′ ə tiv) *adj.* Absolutely necessary; urgent

imperceptible (im′ pər sep′ tə b′l) *adj.* Not plain or distinct to the senses or the mind

imperially (im pir′ ē əl ē) *adv.* Majestically

imperious (im pir′ ē əs) *adj.* Urgent

impertinent (im pur′ t′n ənt) *adj.* Not showing proper respect

impetuous (im peơh′ oo wəs) *adj.* Acting or done suddenly with little thought; rash; impulsive; moving with great force or violence

impious (im′ pē əs) *adj.* Lacking reverence for God

implacable (im plak′ ə b'l) *adj.* Relentless

importunate (im pôr′ chə nit) *adj.* Insistent

importunity (im′ pôr tōōn′ ə te) *n.* A persistent request or demand

imprecation (im′ prə kā′ s/hən) *n.* A curse

impregnable (im preg′ nə b'l) *adj.* Unshakable; unyielding

inanimate (in an′ ə mit) *adj.* Not endowed with life

inauspicious (in ôs pis/h′ əs) *adj.* Not boding well for the future

incessantly (in ses′ 'nt lē) *adv.* Unceasingly

incipient (in sip′ ē ənt) *adj.* Just beginning

incisor (in sī′ zər) *n.* A front tooth

incongruous (in käŋ′ groo wəs) *adj.* Incompatible

incredulously (in krej′ oo ləs lē) *adv.* Skeptically; doubtingly

incubus (iŋ′ kyə bəs) *n.* Something nightmarishly burdensome

inculcation (in′ kul′ kā′ s/hən) *n.* Teaching by repetition and insistent urging

indecorous (in dek′ ər əs) *adj.* Improper

indigenous (in dij′ ə nəs) *adj.* Existing, growing, or produced naturally in a region or country

indigo (in′ di gō′) *n.* A blue dye

ineffable (in ef′ ə b'l) *adj.* Inexpressible

inert (in urt′) *adj.* Motionless

inevitable (in ev′ ə tə b'l) *adj.* Certain to happen; unavoidable

infidel (in′ fə d'l) *n.* A person who holds no religious belief

ingratiating (in grā′ s/hē āt′ iŋ) *adj.* Bringing into favor

inimical (in im′ i k'l) *adj.* Hostile; unfriendly

iniquity (in ik′ wə tē) *n.* A sin

inscrutable (in skrōōt′ ə b'l) *adj.* Not able to be easily understood

insidious (in sid′ ē əs) *adj.* Deceitful; secretly treacherous

insinuate (in sin′ yōō wāt′) *v.* To hint or suggest indirectly; imply

integrity (in teg′ rə tē) *n.* The adherence to a code of values

interminable (in tur′ mi nə b'l) *adj.* Seeming to last forever; without, or apparently without, end

intuitively (in tōō′ i tiv lē) *adv.* Instinctively

invalid (in′ və lid) *v.* To release because of illness or disability

inviolable (in vī′ ə lə b'l) *adj.* Safe from danger

ipecacuanha (ip′ ə kak′ yoo wan′ ə) *n.* A plant with roots used for medicinal purposes

J

jauntily (jôn′ ti lē) *adv.* In a carefree fashion

jocularity (jäk′ yə lar′ ə tē) *n.* A joking good humor

juxtaposition (juk′ stə pə zis/h′ ən) *n.* Placing side by side

L

laggard (lag′ ərd) *adj.* Slow or late in doing things

lamentation (lam′ ən tā′ s/hən) *n.* The outward expression of grief

lariat (lar′ ē it) **rope** *n.* A rope used for tethering grazing horses or cattle

laterally (lat′ ər əl lē) *adv.* In a sideways manner

legacy (leg′ ə sē) *n.* The money or property left to someone by a will

levee (lev′ ē) *n.* A landing place along the bank of a river

licentious (lī sen′ s/həs) *adj.* Disregarding accepted rules

limber (lim′ bər) *adj.* Flexible

list (list′) *v.* To sway

literalist (lit′ ər əl ist) *n.* One who insists on the exact meaning or words

loath (lōt/h) *adj.* Reluctant; unwilling

lubber (lub′ ər) *n.* A slow, clumsy person

lucidity (lōō sid′ i tē) *n.* Brightness

lugubrious (loo gōō′ brē əs) *adj.* Very sad or mournful

lull (lul) *v.* To calm or soothe by gentle sound or motion

luminary (lōō′ mə ner′ ē) *adj.* Giving off light

luminescent (lōō′ mə nes′ 'nt) *adj.* Shining

luminous (lōō′ mə nəs) *adj.* Shining; bright

lurid (lōōr′ id) *adj.* Vivid in a harsh or shocking way

lustrous (lus′ trəs) *adj.* Shining

lusty (lus′ tē) *adj.* Strong; hearty

M

magisterial (maj′ is tir′ ē əl) *adj.* Authoritative

magnanimity (mag′ nə nim′ ə tē) *n.* Ability to rise above pettiness or meanness; generosity

magnanimous (mag nan′ ə məs) *adj.* Noble in mind; rising above pettiness and meanness

mah-jongg (mä′ jôŋ′) *n.* A game of Chinese origin, played with pieces resembling dominoes

malediction (mal′ ə dik′ s/hən) *n.* A curse

malevolent (mə lev′ ə lənt) *adj.* Wishing evil or harm to others

malinger (mə liŋ′ gər) *v.* To pretend to be ill

malign (mə līn′) *adj.* Evil

mammoth (mam′ ət/h) *n.* An extinct elephant with hairy skin

manifest (man′ ə fest′) *n.* A cargo list

manifold (man′ ə fōld′) *adj.* In many ways; plentiful and varied

mansard (man′ särd) *n.* A roof with two slopes on each of the four sides

marrow (mar′ ō) *n.* The soft tissue that fills the cavities of most bones

maverick (mav′ ər ik) *n.* A nonconformist

meander (mē an′ dər) *v.* To move lazily

meditate (med′ ə tāt′) *v.* To think deeply

meditation (med′ ə tā′ s/hən) *n.* A deep reflection

melancholy (mel′ ən käl′ ē) *adj.* Gloomy

melee (mā′ lā) *n.* A noisy, confused fight

mendicant (men′ di kənt) *n.* A beggar

Mesozoic (mes′ ə zō′ ik) *adj.* A geological era characterized by the development and extinction of dinosaurs

mesquite (mes kēt′) *n.* A type of small thorny tree

metamorphosis (met′ ə môr′ fə sis) *n.* A transformation

metate (mā tä′ tä′) *n.* A stone used in the southwestern United States for grinding meal

meticulous (mə tik′ yoo ləs)   *adj.* Extremely careful about details
miasma (mī az′ mə)   *n.* An unwholesome atmosphere
milieu (mēl yoo′)   *n.* The environment
minutia (mi noo′ sһē ə)   *n.* The small and trivial details
mollify (mäl′ ə fī)   *v.* To soothe; calm
monotonous (mə nät′ ′n əs)   *adj.* Having little or no variation or variety; tiresome because unvarying
monotony (mə nät′ ′n ē)   *n.* Tiresome sameness of uniformity
moribund (môr′ ə bund′)   *adj.* Dying; coming to an end
morose (mə rōs′)   *adj.* Gloomy, sullen
mundane (mun dān′)   *adj.* Commonplace; ordinary
munificent (myoo nif′ ə s′nt)   *adj.* Generous
musing (myooz′ iŋ)   *v.* Thinking deeply and at length
myriad (mir′ ē əd)   *adj.* Countless

N

nostalgia (näs tal′ jə)   *n.* A longing

O

obeisance (o′ bā′ s′ns)   *n.* A gesture of respect
obnoxious (əb näk′ sһəs)   *adj.* Very unpleasant; objectionable
obstinacy (äb′ stə nə sē)   *n.* Stubbornness
obstreperous (ə strep′ ər əs)   *adj.* Noisy or unruly
obtuse (äb toos′)   *adj.* Slow to understand or perceive
ominous (äm′ ə nəs)   *adj.* Threatening; sinister
omnipotent (äm nip′ ə tənt)   *adj.* All-powerful
omnipresence (äm′ ni prez′ ′ns)   *n.* A presence in all places at the same time
omniscience (äm nisһ′ əns)   *n.* A knowledge of all things
oppress (ə pres′)   *v.* To weigh heavily on the mind
opprobrious (ə prō′ brē əs)   *adj.* Abusive; disrespectful
ornery (ôr′ nər ē)   *adj.* Having a mean disposition
ornithologist (ôr′ nə tһäl′ ə jəst)   *n.* An expert on birds
oscillation (äs′ ə lā′ sһən)   *n.* The act of swinging regularly back and forth
ostentation (äs′ tən tā′ sһən)   *n.* A boastful display
ostentatious (äs′ tən tā′ sһəs)   *adj.* Intended to attract notice

P

paean (pē′ ən)   *n.* A song of triumph
palisade (pal′ ə sād)   *n.* A large pointed stake set in the ground to form a fence used for defense
pallid (pal′ id)   *adj.* Pale
palpable (pal′ pə b′l)   *adj.* Able to be touched, felt, or handled
paradoxical (par′ ə däks′ i k′l)   *adj.* Expressing an apparent contradiction
Parian (per′ ē ən)   *adj.* Referring to a fine, white marble of the Greek city Paros
parochial (pə rō′ kē əl)   *adj.* Narrow; limited
parsimony (pär′ sə mō′ nē)   *n.* Stinginess
passion (pasһ′ ən)   *n.* An extreme, compelling emotion
pathos (pā′ tһäs)   *n.* The quality in something which arouses pity, sorrow, or compassion
patriarch (pā′ trē ärk)   *n.* The father and ruler of a family or tribe

patrimony (pat′ rə mō′ nē)   *n.* The property inherited from one's father
pelf (pelf)   *n.* The money or wealth regarded with contempt
pensive (pen′ siv)   *adj.* Thinking deeply or seriously
penumbra (pi num′ brə)   *n.* The partly lighted area surrounding the complete shadow of a body in full eclipse
penury (pen′ yə rē)   *n.* A lack of money, property, or necessities
peremptory (pə remp′ tər ē)   *adj.* That cannot be denied, changed, delayed or opposed
perfidy (pur′ fə dē)   *n.* A betrayal of trust; treachery
perfunctory (pər fuŋk′ tər ē)   *adj.* Done without care or interest or merely as a form of routine
periodicity (pir′ ē ə dis′ ə tē)   *n.* A recurrence at regular intervals
periphery (pə rif′ ər ē)   *n.* A surrounding space or area
peroration (per′ ə rā′ sһən)   *n.* The concluding part of a speech
pertinaciously (pur′ tə nā′ sһəs lē)   *adj.* Holding firmly to some purpose
pertinence (pur′ t′n əns)   *n.* Appropriateness; relevance
perturbation (pur′ tər bā′ sһən)   *n.* Agitation
perusal (pə roo′ z′l)   *n.* The act of reading
pervade (pər vād′)   *v.* To pass through; to spread throughout
petulantly (pəcһ′ oo lənt lē)   *adv.* Impatiently or irritably
phantasmagoric (fan taz′ mə gôr′ ik)   *adj.* Fantastic or dreamlike
piety (pī′ ə tē)   *n.* A devotion to religious duties
pilfer (pil′ fər)   *v.* To steal
pimiento (pi men′ tō)   *n.* A red, bell-shaped fruit, used for stuffing green olives
pine (pīn)   *v.* To have an intense longing or desire
pinion (pin′ yən)   *n.* Wing
pinnace (pin′ is)   *n.* A small sailing ship
pinnacle (pin′ ə k′l)   *n.* A lofty peak
pious (pī′ əs)   *adj.* Dutiful
pique (pēk)   *v.* To arouse resentment in
placid (plas′ id)   *adj.* Tranquil; calm
plaguy (plā′ gē)   *adj.* Disagreeable
Pleistocene (plīs′ tə sēn)   *adj.* A geological era characterized by the spreading and recession of continental ice sheets and the appearance of modern man
poignant (poin′ yənt)   *adj.* Sharply painful to the feelings
poise (poiz)   *n.* Balance; stability
pompadour (päm′ pə dôr′)   *n.* A hairdo in which the hair is swept up high from the forehead
portentous (pôr ten′ təs)   *adj.* Ominous
posterity (päs ter′ ə tē)   *n.* All succeeding generations
posture (päs′ cһər)   *v.* To pose
practicable (prak′ ti kə b′l)   *adj.* Capable of being put into practice; feasible; workable
pragmatic (prag mat′ ik)   *adj.* Practical
precept (prē′ sept)   *n.* A rule of conduct
preconception (prē′ kən sep′ sһən)   *n.* An idea formed beforehand
predilection (pred′ ′l ek′ sһən)   *n.* Preference
preposterous (pri päs′ tər əs)   *adj.* Ridiculous
prescient (prē′ sһē ənt)   *adj.* Having foreknowledge

preternatural (prēt′ ər nach′ ər əl) *adj.* Differing from or beyond what is normally expected from nature; supernatural

priggish (prig′ gish) *adj.* Excessively precise

pristine (pris′ tēn) *adj.* Pure, uncorrupted

prodigious (prə dij′ əs) *adj.* Powerful; wonderful

profane (prə fān′) *adj.* Showing disrespect or contempt for sacred things

prophecy (präf′ ə sē) *n.* Prediction of the future

propitiation (prə pə′ tē ā′ shən) *n.* Appeasing

propitious (prə pish′ əs) *adj.* Favorably inclined or disposed

proscenium (prō sē′ nē əm) *n.* The area of the stage in front of the curtain, where action takes place when the curtain is closed

protrude (prō trōōd′) *v.* To jut out

psychology (sī köl′ ə jē) *n.* The science dealing with the mind and with mental and emotional processes

pugilistic (pyōō′ jə lis′ tik) *adj.* Like a boxer

purged (purjt) *v.* Cleansed or rid of impurities

pygmies (pig′ mēz) *n.* Members of African and Asiatic races known for their small stature

Q

quagmire (kwag′ mīr) *n.* A wet, boggy ground

quail (kwāl) *v.* Draw back in fear

quarto (kwôr′ tō) *n.* A book about nine by twelve inches

querulous (kwer′ ə ləs) *adj.* Complaining; inclined to find fault

questing (kwest′ iŋ) *adj.* Searching

quintessentially (kwin′ tə sen′ shə lē) *adv.* Purely

R

radiant (rā′ dē ənt) *adj.* Shining brightly

ramification (ram′ ə fi kā′ shən) *n.* A branchlike division

rampant (ram′ pənt) *adj.* Spreading unchecked

ravenous (rav′ ə nəs) *adj.* Extremely eager

reap (rēp) *v.* To cut or harvest grain from a field

recompense (rek′ əm pens′) *n.* A reward

recondite (rek′ ən dīt′) *adj.* Dealing with very profound, difficult, or abstruse subject matter

recumbent (ri kum′ bənt) *adj.* Resting

redolent (red′ 'l ənt) *adj.* Suggestive

redress (re′ dres) *n.* An atonement; rectification

refluent (ref′ lōō wənt) *adj.* Flowing back

refulgent (ri ful′ jənt) *adj.* Radiant; shining

rehearse (ri hurs′) *v.* To narrate

reiterated (rē it′ ə rāt′ id) *adj.* Repeated

remuda (rə mōō′ də) *n.* A group of extra saddle horses kept as a supply of remounts

repose (ri pōz′) *n.* The state of being at rest

repression (ri presh′ ən) *n.* Restraint

repugnant (ri pug′ nənt) *adj.* Offensive; disagreeable

reverence (rev′ ər əns) *n.* A feeling or attitude of deep respect, love or awe

reverential (rev′ ə ren′ shəl) *adj.* Showing or caused by a feeling of deep respect, love, and awe

reverie (rev′ ər ē) *n.* A daydream

rigor (rig′ ər) *n.* A stiffness; rigidity

rude (rōōd) *adj.* Crude or rough in form or workmanship

rudimentary (rōō də men′ tər ē) *adj.* Elementary

rueful (rōō′ fəl) *adj.* Feeling or showing sorrow or pity

ruminate (rōō′ mə nāt) *v.* To meditate

S

sacrament (sak′ rə mənt) *n.* Something regarded as having a sacred meaning

sagacious (sə gā′ shəs) *adj.* Shrewd

sage (sāj′) *n.* A person widely respected for his or her wisdom

salient (sāl′ yənt) *adj.* Standing out from the rest

sallow (sal′ ō) *adj.* Of a sickly, pale-yellow hue

sardonic (sär dän′ ik) *adj.* Bitterly sarcastic

saturnalia (sat′ ər nā′ lē ə) *n.* A period of unrestrained revelry

savant (sə vänt′) *n.* A learned person; scholar

scorn (skôrn) *v.* To refuse or reject as wrong or disgraceful

scree (skrē) *adj.* A covering of rock fragments on a slope below a rock face

scurvy (skur′ vē) *n.* A disease caused by vitamin-C deficiency

scythe (sīth) *v.* To cut as with a tool with a long single-edged blade set at an angle on a long, curved handle

sedge (sej′) *n.* A grasslike plant

seminal (sem′ ə n'l) *adj.* Highly original and influencing the development of future events

semi-somnambulant (sem′ i säm nam′ byōō lənt) *adj.* Half sleepwalking

sentience (sen′ shəns) *n.* A capacity of feeling

sepulcher (sep′ 'l kər) *n.* A grave; tomb

sequester (si kwes′ tər) *v.* To withdraw; seclude

serenity (sə ren′ ə tē) *n.* Calmness

servile (ser′ v'l) *adj.* Humbly yielding or submissive

sexton (seks′ tən) *n.* A person in charge of the maintenance of a church

shroud (shroud) *n.* 1. A cloth sometimes used to wrap a corpse for burial 2. A set of ropes from a ship's side to the masthead

sibilance (sib′ 'l əns) *n.* A hissing sound

simulacrum (sim′ yoo lā krəm) *n.* A vague representation

sinuous (sin′ yoo wəs) *adj.* Bending or winding in and out; wavy

Skoal (skōl) *interj.* A drinking toast, meaning "to your health"

sleeper (slē′ pər) *n.* A tie supporting railroad tracks

slovenly (sluv′ ən lē) *adj.* Untidy

smite (smīt) *v.* To kill by a powerful blow

solicitous (sə lis′ ə təs) *adj.* Showing concern

somber (säm′ bər) *adj.* Dark and gloomy or dull

somnolent (säm nə lənt) *adj.* Sleepy; drowsy

sovereignty (säv′ rən tē) *n.* The supreme and independent political authority

spartan (spär′ t'n) *adj.* Characteristic of the people of ancient Sparta: hardy, stoical, severe, frugal

specious (spē′ shəs) *adj.* Seeming to be good or sound without actually being so

spurious (spyoor′ ē əs) *adj.* False; artificial

squalor (skäl′ ər) *n.* Filth; wretchedness

squander (skwän′ dər) *v.* To spend or use wastefully

starboard fluke (flook) *n.* The right half of a whale's tail

stark (stärk) *adj.* Severe

staunch (stônch) *adj.* Strong; unyielding

stratosphere (strat′ ə sfir′) *n.* A portion of the upper atmosphere

stringency (strin′ jən sē) *n.* Strictness; severity

stupefaction (stoo′ pə fak′ shən) *n.* Stunned amazement or utter bewilderment

subjugation (sub′ jə gā′ shən) *n.* The act of conquering

sublime (sə blīm′) *adj.* Noble; majestic

subscribe (səb skrīb′) *v.* To give support, sanction, or approval

subservient (səb sʉr′ vē ənt) *adj.* Submissive; servile

subsistence (səb sis′ təns) *n.* The means of support

suffice (sə fīs′) *v.* To be enough

suffrage (suf′ rij) *n.* A vote or voting

suffusion (sə fyoo′ zhən) *n.* A fullness of color

sulfureous (sul fyoor′ ē əs) *adj.* Greenish-yellow

sullen (sul′ ən) *adj.* Sulky; glum

sundry (sun′ drē) *adj.* Various, different

supercilious (soo pər sil′ ē əs) *adj.* Disdainful

superfluous (soo pʉr′ floo wəs) *adj.* Not needed

supposititious (sə päz′ ə tish′ əs) *adj.* Supposed

surmise (sər mīz′) *v.* To guess

sylvan (sil′ vən) *adj.* Characteristic of the forest

synod (sin′ əd) *n.* A high governing body in certain Christian churches

syntax (sin′ taks) *n.* An orderly or systematic arrangement

syringa (sə riŋ′ gə) *n.* A plant with large clusters of tiny white flowers

T

tableau (tab′ lō) *n.* A representation of a silent, motionless scene

tabloid (tab′ loid) *n.* A newspaper with many pictures and short, often sensational, stories

tabula rasa (tab′ yə lə rä′ sə) *n.* A clean slate

taciturn (tas′ ə turn′) *adj.* Almost always silent

tantrum (tan′ trəm) *n.* A childish fit of temper

tarn (tärn) *n.* A small lake

temerity (tə mer′ ə tē) *n.* Foolhardy or heedless disregard of danger; recklessness

tempest (temp′ pist) *n.* A violent storm

tenement (ten′ ə mənt) *n.* A building divided into apartments

teocallis (tē′ ə ka′ lis) *n.* The ancient temples erected by Aztec Indians of Mexico and Central America

termagant (tʉr′ mə gənt) *n.* A quarrelsome woman

terrestrial (tə res′ trē əl) *adj.* Of this world

timorous (tim′ ər əs) *adj.* Full of fear

tortilla (tôr tē′ ə) *n.* A thin, flat cake or cornmeal

tow (tō) *n.* The coarse and broken fibers of hemp or flax before spinning

transient (tran′ shənt) *adj.* Not permanent; passing away with time

translate (trans lāt′) *v.* To transport

transmogrify (trans mäg′ rə fī′) *v.* To transform in a grotesque manner

travail (trə vāl′) *n.* Painfully difficult or burdensome work

tremulous (trem′ yoo ləs) *adj.* Characterized by trembling; quivering

trepidation (trep′ ə dā′ shən) *n.* A fearful anxiety; apprehension

Triton (trīt′ 'n) *n.* A Greek sea god with the body of a man and the tail of a fish, who usually carried a conch-shell trumpet

truncate (truŋ′ kāt) *v.* To cut short

tulle (tool) *n.* A thin, fine netting used for scarves

tumultuous (too mul′ choo wəs) *adj.* Wild and noisy; greatly agitated

turbulence (tʉr′ byə ləns) *n.* A commotion or wild disorder

tyranny (tir′ ə nē) *n.* An oppressive and unjust government

U

unalienable (un āl′ yən ə b'l) *adj.* Not to be taken away

unconscionable (un kän′ shən ə b'l) *adj.* Unreasonable

undulate (un′ doo lāt) *v.* To move in waves

unempathic (un em′ pa′ thik) *adj.* Unable to share in another's emotions

unobstrusively (un əb troo′ siv lē) *adv.* Inconspicuously

unperverted (un′ pər vʉrt′ id) *adj.* Uncorrupted

unscrupulous (un skroop′ yə ləs) *adj.* Not restrained by ideas of right and wrong

unsheathed (un shēt/hd′) *adj.* Removed from its case

unwonted (un wun′ tid) *adj.* Unfamiliar

usurer (yoo′ zhoo rər) *n.* A moneylender who charges very high interest

usurpation (yoo′ sər pā′ shən) *n.* The unlawful seizure of rights or privileges

V

vagary (və ger′ ē) *n.* An unpredictable occurrence; odd, unexpected action or notion

vagrant (vā′ grənt) *n.* An idle wanderer

vagueness (vāg′ nis) *n.* A lack of definition in shape or form

vanquished (vaŋ′ kwisht) *adj.* Defeated

venerable (ven′ ər ə b'l) *adj.* Commanding respect

venomous (ven′ əm əs) *adj.* Spiteful; malicious

venturous (ven′ chər əs) *adj.* Daring

veracious (və rā′ shəs) *adj.* Honest, truthful

verity (ver′ ə tē) *n.* The truth

vernacular (vər nak′ yə lər) *n.* The native speech, language, or dialect of a country or place

vigilance (vij′ ə ləns) *n.* Watchfulness

vigilant (vij′ ə lənt) *adj.* Alert to danger

vignette (vin yet′) *n.* A picture or photograph with no definite border

vigor (vig′ ər) *n.* An active physical or mental force or strength

visage (viz′ ij) *n.* A facial appearance

vituperative (vī too′ prə tiv) *adj.* Spoken abusively

vociferation (vō sif′ ə rā′ shən) *n.* A loud or vehement shouting

vociferous (vō sif′ ər əs) *adj.* Loud, noisy, or vehement in making one's feelings known

voracity   (vô ras′ ə tē)   *n.* Eagerness
votive   (vōt′ iv)   *adj.* Dedicated in fulfillment of a vow or
  pledge
vulcanism   (vul′ kə niz′m)   *n.* The series of phenomena
  connected with the origin and movement of molten rock

W

waggery   (wag′ ər ē)   *n.* A mischievous humor
wampum   (wäm′ pəm)   *n.* Small beads made of shells
wan   (wän)   *adj.* Sickly pale

wanton   (wän t′n)   *adj.* Senseless; unjustified
wily   (wī′ lē)   *adj.* Sly; cunning

X

xenophobic   (zen′ ə fō′ bik)   *adj.* Afraid of strangers or
  foreigners

Z

zither   (zit⁄h′ ər)   *n.* A musical instrument with thirty to
  forty strings stretched across a flat soundboard and
  played with the fingers

INDEX OF FINE ART

Index of Fine Art 1373

1374 *Index of Fine Art*

Index of Fine Art   1375

INDEX OF SKILLS

CRITICAL THINKING AND READING

UNDERSTANDING LANGUAGE

INDEX OF TITLES BY THEMES

INDEX OF AUTHORS AND TITLES

ACKNOWLEDGMENTS (continued)

Elizabeth Barnett, Literary Executor of the Estate of Norma Millay Ellis
Excerpts from "I Shall Go Back Again to the Bleak Shore" and "Recuerdo" by Edna St. Vincent Millay. Copyright 1922, 1923, 1950, 1951 by Edna St. Vincent Millay and Norma Millay Ellis. "Renascence" by Edna St. Vincent Millay. From *Collected Poems*, Harper & Row. Copyright 1912, 1940 by Edna St. Vincent Millay. Reprinted by permission.

Robert Bly
One line from "Solitude Late at Night in the Woods" by Robert Bly, reprinted by permission of the author.

Gwendolyn Brooks
"The Explorer" and lines from "Life for my child is simple and is good" from *Blacks* by Gwendolyn Brooks, published by The David Company, Chicago, IL. Copyright 1987. Reprinted by permission of the author.

Century-Hutchinson Ltd.:
"The Watch" from *Collected Poems* by Frances Cornford, published by Cresset Press Ltd., 1954, now a part of Century-Hutchinson Ltd. Copyright Frances Cornford. Reprinted by permission of Century-Hutchinson Ltd.

Diana Chang
"Most Satisfied by Snow" by Diana Chang. Reprinted by permission of the author.

Curtis Brown Ltd.
Lines from "Untitled" ("the thirty eighth year of my life") from *An Ordinary Woman* by Lucille Clifton. Copyright 1974 by Lucille Clifton. Reprinted by permission of Curtis Brown Ltd.

J. M. Dent & Sons, Ltd.
From "Letters from an American Farmer" by Michel-Guillaume Jean de Crèvecoeur in *An Everyman's Library*.

Dodd, Mead & Company, Inc.
"Douglass" and "We Wear the Mask" reprinted by permission of Dodd, Mead & Company, Inc. from *The Complete Poems of Paul Laurence Dunbar*.

Elizabeth Dos Passos
"Tin Lizzie" from *U.S.A.*, Houghton Mifflin Co. Copyright by John Dos Passos and Elizabeth Dos Passos, Co-Executor of the Estate of John Dos Passos.

Doubleday, a division of Bantam, Doubleday, Dell Publishing Group, Inc.
"Imagined Scenes" by Ann Beattie originally appeared in *The Texas Quarterly*. From the book *Distortions*, copyright © 1974, 1975, 1976 by Ann Beattie. "An Occurrence at Owl Creek Bridge" from *The Complete Stories of Ambrose Bierce*, published by Doubleday & Company, Inc. "The Rain Guitar" by James Dickey first appeared in *The New Yorker*. From the book *The Strength of Fields*, copyright © 1972 by James Dickey. "Night Journey" and "The Waking" copyright 1940, 1948 by Theodore Roethke. "Once More, the Round" copyright © 1962 by Beatrice Roethke as administratrix of the Estate of Theodore Roethke. All poems from the book *The Collected Poems of Theodore Roethke*. Reprinted by permission of Doubleday.

Rita Dove
"This Life" from Rita Dove, *The Yellow House on the Corner*. Carnegie-Mellon University Press, Pittsburgh 1980. Reprinted by permission of the author.

Mari Evans
Lines from "Where Have You Gone" from *I Am a Black Woman* by Mari Evans, published in 1970 by William Morrow & Co., Inc. Reprinted by permission of the author.

Farrar, Straus and Giroux, Inc.
"On the Mall" from *The White Album* by Joan Didion. Copyright © 1975, 1979, 1989 by Joan Didion. "Seal" from *Laughing Time: Nonsense Poems* by William Jay Smith. Copyright © 1955, 1957, 1980 by William Jay Smith. "Engineer-Private Paul Klee Misplaces an Aircraft Between Milbertshofen and Cambrai, March 1916" from *Sadness* by Donald Barthelme. Copyright © 1970, 1971, 1972 by Donald Barthelme. "House Guest" and "Little Exercise" from *The Complete Poems 1927–1979* by Elizabeth Bishop. Copyright 1946, © 1968; renewal copyright © 1980 by Alice Helen Methfessel; copyright © 1983 by Alice Helen Methfessel. Originally appeared in *The New Yorker*. Excerpt from "Visits to St. Elizabeths" from *The Complete Poems 1927–1979* by Elizabeth Bishop. Copyright © 1952, 1965 by Elizabeth Bishop. Copyright © 1979, 1983 by Alice Helen Methfessel. Copyright 1957 by Elizabeth Bishop. Excerpt from *Play It As It Lays* by Joan Didion. Copyright © 1970 by Joan Didion. "The Death of the Ball Turret Gunner" and "Losses" from *The Complete Poems* by Randall Jarrell. Copyright 1945, 1951, © 1955 by Randall Jarrell; copyright renewed 1968, 1969 by Mrs. Randall Jarrell. "Hawthorne" from *Selected Poems* by Robert Lowell. Copyright © 1964 by Robert Lowell; copyright renewed 1972, 1974, 1975 by Robert Lowell. "The First Seven Years" from *The Magic Barrel* by Bernard Malamud. Copyright © 1950, 1958 and renewal copyright © 1978 by Bernard Malamud. Excerpt from *Rising from the Plains* by John McPhee. Copyright © 1986 by John McPhee. Excerpts from "A Far Cry from Africa" and "Codicil" from *Collected Poems, 1948–1984* by Derek Walcott. Copyright © 1962, 1965, 1968 by Derek Walcott. Excerpt from Robert Giroux's Introduction to *The Complete Stories* by Flannery O'Connor. Introduction copyright © by Robert Giroux. Reprinted by permission of Farrar, Straus and Giroux, Inc.

GRM Associates, Inc. Agents for the Estate of Ida M. Cullen
"Any Human to Another" and "Yet Do I Marvel" from *On These I Stand* by Countee Cullen. Copyright © 1925 by Harper & Brothers; copyright renewed 1953 by Ida M. Cullen. Reprinted by permission.

Harcourt Brace Jovanovich, Inc.
"The Life You Save May Be Your Own" copyright 1953 by Flannery O'Connor; renewed 1981 by Mrs. Regina O'Connor. Reprinted from *A Good Man Is Hard to Find and Other Stories* by Flannery O'Connor. "The Jilting of Granny Weatherall" copyright 1930 and renewed 1958 by Katherine Anne Porter. Reprinted from her volume *Flowering Judas and Other Stories*. "Chicago" from *Chicago Poems* by Carl Sandburg, copyright 1916 by Holt, Rinehart and Winston, Inc.; renewed 1944 by Carl Sandburg. "Grass" from *Cornhuskers* by Carl Sandburg, copyright 1918 by Holt, Rinehart and Winston, Inc.; renewed 1946 by Carl Sandburg. Excerpt

from "Lincoln Speaks at Gettysburg" in *Abraham Lincoln: The War Years,* Volume Two, by Carl Sandburg, copyright 1939 by Harcourt Brace Jovanovich, Inc.; renewed 1967 by Carl Sandburg. Excerpts from *The People, Yes* by Carl Sandburg, copyright 1936 by Harcourt Brace Jovanovich, Inc.; renewed 1964 by Carl Sandburg. "Expect Nothing" from *Revolutionary Petunias & Other Poems,* copyright © 1972 by Alice Walker. "A Worn Path" copyright 1941 and renewed 1969 by Eudora Welty. Reprinted from her volume *A Curtain of Green and Other Stories.* "The Beautiful Changes" from *The Beautiful Changes and Other Poems,* copyright 1947 and renewed 1975 by Richard Wilbur. Reprinted by permission of Harcourt Brace Jovanovich, Inc.

Harcourt Brace Jovanovich, Inc. and Faber and Faber Ltd.
"The Love Song of J. Alfred Prufrock" and excerpt from "The Waste Land" from *Collected Poems 1909–1962* by T. S. Eliot, copyright 1936 by Harcourt Brace Jovanovich, Inc.; copyright © 1963, 1964 by T. S. Eliot. Reprinted by permission of the publishers.

Harper & Row, Publishers, Inc.
"The Tooth, the Whole Tooth, and Nothing but the Tooth" from *Inside Benchley* by Robert Benchley. Copyright 1921, 1922, 1925, 1928, and 1942 by Harper & Brothers; copyright © renewed 1970 by Gertrude Benchley. "Traveling Through the Dark" from *Stories That Could Be True: New and Collected Poems* by William Stafford. Copyright © 1960 by William Stafford. "The Boys' Ambition" from *Life on the Mississippi* by Mark Twain. "The Notorious Jumping Frog of Calaveras County" from *Sketches New and Old* by Mark Twain. "Tom Quartz" from *The Complete Short Stories of Mark Twain* edited by Charles Neider. "Walden" from *One Man's Meat* by E. B. White. Copyright 1939, renewed 1967 by E. B. White. First published in *Harper's Magazine.* Reprinted by permission of Harper & Row, Publishers, Inc.

Harper & Row, Publishers, Inc. and Olwyn Hughes & Olwyn Hughes
"Mirror" from *The Collected Poems of Sylvia Plath* edited by Ted Hughes. Copyright © 1963 by Sylvia Plath. First published in *The New Yorker.* Copyright © 1981 by the Estate of Sylvia Plath. Reprinted by permission of Harper & Row, Publisher, Inc.

Harvard University Press
"Upon the Burning of Our House" from *The Complete Works of Anne Bradstreet* edited by Jeannine Hensley. Copyright © 1967 by the President and Fellows of Harvard College. From "History of the Dividing Line" in *The Prose Works of William Byrd of Westover* edited by Louis B. Wright. Copyright 1966 by the President and Fellows of Harvard College. "A narrow Fellow in the Grass," "As imperceptibly as grief," "Because I could not stop for Death—," "'Hope' is the thing with feathers—," "How happy is the little Stone," "I felt a Funeral in my Brain," "I heard a Fly buzz—when I died—," "I like to see it lap the miles—," "I never saw a Moor—," "Much Madness is divinest Sense—," "My life closed twice before its close," "Success is counted sweetest," "Tell all the Truth but tell it slant—," "The Bustle in a House," "The Soul selects her own Society—," "There's a certain Slant of Light," and "This is my letter to the World" reprinted by permission of the publishers and the Trustees of Amherst College from *The Poems of Emily Dickinson* edited by Thomas H. Johnson, Cambridge, Mass.: The Belknap Press

of Harvard University Press, copyright 1951, © 1955, 1979, 1983 by The President and Fellows of Harvard College.

Hill and Wang, a division of Farrar, Straus and Giroux, Inc.
Adapted from "Sinners in the Hands of an Angry God" from *Jonathan Edwards: Representative Selections* by Clarence H. Faust and Thomas H. Johnson. Copyright 1935, © 1962 by Hill and Wang, Inc. Reprinted by permission of Hill and Wang, a division of Farrar, Straus and Giroux, Inc.

Henry Holt and Company, Inc.
"Stopping by Woods on a Snowy Evening" copyright 1923, © 1969 by Holt, Rinehart and Winston. Copyright 1951 by Robert Frost. Reprinted from *The Poetry of Robert Frost* edited by Edward Connery Lathem. "Acquainted with the Night," "After Apple-Picking," "Birches," "Fire and Ice," "Mending Wall," "Nothing Gold Can Stay," "Out, Out—," "The Death of the Hired Man," and "The Wood-Pile" from *The Poetry of Robert Frost* edited by Edward Connery Lathem. Copyright © 1969 by Holt, Rinehart and Winston, Inc. Copyright © 1962 by Robert Frost. Copyright © 1975 by Lesley Frost Ballantine. Reprinted by permission of Henry Holt and Company, Inc.

M. Carl Holman
Lines from "Three Brown Girls Singing" by M. Carl Holman, reprinted by permission of the author.

Houghton Mifflin Company
"A White Heron" from *A White Heron and Other Stories* by Sarah Orne Jewett. "Patterns" from *The Complete Poetical Works of Amy Lowell.* Copyright © 1955 by Houghton Mifflin Company; copyright © renewed 1983 by Houghton Mifflin Company, Brinton P. Roberts, Esquire, and G. D'Andelot Belin, Esquire. "Ars Poetica" from *New and Collected Poems 1917–1976* by Archibald MacLeish. Copyright © 1976 by Archibald MacLeish. From "The Navaho Origin Legend" in *Navaho Legends,* collected and translated by Washington Matthews. From *The Mortgaged Heart* by Carson McCullers. Copyright 1940, 1941, 1942, 1945, 1948, 1949, 1953, © 1956, 1959, 1963, 1971 by Floria V. Lasky, Executrix of the Estate of Carson McCullers; copyright © 1955, 1957, 1963 by Carson McCullers. "The Edge of the Great Rift" from *Sunrise with Seamonsters* by Paul Theroux. Copyright © 1985 by Cape Cod Scriveners Company. "A Noiseless Patient Spider," "Beat! Beat! Drums!" and "When I Heard the Learn'd Astronomer" from *Complete Poetry and Selected Prose of Walt Whitman* edited by J. E. Miller, Jr. Reprinted by permission of Houghton Mifflin Company.

Houghton Mifflin Company and William Collins Sons & Company, Ltd.
Excerpts from *In the Shadow of Man* by Jane van Lawick-Goodall. Copyright © 1971 by Hugo and Jane van Lawick-Goodall. Reprinted by permission.

Johnson Publishing Company, Inc.
From *My Bondage and My Freedom* by Frederick Douglass.

Alfred A. Knopf, Inc.
From *Of Plymouth Plantation 1620–1647* by William Bradford, edited wtih Notes and Introduction by Samuel Eliot Morison. Copyright 1952 by Samuel Eliot Morison and renewed 1980 by Emily Beck. "Katherine Comes to Yellow Sky" from *A Dove of the East and Other Stories* by Mark Helprin. Copyright © 1975 by Mark Helprin. "The Open Boat" from *The Works of Stephen Crane* by Stephen Crane.

Lines from "April Rain Song" from *The Dream Keeper and Other Poems* by Langston Hughes. Copyright 1932 by Alfred A. Knopf, Inc. and renewed 1960 by Langston Hughes. "The Negro Speaks of Rivers" copyright 1926 by Alfred A. Knopf, Inc. and renewed 1954 by Langston Hughes. Reprinted from *Selected Poems of Langston Hughes* by Langston Hughes. "Janet Waking" copyright 1927 by Alfred A. Knopf, Inc. and renewed 1955 by John Crowe Ransom. Reprinted from *Selected Poems, Third Edition, Revised and Enlarged* by John Crowe Ransom. "Anecdote of the Jar" and "Disillusionment of Ten O'Clock" from *The Collected Poems of Wallace Stevens* by Wallace Stevens. Copyright 1923 and renewed 1951 by Wallace Stevens. "The Slump" copyright © 1968 by John Updike. Reprinted from *Museums and Women and Other Stories* by John Updike. Excerpt from *Willa Cather Living* by Edith Lewis. Copyright 1953 by Edith Lewis. Reprinted by permission of Alfred A. Knopf, Inc.

Alfred A. Knopf, Inc. and Olwyn Hughes Literary Agency
Lines from "Mushrooms" copyright © 1960 by Sylvia Plath. Reprinted from *The Colossus and Other Poems* by Sylvia Plath, by permission.

Life Picture Service, a department of Time Inc.
From "A Vision Beyond Time and Place" by N. Scott Momaday, published in *Life* Magazine, 1971, © 1971 Time Inc.

Little, Brown and Company
"There is a solitude of space" from *The Complete Poems of Emily Dickinson* edited by Thomas H. Johnson. Copyright 1914, 1942 by Martha Dickinson Bianchi. By permission of Little, Brown and Company.

Liveright Publishing Corporation
"since feeling is first," "anyone lived in a pretty how town," and "old age sticks" are reprinted from *Complete Poems, 1913–1962*, by E. E. Cummings, by permission of Liveright Publishing Corporation. Copyright © 1923, 1925, 1931, 1935, 1938, 1939, 1940, 1944, 1945, 1946, 1947, 1948, 1949, 1950, 1951, 1952, 1953, 1954, 1955, 1956, 1957, 1958, 1959, 1960, 1961, 1962 by the Trustees for the E. E. Cummings Trust. Copyright © 1961, 1963, 1968 by Marion Morehouse Cummings. Lines from "Astronauts" from *American Journal, Poems* by Robert Hayden, by permission of Liveright Publishing Corporation. Copyright © 1982 by Irma Hayden. Copyright © 1978 by Robert Hayden. "Those Winter Sundays" is reprinted from *Angle of Ascent, New and Selected Poems* by Robert Hayden, by permission of Liveright Publishing Corporation. Copyright © 1975, 1972, 1970, 1966, by Robert Hayden. "Storm Ending" and lines from "Song of the Son", reprinted from *Cane* by Jean Toomer, by permission of Liveright Publishing Corporation. Copyright 1923 by Boni & Liveright. Copyright © renewed 1951 by Jean Toomer.

The Sterling Lord Agency, Inc.
Selections from "The Crisis, Number 1" in *The Selected Work of Tom Paine* edited by Howard Fast. Copyright 1945 by Howard Fast. Reprinted by permission of The Sterling Lord Agency, Inc.

Macmillan Publishing Company
Lines from "Bird-Witted" from *Collected Poems* by Marianne Moore. Copyright 1941, and renewed 1969, by Marianne Moore. Lines from "Nevertheless" from *Collected Poems* by Marianne Moore. Copyright 1944, and renewed 1972 by Marianne Moore. "Poetry" reprinted from *Collected Poems* by Marianne Moore. Copyright 1935 by Marianne Moore, renewed 1963 by Marianne Moore and T. S. Eliot. Lines from "February Twilight", reprinted from *Collected Poems* by Sara Teasdale. Copyright 1926 by Macmillan Publishing Company; renewed 1954 by Mamie T. Wheless. Reprinted with permission of Macmillan Publishing Company.

Naomi Long Madgett
Lines from "Writing a Poem" in *Pink Ladies in the Afternoon* (Detroit: Lotus Press, 1972) by Naomi Long Madgett. Reprinted by permission of the author.

Laureen Mar
Lines from "Chinatown 1" by Laureen Mar, originally published in *The Greenfield Review*. Copyright © by Laureen Mar, and reprinted with her permission.

Ellen C. Masters
"Fiddler Jones" and "Lucinda Matlock" from *Spoon River Anthology* by Edgar Lee Masters, published by Macmillan Publishing Company.

William Morrow & Company, Inc.
"Plucking Out a Rhythm" from *Before the War* by Lawson Fusao Inada. Copyright © 1971 by Lawson Fusao Inada. Reprinted by permission of William Morrow & Company, Inc.

Howard Nemerov
"Storm Windows" from *The Collected Poems of Howard Nemerov*, The University of Chicago Press, 1977. Reprinted by permission of the author.

New Directions Publishing Corporation
"Heat" and "Pear Tree" by H.D., *Collected Poems, 1912–1944.* Copyright © 1982 by The Estate of Hilda Doolittle. "Oread" from H.D., *Selected Poems.* Copyright 1925, 1953, © 1957 by Norman Holmes Pearson. "Merritt Parkway" by Denise Levertov, *Collected Earlier Poems, 1940–1960* of Denise Levertov. Copyright © 1959 by Denise Levertov Goodman. "Canto 13" by Ezra Pound, *The Cantos of Ezra Pound.* Copyright 1934 by Ezra Pound. "In a Station of the Metro" and "The River-Merchant's Wife: A Letter" by Ezra Pound, *Personae.* Copyright 1926 by Ezra Pound. "The Locust Tree," "The Red Wheelbarrow," and "This Is Just to Say" by William Carlos Williams, *Collected Poems Volume I: 1909–1939.* Copyright 1938 by New Directions Publishing Corporation. "Orchard" by H.D. from *Modern American Poetry,* edited by Louis Untermeyer. Copyright 1958 by Harcourt, Brace and World, Inc. Reprinted by permission of New Directions Publishing Corporation.

New York University Press
From the "Preface" to *Walt Whitman: Leaves of Grass, Reader's Comprehensive Edition* edited by Harold W. Blodgett and Sculley Bradley. Copyright © 1965 by New York University. Reprinted by permission of New York University Press.

W. W. Norton & Company, Inc.
"The Observer" is reprinted from *The Fact of A Doorframe, Poems Selected and New, 1950–1984,* by Adrienne Rich, by permission of W. W. Norton & Company, Inc. Copyright ©

1984 by Adrienne Rich. Copyright 1975, 1978 by W. W. Norton & Company, Inc. Copyright © 1981 by Adrienne Rich. From "Civil Disobedience" reprinted from *Walden and Civil Disobedience* by Henry David Thoreau, edited by Owen Thomas. By permission of W. W. Norton & Company, Inc. Copyright © 1966 by W. W. Norton & Company, Inc.

Harold Ober Associates Inc.
"A Black Man Talks of Reaping" and lines from "Southern Mansions" from *Personals* by Arna Bontemps. Copyright © 1963 by Arna Bontemps. Reprinted by permission of Harold Ober Associates Inc.

Simon J. Ortiz
"Hunger in New York City" from *Going For the Rain: Poems* by Simon J. Ortiz. Published by Harper & Row. Reprinted by permission of Simon J. Ortiz

Grace Paley
"Anxiety" from *Later the Same Day* by Grace Paley, published by Farrar, Straus, and Giroux. Copyright © 1985 by Grace Paley; copyright 1985 Farrar, Straus and Giroux, Inc. Reprinted by permission of Grace Paley c/o Elaine Markson Literary Agency, Inc., New York.

Princeton University Press
From "Where I Lived, and What I Lived For" and from "The Conclusion" in *Walden: The Writings of Henry D. Thoreau,* edited by J. Lyndon Shanley. Copyright © 1971 Princeton University Press. Excerpt from "Rhetorical Criticism, Theory of Genres" from *Anatomy of Criticism* by Northrop Frye. Copyright © 1957 by Princeton University Press. All rights reserved. Reprinted with permission of Princeton University Press.

Random House, Inc.
"A Ride Through Spain" copyright 1950 by Truman Capote. Reprinted from *The Dogs Bark: Public People and Private Places* by Truman Capote. Excerpt from "Hidden Name and Complex Fate" from *Shadow and Act* by Ralph Ellison. Copyright 1953, © 1964 by Ralph Ellison. "The Bear" (7,000-word version) by William Faulkner, copyright 1942 and renewed 1970 by Estelle Faulkner and Jill Faulkner Summers. An expanded version of this story appears in *Go Down, Moses* by William Faulkner. "Evening Hawk" copyright © 1975 by Robert Penn Warren, and "Gold Glade" copyright © 1957 by Robert Penn Warren, reprinted from *Selected Poems, 1923–1975* by Robert Penn Warren. Excerpt from *The Dyer's Hand and Other Essays* by W. H. Auden. Copyright 1948, 1950, 1952, 1953, 1954, © 1956, 1957, 1958, 1960, 1962 by W. H. Auden. Excerpt from *The Eye of the Story: Selected Essays and Reviews* by Eudora Welty. Copyright © 1978 by Eudora Welty. Reprinted by permission of Random House, Inc.

Random House, Inc. and Faber and Faber Ltd.
"The Unknown Citizen" copyright 1940 and renewed 1968 by W. H. Auden and "Who's Who" copyright 1937 and renewed 1965 by W. H. Auden, reprinted from *W. H. Auden: Collected Poems* by W. H. Auden, edited by Edward Mendelson. Reprinted by permission of the publishers.

Russell and Volkening, Inc., as agents for the author
"Average Waves in Unprotected Waters" by Anne Tyler, published in *The New Yorker,* February 28, 1977. Copyright © 1977 by Anne Tyler. "The Signature" from *The Riddle of the Fly & Other Stories* by Elizabeth Enright. Copyright 1959 by Elizabeth Enright, renewed 1987 by Oliver Gillham. Re-printed by permission of Russell and Volkening, Inc., as agents for the author.

Charles Scribner's Sons, an imprint of Macmillan Publishing Co.
F. Scott Fitzgerald, "Winter Dreams" from *All The Sad Young Men.* Copyright 1922 by Frances Scott Fitzgerald Lanahan; copyright renewed 1950. Ernest Hemingway, "In Another Country" from *Men Without Women.* Copyright 1927 Charles Scribner's Sons; copyright renewed © 1955 Ernest Hemingway. "Song of the Chattahoochee" from *The Poems of Sidney Lanier.* Barry Lopez, excerpted from *Arctic Dreams.* Copyright © 1986 Barry Holstun Lopez. "Luke Havergal" and "Miniver Cheevy" from *Collected Poems* by Edwin Arlington Robinson, published by Charles Scribner's Sons. "Richard Cory" from *The Children of the Night* by Edwin Arlington Robinson, published by Charles Scribner's Sons. John Hall Wheelock, "Earth" from *The Gardener And Other Poems* by John Hall Wheelock. Copyright © 1961 by John Hall Wheelock. Thomas Wolfe, "The Far And the Near" from *From Death to Morning.* Copyright 1935 by International Magazine Company, Inc.; copyright renewed © 1963 Paul Gitlin. Two excerpts from *Death in the Afternoon* by Ernest Hemingway. Copyright 1932 by Charles Scribner's Sons, re-newed 1960 by Ernest Hemingway. Reprinted with the per-mission of Charles Scribner's Sons, an imprint of Macmillan Publishing Co.

Leslie Marmon Silko
Lines from "Where Mountain Lion Lay Down With Deer" by Leslie Marmon Silko from *Voices of the Rainbow* edited by Kenneth Rosen. Reprinted by permission of Leslie Marmon Silko.

Simon & Schuster, Inc.
From *Lonesome Dove* by Larry McMurtry. Copyright © 1985 by Larry McMurtry. Reprinted by permission of Simon & Schuster, Inc. Pronunciations key from *Webster's New World Dictionary*—Second College Edition. Copyright © 1984 by Simon & Schuster, Inc. Reprinted by permission.

Smithsonian Institution Press
"Song Concerning a Dream of the Thunderbirds" from *Teton Sioux Music* by Frances Densmore. Bureau of American Ethnology Bulletin 61. Smithsonian Institution, Washington, D.C., 1918. "Spring Song" from *Chippewa Music II* by Frances Densmore. Bureau of American Ethnology Bulletin 53. Smithsonian Institution, Washington, D.C., 1913. Re-printed by permission of Smithsonian Institution Press.

Donald E. Stanford
"Huswifery" and "Upon a Wasp Chilled with Cold" reprinted by permission from *The Poems of Edward Taylor* edited by Donald E. Stanford, © 1960 Donald E. Stanford.

Syracuse University Press
From "The Iroquois Constitution" from Arthur C. Parker, "The Constitution of the Five Nations" in *Parker on the Iroquois,* edited with an introduction by William N. Fenton. Syracuse, N.Y.: Syracuse University Press, 1968. By permis-sion of the publisher.

Rosemary A. Thurber
"The Night the Ghost Got In" copyright 1933, © 1961 by James Thurber. From *My Life and Hard Times,* published by Harper & Row. Cartoon caption: "Well, if I called the wrong number, why did you answer the phone?" Copyright 1943 James Thurber; copyright © 1971 Helen Thurber and Rose-